PAGE 40

ON THE ROAD

YOUR COMPLETE DESTINATION GUIDE
In-depth reviews, detailed listings and insider tips

TOP EXPERIENCES MAP NEXT PAGE

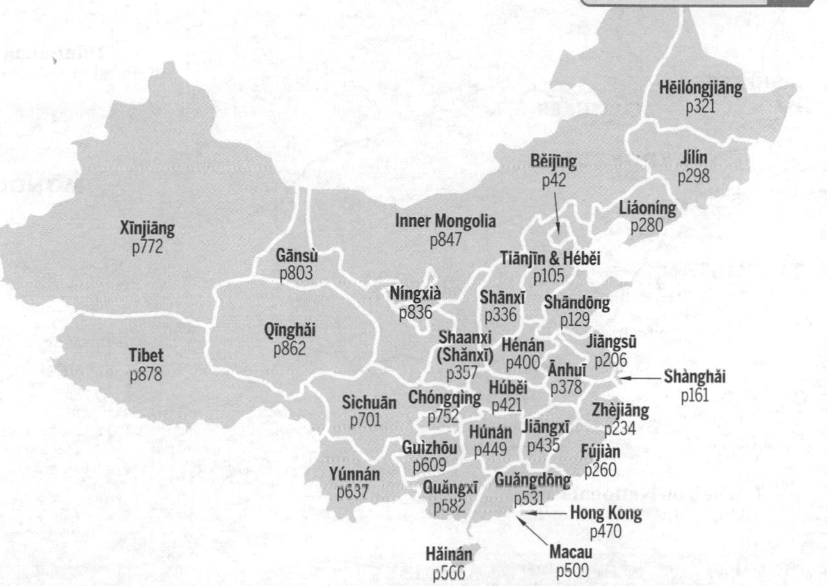

PAGE 979

SURVIVAL GUIDE

YOUR AT-A-GLANCE REFERENCE
How to get around, get a room, stay safe, say hello

Eating & Drinking
What would you recommend?
有什么菜可以推荐的?
What's in that dish?
这道菜用什么东西做的?
That was delicious!
真好吃!

THIS EDITION WRITTEN AND RESEARCHED BY

Damian Harper

Piera Chen, Chung Wah Chow, Min Dai, David Eimer, Robert Kelly, Michael Kohn, Shawn Low, Bradley Mayhew, Daniel McCrohan, Christopher Pitts

❯China

0 500 km
0 250 miles
Silk Road
Camels, deserts and vanished cities (p794)
Dūnhuáng
Silk Road oasis town (p825)
Jiǔzhàigōu National Park
Hiking in the beautiful wilds of Sìchuān (p748)
Lhasa
The land of snows (p882)
Tiger Leaping Gorge
Stunning Yúnnán scenery (p670)
Yuányáng Rice Terraces
For beautiful, iconic views (p652)
RUSSIA
KAZAKHSTAN
MONGOLIA
KYRGYZSTAN
TAJIKISTAN
PAKISTAN
INDIA
NEPAL
BHUTAN
BANGLADESH
MYANMAR (BURMA)
THAILAND
LAOS
TASHKENT
BISHKEK
ISLAMABAD
DELHI
KATHMANDU
THIMPHU
DHAKA
XĪNJIĀNG
TIBET
QĪNGHǍI
GĀNSÙ
SÌCHUĀN
YÚNNÁN
Xīnjiāng
Bólè
Yīníng
Kuqa
Kashgar
Tashkurgan
Yengisar
Yarkand
Dūnhuáng
Zhāngyè
Dégé
Xīníng
Xiàhé
Shílín
Lhasa
Téngchōng
Mènglà
Zhōngdiàn (Shangri-la)
Mèngyǎn
Shíbǎoshān
Xiàguān (Dàlǐ City)
Kūnmíng
Jǐnghóng
Jǐngzhēn
Indus River
Qīnghǎi Hú
Changtang Nature Preserve
Lake Manasarovar
Milam Glacier
Siling-tso
Nam-tso
Ngul-chu
Mt Everest (8488m)
Thimphu Valley
Yangzi River
Bay of Bengal
218
315
109
214
318
ELEVATION
7000m
6000m
5000m
4000m
3000m
2000m
1000m
500m
0

Top Experiences ›

30 TOP EXPERIENCES

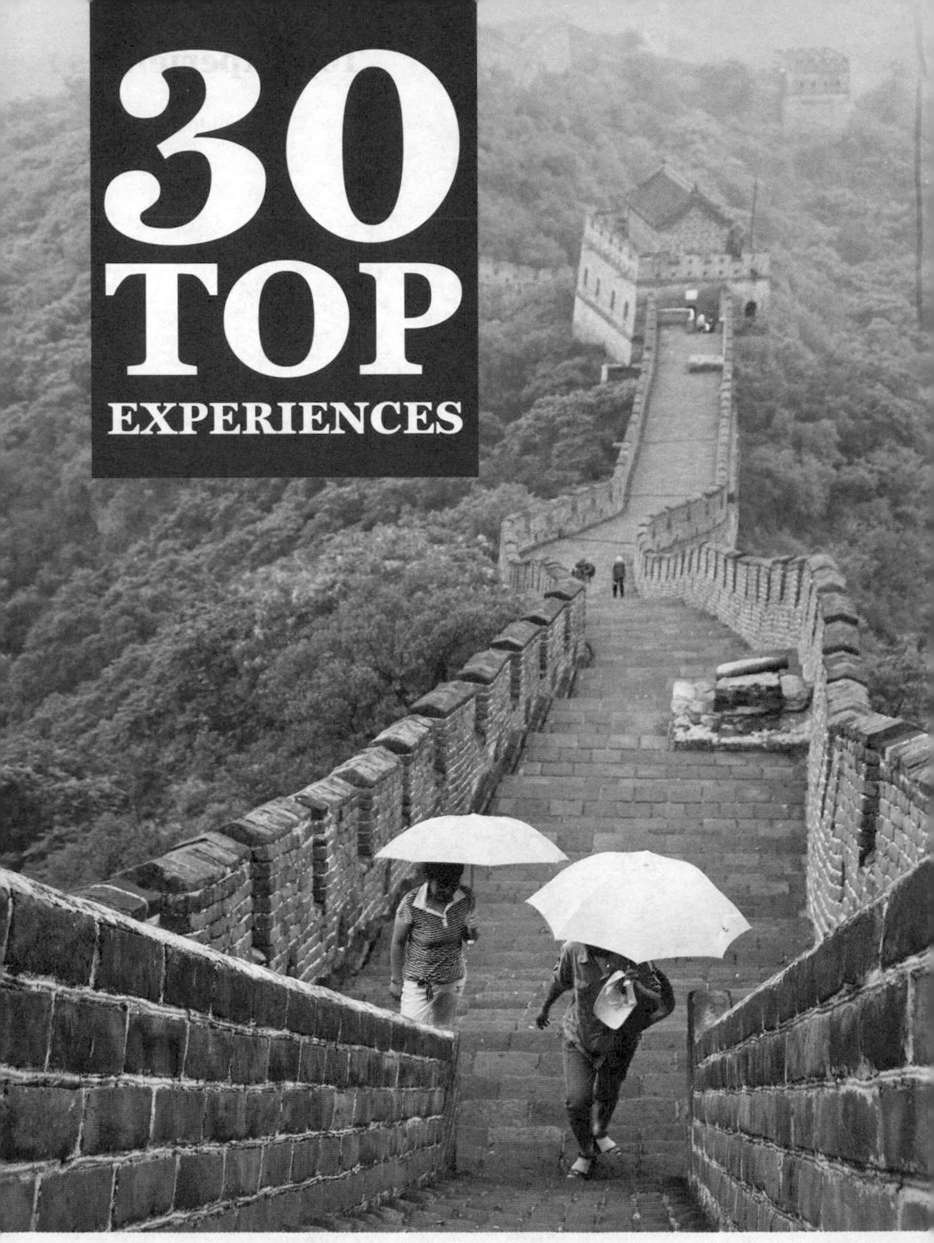

The Great Wall

1 Spotting it from space is both tough and pointless: the only place you can truly put the Great Wall (p98) under your feet is in China. Serve up the Great Wall according to taste: perfectly chiselled, dilapidated, stripped of its bricks, overrun with saplings, coiling splendidly into the hills or returning to dust. Offering an epic journey across north China, the fortification is a fitting symbol of those perennial Chinese traits: diligence, mass manpower, ambitious vision, engineering skill (and distrust of the neighbours).

French Concession, Shànghǎi

2 More than just a city, Shànghǎi (p161) is the country's neon-lit beacon of change, opportunity and sophistication. With its sights set squarely on the not-too-distant future, this is where you come for a taste of all the superlatives China can dare to dream up, from the world's highest observation deck to its largest underground theatre. Whether it's your first stop or you're just pulling in after an epic 40-hour train trip from Xīnjiāng, you'll find plenty to indulge in here. Start with the French Concession, the epicentre of food, fashion and fun.

KEREN SU

The Forbidden City

3 Not a city and no longer forbidden, Běijīng's enormous palace (p47) is the be-all-and-end-all of dynastic grandeur, with its vast halls, splendid gates and age-old relics. No other place in China teems with so much history, legend and good old-fashioned imperial intrigue. From imposing palace halls to dazzling imperial collections, it doesn't come much better. You may get totally lost here but you'll always find something you'll want to write about on the first postcard you can lay your hands on.

YAN LIAO / PHOTOLIBRARY

Tiger Leaping Gorge

4 Picture snowcapped mountains rising on either side of a gorge so deep that you can be 2km above the river rushing across the rocks far below. Then imagine winding up and down trails that pass through tiny farming villages, where you can rest while enjoying views so glorious they defy superlatives. Cutting through remote northwest Yúnnán for 16 stunning kilometres, Tiger Leaping Gorge (p670) is a simply unmissable experience. Trekkers returning from the gorge invariably give it glowing reviews.

MARTIN MOOS

Yangzi River Cruise

5 Snow melting from the world's third pole – the high-altitude Tibet–Qīnghǎi plateau – is the source of China's mighty, life-giving Yangzi. The country's longest river, the Yangzi, surges dramatically west–east across the nation before pouring into the Pacific Ocean. The Yangzi reaches a dramatic crescendo with the Three Gorges, carved over the millennia by the inexorable persistence of the powerful waters. The gorges are a magnificent spectacle and the Yangzi River cruise (p766) is a rare chance to hang up your travelling hat, take a seat and leisurely watch the drama unfold.

Terracotta Warriors

6 Standing silent guard over their emperor for more than 2000 years, the terracotta warriors (p367) are one of the most extraordinary archaeological discoveries ever made. It's not just that there are thousands of the life-sized figures lined up in battle formation; it's the fact that no two of them are alike, with every single one of them bearing a distinct expression. This is an army, but it's one made up of individuals. Gazing at these superbly sculpted faces brings the past alive in an utterly unique way.

SEAN CAFFREY

Hiking Dragon's Backbone Rice Terraces

7 After a bumpy bus ride to the highland in northern Guǎngxī, you'll be dazzled by one of China's most archetypal and photographed landscapes: the splendidly named Dragon's Backbone Rice Terraces (p590). The region is a beguiling patchwork of minority villages, with sparkling layers of waterlogged terraced fields tenaciously climbing the hillsides. You'll be enticed into a game of village-hopping. The most invigorating walk between Píng'ān and Dàzhài villages offers the most spine-tingling views. Visit after the summer rains when the fields are glistening with reflections.

China's Cuisine

8 Say *zàijiàn* to that Chinatown schlock and *nǐhǎo* to a whole new world of food and flavour (see p940). For sure you'll find dim sum, noodles and dumplings aplenty, but there's also the liquid fire of a Chóngqìng hotpot, Tibetan cuisine, or the adventurous flavours of Kāifēng's night market. You'll see things you've never seen before, eat things you've never heard of and drink things *(báijiǔ)* that could lift a rocket into space. And that's just for starters.

ZYSZTOF DYDYNSKI

JULIET COOMBE

Fènghuáng

9 Houses perched precariously on stilts, ancestral halls, crumbling temples and gate towers set amidst a warren of back alleys full of shops selling mysterious foods and medicines – it's enough on its own to make the ancient town of Fènghuáng (p464) an essential stop. Add in the seductive setting on either side of the Tuó River and the chance to stay at an inn right by the water, and you have one of the most evocative towns in China.

JTB PHOTO/ PHOTOLIBRARY

Chángbái Shān

10 China's largest nature reserve (p299) ranges over an eye-opening 2100 sq km. It's not just the birch and pine forests that stretch to the horizon and harbour everything from tigers to rare ginseng; it's not just the endless vistas, the towering waterfalls and the 70km-long canyon with spear-like outcrops. It's volcanic Chángbái Shān itself and the caldera-filling Heaven Lake, a high-mountain body of azure waters revered by Chinese, Koreans and anyone lucky enough to stand on an overlooking peak and take in its awesome size and colours.

TIM MAKINS

Kashgar's Sunday Market

11 Avoid lunchtime, and arrive at the tail end of the Livestock Market (p787), when the crowds are vanishing and the tour buses have rolled on. Wander around and peek over the shoulders of traders as they inspect sheep, goats, camels and other beasts for sale.

Huángshān & Hui Villages

12 Shrouded in mist and light rain over 200 days a year, and maddeningly crowded most of the time, Huángshān (p389) has an appeal that attracts millions of annual visitors. Perhaps it's the barren landscape, or an otherworldly vibe on the mountain. Mist – a fickle mistress – rolls in and out at will; spindly bent pines stick out like lone pins across sheer cragged granite faces. Not far from the base are the perfectly preserved Hui villages including Xīdì (p385) and Hóngcūn (p385). Unesco, Ang Lee and Zhang Yimou were captivated; you'll be too.

KEREN SU

Diāolóu in Kāipíng

MICHAEL COYNE

13 If you only have time for one attraction in Guǎngdōng, Kāipíng's *diāolóu* (p548) should be it. Approximately 1800 outlandishly designed fortress-fashioned residences scatter higgledy-piggledy in the farmland in Kāipíng, a town not far from Guǎngzhōu. These sturdy bastions built in the early 20th century may not be what you'd typically expect in the middle kingdom, but they inspire awe with their eccentric fusion of foreign and domestic architectural styles. Greek, Roman, Gothic, Byzantine and baroque – you name it, they've got it.

Cycling Hǎinán

14 The same blue skies and balmy weather that make China's only tropical island (p566) ideal for a do-nothing holiday, make it superb for exploring on a bicycle. Hit the east for picturesque rice-growing valleys, spectacular bays and some of Asia's finest beaches. And don't miss the sparsely populated central highlands, a densely forested region that's home to the island's original settlers, the Li and the Miao. Here, even the road more taken is still not taken by many at all.

JTB PHOTO/ PHOTOLIBRARY.COM

MERTEN SNIJDERS

Lhasa

15 The holy city of Lhasa (p882) is the perfect introduction to Tibet, and just arriving here can make the hairs stand up on the back of your neck. The spectacular prayer halls of the Potala Palace, the medieval Jokhang Temple and the monastic cities of Drepung and Sera are the big draws, but don't miss the less-visited side chapels and pilgrim paths. The whitewashed winding alleys of the old town hold the real heart of the Tibetan quarter, and you could spend hours here wandering around backstreet handicraft workshops, hidden temples and local teahouses.

Hiking Jiāngxī

16 Jiāngxī (p435) is one of those provinces that you might overlook when planning the itinerary. Jiang-who? Jiang-where? Well, guess what: it's not only full of bucolic scenery, it's also a convenient train ride just west of Shànghǎi. Few people have heard of the Taoist spires of Sānqīng Shān or the ancient post roads of Wùyuán, which link up the whitewashed villages of old Huīzhōu. But if you have a good pair of shoes and are looking to explore China's countryside, Jiāngxī could be for you.

NS CNS/PHOTOLIBRARY

Yuányáng Rice Terraces

17 Hewn out of hills that stretch off into the far distance, the rice terraces of Yuányáng (p652) are testimony to the wonderfully intimate relationship the local Hani people have with the sublime landscape they live in. Rising like giant steps, the intricate terraces are a stunning sight at any time of year. But when they are flooded in winter and the sun's rays are dancing off the water at sunrise or sunset, they're absolutely mesmerising. Just make sure you have enough space on your camera's memory card.

Lí River Scenery, Guǎngxī

18 It's hard to exaggerate the beauty of the Lí River (p597), one of the classic, legendary images travellers tend to have of China, with weeping willow trees leaning over bubbling streams, wallowing water buffalos, and farmers sowing the fields against a backdrop of mossy-green jagged limestone peaks. Ride a bamboo raft along the river and you'll understand why this stunning rural landscape has inspired painters and poets for centuries. Relax, enjoy the tranquility and the dramatic scenery as you float gently down this peaceful river.

MARTIN MOOS

The Great Buddha, Lèshān

19 You can read all the stats you like about Lèshān's Great Buddha (p722) – yes, its ears really are 7m long! – but until you descend the steps alongside the world's tallest Buddha statue and stand beside its feet, with its toenails at the same level as your eyes, you can't really comprehend just how massive it is. Still not impressed? Consider then that this wonderful, riverside stone statue was carved painstakingly into that cliff face above you, more than 1200 years ago.

GREG ELMS

Taichi

20 Ethereal form of moving meditation to some, awesome arsenal of martial-arts techniques to others, taichi (p975) is quintessentially Chinese. Daily practice could add a decade or more to your lifespan or give you some handy moves for getting on those crowded buses. And it's not all slow-going: Chen style has snappy elements of Shàolín boxing and it'll give you a leg-busting workout. Find a teacher – in Běijīng, Shànghǎi, Yángshuò, Wǔdāngshān – and put some magic and mystery into your China adventure.

Labrang Monastery

21 If you can't make it to Tibet, visit this more accessible part of the historic Tibetan region of Amdo in Gānsù. One moment you are in Han China, the next you are virtually in Tibet. Labrang Monastery (p812), in the town of Xiàhé, attracts legions of suntanned Tibetan pilgrims who perambulate single-mindedly around the huge monastery's prayer wheel-lined *kora* (pilgrim path). As a strong source of spiritual power, the monastery casts its spell far and wide, and with great trekking opportunities plus an intriguing ethnic mix, it's a fascinating corner of China.

CHRISTOPHER HERWIG

MARTIN MOOS

Dūnhuáng

22 Where China starts transforming into a lunar desertscape in the far west, the handsome oasis town of Dūnhuáng (p825) is a natural staging post for dusty Silk Road explorers. Mountainous sand dunes swell outside town while Great Wall fragments lie scoured by abrasive desert winds, but it is the magnificent caves at Mògāo (p828) that truly dazzle. Mògāo is the cream of China's crop of Buddhist caves, and its statues are ineffably sublime and perhaps the nation's most superlative cultural treasures.

Cycling Yángshuò

23 Embarking on a full-day bike tour along the Yùlóng River is the ultimate way to enjoy the incredible natural beauty in this verdant valley. Indeed, this is the place that usually leaves the biggest impression on most visitors to Yángshuò (p592). Pack your lunch and some water and enjoy a picnic along the banks. Whether it's just meandering along a small farmer's path between the paddy fields or sitting by the river admiring the rural and karst landscape, you'll fondly remember your time in this river valley.

ROBERT KELLY

Mt Kailash, Western Tibet

24 Worshipped by more than a billion Buddhists and Hindus, Asia's most sacred mountain (p901) rises from the Barkha plain like a giant four-sided 6714m-high *chörten* (stupa). Throw in stunning nearby Lake Manasarovar and a basin that forms the source of four of Asia's greatest rivers, and it's clear that this place is truly special. Travel here to one of the world's most beautiful and remote corners, brings a bonus: the three-day pilgrim path around the mountain erases the sins of a lifetime.

KEREN SU

The Silk Road

25 There are other Silk Road cities in countries like Uzbekistan and Turkmenistan, but it's in China where you really get the feeling of stepping on the actual 'Silk Road'. Travel by bus and experience the route as ancient traders once did – mile by mile, town by town. Kashgar (p786) is the ultimate Silk Road town and today remains a unique melting pot of peoples, but Hotan (p796) is perhaps equally special: a rough-and-tumble town still clinging to bygone days.

Píngyáo

26 Time-warped Píngyáo (p349) is a true gem: an intact, walled Chinese town with an unbroken sense of continuity to its Qing-dynasty heyday. The town ticks most of your China boxes with a convincing flourish: imposing city walls, narrow alleys, ancient shop fronts, traditional architecture, a litter of excellent hotels, a population of hospitable locals and a manageable size. You can literally travel the length and breadth of China and not find another city quite like it. In fact, when you discover Píngyáo, you may never want to leave.

ALDO PAVAN

WIBOWO RUSLI

Hiking in Jiǔzhàigōu National Park

27 Strolling the forested valleys of Jiǔzhàigōu National Park (p748) – past bluer-than-blue lakes and small Tibetan villages, in the shadow of snow-brushed mountains – was always a highlight of any trip to Sìchuān province, but an excellent new ecotourism scheme means travellers can now hike and even camp their way around this stunning part of southwest China. Guides speak English and all camping equipment is provided, so all you need to bring is your sense of adventure and a spare set of camera batteries.

GREG ELMS

Chinese Acrobatics

28 The Chinese are born performers. They may be famed for their fearless and extraordinary martial-arts skills, but the related discipline of acrobatics is equally mind-bending and the two arts frequently cross over. Wherever you go, look out for young street performers, defying physical limitations and doing impossible things with their spines, or watch joint-popping performances from professional troupes in Shànghǎi (p195) or Běijīng (p84) theatres. The Chinese for acrobatics, *zájì,* literally means 'miscellaneous skills', pointing to the art's all-embracing repertoire.

RICHARD I'ANSON

Cruising up Victoria Harbour

29 A buzzer sounds, you bolt for the gangplank. A whistle blows, your boat chugs forward. Beyond the waves, one of the world's most famous views unfolds – Hong Kong's sky-scrapers in their steel and neon splendour, against a backdrop of mountains. You're on the Star Ferry (p508), a legendary service that's been carrying passengers between Hong Kong Island and Kowloon Peninsula since the 19th century. At the end of 10 minutes, a hemp rope is cast, then a bell rings, and you alight. At only HK$2, this is possibly the world's best-value cruise.

Běijīng's Hútòng

30 To truly get under the skin of the capital, you need to get lost at least once in the city's ancient alleyways (p63). Běijīng's DNA can be found here: it's *hútòng* life that makes Běijīng people so warm and fun to be around. The city may be trying to sell itself as a 21st-century metropolis, but Běijīng's true charms – heavenly courtyard architecture, pinched lanes, one-storey higgledy-piggledy rooftops and a strong sense of community – were never high-rise. It's easy: check into a courtyard hotel, stay put for a few days, and true Běijīng will be right on your doorstep.

GREG ELMS

welcome to China

Antique yet up-to-the-minute, familiar yet unrecognisable, outwardly urban but quintessentially rural, conservative yet path-breaking, space-age but old-fashioned, China is a land of mesmerising and eye-opening contradictions.

Awe-Inspiring Antiquity

China may be modernising at a head-spinning pace, but the slick skyscrapers, Lamborghini showrooms and Maglev trains are just eye-catching but wafer-thin gift-wrapping. Let's face it: the world's oldest continuous civilisation is bound to pull an artefact or two out of its hat. Travel selectively around China and you can quickly tap into a rich seam of antiquity: ponder the legends and myths of the Forbidden City, rediscover your sense of wonder on the Great Wall or attempt to fathom the timeless expressions of the silent Terracotta Warriors. Submit to the unique charms of Píngyáo – China's best preserved walled town – or get a glimpse of Nirvana at the serene Mògāo Caves outside Dūnhuáng. Meander among the historic villages of Wùyuán, wake with the cock crow in an ancient Hakka roundhouse or join well-dressed Tibetan pilgrims on their circuitous *kora* around Labrang monastery.

Out-of-This-World Flavours

China is famously fixated with food but do yourself a favour and exchange your meagre local Chinatown menu for the lavish Middle Kingdom cookbook. Wolf down Peking duck, size up a sizzling lamb kebab in Kāifēng or gobble down a bowl of Lánzhōu noodles on the Silk Road. Spicy Húnán food really raises the temperature but find time for *momo* (boiled dumplings), *tsampa* (roasted barley flour porridge) and other titbits from Tibet. Impress your friends as you *gānbēi* (down-in-one) the local firewater, sip a frozen daiquiri in a slick Běijīng bar or survey the Shànghǎi skyline through a raised cocktail glass. Second to none, the never-ending culinary adventure is possibly the most enticing aspect of Middle Kingdom travel and you'll come back from China with highly stimulated taste buds and much-cherished gastronomic memories.

Stupendous Scenery

China is vast. Off-the-scale massive. And you've just got to get outside: island-hop in Hong Kong, gaze out over the epic grasslands of Inner Mongolia or squint up at the mind-blowing peaks of the Himalayas. Trek your way around Tiger Leaping Gorge or cycle between the fairy-tale karst pinnacles of Yángshuò. Ponder the desiccated enormity of the Taklamakan Desert or swoon at Huángshān's preternatural mists. Become entranced by the Yuányáng Rice Terraces of Yúnnán, size up the awesome sand dunes of Dūnhuáng, hike your way around the exquisite landscape of Déhāng or, when your energy fails you, flake out for a tan on the distant beaches of Hǎinán island.

need to know

Currency

» The yuan (Y)

Language

» Mandarin

» Cantonese

When to Go

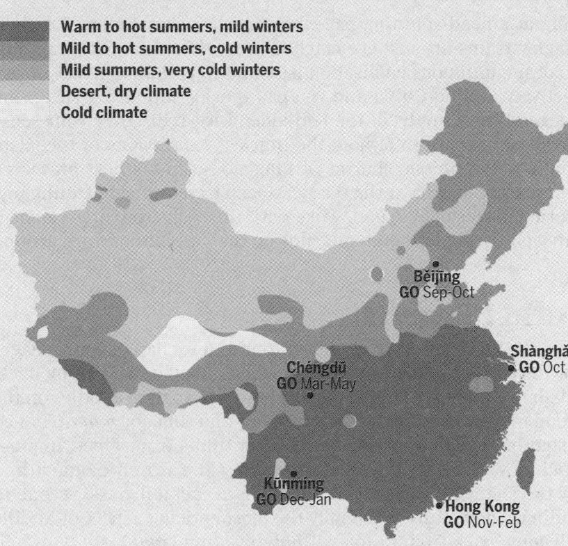

High Season
(May–Aug)

» Prepare for crowds at traveller hot spots and summer downpours.

» Accommodation prices peak during first week of the May holiday period.

Shoulder
(Feb–Apr, Sep & Oct)

» Expect warmer days in spring, cooler days in autumn.

» Autumn in north China is the optimum season weather-wise with clear skies and fresh weather.

» Accommodation prices peak during holidays in October.

Low Season
(Nov–Feb)

» Domestic tourism is at low ebb, but things are busy and expensive for the Chinese New Year.

» Weather is bitterly cold in the north and only warm in the far south.

Set Your Daily Budget

Budget less than
Y200

» Dorm Beds: Y40–Y50

» Excellent, very cheap hole-in-the-wall restaurants and food markets

» Affordable internet access and bike hire

» Some free museums

Midrange
Y200–Y1000

» Double room in a midrange hotel: Y200–Y600

» Lunch and dinner in decent local restaurants

Top end over
Y1000

» Double room in a top-end hotel: start at Y600

» Lunch and dinner in excellent local or hotel restaurants

» Shopping at top-end shops

Money
» ATMs in big cities and towns. Credit cards less widely used; always carry cash.

Visas
» Needed for all visits to China except Hong Kong and Macau. Additional permit required for Tibet and a few other areas.

Mobile Phones
» Inexpensive pay-as-you-go SIM cards can be bought locally for most mobile phones. Buying a local mobile phone is also cheap.

Transport
» The train and bus network is extensive, domestic and air routes are plentiful. Cars can be hired with a temporary Chinese driving licence.

Websites
» **Lonely Planet** (www.lonelyplanet.com/china) Destination information, hotel bookings, traveller forum and more.

» **Ctrip** (www.english.ctrip.com) Excellent hotel booking website and air ticketing.

» **Danwei** (www.danwei.org) Informative perspectives into real China; handy links.

» **Zhongwen** (www.zhongwen.com) Includes a pinyin chat room and online dictionary of Chinese characters.

Exchange Rates

Australia	A$1	Y6.32
Canada	C$1	Y6.70
Euro zone	€1	Y10.36
Hong Kong	HK$1	Y0.98
Japan	¥100	Y6.50
New Zealand	NZ$1	Y5.58
Singapore	S$1	Y5.10
UK	UK£1	Y15.22
USA	US$1	Y7.72

For current exchange rates see www.xe.com.

Important Numbers

Ambulance	☎120
Fire	☎119
Police	☎110
Country code (China/Hong Kong/Macau)	☎86/852/853
International access code	☎00
Directory assistance	☎114

Arriving in China
» **Běijīng Capital Airport**
Airport Express – Every 15 minutes
Express Buses – To centre of Běijīng every 10 to 20 minutes
Taxi – Y85; 30 to 60 minutes to town

» **Shànghǎi Pǔdōng International Airport**
Maglev – Every 20 minutes
Metro – Line 2 to Hóngqiáo Airport; 75 minutes to People's Sq
Airport Buses – Every 15 to 25 minutes
Taxi – Y160; around an hour into town

» **Hong Kong International Airport**
Airport Express – Every 12 minutes
Taxi – About HK$300 (40 minutes) to Central

English in China
English is not widely spoken in China, apart from in Hong Kong. Outside of, and even inside, big cities such as Běijīng and Shànghǎi, you will frequently find English is useless, so avail yourself of the written Chinese in this book for Chinese phrases and as a guide to pronunciation. For first-time users of the language, Chinese pronunciation is tricky and getting the correct tone harder still, while showing the written Chinese to a local person immediately conveys the meaning. Youth hostels often have the best English-speaking staff so never assume the more expensive a hotel, the better the English level of the staff. Even at five-star hotels, you may encounter incomprehension. Restaurants in this book with English menus come with an English menu icon (📋).

if you like...

Imperial Architecture

If ancient monuments are your cup of *chá*, you can't go far wrong in China. Crumbling dynasties have scattered an imposing trail of antiquity across north China from vast imperial palaces to noble ruins of the Great Wall and altars reserved for the emperor. Běijīng should be your first port of call, before exploring the ancient dynastic cities of Kāifēng, Xī'ān and Dàtóng.

Forbidden City China's standout imperial residence, home to two dynasties of emperors and their concubines (p47)

Summer Palace An epic demonstration of traditional Chinese aesthetics with all essential ingredients: hills, lakes, bridges, pavilions and temples (p68)

Imperial Palace Manchu splendour in the former Manchurian heartland of Liǎoníng province (p282)

Kāifēng The funky Northern Song capital survives with its city wall and a winning crop of historic sights (p415)

Chéngdé Summer bolt-hole of the Qing emperors, with palatial remains and a riveting brood of Tibetan-style temples (p118)

The Great Wall

Don't just follow the crowds to Bādálǐng to the over-restored and over-visited sections of wall; get off the beaten path and discover the real wall. Indeed, the wall doesn't just belong to Běijīng: fragments create a long band across much of north China, running from the North Korean border to the windswept deserts of China's wild west.

Jiànkòu Běijīng's prime chunk of Great Wall ruin, a sublime portrait of disintegrating masonry, overgrown with trees and set against a magnificent mountain panorama (p103)

Jiāyùguān Fort Come face-to-face with weathered slogans from Mao's Cultural Revolution scoured by the Gānsù desert winds (p822)

Huánghuā Excellent trekking opportunities along some of the most authentic sections of wall around Běijīng (p103)

Modern Architecture

Befitting its repositioning on the world stage, China is reaching for the stars with some dazzling and funky newfangled architecture. What's more, you don't have to be a building buff to get a buzz from the sleek skyline of Shànghǎi or Hong Kong; all you need is a taste for the up-to-the-minute and unexpected, a fondness for head-spinning heights and a sense of wonder.

Shànghǎi World Financial Center Over a decade in the making, but worth the wait (p175)

CCTV Building 'Big Underpants' to locals, a master class in engineering complexity to others (p65)

National Centre for the Performing Arts The opinion-dividing Běijīng edifice drops jaws whatever your perspective or persuasion (p54)

Bird's Nest Aka the National Stadium, the flagship structure ties top with the medal table as the highlight of the 2008 Olympic Games (p65)

» Watchtowers on Píngyáo's ancient city walls (p349)

SEAN CAFFREY

Ancient Settlements

When you've had enough of the big, big city, China's traditional livelihoods can still be glimpsed in its picturesque, ancient villages. Here Ming- and Qing-dynasty architecture, pinched, narrow lanes and superlative feng shui combine to create a pastoral aesthetic complemented by a relaxed rural tempo. Some rural settlements are home to ethnic minorities and their distinctive building styles.

Píngyáo China's best-looking, best-preserved walled town – by a long shot – warrants thorough exploration (p349)

Hóngcūn Within easy reach of Huángshān, this delightful Ānhuī village is a good-looking primer in the Huīzhōu style (p385)

Wùyuán Take time off to village-hop in the gorgeous Jiāngxī countryside and dream of abandoning urban China for good (p443)

Hakka earth buildings Explore the fortress-like Hakka earthen 'roundhouses', which are found in Guǎngdōng, Fújiàn and Jiāngxī, and are noted for their architectural uniqueness (p269)

Fènghuáng Jump back in time to this funky town in west Húnán (p464)

Urban Extravaganzas

China's most dynamic and stylish dimension belongs to cities like Shànghǎi, where glittering skyscrapers overlook Maglev trains, and tribes of hard-working/hard playing yuppies shop in chic malls, drink at elegant cocktail bars and dine at fashionable restaurants. China's unfathomable reservoirs of energy, manpower and wherewithal are sucked up by its leading cities for transmutation into iconic skylines.

Shànghǎi The city that somehow single-handedly achieved the repositioning of China in the global psyche (p161)

Hong Kong Caught resplendently between China and the West, the ex-British colony still ploughs its own lucrative furrow on the south China coastline (p470)

Běijīng Engaging blend of ancient capital and modern metropolis, China's leading city matches its newfound guise with a bevy of historical sights (p42)

Chóngqìng One of China's fastest-developing urban zones, the megalopolis of Chóngqìng continues its stunning growth but still finds time to send flotillas of tour boats down the unequalled Three Gorges (p752)

Boat Trips

China has some dramatic and breathtaking rivers, including the mighty Yangzi River, which snakes across the width of China from its origins as snowmelt on the Tibet–Qīnghǎi plateau. Occasionally it's time to unplug from travel on the road in China and ease into a totally different experience of its landscapes. Hopping on a riverboat to explore China's riverine panoramas is an excellent way to shift to a lower gear and watch the landscape drift effortlessly by.

Three Gorges China's most awesome riverine panorama (p766)

Lí River The dreamlike karst landscapes of northeast Guǎngxī (p597)

Star Ferry, Hong Kong The short but iconic ferry hop across Victoria Harbour from Tsim Sha Tsui (p508)

Evening river cruise, Chóngqìng Before getting all misty through the Three Gorges, experience Chóngqìng's nocturnal, neon performance (p754)

Qīngyuǎn boat trip, Guǎngdōng Lazily float along the Bei River from Qīngyuǎn past secluded Fēilái Temple and Fēixià monastery (p552)

SEAN CAFFREY

» View of Mt Everest from Everest Base Camp (p898)

Great Food

With its novel flavours, unexpected aromas and tastes, China is as much a culinary as a travel adventure. The big cities – Běijīng, Shànghǎi, Hong Kong – may be stuffed with Chinese and international dining options, but it may well be a meal in a small village tucked away up a distant mountainside that really raises your eyebrows. Head west for zing, zest and spice, north for hearty and salty flavours, east for fresh and lightly flavoured seafood, and south for dim sum. Don't forget China's border regions where ethnic minorities dish up something completely different.

Peking duck Once bitten, forever smitten, and only in Běijīng (p79)

Chóngqìng hotpot Sweat like never before over China's most volcanic culinary creation (p759)

Xiǎolóngbāo Shànghǎi's bite-sized snack packs a lot of flavour (but watch out for the super-heated meat juice)

Street food Across the nation, street snacks fill in between meals and cost a pittance

Museums

Mass modernisation means that collections are often the most observable link to China's past, and fortunately museums are simply everywhere, covering everything from ethnic clothing to Běijīng tap water. And with a growing number of provincial museums waiving the admission fee, they can be an affordable way to learn about local culture and history.

Palace Museum The official and highly prosaic name for the Forbidden City, China's supreme link to its dynastic past (p47)

Shànghǎi Museum A scintillating collection of ceramics, paintings, calligraphy and much more at the heart of Shànghǎi (p166)

Poly Art Museum Bronzes and Bodhisattvas in Běijīng (p65)

Hong Kong Museum of History Entertaining, resourceful and informative leafing through the pages of Hong Kong history (p481)

Cultural Revolution Museum One-of-a-kind in China and a testament to an almost forgotten decade (p562)

Sacred China

Modern China's modern overlays – a curious combination of communism, epic traffic jams and Yves Saint Laurent – cannot conceal the nation's compelling spiritual seam. So get exploring! From the esoteric mysteries of Tibetan Buddhism to the Taoist magic underpinning the soft martial arts and the country's scattered collection of Christian churches, China's sacred realm is the point at which the supernatural and natural worlds converge.

Wǔdāng Shān Commune with the spirit of the Taoist martial arts at the birthplace of taichi (p430)

Pǔníng Temple, Chéngdé Be rendered entirely speechless by China's largest wooden statue, a vast effigy of the Buddhist Goddess of Mercy (p121)

Labrang Monastery Tap into the ineffable rhythms of south Gānsù's place of pilgrimage for legions of Tibetans (p812)

Gyantse Kumbum An overwhelming and monumental sight and experience, the nine-tiered *chörten* is Tibet's largest stupa (p894)

If you like... communist collectives
Spend a day exploring Nánjiēcūn, China's last Maoist collective (p406)

If you like... beer
Head to seaside Dàlián for its International Beer Festival in July (p289)

Trekking

Despite the unremitting media barrage detailing its rapid urbanisation, China is one of the world's largest and most geographically varied nations, so it's hardly surprising that stupendous opportunities exist amid some astonishing scenery. Trekking is perhaps the best way to see China, with its combination of physical exertion, stunning backdrops, ethnic minority life and the chance of encountering the unexpected. Generally speaking, the further west and southwest you travel from Běijīng, the more exciting the trekking opportunities.

Tiger Leaping Gorge Yúnnán's best-known and most enticing trek, but it's not for the faint-hearted (p670)

Dragon's Backbone Rice Terraces Work your way from Dàzhài to Píng'ān through some of China's most delicious scenery (p590)

Wùyuán Follow the old postal roads from village to village in the drop-dead gorgeous Jiāngxī countryside (p446)

Lángmùsì Excellent trekking options radiate in most directions from the charming monastic town on the Gānsù–Sìchuān border (p818)

Ethnic Minorities

Han China hits the buffers around its extensive borderlands, where a colourful patchwork of ethnic minorities preserve distinct cultures, languages, architectural styles and livelihoods. From Yúnnán, Guìzhōu and the southwest to Tibet, Xīnjiāng, Inner Mongolia and the hardy northeast, China is a vibrantly rich nation of contrasting peoples and traditions, all awaiting exploration. Even in the 21st century, you can still encounter people who have never seen Westerners in the flesh (so be on your best behaviour).

Tibet Explore this vast region in the west of China or jump aboard our itinerary (p32) through the easier-to-access regions outside the Tibetan heartland

Déhāng This Miao village in Húnán finds itself delightfully embedded in some breathtaking scenery (p462)

Lìjiāng Yúnnán's famous home of the blue-clothed Naxi folk affords glorious views on to the stunning slopes of Yúlóng Xuěshān (p661)

Kashgar Dusty Central Asian outpost and Uighur China's most famous town, on the far side of the Taklamakan Desert (p786)

Stunning Scenery

You haven't really experienced China until you've had your socks blown off by one of its scenic marvels. China's man-made splendours have lent cities like Shànghǎi head-turning cachet, but Mother Nature yet again steals the show. Get the smog out of your lungs and make a break for the hills (and take along that extra pair of socks).

Yángshuò You've probably seen the karst topography before in picture-perfect photographs; now see the real thing (p592)

Huángshān When suffused in their spectral mists, China's Yellow Mountains enter a different dimension of beauty (p389)

Jiǔzhàigōu Nature Reserve Turquoise lakes, waterfalls, snow-capped mountains and green forests: all this and more (p748)

Chìshuǐ Trek past waterfalls and through ancient forests of fern dating to the Jurassic (p627)

Everest Base Camp Rise early for dramatic images of the mountain in the morning sun (p898)

Yuányáng Rice Terraces Be simply transfixed by the dazzling display of light and water (p652)

month by month

Top Events

1. **Monlam Great Prayer Festival,** February or March
2. **Naadam,** July
3. **Běijīng International Literary Festival,** March
4. **Spring Festival,** January, February or March
5. **Luoyang Peony Festival,** April

January

North China is a deep freeze but the south is much better; preparations for the Chinese New Year get under way well in advance of the festival, which arrives any time between late January and March.

Spring Festival

The Chinese New Year is family-focused, with dining on dumplings and gift-giving of *hóngbāo* (red envelopes stuffed with money). Most families feast together on the New Year's Eve, then China goes on a big week-long holiday. Expect fireworks, parades and temple fairs.

Hā'ěrbīn Ice Festival

Hēilóngjiāng's good-looking capital Hā'ěrbīn is all aglow with rainbow lights refracted through fancifully carved buildings and statues carved from blocks of ice. It's outrageously cold, but that's the whole point.

Yuányáng Rice Terraces

The watery winter is the optimum season for the rice terraces' spectacular combination of liquid and light. Don't forget your camera (or your sense of wonder).

February

North China remains shockingly cold and dry but things are slowly warming up in Hong Kong and Macau. The Chinese New Year could well be firing on all cylinders but sort out your tickets well in advance.

Monlam Great Prayer Festival

Held over two weeks from the third day of the Tibetan New Year and celebrated with spectacular processions across the huge Tibetan world; huge silk *thangka* are unveiled and, on the last day, a statue of the Maitreya Buddha is conveyed around towns and monasteries; catch it in Xiàhé.

Lantern Festival

Held 15 days after the Spring Festival, this celebration was traditionally a time when Chinese hung out highly decorated lanterns. Lantern-hung Píngyáo in Shānxī is an atmospheric place to enjoy the festival (sometimes held in March).

March

China comes back to life after a long winter, although high-altitude parts of China remain glacial. The mercury climbs in Hong Kong and abrasive dust storms billow into Běijīng. Admission prices are still low-season.

Běijīng Book Bash

Curl up with a good book at the Bookworm Cafe (p83) for Běijīng's International Literary Festival, and lend an ear to lectures from international and domestic authors. Also earmark Shànghǎi for its International Literary Festival in the Bund-side Glamour Bar (p194) or the Man Hong Kong International Literary Festival.

Fields of Yellow

Delve into south Chinese countryside and be bowled over by a landscape saturated in bright yellow rapeseed. In some parts of China, such as lovely Wùyuán in Jiāngxī province, it's a real tourist draw.

April

Most of China is warm so it's a good time to be on the road, ahead of the May holiday period and before China's summer reaches its full power.

A Good Soaking

Flush away the dirt, demons and sorrows of the old, old year and bring in the fresh Dai New Year with vast amounts of water at the Water-splashing festival in Xīshuāngbǎnnà. Taking an umbrella is pointless.

Paeon to Peonies

Wángchéng Park in Luòyáng bursts into full-coloured bloom with its Peony Festival: pop a flower garland on your head and join in the floral fun (but don't forget your camera).

Third Moon Festival

This Bai ethnic minority festival is an excellent reason to pitch up in the lovely north Yúnnán town of Dàlǐ. It's a week of horse racing, singing and merrymaking at the end of April and the beginning of May.

Formula One

Petrol heads and aficionados of speed, burnt rubber and hairpin bends flock to Shànghǎi for some serious motor racing at the track near Anting. Get your hotel room booked early: it's one of the most glamorous events on the Shànghǎi calendar.

May

China is in full bloom in mountain regions such as Sìchuān's Wòlóng Nature Reserve. The first four days of May sees China on vacation for one of the three big holiday periods, kicking off with Labour Day (1 May).

Walking Around the Mountain Festival

On Pǎomǎ Shān, Kāngdìng's famous festival celebrates the birthday of Sakyamuni, the historical Buddha, with a magnificent display of horse racing, wrestling and a street fair.

Great Wall Marathon

Experience the true meaning of pain (but get your Great Wall sightseeing done and dusted at the same time). Not for the infirm or unfit (or the cable-car fraternity). See www.great-wall-marathon.com for more details.

June

Most of China is hot and getting hotter. Once-frozen areas, such as Jílín's Heaven Lake, are accessible – and nature springs instantly to life. The great peak season is cranking up.

Dragon Boat Festival

Find yourself the nearest large river and catch all the waterborne drama of Dragon Boat racers in this celebration of one of China's most famous poets. The Chinese traditionally eat *zòngzi* (triangular glutinous rice dumplings wrapped in reed leaves).

July

Typhoons can wreak havoc with travel itineraries down south, lashing the Guǎngdōng and Fújiàn coastlines. Plenty of rain sweeps across China: the big 'plum rains' give Shànghǎi a serious soaking and the grasslands of Inner Mongolia turn green.

Mongolian Merrymaking

Mongolian wrestling, horse racing, archery and more during the week-long Naadam festival on the grasslands of Inner Mongolia at the end of July, when the grasslands are at their summer best.

August

The temperature gauge of the 'three ovens' of Yangzi-region China – Chóngqìng, Wǔhàn and Nánjīng – gets set to blow. Rainstorms hit Běijīng, which is usually way over 40°C; so is Shànghǎi. So head uphill: Lúshān, Mògānshān, Huángshān or Guōliàngcūn.

Qīngdǎo International Beer Festival

Slake that chronic summer thirst with a round of beers and devour a plate of mussels in Shāndōng's best-looking port town, home of the Tsingtao beer brand.

September

Come to Běijīng and stay put – September is part of the fleetingly lovely *tiāngāo qìshuǎng* ('the sky is high and the air is fresh') autumnal season – it's an event in itself.

Mid-Autumn Festival

Also called the Moon Festival. Locals celebrate by devouring daintily prepared moon cakes – stuffed with bean paste, egg yolk, walnuts and more. With a full-moon, it's a romantic occasion for lovers and a special time for families. It's on the 15th day of the eighth lunar month.

October

The first week of October can be hellish if you're on the road: the National Day week-long holiday kicks off, so everywhere is swamped. Go mid-month instead, when everywhere is deserted.

Kurban Bairam (Gu'erbang Jie)

Catch the four-day festivities of the Muslim Festival of Sacrifice in communities across China; the festival is at its liveliest and most colourful in Kashgar.

Hairy Crabs in Shànghǎi

Now's the time to sample delicious hairy crabs in Shànghǎi; they are at their best – male and female crabs eaten together with shots of lukewarm Shàoxīng rice wine – between October and December.

Miao New Year

Load up with rice wine and get on down to Guìzhōu for the ethnic festivities in the very heart of the minority-rich southwest.

November

Most of China is getting pretty cold as tourist numbers drop and holiday-goers begin to flock south for sun and the last pockets of warmth.

Surfing Hǎinán

Annual surfing competition in Shíméi Bay & Sun Moon Bay in Hǎinán as the surfing season gets under way and hordes of Chinese flee the cold mainland for the warmer climes of the southern island.

itineraries

Whether you've got six days or 60, these itineraries provide a starting point for the trip of a lifetime. Want more inspiration? Head online to lonelyplanet.com/thorntree to chat with other travellers.

Four Weeks

Crucial China

Běijīng is fundamental to this tour, so you'll need at least five days to do the **Forbidden City**, size yourself up against the **Great Wall**, wander like royalty around the **Summer Palace** and lose your bearings amid the city's **hútòng** (narrow alleyways). The magnificence of the **Yúngāng Caves** outside Dàtóng should put you in a Buddhist mood, a disposition further heightened by a few nights on monastic **Wǔtái Shān**. We recommend a three-day stopover in **Píngyáo**, an age-old walled town you thought all of China would look like, but actually doesn't. The historic walled city of **Kāifēng** in Hénán is the traditional home of China's small community of Chinese Jews and has a remarkable night market; move on to **Luòyáng** and the Buddhist spectacle of the **Lóngmén Caves** and the **Shàolín Temple**, also within reach. Four days' sightseeing in **Xī'ān** brings you face-to-face with the **Army of Terracotta Warriors** and gives you time for the Taoist mountain of **Huà Shān**. Xī'ān traditionally marked the start of the **Silk Road** which you can follow through **Gānsù** province all the way to the oasis-town of **Dūnhuáng**. From Dūnhuáng you can continue on into **Xīnjiāng** for a taste of the mighty northwest.

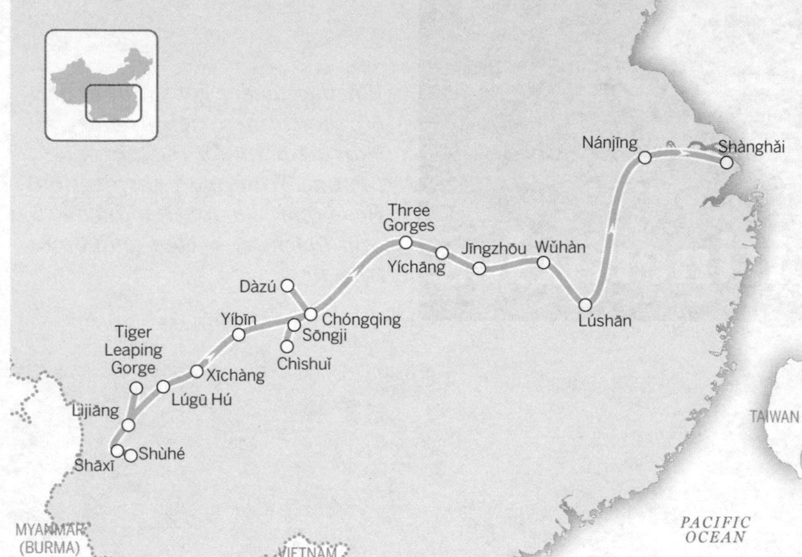

Three to Four Weeks

Yangzi River Tour

After exploring north Yúnnán's ancient Naxi town of **Lìjiāng**, pick up the trail of the **Jīnshā River** (Gold Sand River, which spills down from Tibet and swells into the Yangzi River) on a breathtaking multiday hike along **Tiger Leaping Gorge**. Rest your worn-out legs before discovering the scattered villages and old towns around Lìjiāng, including **Shāxī** and **Shùhé** on the old tea-horse road, and being blown away by the magnificent views of **Yùlóng Xuěshān**. Also consider a trip from Lìjiāng northeast towards west Sìchuān and the gorgeous **Lúgū Hú** on the provincial border, where you can spend several days unwinding by the lakeside. By the time you read this, there may be buses from Lúgū Lake to Xīchāng in Sìchuān and from there on to Yíbīn and then Chóngqìng (but the long route is via Chéngdū); otherwise you may have to return to Lìjiāng to fly to Chóngqìng, home of the spicy and searing Chóngqìng hotpot and gateway to the Three Gorges. Backtrack by bus to the stunning landscapes and natural beauty of Chìshuǐ on the Guìzhōu border to relax, unwind and explore the region before returning by bus to urban Chóngqìng. You'll need around three days in Chóngqìng for the sights in town and for a journey to the Buddhist Caves at Dàzú and a trip to the Yangzi River village of Sōngji to keep a perspective on historic, rural China. Then hop on either a hydrofoil, cruise vessel or passenger boat to Yíchāng in Húběi through the magnificent **Three Gorges**. Journey from Yíchāng to the Yangzi city of **Wǔhàn** via the walled town of **Jīngzhōu**, where it's worth spending the night. After two days in Wǔhàn, hop on a bus to **Lúshān** in Jiāngxī province, from where you can reach **Nánjīng** or make your way to **Huángshān** in the Yangzi River province of Ānhuī. Alternatively, travel direct to Nánjīng – Yangzi River capital of Jiāngsū – and thread your way to **Shànghǎi** via a delightful string of canal towns – **Sūzhōu**, **Tónglǐ**, **Lùzhí** and **Zhūjiājiǎo** – or go direct to Shànghǎi and plug yourself into the **East to South Village tour**.

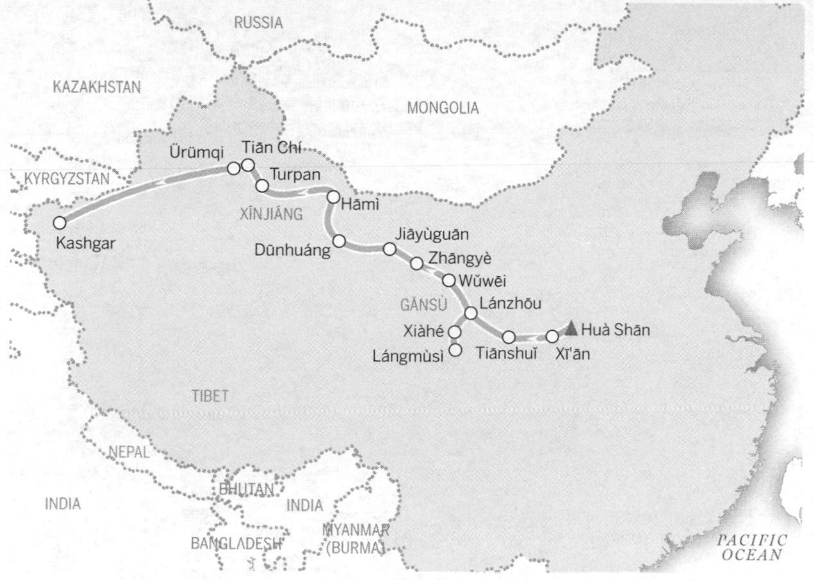

Three Weeks
Silk Road Tour

Picking up roughly where the **Crucial China tour** stops, this journey takes you on an epic and unforgettable journey from **Xī'ān** through **Gānsù** to **Xīnjiāng**. From the southernmost extents of the Silk Road at **Xī'ān**, discover one of imperial China's most iconic remains at the **Army of Terracotta Warriors** and, if you want a major workout, climb the precipitous Taoist mountain of **Huà Shān** – just don't look down. Explore the Muslim Quarter and feast on local Hui specialities. Hop aboard the train to **Lánzhōu** but disembark in southeast Gānsù at **Tiānshuǐ** for the remarkable Buddhist grottoes at verdant **Màijī Shān**. From Lánzhōu you have the option of disembarking temporarily from the Silk Road to ramble along the fringes of Tibet at the Buddhist monastic settlements of **Xiàhé** and **Lángmùsì**. The **Héxī Corridor** naturally draws you on to the ancient Great Wall outpost of **Jiāyùguān**, via the Silk Road stopover town of **Wǔwēi**, and the **Great Buddha Temple** with its outsize effigy of a reclining Sakyamuni in **Zhāngyè**. Stand on the wind-blasted ramparts of **Jiāyùguān Fort**, the last major stronghold of imperial China, and tramp alongside westerly remnants of the **Great Wall**. The delightful oasis outpost of **Dūnhuáng** is one of China's tidiest and most pleasant towns, with the mighty **Singing Sands Mountains** pushing up from the south, a scattered array of sights in the surrounding desert and some excellent food. The town also brings you into contact with perhaps China's most splendid accumulation of Buddhist art, the spellbinding **Mógāo Caves**. Access the mighty northwestern Uighur province of **Xīnjiāng** via the melon-town of **Hāmì** before continuing to **Turpan** and **Ürümqi**; make sure you spend the night in a yurt on the shores of **Tiān Chí**. Thread your way through a string of Silk Road towns by rail to the Central Asian outpost of **Kashgar**, or reach the Uighur town via the Marco Polo–journeyed Southern Silk Road along the cusp of the Taklamakan Desert. From Kashgar, hatch exciting plans to conquer the **Karakoram Highway** or, in the other direction, work out how to get back into China proper.

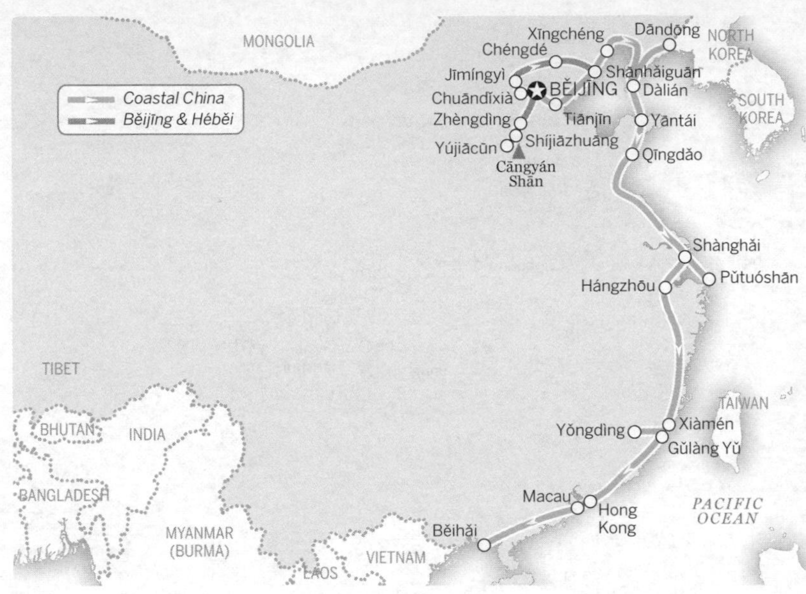

Three to Four Weeks

Coastal China

From **Běijīng**, hop on the high-speed train to face-lifted **Tiānjīn** en route to the Ming-dynasty garrison town of **Shānhǎiguān** on the edge of Manchuria. Beyond the ancient port town of **Xīngchéng** and on around the coast is urbane **Dàlián**, where you can weigh up trips to the North Korean border at **Dāndōng**, or the ferry crossing to **Yāntái** en route to a two-day sojourn around breezy **Qīngdǎo**, the eye-catching Shāndōng port city. Cashing in on dashing **Shànghǎi** is crucial – allow four to five days to tick off surrounding sights, including a mid-week expedition over the waves to insular **Pǔtuóshān** and a trip to the cultured former Song-dynasty capital of **Hángzhōu**. Work your way south around the coast to **Xiàmén** (Amoy) to capture some of the magic of **Gǔlàng Yǔ**, using the port town as a base to explore the **Hakka roundhouses** around **Yǒngdìng**. Conclude the tour feasting on dim sum and getting in step with the rhythms of **Hong Kong** and surrendering to the Portuguese lilt of **Macau**, or go further along the coast to the sleepy port town of **Běihǎi** in Guǎngxī and bounce over the sea in a boat to the volcanic island of **Wéizhōu**.

Ten Days

Běijīng & Héběi

After satiating yourself on Běijīng's many highlights – the **Forbidden City**, **Tiān'ānmén Square**, the **Summer Palace**, the **Great Wall** and the city's charming **hútòng** – hop on an express D-class train to **Shíjiāzhuāng** to ramble round the nearby temple town of **Zhèngdìng**. For some pastoral relaxation, adventurous travellers can make their way west from Shíjiāzhuāng to the small Héběi village of **Yújiācūn**, where you can spend the night immersed in rural simplicity. Head back to Shíjiāzhuāng via the panoramic **Cāngyán Shān**. For more earthy flavours of the surrounding land, head out from Běijīng to the crumbling walled town of **Jīmíngyì** or the snoozy hamlet of **Chuāndǐxià**; you can overnight in each. Northeast from Běijīng towards the Manchurian homelands is easily reached **Chéngdé**, with its grand imperial summer resort and awesome collection of Tibetan-style Buddhist temples, while along the coast is attractive **Shānhǎiguān**, a walled Ming-dynasty garrison town and access point to a cluster of Great Wall sights, from **Jiǎoshān** to **Jiǔménkǒu**, just over the border in **Liáoníng**.

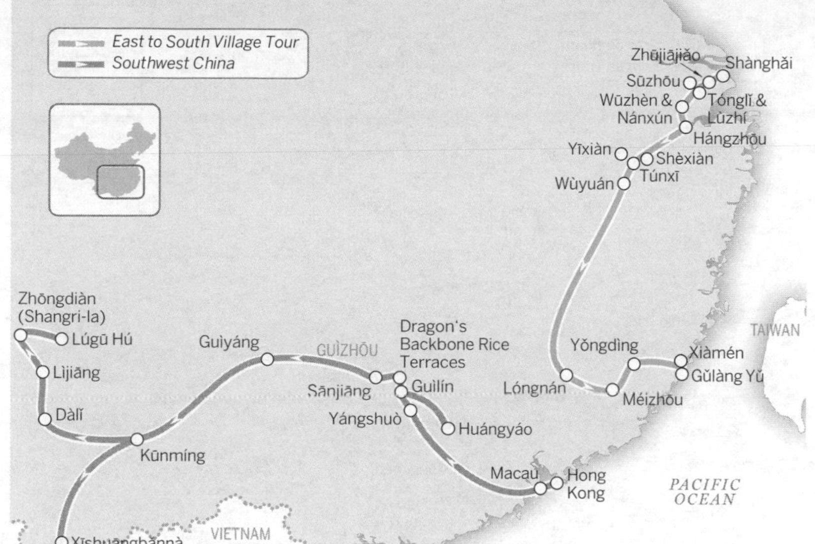

Two Weeks

East to South Village Tour

From **Shànghǎi**, head to **Zhūjiājiǎo** in the municipality's rural west to catch its canal-side charms; if you find yourself in a canal-town mood, the water towns of Jiāngsū and north Zhèjiāng – including **Tónglǐ**, **Lùzhí**, **Wūzhèn** and **Nánxún** – are easy to get to. From either Sūzhōu or Hángzhōu, take a bus to **Túnxī** in Ānhuī to spend several days exploring the delightful clusters of ancient Huīzhōu villages of **Yīxiàn** and **Shèxiàn**. Bus it across the border to Jiāngxī province for two or three days' fabulous trekking from village to village in the gorgeous rural landscape around **Wùyuán**. Work your way to the south of the province to enter Hakka country – a hilly region dotted with fortified villages around **Lóngnán** – and give yourself four days to ramble around the neighbouring Hakka areas of **Méizhōu** and **Yǒngdìng** in Guǎngdōng and Fújiàn, where you can spend the night in an earth building and fully tap into the local rhythms. Round off the tour at coastal **Xiàmén**, spending a night or two amid the colonial remains of **Gǔlàng Yǔ**.

Three Weeks

Southwest China

Four days' wining and dining in **Hong Kong** and **Macau** should whet your appetite, before you head inland to **Guìlín** and three days immersing yourself in the dreamy karst landscape of **Yángshuò**. Jump on a bus to delightful **Huángyáo** before backtracking to Guìlín and journeying north to the **Dragon's Backbone Rice Terraces** and the wind-and-rain bridges and ethnic hues of **Sānjiāng**. Creep over the border to explore the minority-rich villages of eastern **Guìzhōu**, including **Lángdé**, **Shíqiáo**, **Lónglǐ**, **Bāshā** and **Zhàoxīng**, before continuing to **Guìyáng** and on by train to the capital of Yúnnán province, **Kūnmíng**. Spend a few days in Kūnmíng before penetrating north Yúnnán to explore **Dàlǐ**, **Lìjiāng** and **Zhōngdiàn (Shangri-la)**. Consider exploring the border area with Sìchuān at the remote **Lúgū Hú**, from where you can head into Sìchuān. In the other direction, the fertile **Xīshuāngbǎnnà** region lies in the deep south of the province, where Yúnnán's southeast Asian complexion comes to the fore. You'll be rewarded with countless hiking opportunities around China's southwest borders and a profusion of ethnic villages.

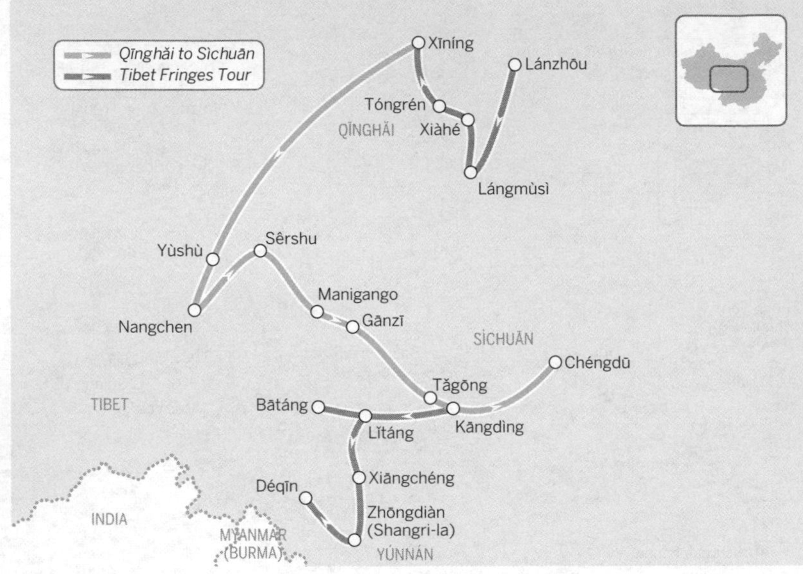

Ten Days
Qīnghǎi to Sìchuān

A component of our **Tibet Fringes tour**, this journey skirts the flanks of Tibet on your way from Xīníng to Chéngdū. The scenery is magnificent but do this trip only in summer (it's too cold even in spring), and take cash and lots of food with you (you won't be able to change money or cash travellers cheques). Be prepared for bus breakdowns, irregular transport connections and simple accommodation. You can jump on a 17-hour sleeper bus or fly from **Xīníng** to the Tibetan trading town of **Yùshù** (Jyekundo), in the south of Qīnghǎi, which suffered a devastating quake in 2010 but is picking itself up. Spend several days visiting the surrounding sights and exploring the deeply Tibetan disposition of the region and its valleys. Trips south into Tibet are feasible but tricky without permits; **Nangchen** is the end of the road if you don't have these. Hop on a bus from Yùshù to **Sěrshu** (Shíqú Xiàn) in northwest Sìchuān, where bus connections run through some stunning scenery past **Manigango** (perhaps with a side trip to Dege), the Tibetan town of **Gānzī** and on past **Tǎgōng** to **Kāngdìng** (Dardo) along the Sìchuān–Tibet Hwy, from where you can head west in the direction of Tibet or east to **Chéngdū**.

Three to Four Weeks
Tibet Fringes Tour

Travel permits are required for the Tibet Autonomous Region (TAR), periodically inaccessible to foreigners and where the effort and cost of travel can be prohibitive. This tour immerses you in areas typically far more straightforward to access yet rewarding with all the colour and vibrancy of Tibet. Only undertake the entire tour in the summer months. From **Lánzhōu** in Gānsù province, go southwest to **Lángmùsì** and **Xiàhé** before penetrating **Qīnghǎi** via the monastery town of **Tóngrén**, where you can pick up a *thangka* (Tibetan sacred art). From here hook up with the **Qīnghǎi to Sìchuān tour** which takes you from **Xīníng** to **Kāngdìng**, from where you can journey by bus west to **Lǐtáng** and on to **Bātáng** within striking distance of the Tibetan border, or travel south to **Xiāngchéng** and on to **Zhōngdiàn (Shangri-la)** and the gorgeous Tibetan region of **north Yúnnán**. From Zhōngdiàn take a bus to high-altitude **Déqīn**, enveloped in gorgeous mountain scenery. Ranging to the borders with Myanmar (Burma), Laos and Vietnam, the rest of this fascinating province beckons. The particularly energetic can join the **Yangzi River tour** which pulls into Shànghǎi.

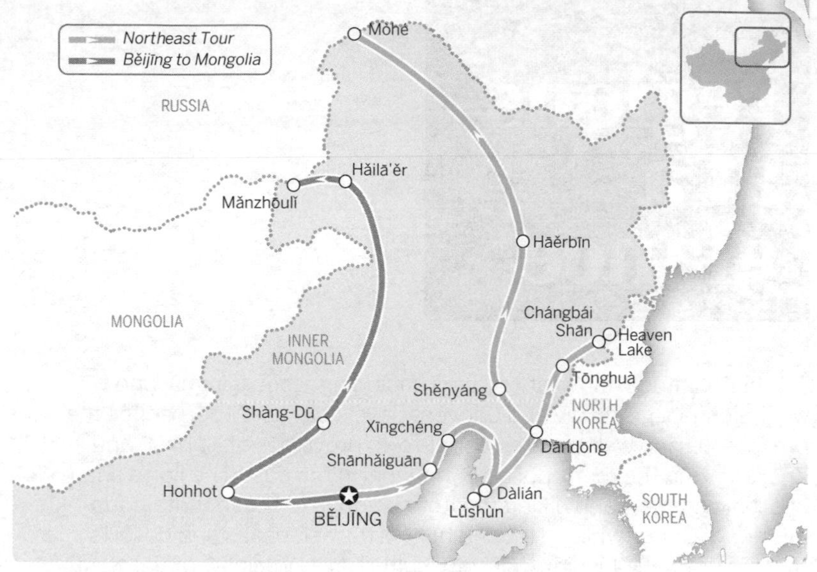

Ten Days
Northeast Tour

With **Běijīng** as a start point, hop on a train to stylish **Dàlián**, but plan to spend a few days exploring the historic walled coastal towns of **Shānhǎiguān** and **Xīngchéng** en route. You'll need several days for Dàlián's sights, including the historic port of **Lǚshùn** and an adorable coastline. Border watchers will be keen to get to **Dāndōng**, on the border with North Korea, for its peculiar frisson. Take a boat tour along the Yālù River, dine on North Korean food and visit **Tiger Mountain Great Wall**. Consider a trip by rail and bus to **Heaven Lake** in **Chángbái Shān** (the largest nature reserve in China) via **Tōnghuà**. Straddling the North Korea border, the volcanic lake is a stunning sight, but is only accessible from mid-June to September. Alternatively, take the train to **Shěnyáng** and visit its Qing dynasty Imperial Palace and the tomb of Huang Taiji, founder of the Qing-dynasty. Hop on a bus or a train to **Hā'ěrbīn** to **Dàolǐqū District** and wonder at the city's Russian and Jewish ancestry. If you simply can't stop travelling, make a meal of it by journeying to China's **North Pole Village** and try to catch the aurora borealis in **Mòhé**.

One Week
Běijīng to Mongolia

After exhausting Běijīng's superb sightseeing, and wining and dining choices, jump aboard a train to **Hohhot** in **Inner Mongolia** where a late-July arrival should coincide with the Naadam festivities at Gegentala to the north, when the grasslands are turning green. Explore Hohhot's lamaseries and temples and make a trip to the grasslands outside town for a taste of the epic Inner Mongolian prairie. From Hohhot you can either directly take the train direct to **Ulaanbataar** in Mongolia, or an alternative route to Mongolia is to first journey by train from Hohhot to **Shàng-Dū** – vanished site of Kublai Khan's celebrated palace at **Xanadu** – and then on to **Hǎilā'ěr** in the far north of Inner Mongolia, towards the border with Mongolia and Russia. The grasslands outside Hǎilā'ěr are a real highlight, so consider spending the night under the stars in a yurt on the prairie. If you are Russia-bound, you can enter the country via the nearby trading town of **Mǎnzhōulǐ** on the border. Alternatively, hop on a train from Hǎilā'ěr to Hā'ěrbīn in Hēilóngjiāng (to hook up with the **Northeast tour**) or jump aboard a flight to Choibalsan in Eastern Mongolia.

regions at a glance

The high-altitude, far west of China, including Tibet, Qīnghǎi and west Sìchuān, gradually and unevenly levels out as it approaches the prosperous and well-watered canal-town provinces of Jiāngsū and Zhèjiāng, and the metropolis of Shànghǎi in the east. The lion's share of scenic marvels and hiking territory belongs to the mountainous interior of China, while in the mighty northwest, peaks and deserts meet in dramatic fashion. Minority culture is a speciality of the west and southwest, and the remote border regions. Different cuisines range across the entire nation, from the hardy northeast to the warm jungles of the far southwest.

Běijīng

History ✓✓✓
Temples ✓✓✓
Food ✓✓✓

Běijīng's imperial pedigree assures it a rich vein of dynastic history, balanced by splendid seams of temple architecture. Wining and dining is another drawcard as the capital is home to an inventive restaurant scene. **p42**

Tiānjīn & Héběi

History ✓✓✓
Temples ✓✓✓
Outdoors ✓✓✓

Tiānjīn's spruced-up foreign concession streetscapes echo stylish Shànghǎi and some standout pagodas and temples can be discovered in Héběi, where the great rural side of China – with excellent village getaways – comes to the fore. **p105**

Shāndōng

History ✓✓✓
Tsingtao ✓✓✓
Mountains ✓✓

Shāndōng groans under the weight of its history-heavy hitters: the revered Confucian home (and tomb) at Qūfù and sacred Tài Shān. Then, of course, there's the home of Tsingtao, Qīngdǎo – today a breezy, laid-back port city. **p129**

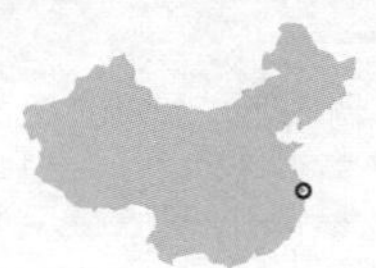

Shànghǎi

Architecture ✓✓✓
Food ✓✓✓
Urban Style ✓✓✓

Shànghǎi exudes a unique style that's unlike anywhere else in China. Business may be its raison d'être, but there's plenty to do here, from nonstop shopping and skyscraper-hopping to stand-out art and fantastic eats. **p161**

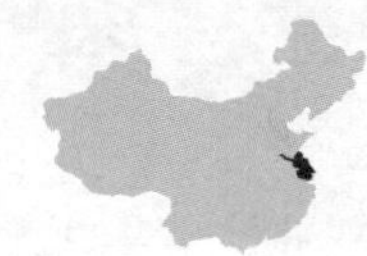

Jiāngsū

Canal Towns ✓✓✓
Outdoors ✓✓
History ✓✓

Locked in a tug-of-war with Hángzhō for the title of 'Heaven on Earth', Sūzhōu is awash with cute-as-pie canal towns and streets. Things get more sombre in Nánjīng, with its WWII past and fabulous Ming wall. **p206**

Zhèjiāng

Canal Towns ✓✓✓
Outdoors ✓✓✓
Islands ✓✓

Flushed with water and vaulted with bridges, Zhèjiāng's water towns are brimful of traditional charm. Pastoral escapes abound further south, Hángzhōu is one of China's most appealing cities and the Buddhist island of Pǔtuóshān is a true getaway. **p234**

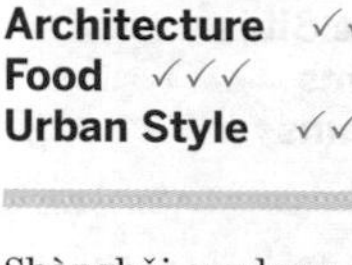

Fújiàn

Architecture ✓✓✓
Food ✓✓
Islands ✓✓

Fújiàn is Hakka heartland and home to the intriguing *tǔlóu* – massive packed stone and mud structures that house hundreds of families. Gǔlàng Yǔ, a tiny island off Xiàmén, has more than 1000 crumbling colonial villas, each one unique. **p260**

Liáoníng

Festivals ✓✓✓
History ✓✓✓
Minority Culture ✓✓✓

In history-rich Liáoníng, imperial relics contend with the legacy of Russian and Japanese colonialism. The North Korean border at Dāndōng is a sobering contrast to the wild beer festival at Dàlián. **p280**

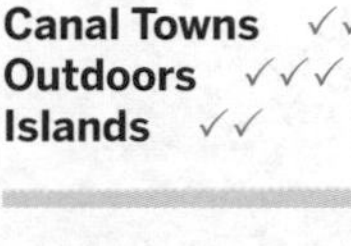

Jílín

Landscapes ✓✓✓
Culture ✓✓✓
Skiing ✓✓

Boasting China's largest nature reserve, and a top ski destination, Jílín exerts a pull on the nature lover. On the trail of the exotic? Head to Jí'ān for the ruins of an ancient Korean empire. **p298**

Hēilóngjiāng

Festivals ✓✓
Culture ✓✓
Nature ✓✓✓

Fire and ice are the highlights in this province where volcanic explosions have left one of China's most mesmerising landscapes, and the winter's bitter climate provides the raw materials for a spectacular ice sculpture festival. **p321**

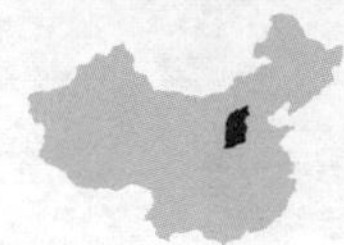

Shānxī

History ✓✓✓
Culture ✓✓✓
Mountains ✓✓✓

Repository of one of China's most superlative Buddhist grottoes, Shānxī also brings you one of its most magical Buddhist mountains. History is on all sides: the walled city of Píngyáo is the most intact of its kind. **p336**

Shaanxi

Historic Sites ✓✓✓
Museums ✓✓✓
Mountains ✓✓

A treasure trove of archaeological sites is scattered across the plains surrounding Shaanxi's capital Xī'ān, where there are museums galore. Blow off all that ancient dust with a trip to Huà Shān, one of China's five holy Taoist peaks. **p357**

Ānhuī

Villages ✓✓✓
Mountains ✓✓✓
Outdoors ✓✓

The amazing Unesco-listed Hui villages of Hóngcūn and Xīdì are some of China's best-preserved. But let's not forget *that* mountain, Huángshān. Its soaring granite peaks have inspired a legion of poets and painters. **p378**

Hénán

History ✓✓✓
Temples ✓✓✓
Mountains ✓✓✓

Hénán's overture of dynastic antiquity is balanced by some excellent mountain escapes and the quirky allure of Nánjiēcūn, China's last Maoist collective. The province's *wǔshù* (martial arts) credentials come no better: the Shàolín Temple is here. **p400**

Húběi

Scenic Wonders ✓✓✓
History ✓✓✓
Rivers ✓✓✓

Slashed by the mighty Yangzi River, history-rich Húběi is one of the gateways to the Three Gorges, but Taoist martial artists may find themselves mustering on Wǔdāng Shān, home of taichi and scenic views. **p421**

Jiāngxī

Scenery ✓✓✓
Mountains ✓✓✓
Ancient Villages ✓✓✓

Communists herald it as the mythic starting point of the Long March, but it's the spectacular mountain scenery and hiking trails past preserved villages and terraced fields that make Jiāngxī truly special. **p435**

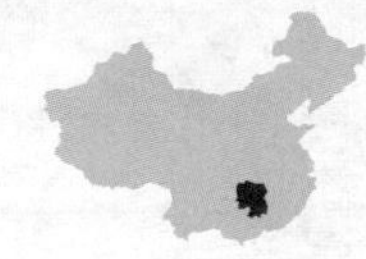

Húnán

Ancient Towns ✓✓✓
Minority Villages ✓✓
Mountains ✓✓

Two of China's most noteworthy ancient towns, Fènghuáng and Hóngjiāng Old Town, are here, as well as the sacred mountain of Héng Shān, the otherworldly karst peaks of Wǔlíngyuán and remote Miao and Dong villages. **p449**

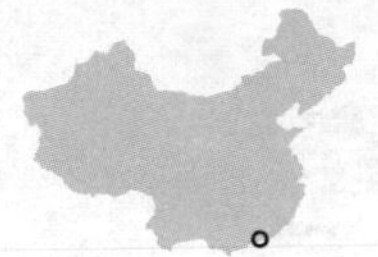

Hong Kong

Food ✓✓✓
Shopping ✓✓✓
Scenery ✓✓✓

This culinary capital offers the best of China and beyond, while a seductive mix of vintage and cutting-edge fashion attracts armies of shoppers. Meanwhile, leafy mountains, shimmering waters, skyscrapers and tenements make an unlikely but poetic match. **p470**

Macau

Food ✓✓✓
Architecture ✓✓✓
Casinos ✓✓✓

Marrying flavours from five continents, Macanese cooking is as unique as the cityscape, where Taoist temples meet baroque churches on cobbled streets with Chinese names. It's also a billionaire's playground with casino-resorts and other luxuries. **p509**

Guǎngdōng

Food ✓✓✓
History ✓✓
Architecture ✓

A strong gastronomic culture offers travellers the chance to savour world-renowned Cantonese cuisine. Guǎngdōng's seafaring temperament has brought the region diverse, exotic architectural styles, including the World Heritage–listed watchtowers. **p531**

Hǎinán

Beaches ✓✓✓
Cycling ✓✓✓
Surfing ✓✓

When it comes to golden sand beaches and warm clear waters, China's only tropical island doesn't disappoint. An ideal cycling destination, Hǎinán attracts in-the-know adventurers with its good roads, balmy winters and varied landscape. **p566**

Guǎngxī

Scenery ✓✓✓
Hiking ✓✓
Cycling ✓✓

Much-loved for its out-of-this-world karst landscape, Guǎngxī offers a superior experience for the adventure-loving traveller with lush green valleys, charming folksy villages and countless walking, cycling and rafting opportunities. **p582**

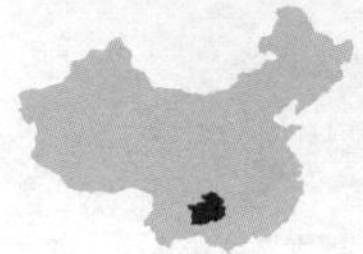

Guìzhōu

Festivals ✓✓✓
Minority Villages ✓✓✓
Waterfalls ✓✓✓

With over a third of the population made up of minorities and more folk festivals than anywhere else in China, in Guìzhōu you can party with the locals all year round. For nature lovers, the stunning countryside features thousands of waterfalls. **p609**

Yúnnán

Ancient Towns ✓✓✓
Mountains ✓✓✓
Minority Villages ✓✓✓

Yúnnán is the province that has it all: towering Himalayan mountains, tropical jungle, sublime rice terraces and over half of China's minority groups. And did we mention gorgeous historic towns like Lìjiāng, the fantastic trekking and the great food? **p637**

Sìchuān

Mountains ✓✓✓
Scenery ✓✓✓
Cuisine ✓✓✓

One province; three regions. Stay in central or southern Sìchuān for steamy bamboo forests and cute Ming-dynasty villages. Head north for stunning lakes set among alpine-esque mountain scenery. Venture west for remote Tibetan-plateau grasslands. **p701**

Chóngqìng

Cuisine ✓✓✓
Ancient Villages ✓✓✓
River Trips ✓✓✓

A unique city with a unique location, hilly Chóngqìng hugs cliffs overlooking the Yangzi, bursts with old-China energy, offers some fascinating day trips and is home to hotpot – the spiciest dish on the planet. **p752**

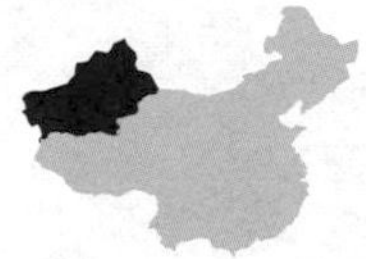

Xīnjiāng

History ✓✓✓
Nature ✓✓
Minority Culture ✓✓✓

Bazaars, kebabs and camels are just a few of the icons that hint at your arrival in Central Asia. Ancient Silk Road towns include Turpan, Kashgar and Hotan, while trekkers gravitate to Kanas Lake and the Tiān Shān. **p772**

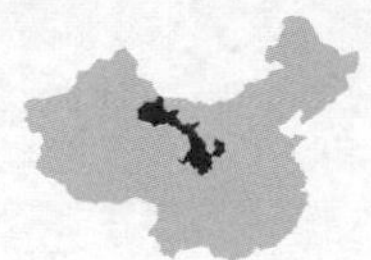

Gānsù

Silk Road ✓✓✓
Tibetan Areas ✓✓✓
Buddhism ✓✓✓

Gānsù is all about diversity: colourful Tibetan regions in the southwest, Mongolia alongside the north and a rich accumulation of Silk Road history running through its middle. Think deserts, mountains, Buddhist artefacts, camels, yaks, pilgrims and nomads. **p803**

Níngxià

History ✓
Activities ✓
Minority Culture ✓

In the designated homeland of the Hui, visit the great tombs of the Xixia, nomadic rock art and the enormous Buddhas of Xūmí Shān. For camel trekking or sliding down the sand dunes, head for the Tengger Desert. **p836**

Inner Mongolia

Food ✓
Activities ✓
Remote Journeys ✓✓

Ride a famed Mongolian horse at a yurt camp near Hohhot and Hǎilā'er and sit down to a Mongolian hotpot (a delicious stew of meat and veggies). Further flung western Inner Mongolia is a hard-to-reach landscape of towering sand dunes, desert lakes and ancient sites. **p847**

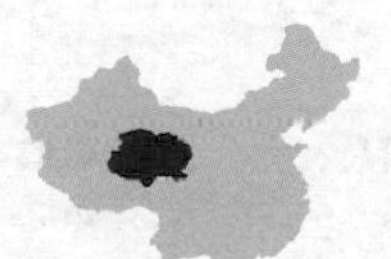

Qīnghǎi

Monasteries ✓✓✓
Scenery ✓✓✓
Culture ✓✓

Vast and remote, the best parts of Qīnghǎi – way up on the Tibetan plateau – are for those who like their travel rough. Need a hot shower and a coffee every morning? Go somewhere else. **p862**

Tibet

Monasteries ✓✓✓
Scenery ✓✓✓
Culture ✓✓

The 'Roof of the World' is a stunningly beautiful high plateau of turquoise lakes, desert valleys and Himalayan peaks, dotted with monasteries, yaks and sacred Buddhist sites. Tight travel regulations currently demand a guide and permits. **p878**

Look out for these icons:

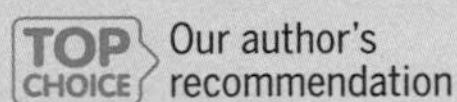
Our author's recommendation

A green or sustainable option

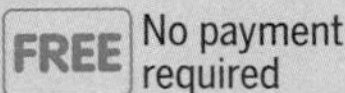
No payment required

See the Index for a full list of destinations covered in this book.

On the Road

Běijīng

POPULATION: 15.6 MILLION / TELEPHONE CODE: 010

Includes »

Best Places to Eat

» Xiao Wang's Home Restaurant (p79)

» Capital M (p81)

» Dàlǐ Courtyard (p79)

» Crescent Moon Muslim Restaurant (p79)

» Vineyard Cafe (p79)

» Element Fresh (p82)

Best Places to Stay

» City Walls Courtyard (p74)

» Opposite House Hotel (p77)

» Peking International Youth Hostel (p74)

» Michael's House (p78)

» Běijīng Downtown Backpackers Accommodation (p74)

Why Go?

Běijīng (北京) is one of China's true ancient citadels. It is also a confident and modern city that seems assured of its destiny to rule over China till the end of time. Its architecture traces every mood swing from Mongol times to the present, from neglected *hútòng* (alleyways) to bomb shelters scooped out during the 1970s and the shimmering baubles of contemporary architects.

It's Běijīng's epic imperial grandeur that is awe-inspiring, and there's still much more substance here than in China's other dynastic capitals, bar Nánjīng or Kāifēng. You just need to do a bit of patient exploration to tap into its historical narrative.

The city's denizens chat in Běijīnghuà – the gold standard of Mandarin – and marvel at their good fortune for occupying the centre of the known world. And for all its gusto, Běijīng dispenses with the persistent pace of Shànghǎi or Hong Kong, and locals instead find time to sit out front, play chess and watch the world go by.

When to Go

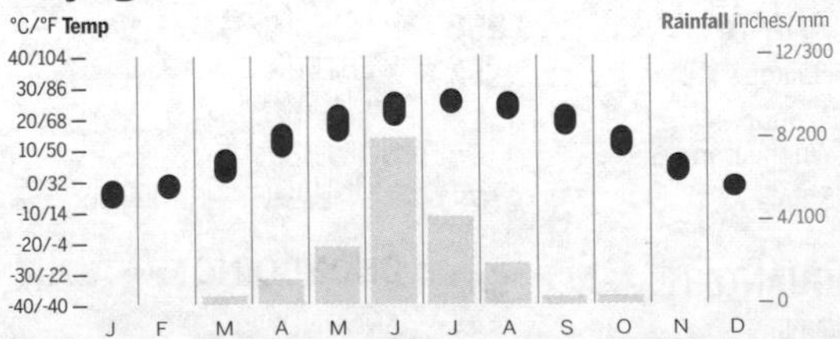

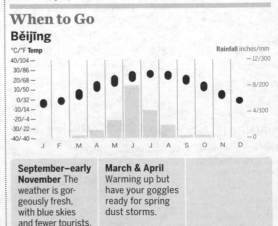

September–early November The weather is gorgeously fresh, with blue skies and fewer tourists.

March & April Warming up but have your goggles ready for spring dust storms.

History

Although seeming to have presided over China since time immemorial, Běijīng (Northern Capital) – positioned outside the central heartland of Chinese civilisation – only emerged as a cultural and political force that would shape the destiny of China with the 13th-century Mongol occupation of China.

Located on a vast plain that extends south as far as the distant Yellow River (Huáng Hé), Běijīng benefits from neither proximity to a major river nor the sea. Without its strategic location on the edge of the North China Plain, it would hardly be an ideal place to locate a major city, let alone a national capital.

Chinese historical sources identify the earliest settlements in these parts from 1045 BC. In later centuries Běijīng was successively occupied by foreign forces: it was established as an auxiliary capital under the Khitan Liao and later as the capital under the Jurchen Jin, when it was enclosed within fortified walls, accessed by eight gates.

In AD 1215 the great Mongol warrior Genghis Khan's army razed Běijīng, an event that was paradoxically to mark Běijīng's transformation into a powerful national capital. Apart from the first 53 years of the Ming dynasty and 21 years of Nationalist rule in the 20th century, it has enjoyed this status to the present day.

The city came to be called Dàdū (大都; Great Capital), also assuming the Mongol name Khanbalik (the Khan's town). By 1279, under the rule of Kublai Khan, grandson of Genghis Khan, Dàdū was the capital of the largest empire the world has ever known.

The basic grid of present-day Běijīng was laid during the Ming dynasty, and Emperor Yongle (r 1403–24) is credited with being the true architect of the modern city. Much of Běijīng's grandest architecture, such as the Forbidden City and the Temple of Heaven, date from his reign.

The Manchus, who invaded China in the 17th century to establish the Qing dynasty, essentially preserved Běijīng's form. In the last 120 years of the Qing dynasty, Běijīng, and subsequently China, was subjected to power struggles and invasions and the ensuing chaos. The list is long: the Anglo-French troops who in 1860 burnt the Old Summer Palace to the ground; the corrupt regime of Empress Dowager Cixi; the catastrophic Boxer Rebellion; General Yuan Shikai; the warlords; the Japanese occupation of 1937; and the Kuomintang. Each and every period left its undeniable mark, although the shape and symmetry of Běijīng was maintained.

Modern Běijīng came of age when, in January 1949, the People's Liberation Army (PLA) entered the city. On 1 October of that year Mao Zedong proclaimed a 'People's Republic' from the Gate of Heavenly Peace to an audience of some 500,000 citizens.

Like the emperors before them, the communists significantly altered the face of Běijīng. The *páilóu* (decorative archways) were brought down and whole city blocks were pulverised to widen major boulevards. From 1950 to 1952, the city's magnificent outer walls were levelled in the interests of traffic circulation. Soviet experts and technicians poured in, bringing their own Stalinesque touches.

The past quarter of a century has transformed Běijīng into a modern city, with skyscrapers, slick shopping malls and heaving flyovers. The once flat skyline is now crenellated with vast apartment blocks and office buildings. Recent years have also seen a convincing beautification of Běijīng: from a toneless and unkempt city to a greener, cleaner and more pleasant place.

The year 2008 was Běijīng's modern coming-of-age. The city spent three times the amount Athens spent on the 2004 Olympics to ensure the Běijīng Olympic Games were the most expensive in history.

As Běijīng continues to evolve, it is shredding its increasingly tenuous links with its ancient past one fibre at a time. Even the old-school *China Daily* has observed that 4.43 million sq metres of old courtyards have been demolished in Běijīng since 1990, or 40% of the downtown area. The historic area

PRICE INDICATORS

The following price indicators are used in this chapter:

Sleeping

$	less than Y400
$$	Y400 to Y1000
$$$	more than Y1000

Eating

$	less than Y40
$$	Y40 to Y100
$$$	more than Y100

Běijīng Highlights

1. Discover the astonishing imperial heritage of the **Forbidden City** (p47)
2. Check into a courtyard hotel, wine, dine and sink a Mongolian yoghurt for breakfast along Běijīng's most famous alley, **Nanluogu Xiang** (p59)
3. Stare into the indefinable gaze of a Tang-dynasty Bodhisattva at the **Poly Art Museum** (p65)
4. Join the art crowd at the former factory site of **798 Art District** (p68) to feel Běijīng's artistic edge
5. Applaud the architectural harmonies of the **Temple of Heaven** (p63), but not *too* loudly
6. Decide if the **National Centre for the Performing Arts** (p54) is a jaw-dropping architectural marvel or metallic carbuncle

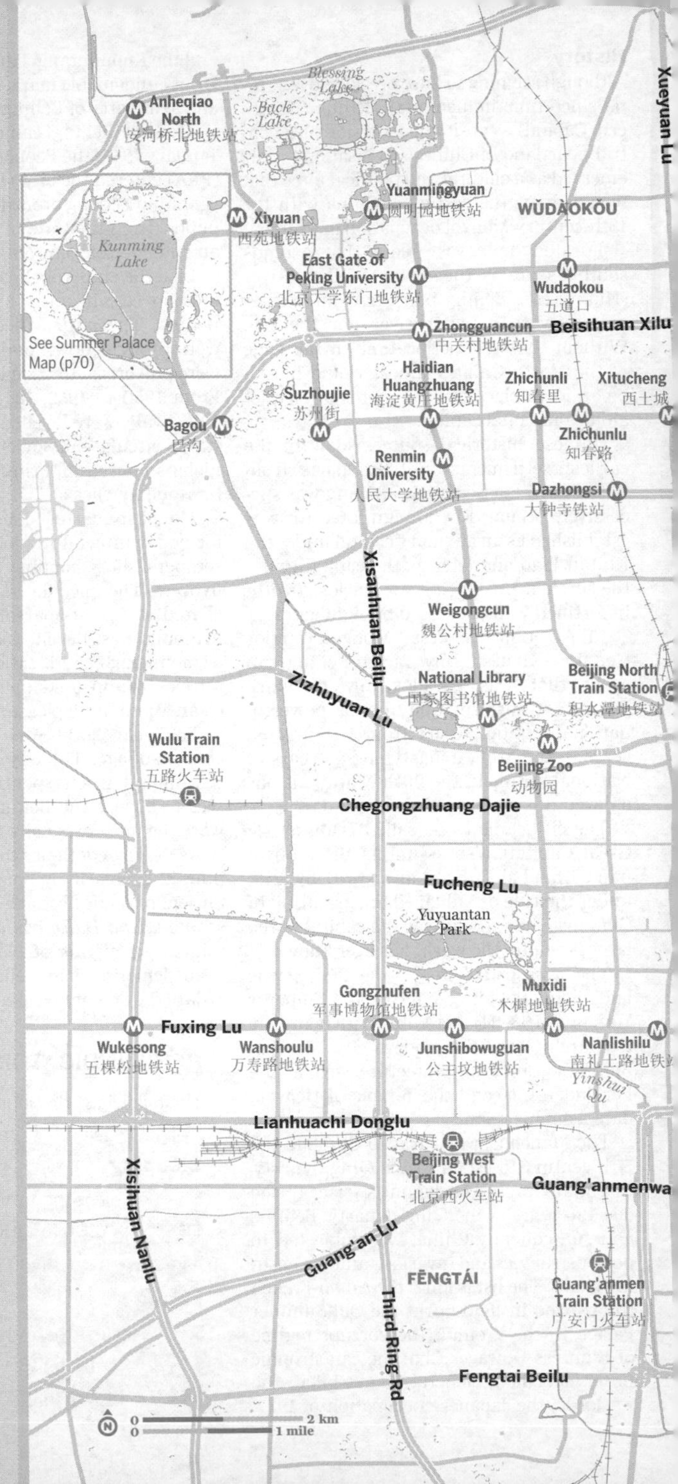

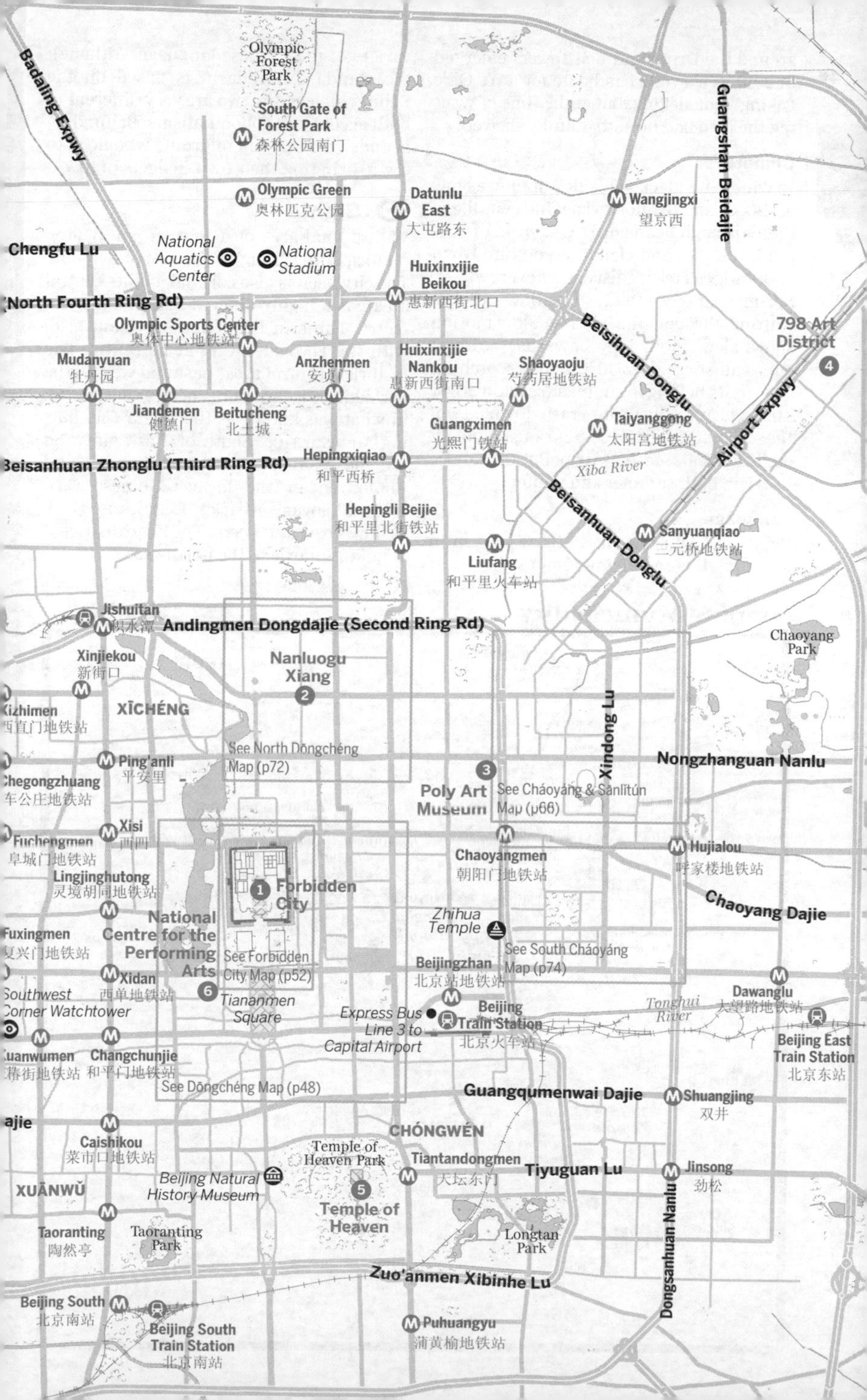

Olympic Forest Park
South Gate of Forest Park
森林公园南门
Badaling Expwy
Guangshan Beidajie
Olympic Green
奥林匹克公园
Datunlu East
大屯路东
Wangjingxi
望京西
Chengfu Lu
National Aquatics Center
National Stadium
Huixinxijie Beikou
惠新西街北口
(North Fourth Ring Rd)
Beisihuan Donglu
798 Art District
4
Olympic Sports Center
奥体中心地铁站
Mudanyuan
牡丹园
Anzhenmen
安贞门
Huixinxijie Nankou
惠新西街南口
Shaoyaoju
芍药居地铁站
Airport Expwy
Jiandemen
健德门
Beitucheng
北土城
Guangximen
光熙门铁站
Taiyanggong
太阳宫地铁站
Beisanhuan Zhonglu (Third Ring Rd)
Hepingxiqiao
和平西桥
Xiba River
Beisanhuan Donglu
Hepingli Beijie
和平里北街铁站
Sanyuanqiao
三元桥地铁站
Liufang
和平里火车站
Jishuitan
积水潭
Andingmen Dongdajie (Second Ring Rd)
Chaoyang Park
Xinjiekou
新街口
Nanluogu Xiang
2
Xizhimen
西直门地铁站
XĪCHÉNG
Xindong Lu
See North Dōngchéng Map (p72)
Ping'anli
平安里
Nongzhanguan Nanlu
Chegongzhuang
车公庄地铁站
3
Poly Art Museum
See Cháoyáng & Sānlǐtún Map (p66)
Fuchengmen
阜城门地铁站
Xisi
西四
Chaoyangmen
朝阳门地铁站
Hujialou
呼家楼地铁站
Lingjinghutong
灵境胡同地铁站
1
Forbidden City
Chaoyang Dajie
National Centre for the Performing Arts
Zhihua Temple
Fuxingmen
复兴门地铁站
See Forbidden City Map (p52)
See South Cháoyáng Map (p74)
Beijingzhan
北京站地铁站
Xidan
西单地铁站
6
Tiananmen Square
Dawanglu
大望路地铁站
Southwest Corner Watchtower
Express Bus Line 3 to Capital Airport
Beijing Train Station
北京火车站
Tonghui River
Beijing East Train Station
北京东站
Xuanwumen
宣武门地铁站
Changchunjie
和平门地铁站
See Dōngchéng Map (p48)
Guangqumenwai Dajie
Shuangjing
双井
CHÓNGWÉN
Caishikou
菜市口地铁站
Temple of Heaven Park
Tiantandongmen
天坛东门
Tiyuguan Lu
Jinsong
劲松
XUĀNWǓ
Beijing Natural History Museum
5
Temple of Heaven
Dongsanhuan Nanlu
Taoranting
陶然亭
Taoranting Park
Longtan Park
Zuo'anmen Xibinhe Lu
Beijing South
北京南站
Beijing South Train Station
北京南站
Puhuangyu
蒲黄榆地铁站

around the Drum and Bell Towers emerged in 2010 as a strong candidate for a 'Ye Olde Peking' remodelling, but at the time of writing the plan had been thankfully shelved.

Climate

In winter, it's glacial outside (dipping as low as -20°C) and the northern winds cut like a knife through bean curd. Arid spring is OK but awesome sand clouds sweep into town and static electricity discharges everywhere. Spring also sees the *liǔxù* (willow catkins) wafting through the air like slow-motion snowflakes. From May onwards the mercury can surge over 30°C and a scorching sun roasts Běijīng in summer (reaching over 40°C); heavy rainstorms crash down late in the season. Summer is also curiously considered the peak season. Air pollution can be heavy in both summer and winter.

Language

Běijīnghuà (北京话), the Chinese spoken in the capital, is seen by purists as the finest variety of the Chinese language. Although the standard Mandarin is based on the Běijīng dialect, the two are very different in both accent and colloquialisms. Běijīnghuà is under threat from migrants who flock to town, bringing their own dialects in tow.

Sights

With a total area of 16,800 sq km, Běijīng municipality is roughly the size of Belgium. The city itself is also colossal, but its central area has a highly ordered design and symmetry. Think of Běijīng as one giant grid, with the Forbidden City at its centre. The historical central areas east and west of the Forbidden City are Dōngchéng and Xīchéng, in what was known as the Tartar City during Manchu rule. South of Tiān'ānmén Sq are the historic districts of Xuānwǔ and Chóngwén in the former Chinese City, while Cháoyáng District occupies much of Běijīng's east and north. The huge district of Hǎidiàn sprawls to the northwest.

Běijīng Municipality

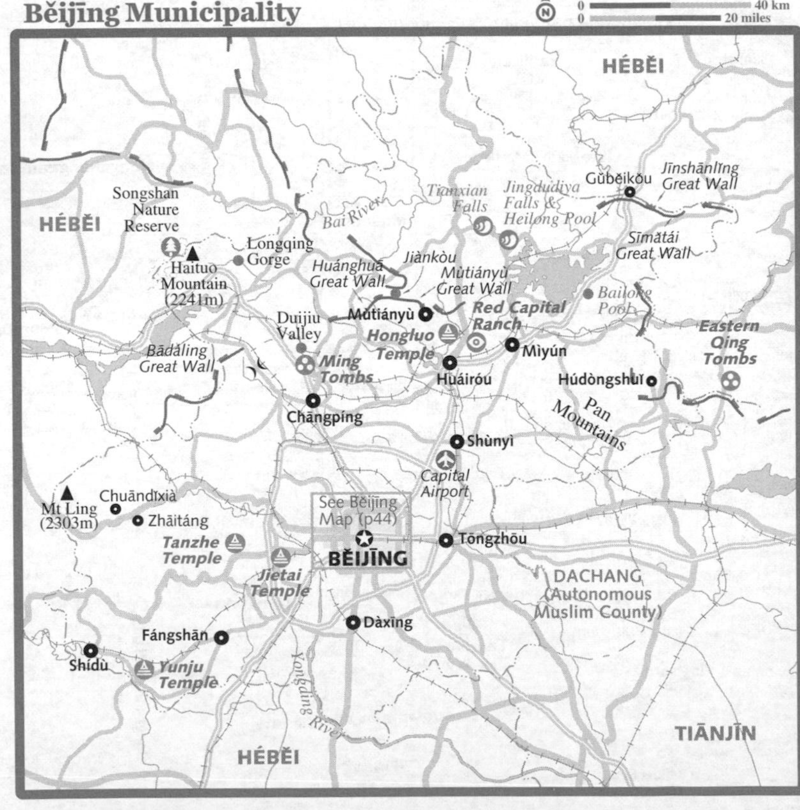

The lion's share of Běijīng's sights lie within the city proper. Notable exceptions are the Great Wall and the Ming Tombs.

DŌNGCHÉNG 东城区

FREE Tiān'ānmén Square SQUARE

(天安门广场; Tiān'ānmén Guǎngchǎng; Map p48; Ⓜ Tiānānmén Xī, Tiānānmén Dōng or Qiánmén) Flanked by stern 1950s Soviet-style buildings and ringed by white perimeter fences, the world's largest public square (440,000 sq metres) is an immense flatland of paving stones at the heart of Běijīng.

Height restrictions have kept surrounding buildings low, allowing largely uninterrupted views of the dome of the sky. Kites flit through the air, children stamp around on the paving slabs and Chinese out-of-towners huddle together for the obligatory photo opportunity with the great helmsman's portrait. On National Day (1 October), Tiān'ānmén Sq heaves with visitors.

In the square, one stands in the symbolic centre of the Chinese universe. The rectangular arrangement, flanked by halls to both east and west, to some extent echoes the layout of the Forbidden City: as such, the square employs a conventional plan that pays obeisance to traditional Chinese culture, but many of its ornaments and buildings are Soviet-inspired. Mao conceived the square to project the enormity of the Communist Party, so it's all a bit Kim Il-Sungish. During the Cultural Revolution, the Chairman, wearing a Red Guard armband, reviewed parades of up to a million people here. In 1976 the 'Tiananmen Incident' is the term given to the near-riot in the square that accompanied the death of Premier Zhou Enlai. Another million people jammed the square to pay their last respects to Mao in the same year. In 1989 army tanks and soldiers forced prodemocracy demonstrators out of the plaza.

Despite being a public place, the square remains more in the hands of the government than the people; it is monitored by closed circuit TV cameras, and plain-clothes police can move faster than the Shànghǎi Maglev if anyone strips down to a Free Tibet T-shirt. The designated points of access, sporadic security checks and twitchy mood cleave Tiān'ānmén Sq from the city. A tangible atmosphere of restraint and authority reigns; in fact, some might say the square symbolises the 'harmonious' China of today.

All this – plus the absence of anywhere to sit – means the square is hardly a place to chill out (don't whip out a guitar), but there's more than enough space to stretch a leg and the view can be simply breathtaking, especially on a clear blue day and at nightfall when the square is illuminated.

If you get up early you can watch the flag-raising ceremony at sunrise, performed by a troop of People's Liberation Army (PLA) soldiers drilled to march at precisely 108 paces per minute, 75cm per pace. The soldiers emerge through the Gate of Heavenly Peace to goosestep impeccably across Chang'an Jie; all traffic is halted. The same ceremony in reverse is performed at sunset. Ask at your hotel for flag-raising/lowering times; rise early, crowds can be intense.

'CON' ARTISTS & TEA MERCHANTS

Beware pesky 'art students' and English students around Wangfujing Dajie, Tiān'ānmén Sq and other tourist areas. They drag Western visitors to exhibitions of overpriced art or extortionate tea ceremonies; the latter may cost Y2000 or more. If approached by over-friendly girls wanting to speak English, refuse to go to a place of their choosing.

Forbidden City HISTORIC SITE

(紫禁城; Zǐjìn Chéng; Map p52; www.dpm.org.cn; admission high/low season Y60/40, Clock Exhibition Hall Y10, Hall of Jewellery Y10, audio tour Y40; ⏲8.30am-4.30pm, last tickets 3.30pm Oct-Mar, 4pm Apr-Sep; Ⓜ Tiānānmén Xī or Tiānānmén Dōng) Ringed by a 52m-wide moat at the very heart of Běijīng, the fantastically named Forbidden City is China's largest and best-preserved complex of ancient buildings. So called because it was off limits for 500 years, when it was steeped in stultifying ritual and Byzantine regal protocol, the otherworldly palace was the reclusive home to two dynasties of imperial rule until the Republic demoted the last Qing emperor to has-been.

The design of the palace was originally closely based on its grand and now dilapidated forerunner in Nánjīng. Today, the Forbidden City is prosaically known as the Palace Museum (故宫博物馆; Gùgōng Bówùguǎn). In former ages the price for uninvited admission was instant execution; these days Y40 will do. It's value for money

Dōngchéng

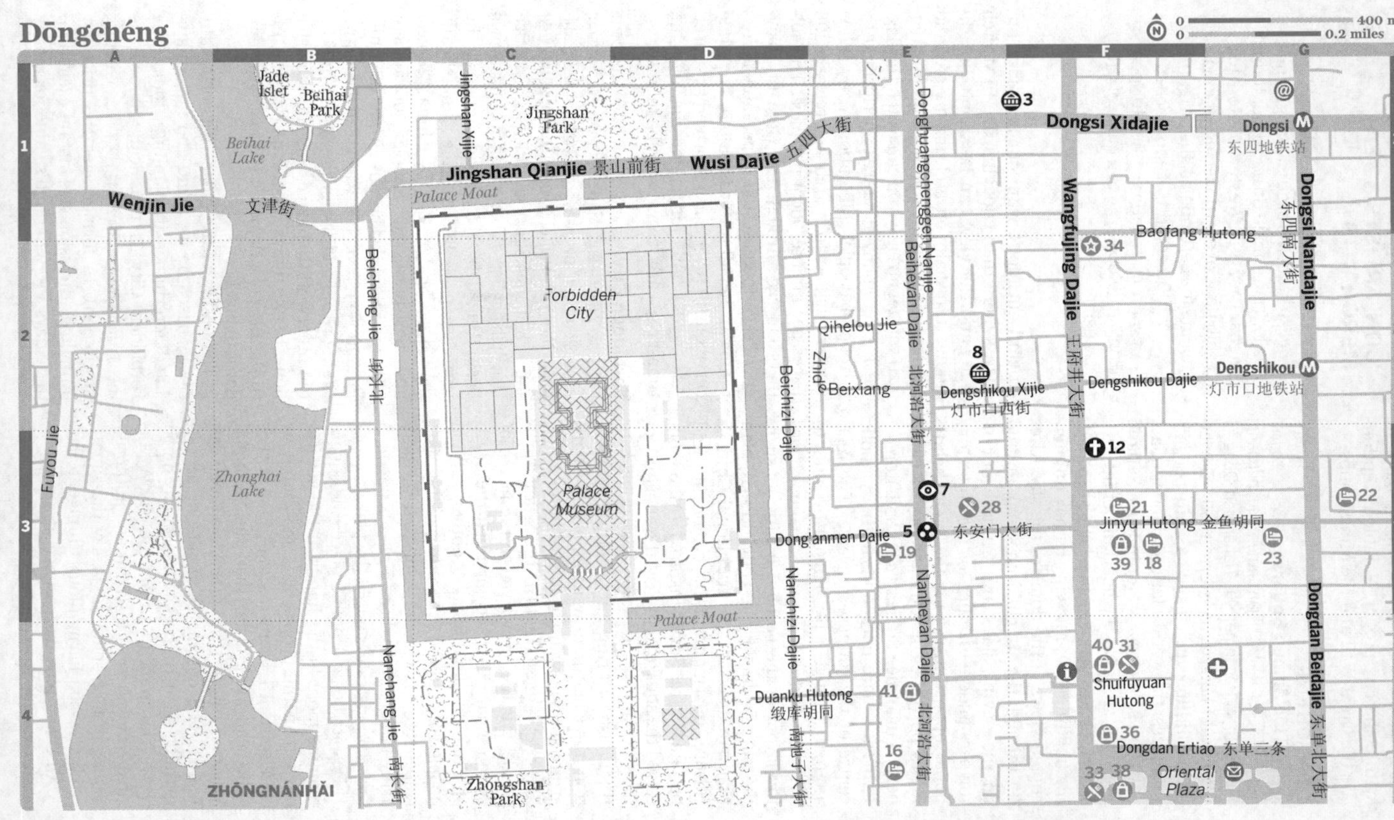
0 400 m
0 0.2 miles
Jade Islet
Beihai Park
Beihai Lake
Jingshan Xijie
Jingshan Park
Jingshan Qianjie 景山前街
Wusi Dajie 五四大街
Dongsi Xidajie
Dongsi
东四地铁站
Dongsi Nandajie
东四南大街
Wenjin Jie
文津街
Palace Moat
Baofang Hutong
Beichang Jie 北长街
Forbidden City
Donghuangchenggen Nanjie
Beiheyan Dajie 北河沿大街
Wangfujing Dajie 王府井大街
Qihelou Jie
Zhide Beixiang
Dengshikou Xijie
灯市口西街
Dengshikou Dajie
Dengshikou
灯市口地铁站
Beichizi Dajie
Palace Museum
Zhonghai Lake
Fuyou Jie
Dong'anmen Dajie
东安门大街
Jinyu Hutong 金鱼胡同
Nanheyan Dajie 北河沿大街
Nanchizi Dajie 南池子大街
Duanku Hutong
缎库胡同
Nanchang Jie 南长街
Zhongshan Park
Shuifuyuan Hutong
Dongdan Ertiao 东单三条
Oriental Plaza
Dongdan Beidajie 东单北大街
ZHŌNGNÁNHǍI
3
34
8
12
7
28
5
19
21
22
23
39
18
41
40
31
36
16
33
38

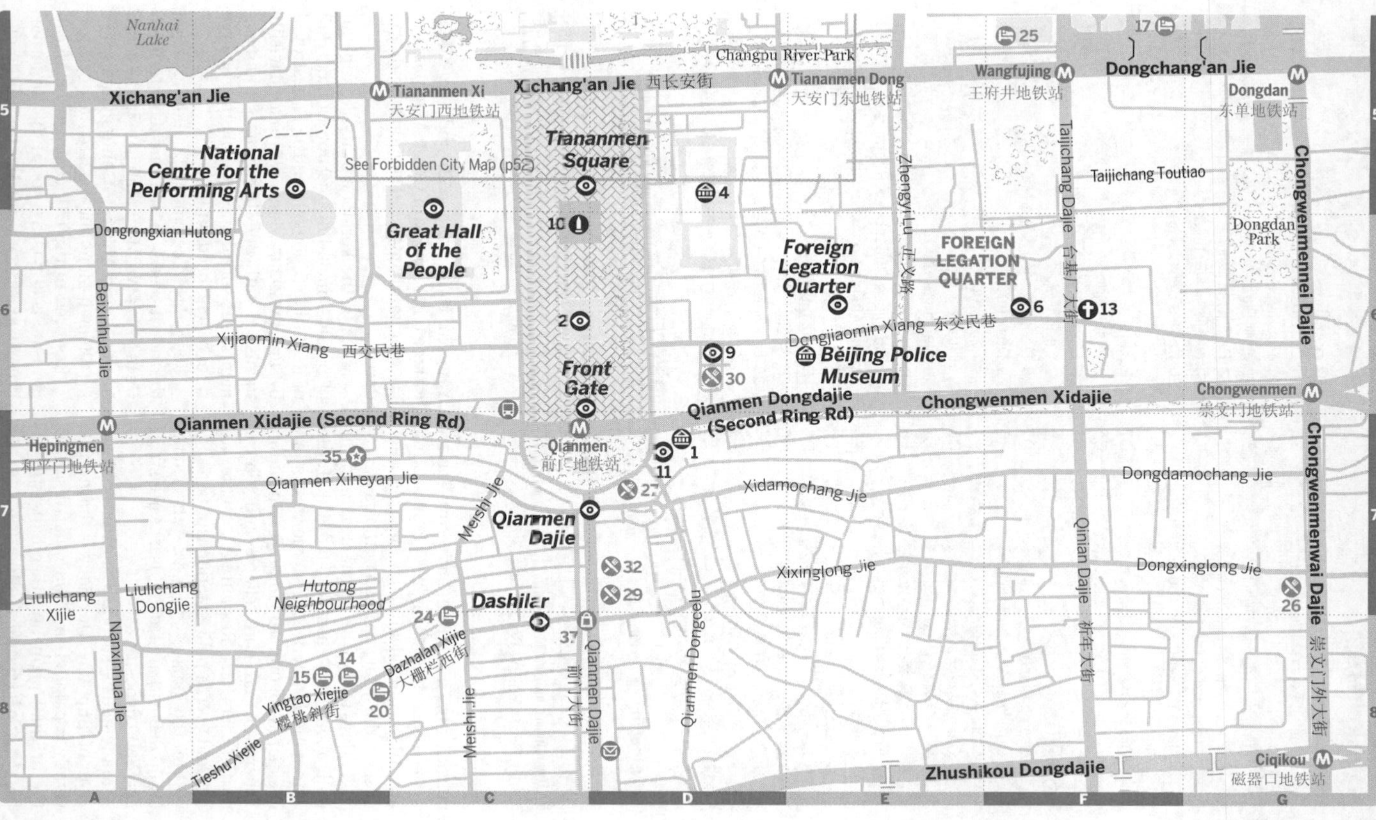
Nanhai Lake
Changpu River Park
Xichang'an Jie
Tiananmen Xi 天安门西地铁站
Xichang'an Jie 西长安街
Tiananmen Dong 天安门东地铁站
Wangfujing 王府井地铁站
Dongchang'an Jie
Dongdan 东单地铁站
National Centre for the Performing Arts
See Forbidden City Map (p52)
Tiananmen Square
Great Hall of the People
Dongrongxian Hutong
Foreign Legation Quarter
FOREIGN LEGATION QUARTER
Zhengyi Lu 正义路
Taijichang Dajie 台基厂大街
Taijichang Toutiao
Dongdan Park
Chongwenmennei Dajie
Beixinhua Jie
Xijiaomin Xiang 西交民巷
Dongjiaomin Xiang 东交民巷
Běijīng Police Museum
Front Gate
Chongwenmen Xidajie
Chongwenmen 崇文门地铁站
Qianmen Xidajie (Second Ring Rd)
Qianmen Dongdajie (Second Ring Rd)
Hepingmen 和平门地铁站
Qianmen 前门地铁站
Qianmen Xiheyan Jie
Meishi Jie
Qianmen Dajie
Xidamochang Jie
Dongdamochang Jie
Chongwenmenwai Dajie 崇文门外大街
Xixinglong Jie
Dongxinglong Jie
Liulichang Xijie
Liulichang Dongjie
Hutong Neighbourhood
Dashilar
Nanxinhua Jie
Dazhalan Xijie 大栅栏西街
Yingtao Xiejie 樱桃斜街
Tieshu Xiejie
Qianmen Dajie 前门大街
Qianmen Dongcelu
Qinian Dajie 祈年大街
Zhushikou Dongdajie
Ciqikou 磁器口地铁站

Dōngchéng

Top Sights

Sights

Sleeping

Eating

Entertainment

Shopping

considering how rampantly over-priced many other tourist sights around China are. Allow yourself a full day for exploration or several trips if you're an enthusiast.

Guides – many with mechanical English – mill about the entrance, but the funky automatically activated audio tours are cheaper (Y40; over 40 languages, including Esperanto) and more reliable (and you can switch them off). Restaurants, a cafe, toilets and even a police station can be found within the palace grounds. Wheelchairs (Y500 deposit) are free to use, as are strollers (Y300 deposit).

Many halls – such as the exterior of the Hall of Supreme Harmony – have been vividly repainted in a way that disguises the original pigment; other halls such as the **Hall of Mental Cultivation** (养心殿; Yǎngxīn Diàn; Map p52) and the **Yìkūn Palace** (翊坤宫; Yìkūn Gōng; Map p52) are far more authentic and delightfully dilapidated.

Much of the Forbidden City is sadly out of bounds, including the now ruined Hall of Rectitude (Zhōngzhèng Diàn), destroyed by fire in 1923, which was once lavishly furnished with Buddhist figures and ornaments. The sound of ping pong may emerge from other closed-off halls.

The palace's ceremonial buildings lie on the north–south axis, from the **Meridian Gate** (午门; Wǔ Mén; Map p52) in the south to the **Divine Military Genius Gate** (神武门; Shénwǔ Mén; Map p52) to the north.

Restored in the 17th century, the Meridian Gate is a massive portal that in former times was reserved for the use of the emperor. Across the Golden Stream, which is shaped to resemble a Tartar bow and is spanned by five marble bridges, towers the **Gate of Supreme Harmony** (太和门; Tàihé Mén; Map p52), overlooking a colossal courtyard that could hold imperial audiences of up to 100,000 people.

Raised on a marble terrace with balustrades are the Three Great Halls (Sān Dàdiàn), which comprise the heart of the Forbidden City. The imposing **Hall of Supreme Harmony** (太和殿; Tàihé Diàn; Map p52) is the most important and the largest structure in the Forbidden City. Originally built in the 15th century, it was used for ceremonial occasions, such as the emperor's birthday, the nomination of military leaders and coronations. Compare the recent recolouring of the outside with the more sombre and natural pigments of the interior.

Inside the Hall of Supreme Harmony is a richly decorated **Dragon Throne** (Lóngyǐ) where the emperor would preside over trembling officials. Bronze *shuǐgāng* (vats) – once containing water for dousing fires – stand in front of the hall; in all, 308 *shuǐgāng* were dotted around the Forbidden City, with fires lit under them in winter to keep them from freezing over (hopefully the flames did not accidentally start larger conflagrations). Water for the Forbidden City was once provided by 72 wells, 30 of which have been preserved.

Behind the Hall of Supreme Harmony is the smaller **Hall of Middle Harmony** (中和殿; Zhōnghé Diàn; Map p52), which served as a transit lounge for the emperor. Here he would make last-minute preparations, rehearse speeches and receive close ministers.

The third hall, which has no support pillars, is the **Hall of Preserving Harmony** (保和殿; Bǎohé Diàn; Map p52), used for banquets and later for imperial examinations. To the rear descends a 250-tonne marble imperial carriageway carved with dragons and clouds, dragged into Běijīng along an ice path. The emperor was conveyed over the carriageway in his sedan chair as he ascended or descended the terrace.

Note the fascinating exhibitions in the halls on the eastern flank of the Three Great Halls, with displays covering the gates and guards in the Forbidden City and an intriguing collection exploring the emperor's Tibetan Buddhist beliefs. In all there were 10 Buddhist chapels in the northwest of the Forbidden City; among them were the **Big Buddha Hall** (Dàfó Táng), the **Rain and Flower Pavilion** (Yǔhuā Gé) – a copy of the Gold Hall from Tholing Monastery in Tibet – and the **Fragrant Clouds Pavilion** (Xiāngyún Tíng), none of which are currently open. Further along in the sequence is an exhibition dedicated to ancestor worship in the palace, and the imperial harem and the lives of imperial concubines. In the next hall along is a detailed diorama of the entire Forbidden City. Halls west of the Three Great Halls exhibit treasures from the palace.

The basic configuration of the Three Great Halls is echoed by the next group of buildings, smaller in scale but more important in terms of real power, which in China traditionally lies in the northernmost part.

The first structure is the **Palace of Heavenly Purity** (乾清宫; Qiánqīng Gōng; Map p52), a residence of Ming and early Qing emperors, and later an audience hall for receiving foreign envoys and high officials.

Beyond the **Hall of Union** (交泰殿; Jiāotài Diàn; Map p52) and the **Earthly Tranquillity Palace** (坤宁宫; Kūnníng Gōng; Map p52) at the northern end of the Forbidden City ranges the much-needed 7000-sq-metre **Imperial Garden** (御花园; Yù Huāyuán; Map p52), a classical Chinese arrangement of fine landscaping, rockeries, walkways and pavilions among ancient and malformed cypresses propped up on stilts. Try to find the **lump tree**, the Elephant Man of the cypress world. Kneeling in front of **Chéngguāng Gate** (承光门; Chéngguāng Mén; Map p52) as you approach the Shénwǔ Gate is a pair of bronze elephants, whose front legs bend in anatomically impossible fashion.

On the western and eastern sides of the Forbidden City range the palatial former living quarters, once containing libraries, temples, theatres, gardens and even the tennis court of the last emperor. Some of these now function as museums with a variety of free exhibitions on everything from imperial concubines to scientific instruments, weapons, paintings, jadeware and bronzes.

The mesmerising **Clock Exhibition Hall** (钟表馆; Zhōngbiǎo Guǎn; Map p52; admission Y10; ⌚8.30am-4pm summer, to 3.30pm winter) is one of the highlights of the Forbidden City. Located in the Fèngxiàn Hall (Fèngxiàn Diàn), the exhibition contains a fascinating array of elaborate timepieces, many of which were gifts to the Qing emperors

Forbidden City

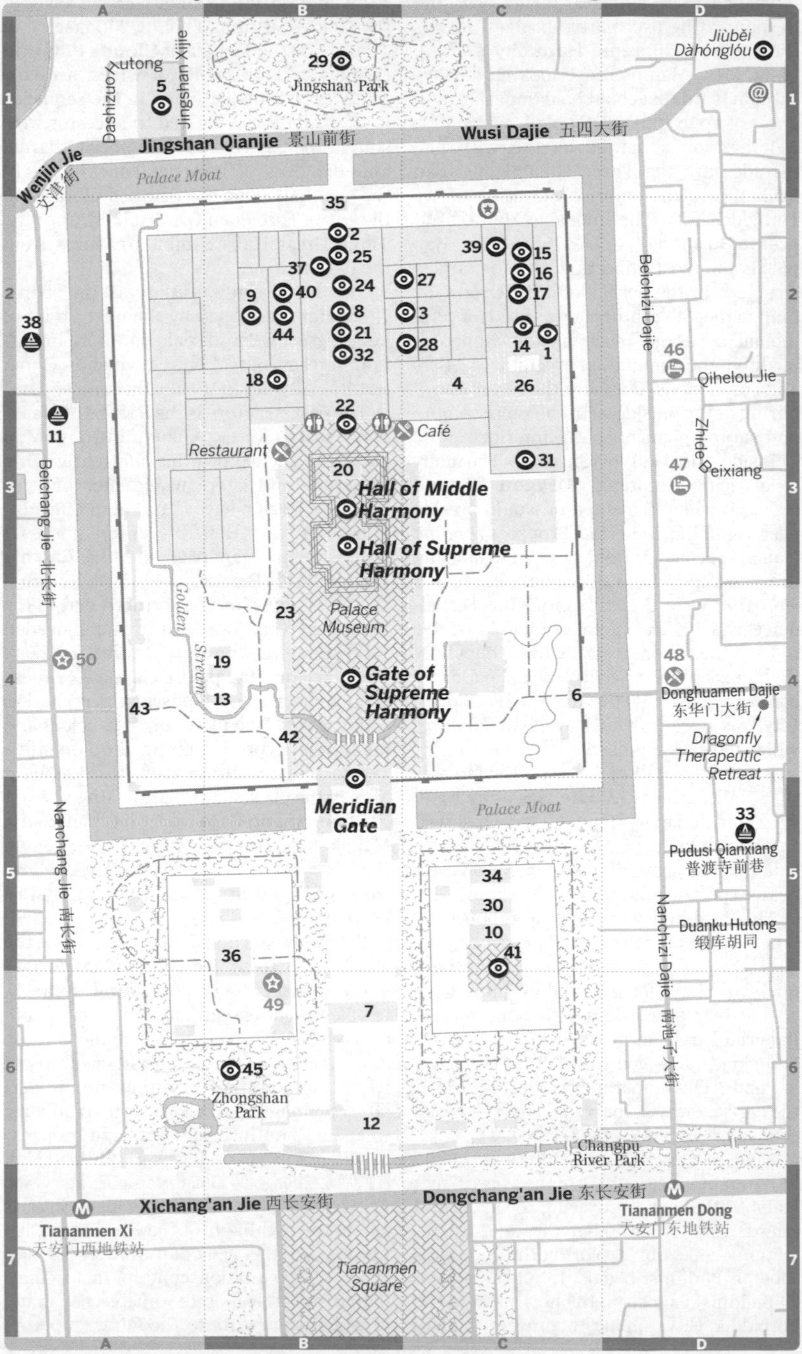

0 200 m
0 0.1 miles

Jiùběi Dàhónglóu
Jingshan Park
Dashizuo Hutong
Jingshan Xijie
Jingshan Qianjie 景山前街
Wusi Dajie 五四大街
Wenjin Jie 文津街
Palace Moat
Beichizi Dajie
Qihelou Jie
Zhide Beixiang
Restaurant
Café
Hall of Middle Harmony
Hall of Supreme Harmony
Palace Museum
Golden Stream
Beichang Jie 北长街
Gate of Supreme Harmony
Donghuamen Dajie 东华门大街
Dragonfly Therapeutic Retreat
Meridian Gate
Palace Moat
Nanchang Jie 南长街
Pudusi Qianxiang 普渡寺前巷
Nanchizi Dajie 南池子大街
Duanku Hutong 缎库胡同
Zhongshan Park
Changpu River Park
Xichang'an Jie 西长安街
Dongchang'an Jie 东长安街
Tiananmen Xi 天安门西地铁站
Tiananmen Dong 天安门东地铁站
Tiananmen Square

Forbidden City

Top Sights

	Gate of Supreme Harmony	B4
	Hall of Middle Harmony	B3
	Hall of Supreme Harmony	B3
	Meridian Gate	B5

Sights

1	Chàngyīn Pavilion	C2
2	Chéngguāng Gate	B2
3	Chengqian Hall	C2
4	Clock Exhibition Hall	C2
	Courtyard Gallery	(see 48)
5	Dagaoxuan Temple	A1
6	Donghua Gate	C4
7	Duān Gate	B6
8	Earthly Tranquillity Palace	B2
9	Eternal Spring Palace	B2
10	Front Hall	C5
11	Fúyòu Temple	A3
12	Gate of Heavenly Peace	B6
13	Gate of Military Prowess	B4
14	Hall of Character Cultivation	C2
15	Hall of Harmony	C2
16	Hall of Jewellery	C2
17	Hall of Joyful Longevity	C2
18	Hall of Mental Cultivation	B2
19	Hall of Military Prowess	B4
20	Hall of Preserving Harmony	B3
21	Hall of Union	B2
22	Heavenly Purity Gate	B3
23	Hongyi Pavilion	B4
24	Imperial Garden	B2
25	Imperial Peace Hall	B2
26	Imperial Supremacy Hall	C2
27	Jadeware Exhibition	C2
28	Jingren Hall	C2
29	Jingshan Park	B1
30	Middle Hall	C5
31	Nine Dragon Screen	C3
32	Palace of Heavenly Purity	B2
33	Pudu Temple	D5
34	Rear Hall	C5
35	Shenwu Gate	B2
36	Square Altar	B5
37	Thousand Autumns Pavilion	B2
38	Wanshou Xinglong Temple	A2
39	Well of Concubine Zhen	C2
40	Western Palaces	B2
41	Workers Cultural Palace	C5
42	Xihe Gate	B4
43	Xihua Gate	A4
44	Yìkūn Palace	B2
45	Zhongshan Park	B6

Sleeping

46	Emperor	D2
47	Peking International Youth Hostel	D3

Eating

48	Courtyard	D4

Entertainment

49	Forbidden City Concert Hall	B6
50	What Bar?	A4

from overseas. Many of the 18th-century examples were imported through Guǎngdōng from England; others are from Switzerland, America and Japan. Exquisitely wrought, fashioned with magnificently designed elephants and other creatures, they all display an astonishing artfulness and attention to detail. Standout clocks include the 'Gilt Copper Astronomy Clock', equipped with a working model of the solar system, and the automaton-equipped 'Gilt Copper Clock' with a robot writing Chinese characters with a brush. Time your arrival for 11am or 2pm and treat yourself to the clock performance in which choice timepieces strike the hour and give a display to wide-eyed children and adults.

Also look out for the excellent **Hall of Jewellery** (珍宝馆; Zhēnbǎo Guǎn; Map p52; admission Y10; ⏲8.30am-4pm summer, to 3.30pm winter), tickets for which also entitle you to glimpse the **Well of Concubine Zhen** (珍妃井; Zhēnfēi Jǐng; Map p52), into which the namesake wretch was thrown on the orders of Cixi, and the glazed **Nine Dragon Screen** (九龙壁; Jiǔlóng Bì; Map p52). The treasures on view are fascinating: within the **Hall of Harmony** (颐和轩; Yíhé Xuān; Map p52) sparkle Buddhist statues fashioned from gold and inlaid with gems, and a gold pagoda glittering with precious stones, followed by jade, jadeite, lapis lazuli and crystal pieces displayed in the **Hall of Joyful Longevity** (乐寿堂; Lèshòu Táng; Map p52). Further objects are displayed within the **Hall of Character Cultivation** (养性殿; Yǎngxìng Diàn; Map p52). The **Chàngyīn Pavilion** (畅音阁; Chàngyīn Gé; Map p52) to the east was formerly an imperial stage.

Gate of Heavenly Peace HISTORIC SITE
(天安门; Tiān'ānmén; Map p52; admission Y15, bag storage Y1-6; ⏲8.30am-4.30pm; Ⓜ Tiānānmén Xī

or Tiānānmén Dōng) Hung with a vast, beatific portrait of Mao and lending its name to the square immediately south, the Gate of Heavenly Peace is a potent national symbol. Built in the 15th century and restored in the 17th century, the double-eaved gate was formerly the largest of the four gates of the Imperial Wall which enveloped the imperial grounds.

The gate is divided into five doors and reached via seven bridges spanning a stream. Each of these bridges was restricted in its use and only the emperor could use the central door and bridge.

Mao proclaimed the People's Republic on 1 October 1949 from here and his gigantic portrait is the dominating feature, with anachronistic slogans on either side.

Climb up for some sweeping views of Tiān'ānmén Sq, and peek inside at the impressive beams and overdone paintwork; in all there are 60 gargantuan wooden pillars and 17 vast lamps suspended from the ceiling. Within the gatetower there is also a fascinating photographic history of the gate (but only in Chinese) and Tiān'ānmén Sq. Yawn-inducing patriotic video presentations celebrating communist events round off the picture.

It's free to walk through the gate, but if you climb it you'll have to pay the admission fee and pay to store your bag at the kiosk (one hour max). Security at the gate is intense and locals are scrupulously frisked. The ticket office only sells tickets for the gate; to visit the Forbidden City, continue north until you can go no further.

Duān Gate HISTORIC SITE

(端门; Duān Mén; Map p52; admission Y10; ⏲8.30am-4.30pm; Ⓜ Tiānānmén Xī or Tiānānmén Dōng) Sandwiched between the Gate of Heavenly Peace and Meridian Gate, Duān Gate was stripped of its treasures by foreign forces quelling the Boxer Rebellion (according to the blurb).

Front Gate HISTORIC SITE

(前门; Qián Mén; Map p48; admission high/low season Y20/10, audioguide Y20; ⏲8.30am-4.30pm; Ⓜ Qiánmén) The Front Gate actually consists of two gates, originally linked by a by a semicircular enceinte, which was swept aside in the early 20th century. Without the city walls, the gate sits entirely out of context, like a door without a wall. The northerly gate, 40m-high **Zhèngyáng Gate** (正阳门; Zhèngyáng Mén) – literally 'Facing the Sun Gate' – dates from the Ming dynasty. The largest of the nine impressive gates of the inner city wall dividing the Inner or Tartar (Manchu) City from the Outer or Chinese City, the gate was partially destroyed during the Boxer Rebellion of 1900 and the temples that flanked it have vanished. Also torched during the Boxer Rebellion, the **Arrow Tower** (箭楼; Jiàn Lóu) to the south is of a similar age and looks down Qianmen Dajie. To the east is the former British-built **Old Station Building** (老车站; Lǎo Chēzhàn; Qián Mén Railway Station), now housing the (unopened) Běijīng Railway Museum.

Běijīng Planning Exhibition Hall MUSEUM

(北京市规划展览馆; Běijīng Shì Guīhuà Zhǎnlǎnguǎn; Map p48; 20 Qianmen Dongdajie; admission Y30; ⏲9am-5pm Tue-Sun, last tickets 4pm) For Chinese cities undergoing a facelift, a planning exhibition hall is de rigeur. The exhibition is all a rather suffocating back-slapping paean to the Běijīng of tomorrow but the detailed diorama of the modern metropolis is worth a look.

National Centre for the Performing Arts THEATRE

(国家大剧院; Guójiā Dàjùyuàn; admission Y30; ⏲1.30-5pm Tue-Fri, 9.30am-5pm Sat & Sun; Ⓜ Tiānānmén Xī) Critics have compared it to an egg, but it's more like a massive mercury bead, an ultramodern missile silo or the futuristic lair of a James Bond villain. To some it's a dazzling work of art, to others it's *the* definitive blot-on-the-landscape. The unmistakable building rises – if that is the word for it – just west of the Great Hall of the People, its glass membrane perennially cleaned by squads of roped daredevil cleaners fending off the Běijīng dust. Despite protestations from designers that its round and square elements pay obeisance to traditional Chinese aesthetics, they're not fooling anyone: the theatre is designed to embody the transglobal (transgalactic perhaps) aspirations of contemporary China.

Examine the bulbous interior, including the titanic steel ribbing of interior bolsters (each of the 148 bolsters weighs eight tonnes). A fascinating exhibition inside displays failed competition conceptions and construction efforts that realised the final building; note how many of the failed entrants (eg the proposal from Obermeyer & Deilmann) incorporated echoes of the Great Hall of the People into their design, something that the winning design (from ADP Aeroports de Paris) avoided at all costs. A noticeboard in the foyer should inform you which of the three halls are open, as they are occasionally shut.

Great Hall of the People HISTORIC SITE
(人民大会堂; Rénmín Dàhuìtáng; Map p48; adult Y30, bag deposit Y2-5; ⌚8.30am-3pm; Ⓜ Tiānānmén Xī) The Great Hall of the People, on the western side of Tiān'ānmén Sq, is where the National People's Congress convenes. The 1959 architecture is monolithic and intimidating; the tour parades visitors past a choice of 29 of its lifeless rooms. Also on the billing is a 5000-seat banquet room and the 10,000-seat auditorium with the familiar red star embedded in a galaxy of lights in the ceiling. It's closed when the National People's Congress is in session. The ticket office is down the south side of the building. Bags must be checked in but cameras are admitted. Hours vary.

FREE **Chairman Mao Memorial Hall** MAUSOLEUM
(毛主席纪念堂; Máo Zhǔxí Jìniàntáng; Map p48; bag storage Y2-10, camera storage Y2-5; ⌚8am-noon Tue-Sun; Ⓜ Tiānānmén Xī, Tiānānmén Dōng or Qiánmén) Chairman Mao died in September 1976 and his Memorial Hall was constructed shortly thereafter on the former site of the Zhōnghuá Gate.

The Chinese display an almost religious respect when confronted with the physical presence of Mao. The Great Helmsman's mummified corpse lies in a crystal cabinet, draped in a red flag emblazoned with hammer and sickle while impatient guards in white gloves brusquely wave the hoi polloi on towards further rooms and Mao memorabilia. At certain times of the year the body requires maintenance and is not on view. Bags must be deposited at the building east of the memorial hall across the road (if you leave your camera in your bag you will be charged for it).

Monument to the People's Heroes MONUMENT
(人民英雄纪念碑; Rénmín Yīngxióng Jìniànbēi; Map p48; Ⓜ Tiānānmén Xī, Tiānānmén Dōng or Qiánmén) Completed in 1958, this 37.9m-high obelisk, made of Qīngdǎo granite, bears bas-relief carvings of key patriotic and revolutionary events (such as Lin Zexu destroying opium at Hǔmén in the 19th century, and Tàipíng rebels).

Foreign Legation Quarter HISTORIC SITE
(Map p48; Ⓜ Qiánmén, Wángfǔjǐng or Chōngwénmén) For grand shades of Europe, the former Foreign Legation Quarter where the 19th-century foreign powers flung up embassies, schools, churches, post offices and banks is well worth a stroll.

BĚIJĪNG MUSEUM PASS

To save money and time queuing for tickets, pocket this **pass** (博物馆通票; Bówùguǎn Tōngpiào; Y80) which allows either complimentary access or discounted admission (typically 50%) to almost 60 museums, temples or tourist sights in and around Běijīng. Not all museums are worth visiting, but you only have to visit a small selection of museums to get your money back. The pass comes in the form of a booklet (Chinese with minimal English), effective from 1 January to 31 December in any one year. You can pick it up from participating museums and sights; it can be hard to find (especially as the year progresses), so phone ☎6222 3793 or ☎6221 3256 (www.bowuguan.com.cn, in Chinese) to locate stocks (free delivery within Fifth Ring Rd).

Access the area walking up the steps east from Tiānānmén Sq into Dongjiaomin Xiang (东交民巷), once called Legation St and renamed 'Anti-Imperialism Road' during the iconoclastic Cultural Revolution. **Legation Quarter** (Map p48; 23 Qianmen Dongdajie) is a classy cluster of elegantly restored legation buildings towards the west end of Dongjiaomin Xiang. The commercial quadrant – which opened straight into the jaws of the credit crunch – is home to several exclusive restaurants (including Maison Boulud), shops and an art gallery. The attractive green-roofed, orange brick building further east at No 40 is the stately former **Dutch Legation**.

The domed building at 4a Zhengyi Lu, on the corner of Zhengyi Lu (正义路) and Dongjiaomin Xiang, is the former **Yokahama Specie Bank**. The grey building at No 19 Dongjiaomin Xiang is the former **French post office**, now the Jingyuan Sichuan Restaurant, not far from the former **French Legation** (法国使馆旧址; Fǎguó Shǐguǎn Jiùzhǐ) at No 15.

Backing onto a small school courtyard, the twin spires of the Gothic **St Michael's Church** (东交民巷天主教堂;

PEKING-KNEES

Běijīng's uncompromising concrete distances can wreak havoc on the body's shock absorbers and bad air days can leave your hair, skin and air sacs worse for wear. Take time out to recharge, revitalise and put that spring back into your step.

Dragonfly Therapeutic Retreat (悠庭保健会所; yōutíng bǎojiàn huìsuǒ; Map p53; ☎6527 9368; 60 Donghuamen Dajie; ⏲11am-1am; Ⓜ Tiānānmén Dōng) is a short walk from the east gate of the Forbidden City. Expect to pay from Y135 for an hour-long body or 'Oriental Foot' massage, or Y270 for a 'Top to Toe'. It has expertly trained masseurs.

Jíxiáng Zhìli Foot Massage Health Centre (吉祥智利; ☎6552 2758; 207 Chaoyangmenwai Dajie; ⏲10am-midnight) is where you can massage away those aches and cramps with the excellent-value Y28 foot massage. You can also treat yourself to a full-body massage for Y66.

Dōngjiàomínxiàng Catholic Church) rises ahead at No 11, facing the green roofs and ornate red brickwork of the former **Belgian Legation**.

North along Taijichang Dajie is a brick street sign embedded in the northern wall of Táijīchǎng Tóutiáo (台基厂头条), carved with the old name of the road, Rue Hart.

Běijīng Police Museum MUSEUM
(北京警察博物馆; Běijīng Jǐngchá Bówùguǎn; 36 Dongjiaomin Xiang; Map p48; admission Y5, through ticket Y20; ⏲9am-4pm Tue-Sun; Ⓜ Qiánmén) Propaganda-infested maybe, but some mesmerising exhibits make this museum a fascinating peek into Běijīng's police force. Learn how Běijīng's first PSB college operated from the Dōngyuè Temple in 1949, and how the Běijīng PSB was destroyed during the 'national catastrophe' of the Cultural Revolution. Upstairs gets to grips with morbid crimes and their investigations; for police weapons, head to the 4th floor. The through ticket includes laser shooting practice and a souvenir. The building was formerly the First National City Bank of New York.

China National Museum MUSEUM
(中国国家博物馆; Zhōngguó Guójiā Bówùguǎn; Map p48; admission Y30, audio tour Y30; ⏲8.30am-4.30pm; Ⓜ Tiānānmén Dōng) This Soviet-style building is due to reopen by 2011 after a massive expansion program that has seen it closed for an interminably long period.

Zhōngshān Park PARK
(中山公园; Zhōngshān Gōngyuán; Map p52; admission Y3; ⏲6am-9pm summer, 6.30am-7pm winter; Ⓜ Tiānānmén Xī) This lovely little park, west of the Gate of Heavenly Peace, has a section hedging up against the Forbidden City moat. Formerly the sacred Ming-style Altar to the God of the Land and the God of Grain (Shìjìtán), where the emperor offered sacrifices, it's tidy and tranquil.

Workers Cultural Palace PARK
(劳动人民文化宫; Láodòng Rénmín Wénhuà Gōng; Map p52; admission Y2; ⏲6.30am-7.30pm; Ⓜ Tiānānmén Dōng) Sounding like a social centre for Leninist labourers, this haven of peace was actually the emperor's premier place of worship, the **Supreme Temple** (太庙; Tài Miào). The often-overlooked temple halls, cloaked in imperial yellow tiles and hunched over expansive courtyards, suggest a mini version of the Forbidden City, sans crowds.

Lao She Museum MUSEUM
(老舍纪念馆; Lǎo Shě Jìniànguǎn; Map p48; 19 Fengfu Hutong; ⏲9am-4pm Tue-Sun; Ⓜ Dēngshìkǒu) Parcelled away down a small *hútòng* off Dengshikou Xijie, this simple museum was the courtyard home of much-loved Běijīng author Lǎo She. Peruse the author's life via newspaper cuttings, first editions, photographs and personal effects. The museum glosses over *the* most salient event in the writer's life: his vituperative beating by Red Guards in August 1966 and his death by drowning in Taiping Lake the following day.

Courtyard Gallery ART GALLERY
(四合院画廊; Sìhéyuàn Huàláng; Map p52; 95 Donghuamen Dajie; Ⓜ Tiānānmén Dōng) A good-looking pit stop on the way to the imperial palace, this micro-gallery and blank white minimalist space in the basement of its namesake moat-side restaurant, across the way from the Forbidden City's Dōnghuá Gate, displays a thoughtful range of contemporary works.

St Joseph's Church CHURCH

(东堂; Dōng Táng; Map p48; 74 Wangfujing Dajie; ⌚6.30-7am Mon-Sat, to 8am Sun; Ⓜ Dēngshìkǒu) Sublimely illuminated at night and called 'East Cathedral' in Chinese, St Joseph's Church was originally built in 1655, damaged by an earthquake in 1720 and rebuilt. The luckless church also caught fire in 1807, was destroyed again in 1900 during the Boxer Rebellion, and restored in 1904, only to be shut in 1966. Now restored, the church is an arresting sight on Wangfujing Dajie, with a large piazza in front swarming with children playing; white doves photogenically flutter about and Chinese models in bridal outfits pose for magazine shots. Avoid being press-ganged into buying tacky oils from the art museum behind the church.

Ancient Observatory HISTORIC SITE

(古观象台; Gǔ Guānxiàngtái; Map p74; admission Y10; ⌚9.30am-4.30pm Tue-Sun; Ⓜ Jiànguómén) Star-gazing is perhaps on the back foot in today's Běijīng – it could take a supernova to penetrate the haze that frequently blankets the nocturnal sky – but the Chinese capital has a sparkling history of astronomical observation. Běijīng's ancient observatory, mounted on the battlements of a watchtower lying along the line of the old Ming city wall, originally dates to Kublai Khan's days when it lay north of the present site.

At ground level is a pleasant courtyard containing a reproduction-looking armillary sphere supported by four dragons and halls housing displays (with limited English captions). At the rear is an attractive garden with grass, sun dials and a further armillary sphere.

Climb the steps to the roof and an array of Jesuit-designed astronomical instruments, embellished with sculptured bronze dragons and other Chinese flourishes – a unique alloy of East and West. The Jesuits, scholars as well as proselytisers, arrived in 1601 when Matteo Ricci and his associates were permitted to work alongside Chinese scientists, becoming the Chinese court's official advisers.

Instruments on display include an azimuth theodolite (1715), an altazimuth (1673) and an ecliptic armilla (1673); of the eight on view, six were designed and constructed under the supervision of the Belgian priest Ferdinand Verbiest. It's not clear which instruments on display are the originals.

Lama Temple BUDDHIST TEMPLE

(雍和宫; Yōnghé Gōng; Map p72; 28 Yonghegong Dajie; admission Y25, English audioguide Y20; ⌚9am-4pm; Ⓜ Yōnghégōng-Lama Temple) This exceptional temple is a glittering attraction in Běijīng's Buddhist firmament. If you only have time for one temple (the Temple of Heaven isn't really a temple) make it this one, where riveting roofs, fabulous frescoes, magnificent decorative arches, tapestries, eye-popping carpentry, Tibetan prayer wheels, tantric statues and a superb pair of Chinese lions mingle with dense clouds of incense.

The most renowned Tibetan Buddhist temple outside the historic lands of Tibet, the Lama Temple was converted to a lamasery in 1744 after serving as the former residence of Emperor Yong Zheng. Today the temple is an active place of worship, attracting pilgrims from afar, some of whom prostrate themselves in submission at full length within its halls.

Resplendent within the **Hall of the Wheel of the Law** (Fǎlún Diàn) is a substantial bronze statue of a benign and smiling Tsong Khapa (1357–1419), founder of the Gelukpa or Yellow Hat sect, robed in yellow and illuminated by a skylight.

A magnificent 18m-high statue of the Maitreya Buddha in his Tibetan form, clothed in yellow satin and reputedly sculpted from a single block of sandalwood, rises up magnificently within the **Wànfú Pavilion** (Wànfú Gé). Each of the Bodhisattva's toes is the size of a pillow. Behind the statue is the Vault of Avalokiteshvara, from where a diminutive and blue-faced statue of Guanyin peeks out. The Wànfú Pavilion is linked by an overhead walkway to the **Yánsuí Pavilion** (Yánsuí Gé), which encloses a huge lotus flower that revolves to reveal an effigy of the longevity Buddha.

Don't miss the collection of bronze Tibetan Buddhist statues within the **Jiètái Lóu**. Most effigies date from the Qing dynasty, from languorous renditions of Green Tara and White Tara to exotic, tantric pieces (such as Samvara) and figurines of the fierce-looking Mahakala. Also peruse the collection of Tibetan Buddhist ornaments within the **Bānchán Lóu**, where an array of *dorje* (Tibetan sceptres), mandalas and Tantric figures are displayed along with an impressive selection of ceremonial robes in silk and satin.

BĚIJĪNG CITY WALLS

Had they been preserved – or even partially protected Nánjīng-style – rather than almost entirely obliterated in the ideological 1950s and '60s, Běijīng's mighty city walls and imposing gates would rank among China's top sights. Their loss is visceral, for they were once a central part of Běijīng's identity and the city's geographic rationale owed so much to their existence. Many Beijingers over the age of 50 lament their destruction in the same way they might deplore the devastation of Běijīng's *hútòng*. A disparate collection of original gates (Qián Mén, Déshèng Mén, the Gate of Heavenly Peace) survive and the occasional portal, such as Yǒngdìng Mén, has been rebuilt, but otherwise the lion's share of Běijīng's grand gates is at one with Nineveh and Tyre.

An epitaph for the city walls, the **Ming City Wall Ruins Park** (明城墙遗志公园; Míng Chéngqiáng Yízhǐ Gōngyuán; Chōngwénmén Dongdajie; admission free; ⏲24hr; Ⓜ Chōngwénmén) runs next to a section of the Ming inner-city wall along the entire length of the northern flank of Chongwenmen Dongdajie. The restored wall stretches for around 2km, rising to a height of around 15m and interrupted every 80m with *dūn tái* (buttresses), which extend south from the wall.

The park extends from the former site of Chōngwén Mén (one of the nine gates of the inner city wall) to the **Southeast Corner Watchtower** (东南角楼;Dōngnán Jiǎolóu; Dongbianmen; admission Y10; ⏲8am-5.30pm; Ⓜ Jiànguómén or Chōngwénmén). Its green-tiled, twin-eaved roof rising up imperiously, this splendid Ming-dynasty fortification is punctured with 144 archer's windows. The highly impressive interior has some staggering carpentry: huge red pillars surge upwards, topped with solid beams. On the 1st floor is the superb **Red Gate Gallery** (红门画廊; Hóngmén Huàláng; www.redgategallery.com; admission free; ⏲10am-5pm); say you are visiting the Red Gate Gallery and the Y10 entry fee to the watchtower is waived. A fascinating exhibition on the 2nd floor within details the history of Běijīng's city gates.

Humble counterpart of the Southeast Corner Watchtower, the **Southwest Corner Watchtower** (Xībiànmén Jiǎolóu; Map p44) is not as impressive as its famous sibling, but you can climb up onto a section of the old city wall amid the roaring traffic. In an excavated pit on Beiheyan Dajie east of the Forbidden City sits a pitiful stump, all that remains of the magnificent **Dōng'ān Mén** (Map p48), the east gate of the Imperial City. The remains are located in the **Imperial Wall Foundation Ruins Park** (Map p48), a slender strip of park following the footprint of the eastern side of the vanished Imperial City Wall.

The street outside the temple entrance heaves with shops piled high with statues of Buddha, talismans, Buddhist charms, incense and keepsakes, picked over by a constant stream of pilgrims.

Confucius Temple & Imperial College

CONFUCIAN TEMPLE

An incense stick's toss away from the Lama Temple, the desiccated **Confucius Temple** (孔庙、国子监; Kǒng Miào; Map p72; 13 Guozijian Jie; admission Y20; ⏲8.30am-5pm; Ⓜ Yonghegong-Lama Temple) had a pre-Olympics spruce up that failed to shift its indelible sense of otherworldly detachment. Like all Confucian shrines, China's second-largest Confucian temple feels rather like a mausoleum, so expect peace and quiet. Some of Běijīng's last remaining *páilóu* bravely survive in the *hútòng* outside (Guozijian Jie) while antediluvian *bìxì* (tortoise-like dragons) glare inscrutably from repainted pavilions. Lumpy and ossified ancient cypresses claw stiffly at the sky while at the rear a numbing forest of 190 stelae (stones or slabs etched with figures or inscriptions) records the 13 Confucian classics in 630,000 Chinese characters.

A ghastly footnote lies unrecorded behind the tourist blurb. Běijīng writer Lao She was dragged here in August 1966, forced to his knees in front of a bonfire of Běijīng opera costumes to confess his 'antirevolutionary crimes', and beaten. The much-loved writer drowned himself the next day in Taiping Lake.

West of the Confucius Temple is the **Imperial College** (国子监; Guózǐjiàn; Map p72), where the emperor expounded the Confucian classics to an audience of thousands of kneeling students, professors and court officials – an annual rite. Built by the grandson of Kublai Khan in 1306, the former college was the supreme academy during the Yuan, Ming and Qing dynasties. On the site is a marvellous glazed, three-gate, single-eaved decorative archway. The Bìyōng Hall beyond is a twin-roofed structure with yellow tiles surrounded by a moat and topped with a shimmering gold knob.

The surrounding streets and *hútòng* are ideal for browsing, harbouring a charming selection of cafes, restaurants and small shops.

Nanluogu Xiang HISTORIC STREET

(南锣鼓巷; Map p72) Once neglected and ramshackle, strewn with spent coal briquettes in winter and silent except for the hacking coughs of old timers or the jangling of bicycle bells, the fun-filled north-south alleyway of Nanluogu Xiang (literally 'South Gong and Drum Alley') underwent accelerated evolution from around 2000 when the pioneering Passby Bar served its first customer. In the mid-noughties, money was tipped into a Nanluogu Xiang facelift: the alley is now the model for how an old *hútòng* haunt can be converted for those in need of decent breakfasts, diverse shopping, appetising lunches, *hútòng* sightseeing, a round of imported beers with dinner and funky courtyard accommodation (in that order). If you're looking to put a pillow under your head, a mushrooming array of fine courtyard hotels has sprung up.

It's quite a carnival. Crowds of Chinese photograph anything that moves (or doesn't) and the alley is perched precariously between its dwindling charm and commercial overload: the impending arrival of its own underground station may be the final straw. Today you can hoover up a miscellany of food from German waffles to crepes, Mongolian, Tibetan or Qīnghǎi yoghurt, fish and chips and cheap alcohol or fork out for toys, trendy T-shirts, ceramics and much more. The shop with the eternal queue is the Wěnyǔ Cheese Shop (No 49), flogging Mongolian cheese. Perceiving a lucrative market, several shops have moved in from Shànghǎi, including Feel Shanghai.

Look out for the 1960s **slogan** on the wall of the Wànqìng Pawnshop, located opposite Plastered T-shirts at 61 Nanluogu Xiang, which exhorts passersby: 'Industry should learn from Dàqìng, agriculture should learn from Dàzhài, the whole nation should learn from the People's Liberation Army'. Just to the north is an earlier slogan from the 1950s, largely obscured with grey paint. Taxis occasionally cruise up the narrow alley, leaving camera-toting pedestrians pinned to the wall.

Do also take time to explore the many *hútòng* that run off east and west from Nanluogu Xiang, if only to fling off the crowds or do our cycling tour in reverse. Mao'er Hutong is one of Běijīng's most famous old alleys, while Dongmianhua Hutong was poetically renamed Great Leap Forward 3rd Alley during the Cultural Revolution.

Drum Tower & Bell Tower HISTORIC SITE

Repeatedly destroyed and restored, the **Drum Tower** (鼓楼; Gǔlóu; Map p72; Gulou Dongdajie; admission Y20, both towers through ticket Y30; ⏲9am-5pm, last tickets 4.40pm) originally marked the centre of the old Mongol capital. The drums of this later Ming-dynasty version were beaten to mark the hours of the day. Stagger up the incredibly steep steps for impressive views over Běijīng's *hútòng* rooftops. Drum performances are given hourly from 9.30am to 11.30am and from 1.30pm to 4.50pm.

Fronted by a stele from the Qing dynasty, the **Bell Tower** (钟楼; Zhōnglóu; Map p72; ☎6401 2674; Zhonglouwan Hutong; admission Y15, both towers through ticket Y30; ⏲9am-5pm, last tickets 4.40pm) originally dates from Ming times. The Ming structure went up in a sheet of flame and the present structure is a Qing edifice dating from the 18th century. Augment visits with drinks at the Drum & Bell Bar.

Both the Drum and Bell Towers can be reached on bus 5, 58 or 107; get off at the namesake Gǔlóu stop.

China Art Gallery ART GALLERY

(中国美术馆; Zhōngguó Měishùguǎn; Map p48; 1 Wusi Dajie; admission Y20; ⏲9am-5pm, last entry 4pm; Ⓜ Dōngsì) The China Art Gallery has a range of modern paintings and hosts occasional photographic exhibitions. The subject matter of art on display is frequently anodyne – especially from Chinese artists – so consider a trip to 798 Art District for something more electrifying. There's no permanent collection so all exhibits are temporary.

Zhìhuà Temple BUDDHIST TEMPLE

(智化寺; Zhìhuà Sì; 5 Lumicang Hutong; admission Y20, audioguide Y10; ⏲8.30am-4.30pm; Ⓜ Jiànguómén or Cháoyángmén) You won't find the coffered ceiling of the third hall (it's

START DONGCHAN'AN JIE
FINISH NANLUOGU XIANG
DISTANCE 6.5KM
DURATION 1½ HOURS

Cycling Tour
Běijīng

❯ Běijīng's spirit-level flatness is tailor-made for cycling, especially if you navigate the *hútòng* that riddle the city. Hop on a pair of wheels and explore some of Běijīng's more historic dimensions on this tour.

Many of Běijīng's *hútòng* have red-painted signs in pinyin and Chinese characters, so following the route should not be too difficult, but we have added *hútòng* names in Chinese characters below to aid navigation. If you get lost, just show these characters to a local and you should be able to get directions.

Set off from Dongchang'an Jie, northeast of Tiān'ānmén Sq. Cycle north through the purple-red archway of Nanchizi Dajie (南池子大街), past the ❶ **Imperial Archives** to your right, a quiet courtyard with echoes of the Forbidden City. On your left you'll pass the eastern entrance to the ❷ **Workers Cultural Palace** from where you can glimpse the imperial yellow roof of the Supreme Temple (太庙; Tài Miào).

The Forbidden City's roofs and towers appear to the west; turn left at Donghuamen Dajie (东华门大街) intersection, then left again to follow the road between the moat and the palace walls. Note the splendid southeastern corner tower of the ❸ **Forbidden City** wall.

The trip around the moat is a spectacular route with unique views of historic Běijīng. Thread through the gate of Quèzuǒ Mén (阙佐门) and the crowded plaza in front of Meridian Gate (午门), imposing portal to the palace. Cycle through the gate of Quèyòu Mén (阙佑门) opposite, by ❹ **Zhōngshān Park**, to continue around the moat, which freezes in winter. To the west lie the eastern gates of Zhōngnánhǎi (中南海), the out-of-bounds nerve centre of political power in Běijīng.

Cycling north onto Beichang Jie (北长街), pass Fúyòu Temple (福佑寺; Fúyòu Sì) to your right – locked away behind closed gates and the palace wall. To your left stand the remains of ❺ **Wànshòu Xīnglóng Temple** (万寿兴隆寺), its band of monks long replaced by lay residents. The temple once housed surviving imperial eunuchs after the fall of the Qing dynasty.

Reaching the T-junction with Jingshan Qianjie (景山前街) and Wenjin Jie (文津街), follow the road right onto Jingshan Qianjie, but disembark at the bend in the road and wheel your bike across the street to enter the first *hútòng* – Dashizuo Hutong (大石作胡同) – heading north on the other side of the road (the *hútòng* opening is in line with the west bank of the palace moat). East of here is the inaccessible Taoist Dàgāoxuán Temple (大高玄殿; Dàgāoxuán Diàn; 23 Jingshan Xijie), its halls visible through the archway opening onto Jingshan Qianjie. Do not attempt to enter as it is a restricted zone.

Wiggling north, Dashizuo Hutong provided carved stone for the Forbidden City. Like many alleys in modern Běijīng, it's a mix of tumbledown dwellings and charmless modern blocks. Follow the alley to the end, and exit opposite ❻ **Jǐngshān Park's** west gate; west along Zhishanmen Jie (陟山门街) is Běihǎi Park's east gate.

Cycle north along Jingshan Xijie (景山西街); at its northern tip enter Gongjian Hutong (恭俭胡同), its entrance virtually straight ahead but slightly west. Exit the alley on Di'anmen Xidajie (地安门西大街); to your west is the north gate of ❼ **Běihǎi Park**; if you push your bike along the southern side of Dianmen Xidajie you'll soon arrive at the park's north gate.

Continuing north, push your bike over the pedestrian crossing then cycle along Qianhai Nanyan (前海南沿) on the eastern shore of Qiánhǎi Lake. On the far side of the lake stretches Lotus Lane, a strip of cafes and restaurants. East of the small, restored white marble Jīndìng Bridge (金锭桥; Jīndìng Qiáo) is Wànníng Bridge (万宁桥;

Wànníng Qiáo), much of which dates to the Yuan dynasty.

Continue north to Yíndìng Bridge (银锭桥; Yíndìng Qiáo) to cycle east along Yandai Xiejie (烟袋斜街) with its shops, bars and cafes. A short diversion from Yíndìng Bridge along Ya'er Hutong (鸦儿胡同) is the Buddhist Guǎnghuà Temple (广化寺) at No 31. Exiting Yandai Xiejie (there are a few steps to negotiate) onto bustling Di'anmenwai Dajie (地安门外大街), the 8 **Drum Tower** rises ahead, obscuring the 9 **Bell Tower** behind; both are worth visiting (but the area is primed for development).

Head south and east through Mao'er Hutong (帽儿胡同) which, despite being quite modern in places, gradually emerges into something more traditional. At the first main junction along Mao'er Hutong, the alley changes its name to Bei Bingmasi Hutong (北兵马司胡同), the two alleys divided by the north-south-running 10 **Nanluogu Xiang**, one of Běijīng's most famous alleyways. If you can weave through the crowds, cycle down Nanluogu Xiang and have a coffee in the relaxed, snug courtyard surrounds of the Passby Bar (108 Nanluogu Xiang) on the corner of the second *hútòng* turning on your left as you cycle south. Alternatively, keep heading south and pop into the micro-sized bar 12sqm (corner of Nanluogu Xiang and Fuxiang Hutong). You can also find a growing glut of courtyard hotels in the small *hútòng* off Nanluogu Xiang. The area is due to have its own namesake metro stop, facilitating access to the rest of the city but guaranteeing a further swelling of visitor numbers and a diminishing of Nanluogu Xiang's charm.

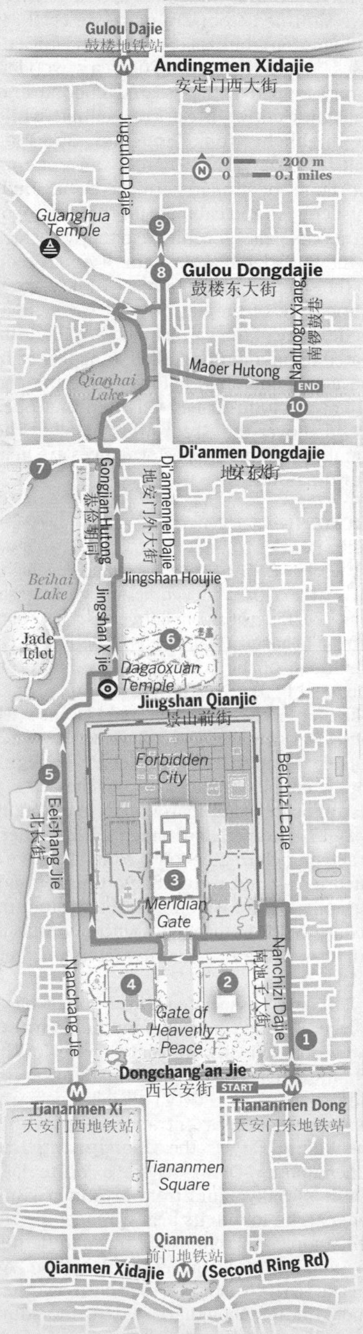

in the USA) and the Four Heavenly Kings have vanished from **Zhìhuà Gate** (智化门; Zhìhuà Mén), but the **Scriptures Hall** encases a venerable Ming-dynasty wooden library topped with a seated Buddha and a magnificently unrestored ceiling, while the highlight **Ten Thousand Buddhas Hall** (万佛殿; Wànfó Diàn) is an enticing two floors of miniature niche-borne Buddhist effigies and cabinets for the storage of sutras (its caisson ceiling currently resides in the Philadelphia Museum of Art). Creep up the steep wooden staircase (if it is open) at the back of the hall to visit the sympathetic effigy of the Vairocana (毗卢) Buddha seated upon a multipetalled lotus flower in the upper chamber, before pondering the fate of the 1000-Armed Guanyin that once presided over the **Great Mercy Hall** at the temple rear. Musical performances are held four times daily.

XĪCHÉNG 西城区

Běihǎi Park PARK

(北海公园; Běihǎi Gōngyuán; admission high/low season Y10/5, through ticket high/low season Y20/15; ⏲6.30am-8pm, buildings until 4pm; Ⓜ Tiānānmén Xī, then bus 5) Běihǎi Park, northwest of the Forbidden City, is largely occupied by the North Sea *(běihǎi),* a huge lake that freezes in winter and blooms with lotuses in summer. Old folk dance together outside temple halls and come twilight, young couples cuddle on benches. It's a restful place to stroll around, rent a rowing boat in summer and watch calligraphers practising characters on paving slabs with fat brushes and water. Some talented calligraphers can fashion characters simultaneously with both hands, with one side in mirror-writing or with characters on their sides!

The site is associated with Kublai Khan's palace, Běijīng's navel before the arrival of the Forbidden City. All that survives of the Khan's court is a large jar made of green jade in the **Round City** (团城; Tuánchéng), near the southern entrance. Also within the Round City is the **Chengguang Hall** (Chéngguāng Diàn), where a white jade statue of Sakyamuni from Myanmar (Burma) can be found, its arm wounded by the allied forces that swarmed through Běijīng in 1900 to quash the Boxer Rebellion. Attached to the North Sea, the South (Nánhǎi) and Middle (Zhōnghǎi) Seas to the south lend their name to the nerve centre of the Communist Party west of the Forbidden City, **Zhōngnánhǎi** (literally 'Middle and South Seas').

Topping **Jade Islet** (琼岛; Qióngdǎo) on the lake, the 36m-high Tibetan-style **White Dagoba** (白塔; Báitǎ) was originally built in 1651 for a visit by the Dalai Lama, and was rebuilt in 1741. Climb up to the dagoba via the **Yǒng'ān Temple** (永安寺; Yǒng'ān Sì).

Xītiān Fánjìng (西天梵境; Western Paradise), situated on the northern shore of the lake, is a lovely temple (admission included in park ticket). The nearby **Nine Dragon Screen** (九龙壁; Jiǔlóng Bì), a 5m-high and 27m-long spirit wall, is a glimmering stretch of coloured glazed tiles depicting coiling dragons, similar to its counterpart in the Forbidden City. West along the shore is the pleasant **Little Western Heaven** (小西天; Xiǎo Xītiān), a further shrine.

Jǐngshān Park PARK

(景山公园; Jǐngshān Gōngyuán; Map p48; admission Y5; ⏲6am-9.30pm; Ⓜ Tiānānmén Xī, then bus 5) A feng shui barrier shielding the Forbidden City from evil spirits (or dust storms), Jǐngshān Park was formed from the earth excavated to create the palace moat. Come here for classic panoramas over the Forbidden City's russet roofing to the south. On the eastern side of the park a locust tree stands in the place where the last of the Ming emperors, Chongzhen, hanged himself as rebels swarmed at the city walls.

Prince Gong's Residence HISTORIC SITE

(恭王府; Gōngwáng Fǔ; ☎6616 8149, 6601 6132; 14 Liuyin Jie; admission Y40, guided tours incl tea & performance Y60; ⏲7.30am-4.30pm summer, 8am-4pm winter; Ⓜ Píng'ānlǐ, then bus 118) Reputed to be the model for the mansion in Cao Xueqin's 18th-century classic *Dream of the Red Mansions,* this residence is one of Běijīng's largest private residential compounds. If you can, get here ahead of the tour buses and admire the rockeries, plants, pools, pavilions, corridors and elaborately carved gateways. Arrive with the crowds and you won't want to stay. Performances of Běijīng opera are held regularly in the Qing-dynasty **Grand Opera House** in the east of the grounds.

Miàoyīng Temple White Dagoba BUDDHIST TEMPLE

(妙应寺白塔; Miàoyīng Sì Báitǎ; 171 Fuchengmennei Dajie; admission Y20; ⏲9am-4pm; Ⓜ Fùchéngmén) Buried away down a ragged *hútòng,* the Miàoyīng Temple slumbers beneath its distinctive, pure-white Yuan-dynasty

BĚIJĪNG'S *HÚTÒNG*

Běijīng's medieval genotype is most discernible down the city's leafy *hútòng* (胡同; narrow alleyways). The spirit and soul of the city lives and breathes among these charming and ragged lanes where a warm sense of community and hospitality survives. Criss-crossing chunks of Běijīng within the Second Ring Rd, the *hútòng* link up into a huge and enchanting warren of one-storey dwellings and historic courtyard homes. Hundreds of *hútòng* survive but many have been swept aside in Běijīng's race to build a modern city. Identified by white plaques, historic homes are protected, but for many others a way of life hangs in a precarious balance.

After Genghis Khan's army reduced the city of Běijīng to rubble, the new city was redesigned with *hútòng*. By the Qing dynasty over 2000 such passageways riddled the city, leaping to around 6000 by the 1950s; now the figure has drastically dwindled. Today's *hútòng* universe is a hotchpotch of the old and the new: Qing-dynasty courtyards are scarred with socialist-era conversions and outhouses while others have been assiduously rebuilt, with a garage perhaps for the Mercedes.

Hútòng nearly all run east–west so that the main gate faces south, satisfying feng shui (wind/water) requirements. This south-facing aspect guarantees sunshine and protection from negative principles amassing in the north.

Old walled *sìhéyuàn* (courtyards) are the building blocks of this delightful universe. Many are still lived in and hum with activity. From spring to autumn, men collect outside their gates, drinking beer, playing chess, smoking and chewing the fat. Inside, scholar trees soar aloft, providing shade and a nesting ground for birds. Flocks of pigeons whirl through the Běijīng skies overhead, bred by locals and housed in coops often buried away within the *hútòng*.

More venerable courtyards are fronted by large, thick red doors, outside of which perch either a pair of Chinese lions or drum stones. The **Lao She Museum** is an excellent example of a courtyard home. To savour Běijīng's courtyard ambience, down a drink at the **Passby Bar**, devour a meal at the **Dàlǐ Courtyard** and sleep it all off at **Courtyard 7** or any number of Běijīng's courtyard hotels.

Tours are easy to find: *hútòng* trishaw drivers lurk in packs around Qiánhǎi Lake: if you are foreign and not walking with real intent, they pounce, waiving flimsy plastic-wrapped cards detailing their tours and repeating the words '*hútòng, hútòng*' (all too often the extent of their 'English').

dagoba (stupa). The **Hall of the Great Enlightened One** (大觉宝殿; Dàjué Bǎodiàn) glitters splendidly with hundreds of Tibetan Buddhist effigies, the highlight of any visit.

In other halls reside a four-faced effigy of Guanyin (here called Parnashavari) and a trinity of past, present and future Buddhas. Exit the temple and wander the tangle of local alleyways for earthy shades of *hútòng* life. Take bus 13, 101, 102 or 103 to Báitǎ Sì bus stop (near Baitasi Lu) or take the subway to Fùchéngmén and walk east.

Běijīng Zoo ZOO

(北京动物园; Běijīng Dòngwùyuán; 137 Xizhimenwai Dajie; admission summer/winter Y15/10, pandas Y5, automatic guide Y40; ⏲7.30am-6pm summer, to 5pm winter; 👪; Ⓜ Běijīng Zoo) The zoo is a pleasant spot for a stroll among the trees, grass and willow-fringed lakes as long as you ignore the animal's pitiful cages and enclosures. If you want to see fauna, it's best just to zero in on the pandas (if you are not going to Sìchuān) or the **Běijīng Aquarium** (adult/child Y120/60; ⏲9am-5pm summer, to 5.30pm winter) in the northeastern corner of the zoo.

Boats to the Summer Palace depart from the **dock** (☎8838 4476; single/return Y40/70) every hour from 10am to 4pm, May to October.

CHŌNGWÉN 崇文区

Temple of Heaven Park PARK

(天坛公园; Tiāntán Gōngyuán; Map p44; Tiantan Donglu; admission park/through ticket high season Y15/35, low season Y10/30, audio tour available at each gate Y40; ⏲park 6am-9pm, sights 8am-6pm; Ⓜ Tiāntándōngmén) A tranquil oasis of peace and methodical Confucian design in one of China's busiest urban landscapes, the 267-hectare Temple of Heaven Park is encompassed by a long wall with a gate at each compass point. The temple – the Chinese actually means 'Altar of Heaven' so don't expect burning incense or worshippers – originally served as a vast stage for solemn rites performed by the Son of Heaven, who prayed here for good harvests, and sought divine clearance and atonement.

The arrangement is typical of Chinese parks, with the imperfections, bumps and wild irregularities of nature largely deleted and the harmonising hand of man accentuated in obsessively straight lines and regular arrangements. This effect is magnified by Confucian objectives, where the human intellect is imposed on the natural world, fashioning order and symmetry. The resulting balance and harmony have an almost haunting – but slightly claustrophobic – beauty. Police whir about in electric buggies as visitors lazily stroll among temple buildings, groves of ancient trees and birdsong. Around 4000 ancient, knotted cypresses (some 800 years old, their branches propped up on poles) poke towards the Běijīng skies within the grounds.

Seen from above, the temple halls are round and the bases square, in accordance with the notion 'Tiānyuán Dìfāng' (天圆地方) – 'Heaven is round, Earth is square'. Also observe that the northern rim of the park is semicircular, while its southern end is square. The traditional approach to the temple was from the south, via **Zhāohēng Gate** (昭亨门; Zhāohēng Mén); the north gate is an architectural afterthought.

The 5m-high **Round Altar** (圜丘; Yuánqiū; admission Y20) was constructed in 1530 and rebuilt in 1740. Consisting of white marble arrayed in three tiers, its geometry revolves around the imperial number nine. Odd numbers possess heavenly significance, with nine the largest single-digit odd number. Symbolising heaven, the top tier is a huge mosaic of nine rings, each composed of multiples of nine stones, so that the ninth ring equals 81 stones. The stairs and balustrades are similarly presented in multiples of nine. Sounds generated from the centre of the upper terrace undergo amplification from the marble balustrades (the acoustics can get noisy when crowds join in).

The octagonal **Imperial Vault of Heaven** (皇穹宇; Huáng Qióngyǔ) was erected at the same time as the Round Altar, its shape echoing the lines of the Hall of Prayer for Good Harvests. The hall contained tablets of the emperor's ancestors, employed during winter solstice ceremonies.

Wrapped around the Imperial Vault of Heaven just north of the altar is the **Echo Wall** (回音壁; Huíyīnbì; admission Y20). A whisper can travel clearly from one end to your friend's ear at the other – unless a cacophonous tour group joins in (get here early for this one).

The dominant feature of the park is the **Hall of Prayer for Good Harvests** (祈年殿; Qíniān Diàn; admission Y20), an astonishing structure with a triple-eaved purplish-blue umbrella roof mounted on a three-tiered marble terrace. The wooden pillars (made from Oregon fir) support the ceiling without nails or cement – for a building 38m high and 30m in diameter, that's quite an accomplishment. Embedded in the ceiling is a carved dragon, a symbol of the emperor. Built in 1420, the hall was reduced to carbon after being zapped by a lightning bolt during the reign of Guangxu in 1889; a faithful reproduction based on Ming architectural methods was erected the following year.

With a green-tiled tow-tier roof, the **Animal Killing Pavilion** (Zǎishēng Tíng) was the venue for the slaughter of sacrificial oxen, sheep, deer and other animals. Today it stands locked and passive but can be admired from the outside. Stretching out from here runs a **Long Corridor** (Chángláng), where Chinese crowds sit out and deal cards, listen to the radio, play keyboards, practise Běijīng opera, dance moves and kick hacky sack. Sacrificial music was rehearsed at the **Divine Music Administration** (Shényuè Shǔ) in the west of the park, while wild cats inhabit the dry moat of the green-tiled Fasting Palace.

FREE **Natural History Museum** MUSEUM
(自然博物馆; Zìrán Bówùguǎn; 126 Tianqiao Nandajie; ⌚8.30am-5pm, last tickets 4pm; Ⓜ Qiánmén) The main entrance hall to the recently restored Natural History Museum is hung with portraits of the great natural historians, including Darwin and Linnaeus. Escort kiddies to the revamped dinosaur hall facing you as you enter, which presents itself with an overarching skellybone of a *Mamenchisaurus jingyanensis* – a vast sauropod that once roamed China – and a much smaller *protoceratops*.

Some of the exhibits, such as the spliced human cadavers and genitalia in the notorious Hall of Human Bodies, are flesh-crawlingly graphic.

CHÁOYÁNG 朝阳区

Rìtán Park PARK

(日坛公园; Map p74; Ritan Lu; 6am-9pm; ; Jiànguómén or Yonganli) Established as an altar for ritual sacrifice to the sun, this is one of Běijīng's oldest and most pleasant parks. The square altar, typically surrounded by kite flyers and playing children, is ringed by a circular wall, while the rest of the park is devoted to pines, quietude, the rituals of taichi practitioners and martial arts shīfu. The park is also home to a decent outdoor **climbing wall** (8563 5038; per climb Y10; 10am-10pm) if you want to climb off calories acquired from the park's gaggle of popular bars and restaurants.

Dōngyuè Temple TAOIST TEMPLE

(东岳庙; Dōngyuè Miào; 141 Chaoyangmenwai Dajie; admission Y10, with guide Y40; 8.30am-4.30pm, last tickets 4pm; Cháoyángmén) Dating to 1607, this active temple's splendid *pǎifāng* (memorial archway) lies to the south, spliced from its shrine by the noisy intervention of Chaoyangmenwai Dajie. Stepping through the entrance pops you into a Taoist Hades, where tormented spirits in numerous halls reflect on their wrongdoing. Visiting during festival time, especially during the Chinese New Year and the Mid-Autumn Festival, sees the temple at its most colourful.

Poly Art Museum MUSEUM

(保利艺术博物馆; Bǎolì Yìshù Bówùguǎn; Map p66; www.polymuseum.com; Poly Plaza, 14 Dongzhimen Nandajie; admission Y20; Dongsishitiao) Caressed with Chinese music, this excellent museum displays a glorious array of ancient bronzes from the Shang and Zhou dynasties and an exquisite gathering of standing Bodhisattva statues. Resembling a semidivine race of smiling humans, most of the statues are from the Northern Qi, Northern Wei and Tang dynasties. It's a sublime presentation and some of the statues have journeyed through the centuries with pigment still attached. In an attached room are four of the Western-styled 12 bronze animals plundered during the sacking of the Old Summer Palace. The pig, monkey, tiger and ox peer out from glass cabinets – you can buy a model for Y12,000 if you want.

National Stadium & National Aquatics Center STADIUM

(国家体育场、国家游泳中心; Guójiā Tǐyùchǎng; Guójiā Yóuyǒng Zhōngxīn; Map p44; National Stadium Y50, National Aquatics Center Y30; 9am-6.30pm; Olympic Sport Center or Olympic Green) It's now hard to imagine that this was the scene of rapturous sporting exultation in August 2008, but such is the fate of most Olympics projects. You can enter the inspiring **National Stadium** – colloquially known as the Bird's Nest – in an attempt to recapture the euphoria of '08 and even ascend the medals podium for a further Y200, or simply admire the architecture for free from the outside. In the winter of 2010, it re-emerged as a snow park; visionaries see its future as a shopping mall and entertainment complex. The nearby **Water Cube** is well worth a gander from the outside, and at the time of writing was set to open as Asia's largest indoor water park.

BIG UNDERPANTS

The outlandish 234m-high CCTV Building (Map p74), as a continuous loop through horizontal and vertical planes, is a unique addition to the Běijīng skyline. Boldy ambitious and designed by Rem Koolhaas and Ole Scheeren of OMA, the building is an audacious statement of modernity, despite being dubbed 'Big Underpants' by locals. In February 2009, stray fireworks from CCTV's own Lantern Festival display sent the costly TV Cultural Center in the north of the complex up in flames. CCTV famously censored its own reporting of the huge conflagration, even though it was visible for miles around. Big Underpants escaped unsinged.

FREE **Olympic Forest Park** PARK

(奥林匹克森林公园; Àolínpǐkè Sēnlín Gōngyuán; Map p44; 9am-5pm; South Gate of Forest Park) The humungous 680-hectare grassy expanse goes on forever so if you're looking for a casual stroll, stick to parks in the centre of town. In summer you can hop on a boat across the lake, which seethes with fat and well-fed fish, hike along brick and concrete paths or simply make a break for the hills. Considering the epic scale of the park, it's a great way to shed a kilo or two but you may end up flagging down a passing electric buggy (Y20; 9am to 5pm) when your shuddering legs start folding at the knees.

Cháoyáng & Sānlǐtún

XUĀNWǓ & FĒNGTÁI 宣武区、丰台区

Capital Museum MUSEUM

(中国首都博物馆; Zhōngguó Shǒudū Bówùguǎn; ☎6337 0491; www.capitalmuseum.org.cn; 16 Fuxingmenwai Dajie; admission Y15; ⏰9am-5pm; Ⓜ Muxidi) This rewarding and impressively styled museum contains a mesmerising collection of ancient Buddhist statues and a lavish exhibition of Chinese porcelain. Further displays are dedicated to a chronological history of Běijīng, cultural relics of Peking Opera, a Běijīng Folk Customs exhibition and exhibits of ancient bronzes, jade, calligraphy and paintings.

Qianmen Dajie HISTORIC STREET

(前门大街; Map p48; Ⓜ Qianmen) Recently reopened after a costly overhaul, this shopping street – now pedestrianised and 'restored' to resemble a late Qing-dynasty street scene – was designed to bring the tourist dollar to a once charmingly tatty area. As late as the 1950s, this road was called Zhengyangmen Dajie (Facing the Sun Gate St), after Front Gate immediately north. Visitors are today treated to the rebuilt **Qiánmén Decorative Arch** (a concrete fake: the original was torn down in the 1950s) and invited to hop on one of the two reproduction trams (Y20) to glide along the street. Qianmen Dajie's former commercial vitality and sense of community is gone and local shops have made way for Zara, H&M et al.

Dashilar HISTORIC STREET

(大栅栏; Dàshílán'er; Map p48; Ⓜ Qianmen) Just west of Qianmen Dajie, this recently restored historic shopping street is a fascinating way to reach the antique shop street of Liulichang to the west. A collection of *lǎozi hào* (shops with history) include Ruifuxiang, Tongrentang, the Neiliansheng Shoe Shop and Liubiju. It's also an excellent place to snack and find accommodation.

Cháoyáng & Sānlǐtún

White Cloud Temple TAOIST TEMPLE
(白云观; Báiyún Guàn; Baiyun Lu; admission Y10; 8.30am-4.30pm May-Sep, to 4pm Oct-Apr; M Muxidi) Founded in AD 739, White Cloud Temple is a lively complex of shrines and courtyards, tended by distinctive Taoist monks with their hair twisted into topknots. Today's temple halls principally date from Ming and Qing times.

Near the temple entrance, a queue snakes slowly through the gate for a chance to rub a polished stone carving for good fortune. Drop by the White Cloud Temple during Chinese New Year for a magnificent *miàohuì* (temple fair).

To find the temple, walk south on Baiyun Lu and cross the moat. Continue south along Baiyun Lu and turn into a curving street on the left; follow it for 250m to the temple entrance.

Cow Street Mosque MOSQUE
(牛街礼拜寺; Niújiē Lǐbài Sì; 88 Niu Jie; admission Y10, Muslims free; 8am-sunset; M Càishìkǒu) Dating back to the 10th century, this Chinese-styled mosque is Běijīng's largest and was the burial site for several Islamic clerics. Surrounded by residential high-rises, the temple is pleasantly decorated with plants and flourishes of Arabic. Look out for the main prayer hall (only Muslims can enter), women's quarters and the Building for Observing the Moon (望月楼; Wàngyuèlóu), from where the lunar calendar was calculated. Dress appropriately (no shorts or short skirts).

Fǎyuán Temple BUDDHIST TEMPLE
(法源寺; Fǎyuán Sì; 7 Fayuansi Qianjie; admission Y5; 8.30-11am & 1.30-3.30pm; M Càishìkǒu) With its air of monastic reverence and busy monks, this bustling temple east of Cow Street Mosque was originally constructed in the 7th century. Now the China Buddhism College, the temple follows a typical Buddhist layout, but make your way to the fourth hall for its standout **copper Buddha** seated atop four further Buddhas, themselves atop a huge bulb of myriad effigies. Within the Guanyin Hall is a Ming-dynasty Thousand Hand and Thousand Eye Guanyin, while a huge supine Buddha reclines in the rear hall.

798 ART DISTRICT

Originally flung up by the East Germans, the disused and sprawling electronics factory known as **798 Art District** (798 艺术新区; Map p44; cnr Jiuxianqiao Lu & Jiuxianqiao Beilu) has for years served as the focus for Běijīng's feisty art community. Standout galleries include **Long March Space** (北京二万五千里文化传播中心; Běijīng Èrwàngwǔqiānlǐ Wénhuà Chuánbō Zhōngxīn; www.longmarchspace.com; ⏲11am-7pm Tue-Sun), where paintings, photos, installations and videos get a viewing; and the well-known **Chinese Contemporary Běijīng** (中国当代; Zhōngguó Dāngdài; www.chinesecontemporary.com; 4 Jiuxianqiao Lu; ⏲11am-7pm). Also check out **Contrasts Gallery** (⏲10am-6pm Tue-Sun), **Běijīng Tokyo Art Projects** (北京东京艺术工程; Běijīng Dōngjīng Yìshù Gōngchéng; www.tokyo-gallery.com; 4 Jiuxianqiao Lu) and the excellent **798 Photo Gallery** (百年印象摄影画廊; Bǎinián Yìnxiàng; www.798photogallery.cn; 4 Jiuxianqiao Lu). For art, architecture and design books, leaf through **Timezone 8** (⏲11.30am-7.30pm) and try one of the super-duper burgers. Several cafes are at hand when your legs give way. **Cave Café** (Dòngfáng Kāfēi) does a fine cuppa and includes a rediscovered, hand-inscribed dedication from Lin Biao on its wall. A further extensive colony of art galleries can be found around 4km northeast of 798 Art District at **Cǎochǎngdì** (草场地). For 798 Art District, ride the subway to Sanyuanqiao station, then jump on bus 401 and get off at Dàshānzi Lúkǒunán (大山子路口南).

HǍIDIÀN 海淀区

Summer Palace HISTORIC SITE

(颐和园; Yíhé Yuán; Map p70; 19 Xinjian Gongmen; ticket Y20, through ticket Y50, audioguide Y40; ⏲8:30am-5pm; Ⓜ Xīyuán or Běigōngmén) Virtually as mandatory a Běijīng sight as the Great Wall or the Forbidden City, the gargantuan Summer Palace easily merits an entire day's exploration, although a (high-paced) morning or afternoon may suffice.

Once a playground for the imperial court fleeing the suffocating summer torpor of the Forbidden City, the palace grounds, temples, gardens, pavilions, lakes, bridges, gate-towers and corridors of the Summer Palace are a marvel of landscaping. Unlike the overpowering flatland of the Forbidden City or the considered harmonies of the Temple of Heaven, the Summer Palace – with its huge lake, hilltop views and energising walks – offers a pastoral escape into the landscapes of traditional Chinese painting.

The domain had long been a royal garden before being considerably enlarged and embellished by Emperor Qianlong in the 18th century. He marshalled a 100,000-strong army of labourers to deepen and expand **Kūnmíng Lake** (昆明湖; Kūnmíng Hú; Map p70), and reputedly surveyed imperial navy drills from a hilltop perch.

Anglo-French troops vandalised the palace during the Second Opium War (1856–60). Empress Dowager Cixi launched into a refit in 1888 with money earmarked for a modern navy; the marble boat at the northern edge of the lake was her only nautical – albeit quite unsinkable – concession.

Foreign troops, angered by the Boxer Rebellion, had another go at torching the Summer Palace in 1900, prompting further restoration work. By 1949 the palace had once more fallen into disrepair, eliciting a major overhaul.

Glittering Kūnmíng Lake swallows up three-quarters of the park, overlooked by **Longevity Hill** (万寿山; Wànshòu Shān). The principal structure is the **Hall of Benevolence and Longevity** (仁寿殿; Rénshòu Diàn; Map p70), by the east gate, housing a hardwood throne and attached to a courtyard decorated with bronze animals, including the mythical *qílín* (a hybrid animal that only appeared on earth at times of harmony). Unfortunately, the hall is barricaded off so you will have to peer in.

An elegant stretch of woodwork along the northern shore, the **Long Corridor** (长廊; Cháng Láng; Map p70) is trimmed with a plethora of paintings, while the slopes and crest of Longevity Hill behind are adorned with Buddhist temples. Slung out uphill on a north–south axis, the **Buddhist Fragrance Pavilion** (佛香阁; Fóxiāng Gé; Map p70) and the **Cloud Dispelling Hall** (排云殿; Páiyún Diàn; Map p70) are linked by corridors. Crowning the peak is the **Buddhist Temple of the Sea of Wisdom** (智慧海; Zhìhuì Hǎi; Map p70), tiled with effigies of Buddha, many with obliterated heads.

Cixi's **marble boat** (清晏船; Qīngyàn Chuán; Map p70) sits immobile on the north shore, south of some fine Qing **boathouses** (船坞; Chuán Wù; Map p70). When the lake is not frozen, you can traverse Kūnmíng Lake by ferry to **South Lake Island** (南湖岛; Nánhú Dǎo; Map p70), where Cixi went to beseech the **Dragon King Temple** (龙王庙; Lóngwáng Miào; Map p70) for rain in times of drought. A graceful **17-arch bridge** (十七孔桥; Shíqīkǒng Qiáo; Map p70) spans the 150m to the eastern shore of the lake. In warm weather, **pedal boats** (4-/6-person boat per hr Y40/60; ⏲8.30am-4.30pm in summer) are also available from the dock.

Try to do a circuit of the lake along the **West Causeway** (Xīdī) to return along the east shore (or vice versa). It gets you away from the crowds, the views are gorgeous and it's a great cardiovascular workout. Based on the Su Causeway in Hángzhōu, and lined with willow and mulberry trees, the causeway kicks off just west of the boathouses. With its delightful hump, the grey and white marble **Jade Belt Bridge** (Yùdài Qiáo) dates from the reign of emperor Qianlong and crosses the point where the Jade River (Yùhé) enters the lake (when it flows).

Towards the North Palace Gate, **Sūzhōu Street** (苏州街; Sūzhōu Jiē; Map p70) is an entertaining and light-hearted diversion of riverside walkways, shops and eateries designed to mimic the famous Jiāngsū canal town.

The Summer Palace is about 12km northwest of the centre of Běijīng, accessed via Xīyuàn station (Exit C2) or Běigōngmén on line 4 of the metro system. In warmer months there's the option of taking a **boat** (☎8836 3576; Houhu Pier; one way/return incl Summer Palace admission Y70/100) from behind the Běijīng Exhibition Center near the zoo; the boat voyages via locks along the canal.

Old Summer Palace HISTORIC SITE
(圆明园; Yuánmíng Yuán; admission Y10, palace ruins Y15; ⏲7am-7pm; Ⓜ Yuánmíngyuán Park) Forever etched on China's national consciousness for its sacking and destruction by British and French forces during the Second Opium War, the old Summer Palace was originally laid out in the 12th century. Resourceful Jesuits were later employed by Emperor Qianlong to fashion European-style palaces for the gardens, incorporating elaborate fountains and baroque statuary. During its looting, much went up in flames and considerable booty was sent abroad, but a melancholic tangle of broken columns and marble chunks from the hardier Jesuit-designed stone palace buildings remain.

The subdued marble ruins of the **Palace Buildings Scenic Area** (Xīyánglóu Jǐngqū) can be mulled over in the **Eternal Spring Garden** (Chángchūn Yuán) in the northeast of the park, near the east gate. There were once over 10 buildings here, designed by Giuseppe Castiglione and Michael Benoist.

The **Great Fountain Ruins** (大水法遗址; Dàshuǐfǎ Yízhǐ) themselves are considered the best-preserved relics. Built in 1759, the main building was fronted by a lion head fountain. Standing opposite is the **Guānshuǐfǎ** (观水法), five large stone screens embellished with European carvings of military flags, armour, swords and guns. The screens were discovered in the grounds of Peking University in the 1970s and later restored to their original positions.

West of the Great Fountain Ruins are the vestiges of the **Hǎiyàntáng Reservoir** (海宴堂蓄水池台基; Hǎiyàntáng Xùshuǐchí Táijī), where the water for the impressive fountains was stored in a tower and huge water-lifting devices were employed. Also known as the Water Clock, the **Hǎiyàntáng**, where 12 bronze human statues with animal heads jetted water in 12 two-hour sequences, was constructed in 1759. The 12 animal heads from this apparatus were distributed among collections abroad, and Běijīng is attempting to retrieve them (four animal heads can be seen at the Poly Art Museum). Just west of here is the Fāngwàiguàn, a building turned into a mosque for an Imperial concubine; an artful reproduction of a former labyrinth called the **Garden of Yellow Flowers** (迷宫; Mígōng) is also nearby.

WANT MORE?

For in-depth information, reviews and recommendations at your fingertips, head to the Apple App Store to purchase Lonely Planet's *Běijīng City Guide* iPhone app.

Alternatively, head to **Lonely Planet** (www.lonelyplanet.com/china/beijing) for planning advice, author recommendations, traveller reviews and insider tips.

Summer Palace

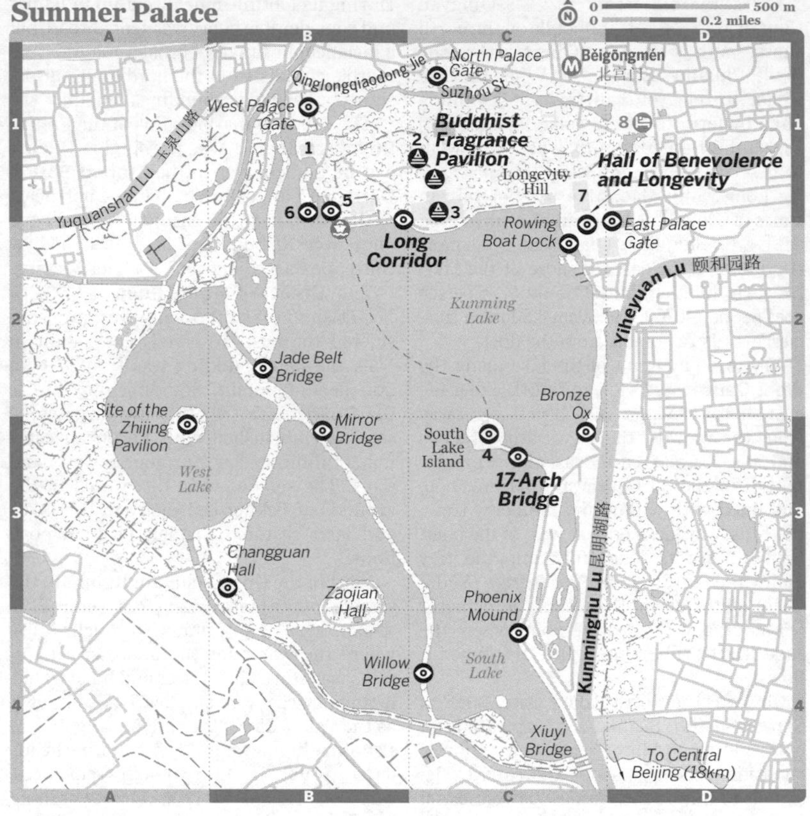

The gardens cover a huge area – some 2.5km from east to west – so be prepared for some walking. Besides the ruins, there's the western section, the **Perfection & Brightness Garden** (圆明园; Yuánmíng Yuán) and the southern compound, the **10,000 Spring Garden** (万春园; Wànchūn Yuán).

Great Bell Temple BUDDHIST TEMPLE
(大钟寺; Dàzhōng Sì; 31a Beisanhuan Xilu; adult Y10; ⌚8.30am-4.30pm; Ⓜ Dazhongsi, 🚌361, 367 or 422) Once a shrine where Qing emperors prayed for rain, the temple today is named after its gargantuan Ming-dynasty bell: 6.75m tall and weighing a hefty 46.5 tonnes, the colossal bell was cast in 1406 and is inscribed with Buddhist sutras, comprising more than 227,000 Chinese characters and decorated with Sanskrit incantations. If you're bell crazy you'll be spellbound by the exhibitions on bell casting, the collection of bells from France, Russia, Japan, Korea and other nations. Also on view are copies of the bells and chimes of the Marquis of Zeng and a collection of Buddhist and Taoist bells including *vajra* bells and the wind chimes (*fēnglíng*) that tinkle from temple roofs and pagodas across China.

Fragrant Hills Park PARK
(香山公园; Xiāngshān Gōngyuán; admission Y10; ⌚7am-6pm) The part of the Western Hills (Xīshān) closest to Běijīng is known as Fragrant Hills Park. It's at its prettiest (and busiest) in autumn, when the maple leaves saturate the hillsides in great splashes of crimson, but the hilly park is a great escape from town any time of year. You can scramble up the slopes to the top of **Incense-Burner Peak** (香炉峰; Xiānglú Fēng) or take the **chairlift** (one way/return Y30/50; ⌚9am-4pm).

Near the north gate of Fragrant Hills Park is the excellent **Azure Clouds Temple** (碧云寺; Bìyún Sì; admission Y10; ⌚8am-5pm), which dates to the Yuan dynasty. The Sun

Summer Palace

Top Sights

- 17-Arch Bridge C3
- Buddhist Fragrance Pavilion C1
- Hall of Benevolence and Longevity C2
- Long Corridor B1

Sights

1. Boathouses B1
2. Buddhist Temple of the Sea of Wisdom C1
3. Cloud Dispelling Hall C1
4. Dragon King Temple C3
5. Marble Boat B1
6. Rowing-Boat Dock B1
7. Theatre Stage C1

Sleeping

8. Aman at Summer Palace D1

Yatsen Memorial Hall contains a statue and a glass coffin donated by the USSR on the death of Sun Yatsen, while at the very back is the marble Vajra Throne Pagoda where Sun Yatsen was interred after he died, before his body was moved to its final resting place in Nánjīng. The Hall of Arhats contains 500 *luóhàn* statues.

To reach Fragrant Hills Park by public transport, take the subway to Běijīng Zoo station and then take fast bus 360; alternatively, you can take bus 318 from Píngguǒyuán underground station.

Běijīng Botanic Gardens PARK

(北京植物园; Běijīng Zhíwùyuán; admission summer/winter Y10/5; 7am-5pm) Located 2km northeast of Fragrant Hills Park, the well-tended Botanic Gardens, set against the backdrop of the Western Hills, make for a pleasant outing among bamboo fronds, pines, orchids and lilacs. The **Běijīng Botanic Gardens Conservatory** (admission Y50) contains 3000 different types of plants and a rainforest house.

About a 15-minute walk north from the front gate (follow the signs) near the Magnolia Garden is the **Temple of the Reclining Buddha** (Wòfó Sì; admission Y5; 8am-4.30pm). First built in the Tang dynasty, the temple's centrepiece is a huge reclining effigy of Sakyamuni weighing in at 54 tonnes, which 'enslaved 7000 people' in its casting. The reclining form of Buddha represents his moment of death, before entering Nirvana. On each side of Buddha are sets of gargantuan shoes, imperial gifts to Sakyamuni.

To get here take the subway to Běijīng Zoo and then hop on fast bus 360; alternatively go to Píngguǒyuán subway station and take bus 318.

Bādàchù BUDDHIST TEMPLE

(八大处; Eight Great Sites; admission Y10; 6am-6pm, later in summer) Named after the eight nunneries and monasteries scattered through its attractive wooded valleys, Bādàchù is an invigoratingly hilly area in the west of Běijīng. Topped with a glittering golden spire, the 13-eaved green tiled brick **Língguāng Temple Pagoda** (Língguāng Sì Tǎ) is also known as the Buddha's Tooth Relic Pagoda; it was built to house a sacred tooth accidentally discovered when the allied powers demolished the place in 1900.

Follow the path up past the small and simple **Sānshān Nunnery** (Sānshān Ān) to the **Dàbēi Temple** (大悲寺; Dàbēi Sì), famed for its 18 arhats (Buddhists who have achieved enlightenment) in the Great Treasure Hall (Dàxióngbǎo Diàn) which were carved by Liu Yuan, a Yuan-dynasty sculptor. Made from a composite of sand and sandalwood, the effigies are over 700 years old. The exterior walls of the hall itself are decorated with slogans from the Cultural Revolution glorifying the supremacy of the Communist Party.

Further slogans adorn the gate to **Lóngquán Nunnery** (Lóngquán Ān; 龙泉庵). Peek into the Longwang Hall (Lóngwáng Táng) where the Dragon King sits with huge, round black eyes. The largest of all the temples is **Xiāngjiè Temple** (Xiāngjiè Sì).

The mountain has plentiful apricot trees, which makes for some cheerful and sweet-smelling scenery around April when the trees briefly bloom. As with other sights, it is inadvisable to visit at weekends, which are busy. A cable car exists for trips to the top of the hill (Y20) and a toboggan (Y40) can sweep you down again. A fast way to reach Bādàchù is to take the underground to Píngguǒyuán station and then jump on bus 958 or 389; alternatively, get bus 347 from the zoo.

Activities

Běijīng Hikers HIKING

(5829 3195; www.beijinghikers.com/home.php; 9am-6pm Tue-Fri) Organises some breathtaking outings out of town.

North Dōngchéng

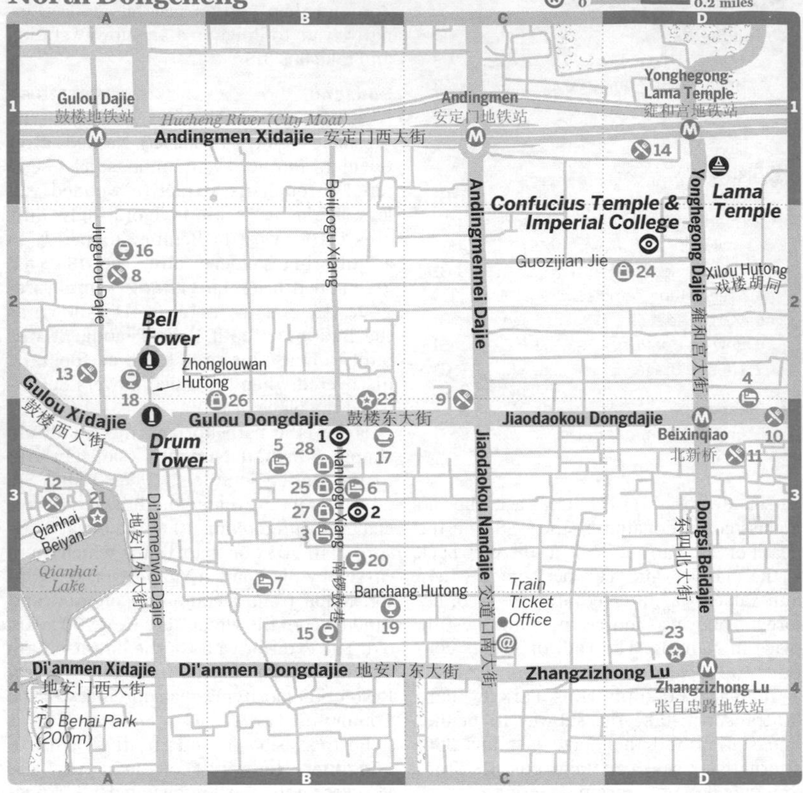

Courses

Culture

China Culture Center CULTURAL PROGRAMS

(☎weekdays 6432 9341, weekends 6432 0141; www.chinaculturecenter.org; Kent Center; 29 Anjialou, Liangmaqiao Lu; Ⓜ Liangmaqiao) Offers a range of cultural programs, taught in English and aimed squarely at foreign visitors and expats. The club also conducts popular tours around Běijīng and expeditions to other parts of China.

Martial Arts

Běijīng is an excellent place to learn taichi and other Chinese martial arts. Several English-speaking instructors teach in Rìtán Park (Map p74); if you are unsure what you want to study, go along and take a look, and then make your choice – mornings and evenings are good times to come and watch. Most schools and teachers accept students at all levels. Alternatively, check under Martial Arts in the classified pages of free expat magazines such as *The Beijinger* (www.thebeijinger.com) or *Time Out* (www.timeout.com/beijing).

Běijīng Milun School of Traditional Kung Fu MARTIAL ARTS

(☎136 2113 3764; www.kungfuinchina.com) Lessons near the west gate of Rìtán Park.

Cooking

Black Sesame Kitchen COOKING CLASSES

(www.blacksesamekitchen,com; ☎136 9147 4408; 3 Heizhima Hutong) Runs popular cooking classes with a variety of recipes from across China; just off Nanluogu Xiang.

Festivals & Events

Spring Festival A week-long holiday commencing at Chinese New Year, usually in late January or February.

North Dōngchéng

Top Sights
Bell Tower ... A2
Confucius Temple & Imperial College ... D2
Drum Tower ... A3
Lama Temple ... D1

Sights
1 Nanluogu Xiang ... B3
2 Slogans from Cultural Revolution ... B3

Sleeping
3 Běijīng Downtown Backpackers Accommodation ... B3
4 Běijīng Lama Temple International Youth Hostel ... D2
5 Courtyard 7 ... B3
Grandma's Kitchen ... (see 11)
Gǔxiàng 20 ... (see 6)
6 Hútòngrén ... B3
7 Mao'er 28 ... B3

Eating
8 Café Sambal ... A2
9 Dàlǐ Courtyard ... C3
10 Ghost Street ... D3
11 Grandma's Kitchen ... D3
12 Hútóng Pizza ... A3
13 Le Little Saigon ... A2
Source ... (see 19)
14 Vineyard Cafe ... D1

Drinking
15 12sqm ... B4
16 Bed Bar ... A2
17 Café Zara ... B3
18 Drum & Bell Bar ... A2
19 Mao Mao Chong Bar ... B4
20 Passby Bar ... B3

Entertainment
21 East Shore Bar ... A3
22 MAO Livehouse ... B3
23 Yúgōng Yíshān ... D4

Shopping
24 Bannerman Tang's Toys & Crafts ... D2
25 Clockwork Monkey ... B3
26 Mega Mega Vintage ... B3
27 Plastered T-Shirts ... B3
28 Pottery Workshop ... B3

Běijīng Literary Festival Local and international writers give talks at the Bookworm Cafe, usually in March.

May Day Kicks-off a three-day holiday on 1 May.

International Music Festival Classical music and opera festival held over five days in May.

National Day Launches a week-long holiday on 1 October.

MIDI Music Festival (☎6259 0101, 6259 0007) Open-air rock festival at the Běijīng MIDI School of Music in October.

Běijīng Pop Festival (www.beijingpopfestival.com/music) Staged every September in Cháoyáng Park.

Běijīng Biennale Arts festival held every two years in September/October.

Běijīng Music Festival (www.bmf.org.cn) Held for around 30 days in October and November.

Sleeping

After its Olympic workout, Běijīng has re-emerged with an impressive bevy of accommodation spanning all budgets. The budget bracket – which once scarcely existed for foreign backpackers – is now a fiercely competitive arena of youth hostels and affordable lodgings. Even the staid midrange bracket has been slapped into shape, while the opening of top-flight courtyard and boutique hotels has added more eye-catching choice to the top end. Value for money is easy to find, whether it's a peaceful courtyard hotel, a resourceful youth hostel, a nifty midrange business hotel, a modish boutique hotel or a five-star luxury tower that pulls out all the stops.

Most travellers aim to stay within the Second Ring Rd, as that's where most of Běijīng's character survives. The historic districts of Xīchéng and especially Dōngchéng are strong areas across all budgets, and Xuānwǔ also has historic charm. Cháoyáng is more modern, with lively nightlife and a crop of stylish boutique hotels but little character or sightseeing. Hǎidiàn is not well supplied with hotels, although the Aman at Summer Palace is tempting for its rarefied sense of seclusion.

South Cháoyáng

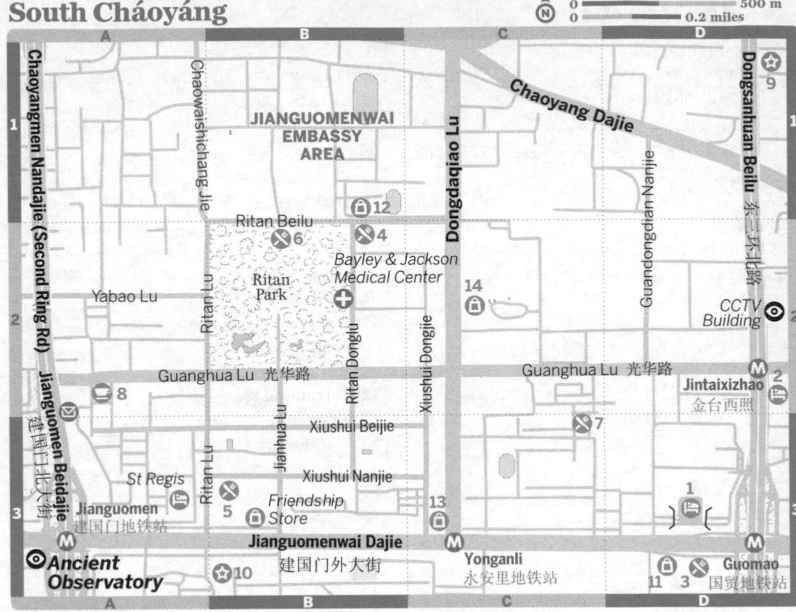

Although most hotels allow Westerners to stay, a hard core of hotels irritatingly survives that does not accept foreigners. The sophisticated bar Face was planning on opening rooms at the time of writing.

For hotel bookings, the online agencies **CTrip** (☎400 619 9999; http://english.ctrip.com) and **Elong** (☎400 617 1717; www.elong.net) are useful.

DŌNGCHÉNG

TOP CHOICE City Walls Courtyard COURTYARD HOTEL $
(☎6402 7805; www.beijingcitywalls.com; 57 Nianzi Hutong; 碾子胡同57号; 8-/4-bed dm Y100/120, d Y380; ❄@) Lovely rooms, crumbling *hútòng* setting, a warm courtyard atmosphere and bubbly owner, this excellent hostel is stuffed away within one of Běijīng's most historic areas. The maze-like web of *hútòng* can be disorientating: from Jingshan Houjie, look for the *hútòng* opening just east of the playground and the Sinopec petrol station. Walk up the *hútòng* and follow it around to the right and then left – the hostel is on the left-hand side. The north gate of the Forbidden City is merely a few minutes' walk away.

TOP CHOICE Peking International Youth Hostel YOUTH HOSTEL $
(北平国际青年旅社; Běipíng Guójì Qīngnián Lǚshè; Map p52; ☎6526 8855; 5 Beichizi Ertiao; 北池子二条5号; 4-/8-/12-bed dm Y100/100/90, d Y400-500; ❄@🛜) The discreet, central alleyway location is the icing on this particular cake, parcelled away off Nanchizi Dajie, a guidebook's throw from the Forbidden City. The highly relaxing *hútòng* aspect maintains just the right vibe – homey lounge area, small and leafy courtyard, good dorms (doubles are small though) and an intimate ambience, although it's a tad pricier than many other hostels. Reserve ahead.

Běijīng Downtown Backpackers Accommodation HOSTEL $
(东堂客栈; Dōngtáng Kèzhàn; Map p72; ☎8400 2429; www.backpackingchina.com; 85 Nanluogu Xiang; 南锣鼓巷85号; s/d/ste Y150/200/300; ❄@🛜) The central location, helpful staff and lively *hútòng* aspect on Nanluogu Xiang are hard to beat. Recently restored doubles are tidy (no TV, some no window), with plastic wood floor and clean shower rooms. Free breakfast and free pick-up from Capital Airport (for stays of four days or more, you pay the toll: Y20), plus bike rental (per day Y20, deposit Y400), inter-

South Cháoyáng

Top Sights

Ancient Observatory A3

Sleeping

1 China World Hotel D3
2 Home Inn D2

Eating

3 China Grill D3
4 Jenny Lou's B2
5 Makye Ame B3
6 Xiao Wang's Home Restaurant B2
7 Xiao Wang's Home Restaurant C3

Drinking

CJW ..... (see 14)
8 Sequoia Café A2

Entertainment

9 Cháoyáng Theatre D1
10 GT Banana B3

Shopping

Chaterhouse Booktrader ..... (see 14)
China World Shopping Mall ..... (see 1)
11 Five Colours Earth D3
Garden Books ..... (see 8)
12 Shard Box Store B1
13 Silk Street C3
14 The Place C2

net access (Y6 per hour) and Great Wall trips.

Mao'er 28 COURTYARD HOTEL **$**
(Map p72; 28 Mao'er Hutong; 帽儿胡同28号; s/d/f Y300/380/580; ❄@) You may need to book a year ahead for a bed at this petite and charming courtyard spot with just three rooms and delightful homestead charm. All the furniture is handmade and Angela the resourceful owner is there for everything, from the cooking to Great Wall trips. The small single has a fan but no air-con. There is no sign outside, just the street number and a bell, which guarantees anonymity.

Courtyard 7 COURTYARD HOTEL **$$$**
(七号院; Qīhàoyuàn; Map p72; ☎6406 0777; www.courtyard7.com; 7 Qiangulouyuan Hutong; 前鼓楼苑胡同7号; d/VIP d Y1180/1400, discounts 45%; ❄@) With tip-top service and three lovely courtyards slung behind a serene old *hútòng* exterior, this is a delightful and fantastically quiet courtyard hotel in a fabulous central location. It's not cheap, but discounts take out a fair amount of the sting.

Raffles Běijīng Hotel HOTEL **$$$**
(北京饭店莱佛士; Běijīng Fàndiàn Láifóshì; Map p48; ☎6526 3388; www.beijing.raffles.com; 33 Dongchang'an Jie; 东长安街33号; d incl breakfast Y4100, normally 30-40% discount; ⊖❄🛜) The seven-storey Raffles oozes cachet and pedigree, lucratively cashing in on a lineage dating to 1900 (when it was the Grand Hotel de Pekin) and an impeccable location. The elegant lobby yields to a graceful staircase leading to immaculate standard doubles which are spacious and well proportioned, decked out with period-style furniture and large bathrooms. The flagship French restaurant Jaan is magnificent. Free wi-fi internet in rooms as well as the lobby.

Park Plaza HOTEL **$$**
(北京丽亭酒店; Běijīng Lìtíng Jiǔdiàn; Map p48; ☎8522 1999; www.parkplaza.com/beijingcn; 97 Jinbao Jie; 金宝街97号; d Y850; ⊖❄@🛜) Appealing midrange value with more than a shot of style in the heart of town, the modish Park Plaza has a tip-top location plus a comfortable, modern and well-presented four-star finish. The lobby is mildly jazzy and sedate – but not subdued – arranged with seats in chocolate brown leather, while rooms are stylish and comfy.

Hilton Běijīng Wángfǔjǐng HOTEL **$$$**
(北京王府井希尔顿酒店; Běijīng Wángfǔjǐng Xī'ěrdùn Jiǔdiàn; Map p48; ☎5812 8888, 800 820 0600; www.wangfujing.hilton.com; 8 Wangfujing Dongdajie; 王府井东大街8号; d Y2300, discounts of 30-50%; ⊖❄@🛜≋) Muted grey and caramel hues come to the fore at this snazzy new signature hotel off Wangfujing Dajie. The sharp and roomy 50-sq-metre standard rooms come with fastidiously neat bathrooms, spacious walk-in wardrobes and iPod docking stations; the 64-sq-metre superior rooms are effortlessly lovely. The 6th-floor swimming pool has outside views, and Macanese and Chinese restaurants assemble on the 5th floor, where you can find the Flames bar.

Grand Hyatt Běijīng HOTEL **$$$**
(北京东方君悦大酒店; Běijīng Dōngfāng Jūnyuè Dàjiǔdiàn; Map p48; ☎8518 1234; www.beijing.grand.hyatt.com; 1 Dongchang'an Jie; 东长安街1号; d Y2600; ⊖❄🛜≋) A crisp freshness keeps things snappy at this smart creation beside Oriental Plaza. Doubles are not very roomy and views can be limited, but are

BĚIJĪNG'S BEST COURTYARD HOTELS

» Courtyard 7 (p75)
» Mao'er 28 (p75)
» City Walls Courtyard (p74)
» Hǎoyuán Hotel (p76)
» Peking International Youth Hostel (p74)

attractively, if rather neutrally, designed. The hotel's range of excellent restaurants, cafes and bars – including the elegant Made in China and the luxuriant Red Moon Bar – are genuine incentives.

Grandma's Kitchen ROOMS **$$$**
(祖母的厨房; Zǔmǔ de Chúfáng; Map p72; ☎8403 9452; 28 Shique Hutong; d Y480; ❄) There's a rack rate as flexible as an iron rod here, with just a handful of rooms slung out in the courtyard behind the restaurant, but this is a quiet and secluded retreat with more than a measure of charm and some excellent food. Another branch is at 47-2 Nanchizi Dajie.

Emperor HOTEL **$$$**
(皇家驿栈酒店; Huángjiā Yìzhàn Jiǔdiàn; Map p52; ☎6526 5566; www.theemperor.com.cn; 33 Qihelou Jie; 骑河楼街; d Y1600; ⊖❄@📶) The location just east of the Forbidden City is certainly regal, although views from the upper floor rooms merely graze the rooftops of the imperial palace. The funkily designed rooms are named after China's emperors; sink a drink in the excellent rooftop bar. Free internet access and wi-fi.

Hǎoyuán Hotel COURTYARD HOTEL **$$**
(好园宾馆; Hǎoyuán Bīnguǎn; ☎6512 5557; www.haoyuanhotel.com; 53 Shijia Hutong; 史家胡同53号; d standard/deluxe Y760/930, ste Y1080-1380, VIP r Y1590; ❄@📶) The eight standard rooms in the red-lantern-hung front courtyard are delightfully arranged, albeit small. The gorgeous leafy rear courtyard is more enchanting still. For more space, the largest suite's bedroom is set off from a Chinese parlour, complete with calligraphic hangings, vases, rugs and lanterns, while the VIP room is huge. The only discernible drawback is the yawning wasteland eyesore opposite the front gate. The hotel is a short walk from the Dengshikou metro station.

Motel 268 HOTEL **$**
(莫泰连锁旅店; Mòtài Liánsuǒ Lǚdiàn; Map p48; ☎5167 1666; www.motel268.com; 19 Jinyu Hutong; 金鱼胡同19号; d Y268-448, f Y538) A tempting central location coupled with dependably clean and well-kept rooms makes this a good choice from the Motel 268 hotel chain. Rooms are unfussy and low on trim, but good value at the lower end of midrange. The hotel can arrange ticketing.

Days Inn HOTEL **$$**
(美国戴斯酒店; Měiguó Dàisī Jiǔdiàn; Map p48; ☎400 881 5555; www.daysinn.cn; 1 Nanwanzi Hutong; 南湾子胡同1号; d/ste Y548/998; ❄@) An enviable location is the main draw at this *hútòng*-corner hotel, finished in grey brick, a few minutes' walk east of the Forbidden City. Some guests may not recommend the tours arranged through the hotel, but seem happy with the clean and restful if uninspiring rooms. There's only one suite, but it ranges over two floors.

Hotel Kapok HOTEL **$$**
(木棉花酒店; Mùmiánhuā Jiǔdiàn; Map p48; ☎6525 9988; www.hotelkapok.com; 16 Donghuamen Dajie; 东华门大街16号; d Y1280; ⊖❄@) Sticking out like a sore but fashionable thumb on Donghuamen Dajie, this trendy and aspiring hotel is popular with the design set and discounts are healthy. A feature of some of the 'fashion rooms' is the overhead atriums for views of the sky.

Also recommended:

Hútòngrén COURTYARD HOTEL **$**
(胡同人; Map p72; ☎8402 5238; hutongren@cchome.com; 71 Xiaoju'er Hutong; 小菊儿胡同71号; s/d Y230/330; ❄) Ensconced quietly away down a small *hútòng* off funky Nanluogu Xiang, this courtyard place has loads of charm with a handful of rooms, decorated with traditional-style furniture and Buddhist carvings.

Gǔxiàng 20 HOTEL **$$**
(古巷20号; Gǔxiàng Èrshí Hào; Map p72; ☎6400 5566; www.guxiang20.com; 20 Nanluogu Xiang; 南锣鼓巷20号; s/d Y888/1280, discounts 35-40%; ❄@) Nanluogu Xiang courtyard-looking hotel with pleasant but small singles decked out in Qing-style furniture and larger doubles; rooftop tennis court.

Běijīng Lama Temple International Youth Hostel HOSTEL **$**
(北京雍和宫国际青年旅社; Běijīng Yōnghégōng Guójì Qīngnián Lǚshè; Map p72; ☎6402 8663; 56 Beixinqiao Toutiao; 北新桥头

条56号; 4-/6-bed dm Y65/60, s/d Y180/220, discounts for members; ❄@📶) Congenial and pleasant hostel south of the Lama Temple; cold in winter.

Běijīng City Central Youth Hostel HOSTEL $
(北京城市国际青年旅社; Běijīng Chéngshì Guójì Qīngnián Lǚshè; ☎8511 5050; www.centralhostel.com; 1 Beijingzhan Qianjie; 北京站前街1号; 4-8 bed dm Y60, s with shower Y298-328, without shower Y120-160, tw with/without shower Y328/160; ❄@) Across the road from Běijīng train station, this hostel compensates for lack of character with a handy location and clean rooms.

XUĀNWǓ

Qiánmén Hostel HOSTEL $
(前门客栈; Qiánmén Kèzhàn; Map p48; ☎6313 2370/2369; www.qianmenhostel.com; 33 Meishi Jie; 煤市街33号; 6-8/4-bed dm Y50/70, tw/d/tr Y200/200/240; ❄@) This heritage hostel combines a relaxing environment with high-ceilinged original woodwork, charming antique buildings and able staff. Affable hostel owner Genghis Kane may show off his environmentally sound heating equipment (fired with dried pellets of plant matter). Heritage rooms are simple; purpose-built rooms are more modern with less character. Western breakfasts, bike hire nearby, laundry available.

Leo Hostel HOSTEL $
(广聚元饭店; Guǎngjùyuán Fàndiàn; Map p48; ☎8660 8923; www.leohostel.com; 52 Dazhalan Xijie; 大栅栏西街52号; 10/12-bed dm Y50, 8-bed dm with toilet Y70, 6-bed dm Y60, q Y60-80, tr Y210-300, d/tw Y240/180; ❄@) Popular and ever busy, it's best to phone ahead to book a room at this bargain hostel tucked away down Dazhalan Xijie. The attractive interior courtyard is decked out with plastic plants; there are OK dorm rooms (pricier dorms with toilet), simple but passable doubles, a lively bar and a fine location.

365 Inn HOSTEL $
(Map p48; ☎6302 8699; 55 Dazhalan Xijie; 大栅栏西街55号; dm with/without shower Y70/50, d/tr Y160/240; ❄@) Popular hostel with a great ground-floor bar area where you can sit and watch life going by on spruced-up Dashilan Xijie. Clean twins are simple but you could cross Běijīng on foot faster than it takes the hot water to kick in.

Chánggōng Hotel HOSTEL $
(长宫饭店; Chánggōng Fàndiàn; Map p48; ☎5194 8204; changgong_hotel@yahoo.com.cn; 1 Yingtao Xiejie; 樱桃斜街11号; 4-/6-bed dm Y40, tw without shower Y60, d/tr with shower Y180/210; ❄@) Opposite the disintegrating Guanyin Temple, the marvellous former Guìzhōu Guild Hall is a cavernous old Qing-dynasty building, arranged over two floors linked by a vertigo-inducing flight of stairs. Excellent-value doubles are spacious, if rather threadbare. Friendly staff speak good English but the hotel's echo-chamber acoustics amplify every murmur and winters can be frosty.

XĪCHÉNG

Red Lantern House COURTYARD HOTEL $
(红灯笼客栈; Hóngdēnglóng Kèzhàn; ☎8328 5771; www.redlanternhouse.com; 5 Zhengjue Hutong; 正觉胡同5号; dm Y55-60, s Y140-180, tw Y160-260, d Y180-260; ❄@📶) Offers homely *hútòng*-located courtyard-style lodgings a short stroll from Hòuhǎi Lake and run by cheerful staff. Doubles are without shower, but are comfy, clean, cheap and charming. If it's booked out, two sibling branches are nearby. Internet (Y1 for 10 minutes), washing (Y10 per kilo), restaurant-bar in main lobby area (Tsingtao beer Y3 per bottle).

Sleepy Inn HOTEL $
(丽舍什刹海国际青年酒店; Lìshè Shíchàhǎi Guójì Qīngnián Jiǔdiàn; ☎6406 9954; www.sleepyinn.com.cn; 103 Deshengmennei Dajie; 德胜门内大街103号, 6-/4-bed dm Y60/80, s & d Y298; ❄@📶) In an adorable perch between Hòuhǎi and Xīhǎi Lakes, congenial Sleepy Inn incorporates one of the halls of the former Taoist Zhēnwǔ Temple into its peaceful formula. Rooms are in the three-storey block, with clean pine-bed dorms and well-looked-after doubles (but rooms come with neither phone nor TV). Free internet access.

CHÁOYÁNG

TOP CHOICE **Opposite House Hotel** HOTEL $$$
(瑜舍; Yúshè; Map p66; ☎6417 6688; wwwtheoppositehouse.com; Bldg 1, The Village, 11 Sanlitun Lu; 三里屯路11号院1号楼; d Y1950; ⊖❄@📶🏊) Artworks litter the lobby area and rooms are top-drawer chic with American oak bathtubs, open-plan bathrooms, underfloor heating and gorgeous mood lighting; the metal basin swimming pool and fastidiously trendy Mesh bar round out a totally sleek boutique picture. Excellent dining options.

Hotel G HOTEL $$
(北京极栈; Běijīng Jízhàn; Map p66; ☎6552 3600; www.hotel-G.com; A7 Gongti Xilu; 工体西路甲7号; d Y1488; ❄@📶) Natty boutique hotel featuring a snappy blend of deep purple, charcoal greys, black, floral print patterns and crushed-velvet textures. Snazzy rooms spoil you with a choice of six different pillows and you won't want to get out of bed they're that comfy. Wi-fi and free breakfast.

China World Hotel HOTEL $$$
(中国大饭店; Zhōngguó Dàfàndiàn; Map p74; ☎6505 2266; www.shangri-la.com; 1 Jianguomenwai Dajie; 建国门外大街1号; d Y2900; 🚭❄📶🏊) The gorgeous five-star China World matches its outstanding level of service to a sumptuous foyer: a masterpiece of Chinese motifs, glittering chandeliers, robust columns and smooth acres of marble. Rooms are modern and amenities extensive, with shopping needs met at the China World Trade Center.

Home Inn HOTEL $
(如家; Rújiā; Map p74; ☎5207 6666; 34 Dongsanhuan Zhonglu; 东三环中路34号; s/d Y259/299, big-bed s & d Y299, business r Y339; ❄@) The location, rising up south of the awesome CCTV Building, is as good as we could find. Handy, neat, crisp, modern, fresh and versatile, it's also a bargain. Regularly shaped, simple and unfussy rooms offer no surprises: we're talking Ikea-style work desks, simple flat-screen TVs and ho-hum artwork on the walls. If space is a high-priority, go for the luxury business rooms

Sānlǐtún Youth Hostel HOSTEL $
(三里屯青年旅馆; Sānlǐtún Qīngnián Lǚguǎn; Map p66; ☎5190 9288; 1 Chunxiu Lu; 春秀路1号; 6-/4-bed dm Y60/70, tw/d Y258/258; ❄@📶) Situated conveniently west of Sānlǐtún, this functional four-floor hostel has clean dorms and hygienic common shower rooms, but little character. The hotel is tucked away in a courtyard east off Chunxiu Lu. Free internet and wi-fi for guests, bike hire (Y20 per day), Great Wall tours, cafe/bar and friendly staff. No lift.

Also recommended:

Zhàolóng International Youth Hostel HOSTEL $
(兆龙青年旅社; Zhàolóng Qīngnián Lǚshè; Map p66; ☎6597 2666; www.zhaolonghotel.com.cn; 2 Gongrentiyuchang Beilu; 工人体育场北路2号; 6-/4-/2-bed dm Y60/70/80; ❄@📶) A six-floor block behind the Zhàolóng Hotel offering clean accommodation.

Holiday Inn Lido HOTEL $$$
(丽都假日饭店; Lìdū Jiàrì Fàndiàn; ☎6437 6688; fax 6437 6237; cnr Jichang Lu & Jiangtai Lu; 近机场路将台路; d Y950; 🚭❄📶) Highly popular and first-rate establishment with excellent amenities and a resourceful shopping mall.

HǍIDIÀN

TOP CHOICE **Michael's House** COURTYARD HOTEL $$
(迈克之家; Màikè Zhījiā; ☎6222 5620; South yard, 1 Zhiqiang Gardens, Xiaoxitian; 小西天志强北园1号南院; d/ste Y608/1008; @) Elegant, quiet and convivial courtyard-style hotel with grey-brick styling and helpful, traditionally attired staff. Modern but quaintly Chinese, the comfy abode is attractively fringed with greenery, offering very pleasant *hútòng* rooms kitted out with a contemporary finish.

Aman at Summer Palace HOTEL $$$
(颐和安缦; Yíhé Ānmàn; Map p70; ☎5987 9999; 15 Gongmenqian Jie; 宫门前街15号; r/courtyard r US$550/650, ste/courtyard ste US$850/$1110; ❄@📶🏊) Just round the corner from the Summer Palace, the elegant Aman resort hotel is an exclusive and palatial escape from Běijīng's fuggy and noisy central districts. Service is discreet and intimate, the courtyard rooms are gorgeous, while choice restaurants, a spa, a library, a cinema, pool and squash courts round off the refined picture, although prices can be heart-stopping.

FURTHER AFIELD

Commune by the Great Wall HOTEL $$$
(长城脚下的公社; Chángchéng Jiǎoxià de Gōngshè; ☎8118 1888; www.communebythegreatwall.com; r Y1890; ❄@📶🏊) It's not cheap but the cantilevered geometric architecture, location and superb panoramas are standout. Positioned at the Shuǐguān section of the Great Wall, Kempinski-managed Commune has a proletarian name but the design is anything but. Treat yourself to a room with the ultimate view.

Red Capital Ranch HOTEL $$$
(☎8401 8886; www.redcapitalclub.com; 28 Xiaguandi village, Yanxi, Huairou County; 怀柔县雁栖镇下关地村28号; d Y1425; ❄@🏊) Běijīng's escapist option, this Manchurian hunting lodge has 10 individually styled villas, a mountain setting, a 20-hectare estate with Great Wall remains and a stress-busting Tibetan Tantric Space Spa. Breakfast included.

 Eating

For a proper handle on Chinese food, get the gloves off and sleeves rolled up in Běijīng. Not only is Běijīng cuisine (京菜; *jīngcài*) one of the major Chinese cooking styles, but chefs from all four corners of the land make the culinary pilgrimage here to serve the faddy masses. Which means you don't really have to leave town to eat your way around China – whether it's Uighur food, Sìchuān hotpot, Lánzhōu Lāmiàn or Cantonese, you can leaf your way through an often-dazzling Chinese atlas of cooking. The international food spectrum is also sorted, so some of your best Běijīng memories could well be table-top ones.

This may be Běijīng, but eating out doesn't necessarily require excessive capital outlays: listed here are restaurants that offer the best food and value within a range of budgets. Supermarkets are plentiful and most visitors will find what they need, but delis stock wider selections of foreign cheeses, cured meats and wines. Street snacking is another way to eat your way around Běijīng, so trust your nostrils to lead you to Běijīng's huge population of tirelessly working street-side chefs.

Supermarkets

Olé Supermarket SUPERMARKET
Handy branches of this well-stocked supermarket can be found in the basement of **Oriental Plaza** (Map p48; ⌚8.30am-10.30pm), the China World Shopping Mall (Map p74) as well as the **Ginza Mall** (basement, 48 Dongzhimenwai Dajie; ⌚10am-10pm) in Dōngzhímén.

Carrefour SUPERMARKET
(家乐福; Jiālèfú; ⌚8.30am-10.30pm) Beisanhuan Donglu (6b Beisanhuan Donglu); Fēngtái (15 No 2 district Fangchengyuan Fangzhuang); Hǎidiàn (54a Zhongguancun Nandajie); Xuānwǔ (11 Malian Dao) Stocks virtually everything you may need, takes credit cards and provides ATMs and a home-delivery service. There are seven branches in town.

April Gourmet DELI
(Map p66; 1 Sanlitun Beixiaojie; ⌚8am-9pm) An expat-oriented deli with fine wines and cheeses; three branches in town. Does deliveries.

Jenny Lou's DELI
(婕妮璐; Jiénílù; Map p74; 6 Sanlitun Beixiaojie; ⌚8am-10pm) Fresh meat, fish, cheeses, wines and a wide array of deli items; six branches in town.

DŌNGCHÉNG

For convenient dining and a Pan-Asian selection under one roof, try one of the ubiquitous food courts that can be found in shopping malls throughout the city.

Dàlǐ Courtyard YUNNAN $$
(大理; Dàlǐ; Map p72; ☎8404 1430; 67 Xiaojingchang Hutong, Gulou Dongdajie; set menu from Y100; ⌚lunch & dinner) Part of the joy of this restaurant is its lovely courtyard setting; the other essential ingredient is the inventive Yúnnán cuisine from China's southwest. It's necessary to book in advance and, unconventionally, there is no menu. Dishes are devised on impulse by the chef, so communicate any dietary requirements up front.

TOP CHOICE **Crescent Moon Muslim Restaurant** MUSLIM $$
(新疆弯弯月亮维吾尔穆斯林餐厅; Xīnjiāng Wānwān Yuèliàng Wéiwú'ěr Mùsīlín Cāntīng; 16 Dongsi Liutiao; dishes from Y18; ⌚lunch & dinner; 📷) The meaty lamb kebabs (羊肉串; *yángròu chuàn*) at this well-known *hútòng*-side Uighur restaurant are the talk of the town and there's a far more intimate feel here than at some of Běijīng's other more high-profile Uighur eateries. The *dàpánjī* (大盘鸡) is a filling dish of potatoes, peppers and vegetables served over thick noodle slices. Picture menu.

TOP CHOICE **Xiao Wang's Home Restaurant** BEIJING $$
(小王府; Xiǎo Wángfǔ; Map p74; ☎6594 3602, 6591 3255; 2 Guanghua Dongli; meals Y70; ⌚lunch & dinner; 📷) Slung out on several floors in an often bewildering maze, this restaurant has enjoyed years of popularity. The deep-fried spare ribs with pepper salt are delectable: dry, fleshy, crispy chops with a small pile of fiery pepper salt, but dig your way through the menu and you'll find many treasures. There's outside seating and a further attractive branch in Rìtán Park (Map p74).

TOP CHOICE **Vineyard Cafe** EUROPEAN $$
(葡萄园; Pútao Yuán; Map p72; ☎6402 7961; 31 Wudaoying Hutong; set lunch Y55/60; ⌚lunch & dinner, closed Mon; 📷👪) Famed for its full-on English breakfasts and excellent pizza, this popular and relaxing *hútòng* cafe is perfect for lunch after seeing the nearby Lama Temple or as a civilised choice for dinner or drinks.

DON'T MISS

GHOST STREET

Hopping at weekends and one of Běijīng's busiest and most colourful restaurant strips at virtually any hour, Ghost St (鬼街; Guǐ Jiē; Map p72) is the nickname of this spirited section of Dongzhimennei Dajie, where scores of restaurants converge to feed legions of locals and out-of-towners. Splendidly lit with red lanterns from dusk to dawn, Ghost St is lined with vocal restaurant staff enticing passersby into hotpot eateries, spicy seafood restaurants and other heaving outfits. The street is always open so you'll always be able to get fed. Take the subway to Běixīnqiáo, head east along Dongzhimennei Dajie and you will find yourself immediately in Ghost St.

Maison Boulud FRENCH **$$$**
(布鲁宫; Bùlǔ Gōng; Map p48; ☎6559 9200; 23 Qianmen Dongdajie; main dishes from Y205; ⊙lunch & dinner; ⓔ) An imposing highlight of the impeccably spruced up Legation Quarter, Daniel Boulud's Běijīng restaurant presents standout French-inspired cuisine in a choice setting overseen by fastidious staff.

Café Sambal MALAYSIAN **$$**
(Map p72; 43 Doufuchi Hutong; set lunch Y80; ⊙11am-midnight; ⓔ) In an uncomplicated but trendy grey-brick, concrete and wood setting with rickety tables, Café Sambal brings Malaysian food to Běijīng with style and panache. The Kumar mutton with vegetables and rice set (Y80) is satisfying, and the menu embraces a wide range of Malaysian treats from Nyonya curry chicken (Y60) to beef rendang (Y60). Good wine list.

Wángfǔjǐng Snack Street STREET FOOD **$**
(王府井小吃街; Wángfǔjǐng Xiǎochījiē; kebabs & dishes from Y5; ⊙9am-10pm) Don't be put off by the starfish (Y20), cicada, seahorse and scorpion kebabs (Y20), this bustling corner of restaurants is a great place to feast elbow-to-elbow with other diners on Xīnjiāng or Muslim Uighur staples such as lamb kebabs (Y5) and flat bread, steaming bowls of *málà tàng* (麻辣烫; spicy noodle soup), *zhájiàngmiàn* (炸酱面; noodles in fried bean sauce; Y12), *Lánzhōu lāmiàn* (兰州拉面; Lánzhōu noodles) and oodles of spicy *chuāncài* (川菜; Sìchuān food). Round it all off with fried ice cream (Y10). Prices are touristy as it's just west off Wangfujing Dajie.

Kǒng Yǐjǐ ZHEJIANG **$$**
(孔乙己酒店; 322 Dongsi Beidajie; dishes from Y18; ⊙lunch & dinner) Classic flavours from the elegant southern canal town of Shàoxīng are the speciality at this much-loved restaurant. Named after a short story from modernist Shàoxīng scribe Lu Xun, Kǒng Yǐjǐ dishes up timeless dishes such as *zuìxià* (drunken shrimps) and the legendary *dōngpō ròu* (dongpo pork), named after poet Su Dongpo. No meal is complete without shots of warming Shàoxīng wine (*huángjiǔ*).

Courtyard FUSION **$$$**
(四合院; Sìhéyuàn; Map p52; ☎6526 8883; 95 Donghuamen Dajie; meals Y400; ⊙6-9.30pm; ⓔ) Discreetly hidden behind a curtain of bamboo, the Courtyard enjoys a virtually unparalleled location perched moat-side opposite the east gate of the Forbidden City; modern menu and scrumptious views for romantic dinners. Book ahead.

Grandma's Kitchen AMERICAN **$$**
(祖母的厨房; Zǔmǔ de Chúfáng; Map p72; 28 Shique Hutong; meals Y50; ⊙7:30am-11pm; ⓔ) 'There's no place like home except Grandma's', goes the blurb, and this place is certainly homely, with a scrummy no-nonsense American menu (steaks, burgers, apple pie and all-day breakfasts), efficient staff and accommodation out the back if you eat so much you'd prefer to be horizontal. There are five branches in town.

Food Republic FOOD HALL **$**
(大食代; Dàshídài; Map p48; basement, Oriental Plaza, 1 Dongchang'an Jie; dishes from Y10; ⊙10am-10pm) Perfect for on-the-spot dining, this huge food court has point-and-serve Chinese and other Asian dining options packed under one roof. Purchase a card at the kiosk at the entrance, load up with credits (Y30 to Y500; Y10 deposit) and browse among the canteen-style outlets for whatever grabs your fancy, from Old Běijīng to Hong Kong, Taiwan and beyond.

Ajisen Noodle NOODLES **$**
(味千拉面; Wèiqiān Lāmiàn; Map p48; FF08, Basement, Oriental Plaza; ⓔ) Ajisen's flavoursome noodles – delivered in steaming bowls by fleet-foot black-clad staff – will have your ears tingling and your tummy quivering. Dishes are inexplicably as tasty as they

BĚIJĪNG'S BEST VEGETARIAN RESTAURANTS

The words *wǒ chīsù* (我吃素; I am a vegetarian) are only understood in their literal sense by the professionals, so if you require your vegetarian food to be 100% meat free, follow your nose to one of the following.

Pure Lotus VEGETARIAN
(净心莲; Jìngxīnlián; Map p66; 12 Nongzhanguan Nanlu; 11am-11pm; mains from Y58; M Tuánjiéhú;) Flee the 'world of dust' (the Buddhist metaphor for the temporal world) to this gracefully presented restaurant run by monks, with an attractive accent on Buddhist cuisine.

Bǎihé Courtyard VEGETARIAN
(百合素食; Bǎihé Sùshí; 23 Caoyuan Hutong; 11am-10pm; M Dōngzhímén or Běixīnqiáo;) This is one place where you can sample Peking duck (Y68) without a major calamity for your karma: all dishes are mock-meat and designed to trick your taste buds.

appear on the photo menu and tea comes free with cups punctiliously refilled. Pay up front.

Dōnghuámén Night Market STREET MARKET $
(东华门夜市; Dōnghuámén Yèshì; Map p48; Dong'anmen Dajie; snacks from Y3; 3-10pm, closed Chinese New Year) A sight in itself, the bustling night market near Wangfujing Dajie is a veritable food zoo: you can choose from lamb kebabs, beef and chicken skewers, corn on the cob, *chòu dòufu* (臭豆腐; smelly tofu), cicadas, grasshoppers, kidneys, quails' eggs, squid, fruit, porridge, fried pancakes, strawberry kebabs, bananas, Inner Mongolian cheese, stuffed aubergines, chicken hearts, pita bread stuffed with meat, shrimps and more. For tourists, expect inflated prices.

Capital M MODERN EUROPEAN $$$
(Map p48; 6702 2727; www.capital-m-beijing.com; 3rd floor, 2 Qianmen Dajie) The latest outpost of Michelle Garnaut's growing empire unsurprisingly offers some iconic views from the terrace over Front Gate and a delectable menu: try the crispy suckling pig.

Source SICHUAN $$$
(都江园; Dūjiāngyuán; Map p72; 14 Banchang Hutong; meals Y188; lunch & dinner) Delightful Dōngchéng courtyard ambience meets the culinary fireworks of Sìchuān province, with great success.

Huáng Tíng CANTONESE $$$
(凰庭; Map p48; Peninsula Palace, 8 Jinyu Hutong; meals Y150; lunch & dinner;) Faux old Peking taken to its most tasteful extreme, Huáng Tíng resembles a Fifth Generation film set. Dim sum (set lunch Y198), but there's also Peking duck (Y280) and dishes from across China.

CHŌNGWÉN

Quánjùdé Roast Duck Restaurant BEIJING $$$
(全聚德烤鸭店; Quánjùdé Kǎoyādiàn; Map p48; 9 Shuaifuyuan Hutong; set menu incl duck, pancakes, scallions & sauce Y168; lunch & dinner;) Less touristy than its revamped Qiánmén sibling, this branch of the celebrated chain has a handy location off Wangfujing Dajie for shopping-laden diners. The roast duck (half duck Y54, minus pancakes, scallions and sauce) is flavoursome and a key ingredient to a Běijīng sojourn.

Dūyīchù DUMPLINGS $$
(都一处; Map p48; 38 Qianmen Dajie; 前门大街38号; dishes from Y26; 7.30am-9pm) Recently reopened, this celebrated *lǎozihào* (established restaurant) located on Qianmen Dajie – finished in grey brick and serenaded with traditional Chinese music – is famed for its *shāomài* dumplings, although service is rather slow. Try the lamb *shāomài* (Y38) or the shrimp and leek *shāomài* (Y36) and pay up front.

Also recommended:

Biànyìfáng Kǎoyādiàn BEIJING $
(便宜坊烤鸭店; Map p48; 3/F China New World Shopping Mall, 5 Chongwenmenwai Dajie; half/whole duck Y94/188; lunch & dinner;) Claiming a pedigree dating to the reign of Qing emperor Xianfeng, Biànyìfáng roasts its fowl in the *menlu* style, in a closed oven.

XĪCHÉNG

Le Little Saigon VIETNAMESE, FRENCH $$
(西贡在巴黎; Xīgòng Zài Bālí; Map p72; meals from Y32;) The French songs and charmingly sedate, easy-going Indo-Chinese vibe are a world away from the fierce traffic noise outside. This yummy corner of French Vietnam hits all the right taste buds: try

scrumptiously scented seafood tamarind soup (Y32), snails in garlic butter (Y48) or Hanoi noodles soup with beef (Y35). Upstairs terrace open in summer.

Hútóng Pizza PIZZA $$
(胡同比萨; Hútóng Bǐsà; Map p72; 9 Yindingqiao Hutong Hou; meals Y80; ⏰11am-11pm; 📋) The Chinese accuse Marco Polo of stealing pizza from China, and it's come back again. This very relaxing spot near the lakes fires up some enormous pizzas (although they are slow in coming). The *hútòng* house interior is funky and the attic room is handsome, with old painted beams.

CHÁOYÁNG

Hatsune JAPANESE $$
(sushi from Y25; ⏰lunch & dinner; 🚭📋) Chaoyang (2/F Heqiao Bldg C, 8a Guanghua Lu); Sānlǐtún (Map p66; 3rd fl, The Village) A stylish and relaxed American-style sushi restaurant much applauded by fickle and picky expat gastronomes for the ambience and the standout and novelty-named hand rolls. Good-value set lunch deals.

Element Fresh WESTERN $$
(新元素; Xīn Yuánsù; Map p66; www.elementfresh.com; 8-3-3 Bldg 8, The Village, 19 Sanlitun Lu; sandwiches from Y39, pasta from Y58; ⏰11am-11pm Mon-Fri, 8am-11pm Sat & Sun; 📶📋) It was only a matter of time before the neat, spic-and-span and perennially popular Shànghǎi outfit migrated to town, bringing its health-giving menu of salads, sandwiches, pastas, smoothies and MSG-free dishes to an eager tribe of Běijīng expats. Branches also at a2-112, Qianmen Dajie and Lido Plaza, 6 Jiangtai Lu.

Běijīng Dàdǒng Roast Duck Restaurant BEIJING $$
(北京大董烤鸭店; Běijīng Dàdǒng Kǎoyādiàn; Map p66; ☎6582 2892/4003; 3 Tuanjiehu Beikou; duck Y98; ⏰lunch & dinner; 📋) A long-term favourite of the Peking duck scene, the hallmark fowl here is a crispy, lean bird without the usual high fat content (trimmed down from 42.38% to 15.22% for its 'Superneat' roast duck, the brochure says), plus plum (or garlic) sauce, scallions and pancakes. Also carved up is the skin of the duck with sugar, an imperial predilection.

Dōngběirén MANCHURIAN $$
(东北人; Map p66; ☎6415 2855; www.dongbeiren.com.cn; 1a Xinzhong Jie; meals Y50; 📋) This hearty Manchurian restaurant, overseen by a smiling gaggle of rouge-cheeked, pig-tailed *xiǎojiě* (waitresses), cooks up flavoursome dumplings (*jiǎozi*) and a fine range of scrummy northeastern fare. Sit back with a Harbin beer (Hāpí; Y12) and enjoy the garrulous atmosphere (with periodic singing from the waitresses).

Also recommended:

Makye Ame TIBETAN $$
(玛吉啊米; Mǎjí Āmǐ; Map p74; 2nd fl, A11 Xiushui Nanjie; dishes from Y30; ⏰11am-midnight; 📋) Comfy restaurant behind the Friendship Store with Tibetan ornaments and a suitably exotic menu: lamb ribs, boiled yak with chilli, tsampa (roasted barley flour porridge), yoghurt, butter tea, cooling salads and evening dancers.

China Grill WESTERN $$$
(66th fl, Park Hyatt, 2 Jianguomenwai Dajie; ⏰lunch & dinner) For high-altitude views of Běijīng and a menu that will take your taste buds to similar heights.

Indian Kitchen INDIAN $$
(印度小厨餐厅; Yìndù Xiǎochú Cāntīng; 2 Sanlitun Beixiaojie; ⏰lunch & dinner) Simple, authentic, popular, strong menu and appealing set lunch buffets.

Drinking

During the past two decades, Běijīng has morphed from a straight-laced and sober citadel into a modern, drink-dependent capital. These days Běijīng bars are easing into a more seasoned furrow after years of energetic experimentation, although the bandwagon forever rolls on to occupy any profitable niche in the easily bored expat scene. Any bar with 10 years on the ticker is a sure-fire veteran.

Available beers range from the mundane (Yanjing, Beijing, Qingdao) to the noteworthy (Guinness, Tetleys) and exotic (Chimay, Kwak); for ale and wine, the more exotic the import, the more outlandish the price. Approach bars selling preposterously cheap (read possibly fake) alcohol, however, with caution.

Main bar areas include a now-scattered and thinned-out colony in Sānlǐtún, a hopping slew of bars along Nanluogu Xiang, a long string of samey bars along the northern and southern shores of Hòuhǎi Lake (Hòuhǎi Nan'àn and Hòuhǎi Běi'àn) and nearby Yandai Xiejie; other outfits do their own thing, in their own part of town, including student dives in Wǔdàokǒu.

Cafes

Bookworm Café CAFE

(书虫; Shūchóng; Map p66; www.beijingbookworm.com; Bldg 4, Nansanlitun Lu; ⌚8am-1am; 📶) Venue of the annual Běijīng Literary Festival in March, the Bookworm is a great place for breakfast, dining, a solo coffee or a major reading binge. Join the swooning bibliophiles perusing the massive English-language book collection and make this place your home whenever your synapses need energising.

Cafe Zara CAFE

(Map p72; www.cafezarah.com; 42 Gulou Dongdajie; coffee Y18, espresso Y15; ⌚10am-midnight Wed-Mon; 📶) Peaceful and serene concrete-floor boho enclave on Gulou Dongdajie tranquilised by ambient/chill-out music (occasionally pierced by the squeal of taxi brakes on the road yonder); you *can* sit outside but you may end up swathed in fumes. Regular coffee comes with its own bottle of warmed, sweetened milk. Winning breakfasts.

Sequoia Café CAFE

(美洲杉咖啡屋; Měizhōu Shān Kafeiwū; Map p74; 44 Guanghua Lu; sandwiches Y25; ⌚8am-8pm) Sequoia has won legions of fans for its cracking coffees and deservedly admired deli-style sandwiches, served on fluffy, delectable bread. There are other branches in Sānlǐtún and the Kerry Mall.

Bars

12sqm BAR

(十二平米酒吧; Shí'èr Píngmǐ Jiǔbā; Map p72; cnr Nanluogu Xiang & Fuxiang Hutong; beers from Y15, cocktails from Y35; ⌚noon-midnight) The once self-proclaimed smallest bar in Běijīng has expanded to the rear but this much-loved watering hole, run by a welcoming husband-and-wife team, has lost none of its pocket-sized Nanluogu Xiang charm.

Passby Bar BAR

(过客; Guòkè; Map p72; 108 Nanluogu Xiang; ⌚9am-2am) One of the original bars on the cafe-bar strip Nanluogu Xiang and still one of the best, with travel-oriented bar staff, a winning courtyard ambience, shelves of books and mags, and a funky ethnic feel.

Tree BAR

(树酒吧; Shù Jiǔbā; Map p66; ☎6415 1954; www.treebeijing.com; 43 Beisanlintun Nan; ⌚11am-2am Mon-Sat, 1pm-late Sun) Seriously popular expat dungeon regularly bursting with gregarious drinkers engrossed in conversation, chomping wood-fired pizza and gulping Leffe (Y40), Duvel (Y40) and over 40 Belgian brews, flogged by skilful bar staff.

Mao Mao Chong Bar BAR

(毛毛虫吧; Máomáochóng Bā; Map p72; 12 Banchang Hutong; ⌚5.30pm-late, closed Tue) Infused with the aroma of freshly baked pizza, this neat and appealing bar in a converted *hútòng* residence oozes style and personality and the location, just off the Nanluogu Xiang drag, enjoys a welcome anonymity. Winning cocktails; homemade vodka.

Bed Bar BAR

(床吧; Chuángbā; Map p72; 17 Zhangwang Hutong; ⌚4pm-late Mon-Tue, noon-late Wed-Sun) One of the few bars where you can get horizontal prior to inebriation, this comfortable bar features beds strewn with cushions, an enticing rear courtyard littered with wobbly tables and repro antique chairs, first-rate music and a small dance floor.

Face BAR

(妃思; Fēisī; Map p66; 26 Dongcaoyuan, Gongrentiyuchang Nanlu; cocktails from Y65; ⌚6pm-late) Sibling of the renowned Shànghǎi French Concession saloon and with the same Southeast Asian accents, Face is elegant if rather pricey (with Tetley's bitter by the pint) but a great bolthole from Běijīng's more sordid taverns. At the time of writing, accommodation was soon to be in the offing.

Yin BAR

(饮; Map p48; 33 Qihelou Jie; cocktails from Y57; ⌚11am-2am Apr-Nov) You don't have to live like royalty to drink like a sovereign on the roof of the Emperor Hotel within earshot of the Forbidden City. Cocktails as the sun dips over the imperial palace at twilight are imperative. Exotic-sounding perhaps, *yǐn* merely means 'drink' in Chinese.

Paddy O'Sheas BAR

(爱尔兰酒吧; Ài'érlán Jiǔbā; Map p66; 28 Dongzhimenwai Dajie; beers from Y20, cocktails from Y40; ⌚10am-2am) Slightly more authentically Irish than a bowl of *jiǎozi*, but it's a close call. Spacious and fun with regulars staring goggle-eyed at live football and rugby (and their bills: pint of Guinness Y55); happy hour till 8pm.

Drum & Bell Bar BAR

(鼓钟咖啡馆; Gǔzhōng Kāfēiguǎn; Map p72; 41 Zhonglouwan Hutong; beers from Y15; ⌚1pm-2am) Clamber to the roof terrace of this bar slung between its namesake towers and, on summer evenings, duck under the thicket of branches and seat yourself amid an idyllic panorama of low-rise Běijīng rooftops. Alternatively, sink without trace into one of the marshmallow-soft sofas downstairs.

Also recommended:

Aperitivo BAR
(意式餐吧; Yìshì Cānbā; Map p66; 43 Sanlitun Beijie; coffee from Y20, wine & cocktails from Y38; ⏲10am-2am) Italian-managed Sānlǐtún bar with a winning continental feel, strong wine list, small terrace and a relaxing measure of style.

CJW WINE BAR
(Map p74; L-137, The Place, 9 Guanghua Lu; ⏲11am-2.30am) With its formula of black velvet sofas and tie-loosening live evening jazz, CJW is a stylish and seductive (but pricey) alternative to Běijīng's full-on beer bars.

☆ Entertainment

Today's Běijīng has seen a revolution in leisure activities as the city's denizens work and play hard. Běijīng opera, acrobatics and kung fu are solid fixtures on the tourist circuit, drawing regular crowds. Classical music concerts and modern theatre reach out to a growing audience of sophisticates, while night owls will find something to hoot about in the live-music and nightclub scene.

Běijīng Opera & Traditional Chinese Music

Chinese opera has probably as many regional variations as there are Chinese dialects, but like Mandarin language, Běijīng opera (京剧; *Jīngjù*) is by far the most famous, with its colourful blend of singing, speaking, swordsmanship, mime, acrobatics and dancing. Sometimes performances can swallow up an epic six hours, but two hours is more common; at most well-known Běijīng opera venues, around 90 minutes is the norm.

Húguǎng Guild Hall CHINESE OPERA
(湖广会馆; Húguǎng Huìguǎn; 3 Hufang Lu; tickets Y160-680; ⏲performances 7.30pm) With a magnificent red, green and gold interior and balconies surrounding the canopied stage, this theatre dates from 1807. There's also a small **opera museum** (admission Y10; ⏲9am to 11am & 3pm to 7.30pm) opposite the theatre.

Lǎo Shě Teahouse TEAHOUSE
(老舍茶馆; Lǎo Shě Cháguǎn; Map p48; 3rd fl, 3 Qianmen Xidajie; evening tickets Y180-380; ⏲performances 7.50pm) This popular teahouse has nightly shows, largely in Chinese. Performances include folk music, tea ceremonies, theatre, puppet shows and matinée Běijīng opera. Evening performances of Běijīng opera, folk art, music, acrobatics, juggling, kung fu and magic are the most popular; phone or check the website for the latest schedule.

Cháng'ān Grand Theatre CHINESE OPERA
(长安大戏院; Cháng'ān Dàxìyuàn; Cháng'ān Bldg, 7 Jianguomennei Dajie; tickets Y80-800; ⏲performances 7.30pm) This theatre offers a genuine experience of Běijīng opera, with an erudite audience chattering knowledgably among themselves during weekend matinée classics and evening performances.

Líyuán Theatre THEATRE
(梨园剧场; Líyuán Jùchǎng; ☎6301 6688, ext 8860; Qiánmén Jiànguó Hotel, 175 Yongan Lu; tickets Y200-500; ⏲performances 7.30pm) Tourist-friendly theatre at the rear of the lobby of the Qiánmén Jiànguó Hotel, with regular performances, matinée kung fu shows and expensive tea ceremony options.

Acrobatics & Martial Arts

Two thousand years old, Chinese acrobatics is one of the best deals in town. Matinée Shàolín performances are held at the **Líyuán Theatre** (梨园剧场; Líyuán Jùchǎng; ☎6301 6688, ext 8860; Qiánmén Jiànguó Hotel, 175 Yongan Lu).

Tiāndì Theatre ACROBATICS
(天地剧场; Tiāndì Jùchǎng; Map p66; 10 Dongzhimen Nandajie; tickets Y100-300; ⏲performances 7.15pm) Young performers from the China National Acrobatic Troupe knot themselves into mind-bending and joint-popping shapes. It's a favourite with tour groups, so book ahead. You can also watch the performers training at the **circus school** (☎6502 3984). Look for the white tower resembling something from an airport – that's where you buy your tickets.

Cháoyáng Culture Center MARTIAL ARTS
(Cháoyáng Qū Wénhuàguǎn; 17 Jintaili; tickets Y180-380; ⏲performances 7.20-8.30pm) Shàolín Warriors perform their punishing stage show here; watch carefully and pick up some tips for queue barging during rush hour in the Běijīng underground.

Cháoyáng Theatre ACROBATICS
(朝阳剧场; Cháoyáng Jùchǎng; Map p74; 36 Dongsanhuan Beilu; tickets Y180-680; performances 5.15pm & 7.30pm) Probably the most accessible place for foreign visitors and often bookable through your hotel, this theatre is the venue for visiting acrobatic troupes filling the stage with plate-spinning and hoop-jumping.

Tiānqiáo Acrobatics Theatre ACROBATICS
(天桥杂技剧场; Tiānqiáo Zájì Jùchǎng; 6303 7449, English 139 1000 1860; tickets Y100-200; performances 7.15-8.45pm) West of the Temple of Heaven, this is one of Běijīng's most popular venues. The entrance is down the eastern side of the building.

Red Theatre KUNG FU
(红剧场; Hóng Jùchǎng; 6714 2473; 44 Xingfu Dajie; tickets Y180-680; performances 7.30-8.50pm) Nightly kung fu shows aimed squarely at tourist groups are performed here.

Nightclubs

Běijīng's nightclub scene ranges wildly from student dives for the lager crowd to snappy venues and top-end clubs for the preening types, urban poseurs and well-heeled fashionistas.

GT Banana CLUB
(吧那那; Bānànà; Map p74; Scitech Hotel, 22 Jianguomenwai Dajie; tickets Y20-50; 8.30pm-4am Sun-Thu, to 5am Fri & Sat) Banana must be doing something right as it's been around for yonks – maybe it's the caged dancers and fire-eaters. Spicy Lounge upstairs brings more variety to the musical mix with regular appearances from international DJs.

MixBěijīng CLUB
(梅克斯; Méikèsī; Map p66; 8pm-late) Major hip-hop and R&B club west of Sānlǐtún with regular crowd-pulling foreign DJs, inside the Workers' Stadium north gate.

Propaganda CLUB
(8.30pm-late) Long-serving Wǔdàokǒu nightclub attracting throngs of *liúxuéshēng* (students), lured by free entry, cheap booze and wildly popular sounds. It's 100m north of Huáqīng Jiāyuán east gate.

Destination CLUB
(目的地; Mùdìdì; Map p66; www.bjdestination.com; 7 Gongrentiyuchang Xilu; admission free weekdays, weekend admission incl a drink Y60; 8pm-2pm) Běijīng's sole gay club, Destination's coarse concrete finish wins few awards for its looks, but the crowds at weekends don't seem to mind.

Live Music

A growing handful of international pop and rock acts make it to Běijīng, but there's still a long way to go, although the live-music scene has evolved dynamically in recent years.

East Shore Bar BAR
(东岸; Dōng'àn; Map p72; 8403 2131; 2nd fl, 2 Shishahai Nanyan; Tsingtao beer Y20; 4pm-3am) With views of Qiánhǎi Lake, this excellent bar hits all the right notes with its low-light candlelit mood and live jazz sounds from 9.30pm (Thursday to Sunday).

Yúgōng Yíshān LIVE MUSIC
(愚公移山; Map p72; 6404 2711; 3 Zhangzi Zhonglu; 7pm-2am) Běijīng's foremost live music venue ensconced within a haunted Qing-dynasty government building and famed for a host of reliably excellent music acts.

2 Kolegas LIVE MUSIC
(两个好朋友; Liǎng Gè Hǎo Péngyǒu; 8196 4820; 21 Liangmaqiao Lu; cover free-Y20; 8pm-2am Mon-Sat, 10am-9pm Sun) Awash with bargain beer and tuned in to independent, rawer sounds, 2 Kolegas is an excellent venue for getting your finger on the pulse of Běijīng's musical fringe; within a drive-in cinema park.

D-22 BAR
(6265 3177; www.d22beijing.com; 242 Chengfu Lu, Haidian; 7pm-2am Wed-Sun) On the music map in Wǔdàokǒu for its excellent crop of top Běijīng bands and no-frills, no-nonsense indie spirit.

MAO Livehouse LIVE MUSIC
(猫; Māo; Map p72; 6402 5080; www.maolive.com; 111 Gulou Dongdajie; 4pm-late) This fantastically popular venue for live sounds is one of the busiest in town.

What Bar? BAR
(什么酒吧; Shénme Bā; Map p52; 133 4112 2757; 72 Beichang Jie; admission on live music nights incl 1 beer Y20; 3pm-late, live music from 9pm Fri & Sat) Microsized and slightly deranged, this broom cupboard of a bar stages regular rotating, grittily named bands to an enthusiastic audience. It's north of the west gate of the Forbidden City.

Classical Music

As China's capital and the nation's cultural hub, Běijīng has several venues where classical music finds an appreciative audience. The annual 30-day **Běijīng Music Festival** (www.bmf.org.cn) is staged between October and November, bringing with it international and home-grown classical music performances.

Běijīng Concert Hall CONCERT HALL
(北京音乐厅; Běijīng Yīnyuètīng; 1 Beixinhua Jie; tickets Y60-580; ⏲performances 7.30pm) The 2000-seat Běijīng Concert Hall showcases evening performances of classical Chinese music as well as international repertoires of Western classical music.

Forbidden City Concert Hall CONCERT HALL
(中山公园音乐堂; Zhōngshān Gōngyuán Yīnyuè Táng; Map p52; Zhōngshān Park; tickets Y50-500; ⏲performances 7.30pm) Located on the eastern side of Zhōngshān Park, this is the venue for performances of classical and traditional Chinese music.

Poly Plaza International Theatre THEATRE
(保利大厦国际剧院; Bǎolì Dàshà Guójì Jùyuàn; Map p66; Poly Plaza, 14 Dongzhimen Nandajie; tickets Y180-1280; ⏲performances 7.30pm) Situated in the old Poly Plaza right by Dōngsìshítiáo subway station, this venue hosts a wide range of performances, including classical music, ballet, traditional Chinese folk music and operatic works.

Theatre

Only emerging in China in the 20th century, *huàjù* (话剧; spoken drama) never made a huge impact. As an art, creative drama is still unable to fully express itself and remains sadly sidelined. But if you want to know what's walking the floorboards in Běijīng, try some of the following. The huge Cháng'ān Grand Theatre largely stages productions of Běijīng opera, with occasional classical Chinese theatre productions.

Capital Theatre THEATRE
(首都剧院; Shǒudū Jùchǎng; Map p48; 22 Wangfujing Dajie; tickets Y80-500; ⏲performances 7pm Tue-Sun) Right in the heart of the city on Wangfujing Dajie, this theatre has regular performances of contemporary Chinese productions from several theatre companies.

China Puppet Theatre THEATRE
(中国木偶剧院; Zhōngguó Mù'ǒu Jùyuàn; 1a Anhua Xili, Beisanhuan Lu; tickets Y30-100;) This popular theatre has regular events, including shadow play, puppetry, music and dance.

Cinemas

The following are two of Běijīng's most central multiscreen cinemas. Only a limited number of Western films are permitted for screening every year.

Star Cinema City CINEMA
(新世纪影城; Xīnshìjì Yǐngyuàn; Map p48; shop BB65, basement, Oriental Plaza, 1 Dongchang'an Jie; tickets Wed-Mon Y50-70, students Y25) This six-screen cinema is centrally located and plush (with leather reclining sofa chairs).

Sundongan Cinema City CINEMA
(新东安影城; Xīndōng'ān Yǐngchéng; Map p48; 5th fl, Sundongan Plaza, Wangfujing Dajie; tickets Y40) Don't expect a huge selection, but you can usually find a Hollywood feature plus other English-language movies.

Shopping

Several vibrant Chinese shopping districts have abundant goods and reasonable prices: Wangfujing Dajie (王府井大街), Xīdān (西单) and reconstructed Qianmen Dajie (前门大街; p66), including Dashilar. The *hútòng* of Dashilar (大栅栏; p66) runs southwest from the northern end of Qianmen Dajie, south of Tiān'ānmén Sq. It's a great jumble of silk shops, old stores, theatres, herbal medicine shops, food and clothing specialists and hostels, slung out along an attractively renovated street. Delve into fun Yandai Xiejie (烟袋斜街), east of Silver Ingot Bridge, for Tibetan trinkets, glazed tiles, T-shirts, paper cuts, teapots, ceramics and even *qípáo* (cheongsam). Nanluogu Xiang (p59) has emerged as a fun shopping enclave of small boutiques and specialist shops.

More luxurious shopping areas can be found in the embassy areas of Jiànguóménwài (建国门外) and Sānlǐtún (三里屯); also check out the five-star hotel shopping malls. Shopping at open-air markets is an experience not to be missed. Běijīng's most popular markets are Silk Street, the Sānlǐtún Yashou Clothing Market, Pānjiāyuán and the Pearl Market. There are also specialised shopping districts such as Liúlíchǎng.

Arts & Crafts

Liulichang Xijie ANTIQUES

Běijīng's premier antique street, not far west of Dashilar, is worth delving along for its quaint, albeit dressed-up, age-old village atmosphere and (largely fake) antiques. Alongside ersatz Qing monochrome bowls and Cultural Revolution kitsch, you can also rummage through old Chinese books, paintings, brushes, ink and paper. Prepare yourself for pushy sales staff and stratospheric prices. If you want a chop (carved seal) made, you can do it here. At the western end of Liulichang Xijie, a collection of ramshackle stalls flog bric-a-brac, Buddhist statuary, Cultural Revolution pamphlets and posters, fake Tang-dynasty *sāncǎi* (three-colour porcelain), shoes for bound feet, silks, handicrafts, Chinese kites, swords, walking sticks, door knockers etc.

Běijīng Curio City ANTIQUES

(北京古玩城; Běijīng Gǔwán Chéng; 21 Dongsanhuan Nanlu; ⌚9.30am-6.30pm) South of Pānjiāyuán, Curio City is four floors of gifts, scrolls, ceramics, carpets, duty-free shopping and furniture. It's an excellent place to turn up knick-knacks and souvenirs, especially on Sundays. Take the subway to Jìngsōng and then hop on bus 28.

Bannerman Tang's Toys & Crafts CRAFTS

(盛唐轩; Shèngtángxuān Chuántǒng Mínjiān Wánjù Kāifā Zhōngxīn; Map p72; 38 Guozijian Jie; ⌚9.30am-7pm) Marvellous collection of handmade toys and delightful collectibles from Chinese weebles (*budao weng;* from Y30), puppets, clay figures, tiger pillows to kites and other gorgeous items; it's just along from the Confucius Temple.

Clockwork Monkey TOYS

(铁皮猴子; Tiěpí Hóuzi; Map p72; 47 Nanluogu Xiang; ⌚10.30am-midnight) Fun and colourful collection of old and reproduction toy tin robots, cars, boats, trains and puppets along bustling Nanluogu Xiang, just north of the corner with Heizhima Hutong and next to the Wěnyǔ Cheese Shop at No 49. Great for children and kiddults alike.

Spin CERAMICS

(旋; Xuán; 6 Fangyuan Xilu; ⌚11am-9.30pm) Jǐngdézhèn ceramics with a funky new imaginative twist; great gift material or for spicing up your dinner table.

Pottery Workshop CERAMICS

(Map p72; Nanluogu Xiang) Another Shànghǎi import on Nanluogu Xiang, this appealing shop sells good-looking ceramics from traditional cool-green celadon tea sets to inventive and artistic creations. It's just north of Qiangulouyuan Hutong, and opens 'when they feel like it'.

Zhāoyuán Gé KITES

(昭元阁; Map p48; 41 Nanheyan Dajie) If you love Chinese kites, you'll enjoy this minute shop on the western side of Nanheyan Dajie. Chinese paper kites range from Y10 for a simple kite, up to around Y300 for a dragon; miniature Chinese kites start from Y25. You can also browse Běijīng opera masks, snuff bottles, chopsticks, Mao badges and *zǐshā* teapots. The owner does not speak much English, but you can look around and make a selection.

Shard Box Store BOXES

(慎德阁; Shèndé Gé; Map p74; 1 Ritan Beilu; ⌚9am-7pm) Captivating collection of boxes intriguingly pieced together from porcelain fragments from ancient vases shattered during the Cultural Revolution.

Clothing

Five Colours Earth CLOTHING

(五色土; Wǔsètǔ; Map p74; 1505, 15/F, Bldg 5, Jianwai Soho, 39 Dongsanhuan Zhonglu; ⌚9am-6pm) Unique, distinctive and stylish clothing items – coats, jackets, lovely skirts and sexy tops – featuring embroideries made by the Miao minority from Guìzhōu.

Mega Mega Vintage CLOTHING

(Map p72; 241 Gulou Dongdajie; ⌚2-10pm) Classic vintage clothing shop hits the nail on the head with a mock-up of an old British red phone box as its fitting room and a great selection of blouses, leather jackets and retro togs galore.

Silk Street CLOTHING

(秀水街; Xiùshuǐ Jiē; Map p74; cnr Jianguomenwai Dajie & Dongdaqiao Lu; ⌚9am-9pm) Seething with shoppers and polyglot (and increasingly tactile) vendors, Silk Street was for long synonymous with fake knock-offs, and some pirated labels survive. The market sprawls from floor to floor, shoving piles of rucksacks, shoes, silk, cashmere and tailor-made *qípáo* into the overloaded mitts of travellers and expats. Haggle fiendishly (credit cards accepted).

Sānlǐtún Yashou Clothing Market CLOTHING
(三里屯雅秀服装市场; Sānlǐtún Yǎxiù Fúzhuāng Shìchǎng; Map p66; 58 Gongrentiyuchang Beilu) After slogging through this hopping, five-floor bedlam of shoes, boots, handbags, suitcases, jackets, silk, carpets, batik, lace, jade, pearls, toys, army surplus and souvenirs, ease the pressure on your bunions with a foot massage (Y50 per hour) or pedicure (Y40) on the 4th floor and restore calories in the 5th-floor food court.

Plastered T-Shirts CLOTHING
(创可贴T-恤; Chuāngkětiē Tìxù; Map p72; 61 Nanluogu Xiang; www.plasteredtshirts.com; ⏲1pm-10pm Mon-Fri, 10am-10pm Sat & Sun) Fun range of tongue-in-cheek, ironic and iconic T-shirts, fitting neatly into the entertaining Nanluogu Xiang mentality.

Books

Bookworm Café BOOKS
(书虫; Shūchóng; ☎6586 9507; www.beijingbookworm.com; Bldg 4, Nansanlitun Lu) Growing section of new and almost new books for sale. Library members can borrow a maximum of two books at a time.

Foreign Languages Bookstore BOOKS
(外文书店; Wàiwén Shūdiàn; 235 Wangfujing Dajie) Third floor for strong children's, fiction and nonfiction sections plus a smattering of travel guides and seats for tired legs.

Chaterhouse Booktrader BOOKS
(Map p74; Basement, The Place, 9a Guanghua Lu; ⏲10am-10pm) Excellent kids section and great range of new fiction, even if prices are high.

Garden Books BOOKS
(Map p74; www.gardenbooks.cn; 44 Guanghua Lu) Sibling of the Shànghǎi branch, above the Sequoia Café.

Department Stores & Malls

Oriental Plaza MALL
(东方新天地; Dōngfāng Xīntiāndì; Map p48; www.orientalplaza.com; 1 Dongchang'an Jie; ⏲9.30am-9.30pm) You could spend a day in this staggeringly large shopping mega-complex at the foot of Wangfujing Dajie. Prices may not be cheap, but window-shoppers will be overjoyed. There's a great range of shops and restaurants and an excellent basement food court. Men, beware of being dragged off to exorbitant cafes and teahouses by pretty English-speaking girls.

The Place MALL
(世贸天阶; Shìmào Tiānjiē; Map p74; 9 Guanghua Lu) With its vast outdoor video screen, snappy shopping plaza The Place has lured big names Zara, French Connection, Miss Sixty and Mango, as well as Chaterhouse Booktrader; there's a good food court in the basement.

The Village MALL
(Map p66; 19 Sanlitun Lu; ⏲10am-10pm) Anchoring Sānlǐtún's expensive commercial facelift, this nifty multistorey mall drags in legions of snappy shoppers and diners to its shops, cafes and restaurants; the world's largest branch of Adidas is here.

Markets

Pānjiāyuán Market MARKET
(潘家园古玩市场; ⏲dawn-6pm Sat & Sun) Hands down the best place to shop for *gōngyì* (crafts) and *gǔwán* (antiques) in Běijīng is Pānjiāyuán (aka the Dirt Market or the Sunday Market). The market only takes place on weekends and sprawls from calligraphy, Cultural Revolution memorabilia and cigarette-ad posters to Buddha heads, ceramics, Tibetan carpets and beyond. Up to 50,000 visitors scope for treasures here: if you want to join them, early Sunday morning is the best time. Also, ignore the 'don't pay more than half" rule here – some vendors may start at 10 times the real price, so aim low. Make a few rounds at Pānjiāyuán before forking out for anything, to compare prices and weigh it all up. It's off Dongsanhuan Nanlu (Third Ring Rd); to get there take the subway to Jìnsōng, then take bus 28.

Pearl Market MARKET
(红桥市场; Hóngqiáo Shìchǎng; Tiantan Donglu; ⏲8.30am-7pm) The cosmos of clutter across from the east gate of Temple of Heaven Park ranges from shoes, leather bags, jackets, jeans, silk by the yard, electronics, Chinese arts, crafts and antiques to a galaxy of pearls (freshwater and seawater, white and black) on the 3rd floor. Prices for the latter vary incredibly with quality and more expensive specimens on the 4th and 5th floors.

Tea

Ten Fu's Tea TEA
(天福茗茶; Tiānfú Míngchá; Map p48; www.tenfu.com; 88 Wangfujing Dajie; 王府井大街88号; ⏲10am-9pm) With perky girls standing outside offering passersby free cups of

tea, Taiwan chain Ten Fu's has a number of branches around town and top-quality loose tea from Tie Guanyin to Pu'er and beyond, with prices starting at Y20 for 1 jīn (500g). There's another branch just west of Ruifuxiang on Dazhalan Jie.

 Information

English-language maps of Běijīng can be grabbed for free at most big hotels and branches of the Běijīng Tourist Information Center. The Foreign Languages Bookstore and other bookshops with English-language titles have maps. Pushy street vendors hawk cheap Chinese character maps (Y1) near subway stations around Tiān'ānmén Sq and Wangfujing Dajie. The *Beijing Tourist Map* (Y8), labelled in both English and Chinese, has little detail but is quite useful.

Internet Access

Internet cafes (网吧; *wǎngbā*) are scarce in the centre of town and tourist areas. Rates are usually Y2 to Y3 (pricier at night). You will need to show your passport and pay a deposit of about Y10; you may be digitally photographed (by the rectangular metallic box on the counter). Many cheaper hotels and youth hostels provide internet access, and numerous bars and cafes around Běijīng now offer wi-fi.

Dáyǔsù Internet Cafe (达宇速网吧; Dáyǔsù Wǎngbā; 2 Hufang Lu; per hr Y3; ⏲8am-midnight) No English sign, but it's around three shops north of the Bank of China on Hufang Lu.

Internet cafe (网吧; wǎngbā; 432-1 Dongsi Beidajie; per hr Y2; ⏲24hr)

Internet cafe (网吧; wǎngba; Wusi Dajie; per hr Y3)

Internet cafe (网吧; wǎngbā; per hr Y5; ⏲24hr) Above the Běijīng City Central Youth Hostel, on the 2nd floor.

Internet cafe (网吧; wǎngbā; per hr Y4; ⏲24hr) It's on the 2nd floor up the fire escape just east of the Bookworm Café.

Internet cafe (网吧; wǎngbā; per hr Y2; ⏲24 hr) Next to the Sānlǐtún Youth Hostel.

Internet cafe (网吧;wǎngbā; per hr Y3; ⏲24 hr) Corner of Dashiqiao Hutong and Jiugulou Dajie.

Sōngjié Internet Cafe (松杰网吧; Sōngjié Wǎngbā; 140-7 Jiaodaokou Nandajie; per hr Y2; ⏲24hr)

Wǎngjù Internet Cafe (网聚网吧; Wǎngjù Wǎngbā; 449 Dongsi Beidajie; per hr Y2; ⏲24hr)

Medical Services

Běijīng has some of the best medical facilities and services in China. Identified by green crosses, pharmacies selling Chinese (中药; *zhōngyào*) and Western medicine (西药; *xīyào*) are widespread. Some pharmacies offer 24-hour service; typically this means you can buy medicine through a window during the night. Branches of **Watson's** (屈臣氏; Qūchénshì) Chaoyangmenwai Dajie (1st fl, Full Link Plaza, 19 Chaoyangmenwai Dajie); Dongchang'an Jie (CC17, 19, CC21, 23, Oriental Plaza, 1 Dongchang'an Jie) purvey some medicines, but are more geared towards selling cosmetics, sunscreens and the like.

Bayley & Jackson Medical Center (庇利积臣医疗中心; Bìlì Jíchén Yīliáo Zhōngxīn; ☎8562 9998; www.bjhealthcare.com; 7 Ritan Donglu) Full range of private medical and dental services.

Běijīng Union Medical Hospital (北京协和医院; Běijīng Xiéhé Yīyuàn; ☎6529 6114, emergencies 6529 5284; 53 Dongdan Beidajie; ⏲24hr) Foreigners' and VIP wing in the back building.

Běijīng United Family Hospital (北京和睦家医院; Běijīng Hémùjiā Yīyuàn; ☎6433 3960, 24hr emergency hotline 6433 2345; www.unitedfamilyhospitals.com; 2 Jiangtai Lu; ⏲24hr) Can provide alternative medical treatments along with a comprehensive range of inpatient and outpatient care, as well as a critical care unit. Emergency room staffed by expat physicians.

International SOS (北京亚洲国际紧急救援医疗中心; Běijīng Yàzhōu Guójì Jǐnjí Jiùyuán Yīliáo Zhōngxīn; ☎clinic appointments 6462 9112, dental appointments 6462 0333, emergencies 6462 9100; www.internationalsos.com; Suite 105, Wing 1 Kūnshā Bldg, 16 Xinyuanli; ⏲9am-6pm Mon-Fri) Expensive, high-quality clinic with English speaking staff.

Wángfǔjǐng Pharmaceutical Store (王府井医药商店; Wángfǔjǐng Yīyào Shāngdiàn; 267 Wangfujing Dajie; ⏲8.30am-10pm) Has a large range of both Western and Chinese medicine, plus wheelchairs.

Money

Foreign currency and travellers cheques can be changed at large branches of the Bank of China, CITIC Industrial Bank, the Industrial & Commercial Bank of China, HSBC, the airport and hotel moneychanging counters, and at several department stores (including the Friendship Store), as long as you have your passport. Hotels give the official rate, but some will add a small commission. Useful branches of the Bank of China with foreign-exchange counters include a branch next to Oriental Plaza on Wangfujing Dajie and in the China World Trade Center. For international money transfers, branches of Western Union can be found in the International Post Office and the Chaoyang branch of **China Post** (3 Gongrentiyuchang Beilu).

ATMs taking international cards are in abundance. The best places to look are in and around the main shopping areas (such as Wangfujing Dajie) and international hotels and their associated shopping arcades; some large department stores also have useful ATMs. There's a Bank of China ATM in the Capital Airport arrivals hall. Other useful ATMs:

Bank of China (中国银行; Zhōngguó Yínháng) Lufthansa Center (1st fl, Lufthansa Center Yǒuyì Shopping City, 50 Liangmaqiao Lu); Novotel Peace Hotel (foyer, Novotel Peace Hotel, 3 Jinyu Hutong); Oriental Plaza (Oriental Plaza, cnr Wangfujing Dajie & Dongchang'an Jie); Sūndōngān Plaza (next to main entrance of Sūndōngān Plaza, Wangfujing Dajie); Swissôtel (2nd fl, Swissôtel, 2 Chaoyangmen Beidajie)

Citibank (花旗银行; Huāqí Yínháng; ☎6510 2933; 6th fl, Tower 2, Bright China Cháng'ān Bldg, 7 Jianguomennei Dajie)

Hong Kong & Shanghai Banking Corporation (汇丰银行; Huìfēng Yínháng; HSBC; ☎6526 0668, 800 820 8878) China World Hotel (Suite L129, Ground fl, China World Hotel, 1 Jianguomenwai Dajie); COFCO Plaza (Ground fl, Block A, COFCO Plaza, 8 Jianguomennei Dajie); Lufthansa Center (Ground fl, Lufthansa Center, 50 Liangmaqiao Lu) All have 24-hour ATMs.

Industrial & Commercial Bank of China (工商银行; Gōngshāng Yínháng; Wangfujing Dajie) Opposite Bank of China ATM at entrance to Sūndōngān Plaza.

Post

The **International Post Office** (国际邮电局; Guójì Yóudiànjú; Jianguomen Beidajie; ⌚8am-7pm) is 200m north of Jiànguóménsubway station; poste restante letters (Y3; maximum one month, take passport for collection) can be addressed here. You can also post letters via your hotel reception desk, which may be the most convenient option, or at green post boxes around town.

Handy branches of **China Post** (中国邮政; Zhōngguó Yóuzhèng) can be found in the CITIC building next to the Friendship Store; in the China World Trade Center basement; in the Silk Street basement; east of Wangfujing Dajie on Dongdan Ertiao; on the south side of Xichang'an Jie, west of the Běijīng Concert Hall; and east of the Qiánmén Jiànguó Hotel, on Yong'an Lu.

Several private couriers in Běijīng offer international express posting of documents and parcels, and have reliable pick-up services as well as drop-off centres.

DHL (敦豪特快专递; Dūnháo Tèkuài Zhuāndì; ☎6466 2211, 800 810 8000; www.dhl.com; 45 Xinyuan Jie) Further branches in the China World Trade Center and COFCO Plaza.

Federal Express (联邦快递; Liánbāng Kuàidì; FedEx; ☎6561 2003, 800 810 2338; 1217, Tower B, Hanwei Bldg, 7 Guanghua Lu) Also in Room 107, No 1 Office Bldg, Oriental Plaza.

United Parcel Service (UPS; ☎6593 2932; Unit A, 2nd fl, Tower B, Běijīng Kelun Bldg, 12a Guanghua Lu)

Public Security Bureau

PSB (公安局; Gōng'ānjú; ☎8402 0101, 8401 5292; 2 Andingmen Dongdajie; ⌚8.30am-4.30pm Mon-Sat) The Foreign Affairs Branch of the PSB handles visa extensions; see p993 for further information. The visa office is on the 2nd floor on the east side of the building. You can also apply for a residence permit and obtain passport photographs here (Y30 for five).

Tourist Information

Běijīng Tourism Hotline (☎6513 0828; ⌚24hr) Has English-speaking operators available to answer questions and hear complaints.

Běijīng Tourist Information Centers (北京旅游咨询服务中心; Běijīng Lǚyóu Zīxún Fúwù Zhōngxīn; ⌚9am-5pm) Běijīng train station (☎6528 8448; 16 Laoqianju Hutong); Capital Airport (☎6459 8148); Cháoyáng (☎6417 6627/6656; Gongrentiyuchang Beilu); Wangfujing Dajie (Wangfujing Dajie); Xuānwǔ (☎6351 0018; xuanwu@bjta.gov.cn; 3 Hufang Lu) English skills are limited and information is basic, but you can grab a free tourist map of town and handfuls of free literature; some offices also have train ticket offices.

Travel Agencies

China International Travel Service (CITS; 中国国际旅行社; Zhōngguó Guójì Lǚxíngshè; ☎8511 8522; www.cits.com.cn; Room 1212, CITS Bldg, 1 Dongdan Beidajie) Useful for booking tours.

Getting There & Away

As the nation's capital, getting to Běijīng is straightforward. Rail and air connections link the city to virtually every point in China, and fleets of buses head to abundant destinations from Běijīng. Using Běijīng as a starting point to explore the rest of the country makes perfect sense.

Air

Běijīng has direct air connections to most major cities in the world. For more information about international flights to Běijīng, see p995.

Daily flights connect Běijīng to every major city in China. There should be at least one flight a week to smaller cities throughout China. The prices listed in this book are approximate only and represent the non-discounted airfare.

Chéngdū Y1440

Chóngqìng Y1660

Dàlián Y780

Guǎngzhōu Y1700
Guìlín Y1440
Guìyáng Y1560
Hángzhōu Y1150
Hārbīn Y1050
Hong Kong Y2860
Kūnmíng Y1630
Lhasa Y2430
Nánjīng Y1010
Qīngdǎo Y710
Shànghǎi Y1220
Shēnzhèn Y1750
Ürümqi Y2410
Wǔhàn Y1080
Xiàmén Y1710
Xī'ān Y840

Purchase tickets for Chinese carriers flying from Běijīng at the **Civil Aviation Administration of China** (中国民航; CAAC; Zhōngguó Mínháng; Aviation Building;民航营业大厦; Mínháng Yíngyè Dàshà; ☎6656 9118, domestic 6601 3336, international 6601 6667; 15 Xichang'an Jie; ⌚7am-midnight) or from one of the numerous other ticket outlets and service counters around Běijīng, and through most midrange and top-end hotels. Discounts are generally available, so it is important to ask. Also book through www.ctrip.com.cn and www.elong.com.

Make enquiries for all airlines at Běijīng's **Capital Airport** (PEK; ☎from Běijīng only 962 580). Call ☎6454 1100 for information on international and domestic arrivals and departures.

Bus

No international buses serve Běijīng, but there are plenty of long-distance domestic routes served by national highways radiating from Běijīng. Běijīng has numerous long-distance bus stations (长途汽车站; *chángtú qìchēzhàn*), positioned roughly on the city perimeter in the direction you want to go.

BĀWÁNGFÉN LONG-DISTANCE BUS STATION Destinations served by **Bāwángfén long-distance bus station** (八王坟长途客运站; Bāwángfén Chángtú Kèyùnzhàn; 17 Xidawang Lu) in the east of town:

Bāotóu sleeper Y150, 12 hours, one daily (6pm)
Chángchūn Y221, 12 hours, four daily
Dàlián Y276, 8½ hours, four daily
Hā'ěrbīn Y301, 14 hours, one daily (8pm)
Qínhuángdǎo Y61 to Y90, 3½ hours, frequent
Shěnyáng Y165, 7½ hours, regular services
Tiānjīn Y31 to Y35

SÌHUÌ LONG-DISTANCE BUS STATION Buses from **Sìhuì long-distance bus station** (四惠长途汽车站; Sìhuì Chángtú Qìchēzhàn):

Bāotóu Y150, 12 hours, one daily (2.30pm)
Chángchūn Y240, 12 hours, one daily (5pm)
Chéngdé Y56 to Y77, four hours, 6am to 4pm
Dàlián Y275, 10 hours, two daily (4.30pm and 6.30pm)
Dāndōng Y180, 12 hours, one daily (4pm)
Jìxiàn Y24, two hours, every 10 minutes (6.15am to 7.30pm)

LIÙLǏQIÁO LONG-DISTANCE BUS STATION Southwest of Běijīng West train station, **Liùlǐqiáo long-distance bus station** (六里桥长途站; Liùlǐqiáo Chángtúzhàn) has buses north, south and west of town:

Bāotóu Y150, four daily
Chéngdé Y73, regular services
Dàlián Y210, one daily (4pm)
Dàtóng Y119, regular services
Héféi Y299, one daily (1.45pm)
Luòyáng Y149, six daily
Shěnyáng Y169, 7½ hours, three daily
Shíjiāzhuāng Y75, regular services
Xiàmén Y579, two daily (11am and 11.30am)
Xī'ān Y259, one daily (5.45pm)
Yínchuān Y239, one daily (5pm)
Zhèngzhōu Y149, 10 daily

LIÁNHUĀCHÍ LONG-DISTANCE BUS STATION The **Liánhuāchí long distance bus station** (莲花池长途汽车站; Liánhuāchí Chángtú Qìchēzhàn) has buses south:

Ānyáng Y84, regular services
Luòyáng Y135, one daily
Shíjiāzhuāng Y59, four to five daily
Yán'ān Y256, one daily

ZHÀOGŌNGKǑU LONG-DISTANCE BUS STATION Another important station is **Zhàogōngkǒu long-distance bus station** (赵公口汽车站; Zhàogōngkǒu Qìchēzhàn) in the south (useful for buses to Tiānjīn and Jǐnán). There are also direct buses to Tiānjīn (Y70, 7am to 11pm) and Qínhuángdǎo from Capital Airport. Lìzéqiáo long-distance bus station on Xīsānhuán in west Běijīng has buses to Tàiyuán and Nánjíng.

Train

Travellers arrive and depart by train at **Běijīng train station** (Běijīng Huǒchēzhàn) near the centre of town, the colossal **Běijīng West train station** (Běijīng Xīzhàn) in the southwest or at the ultra-modern **Běijīng South train station** (Běijīng Nánzhàn) for trains from Tiānjīn,

Shànghǎi and Hángzhōu. Běijīng train station and Běijīng South train station are served by their own underground stations, making access simple. International trains to Moscow, Pyongyang (North Korea) and Ulaanbaatar (Mongolia) arrive at and leave from Běijīng train station; trains for Vietnam leave from Běijīng West train station. Bus 122 (Y1) connects Běijīng train station with Běijīng West train station.

The queues at Běijīng train station can be overwhelming. At the time of writing, there is an English-speaking service window, but it moves around. A **foreigners ticketing office** (⏲24hr) can be found on the 2nd floor of Běijīng West train station.

If you can't face the queues, ask your hotel to book your ticket or try one of the train ticket offices (火车票售票处; Huǒchēpiào Shòupiàochù) around town, where you pay a Y5 commission for your ticket. A handy **train ticket office** (200 Wangfujing Dajie; ⏲9.30am-8.30pm) is at the rear on the right of the 1st floor of the Arts and Crafts Mansion on Wangfujing Dajie; also try the **train ticket office** (9 Zhengjue Hutong; ⏲8am-10.30pm) east of Xinjiekou Nandajie and the **train ticket office** (火车票售票处; 134 Jiaodaokou Nandajie; ⏲8am-9pm) on Jiaodaokou Nandajie. The **Běijīng Tourist Information Office** (北京旅游咨询服务中心; Běijīng Lǚyóu Zīxún Zhōngxīn; ☎6417 6627/6656; Gongrentiyuchang Beilu) near Sānlǐtún also has a train ticket office.

BĚIJĪNG TRAIN STATION Běijīng train station is mainly for T-class trains *(tèkuài)*, slow trains and trains bound for the northeast; most fast trains heading south now depart from Běijīng South train station and Běijīng West train station. Slower trains to Shànghǎi (Y327, 13½ hours) also go from here. The high-speed D-class train to Chángchūn (Y239, 6½ hours) departs from here, while T-class overnight trains take nine hours (Y239). For high-speed trains to Tiānjīn and Shànghǎi, go to Běijīng south train station.

Typical train fares and approximate travel times for hard-sleeper tickets to destinations from Běijīng train station:

Dàlián Y257, 11½ hours

Dàtóng Y108, 5½ hours

Hā'ěrbīn Z-class trains, soft sleeper Y429, under 10 hours; slower train, hard sleeper Y281, 12 hours

Hángzhōu Y353, 15 hours

Jílín Y263, 11½ hours

Jǐ'nán Y137, five hours

Nánjīng Y274, 11 hours

Qīngdǎo Y215, nine hours

Shànghǎi soft-sleeper express Y327, 13½ hours, 12 hours

Tiānjīn hard seat Y58, 80 minutes

BĚIJĪNG WEST TRAIN STATION Fast 'Z' class express trains from Běijīng West train station:

Chángshā soft sleeper only Z17, Y506, 13 hours, one daily (6.10pm)

Fúzhōu Z59, hard seat Y253, hard sleeper Y443, 19 hours 40 minutes, one daily (5.08pm)

Hànkǒu Z77, Y281, 10 hours, one daily (9.12pm)

Lánzhōu Z55, Y377, almost 18 hours, one daily (1.35pm)

Nánchāng Z65, Z67 and Z133, hard sleeper Y308, 11½ hours

Wǔchāng hard sleeper Y281, 10 hours, one daily (Z11 9.06pm, Z37 9pm)

Xī'ān hard sleeper Y265, 11 hours, one daily (Z19 9.18pm, Z53 9.24pm)

Other typical train fares and approximate travel times for hard-sleeper tickets:

Chéngdū Y472, 25 hours

Chóngqìng Y416, 24 hours

Guǎngzhōu Y443, 21 hours

Guìyáng Y490, 29 hours

Hànkǒu Y281, 10 hours 20 minutes

Kowloon Y526, 23 hours 48 minutes

Kūnmíng Y578, 38 hours

Lánzhōu Y377, 20½ hours

Shēnzhèn Y467, 23½ hours

Shíjiāzhuāng D-class trains Y88, two hours; slower train, hard seat Y50, three hours

Ürümqi Y652, 40 hours

Xī'ān Y274, 13 hours

Xīníng Y430, 20½ hours

Yíchāng Y319, 21½ hours

Yínchuān Y301, 19 hours

For Lhasa in Tibet, the T27 (hard seat Y389, hard/soft sleeper Y813/1262, 45 hours) leaves Běijīng West train station at 9.30pm, taking just under two days. In the return direction, the T28 departs Lhasa at 9.20am.

BĚIJĪNG SOUTH TRAIN STATION Most D-class trains and the Tiānjīn C-class train depart from slick, Gattica-like Beijing South train station (Běijīng Nánzhàn) to destinations such as Tiānjīn, Shànghǎi, Hángzhōu and Qīngdǎo.

Hángzhōu D309, Y820, 11½ hours

Jǐnán Y153, three hours

Nánjīng seat/sleeper Y274/520, eight hours

Qīngdǎo Y275, 5½ hours, six daily

BORDER CROSSINGS: GETTING TO MONGOLIA, NORTH KOREA, RUSSIA & VIETNAM

Getting to Mongolia

As well as Trans-Mongolian Railway trains that run from Běijīng to Ulaanbaatar via Dàtóng, the K23 train runs to Ulaanbaatar, departing Běijīng train station at 7.45am every Tuesday, reaching Ulaanbaatar at 1.15pm the next day. In the other direction, the K24 departs from Ulaanbaatar every Thursday at 8.05am, reaching Běijīng the following day at 2.04pm.

Getting to North Korea

There are four international express trains (K27 and K28) between Běijīng and Pyongyang. K27 leaves Běijīng train station at 5.35pm and reaches Pyongyang at 7.30pm the next day (four weekly).

Getting to Russia

The Trans-Siberian Railway runs from Běijīng to Moscow via two routes: the Trans-Mongolian Railway and the Trans-Manchurian Railway. See p1000 for details.

Getting to Vietnam

There are two weekly trains from Běijīng to Hanoi. The GT9 leaves Běijīng West train station at 4.08pm on Thursday and Sunday, arriving in Hanoi at 7am on Saturday and Tuesday. The GT6 departs Hanoi at 6.50pm on Tuesday and Friday, arriving in Běijīng at 12.09pm on Thursday and Sunday. The train stops at Shíjiāzhuāng, Zhèngzhōu, Hànkǒu (in Wǔhàn), Wǔchāng (Wǔhàn), Chángshā, Héngyáng, Yǒngzhōu, Guìlín, Liǔzhōu, Nánníng and Píngxiáng. See p999 for information on visas.

Shànghǎi Hóngqiáo train station eight D-class trains (five night trains), Y499, around 10 hours
Sūzhōu seat/sleeper Y309/620
Tiānjīn C-series, Y58 to Y69, 30 minutes, every 15 minutes (6.35am to 10.10pm)

BĚIJĪNG NORTH TRAIN STATION Inner Mongolia is served by trains from **Běijīng North train station** (Běijīng Běizhàn), including trains to Hohhot (Y170, 11½ hours).

Getting Around

To/From the Airport

Běijīng's Capital Airport is 27km from the centre of town, about 30 minutes to one hour by car depending on traffic.

The 30-minute **Airport Express** (机场快轨; Jīchǎng Kuàiguǐ; Y25; ⏲6am-10.30pm to airport, 6.30am-11pm from airport) runs every 15 minutes, connecting Capital Airport with Line 2 of the underground system at Dōngzhímén and connecting with Line 10 at Sānyuánqiáo.

Several **express bus routes** (fare Y16) run every 10 to 20 minutes during operating hours to Běijīng:

Line 3 (⏲7.30am-last flight from Capital Airport, 5.30am-9pm from Běijīng train station) The most popular with travellers, running to the Běijīng International Hotel and Běijīng train station via Cháoyángmén.

Line 2 (⏲7am-last flight from Capital Airport, 5.30am-9pm from Aviation Building) Runs to the Aviation Building in Xīdàn, via Dōngzhímén.

Line 1 (⏲7am-11pm from Capital Airport, 5.30am-11pm from Fāngzhuāng) Runs to Fāngzhuāng, via Dàběiyáo, where you can get onto the subway Line 1 at Guómào. Buses generally make stops at all terminals, but check with the driver. Bus 359 (Y2, one hour, 5.20am to 10pm) also runs to Capital Airport from Dongzhimenwai Xiejie.

A bus also runs from **Nányuàn Airport** (☎6797 8899) – Běijīng's other airport – to the Aviation Building in Xīdàn, coinciding with departures and arrivals.

Many top-end hotels run shuttle buses from the airport to their hotels.

A taxi (using its meter) should cost about Y85 from the airport to the city centre, including the Y15 airport expressway toll; bank on 30 minutes to one hour to get into town. Join the taxi ranks and ignore approaches from drivers. When you get into the taxi, make sure the driver uses the meter. It is also useful to have the name of your hotel written down in Chinese to show the driver.

TAKEN FOR A RIDE

A well-established illegal taxi operation at the airport attempts to lure weary travellers into a Y300-plus ride to the city, so be on your guard. If anyone approaches you offering a taxi ride, ignore them and insist on joining the queue for a taxi outside.

Bicycle

Flat as a mah jong board, Běijīng was built for bicycling and the ample bicycle lanes are testament to the vehicle's unflagging popularity. The increase in traffic in recent years has made biking along major thoroughfares more dangerous and nerve-racking, however.

Youth hostels often hire out bicycles, which cost around Y20 to Y30 per day; rental at upmarket hotels is far more expensive. A handy network of **bike rental stations** (⏲8am-10pm) can be found outside a few underground stations, principally on Line 2 (including Gulou Dajie). Bikes (per four hours Y10, per day Y20, deposit Y400) can be hired and returned to different underground stations. Otherwise there are plenty of other places you can hire bikes, including the shop at 77 Tieshu Xiejie (Y10 from 7am to 11pm; deposit Y200), one of several along this road. When renting a bike it's safest to use your own lock(s) in order to prevent bicycle theft, a common problem in Běijīng.

Car

Běijīng's Capital Airport has a **Vehicle Administration Office** (车管所; chēguǎnsuǒ; ☎6453 0010; ⏲Mon-Sun 9am-6pm) where you can have a temporary three-month driving licence issued. See p1003 for more information.

Public Transport

A rechargeable **transport card** (公交IC卡; gōngjiāo IC kǎ; deposit Y20) for the underground, buses and taxis is available from subway stations and kiosks. The card typically nets you 60% off the cost of bus trips; merely charge the card at subway stations and swipe as you use.

BUS Buses (公共汽车; *gōnggòng qìchē*) are a reasonable way to get around: there are ample bus lanes, bus routes and fleet numbers are plentiful and prices are low. It can still be slow going, however, compared to the subway. As elsewhere in China, you see precious few foreign faces on town buses: bus routes on bus signs are fiendishly foreigner-unfriendly, although the name of the stop appears in pinyin and announcements are made in English (but try to work out how many stops you need to go before boarding). Getting a seat can verge on the physical, especially at rush hour.

Most fares are typically Y1, although longer trips or journeys on plusher, air-conditioned buses and night buses are more expensive. You generally pay the conductor once aboard the bus, rather than the driver. Using a transport smartcard nets you a big saving of 60% off most bus trips (making most trips just Y0.40); just swipe the touchpad on the bus.

Buses run from 5am to 11pm daily or thereabouts. If you read Chinese, a useful publication (Y5) listing all the Běijīng bus lines is available from kiosks; alternatively, tourist maps of Běijīng illustrate some of the bus routes. See www.bjbus.com/english/default.htm for a map of Běijīng's bus routes in English. If you work out how to combine bus and subway connections, the subway will speed up much of the trip.

Buses 1 to 86 cover the city core; the 200 series are *yèbān gōnggòng qìchē* (night buses), while buses 300 to 501 are suburban lines.

Useful standard bus routes:

1 Runs along Chang'an Jie, Jianguomenwai Dajie and Jianguomennei Dajie, passing Sìhuìzhàn, Bāwāngfén, Yonganli, Dōngdān, Xīdān, Mùxīdì, Jūnshì Bówùguǎn, Gōngzhǔfén and Mǎguānyíng along the way.

5 Déshèngmén, Dì'ānmén, Běihǎi Park, Xīhuámén, Zhōngshān Park and Qiánmén.

15 Běijīng Zoo, Fùxīngmén, Xīdān, Hépíngmén, Liúlíchǎng and Tiānqiáo.

20 Běijīng South train station, Tiānqiáo, Qiánmén, Wāngfǔjǐng, Dōngdān and Běijīng train station.

44 (outer ring) Xīnjiēkǒu, Xīzhímén train station, Fùchéngmén, Fùxīngmén, Changchunjie, Xuānwǔmén, Qiánmén, Táijīchǎng, Chōngwénmén, Dōngbiànmén, Cháoyángmén, Dōngzhímén, Āndìngmén, Déshèngmèn and Xīnjiēkǒu.

103 Běijīng train station, Dēngshìkǒu, China Art Gallery, Forbidden City (north entrance), Běihǎi Park, Fùchéngmén and Běijīng Zoo.

106 Dōngzhímén Transport Hub Station to Běijīng South train station.

126 Useful for the short hop from Qiánmén to Wangfujing Dajie.

332 Běijīng Zoo, Wèigōngcūn, Rénmín Dàxué, Zhōngguāncūn, Hǎidiàn, Běijīng University and Summer Palace.

823 Dōngzhímén Transport Hub Station to Běijīng West train station.

SUBWAY The subway (地铁; *dìtiě*) is fast and reliable. Currently nine lines are operating (including the Airport Line), with two more under construction, including Line 9 which will link Běijīng West train station with Line 1 and

Line 4. The flat fare is Y2 on all lines except the Airport Line (Y25). Trains run every few minutes during peak times, operating from 5am to 11pm daily. Stops are announced in English and Chinese. Subway stations (地铁站; *dìtiě zhàn*) are identified by subway symbols, a blue, encircled English capital 'D'. A further east–west line – Line 6 – was under construction at the time of research. Useful stations should include Beihai North, Nánluógǔ Xiàng, Dōngsī and Cháoyángmén; the line is planned to intersect with numerous other lines, including Lines 10, 2, 5 and 4.

Line 1 (一号线; Yīhàoxiàn) Runs east–west from Píngguǒyuán to Sìhuì East.

Line 2 (二号线; Èrhàoxiàn) The circle line following the Second Ring Rd.

Line 4 (四号线; Sìhàoxiàn) Links Gōngyìxīqiáo and Ānhéqiáo North, connecting with the Summer Palace (Xīyuàn) and the Old Summer Palace (Yuánmíngyuán).

Line 5 (五号线; Wǔhàoxiàn) Runs north–south between Tiāntōngyuàn North and Sōngjiāzhuāng.

Line 8 (八号线; Bāhàoxiàn) Connects Běitǔchéng with South Gate of Forest Park, running through the Olympics Sports Center and Olympic Green.

Line 10 (十号线; Shíhàoxiàn) Follows a long loop from Jìnsōng in the southeast to Bāgōu in the northwest; handy for the Sanlǐtún area.

Line 13 (十三号线; Shísānhàoxiàn) Runs in a northern loop from Xīzhímén to Dōngzhímén.

Batong Line (八通线; Bātōngxiàn) Runs from Sìhuì to Tǔqiáo in the southeastern suburbs.

Airport Line (机场线; Jīchǎngxiàn) Connects Dōngzhímén with the terminals at Capital Airport.

Taxi

Běijīng taxis come in different classes, with red stickers on the side rear window declaring the rate per kilometre. Y2 taxis (Y10 for the first 3km, Y2 per kilometre thereafter) include a fleet of spacious Hyundai cars. The most expensive taxis are Y12 for the first 3km and Y2 per kilometre thereafter. Taxis are required to switch on the meter for all journeys (unless you negotiate a fee for a long journey out of town). Between 11pm and 6am there is a 20% surcharge added to the flag-fall metered fare. For extra room and a sense of style, look out for one of the silver London cabs that cruise the streets.

Běijīng taxi drivers speak little English. If you don't speak Chinese, bring a map or have your destination written down in script. It helps if you know the way to your destination; sit in the front (where the seat belt works) with a map.

Cabs can be hired for distance, by the hour, or by the day (a minimum of Y350 for the day). Taxis can be hailed in the street, summoned by phone or you can wait at one of the designated taxi zones or outside hotels. Call ☎6835 1150 to register a complaint. Remember to collect a receipt (ask the driver to *fāpiào*); if you accidentally leave anything in the taxi, the driver's number appears on the receipt so he or she can be located.

AROUND BĚIJĪNG

Ming Tombs 十三陵

The **Ming Tombs** (Shísān Líng; Map p46; ⌚8am-5pm), located about 50km northwest of Běijīng, are the final resting place of 13 of the 16 Ming emperors. Billed with the Great Wall at Bādálǐng as Běijīng's great double act, the imperial graveyard can unsurprisingly be a rather dormant spectacle, unless you pack a penchant for ceremonial tomb architecture, Confucian symbolism or Ming imperial genealogy.

The Ming Tombs follow the standard plan for imperial tomb design, typically consisting of a *líng mén* (main gate) leading to the first of a series of courtyards and the main hall, the **Hall of Eminent Favours** (灵恩殿; Líng'ēn Diàn). Beyond lie further gates or archways, leading to the **Soul Tower** (明楼; Míng Lóu), behind which rises the burial mound.

Three tombs have been opened up to the public: Cháng Líng, Dìng Líng and Zhāo Líng.

The road leading up to the tombs is the 7km **Spirit Way** (神道; Shéndào; admission winter/summerY20/30; ⌚7am-8pm). Starting with a triumphal arch, the path enters the Great Palace Gate, where officials once had to dismount, and passes a giant *bìxì*, which bears the largest stele in China. A magnificent guard of 12 sets of stone animals and officials ensues.

Cháng Líng (长陵; admission winter/summer Y30/45), burial place of the emperor Yongle, is the most impressive, with its series of magnificent halls lying beyond its yellow-tiled gate. Seated upon a three-tiered marble terrace, the most notable structure is the Hall of Eminent Favours, containing a recent statue of Yongle and a breathtaking interior with vast *nanmu* (cedarwood) columns. The pine-covered burial mound at the rear of the complex is yet to be excavated and is not open to the public.

Dìng Líng (定陵; admission incl museum winter/summer Y40/60), the burial place of the emperor Wanli, contains a series of subterranean interlocking vaults and the remains of the various gates and halls of the complex. Excavated in the late 1950s, this tomb is of more interest to some visitors as you are allowed to descend into the underground vault. Accessing the vault down the steps, visitors are confronted by the simply vast marble self-locking doors that sealed the chamber after it was vacated. The tomb is also the site of the absorbing **Ming Tombs Museum** (Shísān Líng Bówùguǎn; admission Y20).

Zhāo Líng (昭陵; admission winter/summer Y20/30), the resting place of the 13th Ming emperor Longqing, follows an orthodox layout and is a tranquil alternative if you find the other tombs too busy.

Tour buses usually combine visits to one of the Ming Tombs with trips to the Great Wall at Bādálǐng; see p100 for information about buses to and from Bādálǐng. Also see p102 for details of tour buses that include visits to Dìng Líng.

To go independently, take fast bus 345 (345 路快; 345 Lùkuài) from Déshèngménxī, 500m east of Jīshuǐtán subway station, to Chāngpíng (昌平; Y6, one hour, running from 5.30am to 10pm). Get off at the Chāngpíng Dōngguān (昌平东关) stop and change to bus 314 (running 6am to 7pm) for the tombs. Alternatively, take the slower standard bus 345 to Chāngpíng Běizhàn (昌平北站) and similarly transfer to bus 314.

Tánzhè Temple & Jiètái Temple 潭柘寺、戒台寺

Forty-five kilometres west of Běijīng, **Tánzhè Temple** (Tánzhè Sì; Map p46; admission Y35; ⌚8.30am-6pm) is the largest of all of Běijīng's temples. Delightfully climbing the hills amid trees, the temple has a history that extends way back to the 3rd century, although most of what you see is of far more recent construction. The temple grounds are overhung with towering cypress and pine trees; many are so old that their gangly limbs are supported by metal props.

The highlight of a trip to the temple is the small **Tǎlín Temple** (Tǎlín Sì), by the forecourt where you disembark the bus, with its collection of stupas (reliquaries for the cremated remains of important monks) reminiscent of the Shàolín Temple. You can tour them while waiting for the return bus. An excellent time to visit Tánzhè Temple is around mid-April, when the magnolias are in bloom.

About 10km southeast of Tánzhè Temple is the smaller, but more engaging **Jiètái Temple** (Jiètái Sì; Map p46; admission Y35; ⌚8am-6pm). Jiètái (Ordination Terrace) Temple was built around AD 622 during the Tang dynasty, with major modifications made during the Ming dynasty.

The main complex is dotted with ancient pine trees; the **Nine Dragon Pine** is claimed to be over 1300 years old, while the **Embracing Pagoda Pine** does just what it says.

Take Line 1 of the subway west to the Píngguǒyuán stop and hop on bus 931 (Y3), running from 6.15am to 5.35pm, to the last stop for Tánzhè Temple (don't take the bus 931 branch line, zhīxiàn 支线, however). This bus also stops near Jiètái Temple, where it's a 10-minute walk uphill from the bus stop.

Marco Polo Bridge 卢沟桥

Described by the great traveller himself, this 266m-long grey marble **bridge** (Lúgōu Qiáo; 88 Lugouqiaochengnei Xijie; admission Y20; ⌚8am-5pm) is host to 485 carved stone lions. Each animal is different, with the smallest only a few centimetres high, and legend insists they move around during the night.

Dating from 1189, the stone bridge is Běijīng's oldest (but is a composite of different eras; it was widened in 1969), and spans the Yǒngdìng River (永定河) near the small walled town of Wǎnpíng (宛平城), just southwest of Běijīng.

Despite the praises of Marco Polo and Emperor Qianlong, the bridge wouldn't have rated more than a footnote in Chinese history were it not for the famed Marco Polo Bridge Incident, which ignited a full-scale war with Japan. On 7 July 1937, Japanese troops illegally occupied a railway junction outside Wǎnpíng. Japanese and Chinese soldiers started shooting, and that gave Japan enough of an excuse to attack and occupy Běijīng.

WORTH A TRIP

CHUĀNDǏXIÀ (CUÀNDǏXIÀ)

Nestled in a windswept valley 90km west of Běijīng and overlooked by towering peaks is **Chuāndǐxià** (川底下; admission Y20), a gorgeous cluster of historic courtyard homes and old-world charm. The backdrop is lovely: terraced orchards and fields, with ancient houses and alleyways rising up the hillside. The village's real name is Cuàndǐxià (爨底下), but as the first Chinese character 爨 (Cuàn) is so rare, it is colloquially known as Chuāndǐxià.

Chuāndǐxià is also a museum of **Maoist graffiti and slogans**, especially up the incline among the better-preserved houses. Chuāndǐxià's friendly residents long ago flung open their doors to overnighting visitors. The lovely-looking **Bǎishùn Kèzhàn** (百顺客栈), behind the spirit wall at No 43 Chunadixiacun at the foot of the village, is a magnificent old courtyard guesthouse.

To the east of the village is the small Qing-dynasty **Guandi Temple**, making for a delightful walk above the village. For excellent bird's-eye photos, climb the hill south of Chuāndǐxià in the direction of the Niángniáng Temple. Two hours is more than enough time to wander around the village as it's not big.

If taking a taxi, consider paying an extra Y20 or so for your driver to take you back via the nearby village of Língshuǐ Cūn (灵水村), another historic village dating to the Tang dynasty.

A bus (Y10, two hours) leaves for Chuāndǐxià from Píngguǒyuán subway station every day at 7.30am and 12.30pm, returning at 10.30am and 3.30pm. If you take the later bus, you may either need to spend the night or find alternative transport. The other option is to take bus 929 (make sure it's the branch line, or *zhīxiàn* 支线, not the regular bus; runs 7am to 5.15pm) from the bus stop 200m to the west of Píngguǒyuán subway station to Zhāitáng (斋堂; Y8, two hours), then hire a taxi van (Y20). The last bus returns from Zhāitáng to Píngguǒyuán at 4.20pm. If you miss the last bus, a taxi will cost around Y80 to Píngguǒyuán. Taxi drivers waiting at Píngguǒyuán subway station will charge around Y140 to Y150 for a round trip. Some hostels in Běijīng also arrange tours to Chuāndǐxià.

The **Memorial Hall of the War of Resistance Against Japan** is a gory look back at Japan's occupation of China. Also on the site are the Wǎnpíng Castle, Dàiwáng Temple and a hotel.

Take bus 6 from the north gate of Temple of Heaven Park to the last stop at Liùlǐ Bridge (六里桥; Liùlǐ Qiáo) and then either bus 339 or 309 to Lúgōu Xīnqiáo (卢沟新桥); the bridge is just ahead.

Journey to the Great Wall

Includes »

He who has not climbed the Great Wall is not a true man.

Mao Zedong

China's greatest engineering triumph and must-see sight, the Great Wall (万里长城; Wànlǐ Chángchéng) wriggles haphazardly from its scattered Manchurian remains in Liáoníng province to wind-scoured rubble in the Gobi desert and faint traces in the unforgiving sands of Xīnjiāng.

The most renowned and robust examples undulate majestically over the peaks and hills of Běijīng municipality, but the Great Wall can be realistically visited in many North China provinces. It is mistakenly assumed that the wall is one continuous entity; in reality, the edifice exists in chunks interspersed with natural defences (such as precipitous mountains) that had no need for further bastions.

Great Wall History

The 'original' wall was begun more than 2000 years ago during the Qin dynasty (221–207 BC), when China was unified under Emperor Qin Shi Huang. Separate walls that had been constructed by independent kingdoms to keep out marauding nomads were linked together. The effort required hundreds of thousands of workers – many of whom were political prisoners – and 10 years of hard labour under General Meng Tian. An estimated 180 million cu metres of rammed earth was used to form the core of the original wall, and legend tells that one of the building materials used was the bones of deceased workers.

Its beacon tower system, using gunpowder explosions or smoke signals from burning wolves' dung, quickly conveyed news of enemy movements back to the capital. To the west was Jiāyùguān, an important link on the Silk Road, where a customs post of sorts existed and where unwanted Chinese were ejected through the gates to face the terrifying wild west.

Ming engineers made determined efforts to revamp the eroding bastion, facing it with some 60 million cu metres of bricks and stone slabs. This project took over a century, and the cost in human effort and resources was phenomenal. The picture-postcard brick-clad modern day manifestations of the Great Wall date from Ming times.

The wall occasionally served its impractical purpose but ultimately failed as an impenetrable line of defence. Genghis Khan dryly noted, 'The strength of a wall depends on the courage of those who defend it'. Sentries could be bribed. Despite the wall, the Mongol armies managed to impose foreign rule on China from 1279 to 1368 and the bastion failed to prevent the Manchu armies from establishing two and a half centuries of non-Chinese rule on the Middle Kingdom. The wall did not even register with the 19th-century European 'barbarians' who simply arrived by sea, and by the time the Japanese invaded, the wall had been outflanked by new technologies (such as the aeroplane).

The wall was largely forgotten after that. Mao Zedong encouraged the use of the wall as a source of free building material, a habit that continues unofficially today. Its earthen core has been pillaged and its bountiful supply of shaped stone stripped from the ramparts for use in building roads, dams and other constructions.

Without its cladding, lengthy sections have dissolved to dust and the barricade might have vanished entirely without the tourist industry. Several important sections have been rebuilt, kitted out with souvenir shops, restaurants, toboggan rides and cable cars, populated with squads of unspeakably annoying hawkers and opened to the public.

The old chestnut that the Great Wall is the one man-made structure visible from the moon was finally brought down to earth in 2003 when China's first astronaut Yang Liwei failed to spot it from space. The wall is even less visible from the moon, where even individual countries are barely discernible.

Consult William Lindesay's website at www.wildwall.com for reams of info on the Great Wall.

Visiting the Wall

The most touristed area of the Great Wall is at Bādálǐng. Also renovated but less overrun is Mùtiányù, Sīmǎtái and Jīnshānlǐng. Unimpressed with the tourist-oriented sections, explorative travellers have long sought out the authentic appeal of unrestored sections of wall (such as at Huánghuā or Jiànkòu). The authorities periodically isolate such sections or slap fines on visitors. The authorities argue they are seeking to prevent damage to the unrestored wall by traipsing visitors, but they are keener to channel tourist revenue towards restored sections.

When selecting a tour to the Great Wall, it is essential to check that the tour goes where you want to go. Bādálǐng or other tours often combine with trips to the Ming Tombs, so check beforehand; if you don't want to visit the Ming Tombs, choose another tour or go by public transport.

Some tours make hellish diversions (see boxed text, p101) to jade factories, gem exhibition halls, Chinese medicine centres and whatnot. When booking a tour, ensure such scams are not on the itinerary. It can be safest to book through your hotel or youth hostel but always consider going under your own steam by public transport or hiring a car and a driver. As with most popular destinations in China, avoid weekend trips and definitely shun the big holiday periods.

Take shoes with good grip, water, sunscreen and waterproofs in summer.

For a Great Wall step-master, lung-master workout, the 3800 steps and brutal inclines of the **Great Wall Marathon** (www.great-wall-marathon.com) are tackled every May.

Bādálǐng 八达岭

The wall's most-photographed and most-visited manifestation, **Bādálǐng** (Bādálǐng Chángchéng; Map p46; ☎6912 1338, 6912 1423, 6912 1520; adult Y45; ⏰6am-8pm summer, 7am-6pm winter) is 70km northwest of Běijīng.

The raw scenery yields classic views of the bastion snaking into the distance over undulating hills. Nixon, Thatcher, Reagan, Gorbachev and Queen Elizabeth have all paid their respects. The name Bādálǐng sends a shiver down the spines of hard-core wall walkers, however: there are souvenir stalls, T-shirt-flogging hawkers, heavily restored brickwork, guardrails and crowds of sightseers. Chinese guidebooks trumpet that '130 million foreign and domestic tourists have visited Bādálǐng' as if it was a unique selling point. If you're curious to discover how many people can fit on the wall at any one time, choose the big holiday periods. Don't anticipate a one-to-one with the wall unless you visit during the glacial depths of winter.

The wall here was first built during the Ming dynasty (1368–1644), and heavily restored in both the 1950s and the 1980s. Punctuated with *dílóu* (watchtowers), the 6m-wide masonry is clad in brick, typical of Ming engineering.

Two sections of wall trail off in opposite directions from the main entrance. The restored wall crawls for a distance before nobly disintegrating into ruins; unfortunately you cannot realistically explore these more authentic fragments. Cable cars exist for the weary (Y60 round trip).

The admission fee also gets you into the **China Great Wall Museum** (⏲9am-4pm).

Sleeping

Commune by the Great Wall (p78) is located not far from Bādálǐng.

Getting There & Away

Public Transport

The easiest and most reliable way to reach Badaling is on bus 919 (Y12, 80 minutes, every 30 minutes from 7.30am to 7pm) from the old gate of Déshèngmén, about 500m east of the Jīshuǐtán subway stop. Ask for the 919 branch line (919支线). A taxi to the wall and back is a minimum of Y400 (eight-hour hire with maximum of four passengers).

Tour Buses

Hotel tours and hostel tours can be convenient (and should avoid rip-off diversions), but avoid high-price excursions.

Tour buses to Bādálǐng depart from the **Běijīng Sightseeing Bus Centre** (北京旅游集散中心; Běijīng Lǚyóu Jísàn Zhōngxīn; ☎8353 1111), southwest of Tiān'ānmén Sq.

Line C (return Y100, price includes entry to Great Wall; ⏲departures 7.30am-11.30am) Runs to Bādálǐng.

Line A (Y160, includes entrance tickets & lunch; ⏲departures 6am-10.30am) Runs to Bādálǐng and Dìng Líng at the Ming Tombs.

Simple **buses** (Y50) also leave for Bādálǐng and the Ming Tombs from south of Qianmen between 6am and 11am. Everyone else and his dog does trips to Bādálǐng, including **CITS** (☎6512 3075; www.cits.com.cn; 57 Dengshikou Dajie), the Běijīng Tourist Information Center (p90), hotels and hostels.

Mùtiányù 慕田峪

Famed for its Ming-dynasty guard towers and stirring views, the 3km-long section of wall at **Mùtiányù** (Map p46; admission Y45; ⏲6.30am-6pm), 90km northeast of Běijīng in Huáiróu County, dates from Ming-dynasty remains, built upon an earlier Northern Qi-dynasty conception. Bill Clinton came here (Reagan went to Bādálíng), if that's anything to go by. With 26 watchtowers, the wall is impressive and manageable; most hawking is reserved for the lower levels (hawkers go down to around Y15 for cotton 'I climbed the Great Wall' T-shirts). If time is tight, the wall here has a **cable car** (single/return Y35/50; ⏲8.30am-4.30pm); a single trip takes four minutes. You can also sweep down on the **toboggan** (滑道; huádào; single/return Y40/55). October is the best month to visit, with the countryside drenched in autumn hues.

Sleeping & Eating

Red Capital Ranch (p78) is not far from Mùtiányù.

Schoolhouse at Mùtiányù

HOLIDAY HOMES $$$

(小园; Xiǎoyuán; ☎6162 6506; www.theschoolhouseatmutianyu.com; Mutianyu Village; houses per night from Y1800; ❄📶) Magnificent range of thoughtfully designed luxury homes – sleeping up to 10 – with gardens and Great Wall Views. Excellent food.

Getting There & Away

Public Transport

From **Dōngzhímén Transport Hub Station** (东直门枢纽站; Dōngzhímén Shūniǔzhàn), take fast bus 916 (916路快; Jiǔyīliù Lùkuài; Y12, one hour, regular services 6.50am to 7.30pm) to Huáiróu (怀柔), then change for a minibus to Mùtiányù (Y25 to Y30). The normal 916 (Y2, 2½ hours) is much slower. The last fast 916 bus back to Dōngzhímén from Huáiróu is at 5.30pm; the last slow 916 bus is at 7pm. During the summer months, weekend tour bus 6 departs between 7am and 8.30am for Mùtiányù (Y50) from outside the South Cathedral at Xuānwǔmén.

BĀDÁLǏNG BLUES (OR JOURNEY TO THE GREAT MALL) *MIN DAI*

Always try to establish exactly what is on any Great Wall tour before you hand over your cash. Ensure the tour avoids rip-off diversions and goes where you want to go. This cautionary tale is a true account of a budget Great Wall trip undertaken in 2010.

5.20am: Dragged awake from a fog of sleep by my mobile ringing: it's our tour bus driver saying he's almost at our hotel. He was supposed to call at 7am. The bus doesn't eventually depart town until 8.30am. Ye gods.

First Stop: Bādálǐng. Whistlestop 75-minute jaunt with my children on the Great Wall; later I discover it wasn't the proposed Bādálǐng section but another section of wall called Bādálǐng Water Pass (八达岭水关; Bādálǐng Shuǐguān). Ho-hum.

Second Stop: The Ming Tombs. The tour guide announces that the imperial tombs are the same as the graves of ordinary folk. 'Do you really want to be photographed on someone else's grave?' she asks rhetorically, and everyone looks sheepish. She adds that children should not visit the tombs as infants have a 'Third Eye' (天眼; Tiānyǎn) and may see spirits. Neither should old people visit as they will be reminded of their mortality; menstruating women are also disqualified. With loads of kids and pensioners on board, we rocket past the tombs.

Third Stop: The Jade Factory. If we want to *fācái* (become wealthy) or have successful children, it is important to buy a jade *píxiū* (a fierce mythical creature without a bottom), the guide insists. We troop off the bus to a factory crammed with other tourists. Despite my best efforts to resist, I somehow emerge with two jade *píxīu* (the cheapest they had; Y100) and a much lighter pocket.

Lunch: A bread roll, rice, cabbage, potatoes, eggplants and fish that is 90% fishbone.

Fourth Stop: Dried Fruit and Roast Duck Shop. Cheaper and better quality than in town, the guide insists. My guard is somehow down again and I emerge with Y30 worth of dried peaches. A satisfying sense of schadenfreude kicks in when I see fellow travellers forking out Y78 for roast duck.

Fifth Stop: The Third Pole Exhibition Hall. Supposedly an exhibition on Tibetan culture but I quickly find myself Y75 worse off after signing a Buddhist talisman with my name, before discovering there is a levy. A smiling Lama then takes my hands and says I will enjoy good fortune, my son will succeed and my daughter will be blessed with great artistic talent. These blessings all come for a bargain Y1000 to Y9000, he reveals. Haven't got that kind of money on me, I reply. Credit cards are fine, the Lama reassures, still smiling. I only have Y100, I say (I'm loathe to hand it over, but fear bad luck for my family if I don't cough up). The Lama grudgingly waves me to the till for payment.

Sixth Stop: Jade Shop No 2. It's almost 4.30pm now. The tour guide explains that the bus needs to go through a security check before re-entering Běijīng. She tells us we must disembark, but assures us we don't have to buy what's on sale at this stop as it's aimed at foreigners. But the sales team lock us inside and insist the jade pieces we bought at the Third Stop are rubbish, so we should buy theirs instead as they're far superior. In walks the Chinese owner who claims he is from Burma; because his wife has born him a set of twins on this very day, he wants to convey his joy by charging us only Y300 for a normally Y3000 collection of jade. By this time everyone is well and truly 'jaded': we flee without buying anything.

Terminus: We are dropped at the Bird's Nest and told to make our own way back by underground. By the time we get back to the hotel it is 8pm and I have spent just 75 minutes on the Great Wall (plus Y305 on unwanted extras).

Tours

Youth hostels and hotels run tours to Mùtiányù from around Y200; such tours are very convenient, but some hotels charge sky-high prices.

Jūyōngguān 居庸关

Rebuilt by the industrious Ming on its 5th-century remains, the wall at **Jūyōngguān** (Jūyōng Pass; Map p46; admission Y45 ⏲6am-4pm), 50km northwest of Běijīng, is the closest section of the Great Wall to town. The wall's authenticity has been restored out, but it's typically quiet and you can undertake the steep and somewhat strenuous circuit in under two hours.

Getting There & Away

Public Transport

Jūyōngguān is on the road to Bādálǐng, so public buses for Bādálǐng will get you there. Either the slow (慢; *màn*) or fast (快; *kuài*) bus 919 (Y5, one hour, 6am to 4.30pm) from the gate tower of Déshèngmén, 500m east of Jīshuǐtán subway station, stops at Jūyōngguān.

Tour Buses

From the **Běijīng Sightseeing Bus Centre** (北京旅游集散中心; Běijīng Lǚyóu Jísàn Zhōngxīn; ☎8353 1111), southwest of Tiān'ānmén Sq and west of Front Gate, Line B buses go to Jūyōngguān and Dìng Líng at the Ming Tombs (Y125 including entrance tickets; departures 6.30am to 10am).

Sīmătái 司马台

In Mìyún County, 110km northeast of Běijīng, the stirring remains at **Sīmătái** (Map p46; admission Y40; ⏲8am-5pm) make for a more exhilarating Great Wall experience. Built during the reign of Ming-dynasty emperor Hongwu, the 19km section is an invigorating stretch of watchtowers, precarious plunges and scrambling ascents.

This rugged section of wall can be heart-thumpingly steep and the scenery exhilarating. The eastern section of wall at Sīmătái is the most treacherous, sporting 16 watchtowers and dizzyingly steep ascents that require free hands.

Sīmătái has some unusual features, such as 'obstacle-walls'. These are walls-within-walls used for defending against enemies who had already scaled the Great Wall. The cable car (single/return Y30/Y50) saves valuable time and is an alternative to a sprained ankle. Take strong shoes with a good grip. Unperturbed by the dizzying terrain, hawkers make an unavoidable appearance.

The breathtaking (four-hour max) walk between Jīnshānlǐng and Sīmătái is one of the most popular hikes and makes the long journey out here worth it. The walk is possible in either direction, but it's more convenient to return to Běijīng from Sīmătái.

Before heading out to Sīmătái, check if it's open as it was shut for restoration and development at the time of writing.

Sleeping & Eating

Dōngpō Inn GUESTHOUSE $
(东坡驿; Dōngpō Yì; ☎134 826 292 03; www.dongpo.byways.asia; Sīmătái; d/f Y120/230) A whisker within Héběi province, this small, rural guesthouse has access to Sīmătái, organic cooking as well as free pick-up (within locality).

Getting There & Away

Tours

Most travellers get to Sīmătái on early-morning trips with a youth hostel (such as the Běijīng Downtown Backpackers Accommodation), which usually involves being dropped off at Jīnshānlǐng and being picked up at Sīmătái; prices are in the region of Y260, including tickets. The entire journey from Běijīng and back can take up to 12 hours. A taxi from Běijīng for the day costs about Y400.

Tour Buses

Tour buses run to Sīmătái at 9am from the **Běijīng Sightseeing Bus Centre** (北京旅游集散中心; Běijīng Lǚyóu Jísàn Zhōngxīn; ☎8353 1111), northwest of Qianmen alongside Tiān'ānmén Sq, but only if there are enough people. Twelve or more people cost Y160, five to 11 people Y220, and four people Y300; the price includes entrance tickets.

Public Transport

To get here by public transport, take fast bus 980 (980 路快; Jiǔbālíng Lùkuài; Y15, regular services 5.50am to 8pm) to Mìyún (密云) from the **Dōngzhímén Transport Hub Station** (东直门枢纽站; Dōngzhímén Shūniǔzhàn) and change to a minibus to Sīmătái or a taxi (round trip Y120). The last fast 980 bus back from Mìyún is at 6.30pm; the last slow bus returns at 7pm.

Jīnshānlǐng 金山岭

The Great Wall at **Jīnshānlǐng** (Jīnshānlǐng Chángchéng; Map p46; ☎0314 883 0222; admission Y50) marks the starting point of an exhilarating 10km hike to Sīmǎtái. The journey – through some stunning mountainous terrain – takes around four hours as the trail is steep and parts of the wall have collapsed; it can be traversed without too much difficulty, but some find it tiring. Note that some of the watchtowers have been stripped of their bricks. In summer you'll be sweating gallons but unless you carry your body weight in water you will need to turn to the ever-present hawkers for expensive liquid refreshment. Arriving at Sīmǎtái you have to buy another ticket and en route you need to cross a rope bridge (Y5). At the time of writing, the Great Wall at Sīmǎtái was shut so it was not possible to complete the entire hike. Check with your hotel or hostel for the latest. The cable car at the start of Jīnshānlǐng is for the indolent or infirm (one way/return Y30/50).

You can do the walk in the opposite direction, but getting a ride back to Běijīng from Sīmǎtái is easier than from Jīnshānlǐng. Of course, getting a ride should be no problem if you've made arrangements with your driver to pick you up (and didn't pay in advance).

Getting There & Away

Tours

For information on tours to Jīnshānlǐng, see p102.

Public Transport

Take fast bus 980 (980 路快, Y15, regular services 5.50am to 8pm) to Mìyún (密云) from the **Dōngzhímén Transport Hub Station** (东直门枢纽站; Dōngzhímén Shūniǔzhàn) and then hire a minivan to drop you off at Jīnshānlǐng and collect you at Sīmǎtái. This should cost around Y100, but ensure you don't pay the driver in full until he picks you up. If you are heading to Chéngdé (in Héběi province), you will pass Jīnshānlǐng en route. The last fast 980 bus back from Mìyún to Dōngzhímén is at 6.30pm; the last slow bus returns at 7pm.

Jiànkòu 箭扣

For stupefyingly gorgeous hikes along perhaps Běijīng's most incomparable section of wall, head to the rear section of the **Jiànkòu Great Wall** (后箭扣长城; Hòu Jiànkòu Chángchéng; Map p46; admission Y20), accessible from Huáiróu. It's a 40-minute walk uphill from the drop-off at Xīzhàzi Village (西栅子村; Xīzhàzi Cūn) to a fork in the path among the trees which leads you to either side of a collapsed section of wall, one heading off to the east, the other heading west. Tantalising panoramic views spread out in either direction as the brickwork meanders dramatically along a mountain ridge; the setting is truly magnificent.

Tread carefully – sections are collapsing and the whole edifice is overgrown with plants and saplings – but its unadulterated state conveys an awe-inspiring and raw beauty. If you are ambitious and want to continue along the wall, you will need to dismount the wall at several places to skirt brickwork that has either completely disintegrated or plunges almost vertically down mountain sides like a roller-coaster. One of these sections is called the **Heaven's Ladder** (天梯; Tiāntī) – a precipitous section of crumbling bricks. Clamber up to the **Nine Eye Tower** (九眼楼; Jiǔyǎn Lóu) for fantastic views.

Xīzhàzi Village is rudimentary, but if you want to overnight, ask around and a household may put you up very cheaply for a night or more. Some visitors spend weeks here, making a thorough exploration of the surrounding landscape.

Getting There & Away

Public Transport

Take fast bus 916 (ask for the 916路快 or fast bus; the normal 916 is much slower) from **Dōngzhímén Transport Hub Station** (东直门枢纽站; Dōngzhímén Shūniǔzhàn) to Huáiróu (Y12, one hour, regular services 6.30am to 7.50pm). At Huáiróu you will need to hire a minivan to the rear Jiànkòu section; this should cost around Y200 return (one hour each way) as it's a fair distance. Alternatively, hire a van and driver either in Běijīng or Huáiróu for around Y400 for a day-long Great Wall tour, including Jiànkòu, Huánghuā, Mùtiányù, Xiǎngshuǐhú and other sections of wall. The last fast 916 bus back to Dōngzhímén from Huáiróu is at 5.30pm; the last slow 916 bus (Y2, 2½ hours) is at 7pm.

Huánghuā 黄花

The Great Wall at Huánghuā (Map p46), 60km from Běijīng, affords breathtaking panoramas of partially unrestored brickwork and watchtowers snaking off in two directions. There is also a refreshing absence of amusement park rides, exasperating tourist trappings and the full-on commercial mania of Bādálǐng.

Clinging to the hillside on either side of a reservoir, Huánghuā is a classic and well-preserved example of Ming defences with high and wide ramparts, intact parapets and sturdy beacon towers. Periodic but incomplete restoration work on the wall has left its crumbling nobility and striking authenticity largely intact, with the ramparts occasionally collapsing into rubble.

It is said that Lord Cai masterminded this section, employing meticulous quality control. Each *cùn* (inch) of the masonry represented one labourer's whole day's work. When the Ministry of War got wind of the extravagance, Cai was beheaded for his efforts. In spite of the trauma, his decapitated body stood erect for three days before toppling. Years later a general judged Lord Cai's Wall to be exemplary and he was posthumously rehabilitated. The wall was much more impressive before parts of it were knocked down to provide stones for the construction of the dam.

Despite its lucrative tourist potential, the authorities have failed to wrest Huánghuā from local villagers, who have so far resisted incentives to relinquish their prized chunks of heritage. Official on-site signs declare that it's shut and illegal to climb here, but locals pooh-pooh the warnings and encourage travellers to visit and clamber on the wall. Fines are rarely enforced, although a theoretical risk exists.

Shoes with good grip are important for climbing Huánghuā as some sections are either slippery (eg parts of the wall south of the reservoir are simply smooth slopes at a considerable incline) or uneven and crumbling.

From the road, you can go either way along the battlements. Heading east, one route takes you across a small dam, along a path clinging to the side of the wall until the second watchtower where you climb a metal ladder to the masonry. Alternatively, cross a wooden bridge south of the dam (look for the sign to Mr Li's Tavern), pop through an outdoor restaurant and then clamber through someone's back garden to the second watchtower. Whichever route you take, it costs Y2.

Be warned that the wall here is both steep and crumbling, without guard rails. It's possible to make it all the way to the Mùtiányù section of the wall, but it'll take you a few days and some hard clambering (pack a sleeping bag).

In the other direction to the west, climb the steps past the ticket collector (Y2) to the wall, from where an exhilarating walk can be made along the parapet. Things get a bit hairier beyond the third watchtower as there's a steep gradient and the wall is fragile here, but the view of the overgrown bastion winding off into hills is magnificent.

Sleeping & Eating

There are several simple outfits here if you want to spend the night at Huánghuā, with rooms ranging in price from Y50 to around Y150. Many of the restaurants along the road that gives access to the wall offer rooms, so ask around.

Getting There & Away

Public Transport

To reach Huánghuā, take the fast bus 916 (ask for the 916路快 or fast bus; the normal 916 is much slower) from the **Dōngzhímén Transport Hub Station** (东直门枢纽站; Dōngzhímén Shūniǔzhàn) to Huáiróu (怀柔; Y12, one hour, regular services 6.50am to 7.50pm). Get off at Míngzhū Guǎngchǎng (明珠广场), cross the road and take a minibus to Huánghuā (Y10, 40 minutes); ask for Huánghuāchéng (黄花城) and don't get off at the smaller Huánghuāzhèn by mistake. Taxi-van drivers charge around Y40 one way to reach Huánghuā from Huáiróu. The last fast 916 bus back to Dōngzhímén from Huáiróu is at 5.30pm; the last slow 916 (Y2) bus leaves at 7pm.

Tiānjīn & Héběi

POPULATION: 110 MILLION

Includes »

Best Places to Eat

- YY Beer House (p109)
- Quánjùdé (p114)
- Xiǎo Féiyáng (p123)

Best Places to Stay

- Raffles Tiānjīn (p109)
- Orange Hotel (p109)
- Yújiācūn (p118)

Why Go?

A slow-moving panorama of grazing sheep, brown earth and fields of corn and wheat, Héběi (河北) is Běijīng's back garden. Cosmopolitan Tiānjīn (天津) may put on a dazzling show, and providential economic feng shui from Běijīng lends a sparkle here and there, but arid Héběi's main charms are its timeworn and earthy textures. The province is an occasion to decouple from Běijīng's modernity and frantic urban tempo for an encounter with China beyond the sparkly gift wrap. Wander through ancient settlements and walled towns, skirt the wild edges of Manchuria and journey to the majestic 18th-century summer retreat of the Qing emperors in Chéngdé. Put your heart in your mouth standing before the wooden colossus of Guanyin at Pǔníng Temple or head for the hills and the time-warped stone village of Yújiācūn, where changeless ancient rhythms and rural seclusion fashion the perfect retreat.

When to Go

Tiānjīn

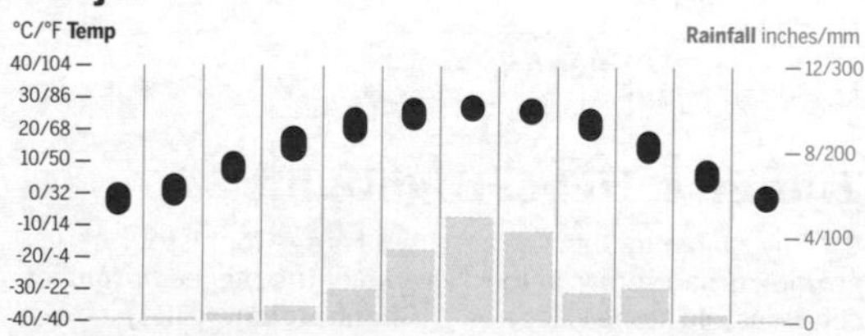

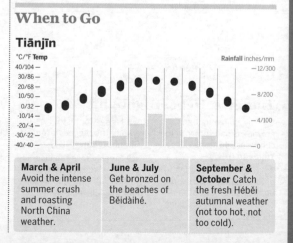

March & April Avoid the intense summer crush and roasting North China weather.

June & July Get bronzed on the beaches of Běidàihé.

September & October Catch the fresh Héběi autumnal weather (not too hot, not too cold).

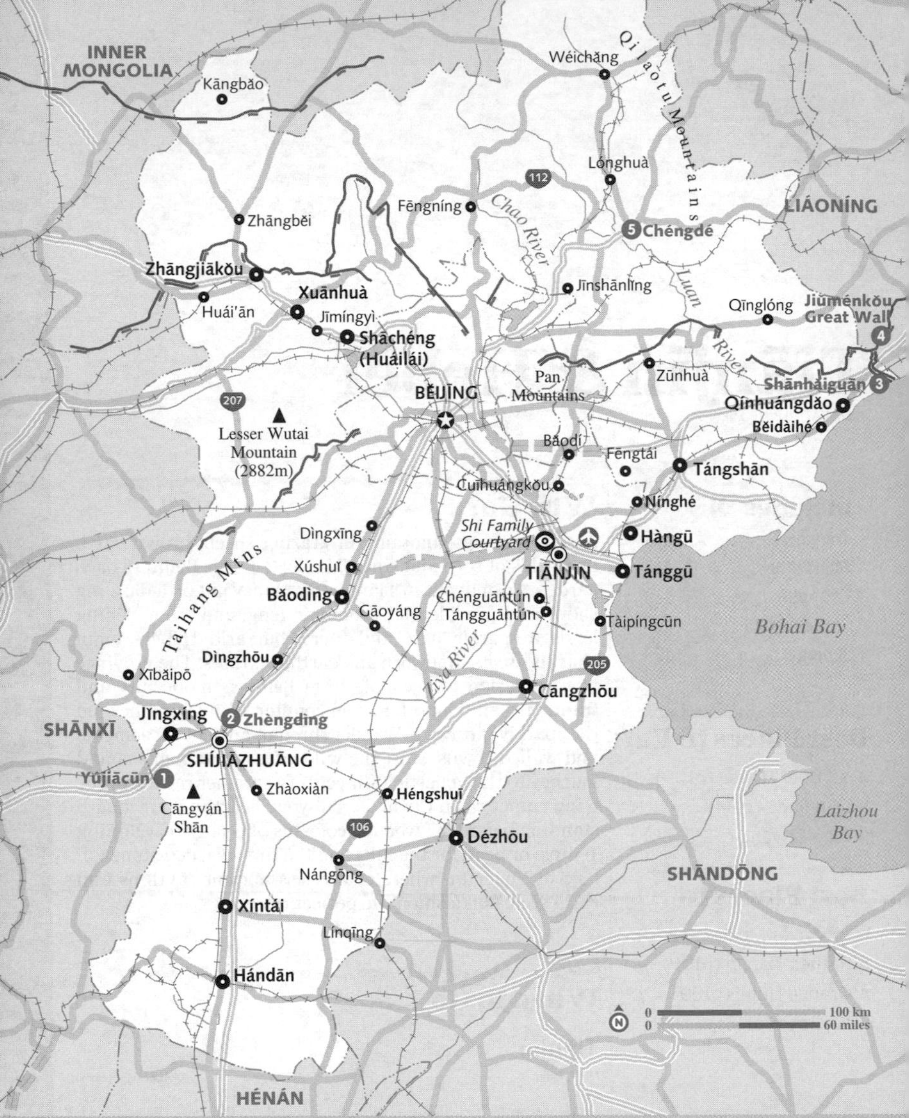

Tiānjīn & Héběi Highlights

1 Say *zàijiàn* to China's growing urban sprawl in the centuries-old stone village of **Yújiācūn** (p117)

2 Explore the temple town of **Zhèngdìng** (p115) and size up the giant metal statue of Guanyin in the Lóngxìng Temple

3 Forage for history among the ragged *hútòng* of **Shānhǎiguān** (p124)

4 Steal across the Liáoníng border to see **Jiǔménkǒu Great Wall** (p126) plunging into the Jiǔjiāng River

5 Be rendered speechless by the colossal multiarmed occupant of **Pǔníng Temple** (p121) in Chéngdé

Climate

Considerable temperature differences exist between the mountainous north and the south of the province, as well as between coastal and inland regions, but Hébĕi generally gets very hot in summer and freezing cold in winter, with dust fallout in spring and heavy rains in July and August.

Language

Although Hébĕi is a Mandarin-speaking region, areas furthest from Bĕijīng have pronounced regional accents and a distinctive argot.

Getting There & Away

Bĕijīng and Tiānjīn are the most convenient bases for exploring the province and the two cities are connected by high-speed express train. Hébĕi is also linked to numerous other domestic destinations by both bus and rail.

Getting Around

The provincial rail hub is Shíjiāzhuang, with rail links to all major towns and cities in Hébĕi. Travel to Chéngdé, Jīmíngyì and Shānhăiguān is best done from Bĕijīng. Bus connections cover the entire province.

> **PRICE INDICATORS**
>
> The following price indicators are used in this chapter:
>
> **Sleeping**
>
> | | |
> |---|---|
> | $ | less than Y400 |
> | $$ | Y400 to Y1000 |
> | $$$ | more than Y1000 |
>
> **Eating**
>
> | | |
> |---|---|
> | $ | less than Y40 |
> | $$ | Y40 to Y100 |
> | $$$ | more than Y100 |

TIĀNJĪN

Tiānjīn

022 / POP 42.1 MILLION

Ambitious Tiānjīn (天津) is a special municipality at the heart of Hébĕi. Its history as a foreign concession, European architecture and port location are redolent of Shànghăi, valuable potential that has been efficiently mined in an impressive facelift of its historic quarters and riverfront. Some stunning modern architecture has been lifted into the Tiānjīn skies, dramatic new bridges span the Hăi River and a dazzling crop of luxury hotels has opened for business. Voted 'Most liveable city in China' by the Economist Intelligence Unit (and 72nd in the world), Tiānjīn clearly has some tricks up its good-looking sleeves. And with the ultra high-speed train whisking you down to Tiānjīn from Bĕijīng faster than you can down a cappuccino, day trips beckon.

History

Tiānjīn rose to prominence as a grain-storage point during the Mongol Yuan dynasty. The city found itself at the intersection of both inland and port navigation routes, and by the 15th century the town had become a walled garrison.

During the foreign concession era, the British and French settled in, joined by the Japanese, Germans, Austro-Hungarians, Italians and Belgians between 1895 and 1900. Each concession was a self-contained world, with its own prison, school, barracks and hospital. During the Boxer Rebellion, the foreign powers levelled the walls of the old Chinese city.

The Tángshān earthquake of 28 July 1976 registered 8.2 on the Richter scale and killed nearly 24,000 people in the Tiānjīn area. The city was badly rocked, but escaped the devastation that virtually obliterated nearby Tángshan, where (according to government estimates) some 240,000 residents died.

Sights

The grandiose vista greeting you as you exit Tiānjīn train station is impressive. Rising crisply to your west towers the glittering **Tiānjīn World Financial Centre** (Jīnróng Dàshà), a singularly bold statement of glass and steel, while facing you across **Liberation Bridge** (解放桥; Jiĕfàng Qiáo) extends a lengthy and ostentatiously rebuilt sweep of red-and-orange Sino-European pomposity in brick, splendidly illuminated at night. A huge and rather surreal mechanical clock tells the time just north of Liberation Bridge, while a bizarre collection of erotic statues do their thing west of the bridge on the south side of the water.

Treaty Port Area HISTORIC SITE

South of the station across Liberation Bridge was the British concession, on and around Jiefang Lu. Cross over the bridge to walk around the newly revamped concession district near the river. An impressively illuminated sight at night from the north side of the river, you need to walk a fair distance south along **Jiefang Beilu** (解放北路) to delve behind the rebuilt riverside facade.

Buildings of note include the **Former French Municipal Administration Council Building** (原法国公议局大楼; Yuán Fǎguó Gōngyìjú Dàlóu), built in 1924, on Chengde Dao; the **Sino-French Industrial and Commercial Bank** (中法工商银行; Zhōngfǎ Gōngshāng Yínháng), dating from 1932; and the **Yokohama Specie Bank Ltd** (横滨正金银行; HéngbīnZhèngjīnYínháng), dating from 1926, next door to the former **Hong Kong & Shanghai Bank Building** (汇丰银行遗址; Huìfēng Yínháng), a pompous creation at No 82, now housing the Bank of China. Also look out for the former address of **Jardine Matheson & Co** (怡和洋行; Yíhé Yángháng), decorated with vast pillars, at No 157. Also worth a peek is the **New World Astor Hotel** (利顺德大饭店; Lìshùndé Dàfàndià), where you can spend the night if you want to be based in the area; alternatively, the Hyatt Regency is nearby at the southern end of Jiefang Beilu.

Old Town HISTORIC SITE

(老城区) Originally enclosed by a wall, Tiānjīn's old town centres on the restored **Drum Tower** (鼓楼; Gǔ Lóu; Chengxiang Zhonglu; admission Y10; ⏲9am-4.30pm). Decorated with *páilou* (decorative archways), the pedestrianised shopping street to the north of the Drum Tower is excellent for buying items such as calligraphy brushes, kites, paper cuts, snuff bottles, fans, silk, ceramics, jade, taichi swords, chops, jewellery, candy floss and sugarcane juice.

Opposite the Drum Tower you'll find the **Guǎngdōng Guild Hall** (广东会馆; Guǎngdōng Huìguǎn; ☎2727 3443; 31 Nanmenli Dajie; admission Y5; ⏲9am-4.30pm Tue-Sun), built in 1907 and also known as the Museum of Opera; it's a lovely old ornate hall with lavishly carved woodwork and performances of traditional music from old-timers. The historic **Confucius Temple** (文庙; Wén Miào; ☎2727 2812; 1 Dongmennei Dajie; admission Y8; ⏲9am-4.30pm Tue-Sun) is also nearby.

Italian Concession HISTORIC AREA

(意式风景区) Like a well-cut suit discovered hanging in the back of its wardrobe, Tiānjīn's newly spruced up **Italian Style District** (意式风景区; Yìshì Fēngjǐngqū) aims to dress up the city as a cosmopolitan and elegant destination. It's probably more for out-of-towners who come here to dine expensively at Italian and French restaurants and daydream they are in Europe. While it's an attractive quadrant for exploration, prices are stratospheric and the blatant commercial bent unnecessarily robs it of some charm.

Monastery of Deep Compassion BUDDHIST TEMPLE

(大悲禅院; Dàbēi Chányuàn; 40 Tianwei Lu; admission Y4; ⏲9am-4.30pm) Tiānjīn's most important Buddhist temple is noted for its **Shìjiā Bǎo Hall** (Shìjiā Bǎodiàn) and the subsequent large hall where a huge and golden multi-armed statue of Guanyin awaits, her eyes following you around the hall. The road leading up to the temple is an extraordinary market of religious paraphernalia, from prayer mats to books, Buddhist rosaries, talismans, statues and incense.

Ancient Culture Street HISTORIC STREET

(古文化街; Guwenhua Jie) Ancient Culture Street is stuffed with vendors flogging Chinese calligraphy, paintings, tea sets, paper cuts, clay figurines, chops and goods from all over China. The fascinating **Tiānhòu Temple** (天后宫; Tiānhòu Gōng; admission Y3; ⏲8.30am-4.30pm) is also here, dedicated to the goddess of seafarers, as well as a shoe museum.

St Joseph's Church CHURCH

(西开天主教堂; Xīkāi Tiānzhǔ Jiàotáng; Binjiang Dao; ⏲5.30am-4.30pm Mon-Sat, 5am-8pm Sun) Erected by the French in 1917, this Catholic church is the largest church in Tiānjīn; pop in to look at the splendid interior. English Mass is at 11.30am on Sundays.

Wǔdàdào HISTORIC SITE

(五大道; Five Large Roads) The area of Wǔdàdào is rich in European-style villas and the pebble-dash former residences of the well-to-do of the early 20th century. Consisting of five roads in the south of the city – Machang Dao, Changde Dao, Munan Dao, Dali Dao and Chengdu Dao – the streetscapes are European, lined with charming houses dating from the 1930s, some art deco. Hop on a clippity-clop horse and carriage for Y30 tours or jump on an electric buggy (Y20 per person).

Tianjin Eye FERRIS WHEEL
(天津之眼; Tiānjīn Zhī Yǎn; Yongle Qiao; adult/child Y50/25; ⌚9.30am-9.30pm Tue-Sun) To get the city's transformation in perspective or for a night-time angle on Tiānjīn, this Ferris wheel is a modern addition to town.

Antique Market MARKET
(古玩市场; Gǔwán Shìchǎng; cnr Shenyang Dao & Shandong Lu; ⌚7.30am-3pm Sat & Sun) Best visited on Sunday, the Antique Market is great for a rifle through its stamps, silverware, porcelain, clocks, Mao badges and Cultural Revolution memorabilia.

Tours

A variety of pleasure boat cruises drift down the Hǎi River during the day and at night. **Haihe Pleasure Boat** (☎5878 9922) offers regular cruises (Y60) from Ěrzhá Gōngyuán to Liberation Bridge, including a night cruise from 7.30pm to 8.30pm (Y80).

Sleeping

Day trips from Běijīng are easy, so sleeping in Tiānjin is inessential. If you miss the last express, a handy branch of Jǐnjiāng Inn (Jǐnjiāng Zhīxīng) is right to the southwest from the main train station.

TOP CHOICE **Raffles Tiānjīn** HOTEL $$$
(天津莱佛士酒店; Tiānjīn Láifóshì Jiǔdiàn; ☎2321 5888; 219 Nanjing Lu; 南京路219号; d Y3000, discounts of 55%) With its seductive lobby-lounge starring beautiful saucer-shaped chandeliers and huge blue cloisonné jars, this penthouse hotel occupies the 36th to 50th floors of the Tiānjīn Centre West Tower. Contemporary and elegant, the rooms are immaculate; king-size rooms are divided into three, with a living area, bedroom and lavish bathrooms. There's 24-hour butler service and spa.

Westin Tiānjīn HOTEL $$$
(天津君隆威斯汀酒店; Tiānjīn Jūnlóng Wēisītīng Jiǔdiàn; ☎2389 0088; www.westin.com/tianjin; 101 Nanjing Lu; 南京路101号;) Rooms are bright and attractively decorated with contemporary furnishings: trademark Heavenly Bed, rainforest shower and modern gadgets. First-rate choice of dining options, from Prego for sumptuous Italian cuisine to Zen5es for innovative Chinese dishes.

TOP CHOICE **Orange Hotel** HOTEL $
(桔子酒店; Júzi Jiǔdiàn; ☎2734 8333; s/tw Y298/328, river-view r Y378, discounts of 25%) Popular and trendy hotel with fashionably geometric styling and fine rooms, a young-professional client base and a handy location near the river. Bicycle hire is available, with the first two hours free. Hop on bus 5 from train station.

Home Inn HOTEL $
(如家; Rújiā; d Y179-199; @) Binjiang Dao (☎5899 6888; 32 Binjiang Dao; 滨江道32号); Xinkai Lu (☎8469 9999; 225 Xinkai Lu; 新开路225号); Ziyou Dao (☎5819 9388; 5 Ziyou Dao; 自由道5号) Friendly staff and a modern attitude make this hotel a great choice on the south side of Liberation Bridge, just off Jiefang Beilu. Rooms are decked out with plastic wood flooring, water cooler, generic artwork and sharp colours, and have bright, well-scrubbed shower rooms. Free broadband; ground-floor restaurant. Other branches are southwest and east of the train station.

Tiānjīn First Hotel HOTEL $
(天津第一饭店; Tiānjīn Dìyī Fàndiàn; ☎2330 9988; 158 Jiefang Beilu; 解放北路158号; s/d Y330/300;) Fuddy-duddy, pleasantly old-fashioned spot in the heart of the concession district with spacious old-world rooms, antique lift and a yesteryear feel.

Hyatt Regency HOTEL $$$
(凯悦饭店; Kǎiyuè Fàndiàn; www.hyatt.com; ☎2330 1234; 219 Jiefang Beilu; 解放北路219号; @) Exceptional central location; undergoing long-awaited refit at the time of writing.

Eating & Drinking

TOP CHOICE **YY Beer House** THAI $$
(粤园泰餐厅; Yuèyuán Tàicāntīng; ☎2339 9634; 3 Aomen Lu; 澳门路3号; meals Y60-70; ⌚11am-2pm;) Often buzzing, this atmospheric place combines a lively and fun vibe with the piquant flavours of Thailand, given a further lift by a heady range of imported beers in the fridge. Wine-tasting parties are held every third Wednesday of the month.

Din Tai Fung DUMPLINGS $$
(鼎泰丰; Dǐngtàifēng; 18 Binshui Dao) No one has a bad word to say about Din Tai Fung's fabulous dumplings. The *xiǎolóngbāo*

Central Tiānjīn

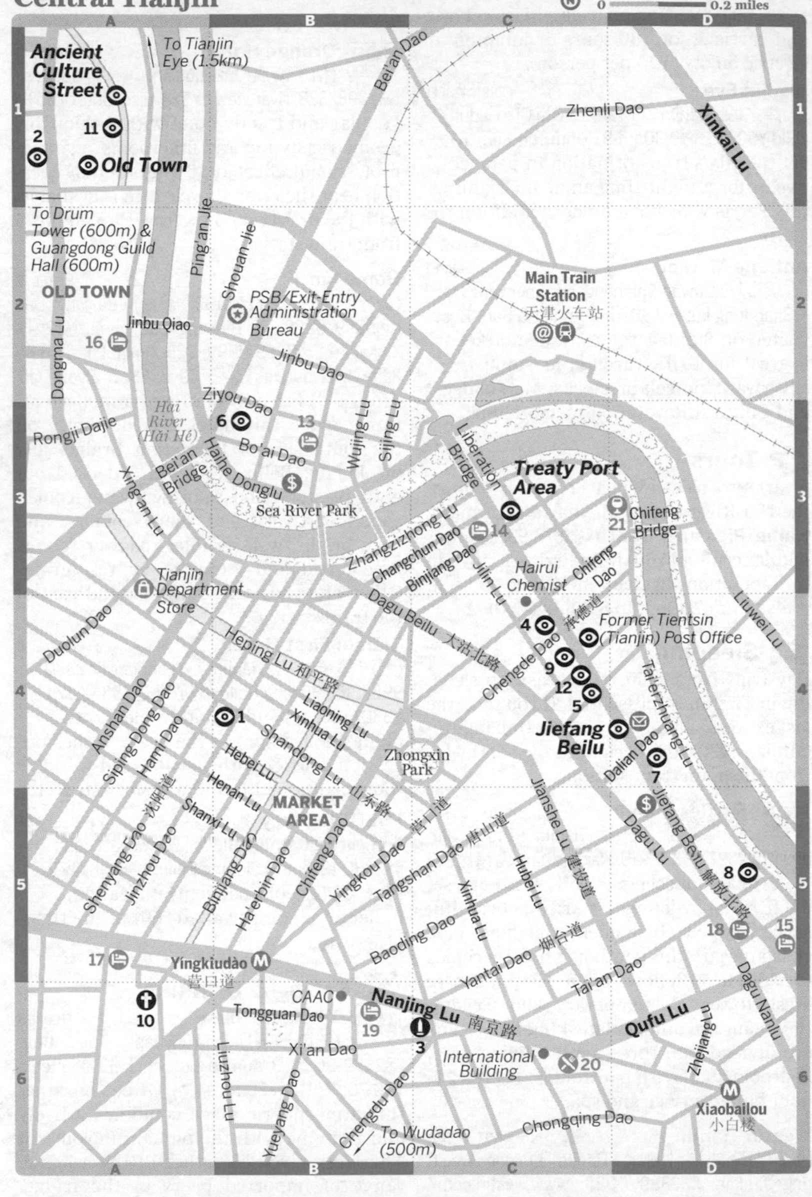

(小笼包; steamed Shanghai dumplings) and steamed shrimp and pork dumplings *(xiāròu zhēngjiǎo)* are delectable, as are the moreish shāomài. The restaurant is located in the south of town.

Drei Kronen 1308 Brauhaus BAR **$$**
(路德维格1308啤酒坊; Lúdé Wéigé 1308 Píjiǔ Fāng; Bldg 5, Jinwan Plaza; 津湾广场5号; ⏰10.30am-1am) Ranging over three floors, with burnished beer vats, outside seating for a river perspective and

Central Tiānjīn

English-speaking staff in fancy Bavarian togs brandishing carnivorous menus, this popular brew house brews its own. It's not cheap (small beer Y38) so target happy hour (6pm to 9pm).

Food Street CHINESE $
(食品街; Shípǐn Jiē) Lively enclosed two-storey emporium of restaurants and outfits flogging noodles, dumplings, tea, seafood plus a panoply of stalls selling dates from Iraq, giant lollipops, squid balls, stinky tofu, ginger sweets, cream puffs and *xìngrénchá* (杏仁茶) – a tasty, warm and super-sweet glutinous paste – ice cream, speciality meats and Tiānjīn delicacies. Food Street is located around 600m west of Beian Bridge.

Information

A handful of internet cafes can be found upstairs in shops around the train station concourse.

Try to score a copy of the magazine *Jin*, which has listings of restaurants, bars and cultural events in town; it also publishes an annual guidebook. A useful expat community website is www.tianjinexpats.net.

Agricultural Bank of China (农业银行; Nóngyè Yínháng; Jiefang Beilu) Has a 24-hour ATM.

Bank of China (中国银行; Zhōngguó Yínháng; 80-82 Jiefang Beilu) The 24-hour ATM takes international cards.

China Post (中国邮政; Zhōngguó Yóuzhèng; 153 Jiefang Beilu)

Hairui Chemist (海瑞药店; Ruìhǎi Yàodiàn; 22 Chifeng Dao; ⊙7.30am-10.30pm)

HSBC (汇丰银行; Huìfēng Yínháng; Ocean Hotel, 5 Yuanyang Guangchang) There's an ATM at the International Building, 75 Nanjing Lu.

Public Security Bureau/Exit-Entry Administration Bureau (PSB; 公安局/出入境管理局; Gōng'ānjú/Chūrùjìng Guǎnlǐjú; ☎2445 8825; 19 Shouan Jie)

Tiānjīn International SOS Clinic (天津国际紧急救援诊所; Tiānjīn Guójì Jǐnjí Jiùyuán Yīliáo Zhěnsuǒ; ☎2352 0143; Sheraton Tianjin Hotel, Zijinshan Lu)

Getting There & Away

Air

Tiānjīn Bīnhǎi International Airport (Tiānjīn Bīnhǎi Guójì Jīchǎng; ☎2490 2950) is 15km east of the city centre. Destinations include Shànghǎi (Y990), Guǎngzhōu (Y1560), Shēnzhèn (Y1510), Xī'ān (Y750) and Chéngdū (Y1020).

Tickets can be bought from **CAAC** (中国民航; Zhōngguó Mínháng; ☎2330 1543, 8331 1666; 103 Nanjing Lu; ⊙8.30am-4pm) or from www.elong.com or www.ctrip.com.

Boat

Tiānjīn's harbour is Tánggū, 50km (30 minutes by train or one hour by bus) from Tiānjīn. See the boxed text, p112 for details of arriving and departing by boat.

Bus

Tiānjīn-bound buses run from the Běijīng's Zhàogōngkǒu bus station (Y30, 1½ hours, every 30 minutes), the Sìhuì bus station (Y23, hourly) or regularly from the Bāwángfén bus station (Y35 to Y40). A shared taxi to Běijīng from the main train station will cost around Y50 per person.

TONGSHA BUS STATION Tiānjín's **Tongsha bus station** (通莎客运站; Tōngshā Kèyùnzhàn; ☎6053 3950; 43 Zhenli Dao) has regular buses:

Běijīng (Bāwángfén, Sìhuì and Zhàogōngkǒu long-distance bus stations) Y35, 1½ hours

Hohhot Y168, two daily

Qīngdǎo Y150, from 8.15am

Qínhuángdǎo Y78, regular services

Shěnyáng Y150, 6pm

Shíjiāzhuāng Y96, four hours

TIANHUAN BUS STATION Bus services from **Tianhuan bus station** (天环客运站; Tiānhuán Kèyùnzhàn; ☎2305 0530; cnr Hongqi Lu & Anshan Xidao):

Běijīng every 30 minutes

Shànghǎi Y295, two daily

Xī'ān 3pm

TIANJIN WEST STATION Bus services from **Tianjin West Station** (天津西站客运站; Tiānjīn Xīzhàn Kèyùnzhàn; ☎2732 1282; Xiqing Dao):

Jǐ'nán Y110

Qínhuángdǎo Y69

Shíjiāzhuāng Y105, four to five hours

Train

Tiānjīn has three train stations: main, north and west. Most trains leave from the **main train station** (Tiānjīn Zhàn; ☎6053 6053). If you have to alight at the **west train station** (☎2618 2662), bus 24 runs to the main train station.

'C'-series trains rapidly connect Tiānjīn train station with Běijīng, making day trips to Tiānjīn feasible. Very regular trains (Y58 to Y69; every 15 minutes) take around 30 minutes to cover the 120km journey, with the first and last train leaving Běijīng South train station at 6.35am and 10.45pm. The last train back to Běijīng leaves Tiānjīn at 10.45pm. A variety of slower trains also link the two cities.

Tiānjīn is a major north–south train junction too:

Hā'ěrbīn hard seat/sleeper Y154/272

Jǐ'nán hard seat/sleeper Y52/97

Nánjīng hard seat/sleeper Y137/242

Qīngdǎo hard seat/sleeper Y103/185

Shànghǎi hard sleeper Y291

Shānhǎiguān hard seat/sleeper Y24/61

Shěnyáng hard seat/sleeper Y99/177

Shíjiāzhuāng hard seat/sleeper Y55/106

Xī'ān hard seat/sleeper Y170/300

Zhèngzhōu hard seat/sleeper Y116/207

Getting Around

To/From the Airport

Taxis ask for Y40 to Y50 to the airport from the city centre. Airport buses for Běijīng's Capital Airport leave from the CAAC ticket office every hour from 4am to 6am and then half-hourly to 6pm (Y80, 2½ hours). From Běijīng Capital Airport to Tiānjīn, buses run hourly from 7am to 9am, then every 30 minutes to 11pm. Bus 678 runs to the airport from Anshan Dao.

Public Transport

Tiānjīn's subway is being extended from one to four lines (Line No 1, 2, 3 and 9); trains run from around 6.30am to just after 10pm (tickets Y2 to Y5). Chargeable transport cards *(chéngcì piào)* are available. Other lines are under consideration, with an ambitious plan to have seven lines in operation. A light rail (Metro Line 9) connects Tiānjīn with the port of Tánggū.

Buses run from 5am to 11pm. Useful routes:

Bus 600 Runs from the square behind Tiānjīn train station to stops for the Tianjin Eye, Ancient Culture Street, the Old Town, Xikai Church, Wǔdàdào, Binjiang Dao, Da Guangming

GETTING TO JAPAN, SOUTH KOREA OR DÀLIÁN

Daily ferries to Dàlián (Y308 to Y1208, 12 hours) and weekly boats to Kōbe (Japan; Y1390 to Y4500, 51 hours) and Incheon (South Korea; Y888 to Y1930, 20 hours, departing Thursday and Sunday) sail from Tánggū (塘沽), about 50km east of Tiānjīn.

In Tiānjīn, buy tickets from the **ticket office** (☎2339 2455; 1 Pukou Dao); in Tánggū, tickets can be bought from the **Passenger Ferry Terminal** (天津港客运站; Tiānjīngǎng Kèyùnzhàn; ☎2587 3261).

Frequent minibuses and buses to Tánggū (Y10) leave from Tiānjīn's main train station; bus 835 (Y5) also runs to Tánggū. In Tánggū, minibuses to Tiānjīn run from outside the train station. A light rail system runs between Zhōngshānmén station in southeast Tiānjīn and Dōnghǎilù station in Tánggū (50 minutes, roughly every 15 minutes, from 7am to 7pm).

Qiao (for Jiefang Beilu and the concession districts) and back again.

Bus 24 Runs between the main and west train stations.

Bus 8 Starts at the main train station then zigzags down to the southwest of town.

Taxi

Flag fall is Y8 for the first 3km, then Y1.70 per kilometre thereafter.

Around Tiānjīn City

SHI FAMILY COURTYARD

In Yángliǔqīng, in the western suburbs of Tiānjīn, is the marvellous **Shi family residence** (石家大院; Shí Jiā Dàyuàn; 47 Yangliuqing Guyi Jie; 杨柳青估衣街47号; admission Y20; ⌚9am-4.30pm), composed of several courtyards. Belonging to a prosperous merchant family, the residence contains a theatre and 278 rooms, some of which are furnished. From Tiānjīn, take bus 153 from the west train station or bus 672 from the Tiānjīn Department Store to Yángliǔqīng. A taxi costs around Y80 return.

HÉBĚI

Shíjiāzhuāng 石家庄

☎0311 / POP 2.2 MILLION

Until relatively recently a small hamlet – the quaint name literally means 'Village of the Shi Family' – Shíjiāzhuāng is today an archetypal Chinese city and the provincial capital of Héběi (河北): a frantic, prosperous and sprawling railway junction town with little sensation of history. But Shíjiāzhuāng's nearby sights – including historic Zhèngdìng and rural Yújiācūn – are more than enough to warrant the short hop down from Běijīng.

Sights

FREE **Héběi Provincial Museum** MUSEUM
(河北省博物馆; Héběi Shěng Bówùguǎn; Zhongshan Donglu; ⌚9am-5pm Tue-Sun) Still undergoing a prolonged renovation and extension at the time of research, Héběi's museum contains limited exhibitions. The standout exhibit – inaccessible until the museum properly reopens – is the excavations from the Mancheng Western Han tombs, including two jade Han burial suits, one of which is sewn with 1.1kg of gold thread.

Revolutionary Martyrs' Mausoleum PARK
(烈士陵园; Lièshì Língyuán; 343 Zhongshan Xilu; park admission Y3, through ticket Y5; ⌚8.30-11.30am & 2.30-5.30pm) With its emphasis on patriotic education, this mausoleum is located in a pleasant tree-shaded park and contains the tomb of Canadian guerrilla doctor Norman Bethune (1890–1939), a surgeon with the Eighth Route Army in the war against Japan.

Sleeping

Home Inn HOTEL $
(如家; Rújiā; ☎8702 8822; www.homeinns.com; 14 Zhanqian Jie; 站前街14号; d from Y209; ❄@) A short walk south from the train station, this branch of Home Inn (almost 20 in town) is cleaner and better-kept than many other budget hotels in the area. Rooms with computer are Y20 extra. Breakfast is Y12 per person. Rooms come with TV, kettle, broadband connection and clean shower.

World Trade Plaza Hotel HOTEL $$
(世贸广场酒店; Shìmào Guǎngchǎng Jiǔdiàn; ☎8667 8888; www.wtphotels.com; 303 Zhongshan Donglu; 中山东路303号; d/ladies room Y940/1056, discounts of 15%; ❄@📶) Shíjiāzhuāng's finest and most elegant hotel is a five-star affair with impressive swaths of marble and ranks of professional staff. Rooms are huge with spick-and-span bathrooms; there's a deli, Chinese restaurant, Brazilian barbecue, cafe, a rather sombre-looking bar, fitness centre, club floor with butler service and ATM. Breakfast is included.

Eating

Minzu Lu (民族路), northwest of the train station area, has a whole crop of busy hotpot, Sìchuān, noodle and dumpling restaurants that kick off from the McDonald's.

Ajisen NOODLES $
(味千拉面; Wèiqiān Lāmiàn; 269 Zhongshan Donglu; meals Y40) If you have blocked sinuses, we can highly recommend the hot and numbing beef noodles (麻辣牛肉拉面; *málà niúròu lāmiàn;* Y29) ferried to your table by perky staff and guaranteed to clear any nasal passages in a shot. The fried dumplings (香辣牛肉煎饺; *xiānglà niúròu jiānjiǎo;* Y12) are also seriously scrummy. Pay up front; photo menu; small interior Japanese garden.

Shíjiāzhuāng

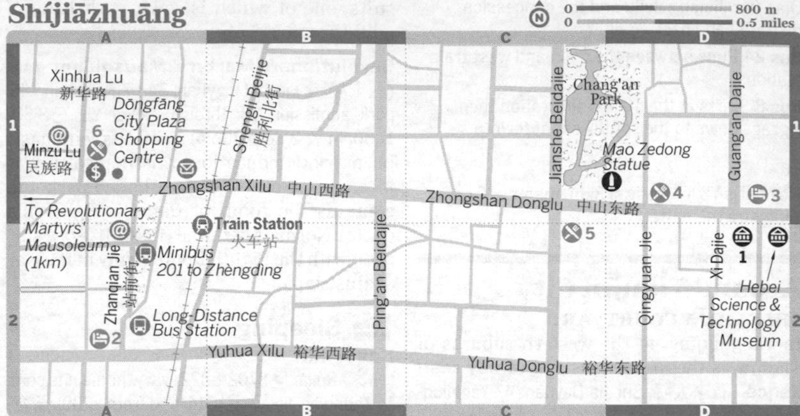

Tudari KOREAN $
(土大力; Tǔdàlì; www.tudari.com.cn; 1 Jinqiao Beijie) A handily located Korean barbecue restaurant with amiable staff and a bubbly atmosphere. Try the lamb kebabs (羊肉串; Y12.50 for five) or swelter over a kimchi hotpot (泡菜火锅; Y22). It's alongside the Dōngfāng City Plaza Shopping Centre (东方大厦; Dōngfāng Dàshà).

TOP CHOICE **Quánjùdé** BEIJING $$
(全聚德; 9 Jianshe Nandajie; roast duck Y148; ⏲10am-2pm & 5-9pm) If you didn't manage your full fix of Peking duck in the capital, this excellent restaurant from Běijīng fires up its duck traditional-style over fruit wood.

Information

Bank of China (中国银行; Zhōngguó Yínháng; Jinqiao Beidajie) Through the west door of the Dōngfāng City Plaza Shopping Centre.

China Post (中国邮政; Zhōngguó Yóuzhèng; cnr Gongli Jie & Zhongshan Xilu; ⏲24hr)

Guānjié Internet Cafe (冠捷网吧; Guānjié Wǎngbā; Minzu Lu; per hr Y2; ⏲24hr)

Jùrén Internet Cafe (巨人网吧; Jùrén Wǎngbā; per hr Y3.5; ⏲24hr) Comfy seats, armchairs and a relaxed atmosphere. It's on the 5th floor, in the building behind the Yanchun Hotel.

Měijué Internet Cafe (美爵网吧; Měijué Wǎngbā; Zhanqian Jie; per hr Y3; ⏲24hr) Just north of the Huiwen Hotel.

Public Security Bureau (公安局; PSB; Gōng'ānjú; Dongfeng Lu)

Shíjiāzhuāng

Sights
1 Héběi Provincial Museum D2

Sleeping
2 Home Inn A2
3 World Trade Plaza Hotel D1

Eating
4 Ajisen D1
5 Quánjùdé C2
6 Tudari A1

Getting There & Away

Air

Flights from Shíjiāzhuāng:

Chéngdū Y1130

Guǎngzhōu Y1560

Kūnmíng Y1020

Shànghǎi Y990

Xī'ān Y750

Bus

Luxury buses depart from the **long-distance bus station** (石家庄客运总站; shíjiāzhuāng kèyùn zǒngzhàn):

Běijīng Y75 to Y90, 3½ hours, every 30 minutes (7am to 6.30pm)

Chéngdé Y150, seven hours, four daily

Jǐ'nán Y75 to Y105, four hours, every 40 minutes (7.20am to 5.30pm)

Kāifēng Y112, eight hours, one daily (11am)

Tiānjīn Y110 to Y120, four hours, every 40 minutes (6.30am to 6.30pm)

Zhèngzhōu Y78 to Y121, six hours, nine daily

For luxury buses, go to the left-hand ticket windows (almost all buses); for old-school clunkers, go to the right-hand side windows.

Train

Shíjiāzhuāng is a major rail hub with D-series express trains from the **train station** (☎8760 0111) to/from Běijīng West (Y88 to Y103, two hours), Zhèngzhōu and Ānyáng. The speed of connections to Běijīng makes Shíjiāzhuāng possible as a day trip. Most trains heading south from Běijīng come via Shíjiāzhuāng.

Chángchūn hard sleeper Y300, 15½ hours
Chéngdé hard sleeper Y83, 11 hours
Dàtóng hard sleeper Y165, 11½ hours
Guǎngzhōu hard sleeper Y395, 20½ hours
Jì'nán hard seat Y47, five hours
Luòyáng hard seat Y76
Nánjīng hard sleeper Y246, 13½ hours
Shànghǎi hard sleeper Y281, 11 hours
Shānhǎiguān hard sleeper Y169, 8½ hours
Tiānjīn hard seat Y55 to Y63

Some trains also stop at or depart from Shíjiāzhuāng North train station (Shíjiāzhuāng Běizhàn).

Getting Around

Shíjiāzhuāng's international airport is 40km northeast of town. Airport buses (Y20, 35 minutes, 6am to 8pm) to the airport depart from the Civil Aviation Hotel next to the **CAAC office** (中国民航; Zhōngguó Mínháng; ☎8505 4084; 471 Zhongshan Donglu). The office can be reached on bus 1. There are numerous buses per day, with departures depending on flights. A taxi to the airport will take about an hour and cost Y130. Taxis are Y5 at flag fall, then Y1.60 per kilometre.

Around Shíjiāzhuāng

ZHÈNGDÌNG 正定

☎0311 / POP 130,300

Its streets littered with needy Taoist soothsayers and temple remains, walled Zhèngdìng is an appetising – albeit incomplete – slice of old China. From atop Zhèngdìng's South Gate, you can see the silhouettes of four distinct pagodas jutting above the sleepy town. Remnants of a traditional skyline in China are a rare sight, and Zhèngdìng is a welcome reminder of the country's former architectural grandeur. Nicknamed the town of 'nine buildings, four pagodas, eight great temples and 24 golden archways', Zhèngdìng has tragically lost many of its standout buildings and archways – Píngyáo it isn't – but enough remains to lend the townscape an air of faded grandeur.

Sights

All attractions are either off the east–west Zhongshan Lu or the north–south Yanzhao Nandajie. Beginning with Lóngxìng Temple, you can see almost everything by walking west until reaching Yanzhao Nandajie, then continuing south tol the city gate.

The **through ticket** (通票; *tōngpiào;* Y85) was not available at the time of writing. Sometimes falling to Y60, it gets you access to all sights except Línjì Temple (free at the time of writing). Opening hours are from 8am to 6pm. During research, the **Zhèngdìng Museum** (正定博物馆; Zhèngdìng Bówùguǎn) was being constructed next to Tiānníng Temple.

Lóngxīng Temple BUDDHIST TEMPLE
(隆兴寺; 109 Zhongshan Donglu; adult/student Y40/30, guide Y40) Of Zhèngdìng's temple tribe, the most notable is this temple, more popularly known as **Dàfó Temple** (大佛寺; Dàfó Sì) or 'Big Buddha Temple', in the east of town.

The time-worn bridge out front constitutes a handsome historical prelude. Dating way back to AD 586, the temple has been much restored and stands divided from its spirit wall by Zhongshan Donglu. Halls such as the Hall of Sakyamuni's Six Teachers await an entire rebuild from the soles up, but still attract a small gathering of glinting Guanyin statues.

You are greeted in the first hall by the jovial Milefo, chubby enough that temple caretakers have pluralised him – he's now the 'Monks with a Bag'. The four Heavenly Kings flanking him in pairs are disconcertingly vast.

Beyond is the **Manichaean Hall**, an astonishingly voluminous hall flagged in smoothed stone with amazing carpentry overhead, a huge gilded statue of Sakyamuni and delectable Ming frescoes detailing Buddhist tales. At the rear of the hall is a distinctly male statue of the goddess Guanyin, seated in a lithe pose with one foot resting on her/his thigh (a posture known as *lalitásana*) and surrounded by *luóhàn* (those freed from the cycle of rebirth).

The **Buddhist Altar** behind houses an unusual bronze Ming-dynasty two-faced Buddha, gazing north and south. Signs say 'no touching' but it's evident that its fingers and thumb have been smoothed by legions of worshippers. There are two halls behind the Buddhist Altar. On the left is the **Revolving Library Pavilion** (Zhuǎnlúnzàng Gé), which contains a revolving octagonal wooden bookcase for the storing of sutras and a stele on the back of a snarling *bìxì* (a mythical tortoiselike dragon). Opposite stands the **Pavilion of Kindness**, containing a 7.4m high statue of Maitreya, one hand aloft.

The blurb introducing the **Pavilion of the Imperial Library** (Yùshū Lóu) draws your attention to a statue of Guanyin and 18 *luóhàn* but they are nowhere to be found. The library is connected by a walkway to the immense **Pavilion of Great Mercy** (大悲阁; Dàbēi Gé), where a bronze colossus of Guanyin rises. At 21.3m high, cast in AD 971 and sporting a third eye, the effigy is wonderful, standing on a magnificently carved base from the Northern Song. Examine the carvings which include myriad characters and musicians, including Buddhist angels and a woman blowing a conch. Overhead towers the dusty goddess with a litter of smaller Guanyin statues at her feet: clamber up into the galleries surrounding Guanyin for free, but the third level is often out of bounds. The wooden hall in which the goddess is housed was rebuilt in 1999 with reference to Song-dynasty architecture manuals.

Circumambulated by worshippers, the **Hall of Vairocana** at the rear contains a four-faced Buddha (the Buddha of four directions), crowned with another four-faced Buddha, upon which is supported a further set. The entire statue and its base contain 1072 statues of Buddha.

Tiānníng Temple BUDDHIST TEMPLE

(天宁寺; Tiānníng Sì; admission Y5) About five minutes west (right as you exit) of Dàfó Temple are the remains of this temple, whose 41m-high Tang-dynasty **Lofty Pagoda** (凌霄塔; Língxiāo Tǎ) – also called Mùtǎ or Wooden Pagoda – originally dates from AD 779; it was later restored in 1045. The octagonal, nine-eaved and spire-topped pagoda is in fine condition and typical of Tang brickwork pagodas. Shut at the time of writing, you can usually clamber up inside and torches are provided (deposit Y10), but mind your head and the steep stairs. The views from the top are not great, as the windows are small.

Further west on Zhongshan Xilu from Tiānníng Temple, past the intersection with Yanzhao Nandajie, is the unassuming **Confucius Temple** (文庙; Wén Miào; admission Y5), though there is little to see here.

Kāiyuán Temple BUDDHIST TEMPLE

(开元寺; Kāiyuán Sì; admission Y15) South on Yanzhao Nandajie this temple originally dates from AD 540 but was destroyed in 1966, the first year of the Cultural Revolution. Little remains apart from some leftover good vibes (it's a popular spot for qì gōng and taichi practitioners), the **Bell Tower** and the drawcard dirt-brown **Xumi Pagoda**, a well-preserved and unfussy early-Tang-dynasty brickwork, nine-eaved structure, topped with a spire. Its round arched doors and carved stone doorway are particularly attractive, as are the carved figures on the base.

Also displayed is a colossal stone *bìxì* statue – China's largest – near the entrance, with a vast chunk of its left flank missing and its head propped up on a plinth. Dating from the late Tang era, the creature was excavated in 2000 from a street in Zhèngdìng.

Línjì Temple BUDDHIST TEMPLE

(临济寺; Línjì Sì; Linji Lu) Normally Y5 to access but free at the time of writing (and attracting scads of beggars in various stages of disfiguration), this active monastery, around 700m southeast of Kāiyuán Temple, is notable for its tall, elegant, carved brick **Chénglíng Pagoda** (澄灵塔; also called the Green Pagoda), topped with an elaborate lotus plinth plus ball and spire. The main hall behind has a large gilt effigy of Sakyamuni and 18 golden *luóhàn*. At the rear of the hall is Puxian astride an elephant, Wenshu on a lion and a figure of Guanyin. In the Tang dynasty, the temple was home to one of Chan (Zen) Buddhism's most eccentric and important teachers, Linji Yixuan, who penned the now famous words 'If you meet the Buddha on the road, kill him!'.

Guǎnghuì Temple BUDDHIST TEMPLE

(广惠寺; Guǎnghuì Sì; admission Y10) Nothing remains of this temple further south, except its unusual Indian-style pagoda decorated with lions, elephants, sea creatures, *púsà* (Bodhisattvas; those worthy of nirvana who remain on earth to help others attain enlightenment) and other figures (some missing). With a brick base and four doors, the pagoda has stone-carved upper storeys and a brickwork cap. You can climb to the top.

City Walls HISTORICAL SITE
(城墙; Chéngqiáng) Part of Zhèngdìng's main street (Yanzhao Dajie) has been restored and is now a pleasant stretch of traditional Chinese roofing, brickwork and willows called the **Zhèngdìng Historical Culture Street** (正定历史文化街; Zhèngdìng Lìshǐ Wénhuà Jiē). At the southern end of the street is **Chánglè Gate** (长乐门; Chánglè Mén; admission Y10; ⌚8am-6pm), also known as Nánchéngmén or South Gate. The original wall (which dates back to the Northern Zhou) was made up of an outer wall *(yuèchéng)* and an inner wall *(nèichéng)*, with enceintes *(wèngchéng)*, and had a total length of 24km. You can climb onto Chánglè Gate, where there is a small exhibition. Extending away from the gate to the east and west are the dilapidated remains of the wall, largely stripped of bricks.

Sleeping & Eating

Loads of restaurants can be found along Zhongshan Donglu, including Sìchuān eateries and cake outlets. Small guesthouses (旅馆; *lǚguǎn*) can also be found along here, charging around Y60 for a simple double room.

Jīnhé Hotel HOTEL $
(金河宾馆; Jīnhé Bīnguǎn; ☎8801 3999; 98 Yanzhao Nandajie; 燕赵南大街98号; s/d/ste Y120/120/180; ❄) Attractive, traditionally styled hotel with fine rooms (all with shower) but let down by indifferent and zero-English-speaking staff.

Information

Chūnxù Internet Cafe (春旭网络广场; Chūnxù Wǎngluò Guǎngchǎng; Yanzhao Nandajie; per hr Y2; ⌚24hr) In a courtyard nine to 10 shops north of Kāiyuán Temple.

Industrial & Commercial Bank of China (工商银行; Gōngshāng Yínháng; cnr Zhongshan Donglu & Yanzhao Nandajie)

Getting There & Away

From Shíjiāzhuāng, minibus 201 (Y2, 45 minutes, 6.30am to 6.30pm) runs regularly to Zhèngdìng from Daocha Jie, slightly south of the main bus stop in the train station square. The minibus runs to Zhèngdìng bus station, from where minibus 1 heads to Dàfó Temple (Y1). Regular train services also run through Zhèngdìng from Shíjiāzhuāng. Minibuses leave from outside Zhèngdìng's Kāiyuán Temple for Shíjiāzhuāng (Y3, last bus 5pm).

Getting Around

Zhèngdìng is not huge and walking is relatively easy as sights are largely clustered together. Taxis within Zhèngding cost around Y10; three-wheel motorcycles cost Y4 for anywhere in town.

Bus 1 Runs from the local bus station to Dàfó Temple

Bus 2 Runs from the local bus station to Kāiyuán Temple and Chánglè Gate

Bus 3 Runs to the train station

Bus 4 Runs along Zhongshan Xilu and Zhongshan Donglu

YÚJIĀCŪN 于家村

POP 1600

Also known as **Stone Village** (石头村; Shítou Cūn) and hidden away in the hills near the Héběi–Shānxī border is the peaceful little settlement of **Yújiācūn** (admission Y20). Nearly everything, from the houses to the furniture inside them, was originally made of stone. As such, Yújiācūn today is remarkably well preserved: bumpy little lanes lead past traditional Ming- and Qing-dynasty courtyard homes, old opera stages and tiny temples. Actually, 'traditional' doesn't quite describe it: this is a model Chinese clan-village, where 95% of the inhabitants all share the same surname of Yu (于).

One of the more unusual sights is inside the **Yu Ancestral Hall** (于氏宗祠; Yúshì Zōngcí), where you'll find the 24-generation family tree, reaching back over 500 years. There are five tapestries, one for the descendants of each of the original Yu sons who founded the village.

Another oddity is the three-storey **Qīngliáng Pavilion** (清凉阁; Qīngliáng Gé), completed in 1581. Supposedly the work of one thoroughly crazed individual (Yu Xichun, who wanted to be able to see Běijīng from the top), it was, according to legend, built entirely at night, over a 16-year period, without the help of any other villagers. It was certainly built by an amateur architect: there's no foundation, and the building stones (in addition to not being sealed by mortar) are of wildly different sizes (some as large as 2m), giving it a higgledy-piggledy look that's quite uncommon in Chinese architecture.

Other buildings worth hunting down are the **Guānyīn Pavilion** (观音阁; Guānyīn Gé) and the **Zhēnwǔ Temple** (真武庙; Zhēnwǔ Miào). Near the primary school is the **Stone Museum** (石头博物馆; Shítou Bówùguǎn) displaying local items made of stone.

Sleeping

The Mandarin accent here is as thick as the coal dust that settles everywhere in the Héběi–Shānxī borderlands, but mercifully Yújiācūn is free of the pollution and it's definitely worth spending the night here. As the sun sets, the sounds of village life – farmers chatting after a day in the fields, clucking hens, kids at play – are miles away from the raging pace of modern Chinese cities.

Villagers rent out rooms for Y10 to Y15 per person; home-cooked meals are another Y10 each, a bottle of beer is Y2. One friendly place is the **Chūnyīng Yuàn** (春英院; ☎0311 8237 6583), which has simple rooms for around Y12.

Getting There & Away

All roads to Yújiācūn pass through Jǐngxíng (井陉), about 35km west of Shíjiāzhuāng. The earliest train (Y8, 50 minutes) leaves Shíjiāzhuāng North train station (Shíjiāzhuāng Běizhàn) at 7.03am, arriving at Jǐngxíng at 8.09am; the next service leaves at 8.50am, arriving at 9.33am. The third train leaves at 2.23pm, arriving at 3.06pm. In the opposite direction, the last train departs from Jǐngxíng at 8.08pm and arrives at Shíjiāzhuāng North train station at 9.13pm. Otherwise, there are regular buses (Y10, one hour) running throughout the day through the industrial countryside between Shíjiāzhuāng's **Xīwáng Station** (西王客运站; Xīwáng Kèyùnzhàn) and Jǐngxíng. Take bus 9 (Y1) to Xīwáng from Shíjiāzhuāng train station.

From Jǐngxíng you can catch buses through a landscape blackened with coal dust to Yújiācūn (Y5, one hour, regular departures 7am to 6.30pm) and Cāngyán Shān (Y5, one hour, departures 9am to 1pm, returns noon to 5pm). Buses arrive at and depart from various intersections in town; you can walk or take a taxi for Y5. Alternatively, hire a taxi for one destination (Y80 return) or for the day (Y200). Be warned that the roads in these parts can be full of coal trucks so travel times are only estimates. To reach Cāngyán Shān from Yújiācūn, take a bus to Bǎishān (柏山; Y2) and change.

CĀNGYÁN SHĀN 苍岩山

Cāngyán Shān (admission Y50) – literally 'Green Crag Mountain' – is the site of the transcendent cliff-spanning Hanging Palace, a Sui-dynasty construction perched halfway up a precipitous gorge. Given its dramatic setting, it must have been an impressive temple complex at one time, though these days the best views after the main hall are of the surrounding canyons. It is a quick, steep jaunt up to the palace, and then another 45 minutes past scattered pagodas and shrines to the new temple at the mountain's summit. The standard lunar festivals see a lot of worshippers and are a good time to visit if you don't mind crowds.

Morning buses (Y26, two hours) for Cāngyán Shān leave from Shíjiāzhuāng's Xīwáng Station at 7am, returning in the late afternoon. It can also be combined with a trip to Yújiācūn and Jǐngxíng.

ZHÀOZHŌU BRIDGE 赵州桥

China's oldest-standing **bridge** (Zhàozhōu Qiáo; admission Y30) has spanned the Jiǎo River (Jiǎo Hé) for 1400 years. In Zhàoxiàn County, about 40km southeast of Shíjiāzhuāng and 2km south of Zhàoxiàn town, this is the world's first segmental bridge (ie its arch is a segment of a circle, as opposed to a complete semicircle) and predates other bridges of its type throughout the world by 800 years. In fine condition, it is 50.82m long and 9.6m wide, with a span of 37m. Twenty-two stone posts are topped with carvings of dragons and mythical creatures, with the centre slab featuring a magnificent *tāotiè* (an offspring of a dragon). The bridge is also known as (安济桥; Ānjì Qiáo) or 'Safe Crossing Bridge'.

To reach the bridge from Shíjiāzhuāng's long-distance bus station, take bus 30 to the **south bus station** (南焦客运站; nánjiāo kèyùnzhàn; ☎8657 3806), then take a minibus to Zhàoxiàn town (赵县; Y9, one hour). There are no public buses from Zhàoxiàn to the bridge, but a *sānlúnchē* (three-wheeled motor scooter) can oblige for Y3.

Chéngdé 承德

☎0314 / POP 457,000

In many respects a typical provincial Chinese town, Chéngdé evolved during the first half of the Qing dynasty from hunting grounds to overblown summer resort and Manchu headquarters of foreign affairs. Beginning with Kangxi, the Qing emperors fled here from the torpid summer heat of the Forbidden City and for closer proximity to the hunting grounds of their northern homelands.

The Bìshǔ Shānzhuāng (Fleeing-the-Heat Mountain Villa) is a grand imperial palace and the walled enclosure behind rings China's largest regal gardens. Beyond the grounds is a remarkable collection of politically chosen temples, built to host dignitaries such as the sixth Panchen Lama.

Autumn visits are recommended, as tourists swarm like termites during summer while winters are face-numbingly cold.

At the time of writing, Chéngdé had stopped allowing foreigners from staying at many cheap hotels. With a vast new retail and hotel complex under construction just south of the Mountain Villa Hotel (with Gucci, Dior and other flash outlets in the pipeline), and commensurate ticket price inflation, the drift is very much in the commercial direction.

History

In 1703, when an expedition passed through the Chéngdé valley, Emperor Kangxi was so enamoured with the surroundings that he had a hunting lodge built, which gradually grew into the summer resort. Rèhé – or Jehol (Warm River; named after a hot spring here) – as Chéngdé was then known, grew in importance and the Qing court began to spend more time here – sometimes up to several months a year, with some 10,000 people accompanying the emperor on his seven-day expedition from Běijīng.

The emperors also convened here with the border tribes – undoubtedly more at ease here than in Běijīng – who posed the greatest threats to the Qing frontiers: the Mongols, Tibetans, Uighurs and, eventually, the Europeans. The resort reached its peak under Emperor Qianlong (r 1735–96), who commissioned many of the outlying temples to overawe visiting leaders.

In 1793 British emissary Lord Macartney arrived to open trade with China. The well-known story of Macartney refusing to kowtow before Qianlong probably wasn't the definitive factor in his inevitable dismissal (though it certainly made quite an impression on the court) – in any case, China, it was explained, possessed all things and had no need for trade.

The Emperor Xianfeng died here in 1861, permanently warping Chéngdé's feng shui and tipping the Imperial Villa towards long-term decline.

Sights

Bìshǔ Shānzhuāng HISTORIC SITE

(避暑山庄; admission Apr-Nov Y120, Dec-Mar Y90; ⌚palace 7am-5pm, park 5.30am-6.30pm)

The imperial summer resort is composed of a main palace complex and vast park-like gardens, all enclosed by a good-looking 10km-long wall. The peak season entrance price is steep, considering the Forbidden City is half the price.

A huge spirit wall shields the resort entrance from the bad spirits and traffic fumes of Lizhengmen Dajie. Through Lìzhèng Gate (丽正门; Lìzhèng Mén), the **Main Palace** (正宫; Zhèng Gōng) is a series of nine courtyards and five elegant, unpainted halls, with a rusticity complemented by towering pine trees. The wings in each courtyard have various exhibitions (porcelain, clothing, weaponry), and most of the halls are decked out in period furnishings.

The first hall is the refreshingly cool **Hall of Simplicity and Sincerity**, built of an aromatic cedar called *nánmù,* and displaying a carved throne draped in yellow silk. Other prominent halls include the emperor's study (Study of Four Knowledges) and living quarters (Hall of Refreshing Mists and Waves). On the left-hand side of the latter is the imperial bedroom. Two residential areas branch out from here: the empress dowager's **Pine Crane Palace** (松鹤斋; Sōnghè Zhāi), to the east, and the smaller Western Apartments, where the concubines (including a young Cixi) resided.

Exiting the Main Palace brings you to the **gardens** and forested hunting grounds, with landscapes borrowed from famous southern scenic areas in Hángzhou, Suzhōu and Jiāxīng, as well as the Mongolian grasslands. The 20th century took its toll on the park, but you can still get a feel for the original scheme of things.

The double-storey **Misty Rain Tower** (烟雨楼; Yānyǔ Lóu), on the northwestern side of the main lake, served as an imperial study. Further north is the **Wénjīn Pavilion** (文津阁; Wénjīn Gé), built in 1773 to house a copy of the *Siku Quanshu,* a major anthology of classics, history, philosophy and literature commissioned by Qianlong. The anthology took 10 years to compile, and totalled an astounding 36,500 chapters. Four copies were made, only one of which has survived (now in Běijīng). In the east, elegant **Yǒngyòusì Pagoda** (永佑寺塔; Yǒngyòusì Tǎ) soars above the fragments of its vanished temple.

About 90% of the compound is taken up by lakes, hills, forests and plains, with the odd vantage-point pavilion. In the northern part of the park, the emperors reviewed displays of archery, equestrian skills and fireworks.

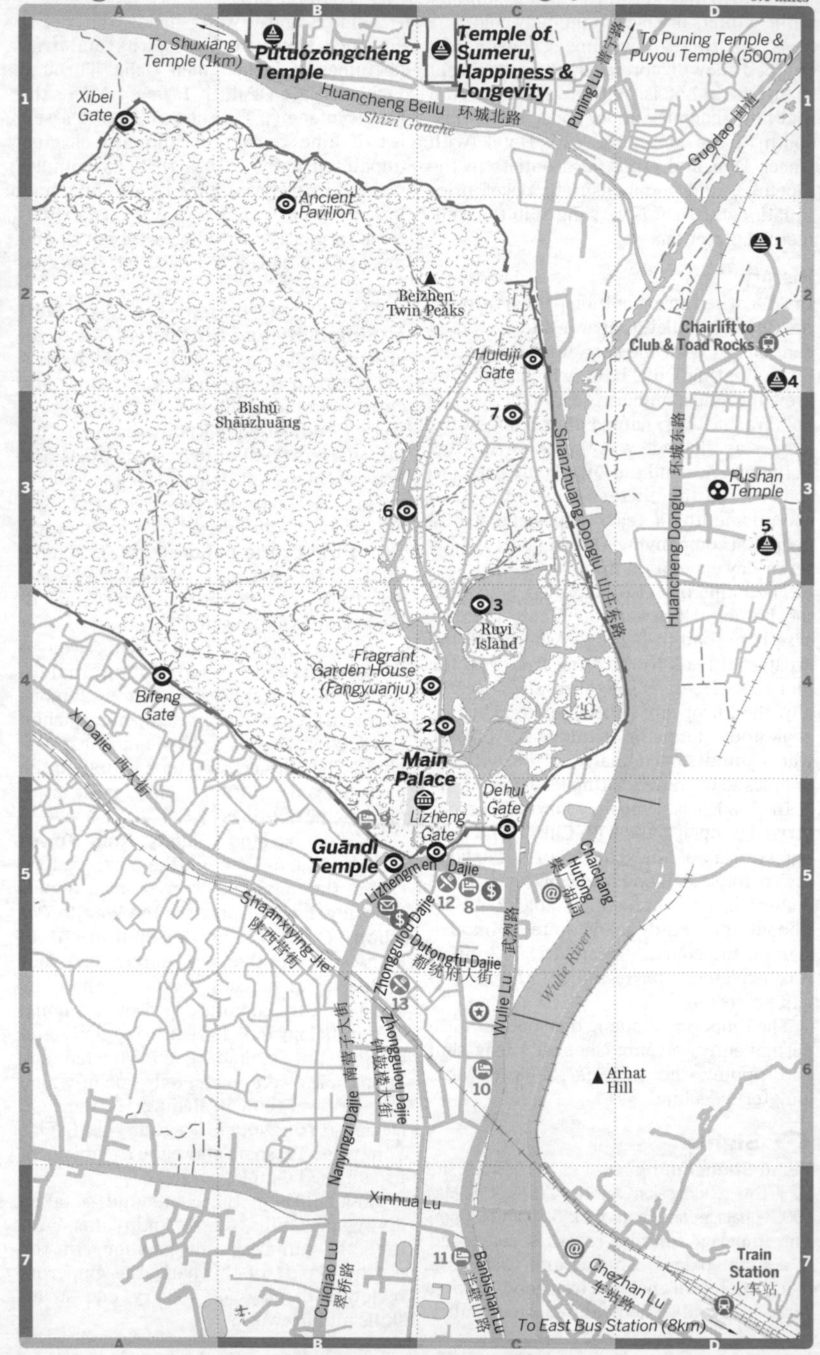

0 600 m
0 0.4 miles
To Shuxiang Temple (1km)
Pǔtuózōngchéng Temple
Temple of Sumeru, Happiness & Longevity
To Puning Temple & Puyou Temple (500m)
Puning Lu 普宁路
Huancheng Beilu 环城北路
Shizi Gouche
Guodao 国道
Xibei Gate
Ancient Pavilion
Beizhen Twin Peaks
Chairlift to Club & Toad Rocks
Huidiji Gate
Bìshǔ Shānzhuāng
Shanzhuang Donglu 山庄东路
Huancheng Donglu 环城东路
Pushan Temple
Ruyi Island
Fragrant Garden House (Fangyuanju)
Bifeng Gate
Xi Dajie 西大街
Main Palace
Dehui Gate
Lizheng Gate
Guāndì Temple
Lizhengmen Dajie
Chaichang Hutong 柴厂胡同
Shaanxiying Jie 陕西营街
Zhonggulou Dajie 钟鼓楼大街
Dutongfu Dajie 都统府大街
Wulie Lu 武烈路
Wulie River
Nanyingzi Dajie 南营子大街
Arhat Hill
Xinhua Lu
Cuiqiao Lu 翠桥路
Banbishan Lu 半壁山路
Chezhan Lu 车站路
Train Station 火车站
To East Bus Station (8km)

Chéngdé

Just beyond the Main Palace are electric carts that whiz around the grounds (Y40); further on is a **boat-rental area** (出租小船; Chūzū Xiǎochuán; per hr Y10-50). Almost all of the forested section is closed from November through May because of fire hazard in the dry months, but fear not, you can still turn your legs to jelly wandering around the rest of the park.

Guāndì Temple TAOIST TEMPLE
(关帝庙; Guāndì Miào; 18 Lizhengmen Dajie; admission Y20; 8am-5pm) The restored Taoist Guāndì Temple was first built during the reign of Yongzheng, in 1732. For years the temple housed residents but is again home to a band of Taoist monks, garbed in distinctive jackets and trousers, their long hair twisted into topknots.

Eight Outer Temples BUDDHIST TEMPLES
(外八庙; *wài bā miào*) Skirting the northern and eastern walls of the Bìshǔ Shānzhuāng, the eight outer temples were, unusually, designed for diplomatic rather than spiritual reasons. Some were based on actual Tibetan Buddhist monasteries but the emphasis was on appearance: smaller temple buildings are sometimes solid, and the Tibetan facades (with painted windows) are often fronts for traditional Chinese temple interiors. The surviving temples and monasteries were all built between 1713 and 1780; the prominence given to Tibetan Buddhism was as much for the Mongols (fervent Lamaists) as the Tibetan leaders.

Bus 6 taken to the northeastern corner will drop you in the vicinity and bus 118 runs along Huancheng Beilu, though pedalling the 12km (round trip) by bike is an excellent idea.

Pǔníng Temple BUDDHIST TEMPLE
(普宁寺; Pǔníng Sì; Puningsi Lu; admission Y50, winter Y40; 7.30am-6pm, winter 8am-5pm) With its squeaking prayer wheels and devotional intonations of its monks, Chéngdé's only active temple was built in 1755 in anticipation of Qianlong's victory over the western Mongol tribes in Xīnjiāng. Supposedly modelled on the earliest Tibetan Buddhist monastery (Samye), the first half of the temple is distinctly Chinese (with Tibetan buildings at the rear).

Enter the temple grounds to a stele pavilion with inscriptions by the Qianlong emperor in Chinese, Manchu, Mongol and Tibetan. The halls behind are arranged in typical Buddhist fashion, with the **Hall of Heavenly Kings** (天王殿; Tiānwáng Diàn) and beyond, the **Mahavira Hall** (大雄宝殿; Dàxióng Bǎodiàn), where three images of the Buddhas of the three generations are arrayed. Some very steep steps rise up behind (the temple is arranged on a mountainside) leading to a gate tower, which you can climb.

On the terrace at the top of the steps is the dwarfing **Mahayana Hall**. On either side are stupas and square blocklike Tibetan-style buildings, decorated with attractive water spouts. Some buildings have been converted to shops, while others are solid, serving a purely decorative purpose.

The mindbogglingly vast gilded statue of **Guanyin** (the Buddhist Goddess of Mercy) towers within the Mahayana Hall. The effigy is astounding: over 22m high, it's the tallest of its kind in the world and radiates a powerful sense of divinity. Hewn from five different kinds of wood (pine, cypress, fir, elm and linden), Guanyin has 42 arms, with each palm bearing an eye and each hand holding instruments, skulls, lotuses and other Buddhist devices. Tibetan touches include the pair of hands in front of the goddess, below the two clasped in prayer, the right one of which holds a sceptre-like *dorje* (*vajra* in Sanskrit), a masculine symbol, and the left a *dril bu* (bell), a female symbol. On Guanyin's head sits the Teacher Longevity Buddha. To the right of the goddess stands a huge male guardian and disciple called Shàncái, opposite his female equivalent, Lóngnǚ (Dragon Girl). Unlike Guanyin, they are both coated in ancient and dusty pigments. On the wall on either side are hundreds of small effigies of Buddha.

If you're fortunate, you may be able to clamber up to the first gallery (Y10) for a closer inspection of Guanyin; torches are provided to cut through the gloom. Sadly, higher galleries are often out of bounds, so an eye-to-eye with the goddess may be impossible. To climb the gallery, try to come in the morning, as it is often impossible to get a ticket in the afternoon, and prepare to be disappointed, as the gallery may simply be shut.

Pǔníng Temple has a number of friendly Lamas who manage their domain, so be quiet and respectful at all times. Take bus 6 from in front of the Mountain Villa Hotel.

Pǔtuózōngchéng Temple BUDDHIST TEMPLE
(普陀宗乘之庙; Pǔtuózōngchéng Zhīmiào; Shizigou Lu; admission Y40, winter Y30; ⌚8am-6pm, winter 8.30am-5pm) Chéngdé's largest temple is a minifacsimile of Lhasa's Potala Palace and houses the nebulous presence of Avalokiteshvara (Guanyin). A marvellous sight on a clear day, the temple's red walls stand out against its mountain backdrop. Enter to a huge stele pavilion, followed by a large triple archway topped with five small stupas in red, green, yellow, white and black. In between the two gates are two large stone elephants whose knees bend impossibly.

Fronted by a collection of prayer wheels and flags, the **Red Palace** (also called the Great Red Platform) contains most of the main shrines and halls. Continue up past an exhibition of *thangka* (sacred Tibetan paintings) in a restored courtyard and look out for the marvellous sandalwood pagodas in the front hall. Both are 19m tall and contain 2160 effigies of the Amitabha Buddha.

Among the many exhibits on view are displays of Tibetan Buddhist objects and instruments, including a *kapala* bowl, made from the skull of a young girl. The main hall is located at the very top, surrounded by several small pavilions and panoramic views. Bus 118 (Y1) runs along Huancheng Beilu past the temple.

Temple of Sumeru, Happiness & Longevity BUDDHIST TEMPLE
(须弭福寿之庙; Xūmífúshòu Zhīmiào; Shizigou Lu; admission Y30, winter Y20; ⌚8am-5.30pm, winter 8.30am-5pm) East of the Pǔtuózōngchéng Temple, this huge temple was built in honour of the sixth Panchen Lama, who stayed here in 1781. Incorporating Tibetan and Chinese architectural elements, it's an imitation of a temple in Shigatse, Tibet. Note the eight huge, glinting dragons (each said to weigh over 1000kg) that adorn the roof of the main hall. Bus 118 (Y1) runs along Huancheng Beilu past the temple.

Pǔlè Temple BUDDHIST TEMPLE
(普乐寺; Pǔlè Sì; admission Y30, winter Y20; ⌚8am-6pm, winter 8.30am-5pm) This peaceful temple was built in 1776 for the visits of minority envoys (Kazakhs among them). At the rear of the temple is the unusual Round Pavilion, reminiscent of the Hall of Prayer for Good Harvests at Běijīng's Temple of Heaven. Inside is an enormous wooden mandala (a geometric representation of the universe).

It's a 30-minute walk to **Hammer Rock** (磬锤峰; Qìngchuí Fēng; admission Y25) from Pǔlè Temple – the rock is said to resemble a kind of musical hammer. There is pleasant hiking and commanding views of the area. Bus 10 will take you to the cable car (return Y45) for Hammer Rock.

Puyou Temple BUDDHIST TEMPLE
(普佑寺; Pǔyòu Sì; admission Y20; ⌚8am-6pm) East of Pǔníng Temple, this temple is dilapidated and missing its main hall, but it has a plentiful contingent of merry gilded *luóhàn* in the side wings, although a fire in 1964 incinerated many of their confrères.

Guǎngyuán Temple BUDDHIST TEMPLE
(广缘寺; Guǎngyuán Sì) Unrestored and inaccessible, the temple's rounded doorway is blocked up with stones and its grounds are seemingly employed by the local farming community.

Ānyuǎn Temple BUDDHIST TEMPLE
(安远庙; Ānyuǎn Miào; admission Y10; ⌚8am-5.30pm) A copy of the Gurza Temple in Xīnjiāng, only the main hall remains, which contains deteriorating Buddhist frescoes. Take bus 10.

Pǔrén Temple BUDDHIST TEMPLE
(普仁寺; Pǔrén Sì) Built in 1713, this is the earliest temple in Chéngdé, but is not open to the public.

Shūxiàng Temple BUDDHIST TEMPLE
(殊像寺; Shūxiàng Si) Surrounded by a low red wall, with its large halls rising on the hill behind and huge stone lions parked outside, this temple is often closed. Just to the west of Shūxiàng Temple is a military-sensitive zone where foreigners are not allowed access, so don't go wandering around.

Sleeping

Chéngdé has an unremarkable and expensive range of tourist accommodation; at the time of writing, foreigners were barred from many cheap hotels. Hotel room prices increase at the weekend and during the holiday periods.

Mountain Villa Hotel HOTEL $$
(山庄宾馆; Shānzhuāng Bīnguǎn; ☎209 1188; www.hemvhotel.com; 11 Lizhengmen Lu; 丽正门路11号; d Y380-680, tr Y400, discounts of 30%; ❄) The Mountain Villa has a plethora of rooms and offers pole position for a trip inside the Bìshǔ Shānzhuāng, making it one of the best choices in town. The cheapest rooms are in the rear block but take a look at rooms first. Take bus 7 from the train station and from there it's a short walk. All major credit cards are accepted.

Qǐwànglóu Hotel HOTEL $$
(绮望楼宾馆; Qǐwànglóu Bīnguǎn; ☎202 2196; 1 Bifengmen Donglu; 碧峰门东路1号; s/d/tr/ste Y480/480/580/1800; ❄) Qǐwànglóu boasts a serene green and traditional setting alongside the Summer Villa's walls, accentuated by the hotel's courtyard gardens and wandering peacocks. Aim for the pleasant rooms backing onto courtyards but avoid downstairs rooms which have bad air.

Yúnshān Hotel HOTEL $$
(云山大酒店; Yúnshān Dàjiǔdiàn; ☎205 5588; 2 Banbishan Lu; 半壁山路2号; d Y880-980, ste Y1600, discounts of 30%; ❄@) The white tile exterior makes it resemble a towering public convenience, and rooms at this four-star hotel are comfortable but once-elegant and now faded, plus bathrooms are small. All in all, comfort but little glamour.

Shùntiānhé Hotel HOTEL $$
(顺天河宾馆; Shùntiānhé Bīnguǎn; ☎203 1966; 13 Wulie Lu; 武烈路13号; s/tw/tr Y480/480/680, discounts of 60%; ❄) Twins are spacious and clean if a bit dated at this serviceable place with good discounts (when it's quiet).

Eating

Chéngdé is famous for wild game (notably venison, *lùròu*, and pheasant, *shānjī*), but don't expect to see too much on the menus these days. There's no shortage of street food; head for Shaanxiying Jie (northern end of Nanyingzi Dajie) for a good choice of barbecue *(shāokǎo)* and Muslim noodle restaurants; Nanxinglong Jie is good for *ròujiāmó* (肉夹馍; meat in a bun) and other snacks. Dongxing Lu (东兴路) is full of big, brash hotpot restaurants.

Xiǎo Féiyáng HOTPOT $
(小肥羊; Xīnyìfùlái Hotel; Lizhengmen Dajie; meals Y40; ⏲11am-9pm) Right across the way from Lìzhèng Gate, this downstairs lamb hotpot restaurant is excellent for post-Imperial Summer Resort ramblings. The two-flavour spicy and mild *yuānyāng* (鸳鸯锅; Y20) base is best, into which you fling plate loads of lamb (羊肉; Y18), cabbage (白菜; Y4), potatoes (土豆片; Y4), eggs (鸡蛋; Y1) and more. Tick the form and hand to the waitress. It's on the ground floor of the Xīnyìfùlái Hotel (新意富来酒店).

Xīláishùn Fànzhuāng MUSLIM $
(西来顺饭庄; ☎202 5554; 6 Zhonggulou Dajie; dishes Y10-40) The gathering place for local Muslims, this unassuming restaurant is a great choice for those undaunted by Chinese-only picture menus. Excellent choices include beef fried with coriander (烤牛肉; *kǎo niúròu;* Y24) and sesame duck kebabs (芝麻鸭串; *zhīma yāchuàn;* Y25). Look for the mosque-style entrance.

Information

Bank of China (中国银行; Zhōngguó Yínháng; 4 Dutongfu Dajie) Also on Xinsheng Lu and Lizhengmen Dajie; 24-hour ATMs.

China Post (中国邮政; Zhōngguó Yóuzhèng; cnr Lizhengmen Dajie & Dutongfu Dajie; ⏲8am-6pm) A smaller branch is on Lizhengmen Dajie, east of the Main Gate of the Imperial Summer Resort.

Public Security Bureau (公安局; PSB; Gōng'ānjú; ☎202 2352; 9 Wulie Lu; ⏲8.30am-5pm Mon-Fri)

Web Cafe (网吧; Wǎngbā; Chaichang Hutong; per hr Y2; ⏲24hr)

Xiàndài Internet Cafe (现代网吧; Xiàndài Wǎngbā; Chezhan Lu; per hr Y2; ⏲24hr) West of the train station.

Getting There & Away

Bus

Buses for Chéngdé leave Běijīng hourly from Liùlǐqiáo bus station (Y56 to Y73, four hours); buses also run from Běijīng's Sìhuì long-distance station (Y50 to Y74, four hours, 6am to 4pm). Minibuses from Chéngdé leave every 20 minutes for Běijīng (Y85, three hours, last bus 6.30pm) from the train station car park, also stopping down the road from the Yúnshān Hotel.

Buses also leave from Chéngdé's **east bus station** (dōng qìchēzhàn; 212 3566), 8km south of town:

Běijīng Y73, four hours, every 20 minutes (6am to 6pm)

Dálián Y178, 13 to 14 hours, one daily (3pm)

Jìxiàn Y52, four hours, two daily (9.30am and 7.30pm)

Qínhuángdǎo Y96, five hours, five daily (for Shānhǎiguān)

Train

The fastest regular trains from Běijīng train station take over four hours (hard/soft seat Y41/92); slower trains take much longer. The first train from Běijīng departs at 8.07am, arriving in Chéngdé at 12.29am. Alternatively, catch the 12.25am train from Běijīng and reach Chéngdé early next morning. In the other direction, the 1.29pm service from Chéngdé is a useful train, arriving in Běijīng at 5.51pm. The first train to Běijīng is at 5.45am, arriving at 11am.

Shěnyáng Y97, 13 hours, one daily (6.53am)

Shíjiāzhuāng hard seat Y80 to Y86, 10 hours

Tiānjīn hard seat Y65, nine hours, one daily (9.53pm)

Getting Around

Taxis are Y6 at flag fall (then Y1.40 per kilometre); on the meter, a taxi from the train station to the Bìshǔ Shānzhuāng should cost around Y7. There are several minibus lines (Y1), including minibus 5 from the train station to Lizhengmen Dajie, minibus 1 from the train station to the east bus station and minibus 6 to the Eight Outer Temples, grouped at the northeastern end of town. Bus 11 also runs from the train station to the Bìshǔ Shānzhuāng. To reach the east bus station, take bus 118 or a taxi (Y20).

Shānhǎiguān 山海关

0335 / POP 19,500

A possible day trip from Běijīng or pit stop on the journey to the Manchurian homelands of the northeast, the drowsy walled town of Shānhǎiguān marks the point where the Great Wall snakes out of the hills to greet the sea.

In a kind of Faustian pact, Shānhǎiguān sold some of its soul trading its shabby charms for a rebuild of the old town's central sections. Thoughtful restoration of Shānhǎiguān's rundown buildings would have been desirable, but their replacement with faux traditional buildings is the typical default mode of tourist developers keen to make a fast buck. Reconstruction is often cheaper than restoration and, as the blurb puts it, 'There are about 90 scenic spots possessing the developing value'.

Shops along Nan Dajie and Bei Dajie have been rebuilt (with lashings of carefully concealed concrete) along with the Drum Tower, rows of *páilou* and a scattering of temples. It is important to keep in mind that these and other traditional buildings in the town are not original. Mercifully, much of the old town has survived, buried away down the *hútòng* running east–west.

History

Guarding the narrow plain leading to northeastern China, the Ming garrison town of Shānhǎiguān and its wall were developed to seal off the country from the Manchu, whose troublesome ancestors ruled northern China during the Jin dynasty (AD 1115–1234). This strategy succeeded until 1644, when Chinese rebels seized Běijīng and General Wu Sangui opted to invite the Manchu army through the impregnable pass to help suppress the uprising. The plan worked so well that the Manchus proceeded to take over the entire country and establish the Qing dynasty.

An ironic footnote: in 1681 Qing rulers finished building their own Great Wall, known as the Willow Palisade (a large ditch fronted by willow trees), which stretched several hundred kilometres from Shānhǎiguān to Jílín, with another branch forking south to Dāndōng from Kāiyuán. The purpose of the Palisade, of course, was to keep the Han Chinese and Mongols out of Manchuria.

Shānhǎiguān fell into gradual dilapidation during the republic and the People's Republic. This charming decay was dramatically reversed when the investment cyclone swept through town before the 2008 Olympics, leaving rows of rebuilt *hútòng*-style shops in its wake, many of which remain empty or sell products targeting tourists.

Sights

First Pass Under Heaven HISTORIC SITE
(天下第一关; Tiānxià Dìyī Guān; cnr Dong Dajie & Diyiguan Lu; adult/student Y40/20; ⏲7am-6.30pm) A restored section of wall studded with watchtowers and tourist paraphernalia, the First Pass Under Heaven is also called East Gate (东门; Dōng Mén). The 12m-high wall's principal watchtower – two storeys with double eaves and 68 arrow-slit windows – is a towering 13.7m high.

The calligraphy at the top (attributed to the scholar Xiao Xian) reads 'First Pass Under Heaven'. Several other watchtowers can also be seen and a *wèngchéng* (enceinte) extends out east from the wall. To the north, decayed sections of battlements trail off into the hills; to the south you can walk to the ramp just east of the South Gate.

The ticket also includes admission to the vaguely interesting 18th-century **Wang Family Courtyard House** (王家大院; Wángjiā Dàyuàn; 29-31 Dongsantiao Hutong; admission Y25; ⏲6.30am-6.30pm), a large residence with an amateur display of period furnishings.

Jiǎo Shān HISTORIC SITE
(角山; admission Y30; ⏲7am-sunset) An excellent hike up the Great Wall's first high peak, Jiǎo Shān affords a telling vantage point over the narrow tongue of land below and one-time invasion route for northern armies. For something more adventurous, follow the wall's unrestored section indefinitely past the watchtowers or hike over to the secluded **Qīxián Monastery** (栖贤寺; Qīxián Sì; admission Y5).

Jiǎo Shān is a 3km bike ride north of town or a half-hour walk from the north gate; otherwise take a *sānlúnchē* (Y10). It's a steep 20-minute clamber from the base, or a cable car can yank you up for Y20.

Old Dragon Head HISTORIC SITE
(老龙头; Lǎolóngtou; admission Y50; ⏲7.30am-5.30pm) The mythic origin/conclusion of the Great Wall at the sea's edge, Old Dragon Head is 4km south of Shānhǎiguān. What you see now was reconstructed in the late 1980s – the original wall crumbled away long ago. The name derives from the legendary carved dragon head that once faced the waves; as attractions go, it's essentially a lot more hype than history. Buses 25 and 21 (Y1) go to Old Dragon Head from Shānhǎiguān's South Gate.

Shānhǎiguān

Top Sights
First Pass Under Heaven ... B1
Great Wall Museum ... B1

Sights
1 Dàbēi Pavilion ... A1
2 Drum Tower ... A1
3 Wang Family Courtyard House ... A1
4 West Gate ... A1

Sleeping
5 Friendly Cooperate Hotel ... B2
6 Shānhǎi Holiday Hotel ... A1
7 Zhòngxìn Hotel ... B2

Eating
8 Shuānghé Shāokǎo ... A2

Other Sights HISTORIC SITES
The wall attached to **North Gate** (北门; Běi Mén) has been partially restored. The city gates once had circular enceintes attached to them, as you can see at the East Gate. The excavated outlines of the enceinte outside the **West Gate** (西门; Xī Mén) are discernible, as are slabs of the original Ming-dynasty road, lying 1m below the current level of the ground.

The **Dàbēi Pavilion** (大悲阁; Dàbēi Gé) in the northwest of town has been rebuilt, as has the Taoist **Sānqīng Temple** (三清观; Sānqīng Guàn; Beihou Jie), outside the walls. Shānghǎiguān's **Drum Tower** (鼓楼; Gǔlóu) has been similarly rebuilt, with a liberal scattering of newly constructed *páilou* running off east and west along Xi Dajie and Dong Dajie.

WORTH A TRIP

JIǓMÉNKǑU GREAT WALL

In a mountain valley 15km north of Shānhǎiguān stretches **Jiǔměnkǒu Great Wall** (九门口长城; Jiǔměnkǒu; admission Y60), the only section of the Great Wall ever built over water. Normally the wall stopped at rivers, as they were considered natural defence barriers all on their own. At Jiǔměnkǒu Great Wall, however, a 100m span supported by nine arches crosses the Jiǔjiāng River, which we can only guess flowed at a much faster and deeper rate than it does today (or else the arches would function more like open gates).

Much effort has gone into restoring this formidable-looking bridge and on both sides the wall continues its run up the steep, rocky hillsides. Heading left, you can quickly see where the wall remains unrestored on the opposite side. Sadly, access to this area is blocked but the distant sight of crumbling stone watchtowers truly drives home the terrible isolation that must have been felt by the guardians of frontier regions such as this.

No buses head to the wall from Shānhǎiguān but taxis will offer their services for Y70 to Y100 as soon as you step off the train. Don't expect to have this place to yourself any more though. The crowds have found their way, as have the hawkers and the cheap amusement attractions, though they're not too hard to escape.

FREE **Great Wall Museum** MUSEUM
(长城博物馆; Chángchéng Bówùguǎn; Diyiguan Lu; ⊙9am-5pm Tue-Sun) Recently rebuilt and expanded into a geometric block of grey stone, this museum provides a resourceful introduction to the Great Wall.

Mèngjiāngnǚ Temple TAOIST TEMPLE
(孟姜女庙; Mèngjiāngnǚ Miào; admission Y40; ⊙7am-5.30pm) A well-known Song-Ming reconstruction, Mèngjiāngnǚ Temple is 6km east of Shānhǎiguān. A taxi here should cost around Y12.

Sleeping

Most of the really cheap hotels in the shabbier part of town south of South Gate do not take foreigners and it's best to do Shānhǎiguān as a day trip from Běijīng. The one decent old town cheapie – the Jīguān Guesthouse – has shut.

Shānhǎi Holiday Hotel HOTEL $$
(山海假日酒店; Shānhǎi Jiàrì Jiǔdiàn; ☎535 2888; www.shanhai-holiday.com; Bei Madao; 北马道; s/d/ste Y680/680/1280; ❄) A traditional-style four-star hotel with attractive courtyard rooms; it's fabricated perhaps, but this is a pleasant and comfortable old town hotel with a good location by the West Gate.

Friendly Cooperate Hotel HOTEL $$
(谊合酒店; Yìhé Jiǔdiàn; ☎593 9777; 4-1 Nanhai Xilu; 南海西路4-1号; tw/tr/q Y380/420/560, discounts of 40%; ❄) This well-maintained two-star hotel has large, clean and reasonably well-maintained double rooms with water cooler, TV, phone and bathroom.

Zhòngxìn Hotel HOTEL $
(众信宾馆; Zhòngxìn Bīnguǎn; ☎507 7698; 1 Nanguan Dajie; 南关大街1号; s Y180, d Y240-328, discounts of 10%; ❄) This place takes foreigners, but has crummy singles at the front or more pleasant (and pricier) doubles in the block at the rear.

Eating

The main eating zone remains in the new town beyond the South Gate.

Shuānghé Shāokǎo ROAST GRILL $
(双和烧烤店; ☎507 6969; Xishun Chengjie; meals Y30; ⊙11am-1am) Ever-bustling kebab restaurant just south of South Gate. Take your seat in a booth with a grill and order up bottles of beer and piles of kebabs (串; *chuàn*): lamb (Y20 per plate), chicken (Y12), eggplant (Y8) or onion (Y6).

Information

Several internet cafes are thrust along Xinglong Jie (兴隆街), east of Nanguan Dajie.

Bank of China (中国银行; Zhōngguó Yínháng; Nanhai Xilu; ⊙8.30am-5.30pm) Foreign exchange, small amounts of US dollars only.

China Post (中国邮政; Zhōngguó Yóuzhèng; Nanhai Xilu; ⊙8.30am-6pm) Just west of the Friendly Cooperate Hotel.

Kodak Express (柯达; Kēdá; Nanhai Xilu) CD burning costs Y15 per disc. Next to the Bank of China.

Public Security Bureau (PSB; 公安局; Gōng'ānjú; ☎505 1163) Opposite the entrance to First Pass Under Heaven, on the corner of a small alleyway.

Zhōngxìng Pharmacy (中兴药店; Zhōngxìng Yàodiàn; Nan Dajie; ⏲7am-9pm) You'll find it just south of Dōngwǔtiáo Hútòng (东五条胡同).

Getting There & Around

The fastest and most convenient train from Běijīng train station is the D5 soft-seat express to Shěnyáng, which leaves Běijīng train station at 9.20am, arriving in Shānhǎiguān at 11.27am (Y118). Other slower trains also pass through Shānhǎiguān from Běijīng and Tiānjīn. Alternatively, trains from Běijīng stop in the larger city of Qínhuángdǎo (Y90, two hours), from where bus 33 (Y2, 30 minutes) connects with Shānhǎiguān. Buses from Běijīng's Bāwángfén Station also run to Qínhuángdǎo (秦皇岛; Y61, 3½ hours).

In the return direction, buses leave for Běijīng's Bāwángfén Station (Y75, three hours, regularly from 7.30am to 6pm) and Běijīng's Capital Airport (Y126, four hours) from Qínhuángdǎo. There are also direct buses from Qínhuángdǎo to Chéngdé (Y96, five hours), departing hourly from 7am to 11am, and at 5pm. From Chéngdé, you can take a bus from the east bus station for Qínhuángdǎo (Y96, five hours).

Cheap taxis are Y5 flag fall and Y1.40 per kilometre after that. Shānhǎiguān has a vast miscellany of motor tricycles, which cost Y2 for trips within town.

Near Shānhǎiguān, Qínhuángdǎo's little airport has flights from Dàlián, Shànghǎi, Tàiyuán, Hā'ěrbīn and Chángchūn.

Jīmíngyì 鸡鸣驿

POP 1000

As ragged and forlorn as a cast-off shoe, sleepy Jīmíngyì is a characteristic snapshot of the Héběi countryside: disintegrating town walls rise above fields of millet and corn, occasional flocks of sheep 'baa' their way through one of the main gates in the early morning and local women sit around peeling garlic. Whipped by dust storms in spring, Jīmíngyì is China's oldest remaining post station; it is also a long, long way from the gleaming capital – much further than the 140km distance would suggest.

During the Ming and Qing dynasties, Jīmíngyì was a place of considerably more bustle and wealth, as evidenced in the numerous surviving temples and its town wall, but most courtyard houses have simply vanished. Today it feels trapped somewhere in the 1970s, a sensation amplified by the peculiarities of its local dialect and the Mao-era slogans on the walls.

History

For more than 2000 years, imperial China employed a vast network of postal routes for conveying official correspondence throughout the land. Post stations, where couriers would change horses or stay the night, were often fortified garrison towns that also housed travelling soldiers, merchants and officials. Marco Polo estimated there were some 10,000 post stations and 300,000 postal-service horses in 13th-century China. While Marco clearly recognised that a little embellishment makes for a good story, there is little doubt the system was well developed by the Yuan dynasty (AD 1206–1368). Jīmíngyì was established at this time under Kublai Khan as a stop on the Běijīng–Mongolia route. In the Ming dynasty, the town expanded in size as fortifying the frontiers with Chinese soldiers became increasingly important.

Sights

The infamous Empress Dowager Cixi passed through here on her flight from Běijīng in 1900; for Y5 you can see the room she slept in, but it's decidedly unimpressive.

Confucius Temple CONFUCIAN TEMPLE
(文昌宫; Wénchāng Gōng; admission Y5) Meandering along the baked-mud-wall warren of Jīmíngyì's courtyard houses takes you past scattered temples, including this simple Ming-dynasty temple which, like many Confucius temples, also doubled as a school.

Tàishān Temple TEMPLE
(泰山行宫; Tàishān Xínggōng; admission Y5) Not far away is this larger temple, whose simply stunning Qing murals depicting popular myths (with the usual mix of Buddhist, Taoist and Confucian figures) were whitewashed – some say for protection – during the Cultural Revolution. A professor from Qīnghuá University helped to uncover them; you can still see streaks of white in places.

Other Temples HISTORIC SITES
Other small temples that can be visited include the **Temple of the God of Wealth** (财神庙; Cáishén Miào; admission Y5) and the **Temple of the Dragon King** (龙王庙; Lóngwáng Miào; admission Y5). You will find the occasional *yǐngbì* (spirit wall) standing alone, its courtyard house demolished, and a few ancient stages. Adding to the time-capsule

BĚIDÀIHÉ

The breezy seaside resort of Běidàihé (北戴河) was first stumbled upon by English railway engineers in the 1890s. To this day it retains a seaside kitsch atmosphere reminiscent of Brighton or Margate (without the fish and chips), even though these days it's flooded with vacationing Russians. During the May to October high season, Běidàihé comes alive with holiday-goers who crowd the beaches and feast on seafood. During the low season, however, the town is a dead zone. Wandering the streets and seafront is enjoyable, or you can hire a bike to wheel around the beachfront roads. Otherwise, fork out for a rubber ring, inner tube and swimming trunks from one of the street vendors and plunge into the sea (after elbowing through the crowds).

Běidàihé can be reached by direct bus or train from Běijīng, or by bus from Qínhuángdǎo. From Shānhǎiguān, the beach resort is a short journey away via Qínhuángdǎo: catch bus 33 (Y2, 30 minutes) to Qínhuángdǎo and then bus 34 to Běidàihé (Y2, 30 minutes) from in front of the train station on Yingbin Lu. Buses to Běijīng's Bāwángfén long-distance bus station (Y95, three hours) from Běidàihé leave from Haining Lu (海宁路) and Bao'er Lu (保二路) at 8.30am, 12.30pm and 4.30pm.

feel are the numerous **slogans** from the Cultural Revolution daubed on walls that seem to have been simply left to fade.

City Walls HISTORIC SITE

Jīmíngyì's walls still stand, although sections have collapsed. Ascend the **East Gate** (东门; Dōng Mén) for fine views of the town, surrounding fields and **Jiming Mountain** (鸡鸣山; Jīmíng Shān) to the north. Across town is the **West Gate**; the **Temple of the Town Gods** (城隍庙; Chénghuáng Miào), overgrown with weeds and in ruins, stands nearby. There are a few intriguing Qing caricatures of Yuan-dynasty crime fighters remaining on the chipped walls. The largest and oldest temple in the area is the **Temple of Eternal Tranquillity** (永宁寺; Yǒngníng Sì), located 12km away on Jīmíng Mountain.

Sleeping & Eating

Most people visit Jīmíngyì as a day trip, but spending the night is a great way to experience village life once others have returned to Běijīng's luxuries. You can arrange to stay with one of the villagers for Y10 to Y15; a home-cooked meal will cost the same. There are a few noodle shops outside the north wall.

Getting There & Away

Jīmíngyì can be reached by bus (Y3, 30 minutes, 8.30am to 5pm) from the town of Shāchéng (沙城). You'll be dropped off along the north wall. Direct buses (Y45, 11.50am and 2pm) to Shāchéng run from Běijīng's Liùlǐqiáo station; otherwise, regular buses run past Shāchéng (Y45, two hours, hourly from 7.40am to 4pm); ask to be dropped off at the Jīmíngyì drop-off, from where it is another 2km walk to Jīmíngyì across the overpass, before turning right at the toll gate. From Shāchéng, buses return to Běijīng from 8.30am to 4pm; alternatively, walk back to the expressway and wait for any Běijīng-bound bus.

Frequent trains run to Shāchéng from Běijīng West and Běijīng Station (hard seat Y9 to Y20, 2½ to three hours). You can also catch a train on to Dàtóng (hard seat Y35, 3½ hours).

You'll need to take a taxi (Y5) or motor tricycle between Shāchéng's train and bus stations. You can store luggage at the bus station for a fee of Y1.

Shāndōng

POPULATION: 93.44 MILLION

Includes »

Best Places to Eat

» Huángdǎo Road Market (p152)

» Bellagio (p152)

» Bǎolóng Hǎixīan Chéng (p159)

Best Places to Stay

» Qūfù International Youth Hostel (p145)

» Kǎiyuè Hostelling International (p151)

» Crowne Plaza (p152)

Why Go?

Steeped in myth and supernatural allure, Shāndōng (山东) is the stuff of legends, where iconic philosophers once pondered. Even the landscape – a fertile flood plain broken by granite massifs and fringed with wild coastline and natural beaches – has a certain strangeness to it, but the region's ancient bedrock is really Confucius, the Yellow River and sacred Tài Shān.

What amateur historian can resist visiting the Apricot Pavilion, where Confucius is said to have taught his students, or the slopes of Tài Shān, where Qin Shi Huang first proclaimed the unity of China? But Shāndōng has modern appeal too. The former concession town of Qīngdǎo ranks as one of the most liveable places and popular beach resorts in northern China. This is the province's real draw: you can climb mountains, explore the cultural legacies of the imperial past and still have time to hit the beach.

When to Go

Qīngdǎo

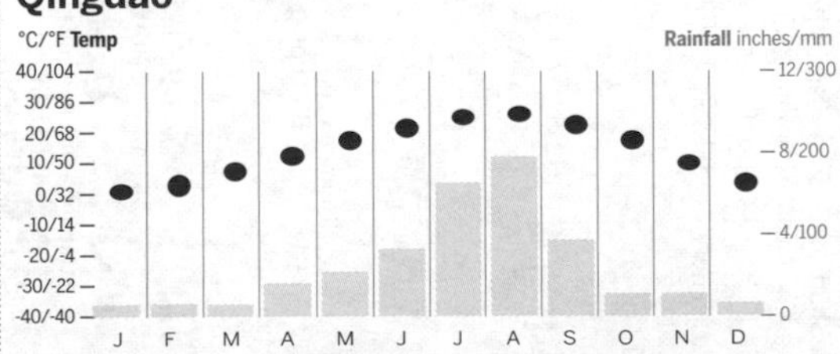

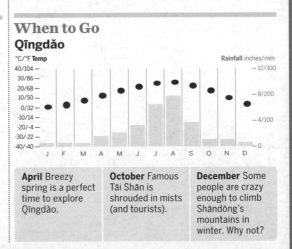

April Breezy spring is a perfect time to explore Qīngdǎo.

October Famous Tài Shān is shrouded in mists (and tourists).

December Some people are crazy enough to climb Shāndōng's mountains in winter. Why not?

Shāndōng Highlights

1 Climb mystical **Tài Shān** (p138) – get ready for a Stairmaster workout!

2 Be charmed by the scenery and friendly residents at the village of **Zhūjiāyù** (p134)

3 Visit **Qūfù** (p142), hometown of the sage Confucius – his family residence and tomb are there

4 Chill out at **Qīngdǎo** (p146), a great combination of German architecture, breezy seaside and modern comforts – and, of course, it's also home to China's famous beer

5 Hike **Láo Shān** (p155), a lovely jumble of granite slabs and thickets of bamboo and pine

6 Slow your pulse by escaping to the former colonial outpost of **Yāntái** (p156)

7 Immerse yourself in the legend of the 'Eight Immortals Crossing the Sea' at **Pénglái Pavilion** (p160), also the site of an ancient military naval base

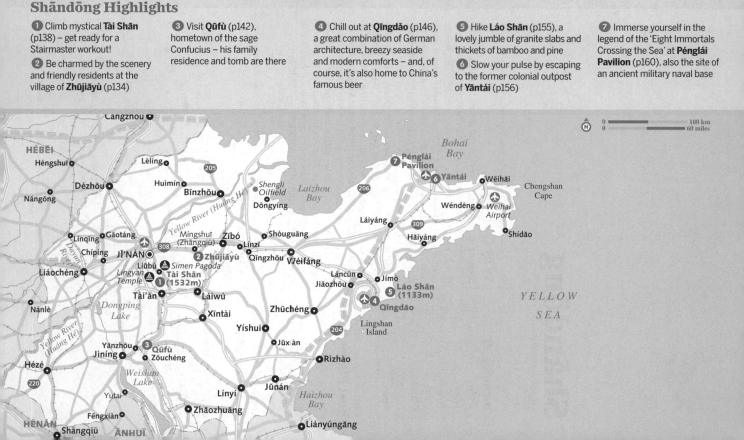

History

Shāndōng has had a tumultuous history. It was victim to the capricious temperament of the Yellow River's floodwaters, which caused mass death, starvation and a shattered economy, and often brought banditry and rebellion in their wake. In 1899 the river (also aptly named 'China's Sorrow') flooded the entire Shāndōng plain; a sad irony in view of the scorching droughts that had swept the area both that year and the previous year. The flood followed a long period of economic depression, a sudden influx of demobilised troops in 1895 after China's humiliating defeat by Japan in Korea, and droves of refugees from the south moving north to escape famines, floods and drought.

To top it all off, the Europeans arrived; Qīngdǎo fell into the clutches of the Germans, and the British obtained a lease for Wēihǎi. Their activities included the building of railroads and some feverish missionary work, which the Chinese believed had angered the gods and spirits. All of this created the perfect breeding ground for rebellion, and in the closing years of the 19th century the Boxers arose out of Shāndōng, armed with magical spells and broadswords.

Today Jǐ'nán, the provincial capital, plays second fiddle to Qīngdǎo, a refrain that has been picked up by the other prospering coastal cities of Yāntái and Wēihǎi.

Getting There & Around

There are airports at Jǐ'nán, Qīngdǎo and Yāntái, with international flights to cities in Japan and South Korea from Qīngdǎo and Yāntái. Ferries run from Yāntái to Dàlián and Incheon in South Korea. There are also boats from Qīngdǎo to South Korea (Incheon and Gunsan) and Japan (Shimonoseki). Shāndōng is linked to neighbouring and more distant provinces by both bus and rail; a rail-ferry service runs between Yāntái and Dàlián, allowing you to book your onward rail tickets from the opposite port.

The provincial rail hub is Jǐ'nán, with rail connections to all major towns and cities in Shāndōng. Bus connections cover the entire province.

PRICE INDICATORS

The following price indicators are used in this chapter:

Sleeping

$	less than Y200
$$	Y200 to Y500
$$$	more than Y500

Eating

$	less than Y20
$$	Y20 to Y50
$$$	more than Y50

Jǐ'nán 济南

0531 / POP 2.27 MILLION

The provincial capital, Jǐ'nán is a modern Chinese city that largely serves travellers as a transit point to other destinations around Shāndōng. It's in a constant state of flux, so expect lots of construction, noise and pollution that is almost on a par with Běijīng. Downplayed in the city's tourist pitch are the celebrities who have come from Jǐ'nán: film idol Gong Li, Bian Que, founder of traditional Chinese medicine, as well as Zhou Yongnian, founder of Chinese public libraries.

Jǐ'nán is a sprawling city, making navigation arduous. The main train station is in the west of town, south of which lies a grid of roads. The east is more developed; the major landmark here is Dàmíng Lake (Dàmíng Hú), south of which can be found the major shopping zone of Quancheng Lu and Quancheng Sq, decked out with flowers and ornamental trees.

Sights

City Parks PARKS
(公园; Gōngyuán) Strolling around willow-filled parks can be a pleasant escape from Jǐ'nán's foot-numbing distances. The most central include the sprawling **Bàotū Spring Park** (趵突泉; Bàotū Quán; Gongqingtuan Lu; admission Y40), **Black Tiger Spring** (黑虎泉; Hēihǔ Quán; Heihuquan Donglu; admission free) and **Five Dragon Pool Park** (五龙潭公园; Wǔlóngtán Gōngyuán; Gongqingtuan Lu; admission Y5). The Five Dragon Pool Park offers a lovely study in local life: residents practise calligraphy on stone steps with water, others sing Chinese folk songs and there are more than a few taichi enthusiasts.

Guāndì Temple & Hui Mosque TEMPLE, MOSQUES
Just west of Five Dragon Pool Park's entrance survives the small **Guāndì Temple** (关帝庙; Guāndì Miào; admission free) where fortunes are told in Chinese (Y10) and the

Jǐ'nán

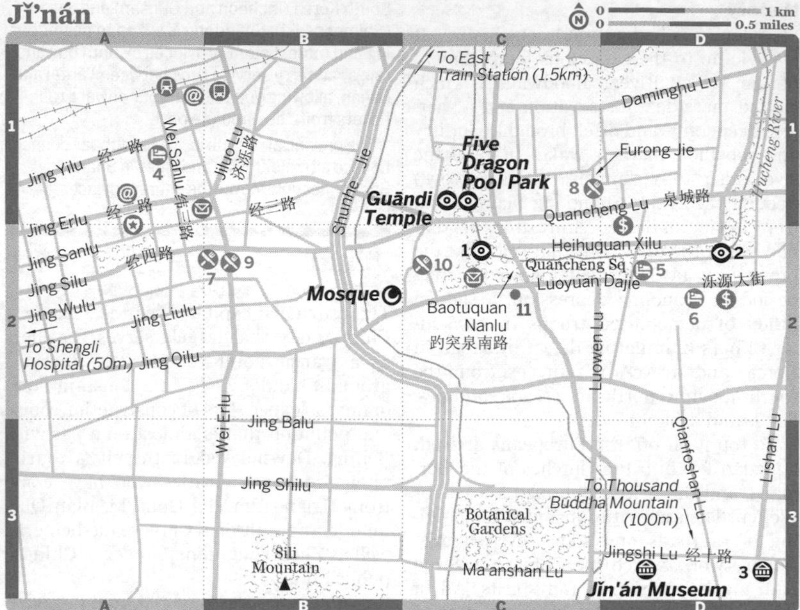

great protector glares out over a row of flickering candles in the main shrine. In the centre of town is a lovely Chinese-style **mosque** (清真寺; Qīngzhēn Sì; 47 Yongchang Jie; admission free) that dates from the late 13th century; a Hui (Muslim Chinese) area stretches north, with butchers, vegetable markets, mosques and kebab stalls.

Thousand Buddha Mountain BUDDHIST MOUNTAIN

(千佛山; Qiānfó Shān; 18 Jingshi Yilu; admission Y30; ⏲6am-9pm) Adding some Buddhist mystery to Jǐ'nán are the statues in this park to the southeast of the city centre. A **cable car** (one way/return Y20/30) runs up the mountain, though the view coming down is better. If you want an adrenalin rush, barrel down the mountain on a **luge** (one way/return Y25/30). At the peak, look south to spot Tài Shān poking out like a giant anthill in the distance…if you can see through the pall of city smog. Bus K51 goes to the park from the train station.

Jǐnán Museums MUSEUMS

Two museums flank the Thousand Buddha Mountain. West along Jingshi Yilu, the **Jǐ'nán Museum** (济南博物馆; Jǐ'nán Bówùguǎn; admission free; ⏲8.30am-4.30pm Tue-Sun) has galleries devoted to painting, calligraphy and ceramics, statues of Buddhist figures from the Tang dynasty and

Jǐ'nán

Top Sights
- Five Dragon Pool Park ... C1
- Guāndi Temple ... C1
- Jǐn'án Museum ... D3
- Mosque ... B2

Sights
1. Bàotū Spring Park ... C2
2. Black Tiger Spring ... D2
3. Provincial Museum ... D3

Sleeping

4 Shāndōng Hotel ... A1
5 Silver Plaza Quancheng Hotel ... D2
6 Sofitel Silver Plaza Jǐn'án ... D2

Eating

7 Dàguān Gardens ... B2
8 Furong Jie Food Street ... C1
Lǔxī'nán Flavor Restaurant ... (see 7)
9 Wei Er Lu Food Street ... B2
10 Yinhuchi Jie Food Street ... C2

Transport

11 Ji'nan International Airport Ticket Office ... C2

a delightful miniature boat carved from a walnut shell.

Five minutes east is the **Provincial Museum** (省博物馆; Shěng Bówùguǎn; Jingshi Yilu; ⌚8.30am-4.30pm Tue-Sun), set to reopen by the time you read this. Future exhibits may include fragments of ancient oracle bones, Kong family clothing, Lóngshān pottery and traditional painting and calligraphy.

Sleeping

Budget hotels are clustered around the main train station. Look at rooms before committing.

Sofitel Silver Plaza Jǐ'nán HOTEL **$$$**
(索菲特银座大饭店; Suǒfēitè Yínzuò Dàfàndiàn; ☎8981 1611; www.sofitel.com; 66 Luoyuan Dajie; 泺源大街66号; d from Y1400, discounts of up to 50%; ❄@🏊) A 49-floor five-star tower in the heart of the commercial district, we wish the Sofitel's standard rooms – smartly decorated in light-wood furniture – were as large as the light-filled lobby. It has European, Japanese and Chinese restaurants.

Silver Plaza Quancheng Hotel HOTEL **$$**
(银座泉城大酒店; Yínzùo Quánchéng Dàjǐudiàn; ☎8629 1911; 2 Nanmen Jie; 南门街2号; d/tr Y480/680; ❄@) You know you are in a Chinese-business hotel when you get blinded by the faux European bling in the lobby. Expect tight rooms with blue bedding and some rooms with a sink outside the bathroom (go figure). Staff are friendly and the location overlooks Quancheng Sq. A new wing was being renovated so expect spiffy rooms.

Shāndōng Hotel HOTEL **$**
(山东宾馆; Shāndōng Bīnguǎn; ☎8606 7000; 92 Jing Yilu; 经一路92号; d/tr Y199/249; ❄@) On the corner of Jing Yilu and Wei Sanlu, this old-timer is well used to dealing with budget travellers. The most convenient choice in town, the Shāndōng's rooms have had a recent makeover. Large toilets, and clean but compact rooms. Get rooms facing away from the noisy main road. No discounts.

Eating

Jǐ'nán is famed as one of the centres of *lǔcài* (Shāndōng cuisine), but much of the eating here seems to take place on the city's food streets.

Food Streets STREET FOOD **$**
A little over 1km south of the main train station is **Dàguān Gardens** (大观园; Dàguān Yuán; Jing Silu), a popular area with modern eateries marked by a large archway. The alley next to it, **Wei Er Lu** (纬二路), is a messy strip of food carts offering up fried noodles, skewers of grilled meats and seafood, lamb soup and pancakes. Y2 for a beer? Who's complaining?

For lamb kebabs and fresh noodles, head to smoky **Yinhuchi Jie** (饮虎池街) in the Muslim Hui minority district east of the mosque. Hawkers toss loads of satay-style skewers on charcoal grills which run for metres along the street.

In the east of town, along the main shopping strip of Quancheng Lu, is **Furong Jie** (芙蓉街), a pedestrian street festooned with hanging lanterns and red banners. Look for the archway, Furong Gang Xiao Chi Guang Chang. The alley next to it, confusingly labelled Furong Jie, also has a large variety of cheap street snacks.

Lǔxī'nán Flavor Restaurant SHANDONG **$$**
(鲁西南老牌坊; Lǔxī'nán Lǎopáifāng; ☎8605 4567; 2 Daguan Yuan; dishes Y28-98; ⌚lunch & dinner; 📖) *The* place to sample Shāndōng cuisine. Try down-home classics like sautéed Chinese cabbage (sweet-and-spicy cabbage with glass noodles; Y16) and sliced lamb served fried, boiled or sautéed (from Y38), accompanied with sesame cakes (Y1) – not rice – and wash it all down with beer (Y9). BYO facemask – the cigarette smoke in the restaurant can be overwhelming.

Information

ATMs (自动取款机; Zìdòng Qǔkuǎn Jī) are available in the lobbies of the Sofitel and Crowne Plaza hotels. There are plenty of banks in town.

Bank of China (中国银行; Zhōngguó Yínháng; 22 Luoyuan Dajie; ⌚9am-5pm Mon-Fri) Foreign exchange and ATMs that take international cards.

China Post (中国邮政; Zhōngguó Yóuzhèng; 162 Jing Erlu; ⌚8am-6.30pm) A red-brick building with pillars, capped with a turret, on the corner of Wei Erlu.

Internet cafe (网吧; wǎngbā; Jing Erlu; per hr Y2; ⌚7am-midnight)

Internet cafe (网吧; wǎngbā; per hr Y3-4; ⌚24hr) Beneath the Tianlong Building opposite the train station.

Public Security Bureau (PSB; 公安局; Gōng'ānjú; ☎8691 5454, visa inquiries ext 2459; 145 Jing Sanlu; ⌚8am-noon & 2-5.45pm Mon-Fri) On the corner of Wei Wulu.

Shěnglì Hospital (省立医院; Shěnglì Yīyuàn; ☎8793 8911; 324 Jing Wulu)

Getting There & Away

Air

Jǐ'nán is connected to most major cities, with daily flights to Běijīng (Y630, one hour), Dàlián (Y910, one hour), Guǎngzhōu (Y1590, 2½ hours), Hā'ěrbīn (Y1130, two hours), Shànghǎi (Y760, 80 minutes), Xī'ān (Y880, 1½ hours) and Yāntái (Y500, 45 minutes).

The **Jǐ'nán International Airport Ticket Office** (济南国际机场售票处; Jǐ'nán Guójì Jīchǎng Shòpiàochù; ☎8611 4750) is at 66 Luoyuan Dajie. Book tickets at **Shèngxiángyuán Hángkōng Tiělù Shòupiàochù** (盛祥源航空铁路售票处; ☎8610 9666; 115 Chezhan Jie, 1st fl, Quánchéng Bīnguǎn; ⏰8am-6pm) beside the train station, or in the lobby of the **Jǐ'nán Railway Hotel** (济南铁道大酒店; Jǐ'nán Tiědào Dàjiǔdiàn), immediately east of the train station.

Bus

Jǐ'nán has at least three bus stations. The most useful for travellers is the efficient **bus station** (汽车站; qìchēzhàn; ☎8830 3030) opposite the main train station, with regular buses:

Běijīng Y124, 5½ hours, eight daily

Qīngdǎo Y79, 4½ hours, every 30 minutes (6.30am to 8pm)

Qūfù Y39, two hours, every 30 minutes

Shànghǎi Y266, 12 hours, two daily (4.30pm and 7pm)

Tài'ān Y21, 1½ hours, every 30 minutes

Tiānjīn Y85, 4½ hours, four daily

Yāntái Y140 to Y160, 5½ hours, 7am to 6.30pm

Train

Jǐ'nán is a major link in the east China rail system. There are two train stations in Jǐ'nán: most trains use the **main train station** *(Jǐ'nán huǒchē zhàn)*, but a handful arrive and depart from the **east train station** *(huǒchē dōngzhàn)*.

Tickets are available from the train station and travel agents on the train station square. **Shèngxiángyuán Hángkōng Tiělù Shòupiàochù** (盛祥源航空铁路售票处; ☎8796 6288; 115 Chezhan Jie, 1st fl, Quánchéng Bīnguǎn; commission Y5; ⏰8am-6pm) is a reliable choice. No English.

Express D trains:

Běijīng 2nd/1st class Y73/114, 3½ hours, 11 daily

Nánjīng 2nd/1st class Y82/127, five hours, one daily (1.06pm)

Qīngdǎo 2nd/1st class Y55/87, 2½ hours, 11 daily

Shànghǎi 2nd/1st class Y115/181, seven hours, one daily (1.06pm)

Tài Shān 2nd/1st class Y13/21, 40 minutes, four daily

Local trains also serve the following destinations:

Běijīng Y55 to Y200, five to seven hours, 15 daily

Qīngdǎo Y41 to Y115, four to five hours, 15 daily

Shànghǎi Y94 to Y236, nine to 14 hours, 17 daily

Tài Shān Y5 to Y96, one hour, more than 15 daily

Xī'ān Y73 to Y529, 15 to 18 hours, five daily

Zhèngzhōu Y92 to Y156, eight to 10½ hours, eight daily

Getting Around

To/From the Airport

Jǐ'nán's **Yáoqiáng airport** (☎8208 6666) is 40km from the city and can be reached in around an hour. Buses (Y20) run to the airport from the **Yùquán Simpson Hotel** (玉泉森信大酒店; Yùquán Sēnxìn Dàjiǔdiàn; Luoyuan Dajie) every hour between 6am and 7pm. A taxi will cost around Y100.

Public Transport

Bus 84 (Y1) connects the long-distance bus station with the main train station. Bus K51 (Y2) runs from the main train station through the city centre and then south past Bàotū Spring Park and on to Thousand Buddha Mountain.

Taxi

Taxis start at Y7.50 for the first 3km, and are Y1.50 per kilometre thereafter.

Around Jǐ'nán

ZHŪJIĀYÙ 朱家峪

☎0531

With its coffee-coloured soil and unspoiled bucolic panoramas, the charming stone village of **Zhūjiāyù** (admission Y15), 80km east of Jǐ'nán, provides a fascinating foray into one of Shāndōng's oldest intact hamlets. Local claims that a settlement has been here since Shang times (1700–1100 BC) might be something of a stretch, but even though most of Zhūjiāyù's buildings date from the more recent Ming and Qing dynasties, walking its narrow streets is a journey way back in time. Residents are also incredibly proud of the village's role as a sometime Chinese movie and TV-drama set and many older locals now eke out a living playing tour guides (Y10, Chinese-speaking only), hired from inside the wall.

Shielded by hills on three sides, Zhūjiāyù can be fully explored in a morning or afternoon. Pay at the main gate in the restored wall enclosing the northern flank of the village and walk along the Ming-dynasty **double track old road** (双轨古道; *shuāngguǐ* *gǔdào*), which leads to the Qing-dynasty **Wénchāng Pavilion** (文昌阁; Wénchāng Gé), an arched gate topped by a single-roofed hall. On your left is **the Shānyīn Primary School** (山阴小学; Shānyīn Xiǎoxué), a series of halls and courtyards, several of which now contain exhibitions detailing local agricultural tools and techniques. Outside the school, a huge painted portrait of Chairman Mao dating from 1966 rears up ahead. The colours are slightly faded, but the image is surprisingly vivid.

The rest of the village largely consists of ancestral temples, including the **Zhu Family Ancestral Hall** (朱氏家祠; Zhūshì Jiācí), packed mudbrick homesteads (many are deserted and collapsing), small shrines and a delightful crop of arched *shíqiáo* (stone bridges). Hunt down the **Lìjiāo Bridge** (立交桥; Lìjiāo Qiáo), a brace of ancient arched bridges dating from 1671.

Zhūjiāyù becomes almost Mediterranean in feel when you reach the end of the village and drystone walls rise in layers up the hills. A further 30-minute climb will take you past a statue of Guanyin to the **Kuíxīng Pavilion** (魁星楼; Kuíxīng Lóu; admission Y2) crowning the hill above the village.

If you want to spend the night, check into the basic **Gǔcūn Inn** (古村酒家; Gǔcūn Jiǔjiā; ☎8380 8135; d with shower Y60), a lovely old building with a courtyard and a spirit wall decorated with a peacock, 80m from the Lìjiāo Bridge. The genial owners provide home-cooked dishes from Y10 (go into the kitchen and point at what you want to eat; beer available). For other eats, there are more than a few restaurants in the old village and streetside chefs fry up live scorpions and offer salty chive-stuffed pancakes for peckish visitors.

To reach Zhūjiāyù from Jǐnán, take a bus headed to BóShān (博山; Y26, 1½ hours) from Jǐnán's bus station (directly opposite the train station) and get the driver to drop you off at the mouth of the village, where it's a further 2km walk.

Buses leave from Zhūjiāyù to Míngshuǐ on the hour or so (Y4, 35 minutes). If there aren't any buses, try getting an outbound visitor to give you a ride (Y15 to Y30). Regular minibuses (Y13, 1½ hours, every 15 minutes, 5am to 6pm) return to Jǐnán from the Míngshuǐ long-distance bus station. You can also try to cross the road from the mouth of the village and flag down any bus heading back to Jǐnán.

Tài'ān 泰安

☎0538 / POP 933,760

Gateway to Tài Shān's sacred slopes, Tài'ān has a venerable tourist industry that has been in full swing since the time of the Ming dynasty. The 17th-century writer Zhang Dai described it as including packaged tours (with sedan chairs for the wealthy), a special mountain-climbing tax (eight *fen* silver), three grades of congratulatory banquets (for having attained the summit) and a number of enormous inns, each with more than 20 kitchens, hundreds of servants and opera performers, and enough courtesans to entertain an entire prefecture.

In comparison, today's Tài'ān is much tamer. Though there's not much to see outside of the magnificent Dài Temple, you will need the better part of a day for the mountain, so spending the night either here or at the summit is advised.

Sights

Dài Temple TEMPLE

(岱庙; Dài Miào; Daibeng Lu; admission Y20; ⏲8.30am-6pm summer, to 5.30pm winter) With its eternal-looking trees and commanding location at the hub of Tài'ān, this magnificent temple complex was a traditional pilgrimage stop on the route to the mountain and the site of sacrifices to the god of Tài Shān. It also forms a delightful portrait of Chinese temple architecture, with birds squawking among the hoary cypresses and ancient stelae looking silently on. Most visitors enter by the north gate (岱庙北入口处; Dài Miào Běi Rùkǒuchù) at the south end of Hongmen Lu, although entering the complex via the south gate allows you to follow the traditional passage through the temple.

You can scale the walls built above the north entrance: there's a weathered cypress tree that the wall was literally built around. The main hall is the colossal twin yellow-eaved, nine-bay-wide **Hall of Heavenly Blessing** (天贶殿; Tiānkuàng Diàn; slippers Y1), which dates to AD 1009. The dark interior is decorated with a marvellous, flaking, 62m-long Song-dynasty fresco depicting Emperor Zhenzong as the god of Tài Shān. Among the cast of characters are elephants, camels and lions, but the gloomy interior makes it hard to discern much.

South of the hall are several stelae supported on the backs of fossilised-looking *bìxì* (mythical tortoiselike dragons). Look out for the scripture pillar, its etched words

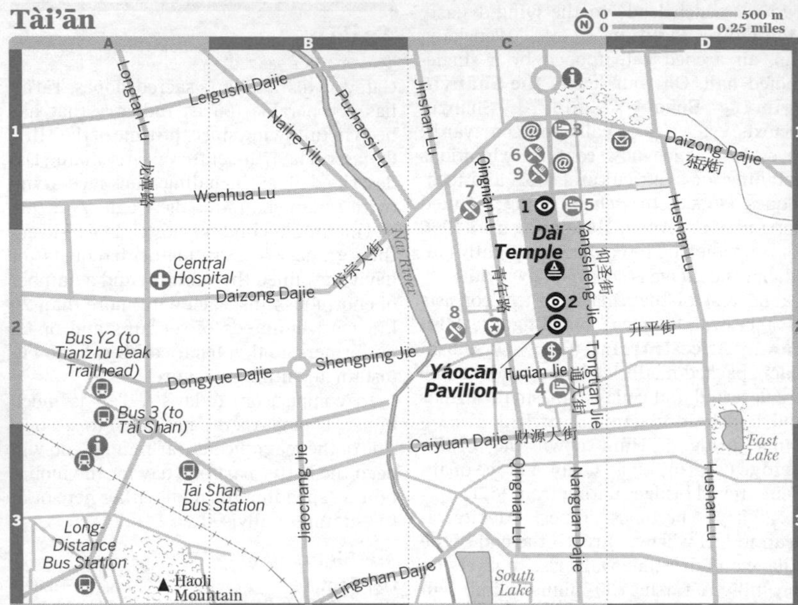

long lost to the Shāndōng winds and inquisitive hands. In the Han Bai courtyard stand cypresses supposedly planted by the Han emperor Wudi. Near the entrance to the courtyard is a vast *bìxì* with five-inch fangs.

To the south of the **south gate** (正阳门; Zhèngyáng Mén) is the splendid Dàimiào Fāng, a *páifāng* (ornamental arch) decorated with four pairs of heavily weathered lions, and dragon and phoenix motifs. Also south of the temple, the **Yáocān Pavilion** (遥参亭; Yáocān Tíng; admission Y1) contains a hall dedicated to effigies of the Old Mother of Taishan (Taishan Laomu), Bixia and a deity (Songzi Niangniang) entreated by women who want children. Further south still, a final memorial arch stands flanked by two iron lions alongside busy Dongyue Dajie.

Sleeping

There are many midrange options in town and a lot are clustered around the train station. Look at rooms and bargain before deciding. The Tài'ān Tourism Information Centre in front of the train station can help you book a room. Basic English is spoken.

Tài'ān

Top Sights
- Dài Temple C2
- Yáocān Pavilion C2

Sights
1. North Entrance to Dài Temple C1
2. South Entrance to Dài Temple C2

Sleeping

3. Roman Holiday C1
4. Tàishān International Youth Hostel C2
5. Yùzuò Hotel C1

Eating

6. Ā Dōng Jīa Cháng Cài C1
7. Beǐxīn Small Eats Street C1
8. Night Market C2
9. Sheng Tao Yang Coffee & Tea C1

Tàishān International Youth Hostel HOSTEL $

(太山国际青年旅舍; Tàishān Guójì Qīngnián Lǚshè; ☎628 5196; 25 Tongtian Jie; 通天街25号; dm Y40-60, d/tw/tr Y228/160/180; ❄@📶) Tài'ān's first youth hostel has clean spartan rooms decked out in pine furnishing and old communist posters, but there are still teething issues. Dorms are great value but avoid rooms on the 3rd floor as they lack internet access and TVs (same price though!). Bike rental, free laundry and a bar on the 3rd floor complete the picture. Limited English.

Yùzuò Hotel HOTEL $$$
(御座宾馆; Yùzuò Bīnguǎn; ☎826 9999; www.yuzuo.cn; 3 Daimiao Beijie; 岱庙北街3号; tw/d/ste Y480/680/780; ❄@) Pleasantly positioned next to the Dài Temple and attractively trimmed with lights at night, this traditionally styled three-star hotel is run by polite staff and ranges among low-rise, two-storey blocks. The imperial-themed rooms are done up in gold and mahogany, though cheaper rooms are rather ordinary. There's an attached bakery and restaurant (cooking up Taoist dishes).

Roman Holiday HOTEL $$
(罗马假日商务酒店; Luómǎ Jiàrì Shāngwù Jiǔdiàn; ☎627 9999; 18 Hongmen Lu; 红门路18号; s & tw Y298, d Y398; ❄@) The small, neat rooms come with see-through showers, glass sinks and striped carpets and wallpaper in this bizarrely named modern four-storey hotel. The location and comfort level are quite good and discounts take prices down to Y158 with breakfast. No Audrey Hepburn. We checked.

Eating

There are two busy streets offering assorted food. The **night market** (夜市; yè shì; ⏲5.30pm-late) located in the centre of town along the Nai River has many hotpot stalls. Pick your ingredients (fish balls, mushrooms, vegetables, noodles etc) then take a seat at a short table by the roadside. A large plastic jug of beer is Y6 and meals should cost Y20 or so. During the day, there's also the **Bèixīn Small Eats Street** (北新小吃步行街;Běixīn Xiǎochī Bùxíng Jīe) where you can find savoury breads, roast-meat skewers, fried chicken and more. Avoid the pedestrian food street to the east of the Dai Temple as prices are increased for tourists.

Ā Dōng Jīa Cháng Cài CHINESE $
(阿东家常菜; 25 Hongmen Lu; meals from Y10; 📖) This handily located, clean restaurant fills you up with *shuǐjiǎo* (水饺; dumplings), including lamb (Y24 per *jīn* – half a *jīn* is enough for one) and vegetable (Y18 per *jīn*) fillings among other choices. There's also a wide range of regular Chinese dishes.

Sheng Tao Yang Coffee & Tea INTERNATIONAL $$
(圣淘缘休闲餐厅; Shèngtáoyuán Xiūxián Cāntīng'; 29 Hongmen Lu; dishes Y25-150; 📶) The ivory baby grand piano beside the toilet may be overkill but the comfy couches, eager staff and huge 36-page menu are lovely. Yummy pizzas. There's also steak, spaghetti and Chinese dishes with rice. Chinese menu with lots of photos.

Information

Bank of China (中国银行; Zhōngguó Yínháng; Tongtian Jie; ⏲8.30am-5pm) The 24-hour ATM accepts foreign cards.

Central Hospital (中心医院; Zhōngxīn Yīyuàn; ☎822 4161; 29 Longtan Lu)

China Post (中国邮政; Zhōngguó Yóuzhèng; 85 Qingnian Lu; ⏲8.30am-5.30pm)

Public Security Bureau (PSB; 公安局; Gōng'ānjú; ☎827 5264; cnr Dongyue Dajie & Qingnian Lu; ⏲8.30am noon & 1-5pm Mon-Fri) Visa office is in the eastern side of this huge building.

Shùyù Píngmín Pharmacy (漱玉平民大药房; Shùyù Píngmín Dàyàofáng; 38 Shengping Jie; ⏲24hr)

Tài'ān Tourism Information Centre (泰安市旅游咨询中心; Tài'ānshì Lǚyóu Zīxún Zhōngxī) Hongmen Lu (22 Hongmen Lu; ☎218 7989; ⏲8am-8pm); Train station (☎688 7358; ⏲6am-midnight) Both offices do hotel, train and plane ticket bookings.

Train & Plane Ticket Bookings (华泰票务; Huátài Piàowù; ☎866 6600; 111 Qingnian Lu) Book air and train tickets (Y5 commission).

Wànjǐng Internet Cafe (万景网吧; Wànjǐng Wǎngbā; 180 Daizong Dajie; per hr Y1.50; ⏲7am-midnight)

World Net Bar Internet (大世界网吧; Dàshìjiè Wǎngbā; 2nd fl, 6 Hongmen Lu; per hr Y1.50; ⏲24hr)

Getting There & Away

You can easily move on to most major destinations from Jǐnán, 90 minutes to the north. Coming from elsewhere, buses and trains often refer to Tài'ān as Tài'shān. There are several places that can help with train and plane ticket bookings.

Bus

Buses leaving from the **long-distance bus station** (长途汽车站; chángtú qìchēzhàn; Panhe Lu), south of the train station:

Běijīng Y134, six hours, two daily (8.30am and 2.30pm)

Jǐ'nán Y22, 1½ hours, every 30 minutes (6.30am to 6pm)

Kāifēng Y98 to Y120, five hours, three daily (6.30am, 9am and 10.30am)

Qīngdǎo Y100, 5½ hours, three daily (6am, 8am and 2.30pm)

Qūfù Y21, one hour, hourly

Shànghǎi Y205, 12 hours, one daily (4.30pm)

Wēihǎi Y139, seven hours

Yāntái Y123, 6½ hours, one daily (7.20am)

From the **Tài Shān Bus Station** (泰山汽车站; Tàishān Qìchēzhàn; Caiyuan Dajie) there are regular buses to Jǐ'nán (Y20, 1½ hours, every 20 minutes, 6am to 6pm).

Train

Tickets can be hard to get here, so book early. Regular trains (hard seat/sleeper):

Běijīng Y158/296, seven to 10 hours, eight daily

Jǐ'nán hard seat Y11, one hour, regular

Nánjīng Y92/254, seven to 10 hours, 25 daily

Qīngdǎo Y70/140, six to seven hours, 11 daily

Shànghǎi Y224/352, eight to 14 hours, 14 daily

Express 'D' trains (hard/soft seat only):

Běijīng Y79/176, four hours, four daily

Nánjīng Y60/96, 4½ hours, five daily

Qīngdǎo Y70/108, 3½ hours, two daily (2.30pm and 7.15pm)

Shànghǎi Y90/140, seven hours, five daily

Getting Around

There are three main bus routes. Bus 3 (三路汽车(往泰山); Y1) runs from the Tài Shān central route trailhead to the western route trailhead at Tiānwài Village (Tiānwài Cūn) via the train station. Buses 1 and 2 also end up near the train station. Bus 4 goes from the train station to the Dai Temple. Bus Y2 (游二路汽车(往天烛峰景区) goes to the Tiānzhú Peak Trailhead.

Taxis start at Y6 (then Y1.50 per kilometre thereafter). Avoid unmetered three-wheelers.

Tài Shān 泰山

☎0538

Sacred mountains are a dime a dozen in China, but when push comes to shove, the one that matters the most is **Tài Shān** (admission Feb-Nov Y125, Dec-Jan Y100). Worshipped since at least the 11th century BC, the mountain rises up like a guardian of the Middle Kingdom, bestowing its divine sanction on worthy rulers and protecting the country from catastrophe. Anyone who's anyone in China has climbed it – from Confucius to Du Fu to Mao Zedong – and Qin Shi Huang, the First Emperor, chose the summit as the place from which to first proclaim the unity of the country in 219 BC.

It may not be as spectacular as Huángshān or as gigantic as Éméi Shān, but its history and supernatural allure more than make up for the lack in altitude. Follow the tribes of wiry grandmothers up the steps and into the mist, where temples to the mountain's daughter, the goddess Bixia, and the Jade Emperor await.

The best time to visit is in autumn when the humidity is low; the clearest weather is from early October onwards. In winter the weather is often fine, but very cold. The tourist season peaks from May to October.

Due to weather changes, you're advised to always carry warm clothing with you. The summit can be very cold, windy and wet; army overcoats are available there for hire (Y20 average) and you can buy waterproof coats from vendors.

Tài Shān itself is 1532m above sea level, with a walking distance of 7.5km from base to summit on the central route and an elevation change of about 1400m. Although it's not a major climb (there aren't any trails on the main route), with well over 6000 steps to the top, it can certainly be exhausting and should not be underestimated.

Avoid coinciding your climb with major public holidays, otherwise you will share the mountain with what the Chinese call *rén shān rén hǎi* – literally 'a mountain of people and a sea of persons'.

Sights & Activities

The climb up Tài Shān is more like one gigantic Stairmaster session than a hiking a trail (though that doesn't seem to stop some visitors from donning their Gore-Tex and CamelBaks). There are three routes up the mountain that can be followed on foot: the main **central route** (sometimes referred to as the east route), the **western route** (often used for bus descents) and the lesser-known **Tiānzhú Peak** route up the back of the mountain. The central and western routes converge at the halfway point (Midway Gate to Heaven), from where it's a final 3.5km of steep steps. Figure on about eight to nine hours round trip (four hours up, one to two hours at the summit, three hours down),

Tài Shān

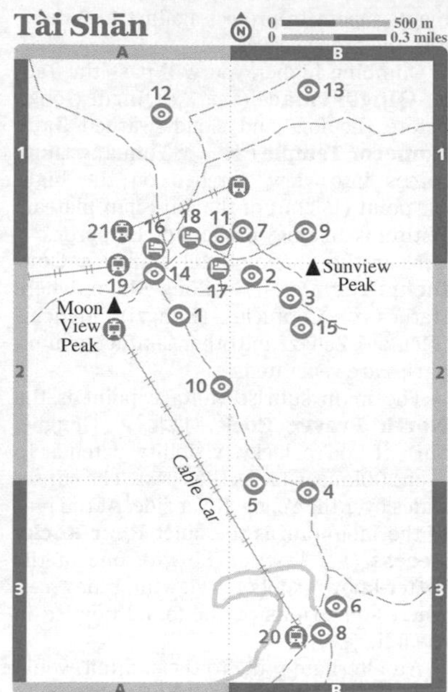

Tài Shān

Sights

1 Archway to Immortality....A2
2 Azure Clouds Temple....B2
3 Bridge of the Gods (Xiānrén Qiáo)....B2
4 Cloud Bridge (Yúnbù Qiáo)....B3
Confucius Temple....(see 17)
5 Five Pine Pavilion....B3
6 God of Wealth Temple....B3
7 Jade Emperor Temple....B1
8 Midway Gate to Heaven....B3
9 North Prayer Rock....B1
10 Opposing Pines Pavilion....A2
11 Qingdi Palace....A1
12 Rear Rocky Recess....A1
13 Rear Temple (Hòushí Wù)....B1
14 South Gate to Heaven....A2
Welcoming Pine....(see 10)
15 Zhanlu Terrace....B2

Sleeping

16 Nán Tiān Mén Bīnguǎn....A1
17 Shénqì Hotel....A2
18 Xiānjū Bīnguǎn....A1

Transport

19 Cable Car to Peach Blossom Park....A2
20 Cable Car to Peak....B3
21 Cable Car to Rear Rocky Access....A1

which includes time to visit the various sights along the way.

If that sounds like too much walking, or if you have bad knees, take a minibus up to Midway Gate to Heaven and then a cable car up to South Gate to Heaven, near the summit area. You can reverse this by climbing up and taking the cable car and then bus down.

As with all Chinese mountain hikes, viewing the sunrise is considered an integral part of the experience. If you want to greet the first rays of dawn, dump your gear at the train station, at a guesthouse in Tài'ān or at the foot of the central route and time your ascent so that you'll reach the summit before sundown. Stay overnight at one of the summit guesthouses and get up early the next morning for the famed sunrise.

CENTRAL ROUTE 中路

This has been the main route up the mountain since the 3rd century BC, and over the past 2000 years or so a bewildering number of bridges, trees, rivers, gullies, inscriptions, caves, pavilions and temples have become famous sights in their own right. Tài Shān essentially functions as an outdoor museum of calligraphic art, with the prize items being the **Rock Valley Scripture** (经石峪; Jīngshí Yù) along the first section of the walk and the **North Prayer Rock** (拱北石; Gǒngběi Shí), which commemorates an imperial sacrifice, at the summit.

Purists can begin their ascents with a south–north perambulation through Dài Temple in Tài'ān, 1.7km south of the trailhead, in imitation of imperial custom. Most climbers, however, begin at the **First Gate of Heaven** (一天门; Yītiān Mén), at the end of Hongmen Lu (at the foot of Taishan). Nearby is the **Guandi Temple** (关帝庙; Guāndì Miào), containing a large statue of Lord Guan. Beyond is a stone archway overgrown with wisteria upon which is written 'the place where Confucius began his ascent'.

Further along is **Red Gate Palace** (红门宫; Hóng Mén Gōng; admission Y5), with its wine-coloured walls. This is the first of a series of temples dedicated to Bixia. After this is a large gate called **Wànxiān Lóu** (万仙楼), and the **ticket office** (售票处; Shòupiào Chù). Further along is **Dǒumǔ Hall** (斗母宫; Dǒumǔ Gōng), first constructed in 1542 and given the more magical name of 'Dragon Spring Nunnery'. Along the way, look out for invocation-inscribed ribbons that festoon the pines and cypresses.

Continuing through the tunnel of cypresses known as Cypress Cave is **Huímǎ Peak** (Huímǎ Lǐng), where Emperor Zhenzong had to dismount and continue by sedan chair because his horse refused to go further. Allow two hours for the climb up to the halfway point, the **Midway Gate to Heaven** (中天门; Zhōng Tiān Mén), where the central and western routes converge. This is where some travellers, after gazing ahead at the steep steps that snake up in the distance, abandon walking for the cable car. Don't be disheartened as it's possible! Rest your legs, buy supplies, allow your pulse to slow and visit the small and smoky **God of Wealth Temple** (财神庙; Cáishén Miào).

Further along is **Five Pine Pavilion** (五松亭; Wǔsōng Tíng), where, in 219 BC, Emperor Qin Shi Huang was overtaken by a violent storm and was sheltered by the pine trees. Today, one lone pine stands, its limbs withered and wiry but still growing.

Ahead is the arduous **Path of Eighteen Bends** (十八盘) that eventually leads to the summit; climbing it is performed in slow motion by all and sundry as legs turn to lead. You'll pass **Opposing Pines Pavilion** (对松亭; Duìsōng Tíng) and the **Welcoming Pine** (迎客松; Yíngkè Sōng) – every mountain worth its salt in China has one – with a branch extended as if to shake hands. Beyond is the **Archway to Immortality** (升仙坊; Shēngxiān Fāng). It was believed that those passing through the archway would become celestial beings (we tried, didn't work). From here to the summit, emperors were carried in sedan chairs. Workers who lug up huge boxes of fruit on their backs give some impression of just how hard this task must have been.

The final stretch takes you to the **South Gate to Heaven** (南天门; Nán Tián Mén), the third celestial gate, which marks the beginning of the summit area. At the summit, bear right and walk along Tian Jie to **Azure Clouds Temple** (碧霞祠; Bìxiá Cí; admission Y5), with its sublime perch in the clouds, where elders offer money and food to the deities of Bixia, Yanguang Nainai and Taishan Songzi Niangniang (the latter helping women bear children). The iron tiling on the temple buildings is intended to prevent damage by strong winds, and *chīwěn* (ornaments meant to protect against fire) decorate the bronze eaves.

Climbing higher, you will pass the Taoist **Qīngdì Palace** (青帝宫; Qīngdì Gōng), before the fog- and cloud-swathed **Jade Emperor Temple** (玉皇顶; Yùhuáng Dǐng) comes into view, perched on the highest point (1532m) of the Tài Shān plateau. Within is an effigy of the Jade Emperor.

Near the Shénqì Hotel stands a **Confucius Temple** (孔庙; Kǒng Miào), where statues of Confucius (Kongzi), Mencius (Mengzi), Zengzi and other Confucian luminaries are venerated.

The main sunrise vantage point is the **North Prayer Rock** (拱北石; Gǒngběi Shí); if you're lucky, visibility extends to over 200km, as far as the coast. The sunset slides over the Yellow River side. At the rear of the mountain is the quiet **Rear Rocky Recess** (后石坞; Hòu Shíwù), one of the better-known spots for viewing pine trees, where some ruins can be found tangled in the foliage.

An alternate route to the summit would be to take a detour before the South Gate to Heaven and hit the Azure Clouds Temple. This is a less popular route as it's another long torturous set of steps to the top but it does allow you to avoid the tourist scrum at the main summit gate.

WESTERN ROUTE 西路

The most popular way to descend the mountain is by bus (Y30) via the western route. If you want to walk, the footpath and road intercept at a number of points, and are often one and the same. Given the amount of traffic, you might prefer to hop on a bus rather than inhale its exhaust. If you choose to hike up or down, you should be aware that unless you walk along the road, the trail is not always clearly marked. Buses will not stop for you once they have left the Midway Gate to Heaven.

Either by bus or foot, the western route treats you to considerable variation in scenery, with orchards, pools and flowering plants. The major attraction along this route is **Black Dragon Pool** (黑龙潭; Hēilóng Tán), which is just below **Longevity Bridge** (长寿桥; Chángshòu Qiáo) and is fed by a small waterfall. Swimming in the waters are rare carp. Mythical tales swarm about the pool, said to be the site of underground carp palaces and of magic herbs that turn people into beasts.

THE FIRST TEACHER

Born into a world of political instability, Confucius (551–479 BC) spent his life in vain, trying to reform society according to traditional ideals. By his own standards he was a failure, but over time he became one of the most influential thinkers the world has ever known – indeed, Confucius' main teachings and ideals continue to form the core of society in East Asia today.

Following a childhood spent in poverty, Confucius (Kongzi or Kongfuzi, literally 'Master Kong') began an unfulfilling government career in his home state of Lǔ. At the age of 50, he resigned and began travelling from state to state, hoping to find a ruler who would put his ideas into practice. He met with an unending string of setbacks and, after 13 years of wandering, returned home to Qūfù. He spent the remainder of his life here as a private teacher, expounding the wisdom of the Six Classics (*The Book of Changes, Songs, Rites, History, Music* and the *Spring and Autumn Annals;* according to legend he compiled all six). He was, notably, the first teacher in China to take on a large number of students, and his belief that everyone, not just the aristocracy, had the right to knowledge was one of his greatest legacies.

Confucius' teachings were recorded in *The Analects (Lúnyǔ)*, a collection of 497 aphoristic sayings compiled by his disciples. Although he drew many of his ideas from an ancient past that he perceived to be a kind of golden age, Confucius was in fact China's first humanist philosopher, upholding morality (humaneness, righteousness and virtue) and self-cultivation as the basis for social order.

For more on Confucian philosophy, see p936.

An enjoyable conclusion to your descent is a visit to **Pǔzhào Temple** (普照寺; Pǔzhào Sì, Pervading Light Temple; admission Y5; ⏲8am-5.30pm). One of the few strictly Buddhist shrines in the area, this simple temple dates to the Southern and Northern dynasties (AD 420–589). Its arrangement of ancient pine trees and small halls rising in levels up the hillside provides a quiet and restful end to the hike.

TIĀNZHÚ PEAK ROUTE 天烛峰景区

The lesser-known route up the back of the mountain through the **Tiānzhú Peak Scenic Area** (Tiānzhú Fēng Jǐngqū) provides more adventurous hikers a rare chance to ascend Tài Shān without the crowds. It's mostly ancient pines and peaks back here; visit the mountain's main sights by taking the central route down. Make sure you get an early start; the bus here takes 45 minutes, and the climb itself can take upwards of four hours. To get to the trailhead, take bus Y2 (游2; *yóu'èr;* Y3) from Caiyuan Dajie opposite the train station in Tài'ān to the terminus, Tiānzhú Fēng Jǐng (天烛峰景).

Sleeping & Eating

There are many hotels at the summit area along Tian Jie, catering to a range of budgets from Y160 and *way* up on weekends. Accommodation prices here don't apply to main holiday periods, when room prices can triple. At other times, always ask for discounts.

There is no food shortage on Tài Shān; the central route is dotted with teahouses, stalls, vendors and restaurants. Your pockets are likely to feel emptier than your stomach, but keep in mind that all supplies are carried up by foot and that the prices rise as you do. Water is Y2 to Y3, instant cup noodles Y5, and fruit ranges from Y5 to Y7 per *jīn*. Dishes at restaurants are priced on a menu and tend to cost at least double what you'd pay in the city.

Nán Tiān Mén Bīnguǎn HOTEL **$$**
(南天门宾馆; ☎833 0988; 1 Tian Jie; 天街1号; tw with shared bathroom Y880, tw/tr Y1480/1680; ❄@) Located smack bang before you turn into Tian Jie. Ignore the ridiculous asking prices, as we were offered Y1480 rooms and breakfast for Y300 (and a further discount when we looked unsure). Rooms are airy with mod cons and squat toilets.

Xiānjū Bīnguǎn HOTEL **$$**
(仙居宾馆; ☎823 9984; fax 822 6877; 2 Tian Jie; 天街2号; tw Y980, d & tr Y1080; ❄) Situated on the left just before the *páilou* marking Tian Jie (a signboard in Chinese marks the entrance), this two-star hotel has a decent

selection of rooms. Ask for a room with a window. Discounts bring a twin room down to Y260.

Shénqì Hotel HOTEL **$$$**
(神憩宾馆; Shénqì Bīnguǎn; ☎822 3866; fax 821 5399; d/ste Y1480/2080; ❄@) The fact that all the important guests to the summit stay here means that prices are inevitably high. It's a reasonably smart hotel with a restaurant (serving Taoist banquets) and a bar, and is reached by steep steps. Rooms are clean with a strange box-like shower hidden in a wooden cubicle.

Getting There & Away

Bus 3 runs from the Tài'ān train station to the Tài Shān central route trailhead via Hongmen Lu (Y1, 10 minutes) and, in the opposite direction, from Tài'ān's train station to the western route trailhead (Y1, 10 to 15 minutes) at Tiānwài Village (Tiānwài Cūn).

Getting Around

At Tiānwài Village (天外村; Tiānwài Cūn), at the foot of the western route, minibuses (Y30 each way) depart every 20 minutes (or when full) to the Midway Gate to Heaven, halfway up Tài Shān. The minibuses operate from 4am to 8pm during high season, less regularly during low season. Frequent buses (旅游客车; Lǚyóu Kèchē) come down the mountain.

The main **cable car** (空中索道; kōngzhōng suǒdào; one way/return Y80/140; ⏲7.30am-5.30pm 16 Apr-15 Oct, 8.30am-5pm 16 Oct-15 Apr) is a five-minute walk from Midway Gate to Heaven. The journey takes around 15 minutes to travel to Moon View Peak (Yuèguān Fēng), near the South Gate to Heaven (Nántiān Mén). Be warned: high-season and weekend queues may force you to wait up to two hours.

There is another **cable car** (桃花源索道; táohuāyuán suǒdào; one way/return Y80/140; ⏲7.30am-5.30pm 16 Apr-15 Oct, 8.30am-5pm 16 Oct-15 Apr) that takes you from north of South Gate to Heaven down to Peach Blossom Park (桃花源; Táohuā Yuán), a scenic area behind Tài Shān that is worth exploring. From here you can take a minibus to Tài'ān (Y25, 40 minutes). You can reverse this process by first taking a minibus from Tài'ān train station to Peach Blossom Park and then ascending by cable car.

A third, shorter **cable car** (后石坞索道; hòushíwù suǒdào; one way Y20; ⏲8.30am-4pm Apr-Oct, closed 16 Oct-15 Apr) comes up from the Rear Rocky Recess (后石坞; Hòu Shíwù) on the back of the mountain.

Qūfù 曲阜

☎0537 / POP 85,700

Hometown of the great sage, Confucius, and his ancestors, the Kong clan, Qūfù is a testament to just how important Confucian thought was in imperial China. The old walled town itself may be small, but everything else here – the temple, residences and even the cemetery – is gargantuan. In 2008 the provincial government revealed plans for a controversial US$4.2 billion 'cultural symbolic city' to be built nearby, beginning in 2010. As of writing, construction had yet to begin. For now, Master Kong's homestead is still king of the hill here.

The old walled core of Qūfù is small and easy to get around, a grid of streets built around the Confucius Temple and Confucius Mansions at its heart, with the Confucius Forest (and cemetery) north of town. Gulou Beijie bisects the town from north to south, and has at its centre the old Drum Tower (Gǔlóu). The city is increasingly modernising within its facade – expect bright lights, and a slew of Chinese clothing stores in the main shopping drag around Wumaci Jie. The bus station is 6km west of town.

⊙ Sights

Collectively, the principal sights – the Confucius Temple, the Confucius Mansions and the Confucius Forest – are known locally as the 'Sān Kǒng' ('Three Confuciuses'). The main ticket office (售票处; Shòupiàochù) is at the corner of Queli Jie and Nanma Dao, east of the Confucius Temple's main entrance. This is where you should purchase a combined ticket (Y150) to all three sights and can hire an English-speaking guide (Y100). From 16 November to 14 February, tickets are Y10 cheaper than those listed and sights close an hour earlier.

Confucius Temple TEMPLE
(孔庙; Kǒng Miào; admission Y90; ⏲8am-5.30pm) China's largest imperial building complex after the Forbidden City, the temple actually started out as a simple memorial hall 2500 years ago, gradually mushrooming into today's compound, which is one-fifth the size of the Qūfù town centre. Like shrines to Confucius everywhere, it has an almost museumlike quality, with none of the worshippers or incense-burning rituals that animate religious temples. There is also little in the way of imagery, and the principal disciples and thinkers of Confucian

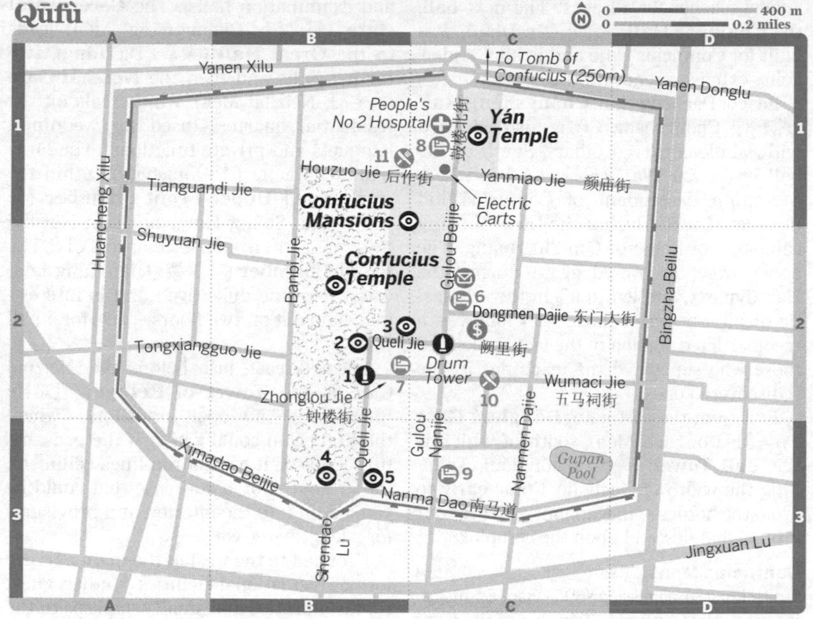

thought are only paid tribute to with simple tablets, in the wings of the main courtyards. It also seems strange that emperors seem to get more mention here than the actual sage himself!

The main entrance in the south passes through a series of triple-door gates, leading visitors to two airy, cypress-filled courtyards. About halfway along the north–south axis rises the triple-eaved **Great Pavilion of the Constellation of Scholars** (奎文阁; Kuíwén Gé), an imposing Jin-dynasty wooden structure containing faded prints illustrating Confucius' exploits in *The Analects*. Beyond lie a series of colossal, twin-eaved stele pavilions, followed by **Dàchéng Gate** (大成门; Dàchéng Mén), north of which is the **Xìngtán Pavilion** (杏坛; Xìng Tán), marking the spot from where Confucius allegedly taught his students.

The core of the complex is the huge yellow-eaved **Dàchéng Hall** (大成殿; Dàchéng Diàn), which, in its present form, dates from 1724; it towers 31m on a white marble terrace. Craftspeople carved the 10 dragon-coiled columns so expertly that they had to be covered with red silk when Emperor Qianlong visited, lest he felt that the Forbidden City's Hall of Supreme Harmony paled in comparison.

Qūfù

Top Sights
- Confucius Mansions ... B1
- Confucius Temple ... B2
- Yán Temple ... C1

Sights
1. Bell Tower ... B2
2. Dōnghuá Gate ... B2
3. Entrance to Confucius Mansions ... B2
4. Entrance to Confucius Temple ... B3
5. Main Ticket Office ... B3

Sleeping
6. Mingya Confucianist Hotel ... C2
7. Quèlǐ Hotel ... B2
8. Qūfù International Youth Hostel ... C1
9. Yǐngshì Bīnguǎn ... C3

Eating
10. Night Market ... C2
11. Yù Shū Fáng ... B1

Inside is a huge statue of Confucius residing on a throne, housed in a red and gold burnished cabinet. Above the sage are the characters for *'wànshì shībiǎo'*, meaning 'model teacher for all ages'. The next hall, the **Chamber Hall** (寝殿; Qǐn Diàn), was built for Confucius' wife and is now undergoing extensive renovations.

East of Dàchéng Hall, **Chóngshèng Hall** (崇圣祠; Chóngshèng Cí) is also adorned with fabulous carved pillars. South of the hall is the **Lǔ Wall** (鲁壁; Lǔ Bì), where the ninth descendant of Confucius hid the sacred texts during the book-burning campaign of Emperor Qin Shi Huang. The books were discovered again during the Han dynasty, and led to a lengthy scholastic dispute between those who followed a reconstructed version of the last books and those who supported the teachings in the rediscovered ones.

Exit from the east gate, **Dōnghuá Gate** (东华门; Dōnghuá Mén), south of which is the **Bell Tower** (钟楼; Zhōnglóu), spanning the width of Queli Jie. Come early to avoid the hordes of megaphone-blaring tour groups that descend upon the complex.

Confucius Mansions MUSEUM

(孔府; Kǒng Fǔ; admission Y60; ⏲8am-6pm) Adjacent to the Confucius Temple are the Confucius Mansions, a maze of 450 halls, rooms, buildings and side passages originally dating from the 16th century.

The mansions were the most sumptuous aristocratic lodgings in China, indicative of the Kong family's former power. From the Han to the Qing dynasties, the descendants of Confucius were ennobled and granted privileges by the emperors. They lived like kings themselves, with 180-course meals, servants and consorts.

Qūfù grew around the Confucius Mansions and was an autonomous estate administered by the Kongs, who had powers of taxation and execution. Emperors could drop in to visit; the Ceremonial Gate near the south entrance was opened only for this event. Because of this royal protection, huge quantities of furniture, ceramics, artefacts and customary and personal effects survived, but many are kept hidden. The Kong family archives are a rich legacy and also survived. As with many 'cultural sights' in China, the mansion is undergoing a makeover and sometimes it's hard to tell what's original and what's a modern alteration.

The Confucius Mansions are built on an 'interrupted' north–south axis. Grouped by the south gate are the former administrative offices (taxes, edicts, rites, registration and examination halls). The **Ceremonial Gate** (重光门; Chóngguāng Mén) leads to the **Great Hall** (大堂; Dà Táng), two further halls and then the **Nèizhái Gate** (内宅门; Nèizhái Mén), which seals off the residential quarters (used for weddings, banquets and private functions). The large *'shòu'* character (寿; longevity) within the single-eaved **Upper Front Chamber** (前上房; Qián Shàng Fáng) north of Nèizhái Gate was a gift from Qing empress Cixi. The **Front Chamber** (前堂楼; Qián Táng Lóu) was where the duke lived and is interestingly laid out on two floors – rare for a hall this size.

Located east just before the Nèizhái Gate is the **Tower of Refuge** (避难楼; Bìnàn Lóu) – not open to visitors – where the Kong clan could gather if the peasants turned nasty. It has an iron-lined ceiling on the ground floor, a staircase that could be yanked up into the interior, and provisions for a lengthy retreat.

Grouped to the west of the main axis are former recreational facilities (studies, guest rooms, libraries and small temples). To the east is the odd kitchen, ancestral temple and the family branch apartments. The last stop is the garden at the rear, where greenery, flowers and a sense of space (but not quiet) await.

Confucius Forest CEMETERY

(孔林; Kǒng Lín; admission Y40; ⏲7.30am-6pm) Around 2km north of town on Lindao Lu is the peaceful Confucius Forest, the largest artificial park and best-preserved cemetery in China.

The pine and cypress forest of over 100,000 trees covers 200 hectares and is bounded by a wall 10km long. Confucius and his descendants have been buried here over the past 2000 years, a tradition that continues today. In summer, wild flowers add a burst of colour amid the sea of green grass which threatens to envelop the haphazard arrangement of tombs and burial mounds.

Flanking the approach to the **Tomb of Confucius** (孔子墓; Kǒngzǐ Mù) are pairs of stone panthers, griffins and larger-than-life guardians. The tomb itself is a simple grass mound enclosed by a low wall and faced with a Ming-dynasty stele. Visitors always seem unsure if they should adopt respectful postures or do the whole 'Look at me! I'm at Confucius' tomb!' poses.

The sage's son and grandson are buried nearby, and scattered through the forest are dozens of temples and pavilions. A slow circuit through the peaceful gardenlike cemetery should take two to three hours. For those in a hurry, small minibuses do a circuit (one way/return Y10/20).

Electric carts (电动旅游车; Diàndòng Lǚyóu Chē; Y15 return) run to the temple from the corner of Houzuo Jie and Gulou Beijie, near the exit of the Confucius Mansions. Otherwise take a pedicab (Y3 to Y5) or bus 1 (Y2) from along Gulou Beijie. To reach the forest on foot takes about 30 minutes.

Yán Temple TEMPLE
(颜庙; Yán Miào; Yanmiao Jie; admission Y50; ⏲8am-5pm) A recent makeover is responsible for the *five-fold* (!) admission increase. The tranquil and little-visited Yán Temple northeast of the Confucius Mansions opens to a large grassy courtyard with some vast stele pavilions sheltering dirty stelae and antediluvian *bìxì*. The main hall, **Fùshèng Hall** (复圣殿; Fùshèng Diàn), is 17.5m high, with a hip and gable roof, and a magnificent ceiling decorated with the motif of a dragon head. Outside the hall are four magnificently carved pillars with coiling dragon designs and a further set of 18 octagonal pillars engraved with gorgeous dragon and floral patterns. The architecture is strikingly similar to that of the Confucius Temple.

Festivals & Events

The Confucius Temple holds two major festivals a year, **Tomb Sweeping Day** (usually 5 April; celebrations may last all weekend) and the **Sage's Birthday** (28 September). There are also two fairs each year in Qūfù – spring and autumn – when the place comes alive with craftspeople, healers, acrobats, peddlers and peasants.

Sleeping

TOP CHOICE **Qūfù International Youth Hostel** HOSTEL $
(曲阜国际青年旅舍; Qūfù Guójì Qīngnián Lǚshè; ☎441 8989; www.yhaqf.com; Gulou Beijie; 鼓楼北街北首路西; dm Y35-45, tw Y100-130, tr Y150; ❄@📶) A fantastic hostel at the northern end of Gulou Beijie. Rooms are so clean you can smell the fresh linen. English-speaking staff, free internet, bike rental, ticket reservations (Y15 to Y20 commission), a cafe/bar (cocktails are Y15!) serving Chinese and Western meals, and free laundry. Dorms have five to eight beds with a shared bathroom. Only fault? Wafer-thin mattresses.

Mingya Confucianist Hotel HOTEL $$
(名雅儒家大饭店; Míngyǎ Rújīa Dàfàndiàn; ☎505 0888; 8 Gulou Beijie; 鼓楼北街8号; s & d Y388, discounts of 35%; ❄@) While we're not sure if the great sage would approve of his name on a hotel banner, we are sure he would like the fab location (smack-bang in the middle of town) and would be more than pleased with the large comfy rooms and well-mannered staff. Free breakfast and discounts offered.

Quèlǐ Hotel HOTEL $$$
(阙里宾舍; Quèlǐ Bīnshè; ☎486 6818; www.quelihotel.com; 15 Zhonglou Jie; 钟楼街15号; s Y398-598, tw Y498-568, ste Y1288; ❄@) The four-star Quèlǐ might be the highest-rated hotel in town, and with its tile roof and ornate decor it looks very much the part as *the* tourist hotel…in reality, it's in dire need of a refurbishment. Rooms are musty and rough round the edges (the door knob nearly fell off when we visited). Even the photos of visiting dignitaries are fading.

Yǐngshì Bīnguǎn HOTEL $$
(影视宾馆; ☎441 1503; Gulou Nanjie; 鼓楼南街南首路东; d, tw & tr Y168-188; ❄) At the southern end of the old town, this place has definitely been around. The tidy rooms are clean with off-white walls, wooden trimming and at times have the usual faint whiff of smoke. Shower and Western toilets are pokey. In low-season, pay Y70 to Y90 for a room if you bargain.

Eating

Head to either the area around **Shendao Lu** (south of the Confucius Temple), or the **night market** (夜市; Yèshì), off Wumaci Jie, east of Gulou Nanjie. In addition to noodles and skewers of meat, look for sellers of *jiānbǐng guǒzi* (煎饼裹子; Y2 to Y3), a steaming crêpelike parcel of egg, vegetables and chilli sauce. If you want a sit-down meal, you can stop at stalls that display raw produce: point at what you want to eat and get the sellers to cook it up. For those with gutsier stomachs, snails and dog meat are available. The **Qūfù International Hostel** also serves up decent Western and Chinese dishes.

Yù Shū Fáng CHINESE BANQUET $$$
(御书房; ☎441 9888; 2nd fl, Houzuo Jie; set meals Y128) With private 2nd-floor rooms overlooking the Confucius Mansions, this

is a fantastic place to take a breather after having successfully navigated several kilometres of courtyards. Recharge with some divine oolong tea (铁观音; *tiě guānyīn*) – cup (杯) from Y10, pot (壶) from Y30; or splash out for a banquet meal where nine (!) Kong family dishes are served in quick succession. No English spoken; enter by the door staffed by *qipao*-clad ladies beside the 1st-floor furniture store (the owner is a woodcarver).

Information

ATMs accepting international credit cards are along or just off Gulou Beijie. Internet cafes are just off Wumaci Jie (Y3 to Y5 per hour; look out for 网吧). Most hotel rooms have an ethernet cable or PC. Surf the net at Qūfù International Youth Hostel (Y5 per hour).

Bank of China (中国银行; Zhōngguó Yínháng; 96 Dongmen Dajie; ⏲8.30am-4.30pm) Foreign exchange and ATM.

China Post (中国邮政; Zhōngguó Yóuzhèng; 8-1 Gulou Beijie; ⏲7.30am-6.30pm summer, 8am-6pm winter)

Gŭlóu Pharmacy (二鲁抗大药店; ÈrlŭKàng Dàyàofáng; ☎442 8167; 12 Gulou Beijie; ⏲7.30am-9pm)

People's No 2 Hospital (第二人民医院; Dì'èr Rénmín Yīyuàn; 7 Gulou Beijie)

Public Security Bureau (PSB; 公安局; Gōng'ānjú; ☎443 0049; 1 Wuyuntan Lu; ⏲8.30am-noon & 2-6pm Mon-Fri)

Getting There & Away

Bus

Qūfú's **long-distance bus station** (汽车站; Qìchēzhàn; ☎441 2554) is 6km southwest of the walled city. **Left luggage** (Y2; ⏲6am-6pm) is available here.

Běijīng Y160 to Y180, six hours, four daily (8.10am, 11.20am, 3pm and 5.30pm)

Jĭ'nán Y44, three hours, every 30 minutes

Qīngdǎo Y125, five hours, five daily (8.30am, 9.30am, 1.30pm, 2.20pm and 4.40pm)

Tài'ān Y21, one hour, every 30 minutes

Yǎnzhōu Y5, 20 minutes, frequent services

Train

When a railway project for Qūfù was first tabled, the Kong family petitioned for a change of routes, claiming that the trains would disturb Confucius' tomb. They won and the nearest tracks were routed to Yǎnzhōu (兖州), 16km west of Qūfù. Eventually another **train station** (☎442 1571) was constructed about 6km east of Qūfù, but only slow trains stop there, so it is more convenient to go to **Yǎnzhōu train station** (☎346 2965), on the line from Běijīng to Shànghǎi. Minibuses connect Yǎnzhōu bus station (walk straight ahead as you exit the train station, cross the car park and turn right; the bus station is 50m on the left) with Qūfù (Y5, 30 minutes, every 15 minutes, 6.30am to 5.30pm). Otherwise, a taxi from Yǎnzhōu train station to Qūfù should cost from Y40 to Y50.

Buy your tickets at the **railway booking office** (火车售票处; huǒchē shòupiào chù; ☎335 2276; 8 Jingxuan Lu; ⏲7am-9pm); Y5 commission. The Qūfù International Youth Hostel also books tickets (Y15 to Y20 commission).

Běijīng D train, 2nd/1st class Y75/100, 4½ hours, two daily, other regular trains

Jĭ'nán Y24, two hours, frequent services

Nánjīng D train, 2nd/1st class Y50/79, four hours, two daily, other regular trains

Qīngdǎo Y48 to Y144, seven to nine hours, 12 daily

Shànghǎi D train, 2nd/1st class Y77/123, six hours, two daily, other regular trains

Tiānjīn Y56 to Y164, six to 8½ hours, regular services

Getting Around

Bus 1 travels along Gulou Beijie and Lindao Lu, connecting the bus station with the Confucius Forest. A taxi from the long-distance bus station to the city should cost Y15 and a pedicab Y5.

Pesky pedicabs (Y2 to Y3 to most sights within Qūfù) infest the streets, chasing all and sundry. Decorated tourist horse carts can take you on 30-minute tours (Y20 to the Confucius Forest from Queli Jie).

Qīngdǎo 青岛

☎0532 / POP 1.73 MILLION

A breath of (literally) crisp sea air for anyone emerging from China's polluted urban interior, Qīngdǎo is hardly old-school China, but its effortless blend of German architecture and modern city planning puts most Chinese white-tile towns to shame. Its German legacy more or less intact, Qīngdǎo takes pride in its unique appearance: the Chinese call the town 'China's Switzerland'. The beaches may be overhyped and the CBD nothing special, but the dilapidated charms of the hillside villas and old town are captivating and the upbeat modern district is a veritable foodie's delight. In certain areas, one certainly gets the feel of concession Shànghǎi, albeit grittier. Of course, it's also home to 'that' beer...the ubiquitous Tsingtao.

Backing onto mountainous terrain to the northeast and hedged in between Jiāozhōu Bay, Láoshān Bay and the Yellow Sea, central Qīngdǎo (the area of interest for more visitors) is divided into three main neighbourhoods. In the west is the old town (the former concession area), with the train and bus stations, historic architecture and budget accommodation. In the centre is upscale Bādàguān, a picturesque residential area dotted with parks and old villas. In the east is the new city, known as the central business district, where Qīngdǎo's office towers and best hotels soar above the trendy restaurants and bars, innumerable malls and shoppers.

History

Before catching the acquisitive eye of Kaiser Wilhelm II, Qīngdǎo was an innocuous fishing village, although its excellent strategic location had not been lost on the Ming, who built a battery here. German forces wrested the port town from the Chinese in 1898 after the murder of two German missionaries, and Qīngdǎo was ceded to Germany for 99 years. Under German rule the famous Tsingtao Brewery opened in 1903, electric lighting was installed, missions and a university were established and the railway to Jǐ'nán was built. The Protestant church was handing out hymnals by 1908, and a garrison of 2000 men was deployed and a naval base established.

In 1914 the Japanese moved into town after the successful joint Anglo-Japanese naval bombardment of the port. Japan's position in Qīngdǎo was strengthened by the Treaty of Versailles, and they held the city until 1922 when it was ceded back to the Kuomintang. The Japanese returned in 1938, after the start of the Sino-Japanese War, and occupied the town until defeated in 1945. Since then, Qīngdǎo's fortunes have risen. It is one of the largest ports in China and a major manufacturing centre (home to both domestic and international brands). Qīngdǎo hosted the Olympic sailing events in 2008.

Sights

Most sights are squeezed into the old town, though walkers will prefer hilly Bādàguān to the west, which is generally more picturesque and a better area to wander. The Qīngdǎo Municipal Government has put up plaques identifying notable historic buildings and sites.

St Michael's Catholic Church CHURCH
(天主教堂; Tiānzhǔ Jiàotáng; 15 Zhejiang Lu; admission Y5; ⏲8am-5pm Mon-Sat, noon-5pm Sun) Completed in 1934, the twin-spired church, up a steep hill off Zhongshan Lu, is a grand edifice with a cross on each spire. The church was badly damaged during the Cultural Revolution and the crosses were torn off. God-fearing locals rescued them, however, and buried them in the hills. The interior is splendid, with white walls, gold piping, sections of stained glass all around and lots of technicolour murals. Look up the back to see an enormous organ that is still used for services. Put aside time to roam the area around here – a lattice of ancient hilly streets where old folk sit on wooden stools in decrepit doorways, playing cards and shooting the breeze.

Protestant Church CHURCH
(基督教堂; Jīdū Jiàotáng; 15 Jiangsu Lu; admission Y7; ⏲8.30am-5pm, weekend services) On a street notable for its German architecture, this church was designed by Curt Rothkegel and built in 1908. The interior is simple and Lutheran in its sparseness, apart from some delightful carvings on the pillar cornices. You can climb up to inspect the mechanism of its clock (Bockenem 1909). It is also well worth wandering along nearby Daxue Lu for a marvellous scenic view of old German Qīngdǎo.

Qīngdǎo Yíng Bīnguǎn CONCESSION BUILDING
(青岛迎宾馆; Qingdǎo Yíng Hotel; admission summer/winter Y15/10; ⏲8.30am-5pm) To the east of Xìnhàoshān Park remains one of Qīngdǎo's most interesting pieces of German architecture – the former German governor's residence and a replica of a German palace. Built in 1903, it is said to have cost 2,450,000 taels of silver. When Kaiser Wilhelm II got the bill, he immediately sacked the extravagant governor. In 1957 Chairman Mao stayed here with his wife and kids on holiday. It's now a museum.

Huāshí Lóu CONCESSION BUILDING
(花石楼; Huāshí Bldg; 18 Huanghai Lu; admission Y6.50; ⏲8am-5.30pm) The castlelike villa built in 1930 was originally the home of a Russian aristocrat, and later the German governor's retreat for fishing and hunting. The Chinese call it the 'Chiang Kaishek Building' as the generalissimo secretly stayed here in 1947. While most of the rooms in the house are closed, what's open is enough to evoke a sense of the

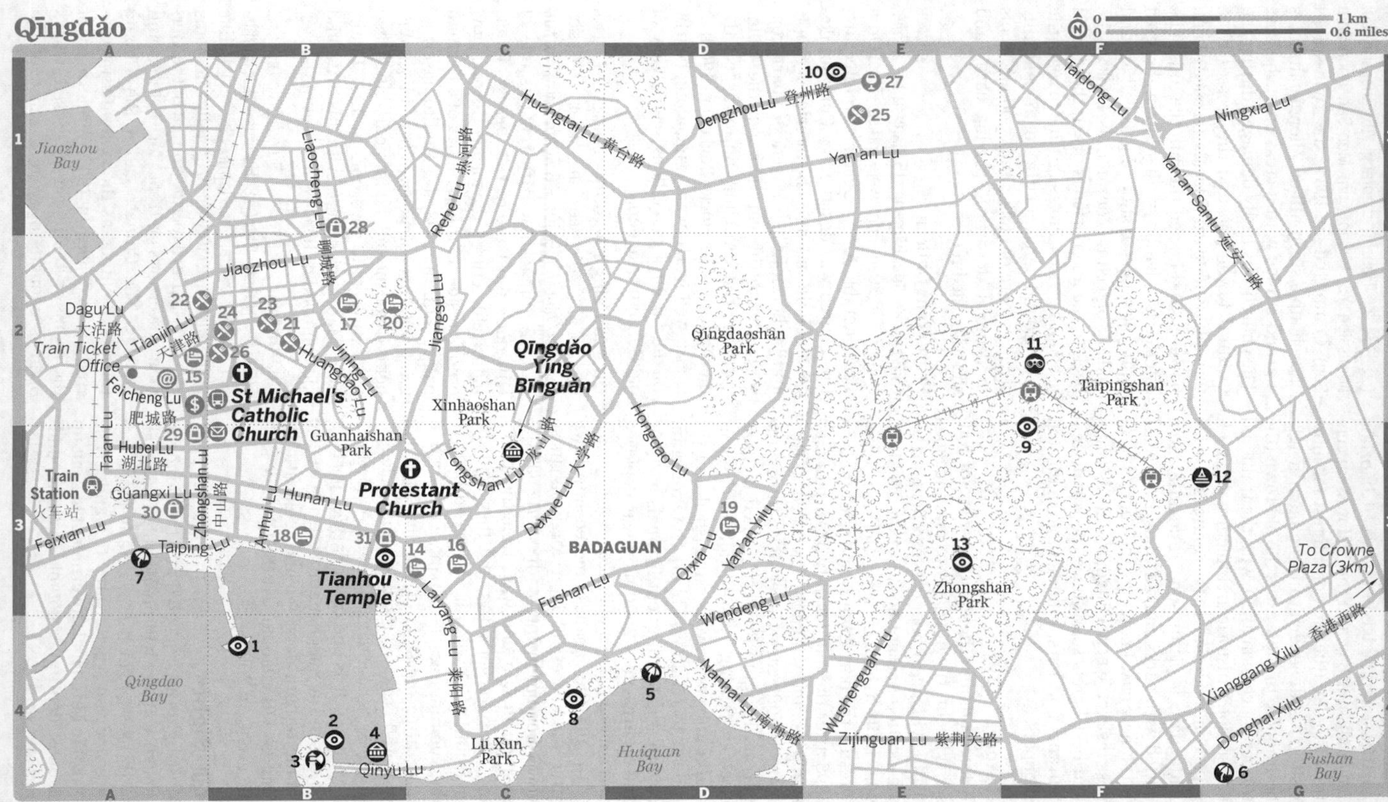
Qīngdǎo
0
1 km
0
0.6 miles
Jiaozhou Bay
Qingdao Bay
Huiquan Bay
Fushan Bay
Dagu Lu
大沽路
Train Ticket Office
Tianjin Lu
天津路
Feicheng Lu
肥城路
Hubei Lu
湖北路
Taian Lu
Train Station
火车站
Guangxi Lu
Feixian Lu
Zhongshan Lu
中山路
Taiping Lu
Anhui Lu
Hunan Lu
Jiaozhou Lu
Huangdao Lu
Jining Lu
Liaocheng Lu
聊城路
St Michael's Catholic Church
Guanhaishan Park
Protestant Church
Tianhou Temple
Xinhaoshan Park
Jiangsu Lu
Rehe Lu
热河路
Qīngdǎo Yíng Bīnguǎn
Longshan Lu
龙山路
Daxue Lu
大学路
Hongdao Lu
BADAGUAN
Fushan Lu
Laiyang Lu
莱阳路
Lu Xun Park
Qinyu Lu
Huangtai Lu
黄台路
Dengzhou Lu
登州路
Yan'an Lu
Qingdaoshan Park
Qixia Lu
Yan'an Xilu
Wendeng Lu
Nanhai Lu
南海路
Wushengguan Lu
Zijinguan Lu
紫荆关路
Zhongshan Park
Taipingshan Park
Taidong Lu
Ningxia Lu
Yan'an Sanlu
延安三路
To Crowne Plaza (3km)
Xianggang Xilu
香港西路
Donghai Xilu
A
B
C
D
E
F
G
1
2
3
4
1
2
3
4
5
6
7
8
9
10
11
12
13
14
15
16
17
18
19
20
21
22
23
24
25
26
27
28
29
30
31

Qīngdǎo

times. Clamber up two narrow stairwells to get to the top of the turret. The surrounding views of the hills behind and the bay in front are stunning. Located at the eastern end of the No 2 Bathing Beach and at the southern tip of Zijingguan Lu.

FREE **Tianhou Temple** TEMPLE
(天后宫; Tiānhòu Gōng; 19 Taiping Lu; ⏲7am-7pm summer, 8am-5pm winter) This small restored temple is dedicated to Tianhou (Heaven Queen), Goddess of the Sea and protector of sailors. The main hall contains a colourful statue of Tianhou, flanked by two figures and a pair of fearsome guardians. Other halls include the Dragon King Hall (龙王殿; Lóngwáng Diàn), where in front of the Dragon King lies a splayed pig, and a shrine to the God of Wealth. What's absolutely incongruous and rather amusing are the many temple attendants who hawk joss sticks to visitors and literally command them to pay their respects.

Little Qīngdǎo LIGHTHOUSE
(小青岛; Xiǎo Qīngdǎo; 8 Qinyu Lu; admission Y10; ⏲7.30am-6.30pm) Poking like a lollipop into Qīngdǎo Bay south of No 6 Bathing Beach, and dominated by its white German-built lighthouse, this spot along the peninsula is excellent for throwing off the crowds battling it out on the beaches. Set your alarm to catch early-morning vistas of the hazy bay and the town coming to life from the promontory's leafy park.

Navy Museum MUSEUM
(海军博物馆; Hǎijūn Bówùguǎn; admission Y50; ⏲8am-5pm) Just adjacent to Little Qīngdǎo, this 'museum' is really a rusty submarine and destroyer permanently anchored in the harbour. There are, of course, displays on the Chinese Navy.

Qingdao Underwater World AQUARIUM
(青岛海底世界; Qīngdǎo Hǎidǐ Shìjie; www.qhdworld.com; 1 Laiyang Lu; summer/winter Y120/100; ⏲8am-6pm) Kids will love this long-standing aquarium, with its spectacular 82m underwater glass-enclosed tunnel and various underwater performances. Just avoid going on the weekend, when the queues are maddening and you get pushed along, production-line style.

Tsingtao Beer Museum MUSEUM
(青岛啤酒博物馆; Qīngdǎo Píjiǔ Bówùguǎn; 56 Dengzhou Lu; admission Y50; ⏲8.30am-4.30pm) For a self-serving introduction to China's

MADE IN TSINGTAO

The beer of choice in Chinese restaurants around the world, Tsingtao is one of China's oldest and most familiar brands. Established in 1903 by a joint German-British beer corporation, the red-brick Tsingtau Germania-Brauerei began its life as a micro-brewery of sorts, producing two varieties of beer (Pilsener Light and Munich Dark) for the concession town, using natural mineral water from nearby Láo Shān. In 1914 the Japanese occupied Qīngdǎo and confiscated the plant, which, as far as the beer was concerned, wasn't such a bad thing: the rechristened Dai Nippon Brewery increased production and began distributing 'Tsingtao' throughout China. In 1949, after a few years under the Kuomintang, the communists finally got hold of the prized brewery, and over the next three decades (marked by xenophobia and a heavily regulated socialist economy) Tsingtao accounted for an astounding 98% of all of China's exports. Today the company continues to dominate China's beer export market and is partly owned by the beer colossus Anheuser-Busch InBev.

You can buy Tsingtao beer by the bag from streetside vendors, but pouring it requires skill. Of course, a visit to the original Tsingtao brewery should be in order too.

iconic beer, head to the original (still functioning) brewery. It's disappointingly comprised of old photos, brewery equipment (the smell of hops has absolutely permeated the place) and statistics, but there are a few glimpses of the modern factory, including a fascinating section overlooking the bottling and packing line. Thankfully, you can stop and sample some product along the way. Alternatively, skip the tour and head straight for Beer St outside the entrance. Bus 221 runs here from Zhongshan Lu; get off at the stop '15中' *(shíwǔ zhōng)*. A taxi from the old town will cost Y10.

Qīngdǎo Beaches BEACHES

(青岛沙滩; Qīngdǎo Shātān) Qīngdǎo is famed for its six beaches, which are pleasant enough, but don't go expecting the French Riviera. Chinese beach culture is low-key, although the main swimming season (June to September) sees hordes of sun-seekers fighting for towel space. Shark nets, lifeguards, lifeboat patrols and medical stations are at hand. If you give in to the many touts in the area, you can take a boat ride around the bay for Y10 to Y20 depending on the size of the boat.

Qīngdǎo's largest beach is draped along the shore, way off in the east of town. **Shílǎorén Bathing Beach** (石老人; Donghai Donglu) is a 2.5km-long strip of clean sand and seawater-smoothed seashells, occasionally engulfed in banks of mist pouring in from offshore. The area around the beach has undergone heavy development in recent years, and has lost some of its charm. The beach gets its name from a hunk of rock sticking out from a rocky strip a few kilometres up the road. If you squint hard enough and have a good imagination, you just might make out a 'Stone Old Man'. Take bus 304 from Zhàn Bridge (Zhàn Qiáo, Y2.50, 45 minutes) or hop in a taxi (Y20). If you take the bus, stop off at the Hái'er Lú (海尔) stop and head east. On the way, look out for the dilapidated Qingdao International Beer City – this once popular amusement park sponsored by the Tsingtao Beer Company now lies in what looks like postapocalyptic ruins.

Close to the train station is the **No 6 Bathing Beach** and neighbouring **Zhàn Bridge** (Zhàn Qiáo), a pier that reaches out into the bay and is tipped with the eight-sided **Huílán Pavilion** (Huílán Gé), constantly packed to the rafters with tourists. The pavilion is the very same one used on the logo of Tsingtao beer labels.

Near the centre of town, the sand of **No 1 Bathing Beach** is coarse-grained, engulfed in seaweed, and bordered by concrete beach huts and bizarre statues of dolphins. The nearby **Bādàguān** area is well known for its sanatoriums and exclusive guesthouses. The spas are scattered in lush wooded zones off the coast, and each street is lined with a different tree or flower, including maple, myrtle, peach, snow pine or crab apple. This is a lovely area in which to stroll.

Heading out of Eight Passes Area, Nos 2 and 3 Bathing Beaches are just east, and the villas lining the headlands are exquisite. **No 2 Bathing Beach** is cleaner, quieter and more sheltered than No 1 Bathing Beach and probably Qīngdǎo's best beach within the city limits. It's not uncommon to see dozens of couples dressed in wedding outfits, getting their photos taken. Huāshí Loú backs onto this beach. You can stroll west along this beach back into town.

Qīngdǎo Parks PARKS
Within this area **Zhōngshān Park** (中山公园; Zhōngshān Gōngyuán; admission free; ⏲6am-6pm) covers a vast 69 hectares, and with its lakes and trees it's almost Europeanlike. There's an amusement park, cherry blossoms, tulip gardens and walking paths. In springtime (late April to early May), the park features a cherry blossom festival and in summer (August) a lantern festival. Buses 26, 203, 214, 231 and 501 travel to the park.

Connected to the Zhōngshān Park, the mountainous area to the northeast is called Tàipíngshān Park (太平山公园; Tàipíngshān Gōngyuán), an area of walking paths, pavilions and the best spot in town for hiking. In the centre of the park is the **TV Tower** (Diànshì Tǎ), with panoramic views out to the bay. You can reach the tower via **cable car** (one way/return Y40/50). Also within the park is Qīngdǎo's largest temple, **Zhànshān Temple** (湛山寺; Zhànshān Sì; admission Y10; ⏲8am-5pm). The entrance is marked with a large pavilion and a huge pagoda standing side-by-side. The temple is actually a huge sprawling complex of restored Míng-style structures. There are a number of dramatic sandalwood Buddhas covered in gold foil scattered throughout the place. Worshippers offer incense while monks scamper about on their business. When you get off the cable car at Zhànshān Temple, look for a round concrete dome on the right. This is the entrance to a former German bunker. The Germans used the bunker as a wine cellar, and today the tunnel leads you past some historical displays into, what else but a wine bar! Fantastic!

Festivals & Events

Lantern Festival SPRING FESTIVAL
Held during the Chinese New Year/Spring Festival in Zhōngshān Park, usually in February/March.

Cherry Blossom Festival BLOSSOM FESTIVAL
The colourful cherry blossom festival is in April/May.

International Beer Festival BEER FESTIVAL
(www.qdbeer.cn) The city's premier party is usually held in August, attracting over three million people.

Sleeping

The old town has excellent budget and midrange options. The central business district has no soul – top-end international chains are located there.

Kǎiyuè Hostelling International HOSTEL $
(凯悦国际青年旅馆; Kǎiyuè Guójì Qīngnián Lǚguǎn; ☎8284 5450; www.yhaqd.com; 31 Jining Lu; 济宁路31号; dm/tw/f from Y25/80/130; ❄@📶) The best hostel in town, with competent staff, a great bar and bike rental in addition to the usual run of services. While we question the taste behind the premium-priced 'Ikea' room, the overall experience will be good for most travellers…one free beer per night! Dorms are roomy; doubles vary in quality. Book in advance.

Big Brother Guesthouse HOSTEL $
(奔之旅青年旅馆; Bēnzhīlǚ Qīngnián Lǚguǎn; ☎8280 2212; 6 Baoding Lu; 保定路6号; dm/tw from Y35/80; ❄📶) The compact cosiness of the place might have something to do with its name, but cameras or no, this is a neat hostel that has tatami mat and bunk-bed dorms as well as midrange en suite twin and double rooms. Staff speak excellent English and even organise dumpling parties. There's another less-attractive branch on the other side of town at 31 Jiangxi Lu (江西路31号).

YHA Old Observatory HOSTEL $
(奥博维特国际青年旅舍; Àobówéitè Guójì Qīngnián Lǚshè; ☎8282 2626; www.hostelqingdao.com; 21 Guanxiang Erlu; 观象二路21号; dm Y25-35, tw & d Y168; ❄@📶) Situated on top of a hill in a former observatory with sweeping panoramas of the city and bay, this is one of the best locales in the city…for views, which are hard to appreciate after a sweaty slog up the hill. The comfort level varies but the rooftop cafe in the parkside setting is good – stop by for a beer or coffee. Consider the pick-up service from the train/bus station (Y20) as it's slightly confusing to find. Even the website (ironically) describes this as a 'hidden gem'.

Qīngdǎo International Youth Hostel HOSTEL $$
(青岛国际青年旅舍; Qīngdǎo Guójì Qīngnián Lǚshè; ☎8286 5177; www.youthtaylor.com; 7a Qixia Lu; 栖霞路7号甲; dm from Y70, tw & tr Y240/320; ❄@📶) Despite the misleading name, this is more of a cosy midrange hotel than hostel. Set inside a renovated villa, the tidy rooms (and bathrooms) are massive.

There's some yesteryear art deco charm, and the location in the plush Bādàguān neighbourhood is ideal for walks through old Qīngdǎo. There's a shared kitchen and limited dorm rooms. Not much English spoken.

Oceanwide Elite Hotel HOTEL **$$$**
(泛海名人酒店; Fànhǎi Míngrén Jiǔdiàn; ☎8299 6699; www.oweh.com.cn; 29 Taiping Lu; 太平路29号; d without/with sea view Y1160/1560, ste Y2800; ❄) This well-maintained five-floor hotel benefits from a superb location overlooking Qīngdǎo Bay (as long as you opt for the pricier sea-view rooms) in the old part of town. Flat-screen TVs and complimentary snacks place it leagues ahead of the surrounding seafront competition. Low-season prices drop to Y850.

Beach Castle Hotel HOTEL **$$**
(青岛海滩古堡酒店; Qīngdaǒ Hǎitān Gúbǎo Jiǔdiàn; ☎8287 8131; beachcastle@163.com; 15 Taiping Lu; 太平路15号; d from Y368; ❄@) This beach-side hotel occupies the grounds of the former Qīngdǎo Prison but we doubt dubbing it Beach Prison Hotel would help its cause much. The standard rooms feature floorboards and basic pine furniture. If you shell out more, you get larger rooms with better furnishing. The location is quite handy as it straddles the Bādàguān neighbourhood and the various sights along Qīngdǎo Bay. The Qīngdǎo German Prison Museum is located on the grounds.

Crowne Plaza HOTEL **$$$**
(青岛颐中皇冠假日酒店; Qīngdǎo Yizhōng Huángguān Jiàrì Jiǔdiàn; ☎8571 8888; www.ichotelsgroup.com; 76 Xianggang Zhonglu; 香港中路76号; d/ste Y1200/2324, discounts up to 40%; ⊖❄@✈≋) At this glittering, 38-floor tower rising above Qīngdǎo's crackling commercial district, you won't be bumping into much old-town charm. Business travellers can content themselves instead with the warm honey-coloured hues of the splendid foyer, the fully equipped rooms, the indoor pool, professional standards of service and a choice of five restaurants – buffets at Café Asia (lunch/dinner Y128/168) are a favourite with expats. Wi-fi in the lobby.

Dōngfāng Fàndiàn HOTEL **$$**
(东方饭店; ☎8286 5888; www.hotel-dongfang.com; 4 Daxue Lu; 大学路4号; tw/d Y280/500; ❄@) A well-maintained but wholly dull four-star hotel. Ask for the east-facing top-floor rooms (same price) which have arguably the best hotel views. Some rooms have PCs with internet access for extra cost.

Eating

Qīngdǎo has no problem keeping even the most fickle diners sated. The waterfront area is brimming with restaurants, from No 6 Bathing Beach almost all the way to No 1 Bathing Beach. Side streets are often peppered with family-run restaurants serving up quick meals. Popular local dining choices, however, are in the business district in **Hong Kong Garden** (香港花园; Xiānggǎng Huāyuán), which consists of several blocks of jam-packed eateries: Korean, Thai, hotpot, Italian and even Russian are just some of the numerous culinary possibilities. Wander at will, or grab a copy of *Red Star* (try the hostels or foreign restaurants) for extensive listings. For the less adventurous budget-conscious, there are food courts in **Jusco** and **Carrefour**. **Café Asia** (亚洲咖啡) in the Crowne Plaza also gets good reviews.

Huángdǎo Road Market STREET MARKET **$**
(Huángdǎo Lù Shìchǎng; meals from Y5; ⌚8am-6pm) A frenetic and fabulous street market chock-a-block with stalls selling raw produce, vegetables and other delights. Every other stall sells food: fried chicken, pancakes, bread, cooked dishes…it's all cheap, so just stop when something catches your fancy. The neighbouring Zhifu Lu has several sit-down kerbside joints serving food and Tsingtao (locals buy it in large plastic bags to takeaway – you can have yours in a glass).

Jiāngníng Road Food Street STREET MARKET **$**
(江宁路小吃街; Jiāngníng Lù Xiǎochī Jiē; meals from Y10; ⌚10am-8pm) A small hole-in-the-wall passageway (below an archway that has a plaster motif '1902') off Zhongshan Lu opens up to a small warren of food stalls. While the whole place is rather 'made up', you can get everything from pancakes to barbecued skewers to live seafood cooked anyway you like. Prices are mostly labelled and many joints have picture menus.

Bellagio TAIWANESE **$$**
(鹿港小镇; Lùgǎng Xiǎozhèn; ☎8387 0877; 19 Aomen Sanlu; dishes from Y15; ⌚10am-midnight) Swish Bellagio serves up excellent Taiwanese cuisine late into the night. There are two equally popular branches in Běijīng, so it must be doing something right! Try the

three-cup chicken (三杯鸡; *sān bēijī*) and save room for the range of delicious sweets. Picture menu. Near the corner of Donghai Xilu (parallel south to Xianggang Xilu) and Shandong Lu.

Lánzhōu Lā Miàn NOODLES **$**
(兰州拉面; Sifang Lu; noodles Y5-6; ⏲9am-11pm) No-frills noodle restaurant run by a family of Chinese-Muslims. Noodles are all handmade on the premises and service is quick and efficient. Order the hearty beef noodle soup (牛肉面; *nĭu ròumìan*) or just point at what the next person's having. You can't go wrong as it's all cheap, cheerful and pretty good. Bottomless refills of soup and raw garlic (that we don't understand) accompaniment if you want it...just don't forget your breath mints.

Cafè Yum INTERNATIONAL **$$$**
(9 Xianggang Zhonglu; buffet lunch/dinner Y168/228; ⏲6am-10pm) Sometimes, you just need a good old burger, or a pig-out-fest at an all-you-can-eat joint. This place in swish Shangri-la in the business district ticks both boxes. Sure, it's a little pricey but service is good and the spread is a veritable feast. As always, we recommend leaving room for dessert. Oh, did we mention the all-you-can-drink beer?

Wángjiě Shāokăo ROAST GRILL **$**
(王姐烧烤; cnr Zhongshan & Dexian Lu; lamb skewers Y2; ⏲10am-6pm) Sooner or later, Qīngdăo's legendary meat skewers will require your undivided attention, and where better to start than to join the throng outside this street-side stall. Squeeze your way to the front and order lamb (羊肉串; *yángròu chuàn;* Y2), pork (猪肉串; *zhūròu chuàn;* Y4) or cuttlefish (鱿鱼串; *yóuyú chuàn;* Y10). Stand with the rest of the punters by the side of the road, finish your meal and toss the skewers into the bucket by the side. There's a sit-down restaurant by the side for the more civilised.

Měidá'ěr Barbecue Restaurant KEBABS **$$**
(美达尔烤肉店; Měidá'ěr Shāokăodiàn; 4 Yan'an Yilu; lamb kebabs Y2-4, meals Y30; ⏲9am-2am) This trusty local chain restaurant just off Beer St serves up lamb (羊肉串; *yángròu chuàn*), pork (猪肉串; *zhūròu chuàn*) or seafood kebabs. If you want cold beer, you might be out of luck. Service is patchy too. There's a branch in the old town along Zhongshan Lu.

Drinking

Qīngdăo wouldn't be Qīngdăo without Tsingtao, and the first stop for any serious beerophile might as well be the many shops along **Beer St** (啤酒街; Píjiŭ Jiē), just outside the brewery's doors, where you can sample the delicious dark *yuánjiāng* (原浆啤酒) brew, which is hard to find elsewhere. The rest of the city's bars are concentrated in the business district in the east of town. Check www.myredstar.com or www.thatsqingdao.com for current listings.

Old Church Lounge BAR
(www.yhaqd.com; 31 Jining Lu; 济宁路31号; beer from Y10) Located on the ground floor of Kăiyuè International Youth Hostel, this is a chilled-out bar set in an old church. Order an ice-cold Tsingtao or cocktail, say a prayer (bless me father for I have sinned) and continue to get hammered. There's a pool table, sheesha and lots of little private spaces if you're feeling antisocial.

Club New York BAR
(纽约吧; Niŭyuē Bā; 2nd fl, 41 Xianggang Zhonglu; beer from Y30) Fuelled by Shakira and company at full blast, this expat favourite is overflowing with late-night revellers on weekends. It's above the lobby of the Overseas Chinese International Hotel in the business district. Out-of-town bands sometimes hold concerts here and there's a cover band from Tuesday to Sunday. Drinks are expensive so come prepared to spend... doesn't seem to stop the expats though!

Entertainment

Huáchén Cinema CINEMA
(华臣影城; Huáchén Yĭngchéng; 8F, 69 Xianggang Zhonglu; tickets from Y50) In the Mykal Department Store in the business district and generally has at least one Hollywood blockbuster playing.

Shopping

Yúngŭ Curios Shop ART
(云古; Yúngŭ; 19 Taiping Lu; ⏲10am-6pm) A fab little shop selling hand-cut paper art. Grab a paper portrait of Chairman Mao or pick up a Zodiac animal paper cut. There are also many other more intricate designs of phoenixes, swallows and auspicious words. The owner and artist, Wenxiang, doesn't speak much English but if you ask nicely she can do a quick demo of her craft. Located beside Tianhou Temple.

Xīnhuá Bookstore BOOKS
(新华书店; Xīnhuá Shūdiàn; 10 Henan Lu; ⏲9am-7pm) On the corner of Guangxi Lu. Sells maps (Y10) and a good range of Chinese books and magazines. Head to Book City (below) for English books.

Carrefour HYPERMART
(家乐福; Jiālèfú; ⏲8.30am-10pm) On the northwest corner of Nanjing Lu and Xianggang Zhonglu. You can buy most everything here.

Jímòlù Market MALL
(即墨路小商品市场; Jímòlù Xiǎoshàngpǐn Shìchǎng; 45 Liaocheng Lu; ⏲9am-6pm) A four-floor shop-till-you-drop bargain bonanza. Pearls, purses, clothing, shoes, backpacks, jade – don't forget to haggle.

Jusco SUPERMARKET
(佳世客; Jiāshìkè; ⏲9am-11pm) Near the southeast corner of Fuzhou Nanlu and Xianggang Zhonglu. Food court and supermarket.

Parkson Building MALL
(Zhongshan Lu; ⏲9am-8pm) Has several floors of shopping and a supermarket in the basement.

Information

Internet Access

Hostels have internet-enabled PCs and wi-fi internet access (网吧). Most hotels have free broadband cables and some have PCs in rooms.

Book City (书城; Shū Chéng; 67 Xianggang Zhonglu; per hr Y2; ⏲9am-midnight) On the 4th floor of Book City at the junction of Xianggang Zhonglu and Yan'erdao Lu; the evening entrance (after Book City closes) is north on Yan'erdao Lu.

Hǎodú Wǎngbā (好读网吧; 2 Dagu Lu; per hr Y2; ⏲24hr)

Internet Resources

My Red Star (www.myredstar.com) Online entertainment guide; the same folks also put out the monthly listings mag *Redstar* – look for it in hotels, bars and foreign restaurants.

That's Qīngdǎo (www.thatsqingdao.com) Online city guide with listings and news clips.

Medical Services

Qīngdǎo Municipal Hospital, International Clinic (青岛市立医院国际门诊; Qīngdǎoshì Shìlì Yīyuàn, Guójì Ménzhěn; ☎international clinic 8593 7690, ext 2266, emergency 8278 9120; 5 Donghai Zhonglu; ⏲8am-noon & 1.30-5.30pm Mon-Sat)

Money

ATMs are fairly easy to find in Qīngdǎo; centrally located machines are listed below.

Bank of China (中国银行; Zhōngguó Yínháng; 66 & 68 Zhongshan Lu; ⏲8.30am-5pm Mon-Fri) On the corner of Feicheng Lu. Foreign-currency exchange. External ATM accepts foreign cards.

Bank of China ATM (中国银行自动取款机; Zhōngguó Yínháng Zìdòng Qǔkuǎnjī; Xianggang Zhonglu; ⏲24hr) East of Book City in the business district.

Jusco (⏲8.30am-10pm) On the 2nd floor of Jusco shopping centre. ATM accepts foreign cards.

Post

China Post (中国邮政; Zhōngguó Yóuzhèng; 51 Zhongshan Lu; ⏲8.30am-6pm) Opposite the large Parkson building.

Public Security Bureau

(PSB; 公安局; Gōng'ānjú; ⏲9am-noon & 1.30-4.30pm Mon-Fri) East branch ☎8579 2555, ext 2860; 272 Ningxia Lu); Old Town (Zhongshan Lu) For the east branch, bus 301 goes from the train station and stops outside the terracotta-coloured building (stop 14).

Travel Agency

China International Travel Service (CITS; 中国国际旅行社; Zhōngguó Guójì Lǚxíngshè; ☎8389 2065/1713; Yuyuan Dasha, 73 Xianggang Xilu; ⏲9am-4pm)

Getting There & Away

Air

There are flights to most large cities in China, including daily services to Běijīng (Y710, 1¼ hours), Shànghǎi (Y740, 1¼ hours) and Hong Kong (Y1810, three hours). International flights include daily flights to Seoul (Y1400) and Tokyo (Y4300) along with four weekly flights to Osaka (Y2700). For flight information call **Liúting International Airport** (☎8471 5139).

Ticket offices:

China Southern (中国南方航空公司; Zhōngguó Nánfāng Hángkōng Gōngsī; ☎8869 8255; Hǎitiān Hotel; 海天大酒店; 48 Xianggang Xilu; ⏲8.30am-5pm)

Civil Aviation Administration of China (CAAC; 中国民航; Zhōngguó Mínháng) Domestic (☎8289 5577; 29 Zhongshan Lu; ⏲8am-6.30pm); International (☎8578 2381; 30 Xianggang Lu; ⏲8.30am-4.30pm)

Dragonair (港龙航空; Gǎnglóng Hángkōng; ☎400 888 6628; Copthorne Hotel; 青岛国敦大酒店; 28 Xianggang Zhonglu; ⏲9am-5pm Mon-Fri)

BORDER CROSSING: JAPAN & SOUTH KOREA

International boats depart from the **passenger ferry terminal** (青岛港客运站; Qīngdǎogǎng Kèyùnzhàn; ☎8282 5001; 6 Xinjiang Lu). There are twice-weekly boats from Qīngdǎo to Shimonoseki (Y1100, 26 hours, 3.30pm Monday and Thursday) in Japan. For South Korea, Qīngdǎo has boats to Incheon (from Y750, 17 hours, 5pm Monday, Wednesday and Friday) and Gunsan (Y920, 16 hours, 2.30pm Monday, Wednesday and Saturday). Boats to Incheon are run by the **Weidong Ferry Company** (www.weidong.com; Incheon (☎8232-777 0490; International Passenger Terminal, 71-2 Hang-dong); Qīngdǎo (☎8280 3574; passenger ferry terminal, 4 Xinjiang Lu); Seoul (☎822-3271 6710; 10th fl, 1005 Sungji Bldg, 585 Dohwa-dong, Mapo-gu).

Korean Air (大韩航空; Dàhán Hángkōng; ☎8387 0088; Hǎitiān Hotel, 48 Xianggang Xilu)

Boat

To reach Dàlián by boat, you will have to go from Yāntái or Wēihǎi; tickets for these trips can be purchased from CITS.

Bus

Most out-of-town buses arrive at Qīngdǎo's **long-distance bus station** (长途汽车站; chángtú qìchēzhàn; ☎8371 3833; 2 Wenzhou Lu) in the Sìfāng District north of town. Daily buses:

Běijīng Y230, nine hours, one daily (8pm)

Hángzhōu Y310, 12 hours, two daily (6pm and 6.30pm)

Héféi Y180, 10 hours, four daily

Jǐ'nán Y78 to Y113, 4½ hours, every 30 minutes

Qūfù Y127, five hours, four daily

Shànghǎi Y286, 11 hours, five daily

Tài'ān Y116, six hours, four daily

Wēihǎi Y93, 3½ hours, hourly

Yāntái Y66, 3½ hours, every 40 minutes

Train

All trains from Qīngdǎo go through Jǐ'nán, except the direct Qīngdǎo to Yāntái and Wēihǎi trains. All prices listed here are for hard seat unless otherwise noted; the express D trains only have 1st- and 2nd-class soft seats. Train tickets can be bought at the train station or for a service charge at several places around town, including a useful **ticket office** (青岛火车航空售票处; Qīngdǎo Huǒchē Hángkōng Shòupiàochù; Feicheng; ⏲24hr) on the north side of Feicheng, just round the corner from the station. Regular trains run to numerous destinations, including:

Tài'ān/Tài'shān Y70, six hours, regular services

Yāntái Y22, 4½ hours, one daily (6am)

Zhèngzhōu soft sleeper Y264, 13 hours, six daily

Express D trains:

Běijīng Y116, six hours, six daily

Jǐ'nán Y55, three hours, regular services

Nánjīng Y137, eight hours, one daily (10.30am)

Shànghǎi Y170, 10 hours, two daily (10.25am and 10.30am)

Tài'ān/Tài'shān Y70, 3½ hours, one daily (10.30am)

Getting Around

To/From the Airport

Qīngdǎo's **Líutíng International Airport** (☎8471 5139) is 30km north of the city. Taxis to/from the airport cost Y50 to Y75. Buses (Y20) leave hourly from the **Green Tea Inn** (格林豪泰商务酒店 (机场巴士); Gélín Háotài Shāngwù Jiǔdiàn (Jīchǎng Bāshì); Zhongshan Lu) in the old town from 5.40am to 7.40pm, and half-hourly from the CAAC office (机场巴士售票处; Jīchǎng Bāshì Shòupiàochù) in the business district from 6am to 9pm.

Public Transport

Bus 501 runs east from the train station, passing Zhōngshān Park and continuing along the entirety of Xianggang Lu in the central business district. Bus 26 from the train station runs a similar route, although it turns north on Nanjing Lu, just before the start of Xianggang Zhonglu. From the long-distance bus station, bus 221 runs to Zhongshan Lu in the old city and bus 366 runs to the CBD. City bus rides cost Y1. Longer-distance buses have conductors who charge and issue tickets according to your destination.

Taxi

Flag fall is Y7 for the first 3km and then Y1.20 per kilometre thereafter, plus fuel tax (Y1).

Láo Shān 崂山

Looking at the jumble of massive granite slabs and boulders capping the hilltops and tumbling down to the sea's edge, it's easy to understand why the stunning landscapes of **Láo Shān** (admission Apr-Oct Y70, Nov-Mar Y50) attracted spiritual seekers throughout the centuries. One of the earliest was the Buddhist pilgrim Faxian, who landed here upon returning from India in the 5th century AD, but the mountain is above all known for its associations with Taoism. Following the establishment of the Quanzhen sect in the 12th century (founded near Yāntái), many adepts later came here to cultivate themselves in the hermitages scattered throughout Láo Shān. Even the emperor Qin Shi Huang ascended the mountain... with the help of a litter party of course.

Today the region is ideal for day hikes, with small dams, temples, thickets of bamboo and pine, and a spectacular coastline in the lower region. There are actually three trails around the mountain, each one leading to a peak. The most picturesque is the **Jùfēng Qū** (巨峰区) trail.

The Jufeng circuit itself takes three to four hours to complete. It's built in the shape of a *báguà,* a Taoist symbol that's supposed to ward off spirits, and there are 'gates' at each of the eight-sided tips of the symbol. Stone steps lead visitors past wind- and water-worked granite. At the peak, there are jaw-dropping views out towards the sea and to the rest of the rocky terrain behind. The trail offers many opportunities to clamber over rocks, stop at temples and a spring, and of course there are many photo opportunities.

There's another trail at **Bāshuǐ Hé** (八水河). It leads up to an old **hermit's cave** (明霞洞; Míngxiá Dòng; admission Y4) at one summit; the route takes a lazy two hours. Alternatively, follow a cliff-side boardwalk a further half-hour down the coast to reach the Song-dynasty **Great Purity Palace** (太清宫; Tàiqīng Gōng; admission Y20), established by the first Song emperor as a place to perform Taoist rites to save the souls of the dead. The Láo Shān park is quite large and merits further exploration – you can easily spend an entire day here.

From Qīngdǎo, bus 304 runs to Láo Shān (Y12, one to two hours). Catch 304 at the Zhàn Qiáo stop by No 6 Bathing Beach from 6.30am; get off at Jùfēng Qū Terminus and get your admission ticket. It's an 8km walk to the cable car station or just shell out for the bus (Guānguāng chē, 观光车, Y15 return). The **cable car** (suǒ dào; one way/return Y40/80) takes you to the base of the purpose-built circuit. It's another 2km slog up to the start of the circuit if you want to save money on the cable car. Note that from November through March, bus 304 only runs as far as Liúqīng Hé (流清河; bus ticket Y4.50), from where you'll need to hire a shared taxi (Y15 to Láo Shān, Y30 back to Liúqīng Hé). Returning, the last bus leaves Láo Shān at 7pm.

Tour buses to Láo Shān (Y25 return excluding entrance fees) ply the streets of Qīngdǎo from 6am onwards, but visit at least four other 'sights' on the way to the mountain and back. If you want to take a tour bus, pick a small one and stay in the bus instead of getting off at the various shops. As one tout proclaimed with an appropriate sense of quasi-mysticism: 'You can spend an entire lifetime looking, but you'll never find a bus that will take you straight there'.

At the time of writing, admission prices were set to increase a whopping 40%!

Yāntái 烟台

☎0535 / POP 0.8 MILLION

Yāntái claims one of the fastest-developing economies in China, which is no small feat in a country renowned for exponential growth. As the investment yuan flow in from entrepreneurs in South Korea and Japan, the port city has somehow managed to look beyond its busy blue-collar roots, simultaneously transforming into an increasingly popular summer beach resort. Meanwhile, the coastline is soaring with a steady development of shiny new high-rise towers that somehow manages to avoid the architectural faux pas of other similar cities. The old residents are staying firm and you'll easily find a warren of old houses nestled a mere block from the bay to the north and the buzzing city to the south. Good for a day or two, the town makes for a relaxed sojourn, with a sprinkling of foreign concession architecture, popular beaches and Pénglái Pavilion not far away.

History

Starting life as a defence outpost and fishing village, Yāntái's name literally means 'Smoke Terrace'; wolf-dung fires were lit on the headland during the Ming dynasty to warn fishing fleets of approaching pirates. Its anonymity abruptly ended in the late 19th century when the Qing govern-

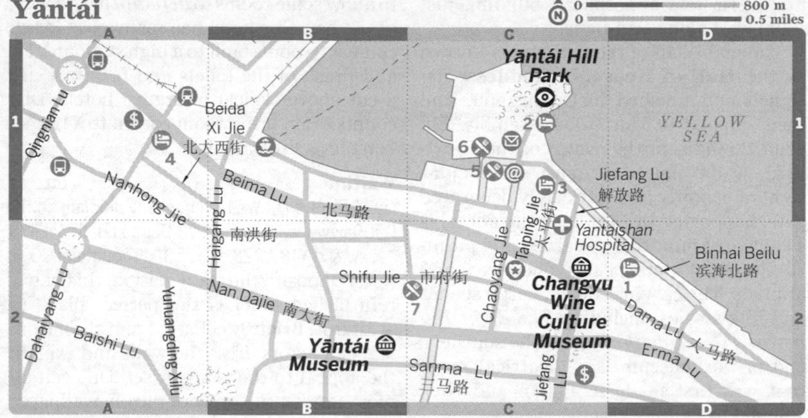

ment, reeling from defeat in the Opium War, handed Yāntái to the British. They established a treaty port here and called it Chefoo (Zhīfú). Several other nations, Japan and the USA among them, had trading establishments here and the town became something of a resort area.

Sights

Yāntái Hill Park PARK

(烟台山公园; Yāntáishān Gōngyuán; admission Y30; ⏲7am-6pm) This quaint park is a veritable museum of well-preserved Western treaty port architecture spread upwards across a maze of stone paths and leafy gardens. Containing a Chinese-only visual exhibition on Yāntái's port days, the **Former American Consulate Building** retains some original interior features. Nearby, the former **Yāntái Union Church** dates from 1875, although it was later rebuilt and now serves as the office for a wedding-planning company. The **Former British Consulate** is perched on the edge of the park overlooking the bay, and the **British Consulate Annexe** looks out onto an overgrown English garden.

Heading northwest, you'll find several points at which to look upon the busy industrial port that is home to Yāntái's fortunes. The northernmost tip has a lonely **pavilion** sticking out into the bay. It's not uncommon to see locals clamber down to the rocks below to fish. Next to the pavilion is a **wooden bridge** with hundreds of heart-shaped lockets attached to it. Couples come here to attach these lockets as a promise of everlasting love.

Yāntái

Top Sights

Changyu Wine Culture Museum C2
Yāntái Hill Park C1
Yāntái Museum B2

Sleeping

1 ACCW D2
2 Golden Gulf Hotel C1
3 Karen Bayview Hotel C1
4 Waitinn A1

Eating

5 Bǎolóng Hǎixiān Chéng C1
6 Brazil Barbecue C1
7 Lǎoyú Lāmiàn C2

At the top of the hill is the Ming-dynasty **Dragon King Temple**, which once found service as a military headquarters for French troops in 1860 and is now home once again to a statue of the Dragon King himself. Directly behind is a **lighthouse** (admission Y5) which you can ascend. The wolf-dung fires were burned from the **smoke terrace** above, dating from the reign of Hongwu. In the west of the park, the 1930s-built **Japanese Consulate** is a typically austere brick lump, equipped with a 'torture inquisition room'.

Yāntái Museum MUSEUM

(烟台博物馆; Yāntái Bówùguǎn; 257 Nan Dajie; admission Y10; ⏲8.30-11.30am & 1.30-5pm) The current home of the museum is a fabulous guildhall built by merchants and sailors of Fújiàn as a place of worship to Tianhou. Sadly, the museum will be moving into a modern, less atmospheric building just 100m west along Nan Dajie.

The main hall of the museum is known as the **Hall of Heavenly Goddess**, designed and finished in Guǎngzhōu, and then shipped to Yāntái for assembly. Beyond the hall, in the centre of the courtyard, is the museum's most spectacular sight: a brightly and intricately decorated gate. Supported by 14 pillars, the portal is a collage of hundreds of carved and painted figures, flowers, beasts, phoenixes and animals. The carvings depict battle scenes and folk stories, including *The Eight Immortals Crossing the Sea*. At the southern end of the museum is a theatrical stage that was first made in Fújiàn and then shipped to Yāntái.

Beaches BEACHES
Of Yāntái's two beaches, **No 1 Beach** (Dìyī Hǎishuǐ Yùchǎng), a long stretch of soft sand along a calm bay area, is superior to **No 2 Beach** (Dì'èr Hǎishuǐ Yùchǎng), which is less crowded, but more polluted. Both beaches can be reached by bus 17.

Changyu Wine Culture Museum MUSEUM
(张裕酒文化博物馆; Zhāngyù Jiǔwénhuà Bówùguǎn; 56 Dama Lu; admission Y30; ⌚8am-5pm) The surprising Changyu Wine Culture Museum introduces the history of China's oldest and largest Western-style winery (founded in 1892), which produces a barely palatable 'Chinese Cabernet' and a sweet riesling (tasting, down in any icy cellar, is included in admission price).

ACCW HISTORIC AREA
East of the Changyu Wine Culture Museum is an attractive but soulless cluster of restored concession buildings, housing a variety of business such as restaurants, clubs, bars and such. It's worth wandering through to have a look at Yāntái's efforts at 'doing' Shànghǎi.

Sleeping

There are many hotels clustered around the train and bus stations but these are often busy, noisy and dull. A better option would be to find a hotel in and around the northern end of Chaoyang Jie, where a lot of old houses still remain. It's a quiet district with an old-world charm.

Karen Bayview Hotel HOTEL $$
(凯琳海景酒店; Kǎilín Háijǐng Jiǔdìan; ☎622 6600; 30 Dongtaiping Jie; 东太平街30号; s/d Y300/380; ❄@) Jutting out at an odd angle to allow some rooms to *actually* have a view of the bay, this hotel has really cosy (read: compact) rooms built to a high standard. Fit and finish of the toilets and furniture are a cut above typical midrange hotels. Discounts often bring rooms down to Y120, so don't forget to bargain.

Waitinn HOTEL $$
(维特风尚酒店; Wéitè Fēngshàng Jiǔdìan; ☎212 0909; www.waitinn.com; 73 Beima Lu; 北马路73号; tw & d Y188-228, tr Y258, discounts of 20%; ❄@) Opposite the train station, this newly refurbished hotel is the perfect place to 'wait inn'. Brightly coloured murals of iconic Asian actors dress the walls and explain the appeal to the younger set. One can almost forgive the eyesore-purple wallpaper as the rooms are comfortable with large beds and flat-screen TVs.

Golden Gulf Hotel HOTEL $$$
(金海湾酒店; Jīnhǎiwān Jiǔdìan; ☎663 6999; fax 663 2699; 34 Haian Lu; 海安路34号; d Y660-1080; ❄@) The six-storey Golden Gulf has a superb sea and parkside location, and falls prey to the Chinese 'let's spend more money on the lobby than on refurbishing rooms' mentality. There's a bar and 'international'-style restaurant attached. Some English is spoken.

Eating & Drinking

Taohua Jie, directly north of the old Yāntái Museum, has a handful of popular local restaurants. South of Yāntái Hill Park, the pedestrian streets Chaoyang Jie and Hai'an Jie have a good pick of bars, cafes, local restaurants, an Irish pub and even a Brazilian barbecue joint, though outside of summer some of the places may be closed. The area surrounding the train station has plenty of eating options, and there's a small strip of street food stalls on the east side of the large Parkson building.

Brazil Barbecue BARBECUE $$
(巴西烤肉主题餐厅; Bāxī Kǎoròu Zhǔtí Cāntīng; ☎661 0185; 22 Hai'an Jie; buffet Y68; ⌚lunch & dinner) The Chinese take on Brazilian *churrascaria* means that you'll get pork slathered in garlic, slices of ox tongue and chicken giblet – all served from long skewers. The all-you-can-eat buffet spread gives you one more reason to delay that diet. Staff offering grilled meats come round once only, so don't feel shy to call out if you want more.

Bǎolóng Hǎixiān Chéng SEAFOOD $$
(宝隆海鲜城; ☎661 1518; 18 Hai'an Jie; meals from Y50) Enter the special seafood-filled room by the entrance where the squirming, crawling and swimming creatures are on display. Vegie and cold dishes have marked prices per serve. Seafood is charged by *jīn* and weighed in front of you. Order what you want and the kitchen will cook it up. Beer is only Y2. Limited English spoken.

Lǎoyú Lāmiàn NOODLES $
(老于拉面; 26-7 Taohua Jie; beef noodles Y6-10; ⏲24hr) This popular joint runs 24 hours so you'll never go hungry. Grab a seat and join the rest of the patrons slurping down noodles. The menu is in Chinese so you'll have to order by pointing at what the people at the next table are having; or you can always go with the *niúròu lāmiàn* (牛肉拉面; beef noodles).

Information

There are numerous internet cafes (网吧; wǎngbā) along Cháoyáng Jie, south of Yańtái Hill Park. Prices per hour are Y2.

Bank of China (中国银行; Zhōngguó Yínháng; 166 Jiefang Lu) ATM accepts all cards. Smaller branch on Beima Lu.

China Post (中国邮政; Zhōngguó Yóuzhèng; Hai'an Jie) It's 25m south of the tourist office.

Chūnhèhéng Pharmacy (春鹤恒药堂; Chūnhèhéng Yàofáng; Beima Lu) Next to the International Seaman's Super 8 Hotel.

Public Security Bureau (PSB; 公安局; Gōng'ānjú; ☎629 7050; 78 Shifu Jie; ⏲8-11.30am & 2-5.30pm Mon-Sat) On the corner of Chaoyang Jie. Office for foreigners is on the 5th floor.

Yāntáishān Hospital (烟台山医院; Yāntáishān Yīyuàn; ☎660 2028; 91 Jiefang Lu)

Getting There & Away

Air

Book tickets at **Yāntái International Airport Group Air Travel Agency** (航空国际旅行有限公司; Yāntái Gúojì Lǚxíngshè Yǒuxiàngōngsī; ☎625 3777; 6 Dahaiyang Lu; ⏲8am-6pm) or at **Shāndōng Airlines** (山东航空公司; Shāndōng Hángkōng; ☎662 2737; 236 Nan Dajie, Bìhaǐ Dàshà; ⏲8am-5pm).

There are daily flights to Běijīng (Y800, one hour), Shànghǎi (Y900, 1½ hours), Guǎngzhōu (Y2080, three hours) and Seoul (Y1000), and thrice-weekly flights to Osaka (Y2500).

Boat

Purchase tickets for fast boats to Dàlián (Y230, 3½ hours, 8.30am, 10am, 1pm and 2pm, May to October only) at the **Yāntái passenger ferry terminal** (烟台港客运站; Yāntáigǎng Kèyùnzhàn; ☎624 2715; 155 Beima Lu) or from numerous ticket offices east of the train station; tickets can only be purchased on the day of travel. There are also numerous slow boats departing daily throughout the year for Dàlián (seat/bed Y125/140, 2nd class Y220, six to seven hours) from 9am to 11.30pm.

Bus

From the **long-distance bus station** (长途汽车站; chánglú qìchē zhàn; cnr Xi Dajie & Qingnian Lu) there are buses to numerous destinations:

Jǐ'nán Y139 to Y149, 5½ hours, hourly

Pénglái Y18, 1½ hours, every 30 minutes

Qīngdǎo Y63 to Y68, 3½ hours, every 40 minutes

Wēihǎi Y27, one hour, every 30 minutes

Sleeper buses also run to destinations further afield:

Běijīng Y224, 13 hours, one daily (10.45am)

Shànghǎi Y302, 11 hours, one daily (7.15am)

Tiānjīn Y184, 11 hours, two daily (10am and 1.30pm

BORDER CROSSING: SOUTH KOREA

Boats to Incheon (from Y960, 16 hours, 5pm Monday, Wednesday and Friday) in South Korea leave from the **Yāntái passenger ferry terminal** (烟台港客运站; Yāntáigǎng Kèyùnzhàn; ☎624 2715; 155 Beima Lu).

The **Weidong Ferry Company** (www.weidong.com; Incheon ☎8232-777 0490; International Passenger Terminal, 71-2 Hang-dong; Seoul ☎822-3271 6710; 10th fl, 1005 Sungji Bldg, 585 Dohwa-dong, Mapo-gu) has boats to Incheon (deluxe/1st/2nd/economy class Y1370/1090/890/750, 15 hours), in South Korea, at 5pm on Tuesday, Thursday and Sunday; check its website for the latest timetables and prices. In Wēihǎi, tickets are available from the ticket office (☎522 6173; 48 Haibin Beilu), south of the passenger ferry terminal (威海港客运码头; wēihǎigǎng kèyùnmǎtóu).

You can also get a boat to Incheon and Busan in South Korea from Qingdao.

WORTH A TRIP

PÉNGLÁI PAVILION

About 65km northwest of Yāntái, the 1000-year-old **Pénglái Pavilion** (蓬莱阁; Pénglái Gé; admission Y100; ⏲7am-6pm summer, 7.30am-5pm winter) is closely entwined in Chinese mythology with the legend of the Eight Immortals Crossing the Sea.

Perched on a cliff top overlooking the waves, the stately pavilion harbours a fascinating array of temples, and what seems like 600 souvenir stalls. The path leading up to the pavilion is a complex that forms China's most complete ancient military naval base, dating back to the Song dynasty. On misty days, fog rolls in over the buildings, giving it an ethereal, otherworldly feel...until you hear the screeching commentary of the next tour guide taking a group through.

En route to the pavilion, you'll find five temples, each one devoted to a different god. There's an old stage where you can watch a performance for Y6. The pavilion looks rather unassuming from the outside as its architecture is rather similar to the rest of the buildings. What's special is a recently installed art installation created by Zhou Jinyun. It's a stunning textured full-colour retelling of the story of the Eight Immortals. Looking at the display from right to left, you'll be able to see all the characters and their adventures.

Once you've toured the pavilion, you can hop on a cable car (Y20 return) to zip across the bay towards, yes, even more temples and pavilions. The ride is quite stunning as part of it takes you over the water and up a forested hill.

Besides the pavilion, Pénglái draws crowds for its optical illusion that locals claim appears every few years or so. The last took place on 7 May 2006 and lasted for some four hours, revealing what appeared to be a mirror image of Pénglái itself, with buildings, cars and people, hovering above the sea.

Pénglái is easily visited as a day trip from Yāntái by bus (Y18, 1½ hours, half-hourly). The pavilion is a 15-minute walk north from the train and bus station. Taxi drivers will want to take you there but will stop you off at several other places prior to the pavilion. The last return bus to Yāntái leaves Pénglái at 6pm.

Minibuses to Pénglái (Y18, 1½ hours, 5.30am to 6pm) also depart every 20 minutes from the **Beima Lu bus station** (北马路汽车站; běimǎlù qìchē zhàn; cnr Beima Lu & Qingnian Lu).

Train

Trains from Yāntái **train station** (Yāntái Hǔochēzhàn; ☎9510 5175; Beiman Lu):

Běijīng hard seat/soft sleeper Y130/365, 14½ hours, one daily (11pm)

Jǐ'nán hard seat/soft sleeper Y67/206, 7½ hours, nine daily

Qīngdǎo hard/soft seat Y22/34, 41½ hours, one daily (2.36pm)

Shànghǎi hard seat/soft sleeper Y161/490, 22 hours, one daily (9.40am)

Xī'ān hard seat/soft sleeper Y176/530, 24½ hours, one daily (3.38pm)

 Getting Around

Yāntái Airport (☎624 1330) is 20km south of town. Airport buses (Y10, 30 minutes) depart from the long-distance bus station around two hours before flights (bus tickets from the arrival hall next door); a taxi will cost around Y40 to Y50.

Bus 17 runs between the two beaches. Taxi flag fall is Y7, and Y1.50 per kilometre thereafter.

Shànghǎi

POPULATION: 19 MILLION / TELEPHONE CODE: 021

Includes »

Best Places to Eat

» Huanghe Rd (p190)
» Bǎoluó Jiǔlóu (p191)
» Lost Heaven (p190)
» Fu 1039 (p192)
» Vegetarian Life Style (p192)

Best Places to Stay

» Urbn (p188)
» Astor House Hotel (p184)
» Park Hyatt (p188)
» Quintet (p186)
» Le Tour Traveler's Rest Youth Hostel (p188)

Why Go?

You can't see the Great Wall from space, but you'd have a job missing Shànghǎi (上海). One of the country's most massive and vibrant cities, Shànghǎi is heading places that the rest of the Middle Kingdom can only fantasise about. Somehow typifying modern China while being unlike anywhere else in the land, Shànghǎi is real China, but perhaps just not the real China you had in mind.

This is a city of action, not ideas. You won't spot many Buddhist monks contemplating the dharma, or wild-haired poets handing out flyers, but skyscrapers will form before your eyes. Shànghǎi is best seen as an epilogue to your China experience: submit to its debutante charms after you've had your fill of dusty imperial palaces and bumpy 10-hour bus rides. From nonstop shopping to skyscraper-hopping to bullet-fast Maglev trains and glamorous cocktails – this is the future that China has long been waiting for.

When to Go

Shànghǎi

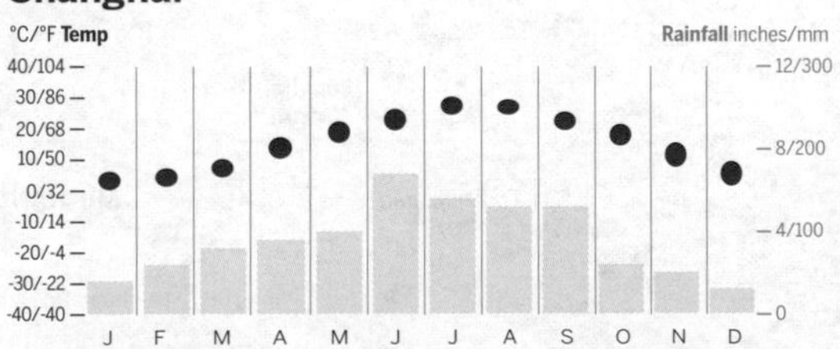

February Visit Yùyuán Gardens for the Lantern Festival, two weeks after Chinese New Year.

April & May March is chilly and 1 May is chaos, but otherwise spring is ideal.

October The optimal season: neither too hot nor too rainy.

Shànghǎi Highlights

1. Stroll down the **Bund promenade** (p165) or raise a glass to the Pǔdōng lights
2. Contemplate the masterpieces of traditional Chinese art in the **Shànghǎi Museum** (p166)
3. Admire the curvature of the earth from atop the **World Financial Center** (p175)
4. Treat your taste buds: from fusion cuisine to Sichuanese peppercorns, **French Concession restaurants** (p191) have you covered
5. Delve into the old alleyways and quirky boutiques at **Tiánzǐfáng** (p173)
6. Put on your best shoes and step out into the **Shànghǎi night** (p195)
7. Bargain-hunt for faux antiques and tailor-made clothes in the **Old Town** (p198)
8. Test your boundaries with the latest in Chinese art at **M50** (p175)
9. Escape the big city for the canal-town vistas of **Zhūjiājiǎo** (p204)

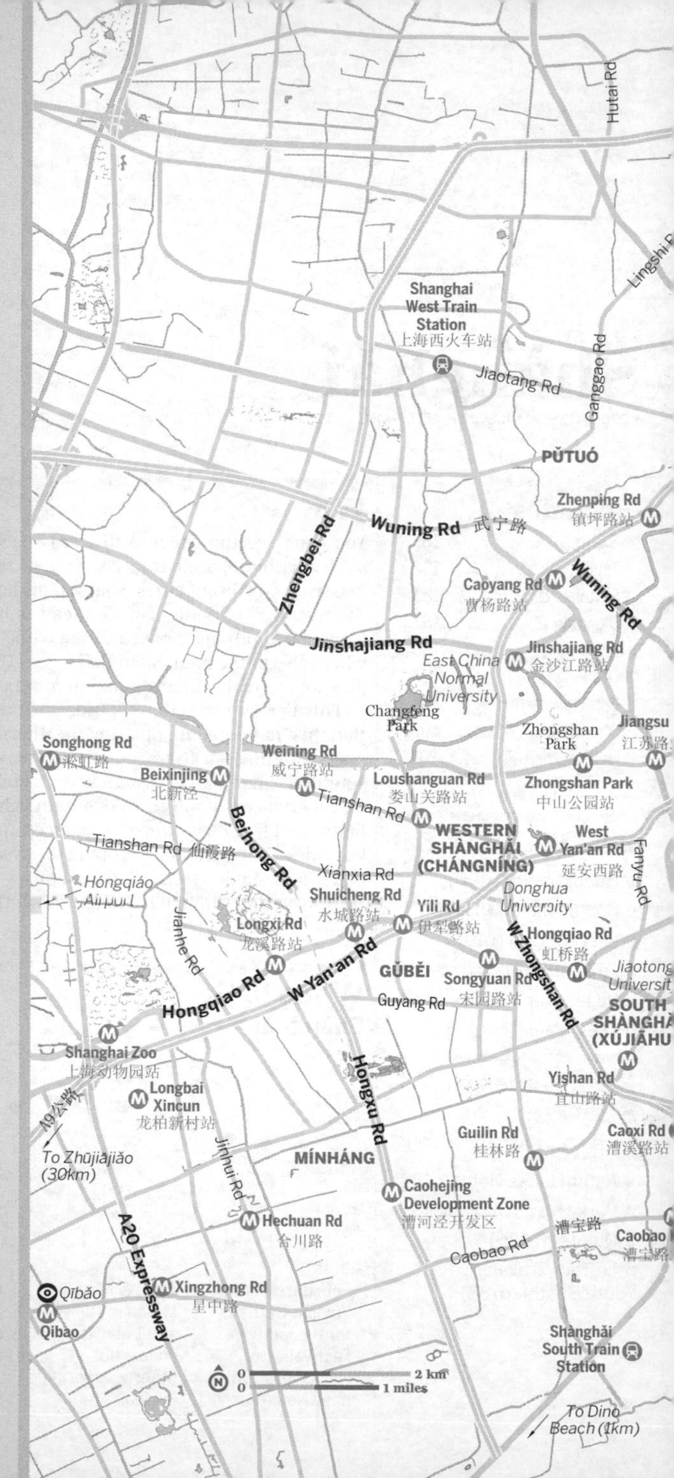

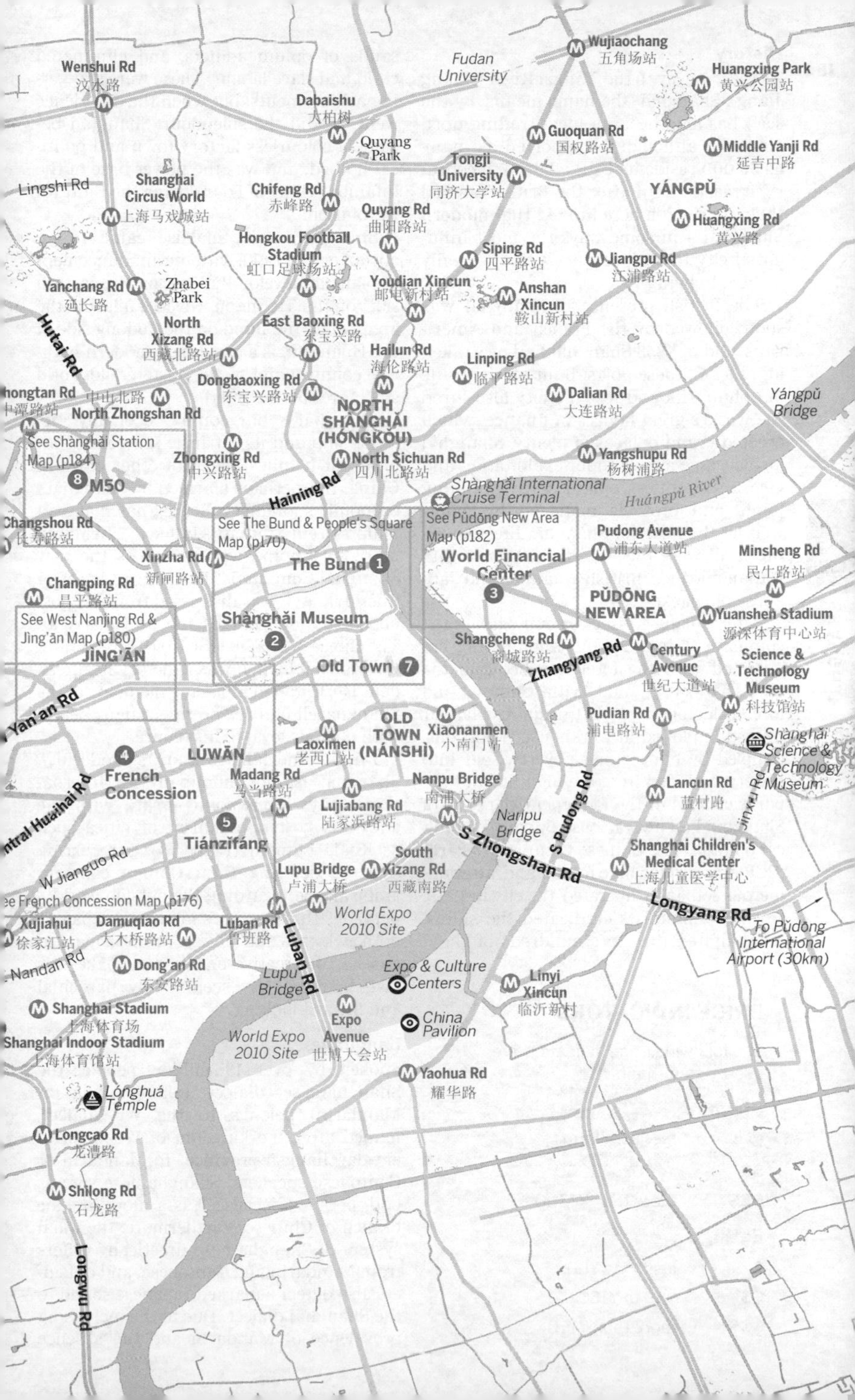

Wujiaochang 五角场站
Fudan University
Huangxing Park 黄兴公园站
Wenshui Rd 汶水路
Dabaishu 大柏树
Quyang Park
Guoquan Rd 国权路站
Middle Yanji Rd 延吉中路
Tongji University 同济大学站
Lingshi Rd
Shanghai Circus World 上海马戏城站
Chifeng Rd 赤峰路
Quyang Rd 曲阳路站
YÁNGPŬ
Huangxing Rd 黄兴路
Hongkou Football Stadium 虹口足球场站
Siping Rd 四平路站
Jiangpu Rd 江浦路站
Yanchang Rd 延长路
Zhabei Park
Youdian Xincun 邮电新村站
Anshan Xincun 鞍山新村站
Hutai Rd
North Xizang Rd 西藏北路站
East Baoxing Rd 东宝兴路
Hailun Rd 海伦路站
Linping Rd 临平路站
Zhongtan Rd 中潭路站
中山北路
North Zhongshan Rd
Dongbaoxing Rd 东宝兴路站
Dalian Rd 大连路站
Yángpŭ Bridge
NORTH SHÀNGHĂI (HÓNGKǑU)
See Shànghǎi Station Map (p184)
M50
Zhongxing Rd 中兴路站
North Sichuan Rd 四川北路站
Yangshupu Rd 杨树浦路
Haining Rd
Shànghǎi International Cruise Terminal
Huángpŭ River
Changshou Rd 长寿路站
See The Bund & People's Square Map (p170)
See Pŭdōng New Area Map (p182)
Pudong Avenue 浦东大道站
Minsheng Rd 民生路站
Xinzha Rd 新闸路站
The Bund
World Financial Center
Changping Rd 昌平路站
PŬDŌNG NEW AREA
Yuanshen Stadium 源深体育中心站
See West Nanjing Rd & Jìng'ān Map (p180)
Shànghǎi Museum
JÌNG'ĀN
Shangcheng Rd 商城路站
Zhangyang Rd
Century Avenue 世纪大道站
Science & Technology Museum 科技馆站
Old Town
Yan'an Rd
OLD TOWN (NÁNSHÌ)
Xiaonanmen 小南门站
Pudian Rd 浦电路站
Shànghǎi Science & Technology Museum
Laoximen 老西门站
LÚWĀN
French Concession
Central Huaihai Rd
Madang Rd 马当路站
Nanpu Bridge 南浦大桥
Lujiabang Rd 陆家浜路站
S Pudong Rd
Lancun Rd 蓝村路
Jinxiu Rd
Nanpu Bridge
Tiánzǐfáng
S Zhongshan Rd
Shanghai Children's Medical Center 上海儿童医学中心
W Jianguo Rd
South Xizang Rd 西藏南路
Lupu Bridge 卢浦大桥
See French Concession Map (p176)
World Expo 2010 Site
Longyang Rd
Xujiahui 徐家汇站
Damuqiao Rd 大木桥路站
Luban Rd 鲁班路
To Pŭdōng International Airport (30km)
Luban Rd
Nandan Rd
Dong'an Rd 东安路站
Expo & Culture Centers
Lupu Bridge
Linyi Xincun 临沂新村
Shanghai Stadium 上海体育场
Expo Avenue 世博大会站
China Pavilion
Shanghai Indoor Stadium 上海体育馆站
World Expo 2010 Site
Yaohua Rd 耀华路
Lónghuá Temple
Longcao Rd 龙漕路
Shilong Rd 石龙路
Longwu Rd

History

As the gateway to the Yangzi River (Cháng Jiāng), Shànghǎi (the name means 'by the sea') has long been an ideal trading port. However, although it supported as many as 50,000 residents by the late 17th century, it wasn't until after the British opened their concession here in 1842 that modern Shànghǎi – in some ways the most influential city in 20th-century China – really came into being.

The British presence in Shànghǎi was soon followed by the French and Americans, and by 1853 Shànghǎi had overtaken all other Chinese ports. Built on the trade of opium, silk and tea, the city also lured the world's great houses of finance, which erected grand palaces of plenty. Shànghǎi also became a byword for exploitation and vice; its countless opium dens, gambling joints and brothels managed by gangs were at the heart of Shànghǎi life. Guarding it all were the American, French and Italian marines, British Tommies and Japanese bluejackets.

After Chiang Kaishek's coup against the communists in 1927, the Kuomintang cooperated with the foreign police and the Shànghǎi gangs, and with Chinese and foreign factory owners, to suppress labour unrest. Exploited in workhouse conditions, crippled by hunger and poverty, sold into slavery, excluded from the high life and the parks created by the foreigners, the poor of Shànghǎi had a voracious appetite for radical opinion. The Chinese Communist Party (CCP) was formed here in 1921 and, after numerous setbacks, 'liberated' the city in 1949.

The communists eradicated the slums, rehabilitated the city's hundreds of thousands of opium addicts, and eliminated child and slave labour. These were staggering achievements; but when the decadence went, so did the splendour. Shànghǎi became a colourless factory town and political hotbed, and was the power base of the infamous Gang of Four during the Cultural Revolution.

Shànghǎi's long malaise came to an abrupt end in 1990, with the announcement of plans to develop Pǔdōng, on the eastern side of the Huángpǔ River. Lùjiāzuǐ, the area facing the Bund on the Pǔdōng side of the Huángpǔ, is a dazzlingly modern high-rise counterpoint to the austere, old-world structures on the Bund.

Shànghǎi's burgeoning economy, its leadership and its intrinsic self-confidence have put it miles ahead of other cities in China. But perhaps alarmed by Shànghǎi's economic supremacy, Běijīng has made attempts to curb the city's influence. In March 2007, Xi Jinping was chosen as the new Shànghǎi Communist Party secretary after Chen Liangyu was dismissed from his post on corruption charges the previous year. The choice of Shaanxi (Shǎnxī)–born Xi Jinping is seen by many as a victory for President Hu Jintao in replacing members of the Shànghǎi clique of ex-president Jiang Zemin with officials loyal to his tenure.

Despite the fanfare and its modernity, Shànghǎi is only nominally an international city; it cannot compare with the effortless cosmopolitanism of cities such as Kuala Lumpur (Malaysia). A recurring sense – deriving from China's constant ambivalence regarding the outside world – pervades that the city's internationalism is both awkward and affected, while a marked absence of creative energy can make this fast-changing city seem oddly parochial and inward-looking.

Language

Spoken by over 13 million people, the Shanghainese dialect (Shànghǎihuà in Mandarin) belongs to the Wú dialect, named after the kingdom of Wú in present-day Jiāngsū province. To Mandarin or Cantonese speakers, Shanghainese sounds odd, perhaps because it is a more archaic branch of Chinese. Furthermore, the tonal system of Shanghainese drastically differs from Mandarin and Cantonese, and outsiders also detect a marked Japanese sound to the Shànghǎi dialect. Due to the increasing prevalence of Mandarin and the absence

PRICE INDICATORS

The following price indicators are used in this chapter:

Sleeping

$	less than Y400
$$	Y400 to Y1300
$$$	more than Y1300

Eating

$	less than Y60
$$	Y60 to Y160
$$$	more than Y160

of a standard form of Shanghainese, the dialect is constantly changing and fewer and fewer young people are able to speak it properly, if at all.

Sights

Shànghǎi municipality covers a huge area, but the city proper is more modest. Broadly, central Shànghǎi is divided into two areas: Pǔxī (west of the Huángpǔ River) and Pǔdōng (east of the Huángpǔ River). The historical attractions belong to Pǔxī, where Shànghǎi's personality is also found: the Bund (officially called East Zhongshan No 1 Rd) and the former foreign concessions, the principal shopping districts, and Shànghǎi's trendiest clusters of bars, restaurants and nightclubs. Pǔdōng is a more recent invention and is the location of the financial district and the famous Shànghǎi skyline. Remember that Shànghǎi is developing at a breakneck pace and there is consequently an even higher rate of change here than in most other major world cities.

The last entrance to many Shànghǎi museums is one hour before closing.

THE BUND 外滩

The area around the Bund is the tourist centre of Shànghǎi and is the city's most famous mile.

The Bund ARCHITECTURE

Symbolic of colonial Shànghǎi, the Bund (Wàitān; Map p170) was the city's Wall St, a place of feverish trading and fortunes made and lost. Coming to Shànghǎi and missing the Bund is like visiting Běijīng and bypassing the Forbidden City or the Great Wall. Originally a towpath for dragging barges of rice, the Bund (an Anglo-Indian term for the embankment of a muddy waterfront) was gradually transformed into a grandiose sweep of the most powerful banks and trading houses in Shànghǎi. The majority of art deco and neoclassical buildings here were built in the early 20th century and presented an imposing – if strikingly un-Chinese – view for those arriving in the busy port.

Today it has emerged as a designer retail and restaurant zone, and the city's most exclusive boutiques, restaurants and hotels see the Bund as the only place to be. The optimum activity here is to simply stroll, contrasting the bones of the past with the futuristic geometry of Pǔdōng's skyline. Evening visits are rewarded by electric views of Pǔdōng and the illuminated grandeur of the Bund. Other options include taking a boat tour on the Huángpǔ River (see p182) or relaxing at some fabulous bars and restaurants. Huángpǔ Park, at the north end of the promenade, features the modest **Bund History Museum** (外滩历史纪念馆; Wàitān Lìshǐ Jìniànguǎn), which has been closed for the past few years for renovations. See the walking tour for a rundown of the area's most famous buildings.

East Nanjing Road ARCHITECTURE

Once known as Nanking Rd, East Nanjing Rd (南京东路; Map p170) was where the first department stores in China were opened in the 1920s, and where the modern era – with its new products and the promise of a radically different lifestyle – was ushered in. A glowing forest of neon at night, it's no longer the cream of Shànghǎi shopping, but it's still one of the most famous and crowded streets in China. Shànghǎi's reputation as the country's most fashionable city was forged in part here, through the new styles and trends introduced in department stores such as the Sun Sun (1926), today the **Shànghǎi No 1 (First) Food Store** (上海市第一食品商店; Shànghǎi Dìyī Shípǐn Shāngdiàn; Map p170; 720 East Nanjing Rd; M People's Sq), and the Sun Company (1936), now the **No 1 Department Store** (上海第一百货商店; Shànghǎi Dìyī Bǎihuò Shāngdiàn; Map p170; 800 East Nanjing Rd; M People's Sq).

Guard against English-speaking Chinese women (or students) shanghaiing you towards extortionate 'tea ceremonies'.

Rockbund Art Museum ART MUSEUM

(上海外滩美术馆; Shànghǎi Wàitān Měishùguǎn; Map p170; www.rockbundartmuseum.org; 20 Huqiu Rd; 虎丘路20号; adult Y15; 10am-6pm Tue-Sun; M East Nanjing Rd) Housed in the former Royal Asiatic Society building (1932) and the adjacent former National Industrial Bank, this private museum behind the Bund focuses on contemporary art, with rotating exhibits year-round. Opened in 2010 as part of the Back Bund renovation project, the Rockbund is off to a promising start as one of the city's top modern-art venues.

FREE **Shànghǎi Post Museum** MUSEUM

(上海邮政博物馆; Shànghǎi Yóuzhèng Bówùguǎn; Map p170; 250 North Suzhou Rd; 北苏州路250号; 9am-5pm Wed, Thu, Sat & Sun; M Tiantong Rd) It may sound like a yawner, but this is actually a pretty good museum, where you can learn about postal history in imperial China, tap your foot to China's

SHÀNGHĂI IN...

One Day

Rise with the sun for early morning riverside scenes on **the Bund** as the vast city stirs from its slumber. Then stroll down East Nanjing Rd to **People's Square** and either the **Shànghǎi Museum** or the **Urban Planning Exhibition Hall**. After a dumpling lunch on Huanghe Rd food street, hop on the metro at People's Sq to shuttle east to Pǔdōng. Explore the fun and interactive **Shànghǎi History Museum** or contemplate the Bund from the breezy Riverside Promenade, then take a high-speed lift to the world's highest observation deck, in the **World Financial Center**, to put Shànghǎi in perspective. Stomach rumbling? Time for dinner in the French Concession, followed by a nightcap on the Bund if you want to go full circle.

Two Days

Pre-empt the crowds with an early start at the Old Town's **Yùyuán Gardens** before poking around for souvenirs on Old St and wandering the alleyways. Make your next stop **Xīntiāndì** for lunch and a visit to the **Shíkùmén Open House Museum**. Taxi it to **Tiánzǐfáng** for the afternoon, before another French Concession dinner. Caught a second wind? Catch the acrobats, hit the clubs or unwind with a traditional Chinese massage.

official postal hymn, *Song of the Mail Swan Geese,* and view rare pre- and post-Liberation stamps (1888–1978). It's located in a magnificent 1924 post office, with panoramic views from the rooftop garden.

Bund Sightseeing Tunnel KITSCH
(外滩观光隧道; Wàitān Guānguāng Suìdào; Map p170; The Bund; one way/return Y45/55; ⏲8am-10.30pm; Ⓜ East Nanjing Rd) The weirdest way to get to Pǔdōng, where train modules convey speechless passengers through a tunnel of garish lights between the Bund and the opposite shore. The entrance is behind the Tourist Information & Service Centre.

FREE **Shànghǎi Gallery of Art** ART GALLERY
(上海沪申画廊; Shànghǎi Hùshēn Huàláng; Map p170; 3rd fl, Three on the Bund; 中山东1路3号3楼; ⏲11am-9pm; Ⓜ East Nanjing Rd) Pop into Shànghǎi's handiest art gallery for glimpses of highbrow and conceptual Chinese art.

PEOPLE'S SQUARE 人民广场
Once the site of the Shànghǎi Racecourse, People's Sq is the modern city's nerve centre. Overshadowed by the dramatic form of **Tomorrow Square** (明天广场; Míngtiān Guǎngchǎng; Map p170), the open space is peppered with museums, performing arts venues and leafy People's Park. Beneath it all, the city's frenetic energy reaches full crescendo amid the tunnels of Shànghǎi's busiest subway interchange.

TOP CHOICE **Shànghǎi Museum** ART MUSEUM
(上海博物馆; Shànghǎi Bówùguǎn; Map p170; www.shanghaimuseum.net; 201 Renmin Ave; 人民大道201号; admission free; ⏲9am-5pm; Ⓜ People's Sq) This must-see Museum guides you through the craft of millennia while simultaneously escorting you through the pages of Chinese history. Expect to spend half, if not most of, a day here (note that entrance is from East Yan'an Rd).

Designed to resemble the shape of an ancient Chinese *dǐng* vessel, the building is home to one of the most impressive collections in China. Take your pick from the archaic green patinas of the **Ancient Chinese Bronzes Gallery** through to the silent solemnity of the **Ancient Chinese Sculpture Gallery**; from the exquisite beauty of the ceramics in the **Zande Lou Gallery** to the measured and timeless flourishes captured in the **Chinese Calligraphy Gallery**. Chinese painting, seals, jade, Ming and Qing furniture, coins and ethnic costumes are also on offer in this museum, intelligently displayed in well-lit galleries. Seats are provided outside galleries on each floor for when lethargy strikes.

Photography is allowed in some galleries. The audio guide (available in eight languages) is well worth the Y40 (deposit Y400 or your passport). The excellent **museum shop** sells postcards, a rich array of books, and faithful replicas of the museum's ceramics and other pieces. There are a few overpriced shops and teahouses inside the museum, as well as a snack bar, a cloakroom and an ATM.

Shànghǎi Urban Planning Exhibition Hall ARCHITECTURE MUSEUM
(上海城市规划展示馆; Shànghǎi Chéngshì Guīhuà Zhǎnshìguǎn; Map p170; www.supec.org; 100 Renmin Ave; 人民大道100号; adult Y30; ⏲9am-5pm Mon-Thu, to 6pm Fri-Sun; Ⓜ People's Sq) Some cities romanticise their past, others promise good times in the present, but only in China are you expected to visit places that haven't even been built yet. The 3rd floor features Shànghǎi's idealised future (c 2020), with an incredible model layout of the megalopolis-to-come plus a dizzying Virtual World 3-D wrap-around tour complete with celebratory fireworks. Balancing it all out are photos and maps of historic Shànghǎi. Entrance is from Xizang Rd.

Shànghǎi Museum of Contemporary Art (Moca Shànghǎi) ART MUSEUM
(上海当代艺术馆; Shànghǎi Dāngdài Yìshùguǎn; Map p170; www.mocashanghai.org; People's Park; 人民公园; adult Y20; ⏲10am-9.30pm; Ⓜ People's Sq) This nonprofit contemporary art centre has an all-glass construction to maximise Shànghǎi's often dismal sunlight and a tip-top location in People's Park. Temporary exhibits here range from the work of local artist Zhou Tiehai and urban dystopia instalments to Japanese ecodesign and multimedia instalments.

Great World ENTERTAINMENT
(大世界; Dà Shìjiè; Map p170; Middle Xizang Rd; 西藏中路; Ⓜ Dashijie) Shànghǎi's famous house of ill repute in the 1930s, Great World has been closed for renovations for a decade. It's unclear when it will reopen.

Shànghǎi Art Museum ART MUSEUM
(上海美术馆; Shànghǎi Měishùguǎn; Map p170; www.sh-artmuseum.org.cn; 325 West Nanjing Rd; 南京西路325号; adult Y20; ⏲9am-5pm, last entry 4pm; Ⓜ People's Sq) The exhibits of modern Chinese art (often 20th century) are hit-and-miss, but the building (the former Shànghǎi Racecourse Club) and its period details are simply gorgeous. English captions are sporadic.

Madame Tussaud's WAX MUSEUM
(上海杜莎夫人蜡像馆; Shànghǎi Dùshā Fūrén Làxiàngguǎn; Map p170; New World Department Store, 2-68 West Nanjing Rd; 南京西路2-68号; adult/child Y135/80; Ⓜ People's Sq) This waxworks museum is largely aimed at locals, but could work for families when a summer downpour inundates town.

OLD TOWN 南市

Known to locals as Nán Shì (Southern City), the Old Town is the most traditionally Chinese part of Shànghǎi. Its circular layout still reflects the footprint of its 16th-century walls, erected to keep marauding Japanese pirates at bay. Sitting on a piece of coveted real estate, and with many residents considering the buildings old and run down, it's not surprising that much of the neighbourhood has been bulldozed over the past decade to make room for developers to build upwards.

Yùyuán Gardens & Bazaar GARDENS, BAZAAR
(豫园、豫园商城; Yùyuán & Yùyuán Shāngchéng; Map p170) With their shaded alcoves, glittering pools churning with carp, pavilions, pines sprouting wistfully from rockeries, and roving packs of Japanese tourists, these **gardens** (豫园; Yùyuán; Map p170; admission Y30; ⏲8.30am-5.30pm, last entry 5pm; Ⓜ Yuyuan Garden) are one of Shànghǎi's premier sights – but are overpoweringly crowded at weekends.

The Pan family, rich Ming-dynasty officials, founded the gardens, which took 18 years (1559–77) to be nurtured into existence before bombardment during the Opium War in 1842. The gardens took another trashing during French reprisals for attacks on their nearby concession by Taiping rebels. Restored, they are a fine example of Ming garden design. The spring and summer blossoms bring a fragrant and floral aspect to the gardens, especially in the heavy petals of its *Magnolia grandiflora*, Shànghǎi's flower. Other trees include the Luohan pine, bristling with thick needles, and willows, gingkos and cherry trees.

Next to the garden entrance is the **Húxīntíng Teahouse** (湖心亭; Húxīntíng; Map p170; ⏲8.30am-9.30pm), once part of the gardens and now one of the most famous teahouses in China.

The adjacent **bazaar** may be tacky, but it's good for a browse if you can handle the push and pull of the crowds and vendors. The nearby Taoist **Temple of the Town God** (城隍庙; Chénghuáng Miào; Map p170; Yùyuán Bazaar; admission Y10; ⏲8.30am-4.30pm) is also worth visiting. Just outside the bazaar is **Old Street** (老街; Lǎo Jiē), known more prosaically as Middle Fangbang Rd, a busy street lined with curio shops and teahouses.

START BROADWAY MANSIONS
FINISH METEOROLOGICAL SIGNAL TOWER
DISTANCE 1.3KM
DURATION ONE HOUR

Walking Tour
The Bund

This comprehensive, easy-to-manage walk guides you along the Bund, Shànghǎi's most memorable mile. The walk can be done either by day or by night; during the evening the buildings are closed but the Bund is spectacularly illuminated and the nocturnal views to Pǔdōng are delicious. Walk along either the west side of East Zhongshan No 1 Rd (the Bund) or along the elevated promenade on the other side of the road overlooking the river.

At the northern end of the Bund, on the north bank of Sūzhōu Creek (also known as Wúsōng River), rises the brick pile of 1 **Broadway Mansions**, built in 1934 as an exclusive apartment block. The Foreign Correspondents' Club occupied the 9th floor in the 1930s and used its fine views to report the Japanese bombing of the city in 1937. The building became the headquarters of the Japanese army during WWII.

Just across Huangpu Rd from the 2 **Russian consulate** is the distinguished 3 **Astor House Hotel**. Opened in 1846 as the Richards' Hotel, this was Shànghǎi's first hotel. The ballroom here hosted the Shanghai stock exchange from 1990 to 1998.

Head south over 4 **Wàibǎidù Bridge** (also called Garden Bridge), which dates from 1907; before 1856 all crossings had to be made by ferry. The first bridge here was the wooden Wills' Bridge, where a charge was levied on users.

Turn west (right) to walk along Sūzhōu Creek until you reach the area known as the Back Bund. The first building you'll see here is the 5 **Union Church**, which dates to 1885. Behind the church, you can catch a glimpse of 6 **the former British Consulate** and gardens. The British Consulate was the first foreign building to go up in Shànghǎi, in the 1840s, though the current structures date to 1873.

Across the road from the former British Consulate is a row of beautiful old buildings, beginning with the Gothamesque 7 **China Baptist Publication Building**. Built in 1930 and home to a Christian printing press, this is one of many art deco structures built by Ladislas Hudec, a Hungarian who was one of Shànghǎi's most famous architects. As you'll notice, the buildings behind the Bund were more diverse in nature then the powerful banks and trading houses on the waterfront itself.

Turn left on East Beijing Rd and head back towards the Bund waterfront. At No 27 on the Bund is the former headquarters of early opium traders 8 **Jardine Matheson**, which became one of Shànghǎi's great *hongs* (trading houses). At No 23 is the imposing 9 **Bank of China** building, which director HH Kung commissioned in 1936, with specific instructions that it should be higher than the adjacent Cathay Hotel. An unusual melange of styles, the top was eventually changed to a blue Chinese roof, and it wound up being one metre shorter than its neighbour. Note the funky art deco lions sitting in front.

The landmark 10 **Peace Hotel** opened in 1929 as the most luxurious hotel in the Far East, when it was known as the Cathay. After three years of renovations, it had just reopened in all its original art deco glory as this book went to press. If you haven't already been to the 11 **Promenade**, this is a good spot to cross over for views of the Pǔdōng skyline.

Originally the Chartered Bank of Australia, India and China, 12 **Bund 18** is a high-profile commercial conversion. In the evening, pop up to Bar Rouge on the 7th floor for sumptuous views.

Next door at No 17 is the former home of the 13 **North China Daily News**. Known as the 'Old Lady of the Bund', the *News* ran from 1864 to 1951 as the main English-language newspaper in China and the mouthpiece of the foreign-run municipality commission. See if you can spot the typo in the paper's motto, etched in stone above the central windows.

Three buildings down, at No 13, the **14 Customs House** was completed in 1927. The building is topped by a clock face (once the largest in East Asia) and 'Big Ching', a bell that was modelled on Big Ben and replaced during the Cultural Revolution by loudspeakers that issued revolutionary slogans and songs.

Next door to the Customs House at No 12 is the grandest building on the Bund, the former **15 Hong Kong & Shanghai Bank**. The bank was established in Hong Kong in 1864 and Shànghǎi in 1865 to finance trade, and soon became one of the richest banks in Shànghǎi, arranging the indemnity paid after the Boxer Uprising (1900). When the current building was constructed in 1923 it was the second-largest bank in the world and reportedly 'the finest building east of Suez'. Enter and marvel at the beautiful mosaic ceiling (no photographs allowed), featuring the 12 zodiac signs and the world's eight great banking centres.

The next few buildings are now upmarket entertainment complexes and retail outlets. The most famous stands at No 3, the impressive restaurant and retail development **16 Three on the Bund**.

The 1911 **17 Shànghǎi Club**, the city's best-known bastion of British snobbery, stood at No 2 on the Bund. The plutocratic club had 20 rooms for residents, but its most famous accoutrement was the bar, which, at 110ft (about 33.6m), was said to be the world's longest. Businessmen would sit here according to rank (no Chinese or women were allowed in the club), with the *taipans* (company bosses) closest to the view of the Bund, sipping chilled champagne and comparing fortunes. It is now the Waldorf Astoria Hotel which, incidentally, had just opened a new Long Bar as this book went to press.

Just across the street is the 49m-tall **18 Meteorological Signal Tower**, originally built in 1908 opposite the French consulate and, in 1993, moved 22m north as part of the revamping of the Bund. Today there is a small collection of old prints of the Bund and an upstairs cafe (Atanu) with fine views from its terrace.

East Yan'an Rd, once a canal and later filled in to become Ave Edward VII, the dividing line between the International Settlement and the French Concession, marks the end of the walk.

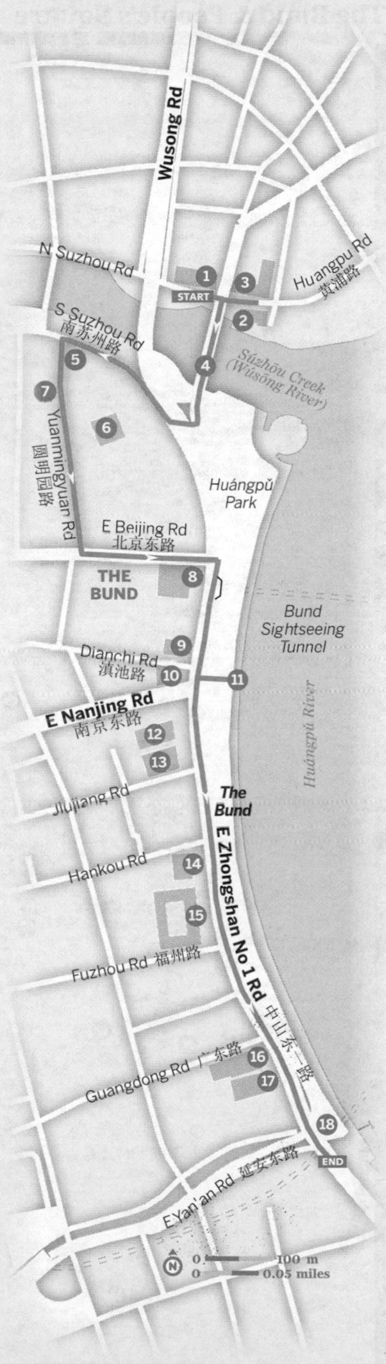

The Bund & People's Square

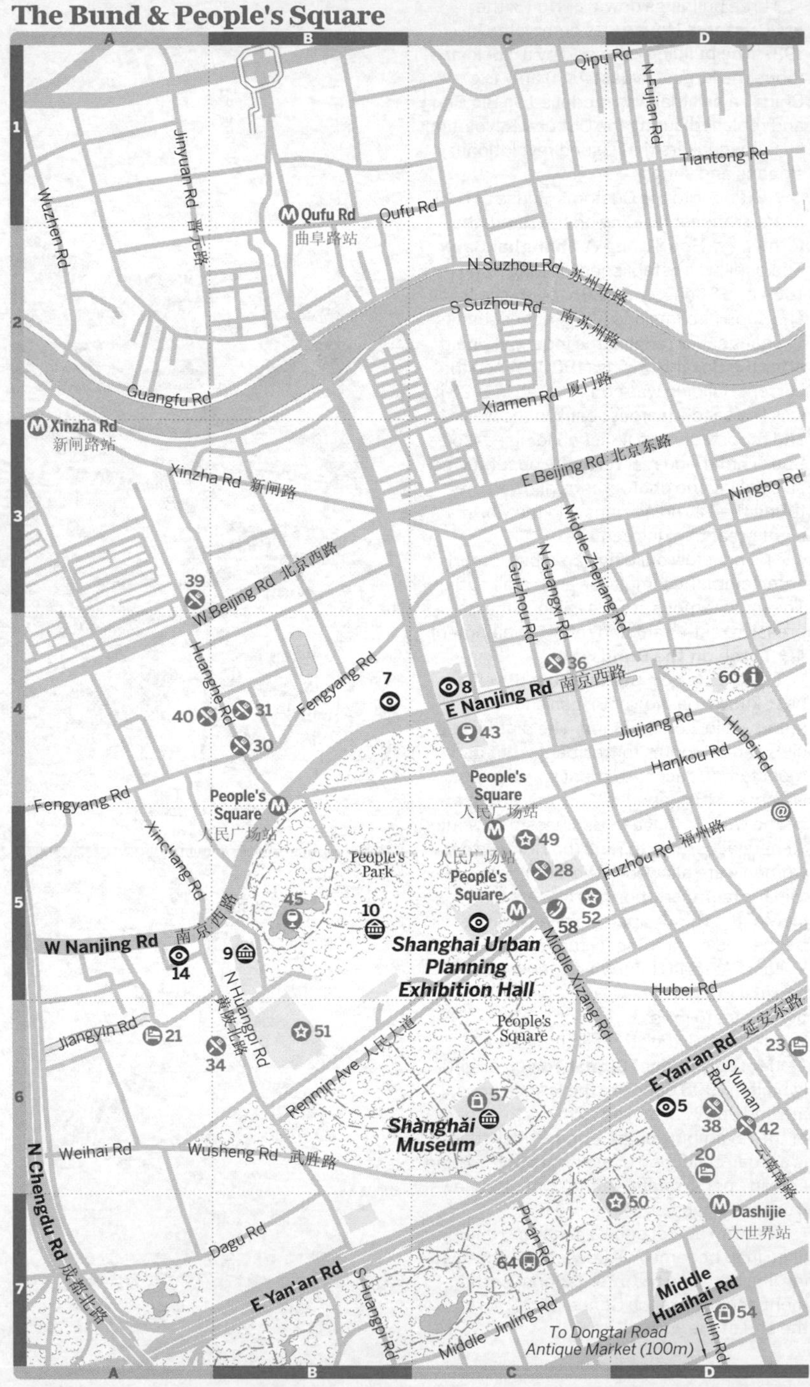

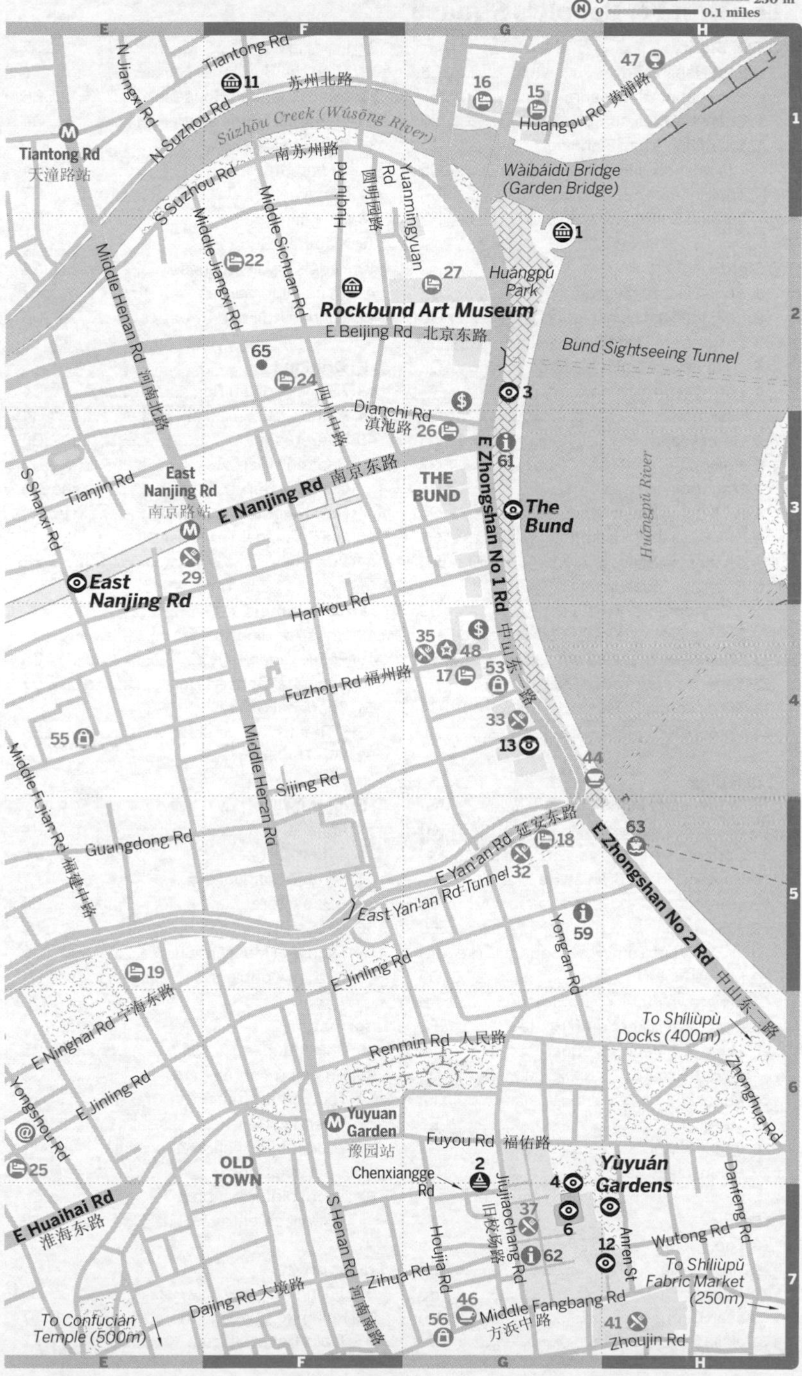
0 250 m
0 0.1 miles
Tiantong Rd
苏州北路
N Jiangxi Rd
N Suzhou Rd
Súzhōu Creek (Wúsōng River)
Huangpu Rd 黄浦路
Tiantong Rd
天潼路站
S Suzhou Rd
南苏州路
Middle Jiangxi Rd
Middle Sichuan Rd
Huqiu Rd
圆明园路
Yuanmingyuan Rd
Wàibáidù Bridge
(Garden Bridge)
Huángpǔ Park
Middle Henan Rd
Rockbund Art Museum
E Beijing Rd 北京东路
Bund Sightseeing Tunnel
河南北路
四川中路
Dianchi Rd
滇池路
E Zhongshan No 1 Rd
Huángpǔ River
S Shanxi Rd
Tianjin Rd
East Nanjing Rd
南京路站
E Nanjing Rd 南京东路
THE BUND
The Bund
East Nanjing Rd
Hankou Rd
中山东一路
Fuzhou Rd 福州路
Middle Fujian Rd
Middle Henan Rd
Sijing Rd
Guangdong Rd
福建中路
E Yan'an Rd 延安东路
E Zhongshan No 2 Rd
E Yan'an Rd Tunnel
East Yan'an Rd Tunnel
Yong'an Rd
E Jinling Rd
中山东二路
E Ninghai Rd 宁海东路
Renmin Rd 人民路
To Shílìùpù Docks (400m)
Zhonghua Rd
Yongshou Rd
E Jinling Rd
Yuyuan Garden
豫园站
Fuyou Rd 福佑路
OLD TOWN
Chenxiangge Rd
Yùyuán Gardens
E Huaihai Rd
淮海东路
S Henan Rd
Houjia Rd
Jiujiaochang Rd
旧校场路
Anren St
Wutong Rd
Danfeng Rd
To Shíliùpǔ Fabric Market (250m)
Zihua Rd
Dajing Rd 大境路
河南南路
Middle Fangbang Rd
方浜中路
Zhoujin Rd
To Confucian Temple (500m)
SHÀNGHĂI

The Bund & People's Square

Top Sights

East Nanjing Rd ... E3
Rockbund Art Museum ... F2
Shànghǎi Museum ... C6
Shànghǎi Urban Planning Exhibition Hall ... C5
The Bund ... G3
Yùyuán Gardens ... H7

Sights

1 Bund History Museum ... G2
2 Chénxiānggé Nunnery ... G6
3 Entrance to Bund Sightseeing Tunnel ... G2
4 Entrance to Yùyuán Gardens & Bazaar ... G6
5 Great World ... D6
6 Húxīntíng Teahouse ... G7
7 Madame Tussaud's ... B4
8 No 1 Department Store ... C4
9 Shànghǎi Art Museum ... B5
Shànghǎi Gallery of Art ... (see 13)
10 Shànghǎi Museum of Contemporary Art ... B5
Shànghǎi No 1 (First) Food Store (see 36)
11 Shànghǎi Post Museum ... F1
12 Temple of the Town God ... H7
13 Three on the Bund ... G4
14 Tomorrow Square ... A5

Sleeping

15 Astor House Hotel ... G1
16 Broadway Mansions ... G1
17 Captain Hostel ... G4
18 Captain Hostel (Yan'an Rd Branch) ... G5
19 Jinjiang Inn ... E5
JW Marriott Tomorrow Square ... (see 14)
20 Marvel Hotel ... D6
21 Mingtown Etour Youth Hostel ... A6
22 Mingtown Hiker Youth Hostel ... F2
23 Mingtown People's Square Youth Hostel ... D6
24 Motel 268 ... F2
25 Motel 268 ... E6
26 Peace Hotel ... G3
27 Peninsula Hotel ... G2

Eating

28 Food Republic ... C5
29 Hóngyī Plaza ... E3
30 Huanghe Rd Food Street ... B4
Jean Georges ... (see 13)
31 Jiājiā Soup Dumpings ... B4
32 Lost Heaven ... G5
33 M on the Bund ... G4
34 Nina's Sìchuān House ... B6
35 Shànghǎi Grandmother ... G4
36 Shànghǎi No 1 (First) Food Store ... C4
37 Sōngyuèlóu ... G7
38 Wǔ Fāng Zhāi ... D6
39 Xiǎo Nán Guó ... A3
40 Yang's Fry Dumpings ... A4
41 Yù Fashion Garden ... H7
42 Yunnan Rd Food Street ... D6

Drinking

43 789 Nanjing Lu Bar ... C4
44 Atanu ... G4
45 Barbarossa ... B5
Captain's Bar ... (see 17)
Glamour Bar ... (see 33)
New Heights ... (see 13)
46 Old Shànghǎi Teahouse ... G7
47 Vue ... H1

Entertainment

48 House of Blues & Jazz ... G4
49 Peace Cinema ... C5
50 Shànghǎi Concert Hall ... D7
51 Shànghǎi Grand Theatre ... B6
52 Yìfū Theatre ... C5

Shopping

53 Annabel Lee ... G4
54 Cybermart ... D7
55 Foreign Languages Bookstore ... E4
56 Old Street ... G7
57 Shànghǎi Museum Shop ... C6
Sūzhōu Cobblers ... (see 17)

Information

58 China Mobile ... C5
59 Huángpǔ Tourist Centre ... G5
60 Tourist Information & Service Centre ... D4
61 Tourist Information & Service Centre ... G3
62 Tourist Information & Service Centre ... G7

Transport

63 Jīnlíng Rd Ferry ... H5
64 Pu'an Rd Bus Station ... C7
65 Train Ticket Office ... F2

Chénxiānggé Nunnery BUDDHIST TEMPLE
(沉香阁; Chénxiāng Gé; Map p170; 29 Chenxiangge Rd; 沉香阁路29号; admission Y10; ⏲7am-4pm; Ⓜ Yuyuan Garden) Sheltering a community of around 40 dark-brown-clothed nuns, this gorgeous yellow-walled temple is a tranquil portal to a devout existence far from the city's frantic temporal realm. Climb the **Guanyin Tower** (观音楼; Guānyīn Lóu; admission Y2) at the rear hall to view an exquisite statue of Guanyin, the Buddhist goddess of compassion.

Confucian Temple CONFUCIAN TEMPLE
(文庙; Wén Miào; 215 Wenmiao Rd; 文庙路215号; admission Y10; ⏲9am-5pm; Ⓜ Laoximen) This well-tended temple to the dictum-coining sage-cum-social theorist is a cultivated acreage of maples, pines, magnolias and birdsong. Originally dating from 1294, the temple was moved to its current site in 1855. There's a secondhand book market here on Sunday mornings.

FRENCH CONCESSION 法租界

Once home to the bulk of Shànghǎi's adventurers, revolutionaries, gangsters, prostitutes and writers, the French Concession is the most graceful part of the city. Today a residential, retail and restaurant district with atmospheric tree-lined streets, the French Concession is a name you won't find appearing on any Chinese maps, but it ranges elegantly through the districts of Lúwān and Xúhuì, also taking in slices of Chángníng and Jìng'ān. The cream of Shànghǎi's old residential buildings and art deco apartment blocks, hotels and edifices are preserved here, while commercial Huaihai Rd teems with shoppers. The district naturally tends towards gentrification, but it's also a trendy and happening enclave, excellent for random exploration in a slow progression or by full immersion in Tiánzǐfáng, a hip quadrant of lane housing overflowing with shops and cafes, which has overtaken Xīntiāndì as one of the latest retail and entertainment hot spots.

Tiánzǐfáng ART GALLERIES, SHOPS
(田子坊; Map p176; Lane 210, Taikang Rd; 泰康路210弄; Ⓜ Dapuqiao) Xīntiāndì and Tiánzǐfáng are based on a similar idea – an entertainment complex housed within a warren of traditional *lòngtáng* (alleyways) – but when it comes to genuine charm and vibrancy, Tiánzǐfáng is the one that delivers. Also known as Taikang Lu (泰康路) or Taikang Rd, this community of design studios, wi-fi cafes and boutiques is the perfect antidote to Shànghǎi's oversized malls and intimidating skyscrapers. With some families still residing in neighbouring buildings, a community mood survives.

There are three main north–south lanes (Nos 210, 248, 274) criss-crossed by irregular east–west alleyways, which makes exploration slightly disorienting and fun. On the main lane is the excellent **Deke Erh Art Centre** (尔冬强艺术中心; Ěr Dōngqiáng Yìshù Zhōngxīn; Map p176; No 2, Lane 210), owned by a local photographer and author. Another gallery is **Unique Hill** (奇岗草堂; Qígǎng Cǎotáng; Map p176; No 10, Lane 210), with a collection of old Shànghǎi photos and posters.

Of course, the real activity here is shopping, and the recent explosion of creative start-ups makes for some interesting finds, from ethnic embroidery and hand-wrapped pu-erh teas to retro communist dinnerware. Elsewhere, a growing band of cool cafes, such as Kommune (p194), can sort out meals and drinks and take the weight off your feet. Don't bother looking for Chinese food here; there isn't any.

Xīntiāndì SHOPS
(新天地; Map p176; www.xintiandi.com; cnr Taicang & Madang Rds; 太仓路与马当路路口; Ⓜ South Huangpi Rd, Xintiandi) Xīntiāndì hasn't even been around for a decade yet and already it's a Shànghǎi icon. An upmarket retail and dining complex consisting of largely rebuilt *shíkùmén* houses (low-rise tenement buildings built in the early 1900s), this was the first development in the city to prove that historic architecture does, in fact, have economic value. Well-heeled shoppers and alfresco diners keep the place busy until late, while two museums add a dash of culture to the mix.

The north block is where most of the action is. The small **Shíkùmén Open House Museum** (屋里厢石库门民居陈列馆; Wūlǐxiāng Shíkùmén Mínjū Chénlièguǎn; Map p176; admission Y20; ⏲10.30am-10.30pm Sun-Thu, 11am-11pm Fri & Sat) depicts traditional life in a 10-room Shànghǎi *shíkùmén*. Beyond this, it's best for strolling the prettified alleyways and enjoying a summer's evening over drinks or a meal.

FREE **Site of the 1st National Congress of the CCP** COMMUNISM MUSEUM
(中共一大会址纪念馆; Zhōnggòng Yīdà Huìzhǐ; Map p176; 76 Xingye Rd; 兴业路76号; ⏲9am-5pm; Ⓜ South Huangpi Rd, Xintiandi) The CCP was founded in July 1921 in this French

SEDUCTION & THE CITY

Shànghǎi owes its reputation as the most fashionable city in China to the calendar poster, whose print runs once numbered in the tens of millions and whose distribution reached from China's interior to Southeast Asia. The basic idea behind the poster – associating a product with an attractive woman to encourage subconscious desire and consumption – today sounds like Marketing 101, but in the early 20th century it was revolutionary. Calendar posters not only introduced new products to Chinese everywhere, their portrayal of Shànghǎi women – wearing makeup and stylish clothing, smoking cigarettes and surrounded by foreign goods – set the standard for modern fashion that many Chinese women would dream of for decades. Today, reproduction posters are sold throughout the Old Town for as little as Y10, though finding a bona fide original is quite a challenge. For an in-depth look at calendar posters and Shànghǎi's role in shaping modern China, see Wen-hsin Yeh's *Shanghai Splendor.*

Concession *shíkùmén* building in one fell swoop, converting an unassuming block into one of Chinese communism's holiest shrines. Now a museum, its dizzying Marxist spin and communist narcissism is irritating, but you can nonetheless visit the room where the Party began.

Propaganda Poster Art Centre ART GALLERY
(宣传画年画艺术中心; Xuānchuánhuà Niánhuà Yìshù Zhōngxīn; Map p176; www.shanghaipropagandaart.com; Room B-OC, President Mansion, 868 Huashan Rd; 华山路868号B-OC室; admission Y20; ⌚10am-5pm; Ⓜ Shanghai Library, Jiangsu Rd) If phalanxes of red tractors, bumper harvests, muscled peasants and lantern-jawed proletariat get you going, this small gallery in the bowels of a residential block will truly fire you up. Go weak-kneed at the cartoon-world of anti-US defiance, and size up a collection of 3000 original posters from the 1950s, '60s and '70s – the golden age of Maoist poster production. The centre divides into a showroom and a shop featuring posters and postcards for sale. Once you find the main entrance, a guard will point the way.

Sun Yatsen's Former Residence HISTORIC RESIDENCE
(孙中山故居; Sūn Zhōngshān Gùjū; Map p176; 7 Xiangshan Rd; 香山路7号; admission Y20; ⌚9am-4.30pm; Ⓜ South Shaanxi Rd, Xīntiāndì) China is stuffed to the gills with Sun Yatsen memorabilia, and this former residence, on what was previously rue Molière, is where the founder of modern China (posthumously dubbbed Guófù, Father of the Nation) lived for six years. After Sun's death, his wife, Song Qingling (1893–1981) remained here until 1937, watched by plain-clothes Kuomintang and French police. The two-storey house is decorated with period furnishings, despite looting by the Japanese.

Wukang Road Tourist Information Center ARCHITECTURE
(武康路旅游咨询中心; Wǔkāng Lù Lǚyóu Zīxún Zhōngxīn; Map p176; www.qjtrip.com/wukangroad; 393 Wukang Rd; 武康路393号; ⌚9am-5pm; Ⓜ Shanghai Library) On one of the French Concession's best-preserved streets, this centre displays scale-model concession buildings, and maps for self-guided walking tours of Wukang Rd.

WEST NANJING ROAD & JÌNG'ĀN
南京西路、静安

Lined with sharp top-end shopping malls, clusters of foreign offices and a dense crop of embassies and consulates, West Nanjing Rd is where Shànghǎi's streets are paved with gold, or at least Prada and Gucci.

But head north of West Nanjing Rd and you're plunged into a grittier and more absorbing section of Jìng'ān, which extends until reaching the Shànghǎi Railway Station. Like Hóngkǒu (north of the Bund), this area is primed for development.

Jade Buddha Temple BUDDHIST TEMPLE
(玉佛寺; Yùfó Sì; Map p180; 170 Anyuan Rd; 安远路170号; adult Y20; ⌚8am-4.30pm; Ⓜ Changshou Rd) One of Shànghǎi's few active Buddhist monasteries, this temple was built between 1911 and 1918. The centrepiece is the 1.9m-high pale green **Jade Buddha** (Yùfó), seated upstairs in his own hall. It is said that Hui Gen (Wei Ken), a Pǔtuóshān monk, travelled to Myanmar (Burma) via Tibet, lugged five jade Buddhas back to China and then sought alms to build a temple for them. The beautiful effigy of Sakyamuni, clearly Southeast Asian in style,

gazes ethereally from a cabinet. Visitors are not able to approach the statue, but can admire it from a distance. An additional charge of Y10 is levied to see the statue (no photographs).

An equally elegant **reclining Buddha** is downstairs, opposite a much more substantial copy in stone. A large **vegetarian restaurant** (素菜餐厅; sùcài cāntīng; Map p184; 999 Jiangning Rd) is attached to the temple around the corner.

In February the temple is very busy during the Lunar New Year, when some 20,000 Chinese Buddhists throng to pray for prosperity.

FREE **M50** ART GALLERIES

(创意产业集聚区; M50 M Wǔshí Chuàngyì Chǎnyè Jíjùqū; Map p180; 50 Moganshan Rd; 莫干山路50号; ⏲10am-6pm Tue-Sun; Ⓜ Shanghai Railway Station) Běijīng may dominate the art scene in China, but Shànghǎi has its own thriving gallery subculture, centred on this complex of industrial buildings down dusty Moganshan Rd in the north of town. Although the artists who originally established the enclave are long gone, it is well worth putting aside a half-day to poke around the many galleries here.

Like all of Shànghǎi's galleries, cutting-edge work is often surrounded by mediocrity, so prepare to sift if you're in a buying frame of mind. The best of the bunch include old timer **ShanghART** (香格纳画廊, Xiānggénà Huàláng; www.shanghartgallery.com; Bldg 16 & 18), the collaborative and provocative **island6** (www.island6.org; 2nd fl, Bldg 6), and photography from **OFoto** (www.ofoto-gallery.com; 2nd fl, Bldg 13) and **m97** (www.m97gallery.com; 2nd fl, 97 Moganshan Rd), the latter of which is across the street. When your legs finally give way, flop down at **Bāndù Cabin** (Map p184). Evening entertainment includes **Image Tunnel** (Map p184; 2nd fl, Bldg 19; admission Y30), which shows independent Chinese films on Saturdays (7pm).

Jìng'ān Temple BUDDHIST TEMPLE

(静安寺; Jìng'ān Sì; Map p179; 1686-88 West Nanjing Rd; 南京西路1686-1688号; admission Y30; ⏲7.30am-5pm; Ⓜ Jing'an Temple) A skyscraper only needs a few years to go up in Shànghǎi, but the rebuilding of Jìng'ān Temple (largely destroyed in 1851) seems an eternal work in progress. The recent add-ons are eye-catching and make for some great photos when contrasted with the surrounding supertowers, but the main temple hall remains under construction. The temple manages to somehow sum up Shànghǎi: 5% traditional, 95% rebuild.

Shànghǎi Natural History Museum SCIENCE MUSEUM

(上海自然博物馆; Shànghǎi Zìrán Bówùguǎn; Diaosu Park; 雕塑公园; Ⓜ Shanghai Natural History Museum) The city's new natural history museum is expected to open in 2012.

PŬDŌNG NEW AREA 浦东新区

The colossal concrete-and-steel Pǔdōng New Area (Pǔdōng Xīnqū), which was, until recently, 350 sq km of boggy farmland, stretches off to the East China Sea from the skyscraper-fragmented skyline of Lùjiāzuǐ, one of Shànghǎi's most photographed panoramas.

Its main attractions include some fine museums, the simply stratospheric Shànghǎi World Financial Center and Jīnmào Tower, delicious views across to the Bund, and some of Shànghǎi's best hotels. It is not, however, very pedestrian friendly; the most interesting area for visitors is around the Lujiazui metro station.

Shànghǎi World Financial Center SKYSCRAPER

(SWFC; 上海环球金融中心; Shànghǎi Huánqiú Jīnróng Zhōngxīn; Map p182; www.swfc-observatory.com; 100 Century Ave; 世纪大道100号; observation deck 94th/97th/100th fl, adult Y100/110/150; ⏲8am-midnight; Ⓜ Lujiazui) The neck-craning 492m-high Shànghǎi World Financial Center was never able to grab the ever-elusive title of world's tallest building, but it is nonetheless a stunning addition to the Pǔdōng skyline. With the world's highest observation deck (there are three decks in total, on the 94th, 97th and 100th floors) and the world's 2nd-highest hotel above ground level (at research time), even the

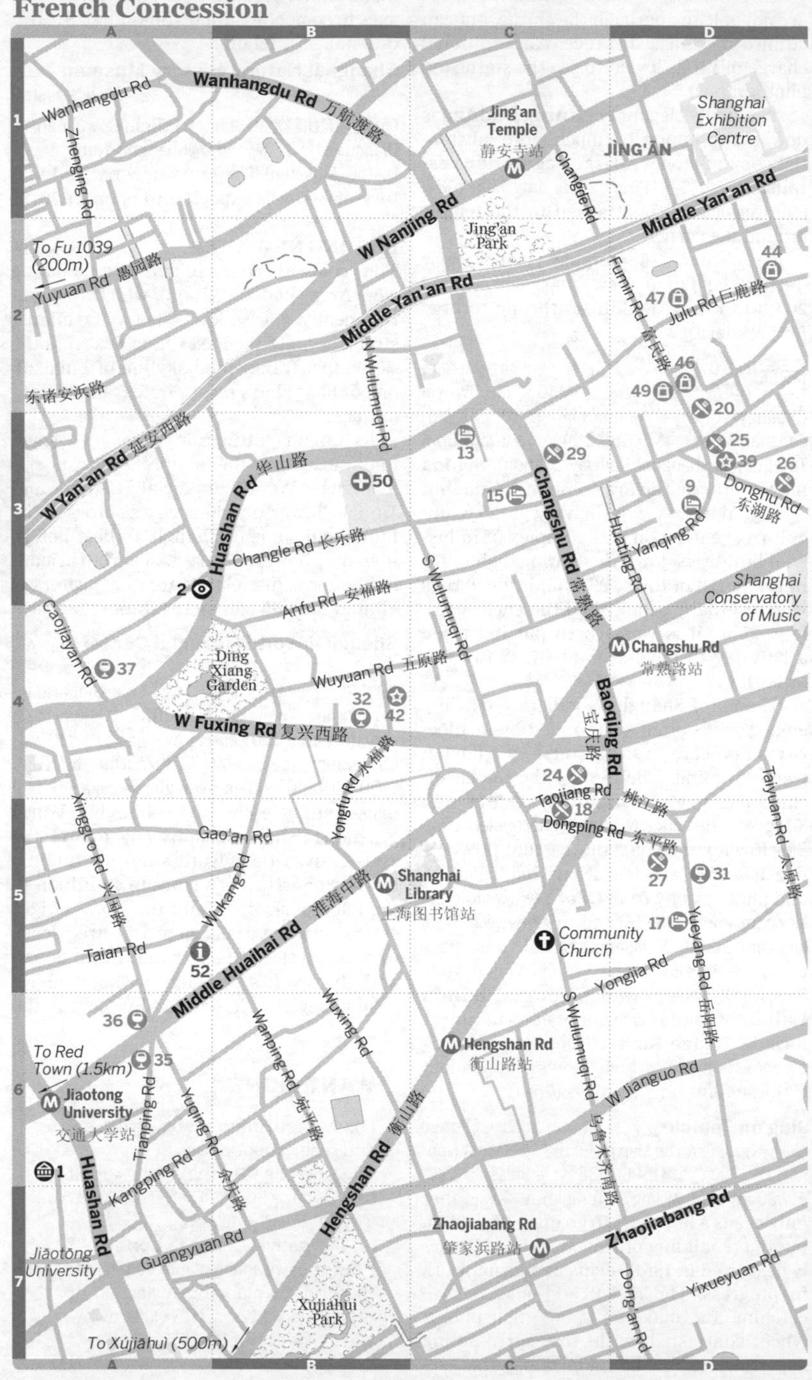
Wanhangdu Rd 万航渡路
Wanhangdu Rd
Zhenging Rd
Jing'an Temple
静安寺站
Shanghai Exhibition Centre
JÌNG'ĀN
Changde Rd
W Nanjing Rd
Middle Yan'an Rd
Jing'an Park
To Fu 1039 (200m)
Yuyuan Rd 愚园路
Middle Yan'an Rd
Fumin Rd 富民路
Julu Rd 巨鹿路
N Wulumuqi Rd
东诸安浜路
W Yan'an Rd 延安西路
华山路
Huashan Rd
Changshu Rd 常熟路
Donghu Rd 东湖路
Huating Rd
Yanqing Rd
Changle Rd 长乐路
Anfu Rd 安福路
S Wulumuqi Rd
Shanghai Conservatory of Music
Caojiayan Rd
Ding Xiang Garden
Wuyuan Rd 五原路
Changshu Rd
常熟路站
Baoqing Rd
宝庆路
W Fuxing Rd 复兴西路
Yongfu Rd 永福路
Taojiang Rd 桃江路
Dongping Rd 东平路
Taiyuan Rd 太原路
Xingguo Rd 兴国路
Gao'an Rd
Wukang Rd
Middle Huaihai Rd 淮海中路
Shanghai Library
上海图书馆站
Community Church
Taian Rd
Yueyang Rd 岳阳路
Yongjia Rd
Wuxing Rd
Wanping Rd 宛平路
S Wulumuqi Rd 乌鲁木齐南路
Hengshan Rd
衡山路站
To Red Town (1.5km)
Jiaotong University
交通大学站
Tianping Rd
Yuqing Rd 余庆路
W Jianguo Rd
Hengshan Rd 衡山路
Kangping Rd
Huashan Rd
Zhaojiabang Rd
肇家浜路站
Zhaojiabang Rd
Guangyuan Rd
Jiāotōng University
Dong'an Rd
Yixueyuan Rd
Xujiahui Park
To Xújiāhuì (500m)
SHÀNGHĂI

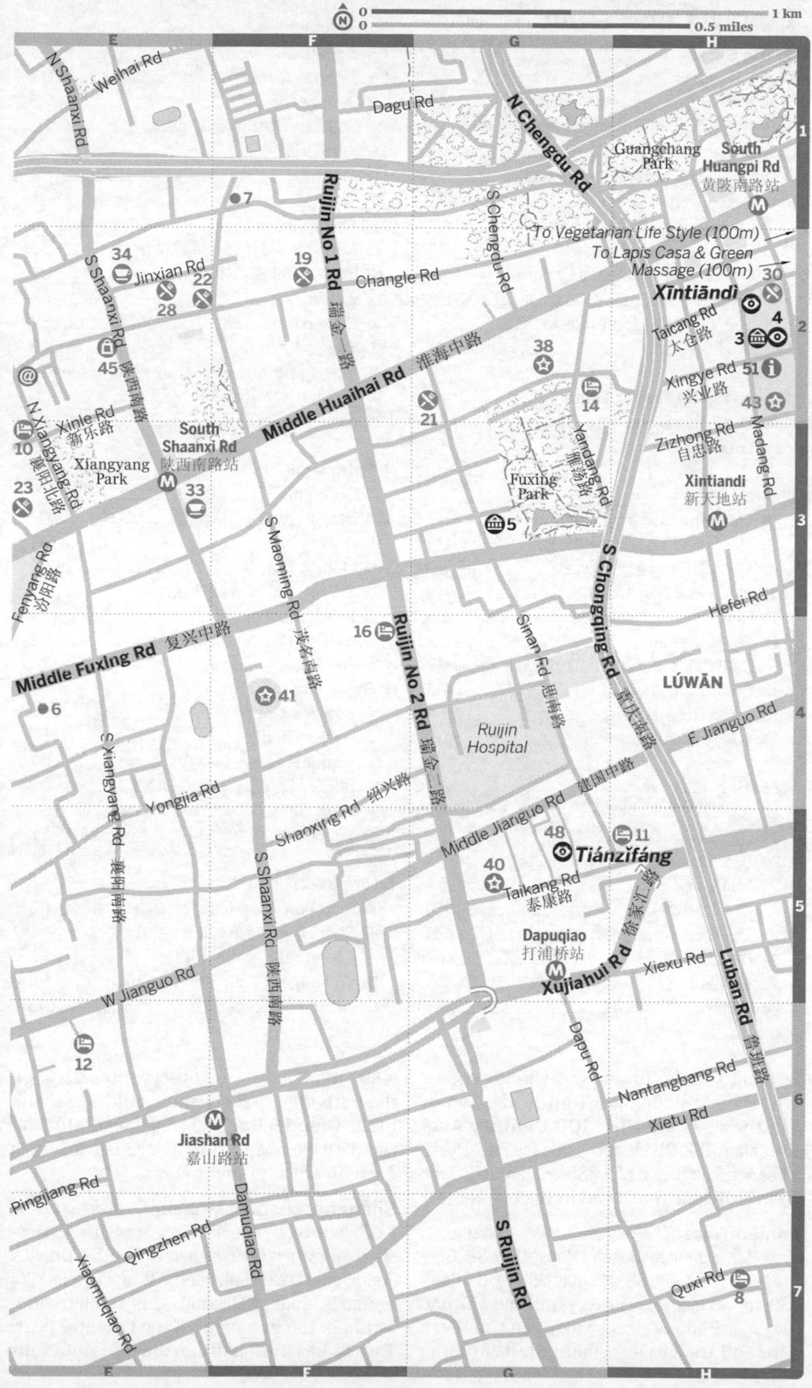
0 1 km
0 0.5 miles
Weihai Rd
N Shaanxi Rd
Dagu Rd
N Chengdu Rd
Guangchang Park
South Huangpi Rd
黄陂南路站
Ruijin No 1 Rd
瑞金一路
S Chengdu Rd
To Vegetarian Life Style (100m)
To Lapis Casa & Green Massage (100m)
Jinxian Rd
Changle Rd
Xīntiāndì
S Shaanxi Rd
陕西南路
Taicang Rd
太仓路
Middle Huaihai Rd
淮海中路
Xingye Rd
兴业路
Xinle Rd
新乐路
N Xiangyang Rd
襄阳北路
South Shaanxi Rd
陕西南路站
Xiangyang Park
Zizhong Rd
自忠路
Yandang Rd
雁荡路
Madang Rd
Fuxing Park
Xintiandi
新天地站
S Maoming Rd
茂名南路
Fenyang Rd
汾阳路
S Chongqing Rd
重庆南路
Hefei Rd
Middle Fuxing Rd
复兴中路
Ruijin No 2 Rd
瑞金二路
Sinan Rd
思南路
LÚWĀN
Ruijin Hospital
E Jianguo Rd
S Xiangyang Rd
襄阳南路
Yongjia Rd
Shaoxing Rd
绍兴路
Middle Jianguo Rd
建国中路
Tiánzǐfáng
Taikang Rd
泰康路
徐家汇路
Dapuqiao
打浦桥站
Xujiahui Rd
Xiexu Rd
Luban Rd
鲁班路
S Shaanxi Rd
陕西南路
W Jianguo Rd
Dapu Rd
Nantangbang Rd
Xietu Rd
Jiashan Rd
嘉山路站
Damuqiao Rd
Pingjiang Rd
Qingzhen Rd
Xiaomuqiao Rd
S Ruijin Rd
Quxi Rd
SHÀNGHǍI

French Concession

dazzling Jīnmào Tower is now in the shade. Take the ear-popping lift up to the top or visit the restaurant/bar **100 Century Avenue** (Map p182; 91st fl, access via the Park Hyatt; coffee/weekday lunch Y55/180; ⌚11am-10.30pm; 📶) to truly put your head in the clouds.

Jīnmào Tower SKYSCRAPER
(金茂大厦; Jīnmào Dàshà; Map p182; 88 Century Ave; 世纪大道88号; adult Y88; ⌚8.30am-9.30pm; Ⓜ Lujiazui) The crystalline Jīnmào Tower is Pǔdōng's most arresting modern spire and the city's second-tallest building (420.5m). There's an observation deck on the 88th floor, but consider sinking a drink in the **Cloud 9 Bar** (see boxed text, p193) on the 87th floor and time your visit for dusk for both day and night views.

Shànghǎi History Museum HISTORY MUSEUM
(上海城市历史发展陈列馆; Shànghǎi Chéngshì Lìshǐ Fāzhǎn Chénlièguǎn; Map p182; Oriental Pearl Tower basement; adult Y35, audio tour Y30; ⌚8am-9.30pm; Ⓜ Lujiazui) This modern museum, in the basement of the Oriental Pearl Tower, has fun multimedia presentations

and imaginative displays that recreate the history of Shànghǎi, with an emphasis on the pre-1949 era. Find out how the city prospered on the back of the cotton trade and junk transportation, when it was known as 'Little Sūzhōu'. Life-size models of traditional shops are inhabited by realistic wax figures, and there's a wealth of historical detail, including a boundary stone from the International Settlement, and one of the pair of bronze lions that originally guarded the entrance to the Hong Kong & Shanghai Bank on the Bund.

World Expo Site ARCHITECTURE
(世博会区; Shìbó Huì Qū; Ⓜ South Yaohua Rd, lines 7 & 8) Most of the pavilions at the site of the 2010 World Expo were designed as temporary structures and were dismantled shortly after the event's completion. However, at least five structures on the Pǔdōng side will remain standing and continue to host exhibits and events, including the iconic **China Pavilion** (中国国家馆; Zhōngguó Guójiā Guǎn), the **Expo Center** (世博中心; Shìbó Zhōngxīn) and the **Cultural Center** (世博文化中心; Shìbó Wénhuà Zhōngxīn).

Some 4000 Expo highlights will be on display at the Expo Museum (世博博物馆; Shìbó Bówùguǎn), which is slated to open on the Pǔxī side (across the river from Pǔdōng) in 2012.

Oriental Pearl Tower SKYSCRAPER
(东方明珠电视塔; Dōngfāng Míngzhū Diànshì Tǎ; Map p182; 1 Century Ave; 世纪大道1号; tickets Y100-150; ⏲8am-10pm; Ⓜ Lujiazui) Best viewed when it's illuminated at night, this poured-concrete shocker of a tripod TV tower has become symbolic of the Shànghǎi renaissance. The Shànghǎi History Museum in the basement is well worth exploring, and not just because it's the one part of Pǔdōng where you can't see the tower itself.

Science & Technology Museum SCIENCE MUSEUM
(上海科技馆; Shànghǎi Kējìguǎn; www.sstm.org.cn; 2000 Century Ave; 世纪大道2000号; adult Y60; ⏲9am-5.15pm Tue-Sun; Ⓜ Science & Technology Museum) Some exhibits are past their prime here, but it's still a fun outing for kids. There are also four theatres (two IMAX, one 4-D and one outer space) that show themed 15- to 40-minute **films** (tickets Y20 to Y40) throughout the day.

Riverside Promenade PROMENADE
(滨江大道; Bīnjiāng Dàdào; Map p182; ⏲6.30am-11pm; Ⓜ Lujiazui) The best stroll in Pǔdōng, the promenade alongside Riverside Ave offers splendid views to the Bund across the water and choicely positioned riverfront cafes.

THE ONLY WAY IS UP

The 'No Climbing' signs at the foot of the Jīnmào Tower recall the French 'Spiderman' Alain Robert's 90-minute scaling of the tower in May 2007. Dressed as his arachnid hero, the climber was immediately arrested upon descent, having failed to gain authorisation (he had made two previous applications, both refused). Glance up the side of the building and you're spoiled for choice for handholds (Robert apparently said he could climb it with one arm). A shoe salesman from Ānhuī province has also climbed the tower, on impulse in 2001.

Shànghǎi Ocean Aquarium AQUARIUM
(上海海洋水族馆; Shànghǎi Hǎiyáng Shuǐzúguǎn; Map p182; www.sh-aquarium.com; 1388 Lujiazui Ring Rd; 陆家嘴环路158号; adult Y135; ⏲9am-6pm; Ⓜ Lujiazui) Education meets entertainment in this slick and intelligently designed aquarium.

NORTH SHÀNGHǍI (HÓNGKǑU) 虹口

The gritty northeast districts of Hóngkǒu and Zháběi are little visited but offer some interesting backstreets and a handful of minor sights. Originally the American Settlement before the Japanese took over, Hóngkǒu also welcomed thousands of Jewish refugees fleeing persecution.

Ohel Moishe Synagogue HISTORY MUSEUM
(摩西会堂; Móxī Huìtáng; 62 Changyang Rd; 长阳路62号; admission Y50; ⏲9am-4.30pm; Ⓜ Dalian Rd) This synagogue was built by the Russian Ashkenazi Jewish community in 1927 and lies in the heart of the 1940s Jewish ghetto. Today it houses the Shànghǎi Jewish Refugees Museum, which is an excellent introduction to the lives of the approximately 20,000 Central European refugees who fled to Shànghǎi to escape the Nazis. You can also visit the synagogue.

Duolun Road Cultural Street ARCHITECTURE
This restored **street** (多伦文化名人街; Duōlún Wénhuà Míngrén Jiē; Ⓜ Dongbaoxing Rd) of fine old houses was once home to several

West Nanjing Rd & Jìng'ān

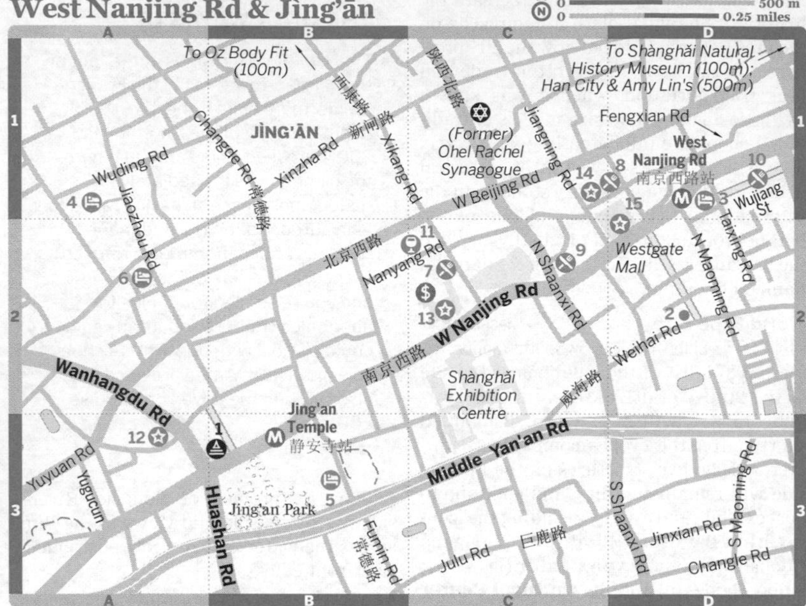

of China's most famous writers (as well as Kuomintang generals). Today it has a few excellent antique shops (No 181 is the best), some historic architecture (the brick Hóngdé Temple at No 59 is a Christian church) and a few cafes – the **Old Film Cafe** (No 123; ⏲10am-midnight), next to the bell tower at the bend in the road, shows old Chinese films. The **Shànghǎi Duōlún Museum of Modern Art** (上海多伦现代美术馆; Shànghǎi Duōlún Xiàndài Měishùguǎn; No 27; admission Y10; ⏲10am-6pm Tue-Sun) occasionally gets decent exhibits of contemporary Chinese art, but quality varies. The street ends in the north at the Moorish-looking **Kong Residence** (No 250), built in 1924, with its Middle Eastern tiles and windows.

SOUTH SHÀNGHǍI (XÚJIĀHUÌ) 徐家汇

Originally a Jesuit settlement dating back to the 17th century, Xújiāhuì was known to 1930s expat residents as Ziccawei or Sicawei. These days it's more of a monument to capitalism than Catholicism, however, and the main intersection is encircled by shopping malls, including the massive Grand Gateway.

Lónghuá Temple BUDDHIST TEMPLE
(龙华寺; Lónghuá Sì; 2853 Longhua Rd; 龙华路2853号; admission Y10; ⏲7am-4.30pm; Ⓜ Longcao Rd) Southwest of central Shànghǎi, this is the oldest and largest temple in the city; it's said to date from the 10th century. Opposite the temple stands a seven-storey pagoda, originally built in AD 977 and much restored. From the Longcao Rd metro station, head east along North Longshui Rd for about 1km.

FREE **CY Tung Maritime Museum** HISTORY MUSEUM
(董浩云航运博物馆; Dǒng Hàoyún Hángyùn Bówùguǎn; Map p176; 1954 Huashan Rd, Jiāotōng University campus; 华山路1954号交通大学内; ⏲1.30-5.30pm Tue-Sun; Ⓜ Jiaotong University) This small but fascinating museum features exhibits on the legendary explorer Zheng He and the often overlooked world of Chinese maritime history.

Bibliotheca Zi-Ka-Wei LIBRARY
(徐家汇藏书楼; Xújiāhuì Cángshūlóu; ☎6487 4095, ext 208; 80 North Caoxi Rd; 漕溪北路80号; ⏲library tour 2pm Sat; Ⓜ Xujiahui) This former Jesuit library has a free 15-minute tour of the main library and its collection of antiquarian tomes on Saturdays. Reservations are essential.

St Ignatius Cathedral CATHEDRAL
(天主教堂; Tiānzhǔ Jiàotáng; 158 Puxi Rd; 蒲西路158号; ⏲1-4.30pm Sat & Sun; Ⓜ Xujiahui)

West Nanjing Rd & Jìng'ān

Sights

1 Jing'an Temple B3

Activities, Courses & Tours

2 Chinese Cooking Workshop D2

Sleeping

3 Jia Shànghǎi D1
4 Le Tour Traveler's Rest Youth Hostel A1
5 Púlì B3
6 Urbn A2

Eating

Element Fresh .... (see 13)
7 Lynn C2
8 Vegetarian Life Style D1
9 Wagas C2
10 Wujiang Rd Food Street D1

Drinking

11 Big Bamboo C2

Entertainment

12 Paramount Ballroom A3
13 Shànghǎi Centre C2
14 Shànghǎi Cultural Information & Booking Centre C1
15 Studio City D2

Shopping

Chaterhouse Booktrader .... (see 13)

This dignified twin-spired cathedral (1904) is a major Xújiāhuì landmark. Across the road stands the former St Ignatius Convent, now a restaurant.

WEST SHÀNGHǍI

West Shànghǎi includes a large area made up of the districts of Mǐnháng (闵行) and Chángníng (长宁), which envelops the smaller residential community of Gǔběi (古北). It is mainly of interest for long-term expats and those on business. That said, there are a few sites in the area, as well as Hóngqiáo Airport.

Qībǎo HISTORIC VILLAGE
(七宝; Mǐnháng district; admission Y30; Ⓜ Qibao, line 9) When you tire of Shànghǎi's incessant quest for modernity, this tiny town is only a hop, skip and metro ride away. An ancient settlement that prospered during the Ming and Qing dynasties, it is littered with traditional historic architecture, threaded by small, busy alleyways and cut by a picturesque canal. If you can somehow blot out the crowds, Qībǎo brings you the flavours of old China along with huge doses of entertainment.

There are nine official sights included in the through ticket, though you can also skip the ticket and just pay Y5 per sight as you go. The best of the bunch include the **Cotton Textile Mill**, the **Shadow Puppet Museum** (performances from 1pm to 3pm Wednesday and Sunday), **Zhou's Miniature Carving House** and the **Old Wine Shop** (still an active distillery and a good lunch spot). Half-hour **boat rides** (per person Y10; ⌚8.30am-5pm) along the canal slowly ferry passengers from Number One Bridge to Dōngtángtān (东塘滩) and back. Also worth ferreting out is the **Catholic Church** (天主教堂; 50 Nanjie), adjacent to a convent off Qibao Nanjie, south of the canal.

Wander along Bei Dajie north of the canal for souvenirs; Nan Dajie south of the canal is full of snacks and small eateries such as No 14, which sells sweet *tāngyuán* dumplings, and No 19, which is a rarely seen traditional teahouse.

Mínshēng Art Museum & Red Town ART MUSEUM
(民生现代美术馆、红坊; Mínshēng Xiàndài Měishùguǎn, Hóng Fāng; Bldg F, 570 West Huaihai Rd; 淮海西路570号F座; admission Y20; ⌚10am-9pm Tue-Sun; Ⓜ Hongqiao Rd, lines 3, 4 & 10) Part of Shànghǎi's bid to give the local arts scene some street cred has been the continual addition of new museums over the past decade. The Mínshēng, which opened in 2010, got off to a good start with an acclaimed retrospective of modern Chinese art. It also has a prime location in the sculpture-dotted creative complex of Red Town (formerly the No 10 Steel Factory).

Courses

Learn how to balance your yin and yang with the following courses.

Chinese Cooking Workshop COOKING
(Map p179; ☎5404 3181; www.chinesecookingworkshop.com; Room 307, No 696, Weihai Rd; 威海路696号307室; Ⓜ West Nanjing Rd)

Pŭdōng New Area

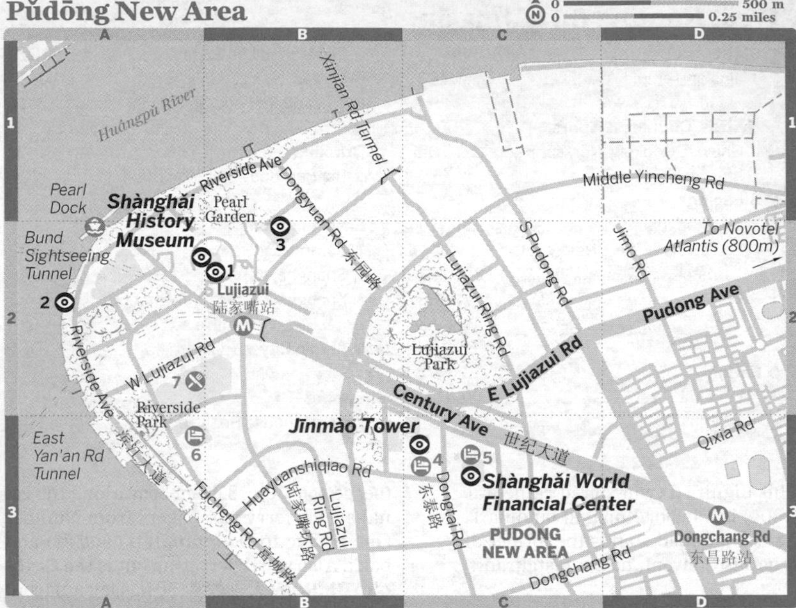

The Kitchen at... COOKING
(Map p176; ☎6433 2700; www.thekitchenat.com; Bldg 101, No 75, Lane 1295, Middle Fuxing Rd; 复兴中路1295弄75号101; Ⓜ Changshu Rd)

Lóngwŭ Kungfu Center MARTIAL ARTS
(龙武功夫馆; Lóngwŭ Gōngfū Guǎn; Map p176; ☎6287 1528; www.longwukungfu.com; 1 South Maoming Rd; 茂名南路1号; Ⓜ South Shaanxi Rd)

Oz Body Fit MARTIAL ARTS
(☎6288 5278; www.ozbodyfit.com; 528 Kangding Rd; 康定路528号; Ⓜ Jing'an Temple)

Tours

From boats to bikes to buses, various organised tours offer a great introduction to Shànghǎi.

Sūzhōu Creek Boat Tours BOAT
(苏州河游览船; Sūzhōuhé yóulǎnchuán; Changhua Rd Dock; 昌化路码头; Map p180; tickets day/night Y50/70; Ⓜ Zhongtan Rd, taxi) Forty-five-minute boat tours running in between the M50 art galleries and Chángfēng Park (长风公园; Chāngfēng Gōngyuán) to the west. As this is a brand-new service, research it ahead of time in case of changes.

Big Bus Tours BUS
(www.bigbustours.com; tickets US$44) Shànghǎi's first hop-on, hop-off bus service (22 stops). Tickets are valid for 24 hours and include a boat tour.

BOHDI CYCLING
(☎5266 9013; www.bohdi.com.cn; tours Y150) Night-time cycling tours on Tuesdays and Thursdays.

Pŭdōng New Area

Top Sights

	Jīnmào Tower	C3
	Shànghǎi History Museum	A2
	Shànghǎi World Financial Center	C3

Sights

1	Oriental Pearl Tower	B2
2	Riverside Promenade	A2
3	Shànghǎi Ocean Aquarium	B2

Sleeping

4	Grand Hyatt	C3
5	Park Hyatt	C3
6	Pŭdōng Shangri-La	A3

Eating

	100 Century Avenue	(see 5)
7	Superbrand Mall	A2

Drinking

	Cloud 9	(see 4)

Huángpǔ River Cruise (The Bund) BOAT
(黄浦江游览船; Huángpǔjiāng yóulǎnchuán; 501 East Zhongshan No 2 Rd; 中山东二路501号; tickets Y100; ⌚10.30am-10.15pm) The classic Shànghǎi tour. Fifty-minute cruises run from the Shíliùpù Docks (aka 'The 16 Pu'; 十六铺; Shíliùpù) south of the Bund.

Huángpǔ River Cruise (Pǔdōng) BOAT
(黄浦江游览船; Huángpǔjiāng yóulǎnchuán; Pearl Dock; 明珠码头; tickets Y50-70; ⌚10am-8pm; Ⓜ Lujiazui) Forty-minute cruises departing hourly in Pǔdōng.

Shanghai Sideways MOTORCYCLE
(www.shanghaisideways.com) Unusual motorcycle-sidecar tours of the city.

Shànghǎi Sightseeing Buses BUS
(上海旅游集散中心; Shànghǎi Lǚyóu Jísàn Zhōngxīn; www.chinassbc.com; Ⓜ Shanghai Stadium) Daily tours from Shànghǎi Stadium to nearby canal towns (eg Tónglǐ, Nánxún). Convenient but less fun than visiting on your own.

SISU CYCLING
(☎5059 6071; www.sisucycling.com; tour Y150) Night-time cycling tours on Wednesdays.

Festivals & Events

Lantern Festival TRADITIONAL
A colourful time to visit Yùyuán Gardens. People make *yuánxiāo* or *tāngyuán* (glutinous rice dumplings with sweet fillings) and some carry paper lanterns on the streets. The Lantern Festival (元宵节; *yuánxiāo jié*) falls on the 15th day of the first lunar month (6 February 2012, 24 February 2013).

Shànghǎi International Literary Festival LITERARY
Held in March or April, this highly popular festival (上海国际文学艺术节; Shànghǎi Guójì Wénxué Yìshù Jié) for bibliophiles is staged in the Glamour Bar (Map p170), with international and local authors in attendance.

Lónghuá Temple Fair TRADITIONAL
This fair (龙华寺庙会; Lónghuá Sì Miàohuì) at Lónghuá Temple, held for several weeks during the 3rd lunar month (late March, April or early May), is eastern China's largest and oldest folk gathering, with all kinds of snacks, stalls, jugglers and stilt walkers.

Formula 1 SPORT
(www.formula1.com; 2000 Yining Rd, Jiādìng; Ⓜ Shanghai International Circuit, Line 11) The slick new Shànghǎi International Circuit hosts several high-profile motor-racing competitions, including the hotly contested Formula 1 in April.

Dragon Boat Festival TRADITIONAL
Celebrated on the fifth day of the fifth lunar month (23 June 2012, 12 June 2013), this festival (端午节; Duānwǔ Jié) sees dragon boats raced along Sūzhōu Creek and, more importantly for most, *zòngzi* (glutinous rice dumplings steamed in bamboo leaves) go on sale everywhere.

Shànghǎi International Film Festival FILM
(上海国际电影节; Shànghǎi Guójì Diànyǐng Jié; www.siff.com) With screenings at several cinemas around town, this movie-going festival brings a range of international and locally produced films to town in June. For international flicks, make sure it's the original version you're going to see (原版; *yuánbǎn*), and not dubbed into Chinese.

China Shànghǎi International Arts Festival ART
(中国上海国际艺术节; Zhōngguó Shànghǎi Guójì Yìshù Jié; www.artsbird.com) A month-long program of cultural events held in October and November, including the Shànghǎi Art Fair, international music, dance, opera, acrobatics and the **Shànghǎi Biennale** (www.shanghaibiennale.org; 2012).

Sleeping

Shànghǎi's sleeping options are excellent at both ends of the spectrum, though quality in the midrange market is definitely in short supply – it's best to do your homework and secure a room well ahead of time. Don't forget to enquire about rates at the top-end hotels, as the discounts in these places often make them considerably more affordable. In general, hotels fall into five main categories: slick new skyscraper hotels, historic hotels in old villas or apartment blocks, boutique hotels, Chinese chain hotels, and hostels. There are additionally a handful of new B&Bs, though these are relatively scarce.

The most central neighbourhoods are the Bund and People's Sq. If you'd rather be based in a more residential area, you'll want to look at options in the French Concession, Jìng'ān or Hóngkǒu, all of which have some unique choices. Pǔdōng is interesting if a night in one of the world's highest hotels sounds appealing, but keep in mind that it

Shànghǎi Station

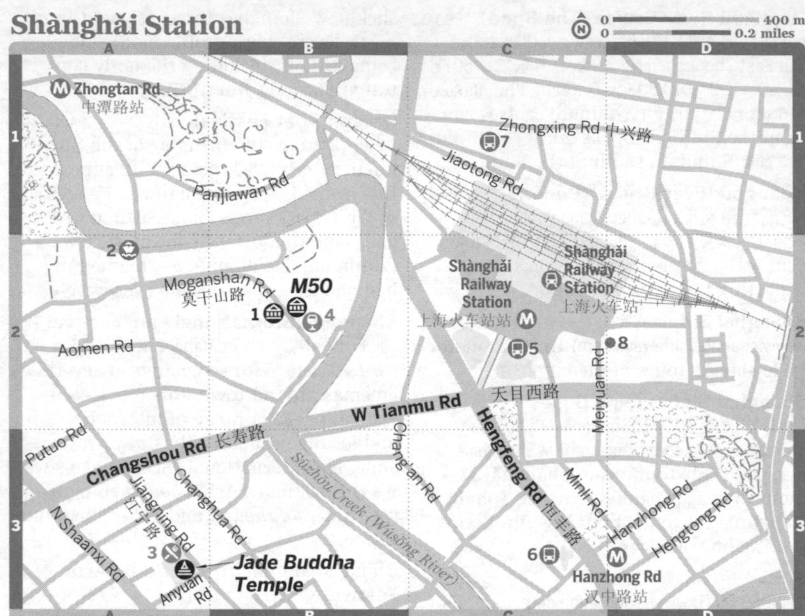

is a business district and thus not too exciting from a cultural perspective. Nevertheless, if you're near the Lujiazui metro stop, it is easy to get to.

Rack rates are listed here, but, as you'll notice when you book online, discounts are standard in many establishments outside holiday periods. Four- and five-star hotels add a 10% or 15% service charge, which is sometimes negotiable. Most hotels listed here have air-conditioning and broadband internet access.

For hotel bookings, the online agencies **CTrip** (☎400 619 9999; http://english.ctrip.com) and **Elong** (☎400 617 1717; www.elong.net) are good choices.

THE BUND & PEOPLE'S SQUARE

TOP CHOICE **Astor House Hotel** HISTORIC HOTEL **$$**
(浦江饭店; Pǔjiāng Fàndiàn; Map p170; ☎6324 6388; www.astorhousehotel.com; 15 Huangpu Rd; 黄浦路15号; d Y1280, discounts 40%; ❄@) Etched with history, this venerable old-timer is a dream come true for travellers requiring a perch near the Bund, a yesteryear nobility and a pedigree that reaches back to the early days of concession-era Shànghǎi. Rooms are colossal (you could fit a bed in the capacious bathrooms) and no other hotel has its major selling

Shànghǎi Station

Top Sights
Jade Buddha Temple A3
M50 .... B2

Sights
island6 .... (see 4)
1 m97 .... B2
OFoto .... (see 4)
ShanghART .... (see 4)

Activities, Courses & Tours
2 Sūzhōu Creek Boat Tours A2

Eating
3 Jade Buddha Temple Vegetarian Restaurant A3

Drinking
4 Bāndù Cabin B2

Entertainment
Image Tunnel .... (see 4)

Transport
5 Bus to Pǔdōng Airport C2
6 Hengfeng Road Bus Station C3
7 Shànghǎi Long-Distance Bus Station C1
8 Train Ticket Office D2

points: doormen wearing kilts, original polished wooden floorboards and the overall impression of British public school meets Victorian asylum.

Mingtown Etour Youth Hostel HOSTEL $
(上海新易途国际青年旅舍; Shànghǎi Xīnyìtú Guójì Qīngnián Lǚshè; Map p170; ☎6327 7766; 55 Jiangyin Rd; 江阴路55号; 6-bed dm Y65, d Y220-340; ❄@📶; Ⓜ People's Sq) The Etour has a choice location just behind People's Sq, and pleasant rooms (many with reproduction antique furniture) to boot. But it's the tranquil courtyard with fish pond and split-level bar-restaurant that really sells this one. The superb communal area comes with computers (free for one hour), a projector-screen DVD player, free pool table and plenty of outdoor seating.

Peace Hotel HISTORIC HOTEL $$$
(和平饭店; Hépíng Fàndiàn; Map p170; ☎6321 6888; www.fairmont.com; 20 East Nanjing Rd; 南京东路20号; d Y2500-3100, discounts 20%; ⊖❄@📶≋; Ⓜ East Nanjing Rd) After three-plus years of renovations, the city's definitive art deco building, the Peace Hotel, reopened in 2010 under the direction of the Fairmont group. The main challenge in modernising the building was balancing out the architectural integrity of such a historic place with the need to upgrade a building that was not originally designed to be a hotel. Connoisseurs of old Shànghǎi will be pleased to know that the famous antediluvian jazz band is back in action.

Marvel Hotel HOTEL $$
(商悦青年会大酒店; Shāngyuè Qīngniánhuì Dàjiǔdiǎn; Map p170; ☎3305 9999; www.marvelhotels.com.cn; 123 South Xizang Rd; 西藏南路123号; d Y1080-1580; ❄@📶; Ⓜ Dashijie) Occupying the former YMCA building (1931) just south of People's Sq, the Marvel is one of the city's standout midrange hotels. The successful mix of history, central location and modern comfort (broadband access via the TV, soundproofed windows, comfy down pillows) makes it one of Shànghǎi's best-value hotels.

Mingtown Hiker Youth Hostel HOSTEL $
(上海旅行者青年旅舍; Shànghǎi Lǚxíngzhě Qīngnián Lǚshè; Map p170; ☎6329 7889; 450 Middle Jiangxi Rd; 江西中路450号; 6-bed dm Y55-60, d Y150-280; ❄@📶; Ⓜ East Nanjing Rd) A short hike from the Bund, this is another well-located hostel. Rooms include tidy four- and six-bed dorms (some with shower, cheapest without windows) and a handful of good-value luxury doubles, decorated in a Chinese style. There's a bar with pool table, free movies, and internet access (first hour free for guests).

JW Marriott Tomorrow Square LUXURY HOTEL $$$
(明天广场JW万怡酒店; Míngtiān Guǎngchǎng JW Wànyí Jiǔdiàn; Map p170; ☎5359 4969; www.marriotthotels.com/shajw; 399 West Nanjing Rd; 南京西路399号; d Y2600-3550, discounts 20%; ⊖❄@📶≋; Ⓜ People's Sq) Victor Sassoon probably would have traded in his old digs in a heartbeat if he could have stayed in the chairman's suite here. Housed across the upper 24 floors of one of Shànghǎi's most dramatic towers, the JW Marriott boasts marvellously appointed rooms with spectacular vistas (the view over People's Sq from the 38th-floor lobby cafe is something in itself) and showers with hydraulic massage functions to soak away the stress. Internet access in rooms is an extra Y120.

Peninsula Hotel LUXURY HOTEL $$$
(上海半岛酒店; Shànghǎi Bàndǎo Jiǔdiàn; Map p170; ☎2327 2888; www.peninsula.com; 32 East Zhongshan No 1 Rd; 中山东一路32号; d Y3200-5400, discounts 40%; ⊖❄@📶≋; Ⓜ East Nanjing Rd) This new luxury hotel on the Bund combines art deco motifs with Shànghǎi modernity, but it's the little touches that distinguish it from the numerous other five-star places in the neighbourhood: a TV in the tub, valet box and fabulous views across the river or out onto the gardens of the former British consulate.

Motel 268 CHAIN HOTEL $
(莫泰连锁旅馆; Mòtài Liánsuǒ Lǚguǎn; Map p170; ☎5179 3333; www.motel168.com; 50 Ningbo Rd; 宁波路50号; dY268-318; ❄📶; Ⓜ East Nanjing Rd) The ever-dependable Motel 268 comes through with modern doubles near the Bund, with huge beds, wood-trimmed furnishings and smartly tiled chrome-and-glass bathrooms. Check the website for other locations around Shànghǎi, including the one near People's Sq (Map p170; ☎5153 3333; 531 East Jinling Rd; 金陵东路531号; dY268-318; ❄📶; Ⓜ Dashijie).

Jǐnjiāng Inn CHAIN HOTEL $
(锦江之星旅馆; Jǐnjiāng Zhīxīng Lǚguǎn; Map p170; ☎6326 0505; www.jj-inn.com; 33 South Fujian Rd; 福建南路33号; d Y229-289; ❄; Ⓜ Dashijie) The central branch of this hotel chain, which looks like it struck a deal with Ikea, has bright, airy rooms (some doubles, but mostly twins). Rooms facing inwards are

smaller, cheaper and quieter; the higher-floor rooms are generally best.

Captain Hostel HOSTEL $
(船长青年酒店; Chuánzhǎng Qīngnián Jiǔdiàn; Map p170; ☎6323 5053; www.captainhostel.com.cn; 37 Fuzhou Rd; 福州路37号; dm/d Y70/400; ❄@📶) Hands down the least-friendly youth hostel in Shànghǎi, this state-run place still reels in punters by the boatload with its fantastic location off the Bund and spot-on rooftop bar. There's a newer branch on **Yan'an Rd** (Map p170; ☎3331 0000; 7 East Yan'an Rd; 延安东路7号; dm Y100, d Y500-600; ❄@📶) two blocks south.

Broadway Mansions HOTEL $$$
(上海大厦; Shànghǎi Dàshà; Map p170; ☎6324 6260; www.broadwaymansions.com; 20 North Suzhou Rd; 苏州北路20号; d Y2200, river-view d Y2500, discounts 40%; ❄@) Originally built as a luxury apartment block in the 1930s before being taken over by first the Japanese and then the US military, this classic art deco brick pile north of the Bund has elegantly refurbished rooms. Aim for river-view rooms on higher floors to get fantastic panoramas.

Mingtown People's Square Youth Hostel HOSTEL $
(人民广场青年旅舍; Rénmín Guǎngchǎng Qīngnián Lǔshè; Map p170; ☎6320 1114; 35 Yongshou Rd; 永寿路35号; 6-bed dm Y60, d Y220-300; ❄@📶; Ⓜ People's Sq) Although a bit less convenient than the other Mingtown hostels, the facilities are nonetheless excellent.

FRENCH CONCESSION

Old House Inn BOUTIQUE HOTEL $$
(老时光酒店; Lǎoshíguāng Jiǔdiàn; Map p176; ☎6248 6118; www.oldhouse.cn; 16, Lane 351, Huashan Rd; 华山路351弄16号; s incl breakfast Y580, d Y880-1250; ❄@📶; Ⓜ Changshu Rd) This 1930s red-brick building has been restored to create an exclusive, yet affordable place to stay. All 12 rooms are decorated with care and attention and come with wooden floors, traditional Chinese furniture, stylish artwork and a few antiques.

Mansion Hotel HISTORIC HOTEL $$$
(首席公馆酒店; Shǒuxí Gōngguǎn Jiǔdiàn; Map p176; ☎5403 9888; www.mansionhotelchina.com; 82 Xinle Rd; 新乐路82号; d Y1980-2770, discounts 10%; ⊝❄📶; Ⓜ South Shaanxi Rd) Combining historic charm and modern luxury like no other hotel in Shànghǎi, this truly exceptional place was originally the residence of Sun Tingsun, a business partner of two of Shànghǎi's most powerful gangsters. Stepping through the front door is like stepping back in time to the city's glorious, notorious past: rooms are antique-filled and exquisitely luxurious.

Quintet B&B $$
(Map p176; ☎6249 9088; www.quintet-shanghai.com; 808 Changle Rd; 长乐路808号; d Y800-1200; ⊝❄📶; Ⓜ Changshu Rd) This chic B&B has six beautiful double rooms in a 1930s town house not short on character. Some of the rooms are on the small side, but each is decorated with style, incorporating modern luxuries such as big-screen satellite TV, wi-fi and laptop-sized safes with more classic touches like wood-stripped floorboards and deep porcelain bathtubs. Staff members sometimes get a BBQ going on the roof terrace, but there's an excellent restaurant on the ground floor. There's no sign – buzz on the gate marked 808 to be let in.

Púdǐ Boutique Hotel BOUTIQUE HOTEL $$$
(璞邸精品酒店; Púdǐ Jīngpǐn Jiǔdiàn; Map p176; ☎5158 5888; www.boutiquehotel.cc; 99 Yandang Rd; 雁荡路99号; d from Y1577, discounts 20%; ❄@📶; Ⓜ Xintiandi) This exquisite 52-room boutique hotel gets excellent reviews for its trendy, ultramodern rooms, professional staff and elite but accessible atmosphere. The interior is superstylish and alluringly dark hued; rooms are beautifully attired and spacious.

Magnolia Bed & Breakfast B&B $$
(Map p176; www.magnoliabnbshanghai.com; 36 Yanqing Rd; 延庆路36号; r Y650-1200; ⊝❄📶; Ⓜ Changshu Rd) Opened by the duo that started the cooking school The Kitchen at..., this cosy little B&B is located in a 1930s French Concession home. It's Shànghǎi all the way, with an art deco starting point followed by a stylish quest for modernity in both comfort and design. There are only five rooms, so make sure you book well in advance.

Blue Mountain Youth Hostel HOSTEL $
(蓝山国际青年旅舍; Lánshān Guójì Qīngnián Lǔshě; Map p176; ☎6304 3938; www.bmhostel.com; Bldg 1, 2nd fl, 1072 Quxi Rd; 瞿溪路1072号1号甲2楼; 8-bed dm Y50-60, d without/with bathroom Y140/200; ❄@📶; Ⓜ Luban Rd) A good hostel that's not exactly in the thick of things, but it is next to a metro station so transport is at least convenient. Rooms are simple but clean and there are women-only,

SHÀNGHǍI FOR CHILDREN

Shànghǎi isn't exactly at the top of most kids' holiday wish-list, but the new Disney theme park in Pǔdōng (estimated completion date is 2014) will no doubt improve its future standing. In the meantime, if you're passing through the city with children, the following sights should keep the entire family entertained.

In Pǔdōng:

» Shànghǎi World Financial Center or Jīnmào Tower

» Shànghǎi History Museum

» Shànghǎi Ocean Aquarium

» Science & Technology Museum

» A ride on the Maglev train

In central Shànghǎi:

» River cruise

» Acrobatics show

» Madame Tussaud's

» Shànghǎi Natural History Museum

Note that in general, 1.4m (4ft 7in) is the cut-off height for children's tickets. Children under 0.8m (2ft 7in) normally get in for free.

If sightseeing mutiny strikes, you can also check out these amusement parks:

» **Happy Valley** (欢乐谷; Huānlè Gǔ; http://sh.happyvalley.com.cn, in Chinese; adult/child 1.2-1.4m Y200/100; Linyin Ave, Sheshan, Songjiang County; 松江区佘山林荫大道; ⊙9am-6pm; MSheshan, line 9) Popular national amusement park an hour from Shànghǎi by metro.

» **Dino Beach** (热带风暴; Rèdài Fēngbào; www.dinobeach.com.cn; 78 Xinzhen Rd; 新镇路78号; admission Y100-200; ⊙10am-11pm Tue-Sun, 2-11pm Mon Jun-Sep; MXinzhuang line 1, then bus Nos 763 or 173) Way down in south Shànghǎi, this water park has a beach, a wave pool and water slides.

men-only and mixed dorms. The communal facilities are excellent, including a bar-restaurant area with free pool table, internet and films, plus a kitchen and washing machines.

Ruìjīn Guesthouse HISTORIC HOTEL **$$**
(瑞金宾馆; Ruìjīn Bīnguǎn; Map p176; ☎6472 5222; www.ruijinhotelsh.com; 118 Ruijin No 2 Rd; 瑞金二路118号; d Y1200-2000; ❄) There are four buildings in this lovely garden estate, housing a range of rooms, but the one you want is Bldg No 1, a 1919 red-brick mansion and the former residence of Benjamin Morris, one-time owner of *North China Daily News*.

Yuèyáng Hotel HOTEL **$**
(悦阳商务酒店; Yuèyáng Shāngwù Jiǔdiàn; Map p176; ☎6466 6767; 58 Yueyang Rd; 岳阳路58号; d & tw Y218-398; ❄; MHengshan Rd) One of the best budget options in the French Concession that's both central and within easy walking distance of a metro station, Yuèyáng has decent rooms, though you'll want to look at a few first.

Nine BOUTIQUE HOTEL **$$**
(Map p176; ☎6471 9950; 355 West Jianguo Rd; 建国西路355号; r Y800-1500; ❄; MJiashan Rd) Book waaaaay in advance for Shànghǎi's most exclusive boutique hotel. Six rooms, no website and impossible to find unless you're one of the guests.

Lapis Casa BOUTIQUE HOTEL **$$$**
(☎5382 1600; lapiscasahotel@yahoo.com; 68 Taicang Rd; 台仓路68号; d Y1500, discounts 40%; ❄📶; MSouth Huangpi Rd) Although it doesn't really say 'Shànghǎi', this spacious boutique hotel stuffed with antiques is still an excellent choice.

Motel 268 CHAIN HOTEL $
(莫泰连锁旅店; Mòtài Liánsuǒ Lǚdiàn; Map p176; ☎5170 3333; www.motel168.com; 113 Sinan Rd; 思南路113号; r from Y198; Ⓜ Dapuqiao) This dependable chain on leafy Sinan Rd is ideally located for those wanting to explore the maze of charming alleyways known as Tiánzǐfáng. English is limited.

WEST NANJING ROAD & JÌNG'ĀN

TOP CHOICE **Le Tour Traveler's Rest Youth Hostel** HOSTEL $
(乐途静安国际青年旅舍; Lètú Jìng'ān Guójì Qīngnián Lǚshè; Map p180; ☎6267 1912; www.letourshanghai.com; 36, Alley 319, Jiaozhou Rd; 胶州路319弄36号; dm Y60, d Y220-300; Ⓜ Jìng'ān Temple) Housed in a former towel factory, this fabulous youth hostel leaves most others out to dry. Sitting quietly in a *lǐlòng* (alleyway), this great place has bundles of space, and the old-Shànghǎi textures continue once inside, with red-brick interior walls and reproduced stone gateways above doorways. It's bright, spacious and airy with attractive, gaily painted rooms and amiable staff. Internet, laundry, kitchen, free umbrella loan, ping pong and a pool table.

Urbn BOUTIQUE HOTEL $$$
(Map p180; ☎5153 4600; www.urbnhotels.com; 183 Jiaozhou Rd; 胶州路183号; d & tw Y2000-2500, discounts 30%; Ⓜ Changping Rd) China's first carbon-neutral hotel not only uses recyclable materials and low-energy products where possible, it also calculates its complete carbon footprint – including staff commutes and delivery journeys – then offsets it by donating money to environmentally friendly projects. The 26 open-plan rooms are beautifully designed with low furniture and sunken living areas exuding space.

Jia Shànghǎi BOUTIQUE HOTEL $$$
(Map p180; ☎6217 9000; www.jiashanghai.com; 931 West Nanjing Rd; 南京西路931号; studio Y1955-3860, discounts 25%) It's easy to miss the understated and anonymous front door of this chic boutique hotel (entrance down Taixing Rd), announced with an unassumingly minute plaque. Offbeat, fun and modish, the lobby ornaments (funky birdcages, amusingly designed clocks) and dapper staff prepare you for the colourful and supertrendy kitchenette-equipped studio rooms (bathrooms glinting with gold mosaics) in this 1920s building. Shànghǎi badly needs this kind of place, which delivers style, comfort and flair.

Púlì LUXURY HOTEL $$$
(璞丽酒店; Púlì Jiǔdiàn; Map p180; ☎3203 9999; www.thepuli.com; 1 Changde Rd; 常德路1号; d from Y3380, discounts 38%; Ⓜ Jing'an Temple) A future-forward Shànghǎi edifice, with open-space rooms divided by hanging screens, and an understated beige-and-mahogany colour scheme accentuated by the beauty of a few well-placed orchids. Twenty-five storeys high, the Púlì makes another strong case for stylish skyscrapers.

PŬDŌNG NEW AREA

TOP CHOICE **Park Hyatt** LUXURY HOTEL $$$
(柏悦酒店; Bóyuè Jiǔdiàn; Map p182; ☎6888 1234; www.parkhyattshanghai.com; 100 Century Ave; 世纪大道100号; d from Y3600, discounts 20%; Ⓜ Lujiazui) Spanning the 79th to 93rd floors of the towering Shànghǎi World Financial Center, this jaw-dropper is the world's highest hotel above ground level and could easily lay claim to being the coolest hotel in China, never mind Shànghǎi. High-walled corridors with brown-fabric and grey-stone textures lead to luxurious rooms with quirky features such as a mist-free bathroom mirror containing a small TV screen, a rainforest shower in the bathroom ceiling, a plug socket in the safe for your laptop, and a toilet seat that opens automatically as you approach it. The Park Hyatt is accessed from the south side of the tower.

Grand Hyatt LUXURY HOTEL $$$
(金茂凯悦大酒店; Jīnmào Kǎiyuè Dàjiǔdiàn; Map p182; ☎5049 1234; www.shanghai.grand.hyatt.com; 88 Century Ave; 世纪大道88号; d from Y2500) One of Shànghǎi's best-known hotels, the Grand Hyatt commences on the 54th floor of the standout Jīnmào Tower before shooting up another 33 stylish storeys; put a serious crick in your neck checking out the atrium. Rooms are packed with gadgets (TV internet access, three-jet showers and sensor reading lamps), but keeping the glass basins spotless must keep the cleaning staff cursing.

Pŭdōng Shangri-La LUXURY HOTEL $$$
(浦东香格里拉大酒店; Pǔdōng Xiānggélǐlā Dàjiǔdiàn; Map p182; ☎6882 8888; www.shangri-la.com; 33 Fucheng Rd; 富城路33号; d from Y2650; Ⓜ Lujiazui) With its muted Chinese motifs and spectacular views of the Bund, the 28-floor Shangri-La is an elegant luxury choice in the heart of Lùjiāzuǐ, backed up by a towering V-topped annexe.

PEACE HOTEL

The Peace Hotel (p185), originally known as the Cathay Hotel, is a ghostly reminder of the immense wealth of Victor Sassoon. From a Baghdad Jewish family, Sassoon made millions out of the opium trade and then ploughed it back into Shànghǎi real estate and horses.

Sassoon's quote of the day was: 'There is only one race greater than the Jews, and that's the Derby'. His office-cum-hotel was completed in 1930 and was known as Sassoon House, incorporating the Cathay Hotel from the 4th to 7th floors. From the top floors Sassoon commanded his real estate – he is estimated to have owned 1900 buildings in Shànghǎi.

Like the Taj in Bombay, the Raffles in Singapore and the Peninsula in Hong Kong, the Cathay was *the* place to stay in Shànghǎi. The guest list included Charlie Chaplin, George Bernard Shaw and Noël Coward, who wrote *Private Lives* here in four days in 1930 when he had the flu. Sassoon himself resided in a suite on the top floor, with its unsurpassed 360-degree views, just below the green pyramidal tower. He also maintained Sassoon Villa, a Tudor-style villa out near Hóngqiáo Airport.

After the communists took over the city, the troops were billeted in places such as the Cathay and Picardie (now the Hengshan Picardie Hotel), where they spent hours experimenting with the elevators, used bidets as face-showers and washed rice in the toilets – which was all very well until someone pulled the chain.

In 1953 foreign owners tried to give the Cathay to the Chinese Communist Party in return for exit visas. The government refused at first, but finally accepted after the payment of 'back taxes'. It was renamed the Peace Hotel in 1956.

Novotel Atlantis HOTEL **$$**
(海神诺富特大酒店; Hǎishén Nuòfùtè Dàjiǔdiàn; ☎5036 6666; www.novotel.com; 728 Pudong Ave; 浦东大道728号; d Y1035-1495, discounts 10%; ❄@📶🏊; Ⓜ Pudong Ave) One of the few midrange hotels in Shànghǎi with a pool, this is an excellent choice for families.

NORTH SHÀNGHǍI (HÓNGKǑU)

Koala Garden House (Duōlún Branch) B&B **$**
(考拉旅舍上海多伦路店; Kǎolā Lǚshè Shànghǎi Duōlún Lù Diàn; ☎5671 1038; www.koala-house.com; 240 Duolun Rd; 多伦路240号; dm Y70, d from Y196; ❄@📶; Ⓜ Dongbaoxing Rd) More of a B&B than a youth hostel, this is one of the most charming budget sleeps in the city. Even the lobby – which doubles up as a chic wi-fi cafe – is a joy to be in, with its high ceilings and brightly painted walls. But it's the rooms, all slightly different, that really stand out. Although on the small side, all are thoughtfully decorated (flower-patterned wallpaper) and come with wall-mounted flat-screen TV and funky little bathroom.

InnJoy International Youth Hostel HOSTEL **$**
(九屋国际青年旅舍; Jiǔwū Guójì Qīngnián Lǚshè; ☎6535 1562; 394 Zhoushan Rd; 舟山路394号; 12-bed dm Y50, d from Y100; ❄@📶; Ⓜ Linping Rd) Housed in a fabulous three-storey 1924 *shíkùmén* house, with original wooden floorboards and staircases, and a gorgeous stone gateway over the back door, this hostel is another great choice. There's free use of a kitchen, free internet, wi-fi on the ground floor, bicycles to rent (Y30) and very friendly staff. Just outside is a nice residential area with a bustling street market.

Eating

In true Shànghǎi style, today's restaurant scene is a reflection of the city's craving for foreign trends and tastes, whether it comes in the form of Hunanese chilli peppers or French foie gras. Most visitors will be interested in the Chinese end of the spectrum, of course, for that's where the best cooking is, as well as the most variety.

While a dinner overlooking the Huángpǔ River or safe in the Xīntiāndì bubble makes for a nice treat, real foodies know that the best restaurants in China are often where you least expect to find them. Part of the fun of eating out in Shànghǎi is stumbling across those tiny places in malls, metro stations or down backstreets that offer an inimitable dining experience. Nor should you be put off by eating in chain restaurants;

FOOD STREETS

Shànghǎi's food streets are great spots for gourmands to search for something new. It's not really street food like elsewhere in Asia, but rather a collection of tiny restaurants, each specialising in a different Chinese cuisine.

With a prime central location near People's Park, **Huanghe Road** (黄河路美食街; Huánghé Lù Měishí Jiē; Map p170; Ⓜ People's Sq) covers all the bases from cheap lunches to late-night post-theatre snacks. You'll find excellent Shanghainese further north at **Xiǎo Nán Guó** (小南国; No 214), but it's best for dumplings – get 'em fried at **Yang's Fry Dumplings** (小杨生煎馆; No 97) or served up in bamboo steamers across the road at **Jiājiā Soup Dumplings** (佳家汤包; No 90).

South Yunnan Road (云南路美食街; Yúnnán Lù Měishí Jiē; Ⓜ Dashijie) has some interesting speciality restaurants and is just the spot for an authentic meal after museum-hopping at People's Sq. Look out for Shaanxi cuisine at No 15 and five-fragrance dim sum at **Wǔ Fāng Zhāi** (五芳斋; Map p170; No 28). You can also find cold salted chicken (咸鸡; *xiánjī*) – it's better than it sounds – and Uighur kebabs here.

many of Shànghǎi's better eateries have branches scattered across town.

Shànghǎi cuisine itself is generally sweeter than other Chinese cuisines, and is heavy on fish and seafood. Classic dishes and snacks to look for include smoked fish (熏鱼; *xūnyú*), braised pork belly (红烧肉; *hóngshāo ròu*), fried dumplings (生煎; *shēngjiān*) and Shànghǎi's steamed dumpling, the *xiǎolóngbāo* (小笼包), copied everywhere else in China but only true to form here. Make sure to reserve at fancier places.

THE BUND & PEOPLE'S SQUARE

A lot's cooking near the Bund: from elegant gourmet palaces to delicious local restaurants hidden in malls, all are staking out a spot along the sumptuous skyline.

Lost Heaven YUNNANESE $$$
(花马天堂; Huāmǎ Tiāntáng; Map p170; www.lostheaven.com.cn; ☎6330 0967; 17 East Yan'an Rd; 延安东路17号; dishes Y30-90; 🄴; Ⓜ East Nanjing Rd) Lost Heaven might not have the views that keep its rivals in business, but why go to the same old Western restaurants when you can get sophisticated Bai, Dai and Miao folk cuisine from China's mighty southwest? Specialities are flowers (banana and pomegranate), wild mushrooms, chillies, Burmese curries, Bai chicken and superb pu-erh teas, all served up in gorgeous Yúnnán-meets-Shànghǎi surrounds.

TOP CHOICE **Hóngyī Plaza** CHINESE $$
(宏伊国际广场; Hóngyī Guójì Guǎngchǎng; Map p170; 299 East Nanjing Rd; 南京东路299号; meals from Y30; 🄴; Ⓜ East Nanjing Rd) Not all malls are created equal: the Hóngyī effortlessly slices and dices the competition with its star-studded restaurant line-up, and the whole shebang is a mere stone's throw from the waterfront. Top picks here are **South Memory** (6th floor), which specialises in spicy Hunanese drypots (a kind of personal miniwok); **Dolar Hotpot** (5th floor), whose delicious sauce bar makes it popular even outside of winter; **Charme** (4th floor), a Taiwanese restaurant with try-it-to-believe-it shaved-ice desserts; **Wagas** (ground floor), Shànghǎi's own wi-fi cafe chain; and **Ajisen** (basement), king of Japanese ramen.

Shànghǎi Grandmother SHANGHAINESE $$
(上海姥姥; Shànghǎi Lǎolao; Map p170; 70 Fuzhou Rd; 福州路70号; dishes from Y20; 🄴; Ⓜ East Nanjing Rd) This packed home-style Shanghainese eatery is within easy striking distance of the Bund and handy for a casual lunch or dinner. You can't go wrong with the classics, like Grandma's braised pork and fried tomato and egg.

Food Republic FOOD COURT $
(大食代; Dàshídài; Map p170; www.dashidai.com; 6th fl, Raffles City, 268 Middle Xizang Rd; 西藏中路268号; meals from Y35; Ⓜ People's Sq) King of the food courts, Food Republic offers Asian cuisines in abundance for busy diners, with handy branches around town – this one overlooks the nonstop action on People's Sq. Prepay, grab a card (Y10 deposit) and head to the stall of your choice for on-the-spot service.

Nina's Sìchuān House SICHUANESE $$
(蜀菜行家; Shǔcài Hángjiā; Map p170; 227 North Huangpi Rd, inside Central Plaza; 黄陂北路227号; dishes Y18-88; 🄴; Ⓜ People's Sq) The best

Sichuanese restaurant in the neighbourhood, Nina's is as authentic as they come, with lines out the door and few foreigners in on the secret.

Jean Georges FUSION $$$
(法国餐厅; Făguó Cāntīng; Map p170; ☎6321 7733; www.jean-georges.com; 4th fl, Three on the Bund, 3 East Zhongshan No 1 Rd; 中山东一路3号4楼; mains from Y148, 3-course lunches Y188; ⓔ; ⓂEast Nanjing Rd) Divine palate-pleasers such as pickled peach, goat's cheese and crystallised wasabi salad, and crunchy tiger prawns.

M on the Bund CONTINENTAL $$$
(米氏西餐厅; Mǐshì Xīcāntīng; Map p170; ☎6350 9988; www.m-onthebund.com; 7th fl, 20 Guangdong Rd; 广东路20号7楼; mains from Y198, 2-course lunches Y186; ⓔ; ⓂEast Nanjing Rd) With table linen flapping in the breeze alongside exclusive rooftop views to Pǔdōng, the grand dame of the Bund still elicits applause from Shànghǎi's gastronomes.

OLD TOWN

Yù Fashion Garden CHINESE $$
(豫城时尚; Yùchéng Shíshàng; Map p170; Middle Fangbang Rd; 方浜中路; meals from Y58; ⓂYuyuan Bazaar) True, eating in a mall isn't quite the same as braving the crowds at the Yùyuán Bazaar – and if you're up for it, by all means give it a try – but if you'd prefer to dine in more-relaxed surrounds, there are a few good choices here, notably **Din Tai Fung** (2nd floor), whose tender dumplings knock the stuffing out of the overrated ones at the bazaar.

Sōngyuèlóu VEGETARIAN, CHINESE $
(松月楼; Map p170; 99 Jiujiaochang Rd; dishes Y25-48; ⊙7am-10pm; ⓥⓔ; ⓂYuyuan Bazaar) This humble spot is Shànghǎi's oldest veggie restaurant, with the usual mix of tofu masquerading as meat. English menu on the 2nd floor.

FRENCH CONCESSION

TOP CHOICE **Bǎoluó Jiǔlóu** SHANGHAINESE $$
(保罗酒楼; Map p176; ☎6279 2827; 271 Fumin Rd; 富民路271号; dishes Y18-68; ⊙11am-3am; ⓔ; ⓂChangshu Rd, Jing'an Temple) Gather up a boisterous bunch of friends for a fun-filled meal at this typically chaotic and cavernous Shànghǎi institution, which has lines out the door late into the night. Try the excellent lion's head meatballs, lotus-leaf roasted duck or the *bǎoluó kǎomàn* (保罗烤鳗; baked eel).

Crystal Jade DIM SUM $$
(翡翠酒家; Fěicuì Jiǔjiā; Map p176; ☎6385 8752; Xīntiāndì, South Block, 2nd fl, Bldg 6; 兴业路123弄新天地南里6号2楼; noodles & dim sum Y20-40; ⓔ; ⓂSouth Huangpi Rd, Xīntiāndì) What distinguishes Crystal Jade from other dim sum restaurants is the dough: dumpling wrappers are perfectly tender, steamed buns come out light and airy, and the fresh noodles have been pulled to perfection. Go for lunch, when both Cantonese and Shanghainese dim sum are served. Located in the mall.

Sìchuān Citizen SICHUANESE $
(龙门陈茶屋; Lóngmén Chénchá Wū; Map p176; ☎5404 1235; 30 Donghu Rd; 东湖路30号; dishes Y18 58; ⓦⓔ; ⓂSouth Shaanxi Rd) Citizen has opted for the 'rustic chic' look, the wood panelling and whirring ceiling fans conjuring up visions of an old-style Chéngdū teahouse that's been made over for an *Elle* photoshoot. But the food is the real stuff, prepared by a busy Sìchuān kitchen crew to ensure no Shanghainese sweetness creeps into the peppercorn onslaught.

Dīshuǐdòng HUNANESE $$
(滴水洞; Map p176; ☎6253 2689; 2nd fl, 56 South Maoming Rd; 茂名南路56号2层; dishes Y18-58; ⓔ; ⓂSouth Shaanxi Rd) Shànghǎi's oldest Hunanese restaurant is surprisingly down-home, but the menu is sure-fire, albeit mild for one of China's spiciest culinary traditions. The spicy bean curd and *zīrán* (cumin) ribs hit the mark; flesh out the meal with Mao's stewed pork.

Southern Barbarian YUNNANESE $$
(南蛮子; Nánmánzi; Map p176; ☎5157 5510; E7, 2nd fl, 169 Jinxian Rd; 进贤路169号2楼E7; dishes Y18-45; ⓔ; ⓂSouth Shaanxi Rd) Despite the alarming name, there's nothing remotely barbaric about the food here. Instead you get superb MSG-free Yúnnán cuisine: barbecued snapper, beef-and-mint casserole, chicken wings and the famous Yúnnán goat cheese. Enter through the mall.

Din Tai Fung DUMPLINGS $$
(鼎泰丰; Dǐng Tài Fēng; Map p176; ☎6385 8378; Xīntiāndì, South Block, 2nd fl, Bldg 6; 兴业路123弄新天地南里6号楼2楼; 10 dumplings from Y56; ⓥⓔ; ⓂSouth Huangpi Rd, Xīntiāndì) Come here for different dumpling styles from across China. Critics harp that it charges high prices (true), but the throngs inside make a convincing riposte: the food here really is that good. Located in the mall.

El Willy SPANISH $$$

(Map p176; ☎5404 5757; www.elwilly.com.cn; 20 Donghu Rd; 东湖路20号; tapas Y65-165, rice for 2 Y188-218; ; South Shaanxi Rd) The unstoppable energy of colourful-sock-wearing Barcelona chef Willy fuels this restored 1920s villa, which ups its charms with creative tapas and succulent rice dishes. The set lunch (Y78) is a steal.

Simply Thai THAI $$

(天泰餐厅; Tiāntài Cāntīng; Map p176; ☎6445 9551; www.simplythai-sh.com; 5c Dongping Rd; 东平路5号C座; mains Y45-65; ; Changshu Rd) Everyone raves about this place for its delicious, MSG-free curries and salads, and crisp decor. There's nice outdoor seating, a choice of 55 different wines and lunch specials are good value. Another branch is in Xīntiāndì.

Xīnjíshì SHANGHAINESE $$

(新吉士; Map p176; ☎6336 4746; Xīntiāndì, North Block, Bldg 9; 新天地北里9号楼; dishes from Y28; ; South Huangpi Rd, Xīntiāndì) Sweet Shanghainese home cooking in swish surrounds: specialities include crab dumplings, stuffed red dates and the classic Grandma's braised pork. Several branches.

Noodle Bull NOODLES $

(狠牛面; Hěnniú Miàn; Map p176; 3b, 291 Fumin Rd; 富民路291号1F3b室; noodles Y25-30; ; Changshu Rd, South Shaanxi Rd) Far cooler than your average street-corner noodle stand (minimalist concrete chic and funky bowls), Noodle Bull's secret ingredient is the super-slurpable MSG-free broth. Entrance is from Changle Rd.

Chá's DIM SUM $

(查餐厅; Chá Cāntīng; Map p176; 30 Sinan Rd; 思南路30号; dishes Y18-50; ; South Shaanxi Rd) Absolutely packed no-frills dim sum diner (sweet-and-sour pork, baked salt chicken, noodles). Plan on a minimum 15-minute wait.

Bankura JAPANESE $$

(万藏; Wànzàng; Map p176; ☎6215 0373; 344 Changle Rd; 长乐路344号; noodles Y30-55; ; South Shaanxi Rd) Underground Japanese noodle bar, with delectable extras such as grilled fish, curried shrimp and fried shiitake mushrooms.

Haiku JAPANESE $$

(隐泉之语; Yǐnquán Zhī Yǔ; Map p176; ☎6445 0021; 28b Taojiang Rd; 桃江路28号乙; maki rolls Y60-98; ; Changshu Rd) Wacky maki rolls from the Ninja (shrimp, crab and killer spicy sauce) and the Philly (cream cheese and salmon) to the Pimp My Roll (everything).

Xībó Grill CENTRAL ASIAN $$

(锡伯餐厅; Xībó Cāntīng; Map p176; ☎5403 8330; 3rd fl, 83 Changshu Rd; 常熟路83号3楼; dishes Y15-68; ; Changshu Rd) If you're in need of a mutton fix, try out the rooftop terrace of this stylish Xīnjiāng joint.

Azul FUSION $$$

(Map p176; ☎6433 1172; 18 Dongping Rd; 东平路18号; tapas from Y78, mains from Y148; ; Changshu Rd) This Latin place is a favourite for its fresh New World cuisine and hip decor, but it's the smoothie-driven weekend brunches that elicit the most praise.

WEST NANJING ROAD & JÌNG'ĀN

TOP CHOICE **Fu 1039** SHANGHAINESE $$$

(福一零三九; Fú Yāo Líng Sān Jiǔ; ☎6288 1179; 1039 Yuyuan Rd; 愚圆路1039号; dishes Y40-288; 11am-2.30pm & 5-11pm; ; Jiangsu Rd) Set in a three-storey 1913 villa, Fu is upmarket Shanghainese all the way, with an unusual old-fashioned charm in a city hell-bent on modern design. Not easy to find, it rewards the persistent with succulent standards such as the smoked fish starter and stewed pork in soy sauce. The entrance, down an alley and on the left, is unmarked. To get here, follow Yuyuan Rd west from the metro station for about 200m (after crossing Jiangsu Rd) and then turn south (left) down an alley. The unmarked entrance will be the first on your left.

Lynn SHANGHAINESE $$

(琳怡; Lín Yí; Map p180; ☎6247 0101; 99-1 Xikang Rd; 西康路99-1号; dishes Y35-90; ; West Nanjing Rd) Another one of the growing number of restaurants pushing the boundaries between Shanghainese and Cantonese cuisine, Lynn offers consistently good, cleverly presented dishes at reasonable prices in plush but unfussy surroundings. The lunch dim sum menu offers a range of delicate dumplings, while for dinner there are more adventurous standouts including sautéed chicken with sesame pockets and deep-fried spare ribs with honey and garlic.

Vegetarian Life Style CHINESE $$

(枣子树; Zǎozi Shù; Map p180; ☎6215 7566; 258 Fengxian Rd; 奉贤路258号; dishes Y20-48; ; West Nanjing Rd) For light and healthy organic vegetarian Chinese food, with zero meat and precious little oil, this

SHANG HIGH

Much like Babel, Shànghǎi yearns to reach the heavens, and not in a spiritual sense. With so many towers scattered around town, a high-altitude view of the metropolis is inevitable, so why not choose a spot where you can relax with a drink? Bund bars have fantastic views, of course, but if you want to get really high, you'll need to hit the hotel bars. Don't yawn yet – they're cheaper (coffee from Y55, cocktails from Y70) and often more congenial than the crowded viewing platforms. Smog can obscure daytime views, so time your visit for dusk.

» **Cloud 9** (九重天酒廊; Jiǔchóngtiān Jiǔláng; Map p181; 87th fl, Jīnmào Tower, 88 Century Ave; 世纪大道88号金茂大厦87; ⏲5pm-1am Mon-Fri, 11am-2am Sat & Sun; Ⓜ Lujiazui) Atop the Grand Hyatt, this is no longer the highest bar in the city, but it's still the coolest in the stratosphere.

» **Vue** (非常时髦; Fēicháng Shímáo; Map p170; 32nd & 33rd fl, Hyatt on the Bund, 199 Huangpu Rd; 外滩茂悦大酒店黄浦路199号32-33楼; ⏲6pm-1am; Ⓜ Tiantong Rd) Fabulous views down the Bund and an outdoor jacuzzi to accompany bottles of bubbly and Vue martinis (vodka and mango purée).

» **789 Nanjing Lu Bar** (789南京路酒吧; Qībǎi Bāshíjiǔ Nánjīng Lù Jiǔbā; Map p170; 64th-66th fl, Le Royal Meridien, 789 East Nanjing Rd; 南京东路789号64-66楼; ⏲3pm-1am; Ⓜ People's Sq) Chocolate martinis and 360-degree views are the specialities at the apex of this People's Sq skyscraper.

welcoming place has excellent fare. The health-conscious, ecofriendly mentality extends all the way to the toothpicks, made of cornflour. There's another **branch** (☎6384 8000; 77 Songshan Rd; 嵩山路77号; Ⓜ South Huangpi Rd) in the French Concession.

Element Fresh CAFE $$
(新元素餐厅; Xīnyuánsù; Map p180; ☎6279 8682; www.elementfresh.com; Shànghǎi Centre, 1376 West Nanjing Rd; sandwiches Y38-88, dinners from Y128; ⏲7am-11pm; 📶🖉📋; Ⓜ West Nanjing Rd) The focus at this bright Shànghǎi institution is on healthy sandwiches, fresh salads and imaginative smoothies for the young laptop crowd. Eight branches around town, including at the Superbrand Mall in Pǔdōng (Map p181).

Wagas CAFE $
(沃歌斯; Wògēsī; Map p180; www.wagas.com.cn; B11a, Citic Square, 1168 West Nanjing Rd; 南京西路1168号下一层11a室; meals from Y48; ⏲7am-9.30pm; 📶📋; Ⓜ West Nanjing Rd) Breakfasts are 50% off before 10am, pasta is Y33 after 6pm, you can hang out here for hours with your laptop and no one will shoo you away – need we say more? Locations abound.

Wujiang Road Food Street FOOD STREET $
(Map p180; Wujiang Rd; 吴江路; meals from Y30; Ⓜ West Nanjing Rd) The original Wujiang food street is long gone, replaced by a modern version, with chain cafes, noodle bars and various other cheap options.

PǓDŌNG NEW AREA

Superbrand Mall FOOD COURT $$
(正大广场; Zhèngdà Guǎngchǎng; Map p182; 168 West Lujiazui Rd; 陆家嘴西路168号; ⏲10am-10pm; Ⓜ Lujiazui) This gargantuan shopping mall has the best selection of eats in Pǔdōng, with everything from cheap Thai and healthy sandwiches to the swish Sichuanese-Cantonese combo on the 10th floor (South Beauty).

Drinking

Shànghǎi is awash with watering holes, their fortunes cresting and falling with the vagaries of the latest vogue. Perhaps because of Shànghǎi's notoriously boggy foundations, bars regularly sink without a trace, while others suddenly pop up like corks from nowhere. Today the city has an inventive and wide-ranging concoction of different bar types, from gritty student dives through solid Irish pubs and sports bars to jazzy cocktail bars, seductive wine lounges and elegant, fashion-conscious establishments operating from grandiose concession-era buildings. Drinks are pricier here than in the rest of China, retailing from around Y40 (beer) or Y60 (cocktails) at most places, so happy-hour visits (typically 5pm to 8pm) can be crucial. Bars usually open late afternoon (but many open earlier), calling it a night at around 2am.

The Bund

Glamour Bar COCKTAIL BAR
(魅力酒吧; Mèilì Jiǔbā; Map p170; www.m-theglamourbar.com; 6th fl, 20 Guangdong Rd; 广东路20号6楼; ⏲5pm-late; Ⓜ East Nanjing Rd) Michelle Garnaut's stylish bar is set in a splendidly restored space just beneath M on the Bund. In addition to mixing great drinks, it hosts film screenings, an annual literary festival, music performances and China-related book launches.

Captain's Bar BAR
(船长青年酒吧; Chuánzhǎng Qīngnián Jiǔbā; Map p170; 6th fl, 37 Fuzhou Rd; 福州路37号6楼; ⏲11am-2am; 📶; Ⓜ East Nanjing Rd) There's the odd drunken sailor and the crummy lift needs a rethink, but this is a fine Bund-side terrace-equipped bar atop the Captain Hostel. Come for cheap drinks and phosphorescent nocturnal Pǔdōng views, with pizza and without wall-to-wall preening sophisticates.

Barbarossa BAR
(芭芭露莎会所; Bābālùshā Huìsuǒ; Map p170; People's Park, 231 West Nanjing Rd; 南京西路231号人民公园内; ⏲11am-2am; 📶; Ⓜ People's Sq) Bringing a whiff of Middle Eastern promise to the Pearl of the Orient, this Moroccan-styled bar-restaurant sits pondside in People's Park like something from a mirage. It's more than a mere novelty: there's excellent music, outside seating and evening views.

New Heights BAR
(新视角; Xīn Shìjiǎo; Map p170; 7th fl, Three on the Bund, 3 East Zhongshan No 1 Rd; 中山东一路3号7楼; ⏲11am-1.30am; 📶; Ⓜ East Nanjing Rd) The terrace of this casual Three on the Bund bar pretty much has *the* definitive angle on Lùjiāzuǐ's neon nightfall overture. Try the cocktails, skip the food.

Atanu BAR/CAFE
(阿塔努咖啡酒吧; Ātǎnǔ Kāfēi Jiǔbā; Map p170; 1 Zhongshan East No 2 Rd; 中山东二路1号; ⏲10am-2am; Ⓜ East Nanjing Rd) Located on the top two floors of the former signal tower, this is an ideal pit stop for those strolling the Bund.

Old Town

Old Shànghǎi Teahouse TEAHOUSE
(老上海茶馆; Lǎo Shànghǎi Cháguǎn; Map p170; 385 Middle Fangbang Rd; 方浜中路385号; ⏲9am-9pm; Ⓜ Yuyuan Garden) Heading up here is like barging into someone's attic, where ancient gramophones, records, typewriters, fire extinguishers and even an ancient Frigidaire refrigerator share space with the aroma of Chinese tea and tempting snacks.

French Concession

Citizen Cafe CAFE
(天台餐厅; Tiāntái Cāntīng; Map p176; 222 Jinxian Rd; 进贤路222号; ⏲11am-12.30am; 📶; Ⓜ South Shaanxi Rd) Citizen's burgundy-and-cream colours, antique ceiling fans and well-worn parquet offer calming respite from the Shànghǎi crush. Cappuccinos, cocktails and club sandwiches.

Cafe 85°C CAFE
(85度咖啡店; Bāshíwǔ Dù Kāfēidiàn; Map p176; 117 South Shaanxi Rd; 陕西南路117号; ⏲24hr; Ⓜ South Shaanxi Rd) The cheapest caffeine fix (and breakfast) in town, with quality coffee, tea and never-before-seen Taiwanese pastries. Dozens of branches in town.

Kommune CAFE
(公社酒吧; Gōngshè Jiǔbā; Map p176; 7, Lane 210, Taikang Rd; 泰康路210弄7号田子坊; ⏲8am-midnight; 📶; Ⓜ Dapuqiao) The original Tiánzǐfáng cafe, Kommune is a consistently packed hang-out with outdoor courtyard seating, drinks, big breakfasts, and sandwiches on the menu.

Boxing Cat Brewery BAR
(拳击猫啤酒屋; Quánjīmāo Píjiǔwū; Map p176; www.boxingcatbrewery.com; 82 West Fuxing Rd; 复兴西路82号; ⏲5pm-2am Mon-Fri, 11am-2am Sat & Sun; 📶; Ⓜ Shanghai Library/Changshu Rd) Deservedly popular three-floor microbrewery with Southern-style grub.

Time Passage BAR
(昨天今天明天; Zuótiān Jīntiān Míngtiān; Map p176; 183 Lane 1038, Caojiayan Rd; 曹家堰路1038弄183号; ⏲5.30pm-2am; 📶; Ⓜ Jiangsu Rd) If you like cheap beer, an undemanding, lived-in ambience and John and Yoko posters, this businessman-free bar has been charting its passage since 1994.

Abbey Road BAR
(艾比之路; Àibǐ Zhī Lù; Map p176; 45 Yueyang Rd; 岳阳路45号; ⏲4pm-late Mon-Fri, 8.30am-late Sat & Sun; 📶; Ⓜ Changshu Rd) The cheap beer–classic rock combination works its stuff again, attracting plenty of regulars to this French Concession favourite.

Jìng'ān

Big Bamboo SPORTS BAR
(Map p179; 132 Nanyang Rd; 南阳路132号; ⏲11am-2am; 📶; Ⓜ Jing'an Temple) Huge, extro-

verted sports bar ranging over two floors with beefy American menu (set lunches 11am to 3pm), mammoth sports screen backed up by a constellation of TV sets, Guinness, pool, darts, DJ and live-music nights.

Bàndù Cabin CAFE
(半度雨棚; Bàndù Yǔpéng; Map p180; ☎6276 8267; Bldg 11, 50 Moganshan Rd; 莫干山路50号11号楼; ⏲10am-6.30pm; 📶; Ⓜ Shanghai Railway Station) Welcoming low-key Moganshan Rd Art Centre enclave with pine tables, low-cost menu (noodles, sandwiches, coffee) and traditional Chinese musical events on Saturday evenings at 8pm (phone ahead).

☆ Entertainment

There's something for most moods in Shànghǎi: opera, rock, hip hop, techno, salsa and early-morning waltzes in People's Sq. None of it comes cheap, however (except for the waltzing, which is free). Expect a night on the town in Shànghǎi to be comparable to a night out in Hong Kong or Taipei.

Venues open and close all the time. Check out Shànghǎi's entertainment websites and magazines for guidance.

Traditional Performances

Chinese acrobatic troupes are among the best in the world, and Shànghǎi is a good place for performances.

Yìfū Theatre CHINESE OPERA
(逸夫舞台; Yìfū Wǔtái; Map p170; ☎6322 5294; www.tianchan.com; 701 Fuzhou Rd; tickets Y30-280; Ⓜ People's Sq) A block east of People's Sq, this is the main opera theatre in town, staging a variety of regional operatic styles, including Běijīng opera, Kunqu opera and Yue opera, with a Běijīng opera highlights show several times a week. A shop in the foyer sells CDs.

Paramount Ballroom BALLROOM DANCING
(百乐门; Bǎilèmén; Map p179; ☎6322 5294; 218 Yuyuan Rd, Jìng'ān; 豫园路218号; afternoon-tea dances Y80, evening ballroom dancing Y250; ⏲1-4.30pm & 8.20pm-1.30am; Ⓜ Jing'an Temple) This old art deco theatre was the biggest nightclub in the 1930s, and today has sedate afternoon-tea dances to the sounds of old-school jazz and tango, as well as ballroom dancing in the evening. It makes for a nice nostalgia trip for those with a sense of humour (dance partners cost extra).

TICKETS

Tickets for all of Shànghǎi's performing-arts events can be purchased at the venues where the performances take place. Tickets are also available from **Smart Ticket** (www.smartshanghai.com/smartticket) and the **Shànghǎi Cultural Information & Booking Centre** (上海文化信息票务中心; Shànghǎi Wénhuà Xìnxī Piàowù Zhōngxīn; Map p179; ☎6217 2426; www.culture.sh.cn; 272 Fengxian Rd; 奉贤路272号; ⏲9am-7pm; Ⓜ West Nanjing Rd), which is directly behind the Westgate Mall on West Nanjing Rd. It often has tickets available when other places have sold out.

Shànghǎi Circus World ACROBATICS
(上海马戏城; Shànghǎi Mǎxìchéng; ☎6652 7501; 2266 Gonghexin Rd; 闸北区共和新路2266号; admission Y180-580; Ⓜ Shanghai Circus World) Elegant modern acrobatics with multimedia elements and an impressive modern venue north of town. Nightly shows (currently known as ERA) at 7.30pm.

Shànghǎi Centre ACROBATICS
(上海商城剧院; Shànghǎi Shāngchéng Jùyuàn; Map p179; ☎6279 8948; www.pujiangqing.com; 1376 West Nanjing Rd; 南京西路1376号; tickets Y100-280; Ⓜ Jing'an Temple) The Shànghǎi Acrobatic Troupe (Shànghǎi Zájì Tuán) has short but entertaining performances here most nights at 7.30pm.

Live Music

In addition to the places listed here, other bars, cafes and restaurants, such as the Glamour Bar and Bāndù Cabin (traditional Chinese music), stage musical performances. The Peace Hotel jazz band had just been resuscitated as this book went to press.

Yùyīntáng ROCK
(育音堂; www.yuyintang.org; 1731 West Yan'an Rd, 延安西路1731号; cover Y40; ⏲Thu-Sun 8pm-midnight; Ⓜ West Yan'an Rd) Small enough to feel intimate, but big enough for a sometimes pulsating atmosphere, Yùyīntáng has long been the place in the city to see live music. Rock is the staple diet, but anything goes, from hard punk to gypsy jazz. It's west of the city, on lines 3 and 4. The entrance is on Kaixuan Rd.

ACCUPRESSURE MASSAGE

Shànghǎi's midrange massage parlours are a must – for the price of a cocktail or three, you get your own set of PJs, some post-therapy tea and Chinese flute music to chill out with. Just don't expect the masseuses to be gentle. As they say: no pain, no gain. Reserve in advance.

Dragonfly (悠庭保健会所; Yōutíng Bǎojiàn Huìsuǒ; Map p176; www.dragonfly.net.cn; massages from Y150; ⏲10am-2am) Donghu Rd (☎5405 0008; 20 Donghu Rd; 东湖路20号; Ⓜ South Shaanxi Rd); Xinle Rd (☎5403 9982; 206 Xinle Rd; 新乐路206号; Ⓜ South Shaanxi Rd); Nanchang Rd (☎5386 0060; 84 Nanchang Rd; 南昌路84号; Ⓜ South Huangpi Rd) offers hour-long Chinese body massages, Japanese-style shiatsu and traditional foot massages in soothing surroundings. There are several French Concession branches around town.

Green Massage (青专业按摩; Qīng Zhuānyè Ànmó; ☎5386 0222; 58 Taicang Rd; 太仓路58号; massages from Y98; ⏲10.30am-2am; Ⓜ South Huangpi Rd) has 45-minute *tuīná* and shiatsu massages with Chinese cupping and hour-long foot massages.

Melting Pot ROCK, FOLK
(Map p176; No 288, Taikang Rd; 泰康路288号; ⏲5.30pm-1am; Ⓜ Dapuqiao) This friendly bar has an eclectic line-up of local musicians – some good, some bad – every night of the week. It's a good spot to hear some tunes after an afternoon or evening at the Taikang Rd Art Centre.

House of Blues & Jazz JAZZ
(布鲁斯与爵士之屋; Bùlǔsī Yǔ Juéshì Zhī Wū; Map p170; ☎6323 2779; 60 Fuzhou Rd; 福州路60号; ⏲4.30pm-2am; Ⓜ East Nanjing Rd) Jazz- and blues-lovers should make a beeline to this classy restaurant and bar where the in-house band (which changes every three months) whips up live music from 10pm to 1am.

MAO Livehouse ROCK
(www.maolive-sh.org; Bldg 32, 570 West Huaihai Rd; 淮海西路570号32栋,红坊内; Ⓜ Hongqiao Rd) One of Shànghǎi's best music venues, MAO is west of the city on lines 3, 4, and 10, in the Red Town complex. Check the website for schedules and ticket prices.

Nightclubs

Shànghǎi's swift transition from dead zone to party animal and its reputation as a city on the move forges an inventive clubbing attitude and a constant stream of clubbers. Clubs range from huge, swanky spaces dedicated to the preening Hong Kong and white-collar crowd to more relaxed, intimate spots and trendy bars that rustle up weekend DJs. There's a high turnover, so check listings websites and magazines for the latest on the club scene.

Shelter CLUB
(Map p176; 5 Yongfu Rd; 永福路5号; ⏲9pm-4am Wed-Sun; Ⓜ Shanghai Library) The darling of the underground crowd, Shelter is a converted bomb shelter where you can count on great music and cheap drinks. A good line-up of DJs and hip-hop artists pass through; cover for big shows is around Y30.

Muse CLUB
(www.museshanghai.cn; New Factories, 68 Yuyao Rd; 余姚路68号同乐坊; ⏲8.30pm-4.30am; Ⓜ Changping Rd) One of the city's hottest clubs (house, hip hop) over the past few years, Muse has three locations. The main club is in north Jìng'ān, the other two (both smaller) are in the French Concession; check the website for details.

Chinatown BURLESQUE
(☎6258 2078; www.chinatownshanghai.com; 471 Zhapu Rd, Hóngkǒu; 乍浦路471号; ⏲8pm-2am Wed-Sat; Ⓜ North Sichuan Rd) The Chinatown Dolls take to the stage in an old Buddhist temple north of the Bund. The show itself is somewhat tame; the first-rate cocktails ain't. There's a minimum spend of Y250 on weekend nights; reserve.

Gay & Lesbian Venues

Shànghǎi has a few places catering to gay patrons, but locales keep moving around, so check the listings.

Shànghǎi Studio BAR
(嘉浓休闲; Jiānóng Xiūxián; Map p176; No 4, Lane 1950, Middle Huaihai Rd; 淮海中路1950弄4号; ⏲9pm-2am; Ⓜ Jiaotong University) This hip newcomer to the Shànghǎi gay scene has transformed the cool depths of a for-

mer bomb shelter into a laid-back bar, art gallery and men's underwear shop.

Eddy's Bar BAR
(嘉浓咖啡; Jiānóng Kāfēi; Map p176; 1877 Middle Huaihai Rd; ⏲8pm-2am; Ⓜ Jiaotong University) A gay-friendly bar-cafe attracting a slightly more mature Chinese and international gay crowd with inexpensive drinks and neat decor.

Classical Music, Opera & Theatre

Oriental Art Center CLASSICAL, OPERA
(东方艺术中心; Dōngfāng Yìshù Zhōngxīn; ☎6854 7796; www.shoac.com.cn; 425 Dingxiang Rd, Pǔdōng; 浦东丁香路425号; tickets Y30-680; Ⓜ Science & Technology Museum) Home of the Shànghǎi Symphonic Orchestra, the Oriental Art Center was designed to resemble five petals of a butterfly orchid. There are three main halls that host classical, jazz, dance, and Chinese and Western opera performances.

Shànghǎi Cultural Plaza CLASSICAL
(上海文化广场; Shànghǎi Wénhuà Guǎngchǎng; Map p176; www.shculturesquare.com, in Chinese; 36 Yongjia Rd; 永嘉路36号; Ⓜ South Shaanxi Rd) This new 2000-seat music and dance venue is the world's largest underground theatre, built on the site of the former dog-racing stadium (Canindrome). It should be open by the time you read this.

Shànghǎi Grand Theatre CLASSICAL, OPERA, DANCE
(上海大剧院; Shànghǎi Dàjùyuàn; Map p170; ☎6386 8686; www.shgtheatre.com; 300 Renmin Ave; 人民大道300号; tickets Y50-2280; Ⓜ People's Sq) This state-of-the-art venue is in People's Sq and features both national and international opera, dance, music and theatre performances.

Shànghǎi Concert Hall CLASSICAL
(上海音乐厅; Shànghǎi Yīnyuè Tīng; Map p170; ☎6386 2836; 523 East Yan'an Rd; 人民广场延安东路523号; tickets Y50-680; Ⓜ Dashijie) Equipped with fine acoustics, this 75-year-old building is the venue for regular performances by orchestras including the Shànghǎi Symphony Orchestra and the Shànghǎi Broadcasting Symphony Orchestra.

Cinemas

Only a limited (and generally late) selection of foreign-language films make it to cinemas; they are often dubbed into Chinese, so ensure your film is the English version (英文版; *yīngwénbǎn*). Tickets cost Y40 to Y60.

Peace Cinema CINEMA
(和平影都、巨幕影院; Hépíng Yǐngdū; Map p170; 290 Middle Xizang Rd; 西藏中路290号; tickets Y50; Ⓜ People's Sq) A useful location at People's Sq, with an IMAX cinema (Y80).

Studio City CINEMA
(环艺电影城; Huányì Diànyǐngchéng; Map p179; 10th fl, Westgate Mall, 1038 West Nanjing Rd; 南京西路1038号10楼; Ⓜ West Nanjing Rd)

UME International Cineplex CINEMA
(UME; 国际影城; Guójì Yǐngchéng; Map p176; www.ume.com.cn; Xīntiāndì, South Block, No 6, 5th fl; 新天地南里6号楼5楼; Ⓜ South Huangpi Rd, Xīntiāndì)

Shopping

It's no exaggeration to say that some people come to Shànghǎi specifically to shop. What the city lacks in terms of historic sights, it makes up for with its fashion-forward attitude and great bargains. From megamalls to independent boutiques and haute couture, Shànghǎi is once again at the forefront of Chinese fashion and design.

The Bund & People's Square

The Bund is all about luxury shopping.

Annabel Lee FASHION
(安梨家居; Ānlí Jiājū; Map p170; www.annabel-lee.com; 1, Lane 8, East No 1 Zhongshan Rd; ⏲10am-10pm; Ⓜ East Nanjing Rd) On the Bund, Annabel Lee sells a lovely range of playfully designed, soft-coloured accessories in silk, linen and cashmere, many of which feature delicate embroidery. There's another branch in Xīntiāndì.

Shànghǎi No 1 (First) Food Store SNACKS
(上海市第一食品商店; Shànghǎishì Dìyī Shípǐn Shāngdiàn; Map p170; 720 East Nanjing Rd; ⏲9.30am-10pm; Ⓜ East Nanjing Rd) It's bedlam, but this is how the Shanghainese shop and it's a lot of fun. Trawl the ground floor for egg tarts, moon cakes, dried mushrooms, ginseng and dried seafood, or pop a straw into a thirst-quenching coconut.

Shànghǎi Museum Shop ART
(上海博物馆商店; Shànghǎi Bówùguǎn Shāngdiàn; Map p170; 201 Renmin Ave; ⏲9am-5pm; Ⓜ People's Sq) This shop sells excellent but expensive imitations of museum pieces, which are far superior to the mediocre clutter in tourist shops.

Sūzhōu Cobblers SHOES
(上海起想艺术品; Shànghǎi Qǐxiǎng Yìshùpǐn; Map p170; www.suzhou-cobblers.com; Room 101,

WHERE CAN I FIND...

» **Faux antiques and souvenirs?** Head to Old Street or the Dongtai Rd Antique Market in the Old Town.

» **Local fashion?** Tiánzǐfáng and the French Concession (Xinle Rd and Changle Rd).

» **Tailor-made clothing and fabric?** Shíliùpù Fabric Market in the Old Town.

» **Discount (OK, fake) clothing and accessories?** Han City Fashion and Accessories Plaza in Jìng'ān or the A.P. Xinyang Fashion & Gifts Market in Pǔdōng.

» **Real pearls?** Amy Lin's Pearls in Jìng'ān.

» **Handicrafts?** Brocade Country, Yú or Sūzhōu Cobblers.

» **Electronics? My laptop crashed in Sìchuān!** Head to Cybermart in the French Concession or China's largest Apple store (next to the IFC Mall, 8 Century Ave) in Pǔdōng.

17 Fuzhou Rd; ⏲10am-6pm; Ⓜ East Nanjing Rd) For hand-embroidered silk slippers and shoes, pop into this minute shop just off the Bund.

Cybermart ELECTRONICS
(赛博数码广场; Sàibó Shùmǎ Guǎngchǎng; Map p170; 1 Middle Huaihai Rd; 淮海中路1号; ⏲10am-8pm; Ⓜ Dashijie) Cybermart is the most central and reliable location for all sorts of gadgetry, including laptops, digital cameras and memory sticks. You can bargain, but don't expect enormous discounts.

Foreign Languages Bookstore BOOKS
(外文书店; Wàiwén Shūdiàn; Map p170; 390 Fuzhou Rd; ⏲9.30am-6pm Sun-Thu, to 7pm Fri & Sat; Ⓜ East Nanjing Rd) Hit the 1st floor for guidebooks and China-related material, the 4th floor for imported nonfiction and novels.

Old Town

Yùyuán Bazaar in the Old Town is a magnificent sprawl of shops satisfying virtually every souvenir requirement. Shops along nearby Old Street (老街; aka Middle Fangbang Rd; Map p170) are slightly better, selling everything from calligraphy, teapots and memorabilia to woodcuts and reproduction 1930s posters. It's all fun, but haggle hard and tie in lunch by snacking.

Shíliùpǔ Fabric Market FABRIC
(十六铺面料城; Shíliùpǔ Miánliào Chéng; 2 Zhonghua Rd; 中华路2号; ⏲8.30am-6.30pm; Ⓜ Xiaonanmen) Expats and travellers line up for made-to-measure clothing at this market, popular for its bolts of cheap silk, cashmere, wool, linen and cotton. Follow Middle Fangbang Rd from the Yùyuán Bazaar east towards the river and you'll reach it after about 10 minutes (500m).

Dongtai Road Antique Market SOUVENIRS
(东台路古商品市场; Dōngtáilù Gǔshāngpǐn Shìchǎng; Dongtai Rd; 东台路; ⏲8.30am-6pm) A short shuffle west of the Old Town towards Xīntiāndì, the Dongtai Rd Antique Market is a hefty sprawl of curios, knick-knacks and Mao-era nostalgia, though only a fraction of the items qualify as antique. Haggle hard.

French Concession

The French Concession is where it's at for shoppers; there are boutiques on almost every corner. For a one-stop trip head to Tiánzǐfáng. With more time, start near the South Shaanxi metro station and try South Maoming Rd for tailor-made *qípáo* (a tight-fitting Chinese-style dress that came into fashion in 1920s Shànghǎi), and Xinle Rd and Changle Rd (between Ruijin No 1 Rd and S Chengdu Rd) for more contemporary fashion. Middle Huaihai Rd is lined with malls and international chains. Afternoon and evening are the best hours for browsing: some smaller shops don't open their doors until noon, but most stay open until 10pm.

Tiánzǐfáng FASHION, SOUVENIRS
(田子坊; Map p176; Taikang Rd; 泰康路; Ⓜ Dapuqiao) Burrow into the *lìlòng* here for a rewarding haul of creative boutiques, selling everything from hip jewellery and yak-wool scarves to retro communist dinnerware. Stores get shuffled around about as regularly as mahjong tiles, but keep your eyes peeled for **Feel Shanghai** (Unit 110, No 3, Lane 210) offering tailored Chinese clothing, **InSH** (Unit 306, No 3, Lane 210) for contemporary local fashion, **Chouchou Chic** (No 47, Lane 248) with kid's clothes, as well as arty tea shop **Zhenchalin Tea** (No 13, Lane 210).

Xīntiāndì FASHION
(新天地; Cnr Taicang & Madang Rds; 太仓路与马当路路口; ⏲11am-11pm; Ⓜ South Huangpi Rd, Xīntiāndì) Browse the north block for upmarket boutiques, from the fluorescent chic of **Shanghai Tang** (Bldg 15) and clever design at **Simply Life** (Unit 101, 159 Madang Rd) to the eco-fabrics of **Shanghai Trio** (No 4, enter via Taicang Rd), iridescent glass sculptures at **Líuligōngfáng** (Bldg 11) and embroidered accessories at **Annabel Lee** (Bldg 3).

Yú CERAMICS
(萸; Map p176; 164 Fumin Rd; 富民路164号; ⏲11am-9pm; Ⓜ Changshu Rd) Man Zhang and her husband create the personable porcelain at this tiny shop, the latest link in the Shànghǎi–Jǐngdézhèn connection, which is an excellent place to browse for handmade and hand-painted teaware, bowls and vases.

Spin CERAMICS
(旋; Xuán; Map p176; Bldg 3, 758 Julu Rd; 巨鹿路758号3号楼; ⏲noon-10pm; Ⓜ Jing'an Temple) New-wave and snazzy Jǐngdézhèn ceramics, from cool celadon tones and oblong teacups to 'kung-fu' vases, presented in a sharp and crisp showroom.

Brocade Country HANDICRAFTS
(锦绣纺; Jǐnxiù Fǎng; Map p176; 616 Julu Rd; 巨鹿路616号; ⏲10.30am-7pm; Ⓜ Changshu Rd) Exquisite collection of minority handicrafts from China's southwest, personally selected by the owner Liu Xiaolan, a Guìzhou native.

Madame Mao's Dowry SOUVENIRS
(毛太设计; Máotài Shèjì; Map p176; ☎5403 3551; 207 Fumin Rd; 富民路207号; ⏲10am-7pm; Ⓜ Changshu Rd, Jing'an Temple) The Maoist era repackaged as a chic accessory; pick up a bust of the Chairman, a repro revolutionary tin mug, Cultural Revolution prints or an antique lacquered Ming cabinet.

Garden Books BOOKS
(韬奋西文书局; Tāofèn Xīwén Shūjú; Map p176; 325 Changle Rd; 长乐路325号; ⏲10am-10pm; 📶; Ⓜ South Shaanxi Rd) Ice-cream parlour or bookshop? You decide.

Jīng'àn

Amy Lin's Pearls PEARLS
(艾敏林氏珍珠; Àimǐn Línshì Zhēnzhū; Room 30, 3rd fl, 580 West Nanjing Rd; 南京西路580号3楼30号; ⏲10am-8pm; Ⓜ West Nanjing Rd) Shànghǎi's most reliable retailer of pearls of all colours and sizes, which come for a fraction of the price that you'd pay back home.

Han City Fashion & Accessories Plaza CLOTHES, SOUVENIRS
(韩城服饰礼品广场; Hánchéng Fúshì Lǐpǐn Guǎngchǎng; 580 West Nanjing Rd; 南京西路580号; ⏲9am-9pm; Ⓜ West Nanjing Rd) This unassuming-looking building is one of the best locations to pick up bargain T-shirts, jackets, shoes and so on, with hundreds of stalls spread across several floors. Bargain hard.

Chaterhouse Booktrader BOOKS
(Map p180; Shanghai Centre, Unit 104, 1376 West Nanjing Rd; 南京西路1376号104室; ⏲9am-9pm; Ⓜ Jing'an Temple) A great hit with literature-starved expats for its selection of books and mags.

Pǔdōng

A.P. Xīnyáng Fashion & Gifts Market CLOTHES, SOUVENIRS
(亚大新阳服饰礼品市场; Yàdà Xīnyáng Fúshì Lǐpǐn Shìchǎng; ⏲10am-8pm; Ⓜ Science & Technology Museum) Below ground in the Science & Technology Museum metro station is Shànghǎi's largest collection of discount shopping stalls, including a branch of the Old Town fabric market and a separate area devoted exclusively to pearls. Bargain hard.

Hóngkǒu

Qīpǔ Market CLOTHES
(七浦服装市场; Qīpǔ Fúzhuāng Shìchǎng; 168 & 183 Qipu Rd; 七浦路168 & 183号; ⏲7am-5pm; Ⓜ Tiantong Rd) One big 'everything must go now' sale, this is the cheapest and most entertaining clothes-and-shoes market in the city. Haggle hard.

ℹ Information

Free English and bilingual maps of Shànghǎi are available at the airports, Tourist Information & Service Centres, bookshops and many hotels. Metro maps (地铁线路图; *dìtiě xiànlùtú*) are usually available at all stations. Quality online maps are available through Google.

Internet Access

Internet cafes have become much more scarce in touristy areas – it's generally more convenient to get online at your hotel or at a wi-fi hotspot if you have a laptop. Otherwise, ask your hotel for the closest internet cafe (网吧; *wǎngbā*) and bring your passport.

Jiāyì Internet Cafe (佳毅网吧; Jiāyì Wǎngbā; East Jinling Rd, near Guangxi Rd; 金陵东路、靠近广西路; per hr Y4; ⏲24hr)

Jídù Kōngjiān Internet Café (Jídù Kōngjiān Wǎngbā; cnr North Xiangyang & Changle Rds; 襄阳北路、长乐路交叉口; per hr Y3; ⌚24hr)

Míngwàng Internet Cafe (名旺网吧; Míngwàng Wǎngbā; 515 Fuzhou Rd; 福州路515号; per hr Y3.50; ⌚24hr) On the corner of Hubei Rd.

Media

Grab a free copy of the monthly *That's Shanghai* from an expat-centric restaurant or bar, followed swiftly by issues of *City Weekend* and *Time Out* for an instant plug into what's on in town, from art exhibitions and club nights to restaurant openings.

Foreign newspapers and magazines are available from the larger tourist hotels and some foreign-language bookshops. The local government publishes the *Shanghai Daily* (Y2).

Medical Services

Huàshān Hospital (华山医院; Huàshān Yīyuàn; Map p176; ☎5288 9998; www.sh-hwmc.com.cn; 12 Middle Wulumuqi Rd; 乌鲁木齐中路12号; Ⓜ Changshu Rd) Hospital treatment and outpatient consultations are available at the 8th-floor foreigners' clinic (open 8am to 10pm daily), with 24-hour emergency treatment on the 15th floor in Building 6.

Parkway Health (以极佳医疗保健服务;Yǐjíjiā Yīliáo Bǎojiàn Fúwù; ☎24hr hotline 6445 5999; www.parkwayhealth.cn) Seven locations around Shànghǎi, including at the **Shànghǎi Centre** (上海商城; Shànghǎi Shāngchéng; Suite 203, Shànghǎi Centre, 1376 West Nanjing Rd; 南京西路1376号203室; Ⓜ West Nanjing Rd). Private medical care by expat doctors, dentists and specialists.

Shànghǎi United Family Hospital (上海和睦家医院; Shànghǎi Hémùjiā Yīyuàn; ☎2216 3900, 24hr emergency 2216 3999; www.unitedfamilyhospitals.com; 1139 Xianxia Rd; 仙霞路1139号; Ⓜ Beixinjing, line 2) Complete private hospital, staffed by doctors trained in the West. Located near Hóngqiáo Airport.

Watson's (屈臣氏; Qūchénshì) French Concession (787 Middle Huaihai Rd; 淮海中路787号; Ⓜ South Shaanxi Rd); West Nanjing Rd (Westgate Mall, 1038 West Nanjing Rd; 南京西路1038号; Ⓜ West Nanjing Rd) This pharmacy has Western cosmetics, over-the-counter medicines and health products, with numerous outlets around the city.

Money

Almost every hotel has money-changing counters. Most tourist hotels, upmarket restaurants and banks accept major credit cards. ATMs are everywhere; most accept major cards.

Bank of China (中国银行; Zhōngguó Yínháng; The Bund; ⌚9am-noon & 1.30-4.30pm Mon-Fri, 9am-noon Sat) Right next to the Peace Hotel. Tends to get crowded, but is better organised than Chinese banks elsewhere around the country (it's worth a peek for its grand interior). Take a ticket and wait for your number. For credit-card advances, head to the furthest hall (counter No 2).

Citibank (花旗银行; Huāqí Yínháng; The Bund) Useful ATM open 24 hours.

Hong Kong & Shanghai Bank (汇丰银行; HSBC; Huìfēng Yínháng) Shànghǎi Centre (West Nanjing Rd); The Bund (15 East Zhongshan No 1 Rd) Has ATMs in the above locations; also an ATM at Pǔdōng Airport arrivals hall.

Post

Larger tourist hotels have post offices where you can mail letters and small packages; this is by far the most convenient option. China Post offices and postboxes are green. The **International Post Office** (国际邮局; Guójì Yóujú; 276 North Suzhou Rd; 苏州北路276号; ⌚7am-10pm; Ⓜ Tiantong Rd) is just north of Sūzhōu Creek in Hóngkǒu.

Public Security Bureau

(PSB;公安局;Gōng'ānjú; ☎2895 1900, ext 2; 1500 Minsheng Rd; 民生路1500号; ⌚9am-4.30pm Mon-Sat; Ⓜ Science & Technology Museum) Handles visas and registrations; 30-day visa extensions cost around Y160. In Pǔdōng.

Telephone

After Skype (www.skype.com), internet phone (IP) cards are the cheapest way to call internationally (Y1.80 per minute to the US), but may not work with some hotel phones. Using a mobile phone is naturally the most convenient option. For mobile phone SIM cards, China Mobile shops are ubiquitous; cards can also be bought from newspaper kiosks with the China Mobile sign.

China Mobile (中国移动通信; Zhōngguó Yídòng Tōngxìn; Map p170; 200 Middle Xizang Rd; 西藏中路200号; ⌚10am-8.30pm; Ⓜ People's Sq) Central branch off People's Sq.

Tourist Information

Your hotel should be able to provide you with maps and most of the tourist information you require. Also consult the websites listed under Websites opposite.

Shànghǎi Call Centre (☎962 288; ⌚24hr) This toll-free English-language hotline is possibly the most useful telephone number in Shànghǎi – it can even give your cab driver directions if you've got a mobile phone.

Shànghǎi Information Centre for International Visitors (Map p176; ☎6384 9366; No 2, Alley 123, Xingye Rd) Xīntiāndì information centre.

Tourist Information & Service Centres (旅游咨询服务中心; Lǚyóu Zīxún Fúwù Zhōngxīn; Map

BORDER CROSSING: GETTING TO JAPAN

Weekly ferries to Osaka in Japan depart from the **Shànghǎi Port International Cruise Terminal** (上海港国际客运中心; Shànghǎi Gǎng Guójì Kèyùn Zhōngxīn; Gaoyang Rd; 高阳路). Tickets are sold by the two boat operators: **China-Japan International Ferry Company** (☎6595 6888/6325 7642; www.chinajapanferry.com; 18th fl), with departures on Saturdays, and **Shànghǎi International Ferry Company** (☎6595 8666; www.shanghai-ferry.co.jp; 15th fl), with departures on Tuesdays. Both are in the Jin'an Building (908 Dongdaming Rd; 东大明路908号金岸大厦) north of the Bund. Tickets to either destination (44 hours) range from Y1300 in an eight-bed dorm to Y6500 in a deluxe twin cabin. Reservations are recommended in July and August. Passengers must be at the harbour three hours before departure to get through immigration.

p170) The Bund (beneath the Bund promenade, opposite the intersection with East Nanjing Rd); East Nanjing Rd (Century Sq, 518 Jiujiang Rd); Old Town (149 Jiujiaochang Rd) These centres are conveniently located near major tourist sights. The standard of English varies from good to non-existent, but free maps and some information are available.

Travel Agencies

See p202 for details on train and ferry ticket agencies.

CTrip (☎400 619 9999; http://english.ctrip.com) Online agency good for hotel and flight bookings.

Elong (☎400 617 1717; www.elong.net) Online agency good for hotel and flight bookings.

STA Travel (☎2281 7723; www.statravel.com.cn; Room 919, Zi An Bldg, 309 Yuyuan Rd; 愚园路309号紫安大厦919室; ⊙Mon-Sat; Ⓜ Jing'an Temple) Sells train and air tickets, and can issue International Student Identity Cards.

Websites

City Weekend (www.cityweekend.com.cn) Listings website.

Shanghai Daily (www.shanghaidaily.com) (Censored) coverage of local news.

Shanghai Expat (www.shanghaiexpat.com) A must-see if you are thinking of relocating to Shànghǎi; useful forum.

Shanghaiist (www.shanghaiist.com) Local entertainment and news blog.

SmartShanghai (www.smartshanghai.com) For food, fun and frolicking. Good entertainment coverage.

Tales of Old China (www.talesofoldchina.com) Lots of reading on Old Shànghǎi, with the text of hard-to-find books online.

Urbanatomy (www.urbanatomy.com) Listings website from *That's Shanghai*.

Virtual Shanghai (http://virtualshanghai.ish-lyon.cnrs.fr) Amazing database of old photos, maps and texts.

ℹ Getting There & Away

Shànghǎi is straightforward to reach. With two airports, rail and air connections to places all over China, and buses to destinations in adjoining provinces and beyond, it's a handy springboard to the rest of the land.

Air

Shànghǎi has international flight connections to most major cities, many operated by China Eastern, which has its base here.

All international flights (and a few domestic flights) operate out of **Pǔdōng International Airport** (PVG; 浦东国际机场;Pǔdōng Guójì Jīchǎng; ☎96990 flight information; www.shairport.com; Ⓜ Pudong International Airport), with most (but not all) domestic flights operating out of **Hóngqiáo Airport** (SHA; 虹桥机场; Hóngqiáo Jīchǎng; ☎96990 flight information; www.shairport.com; Ⓜ Hongqiao Airport) on Shànghǎi's western outskirts. If you are making an onward domestic connection from Pudong it is essential that you find out whether the domestic flight leaves from Pǔdōng or Hóngqiáo, as the latter will require *at least* an hour to cross the city.

Daily (usually several times) domestic flights connect Shànghǎi to major cities in China:

Běijīng Y1220, 1½ hours

Chéngdū Y1700, two hours 20 minutes

Guǎngzhōu Y1370, two hours

Guìlín Y1390, two hours

Qīngdǎo Y810, one hour

Xī'ān Y1350, two hours

You can buy air tickets almost anywhere, including at major hotels, travel agencies and online sites such as ctrip.com and elong.net. Discounts of up to 40% are standard. Minor cities are less likely to have daily flights, but chances are there will be at least one flight a week, probably more, to Shànghǎi.

Boat

Domestic boat tickets can be bought from the **Huángpŭ Tourist Centre** (黄浦旅游集散中心; Huángpŭ Lǚyóu Jísàn Zhōngxīn; Map p170; ☎6336 9051; 21 East Jinling Rd; 金陵东路21号; ⏰9am-6pm; Ⓜ East Nanjing Rd).

Overnight boats (Y109 to Y499, 10½ hours) to Pŭtuóshān depart every day at 8pm from the **Wúsōng Wharf** (吴淞码头; Wúsōng Mătou; Ⓜ Songbing Rd), almost at the mouth of the Yangzi River; to reach Wúsōng Wharf take metro line 3 to Songbing Rd and then walk or hail a taxi.

A high-speed ferry service (Y258, three hours, 9.30am) to Pŭtuóshān departs twice daily from Xiăo Yáng Shān (小洋山). A bus (price included in ferry ticket, two hours, departs 7.20am) runs to Xiăo Yáng Shān from Nánpŭ Bridge (南浦大桥; by the bridge).

Bus

Shànghăi has a number of long-distance bus stations, though given the traffic gridlock it's best to take the train when possible. The massive **Shànghăi Long-Distance Bus Station** (上海长途汽车总站; Shànghăi Chángtú Qìchē Kèyùn Zŏngzhàn; Map p180; 1666 Zhongxing Rd; Ⓜ Shanghai Railway Station), north of Shànghăi train station, has buses to destinations as far away as Gānsù province and Inner Mongolia. Regular buses run to Sūzhōu (frequent) and Hángzhōu (frequent), as well as Nánjīng (12 daily) and Bĕijīng (Y311, 4pm). Although it appears close to the train station, it is a major pain to reach on foot. It's easiest to catch a cab here.

Handier is the **Hengfeng Road Bus Station** (恒丰路客运站; Héngfēnglù Kèyùnzhàn; Map p180; Ⓜ Hanzhong Rd), which serves cities including Bĕijīng (Y311, 5pm), Hángzhōu (eight daily), Nánjīng (frequent) and Sūzhōu (frequent).

The vast **Shànghăi South Long-Distance Bus Station** (上海长途客运南站;Shànghăi Chángtú Kèyùn Nánzhàn; 666 Shilong Rd; Ⓜ Shanghai South Railway Station) serves cities in south China, including Hángzhōu (frequent), Nánjīng (four daily), Níngbō (frequent), Sūzhōu (frequent), Túnxī/Huáng Shān (Y135, six hours, eight daily) and Wùyuán (Y175, five hours, two daily).

Buses also depart for Hángzhōu and Sūzhōu from the long-distance bus stations at Hóngqiáo Airport and Pŭdōng International Airport.

Some sample fares and trip durations (may vary from station to station):

Hángzhōu Y68, two hours

Nánjīng Y105, four hours

Níngbō Y99, three hours

Sūzhōu Y38, 90 minutes

Shànghăi Sightseeing Buses run to the canal towns outside Shànghăi; see p183 for details.

Train

Many parts of the country can be reached by direct train from Shànghăi. The city has three useful stations: the main **Shànghăi railway station** (Shànghăi zhàn; Ⓜ Shanghai Railway Station), the **Shànghăi South railway station** (Shànghăi Nánzhàn; Ⓜ Shanghai South Railway Station) and the **Hóngqiáo railway station** (上海虹桥站; Shànghăi Hóngqiáo zhàn; Ⓜ Hongqiao Railway Station) near Hóngqiáo Airport. Most trains depart from the main station, though for some southern destinations, like Hángzhōu, they leave from Shànghăi South. The Hóngqiáo station is for new express trains (many Nánjīng and Sūzhōu trains leave from here) and will ultimately serve as the terminus for the Shànghăi–Bĕijīng express, which is estimated to begin in 2012. Wherever you're going, make sure to get your tickets as early as possible. If you're arriving in Shànghăi, don't get off at Shànghăi West (上海西站; Shànghăi Xīzhàn), which is not convenient for travellers.

There are several ways to purchase tickets: at the station (generally stressful), via your hotel or a travel agency (much easier but expect a commission charge), or at train ticket offices around town.

At the main station there are two ticket halls (售票厅; *shòupiàotīng*), one in the main building (same-day tickets) and another on the east side of the square (advance tickets). One counter will claim to have English-speakers. **Bilingual automated machines** (自助售票处; *zìzhù shòupiàochù;* ⏰24hr) just east of the same-day ticket hall sell tickets to many major destinations. They seem to work well, though remember to bring cash.

Alternatively, tickets can also be purchased from one of the numerous **train ticket offices** (火车票预售处; *huŏchēpiào yùshòuchù*) Bund (384 Middle Jiangxi Rd; 江西中路384号; ⏰8am-8pm); Jìng'ān (77 Wanhangdu Rd; 万航渡路77号; ⏰8am-5pm); Pŭdōng (1396 Lujiazui Ring Rd; 陆家嘴环路1396号; ⏰8am-7pm) around town.

Prices and times listed here are always for the fastest train. Slower, less expensive trains have not been listed. Some trains leaving from Shànghăi Railway Station:

Bĕijīng (D train) seat/sleeper Y327/Y655, 10 hours, seven daily

Chéngdū Y352, 35 hours, three daily

Hong Kong Y395, 18½ hours, one daily

Huángshān Y169, 12 hours, two daily

Guăngzhōu East Y367, 16 hours, two daily

Lhasa Y821, 49 hours, one every other day

Nánjīng Y146, one hour 15 minutes, frequent services

Sūzhōu Y41, 30 minutes, frequent services

Xī'ān Y323, 14 hours, 10 daily

A note on the Běijīng-bound trains: schedules will probably change once the new express starts service from Hóngqiáo (estimated 2012), which will cut the trip down to four hours and stop off at several cities, including Nánjīng. If the D trains (the ones listed here) are still in service be aware that you'll want to get a bed (soft sleeper only) instead of a seat if you're on an overnight train. There are/were three slower sleeper trains that require 10 days advance booking.

Some trains leaving from Shànghǎi South Railway Station:

Hángzhōu Y58, 1½ hours, frequent
Kūnmíng Y491, 38 hours, three daily
Shàoxīng Y68, two hours, 10 daily
Yùshān (Sānqīng Shān) Y130, six hours, six daily

Getting Around

The best way to get around Shànghǎi is the metro, which now gets to most places in the city, followed by cabs, which are reasonably cheap and easy to flag down unless it's raining. In general, buses (Y2) should be avoided as they're hard to figure out, even for Mandarin speakers. Whatever mode of transport you use, try to avoid rush hours between 8am and 9am, and 4.30pm and 6pm.

Although there are some fascinating areas to stroll around, new road developments, building sites and traffic conditions conspire to make walking from A to B an exhausting and sometimes stressful experience.

To/From the Airport

Pǔdōng International Airport handles most international flights and some domestic flights. There are four ways to get from the airport to the city: taxi, Maglev train, metro and bus.

A taxi ride into central Shànghǎi will cost around Y160 and take about an hour; to Hóngqiáo Airport costs around Y200. Most taxi drivers in Shànghǎi are honest, though make sure they use the meter; avoid monstrous overcharging by using the regular taxi rank outside the arrivals hall. Regular buses also run to Sūzhōu (Y84) and Hángzhōu (Y100).

The bullet-fast **Maglev train** (www.smtdc.com) runs from Pǔdōng Airport to its terminal in Pǔdōng in just eight minutes, from where you can transfer to the metro (Longyang Rd station) or take a taxi (Y40 to People's Sq). It is a significant time saver. Economy single/return tickets cost Y50/80; but show your same-day air ticket and it's Y40 one way. Children under 1.2m travel free (kids taller than this are half-price). The train departs every 20 minutes from roughly 6.45am to 9.40pm.

Metro line 2 runs from Pǔdōng Airport to Hóngqiáo Airport, passing through central Shànghǎi. It is certainly convenient, though not for those in a hurry. From Pǔdōng Airport, it takes about 75 minutes to People's Sq (Y6) and one hour 45 minutes to Hóngqiáo Airport (Y8).

There are also numerous **airport buses**, which take between 60 and 90 minutes to run to their destinations in Pǔxī. Buses leave to the airport roughly every 15 to 25 minutes from 6.30am to 11pm; they go to the airport from roughly 5.30am to 9.30pm (bus 1 runs till 11pm). The most useful buses are airport bus 1 (Y30), which links Pǔdōng International Airport with Hóngqiáo Airport, and airport bus 2 (Y22), which links Pǔdōng International Airport with the Airport City Terminal (上海机场城市航站楼; Shànghǎi Jīchǎng Chéngshì Hángzhàn Lóu) on West Nanjing Rd, east of Jìng'ān Temple. Airport bus 5 (Y16 to Y22) links Pǔdōng International Airport with Shànghǎi train station via People's Sq.

Hóngqiáo Airport is 18km from the Bund, a 30- to 60-minute trip. Most flights now arrive at Terminal 2, which is connected to downtown via metro lines 2 and 10 (30 minutes to People's Sq). If you arrive at Terminal 1, you can also catch the airport shuttle bus (Y4, 7.50am to 11pm) to the Airport City Terminal on West Nanjing Rd. Airport bus 1 (Y30, 6am to 9.30pm) runs to Pǔdōng International Airport. Taxis cost Y70 to Y100 to central Shànghǎi.

Major hotels run airport shuttles to both airports (generally free to Hóngqiáo; Y30 to Pǔdōng).

TRANSPORT CARD

If you are going to be doing a lot of travelling in Shànghǎi, it's worth investing in a transport card (交通卡; *jiāotōng kǎ)* as it can save you queuing. Sold at metro stations and some convenience stores, cards can be topped up with credits and used on the metro, most buses and in taxis. Credits are electronically deducted from the card as you swipe it over the sensor at metro turnstiles and near the door on buses; when paying your taxi fare, hand the card to the driver, who will swipe it for you. You'll need to pay a deposit of Y20, which can be refunded before you leave at the East Nanjing Rd metro station.

Public Transport

FERRY The **Jīnlíng Rd Ferry** (金陵路轮渡站; Jīnlíng Lù Lúndù Zhàn), running between the southern end of the Bund and the Dongchang Rd dock in Pǔdōng, is of minimal use to travellers. Ferries (Y2) run every 10 minutes from 7am to 10pm.

METRO The Shànghǎi metro system (indicated by a red M) currently runs to 11 lines after huge expansion; three additional lines (12, 13, 21) are expected to open in 2012. Lines 1, 2 and 10 are the principal lines that travellers will use. Tickets cost between Y3 and Y10 depending on the distance and are only sold from bilingual automated machines (except in rare cases); keep your ticket until you exit. Transport cards are available from information desks for Y50 and Y100; they don't offer any savings, but are useful for avoiding queues and can also be used in taxis and on most buses. A one-day metro pass is also sold from information desks for Y18.

You should be able to pick up a metro map at most stations; the free tourist maps also have a small metro map printed on them. Check out exploreshanghai.com for online maps and apps.

Taxi

Shànghǎi's taxis are reasonably cheap, hassle-free and easy to flag down outside rush hour, although finding a cab during rainstorms is impossible. Flag fall is Y12 (for the first 3km) and Y16 at night (11pm to 5am).

Major taxi companies:

Bàshì (☎96840)

Dàzhòng (☎96822)

Qiángshēng (☎6258 0000)

AROUND SHÀNGHĂI

The most popular day trips from Shànghǎi are probably to the canal towns of Mùdú and Tónglǐ (in Jiāngsū), and Nánxún and Wūzhèn (in Zhèjiāng).

Zhūjiājiǎo

朱家角

Thirty kilometres west of Shànghǎi, **Zhūjiājiǎo** (optional ticket incl entry to 4/8 sights Y30/60) is both easy to reach and truly delightful – as long as your visit does not coincide with the arrival of phalanxes of tour buses. Select an off-season rainy weekday, pack an umbrella and pray the sky clears before others get wind of sunshine over town.

Chinese guidebooks vaguely identify human activity in these parts 5000 years ago and a settlement was here during the Three Kingdoms period 1700 years ago. It was during the Ming dynasty, however, that a commercial centre built on Zhūjiājiǎo's network of waterways was truly developed. What survives today is a charming tableau of Ming- and Qing-dynasty alleys, bridges and old-town (古镇; *gǔzhèn*) architecture.

Paper maps of Zhūjiājiǎo may be hard to find, but ample stone maps of town are affixed to street walls in the old town. In any case, the riverside settlement is small enough to wander around completely in three hours, by which time you will have developed a very precise mental map.

On the west side of the recently built City God Temple bridge stands the **City God Temple** (城隍庙; Chénghuáng Miào; admission Y5; ⌚7.30am-4pm), moved here in 1769 from its original location in Xuějiābāng. Further north along Caohe St (漕河街), running alongside the canal, is the **Yuánjīn Buddhist Temple** (圆津禅院; Yuánjīn Chányuàn; admission Y5; ⌚8am-4pm) near the distinctive **Tài'ān Bridge** (泰安桥; Tài'ān Qiáo). Pop into the temple to climb the **Qīnghuá Pavilion** (清华阁; Qīnghuá Gé) at the rear, a towering hall visible from many parts of town, containing a multiarmed statue of Guanyin on the ground floor, a pagoda studded with multiple effigies of the goddess above and a recently cast bell on the top floor that you can strike for good luck (Y5).

Earmark a detour to the magnificent **Zhūjiājiǎo Catholic Church of Ascension** (朱家角耶稣升天堂; Zhūjiājiǎo Yēsū Shēngtiāntáng; No 317 Alley, 27 Caohe Jie; 漕河街27号317弄), a gorgeous church with its belfry rising in a detached tower by the rear gate. Built in 1863, the brick church stands alongside a lovingly cultivated courtyard decorated with a statue of Joseph holding a baby Jesus.

Of Zhūjiājiǎo's quaint band of ancient bridges, the standout **Fàngshēng Bridge** (放生桥; Fàngshēng Qiáo), first built in 1571 and linking Bei Dajie (北大街) and Dongjing Jie (东井街) with its long and graceful 72m span, is the most photogenic. The five-arched bridge was originally assembled with proceeds from a monk's 15 years of alms gathering. You can jump on boats for comprehensive tours of town at various points, including Fàngshēng Bridge. Tickets are Y60/120 per boat for the short/long tour.

In the past few years, Zhūjiājiǎo has developed into something of a bohemian getaway from busy Shànghǎi, and there's now an admirable selection of tiny hotels, cafes and arty shops scattered around town. Top picks for overnighting are the quaint **1, 2, 3**

(☎5923 2101; www.byways.asia; No 3, Lane 123, Xijing St; 西井街123弄3号; dm/d Y60/150) and the **Uma Hostel** (☎189 1808 2961; umahostel@gmail.com; 103 Xijing St; 西井街103号; dm/d Y50/200), both near the Kèzhí Gardens (课植园; Kèzhí Yuán). A bit fancier is **West Well** (☎5924 2675; xijinghui@gmail.com; 54 Xijing St; 西井街56号; d Y350), set in a huge old courtyard house.

To get to Zhūjiājiǎo, it's easiest to go to the **Pu'an Rd Bus Station** (普安路汽车站; Pǔ'ān Lù Qìchē Zhàn; ⓂDashijie) just south of People's Sq, where you can take the Hùzhū Gāosù Kuàixiàn bus (沪朱高速快线; Y12, one hour, every 30 minutes from 6am to 10pm) direct to the village. Alternatively, you can take the Shànghǎi Sightseeing Bus day tour (Y85, departs 9am and 10am); it returns for Shànghǎi at 3.45pm and 4.45pm. The ticket includes admission to the town. Zhūjiājiǎo can also be reached from the bus station in Tónglǐ (Y15, 90 minutes, nine buses daily).

Jiāngsū

POPULATION: 75.5 MILLION

Includes »

Best Places to Eat

» Pingvon (p225)

» Xīshèngyuán (p225)

» Sìchuān Jiǔjiā (p216)

Best Places to Stay

» Píngjiāng Lodge (p225)

» Sūzhōu Mingtown Youth Hostel (p224)

» Zhèngfú Cǎotáng (p229)

Why Go?

Bordering the East China Sea and dubbed the 'land of fish and rice' since antiquity, Jiāngsū (江苏) originally owed its wealth to the waterways of the Yangzi River (Cháng Jiāng) and the Grand Canal, and also through silk, as well as salt panned off its low-lying marshy coast.

Defended by a magnificent Ming city wall and situated on the south bank of the Yangzi River, Nánjīng is one of China's most pleasant provincial capitals, though the shadow of its military suffering hangs like a pall over its collective consciousness.

A fleeting train trip from Shànghǎi, Sūzhōu – famed for its lilting canal views and elaborate gardens – is an unbeatable base for exploring the water towns in the region. Dressed in old-world charm, Tónglǐ, Lùzhí and Mùdú are perfect for slow meanderings. These canal towns will force you to take an unhurried appreciation of a disappearing side of China.

When to Go

Nánjīng

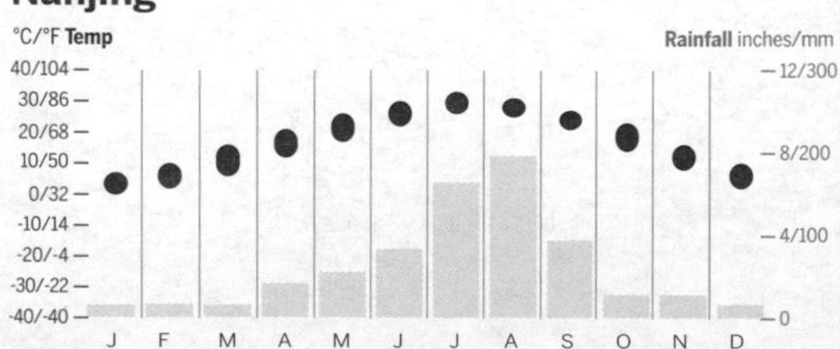

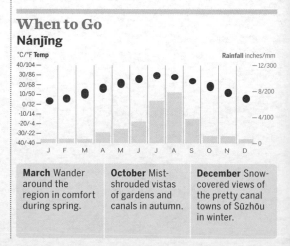

March Wander around the region in comfort during spring.

October Mist-shrouded vistas of gardens and canals in autumn.

December Snow-covered views of the pretty canal towns of Sūzhōu in winter.

Jiāngsū Highlights

1 Nánjīng is packed with key historical sights, including the sombre **Memorial Hall of the Nánjīng Massacre** (p209)

2 Pour over historical artefacts at the IM Pei–designed **Sūzhōu Museum** (p221)

3 The gorgeous **gardens of Sūzhōu** (p221) are too many to list, each one different

4 Sūzhōu's 'Venice of the East' moniker becomes clear along **Píngjiāng Lù** and **Shàngtáng Jīe** (p222)

5 Appreciate a traditional píngtán performance at the **Pingtan Teahouse** (p227)

6 If you only have time for one canal town, it has to be **Tónglǐ** (p228)

7 Four words: **Chinese Sex Culture Museum** (p229) – yes, you can giggle now

8 Complete the canal-town experience by visiting **Lùzhí** (p229) and **Mùdú** (p230)

9 Unheralded Yángzhōu is home to the gorgeous **Slender West Lake Park** (p231)

History

Jiāngsū was a relative backwater until the Song dynasty (960–1279), when it emerged as an important commercial centre because of trading routes opened up by the Grand Canal. The province particularly flourished in the south, where the towns of Sūzhōu and Yángzhōu played an important role in silk production and began to develop a large mercantile class.

Prosperity continued through the Ming and Qing dynasties, and with the incursion of Westerners into China in the 1840s, southern Jiāngsū opened up to Western influence. During the Taiping Rebellion (1851–64), the Taiping established Nánjīng as their capital, calling it Tiānjīng (Heavenly Capital).

Jiāngsū was also to play a strong political role in the 20th century, when Nánjīng was established as the capital by the Nationalist Party until taken over by the communists in 1949, who moved the capital to Běijīng.

Today, because of its proximity to Shànghǎi, southern Jiāngsū benefits from a fast-growing economy and rapid development, although northern Jiāngsū still lags behind.

Climate

Jiāngsū is hot and humid in summer (May to August), yet has temperatures requiring coats in winter (December to February, when visibility can drop to zero because of fog). Rain or drizzle can be prevalent in winter, adding a misty touch to the land. The natural colours can be brilliant in spring (March and April). Heavy rains fall in spring and summer; autumn (September to November) is the driest time of year, and the best time to visit.

PRICE INDICATORS

The following price indicators are used in this chapter:

Sleeping

$	less than Y200
$$	Y200 to Y800
$$$	more than Y800

Eating

$	less than Y20
$$	Y20 to Y50
$$$	more than Y50

Getting There & Around

Jiāngsū is well connected to all major cities in China. There are numerous flights daily from Nánjīng and Sūzhōu to points around the country, as well as frequent bus and train connections.

Jiāngsū has a comprehensive bus system that allows travellers to get to most destinations within the province without difficulty. Travelling by train is also largely straightforward.

Nánjīng 南京

025 / POP 3.39 MILLION

Largely enclosed within a magnificent Ming-dynasty city wall, Nánjīng, Jiāngsū's capital, lies on the lower stretches of the Yangzi River. One of China's more pleasant and prosperous cities, the famous university town has wide, tree-lined boulevards, chic apartment blocks and mile-high office towers, set among a beautiful landscape of lakes, forested parks and rivers.

The city sports a long historical heritage and has twice served briefly as the nation's capital, first in the early years of the Ming dynasty (1368–1644) and then as the capital of the Republic of China in the early years of the 20th century. Most of Nánjīng's major attractions are reminders of the city's former glory under the Ming dynasty.

Although many have been uprooted in recent years for road widening, the city's pleasant *wutong* trees afford glorious shade in the summer and lend the city a leafy complexion.

History

During the Qin dynasty (221–207 BC), Nánjīng prospered as a major administrative centre. Nánjīng fell during the Sui dynasty (AD 589–618) and later enjoyed a period of prosperity under the long-lived Tang dynasty, before slipping into obscurity.

In 1356 a peasant rebellion led by Zhu Yuanzhang against the Mongol Yuan dynasty was successful but Nánjīng's glory as imperial capital was shortlived. In 1420 the third Ming emperor, Yongle, moved the capital back to Běijīng. From then on Nánjīng's fortunes variously rose and declined as a regional centre, but it wasn't until the 19th and 20th centuries that the city again entered the centre stage of Chinese history.

In the 19th century the Opium Wars brought the British to Nánjīng and it was here that the first of the 'unequal treaties' were signed, opening several Chinese ports to foreign trade, forcing China to pay a huge war indemnity, and officially ceding the island of Hong Kong to Britain. Just a few years later Nánjīng became the Taiping capital during the Taiping Rebellion, which succeeded in taking over most of southern China.

In 1864 the combined forces of the Qing army, British army, and various European and US mercenaries surrounded the city. They laid siege for seven months, before finally capturing it and slaughtering the Taiping defenders.

During the 20th century Nánjīng was the capital of the Republic of China – the site of the worst war atrocity in Japan's assault on China – and the Kuomintang capital from the period of 1928–37, and again between 1945 and 1949, before the communists 'liberated' the city and made China their own.

Sights

TOP CHOICE Memorial Hall of the Nánjīng Massacre — MEMORIAL

(南京大屠杀纪念馆; Nánjīng Dàtúshā Jìniànguǎn; 418 Shuiximen Dajie; admission free; ⌚8.30am-4.30pm Tue-Sun; Ⓜ Yunjin Lu) Hands down the best 'sight', if it can be called such, in Nánjīng. The unsettling exhibits at the Memorial Hall of the Nánjīng Massacre document the atrocities committed by Japanese soldiers against the civilian population during the occupation of Nánjīng in 1937 (see boxed text, p210). They include pictures of actual executions – many taken by Japanese army photographers – and a gruesome viewing hall built over a mass grave of massacre victims. Detailed captions are in English, Japanese and Chinese, but the photographs, skeletons and displays tell their own haunting stories without words. At times it feels a little overwhelming but visitors might begin to understand that the massacre is deeply linked to the identity of the city. Get there early to beat the surge of people.

It's in the city's southwestern suburbs; take bus Y4 from Zhōnghuá Gate or Nánjīng west train station (南京西站;Nánjīng Xīzhàn). Get off at subway line 2 Jíqìngdàjīe station (集庆门大街站).

Zǐjīn Mountain Scenic Area — PARK

Dominating the eastern fringes of Nánjīng is Zǐjīn Mountain (紫金山; Zǐjīn Shān), or 'Purple-Gold Mountain', a heavily forested area of parks and the site of most of Nánjīng's historical attractions – Sun Yatsen Mausoleum, Míng Xiàolíng Tomb, Línggǔ Temple Scenic Area and the Botanic Gardens (植物园; Zhíwù yuán). It's also one of the coolest places to escape from the steamy summers. There are discounts if tickets to various sights are purchased together.

Buses 9, Y2 or Y3 go from the city centre to the Sun Yatsen Mausoleum at the centre of the mountain. From here, tourist buses labelled Y2 and Y3 also run between all the sites on the mountain, Y1 per ride.

Sun Yatsen Mausoleum — MEMORIAL

(中山陵; Zhōngshān Líng; admission Y80; ⌚6.30am-6.30pm) Dr Sun is recognised by the communists and Kuomintang alike as the father of modern China. He died in Běijīng in 1925, leaving behind an unstable Chinese republic. He had wished to be buried in Nánjīng, no doubt with greater simplicity than the Ming-style tomb his successors built for him. Despite this, less than a year after his death, construction of this mausoleum began.

The tomb itself lies at the top of an enormous stone stairway – a breathless 392 steps. At the start of the path stands a dignified stone gateway built of Fújiàn marble, with a roof of blue-glazed tiles. The blue and white of the mausoleum symbolise the white sun on the blue background of the Kuomintang flag.

The crypt is at the top of the steps at the rear of the memorial chamber. A tablet hanging across the threshold is inscribed with the 'Three Principles of the People', as formulated by Dr Sun: nationalism, democracy and people's livelihood. Inside is a statue of Dr Sun seated. The walls are carved with the complete text of the Outline of Principles for the Establishment of the Nation put forward by the Nationalist government, and Dr Sun devotees are often seen copying these principles by hand. A prostrate marble statue of Dr Sun seals his copper coffin.

There's a free shuttle bus (it looks like a red steam train) that goes to the Línggǔ Temple Scenic Area.

Míng Xiàolíng Tomb — TOMB

(明孝陵; admission Y70; ⌚8am-5.30pm, to 6.30pm summer) On the southern slope of Zǐjīn Mountain is the 14th-century Míng Xiàolíng of Emperor Zhu Yuanzhang, the only Ming emperor to be buried outside of Běijīng.

The first section of the 618m avenue leading up to the mausoleum takes you along

THE RAPE OF NÁNJĪNG

In 1937, with the Chinese army comparatively weak and underfunded and the Japanese army on the horizon, the invasion into, and occupation of, Nánjīng by Japan appeared imminent. As it packed up and fled, the Chinese government encouraged the people of Nánjīng to stay, saying, 'All those who have blood and breath in them must feel that they wish to be broken as jade rather than remain whole as tile.' To reinforce this statement, the gates to the city were locked, trapping over half a million citizens inside.

What followed in Nánjīng was six weeks of continuous, unfathomable victimisation of civilians to an extent unwitnessed in modern warfare. According to journalists and historians such as Iris Chang and Joshua Fogel, during Japan's occupation of Nánjīng between 200,000 and 300,000 Chinese civilians were killed, either in group massacres or individual murders. Within the first month, at least 20,000 women between the ages of 11 and 76 were brutally raped. Women who attempted to refuse or children who interfered were often bayoneted or shot.

The Japanese, however, underestimated the Chinese. Instead of breaking the people's will, the invasion fuelled a sense of identity and determination. Those who did not die – broken as jade – survived to fight back.

Iris Chang's highly acclaimed *The Rape of Nanjing* details the atrocities suffered by Chinese civilians under the occupation of the Japanese. The dark nature of the massacre seemed to have played heavily on Chang and she later committed suicide. But Chang wasn't the first suicide linked to massacre: Minnie Vautrin, an American missionary, killed herself after the massacre.

the 'spirit path', lined with stone statues of lions, camels, elephants and horses. There's also a mythical animal called a *xiè zhì* – which has a mane and a single horn on its head – and a *qílín*, which has a scaly body, a cow's tail, deer's hooves and one horn. These stone animals drive away evil spirits and guard the tomb.

As you enter the first courtyard, a paved pathway leads to a pavilion housing several stelae. The next gate leads to a large courtyard with the **Línghún Pagoda** (Línghún Tǎ), a mammoth rectangular stone structure. Look for the stalactites and stalagmites formed by years of water dripping down the walls. Walk through a long tunnel and up a wall, 350m in diameter, to get to a huge earth mound. Beneath this mound is the unexcavated tomb vault of Hongwu.

The area surrounding the tomb is the **Míng Xiàolíng Scenic Area** (明孝陵风景区; Míng Xiàolíng Fēngjǐngqūf). A tree-lined pathway winds around pavilions and picnic grounds and ends at scenic **Zǐxiá Lake** (Zǐxiá Hú; admission Y10), ideal for strolling.

Línggǔ Temple Scenic Area TEMPLE
(灵谷寺风景区; Línggǔ Sì Fēngjǐng Qū; admission included with Sun Yatsen Mausoleum; ⏲7am-6.30pm) The large Ming Línggǔ Temple complex has one of the most interesting buildings in Nánjīng – the **Beamless Hall** (Wúliáng Diàn), built in 1381 entirely out of brick and stone and containing no beam supports. Buildings during the Ming dynasty were normally constructed of wood, but timber shortages meant that builders had to rely on brick. The structure has a vaulted ceiling and a large stone platform where Buddhist statues once sat. In the 1930s the hall was turned into a memorial to those who died resisting the Japanese. One of the inscriptions on the inside wall is the old Kuomintang national anthem.

A road runs on both sides of the hall and up two flights of steps to the graceful **Pine Wind Pavilion** (Sōngfēng Gé), originally dedicated to Guanyin as part of **Línggǔ Temple**. The temple itself (Y5 admission) and a memorial hall to Xuan Zang (the Buddhist monk who travelled to India and brought back the Buddhist scriptures) are close by; after you pass through the Beamless Hall, turn right and then follow the pathway. Inside the memorial hall is a golden scale model of a 13-storey wooden pagoda that contains part of Xuan Zang's skull, a sacrificial table and a portrait of the monk.

Nearby is the colourful **Línggǔ Pagoda** (Línggǔ Tǎ). This nine-storey, 60m-high, octagonal pagoda was finished in 1933 under the direction of a US architect to remember those who died during the Kuomingtang revolution. Tour bus Y2 and Y3 runs to the Línggǔ Temple from Nánjīng train station. A free shuttle bus connects the area to the Sun Yatsen Mausoleum.

Ming Palace Ruins PARK

(明故宫; Míng Gùgōng) **Wǔcháomén Park** (Wǔcháomén Gōngyuán; Zhongshan Donglu; admission free; ⏲6.30am-9.30pm), in which the Ming Palace Ruins are scattered, is a peaceful but maudlin place. Built by Hongwu, the imperial palace is said to have been a magnificent structure after which the Imperial Palace in Běijīng was modelled. Anyone familiar with the layout of the Forbidden City will see similarities in the arrangement.

You can clamber into the ruined **Meridian Gate** (Wǔ Mén). It's not as magnificent as its namesake portal in the Forbidden City, but it, too, once had huge walls jutting out at right angles from the main structure, along with watchtowers. Today, the park is filled with locals practicing ballroom dancing (not quite what the emperor had in mind) to dance-music soundtracks.

You can reach the Ming Palace Ruins by catching bus Y1 from Nánjīng train station or bus 9 from Zhongyang Lu. Subway line 2 stops at Míng Gùgōng (明故宫站).

Jīmíng Temple TEMPLE

(鸡鸣寺; Jīmíng Sì; admission Y5; ⏲7.30am-5pm winter, to 5.30pm summer) Close to the Ming walls and Xuánwǔ Lake (Xuánwǔ Hú) is the Buddhist Jīmíng Temple, which was first built in AD 527 during the Three Kingdoms period. It's been rebuilt many times since, but has retained the same name (which literally translates as 'rooster crowing') since 1387. This temple is the most active temple in Nánjīng and is packed with worshippers during the Lunar New Year. The seven-story tall Yàoshīfótǎ Pagoda (药师佛塔) offers views over Xuánwǔ Lake. Walk up to the rear of the temple and out onto the **city wall** (admission Y15). Tufts of grass poke out from between the stones and you can embark on a lengthy and fabulous jaunt east along the overgrown ramparts; see the boxed text on p215. Bus Y1 and 304 can get you here.

Fūzǐ Temple TEMPLE

(夫子庙; Fūzǐ Miào; Gongyuan Jie; admission Y30; ⏲9am-10pm Mon-Thu & Sun, to 10.30pm Fri & Sat; Ⓜ Sanshan Jie) The Confucian Fūzǐ Temple, in the south of the city in a pedestrian zone, was a centre of Confucian study for more than 1500 years. This temple has been damaged and rebuilt repeatedly; what you see here today are newly restored, late-Qing-dynasty structures or wholly new buildings reconstructed in traditional style.

Across from the temple complex to the east is the **Imperial Examinations History Museum** (江南贡院历史陈列馆; Jiāngnán Gòngyuàn Lìshǐ Chénlièguǎn; 1 Jinling Lu; admission Y20; ⏲8.30am-10pm). This is a recent reconstruction of the building where scholars once spent months – or years – in tiny cells studying Confucian classics in preparation for civil service examinations.

Today the area surrounding Fūzǐ Temple has become Nánjīng's main amusement quarter and is a particularly lively, crowded and fairly unattractive place. On weekends and public holidays, it seems like the whole of Nánjīng throngs here. It's littered with restaurants and rows upon rows of souvenir and fashion shops and even pet stores. The whole area is lit up at night, adding to the kitsch ambience. **Tour boats** *(yóuchuán)* leave from the dock across from the temple itself for 30-minute day (Y50 to Y60) and evening (Y60 to Y80) trips along the Qínhuái River (秦淮河; Qínhuái Hé).

Catch bus 1 or Y2 from Xīnjīekǒu here.

FREE **Nánjīng Museum** MUSEUM

(南京博物馆; Nánjīng Bówùguǎn; 321 Zhongshan Donglu; ⏲9am-4.30pm; Ⓜ Minggugong) Just east of Zhōngshān Gate, the Nánjīng Museum displays artefacts from Neolithic times right through to the communist period…when it's not under renovation. The main building was constructed in 1933 in the style of a Ming temple with yellow-glazed tiles, red-lacquered gates and columns. While this building is being tinkered with, a small collection has moved to the **Art Gallery** (艺术陈列馆; Yīshùchénlièguǎn) building next door.

The limited offerings include a haphazardly arranged collection of porcelain, textiles, bronze ware, earthen ware and folk art. Some of the 500-plus-year-old porcelain, with striking colours, looks startlingly contemporary, while a large wooden weaving machine boggles the imagination (how did they get up there to thread the looms?). Some displays are labelled in (bad) English. An example would be the 'keep quiet' notice translated as 'the subliminal of thought has started while the noisy has stopped'.

Nánjīng

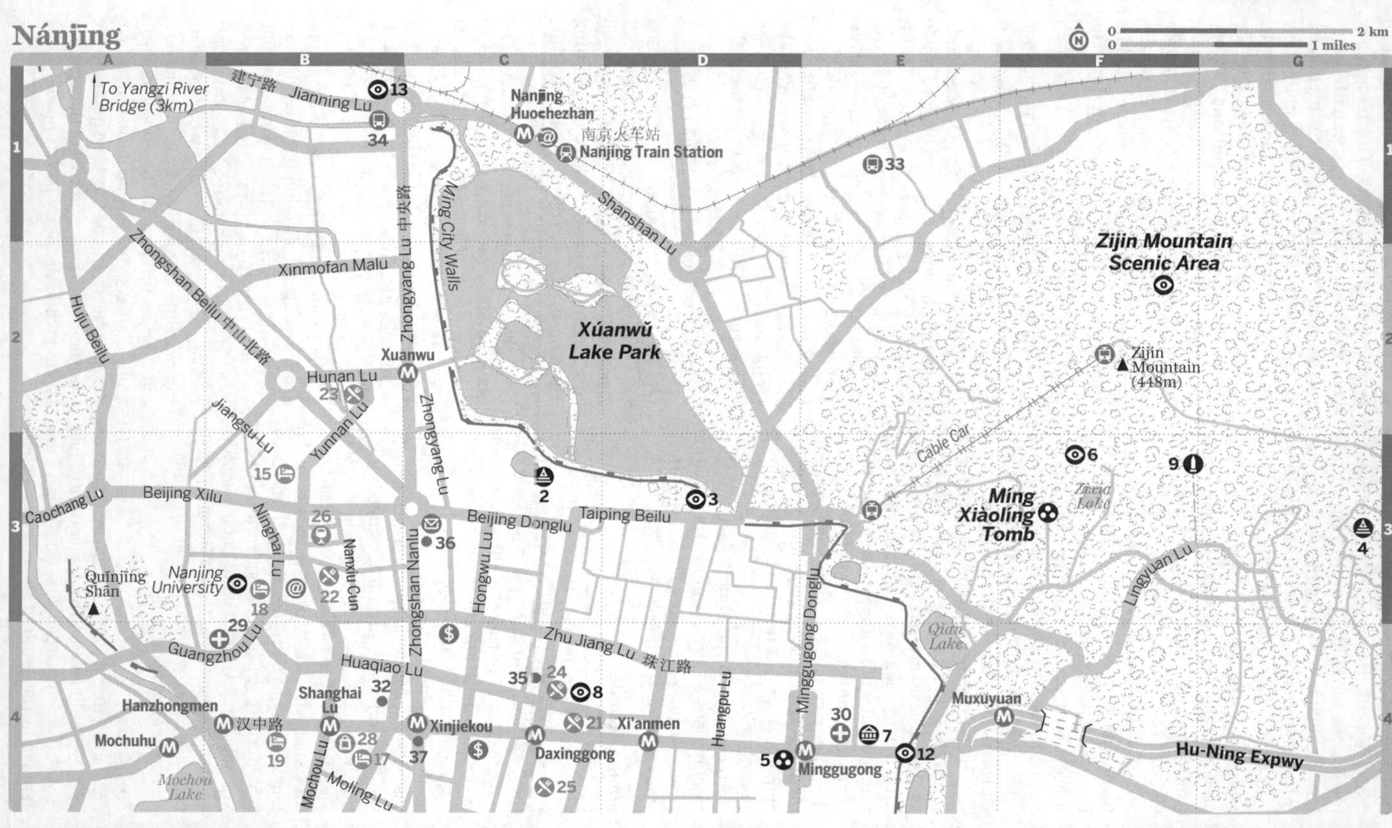
0 2 km
0 1 miles
To Yangzi River Bridge (3km)
建宁路 Jianning Lu
13
34
Nanjing Huochezhan
南京火车站
Nanjing Train Station
33
Shanshan Lu
Ming City Walls
Zhongyang Lu 中央路
Xinmofan Malu
Zhongshan Beilu 中山北路
Hujü Beilu
Xuanwu
Hunan Lu
23
Xúanwǔ Lake Park
Zijin Mountain Scenic Area
Zijin Mountain (448m)
Cable Car
6
9
Jiangsu Lu
Yunnan Lu
Zhongyang Lu
15
2
3
Míng Xiàolíng Tomb
Zixia Lake
4
Caochang Lu
Beijing Xilu
Ninghai Lu
26
36
Beijing Donglu
Taiping Beilu
Nanxiu Cun
Zhongshan Nanlu
Hongwu Lu
Lingyuan Lu
Quīnjīng Shān
Nanjing University
18
22
29
Guangzhou Lu
Zhu Jiang Lu 珠江路
Qian Lake
Huaqiao Lu
35
24
8
Huangpu Lu
Minggugong Donglu
Hanzhongmen
Shanghai Lu
32
汉中路
Xinjiekou
21
Xi'anmen
30
7
Muxuyuan
Mochuhu
19
28
17
37
Daxinggong
5
Minggugong
12
Hu-Ning Expwy
Mochou Lu
Moling Lu
25
Mochou Lake

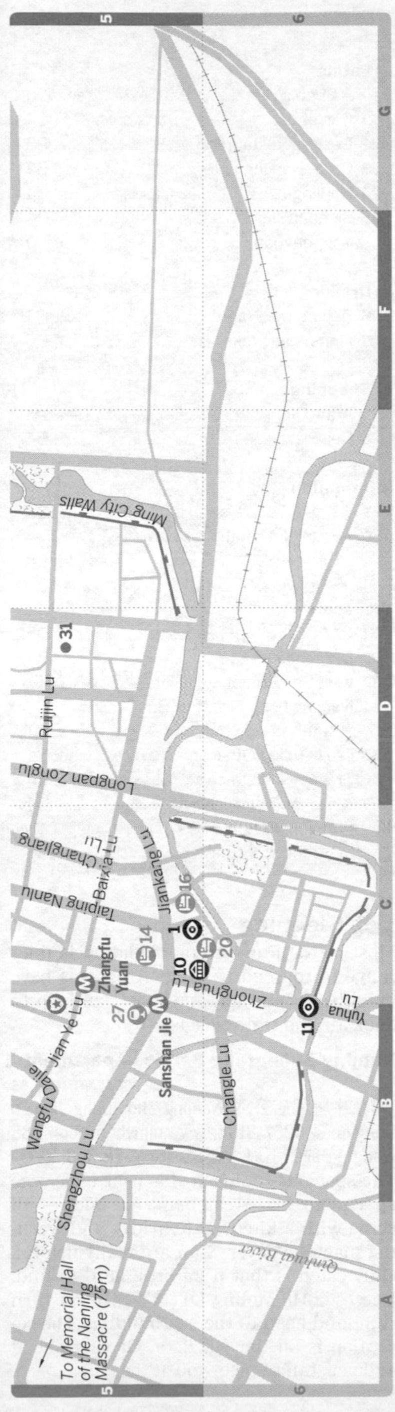

Xuánwǔ Lake Park PARK
(玄武湖公园; Xuánwǔhú Gōng Yuán; admission 1 Mar-1 May & 1 Sep-30 Nov Y30, 1 Dec-29 Feb & 1 Jun-31 Aug Y20; ⏲7am-9pm) This verdant 530-hectare park, backing onto the Ming-dynasty city wall, has a connected network of five isles spread across its lake. Scattered on the isles are bonsai gardens, camphor and cherry-blossom trees, temples and bamboo forests. The entire lake circuit is 9.5km for those inclined to a long jaunt. For the lazy, take a languid boat ride (Y60 per hour) around the lake – just make sure your boat steers properly before taking off.

Taiping Heavenly Kingdom History Museum MUSEUM
(太平天国历史博物馆; Tàipíng Tiānguó Lìshǐ Bówùguǎn; 128 Zhonghua Lu; admission Y30; ⏲8am-5pm; Ⓜ Sanshan Jie) Hong Xiuquan, the leader of the Taiping, had a palace built in Nánjīng, but the building was completely destroyed when Nánjīng was taken in 1864.

The Taiping Heavenly Kingdom History Museum (no English sign) was originally a garden complex, built in the Ming dynasty, which housed some of the Taiping officials before their downfall. There are displays of maps showing the progress of the Taiping army from Guǎngdōng, Hong Xiuquan's seals, Taiping coins, weapons and texts that describe the Taiping laws on agrarian reform, social law and cultural policy. Daily opera performances (Y70) are held in the evening.

Bus Y2 goes to the museum from the Ming Palace Ruins or Taiping Nanlu.

Yangzi River Bridge BRIDGE
(南京长江大桥; Nánjīng Chángjiāng Dàqiáo) Opened on 23 December 1968, the Yangzi River Bridge is one of the longest bridges in China – a double-decker with a 4500m-long road on top and a train line below. Wonderful socialist realist sculptures can be seen on the approaches. Odds are that you'll probably cross the bridge if you take a train from the north. Probably the easiest way to get up on the bridge is to go through the **Bridge Park** (Dàqiáo Gōngyuán; adult/child Y12/10; ⏲7.30am-6.30pm). Catch bus 67 from Jiangsu Lu, northwest of the Drum Tower (鼓楼; Gǔlóu), to its terminus opposite the park.

Presidential Palace PALACE
(总统府; Zǒngtǒng Fǔ; 292 Changjiang Lu; admission Y40; ⏲8am-5.30pm; Ⓜ Daxinggong) After the Taiping took over Nánjīng, they

Nánjīng

Top Sights

Míng Xiàolíng Tomb F3
Xúanwǔ Lake Park C2
Zijin Mountain Scenic Area F2

Sights

1 Fūzǐ Temple C5
Imperial Examinations History Museum (see 1)
2 Jīmíng Temple C3
3 Jiǔhúashān Park D3
4 Línggǔ Temple G3
5 Ming Palace Ruins D4
6 Míng Xiàolíng Scenic Area F3
7 Nánjīng Museum E4
8 Presidential Palace C4
9 Sun Yatsen Mausoleum F3
10 Taiping Heavenly Kingdom History Museum C5
11 Zhōnghuá Gate B6
12 Zhōngshān Gate E4
13 Zhōngyāng Gate B1

Sleeping

14 Jin's Inn (Fūzǐ Temple) C5
15 Jin's Inn (Yunnan Lu) B3
16 Nánjīng Fūzǐmiào International Youth Hostel C5
17 Nánjīng Zhōngfáng Service Apartment B4
18 Nánshān Experts Building B3
19 Sheraton Nánjīng Kingsley B4
20 Sunflower Youth Hostel C6

Eating

A Simple Diet (see 23)
21 Carrefour C4
22 Cosima Restaurant B3
23 Great Nánjīng Eatery B2
24 Nanjing 1912 C4
25 Sìchuān Jiǔjiā C4
Yǒnghéyuán (see 1)

Drinking

26 Behind the Wall B3
27 Finnegans Wake B5

Shopping

Aqua City (see 14)
28 Deji Plaza B4

Information

29 Jiāngsū People's Hospital B4
30 Nánjīng International SOS Clinic E4

Transport

31 CAAC D5
32 Dragonair B4
33 East Bus Station E1
34 Nánjīng Long-Distance Bus Station B1
35 Train Ticket Office C4
36 Train Ticket Office C3
37 Xīnjīekǒu Roundabout C4
Zhongshan Nanlu Bus Station (see 27)

built the Mansion of the Heavenly King (Tiānwáng Fǔ) on the foundations of a former Ming-dynasty palace. This magnificent palace did not survive the fall of the Taiping, but there is a reconstruction and a classical Ming garden, now known as the Presidential Palace. Other buildings on the site were used briefly as presidential offices by Sun Yatsen's government in 1912 and by the Kuomintang from 1927 to 1949. Bus Y1 travels here.

Festivals & Events

The **Nánjīng International Plum Blossom Festival**, held yearly from the last Saturday of February to early March, takes place on Zǐjīn Mountain near the Míng Xiàolíng Tomb when the mountain bursts with pink and white blossoms.

Sleeping

Most of Nánjīng's accommodation is midrange to top end in price. All rooms have broadband internet, and most can help to book air and train tickets.

Nánjīng Zhōngfáng Service Apartment
SERVICE APARTMENT **$$**

(南京中房酒店公寓; Nánjīng Zhōngfáng Jiǔdiàn Gōngyù; ☎6867 8188; www.njmyhome.com; 88 Wangfu Dajie; 王府大街88号; r Y328-368; ❄@) The spacious rooms at this central service apartment are great bang for buck – all come with a kitchenette, fridge and washing machine/dryer. Staff are really helpful. Only catch is that it's a little hard to find. Enter via 118 Moling Lu (秣陵路118号), turn right and head to the last building. The reception is on the 4th floor. Or ring ahead and get staff to meet you at the gate.

MING CITY WALLS

Běijīng will be forever haunted by the communists' destruction of its awe-inspiring city walls. Xī'ān's mighty Tang-dynasty wall – which was far, far larger than its current wall – is a mere memory. Even Shànghǎi's modest city wall came down in 1912.

The same story is repeated across China, but Nánjīng's fabulous surviving city wall is a constant reminder of its former glories. The wall may be overgrown, but this neglect – in a land where historic authenticity has too often courted destruction – has helped ensure its very survival.

Perhaps the most impressive remnant of Nánjīng's Ming-dynasty golden years, the impressive, five-storey Ming bastion, measuring over 35km, is the longest city wall ever built in the world. About two-thirds of it still stands.

Built between 1366 and 1393, by more than one million labourers, the layout of the wall is irregular, an exception to the usual square format of these times; it zigzags around Nánjīng's hills and rivers, accommodating the local landscape. Averaging 12m high and 7m wide at the top, the fortification was built of bricks supplied from five Chinese provinces. Each brick had stamped on it the place it came from, the overseer's name and rank, the brick-maker's name and sometimes the date. This was to ensure that the bricks were well made; if they broke they had to be replaced. Many of these stamps remain intact.

Some of the original 13 Ming city gates remain, including the **Zhōngyāng Gate** (中央门; Zhōngyāng Mén) in the north, **Zhōnghuá Gate** (中华门; Zhōnghuá Mén; admission Y20) in the south and **Zhōngshān Gate** (中山门; Zhōngshān Mén) in the east. The city gates were heavily fortified; built on the site of the old Tang-dynasty wall, Zhōnghuá Gate has four rows of gates, making it almost impregnable, and could house a garrison of 3000 soldiers in vaults in the front gate building. When walking through, observe the trough in either wall of the second gate, which held a vast stone gate that could be lowered into place. The gate is far more imposing than anything that has survived in Běijīng.

You can climb onto the masonry for exploration at several points. Long walks extend along the wall from Zhōngshān Gate in the east of the city and it's quite common to see locals walking their dogs or taking post-dinner walks along the weathered path; there is no charge for climbing the wall here.

One of the best places to access the gate is from the rear of Jīmíng Temple. Walk to Jiǔhúashān Park off Taiping Beilu, looking out over huge **Xúanwǔ Lake Park** (玄武湖公园) and passing crumbling hillside pagodas.

Sheraton Nánjīng Kingsley HOTEL $$$
(南京金丝利喜来登酒店; Nánjīng Jīnsīlì Xǐláidēng Jiǔdiàn; ☎8666 8888, 800 810 3088; www.sheraton.com/nanjing; 169 Hanzhong Lu; 汉中路169号; d Y1580-2080, discounts of almost 50%) The centrally located Sheraton is a dependably smart choice for business travellers, with four restaurants and two bars, indoor pool and tennis court.

Nánshān Experts Building HOTEL $$
(南山专家楼; Nánshān Zhuānjiā Lóu; ☎8329 2888; 122 Ninghai Lu; 宁海路122号; s/d/tr Y120/200/240; ❄@) Located on the lovely grounds of Nánjīng University, rooms have been tastefully redecorated with newish furniture. The campus setting is fantastic. Enter through the university's main gate, walk up the main lawn, turn left and take the third turning on the left; it's up the hill on the left. If you get lost, just ask a student for directions.

Jin's Inn HOTEL $$
(金一村; Jīnyī Cūn; ☎8375 5666; www.jinsinn.com; 26 Yunnan Lu; 云南路26号; s/d/f Y148/188/218; ❄) It's hard to miss this eye-popping orange-and-yellow hotel, where rooms are simple, clean and well-looked after. Free washing machine use and free internet for 30 minutes is available. The inn has stitched up the midrange market and there are 10 other branches around the city, including one just north of the Fūzǐ Temple area.

Sunflower Youth Hostel HOSTEL $
(南京瞻园国际青年旅舍; Nánjīng Zhānyuán Guójì Qīngnián Lǚshè; ☎5226 6858; 80 Zhanyuan

Lu; 瞻园路80号; dm Y40, d Y130-150; ❄@📶) You won't get any flowers on arrival and dorms are tight but the cosy singles and doubles have startling mosaic-tiled toilets and artwork doodled by former visitors on the yellow walls. Sadly, all the beds are thin foam on wood. The 4th-floor bar (table football, pool, movies, wi-fi) is great and it's open 24 hours. The pleasant staff are the best resource. Internet is Y5 per hour.

Nánjīng Fūzǐmiào International Youth Hostel HOSTEL $
(南京夫子庙国际青年旅舍; Nánjīng Fūzǐmiào Guójì Qīngnián Lǚguǎn; ☎8662 4133; 68 Pingjiangfu Lu; 平江府路68号; dm Y45-60, d & tw Y158-180; ❄@) Highly popular with Chinese backpackers (so book ahead), this place by the river has friendly staff. Rooms are old but fine, although aim for one overlooking the water as the others are windowless. Offers bike rental, DVD burning and laundry, plus a small area for watching DVDs. Internet is Y5 per hour.

Eating

The two main eating quarters in Nánjīng are at Fūzǐ Temple and Shīzǐqíò (狮子桥) off Hunan Lu. Both are lively pedestrian areas that come alive at night, packed with people, snack stands and small restaurants. You'll also find a scattering of family-run restaurants in the small lanes around the Nánjīng University district. Shanghai Lu is home to a strip of restaurants popular with the university crowd. Near the Presidential Palace, **Nánjīng 1912** (corner Taiping Beilu and Changjiang Lu) is a compound of shiny neon-lit bars, clubs, coffee houses and upscale restaurants.

Sìchuān Jiǔjiā SICHUANESE, JIANGSU $
(四川酒家; 171 Taiping Nanlu; meals from Y15; ⌚10.30am-10.30pm) This is a terrific place to sample local dishes and rub shoulders with locals. Cheap, local dining is on the 1st floor: there's *yánshuǐ yā* (盐水鸭; Nánjīng pressed duck; Y10), *dàndànmiàn* (担担面; spicy noodles; Y3.50), *chā shāo* (叉烧; pork slices; Y10), *tèsè tāngpā* (煎饺; special soup dumplings; Y5) and *jiānjiǎo* (煎饺; fried dumplings; Y4.50), *Suāncàiyú* (酸菜鱼; fish-and-cabbage soup; Y28) and other Sìchuān dishes are on the smarter, much pricier 2nd floor. There's no English sign, so look for the bright-red building and the sign with dancing chilli peppers. Order and pay at the counter, and watch the chefs bustle around the kitchen.

A Simple Diet JIANGSU $$
(粗茶淡饭; Cūchá Dànfàn; 32 Shiziqiao; mains Y8-20; ⌚11am-9pm) If stuffing your face with some of the best *xiǎolóng tāngbāo* (小笼汤包; *xiaolong* dumplings; Y14) in town constitutes a simple diet, it's time to cancel that gym membership. Dishes are displayed and prices are labelled. Get some Tsingtao (Y6) to wash it all down. Ahh, to hell with that diet.

Great Nánjīng Eatery JIANGSU $$
(南京大牌档; Nánjīng Dàpáidàng; 2 Shiziqiao; dishes Y12-46; ⌚11am-2pm & 5-11pm) This old-style teahouse is a popular place to try yummy local snacks, such as *yāxiě fěnsī tāng* (鸭血粉丝汤; duck-blood soup with rice noodles) or *dòufu nǎo* (豆腐脑; salty custardlike tofu). There's no English sign, so look for the two large stone lions out the front and the wooden bridge (!) just behind the huge red double doors.

Yǒnghé Yuán JIANGSU, SHANGHAINESE $
(永和园; 122 Gongyuan Jie; mains Y15; ⌚8.30am-9pm) Not far from the decorative arch roughly halfway along Gongyuan Jie, this long-serving food court is low on decor but that doesn't stop the crowds from packing in. It serves a great range of tasty snacks, from *páigǔ miàn* (排骨面; spare ribs and noodles; Y15) and *xiānròu húntun* (鲜肉馄饨; meat dumplings; Y5) to *wǔxiāng dàn* (五香蛋; five-flavour eggs; Y1), *xiaolong* dumplings (Y14) and the local favourite *yāxiě fěnsī tāng* (Y8). Grab a tray, order your dishes, take them to the cashier and pay.

Cosima Restaurant PIZZA, TAPAS $$
(120 Shanghai Lu; pizza Y38-58, tapas Y6.50-48; ⌚10am till late; 📋) Part Spanish, part Italian, 100% atmosphere. There are only three tables in this tiny no-bookings restaurant so most punters end up ringing ahead to order their pizzas for takeaway. If you sit down, order some tapas and a bottle of Spanish red...you might soon forget you're in China, until someone on the next table jabs you in the ribs while lifting their pizza slice.

Carrefour SUPERMARKET $
(Jiālèfú; 235 Zhongshan Donglu; ⌚8am-10pm) Located underground, this French hypermart stocks everything you would need and some things you don't (blueberry-flavoured chips).

Drinking

Nánjīng's bar and club scene has exploded over the past few years, though it's still not as vibrant or imaginative as in Shànghǎi. There are bars and clubs in **Nánjīng 1912** (corner Taipei Beilu and Changjiang Lu).

Behind the Wall BAR

(答案; Dá'àn; 150 Shanghai Lu; pint Y30;) Very laid-back and comfortable with outside seating, convivial atmosphere and draught beer. A talented guitar duo performs most nights. The bar doubles as a Mexican restaurant and servings (from Y48) are huge. It's literally 'behind the wall'.

Finnegans Wake BAR

(cnr Shengzhou & Zhongshan Nan Lu; Guinness draft pint Y68; 10am-4am) Great, if pricey, food and drinks. Guinness on tap and an Irish bartender who also belts out the tunes. Quiet except for the weekends and Monday (half-price burgers). *Don't* try the chilli vodka unless you want to spend the night writhing on the ground.

Shopping

The area surrounding **Fūzǐ Temple** is a pedestrian zone with souvenirs, clothing, shoes, antiques and even animals for sale. You'll find many major department stores around Hanzhong Lu and Zhongshan Lu. These are some of the more popular malls:

Aqua City MALL

(水游城; Shuǐ Yóu Chéng; 1 Jiankang Lu) No water in sight but Nánjīng's newest mall is packed with midrange name brands.

Deji Plaza MALL

(德基广场; Déjī Guǎngchǎng; 89 Hanzhong Lu) Top brands such as Louis Vuitton. Cinema on top floor.

Foreign Languages Bookstore BOOKSHOP

(外文书店; Wàiwén Shūdiàn; 218 Zhongshan Donglu; 9am-7pm)

Popular Book Mall BOOKSHOP

(大众书局; Dàzhòng Shūjú; Xīnjīekǒu; 9am-9pm) Has a range of English fiction on the 4th floor.

Information

Internet Access

Internet cafe (网吧; wǎngbā; per hr Y4; 24hr) In an alley between KFC and McDonald's at Nánjīng train station.

Jīnsuǒ Internet Cafe (金锁网洛; Jīnsuǒ Wǎngluò; 85 Shanghai Lu; per hr Y3; 24hr)

Internet resources

Nanjing Expats (www.nanjingexpat.com) Active forum, events and listings in Nánjīng. It also distributes a magazine around the city.

Media

Map (www.mapmagazine.com.cn) Expat listings magazine.

Nanjing Expats (www.nanjingexpat.com) Another expat listings magazine available at restaurants and bars.

Medical services

Jiāngsū People's Hospital (江苏省人民医院; Jiāngsū Shěng Rénmín Yīyuàn; 8371 8836; 300 Guangzhou Lu; 8am-noon & 2-5.30pm) Runs a clinic for expats and has English-speaking doctors available.

Nánjīng International SOS Clinic (南京国际SOS 紧急救援诊所; Nánjīng Guójì SOS Jǐnjí Jiùyuán Zhěnsuǒ; 8480 2842, 24hr alarm centre 010 6462 9100) On the ground floor of the Grand Metropark Hotel. Staff on duty speak English.

Money

An ATM taking international cards can be found in the Sheraton Nánjīng Kingsley. Most bank ATMs are open 24 hours and take international cards. Banks below change major currency and travellers cheques.

Bank of China (中国银行; Zhōngguó Yínháng; 29 Hongwu Lu; 8am-5pm Mon-Fri, to 12.30pm Sat)

Bank of China (中国银行; Zhōngguó Yínháng; 148 Zhonghua Lu; 8am-5pm Mon-Fri, to 12.30pm Sat)

Post

China Post (中国邮政; Zhōngguó Yóuzhèng; 2 Zhongshan Nanlu; 8am-6.30pm) Postal services and international phone calls.

Public Security Bureau

(PSB;公安局; Gōng'ānjú) On a small lane called Sanyuan Xiang down a nest of streets west off Zhongshan Nanlu.

Travel Agencies

Most hotels have their own travel agencies and can book tickets for a service charge. They can also arrange tours around town and to neighbouring sights.

China International Travel Service (CITS; 中国国际旅行社; Zhōngguó Guójì Lǚxíngshè; 8342 1125; 202 Zhongshan Beilu; 9am-4pm) Across from the Nánjīng Hotel; arranges tours, and books air and train tickets.

Getting There & Away

Air

Nánjīng has regular air connections to all major Chinese cities. The main office for the **Civil Aviation Administration of China** (CAAC; 中国民航; Zhōngguó Mínháng; ☎8449 9378; 50 Ruijin Lu) is near the terminus of bus 37, but you can also buy tickets at most top-end hotels.

Dragonair (港龙航空; Gǎnglóng Hángkōng; ☎8471 0181; Room 751-53, World Trade Centre, 2 Hanzhong Lu) has daily flights to Hong Kong.

Boat

Several ferries depart daily from Yangzi port downriver (eastward) to Shànghǎi (about 10 hours) and upriver (westward) to Wǔhàn (two days); a few boats also go to Chóngqìng (five days). The passenger dock is in the northwest of the city at **No 6 dock** (六号码头; Liù Hào Mǎtóu). Tickets can be booked at the dock in the terminal building.

Bus

Of Nánjīng's numerous long-distance bus stations, **Nánjīng long-distance bus station** (南京门长途汽车站; Nánjīng Chángtú Qìchēzhàn; ☎8533 1288) is the largest, located southwest of the wide-bridged intersection with Zhongyang Lu. It is sometimes referred to as the Zhōngyángmén long distance station. Regular buses departing from here:

Hángzhōu Y100, four hours

Héféi Y45, 2½ hours

Huángshān (Túnxī) Y76, four hours

Shànghǎi Y95, four hours

Sūzhōu Y70, 2½ hours

Buses departing the **east bus station** (长途汽车东站; *chángtú qìchē dōngzhàn*):

Sūzhōu Y70, three hours

Wúxī Y17, 1½ hours

Yángzhōu Y34, 1½ hours

Zhènjiāng Y24, 1½ hours

From Nánjīng train station, take bus 13 north to Zhōngyāngmén long-distance bus station. Bus 2 from Xīnjīekǒu goes to the east bus station. A taxi from town will cost Y20 to Y25 to either station.

Train

Nánjīng is a major stop on the Běijīng–Shànghǎi train line, and **Nánjīng train station** (☎8582 2222) is mayhem. Heading eastward from Nánjīng, the line to Shànghǎi connects with Zhènjiāng, Wúxī and Sūzhōu. Some trains may terminate at Nánjīng west train station (南京西站; Nánjīng *xīzhàn*), so check when you buy your ticket.

More than 10 daily express D trains run between Nánjīng and Shànghǎi (Y80, 2½ hours), stopping at Sūzhōu (Y33, two hours). There are six D trains to Běijīng (Y274, 8½ hours). There are two D trains to Hángzhōu (Y114, five hours) that go via Shànghǎi . Regular trains also go to Huángshān City (Túnxī) in Ānhuī province (Y54 to Y159, seven hours).

A slow train to Guǎngzhōu (Y238 to Y658, 28 hours, three daily) goes via Shànghǎi.

Try to get tickets via your hotel or the **train ticket office** (火车票售票处; huǒchēpiào shòupiàochù; 2 Zhongshan Nanlu; ⌚8.30am-5pm) on the 3rd floor of the post office, and the **train ticket office** (huǒchēpiào shòupiào chù; 35 Taiping Beilu) on Taiping Beilu.

Getting Around

To/From the Airport

Nánjīng's Lùkǒu airport is approximately one hour south of the city. Buses (Y25) run to the airport every 30 minutes between 6am and 7.30pm from the **Zhongshan Nanlu bus station** (中山南路客运站; Zhōngshān Nánlù Kèyùnzhàn) next to the Sanshan Jie subway station (三山街). Most hotels have hourly shuttle buses to and from the airport. A taxi will cost around Y125.

Public Transport

Nánjīng has an efficient **metro system** that cuts through the city centre. Line No 1 runs from Màigāoqiáo in the north to the Olympic Sports Stadium in the southwest between 6.41am and 10pm. Line No 2 opened mid-2010 and makes getting to some sights more convenient. It goes east from Jīngtīanlù to Yóufāngqío in the west. Tickets are Y2 to Y4.

You can get to Xīnjīekǒu, in the heart of town, by jumping on bus 13 from Nánjīng train station or from Zhōngyāng Gate. There are also tourist bus routes that visit many of the sights:

Bus Y1 Goes from Nánjīng train station and Nánjīng long-distance bus station through the city to the Sun Yatsen Mausoleum.

Bus Y2 Starts in the south at the Martyrs' Cemetery (烈士墓地; Lièshì Mùdì), passes Fūzǐ Temple and terminates halfway up Zǐjīn Mountain.

Bus Y3 Passes by Nánjīng train station en route to the Míng Xiàolíng Tomb and Línggǔ Temple.

Bus 16 Links the Fūzǐ Temple area and Nánjīng west train station (南京西站; Nánjīng Xīzhàn), passing by the Drum Tower (鼓楼; Gǔlóu).

Many local maps contain bus routes. Normal buses cost Y1 and tourist buses cost Y2.

Taxi

Taxi fares start at Y9 and it's Y2.40 for each 3km thereafter. Trips to most destinations in the city are Y10 to Y14. Taxis are easy to flag down anywhere in the city.

Around Nánjīng

On Qīxiá Mountain, 22km northeast of Nánjīng, **Qīxiá Temple** (栖霞寺; Qīxiá Sì; admission Y20; ⏲7am-5.30pm) was founded by the Buddhist monk Ming Sengshao during the Southern Qi dynasty, and is still an active place of worship. It's long been one of China's most important monasteries, and even today is one of the largest Buddhist seminaries in the country. In mid-2010, relics believed to be part of the skull of Gautama Buddha were unveiled and interred here. There are two main temple halls: the Maitreya Hall, with a statue of the Maitreya Buddha sitting cross-legged at the entrance; and, behind this one, the Vairocana Hall, housing a 5m-tall statue of the Vairocana Buddha.

Behind Qīxiá Temple is the **Thousand Buddha Cliff** (Qiānfó Yá). Several small caves housing stone statues are carved into the hillside, the earliest of which dates as far back as the Qi dynasty (AD 479–502), although there are others from succeeding dynasties through to the Ming. There is also a small stone pagoda, **Shělì Pagoda** (舍利; Shělì Tǎ), which was built in AD 601, and rebuilt during the late Tang period. The upper part has engraved sutras and carvings of Buddha; around the base, each of the pagoda's eight sides depicts Sakyamuni.

The temple is built on a scenic area, and if you continue northwards there's a whole heap of areas behind the temple to stop and admire. The (sometimes steep) path meanders along an array of pavilions and rocky outcrops which you climb between. The entire area is rather serene and you could bring your lunch and spend the better part of your day here.

You can reach this temple from Nánjīng by a public bus (南上, Nán Shàng, Y2.50, one hour) that departs from a station beside the Nánjīng train station. When you get off the bus, you will be approached by motorcycle taxis that will offer to take you into the temple the 'back' way for Y10. Be warned, it's an arduous hike up and down a large hill to the temple if you take this option.

Sūzhōu 苏州

☎0512 / POP 1.6 MILLION

Sūzhōu's fame was immortalised in the proverb 'In heaven there is paradise, on earth Sūzhōu and Hángzhōu' – a line still very much plugged in the tourist campaigns. Sadly, this isn't nearly the case anymore. Communist rule has spawned some mightily unattractive cities and disfigured many more, and like all modern Chinese towns, Sūzhōu has had to contend with destruction of its heritage and its replacement with largely arbitrary chunks of modern architecture. But while you won't fall for its hackneyed 'Venice-of-the-East' chat-up line, Sūzhōu – described by Marco Polo as one of the most beautiful cities in China – still contains enough pockets of charm to warrant two to three days' exploration. It's not uncommon for visitors to end up staying for over a week, such is the charm of its canals and gardens.

Sūzhōu's gardens, a symphonic combination of rocks, water, trees and buildings, reflect the Chinese appreciation of balance and harmony. You could easily spend an enjoyable several days wandering through gardens, visiting some excellent museums, and exploring some of Sūzhōu's surviving canal scenes, pagodas and humpbacked bridges.

History

Dating back some 2500 years, Sūzhōu is one of the oldest towns in the Yangzi Basin. With the completion of the Grand Canal during the Sui dynasty, Sūzhōu began to flourish as a centre of shipping and grain storage, bustling with merchants and artisans.

By the 14th century, Sūzhōu had become China's leading silk-producing city. Aristocrats, pleasure seekers, famous scholars, actors and painters arrived, constructing villas and garden retreats.

The town's winning image as a 'Garden City' or a 'Venice of the East' drew from its medieval blend of woodblock guilds and embroidery societies, whitewashed housing, cobbled streets, tree-lined avenues and canals. The local women were considered the most beautiful in China, largely thanks to the mellifluous local accent, and the city was home to a variety of rich merchants and bookish scholars...no doubt drawn by the beautiful women.

In 1860 Taiping troops took the town without a blow and in 1896 Sūzhōu was opened to foreign trade, with Japanese and other international concessions. Since 1949 much of the historic city, including its city walls, has vanished (yes, blame development and the Cultural Revolution).

Sūzhōu

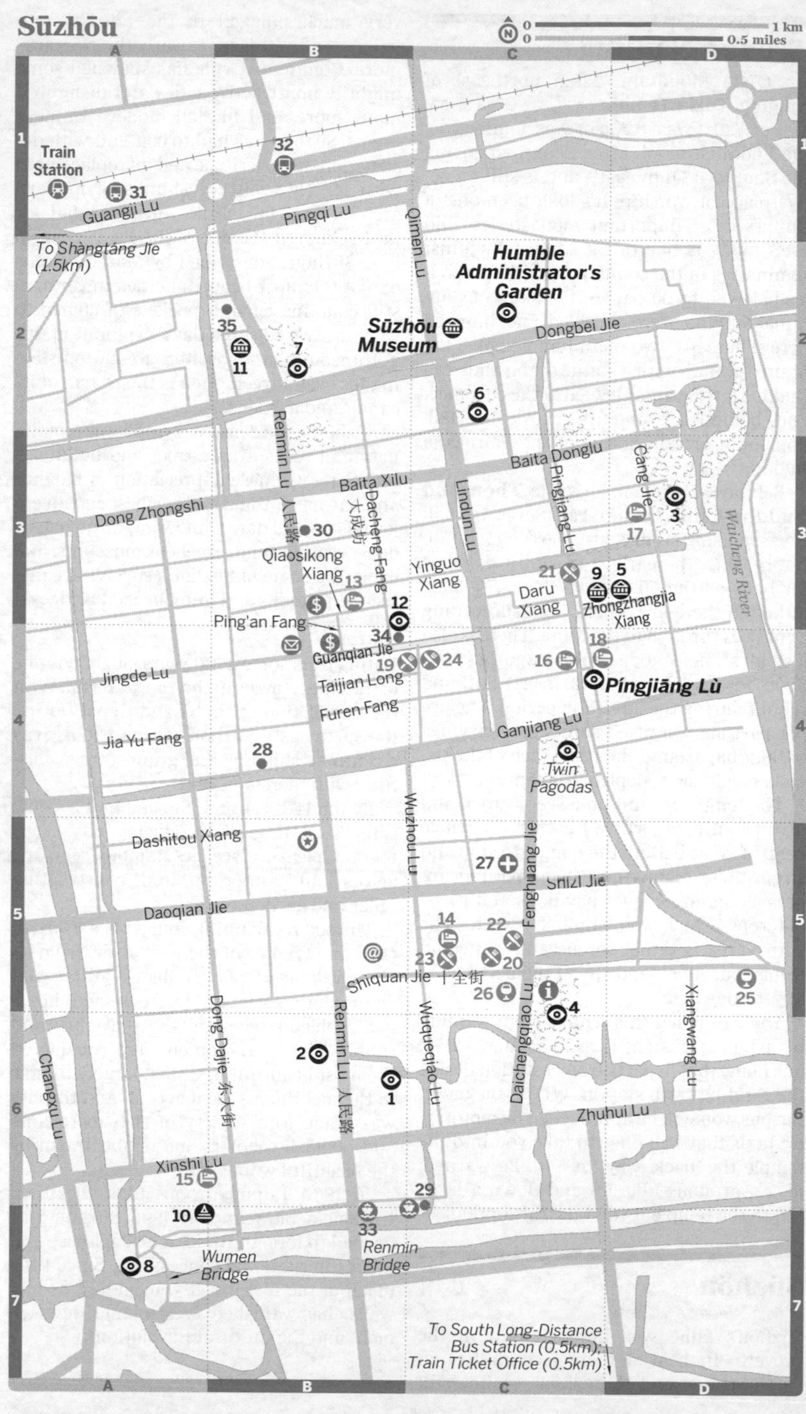
0 1 km
0 0.5 miles
Train Station
31
32
Guangji Lu
Pingqi Lu
To Shàngtáng Jie (1.5km)
Qimen Lu
Humble Administrator's Garden
Sūzhōu Museum
Dongbei Jie
35
11
7
6
Renmin Lu
Baita Donglu
Baita Xilu
Dong Zhongshi
Dacheng Fang 大成坊
人民路
30
Lindun Lu
Pingjiang Lu
Cang Jie
3
17
Waicheng River
Qiaosikong Xiang
Yinguo Xiang
21
9
5
13
12
Daru Xiang
Zhongzhangjia Xiang
Ping'an Fang
34
18
Guanqian Jie
19
24
16
Jingde Lu
Taijian Long
Píngjiāng Lù
Furen Fang
Ganjiang Lu
Jia Yu Fang
28
Twin Pagodas
Wuzhou Lu
Dashitou Xiang
Fenghuang Jie
27
Shizi Jie
Daoqian Jie
14
22
23
20
Shiquan Jie 十全街
26
25
Dong Dajie 东大街
Renmin Lu 人民路
Wuqueqiao Lu
Daichengqiao Lu
4
Xiangwang Lu
2
1
Changxu Lu
Zhuhui Lu
Xinshi Lu
15
29
10
33
Renmin Bridge
8
Wumen Bridge
To South Long-Distance Bus Station (0.5km); Train Ticket Office (0.5km)

Sūzhōu

Top Sights

Humble Administrator's Garden C2
Píngjiāng Lù C4
Sūzhōu Museum C2

Sights

1 Blue Wave Pavilion B6
2 Confucian Temple B6
3 Couple's Garden D3
4 Garden of the Master of the Nets C5
5 Kūnqǔ Opera Museum D3
6 Lion's Grove Garden C2
7 North Temple Pagoda B2
8 Pán Gate A7
9 Píngtán Museum C3
10 Ruìguāng Pagoda A7
11 Sūzhōu Silk Museum B2
12 Temple of Mystery B3

Sleeping

13 Hotel Soul B3
14 Nánlín Hotel C5
15 Pan Pacific Sūzhōu A6
16 Píngjiāng Lodge C4
17 Sūzhōu Joya Youth Hostel D3
18 Sūzhōu Mingtown Youth Hostel C4

Eating

19 Déyuè Lóu B4
20 Pingtan Teahouse C5
21 Pingvon C3
22 Xīshèngyuán C5
23 Yàkèxī C5
24 Zhūhóngxìng Miànguǎn C4

Drinking

25 Bookworm D5
26 Jane's Pub C5

Entertainment

Garden of the Master of the Nets . (see 4)
Kūnqǔ Opera Museum .... (see 5)
Pingtan Museum .... (see 9)

Information

27 No 1 Hospital C5

Transport

28 China Eastern Airlines B4
29 Grand Canal Boat Ticket Office C6
30 Liánhé Ticket Centre B3
31 Local Buses A1
32 North Long-Distance Bus Station B1
33 Sūzhōu to Hángzhōu Boat Wharf B7
34 Train Ticket Office (Guanqian Jie) B4
35 Yángyáng Bike Rental Shop B2

Sights & Activities

Children under 1.2m get in for half-price to all gardens and into other sights for free. High-season prices listed are applicable from March to early May and September to October. Gardens and museums stop selling tickets 30 minutes before closing.

FREE **Sūzhōu Museum** MUSEUM

(苏州博物馆; Sūzhōu Bówùguǎn; 204 Dongbei Jie; audioguide Y30; ⏲9am-5pm) This IM Pei–designed museum is a soothing contrast of water, bamboo and straight lines in a stunning geometric interpretation of a Sūzhōu garden. Inside is a fascinating array of jade, ceramics, wooden carvings, textiles and other displays, all with good English captions. Look out for the Boxwood statue of Avalokiteshvara (Guanyin), dating from the republican period. An in-depth look at the scholars and their lifestyle of the period is particular fascinating (containers for crickets? A mahogany birdcage with a dainty porcelain water cup? Did these guys actually do any study?). Draconian entry rules apply: flip-flops wearers get turned away. Come early as there are limited 'tickets' each day.

Garden of the Master of the Nets CLASSICAL GARDEN

(网师园; Wǎngshī Yuán; high/low season Y30/20; ⏲7.30am-5pm) Off Shiquan Jie, this pocket-sized garden, the smallest in Sūzhōu, is considered one of the best preserved in the city. It was laid out in the 12th century, went to seed and was later restored in the 18th century as part of the home of a retired official turned fisherman (thus the name). The central section is the main garden. The western section is an inner garden where a courtyard contains the **Spring Rear Cottage** (Diànchūn Yì), the master's study.

The most striking feature of this garden is its use of space: the labyrinth of courtyards, with windows framing other parts of the garden, is ingeniously designed to give the illusion of a much larger area. Trivia nuts: the **Peony Study** is used as the model for the Astor Court and Ming Garden in the Museum of Modern Art, New York.

There are two ways to the entry gate, with English signs and souvenir stalls marking the way: you can enter from the alley on Shiquan Jie or via Kuòjiātóu Xiàng (阔家头巷), an alley off Daichengqiao Lu. Music performances are held for tourists in the evening (see p226).

Humble Administrator's Garden CLASSICAL GARDEN

(拙政园; Zhuōzhèng Yuán; 178 Dongbei Jie; high/low season Y70/50, audioguide free; ⊙7.30am-5.30pm) First built in 1509, this 5.2-hectare garden is clustered with water features, a museum, a teahouse and at least 10 pavilions such as 'the listening to the sound of rain' and 'the faraway looking' pavilions – hardly humble, we know. It is the largest of all the gardens and considered by many to be the most impressive. With its zigzagging bridges, pavilions, bamboo groves and fragrant lotus ponds, it should be an ideal place for a leisurely stroll...sadly you'll have to battle with crowds for right of way!

Lion's Grove Garden CLASSICAL GARDEN

(狮子林; Shīzi Lín; 23 Yuanlin Lu; high/low season Y30/20; ⊙7.30am-5.30pm) Near the Humble Administrator's Garden is the Lion's Grove Garden, constructed in 1342 by the Buddhist monk Tianru to commemorate his master, who lived on Lion Cliff in Zhèjiāng's Tīanm' Mountain. The garden is most notable for its legion of curiously shaped rocks, meant to resemble lions, protectors of the Buddhist faith. If the Humble Administrator's Garden was crowded, get ready to be pushed along by the tide of tourists here.

Garden to Linger In CLASSICAL GARDEN

(留园; Liú Yuán; 79 Liuyuan Lu; high/low season Y40/30; ⊙7.30am-5pm) One of the largest gardens in Sūzhōu, this 3-hectare garden was originally built in the Ming dynasty by a doctor as a relaxing place for his recovering patients. It's easy to see why the patients took to the place: the winding corridors are inlaid with calligraphy from celebrated masters, their windows and doorways opening onto unusually shaped rockeries, ponds and dense clusters of bamboo. Stone tablets hang from the walls, inscribed by patients recording their impressions of the place. The teahouse is a fantastic place to recover from crowd overload. Order a cup of *lóngjǐng* (龙井; Y15) and feel time slow down.

The garden is about 3km west of the city centre and can be reached on tourist bus Y1 from the train station or Renmin Lu.

West Garden Temple CLASSICAL GARDEN

(西园寺; Xīyuán Sì; Xiyuan Lu; admission Y25; ⊙8am-5pm) This attractive temple was once part of the Garden to Linger In, but was given to a Buddhist temple in the early 17th century. The West Garden Temple, with its mustard-yellow walls and gracefully curved eaves, was burnt to the ground during the Taiping Rebellion and rebuilt in the late 19th century.

Greeting you upon entering the magnificent **Arhat Hall** (罗汉堂; Luóhàn Táng) within the temple is a stunning four-faced and thousand-armed statue of Guanyin, leading to mesmerising and slightly unnerving rows of 500 glittering *luóhàn* (Buddhists, especially a monk who has achieved enlightenment and passes to nirvana at death) – each one unique and near life-size. Kids might get scared.

There's a fantastic **vegetarian restaurant** serving noodles (Y7 to Y9).

Old Streets (Píngjiāng Lù & Shàngtáng Jīe) OLD STREETS

While most of the canals in the city have been sealed and paved into roads, there are two outstanding areas which give visitors a clue to Suzhou's 'Venice of the East' moniker. On the eastern side of the city, **Píngjiāng Lù** (平江路) is undoubtedly the prettier and more popular of the two. This pedestrian road (watch out for electric bikes though!) is set alongside a canal. Whitewashed local houses and trendy cafes selling overpriced lattes sit comfortably side-by-side – locals wring their dirty mops into the canal and are completely oblivious to the hordes of tourist jostling to get their *National Geographic*-worthy snapshots. Had enough of makeover studios and Tsingtao-swilling tourists? Duck down some of the side streets that jut out from the main path for a glimpse at the slow-paced local life.

At the foot of Tiger Hill is the start of a grittier version of Píngjiāng Lù. **Shàngtáng Jīe** (上塘街) eschews espresso and beer for tacky souvenir shops but keep on walking and the dross is soon replaced by grimy Ming- and Qing-dynasty houses and locals pottering about. Sure, it lacks the touristy sheen but there's just something about the dirty cobblestone paths that appeals. You can get a ticket (Y45) to several tourist spots including old residences, but you can do without that. The walk will take you 2.5km down to Xīzhōngshì at the edge of central Sūzhōu. Boat rides along the canal are Y34 to Y45, but why miss out on all the close action?

Blue Wave Pavilion CLASSICAL GARDEN

(沧浪亭; Cānglàng Tíng; Renmin Lu; high/low season Y20/15; ⏲7.30am-5pm) Overgrown and wild, the 1-hectare garden around the Blue Wave Pavilion is one of Sūzhōu's oldest. The buildings date from the 11th century, although they have been repeatedly rebuilt. The entrance sits across a bridge that straddles the small lake out the front. Originally the home of a prince, the property passed into the hands of the scholar Su Zimei, who named it after a poem by Qu Yuan (340–278 BC).

Lacking a northern wall, the garden creates the illusion of space by borrowing scenes from the outside. A double verandah out the front pavilion wends its way along a canal. From the outer path, you'll see green space inside and from the inner path you can see views of the water. Look out for a 'temple' whose dark walls are carved with the portraits of over 500 sages, and the 'pure fragrance house' has some impressive furniture made from the gnarled roots of banyan trees.

FREE **Confucian Temple** TEMPLE

(文庙; Wénmiào; 613 Renmin Lu; ⏲8.30-11am & 12.30-4.30pm) The main building of this former Confucian Temple is currently under renovation and should look stunning when complete. Visitors are still able to enter the compound and should look out for some fabulous stelae carved during the Southern Song dynasty (1137–1279). One features a map of old Sūzhōu – it details the canal system (much of which is now paved over and blocked), old roads and the city walls dating to 1229. Surprisingly, the whole city grid is relatively unchanged from 800 years ago. There's also an astronomy stelae from 1190 – one of the oldest astronomy charts in the world.

Sūzhōu Silk Museum MUSEUM

(丝绸博物馆; Sūzhōu Sīchóu Bówùguǎn; 2001 Renmin Lu; admission Y15; ⏲9am-5pm) Sūzhōu was the place for silk production and weaving, and the Sūzhōu Silk Museum houses a number of fascinating exhibitions that detail the history of Sūzhōu's 4000-year-old silk industry. Exhibits include a section on silk-weaving techniques and a room with live silk worms munching away on mulberry leaves and spinning cocoons. There are many functioning looms and its not uncommon to see staff at work on, say, a large brocade. Magnificent. Many of the captions are in English.

North Temple Pagoda PAGODA

(北寺塔; Běisì Tǎ; 1918 Renmin Lu; admission Y25; ⏲7.45am-5.30pm) The tallest pagoda south of the Yangzi, at nine storeys North Temple Pagoda dominates the northern end of Renmin Lu. Climb it for sweeping views of hazy modern-day Sūzhōu.

The temple complex goes back 1700 years and was originally a residence; the current reincarnation dates back to the 17th century. Off to the side is **Nánmù Guānyīn Hall** (Nánmù Guānyīn Diàn), which was rebuilt in the Ming dynasty with some features imported from elsewhere.

Pán Gate ANCIENT WALL

(盘门; Pán Mén; 1 Dong Dajie; admission Pán Gate only/with Ruìguāng Pagoda Y25/31; ⏲7.30am-6pm) Straddling the outer moat in the southwest corner of the city, this stretch of the city wall has Sūzhōu's only remaining original coiled gate, Pán Gate, which dates from 1355. This overgrown gate, actually really a wall, straddles the canal and it's the only remaining land-and-water gate in China. The double-walled water gate was used for controlling waterways and has many defensive positions at the top. From the atmospheric gate, you can spy the exquisite arched Wúmén Bridge (Wúmén Qiáo) to the east and there are great views of the moat and the crumbling **Ruìguāng Pagoda** (瑞光塔; Ruìguāng Tǎ), constructed in 1004. The pagoda can be climbed. The gate is also connected to 300m of the ancient city wall which visitors can walk along.

To get there, take tourist bus Y5 from the train station or Changxu Lu.

Tiger Hill HILL PARK

(虎丘山; Hǔqiū Shān; Huqiu Lu; admission high/low season Y60/40; ⏲7.30am-6pm, to 5pm winter) In the far northwest of town, Tiger Hill is popular with local tourists. The hill itself is artificial and is the final resting place of He Lu, founding father of Sūzhōu. He Lu died in the 6th century BC and myths have coalesced around him – he is said to have been buried with a collection of 3000 swords and to be guarded by a white tiger.

The most popular point (and a sort of beacon drawing the visitors) is the leaning **Cloud Rock Pagoda** (云岩塔; Yúnyán Tǎ) atop Tiger Hill. The octagonal seven-storey pagoda, also known as Hǔqīu Pagoda, was built in the 10th century entirely of brick, an innovation in Chinese architecture at the time. The pagoda began tilting over 400 years ago, and today the highest point is displaced more than 2m from its original position. Comparisons by local guides to the Leaning Tower of Pisa are inevitable though the tower cannot be climbed.

Tourist buses Y1 and Y2 from the train station go to Tiger Hill.

Couple's Garden CLASSICAL GARDEN
(耦园; Ǒu Yuán; high/low season Y20/15; ⌚8am-4.30pm) The tranquil Couple's Garden is off the main tourist route and sees fewer visitors (a relative concept in China), though the gardens, pond and courtyards are quite lovely. Surrounding the garden on Píngjiāng Lù are some fine examples of traditional Sūzhōu architecture, bridges and canals. Short boat rides (Y10) launch from the private dock at the rear of the compound.

FREE **Kūnqǔ Opera Museum** MUSEUM
(戏曲博物馆; Xìqǔ Bówùguǎn; 14 Zhongzhangjia Xiang; ⌚8.30am-4pm) Down a warren of narrow lanes, the small Kūnqǔ Opera Museum is dedicated to *kūnqǔ,* the opera style of the region. The beautiful old theatre houses a stage, old musical instruments, costumes and photos of famous performers. It also puts on occasional performances of *kūnqǔ.* and *shūoshū* (storytelling).

Píngtán Museum MUSEUM
(评弹博物馆; Píngtán Bówùguǎn; 3 Zhongzhangjia Xiang; admission Y4; ⌚8.30am-4pm) Up the same street, west of the Kūnqǔ Opera Museum, is the Píngtán Museum, which puts on wonderful performances of *píngtán,* a singing and storytelling art form sung in the Sūzhōu dialect. Shows are at 1.30pm daily.

Temple of Mystery TEMPLE
(玄妙观; Xuánmiào Guàn; Guanqian Jie; admission Y10, incl performance Y30; ⌚7.30am-5.30pm) The Taoist Temple of Mystery stands in what was once Sūzhōu's old bazaar, a rowdy entertainment district with travelling showmen, acrobats and actors. The temple's present surroundings of Guanqian Jie are just as boisterous, but the current showmen are more likely to sell you a fake designer watch than balance plates on their heads.

The temple was founded during the Jin dynasty in the 3rd century AD, and restored many times over its long history. The complex contains several elaborately decorated halls, including **Sānqīng Diàn** (Three Purities Hall), which is supported by 60 pillars and capped by a double roof with upturned eaves. The temple dates from 1181 and is the only surviving example of Song architecture in Sūzhōu. Your extra Y20 buys you a short music and cymbal performance.

Tours

Evening boat tours wind their way around the outer canal leaving nightly from 7pm to 8.30pm (Y35, 80 minutes, half-hourly). The trips are good fun and a great way to experience old Sūzhōu. Remember to bring bug repellent as the mosquitos are tenacious. Tickets can be bought at the port near Rénmín Bridge, which shares the same quarters with the Grand Canal boat ticket office (划船售票处; Huáchuán Shòupiàochù).

Festivals & Events

Every September Sūzhōu hosts the **Sūzhōu Silk Festival**. There are exhibitions devoted to silk history and production, and silk merchants get to show off their wares to crowds of thousands.

Sleeping

Sūzhōu has little to offer in the way of cheap accommodation. Hotels, in general, are terribly overpriced for what you get. On a more positive note, it's often possible to bargain room prices down, so don't be immediately deterred by the posted rates.

Sūzhōu Mingtown Youth Hostel HOSTEL $
(苏州浮生四季青年旅舍; Sūzhōu Míngtáng Qīngnián Lǚshè; ☎6581 6869; 28 Pingjiang Lu; 平江路28号; 6-bed dm Y50, r Y140-180; ❄@) Sūzhōu's most pleasant youth hostel by a long shot, this lovely place is located canalside in a traditional part of town rich in old-world flavour (if you overlook the trendy cafes). No effort has been spared to create an elegant atmosphere, and even dorms come with dark wooden 'antique' furniture. The only thing that bugs us is hot water: it's only on in the mornings and after 7pm. There's free internet, free washing, and bike rental (Y10 for four hours); the inhouse Mingtown Cafe is next door.

Píngjiāng Lodge BOUTIQUE HOTEL $$$
(苏州平江客栈; Sūzhōu Píngjiāng Kèzhàn; ☎6523 2888; www.pingjianglodge.com; 33 Niujia Xiang; 钮家巷33号; r Y988-2588, discounts of up to 50%; ❄@) Fab little hotel spread across two 400-year-old residences. There are well-kept gardens, quiet courtyards and rooms are splashed out in traditional furniture. Rooms at the pointy end are suites with split-level living spaces and beautiful bathrooms. Standard rooms are lovely too.

Pan Pacific Sūzhōu HOTEL $$$
(苏州吴宫泛太平洋酒店; Sūzhōu Wúgōng Fàntàipíngyáng Dàjiǔdiàn; ☎6510 3388; www.panpacific.com/Suzhou; 259 Xinshi Lu; 新市路259号; d Y1268) While this former Sheraton hotel has been rebranded, its five-star luxury still makes the grade. We can't decide if the place looks like the Forbidden City or the US Embassy, but its pseudo-Ming-style rooms are luxurious and fitted with all the latest gadgets to make you happy. Porcelain vases and a small garden connected to each room are nice touches that you won't see elsewhere.

Sūzhōu Joya Youth Hostel HOSTEL $
(苏州小雅国际青年旅舍; Sūzhōu Xiǎoyǎ Guójì Qīngnián Lûshè; ☎6755 1752; www.joyahostel.com; 1/21 Daxinqiao Xiang; 大新桥巷1/21号; dm/d/tr Y60/120/180; ❄@) A good alternative if Mingtown is booked out. Joya is set off the main strip in a quiet lane in an 1883 residence, complete with floral lattice windows and many original wooden beams. Rooms are small, but have high ceilings and open out onto courtyards. Wi-fi, internet (Y3 per hour) and bike rental.

Hotel Soul HOTEL $$$
(苏哥李酒店; Sūgēlǐ Jiǔdiàn; ☎6777 0777; www.hotelsoul.com.cn; 27-33 Qiaosikong Xiang; 乔司空巷27-33号, d & tw Y1080-1680; ❄) This brand-spanking-new Philippe Starck–wannabe has a lot of sharp angles and neon blue lights but not much soul. It is, however, very good value. Rooms are huge with textured wallpaper, plush beds and tones that make you want to order a martini. Service staff are eager and attentive. There were buy one night, get one night free specials during the time of research.

Nánlín Hotel HOTEL $$
(南林饭店; Nánlín Fàndiàn; ☎6519 6333; 20 Gunxiufang; 滚绣坊20号; d incl breakfast Y1380) Set in a large, tree-filled compound entered off Shiquan Jie and surrounded by gardens, the tasteful rooms in this modern hotel are dressed in shades of mahogany and cream. Management is courteous and helpful. Discounts knocked rooms down to Y588 during time of research.

Eating

Plentiful restaurants can be found along Guanqian Jie, especially down the road from the Temple of Mystery. Shiquan Jie, between Daichengqiao Lu and Xiangwang Lu, is lined with bars, restaurants and bakeries.

Some local delicacies to try are *sōngshǔ guìyú* (松鼠鳜鱼; sweet-and-sour mandarin fish), *xiāngyóu shànhú* (香油鳝糊; stewed shredded eel) and *xīguā jī* (西瓜鸡; chicken placed in watermelon rind and steamed).

Pingvon TEAHOUSE $
(品芳; Pǐnfāng; 94 Pingjiang Lu; dishes from Y4; 📋) A cute little teahouse perched beside one of Sūzhōu's most popular canalside streets. Pingvon serves up excellent dumplings and delicate little morsels in baskets and on small plates. Try the green tea Buddha biscuit and pan-fried dumplings.

Xīshèngyuán DUMPLINGS $
(熙盛源; 43 Fenghuang Jie; dumplings from Y6) Crowds pay and gather near the entrance to wait for the steaming fresh *xiǎolóng bāo* (小龙包; soup dumplings; Y6) to come out of the kitchen. If you don't want to jostle, grab a seat and order several other great dishes including assorted *húntūn* (馄饨; dumplings; Y6 to Y10).

Yàkèxī UIGHUR $$
(亚克西酒楼; Yàkèxī Jiǔlóu; 768 Shiquan Jie; mains Y40; ⏲10am-2am) The Uighur kitsch atmosphere is entertaining and the Xīnjiāng staples – lamb kebabs (Y2.50), hot and spicy lamb soup (Y16) and *nang* bread (Y3) – all tasty. Round it off with a bottle of SinKiang beer (Y10) or a sour milk drink (Y8) and dream of Kashgar. No time to sit down? The lamb kebabs are grilled just outside.

Zhūhóngxìng Miànguǎn NOODLES $
(朱鸿兴; Taijian Long; mains Y20-30) Popular with locals, this eatery, with several branches across town, has a long history and wholesome, filling noodles – try the *xiānglà páigǔmiàn* (香辣排骨面; salty pork and noodles; Y15) or the scrummy *cōngyóu xiānggūmiàn* (葱油香菇面, onion oil and mushroom noodles, Y10). Note: there's no English menu.

Déyuè Lóu CHINESE $$$

(得月楼; ☎6523 8940; 43 Taijian Long; mains Y30-120; ⏰24hr; 📋) Across the way from Zhūhóngxìng Miànguǎn, this place has been around since the Ming dynasty, with a menu featuring over 300 items and an emphasis on freshwater fish. It's a popular stop for tour groups and for large wedding parties, and feels a little over the top at times.

Drinking

Bustling Shiquan Jie surges late into the night, but prices are dear. There are also stacks of trendy cafe-bars scattered along Pingjiang Lu.

Bookworm CAFE-BAR

(老书虫; Lǎo Shūchóng; 77 Gunxiu Fang; ⏰9am-1am) Beijing's Bookworm has wormed its way down to Sūzhōu, although the selection isn't as good as Beijing's. The service could be a little quicker but the food is crowd pleasers (lots of Western options) and the beer is cold and includes Tsingtao (Y15) and Erdinger (Y45), as well as coffee (from Y10). There are occasional events and books you can borrow or buy. Just off Shiquan Jie.

Jane's Pub PUB

(621 Shiquan Jie; ⏰7pm-3am) With Guinness on tap (per pint Y55), Chimay and Duvel for more discerning palates, obligatory foreign banknotes stapled to the bar, pool and the occasional live singer (from 9pm), Jane's musters enough appeal for those that like an old-fashioned rough and tumble bar.

☆ Entertainment

Kūnqǔ Opera Museum CHINESE OPERA

(昆曲博物馆; Kūnqǔ Bówùguǎn; 14 Zhongzhangjia Xiang; tickets Y20) Puts on occasional performances of *kūnqǔ*. At the time of publication, there were *shūoshū* (说书, storytelling, including tea Y20) sessions.

Garden of the Master of the Nets MUSIC

(网师园; Wǎngshī Yuán; tickets Y100) From March to November, music performances are held nightly from 7.30pm to 9.30pm for tourist groups at this garden. Don't expect anything too authentic.

Píngtán Museum TRADITIONAL SINGING

(评弹博物馆; Píngtán Bówùguǎn; 3 Zhongzhangjia Xiang; tickets Y4-5) Better shows than at 'Garden of the Master of the Nets' are performed here at 1.30pm daily. Tickets on sale at noon.

Shopping

Sūzhōu-style embroidery, calligraphy, paintings, sandalwood fans, writing brushes and silk underclothes are for sale nearly everywhere. For good-quality items at competitive rates, shop along Shiquan Jie, east off Renmin Lu, which is lined with shops and markets selling souvenirs. The northern part of Renmin Lu has a number of large silk stores (丝绸商店; Sīchóu Shāngdiàn).

Xīnhuá Bookshop BOOKS

(新华书店; Xīnhuá Shūdiàn; 166 Guanqian Jie; ⏰9am-9pm) Sells a variety of English- and Chinese-language maps. Stodgy English novels on the 4th floor.

Information

Major tourist hotels have foreign-exchange counters.

Bank of China (中国银行; Zhōngguó Yínháng; 1450 Renmin Lu) Changes travellers cheques and foreign cash. There are ATMs that take international cards at most larger branches of the Bank of China.

China Post (中国邮政; Zhōngguó Yóuzhèng; cnr Renmin Lu & Jingde Lu)

Hóng Qīngtíng Internet Cafe (红蜻蜓网吧; Hóng Qīngtíng Wǎngbā; 916 Shiquan Jie; per hr Y2.50; ⏰24hr)

Industrial & Commercial Bank of China (工商银行; Gōngshāng Yínháng; 222 Guanqian Jie) 24-hour ATM.

No 1 Hospital (苏大附一院; Sūdà Fùyīyuàn; 96 Shizi Jie) There are numerous other hospitals in Sūzhōu.

Public Security Bureau (PSB; 公安局; Gōng'ānjú; ☎6522 5661, ext 20593; 1109 Renmin Lu) Can help with emergencies and visa problems. The visa office is about 200m down a lane called Dashitou Xiang.

Sūzhōu Tourism Information Center (苏州旅游咨询中心; Sūzhōu Lǚyóu Zīxún Zhōngxīn; ☎6530 5887; www.classicsuzhou.com; 345 Shiquan Jie) Several branches in town including bus stations. Can help with booking accommodation and tours. Festival listings and general information on website.

Getting There & Away

Air

Sūzhōu does not have an airport, but **China Eastern Airlines** (东方航空公司; Dōngfāng Hángkōng Gōngsī; ☎6522 2788; 115 Ganjiang Lu) can help with booking flights out of Shànghǎi. Buses leave here frequently for Hóngqiáo Airport in Shànghǎi. Tickets are Y50.

PÍNGTÁN: TRADITIONAL STORYTELLING IN SŪZHŌU'S HEART

SHAWN LOW

One of the great beauties of the job is stumbling upon a hidden gem when you least expect it. In this case, tiny words in Chinese which said 'tea' and '*pingtan*' caught my eye. Curiosity followed by 'Oh, what the hell' led me into a tiny corridor and up a creaky staircase into a delightful **Pingtan Teahouse** (评弹茶馆; Píngtán Cháguǎn; 2nd fl, 626 Shiquan Jie).

The owner, Mei Mei, was quick to explain. Each night, a *píngtán* master takes the stage from 8pm to 10pm. Customers order tea (the speciality is Yunnan pu'er, unlimited serves from Y100) and pick songs (from Y45) for the master to play.

For the uninitiated (myself included), *píngtán* is a 400-year-old storytelling and singing art form, sung in the local dialect and often accompanied by traditional instruments. The stories tend to revolve around Chinese classics such as *The Three Kingdoms* (a warring period from AD 220 to 280). Done well, it's an enchanting blend of singing and strings that emotes the themes behind most of these tunes. Done poorly? Think wailing cats.

I lucked out. It seems that the teahouse is a favourite gathering spot for *píngtán* enthusiasts and local musicians. That night, while the tea flowed, different masters continually took to the stage and sang a large variety of songs until it was past 11pm. When they all left, drunk on tea and music, Mei Mei took it upon herself to give me a quick music lesson on the *gǔzhēng* (zither) and *pípá* (lute). I finally made it out past midnight with a three-note repertoire, and ancient tunes in my head that kept steady time with my heartbeat.

Mei Mei left me with this parting quote, 'I'm not doing this for the money...I really like folk music and pu'er tea. It seemed to make sense to put the two together. And I get to provide a place where *píngtán* enthusiasts can meet to keep the traditions alive.'

Rock on...I mean, sing and strum on!

Boat

You can get tickets for the Sūzhōu to Hángzhōu boat (Y80 to Y210, 11 hours, 5.30pm daily) at the **Liánhé Ticket Centre** (联合售票处; Liánhé Shòupiàochù; ☎6520 6681; 1606 Renmin Lu; ⏲8am-5pm). Boats leave from the wharf at 306 Renmin Lu.

Bus

Sūzhōu has three long-distance bus stations and the two listed are the most useful. Tickets for all buses can also be bought at the **Liánhé Ticket Centre** (Liánhé Shòupiàochù; 1606 Renmin Lu; ⏲bus tickets 8.30-11.30am & 1-5pm).

The principal station is the **North long-distance bus station** (汽车北站; qìchē běizhàn; ☎6577 6577) at the northern end of Renmin Lu, next to the train station:

Hángzhōu Y69, two hours, regular services

Nánjīng Y70, 2½ hours, regular services

Níngbō Y119, four hours, seven daily

Yángzhōu Y71, three hours, regular services

Buses from the **South long-distance bus station** (汽车南站; qìchē nánzhàn; cnr Yingchun Lu & Nanhuan Donglu) has buses to:

Hángzhōu Y70, two hours, every 20 minutes

Nánjīng Y70, two hours, every 20 minutes

Shànghǎi Y33, 1½ hours, every 30 minutes

Shèngzén Y14.50, one hour, every 15 minutes

Yángzhōu Y71, two hours, hourly

Train

Sūzhōu is on the Nánjīng–Shànghǎi express D line. Book train tickets on the 2nd floor of the **Liánhé Ticket Centre** (Liánhé Shòupiàochù; 1606 Renmin Lu; ⏲train tickets 7.30-11am & noon-5pm). There's also a **ticket office** along Guanqian Jie across from the Temple of Mystery. Another **ticket office** can be found on the other side of the road from the South bus station.

Běijīng hard/soft sleeper Y158/256, 10 hours, one daily (1.10pm)

Nánjīng Y33, 2½ hours, frequent services

Shànghǎi Y31, 30 minutes, 20 daily

Wúxī Y12, 30 minutes, frequent services

ℹ Getting Around

Bicycle

Riding a bike is the best way to see Sūzhōu, though nutty drivers and traffic can be nerve jangling, especially around the train station. Search out the quieter streets and travel along the canals to get the most of what this city has to offer.

The **Yángyáng Bike Rental Shop** (洋洋车行; Yángyáng Chēháng; 2061 Renmin Lu; ⏲7am to 6pm), a short walk north of the Silk Museum, offers bike rentals (Y20 per day plus Y200 deposit). Check out the seat and brakes carefully before you pedal off.

Public Transport

Sūzhōu has some convenient tourist buses that visit all sights and cost Y2. They all pass by the train station. Buses with a snowflake motif are air-conditioned.

Bus Y5 Goes around the western and eastern sides of the city.

Bus Y2 Travels from Tiger Hill, Pán Gate and along Shiquan Jie.

Buses Y1 & **Y4** run the length of Renmin Lu.

At the time of writing, Sūzhōu was constructing its first metro line. The first line is expected to be completed by the end of 2010.

Taxi

There are plenty of taxis in Sūzhōu. Fares start at Y10 and drivers generally use their meters. A trip from Guanqian Jie to the train station should cost around Y15. Pedicabs hover around the tourist areas and can be persistent (Y5 for short rides is standard). There are also drivers who might offer you rides – avoid unless you know how much a taxi ride costs and get offered that.

Around Sūzhōu

Sūzhōu's tourist brochures offer a mind-boggling array of sights around the town. Sadly, not all are great, and noteworthy ones are often overrun by tourists. Go early to avoid the crowds.

TÓNGLǏ 同里

☎0512

The lovely canal town of Tónglǐ, only 18km southeast of Sūzhōu, has been around since at least the 9th century and is *the* sight to visit outside Sūzhōu. Rich in historic canal-side atmosphere and weather-beaten charm, many of Tónglǐ's buildings have kept their traditional facades, with stark whitewashed walls (faded white if you venture off the tourist trails), black-tiled roofs, cobblestone pathways and willow-shaded canal views adding to a picturesque allure.

You can reach Tónglǐ from either Sūzhōu or Shànghǎi, but aim for a weekday visit.

Sights

The **Old Town** (老城区; Lǎochéngqū; ☎6333 1140; admission Y80; ⏲7.30am-5.30pm) of Tónglǐ is best explored the traditional way: aimlessly meandering the canals and alleys until you get lost. The whitewashed houses and laundry hanging out to dry are all so charming that it doesn't really matter where you go, as long as you can elude the crowds.

There are three old residences that you'll pass at some point (unless you're really lost), the best of which is **Gēnglè Táng** (耕乐堂), a sprawling Ming-dynasty estate with 52 halls spread out over five courtyards in the west of town. The buildings have been elaborately restored and redecorated with paintings, calligraphy and antique furniture to bring back the atmosphere of the original buildings.

In the north of town is the **Pearl Pagoda** (珍珠塔; Zhēnzhū Tǎ), which dates from the Qing dynasty but has recently been restored. Inside, you'll find a large residential compound decorated with Qing-era antiques, an ancestral hall, a garden and an opera stage. The place gets its name from a tiny pagoda draped in pearls.

In the east of the Old Town you'll find **Tuìsī Garden** (退思园; Tuìsī Yuán), a gorgeous 19th-century garden that delightfully translates as the 'Withdraw and Reflect Garden', so named because it was a Qing government official's retirement home. The Tower of Fanning Delight served as the living quarters, while the garden itself is a lovely portrait of pond water churning with outsized goldfish, rockeries and pavilions, caressed by traditional Chinese music. It's a lovely place to find a perch and drift into a reverie, unless you are outflanked by a marauding tour group.

Last but not least and definitely not for infant Tónglǐ-goers, you can't miss the **Chinese Sex Culture Museum** (中华性文化博物馆; Zhōnghuá Xìngwénhuà Bówùguǎn; admission Y20; ⏲9am-5.30pm). If you thought Confucius was a prude, think again.

Slow-moving **six-person boats** (Y40/70 for 30/60 minutes) ply the waters of Tónglǐ's canal system. The boat trip on Tónglǐ Lake is free, though of no particular interest.

Sleeping & Eating

Guesthouses (客栈, *kèzhàn*) are plentiful, with basic rooms starting at about Y80. Restaurants are everywhere, but resist being steered towards the priciest dishes. Some local dishes to try include *méigāncàishāoròu*

FIVE THOUSAND YEARS OF EROTICA

Overall, there's not a whole lot distinguishing one canal town from another, and whichever one you choose to visit is ultimately a matter of either convenience or fate (or both). Tónglǐ, however, does have an X-rated trump card up its sleeve, it's the **Chinese Sex Culture Museum**. Unfortunately, the name deters most people from even considering a visit (visitors tentatively approach, see the sign, giggle, blush and turn around), though in reality it is not that racy.

Founded by sociology professors Liu Dalin and Hu Hongxia, the museum's aim is not so much to arouse, but rather to reintroduce an aspect of the country's culture that, ironically, has been forcefully repressed since China was 'liberated' in 1949. The pair have collected several thousand artefacts relating to sex, from the good (erotic landscape paintings, fans and teacups) to the bad (chastity belts and saddles with wooden dildos used to punish 'licentious' women and 'zoophilia' statues), and the humorous (satirical Buddhist statues) to the unusual (a pot-bellied immortal with a penis growing out of his head topped by a turtle). This is also one of the only places in the country where homosexuality is openly recognised as part of Chinese culture.

Though some of the exhibits seem a little forced (a stone pillar displayed represents a 'penis'? That's stretching it), and the one-too-many pictures of penis- and vagina-shaped rocks will elicit schoolboy giggles, it's worth a visit simply because there isn't anything like this anywhere else in China.

(梅干菜烧肉; stewed meat with dried vegetables), *yínyúchǎodàn* (银鱼炒蛋; silver fish omelette) and *zhuàngyuángtí* (状元蹄; stewed pig's leg). Annoyingly, food prices here are much dearer than Sūzhōu.

Zhèngfú Cǎotáng BOUTIQUE HOTEL $$$
(正福草堂; ☎6333 6358; www.zfct.net; 138 Mingqing Jie; 明清街138号; d Y380-1380; ❄@) The best accommodation in town. There are 14 deluxe rooms, all tastefully furnished in Qing-style furniture and antiques. Rooms wouldn't be out of place in a *Wallpaper* spread, with hues of gold and brown, and ultramodern toilets. The larger, more expensive rooms have private spaces for musing.

Tongli International Youth Hostel HOSTEL $
(同里国际青年旅舍; ☎6333 9311; 210 Xintian Jie; 新填街210号; dm Y40, r Y100-160; ❄@📶) Rejoice! Tónglǐ finally has a youth hostel! The main location is hard to find (walk across the main bridge onto 中川北路, look on your right for a sign that says 根和民居 and walk inside the tiny alley), but it's a stunner. Rooms are decked out in the owner's antique Ming furniture, and the wooden pillars and stone courtyard ooze atmosphere. Dorms were being built at the time of research but will lack the antique charm of the regular rooms. The alternate location beside Taiping bridge only has tight dorm beds.

ℹ Getting There & Away

From Sūzhōu, take a bus (Y8, 50 minutes, every 30 minutes) from the South long-distance bus station to Tónglǐ. Grab an electric cart (Y2) from beside the Tongli bus station to the Old Town, or you can walk it in about 15 minutes. Pedicabs might offer you rides into town to dodge the entry fee but you really need the ticket to see the sights in the town so avoid them.

Buses return to Sūzhōu every 30 minutes (last bus 7.25pm). The last bus to drop you at the South long-distance bus station departs at 4.30pm. Buses thereafter drop you off behind Súzhóu's train station.

From Shànghǎi, sightseeing buses depart daily from the Shànghǎi Stadium at 8.30am (and depart from Tónglǐ at 4.30pm); the journey takes up to 1¾ hours depending on traffic. Tickets are Y130 and include admission to Tónglǐ and its sights, bar the Chinese Sex Culture Museum. Ten daily buses (Y32) leave Tónglǐ bus station for Shànghǎi.

LÙZHÍ 甪直

Only a 25km public bus trip southeast of Sūzhōu, this minute canal town has bundles of charm. The entrance ticket of Y60 can be skipped if you just want to wander the streets, alleys and bridges – you only have to pay if you enter the top **tourist sights** (⏲8am-5pm), such as the **Wànshèng Rice Warehouse** (万盛米行; Wànshèng Mǐháng) and the **Bǎoshèng Temple** (保圣寺; Bǎoshèng Sì), but these can be missed without detracting from the overall experience.

Lùzhí's bridges are delightful: the **Jìnlì Bridge** (进利桥; Jìnlì Qiáo) is a typically attractive humpbacked bridge and the **Xīnglóng Bridge** (兴隆桥; Xīnglóng Qiáo) dates to the 15th century. Taking a half-hour **boat ride** (Y40) is an excellent way to sample the canal views. Boats depart from several points, including the Yǒng'ān Bridge (永安桥; Yǒng'ān Qiáo).

The place is popular with local teenagers who come to get photos taken in period dresses so don't feel like you've stepped into a time warp when you encounter a lady, dressed in silk, plucking a *gǔzhēng* (zither) – look closely and you'll see sport shoes under the dress. At the time of research, a huge faux Ming-dynasty complex, the **Lùzhí Cultural Park** (甪直文化园), was due for completion. Expect a variety of tourist shops, landscaped gardens, ponds and pavilions upon completion in 2011.

There are very few places to spend the night in Lùzhí, but the town easily works as a day trip. **Lóngxìng Kèzhàn** (龙兴客栈; ☎6501 0749; 53 Zhongshi Jie; 中市街53号; d with shower Y80) is a quiet place with basic rooms, just by the canal. There are also various other guesthouses with similar rates.

To get to Lùzhí, take bus 518 from Sūzhōu's train station (Y4, one hour, first/last bus 6am/8pm) or from the bus stop on Pingqi Lu (平齐路) to the last stop. When you get off, take the first right along Dasheng Lu (达圣路) to the decorative arch; crossing the bridge takes you into the back of the old town, a five-minute walk. Hordes of pedicabs will descend upon you offering to take you to the main entrance. Pay no more than Y5.

The last bus back from Lùzhí is at 7.30pm. If you want to continue to Shànghǎi from Lùzhí, buses (Y18, two hours) from the Lùzhí bus station run from 6.20am to 5pm to the bus station at 806 North Zhongshan Rd in Shànghǎi (from where buses also regularly run to Lùzhí).

MÙDÚ 木渎

Easily reached from the city centre, Mùdú adds a further dimension to the Sūzhōu experience. Originally dating to the Ming dynasty and once the haunt of wealthy officials, intellectuals and artists, the village of Mùdú has been swallowed up by Sūzhōu's growing urban sprawl. Mùdú even attracted the Qing Emperor Qianlong, who visited six times. While Mùdú is neither the largest nor the most appealing of Jiāngsū's canal towns, it makes for a convenient half-day tour.

Mùdú is free if you merely want to soak up the atmosphere – the entrance fee is for the top sights. Sadly, as most of the buildings along the canal are now modern structures, it's actually worth shelling out the admission fees.

Sights

Near the entrance to the **Old Town** (老城区; Lǎochéngqū; ☎6636 8225; admission Y60; ⏲8am-4.30pm) is the dignified **Bǎngyǎn Mansion** (榜眼府第; Bǎngyǎn Fǔdì) of the 19th-century writer and politician Feng Guifen. It has a rich collection of antique furniture and intricate carvings of stone, wood and brick – it often does part-time duties as a movie set. The surrounding garden is pretty but fairly typical – lotus ponds, arched bridges, bamboo – and can't compare to the more ornate gardens of Sūzhōu.

By far the most interesting place in Mùdú is the **Hóngyǐn Mountain Villa** (虹饮山房; Hóngyǐn Shānfáng), with its elaborate opera stage, exhibits and even an imperial pier where Emperor Qianlong docked his boat. The stage in the centre hall is impressive; honoured guests were seated in front and the galleries along the sides of the hall were for women. The emperor was a frequent visitor and you can see his uncomfortable-looking imperial chair, which faces the stage. Said chair is over 1000 years old, worn smooth in spots where hands have touched it. Operas are still performed here during the day. Surrounding the stage are some carefully arranged gardens, criss-crossed with dainty arched bridges and walkways. The old residence halls have been wonderfully preserved and have some interesting exhibits, including displays of dusty hats and gowns worn by imperial officers. Look out for the display on the Manchu-Han imperial feast: 111 faux-plastic dishes (we counted!) are on display. There's everything from abalone to fish, whole suckling pig and dainty bread buns made to look like rabbits!

In the middle of Shantang Jie is the **Ancient Pine Garden** (古松园; Gǔsōngyuán), known for its intricately carved beams. Look out for wooden impressions of officials, hats, phoenixes, flowers and stuff most people can't identify.

In the northwest corner of the Old Town is the **Yan Family Garden** (严家花园; Yánjiā Huāyuán), which dates back to the

Ming dynasty and was once the home of a former magistrate. The garden, with its rockeries and a meandering lake, is separated into five sections and divided by walls, with each section meant to invoke a season. Flowers, plants and rocks are arranged to create a 'mood'. If you come during the weekend, the only mood the crowds might invoke is exasperation – it's more inspiring to come on a weekday, when you can enjoy the surroundings in peace.

The most pleasurable way to experience Mùdú is by **boat**. You'll find a collection of traditional skiffs docked outside the Bǎngyǎn Mansion. A ride in one of these will take you along the narrow canals, shaded by ancient bridges and battered stone walls. Boat rides are Y10 per person (Y30 per boat minimum charge).

Getting There & Away

From Sūzhōu, tourist bus Y4 runs from the train station to Mùdú (Y3). Get off at Mùdú Yánjiā Huāyuán Zhàn (木渎严家花园站), across from a small road (明清街; Míngqīng Jīe) leading to the main entrance. You'll see a big sign and a parking lot full of tour buses. The ride takes about 45 minutes.

From Shànghǎi, deluxe buses (Y120, two hours) run from the Shànghǎi Sightseeing Bus Centre directly to Mùdú every other Saturday at 8.30am, returning from Mùdú at 3.30pm; the ticket price includes entrance to Mùdú's sights. Alternatively, take a bus or train to Sūzhōu and switch to tourist bus 4 at the train station.

TIĀNPÍNGSHĀN & LÌNGYÁNGSHĀN 天平山、灵岩山

These two mountains (OK, so they're really large hills) are along the same bus route to Mùdú and can be combined in one long day trip. Scenic **Tiānpíngshān** (Lingtian Lu; admission Y18; 7.30am-5pm) is a low, forested hill about 13km west of Sūzhōu. It's a wonderful place for hiking or just meandering along one of its many wooded trails. It's also famous for its medicinal spring waters.

Eleven kilometres southwest of Sūzhōu is **Língyánshān** (Lingtian Lu; admission Y20; 8am-4.30pm winter, to 5pm summer), or 'Cliff of the Spirits', once the site of a palace where Emperor Qianlong stayed during his inspection tours of the Yangzi River valley. Now the mountain is home to an active Buddhist monastery. It's a gorgeous place and the climb to the peak is exhausting in a really good way. On the way up, take the path on the left for an exciting clamber over rough-hewn stone and paths. The summit offers panoramic views of the area: you'll note the alarming encroachment of industry onto green spaces.

Tourist bus 4 goes to Língyánshān and Tiānpíngshān from Sūzhōu's train station.

Yángzhōu 扬州

0514 / POP 0.55 MILLION

Yángzhōu, a modern city near the junction of the Grand Canal and the Yangzi River, was once an economic and cultural centre of southern China. The city prospered on the salt trade, attracting merchants and artisans who established residences and gardens. Today, the central portion of the city is a fairly sedate area with pockets of old buildings. The main drawcard here is the large and delightful Slender West Lake Park. Yángzhōu can be visited on a day or overnight trip from Nánjīng.

Sights & Activities

Yángzhōu's sights are concentrated around the Grand Canal in the north and northwest parts of the city, where you'll find Slender West Lake Park and Dàmíng Temple. The main shopping area radiates out from Wénchāng Gé (文昌阁), an old bell tower in the centre of town.

A combined ticket to the city sights includes Slender West Lake Park, a canal boat ride, Dàmíng Temple, Hé, Gè and Potted Plant gardens and is Y180.

Slender West Lake Park GARDEN
(瘦西湖公园; Shòuxīhú Gōngyuán; 28 Da Hongqiao Lu; admission Y90; 6.30am-5pm) Stretching noodle-like northwards from Da Hongqiao Lu towards Dàmíng Temple, this park is decorated with pretty willow- and peach-tree-lined banks dotted with pavilions and gardens. It was a favourite vacationing spot of Emperor Qianlong in the 18th century and it's not hard to imagine why as it's particular moving and moody on a misty day, yet cheerful and colourful in good light.

A highlight is the exquisite triple-arched **Five Pavilion Bridge** (五亭桥; Wǔtíng Qiáo), built in 1757. Another interesting structure is the **24 Bridge** (二十四桥; Èrshísì Qiáo), its back arched high enough to almost form a complete circle, allowing boats easy passage.

The combined ticket to Slender West Lake Park includes a **river cruise** along the Grand Canal (which looks like one huge

THE GRAND CANAL

The world's longest canal, the Grand Canal (大运河; Dàyùnhé) once meandered for almost 1800km from Běijīng to Hángzhōu, and is a striking example of China's engineering prowess. Sections of the canal have been silted up for centuries and today perhaps half of it remains seasonally navigable.

The Grand Canal's construction spanned many centuries. The first 85km were completed in 495 BC, but the mammoth task of linking the Yellow River (Huáng Hé) and the Yangzi River (Cháng Jiāng) was undertaken between AD 605–609 by a massive conscripted labour force during Sui times. It was developed again during the Yuan dynasty (1271–1368). The canal enabled the government to capitalise on the growing wealth of the Yellow River basin and to ship supplies from south to north.

The Jiāngnán section of the canal (Hángzhōu, Sūzhōu, Wúxī and Chángzhōu) is a skein of canals, rivers and branching lakes. Passenger vessels run between Sūzhōu and Hángzhōu (see p227).

There are boat rides along certain sections of the canal in Sūzhōu (p224) and Yángzhōu – with all the surrounding modernity though the grandness of the project seems to have all but faded.

drain) on the eastern length of the city. Board on the docks in the northeastern point of the city along Tàizhōlù (泰州路). The trip takes you under several bridges and past condominiums and city life. Boy, things sure have changed since the old days.

Gè Garden GARDEN

(个园;Gè Yuán; 10 Yanfu Donglu; admission Y45; ⌚7.15am-5.45pm) With its crooked pathways, dense bamboo groves and humpback bridges, this garden, east of the city centre, is typically southern-styled. Built in 1883, it was once the home of the painter Shi Tao and was later acquired by an affluent salt merchant. The traditional residences at the rear are well restored and offer a glimpse into Yangzhou's former affluence. Bus Y1 and Y2 pass the garden.

The entrance to the main south gate of Gè Garden sits on a particularly atmospheric old street. **Dōngguān Jīe** (东关街) is a restored strip of grey brick houses dating back to the Yuan dynasty. These days, it's packed with stores selling souvenirs, peanut candy and snacks. You can venture into the side alleys to get a glimpse of local life. The large city gate marking the start of the street used to be where traders would enter the city when they disembarked from the Yangzhou section of the Grand Canal.

Hé Garden GARDEN

(何园;Hé Yuán; 77 Xuningmen Jie; admission Y45; ⌚7.30am-6pm) This tiny garden in the south of the city was built by a Qing-dynasty salt merchant. It boasts more buildings than actual garden, with airy pavilions and halls surrounded by tree-lined pathways, bamboo and convoluted rockery. The central portion is home to a Frankenstein 'West meets East' building, an architectural style popular in the late Qing period.

Sleeping

Yángzhōu is tragically lacking in anything more than midrange Chinese-style hotels. Your best bet are midrange chain hotels.

Yuqinting Boutique Hotel HOTEL $$

(玉蜻蜓雅致酒店; Yùqīngtíng Yǎzhìjiǔdiàn; ☎8736 0000; 42 Wenhe Beilu; 汶河北路52号; d & tw Y480-680; ❄@) More tacky, less boutique Yuqinting offers large rooms (Y300 discounted) with flat-screen TVs and smart modern bathrooms. The cheaper unrenovated rooms (Y259 discounted) are ordinary and some are windowless. The hotel still has the old 'Lantian Hotel' sign and the unmissable lobby is decked out in gaudily coloured lights and faux Louis XIV furnishings.

Bǎihuì International Youth Hostel HOSTEL $

(百汇国际青年旅舍; Bǎihuì Guójì Qīngnián Lûshè; ☎130 5633 8583; 148 Daxue Beilu; 大学北路148号; 4-bed dm Y35-50, s Y80-128, d 80-138; ❄@📶) Quite hard to spot as it's tucked away down an alley, this place has decent (if old) rooms and friendly staff. It also has a pool table and a kitchen, and there's free internet and wi-fi. Lots of eating options nearby and it's walking distance to Slender West Lake Park.

Motel 168 HOTEL $$
(莫泰连锁旅店; Mòtài Liánsuǒ Lǚdiàn; ☎8793 9555; www.motel168.com; 52 Wenhe Beilu; 汶河北路52号; d Y208-228; ❄) Pretty much offering the same kind of rooms as the other budget chain Home Inn (and in virtually the same spot), but right on Wenhe Beilu. No-frills convenience.

Eating

Along Da Hongqiao Lu, leading to the entrance to Slender West Lake Park, are a string of small restaurants selling fried rice and other dishes. Wenhe Beilu in the heart of the city is also plastered with food shops of all sorts.

Chóngqìng Tiāncì CHONGQING & SICHUAN $$
(重庆天赐; ☎8723 3198; 154 Siwangting Lu; dishes Y8-38; ⏰10am-9pm) This busy restaurant serves up a range of Chongqing and Sichuan dishes. Particularly popular are the fish dishes such as the stingingly spicy water-cooked fish (水煮鱼; *shuǐzhǔyú*). After you decide how heavy the fish should be, staff will take you round the back, where a lady picks out a live one, weighs it and thumps it on the head. Thankfully, there's ice-cold Tsingtao (Y8). Picture menu.

Fùchūn Cháshè TEAHOUSE $$
(富春茶社; ☎723 3326; 35 Desheng Qiao; mains Y10-30; ⏰8am-9pm) One of Yángzhōu's most famous and crowded teahouses, this place is on a lane just off Guoqing Lu, in an older section of town. Try an assorted plate of its famous dumplings for Y30.

Information

Bank of China (中国银行; Zhōngguó Yínháng; 279 Wenchang Zhonglu) Will change travellers cheques and cash. There's an ATM.

China Post (中国邮政; Zhōngguó Yóuzhèng; 162 Wenchang Zhonglu) In the city centre.

Fēishí Internet Cafe (飞时网吧; Fēishí Wǎngbā; Daxue Beilu; per hr Y2; ⏰24hr) Just north of the Bǎihuì International Youth Hostel.

Public Security Bureau (PSB; 公安局; Gōng'ānjú; 1 Huaihai Lu) Can help with visa extensions.

Getting There & Away

From the **Yángzhōu long-distance bus station** (扬州汽车站; Yángzhōu Qìchēzhàn; Jiangyang Zhong Lu; ☎8796 3658) in the west of town, there are buses to the following destinations:

Shànghǎi Y101, 4½ hours, two to four daily

Sūzhōu Y78, three hours, regular services

Nánjīng Y34, two hours, regular services

The **train station** (扬州火车站; Yángzhōu Huǒchēzhàn; Wenchang Xilu) is west of town. There are trains to Guǎngzhōu (Y219 to Y600, 26 hours, 4.14pm) that pass through Nánjīng and Huángshān. Trains to Shànghǎi (Y97, 5½ hours, 12.16pm) pass through Nánjīng, Zhènjiāng, Wúxī and Sūzhōu. There's a direct train to Běijīng (Y272 to Y429, 14 hours, 8.30pm).

Getting Around

Bus 20 (Y1) runs to the long-distance bus station along Siwangting Lu. The tourist buses Y1 and Y2 start from the long-distance bus station and do loops around the city, hitting many of the sights. Taxis are cheap and start at Y7.

Zhèjiāng

POPULATION: 47 MILLION

Includes »

Best Places to Eat

» Grandma's Kitchen (p242)

» Moganshan Lodge (p246)

» Zhōujiā Shípǐn (p250)

Best Places to Stay

» Mingtown Youth Hostel (p241)

» Moganshan House 23 (p246)

» Shaoxing International Youth Hostel (p250)

Why Go?

Zhèjiāng's prized drawcard is its good-looking and much-visited capital, Hángzhōu. But while Hángzhōu – a quick trip down from Shànghǎi – is in a league of its own, Zhèjiāng's other sights demonstrate the sheer variety of the small and wealthy coastal province. With arched bridges and charming canal scenes, the small water towns of Wūzhèn and Nánxún typify the lushly watered northern Zhèjiāng (浙江) with its sparkling web of rivers and canals. The Buddhist island of Pǔtuóshān is the best-known of the thousands of islands dotting a ragged and fragmented shoreline.

Southern Zhèjiāng is, however, a region of wild beauty, with jagged mountain peaks and rocky, unspoiled valleys. The charming villages of Yántóucūn, Fúróngcūn, Cāngpōcūn and other settlements along the stunning Nánxījiāng form a great introduction. Zhèjiāng's rural aspect furthermore comes to the fore in the less-visited ancient villages of Guōdòng and Yúyuán outside Wǔyì.

When to Go

Hángzhōu

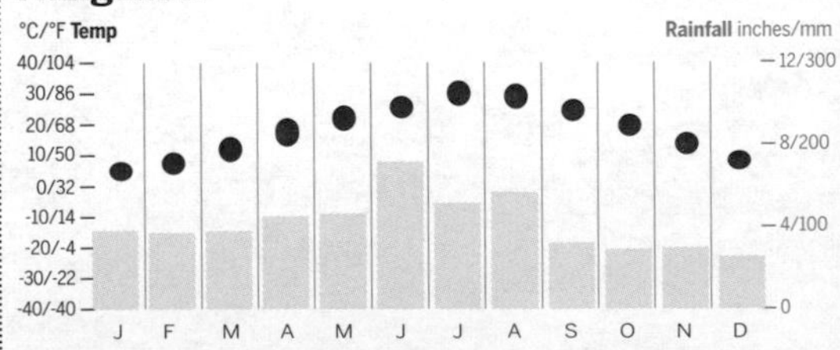

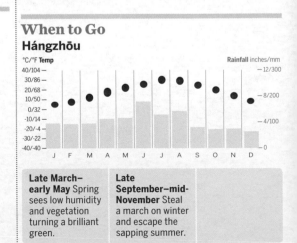

Late March–early May Spring sees low humidity and vegetation turning a brilliant green.

Late September–mid-November Steal a march on winter and escape the sapping summer.

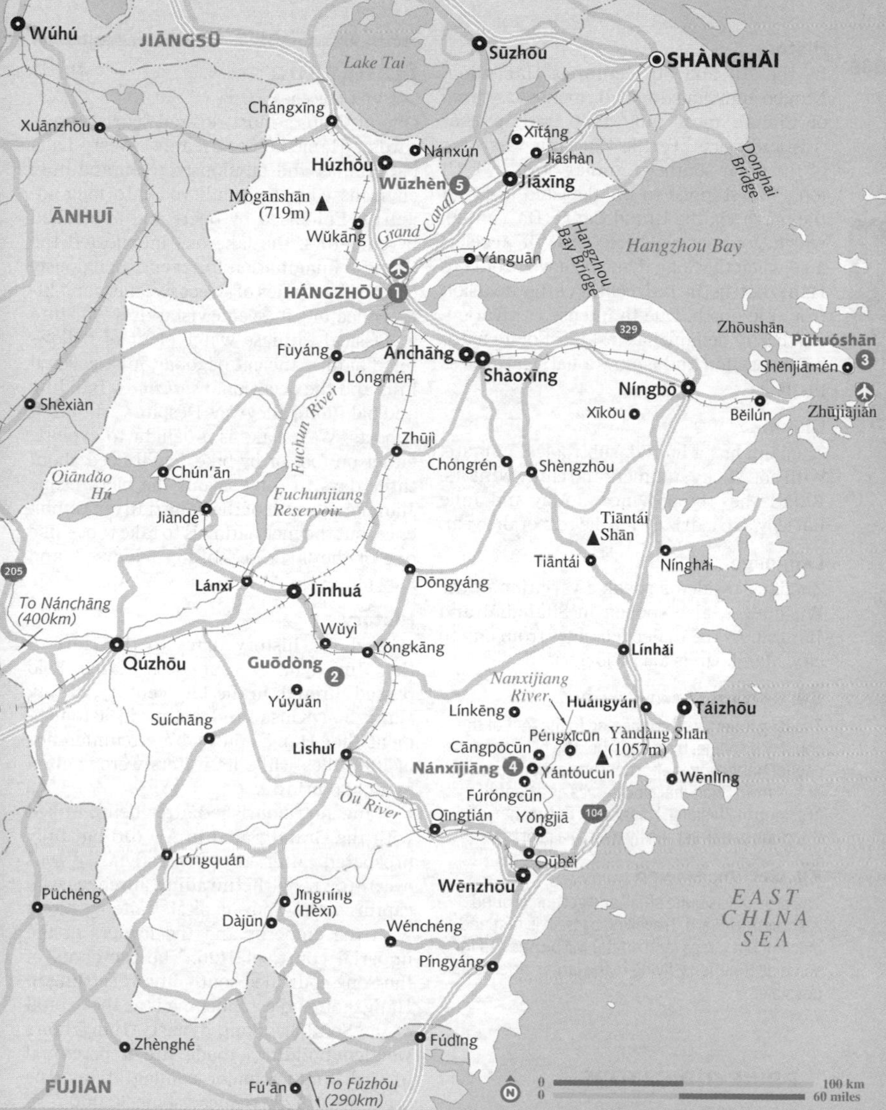

Zhèjiāng Highlights

1. Grab a bike and make a leisurely circuit of Hángzhōu's splendid **West Lake** (p235)
2. Escape to the small village charms and pastoral allure of **Guōdòng** (p252)
3. Take a boat to **Pŭtuóshān** (p253) to explore its Buddhist mysteries
4. Village-hop through the sparkling **Nánxījiāng** (p258) valley outside Wēnzhōu
5. Discover Zhèjiāng's picturesque canal town culture at **Wūzhèn** (p246)

History

By the 7th and 8th centuries Hángzhōu, Níngbō and Shàoxīng had emerged as three of China's most important trading centres and ports. Fertile Zhèjiāng was part of the great southern granary from which food was shipped to the depleted areas of the north via the Grand Canal (Dà Yùnhé), which commences here. Growth accelerated when the Song dynasty moved court to Hángzhōu in the 12th century after invasion from the north. Due to intense cultivation, northern Zhèjiāng has lost most of its natural vegetation and is now a flat, featureless plain.

Climate

Zhèjiāng has a humid, subtropical climate, with hot, sticky summers and chilly winters. Rain lashes the province in May and June but slows to a drizzle for the rest of the year.

Language

Zhèjiāng residents speak a variation of the Wu dialect, also spoken in Shànghǎi and Jiāngsū. As the dialect changes from city to city, Mandarin is also widely used.

Getting There & Away

Zhèjiāng is very well connected to the rest of the country by plane, train and bus. The provincial capital Hángzhōu is effortlessly reached by train or bus from Shànghǎi, and serves as a useful first stop in Zhèjiāng. Hángzhōu, Pútuóshān and Wēnzhōu are all served by nearby airports.

Getting Around

The province is quite small and getting around is straightforward. Travelling by train is fast and efficient but buses (and boats) will be needed for some destinations; flying to the larger cities is also possible.

PRICE INDICATORS

The following price indicators are used in this chapter:

Sleeping

$	less than Y200
$$	Y200 to Y500
$$$	more than Y500

Eating

$	less than Y40
$$	Y40 to Y100
$$$	more than Y100

Hángzhōu 杭州

0571 / POP 6.16 MILLION

One of China's most revered tourist drawcards, Hángzhōu's dreamy West Lake panoramas and fabulously green and hilly environs can easily lull you into long sojourns. Eulogised by poets and applauded by emperors, the lake has intoxicated the Chinese imagination for aeons. Religiously cleaned by armies of street sweepers and litter collectors, its scenic vistas draw you into a classical Chinese watercolour of willow-lined banks, ancient pagodas, mist-covered hills and the occasional *shíkùmén* building and old *lĭlòng* alleyway. Despite vast tourist cohorts, West Lake is a delight to explore, either on foot or by bike. You'll need about three days to fully savour the picturesque Jiāngnán ('south of the Yangzi River') ambience, but the inclination is to take root – like one of the lakeside's lilting willows – and stay put.

History

Hángzhōu's history dates to the start of the Qin dynasty (221 BC). Marco Polo passed through in the 13th century, calling Hángzhōu Kinsai and noting in astonishment that Hángzhōu had a circumference of 100 miles while its waters were vaulted by 12,000 bridges.

Hángzhōu flourished after being linked with the Grand Canal in AD 610 but fully prospered after the Song dynasty was overthrown by the invading Jurchen, who captured the Song capital Kāifēng, along with the emperor and the leaders of the imperial court, in 1126. The remnants of the Song court fled south, finally settling in Hángzhōu and establishing it as the capital of the Southern Song dynasty. Hángzhōu's wooden buildings made fire a perennial hazard; among major conflagrations, the great fire of 1237 reduced some 30,000 residences to piles of smoking carbon.

When the Mongols swept into China they established their court in Běijīng, but Hángzhōu retained its status as a prosperous commercial city. With 10 city gates by Ming times, Hángzhōu took a hammering from Taiping rebels, who besieged the city in 1861 and captured it; two years later the imperial armies reclaimed it. These campaigns reduced almost the entire city to ashes, led to the deaths of over half a million of its residents through disease, starvation and warfare, and finally ended

Hángzhōu's significance as a commercial and trading centre.

Few monuments survived the devastation; much of what can be seen in Hángzhōu today is of fairly recent construction.

Sights & Activities

Hángzhōu grants free admission to all museums and gardens. Other sights offer half-price tickets for children between 1m to 1.3m, free for shorties under 1m.

West Lake LAKE

(西湖; Xīhú) The saccharine Chinese tourist brochure hyperbole extolling West Lake is almost justified in its cloying accolades. The very definition of classical beauty in China, West Lake continues to mesmerise and methodical prettification has worked a cunning magic. Pagoda-topped hills rise over willow-lined waters as boats drift slowly through a vignette of leisurely charm. With history heavily repackaged, it's not that authentic – not by a long shot – but it's still a grade-A cover version of classical China.

Originally a lagoon adjoining the Qiántáng River, the lake didn't come into existence until the 8th century, when the governor of Hángzhōu had the marshy expanse dredged. As time passed the lake's splendour was gradually cultivated: gardens were planted, pagodas built, and causeways and islands were constructed from dredged silt.

Celebrated poet Su Dongpo himself had a hand in the lake's development, constructing the **Su Causeway** (苏堤; Sūdī) during his tenure as local governor in the 11th century. It wasn't an original idea – the poet-governor Bai Juyi had already constructed the **Bai Causeway** (白堤; Báidī) some 200 years earlier. Lined by willow, plum and peach trees, today the traffic-free causeways with their half-moon bridges make for restful outings, particularly on a bike.

Connected to the northern shores by the Bai Causeway is **Gūshān Island** (孤山岛; Gūshān Dǎo), the largest island in the lake and the location of the **Zhèjiāng Provincial Museum** (浙江省博物馆; Zhèjiāng Shěng Bówùguǎn; 25 Gushan Lu; admission free, audioguide Y10; ⌚8.30am-4.30pm Tue-Sun), **Zhōngshān Park** (中山公园; Zhōngshān Gōngyuán) and the Lóuwàilóu Restaurant (p243). The island's buildings and gardens were once the site of Emperor Qianlong's 18th-century holiday palace and gardens. Also on the island is the intriguing **Seal Engravers' Society** (西泠印社; Xīlíng Yìnshè), dedicated to the ancient art of carving the name seals (chops) that serve as personal signatures.

In the northwest is the lovely **Qūyuàn Garden** (曲院风荷; Qūyuàn Fēnghé), a collection of gardens spread out over numerous islets and renowned for their fragrant spring lotus blossoms. Near **Xīlíng Bridge** (Xīlíng Qiáo) is the tomb of **Su Xiaoxiao** (苏小小墓;Sū Xiǎoxiǎo Mù), a 5th-century courtesan who died of grief while waiting for her lover to return. It's been said that her ghost haunts the area and the tinkle of the bells on her gown can be heard at night.

The smaller island in the lake is **Xiǎoyíng Island** (小瀛洲; Xiǎoyíng Zhōu), where you can look over at **Three Pools Mirroring the Moon** (三潭印月; Sāntán Yìnyuè), three small towers in the water on the south side of the island; each has five holes that release shafts of candlelight on the night of the mid-autumn festival. From Lesser Yíngzhōu Island, you can gaze over to **Red Carp Pond** (花港观鱼; Huāgǎng Guānyú), home to a few thousand red carp.

Cruise boats (游船; yóuchuán; incl entry to Three Pools adult/child Y45/22.50; ⌚7am-4.45pm) shuttle frequently from four points (Hubin Park, Red Carp Pond, Zhōngshān Park and the Mausoleum of General Yue Fei) to the Mid Lake Pavilion (Húxīn Tíng) and Xiǎoyíng Island (Xiǎoyíng Zhōu). Trips take one and a half hours and depart every 20 minutes. Alternatively, hire one of the six-person boats (小船; *xiǎo chuán*; Y80 per person or Y160 per boat) rowed by boatmen. Look for them across from the Overseas Chinese Hotel or along the causeways. Paddle boats (Y15 per 30 minutes, Y200 deposit) on the Bai Causeway are also available for hire.

Impromptu opera singing and other cultural activities may suddenly kick off around the lake and if the weather's fine, don't forget to earmark the east shore for sunset-over-West-Lake photos. Walking around West Lake at night is also gorgeous and very romantic, with loads of benches and seats facing the still waters.

Buggies (⌚8am-6.30pm) speed around West Lake; just raise your hand to flag one down. A complete circuit is Y40, otherwise Y10 takes you to the next stop. Tourist buses Y1 and Y2 also run around West Lake.

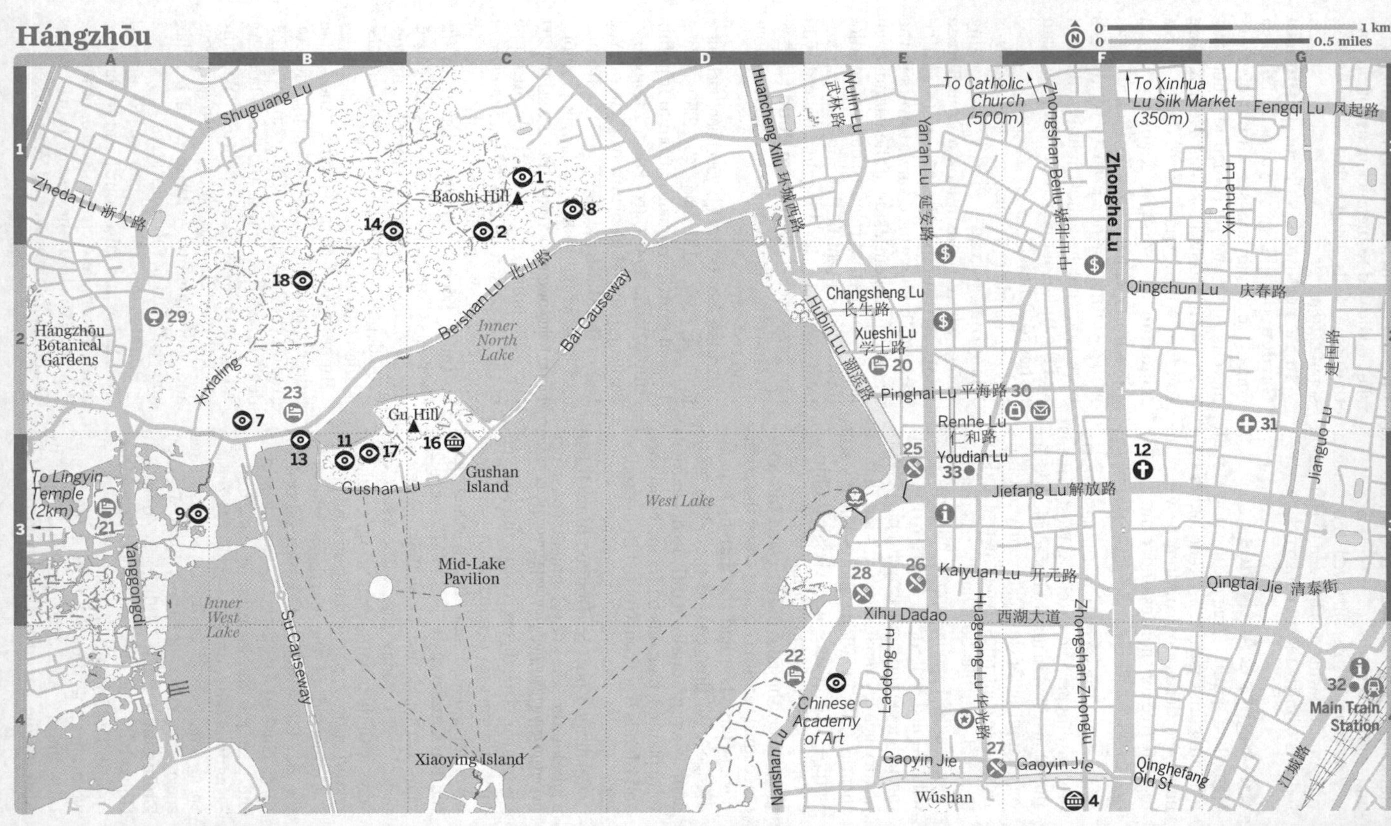

Hángzhōu
To Catholic Church (500m)
To Xinhua Lu Silk Market (350m)
Fengqi Lu 凤起路
Shuguang Lu
Zheda Lu 浙大路
Baoshi Hill
Huancheng Xilu 环城西路
Wulin Lu 武林路
Yan'an Lu 延安路
Zhongshan Beilu 中山北路
Zhonghe Lu
Xinhua Lu
Qingchun Lu 庆春路
Changsheng Lu 长生路
Xueshi Lu 学士路
Hubin Lu 湖滨路
Beishan Lu 北山路
Inner North Lake
Bai Causeway
Hángzhōu Botanical Gardens
Xixialing
Pinghai Lu 平海路
Renhe Lu 仁和路
Youdian Lu
Jianguo Lu
Gu Hill
Gushan Lu
Gushan Island
West Lake
Jiefang Lu 解放路
To Lingyin Temple (2km)
Yanggongdi
Mid-Lake Pavilion
Inner West Lake
Su Causeway
Kaiyuan Lu 开元路
Qingtai Jie 清泰街
Xihu Dadao 西湖大道
Laodong Lu
Huaguang Lu 华光路
Zhongshan Zhonglu
Chinese Academy of Art
Nanshan Lu
Xiaoying Island
Gaoyin Jie
Wúshan
Qinghefang Old St
Main Train Station

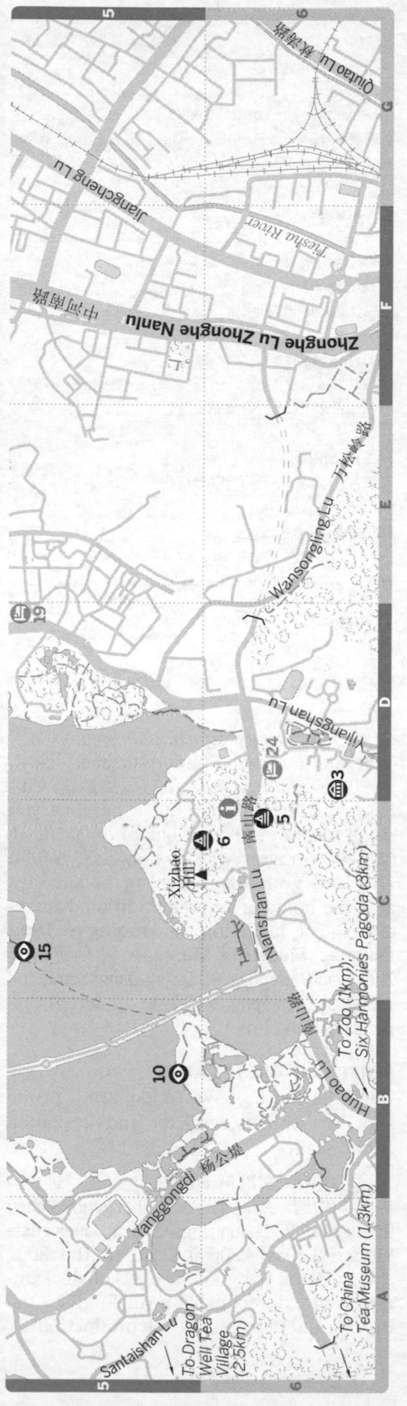

Mausoleum of General Yue Fei TEMPLE
(岳庙; Yuè Fēi Mù; Beishan Lu; admission Y25; ⌚7am-6pm) Commander of the southern Song armies, General Yue Fei (1103–42) led a series of successful battles against Jurchen invaders from the north in the 12th century. Despite his initial successes, he was recalled to the Song court, where he was executed, along with his son, after being deceived by the treacherous prime minister Qin Hui. In 1163 Song emperor Gao Zong exonerated Yue Fei and had his corpse reburied at the present site.

Léifēng Pagoda PAGODA
(雷峰塔; Léifēng Tǎ Jǐngqū; admission Y40; ⌚7.30am-9pm Mar-Nov, 8am-5.30pm Dec-Feb) Topped with a golden spire, the eye-catching Léifēng Pagoda can be climbed for fine views of the lake. The original pagoda, built in AD 977, collapsed in 1924. During renovations in 2001, Buddhist scriptures written on silk were discovered in the foundations, along with other treasures.

Jìngcí Temple BUDDHIST TEMPLE
(净慈寺; Jìngcí Sì; admission Y10; ⌚6am-5.30pm) The serene Chan (Zen) Jìngcí Temple was originally built in AD 954 and is now fully restored. The splendid first hall is home to the massive and foreboding Heavenly Kings and a magnificent red-and-gold case encapsulating Milefo and Weituo. The main hall – the **Great Treasure Hall** – contains a simply vast seated effigy of Sakyamuni. Hunt down the awesome **1000-arm Guanyin** (千手观音) in the Guanyin Pavilion with her huge fan of arms. The temple's enormous bronze bell is struck 108 times for prosperity on the eve of the Lunar New Year.

Língyǐn Temple BUDDHIST TEMPLE
(灵隐寺; Língyǐn Sì; Lingyin Lu; grounds Y35, grounds & temple Y65; ⌚7am-5pm) Hángzhōu's most famous Buddhist temple, Língyǐn Temple was built in AD 326. Due to episodes of war and calamity, it has been destroyed and restored no fewer than 16 times.

The main **temple buildings** are restorations of Qing-dynasty structures. Behind the Hall of the Four Heavenly Guardians stands the Great Hall and a magnificent 20m-high statue of Siddhartha Gautama (Sakyamuni), sculpted from 24 blocks of camphor wood in 1956 and based on a Tang-dynasty original. Behind the giant statue is a startling montage of 150 small figures, which charts the journey of 53 children on the road to Buddhahood.

Hángzhōu

Sights

1 Baochu Pagoda........C1
2 Baopu Taoist Temple........C1
3 China Silk Museum........D6
4 Húqìngyú Táng Chinese Medicine Museum........F4
5 Jìngcí Temple........C6
6 Léifēng Pagoda........C6
7 Mausoleum of General Yue Fei........B2
8 Ming Dynasty Effigies........C1
9 Quyuan Garden........A3
10 Red Carp Pond........B5
11 Seal Engravers' Society........B3
12 Si-Cheng Church........F3
13 Su Xiaoxiao's Tomb........B3
14 Sunrise Terrace........B1
15 Three Pools Mirroring the Moon........C5
16 Zhèjiāng Provincial Museum........C3
17 Zhōngshān Park........B3
18 Ziyun Cave........B2

Sleeping

19 Crystal Orange Hotel........D5
20 Grand Hyatt Regency........E2
21 Mingtown Garden Hostel........A3
22 Mingtown Youth Hostel........D4
23 Shangri-La Hotel........B2
24 West Lake Youth Hostel........D6

Eating

25 Ajisen........E3
26 Carrefour........E3
27 Lǎo Hángzhōu Fēngwèi........E4
28 Lǎomǎjiā Miànguǎn........E3

Drinking

29 1944 Bar........A2
Mingtown Youth Hostel........(see 22)

Shopping

30 Wúshān Lù Night Market........F2

Information

31 Zhèjiāng University First Affiliated Hospital........G2

Transport

32 Bus Ticket Office........G4
33 Train Ticket Office........E3

During the time of the Five Dynasties (907–60) about 3000 monks lived in the temple.

The walk up to the temple skirts the flanks of **Fēilái Peak** (Fēilái Fēng; Peak Flying from Afar), magically transported here from India according to legend. The **Buddhist carvings** lining the riverbanks and hillsides, all 470 of them, date from the 10th to 14th centuries. To get a close-up view of the best carvings, including the famed 'laughing' Maitreya Buddha, follow the paths along the far (east) side of the stream.

Behind Língyǐn Temple is the **Northern Peak** (Běi Gāofēng), which can be scaled by cable car (up/down Y30/40). From the summit there are sweeping views across the lake and city.

Bus K7 and tourist bus Y2 (both from the train station), and tourist bus Y1 from the roads circling West Lake, go to the temple.

Qīnghéfāng Old Street SHOPPING STREET

At the south end of Zhongshan Zhonglu is this fun and fascinating bustling pedestrian street (清河坊历史文化街; Qīnghéfāng Lìshǐ Wénhuà Jiē), with makeshift puppet theatres, teahouses and curio stalls. Chomp on a chewy *nánsòng dìngshèng gāo* (南宋定胜糕; southern Song dingsheng cake, Y1.50), or a *guǐcài jiānbing* (鬼菜煎饼; Chinese burrito; Y3), pick up a hand-carved stone teapot (Y29) or a box of *lóngxūtáng* (龙须糖; dragon whiskers sweets; Y10 a box) and grab some ginseng or silk. It's also the home of several traditional medicine shops, including the **Húqìngyú Táng Chinese Medicine Museum** (中药博物馆; Zhōngyào Bówùguǎn; 95 Dajing Gang; admission Y10; ⌚8.30am-5pm), which is an actual dispensary and clinic.

SOUTH OF WEST LAKE

The hills south of West Lake are a prime spot for walkers, cyclists and green-tea connoisseurs.

FREE **China Silk Museum** MUSEUM

(中国丝绸博物馆; Zhōngguó Sīchóu Bówùguǎn; 73-1 Yuhuangshan Lu; audioguide Y100; ⌚8.30am-4.30pm) Close to the lake, this museum has good displays of silk samples, and exhibits explain (in English) the history and processes of silk production.

FREE **China Tea Museum** MUSEUM (中国茶叶博物馆; Zhōngguó Cháyè Bówùguǎn; Longjing Lu; ⏲8.30am-4.30pm Tue-Sun) Not far into the hills, you'll begin to see fields of tea bushes planted in undulating rows, the setting for the China Tea Museum – 3.7 hectares of land dedicated to the art, cultivation and tasting of tea. Further up are several tea-producing villages, all of which harvest China's most famous variety of green tea, *lóngjǐng* (dragon well), named after the spring where the pattern in the water resembles a dragon. You can enjoy one of Hángzhōu's most famous teas at the **Dragon Well Tea Village** (龙井问茶; Lóngjǐng Wènchá; ⏲8am-5.30pm), near the first pass. Tourist bus Y3 will take you to the museum and the village.

Six Harmonies Pagoda PAGODA (六和塔; Liùhé Tǎ; 16 Zhijiang Lu; grounds Y20, grounds & pagoda Y30; ⏲6am-6.30pm) Three kilometres southwest of the lake, an enormous rail-and-road bridge spans the Qiántáng River. Close by is the 60m-high octagonal Six Harmonies Pagoda, first built in AD 960. The pagoda also served as a lighthouse, and was supposed to have magical power to halt the 6.5m high tidal bore that thunders up Qiántáng River (see p245). Behind the pagoda stretches a charming walk, through terraces dotted with sculptures, bells, shrines and inscriptions. Take bus K4 from Nanshan Lu.

OTHER SIGHTS

Hidden away behind sheet-metal gates, the blue-and-white **Catholic Church** (天主堂; Tiānzhǔ Táng; 415 Zhongshan Beilu; admission free) is a lovely old building, with a compassionate effigy of Mary above the door. Knock on the gate and the gatekeeper may let you in. Chinese-built, the brick Protestant **Si-Cheng Church** (思澄堂; Sīchéng Táng; 132 Jiefang Lu; admission free) is a more Chinese-style church, with a loyal and welcoming congregation; if it looks shut, try the entrance along Jueyuansi Alley (觉苑寺巷) down the east side of the church.

Tours

Just about every midrange and top-end hotel offers tours to West Lake and the surrounding areas. Frequent tours also run from the Hángzhōu Tourist Information Centre.

Festivals & Events

The **International Qiántáng River Tide-Observing Festival** every autumn in Yánguān, outside Hángzhōu, is a top event. See p245 for more details.

Sleeping

Hángzhōu's hotels have expanded in recent years across all budgets; youth hostels are now plentiful. Book well ahead in the summer months, at weekends and during the busy holiday periods. Look out for 住宿 and 客房 signs (meaning 'rooms available'), which identify cheap guesthouses which may take foreigners.

TOP CHOICE **Mingtown Youth Hostel** HOSTEL $ (明堂杭州国际青年旅社; Míngtáng Hángzhōu Guójì Qīngnián Lǚshè; ☎8791 8948; 101-11 Nanshan Lu; 南山路101-11号; dm/s Y50/180, d Y130-240; ❄@) With its handy lakeside location, this friendly hostel is often booked out so reserve well ahead. It offers ticket booking, internet access, and rents bikes and camping gear.

TOP CHOICE **West Lake Youth Hostel** HOSTEL $ (杭州过客青年旅社; Hángzhōu Guòkè Qīngnián Lǚshè; ☎8702 7027; www.westlakehostel.com; 62-3 Nanshan Lu; 南山路62-3号; dm Y45-50, s/d Y160/200; ❄@) Tucked away among the trees and foliage east of Jìngcí Temple, with pleasant rooms and comfy lounge-bar area (Tstingtao Y10) hung with lanterns, this place enjoys both character and a sense of seclusion; reserve ahead. Take bus K4 from Yanan Nanlu and get off at the Chángqiáo (长桥) stop.

Crystal Orange Hotel HOTEL $$$ (桔字水晶酒店; Júzi Shuǐjīng Jiǔdiàn; ☎2887 8988; www.orangehotel.com; 122 Qingbo Jie; 清波街122号; tw/ste Y788/1388, discounts of 50%; ❄@) Uncluttered and modern business hotel with a crisp and natty interior, Warhol prints in the lobby, glass lift and only four floors, but sadly no views of West Lake from the neat rooms.

Grand Hyatt Regency HOTEL $ (杭州凯悦酒店; Hángzhōu Kǎiyuè Jiǔdiàn; ☎8779 1234; www.hangzhou.regency.hyatt.com; 28 Hubin Lu; 湖滨路28号; s/d Y1800/1800, lake view Y2250/2250, discounts of 10-30%; ❄@) The huge megacomplex of the Hyatt dominates the eastern lakeshore; in addition to international-standard rooms, the hotel offers five-star luxuries such as a

WEST LAKE WALK

For a breathtaking trek into the hills above the lake, take Xixialing Lu (栖霞岭路; also called Qixialing Lu) just west of the Mausoleum of General Yue Fei. The road runs past the west wall of the temple before entering the shade of towering trees to climb stone steps. At **Ziyun Cave** (紫云洞; Zǐyún Dòng), the road forks; take the right-hand fork towards **Baopu Taoist Temple** (Bàopǔ Dàoyuàn) 1km away and the **Baochu Pagoda** (保俶塔; Bǎochù Tǎ). At the top of the steps turn left and, passing the **Sunrise Terrace** (初阳台; Chūyáng Tái), again bear left. Down the steps bear right to the **Baopu Taoist Temple** (抱朴道院; Bàopǔ Dàoyuàn; admission Y5; ⊙6am-5pm), whose first hall contains a statue of Guanyin (Buddhist goddess nonetheless) before a yin-yang diagram; an effigy of Taoist master Gehong (葛洪) – who once smelted cinnabar here – resides in the next hall, behind a fabulously carved altar decorated with figures. Return the way you came to continue east to the Baochu Pagoda and after hitting a confluence of three paths, take the middle track. Squeeze into a gap between some huge boulders and you will spot the Baochu Pagoda rising up ahead. Repeatedly restored, the seven-storey brick pagoda was last rebuilt in 1933, although its spire tumbled off in the 1990s. Continue on down and you will pass through a *páilou* – or decorative arch – erected during the Republic (with some of its characters scratched off) to a series of cliff-side Ming-dynasty effigies, all of which were vandalised in the tumultuous 1960s, apart from two effigies on the right which were left untouched. Bear right and head down to Beishan Lu (北山路), emerging from Baochutaqianshan Lu (保俶塔前山路).

swimming pool, sauna and health club, and wireless connection.

Shangri-La Hotel HOTEL **$$$**
(杭州香格里拉饭店; Hángzhōu Xiānggélǐlā Fàndiàn; ☎8797 7951; www.shangri-la.com; 78 Beishan Lu; 北山路78号; d Y1650, with lake view Y2500, discounts of 30%; ❄@📶🏊) Surrounded by forest on the north shore of the lake, this hotel enjoys a winning, picturesque location. The hotel has been around for a long time, so view rooms first, as quality varies. Wireless connection, swimming pool and health club.

Mingtown Garden Hostel HOSTEL **$**
(明堂湖中居旅社; Míngtáng Húzhōngjū Lǚshè; ☎8797 5883; fax 8796 8819; 4 Yanggongdi, Zhaogongdi Lu; 杨公堤赵公堤路4号; dm/s/d Y45/158/208; ❄@) Popular hostel attractively located on the west side of the lake. It's clean, well kept and very near the water; traditional styling and friendly staff.

Eating

Hángzhōu cuisine emphasises fresh, sweet flavours and makes good use of freshwater fish, especially eel and carp. Dishes to watch for include *dōngpō ròu* (东坡肉; braised pork), named after the Song-dynasty poet Su Dongpo, and *jiàohuā tóngjī* (叫花童鸡; chicken wrapped in lotus leaves and baked in clay), known in English as 'beggar's chicken'. Bamboo shoots are a local delicacy, especially in the spring when they're most tender. Hángzhōu's most popular restaurant street is Gaoyin Jie, parallel to Qīnghéfāng Old St. Hángzhōu's leafy answer to Shànghǎi's Xīntiāndì, **Xīhú Tiāndì** (西湖天地; 147 Nanshan Lu) has an attractive panoply of smart cafes and restaurants.

TOP CHOICE **Grandma's Kitchen** HANGZHOU **$**
(外婆家; Wàipójiā; 8 fl, Bldg B, Hangzhou Tower, Huancheng Beilu; mains Y6-55; ⊙10.30am-2pm & 4-9pm; 📋) Highly popular with locals, this chain restaurant cooks up classic Hángzhōu favourites; try the *hóngshāo dōngpō ròu* (红烧东坡肉; braised pork). There are several other branches in town.

Lǎomǎjiā Miànguǎn NOODLES **$**
(老马家面馆; 232 Nanshan Lu; meals Y15; ⊙7am-10.30pm) Simple, popular and unfussy Muslim restaurant stuffed into an old *shíkùmén* tenement building with a handful of tables and spot-on *niúròu lāmiàn* (牛肉拉面; beef noodles; Y7) and super-scrummy *ròujiāmó* (肉夹馍; meat in a bun; Y5).

Ajisen NOODLES **$**
(味千拉面; Wèiqiān Lāmiàn; 10 Hubin Lu; meals Y20-30; ⊙10am-11pm) The reading is high on the chilli-ometer for Ajisen's tasty noodles, but the West Lake perspective offers cool-

ing relief. Ajisen's photo menu makes ordering a breeze, there's free tea and busy, efficient staff. Pay up front.

Lǎo Hángzhōu Fēngwèi HANGZHOU $$
(老杭州风味; 141 Gaoyin Jie; mains Y20; ⌚11.30am-9pm) This local watering hole serves tasty home-style dishes, including *zāohuì biānsǔn* (糟烩鞭笋; wine-braised bamboo shoots) and *dōngpō* pork. Make sure to try the *pópoqiāo tǔdòu bǐng* (婆婆敲土豆饼; crispy potato cakes with garlic and chilli).

Lóuwàilóu Restaurant HANGZHOU $$$
(楼外楼; Lóuwàilóu; 30 Gushan Lu; mains Y30-200; ⌚10.30am-3.30pm & 4.30-8.45pm; ▣) Founded in 1838, this is Hángzhōu's most famous restaurant. The local speciality is *xīhú cùyú* (西湖醋鱼; sweet and sour carp) and *dōngpō* pork, but there's a good choice of other well-priced standard dishes.

Carrefour SUPERMARKET $
(家乐福; Jiālèfú; 135 Yan'an Lu; 延安路135号; ⌚9am-9pm) Can be found at the northwest corner of Yan'an Lu and Xihu Dadao.

Drinking

For drinking, Shuguang Lu north of West Lake is the place; a brash clutch of lesser bars also operates opposite the China Academy of Art on Nanshan Lu (南山路). For a comprehensive list of Hángzhōu bars and restaurants, grab a copy of *More – Hangzhou Entertainment Guide* (www.morehangzhou.com), available from bars and concierge desks at good hotels.

Mingtown Youth Hostel BAR
(明堂杭州国际青年旅社; 101-11 Nanshan Lu; ⌚7pm-1am) The hostel's lovely bar area is one of the most chilled-out spots in town, with comfy sofas, sensuous music, great atmosphere and a roof garden. Great range of brews, including Franziskaner Weissbier (Y32), or you can just sit back with a Tsingtao (Y18).

1944 Bar BAR
(酒吧; 119 Shuguang Lu; ⌚8pm-2.30am)
Darkly lit, all-wood and brickwork bar, cluttered with assorted bar artefacts from animal horns to an unemployed dart board; popular with locals. Carlsberg Y22, Budweiser Y20.

Shopping

Hángzhōu is famed for its tea, in particular *lóngjǐng* green tea, as well as silk, fans and, of all things, scissors. All of these crop up in the **Wúshān Lù night market** (吴山路夜市; Wúshān Lù Yèshì), now on Huixing Lu (惠兴路) between Youdian Lu (邮电路) and Renhe Lu (仁和路), where fake ceramics jostle with ancient pewter tobacco pipes, Chairman Mao memorabilia, silk shirts and pirated CDs. Qīnghéfāng Old St (see p240) has loads of possibilities, from Chinese tiger pillows to taichi swords.

Xinhua Lu Silk Market SILK
(新华路市场丝绸市场; Sīchóu Shìchǎng; Xinhua Lu; ⌚8am-5pm) For silk, try this string of silk shops strung out along the north of Xinhua Lu. Check out the **Ming-dynasty residence** (明宅; Míng Zhái; 227 Xinhua Lu), now a silk emporium.

Information

Internet Access

Twenty-four-hour internet cafes are in abundance around the train station (typically Y4 or Y5 per hr); look for the neon signs '网吧'.

Internet Resources

Hángzhōu City Travel Committee (www.gotohz.com) Current information on events, restaurants and entertainment venues around the city.

Hángzhōu News (www.hangzhou.com.cn/english) News-oriented website with travel info.

More Hángzhōu (www.morehangzhou.com) Handy website with restaurant, nightlife reviews, forums and classifieds

Medical Services

Zhèjiāng University First Affiliated Hospital (浙江大学医学院附属第一医院; Zhèjiāng Dàxué Yīxuéyuàn Fùshǔ Dìyī Yīyuàn; 79 Qingchun Lu)

Money

Bank of China (中国银行; Zhōngguó Yínháng; 177 Laodong Lu) Offers currency exchange plus 24-hour ATM.

HSBC (汇丰银行; Huìfēng Yínháng; cnr Qingchun Lu & Zhonghe Lu) Has a 24-hour ATM.

Industrial & Commercial Bank of China (工商银行; Gōngshāng Yínháng; 300 Yan'an Lu) Has a 24-hour ATM.

Post

China Post (中国邮政; Zhōngguó Yóuzhèng; Renhe Lu) Close to West Lake.

Public Security Bureau

Public Security Bureau Exit & Entry Administration Service Center (PSB; 公安局; Gōng'ānjú Bànzhèng Zhōngxīn; ☎8728 0600; 35 Huaguang Lu; ⌚8.30am-noon & 2-5pm Mon-Fri) Can extend visas.

Tourist Information

Hángzhōu Tourist Information Centre (杭州旅游咨询服务中心; Hángzhōu Lǚyóu Zīxún Fúwù Zhōngxīn; Hángzhōu train station) Provides basic travel info, free maps and tours. Other branches include one at Léifēng Pagoda and at 228 Yan'an Lu.

Tourist Complaint Hotline (☎8796 9691)

Travellers Infoline (☎96123) Helpful 24-hour information with English service from 6.30am to 9pm.

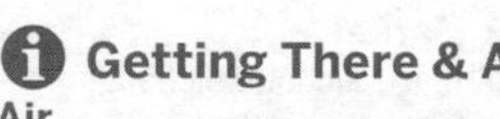

Getting There & Away

Air

Hángzhōu has flights to all major Chinese cities (bar Shànghǎi) and international connections to Hong Kong, Macau, Tokyo, Singapore and other destinations. Several daily flights connect to Běijīng (Y1050) and Guǎngzhōu (Y960).

One place to book air tickets is at the **Civil Aviation Administration of China** (CAAC; 中国民航; Zhōngguó Mínháng; ☎8666 8666; 390 Tiyuchang Lu; ⏲7.30am-8pm). Most hotels will also book flights, generally with a Y20 to Y30 service charge.

Bus

All four bus stations are outside the city centre; tickets can be conveniently bought for all stations from the **bus ticket office** (长途汽车售票处; Chángtú Qìchē Shòupiàochù; ⏲6.30am-5pm) right off the exit from Hángzhōu's main train station.

The **east bus station** (汽车东站; Qìchē Dōngzhàn; 71 Genshan Xilu) is the most comprehensive, with frequent deluxe buses:

Níngbō Y52, two hours

Shànghǎi Y54, 2½ hours

Shàoxīng Y22, one hour

Wūzhèn Y25, one hour

Buses from the **south bus station** (汽车南站; Qìchē Nánzhàn; 407 Qiutao Lu):

Níngbō Y52, two hours

Shàoxīng Y24, one hour

Wēnzhōu Y140, 4½ hours

Wǔyì Y59, six daily

From the **north bus station** (汽车北站; Qìchē Běizhàn; 766 Moganshan Lu):

Běijīng Y410, 15 hours, one daily (3.15pm)

Nánjīng Y120, four hours, every 30 minutes

Wǔkāng Y15, 45 minutes

From Shànghǎi, buses leave frequently for Hángzhōu's **east bus station** (Y65, 2½ hours) from Shànghǎi's Hengfeng Rd bus station, the Shànghǎi south bus station and the main long-distance bus station. Buses (Y85, two hours) to Hángzhōu also run every 30 minutes between 10am and 9pm from the Hóngqiáo airport long-distance bus station. Regular buses (Y100, three hours) also run to Hángzhōu from Shànghǎi's Pǔdōng International Airport long-distance bus station.

Buses for Huángshān (Y59 to Y88, six hours) leave from the **west bus station** (汽车西站; Qìchē Xīzhàn; 357 Tianmushan Lu).

Train

Regular D-class express trains (Y54, 75 to 90 minutes) run daily to Hángzhōu from Shànghǎi South train station (Shànghǎi Nánzhàn); book weekend tickets in advance. The earliest train leaves Shànghǎi at 7.20am and the last is soon after 8pm. The last express train back to Shànghǎi South train station is at 8.40pm. Numerous other slow trains run between the two cities.

A handy evening express D-class train runs to Běijīng (soft seat/soft sleeper Y354/821, 11 hours, 8.15pm); book in advance. Z class and T class trains to Běijīng cost Y539 and take 13 hours.

Other trains from Hángzhōu:

Guǎngzhōu Y383, 16 to 23 hours

Nánjīng D-class hard/soft seat Y156/187, 4½ hours

Xiàmén D class Y309, 6½ hours

Xī'ān Y341, 19 to 23 hours

Trains from Hángzhōu's main train station also run to Wēnzhōu and east to Shàoxīng and Níngbō. Most trains heading north go via Shànghǎi.

Booking sleepers can be difficult at Hángzhōu train station, especially to Běijīng. Most hotels can do this for you for a service charge. A handy **train ticket office** (火车票售票处; Huǒchēpiào Shòupiàochù; Huansha Lu) can be found north of Jiefang Lu, just east of West Lake.

Getting Around

To/From the Airport

Hángzhōu's airport is 30km from the city centre; taxi drivers ask around Y100 to Y130 for the trip. Shuttle buses (Y20, one hour) run every 15 minutes between 5.30am and 9pm from the CAAC office.

Bicycle

You'll be tripping over bike-hire outfits around West Lake (Y5 to Y10 per hour); the city's public bicycle scheme is cheaper. Youth hostels also rent out bikes.

Public transport

BUS Hángzhōu has a clean, efficient bus system and getting around is easy. 'Y' buses are tourist buses; 'K' is simply an abbreviation of '*kōngtiáo*' (air-con). Tickets are Y2 to Y5. Following are popular bus routes:

Bus K7 Usefully connects the main train station to the western side of West Lake and Língyǐn Temple.

Tourist bus Y1 Circles West Lake in a return loop to Língyǐn Temple.

Tourist bus Y2 Goes from the main train station, along Beishan Lu and up to Língyǐn Temple.

Tourist bus Y3 Travels around West Lake to the China Silk Museum, China Tea Museum, Dragon Well Tea Village and the Southern Song-dynasty Guan Kiln.

Bus K56 Travels from the east bus station to Yan'an Lu.

Buses 15 & K15 Connects the north bus station to the northwest area of West Lake.

Bus K95 Links Hángzhōu train station with the north bus station.

Bus K518 Connects the east train station with the main train station, via the east bus station.

METRO The No 1 Line of Hángzhōu's new metro system is due to open by 2012 and will run through the main train station.

Taxi

Metered Hyundai taxis are ubiquitous and start at Y10; figure on around Y20 to Y25 from the main train station (queues can be horrendous though) to Hubin Lu.

Around Hángzhōu

QIÁNTÁNG RIVER TIDAL BORE 钱塘江潮

A spectacular natural phenomenon occurs when the highest tides of the lunar cycle sweep a wall of water up the narrow mouth of the Qiántáng River from Hángzhōu Bay (Hángzhōu Wān) at thundering speeds of up to 40km per hour.

Although the tidal bore can be viewed from the riverbank in Hángzhōu, the best place to witness this amazing phenomenon is on either side of the river at Yánguān (盐官), a lovely ancient town about 38km northeast of Hángzhōu. The most popular viewing time is during the **Mid-Autumn Festival**, around the 18th day of the eighth month of the lunar calendar, when the **International Qiántáng River Tide Observing Festival** takes place. However, you can see it throughout the year when the highest tides occur at the beginning and middle of each lunar month. For tide times, check with the Hángzhōu Tourist Information Centre.

Hotels and travel agencies offer tours to see the bore during the Mid-Autumn Festival, but you can visit just as easily on your own. To reach Yánguān, take a bus from Hángzhōu's east bus station to Guōdiàn (郭店; Y14, one hour, 7am to 5.25pm) and change to local bus 109 (25 minutes).

MÒGĀNSHĀN 莫干山

☎0572

A blessed release from the suffocating summer torpor roasting north Zhèjiāng, this delightful **hilltop resort** (admission Y80) was developed as a resort by 19th-century Europeans from Shànghǎi and Hángzhōu during the concession era, in the style of Lúshān and Jīgōngshān in Hénán. Refreshingly cool in summer and sometimes smothered in spectral fog, Mògānshān is famed for its scenic, forested views, towering bamboo and stone villa architecture; the mountain remains a weekend bolthole for expat *tàitai*'s (wives) fleeing the simmering lowland heat.

The best way to enjoy Mògānshān is just to wander the winding forest paths and stone steps, taking in some of the architecture en route. There's Shànghǎi gangster **Du Yuesheng's old villa** (杜月笙别墅; Dù Yuèshēng Biéshù) – now serving as a hotel – Chiang Kaishek's lodge, a couple of churches (375 Moganshan and 419 Moganshan) and many other villas linked (sometimes tenuously) with the rich and famous, including the **house** (毛主席下榻处; Máo Zhǔxí Xiàtàchù; 126 Moganshan) where Chairman Mao rested his chubby limbs.

Apart from the gaunt villa architecture, more recent construction has flung up less attractive villas made of more regular blocks; the genuine older villas are made of irregularly shaped stone. Sadly many of the original interiors have been ripped out, so much of the period charm is absent. Mock classical porticos have been bolted on to other villas in a clumsy Chinese interpretation of European style. The blue and red corrugated-iron roofing looks new, but is actually the original roofing material. Containing **Ta Mountain** (塔山; Tǎshān) in the northwest, the **Da Keng Scenic Area** (大坑景区; Dàkēng Jǐngqū) is great for rambling. You can pick up a Chinese map (Y4) at your hotel for some sense of orientation, otherwise there are billboard maps dotted about.

The **main village** (Mògānshān Zhèn) is centred around **Yinshan Jie** (荫山街), where you will find the **China Post** (40 Moganshan; ⊙8.30-11am & 1-4pm), a branch of the PSB (opposite the post office) and several hotels. For information on hikes or for suggestions for activities on Mògānshān, contact well-informed Mark Kitto, author of the riveting *China Cuckoo*, at Moganshan Lodge, but he may appreciate it if you bought a coffee.

Sleeping

Mògānshān is full of hotels of varying quality, most housed in crumbling villas; room prices peak at weekends (Friday to Sunday). Don't expect to find any backpacker spots, but haggle your socks off to drive prices down; if you come off-season (eg early spring) you can expect good rates, but be warned that many hotels either shut up shop or close for renovation over the winter.

TOP CHOICE **Moganshan House 23** HOTEL $$$
(莫干山杭疗23号; Mògānshān Hángliáo 23 Hào; ☎803 3822; 23 Moganshan; 莫干山23号; weekday/weekend d Y900/1200, family r Y1250/1500; ❄📶) This exquisitely restored villa hits the Mògānshān nail squarely on the head, bursting with period charm, from art-deco-style sinks, black-and-white-tiled bathroom floors, wooden floorboards, the original staircase to a lovely English kitchen. It's also kid friendly with a family room, baby chairs and swings in the garden. With only six rooms, book well in advance, especially for weekend stays. Breakfast included in room price.

Naked Retreats FARM HOUSES $$
(☎021 5465 9577; www.nakedretreats.cn; 329 Moganshan; 莫干山329号; per person weekday lodge/bungalow Y350/520, weekend Y450/750; ❄) Naked Retreats is at the top of a gully below the village, offering a selection of eco-lodges, farm houses and bungalows enveloped in bamboo forest sleeping anything from a couple to a crowd; lovely views. Range of activities also organised, from biking to fishing, trekking, star gazing, yoga and massage. Note: phone calls only answered Monday to Friday 9am to 6pm. Rates are for a minimum double occupancy.

Jiànquán Shānzhuāng HOTEL $$
(剑泉山庄; ☎803 3607; 91 Moganshan; 莫干山91号; d Y480-680; ❄) A cheap option sitting below the village.

Eating

Yinshan Jie has a number of restaurants and hotels with restaurants.

TOP CHOICE **Moganshan Lodge** INTERNATIONAL $$
(马克的咖啡厅; Mǎkè de Kāfēitīng; ☎803 3011; www.moganshanlodge.com; Songliang Shanzhuang, just off Yinshan Jie; ⊙9am-11pm; 📶) English Mògānshān resident Mark Kitto can cook up a treat, brew up a fine coffee and give you the low-down on Mògānshān's charms at this elegantly presented villa up some steps from Yinshan Jie.

Getting There & Away

From Hángzhōu, buses leave from the north bus station to Wǔkāng (武康; Y15, 40 minutes, every 30 minutes) from 6.20am to 7pm; in the other direction, buses run every 30 minutes from 6.30am till 7pm; note that Wǔkāng is also known as Déqīng (德清).

From Wǔkāng minivans run to the top of Mògānshān for around Y50; a taxi will cost around Y70 to Y80. Buses from Shànghǎi run to Wǔkāng (Y53, four hours) and leave from the old north bus station near Baoshan Rd metro, at 80 Gongxing Rd. Buses depart from Shànghǎi at 6.30am, 11.50am and 12.50pm; buses depart from Wǔkāng for Shànghǎi at 6.30am, 7.40am, 1pm and 3.30pm. Buses also run between Shànghǎi north bus station and Wǔkāng (Y60).

Wūzhèn 乌镇

☎0573

With origins dating from the late Tang dynasty, Wūzhèn is a historic town that has been resurrected as a tourist destination. Like Zhōuzhuāng and other places in southern Jiāngsū, Wūzhèn is a water town whose network of waterways and access to the Grand Canal once made it a prosperous place for its trade and production of silk. An ambitious restoration project re-creates what Wūzhèn would have been like in the late Qing dynasty.

Sights

Wūzhèn is tiny and it's possible to see everything in a couple hours. Most people come here on a day trip from Hángzhōu or Shànghǎi. The main street of the old town, Dongda Jie, is a narrow path paved with stone slabs and flanked by wooden buildings. You pay an exorbitant entrance fee at the **main gate** (入口; rùkǒu; Daqiao Lu; through ticket Y150; ⏲8am-5pm), which covers entry to all of the exhibits. Some of these are workshops, such as the **Gongsheng Grains Workshop** (三白酒坊; Sānbái Jiǔfáng), an actual distillery churning out a pungent rice wine ripe for the sampling. Next door, the **Blue Prints Workshop** (蓝印花布作坊; Lán Yìnhuābù Zuōfang) shows the dyeing and printing process for the traditional blue cloth of the Jiāngnán region.

Further down the street and across a small bridge is **Mao Dun's Former Residence** (茅盾 故居; Máo Dùn Gùjū). Revolutionary writer Mao Dun is a contemporary of Lu Xun and the author of *Spring Silkworms* and *Midnight*. Mao Dun's great-grandfather, a successful merchant, bought the house in 1885 and it's a fairly typical example from the late Qing dynasty. There are photographs, writings and other memorabilia of Mao Dun's life, though not much explanation in English.

At the western end of the old town, around the corner on Changfeng Jie, is an interesting exhibit many visitors miss. The **Huìyuán Pawn House** (汇源当铺; Huìyuán Dàngpù) was once a famous pawnshop that eventually expanded to branches in Shànghǎi. It has been left intact, and despite the lack of English captions the spartan decor gives a Dickensian feel to the place.

One of the best reasons to visit Wūzhèn is for the regular live performances of local **Flower Drum opera** (Huāgǔ xì) held throughout the day in the village square, and shadow puppet shows *(píyǐngxì)* in the small theatre beside the square. The puppet shows in particular are great fun and well worth watching. There are also **martial arts performances** on the 'boxing boats' in the canal every half-hour from 8.30am to 4.30pm. You can hire a boat at the main gate (Y80 per person) for a ride down the canal.

Getting There & Away

From Hángzhōu, buses run from the east bus station to Wūzhèn (Y26, 1½ hours) leaving every hour or so from 6.25am to 6.25pm.

From Shànghǎi, the easiest (but most expensive) way is to take a tour bus (Y165 return, ticket includes the entrance fee to Wūzhèn and a Chinese-speaking guide, 9am and 9.30am, two hours) from Shànghǎi Stadium. A cheaper option is to take a bus from Shànghǎi's south bus station (Y46).

Minibuses (Y10) connect Wūzhèn with the canal town of Nánxún.

Nánxún 南浔

☎0572

Nestled on the border with Jiāngsū province, about 125km from Hángzhōu and only 20km from Wūzhèn, Nánxún is a water town whose contemporary modest appearance belies its once glorious past. Established over 1400 years ago, the town came to prominence during the Southern Song dynasty due to its prospering silk industry. By the time the Ming rolled around, it was one of Zhèjiāng's most important commercial centres. The town shares the typical features of other southern water towns – arched bridges, canals, narrow lanes and old houses – but what sets it apart is its intriguing mix of Chinese and European architecture, introduced by affluent silk merchants who once made their homes here.

Sights

Since **Nánxún** (adult/student through ticket Y100/50; ⏲8am-5pm summer, to 4.30pm winter) isn't large, it won't take more than a couple of hours to see everything. The entrance fee includes all sights. On the back of your ticket is a small map to help you find your way around.

Nánxún's most famous structure is the rambling **100 Room Pavilion** (百间楼; Bǎijiān Lóu) in the northeast corner of town. It was built 400 years ago by a wealthy Ming official to supposedly house his servants. It's a bit creaky but in amazingly good shape for being so old.

Nánxún has some attractive gardens; the loveliest is **Little Lotus Villa** (小莲庄; Xiǎolián Zhuāng), once the private garden of a wealthy Qing official. The villa gets its name from its pristine lotus pond surrounded by ancient camphor trees. Within the garden are some elaborately carved stone gates and a small family shrine.

Close by is the **Jiāyè Library** (嘉业堂藏书楼; Jiāyètáng Cángshūlóu), once one of the largest private libraries in southeast China. It was home to over 30,000 books, some dating back to the Tang dynasty. Inside is a large woodblock collection and displays of manuscripts. The library is surrounded by a moat – an effective form of fire prevention in the Qing.

The **Zhang Family Compound** (张石铭旧宅; Zhāngshímíng Jiùzhái) is one of the more interesting old residences in Nánxún. Once owned by a wealthy silk merchant, it was the largest and most elaborate private residence in southeastern China during the late Qing dynasty. The home was constructed with wood, glass, tiles and marble, all imported from France. The buildings are an intriguing combination of European and Chinese architecture surrounded by delicate gardens, fishponds and rockeries. Most incongruous is a French-style mansion with red-brick walls, wrought-iron balconies and louvred shutters. Amazingly there's even a ballroom inside, complete with bandstand. This fondness for Western architecture is also seen in the **Liu Family Compound** (刘氏梯号; Liúshì Tīhào) with its imported stained glass, heavy wooden staircases and red-brick exterior.

It's pleasant after a day of walking to relax at one of the small restaurants facing the canal for a snack or some tea. You'll need to bargain for your meal; don't accept the first price you're told.

Getting There & Away

Buses leave hourly from Hángzhōu's north bus stations for Nánxún (Y39, 10 daily). Buses (Y10) also link Nánxún and Wūzhèn. Regular buses (Y43, 2½ hours, 6am to 7.30pm) run from Shànghǎi south station, and from Sūzhōu's south bus station from 7am to 5.50pm.

Nánxún has two bus stations: the **Tài'ān Lù station** (Tài'ān Lù chēzhàn) and another **station** by the expressway *(nánxún qìchēzhàn)*. Both stations have buses from 5.50am to 5pm:

Shànghǎi Y30 to Y50, 2½ hours

Sūzhōu Y21, one hour

Shàoxīng 绍兴

☎0575 / POP 4.3 MILLION

With its winding canals, arched bridges and antiquated homesteads, Shàoxīng is a large water town 67km southeast of Hángzhōu. Being more spread out and developed, Shàoxīng has less of the concise canal-side magic of the smaller water towns, but a stay is worthwhile, especially for excursions out of town. Shàoxīng is known to all Chinese for its *huángjiǔ* (yellow wine), a warming spirit often used in cooking. Computer hacking is apparently another famous local industry: international newspaper reports in 2010 identified Shàoxīng as *the* hacking capital of China.

History

Capital of the Yue kingdom from 770 to 211 BC, Shàoxīng was a flourishing administrative and agricultural centre for much of its history. The town has also been the birthplace of many influential and colourful figures, including mythical 'flood tamer' the Great Yu, painter and dramatist Xu Wei, female revolutionary hero Qiu Jin and Lu Xun, China's first great modern novelist.

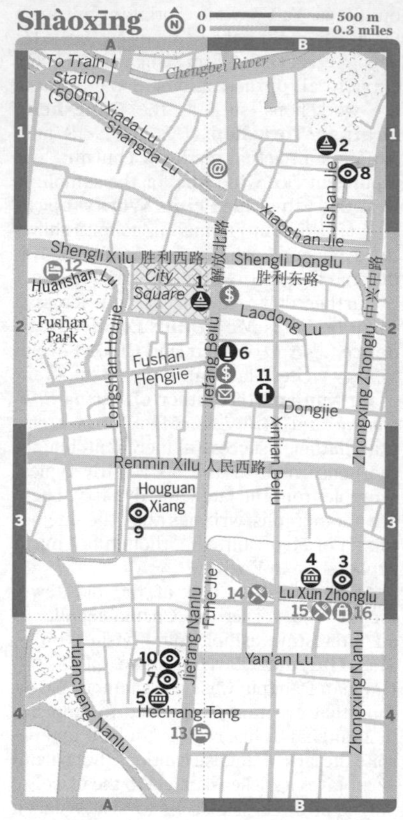

Sights

Wandering Shàoxīng's more historic lanes is charming and restful. The area around Jishan Jie (蕺山街), the vegetation-covered **Tíshān Bridge** (Tíshān Qiáo) and the **Jièzhū Temple** (Jièzhū Sì), just north of Shengli Donglu and east of Jiefang Beilu, is a typically charming zone of mouldering old low-rise whitewashed houses, shops and residences. Nearby Xiaoshan Jie (萧山街) is also a picture, stuffed with goods for sale from old shops and locals sitting out on bamboo stools in front of crumbling canal-side dwellings.

Shàoxīng

Lu Xun's Former Residence MUSEUM

(鲁迅故居; Lǔ Xùn Gùjū; 393 Lu Xun Zhonglu; ⌚8.30am-5pm) Lu Xun (1881–1936), one of China's most mould-breaking and talented modern writers and author of such seminal works as *Diary of a Madman* and *Medicine,* was born in Shàoxīng and lived here until he went abroad to study. He later returned to China, but was forced to hide out in Shànghǎi's French Concession when the Kuomintang decided his books were too dangerous. His tomb is in Shànghǎi.

Sights linked to Lu Xun are clustered along Lu Xun Zhonglu, which these days is more like a carnival street in a permanent state of festivity and tourist mayhem. You can visit Lu Xun's Former Residence; the **Lu Xun Memorial Hall** (鲁迅纪念馆; Lǔ Xùn Jìniànguǎn; ⌚8am-5pm), at the same location; and the **Lu Xun Ancestral Residence** (鲁迅祖居; Lǔxùn Zǔjū; 237 Lu Xun Zhonglu). Opposite is the **one-room school** (Sānwèi Shūwū) the writer attended as a young boy. The captions at the **Yellow Rice Wine Museum** (黄酒馆; Huángjiǔ Guǎn; Lu Xun Zhonglu; ⌚8.30am-7.30pm) are all in Chinese. All sights are free but you need to register by showing your passport at the **Tourist Centre Ticket Office** (免费领票处; Miǎnfèi Lǐngpiàochù; ⌚8.30am-5pm).

Ancestral Homes MUSEUMS

The **studio** (青藤书屋; Qīngténg Shūwū; Qianguan Xiang; admission Y5; ⌚8am-4pm) of controversial Ming painter, poet and dramatist Xu Wei (1521–93) is off Renmin Xilu in a small alley. Born in Shàoxīng, Xu's artistic talents brought him early fame and later he served as a personal assistant to the governor of the southeastern provinces. When the governor was killed for treason, Xu spiralled into madness. Over a period of years, he attempted suicide nine times, once by trying to split his skull with an axe. Later, in a fit of rage he beat his wife to death and was sent to prison. Skilful manoeuvring on the part of his friends got him free. In his later years Xu remained in Shàoxīng, living in this study where he spent the remainder of his life painting and writing plays.

The studio, surrounded by a tranquil bamboo garden, is a well-maintained example of 16th-century architecture, with its ivy-covered, whitewashed walls and black-tiled roof. Inside are displays of the artist's paintbrushes, painting and calligraphy.

Qiu Jin's Former Residence (秋瑾故居; Qiū Jǐn Gùjū; 35 Hechang Tang; admission Y10; ⌚8am-5pm) is where pioneering female revolutionary Qiu Jin was born. Qiu Jin studied in Japan, and was active in women's rights and the revolutionary movement against the Qing government. She was beheaded in 1907 by Qing authorities at the age of 29. A memorial **statue of Qiu Jin** (秋瑾像; Qiūjǐn Xiàng; Jiefang Beilu) stands near Fushan Hengjie.

Yìngtiān Pagoda PAGODA

(应天塔;Yìngtiān Tǎ) Rising up within **Tǎshān Park** (Tǎshān Gōngyuán; admission Y2) and originally part of a Song-dynasty temple, Yìngtiān Pagoda stands gracefully on a hill overlooking modern-day Shàoxīng. Destroyed during the Taiping Rebellion (1850–64) and later rebuilt, the pagoda offers good views from the top.

King Yu's Mausoleum HISTORIC SITE

(大禹陵;Dà Yǔ Líng; admission Y50; ⌚7.30am-5.30pm) According to legend, in 2205 BC the Great Yu became the first emperor of the Xia dynasty, and earned the title 'tamer of floods' after he conquered the dragons that lived underground and caused floods.

A temple and mausoleum complex to honour the 'great-grandfather of China' was first constructed in the 6th century and was added to over the centuries that followed. King Yu's Mausoleum is about 4km southeast of the city centre and is composed of a huge 24m-tall Main Hall, a Memorial Hall and Meridian Gate (Wǔ Mén). A statue of Yu graces the Main Hall.

Bus 2 will get you to King Yu's Mausoleum from the train station area or from Jiefang Beilu (get off at the last stop).

OTHER SIGHTS

Sprouting a crop of saplings, the picturesque seven-storey **Dàshàn Pagoda** (大善塔; Dàshàn Tǎ) by City Sq (Chéngshì Guǎngchǎng) sadly cannot be climbed, even though steps lead up from its 2nd-floor portal. The brick Protestant **Zhēnshén Church** (真神堂; Zhēnshén Táng; 81 Dongjie) records a historic Christian presence in Shàoxīng. For a canal-borne perspective of Shàoxīng, you can hop on an expensive *wūpéng chuán* (乌篷船; narrow canal boat, Y50) for a 20-minute journey from the Lu Xun one-room school on Lu Xun Lu.

Festivals & Events

The **Orchid Pavilion Calligraphy Festival** is held each year on the third day of the third lunar month at the Orchid Pavilion (p251). Shàoxīng wine enjoys its own festival in autumn with the **Yellow Wine Festival** (Huángjiǔ Jié). Calligraphy exhibitions and contests are also held.

Sleeping

Shàoxīng can be done as a day trip from Hángzhōu or used as a stopover if you want to spend some time at the outlying sights.

Shaoxing International Youth Hostel HOSTEL $
(绍兴国际青年旅社; Shàoxīng Guójì Qīngnián Lǚshè; ☎8515 1780; 11 Huanshan Lu; 4- & 10-bed dm Y40, s/d Y120/160; ❄@📶) Excellent hostel in a great location down leafy Huanshan Lu (next to the Shaoxing Hotel) with a very relaxing and cultured feel, this is the place to come in Shàoxīng. Rooms are clean and comfy; free internet.

Shàoxīng Hotel HOTEL $$$
(绍兴饭店; Shàoxīng Fàndiàn; ☎515 5858; www.hotel-shaoxing.com; 9 Huanshan Lu; 环山路9号; d Y660-980, ste Y1280-9800; ❄@) One of the nicest places to stay in town, this modern hotel has well-equipped, comfortable rooms in several buildings surrounded by gardens. The restaurant has an excellent reputation. Discounts of 30% are typical.

Xiánhēng Hotel HOTEL $$$
(咸亨大酒店; Xiánhēng Dàjiǔdiàn; ☎806 8688; www.xianhengchina.com; 680 Jiefang Nanlu; 解放南路680号; s & d Y980, ste Y1680) Tall tower in the south of town with – apart from the fake bamboo rising over the lobby bar – an elegant interior and professional service.

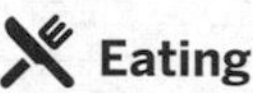

Eating

The overpowering fumes of stinky tofu (臭豆腐; *chòu dòufu*) eye-wateringly waft down Shàoxīng's streets. The pungent snack tastes better than it smells.

Zhōujiā Shípǐn SNACKS $
(周家食品; 25 Lu Xun Lu; snacks from Y5; ⏲8.30am-5pm) Very popular and busy place for local specialities opposite Lu Xun's Former Residence; just look at what's on the corner and point, but try to aim for the lovely creamy tarts (奶油小攀; *nǎiyóu xiǎopān*; Y5). Friendly chefs may entice you in the direction of stinky tofu: tame its flavour with a shot of Shàoxīng rice wine (Y3).

Āpó Miànguǎn NOODLES $
(阿婆面馆; ☎8513 0826; 100 Lu Xun Zhonglu; meals Y20; ⏲9am-11pm) With excellent noodle dishes and outside seating, order up the trademark Apo Noodles (Āpó Miàn; Y18), a steaming and filling bowl of noodles, carrots, greens, egg yolk, mushroom, shrimps and cabbage; down it with a glass of heartwarming and pink alcohol-infused *Nǚer hóng* (Y28 to Y48).

Ajisen NOODLES $
(味千拉面; Wèiqiān Lāmiàn; meal Y30) Just south of the train station, next to a branch of the fast food chain Dicos.

Shopping

Jia Dan's Papercut Shop PAPERCUTS
(佳丹剪画社; Jiādān Jiǎnhuàshè; ☎8536 3376; 246 Luxun Guli; ⏲8.30am-6pm) With prices starting at around Y17, Jia Dan sells some exquisite red and black traditional paper cuts; she also runs Chinese-language classes in paper-cutting.

Information

Bank of China (中国银行; Zhōngguó Yínháng; 9 Laodong Lu; ⏲8.30am-5pm) Foreign exchange in major currencies; 24-hour ATM. There's also a branch at 472 Jiefang Beilu.

China Post (邮局; Zhōngguó Yóuzhèng; 1 Dongjie; ⌚8am-5pm) Centrally located on the corner of Dongjie and Jiefang Beilu.

Míngxīng Internet Cafe (明星网吧; Míngxīng Wǎngbā; 121 Jiefang Beilu; per hr Y2)

Net Bar (Net Bar网吧; Net Bar wǎngbā; per hr Y3) Opposite the train station.

Public Security Bureau (PSB; 公安局; Gōng'ānjú; ☎865 1333, ext 2104) About 2km east of the city centre on Renmin Donglu, near Huiyong Lu.

Shàoxīng Travel Guide (www.travelchinaguide.com/cityguides/zhejiang/Shaoxing) Provides general background information on Shàoxīng.

Getting There & Away

All trains and buses travelling between Hángzhōu and Níngbō stop in Shàoxīng. Shàoxīng has three bus stations, the most useful is the **long-distance bus station** in the northeast of town:

Hángzhōu Y23, 45 minutes

Níngbō Y43, 1½ hours

Shànghǎi Y80, three hours

Shěnjiāmén Y85, three hours (for boats to Pǔtuóshān)

Wēnzhōu Y134

A ticket office for the long-distance bus station can be found in the train station. Buses also travel to most tourist cities in Jiāngsū.

Getting Around

The bus system in Shàoxīng is fairly straightforward. Bus 1 travels from the train station down Jiefang Beilu and then east to East Lake. Bus 3 and bus 8 can get you to the long-distance bus station. Taxis are cheap, starting at Y5.

Around Shàoxīng

ORCHID PAVILION 兰亭

Considered by many Chinese to be one of Shàoxīng's 'must see' spots, this **site** (Lán Tíng; admission Y40; ⌚7am-5pm) is where the famous calligrapher Wang Xizhi (AD 321–79) gathered with 41 friends and composed the collection of poetry called the *Orchid Pavilion*. At the pavilion you'll see gardens, Wang's ancestral shrine and stelae with his calligraphy. A **calligraphy festival** is held yearly in March. The Orchid Pavilion is around 10km southwest of the city centre and can be reached by bus 3 from Shengli Lu.

Ānchāng 安昌

☎0575

About 40 minutes west of Shàoxīng by bus is the peaceful little water town of **Ānchāng** (admission Y35; ⌚8am-4.30pm). An ancient settlement, Ānchāng has few sites; there's little to do but explore the two main streets along the canal, which are linked by a series of 17 stone bridges. The Ming- and Qing-style stone houses and shops that line the canal front have seen little restoration; townsfolk gather along the canal to play mahjong, cobblers sew cloth shoes and elderly women sit in doorways spinning cotton into yarn.

Some old buildings have opened to the public and are interesting to peruse; the map on the back of your entry ticket has them marked in Chinese. Close to the entrance is a former **bank** (穗康钱庄, *suìkāng qiánzhuāng*), with displays of abacuses and Nationalist-era bank notes in its gloomy, cobwebbed interior. Also interesting and a few minutes' walk from the bank is an old **mansion** (斯干堂, *sīgān táng*) with three large courtyards that have interesting displays of beds, chairs and other Qing-style furnishings.

Riding on oilcloth-covered boats down the canal is fun; Y10 per person is a reasonable bargaining price.

Bus 118 from Shàoxīng's long-distance bus station will take you on a bumpy roundabout tour of the countryside before dropping you off at Ānchang's entrance, marked by an arch. The trip costs Y5.

Wǔyì 武义

☎0579

Located far inland, Wǔyì is itself an uninteresting city, but it is the gateway to the two villages of Yúyuán and Guōdòng in the surrounding scenic hilly countryside. It is far preferable to spend the night in Guōdòng, which has so much more character and charm, but if you wish to stay in Wǔyì, hotels can be found near the long-distance bus station.

The **Hóngdá Hotel** (鸿达大酒店; Hóngdá Dàjiǔdiàn; ☎8762-2001; d Y380, discounts of 60%; ❄) has decent and spacious wood-floored rooms, although the hotel is a bit murky.

Information

Bank of China (中国银行; Zhōngguó Yínháng; 71 Hushanxia Jie) In the south of town.

Industrial & Commercial Bank of China (工商银行; Gōngshāng Yínháng; Wuyang Lu) Has a 24hr ATM.

Péngkè Wǎngbā (朋客网吧; Jiefang Beijie; per hr Y2.50; 24hr) For internet access.

Getting There & Away

Bus

Buses run to and from Wǔyì's **main bus station** (客运中心; kèyùn zhōngxīn; 8851 5959) from Hángzhōu south bus station (Y76, six per day from 7.10am to 4.40pm), Níngbō (Y85, three per day) and Wénzhōu (8.30am).

Train

Wǔyì is easy to reach by train from a number of destinations:

Hángzhōu seat/sleeper Y38/89, 3½ to four hours, seven daily

Nánjīng seat/sleeper Y94/188, 9½ to 13 hours, three daily

Shànghǎi hard seat/sleeper Y63/124, six hours

Wēnzhōu seat/sleeper Y38/79, four to five hours, 12 daily

Around Wǔyì

GUŌDÒNG 郭洞

Embraced by bamboo-clad hills and dating to the Song dynasty, this lovely old Zhéjiāng **village** (through ticket Y30) is miles away from it all south of Wǔyì. Exquisite in parts, Guōdòng offers ample opportunity for threading through ancient and cramped **Ming-dynasty lanes** with their even brickwork and mud-packed walls, past washer women, ancient wells and antique shops, and trekking in the surrounding scenery. Note the lovely brickwork along **Qīngyuán Lù** (清源路), which is where you also find a small **church** (in a courtyard, next to 20 Qingyuan Lu). The **Ancestral Hall of the He Clan** (何氏宗祠; Héshì Zōngcí) is a huge affair at the heart of the village originally dating to the Ming dynasty. Also worth looking out for are the **Fanyu Hall** and the **Rènlán Hall** (纫兰堂; Rènlán Táng). If you have a fear of canines, note that Guōdòng has a large population of barking dogs.

Some homesteads are graced with Christian posters on their doors, while others are decorated with lovely poetic couplets celebrating the rhythms of nature, such as '近山识鸟音、临水知鱼性' (Enter the mountains to know the sounds of birds, face the water to know the nature of fish). After you have explored the village, wander along **Lóngshān Lù** (龙山路) and up into the bamboo and woods in the hill above the village (admission included in ticket).

A highlight is the **Dawan Lake Scenic Area** (大弯湖景区; Dàwānhú Jǐngqū; Y5), a 30-minute walk out of the village (follow the signs) past the **Wenchang Pavilion** (文昌阁; Wénchāng Gé) and a vast, 600-year old fir tree. At the lake, cross over the dam and wander round the lake with its dark pine-green waters picturesquely surrounded by forests of bamboo.

It's well worth spending the night in Guōdòng (rather than Wǔyì) and the village has more character than Yúyuán. Near the bus drop-off is the **Guōdòng Kèzhàn** (郭洞客栈; 0579-8773 6077 or 139 5847 4997; d Y70;) with large and pleasant rooms, with TV and shower. Another possibility is the **Guōdòng Bīnguǎn** (郭洞宾馆; 136 0572 8043). All hotels either have restaurants or can fix you a meal, but avoid being pushed towards *tǔjī* (free-range chicken) unless you really want it, as it is expensive. A small plate of *xiǎo xīyú* (小溪鱼; grilled river fish) should cost around Y18.

To reach Guōdòng, take bus 5 (Y1.50) to the **east bus station** (客运东站; *kèyùn dōngzhàn*) in Wǔyì and hop on a Guōdòng-bound bus (Y3, one hour, every 30 minutes) collecting passengers across the road. Returning to Wǔyì, the first/last bus from Guōdòng is at 6.30am/5.50pm.

YÚYUÁN 俞源

A 20km trip through the glittering Zhèjiāng countryside from Wǔyì past mountains, fields of tea bushels, yellow and green bamboo, old bridges and fields of rapeseed brings you to the riverside village of Yúyuán. Surrounded by hills striated with fields, the **ancient village** (admission Y30) is famously based on the arrangement of the Taoist Taiji (twin fish) diagram, although this can be hard to discern for those without a definitive interest in feng shui.

Nonetheless, with its whitewashed residences, ancient halls, old doorways decorated with hanging red couplets, carved woodwork, cobbled lanes, crowing cocks and waddling geese, the village has an abundance of historic charm. Originally dating to 1374, the **Ancestral Hall of the**

Yu Clan (俞氏宗祠; Yúshì Zōngcí) is a lovely and unrestored collection of halls around a magnificently carved stage daubed at the rear with a conspicuous slogan from the Cultural Revolution. At the rear is the **Qǐn Táng** (寝堂) where the tablets of the ancestors resided. The hall once burned down and was rebuilt, a battalion camped in the hall in 1930 and it served as a grain storage depot in 1951. Also track down the **Ancestral Hall of the Li Clan** (李氏宗祠; Lǐshì Zōngcí), with its light well *(tiānjǐng)* courtyard and side halls bedecked with folk articles. Several of the village's old residences – many in need of restoration – are still occupied, such as **Dūnhòu Táng** (敦厚堂) and the **Xiàtài Lóu** (下态楼). Also look out for the lovely wood-fronted **Hóngbīn Lóu** (鸿宾楼) by the **Yín River** (银河; Yín Hé), the lovely **Jīngshēn Lóu** (精深楼), the ample **Yùhòu Táng** (裕后堂) – occupying 2560 sq metres – and the **Shēngyuǎn Táng** (声远堂; also called Liufeng Hall), one of the most ambitious and best-preserved of Yúyuán's halls. A fair amount of Yúyuán's feng shui charm has been irreversibly ruined by modern eyesore attachments thrown up willy-nilly and white tile buildings with aluminium shuttering that viciously overlook old residences.

Next to a bridge by the river on the outskirts of Yúyuán, the lovely Taoist **Temple of the Cave Host** (洞主庙; Dòngzhǔ Miào) originally dates to the Northern Song and is seemingly one of the best preserved buildings in the village.

To reach Yúyuán, take a direct bus (Y4, 25 minutes, every 20 minutes, last bus 5.30pm) from the west bus station (西站; Xīzhàn) in Wǔyì. Bus 5 (Y1.50) runs between the main bus station in Wǔyì and the west bus station.

Pǔtuóshān 普陀山

☎0580

The lush and well-tended Buddhist island of Pǔtuóshān – the Zhōushān Archipelago's most famed isle – is the enchanting abode of Guanyin, the eternally compassionate Goddess of Mercy. One of China's four sacred Buddhist mountains, Pǔtuóshān is deeply permeated with the aura of the goddess and the devotion her worshippers bring to this gorgeous island. With its clean beaches and fresh air, it's a perfect retreat, but try to visit midweek, as the island is bombarded by tourists come weekends. Spring can be fogged out with sporadic boat services, so phone ahead. Guanyin's three birthdays (19 February, 19 June and 19 September) are naturally celebrated with gusto across the island.

Sights

Images of Guanyin are ubiquitous and Pǔtuóshān's temples are all shrines for the merciful goddess. Besides the three main temples, you will stumble upon nunneries and monasteries everywhere, although several have been converted from their original purpose.

The central part of town is around Pǔjì Temple about 1km north of the ferry terminal. This is where many hotels are located. You can reach the central square by taking the roads leading east or west from the ferry terminal; either way takes about 20 minutes. Alternatively, minibuses from the ferry terminal run to Pǔjì Temple and to other points of the island.

The first thing you see as you approach the island by boat is a 33m-high glittering statue of Guanyin, the **Nánhǎi Guānyīn** (南海观音; admission Y6), overlooking the waves at the southernmost tip of the island.

An entrance fee (summer/winter Y160/140) is payable when you arrive; entry to some other sights is extra.

Pǔjì Temple TEMPLE
(普济禅寺; Pǔjì Sì; admission Y5; ⏰5.30am-6pm) Fronted by large ponds and overlooked by towering camphor trees and Luóhàn pines, this temple stands by the main square and dates to at least the 17th century. Past chubby Milefo – the future Buddha – sitting in a red, gold and green burnished cabinet in the Hall of Heavenly Kings, throngs of worshippers stand with flaming incense in front of the stunning main hall. Buses leave from the west side of the temple to various points around the island. Built in 1334 is the nearby five-storey **Duōbǎo Pagoda** (多宝塔; Duōbǎo Tǎ; admission Y15).

Fǎyǔ Temple TEMPLE
(法雨禅寺; Fǎyǔ Chánsì; admission Y5; ⏰5.30am-6pm) Colossal camphor trees and a huge gingko tree tower over this temple, where a vast glittering statue of Guanyin is seated in the main hall, flanked by rows of histrionic *luóhàn* (arhat) effigies. In the hall behind stands a 1000-arm Guanyin. Get to the temple by bus from the ferry terminal (Y6).

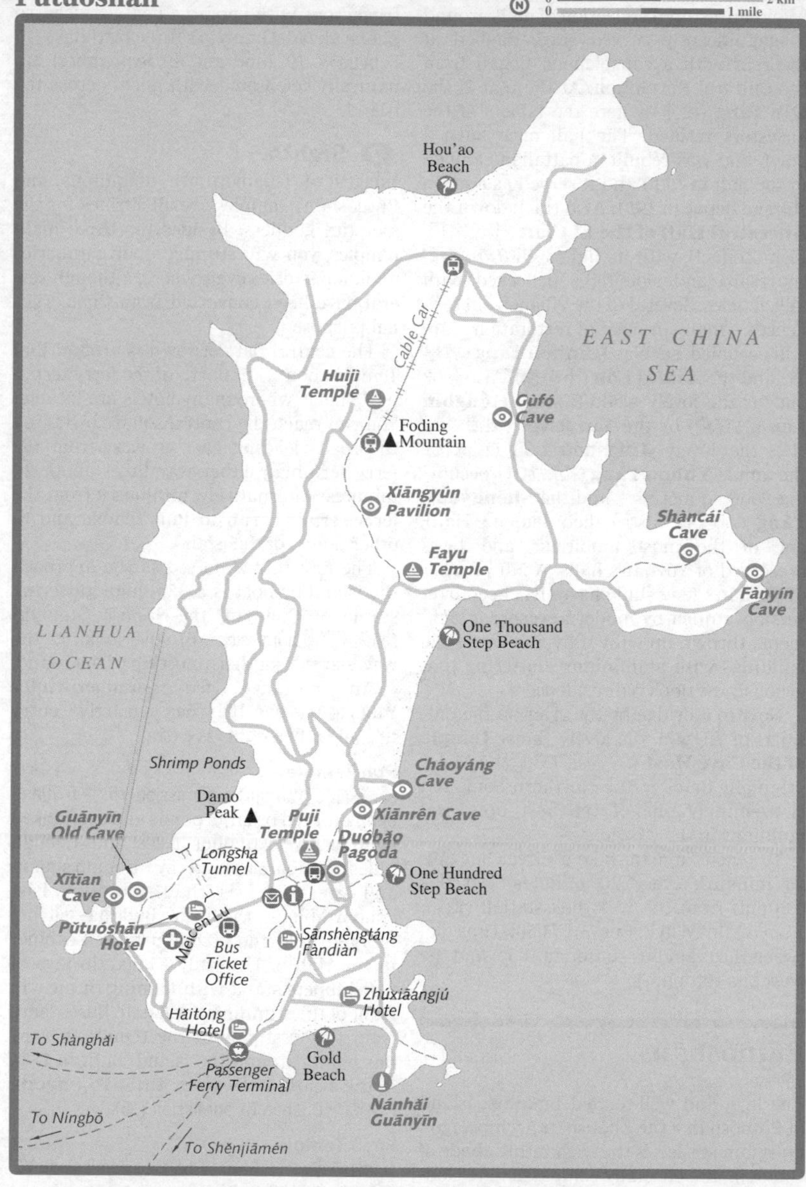

Fódǐng Mountain MOUNTAIN
(佛顶山; Fódǐng Shān; admission Y5) A fantastic, shaded half-hour climb can be made from Fǎyǔ Temple to Fódǐng Mountain – Buddha's Summit Peak – the highest point on the island. This is also where you will find the less elaborate **Huìjì Temple** (慧济禅寺; Huìjì Chánsì; admission Y5; ⏲5.30am-6.30pm). In summer the climb is much cooler in the late afternoon; watch devout pilgrims and Buddhist nuns stop every three steps to either bow or kneel in supplication. The less

motivated take the **cable car** (one way/return Y30/50; ⏲6.40am-5pm). The **Xiāngyún Pavilion** (香云亭; Xiāngyún Tíng) is a pleasant spot for a breather.

Beaches BEACHES

Pǔtuóshān's two large beaches, **One Hundred Step Beach** (百步沙; Bǎibùshā; ⏲6am-6pm) and **One Thousand Step Beach** (千步沙; Qiānbùshā) on the east of the island are attractive and largely unspoilt, although periodically you may have to pay for access (admission Y15); swimming (May through August) is not permitted after 6pm.

Caves CAVES

Fànyīn Cave (梵音洞; Fànyīn Dòng; admission Y5; ⏲5.30am-6pm), on the far eastern tip of the island, has a temple dedicated to Guanyin perched between two cliffs with a seagull's view of the crashing waves below. The sound of the roaring waves in **Cháoyáng Cave** (朝阳洞; Cháoyáng Dòng; admission Y12), which overlooks the sea, is said to imitate the chanting of the Buddha. A fully fledged temple has been assembled around the small grotto of the **Guānyīn Old Cave** (观音古洞; Guānyīn Gǔdòng). Other natural wonders include the **Shàncái Cave** (善财洞; Shàncái Dòng; admission Y5), **Gǔfó Cave** (古佛洞; Gǔfó Dòng; admission Y5), **Xiānrén Cave** (仙人洞; Xiānrén Dòng; admission Y5) and **Xītiān Cave** (西天洞; Xītiān Dòng; admission Y5).

Sleeping

Room prices are generally discounted from Sunday to Thursday; the prices given here refer to Friday and Saturday and holiday periods. As you get off the boat, you'll be greeted by hotel touts who can fix you up with a place to stay, but it pays to compare places and rooms. Several hotels have shuttle buses to and from the pier. For inexpensive rooms, try one of the cheap hotels that cluster along Meicen Lu in Xīshān Xīncūn (西山新村), a short walk over the hill to the west from the ferry terminal. Some hotels don't take foreigners, but others do (speaking Chinese helps); rooms go for around Y120/300 per weekday/weekend. Look for the characters '内有住宿', which means rooms are available.

Pǔtuóshān Hotel HOTEL $$$

(普陀山大酒店; Pǔtuóshān Dàjiǔdiàn; ☎609 2828; www.putuoshanhotel.com; 93 Meicen Lu; 梅岑路93号; d Y1188-1288, ste Y1988; ❄@) Backing onto a green hill, Pǔtuóshān's best hotel has a pleasant and uncluttered feel, with decent amenities and service to match. Midweek rooms are discounted to Y650.

Sānshèngtáng Fàndiàn HOTEL $$$

(三圣堂饭店; ☎609 3688; 121 Miaozhuang Yanlu; 妙庄严路121号; d Y720-980; ❄) Often full, this traditional-style place is attractively set off a small path near the Pǔjì Temple and is shaded by trees. Rooms generally go for around Y300 during slack times, but foreigners can be overcharged.

Zhúxiāngjū Hotel HOTEL $$$

(竹香居宾馆; Zhúxiāngjū Bīnguǎn; ☎669 8080; 20 Jinsha Lu; 金沙路20号; s/d Y1880/1680, seaview d Y1880; ❄) Decked out with gold and occasional Buddhist ornaments, this pleasant hotel is just across the road from the sands of Gold Beach in a cove on the south of the island, with lovely sea views. The cheapest rooms are discounted to Y380 midweek. No English sign.

Hǎitōng Hotel HOTEL $$$

(海通宾馆; Hǎitōng Bīnguǎn; ☎609 2569; d Y680-780, t with seaview Y980, midweek/weekend discounts of 60%/30%; ❄) Across the road as you exit the ferry terminal, this agreeable place has helpful staff and a tempting traditional feel.

Eating

Pǔtuóshān isn't famed for its food; what you get is generally brought in from the mainland and is expensive. Seafood is pretty much the staple. Some of the best places to eat are in the temples, where vegetarian meals are usually served at lunch and sometimes at breakfast and dinner for Y2 to Y10.

Information

Bank of China (中国银行; Zhōngguó Yínháng; Meicen Lu; ⏲8-11am & 2-5pm) Has Forex currency exchange. ATMs (24-hour) taking international cards are close by down the side of the block.

China Mobile (中国移动; Zhōngguó Yídòng; Meicen Lu) For mobile-phone SIM cards. Located near the banks.

China Post (中国邮政; Zhōngguó Yóuzhèng; 124 Meicen Lu) Southwest of Pǔjì Temple.

Clinic (诊所; Zhěnsuǒ; ☎609 3102; Meicen Lu) Situated behind the Bank of China.

Industrial & Commercial Bank of China (工行; Gōngháng; Meicen Lu; ⏲8-11am & 2-5pm)

Left-luggage office (寄存处; jìcúnchù; per luggage piece Y4;⏲6.30am-5pm) At the ferry terminal, this handy service allows you to ditch your bag and hunt for a room.

Tourist Service Centre (旅游咨询中心; Lŭyóu Zīxún Zhōngxīn; ☎609 4921) Near Pŭjì Temple.

Getting There & Away

The nearest airport is Zhōushān (Pŭtuóshān) airport on the neighbouring island of Zhūjiājiān (朱家尖).

Regular boats link Pŭtuóshān and Zhūjiājiān. Pŭtuóshān can be reached by boat from either Níngbō or Shànghăi; Níngbō is closer and offers more frequent services.

Fast ferries (Y73, first bus/boat around 6.20am/7.35am, last bus 3.10pm, every 30 minutes) for Pŭtuóshān leave Níngbō's **passenger ferry terminal** (lúnchuán mătou; ☎0574 2769 1132; 380 Zhongma Lu; ⏱5.45am-4.15pm summer, 6.15am-4.15pm winter); the trip takes about 2½ hours, including the bus ride to the fast boat wharf outside Níngbō. From Pŭtuóshān to Níngbō boats leave every half-hour from 7.30am to 4.50pm. Note: buses and boats can be cancelled during fog (common in spring months). At the time of writing, the ticket office had moved 100m north up the road from its former address.

Buses (Y41, three hours, every 30 minutes) also run from the **north bus station** (qìchē bĕizhàn; ☎8735 5321; 122 Taodu Lu) in Níngbō to Shĕnjiāmén (沈家门) on the island of Zhōushān (舟山岛), from where fast boats (Y19.5) run every 10 minutes for the short hop to Pŭtuóshān.

A nightly boat leaves Pŭtuóshān at 4.40pm for the 12-hour voyage to Shànghăi's Wúsōng Wharf. Tickets cost Y109 to Y499, offering numerous grades of comfort; it's easy to upgrade once you're on board. From Shànghăi, the boat leaves Wúsōng Wharf at 8pm, with an extra two services on Friday at 7.20pm and 8.40pm. To reach Wúsōng Wharf, take metro line 3 to Songbin Lu from where it's a 15-minute walk. Cross the eight-lane highway and follow the signs to the wharf. Bank on a 90-minute journey from People's Square.

A fast boat (Y258) departs Pŭtuóshān for the port of Xiăo Yáng Shān (小洋山) south of Shànghăi at 1pm, where passengers are then bussed to Nánpŭ Bridge; the whole trip takes four hours. The twice-daily bus/ferry from Shànghăi to Pŭtuóshān departs from Xiăo Yáng Shān; shuttle buses leave depart Nánpŭ Bridge in Shànghăi at 7.20am and 8am to connect with them.

Tickets for both ferry and bus/ferry services are available at the **Huángpŭ Tourist Centre** (黄浦旅游集散中心; Huángpŭ Lŭyo'u Jísàn Zhōngxīn; ☎6336 9051; 21 East Jinling Rd;金陵东路21号; ⏱9am-6pm).

You can also reach Shànghăi by taking one of the **regular boats** to Shĕnjiāmén and jumping on a bus (Y125, five hours, several departures daily); buses also run to Hángzhōu (Y90, frequent). Bus tickets are available from the **passenger ferry terminal ticket office** (☎609 1186), and the bus ticket office next to the Hăitōng Hotel; another **bus ticket office** (⏱8-10.40am & 1.20-4.15pm) can be found opposite the Pŭtuóshān Hotel.

Getting Around

Walking around Pŭtuóshān is the most relaxing option if you have time. If not, minibuses zip from the passenger ferry terminal to various points around the island, including Pŭjì Temple (Y5), One Thousand Step Beach (Y6), Făyŭ Temple (Y6), Fànyīn Cave (Y8) and the cable car station (Y10). There are more bus stations at Pŭjì Temple, Făyŭ Temple and other spots around the island serving the same and other destinations.

Wēnzhōu 温州

☎0577 / POP 7.4 MILLION

A thriving and bustling seaport on the Zhèjiāng coastline, Wēnzhōu is trumpeted as one of China's economic success stories, built upon a solid manufacturing base. Strong business and historic ties to Europe and North America have given the city prosperity (and endless shoe factories) but little character. There's an abiding sense that something has been trampled underfoot: a proliferation of beggars sprawls in front of hand-written notes relating tales of personal tragedy while Wēnzhōu's money-making reputation (and pitiless economic environment) has lent the city a spiteful edge. There's no reason to hang about in town: get out to the lovely historic villages and surrounding scenery of the Nánxījiāng region.

Sights

Jiāngxīn Island (江心岛; Jiāngxīn Dăo; adult/child Y20/10; ⏱8am-10pm, 1st/last ticket 7.45am/8.30pm), in the middle of the **Ōu River** (Ōu Jiāng), is dotted with pagodas (including one capped with a tree), a lake, footbridges and a main temple. It's easily reached by ferry, included in the admission, from Jiāngxīn Pier (江心码头; Jiāngxīn Mătóu) on Wangjiang Donglu. The river itself is more of an eyesore, with pungent Dickensian fumes wafting from its surface in patches.

Surrounded by high-rise residential blocks, the **Catholic Church** (周宅寺巷天主教堂; Zhōuzhái Sì Xiàng Tiānzhǔ Jiàotáng) was moved to its present site in 1866 and rebuilt in 1888 after being burned down during the Opium War. Stripped of its pews and stained glass, the musty, whitewashed and mildewed interior has been damaged by rain penetration and neglect; climb up the stairs to the gallery above and the belfry.

The grey-brick **Chéngxī Christian Church** (城西基督教堂; Chéngxī Jīdū Jiàotáng; 107 Chengxi Jie) is decorated with Gothic arched windows.

Wēnzhōu's Buddhist '*xiāngkè*' (incense-toting worshippers) head to **Miàoguǒ Temple** (Miàoguǒ Sì; admission Y3).

Sleeping

Wēnzhōu is significantly lacking in budget options, although cheaper hotels can be found in the vicinity of the train station and Xīnchéng bus station.

Jīnwàngjiǎo Seaview Hotel HOTEL $$
(金旺角海港大酒店; Jīnwàngjiǎo Hǎigǎng Dàjiǔdiàn; ☎8803 8888; Wangjiang Lu; 望江路; s Y188, d Y498 568) Try to get a river-view room at this well-located, clean and well-kept hotel, otherwise the cheaper rooms are all south facing. Discounts bring the cheapest rooms here down to around Y280.

Wēnzhōu International Hotel HOTEL $$$
(温州国际大酒店; Wenzhou Guoji Dajiudian; ☎8825 1111; www.wzihotel.com; 1 Renmin Donglu; 人民东路1号; s/d/ste Y530/780/1200, discounts of 30%) This 26-storey four-star hotel has a rather featureless interior, but rooms are comfortable and the English-speaking staff are friendly.

Jiàoyù Hotel HOTEL $
(教育宾馆; Jiàoyù Bīnguǎn; ☎8822 7890; 32 Chan Jie; 蝉街32号; s/d/tr/ste Y228/228/248/288, discounts of 20%; ❄) Clean lower-rung business hotel with well-kept but rather smallish rooms with shower; central, convenient and friendly. No English sign.

Eating

Wēnzhōu is well known for its seafood, with restaurants running along Jiefang Jie and by the river. Another good place to look for food is on Wuma Jie, a busy pedestrian shopping street in the middle of town.

Chángrén Huntun NOODLES $
(常人馄饨; 195 Jiefang Jie; noodles from Y5; ⏲6am-11pm) Busy spot with a long history and clean interior; the *jīdàn miàn* (鸡蛋面; egg and noodles; Y5.50) is salty and tasty, the *xīhóngshì dàntāng* (西红柿蛋汤; egg and tomato soup; Y5) ample and filling.

Information

Bank of China (中国银行; Zhōngguó Yínháng; 129 Chan Jie; ⏲9am-5pm) Changes travellers cheques and major currency. There's another branch on Lucheng Lu with an ATM.

China Post (Xinhe Jie; ⏲8.30am-5.30pm) Next to the China Telecom office.

Public Security Bureau (PSB; 公安局; Gōng'ānjú; cnr Jinxiu Lu & Jinqiao Lu) In the east of town.

Pǔfā Internet Cafe (浦发网吧; Pǔfā Wǎngbā; per hr Y4; ⏲24hr)

Xīngjiàn Internet Cafe (星箭网吧; Xīngjiàn Wǎngbā; Renmin Donglu; per hr Y3; ⏲24hr) Opposite Wēnzhōu International Hotel.

Getting There & Away

Air

Wēnzhōu's airport has good connections to other Chinese cities. Keep in mind that flights are often delayed or cancelled because of heavy fog. The **CAAC** (Zhōngguó Mínháng; ☎8833 3197) is in the southeast section of town.

Bus

For long-haul destinations, you're better off taking the train. Wēnzhōu has several bus stations including the useful **Xīnnán bus station** near the old train station:

Fúzhōu Y135 to Y145, 4½ hours, frequent
Nánjīng Y170 to Y220, eight hours, five daily
Shànghǎi Y185, six hours, frequent
Sūzhōu Y318, seven hours, three daily
Xiàmén Y200, eight hours, three daily

The **Xīnchéng bus station** in the east of town also has buses:

Hángzhōu Y140, 4½ hours
Níngbō Y110, 3½ hours
Shěnjiāmén Y160, six hours, three daily

Train

Wénzhōu's colossal new **South train station** (南站; Nánzhàn) is out in the blighted suburbs. Take bus 15 (Y2, 45 minutes) from Renmin Lu, Miàoguǒ Temple or Zhōngshān Park. Express trains, including high speed D-class trains:

Běijīng sleeper Y405, 28 hours
Fúzhōu Y92, 1½ to two hours

Hángzhōu 1st-/2nd-class seat Y130/156, three to five hours

Níngbō 1st-/2nd-class seat Y85/102, 1½ hours

Shànghǎi South train station 1st-/2nd-class seat Y188/225, 4½ to five hours

Getting Around

Wēnzhōu airport is 27km east of the city centre and taxis charge Y100 to Y120 for the trip. A bus goes from the CAAC to the airport for Y10. Taxis around the city centre start at Y10. A pedicab should cost around Y6 from Renmin Lu to the Ōu River. Bus 32 links the train station and Xīnchéng bus station.

Around Wēnzhōu

NÁNXĪJIĀNG 楠溪江

The gorgeous river waters of the Nánxījiāng region, speckled with ancient, picturesque villages that lie clustered within easy reach of town, make for fantastic exploration.

YÁNTÓUCŪN 岩头村

An enchanting system of waterways at its heart and backing onto green mountains, this ancient village is charming. The first thing to do is to find the **old town** (admission Y15), a settlement that originally dates to the end of the Five Dynasties. Covered, bow-shaped and red-lantern-hung **Lishui Jie** (丽水街) is a pleasingly cobbled curve of a street alongside a glistening stretch of water lined with willows. More of a wooden corridor, the street – several hundred metres in length – is lined with old shops, the occasional pavilion and water wheel.

Near Lishui Jie, the **Ancestral Hall** is a picture with a cobbled courtyard, stage and fine original woodwork. On the other side of the bridge at the end of Lishui Jie stands the smoky and vibrant Taoist **Tǎhu' Temple** (Tǎhu' Miào), facing an old stage.

With its belfry and small white interior, the **Catholic Church** (天主教堂; Tiānzhǔ Jiàotáng; 8 Heng Jie; 横街8号) is a sweet brick edifice. The whitewashed **Jesus Church** (耶稣教堂; Yēsū Jiàotáng; Qianyang Xiang), opposite No 7, is in a state of neglect.

There are not many places to stay in the old town, but the small and simple **guesthouse** (☎6715 2602; 153 Lishui Jie; r Y60) is very attractively located, with clean rooms (common shower). Next door at No 155 is another small guesthouse.

The quickest way to reach Yántóucūn is to take a river ferry (Y1.50, the first boat leaves at 5.50am, the last boat at 10.40pm, every 15 minutes) from the wharf from Wēnzhōu to Ōuběi; then hop on a waiting minibus to Yántóucūn (Y11, one hour). Alternatively, take bus 51 (Y3.50, one hour) from Wēnzhōu to Ōuběi and wait for the minibus to Yántóucūn, which runs along Luofu Dajie (罗浮大街). The last bus back from Yántóucūn to Ōuběi leaves at around 5pm, but check with the driver when you disembark.

FÚRÓNGCŪN 芙蓉村

A short walk south along the road from Yántóucūn, this picturesque **village** (admission Y20) originally dates to the Tang dynasty. A considerable amount of history survives within the village, although much has been lost in recent decades.

Near the main gate to the village is the Ming-dynasty **Chen Clan Ancestral Hall** (陈氏大宗; Chénshì Dàzōng), liberally plastered in **Maoist slogans** (on the door posts). The slogan on the left of the door reads '毛泽东思想是我们的命根子' (which translates as 'Mao Zedong thought is the core of our life'), while the matching slogan to the right proclaims '毛主席是我们心中的红太阳' ('Chairman Mao is the red sun in our hearts'). Interestingly, Maoist slogans are also daubed on the supporting pillars in front of the shrine altar, where devotional couplets would normally hang.

The village pond lies further up the road; here water buffalo cool off in the water during summer, with their flaring nostrils just above the water line. Complete with desks and a portrait of Confucius, the nearby **Fúróng Academy of Classical Learning** (Fúróng Shūyuàn) stands nobly alongside a lovely bamboo grove.

If you want to spend the night, cross the courtyard opposite the academy to the road on the other side to find the **Dàwū Rénjiā Kèzhàn** (大屋人家客栈; ☎0577 6715 2777, 8299 0002; r with bathroom Y100; ❄), a great old courtyard residence with marvellous rooms fashioned in wood, but phone ahead as it's often booked out.

CĀNGPŌCŪN 苍坡村

A 20-minute trip by *sānlúnchē* (pedicab, Y5 to Y10) past rice fields brings you to this nearby ancient **village** (admission Y15) of cypresses, pavilions and old China charm. Enter the village through **Xī Gate** (溪门; Xīmén). Alongside the large **West Pond** (西池; Xīchí), the most impressive building is the unrestored **Li Family Ances-**

tral Shrine (Lǐshì Dàzōng), with its old stage. Ornamental gates lie dotted around the village, along with a substantial number of old courtyard residences. The small **Water-moon Hall** (水月堂; Shuǐyuè Táng) originally dated all the way back to 1124, but is a Qing-dynasty restoration. Figure on around Y5 to 10 for a *sānlúnchē* trip from Yántóucūn to Cāngpōcūn and Y10 to 15 between Fúróngcūn and Cāngpōcūn.

OTHER VILLAGES

Other attractive settlements in the area that you can reach from Yántóucūn include **Péngxīcūn** (蓬溪村). To reach Péngxīcūn, get on a bus (Y2.50) to Hèshèng (鹤盛) from the Yántóucūn bus station on Xianqing Lu (仙清路) and ask to get off at the drop-off, from where you can hop on a *sānlúnchē* (Y5) to the village. The historic village of **Línkēng** (林坑) can be reached by bus (Y9.50, four departures daily) from Yántóucūn.

Fújiàn

POPULATION: 36.6 MILLION

Includes »

Best Places to Eat

» Gŭlàng Yŭ (p269)

» Huángzéhé Peanut Soup Shop (p265)

» Lucky Full City Seafood (p265)

Best Places to Stay

» 46Howtel (p268)

» Hakka Tŭlóu (p272)

» Lùjiāng Harbourview Hotel (p265)

Why Go?

Directly facing Taiwan across the Taiwan Strait, the southern province of Fújiàn (福建) is a lushly mountainous, coastal region of China. Well watered and lashed by summer typhoons that sweep along the coastline, the province is also renowned for an outward-looking mentality that has prompted centuries of migration to Malaysia, Singapore, the Philippines and Taiwan.

One of China's most attractive harbour cities, Xiàmén is a useful first port of call. The hypnotically slow tempo, gorgeous colonial architecture and meandering, hilly lanes of offshore Gŭlàng Yŭ make it an ideal place to unwind.

Heading into the hilly interior, travellers will find some of the most unique buildings in China. Rising like medieval forts, the astonishing Hakka *tŭlóu* (roundhouses) in Fújiàn's southwest present a mind-boggling dimension to the China experience. The province's rugged mountainous dimension can be explored at Wŭyí Shān in the northwest, where hiking opportunities await.

When to Go

Xiàmén

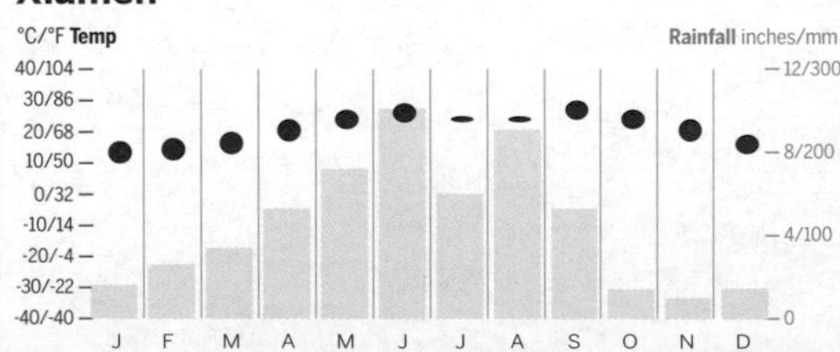

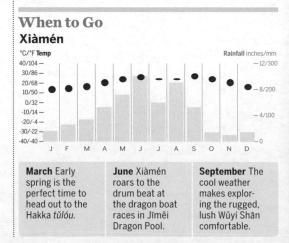

March Early spring is the perfect time to head out to the Hakka *tŭlóu.*

June Xiàmén roars to the drum beat at the dragon boat races in Jīměi Dragon Pool.

September The cool weather makes exploring the rugged, lush Wŭyí Shān comfortable.

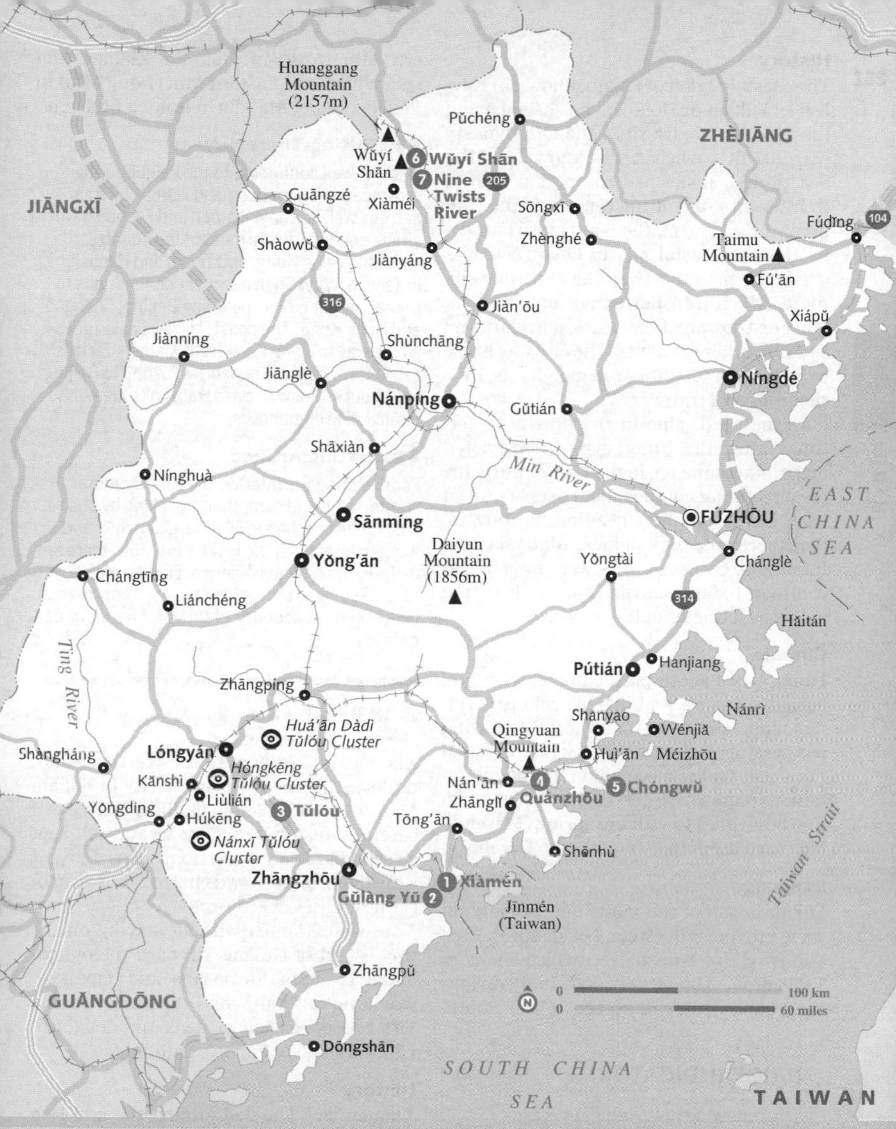

Fújiàn Highlights

1 Base yourself in breezy **Xiàmén** (p261), one of Fújiàn's most attractive cities

2 Explore **Gǔlàng Yǔ** (p267), an island packed with crumbling colonial villas

3 Head out to see some **tǔlóu** (p270), the massive packed-earth structures that are the ancient equivalents of modern-day apartments

4 Glimpse China's historical maritime past in **Quánzhōu** (p273)

5 Get lost in the walled city of **Chóngwǔ** (p276) – one of the best preserved in China

6 Hike and explore some of Fújiàn's most magnificent terrain at **Wǔyí Shān** (p278)

7 Float on a raft down the **Nine Twists River** (p278) – look for boat-shaped coffins stuck in cavities along the surrounding rock faces

History

The coastal region of Fújiàn, known in English as Fukien or Hokkien, has been part of the Chinese empire since the Qin dynasty (221–207 BC), when it was known as Min. Sea trade transformed the region from a frontier into one of the centres of the Chinese world. During the Song and Yuan dynasties the coastal city of Quánzhōu was one of the main ports on the maritime silk route, which transported not only silk but other textiles, precious stones, porcelain and a host of other valuables. The city was home to more than 100,000 Arab merchants, missionaries and travellers.

Despite a decline in the province's fortunes after the Ming dynasty restricted maritime commerce in the 15th century, the resourcefulness of the Fújiàn people proved itself in the numbers heading for Taiwan, Singapore, the Philippines, Malaysia and Indonesia. Overseas links were forged that continue today, contributing much to the modern character of the province.

Climate

Fújiàn has a subtropical climate, with hot, humid summers and drizzly, cold-ish winters. June through August brings soaring temperatures and humidity, with torrential rains and typhoons common. In the mountainous regions, winters can be fiercely cold. The best times to visit are spring (March to May) and autumn (September to October).

Language

Fújiàn is one of the most linguistically diverse provinces in China. Locals speak variations of the Min dialect, which includes Taiwanese. Min is divided into various subgroups – you can expect to hear Southern Min (Mǐnnán Huà) in Xiàmén and Quánzhōu, and Eastern Min (Dōng Mǐn) in Fúzhōu. Using Mandarin is not a problem.

PRICE INDICATORS

The following price indicators are used in this chapter:

Sleeping

$	less than Y200
$$	Y200 to Y400
$$$	more than Y400

Eating

$	less than Y20
$$	Y20 to Y60
$$$	more than Y60

Getting There & Away

Fújiàn is well connected to the neighbouring provinces of Guǎngdōng and Jiāngxī by train and coastal highway. Xiàmén and Fúzhōu have airline connections to most of the country, including Hong Kong, and Taipei and Kaohsiung in Taiwan. Wǔyí Shān has flight connections to China's larger cities, including Běijīng, Shànghǎi and Hong Kong. The coastal freeway also goes all the way to Hong Kong from Xiàmén. Z-class express trains link Xiàmeń via Fúzhōu to Běijīng in 19 hours. A new D-class train links Xiàmén to Shànghǎi in eight hours.

Getting Around

For exploring the interior, D trains are more comfortable and safer than travelling by bus. Wǔyí Shān is linked to Fúzhōu, Quánzhōu and Xiàmén by train. If the train is too slow, there are daily flights between Xiàmén, Fúzhōu and Wǔyí Shān. See the Getting There & Away information in the relevant sections of this chapter for more details.

Xiàmén 厦门

0592 / POP 637,000

Xiàmén, also known to the West as Amoy, ranks as the most attractive city in Fújiàn. Many of its old colonial buildings have been carefully restored, and its clean, well-kept streets and lively waterfront district give it a captivating old-world charm rarely seen in Chinese cities.

To visit Xiàmén without staying on the tiny island of Gǔlàng Yǔ, once the old colonial roost of Europeans and Japanese, would be to totally miss the point. Gǔlàng Yǔ's breezy seaside gardens and delightful villas are one of Fújiàn's highlights.

History

Xiàmén was founded around the mid-14th century in the early years of the Ming dynasty, when the city walls were built and the town was established as a major seaport and commercial centre. In the 17th century it became a place of refuge for the Ming rulers fleeing the Manchu invaders. Xiàmén and nearby Jīnmén were bases for the Ming armies who, under the command of the pirate-general Koxinga, raised their anti-Manchu battle-cry, 'resist the Qing and restore the Ming'.

The Portuguese arrived in the 16th century, followed by the British in the 17th century, and later by the French and the Dutch, all attempting, rather unsuccessfully, to establish Xiàmén as a trade port. The port was closed to foreigners in the 1750s and it was not until the Opium Wars that the tide turned. In August 1841 a British naval force of 38 ships carrying artillery and soldiers sailed into Xiàmén harbour, forcing the port to open. Xiàmén then became one of the first treaty ports.

Japanese and Western powers followed soon after, establishing consulates and making Gǔlàng Yǔ a foreign enclave. Xiàmén turned Japanese in 1938 and remained that way until 1945.

Sights & Activities

The town of Xiàmén is on the island of the same name. It's connected to the mainland by a 5km-long causeway bearing a train line, road and footpath. The most absorbing part of Xiàmén is near the western (waterfront) district, directly opposite the small island of Gǔlàng Yǔ. This is the old area of town, known for its colonial architecture, parks and winding streets.

Nánpǔtuó Temple TEMPLE
(南普陀寺; Nánpǔtuó Sì; Siming Nanlu; admission Y3; ⏲8am-6pm) On the southern side of Xiàmén, this Buddhist temple was originally built over a millennium ago but has been repeatedly destroyed and rebuilt. Its latest incarnation dates to the early 20th century, and today it's an active and busy temple with chanting monks and worshippers lighting incense.

The temple is fronted by a lovely lotus-flower-filled lake. In front of the courtyard is the twin-eaved **Big Treasure Hall** (Dàxióng Bǎodiàn), presided over by a trinity of Buddhas representing his past, present and future forms. Behind rises the eight-sided **Hall of Great Compassion** (Dàbēi Diàn), in which stands a golden 1000-armed statue of Guanyin, facing the four directions.

The temple has an excellent **vegetarian restaurant** (dishes Y20-50; ⏲10.30am-4pm) in a shaded courtyard where you can dine in the company of resident, mobile-phone toting monks. Round it all off with a hike up the steps behind the temple among the rocks and the shade of trees.

Take bus 1 from the train station or bus 21, 45, 48 or 503 from Zhongshan Lu to reach the temple.

Xiàmén University HISTORICAL BUILDINGS
(厦门大学; Xiàmén Dàxué) Next to Nánpǔtuó Temple and established with overseas Chinese funds, the university has well-maintained grounds featuring an attractive lake. It's a good place for a pleasant, shady stroll. The campus entrance is next to the stop for bus 1.

Húlǐ Shān Fortress MILITARY BUILDING
(胡里山炮台; Húlǐ Shān Pàotái; admission Y25; ⏲7.30am-5.30pm) Across Daxue Lu, south of the university, is this gigantic German gun artillery built in 1893. You can rent binoculars to peer over the water to the Taiwanese-occupied island of Jīnmén (金门), formerly known as Quemoy, claimed by both mainland China and Taiwan. Boats (Y106 to Y126) do circuits of Jīnmén from the **passenger ferry terminal** (客运码头; kèyùn mǎtou; ☎298 5551) off Lujiang Lu.

FREE **Overseas Chinese Museum** MUSEUM
华侨博物馆; Huáqiáo Bówùguǎn; 73 Siming Nanlu; ⏲9.30am-4.30pm Tue-Sun) A fascinating and ambitious celebration of China's communities abroad, with models, street scenes, photos and props. Close to the university.

Tours

China International Travel Service (CITS; p266) and many larger hotels can also help with tours.

Apple Travel TRAVEL AGENCY
(☎505 3122; www.appletravel.cn; Shop 20, Guanren Lu) Pricey but can can help arrange tours around Xiàmén, Gǔlàng Yǔ and to the Hakka *tǔlóu*. Also organises English-speaking guides.

Festivals & Events

Xiàmén International Marathon MARATHON
Held in spring, and draws local and international participants. Runners race around the coastal ring road that circles the island.

Dragon-boat races DRAGON-BOAT RACES
Held in Xiàmén at the Dragon Pool (Lóngzhōu Chí, 龙舟池) in Jīměi (集美) every June and are quite a sight.

Sleeping

For ambience, Gǔlàng Yǔ beats Xiàmén hands down as a more memorable and relaxing place to stay. In Xiàmén, hotels are clustered around the harbour and in the

Xiàmén & Gŭlàng Yŭ

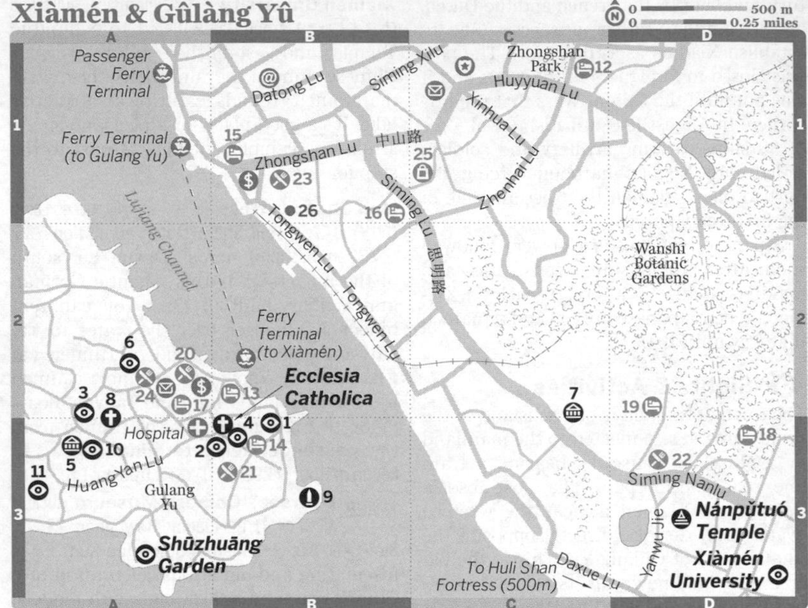

far-eastern section of town near the train station. Most accommodation in Xiàmén is midrange, shading top end. Many hotels in this range are equipped with free broadband internet (BYO computer).

There's a wide range of top-end accommodation in Xiàmén, but much of it is badly located in the eastern part of town. Most places offer 50% discounts. Some places levy service charges to prices, so check.

Shángkètáng HOTEL **$$**
(上客堂; Shángkètáng; ☎252 1988; 515 Siming Nanlu; 思明南路515号; s Y280, tw Y260-380, discounts of 20% available; ❄@) It could be us, but we swear the soap at this Buddhist-run hotel smells like incense. An excellent midrange choice perched on a small hill right beside the Nánpŭtuó Temple. You get large flat-screen TVs, plush carpets and friendly, helpful staff. Consider the Guanyin-engraved table lamp a bonus. Note: access to the hotel is via Nanhua Lu after 8pm.

Lùjiāng Harbourview Hotel HOTEL **$$$**
(鹭江宾馆; Lùjiāng Bīnguǎn; ☎202 2922; www.lujiang-hotel.com; 54 Lujiang Dao; 鹭江道54号; s Y600-800, sea-view d Y920-1070, discounts of 30% available; ❄@) This 1940s-era four-star hotel has great panoramas from its more spacious sea-view rooms, some with balcony. Rooms are large and complete with spiffy orange-coloured walls and chairs. Staff are helpful and the rooftop restaurant is excellent.

Xiàmén International Youth Hostel HOSTEL **$**
(厦门国际青年旅舍; Xiàmén Guójì Qīngnián Lǚshè; ☎208 2345; www.yhaxm.com; 41 Nanhua Lu; 南华路41号; dm from Y50, s Y95-160, d Y160-240; ❄@) With clean dorm rooms, doubles and showers, this compact but pleasant place is run by amiable staff. There's also bike rental, a kitchen, a ticket-booking service, internet access (Y2 per hour) and the small but cosy Anywhere Pub (Tsingtao Y5; open until midnight).

Bǎijiācūn International Youth Hostel HOSTEL **$**
(百家村国际青年旅舍; Bǎijiācūn Guójì Qīngnián Lǚshè; ☎213 1010; www.yhaxiamen.com; 20 Liaohua Lu; 寥华路20号; 4-/6-bed dm Y55/50, s/d & tw Y200/220; ❄@) Similarly housed in a large old colonial-style villa, this hostel runs a close race with the Xiàmén International Youth Hostel. Cosy (read: small) rooms are decorated in pine furniture and there are little nooks to curl up in with a book. Some staff need to realise that the gated compound shouldn't necessarily equate to guarded service.

Xiàmén & Gûlàng Yû

Top Sights

	Ecclesia Catholica	B3
	Nánpǔtuó Temple	D3
	Shūzhuāng Garden	A3
	Xiàmén University	D3

Sights

1	Bo'ai Hospital	B3
	British Consulate	(see 1)
2	Former Japanese Consulate	B3
3	Former Law Court	A2
	Former Spanish Consulate	(see 2)
	Guāncǎi Lóu	(see 3)
4	Huang Rongyuan Villa	B3
5	Koxinga Memorial Hall	A3
6	Organ Museum	A2
7	Overseas Chinese Museum	C2
8	Sanyi Church	A2
9	Statue of Koxinga	B3
	Sunlight Rock	(see 10)
10	Sunlight Rock Park	A3
11	Yīngxióng Hill	A3
	Yìzú Shānzhuāng	(see 3)

Sleeping

	46Howtel	(see 4)
12	Bǎijiācūn International Youth Hostel	C1
13	Gǔlàng Yǔ International Youth Hostel	B2
14	Gǔlàng Yǔ Lù Fēi International Youth Hostel	B3
15	Lùjiāng Harbourview Hotel	B1
16	Millennium Harbour View Hotel	B1
17	Mogo Cafe Hotel	A2
18	Shángkètáng	D3
19	Xiàmén International Youth Hostel	D2

Eating

20	Babycat Café	A2
21	Black Cat Club	B3
22	Dàfāng Sùcàiguǎn	D3
23	Huángzéhé Peanut Soup Shop	B1
24	Liji Mudan Fishball	A2

Shopping

25	Yèshì (Night Market)	C1

Transport

26	Silk Air	B1
	Thai Airways International	(see 26)

Millennium Harbour View Hotel HOTEL $$$
(厦门海景千禧大酒店; Xiàmén Hǎijǐng Qiānxǐ Dàjiǔdiàn; ☎202 3333; www.millenniumxiamen.com; 12-8 Zhenhai Lu; 镇海路12号之8; d Y1500-2000, discounts of around 50%;) This ex–Holiday Inn is a smart option, with efficient staff, and Italian, Japanese and Chinese restaurants. Discounts bring a deluxe sea-view room down to around Y650.

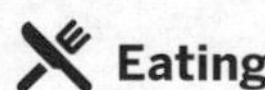

Eating

Being a port city, Xiàmén is known for its fresh fish and seafood, especially oysters and shrimp. You'll find good places to eat around Zhongshan Lu near the harbour. **Jukou Jie**, near the intersection of Siming Beilu and Zhongshan Lu, has a bunch of Sìchuān and Taiwanese restaurants. Nánpǔtuó Temple has an excellent vegetarian restaurant. **Yundang Lu** (筼筜路), near Marco Polo Hotel, has a long strip of cafes and restaurants popular with expats and trendy locals.

Huángzéhé Peanut Soup Shop SNACKS $
(黄则和花生糖店; Huángzéhé Huāshēng Tángdiàn; 20 Zhongshan Lu; snacks Y1-6; 6.30am-10.30pm) Very popular restaurant with basic service and seating, famed for its delectably sweet *huāshēng tāng* (花生汤; peanut soup; Y2) and popular snacks including *zhūròu chuàn* (猪肉串; pork kebabs; Y3) and *xiǎolóngbāo* (小笼包; Shanghai dumplings; Y3 for four). You need to purchase coupons that you hand over when you order food.

Lucky Full City Seafood DIM SUM $$
(潮福城; Cháofú Chéng; 28 Hubin Bei Lu; dim sum from Y10; 10am-10pm;) You'll have to either be really lucky (or wait at least 30 minutes) for a table at this popular dim sum restaurant. You will, however, leave really full after digging into roast meats, *chār shāo bāo* and *shāo mài*; English and picture menu available. Catch a taxi here: the driver will know where it is.

Dàfāng Sùcàiguǎn VEGETARIAN **$$**
(大方素菜馆; ☎209 3236; 3 Nanhua Lu; dishes Y28-68; ⏲9am-9.30pm;) This vegetarian restaurant near Nánpǔtuó Temple has gone upmarket. Formerly the domain of a budget-conscious crowd, the temple has priced them out with a very wide range of vegetarian dishes including hotpots and mock meat. Try the *tiěbǎn hēijiāo niúpái* (铁板黑椒牛排; vegetable 'beef' strips with pepper).

Food Hall, World Trade Centre INTERNATIONAL **$$**
(新食尚文化美食广场世界商城; Xīnshíshàng Wénhuà Měishí Guǎngchǎng; Xiahe Lu; meals Y25; ⏲10am-10pm) Head up to the 5th floor for this brash, bright and lively food hall crammed with Asian flavours from Hong Kong to Korea and beyond, and sit down with a clay pot (Y15), lamb kebabs (Y2.50) or whatever takes your fancy. Pay with charge cards (Y10 to Y200), available at the kiosk. You can return cards when you leave. Located next to the long-distance bus station.

Shopping

There's a crowded **yèshì** (夜市场; night market) on Ding'an Lu, between Zhongshan Lu and Zhenhai Lu. Zhongshan Lu is essentially a long shopping strip filled with the latest brands.

Information

Pickpockets, both individuals and groups, operate around the popular areas in Xiàmén. This includes Zhongshang Lu and the ferry to/from Gǔlàng Yǔ and also around train and bus stations.

Amoy Magic (www.amoymagic.com) One of the most comprehensive websites on Xiàmén.

Bank of China (中国银行; Zhōngguó Yínháng; 6 Zhongshan Lu) The 24-hour ATM accepts international cards.

China International Travel Service (CITS; 中国国际旅行社; Zhōngguó Guójì Lǚxíngshè; 335 Hexiang Xilu) There are several offices around town. This branch near Yundang Lake is recommended.

China Post (中国邮政; Zhōngguó Yóuzhèng; cnr Xinhua Lu & Zhongshan Lu) Telephone services available.

Life Line Medical Clinic (Mǐfú Zhénsuǒ; ☎532 3168; 123 Xidi Villa Hubin Beilu; ⏲8am-5pm Mon-Fri, to noon Sat) English-speaking doctors; expat frequented. Telephone-operated 24 hours.

Public Security Bureau (PSB; 公安局外事科; Gōng'ānjú; ☎226 2203; 45-47 Xinhua Lu) Opposite the main post and telephone office. The visa section (*chūrùjìng guǎnlǐchù;* open 8.10am to 11.45am and 2.40pm to 5.15pm Monday to Saturday) is in the northeastern part of the building on Gongyuan Nanlu.

What's On Xiamen (www.whatsonxiamen.com) Up-to-date information on Xiamen.

Yúyuè Internet Cafe (娱悦网吧; Yúyuè Wǎngbā; 113 Datong Lu; per hr Y4; ⏲24hr) Gaming hall.

Getting There & Away

Air

Air China, China Southern, Xiàmén Airlines and several other domestic airlines operate flights to/from Xiàmén to all major domestic airports in China. There are innumerable ticket offices around town, many of which are in the larger hotels, such as the Millennium Harbour View Hotel (p265). There are international flights to/from Bangkok, Hong Kong, Jakarta, Kuala Lumpur, Los Angeles, Manila, Osaka, Penang, Singapore and Tokyo.

All Nippon Airways (☎573 2888) In the Lùjiāng Harbourview Hotel.

Apple Travel (☎505 3122; www.appletravel.cn; Shop 20, Guanren Lu) Flight bookings.

Silk Air (胜安航空; Shèng'ān Hángkōng; ☎205 3280; International Plaza, 15th fl, Unit H, 8 Lujiang Dao)

Thai Airways International (泰国航空公司; Tàiguó Hángkōng Gōngsī; ☎226 1688) In the International Plaza.

Boat

Fast boats (Y10, 20 minutes) leave for the nearby coastal Fújiàn town of Zhāngzhōu (漳州) from the **passenger ferry terminal** (客运码头; Kèyùn Mátóu). Boats run every 15 minutes between 7am and 5.45pm. Buses (Y12, one hour) then run from Zhāngzhōu's harbour to Zhāngzhōu. There is also a ferry service to Jīnmén, Taiwan (Y180, one hour, hourly), though you need a multiple-entry visa if you want to return to Xiàmén. You will get a Taiwanese visa upon arrival.

Bus

Destinations from the **long-distance bus station** (长途汽车站; chángtú qìchēzhàn; 58 Hubin Nanlu):

Fúzhōu Y60, four hours, every 10 minutes

Guǎngzhōu Y208, nine hours, two daily

Guìlín Y253,one daily (8.50am)

Kūnmíng Y474, 15 hours, two daily

Lóngyán Y46, three hours, regular services

Quánzhōu Y37, two hours, every 20 minutes

Wǔyí Shān Y124 to Y202, nine hours, two daily

Yǒngdìng Y65, four hours, four daily

Train

Book tickets at the train station or through CITS (p266), which charges a Y35 service fee. Services from Xiàmén's **train station** (Xiahe Lu), in the northeast of the city (prices range from hard seat to soft sleeper tickets):

Běijing West Y253 to Y705, 34 hours
Hángzhōu (D train) Y198, six hours
Kūnmíng Y271 to Y754, 41 hours
Nánjīng Y150 to Y452, 30 hours
Shànghǎi (D train) Y237, 7½ hours
Wǔyí Shān Y149 to Y232, 13½ hours

Getting Around

Xiàmén airport is 15km from the waterfront district, about 8km from the eastern district. From the waterfront, taxis cost around Y35. Bus 27 travels to the airport from the ferry terminal. Bus 19 runs to the train station from the ferry terminal (Y1). Frequent minibuses also run between the train station and ferry terminal (Y1). Buses to Xiàmén University go from the train station (bus 1) and from the ferry terminal (bus 2). Taxis start at Y8.

Gǔlàng Yǔ 鼓浪屿

0592

If you think about it, it's almost funny to visit an island (Xiàmén), only to jump on a 10-minute boat ride to *another* island (Gǔlàng Yǔ). But people do it in droves. In fact, the tiny island of Gǔlàng Yǔ has bucket loads more charm than, gasp, Xiàmén. Even locals are enamoured with the darn place. We'd go so far as to say that you could safely skip Xiàmén altogether and spend your entire time in Gǔlàng Yǔ.

And it's not hard to see why. Gǔlàng Yǔ is a sedate retreat of meandering lanes and shaded warrens of backstreets, set in an architectural twilight of more than 1000 (!) colonial villas, crumbling buildings and ancient banyan trees, and it's well worth spending a few days soaking up its charms. There really isn't anything quite like it anywhere else in China: think of it as a living time capsule which offers the best of the colonial and Chinese intersection.

The foreign community was well established on Gǔlàng Yǔ by the 1880s, with a daily English newspaper, churches, hospitals, post and telegraph offices, libraries, hotels and consulates. In 1903 the island was officially designated an International Foreign Settlement, and a municipal council with a police force of Sikhs was established to govern it. Today, memories of the settlement linger in the many charming colonial buildings and the sound of classical piano wafting from speakers (the island is nicknamed 'piano island' by the Chinese). Many of China's most celebrated musicians have come from Gǔlàng Yǔ, including the pianists Yu Feixing, Lin Junqing and Yin Chengzong.

The best way to enjoy the island is to wander along the streets, peeking into courtyards and down alleys to catch a glimpse of colonial mansions seasoned by local life before popping into one of the many cute cafes for a beer or milk tea.

Sights

Old colonial residences and **consulates** are tucked away in the maze of streets leading from the pier, particularly along Longtou Lu and the back lanes of Huayan Lu. Many of Gǔlàng Yǔ's buildings are deserted and tumbledown, with trees growing out of their sides, as residents cannot afford their upkeep. You can buy a through ticket to the island's main sights for Y80, but you can skip these without detracting too much from the overall experience.

Southeast of the pier you will see the two buildings of the former **British Consulate** (原英国领事馆; 14-16 Lujiao Lu) above you, while further along at 1 Lujiao Lu (鹿礁路) is the cream-coloured former Japanese **Bo'ai Hospital**, built in 1936. Residents have now barred access to the public via a warning near the entrance slathered in black paint. Up the hill on a different part of Lujiao Lu at No 26 stands the red-brick **former Japanese Consulate**, just before you reach the magnificent snow-white **Ecclesia Catholica** (天主堂; Roman Catholic Church; Tiānzhǔtáng; 34 Lujiao Lu), dating from 1917. The white building next to the church is the **former Spanish Consulate**. Just past the church on the left is the **Huang Rongyuan Villa**, a marvellous pillared building, now the **Puppet Art Center** (adult/child Y60/30). The entry gate is topped, nay, enveloped by a banyan tree!

There is also some **art deco architecture**. Take a look at the building at 28 Fujian Lu. Other buildings worth looking at include the Protestant **Sanyi Church** (三一堂), a red-brick building with a classical portico and cruciform-shaped interior on the corner of Anhai Lu (安海路) and Yongchun Lu (永春路). Where Anhai Lu meets

Bishan Lu (笔山路) is the former **Law Court** (1-3 Bishan Lu), now inhabited by some local residents.

For a sign of how badly some buildings have been looked after, look out for the **old building** on Neicuo'ao Lu (内厝澳路), where old interior doors have been ripped out to make a garden fence! Doing a circuit of Bishan Lu will take you past a not-oft-visited part of the island. **Guāncǎi Lóu** (观彩楼; 6 Bishan Lu), a residence built in 1931, ha a magnificently dilapidated interior with a wealth of original features and – like so many other buildings here – is crying out to be preserved. The building stands in stark contrast next to the immaculate **Yìzú Shānzhuāng** (亦足山庄; 9 Bishan Lu), a structure dating from the 1920s.

The highly distinctive **Bāguà Lóu** (八卦楼) at No 43 Guxin Lu (鼓新路) is now the **Organ Museum** (风琴博物馆; Fēngqín Bòwùguǎn; admission Y20, incl in through ticket for island; ⌚8.40am-5.30pm), with a fantastic collection including a Norman & Beard organ from 1909.

Hàoyuè Garden (皓月园; Hàoyuè Yuán; admission Y15, incl in through ticket; ⌚6am-7pm) is a rocky outcrop containing an imposing **statue of Koxinga** in full military dress. **Sunlight Rock** (Rìguāng Yán) is the island's highest point at 93m. On a clear day you can see the island of Jīnmén. At the foot of Sunlight Rock is a large colonial building known as the **Koxinga Memorial Hall** (郑成功纪念馆; Zhèngchénggōng Jìniànguǎn; ⌚8-11am & 2-5pm). Both sights are in **Sunlight Rock Park** (日光岩公园; Rìguāng Yán Gōngyuán; admission Y60, incl in through ticket; ⌚8am-7pm). Also in the park is **Yīngxióng Hill** (Yīngxióng Shān), near the memorial hall and connected via a free cable-car ride. It has an **open-air aviary** (admission free) with chattering egrets and parrots, and a terrible bird 'show'.

The waterfront **Shūzhuāng Garden** (菽庄花园; Shūzhuāng Huāyuán; admission Y30, incl in through ticket) on the southern end of the island is a lovely place to linger for a few hours. It has a small *pénzāi* (bonsai) garden and some delicate-looking pavilions. The piano theme is in full effect at the piano museum housed within the grounds. One piano has its original bill of sale from Melbourne at the turn of the last century.

Sleeping

Gǔlàng Yǔ groans under the weight of its accommodation choices. However, its popularity means that you should book in advance, especially if you're visiting over the weekend. Although the island is small, cars aren't allowed, so try to book a hotel closer to the ferry terminal if you've got a lot of luggage.

46Howtel HOTEL $$$
(☎206 5550; www.46howtel.com; 46 Fujian Lu; 福建路46号; r Y360-780; ❄@) While the rest of the hotels on the island are happy with quirky and antique styles (oh, how plebeian), this 'howtel' opts for cutting-edge modern. Expect rooms straight out of a *Wallpaper* spread: sharp lines, glossy surfaces and plush carpets. Service is top notch too.

Mogo Cafe Hotel HOTEL $$
(蘑菇旅馆; Mógū Lǚguǎn; ☎208 5980; www.mogo-hotel.com; 3-9 Longtou Lu; 龙头路3-9号; r Y280-580; ❄@) Book ahead if you want rooms at this fab joint, perched just 100m from the ferry terminal. Each of the 19 rooms has designer flair: textured wallpaper, mood lighting, rain showers. You've got to lug your luggage up three flights of stairs, though, so pack light.

Gǔlàng Yǔ International Youth Hostel HOSTEL $
(鼓浪屿国际青年旅馆; Gǔlàng Yǔ Guójì Qīngnián Lǚguǎn; ☎206 6066; www.yhagly.com; 18 Lujiao Lu; 鹿礁路18号; 6-bed/4-bed dm Y50/75, s Y110, d Y270 & Y370; @) The best-located hostel has large rooms with high, beamed ceilings and strange toilets that seem to channel a nautical theme. During winter the place is damp and chilly. There's a cute little TV room and a relaxing garden courtyard, as well as internet access (Y5 per hour), a laundry (Y5) and lots of company.

Gǔlàng Yǔ Lù Fēi International Youth Hostel HOSTEL $
(鼓浪屿鹭飞国际青年旅舍; Gǔlàng Yǔ Lù Fēi Guójì Qīngnián Lǚshè; ☎208 2678; www.yhalf.cn; 20 Guxin Lu; 鼓新路20号; dm Y60, s & d Y270-370; ❄@) Positives: totally cute rooms, each one unique. Pastel hues, flat-screen TVs, wrought-iron beds. Negatives: 400m from the ferry terminal; prices increase 10% on weekends.

Eating

Gŭlàng Yŭ is a great place for fish and seafood, especially at the restaurants in the centre of town. You'll find a collection of small eateries in the streets around the ferry terminal, and off Longtou Lu there are many small restaurants and stalls. Try the shark fishballs (go on, make a joke) and the Amoy pie (sweet, filled pastry). There are plenty of trendy cafe-bars dotted around the island.

Babycat Café CAFE $$
(☎206 4119; 8 Longtou Lu; ⌚10.30am-11pm;) Trendy cafe (that actually reminds us of Luke Skywalker's home on Tattoine) with a large range of coffees, Amoy handmade pie, Tsingtao beer (Y15) and smoothies (from Y18). Further, non-Tattoine-style branch at 143 Longtou Lu. Free wi-fi.

Liji Mudan Fishball LOCAL $$
(林记鱼丸汤; Línjìyúwántāng; 56 Longtou Lu; dishes from Y8; ⌚10am-9pm) Pull up a bench and order some local specialities: shark fishball noodles (鲨鱼丸粉丝; Y8) and a serve of oyster omelette (海蛎煎; Y15). Slurp it down and order a second serve.

Black Cat Club FUSION $$$
(Hēimāo Jùlèbù; ☎206 6158; www.blackcat1920.com; 14 Yongchun Lu; set meals Y88-168; ⌚10am-10pm) The modern cuisine is quite passable at this posh joint, as is the service. The real charm comes from the setting: you're seated in an old villa decked out in the owners' antique furniture. Dine on a highback chair while admiring the calligraphy on the walls and imagining yourself in swinging colonial times.

Information

There are different maps on sale (Y10). The flavour of the month seems to be a hand-drawn Chinese version printed on brown paper; while it lists all the sights of interest, it's not to scale and useless when you get lost.

Bank of China (中国银行; Zhōngguó Yínháng; 2 Longtou Lu; ⌚9am-7pm) Forex and 24-hour ATM.

China Post (中国邮政; Zhōngguó Yóuzhèng; 102 Longtou Lu)

Hospital (Yīyuàn; 60 Fujian Lu) Has its own miniature ambulance for the small roads.

Xiàmén Gŭlàng Yŭ Visitor Center (Xiàmén Gŭlàng Yŭ Yóukè Zhōngxīn; Longtou Lu) Left luggage Y2 to Y5.

Getting There & Around

Ferries for the five-minute trip to Gŭlàng Yŭ leave from the ferry terminal just west of Xiàmén's Lùjiāng Harbourview Hotel. Outbound, it's a free ride on the bottom deck and Y1 for the upper deck. Xiàmén-bound it's Y8 (free between 10pm and midnight). Boats run between 5.30am and midnight. Waterborne circuits of the island can be done by boat (Y15), with hourly departures from the passenger ferry terminal off Lujiang Lu between 7.45am and 8.45pm. Round-island buggies take 30 minutes for a circuit (Y10 to Y40).

Hakka Tŭlóu 客家土楼

☎0597 / POP 40,200

The stunning rural area of rolling farmland and hills in southwestern Fújiàn is the heartland of the Hakka (客家; *kèjiā*) people and their remarkable *tŭlóu* (土楼). These vast, packed-earth edifices resembling fortresses are scattered throughout the surrounding countryside. Today over 30,000 survive, many still inhabited and open to visitors.

OK, you're sold and you want to visit. And you're left confused by the plethora of names, villages and options available. Don't worry, because we are too. Ever since Unesco status was conferred on some roundhouse clusters, the local government has been in a flap revamping. China's President Hu Jintao visited in early 2010 and things reached fever pitch: roads leading to and around these roundhouses are being widened, new buildings (presumably hotels and shops) are being erected, and entry fees have increased. Don't be surprised if things change by the time this book goes to print. At the time of research, a tourist bus line was being installed in-between the Hóngkēng and Tiánluókēng clusters. These buses were set to do circuits of several clusters.

Sights

There are thousands of *tŭlóu*, some a few centuries old, but the big-ticket ones are lumped into various clusters. There are three main counties that you will often see referred to: the **Yŏngdìng**, **Nánjìng** and **Huá'ān**. Except for the Huá'ān cluster, the rest can be visited in a few days. The first two are in the general vicinity of each other and you can base yourself in the small village of Liùlián (六联), also called the Tŭlóu Mínsú Wénhuàcūn (土楼民俗文化村), which you can reach by bus from Xiàmén,

JUST WHAT IS A *TǓLÓU*?

The Hakka have inhabited Yǒngdìng County and its neighbouring villages for hundreds of years. During the Jin dynasty (AD 265–314) the Hakka peoples of northwest China began a gradual migration south to escape persecution and famine. They eventually settled in Jiāngxī, Fújiàn and Guǎngdōng, where they began to build *tǔlóu* to protect themselves from bandits and wild animals.

The walls are made of rammed earth and glutinous rice, reinforced with strips of bamboo and wood chips. These structures are large enough to house entire clans, and they did, and still do! The buildings were communal, with interior buildings enclosed by enormous peripheral structures that could accommodate hundreds of people. Nestled in the mud walls were bedrooms, wells, cooking areas and storehouses, circling a central courtyard. The later *tǔlóu* had stone fire walls and metal-covered doors to protect against blazes.

The compartmentalised nature of the building meant that these structures were the ancient equivalent of modern apartments! A typical layout would be the kitchens on the 1st floor, storage on the second level and accommodation on the third level onwards. Some *tǔlóu* have multiple buildings built in concentric rings within the main enclosure. These could be guest rooms and home schools. The centre is often an ancestral hall or a meeting hall used for events such as birthdays and weddings. The only thing missing is a shopping mall.

Today, many *tǔlóu* are still inhabited, often by a single clan, and residents depend on a combination of tourism and farming for a living. The *tǔlóu* are surprisingly comfortable to live in, being '*dōng nuǎn, xià liáng*' (冬暖夏凉), or 'warm in winter and cool in summer'. These structures were built to last and they're not going away any time soon.

Lóngyán or Yǒngdìng. Consisting of little more than a small bus station and some hotels and restaurants, it's also within walking distance of Zhènchéng Lóu, the most famous and impressive *tǔlóu* in the area. It is also possible to base yourself in the larger nearby small town of Húkēng (湖坑), which has more facilities but isn't very attractive.

Huá'ān is over 100km northeast away and is best visited as a separate trip if you're not hiring a vehicle. See p272 for details on how to get to the various *tǔlóu*.

HÓNGKĒNG TǓLÓU CLUSTER 洪坑土楼群

Cluster admission is Y90.

Zhènchéng Lóu TǓLÓU

(振成楼) A short walk from Liùlián, this is a grandiose structure built in 1912, with two concentric circles and a total of 222 rooms. In the centre of the *tǔlóu* is a large ancestral hall, complete with Western-style pillars, for special ceremonies and greeting guests. The locals dub this *tǔlóu wángzǐ* (土楼王子), the prince *tǔlóu*.

Kuíjù Lóu TǓLÓU

(奎聚楼) Near Zhènchéng Lóu, this much older, square *tǔlóu* dates back to 1834.

Rúshēng Lóu TǓLÓU

(如升楼) The smallest of the roundhouses, this late-19th-century, pea-sized *tǔlóu* has only one ring and 16 rooms.

Fúyù Lóu TǓLÓU

(福裕楼) Along the river, this five-storey square *tǔlóu* boasts some wonderfully carved wooden beams and pillars. Rooms are available here for Y60.

GĀOBĚI TǓLÓU CLUSTER 高北土楼群

Cluster admission is Y50.

Chéngqǐ Lóu TǓLÓU

(承启楼) In the village of Gāoběi (高北) and built in 1709, this granddaddy *tǔlóu* has 400 rooms and once had 1000 inhabitants. It's built with elaborate concentric rings within the outside walls, and circular passageways between them and a central shrine – like a village within a village; it's simply astonishing. It's one of the most iconic and photographed *tǔlóu* and we're not surprised that it has been dubbed *tǔlóu wáng* (土楼王), the king *tǔlóu*.

Wǔyún Lóu TǓLÓU

(五云楼) Deserted and rickety, this square building took on a slant after an earthquake in 1918.

Qiáofú Lóu TŮLÓU

(桥福楼) A modern *tǔlóu* constructed in 1962, housing 90 rooms across three levels. Decent rooms are available for Y100.

Yíjīng Lóu TŮLÓU

(遗经楼) In the village of Gāoběi. A massive, crumbling structure with 281 rooms, two schools and 51 halls. Built in 1851.

TIÁNLUÓKĒNG TŮLÓU CLUSTER 田螺坑土楼群

Perhaps the most photogenic cluster of *tǔlóu* in the area, the five noble buildings at **Tiánluókēng** (田螺坑) consist of three types of *tǔlóu:* circular, square and oval. You can spend the night in one of the *tǔlóu,* for example in the **Ruìyún Lóu** (瑞云楼), where simple fan rooms are available for Y60 to Y80. If you hire a driver, make sure they take you up a neighbouring hill for picture-postcard snaps of Tiánluókēng. Cluster admission is Y100.

Yùchāng Lóu TŮLÓU

(裕昌楼) Located in the general direction of Tiánluókēng and originally built between 1308 and 1338, this vast five-floor structure has an observation tower (to check for marauding bandits) and 270 rooms. Notice how the pillars bend at an angle on the 3rd floor and at the opposite angle on the 5th floor! Guides like to joke and say that disgruntled builders did this on purpose because of some issues with their pay.

Tǎxià VILLAGE

(塔下村) This nearby village is also worth exploring – it's a delightful settlement alongside a river, with several *tǔlóu,* including the **Shùnqìng Lóu**, where you can spend the night in a modern *tǔlóu* room (Y100). Another highlight of the village is the **Zhang Ancestral Hall**. It's surrounded by 23 elaborately carved spear-like stones which celebrate achievements of prominent villagers.

Bùyún Lóu TŮLÓU

(步云楼) At the heart of the Tiánluókēng cluster (*tǔlóu* clusters are called *tǔlóu qún;* 土楼群) is this square building. First built in the 17th century, it burnt down in 1936 and was rebuilt in the 1950s.

Wénchāng Lóu TŮLÓU

(文昌楼) The Tiánluókēng cluster's oval-shaped building.

NÁNXĪ TŮLÓU CLUSTER 南溪土楼群

Cluster admission is Y70.

Huánjí Lóu TŮLÓU

(环极楼) In the direction of Pínghé (平和), this four-storey-high building is a huge circular affair with inner concentric passages, tiled interior passages, a courtyard and halls. The doughnut-shaped *tǔlóu* still delightfully buzzes with family life and also sports a *huíyīnbì* (回音壁) – a wall that echoes and resonates to sharp sounds.

Yǎnxiāng Lóu TŮLÓU

(衍香楼) In the same direction as Huánjí Lóu and rising up next to a river, this impressive four-storey *tǔlóu* has an ancestral hall standing in the middle of the courtyard.

Lìběn Lóu TŮLÓU

To the rear of Yǎnxiāng Lóu is this derelict *tǔlóu* with crumbling walls. It was burnt down during civil war and stands without its roof.

Qìngyáng Lóu TŮLÓU

(庆洋楼) Also not far from Yǎnxiāng Lóu, this huge, rectangular, semidecrepit structure was built between 1796 and 1820.

HUÁ'ĀN DÀDÌ TŮLÓU CLUSTER 华安大地土楼群

Located 142km northwest of Xiàmén, the Huá'ān cluster is set in gorgeous surrounds. Rolling green hills and soporific streams encase the *tǔlóu* here and gives them an idyllic vibe. Cluster admission is Y90.

Èryì Lóu TŮLÓU

(二宜楼) The centrepiece of the cluster, this 1740 building has 2.53m-thick walls and a whole host of features, including escape tunnels, sound holes (to communicate through the walls) and a large ancestral hall on the top floor. It may be the best preserved of all the round *tǔlóu*. One unique feature of this *tǔlóu* is found on the upper floors: walls of several rooms are plastered with pages from *New York Times* issues dated 1931. The walls are painted with murals depicting a lady in Western dress and even Indian goddesses in blush-worthy poses: these are marks of a later descendant who was certainly a lot more worldly than his forefathers. Fan-only rooms are available here from Y60.

Nányáng Lóu TŮLÓU

(南阳楼) Next door to Èryì Lóu and built in 1817 by the great-grandson of Èryì Lóu's builder, this is now a *tŭlóu* museum. Displays showcase life in these buildings: mock bedroom, kitchen, dining hall – you get the idea.

Dōngyáng Lóu TŬLÓU
(东阳楼) This tiny square building is also nearby.

Sleeping & Eating

Spending the night in a *tŭlóu* will reward you with unforgettable memories of a vanishing dimension of life in China. Bring a torch (flashlight) and bug repellent. Some families also include meals in the room price, or can cook one up for you. Prices vary depending on how much meat you order, but expect to pay Y15 upwards for a dish.

You will be able to find a room in most of the *tŭlóu* you visit as many families have now moved out. Residents will offer rooms – look it over before you agree to a price. Don't expect accommodation to be anything but basic – a bed, a thermos of hot water, a fan and not much else. Some rooms might have a small TV. You might also find that the toilets are on the outside, and the huge gates to the *tŭlóu* shut around 8pm, so plan ahead.

There are many hotels in Yŏngdìng, such as the **Dōngfŭ Hotel** (Dōngfŭ Bīnguǎn; ☎583 0668), and there are plenty of hotels in Húkēng as well, but neither town is particularly attractive. We recommend you base yourself in a *tŭlóu*.

Fúyù Lóu Chángdì Inn TŬLÓU $
(福裕楼常棣客栈; ☎553 5900, 1386 0221 798; tulou@126.com; d incl breakfast Y60) The owners of the Fúyù Lóu (p270) have converted some rooms at the rear into basic but comfy doubles complete with fan and small TV. The owners are friendly, speak some English and serve tasty Hakka food (dishes from Y20). They can also organise a pick-up from Xiàmén and transport for touring the area.

Qiáofú Lóu TŬLÓU $
(桥福楼; ☎557 3777, 1335 0836 981; d Y30-100) The owners of this *tŭlóu* (p272) come from a line of professors and you'll be shown a happy family photo where everyone's dressed in their PhD best. That aside, this cosy place has plain but adequate rooms. In the evenings, the red-lantern-lit courtyard becomes the scene for home-cooked dinner, beer and conversation. BYO mosquito repellent.

Tŭlóu Rénjiā MOTEL $
(土楼人家; ☎553 2764; d Y100; ❄@) Just up from the small bus station in Liùlián, Tŭlóu Rénjiā has decent rooms in a modern building. It can arrange drivers for tours of the region's *tŭlóu*. There's a variety of rooms, with hot water, air-con and shower, a downstairs restaurant and a computer terminal for internet access. It also has accommodation in a lovely *tŭlóu* in Tǎxià village, Sōngxīng Lóu (塔下村松兴楼; rooms from Y100).

Getting There & Away

Transport to the area is fast changing and new roads have halved the travel times. However, the region is prone to landslides, so check if you're there during rainy season.

Bus

YŎNGDÌNG From Xiàmén long-distance bus station, take a bus headed to Yŏngdìng (永定县; Y65, four hours, four daily from 5.30am to 12.30pm). It will pass Liùlián and Húkēng and also pass by the Gāoběi *tŭlóu* cluster. In the other direction, there is a bus at 7.20am and 12.20pm from Yŏngdìng. Check with local bus stops for timings closer to departure. Yŏngdìng can also be accessed by bus from Guǎngdōng and Lóngyán (Y15, one hour, regular). Regular buses run between Húkēng and Yŏngdìng (Y14) between 7.30am and 4.10pm.

LÓNGYÁN Alternatively, first catch a bus from Xiàmén to Lóngyán (Y54, three hours, regular) and then switch to a minibus (Y21, two hours) to Liùlián or Húkēng, or a bus to Yŏngdìng. The bus for Liùlián from the bus station in Lóngyán is the *tŭlóu zhuānxiàn* (土楼专线), which passes the town of Húkēng (where you can also stay) and will drop you off at Liùlián. The bus also passes through other villages and *tŭlóu* areas such as Fŭshì (抚市), Chéndōng (陈东), Dàxī (大溪) and Qílǐng (岐岭). Lóngyán has regular buses to Fúzhōu, Quánzhōu, Xiàmén and other destinations.

HUÁ'ĀN To get to the Huá'ān Dàdì *tŭlóu* cluster, get a bus from the Xiàmén long-distance bus station (Y25, three hours, 8.10am, 11.20am, 2.30pm, 5.50pm). From the last stop at Huá'ān County centre (华安县; ☎0596-7362677), you need to get a local bus (Y5, 40 minutes, half-hourly) to take you to Xiāndū (仙都), where the cluster is. Return buses from the Huá'ān cluster to Xiàmén run at 7.40am, 11am, 2.15pm and 5.40pm.

Tours & Private Transport

With the infrastructure still in flux, the easiest way to see the *tŭlóu* is to book a tour or hire a vehicle from Xiàmén. You'll most probably need to find transport at the *tŭlóu* areas, so it might make fiscal sense to just get transport from Xiàmén (haggle but expect to pay Y500 a day to/from Xiàmén).

Apple Travel (p266) can organise English-guided tours. Otherwise, any of the accommodation places can help with transport and Xiàmén pick-up if required.

Getting Around

Hiring a driver to take you around the countryside on a *tǔlóu* tour is the most convenient approach. You'll find taxi drivers in Yǒngdìng, Húkēng or Liùlián who will offer their services for around Y400 a day, setting off early in the morning and returning in the late afternoon. Expect to see two clusters per day.

Quánzhōu 泉州

0595 / POP 179,900

Quánzhōu was once a great trading port and an important stop on the maritime silk route. Back in the 13th century, Marco Polo informed his readers that 'it is one of the two ports in the world with the biggest flow of merchandise'. The city reached its zenith as an international port during the Song and Yuan dynasties, drawing merchants from all over the world to its shores. By the Qing, however, it was starting to decline and droves of residents began fleeing to Southeast Asia to escape the constant political turmoil.

Today Quánzhōu is smaller than Fúzhōu and Xiàmén and has a small-town feel. Evidence of its Muslim population can still be detected among the city's residents and buildings. It still has a few products of note, including the creamy-white *déhuà* (or 'blanc-de-Chine' as it is known in the West) porcelain figures, and locally crafted puppets.

Quánzhōu

Sights

The centre of town lies between Zhongshan Nanlu, Zhongshan Zhonglu and Wenling Nanlu. This is where you'll find most of the tourist sights, the bank and the post office. The oldest part of town is to the west, where there are many narrow alleys and lanes to explore that still retain their traditional charm.

Kāiyuán Temple MUSEUM

(开元寺; Kāiyuán Sì; 176 Xi Jie; admission Y8; 7.30am-7pm) In the northwest of the city is one of the oldest temples in Quánzhōu, dating back to AD 686. Surrounded by trees, the temple is serene and famed for its pair of rust-coloured five-storey stone pagodas, stained with age and carved with figures, which date from the 13th century. Behind the eastern pagoda is a **museum** containing

Quánzhōu

Top Sights

Guandi Temple	B3
Jǐnxiùzhuāng Puppet Museum	B3
Kāiyuán Temple	A1

Sights

1 Qīngjìng Mosque	B3

Sleeping

2 Bǎoqí Zhāodàisuǒ	B3
3 Jīnzhōu Hotel	B4

Eating

4 Ānjìkèwáng	B3
5 Gǔcuò Cháfáng	B3

the enormous hull of a Song-dynasty seagoing junk, which was excavated near Quánzhōu in 1974. The temple's **Great Treasure Hall** (Dàxióng Bǎodiàn) and the hall behind are decorated with marvellous overhead beams and brackets. The main courtyard is flanked by a row of wizened banyan trees; one is 800 years old! Take bus 2 (Y2) from Wenling Nanlu.

Qīngjìng Mosque MOSQUE
(清净寺; Qīngjìng Sì; 108 Tumen Jie; admission Y3; ⌚8am-5.30pm) This stone edifice is one of China's only surviving mosques from the Song dynasty, built by Arabs in 1009 and restored in 1309. Only a few sections (mainly walls) of the original building survive, largely in ruins.

Guandi Temple TEMPLE
(关帝庙; Guāndì Miào; Tumen Jie) This smoky and fabulously carved temple is southeast of the mosque. It's dedicated to Guan Yu, a Three Kingdoms hero and the God of War, and inside the temple are statues of the god and panels along the walls that detail his life.

FREE **Maritime Museum** MUSEUM
(泉州海外交通史博物馆; Quánzhōu Hǎiwài Jiāotōngshǐ Bówùguǎn; Donghu Lu; ⌚8.30am-5.30pm Tue-Sun) On the northeast side of town, this museum explains Quánzhōu's trading history and the development of Chinese shipbuilding. There are wonderfully detailed models of Chinese ships, from junks to pleasure boats.

FREE **Jǐnxiùzhuāng Puppet Museum** MUSEUM
(錦绣庄木偶艺术馆; Jǐnxiùzhuāng Mù'ǒu Yìshùguǎn; 10-12 Houcheng; ⌚9am-9pm) Has displays of puppet heads, intricate 30-string marionettes and comical hand puppets. There are over 3000 puppet heads, though at times the service is rather wooden.

Sleeping

There aren't any hostels or top-end international hotels in Quánzhōu. If the options below are booked out, there are plenty of nondescript midrange Chinese hotels along Wenling Nanlu heading north.

Jīnzhōu Hotel HOTEL $$$
(金洲大酒店; Jīnzhōu Dàjiǔdiàn; ☎2258 6788; fax 2258 1011; 615 Quanxiu Jie; 泉秀路615号; s & d Y458-538, discounts available; ❄@) A smart three-star place perfectly poised for the long-distance bus station. Bathrooms are Lilliputian, but rooms are really comfortable. Discounts knock room prices down to Y168 to Y228. There's a ticket-booking desk in the lobby.

Jǐnjiāng Hotel HOTEL $
(锦江之星旅馆; Jǐnjiāng Zhīxīng Lǚguǎn; ☎2815 6355; 359 Wenling Beilu; 温陵北路359号; tw/d Y169/179; ❄@) Located right across a lovely park, this midrange chain has decently sized rooms and clean bathrooms. It's a notch above similar Chinese hotel chains in the midrange category, such as Motel 168.

Bǎoqí Zhāodàisuǒ HOTEL $
(宝琦招待所; ☎2228 2903; 198 Wenling Nanlu; 温陵南路198号; tr per bed Y25, s/d without bathroom Y30/40, s/d with bathroom Y60/70; ❄) It looks scuzzy on the outside, but rooms are small, cheap and clean. There's no English spoken here and no English sign, but it's next to the flyover. Yes, it's the dodgy-looking entrance with a staircase leading upstairs.

Eating & Drinking

You can find the usual noodle and rice dishes served in the back lanes around Kāiyuán Temple and also along the food street close to Wenling Nanlu.

Ānjìkèwáng HAKKA $$
(安记客王; 453-461 Tumen Jie; meals from Y50; ⌚11am-9.30pm) This is an excellent restaurant, if a little overdressed, for sampling some of the traditional Hakka dishes, including the lovely *kèjiā jiānniàng dòufu* (客家煎酿豆腐; soft cubes of tofu impregnated with crumbs of pork; Y22) and the delectable *tiěpén jiāngcōng niúròu* (铁盆姜葱牛肉; Y38), a sizzling iron plate of beef strips tossed with ginger, onions and shallots. The roast duck and dim sum selection are good options too.

Gǔcuò Cháfāng TEA $$
(古厝茶坊; 44 Houcheng Xiang; tea Y10-280, snacks Y7-15; ⌚9am-1am) This lovely teahouse in the alley behind the Guandi Temple has a refreshing old-time courtyard ambience, hung with red lanterns, paved with flagstones and laid out with traditional wooden halls and bamboo chairs. There are puppet shows every Friday (8.30pm, Y15 to Y50).

Information

You'll find **internet cafes** near the PSB on Dong Jie and in the small lanes behind Guandi Temple. Most charge Y2 to Y3 an hour.

Bank of China (中国银行; Zhōngguó Yínháng; 9-13 Jiuyi Jie; ⏲9am-5pm) This branch also exchanges travellers cheques; 24-hour ATM.

Chíchí Internet Cafe (池池网吧; Chíchí Wǎngbā; Xianhou Lu; per hr Y3; ⏲24hr)

China Post (中国邮政; Zhōngguó Yóuzhèng; cnr Dong Jie & Nanjun Lu; ⏲8.30am-6pm)

Fēiténg Xiūxián Internet Cafe (飞腾休闲网吧; Fēiténg Xiūxián Wǎngbā; Xi Jie; per hr Y3; ⏲24hr)

Public Security Bureau (PSB; 公安局; Gōng'ānjú; ☎2218 0323; 62 Dong Jie; ⏲visa section 8-11.30am & 2.30-5.30pm)

Quánzhōu Xiéhé Hospital (Quánzhōu Xiéhé Yīyuàn; Tian'an Nanlu) In the southern part of town.

Getting There & Around

BUS The **long-distance bus station** (泉州汽车站; Quánzhōu qìchēzhàn; cnr Wenling Nanlu & Quanxiu Jie) is in the southern corner of town.

Guǎngzhōu Y250, nine hours, two daily

Shēnzhèn Y250, eight hours, one daily (9.40pm)

Regular deluxe buses:

Fúzhōu Y62, 3½ hours

Lóngyán Y91

Xiàmén Y37 to Y40, 1½ hours

There's a **new long-distance bus station** (kèyùn xīnzhàn; Quanxiu Jie) further east along Quanxiu Jie with buses to similar destinations. Take bus 15 to get there.

Local bus 2 (Y2) goes from the bus station to Kāiyuán Temple. Buses 19 and 23 run from the train station to the centre of town. Taxi flag fall is Y6, then Y1.60 per kilometre.

TRAIN The small train station is in the northeast of town for Wǔyí Shān (hard sleeper Y149, 12½ hours, 5pm). Buses 7, 19, 23 and 25 go to the station. D trains depart from the high-speed rail station, 15km from the town centre:

Fúzhōu Y29, one hour, every 30 minutes

Shànghǎi Y237, seven hours, one daily (11.50am)

Xiàmén Y28, 45 minutes, every 30 minutes

You have to take a taxi (Y30 to Y40) there. In town, train tickets can be bought at the Wenling Nanlu **ticket office** (铁路火车票代售点; tiělù huǒchēpiào dàishòudiǎn; 166 Wenling Nanlu; ⏲9am-6pm) or from the **ticket office** (火车售票亭; huǒchē shòupiàotíng; 675 Quanxiu Jie;

WORTH A TRIP

CHÓNGWǓ

About 50km east of Quánzhōu is the **ancient 'stone city'** (Gǔchéng; admission free) of Chóngwǔ (崇武), with one of the best-preserved city walls in China. The granite walls date back to 1387, stretch over 2.5km long and average 7m in height. Scattered around the walls are 1304 battlements and four gates into the city.

The town wall was built by the Ming government as a frontline defence against marauding Japanese pirates, and it must be said that it has survived the last 600 years remarkably well. Meander around perusing the old halls and courtyard residences – but perhaps the wall has fostered a siege mentality as not all locals are friendly. Still, it's an amazing bit of architecture and the warren of lanes and cul-de-sacs are maddeningly unique. You can also walk along the top of the wall at some points.

Next to the stone city is **Scene of Chóngwǔ** (崇武城成传统民居游览区; Chóngwǔ Gǔchéng Chuántǒng Mínjū Yóulǎnqū; admission Y25), a large park filled with over 500 stone sculptures made by local craftspeople. There's a small beach inside, along with access to a lighthouse and some seafood restaurants. You can enter the stone city from inside the park.

Frequent minibuses depart Quánzhōu's new long-distance bus station (Y12, 1½ hours), taking you past amazing arrays of stone statues (the area is famed for its stone-carving workshop) before ending up in Chóngwǔ.

Motorbikes (Y1 to Y3) will take you from the bus drop-off to the Scene of Chóngwǔ entrance. From here, walk along the stone wall away from this entrance to find access to the stone city via a city gate. Refuse the motorbike rider's offer to take you the 'back way' for 'free admission' into the stone city.

⏲7am-6pm) just east of the long-distance bus station. There's a Y5 booking fee.

Fúzhōu 福州

☎0591 / POP 1.26 MILLION

Fúzhōu, capital of Fújiàn, is a prosperous modern city that attracts a significant amount of Taiwanese investment, reflected in innumerable shopping centres and expensive restaurants. Unless you're on business or en route to Wǔyí Shān, the city can be safely skirted. Fúzhōu's city centre sprawls northwards from the Mǐn River (Mǐn Jiāng).

Sights & Activities

FREE **Jade Hill Scenic Area** PARK
(于山风景区; Yú Shān Fēngjǐngqū) This rocky hill park in the centre of Fúzhōu rises above a snow-white **statue of Mao Zedong** (毛主席像; Máo Zhǔxí Xiàng) playing 'traffic cop'. Check out the seven-storey **White Pagoda** (白塔; Bái Tǎ), built in AD 904. At the foot of Jade Hill are the wretched remains of Fúzhōu's **Ming dynasty city wall** (明代古城墙遗迹; Míngdài Gǔchéngqiáng Yíjì); originally boasting seven gates, the wall was pulled down for road widening.

FREE **West Lake Park** PARK
(西湖公园; Xīhú Gōngyuán; ⏲6am-10pm) In the northwest of Fúzhōu, this park with a large artificial lake is a popular hang-out for locals on the weekends. The park is modelled on Hángzhōu's West Lake. This is a fab little spot for chilling out, or you can hire a paddleboat (Y20 to Y50 per hour) if you're feeling energetic.

FREE **Fújiàn Provincial Museum** MUSEUM
(省博物馆; Fújiàn Shěng Bówùguǎn; ⏲9am-4pm Tue-Sun) Despite its tacky exterior, this museum in the park has good exhibits, including a fascinating 3445-year-old 'boat coffin' unearthed from a cliff in Wǔyí Shān and a rundown of Fujian's history. The surrounding buildings are chameleonic in nature and you might expect to find art exhibitions of various sorts at any given time. Bus 100 from the main bus station goes to the museum.

Sleeping

Fúzhōu accommodation falls mainly in the midrange and top-end categories. Many hotels offer discounts. Wusi Lu and Dongda Lu are the best places to look for places to stay. Most hotels are equipped with broadband internet.

Budget hotels are scarce, but you can try one of the cheapie guesthouses.

Shangri-La Hotel HOTEL $$$
(香格里拉大酒店; Xiānggélǐlā Dàjiǔdiàn; ☎8798 8888; www.shangri-la.com; 9 Xinquan Nanlu; 新权南路9号; d Y1250;) Fantastic and classy tower right at the heart of town overlooking Wuyi Sq, bringing the chain's high standards of hospitality and rooms to Fúzhōu.

Jīnhuī Hotel HOTEL $$$
(金辉酒店; Jīnhuī Dàjiǔdiàn; ☎8759 9999; 492 Hualin Lu; 华林路492号; d Y395-520;) Spiffing lobby and good discounts that take prices down to around Y188 (including breakfast) make this a good option, though the rooms could do with minor renovations. Directly opposite the train station, north of town.

Yúshān Hotel HOTEL $$$
(于山宾馆; Yúshān Bīnguǎn; ☎8335 1668; www.yushan-hotel.com; 10 Yushan Lu; 于山路10号; s Y638, d Y498-698, discounts of 20%;) Surrounded by trees next to the White Pagoda in the grassy, parklike grounds of Jade Hill, the Yúshān offers large and peaceful, if plain-Jane, rooms.

Home Inn HOTEL $$
(如家; Rújiā; ☎297 8222; www.homeinns.com; 195 Wuyi Zhonglu; 五一中路195号; d & tw Y189-239;) Budget chain with passable rooms that channel a high-school vibe: garish coloured walls, cheap fibreboard tables and kitschy, patterned sheets. A good, if safe, fallback if all else is booked out.

Jīnshān Dàfàndiàn BUDGET HOTEL $$
(金山大饭店; ☎8310 0366; 472 Hualin Lu; 华林路472号; d & tw Y88-138;) North of town near the train station.

Eating

Fúzhōu is not strong on recommended restaurants, and never has been. For cheap noodles and dumplings in a lively nocturnal environment, locals head south to Taijiang Lu, a **pedestrianised food street** (食品步行街; *shípǐn bùxíngjiē*) lined with slightly dilapidated Ming dynasty–style wooden buildings and lanterns. It's dead during the day. Take bus 51 from Wusi Lu to get there.

The Dong Jie and Bayiqi Lu intersection is a good place to hunt for restaurants. The area north of town around the train station is also home to many fast-food restaurants and local noodle-type joints.

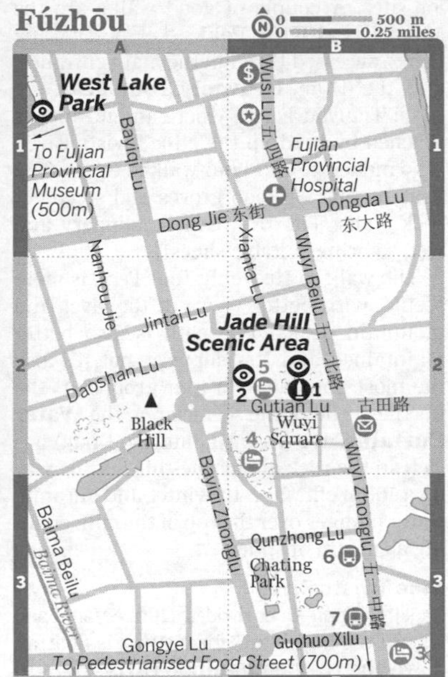

Fúzhōu

Top Sights

- Jade Hill Scenic Area ... B2
- West Lake Park ... A1

Sights

1 Mao Zedong Statue ... B2
Ming Dynasty City Wall Remains ... (see 1)
2 White Pagoda ... B2

Sleeping

3 Home Inn ... B3
4 Shangri-La Hotel ... B2
5 Yúshān Hotel ... B2

Transport

6 North Long-Distance Bus Station ... B3
7 South Long-Distance Bus Station ... B3

Information

Bank of China (中国银行; Zhōngguó Yínháng; 136 Wusi Lu; ⏰8am-6pm) Changes travellers cheques and cash; ATM handles foreign cards.

China Post (中国邮政; Zhōngguó Yóuzhèng; 101 Gutian Lu; ⏰7.30am-7.30pm) Has telephone service.

China Travel Service (CTS; 中国旅行社; Zhōngguó Lǚxíngshè; ☎8753 6250; 128 Wusi Lu) Airline tickets, tours to Wǔyí Shān.

Fújiàn Provincial Hospital (福建省立医院; Fújiàn Shěnglì Yīyuàn; 134 Dong Jie) In the city centre.

Internet access Places come and go around the train station; Y2 to Y3 per hour is standard.

Public Security Bureau (PSB; 公安局; Gōng'ānjú; 107 Beihuan Zhonglu) Opposite the sports centre in the northern part of town.

Getting There & Away

Air

The **Civil Aviation Administration China** (CAAC; 民航售票处; Zhōngguó Mínháng; ☎8334 5988; 18 Wuyi Zhonglu) sells tickets for daily flights to Běijīng (Y1550, 2½ hours), Guǎngzhōu (Y830, one hour), Shànghǎi (Y780, 70 minutes), Hong Kong (Y1810, 80 minutes), Wǔyí Shān (Y490, 30 minutes) and Xiàmén (Y250, 35 minutes).

Airport buses (Y20) leave from the Apollo Hotel (Ābōluó Dàjiǔdiàn) on Wuyi Zhonglu every 25 minutes between 5.30am and 7.30pm. The 50km trip takes about an hour.

Bus

The **north long-distance bus station** (长途汽车北站; chángtú qìche běizhàn; 317 Hualın Lu) services the following destinations:

Guǎngzhōu Y250, 12 hours, eight daily
Lóngyán Y150, four to five hours, seven daily
Quánzhōu Y62, two hours, six daily
Shànghǎi Y230, 10 hours, three daily
Wēnzhōu Y125, four hours, two daily
Wǔyí Shān Y86 to Y90, eight hours, night bus
Xiàmén Y65, three hours, every 15 minutes

The **south long-distance bus station** (长途汽车南站; chángtú qìchē nánzhàn; cnr Guohuo Xilu & Wuyi Zhonglu) services the following destinations:

Guǎngzhōu Y290 to Y350, 12 hours, eight daily
Hong Kong Y290, 15 hours, two daily (6.10pm and 7pm)
Shēnzhèn Y230, 12 hours, six daily
Xiàmén Y65 to Y75, 3½ hours, every 30 minutes

Train

Fúzhōu has a good network of trains to most many major cities. D trains:

Xiàmén Y42, 1½ hours, every 30 minutes
Quánzhōu Y29, one hour, every 30 minutes
Shànghǎi Y282, 6½ hours, two daily (9.52am and 3.14pm)

There are also regular trains from Fúzhōu to Wǔyí Shān (Y47 to Y161, 4½ to 6½ hours, eight daily). There's a direct high-speed Z60 overnight express to Běijīng (soft sleeper Y705, 19 hours, 4.52pm).

Many hotels will book train tickets for a service fee, and there's also a **train-ticket booking office** (火车票售票处; Huǒchēpiào Shòupiàochù; ⏲8am-5pm) on the west side of the Xīnhuádū Bǎihuò (新都百货) at the corner of Bayiqi Lu and Dong Jie. Tickets are also available at the station, north of town.

Getting Around

Taxi flag fall is Y8. There's a good bus network, and Chinese bus maps are available at the train station. The local bus terminal is 100m west of the train station. Bus 51 travels from the train station along Wusi Lu, and bus 1 goes to West Lake Park from Bayiqi Lu.

Wǔyí Shān 武夷山

☎0599 / POP 22,000

Wǔyí Shān, in the far northwest corner of Fújiàn, has some of the most spectacular, unspoilt scenery in the province. With its rivers, waterfalls, mountains and protected forests, it's a terrific place for hiking and exploring. Try to come midweek or in low season (November, March and April) and you might have the area to yourself.

The scenic part lies on the west bank of Chóngyáng Stream (Chóngyáng Xī), and some accommodation is located along its shore. Most of the hotels are concentrated in the *dù jià qū* (resort district) on the east side of the river. The main settlement is Wǔyí Shān city, about 10km to the northeast, with the train station and airport roughly halfway between.

During research, Wǔyí Shān was flooded: multiple areas were damaged and trails were washed out. The area should be repaired and ready for tourists by the time this book goes to print. Avoid the area during heavy rain even if the hotels and tour organisers advise otherwise.

Sights & Activities

Wǔyí Shān Scenic Area — MOUNTAIN PARK

(武夷宫; 1-/2-/3-day access Y140/150/160; ⏲6am-8pm) Enter the area via **Wǔyí Gōng**, about 200m south of the Wǔyí Mountain Villa, near the confluence of the Chóngyáng Stream and the Nine Twists River. Trails within the scenic area connect all the major sites. A couple of good walks are the 530m **Great King Peak** (大王峰; Dàwáng Fēng), accessed through the main entrance, and the 410m **Heavenly Tour Peak** (天游峰; Tiānyóu Fēng), where an entrance is reached by road up the Nine Twists River. It's a moderate two-hour walk to Great King Peak among bamboo groves and steep-cut rock walls. The trail can be slippery and wet, so bring suitable shoes.

The walk to Heavenly Tour Peak is more scenic, with better views of the river and mountain peaks. The path is also better maintained and less slippery, but it's also the most popular with tour groups. At the northern end of the scenic area, the **Water Curtain Cave** (水帘洞; Shuǐlián Dòng) is a cleft in the rock about one-third of the way up a 100m cliff face. In winter and autumn, water plunges over the top of the cliff, creating a curtain of spray.

Nine Twists River — RIVER

(九曲溪; Jiǔqū Xī; boat rides Y100; ⏲7am-5pm) One of the highlights for visitors is floating down the river on **bamboo rafts** *(zhúpái)* fitted with rattan chairs. Departing from Xīngcūn (星村), a short bus ride west of the resort area, the trip down the river takes over an hour. The boat ride takes you through some magnificent gorge scenery, with sheer rock cliffs and lush green vegetation.

One of the mysteries of Wǔyí Shān is the cavities, carved out of the rock faces at great heights, which once held boat-shaped coffins. Scientists have dated some of these artefacts back 4000 years. If you're taking a raft down the river, it's possible to see some remnants of these coffins on the west cliff face of the fourth meander or 'twist', also known as **Small Storing Place Peak** (小藏山峰; Xiǎozàngshān Fēng).

Xiàméi — ANCIENT VILLAGE

(下梅; admission Y26) This village dates to the Northern Song dynasty, and boasts some spectacular Qing-dynasty architecture from its heyday as a wealthy tea-trading centre. To reach Xiàméi, hop on a minibus (Y4) from Wǔyí Shān city for the 12km journey. Minibuses also run to Xiàméi (Y3) from the Wǔyí Shān Scenic Area.

Sleeping

Most of the accommodation in Wǔyí Shān is midrange in price, and room rates rise and fall according to demand and season. Hotels are mostly on the east side of the river, though there are a few on the quieter west side. Discounts are often available.

Wǔyí Mountain Villa HOTEL **$$$**
(武夷山庄; Wǔyí Shānzhuāng; ☎525 1888; Wuyi Gong; 武夷宫; d Y888-988, ste Y1388-2888, discounts of 40%;) This is the most upmarket hotel in Wǔyí Shān and its secluded location on the west side of the river at the foot of Great King Peak makes it (almost) worth the price. Buildings are chalet-style and surrounded by peaceful gardens, a swimming pool and a waterfall.

Bǎodǎo Dàjiǔdiàn HOTEL **$$$**
(宝岛大酒店; ☎523 4567; fax 525 5555; Wangfeng Lu; 望峰路; s/d Y780/880) Situated next to the Bank of China, this centrally located hotel has a curiously arrayed lobby decorated with chunky tree-trunk furniture. Rooms are respectable and good sized, with clean bathrooms. It's place with tour groups, so you may need to book ahead.

International Trade Hotel HOTEL **$$**
(国贸大酒店; Guómào Dàjiǔdiàn; ☎525 2521; fax 525 2521; Wangfeng Lu; 望峰路; d Y240-580) On the eastern side of the resort area, this well-managed hotel gives good discounts midweek for its serviceable, though uninspired, guest rooms.

Eating

Frogs, mushrooms, bamboo rice and bamboo shoots are the specialities of Wǔyí Shān's cuisine. In town, there are food stalls along the streets in the evening. As to be expected, restaurants are overpriced.

Information

Maps of the Wǔyí Shān area are available in bookshops and hotels in the resort district.

There are some grubby **internet cafes** in the back alleys south of Wangfeng Lu (望峰路), charging Y2 to Y4 an hour.

Bank of China (中国银行; Zhōngguó Yínháng; Wujiu Lu; ⏲9am-5pm) In Wǔyí Shān city, this branch changes travellers cheques and has an ATM.

China International Travel Service (CITS; 中国国际旅行社; Zhōngguó Guójì Lǚxíngshè; ☎525 0380; 35 Guanjing Lu; ⏲9am-4pm Mon-Sat) The staff are helpful and can arrange train tickets and tours.

Getting There & Away

AIR Wǔyí Shān has air links to several cities.

Běijīng Y1350, two hours
Fúzhōu Y490, 35 minutes
Guǎngzhōu Y890, 2½ hours
Hong Kong Y1300, two hours
Shànghǎi Y660, one hour
Xiàmén Y720, 50 minutes

BUS Buses run from the **long-distance bus station** in Wuyi Shan city.

Fúzhōu Y86 to Y90, eight hours
Nánpíng Y37, three hours
Shàngráo Y26, two hours
Shàowǔ Y15, 1½ hours
Xiàmén regular/deluxe Y124/202, nine hours

TRAIN Direct trains go to Wǔyí Shān from Quánzhōu (Y158 to Y365, 13 hours) and Xiàmén (Y149 to Y232, 12 hours).

Getting Around

Bus 6 runs between the airport, the resort area and the train station. Minivans or a public bus (Y2) shuttle between Wǔyí Shān city and the resort district, and there are minibuses between Wǔyí Shān city and Xīngcūn. The resort area is small enough to walk everywhere, so ignore pesky trishaw drivers who insist everything is 'too far'.

Expect to pay about Y10 for a motorised trishaw from the resort district to most of the scenic area entrances. A ride from the train station or airport to the resort district will cost Y10 to Y20 – haggle.

Liáoníng

POPULATION: 43 MILLION

Includes »

Best Places to Eat

» Lǎobiān Dumplings (p285)

» View & World Vegetarian Restaurant (p285)

» Pyongyang North Korean Restaurant (p295)

» Dàbáicài Gǔtouguǎn (p289)

Best Places to Stay

» Liáoníng Bīnguǎn (p284)

» Traders Hotel (p284)

» City Central Youth Hostel (p284)

» Dàlián Bīnhǎi Hotel (p288)

Why Go?

History and hedonism are side by side in Liáoníng (辽宁). Walled Ming-dynasty cities rub up against booming beach resorts, while imperial palaces sit in the centre of the bustling modern cities. Nothing quite captures the fun and distinction, however, as much as seaside Dàlián with its golden coastline and summer beer festival (or is that bacchanalia?), but also former battlegrounds where Russian and Japanese armies wrestled for control of the region in the early 20th century.

Outside of the major cities, Liáoníng is largely expanses of farmland, forest and smokestack towns. The North Korean border runs alongside the province and is an intriguing area, not simply because it's as close as you can get to the Democratic People's Republic of Korea (DPRK) without actually going there. The heavy Korean population and the easy mix of cultures provides a ready example that China is only a land of stereotypes if you never venture far into it.

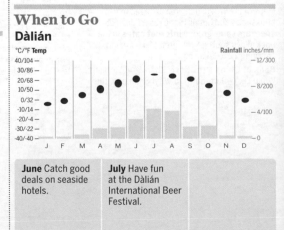

When to Go

Dàlián

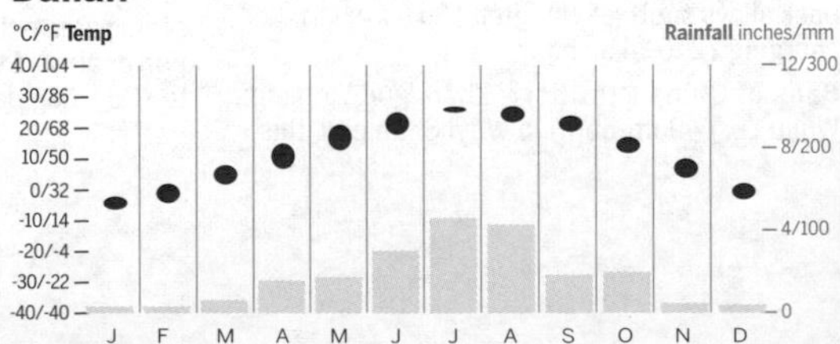

June Catch good deals on seaside hotels.

July Have fun at the Dàlián International Beer Festival.

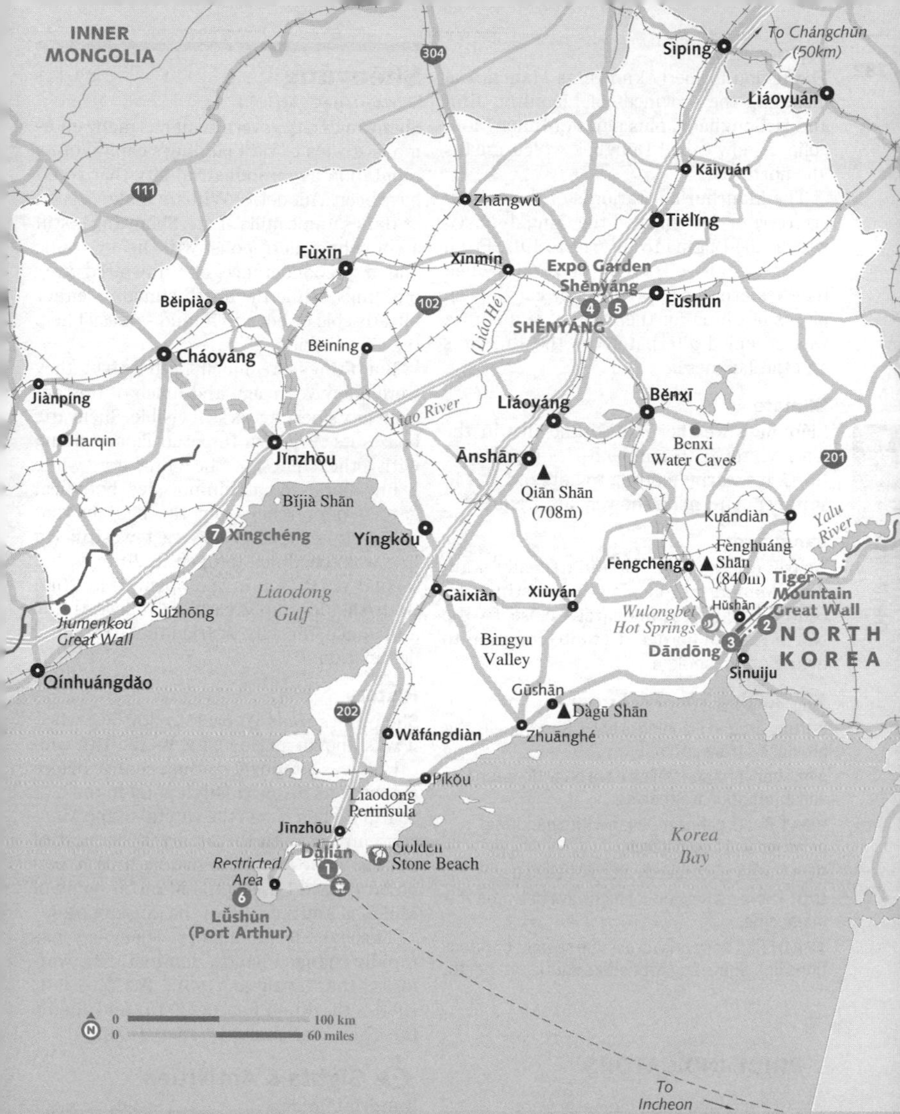

Liáoníng Highlights

1. Kick back in **Dàlián** (p286), enjoy the beaches and a beer festival
2. Climb the easternmost stretch of the Great Wall at **Tiger Mountain Great Wall** (p294), near Dāndōng
3. Cruise the Yālù River close to North Korea and experience the mix of Korean and Chinese culture in **Dāndōng** (p293)
4. Explore the tomb of Huang Taiji, founder of the Qing dynasty, in **Shěnyáng** (p283)
5. Lose yourself in nature at the enormous **Expo Garden Shěnyáng** (p284)
6. Wander the old battlefields and graves of **Lǚshùn** (p291), fought over by rival Japanese and Russian Empires
7. Laze on the beach and stroll the old city of historic, little-visited **Xīngchéng** (p296)

History

The region formerly known as Manchuria, including the provinces of Liáoníng, Jílín and Hēilóngjiāng, plus parts of Inner Mongolia, is now called Dōngběi, which means 'the northeast'.

The Manchurian warlords of this northern territory established the Qing dynasty, which ruled China from 1644 to 1911. From the late 1800s to the end of WWII, when the Western powers were busy carving up pieces of China for themselves, Manchuria was occupied alternately by the Russians and the Japanese.

Climate

Liáoníng's weather is cold and dry in the long winter with temperatures dipping to -15°C. It's warm (tending to hot) and wet in summer. Afternoon showers are frequent.

Language

Nearly everyone in Liáoníng speaks standard Mandarin, albeit with a distinct accent. In Dāndōng and areas close to the North Korean border, it's quite common to hear Korean spoken.

Getting There & Around

Getting around Liáoníng is easy. Shěnyáng is the province's transport hub.

AIR Shěnyáng and Dàlián have busy domestic and international airports.

BOAT Boats connect Dàlián with Shāndōng province and South Korea.

BUS Buses are a speedy alternative to trains.

CAR There's a network of highways between the major cities.

TRAIN Rail lines crisscross the region; connections link Shěnyáng with cities south and north.

PRICE INDICATORS

The following price indicators are used in this chapter:

Sleeping

$	less than Y200
$$	Y200 to Y400
$$$	more than Y400

Eating

$	less than Y10
$$	Y10 to Y40
$$$	more than Y40

Shěnyáng 沈阳

024 / POP 7.2 MILLION

Shěnyáng's city government has made enormous strides to rid Liáoníng's capital of its reputation as an industrial city that could have been a model for William Blake's vision of 'dark satanic mills'. True, Shěnyáng is still a sprawling metropolis, with heavy traffic and a preponderance of uninspired grey buildings, while the harsh climate – either bitterly cold or hot and humid – doesn't help the air pollution.

But things are much better than they were a few years ago and much of this ancient city's heritage is still visible. Shěnyáng boasts its very own Imperial Palace, along with other relics of the Qing era, while a fine park and an impressive botanical garden offer relief from the bedlam that is the city's roads. A new east–west metro line was scheduled to open in 2010, with a second north–south line opening in 2012. Both should help greatly to relieve traffic and make the city a friendlier travelling destination.

History

Shěnyáng's roots go back to 300 BC, when it was known as Hou City. By the 11th century it was a Mongol trading centre, before reaching its historical high point in the 17th century when it was the capital of the Manchu empire. With the Manchu conquest of Běijīng in 1644, Shěnyáng became a secondary capital under the Manchu name of Mukden, and a centre of the ginseng trade.

Throughout its history Shěnyáng has rapidly changed hands, dominated by warlords, the Japanese (1931), the Russians (1945), the Kuomintang (1946) and finally the Chinese Communist Party (1948).

Sights & Activities

Imperial Palace HISTORICAL SITE
(故宫; Gùgōng; 171 Shenyang Lu; admission Y60; 8.30am-6pm, last entry 5.15pm) Shěnyáng's main attraction is this impressive palace complex, which resembles a small-scale Forbidden City. Constructed between 1625 and 1636 by Manchu emperor Nurhachi (1559–1626) and his son, Huang Taiji, the palace served as the residence of the Qing-dynasty rulers until 1644.

The central courtyard buildings include ornate ceremonial halls and imperial living quarters, including a royal baby cradle. In

Shěnyáng

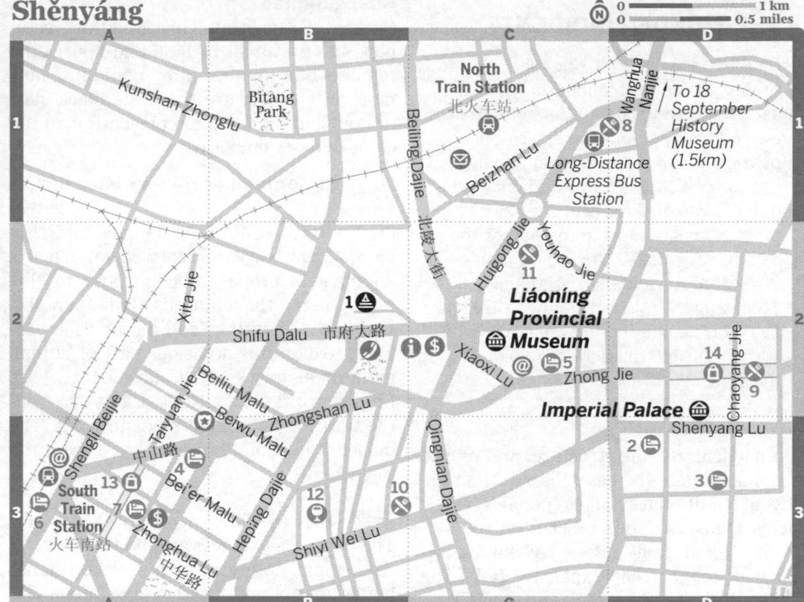

all, there are 114 buildings, not all of which are open to the public.

Don't miss the double-eaved octagonal **Dàzhèng Hall** (at the rear of the complex), which has two gold dragons curled around the pillars at the entrance, a deep interior plafond ceiling and an elaborate throne, where Nurhachi's grandson, Emperor Shunzhi, was crowned. At **Chóngzhèng Hall**, the first large building as you enter, the beams over the entrance portico are all carved in the shape of five-fingered dragons.

The palace is in the oldest section of the city. Take bus 237 from the south train station, or bus 227 from the North Tomb via the east side of the north train station.

North Tomb HISTORICAL SITE

(北陵; Běi Líng; 12 Taishan Lu; park/tombs Y6/30; ⌚6am-6pm) Another Shěnyáng highlight is this extensive tomb complex, the burial place of Huang Taiji (1592–1643), founder of the Qing dynasty. The tomb's animal statues lead up to the central mound known as the Luminous Tomb (Zhāo Líng).

In many ways a better-preserved complex than the Imperial Palace, the tomb site is worth a few hours examining the dozens of buildings with their traditional architecture and ornamentation. **Lóng'ēn Hall**

Shěnyáng

Top Sights
Imperial Palace ... D2
Liáoníng Provincial Museum ... C2

Sights
1 Huáng Sìmiào ... B2

Sleeping
2 City Central Youth Hostel ... D3
3 Home Inn ... D3
4 Liáoníng Bīnguǎn ... A3
5 Méishān Bīnguǎn ... C2
6 Shěntiě Shěnzhàn Bīnguǎn ... A3
7 Traders Hotel ... A3

Eating
8 Carrefour Supermarket ... D1
9 Lǎobiān Dumplings ... D2
10 View & World Vegetarian Restaurant ... B3
11 Yúfū Mǎtóu Shāokǎo ... C2

Drinking
12 Stroller's ... B3

Shopping
13 Night Market ... A3
14 Zhong Jie ... D2

THE 'MUKDEN INCIDENT'

By 1931 Japan was looking for a pretext to occupy Manchuria. The Japanese army took matters into their own hands by staging an explosion on the night of 18 September at a tiny section of a Japanese-owned railway outside Mukden, the present-day city of Shěnyáng. Almost immediately, the Japanese attacked a nearby Chinese army garrison and then occupied Shěnyáng the following night. Within five months, they controlled all of Manchuria and ruled the region until the end of WWII.

is a particularly fine structure, and as you circumambulate the base observe the richness of traditional symbols (peonies, vases, lucky clouds) carved in relief.

The North Tomb sits a few kilometres north of town inside expansive **Běi Líng Park**. With its pine trees and large lake, the park is an excellent place to escape Shěnyáng's hubbub. Locals come here to promenade, sing or just kick back.

Take bus 220 from the south train station or bus 217 from the north train station. Bus 227 from the Imperial Palace via the east side of the north train station also travels to and from the North Tomb.

Expo Garden Shěnyáng GARDENS
(沈阳世博园; Shěnyáng Shìbó Yuán; admission Y35; ⏲9am-5pm) These vast gardens on the eastern outskirts of Shěnyáng have dozens of elaborate exhibition gardens featuring plants and flowers from almost every region of China, as well as some from overseas. With restaurants and snack stops scattered throughout, you can easily spend a day wandering.

Trains leave the north station at 6.15am and 9.15am (Y3.50, 30 minutes) and return at 6.15pm and 7.30pm, but you can catch bus 168 back to the city or a taxi (Y50 to Y70).

FREE **Liáoníng Provincial Museum** MUSEUM
(辽宁省博物馆; Liáoníng Shěng Bówùguǎn; SE cnr Government Sq; ⏲9am-noon & 1-5pm, last entry 3.30pm, closed Mon & public holidays) Three floors of exhibits highlight the region's prehistoric culture, Liao-dynasty ceramics, ancient Chinese money and carved stone tablets illustrating the evolution of Chinese calligraphy.

Huáng Sìmiào BUDDHIST TEMPLE
(皇寺庙; ⏲8am-9pm) This Buddhist complex was first built in 1636 and houses the remains of a high-ranking monk. Probably more interesting are the large black statues outside the temple representing all the Qing-dynasty emperors.

FREE **18 September History Museum** MUSEUM
(九一八历史博物馆; Jiǔ Yī Bā Lìshǐ Bówùguǎn; 46 Wanghua Nanjie; ⏲9am-5.30pm) There's an obvious propagandic purpose to this museum, but the hundreds of photographs, sculptures, paintings and dioramas are informative on this notorious part of China's modern history (see the boxed text, left). English captions are limited. Bus 325 from the north train station stops in front. The museum is about 2km northeast from the town centre.

Sleeping

The best area to stay is around the Imperial Palace, but note that many of the smaller hotels are not permitted to take foreigners.

Liáoníng Bīnguǎn HOTEL $$
(辽宁宾馆; Liaoning Hotel; ☎2383 9104; 97 Zhongshan Lu; 中山路97号; incl breakfast s Y298, d Y358-498; ❄@) This grand old Japanese-built hotel dates back to 1927. Recently refurbished, it retains many of its period details – the marbled lobby is particularly impressive – but also offers comfortable modern rooms, some of which offer a fine view of Zhongshan Sq.

Traders Hotel HOTEL $$$
(商贸饭店; Shāngmào Fàndiàn; ☎2341 2288; www.shangri-la.com; 68 Zhonghua Lu; 中华路68号; d Y698-1238; ⊖❄@) Owned by the Shangri-La chain, this is Shěnyáng's best luxury hotel, with big rooms and efficient, English-speaking staff delivering top-notch service. Room rates vary depending on the season. Book online for good deals. Add a 15% service charge to room rates.

Home Inn HOTEL $
(如家快捷酒店; Rújiā Kuàijié Jiǔdiàn; ☎8295 0925; 7 Donghua Lane, Shenyang Lu; 沈阳路东华南巷7号; d from Y166; 📶) Bright, spotless rooms feature free broadband, and the ones that face the alley are surprisingly quiet. Given the doubles here are just a few dollars more than the hostel rooms, and are in the same neighbourhood as the Imperial Palace, this is a solid budget choice.

City Central Youth Hostel HOSTEL $
(帅府国际青年旅舍; Shuàifǔ Guójì Qīngnián Lǚshè; ☎2484 4868; www.chinayha.com; 103 Shenyang Lu; 沈阳路103号; dm Y40, d without bathroom Y100, s & d with bathroom Y158) This historic building was built to house officers from the army of notorious warlord Zhang Zuo Lin. A stone's throw from the Imperial Palace, it's popular with Chinese travellers and has four- or six-bed dorm rooms that are good value, though there are no hostel standards like laundry and internet. The singles and doubles are getting pretty scuffed and need a new paint job. Book ahead here.

Méishān Bīnguǎn HOTEL $
(梅杉宾馆; Main Sun Hotel; ☎2278 3399; 48 Xiaoxi Lu; 小西路48号; s Y60-100, d Y80-120; ❄) The cheaper, single rooms are rather cell-like and have no attached bathrooms; it's worth splashing out for the more spacious doubles, though in general the hotel is in need of an update.

Shěntiě Shěnzhàn Bīnguǎn HOTEL $
(沈铁沈站宾馆; Shěnyáng Railway Station Hotel; ☎2358 5888; 2 Shengli Dajie; 胜利大街2号; s without bathroom Y80, d Y168-188; ❄@) A convenient if ageing place next to the south train station. Some of the singles without bathrooms have no windows.

Eating

Both the north and south train stations are cheap-restaurant zones. You'll also find lots of reasonably priced restaurants around the Imperial Palace. Most have picture menus.

TOP CHOICE **Lǎobiān Dumplings** DUMPLINGS $$
(老边饺子馆; Lǎobiān Jiǎoziguǎn; 2f 208 Zhong Jie; dumplings Y8-35; ⏰10am-10pm) Shěnyáng's most famous restaurant has been packing in the locals since 1829, and they continue to flock here for the fine dumplings. But the soups are equally impressive. The restaurant is on the 2nd floor of the Lǎobiān Hotel.

View & World Vegetarian Restaurant VEGETARIAN $$
(宽巷子素菜馆; Kuān Xiàngzi Sùcàiguǎn; 202 Shiyi Wei Lu; dishes Y8-38; ⏰10am-10.30pm; ✓📋) Peking duck (Y28) and meatballs (Y24) are on the menu here, but there won't be any actual meat on your plate. Everything is meat-free at this nearly vegan paradise, which claims to be the only non-MSG restaurant in all northeast China (an astonishing claim if true). The fruit and vegie drinks pair up nicely with the main courses.

Yúfū Mǎtóu Shāokǎo SEAFOOD $$
(沈阳渔夫码头烧烤; Fisherman's Harbour Barbecue; 75 Huigong Jie; dishes Y6-38; ⏰11.30am-midnight) A friendly, fun, three-floor restaurant with a nautical theme. The seafood platter (Y118) arrives in a boat-shaped dish and satisfies two or three people easily. Plenty of meat is available, plus hotpot, and some very filling and cheap noodle and vegie dishes with an emphasis on spice. There's also a proper bar where you can sip a Harbin beer. Picture menu available.

Carrefour Supermarket SUPERMARKET $
(家乐福; Jiālèfú; Beizhan Lu; ⏰7.30am-10pm) Near the long-distance bus station. You can pack a picnic for your travels here or grab a quick bite from the noodle joints on the ground floor.

Drinking

Stroller's BAR
(流浪者餐厅; Liúlàngzhě; 36 Beiwu Jing Jie) It looks more like a superior junk shop than a bar, with the walls and ceiling covered with old posters, helmets, bikes and seemingly anything they could find. A popular spot with both locals and expats, it does reasonable Western food, too. The street is not signed, so look for the Royal Hotel on Shiyi Wei Lu. Stroller's is about a block north.

Shopping

Near the south train station is Taiyuan Jie, one of Shěnyáng's major shopping streets, with department stores and a bustling **night market**. Below Taiyuan Jie is an extensive underground shopping street.

Zhong Jie, near the Imperial Palace, is another popular pedestrianised shopping zone that was getting a full revamping at the time of writing to make it ready to host the hordes who will be flocking here soon on the new metro.

Information

ATMs accepting foreign cards can be found all over the city.

Bank of China (中国银行; Zhōngguó Yínháng) Government Sq (253 Shifu Dalu; ⏰8.30-5pm Mon-Fri); south train station area (96 Zhonghua Lu; ⏰8am-noon & 1-4pm Mon-Fri) South station area branch has 24-hour ATM. Both will change travellers cheques.

Internet cafe (网吧;wǎngbā; main level, south train station; per hr Y3; ⏲24hr)

Photo shop (64 Xiaoxi Lu; CDs Y10) For CD burning; near the Méishān Bīnguǎn.

Public Security Bureau (PSB; 公安局; Gōng'ānjú; ☎2253 4850; Zhongshan Sq)

Getting There & Away

Large hotels can book airline and train tickets, as can **China Travel Service of Shenyang** (沈阳市中国旅行社; Shěnyáng Shì Zhōngguó Lǚxíngshè; ☎13700-000-681; 1 Shifu Lu; ⏲8.30am-5pm).

Air

Shenyang Taoxian International Airport (www.taoxianairport.com) has flights to Seoul (return Y3200) as well as the domestic cities listed below. There are no direct flights to Russia.

Běijīng Y770

Hā'ěrbīn Y580

Shànghǎi Y1390

Bus

The **long-distance express bus station** (长途汽车快速客运站; Chángtú qìchē kuàisù kèyùnzhàn; Huigong Jie) is south of Beizhan Lu, about a five-minute walk from the north train station and close to the Carrefour Supermarket. Buses service the following destinations:

Běijīng Y129, 7½ hours, six daily (8am to 10pm)

Chángchūn Y68, 4½ hours, hourly (7am to 6pm)

Dāndōng Y77, three hours, every 30 minutes (6am to 7pm)

Hā'ěrbīn Y76, 6½ hours, four daily (8.10am to 2.30pm)

Jílín Y105, 4½ hours, six daily (7.30am to 4.30pm)

Xīngchéng Y78.50, 3½ hours, two daily (8.50am and 3.40pm)

Train

Shěnyáng's major train stations are the north and south stations. Many trains arrive at one station, stop briefly, then travel to the next; it may be different when departing – always confirm which station you need. Buy sleeper or D-train tickets (to Běijīng or Shànghǎi) as far in advance as possible. Bus 262 runs between the north and south train stations.

SOUTH STATION TRAINS

Báihé seat/sleeper Y50/100, one daily (departs 9.30am, arrives just past midnight)

Běijīng seat/sleeper Y96/218, eight to 10 hours

Chángchūn Y47, four to six hours

Dàlián Y49 to Y65, four hours

Dāndōng Y24 to Y37, four hours

Hā'ěrbīn Y38 to Y67, five to seven hours

Xīngchéng Y28 to Y41, four hours, eight daily

NORTH STATION TRAINS

Běijīng (D train) Y218 to Y261, four hours

Shànghǎi seat/sleeper Y231/401, 27 hours

Shànghǎi (D train) seat Y410 to Y511, 14 hours

Getting Around

TO/FROM THE AIRPORT The airport is 25km south of the city. Taxis to Shěnyáng are Y50 to Y80.

BUS Buses are cheap, frequent and cover the city. Maps of the routes (Y5) are sold at train stations.

SUBWAY A new subway system is under construction in Shěnyáng. The first line (green; to run east–west) is scheduled to open late 2010, with a second in 2012. Expect stations at south train station and Zhong Jie (for the Imperial Palace).

TAXI Taxis cost Y8 for the first 3km.

Dàlián 大连

☎0411 / POP 3.4 MILLION

Dàlián is one of the most relaxed and liveable cities in the northeast, if not all of China. Tree-lined, hilly streets, plenty of early-20th-century architecture, an impressive coastline complete with beaches, manageable traffic and (relatively) clean air, as well as the booming local economy and some serious shopping, have resulted in the city being dubbed the 'Hong Kong of the North'.

Perched on the Liáodōng Peninsula and bordering the Yellow Sea, Dàlián is a fine city to relax in for a few days (once you get away from the train-station area). As well as lazing on the beach, strolling for hours along the southwest coastline, and exploring the formerly closed historic port town of Lǚshùn, there are good seafood restaurants, plus cafes and a buzzing bar scene to enjoy.

Sights & Activities

TOP CHOICE **Southwest Coastline** SCENIC COASTLINE

(Map p292) Dàlián's southwest coast is dotted with pleasant beaches that boast both a laid-back community feel and a subtly exotic distinction. At **Fùjiāzhuāng Beach** (傅家庄海滨; Fùjiāzhuāng Hǎitān), a popular beach set in a deep bay, junks float just offshore, small broken islands dot the horizon, and loads of families can be seen

Dàlián

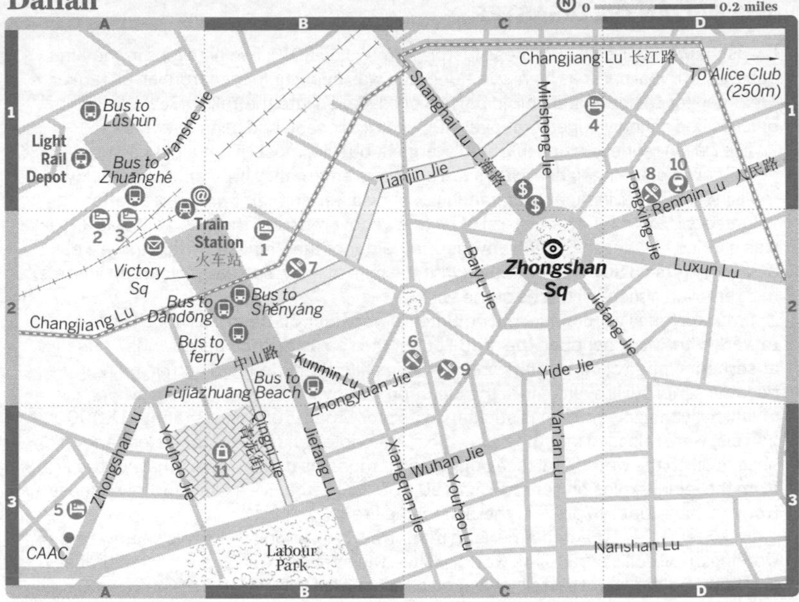

having fun. Take bus 5 from Jiefang Lu (Y1, 20 to 30 minutes) and get off at the square across from the beach.

From Fùjiāzhuāng you can walk to **Xīnghǎi Sq** along a combination of sidewalks and boardwalks that runs along the contours of the coast. At Xīnghǎi Sq, which is sporting some heady architecture these days, the path crosses a pedestrian bridge, widens and continues for another hour alongside the sea (it looked like it would soon go even further). This has to be one of the longest (to say nothing of most scenic) continuous coastal walks you can do in China without interference from motor vehicles.

On the other side of Xīnghǎi Sq look for the tram line on Zhongshan Lu to take you back to the city centre.

Golden Stone Beach BEACH

(Map p281; Jīnshítān) The coast around Golden Stone Beach, 60km north of the city, is in the process of being turned into a domestic tourist mecca with a number of theme parks, and rock formations commanding inflated entrance fees. The long pebbly beach itself is free and quite pretty, set in a wide bay with distant headlands.

To get there take the light rail, known by the locals as Line 3 (轻轨三号线; Qīngguǐ Sānhàoxiàn), from the depot on the east side of Triumph Plaza, behind the Dàlián train station (Y8, 50 minutes). From the beach station it's a 10-minute walk to the beach, or catch a tourist shuttle bus (Y20,

Dàlián

Top Sights
- Zhongshan Sq ... C2

Sleeping
1. Bóhǎi Pearl Hotel ... B2
2. Broadway Hotel ... A2
3. Dōng Hào Hotel ... A2
4. Home Inn ... C1
5. Nóngkěn Hotel ... A3

Eating
6. Dàbáicài Gǔtouguǎn ... C2
7. Night Market ... B2
8. Tiántián Yúgǎng ... D1
9. Xiǎo Yāogǔ Shǎnxī Miàn Zhuāng ... C2

Drinking
10. Meeting Place Bar ... D1

Shopping
11. New Mart Shopping Mall ... B3

THE DÀLIÁN OIL DISASTER

It was the worst oil spill in Chinese history. On 16 July 2010, two pipelines in the Xingang oil terminal burst as high-sulphur crude was being unloaded from an oil tanker. A fire raged for 15 hours and untold barrels of oil leaked into the Yellow Sea. Within days officials had acknowledged that over 400 sq km of ocean had been affected.

The Dàlián refinery is one of China's largest, but like most (if not all) it had no contingency planning to deal with such a serious emergency. City officials, quickly realising they were incapable of handling the disaster on their own, started offering volunteers US$44 for every barrel of oil they recovered from the sea. That was all that was needed to unleash the entrepreneurial valour of the Chinese. Within three weeks 8000 workers on 800 fishing boats (with the help of a few specialist clean-up vessels) had removed almost all traces of the spill.

Small fortunes were made, but volunteers were lucky if they had rubber gloves to work with. Many scooped the crude out of the sea using their bare hands or used absorbents made of straw mats and stockings filled with donated human hair. Some became seriously ill even before the clean-up was over.

Officially the government is sticking to its story that 1500 tonnes (about 11,000 barrels) were released into the Yellow Sea. Anecdotal evidence of the extent and thickness of oil on the water's surface suggests far more, as does a report that, as the fire from the initial explosion spread, up to 50,000 tonnes of oil was deliberately released from onshore tanks to prevent them catching fire.

Rick Steiner, a respected American marine conservationist who has spent years working on oil spills around the world, visited the affected area and reported that several hundred thousand barrels of leaked oil is a more likely figure. This puts the Dàlián spill on a comparable scale with the Exxon Valdez disaster (which Steiner studied) off Alaska in 1989.

For now, the Dàlián coastline shows few signs of the spill, and swimmers have gone back to enjoying the gold-sand beaches and warm waters. The long-term effects on the coastal environment, the fisheries and the locals, who suffered both from direct contact with the oil and from the toxic air that hung over the city for days, remains uncertain.

30 minutes) which winds round the coast first before dropping you off at the beach. There's a **visitor centre** to the right of the train station as you exit, with English-speaking staff if you need help.

Labour Park PARK
(Map p292; 劳动公园; Láodòng Gōngyuán) In the centre of this hilly park is a giant football, a reminder of the time at the turn of the century when the local soccer team, Dàlián Shi'de, was the best in China. There are good views of the city from the TV Tower.

Zhongshan Sq SQUARE
(Map p287; 中山广场; Zhōngshān Guǎngchǎng) This is Dàlián's hub, with grand buildings, mostly from the early 1900s, encircling a huge roundabout. Dàlián Bīnguǎn, a dignified hotel on the square's south side, appeared in the movie *The Last Emperor*.

Sleeping

Dàlián Bīnhǎi Hotel HOTEL **$$$**
(Map p292; 大连滨海大厦; Dàlián Bīnhǎi Dàshà; ☎8240 6666; fax 8240 6670; 2 Binhai Xilu; 滨海西路2号; d Y398-588; ❄📶) A favourite with visiting Russians, this high-rise place looks slightly rundown on the outside but is one of the best-value options if you want to stay by the coast. The hotel is literally across the road from Fùjiāzhuāng Beach and decent-sized rooms with a sea view are about Y498 in summer.

Home Inn HOTEL **$$**
(Map p287; 如家快捷酒店; Rújiā Kuàijié Jiǔdiàn; ☎8263 9977; www.homeinns.com; 102 Tianjin Jie; 天津街102号; d from Y228; ❄@) With its brightly coloured and tidy little rooms, free broadband and in-house restaurant serving cheap but tasty dishes, this is a good choice for the city centre. It's popular with Chinese travellers, so book ahead. If you stay more than a night it's worthwhile to get a mem-

bership card (Y40) as it drops the room rate down.

Bóhǎi Pearl Hotel HOTEL $$$
(Map p287; 渤海明珠酒店; Bóhǎi Míngzhū Jiǔdiàn; ☎8812 8888; www.bohaipearl.com; 8 Victory Sq; 胜利广场8号; d/tw/tr Y578/478/678;) This 30-storey tower with a kitschy revolving restaurant faces the train station, but the large lobby area means you are spared the madness of the outside world. Rooms have generic midrange comfort, large bathrooms and broadband internet. A few unexpected services include spa and pool.

Nóngkěn Hotel HOTEL $$
(Map p287; 农垦宾馆; Nóngkěn Bīnguǎn; ☎8886 7888; www.nongkenhotel.com; 141-3 Zhongshan Lu; 中山路141-3号; d/tw Y420/480) Rooms have a suburban notion of cosy comfort (think striped wallpaper, dim lights) but the location is great, close to Labour Park and the start of the leafy section of Dàlián.

Broadway Hotel HOTEL $$
(Map p287; 四方盛世酒店; Sìfāng Shèngshì Jiǔdiàn; ☎6262 8988; www.4Fhotel.com; 26-28 Jianshe Jie; 建设街26-28号; d Y328, discounts of 50%;) Rooms are bland, and the sheet thread count is low, but the place is clean and, with the price usually discounted 50%, fine for a night's stay. To find the hotel, take the underground passageway to the right as you exit the train station. When you pop out on the other side, look for a tall building to the left across from where the buses park. The Chinese characters run down the side, but the English says You Ho.

Dōng Hào Hotel HOTEL $$
(Map p287; 东浩大酒店; Dōnghào Dàjiǔdiàn; ☎3965 9888; 12 Jianshe Jie; 建设街12号; d Y368-398, discounts of 30%) Also on the back side of the train station, Dōng Hào features standard rooms that vary in their level of upkeep. Look for the hotel entrance just past the Kentucky Fried Chicken to the left as you exit the underpass.

Eating

There are plenty of small restaurants on the roads leading off Zhongshan Sq and Friendship Sq. The upscale New Mart Shopping Mall has a spiffy food court (dishes from Y8 to Y38) on the 5th floor with a huge range of eating and drinking options. It's a good choice for a single traveller in a city where most restaurants are set up for groups. There's also a well-provisioned supermarket on the lower level. Note that Friendship Sq has numerous buildings crowded in the plaza, so look for the big mall directly across from Starbucks. The food court in the nearby underground mall in Victory Sq is older and a bit cheaper.

Both sides of the plaza outside the train station are lined with fruit vendors and shops selling cheap *bàozi* (steamed meat buns).

Dàbáicài Gǔtouguǎn DONGBEI $$
(Map p287; 大白菜骨头馆; 21 Zhongyuan Jie, btwn Youhao Lu & Xiangqian Jie; dishes Y14-36; ⌚9.30am-10pm) This home-style restaurant with a friendly and loud atmosphere serves fresh seafood and fiery northern-style fare. Look for the sign high up with a green cabbage on it. Note that the restaurant is located on a corner and you must walk up the stairs to get to it. Otherwise it's easy to pass by.

Xiǎo Yāogǔ Shǎnxī Miàn Zhuāng SHAANXI $
(Map p287; 小腰鼓陕西面庄; dishes Y3-10; ⌚8am-9.30pm) At the end of Zhongyuan Jie, one block past Dàbáicài Gǔtouguǎn, is this Shaanxi restaurant that serves great dishes such as lamb *jiāmó* (羊肉夹馍; lamb in pita bread) or *pàomó* (泡馍; bread stew) at a ridiculously low price. A light meal will set you back under Y10. Look for the red lanterns outside and place your order at the front desk beside the picture menu.

Tiāntiān Yúgǎng SEAFOOD $$$
(Map p287; 天天鱼港; 10 Renmin Lu; dishes Y12-88; ⌚11am-10pm) Choose your meal from the many sea creatures swimming in the tanks at this upscale seafood restaurant. Most

BEER MANIA

For 12 days every July, Dàlián stages the **Dàlián International Beer Festival** (www.12chinabeer.com), its very own version of Munich's Oktoberfest. Beer companies from across China and around the world set up tents at the vast Xīnghǎi Sq (Map p292), near the coast, and locals and visitors flock there to sample the brews, snack on seafood, listen to live music and generally make whoopee. Entrance tickets are a low Y10 and in 2010 there were over 400 brands of beer for sampling.

dishes are set out in refrigerated levels for you to choose, making this a rare easy seafood-eating experience in China.

Night market MARKET $
(Map p287; Tianjin Jie) Near the Home Inn. You can sit outside and eat barbecue seafood with a beer.

Drinking & Entertainment

For what it's worth, Dàlián has the most happening bar and club scene of any city in the northeast. Check out *Focus on Dalian* magazine for more.

Changjiang Lu is home to a host of clubs, ranging from the upmarket and sleazy to the downright seedy. A couple of upscale bars with outdoor patios sit almost next door to I-55 bakery.

I-55 Coffee Stop & Bakery BAKERY
(Map p292; Àiwǔwǔ Měishì Kāfēizhàn; 67 Gao'erji Lu; ⌚8.30am-midnight; 📶) For coffee, cakes and sandwiches, try the I-55. There's a cosy upscale atmosphere here with throw-cushion-decked lounges, jazzy music and a nice leafy outdoor patio.

Alice Club CLUB
(艾丽丝; Dàlián Àilìsī; 8 Zhi Fu Lu) Behind the Furama Hotel. A long-term favourite.

Noah's Ark BAR
(Map p292; Nuòyà Fāngzhōu; 32 Wusi Lu; ⌚12.30pm-2am; 📶) A good, long-standing place to catch some fine local musicians and grab a beer. Mix of locals and expats. Very strong wireless connection.

Meeting Place Bar BAR
(Map p287; 互动酒吧; Hùdòng Jiǔbā; 12 Renmin Lu) Sports-bar styling with a Chinese house band. Popular with locals.

Shopping

There are malls all over Dàlián. The **New Mart Shopping Mall** (Map p287), south of Victory Sq, is a pedestrian plaza lined with upscale department stores. Across from the train station there's an enormous underground shopping centre below Victory Sq.

Information

There are ATMs all around town. Zhongshan Sq has a number of large bank branches including **Bank of China** (中国银行; Zhōngguó Yínháng; 9 Zhongshan Sq; ⌚8.30-11.30am & 1-7pm Mon-Fri), where you can change currency and travellers cheques.

China International Travel Service (CITS; 中国国际旅行社; Zhōngguó Guójì Lǚxíngshè; ☎8367 8019; www.citsdl.net; 145 Zhongshan Lu; ⌚8.30am-5.30pm Mon-Fri) On the 2nd floor of the Central Plaza Hotel (Xiāngzhōu Dàfàndiàn). Has tours to Bingyu Valley (Y260) in summer.

Dàlián Xpat (www.dalianxpat.com) A good source of English-language information about restaurants, bars and clubs in Dàlián.

Focus on Dalian New bilingual magazine with good articles and restaurant and bar recommendations. Has a local perspective, though, so directions to places are poor.

Internet cafe (网吧; wǎngbā; lower level, train station; per hr Y2) Exit the train station and turn right. The entrance is on the corner of the west side of the building, downstairs.

Getting There & Away

Air

Dàlián International Airport (www.dlairport.com/wyweb/YW_index.asp) is 12km from the city centre and well connected to most cities in China and the region. Tickets can be purchased at the **Civil Aviation Administration of China** (CAAC; 中国民航; Zhōngguó Mínháng; ☎8361 2888; www.tickets.dlairport.com; Zhongshan Lu; ⌚8am-4pm) or any of the travel offices nearby.

DOMESTIC FLIGHTS

Běijīng Y780, one hour

Hāěrbīn Y930, 1½ hours

Hong Kong Y2400, 3½ hours

INTERNATIONAL FLIGHTS

Khabarovsk Y2800, two flights weekly

Tokyo Y2450, four flights weekly

Vladivostok Y2600, two flights weekly

Boat

There are several daily boats to Yāntái (Y140 to Y600, four to seven hours) and two daily boats to Wēihǎi (Y160 to Y260, seven hours, 10.30am and 9pm). Buy tickets at the passenger ferry terminal in the northeast of Dàlián or from one of the many counters in front of the train station. To the ferry terminal, take bus 13 from the northeast corner of Shengli Guangchang and Zhongshan Lu near the train station.

Bus

Long-distance buses leave from various points around the train station. It can be tricky to find the correct ticket booths, and they do occasionally move.

BORDER CROSSING: GETTING TO SOUTH KOREA FROM DÀLIÁN

The Korean-run **Da-in Ferry** (☎Dàlián 8270-5082, Incheon 8232-891 7100, Seoul 822-3218 6551; www.dainferry.co.kr) to Incheon in South Korea departs from Dàlián on Monday, Wednesday and Friday at 3.30pm (Y920 to Y1848, 19 hours).

Dāndōng (Y92, four hours, eight daily) Buses leave from stand No 2 on Shengli Guangchang just south of Changjiang Lu.

Lǚshùn (旅顺; Y7, one hour, every 10 minutes) Buses leave from the back of the train station, across the square.

Shěnyáng (沈阳; Y122, 4½ hours, every 30 minutes) Buses depart from the south side of Changjiang Lu, directly across from the train station. Buy tickets in a booth just at the top of the stairs leading into the underground mall.

Zhuānghé (庄河; Y43, 2½ hours, 15 daily) Buses leave from in front of the ticket booth on Jiangshe Jie, the first street behind the train station.

Train

Buy your ticket as early as possible for long-distance trains.

Běijīng seat/sleeper Y140/247, 10 to 12 hours

Chángchūn seat/sleeper Y94/168, seven to 10 hours

Hā'ěrbīn seat/sleeper Y125/223, nine to 13 hours

Shěnyáng Y49 to Y65, four hours

Getting Around

Dàlián's central district is not large and can be covered on foot.

TO/FROM THE AIRPORT A taxi from the city centre costs Y30 to Y60 depending on the time of day. No shuttle buses.

BUS Buses are plentiful and stops have English signboards explaining the route.

TAXI Fares start at Y8; most trips aren't more than Y15.

TRAM Dàlián has a very slow tram, with two lines, the 201 and the 202 (Y1 each) – 201 runs past the train station on Changjiang Lu; 202 runs out to the ocean and Xīnghǎi Sq (you must take 201 first and transfer).

AROUND DÀLIÁN

Lǚshùn 旅顺

With its excellent port, and strategic location on the northeast coast, Lǚshùn (formerly Port Arthur) was the focal point of both Russian and Japanese expansion in the late 19th and early 20th centuries. The bloody 1904–05 Russo-Japanese War finally saw the area fall under Japanese colonial rule, which would continue for the next 40 years.

Only recently opened to foreign tourists, Lǚshùn is a must see during any visit to Dàlián. It's a relaxed town built on the hills and, while most sites are related to military history, there's an excellent museum on Liáoníng, as well as a number of scenic lookouts and parks.

As soon as you exit the bus station at Lǚshùn, taxis will cry out for your business. A few hours touring the sights will cost Y100 to Y150. Pick up a bilingual English-Chinese map at the newsstand at the station to help you negotiate.

Sights

TOP CHOICE **Soviet Martyrs Cemetery** CEMETERY
(苏军烈士陵园; Sūjūn Lièshì Língyuán) The largest cemetery in China for foreign-born nationals honours Soviet soldiers who died in the liberation of northeast China at the end of WWII, as well as pilots killed during the Korean War (known as the War against US Aggression). Designed by Soviet advisers, the cemetery is heavy with communist-era iconography. A giant rifle-holding soldier guards the front, while inside are memorials to the sacrifice of Soviet soldiers and rows of neatly tended gravestones.

Lǚshùn Museum MUSEUM
(旅顺博物馆; Lǚshùn Bówùguǎn; admission Y20; ⏰9am-4.30pm) The history of Liáoníng province is covered in this stylish old museum in a building erected in 1917. Among the thousands of artefacts on display are ancient bronzes, coins and paintings, as well as several mummies.

Hill 203 WAR MEMORIAL
(二0三景区; Èr Líng Sān Jǐngqū; admission Y30) During the 1904–05 Russo-Japanese War, troops fought like wildcats for control of this strategic hill (when you get to the top you'll see why). Over 5000 Russian and 10,000

Around Dàlián

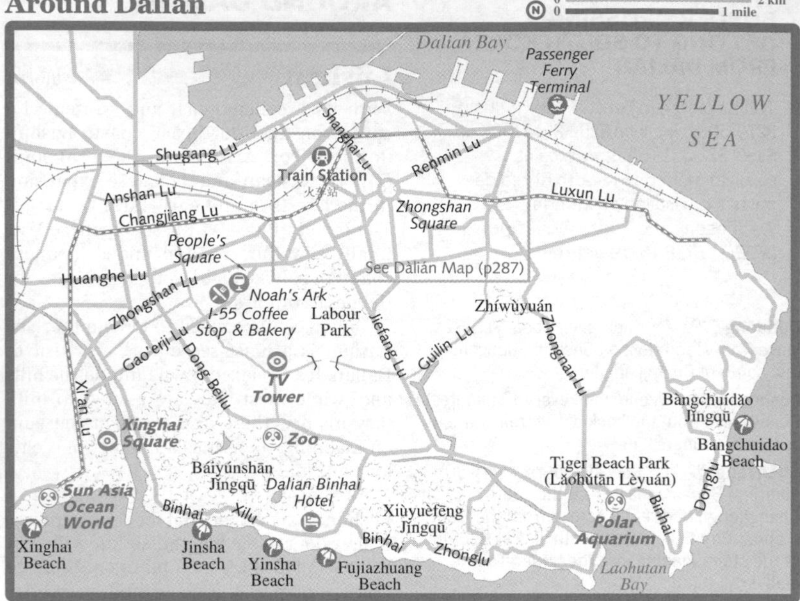

Japanese soldiers lost their lives in the battle, which eventually went to the Japanese. Afterwards the victors erected a 10m-high bullet-shaped memorial (constructed from shell casings) and, remarkably, it still stands to this day.

Lǔshùn Railway Station OLD RAILWAY STATION (旅顺火车站; Lǔshùn Huǒchēzhàn) Built in 1903 during Russia's brief control of the area, the handsome station was rebuilt in 2005 following the original design. It's worth a pop by on your way to other sights.

Getting There & Away

Buses to Lǔshùn (Y7, one hour) leave every 10 minutes from a stop across the square at the back of the Dàlián train station (see Map p287). Buses run from early morning to evening.

Bīngyù Valley

If you can't travel south to Guìlín (p584), the **Bīngyù Valley Geopark** (冰峪沟; Bīngyù Gōu; www.dlby.com; admission Y120) offers a taste of what you're missing. About 250km northeast of Dàlián, this park has tree-covered limestone cliffs set alongside a river and is similar to Guìlín, if not nearly as dramatic. A boat from the ticket office takes you along a brief stretch of the river, where rock formations rise steeply along the banks, before depositing you at a dock. From there, you can hire your own little boat and paddle around the shallow waters, or follow some short trails along the river and up to some lookouts.

The park is increasingly popular with big tour groups, who come for the zip lines, tame amusement-park rides, and even jet skiing. Given the rather small area you can explore it can be tough to find any tranquillity in this otherwise lovely environment.

In summer Dàlián CITS arranges tours (Y260) leaving at 7am and returning around 7pm. Otherwise, catch the bus to Zhuānghé (Y43, 2½ hours, 15 daily, 6.20am to 4.30pm) behind Dàlián station. From Zhuānghé bus station, minibuses to Bīngyù Valley's east gate (Y10, one hour) leave frequently.

Accommodation in the park is poor value (you'll spend several hundred if you want a room with a shower). Outside the park gate are several small guesthouses including **Sūnjié Nóngjiāyuàn Lǚfàndiàn** (孙杰农家院旅饭店; ☎1300-9432 249; d Y100), a popular family-run place in a farming village about five minutes' walk from the park. Rooms are small and nondescript but face out into the courtyard, and the whole complex is surrounded by forest. Some very fine homemade meals (dishes Y12 to Y38) from fresh local ingredients are available.

Buses from Zhuānghé back to Dàlián leave about every 20 minutes until 4.30pm. If you're travelling north to Dāndōng, buses depart Zhuānghé (Y35, three hours) at 6.29am, 7.16am, 8.17am and 1.18pm.

Dāndōng 丹东

☎0415 / POP 752,200

The principal gateway to North Korea (Cháoxiǎn) from China, Dāndōng has a buzz unusual for a Chinese city of its size. Separated from the DPRK by the Yālù River (Yālù Jiāng), Dāndōng thrives on trade, both illegal and legal, with North Korea.

For most visitors to Dāndōng, this is as close as they will get to the DPRK. While you can't see much, the contrast between Dāndōng's lively, built-up riverfront and the desolate stretch of land on the other side of the Yālù River speaks volumes about the dire state of the North Korean economy and the restrictions under which its people live.

Although CITS runs tours to the DPRK, they are aimed at Chinese nationals. If you want to visit, then you'll do far better to travel with the reputable Běijīng-based **Koryo Tours** (☎010-6416 7544; www.koryogroup.com; 27 Beisanlitun Nan, Běijīng), which can help you organise visas and offers trips designed for Westerners. At the time of writing, US citizens could fly into North Korea but not take the train.

The river is about 700m southeast of the train station. The Business and Tourism District (Shāngmào Lǚyóuqū), lined with riverfront restaurants and many KTV joints, is southwest of the Yālù River bridge. The main shopping district is just east of the station.

Sights & Activities

North Korean Border BORDER

(北朝鲜边界; Běi Cháoxiǎn Biānjiè) For views of the border, stroll along the riverfront **Yālùjiāng Park** that faces the North Korean city of Sinuiju.

In 1950, during the Korean War, American troops 'accidentally' bombed the original steel-span bridge between the two countries. The North Koreans dismantled the bridge less than halfway across the river, leaving a row of support columns. You can wander along the shrapnel-pockmarked **Broken Bridge** (Yālùjiāng Duànqiáo; admission Y35; ⊙7am-7pm) and get within the distance of a good toss of a baseball to the North Korea shoreline. The Sino-Korean Friendship Bridge, the official border crossing between China and North Korea, is next to the old one, and trains and trucks rumble across it on a regular basis.

To get closer to North Korea, take a **boat cruise** (guānguāng chuán; ⊙7am-6pm) from the tour-boat piers on either side of the bridges. The large boats (Y50) are cheaper than the smaller speedboats (Y70), but you have to wait for them to fill up with passengers. In the summer, you can sometimes see kids splashing about in the river, as well as fishermen and the crews of the boats moored on the other side.

Jǐnjiāng Pagoda PAGODA

(锦江塔; Jǐnjiang Tǎ) The highest point around for miles, the pagoda sits atop Jǐnjiāngshān in a park of the same name. The views across to North Korea are unparalleled and the park itself (a former military zone) is a well-tended expanse of forested slopes. You can take a taxi to the entrance or easily walk there in 20 minutes from the train station, though it's another steep kilometre uphill to the pagoda.

FREE **Museum to Commemorate US Aggression** MUSEUM

(抗美援朝纪念馆; Kàngměi Yuáncháo Jìniànguǎn; ⊙9am-4pm Tue-Sun) With everything from statistics to shells, this comprehensive museum offers Chinese and North Korean perspectives – they won it! – on the war with the US-led UN forces (1950–53). There are good English captions here. The adjacent North Korean War Memorial Column was built 53m high, symbolising the year the Korean War ended.

A taxi here will cost Y7 from downtown, or you can walk there as part of a trip to the pagoda. From the entrance to the park on Shanshang Jie, it's about 1.5km to the entrance to the memorial.

TOP CHOICE **Tiger Mountain Great Wall** GREAT WALL

(虎山长城; Hǔshān Chángchéng; admission Y60; ⊙8am-dusk) About 12km northeast of Dāndōng, this steep, restored stretch of the wall, known as Tiger Mountain Great Wall, was built during the Ming dynasty and runs parallel to the North Korean border.

Dāndōng

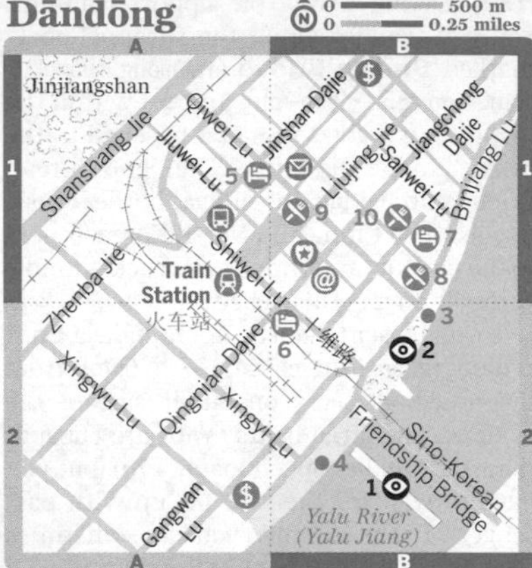

Dāndōng

Sights

1 Broken Bridge B2
2 Yālùjiāng Park B2

Activities, Courses & Tours

3 Tour-Boat Pier B2
4 Tour-Boat Pier B2

Sleeping

5 Huá Xià Cūn Bīnguǎn A1
6 Lǜyuàn Bīnguǎn B2
7 Oriental Cherry Hotel B1

Eating

8 Ālǐláng Xiǎnzú Fēngwèi B1
9 Pyongyang North Korean Restaurant B1
10 Tesco's B1

Unlike other sections of the wall, this one sees comparatively few tourists.

The wall ends at a small **museum** (admission Y10) with a few weapons, vases and wartime dioramas. From here three paths loop back to the entrance. Avoid heading right, as it's simply a road. Going left you can either follow the river on a narrow dirt path (North Korea is just on the other side) or climb back up the wall stairs and look for a path on the right that literally runs along the cliff face. There are some good scrambles and in 20 minutes or so you'll get to a point called Yībùkuà – 'one step across' – marking an extremely narrow part of the river between the two countries.

Close up, the border fence on the DPRK side looks like a less-than-effective barrier, but don't try to test it; a gun-toting soldier may suddenly appear. Boats (Y20, 10 minutes) wait on the water. It's OK to pass through the barbed-wire gate and take them either back to the museum or onward to the end of the path just a minute from the entrance. You can also walk this last stretch. Note that if you walk along the dirt river path from the museum you will also reach this same point.

Buses to the wall (Y5.50, 45 minutes) run about every hour from the Dāndōng long-distance bus station.

Sleeping

There are many hotels in Dāndōng, most for around Y200 a night.

Huá Xià Cūn Bīnguǎn HOTEL **$**
(华夏村宾馆; ☎212 1999; fax 2123 5266; 11 Bajing Jie; 八经街11号; d incl breakfast from Y160, discounts of 25%; ❄ @) This is a good budget option, with rooms sporting comfort far above their price level, broadband internet and a location smack in the middle of town. The restaurant on the ground floor serves a range of tasty northern dishes (Y10 to Y30) and has a picture menu wall. Portions are large.

Oriental Cherry Hotel HOTEL **$$**
(樱桃大酒店; Yīngtáo Dàjiǔdiàn; ☎210 0099; 2 Liuwei Lu; 六纬路2号; d/tr Y398/480, discounts of 30-40%; ❄ @) With the discounts that are regularly on offer here, the large double rooms are decent value, especially if you ask for the ones with views of the river and the DPRK. The hotel is a half-block from the riverfront and has broadband internet.

Lǜyuàn Bīnguǎn HOTEL **$**
(绿苑宾馆; ☎212 7777; fax 210 9888; cnr Shiwei Lu & Sanjing Jie; 三经街十纬路交界处; dm Y80-90, s/d Y160/188; ❄) There are reasonable three- and four-bed dorms at this slightly gloomy guesthouse located close to the riverfront, but the more expensive doubles are overpriced.

Eating & Drinking

On summer nights, the smoke from hundreds of barbecues drifts over Dāndōng as street corners become impromptu restaurants serving up fresh seafood and bottles of Yālù River beer, the excellent local brew. One of the best places for barbecue is on the corner of Bawei Lu and Qijing Jie. More conventional restaurants, including a range of Korean, and a number of cafes where you can sip coffee and watch how the other half lives, line the riverfront on either side of the bridges. There's a big **Tesco's** (Lègòu; cnr Liuwei Lu & Sanjing Jie) supermarket.

Pyongyang North Korean Restaurant NORTH KOREAN **$$**
(平壤高丽饭店; Píngrǎng Gāolì Fàndiàn; Bawei Lu; dishes Y18-58; ⏱11am-11pm) A big part of the experience for many travellers to this region is eating at a North Korean restaurant with real North Korean waitresses. At Pyongyang, waitresses clad in air hostess–style uniforms are a chirpy lot and will happily suggest a meal, normally grilled beef or fish. To find this place, look for the sign with the DPRK flag on it. The restaurant's characters are actually displayed on the 2nd floor. Picture menu available.

Ālǐláng Xiānzú Fēngwèi HOTPOT **$$**
(阿里郎鲜族风味; Binjiang Lu; ⏱9am-9.30pm) Your basic hotpot costs Y18; after that the sky's the limit as you choose from a huge array of marine life as well as vegie and meat dishes.

Information

Bank of China (中国银行; Zhōngguó Yínháng; 60 Jinshan Dajie) Has ATM. Also ATM and currency-exchange at branch in business and tourist district.

China International Travel Service (CITS; 中国国际旅行社; Zhōngguó Guójì Lǚxíngshè; ☎213 2196; 20 Shiwei Lu, at Jiangcheng Dajie; ⏱8am-5.30pm) Can arrange DPRK visits with Chinese tours. Email English-speaking Jackie Zhang for details (jacky790117@hotmail.com).

Internet cafe (wǎngbā; 26 Jiangcheng Dajie; per hr Y3; ⏱8am-midnight)

Public Security Bureau (PSB; 公安局; Gōng'ānjú; ☎210 3138; 15 Jiangcheng Dajie; ⏱8am-12.30pm & 1.30-5.30pm Mon-Fri)

Getting There & Away

Dāndōng airport has infrequent flights to a few cities in China, but most travellers arrive by bus or train.

Bus

The **long-distance bus station** (98 Shiwei Lu) is near the train station.

Dàlián Y91, 3½ hours, eight daily (6am to 2.50pm)

Jí'ān Y60, 6½ hours, one daily (8.30am)

Shěnyáng Y76, three hours, every 30 minutes (5.10am to 6.30pm)

Tōnghuà Y72, eight hours, two daily (6.30am and 8.50am)

Train

The train station is in the centre of town, north of the river. A lofty Mao statue greets arriving passengers.

Běijīng seat/sleeper Y132/256, 14 hours

Dàlián seat/sleeper Y47/99, 10 hours

Shěnyáng seat Y24 to Y37, four hours

The K27 train from Běijīng to Pyongyang stops at Dāndōng at 7.17am on Monday, Wednesday, Thursday and Saturday (Dāndōng to Pyongyang takes 14 hours). If you have the necessary visas (normally requiring that you travel with a tour group), you can hop aboard.

TRICKS OF THE TRADE

It's no exaggeration to say that, without China, the North Korean regime would not survive. The DPRK relies on China for food, fuel and arms. For China, keeping North Korea's leader, Kim Jung-il (or likely his son Kim Jong-un by the time you read this), in power is a way of maintaining the delicate power balance in North Asia, where South Korea and Japan are both strong allies of the US. Equally important, though, is the fact that the DPRK is a captive market for Chinese companies and one worth an estimated US$2 billion a year.

Dāndōng is the hub of Sino–North Korean trade. Local Chinese websites advertise business opportunities across the border, while North Korean officials come looking for raw materials and machinery, as well as access to Chinese markets. But there's a thriving black-market economy too. Everything from cigarettes and mobile phones to TVs and furs (a UN resolution bans the export of luxury goods to the DPRK) makes its way across the Yālù River.

This illicit trade is having a significant impact on life inside the DPRK. Mobile phones enable people to communicate outside their local areas and, in some cases, abroad (they are officially banned), while the yuán is now an alternative currency to the inflation-prone won in many regions. If and when North Korea does open up to the outside world, China will be ready to take full advantage.

BORDER CROSSING: GETTING TO SOUTH KOREA FROM DĀNDŌNG

The **Dāndōng International Ferry Co** (cnr Xingwu Lu & Gangwan Lu; www.dandongferry.co.kr; ⌚8am-5pm) runs a boat to Incheon in South Korea, departing 4pm on Tuesday, Thursday and Sunday (Y810 to Y1270, 17 hours). Buy tickets at the company's office on Xingwu Lu.

Xīngchéng 兴城

☎0429 / POP 110,000

Despite being one of only four Ming-dynasty cities to retain their complete outer walls and boasting the oldest surviving temple in all of northeastern China, as well as an up-and-coming beach resort, Xīngchéng has stayed well off the radar of most travellers. In truth it's still a bit dusty and rough round the edges, and the old city is as notable for its rows of jeans shops as Ming gates, but conditions are improving and historians and aficionados will have a field day here.

Xīngchéng's main drag is Xīnghǎi Lù Èrduàn (兴海路二段), where you'll find hotels, a **Bank of China** (中国银行; Zhōngguó Yínháng) with a 24-hour ATM, and restaurants. From the train station head right, take the first left, and then a quick right to get onto Xing Hai Lu Yi Duan. This merges into Er Duan (Section 2) in a kilometre.

Sights

Old City OLD CITY

(老城; Lǎo Chéng) The principal reason to visit Xīngchéng, this walled city dates back to 1430. Modern Xīngchéng has grown up around it, but it's still home to around 3000 people. You can enter by any of the four gates, but the easiest one to find is the **south gate** (南门; *nánmén*), which is just off Xing Hai Lu Er Duan. There are signs in English and Chinese pointing the way.

In addition to the **City Walls** (城墙; Chéngqiáng; admission Y25; ⌚8am-5pm), the **Drum Tower** (鼓楼; Gǔlóu; admission Y20; ⌚8am-5pm), which sits slap in the middle of the Old City, and the watchtower on the southeastern corner of the city are all intact. You can do a complete circuit of the walls in around an hour.

Also inside the Old City are the **Gao House** (将军府; Jiāngjūn Fǔ; admission Y10; ⌚8am-5pm), the former residence of General Gao Rulian, who was one of Xīngchéng's most famous sons. The impressive and well-maintained **Confucius Temple** (文庙; Wénmiào; admission Y35; ⌚8am-5pm), built in 1430, is reputedly the oldest temple in northeastern China.

BEACHES

Xīngchéng's imaginatively named **Beach 1** (第一浴场), **Beach 2** (第二浴场) and **Beach 3** (第三浴场) are pretty enough, with golden sands and calm waters, but are not particularly special.

At Beach 1 look for a statue honouring **Juhua Nu** (the Chrysanthemum Woman). According to local legend, she changed herself into an island to protect Xīngchéng from a sea dragon. This island, **Júhuā Dǎo**, lies 9km off the coast and is home to a fishing community, a small beach and a couple of temples. Daily **ferries** (round trip Y175; ⌚depart 8.30am & 10am, return noon, 2pm & 5pm) leave from the northern end of Beach 1.

Bus 1 (Y1) travels from Xing Hai Lu Er Duan to Beach 1 (9km from the city centre) in about 30 minutes, and then further north to Beach 2 and Beach 3. A taxi to the area costs Y15 to Y20.

Sleeping

Beach hotels are aimed at the domestic tourist market and budget options are limited from early July to September. In the short low season this is the best area to stay, as rooms are often cheaper than in the city.

Bāyī Bīnguǎn HOTEL $$

(八一宾馆; ☎385 2888; d Y298; ❄) A cosy little place just off Beach No 1 with simple rooms that go for Y100 in low season but up to Y400 in summer. To get here turn right when you hit the beach strip and walk 200m.

Jīn Zhǒng Zi Dà Shà HOTEL $$

(☎352 1111; 9 Xing Hai Lu Yi Duan; 兴海路一段9号; r from Y298, discounts available; ❄@) Right in the heart of the city on a busy intersection, this hotel offers comfortable rooms, free broadband internet and a good restaurant (dishes from Y8 to Y25). With the standard discount a double goes for around Y200.

Kǎilái Bīnguǎn HOTEL $

(凯莱宾馆; Xing Hai Lu Er Duan; ☎385 7168; d Y108-168; @❄) Very basic rooms (though with broadband internet) on the main drag in Xīngchéng. The cheapest doubles usually go early.

Eating

Unsurprisingly, seafood is big here. Restaurants line the beachfront at No 1 Beach, where you can pick your crustacean or fish of choice from the tanks in which they await their death.

Xing Hai Lu Er Duan is home to many restaurants, including **Tiānhé Féiniú** (天和肥牛; dishes Y5-28), a bright, modern hotpot place on the left a couple of hundred metres before the turn for the south gate.

There are street-food stalls outside the south gate of the Old City that stay open until late, and a number of barbecue places that only open up in the evening. The Hui Muslim stalls always have the best lamb skewers (Y1).

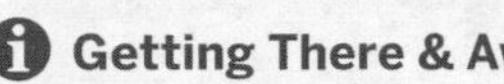

Getting There & Away

Xīngchéng is a stop for many trains between Běijīng and Hā'ěrbīn (and all cities in between), but it's usually easier to get a bus out than a train.

Bus

Destinations from Xīngchéng Bus Station (兴城市客运站; Xīngchéng Shì Kèyùn Zhàn):

Běijīng Y117, one daily (8.10am)

Jǐnzhōu Y15, two hours, every 30 minutes

Shānhǎiguān Y20.50, two hours, two daily (6.50am and 8am)

Shěnyáng Y78.50, 3½ hours, three daily (7.50am, 2pm and 3.40pm)

Train

Běijīng seat/sleeper Y55/103, six to seven hours, five to six daily

Shānhǎiguān Y9 to Y27, 1½ hours

Shěnyáng Y28 to Y41, four hours

Jílín

POPULATION: 27.9 MILLION

Includes »

Best Places to Eat

» Héshèngyuán Yěshēng Xiǎoyúguǎn (p303)
» Gāolí Fàndiàn (p304)
» Xīnxīngyuán Jiǎoziguǎn (p308)
» French Bakery (p311)

Best Places to Stay

» Woodland Youth Hostel (p302)
» Landscape Resort (p304)
» Yánbiān Diànlì Dàshà (p305)
» Chūnyì Bīnguǎn (p311)

Why Go?

A flirty province, Jílín (吉林) teases with the ancient and the modern, the artificial and the supernatural. Travellers tired of great walls and imperial facades can explore Western-influenced palaces and the ruins of an ancient Korean kingdom. In fact much of the far-eastern region comprises the little-known Korean Autonomous Prefecture, home to more than one million ethnic Koreans. Kimchi and cold noodles dominate the menu here and there's an easy acceptance of outsiders.

Known for its motor cities and smokestack towns, Jílín is also a popular ski destination and boasts China's largest nature reserve. So go for the contrasts? No, go for the superlatives. Heaven Lake, a stunning, deep-blue volcanic crater lake within the country's largest reserve, is one of China's most mesmerising natural wonders. Jílín can be a little rough around the edges at times, but its rewards are pure polished jewels.

When to Go

Jílín City

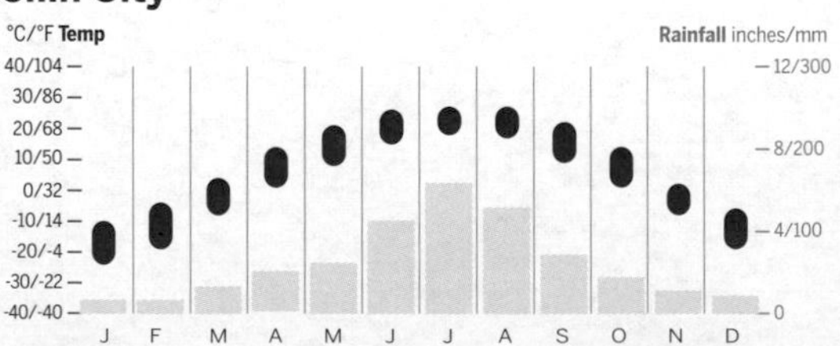

January Ice Lantern Festival in Jílín.

June–September Best months to visit Chángbái Shān.

November–March Ski season at Běidàhú Ski Resort.

History

Korean kings once ruled parts of Jílín and the discovery of important relics from the ancient Koguryo kingdom (37 BC–AD 668) in the small southeastern city of Jí'ān has resulted in the area being designated a World Heritage Site by Unesco.

The Japanese occupation of Manchuria in the early 1930s pushed Jílín to the world's centre stage. Chángchūn became the capital of what the Japanese called Manchukuo, with Puyi (the last emperor of the Qing dynasty) given the role of figurehead of the puppet government. In 1944 the Russians wrested control of Jílín from the Japanese and, after stripping the area of its industrial base, handed the region back to Chinese control. For the next several years Jílín would pay a heavy price as one of the frontlines in the civil war between the Kuomintang and the Chinese Communist Party (CCP).

Jílín's border with North Korea has dominated the region's more recent history. Since the mid-1990s, thousands of North Koreans have fled into China to escape extreme food shortages. The Chinese government has not looked favourably on these migrants, refusing to grant them protected refugee status.

Climate

Jílín is bitterly cold during its long winter, with heavy snow, freezing winds and temperatures as low as -20°C. In contrast, summer is pleasantly warm, especially along the coastal east, but short. Rainfall is moderate.

Language

Mandarin is the standard language across Jílín. Korean is widely spoken in Yánjí and the Korean Autonomous Prefecture in the east of the province.

Getting There & Around

The rail and bus network connects all major cities and towns, but not many daily trains head east. The new airport connects Chángbái Shān with Chángchūn and other major Chinese cities.

Chángbái Shān 长白山

0433 BÁIHÉ & THE NORTHERN SLOPE

0439 SŌNGJIĀNGHÉ & THE WESTERN SLOPE

Chángbái Shān (Ever-White Mountains), China's largest nature reserve, covers 2100 densely forested sq km on the eastern edge of Jílín. By far the region's top attraction, the park's greenery and open space offers a very welcome contrast to Jílín's industrial cities.

The centrepiece of Chángbái Shān is the spellbinding **Heaven Lake** (天池; Tiān Chí), whose blue waters stretch across an outsized volcanic crater straddling the China–North Korea border. Heaven Lake's beauty and mystical reputation, including its Loch Ness style monster *(guàiwu)*, lures visitors from all over China, as well as many South Koreans. For the latter, the area is known as Mt Paekdu, or Paekdusan. North Korea claims that Kim Jung-il was born here (although he's believed to have entered the world in Khabarovsk, Russia).

At lower elevations, the park's forests are filled with white birch, Korean pines and hundreds of varieties of plants, including the much-prized Chángbái Shān ginseng. Above 2000m the landscape changes dramatically into a subalpine zone of short grasses and herbs. Giant patches of ice cover parts of the jagged peaks even in mid-June, and mountain streams rush down the treeless, rocky slopes. With the lake at an altitude of nearly 2200m, visitors should be prepared for lower temperatures. It might be sunny and hot when you enter the reserve, but at higher altitudes strong winds, rain and snow are possible.

Chángbái Shān has two main recreation areas: the northern slope (Běi Pō) and the western slope (Xī Pō). As the entrances to these areas are separated by 100km by road, we treat them as distinct destinations below for the sake of clarity.

Visitors to either area are limited to a few sights and a few short walks. Chángbái Shān is geared towards Chinese tour

PRICE INDICATORS

The following price indicators are used in this chapter:

Sleeping

$	less than Y200
$$	Y200 to Y400
$$$	more than Y400

Eating

$	less than Y20
$$	Y20 to Y50
$$$	more than Y40

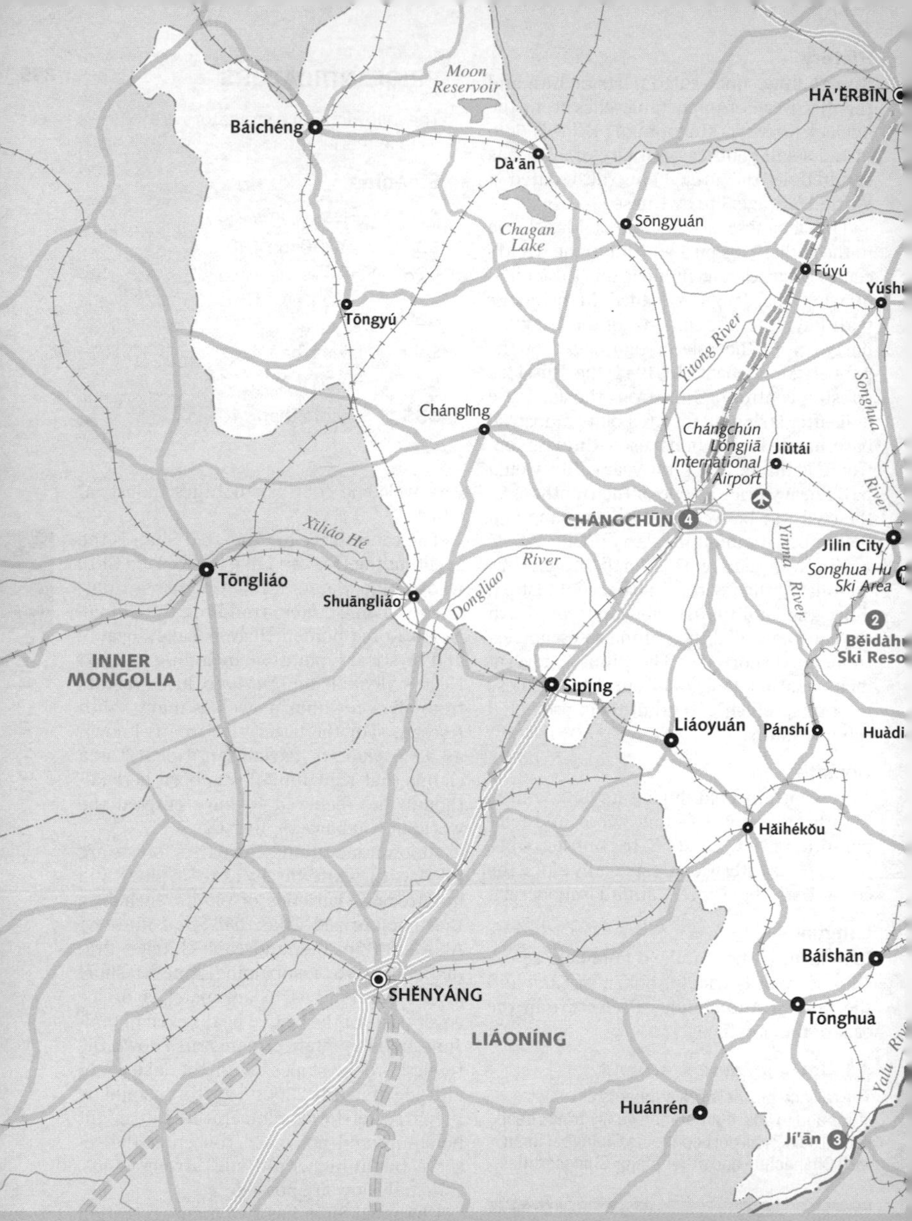

Jílín Highlights

❶ Visit China's largest nature reserve, **Chángbái Shān** (p299), with its waterfalls, hot springs and aptly named Heaven Lake (p302 and p303)

❷ Hit the slopes at the **Běidàhú Ski Resort** (p309), one of China's premier skiing spots

❸ Explore the mysterious remains of the ancient Koguryo kingdom in **Jí'ān** (p306), just across the Yālù River from North Korea

4 Go on the trail of Puyi, the last emperor of China, at the Imperial Palace of Manchu State in **Chángchūn** (p309)

5 See China's ethnic Korean culture in **Yánjí** (p304)

BEWARE OF THE BORDER

The China–North Korea border cuts across Heaven Lake. As the border isn't clearly marked, and detailed maps of the area are unavailable, it's possible to accidentally end up in North Korea. The border guards will not welcome you with open arms; at least one traveller has ended up in a North Korean prison.

Approximately one-third of the lake, the southeastern corner, is on the North Korean side and off limits. These days, with most trails around Chángbái Shān closed or limited to short walks, it's hard to venture very far, but at any time if you think you are nearing the border or are unsure where exactly it lies, do not proceed further!

groups rather than independent travellers and a multibillion-yuán project is under way to turn the park into a luxury sightseeing zone – a Banff of sorts, with hot springs and golf courses but no DIY hiking or camping.

The only really feasible time to visit Chángbái Shān (unless you are coming to ski the western slope) is from mid-June to early September. Accommodation is available on both the northern and western slopes, as well as in the nearby gateway towns of Báihé and Sōngjiānghé. See www.cbs.travel for more information.

NORTHERN SLOPE 北坡

The views of Heaven Lake from the **northern slope** (Běi Pō; admission Y100, transport fee Y68; ⏰7am-6pm) are the best. The gateway town for this area, where most travellers spend the night, is Báihé.

You can see all the sights in a day.

Sights & Activities

Heaven Lake SCENIC AREA

(天池; Tiān Chí) This two-million-year-old crater lake, 13km in circumference, sits at an altitude of 2194m and is surrounded by rock outcrops and 16 mountainous peaks. The highest, **White Rock Peak** (Báiyán Fēng), soars to 2749m and can be climbed if you have permits and are with a Chinese tour group. Legend has it that the lake is home to a large, but shy, beastie that has the magical power to blur any photo taken of him.

You can no longer hike to the lakeside area but may only enjoy the panoramic views from the crater lip.

Yuèhuà Plaza HOT SPRINGS

(岳桦广场; Yuèhuà Guǎngchǎng) The road forks at a junction called *dàozhànkǒu*, with one branch climbing steeply to Heaven Lake, and the other leading past several hotels to Yuèhuà Plaza, in essence a big parking lot. On the edge of the lot is a small area of **hot springs** where you can soak your feet, or boil an egg.

A short trail leads quickly to the viewpoint for the magnificent 68m **Changbai Waterfall** (长白瀑布; Chángbái Pùbù).

Green Deep Pool POOL

(绿渊潭; Lû Yuān Tán) From Yuehua Plaza, cross the river and head downstream on a plank walkway through the juniper forests. At the end of the walkway, where it joins the main road, cross the lot and head up to see this pool, which is rather aptly named. Buses run from here down to the *dàozhànkǒu* junction and the Dell Forest park.

Dell Forest FOREST PARK

(谷底森林; Gǔdǐ Sēnlín) Lying between the park entrance and *dàozhànkǒu*, this verdant woodland area has a few trails with an hour's worth of hiking. Buses run from here back to the north gate.

Sleeping & Eating

At the northern slope there are several hotels and restaurants inside the park along the road to the waterfall. But most people stay in Èrdào Báihé, generally called Báihé (白河), about 20km north of the reserve. The town is divided into two sections: the train station area and the main drag a few kilometres away. There's lodging and small restaurants in both areas. The main drag has a number of supermarkets and fruit stands to pick up supplies for the day at Chángbái Shān.

A taxi from the train station into town is Y10.

BÁIHÉ

On your arrival at the train station, touts for cheap guesthouses will most likely approach you when you arrive: one of the better guesthouses in town is Chángfā Lûdiàn.

Woodland Youth Hostel HOSTEL $
(望松国际青年旅舍; Wàngsōng Guójì Qīngnián Lǚshè; ☎571 0800; www.cbshan.net; dm/d Y45/120; ❄@) This friendly hostel offers four-bed dorms, as well as basic, clean doubles. Follow the directions for Chángfā Lǚdiàn to reach it.

Xìndá Bīnguǎn HOTEL $$
(信达宾馆; ☎572 0444; d incl breakfast Y280-380; ❄) On Báihé's main drag, at the north end of town, this hotel offers a pleasant environment and cosy rooms. Small discounts are sometimes available.

Chángfā Lǚdiàn GUESTHOUSE $
(长发旅店; ☎135 9659 5253; r Y80; @❄) One of the better guesthouses in town. From the train station exit turn right, then left and walk to the main road. Turn right and walk about 200m. Just past the Woodland Youth Hostel sign turn right down a narrow alley. The guesthouse is at the end on the left.

Hǎowànjiā Hotel HOTEL $$
(好万家大酒店; ☎617 9666; fax 617 9886; d incl breakfast Y360; @❄) The hallway carpeting may remind you of Bert's (of Bert and Ernie fame) striped shirt, but the rooms sadly don't have that flair. But they are new and clean and offer free broadband. The hotel is a few hundred metres south of Xìndá Bīnguǎn in the middle of town on the west side of the road.

Héshèngyuán Yěshēng Xiǎoyúguǎn SEAFOOD $$
(合盛源野生小魚館; dishes Y8-30) Next to the Woodland Hostel in Báihé, just at the entrance of the alley to Chángfā Lǚdiàn, this primarily seafood restaurant matches flashy lights and good food. Staff are friendly but speak no English.

WITHIN THE PARK

Chángbái Shān Yùndòngyuán Cūn HOTEL $$$
(长白山运动员村; Mt Changbai Athletes Village; ☎574 6008; fax 574 6055; d Y780) Clean and simple rooms are on offer here for a rather inflated price. The hotel is on the right at the *dàozhànkǒu* and has its own restaurant.

Tours

China International Travel Service (CITS; 中国国际旅行社; Zhōngguó Guójì Lǚxíngshè; ☎0432-244 2907; 2222 Chongqing Jie, Jílín; ⏲8.30am-5pm) Runs three-day, two-night trips. Prices start at Y480, including transport, lodging and park admission.

CITS (☎0433-271 0018; www.ybcits.com; 558 Yixie Jie, Yánjí) Organises one-/two-day tours (Y280/400). Does not include the Y80 4WD fee.

Information

Bank of China (中国银行; Zhōngguó Yínháng) On the main street in Báihé.

Internet cafe (网吧; wǎngbā; per hr Y2) About 100m south and on the opposite side of the road from Xìndá Bīnguǎn. It's on the 3rd floor.

Getting There & Away

Public transport only goes as far as Báihé.

BUS Buses leave from the **long-distance bus station** *(kèyùnzhàn)*. From the train station head to the main road; the station is across the main road just to the left. Destinations include Yánjí (Y39, three hours, six daily).

TRAIN There's one direct daily train from Shěnyáng to Báihé (seat/sleeper Y50/100) leaving at 9.30am and arriving just past midnight. Trains from Báihé:

Shěnyáng seat/sleeper Y50/100, 15 hours, two daily (6.40am and 7pm)

Sōngjiānghé seat Y8, two hours, three daily (6.40am, 3.30pm and 7pm)

Tōnghuà seat/sleeper Y24/58, six to seven hours, two daily (6.40am and 7pm). More trains to Tōnghuà leave from Sōngjiānghé.

Getting Around

Hotels and hostels in Báihé organise cheap transport to the reserve (Y20), which usually leaves at 6am and 8.30am and has a set time for returning; the only other option is to take a taxi (Y50 one way).

At the reserve's north gate, you change to a park bus. Park buses go to *dàozhànkǒu* junction, where you can board a 4WD for the final 16km trek to Heaven Lake. You can also take other park buses to the waterfall, the Green Deep Pool and Dell Forest. The park bus rides are all included in your ticket, but the 4WD is another Y80.

WESTERN SLOPE 西坡

The **western slope** (Xī Pō; admission Y100, transport fee Y68; ⏲7am-6pm) is set up much like a Western-style national park, with a big wooden A-frame visitor centre and infrastructure that blends into the environment. Unfortunately you have no chance of getting away from the crowds here.

The gateway town for the western slope is Sōngjiānghé (see p304 for transport information). You can see all the sights from here in a day.

Sights & Activities

Heaven Lake SCENIC AREA
(天池; Tiān Chí) It's a lovely ride up the mountain's western slope to the lake. You pass through dense deciduous forest that suddenly gives way around 1900m to an alpine tundra zone of scrubby grass and flowers. Enjoy the big views over the forested plains from up here.

From the lot where buses drop you off it's a 30-minute walk up 1236 steps to the viewpoint for the lake. Seen from the peaks that surround it, at a height of about 2500m, it's a stupendous sight.

Chángbái Shān Canyon SCENIC AREA
(长白山大峡谷; Chángbái Shān Dàxiágǔ) Filled with dramatic rock formations, the 70km-long, 200m-wide and 100m-deep canyon really deserves more fame, but it's tough to measure up against the lake. There's an easy 40-minute walk along a boardwalk that follows the canyon rim through the forest.

Sleeping & Eating

When visiting the western slope, most people stay in dusty, traffic-snarled Sōngjiānghé (松江河), about 40km northwest. A new airport halfway between the park and Sōngjiānghé has recently opened and a number of hotels and resort villages are being built up nearby. In the future it seems likely that most visitors will bypass Sōngjiānghé completely.

One block west of Sōngjiānghé's main square is a busy market lane. Wander around and look at some of the impressive mushrooms. All around the main square you'll find small family-run restaurants (dishes from Y8). Within the park you'll find a couple of snack shops.

Changbai Shan Fashion Hostel HOTEL $$
(长白山时尚宾馆; Chángbái Shān Shíshàng Bīnguǎn; ☎625 3111; www.go2changbaishan.com; Songjiang Dajie; d Y238-328; @) Half a kilometre up the road from the train station on Songjiang Dajie is this modern hotel with a dash of urban styling. Friendly staff are thrown in for free, but a hearty breakfast goes for an extra Y15. Check the website for good discounts off the rack rates.

Landscape Resort HOTEL $$$
(蓝景戴斯度假酒店; Lánjǐngdàisī Dùjià Jiǔdiàn; ☎633 7999; www.ljdsh.cn; r from Y1068) The top accommodation near the park, the lodge-like Landscape with its lobby fireplace, stylish eating and drinking venues, and wood, glass and stone decor wouldn't look out of place at Lake Louise. Landscape is set back from the park entrance, about a five-minute walk away from it. In the winter the hotel offers ski packages.

Gāolí Fàndiàn KOREAN $$
(高丽饭店; ☎663 7377; dishes Y18-48; ⊙lunch & dinner) Friendliness and fine food complement each other perfectly at this extremely popular Korean-barbecue restaurant in Sōngjiānghé. From the main square tower, go one block east and turn right at the first alley. The restaurant is up one block on the right. You must make reservations.

Information

Bank of China (中国银行; Zhōngguó Yínháng) Off the main square in Sōngjiānghé; 24-hour ATMs.

Internet cafe (网吧; wǎngbā; per hr Y3; ⊙24hr) West of the main square on the north side of the road.

Getting There & Away

Public transport only goes as far as Sōngjiānghé.

AIR There are several flights a week from Běijīng (Y1700) and Chángchūn (Y650) to the airport halfway between Sōngjiānghé and the western-slope entrance. Expect more flights in the coming years as the villages around the airport are completed.

BUS Two buses a day run to Tōnghuà (Y47, four hours, 6am and 1pm).

TRAIN The station is at the north end of town, about 2km from the main square. A new station is being built beside it and traffic is messy. Trains to Shěnyáng and Tōnghuà originate in Báihé. Trains from Sōngjiānghé:

Báihé seat Y8, two hours

Shěnyáng seat/sleeper Y38/79, two daily (8.51am and 9.03pm)

Tōnghuà seat Y26, four hours, three daily (8.51am, 4.41pm and 9.03pm)

Getting Around

From Sōngjiānghé, taxis make the return trip to the western slope for Y100 though some may ask for twice this. Taxis will also do a day trip from Báihé (Y240).

At the park, shuttle buses take you from the main gate to a big lot (33km) where you start the stairs to Heaven Lake. Shuttle buses then take you back to a junction where you switch buses for the short distance to the canyon. Buses from the canyon head back directly to the main gate.

Yánjí 延吉

☎0433 / POP 399,000

Although Yánjí has the typical layout and appearance of a Chinese city, the capital of China's Korean Autonomous Prefecture has one foot across the nearby border with North Korea. About a third of the population is ethnic Korean, many more are of Korean descent, and it's common to hear people speaking Korean rather than Mandarin. If you're intent on exploring the prefecture, this is the ideal starting point. Yánjí is also a transport hub for trips to Chángbái Shān.

The Bù'ěrhātōng River (Bù'ěrhātōng Hé) bisects the city. The train and bus stations are south, while the commercial district is north. Taxi fares start at Y5, and most rides cost between Y5 and Y10.

Sleeping & Eating

Yánbiān Diànlì Dàshà HOTEL $
(延边电力大厦; ☎291 1881; 399 Guangming Lu; 光明街399号; incl breakfast d Y148-168, tr Y228; ❄📶) Even the cheaper rooms are huge, clean and cosy, and that goes for the bathrooms too. With a great restaurant on the ground floor and wireless in-room, this hotel is an ideal spot to hang out in if you need a bit of time to unwind after a long haul on the road.

The hotel's restaurant (dishes Y10 to Y45; open 6am to 9pm) is packed every meal with outside guests devouring a range of excellent Korean dishes. There's a big picture-menu wall and plenty of side dishes you can point to. The staff are very friendly and this is one of the few places in China they won't let you over-order.

Tiě Dào Dàshà HOTEL $
(铁道大厦; ☎611 2000; 63 Zhanqian Jie; d without/with bathroom Y50/100; ❄) Basic, reasonably clean doubles are available. Turn right immediately as you exit the train station. Look for the green glass windows.

Information

Bank of China (中国银行; Zhōngguó Yínháng; cnr Changbaishan Lu & Zhanqian Jie) Two blocks up from the train station on the right; 24-hour ATM.

CITS (中国国际旅行社; Zhōngguó Guójì Lǚxíngshè; ☎271 0166; 6th fl, 558 Yixie Jie; ⏲8am-5pm) Arranges flight tickets and tours to Chángbái Shān.

Internet cafe (网吧; wǎngbā; cnr Zhanqian Jie & Gianjin Lu; per hr Y2; ⏲24hr) A block north of the train station.

Getting There & Away

AIR Yánjí airport is 5km west of the city centre.

Běijīng Y1220, one hour 40 minutes

Dàlián Y1190, 2½ hours

Shěnyáng Y810, one hour

BUS Buses from the long-distance bus station (客运站; *kèyùn zhàn*) at 2319 Changbaishan Xilu:

Èrdào Báihé Y40, three hours, six daily

Húnchūn Y23, two hours, every 30 minutes

Mǔdānjiāng Y56, five hours, two daily (6.30am and 9.50am)

Buses from the long-distance bus station at the train station:

Chángchūn Y95, 8½ hours, four daily

Jílín Y71, six hours, two daily (8am and 9am)

TRAIN

Chángchūn seat/sleeper Y39/124, eight to nine hours

Jílín seat/sleeper Y30/78, six to eight hours

Around Yánjí

The **Korean Autonomous Prefecture** (延边朝鲜族自治州; Yánbiān Cháoxiǎnzú Zìzhìzhōu) has China's greatest concentration of ethnic Koreans. The majority inhabit the border areas northeast of Báihé, up to the capital Yánjí and the border city of Túmén (图门).

To explore the region, head east from Yánjí to Túmén or even further east to Fángchuān (防川), a sliver of land where China meets North Korea and Russia. To reach Fángchuān, take a bus from Yánjí to Húnchūn (混春; Y23, every 30 minutes, two hours), from where you take another bus to the border town. Buses to Túmén and Húnchūn leave from Yánjí's long-distance bus station at Changbaishan Xilu.

Jí'ān 集安

☎0435 / POP 240,000

This small city, just across the Yālù River from North Korea, was once part of the Koguryo (高句丽; Gāogōulì) kingdom, a Korean dynasty that ruled areas of northern

CROSSING THE BORDER

Every year thousands of North Koreans slip across the border to China – on their own, with the help of relatives, or aided by people smugglers and Christian groups. Some return to the Democratic People's Republic of Korea (DPRK) after earning more money than they ever could at home. The lucky few move on to South Korea, but an estimated 100,000 are stuck in the Korean Autonomous Prefecture, where they live a precarious, paperless existence.

In recent years women have made up the majority of escapees and their situation is especially difficult. Some end up sold as wives to local farmers; others can be found living a dismal existence as prostitutes in the karaoke TV (KTV) joints of towns like Yánjí. Their plight, and that of other North Korean refugees, draws little attention in the West.

China and the Korean peninsula from 37 BC to AD 668. Jí'ān's extensive Koguryo pyramids, ruins and tombs resulted in Unesco designating it a World Heritage Site in 2004. Archaeologists have unearthed remains of three cities plus some 40 tombs around Jí'ān and the town of Huánrén (in Liáoníng province).

With a drive to capitalise on its Korean heritage's tourism potential, modern-day Jí'ān is fast transforming itself into one of China's most pleasant modern towns, with well-tended parks, cobbled streams running through town, leafy streets and a beautiful new riverfront area where you can gaze across to North Korea. Add in the town's 360-degree mountain backdrop, excellent Korean food and friendly locals, and you have an up-and-coming hot spot that for now is completely under the radar.

Shengli Lu runs east–west through town, with the long-distance bus station at the west end. The main north–south road is Li Ming Jie, which ends at the river park. It's easy to walk around town and you can pick up a good English-language map of Jí'ān and the surrounding area at any hotel.

Sights

The main sights other than the river park are scattered on the outskirts of the city. You could cover them on foot in a long day, but most people hire a taxi. Expect to pay Y50 to Y80 for a half-day tour of three to five locations.

The **Koguryo sites** (8.30am-5.20pm) are spread around the very lovely green hills surrounding Jí'ān. Despite their historical significance, most sites don't have a terrible amount of detail to examine, however. Many of the tombs are cairns – essentially heaps of stones piled above burial sites – while others are stone pyramids. But there is something magical about the open fields and high terraces they were constructed on that makes you want to linger. The most impressive site, Wandu Mountain City, needs a couple of hours to cover its expansive grounds. It's best to get your taxi to drop you off here at the end. You can easily walk back to Jí'ān on Shancheng Rd in less than an hour, following the river down the valley.

A Y100 ticket gets you into the four most important sites; you can also buy separate tickets for each sight for Y30.

Jiāngjūnfén (General's Tomb) TOMB
(将军坟) One of the largest pyramid-like structures in the region, the 12m-tall Jiāngjūnfén was built during the 4th century for a Koguryo ruler; a smaller tomb 100m nearby on the same site is the resting place of a family member. The site is set among the hills 4km northeast of town.

Hǎotàiwáng Stele STELE
(好太王碑; Hǎotàiwáng Bēi) Inscribed with 1775 Chinese characters, the Hǎotàiwáng Stele, a 6m-tall stone slab that dates to AD 415, records the accomplishments of Koguryo king Tan De (AD 374–412), known as Hǎotàiwáng. Tan De's tomb (labelled 'Tàiwáng Tomb') is on the same site, and you can enter and see the stone burial slabs.

The stele and tomb are quite close to Jiāngjūnfén.

Cemetery of Noblemen at Yushan TOMBS
(禹山贵族墓地; Yǔshān Guìzú Mùdì) In this small gated park the stone crypts of various noblemen are open for visitors, though the only one you could actually enter at the time of writing was Tomb No 5 (wait for the guard to take you). It's a creepy descent underground into the chilly stone chamber,

but as your eyes adjust to the light there are some intriguing wall paintings to behold.

Wandu Mountain City ANCIENT CITY
(丸都山城; Wándū Shānchéng) The capital of the Koguryo kingdom in its early and middle period, this city was first built in AD 3 but was destroyed in the 3rd century. There's little left of the original buildings, but the layout has been cleared and it's still immensely enjoyable scrambling about the terraces and enjoying the views that surely must have been a deciding factor in establishing the capital here.

Giant cairns CAIRNS
Down on the plains, on a large shelf above the river is Jí'ān's largest collection of giant stone cairns. Erected after the destruction of the city, the group is so far unaffected by tourists or tourism infrastructure. It's another beautiful area and the sight of these massive rock piles in fields of Spanish needle *(bidens pilosa)* is probably the most photogenic in all Jí'ān.

Riverside Plaza PARK
Where on earth did the budget come from to transform the formerly dour Jí'ān riverside into this dazzling new waterfront park? Miragelike, the park features stone fountains, landscaped gardens, cobbled walkways, carp pools, statues and riverside decks where you can view North Korea across the Yālù River. At night the stylish modern apartments surrounding the park light their rooftops, while a small lotus pond opens out to a wooden junk for visitors to row themselves out to. It's all terribly romantic – all the more so because completely unexpected.

The centrepiece of the park is the very sleek looking **Jí'ān Museum** (集安博物馆; Jí'ān Bówùguǎn), sporting a brown stone base and a glass top with sails that open up like leaves. The museum itself hadn't opened at the time of writing, but we were told it would soon. Naturally, it will display artefacts from the Koguryo era.

To get to Riverside Plaza walk east on Shengli Lu to the corner of Jian She Jie.

Sleeping & Eating

Lùmíng Bīnguǎn HOTEL $$
(鹿鸣宾馆; ☎625 6988; 653 Shengli Lu; 胜利路653号; dm/d without bathroom Y30/80, d with bathroom & incl breakfast Y150-188; @) Friendly staff and well-kept rooms make this Jí'ān's best budget option. It's three blocks east of the bus station on the north side of Shengli Lu just before you reach Liming Jie. Look for the English sign reading 'Guesthouse' above the entrance. Some rooms have their own computer.

Cuìyuán Bīnguǎn HOTEL $$
(翠园宾馆; ☎622 2123; 888 Shengli Lu; 胜利路888号; s/d & tr Y288/388, discounts available) Two blocks east of the bus station, and across from a cute park with a cobbled stream running through it, Cuìyuán Bīnguǎn offers good midrange comfort, though the singles are a bit on the small side. Expect big discounts off the rack rates.

Head to the market off Shengli Lu before Liming Jie (just past the Lùmíng Bīnguǎn); it sells fruit, nuts, dumplings, bread and barbecued meats, and has a couple of restaurants selling Korean cold-noodle dishes.

There are two sets of outdoor barbecue eating areas at Riverside Plaza. If you want a proper sit-down meal head to Dongsheng Jie.

Information

Bank of China (中国银行; Zhōngguó Yínháng; Shengli Lu) Located just east of the junction of Shengli Lu and Li Ming Jie; 24-hour ATM.

Internet bar (网吧; wǎngbā; Dongsheng Jie; per hr Y2) One block north of Shengli Lu.

Public Security Bureau (PSB; 公安局; Gōng'ānjú; Li Ming Jie) Between Shengli Lu and the river.

Getting There & Away

The main routes to Jí'ān are via Tōnghuà to the north or Shěnyáng and Dāndōng in Liáoníng province. If you're travelling to Chángbái Shān, you can make connections in Tōnghuà. If travelling up to Chángchūn it's probably faster to take a bus as trains only go to Tōnghùa.

BUS The **long-distance bus station** (客运站; kèyùn zhàn; Shengli Lu) is in the west part of town.

Chángchūn Y98, 5½ hours, two daily (5.30am and 2.50pm)

Dāndōng Y58, six hours, two daily (7.30am and 12.20pm)

Huánrén Y29, 3½ hours, two daily (6.30am and 6.55am)

Shěnyáng Y90, six hours, two daily (6.20am and 11.20am)

Tōnghuà Y22, two hours, every hour

TRAIN The **station** (Yanjiang Lu) is in the northeast part of town. One slow train a day travels from Jí'ān to Tōnghuà (Y8, 2½ to three hours, 11.40am).

Jílín City 吉林市

☎0432 / POP 1.98 MILLION

Industrial Jílín isn't exactly a winter wonderland, but it's fast improving, and the city is at its best during the coldest months of the year when the spectacular and peculiar phenomenon of needle-like frost covers the trees along the Sōnghuā River promenade. There's also a popular **Ice Lantern Festival** (Bīngdēng Jié; see CITS, opposite, for dates), and nearby there's some of China's best skiing.

It's easy to walk around the downtown area. Traffic is light and the sidewalks are wide.

Sights & Activities

Walking along the Sōnghuā River promenade is a pleasant way to spend some time.

Catholic Church CHURCH

(天主教堂; Tiānzhǔ Jiàotáng; 3 Songjiang Lu) Jílín's most distinctive building, the church was built in 1917 in the Gothic style and was completely ransacked during the Cultural Revolution. In 1980 it reopened and now holds regular services.

Wén Miào TEMPLE

(文庙; Confucius Temple; Wenmiao Hutong; admission Y15; ⏲8.30am-4pm) Set in three courtyards, the temple was originally constructed in 1736 and rebuilt in 1907.

Sleeping

Guǎngdiàn Bīnguǎn HOTEL $$

(广电宾馆; ☎6615 9888; 2 Nanjing Jie; 南京街2号; d Y158-228; ❄@) A great location near the river (and the CITS office if you are using its daily ski service). Rooms could be pulled from any midrange hotel but are cosy enough, have free broadband internet, and some their own computer.

Jīnchí Shāngwù Bīnguǎn HOTEL $$

(金池商务宾馆; ☎6111 4778; Chongqing Jie; d incl breakfast Y169-190; ❄@) A newly opened hotel with fresh, clean rooms and friendly staff.

Central Jílín City

Top Sights

	Catholic Church	C3
	Wén Miào	D2
Sleeping		
1	Guǎngdiàn Bīnguǎn	C2
2	Jīnchí Bīnguǎn	D1
Eating		
3	Xīnxīngyuán Jiǎoziguǎn	B2

Central Jílín City

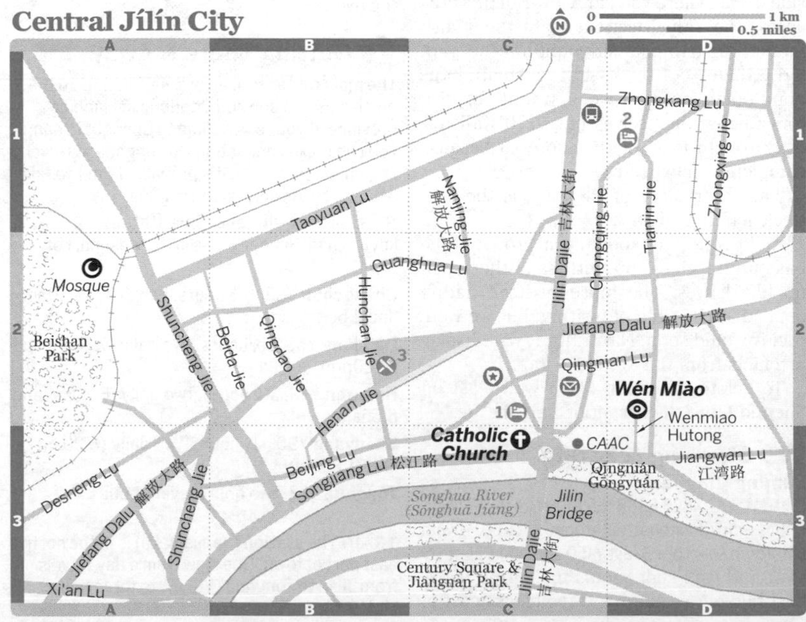

Eating

Jílín's pedestrian street is loaded with restaurants and stalls, and there are even a few places to snack along the river.

Xīnxīngyuán Jiǎoziguǎn DUMPLINGS $$
(新兴园饺子馆; 399 Henan Jie; dumplings Y11-20; ⊙9am-8pm) Choose from the cold plates on display and pair them with first-rate *jiǎozi* (dumplings) at this 2nd-floor restaurant on a pedestrian street. Look for a building with traditional overhanging eaves and red lanterns; Xīnxīngyuán Jiǎoziguǎn is to the right of this.

Information

ATMs and banks are all around, though internet cafes can be hard to find.

CITS (中国国际旅行社; Zhōngguó Guójì Lǚxíngshè; ☎244 2907; 2222 Chongqing Jie; ⊙8.30am-5pm) Near the CAAC. Organises ski trips, and tours to Chángbái Shān's northern slope.

Getting There & Around

AIR Flights to/from Jílín use Chángchūn's airport, about 60km west. For flight information and tickets, contact **Civil Aviation Administration of China** (CAAC; 中国民航; Zhōngguó Mínháng; ☎651 8888; 2288 Chongqing Jie; ⊙8am-5pm). Airport shuttle buses from the CAAC office start at 5.30am (Y40, 1½ hours, 10 a day).

BUS Destinations from the **long-distance bus station** (kèyùnzhàn; Zhongkang Lu):

Běidàhú Y11.50, three hours, five daily

Chángchūn Y37, 1½ hours, every 15 minutes

TAXI Fares start at Y5.

TRAIN The station (江北站) is to the northeast, 20 minutes away by taxi (about Y20).

Chángchūn Y11 to Y22, two hours

Hā'ěrbīn Y25, five hours

Běidàhú Ski Resort 北大湖滑雪场

Since it hosted the 2007 Asian Winter Games, **Běidàhú** (Běidàhú Huáxuěchǎng; www.beidahuski.com; admission to park area Y20; ⊙park 8.30am-4.30pm yr round, ski area Nov-Mar) has established itself as one of China's premier ski resorts, though there are indications that it may be slipping owing to a lack of continued investment. Located in a tiny village 53km south of Jílín, the resort has runs on two mountains ranging from beginner to advanced. Rental and day passes are around Y400 per day.

If you're keen on a few days' skiing, it's more economical to stay in Jílín than on the mountain. CITS in Jílín has daily ski packages for Y188 that include transport, lunch and a four-hour ski pass. Otherwise try **Běidàhú Yàyùncūn** (北大湖亚运村; Beidahu Asian Games Village; ☎0432-6420 2023; ❄), the athletes' village for the Asian Games and now the main accommodation on the mountain. At the time of writing dorm rooms were being added, though there was no word on when they would be finished. Posher doubles went from Y480 to Y1380, but you can expect winter prices (which change every year) to be higher.

Getting to Běidàhú by public transport is problematic. There are several daily ski shuttle buses from Jílín bus station, but the last return is 2.30pm, so the chances of getting stuck on the mountain are good. A taxi is about Y150 each way. Some skiers fly into Chángchūn and take a taxi directly to the mountain (Y350, two hours).

Chángchūn 长春

☎0431 / POP 3.22 MILLION

The Japanese capital of Manchukuo between 1933 and 1945, Chángchūn was also the centre of the Chinese film industry in the 1950s and '60s. Visitors expecting a Hollywood-like backdrop of palm trees and beautiful people will be disappointed, though. Chángchūn is now better known as China's motor city because of the many car manufacturers who have factories here, and, appropriately enough, it's a traffic-snarled, smoggy place.

But for people on the trail of Puyi, China's last emperor, it's an essential stop. There are also a fair few historic buildings dating back to the early days of the 20th century, mostly along and off Renmin Dajie.

Chángchūn sprawls from north to south. The long-distance bus station and the train station are in the north of the city.

Sights

TOP CHOICE **Imperial Palace of Manchu State (Puppet Emperor's Palace)** MUSEUM
(伪满皇宫博物院; Wěimǎn Huánggōng Bówùyuàn; 5 Guangfu Lu; admission Y80; ⊙8.30am-4.20pm, last entry 40min before closing) Chángchūn's main attraction is the former residence of Puyi, who was the Qing dynasty's final emperor. His story was the

Chángchūn

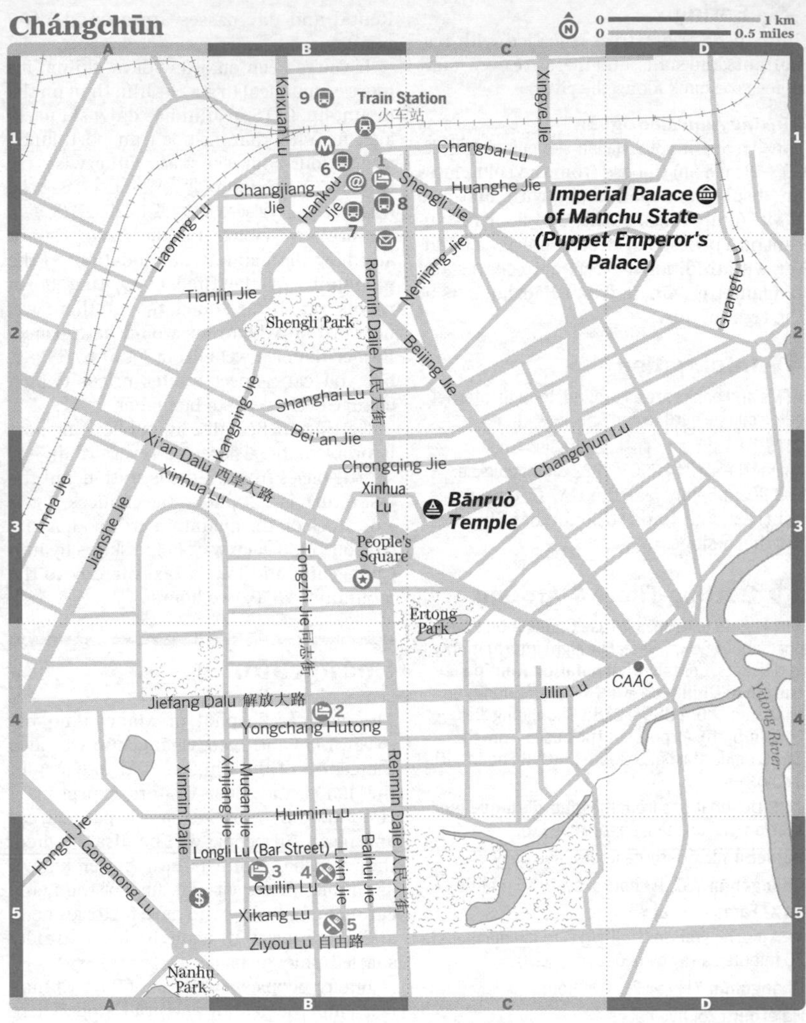

basis for the 1987 Bernardo Bertolucci film *The Last Emperor*.

In 1908, at age two, Puyi became the 10th Qing emperor. His reign lasted just over three years, but he was allowed to remain in the Forbidden City until 1924. Subsequently, he lived in Tiānjīn until 1932, when the Japanese installed him at this palace as the 'puppet emperor' of Manchukuo. After Japan's defeat in 1945, Puyi was captured by Russian troops. In 1950 he was returned to China, where he spent 10 years in a re-education camp before ending his days as a gardener in Běijīng. Puyi died in 1967.

Puyi's study, bedroom and temple, as well as his wife's quarters (including her opium den) and his concubine's rooms, have all been elaborately re-created. His American car is also on display, but it's the exhibition on his extraordinary life, which has a large collection of photos, that is most enthralling.

Bānruò Temple BUDDHIST TEMPLE

(般若寺; Bānruò Sì, 137 Changchun Lu) One of the largest Buddhist temples in the north-east, Bānruò is a lively place of worship for locals and pilgrims alike. Wander around the temple back alleys and you'll find mer-

Chángchūn

Top Sights

Sleeping

Eating

Transport

chants selling any number of charms, statues, shrines and incense. This religious entrepreneurial spirit is as interesting to observe as the more faith based.

To get here take bus 6 (10 minutes) from Renmin Dajie across from the main bus station and get off at Renmin Guangchang (Renmin Sq; 'People's Sq' on our map). You can also walk from the train-station area in about 30 minutes. The temple was closed at the time of writing but should be reopen by the time you read this.

Jìngyuètán SCENIC AREA
(净月潭旅游区; Jìngyuètán Lǚyóuqū; admission Y30; 24hr) This massive lakeside park on the southeast outskirts of Chángchūn encompasses over 90 sq km and is a most welcome break if you have to spend any time in the motor city. Established in 1934, it features well-tended gardens, pavilions, lookouts and a 20km round-the-lake bike path. Shuttle buses (Y10) take you to the dam, where you can catch boats (Y30 per trip). At the front gate there are bike rentals (Y20 per hour).

The easiest way to get here is to take the light rail from the station on Liaoning Lu (Y4, 55 minutes).

Sleeping

Chūnyì Bīnguǎn HOTEL $$
(春谊宾馆; 8209 6888; www.chunyihotel.com; 80 Renmin Dajie; 人民大街80号; d/tr incl breakfast Y348/388, discounts available; ❄@) The old-school charm has diminished a little since this place was built in 1909, but it retains a gorgeous marble staircase and foyer. Rooms and bathrooms are huge, and as a sop to modern times feature broadband internet. Some doubles are holding up better than others, so if you are shown one a little tatty ask to see another.

The hotel is opposite the train station. Expect to pay about half the posted rack rates.

Elan Fashion Inn HOTEL $
(米兰花时尚酒店; Mǐlánhuā Shíshàng Jiǔdiàn; 8564 4588; cnr Tongzhi Jie & Yongchang Hutong; 同志街与永昌胡同交汇处; d Y98-138; ❄@) Rooms are reliably spick and span, although the ones facing Tongzhi Jie are a little noisy. From the train station, take bus 62 or 362 and get off on Tongzhi Jie just south of Jiefang Dalu.

Star Moon Fashion Inn HOTEL $$
(星月时尚酒店; Xīngyuè Shíshàng Jiǔdiàn; 8509 0555; www.starmoon.inn.com.cn; 1166 Longli Lu; 隆礼路１１６６号; d from Y138; ❄@) For a grey industrial city, Chángchūn has its share of fashion inns. This modern hotel is in a great location near shops, restaurants and nightlife.

Eating & Drinking

Tongzhi Jie between Huimin Lu and Ziyou Lu is the most happening part of Chángchūn come nightfall. The streets off here are packed with inexpensive restaurants and music and clothes shops. Guilin Lu and Xikang Lu are good places to head for a meal, while Longli Lu is lined with bars, mostly sleazy but some clearly fine for a casual drink.

Yánbiān Xìnzǐ Fàndiàn KOREAN $$
(延边信子饭店; 728 Xikang Lu; dishes Y6-28; 10am-midnight) This place offers Korean classics such as *shí guō bàn fàn* (rice, vegetable and eggs served in a clay pot) and cold noodle dishes. Korean beers from Y10.

French Bakery WESTERN $$
(红磨坊; Hóng Mòfáng; 745 Guilin Lu; 9am-10pm) With its wood-panelled design, laid-back atmosphere, good coffee (Y15) and Western dishes (mains from Y30), this is an unusual find in Chángchūn. Try the huge, filling breakfast omelettes (from Y25) to start your day.

Information

There are 24-hour ATMs all over town. You can pick up a Chinese map with train and bus info at the train or bus stations.

Bank of China (中国银行; Zhōngguó Yínháng; 1296 Xinmin Dajie; ⌚8.30-11.30am & 1-4.30pm) Near Nánhú Park (Nánhú Gōngyuán). Will change travellers cheques. No 24-hour ATM.

CAAC (中国民航; Zhōngguó Mínháng; ☎8298 8888; 480 Jiefang Dalu) In the CAAC Hotel. For air tickets and shuttle buses to airport.

Internet cafe (网吧; wǎngbā; cnr Hankou Jie & Changjiang Jie; per hr Y3; ⌚24hr) One of several around the train station.

Public Security Bureau (PSB; 公安局; Gōng'ānjú; 2627 Renmin Dajie) On the southwestern corner of People's Sq, in a building that dates from the Japanese occupation.

Getting There & Away

AIR **Chángchūn Lóngjiā International Airport** has daily flights to major cities including Běijīng (Y760, 1½ hours); Sōngjiānghé (Y650, Tuesday and Thursday to Sunday), near Chángbái Shān; and Seoul (Y3300 return, two hours).

BUS The **long-distance bus station** (长途汽车站; chángtú qìchézhàn; 226 Renmin Dajie) is two blocks south of the train station. Buses to Hā'ěrbīn leave from the north bus station (*běizhàn*) behind the train station. Facing the station, head left and take the underpass near the *wǎngbā* (internet cafe) sign.

Běidàhú Y30, four hours, one daily (3.10pm)

Běijīng Y241, 7½ hours, two daily (3pm and 6pm)

Hā'ěrbīn Y75.50, 3½ hours, every 30 minutes

Jí'ān Y99, 5½ hours, two daily (7.45am and 5.30pm)

Jílín Y22.50, 1½ hours, every 30 minutes

Shěnyáng Y67, 3½ hours, hourly

TRAIN

Běijīng (D train) seat Y311 to Y373, five to six hours

Běijīng seat/sleeper Y130/207, nine to 12 hours

Hā'ěrbīn (D train) seat Y77 to Y93, two hours

Hā'ěrbīn seat Y20 to Y57, three hours

Jílín seat Y12 to Y35, two hours

Shěnyáng (D train) seat Y94 to Y113, two hours

Shěnyáng seat Y22 to Y38, 3½ to four hours

Getting Around

TO/FROM THE AIRPORT The airport is 20km east of the city centre, between Chángchūn and Jílín. Shuttle buses to the airport (Y20, 50 minutes) leave from the **CAAC Hotel** (民航宾馆; Mínháng Bīnguǎn; 480 Jiefang Dalu) on the east side of town. Taxi fares to the airport are Y80 to Y100 for the one-hour trip.

BUS Bus 6 follows Renmin Dajie south from a stop across from the long-distance bus station. Other city buses leave from a stand across the road in front of the train station. Buses 62 and 362 travel between the train station and Nánhú Park via the Chongqing Lu and Tongzhi Jie shopping districts.

LIGHT RAIL The **Chángchūn Light Rail** (⌚6.30am-9pm) service is only useful for getting to Jìngyuètán park.

TAXI Fares start at Y5, but you can often wait a long time for an empty cab.

Essential China

Cuisine »
The Great Wall »
Temples »
Hiking »
Festivals »

unrise over Lí River, Guǎngxī (p597)

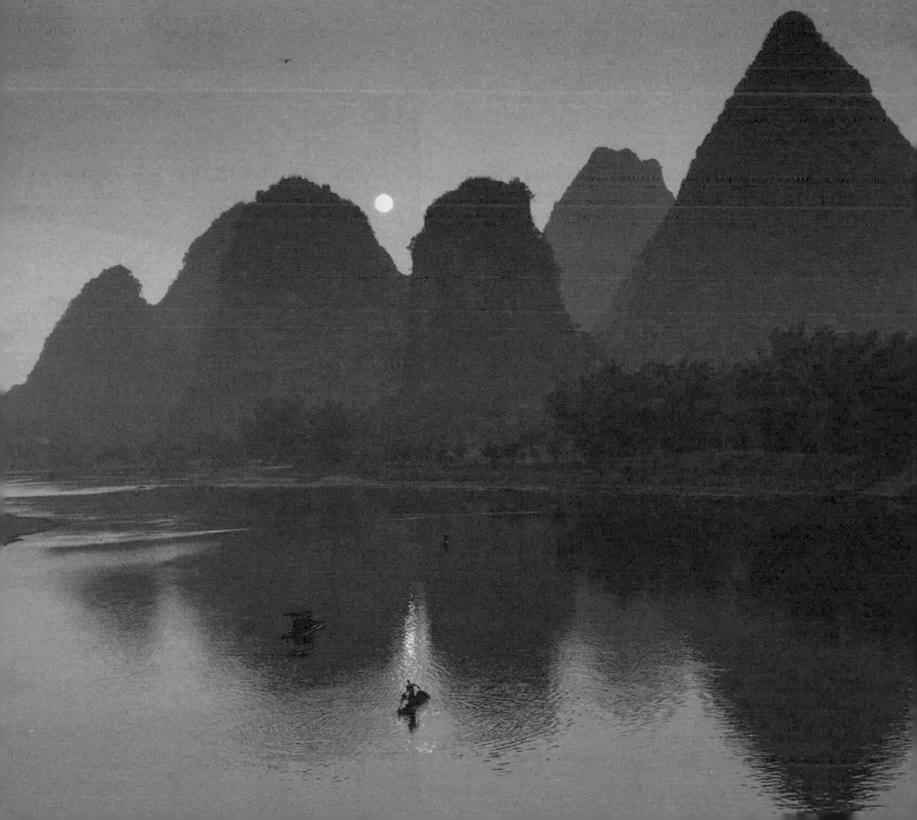

Cuisine

To the Chinese, food is life. Dining is the cherished high point of the daily social calendar and often the only occasion to stop work and fully relax. The only problem is knowing where to begin: the sheer variety on offer can have your head spinning and your tummy quivering.

Noodles

1 Marco Polo may have nicked the recipe to make spaghetti (so they say), but he didn't quite get the flavouring right. Noodles range across an exciting spectrum of taste, from the wincingly spicy *dàndan miàn* through to the supersalty *zhájiàng miàn*.

Dumplings

2 Set your compass north and northeast for the best dumplings *(jiǎozi)*. Pork, leek, lamb and crab meat, all wrapped up in a small envelope of dough. If you like them crispy, get them fried *(guōtiē)*. Shànghǎi's interpretation is *xiǎolóngbāo* – steamed and scrummy.

Dim Sum

3 Dim sum is steamed up across China, but like the Cantonese dialect, it's best left to the masters of the south to get right. Hong Kong (p470), Macau (p509) and Guǎngzhōu (p533) should be your first ports of call – they set the dim sum benchmark.

Peking Duck

4 Purists insist you have to be in Běijīng for true Peking duck, roasted to an amber hue over fruit tree wood, and you might as well take their advice as that's where you'll find the best Peking-duck restaurants (p79).

Hot Pot

5 It's ideal for banishing the bitter cold of a northern winter, but in steamy Chóngqìng (p752) old folk devour the spiciest variety at the height of summer – clearly an all-weather meal. There are two main varieties: Sìchuān hotpot (spicy) and Mongolian hotpot (non-spicy).

Clockwise from top left

1. Rice noodles **2.** Steamed dumplings **3.** Dim sum **4.** Peking duck

GREG ELMS

1

LEE FOSTER

4

GREG ELMS

3

The Great Wall

China's elongated bastion ranges in fragments across a huge northern belt, stretching from the North Korean border, vaulting rivers, poking down to the sea, snaking over mountains around Běijīng, disappearing here, reappearing there before finally being ground down by the remorseless desert winds of the northwest.

Jīnshānlǐng

1 The magnificent hike from Jīnshānlǐng (p102) towards Sìmǎtái is ideal in late autumn, when Běijīng's weather is at its best; in the hammering heat of summer you'll need a lot of water and an effective sunhat.

Jiāyùguān Fort

2 Jiāyùguān Fort (p824) in Gānsù offers unique images of the wind-blasted desert fort set against the snowcapped Qílián mountains. China's Wild West truly kicks off here and you can explore vestiges of the wall running between ancient and disintegrating watchtowers.

Jiànkòu

3 Běijīng's most exciting and authentic part of the Great Wall is, not surprisingly, not the easiest to reach. But it's worth the effort: Jiànkòu (p103) will give you the best experience, the finest photos, an excellent workout and almost certainly unforgettable memories.

Huánghuā

4 A much-needed alternative to over-commercialised and overdone sections of wall, Huánghuā (p103) is an impressively authentic rendition of the Great Wall. Excellent hiking awaits if you have time, shoes with good grip and a sense of exploration.

Jiǔménkǒu

5 A chance to make an adventurous outing into China's Manchurian northeast, Jiǔménkǒu (p126) is the country's sole section of wall straddling a river. Being somewhat far from Běijīng, it's less visited and offers unique images of the brick bastion.

TIM MAKINS

1

3

DAMIAN HARPER

Clockwise from top left

1. The Great Wall at Jīnshānlǐng **2.** Jiāyùguān Fort's temple **3.** The Jiànkòu section of the Great Wall

Temples

Divided between the Buddhist, Taoist and Confucian faiths, China's temples are places of quietude, introspection, peace and absolution. Find them on mountain peaks, in caves, down side streets, hanging precariously on cliffsides or occupying the epicentre of town, from far-off Tibet to Běijīng and beyond.

Temple of Heaven, Běijīng

1 Not really a temple, but let's not quibble. Běijīng's Temple of Heaven (p63) was China's most graceful place of worship for the Ming and Qing emperors, fully encapsulating the Confucian desire for order and symmetry, and harmony between heaven and earth.

Confucius Temple, Qūfù

2 This is China's largest and most important Confucius Temple (p142). The Shāndōng sage has had an immeasurable influence on the Chinese persona through the millennia – visit the town where it all began and try to put his teachings in perspective.

Labrang Monastery, Xiàhé

3 If it's too much hassle to rustle up a Tibet travel permit, pop down to this gargantuan Tibetan monastery (p812) in the scenic southwest corner of Gānsù. Its aura of devotion is amplified by the nonstop influx of Tibetan pilgrims and worshippers.

Pǔníng Temple, Chéngdé

4 On a clear day, the temple (p121) stands beautifully against the hills around Chéngdé, but nothing compares to the Guanyin statue in its Mahayana Hall, a 22m-high, multiarmed embodiment of Buddhist benevolence and perhaps China's most astonishing statue.

Jokhang Temple, Lhasa

5 Tibet's holiest place of worship, the Jokhang Temple (p884) in Lhasa is a powerful source of sacred power. A place of pilgrimage for every Tibetan Buddhist at least once in their lifetime, the beguiling temple is rewarded by repeat visits.

Right
1. Hall of Prayer for Good Harvests, Temple of Heaven, Běijīng **2.** Dàchéng Hall, Confucius Temple, Qūfù

MERTEN SNIJDERS

1

KRZYSZTOF DYDYNSKI

2

Hiking

If you're keen to escape the cities into the great outdoors, China's dramatic variety of landscapes is the perfect backdrop for bracing walks – whether island-hopping in Hong Kong, exploring the foothills of the Himalayas or trekking through gorges in Yúnnán province.

Ganden to Samye, Tibet

1 You'll need four to five days for this glorious high-altitude trek connecting two of Tibet's most splendid monasteries (p893). The landscape is beautiful, but the trek requires preparation both physically and mentally, plus a Tibet travel permit.

Tiger Leaping Gorge, Yúnnán

2 The mother of all southwest China's treks, this magnificently named Yúnnán hike (p670) is at its most colourful and picturesque in early summer. It's not a walk in the park, so plan ahead and give yourself enough time.

Yángshuò, Guǎngxī

3 Yángshuò's karst topography (p592) is astonishing, a landscape of endless surprises. Base yourself in town, give yourself three or four days, and walk your socks off (or hire a bike). Adventurous types can even try rock climbing.

Huángshān, Ānhuī

4 Sooner or later you'll have to hike uphill, and where better than up China's most beautiful mountain (p389). The steps may be punishing, but just focus on the scenery: even if the fabled mists are nowhere to be seen, the views are incredible.

Hong Kong's Outlying Islands & New Territories

5 A whopping 70% of Hong Kong is trekking territory, so fling off your Gucci loafers and grab your trusty boots. Hop from island to island and make a break for the New Territories where some fantastic hiking trails await (p487).

Left

1. Kyi-chu Valley views from Ganden Monastery **2.** View of the Yangzi River at Tiger Leaping Gorge

Festivals

China is a nation of hard workers and enterpreneurs, but considerable energy is reserved for its festivals and celebrations. Festivals can be religious, fun-filled, commemorative or seasonal. Locals don their best clothes and get seriously sociable. Join in and be part of the party.

Third Moon Fair, Dàlǐ

1 One of China's countless ethnic minority festivals is usually held in April. Try to time your visit to Dàlǐ (p656) in Yúnnán to coincide with this Bai festival that commemorates the appearance of Guanyin, the Bodhisattva of Mercy, to the people of the Nanzhao kingdom.

Dragon Boat Festival

2 Commemorating the death of Qu Yuan (the celebrated 3rd-century-BC poet and statesman), dramatic and muscle-powered dragon-boat races can be seen in May or June churning up the waterways across China, including Shànghǎi, Hong Kong and Tiānjīn.

Spring Festival

3 China's most commercially driven and full-on celebration takes the entire nation by storm at the stroke of midnight on the first day of the first lunar month, when the fuse is lit on a nationwide arsenal of fireworks.

Monlam (Great Prayer) Festival, Xiàhé

4 Celebrated across Tibet, the highlight Buddhist festival (in February or March) is easiest to witness in the monastic town of Xiàhé (p814), where a host of celebrations include the unfurling of a huge, sacred *thangka* (sacred painting) on the hillside.

Ice & Snow Festival, Hāěrbīn

5 The arctic temperatures may knock the wind from your lungs, but every January the frost-bitten capital of Hēilóngjiāng province (p327) twinkles with an iridescent collection of magnificently carved ice sculptures.

Right
1. Third Moon Fair, Dàlǐ, Yúnnán **2.** Dragon-boat races at Stanley Main Beach, Hong Kong Island

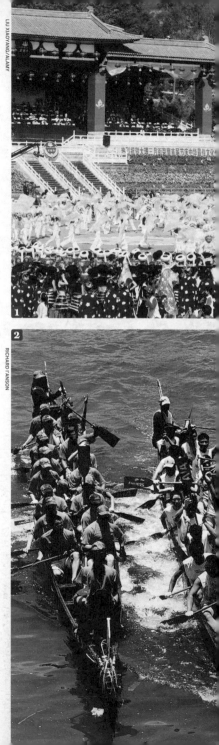

LIU XIAOYANG/ALAMY

1

2

RICHARD I'ANSON

Hēilóngjiāng

POPULATION: 38.2 MILLION

Includes »

Best Places to Eat

» Cafe Russia 1914 (p321)

» Dōngfāng Jiǎozi Wáng (p320)

» Dǐng Dǐng Xiāng (p321)

» Shuānglóng Jiǎozi Wáng (p324)

Best Places to Stay

» Kazy International Youth Hostel (p319)

» Modern Hotel (p320)

» Jìngpò Hú Shānzhuāng Jiǔdiàn (p324)

» Dàqìng Yóutián Liáoyǎngyuàn (p326)

Why Go?

It's cold in China's northernmost province, sub-Arctic cold – but that frigid weather is put to good use. Winter is peak tourist season, and with a world-renowned ice sculpture festival and China's finest ski runs it's worth swaddling yourself in layers and joining the crowds.

Hēilóngjiāng (黑龙江) means Black Dragon River, and this particular coiling dragon is the separating line between China and Russia. Across the province a neighbourly influence is evident in architecture, food and even souvenirs. Hā'ěrbīn's famed cobblestone streets and European-style facades are just the beginning.

Outside the cities, Hēilóngjiāng is a rugged, beautiful landscape of forests, lakes, mountains and dormant volcanoes. In Mòhé, China's North Pole village, the meadows and marshes have a magnetic pull all their own and the bragging rights to say you have stood at the very northern tip of China is well worth the 21-hour train ride to get there.

When to Go

Hā'ěrbīn

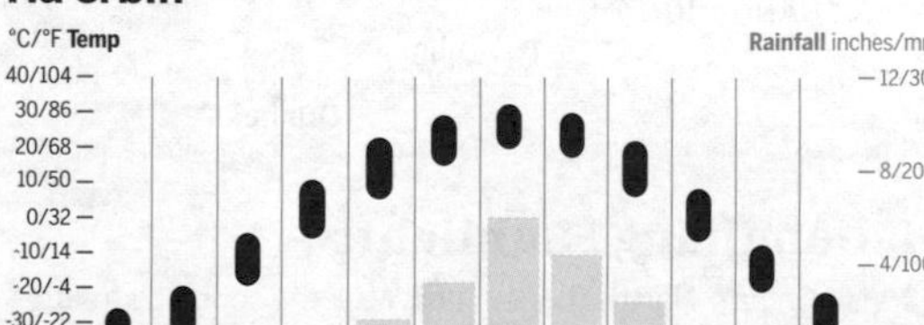

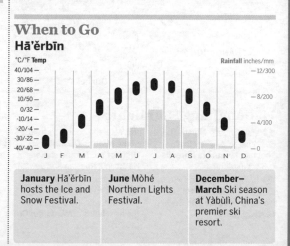

January Hā'ěrbīn hosts the Ice and Snow Festival.

June Mòhé Northern Lights Festival.

December–March Ski season at Yàbùlì, China's premier ski resort.

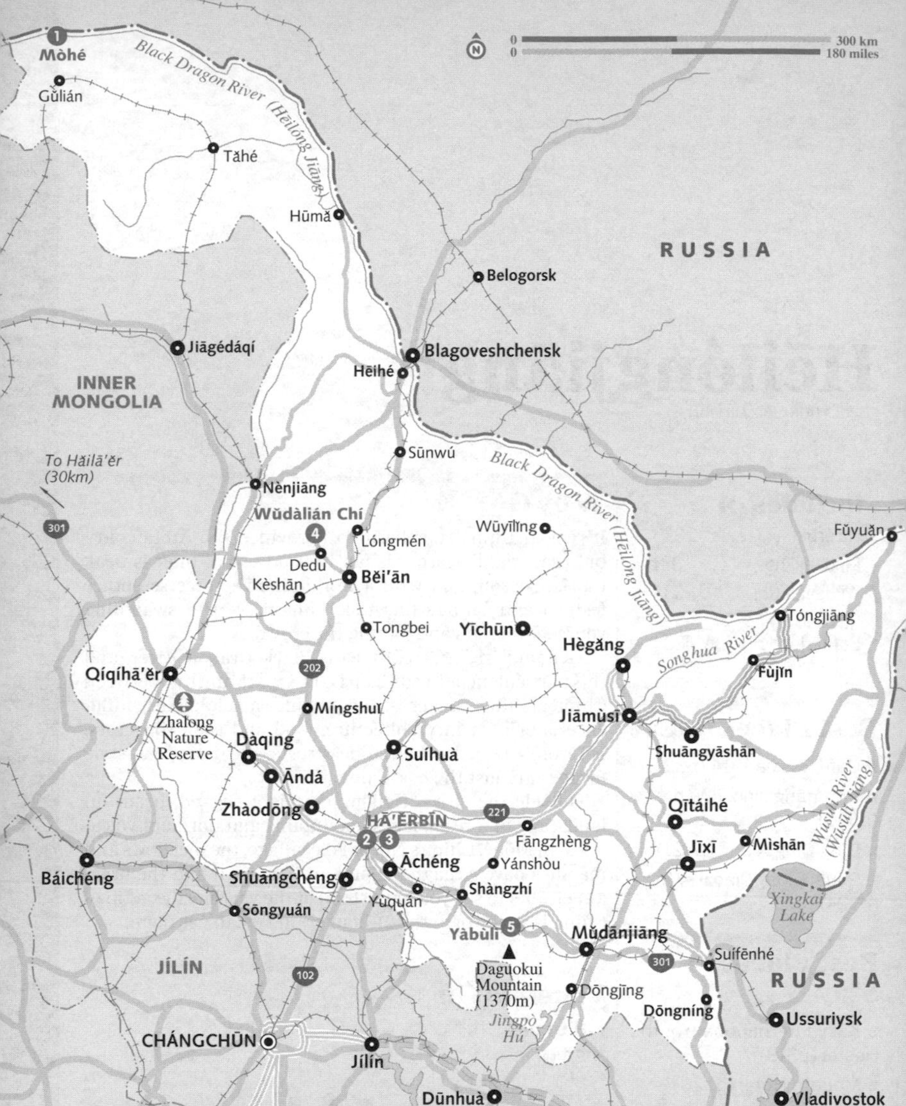

Hēilóngjiāng Highlights

1. Visit China's 'North Pole Village' and see the spectacular **aurora borealis** (p327) in Mòhé
2. Brave the cold and join the crowds who flock to Hā'ěrbīn's world-famous **Ice and Snow Festival** (p319)
3. Walk the cobbled streets of the historic **Dàolǐqū District** (p314) and explore Hā'ěrbīn's Russian and Jewish past
4. Hike to the top of a dormant volcano and through the lava fields of **Wǔdàlián Chí** (p325)
5. Ski and snowboard at **Yàbùlì** (p322), China's finest ski resort

History

Hēilóngjiāng forms the northernmost part of Dōngběi, the region formerly known as Manchuria. Its proximity to Russia has long meant strong historical and trade links with its northern neighbour. In the mid-19th century, Russia annexed parts of Hēilóngjiāng, while in 1897 Russian workers arrived to build a railway line linking Vladivostok with Hā'ěrbīn. By the 1920s well over 100,000 Russians resided in Hā'ěrbīn alone.

Like the rest of Manchuria, Hēilóngjiāng was occupied by the Japanese between 1931 and 1945. After the Chinese Communist Party (CCP) took power in 1949, relations with Russia grew steadily frostier, culminating in a brief border war in 1969. Sino-Russian ties have improved much in recent years and the two sides finally settled on the border in July 2008, after 40-odd years of negotiation.

Climate

Long freezing winters, with temperatures dropping below -30°C. Short summers are pleasantly warm, especially in the south and east, though mid to high 30's temperatures possible. Afternoon showers are common.

Language

The vast majority of people in Hēilóngjiāng speak northeast Mandarin, which is the same as standard Mandarin, apart from the accent. You're also likely to hear a lot of Russian. In the far northwest, tiny numbers of the Oroqen, Daur, Ewenki and Hezhen ethnic minorities still speak their own languages. A handful of people can speak Manchu, once the dominant tongue of the region.

Getting There & Around

Hā'ěrbīn is the logistical hub for the region and has extensive links with the rest of China. Buses are often the quicker way of getting around, rather than local trains which are slow. A new network of highways is set to open in the coming years which will shorten bus/driving travel times considerably. If you're headed for Inner Mongolia, direct trains run from Hā'ěrbīn to the cities of Hǎilā'ěr and Mǎnzhōulǐ.

PRICE INDICATORS

The following prices indicators are used in this chapter:

Sleeping

$	less than Y150
$$	Y150 to Y300
$$$	more than Y300

Eating

$	less than Y10
$$	Y10 to Y40
$$$	more than Y40

Hā'ěrbīn 哈尔滨

☎0451 / POP 3.2 MILLION

For a city of its size, Hā'ěrbīn is surprisingly easygoing. Cars (and even bicycles) are barred from Zhongyang Dajie, the main drag of the historic Dàolǐqū District, where most of Hā'ěrbīn's old buildings can be found. The long riverfront also provides sanctuary for walkers, as does Sun Island on the other side.

The city's sights are as varied as the architectural styles on the old street. Temples, old churches and synagogues coexist, while deep in the southern suburbs a former Japanese germ-warfare base is a sobering reminder of less harmonious times. Hā'ěrbīn's rich Russian and Jewish heritage makes it worth visiting at any time of year, but winter is tops with the world-class ice sculpture festival turning the frosty riverfront into a multicoloured wonderland.

History

In 1896 Russia negotiated a contract to build a railway line from Vladivostok to Hā'ěrbīn, then a small fishing village, and Dàlián (in Liáoníng province). The subsequent influx of Russian workers was followed by Russian Jews and then by White Russians escaping after the 1917 Russian Revolution.

These days, Hā'ěrbīn, whose name comes from a Manchu word meaning 'a place to dry fishing nets', is an ever-expanding, largely industrial city, and while Chinese are of course the majority, with Russia so close foreign faces are still common on the streets.

Sights

Dàolǐqū OLD DISTRICT

The cobblestone street of Zhongyang Dajie is the most obvious legacy of Russia's involvement with Hā'ěrbīn. Now a pedestrian-only zone, the street, and those nearby, are lined with buildings that date back to the early 20th century. Some are imposing,

Hā'ěrbīn

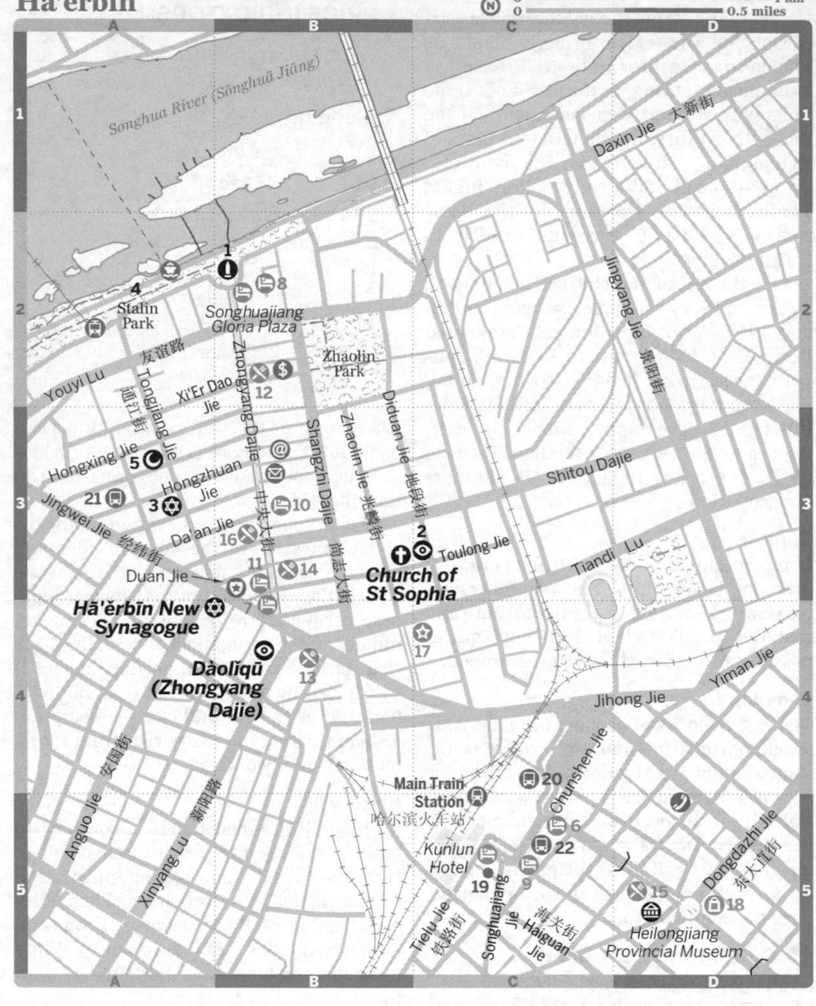

others distinctly dilapidated, but the mix of architectural styles is fascinating.

Church of St Sophia RUSSIAN CHURCH

(圣索菲亚教堂; Shèng Suǒfēiyà Jiàotáng; cnr Zhaolin Jie & Toulong Jie; admission Y20; ⌚8.30am-5.30pm) The red-brick Russian Orthodox Church of St Sophia, with its distinctive green 'onion' dome, is Hā'ěrbīn's most famous landmark while the surrounding square a prime spot to watch the crowds. Built in 1907, the church is now home to the **Hā'ěrbīn Architecture Arts Centre**, which displays charming black-and-white photographs of Hā'ěrbīn from the early 1900s. It's interesting to note that the captions display a very positive attitude towards the foreign influence on the city.

Stalin Park PARK

(斯大林公园; Sīdàlín Gōngyuán) Locals and visitors alike congregate year-round in Stalin Park. The tree-lined promenade, dotted with statues, playgrounds and cafes, runs along a 42km-long embankment that was built to curb the unruly Sōnghuā River. The odd **Flood Control Monument** (防洪胜利纪念塔; Fánghóng Shènglì Jìniàntǎ), from 1958, commemorates the thousands of

Hā'ěrbīn

Top Sights
Church of St Sophia B3
Dàolǐqū (Zhongyang Dajie) B4
Hā'ěrbīn New Synagogue A4

Sights
1 Flood Control Monument B2
2 Hā'ěrbīn Architecture Arts Centre C3
Jewish Middle School .... (see 3)
3 Old Main Synagogue A3
4 Stalin Park A2
5 Turkish Mosque A3

Sleeping
6 Běiběi Hotel C5
7 Běiběi Hotel B4
8 Jīndì Bīnguǎn B2
Kazy International Youth Hostel ... (see 3)
9 Lóngyùn Hotel C5
10 Modern Hotel B3
11 Zhōngdà Hotel B3

Eating
Bì Fēng Táng .... (see 12)
12 Cafe Russia 1914 .... B2
13 Dǐng Dǐng Xiāng B4
14 Dōngfāng Jiǎozi Wáng B3
15 Dōngfāng Jiǎozi Wáng D5
16 Food Market B3

Entertainment
17 Éluósī Jiǔbā C4

Shopping
18 Hóngbó Century Square D5

Information
19 Hā'ěrbīn Railway International Travel Service C5

Transport
20 Bus stop C4
21 Bus stop to Siberian Tiger Park A3
22 Long Distance Bus Station C5

people who died in years past when the river overflowed its banks.

During summer, it's a spot to sample snacks and sip a beer under the trees. In winter, the Songhua River becomes the local sports centre, with **ice skating**, **ice hockey** and **ice sailing** all options. You can hire the gear you'll need from vendors along the riverbank. If you really want to show off, join the people who like to swim in the gaps in the ice.

Sun Island Park — PARK

(太阳岛公园; Tàiyángdǎo Gōngyuán) Across the river from Stalin Park is Sun Island Park, a 38-sq-km recreational zone with landscaped gardens, miniforests, a 'water world', a Russian Style Town, and various small galleries and museums. It's a pleasant place to walk around, though as usual you need to pay extra to get into many areas.

You can boat across (Y10 return) from the dock directly north of the Flood Control Monument or catch the nearby **cable car** (one way/return Y50/100; ⌚8.30am-6.30pm).

Siberian Tiger Park — ANIMAL PARK

(东北虎林园; Dōngběihǔ Línyuán; www.dongbeihu.net.cn; 88 Songbei Jie; admission Y65; ⌚8am-4.30pm, last tour 4pm) At the Siberian Tiger Park, visitors get the chance to see one of the world's rarest animals (and largest felines) close-up. This breeding centre and urban park is not the most edifying spectacle, however, with the tigers fenced in and visitors, who tour safari-style in buses, encouraged to buy (live!) chickens (Y100), ducks and even cows (Y1500) to throw to the animals. The feeding takes place during the ride around the park, so if you don't think you can handle the spectacle (of cheering locals as much as tigers mauling their prey), consider not taking the ride.

The park is located roughly 15km north of the city. From Zhongyang Dajie walk down Hongzhuan Jie five minutes to just past Gaoyi Jie and catch bus 67 to the Gonglu Da Qiao stop just before the bridge over the Songhua River. Here, change to bus 54, which drops you off at the entrance to the park (look for a statue of a tiger). Alternatively, a taxi from the city centre is about Y40 one way.

After buying your ticket, head across the lot to the building across from the booth and register for a seat on one of the safari buses.

Jewish Hā'ěrbīn — JEWISH SIGHTS

The Jewish influence on Hā'ěrbīn was surprisingly long lasting; the last Jewish resident of the city died in 1985. In the 1920s Hā'ěrbīn was home to some 20,000 Jews, the largest Jewish community in the Far East at the time.

If you're on the trail of Hā'ěrbīn's Jews, then the **Hā'ěrbīn New Synagogue** (哈尔滨犹太新会堂; Hā'ěrbīn Yóutài Xīnhuìtáng; 162 Jingwei Jie; admission Y25; ⊙8.30am-5pm) is the place to start. The synagogue was built in 1921 by and for the community, the vast majority of which had emigrated from Russia. Restored and converted to a museum in 2004, the 1st floor is an art gallery with pictures and photos of old Hā'ěrbīn. The 2nd and 3rd floors feature photos and exhibits that tell the story of the history and cultural life of Hā'ěrbīn's Jews. From all accounts they had a splendid life centred on sports, music and business.

Tongjiang Jie was the centre of Jewish life in the city till the end of WWII, and many of the buildings on the street date back to the early 20th century. The museum can clue you in to the former location of bakers, kosher butchers and furriers. The old **Main Synagogue** (Yóutài Jiùhuìtáng; 82 Tongjiang Jie), built in 1909, now houses a cafe, shops and excellent little hostel. Close by is the former **Jewish Middle School** (犹太中学; Yóutài Zhōngxué), now home to an arts group.

Further up Tongjiang Jie is the interesting **Turkish Mosque** (土耳其清真寺; Tú'ěrqí Qīngzhēn Sì); built in 1906, it's no longer operating and is closed to visitors.

In the far eastern suburbs of Hā'ěrbīn is the **Huángshān Jewish Cemetery**, the largest in the Far East. There are over 600 graves here, all very well maintained. A taxi here takes around 45 minutes and will cost about Y50.

FREE **Japanese Germ Warfare Experimental Base** WAR MUSEUM
(侵华日军第731部队遗址;Qīnhuá Rìjūn Dì 731 Bùduì Yízhǐ; Xinjiang Dajie; ⊙9-11am & 1-3.30pm Tue-Sun) There are museums highlighting Japanese wartime atrocities all over Dongbei, but this is one is actually set in the notorious Japanese Germ Warfare Experimental Base – 731 Division used to inflict some of those atrocities. Between 1939 and 1945, Chinese prisoners of war and civilians were frozen alive, subjected to vivisection or infected with bubonic plague, syphilis and other virulent diseases. Three to four thousand people died here in the most gruesome fashion, including Russians, Koreans, Mongolians and, it is believed, a few American airmen.

The main building of the base is now a museum complete with photos, sculptures and exhibits of the equipment used by the Japanese. There are extensive English captions.

The base is in the far south of Hā'ěrbīn and takes about an hour to get to by bus. To the left of the post office on Tielu Jie, catch bus 343 (Y2). Get off at the stop called Xinjiang Dajie and walk back for about five minutes. The base is on the left-hand side of the road. If you get lost, just ask the locals the way to 'Qi San Yi' or '731'.

Temples

With Dongdazhi Jie all chewed up with subway construction, bus routes are tricky and it's best to take a taxi (Y10 from the Dàolǐqū district) to the entrance of the pedestrian street where the Buddhist temples are located.

For the Confucius Temple, look for an arch to the right of the pedestrian street. Pass through this and then a second arch on the left. The temple is a 10-minute walk along Wen Miao Jie.

Seven-Tiered Buddhist Pagoda PAGODA
(七级浮屠塔; Qījí Fútú Tǎ; 15 Dongdazhi Jie; admission Y10; ⊙8.30am-4pm) Hēilóngjiāng's largest temple complex, the Seven-Tiered Buddhist Pagoda was built in 1924 and is dominated by a giant statue of the Buddha. Tickets include admission to the Temple of Bliss next door.

Temple of Bliss BUDDHIST TEMPLE
(吉乐寺; Jí Lè Sì; 9 Dongdazhi Jie; ⊙8.30am-4pm) The active Buddhist community in residence gives this temple a genuine religious atmosphere despite the ticket sales. Among the many large statues here include Milefo (Maitreya), the Buddha yet-to-come, whose arrival will bring paradise on earth.

Confucius Temple CONFUCIUS TEMPLE
(文庙; Wén Miào; 25 Wen Miao Jie; admission Y15; ⊙8.30am-4pm, closed Wed) This peaceful and little-visited temple was built in 1929 and is said to be the largest Confucian temple in northeastern China. Restoration work was ongoing at the time of writing.

Other Sights

Hēilóngjiāng Science & Technology Museum MUSEUM
(黑龙江省科技馆; Hēilóngjiāngshěng Kējìguǎn; admission Y20; ⊙9am-4.30pm Tue-Sun) This children's museum is west of Sun Island Park and features excellent hands-on dis-

THE GREAT CATS

Only around 400 Siberian tigers are believed to still prowl the wilds with about 20 divided between Hēilóngjiāng and Jílín provinces. It's a dismal figure, and in 1986 the Chinese government set about to boost numbers by establishing the world's largest tiger breeding centre. Beginning with only eight tigers, the centre has been so successful that the worldwide number of Siberian tigers was expected to top 1000 in 2010.

Almost all of these are of course in captivity, which makes any wild sighting a cause for celebration. In June 2010, the figurative champagne flowed when tracks of a wild female Siberian tiger were found in Yongfeng Forest Farm in eastern Hēilóngjiāng. Senior researcher Dong Hongyu believed the tracks belonged to the mother of a one-year-old tiger found trapped in a fence in February of the same year.

Discovering the baby tiger, just days after the start of the Year of the Tiger, seemed like a favourable omen. The malnourished cub died after two days, however, and more bad news came in the following months when it was discovered that 11 Siberian tigers had died in a zoo in Shěnyáng.

It seemed like a double blow to conservation but in truth the incidents have nothing in common. The zoo in Shěnyáng is private and the cats were consistently underfed because of budget shortfalls. Though China's law makes killing a Siberian tiger punishable by death, property laws protect unscrupulous zoo owners in the case of negligence. There is no reason to think Siberian tigers (in captivity anyway) are in any danger because of such incidents. Breeding the cats is actually quite easy; reintroducing them to the forests they belong to is another story. The loss of the little cub was something the wild population could ill afford.

plays highlighting the principles of aviation, acoustics, transportation, energy and aeronautics. The museum can be reached either by taxi or by following the road west (left) about 4km after you get off the boat to the island.

Festivals & Events

The **Ice & Snow Festival** (冰雪节; Bīngxuě Jié; ☎8625 0068; admission to main area Y200) is Hā'ěrbīn's main claim to fame these days. Every January, Zhāolín Park (照林公园) and the banks of the Sōnghuā River, as well as Sun Island Park, become home to extraordinarily detailed, imaginative and downright wacky snow and ice sculptures. They range from huge recreations of iconic buildings, such as the Forbidden City and European cathedrals, to animals and interpretations of ancient legends. At night they're lit up with coloured lights to create a magical effect.

It might be mind-numbingly cold and the sun disappears mid-afternoon, but the festival, which also features figure-skating shows and a variety of winter sports, is Hā'ěrbīn's main tourist attraction – and prices jump accordingly. Officially, the festival gets going on 5 January and runs for a month, but it sometimes starts earlier and often lasts longer, weather permitting.

The main entrance is by the Flood Control Monument. Afterwards you can walk across the frozen Sōnghuā River to Sun Island Park to visit its ice sculptures.

Sleeping

The most convenient places to stay are along Zhongyang Dajie in Dàolǐqū district or in one of the many hotels that surround the train station. During the Ice and Snow Festival, expect hotel prices to go up by at least 20%.

Kazy International Youth Hostel HOSTEL **$**
(卡兹国际青年旅舍; Kǎzī Guójì Qīngnián Lǚshè; ☎8765 4211; www.snowtour.cn; dm/s/d shared bathroom Y40/60/100, d with bathroom Y120; 📶) This hostel has taken over the lower floors of the old Main Synagogue, giving it the largest and highest ceiling lobby of any hostel we've seen. Dorm rooms are bright and clean, but the singles and doubles in the garret with Star of David frame windows are a treat to stay in, even if (or maybe because) they lack aircon. Staff are friendly and a great source of travel information around the city and province. The hostel, with a laundry and a cafe, is popular with Chinese travellers.

Modern Hotel HOTEL $$$

(马迭尔宾馆; Mǎdié'ěr Bīnguǎn; ☎8488 4199; http://hotel.hrbmodern.com; 89 Zhongyang Dajie; 中央大街89号; s/d from Y680/980; ❄@≋) One of the more imposing buildings on Zhongyang Dajie, this 1906 construction still features some of its original marble, blond wood accents and art nouveau touches. Go for the Euro Standard rooms which are just Y100 more than the standard but almost twice the size.

All rooms include free broadband, and a breakfast buffet. Note that the entrance to the hotel is around the back.

Zhōngdà Hotel HOTEL $$

(中大大酒店; Zhōngdà Dàjiǔdiàn; ☎8463 8888; fax 8465 2888; 32-40 Zhongyang Dajie; 中央大街32-40号; d & tw Y198-298; ❄@) With a prime location on Zhongyang Dajie, and comfortable rooms flooded with light, this heritage hotel is your best midrange choice in Hā'ěrbīn. Corners rooms are the best, with large windows on two sides of the room, views over Zhongyang Dajie, free computers and large bathrooms. All rooms include free broadband and Chinese breakfast. The hotel is about one block up from the start of Zhongyang Dajie.

Běiběi Hotel HOTEL $$

(北北快捷宾馆; Běiběi Kuàijié Bīnguǎn; ☎8785 2222; www.beibeihotel.com; 10 Hongxing Jie; 红星街10号; s Y228, tw Y228-288; ❄@) Just off Zhongyang Dajie and almost opposite the Zhōngdà Hotel, the Běiběi's bright spic-and-span rooms have computers and big glass-walled bathrooms to please voyeurs.

Běiběi Hotel HOTEL $$

(北北大酒店; Běiběi Dàjiǔdiàn; ☎8257 0960; www.beibeihotel.com; 2 Chunshen Jie; 春申街2号; s Y128-168, tw Y168-228; ❄@) Just to the left of the bus station as you face it is another branch of Běiběi, a little more worn with traffic but a good deal if you need to be by the bus or train. The lowest singles go quickly but the nicest rooms are the twins for Y228 which have clean tiled bathrooms and their own computers.

Jīndì Bīnguǎn HOTEL $

(金地宾馆; ☎5551 7717; 261 Zhongyang Dajie; 中央大街261号; s Y120, tw Y160-180, tr Y288; ❄@) If you're looking for a river view on the cheap, then this is the place to come. The rooms are fairly spacious, and there's broadband available in some. The more expensive twins face the river and the triples come with a separate living room with a giant TV.

Though the address is on Zhongyang Dajie, turn right at the very end of that road before the park. Jīndì sits just beside the pricey Gloria Plaza Hotel, which glitters but is not truly gold.

Lóngyùn Hotel HOTEL $$

(龙运宾馆; Lóngyùn Bīnguǎn; ☎8283 0102; Huochezhan Zhanqian Guangchang; 火车站站前广场; s with shared bathroom Y158, d & tw Y308-328, tr Y388; ❄@) Next to the long-distance bus station and opposite the train station, this tower is a good choice if you're just passing through and want a bit more comfort than a usual train station hotel. Avoid the cramped, tatty singles without bathrooms and instead go for the nicer twins. The more expensive rooms come with computers. Rates include breakfast.

Little Fir International Youth Hostel HOSTEL $

(小杉树国际青年旅馆; Xiǎo Shānshù Guójì Qīngnián Lǚguǎn; ☎8664 6192; www.yhhrb.com, in Chinese; 83 Xuefu Lu; 学府路83号; dm/s/tr Y35/60/90, tw & d Y120; @) The dorm beds and doubles are a good deal at this HI affiliate but the location is very inconvenient unless you simply want to take advantage of the hostel's usual good deals on one- and two-day trips to the Yàbùlì Ski Resort (prices vary each year).

To get here take bus 11 from the bus stand to the far right as you exit the train station. In 20 minutes get off opposite the Second Hospital of Hā'ěrbīn Medical University (医大二院; Yīdà Èryuàn). Walk back for a couple of blocks and look for the hostel's sign.

Eating

Zhongyang Dajie and its side alleys are full of small restaurants and bakeries. Tongjiang Jie is also a good place to look for somewhere to eat and has an abundance of fruit stands.

Dōngfāng Jiǎozi Wáng DUMPLINGS $

(东方饺子王; Kingdom of Eastern Dumplings; dumpling plate Y2-20; ⏲10.30am-9.30pm; ▣) Dàolǐqū District (51 Zhongyang Dajie); train station area (72 Hongjun Jie) It's not just the cheap *jiǎozi* (饺子; dumplings) that are good at this always busy chain: there are plenty of tasty vegie dishes, too, and excellent fresh fruit drinks. The Hongjun Jie branch is a 10-minute walk southeast of the train station, next to the Overseas Chinese Hotel down the alley. Both branches have English menus if you can get the staff to understand you want one.

Cafe Russia 1914 RUSSIAN RESTAURANT/CAFE $$
(露西亚咖啡西餐厅; Lùxīyà kāfēi Xīcān Tīng; 57 Xitoudao Jie; dishes Y12-48; ⊙10am-midnight) Step back in time at this tranquil, ivy-covered teahouse-cum-restaurant and cafe. Black-and-white photos illustrating Hā'ěrbīn's Russian past line the walls, while the old school furniture and fireplace evoke a different era. The food is substantial Russian fare, such as borscht and *piroshki* (cabbage, potato and meat puffs). It serves Russian vodka, too.

The restaurant is off Zhongyang Dajie in a little courtyard. Look for the sign reading 'Russian Food and Tea'.

Bì Fēng Táng RESTAURANT $$
(避风塘; 185 Zhongyang Dajie; dishes Y12-38; ⊙7am-2am) A northern outpost of the popular Shànghǎi restaurant empire. Come here for delicate, southern-style dumplings, as well as rice noodles, clay pot dishes and excellent desserts. It's good for late-night munchies. Note that the restaurant address is the same as the Jin Gu Hotel, but it's around to the side across from Cafe Russia 1914.

TOP CHOICE **Dǐng Dǐng Xiāng** HOTPOT $$
(Hotpot Paradise; 鼎鼎香; 58 Jingwei Jie; dishes Y10-68; ⊙10.30am-11pm) In winter, Hā'ěrbīn and hotpot go together like strawberries and cream. This three-storey hotpot restaurant, which looks like a KTV palace, can get very pricey if you order some of the face-giving seafood and Japanese beef dishes, but you can also dine well on normal beef, lamb and seafood for a modest outlay. Just make sure you order the special sauces (from Y5) to accompany your hotpot.

During summer, the streets off Zhongyang Dajie come alive with open-air food stalls and beer gardens, where you can sip a Hāpí, the local beer, while chewing squid on a stick, or *yángròu chuàn* (lamb kebabs) and all the usual street snacks.

The year-round indoor **food market** (小吃城; xiǎochī chéng; 96 Zhongyang Dajie; ⊙8.30am-8pm) has stalls selling decent bread, smoked meats, sausages, wraps, fresh dishes, as well as nuts, cookies, fruits and sweets. It's a great place to stock up on food for a long bus or train ride or when you just want to have a meal in your own room.

Drinking & Entertainment

Hā'ěrbīn has the usual collection of karaoke TV (KTV) joints. If communal singing isn't your bag, there are a few bars on and off Zhongyang Dajie and Tiandi Lu. Zhongyang Dajie and Stalin Park also have beer gardens in the summer with cheap draft and plenty of snack food to enjoy as you watch sports on the big screens.

The flashy **Éluósī Jiǔbā** (Russian Disco bar; 俄罗斯酒吧; 112 Tiandi Lu) attracts a young crowd of Russians and locals.

Shopping

There's a distinctly martial-arts bent to some of the shops along **Zhongyang Dajie**, with imitation Russian and Chinese camouflage uniforms on sale alongside the sort of fearsome-looking knives you shouldn't attempt to take on a plane. But there are also department stores, boutiques and many Western clothes chains here. Many souvenir shops have Russian knickknacks worth a look at simply because you so seldom see them anywhere else.

Locals head to Dongdazhi Jie for their shopping needs, as well as the **Hóngbó Century Square** (红博世纪广场; Hóngbó Shìjì Guǎngchǎng), a huge subterranean shopping complex.

Information

There are ATMs all over town. Most large hotels will also change money. Most midrange and top end hotels have travel services that book tickets and arrange tours throughout the province.

Bank of China (中国银行; Zhōngguó Yínháng; Xi'Er Dao Jie) Has a 24-hour ATM and will cash travellers cheques. Easy to spot on a (right) side road as you walk up Zhongyang Dajie.

Civil Aviation Administration of China (CAAC; Zhōngguó Mínháng; 101 Zhongshan Lu) In the CAAC Hotel, for flight tickets and airport shuttle buses.

Harbin Modern Travel Company (哈尔滨马迭尔旅行社; Hā'ěrbīn Mǎdié'ěr Lǚxíngshè; www.hrbmodern.com; 89 Zhongyang Dajie) This travel agent (with some English-speaking staff) at Modern Hotel offers one- and two-day ski trips to Yàbùlì and can handle flight tickets to Mòhé.

Internet bar (网吧; wǎngbā; 32 Xiliu Dajie; per hr Y3; ⊙24hr) Off Zhongyang Dajie. Also several in and around the train station.

Public Security Bureau (PSB; 公安局; Gōng'ānjú; 26 Duan Jie; ⊙8.40am-noon & 1.30-4.30pm Mon-Fri)

Getting There & Away

Air

Harbin Taiping International Airport (www.hljairport.com/jichang_english/hrbairport.asp) has flights to domestic destinations:

Běijīng Y1050, one hour 50 minutes

Dàlián Y930, 1½ hours

Mòhé Y1740, 2½ hours, two flights daily (8.20am and 1pm)

Russia and South Korea are also popular routes from Hā'ěrbīn.

Bus

The main long-distance bus station is directly opposite the train station.

Chángchūn Y76, 3½ hours, hourly

Jílín Y50 to Y66, four hours, hourly

Mǔdānjiāng Y67, 4½ hours, every 30 minutes

Qíqíhā'ěr Y64, four hours, hourly

Wǔdàlián Chí Y70, six hours, three daily (7.30am, 10.30am and 2.30pm) When the new freeway opens in 2012, travel time should be reduced to two to three hours.

Yàbùlì Y39, 3½ hours, three daily (7.30am, 10am and 1.20pm)

Train

Hā'ěrbīn is a major rail transport hub with routes throughout the northeast and beyond, including daily services:

Běi'ān seat Y46 to Y76, five to seven hours

Běijīng seat/sleeper Y154/262, 10 to 15 hours

Chángchūn seat Y20 to Y57, 2½ to three hours

Dàlián seat/sleeper Y125/215, nine to 10 hours

Mòhé hard/soft sleeper Y244/382, 21 hours, one daily (9.55pm)

Mǔdānjiāng seat Y26 to Y46, 4½ to five hours

Qíqíhā'ěr Y22 to Y68, 2½ to four hours

Shěnyáng seat Y39 to Y67, five to six hours

Suífēnhé seat/sleeper Y67/130, 10 hours

There are also D class trains to Běijīng (seat Y387 to Y464, eight hours) and Shěnyáng (seat Y170 to Y204, four hours)

BORDER CROSSING: GETTING TO RUSSIA

The N23 train departs from Hā'ěrbīn to Vladivostok (Y642) via Suífēnhé every Wednesday night at 9pm, arriving in Vladivostok the following Friday at 8am (Russian time); in the opposite direction, the N24 leaves Vladivostok on Monday and Thursday.

Travellers on the Trans-Siberian Railway to or from Moscow can start or finish in Hā'ěrbīn (six days). Contact the **Hā'ěrbīn Railway International Travel Service** (哈尔滨铁道国际旅行社; Hā'ěrbīn Tiědào Guójì Lǚxíngshè; ☎5361 6717; www.ancn.net; Kunlun Hotel, 8 Tielu Jie) for information on travelling through to Russia.

Getting Around

To/From the Airport

Hā'ěrbīn's airport is 46km from the city centre. From the airport, shuttle buses (Y20) will drop you at the railway station or the CAAC office. To the airport, shuttles leave every 30 minutes from the CAAC office until 6.30pm. A taxi (Y100 to Y125) will take 45 minutes to an hour.

Public Transport

Buses 101 and 103 run from the train station to Shangzhi Dajie, dropping you off at the north end of Zhongyang Dajie (the old street). Buses leave from a stop across the road and to the left as you exit the train station (where Chunshen Jie and Hongjun Jie meet).

There have been plans for a subway for some time. Work resumed in 2010 but there is no current deadline for opening.

Taxi

Taxis are fairly plentiful though they fill up quickly when it's raining. Taxi flag fall is Y8.

Around Hā'ěrbīn

The biggest ski resort in China and the training centre for the Chinese ski team, **Yàbùlì Ski Resort** (亚布力滑雪中心; Yàbùlì Huáxuě Zhōngxīn; www.yabuliski.com), 200km southeast of Hā'ěrbīn, has runs ranging from beginner to advanced, and is divided into competitive and leisure areas. Snow permitting, the ski season lasts from December through March. You can cross-country ski, snowboard and toboggan here, too.

Travel agencies and some hotels in Hā'ěrbīn offer ski packages that include transport, ski passes, equipment and clothing rental and accommodation (ranging from Y600 to Y2000). One-day trips have become more expensive as lift tickets were increased after a substantial upgrading of the facilities in 2009. In 2010 they were around Y400 per day, which gave you a couple of hours' skiing.

If you want to head up on your own, buses to Yàbùlì village depart from Hā'ěrbīn (Y39, three hours, 7.30am, 10am, 1.20pm). Minibuses and taxis take you the rest of the way to the ski resort.

There are also trains from Hā'ěrbīn (seat Y30 to Y48, three to four hours), including a special 'skiing' train that goes to the new Yàbùlì Nán station just at the base of the resort area. You'll probably need to book tickets for the latter through an agent.

Trains and buses are very limited from Mǔdānjiāng (Y10 to Y24, two hours, 5.50am and 6.10am).

Mǔdānjiāng 牡丹江

☎0453 / POP 850,000

A nondescript city surrounded by some lovely countryside, Mǔdānjiāng is the jumping-off point for nearby Jìngpò Hú (Mirror Lake) and the Underground Forest. Taiping Jie is the main drag in town and runs directly south of the train station.

Sleeping & Eating

For higher-end hotels, head up Taiping Jie. There are plenty of cheap restaurants in the alleys off Qixing Jie which intersects with Taiping Jie half a kilometre up from the train station. Dongyitiao Lu (off Qixing Jie) is a lively pedestrian-only street with a wide range of BBQ, noodle and snack venues open in the evening.

Kǎijié Bīnguǎn HOTEL $$
(凯捷宾馆; ☎893 8218; 128 Guanghua Jie; 光花街138号; d Y238-288, 40% discounts usual; ❄@) Rooms are massive, though sparely furnished, and come with free broadband. Unless you really need a bit of luxury they should be fine for a night or two. The hotel is almost directly across from the train station on the far right of the row of buildings set back from a park.

Mǔdānjiāng Fàndiàn HOTEL $
(牡丹江饭店; ☎692 5833; 128 Guanghua Jie; 光花街128号; d without bathroom Y60-100, r with bathroom Y120-280; ❄) Consider these run-down but reasonably clean rooms only if you need the cheapest option. Otherwise, better deals are around if you are willing to pay more than Y100 for a room. To reach the hotel, cross the road in front of the train station, turn left and walk one block.

Shuānglóng Jiǎozi Wáng DUMPLINGS $$
(双龙饺子王; cnr Qixing Jie & Taiping Jie; dishes Y6-28) There's a wide selection of *jiǎozi* (饺子; dumplings), as well as the usual Dōngběi classics. As you turn left off Taiping, Jie Shuānglóng is the big glass building on the right. There's an English sign out front and a partial picture menu to help you order.

Information

Bank of China (中国银行; Zhōngguó Yínháng; Taiping Lu) This huge branch, two blocks up from the train station, will cash travellers cheques and has a 24-hour ATM.

China International Travel Service (CITS; 中国国际旅行社; Zhōngguó Guójì Lǚxíngshè; 34 Jingfu Jie; ⏲8am-5pm Mon-Fri) For daily tours to Jìngpò Hu (Y300) call one or two days beforehand to make a reservation.

Getting There & Away

Long-distance buses arrive and depart from in front of the train station.

Mǔdānjiāng has rail connections to the following places:

Dōngjīng Y4.50, 1¼ hours

Hā'ěrbīn Y87, 4½ hours, frequent services

Suífēnhé Y27, four to five hours

Yàbùlì Y10 to Y24, two hours, two daily (5.50am and 6.10am)

Around Mǔdānjiāng

JÌNGPÒ HÚ

Formed on the bend of the Mǔdān River 5000 years ago by the falling lava of five volcanic explosions, **Jìngpò Hú** (镜泊湖; Mirror Lake; www.jinpohu.com.cn; admission Y80), 110km south of Mǔdānjiāng, gets its name from the unusually clear reflections of the surrounding lush green forest in its pristine blue water.

Hugely popular in the summer with Chinese day trippers who come to paddle or picnic by the lakeside, it's a pleasant spot if you hike along the lake and escape the crowds. Alternatively, ferries (Y80 to Y100 one way) make leisurely tours of the lake.

Sights

Diàoshuǐlóu Waterfall WATERFALL
(吊水楼瀑布; Diàoshuǐlóu Pùbù) One of the area's biggest attractions is this fall with a 12m-drop and 300m span. In the rainy season when Diàoshuǐlóu is in full throat, it's a spectacular raging beauty, but during the summer it's little more than a drizzle.

CRANE COUNTRY

Northeastern China is home to several nature reserves established to protect endangered species of wild cranes. **Zhālóng Nature Reserve** (扎龙自然保护区; Zhālóng Zìrán Bǎohùqū) near Qíqíhā'ěr is the most accessible and most visited of these sanctuaries. The reserve is home to some 260 bird species, including several types of rare cranes. Four of the species that migrate here are on the endangered list: the extremely rare red-crowned crane, the white-naped crane, the Siberian crane and the hooded crane.

The reserve comprises some 2100 sq km of wetlands that are on a bird migration path extending from the Russian Arctic down into Southeast Asia. Hundreds of birds arrive from April to May, rear their young from June to August and depart from September to October. Unfortunately, a significant percentage of the birds you can see live in zoolike cages and are released once a day so that visitors can take photos.

The best time to visit Zhālóng is in spring. In summer the mosquitoes can be more plentiful than the birds – take repellent!

The **Xiànghǎi National Nature Reserve** (向海; Xiànghǎi Guójiā Zìrán Bǎohùqū), 310km west of Chángchūn in Jílín province, is on the migration path for Siberian cranes, and the rare red-crowned, white-naped and demoiselle cranes breed here. More than 160 bird species, including several of these cranes, have been identified at the **Horqin National Nature Reserve** (科尔沁; Kērqìn Guójiā Zìrán Bǎohùqū), which borders Xianghai in Inner Mongolia. The **Mòmògé National Nature Reserve** (莫莫格; Mòmògé Guójiā Zìrán Bǎohùqū) in northern Jílín province is also an important wetlands area and bird breeding site.

For more information about China's crane population and these nature reserves, contact the **International Crane Foundation** (www.savingcranes.org) or see the website of the **Siberian Crane Wetland Project** (www.scwp.info).

You can walk to the waterfall from the north-gate entrance in about 10 minutes. Just stay on the main road and follow the English signs.

Underground Forest SCENIC AREA
(地下森林; Dìxià Sēnlín; admission Y40) Despite its name, the Underground Forest isn't below the earth; instead it has grown within the craters of volcanoes that erupted some 10,000 years ago. Hiking around the thick pine forest and several of the 10 craters takes about an hour.

The forest is 50km from Jìngpò Hú. Most day tours to the lake include it on their itinerary; check before you set out. Otherwise, you have to take a bus from the north gate of Jìngpò (one hour), which is not really viable if you only have a day at the lake.

Sleeping & Eating

It's pleasant to spend the night in the park and enjoy the lake when the crowds return to their hotels in Mǔdānjiāng. Expect to pay between Y100 and Y400 a night for a room in the park.

Jìngpò Hú Shānzhuāng Jiǔdiàn HOTEL $$
(镜泊湖山庄酒店; ☎627 0039, 139 0483 9459; r Y200-300) One place to try is this hotel which is just back from the water at the first lakeside drop-off point for the shuttle buses. There's a small beach here you can swim off. The hotel's restaurant has decent food if a little overpriced.

Getting There & Away

The easiest way to get to Jìngpò Hú is on the one-day tours run by CITS and other travel agencies in Mǔdānjiāng. Some hotels also run trips. Unless you are going to stay overnight, it really isn't worth all the trouble of getting there on your own.

If you want to head out here under your own steam, first get to dusty Dōngjīng. Buses to Dōngjīng (Y12, 1½ hours, frequent) leave from Mǔdānjiāng's local bus station (客车站; kè chēzhàn); take a taxi here (Y6). Cramped minibuses (Y8, 40 to 60 minutes) to the lake leave from outside Dōngjīng train station about 5km down the road from where the bus from Mǔdānjiāng drops you off. There are sometimes direct buses back to Mǔdānjiāng from the lake in the afternoon (Y20).

Getting Around

The ticket centre for the lake is at the North Gate (Běimén). From here walk about five minutes to a parking lot where there are shuttle buses to take you to the lake and other sights (Y12 per ride). Diàoshuǐlóu Waterfall is just behind this lot.

Wǔdàlián Chí 五大连池

☎0456

Formed by a series of volcanic eruptions, the Wǔdàlián Chí nature reserve boasts one of China's most mesmerising landscapes. It's a genuine Lost World with vast fields of hardened lava, rivers of basalt, volcanic peaks, azure lakes and the odd little reed-lined pond. You could spend days exploring.

The last time the volcanoes erupted was 1720 and the lava flow blocked the nearby North River (Běi Hé), forming the series of five interconnected lakes that give the area its name. Wǔdàlián Chí is about 250km northwest of Hā'ěrbīn, and in addition to the volcanic landscape is home to mineral springs that draw busloads of Chinese and Russian tourists to slurp the allegedly curative waters. So many Russians roll up that the town's street signs are in both Chinese and Russian.

Except there's no real town here, just a long pleasant tree-lined street called Yaoquan Lu. Everything you want is on a section that runs west of the bus station. The intersection of Yaoquan Lu and Shilong Lu (about 3km to 4km from the bus stop) is the main crossroad and smack in the middle of the hotel area. Taxis make the trip from the bus station to the hotel area for Y5.

It's only really viable to visit Wǔdàlián Chí between May and October.

Sights & Activities

A bike would be the perfect way to take in the sights in this flat landscape but no one seems to be renting. For now you must hire a taxi and expect to pay around Y120 to Y200 for a day-long loop taking in the lakes, volcanoes and caves.

Lǎohēi Shān SCENIC AREA

(老黑山; admission Y80 plus Y25 shuttle fee; ⏲7.30am-6pm May-Oct; 👪) It's a mostly uphill 1km stair climb to the summit of Lǎohēi Mountain, one of the area's 14 volcanoes. From the lip of the crater you will have panoramic views of the lakes and other volcanoes.

Taxis drop you at the ticket booth (though you could walk here from Wǔdàlián Chí in two hours). From here park shuttle buses take you to a lot at the start of the trail. To the left is the trail up the mountain, to the right a boardwalk to the aptly named **Shí Hǎi** (石海; Stone Sea), a magnificent lava field.

Back in the parking lot smaller green shuttle buses take you to **Huǒshāo Shān** (火烧山) and the end of the road at another collection of weirdly shaped lava stones. This stretch is one of Wǔdàlián Chí's most enchanting, with lava rock rivers, **birch forests**, grassy fields, ponds and more wide stretches of lava fields. It's about 5km from the start to the end, meaning you could walk it back but be careful as the shuttle drivers go fast.

Lóngmén 'Stone Village' SCENIC AREA

(龙门后塞奇观观光区; Lóngmén Hòusài Qíguān Guānguāngqū; admission Y50; ⏲7.30am-6pm May-Oct; 👪) At this impressive lava field, you walk through a forest of white and black birch trees on a network of boardwalks, with the lava rocks stretching away in the distance on either side.

Ice Caves CAVES

(熔岩冰洞; Róngyán Bīngdòng; admission Y30; ⏲7.30am-6pm May-Oct; 👪) At the Lava Ice Cavern, elaborate ice sculptures, including temples and a Buddha lit by coloured lights, are on show in a chilly year-round -5°C environment. The nearby **Lava Snow Cavern** (熔岩雪洞; Róngyán Xuědòng; admission Y30; ⏲7.30am-6pm) has more of the same, although it's not as good. A ticket to one of the caverns will get you into the other. Rent a warm coat (Y5) if you don't have your own.

Sleeping & Eating

The following hotels are all on Yaoquan Lu, the main east–west drag. From October to May most places shut, while during the summer months you need to book in advance to avoid getting stranded without a room.

At the time of writing, Wǔdàlián Chí Shì (the town 20km away) was seeing some work done to improve its look as the new highway from Hā'ěrbīn was being run through. Seeing as you can't explore Wǔdàlián Chí without a taxi, this town might be a viable option for sleeping in the future. The new highway may also make it possible to visit from Hā'ěrbīn as a day trip.

Wǔdàlián Chí caters to group tours, and single travellers who aren't staying at a hotel with a restaurant will have to go for the local restaurants just south of the main intersection at Yaoquan and Shilong Lu. There are two dozen greasy-spoon choices (dishes Y5 to Y48), largely serving the five types of local fish the area is famous for. Of course, you can also get cheap *jiǎozi* (dumplings) and BBQ. Several grocery stores sell fruit and imported snacks including real chocolate.

Gōngrén Liáoyǎngyuàn HOTEL **$$**
(Workers Sanatorium; 工人疗养院; ☎722 1569; tw Y280-480; ❄@) This cavernous complex with long corridors reminiscent of *The Shining* is popular with Russian tourists. The parklike grounds are pleasant and the restaurant, which serves both Chinese and Russian food, is decent value (but will only serve guests).

Dàqìng Yóutián Liáoyǎngyuàn HOTEL **$$**
(大庆油田疗养院; ☎729 6333; tw Y280-380; ⏲May-Sep; ❄) Across the road from the Gōngrén Liáoyǎngyuàn, this is a more modern option with bright, clean rooms and friendly staff.

Information

There's a 24-hour **internet cafe** (per hr Y3) one block south of Yaoquan Lu on Shilong Lu, and a visitor centre between the bus station and hotel area with good English maps of the area.

There are no banks or ATMs accepting foreign cards in Wǔdàlián Chí.

Getting There & Away

You have a few options to get here. When the new freeway opens in 2012, driving times from Hā'ěrbīn should be two to three hours.

Bus

There are buses direct from Hā'ěrbīn (Y70, six hours, 7.30am, 10.30am and 2.30pm). Buses from Hā'ěrbīn (Y60, 5½ hours) via Běi'ān travel at 7am, 8.30am, 12.30pm, 3pm and 4pm. There are also several daily trains from Hā'ěrbīn (Y25, 5½ to six hours) via Běi'ān.

Běi'ān's bus station is one block straight ahead from the train station up the main road. At Běi'ān buses depart for Wǔdàlián Chí (Y15, 1½ hours) at 5.40am, 10am, 12.40pm, 1.40pm and 2.40pm.

After 2.40pm you can catch a bus on the street to Wǔdàlián Chí Shì (not the same as Wǔdàlián Chí), where taxis will take you the rest of the way for Y40.

Going the other way, buses leave for Hā'ěrbīn (Y60 to Y93, 5am and 8.10am) and Hēihé (Y51, 7.10am) .There are also buses to Běi'ān if you want to catch a train.

Russian Borderlands

Much of the northeastern border between China and Siberia follows the Black Dragon River (Hēilóng Jiāng), known to the Russians as the Amur River. Along the border it's possible to see Siberian forests and dwindling settlements of northern minorities, such as the Daur, Ewenki, Hezhen and Oroqen.

At the time of writing, you didn't need permits to visit any areas along the border but it would be good to check with the PSB in Hā'ěrbīn nonetheless.

Major towns in the far north include Mòhé and Hēihé, a popular shopping destination for people in the province. On the eastern border, Suífēnhé is a gateway to Vladivostok.

MÒHÉ 漠河

China's a big place, if you haven't noticed. And that vastness contains a multitude of landscapes, ecosystems and climates. China's northernmost town, Mòhé, standing amidst spindly pine forests and vast bogs, holds the record for the lowest plunge of the thermometer: -52.3°C, recorded in 1956. That same day in the southern extreme at Sānyà, a tropical beach paradise of azure waters and coconut palms, the temperature was likely in the high 20s.

Mòhé is one of China's most fascinating outliers, sharing not just a border with Russia, but architecture as well.

Sights & Activities

Russian Architecture STREETS
In 1985, Mòhé burned to the ground in a raging forest fire. When it came time for rebuilding, a curious decision was made: given the town's proximity to Russia, and Hēilóngjiāng's long close relations with that country, the main streets would be rebuilt in an imperial-era style with spired domes, pillared entrances and facades with rows of narrow windows. For an overview of the town climb, the stairs at the start of Zhenxing Jie to the **North Pole Star Park** (北极星公园; Běijí Xīng Gōngyuán).

North Polar Pine Trees Park PARK
(北极松苑; Běijí Sōngyuàn) This small forest park in the dead centre of town is locally famous for having somehow survived the big fire of 1985. To visitors, the rare two-coloured pines will be of more interest. Brown on the bottom and red-rust on the

top half, these are like no trees you've seen before. And despite the thin trunks, most pines are hundreds of years old; the growing season up here is very short!

Festivals

In mid-June, the sun is visible for as long as 22 hours and the annual **Festival of Aurora Borealis** (北极光节; Běijíguāng Jié), held from 15 to 25 June, attracts visitors hoping to see the spectacular northern lights after sunset. Oddly, this is one of the few times you can see the lights according to locals. Later in the summer, when there are more hours of darkness, the lights don't appear.

Sleeping & Eating

At the time of writing, foreign travellers faced restrictions on where they could stay in Mòhé. Check in at the PSB when you arrive to find out where is legal. You can try to stay in an unapproved hotel, but with the police station on the main road and foreign travellers a rarity, it's difficult to escape notice, as we found out the hard way.

For eating head to **Fanrong Xiang**. From the North Pole Star Park, head up Zhenxing Jie two blocks and turn right. There are half a dozen cheap noodle shops (dishes Y5 to Y18) and most have picture menus on the walls. The alley just prior to Fanrong Xiang is the town's **fruit street** with BBQ joints further down. In summer look for wild blueberries for sale as well as some of the oddest-looking mushrooms you've ever seen.

Information

The main street in town is Zhenxing Jie, where you'll find an **ICBC** (中国工商银行; Zhōnguó Gōngshāng Yínháng) with a 24-hour ATM (though you're still advised to bring whatever money you might need) as well as the local **Public Security Bureau** (PSB; 公安局; Gōng'ānjú).

Getting There & Away

You can fly to Mòhé's new airport from Hā'ěrbīn (Y1740, 2½ hours). There are usually two flights a day and the morning flight is cheaper. From the airport to the centre of Mòhé by taxi is Y20.

From Hā'ěrbīn one train (hard/soft sleeper Y237/382) runs daily at 9.55pm, arriving in Mòhé at 6.30pm the next day. Heading back, the train leaves at 7.27pm, arriving in Hā'ěrbīn at 2.20pm.

Mòhé's train station is about 2km from the centre of town. A taxi will cost Y10.

BĚIJÍCŪN (NORTH POLE VILLAGE) 北极村

Even more northerly than Mòhé is this sprawling **village/recreation area** (admission Y60, shuttle bus Y20) on the very banks of the Hēilóng Jiāng River separating China and Russia. There's nowhere to go but back south here and one house has even been labelled **China No 1** (中国最北一家; ie China's furthest north house).

Běijícūn covers an area of forest, meadowland and bog, with the occasional hamlet, log cabin or Russian-style structure dotting the pretty surroundings. Even taking the shuttle bus between areas and sights will take half a day. If you wish to spend the night, ask your driver about homestays.

Sights

Sandbar

(北极沙洲; Běijí Shāzhōu) This peaceful meadowland bordering the Hēilóng Jiāng River is the end of the line. Boardwalks run across the fields at Sandbar and at the far end a **map of China** has been etched into a square. Step up on the podium and you are at the most northerly point one can be within 9,671,018 sq km of the earth's surface. It's kitschy but profound at the same time and few other countries could pull something like this off at all. For pure kitsch look for the giant **dragon chop** (金鸡之冠; Jīnjī Zhī Guàn) on a tripod.

Prostitutes Graveyard GRAVEYARD

(胭脂沟妓女坟; Yānzhī Gōu Jìnǔ Fén) Outside Běijícūn, about a 30-minute drive down a side road to the **source of the Hēilóng Jiāng River** (黑龙江源头; Hēilóngjiāng Yuántóu) is a quiet glade. Within is the Prostitutes Graveyard, the burial mounds of dozens of destitute women who worked as prostitutes during Mòhé's gold rush in the late 19th century. It's a sombre place to say the least and more so as a small **museum** at the start contains black-and-white photographs of some of the women, as well as articles of clothing and jewellery once belonging to them.

Getting There & Away

Taxis from Mòhé to Běijícūn charge Y240 return, Y200 one way.

There are two morning buses (Y15, two hours) from Mòhé. Facing the North Pole Park head left, walk one block to Shangmao Lu and turn left. The station (87 Shangmao Lu) is on the right.

Shānxī

POPULATION: 35 MILLION

Includes »

Best Place to Eat

» Tàiyuán Noodle House (p347)

Best Places to Stay

» Jing's Residence (p351)

» Harmony Guesthouse (p351)

» Fóyuán Lóu (p345)

Why Go?

Waist-deep in handsome history, mountainous Shānxī (山西) meets virtually all your China travel expectations – and throws in a few surprises. If you only visited Píngyáo and jetted home, you might assume China was bursting with picture-perfect ancient walled settlements oozing character and charm from each nook and adorable cranny. For sure, basing yourself here and jumping to Píngyáo's surrounding sights is practically all you need, with time-worn temples, fastidiously arranged Qing-dynasty courtyard architecture and some of the warmest people in the Middle Kingdom. The mountain fastness of Wǔtái Shān, however, reveals Shānxī's other great source of magic, a Buddhist leaning that fashions some magnificent monastic architecture, a disposition further concentrated in the astonishing Buddhist cave sculpture at Yúngāng. The good-looking portrait is rounded out by the cities of Dàtóng and Tàiyuán, where history and modernity reach an engaging balance.

When to Go

Dàtóng

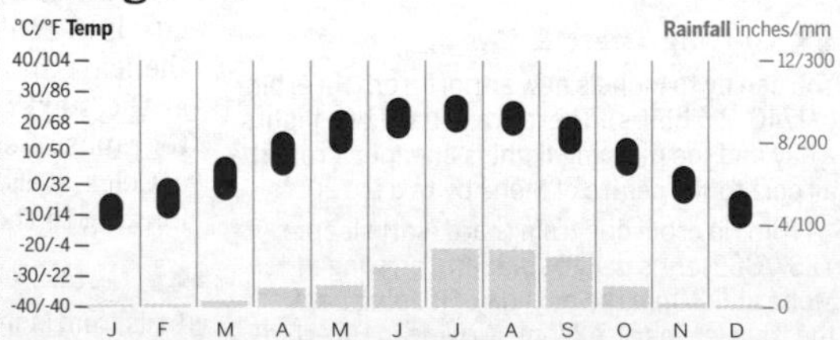

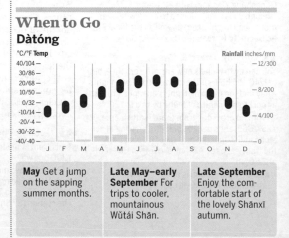

May Get a jump on the sapping summer months.

Late May–early September For trips to cooler, mountainous Wǔtái Shān.

Late September Enjoy the comfortable start of the lovely Shānxī autumn.

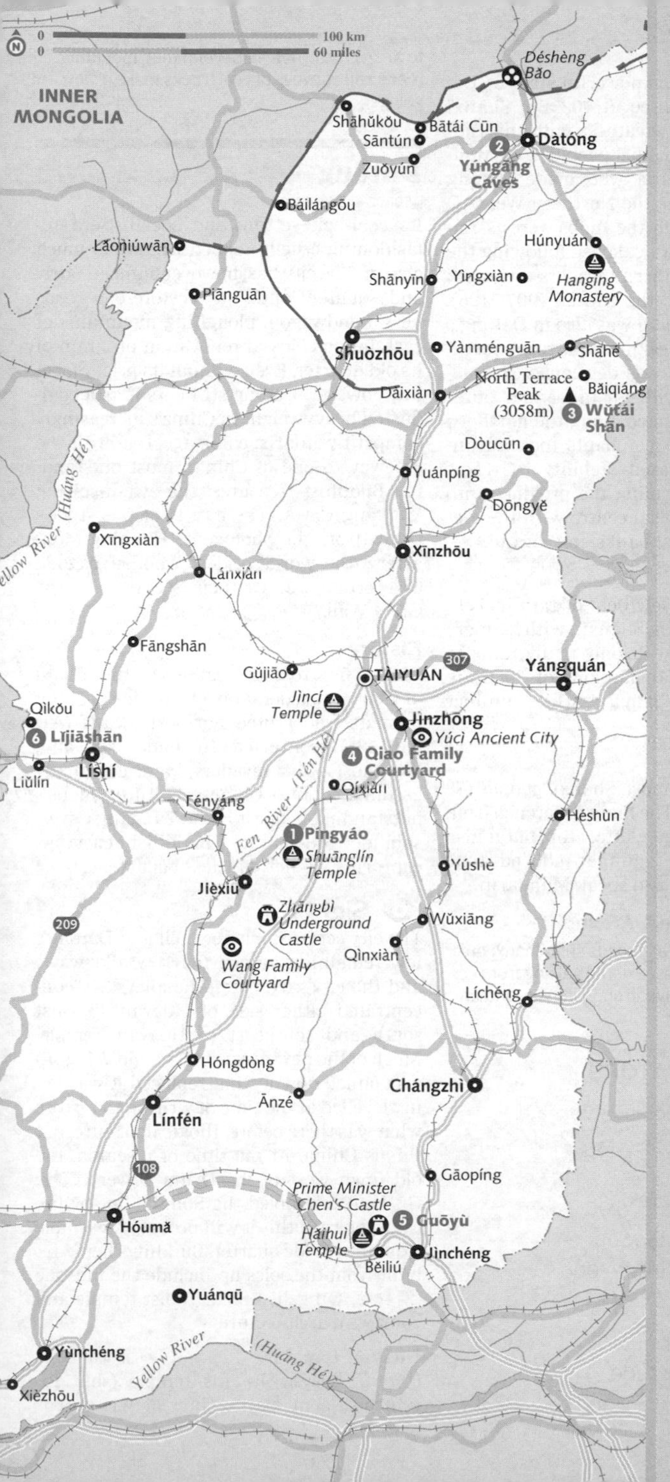

Shānxī Highlights

1. Fall head over heels for time-warped **Píngyáo** (p349)
2. Discover the indescribable beauty of the Buddhist statues at the **Yúngāng Caves** (p341)
3. Hang up your traveller's hat in the monastic enclave of **Wǔtái Shān** (p343)
4. Explore some of China's best-preserved courtyard architecture at the **Qiao Family Courtyard** (p349)
5. Journey to the still-inhabited ancient walled village of **Guōyù** (p356) in Shānxī's remote southeast
6. Burrow your way into Shānxī's past with an overnight stay in the ancient cave village of **Lǐjiāshān** (p354)

History

Though home to the powerful state of Jin, which split into three in 403 BC, Shānxī only really rose to greatness with the Tuoba, a clan of the Xianbei people from Mongolia and Manchuria who made Dàtóng their capital during the Northern Wei (AD 386–534). Eventually the Tuoba were assimilated, but as China weakened following the Tang collapse, northern invaders returned; most notable were the Khitan (907–1125), whose western capital was also in Dàtóng.

After the Ming regained control of northern China, Shānxī was developed as a defensive outpost, with an inner and outer Great Wall constructed along the northern boundaries. Local merchants took advantage of the increased stability to trade, eventually transforming the province into the country's financial centre with the creation of China's first banks, in Píngyáo.

Climate

Dry as dust, precisely 0cm of rain in February is normal in Shānxī, with a mere 35cm of rain a year. It only really rains in July (just 12cm). Tàiyuán lows of -10°C are not uncommon in January, while summer highs exceed 30°C.

Language

Jin is spoken by most Shānxī people (45 million speakers). The main difference from Mandarin is its final glottal stop, but it also features complex grammar-induced tone shifts. Most locals also speak Mandarin.

Getting There & Around

Modern railway lines and roads split Shānxī on a northeast–southwest axis, so getting from Běijīng to Dàtóng, Tàiyuán and Píngyáo, and on to Xī'ān is no problem. Beyond that, mountain roads and convoys of coal trucks make it slow going.

PRICE INDICATORS

The following price indicators are used in this chapter:

Sleeping

$	less than Y200
$$	Y200 to Y500
$$$	more than Y500

Eating

$	less than Y40
$$	Y40 to Y100
$$$	more than Y100

Dàtóng 大同

0352 / POP 1.1 MILLION

Its coal-belt setting and socialist-era refashioning cruelly robbed Dàtóng of much charm. The city has, however, jumped fairly and squarely onto the 'restore-our-greatness' bandwagon, ploughing mountains of cash into a colossal renovation program of its old quarter. Even without its pricey facelift, however, Dàtóng still cuts it as a coal-dusted heavyweight in China's increasingly competitive tourist challenge. Dàtóng is the gateway to one of China's most outstanding Buddhist treasures: the awe-inspiring Yúngāng Caves. The city is also a stone's throw from the photogenic Hanging Monastery, the world's oldest wooden pagoda and crumbling earthen sections of the Great Wall.

History

Dàtóng first rose to greatness as the capital of Tuoba, a federation of Turkic-speaking nomads who united northern China (AD 386–534), converted to Buddhism and, like most other invaders, were eventually assimilated into Chinese culture. Tuoba's outstanding bequest is the Yúngāng Caves, sublime 5th-century Buddhist carvings capturing a quiet, timeless beauty.

Sights

The city centre is where you'll find Dàtóng's few remaining *hútòng* (narrow alleyways) and the city's old core. The alleys are concentrated either side of Huayan Jie, just south and southeast of Huáyán Temple. Much of the **old town** (老城区; *lǎochéngqū*) was pulled down; what replaced it was being levelled at the time of writing to restore what was there before. Illogical for sure, but this is China. At the time of research, the old town west of the Drum Tower (鼓楼; Gǔ Lóu) resembled the Somme but by the time you read this it will probably resemble a quaint ye olde quarter. Buildings being rebuilt from the soles up include the mosque (清真寺; Qīngzhēn Sì), a Taoist temple and courtyard architecture.

Huáyán Temple BUDDHIST TEMPLE

(华严寺; Huáyán Sì) This temple (shut for refurbishment at the time of writing) is divided into two separate complexes, one of which is an active monastery (upper temple), while the other is a museum (lower temple). Built by the Khitan during the Liao dynasty (AD 907–1125), the temple faces east, not south (it's said the Khitan were sun worshippers).

Dating to 1140, the impressive main hall of the **upper temple** (上华严寺; Shàng Huáyán Sì; Huayansi Jie; admission Y20; ⌚8am-6pm summer, to 5.30pm winter) is one of the largest Buddhist halls in China, with Ming statues and Qing murals within. The rear hall of the **lower temple** (下华严寺; Xià Huáyán Sì; Huayansi Jie; admission Y20; ⌚8am-6pm summer, to 5.30pm winter) is the oldest building in Dàtóng (1038), containing some remarkable Liao-dynasty wooden sculptures. Side halls contain assorted relics from the Wei, Liao and Jin dynasties.

Take bus 4 (Y1) from the train station to get here.

Dàtóng

Nine Dragon Screen — ANCIENT SITE

(九龙壁; Jiǔlóng Bì; Da Dongjie; admission Y10; ⌚8am-6pm) With its nine beautiful multicoloured coiling dragons, this 45.5m long, 8m high and 2m thick Ming-dynasty spirit wall was built in 1392. It's the largest glazed-tile wall in China and is an amazing sight; the palace it once protected burnt down years ago.

Shànhuà Temple — BUDDHIST TEMPLE

(善化寺; Shànhuà Sì; Nansi Jie; admission Y20; ⌚8am-6pm summer, 8.30am-5.30pm winter) This temple was originally built in 713; the current temple is a Jin rebuild. The grandiose wooden-bracketed rear hall contains five beautiful central Buddhas and expressive statues of celestial generals in the wings.

FREE Planning Exhibition Hall — MUSEUM

Decorated with Maoist slogans, the vast 1950s socialist edifice north of Hóngqí Guǎngchǎng (红旗广场; Red Flag Sq) was designed around the same time as the Great Hall of the People (p55) in Běijīng. Its **exhibition hall** (大同规划展览馆; Dátóng Guīhuà Zhǎnlǎnguǎn; ⌚9am-5pm Tue-Sun) presents Dátóng's future guise in a huge illuminated diorama, but it's more interesting to look at the photos of old Dátóng. The vast building also houses the library and the town museum.

Tours

China International Travel Service (see p340) offers various day trips with an English-speaking guide for Y100 (transport only) or Y225 (transport, lunch and

Dàtóng

entrance tickets). Mr Gao, the manager of the train station branch, speaks excellent English and is very helpful.

Sleeping

Most hotels are situated around the train station, although there are a couple in the city centre.

TOP CHOICE **Tóngtiě Bīnguǎn** HOTEL $$
(同铁宾馆; ☎713 0768; 15 Zhanbei Jie; 站北街15号; s/d/ste Y280/280/398, discounts of 30%; ❄) There are excellent, spacious and modern rooms with traditional furnishings and elegant touches at this smart, fantastic-value hotel north of the train station. Rooms are clean and well kept, and shower rooms come with heat lamps.

Fēitiān Hotel HOTEL $
(飞天宾馆; Fēitiān Bīnguǎn; ☎281 5117; 1 Zhanqian Jie; 站前街1号; dm/tw/tr Y35/160/280, discounts of 30%; ❄) Right by the train station, this old favourite is a comfortable budget choice but was shut for a refit at the time of writing. Pre-refit staff could not speak English but were used to dealing with foreigners.

Garden Hotel HOTEL $$$
(花园大饭店; Huāyuán Dàfàndiàn; ☎586 5825; www.huayuanhotel.com.cn; 59 Da Nanjie; 大南街59号; d & tw Y880-1180, discounts of 25%; ❄@) Impeccable rooms at this intimate hotel feature goose-down quilts, carved pear-wood bed frames, reproduction antique furnishings and lovely bathrooms. It has a lovely atrium, Latin American and Chinese restaurants plus excellent staff; and a Bank of China ATM.

Eating

The local treat is *shāomài* (烧麦; Y3.50), a steamed pork dumpling with a crinkled top that's dipped in Shānxī vinegar. Most places that sell ordinary dumplings also do *shāomài*. Look for the bamboo basket steamers.

There are plenty of restaurants around the train station.

Tónghé Dàfàndiàn CHINESE $
(同和大饭店; Zhanqian Jie; meals Y20-30; ⏲10am-2pm & 5-9pm; 📖) This popular, bright and cheery spot next to the Hongqi Hotel is perfect for a meal before catching the train. Its big round tables may look intimidating, but solo diners can still take a seat; try the Shānxī fried noodles (Y12), the pancake with meat filling (Y3.50), the tasty stir-fried mutton slices with Chinese onion, or the egg soup (Y8).

Yǒnghé Fast Food CHINESE FAST FOOD $
(永和快餐; Yǒnghé Kuàicān; Xiao Nanjie; meals Y20; ⏲6.50-9.30am & 11am-10pm; 📖) Next to the more expensive Yonghe Chinese Food Hall just north of the city wall, this is a handy place for a quick meal. Tick off a form and hand it to the waitress. Try the *málà niúròu miàn* (麻辣牛肉面; Y12), a spicy steaming bowl of beef noodles and a fried egg (煎蛋; *jiāndàn;* Y1), or a *xiāngjiān cōngyóu bǐng* (香煎葱油饼; deep-fried pancake; Y3). Yanjing beer comes by the pint (Y7). Photo menu at the service desk.

Information

Bank of China (中国银行; Zhōngguó Yínháng; Xiao Nanjie) ATM; for travellers cheques, you need the Yingbin Xilu branch (open 8am to noon and 2.30pm to 6pm weekdays).

China Construction Bank (中国建设银行; Zhōngguó Jiànshè Yínháng; Xinjian Beilu) ATM near the train station; another branch is by Red Flag Sq.

China International Travel Service (CITS; 中国国际旅行社; Zhōngguó Guójì Lǚxíngshè; ☎712 4882, 130 0808 8454; Tàijiā Hotel, 泰佳宾馆; ⏲6.30am-6.30pm) Helpful tourist information branch in the Tàijiā Hotel just north of the train station.

China Post (中国邮政; Zhōngguó Yóuzhèng; cnr Da Xijie & Xinjian Nanlu; ⏲8am-6.30pm) South of Red Flag Sq; there's another branch near the train station.

Dōngfāng Internet Cafe (东方网络; Dōngfāng Wǎngluò; 6th fl, cnr Qingyuan Jie & Shitou Xiang; per hr Y3; ⏲24hr) Take the crummy lift to the 6th floor then go through the noisy amusement arcade to the end.

Internet cafe (网吧; wǎngbā; Xinjian Beilu; per hr Y3; ⏲24hr) West of Fēitiān Hotel.

Mènglàng Internet Cafe (梦浪网吧; Mènglàng Wǎngbā; Da Beijie; per hr Y2; ⏲24hr)

Public Security Bureau Entry & Exit Office (PSB; 公安局出入境接待处; Gōng'ānjú Chūrùjìng Jiēdàichù; Weidu Dadao; ⏲9am-noon & 3-5.30pm Mon-Fri)

Getting There & Away

Air

Located 20km east of the city, Dàtóng's small airport has flights to Běijīng (Y400), Shànghǎi (Y1450), Hǎinán Island (Y2500) and Guǎngzhōu (Y1630). Buy tickets at **Aviation Travel Service** (航空售票处; Hángkōng Shòupiàochù; Nanguan Xijie; ⏲8am-7pm). No public transport goes to the airport. A taxi costs around Y40.

Bus

Example routes and fares from the **new south bus station** (新南站; Xīnnán Zhàn; ☎503 2555):

Běijīng Y120, 4½ hours, eight daily

Mùtǎ Y20, 1½ hours, every 20 minutes (6.50am to 7pm)

Tàiyuán Y92 to Y120, three hours, every 20 minutes (6.50am to 6.30pm)

Wǔtái Shān Y66, 3½ hours, two daily (8.30am and 2pm; summer only)

Example routes and fares from the **main bus station** (大同汽车站; Dàtóngqìchēzhàn; ☎246 4464; 20 Yantong Xilu):

Déshèngbǎo Y15, 40 minutes, regular services (7am to 5pm)

Hanging Monastery Y35, 1½ hours, regular serivces (6.30am to 6pm)

Hohhot Y70, 3½ hours, hourly (9am to noon)

Zuǒyún Y16, 1½ hours, regular services (6.30am to 6pm)

Train

Běijīng Y64 to Y105, six to 7½ hours, frequent services

Hohhot Y59 to Y95, four hours, frequent services

Píngyáo Y75 to Y80, seven to eight hours, five daily

Tàiyuán Y63 to Y85, six to seven hours, 10 daily

Xī'ān Y135, 16½ hours, two daily

Getting Around

Bus 4 (Y1) runs from the train station through the centre of town, down Da Beijie before turning west along Da Xijie. Bus 30 (Y1, 30 minutes) runs from the train station to the new south bus station. Buses 2 and 15 (Y1, 10 minutes) run from the train station to the main bus station.

Dàtóng has an infestation of hand-me-down taxis from the rest of China which swarm across town.

Around Dàtóng

YÚNGĀNG CAVES 云冈石窟

One of China's most superlative examples of Buddhist cave art, these 5th-century **caves** (Yúngāng Shíkū; ☎0352-302 6230; admission Y100, guide Y80; ⏲8.30am-5.20pm summer, 9am-4.20pm winter) are ineffably sublime. With 51,000 ancient statues, they put virtually everything else in the Shānxī shade.

Carved by the Turkic-speaking Tuoba, the Yúngāng Caves draw their designs from Indian, Persian and even Greek influences that swept along the Silk Road. Work began in AD 460, continuing for 60 years before all 252 caves, the oldest collection of Buddhist carvings in China, had been completed.

At the time of writing only 39 of the 45 caves were open, showcasing some of the most precious and elegant Buddhist artwork in China. Despite weathering, many of the statues at Yúngāng still retain their gorgeous pigment, unlike the slightly more recent statues at Lóngmén (p412). Note that some of these caves still attract worshippers (prayer cushions are laid out in Cave 20), which of course was their original purpose. Some of the caves were once covered by wooden structures, but many of these are long gone, although **Caves 5**, **6**, **7** and **8** are fronted by wooden temples.

Some caves contain intricately carved square-shaped pagodas, while others depict the inside of temples, carved and painted to look as though made of wood. Frescos are in abundance and there are graceful depictions of animals, birds and angels, some still brightly painted, and almost every cave contains the 1000-Buddha motif (tiny Buddhas seated in niches).

Eight of the caves contain enormous Buddha statues; the largest can be found in **Cave 5**, an outstanding 17m-high, seated effigy of Sakyamuni with a gilded face. The frescos in this cave are badly scratched, but note the painted vaulted ceiling. Bursting with colour, **Cave 6** is also stunning, resembling a set from an *Indiana Jones* epic with legions of Buddhist angels, Bodhisattvas and other figures. In the middle of the cave, a square block pagoda connects with the ceiling, with Buddhas on each side over two levels. Most foreign visitors are oblivious to the graffiti in bright red oil paint on the right-hand side of the main door frame within the cave, which reads 大同八中 (Dàtóng Bāzhōng; Datong No 8 Middle School), courtesy of pupils probably during the Cultural Revolution. On the priceless fresco to the right is further graffiti in red paint, left by what appears to be a contingent from Píngyáo.

Further damage is much in evidence. Chronic weathering has afflicted **Cave 7** (carved between 470 and 493) and **Cave 8**, both scoured by the Shānxī winds. Atmospheric pollution has also taken its toll.

Caves 16 to 20 are the earliest caves at Yúngāng, carved under the supervision of monk Tanyao. Examine the exceptional quality of the carvings in **Cave 18**; some of the faces are perfectly presented. **Cave 19** contains a vast 16.8m high effigy of Sakyamuni. The Maitreya Buddha is a popular subject for Yúngāng's sculptors, for example in the vast seated form in **Cave 17** and **Cave 13**; the latter statue has been carved with graffiti by workers from Hohhot (p850) and other miscreants.

Cave 20 is similar to the Ancestor Worshipping Cave at Lóngmén, originally depicting a trinity of Buddhas (the past, present and future Buddhas). The huge seated Buddha in the middle is the representative icon at Yúngāng, while the Buddha on the left has somehow vanished. Many caves in the western end of Yúngāng have Buddhas with their heads smashed off, as in **Cave 39**. Buddhist figures exposed to the elements, especially near doorways, have been almost totally weathered away.

English-speaking guides are available, although almost every cave comes with English captions. Photography is permitted in some caves but not in others. For Y10 you can get your photo taken on the back of a flea-bitten camel.

ℹ Getting There & Away

At the time of writing, getting to Yúngāng was a nightmare due to roadworks. Things should have eased by the time you read this and bus 3-2 (Y2.50, 50 minutes, from 6am to 6pm) from Dàtóng train station should be running again. At research time you had to take bus 4 (Y1, 30 minutes) to Xīnkāilǐ (新开里), then bus 3-1 (Y1.50) to Jìnhuá Gōng (晋华宫), followed by a taxi (Y10) to the drop-off from where it is a further 1km walk; due to traffic jams, the entire journey was taking 2½ hours or more. A taxi from Dàtóng will cost around Y80.

GREAT WALL 长城

The Great Wall (Chángchéng) is far less spectacular here than the restored sections found near Běijīng. Its Ming bricks – too useful for local farmers to leave alone – have all but disappeared, so just picture rammed earthen mounds, parts of which have crumbled away into nothing.

A rewarding half-day trip from Dàtóng is the wall a few hundred metres north of **Déshèng Bǎo** (得胜堡), a 16th-century walled fort containing a small farming village. Buy a ticket to Fēngzhèn (丰镇; Y15, 40 minutes, from 7am to 5pm) on any bus to Jíníng (集宁); tell the driver to drop you at Déshèng Bǎo. Buses leave from the main bus station, but it's quicker to catch them at the train station, where they spend up to an hour trawling for passengers. The last bus back is around 6.30pm.

For something more remote, and with great hiking possibilities, try getting to **Bātái Village** (八台村; Bātái Cūn), behind which the wall snakes its way east towards Běijīng and west into the hills before turning south towards the Yellow River (Huáng Hé). Take a bus (Y16, 90 minutes, from 7am to 5pm) from Dàtóng's main bus station to Zuǒyún (左云), then change to a minibus to Sāntún (三屯; Y4, 15 minutes). If you ask, the driver should be happy to take you on to Bātái (Y20 to Y30 per vehicle each way, 30 minutes). Just make sure you arrange to be picked up again!

HANGING MONASTERY 悬空寺

Built precariously into the side of a cliff, the Buddhist **Hanging Monastery** (Xuánkōng Sì; admission Y130; 7am-7pm summer, 8am-6pm winter) is made all the more stunning by its long support stilts. The halls have been built along the contours of the cliff face, connected by rickety catwalks and corridors.

If passengers on the bus from Dàtóng are scarce you may be transferred into a free taxi for the last 5km from Húnyuán (浑源). The same should, in theory, apply in the opposite direction. To go from the Hanging Monastery to Mùtǎ, you'll need a taxi (Y10) to Húnyuán, from where there are regular buses to Mùtǎ (Y12, 25 minutes, last bus 6pm).

MÙTǍ 木塔

Built in 1056, this charming five-storey **tower** (admission Y60; 7am-7pm summer, 8am-6pm winter) is the world's oldest and tallest (67m) wooden pagoda. The clay Buddhist carvings it houses, including an 11m-high Sakyamuni on the 1st floor, are as old as the pagoda itself. Sadly, visitors are not allowed beyond the 2nd floor, but photos of the higher floors can be viewed on a noticeboard to the side of the pagoda.

Mùtǎ is located in Yìngxiàn (应县). Buses from Dàtóng's new south bus station (Y20) go right past the tower. To carry on to Wǔtái Shān (Y57, two hours), or to go back to Dàtóng, take a taxi (Y5) from Mùtǎ to the east bus station (东站; Dōngzhàn). It's more of a crossroads than a bus station, and buses stop running by about 3pm. To go to Tàiyuán, take a taxi (Y3) to the west bus station (西站; Xīzhàn), from where there are regular buses until 1.30pm.

Wǔtái Shān 五台山

0350

The gorgeous mountainous, monastic enclave of Wǔtái Shān (Five Terrace Mountains; www.wutaishan.cn) is Buddhism's sacred northern range and the earthly abode of Manjusri (文殊; Wénshū), the Bodhisattva of Wisdom. Chinese students sitting the ferociously competitive *gāokǎo* exams troop here for a nod from the learned Bodhisattva, proffering incense alongside saffron-robed monks and octogenarian pilgrims. A powerful sense of the divine holds sway in Wǔtái Shān, emanating from the port-walled monasteries – the principal sources of spiritual power – and finding further amplification in the astonishing mountain scenery.

The forested slopes overlooking the town eventually give way to alpine meadows where you'll find more temples and great hiking possibilities. Wǔtái Shān is also famed for its mysterious rainbows, which can appear without rain and are said to contain shimmering mirages of Buddhist beings, creatures and temple halls.

There's a steep Y218 entrance fee for the area – including a mandatory Y50 'sightseeing bus' ticket (旅游观光车票; *lǚyóu guānguāng chēpiào*) for transport within the area, valid for three days – valid throughout the duration of your stay. Some of the more popular temples charge an additional small entrance fee.

Avoid Wǔtái Shān during the holiday periods and high-season weekends; temperatures are often below zero from October to March and roads can be impassable.

History

It's believed that by the 6th century there were already 200 temples in the area, although all but two were destroyed during the official persecution of Buddhism in the 9th century. In the Ming dynasty, Wǔtái Shān began attracting large numbers of Tibetan Buddhists (principally from Mongolia) for whom Manjusri holds special significance.

Climate

Wǔtái Shān is at high altitude and powerful blizzards can sweep in as late as May and as early as September. Winters are freezing and snowbound; the summer months are the most pleasant, but always pack waterproofs and waterproof shoes or boots for rain, as well as warm clothing, as temperatures can still fall rapidly at night. If you are climbing up the peaks to see the sunrise, warm coats can be hired.

Sights

Enclosed within a lush valley between the five main peaks is an elongated, unashamedly touristy town, called **Táihuái** (台怀) but which everyone simply calls Wǔtái Shān. It's here that you'll find the largest concentration of temples, as well as all the area's hotels and tourist facilities. The five main peaks are north (北台顶; *běitái dǐng*), east (东台顶; *dōngtái dǐng*), south (南台顶; *nántái dǐng*), west (西台顶; *xītái dǐng*) and central (中台顶; *zhōngtái dǐng*).

Over 50 temples lie scattered in town and across the surrounding countryside, so knowing where to start can be a daunting prospect. Most travellers limit themselves to what is called the **Táihuái Temple Cluster** (Táihuái Sìmiàoqún; 台怀寺庙群), about 20 temples around Táihuái itself, among which Tǎyuàn Temple and Xiǎntōng Temple are considered the best. Many temples in Táihuái contain a statue of Manjusri, generally depicted riding a lion and holding a sword used to cleave ignorance and illusion. You could spend weeks exploring the mountain area, investigating temple after temple.

Tǎyuàn Temple BUDDHIST TEMPLE

(塔院寺; Tǎyuàn Sì; admission Y7) At the base of **Spirit Vulture Peak** (灵鹫峰; Língjiù Fēng), the distinctive white stupa rising above, Tǎyuàn Temple is the most prominent landmark in Wǔtái Shān and virtually all pilgrims come through here to spin the prayer wheels at its base or to prostrate themselves, even in the snow. Beyond the **Devaraja Hall** (Hall of Heavenly Kings) with its candlelit gilded statue of Avalokitesvara (instead of Milefo, who you usually find in this position), at the rear of the **Dàcí Yánshòu Hall** is an altar where worshippers leave tins of instant coffee to Guanyin. Hung with small yellow bells chiming in the Wǔtái Shān winds, the marvellous **Great White Stupa** (大白塔; Dàbái Tǎ) dates originally from 1301 and is one of 84,000 dagobas built by King Asoka, 19 of which are in China. The **Great Sutra-Keeping Hall** is a magnificent sight; its towering

Wǔtái Shān

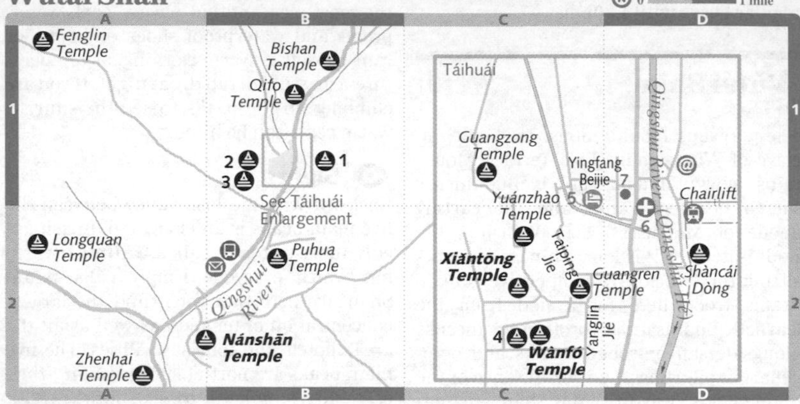

9th-century revolving Sutra case originally held scriptures in Chinese, Mongolian and Tibetan.

Xiǎntōng Temple BUDDHIST TEMPLE
(显通寺; Xiǎntōng Sì; admission Y10) Xiǎntōng Temple – the largest and most captivating temple in town – embraces more than 100 halls and rooms. The **Qiānbō Wénshū Hall** contains a 1000-armed, multifaced Wenshu, whose every palm supports a miniature Buddha. The astonishing brick **Beamless Hall** (无梁殿; Wúliáng Diàn) holds a miniature Yuan-dynasty pagoda, remarkable statues of contemplative monks meditating in the alcoves and a vast seated effigy of Wenshu. Further on, up some steps is the blindingly beautiful **Golden Hall**, enveloped in a constellation of small Buddhas covering all the walls. Five metres high and weighing 50 tonnes, the metal hall was cast in 1606 before being gilded; it houses an effigy of the Wenshu of Wisdom seated atop a lion.

OTHER SIGHTS

You can continue exploring the cluster of temples north beyond Xiǎntōng Temple. **Yuánzhào Temple** (圆照寺; Yuánzhào Sì) contains a smaller stupa than the one at Tǎyuàn Temple. A 10-minute walk south down the road, **Shūxiàng Temple** (殊像寺; Shūxiàng Sì) can be reached up some steep steps beyond its spirit wall by the side of the road; the temple contains Wǔtái Shān's largest statue of Wenshu riding a lion. You can spend the night here at the excellent Fóyuàn Lóu. Before you go looking for St Nicholas at **Sāntǎ Temple** (三塔寺; Sāntǎ Sì) to the east of Táihuái, the name actually means Three Pagoda Temple.

For great views of the town, you can trek, take a chairlift (up/down Y35/30, return Y60) or ride a horse (Y30) up to the temple on **Dàiluó Peak** (黛螺顶; Dàiluó Dǐng; admission Y6), on the eastern side of Qīngshuǐ River (清水河; Qīngshuǐ Hé). For even better views of the surrounding hills, walk 2.5km south to the isolated, fortress-like **Nánshān Temple** (南山寺; Nánshān Sì; admission Y4) and its beautiful stone carvings. **Wànfó Temple** (万佛阁; Wànfó Gé) is perfect for a pit stop; during the summer months, there are fabulous, free performances of Shānxī opera on its outdoor stage that run all morning and from 3pm to 6pm.

Activities

Opportunities for hiking are immense, but sadly no facilities are in place to help. There are no good maps, no marked trails and no locals with any interest in hiking to show you the way. You're on your own here, so pack some food and plenty of water. A good place to start is the hills behind Shūxiàng Temple. Walk past the temple on the small road leading to the central and western peaks, and turn left immediately after the small bridge. You'll find a trail behind the houses that leads up the hillside before heading west on top of the hill. Roads lead to the summits of the five main peaks, so another option is to take a taxi up to one of them before hiking back into town using the road as a bearing.

Wǔtái Shān

Top Sights

Sights

Sleeping

Information

Tours

CITS (中国国际旅行社; Zhōngguó Guójì Lǚxíngshè; ☎139 9410 4419; ⏲7am-9pm) has guides for Y300 per day. It can run tours to the five main peaks; so can other tour companies, but most do not have their own transport and just use local taxis, which you may as well arrange yourself. Return trips cost Y60 (south and east) or Y70 (north, west, central) per person, including waiting time at the top. It's on the main strip.

Sleeping

Cheaper guesthouses can be found in the vicinity of the restaurants and shops in the north of the village.

TOP CHOICE **Fóyuán Lóu** HOTEL $$
(佛缘楼; ☎654 2659; Shūxiàng Temple; r standard/deluxe Y260/360, ste Y480, discounts of 40%; ❄) There are lovely and spacious rooms with elegant furnishings at this hotel with a gorgeous monastic aspect behind Shūxiàng Temple. Take the steep flight of steps up to the temple; the hotel is to the rear. Staff are friendly but slow; note the impressive stone staircase leading to the 2nd floor. Room prices drop when it's quiet.

Fóguó Bīnguǎn HOTEL $
(佛国宾馆; ☎654 5962; Zhenjianfang Jie; tw & q/s without shower Y20/40, tw with shower Y80-100, tr Y120) Off a kind of modern grey courtyard, the cheapest rooms are very simple so it's worth spending a bit more for comfort. The Y100 twin rooms are clean and well kept; the Y5 breakfast includes rice porridge, bread rolls and a boiled egg. Walk to the end of Yingfang Beijie alley, turn left and it's on your left (not far from the bridge).

Eating

Loads of small family-run restaurants are tucked away behind hotels and down small alleys off the main strip where you can find standard fare. *Táimó* (台蘑), the much-revered Wǔtái Shān mushroom, is the local treat. Several restaurants serve up *táimó* dishes, including *táimódùn jīkuài* (台蘑炖鸡块; *táimó* stewed chicken; Y50) and *táimódùn tǔ jī* (台蘑炖土鸡; *táimó* stewed wild chicken; Y80). Also look out for the cheaper *táimódùn dòufu* (台蘑炖豆腐; *táimó* stewed tofu; Y20). Babelfish has left its mark on some restaurant names, including the 'Farm Soil Restaurant'.

Information

Bring cash, as there's nowhere to change money and ATMs only accept Chinese cards. There are no proper hiking maps available, but you can pick up an OK tourist map (Y5) from Fǎyīn Bookshop (法音书社; Fǎyīn Shūshè) and other shops.

Bǎiróng Dàyàofáng (百荣大药房; ⏲8am-9pm) Small chemist on the main strip.

China Post (中国邮政; Zhōngguó Yóuzhèng; ⏲8am-7pm) By the bus station, half an hour's walk south, just north of a China Mobile shop.

Tiānyuán Internet (天缘网吧; Tiānyuán Wǎngbā; per hr Y3; ⏲24hr) At the back of a courtyard off the road east of the Qīngshuǐ River.

Getting There & Away

Bus

Example routes and fares from **Wǔtái Shān bus station** (汽车站; Qìchē zhàn; ☎654 3101):

Běijīng Y131, 6½ hours, one to two daily

Dàtóng Y67, four hours, regular (7.30am to 2.30pm; summer only)

Hanging Monastery Y56, three hours, one daily (7.40am)

Shāhé Y20, 1½ hours, hourly (8am to 6pm)

Tàiyuán Y74, four hours, eight daily (5.40am to 3.40pm)

Xīnzhōu Y43, three hours, one daily

Tàiyuán buses all stop in Dòucūn (Y15) and Dōngyě (Y30), small towns close to Fóguāng Temple and Nánchán Temple, respectively. Dàtóng buses should pass by Húnyuán (浑源), a short taxi ride (Y10) from the monastery. From

Dàtóng in winter, first go to Shāhé (Y42, 3½ hours, every 15 minutes, 7am to 4.30pm) then take a minibus taxi (around Y70).

Train

The station known as **Wǔtái Shān** is actually 50km away in the town of Shāhé (砂河). All Dàtóng buses go via here (Y20). Example routes and fares:

Běijīng Y58, six to seven hours, two daily (8.38pm and 1.37am)

Tàiyuán Y16, four hours, regular services (8.30am to 3.52pm)

Around Wǔtái Shān

Two of the oldest wooden buildings in China, dating from the Tang dynasty, are at Fóguāng Temple and Nánchán Temple; so few visitors go you may have to ask the caretaker to unlock the gates. All Wǔtái Shān–Tàiyuán buses should pass through the small towns where the temples are located, so both can be seen as a day trip.

FÓGUĀNG TEMPLE 佛光寺

The elongated main hall of this Buddhist **temple** (Fóguāng Sì; admission Y15) dates to 857. It contains a central Sakyamuni surrounded by 17 other colourful Tang statues with 296 intriguing Ming arhat statues in the flanks. Fóguāng Temple is set among farmland 6km outside the small town of Dòucūn (豆村). From Wǔtái Shān, take a Tàiyuán-bound bus to Dòucūn (Y15, one hour) then a minibus taxi (Y20 return, including waiting time) to the temple, or a local bus (Y1) part of the way, leaving you with a pleasant 2km walk.

NÁNCHÁN TEMPLE 南禅寺

A further 45km southwest of Fóguāng, near Dōngyě (东冶), this even quieter **temple** (Nánchán Sì; admission Y15) contains a smaller but strikingly beautiful hall built in 782, one of China's oldest temple halls. From Dòucūn, take a bus (Y12, one hour) to Dōngyě then a minibus taxi (Y20 return). The last bus from here to Tàiyuán (Y36, two hours) leaves around 4pm.

Tàiyuán 太原

☎0351 / POP 2.8 MILLION

Most travellers pass through Tàiyuán en route to Píngyáo, but the city has enough to keep you occupied for a day or two, from its excellent museum to a crop of handsome temples, pagodas and historical buildings.

Sights

FREE **Shānxī Museum** MUSEUM
(山西博物馆; Shānxī Bówùguǎn; ☎878 9555; Binhe Xilu Zhongduan; English-speaking guide Y100, audioguide Y10; ⏰9am-5pm, last entrance 4pm, closed Mon) This top-class museum has three floors that walk you through all aspects of Shānxī culture, from prehistoric fossils to detailed local opera and architecture exhibits. All galleries are imaginatively displayed and most contain English captions. Take bus 6 (Y1) from the train station, get off at Yifen Qiaoxi (漪汾桥西) bus stop across the river and look for the inverted pyramid.

Twin Pagoda Temple/Yǒngzuò Temple BUDDHIST TEMPLE
(双塔寺/永祚寺; Shuāngtǎ Sì/Yǒngzuò Sì; admission Y30; ⏰8.30am-5.30pm) This gor-

Tàiyuán

0 500 m
0 0.25 miles
A B C D
1 2
4 Shipin Jie
Zhonglou Jie 钟楼街
To World Trade Hotel (500m)
Qiaotou Jie 桥头街
Shangma Jie 上马街
Chóngshàn Temple
Confucian Temple
Jianshe Beilu 建设北路
Dilianggong Jie 狄梁公街
Children's Park
Kaihuasi Jie
Liuxiang Nanlu
Wuyi Lu
Jiefang Lu
Kodak
2
Wuyi Dongjie 五一东街
Train Station 火车站
5
Houtie Jianxiang
Qifeng Jie 起风街
Wǔyī Guǎngchǎng
Yingze Dajie 迎泽大街
1
Jianshe Nanlu 建设南路
Yingze Park
Hubin Sq
Qingnian Lu
China Eastern Airlines Booking Office
Yingze Nanjie 迎泽南街
3

geous pair of namesake twin pagodas rises up south of the Nansha River in Tàiyuán's southwest. Not much of the temple itself is left but the area is well tended with shrubs and greenery; with the wind in their tinkling bells, the highlight brick pagodas are lovely. The 13-storey **Xuānwén Pagoda** (宣文塔; Xuānwén Tǎ) dates from the reign of Ming emperor Wanli and can be climbed. The adjacent pagoda dates from the same period but cannot be climbed. Take bus 820 or 812 from the train station.

Chóngshàn Temple BUDDHIST TEMPLE
(崇善寺; Chóngshàn Sì; Dilianggong Jie; admission Y2; ⌚8am-4pm) Lovely and cool in summer, the double-eaved wooden hall in this Ming temple contains three magnificent statues: Samantabhadra (the Bodhisattva of Truth), Guanyin (the Goddess of Mercy with 1000 arms) and Manjusri (the Bodhisattva of Wisdom with 1000 alms bowls). The hall at the rear is in the first stages of a rebuild. The entrance is down an alley off Dilianggong Jie behind the captivating **Confucian Temple** (文庙; Wén Miào; 3 Wen Miao Xiang; admission free; ⌚9am-5pm, closed Mon), the main hall of which has been converted to a museum to the Shandōng sage.

Sleeping

World Trade Hotel HOTEL $$$
(山西国贸大饭店; Shānxī Guómào Dàfàndiàn; ☎868 8888; www.sxwtc.com; 59 Fuxi Jie; 府西街59号; d Y1258-1338, ste 2478;) Its marbled lobby a vast atrium-lit space slung out between its two towers (bizarrely named after – and resembling – New York's former World Trade Center), this efficient five star hotel has dapper, well-equipped rooms, but you'll need to pay extra for a view not looking straight into the neighbouring tower.

Jǐnlín Oriental Hotel HOTEL $$
(锦麟东方酒店; Jǐnlín Dōngfāng Jiǔdiàn; ☎839 0666; Yingze Nanjie; 迎泽南街; d & tw Y418, ste Y588, discounts of 30%;) A decent midrange choice, this four-star hotel has respectably furnished, decent-sized rooms with attractive shower. Rooms with computer cost Y30 more. The friendly staff members speak good English.

Chángtài Fàndiàn HOTEL $
(长泰饭店; ☎223 0888; fax 403 4931; 60 Yingze Dajie; 迎泽大街60号; s /tr/ste Y180/298/500, tw Y238-330, discounts of 15%;) Chángtài has spacious rooms, clean floors, reasonably new furnishings and chirpy staff.

Hénghuī Zhāodàisuǒ GUESTHOUSE $
(恒辉招待所; ☎416 9490 8988; 99 Wuyi Dongjie; 五一东街99号; s/tw without bathroom Y30/40, d with bathroom Y60) Very basic rooms with TVs at this friendly guesthouse, but the communal shower room isn't pretty. No English spoken.

Eating

Shānxī is famed for its noodles – including *dāoxiāo miàn* (刀削面; knife-pared noodles) and *lamiàn* (拉面; hand-pulled noodles) – and vinegar, both in abundance in Tàiyuán. Mutton soup is lapped up by locals for breakfast. For more than noodles to fuel your stay, visit **food street** (食品街; Shípǐn Jiē; Shipin Jie) and restaurants of all flavours housed in Ming-style buildings.

TOP CHOICE **Tàiyuán Noodle House** NOODLES $
(太原面食店; Tàiyuán Miànshí Diàn; 5 Jiefang Lu; meals from Y20; ⌚lunch & dinner) *The* place to try Shānxī's famous vinegar/noodle combo: classic forms (named after their shape, not ingredients) include *māo'ěrduo* (猫耳朵; cat's ears) and *cuōyú* (搓鱼; rolled fish). Garnishes include *ròuzhàjiàng* (肉炸酱; pork) and *yángròu* (羊肉; mutton).

Hǎo Gānggāng Yángzá Gēdiàn LAMB NOODLES $
(郝刚刚羊杂割店; cnr Fudong Jie & Liu Xiang; 府东街和柳巷的交叉口; meals Y12; ⌚6am-2pm & 6-9pm) With chefs slaving over a huge vat of lamb soup near the door, this very popular restaurant specialises in tasty lamb snacks. A large bowl of *dàwǎn ròu* (大碗肉; lamb and noodles with onion; Y11) is filling, especially with a tasty *yóusū bǐng* (油酥饼; fried crisp bread; Y1). Add chilli and vinegar as you see fit. No English sign. The restaurant is around 500m northwest of Children's Park along Liu Xiang.

Tàiyuán

Information

Streets around the train station seethe with internet cafes (Y3 per hour).

Bank of China (中国银行; Zhōngguó Yínháng; 169 Yingze Dajie; ⏲8.30am-5.30pm) ATM accepts foreign cards. Can change travellers cheques (Monday to Friday).

China Post (中国邮政; Zhōngguó Yóuzhèng; ⏲8am-7pm) Opposite the train station.

Industrial & Commercial Bank of China (ICBC; 工商银行; Gōngshāng Yínháng; Yingze Dajie) The 24-hour ATM accepts foreign cards.

Internet cafe (网吧; wǎngbā; 3rd fl, cnr Jianshe Nanlu & Yingze Nanjie; per hr Y3; ⏲24hr)

Kodak (柯达; Kēdá; Wuyi Guangchang; ⏲8am-9.30pm) Southwest end of walkway bridge north of Wǔyī Guǎngchǎng; CD burning costs Y10 per disc.

Lǜsè Dònglì Internet (绿色动力网吧; Lǜsè Dònglì Wǎngbā; Yingze Dajie; per hr Y3; ⏲24hr) On the 3rd floor.

Public Security Bureau Exit & Entry Office (PSB; 公安局出入境接待处; Gōng'ānjú; Wuyi Dongjie; ☎895 5355; ⏲8-11.30am & 2.30-5.30pm Mon-Fri winter, 8-11.30am & 3pm-5.30pm summer) Can extend visas. 'Out of Work' Saturday and Sunday. If you walk east along Wuyi Dongjie from Wǔyī Guāngchāng, you'll find the office about 100m up on your left on the corner.

Tàiyuán Tourist Information Centre (太原旅游中心; Tàiyuán Lǚyóu Zhōngxīn; 88 Yingze Dajie; ☎567 9966; ⏲8am-7.30pm) Next to the long-distance bus station; not much use.

Getting There & Away

Air

You can buy tickets at the **China Eastern Airlines booking office** (东方航空公司; Dōngfāng Hángkōng Gōngsī; ☎404 2903; 158 Yingze Dajie; ⏲8am-6.30pm). Bus 201 (Y2, 40 minutes, first/last bus 6am/8pm) runs from the train station to the airport, 15km southeast of town; bus 901 (Y2) to Yúcì also runs to the airport from the train station. In addition, shuttle buses (Y15) also run to the airport from the China Eastern Airlines booking office. A taxi costs around Y50. Example flights and fares:

Běijīng Y660, eight daily

Hángzhōu Y1150, one daily

Hong Kong Y2390, two flights a week (Monday and Friday)

Kūnmíng Y1640, two daily

Nánjīng Y880, one daily

Shànghǎi Y1290, 14 daily

Shēnzhèn Y1240, one daily

Bus

Frequent departures from Tàiyuán's **long-distance bus station** (长途汽车站; chángtú qìchēzhàn; ☎404 2346):

Běijīng Y119, seven hours, every two hours (7.30am to 10pm)

Dàtóng Y92 to Y120, 3½ hours, every 20 minutes (6.40am to 7pm)

Shànghǎi Y409, 17 hours, one daily (2.30pm)

Shíjiāzhuāng Y60, 3½ hours, every 20 to 30 minutes (6.30am to 7.30pm)

Xī'ān Y180 to Y190, eight hours, six daily (7am to 10pm)

Zhèngzhōu Y139, seven hours, 11 daily (7.30am to 10.30pm)

Buses from the **Jiànnán bus station** (建南站; Jiànnán Zhàn, ☎707 1219), 3km south of the train station:

Jièxiū Y37, two hours, regular services

Jìnchéng Y96, four hours, every 30 minutes (6.40am to 7.30pm)

Píngyáo Y25, two hours, regular services (7.20am to 8pm)

The **east bus station** (东客站; Dōng Kèzhàn; ☎238 9025) has buses to Wǔtái Shān (Y74, four hours, every 50 minutes, 6.40am to 6.30pm).

The **west bus station** (客运西站; Kèyùn Xīzhàn, ☎655 2571) services:

Líshí Y70, two hours, regular services (7am to 7.30pm)

Qìkǒu Y67, five hours, three daily (7.30am, 10.30am and noon)

Train

Direct routes from **Tàiyuán train station** (火车站; huǒchēzhàn; ☎9510 5688):

Běijīng Y87 to Y165, 3½ to 14½ hours, 12 daily

Dàtóng Y63 to Y102, five to seven hours, 10 daily

Jìnchéng Y64, seven hours, two daily (9.41am and 7.42pm)

Píngyáo Y8, 1½ hours, frequent services

Wǔtái Shān Y53 to Y89, four hours, eight daily

Xī'ān Y97 to Y106, nine to 11 hours, five daily

Getting Around

Bus 1 (Y1) runs the length of Yingze Dajie. Take bus 611 (Y1.50) from the train station to Jiànnán bus station. For the east bus station take any bus (Y1.50) or rickshaw (Y2) heading east from Wulongkou Jie. For the west bus station take bus 611 (Y1.50) from the train station. Taxis are Y8 at flag fall.

Around Tàiyuán

JÌNCÍ TEMPLE 晋祠

The highlight of this sprawling Buddhist **temple complex** (Jìncí; admission Y70; 8am-6pm) is the **Hall of the Sacred Mother** (圣母殿; Shèngmǔ Diàn), a magnificent wooden structure first built (nail less) in 984, then renovated in 1102. Eight dragons twine their way up the first row of pillars. Inside are 42 Song-dynasty clay maidservants of the sacred lady, the mother of Prince Shuyu, who founded the state of Jin (772–403 BC). Adjacent is the **Zhou Cypress**, an unusual tree that has been growing at an angle of about 30 degrees for the last 900 years. Take bus 804 or 308 from the train station (Y2.50, 45 minutes).

YÚCÌ ANCIENT CITY 榆次老城

A favourite location for Chinese film producers, there are over 400 rooms and halls to explore in the preserved section of this **Ming town** (Yúcì Lǎochéng; admission Y60). Walk the streets and some of the gardens for free, but buy a ticket to enter the temples or the numerous former government offices. The oldest building is the impressive **God Temple** (隍庙; Huáng Miào), built in 1362. Take bus 901 (Y3, 80 minutes, first/last bus 6am/8pm) from near Tàiyuán train station.

QIAO FAMILY COURTYARD 乔家大院

Completely devoid of vegetation, this ornately decorated Qing-dynasty merchant's **residence** (Qiáojiā Dàyuàn; admission summer/winter Y60/40; 8am-6pm) contains six courtyards and more than 300 rooms. The complex is famously where Zhang Yimou's lush fifth-generation tragedy *Raise the Red Lantern* was filmed. All Tàiyuán–Píngyáo buses (Y25) pass by, or you can take a bus heading for Qíxiàn (祁县; Y18, one hour) from Jiànnán Bus Station.

Píngyáo 平遥

0354 / POP 450,000

China's best-preserved ancient walled town, Píngyáo is fantastic. Anyone with China mileage under their belt will be bewitched by the town's age-old charms, charms squandered away – or forever lost – elsewhere across the Middle Kingdom. While other 'ancient' cities in China rustle together an unconvincing display of old city walls, sporadic temples or the occasional ragged alley thrust beneath an unsightly melange of white-tile architecture and socialist-era workers' housing, Píngyáo has kept its beguiling narrative largely intact. This is the China we all think of in flights of fancy: red-lantern-hung lanes set against night-time silhouettes of imposing town walls, elegant courtyard architecture, ancient towers poking into the north China sky and an entire brood of creaking temples and old buildings. Píngyáo is also a living-and-breathing community: locals hang laundry in courtyards, career down alleyways on bicycles, simply sun themselves in doorways or chew the fat with neighbours. The only traffic jams you'll see are tour buggies bumping head-on at a corner; the town is also perfectly placed for some great day trips, with the enchanting village of Zhāngbì Cūn and its 1400-year-old underground castle the icing on Píngyáo's cake.

History

Already a thriving merchant town during the Ming dynasty, Píngyáo's ascendancy came during the Qing when merchants created the country's first banks and cheques to facilitate the transfer of vast amounts of silver from one place to another. The city eschewed the shocking reshaping much loved by communist town planners, and almost 4000 Ming- and Qing-dynasty residences remain within the city walls.

Sights & Activities

Bounded by an intact city wall, gates access the old town at various points in the east, west, north and south. The old town's main drag is Nan Dajie (南大街), where you'll find guesthouses, restaurants, museums, temples and souvenir shops galore. For anyone used to exploring the hard-edged white-tile hinterlands of Hénán or Jiāngxī, Píngyáo is a dream. If you have even the remotest interest in Chinese history, culture or architecture, you could easily spend a day wandering the pinched lanes of Píngyáo, stumbling across hidden gems while ticking off the well-known sights. It's free to walk the streets, but you must pay Y120 to climb the city walls or enter any of the 18 buildings deemed historically significant. Tickets are valid for two days; electronic audio tours are Y40 (Y100 deposit). Opening hours for the sights are from 8am to 7.30pm from 1 May to 30 September, and from 8am to 6.30pm from 1 October to 30 April.

Píngyáo

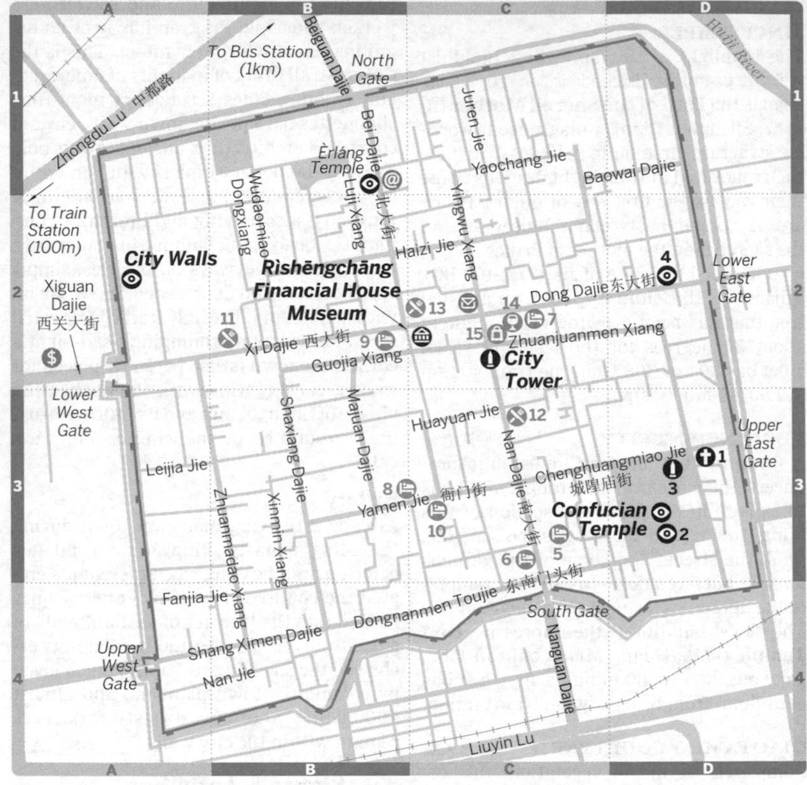

City Walls HISTORIC WALLS

(城墙; *chéng qiáng*) A good place to start is the magnificent city walls, which date from 1370. At 10m high and more than 6km in circumference, they are punctuated by 72 watchtowers, each containing a paragraph from Sunzi's *The Art of War*. Part of the southern wall, which collapsed in 2004, has been rebuilt, but the rest is original. Píngyáo's **city gates** (城门; *chéngmén*) are fascinating and are some of the best preserved in China; the **Lower West Gate** (also called Fèngyì Mén, or Phoenix Appearing Gate) has a section of the original road, deeply grooved with the troughs left by cartwheels (also visible at the South Gate).

Rìshēngchāng Financial House Museum MUSEUM

(日升昌; Rìshēngchāng; 38 Xi Dajie; 西大街38号) Also not to be missed, this museum began life as a humble dye shop in the late 18th century before its tremendous success as a business saw it transform into China's first draft bank (1823), eventually expanding to 57 branches nationwide. The museum has nearly 100 rooms, including offices, living quarters and a kitchen, as well as several old cheques.

Confucian Temple CONFUCIAN TEMPLE

Píngyáo's oldest surviving building is **Dàchéng Hall** (大成殿; Dàchéng Diàn), dating from 1163 and found in the **Confucian Temple** (文庙; Wén Miào), a huge complex where bureaucrats-to-be came to take the imperial exams.

Slogans COMMUNIST HERITAGE

Pop into No 153 Xi Dajie for two red-blooded slogans from the Cultural Revolution that have survived on buildings within the courtyard. The one on the left intones: 工业学大庆 ('Industry should learn from Dàqìng'); the rarer slogan on the right proclaims: 认真

Píngyáo

Top Sights

City Tower C2
City Walls A2
Confucian Temple D3
Rìshēngchāng Financial House Museum C2

Sights

1 Catholic Church D3
2 Dàchéng Hall D3
3 Nine Dragon Screen D3
4 Qīngxū Guàn D2

Sleeping

5 Cuì Chénghǎi Hotel C3
6 Harmony Guesthouse C3
7 Jing's Residence C2
8 Yámén Youth Hostel B3
9 Yúnjǐnchéng Hotel B2
10 Zhèngjiā Kèzhàn C3

Eating

11 Big Bowl Noodles B2
12 Déjūyuán C3
13 Déjūyuán Bīnguǎn C2

Drinking

14 Sakura Café C2

Shopping

15 Tip-toe Tapestry C2

搞好斗批改 ('Earnestly undertake struggle, criticism and reform').

City Tower TOWER

(市楼; Shì Lóu; Nan Dajie; admission Y5; ⊙8am-7pm) Tallest building in the old town. Climb its smooth stone steps for fine views over Píngyáo's magnificent rooftops and inspect its ragged and forlorn shrine to a severe-looking Guandi.

Nine Dragon Screen ANCIENT MONUMENT

(九龙壁; Jiǔlóng Bì; Chenghuangmiao Jie) In front of the old Píngyáo Theatre (大戏堂; Dàxìtáng).

Qīngxū Guàn TAOIST TEMPLE

(清虚观; Dong Dajie) Shānxī dust has penetrated every crevice of this ancient and partly fossilised Taoist temple. With 10 halls and originally dating to the Tang dynasty, it's an impressive complex.

Catholic Church CHURCH

(天主堂; Tiānzhǔ Táng; 2 Anjia Jie) With a brand-new snow-white statue of the Virgin Mary outside, this historic church is the focal point for Píngyáo's Catholic Christians.

Tours

Mr Deng, who runs the Harmony Guesthouse, gives reader-recommended day-long tours of the city, or any of the surrounding sights, for Y150. Also look out for **Mr Liu Wei Zhang** (☎568 5116, 137 5342 9854; 138 Chenghuangmiao Jie), a Píngyáo resident who speaks rather basic English, but she is very kind-hearted and welcoming, and can offer tours.

Sleeping

Many of Píngyáo's hotels are delightfully converted from courtyard homes, and finding a bed for the night is not hard. Píngyáo courtyards differ from their squarer Běijīng equivalents; courtyards in Píngyáo are 目字形, meaning 'shaped like the character 目', and are more rectangular in shape. Píngyáo hoteliers are tuned in to the needs of Western travellers, which means a fair amount of English is spoken and Western breakfasts make a fair stab at mimicking the original. If you head down the back alleys, you can find rooms for around Y30 (without shower). Many hotels and hostels can arrange pick up from the train or bus station.

TOP CHOICE **Harmony Guesthouse** COURTYARD HOTEL $

(和义昌客栈; Héyìchāng Kèzhàn; ☎568 4952; www.py-harmony.com; 165 Nan Dajie; 南大街165号; dm Y30-50, s & tw Y80-100, d Y100-180, tr Y150-200; ❄@☎) Ever popular, Harmony Guesthouse offers rooms off two beautifully preserved courtyards in a lovely 300-year-old Qing building. The unflagging English-speaking husband-and-wife team have created a hospitable and entertaining environment. Rooms are off two beautifully preserved courtyards. Most come with traditional stone *kang* beds, wooden bed-top tea tables and delightful wooden inlaid windows. Dorm accommodation can be found in their old guesthouse. Harmony also has a recently opened bar up the road. There's ticketing, bike rental (Y10 per day), laundry (Y10 per kg), internet (30 minutes free, till 10pm), wi-fi and pick-up.

TOP CHOICE **Jing's Residence** COURTYARD HOTEL $$$

(锦宅; Jǐn Zhái; ☎584 1000; www.jingsresidence.com; 16 Dong Dajie; 东大街16号; r Y1660, discounts of 50%; ❄@☎) This supremely classy abode features a soothing blend of old Píngyáo and modern flair: it's sleek, modish and fastidiously well finished. The themed courtyards are an absolute picture and the rooms are elegant and stylish, while the upstairs bar is the last word in nattiness. The 260-year old building is the former home of a Qing-dynasty silk merchant; views from the suites upstairs stretch out over the Píngyáo rooftops. Reserve ahead as there are only 19 rooms.

Yámén Youth Hostel YOUTH HOSTEL **$**
(衙门官舍青年旅社; Yámén Guānshè Qīngnián Lûshè; ☎568 3539; 69 Yamen Jie; 衙门街69号; 7-/3-bed dm Y30/40, s & tw Y120, d/tr Y160/210; ❄@📶) Also set around a gorgeous Qing courtyard, rooms here are much larger than Harmony's but rather done in, although the courtyard ambience is pleasant and quiet, if threadbare. Dorms under the eaves are clean, with OK toilets downstairs. Staff are friendly and the usual hostel favourites are here: DVD room, ticketing, laundry (Y10), free internet, wi-fi, bike hire (Y1 per hour), pool table and pick-up.

Zhèngjiā Kèzhàn COURTYARD HOTEL **$**
(郑家客栈; ☎568 4466; 68 Yamen Jie; 衙门街68号; dm/d Y40/168, discounts of 20%; @) All the dorms (no shower) are upstairs under the eaves at this pleasant place with a courtyard atmosphere just east of Listen to the Rain Pavilion. Downstairs doubles are spacious and pleasantly arranged, with shower. Next door there's another lovely courtyard belonging to the same outfit; arranged on two levels, it has pricier double rooms (Y258) elegantly decorated with period furniture, and a gracefully presented main area. Internet and pick-up.

Cuì Chénghǎi Hotel COURTYARD HOTEL **$$**
(翠成海客栈; Cuì Chénghǎi Kèzhàn; ☎577 7888; www.pycch.com; 178 Nan Dajie; 南大街178号; tw & d Y388-568, ste from Y868, discounts of 30-50%; ❄@) With three courtyards and more spacious and more elegantly furnished rooms than in hostels mentioned here, this decent midrange option is worth trying. The cheapest rooms off a more modern building to the side are nothing special, but the ones off the central Ming-dynasty courtyard are lovely.

Yúnjǐnchéng Hotel COURTYARD HOTEL **$$$**
(云锦成宾馆; Yúnjǐnchéng Bīnguǎn; ☎568 9220; www.pibc.cn; 56 Xi Dajie; 西大街56号; d/ste Y1080/1480, discounts of 30%; ❄) Good-looking courtyard compound, replete with carved wooden screens and lacquered furniture.

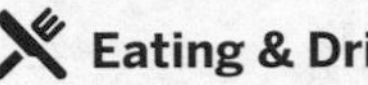

Eating & Drinking

Most hotels can rustle up (Western or Chinese) breakfast, lunch and dinner. Píngyáo does not have too many bars, but courtyard hotels provide virtually all you need: bottles of chilled beer, a gorgeous courtyard to sit in, a chair and table, some grilled peanuts, the Shānxī night sky above your head, a book and some candlelight. The Chinese fast-food chain Dico's has the smallest branch imaginable next to number 49 Xi Dajie; otherwise *xiǎochī* (小吃; hole-in-the-wall restaurants) are everywhere. Some of Píngyáo's English menus are highly inventive ('clear cooks the bull's penis', 'photo meatball' and 'roast chicken skeleton', anyone?). Look out for heart-warming, soothing alcoholic infusions such as the pink *nǚ'er hóng* (女儿红) or the clear *méiguì* (玫瑰), available for sale at the Harmony Guesthouse and other hotels and restaurants.

Déjūyuán HOMESTYLE FOOD **$$**
(德居源; 82 Nan Dajie; ⌚8.30am-10pm; 📋) This welcoming and popular little Nan Dajie restaurant has a simple and tasty menu of affordable dishes from lamb dumplings (Y15) to stewed eggplant (Y10). It's opposite the Tian Yuan Kui Guesthouse.

Big Bowl Noodles NOODLES **$**
(大碗面; Dàwǎn Miàn; Xi Dajie; dishes from Y6; ⌚10am-10pm; 📋) Down-to-earth, no-nonsense noodle joint with tasty pork noodles (Y4 to Y6), braised pork noodles (Y10 to Y12), braised pork ribs (Y25) and roast-beef kebabs (Y2).

Déjūyuán Bīnguǎn SHANXI **$$**
(德居源宾馆; Xi Dajie; dishes Y10-35; 📋) Superb Shānxī cuisine served in a traditional courtyard.

Sakura Cafe BAR **$**
(樱花屋西餐酒吧; Yīnghuāwū Xīcān Jiǔbā; 6 Dong Dajie; beers from Y10; ⌚9am-late; 📋) Lively, fun and adorned with red lanterns and flags, this gregarious, warm, entertaining and affordable cafe/bar has good music and is popular with local Chinese.

Shopping

Part of Píngyáo's charms lie in its peeling and weather-beaten shopfronts, yet to be mercilessly restored. Nan Dajie is stuffed with wood-panelled shops selling ginger sweets (marvel at vendors pulling the golden sugary ginger mass into strips), moon cakes, Píngyáo snacks, knick-knacks and bric-a-brac, Cultural Revolution posters, jade, shoes and slippers, and loads more. Look out for red and black Shānxī paper cuts, which make excellent presents; a shop can be found at No 25 Chenghuangmiao Jie. Also look out for more hats, shoes, slippers, lacquerware and what-not along Xi Dajie. Shānxī vinegar is on sale in vinegar shops in hefty brown jars (you may not want to load one of those into your rucksack). The shutters start closing around 9pm.

Tip-toe Tapestry SHOES
(绣品行; Xiùpǐn Háng; 122 Nan Dajie; ⌚8.30am-9pm) Gorgeous hand-embroidered, hand-washable ladies shoes and slippers from Y45 a pair. Further branch at 18 Nan Dajie.

Information

China Post (中国邮政; Zhōngguó Yóuzhèng; Xi Dajie; ⌚8am-6pm)

Industrial & Commercial Bank of China (ICBC; 工商银行; Gōngshāng Yínháng; Xiguan Dajie) Has an ATM that accepts Visa but, like all other Píngyáo banks, does not change money or travellers cheques.

Internet cafe (网吧; wǎngbā; per hr Y2; ⌚24hr) Beyond the Lower West Gate.

Public Security Bureau (PSB; 公安局; Gōng'ānjú; ☎563 5010; Shuncheng Lu; ⌚8am-12pm & 3-6pm Mon-Fri) Around 3km south of the train station, on the corner of the junction with Shuguang Lu. Cannot extend visas.

Xīngténg Internet cafe (兴腾网吧; Xīngténg Wǎngbā; per hr Y2; ⌚24hr) Opposite the Èrláng Temple on Bei Dajie.

Getting There & Away

Bus

Buses to local destinations such as Jiéxiū (Y9, 40 minutes) usually trawl for passengers at the train station, so it's normally quicker to catch them there.

Píngyáo's **bus station** (汽车新站; qìchēxīnzhàn, ☎569 0011) has buses to Tàiyuán (Y25, two hours, frequent, 6.45am to 7.20pm) and Líshí (Y36, three hours, 7am to 12.30pm).

Train

Tickets for trains are tough to get, especially for sleepers, so plan ahead. Your hotel/hostel should be able to help.

Direct trains:

Běijīng Y117 to Y154, 11 to 12 hours, three daily

Dàtóng Y75 to Y80, seven to 8½ hours, four daily

Tàiyuán Y8 (hard seat), 1½ to two hours, frequent services (6.14am to 9.53pm)

Xī'ān Y83 to Y95, 8½ to 10½ hours, five daily

Getting Around

Píngyáo can be easily navigated on foot or bicycle (Y10 per day). Bike rental is all over the place; Xi Dajie has several bike-rental spots, including one by the Lower West Gate. Electric carts whiz around town (Y5 to Y10). Some hostels will pay the driver when you first arrive as part of their free pick-up promise.

Around Píngyáo

Check with your hostel (or other hostels), as other travellers may be looking for fellow passengers to hire a car for the day to take in the surrounding sights. Hostels also arrange tours.

SHUĀNGLÍN TEMPLE 双林寺

Within easy reach of Píngyáo, this **Buddhist temple** (Shuānglín Sì; admission Y25; ⌚8am-7pm), rebuilt in 1571, houses a number of rare, intricately carved Song and Yuan painted statues. The interiors of the Sakyamuni Hall and flanking buildings are particularly exquisite. A rickshaw will cost about Y40 return and a taxi Y50 (but consider cycling out there instead).

WANG FAMILY COURTYARD 王家大院

More castle than cosy home, this Qing-dynasty **former residence** (Wángjiā Dàyuàn; admission Y66; ⌚8am-7pm) is grand (123 courtyards) if rather redundant. Of more interest perhaps are the still-occupied **cave dwellings** (窑洞; *yáodòng*) behind the castle walls. Two direct buses (8.20am and 2.40pm) leave from Píngyáo bus station. Regular buses go to Jièxiū (介休; Y7, 40 minutes), where you can change to bus 11 (Y4, 40 minutes), which terminates at the complex. The Wang residence is behind the Yuan-dynasty **Confucian Temple** (文庙; Wén Miào; admission Y10), housing a beautiful four-storey pagoda. The last bus back to Jièxiū leaves at 6pm.

ZHĀNGBÌ UNDERGROUND CASTLE 张壁古堡

This fascinating 1400-year-old network of **defence tunnels** (Zhāngbì Gǔbǎo; admission Y40, guide Y20; ⌚8am-6.30pm), built at the end of the Sui dynasty, was never employed for its intended use against possible attack from Tang-dynasty invaders, and subsequently fell into disrepair. Guides speak only Chinese but are essential to prevent you from getting lost inside more than 1500m of tunnels on three levels, the deepest of which drops 26m. Small caves off the pathways were storage rooms and bedrooms, while peepholes in the floor of some of the upper levels were made to spy on and attack would-be invaders.

The guided tour includes a visit to **Zhāngbì Cūn** (张壁村), an enchanting, still-occupied Yuan-dynasty village above the tunnels. You can wander its cobblestoned streets and 800-year-old buildings for free if you don't mind skipping the underground castle.

You can only get here by taxi. To cut the cost, take a bus or a train halfway to Jièxiū (介休; Y9, 40 minutes). A return taxi from Jièxiū, including waiting time, is around Y70. Expect to pay at least double that from Píngyáo.

Qìkǒu 碛口

0358 / POP 32,000

This tiny Ming river port on the banks of the Yellow River (黄河; Huáng Hé) found prosperity during its Qing heyday and is well worth visiting for its stone courtyards and enchanting cobbled pathways, which wind their way up from the banks of the river to the Black Dragon Temple. The main draw is the nearby ancient village of Lǐjiāshān, a seemingly long-forgotten settlement of hundreds of cave dwellings (窑洞; *yáodòng*), some of which remain inhabited today.

Sights

Black Dragon Temple TAOIST TEMPLE

(黑龙庙; Hēilóng Miào) They say the acoustics of this Ming Taoist temple, with wonderful views of the Yellow River, were so excellent that performances held on its stage were audible in Shaanxi (Shǎnxī) province (on the far side of the river). From Qìkǒu's bus stop, follow the road down to the river, then take any number of old cobbled pathways up the hill, via the odd courtyard or two.

Lǐjiāshān MOUNTAIN CAVES

(李家山) An absolute dream for travellers wanting to experience Shānxī's cave houses, this remote 550-year-old village, hugging a hillside set back from the Yellow River, has hundreds of cave dwellings scaling nine storeys. Once home to more than 600 families, most surnamed Li, today's population numbers just over 40; the local school, with caves for classrooms, has just four pupils. Some of the stone paths and stairways that wind their way up the hill also date from Ming times. Note the stone rings on some walls that horses were tied to.

To get here, cross the bridge by Qìkǒu's bus stop and follow the river for about 30 minutes until you see a blue sign with '李家山' on it. Then follow the dirt track up the hill for about 20 minutes until you reach the old village.

Sleeping & Eating

Qìkǒu Kèzhàn GUESTHOUSE $

(碛口客栈; 446 6188; d/tw Y188/218; @) Overlooking the river in Qìkǒu, this place has comfortable, *yáodòng*-style rooms with *kang* beds off two 300-year-old courtyards. It also does decent food, although there are cheaper places to eat behind the bus stop. Free internet connection in each room.

Sìhéyuàn Lǚdiàn COURTYARD $

(四合院旅店; 138 3583 2614; r per person Y40 with meals) In Lǐjiāshān, some locals have spare caves that they will let you stay in for around Y40, including basic meals. If you can't wrangle one, fear not: this 180-year-old, wonderfully rustic courtyard has a handful of cave bedrooms that burrow into the hillside behind it. Run by Mr Li and his wife, whose family have lived here for six generations, rooms come with huge, chunky, stone *kang* beds and traditional Chinese paper window panes. There's electricity (most of the time), but no running water. Apart from Mr Li, who speaks good Mandarin, most residents speak only Jin. The guesthouse is up to your left as you enter the village. Look for the big red banner with '四合院旅店' on it.

Getting There & Away

Two direct buses run from Tàiyuán to Qìkǒu (Y67, four hours, 7.30am, 10.30am and noon). If you miss these, or are coming from Píngyáo, you will have to take the more complicated route through Líshí (离石).

Regular buses go from Tàiyuán to Líshí (Y70, two hours, from 7am to 7.30pm). Two go from Píngyáo (Y29, 2½ hours, 7.30am and noon). From Líshí's long-distance bus station (长途汽车站; *chángtú qìchēzhàn*), take bus 1 (Y1, 20 minutes) to the west bus station (西客站; *xī kèzhàn*) then change for Qìkǒu (Y15, two hours).

CAVE DWELLINGS

People have been living in caves in Shānxī for almost 5000 years, and it's believed that at one stage a quarter of the population lived underground. Shānxī's countryside is still littered with (窑洞; *yáodòng*), especially around the Yellow River area, and Lǐjiāshān is a wonderful example. These days, most lie abandoned but, incredibly, almost three million people still live in Shānxī caves. And who can blame them? Compared to modern houses, they're cheaper and easier to make, far better insulated against freezing winters and scorching summers, much more soundproof and afford better protection from natural disasters such as earthquakes or forest fires. Furthermore, with far fewer building materials needed to construct them, they're a whole lot more environmentally friendly. So why isn't everyone living in them? Well, although most are now connected to the national grid, the vast majority of cave communities have no running water or sewerage system, turning simple daily tasks like washing or going to the toilet into a mission and suddenly making even the ugliest tower block seem a whole lot more attractive.

There's one daily bus from Qìkǒu to Tàiyuán, but it leaves at 5.30am, while buses to Líshí from Qìkǒu stop running at 12.30pm. After that, though, you should still be able to land a seat in a minibus for about Y20. From Líshí, there are regular buses back to Tàiyuán (from 6.30am to 8pm), two to Píngyáo (7.30am and noon) and two to Xī'ān (Y151, eight hours, 7am and 2.30pm).

Jìnchéng 晋城

☎0356 / POP 395,000

One snug, 450-year-old pagoda aside, Jìnchéng has few sights, but this small industrial town is the launch pad for a historical adventure into Shānxī's southeast. The surrounding countryside is bursting with ancient architecture, making this a rewarding stop, particularly if you are continuing south into Hénán.

The only sight of note in town is **Bǐfēng Temple** (笔峰寺; Bǐfēng Sì; ⌚dawn-dusk), 300m in front of the train station. The dark, narrow and, quite frankly, scary steps inside its Ming pagoda can be climbed for Y3.

For accommodation, hop on bus 2 to **Zhōngyuán Bīnguǎn** (中原宾馆; ☎888 0700; Wengchang Dongjie; 文昌冻街; d & tw Y98, discounts 20%; ❄), a friendly hotel set back from the road through an open gateway, opposite the People's Hospital (人民医院; Rénmín Yīyuàn). There are a few restaurants opposite the hotel, with tables spilling out onto the pavement come evening.

Internet cafes can be found near the train station. The **Bank of Communications** (交通银行; Jiāotōng Yínháng; cnr Jianshe Lu & Hongxing Xijie), is further along the bus 2 route, a couple of minutes' walk down the hill from the long-distance bus station. It has a 24-hour ATM. **Maps** (地图; dìtú; Y4) of Jìnchéng can be bought at kiosks outside the bus and train stations.

Bus 2 (Y1, 6.30am to 8pm) runs from the train station, past the Central Bus Station, along Wencheng Dongjie, where hotels and restaurants can be found, past the Bank of Communications and on to the long-distance bus station.

Buses to Tàiyuán (Y107, four hours, from 6am to 7.15pm) leave frequently from the Central Bus Station, a 20-minute walk straight along the road from the train station. Buses to other destinations, including Píngyáo (Y104, 5½ hours, 8am and 9.30am), Xī'ān (Y159, seven to eight hours, three daily), Běijīng (Y240, 10 hours, 8pm) and Zhèngzhōu in Hénán (Y60, three hours, frequently), leave from the long-distance bus station.

The few trains that pass Jìnchéng shuttle between Tàiyuán (Y64, seven hours, 1.17am and 4.06am) and Zhèngzhōu (Y54, 3½ hours, 2.49am and 4.57pm), from where you can change to onward destinations.

Around Jìnchéng

PRIME MINISTER CHEN'S CASTLE 皇城相府

This beautifully preserved Ming-dynasty **castle** (Huángchéng Xiàngfǔ; admission Y60) is the former residence of Chen Tingjing, prime minister under Emperor Kangxi in the late 17th century, and co-author of China's most famous dictionary. It comes with tourist trappings – souvenir sellers,

FOR REFERENCE

Prime Minister Chen Tingjing was undoubtedly a man of many talents. Outside his governmental responsibilities he also inspired as a teacher, poet and musician. His surviving legacy, however, was not one of China's great works of creativity, but a dictionary. Not just any dictionary, mind. China's most famous and most comprehensive, and the last one ever to be commissioned by an emperor. Named after that emperor, the Kangxi Dictionary was a mammoth undertaking put together by Chen and Zhang Yushu, both of whom died before its completion in 1716. Multivolumed, and containing 49,030 characters, it was, until 1993, the largest Chinese dictionary ever compiled.

Appropriately enough, Chen's former residence (p355) now houses China's only dictionary museum which includes amongst its exhibits 39 versions of the Kangxi Dictionary, the oldest being a 42-volume, 47,035-character edition of 1827. Modern reprints (Y580 to Y2000) can be bought in the small dictionary shop, although you might need a spare rucksack to get one back to the hotel!

megaphone-wielding guides – but remains an intriguing maze of courtyards, gardens and stone archways, and is home to China's only dictionary museum! Frequent buses (Y12, 75 minutes, from 6am to 6.30pm) run from the long-distance station. Return transport is scarce, so it's best to take a minibus to the small town of Běiliú (北留; Y3, 15 minutes) then catch an ordinary bus back to Jìnchéng (Y10).

HǍIHUÌ TEMPLE 海会寺

The highlights of this active Buddhist **temple** (Hǎihuì Sì; admission Y30), where Minister Chen used to study, are its twin brick pagodas. The 20m-high **Shělì Tǎ** (舍利塔) is almost 1100 years old. Towering above it is the octagonal **Rúlái Tǎ** (如来塔), built in 1558, which can be climbed for an extra Y10. To get here, take the bus to the castle but tell the driver you want to get off at Hǎihuì. To continue to the castle or Guōyù Ancient Village, take a minibus from the main road (Y2) or walk (45 minutes).

GUŌYÙ ANCIENT VILLAGE 郭峪古城

This enchanting walled village (Guōyù Gǔchéng) is, for some, the highlight of a trip to this part of Shānxī. There's no entrance fee and no tourist nonsense, just the genuine charm of a still-inhabited Ming-dynasty settlement. It's best simply to wander the streets aimlessly, but don't miss **Tāngdì Miào** (汤帝庙), a 600-year-old Taoist temple and the village's oldest building. It's also worth poking your nose inside the former courtyard residence of Minister Chen's grandfather at **1 Jingyang Beilu** (景阳北路1号). Guōyù is a 10-minute walk down the hill from the castle. The bus will drop you off here if you ask.

Shaanxi (Shǎnxī)

POPULATION: 37 MILLION

Includes »

Best Places to Eat

» Xī'ān's Muslim Quarter (p8)

» First Noodle Under the Sun (p9)

» Máogōng Xiāngcàiguǎn (p9)

» Yán'ān's Night Market (p20)

Best Places to Stay

» Hàn Táng Inn (p7)

» Xiāngzǐmén Youth Hostel (p7)

» Sofitel (p8)

» A courtyard house in Dǎngjiācūn (p18)

Why Go?

Shaanxi (陕西) is where it all started for China. As the heartland of the Qin dynasty, whose warrior emperor set out to unite much of China for the first time, Shaanxi was the cradle of Chinese civilisation. Later on, Xī'ān was the beginning and end of the Silk Road and a buzzing, cosmopolitan capital long before anyone had heard of Běijīng.

It's Shaanxi's treasure trove of archaeological sites that make it such an essential destination. Nor is it all ancient history; the caves around Yán'ān were the Chinese Communist Party's (CCP) base in the 1930s and '40s.

But there's much more to Shaanxi than just its storied past. There are farm villages barely touched by modern life, and mountains that were once home to hermits and sages waiting to be explored. So wherever you go, the sights and views will knock you out.

When to Go

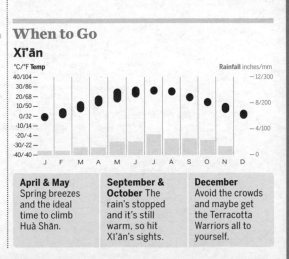

Xī'ān

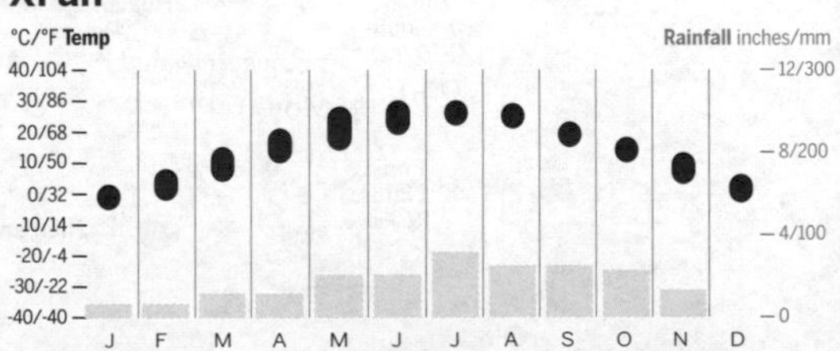

April & May Spring breezes and the ideal time to climb Huà Shān.

September & October The rain's stopped and it's still warm, so hit Xī'ān's sights.

December Avoid the crowds and maybe get the Terracotta Warriors all to yourself.

Shaanxi Highlights

1. See what an emperor takes with him to the grave at the extraordinary **Army of Terracotta Warriors** (p11)
2. Contemplate Xī'ān's fabled past from its formidable old **city walls** (p4)
3. Watch the sun rise over the Qínlǐng Mountains from atop Taoism's sacred western peak, **Huà Shān** (p15)
4. Step back in time in the perfectly preserved Ming-dynasty village of **Dǎngjiācūn** (p17)
5. Take a different look at China's past by gazing down on the enthralling excavations at the **Tomb of Emperor Jingdi** (p14)
6. Get lost wandering the backstreets of Xī'ān's ancient **Muslim Quarter** (p2)
7. Check out the **cave** where Mao Zedong lived in Yán'ān and the red tourists who flock to see it (p19)

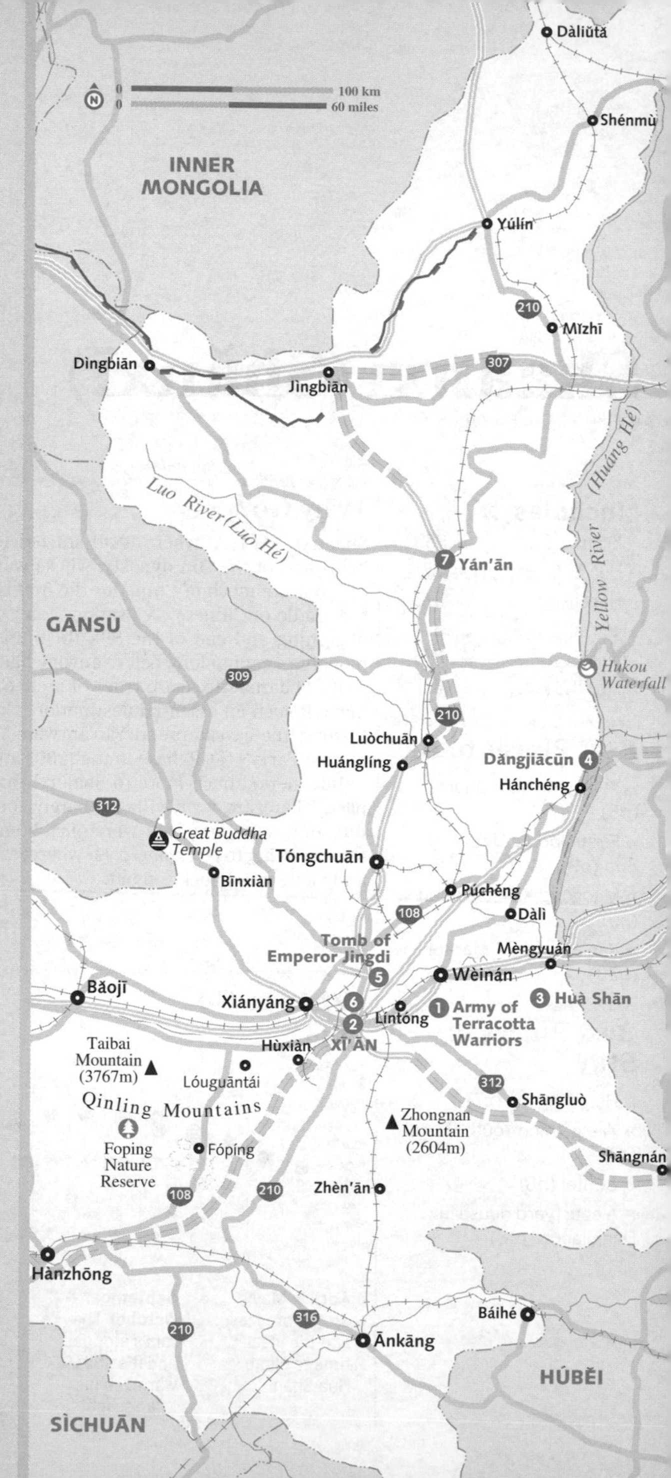

History

Around 3000 years ago, the Zhou people of the Bronze Age moved out of their Shaanxi homeland, conquered the Shang and became dominant in much of northern China. Later the state of Qin, ruling from its capital Xiányáng (near modern-day Xī'ān), became the first dynasty to unify much of China. Subsequent dynasties, including the Han, Sui and Tang, were based in Xī'ān, then known as Cháng'ān, which was abandoned for the eastern capital of Luòyáng (in Hénán) whenever invaders threatened.

Shaanxi remained the political heart of China until the 10th century. However, when the imperial court shifted eastward, the province's fortunes began to decline. Rebellions and famine were followed in 1556 by the deadliest earthquake in history, when an estimated 830,000 people died. The extreme poverty of the region ensured that it was an early stronghold of the CCP.

Language

Locals like to joke that Xī'ān's dialect is the 'real' standard Mandarin – after all, the city was one of the ancient capitals of China. Those pedantic linguists, however, prefer to classify the Shaanxi dialect as part of the central Zhōngyuān Mandarin group. Jin is also spoken in some parts of the province.

Getting There & Around

Xī'ān has one of China's best-connected airports. Roads are good north, east and west of Xī'ān; travelling south is more problematic. Rail links within the province are slow.

PRICE INDICATORS

The following price indicators are used in this chapter:

Sleeping

$	less than Y160
$$	Y160 to Y400
$$$	more than Y400

Eating

$	less than Y50
$$	Y50 to Y100
$$$	more than Y100

Xī'ān 西安

029 / POP 4.5 MILLION

Xī'ān's fabled past is a double-edged sword. Primed with the knowledge that this legendary city was once the terminus of the Silk Road and a melting pot of cultures and religions, as well as home to emperors, courtesans, poets, monks, merchants and warriors, visitors can feel let down by the roaring, modern-day version. But even though Xī'ān's glory days ended in the early 10th century, many elements of ancient Cháng'ān, the former Xī'ān, are still present.

The city walls remain intact, vendors of all descriptions still crowd the narrow lanes of the warrenlike Muslim Quarter, and there are enough places of interest to keep even the most diligent amateur historian busy. There's still a vital feel to Xī'ān, too, as if the ghosts of the ancient traders, sages, soldiers and officials were sitting up on the ramparts of the city walls demanding not to be forgotten.

While Xī'ān is no longer China's political capital, it's woken up to the potential value of its hallowed history. In the last few years, the city has been campaigning for the Silk Road to be added to the UN's World Heritage List, and at the time of writing there were ambitious plans to revitalise the Muslim Quarter. Whether that means a Silk Road-meets-Disney tourist trap or something less tacky remains to be seen, but expect some changes.

Most people only spend two or three days in Xī'ān; history buffs could easily stay busy for a week. Of course, nearby are some of the most spectacular and essential sights in all China; topping the list in and around the city are the Terracotta Warriors, the Tomb of Emperor Jingdi, the Muslim Quarter and the city walls. With a little more time, check out the pagodas, museums and any number of other sights outside the city. Better still, arrange an overnight trip to nearby Huà Shān or Hánchéng.

Sights

INSIDE THE CITY WALLS

Muslim Quarter HISTORIC SITE

(回族区) The backstreets leading north from the Drum Tower have been home to the city's Hui community (Chinese Muslims) for centuries. Although Muslims have been here since at least the 7th century,

Xī'ān

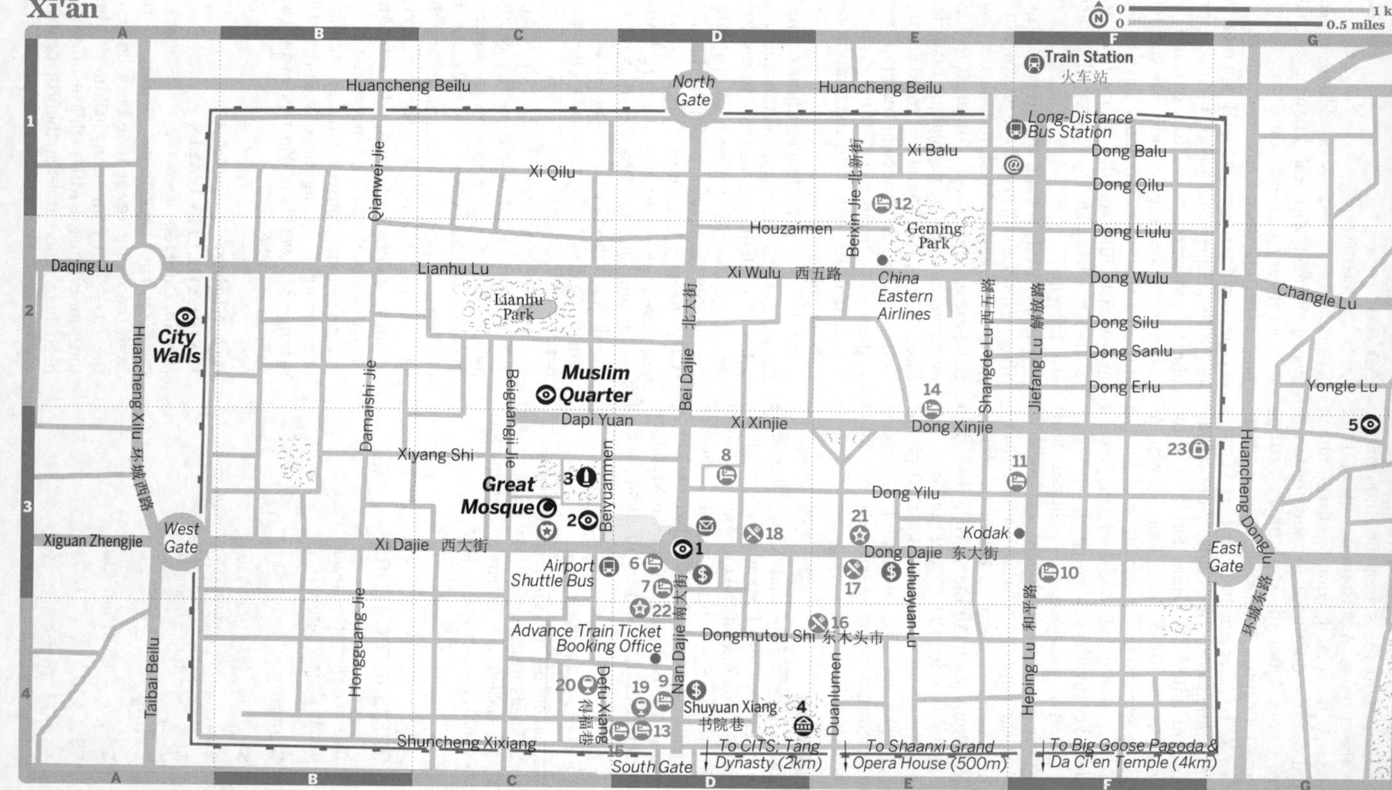
Train Station
火车站
Long-Distance Bus Station
Huancheng Beilu
North Gate
Xi Balu
Dong Balu
Xi Qilu
Dong Qilu
Qianwei Jie
Houzaimen
Beixin Jie 北新街
Geming Park
Dong Liulu
Daqing Lu
Lianhu Lu
Xi Wulu 西五路
China Eastern Airlines
Dong Wulu
Changle Lu
Lianhu Park
City Walls
Huancheng Xilu 环城西路
Bei Dajie 北大街
Shangde Lu 西五路
Jiefang Lu 解放路
Dong Silu
Dong Sanlu
Dong Erlu
Yongle Lu
Muslim Quarter
Damaishi Jie
Beiguangji Jie
Dapi Yuan
Xi Xinjie
Dong Xinjie
Xiyang Shi
Beiyuanmen
Great Mosque
Dong Yilu
Kodak
West Gate
Xiguan Zhengjie
Xi Dajie 西大街
Dong Dajie 东大街
East Gate
Huancheng Donglu 环城东路
Airport Shuttle Bus
Juhuayuan Lu
Heping Lu 和平路
Advance Train Ticket Booking Office
Nan Dajie 南大街
Dongmutou Shi 东木头市
Taibai Beilu
Hongguang Jie
Defu Xiang 得福巷
Shuyuan Xiang 书院巷
Duanlumen
Shuncheng Xixiang
South Gate
To CITS; Tang Dynasty (2km)
To Shaanxi Grand Opera House (500m)
To Big Goose Pagoda & Da Ci'en Temple (4km)
1 km
0.5 miles

some believe that today's community didn't take root until the Ming dynasty.

The narrow lanes are full of butcher shops, sesame-oil factories, smaller mosques hidden behind enormous wooden doors, men in white skullcaps and women with their heads covered in coloured scarves. It's a great place to wander and especially atmospheric at night. Good streets to stroll down are Xiyang Shi, Dapi Yuan and Damaishi Jie, which runs north off Xi Dajie through an interesting Islamic food market.

Great Mosque MOSQUE
(清真大寺; Qīngzhēn Dàsì; Huajue Xiang; admission Mar-Nov Y25, Dec-Feb Y15, Muslims free; ⏲8am-7.30pm Mar-Nov, to 5.30pm Dec-Feb) One of the largest mosques in China, the Great Mosque is a fascinating blend of Chinese and Islamic architecture. Facing west (towards Mecca) instead of the usual south, the mosque begins with a classic Chinese temple feature, the spirit wall, designed to keep demons at bay. The gardens, too, with their rocks, pagodas and archways are obviously Chinese, with the exception of the four palm trees at the entrance. Arab influence, meanwhile, extends from the central minaret (cleverly disguised as a pagoda) to the enormous turquoise-roofed Prayer Hall (not open to visitors) at the back of the complex, as well as the elegant calligraphy gracing most entryways. The present buildings are mostly Ming and Qing, though the mosque is said to have been founded in the 8th century.

To get here, follow Xiyang Shi several minutes west and look for a small alley leading south past a gauntlet of souvenir stands.

Forest of Stelae Museum MUSEUM
(碑林博物馆; Bēilín Bówùguǎn; 15 Sanxue Jie; admission Mar-Nov Y45, Dec-Feb Y30; ⏲8am-6.15pm Mar-Nov, to 5.15pm Dec-Feb) Housed in Xī'ān's Confucius Temple, this museum holds over 1000 stone stelae (inscribed tablets), including the nine Confucian classics and some exemplary calligraphy. The second gallery holds a Nestorian tablet (AD 781), the earliest recorded account of Christianity in China. (The Nestorians professed that Christ was both human and divine, for which they were booted out of the Church in 431.) The fourth gallery holds a collection of ancient maps and portraits, and is where rubbings (copies) are made, an interesting process to watch.

The highlight, though, is the fantastic sculpture gallery (across from the gift shop), which contains animal guardians from the Tang dynasty, pictorial tomb stones and Buddhist statuary.

To get to the museum, follow Shuyuan Xiang east from the South Gate.

Bell Tower & Drum Tower HISTORIC SITES
Now marooned on a traffic island, the **Bell Tower** (钟楼; Zhōng Lóu; admission Y27,

Xī'ān

Top Sights
- City Walls ... A2
- Great Mosque ... C3
- Muslim Quarter ... C2

Sights
- 1 Bell Tower ... D3
- 2 Drum Tower ... C3
- 3 Folk House ... C3
- 4 Forest of Stelae Museum ... D4
- 5 Temple of the Eight Immortals ... G3

Sleeping
- 6 Bell Tower Hotel ... D3
- 7 City Hotel Xī'ān ... D3
- 8 Hàn Táng Inn ... D3
- 9 Héjiā Shāngwù Hotel ... D4
- 10 Hyatt Regency Xī'ān ... F3
- 11 Jǐnjiāng Inn ... F3
- 12 Qīxián Youth Hostel ... E1
- 13 Shūyuàn Youth Hostel ... D4
- 14 Sofitel ... E2
- 15 Xiāngzǐmén Youth Hostel ... D4

Eating
- 16 First Noodle Under the Sun ... E4
- 17 Lǎo Sūn Jiā ... E3
- 18 Wǔyī Fàndiàn ... D3

Drinking
- 19 Moonkey Music Bar ... D4
- 20 Old Henry's Bar ... C4

Entertainment
- 21 1+1 ... E3
- 22 Song & Song ... D4

Shopping
- 23 Northwest Antique Market ... F3

combined Drum Tower ticket Y40; ⌚8.30am-9.30pm Mar-Nov, to 6pm Dec-Feb) sits at the heart of Xī'ān and originally held a large bell that was rung at dawn, while its alter ego, the **Drum Tower** (鼓楼; Gǔ Lóu; Beiyuanmen; admission Y27, combined Bell Tower ticket Y40; ⌚8.30am-9.30pm Mar-Nov, to 6pm Dec-Feb), marked nightfall. Both date from the 14th century and were later rebuilt in the 1700s (the Bell Tower initially stood two blocks to the west). Musical performances, included in the ticket price, are held inside each at 9am, 10.30am, 11.30am, 2.30pm, 4pm and 5pm. Enter the Bell Tower through the underpass on the north side.

Folk House HISTORIC SITE

(高家大院; Gāojiā Dàyuàn; 144 Beiyuanmen; admission Y15, with tea Y20; ⌚8.30am-11pm) This well-rounded historic residence also serves as an art gallery, entertainment centre and teahouse. Originally the home of the Qing bureaucrat Gao Yuesong, it's a fine example of a courtyard home and has been tastefully restored. There are reception rooms, bedrooms, servants' quarters, an ancestral temple and a study (now the teahouse).

Tours start with an optional marionette or shadow-puppet demonstration (Y10). As the complex currently belongs to the Shaanxi Artists Association, there's an art gallery here where you can pick up reasonably priced traditional Chinese art. Confusingly, despite the address, this place isn't at No 144, but is about 20m down the street.

OUTSIDE THE CITY WALLS

City Walls HISTORIC SITE

(城墙; Chéngqiáng; admission Y40; ⌚8am-8.30pm Apr-Oct, to 7pm Nov-Mar) Xī'ān is one of the few cities in China where the old city walls are still standing. Built in 1370 during the Ming dynasty, the 12m-high walls are surrounded by a dry moat and form a rectangle with a perimeter of 14km.

Most sections have been restored or rebuilt, and it is now possible to walk the entirety of the walls in a leisurely four hours. You can also cycle from the South Gate (bike hire Y20 for 100 minutes, Y200 deposit). The truly lazy can be whisked around in a golf cart for Y200. Access ramps are located inside the major gates, with the exception of the South Gate, where the entrance is outside the walls; there's another entrance inside the walls beside the Forest of Stelae Museum.

To get an idea of Xī'ān's former grandeur, consider this: the Tang city walls originally enclosed 83 sq km, an area seven times larger than today's city centre.

FREE **Shaanxi History Museum** MUSEUM

(陕西历史博物馆; Shǎnxī Lìshǐ Bówùguǎn; 91 Xiaozhai Donglu; ⌚8.30am-6pm Tue-Sun Apr-Oct, last admission 4.30pm, 9.30am-5pm Tue-Sun Nov-Mar, last admission 4pm) Shaanxi's museum is often touted as one of China's best, but if you come after visiting some of Xī'ān's surrounding sights you may feel you're not seeing much that is new. Nevertheless, the museum makes for a comprehensive and illuminating stroll through ancient Cháng'ān, and most exhibits include labels and explanations in English.

The ground floor covers prehistory and the early dynastic period. Particularly impressive are several enormous Shang- and Western Zhou-dynasty bronze tripods *(dǐng),* Qin burial objects, bronze arrows and crossbows, and four original terracotta warrior statues.

Upstairs, the second section is devoted primarily to Han-dynasty relics. The highlights include a collection of about 40 terracotta figurines from the tomb of the first Han emperor Liu Bang. There's also an imaginative collection of bronze lamps, Wei figurines and mythological animals.

The third section focuses primarily on Sui and Tang artefacts: expressive tomb guardians; murals depicting a polo match; and a series of painted pottery figurines with elaborate hairstyles and dress, including several bearded foreigners, musicians and braying camels.

The number of visitors is limited to 4000 a day, so get here early and expect to queue for at least 30 minutes. Make sure you bring your passport to claim your free ticket. Take bus 610 from the Bell Tower or bus 701 from the South Gate.

Big Goose Pagoda BUDDHIST TEMPLE

(大雁塔; Dàyàn Tǎ; Yanta Nanlu; admission Y50, incl pagoda climb Y80; ⌚8am-7pm Apr-Oct, to 6pm Nov-Mar) Xī'ān's most famous landmark, this pagoda dominates the surrounding modern buildings. One of China's best examples of a Tang-style pagoda (squarish rather than round), it was completed in AD 652 to house the Buddhist sutras brought back from India by the monk Xuan Zang. Xuan spent the last 19 years of his life translating scriptures with a crack team of linguist monks; many of these translations

MONKEY BUSINESS

Xuan Zang's epic 17-year trip to India, via Central Asia and Afghanistan, in search of Buddhist enlightenment was fictionalised in *Journey to the West*, one of Chinese literature's most enduring texts. The Ming-dynasty novel gives the monk Xuan three disciples to protect him along the way, the best-loved of which is the Monkey King.

The novel, which is attributed to the poet Wu Cheng'en, has inspired many films, plays and TV shows, including the cult '70s series *Monkey*. More recently, the Gorillaz team of Damon Albarn and Jamie Hewlett collaborated with opera director Chen Shi-Zheng on a popular 2007 stage version.

are still used today. His travels also inspired one of the best-known works of Chinese literature, *Journey to the West*.

Surrounding the pagoda is **Dà Cí'ēn Temple** (大慈恩寺; Dàcí'ēn Sì), one of the largest temples in Tang Cháng'ān. The buildings today date from the Qing dynasty.

Bus 610 from the Bell Tower and bus 609 from the South Gate drop you off at the pagoda square; the entrance is on the south side. An evening fountain show is held on the square.

FREE **Xī'ān Museum** MUSEUM

(西安博物馆; Xī'ān Bówùguǎn; 76 Youyi Xilu; ⌚8.30am-7pm, closed Tue) Housed in the pleasant grounds of the Jiànfú Temple is this new-ish museum featuring relics unearthed in Xī'ān over the years. There are some exquisite ceramics from the Han dynasty, as well as figurines, an exhibition of Ming-dynasty seals and jade artefacts. Don't miss the basement, where a large-scale model of ancient Xī'ān gives a good sense of the place in its former pomp.

Also in the grounds is the **Little Goose Pagoda** (小雁塔; Xiǎoyàn Tǎ; ⌚8.30am-7pm, closed Tue). The top of the pagoda was shaken off by an earthquake in the middle of the 16th century, but the rest of the 43m-high structure is intact. Jiànfú Temple was originally built in AD 684 to bless the afterlife of the late Emperor Gaozong. The pagoda, a rather delicate building of 15 progressively smaller tiers, was built from AD 707 to 709 and housed Buddhist scriptures brought back from India by the pilgrim Yi Jing. At the time of writing, it was no longer possible to climb the pagoda.

Bus 610 runs here from the Bell Tower; from the South Gate take bus 203.

Temple of the Eight Immortals TAOIST TEMPLE

(八仙庵; Bāxiān Ān; Yongle Lu; admission Y3; ⌚7.30am-5.30pm Mar-Nov, 8am-5pm Dec-Feb) Xī'ān's largest Taoist temple dates back to the Song dynasty and is still an active place of worship. Supposedly built on the site of an ancient wine shop, it was constructed to protect against subterranean divine thunder. Scenes from Taoist mythology are painted around the courtyard. Empress Cixi, the mother of the Last Emperor, stayed here in 1901 after fleeing Beijing during the Boxer Rebellion. There's a small **antique market** opposite, which is busiest on Sundays and Wednesdays.

Bus 502 runs close by the temple (eastbound from Xi Xinjie).

Sleeping

If you're arriving by air and have not yet booked accommodation, keep in mind that representatives at the shuttle bus drop-off (outside the Melody Hotel) can often get you discounted rooms at a wide selection of hotels.

All hostels in the city offer a similar range of services, including bike hire, internet, laundry, restaurant and travel services. Ask about free pick-up from the train station and book ahead at the most popular places.

TOP CHOICE **Hàn Táng Inn** HOSTEL $

(汉唐驿; Hàntáng Yì; ☎8728 7772, 8723 1126; www.hostelxian@yahoo.com.cn; 7 Nanchang Xiang; 南长巷7号; dm/s/d Y50/70/160; ⊖❄@) Newly ensconced in a more convenient central location, the dorms here are compact but spotless and come with en suite bathrooms. Smaller and more homely than the other hostels in town – the roof terrace provides space to spread out – the staff know what travellers want and do their best to satisfy them. It's tucked down an alley off Bei Dajie; look for the two terracotta warriors standing guard outside.

Xiāngzǐmén Youth Hostel HOSTEL $

(湘子门国际青年旅舍; Xiāngzǐmén Guójì Qīngnián Lǚshè; ☎6286 7999/7888; www.yhaxian.com; 16 Xiangzimiao Jie; 南门里湘子庙街16号; dm Y50, s, d & tr Y120-220; ❄@) Lively and loud, this is the hostel of the moment. Set around an impressive series of interconnected courtyards, it's a big, sprawling place with friendly staff and attracts a good mix of local and foreign travellers. Avoid the windowless basement rooms. Take bus 603 from opposite the train station to the South Gate and walk 100m west.

Sofitel HOTEL $$$
(索菲特人民大厦; Suǒfēitè Rénmín Dàshà; ☎8792 8888; sofitel@renminsquare.com; 319 Dong Xinjie; 东新街319号; d/ste Y1242/1814;) Xī'ān's self-proclaimed 'six-star' hotel is undoubtedly the most luxurious choice in the city and has a soothing, hushed atmosphere. The bathrooms are top-notch. Cantonese, Japanese and Moroccan restaurants are on-site, as well as a South American–themed bar. Reception is in the east wing and room rates change daily, so you can score a deal when business is slow.

Shūyuàn Youth Hostel HOSTEL $
(书院青年旅舍; Shūyuàn Qīngnián Lǚshè; ☎8728 7721; shuyuanhostel@yahoo.com.cn; 2a Shuncheng Xixiang; 南门里顺城西巷甲2号; dm Y30-50, s & d Y160;) The longest-running hostel in Xī'ān and still one of the most amenable, the Shūyuàn is located in a converted courtyard residence near the South Gate. The pleasant cafe, with wi-fi access, is a good place to hang out with fellow travellers. The hostel is 20m west of the South Gate along the city walls and bus 603 runs close to it.

Jǐnjiāng Inn HOTEL $$
(锦江之星; Jǐnjiāng Zhīxīng; ☎8745 2288; www.jj-inn.com; 110 Jiefang Lu; 解放路110号; d/tw/ste Y179/199/219;) By Xī'ān's standards, the prices are close to budget, but the clean and bright modern rooms, all with ADSL, make this a better option than most three-star places. There's a cheap restaurant here, too.

Hyatt Regency Xī'ān HOTEL $$$
(西安凯悦（阿房宫）酒店; Xī'ān Kǎiyuè Jiǔdiàn; ☎8769 1234; 158 Dong Dajie; 东大街158号; d Y1600, discounts of up to 40%;) Slap in the centre of downtown, the Hyatt has big, rather characterless rooms with all the trimmings, as well as efficient staff, a spa and Western and Chinese restaurants. Add a 15% service charge to the bill.

Bell Tower Hotel HOTEL $$$
(西安钟楼饭店; Xī'ān Zhōnglóu Fàndiàn; ☎8760 0000; www.belltowerhtl.com; 110 Nan Dajie; 南大街110号; d Y850-1080, discounts of 33%;) Big discounts are on offer during slack periods, making this state-owned, four-star more affordable. Some rooms have a bird's-eye view of the Bell Tower and all are spacious and comfortable with cable TV and broadband internet connections.

Qīxián Youth Hostel HOSTEL $
(七贤庄; Qīxián Zhuāng; ☎6229 6977; www.7sages.com.cn; 1 Beixin Jie; 北新街1号; dm Y40-60, s & d Y120-150;) This is the most secluded hostel, set in a traditional courtyard house, and popular with Chinese travellers. The rooms are a little faded, but there's a decent communal cafe and restaurant, and the staff are helpful. Take bus 610 from opposite the train station.

Héjiā Shāngwù Hotel HOTEL $$
(和嘉商务宾馆; ☎8728 2200/8919; www.hj600.cn; 16 Nan Dajie; 南大街16号; s/d/tr Y280/298/368, discounts of 30%;) The great location means this new place can be noisy, but the rooms are decent-sized with clean bathrooms and they all come with ADSL connections.

City Hotel Xī'ān HOTEL $$
(西安城市酒店; Xī'ān Chéngshì Jiǔdiàn; ☎8721 9988; www.cityhotelxian.com; 70 Nan Dajie; 南大街70号; s/tw/d Y266/488/588, discounts of 25%;) Despite the dreary decor, this is a reliable midrange choice popular with tour groups. The entrance is down an alley 20m west off Nan Dajie.

Eating

Hit the **Muslim Quarter** for fine eating in Xī'ān. Common dishes here are *májiàng liángpí* (麻酱凉皮; cold noodles in sesame sauce), *fěnzhēngròu* (粉蒸肉; chopped mutton fried in a wok with ground wheat), *ròujiāmó* (肉夹馍; fried pork or beef in pitta bread, sometimes with green peppers and cumin), *càijiāmó* (菜夹馍; the vegetarian version of *ròujiāmó*) and the ubiquitous *ròuchuàn* (肉串; kebabs).

Best of all is the delicious *yángròu pàomó* (羊肉泡馍), a soup dish that involves crumbling a flat loaf of bread into a bowl and adding noodles, mutton and broth. You can also pick up mouth-watering desserts such as *huāshēnggāo* (花生糕; peanut cakes) and *shìbǐng* (柿饼; dried persimmons), which can be found at the market or in Muslim Quarter shops.

A good street to wander for a selection of more typically Chinese restaurants is Dongmutou Shi, east of Nan Dajie.

SHAANXI (SHǍNXĪ)

All the hostels serve up Western breakfasts and meals with varying degrees of success. For something more refined, try the buffet at the **Sofitel** (lunch/dinner incl service charge Y128/208).

First Noodle Under the Sun NOODLES **$**
(天下第一面酒楼; Tiānxià Dìyī Miàn Jiǔlóu; ☎8728 6088; 19 Dongmutou Shi; dishes Y6-58; ⏲9am-10.30pm; 🗐) The speciality at this busy place is *biáng biáng miàn,* a giant, 3.8m strip of noodle that comes folded up in a big bowl with two soup side dishes (Y10). But all sorts of excellent noodle, meat and vegie dishes are available here.

Máogōng Xiāngcàiguǎn HUNAN **$$**
(毛公湘菜馆; ☎8782 0555; 99 Youyi Xilu; mains from Y26; ⏲11am-10pm; 🗐) A statue of the Chairman overlooks diners at this slick place across the road from the Little Goose Pagoda. The menu features Húnán classics, such as spicy chicken and boiled frog (Y38), most of which have a fiery kick that Mao, who liked his food hot, would have approved of.

Lǎo Sūn Jiā SHAANXI **$**
(老孙家; ☎8240 3205; 2nd fl, Dong Dajie; dishes Y12-40; ⏲8am-9pm; 🚭) Xī'ān's most famous restaurant (over a century old) is as well known for its perfunctory service as it is for the steaming bowls of *yángròu pàomó* it specialises in. They still go down a treat. There's no English sign; look for the big red characters on the 2nd-floor window.

Green Molly Restaurant & Bar WESTERN **$$**
(绿茉莉; Lǜ Mòlì; ☎8188 3339; Keji Lu; 世纪金花商厦后门右200米; mains from Y52; ⏲7pm-3am; 🗐) It's a bit of a trek southwest of the city walls (Y20 in a taxi), but if you're craving authentic Western food and beers on tap, then this wood-panelled pub behind the Ginwa Shopping Centre is the place to come. The menu covers all the bases, from steaks and pizzas to Mexican. The beers are expensive, but it's buy one, get one free all the time. It's hard to find, so get your taxi driver to call for directions.

Wǔyī Fàndiàn CHINESE **$**
(五一饭店; 351 Dong Dajie; dishes Y8-22; ⏲7.30am-9.30pm) This frenetic and noisy cafeteria-style restaurant is good for northern staples, such as dumplings and noodles, and the pick-and-choose format is perfect for the Chinese-challenged. It's normally packed out with locals craving postshopping sustenance.

Drinking

Xī'ān's nightlife options range from bars and clubs to cheesy but popular tourist shows.

The main bar strip is Defu Xiang, close to the South Gate. The top end of the street has coffee shops and teahouses. The bars get more raucous the closer to the South Gate you get, but it's still fairly tame.

Old Henry's Bar BAR
(老亨利酒吧; Lǎohēnglì Jiǔbā;48 Defu Xiang; ⏲8pm-3am) Always busy and has outside seating.

Moonkey Music Bar BAR
(月亮钥匙音乐酒吧; Yuèliàng Yàoshi Yīnyuè Jiǔbā; ⏲5pm-2am) Opposite the South Gate, this is an appropriately grungy spot to hear local bands while downing a beer.

Entertainment

Clubs get going early in Xī'ān, in part because they're as much places to drink as to dance. They are free to get into, but expect to pay at least Y30 for a beer. Most are located along or off Nan Dajie.

Some travellers enjoy spending the evening at the **fountain & music show** (⏲9pm Mar-Nov, 8pm Dec-Feb) on Big Goose Pagoda Sq; it's the largest in Asia. Xī'ān also has a number of dinner-dance shows, which are normally packed out with tour groups. They can be fun if you're in the mood for a bit of kitsch.

Song & Song CLUB
(上上酒吧乐巢会; Shàngshàng Jiǔbā Lècháohùi; 109 Ximutou Shi; ⏲7pm-late) More of a big bar with DJs than a genuine club.

1+1 CLUB
(壹加壹俱乐部; Yījiāyī Jùlèbù; 285 Dong Dajie; ⏲7pm-late) The ever-popular 1+1 is a neon-lit maze of a place that pumps out party hip-hop tunes well into the early hours.

Tang Dynasty DINNER SHOW
(唐乐宫; Tángyuè Gōng; ☎8782 2222; www.xiantangdynasty.com; 75 Chang'an Beilu; performance with/without dinner Y500/220) The most famous dinner theatre in the city stages an over-the-top spectacle with Vegas-style costumes, traditional dance, music and singing. It's dubbed into English.

Shaanxi Grand Opera House DINNER SHOW
(陕歌大剧院; Shǎngē Dàjùyuàn; ☎8785 3295; www.xiantangdynasty.com; 165 Wenyi Lu; performance with/without dinner Y198/128) Also known as the Tang Palace Dance Show, this is a cheaper, less flashy alternative to the Tang Dynasty show.

Shopping

Stay in Xī'ān for a couple of days and you'll be offered enough sets of miniature terracotta warriors to form your own army. The souvenir industry is big business here, with everyone from the major museums to street vendors doing their best to separate you from your cash. A good place to search out gifts is the Muslim Quarter, where prices are generally cheaper than elsewhere.

Xiyang Shi is a narrow, crowded alley running north of the Great Mosque where terracotta warriors, Huxian farmer paintings, shadow puppets, lanterns, tea ware, 'antiques', Mao memorabilia and T-shirts are on offer. Bear in mind that most of it is fake, so check the quality of what you're buying and bargain hard. Remember, though, the purpose of haggling is to achieve a mutually acceptable price and not to screw the vendor into the ground. It always helps to smile.

Near the South Gate is the Qing-style Shuyuan Xiang, the main street for art supplies, paintings, calligraphy, paper cuts, brushes and fake rubbings from the Forest of Stelae Museum. Serious shoppers should also visit the **Northwest Antique Market** (西北古玩城; Xīběi Gǔwán Chéng; Dong Xinjie; ⏲10am-5.30pm), by the Zhongshan Gate. This three-storey warren of shops selling jade, seals, antiques and Mao memorabilia sees far fewer foreign faces than the Muslim Quarter.

There's a much smaller antique market by the Temple of the Eight Immortals on Sunday and Wednesday mornings.

Information

Pick up a copy of the widely available *Xi'an Traffic & Tourist Map* (Y8). This bilingual publication has exhaustive listings and is regularly updated – even the bus routes are correct. Chinese-language maps with the bus routes are sold on the street for Y5.

All hostels and most hotels offer internet access. You can burn digital photos onto CDs at the youth hostels (per disc Y20).

In the event of an emergency, call ☎120.

ATM (自动柜员机; Zìdòng Guìyuánjī; ⏲24hr) You should have no trouble finding usable ATMs. When in doubt, try the southeast corner of the Bell Tower intersection.

Bank of China (中国银行; Zhōngguó Yínháng) Juhuayuan Lu (38 Juhuayuan Lu; ⏲8am-8pm); Nan Dajie (29 Nan Dajie; ⏲8am-6pm) You can exchange cash and travellers cheques and use the ATMs at both of these branches.

China International Travel Service (CITS; 中国国际旅行社; Zhōngguó Guójì Lǚxíngshè) Branch office (2nd fl, Bell Tower Hotel, 110 Nan Dajie); Main office (48 Chang'an Beilu) The Bell Tower Hotel office is best for organising tours.

China Post (中国邮政; Zhōngguó Yóuzhèng; Bei Dajie; ⏲8am-8pm)

Internet cafe (网吧; wǎngbā; 21 Xi Qilu; per hr Y3; ⏲24hr) Around the corner from the long-distance bus station. There are also other internet cafes in this area.

Kodak (柯达数码中心; Kēdá Shùmǎ Zhōngxīn; cnr Jiefang Lu & Dong Dajie; per disc Y10; ⏲8am-9pm) Offers CD burning.

Public Security Bureau (PSB; 公安局; Gōng'ānjú; ☎1682 1225; 63 Xi Dajie; ⏲8.30am-noon & 2-6pm Mon-Fri)

Getting There & Away

Air

Xī'ān's Xiányáng Airport is one of China's best connected – you can fly to almost any major Chinese destination from here, as well as several international ones.

China Eastern Airlines (中国东方航空公司; Zhōngguó Dōngfāng Hángkōng; ☎8208 8707; 64 Xi Wulu; ⏲8am-9pm) operates most flights to and from Xī'ān. Daily flights include Běijīng (Y840), Chéngdū (Y630), Guǎngzhōu (Y890), Shànghǎi (Y1160), Shēnzhèn (Y980) and Ürümqi (Y1640). On the international front, China Eastern has flights from Xī'ān to Hong Kong (Y1410), Seoul, Bangkok, Tokyo and Nagoya.

Most hostels and hotels and all travel agencies sell airline tickets.

Bus

The most central **long-distance bus station** (长途汽车站; *chángtú qìchēzhàn*) is opposite Xī'ān's train station. It's a chaotic place. Note that buses to Huà Shān (6am to 8pm) depart from in front of the train station.

Other bus stations around town where you may be dropped off include the **east bus station** (城东客运站; chéngdōng kèyùnzhàn; Changle Lu) and the **west bus station** (城西客运站; chéngxī kèyùnzhàn; Zaoyuan Donglu). Both are located outside the Second Ring Rd. Bus 605 travels between the Bell Tower and the east bus station, and bus 103 travels between the train station and the west bus station. A taxi into the city from either bus station costs between Y15 and Y20.

Buses from Xī'ān's long-distance bus station go to:

Hánchéng Y62.50, four hours, every 30 minutes (7am to 4pm)

Huà Shān one way/return Y33/55, two hours, three daily (11am, noon and 2.30pm)

Luòyáng Y60.50, four hours, every 40 minutes (7am to 7.30pm)

Píngyáo Y180, seven hours, hourly (8am to 4pm)

Yán'ān Y82.50, 5½ hours, every 40 minutes (6.40am to 4.20pm)

Zhèngzhōu Y120, 6½ hours, hourly (7am to 4.30pm)

Train

Xī'ān's main train station *(huǒchē zhàn)* is just outside the northern city walls. It's always busy. Buy your onward tickets as soon as you arrive. Most hotels and hostels can get you tickets (Y40 commission); there's also an **Advance Train-Ticket Booking Office** (代售火车票; Dàishòu Huǒchēpiào; Nan Dajie; ⌚8.30am-noon & 2-5pm) in the ICBC Bank's south entrance. Otherwise, brave the crowds in the main ticket hall.

Xī'ān is well connected to the rest of the country. Deluxe Z-trains run to/from Běijīng West (soft sleeper only Y417, 11½ hours), leaving Xī'ān at 7.23pm and Běijīng at 9.24pm. Several express trains also make the journey (Y265, 12½ hours); departures begin late afternoon.

All prices listed below are for hard sleeper *(yìng wò)* tickets.

Chéngdū Y201, 16 ½ hours

Chóngqìng Y191, 14 hours

Guǎngzhōu Y416, 26 hours

Guìlín Y385, 27 hours

Jì'nán Y265, 16 to 18 hours

Kūnmíng Y385, 36 hours

Lánzhōu Y169, 7 ½ to nine hours

Luòyáng Y106, five hours

Píngyáo Y95, nine hours

Shànghǎi Y323, 15 to 22 hours

Tàiyuán Y106, 10 to 12 hours

Ürümqi Y483, 27 to 39 hours

Zhèngzhōu Y133, six to eight hours

Within Shaanxi, there is an overnight train to Yúlín (Y165, 12 to 14 hours) via Yán'ān (Y103, five to nine hours). Buy tickets in advance. There is also an early-morning train to Hánchéng (Y19, 4½ hours).

Getting Around

Xī'ān's Xiányáng Airport is about 40km northwest of Xī'ān. Shuttle buses run every 20 to 30 minutes from 5.40am to 8pm between the airport and the Melody Hotel (Y25, one hour). Taxis into the city charge over Y100 on the meter.

If you're itching to try out the public buses, they go to all the major sights in and around the city. Bus 610 is a useful one: it starts at the train station and passes the Bell Tower, Little Goose Pagoda, Shaanxi History Museum and Big Goose Pagoda. Remember that packed buses are a pickpocket's paradise, so watch your wallet.

The official word on the city's much-needed and much-delayed first subway line is that it should open in 2011.

Taxi flagfall is Y6. It can be very difficult to get a taxi in the late afternoon, when the drivers change shifts. If you can cope with the congested roads, bikes are a good alternative and can be hired at the youth hostels.

Around Xī'ān

The plains surrounding Xī'ān are strewn with early imperial tombs, many of which have not yet been excavated. But unless you have a particular fascination for burial sites, you can probably come away satisfied after visiting a couple of them.

The Army of Terracotta Warriors is obviously the most famous site, but it's really worth the effort to get to the Tomb of Emperor Jingdi as well.

Tourist buses run to almost all of the sites from in front of Xī'ān train station, with the notable exception of the Tomb of Emperor Jingdi.

Sights

EAST OF XĪ'ĀN

Army of Terracotta Warriors MUSEUM
(兵马俑; Bīngmǎyǒng; www.bmy.com.cn; admission Mar-Nov Y90, students Y45, Dec-Feb Y65; ⌚8.30am-5.30pm Mar-Nov, to 5pm Dec-Feb) The Terracotta Army isn't just Xī'ān's premier site, but one of the most famous archaeological finds in the world. This subterranean life-size army of thousands has silently stood guard over the soul of China's first unifier for over two millennia. Either Qin Shi Huang was terrified of the vanquished spirits awaiting him in the afterlife, or, as most archaeologists believe, he expected his rule to continue in death as it had in life – whatever the case, the guardians of his tomb today offer some of the greatest insights we have into the world of ancient China.

The discovery of the army of warriors was entirely fortuitous. In 1974, peasants drilling a well uncovered an underground vault that eventually yielded thousands of terracotta soldiers and horses in battle formation. Over the years the site became so famous that many of its unusual attributes are now well known, in particular the fact that no two soldier's faces are alike.

Around Xī'ān

To really appreciate a trip here, it helps to understand the historical context of the warriors. If you don't want to employ a guide (Y100) or use the audioguide (Y40), the on-site theatre gives a useful primer on how the figures were sculpted. Then visit the site in reverse, which enables you to build up to the most impressive pit for a fitting finale.

Start with the smallest pit, **Pit 3**, containing 72 warriors and horses, which is believed to be the army headquarters due to the number of high-ranking officers unearthed here. It's interesting to note that the northern room would have been used to make sacrificial offerings before battle. In the next pit, **Pit 2**, containing around 1300 warriors and horses, which is still being excavated, you get to examine five of the soldiers up close: a kneeling archer, a standing archer, a cavalryman and his horse, a mid-ranking officer and a general. The level of detail is extraordinary: the expressions, hairstyles, armour and even the tread on the footwear are all unique.

The largest pit, **Pit 1**, is the most imposing. Housed in a building the size of an aircraft hangar, it is believed to contain 6000 warriors (only 2000 are on display) and horses, all facing east and ready for battle. The vanguard of three rows of archers (both crossbow and longbow) is followed by the main force of soldiers, who originally held spears, swords, dagger-axes and other long-shaft weapons. The infantry were accompanied by 35 chariots, though these, made of wood, have long since disintegrated.

Almost as extraordinary as the soldiers is a pair of bronze chariots and horses unearthed just 20m west of the Tomb of Qin Shi Huang. These are now on display, together with some of the original weaponry, in a small **museum** to the right of the main entrance.

The Army of Terracotta Warriors is easily reached by public bus. From the car park at Xī'ān train station, take one of the green Terracotta Warriors minibuses (Y7, one hour) or bus 306 (Y7, one hour), both of which travel via Huáqīng Hot Springs and the Tomb of Qin Shi Huang. The car park for all vehicles is a good 15-minute walk from the Terracotta Warriors site. Electric carts do the run for Y5. If you want to eat here, go for the restaurants across from the car park.

Huáqīng Hot Springs HISTORIC SITE

(华清池; Huáqīng Chí; admission Mar-Nov Y70, Dec-Feb Y40; ⏲7am-7pm Mar-Nov, 7.30am-6.30pm Dec-Feb) The natural hot springs in this park were once the favoured retreat of emperors and concubines during the Tang dynasty.

An obligatory stop for Chinese tour groups, who pose for photos in front of the elaborately restored pavilions and by the ornamental ponds, it's a pretty place but not really worth the high admission price. You can, though, hike up to the **Taoist temple** on Black Horse Mountain (Lí Shān). The temple is dedicated to Nuwa, who created the human race from clay and also patched up cracks in the sky. There's also a **cable car** (one way/return Y45/70) to the temple, but note that the stop is outside the park, so you won't be able to get back in unless you buy another ticket.

Tomb of Qin Shi Huang HISTORIC SITE
(秦始皇陵; Qín Shǐhuáng Líng; admission Mar-Nov Y40, Dec-Feb Y20; ⊙8am-6pm Mar-Nov, to 5pm Dec-Feb) In its time, this tomb must have been one of the grandest mausoleums the world had ever seen.

Historical accounts describe it as containing palaces filled with precious stones, underground rivers of flowing mercury and ingenious defences against intruders. The tomb reputedly took 38 years to complete, and required a workforce of 700,000 people. It is said that the artisans who built it were buried alive within, taking its secrets with them.

Considered too dangerous to excavate, the tomb has little to see but you can climb the steps to the top of the mound for a fine view of the surrounding countryside. The tomb is about 2km west of the Army of Terracotta Warriors. Take bus 306 from Xī'ān train station.

Bànpō Neolithic Village ANCIENT VILLAGE
(半坡博物馆; Bànpō Bówùguǎn; admission Mar-Nov Y35, Dec-Feb Y25; ⊙8am-6pm) This village is of enormous importance for Chinese archaeological studies, but unless you're desperately interested in the subject it can be an underwhelming visitor experience.

Bànpō is the earliest example of the Neolithic Yangshao culture, which is believed to have been matriarchal. It appears to have been occupied from 4500 BC until around 3750 BC. The excavated area is divided into three parts: a pottery-manufacturing area, a residential area complete with moat, and a cemetery. There are also two exhibition halls that feature some of the pottery, including strange-shaped amphorae, discovered at the site.

The village is in the eastern suburbs of Xī'ān. Bus 105 (Y1) from the train station runs past (ask where to get off); it's also often included on tours.

NORTH & WEST OF XĪ'ĀN

Tomb of Emperor Jingdi HISTORIC SITE
(汉阳陵; Hàn Yánglíng; admission Mar-Nov Y90, Dec-Feb Y65; ⊙8.30am-7pm Mar-Nov, to 6pm Dec-Feb) This tomb (also referred to as the Han Jing Mausoleum, Liu Qi Mausoleum and Yangling Mausoleum) is easily Xī'ān's most underrated highlight. If you only have time for two sights, then it should be the Army of Terracotta Warriors and this impressive museum and tomb. And unlike the warriors, there are relatively few visitors here so you have the space to appreciate what you're seeing.

A Han-dynasty emperor influenced by Taoism, Jingdi (188–141 BC) based his rule upon the concept of *wúwéi* (nonaction or noninterference) and did much to improve the life of his subjects: he lowered taxes greatly, used diplomacy to cut back on unnecessary military expeditions and even reduced the punishment meted out to criminals. The contents of his tomb are particularly interesting, as they reveal more about daily life than martial preoccupations – a total contrast with the Terracotta Army.

The site has been divided into two sections: the museum and the excavation area. The **museum** holds a large display of expressive terracotta figurines (over 50,000 were buried here), including eunuchs, servants, domesticated animals and even female cavalry on horseback. The figurines originally had movable wooden arms (now gone) and were dressed in colourful silk robes.

But it's the **tomb** itself, which is still being excavated, that's the real reason to make the trip out here. Inside are 21 narrow pits, some of which have been covered by a glass floor, allowing you to walk over the top of ongoing excavations and get a great view of the relics. In all, there are believed to be 81 burial pits here.

Unfortunately, getting here by public transport is a pain. First, take bus 4 (Y1) from Xī'ān's North Gate. After 30 minutes, it reaches the end of its line at the Zhang Jiabu roundabout. Get off and walk 100m right of the roundabout, where another bus, also numbered 4 (Y2), leaves for the tomb. The catch is that while there are many buses to the roundabout, only three a day do the second leg to the tomb. At the time of writing, they were leaving at 8.30am, 10.50am and 2.30pm, returning to Xī'ān at 12.30pm, 3.30pm and 5.30pm.

Alternatively, you can try to find a Western Tour that visits the site, or hire a taxi (figure on Y200 for a half-day). The tomb is also close to the airport, so you could stop here on your way to or from there.

Fǎmén Temple BUDDHIST TEMPLE
(法门寺; Fǎmén Sì; admission Mar-Nov Y120, Dec-Feb Y90; ⊙8am-6pm) This temple dating back to the 2nd century AD was built to

THE MAN BEHIND THE ARMY

History is written by the winners. But in China, it was penned by Confucian bureaucrats and for Qin Shi Huang that was a problem, because his disdain for Confucianism was such that he outlawed it, ordered almost all its written texts to be burnt and, according to legend, buried 460 of its top scholars alive. As a result, the First Emperor went down in history as the sort of tyrant who gives tyrants a bad name.

At the same time, though, it's hard to overstate the magnitude of his accomplishments during his 36 years of rule (which began when he was just 13). A classic overachiever, he created an efficient, centralised government that became the model for later dynasties; he standardised measurements, currency and, most importantly, writing; he built over 6400km of new roads and canals; and, of course, he conquered six major kingdoms before turning 40.

The fact that Qin Shi Huang did all this by enslaving hundreds of thousands of people helped ensure that his subsequent reputation would be as dark as the black he made the official colour of his court. But in recent years, there have been efforts by the China Communist Party (CCP), no strangers to autocratic rule themselves, to rehabilitate him, by emphasising both his efforts to unify China and the far-sighted nature of his policies.

Nevertheless, he remains a hugely controversial figure in Chinese history, but also one whose presence permeates popular culture. The First Emperor pops up in video games, in literature and on TV shows. He's also been the subject of films by both Chen Kaige and Zhang Yimou (*The Emperor and the Assassin* and *Hero*), while Jet Li played a thinly disguised version of him in the 2008 Hollywood blockbuster *The Mummy: Tomb of the Dragon Emperor*.

house parts of a sacred finger bone of the Buddha, presented to China by India's King Asoka. In 1981, after torrential rains had weakened the temple's ancient brick structure, the entire western side of its 12-storey pagoda collapsed. The subsequent restoration of the temple produced a sensational discovery. Below the pagoda in a sealed crypt were over 1000 sacrificial objects and royal offerings – all forgotten for over a millennium.

Scenting a cash cow, the local authorities have recently started enlarging the temple complex, an ongoing process. You can join the queue of pilgrims who shuffle past the finger bone, but the real reason to make the trip out here is the superb **museum** and its collection of Tang-dynasty treasures. Arguably, what's on display here is more impressive than the collection at the Shaanxi History Museum. There are elaborate gold and silver boxes (stacked on top of one another to form pagodas) and tiny crystal and jade coffins that originally held the four sections of the holy finger.

Other notable exhibits are ornate incense burners, glass cups and vases from the Roman Empire, statues, gold and silver offerings, and an excellent reproduced cross-section of the four-chamber crypt, which symbolised a tantric mandala (a geometric representation of the universe).

Fǎmén Temple is 115km northwest of Xī'ān. Tour bus 2 (Y25, 8am) from Xī'ān train station runs to the temple and returns to Xī'ān at 5pm. The temple is also generally included on Western Tours.

FREE Xiányáng City Museum MUSEUM
(咸阳市博物馆; Xiányáng Shì Bówùguǎn; Zhongshan Jie; ⏲9am-5.30pm) Over 2000 years ago, Xiányáng was the capital of the Qin dynasty. These days, it's just a dusty satellite of Xī'ān. Its chief attraction is this museum, which houses a remarkable collection of 3000 50cm-tall terracotta soldiers and horses, excavated from the tomb of Liu Bang, the first Han emperor, in 1965. Set in an attractive courtyard, the museum also has bronze and jade exhibits and good English captions.

Buses run every 15 minutes to Xiányáng (Y8.50, one hour) from Xī'ān's long-distance bus station. Ask to be dropped off at the museum. To get back to Xī'ān, just flag down buses going in the opposite direction.

Imperial Tombs HISTORIC SITES
A large number of imperial tombs (皇陵; *huáng líng*) dot the Guānzhōng plain around Xī'ān. They are sometimes in-

cluded on tours from Xī'ān, but most aren't so remarkable as to be destinations in themselves. By far the most impressive is the **Qián Tomb** (乾陵; Qián Líng; admission Mar-Nov Y45, Dec-Feb Y25; ⏲8am-6pm), where China's only female emperor, Wu Zetian (AD 625–705), is buried together with her husband Emperor Gaozong, whom she succeeded. The long **Spirit Way** (Yù Dào) here is lined with enormous, lichen-encrusted sculptures of animals and officers of the imperial guard, culminating with 61 (now headless) statues of Chinese ethnic group leaders who attended the emperor's funeral. The mausoleum is 85km northwest of Xī'ān. Tour bus 2 (Y25, 8am) runs close to here from Xī'ān train station and returns in the late afternoon.

Nearby, are the **tomb of Princess Yong Tai** (永泰幕; Yǒng Tài Mù) and **tomb of Princess Zhang Huai** (章怀幕; Zhāng Huái Mù), both of whom fell foul of Empress Wu, before being posthumously rehabilitated. Other notable tombs are the **Zhao Tomb** (昭陵; Zhāo Líng), where the second Tang emperor Taizhong is buried, and the **Mao Tomb** (茂陵; Mào Líng), the resting place of Wudi (156–87 BC), the most powerful of the Han emperors.

Tours

One-day tours allow you to see all the sights around Xī'ān more quickly and conveniently than if you arranged one yourself. Itineraries differ somewhat, but there are two basic tours: an Eastern Tour and a Western Tour.

Most hostels run their own tours, but make sure you find out what is included (admission fees, lunch, English-speaking guide) and try to get an exact itinerary, or you could end up being herded through the Terracotta Warriors before you have a chance to get your camera out.

Eastern Tour

The Eastern Tour (Dōngxiàn Yóulǎn) is the most popular as it includes the Army of Terracotta Warriors, as well as the Tomb of Qin Shi Huang, Bànpō Neolithic Village, Huáqīng Hot Springs and possibly the Big Goose Pagoda. Most travel agencies and hostels charge around Y300 for an all-day, all-in excursion, including admission fees, lunch and guide, although sometimes the hostel tours skip Bànpō. Tours to the Terracotta Warriors only are also available for around Y160.

It's perfectly possible to do a shortened version of the Eastern Tour by using the tourist buses or bus 306, all of which pass by Huáqīng Hot Springs, the Terracotta Warriors and the Tomb of Qin Shi Huang. If you decide to do this, start at the hot springs, then travel to Qin Shi Huang's tomb and end at the Terracotta Warriors.

Western Tour

The longer Western Tour (Xīxiàn Yóulǎn) includes the Xiányáng City Museum, some of the imperial tombs, and possibly also Fǎmén Temple and (if you insist) the Tomb of Emperor Jingdi. It's far less popular than the Eastern Tour and consequently you may have to wait a couple of days for your hostel or agency to organise enough people. It's also more expensive; expect to pay Y600.

Huà Shān 华山

One of Taoism's five sacred mountains, the granite domes of Huà Shān used to be home to hermits and sages. These days, though, the trails that wind their way up to the five peaks are populated by droves of day trippers drawn by the dreamy scenery. And it is spectacular. There are knife-blade ridges and twisted pine trees clinging to ledges as you ascend, while the summits offer transcendent panoramas of green mountains and countryside stretching away to the horizon. Taoists hoping to find a quiet spot to contemplate life and the universe will be disappointed, but everyone else seems to revel in the tough climb and they're suitably elated once they reach the top. So forget all that spiritual malarkey and get walking.

Sights & Activities

There are three ways up the mountain to the **North Peak** (北峰; Běi Fēng), the first of five summit peaks. Two of these options start from the eastern base of the mountain, at the cable-car terminus. The first option is handy if you don't fancy the climb: an Austrian-built **cable car** (one way/return Y80/150; ⏲7am-7pm) will lift you to the North Peak in 10 scenic minutes.

The second option is to work your way to the North Peak under the cable-car route. This takes a sweaty two hours, and two sections of 50m or so are quite literally vertical, with nothing but a steel chain to grab onto and tiny chinks cut into the rock

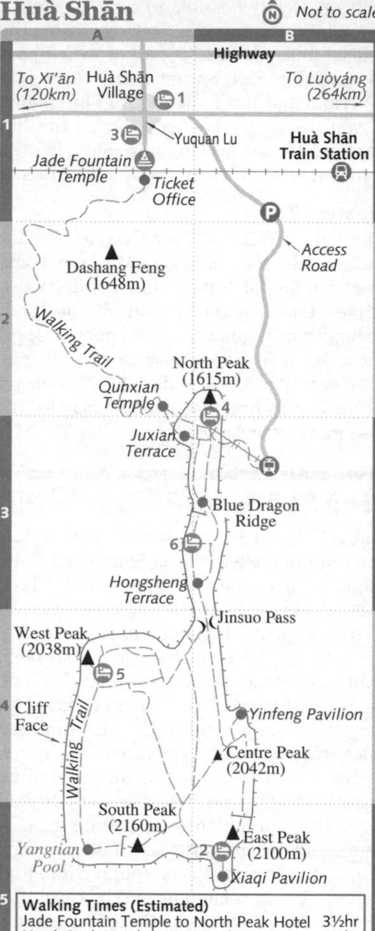

Huà Shān

Sleeping

1 Bǔjiāyí Inn A1
2 Dōngfēng Bīnguǎn B5
3 Huáyáng Hotel A1
4 North Peak Hotel B2
5 West Peak Hostel A4
6 Wǔyúnfēng Fàndiàn A3

for footing. Not for nothing is this route called the 'Soldiers Path'.

The third option is the most popular, but it's still hard work. A 6km path leads to the North Peak from the village of Huà Shān, at the base of the mountain. It usually takes between three and five hours to reach the North Peak via this route. The first 4km up are pretty easy going, but after that it's all steep stairs.

If you want to carry on to the other peaks, then count on a minimum of eight hours in total from the base of Huà Shān. If you want to spare your knees, then another option is to take the cable car to the North Peak and then climb to the other peaks, before ending up back where you started. It takes about four hours to complete the circuit in this fashion and it's still fairly strenuous. In places, it can be a little nerve-racking, too. Huà Shān has a reputation for being dangerous, especially when the trails are crowded, or if it's wet or icy, so exercise caution.

But the scenery is sublime. Along **Blue Dragon Ridge** (苍龙岭; Cānglóng Lǐng), which connects the North Peak with the **East Peak** (东峰; Dōng Fēng), **South Peak** (南峰; Nán Fēng) and **West Peak** (西峰; Xī Fēng), the way has been cut along a narrow rock ridge with impressive sheer cliffs on either side.

The South Peak is the highest at 2160m and the most crowded. The East Peak is less busy, but all three rear peaks afford great views when the weather cooperates.

There is accommodation on the mountain, most of it basic and overpriced, but it does allow you to start climbing in the afternoon, watch the sunset and then spend the night, before catching the sunrise from either the East Peak or South Peak. Some locals make the climb at night, using torches (flashlights). The idea is to start around 11pm and be at the East Peak for sunrise; you get to see the scenery on the way down.

Admission is Y100. To get to the cable car *(suǒdào)*, take a taxi from the village to the ticket office (Y10) and then a shuttle bus (one way/return Y10/20) the rest of the way.

Sleeping & Eating

You can either spend the night in Huà Shān village or on one of the peaks. Take your own food or eat well before ascending, unless you like to feast on instant noodles and processed meat – proper meals are very pricey on the mountain. Don't forget a torch and warm clothes. Bear in mind that prices for a bed triple during public holidays. Some of the mountain hotels are also reluctant to give out dorm beds to solo travellers. If that happens, head to the West Peak Hostel.

In the village, there are a number of dingy, none-too-clean hotels along Yuquan Lu, the road leading up to the trailhead, that offer beds from Y50 upwards. There are smarter places on Yuquan Donglu. On the mountain, expect nothing remotely luxurious, especially not a private bathroom.

Bǐjiāyí Inn HOTEL $$
(比家宜快捷酒店; Bǐjiāyí Kuàijié Jiǔdiàn; ☎0913-465 8000; Yuquan Donglu; 玉泉东路; s & d Y238-281; ❄) A new and welcome choice in a town crying out for a decent midrange hotel. Big, modern rooms and the best option if you want a modicum of comfort without breaking the bank.

Wǔyúnfēng Fàndiàn HOTEL $
(五云峰饭店; dm Y100-180, tr/d Y210/280) If you're planning on doing a circuit of the rear peaks the next day, or want to catch the sunrise at the East or South Peak, this is a good choice.

Huáyáng Hotel HOTEL $
(华洋大酒店; Huáyáng Dàjiǔdiàn); ☎0913-436 5288; Yuquan Lu; 玉泉路; s & d Y120) Clean and simple rooms with OK bathrooms make this the pick of the admittedly poor hotels on offer on Yuquan Lu.

Dōngfēng Bīnguǎn HOTEL $
(东峰宾馆; dm Y100-220, tr/d Y260/320) The top location for watching the sun come up and the best restaurant.

West Peak Hostel HOSTEL $
(西峰旅社; Xīfēng Lǚshè; dm Y80) Rustic and basic, but also the friendliest place on the mountain. It shares its premises with an old Taoist temple.

North Peak Hotel HOTEL $
(北峰饭店; Běifēng Fàndiàn; dm Y60-180, d Y240-260) The busiest of the peak hotels.

Getting There & Away

From Xī'ān to Huà Shān, catch one of the private buses (one way/return Y33/55, two hours, 6am to 8pm) that depart from in front of Xī'ān train station. You'll be dropped off on Yuquan Lu, which is also where buses back to Xī'ān leave from 7.30am to 7pm. Coming from the east, try to talk your driver into dropping you at the Huà Shān highway exit if you can't find a direct bus. Don't pay more than Y10 for a taxi into Huà Shān village. There are few buses (if any) going east from Huà Shān; pretty much everyone catches a taxi to the highway and then flags down buses headed for Yùnchéng, Tàiyuán or Luòyáng. If you can't read Chinese, try to find someone to help you out.

Hánchéng 韩城

☎0913 / POP 59,000

Hánchéng is best known for being the hometown of Sima Qian (145–90 BC), China's legendary historian and author of the *Shiji* (Records of the Grand Historian). Sima Qian chronicled different aspects of life in the Han dynasty and set about arranging the country's already distant past in its proper (Confucian) order. He was eventually castrated and imprisoned by Emperor Wudi, after having defended an unsuccessful general.

Hánchéng makes for a good overnight trip from Xī'ān. Built upon a hill, the new town (新城; *xīnchéng*) located at the top is dusty and unremarkable and is where you'll find hotels, banks and transport. But the more atmospheric old town (古城; *gǔchéng*) at the bottom of the hill boasts a handful of historic sights that are well off the main tourist circuit. The principal reason to visit, though, is to head to the nearby Ming-dynasty village of Dǎngjiācūn.

Sights

Dǎngjiācūn ANCIENT VILLAGE
(党家村; admission Y40; ⏰7.30am-6.30pm) This remarkable, perfectly preserved, 14th-century village nestles in a sheltered location in a loess valley. Once the home of the Dang clan, successful merchants who ferried timber and other goods across the Yellow River, it's since evolved into a quintessential farming community. Three hundred and twenty families live here in 125 grey-brick courtyard houses, which are notable for their carvings and mix of different architectural styles. The elegant six-storey tower is a **Confucian pagoda** (Wénxīng gé). With its sleepy, timeless atmosphere, it's a fine place to escape the hustle of modern China.

Dǎngjiācūn is 9km northeast of Hánchéng. To get here, take a minibus (Y3, 20 minutes) from the bus station to the entrance road, from where it's a pleasant 2km walk through fields to the village. Otherwise, you can take a taxi from Hánchéng (Y20).

Confucius & Chénghuáng Temples CONFUCIAN TEMPLES

In the heart of the old town, the tranquil **Confucius Temple** (文庙; Wén Miào; admission Y15; ⌚8am-5.30pm) is the pick of the sights in Hánchéng itself. The dilapidated Yuan, Ming and Qing buildings could do with a fresh coat of paint, but there's a half-moon pool, towering cypress trees and glazed dragon screens. The city museum holds peripheral exhibits in the wings.

At the back of the Confucius Temple is the **Chénghuáng Temple** (城隍庙; Chénghuáng Miào; admission Y15; ⌚8am-5.30pm), in a lane lined with Ming-dynasty courtyard houses. There has been a temple here since the Zhou dynasty, but the whole site has undergone extensive renovation in recent years. The main attraction is the **Sacrificing Hall**, with its intricate roof detail, where gifts were offered to the gods to protect the city.

Buying a ticket to either temple gets you into the other as well. Bus 102 (Y1) runs here from the southwest corner of Huanghe Dajie, close to the bus station. A taxi is Y10.

Yuánjué Pagoda MONUMENT

(园觉寺塔; Yuánjué Sìtǎ; ⌚6am-6pm) Looming over the old town and dating back to Tang dynasty, but rebuilt in 1958, this pagoda also acts as a memorial to Red Army soldiers killed fighting the KMT. It's not possible to climb the pagoda itself, but the steep ascent to it offers panoramic views over the old town. To get here, turn sharp right when leaving the Chénghuáng Temple and then take the first major right you come to. The walk takes you through the most evocative part of the old town; exit the pagoda through the park on the other side and you're back in the new town.

Tomb of Sima Qian HISTORIC SITE

(司马迁祠; Sīmǎqiān Cí; admission Y35; ⌚8am-6pm) With its dramatic location atop a hill overlooking fields and the nearby Yellow River, the Tomb of Sima Qian is an imposing sight, even if there's an elevated freeway close by. Despite that, it's still a popular spot with picnickers. The actual tomb, though, isn't much to look at.

The tomb is 10km south of town. To get here, take bus 1 (Y1, 10 minutes) from the train station to its terminus at Nánguān, and then switch to the green Sīmǎ Miào bus (Y3, 20 minutes). You'll have to catch a taxi back (Y30).

Sleeping

For something completely different, spend the night in Dǎngjiācūn, where basic dorm beds in some of the courtyard houses are available for Y15. If a local doesn't approach you, just ask and you'll be pointed in the right direction. They also offer simple and cheap home cooking.

If you'd prefer to spend the night in town try one of the following:

Tiānyuán Bīnguǎn HOTEL $

(天园宾馆; ☎529 9388; Longmen Dajie Beiduan; 龙门大街北段; s & d Y120-130; ❄@) Across from the train station.

Yínhé Dàjiǔdiàn HOTEL $$

(银河大酒店; ☎529 2555; Longmen Dajie Nanduan; 龙门大街南段; r Y398, discounts of up to 33%; ❄@) More upmarket.

Information

There's a branch of the **Bank of China** (中国银行; Zhōngguó Yínháng; cnr Huanghe Dajie & Jinta Zhonglu; ⌚8am-6pm) close to the bus station that has a 24-hour ATM and will change cash. There are other ATMs that take foreign cards, too.

Getting There & Away

Buses leave Xī'ān's long-distance bus station for Hánchéng (Y62.50, three hours, seven daily) from 7am onwards. Buses back to Xī'ān run until 6pm – though these may drop you off at the east bus station. You can catch them from opposite the train station on Longmen Dajie Beiduan, as well as from the bus station. If you're in an exploratory mood, you can also cross over the Yellow River into Shānxī from here.

An early-morning train runs from Xī'ān to Hánchéng (Y19, 4½ hours) at 2.50am. From Hánchéng, a daily local train rumbles towards Běijīng via Píngyáo and Tàiyuán at 4.10pm (Y217, 18 hours).

Yán'ān 延安

☎0911 / POP 107,000

When the diminished communist armies pitched up here at the end of the Long March, it signalled the beginning of Yán'ān's brief period in the sun. For 12 years, from 1935 to 1947, this backwater town was the CCP headquarters, and it was in the surrounding caves that the party thrashed out much of the ideology that was put into practice during the Chinese revolution.

These days, Yán'ān's residents seem to be more interested in consumerism than communism; for a small place, there are a surprising number of shopping malls. But its livelihood is still tied to the CCP; endless tour groups of mostly middle-aged 'red tourists' pass through each year on the trail of Mao and his cohorts. Few foreigners make it here, so expect some attention.

Sights

FREE **Yán'ān Revolution Museum** MUSEUM
(延安革命简史陈列馆; Yán'ān Gémìng Jiǎnshǐ Chénlièguǎn; Shengdi Lu; 8am-5pm) By far the most flash building in town is the new **Yán'ān Revolutionary Memorial Hall** (延安革命纪念馆; Yán'ān Gémìng Jìniànguǎn), fronted by a statue of Mao and housing this museum. It offers an excellent, if obviously one-sided, account of the CCP's time in Yán'ān and the Sino-Japanese War. More English captions would be nice, but there are plenty of photos of the good old days and other exhibits that are self-explanatory. Bus 1 (Y1) runs here.

FREE **Yángjiālǐng Revolution Headquarters Site** HISTORIC SITE
(杨家岭革命旧址; Yángjiālǐng Gémìng Jiùzhǐ; Yangjialing Lu; 8am-6pm Mar-Nov, 8.30am-5pm Dec-Feb) During their extended stay, the communist leadership shifted around Yán'ān. As a result there are numerous former headquarters sites. The most interesting, this site is located 3km northwest of the town centre. Here you can see the assembly hall where the first central committee meetings were held, including the seventh national plenum, which formally confirmed Mao as the leader of the party and the revolution. It's fun watching the red tourists pose in old CCP uniforms in front of the podium.

Nearby are simple **dugouts** built into the loess earth where Mao, Zhu De, Zhou Enlai and other senior communist leaders lived, worked and wrote.

FREE **Wángjiāpíng Revolution Headquarters Site** HISTORIC SITE
(王家坪革命旧址; Wángjiāpíng Gémìng Jiùzhǐ; Wangjiaping Lu; 8am-6pm Mar-Nov, 8.30am-5pm Dec-Feb) Further south, this was the last site occupied by the communist leadership in Yán'ān. The improved living conditions at this site – houses rather than dugouts – indicate the way the CCP's fortunes were rising by the time it moved here.

Both Revolution Headquarters Sites can be reached by taking bus 1, which runs along the road east of the river and then heads up Shengdi Lu. Bus 3 runs along the other side of the river along Zhongxin Jie; get off when it crosses north over the river. Both of these buses start at the train station. Bus 8 also passes by these places and can be caught from Da Bridge (大桥). The taxi flag fall is Y5.

FREE **Fènghuángshān Revolution Headquarters Site** HISTORIC SITE
(凤凰山革命旧址; Fènghuángshān Gémìng Jiùzhǐ; 8am-5pm Mar-Nov) More accessible from town, this Revolution Headquarters Site is about 100m west of the post office. This was the first site occupied by the communists after their move to Yán'ān, before being abandoned because it was too easy for enemy planes to attack it. There's a photo exhibit about Norman Bethune, the Canadian doctor who became a hero in China for treating CCP casualties in the late 1930s.

Treasure Pagoda MONUMENT
(宝塔; Bǎo Tǎ; admission Y65; 6.30am-9pm Mar-Nov, to 8pm Dec-Feb) Yán'ān's most prominent landmark, Treasure Pagoda dates back to the Song dynasty. For an extra Y10, you can climb the very narrow steps and ladders of the pagoda for a restricted view of the city.

Qīngliáng Mountain PARK
(清凉山; Qīngliáng Shān; admission Y31; 8am-7pm Mar-Nov, to 5.30pm Dec-Feb) This was the birthplace of the CCP propaganda machine; *Xinhua* News Agency and the *Liberation Daily* both started life here when the place was known as 'Information Mountain'. Now, it's a pleasant hillside park with some nice trails and a few sights, including **Ten Thousand Buddha Cave** (万佛洞; Wànfó Dòng) dug into the sandstone cliff beside the river. The cave has relatively intact Buddhist statues.

Sleeping & Eating

There are few budget options in Yán'ān. Most hotels, though, offer discounts. It's also not a gourmet's paradise, though the night market, just off the small square in the centre of town, is a fine spot for eating al fresco and meeting the locals. Try the very tasty handmade noodles.

Yán'ān Shénzhōu Guójì Hotel HOTEL $$
(延安神舟国际大酒店; Yán'ān Shénzhōu Guójì Dàjiǔdiàn; 298 0888; Dong Dajie; 东大街; s/d Y538/698, discounts of 60%;) With its dim lighting and red-themed decor, this

new place close to the east bus station looks distinctly dodgy at first glance. But it's not a love hotel and the rooms are modern and spacious. Ignore the ludicrously optimistic prices.

Yàshèng Dàjiǔdiàn HOTEL **$$**
(亚圣大酒店; ☎266 6000; Erdaojie Zhongduan; 二道街中段; tw Y328-368, discounts of 40%; ❄) Located in the centre of town, the rooms here are clean and comfortable, if slightly gloomy. There's an OK restaurant (dishes Y14 to Y40) on the top floor.

 Information

Bank of China (中国银行; Zhōngguó Yínháng; Daqiao Jie; ⏲8am-5pm) On the corner of Daqiao Jie and Erdao Jie, this branch has a 24-hour ATM. There are other ATMs around town, too.

China Post (中国邮政; Zhōngguó Yóuzhèng; Yan'anshi Dajie) Post and telephone office.

Internet cafe (wǎngbā; per hr Y3; ⏲24hr) On the 2nd floor, down an alley just to the left of the Yàshèng Dàjiǔdiàn.

Public Security Bureau (PSB; 公安局; Gōng'ānjú; 56 Yan'anshi Dajie) There is an office at the Yán'ān Bīnguǎn.

 Getting There & Away

Air

There are daily flights to Xī'ān (Y380) and Běijīng (Y850) from the airport (飞机场), 7km northeast of the town.

The airline booking office, the **Civil Aviation Administration of China** (CAAC; 中国民航; Zhōngguó Mínháng; ☎211 1111; ⏲8am-noon & 2.30-5.30pm), is located on Baimi Dadao.

Bus

From Xī'ān's east bus station, there are buses to Yán'ān (Y82.50, four to five hours) every 40 minutes from 6.30am to 4.20pm. The schedule back to Xī'ān is essentially the same. Buses arrive and depart from the south bus station (汽车南站; *qìchē nánzhàn*).

At Yán'ān's east bus station *(qìchē dōngzhàn)*, there are buses to Yúlín (Y69.50, five hours) every 50 minutes from 7.25am to 6pm. Heading west, there are departures to Yínchuān in Níngxià (Y107, eight hours); buses leave at 8am, 9.30am and 10.30am, while sleepers leave at 4pm and 5.30pm. You can also get into Shānxī and Hénán from here.

Train

The quickest overnight train back to Xī'ān leaves at 10.28pm (Y106, eight hours). Advance tickets in Yán'ān can be hard to come by – consider taking the bus instead. A taxi from the train station into town costs Y10.

Yúlín 榆林

☎0912 / POP 92,000

Thanks to extensive coal mining and the discovery of natural gas fields nearby, this one-time garrison town on the fringes of Inner Mongolia's Mu Us Desert is booming. Despite all the construction, there's still enough of interest to make this a good place to break a trip if you're following the Great Wall or heading north on the trail of Genghis Khan.

Parts of the earthen **city walls** are still intact, while the main north–south pedestrian street in the elongated old town (divided into Beidajie and Nandajie) has several restored buildings, including what appears to be an early-20th-century **Bell Tower** (钟楼; Zhōng Lóu). With several restaurants and antique shops, it's a nice street to wander at night, when it's lit by lanterns.

West of Beidajie and Nandajie and running parallel to it is Xinjian Nanlu, where you can find ATMs, internet cafes and a post office. The streets running off it are good for cheap restaurants.

Four kilometres north of Yúlín are some badly eroded 15th-century sections of the Great Wall and a prominent four-storey **beacon tower** (镇北台; zhènběitái; admission Y20; ⏲8am-6pm). Bus 11 (Y1) runs here from Changcheng Nanlu, about 200m west of the main bus station.

Sleeping

Xīyà Hotel HOTEL **$$**
(西亚大酒店; Xīyà Dàjiǔdiàn; ☎368 4000; 59 Xinjian Nanlu; 新建南路59号; s/d Y238/268, discounts of 30%; ❄@) The Xīyà's huge rooms have comfy beds and all come with computers, while some of the bathrooms feature cool whirlpool baths. With the discounts on offer, it's a good deal. The easy-to-miss entrance is two doors down from a China Mobile store.

Shùnfā Zhāodàisuǒ HOTEL **$**
(顺发招待所; ☎326 8958; 2nd fl, 5 Yuyang Zhonglu; 榆扬中路5号二楼; r with shared bathroom Y60) Five minutes' walk from the main bus station and just east of Xinjian Nanlu, this place offers OK basic accommodation and is one of the few cheapies that will take foreigners. Look for the red doors and head up the stairs.

FROM FARM BOY TO EMPEROR

Li Zicheng enjoyed a remarkable rise from shepherd to sitting on the imperial throne and led the most successful of the many peasant rebellions that took place in the dying days of the Ming dynasty. Born in 1606, Li drew tens of thousands of followers in famine-racked, 1630s Shaanxi by advocating equal shares of land for all and no taxes. Having taken over large parts of Shaanxi, Shānxī and Hénán, Li and his army sacked Běijīng and, after the suicide of the last Ming emperor, Li proclaimed himself Emperor of the Shun dynasty in April 1644.

His reign was short-lived. Less than two months later, the invading Manchu forces defeated his army and Li retreated back to Shaanxi and subsequently to Húběi, where he either committed suicide or was killed in 1645. Four centuries later, Li's impeccable socialist credentials, as well as his megalomania, made him an ideal role model for the CCP, who continue to laud his exploits as an early revolutionary.

Getting There & Around

There is a daily flight from Yúlín to Xī'ān (Y400).

Yúlín has two bus stations. If you get off the bus inside the town walls (near the south gate), you are at the **main (south) bus station** (汽车站; *qìchē zhàn*); the **regional (north) bus station** (客运站; *kèyùn zhàn*) is located 2km northwest on Yingbin Dadao.

The main bus station has regular buses to Xī'ān (Y155, 10 hours) from 7am to 7.30pm. You can also get frequent buses to Yán'ān (Y69, five hours), and morning buses to Tàiyuán (Y122, eight hours) and Yínchuān (Y127, five to six hours).

The **regional bus station** has hourly buses to Bāotóu in Inner Mongolia (Y84, five hours) and half-hourly buses to Dàliǔtǎ (Y10, 1½ hours), from where you can travel on to Dōngshèng. Note that the buses to Dōngshèng pass by Genghis Khan's Mausoleum.

The **train station** is 1km west of town. There are two trains a day to Xī'ān (Y101 to Y165, 12 to 14 hours) via Yán'ān, but sleeper tickets are hard to come by.

Bus 1 (Y1) runs between the two bus stations. Taxis around town and to the train station will cost you Y5.

Mǐzhǐ 米脂

0912

About 70km south of Yúlín, Mǐzhǐ is best known as the hometown of Li Zicheng, protocommunist and would-be emperor, as well as for the alleged beauty of its female residents.

Despite those twin draws, it's a sleepy place with a small Hui presence and way off the tourist circuit; you will be the sole foreigner in town and likely the only visitor of any description. Some of the local population still live in caves and homes carved out of the surrounding hillsides, while the small old quarter, with its narrow alleys and dilapidated courtyard homes, is a fascinating place to wander.

The principal sight, though, is the **Li Zicheng Palace** (李自成行宫; Lǐ Zìchéng Xínggōng; Xinggong Lu; admission Y20; 8.30am-5.30pm). This well-preserved and compact palace was built in 1643 at the height of Li's power. Set against a hillside, there's a statue of the man himself, as well as pavilions, which house exhibits about Li and notable Mǐzhǐ women, and a pagoda. There's also a fine theatre, where music performances and plays were held, sometimes for three days at a time, to celebrate Li's victories. To reach the palace, walk east on Xinggong Lu.

Turn left immediately after leaving the palace and you are in the heart of the **old quarter** of Mǐzhǐ. Many of the original, late-Ming-dynasty courtyard homes survive, albeit in a rundown condition.

There's no reason to stay the night, but if you want to break the trip to Yán'ān then try the **Bǎoshān Bīnguǎn** (宝山宾馆; 621 3987; Zhihuang Xilu; 治黄西路; s & d Y50-100;), or the posher **Jīntài Hotel** (金泰大酒店; Jīntài Dàjiǔdiàn; 621 1999; Jiulong Qiao; 九龙桥北侧; s/d/tr Y168/218/228;) on the north side of Jiulong Qiao.

Mǐzhǐ makes an easy day trip from Yúlín. Buses (Y19, 1½ hours) run from Yúlín's main, or south, bus station. Ask to get off at Jiulong Qiao. Local buses to Yán'ān will also drop you here. At the time of writing, road repairs meant the journey was taking three to four hours.

Ānhuī

POPULATION: 63.2 MILLION

Includes »

Best Places to Eat

» Měishí Rénjiā (p382)
» Pig's Heaven Inn (p386)
» Qīuyùn Kèzhàn (p387)

Best Places to Stay

» Pig's Heaven Inn (p386)
» Qīuyùn Kèzhàn (p387)

Why Go?

Well-preserved villages and fantastical mountain scapes are the principal draw for visitors to Ānhuī (安徽). The main attraction of this southern Huīzhōu region is unquestionably Huángshān, a jumble of sheer granite cliffs wrapped in cottony clouds that inspired an entire school of ink painting during the 17th and 18th centuries. But the often-overlooked peaks of nearby Jiǔhuá Shān, where Buddhists bless the souls of the recently departed, are much quieter, with a hallowed aura that offers a strong contrast to Huángshān's stunning natural scenery. At the foot of these ranges are strewn the ancient villages of Huīzhōu; their distinctive whitewashed walls and black-tiled roofs stand out against a verdant backdrop of green hills and terraced tea gardens.

Ānhuī's lush mountains and slower pace of life are the perfect antidote to the brashness of China's larger cities. Yes, you have to visit.

When to Go

Túnxī

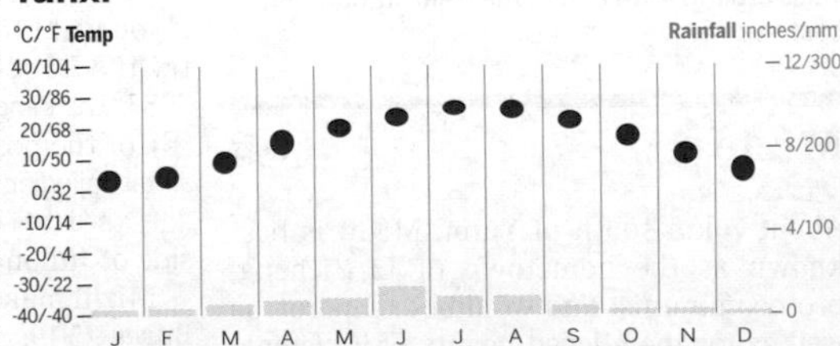

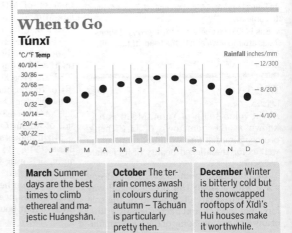

March Summer days are the best times to climb ethereal and majestic Huángshān.

October The terrain comes awash in colours during autumn – Tǎchuān is particularly pretty then.

December Winter is bitterly cold but the snowcapped rooftops of Xīdì's Hui houses make it worthwhile.

Ānhuī Highlights

1. Soak up the Ming-dynasty vibe along Túnxī's **Old Street** (p380)
2. Explore the grottoes and dilapidated temples at the Taoist **Qíyún Shān** (p383)
3. Climb up and stay on **Huángshān** (p389), an iconic Chinese mountain
4. Join the Buddhist pilgrims at the active, fog-shrouded **Jiǔhuá Shān** (p394)
5. Don't miss the World Heritage–listed village of **Hóngcūn** (p385)
6. Eschew crowds and get a feel of authentic village life at **Chéngkǎn** (p387)
7. Soar down across heavy plumes of feathery bamboo in Mùkēng…on a **flying fox** (p386)
8. Seek out the unmarked **Pig's Heaven Inn** (p386) in Xīdì for a fantastic meal, and consider staying the night

History

The provincial borders of Ānhuī were defined by the Qing government, bringing together two disparate geographic regions and cultures: the arid, densely populated North China Plain and the mountainous terrain south of the Yangzi River (Cháng Jiāng), which wasn't settled until the late Tang dynasty. Prior to the 20th century, the two areas – separated by the mighty Yangzi – had little contact with one another.

Traditionally impoverished, Ānhuī's fortunes have begun to reverse. Some say the massive infrastructure improvements in the hitherto remote areas are partly due to president Hu Jintao, whose ancestral clan hails from Jìxī County. Hu comes from a long line of Huīzhōu merchants, who for centuries left home to do business or fill official posts elsewhere, but throughout their lifetimes would never fail to complete their filial duty and send their profits back home (much of it by way of large homes and ceremonial structures).

These days, locals often leave the region to seek work and fortune elsewhere (no different from their ancestors). However, they are never ashamed to declare their origins. And rightly so.

Climate

Ānhuī has a warm-temperate climate, with heavy rain in spring and summer that brings plenty of flooding. Winters are damp and very cold. When travelling through Ānhuī at any time of year, bring rain gear and a warm jacket for the mountain areas.

Getting There & Away

The historical and tourist sights of Ānhuī are concentrated in the south around the town of Túnxī and are easily accessible by bus, train or plane from Hángzhōu, Shànghǎi and Nánjīng.

PRICE INDICATORS

The following price indicators are used in this chapter:

Sleeping

$	less than Y200
$$	Y200 to Y550
$$$	more than Y550

Eating

$	less than Y20
$$	Y20 to Y60
$$$	more than Y60

Túnxī 屯溪

0559 / POP 75,000

Ringed by low-lying hills, the old trading town of Túnxī (also called Huángshān Shì) is the main springboard for trips to Huángshān and the surrounding Huīzhōu villages. If you stay in the Old, Town, it's an agreeable place with good transport connections to the Yangzi River delta area. Compared with the region's capital, Héféi, Túnxī makes for a better base from which to explore southern Ānhuī.

Sights

Túnxī is located at the junction of the Xīn'ān River (Xīn'ān Jiāng) and Héng River (Héng Jiāng). The oldest and most interesting part of town is in the southwest, around Huangshan Lu and Xin'an Lu. Most travellers sequester themselves in Old St (Lao Jie). The newer part of town is in the northeast, near the train station.

Túnxī is a small town that isn't big on sights. Running a block in from the river, **Old Street** (老街; Lao Jie) is a souvenir street lined with wooden shops and restored Ming-style Huīzhōu buildings open till late at night. Duck into the side alleys for a glimpse at the local life and to find small eateries. Also on Lao Jie, **Wàncuìlóu Museum** (万粹楼博物馆; Wàncuìlóu Bówùguǎn; 143 Lao Jie; admission Y50; 8.30am-9.30pm) displays a private antiques collection, offering an introduction to Huīzhōu architecture and furniture over four floors.

Tours

Youth hostels offer a day-long village tour to Xīdì and Hóngcūn (Y180 including transport, admission fees and lunch) and a direct bus to Huángshān (Y18, one hour, 6.10am). The Huāngshān Tourist Distribution Center also offer tours and discounted tickets.

Sleeping

Old Street Hostel HOSTEL $
(老街国际青年旅舍; Lǎojiē Guójì Qīngnián Lǔshè; 254 0386; www.hiourhostel.com; 266 Lao Jie; 老街266号; dm/d/tw/tr/f Y40/129/149/188/200;) With its convenient location and decent rooms – the four-person dorms come with proper mattresses and private bathrooms, while the private rooms sport wood-lattice decor and

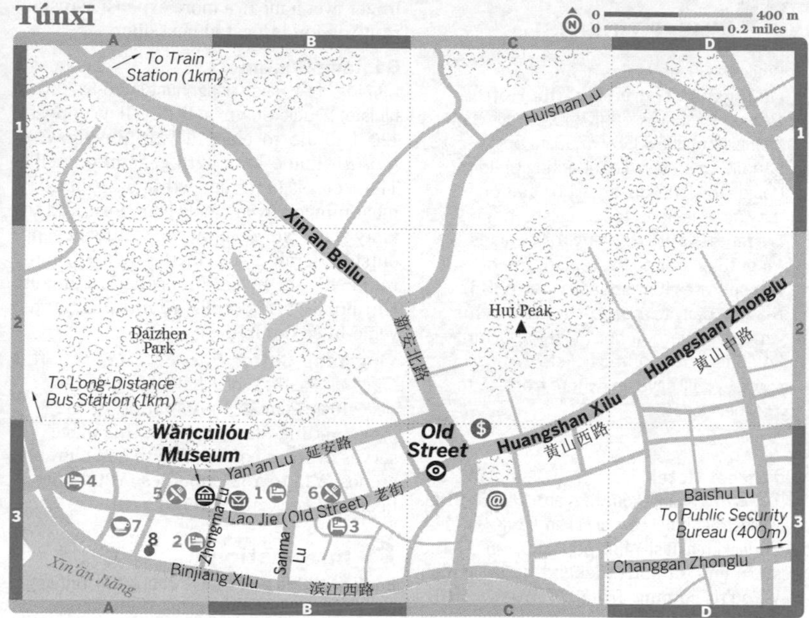

flat-screen TVs – this place clearly has an appeal that extends beyond the backpacking crowd. The 2nd floor houses a cafe overlooking Lao Jie with wi-fi, plush couches, overpriced beer and an outdoor balcony. Staff speak English, though they tend to blow hot and cold.

Ancient Town Youth Hostel HOSTEL $
(小镇国际青年旅舍; Xiǎozhèn Guójì Qīngnián Lǚshè; ☎252 2088; www.yhaha.com; 11 Sanma Lu; 三马路11号; dm Y40, d & tw Y145-198; ❄@) Started by some former tour guides, this hostel ticks all the right boxes, with a well-stocked bar, movie room, friendly and helpful staff, bike rental and so on. The rooms also pass muster. Dorm beds are huge and comfy, while the cheaper twin rooms are clean though lacking in natural light. The more expensive doubles are hotel quality. Go for the rooms with the Chinese decor to match the mood of Old St. Staff speak English.

Harbour Inn & Bar HOTEL $$
(夜泊客栈; Yèbó Kèzhàn; ☎252 2179; 29 Zhongma Lu; 中马路29号; tw Y160-200; ❄@) We're not sure where to set sail from, but the rooms in this renovated traditional building in Túnxī's old town are a notch above the typical midrange options. Get a twin that overlooks the street or splash out for the deluxe room for a chance to sleep in a traditional wooden Chinese canopy bed. A bar is conveniently located downstairs, for when you get bored with looking at the floral wallpaper and matching bed sheets in the rooms.

Túnxī

Top Sights
- Old Street C3
- Wàncuìlóu Museum A3

Sleeping
1. Ancient Town Youth Hostel B3
2. Harbour Inn & Bar A3
3. Old Street Hostel B3
4. Old Street Hotel A3

Eating
5. Gāotāng Húntūn A3
6. Měishí Rénjiā B3

Drinking
7. Ying Yang Coffee Bar A3

Transport
8. Huángshān Air Travel Agency A3

CHEAP TICKETS!

While the lovely ladies at the **Huāngshān Tourist Distribution Center** (黄山市旅游集散中心; Lǚyóu Jísàn Zhōngxīn; ☎255 8358; ⏰7.30am-6pm) – handily located in a connecting building beside the long-distance bus station – may not speak perfect English, they are fantastic at arranging travel plans for getting around the region. The office operates tourist buses (see p383) that run daily to most of the attractions within southern Ānhuī. Most importantly, it offers discounted tickets to most sights: you'll save anywhere from Y5 to Y50 per ticket.

Old Street Hotel HOTEL $$$
(老街口客栈; Lǎojiēkǒu Kèzhàn; ☎233 9188; www.oldstreet-hotel.com.cn; 1 Lao Jie; 老街口1号; s/d/tr incl breakfast Y480/580/680; ❄) At the western end (or start, depending on which way you're coming from) of Lao Jie, this stylish hotel gets guests in the right mood with its Huīzhōu interior. The traditionally styled rooms have wood covers for the air-conditioners, lovely beds, wood-strip flooring and clean, bright showers. Make sure to get a room that offers views of the river. Limited English spoken. Discounts knock a double down to Y240. Ticket-booking office in lobby.

Eating & Drinking

There are cheap street eats and a variety of local restaurants in the area just east of the eastern end of Old St. The streets abutting Old Street are constantly being renovated and are home to a bunch of restaurants and cute coffee shops and bars.

TOP CHOICE **Měishí Rénjiā** HUI CUISINE $
(美食人家; Lao Jie; dishes Y6-38; ⏰lunch & dinner) At the offical entrance to Lao Jie, this bustling restaurant – spread over two floors and hung with traditional Chinese *mǎdēng* lanterns – seethes with satisfied customers. Peruse the counter for a range of dishes – *húntūn* (wontons; dumpling soup), *jiǎozi* (stuffed dumplings), *bāozi* (steamed buns stuffed with meat or vegetables), noodles, clay pot and more – on display, have them cooked fresh to order and sink a delicious glass of sweet *zǐmǐlù* (紫米露), made from purple glutinous rice. If you want to linger over a meal, a more expensive restaurant version is located next door.

Gāotāng Húntūn WONTONS $
(高汤馄饨; 1 Haidi Xiang; húntūn Y6-8; ⏰10am till late) Duck down a little alley opposite 120 Lao Jie to enjoy a warming bowl of *húntūn* made by a 12th-generation seller. The secret is in the superthin *húntūn* skins, meat minced from whole lean pork, and the tasty soup. No room on the skinny benches outside? Grab a seat in the owner's living room: it's set in an atmospheric Qing-era Hui home. It also sells *dà húntūn* (larger, vegie-filled dumplings).

Ying Yang Coffee Bar CAFE $
(轮回咖啡酒吧; Lúnhuí Kāfēi Jiǔbā; 44 Lao Jie; ⏰10am-2am; @📶) A spin-off of the longstanding Shànghǎi bar, this place serves average coffee (Y20 to Y25), French crêpes (Y15 to Y35), noodles (Y20), juice, beer and cocktails (Y35 to Y40).

Information

Bank of China (中国银行; Zhōngguó Yínháng; cnr Xin'an Beilu & Huangshan Xilu; ⏰8am-5.30pm) Changes travellers cheques and major currencies; 24-hour ATM takes international cards.

China Post (中国邮局; Zhōngguó Yóuqū; 183 Lao Jie)

Dàwèi Internet Cafe (大卫网吧; Dàwèi Wǎngbā; per hr Y2; ⏰8am-midnight) Opposite the Bank of China along a dodgy-looking alley south of Yuzhong Garden (昱中花园). There are plenty of other internet cafes around nearby Xin'an Beilu (新安北路).

Public Security Bureau (PSB; 公安局; Gōng'ānjú; ☎232 3093; 1st fl, 108 Changgan Zhonglu; ⏰8am-noon & 2.30-5pm)

Getting There & Away

Air

Daily flights from **Huángshān City Airport** (黄山市飞机场; Huángshānshì Fēijīchǎng):

Běijīng Y1090, two hours, one daily

Guǎngzhōu Y960, 1½ hours, one daily

Hong Kong Y2188, 1¾ hours, three times a week

Shànghǎi Y580, one hour, one daily

You can buy tickets at the **Huángshān Air Travel Agency** (黄山航空旅游公司; Huángshān Hángkōng Lǚyóu Gōngsī; ☎251 7373; 1-1 Binjiang Xilu, ⏰8am-5.30pm).

Bus

The **long-distance bus station** (客运总站; kèyùn zǒngzhàn; Qiyun Dadao) is roughly 2km west of the train station on the outskirts of town. Destinations include the following:

Hángzhōu Y85, three hours, hourly (6.50am to 5.50pm)

Jǐngdézhèn Y55, 3½ hours, three daily (9.15am, noon and 2.10pm)

Nánjīng Y95, 5½ hours, two daily (7.25am and 12.10pm)

Shànghǎi Y132, five hours, five daily (last bus 3.50pm)

Sùzhōu Y100, six hours, one daily (6am)

Wùyuán Y34, two hours, two daily (8.20am and 12.30pm)

Within Ānhuī, buses go to the following destinations:

Héféi Y110, four hours, hourly

Jiǔhuá Shān Y51, 3½ hours, one daily (1.30pm)

Shèxiàn Y6, 45 minutes, frequent services

Yīxiàn Y12.50, one hour, frequent services (6am to 5pm)

Buses to Huángshān go to the main base at Tāngkǒu (Y13, one hour, frequent, 6am to 5pm) and on to the north entrance, Tàipíng (Y20, two hours). There are also minibuses to Tāngkǒu (Y15) from in front of the train station.

Inside the bus station (to the right as you enter) is the separate **Huāngshān Tourist Distribution Center** (黄山市旅游集散中心; Lǚyóu Jísàn Zhōngxīn; ☎255 8358; ⊙7.30am-6pm) with special tourist buses to to popular destinations. Return buses operate hourly from 8am to 4pm, with a two-hour break from 11am to 1pm. Some places visited:

Hóngcūn Y14, 1½ hours

Qíyún Shān Y7, 40 minutes

Xīdì Y12, one hour

Bus 9 (Y1) runs between the bus station and train station; otherwise, a taxi should cost Y7 to Y10.

Train

Train connections are abysmal. Trains from Běijīng (Y195 to Y330, 20 hours, 9.21am), Shànghǎi (Y94 to Y175, 13 hours, 7.10pm and 10.11pm) and Nánjīng (Y64 to Y108, six to 7½ hours, 15 daily) stop at Túnxī (generally called Huángshān). There is also service to Jǐngdézhèn (Y19 to Y65, three to five hours, 11 daily). For better connections to southern destinations, first go to Yīngtán (Y51 to Y196, five to seven hours, nine daily) in Jiāngxī and change trains there.

Getting Around

Taxis are Y5 at flag fall, with the 5km taxi ride to the airport costing about Y30. Competition among pedicab drivers is fierce, so they are the cheapest way of getting around, costing approximately Y4 for a trip to Old St from the train station area. Short rides start at Y2.

Around Túnxī

QÍYÚN SHĀN 齐云山

A 40-minute bus trip west of Túnxī brings you to the lush mountain panoramas of **Qíyún Shān** (admission 1 Mar–30 Nov Y75, 1 Dec–28 Feb Y55; ⊙8am-5pm Mon-Fri, 7.30am-5.30pm Sat & Sun). Long venerated by Taoists, the reddish sandstone rock provides a mountain home to the temples and the monks who tend to them, while mountain trails lead hikers through some stupendous scenery.

From the bus drop-off, cross the **Dēngfēng Bridge** (登封桥; Dēngfēng Qiáo) – dwelling on the luxuriant river views – and turn right through the village at the foot of the mountain for a 75-minute clamber up stone steps to the ticket office. Or you can take a **cable car** (up Y26, down Y14) from the station located 500m from where the bus drops you off.

Beyond the ticket office, the **Zhēnxiān Cave** (真仙洞府; Zhēnxiān Dòngfǔ) houses a complex of Taoist shrines in grottoes and niches gouged from the sandstone cliffs. Seated within the smoky interior of the vast and dilapidated **Tàisù Gōng** (太素宫) further on is an effigy of Zhengwu Dadi, a Taoist deity. A further temple hall, the **Yùxū Gōng** (玉虚宫), is erected beneath the huge brow of a 200m-long sandstone cliff, enclosed around effigies of Zhengwu Dadi and Laotze.

There's a completely charming village, Qíyún Village (Qíyún Cūn), seemingly plonked in the middle of the mountain range. Its whitewashed buildings are home to a variety of restaurants, souvenir stalls and friendly residents.

Getting There & Away

Tourist buses run directly to Qíyún Shān (Y8, 45 minutes) from the Túnxī long-distance bus station tourist centre, leaving hourly from 8am to 4pm. This bus can drop you at the Dēngfēng Bridge or the cable-car station. Otherwise, take any Yīxiàn-bound bus from Túnxī and ask the driver to stop at Qíyún Shān. Returning to Túnxī, wait at the side of the road for buses coming from Yīxiàn, but note that the last bus from Yīxiàn to Túnxī departs at 5pm. The last tourist bus departs at 4pm.

HUĪZHŌU STYLE

Huīzhōu architecture is the most distinctive ingredient of the regional personality, representative of the merchant class that held sway in this region during the Ming and Qing dynasties. The residences of Yīxiàn and Shèxiàn are the most typical examples of Huīzhōu architecture; their whitewashed walls topped on each flank by horse-head gables, originally designed to prevent fire from travelling along a line of houses, and later evolving into decorative motifs. Strikingly capped with dark tiles, walls are often punctured by high, narrow windows, designed to protect the residence from thieves (and lonely wives from illicit temptations).

Exterior doorways, often overhung with decorative eaves and carved brick or stone lintels, are sometimes flanked by drum stones *(gǔshí)* or mirror stones *(jìngshí)* and lead onto interior courtyards delightfully illuminated by light wells *(tiānjǐng)*, rectangular openings in the roof. The doors are a talking point in themselves. It's said that an owner would have spent 1000 taels of silver on the decorative archway and carvings but only four taels on the actual door!

Many Huīzhōu houses are furnished with intricately carved wood panels and extend to two floors, the upper floor supported on wooden columns. Even the furnishing holds much meaning. The main hall for taking visitors has several elements worth keeping an eye out for. You might notice semicircle half-tables against the walls: if the master of the house is in, the tables would be combined; if they are split, it's a subtle hint for male visitors to not intrude upon the wife. There might also be a mantlepiece where you will see a clock, vase and mirror. This symbolises peace and harmony in the house. The Chinese words for these items translate as: *zhong shēng* (钟声; hourly chiming on clock), *píng* (平; harmony), *jìng* (静; peace).

Another characteristic element of regional architecture is the obsession with decorative archways (*páifāng* or *páilou*), which were constructed by imperial decree to honour an individual's outstanding achievement. Examples include becoming a high official (for men; *páifāng*) or leading a chaste life (for women; *páilou*). Archways are common throughout China and don't always carry symbolic meaning, but in Huīzhōu they were of great importance because they gave the merchants – who occupied the bottom rung of the Confucian social ladder (under artisans, peasants and scholars) – much-desired social prestige. Roads were built to pass under a *páifāng* but around a *páilou*, so that a man would never feel that his status was beneath that of a woman's.

Huīzhōu Villages

0559

In Ānhuī, there's a traditional saying: 'In your past life you failed to cultivate yourself; thus you were born in Huīzhōu' (*Qián shì bù xiū, shēng zài Huīzhōu*). The home of highly successful merchants who dealt in lumber, tea and salt – in addition to running a string of lucrative pawnshops throughout the empire – Huīzhōu was a double-edged sword: the inhabitants were often quite wealthy, but they were also mostly absent. At age 13, many young men were shunted out the door for the remainder of their lives to do business elsewhere, sometimes returning home only once per year. Rather than uproot their families and disrespect their ancestral clans, these merchants remained attached to the home towns they rarely saw, funnelling their profits into the construction of lavish residences and some of China's largest ancestral halls.

Consequently, the villages scattered throughout southern Ānhuī (also known as Wǎnnán; 皖南) and northern Jiāngxī are some of the country's loveliest, augmented by the fact that they are often set in the lush surroundings of buckling earth and bamboo-and-pine forest, the silhouettes of stratified hills stacked away into the distance.

WESTERN VILLAGES (YĪXIÀN) 黟县

Yīxiàn is home to the two most picturesque communities in Ānhuī: Xīdì and Hóngcūn. Even when spilling over with crowds (most of the time), these are hands down the most impressive sights in the Huīzhōu area. Staying overnight is recommended.

Sights

Xīdì HISTORICAL VILLAGE

(西递; admission Y80) Dating to AD 1047, the village of Xīdì has for centuries been a stronghold of the Hu (胡) clan, descended from the eldest son of the last Tang emperor who fled here in the twilight years of the Tang dynasty. Typical of the elegant Huīzhōu style (see the boxed text, p384), Xīdì's 124 surviving buildings reflect the wealth and prestige of the prosperous merchants who settled here.

Xīdì has flirted gaily with its increasing popularity and, as a Unesco World Heritage site, enjoys an increasingly lucrative tourist economy. The village nevertheless remains a picturesque tableau of slender lanes, cream-coloured walls topped with horse-head gables, roofs capped with dark tiles, and doorways ornately decorated with carved lintels.

Wander around the maze of flagstone lanes, examining lintel carvings above doorways decorated with vases, urns, animals, flowers and ornamental motifs, and try to avoid tripping over hordes of high-school artists consigning scenes of stone bridges spanning small streams to canvas.

Xīdì's magnificent three-tiered Ming-dynasty decorative arch, the **Húwénguāng Páifāng** (胡文光牌坊), at the entrance to the village, is an ostentatious symbol of Xīdì's former standing. Numerous other notable structures are open to inspection, including the **Dìjí Hall** (迪吉堂; Dìjí Táng) and the **Zhuīmù Hall** (追慕堂; Zhuīmù Táng), both on Dalu Jie (大路街). **Jìng'ài Hall** (敬爱堂; Jìng'ài Táng), is the town's largest building and was used for meetings, weddings and, of course, meting out punishment. Back in the day, women weren't allowed in the hall; oh, how things have changed. **Xīyuán** (西园) is a small house known for its exquisite stone carvings on the windows. Unlike regular carvings, these are carved on both sides. The owner has previously rejected offers of US$10,000 (each!) for them.

When you're done with the village, pop out on paths leading out to nearby hills where there are suitable spots for your picture-postcard panoramas of the village.

Hóngcūn HISTORICAL VILLAGE

(宏村; admission Y80) Dating to the southern Song dynasty, the delightful village and Unesco World Heritage site of Hóngcūn, 11km northeast of Yīxiàn, has at its heart the crescent-shaped Moon Pond (月沼; Yuè Zhǎo) and is encapsulated by South Lake (南湖; Nán Hú), West Stream (西溪; Xī Xī) and Léigǎng Mountain (雷岗山; Léigǎng Shān). Famously conceived to resemble an ox, with its still-functioning waterway system representing the entrails, Hóngcūn is home to members of the traditionally wealthy Wang (汪) clan. The village is a charming and unhurried portrait of bridges, lakeside views, narrow alleys and traditional halls. Alleyway channels flush water through the village from West Stream to Moon Pond and from there on to South Lake, while signs guide visitors on a tour of the principal buildings. Lost? Just follow the waterflow.

If the bridge at the entrance to the village looks familiar, it's because it featured in a scene from Ang Lee's *Crouching Tiger, Hidden Dragon*. The **Chéngzhì Hall** (承志堂; Chéngzhì Táng) on Shangshuizhen Lu (上水圳路) dates from 1855 and was built by a salt merchant. It has 28 rooms, adorned with fabulous woodcarvings, 2nd-floor balconies and light wells. Peepholes on top-floor railings are for girls to peek at boy visitors and the little alcove in the mahjong room was used to hide the concubine. The now-faded gold-brushed carvings are said to have required 100 taels of the expensive stuff.

Other notable buildings include the **Hall of the Peach Garden** (桃源居; Táoyuán Jū), with its elaborate carved wood panels, and the **South Lake Academy** (南湖书院; Nánhú Shūyuàn), which enjoys a delicious setting on tranquil South Lake. Overlooking picturesque Moon Pond is a gathering of further halls, chief among which is the dignified **Lèxù Hall** (乐叙堂; Lèxù Táng), a hoary and dilapidated Ming antique from the first years of the 15th century. Turn up bamboo carvings, trinkets and a large selection of tea at the **market** west of Moon Pond. The busy square by Hóngjì Bridge (宏际桥; Hóngjì Qiáo) on the West Stream is shaded by two ancient trees (the 'horns' of the ox), a red poplar and a gingko. Admission includes a guide with limited English-speaking skills.

Tǎchuān HISTORICAL VILLAGE

(塔川; admission Y20) Located 3km northwest of Hóngcūn is the tiny little village of Tǎchuān. It's set at the base of a valley and noted for its stunning autumn scenery. Each year, the leaves on old-growth trees in and around the village change colours for anywhere between 10 to 30 days. The entire valley comes ablaze in shades of orange, green and brown, much to the delight of photographers. On other days, the villagers eke out their living by planting rice and tea. From afar, the village looks like a pagoda as it's built across the steps of foothills. House 18 has some of the most exquisite wooden carvings in the region. Admission includes a guide with limited English-speaking skills.

Nánpíng HISTORICAL VILLAGE

(南屏; admission Y43) With a history of over 1100 years, this intriguing and labyrinthine village, 5km to the west of Yīxiàn town, is famed as the setting of Zhang Yimou's 1989 tragedy *Judou*. Numerous ancient ancestral halls, clan shrines and merchant residences survive within Nánpíng's mazelike alleys, including the **Chéngshì Zōngcí** (程氏宗祠) and the **Yèshì Zōngcí** (叶氏宗祠). The **Lǎo Yáng Jiā Rǎnfáng** (老杨家染坊) residence that served as the principal household of dyer Gongli and her rapacious husband in *Judou* remains cluttered with props, and stills from the film hang from the walls. Admission includes a guide with limited English-speaking skills.

Guānlù HISTORICAL VILLAGE

(关麓; admission Y35) Around 8km west of Yīxiàn and further along the road beyond Nánpíng, this small village's drawcard sights are the fabulous households – **Bādàjiā** (八大家) – of eight rich brothers. Each Qing-dynasty residence shares similar elegant Huīzhōu features, with light wells, interior courtyards, halls, carved wood panels and small gardens. Each an independent entity, the households are interconnected by doors and linked together into a systemic whole. A distinctive aspect of the residences is their elegantly painted ceilings, the patterns and details of which survive. The houses have now been subdivided among the decendants' families. Sadly, many wings are in disrepair as many of the younger villagers have left for more modern abodes. Admission includes a guide with limited English-speaking skills.

Activities

A hike through Mùkēng's **bamboo forest** (木坑竹海; Mùkēng Zhúhǎi; admission Y30) is an excellent way to escape the megaphones and roving packs of art students in the nearby towns. Remember *Crouching Tiger, Hidden Dragon*'s breathtaking fight scenes? Yep, they were filmed here. The two-hour circuit along a ridgeline leads past the top-heavy plumes of feathery bamboo, trickling streams and hillside tea gardens, past a small village where you can get a clean room with bath for Y30, and eventually coming to a small hamlet where you can break for a cup of *chá* (tea) or a filling lunch. Perhaps inspired by the aforementioned movie, a **flying fox** (Y40) has been built near the highest point in the trail; it's a 30-second zip to the bottom from over 50m above the ground! The forest is 5km northeast of Hóngcūn; a taxi or pedicab there/return will cost Y10/20.

You can also cycle there – or anywhere you want in the surrounding countryside – by renting **bikes** (出租自行车; chūzū zìxíngchē; per hr Y2) on the modern street opposite Hóngcūn's Hóngjì Bridge (宏际桥; Hóngjì Qiáo).

Sleeping & Eating

It's quite possible to just turn up and find simple homestay-style accommodation (住农家; *zhù nóngjiā*) in Xīdì and Hóngcūn from Y60 to Y80, which is a great way to get a glimpse of local life as well as sample some excellent home cooking (meals are generally around Y20, unless you have a chicken slaughtered, which will cost Y50 to Y100). Restaurants abound; in spring, succulent bamboo shoots (竹笋; *zhúsǔn*) figure prominently in many dishes.

Pig's Heaven Inn BOUTIQUE HOTEL **$$**

(猪栏酒吧; Zhūlán Jiǔbā; ☎515 4555; http://blog.sina.com.cn/zhulanjiuba; Renrang Li, Xīdì; 西递镇仁让里; d incl breakfast Y300, ste Y680-800; ❄@) The place to splurge, this is a truly gorgeous 400-year-old house in Xīdì that has been brilliantly restored, with a study, two terraces and six distinctive rooms. Reservations are essential (the entrance is unmarked); gourmet sleuths can seek it out for a fantastic lunch (dishes Y15 to Y30) in the courtyard. The owners have developed a larger, pricier property in Bìshān (碧山), several kilometres away. This is a great place to just unwind for a day or three; grab one of their bicycles and explore the surrounding area. Transfers to both properties are available. Limited English.

Xīdì Travel Lodge HOTEL **$$$**

(西递行馆; Xīdì Xíngguǎn; ☎515 6999; www.xidilodge.com, Xīdì; 西递; d incl breakfast Y368-488, ste Y608-1288, discounts of 20%; ❄@) If Pig's Heaven Inn is intimate, Xīdì Travel Lodge is quite the opposite. This newly constructed can't-miss-it property just behind the main gate to the Xīdì village, is a glamorous, multibuilding affair complete with glossy rooms and its own restaurant and alfreso cafe. All rooms have modern showers, flat-screen TVs and faux antique furnishing, while some have balconies. Get a room facing the small tea garden. The restaurant serves local fare (dishes Y12 to Y78) and there's cheap Y6 beer at the cafe.

Hóngdá Tíngyuàn HOMESTAY **$**
(宏达庭院; ☎554 1262; 5 Shangshui Zhen, Hóngcūn; 宏村上水圳5号; r Y100) The draw of this Hóngcūn home is the verdant courtyard filled with potted daphne, heavenly bamboo and other flowering shrubs, all set around a small pool and pavilion. Its rooms are unadorned, but the peaceful location in the upper part of the village is ideal. You can stop by for lunch (meals from Y20), space permitting. No English.

Qīuyùn Kèzhàn BOUTIQUE HOTEL **$$**
(秋韵客栈; ☎554 6099; Tǎchuān; 塔川; d/tw/tr/ste Y240/320/400/880) Located at the back of Tǎchuān village, this truly beautiful hotel is set in a restored Hui home. Furnishing ranges from old four-poster Chinese beds to silk bedspreads and ornate dressing tables. The multiroomed suite is quite a sight to behold. When you get tired of the rooms, wander out to one of the many quiet stone courtyards for tea. The attached restaurant whips up good local cuisine (dishes Y15 to 78). Limited English.

Getting There & Around

BUS Tourist buses run directly to Xīdì (Y12, one hour) and then to Hóngcūn (Y14, 1½ hours) from the Túnxī long-distance bus station's tourist centre, leaving hourly from 8am to 4pm. Otherwise, catch a local bus from the long-distance bus station to Yīxiàn (Y12.50, one hour, frequent, 6am to 5pm), the transport hub for public transport to the surrounding villages.

From Yīxiàn there are green minibuses (Y2, half-hourly, 7am to 5pm) to Xīdì (15 minutes), Nánpíng (15 minutes) and Guānlù (20 minutes). The bus to Hóngcūn (20 minutes) leaves from outside the bus station; make two rights upon exiting and cross the bridge – but to be sure, ask first at the station: '*Qù Hóngcūn de gōngjiāochē zài nǎli?*' (去宏村的公交车在哪里). You may need to return to Yīxiàn to get between the different villages, with the exception of Nánpíng and Guānlù, which are both in the same direction. From Yīxiàn, it's possible to travel on to Tāngkǒu (Y11, one hour, four daily) and Qīngyáng (Y34, 2½ hours, three daily).

TAXI Taxis and pedicabs go to Xīdì (Y10), Hóngcūn (Y15), Nánpíng (Y20) and Guānlù (Y25) from Yīxiàn. Booking a taxi to take you to all four villages from Yīxiàn can cost as little as Y150 for the day, depending on your bargaining skills. A minivan for the day will cost Y400. Most accommodation places can help with transport bookings.

NORTHERN VILLAGES

Rarely visited by individual travellers, the villages north of Túnxī can serve as a quieter antidote to the much-hyped and crowded towns to the west.

Sights

Chéngkǎn HISTORICAL VILLAGE
(呈坎; admission Y80; ⏲8am-5pm) A real working community, Chéngkǎn presents a very different picture from its more affluent cousins in Shèxiàn – farmers walk through town with hoes slung over their shoulders, tea traders dump baskets of freshly picked leaves straight out onto the street, quacking ducks run amok in streams and there's the unmistakable smell of pig manure in the air: a bona fide slice of life in rural China. Most visitors come to see southern China's largest **ancestral temple** (罗东舒祠; Luó Dōngshū Cí), a massive wooden complex several courtyards deep that took 71 years (1539–1610) to build. It has a mixed bag of architectural styles: from Graeco-Roman columns to Persian patterns on overhead beams. There are other venerable structures in town, such as the three-storey **Yànyì Táng** (燕翼堂), which is nearly 600 years old; however, many residences are in poor condition. Look out for a house where the owner still gives haircuts (Y2) on his 100+-year-old chair. The mirror is just as old! Another big appeal lies in the lush panoramas of the surrounding Ānhuī countryside.

Tángmó HISTORICAL VILLAGE
(唐模; admission Y55, incl electronic guide deposit Y300; ⏲8am-5pm) A narrow village that extends 1km along a central canal, Tángmó was originally established during the late Tang dynasty. A pathway follows the waterway from the entrance at the east gate (东门; *dōng mén*) into the village, leading past the large **Tán'gàn Garden** (檀干园; Tán'gàn Yuán), which was modelled after Hángzhōu's West Lake. Here you'll enter the village proper, passing canalside Qing residences along **Shui Jie** (水街) before coming to the covered **Gāoyáng**

Bridge (高阳桥; Gāoyáng Qiáo), built in 1733 and now home to a small teahouse. At the end of town is the **Shàngyì Ancestor Hall** (尚义堂; Shàngyì Táng), with 199 peony blossoms carved into the entrance beam. There's a string of traditional workshops and stalls near the east gate. Sample homemade *dòujiāng* (豆浆; soya bean milk; Y1) and pick up a traditional Ānhuī ink stone (砚台; *yàntái*).

It's possible to sleep here at a villager's house for about Y60. Note that the public bus will probably drop you off at the west gate (where the ticket office is located), but there should be onward transport of some kind to the east gate, or just backtrack.

Getting There & Around

There's an hourly **tourist bus** from the Túnxī long-distance bus station that stops at Qiánkǒu (Y12, one hour) and Tángmó (Y14, 1½ hours). It runs from 8am to 4pm with a two-hour break from 11am to 1pm.

Getting to Chéngkǎn is slightly complicated. Start by taking a bus to Yánsì (岩寺; Y4, 30 minutes, frequent) from the Túnxī long-distance bus station. From the Yánsì bus terminus, you'll need to proceed to the town's north bus station (北站; *běi zhàn*) by public bus (Y1) or a pedicab (Y3). From the north bus station, you can take another bus to Chéngkǎn (Y3.50, 20 minutes). You can also get to either Qiánkǒu (Y1.50, 10 minutes) or Tángmó (Y2.50, 20 minutes) though the wait for the buses can be long.

It's also possible to hire a **pedicab** here to Qiánkǒu (Y10), Chéngkǎn (Y20) or Tángmó (Y10). If you're a decent bargainer, you can get one for the day for as little as Y60. To get between the villages on public transport, you'll need to return to Yánsì. Note that the last buses are at 5pm, and transport stops for at least an hour around noon.

EASTERN VILLAGES

The appeal of the eastern villages is also in their less-touristy vibe. Shèxiàn is a decent-sized provincial town that hides some interesting historic sights, while the neighbouring port of Yúliáng presents an architectural heritage entirely different from the other Huīzhōu villages.

Sights

Shèxiàn HISTORICAL VILLAGE

Historic seat of the Huīzhōu prefecture, Shèxiàn (歙县) is 25km east of Túnxī and can be visited as a day trip from there. The town was formerly the grand centre of the Huīzhōu culture, serving as its capital. Today, the **Ancient City** (徽州古城; Huīzhōu Gǔchéng; admission incl entry to Yùliáng & guide Y80, without entry to Yùliáng Y60) serves as the town's main sight.

From the Shèxiàn bus station, cross the bridge over the river and go through the modern gate tower and along to **Yánghé Mén** (阳和门), a double-eaved gate tower constructed of wood. Get your admission ticket and climb the gate to examine a Ming-dynasty stone *xièzhì* (獬豸; a legendary beast) and elevated views of the magnificent **Xǔguó Archway** (许国石坊; Xǔguó Shífáng) below. Fabulously decorated, this is China's sole surviving four-sided decorative archway, with 12 lions (18 in total if you count the cubs) seated on pedestals around it and a profusion of bas-relief carvings of other mythical creatures.

Continue in the same direction to reach the alleyway to the old residential area of **Doushan Jie** (斗山街古民居; Dòushānjiē Gǔmínjū), a marvellous street of Huīzhōu houses, with several courtyard residences open to visitors and decorated with exquisitely carved lintels, beautiful interiors and occasional pairs of leaping-on blocks for mounting horses. Look out for the *páifāng* (decorative archway) that has been filled in and incorporated into a wall.

At the time of research, massive construction in the Ancient City was under way. When complete, a replica of the original capital city complex will be open to the public.

Yúliáng HISTORICAL VILLAGE

(渔梁; admission Y30) Little-visited Yúliáng is a historic riverine port village on the Liàn River (Liàn Jiāng). Cobbled **Yuliang Jie** (渔梁街) is a picturesque alley of buildings and former transfer stations for the wood, salt and tea that plied the Liàn River and was shipped to north China; the **teashop** at No 87 is an example. Note the firewalls separating the houses along the road. Examine the traditional Huīzhōu arrangement of the **Bāwèizǔ Museum** (巴慰祖纪念馆; Bāwèizǔ Jìniànguǎn), also on Yuliang Jie.

The **Lion Bridge** (狮子桥; Shizi Qiao) dates to the Tang dynasty, a time when the 138m-long granite **Yúliáng Dam** (渔梁坝; Yúliáng Bà) across the river was first constructed. Boats can ferry you from the dam for short 15-minute trips up river (Y15 to Y20).

Tranquil Yúliáng is a good place to recharge your batteries. There are rooms with lovely views at a small **inn** (☎0559-653 9731; 147 Yuliang Jie; 渔梁街147号; d without/with bathroom Y50/60; ❄). There's also another similar **inn** (☎0559-653 8024; 145 Yuliang Jie; 渔梁街145号; d without/with bathroom Y60/80; ❄) two doors along. Both serve meals with dishes starting at Y15. The innkeepers will take you into the village if you book ahead.

Getting There & Away

Buses from Túnxī's long-distance bus station run regularly to Shèxiàn (Y6, 45 minutes, frequent). To reach Yúliáng, take a pedicab (Y5) from Shèxiàn's bus station (by the bridge), or hop on bus 1, which runs to Yúliáng (Y1) from outside the bus station. The last bus back to Túnxī departs at 6pm.

Huángshān 黄山

☎0559 / ELEV 1873M

When its archetypal granite peaks and twisted pines are wreathed in spectral folds of mist, Huángshān's idyllic views easily nudge it into the select company of China's top 10, nay, top five, sights. Legions of poets and painters have drawn inspiration from Huángshān's iconic beauty. Yesterday's artists seeking an escape from the hustle and bustle of the temporal world may have been replaced by crowds of tourists, who bring the hustle and bustle with them, but Huángshān still rewards visitors with moments of tranquillity, and the unearthly views can be simply breathtaking.

Climate

Locals claim that it rains over 200 days a year up on the mountain. For this reason give yourself several days in the area and head to the mountain when the forecast is best. Spring (April to June) generally tends to be misty, which means you may be treated to some stunning scenery, but you're just as likely to encounter a thick fog that obscures everything except for a line of yellow ponchos extending up the trail. Summer (July to August) is the rainy season, though storms can blow through fairly quickly. Autumn (September to October) is generally considered to be the best travel period. Even at the height of summer, average temperatures rarely rise above 20°C at the summit, so come prepared.

Sights & Activities

Buses from Túnxī (Huángshān Shì) drop you off in Tāngkǒu, the sprawling town at the foot of Huángshān. A base for climbers, this is the place to stock up on supplies (maps, raincoats, food, money), store your excess luggage and arrange onward transport. It's possible to spend time in Tāngkǒu, but unless you're on a tight budget, you might as well stay on the mountain.

The town consists of two main streets, the larger Feicui Lu – a strip of restaurants, supermarkets and hotels – and the more pleasant Yanxi Jie, which runs along the river perpendicular to Feicui Lu and is accessed by stairs leading down from the bridge.

ASCENDING & DESCENDING THE MOUNTAIN

Regardless of how you ascend **Huángshān** (admission 1 Mar–30 Nov Y230, 1 Dec–29 Feb Y130, seniors year-round Y60, child 1.1-1.3m Y60), you will be stung by the dizzying entrance fee. You can pay at the eastern steps near the **Yúngǔ Station** (云谷站; Yúngǔ Zhàn) or at the **Mercy Light Temple Station** (慈光阁站; Cíguāng Gé Zhàn), where the western steps begin. Shuttle buses (Y13) run to both places from Tāngkǒu.

Three basic routes will get you up to the summit: the short, hard way (eastern steps); the longer, harder way (western steps); and the very short, easy way (cable car). The eastern steps lead up from the Yúngǔ Station; the western steps lead up from the parking lot near Mercy Light Temple. It's possible to do a 10-hour circuit going up the eastern steps and then down the western steps in one day, but you'll have to be slightly insane, in good shape and you'll definitely miss out on some of the more spectacular, hard-to-get-to areas.

A basic itinerary would be to take an early-morning bus from Túnxī, climb the eastern steps, hike around the summit area, spend the night at the top, catch the sunrise and then hike back down the western steps the next day, giving you time to catch an afternoon bus back to Túnxī. Most travellers do opt to spend more than one night on the summit to explore all the various trails. Don't underestimate the hardship involved; the steep gradients and granite steps can wreak havoc on your knees, both going up and down.

Most sightseers are packed (and we mean *packed*) into the summit area above the upper cable car stations, which consists of a network of trails running between various

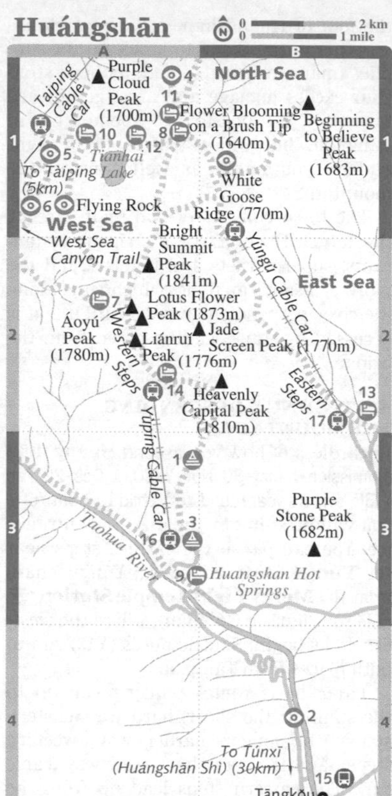

Huángshān

Sights

1	Bànshān Temple	A3
2	Front Gate	B4
3	Mercy Light Temple	A3
	Mt Huángshān Visitors Centre	(see 3)
4	Refreshing Terrace	A1
5	West Sea Canyon (Ring Road 1)	A1
6	West Sea Canyon (Ring Road 2)	A1

Sleeping

7	Báiyún Hotel	A2
8	Běihǎi Hotel	A1
	Běihǎi Hotel (three-star wing)	(see 8)
9	Best Western Resort and Spa	A3
10	Páiyúnlóu Hotel	A1
11	Shīlín Hotel	A1
12	Xīhǎi Hotel	A1
13	Yúngǔ Hotel	B2
14	Yùpínglóu Hotel	A2

Information

	Bank of China	(see 8)
	Police Station	(see 8)

Transport

15	Long-Distance Bus Station	B4
16	Merci Light Temple Station	A3
17	Yungu Station	B2

peaks. The highlight of the climb for many independent travellers is the lesser-known West Sea Canyon hike (p392), a more rugged, exposed section where tour groups and megaphone wielders dare not venture.

Make sure to bring enough water, food, warm clothing and rain gear before climbing. Bottled water and food prices increase the higher you go. As mountain paths are easy to follow and English signs plentiful, guides are unnecessary.

Hot Springs HOT SPRINGS

(黄山温泉; Huángshān Wēnquán; admission Y238; ⏲10.30am-10.30pm) After years of renovation, the hot springs area is finally open. If you want a soak after the strenuous climbing, this place offers a mind-boggling variety of themed springs. Soak in a coffee-infused pool or get heady in the wine- or alcohol-infused spring. There's also a pool with fish that nibble away dead skin on your feet. Follow it all up with a foot massage. Entry includes complimentary snacks and tea.

The best way to get to the springs is to arrange for a free transfer and pick-up via your hotel. Shuttle buses (Y7) run to the Yúngǔ Station, from where it's a short walk downhill to the hot springs.

Eastern Steps TRAIL

A medium-fast climb of the 7.5km eastern steps from **Yúngǔ Station** (890m) to **White Goose Ridge** (白鹅峰; Bái'é Fēng; 1770m) can be done in 2½ hours. The route is pleasant, but lacks the awesome geological scenery of the western steps. In spring wild azalea and weigela add gorgeous splashes of colour to the wooded slopes of the mountain.

Much of the climb is comfortably shaded and although it can be tiring, it's a doddle compared with the western steps. Slow-moving porters use the eastern steps for ferrying up their massive, swaying loads of food, drink and building materials, so considerable traffic plies the route. While clambering up, note the more ancient flight of steps that makes an occasional appearance alongside the newer set.

Purists can extend the eastern steps climb by several hours by starting at the **Front Gate** (黄山大门; Huángshān Dàmén), where a stepped path crosses the road at several points before linking with the main eastern steps trail.

Western Steps TRAIL

The 15km western steps route has some stellar scenery, but it's twice as long and strenuous as the eastern steps, and much easier to enjoy if you're clambering down rather than gasping your way up. If you take the cable car up, just do this in reverse.

The western steps descent begins at the **Flying Rock** (飞来石; Fēilái Shí), a boulder perched on an outcrop half an hour from Běihǎi Hotel, and goes over **Bright Summit Peak** (光明顶; Guāngmíng Dǐng; 1841m). Look out from Bright Summit Peak to **Áoyú Peak** (鳌鱼峰; Áoyú Fēng; 1780m): you'll notice that it looks like two turtles!

South of Áoyú Peak en route to Lotus Flower Peak, the descent funnels you down through a **Gleam of Sky** (一线天; Yīxiàn Tiān), a remarkably narrow chasm – a vertical split in the granite – pinching a huge rock suspended above the heads of climbers. Further on, **Lotus Flower Peak** (莲花峰; Liánhuā Fēng; 1873m) marks the highest point, but is occasionally sealed off, preventing ascents. **Liánruì Peak** (莲蕊峰; Liánruì Fēng; 1776m) is decorated with rocks whimsically named after animals, but save some energy for the much-coveted and staggering climb – 1321 steps in all – up **Heavenly Capital Peak** (天都峰; Tiāndū Fēng; 1810m) and the stunning views that unfold below. As elsewhere on the mountain, young lovers bring padlocks engraved with their names up here and lash them for eternity to the chain railings. Successful ascents can be commemorated with a gold medal engraved with your name (Y10). Access to Heavenly Capital Peak (and other peaks) is sometimes restricted for maintenance and repair, so keeps those fingers crossed when you go!

Further below, the steps lead to **Bànshān Temple** (半山寺; Bànshān Sì) and below that the **Mercy Light Temple** (慈光阁; Cíguāng Gé), where you can pick up a minibus back to Tāngkǒu (Y13) or continue walking to the hot springs area.

Huángshān is not one of China's sacred mountains, so little religious activity is evident. The Cíguāng Temple at the bottom of the western steps is one of the few temples on the mountain whose temple halls survive, although they have been converted to more secular uses. The first hall now serves as the **Mt Huángshān Visitors Centre** (黄山游人中心; Huángshān Yóurén Zhōngxīn), where you can pore over a diorama of the mountain ranges. Now head to Tāngkǒu to find yourself some beer as a reward.

Yúngǔ Cable Car CABLE CAR

(云谷索道; Yúngǔ Suǒdào; one way 1 Mar–20 Nov Y80, 1 Dec–29 Feb Y65; ⏲7am-4.30pm) Shuttle buses (Y13) ferry visitors from Tāngkǒu to the cable car. Either arrive very early or late (if you're staying overnight) as long queues are the norm. Thankfully, a new cable-car station has shorted what was once three-hour queues to nothing more than 45 minutes.

Shuttle buses (Y13) also run from Tāngkǒu to Mercy Light Temple, which is linked by the **Yùpíng Cable Car** (玉屏索道; Yùpíng Suǒdào; one way 1 Mar–20 Nov Y80, 1 Dec–29 Feb Y65; ⏲7am-4.30pm) to the area just below the Yùpínglóu Hotel.

ON THE SUMMIT

The summit is essentially one huge network of connecting trails and walks that meander up, down and across several different peaks. More than a few visitors spend several nights on the peak, and the North Sea (北海; Běihǎi) sunrise is a highlight for those staying overnight. **Refreshing Terrace** (清凉台; Qīngliáng Tái) is five minutes' walk from Běihǎi Hotel and attracts sunrise crowds (most hotels supply thick padded jackets for the occasion). Lucky visitors are rewarded with the luminous spectacle of *yúnhǎi* (literally 'sea of clouds'): idyllic pools of mist that settle over the mountain, filling its chasms and valleys with fog.

The staggering and otherworldly views from the summit reach out over huge valleys of granite and enormous formations of rock, topped by gravity-defying slivers of stone and the gnarled forms of ubiquitous Huángshān pine trees *(Pinus taiwanensis)*. Many rocks have been christened with fanciful names by the Chinese, alluding to figures from religion and myth. **Beginning to Believe Peak** (始信峰; Shǐxìn Fēng; 1683m), with its jaw-dropping views, is a major bottleneck for photographers. En route to the North Sea, pause at the **Flower Blooming on a Brush Tip** (梦笔

生花; Mèngbǐ Shēnghuā; 1640m), a granite formation topped by a pine tree. Clamber up to **Purple Cloud Peak** (丹霞峰; Dānxiá Fēng; 1700m) for a long survey over the landscape and try to catch the sun as it descends in the west. Aficionados of rock formations should keep an eye out for the poetically named **Mobile Phone Rock** (手机石; Shǒujī Shí), located near the top of the western steps.

WEST SEA CANYON 西海大峡谷

A strenuous and awe-inspiring 8.5km hike, this route descends into a **gorge** (Xīhǎi Dàxiágǔ) and has some impressively exposed stretches (it's not for those afraid of heights), taking a minimum four hours to complete. You can access the canyon at either the northern entrance (near the Páiyúnlóu Hotel) or the southern entrance (near the Báiyún Hotel aka White Clouds Hotel). It's sometimes indicated on maps as the Illusion Scenic Area (梦幻景区; Mènghuàn Jǐngqū).

A good option to start would be at the northern entrance. From there, you'll pass through some rock tunnels and exit onto the best bits of the gorge. Here, stone steps have been attached to the sheer side of the mountain! Peer over the side for some serious butt-clenching views down. Don't worry, there are handrails. If you're pressed for time or don't have the energy to stomach a long hike, do a figure-eight loop of **Ring Rd 1** (一环上路口) and **Ring Rd 2** (二环上路口), and head back to the northern entrance. Sure, you'll miss some stunning views across lonely, mist-encased peaks, but you'll also miss the knee-killing dip into the valley and the subsequent thigh-killing climb out.

Avoid the area in bad weather.

Sleeping & Eating

Huángshān has five locations where hotels can be found. Prices and bed availability vary according to season; it's a good idea to book ahead for summit accommodation, especially so for dorms. Note that prices for hotels tend to cost at least double what you'd pay in a nonmountain setting. If you're on a tight budget, make sure to take plenty of food to the summit. You won't be able to get a hot meal there for under Y30.

TĀNGKǑU 汤口

Mediocre midrange hotels line Tāngkǒu's main strip, Feicui Lu; remember to look at rooms first and ask for discounts before committing. There are also a host of budget choices along Tiandu Lu. Restaurants cluster along Yanxi Jie, which runs along the river perpendicular to Feicui Lu. There are also several useful restaurants that can help with trip preparations and onward ticket bookings, including the central **Quánxīng Big Restaurant** (全兴大酒店; Quánxīng Dàjiǔdiàn; 50 Yanxi Jie; 沿溪街50号; dishes Y5-30) and **Mr Cheng's Restaurant** (☎130 8559 2603; dishes Y5-30), located at the western entrance to town, near the bridge. All speak English.

Huángshān Hot Springs Youth Hostel HOSTEL $
(黄山温泉国际青年旅社; Huángshān Wēnquán Guójì Qīngnián Lǚshè; ☎556 2478; Tiandu Lu; 天都路; dm/tw Y40/200) An unexceptional hostel, with few English speakers. However, rooms are cheap and clean, and the owner does her very best to accommodate you. She'll help with ticket bookings, laundry, transfers and offer information. Her son speaks OK English. Despite the name, it's not located in the hot springs area.

Huáyì Bīnguǎn HOTEL $$
(华艺宾馆; ☎556 6888; South Gate; 南大门; tw Y480-680; ❄) A large white edifice on the west side of the river on the Huángshān access road, this four-star hotel offers the priciest and nicest (the word being relative in this context) accommodation in Tāngkǒu. Prices in the three-star building are lower. Staff can help with bus and flight bookings.

HOT SPRINGS AREA 温泉区

The hot springs area, 4km further uphill and accessible by shuttle or taxi, is only worth staying in if you want to spend time soaking in the springs.

Best Western Resort and Spa HOTEL $$
(最佳西方酒店; Zuìjiā Xīfāng Jiǔdiàn; ☎558 5030; www.bestwestern.com; r incl breakfast from Y550; ❄@) A newish five-star resort, and operator of the outdoor hot springs. The complex is sequestered along a lovely wooded hill and is a fantastic place to unwind. Rooms are small but cosy, with brown trim, and soft beds.

YÚNGǓ STATION 云谷索道站

Yúngǔ Hotel HOTEL $$
(云谷山庄; Yúngǔ Shānzhuāng; ☎558 6444; s & d Y580, discounts of 35%; ❄) With a lovely

but inconveniently located setting looking out onto bamboo and forest, this traditionally styled hotel has fine, clean rooms, with 35% discounts frequently given. Walk down from the car park in front of the cable-car station.

WESTERN STEPS 西线台阶

Yùpínglóu Hotel HOTEL **$$$**
(玉屏楼宾馆; Yùpínglóu Bīnguǎn; ☎558 2288; fax 558 2258; d/q/tr Y1480/1600/1680; ❄@) A 10-minute walk from the Yùpíng Cable Car (go to your right), this four-star hotel is perched on a spectacular 1660m-high lookout just above the Welcoming Guest Pine Tree. Aim for the doubles with the good views at the back, as some rooms have small windows with no views. Discounted doubles are Y880.

Báiyún Hotel HOTEL **$$$**
(白云宾馆; Báiyún Bīnguǎn; ☎558 2708; fax 558 2602; dm Y280-360, d/tr Y1480/1680; ❄@) Dorms come with TV and shower, but are a bit old and worn; doubles (with private bathroom) pass muster but the hotel is sorely lacking compared with its competition. It seems to be happy to just rely on large tour groups. No English sign, but the hotel is well signposted in English as White Clouds Hotel. Discounts knock dorms to Y200 and doubles to Y980.

THE SUMMIT 山顶

Ideally, Huángshān visits include nights on the summit. Note that room prices will rise on Saturday and Sunday, and are astronomical during major holiday periods. Most hotel restaurants offer buffets (breakfast Y40 to Y50, lunch/dinner Y80 to Y100) plus a selection of standard dishes (fried rice Y40), though it can be difficult to get service outside meal times. Hotels in Tāngkǒu can arrange tents (*zhàngpeng;* 帐篷; Y180) for camping at selected points on the summit.

Shīlín Hotel HOTEL **$$**
(狮林饭店; Shīlín Fàndiàn; ☎558 4040; www.shilin.com; dm without/with bathroom Y200/400, d Y1680; @) Cheaper rooms are devoid of views, but the pricier doubles are bright and clean and have flat-screen TVs. Cramped nine-bed dorms are also well kept, with bunk beds and shared bathroom; the block up the steps from the hotel has good views, as do some of the newer rooms in the main block. Staff might offer you basic staff rooms on the side. Haggle. Discounted doubles are Y880.

Běihǎi Hotel HOTEL **$$$**
(北海宾馆; Běihǎi Bīnguǎn; ☎558 2555; www.hsbeihaihotel.com; dm Y200, s & d Y1680, discounts of 30%; @) The four-star Běihǎi comes with professional service, money exchange, a mobile-phone charging point, cafe and 30% discounts during the week. Larger doubles with private bathroom have older fittings than the smaller, better-fitted-out doubles (same price). There are Y800 doubles in the three-star compound on a hill across the main square. Although the best-equipped hotel, it's also the busiest and least charming.

Páiyúnlóu Hotel HOTEL **$$**
(排云楼宾馆; Páiyúnlóu Bīnguǎn; ☎558 1558; dm/d/tr Y280/1280/1480; @) With an excellent location near Tiānhǎi Lake (Tiānhǎi Hú) and the entrance to the West Sea Canyon, plus four-star comfort, this place is recommended for those who prefer a slightly more tranquil setting. Ironically, none of the regular rooms has *any* views, but the newer dorms are unobstructed and come with attached showers. Discounted dorms are Y160 and doubles Y780.

Xīhǎi Hotel HOTEL **$$**
(西海饭店; Xīhǎi Fàndiàn; ☎558 8888; www.hsxihaihotel.cn; dm/d Y240/1280; @) Warm jackets are supplied in rooms for sunrise watchers, bathrooms are clean and all rooms come with heating and 24-hour hot water, but take a look at the doubles first, as some face inwards. Discounts knock dorms to Y200 and doubles to Y1000. A new five-star block was under construction at the time of research. It will be completed in 2011.

Information

Tāngkǒu

If you have extra luggage, leave your bags (Y2 to Y5) at one of the travellers' restaurants, which are also good sources of information.

Bank of China (中国银行; Zhōngguó Yínháng; ⏲8am-5pm) Southern end of Yanxi Jie.

Jiǎqiàochóng Internet Cafe (甲壳虫网吧; Jiǎkéchóng Wǎngbā; per hr Y3; ⏲24hr) A blue sign on the east side of the river.

Língdiǎn Internet Cafe (零点网吧; Língdiǎn Wǎngbā; per hr Y3; ⏲8am-midnight) On the west side of the river, 2nd floor.

Public Security Bureau (PSB; 公安局; gōng'ānjú; ☎556 2311) Western end of the bridge.

On the Mountain

Most hotels on the mountain have internet access areas for guests and nonguests, with hourly rates of Y15 to Y20.

Bank of China (中国银行; Zhōngguó Yínháng; ⏲8-11am & 2.30-5pm) Opposite Běihǎi Hotel. Changes money. ATM that accepts international cards.

Police station (派出所; pàichūsuǒ; ☎558 1388) Beside the bank.

Getting There & Away

Buses from Túnxī (aka Huángshān Shì) take around one hour to reach Tāngkǒu from either the long-distance bus station (Y13, one hour, frequent, 6am to 5pm) or the train station (Y15, departures when full, 6.30am to 5pm, may leave as late as 8pm in summer). Buses back to Túnxī from Tāngkǒu are plentiful, and can be flagged down on the road to Túnxī (Y13). The last bus back leaves at 5.30pm.

Tāngkǒu's **long-distance bus station** (东岭换乘分中心; Dōnglǐng Huànchéng Fēnzhōngxīn) is east of the town centre. Your hotel should be able to help with bookings and even pick-up or transfers. Buses run to the following destinations:

Hángzhōu Y90 to Y95, 3½ hours, seven daily

Héféi Y77, four hours, four daily

Jiǔhuá Shān Y41, 2½ hours, two daily (6.10am and 2.40pm)

Nánjīng Y86, five hours, three daily

Qíngyáng Y24, two hours, four daily

Shànghǎi Y120, 6½ hours, one daily (6.30am)

Tàipíng Y10, one hour, four daily

Wǔhàn Y220, nine hours, two daily

Yīxiàn Y15, one hour, four daily

Getting Around

Official tourist shuttles run between the bus station and the hot springs area (Y7), Yúngǔ Station (云谷站; Yúngǔ Zhàn; eastern steps, Y13) and Mercy Light Temple Station (慈光阁站; Cíguānggé Zhàn; western steps, Y13). Officially they depart every 20 minutes from 6am to 5.30pm, though they usually don't budge until enough people are on board. Taking a taxi to the eastern or western steps will cost Y50; to the hot springs area Y30.

Jiǔhuá Shān 九华山

☎0566

The Tang-dynasty Buddhists who determined Jiǔhuá Shān to be the earthly abode of the Bodhisattva Dizang (Ksitigarbha), Lord of the Underworld, chose well. Often shrouded in a fog that pours in through the windows of its cliffside temples, Jiǔhuá Shān exudes an aura of otherworldliness, heightened by the devotion of those who come here to pray for the souls of the departed. At times, though, it seems that the commerce that drives the religion – religious trinkets, good-luck charms and overpriced joss sticks abound – detracts from the overall experience. However, true believers seem to be able to brush it all off with their fervency. With its yellow-walled monasteries, flickering candles and the steady drone of Buddhist chanting emanating from pilgrims' MP3 players, the mountain is an entirely different experience from neighbouring Huángshān.

History

One of China's four Buddhist mountain ranges, Jiǔhuá Shān was made famous by the 8th-century Korean monk Kim Kiao Kak (Jīn Qiáojué), who meditated here for 75 years and was posthumously proclaimed to be the reincarnation of Dizang. Jiǔhuá Shān receives throngs of pilgrims for annual festivities held on the anniversary of Kim's death, which falls on the 30th day of the seventh lunar month. In temples, Dizang is generally depicted carrying a staff and a luminous jewel, used to guide souls through the darkness of hell.

Sights & Activities

Buses will let you off at Jǐhuáshān Xīnqūzhàn (九华山新区站). It's the local bus terminus and main ticket office where you purchase your ticket for the **mountain** (admission 1 Mar–30 Nov Y190, 1 Dec–29 Feb Y140); proceed to the right of the ticket office for shuttle buses on to **Jiǔhuájiē village** (included in ticket price; every 30 minutes). The village is the main accommodation area and is about halfway up the mountain (or, as locals say, at roughly navel height in a giant Buddha's potbelly). The shuttle terminates at the bus station just before the gate (大门; *dàmén*) leading to the village, from where the main street (芙蓉路; Furong Lu) heads south past hotels and restaurants. The main square is on the right off Furong Lu as you proceed up the street. The small street off the main square leads to Jiuhua Lao Jie, a street filled with cheaper home-style accommodation, shops and restaurants.

FREE **Zhīyuán Temple** TEMPLE
(祇园寺; Zhīyuán Sì; ⏲6.30am-8.30pm) Just past the village's main entrance on

your left, worshippers hold sticks of incense to their foreheads and face the four directions at this enticingly esoteric yellow temple. There are chanting sessions in the evening that pilgrims can join.

FREE **Huàchéng Sì** TEMPLE
(化成寺; ⏲6.30am-8.30pm) The largest, most colouful and elaborate temple in town. Ornately carved dragons serve as handrails up the main steps. The eaves and beams of the buildings are painted in every colour imaginable and the icing on the cake is the three huge golden bodhisattvas that greet visitors: each one sits at least 25m tall.

Mountain Summit TRAIL
The real highlight is walking up the mountain alongside the pilgrims, following a trail (天台正顶) that passes waterfalls, streams, and countless nunneries, temples and shrines. The summit is on a mountain range behind the village. The hike up takes a leisurely four hours; count on about two to three hours to get back down to the village.

You can begin just after the village's main entrance, where a 30-minute hike up the ridge behind Zhìyuán Temple leads you to **Bǎisuì Gōng** (百岁宫; admission free; ⏲6am-5.30pm), an active temple built into the cliff in 1630 to consecrate the Buddhist monk Wu Xia, whose shrunken, embalmed body is coated in gold and sits shrivelled within an ornate glass cabinet in front of a row of pink lotus candles. If you don't feel like hiking, take the **funicular** (express/ordinary return Y150/100, one way Y55; ⏲7am-5.30pm) to the ridge.

From the top, walk south along the ridge past the **Dōngyá Temple** (东崖禅寺; Dōngyá Chánsì) to the **Huíxiāng Pavilion** (回香阁; Huíxiāng Gé), above which towers the seven-storey **10,000 Buddha Pagoda** (万佛塔; admission Y10; ⏲6am-5.30pm), fashioned entirely from bronze and prettily lit at night. A western path leads to town, while the eastern one dips into a pleasant valley and continues past the **Phoenix Pine** (凤凰松; Fènghuáng Sōng) and the **cable-car station** (one-way/return Y75/140) to **Tiāntái Peak** (天台正顶; Tiāntái Zhèng Dǐng; 1304m). The two-hour walk to the summit is tough going, passing small temples and nunneries. The cable-car ride takes 10 minutes each way. The summit is slightly damp, with incense-like mist shrouding the area.

Within the faded **Tiāntái Temple** (天台寺; Tiāntái Sì) on Tiāntái Peak, a statue of the Dizang Buddha is seated within the **Dìzàng Hall** (Dìzàng Diàn), while from the magnificent **10,000 Buddha Hall** (Wànfó Lóu) above, a huge enthroned statue of the Dìzàng Buddha gazes at the breathless masses appearing at his feet. Note the beams above your head that glitter with rows of thousands of Buddhas.

There's another trail to your right before the main stairs to the Tiāntái Temple. This one leads you to one of the highest and quietest points of the mountain, Shíwáng Peak (十王峰; Shíwáng Fēng; 1344m), where you can stop and let the rolling fog sweep past you.

An easier route is to take a bus (return trip included with the ticket) from Jiǔhuájiē village up to the **Phoenix Pine area** (凤凰松; Fènghuáng Sōng) to take the cable car. You can also walk to the summit in two hours from here. The bus option does not pass Bǎisuì Gōng.

Sleeping & Eating

There are a large number of hotels in Jiǔhuájiē village along Furong Lu. Outside of major holiday periods, most dorm beds go for Y30, while basic twins can be had from Y80. Prices often double during weekends and public holidays, but haggle during other times. Cheap guesthouses can be found along Jiuhua Lao Jie.

There are plenty of restaurants in the village around the main square and along Furong Lu and Huacheng Lu, which serve variously priced local dishes. Food is plentiful on the way up; stop at one of the inexpensive restaurants near the Phoenix Pine (about halfway up). As on other mountains, food costs rise the higher you climb.

Lóngquán Hotel HOTEL $$
(龙泉饭店; Lóngquán Fàndiàn; ☎328 8888; Furong Lu; s/tw incl breakfast Y580/980, discounts of 30%; ❄@) Located at the end of Furong Lu, this corner-block hotel has compact but smartly renovated rooms. Comfy beds, modern showers that don't choke, Chinese cable TV and terrible breakfast.

Shàngkètáng Hotel HOTEL $$$
(上客堂; Shàngkètáng Bīnguǎn; ☎283 3888; 1 Furong Lu; 芙蓉路1号; d & tw Y1280; ❄@) Brand-spanking new, get this, Buddhist-themed hotel in a prime location. Rooms are splashed out in rosewood furniture, flat-screen TVs and plush carpets. If you

don't get bugged by golden Buddhas staring you down outside elevators, then this is probably the best high-end accommodation in town. Discounts knock rooms down to Y780. The in-house vegetarian restaurant (dishes from Y15) is very good.

Bǎisuìgōng Xiàyuàn Hotel HOTEL $$
(百岁宫下院; Bǎisuìgōng Xiàyuàn; ☎283 3118; dm Y30, d Y160-200, tr Y240-300; ❄) Pleasantly arranged around an old temple, this hotel definitely has the right atmosphere. Standard rooms are unfortunately in very poor shape, although the dorms (common shower) are appropriately priced. It's opposite Zhīyuán Temple, off Furong Lu.

Information

Bank of China (中国银行; Zhōngguó Yínháng; 65 Huacheng Lu; ⊙9am-5pm) Changes travellers cheques and foreign exchange; west of main square.

China Post (中国邮政; Zhōngguó Yóuzhèng; 58 Huacheng Lu) Off the main square.

China Travel Service (CTS; 中国旅行社; Zhōngguó Lǚxíngshè; ☎283 1890; 3rd fl, 135 Baima Xincun) Located on the far side of a school field.

Huáyǒng Internet Cafe (华湧网吧; Huáyǒng Wǎngbā; per hr Y5; ⊙8am-midnight) On the right, before the pond on Baima Xincun.

Jiǔhuáshān Red Cross Hospital (九华山红十字医院; Jiǔhuáshān Hóngshízì Yīyuàn; ☎283 1330) After the pond on Baima Xincun.

Public Security Bureau (PSB; 公安局; Gōng'ānjú) Next to the main ticket office at the base of the mountain.

Getting There & Away

Buses from the Jiǔhuáshān Xīnqūzhàn (九华山新区站) – the bus terminus and main Jiǔhuá Shān ticket office – run to/from the following destinations:

Héféi Y77, 3½ hours, 18 buses daily

Huángshān Y50, three hours, two daily (7am and 2.30pm)

Qīngyáng Y7, 30 minutes, frequent services (7am to 5pm)

Shànghǎi Y100, six hours, one daily (7am)

Tónglíng Y21, one hour, two daily(10am and 12.40pm)

Túnxī Y60, 3½ hours, one daily (7am)

Wǔhàn Y129, six hours, one daily (7am)

More frequent buses leave from nearby Qīngyáng:

Hángzhōu Y82, five hours, hourly

Héféi Y65, two to three hours, hourly

Huángshān Y40, three hours, three daily (7.30am, 9.30am and 2pm)

Nánjīng Y63, three hours, hourly

Shànghǎi Y80, six hours, hourly

Túnxī Y45, two hours, two daily (7.30am and 2pm)

Yīxiàn Y34, 2½ hours, two daily (8.30am and 1.30pm)

Getting Around

The ticket includes four bus rides: from the main ticket office to Jiǔhuájiē village (base for mountain ascent), from the village to Phoenix Pine (cable-car station) and back to the village, and from the village back to the main ticket office.

To get to Phoenix Pine, catch the bus (every 30 minutes or when full) from the bus station north of the main gate (take the first road on the right after the Jùlóng Hotel). On busy days, you may need to queue for over two hours for the cable car to the peak.

Héféi 合肥

☎0551 / POP 1.44 MILLION

The provincial capital, Héféi is a pleasant and friendly city with lively markets, attractive lakes and parks but few scenic attractions. It's better used as a transport hub to the rest of Ānhuī.

Sights

Shengli Lu leads from the train station down to the Nánféi River (Nánféi Hé) then meets up with Shouchun Lu. Changjiang Zhonglu is the main commercial street and cuts east–west through the city. Between Suzhou Lu and Huancheng Donglu is Huaihe Lu Buxing Jie, a busy pedestrian shopping street.

Parks PARKS
Among Héféi's green spaces, **Xiāoyáojīn Park** (Xiāoyáojīn Gōngyuán; Shouchun Lu; admission free; ⊙6am-7pm) and **Bāohé Park** (Bāohé Gōngyuán; admission free; ⊙6am-10pm) are the most pleasant. Bāohé Park contains various sights (see the boxed text, p398) worth paying for.

Míngjiào Temple TEMPLE
(明教寺; Míngjiào Sì; Huaihe Lu; admission Y10; ⊙6am-6pm) Small and atmospheric and looking out of place, this temple sits 5m above ground on the pedestrianised section of Huaihe Lu.

Former Residence of Li Hongzhang HISTORIC HOME
(李鸿章故居; Lǐ Hóngzhāng Gùjū; Huaihe Lu; admission Y20; ⊙8.30am-6.30pm) Further west

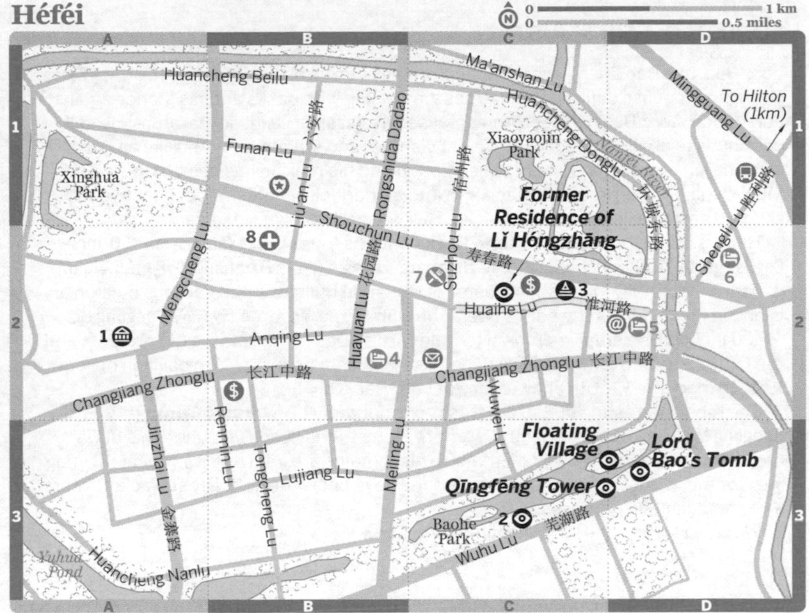

along Huaihe Lu, this restored home of a local official from the late Qing dynasty sits stoically amid the hubbub of commercial activity all around.

FREE **Ānhuī Provincial Museum** MUSEUM
(安徽省博物馆; Ānhuī Shěng Bówùguǎn; 268 Anqing Lu; ⊙9am-5pm Tue-Sun) Contains displays of bronzes, Han-dynasty tomb rubbings and some fine examples of the wooden architectural style found around Huángshān.

Sleeping & Eating

The city is awash with a range of hotels (but there are no hostels!). The area around the train station has Chinese midrange-category places (from Y150 upwards) and the main commercial street of Changjiang Zhonglu is where you'll find the midrange hotel chains such as 7 Days, Home Inn and Hanting. For food, head to the pedestrianised Huaihe Lu Buxing Jie. The side streets have cheap eats and there's everything from fast-food chains to noodle shops.

Héféi

Top Sights
- Floating Village D3
- Former Residence of Lǐ Hóngzhāng C2
- Lord Bao's Tomb D3
- Qīngfēng Tower C3

Sights
- 1 Ānhuī Provincial Museum A2
- 2 Bāo Gōng Temple C3
- 3 Míngjiào Temple C2

Sleeping
- 4 Huádū Hotel B2
- 5 Motel 168 .... D2
- 6 Xīnyà Hotel D2

Eating
- 7 Lúzhōu Kǎoyā C2

Information
- 8 First People's Hospital B2

Transport
- China Eastern Airlines .... (see 4)

Hilton HOTEL $$$
(合肥希尔顿酒店; Héféi Xī'ěrdùn Jiǔdiàn; ☎280 8888; www.hilton.com/hefei; 198 Shengli Lu; 胜利路198号; d from Y498; ❄@≋) The nicest choice in the city, with a full range of modern facilities, including flat-screen TV, fitness centre and tennis courts. It's out by the

LORD BAO: FAIR & JUST

Lord Bao, aka Bāo Zhěng, was an official in the Northern Song dynasty (960–1279). Owing to his sense of filial piety, fairness in dealing with cases and his stance against corruption, Lord Bao has been immortalised in classical Chinese literature. He still continues to be the subject of movies, TV shows and stage plays. And like all good classical characters, the line between fiction and his real life has been blurred. The Ming-dynasty interpretation made him into a Sherlock Holmes–type detective with several martial-arts capable sidekicks. He even had his own video game.

Héféi is his birthplace and **Bāohé Park** contains four **sights** (admission Y50, incl English guide Y100; ⏲8am-6pm). The **floating village** (浮庄; Fúzhuāng; ⏲8am-5.45pm) is an architecturally interesting cluster of Hui-style buildings and gardens built on an island in the middle of the park's river. The **Bāo Gōng Temple** (包公祠; Bāogōng Cí; ⏲7.30am-6pm) is a small memorial temple with a huge 9ft-tall statue of Lord Bao, and the **Qīngfēng Tower** (清风园; Qīngfēng Yuán; ⏲7.30am-6pm) is a 42m pavilion built in 1999 to mark the 1000th anniversary of Lord Bao's birth.

The most interesting of these sights is undoubtedly **Lord Bao's Tomb** (包公墓园; Bāogōng Mùyuán; ⏲8am-5.45pm). A sombre stone tunnel leads you under his burial mound and to a large brown coffin where his remains are interred. As you might imagine, not much is left and various bits of bone have been hermetically sealed and stored away for scientific purposes.

We're waiting for the Lord Bao amusement park...

train station; ask about discounts or book online for better rates.

Motel 168 HOTEL $$
(莫泰连锁旅店; Mòtài Liánsuǒ Lǚdiàn; ☎216 1111; www.motel168.com; 1 Huaihe Lu; 淮河路1号; tw Y198-228, d Y218-238; ❄@) This reliable, modern midrange chain hotel offers cheap, clean doubles in a five-floor branch at the beginning of the pedestrian street. More-expensive rooms have PCs and eye-hurting orange furniture.

Huádū Hotel HOTEL $$
(华都宾馆; Huádū Bīnguǎn; ☎262 2988; 158 Changjiang Zhong Lu; 长江中路158号; s incl breakfast Y215, d & tw Y268-368; ❄@) Good discounts bring the spacious rooms at this Chinese three-star hotel well within range of most budgets. The rooms are slightly tattered, and more-expensive rooms are on higher floors with slightly newer carpets, furnishing and toilets. Get a quieter north-facing room. Prices include Chinese breakfast. Hotel entrance is off the main road.

Xīnyà Hotel HOTEL $$
(新亚大酒店; Xīnyà Dàjiǔdiàn; ☎220 3088; www.xinyahotel.cn; 18 Shengli Lu; 胜利路18号; d/ste incl breakfast Y298/418, discounts of 30%; ⊖❄) Another Chinese-style business hotel that offers good value once discounts are applied. Rooms are bog-standard but the location is a good compromise between the bus and train stations, and town.

Lúzhōu Kǎoyā ROAST DUCK $
(庐州烤鸭; 107 Suzhou Lu; dishes from Y6) Sample some of Ānhuī's traditional roast duck (烤鸭; Y18.50 per 500g), plus plenty of other noodle and dumpling dishes (from Y6) at this buzzy eatery. Order at the counter and show the slip to the server, then take a seat. Grab some of the savoury roasted biscuits (look for the queue outside) to go.

ℹ Information

Bank of China (中国银行; Zhōngguó Yínháng) Main branch (155 Changjiang Zhonglu); Shouchun Lu (Shouchun Lu) The main branch changes currency and has an ATM that takes international cards. The Shouchun Lu branch is north of Míngjiào Temple and has a 24-hour ATM.

China International Travel Service (CITS; 中国国际旅行社; Zhōngguó Guójì Lǚxíngshè; ☎282 3100; 8 Meishan Lu; ⏲9am-6pm) Situated next to Ānhuī Hotel. Can book air tickets

China Post (中国邮政; Zhōngguó Yóuzhèng; Changjiang Zhonglu) There's also a branch just beside the train station.

First People's Hospital (第一人民医院; Dìyī Rénmín Yīyuàn; ☎265 2893; 322 Huaihe Lu)

Internet cafes (网吧; wǎngbā; per hr Y2; ⏲8am-midnight) A cluster of them is located about 80m west of Motel 168, off Huaihe Lu.

Public Security Bureau (PSB; 公安局; Gōng'ānjú) Located on the northwest corner of the intersection of Shouchun Lu and Liu'an Lu.

 Getting There & Away

Air

Daily flights:

Běijīng Y990, 1½ hours

Guǎngzhōu Y1040, two hours

Hángzhōu Y580, 45 minutes

Shànghǎi Y490, one hour

Xiàmén Y860, 1½ hours

Bookings can be made at **China Eastern Airlines** (东方航空售票处; Dōngfāng Hángkōng Shòupiàochù; ☎262 9955; 158 Changjiang Zhonglu), situated next to the Húadū Hotel, through CITS, and at the train station's ticket-booking office.

Bus

Héféi has way too many bus stations for its relatively small size, but thankfully the organisation makes sense (so far).

The **Héféi long-distance bus station** (合肥长途汽车站; Héféi chángtú qìchēzhàn; 168 Mingguang Lu) has buses to numerous destinations in the surrounding provinces:

Hángzhōu Y128, 5½ hours, six daily

Nánjīng Y48 to Y55, 2½ hours, every 30 minutes

Shànghǎi Y160, seven hours, 12 daily (including sleeper)

Wǔhàn Y185, 6½ hours, eight daily

The **east bus station** (汽车东站; qìchē dōngzhàn; Changjiang Donglu) runs buses to most destinations in Ānhuī:

Huángshān Y95, four hours, four daily

Túnxī Y115, four hours, hourly

Buses to Jiǔhuá Shān (Y80, 3½ hours, half-hourly) leave from the **tourist bus station** (旅游汽车站; lǚyóu qìchēzhàn; Zhanqian Jie) near the train station. The so-called **main bus station** (客运总站; kèyùn zǒngzhàn; Zhanqian Jie), just outside the train station, is for local buses only.

Train

The train station is 4km northeast of the city centre. Express D trains:

Nánjīng Y59, one hour, 11 daily

Shànghǎi Y65 to Y101, 3½ hours, 10 daily

Regular service destinations:

Běijīng Y136 to Y411, 10 to 15 hours, six daily

Shànghǎi Y106 to Y127, 6½ to 8½ hours, eight daily

Túnxī Y64 to Y196, six to eight hours, four daily

 Getting Around

Taxis are cheap, starting at Y6. Taking a taxi (Y25, 30 minutes) is the best way to the airport, 11km south of the city centre. Rides from the city to the train station should cost Y10.

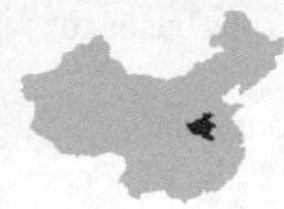

Hénán

POPULATION: 100 MILLION

Includes »

Best Places to Eat

- » Kāifēng Night Market (p419)
- » Hénán Shífǔ (p403)

Best Places to Stay

- » Nanjiecun Hotel (p406)
- » Sofitel (p403)
- » Guōliàngcūn (p414)
- » Kāifēng Hotel (p419)

Why Go?

Affluent Chinese roll their eyes at the mention of impoverished and land-locked Hénán (河南), yet the province's heritage takes us back to the earliest days of Chinese antiquity. Ancient capitals rose and fell in Hénán's north, where the capricious Yellow River (Huáng Hé) nourished the flowering of a great civilisation. Hénán is home to China's oldest surviving Buddhist temple and one of the country's most astonishing collections of Buddhist carvings, the Lóngmén Caves. There is also the Shàolín Temple, that legendary institution where the martial way and Buddhism found an unlikely but effective alliance. Hénán's inability to catch up with the rest of the land helps explain why the unusual village of Nánjiēcūn still sees a future in Maoist collectivism. Hénán is also home to China's oldest settlement of Jews, which established itself in the excellent walled town of Kāifēng.

When to Go

Zhèngzhōu

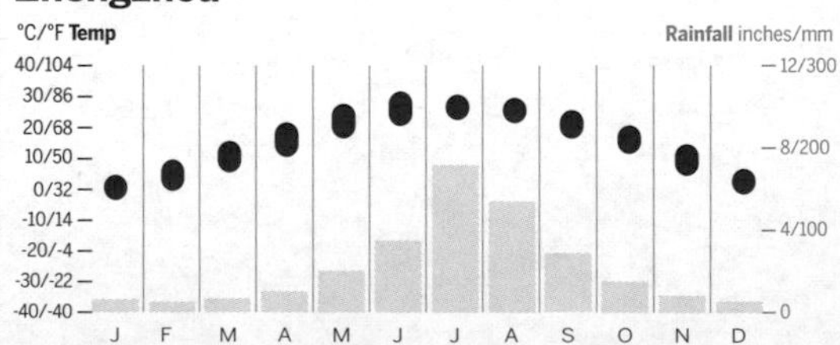

April Wángchéng Park in Luòyáng is a blaze of floral colour during the Peony Festival.

June For trips to cool Guōliàngcūn up in the Ten Thousand Immortals Mountains.

September & October Catch the lovely and fleeting north China autumn.

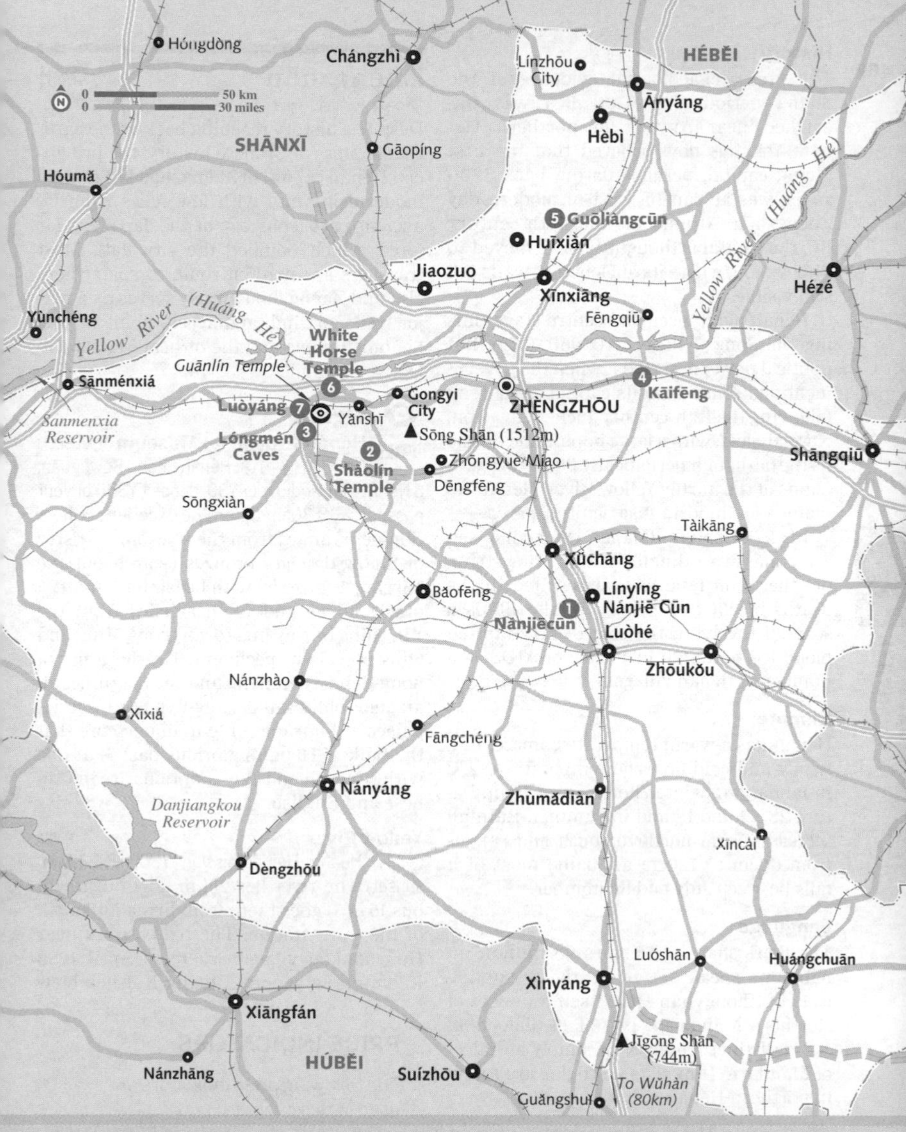

Hénán Highlights

1 Rediscover communism with Chinese characteristics at **Nánjiēcūn** (p406)

2 Fathom the martial mysteries of Shàolín boxing at the **Shàolín Temple** (p407)

3 Seek enlightenment among the carved Bodhisattvas at the **Lóngmén Caves** (p412)

4 Take a trip back in time to **Kāifēng** (p415) and engage in some adventurous snacking at the night market

5 Hide away in cliff-top **Guōliàngcūn** (p414) – but don't forget your sketchpad

6 Explore China's oldest Buddhist shrine: the **White Horse Temple** (p413) outside Luòyáng

7 Catch Luòyáng in full bloom at the annual **Peony Festival** (p409) in April

History

The first archaeological evidence of the Shang period (1700–1100 BC) was unearthed near Ānyáng in northern Hénán. Yet it is now believed that the first Shang capital, perhaps dating back 3800 years, was at Yǎnshī, west of modern-day Zhèngzhōu. Around the mid-14th century BC, the capital is thought to have moved to Zhèngzhōu, where its ancient city walls are still visible.

Hénán again occupied centre stage during the Song dynasty (AD 960–1279), but political power deserted it when the government fled south from its capital at Kāifēng following the 12th-century Juchen invasion. Nevertheless, with a large population on the fertile (although periodically flood-ravaged) plains of the unruly Yellow River, Hénán remained an important agricultural area.

In 1975 Hénán's Bǎnqiáo Dam collapsed after massive rainfall, leading to a string of other dam failures that resulted in the deaths of 230,000 people. In the 1990s a scandal involving the sale of HIV-tainted blood led to a high incidence of AIDS in a number of Hénán villages.

Climate

Hénán has a warm-temperate climate: dry, windy and cold (average temperature -2°C in January) in winter, hot (average temperature 28°C) and humid in summer. Rainfall increases from north to south and ranges from 60cm to 120cm annually; most of it falls between July and September.

Language

The lion's share of Hénán's 93 million inhabitants speak one of nearly 20 subdialects of Zhōngyuán Huà, itself a dialect of Northern Mandarin. Two of 15 dialects of Jin, a distinct language or simply a dialect of Mandarin (linguists wrangle), are found in northern Hénán.

Getting There & Around

Hénán is that rarity in China: a province in which travellers can get from point A to point B (inside or outside the province) with ease. Zhèngzhōu is a major regional rail hub, and expressways laden with comfy express buses run parallel to rail lines and stretch into southern parts of the province.

Zhèngzhōu is the main hub for flying to/from Hénán. Luòyáng has a smaller airport, but it's recommended that you use Zhèngzhōu.

Zhèngzhōu 郑州

0371 / POP 2 MILLION

Despite a history reaching back to the earliest chapters of Chinese history, the provincial Hénán capital of Zhèngzhōu is a rapidly modernising city with few relics from its ancient past (courtesy of the Japanese air force, which bombed the city flat). Most travellers are here en route to somewhere else and Zhèngzhōu largely serves as a major transport hub and access point for the Shàolín Temple and the offbeat Maoist collective of Nánjiē.

Sights

FREE **Hénán Provincial Museum** MUSEUM
(河南省博物馆; Hénán Shěng Bówùguǎn; 8 Nongye Lu; audio tour Y30, deposit Y300 or your passport; 8.30am-6pm) The excellent collection here ranges from the awesome artistry of Shang-dynasty bronzes (search out the stirring 'Bronze *bu* with beast mask motif'), oracle bones and further relics from the Yīn ruins in Ānyáng, to gorgeous Ming and Qing porcelain specimens. The dioramas of Song-dynasty Kāifēng and the magnificent, and now obliterated, Tang-dynasty imperial palace at Luòyáng serve to underscore that the bulk of Hénán's glorious past is at one with Nineveh and Tyre. Captions are in Chinese and English.

Yellow River RIVER
(黄河; Huáng Hé; admission Y30; 6.30am-sunset) The river lies 25km north of town; bus 16 (Y5) goes there from Erma Lu, north of the train station. The road passes near Huāyuánkǒu village, where in April 1938 Kuomintang general Chiang Kaishek blew

PRICE INDICATORS

The following price indicators are used in this chapter:

Sleeping

$	less than Y200
$$	Y200 to Y500
$$$	more than Y500

Eating

$	less than Y40
$$	Y40 to Y100
$$$	more than Y100

a dyke to flood Japanese troops. This desperate, ruthless tactic drowned about one million Chinese people and left another 11 million homeless and starving.

FREE **Shang City Walls** CITY WALL RUINS
(商代城墙遗址; Shāngdài Chéngqiáng Yízhǐ) Zhèngzhōu's eastern outskirts are marked by long, high mounds of earth, the remains of the old city walls, which can be clambered upon for walks.

FREE **Chénghuáng Temple** TAOIST TEMPLE
(城隍庙; Chénghuáng Miào; Shangcheng Lu; 9am-6pm) Bustles with worshippers who leave its trees festooned with red ribbons.

FREE **Confucius Temple** TEMPLE
(文庙; Wén Miào; 24 Dong Dajie; 8.30am-5pm) Massively restored; take bus 60 from 7 February Sq.

Mao Zedong Statue STATUE
(毛泽东像; Máo Zédōng Xiàng) Standing like a triumphant throwback at the Jinshui Lu and Renmin Lu intersection, the imposing statue of Mao gesticulates to a tangled web of flyovers. Come here just before twilight for iconic 'the sun sets over Chairman Mao' photo ops.

Sleeping

Sofitel HOTEL $$$
(索菲特国际饭店; Suǒfēitè Guójì Fàndiàn; 6595 0088; www.sofitel.com; 289 Chengdong Lu; d incl breakfast Y2722, discounts of 40%;) On balance, the five-star Sofitel may be more goodish four-star, but rooms are excellent. The funky atrium area bathes the cafe (with a popular afternoon-tea buffet), bar and restaurants below in natural light. There's also wi-fi access and free English maps from the concierge, swimming pool and health club.

Express by Holiday Inn HOTEL $$$
(中州快捷假日酒店; Zhōngzhōu Kuàijié Jiàrì Jiǔdiàn; 6595 6600; 115 Jinshui Lu; s & d Y988, ste Y1388, discounts of 40%;) Linked to the Sofitel by a connecting walkway, this is a neat and snappy midrange option with a selection of modern rooms. Breakfast is included, and there's free broadband in business-class rooms and wireless connection in the lobby and dining room.

Jǐnjiāng Inn HOTEL $
(锦江之星; Jǐnjiāng Zhīxīng; 6693 2000; Erma Lu; s/d Y179) Modern and swish looking, with crisp, sharp and well-looked-after rooms (work desks, flat-screen TVs) in a block set back from the road.

Yíngbīn Zhāodàisuǒ GUESTHOUSE $
(迎宾招待所; Yíngbīn Guest House; 6699 6858; 2nd fl, off ticket office No 1, train station; r Y30-120) Slap-bang in the train station with a highly affordable variety of sparsely furnished rooms and an internet cafe right next door.

Eating & Drinking

Hénán Shífǔ HENAN $
(河南食府; 6622 2108; 25 Renmin Lu; meals Y25; 10am-2pm & 5-9.30pm) Tucked away in a courtyard off Renmin Lu, this well-known restaurant's photo menu is full of exotic-looking dishes, but turn to the rear pages for cheap, tasty and wholesome fare. Try the *Shànghǎi xiǎolóngbāo* (上海小笼包; Shànghǎi steamed dumplings; meat/vegie Y12/10) or the tasty and cheap *yángròu huìmiàn* (羊肉烩面; lamb-braised noodles; small/large Y4/8).

Guāngcǎi Market MARKET $
(光彩市场; Guāngcǎi Shìchǎng; snacks Y1-5; 8am-9pm) Gritty, perhaps, but this crowded warren of food and clothes stalls in the block northeast of Èrqī Tǎ is always stuffed with diners. Join the crowds for *málà tàng* (麻辣烫; spicy soup with skewered vegies and meat), *chūn juǎn* (春卷; spring rolls), *ròujiāmó* (肉夹馍; spicy meat in a bun), *càijiābǐng* (菜夹饼; vegetables in a bun); *guōtiē* (锅贴; fried dumplings), *bàokǎo xiān yóuyú* (爆烤鲜鱿鱼; fried squid kebabs), *règānmiàn* (热干面; hot, dry noodles), sweet *xìngrén chá* (杏仁茶; almond tea), *làjiāobǐng* (辣椒饼; bread with chilli), *yángròu tāng* (羊肉汤; lamb soup) and much more.

Roast Duck Restaurant ROAST DUCK $$
(烤鸭店; Kǎoyādiàn; 6623 5108; 108 Erqi Lu; half duck Y38) Escape the noise and fumes at street level for some scrumptious duck in a smart upstairs setting just north of the Tianhe Hotel. Flick through the photo menu, attended to by polite and efficient staff, and watch chefs firing up the ovens through a glass screen.

Target Pub PUB
(目标酒吧; Mùbiāo Jiǔbā; 138 0385 7056; 10 Jingliu Lu; 8pm-last customer) The triumphant Target Pub, a seasoned panorama of flags, old banknotes, rattan chairs, lazy mezzanine and half a car pinned to the ceiling, hits the bullseye with excellent music,

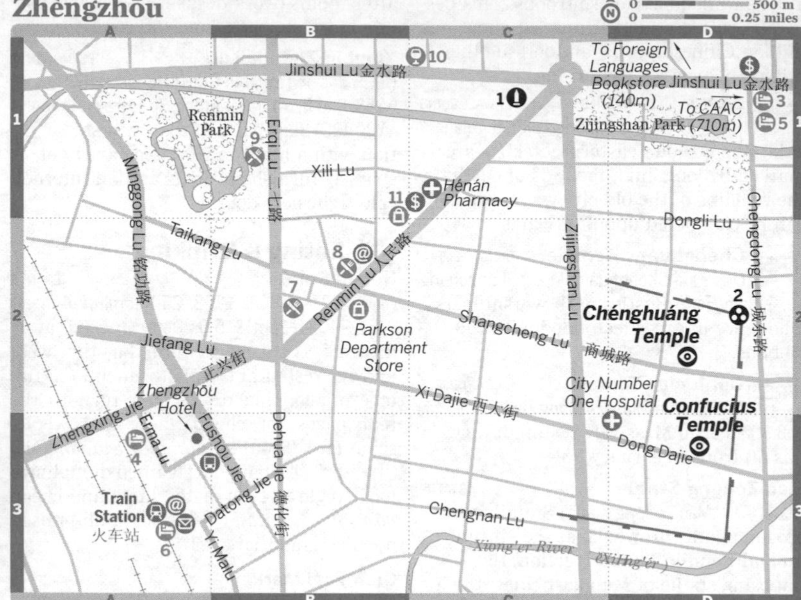

an outstanding selection of spirits and a laid-back vibe. Seize a chilled beer and allow proprietor Lao Wang to regale you with his tales of taming the Taklamakan Desert and wheeling it to Paris.

Shopping

Book Plaza BOOKS
(中原图书大厦; Zhōngyuán Túshū Dàshà; ☎6628 7809; 22 Renmin Lu; ⏲9am-7.30pm) Limited selection of English-language titles on the 3rd floor.

Foreign Languages Bookstore BOOKS
(外文书店; Wàiwén Shūdiàn; Zhengsan Jie; ⏲8.30am-6pm)

Information

Internet Access

Internet cafes (rates Y3 to Y5 per hour) cluster near the train station.

Internet cafe (网吧; wǎngbā; per hr Y2-3; ⏲24hr) Next to Hénán Shífǔ.

Internet cafe (网吧; wǎngbā; 2nd fl, ticket hall No 1, train station; per hr Y3-5; ⏲8am-midnight)

Tiānyá Internet Cafe (天涯网吧; Tiānyá Wǎngbā; 2nd fl, Jiankang Lu; per hr Y2; ⏲24hr) About 1km due north of Renmin Park; look for the Winnie-the-Pooh sign.

Yìlóng Wǎngjiā (176 Jiankang Lu; per hr Y2.50; ⏲24hr) Around 1.5km north of Renmin Park.

Zhèngzhōu

Top Sights
- Chénghuáng Temple ... D2
- Confucius Temple ... D3

Sights
- 1 Mao Zedong Statue ... C1
- 2 Shang City Walls ... D2

Sleeping
- 3 Express by Holiday Inn ... D1
- 4 Jǐnjiāng Inn ... A3
- 5 Sofitel ... D1
- 6 Yíngbīn Zhāodàisuǒ ... A3

Eating
- 7 Guǎngcǎi Market ... B2
- 8 Hénán Shífǔ ... B2
- 9 Roast Duck Restaurant ... B1

Drinking
- 10 Target Pub ... C1

Shopping
- 11 Book Plaza ... B1

Medical Services

City Number One Hospital (市一院; Shì Yīyuàn; Dong Dajie)

Hénán Pharmacy (河南大药房; Hénán Dàyàofáng; ☎6623 4256; 19 Renmin Lu; ⏰24hr)

Money

Bank of China (中国银行; Zhōngguó Yínháng; 8 Jinshui Lu; ⏰9am-5pm)

Industrial & Commercial Bank of China (工商银行; Gōngshāng Yínháng; Renmin Lu) Has a 24-hour ATM.

Post

China Post (中国邮政; Zhōngguó Yóuzhèng; ⏰8am-8pm) South end of train-station concourse.

Public Security Bureau

PSB Exit-Entry Administrative Office (公安局出入境管理处; Gōng'ānjú Chūrùjìng Guǎnlǐchù; ☎6962 0350; 90 Xihuanghe Donglu; ⏰8.30am-noon & 3-6.30pm Jun-Aug, 2-5.30pm Mon-Fri Sep-May) For visa extensions; take bus 135 or 114.

Getting There & Away

Air

The **Civil Aviation Administration of China** (CAAC; 中国民航; Zhōngguó Mínháng; ☎6599 1111; 3 Jinshui Lu, at Dongmin Lu), just east of the centre, sells tickets, as does the **ticket office** (售票处; shòupiàochù; ☎6672 0111) at the **Zhèngzhōu Hotel** (郑州大酒店; Zhèngzhōu Dàjiǔdiàn; ☎6677 7111; 8 Xinglong Jie). Look for the sign that reads 'Zhengzhou Airport Ticket Office'. Daily flights include the following:

Běijīng Y690, eight flights daily

Guǎngzhōu Y1760, 11 flights daily

Guìlín Y1200, two flights daily

Hong Kong Y2200, one flight daily

Shànghǎi Y800, 14 flights daily

Shēnzhèn Y1410, nine flights daily

Bus

The most useful **long-distance bus station** (长途汽车站; *chángtú qìchēzhàn*) is opposite the train station, with regular buses:

Dēngfēng Y26, one hour, every 30 minutes

Gǒngyì Y24, one hour, every 30 minutes

Línyǐng Y31, two hours, hourly

Luòyáng Y38 to Y50, two hours, every 15 minutes

Shàolín Temple Y25, 1½ to 2½ hours, every 20 to 30 minutes (6.30am to 11.30pm)

Xī'ān Y120, 6½ hours, hourly

Check at the long-distance bus station to see if there are buses to Kāifēng (Y7); otherwise, buses (Y7, 9½ hours) run from the **north bus station** (*qìchē běizhàn*), reachable on bus 520 (Y1.50).

Train

Zhèngzhōu is a major rail hub with trains to virtually every conceivable destination, including the Běijīng–Kowloon express.

For a Y5 commission, tickets are easy to buy at the **advance-booking office** (火车预售票处; Huǒchē Yùshòupiàochù ☎6835 6666; cnr Zhengxing Jie & Fushou Jie; ⏰8am-5pm).

There are nine G-class high-speed trains to Luòyáng (Lóngmén) between 7.55am and 8.25pm; tickets cost Y61/97 (2nd/1st class).

D-class express trains:

Ānyáng hard/soft seat Y58/69, two daily (7.22am and 8.51am).

Běijīng hard/soft seat Y213/256, five hours, one daily (7.22am). Via Ānyáng and Shíjiāzhuāng; D134. To Běijīng West train station; three other D trains run to this station.

Hànkǒu hard/soft seat Y160/192

Jǐnán hard/soft seat Y207/248

Kāifēng hard/soft seat Y22/27, 30 minutes, one daily (8.23am)

Luòyáng Y17 to Y20, 2½ hours

Nánjīng hard/soft seat Y205/247, one daily (8.23am)

Shànghǎi hard/soft seat Y239/299, 6½ hours, one daily (8.23am). Via Kāifēng and Nánjīng.

Shíjiāzhuāng hard/soft seat Y128/153, two daily (7.22am and 8.51am).

Tàiyuán hard/soft seat Y199/239, 4½ hours, one daily (8.51am). Via Ānyáng and Shíjiāzhuāng.

Xī'ān hard seat Y78, 7½ hours

Xīnxiāng Y13, 1½ hours

Getting Around

TO/FROM THE AIRPORT Airport buses (Y15, one hour, from 6.30am to 7pm) leave every hour from the Zhèngzhōu Hotel. A taxi to the airport (40 minutes) costs around Y100.

BUS

Bus 2 Runs to near the Shang City Walls.

Bus 39 Runs from the train station to Hénán Provincial Museum.

Bus 26 Runs from the train station past 7 February Sq and along Jinshui Lu to the CAAC office.

LIGHT RAIL Line 1 is under construction along Renmin Lu. The north–south Line 2 following Zijingshan Lu is also under construction.

TAXI Fares start at Y6 (Y8 at night).

PASSING THROUGH CHÁOYÁNG GATE

To walk through Nánjiēcūn's Cháoyáng Gate is to depart one world and enter another. Amble south through the gate from the boisterous and tatty market road in real China and observe how the unruly sounds of capitalist China are quickly smothered by jubilant Maoist propaganda blaring from speakers in Nánjiēcūn. There is no shouting, no spitting, no hawking, no swindling and there are no beggars or massage parlours in Nánjiēcūn. A powerful sense of decency and socialist civilisation prevails on its streets, which is conspicuous if you have spent time contending with the abrasiveness and squalor of the modern Chinese economy. Do take time, however, to wander to the outskirts of town. Although considerable activity animates the centre of Nánjiēcūn, things can appear surprisingly deserted on its peripheries. When we visited, these streets seemed empty, with no one entering or leaving the flats and just the occasional bicycle rattling by empty-looking and idle factories. In fact parts of Nánjiēcūn create a feeling of unreality reminiscent of *The Truman Show*. In 2008 reports suggested that Nánjiēcūn was a costly fraud, after amassing debts of over 1 billion yuán and effectively being funded by the Agricultural Bank of China. Perhaps attempting to clarify, the tourist-brochure blurb notes that Nánjiēcūn is 'neither myth nor Eutopia (sic), but is in existence, growing and advancing' and can 'enrich people's connotation' while helping you to feel the 'superiority complex of collectivity'.

Around Zhèngzhōu

NÁNJIĒCŪN 南街村

South of Zhèngzhōu, **Nánjiēcūn** (www.nanjiecun.cn; admission free) is China's very last Maoist collective (*gōngshè*). There are no Buddhist temples or mist-wreathed mountain panoramas, but a trip to Nánjiē is nonetheless one back in time: this is a journey to the puritanical and revolutionary China of the 1950s, when Chairman Mao was becoming a supreme being, money was yesterday's scene and the menace of karaoke had yet to be prophesied by even the most paranoid party faithful.

The first inkling you are stepping into an entirely different world may appear if you drop your bag off at the Nánjiēcūn Supermarket (南街村超市; Nánjiēcūn Chāoshì) on the western edge of town, where smiling young girls in revolutionary greens accept no fee for bag storage. Wow.

Nánjiēcūn perhaps resembles an average town in North Korea: the perfectly clean streets run in straight lines with a kind of austere socialist beauty, past noodle factories, schools and rows of identikit blocks of workers' flats emblazoned with vermillion communist slogans. One slogan reads: 'A drop of water only needs to be part of a great ocean to never dry up; a person can only have its greatest strength when part of a collective body'. Beatific portraits of Chairman Mao gaze down, while occasional flocks of white doves add to a surreal mood.

Make your way east along Yingsong Dadao (颍松大道) to **East is Red Sq** (东方红广场; Dōngfānghóng Guǎngchǎng), where two armed guards maintain a 24-hour vigil at the foot of a statue of Chairman Mao, and portraits of Marx, Engels, Stalin and Lenin (the original 'Gang of Four') rise up on all four sides. The square is deluged in shrill propaganda broadcast from speakers in true 1950s style. A short stroll north brings you to **Cháoyáng Gate Sq** (朝阳门广场; Cháoyángmén Guǎngchǎng) and the rebuilt, traditional architecture of **Cháoyáng Gate** (朝阳门; Cháoyáng Mén), topped with a portrait of Sun Zhongshan.

Indefatigable party loyalists troop to facsimiles of Chinese communist icons (Yan'an Pagoda, Chairman Mao's Sháoshān home and others) in the south of the village by the **Nánjiēcūn Botanic Gardens** (Nánjiēcūn Zhíwùyuán).

Sleeping & Eating

A day trip from Zhèngzhōu should suffice, but if you find Nánjiēcūn's nostalgic kitsch hard to abandon, check into the white-tile **Nanjiecun Hotel** (南街村宾馆; ☎0395-885 1271; r Y40, d/tr Y160/180, discounts of 25%; ❄), where the carpets are revolutionary red and girls in combat greens can lead you to classically old-style two-star hotel rooms. The hotel, with a restaurant, is on the northwest side of East is Red Sq.

A clutch of restaurants can be found along the western end of Zhongyuan Lu (中原路), to the south of and parallel with Yingsong Dadao. Alternatively, head north through Cháoyáng Gate to the boisterous market street in real China beyond, which is peppered with restaurants.

Information

Take money with you to Nánjiēcūn, as the ATM at the **Agricultural Bank of China** (农业银行; Nóngyè Yínháng) on Yingsong Lu may not take your card and there is nowhere to change money. The **Tourist Service Center** (旅游接待处; Yóukè Jiēdàichù; ⌚7.30am-5.30pm) at the west end of Yingsong Dadao can provide you with a booklet and a map (in Chinese) to prepare you for exploration.

Getting There & Away

From Zhèngzhōu bus station, buses (Y31, two hours) run south every hour between 6.40am and 6.10pm to the bus station at Línyǐng (临颍), from where it's a 2km or so walk or *sānlúnchē* (pedal-powered tricycle) journey south to Nánjiēcūn on the east side of the road.

Sōng Shān & Dēngfēng

嵩山、登封

☎0371

In Taoism, Sōng Shān is regarded as the central mountain, symbolising earth *(tǔ)* among the five elements and occupying the axis directly beneath heaven. Despite this Taoist affiliation, the mountains are also home to one of China's most famous and legendary Zen (Chan) Buddhist temples, the Shàolín Temple. Three main peaks compose Sōng Shān, rising to 1512m about 80km west of Zhèngzhōu.

At the foot of 1494m-high **Tàishì Shān** (太室山), a short ride southeast of the Shàolín Temple and 74km from Zhèngzhōu, sits the squat little town of Dēngfēng. Tatty and squalid in parts, it is used by travellers as a base for trips to surrounding sights or exploratory treks into the hills.

The main bus station is in the far east of town. Most hotels and restaurants are strung out on or near Zhongyue Dajie (中岳大街), the main east–west street, and Shaolin Dadao (少林大道), parallel to the south. The Shàolín Temple is a 15-minute bus ride northwest of town.

Sights & Activities

Shàolín Temple BUDDHIST TEMPLE
(少林寺; Shàolín Sì; ☎6370 2503; admission Y120; ⌚8am-6.30pm) The largely rebuilt Shàolín Temple, some 80km southwest of Zhèngzhōu, is a victim of its own success. A frequent target of war, the temple was last torched in 1928, and the surviving halls – many of recent construction – are today besieged by marauding tour groups.

Note that most, if not all, of the temple halls are very recent rebuilds, as many – such as the main **Great Treasure Hall** (大雄宝殿; Dàxióng Bǎodiàn; reconstructed in 1985) – were levelled by fire in 1928. Some halls only date back as far as 2004. Among the oldest structures at the temple are the **decorative arches** and **stone lions**, both outside the main gate.

Enter the temple past stelae of dedication – many, such as one from the Tang Soo Do Association, from abroad – and make for the temple's signature sights. At the rear, the **Pilu Pavilion** (西方圣人殿; Xīfāng Shēngrén Diàn) contains the famous depressions in the floor, apocryphally the result of generations of monks practising their stance work, and huge colour frescos. The **Guanyin Hall** (观音殿; Guānyīn Diàn) contains the celebrated frescos of fighting Shàolín monks. Always be on the lookout for the ubiquitous Damo (Bodhidharma), founder of Shàolín boxing, whose bearded Indian visage gazes sagaciously from stelae or peeks out from temple halls.

Across from the temple entrance, the Arhat Hall within the **Shífāng Chányuàn** (十方禅院) contains legions of crudely fashioned *luóhàn* (monks who have achieved enlightenment and passed to nirvana at death). The **Pagoda Forest** (少林塔林; Shàolín Tǎlín), a cemetery of 246 small brick pagodas including the ashes of an eminent monk, is well worth visiting if you get here ahead of the crowds. As you face the Shàolín Temple, paths on your left lead up **Wǔrǔ Peak** (五乳峰; Wǔrǔ Fēng). Flee the tourist din by heading into the hills to see the **cave** (达摩洞; Dámó Dòng) where Damo meditated for nine years; it's 4km away, so viewing it through high-powered binoculars (Y2) is an option. All of the sights mentioned so far are included in the main ticket price.

At 1512m above sea level and reachable on the Sōngyáng Cableway (Sōngyáng Suǒdào; Y30 return), **Shàoshì Shān** (少室山) is the area's tallest peak, with a scenic trek beside craggy rock formations along a path that often hugs the cliff. The trek takes about six hours return, covers 15km and takes you to the 782-step **Rope Bridge** (索桥; Suǒ Qiáo). For safety reasons, monks recommend trekking with a friend. The Shàolín Cableway (Shàolín Suǒdào; Y60 return) leads to the **Sānhuángzhài Scenic Area** (三皇寨景区; Sānhuángzhài Jǐngqū). Both cableways can be found just beyond the Pagoda Forest. Maps in Chinese are available at souvenir stalls.

To reach the Shàolín Temple, take a bus (Y3, 15 minutes) from Dēngfēng's west bus station (西站; *xīzhàn*) on Zhongyue Dajie to the drop-off point and then a buggy (Y5, from 8am to 6pm) to the temple entrance, or walk (20 minutes). Alternatively, take a minibus from either Luòyáng or Zhèngzhōu (Y17 to Y20, 1½ to 2½ hours) to the drop-off, although some make detours, so ask. From the temple, return buses leave from the drop-off point (last bus at around 8pm). A taxi to the temple from Dēngfēng will cost around Y30.

Sōngyáng Academy ACADEMY
(嵩阳书院; Sōngyáng Shūyuàn; admission Y30; ⏲8am-6pm) At the foot of Tàishì Shān sits one of China's oldest academies, the lush and well-tended Sōngyáng Academy, which dates to AD 484 and rises up the hill on a series of terraces. In the courtyard are two cypress trees believed to be around 4500 years old – and they're still alive! Within walking distance of the academy, the **Sōngyuè Pagoda** (嵩岳塔; Sōngyuè Tǎ; admission Y25; ⏲8am-6.30pm), built in AD 509, is China's oldest brick pagoda.

Both bus 2 and bus 6 (Y1) from Dēngfēng run to the Sōngyáng Academy.

Zhōngyuè Temple TAOIST TEMPLE
(中岳庙; Zhōngyuè Miào; admission Y30; ⏲6.30am-6.30pm) A few kilometres east of Dēngfēng, the ancient and hoary Zhōngyuè Miào is a colossal active Taoist monastery complex that originally dates back to the 2nd century BC. Less visited, the complex – set against a mountainous background – exudes a more palpable air of reverence than its Buddhist sibling, the Shàolín Temple. Besides attending the main hall dedicated to the Mountain God, walk through the **Huàsān Gate** (化三门; Huàsān Mén) and expunge *pengju, pengzhi* and *pengjiao* – three pestilential insects that respectively inhabit the brain, tummy and feet. Pay a visit to the **Ministry of Hades** (七十二司; Qīshí'èr Sī) and drop by the four **Iron Men of Song**, rubbed by visitors to cure ailments. From Dēngfēng, take the green bus 2 along Zhongyue Dajie.

Guānxīng Tái Observatory OBSERVATORY
(观星台; admission Y10; ⏲8am-6.30pm) In the town of Gàochéng, 15km southeast of Dēngfēng, is China's oldest surviving observatory. In 1276 the emperor ordered two astronomers to chart a calendar. After observing from the stone tower, they came back in 1280 with a mapping of 365 days, five hours, 49 minutes and 12 seconds, which differs from modern calculations by only 26 seconds. Regular southbound buses from Dēngfēng can take you here; catch them from any large intersection in the southeastern part of town.

Sleeping

Shàolín Hotel HOTEL $$
(少林宾馆; Shàolín Bīnguǎn; ☎6016 1616; 66 Zhongyue Dajie; 中岳大街66号; d Y288, business r Y300, discounts of 50%; ❄) Bright and cheery staff, good discounts and clean rooms make this neat and trim hotel on Zhongyue Dajie a good choice. There's no English sign, so look for the four-storey white building east of Dicos (a fast-food restaurant).

Shàolín International Hotel HOTEL $$$
(少林国际大酒店; Shàolín Guójì Dàjiǔdiàn; ☎6285 6868; www.shaolinhotel.com; 20 Shaolin Dadao; 少林大道20号; s/d/ste Y680/780/1180; ❄) Calling itself a four-star hotel, this is more like a smartish three-star, with obligatory scads of black Buicks parked outside. Jiang Zemin stayed here, leaving his photo in the lobby and making the hotel popular with visiting Chinese.

Dēng Fēng Shàolín Temple Traveler's Hostel HOSTEL $
(旅行家青年旅舍; Lǚxíngjiā Qīngnián Lǚshè; ☎6288 6799, 159 8188 3801; Chonggao Luxi; 崇高路西308号; dm Y30, d with/without bathroom Y160/100; ❄@) English-speaking staff.

Information

Bank of China (中国银行; Zhōngguó Yínháng) 52 Zhongyue Dajie (⏲9am-5pm Mon-Fri); 186 Shaolin Dadao (⏲9am-noon & 2-5pm Mon-Fri) Both have 24-hour ATM and forex.

China International Travel Service (CITS; 中国国际旅行社; Zhōngguó Guójì Lǚxíngshè; ☎6288 3442; Beihuan Lu Xiduan) Has helpful, English-speaking staff.

China Post (中国邮政; Zhōngguó Yóuzhèng; cnr Zhongyue Dajie & Wangji Lu)

No 2 People's Hospital (第二人民医院; Dì'èr Rénmín Yīyuàn; ☎6289 9999; 189 Shaolin Dadao) Located on the main road.

Getting There & Around

The Dēngfēng bus station is in the east of town; jump on bus 1 (Y1) to reach Zhongyue Dajie and the town centre. Buses to/from Zhèngzhōu (Y26, 1½ hours) and Luòyáng (Y20, two hours) run every 30 minutes. Hotels in Zhèngzhōu and Luòyáng often arrange day tours (Y40, excluding entrance fees) that include sites along the way. To purchase tickets for trains departing from Zhèngzhōu, go to the **train ticket office** (⏲8am-noon & 2-5pm) at the gate of the Sōngyáng Yingbin Hotel (130 Shaolin Dadao). Taxis start at Y5.

Luòyáng 洛阳

☎0379 / POP 1.4 MILLION

Capital of 13 dynasties until the Northern Song dynasty shifted its capital to Kāifēng in the 10th century, Luòyáng was one of China's true dynastic citadels. Charted on maps of the town, the mighty Sui- and Tang-dynasty walls sat in an imposing rectangle north and south of the Luò River, while the city boasted 1300 Buddhist temples. A leaflet at the Luòyáng Museum trumpets: 'Luòyáng has been the centre of the world since ancient times...it is a resplendent pearl'. It's impossible today to conceive that Luòyáng was once the very centre of the Chinese universe and the eastern capital of the great Tang dynasty. The heart of the magnificent Sui-dynasty palace complex was centred on the point where today's Zhongzhou Lu and Dingding Lu intersect in a frenzy of honking traffic.

Luòyáng is now largely indistinguishable from other fume-laden modern Chinese towns. Nonetheless, the magnificently sculpted Lóngmén Caves by the banks of the Yī River remain one of China's most prized Buddhist treasures and the annual **Peony Festival**, centred on Wángchéng Park in April, is colourful fun. The old town, where the bulk of Luòyáng's history survives, is in the east.

Sights & Activities

FREE **Luòyáng Museum** MUSEUM
(洛阳博物馆; Luòyáng Bówùguǎn; 298 Zhongzhou Zhonglu; ⏲8.30am-5.30pm Apr-Oct, to 5pm Nov-Mar) One of the few places you can get your finger on the pulse of ancient Luòyáng, this museum has an absorbing collection of Tang-dynasty three-colour *sāncǎi* porcelain and dioramas of the Sui- and Tang-dynasty city: the outer Tang wall was punctured by 18 magnificent gates and embraced the Imperial City with the colossal, five-eaved and circular Tiāntáng (Hall of Heaven) at its heart. Despite plentiful explanations concerning Luòyáng's former grandeur, there is little info on its subsequent loss. Take bus 4 or 11.

Old Town HISTORIC AREA
(老城区; *lǎochéngqū*) Any Chinese city with any sense of history has its old town. Luòyáng's old town lies east of the rebuilt **Lìjīng Gate** (丽京门; Lìjīng Mén; gate tower admission Y30; ⏲8am-10pm), where a maze of narrow and winding streets rewards exploration, and old courtyard houses survive amid modern outcrops. Climbable for Y2, originally dating to 1555 and moved to this location in 1614, the old **Drum Tower** (鼓楼; Gǔ Lóu) rises up at the east end of Dong Dajie (东大街), itself lined with traditional rooftops. The square, brick **Wénfēng Pagoda** (文峰塔; Wénfēng Tǎ; 6 Donghe Xiang) has a 700-year history, with an inaccessible door on the 2nd floor and a brick shack built onto its south side. A notable historic remnant survives in the two halls of the former **City God Temple** (城隍庙; Chénghuáng Miào), east of the corner of Zhongzhou Donglu and Jinye Lu, although it is not open to visitors. Note the intriguing roof ornaments of the green-tiled first hall facing the street.

Wángchéng Park PARK
(王城公园; Wángchéng Gōngyuán; Zhongzhou Zhonglu; admission Y3, park & zoo Y15, Peony Festival Y50-55) One of Luòyáng's indispensable green lungs, this attractive park is the site of the annual Peony Festival; held in April, the festival sees the park flooded with colour, floral aficionados, photographers, girls with garlands on their heads and hawkers selling huge bouquets of flowers. During the festival, the park is open late for a light show.

Sleeping

Luòyáng has a largely unappealing choice of hotels in every budget bracket.

Luòyáng Youth Hostel HOSTEL $
(洛阳国际青年旅社; Luòyáng Guójì Qīngnián Lǚshè; ☎6526 0666; 3rd fl, Binjiang Dasha, 72 Jinguyuan Lu; 金谷园路72号滨江大厦3楼;

Luòyáng

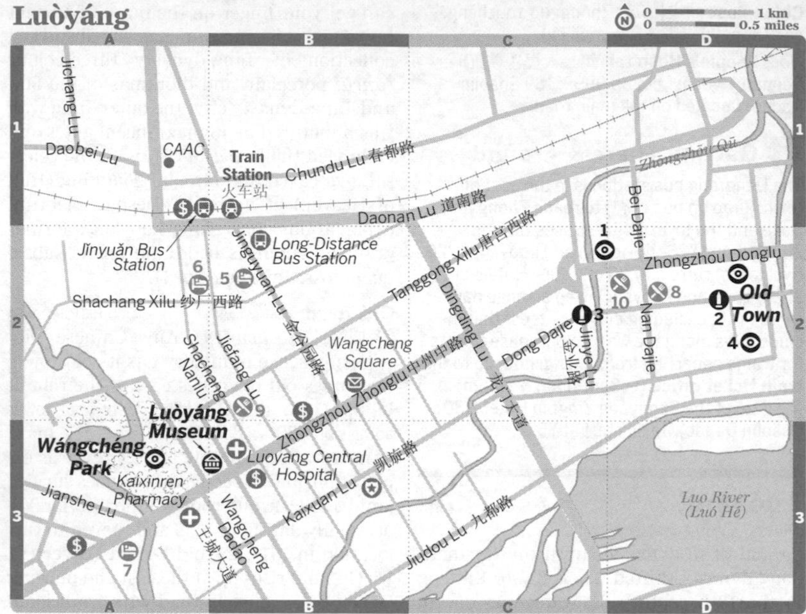

6-/8-person dm Y60/55, common r Y140, s/d Y238/228, discounts on d of 40%; ❄@) This rather sterile hostel, a short walk from the train station, has very tidy, bright and clean bunk-bed dorms. Tiled-floor doubles are clean and simple; some rooms come with computers. Internet access available at Y2 per hour.

Míngyuàn Hotel HOTEL $
(明苑宾馆; Míngyuàn Bīnguǎn; ☎6319 0378; lymingyuan@163.com; 20 Jiefang Lu; 解放路20号; dm Y50, s & d Y328; ❄@) Once a popular and efficient backpacker hotel, this place has morphed into a more average two-star affair with an imitation-leather suite in the foyer and less responsive service, but standard rooms are comfortable enough.

Peony Hotel HOTEL $$
(牡丹大酒店; Mǔdān Dàjiǔdiàn; ☎6468 0000; www.peonyhotel.net; dept@yahoo.com.cn; 15 Zhongzhou Xilu; 中州西路15号; standard d Y550-660, discounts of 30%; ❄@) Renovated in 2004, standard 'A' doubles are small, with midget bathrooms, but are prettily laid out and attractively furnished, with free broadband. Nonsmoking rooms available.

Eating

Luòyáng's famous 'water banquet' resonates along China's culinary grapevine. The main dishes of this 24-course meal are soups and are served up with the speed of flowing water – hence the name. A handy branch of Carrefour (家乐福; Jiālèfú) can be found near the corner of Tanggong Xilu and Jiefang Lu.

Luòyáng

Tudali KOREAN $
(土大力; Tǔdàlì; ☎6312 0513; www.tudali.com, in Chinese; Xinduhui, cnr Jiefang Lu & Tanggong Xilu; meals Y30; ⊙11.30am-2am) With the accent on spiciness, this popular Korean restaurant brings out patrons in a sweat. The *pàocàitāng* (泡菜汤; kimchi soup; Y15) is refreshingly piquant, as is the *làwèi niúròutāng* (辣味牛肉汤; spicy beef soup; Y22), or you can get your metal chopsticks around a plate of chips (Y10). Handy photo menu and helpful staff in red and black tops.

Old Town Market MARKET $
(南大街夜市; Nándàjiē yèshì; cnr Xi Dajie & Dong Dajie & north to Zhongzhou Donglu; ⊙10am-10pm) Lively street market with a cornucopia of snacks from *cuìpí xiānnǎi* (脆皮鲜奶; crispy milk nuggets; Y2), *yángròu chuàn* (羊肉串; lamb kebabs; Y2), sweet, gelatinous bowls of *xìngrénchá* (杏仁茶; almond dessert; Y5) and super-sweet *gānzhe zhī* (甘蔗汁; sugar-cane juice; Y1 to Y2).

Zhēn Bù Tóng Fàndiàn HENAN $$
(真不同饭店; One of a Kind Restaurant; ☎6399 5080; 369 Zhongzhou Donglu; dishes Y15-45, water banquet from Y60) Huge place behind a colourful green, red, blue and gold traditional facade. This is the place to come for a water-banquet experience; if 24 courses seems a little excessive, you can opt to pick individual dishes from the menu.

Information

Internet cafes (per hour Y2) are scattered around the train station and sprinkled along nearby Jinguyuan Lu.

Bank of China (中国银行; Zhōngguó Yínháng; ⊙8am-4.30pm) The Zhongzhou Xilu office exchanges travellers cheques and has an ATM that accepts MasterCard and Visa. There's also a branch on the corner of Zhongzhou Lu and Shachang Nanlu that's open until 5.30pm. Another branch just west of the train station has foreign-exchange services.

China Post (中国邮政; Zhōngguó Yóuzhèng; cnr Zhongzhou Zhonglu & Jinguyuan Lu)

Industrial & Commercial Bank of China (ICBC; 工商银行; Gōngshāng yínháng; Zhongzhou Zhonglu) Huge branch; forex and 24-hour ATM.

Kāixīnrén Pharmacy (开心人大药房; Kāixīnrén Dàyàofáng; ☎6392 8315; 483 Zhongzhou Zhonglu; ⊙24hr)

Luòyáng Central Hospital (洛阳市中心医院; Luòyáng Shì Zhōngxīn Yīyuàn; ☎6389 2222; 288 Zhongzhou Lu) Works in cooperation with SOS International; also has a pharmacy.

Public Security Bureau (PSB; 公安局; Gōng'ānjú; ☎6393 8397; cnr Kaixuan Lu & Tiyuchang Lu; ⊙8am-noon & 2-5.30pm Mon-Fri) The exit-entry department (Chūrùjìng Dàtīng) is in the south building.

Western Union (全球汇款特快; Quánqiú Huìkuǎn Tèkuài; ☎800 820 8668; Zhongzhou Xilu) Next door to the Bank of China.

Getting There & Away

Air

You would do better to fly into or out of Zhèngzhōu. The **CAAC** (中国民航; Zhōngguó Mínháng; ☎6231 0121, 24hr 6539 9366; 196 Chundu Lu) is in an ugly white-tile building north of the railway line, but tickets can be obtained through hotels. Daily flights operate to Běijīng (Y890, one hour), Shànghǎi (Y890, one hour) and other cities.

Bus

Regular departures from the **long-distance bus station** (长途汽车站; chángtú qìchēzhàn; 51 Jinguyuan Lu) across from the train station includethe following:

Dēngfēng Y20, two hours, every 30 minutes

Kāifēng Y50, three hours, hourly (7.15am to 6pm)

Línyǐng Y51, four hours, one daily (2pm)

Shàolín Temple Y17, 1½ hours, every 20 minutes (5.20am to 6pm)

Xī'ān Y90, four hours, hourly (8am to 6pm)

Zhèngzhōu Y40, 1½ hours, every 20 minutes

Buses to similar destinations depart from the **Jǐnyuǎn bus station** (锦远汽车站; Jǐnyuǎn *qìchēzhàn*), just west of the train station.

Fast buses to Shàolín (Y20, one to 1½ hours) leave from outside the train station every half-hour until 4.30pm; otherwise, take a bus for Xǔchāng from the long-distance bus station and get off at the temple (Y22, 1½ hours). You can also get to Shàolín on buses to Dēngfēng (Y20, two hours).

Train

Luòyáng's new **Luòyáng Lóngmén Station** (洛阳龙门站; Luòyáng Lóngmén Zhàn) over the river in the south of town has extra-high-speed trains to Zhèngzhōu and Xī'ān.

Regional destinations include Kāifēng (hard seat Y30, three hours) and Zhèngzhōu (hard seat Y10 to Y20, 1½ hours).

Hard-sleeper destinations:

Běijīng West seat/sleeper Y106/191, seven to 10 hours

Nánjīng seat/sleeper Y113/201, 10 to 12 hours

Shànghǎi seat/sleeper Y153/254, 13 to 16 hours

Wǔhàn seat/sleeper Y87/157, nine hours

Xī'ān 2nd/1st class Y184/294, two hours. There are eight G-class trains to Xī'ān daily.

Zhèngzhōu 2nd/1st class Y61/97, 40 minutes, eight daily. G train. From Lùoyáng Lóngmén Station.

 Getting Around

There is no shuttle bus from the CAAC office to the airport, 12km north of the city, but bus 83 (Y1, 30 minutes) runs from the parking lot to the right as you exit the train station; a taxi from the train station will cost about Y30.

Buses 5 and 41 go to the Old Town from the train station, running via Wángchéng Sq. Buses 26, 28, 33, 65 and 66 run to Lùoyáng Lóngmén Station.

Taxis are Y5 at flag fall, making them good value and a more attractive option than taking motor-rickshaws, which will cost you around Y4 from the train station to Wángchéng Sq.

Around Luòyáng

LÓNGMÉN CAVES 龙门石窟

A priceless Unesco World Heritage Site, the ravaged grottoes at Lóngmén constitute one of China's handful of surviving masterpieces of Buddhist rock carving. A Sutra in stone, the epic achievement of the **Lóngmén Caves** (Dragon Gate Grottoes; Lóngmén Shíkū; admission Y120, English-speaking guide Y100; ⏲6am-8pm summer, 6.30am-7pm winter) was first undertaken by chisellers from the Northern Wei dynasty, after the capital was relocated here from Dàtóng in AD 494. Over the next 200 years or so, more than 100,000 images and statues of Buddha and his disciples emerged from over a kilometre of limestone cliff wall along the Yī River (Yī Hé).

A bewildering amount of decapitation disfigures the statuary. In the early 20th century, many effigies were beheaded by unscrupulous collectors or simply extracted whole, many ending up abroad in such institutions as the Metropolitan Museum of Art in New York, the Atkinson Museum in Kansas City and the Tokyo National Museum. A noticeboard at the site lists significant statues that are missing and their current whereabouts. Some effigies are returning and severed heads are gradually being restored to their bodies, but many statues have clearly just had their faces crudely bludgeoned off, vandalism that dates to the Cultural Revolution (the Ten Thousand Buddha Cave was particularly badly damaged during this period) and earlier episodes of anti-Buddhist fervour. Weather has also played its part, wearing smooth the faces of many other statues.

The caves are scattered in a line on the west and east sides of the river. Most of the significant Buddhist carvings are on the west side, but a notable crop can also be admired after traversing the bridge to the east side. Surprisingly, English captions are rudimentary despite the caves being a major tourist drawcard. The caves are numbered and illuminated at night.

The Lóngmén Caves are 13km south of Luòyáng and can be reached by taxi (Y30) or bus 81 (Y1.50, 40 minutes) from the east side of Luòyáng's train station. The last bus 81 returns to Luòyáng at 8.50pm. Buses 53 and 60 also run to the caves.

WEST SIDE

Three Bīnyáng Caves CAVES

(宾阳三洞; Bīnyáng Sān Dòng) Work began on the Three Bīnyáng Caves during the Northern Wei dynasty. Despite the completion of two of the caves during the Sui and Tang dynasties, statues here all display the benevolent expressions that characterised Northern Wei style. Traces of pigment remain within the three large grottoes and other small niches honeycomb the cliff walls. Nearby is the **Móyá Three Buddha Niche** (摩崖三佛龛; Móyá Sānfó Kān), with seven figures that date to the Tang dynasty.

Ten Thousand Buddha Cave CAVE

(万佛洞; Wànfó Dòng) South of Three Bīnyáng Caves, the Tang-dynasty Ten Thousand Buddha Cave dates from 680. In addition to its namesake galaxy of tiny bas-relief Buddhas, there is a fine effigy of the Amitabha Buddha. Note the red pigment on the ceiling.

Lotus Flower Cave CAVE

(莲花洞; Liánhuā Dòng) Cave No 712, also called Lotus Flower Cave, was carved between 525 and 527 during the Northern Wei dynasty. The cave contains a large standing Buddha, now faceless and handless. On the cave's ceiling wispy apsaras (celestial nymphs) drift around a central lotus flower, itself a Buddhist metaphor for purity and serenity. Note the gorgeous, ornate, cloud-like scrolling decoration above the entrance.

Ancestor Worshipping Temple CAVE TEMPLE
The most physically imposing of all the Lóngmén caves, this vast cave temple (奉先寺; Fèngxiān Sì) was carved during the Tang dynasty between 672 and 675; it contains the best examples of sculpture, despite evident weathering.

Nine principal figures dominate the Ancestor Worshipping Temple. Tang figures tend to be more three-dimensional than the Northern Wei figures, while their expressions and poses also seem more natural. In contrast to the other-worldly effigies of the Northern Wei, many Tang figures possess a more fearsome ferocity and muscularity, most noticeable in the huge guardian figure in the north wall.

The 17m-high seated central Buddha is said to be Losana, whose face is allegedly modelled on Tang empress and Buddhist patron Wu Zetian, who funded its carving. In the corner of the south wall of the temple, next to the semi-obliterated guardian figure, are three statues that have simply been smashed away.

Medical Prescription Cave CAVE
(药方洞; Yàofāng Dòng) Located south of Ancestor Worshipping Temple is the tiny Medical Prescription Cave, begun in the Northern Wei and completed in the Northern Qi. The entrance to this cave is carved with 6th-century stone stelae inscribed with remedies for a range of common ailments.

Earliest Cave CAVE
(古阳洞; Gǔyáng Dòng) Next door to the Medical Prescription Cave is the larger Earliest Cave, begun in 493. It's a narrow, high-roofed cave featuring a Buddha statue and a profusion of sculptures, particularly of flying apsaras.

Huǒshāo Cave CAVE
(火烧洞; Huǒshāo Dòng) This largely damaged cave is followed by a string of smaller grottoes that are all in miserable condition.

Cave 1628 CAVE
Contains a row of largely headless Tang figures.

Carved Cave CAVE
(石窟洞; Shíkū Dòng) The last major cave in the Lóngmén complex. Features intricate carvings depicting religious processions of the Northern Wei dynasty.

EAST SIDE

When you have reached the last cave on the west side, cross the bridge and walk back north along the east side. The lovely **Thousand Arm and Thousand Eye Guanyin** (千手千眼观音龛; Qiānshǒu Qiānyǎn Guānyīn Kān) in Cave 2132 is a splendid bas-relief dating to the Tang dynasty, revealing the Goddess of Mercy framed in a huge fan of carved hands, each sporting an eye. Cave 2139, the **Worshipping Pure Land Niche** (西方净土变龛; Xīfāng Jìngtǔ Biànkān), also dates to the Tang dynasty. Up the steps, two Tang-dynasty guardian deities stand outside the sizeable **Lord Gāopíng Cave** (高平郡王洞; Gāopíng Jùnwáng Dòng). Further along are several empty niches before you reach the most impressive cave on the east side, the large **Reading Sutra Cave** (看经寺洞; Kàn Jīng Sìdòng), with a carved lotus on its ceiling and 29 *luóhàn* around the base of the walls. There is also a large **viewing terrace** for sizing up the Ancestor Worshipping Temple on the far side of the river.

WHITE HORSE TEMPLE

Although its original structures have largely been replaced and it is likely older temples have vanished, this active **monastery** (白马寺; Báimǎ Sì; admission Y50; ⏲7am-7pm) is regarded as the first surviving Buddhist temple erected on Chinese soil, originally dating from the 1st century AD.

When two Han-dynasty court emissaries went in search of Buddhist scriptures, they encountered two Indian monks in Afghanistan; the monks returned to Luòyáng on two white horses carrying Buddhist Sutras and statues. The impressed emperor built the temple to house the monks; it is also their resting place.

In the **Hall of the Heavenly Kings**, Milefo laughs from within a wonderful old burnished cabinet. Structures of note include the **Big Buddha Hall**, the **Hall of Mahavira** and the **Pilu Hall** at the very rear, while the standout **Qíyún Pagoda** (齐云塔; Qíyún Tǎ), an ancient 12-tiered brick tower, is a pleasant five-minute walk away.

The temple is located 13km east of Luòyáng, around 40 minutes away on bus 56 from the Xīguān (西关) stop.

GUĀNLÍN TEMPLE

North of the Lóngmén Caves, this **temple** (关林寺; Guānlín Sì; admission Y30; ⊙8am-5pm) is the burial place of the legendary general Guan Yu of the Three Kingdoms period (AD 220–265). The temple buildings were built during the Ming dynasty and Guan Yu was issued the posthumous title 'Lord of War' in the early Qing dynasty. Buses 81 (Y1.50) and 55 (Y1.50) run past Guānlín Temple from the train station in Luòyáng. Bus 81 stops at the temple on its return from the Lóngmén Caves. Bus 58 connects Guānlín Temple and the White Horse Temple.

Guōliàngcūn 郭亮村

☎0373 / POP 300

On its clifftop perch high up in the Wànxiān (Ten Thousand Immortals) Mountains in north Hénán, this delightful high-altitude stone hamlet was for centuries sheltered from the outside world by its combination of inaccessibility and anonymity. Guōliàngcūn shot to fame as the bucolic backdrop to a clutch of Chinese films, which firmly embedded the village in contemporary Chinese mythology.

Today the village attracts legions of artists, who journey here to capture the unreal mountain scenery on paper and canvas. New hotels have sprung up at the village's foot, but the original dwellings – climbing the mountain slope – retain their simple, rustic charms. Long treks through the lovely scenery more than compensate you for the effort of journeying here.

Approximately 6°C colder than Zhèngzhōu, Guōliàngcūn is cool enough to be devoid of mosquitoes year-round (some locals say), but pack very warm clothes for winter visits, which can be bone-numbing. Visiting in low season may seem odd advice, but come evening the village can be utterly tranquil, and moonlit nights are intoxicating. Occasional power cuts plunge the village into candlelight, so pack a small torch.

Officially, the entrance charge for Guōliàngcūn is Y60 (admission to the Wànxiān Mountains Scenic Area). There is nowhere to change money in Guōliàngcūn, so take money with you. A small **clinic** (☎671 0303) can be found in the village.

Sights & Activities

All of the delightful **village dwellings**, hung with butter-yellow *bàngzi* (sweet-corn cobs), are hewn from the same local stone that paves the slender alleyways, sculpts the bridges and fashions the picturesque gates of Guōliàngcūn. Walnut-faced old women peek from doorways and children scamper about, but locals are well used to outsiders.

You will have passed by the **Precipice Gallery** (绝壁长廊; Juébì Chángláng) en route to the village, but backtrack down for a closer perspective on these plunging cliffs, with dramatic views from the tunnel carved from the rock face. Before this tunnel was built (between 1972 and 1978) by a local man called Shen Mingxin and others, the only way into the village was via the **Sky Ladder** (天梯; Tiān Tī), Ming-dynasty steps hewn from the local pink stone, with no guard rails but amazing views. You pass the Sky Ladder after about 30 to 40 minutes if walking along the path to the charming village of **Huìtáo Zhài** (会逃寨), with its cliff-top cottages. It's hard to imagine that this area was largely under the sea 500 million years ago.

Over the bridge on the other side of the precipice from the village, walk past the small row of cottages almost on the edge of the cliff called **Yáshàng Rénjiā** (崖上人家) and you can step onto a platform atop a pillar of rock for astonishing views into the canyon.

Continuing along the road out of Guōliàngcūn, past the hotels and away from the Sky Ladder, you can do a bracing 5km loop through the mountain valley and past the awe-inspiring curtain of rock above the **Shouting Spring** (喊泉; Hǎn Quán); its flow responds to the loudness of your whoops, so the story goes. You'll also pass the **Old Pool** (老潭; Lǎo Tán) and two caves: the **Red Dragon Cave** (红龙洞; Hónglóng Dòng) and the **White Dragon Cave** (白龙洞; Báilóng Dòng). Vehicles whiz travellers along the route for Y5. Once you've seen the big sights, get off the beaten trail and onto one of the small paths heading into the hills (such as the boulder-strewn brookside trail along the flank of Guōliàngcūn that leads further up into the mountain), but take water.

Sleeping & Eating

Many homesteads in Guōliàngcūn proper have thrown open their doors to wayfarers, offering cheap and simple beds for Y20 to Y40. Prices can be a bit higher during the summer but are negotiable in the low season. The strip of hotels at the foot of the village offer more spacious rooms, some with showers and TVs (from Y40). There are no restaurants per se, but hoteliers will cook up simple meals on request and a couple of shops sell snacks and essentials.

Getting There & Away

Reach Guōliàngcūn from Xīnxiāng (新乡), between Ānyáng and Zhèngzhōu. Fast trains run to Xīnxiāng from Zhèngzhōu (Y18, one hour), as do regular buses (Y25, 1½ hours). Exit Xīnxiāng train station, head straight ahead and take the first left onto Ziyou Lu (自由路) for buses to Huīxiàn (辉县; Y6, 45 minutes, regular). Six buses (Y11, one hour 40 minutes, first/last bus 7.30am/4.30pm) from Huīxiàn's east bus station (辉县东站; Huīxiàn Dōngzhàn) pass by the mountain road to Guōliàngcūn. Note that buses from Huīxiàn may have the characters for Guōliàng (郭亮) on the window, but may only stop at Nánpíng (南坪), a village beyond the base of the road to Guōliàngcūn, depending on passenger numbers.

From Nánpíng it is a steep 3km walk to Guōliàngcūn up the mountain road (not recommended with a heavy backpack); otherwise, taxis or local drivers are prone to fleecing for the steep haul (Y40), especially if travellers are scarce. In the other direction, Huīxiàn-bound minibuses (Y11) run from the bottom of the mountain road from Guōliàngcūn at 9am, noon and 3pm. Guesthouse owners should be able to run you down to the drop-off point for around Y30 if you spend the night in their lodgings.

Kāifēng 开封

☎0378 / POP 581,000

Of all China's provinces, Hénán perhaps best typifies the contradictions of a nation that loves to boast of a staggeringly long history which it has also so effectively managed to bury, overlay or destroy. More than any other of Hénán's ancient capitals, however, Kāifēng has preserved a semblance of its original grandeur. Kāifēng has character: you may have to squint a bit and learn to sift the fakes from the genuine historical fragments, but the city still offers up a riveting display of age-old charm, magnificent market food, relics from its long-vanished apogee and colourful chrysanthemums (the city flower; Kāifēng is also known as Júchéng, or 'Chrysanthemum Town').

It's no Píngyáo – the city is hardly knee-deep in history, and white-tile buildings blight the low skyline – but enough survives above ground level to hint at past glories and reward ambitious exploration. One reason you won't see soaring skyscrapers here is because buildings requiring deep foundations are prohibited, for fear of destroying the ancient Northern Song–dynasty city below. Large public buildings, ministries and academies such as Hénán University are all outside the city walls.

History

Once the prosperous capital of the Northern Song dynasty (960–1126), Kāifēng was established south of the Yellow River, but not far enough to escape the river's capricious wrath. After centuries of flooding, the city of the Northern Song largely lies buried 8m to 9m deep. Between 1194 and 1938 the city flooded 368 times, an average of once every two years.

Kāifēng was also the first city in China where Jewish merchants settled when they arrived, along the Silk Road, during the Song dynasty. A small Christian community also lives in Kāifēng alongside a much larger local Muslim Hui community.

Sights

For ancient Kāifēng architecture, the trick is to wander along small streets off the main drag within the city walls, where you can find old, tumbledown, one-storey buildings with misshapen tiled roofs. Beishudian Jie has a collection of ancient, lopsided and sunken rooftops sprouting dry grass.

Temple of the Chief Minister

BUDDHIST TEMPLE

(大相国寺; Dà Xiàngguó Sì; Ziyou Lu; admission Y30; ⏲8am-6pm) First founded in AD 555, this frequently rebuilt temple was destroyed along with the city in the early 1640s when rebels breached the Yellow River's dykes. During the Northern Song, the temple covered a massive 34 hectares and housed over 10,000 monks.

Within the **Hall of the Heavenly Kings** (天王殿; Tiānwáng Diàn), the mission of chubby Milefo (the Laughing Buddha) is proclaimed in the attendant Chinese characters: 'Big belly can endure all that is hard to endure in the world'. But the temple showstopper is the mesmerising **Four-Faced Thousand Hand Thousand Eye Guanyin** (四面千手千眼观世音), towering

Kāifēng

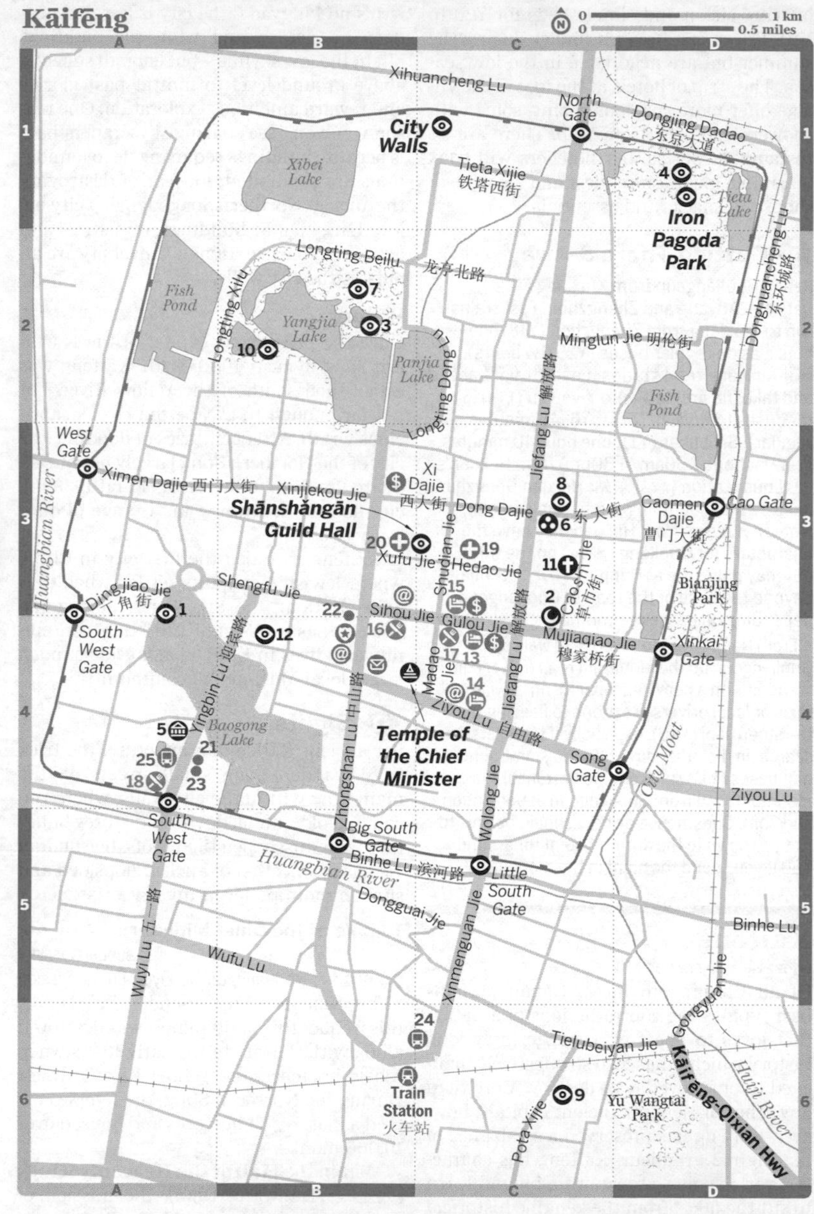

within the octagonal Arhat Hall (罗汉殿; Luóhàn Diàn), beyond the **Hall of Tathagata** (大雄宝殿; Dàxióng Bǎodiàn). Fifty-eight years in the carving, the 7m-tall gilded statue bristles with giant fans of 1048 arms, an eye upon each hand; the arhats themselves are presented with considerably less artistry. Jade Buddhas assemble within the **Hall of Tripitaka** (Cángjìng Lóu), where scriptures were stored, and a multitude of side halls can be explored as well as numerous shops where you can pick up

Kāifēng

Buddhist talismans and knick-knacks. Recent additions include some rather crudely fashioned pagodas and at the rear is a further hall awaiting construction. Elsewhere in the temple you can divine your future by drawing straws *(chōuqiān)*, dine at the on-site **vegetarian restaurant** (斋堂) or listen to the song of caged birds.

Shānshǎngān Guild Hall GUILDHALL
(山陕甘会馆; Shānshǎngān Huìguǎn; 85 Xufu Jie; admission Y20; ⏲8.30am-6.30pm summer, 8am-5pm winter) The elaborately styled guildhall was built as a lodging and meeting place during the Qing dynasty by an association of merchants from Shānxi, Shǎnxi (Shaanxi) and Gānsù provinces. Note the carvings on the roofs, and delve into the exhibition on historic Kāifēng. Check out the fascinating diorama of the old Song city – with its palace in the centre of town – and compare it with a model of modern Kāifēng. There are also some excellent photographs of the city's standout historic monuments, but captions are in Chinese.

Iron Pagoda Park PARK
(铁塔公园; Tiě Tǎ Gōngyuán; 210 Beimen Dajie; admission Y20; ⏲7am-7pm) Rising up within Iron Pagoda Park is a magnificent 55m, 11th-century pagoda, a gorgeous, slender brick edifice wrapped in glazed rust-coloured tiles (hence the name); it's climbable for Y10. West of the pagoda is the **Jiēyǐn Hall** (接引殿; Jiēyǐn Diàn), where a bronze statue of Buddha from the Song/Jin era stands. The park hedges up against sections of the **city wall**.

Take bus 3 from the train station via Jiefang Lu to the route terminus; it's a short walk east to the park's entrance from here.

Pó Pagoda BUDDHIST PAGODA
(繁塔; Pó Tǎ; Pota Xijie; admission Y10; ⏲8am-6pm) This stumpy pagoda is the oldest Buddhist structure in Kāifēng (from 974). The original was a nine-storey hexagonal building, typical of the Northern Song style. The pagoda is clad in tiles decorated with 108 different Buddha images – note that all the Buddhas on the lower levels have had their faces smashed off. The pagoda is all that survives of Tiānqīng Temple (天清寺; Tiānqīng Sì), but worshippers still flock here to burn incense and pray. The Pó Pagoda Temple Fair is held here in April.

You'll find the pagoda hidden down alleyways east of the train station. Cross southward over the railway tracks from Tielubeiyan Jie and take the first alleyway on your left. From here follow the red arrows spray-painted on the walls. Bus 15 gets relatively close; ask the driver to let you off at the right stop, or grab a taxi.

FREE **Kāifēng Museum** MUSEUM
(开封博物馆; Kāifēng Bówùguǎn; 26 Yingbin Lu; ⏲9am-noon & 2.30-5.30pm Tue-Sun) The

highlight of the museum is the two notable Jewish stelae on the 4th floor, managed by the **Kāifēng Institute for Research on the History of Chinese Jews** (☎393 2178, ext 8010), but you will have to pay Y50 to see them. Buses 1, 4, 9 and 23 all travel past here.

City Walls HISTORIC SITE
(城墙) Kāifēng is ringed by a relatively intact, much-restored Qing-dynasty wall. Encased with grey bricks, rear sections of the ramparts have been recently buttressed very unattractively with concrete. Today's bastion was built on the foundations of the Song-dynasty **Inner Wall** (内城; Nèichéng). Rising up beyond was the mighty, now buried **Outer Wall** (外城; Wàichéng), a colossal construction containing 18 gates, which looped south of the Pó Pagoda, while the **Imperial Wall** (皇城; Huángchéng) protected the imperial palace.

Lóngtíng Park PARK
(龙亭公园; Lóngtíng Gōngyuán; ☎566 0316; Zhongshan Lu; admission Y45; ⏲7am-6.30pm) Site of the former imperial palace, this park is largely covered by lakes, into which hardy swimmers dive in winter. Climb the **Dragon Pavilion** (龙亭; Lóng Tíng) for town views.

Riverside Scenic Park Qīngmíng Garden PARK
(清明上河园; Qīngmíng Shànghéyuán; admission Y80; ⏲9am-10pm, performances 9am-7.50pm) High on historical kitsch, this theme park recreates Kāifēng in its heyday, complete with cultural performances, folk art and music demonstrations. Within the park, the **Jewish Cultural Exhibit Center** (⏲9am-6.30pm) is a fascinating foray into Kāifēng's Jewish culture.

Yánqìng Temple TAOIST TEMPLE
(延庆观; Yánqìng Guàn; 53 Guanqian Jie; admission Y15; ⏲8am-5.30pm) The modest Taoist Yánqìng Temple dates to 1233. The intriguingly shaped **Tower of the Jade Emperor**, repeatedly buried during the floods, contains a domed ceiling. At the rear is the **Hall of the Three Clear Ones** (三清殿; Sānqīng Diàn), where a trinity of Taoist deities welcomes worshippers.

Kāifēng Synagogue RUINS
(开封犹太教堂; Kāifēng Yóutài Jiàotáng Yízhǐ; 59 Beitu Jie) Sadly, nothing remains of the synagogue except a well with an iron lid in the boiler room of the No 4 People's Hospital. The spirit of it lingers, however, in the name of the brick alley immediately south of the hospital – **Jiaojing Hutong** (教经胡同; Teaching the Scripture Alley).

Sacred Heart of Jesus Church CHURCH
(耶酥圣心堂; Yēsū Shèngxīntáng; cnr Caoshi Jie & Lishiting Jie) Delve along Jiaojing Hutong until it meets the small Caoshi Jie (草市街), then head south and you will soon see the 1917 church's 43m-high spire. If you find the building open, pop in, take a pew and admire the grey-and-white interior.

Dōngdà Mosque MOSQUE
(东大寺; Dōngdà Sì; 39 Mujiaqiao Jie) South is Kāifēng's main Muslim district, whose landmark place of worship is this Chinese temple-styled mosque. Streets here have colourful names, such as Shaoji Hutong (Roast Chicken Alley).

Old Guanyin Temple MONASTERY
(古观音堂; Gǔ Guānyīn Táng; Baiyige Jie; ⏲7.30am-4.20pm) Just northeast of the No 4 People's Hospital is this active and recently rebuilt monastery. The large temple complex includes a notable hall with a twin-eaved umbrella roof, and a sizeable effigy of a recumbent Sakyamuni in its **Reclining Buddha Hall** (卧佛殿; Wòfó Diàn).

Yellow River Sightseeing Area SIGHTSEEING AREA
(黄河游览区; Huánghé Yóulǎnqū) This area is about 8km north of North Gate (安达门; Āndá Mén), although there is little to see as the water level is low these days. Bus 6 runs from near the Iron Pagoda to the Yellow River twice daily. A taxi will cost Y50 to Y60 for the return trip.

Bāogōng Temple TEMPLE
(包公祠; Bāogōng Cí; admission Y20) Attractively situated on the west shore of Bāogōng Lake.

Sleeping

Kāifēng's hotel industry is diverse, befitting the town's popularity with travellers. Those on very tight budgets can try their luck at one of the cheap flophouses identified by Chinese signs (look for the characters 住宿); otherwise aim for one of the following. Right at the heart of town, the smart **Soluxe Hotel Kāifēng** (开封阳关道酒店; Kāifēng Yángguāng Jiǔdiàn; ☎150 9369 6779; Gulou Jie; 鼓楼街) was yet to open at the time of writing but should offer modern business-style rooms at around the Y300 mark. On the ground floor is an attractive and plush-looking roast-duck restaurant.

Dàjīntái Hotel HOTEL $
(大金台宾馆; Dàjīntái Bīnguǎn; ☎255 2888; fax 255 5189; 23 Gulou Jie; 鼓楼街23号; r Y60, s & d Y130-160; ❄) Two-star old-timer combining excellent value with a central location on the very fringe of the bustling night market. Rooms in the No 5 block are cheaper, but grim; rooms in the No 2 block are set back from the street and more pleasant. Winter heating can be sluggish coming on. Breakfast (from 7am to 9am) is included.

Kāifēng Hotel HOTEL $$
(开封宾馆; Kāifēng Bīnguǎn; ☎595 5589; fax 595 3086; 66 Ziyou Lu; 自由路66号; s Y260, d Y260-380, deluxe d Y438, discounts of 25%; ❄) With its harmonious Chinese roofing and well-tended magnolias, this inviting Russian-built hotel offers a variety of rooms and a central location. The pricier deluxe rooms in the attractive Mènghuá Lóu (Building Two) are lovely, arranged with traditional furniture and large, clean bathrooms; cheaper rooms are in Building Three at the rear.

Eating & Drinking

Night Market STREET MARKET $
(古楼夜市; Gǔlóu Yèshì; cnr Gulou Jie & Madao Jie; snacks from Y2; ⏲6.30pm-late) Kāifēng's steaming, bustling and bellowing night market is a brilliant performance, especially at weekends. Join the scrum weaving between stalls busy with red-faced popcorn sellers and hollering Hui Muslim chefs cooking up kebabs and *náng* bread. There are also loads of rowdy vendors, from whom you can buy *shāo bǐng* (sesame-seed cakes), cured meats, *chòu gānzi* (臭干子; dry strips of tofu), hearty *jiānbǐng guǒzi* (煎饼裹子; pancake with chopped onions), sweet potatoes, crab kebabs, lamb kebabs, roast rabbit, lobster, *xiǎolóngbāo* (Shànghǎi-style dumplings), sugar-coated pears, peanut cake, Thai scented cakes and throwaway cups of sugar-cane juice. Also look out for *yángròu kàngmó* (羊肉炕馍; lamb in a parcel of bread), a local Kāifēng Muslim speciality. Or opt for *yángròu chuàn* (羊肉串; lamb kebabs) and ask the chef to stuff them into some *shāobǐng* (bread). The adventurous might slurp *yāxiě tāng* (鸭血汤; duck-blood soup) or try a *yángyǎnchuàn* (羊眼串; sheep's-eye kebab).

Among the flames jetting from ovens and clouds of steam slave vocal vendors of *xìngrén chá* (杏仁茶; almond tea), a sugary paste made from boiling water thickened with powdered almond, red berries, peanuts, sesame seeds and crystallised cherries. A bowl costs a mere Y4 or so. Two to three bowls constitute a (very sweet) meal. *Xìngrén chá* stalls stand out for their unique red pompom-adorned, dragon-spouted copper kettles. Also set out to sample *ròuhé* (肉合), a local snack of fried vegetables and pork or mutton in flat bread; there's also a good vegie version. Join the locals at one of the rickety tables. The market slowly peters out into stalls selling clothes, toys and books.

Dìyīlóu Bāozi Guǎn BUNS $
(第一楼包子馆; 8 Sihou Jie; 10 dumplings Y12; ⏲7am-10.30pm) Famed for its *bāozi* (包子; meat-filled buns), this cavernous Kāifēng institution at the centre of town has been in business for years. With cabbage, mushroom and bamboo shoots, the egg soup (鸡蛋汤; *jīdàn tāng;* Y10) alone can feed an army, while the *xiǎolóngbāo* (小笼包; Y12 a steamer), *yángròu bāozi* (羊肉包子; lamb buns) or *hǎimǐ bāozi* (海米包子; shrimp buns) are all tasty. Sit back with a Bianjing Old Beer (Y12) and listen to evening singers crooning soppy songs.

Xiǎo Féiyáng HOTPOT $$
(小肥羊; 1 Yingbin Lu; meals Y50) By the South West Gate, this friendly hotpot restaurant is great if you're a gang of diners. Order up a soup base (Y18 to Y22) – for spicy ask for *là* (辣), for nonspicy *bú là* (不辣); for one half spicy, one half nonspicy ask for *yuānyāng* (鸳鸯) – and fling in strips of lamb (羊肉片; *yángròu piàn;* Y22) and vegetables.

Information

A number of travellers recommend a local tour guide called Jason (☎159 3850 5092 or 293 3844), who speaks reasonable English and owns a pedicab, with whom you can negotiate a price for tours of Kāifēng. The train-station area is infested with internet cafes.

Bank of China (中国银行; Zhōngguó Yínháng) Gulou Jie (64 Gulou Jie); Xi Dajie (cnr Xi Dajie & Zhongshan Lu) There's a 24-hour ATM (MasterCard and Visa) at the Xi Dajie branch.

CITS (中国国际旅行社; Zhōngguó Guójì Lǚxíngshè; ☎393 4702; 98 Yingbin Lu; ⏲9am-5pm) Just north of the Dōngjīng Hotel, opposite the west long-distance bus station. No maps, and little English spoken.

China Post (中国邮政; Zhōngguó Yóuzhèng; Ziyou Lu; ⏲8am-5.30pm) West of the Temple of the Chief Minister.

Industrial & Commercial Bank of China (工商银行; Gōngshāng Yínháng; Gulou Jie) Has a 24-hour ATM.

Jīdì Internet Cafe (基地网吧; Jīdì Wǎngbā; per hr Y3; ⏲24hr) Off Zhongshan Lu, just south of the PSB.

First People's Hospital of Kāifēng (开封第一人民医院; Kāifēng Dìyī Rénmín Yīyuàn; ☎567 1288; 85 Hedao Jie)

Public Security Bureau (PSB; 公安局; Gōng'ānjú; ☎532 2242; 86 Zhongshan Lu; ⏲8.30am-noon & 2.30-6pm Mon-Fri) Gets fairly good reviews on visa renewals.

Xīngjì Internet Cafe (星际网吧; Xīngjì Wǎngbā; Sihou Jie; per hr Y3; ⏲24hr)

Zhōngxīn Internet Cafe (中心网吧; Zhōngxīn Wǎngbā; Ziyou Lu; per hr Y2; ⏲24hr) West of the Kāifēng Hotel.

Zhāngzhòngjǐng Pharmacy (张仲景大药房; Zhāngzhòngjǐng Dàyàofáng; ⏲7.30am-10pm summer, 8am-9pm winter) Next to Shānshǎngān Guild Hall.

Getting There & Away

Air

The nearest airport is at Zhèngzhōu. Air tickets can be bought at the **IATA Air Ticket Office** (☎595 5555; Hángkōng Dàshà) next to the PSB; two free daily buses (7am and noon) run to Zhèngzhōu airport from here.

Bus

Buses run from the **west long-distance bus station** (长途汽车西站; Chángtú Qìchē Xīzhàn):

Dēngfēng Y28, four hours, two daily (9.30am and 1pm)

Luòyáng Y50, three hours, regular services

Xīnxiāng Y32, two hours, regular services

Zhèngzhōu Y7, 1½ hours, every 15 minutes (6.20am to 7.30pm)

Buses from the **south long-distance bus station** (长途汽车南站; Chángtú Qìchē Nánzhàn), opposite the train station:

Ānyáng Y54, four hours, regular services

Luòyáng Y50, three hours, hourly

Xīnxiāng Y32, two hours, every 40 minutes

Zhèngzhōu Y7, 1½ hours, every 15 minutes

From Zhèngzhōu, buses to Kāifēng leave from the north bus station (p405), but some may leave from the long-distance bus station. When you board in Zhèngzhōu, check where the bus terminates in Kāifēng, as some buses stop at the Temple of the Chief Minister, while others stop at the train station or the west long-distance bus station.

Train

Kāifēng is on the railway line between Xī'ān and Shànghǎi, with several D-class trains passing through.

Běijīng seat/sleeper Y94/179, 12 hours; goes to Běijīng West station.

Luòyáng Y30, 2½ hours

Shànghǎi hard/soft seat Y222/278, 6½ hours

Shíjiāzhuāng Y128, 80 minutes

Xī'ān seat/sleeper Y82/149, eight hours

Zhèngzhōu Y22/27, 30 minutes

Tickets can be bought at the **rail-ticket office** (铁路票务中心; Tiělù Piàowù Zhōngxīn; 99 Yingbin Lu; ⏲8am-noon & 2-5pm) north of the South West Gate or at the **railway ticket office** (火车票代售点; huǒchēpiào dàishòudiǎn; ⏲8am-noon & 1.30-5.30pm) down the road opposite the Shānshǎngàn Guild Hall.

Getting Around

Gulou Jie, Sihou Jie and Shudian Jie are all good for catching buses (Y1). Taxis (flag fall Y5) are the best way to get about; a journey from the train station to the Dàjīntái Hotel should cost around Y5. Avoid pedicabs, as they frequently rip off tourists. Budget hotels may help you rent a bike (Y10 per day).

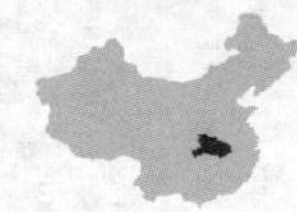

Húběi

POPULATION: 61.8 MILLION

Includes »

Best Places to Eat

» Xiǎo Bèiké (p426)

» Crown Bakery (p427)

Best Places to Stay

» Pathfinder Youth Hostel (p425)

» Tomolo (p425)

Why Go?

Sliced by rivers – including the prodigious Yangzi (Cháng Jiāng) – and dappled with lakes, Húběi (湖北) is one of the lushest and most fertile of China's provinces. Vast hordes of Western travellers find themselves drifting into Húběi through the Three Gorges, the precipitous geological marvel that begins in neighbouring Chóngqìng and concludes here. The gorges introduce Húběi's natural dramatic beauty, typified by the Taoist mountains of Wǔdāng Shān and the wild forests of Shénnóngjià. Another tempting piece in Húběi's travel mosaic is history: its central location gave the province a key role in Chinese history, with plenty of evidence around the ancient city of Jīngzhōu of the great Chu kingdom that ruled this part of China more than 2000 years ago. Straddling the Yangzi River, the dynamic capital Wǔhàn – aptly referred to as one of the country's 'three furnaces' for its soaring summer temperatures – is similarly awash with both water and history.

When to Go

Wǔhàn

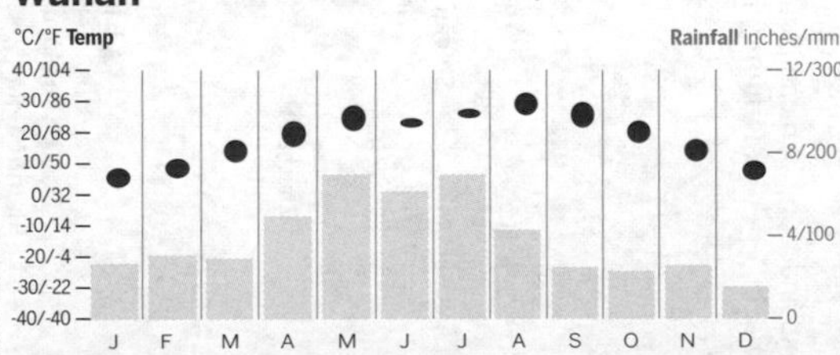

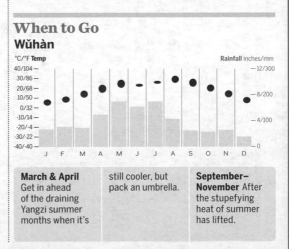

March & April Get in ahead of the draining Yangzi summer months when it's still cooler, but pack an umbrella.

September–November After the stupefying heat of summer has lifted.

Húběi Highlights

1. Commune with supernatural views and find yourself a taichi teacher in **Wǔdāng Shān** (p430)
2. Flee China's urban sprawl and camp out in the wilds of **Shénnóngjià** (p433)
3. Find a bar and knock back a beer in the riverside concession district of mighty **Wǔhàn** (p427)
4. Explore the historic gates, walls and temples of **Jīngzhōu** (p428)

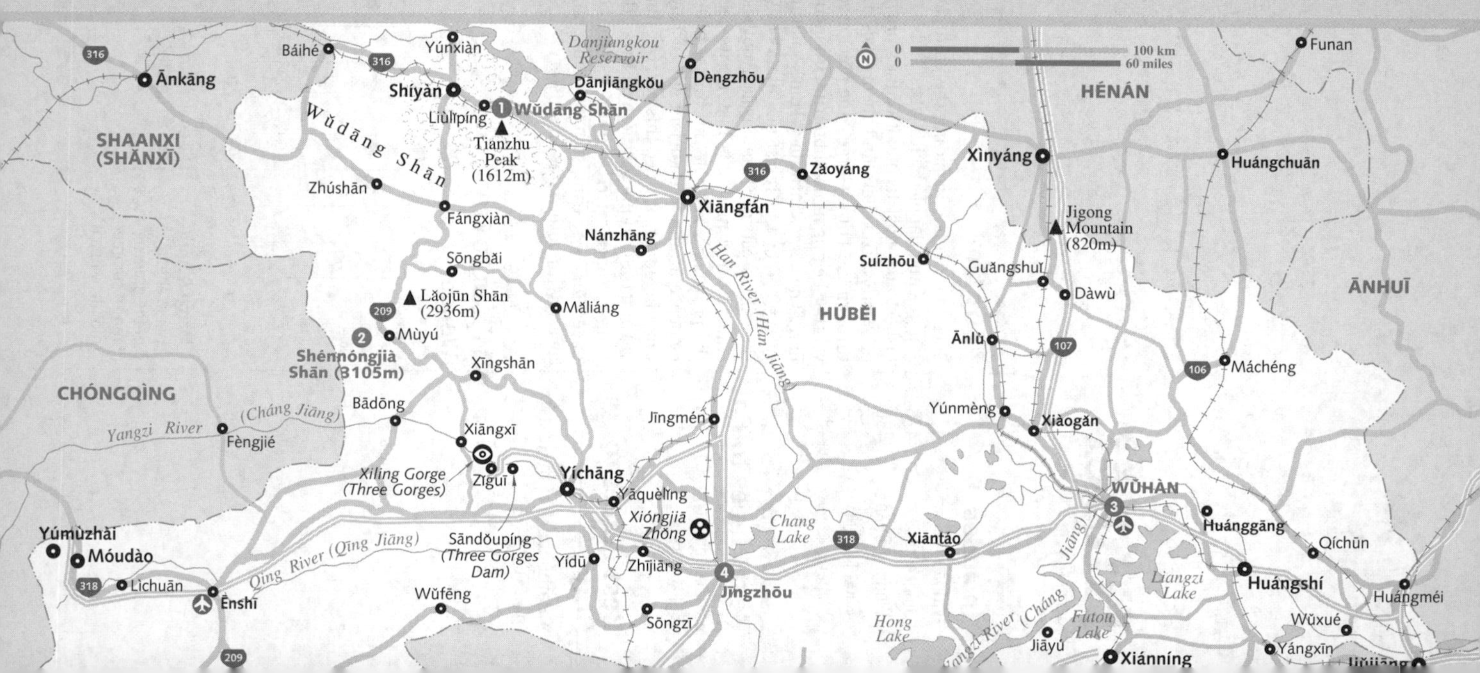

History

The Húběi area first came to prominence during the Eastern Zhou (700–221 BC), when the powerful Chu kingdom, based in present-day Jīngzhōu, was at its height. Húběi again became pivotal during the Three Kingdoms (AD 220–280). The Chinese classic *The Romance of the Three Kingdoms (Sān Guó Yǎnyì)* makes much reference to Jīngzhōu. The mighty Yangzi River ensured prosperous trade in the centuries that followed, especially for Wǔhàn, China's largest inland port and stage of the 1911 uprising, which led to the fall of the Qing and the creation of the Republic of China.

Climate

Even Húběi's 'furnace', Wǔhàn, is only stupidly hot in July and August. Other months are much more pleasant, while the western mountains are more temperate generally. Rainfall is heavy in the southeast but decreases north and west. Expect most of it from April to July.

Language

Húběi has two dialects of Northern Mandarin – Southwest Mandarin and Lower-Mid Yangzi Mandarin – while in the southeast many people speak Gàn, a Mandarin dialect from Jiāngxī.

Getting There & Around

Wǔhàn is one of the best-connected cities in China, and travelling round east and central Húběi is generally easy. Better roads have seen demand for boat travel fall in recent years. It used to be popular to cruise the Yangzi from Chóngqìng right the way across Húběi and on towards Shànghǎi. Now standard passenger boats only go as far as Yíchāng.

PRICE INDICATORS

The following price indicators are used in this chapter:

Sleeping

$	less than Y200
$$	Y200 to Y500
$$$	more than Y500

Eating

$	less than Y40
$$	Y40 to Y100
$$$	more than Y100

Wǔhàn 武汉

027 / POP 4.26 MILLION

A gargantuan alloy of three formerly independent cities (Wǔchāng, Hànkǒu and Hànyáng), Wǔhàn is huge, but thanks to the Yangzi River, and an abundant supply of lakes, it's more comfortable than you might imagine. The Yangzi thrusts its way through the centre, carving the city in two and allowing for some breathing space between towering buildings and gnarling traffic, while Wǔhàn's numerous lakes and a smattering of decent sights also provide visitors with welcome retreats.

Chinese quip that 'In Heaven there are nine-headed birds, on earth there are Húběi folk' (an accusation that locals are a bit crafty). Wǔhàn is also famed for its pretty women, whose lovely skin is nourished by the damp climate.

Don't ignore the city itself. Largely characterless pedestrianised zones are offset with narrow lanes bursting with life and full of fun places to eat, while the former concession area provides a pleasant, tree-covered base from which to explore Wǔhàn's thriving nightlife. Hànkǒu is where you'll find the main areas for shopping (Jianghan Lu), eating (Zhongshan Dadao) and drinking (Yanjiang Dadao), as well as a liberal sprinkling of 19th-century colonial buildings.

History

Although not actually named Wǔhàn until 1927, the city's three mighty chunks trace their influential status back to the Han dynasty, with Wǔchāng and Hànkǒu vying for political and economic sway. The city was prised open to foreign trade in the 19th century by the Treaty of Nanking.

The 1911 uprising sparked the beginning of the end for the Qing dynasty. Much that wasn't destroyed then was flattened in 1944 when American forces fire-bombed the city after it had fallen under Japanese control.

Sights

The area around Zhongshan Dadao and Yanjiang Dadao remains a hodgepodge of concession-era architecture and old consulate buildings interspersed with modern towers and the occasional lump of bizarre, kitschy nautical architecture. Models pose for photos outside historic buildings, but the city is ramshackle and badly needs a

Wǔhàn

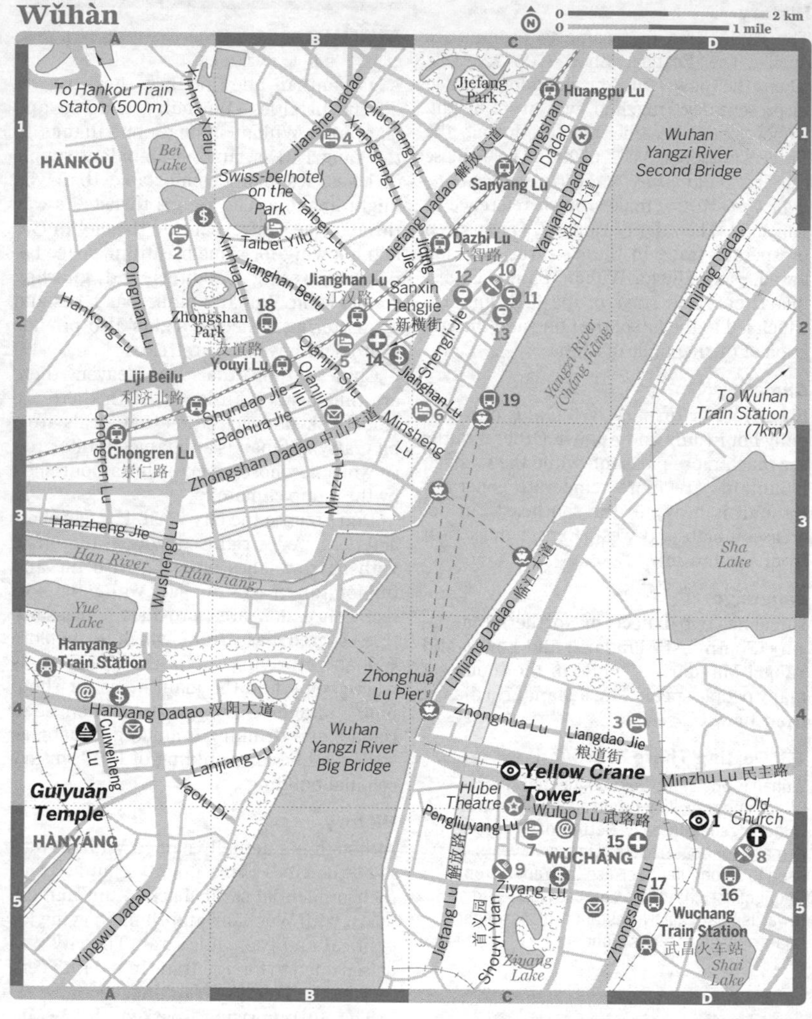

Shànghǎi Bund–style spruce up. While buildings like the old **National City Bank of New York** are shut and signal a closed book, the new chapter has apparently yet to open.

Yellow Crane Tower HISTORIC SITE
(黄鹤楼; Huánghè Lóu; Wuluo Lu; admission Y80; ⏲7.30am-5.30pm, to 6.30pm summer) Wǔhàn's magical dancing crane, immortalised in the poetry of Cui Hao, has long flown but the city's pride and joy remains perched on top of Snake Hill. The tower has had its history rebuilt out of it since the original was constructed in AD 223, and today's beautiful five-storey, yellow-tiled version is a 1980s remake of the Qing tower that combusted in 1884. Trolley bus 1 and bus 10 go here.

FREE **Húběi Provincial Museum** MUSEUM
(湖北省博物馆; Húběi Shěng Bówùguǎn; 156 Donghu Lu; 东湖路156号; ⏲9am-5pm, no admission after 3.30pm) The centrepiece of this fabulous museum is the exhibition of the tomb of Marquis Yi of Zeng, which includes one of the world's largest musical instruments, a remarkable 5-tonne set of 64 double-tone bronze bells. The museum is beside the enormous **East Lake** (东湖; Dōng

Wǔhàn

Hú), a pleasant area for cycling. Take bus 402 or 411.

Chángchūn Temple TAOIST TEMPLE
(长春观; Chángchūn Guàn; ☎8280 1399; admission Y10; ⊙8am-5pm) This charming Taoist temple dates back to the Han dynasty. The **Hall of Supreme Purity** (Tàiqīng Diàn), containing a white-bearded statue of Laotzu, is the centrepiece. Other halls lead up the steep steps behind it. There's a good vegetarian restaurant next door. Buses 411, 401 and 402 all go here.

Guīyuán Temple BUDDHIST TEMPLE
(归元寺; Guīyuán Sì; 20 Cuiweiheng Lu; 翠微横路20号; admission Y10; ⊙8am to 5pm) Pass a large rectangular pond where turtles cling like shipwrecked survivors to two metal lotus flowers and examine the magnificently burnished cabinet housing Milefo in the first hall. Also seek out this 350-year-old Buddhist temple's collection of more than 500 statues of enlightened disciples in the **Hall of Arhats** (罗汉堂; Luóhàn Táng). Completed in 1890, after nine years in the making, they remain in pristine condition. In the **Mahasattva Pavilion** (大士阁; Dàshì Gé), the 2m-high Tang-dynasty tablet carved with an image of Guanyin holding a willow branch is impressive and a jade Buddha can be found in the **Cángjīng Pavilion** (藏经阁; Cángjīng Gé). Bus 401 (Y2) from Yellow Crane Tower goes here.

Sleeping

TOP CHOICE **Pathfinder Youth Hostel** HOSTEL $
(探路者国际青年旅社; Tànlùzhě Guójì Qīngnián Lǚshè; ☎8884 4092; 368 Zhongshan Lu; 中山路368号; 6-bed dm without bathroom Y40, 4-/3-/2-bed dm with bathroom Y58/68/78, d/tw Y158/198; ❄@📶) Next to the Húběi Art Gallery (湖北美术馆; Húběi Měishùguǎn), Wǔhàn's best budget option has an art-warehouse feel to it where guests add graffiti to the walls. Pinewood-decorated rooms are basic but clean; bathrooms are small with squat loos (communal bathrooms have sit-down versions), but the rest of the place oozes space. There's internet (first hour free then Y3 per hour, free wi-fi), bike rental (Y20 per day), real coffee and very helpful, English-speaking staff.

TOP CHOICE **Tomolo** BOUTIQUE $$$
(天美乐饭店; Tiānměilè Fàndiàn; ☎8275 7288; 56 Jianghan Sanlu; 江汉三路56号; d & tw Y698, discounts of 50%; ❄@) Tucked away in an alley off the bustling pedestrianised zone, this excellent-value boutique hotel has a prime location and a natty finish throughout. Big rooms come with sofas, wide-screen TVs, internet access and lush carpets, while the bathrooms, complete with mosaic tiling and power showers,

WŬHÀN WORDS

Wǔhàn locals speak Hànqiāng (汉腔) or 'Wǔhàn speak', a local speciality. To locals, shoes are *haizi* (sounding like the word for 'child') rather than the more standard *xiézi*, so Wǔhàn's ubiquitous shoe cleaners shout *'ca haizi'* ('clean shoes') instead of *'cā xiézi'* (in this respect the word is similar to the Cantonese). Another lovely peculiarity you don't hear in many other parts of China is the word *fúzi* (服子) for towel and *mámù* (麻木) for a pedicab, more prosaically called a *sānlúnchē* (三轮车) elsewhere across the land. To show off is to *fapao* (create a froth) while 'inside' (里面) is inexplicably *'dòulǐ'* (豆里) (literally 'inside the bean'). 'Clean' in Wǔhàn is not *'gānjìng'* but *'línxīn'* (林新). Wǔhàn folk end their sentences with a *sa* (撒) particle, instead of the far more usual *a* (啊) sound you hear elsewhere in China.

are in pristine condition; staff make a real effort. Excellent discounts.

Shangri-La Hotel HOTEL **$$$**
(香格里拉大饭店; Xiānggélǐlā Dàfàndiàn; ☎8580 6868; 700 Jianshe Dadao; 建设大道700号; s/d Y1078/1193;) A strong smell of air-freshener hits you when you enter, but the trademark golden-honey hues are always a welcoming sight, as is the usual Shangri-La comfort and excellence (although the spoken English is surprisingly feeble).

Yangzi River International Youth Hostel HOSTEL **$**
(扬子江国际青年旅社; Yángzǐjiāng Guójì Qīngnián Lǚshè; ☎8275 7188; 47 Jianghan Lu; 江汉路47号; d & tw from Y178, tr Y198;) A decent budget choice, this shipshape, river-boat-themed hostel has good rooms with oceans of space, wood flooring and tastefully designed bathrooms. Portholes are dotted around, life jackets are in the hallways but things are capsized rather by the zero spoken English and no dorms. Set back from the road through an archway with an internet cafe above.

Zhōng Huì Hotel HOTEL **$**
(中惠宾馆; Zhōnghuì Bīnguǎn; ☎8805 9288; 188 Shouyi Xincun; 首义新村188号; s/d Y98/168;) This three-star hotel has well-kept rooms with clean bathrooms. The cheapest singles have no windows, but are still comfortable, and you'll have fun getting to them in the exterior brass lift. Rates include breakfast; the Y168 rooms come with computer.

Novotel HOTEL **$$$**
(新华诺富特大饭店; Xīnhuá Nuòfùtè Dàfàndiàn; ☎8555 1188; 558 Jianshe Dadao; 建设大道558号; s/d Y1340/1380, discounts of 30-40%, more in summer;) With rather bland cream-caramel tones, the Novotel nonetheless has a kind of functional elegance and good-value post-discount rooms – blond wood with compact bathrooms – in the business end of town. Tennis courts, swimming pool, bistro, bar, deli, ATM.

Eating

The Chinese say 'Eat in Guǎngdōng, get dressed up in Shànghǎi, but eat and wear your best in Wǔhàn', so get your best togs on and go for a feast. Both Hànkǒu and Wǔchāng are littered with restaurants that spill out onto the streets as early evening approaches. In Hànkǒu, the alleyways north of Zhongshan Dadao, between Qianjin Yilu and Qianjin Silu, are particularly lively. Jiqing Jie (吉庆街) has numerous *dàpáidǎng* (open-air food stalls or restaurants) selling seafood and duck, especially at the Dazhi Lu end. In Wǔchāng, follow your nose around the alleys south of Zhonghua Lu as it leads away from the ferry terminal, or head to **Shǒuyì Garden Snack Street** (Shǒuyìyuán Xiǎochījiē). Vegetarian restaurants cluster near the Guīyuán Temple.

Breakfast – called *guòzǎo* (过早) in Wǔhàn – is all about *règān miàn* (热干面; literally 'hot-dry noodles'; Y4).

TOP CHOICE **Xiǎo Bèiké** CHINESE **$$**
(小贝壳; 129 Dongting Jie; 洞庭街129号; ⏲10.30am-9.30pm; meal Y50) Also called the Petite Coquille Restaurant and overseen by staff in purple tops, this stylish restaurant has melt-in-the-mouth *méicài kòuròu* (梅菜扣肉; stewed pork with preserved vegetables; Y25) and *jiǔcài hézi* (韭菜盒子; fried chive dumplings; Y18 a portion) plus loads of other tasty dishes. Try and grab an outside table. It's the yellow building on the corner of Dongting Jie and Cai'e Lu.

Crown Bakery BAKERY $
(皇冠蛋糕; Huángguān Dàngāo; 359 Wuluo Lu; 武珞路359号; ⏲6am-9.30pm) Fabulously located in an old cruciform church (built in 1907) with its original wood ceiling intact (and loads of portraits of Jesus), come here for ambience, take a seat in the apse to break bread and order egg tarts (Y1), tea (Y3.50) or loads of cakes.

Chángchūn Temple Vegetarian Restaurant VEGETARIAN $
(长春观素菜餐厅; Chángchūnguān Sùcài Cāntīng; 145 Wuluo Lu; 武珞路145号; ⏲9am-8.30pm; ✎) Delightful restaurant attached to a Taoist temple priding itself on bizarre mock-meat creations but also serving mouth-watering fish dishes. There's a handy photo menu.

Drinking

Hànkǒu is the place to go for a night out; Yanjiang Dadao (沿江大道) is probably the best place to start.

Café Brussels BAR
(布鲁塞尔咖啡馆; Bùlǔsāi'ěr Kāfēiguǎn; 183 Shengli Jie; Tsingtao Y20; ⏲5pm-late Mon-Fri, from 11am Sat & Sun) With more than 40 Belgian brews (Chimay Red Y40), Guinness (Y35) and sports TV, this cavernous bar-restaurant is run by a friendly Belgian bloke who also brews his own (Y20). At the time of writing, the owner was set to move to a new location.

York Teahouse BAR
(约克英式茶馆; Yuēkè Yīngshì Cháguǎn; 162 Yanjiang Dadao; ⏲1pm-3am) Run by the fun 'Mr Sugar' (Tang Xiansheng), this old-timer has been doing its thing on the riverfront since 2001. Inside is a warren of rooms, or you can just sit outside with a draught Bud (Y30), a bottle of Snowflake (Y20) or a Sol (Y25).

Bordeaux Bar BAR
(波尔多酒廊; Bō'ěrduō Jiǔláng; 173 Yanjiang Dadao; ⏲1pm-2am) A short walk north of the York Teahouse, set back from the road, is this unassuming, pocket-sized French-style cafe.

Information

Maps (地图; *dìtú;* Y2 to Y4) of the city can be bought at bookstores, at newspaper kiosks or from hawkers outside tourist sights.

Bank of China (中国银行; Zhōngguó Yínháng; cnr Zhongshan Dadao & Jianghan Lu) Foreign exchange and credit-card advances, plus 24-hour ATM for foreign cards.

Bank of China (中国银行; Zhōngguó Yínháng; Hanyang Dadao) Has a 24-hour ATM for foreign cards.

China International Travel Service (CITS; 中国国际旅行社; Zhōngguó Guójì Lǚxíngshè; ☎5151 9953; 173 Yangjiang Dadao; ⏲9am-6pm)

China Merchants Bank (招商银行; Zhāoshāng Yínháng; cnr Ziyang Lu & Shouyi Lu) Has a 24-hour ATM for foreign cards.

China Post (中国邮政; Zhōngguó Yóuzhèng) Hànkǒu (Zhongshan Dadao; ⏲8.30am-6.30pm); Hànkǒu train station (⏲8.30am-6pm); Hànyáng (Hanyang Dadao; ⏲8.30am-6pm); Wǔchāng (Ziyang Lu; ⏲8.30am 4.30pm)

Fēibǎo Internet Cafe (飞宝网吧; Fēibǎo Wǎngbā; Shouyi Lu; per hr Y2; ⏲24hr)

HSBC (汇丰银行; Huìfēng Yínháng; Jianshe Dadao) Has an ATM.

Pǔ'ān Pharmacy (普安大药房; Pǔ'ān Dàyàofáng; cnr Jianghan Lu & Jianghan Silu; ⏲24hr)

Public Security Bureau (PSB; 公安局; Gōng'ānjú; ☎8539 5351; Zhangzizhong Lu; 张自忠路; ⏲8.30am-noon & 2.30-5.30pm) Can extend visas.

Xīngāosù Shídài Internet Cafe (新高速时代网吧; Xīnggāosù Shídài Wǎngbā; Hanyang Dadao; per hr Y3; ⏲24hr) North of Guīyuán Temple.

Zhōnglián Pharmacy (中联大药店; Zhōnglián Dàyàodiàn; Zhongshan Lu; 中山路; ⏲24hr)

Getting There & Away

Air

Tiānhé International Airport (天河飞机场; Tiānhé Fēijīchǎng; ☎8581 8888) is 30km northwest of town. You can book tickets at the CAAC office in the Swiss-belhotel on the Park. Daily flights go to Běijīng (Y650), Hong Kong (Y1000), Shànghǎi (Y410) and Xī'ān (Y480).

Regular airport shuttle buses go to and from Hànkǒu train station (Y15, 45 minutes) and Fùjiāpō long-distance bus station (Y30, one hour). A taxi is about Y80.

Bus

In Hànkǒu the main **long-distance bus station** (长途汽车站(汉口; chángtú qìchēzhàn; ☎8572 5507; cnr Jiefang Dadao & Xinhua Lu) has regular buses to the following destinations:

Běijīng Y280, 17 hours, one daily (1.30pm)

Jīngzhōu Y74, three hours

Wǔdāng Shān Y130, five hours, one daily (8.40am)

Xī'ān Y190, 12 hours, one daily (4.10pm)

Yíchāng Y95, four to five hours

Buses from the **ferry terminal bus station** (武汉港长途汽车站; Wǔhàngǎng chángtú qìchēzhàn):

Ēnshī Y221

Nánjīng Y230

Shànghǎi Y355 to Y380, 12 hours

Yíchāng Y139, four hours

Wǔchāng's main bus stations are **Fùjiāpō long-distance bus station** (傅家坡汽车客运站; Fùjiāpō qìchē kèyùnzhàn) and **Hóngjī long-distance bus station** (宏基长途汽车站; Hóngjī chángtú qìchēzhàn). Hóngjī is handier with several bus services:

Jīngzhōu Y88, three hours, regular services

Shànghǎi Y330 to Y410, 12 hours, two daily (4.30pm & 7.20pm)

Yíchāng Y95, four hours, regular services

Zhāngjiājiè Y187 to Y201, 13 hours, two daily (9.40am and 5.30pm)

Train

Wǔhàn has three train stations, including the new **Wǔhàn Train Station** (武汉火车站; Wǔhàn Huǒchēzhàn) which opened in 2010, from where regular high-speed G-class trains rocket to Guǎngzhōu in four hours, via Chángshā. D-class trains also run to Shànghǎi (Y273 to Y327, five to six hours), Běijīng West train station and Zhèngzhōu from here. The new station is located in northeast Wǔchāng, and will be linked to Line 4 of the subway system when the first section opens in 2012.

The other two train stations are **Hànkǒu train station** and **Wǔchāng train station**. Few destinations cannot be reached directly from both, the exception being Yíchāng, which can only be reached directly from Hànkǒu (seat/sleeper Y54/105, five hours). Useful destinations from either station:

Běijīng D-class hard/soft seat Y281/351, 8½ hours

Kūnmíng Y219 to Y385, 26 to 31 hours, four daily

Shànghǎi D-class hard/soft seat Y225/279, five to six hours

Wǔdāng Shān Y57 to Y64, five to nine hours, five daily

Xī'ān Y137 to Y242, 11 to 16 hours, frequent

There's a handy **Train Ticket Agency** (铁路客票代售; Tiělù Kèpiào Dàishòu; cnr Zhongshan Dadao & Cai'e Lu; 中山大道和蔡锷路的交叉口; commission Y5; ⊙8.30am-6.30pm) in central Hànkǒu.

Getting Around

Despite being raised above the city streets, Hànkǒu's modern light rail line is classed as Line 1 of the subway system. It is due to be extended slightly, before being linked up with two underground subway lines, Lines 2 and 4 (both due to be operational by 2012), which will connect Hànkǒu and Wǔchāng, as well as the new Wǔhàn Train Station (reachable on bus 610 from Hànkǒu train station). A further nine subway lines are planned for the coming years.

Useful buses:

Bus 10 (Y1.50) Connects the two main train stations.

Bus 401 (Y2) From Hànyáng past Guīyuán Temple, Yellow Crane Tower and Chángchūn Temple to East Lake.

Bus 402 (Y2) From Wǔchāng train station to Chángchūn Temple and Yellow Crane Tower, then via Hànyáng to Yanjiang Dadao in Hànkǒu before returning over the river for the museum and East Lake.

Bus 411 (Y1.50) Travels a more direct route from the museum to Yellow Crane Tower and Chángchūn Temple before carrying on to Hànkǒu train station.

Ferries (Y1, every 20 minutes from 6.30am to 8pm) make swift daily crossings of the Yangzi between Zhonghua Lu pier in Wǔchāng and the Wǔhàn Ferry Terminal in Hànkǒu.

Wǔhàn's one light rail line (Y1.50 to Y2, every nine minutes from 6.30am to 9.30pm) in Hànkǒu has 10 stations (to be expanded to 16 before being linked up with the new subway system).

Taxis start at Y6.50.

Jīngzhōu 荆州

☎0716 / POP 1.5 MILLION

Capital of the Chu kingdom during the Eastern Zhou, Jīngzhōu has an ancient history and a homely small-town feel. One of the few Chinese cities still ringed by an intact city wall, Jīngzhōu has managed to cling on to a few temples of note and boasts a noteworthy museum. The surrounding farmlands are home to several ancient burial sites, including Xióngjiā Zhǒng, the largest collection of Chu kingdom tombs ever discovered.

Sights

Jīngzhōu is approximately 3.75km from east to west and 2.4km from north to south, with city gates dotted around at the cardinal points (and several lesser gates). South St (荆州南路; Jingzhou Nanlu) runs west from the new east gate (新东门; *xīn dōngmén*); Zhangjuzheng Jie (张居正街), where you'll find accommodation and restaurants, is parallel to South St. Following the wall further north will bring you to East St (荆州东路; Jingzhou Donglu), which runs all the way to the west gate (西门; *xīmén*), not far from the city's superb museum.

FREE **Jīngzhōu Museum** MUSEUM
(荆州博物馆; Jīngzhōu Bówùguǎn; Jingzhou Zhonglu; 荆州中路; audio tour Y20, English tour guide Y200; ⏲9am-5pm Tue-Sun) The highlight of this excellent museum is the incredibly well preserved 2000-year-old body of a man found in his **tomb** with ancient tools, clothing and even food; the airtight mud seal around his crypt helped preserve him. It's in a small exhibition hall by the lake behind the main building. The museum also houses China's largest exhibition of jade, unearthed from the nearby site of Xióngjiā Zhǒng. All displays have English captions.

City Wall HISTORIC SITE
Jīngzhōu's original mud wall (城墙; *chéngqiáng*) was Eastern Han, with the first stone version coming during the Five Dynasties and Ten Kingdoms. Today, the oldest surviving sections, around the **south gate** (南门; *nánmén*), are Song, but most of what you'll see is Ming and Qing. The south gate, with its enceinte still attached, is best for flavours of medieval Jīngzhōu and swarms with Taoist soothsayers, outdoor hairdressers offering cutthroat shaves and vegetable sellers. A similar carnival feel accompanies the **east gate** (老东门; Lǎo Dōngmén), which also has an enceinte and a fairground feel with bouncing castles and costume hire. You can walk on parts of the wall, sometimes for a small fee, but the best way to see it is to rent a bike and cycle around the outside (1½ hours) between the wall and the city moat.

Kāiyuán Temple TAOIST TEMPLE
(开元观; Kāiyuán Guàn) Explore the empty remains attached to the Jīngzhōu Museum.

Guāndì Temple TAOIST TEMPLE
(关帝庙; Guāndì Miào) Up the road from the south gate.

Tiěnǚ Temple BUDDHIST TEMPLE
(铁女寺; Tiěnǚ Sì; off Jingbei Lu) The intriguingly named Iron Girl Temple.

Xuánmiào Temple TAOIST TEMPLE
(玄妙观; Xuánmiào Guàn; north of Jingbei Lu) This Taoist temple literally translates as the 'Temple of Mystery'.

Confucian Temple CONFUCIAN TEMPLE
(文庙; Wén Miào) Now part of the Shíyàn Zhōngxué (Experimental Middle School) on Jingzhou Zhonglu.

Sleeping & Eating

Bāyī Bīnguǎn HOTEL $
(八一宾馆; ☎846 4501; 14-4 Zhangju Zhengjie; 张居正街14-4号; s Y70-100, d Y100, discounts of 20%; ❄) No lift, but rooms are perfectly fine; one of several cheap hotels on Zhangju Zhengjie.

Gǔchéng Bīnguǎn HOTEL $
(古城宾馆; ☎843 6199; 162 Jingzhong Lu; 荆中路612号; s/d Y138/158, discounts of 30%; ❄) Comfortable rooms with flat-screen TVs, computer and shower room; it's next to the Fifth Hospital.

Zhangju Zhengjie has several restaurants, with *shāokǎo* (barbecue) restaurants clustering near the east gate. The lamb restaurant opposite the Bāyī Bīnguān does excellent lamb kebabs and lamb soup. Local specialities include *niúròu miàn* (牛肉面; spicy beef noodles), *yúgāo* (鱼糕; fish cakes) and *yóumèn dàxiā* (油焖大虾; spicy braised shrimp).

Information

Industrial & Commercial Bank of China (ICBC; 工商银行; Gōngshāng Yínháng; cnr Quyuan Lu & Zhangju Zhengjie; 屈原路和张居正街的交叉口) Has a 24-hour ATM.

Police station (派出所; pàichūsuǒ; 5 Zhangju Zhengjie)

Yǒngxìng Internet Cafe (永兴网吧; Yǒngxìng Wǎngbā; 14-9 Zhangju Zhengjie; per hr Y1.5; ⏲24hr) Near the Bāyī Bīnguǎn.

Getting There & Around

Jīngzhōu is due to be linked up by rail to Wǔhàn and Yíchāng by 2012. Buses from Yíchāng or Wǔhàn usually drop you at Shāshì Central Bus Station (沙市中心客运站; Shāshì Zhōngxīn Kèyùnzhàn), a few kilometres outside the old city. Exit the station to the first stop on your right for bus 101 or 1 (Y1, 30 minutes) to the old city; both enter via the new east gate, running to the west gate. Regular buses run from Shāshì Central Bus Station to Yíchāng (Y38, two hours) and Wǔhàn (Y70 to Y75, four hours) from 7am to 8pm.

You can also reach Wǔhàn from Jīngzhōu bus station (荆州车站; Jīngzhōu *chēzhàn*), inside the east gate on Jingzhou Nanlu, and for Yíchāng from *shāyí liányíng chēduì* (沙宜联营车队), more of a bus stop than a station, outside the city moat just to your left as you exit the new east gate.

Just inside the wall on South St is a **bike rental place** (per day Y15). Electric buggies can whisk you on tours around town for Y5 to Y30 from the east gate.

Around Jīngzhōu

A visit to the 2300-year-old tombs of **Xióngjiā Zhǒng** (熊家冢; admission Y30, ⏲9.30am-4.30pm) is a rare opportunity to witness archaeology in progress, as most of them, including the main tomb itself, have yet to be opened. Artefacts already excavated include China's largest collection of jade (on display at the Jīngzhōu Museum) and the fascinating skeletal remains of two horses pulling a chariot, which have been left in their small, open tomb for visitors to see. At the time of research, only Chinese-speaking guides were available.

The tombs are 40km north of Jīngzhōu. Take a bus (Y6, one hour) from Jiānglíng Bus Station (江陵车站; Jiānglíng *chēzhàn*), on South St (Jingzhou Nanlu), to Chuāndiàn (川店). A taxi should be Y100 return, including waiting time.

Wǔdāng Shān 武当山

☎0719

Wǔdāng Shān may not be one of China's five sacred Taoist mountains but it's paradoxically known as the No 1 Taoist Mountain in the Middle Kingdom. Sacrosanct in martial arts circles, it is acknowledged that 'in the north they esteem Shàolín, in the south they revere Wǔdāng'. The Unesco World Heritage Site of Wǔdāng Shān is the apocryphal birthplace of taichi, and possesses supernaturally good-looking vistas and an abundance of medicinal plants that naturally find their way into a panoply of Taoist medicinal potions. The mountain is also sadly overpriced and over-commercialised, with new developments afoot, so expect the magic of Taoist chanting to be occasionally perforated by the squeal of buzz saws.

Sights & Activities

The town's main road, Taihe Lu (太和路), runs east–west on its way towards the main gate of the mountain, about 1km east of the town. The train station is a few hundred metres south of Taihe Lu on Chezhan Lu (车站路). The bus station is at the junction of these two roads. You can buy Chinese (Y3) or English (Y8) maps at the main gate of the mountain or at Jīnlóngdiàn Hotel.

FREE **Wǔdāng Museum of China** MUSEUM
(武当博物馆; Wǔdāng Bówùguǎn; audio tour Y20, deposit Y200; ⏲9-11am & 2.30-5pm) This is a great opportunity to get to grips with Wǔdāng Shān history, lore and architecture. There's a whole pantheon of gods, including the eminent Zhenwu (patriarch of the mountain) and a section of Taoist medicine including the fundamentals of *nèidān Xué* (内丹学; internal alchemy). There are also some stunning bronze pieces. From the train station turn left onto Taihe Lu, take the first right and continue to Culture Sq (文化广场; Wénhuà Guǎngchǎng).

Yùxū Temple TAOIST TEMPLE
(玉虚宫; Yùxū Gōng; Gongyuan Lu; admission Y20; ⏲8am-5.30pm) This colossal temple with pavilions in a vast courtyard was first built in 1413. Turn immediately right out of the train station, take the first right and go through the tunnel.

Climbing Wǔdāng Shān TAOIST MOUNTAIN
(admission Y140, bus Y70, optional insurance Y2) The mountain attracts a diverse array of climbers: Taoist nuns with knapsacks, workers shouldering paving slabs and sacks of rice, businessmen with laptops and bright-eyed octogenarians hopping along. Take bus 2 (Y2) or pedicab (Y2) from Taihe Lu to the main gate (山门口; Shān Ménkǒu) and ticket office. The bus ticket you must buy with your admission gives you unlimited use of shuttle buses (from 6am to 6.30pm). Note that everything added together (including buses and temple tickets) will cost you Y245; presumably this funded the construction of the expensive-looking ticket hall. The ticket-checking guards in black quasi-military outfits and red berets are curious in such a sacred place. Before buying your ticket you are funnelled mercilessly past shops selling Wǔdāng swords and the like.

One bus – often only leaving when full – runs to the start of the **cable car** (索道; suǒdào; up/down Y50/45). For those who don't mind steps, take the bus to South Cliff (南岩; Nányán), where the trail to 1612m **Heavenly Pillar Peak** (天柱峰; Tiānzhù Fēng), the highest peak, begins. Con-

LYING IN WAIT

Despite being discovered 30 years ago, when canal diggers dug up the remains of a horse and chariot, mystery still surrounds the potentially momentous tomb site at Xióngjiā Zhǒng. Fears of insufficient preservation techniques meant excavation only began in 2006, and only a fraction of its more than 100 tombs have been opened. Finds already unearthed include one of China's finest collections of jade, but potentially there's a lot more to come. Work began in 2008 on excavating the huge, 130m-long horse and chariot tomb, while the main tomb itself, which is believed to contain the largest royal coffin ever discovered in China (248 sq metres, if estimates are accurate), still hasn't been touched. Exactly whose body is lying in it, waiting to be discovered, is still unknown. The site is believed to be named after the surname of the person buried in it (Xióng; 熊). No accounts specify who that person is, but Xióng was a royal family name of the Chu Kingdom (722–221 BC) so it's widely assumed the tomb belongs to one of the 20 Chu kings who used to rule the area. If so, it would be the first Chu king tomb ever discovered. Experts date the site at around 2300 years old, which points to the last Chu king, Chǔ Zhāowáng (楚昭王), also known as Xióng Zhēn (熊珍). No documents link him with the site, but he was known to have been so popular that people were willing to die for him, which is perhaps why the main tomb comes with at least 92 accompanying tombs, all thought to contain human remains.

sider disembarking early at the beautiful, turquoise-tiled **Purple Cloud Temple** (紫霄宫; Zǐxiāo Gōng; admission Y20), from where a small stone path leads up to South Cliff (45 minutes). From South Cliff, it's an energy-sapping, two-hour, 4km climb to the top, but the scenery is worth every step and there are plenty of Taoist temples en route where you can take contemplative breathers. Note the occasional Taoist cairn and trees garlanded with scarlet ribbons weighed with small stones.

The enchanting red-walled **Cháotiān Temple** (朝天宫; Cháotiān Gōng) is about halfway up, housing a statue of the Jade Emperor and standing on an old, moss-hewn stone base with 4m-high tombstones guarding its entrance. From here you have a choice of two ascent routes, via the 1.4km Ming-dynasty route (the older, Back Way) or the 1.8km Qing-dynasty path (the 'Hundred Stairs'). The shorter, but more gruelling Ming route ascends via the **Three Heaven's Gates**, including the stupefying climb to the **Second Gate of Heaven** (二天门; Èrtiān Mén). You can climb by one route and descend by the other. Temple ruins, fallen trees, shocking inclines and steep steps misshapen by centuries of footslogging await you. Either way it's tempting to reach for a Red Bull, until you hear the price tag (Y15); if you're flush, a sedan chair from Cháotiān Temple to the summit is Y380 (one way).

Near the top, beyond the cable-car exit, is the magnificent **Forbidden City** (紫金城; Zǐjīn Chéng; admission Y20) with its 2.5m-thick stone walls hugging the mountainside and balustrades festooned with lovers' locks. From here you can stagger to magnificent views from the **Golden Hall** (金殿; Jīn Diàn; admission Y20), constructed entirely from bronze, dating from 1416 and in dire need of some buffing up. A small statue of Zhenwu Ming emperor and Wǔdāngshān's presiding Taoist deity – is enclosed within. On the way down, note how some pilgrims descend backwards!

Courses

If you're going to dabble in taichi (太极拳), why not try it where it all began? There are many schools around, but the following both have English speakers. Standard fees are US$50 per day.

Academy of Wǔdāng Taoism Wǔshù TAICHI
(道教武术院; Dàojiào Wǔshùyuàn; ☎568 9185; www.wudang.org) The pick in terms of ambience alone. Its grand old red building stands halfway up the mountain, a short walk from Purple Cloud Temple. Call ahead to be picked up from town.

Wǔdāng Shān Dàojiào Tàihé Wǔshùyuàn TAICHI
(武当山道教太和武术院; ☎5666 653; www.wudangwushu.net) In the town itself is this smaller school. The office is in a

THE BIRTH OF TAICHI

Zhang San Feng (张三丰), a semi-legendary Wǔdāng Shān monk from the 10th or 13th century (depending what source you read), is reputed to be the founder of the martial art *tàijíquán*, or taichi. Zhang had grown dissatisfied with the 'hard' techniques of Shaolin boxing and searched for something 'softer'. Sitting on his porch one day, he became inspired by a battle between a huge bird and a snake. The sinuous snake used flowing movements to evade the bird's attacks. The bird, exhausted, eventually gave up and flew away. Taichi is closely linked to Taoism, and many priests on Wǔdāng Shān practise some form of the art.

junior school on your right as you walk towards the museum.

Sleeping

Room prices peak at the weekends.

IN TOWN

Jīnlóngdiàn Hotel HOTEL **$$**
(Jīnlóngdiàn Bīnguǎn; 金龙殿宾馆; ☎566 8919; 1 Yongle Dadao; 永乐大道1号; s Y240, d Y180-260, discounts of 40%; ❄) This four-storey place has seen better days but it's OK for the night. From the train station, turn right onto Taihe Lu and it's on the corner of the second turning on your left.

Shèngjǐngyuàn Bīnguǎn HOTEL **$$**
(圣景苑宾馆; ☎566 2118; Taihe Lu; 太和路; r with shared/private bathroom Y268/358, discounts of 70%; ❄) Bright and pleasant rooms come with comfortable mattresses and good bathrooms. The cheapest rooms often go for Y80; no lift but smiling staff. A bit further along from the Jīnlóngdiàn Hotel.

ON THE MOUNTAIN

Nányán Hotel HOTEL **$$**
(南岩宾馆; Nányán Bīnguǎn; ☎568 9182; d Y380-486, tr Y486, discounts of 60-70%) This hotel at South Cliff has acceptable rooms with comfy and spacious doubles; cheaper rooms have squat loo but low-season prices are attractive all round.

Taihé Bīnguǎn HOTEL **$$**
(太和宾馆; ☎568 9189; d Y238-398) The best doubles normally go for Y120 and are clean and bright with great views but service is a big letdown at this South Cliff choice. Grubby cheapies slide to Y80.

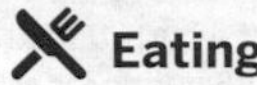

Eating

The night market, on a small, unnamed lane off Taihe Lu, is a fun place to eat. There are plenty of varieties of *chuàn* (串; kebab sticks; from Y1) or else chefs will fry up in front of you whatever you point at. It's also a good place to stock up on fruit and snacks for next day's mountain assault. Coming from the train station, it's on your right, just before the hospital.

Information

Several internet cafes are on Yuxu Lu.

China Construction Bank (中国建设银行; Zhōngguó Jiànshè Yínháng; Taihe Lu) Has a 24-hour ATM for foreign cards. From the train station, turn right onto Taihe Lu; it's on your left after the first junction.

China Post (中国邮政; Zhōngguó Yóuzhèng; 40 Yongle Lu; ⏲8am-6pm) Take the next left after the Construction Bank and it's on your left. Closes for lunch.

Net Bar (网吧; Wǎngbā; 3rd fl, Yuxu Lu; per hr Y2; ⏲24hr) Just south of the junction with Taihe Lu.

Public Security Bureau (PSB; 公安局; Gōng'ānjú; Yuxu Lu; ⏲8-11.30am & 2.30-6pm) From the train station, turn right onto Taihe Lu, take the first left and it's on the next corner.

Wǔdāng Shān Hospital (特区医院; Tèqū Yīyuàn; Taihe Lu) From the train station, turn right onto Taihe Lu and it's on your right before the river.

Getting There & Away

Bus

Coming from Shíyàn (十堰), regular buses run to Wǔdāng Shān (Y8, one hour) from the road on the left of the train station. The road to Wǔdāng Shān is being widened to accommodate more vehicles so the trip should become faster.

Shíyàn Y8, one hour, regular services

Wǔhàn Y120 to Y150, five hours, 9.20am & 11.30am, then regularly 4.30pm to 6.30pm

Yíchāng Y110, five hours, two daily (8.50am and 7pm)

Train

Wǔdāng Shān town is on the railway between Wǔhàn and Chóngqìng. At the time of writing, Wǔdāng Shān was awaiting a new train station and it was quicker to take the train to nearby Shíyàn, followed by a bus. An early-morning express 'D' train (3½ hours) from Hànkǒu leaves for Shíyàn at 8.20am; ask if it stops at Wǔdāng Shān.

Shénnóngjià 神农架

☎0719

Famed for its medicinal plants and legendary ape-man (野人; *yěrén*), Shénnóngjià is likely to be the wildest of your experiences in Húběi. Fir and pine forests flourish among more than 1300 species of medicinal plants across picturesque mountains and valleys. Foreigners are only allowed into one of the four sections of the national park, at **Yāzikǒu** (鸭子口; admission Y140), but the area is big enough to offer good trekking and cycling options. You can also camp here. Areas worth checking out are **Xiǎolóngtán** (小龙潭) and **Dàlóngtán** (大龙潭), the best two places to spot monkeys, and **Shénnóngdǐng** (神农顶), the highest peak (3105m). Winter here is bitterly cold and snow often blocks roads.

The only area not off limits to foreigners is accessed from **Mùyú** (木鱼), a small but well-developed tourist village about 14km down from Yāzikǒu. Despite the Visa signs, none of the ATMs accepts foreign cards.

The **Shuānglín Hotel** (双林酒店; Shuānglín Jiǔdiàn; ☎345 3800; tw Y160) has tidy rooms with TVs and clean bathrooms, and they usually go for Y50. It's up towards the top of the village on the right-hand side of the road. Down the hill a bit, across the road, the **Shénnóngjià Characteristic Restaurant** has a terrace where you can sample the area's delicious wild mushrooms. Try the *shānyào chǎomù'ěr* (山药炒木耳; stir-fried mushrooms with ginger, peppers and chilli; Y18). Further down the hill, on the same side of the road, is **Yuánmèng Hùwài Yùndòng Lǚyóu** (神农架圆梦户外运动旅游; ☎345 2518; ⏲7.30am-9pm), where you can rent mountain bikes (Y50 per day) and tents (also Y80 per day), but prepare yourself for the Y1000 deposits! On the same side of the road is **YTS tourist office** (青年旅行社; qīngnián lǚxíngshè; ☎345 2879; ⏲8am-6pm), which offers a car and driver for Y300 per day. Expect to pay an extra Y300 per day for an English-speaking guide.

Minibuses run when full from Mùyú to Yāzikǒu (Y10) or else it's a lung-busting, but very rewarding, three-hour 14km cycle. There are three daily buses from Mùyú to Yíchāng (Y50, three hours, 7am and 1pm). You can buy tickets from the Shuānglín Hotel. Foreigners are not allowed to continue north to Wǔdāng Shān from Mùyú.

Yíchāng 宜昌

☎0717 / POP 4 MILLION

A nondescript and scruffy city of four million souls, Yíchāng is on the map as a hopping-on or hopping-off point for ferries to the spectacular Three Gorges.

Sights

Yíchāng hugs a bend in the Yangzi, east of the Three Gorges (三峡; Sānxiá). Its heartbeat is between Yanjiang Dadao (沿江大道), running alongside the river, and Dongshan Dadao (东山大道), running parallel 1.5km to the north. The old train station, perched above Dongshan Dadao up a punishing flight of stairs, looks south along the length of Yunji Lu (云集路), which runs towards the river. Heading south along Yunji Lu, turn left into Jiefang Lu (解放路) or Zili Lu (自立路) to find a cluster of bars, clubs and restaurants. The new train station is east of town.

Three Gorges Dam SCENIC AREA

(三峡大坝; Sanxiá Dàbà; admission Y105) The huge Three Gorges Dam hulks away upstream. The world's largest due to length (2.3km) rather than height (101m), it isn't the most spectacular, but is worth a peek. You can't walk on it, but there's a tourist viewing area to the north. The view from the south is much the same, and free. Take a bus from the long-distance station to Máopíng (茅坪; Y15), but get off at Bālù Chēzhàn (八路车战). Alternatively, take bus 4 from the ferry terminal to Yèmíngzhū (夜明珠; Y1) then change to bus 8 (Y10), which terminates at Bālù Chēzhàn. Tours (Y150 inclusive of admission) also leave at 8.30am and 1pm from **Hubei Xiazhou International Travel Service** (☎644 0001; 78 Yiling Lu).

Sleeping & Eating

Yíchāng Hotel HOTEL $$

(宜昌饭店; Yíchāng Fàndiàn; ☎644 1616; 113 Dongshan Dadao; 东山大道113号; s/d Y268/288, discounts of 10%; ❄@) This jolly friendly place has an elegant foyer, large and pleasant rooms (standard doubles come with computer). English is shaky but it's all smiles; exit the train station and take the left-hand road down to the hotel.

25 Hours Hotel HOTEL **$$**
(25 Hours 块捷酒店; 25 Hours Kuàijié Jiǔdiàn; ☎691 0000; 1 Guoyuan Lu; 果园路1号; s/d Y288/298, discounts of 40%; ❄📶) Nifty business hotel with a decent sense of style, tidy rooms with computer, flat-screen TVs and clean shower rooms. Lift from 2nd floor; good discounts.

Zili Lu has loads of cheap restaurants offering filling bowls of *zhōu* (粥; porridge; Y4) and various noodle dishes. Try spicy *niúròu miàn* (牛肉面; beef noodles; Y5). Guoyuan Yilu (果园一路) – its entrance is opposite the Yíchāng Hotel – also has loads of restaurants and fruit stalls. Also look out for street sellers of fantastic *kàng tǔdòu* (cooked potatoes with chilli; Y2).

 Information

Guoyuan Yilu has loads of internet cafes.

China Construction Bank (中国建设银行; Zhōngguó Jiànshè Yínháng; Yunji Lu; ⊙8am-5.30pm) Foreign exchange and 24-hour ATM. It's 700m south of the train station, on your left.

China International Travel Service (CITS; 中国国际旅行社; Zhōngguó Guójì Lǚxíngshè; ☎625 3088; Yunji Lu; ⊙8.30am-5.30pm) Can arrange Three Gorges tours. Some English spoken. It's beside the China Construction Bank.

China Post (中国邮政; Zhōngguó Yóuzhèng; 99 Yiling Dadao) On the corner of Yunji Lu.

Haixing Internet Cafe (海星网吧; Hǎixīng Wǎngbā; Guoyuan Yilu; per hr Y2.5; ⊙24hr) Behind the 25 Hours Hotel.

Industrial & Commercial Bank of China (ICBC; 工商银行; Gōngshāng Yínháng; crn Yunji Lu & Yiling Dadao) Has a 24-hour ATM.

Public Security Bureau (PSB; 公安局; Gōng'ānjú; 14 Xueyuan Jie; 学院街14号; ⊙8-11.30am & 2.30-5pm Mon-Fri) Head south from the train station down Yunji Lu for about 1km, turn right into Jiefang Lu, then left into Xueyuan Jie.

 Getting There & Around

Bus 4 (Y1) goes from one block north of the train station to the ferry terminal. Taxis start at Y3.

Air

Daily flights from Three Gorges Airport (三峡机场; Sānxiá Jīchǎng) go to Běijīng (Y1200), Shànghǎi (Y1000) and Xī'ān (Y800).

Shuttle buses (Y20, 40 minutes, 8am to 6.30pm) run to and from the Qīngjiāng Building (清江大厦; Qīngjiāng Dàshà). Flight tickets can be bought from the Air China office inside. Come down the train station steps, turn right and it's on your right after 800m.

Boat

Westbound-only boats leave daily from the **Yíchāng Ferry Terminal** (宜昌港客运站; Yíchāng Gǎng Kèyùnzhàn; Yanjing Dadao), where tickets are sold.

Chóngqìng Y152 to Y884, 38 hours, one daily (4.30pm)

Wànxiàn Y148 to Y498, 24 hours

Speedier hydrofoil services:

Fēngjié Y220, hourly (6.50am to 1.20pm)

Wànxiàn Y300, six hours, hourly (6.50am to 1.20pm)

Wūshān Y190, hourly (6.50am to 1.20pm)

Bus

Services from the **long-distance bus station** (长途汽车站; chángtú qìchēzhàn; Dongshan Dadao):

Jīngzhōu Y38, two hours, frequent

Lìchuān Y135, five hours, one daily (6.30pm)

Mùyú Y57, six hours, three daily

Shíyàn Y100

Wǔchāng Y102 to Y142, 4½ hours, every hour (7am to 8pm)

Wǔdāng Shān Y93, six hours, two daily (8am and 1pm)

Services from the **ferry terminal bus station**:

Chóngqìng Y235, 14 to 16 hours, one daily (4pm)

Wǔhàn Y70, 4½ hours

Train

Yíchāng has a brand-new train station east of town as well as the old train station. Train tickets (Y5 service charge) can be bought at window 1 of the long-distance bus station.

Luòyáng Y76/146, 8½ to 10 hours

Shíyàn Y63, six hours

Wǔhàn seat/sleeper Y55/105, 4½ hours

Wǔdāng Shān Y62, five hours

Zhèngzhōu Y103/185, 9½ to 12 hours

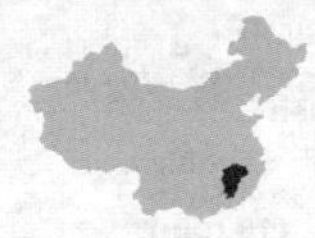

Jiāngxī

POPULATION: 44 MILLION

Includes »

Best Places to Eat

» Xiánhēng Jiǔdiàn (p439)
» Yangzi Jie (p439)
» Luótiáncūn (p440)

Best Places to Stay

» Guangmíng Chálóu (p445)
» Cháxiāng Kèlóu (p445)
» Sānqīng Shān (p442)

Why Go?

An interconnected web of rivers, lakes and shimmering rice paddies, Jiāngxī (江西) is defined by its water. Farmers in slickers and heavy boots till the fields in drizzling rain as snow-white herons whirl overhead, and off at the edges of the province, low-lying hills of pencil-thin pines give way to more substantial mountain ranges, seemingly shrouded in perpetual mist. At the northern border is Póyáng Lake, a wetlands area that swells to become the country's largest freshwater lake in summer.

While it certainly doesn't wind up on many people's must-see list, the province has its surprises, and it can be just the spot if you're after a more remote corner of the country. Hikers should lace up their boots immediately; almost all of the major attractions are off in the mountains or verdant rolling countryside. And with several high-speed train connections from Shànghǎi and Hángzhōu, getting here has never been easier.

When to Go

Nánchāng

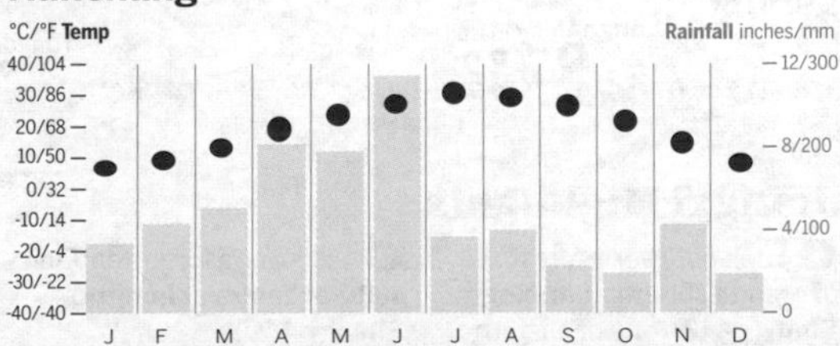

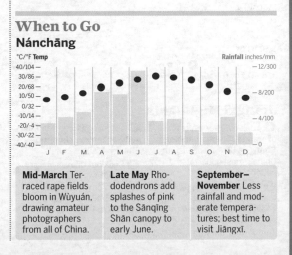

Mid-March Terraced rape fields bloom in Wùyuán, drawing amateur photographers from all of China.

Late May Rhododendrons add splashes of pink to the Sānqīng Shān canopy to early June.

September–November Less rainfall and moderate temperatures; best time to visit Jiāngxī.

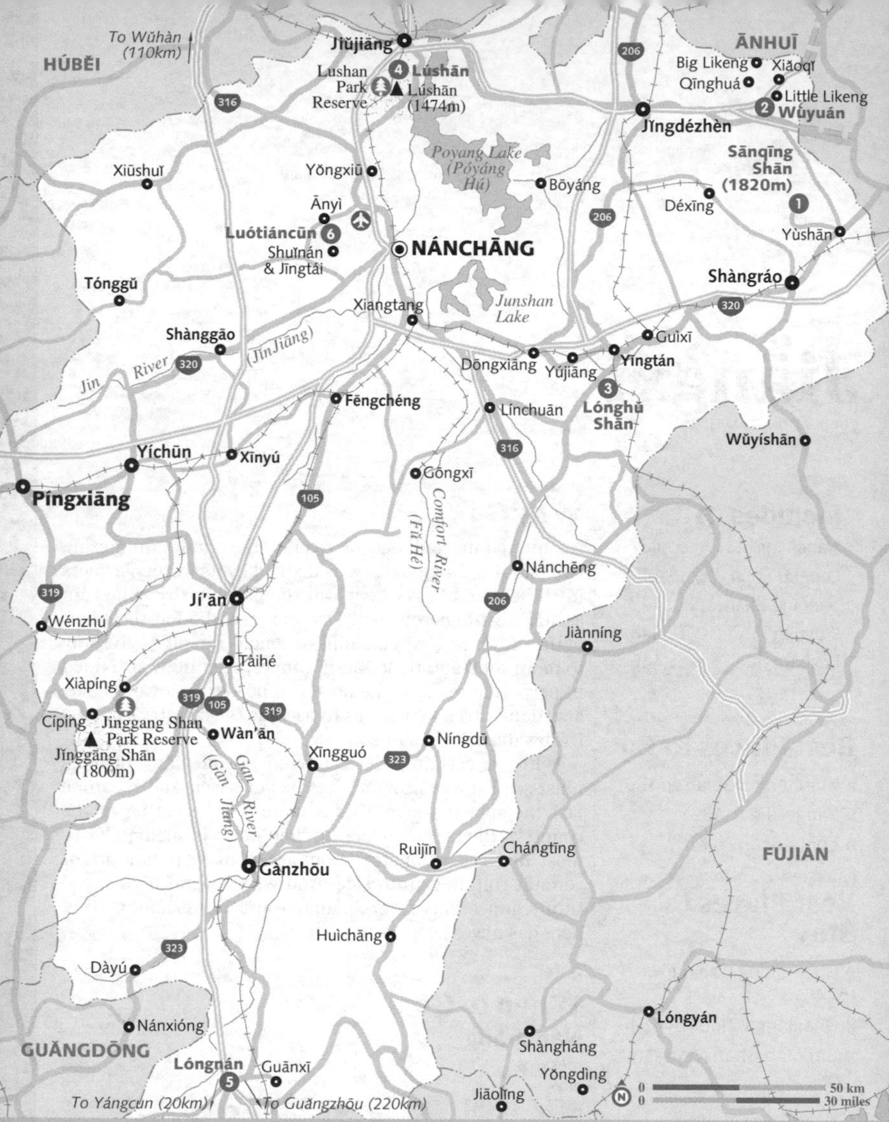

Jiāngxī Highlights

1 Look out over a forest of granite spires in **Sānqīng Shān** (p442), one of eastern China's most underrated national parks

2 Walk the ancient postal roads linking the Huīzhōu-style villages around **Wùyuán** (p444)

3 Discover a forgotten Taoist cultural centre at **Lónghŭ Shān** (p440)

4 Seek out China's literary muse, unravel political scandals or wait for the ethereal mists to clear on **Lúshān** (p446)

5 Explore Hakka country around **Lóngnán** (p447), where fortified villages and subtropical forest await

6 Escape the urban greys of Nánchāng in the traditional alleyways of **Luótiáncūn** (p440)

History

Jiāngxī's Gàn River Valley was the principal trade route that linked Guǎngdōng with the rest of the country in imperial times. Its strategic location, natural resources and long growing season ensured that the province has always been relatively well off. Jiāngxī is most famous for its imperial porcelain (from Jǐngdézhèn), although its contributions to philosophy and literature are perhaps more significant, particularly during the Tang and Song dynasties. Lúshān was an important Buddhist centre, and also served as the home to the famous White Deer Grotto Academy, re-established by the founder of neo-Confucianism, Zhu Xi (1130–1200), as the pre-eminent intellectual centre of the time. Taoism also played a role in Jiāngxī's development after Lónghǔ Shān became the centre of the powerful Zhèngyī sect in the Song dynasty (960–1279).

Peasant unrest arose during the 16th century and again in the 19th century when the Taiping rebels swept through the Yangzi River Valley. Rebellion continued into the 20th century, and Jiāngxī became one of the earliest bases for the Chinese communists.

Climate

Central Jiāngxī lies in the Gàn River plain (formerly the main trade route linking Guǎngdōng with the rest of China) and experiences a four-season, subtropical climate. Mountains encircle the plain and locals flock here to escape the summer heat, which averages over 30°C in July. Rainfall averages 120cm to 190cm annually and is usually heaviest in the northeast; half falls between April and June.

PRICE INDICATORS

The following price indicators are used in this chapter:

Sleeping

$	less than Y100
$$	Y100 to Y400
$$$	more than Y400

Eating

$	less than Y30
$$	Y30 to Y60
$$$	more than Y60

Language

Most Jiāngxī natives speak one of innumerable local variants of Gàn (赣), a dialect whose name is also used as a shorthand for the province. Gàn is similar (some say related) to the Hakka language, spoken in southern Jiāngxī.

Getting There & Around

Nánchāng is connected by air to most major cities in China, including Hong Kong. The capital has several express trains linking it with Běijīng to the north, Chángshā to the west, and Hángzhōu and Shànghǎi to the east. A sleeper train connects the capital with Guǎngzhōu to the south. Getting around the province and on to neighbouring provinces by bus is generally fast and reliable.

Nánchāng 南昌

0791 / POP 2.15 MILLION

A bustling, busy and booming town, Nánchāng is branded on Chinese consciousness as a revolutionary torchbearer and applauded in China's history books for its role in consolidating the power of the Chinese Communist Party (CCP). It may come as little surprise, therefore, that Western travellers, unless otherwise detained, should jump on the first connection out of town to the bucolic charms of Luótiáncūn, stupendous Wùyuán or Sānqīng Shān.

Sights

Téngwáng Pavilion MONUMENT

(滕王阁; Téngwáng Gé; Rongmen Lu; 榕门路; admission Y50; 7.30am-6.50pm summer, 8am-5.30pm winter) This nine-storey pagoda is the city's drawcard prerevolutionary monument, first erected during Tang times.

Yòumín Temple BUDDHIST TEMPLE

(佑民寺; Yòumín Sì; 181 Minde Lu; 民德路181号; admission Y2; 7am-5.30pm) This huge temple was heavily damaged during the Cultural Revolution, but contains some notable statuary.

FREE **Zhu De's Former Residence** MUSEUM

(朱德旧居; Zhū Dé Jiùjū; 2 Huayuanjiao Jie; 花园角街2号; 9am-5pm, closed Mon) The former communist general lived here for several months in 1927. It's now a revolutionary history museum, though the commentary is in Chinese only.

Nánchāng

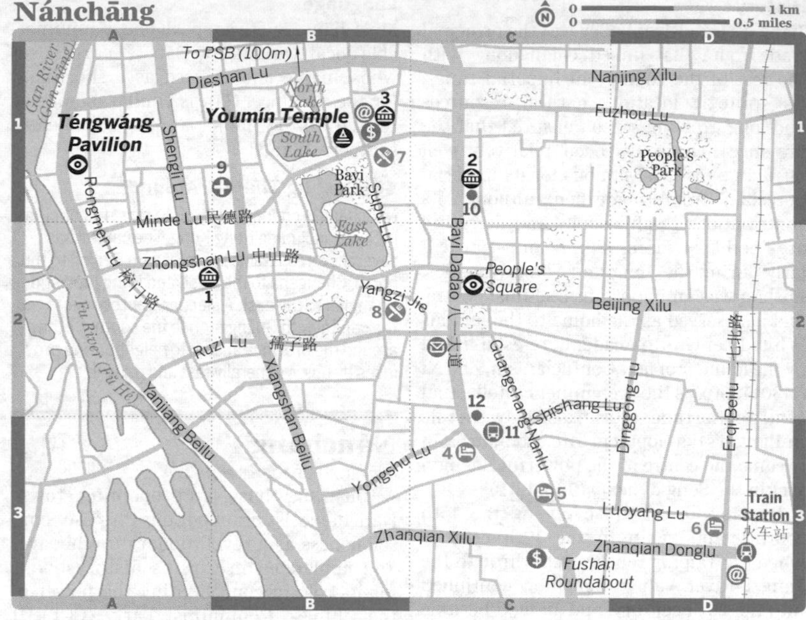

Nánchāng

FREE **Memorial Hall to the Martyrs of the Revolution** MUSEUM
(革命烈士纪念馆; Gémìng Lièshì Jìniànguǎn; 399 Bayi Dadao; 八一大道399号; ⌚8am-5pm) Archival photos from the 1920s to the 1940s.

FREE **Former Headquarters of the Nánchāng Uprising** MUSEUM
(八一南昌起义纪念馆; Bāyī Nánchāng Qǐyì Jìniànguǎn; 380 Zhongshan Lu; 中山路380号; ⌚9-11.30am & 1-3.30pm) Wartime paraphernalia for rainy days and enthusiasts of the CCP. Admission free with passport.

Sleeping

7 Days Inn HOTEL **$$**
(七天连锁酒店; Qītiān Liánsuǒ Jiǔdiàn; ☎885 7688; www.7daysinn.cn; 142 Bayi Dadao; 八一大道142号; r Y168-218; ❄@) With its handy location across from the long-distance bus station, this popular chain (the orange and yellow building) fills up quickly. Interiors are bright and spiffy, and you can usually get a member discount, which drops cheaper rooms to Y157. Added bonus: there's a good restaurant right next door. Reservations are recommended (rooms start at Y137 online, though it's Chinese only).

Welcome Inn HOTEL **$$**
(唯客大酒店 Wéikè Dàjiǔdiàn; ☎816 8168; 70 Luoyang Lu; 洛阳路70号; d Y269-339, discounts of 25%; ❄) Across from the train station is this dependable and modern midrange chain.

Xīngqiú Bīnguǎn HOTEL **$$**
(星球宾馆; ☎612 6555; Train Station Sq; 火车站广场; r Y238-328, discounts of 38%) This is an acceptable budget choice across from the train station. Its gigantic (but weathered) rooms usually start at Y148.

Galactic Peace Hotel HOTEL **$$$**
(嘉莱特和平国际酒店; Jiāláitè Hépíng Guójì Jiǔdiàn; ☎611 1118; www.glthp.com; 10 Guangchang Nanlu; 广场南路10号; d incl breakfast Y1090-1580, discounts of 50%; ⊖❄@︎📶≋) Though there's no particular charm here, this is as comfortable as it gets in Jiāngxī. The facilities are top-notch and the refurbished rooms spacious (the best are in Block B).

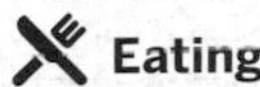

Eating

The area south of Bāyī Park (八一公园) is one of the more fun places to search for food and drink. Yangzi Jie (羊子街), particularly the western end, is lined with tiny inexpensive restaurants. There's also a handful of cafes (internet and coffee) and clubs scattered in the area and further west along Minde Lu.

Xiánhēng Jiǔdiàn SOUTHERN CHINESE **$$**
(咸亨酒店; 48 Minde Lu; 民德路48号; dishes Y12-42; 📋) Contemporary two-floor restaurant, with an intriguing mix of southern cuisines (Jiāngxī, Cantonese and Zhèjiāng); try the spicy, peanut-laden drunken beef (酒鬼牛肉; *jiǔguǐ niúròu*).

Information

007 Wǎngchéng (007网城; Train Station Sq, 4th fl; per hr Y3; ⊙24hr) Internet access in a postapocalyptic building.

ABC Internet Bar (ABC网城; ABC Wǎngchéng; 225 Supu Lu; 苏圃路225号; per hr Y2; ⊙24hr)

Bank of China (中国银行; Zhōngguó Yínháng) Main branch (Zhanqian Xilu; 站前西路); ATM branch (Erqi Nanlu, next to 007 Wǎngchéng; 二七南路; ⊙24hr); ATM branch (161 Minde Lu; 民德路161号; ⊙24hr) The main branch has foreign exchange and an ATM (open office hours only). ATMs throughout Nánchāng accept all major cards.

China Post (邮局; Zhōngguó Yóuzhèng; cnr Bayi Dadao & Ruzi Lu; 八一大道, 近孺子路)

Nánchāng No 1 People's Hospital (南昌市第一人民医院; Nánchāng Shì Dìyī Rénmín Yīyuàn; 128 Xiangshan Beilu; 象山北路128号)

Public Security Bureau (PSB; 公安局; Gōng'ānjú; ☎728 8493; 131 Yangming Lu; 阳明路131号; ⊙8am-noon & 2.30-6pm)

Getting There & Away

Air

Chāngběi airport is 28km north of the city, with flights to the following:

Běijīng Y1300, two hours
Guǎngzhōu Y800, 1½ hours
Hong Kong Y1200, two hours
Shànghǎi Y710, one hour
Xī'ān Y1010, 1½ hours

Air tickets can be purchased from travel agents next to the long-distance bus station or in the train station area.

Bus

The Nánchāng **long-distance bus station** (长途汽车站; Chángtú Qìchēzhàn; Bayi Dadao) has regular buses:

Lúshān Y50, 2½ hours, three daily
Nánjīng Y191, eight hours, two daily
Shàngráo Y80, three hours, regular services
Wùyuán Y95, five hours, four daily
Yīngtán Y45, two hours, hourly
Yùshān Y94, four hours, one daily

Train

Buy train tickets at the **Advance Rail Ticket Office** (铁路售票处; Huǒchē Shòupiàochù; 393 Bayi Dadao; 八一大道393号; ⊙8am-noon & 12.30-5pm) or at the **Rail Ticket Office** (铁路售票处; Tiělù Shòupiàochù; Bayi Dadao), down an alleyway next to the long-distance bus station. The following destinations have rail connections with Nánchāng.

Běijīng West Y308, 12 to 22 hours, 12 daily
Chángshā (express) Y130, three hours, one daily
Fúzhōu Y157, 10 hours, eight daily
Guǎngzhōu East Y272, 12 hours, six daily
Hángzhōu (express) Y199, four hours, two daily; (sleeper) Y157, nine hours, 12 daily
Shànghǎi South (express) Y253, 5½ hours, one daily; (sleeper) Y191, 10 hours, eight daily
Shàngráo Y36, two to four hours, regular services
Wǔhàn Y52, 3½ to five hours, regular services
Yīngtán Y12 to Y45, one to two hours, regular services
Yùshān Y39, four hours, six daily

Getting Around

Airport buses (Y10, one hour, half-hourly from 6am to 8pm) leave from in front of the train station. A taxi to the airport costs around Y100.

From the train station, bus 2 goes up Bayi Dadao past the long-distance bus station. Taxis are Y6 at flag fall.

Around Nánchāng

Northwest of town and faced on all sides by imposing ornamental gateways *(ménlóu),* the 1120-year-old village of **Luótiáncūn** (罗田村; admission Y30), its uneven stone-flagged alleys etched with centuries of wear, makes an ideal day out and rural escape from urban Nánchāng. A disorientating labyrinth of tight, higgledy-piggledy lanes, disused halls and ancient homesteads assembled from dark stone, Luótiáncūn is set among a picturesque landscape of fields and hills that maximise its pastoral charms.

A self-guided tour (beginning at the square with the pond) will take you through a tight maze of lanes, past hand-worked pumps, ancient wells, stone steps, scattering chickens, lazy cows and conical haystacks. There are some lovely buildings here, including the former residence **Dàshìfūdì** (大世夫第) on Hengjie (横街; Cross St). On the fringes of the village is a fat old camphor tree dating from Tang days; also hunt down the **old well** (古井; *gǔjǐng*), which locals swear is 1000 years old.

From the waterwheel at the foot of Qianjie, a flagstone path links Luótiáncūn with its sibling village, **Shuǐnán** (水南). In Shuǐnán, follow the signs to the **Shuǐnán Folk Museum** (水南民俗馆; Shuǐnán Mínsúguǎn), another old residence consisting of bedchambers and threadbare exhibits. Towards the edge of the village, the **Guīxiù Lóu** (闺秀楼) is another notable building.

A further 500m down the stone path (and across the road) is forlorn **Jīngtái** (京台), whose gap-toothed and largely non-Mandarin-speaking denizens are all surnamed either Liu (刘) or Li (李).

Simple, peasant-family (农家; *nóngjiā*) **accommodation** (bed Y30) is available in Luótiáncūn, but all three villages can be done as a day trip from Nánchāng. Avoid eating on the main square – seek out the local families instead.

Take a bus to Ānyì (安义; Y17, one hour, frequent buses 6am to 6pm) from the Nánchāng long-distance bus station. Across from the Ānyì long-distance bus station, buses leave regularly (when full) for Shíbí (石鼻; Y3.50, 20 minutes), from where *sānlúnchē* (a cross between a motorcycle and mini pickup truck) muster for trips to Luótiáncūn (Y5, 10 minutes). Alternatively, you can take a cab direct to Luótiáncūn from Ānyì for Y40.

Lónghǔ Shān 龙虎山

☎0701

From powerful Taoist priests to the opening scenes of the martial-arts novel *Outlaws of the Marsh,* Lónghǔ Shān (Dragon and Tiger Mountain) left a distinct mark on traditional Chinese culture in its heyday during the Song, Yuan and Ming dynasties. The Cultural Revolution may have wiped clean the physical traces of this past, but with a setting reminiscent of a landscape painting – a winding river, cluster of red sandstone peaks, grazing water buffaloes and solitary herons – this is as good a place as any to discover the lush Jiāngxī countryside.

In the Song dynasty (960–1279), Lónghǔ Shān became the centre of the emergent Zhèngyī sect, which claimed to represent the teachings of religious Taoism's founder, Zhang Daoling (34–156). Together with the Quánzhēn sect, Zhèngyī Taoism was one of the most prominent schools of Taoism in late imperial China, and there were once over 100 temples and monasteries here. Zhèngyī Taoists were active in society, selling protective talismans (still for sale) and performing religious services for the general populace. The head of the Zhèngyī sect was known as the Celestial Master, a lineage that was traced back to Zhang Daoling.

Sights & Activities

The Lónghǔ Shān scenic area encompasses 200 sq km, most of which is located along the eastern bank of the Lúxī River. A **ticket** (www.longhushan.com; without/with raft trip Y150/225) includes admission to seven sites and a raft ride, as well as transport on miniature trains (main entrance to Zhèngyī Temple) and shuttle buses (from Zhèngyī Temple to the Residence of the Celestial Masters). To get the most out of your visit, narrow down your sightseeing options to two main areas: the Residence of the Celestial Masters and Elephant's Trunk Hill.

Residence of the Celestial Masters TAOIST TEMPLE

(天师府; Tiānshī Fǔ) About 28km from the main entrance, this is the largest and best-preserved temple in the area. It was originally built in the Song dynasty as Zhèngyī's main temple complex, thoroughly renovated in the Qing dynasty and then again in the 1990s. The oldest building still standing is the **Sanctuary of Triple Introspection** (三省堂; Sān Xǐng Táng), which dates to 1865. To get here, walk 15 minutes through old Shàngqīng village from the shuttle drop-off. Another 500m along Fuqian Jie (府前街) is an abandoned **Catholic church** (天主教堂; Tiānzhǔjiào Táng), a wonderfully bizarre building and strange relic of colonial missionary days.

Shàngqīng Palace TAOIST TEMPLE

(大上清宫; Dà Shàngqīng Gōng) Five hundred metres past the church, this temple complex was almost entirely destroyed by fire; only the entrance gate, first courtyard (with the drum and bell tower) and a few side halls remain. A mythic spot, Shàngqīng Palace is both the alleged site of the residence of the first Celestial Master (Zhang Daoling) as well as the place from which the spirits of the 108 demons were accidentally released in *Outlaws of the Marsh*.

Elephant's Trunk Hill SCENIC AREA

(象鼻山; Xiàngbí Shān) Closer to the main entrance, this is the first stop you'll reach on the miniature train. Here you can hike a loop past rock formations and rebuilt temples, then descend to the river from where you'll be able to spy Lónghǔ Shān's **hanging coffins** (悬棺; xuán guān) on the opposite side of the bank. About 2500 years ago, the original inhabitants of the area, the Guyue, buried their dead in grottoes located high up on the cliff face. A hanging coffin performance (it's a liberal reinterpretation) is staged three times a day here at 8.30am, 1.30pm and 4.30pm; a ferry also crosses the river for free.

At the main entrance are two small museums, the **Taoist Museum** (⏲8am-5pm), with information in Chinese only, and the **Geology Museum** (⏲8am-5pm), with detailed explanations of Lónghǔ Shān's formation.

Sleeping & Eating

Hotels and restaurants are conveniently based near the main entrance. Construction was in a frenzy when we visited: expect to find a bevy of new midrange hotels. There are smaller restaurants in Shàngqīng village, at the opposite end of the scenic area.

Róngshèng Bīnguǎn HOTEL $$

(荣盛宾馆; Róngshèng Bīnguǎn; ☎665 7669; 龙虎山新大门对面; tw from Y200, discounts of 20%; ❄@) Tasteful and surprisingly sophisticated, the Róngshèng has hardwood floors, flat-screen TVs and traditional Chinese-style sinks in the bathrooms. It's opposite the park entrance.

Lónghǔ Shān Nóngjiālè HOTEL $

(龙虎山农家乐; ☎665 9506; 39 Xianrencheng Lu; 仙人城路15号; tw Y60; ❄) Down a side street, this clean and friendly place is more a homestay than a hotel.

Information

The most convenient bank is the **China Construction Bank** (中国建设银行; Zhōngguó Jiànshè Yínháng; ⏲24hr ATM) in Yīngtán, but note it's a good 15-minute walk from the train station up Zhanjiang Lu (站江路). There are **internet cafes** (网吧; *wǎngbā*) across from the train station in Yīngtán.

Getting There & Around

Lónghǔ Shān is near the city of Yīngtán (鹰潭), which is on the Shànghǎi–Nánchāng railway line. To get to Lónghǔ Shān from Yīngtán, take bus K2, which runs from in front of the train station, past the bus station and on to the main entrance (Y3, 20 minutes, 8am to 8pm). Minibuses also make the trip for Y8.

Services from **Yīngtán's train station** (火车站; huǒchē zhàn):

Hángzhōu Y70, six hours, frequent services

Nánchāng from Y12, 1½ hours, frequent services

Shànghǎi South Y169, from eight hours, frequent services

Shàngráo from Y9, 75 minutes, frequent services

Two express trains also run to/from Shànghǎi South (soft seat Y250, 4½ hours) via Hángzhōu (Y180, three hours).

Services from the bus station (客运站; kèyùn zhàn) are less practical:

Nánchāng Y50, two hours, regular services

Shàngráo Y34, two hours, regular services

Wùyuán Y37, three hours, four daily

Sānqīng Shān 三清山

☎0793

Imagine a hiking trail built into sheer rock face, looking out onto a forest of fantastical granite spires and a gorgeous canopy sprinkled with white rhododendron blooms. This is one of the many walks you can do at **Sānqīng Shān** (www.sanqingshan.com.cn; admission Y150), one of the most underrated national parks in eastern China. It's underrated not just because of the unique scenery, but also because it's relatively unknown and less crowded than other Chinese mountains.

Unlike its more famous neighbour to the north, Huángshān, Sānqīng Shān has a spiritual legacy and has been a place of retreat for Taoist adepts for centuries. The name Sānqīng means 'The Three Pure Ones', in reference to the three main peaks, which are believed to resemble Taoism's three most important deities. Views are spectacular in any season, reaching a climax when the rhododendrons start to bloom in late May.

There are enough trails that you could easily spend two days up here, though a strenuous day hike (roughly 13km) is also doable. There are two main access points: the southern route (南部; *nán bù*) and the eastern route (东部; *dōng bù*). Yùjīng Peak is the highest point in the area, with an altitude of 1820m.

Sights & Activities

Nánqīng Garden HIKING TRAIL
(南清苑; Nánqīng Yuàn) The main summit area is known as the Nánqīng Garden, a looping trail that wends beneath strange pinnacles and connects the southern and eastern routes.

West Coast Trail HIKING TRAIL
(西海岸; Xī Hǎi'àn) From the Nánqīng Garden loop you can take the spectacularly exposed West Coast Trail, which was built into the cliff face at an average altitude of 1600m. This trail eventually leads to the secluded **Taoist Sānqīng Temple** (三清宫; Sānqīng Gōng), established in the Ming dynasty. It's one of the few Taoist temples in Jiāngxī to have survived the Cultural Revolution.

Sunshine Coast Trail HIKING TRAIL
(阳光岸; Yángguāng Àn) Returning from the temple, the Sunshine Coast Trail winds through a forest of ancient rhododendrons, sweet chestnut, bamboo, magnolia and pine, and even features a glass-floored observation platform. There are lots of steps here; make sure you take it on the way back from the temple.

Sleeping

You can sleep in three areas: on the mountain, at the foot of the mountain (south or east) or in the town of Yùshān. Hotels here provide you with a roof over your head, not luxury. Prices rise on weekends.

YÙSHĀN

Guófù Bīnguǎn HOTEL $
(国富宾馆; Guófù Bīnguǎn; ☎255 5909; Renmin Lu, Xishangyuan; 人民路西商苑1区外; tw Y60; ❄) Simple rooms and a few gods and goddesses behind reception to welcome travellers. A good 10-minute walk from the bus station.

Péngfā Hotel HOTEL $$
(蓬发宾馆; Péngfā Bīnguǎn; ☎220 6666; Xiufeng Lu; 秀峰路; tw from Y120; ❄@) Dependable rooms. It's located around the corner from the Yùshān bus station.

AT THE TRAILHEADS

Holiday Hotel HOTEL $$$
(假日酒店; Jiàrì Jiǔdiàn; ☎218 1186; tw from Y680, discounts from 72%) The nicest hotel at the southern trailhead, often offering incredible discounts.

Shuāngxī Hotel HOTEL $$
(双溪寒舍; Shuāngxī Hánshè; ☎218 0788; tw from Y100) Cheap rooms. It's at the southern trailhead.

ON THE SUMMIT

Tents CAMPING $$
(帐篷; zhàngpeng; tents Y120) You can rent a tent and blankets from the Sānqīng Temple caretakers. If you have your own equipment you can also set it up here. It's a minimum 3km walk from the southern chairlift.

Nǚshén Hotel HOTEL $$$
(女神酒店; Nǚshén Jiǔdiàn; ☎218 9300; discounted tw from Y400) One of two hotels at the summit; located at the top of the eastern chairlift.

Information

Bank of China (Zhōngguó Yínháng; 101 Renmin Dadao; 人民大道101号) In Yùshān.

Sānqīng Shān Tourist Office (三清山旅游集散中心; Sānqīng Shān Lǚyóu Jísàn Zhōngxīn;

⏲8am-5pm) Small desk located in the bus station. Sells so-so maps and can help with hotel bookings. No English.

Getting There & Away

Sānqīng Shān is accessed via the town of Yùshān (玉山), accessible by both bus and train. If you can't get to Yùshān directly, go to the nearby city of Shàngráo (上饶) instead and then take a connecting train or bus.

Bus

Yùshān bus station (汽车站; *qìchēzhàn*) connections:

Hángzhōu Y80, four hours, four daily

Nánchāng Y70, three hours, two daily

Shàngráo Y10, one hour, frequent

Wùyuán Y40, 2½ hours, two daily

Train

Yùshān is on the Shànghǎi–Nánchāng line. A taxi to the train station (火车站; *huǒchēzhàn*) costs Y10. Destinations from Sānqīng Shān:

Hángzhōu from Y25, four hours, nine daily

Nánchāng from Y22, four hours, six daily

Shànghǎi South Y130, seven hours, six daily

Shàngráo from Y3.50, 20 minutes, frequent services

Yīngtán from Y12, two hours, frequent services

Getting Around

Minibuses (Y15, 80 minutes, 6am to 5.20pm) run from the Yùshān bus station to the start of both the eastern route (东部) and southern route (南部) – make sure you specify your destination. A **chairlift** (索道; up/return Y70/125) leaves from both places. Otherwise, the porter's trail – a sweaty 90-minute walk (2.5km) that snakes under the chairlift – ascends the southern route.

Wùyuán 婺源

☎0793 / POP 81,200

The countryside around Wùyuán is home to some of southeastern China's most immaculate views. Parcelled away in this hilly pocket is a scattered cluster of picturesque Huīzhōu villages, where old China remains preserved in enticing panoramas of ancient bridges, glittering rivers and stone-flagged alleyways.

Despite lending its name to the entire area, Wùyuán itself – also called Zīyángzhèn (紫阳镇) – is a far-from-graceful town and best avoided. The **museum** (博物馆; bówùguǎn; Wengong Beilu; admission free; ⏲8.30am-noon & 2.30-5pm), 1km north of town, is worth a look if you have time to kill, but most travellers will need no excuses before immersing themselves in the region's tantalising bucolic charms way out beyond the shabby suburbs.

Maps in English are nonexistent, but if you need to find your way around town, look for Wengong Lu (文公路), the main north–south drag.

Tours

Hire an English-speaking guide (Y200 per day) and driver at the **CITS office** (中国国际旅行社; Zhōngguó Guójì Lǚxíngshè; ☎0798 862 9999) in nearby Jǐngdézhèn.

Sleeping

It's preferable to stay in one of the villages, but if you arrive in the middle of the night there are several hotels along Wengong Lu.

Yíngdū Bīnguǎn HOTEL $
(迎都宾馆; ☎734 8620; 13 Wengong Nanlu; 文公南路13号; s & tw Y80-100; ❄@) Centrally located hotel in reasonable condition. More expensive rooms come with a computer.

Tiānmǎ Hotel HOTEL $$
(天马大酒店; Tiānmǎ Dàjiǔdiàn; ☎736 7123; www.wytm.cn; 119 Wengong Beilu; 文公北路119号; d Y160-180; ❄📶) This smart hotel is the most comfortable option in the area; prices rise by about Y100 during the high season (March, April and major holidays).

Information

Bank of China (中国银行; Zhōngguó Yínháng; 1 Dongxi Lu) The 24-hour ATM accepts international cards.

China Post (邮局; Zhōngguó Yóuzhèng; cnr Tianyou Donglu & Lianxi Lu)

People's Hospital (人民医院; Rénmín Yīyuàn; Wengong Nanlu)

Public Security Bureau (PSB; 公安局; Gōng'ānjú; 2 Huancheng Beilu; ⏲8-11.30am & 2.30-5.30pm)

Qǐháng Wǎngbā (启航网吧; Wengong Nanlu; per hr Y3; ⏲24hr) Internet cafe; located next to the People's Hospital.

Getting There & Away

The Wùyuán **main bus station** (婺源汽车站; Wùyuán qìchēzhàn) is located west of town; a motorbike or taxi here should cost you Y5. Note that buses that arrive at night (such as the Shànghǎi one) will drop you off at the north end of town, not at the station.

Jiǔjiāng Y83, three hours, two daily

Hángzhōu Y123, 3½ hours, two daily
Nánchāng Y103, four hours, four daily
Shànghǎi South Y183, six hours, two daily
Shàngráo Y54, 3½ hours, 6am to 4.30pm
Túnxī Y40, 2½ hours, two daily
Yùshān (Sānqīng Shān) Y42, 2½ hours, two daily

Around Wùyuán

Wùyuán has become a massively popular destination with domestic tourists in the past few years, but as it's such a large area, it's easy enough to escape the crowds with a little bit of determination.

There are two main ticketing options: either a **five-day pass** (Y180), which grants you admission to 12 sights, or the **single tickets** at each village (Y60 each). The pass covers a number of villages (only the most interesting are listed here), including Sīxī/Yáncūn, Little Lǐkēng (Xiǎo Lǐkēng) and Xiǎoqǐ, plus various other sights such as the Rainbow Bridge (Qīnghuá). Big Lǐkēng (Dà Lǐkēng) has a separate admission fee. The lesser-known outer villages – including Guānkēng, Lǐngjiǎo, Qìngyuán and Chángxī – were free at the time of writing. They are best visited in two days.

Getting Around

Transport throughout the region can be frustrating, unless you plan on spending the night, as villages are spaced apart and are not always linked by reliable bus connections. Hiring a motorbike (摩的; *módī*) in either Wùyuán or Qīnghuá is easier than getting a bus. A full day (Y120, plus lunch for your driver) will give you enough time to get to four or five villages. Otherwise, sample one-way fares for individual trips by motorbike (from Wùyuán) include: Qīnghuá (Y20), Little Lǐkēng (Y15) and various outer villages (Y60). From Qīnghuá to Big Lǐkēng is Y30, and Xiǎoqǐ to Little Lǐkēng Y20. If you're in a group, it's worth negotiating with taxi and minivan drivers. They generally start out asking around Y300 for a full day, but they may go as low as Y200 when business is slow.

If you take the bus, be aware there are three possible departure points, depending on where you want to go. From the main bus station you can get to the northern villages:

Big Lǐkēng Y13, one hour, two daily
Guānkēng Y20, 50 minutes, two daily
Lǐngjiǎo Y16, two hours, two daily
Qīnghuá Y7, 30 minutes, 6.30am to 5.30pm, frequent services

From in front of Wùyuán's old north bus station (老北站; *lǎo běizhàn*), at the northern end of Wengong Beilu, frequent buses run to Qīnghuá and various eastern villages:

Little Lǐkēng Y5, 20 minutes, 6.40am to 4.20pm, frequent services
Qīnghuá Y7, 30 minutes, 6.30am to 5.30pm, frequent services
Xiǎoqǐ Y12, one hour, 6.40am to 4.20pm, frequent services

To catch transport to Qìngyuán, you need to go to the fruit market (水果市场; *shuǐguǒ shìchǎng*) and ask around – it should cost Y30. Before you actually go to any of these places, make sure to confirm first, as departure points change.

EASTERN VILLAGES

LITTLE LǏKĒNG 李坑

The most picturesque village in the area, Little Lǐkēng (known as Xiǎo Lǐkēng) enjoys a stupendous riverside setting, hung with lanterns, threaded by tight alleys and tightly bound together by quaint bridges. Come night-time, Little Lǐkēng is even more serene, its riverside lanes glowing softly under red lanterns and old-fashioned street lamps

Little Lǐkēng's highly photogenic focal point hinges on the confluence of its two streams, traversed by the bump of the 300-year-old **Tōngjì Bridge** (通济桥; Tōngjì Qiáo) and signposted by the **Shēnmíng Pavilion** (申明亭; Shēnmíng Tíng), one of the village's signature sights, its wooden benches polished smooth with age.

Among the *báicài* (Chinese cabbage) draped from bamboo poles and chunks of cured meat hanging out in the air from crumbling, mildewed buildings, notable structures include the **Patina House** (铜录坊; Tónglù Fáng), erected during Qing times by a copper merchant, the rebuilt **old stage** (古戏台; *gǔxìtái*), where Chinese opera and performances are still held during festivals, and spirit walls erected on the riverbank to shield residents from the sound of cascading water.

Cross one of the bridges just beyond the old stage and take the stone-flagged path up the hill, past an old camphor tree and terraced fields, through bamboo and firs, and down to the river and the **Li Zhicheng Residence** (李知诚故居; Lǐ Zhīchéng Gùjū), the residence of a military scholar from the Southern Song. Walk in any direction and you will hit the countryside.

Around Wùyuán

Accommodation is easy to find; try the teahouses **Cháxiāng Kèlóu** (茶香客楼; ☎0793-737 0291; d Y80; ❄@📶) at the Tōngjì Bridge (bring a towel) or **Guāngmíng Chálóu** (光明茶楼; ☎0793-737 0999; d Y60; ❄📶🍴), overlooking the river further up from the Shénmíng Pavilion.

Buses drop you off at the village turn-off, from where it's a five-minute walk to the ticket office.

XIǍOQǏ 晓起

About 36km from Wùyuán, Xiǎoqǐ dates back to 787. There are actually two villages here: the tacky and overcrowded lower Xiǎoqǐ (下晓起) and the more pleasant upper Xiǎoqǐ (上晓起), where you'll find a fascinating old **tea factory** (传统生态茶作仿; *chuántǒng shēngtài chá zuòfáng*).

Accommodation is plentiful. In lower Xiǎoqǐ try the **Jìxùtáng Hotel** (继序堂饭店; Jìxùtáng Fàndiàn; ☎0793-729 7014; d Y60; ❄) in an old Qing-dynasty building by the river, equipped with a downstairs restaurant. In upper Xiǎoqǐ, stay with a local family for around Y20.

QÌNGYUÁN 庆源

If you've had enough of the jostling tour groups, the isolated village of Qìngyuán is a good place to escape to. It doesn't have the architectural beauty of the other villages in the Huīzhōu area; it's quite poor and it looks like it always has been. But unlike most of the surrounding villages, it is entirely undeveloped and has never been repackaged for the tour bus crowd. Infinitely more peaceful, a trip here will nonetheless help you to appreciate the benefits of organised tourism – namely the economic ones for local villagers – in China. A popular destination for independent Chinese travellers, you can easily find accommodation here (homestay per person Y20); otherwise hire a driver and visit as a day trip.

NORTHERN VILLAGES

QĪNGHUÁ 清华

Qīnghuá is the largest and least-captivating place in Wùyuán, but because of its central location, it can make a good base. The main sight is the 800-year-old Southern Song-dynasty **Rainbow Bridge** (彩虹桥; Cǎihóng Qiáo), with its gorgeous riverine views, but also wander along the old street **Qinghua Laojie** (清华老街), a dilapidated portrait of time-worn stone architecture with carved wood shopfronts, lintels, decorative architraves and old folk stripping bamboo. The hospitable **Lǎojiē Kèzhàn** (老街客栈; ☎0793-724 2359; 355 Qinghua Laojie; 清华老街355号; s/d Y35/50, ❄) has basic, clean rooms.

It's possible to hire motorbike taxis here; buses depart for Sīkǒu (Y3, 10 minutes), Wùyuán (Y6, 30 minutes) and Jǐngdézhēn (Y22, two hours, two daily), among other places.

SĪXĪ & YÁNCŪN 思溪、延村

The village of Sīxī is a delightful little place favoured by film crews, with the prow-shaped, covered wooden **Tōngjì Bridge** (通济桥; Tōngjì Qiáo) at its entrance, dating back to the 15th century and adorned with a large *bāguà* (eight trigrams) symbol. Follow the self-guided tour past the numerous Qing residences, many of which are open to the public, and make sure not to miss the large **Jìngxù Hall** (敬序堂; Jìngxù Táng)

WALKING WÙYUÁN

Many of Wùyuán's villages are linked by timeworn **postal roads** (驿道; *yìdào*) that today provide hikers with the perfect excuse to explore the area's gorgeous backcountry: imagine wild azalea, wisteria and iris blooms dotting steep hills cut by cascading streams, and you're off to the right start. You'll have to find a villager willing to guide you and be forewarned that it can be quite difficult – but not impossible – to arrange without Chinese-language skills. For a half-/full-day hike, figure on spending about Y60/120, including meal(s) for your guide, and Y20 for accommodation (if you strand him). Note: do not hike from one village to another without a guide; you will get lost.

You can start by asking around for a guide in the village you're staying in. (我要步行去X. 这里有没有一个人可以带我去?/*Wǒ yào bùxíng qù X. Zhèlǐ yǒu méiyǒu yī gè rén kěyǐ dài wǒ qù?*/I want to hike to X. Can someone here guide me?) Otherwise, in Big Lǐkēng look for **Yu Xiaobin** (余小宾; ☎139 7937 3570), who has excellent knowledge of the surrounding paths and can take you (when available) to either Qīnghuá, Dàzhāng Shān (大鄣山; 13km) or Hóngguān (虹关; 15km). He speaks no English.

Recommended hikes:

» **Big Lǐkēng to Qīnghuá** (理坑-清华; 15km, minimum 4½ hours) This walk wends through typical countryside and over a low pass before descending into a secluded river valley.

» **Guānkēng to Lǐngjiǎo** (官坑-岭脚; 8km, minimum three hours) A straightforward hike over a high ridge, from one remote village to another. You'll need at least two days. A 9am bus leaves Wùyuán for Guānkēng (Y20, two hours). That night you can arrange a simple homestay (住农家; *zhù nóngjiā;* about Y20) in either Lǐngjiǎo or Hóngguān, 30 minutes' walk down the road. Buses leave the next morning for Wùyuán (Y13, two hours).

If all this sounds too complicated for your tastes, remember that you can simply walk into the tea terraces or rapeseed fields outside any of the villages for a much shorter and equally beautiful day hike.

upstream. A 15-minute walk downstream brings you to Yáncūn, Sīxī's more homely sibling. To get here, take any Wùyuán-Qīnghuá bus (Y3) and get off at Sīkǒu (思口). Motorbikes (if you can find one) will take you the rest of the way for Y5.

BIG LǏKĒNG 理坑

This riverside hamlet of around 300 homesteads is popularly called **Dà Lǐkēng** (admission Y60), not to be confused with Little Lǐkēng to the east. Perhaps the most splendid aspect of a visit here is traversing the hilly countryside from Qīnghuá, a beautiful landscape of fields and valleys cut by shimmering streams.

Although the village itself has been subjected to some arguably dodgy redevelopment – it's a private enterprise that exists outside of the official Wùyuán network – it is a good base for hiking trips. As in Qīnghuá, several local households have opened their doors to travellers, with simple beds available from around Y20 per night.

Motorbikes can take you here from Qīnghuá for as little as Y30. Alternatively, take a bus here (Y13, one hour, twice daily) from the main bus station in Wùyuán.

Lúshān 庐山

☎0792

One of the great early cultural centres of Chinese civilisation, the dramatic fog-enshrouded cliffs of **Lúshān** (admission Y180) attracted large numbers of monastics and thinkers for some 1500 years. The monk Hui Yuan, one of the first Chinese teachers to emphasise the importance of meditation, founded Pure Land Buddhism here in the 4th century AD. His contemporary and acquaintance, Tao Yuanming, who lived at the foot of the mountain, is generally regarded as China's first landscape poet.

Numerous other writers resided on Lúshān's slopes in the centuries that followed – notably Bai Juyi, Zhu Xi and Su Dongpo – but unfortunately the Taiping

Rebellion destroyed almost everything of note in the mid-19th century. Western colonialists and missionaries followed in the rebels' wake and built the retreat town of Gŭlĭng (Kuling; altitude 1167m), where Nobel Prize–winner Pearl S Buck spent her childhood summers and Mervyn Peake (author of the *Gormenghast* novels) was born.

Following the CCP's rise to power, the European-style villas of Gŭlĭng were subsequently transformed into an infamous political conference centre, which, together with the stunning scenery, is what most visitors today come to see.

Sights & Activities

The main attraction here is exploring the mountain roads and paths on your own – generally, any place you have to walk to will be significantly less crowded. The **Xīnhuá Bookshop** (新华书店; Xīnhuá Shūdiàn; 11 Guling Zhengjie) sells detailed maps showing roads and walking paths.

Měilú Villa HISTORIC RESIDENCE
(美庐别墅; Měilú Biéshù; 180 Hedong Lu; admission Y25; ⌚8am-6pm) Built by Chiang Kaishek in the 1930s and named after his wife, Song Meiling.

Zhōu Ēnlái Residence HISTORIC RESIDENCE
(周恩来纪念室; Zhōu Ēnlái Jìniàn Shì; admission incl with Měilú Villa) The former premier's residence stands defiantly across the stream from the Měilú Villa.

Site of the Lúshān Conference MUSEUM
(庐山会议旧址; Lúshān Huìyì Jiùzhǐ; 504 Hexi Lu; admission Y50; ⌚8am-5pm) Also called the People's Hall, this was the venue for the CCP's historic confabs in 1959 and 1970.

FREE **Lúshān Museum** MUSEUM
(庐山博物馆; Lúshān Bówùguǎn; 1 Lulin Lu; ⌚8am-5.30pm) Mao's former residence, littered with paraphernalia detailing the Lúshān communist connection.

One excellent destination for hikers is **Wŭ Lăo Fēng** (五老峰; Five Old Men Peak; 1358m). A bit less remote but a favourite with photographers is the **Three Step Waterfall** (三叠泉; Sāndié Quán).

At Lúshān's northwestern rim, the land falls away abruptly to spectacular views across Jiāngxī's densely settled plains. A long walking track south (about one hour from Gŭlĭng) around these precipitous slopes leads to **Dragon Head Cliff** (龙首崖; Lóngshǒu Yá), a natural rock platform tilted above an eye-popping vertical drop.

> **JĬNGDÉZHÈN: CHINA'S CHINA**
>
> Jĭngdézhèn (景德镇) is a name known to many: it's where China's much-coveted porcelain is fired up, although the imperial kilns that manufactured ceramics for the occupants of the Forbidden City were long ago extinguished. With more china here than the rest of China put together, travellers can rapidly feel glazed: Jĭngdézhèn is hardly an oil painting and is strictly for those in the business. If you're a porcelain buff, visit Shànghǎi instead: the collection at the Shànghǎi Museum is China's best, and shops such as Spin and Yú sell standout pieces in all styles.

Lúshān's old places of worship include the **Protestant Church** (基督教堂; Jīdūjiào Táng; 23 Hexi Lu) and **Catholic Church** (天主教堂;Tiānzhǔjiào Táng; 12 Xiangshan Lu).

Sleeping & Eating

July and August is the Lúshān peak season, and if you are coming then – particularly on a weekend – you should book in advance. Outside of this time period though, it's quite possible to just show up and find a room.

Lúshān Yúntiān Villa HOTEL $$
(庐山云天别墅; Lúshān Yúntiān Biéshù; ☎829 3555; Guling Zhengjie; 牯岭正街; d/tr Y180/260, in Jul & Aug Y300/400; ❄) A move away from Lúshān's typically musty and worn lodging options, this place offers old villa atmosphere with roomy, fresh accommodation and a crisp finish.

Jīnyì Hotel HOTEL $
(金艺宾馆; Jīnyì Bīnguǎn; ☎135 079 2504; 18 Guling Zhengjie; 牯岭正街18号; d Y60-120, in Jul & Aug Y100-200) Although you probably couldn't convince your mother to stay here, it's still a perfectly acceptable budget hotel with 24-hour hot water and inviting white sheets. No towels.

Jùdĭngxuān CHINESE $
(聚鼎轩; 39 Guling Zhengjie; 牯岭正街39号; dishes Y5-36) An open kitchen and juice bar make this place stand out from the 50-odd basic eateries lining Guling Zhengjie.

WORTH A TRIP

LÓNGNÁN

In the deep south of Jiāngxī lies the rarely visited Hakka country, a region of lush hills peppered with fortified villages, unusually built in rectangular shapes, unlike the mostly circular *tŭlóu* (roundhouse) of Fújiàn. Although there are estimates of some 370 such dwellings in Lóngnán (龙南) County, travellers can safely narrow down the choices to two main areas, both of which can be visited from the busy town of Lóngnán.

Built by a lumber merchant in the early 19th century, **Guānxī New Fort** (关西新围; Guānxī Xīn Wéi; admission Y10; ⊙8am-5pm) is the largest and most ornate fortified village in the county. Nearby is the **Hakka Wine Castle** (客家酒堡; Kèjiā Jiŭbăo; admission Y15), built at the same time by a rich wine producer. Bus 4 from Binjiang Sq in Lóngnán runs to Guānxī (Y5, 50 minutes, hourly), passing by the Hakka Wine Castle (Y3).

A number of crumbling old fortified villages lie in the vicinity of Yángcūn town (杨村), including the 350-year-old **Yànyì Wéi** (燕翼围; admission Y10), the tallest such residence in the county (four storeys). However, more striking is nearby **Wŭdāng Shān** (武当山; admission Y15; ⊙8am-6pm), a group of weathered sandstone domes poking above subtropical forest (not to be confused with Húběi's Wŭdāng Shān). To get to Yángcūn, take a bus (Y8.50, 1½ hours, frequent) from 99 Longding Dadao (龙鼎大道99号) in Lóngnán. Buses in both directions pass Wŭdāng Shān on the way; drivers will let you off at the entrance.

Trains to Lóngnán run from Nánchāng (Y143, 7½ hours) and Guăngzhōu (Y69, 5½ hours); otherwise take a bus from Nánchāng to Gànzhōu (Y120, 4½ hours), where you can transfer to a Lóngnán-bound bus (Y43, two hours). Five daily buses run to Guăngzhōu (Y90, five hours). Bus 1 runs from the train station past the bus station to the centre of town.

In Lóngnán, you can stay at the **Xīnxìng Bīnguăn** (新兴宾馆; ☎353 6288; Binjiang Sq; 滨江广场; tw Y80-120; ❄@).

Information

Bank of China (中国银行; Zhōngguó Yínháng; 13 Hemian Jie) Change money or use the 24-hour ATM here.

Internet cafe (网吧; Wăngbā; Guling Zhengjie; per hr Y3; ⊙8am-midnight) Located obliquely opposite the PSB at the bottom of the steps (ask for directions).

Public Security Bureau (PSB; 公安局; Gōng'ānjú; 20 Guling Zhengjie)

Getting There & Around

Travellers generally arrive in Lúshān from either Nánchāng or Jiŭjiāng. In July and August hourly buses leave for Nánchāng (Y50, 2½ hours, 7.50am to 5.30pm) from the bus station on Hexi Lu. Only three daily buses make the trip in the low season (last bus 3.30pm).

Buses to Jiŭjiāng (Y12, one hour, 7.50am to 4.30pm) are more dependable, departing regularly from the small ticket office on Guling Jie. Other buses from this office:

Héféi Y120, four hours, three daily

Nánjīng Y165, seven hours, four daily

Shànghăi Y230, six hours, one daily (8pm)

Wŭhàn Y100, four hours, hourly

Wùyuán Y100, four hours, three daily

In summer it may be a good idea to book your return seat upon arrival, particularly for day trippers.

From Jiŭjiāng, buses leave hourly from 6.50am for Lúshān from the long-distance bus station (长途汽车站; *chángtú qìchē zhàn*), with other connections:

Nánchāng Y45, two hours, half-hourly

Nánjīng Y150, six hours, hourly

Shànghăi Y218, 10 hours, one daily

Wŭhàn Y80, three hours, hourly

Lúshān's myriad footpaths and bus-bound tour groups make explorations on foot the most enjoyable way to go. However, there is also a hop-on hop-off **shuttle service** (旅游观光车; *lǚyóu guānguāng chē*; 1-/3-day pass Y65/80) that goes to most sights and which can be convenient – the main drawback being that you won't escape the crowds. Buy the pass at the bus station that serves Nánchāng. Taxi service is of no use here as private vehicles are barred from entering most roads. Lúshān has several cable cars (return Y80).

Húnán

POPULATION: 64 MILLION

Includes »

Best Places to Eat

» Night market in Fènghuáng (p467)

» Huǒgōngdiàn (p454)

» Miáozú Fēngwèi Guǎn (p464)

Best Places to Stay

» Koolaa's Home (p466)

» Xiāngdiàn International Hotel (p461)

» Liú Sōngxiū Guest House (p469)

Why Go?

Communist Party cadres might wax lyrical about the sacred standing of Húnán (湖南) in the annals of Chinese history, as the birthplace of Mao Zedong, but it's the dramatic and fecund scenery of Húnán that is the real draw. Spreading east, west and south from the province's Yangzi River basin plain (and Chángshā) is an astonishing landscape of rough, isolated mountain ranges, forests, lush rice terraces, waterfalls and karst peaks.

Scattered amidst this natural bounty are welcoming minority villages, wind-and-rain bridges, Taoist temples and the ancient riverside towns of Fènghuáng and Hóngjiāng. In complete contrast, the capital Chángshā has some of the most vibrant nightlife outside Běijīng and Shànghǎi.

Alongside the combustible thought of firebrand Mao Zedong, Húnán's other potent export is its fiery food. *Xiāngcài* restaurants have eyes streaming and faces glowing across China, but the peppery cuisine is best sampled on its home turf. For the locals, spice truly is life.

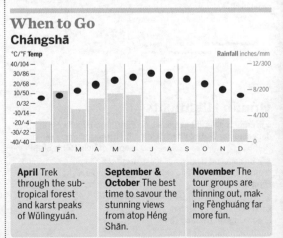

When to Go

Chángshā

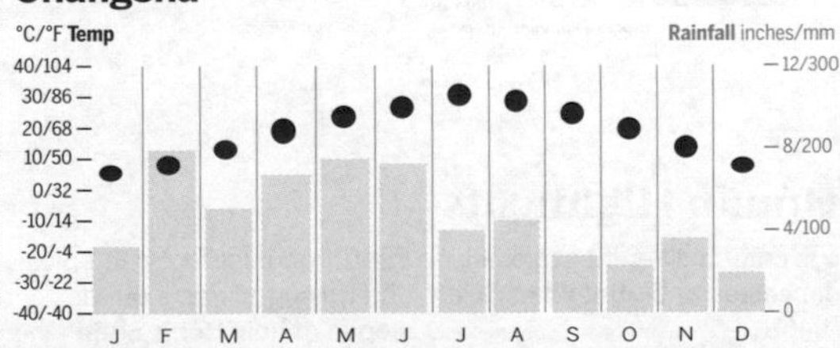

April Trek through the subtropical forest and karst peaks of Wǔlíngyuán.

September & October The best time to savour the stunning views from atop Héng Shān.

November The tour groups are thinning out, making Fènghuáng far more fun.

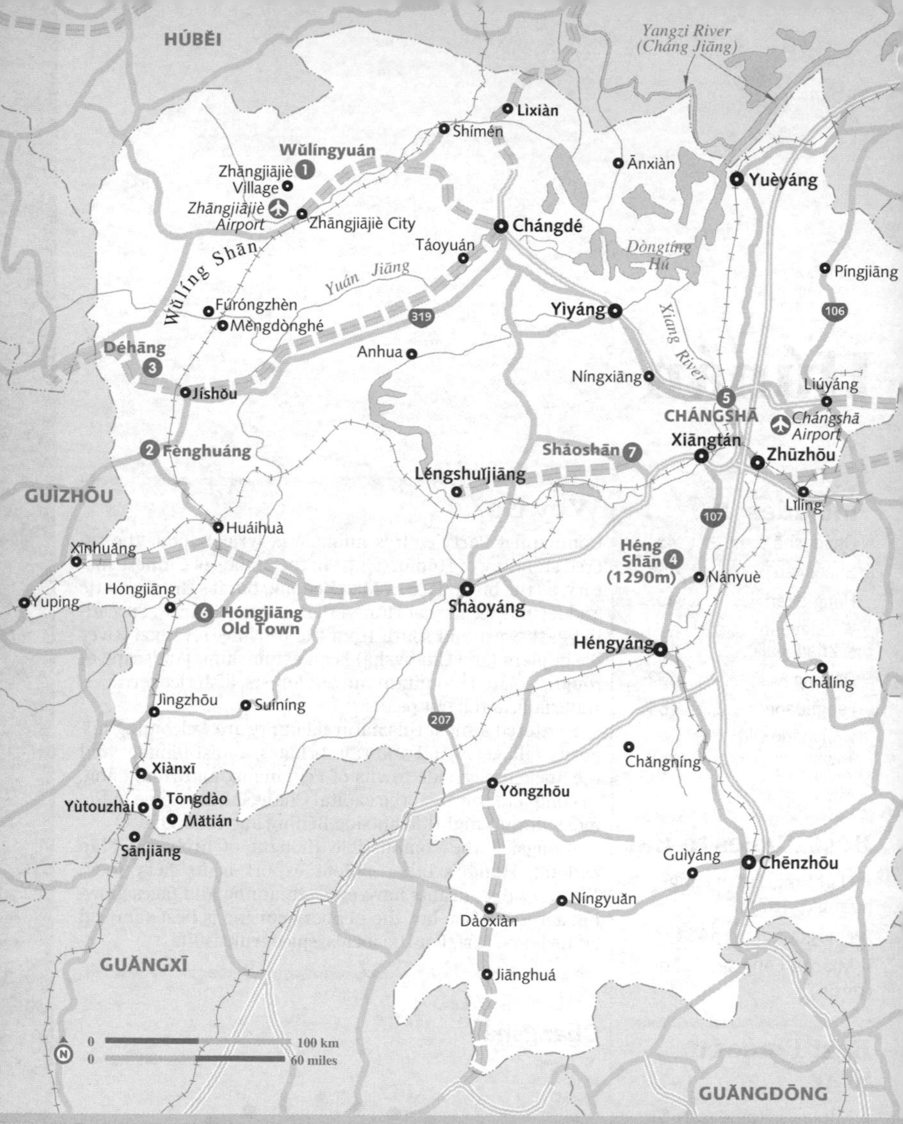

Húnán Highlights

1. Enter a different geological dimension at **Wǔlíngyuán** (p459)
2. Be seduced by the crumbling charm of ancient **Fènghuáng** (p464)
3. Hike into the extraordinary karst scenery surrounding the Miao village of **Déhāng** (p462)
4. Climb past Taoist temples and through forests on the slopes of holy **Héng Shān** (p457)
5. Spend a night on the tiles in Chángshā's happening **bars** and **clubs** (p454)
6. Explore the maze-like alleys and former opium shops of **Hóngjiāng Old Town** (p468)
7. Mingle with the masses paying homage to Mao in **Sháoshān** (p455)

History

Under the Ming and Qing dynasties, Húnán was one of the empire's granaries, and vast quantities of rice were transported to the depleted north. By the 19th century, land shortages and landlordism were causing widespread unrest among farmers and hill-dwelling minorities. This contributed to the Taiping Rebellion in 1856 and later ensured strong support for the Chinese Communist Party (CCP) in the 1920s.

Language

Hunanese *(xiāng)* is a Northern Mandarin dialect and has six to eight 'dialects' of its own. Gàn, another Northern Mandarin dialect, is spoken in the west and south. The border regions are home to a mosaic of local dialects and minority languages which defy family-group classification.

Getting There & Around

The airports at Chángshā, Zhāngjiājiè and Huáihuà are useful points of access for air passengers, opening up the east, west and northwest. All of Húnán's sights can be reached by either train or bus but, with new expressways tightening up travel times, it's normally quicker to travel by road.

PRICE INDICATORS

The following price indicators are used in this chapter:

Sleeping

$	less than Y150
$$	Y150 to Y550
$$$	more than Y550

Eating

$	less than Y50
$$	Y50 to Y100
$$$	more than Y100

Chángshā 长沙

0731 / POP 2.3 MILLION

Although British philosopher Bertrand Russell compared it to 'a mediaeval town' when passing through in the 1920s, virtually all of old Chángshā was destroyed by fire in 1938 during the Sino-Japanese War. Consequently, there's little to distinguish it visually from other second-tier Chinese cities. The upside is that it has more parks and less congested traffic than most places of its size. But Chángshā remains known mainly for its sights related to a certain Mr Mao and as the gateway to his rustic birthplace, Sháoshān.

Sights

FREE **Húnán Provincial Museum** MUSEUM
(湖南省博物馆; Húnán Shěng Bówùguǎn; 50 Dongfeng Lu; 9am-5pm Tue-Sun) Not to be missed, this first-rate museum has fascinating exhibits from the 2100-year-old Western Han tombs of Mǎwángduī, some 5km east of the city.

The items on show allow you to get a rare handle on Western Han aesthetics – check out the astonishing expressions on the faces of some of the wooden figurines. Also excavated are more than 700 pieces of lacquerware, Han silk textiles and ancient manuscripts on silk and bamboo wooden slips, including one of the earlier versions of the Zhōuyì (Yìjīng, also called I Ching), written in formalised Han clerical script.

But the highlight is the body of the Marquess of Dai, extracted from her magnificent multilayered lacquered coffin after 2100 years. Due to the air-tight seal and 80L of preserving fluid, her body is marvellously well pickled.

A set number of visitors are allowed in each day and tickets are given out on a first come, first served basis, so it's best to get here early in the morning. Buses 112, 113 and 136 all run here from the train station.

FREE **Chángshā City Museum** MUSEUM
(市博物馆; Shì Bówùguǎn; 480 Bayi Lu; 9am-4.30pm Tue-Sun) A colossal 1968 statue of Mao – cast out of an aluminium-magnesium alloy in Hēilóngjiāng – affably greets you at the entrance to the museum's pleasant grounds. Compare his carriage – right arm raised aloft, heralding a new dawn – with that of his more demure statue erected in Sháoshān in 1993, when the reform drive had long kicked in and Mao was a demigod no more.

The statue is the first clue that this hammer and sickle–decorated museum is essentially a shrine to Chángshā's most famous adopted son, despite the paintings, ceramics and jade on display here. Check out the huge portrait of the young Mao, with shafts of light emanating from his head, which hangs over the entrance.

Also in the museum grounds is the former site of the **Húnán CCP Committee**

Chángshā

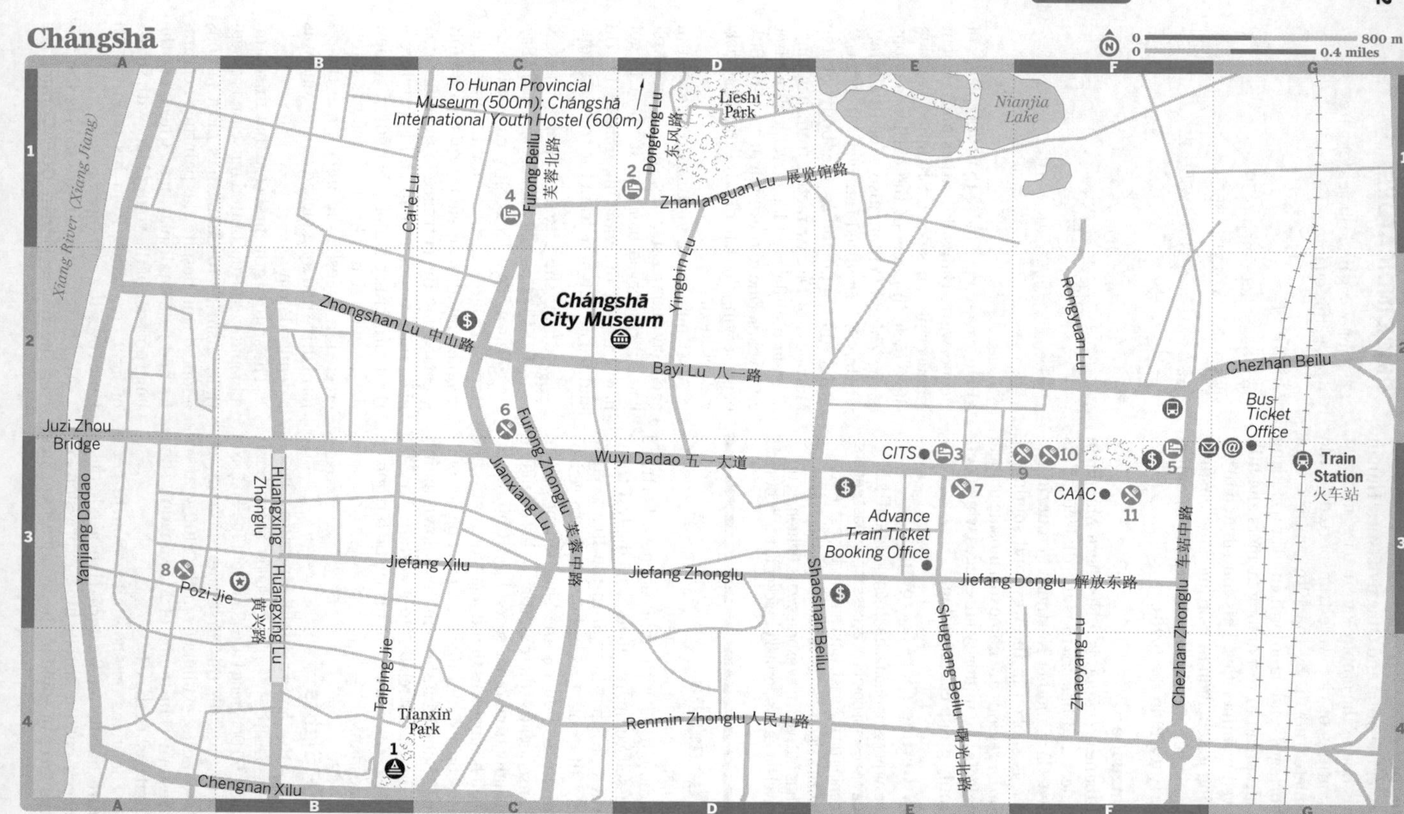

0 800 m
0 0.4 miles
To Hunan Provincial Museum (500m); Chángshā International Youth Hostel (600m)
Lieshi Park
Niànjia Lake
Xiang River (Xiang Jiang)
Furong Beilu 芙蓉北路
Dongfeng Lu 东风路
Zhanlanguan Lu 展览馆路
Cai'e Lu
Yingbin Lu
Chángshā City Museum
Zhongshan Lu 中山路
Bayi Lu 八一路
Rongyuan Lu
Chezhan Beilu
Bus Ticket Office
Train Station 火车站
Juzi Zhou Bridge
Wuyi Dadao 五一大道
CITS
CAAC
Furong Zhonglu 芙蓉中路
Jianxiang Lu
Huangxing Zhonglu
Huangxing Lu 黄兴路
Yanjiang Dadao
Jiefang Xilu
Jiefang Zhonglu
Jiefang Donglu 解放东路
Advance Train Ticket Booking Office
Shaoshan Beilu
Shuguang Beilu 曙光北路
Zhaoyang Lu
Chezhan Zhonglu 车站中路
Pozi Jie
Taiping Jie
Tianxin Park
Renmin Zhonglu 人民中路
Chengnan Xilu

Chángshā

Top Sights

Sights

Sleeping

Eating

(Zhōng Gòng Xiāngqū Wěiyuánhuì Jiùzhǐ; admission free; ⏲9am-4.30pm Tue-Sun), where Mao lived from 1921 to 1923 with his first wife while secretly running the local CCP. The spartan family living quarters, along with a few photos and historical items, are on view.

Húnán No 1 Teachers' Training School HISTORIC SITE
(第一师范学校; Dìyī Shīfàn Xuéxiào; 324 Shuyuan Lu; admission Y15; ⏲8.30am-5.30pm) Mao attended classes here between 1913 and 1918; he returned to teach Chinese from 1920 to 1922. It's still a working college and if you're lucky a student keen to practise their English will show you around the place, including Mao's dormitory, his old classrooms, halls where he held some of his first political meetings and an open-air well where he enjoyed taking cold baths. Otherwise, there are a few English captions. Take bus 1 from the train station.

Tiānxīn Gé HISTORIC SITE
(天心阁; Heart of Heaven Pavilion; park admission free, pavilion Y16; ⏲7.30am-10pm, pavilion 7.30am-6pm) The only remaining part of the old city walls is a popular place to escape the summer heat. It's off Chengnan Xilu. Catch bus 212 from the train station.

Sleeping

Chángshā is short on decent budget options, but there are basic places around the train station.

Chángshā International Youth Hostel YOUTH HOSTEL $
(长沙国际青年旅舍; Chángshā Guójì Qīngnián Lǚshè; ☎8299 0202; www.hnhostel.com; 61 Gongshang Lane, Dongfeng Lu; 东风路下大陇工商巷61号; dm Y40-45, s/d/tr Y88/108/128; ⊖❄@) Tucked away down a quiet, tree-lined street, this is the only hostel in town. The dorms are clean and airy and the doubles spacious; some of the singles have squat toilets. There's a nice garden area, helpful staff and the only downside is that there's an extra Y20 a night charge for air-con. Take bus 136 from the train station and get off at the Xiadalong stop on Dongfeng Lu. Look for the YHA sign to guide you here.

Lotus Huátiān Hotel HOTEL $$
(芙蓉华天大酒店; Fúróng Huátiān Dàjiǔdiàn; ☎8440 1888; fax 8440 1889; 176 Wuyi Dadao; 五一大道176号; d Y518-798, discounts of 25%; ❄@) The concrete-and-glass exterior is unprepossessing, but inside this is a well-run and well-maintained hotel with affable staff. The discounts on offer make it a very comfortable midrange choice, especially if you go for the pricier doubles, which come with computers and nice showers.

Sheraton Chángshā HOTEL $$$
(喜来登; Xǐláidēng; ☎8488 8888; www.starwoodhotels.com; Yunda International Plaza, 478 Furong Zhonglu; 芙蓉中路一段478号运达国际广场; d Y1088; ⊖❄@≋) The finest hotel in Chángshā offers international levels of comfort and top-notch service. The beds are great and there's a spa, gym and pool, as well as a choice of Cantonese, Hunan and Western restaurants. Rates change daily, so you might catch a deal in slack periods.

Jǐnjiāng Inn HOTEL $$
(锦江之星宾馆; Jǐnjiāng Zhīxīng Bīnguǎn; ☎8828 1888; www.haotian1019@163.com; 1 Dongfeng Lu; 东风路1号; d/tw Y169/189; ❄@) Part of a chain that covers most of China, the Jǐnjiāng is generic, but in a good way: bright rooms with modern bathrooms and internet access. This one is near to the centre of town, while leafy Lièshì Park is very close.

Tàichéng Hotel HOTEL $
(泰成大酒店; Tàichéng Dàjiǔdiàn; ☎8217 9999; 309 Chezhan Zhonglu; 车站中路309号; s & d Y238-288, tr Y358, discounts of 50%; ❄@) A standard Chinese cheapie popular with domestic tour groups. The tiny bathrooms here have seen better days, but the rooms

themselves are clean and the location, opposite the train station, is very handy. The more expensive rooms have ADSL access.

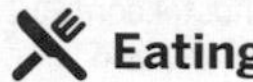

Eating

Zhaoyang Lu and the lanes off Huangxing Zhonglu are good places for street food. **Carrefour** (家乐福; Jiālèfú; Wuyi Dadao; ⏲8am-10pm) is a lifesaver for those in search of Western eats.

TOP CHOICE **Huǒgōngdiàn** HUNAN $$
(火宫殿; ☎8581 4228; 78 Pozi Jie; dim-sum dishes from Y5; ⏲6am-2am) There's a great buzz at this landmark Chángshā restaurant – Mao was a fan of its stinky *dòufu* (tofu). A huge selection of steaming dim sum–style dishes are wheeled around by ladies who like to tempt foreigners into trying such delights as chicken feet. Make sure to order the excellent *máoshì hóngshāoròu* (毛氏红烧肉; Mao-style braised pork; Y48) off the menu. There's a less atmospheric branch near the train station at 93 Wuyi Dadao (call (☎8412 0580).

Sun River Dumpling Restaurant DUMPLINGS $
(松花江饺子馆; Sōnghuājiāng Jiǎoziguǎn; ☎8446 1492; 102 Wuyi Dadao; dumplings from Y3; ⏲9am-1.20am) Need a break from chewing chillis? If so, then try this big, bustling place that specialises in the far less fiery cuisine of northern China. Dumplings *(jiǎozi)* are the house speciality, and there are seemingly endless varieties, including vegie options, on offer. The picture menu has many other dishes to choose from too.

Xīnhuá Lóu HUNAN $
(新华楼; ☎8415 2057; 35 Wuyi Dadao; dishes Y4-25; ⏲6.30am-1.30am) This long-time favourite is a can't-miss option for local dishes; harried middle-aged ladies wheel around trolleys of cold and hot dishes for patrons to pick and choose. It also does great noodles (from Y7). Another branch is across the way at 108 Wuyi Dadao.

Drinking & Entertainment

Chángshā comes alive after dark. Every day of the week, the bars and clubs jump as the locals let off steam. The following is just a guide; places open and shut quicker than you can down a drink.

A good place to start the night is redeveloped Taiping Jie (太平街), which runs parallel to the top end of Huangxing Lu. One of Chángshā's oldest surviving streets, it has a nice mix of bars, as well as boutiques, internet cafes and tea and souvenir shops. From there, it's a short walk around the corner to Jiefang Xilu (解放西路), Chángshā's club central. There are all manner of KTV (karaoke) joints and nightclubs here. They're free to get into, which makes it easy to club-hop, although drinks are expensive.

There's also a busy bar street that runs south off Huangxing Zhonglu. Turn left at the big stage on Huangxing Zhonglu and then right after 100m.

Information

ATMs all over town take foreign cards. The train-station area is heavily pixelated with internet cafes.

Bank of China (中国银行; Zhōngguó Yínháng; 43 Wuyi Dadao) This big branch next door to the Civil Aviation Hotel will change travellers cheques and money, and has a 24-hour ATM.

China International Travel Service (CITS; 中国国际旅行社; Zhōngguó Guójì Lǚxíngshè; ☎8446 8929; 160 Wuyi Dadao; ⏲8.30am-6pm) On the corner of Changdao Lu and Wuyi Dadao, just east of Lotus Huátiān Hotel.

China Post (中国邮政; Zhōngguó Yóuzhèng) To the right of the train-station exit.

HSBC (汇丰银行; Huìfēng Yínháng; 159 Shaoshan Lu) Inside the Dolton Hotel; has 24-hour ATM.

Liányíng Internet Cafe (联赢网吧; Liányíng Wǎngbā; per hr Y3; ⏲24hr) North section of train-station concourse. Bring your passport.

Public Security Bureau (PSB; 公安局; Gōng'ānjú; ☎8589 5000; 1 Dianli Lu)

Getting There & Away

Air

The **Civil Aviation Administration of China** (CAAC; 中国民航售票处; Zhōngguó Mínháng Shòupiàochù; ☎8411 2222; Wuyi Dadao) is one block west of the train station, next to the Civil Aviation Hotel.

From Chángshā, there are daily flights to major cities such as Běijīng (Y970), Chéngdū (Y730), Kūnmíng (Y950), Qīngdǎo (Y1040), Shànghǎi (Y670), Xiàmén (Y690) and Xī'ān (Y710). Flights going to Zhāngjiājiè (Y490) officially (but occasionally optimistically) run daily.

Bus

Services leaving from the **bus station** (汽车站; *qìchēzhàn*) across from the train station:

Jíshǒu Y110, seven hours, every 40 minutes (7.40am to 6.40pm)

Sháoshān Y34, two hours, three daily (7.30am, 9am and 1.30pm)

Zhāngjiājiè Y104, four hours, hourly (8.30am to 6pm)

The **south bus station** *(qìchēnánzhàn)* is way down in the southern suburbs. Take bus 107 or bus 7 (Y2) from the train station; a taxi is Y35 to Y40.

Guìlín Y171, six hours, two daily (8.30am and 4pm)

Héng Shān Y46, three hours, every 40 minutes (8.10am to 4pm)

Hóngjiāng City Y136, seven hours, one daily (9am)

Jǐnggāng Shān Y107, five hours, one daily (12.35pm)

Sháoshān Y31, two hours, every 30 minutes (8am to 5.30pm)

Also from the train station, bus 126 goes to the **east bus station** *(dōngzhàn)*.

Wǔhàn Y119, four hours, hourly (from 8am)

Yuèyáng Y55, two hours, every 40 minutes (from 8.30am)

Take bus 12 from the train station, then change to bus 315 to get to the **west bus station** *(xīzhàn)*.

Chóngqìng Y233, 16 hours, one daily (2.20am)

Huáihuà Y147, 11 hours, one daily (8.20am)

Zhāngjiājiè Y117, four hours, 10 daily (8.10am to 7pm)

Train

There's an advance **train-ticket booking office** (火车售票处; Hǔochē Shòupiàochù; ☎8263 0150; 278 Jiefang Donglu; ⊙8am-5.30pm) at the Lotus Huátiān Hotel. Otherwise, counter 7 at the train station booking hall is supposedly for foreigners.

There are two Guǎngzhōu–Chángshā–Běijīng express trains daily in each direction and a daily train to Shànghǎi (Y265, 15 hours). Other routes via Chángshā are Běijīng–Guìlín–Kūnmíng and Guǎngzhōu–Xī'ān–Lánzhōu. Two morning trains run to Zhāngjiājiè (Y106, six hours), while new high-speed ones make the run to Wǔhàn (Y175) in an expensive 1½ hours.

If you're heading to Hong Kong, you can take one of a few overnight Chángshā–Shēnzhèn air-conditioned express trains. The Běijīng–Kowloon express train also passes through Chángshā.

Getting Around

TO/FROM THE AIRPORT Huánghuā International Airport (黄花国际 机场; Huánghuā Guójì Jīchǎng) is 26km from the city centre. CAAC shuttle buses (Y16, 40 minutes) depart every 20 minutes between 6.30am and 10pm from the Civil Aviation Hotel, next to the CAAC on Wuyi Dadao.

BUS Bus 502 (Y2) runs between the east bus station and the south bus station. Bus 168 (Y2) connects the west bus station and the east bus station.

TAXI Flagfall is Y6.

Sháoshān 韶山

☎0732

In May 2010 a popular Chinese historian suggested tongue-in-cheek that a trip to Sháoshān, Mao Zedong's birthplace, was akin to visiting the notorious Yasukuni Shrine in Tokyo, where war criminals are among the honoured Japanese dead from WWII. His comments sparked online outrage and saw him officially censured, a sign of how much the Great Helmsman is still revered in China, as well as of how many Chinese shrug off the fact that some of Mao's policies caused the deaths of tens of millions of people. At one time, three million red tourists a year (including the man himself in 1959 and 1966) made the pilgrimage to surprisingly pretty Sháoshān, about 130km southwest of Chángshā. Swarms of people, both young and old, still come, so expect queues for the key sights and many, many tour groups.

Sights & Activities

Sháoshān has two distinct parts: the new town clustered around the train and bus stations, and the original Sháoshān village about 5km away, which is where the sights are. The number of these has mushroomed over the years in a lucrative bid to separate tourists from their hard-earned máo, but only a handful have a genuine connection with the man. In particular, guides on the minibuses that connect new and old Sháoshān give the **Mao Zedong Memorial Park** (admission Y60) the hard sell. It's not worth it.

FREE **Mao's Childhood House** HISTORIC SITE (毛泽东故居; Máo Zédōng Gùjū; ⊙8.30am-5pm) Sited in front of a pond, this simple mud-brick house with a thatched roof and stable is the village's shrine. Mao was born here in 1893 and returned to live here briefly in 1927. Among the paraphernalia are kitchen utensils, original furnishings, bedding and photos of Mao's parents, with facilities including a small barn and cattle pen. No photography is allowed inside.

THE GREAT HELMSMAN

Mao Zedong was born in Sháoshān, not far from Chángshā, in 1893. Once poor, his father served in the military to make money, and his efforts ultimately raised the family's status to 'rich' peasants. At 16, Mao left Sháoshān to enter middle school in Chángshā.

In Chángshā, Mao was first exposed to the ideas of Sun Yatsen's revolutionary secret society. Later that year, the Qing dynasty collapsed and Mao joined the regular army. He resigned six months later, thinking the revolution was over when Sun handed the presidency to Yuan Shikai and the war between the north and south of China did not take place.

Voraciously reading newspapers, Mao was introduced to socialism. While at the Húnán No 1 Teachers' Training School (p453), he inserted an advertisement in a Chángshā newspaper 'inviting young men interested in patriotic work to make contact with me'. Among those who got in touch were Liu Shaoqi, who later became president of the People's Republic of China (PRC), and Xiao Chen, who became a founding member of the Chinese Communist Party (CCP).

Mao graduated in 1918 and went to Běijīng, where he worked as an assistant librarian at Peking University. In Běijīng he met future co-founders of the CCP: the student leader Zhang Guodao, Professor Chen Duxiu and university librarian Li Dazhao. Chen and Li are regarded as the founders of Chinese communism. On returning to Chángshā, Mao became increasingly active in communist politics. He edited the *Xiang River Review*, a radical Húnán students' newspaper, and began teaching. By 1920 he was organising workers and truly felt himself a Marxist. In Shànghǎi in 1921 Mao attended the founding meeting of the CCP and helped organise Húnán's provincial branch. Differing from orthodox Marxists, Mao saw the peasants as the lifeblood of the revolution, and from 1922 to 1925 the CCP organised its first unions of peasants, workers and students. Vengeful warlords impelled Mao's flight to Guǎngzhōu (Canton).

In April 1927, following Kuomintang leader Chiang Kaishek's massacre of communists, Mao was dispatched to Chángshā to organise what became known as the 'Autumn Harvest Uprising'. Mao's army scaled Jǐnggāng Shān to embark on a guerrilla war – step one towards the communist takeover.

Mao became the new chairman of the PRC in 1949 and embarked on radical campaigns to repair his war-ravaged country. In the mid-1950s he became disillusioned with the Soviets and began to implement peasant-based and decentralised socialist development. The outcome was the ill-fated Great Leap Forward and, later, the chaos of the Cultural Revolution (for details, see p922).

The current regime officially says Mao was 70% correct and 30% wrong. Upwards of 70 million Chinese died during his rule, but he remains revered as the man who united the country. 'Great Leader', 'Great Teacher' and 'supremely beloved Chairman' are oft-used monikers; his ubiquitous images reveal a saint who will protect people (or make them rich).

By far the most controversial dissection of his life and purpose came with the publication of *Mao: The Unknown Story* by Jung Chang and Jon Halliday, the fruit of 10 years' research. Seeking to balance the hagiographical bias of much Chinese commentary on Mao, Chang and Halliday endeavoured to demolish the myth of the Long March and portray Mao as an unscrupulous schemer, whose collusion with communist ideology simply served as a route to total supremacy.

Nán'àn School HISTORIC SITE
(南岸私塾; Nán'àn Sīshú; admission Y10; ⏲8.30am-5pm) Shut for repairs at the time of writing, this frugal school, its interior illuminated by light wells, is where Mao began his education. Climb the stairs to glimpse Mao's place of study, eyeball the teacher's bed downstairs and peer at fading photos of relatives and descendants.

FREE **Museum of Comrade Mao** MUSEUM
(毛泽东同志纪念馆; Máo Zédōng Tóngzhì Jìniànguǎn; ☎568 5127; ⏲9am-4.30pm) One of the few freebies in Sháoshān, this

museum lacks English captions, but the photos of Mao's life and exhibits of his belongings are self-explanatory. To the right as you face the museum and opposite the bronze statue of Mao Zedong (decorated with calligraphy by Jiang Zemin) is the **Mao Family Ancestral Hall** (毛氏宗祠; Máo Shì Zōngcí), which is now closed to visitors.

Dripping Water Cave RETREAT
(滴水洞; Dī Shuǐ Dòng; admission Y50; ⌚7am-6.30pm spring-summer, 7.30am-5.30pm autumn-winter) Some 3km up from Sháoshān village is the retreat (no, it's not a cave, but his villa was quite bunkerlike) where Mao lived for 11 days in June 1966. The Mao clan are entombed nearby. Buses and motorbikes head here from the car park opposite Sháoshān Bīnguǎn.

Sháo Peak MOUNTAIN
(韶峰; Sháo Fēng; admission Y40, cable car Y40) This cone-shaped mountain is visible from the village. The summit has a lookout pavilion, and the '**forest of stelae**' (毛泽东诗词碑林; Máo Zédōng Shīcí Bēilín; admission Y17) on the lower slopes has stone tablets engraved with Mao's poems. From Sháoshān village you can take a minibus or motorcycle taxi (Y5) south to the end of the road at the cable-car station. Hiking to the top of the mountain takes about an hour.

Sleeping & Eating

Sháoshān can be easily done as a day trip from Chángshā, so there's little reason to spend the night here. Close to the bus station in the new town, various nondescript hotels offer rooms for Y120 after discounts. In the village itself, touts can lead you to stay with a local family or *nóngjiā* (农家).

Restaurants are all over the place in the village, all typically cooking up Mao's favourite dish, Mao family braised pork, and selling it for Y35 and up.

Sháoshān Bīnguǎn HOTEL $$
(韶山宾馆; ☎568 5262; 16 Guyuan Lu; 故园路16号; s/d Y368/398; ❄@) Most rooms here are in the new block and are overpriced; you're paying for the location. For the older, historic buildings that housed Mao on his 1959 return visit, as well as various CCP bigwigs over the years, prices go stratospheric (Y8000 to stay in Mao's old digs).

Getting There & Away

BUS Three daily buses (Y34, 90 minutes, 7.30am, 9am and 1.20pm) leave for Sháoshān from the bus station opposite Chángshā's train station, although you may have to switch to a different bus at Chángshā's south bus station (*qìchēnánzhàn*), where buses run to Sháoshān every half-hour (Y31, two hours) from 8am onwards. Buses return to Chángshā from Sháoshān's **long-distance bus station** (长途汽车站; chángtú qìchēzhàn; Yingbin Lu), just north of the train station, with the last bus leaving at around 5.30pm.

TRAIN A handy daily train (Y10, 2½ hours) to Sháoshān runs from Chángshā, departing at 6.30am; the train returns from Sháoshān at 4.38pm.

Getting Around

Minibuses (Y2.50) head to village sites from the train station. Some minibuses will take you to all the key sites and back for Y10.

Héng Shān 

☎0734

Lying 127km south of Chángshā, this mountain is also known as **Nányuè** (南岳; Southern Peak), the name given to the town that marks the start of the climb. The southernmost of China's five Taoist mountains, where emperors once came to hunt and make sacrifices to heaven and earth, Héng Shān has superb scenery: you climb past gushing waterfalls and streams, small farms hacked out of the lushly forested slopes, and Taoist shrines.

Sights & Activities

Héng Shān MOUNTAIN
(☎567 5588; admission Y100) To reach the mountain from Nányuè, follow Yanshou Lu (延寿路) north of Nányuè Temple until it curves to your right. Hiking on the paved road or sometimes steep paths to **Wishing Harmony Peak** (祝融峰; Zhùróng Fēng), the mountain's highest point, takes four hours, and it's another four hours to descend, although visiting the monasteries, temples, villas and gardens on the mountain takes longer.

If walking, don't take the road uphill beyond the ticket office and entrance, but take the steps that go along **Fànyīn Valley** (梵音谷; Fànyīn Gǔ) and follow it up. After about half an hour, you'll reach the **Shénzhōu Temple** (神州祖庙; Shénzhōu Zǔmiào). Past the cable-car departure point at **Bànshān Tíng** (半山亭), you'll have to take to the road more frequently, but look out for steps among the pines leading uphill from the wayside. A **stele** on the way up is inscribed with a dedication from Kuomintang leader Chiang Kaishek celebrating the pine forest. The dignified and lovingly tended **Nányuè Martyrs Memorial Hall** (南岳忠烈祠; Nányuè Zhōnglièci) is a grand design, with an impressive gateway and a series of halls dedicated to the anti-Japanese resistance. The hall is just before Bànshān Tíng.

Bànshān Tíng is also the location of the **Xuándū Guàn** (玄都观), an impressive active Taoist temple. From Bànshān Tíng it's a further 7km walk to Wishing Harmony Peak.

Built during the Ming dynasty, **Wishing Harmony Palace** (祝融殿; Zhùróng Diàn) is the resting place of Zhu Rong, an official 'in charge of fire' during one of China's early periods. Zhu Rong used to hunt on Héng Shān, so Taoists selected the mountain to represent fire, one of the five primordial elements of Chinese philosophy.

From 7am to 5.30pm minibuses run to **Nántiānmén** (南天门), a couple of kilometres from the summit, for Y40/70 one way/return, which allows you to walk up and ride most of the way down. Alternatively, there's a **cable car** (one way/return Y40/70; ⏲7am-5.30pm) that starts midway up the mountain and takes 10 minutes to get to Nántiānmén. If taking the cable car, free minibuses (queues can get long) run to and from Bànshān Tíng. Thick PLA surplus coats (Y20) are hired out at the Nántiānmén Cable Car Station (南天门索道站; Nántiānmén Suǒdàozhàn) and other points, as it can be bone-numbingly chilly and foggy outside the warm months.

Nányuè Temple TEMPLE
(南岳大庙; Nányuè Dàmiào; ☎567 3658; admission Y40; ⏲7am-6pm) Located in Nányuè, this vast temple dates from the Tang dynasty and was rebuilt during the Qing dynasty. Take note of the column supports, one for each of the mountains in the Taoist range, purportedly.

Zhùshèng Temple TEMPLE
(祝圣寺; Zhùshèng Sì; 67 Dong Jie; admission Y5; ⏲5am-9pm) In Nányuè, this temple dates back to the Tang dynasty.

FREE **Dàshàn Chán Temple** TEMPLE
(大善禅寺; Dàshàn Chánsì; off Zhurong Beilu; ⏲7.30am-6pm) Also in Nányuè.

Sleeping & Eating

The cheapest rooms can be found in Nányuè's many small family-run **inns** (客栈; *kèzhàn*), where you can get a bed for Y50 (or Y80 with air-con and a shower). Ask at the bus station; many restaurants around town also offer rooms. Otherwise, there are hotels all along Zhurong Beilu (祝融北路).

There are many hotels on the mountain itself, most of them basic. The majority are clustered around Bánshān Tíng. Expect prices to rocket during holiday periods.

Numerous restaurants can be found in the village of Nányuè, although the presence of so many tourists means they're pricey. Food on the mountain is even more expensive; take snacks and water with you.

Zhěnyùe Lóu Dàjiǔdiàn HOTEL $$
(枕岳楼大酒店; ☎567 7777; Hengshan Lu; 衡山路; s/d Y298/368, discounts of 50-60%; ❄@) A good option with comfortable rooms that are discounted during slow periods. To find it, turn right out of the bus station and it's a 100m walk on the other side of the road at the junction of Zhurong Beilu and Hengshan Lu.

Yánshòu Hotel HOTEL $
(d/tr Y100/120) Clean doubles with so-so bathrooms; triples also available.

Dúxiù Bīnguǎn HOTEL $$
(独秀宾馆; ☎566 1541; d Y318-368, tr Y428) Near Yánshòu Hotel, and smarter, but doubles with great views can still be had for Y200 after a discount.

Information

Near the bus station, there's a branch of the **Bank of China** (中国银行; Zhōngguó Yínháng; 270 Hengshan Lu) with a 24-hour ATM. It will change currency but not travellers cheques. The **PSB** is on Xijie (西街).

Getting There & Around

From the archway (牌坊; *páifāng*) at the intersection of Zhurong Beilu and Hengshan Lu, turn right and the **long-distance bus station** is a few minutes' walk along on your left. There are 12 buses a day to Chángshā (Y42, two to three hours, every 40 minutes between 7am and 4pm).

Trains from Chángshā (Y22, two hours) are another option, but they're slower than buses on the new expressways and require switching to a minibus for a half-hour ride from the railhead. Dinky green baby buses, which look like elongated golf carts, connect the bus station with the Héng Shān entrance and **ticket office** (进山门票处; *jìnshān ménpiàochù*) and Nányuè Temple. They're free and run between 7am and 7pm.

Wŭlíngyuán & Zhāngjiājiè 武陵源、张家界

☎0744

Rising from the misty subtropical forest of northwest Húnán are 243 peaks, surrounded by over 3000 karst upthrusts, a concentration not seen elsewhere in the world. The sublime picture is completed by waterfalls, limestone caves (including Asia's largest chamber) and rivers suitable for organised rafting trips. Nearly two dozen rare species of flora and fauna call the region home and botanists will delight in the 3000-odd plant species present. Monkeys gambol around the sides of the paths, or hang from the trees, and more exotic animals such as clouded leopards and pangolins lurk deeper in the park.

Known as the **Wŭlíngyuán Scenic Area** (Wŭlíngyuán Fēngjĭngqū; www.zhangjiajie.com.cn) and recognised by Unesco in 1990 as a World Heritage Site, Wŭlíngyuán is home to three minority peoples: Tujia, Miao and Bai. The region encompasses the localities of Zhāngjiājiè, Tiānzĭshān and Suŏxīyù. **Zhāngjiājiè city** (张家界市; Zhāngjiājiè *shì*) is the best known (many Chinese refer to the region by that name) and has the most useful transport links, as well as plenty of places to stay overnight and to stock up on provisions.

Sights & Activities

Wŭlíngyuán SCENIC AREA

(adult/student Y248/160) There are two principal access points to Wŭlíngyuán. **Zhāngjiājiè village** (张家界村; Zhāngjiājiè *cūn*), the site of the south entrance, is the more appealing option, situated nearly 600m above sea level in the Wŭlíng foothills, surrounded by sheer cliffs and vertical rock outcrops. It's technically known as the **Zhāngjiājiè National Park Entrance** (张家界公园门票站; Zhāngjiājiè Gōngyuán Ménpiàozhàn), but the locals mostly refer to it as simply **Forest Park** (森林公园; Sēnlín Gōngyuán).

From the east, you can use the **Wŭlíngyuán Entrance** (武陵源门票站; Wŭlíngyuán Ménpiàozhàn), east of Suŏxī Lake (索溪湖; Suŏxī Hú). In the north of Wŭlíngyuán is a further way in, the **Tiānzĭ Mountain Entrance** (天子山门票站; Tiānzĭshān Ménpiàozhàn).

A staggering admission fee includes Y3 compulsory insurance and buys a ticket that is valid for two days. It must be used on consecutive days, and thumb prints are taken at the entrance, so tickets can't be resold or passed on. There are admission fees to some other sights within the park as well. Available from the ticket office, and hotels in the village and city, the *Tourist Map of Wulingyuan Scenic Zone* (武陵源景区导游图; Y5) contains an English-language map of the scenic area and a Chinese-language map of Zhāngjiājiè city.

The highest area closest to Zhāngjiājiè village is **Huángshízhài** (黄石寨), and at 1048m it's a two-hour hike up 3878 stone steps (cable car up/down Y48/48). It takes two to three hours to follow the **Golden Whip Stream Scenic Route** (金鞭溪精品游览线; Jīnbiānxī Jīngpĭn Yóulăn Xiàn), which follows its namesake stream to the **Suŏxī Valley Nature Reserve** (索溪峪自然保护区; Suŏxīyù Zìrán Băohù Qū) in the east of the reserve. From there it's a short walk to the dramatic and very popular **Bailong Sky Lift** (百龙天梯; Băilóng Tiāntī; up/down Y56/56), which transports visitors up to the **Yuánjiājiè** (袁家界) area, the heart of the park.

From there, you can hike or take the sightseeing tram (观光电车; Guānguāng Diànchē) along the **Ten Mile Gallery** (十里画廊; Shílĭ Huàláng) towards the **Tiānzĭ Shān Nature Reserve** (天子山自然保护区; Tiānzĭ Shān Zìrán Băohù Qū), a popular expedition in the northern section of the reserve; a **cable car** (up/down Y52/52) also services the region. The Tiānzĭ Shān area can also be accessed by minibus to the entrance at **Tiānzĭshān village** (天子山镇; Tiānzĭshān Zhèn), where you can also overnight.

Organised tours to the park and **Jiŭtiān Cave** (九天洞; Jiŭtiān Dòng; admission Y62) often include a **rafting trip** *(piāoliú)*, or you can join a tour and just do the rafting trip. While good white-water rafting trips are possible northwest of Zhāngjiājiè near the Húběi border, you'll have to make special arrangements for the equipment and transport.

Most rivers are pretty tame, so don't expect great thrills, but the scenery is fantastic. The actual rafting usually lasts about four hours, with about the same amount of time taken up in travel to and from the launch area.

Pŭguāng Temple TEMPLE

(普光禅寺; Pŭguāng Chánsì; 20 Jiefang Lu; admission Y20; ⏲8am-5.30pm) Within

Wŭlíngyuán

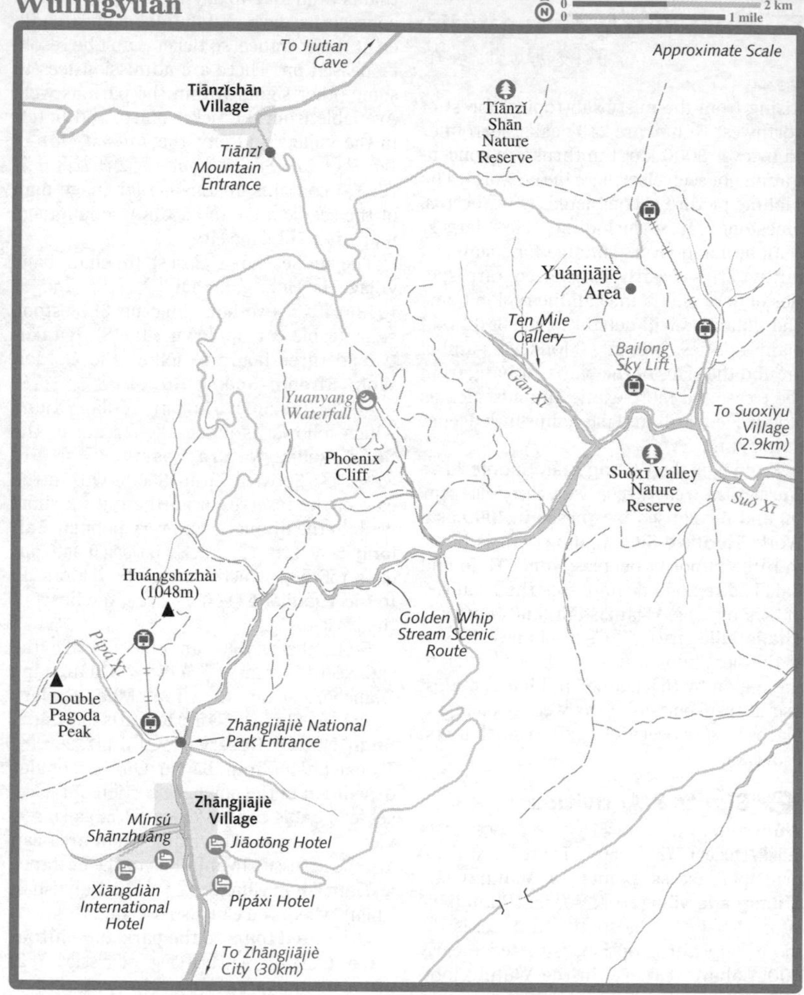

Zhāngjiājiè city, this temple is a well-preserved historic Buddhist shrine.

Tours

You can join tours of the park and rafting trips, or arrange your own through hotels and travel agencies in Zhāngjiājiè city. Both the Zhōngtiān International Youth Hostel and **CITS** (中国国际旅行社; Zhōngguó Guójì Lǚxíngshè; ☎820 0885; www.cits999.com; 631 Ziwu Lu; ⏲8am-9pm) offer one-day rafting tours on the Měngdòng River (猛洞河; Měngdòng Hé) for Y200 per person.

Sleeping

Staying in Zhāngjiājiè village puts you right next to the park – and it's a gorgeous setting, with karst peaks soaring above – but it's more expensive and there's a much greater selection of hotels in Zhāngjiājiè city. A large choice of hotels and inns (客栈; *kèzhàn*) can also be found at Suŏxī at the eastern entrance to Wŭlíngyuán, particularly handy before or after exploring this part of the reserve.

ZHĀNGJIĀJIÈ CITY 张家界市

There are cheapies scattered around the bus station and on Bei Zhengjie (北正街),

where you can find a room for around Y80 with a discount.

Zhōngtiān International Youth Hostel YOUTH HOSTEL $

(中天国际青年旅舍; Zhōngtiān Guójì Qīngnián Lǚshè; ☎832 1678; www.zjjztqnls.com; Room 4 A1, Zhongtian Bldg, Ziwu Rd; 子午路中天大厦4楼A1室; dm Y40-50, d Y128-148; ❄@) Despite the location in an anonymous office block, this pleasant place has a rooftop garden, a small bar and restaurant, table football and clean rooms, although there's not much English spoken. There's a more basic branch in the Yuánjiājiè area of Wǔlíngyuán itself.

Jǐnjiāng Inn HOTEL $$

(锦江之星; Jǐnjiāng Zhīxīng; ☎839 8888; 51 Ziwu Lu; 子午路51号; d/tw Y219/229; ❄@) This Jǐnjiāng has larger rooms than the ones found in its big-city cousins. All come with decent bathrooms and broadband access.

Mǐnnán (GDH) International Hotel HOTEL $$$

(闽南(粤海)国际酒店; Mǐnnán Yùehǎi Gúojì Jiǔdiàn; ☎822 8888; www.zjjmnhotel.com; 18 Ziwu Lu; 子午路18号; d & tw Y1380, discounts of 50-60%; ❄@) Zhāngjiājiè's five star choice has spacious, modern rooms and on-site Western and Chinese restaurants. Discounts available out of season.

ZHĀNGJIĀJIÈ VILLAGE 张家界村

Some places in the village take foreigners, but look around and compare prices. It is possible to stay with local families within the park, but don't bank on it. Your best bet is to ask the ladies who staff the various food, drink and souvenir stalls in the park. Expect to pay Y60 to Y80. For those hiking overnight, there are places to stay inside the park along the popular trail routes, including an outpost of the **Zhōngtiān International Youth Hostel** (☎590 3315). Local visitors often do a two- to three-day circuit hike, going in at Zhāngjiājiè village and hiking or bussing it to villages within the park boundaries, such as Tiānzǐshān and Suǒxīyù, which each have a bewildering choice of hotels and hostels. All of the following hotels are on the main road, called Jinbian Lu (金鞭路); other places lurk down the road beyond the Xiāngdiàn International Hotel.

Xiāngdiàn International Hotel HOTEL $$$

(湘电国际酒店; Xiāngdiàn Guójì Jiǔdiàn; ☎571 2999; www.xiangdianhotel.com; s & d Y680-1080, ste Y1280, discounts of 30-40%; ⊖❄@) The posh option in the village, this good-looking and professional four-star hotel has an attractive courtyard garden aspect at the rear, complete with water features. The atmosphere is relaxed and most rooms have balconies and at least partial views.

Pípáxī Hotel HOTEL $$

(琵琶溪宾馆; Pípáxī Bīnguǎn; ☎571 8888; www.pipaxi-hotel.com; d Y580-680, discounts of 33%; ❄) Tucked away from the action, this quiet hotel in the modernist style is well tended, with magnolias and other flowering trees. The rooms are large, bright and clean.

Jiāotōng Hotel HOTEL $$

(交通宾馆; Jiāotōng Bīnguǎn; ☎571 8188; s/d Y258/268, discounts of 40%) Located in an ugly car park north of the Pípáxī Hotel, this is the cheapest acceptable place in the village, but only just. It's very rudimentary, with tiny, grimy bathrooms.

Eating

Simple eating houses are scattered around Zhāngjiājiè village, cooking up Tujia dishes; you may well be steered towards expensive *tǔjī* (土鸡; free-range chicken), but there will be many other cheaper dishes. Fruit and snack stalls set up just south of the main entrance in Zhāngjiājiè village.

Information

The **Agricultural Bank of China** branch in Zhāngjiājiè village has an ATM that accepts foreign cards but will not change money.

2 in 1 Internet Cafe (二合一网吧; Èrhéyī Wǎngbā; per hr Y2; ⌚24hr) On the corner of Bei Zhengjie and Ziwu Lu in Zhāngjiājiè city.

Bank of China (中国银行; Zhōngguó Yínháng; Ziwu Lu, Zhāngjiājiè city) This branch close to the Zhōngtiān International Youth Hostel will change money and travellers cheques, and has a 24-hour ATM.

China Post (中国邮政; Zhōngguó Yóuzhèng; ⌚8am-5.30pm) On Jinbian Lu, just north of the Xiāngdiàn International Hotel in Zhāngjiājiè village.

CITS (中国国际旅行社; Zhōngguó Guójì Lǚxíngshè; ☎820 0885; www.cits999.com; 631 Ziwu Lu, Zhāngjiājiè city)

Forest Park First Aid Centre (☎571 8819)

Industrial & Commercial Bank of China (ICBC; 工商银行; Gōngshāng yínháng; Huilong Lu, Zhāngjiājiè city) Lies 250m east of the bus station.

Public Security Bureau (PSB; 公安局; Gōng'ānjú; ☎571 2329; Jinbian Lu, Zhāngjiājiè village)

THE INSPIRATION FOR *AVATAR*

Ever wondered where James Cameron got the idea for the floating mountains on Pandora, the fictional planet in his record-breaking blockbuster *Avatar*? Well, according to Zhāngjiājiè's local government, it was Wǔlíngyuán's karst peaks that inspired Pandora's Hallelujah Mountains. And with *Avatar* the most successful film ever released in China, Zhāngjiājiè officials decided in January 2010 to rename one of Wǔlíngyuán's peaks the 'Avatar Hallelujah Mountain', in an effort to boost tourism.

It was a move that provoked controversy, with some people wondering why a Chinese mountain should be given a Christian name. But there's no doubt that the area has benefited from the fact that *Avatar* was such a phenomenon in China. Many local viewers saw the plight of the Na'vi tribe in the movie, who face being thrown off their planet by an evil mining corporation, as a metaphor for the huge numbers of forced evictees in China.

As for whether the floating mountains were actually based on Wǔlíngyuán, the jury is still out. Zhāngjiājiè officials point to the fact that the area was scouted by a team from Hollywood in 2008. However, when Cameron came to China to promote *Avatar* he said the inspiration was actually Huángshān, the ethereal peak in Ānhuī province. Either way, there's no doubt that Wǔlíngyuán is one of the few places on earth where you can imagine you're on Pandora.

Getting There & Away

AIR Zhāngjiājiè Airport is 4km southwest of Zhāngjiājiè city and 40km from the park entrance; a taxi should cost around Y100 to the park. More and more flights link Zhāngjiājiè city with the rest of China; current destinations include Běijīng (Y1340), Chángshā (Y490), Chóngqìng (Y520), Guǎngzhōu (Y600), Shànghǎi (Y800) and Xī'ān (Y690).

BUS Buses leave from the **long-distance bus station** (☎822 2417) on Huilong Lu in Zhāngjiājiè city.

Chángshā Y104, 3½ to four hours, regular service (7am to 7pm)

Fènghuáng via Jíshǒu Y60, four hours, three daily (8.30am, 9.30am and 10.30am)

Jíshǒu Y45, two hours, hourly

Shànghǎi Y309, 20 hours, one daily (10.30am)

Wǔhàn Y175, 12 hours, three daily (8.30am, 5.30pm and 6pm)

Xī'ān Y292, 20 hours, one daily (1.30pm)

Yuèyáng Y100, seven hours, one daily (8.30am)

TRAIN The station is 8km southeast of the city; buy tickets well in advance. There are two morning trains from Chángshā at 7.37am and 8.16am (Y49, six hours). In the other direction, there are five trains during the day and one overnight sleeper (Y177, 11 hours). Other services:

Běijīng Y341, 22 to 27 hours, three daily

Guǎngzhōu Y254, 14 hours, twice daily

Huáihuà Y19 to Y38, four to 5½ hours, 11 daily

Jíshǒu Y10 to Y22, two hours, 12 daily

Yíchāng Y24, five hours, five daily

Getting Around

Minibuses to Zhāngjiājiè village (Y10, 40 minutes) – also called Forest Park (森林公园; Sēnlín Gōngyuán) – leave every 15 minutes from the long-distance bus station on Huilong Lu. The last bus back to Zhāngjiājié city leaves at 7pm. Ensure you get on the right bus, as some buses go to the eastern Wǔlíngyuán entrance at Suǒxī (buses run between these two entrances; they're free as long as you have purchased an entrance ticket). Buses to Tiānzǐshān (Y13, every hour) in the north also leave from here.

Taxi flagfall in Zhāngjiājiè city is Y4.

Déhāng

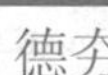

In a seductive riverine setting overlooked by towering, other-worldly karst peaks, the Miao hamlet of **Déhāng** (admission Y60), to the northwest of Jíshǒu in western Húnán province, offers a tantalising spectrum of treks into picturesque countryside. Rising into columns, splinters and huge foreheads of stone, the local karst geology climbs over verdant valleys layered with terraced fields and flushed by waterfalls and clear streams. Side-stepping the bovine traffic could be the only thing distracting you from the gorgeous scenery.

The village itself has been partially dolled up for domestic tourism, but on its fringes the feeling survives of a pleasant riverside minority Miao village, where wood-constructed and highly affordable hotels turn Déhāng into an inexpensive and alluring retreat. Avoid the inauthentic, tourist crowd-oriented Déhāng Miáozhài (德夯苗寨) hub, where evening shows are staged, and keep to the narrow lanes and riverside views of the old village leading to the arched **Jiēlóng Bridge** (接龙桥; Jiēlóng Qiáo), where old folk decked out in blue Miao outfits and bamboo baskets cluster, and cows and water buffalo wander quietly around chewing the cud.

Sights & Activities

Surplus to its charming village views, Déhāng is itself located within a huge 164-sq-km geological park, where some delightful treks thread into the hills.

Nine Dragon Stream Scenic Area WALK
(九龙溪景区; Jiǔlóngxī Jǐngqū) This beautiful area winds along a stream out of the village, past Miao peasants labouring in the terraced fields, over bridges, alongside fields croaking with toads or seething with tadpoles (depending on the season), and into an astonishing landscape of peaks blotched with green and valleys carpeted with lush fields. At a bend in the path you will come to a point of entry for the **Nine Dragon Waterfall** (九龙瀑布; Jiǔlóng Pùbù; admission Y15), which leads to a fun 1.5km clamber past gullies and falls; however, if the weather is wet (when the falls are at their best), the climb is slippery and potentially dangerous, especially the slimy bridges. Continue to the end of the trail for the fantastic **Liúshā Waterfall** (流沙瀑布; Liúshā Pùbù; admission free) – China's highest waterfall at 216m – which descends in fronds of spray onto rocks above a green pool at its foot. Climb the steps behind the waterfall for stirring views through the curtain of water (a small umbrella is handy at this point) – the sight is particularly impressive after rainfall. The return walk to the Liúshā Waterfall takes about two hours.

Yùquánxī Scenic Area WALK
(玉泉溪景区; Yùquánxī Jǐngqū) Cross the bridge over the river to visit this 2.6km-long scenic area, where you follow a path along a valley by the Yùquán Stream, past haystacks (consisting of stout wooden poles sunk into the ground onto which are tossed clumps of hay) and gorgeous belts of layered terraced fields. Walk along the valley for a good 1.5km before the path ducks into a small gorge, where you will traverse the river at several points, and continue on into a thick profusion of green. Cross the **Jade Fountain Gate** (玉泉门; Yùquán Mén) and follow the path to the waterfall, which spills down in a single thread of water. If you have the energy, climb the steps up to the **Tiānwèn Platform** (天问台; Tiānwèn Tái), where fabulous views span out through the gorge above the waterfall and a few simple Miao homesteads find a perch. Note how a whole new series of terraced slopes commences at this altitude.

Jiēlóng Bridge walk WALK
Another pleasant walk can be made by crossing the river over Jiēlóng Bridge and climbing up the stone-flagged steps through the bamboo for views over the village.

Sleeping & Eating

Several simple inns (客栈; *kèzhàn*) can be found in the village, near the square, stuffed down alleyways or picturesquely suspended over the river. You'll need a torch (flashlight) to avoid tumbling into the water at night. Travellers aiming for more midrange comfort can stay overnight in nearby (and unattractive) Jíshǒu.

Most inns around the village have small restaurants serving local dishes, but meals are often more expensive than their rooms. Hawkers proffer skewers of grilled fish (*táohuāyú;* Y1) and baby crab (Y2). Restaurants are also clustered around the square and the road leading off it to the east.

Jiēlóngqiáo Inn INN $
(接龙桥客店; Jiēlóngqiáo Kèdiàn; ☎135 1743 0915; s/d Y40/50) This small, all-wood inn is next door to the Jiēlóng Inn – the owners play mah jong together much of the time – and the well-kept, heavily varnished rooms, with fan and TV, are the best in the village. The drawback is the communal shower and toilet, located two flights down in the dank basement.

Fēngyǔqiáo Inn INN $
(风雨桥客栈; Fēngyǔqiáo Kèzhàn; ☎135 7430 9026; dm/d Y15/40) This is another friendly riverside alternative and the first you'll see when you arrive, over the bridge from the square and at the start of the Yùquánxī Scenic Area trail. There's no air-con or heating, so you'll need to pile on the quilts during colder months.

Jiēlóng Inn INN $
(接龙客栈; Jiēlóng Kèzhàn; ☎135 7432 0948; s/d Y40/60; ❄) Right next to the Jiēlóng

Bridge, this popular spot has a handful of air-con rooms with shared shower and toilet, and a restaurant-seating area with views along the river.

Miáozú Fēngwèi Guǎn RESTAURANT
(苗族风味馆; ☎0743-866 5520; meals Y40) At this amiable village place you can perch on an old Miao wooden stool, fill up on very tasty local dishes and sample the village firewater.

Getting There & Away

The best way to reach Déhāng is to travel via Jíshǒu, a railway town to the south of the village. Regular buses to Déhāng (Y6, 50 minutes) leave from outside Jíshǒu's train station, arriving at and departing (every 20 minutes) from the square/parking lot in Déhāng. The last third of the journey is spectacular, as the bus hugs the river and the karst peaks tower overhead.

Fènghuáng 凤凰

☎0743

Under round-the-clock siege from domestic tourists – the Taiping Rebellion of the modern age – this riveting riverside town of ancient city walls, disintegrating gate towers, rickety houses on stilts and hoary temples can easily fill a couple of days. Home to a lively population of Miao (苗) and Tujia (土家) minorities, the architectural legacy of Fènghuáng's old town (凤凰古城; Fènghuáng Gǔchéng) shows distressing signs of neglect, as tourism-orientated development takes precedence over preservation, so get here to see it before it crumbles away completely.

Sights & Activities

Strolling willy-nilly is the best way to see Fènghuáng. Many of the back alleys in the old town maintain an intriguing charm, a treasure trove of old family pharmacists, traditional shops, temples, ancestral halls and crumbling dwellings. Restored fragments of the city wall lie along the south bank of the Tuó River (Tuó Jiāng) in the old town and a few dilapidated chunks survive elsewhere.

Strips of riverweed hang out to dry and cured meats (including flattened pig faces!) swing from shopfronts. Elsewhere, platters of garlic, peanuts and fish are left out to dry. You can buy virtually anything from the clutter of tourist shops and stalls, from crossbows to walking sticks, wooden combs, ethnic flip-flops, embroidered Miao clothes and silver jewellery.

Most sights can only be visited if you buy the Y148 **through ticket** (通票; *tōngpiào*), which includes entrance to the Yang Family Ancestral Hall, the Former Home of Shen Congwen, the Former Home of Xiong Xiling (熊希龄故居), Gǔchéng Museum, Wànshòu Temple, a boat ride along the Tuó River, the East Gate Tower and a few other sights. You don't have to buy the through ticket, and much of Fènghuáng can be seen for free, but you will need it if you simply have to see the included sights. Through tickets are sold at several places in town, including the North Gate Tower and the Tourism Administrative Bureau of Fènghuáng. Boat trips ferry passengers along the river for Y30 from the North Gate Tower (atmospheric night trips included). Sights are generally all open from 8am to 5.30pm. Much of Fènghuáng is dazzlingly illuminated come nightfall.

SOUTH OF THE RIVER

City Wall HISTORIC SITE
(城墙; *chéngqiáng*) Wander along Fènghuáng's restored salmon-pink city wall with its defensive aspect along the southern bank of the Tuó River. Halfway along its length, the **North Gate Tower** (北门城楼; Běimén Chénglóu) is in a tragic state of neglect, downtrodden and scratched with names, but it remains a magnificent structure. While perusing this area, look up at the distinctive roof ridges on buildings above – many adorned with carvings of creatures and fish – which are far better preserved than much at ground level.

Yang Family Ancestral Hall HALL
(杨家祠堂; Yángjiā Cítáng) Further along the wall is this building, its exterior still decorated with Maoist slogans from the Cultural Revolution.

East Gate Tower TOWER
(东门城楼; Dōngmén Chénglóu) This Qing-dynasty twin-eaved tower dates from 1715.

Hóng Bridge BRIDGE
(虹桥; Hóng Qiáo) This magnificent covered bridge spans the river. The upstairs galleries are covered by the through ticket.

Jiāngxīn Buddhist Temple TEMPLE
(江心禅寺; Jiāngxīn Chánsì) This temple is on Huilong Ge, a narrow alley of shops, hotels and restaurants east of Hóng Bridge.

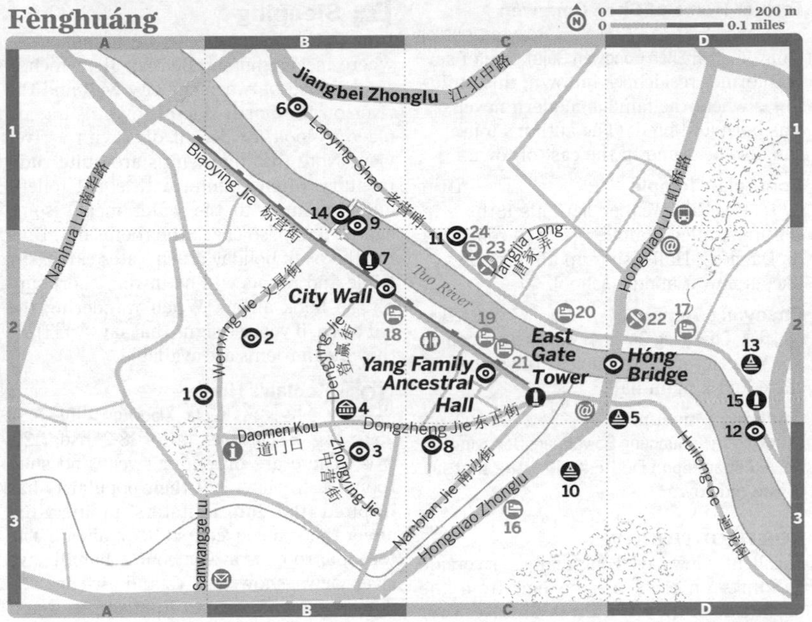

Fènghuáng

Top Sights
- City Wall B2
- East Gate Tower C2
- Hóng Bridge D2
- Yang Family Ancestral Hall C2

Sights
- 1 Cháoyáng Temple A2
- 2 Confucian Temple B2
- 3 Former Home of Shen Congwen B3
- 4 Gǔchéng Museum B2
- 5 Jiāngxīn Buddhist Temple D2
- 6 Laoying Shao B1
- 7 North Gate Tower B2
- 8 Queen of Heaven Temple C3
- 9 Stepping Stones B1
- 10 Three Kings Temple C3
- 11 Tian Family Ancestral Temple C2
- 12 Wànmíng Pagoda D3
- 13 Wànshòu Temple D2
- 14 Wooden Footbridge B1
- 15 Yíngxī Gate D2

Sleeping
- 16 Border Town International Youth Hostel C3
- 17 Fènghuáng International Youth Hostel D2
- 18 Gǔyùn Hotel B2
- 19 Koolaa's Home C2
- 20 Phoenix Jiāngtiān Holiday Village C2
- 21 Túoshuǐ Rénjiā Kèzhàn C2

Eating
- 22 Night Market D2
- 23 Soul Too C2

Drinking
- 24 Elope Bar C2

Three Kings Temple TEMPLE
(三皇庙; Sānhuáng Miào) A welcome respite from the crowds and good views over town await at this temple, up a steep flight of steps off Jianshe Lu.

Queen of Heaven Temple TEMPLE
(天后宫; Tiānhòu Gōng) Off Dongzheng Jie, this simple temple is dedicated to the patron deity of seafarers.

Former Home of Shen Congwen FORMER RESIDENCE

(沈从文故居; Shěn Cóngwén Gùjū) One of several former residences in town, this building is where the famous modern novelist was born and bred. (The author's tomb can also be found in the east of town.)

Confucian Temple TEMPLE

(文庙; Wén Miào; Wenxing Jie) This 18th-century walled temple, the twin roofs of its Dàchéng Hall rising up almost claw-like, is now a middle school.

Cháoyáng Temple TEMPLE

(朝阳宫; Cháoyáng Gōng; 41 Wenxing Jie; admission Y10) Home to an ancient theatrical stage and a main hall.

Gǔchéng Museum MUSEUM

(古城博物馆; Gǔchéng Bówùguǎn; Dengying Jie; ⏲7.30am-6pm) Dedicated to the history of the old town.

NORTH OF THE RIVER

Excellent views of Fènghuáng's riverside buildings on stilts can be had from the north side of the river. Cross the river over the **stepping stones** (跳岩; *tiàoyán*), best navigated when sober, or by the **wooden footbridge** (木头桥; Mùtou Qiáo).

Laoying Shao STREET

Ever-developing street of bars, cafes and shops overlooking the river.

Tian Family Ancestral Temple TEMPLE

(田家祠堂; Tiánjiā Cítáng; Laoying Shao) Currently shut, this temple is a portrait of Fènghuáng in neglect: it's overgrown with weeds.

Wànshòu Temple TEMPLE

(万寿宫; Wànshòu Gōng) This temple isn't far from Wànmíng Pagoda.

Yíngxī Gate GATE

(迎曦门; Yíngxī Mén) This small gate near the pagoda dates from 1807.

Southern Great Wall DEFENSIVE WALL

(南长城; Nán Chángchéng; admission Y45) This Ming-dynasty construction is 13km outside town – reach it by bus (Y5) from Fènghuáng – but it doesn't compare with the bastion that fortified north China.

Huángsī Bridge Old Town VILLAGE

(黄丝桥古城; Huángsī Qiáo Gǔchéng; admission Y20) Also outside town, this village is similar in character to Fènghuáng.

Sleeping

Inns (客栈; *kèzhàn*) can be found everywhere in Fènghuáng. Beibian Jie, which is sandwiched between the city wall and the river on the north side of town, is a good place to look for decent digs with a river view. Note that many inns are quite rudimentary, often coming with squat toilets, and proximity to the water means some can be damp, so check the rooms out. During the peak holiday crush, rates can easily triple and rooms will be in very short supply, so book ahead. When wandering the old town, if you see signs that say '今日有房', they mean rooms are available.

TOP CHOICE **Koolaa's Home** INN $

(考拉小屋; Kǎolā Xiǎowū; ☎151 7433 9597; 18-2 Beibian Jie; 北边街18-2号; d Y120; ❄@) There are only four sweet and snug rooms at Koolaa's, but their popularity has inspired the inn imitators proliferating along the same street, so book ahead. The top-floor rooms have balconies, but all have river views, showers, TVs and air-con. The downstairs cafe has an English menu and wi-fi. To reach Koolaa's, walk through the North Gate Tower and turn right, walking down the alley between the city wall and the river. It's around 200m along on your left – look for the English sign.

Border Town International Youth Hostel YOUTH HOSTEL $

(边城国际青年旅舍; Biānchéng Gúojì Qīngnián Lǚshè; ☎322 8698; Hongqiao Zhonglu; 虹桥中路; dm/s Y20/78, d Y100-130, tr Y138; ❄@) Named after a novel by Fènghuáng's most famous son, Shen Congwen, this newly opened hostel is located a few minutes south of the Hóng Bridge in a former hotel. That means the rooms are bigger than in many hostels, especially the more expensive twins, which come with computers. The amiable staff make a stay here a pleasant experience, but there are squat toilets throughout.

Phoenix Jiāngtiān Holiday Village HOTEL $$$

(凤凰江天旅游度假村; Fènghuáng Jiāngtiān Lǚyóu Dùjiàcūn; ☎326 1998; www.fhjt-hotel.com; Jiangtian Sq; 虹桥路江天广场; s & d Y588, tr Y688, discounts of 40%; ❄@) Tucked behind Laoying Shao in a square that can also be accessed from Hongqiao Lu, the Phoenix offers spacious rooms with decent bathrooms, all with ADSL. Discounts outside of peak periods make it an attractive choice, although there are no river views. To get here, turn right at the arch on Laoying Shao.

Túoshuǐ Rénjiā Kèzhàn INN $
(沱水人家; ☎350 1690; 14 Beibian Jie; 北边街14号; d Y50-120; ❄@) The best of the Koolaa clones on Beibian Jie, the Túoshuǐ has a similar wood finish throughout and five rooms, four of which come with balconies, river views and computers. No sit-down toilets, though. The single cheap room is less appealing.

Gǔyùn Hotel HOTEL $$
(古韵宾馆; Gǔyùn Bīnguǎn; 52 Laocai Jie; 老菜街52号; ☎350 0077; s/d/tr Y258/268/368; ❄@) Just east of the North Gate Tower, there are no river views here, but you do get air-con, shower-equipped, albeit drab, rooms that come with broadband access. Big discounts are available outside of holiday season.

Fènghuáng International Youth Hostel YOUTH HOSTEL $
(凤凰国际青年旅馆; Fènghuáng Guójì Qīngnián Lǚguǎn; ☎326 0546; yhaphoenix@163.com; 11 Shawan; 沙湾11号; dm Y25, s & d Y108-148; ❄@) Well sited on the north side of the Tuó River, next to East Pass Gate (东关门; Dōgguā Mén) and not far from the Wànshòu Temple, this quaint-looking place with a small communal area is blighted by sleepy service and a curiously deadened atmosphere. The shared bathrooms have squat toilets.

Eating

Fènghuáng's restaurants tend to be pricey; the ones to the west of the North Gate Tower are less touristy and so cheaper. You'll also see some less-than-appetising food on display, including rats and snakes in cages. The good news is that it's a great town for street snacks. There are vendors down every alley selling a ton of takeaway options, from crab, fish or potato kebabs and snails to spicy fried *dòufu* and cooling bowls of *liángfěn* (bean-starch jelly).

Night Market STREET MARKET $
(虹桥夜市; Hóngqiáo Yèshì; Hongqiao Donglu; ⌚5pm-1am) Hands down the best place to eat in Fènghuáng is this fantastic, lively night market. From the late afternoon, just north of the Hóng Bridge, food stalls set up shop ready to barbecue all manner of meat, fish and vegies. Everything is on display, so just pick what you want, grab a beer from the shops across the way and take a seat at the covered tables.

Soul Too WESTERN $$
(亦素咖啡; Yìsù Kāfēi; ☎326 0396; 18 Laoying Shao; ⌚8am-midnight) An upmarket cafe serving a wide variety of proper coffee (from Y25), as well as good pizza (from Y45), pasta and tempting chocolate cake, Soul Too makes for a nice pit stop away from the tour-group madness. It's not cheap, but then there aren't many places in Fènghuáng with an extensive list of foreign wines and a choice of Cuban cigars

Drinking

Laoying Shao is full of extremely loud bars with river views, live music and throngs of vacationing Chinese letting their hair down. Some bars don't welcome foreigners. There are also a few cafes here. Other bars can be found along Huilong Ge on the other side of the river.

Vendors of local Miao spirits *(miáo jiǔ)* are plentiful; expect to pay Y10 to Y15 for a *jīn* of 53°-proof mind-warping alcohol.

Elope Bar BAR
(25 Laoying Shao; ⌚1pm-2am) More mellow than most of the bars on the Laoying Shao strip, and with a raised balcony that enables you to sip a drink while contemplating the river. Beers start at Y20, cocktails at Y35.

Information

Note that no banks can exchange foreign currency in Fènghuáng, so change money before you arrive. The nearest bank that can exchange money is in Jíshǒu.

China Post (中国邮政; Zhōngguó Yóuzhèng)

Chūnyì Pharmacy (春意大药房; Chūnyì Dàyàofáng; Nanhua Lu; ⌚8am-10pm) Southwest of town, near the corner with Jianshe Lu.

Industrial & Commercial Bank of China (ICBC:工商银行; Gōngháng; Nanhua Lu) Has a 24-hour ATM.

Internet cafe (wǎngbā; Hongqiao Donglu; per hr Y2; ⌚24hr)

Tourism Administrative Bureau of Fènghuáng (凤凰旅游中心; Fènghuáng Lǚyóu Zhōngxīn; ☎322 9364; 46 Daomen Kou) Alongside Culture Sq.

Xīndōnglì Internet Cafe (新动力网吧; Xīndōnglì Wǎngbā; 2nd fl, Jianshe Lu; per hr Y2; ⌚24hr) Just west of the road at the southern foot of Hóng Bridge.

Getting There & Around

Buses to and from Jíshǒu stop outside the old town. A motorcycle taxi will ferry you in for Y5.

MINORITIES & MISSILES

Way down in the southwest corner of Húnán is the Tōngdào Dong Minority Autonomous County (通道侗族自治区; Tōngdào Dòngzú Zìzhìqū). Close to the borders with both Guǎngxī and Guìzhōu, this is the Húnán heartland of the Dong minority, famed for their distinctive drum towers, wind-and-rain bridges and dark wooden buildings. The hills surrounding the town of Tōngdào are full of little-visited villages, whose residents communicate in the Dong language rather than Mandarin (although they understand it).

Particularly picturesque is **Yùtouzhài** (芋头寨), which has a charming collection of drum towers, bridges and buildings climbing the pine- and bamboo-covered hillsides. Look out for the tall and imposing **Lúshēng Lóu** (芦笙楼), a nine-tiered drum tower. Also worth a visit is **Píngrì** (坪日)and its **Huílóng Bridge** (回龙桥; Huílóng Qiáo), a magnificent wind-and-rain bridge first built in 1761.

About 1km north of Píngrì is **Hénglǐngzhài** (横岭寨), which is set in a lovely landscape of paddies and hill slopes layered with terraced fields. Many other villages in the area are worthy of exploration as well. Nondescript **Tōngdào** can be used as a base for exploring the area; it's possible to stay in local houses, but don't expect much in the way of comfort. Bear in mind, too, that some villages may levy an entrance fee and that irregular bus schedules mean moving between the villages is time-consuming.

However, the biggest problem travellers face here is that the region, including the neighbouring county of Jìngzhōu, is also home to a sizeable proportion of China's intercontinental ballistic missiles. While you won't see any evidence of this, as the missile silos are buried in hillsides or cunningly camouflaged as wind-and-rain bridges (not really), the authorities can't seem to make up their minds about whether foreigners should be allowed here. Consequently, the area has been both opened and closed in recent years.

At the time of writing, it was closed and foreigners who unwittingly strayed into the region were being put on the first bus out. That may well have changed by the time you read this, so check with the local PSB. If it is still closed, you will have better luck sneaking in from Guǎngxī than heading south from Jìngzhōu, where the bus drivers will tell the police they have a foreigner on board.

Regular buses run to Jíshǒu throughout the day (Y15, 70 minutes).

Chángshā Y120, five hours, eight daily (8.30am to 5.30pm)

Huáihuà Y33, two hours, every 20 minutes. Depart from a car park off Hongqiao Donglu.

Wǔhàn Y200, eight hours, one daily (3.10pm)

Zhāngjiājiè Y60, four hours, four daily (8.30am, 9.30am, 2.30am and 4.30pm)

There's no train station in Fènghuáng, but you can book tickets for elsewhere at the **Train Ticket Booking Office** (火车售票处; Huǒchē Shòupiàochù; ☎322 2410; Hongqiao Zhonglu; ⏰8am-10pm). It's just south of Hóng Bridge opposite the Xīndōnglì Internet Cafe.

To get around locally, taxis start at Y3.

Hóngjiāng Old Town 洪江古商城

☎0745

This little-known town 55km south of Huáihuà boasts an extraordinary history as a Qing-dynasty financial and trading centre, thanks to its fortuitous location at the confluence of the Yuán (沅江; Yuán Jiāng) and Wū (巫水; Wū Shuǐ) Rivers. At one time, it was the main opium-distribution hub in southwest China. Dating as far back as the Northern Song dynasty, the city is mostly modern now, but the past lives on in the remarkable old town (Hóngjiāng Gǔshāngchéng), which is still home to a few thousand people. As it's far less touristy than Fènghuáng, you're likely to be exploring the place on your own.

Sights

The old town is the principal reason to come here and can be visited in half a day. Essentially enclosed within Xinmin Lu (新民路), Yuanjiang Lu (沅江路) and Xiongxi Lu (雄溪路), which turns into Xingfu Lu (幸福路), the old town undulates in a delightfully higgledy-piggledy, often steep, maze of narrow stone-flagged alleys and lanes. Signposts in English and Chinese point the way to the notable buildings, some of which have been restored, including the town brothel, tax office, opium stores, newspaper office, shrines and the courtyard homes of prominent merchants. Nearly all were constructed in the Yìnzǐwū (窨子屋) style, where the interiors are lit by light wells in the roofs, which could be opened and closed depending on the season.

Getting lost in this labyrinth is inevitable, but the locals who live in some of the 380 historic structures, as well as in newer dwellings, can point the way. Make sure to check out the **Taiping Temple** (太平宫; Tàipíng Gōng), built in 1723 but largely destroyed during the Cultural Revolution.

There's an official **ticket office** (⏲8am-5pm) on Yuanjiang Lu. You can avoid paying the hefty admission price of Y100 by simply wandering into the old town via the many alleys that connect it to Xinmin Lu, including one opposite the Hóngjiàng Hotel, Yuanjiang Lu and Xiongxi Lu. However, you won't be allowed into some of the key sights without a ticket.

Sleeping & Eating

For restaurants, head to the riverbank on the left-hand side of the Hóng Bridge, where a strip of places cook up the catch of the day.

Liú Sōngxiū Guest House GUESTHOUSE **$**
(刘松修商宅; Liú Sōngxiū Shāngzhái; ☎763 6222; 9 Liren Alley; 古商城里仁巷9号; d/ste Y88/168; ❄) This tastefully restored former inn sits at the heart of the old town and offers the chance to experience a taste of Hóngjiāng's glory days. The huge skylight illuminates the two-storey, nicely furnished all-wood interior. There are only two rooms here; the double is a very comfortable option with TV, but splash out on the suite and you get to sleep on a Qing dynasty-style emperor bed. The showers and toilets are shared.

Hóngjiāng Hotel HOTEL **$$**
(洪江大酒店; Hóngjiāng Dàjiǔdiàn; ☎766 2999; Xinmin Lu; 新民路; s/d Y168/188, discounts of 20%; ❄) Towering two-star next door to the Bank of China. Clean and comfortable, it's just across the road from an entrance to the old town and three minutes' walk from the Hóng Bridge.

Information

Bank of China (中国银行; Zhōngguó Yínháng) Has a 24-hour ATM and will change currency.

Getting There & Away

Do not confuse Hóngjiāng Old Town with Hóngjiāng City (洪江市; Hóngjiāng Shì), the town on the railway to the west. The old town is best accessed via Huáihuà (怀化). Buses leave from Huáihuà's south bus station (Y20, 80 minutes, every 40 minutes) between 6.50am and 6pm. Numerous buses return to Huáihuà from the bus station on Yuanjiang Lu opposite the main entrance to the old town.

Hong Kong

POPULATION: 7 MILLION / TELEPHONE CODE: 852

Includes »

Best Places to Eat

» Luk Yu Teahouse (p496)

» Pure Veggie House (p497)

» Ye Shanghai (p498)

» Tung Po Seafood Restaurant (p497)

» L'Atelier de Joel Robuchon (p497)

Best Places to Stay

» Hyatt Regency TST (p491)

» Upper House (p489)

» Peninsula Hong Kong (p491)

» Y-Loft Youth Square Hostel (p489)

» Hop Inn (p491)

Why Go?

Like a shot of adrenalin, Hong Kong quickens the pulse. Skyscrapers march up jungle-clad slopes by day and blaze neon by night across a harbour criss-crossed by freighters and motor junks. Above streets teeming with traffic, five-star hotels stand next to ageing tenement blocks.

The very acme of luxury can be yours in this billionaires' playground, though enjoying the city need not cost the earth. A HK$2 ride across the harbour must be the best-value cruise in the world. A meander through a market offers similarly cheap thrills. You can escape the crowds – just head for one of the city's many country parks.

This is also a city that lives to eat, offering diners the very best of China and beyond. Hong Kong, above all, rewards those who grab experience by the scruff of the neck, who'll try that jellyfish, explore half-deserted villages or stroll beaches far from neon and steel.

When to Go

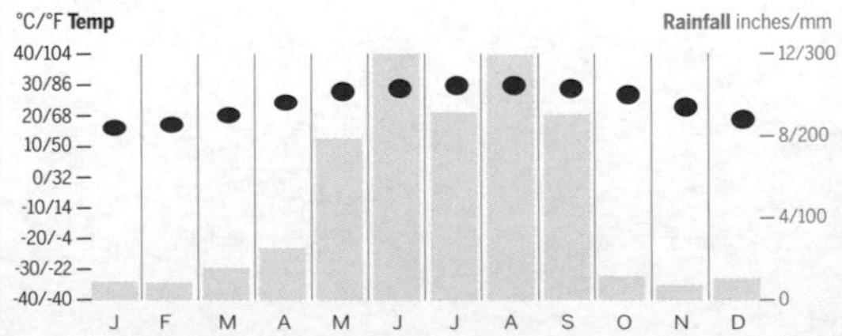

March–May Asia's top film festival and deities' birthday festivities beckon beyond a sea of umbrellas.

June–September Get hot (sunbathing, clothes), get wet (boat racing, cocktails): sultry summer.

November–February Mountains by day, Arts Festival by night, plus Chinese New Year celebrations.

History

Until European traders started importing opium into the country, Hong Kong really was an obscure backwater in the Chinese empire. The British, with a virtually inexhaustible supply from the poppy fields of Bengal, developed the trade aggressively and by the start of the 19th century traded this 'foreign mud' for Chinese tea, silk and porcelain.

China's attempts to stamp out the opium trade gave the British the pretext they needed for military action. Gunboats were sent in. In 1841, the Union flag was hoisted on Hong Kong Island and the Treaty of Nanking, which brought an end to the so-called First Opium War, ceded the island to the British crown 'in perpetuity'.

At the end of the Second Opium War in 1860, Britain took possession of Kowloon Peninsula, and in July 1898 a 99-year lease was granted for the New Territories.

Through the 20th century Hong Kong grew in fits and starts. Waves of refugees fled China for Hong Kong during times of turmoil. Trade flourished along with Hong Kong's vibrant British expat social life until the Japanese army crashed the party in 1941.

By the end of the war Hong Kong's population had fallen from 1.6 million to 610,000. But trouble in China soon swelled the numbers again as refugees (including industrialists from Shànghǎi) from the communist victory in 1949 increased Hong Kong's population beyond two million. This, together with a UN trade embargo on China during the Korean War and China's isolation in the next three decades, enabled Hong Kong to reinvent itself as one of the world's most dynamic ports and manufacturing and financial-service centres.

PRICE INDICATORS

The following price indicators are used in this chapter:

Sleeping

$	less than HK$900
$$	HK$900 to HK$1500
$$$	more than HK$1500

Eating

$	less than HK$200
$$	HK$200 to HK$400
$$$	more than HK$400

In 1984 Britain agreed to return what would become the Special Administrative Region (SAR) of Hong Kong to China in 1997, on the condition it would retain its free-market economy as well as its social and legal systems for 50 years. China called it 'One country, two systems'. On 1 July 1997, in pouring rain outside the Hong Kong Convention & Exhibition Centre, the British era ended.

In the years that followed, Hong Kong weathered several major storms – an economic downturn sparked by the Asian financial crisis of 1997, the outbreak of the deadly SARS virus and general mistrust of the government.

At the end of the decade, Hong Kong's economy is recuperating. However, Donald Tsang's leadership has become almost as weak as that of his oft-criticised predecessor Tung Chee Hwa. The dowdy Tsang has made the mistake of wanting to become a populist politician despite his lack of the qualities required.

Climate

Hong Kong rarely gets especially cold, but it would be worth packing something at least a little bit warm between November and March. Between May and mid-September temperatures in the mid-30s combined with stifling humidity can turn you into a walking sweat machine. This time is also the wettest, accounting for about 80% of annual rainfall – partly due to typhoons.

The best time to visit Hong Kong is between mid-September and February. At any time of the year pollution can be diabolical, most of it pouring across the border from the coal-powered factories of Guǎngdōng, many of which are Hong Kong owned.

Language

Almost 95% of Hong Kongers are Cantonese-speaking Chinese, though Putonghua (Mandarin) is increasingly used. Visitors should have few problems, however, because English is widely spoken and the city's street signs are bilingual. Written Chinese in Hong Kong uses traditional Chinese characters, some of which are more complicated than the simplified Chinese used on the mainland.

Sights

Hong Kong is divided into four main areas: Hong Kong Island, Kowloon, the New Territories and the Outlying Islands. Most of

Hong Kong Highlights

1. Cross Victoria Harbour on the iconic **Star Ferry** (p508)
2. Ride the historic **Peak Tram** (p474) up Victoria Peak
3. Enjoy yum cha under fans at **Luk Yu Teahouse** (p496)
4. Soak up the incensed air at **Man Mo Temple** (p474)
5. Lose yourself in a walled village on the **Ping Shan Heritage Trail** (p484)
6. Get some context for it all at the **Museum of History** (p481)
7. Pay your respects to the **Big Buddha** (p485)

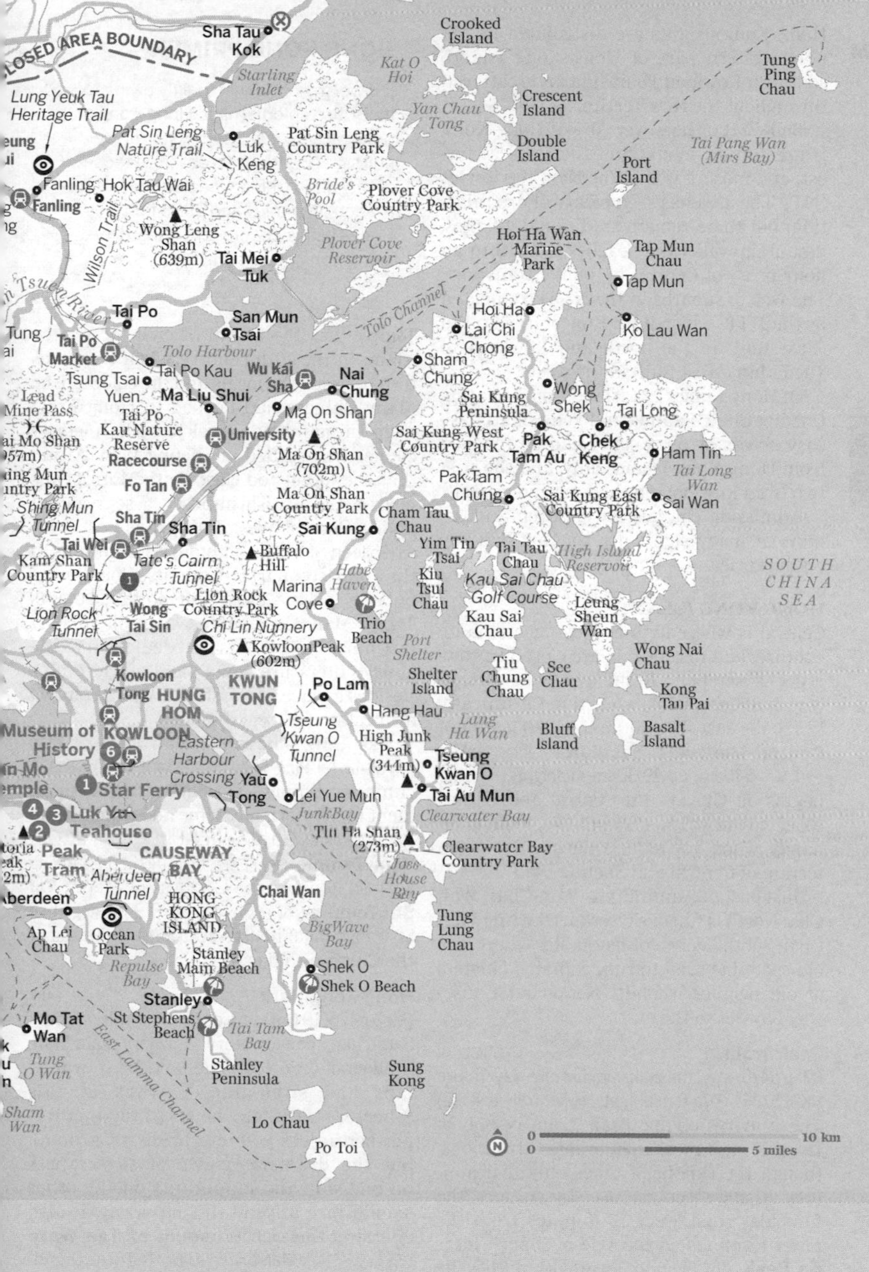

CLOSED AREA BOUNDARY
Sha Tau Kok
Crooked Island
Kat O Hoi
Starling Inlet
Tung Ping Chau
Lung Yeuk Tau Heritage Trail
Crescent Island
Yan Chau Tong
Double Island
Pat Sin Leng Nature Trail
Luk Keng
Pat Sin Leng Country Park
Tai Pang Wan (Mirs Bay)
Port Island
Fanling
Hok Tau Wai
Bride's Pool
Plover Cove Country Park
Wong Leng Shan (639m)
Wilson Trail
Plover Cove Reservoir
Hoi Ha Wan Marine Park
Tap Mun Chau
Tai Mei Tuk
Tap Mun
Tai Po
Tolo Channel
Hoi Ha
San Mun Tsai
Lai Chi Chong
Ko Lau Wan
Tai Po Market
Tolo Harbour
Sham Chung
Tai Po Kau
Tsung Tsai Yuen
Wu Kai Sha
Nai Chung
Wong Shek
Ma Liu Shui
Ma On Shan
Sai Kung Peninsula
Lead Mine Pass
Tai Po Kau Nature Reserve
Tai Long
University
Sai Kung West Country Park
Pak Tam Au
Chek Keng
Ham Tin
Ma On Shan (702m)
Racecourse
Tai Long Wan
Fo Tan
Pak Tam Chung
Ma On Shan Country Park
Sai Kung East Country Park
Sai Wan
Shing Mun Tunnel
Cham Tau Chau
Sha Tin
Sha Tin
Sai Kung
Tai Wai
Buffalo Hill
Yim Tin Tsai
Tai Tau Chau
High Island Reservoir
Kam Shan Country Park
Tate's Cairn Tunnel
Habe Haven
SOUTH CHINA SEA
Kiu Tsui Chau
Kau Sai Chau Golf Course
Lion Rock Country Park
Marina Cove
Leung Sheun Wan
Lion Rock Tunnel
Wong Tai Sin
Kau Sai Chau
Trio Beach
Chi Lin Nunnery
KowloonPeak (602m)
Port Shelter
Wong Nai Chau
Kowloon Tong
Tiu Chung Chau
See Chau
HUNG HOM
KWUN TONG
Po Lam
Shelter Island
Kong Tau Pai
Hang Hau
Tseung Kwan O Tunnel
Lang Ha Wan
Museum of History
KOWLOON
Bluff Island
Basalt Island
High Junk Peak (344m)
Eastern Harbour Crossing
Tseung Kwan O
Yau Tong
Star Ferry
Tai Au Mun
Lei Yue Mun
Luk Yu Teahouse
Junk Bay
Clearwater Bay
Tin Ha Shan (273m)
Peak Tram
CAUSEWAY BAY
Clearwater Bay Country Park
Aberdeen Tunnel
Jass House Bay
Aberdeen
Chai Wan
HONG KONG ISLAND
Tung Lung Chau
Ap Lei Chau
Ocean Park
Big Wave Bay
Stanley Main Beach
Repulse Bay
Shek O
Shek O Beach
Stanley
Mo Tat Wan
St Stephens Beach
Tai Tam Bay
East Lamma Channel
Tung O Wan
Stanley Peninsula
Sung Kong
Sham Wan
Lo Chau
Po Toi
0
10 km
0
5 miles

Hong Kong's sights are distributed in the northwestern part of Hong Kong Island, southern Kowloon Peninsula and scattered throughout the New Territories.

Believe it or not, over 70% of Hong Kong is green hills, mountains and tropical forest, and most of it is in the New Territories (NT). The area has seen plenty of urbanisation, but there remain traditional villages, mountain walks and beaches, all within an hour or so of Central by public transport. The web of suburbs in the NT is connected by the MTR, which links Kowloon to Lo Wu (East Rail) in the north and Kowloon to Tuen Mun (West Rail) in the west.

Of Hong Kong's 234 islands, only Lantau, Cheung Chau, Lamma and Peng Chau have easy access by ferry. They can be reached from Hong Kong Island daily, and the first two from Kowloon on the weekend as well.

Admission charges for children and seniors at many sights are roughly half the regular price.

HONG KONG ISLAND

Central is where high finance meets haute couture, and mega deals are closed in towering skyscrapers. To the west is historically rich Sheung Wan, while quiet Admiralty lies to the east. The 800m-long, 20-segment **Central-Midlevels Escalator** (Map p476; ⌚down 6-10am, up 10.30am-midnight), which begins on Queen's Rd Central and climbs 135m to finish at Conduit Rd, comes in handy when you're negotiating the steep terrain of Central and Sheung Wan.

Just east of Admiralty is Wan Chai. Wan Chai North is full of skyscrapers, while Wan Chai South, near Johnston Rd where the old coastline used to run, contains clusters of old neighbourhoods. Neon-clad Causeway Bay lies to the east.

Peak Tram — FUNICULAR

(Map p476; www.thepeak.com.hk; one-way/return HK$25/36; ⌚7am-midnight; Ⓜ Central, exit J2) The gravity-defying Peak Tram is one of Hong Kong's most memorable attractions, though the ride itself takes only five minutes. Rising steeply above skyscrapers, the funicular runs every 15 minutes from the lower terminus up the side of 552m **Victoria Peak**. On clear days and at night, the view from the top is spectacular.

TOP CHOICE Man Mo Temple — TEMPLE

(文武廟; Map p476; 124-126 Hollywood Rd, Sheung Wan; ⌚8am-6pm; bus 26) Hong Kong's most important temple, Man Mo Temple was the centre of civil life on the island in the 19th century when trust was thin between the locals and the colonialists. Many Chinese had flocked to Hong Kong from the mainland to seek jobs, the majority coolies who settled in Sheung Wan. Afraid that they'd get too close to the Europeans nearby, the British imposed a segregation policy: Chinese West, Europeans East, with Aberdeen St as the boundary. Conditions in the Chinese quarter were atrocious and a bubonic plague broke out, killing 20,000. Taoist Man Mo Temple was built in 1847 by Chinese merchants and dedicated to the gods of literature ('man') and of war ('mo'). Besides a place of worship, it was a court of arbitration for local disputes.

Pak Sing Ancestral Hall (百姓廟; Map p476; 42 Tai Ping Shan St; ⌚8am-6pm) was a clinic for Chinese patients refusing treatment by Western medicine and a storeroom for bodies awaiting burial in China. **Kwun Yam Temple** (觀音堂; Map p476; 34 Tai Ping Shan St) honours the Goddess of Mercy. **Tai Sui Temple** (太歲廟; Map p476; 9 Tai Ping Shan St; ⌚8am-6pm) houses statues of animals of the Chinese zodiac.

> **HONG KONG PRIMER**
>
> It's worth noting that, partly owing to its British colonial past, Hong Kong's political and economic systems are still significantly different from those of mainland China. See p988 for information on money and p993 for visas. Prices in this chapter are quoted in Hong Kong dollars (HK$).

Hong Kong Park — PARK

(Map p476; 19 Cotton Tree Dr, Admiralty; ⌚park 6am-11pm, conservatory & aviary 9am-5pm; Ⓜ Admiralty, exit C1) The artificial waterfalls and swan-graced ponds in this 8-hectare park may be a tad too picture-perfect unless you're a bride (or groom), but the dramatic views of skyscrapers on one side and mountains on the other should lure anyone to snap away. It also contains the rich **Museum of Tea Ware** (茶具文物館; Map p476; 10 Cotton Tree Dr, Admiralty; ⌚10am-5pm Wed-Mon).

Central Police Station Compound — HERITAGE BUILDING

(前中區警署; Map p476; 10 Hollywood Rd; Ⓜ Central, exit D1) Hong Kong's oldest symbol of law and order, this now disused police-magistracy-prison complex modelled after London's Old Bailey offered streamlined, one-stop 'service' to criminals. Visitors are not allowed inside the sprawling complex.

Hong Kong Zoological & Botanical Gardens PARK
(Map p476; Albany Rd, Central; ⏲terrace gardens 6am-10pm, zoo & aviaries to 7pm; 🚌buses 3B, 12) Built over a century ago in the style of an English park, the gardens feature a pleasant collection of arboured paths, fountains and aviaries and a zoo. It's ideal for a walk, if you can ignore the smell of flamingo droppings.

Statue Square HISTORIC MONUMENTS
(Map p476; Edinburgh Pl, Central; Ⓜ Central, exit K) This leisurely square used to house effigies of British royalty. Now it pays tribute to a single sovereign – the founder of HSBC, the banking giant which owns the square. To the east is the **Legislative Council Building** (立法會大樓; Map p476; 8 Jackson Rd), a neoclassical edifice. To the north is the **Cenotaph** (和平紀念碑; Map p476; Chater Rd), a memorial to Hong Kong residents killed during the two world wars.

Dr Sun Yatsen Museum MUSEUM
(孫中山紀念館; Map p476; 7 Castle Rd, Midlevels, Central; admission HK$10; ⏲10am-6pm Mon-Wed, Fri & Sat, to 7pm Sun; 🚌buses 3B, 12) Photographs and archival materials related to the father of modern China and his time in Hong Kong are respectfully displayed inside a historic house. The museum also publishes a guidebook on the **Dr Sun Yatsen Historical Trail** – most sites only have a plastic plaque to evoke their former identities, so bring your imagination.

St John's Cathedral CATHEDRAL
(聖約翰座堂; Map p476; www.stjohnscathedral.org.hk; 4-8 Garden Rd, Central; ⏲7am-6pm; Ⓜ Central, exit K) An elegant Anglican cathedral consecrated in 1849.

Hong Kong Catholic Cathedral of the Immaculate Conception CATHEDRAL
(天主教聖母無原罪主教座堂; Map p476; http://cathedral.catholic.org.hk; 16 Caine Rd, Central; ⏲7am-7pm) Hong Kong's most representative Catholic building, built in 1888.

Jamia Mosque MOSQUE
(回教清真禮拜堂; Map p476; ⏲2523 7743; 30 Shelley St, Central) Hong Kong's oldest mosque is closed to non-Muslims.

SIGHTS WEBSITES

Handy websites for sights listed in this book:

» **Antiquities & Monuments Office** (http://amo.gov.hk) All villages, heritage trails, and some historic structures.

» **Chinese Temple Committee** (www.ctc.org.hk) Most temples.

» **Leisure & Cultural Services Department** (www.lcsd.gov.hk) All public parks and museums.

Ohel Leah Synagogue SYNAGOGUE
(猶太教莉亞堂; Map p476; ⏲2589 2621; www.ohelleah.org; 70 Robinson Rd, Midlevels; ⏲10.30am-7pm Mon-Thu) This Moorish temple is the territory's earliest synagogue. Bring ID if you want to visit the interior; open by appointment only.

Old Wan Chai OLD NEIGHBOURHOODS
The area around Queen's Rd E (Wan Chai metro station, exit A3) is filled with pockets of local culture that are best explored on foot. The historic **Blue House** (Map p480; 72-74a Stone Nullah Lane) is a prewar building with cast-iron Spanish balconies reminiscent of those found in New Orleans. Conservationists love it; tenants loathe it (old Bluesy's loos don't flush!). **Old Wan Chai Post Office** (舊灣仔郵政局; Map p480; 221 Queen's Rd E; ⏲10am-5pm Wed-Mon) is Hong Kong's oldest post-office building. The area sandwiched by Queen's Rd E and Johnston Rd is a lively outdoor bazaar. **Wan Chai market** (p480; ⏲7.30am-7pm) vendors flaunt their wares on Cross St and Stone Nullah Lane. **Tai Yuen St** has goldfish, plastic flowers and granny underwear for sale but is best known for its **toy shops** (14-19 Tai Yuen St; ⏲10am-8.30pm) selling collectibles such as clockwork tin.

Pak Tai Temple TEMPLE
(2 Lung On St, Wan Chai; ⏲8am-5pm; Ⓜ Wan Chai, exit A3) A short stroll up Stone Nullah Lane takes you to a majestic Taoist temple built 140 years ago to honour a god of the sea and recently given a facelift. The temple is impressive, but the waxy likeness of the immortal makes one wonder if the contractor had taken the facelift a little too literally.

Tin Hau Temple TEMPLE
(天後廟; Map p480; 10 Tin Hau Temple Rd, Causeway Bay; ⏲7am-5pm; Ⓜ Tin Hau, exit B) This listed

Sheung Wan, Central & Admiralty

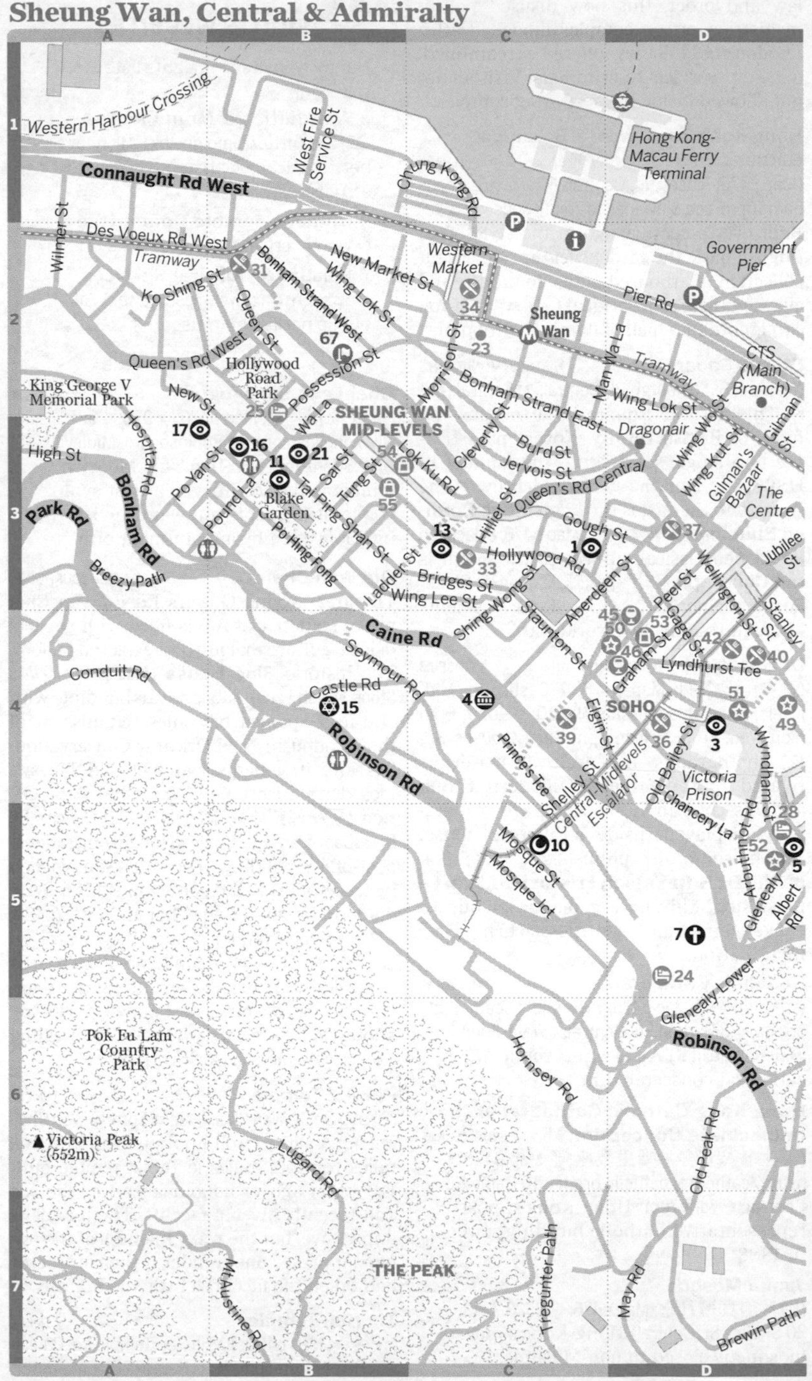

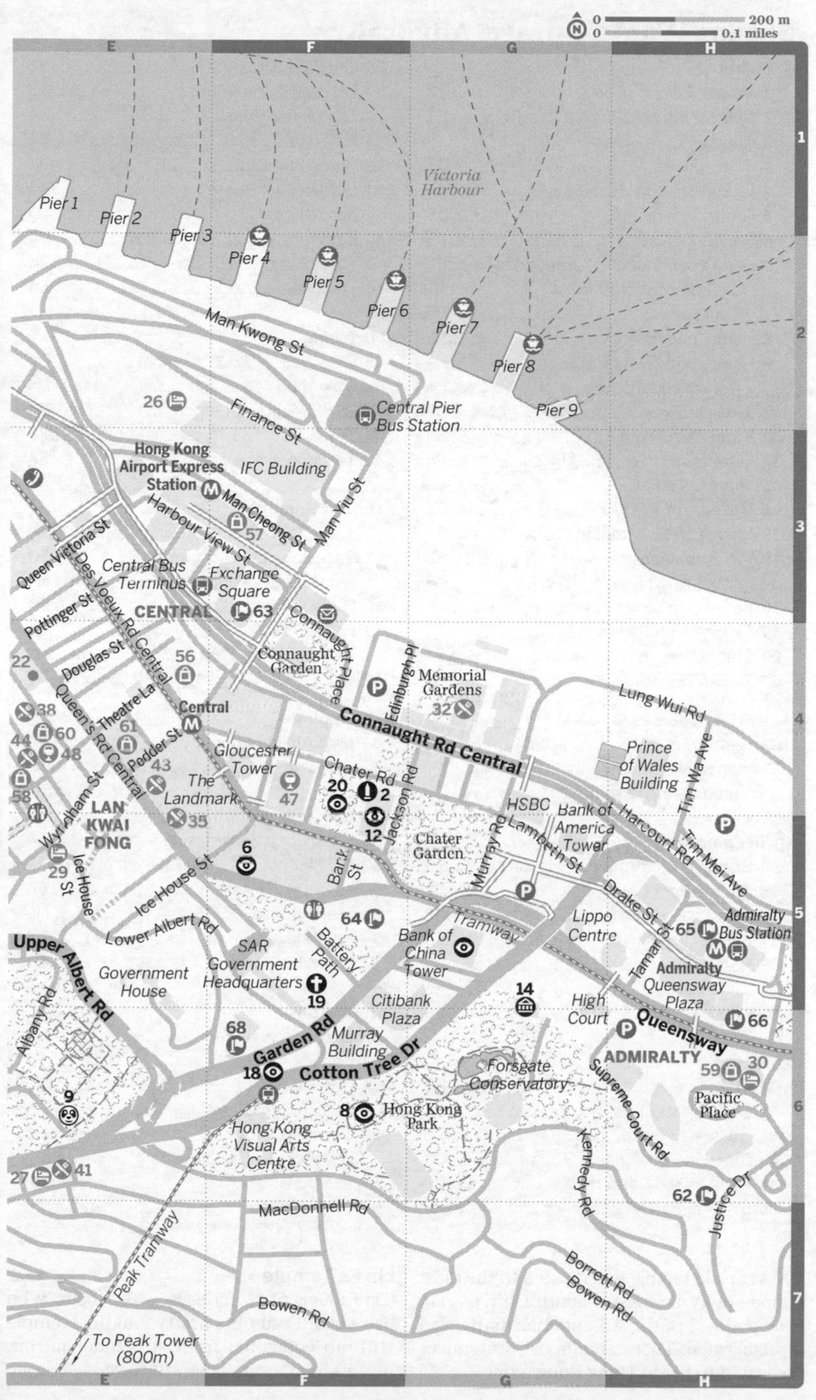

0 200 m
0 0.1 miles
Victoria Harbour
Pier 1
Pier 2
Pier 3
Pier 4
Pier 5
Pier 6
Pier 7
Pier 8
Pier 9
Man Kwong St
Finance St
Central Pier Bus Station
Hong Kong Airport Express Station
IFC Building
Man Cheong St
Man Yiu St
Harbour View St
Queen Victoria St
Des Voeux Rd Central
Central Bus Terminus
Exchange Square
CENTRAL
Connaught Place
Pottinger St
Douglas St
Connaught Garden
Memorial Gardens
Edinburgh Pl
Connaught Rd Central
Lung Wui Rd
Queen's Rd Central
Theatre La
Central
Pedder St
Gloucester Tower
Chater Rd
Jackson Rd
Prince of Wales Building
Tim Wa Ave
The Landmark
LAN KWAI FONG
Wyndham St
HSBC
Bank of America Tower
Harcourt Rd
Lambeth St
Murray Rd
Chater Garden
Tim Mei Ave
Ice House St
Bank St
Drake St
Lower Albert Rd
Tramway
Lippo Centre
Admiralty Bus Station
Battery Path
Bank of China Tower
Tamar St
Admiralty
Queensway Plaza
Upper Albert Rd
Government House
SAR Government Headquarters
Albany Rd
Citibank Plaza
High Court
Queensway
Garden Rd
Murray Building
ADMIRALTY
Cotton Tree Dr
Forsgate Conservatory
Supreme Court Rd
Pacific Place
Hong Kong Park
Hong Kong Visual Arts Centre
Kennedy Rd
Justice Dr
MacDonnell Rd
Peak Tramway
Borrett Rd
Bowen Rd
To Peak Tower (800m)
HONG KONG

Sheung Wan, Central & Admiralty

Sights

1 Amelia Johnson Contemporary........... C3
2 Cenotaph..F4
3 Central Police Station Compound.. D4
4 Dr Sun Yat-sen Museum..................... C4
5 Grotto Fine Art.................................. D5
6 Hanart TZ Gallery F5
7 Hong Kong Catholic Cathedral of the Immaculate Conception.................................. D5
8 Hong Kong Park..................................F6
9 Hong Kong Zoological & Botanical Gardens.............................E6
10 Jamia Mosque.................................. C5
11 Kwun Yam Temple B3
12 Legislative Council Building.................F5
13 Man Mo Temple C3
14 Museum of Tea Ware G5
15 Ohel Leah Synagogue B4
16 Pak Sing Ancestral Hall........................ B3
17 Para/Site Art Space............................ A3
18 Peak Tram Lower Terminus F6
19 St John's Cathedral..............................F5
20 Statue Square......................................F4
21 Tai Sui Temple B3

Activities, Courses & Tours

22 Fightin' Fit...E4
23 Wan Kei Ho International Martial Arts Association.................... C2

Sleeping

24 Bishop Lei International House............ D5
25 Central Park Hotel.............................. B2
26 Four Seasons Hotel E2
27 Garden View YWCA E6
28 Hotel LKF... D5
29 Ice House..E5
30 Upper House H6

Eating

31 ABC... B2
32 City Hall Maxim's Palace...................... G4
city'super.......................................(see 57)
33 Classified The Cheese Room................ C3
34 Honeymoon Dessert C2
35 L'Atelier de Joel Robuchon...................E5
36 Life Cafe...D4
37 Lin Heung Tea House............................D3
38 Luk Yu Tea House E4
39 Magushi...C4
40 Nha Trang D4
41 Pure Veggie House...............................E6
San Xi Lou....................................(see 41)
42 Ser Wong Fun D4
43 ThreeSixty E4
44 Yung Kee..E4

Drinking

45 Club 71...D4
46 Makumba D4
Pacific Coffee Company .... (see 57)
47 Sevva..F4
48 Tastings Wine Bar E4

Entertainment

Azure ....(see 28)
49 Backstage Live Restaurant D4
Gecko Lounge...............................(see 51)
50 Peel Fresco D4
51 Propaganda D4
Tazmania Ballroom......................(see 28)
52 Works D5

Shopping

53 Arch Angel Antiques D4
54 Cat Street B3
Dymocks .... (see 57)
55 Hollywood Rd..B3
56 Hong Kong Book Centre........................E4
57 IFC Mall F3
58 Mountain Folkcraft...............................E4
59 Pacific Place H6
60 Photo Scientific E4
61 Shanghai Tang.......................................E4

Information

62 British Consulate.................................. H6
63 Canadian Consulate..............................F3
64 Dutch Consulate....................................F5
65 French Consulate.................................H5
66 German Consulate H6
Japanese Consulate.......................(see 63)
67 Lao Consulate.......................................B2
68 US Consulate..F6

300-year-old temple is dedicated to the most famous deity in coastal South China – Tin Hau, goddess of the sea and guardian angel for fishermen. There are almost 60 temples dedicated to her in Hong Kong alone.

Lin Fa Temple TEMPLE
(Lin Fa Kung St W, Tai Hang; ⏲8am-5pm; Ⓜ Tin Hau, exit B) 'Lotus' is a pretty Buddhist temple with an octagonal front, a boulder jutting into its rear, and elaborate frescos. A stone

staircase leads to the altar. The temple's neighbourhood, Tai Hang, is famous for the **Fire Dragon Dance**. For three days beginning at 8pm, during the Mid-Autumn Festival, a 70m 'dragon' made of thousands of burning incense sticks is paraded by barebacked men through the neighbourhood.

Hung Shing Temple TEMPLE

(Map p480; 129-131 Queen's Rd E, Wan Chai; 8am-5.30pm; M Wan Chai, exit A3) Once a seaside shrine, this tiny temple is dedicated to the worship of a deified official. It also offers **villain exorcism** (打小人; *da siu yan*; HK$100), a type of folk sorcery that removes adversaries for clients through an exorcist, who strikes with a symbolic weapon an allegory of that hated boss or pestering ex. This presumably will get rid of him or her for good.

Victoria Park PARK

(Map p480; Causeway Rd, Causeway Bay; M Tin Hau, exit B) Hong Kong's largest patch of public greenery is best visited on weekday mornings, when it becomes a slow-motion forest of taichi practitioners. You can join the (non)action if you like.

Stanley MARKET, BEACH

This crowd pleaser is best visited on weekdays. Its maze of covered alleyways is called **Stanley Market** (Map p472; Stanley Village Rd; 10am-6pm), which has (pricey) bargain clothing, including a variety of children's wear (haggling a must!). **Stanley Main St** is a wood-planked, waterfront promenade with all the works of a prototype beach town, views included. **Stanley Main Beach** is where to go for beach-bumming and windsurfing.

Aberdeen TYPHOON SHELTER

(Map p472) Aberdeen's main attraction is the typhoon shelter it shares with sleepy **Ap Lei Chau**, where the sampans of Hong Kong's boat-dwelling fisherfolk used to moor. On weekday evenings, you may spot dragonboat teams practising here. The best way to see the area is by sampan. A half-hour tour of the typhoon shelter costs about HK$55 per person. Embark from **Aberdeen Promenade**. You can also hop on the commuter boats plying the waters between Aberdeen Promenade and Ap Lei Chau (HK$1.80, five minutes).

Repulse Bay BEACH

(Map p472) At the southeastern end of Hong Kong's most popular beach stand the eccentric **Kwun Yam shrine** (觀音廟) and a garish gallery of deities – from goldfish and a monkey god to the more familiar Tin Hau. Crossing Longevity Bridge (長壽橋) is supposed to add three days to your life. There's no word, however, on whether running back and forth all day will add years.

Ocean Park AMUSEMENT PARK

(香港海洋公園; Map p472; www.oceanpark.com.hk; Ocean Park Rd; admission HK$250; 10am-6pm) Ocean Park, the worthy nemesis of Hong Kong Disneyland, is a massive marine-themed amusement park complete with white-knuckle rides, giant pandas, an **atoll reef** and an amazing **aquarium**. Kidults will have a blast at the park's annual **Halloween Bash** (5.30pm-midnight late Sep-Oct). Bus 629 from Admiralty MTR Station (Map p476) or Central Pier No 7 (Map p476) takes you there.

Hong Kong Film Archive FILM ARCHIVE

(2739 2139; www.filmarchive.gov.hk; 50 Lei King Rd; main foyer 10am-8pm, closed Thu, box office noon-8pm, closed Thu, resource centre 10am-7pm Mon-Wed & Fri, 10am-5pm Sat, 1-5pm Sun; M Sai Wan Ho, exit A) The excellent archive which catalogues and studies Hong Kong cinema is well worth a visit for anyone who likes films. There are over 6300 reels and tapes in the vaults and 300,000 pieces of related material. The archive's collection of Hong Kong's historical films is one of the world's largest.

Shek O BEACH

(Map p472) Shek O is the kind of place where villagers drying algae on clothes-lines live alongside Vespa-riding 'bourgeois bohemians'. Ragged cliffs and a laid-back vibe complete the picture.

KOWLOON

Tsim Sha Tsui, known for its dining and shopping options, is Hong Kong's most (charmingly) eclectic district, with a population comprising Chinese, Indians, Filipinos, Nepalese, Africans and Europeans, and the glamorous often only a stone's throw from the pedestrian.

Just north of Tsim Sha Tsui is Yau Ma Tei, whose grid layout strikes a contrast to TST's meandering streets. The Chinese characters refer to the place *(tei)* where fishermen waterproofed their boats with oil *(yau)* and repaired their hemp ropes *(ma)*. Traffic- and pedestrian-choked Mong Kok is the world's most densely populated place.

Wan Chai & Causeway Bay

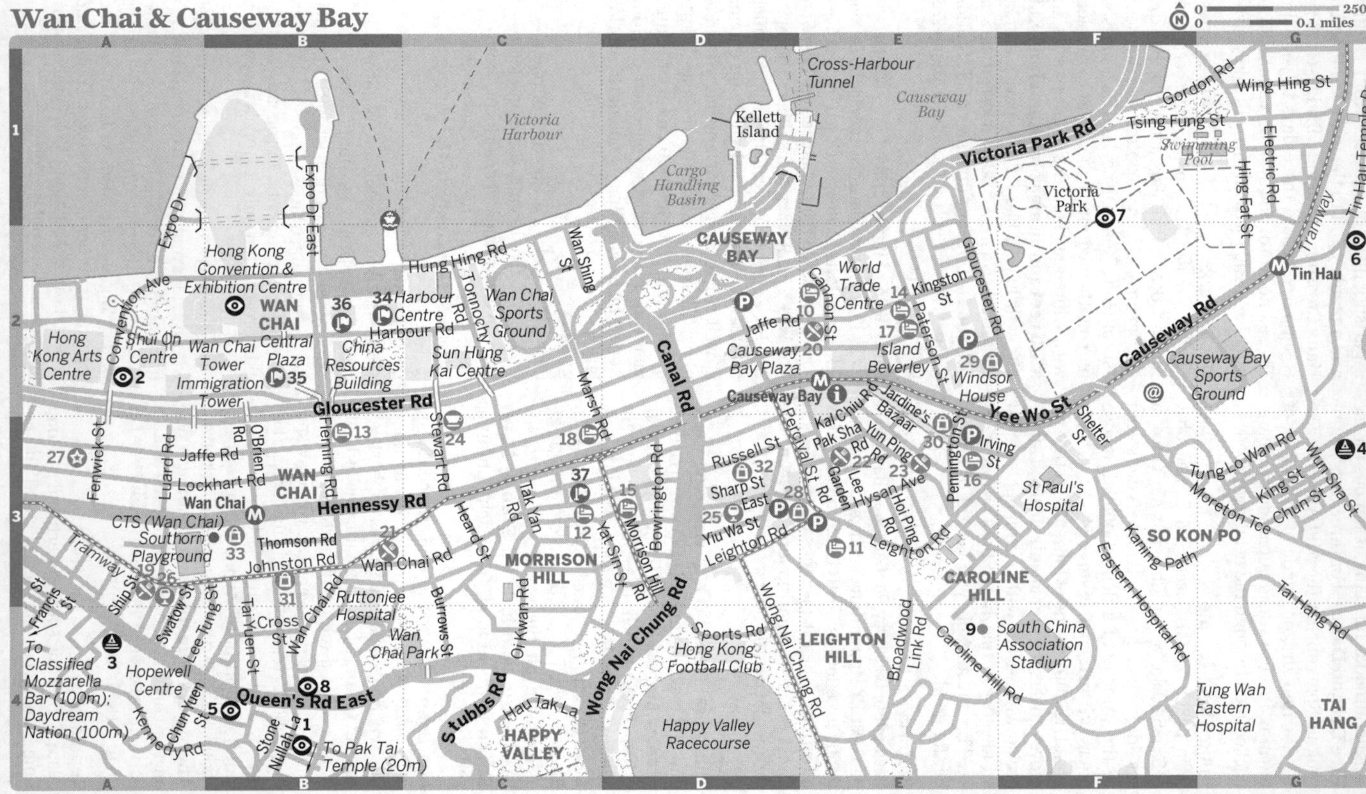

Wan Chai & Causeway Bay

Sights

1 Blue House B4
2 Hong Kong Arts Centre A2
3 Hung Shing Temple A4
4 Lin Fa Temple G3
5 Old Wan Chai Post Office B4
6 Tin Hau Temple G2
7 Victoria Park F1
8 Wan Chai Market B4

Activities, Courses & Tours

9 South China Athletic Association E4

Sleeping

10 Alisan Guest House E2
11 Causeway Bay Guest House E3
12 Charterhouse Hotel C3
13 Fleming B3
14 Hong Kong Hostel E2
15 Hotel Bonaparte D3
16 Jia E3
17 Noble Hostel E2
18 Wifi Boutique Hotel C3

Eating

19 Bo Innovation A3
20 Changwon Korean Restaurant E2
21 Hang Zhou Restaurant B3
22 Tai Ping Koon E3
23 West Villa E3

Drinking

24 Cafe Zambra C3
25 Executive B.A.R. D3
26 Pawn A3

Entertainment

27 Wanch A3

Shopping

28 G.O.D. D3
29 In Square E2
30 Jardine's Bazaar E3
31 Johnston Rd B3
32 Page One D3
33 Wan Chai Computer Centre B3

Information

34 Australian Consulate B2
35 New Zealand Consulate B2
36 South African Consulate B2
37 Vietnamese Consulate C3

TOP CHOICE **Tsim Sha Tsui East Promenade & Star Ferry** HARBOUR
(尖沙嘴東部海濱花園和天星小輪; Map p492; Salisbury Rd; Ⓜ Tsim Sha Tsui, exit E) The resplendent views of Victoria Harbour make this walkway one of the best strolls in Hong Kong. Begin your journey at the old **Kowloon-Canton Railway clock tower**, a landmark of the Age of Steam, near the **Star Ferry concourse**. To your left is the windowless **Hong Kong Cultural Centre** (香港文化中心), passing which you'll arrive at the **Avenue of the Stars** (星光大道), Hong Kong's tribute to its film industry. Though uninspiring, it's the vantage point for watching the **Symphony of Lights** (⌚8-8.20pm), a laser-light show à la *Star Wars* projected from atop skyscrapers. The walk then takes you past the hotels of the reclaimed area known as **Tsim Sha Tsui East** to **Hung Hom train station**.

TOP CHOICE **Hong Kong Museum of History** MUSEUM
(香港歷史博物館; Map p492; 100 Chatham Rd South; admission HK$10; ⌚10am-6pm Mon & Wed-Sat, to 7pm Sun; Ⓜ Tsim Sha Tsui, exit B2) If you only have time for one museum, do make it this one. It takes you on a fascinating journey through Hong Kong's past, from prehistoric times to 1997. The colourful 'Hong Kong Story' shows with interesting artefacts the customs of the territory's earliest inhabitants and the development of its urban culture. Film buffs can join spritely seniors for an old Cantonese flick in the '60s-style cinema.

Temple Street Night Market STREET MARKET
(廟街夜市; Map p494; ⌚6pm-midnight; Ⓜ Yau Ma Tei, exit C) Extending from Man Ming Lane (north) to Nanking St (south), this famous bazaar hawks everything under the moon from pirated designer bags to sex toys. Remember to bargain. There are also Cantonese opera performances, and fortune-tellers, many of them English-speaking. Night owls should saunter to the historic **wholesale fruit market** (cnr Shek Lung & Reclamation Sts; ⌚midnight-dawn; Ⓜ Yau Ma Tei, exit B2) nearby with its spectacle of trucks off-loading fresh fruit and workers manoeuvring boxes in front of century-old stalls.

ART GALLERIES

Besides the commercial galleries listed below, you should also check out the nonprofit **Para/Site Artspace** (藝術空間; Map p476; www.para-site.org.hk; 4 Po Yan St, Sheung Wan; ⏲noon-7pm Wed-Sun).

Amelia Johnson Contemporary (Map p476; www.ameliajohnsoncontemporary.com; 6-10 Sin Hing St, Central; ⏲11am-7pm Tue-Fri, to 6pm Sat) Showcases the works of artists from Hong Kong and overseas.

Grotto Fine Art (Map p476;www.grottofineart.com; 2nd fl, 31C-31d Wyndham St, Central; ⏲11am-7pm Mon-Sat) The only gallery that represents exclusively Hong Kong artists.

Hanart TZ Gallery Map p476; www.hanart.com; Room 202, 2nd fl, Henley Bldg, 5 Queen's Rd, Central; ⏲10am-6.30pm Mon-Fri, to 6pm Sat) Hanart was instrumental in introducing contemporary Chinese art to the world.

Osage Gallery (www.osagegallery.com; 5th fl, Kian Dai Industrial Bldg, 73-75 Hung To Rd; ⏲10am-7pm Tue-Sun & public holidays) This gallery specialises in Hong Kong, Chinese and Asian art.

Jade Market & Shanghai St
JADE MARKET, OLD STREETS

(玉器市場和上海街; Map p494; cnr Kansu & Battery Sts, Yau Ma Tei; ⏲10am-5pm; Ⓜ Yau Ma Tei, exit C) Some 450 stalls sell all varieties and grades of jade, but unless you know your nephrite from your jadeite, it's wise not to buy expensive pieces here. Walking down Shanghai St on the other side of Kansu St, however, is free. Once Kowloon's main drag, it's lined with stores selling embroidered Chinese wedding gowns, sandalwood incense, kitchenware, herbal medicine and Buddhist provisions; there's even a pawn shop (at the junction with Saigon St).

Tin Hau Temple
TEMPLE

(天后廟; Map p494; cnr Temple & Public Square Sts; ⏲8am-5pm; Ⓜ Yau Ma Tei, exit C) This large, incense-filled sanctuary built in the 19th century is one of Hong Kong's most famous Tin Hau temples. The square in front is Yau Ma Tei's communal heart, where fishermen once laid out their hemp ropes to sun next to banyans that today shade chess players, retirees and gangsters.

Middle Road Children's Playground
PARK, PLAYGROUND

(中間道遊樂場; Map p492; Middle Rd; ⏲7am-11pm; Ⓜ East Tsim Sha Tsui) You don't have to be 10 to appreciate this hidden gem. Besides play facilities, the spacious park has shaded seating, greenery and views of the waterfront. It's usually quiet, but on weekends it attracts children and picnickers of as many ethnicities as there are ways to go down a slide. The park sits on the podium of the MTR Tsim Sha Tsui East station. Its eastern exit is connected to the handsome **Tsim Sha Tsui East Waterfront Podium Garden** (尖沙咀東海濱平台花園; Map p492).

Signal Hill Garden & Blackhead Point Tower
PARK, TOWER

(訊號山公園和訊號塔; Map p492; Minden Row; ⏲tower 9-11am & 4-6pm) The views at the top of this knoll are quite spectacular, though if this were the 1900s all the ships in the harbour could be returning your gaze – a copper ball in the handsome Edwardian-style tower was dropped at 1pm daily so seafarers could adjust their chronometers. The garden is perched above the Middle Road Children's Playground. Enter from Minden Row (off Mody Rd).

Hong Kong Museum of Art
MUSEUM

(香港藝術博物館; Map p492; 10 Salisbury Rd; admission HK$10; ⏲10am-6pm Fri-Wed, to 8pm Sat; Ⓜ Tsim Sha Tsui, exit J) The museum's six floors of Chinese antiquities, paintings, calligraphy and contemporary Hong Kong art are a must if you're remotely interested in art. Thematic exhibitions featuring modern works by local and overseas artists are also inspiring. Free English-language tours at 11am.

Yuen Po St Bird Garden
GARDEN

(園圃街雀鳥花園; Flower Market Rd, Mong Kok; ⏲7am-8pm; Ⓜ Prince Edward, exit B1) To the east of the Prince Edward MTR station is this delightful place where birds are preened, bought, sold and fed bugs with chopsticks by their fussy owners (usually men). Nearby is the **flower market**, which keeps the same hours but is busiest after 10am.

Kowloon Park
PARK

(九龍公園; Map p492; 22 Austin Rd; ⏲6am-midnight; Ⓜ Jordan, exit E) This green oasis is great for people-watching, particularly on Sunday when it's packed with migrant domestic workers enjoying their day off singing, dancing and flirting. Sunday is also the day for Kung Fu Corner, a display of Chinese martial arts.

Fook Tak Ancient Temple TEMPLE
(福德古廟; Map p492; 30 Haiphong Rd; 6am-8pm; M Tsim Sha Tsui, exit A1)
Built in 1900, Tsim Sha Tsui's only temple is a smoky hole-in-the-hall with a hot tin roof. Most incense offerers are white-haired octogenarians – Fook Tak specialises in longevity.

Kowloon Mosque & Islamic Centre MOSQUE
(九龍清真寺暨伊斯蘭中心; Map p492; 105 Nathan Rd; 5am-10pm; M Tsim Sha Tsui, exit A1) This edifice with its gleaming dome and carved marble accommodates up to 2000 worshippers. Non-Muslims should ask for permission to enter.

Hong Kong Space Museum MUSEUM
(香港太空館; Map p492; 10 Salisbury Rd; admission HK$10, Wed free; 1-9pm Mon & Wed-Fri, 10am-9pm Sat & Sun; M East Tsim Sha Tsui, exit J) The museum has a dated feel, but simulators such as the virtual paraglider seem to hold a timeless fascination for overaged nerds. The gift shop has dehydrated 'astronaut' ice cream.

NEW TERRITORIES

The southernmost 31 sq km of the New Territories is officially called New Kowloon. Full of high-rise apartments, it's less frantic than its neighbours to the south.

Tuen Mun is the largest town in western New Territories. Yuen Long, the springboard for Hong Kong's most important cluster of walled villages as well as a world-class nature reserve, is on both the West Rail and the Light Rail Transit (LRT) lines. To reach Kam Tin, where some of the villages are located, take bus 64K (which stops along Kam Tin Rd), 77K or 54 from Yuen Long.

Sha Tin was designed on a model of the vertical futuristic city inspired by Swiss-French architect Le Corbusier. That's why skyscrapers overshadow many rural villages and also why, despite its huge population, Sha Tin doesn't feel very crowded.

The Sai Kung Peninsula is the garden spot of the New Territories and is great for hiking, sailing and seafood. The New Territories' best beaches are here, some reachable only by sampan.

HONG KONG MUSEUMS

The **Hong Kong Museum Pass** (7 days HK$30), which allows multiple entries to all museums mentioned in this book, is available from the participating museums – see www.discoverhongkong.com/eng/attractions/museum-major.html.

Museums are free on Wednesday.

TOP CHOICE **Chi Lin Nunnery** TEMPLE
(志蓮淨苑; www.chilin.org; 5 Chin Lin Dr, Diamond Hill; 9am-4.30pm; M Diamond Hill, exit C2) This beautiful replica of a Tang-dynasty monastery comes complete with temples, lotus ponds, Buddhist relics and timber structures assembled without the use of a single iron nail. It's the world's largest cluster of handcrafted timber buildings. Connected to the nunnery is **Nan Lian Garden** (www.nanliangarden.org; 10am-6pm), a Tang-style garden featuring a pagoda, a tea pavilion, a koi pond and a bizarre collection of petrified wood.

Cattle Depot Artist Village ARTIST VILLAGE
(牛棚藝術村; 63 Ma Tau Kok Rd, To Kwa Wan) A century-old slaughterhouse deep in the entrails of Kowloon has reincarnated into an artists' village, its 14 red-bricked buildings housing studios and exhibition halls. Though many are closed during the day, the depot itself is an interesting place to explore. To ensure the doorman lets you in, call a tenant ahead to let them know you're coming. Friendly **1a Space** (2529 0087; www.oneaspace.org.hk; Unit 14, Cattle Depot Artist Village; noon-8pm Tue-Sun) welcomes visitors and keeps regular opening times. Buses 106, 12A and 5C go to Ma Tau Kok Rd.

Sik Sik Yuen Wong Tai Sin Temple TEMPLE
(嗇色園黃大仙祠; www.siksikyuen.org.hk; Lung Cheung Rd, Wong Tai Sin; admission by donation HK$2; 7am-5.30pm; M Wong Tai Sin, exit B3) This Taoist temple is dedicated to Wong Tai Sin, who was said to have transformed boulders into sheep. In fact, the whole area, an MTR station and a residential property near the temple are all named after this poor immortal who was supposed to have been a hermit. Just below the temple is an arcade of fortune-tellers, some of whom speak English.

Jockey Club Creative Arts Centre ARTIST STUDIOS

(賽馬會創意藝術中心; www.jccac.org.hk; 30 Pak Tin St, Shek Kip Mei; ⊙10am-10pm; Ⓜ Shek Kip Mei, exit C) Over 150 artists have moved into these factory premises that used to churn out shoes and watches. Many studios are closed on weekdays, but you can visit the breezy communal areas and **G.O.D. Street Culture Museum & Store** (Unit L2-09; ⊙12.30-6.30pm, closed Mon & Tue), which has an attractive 'old Hong Kong' display and regular opening hours.

TOP CHOICE **Ping Shan Heritage Trail** HERITAGE TRAIL

(屏山文物徑; Map p472; Ⓜ West Rail Tin Shui Wai station, exit E) At 1km, Hong Kong's first heritage trail includes the territory's **oldest pagoda** (⊙9am-1pm & 2-5pm, closed Tue), a magnificent **ancestral hall** (⊙9am-1pm & 2-5pm), a **temple**, a **study hall** and a **gallery** (⊙10am-5pm, closed Mon) inside an **old police station**, all built by the Tang clan, the first and the most powerful of the 'Five Clans' who began settling in the New Territories around the 11th century. Cross Tsui Sing Rd from the ground floor of the MTR station and you'll see the pagoda.

Shui Tau Tsuen WALLED VILLAGE

(水頭村; Map p472) This 17th-century village, more substantial than Kat Hing Wei, is famous for its prow-shaped roofs decorated with dragons and fish. During opening hours, you can obtain a map detailing an hour-long heritage trail through the village. At other times, the village is still an interesting place to explore if you don't mind not knowing which building is which. Shui Tau Tsuen is signposted from Kam Tin Rd.

Kat Hing Wai WALLED VILLAGE

(吉慶圍; Map p472) This tiny (100m by 90m), once-moated hamlet on Kam Tin Rd is the domicile of the Tang clan, though some Hakka villagers also live here. Visitors are asked to make a donation as they enter. For HK$10, you can take pictures of the old Hakka ladies near the entrance. If you don't pay, they'll hide their faces.

Hong Kong Wetland Park PARK

(香港濕地公園; Map p472; www.wetlandpark.com; Wetland Park Rd, Tin Shui Wai; admission HK$30; ⊙10am-5pm) This wonderful 61-hectare park is located on one of the most important bird-migration routes in Asia, offering serenity, award-winning architecture and a fascinating look into wetland ecosystems. Take the West Rail line to Tin Shui Wai and board MTR Light Rail line 705 or 706.

Mai Po Marsh Nature Reserve NATURE RESERVE

(米埔自然保護區; Map p472; ☎2471 3480, www.wwf.org.hk; San Tin, Yuen Long; ⊙9am-5pm Mon-Fri) The 27-sq-km protected wetland is home to an amazing range of flora and fauna, including up to 300 species of birds. Three-hour guided tours (HK$70), most in Cantonese, leave the visitor centre four times between 9am and 2.30pm on weekends. Groups of five or more can book two weeks in advance for a private tour. Call, or register online. Take bus 76K from Fanling or Sheung Shui MTR East Rail stations.

Lung Yeuk Tau Heritage Trail HERITAGE TRAIL

(龍躍頭文物徑; Ⓜ East Rail Fan Ling station, then bus 54K or 56K) Crouching under 'leaping dragon' ('Lung Yeuk') are 11 villages belonging to – you guessed it – the mighty Tang clan. The most impressive of the lot are the **Tang Chung Ling Ancestral Hall** (⊙9am-1pm & 2-5pm, closed Tue) and the grey-bricked **Lo Wai** (⊙9am-5pm).

Sheung Shui Heung OLD VILLAGE

(上水鄉; Mun Hau Tsuen, Sheung Shui Heung, Sheung Shui; ⊙9am-1pm & 2-5pm Wed, Thu, Sat & Sun; Ⓜ East Rail Sheung Shui station, exit B) During the Ming dynasty, the Liu clan from Fujian settled in Sheung Shui, where they carved out a nifty niche for themselves that included the ancestral hall here – a large structure richly embellished with carvings and murals. From the MTR station, follow the sign for Liu Man Shek Tong. Then from San Fung Ave, turn into Po Shek Wu Rd, make a left into Jockey Club Rd, then another left into Sheung Shui Heung, and head for the sound of clacking mah-jong tiles.

Fung Ying Seen Temple TEMPLE

(蓬瀛仙館; 66 Pak Wo Rd, Fanling; ⊙8am-6pm; Ⓜ East Rail Fan Ling station) For all its cheerful colours, this Taoist temple is a little morbid. It contains a dozen columbaria for cremated ancestral remains. If you venture into the hills behind the complex, you'll see graves flung all over the slopes, Tim Burton style.

TOP CHOICE **Hong Kong Heritage Museum** MUSEUM

(香港文化博物館; 1 Man Lam Rd; admission HK$10; ⊙10am-6pm Mon & Wed-Sat, to 7pm Sun; Ⓜ East Rail Sha Tin station) The impressive displays on Cantonese opera and New Territories heritage feature replicas of traditional

HONG KONG IN...

One Day

Catch a tram up to **Victoria Peak** for a great view of the city, stopping in **Central** for lunch on the way down. Then head to **Man Mo Temple** for a taste of history before taking the **Star Ferry** to Kowloon. Enjoy the views along **Tsim Sha Tsui East Promenade** as you make your way to the **Museum of History** for some context to all you've seen. After dinner in Tsim Sha Tsui, take the MTR to **Lan Kwai Fong** for drinks and dancing.

Two Days

In addition to the above, you could head to **Aberdeen** for a boat ride and some shopping at **Horizon Plaza** in **Ap Lei Chau**, or go hiking in **Sai Kung** followed by a late seafood lunch on the Sai Kung waterfront. After dark, make your way to the **Temple Street Night Market**.

villages and bamboo theatres, and stunning costumes once worn by opera artists. From time to time, the museum also showcases the works of Hong Kong's excellent but little-known photographers. Kids will love the large **Children's Discovery Gallery** on the ground floor. There are free **Cantonese opera** performances every Saturday from 3pm to 5.30pm.

Ten Thousand Buddhas Monastery MONASTERY
(萬佛寺; www.funeralservice.com.hk/2/index.htm; 221 Pai Tau Village; ⌚9am-5pm; Ⓜ Sha Tin, exit B) This large monastery with its red pagoda and statues swathed in gold calls to mind a dated movie set. The only exception is the main temple, where 12,800 Buddha statues line the walls like intricate lacework. Even so, the founder's body sits up to his eyeballs in gold before the altar. From the MTR exit, walk down the ramp, turning left onto Pai Tau St. After a short distance, turn right onto Sheung Wo Che St, walk to the end and follow the signs up the 400 steps.

Dragon Garden PRIVATE GARDEN
(龍圃; Sham Tseng; heritage@dragongarden.hk; http://dragongarden.hk) Hong Kong's largest remaining private garden has gorgeous faux-ancient architecture inspired by period styles of the Song, Ming and Qing dynasties, lovely fauna and flora, and a few quirky features thrown in for good measure. A philanthropist's weekend villa, it appeared in the Bond classic *Man with the Golden Gun* (1974) and the mini-series *Noble House* starring Pierce Brosnan (1988). There are monthly guided tours. Email for details.

OUTLYING ISLANDS

Twice the size of Hong Kong Island, **Lantau** has only about 50,000 residents and you could easily spend a day exploring its trails and enjoying its beaches. **Mui Wo** (Map p472) or Silver Mine Bay is the arrival point for ferries from Central.

TOP CHOICE **Po Lin Monastery** MONASTERY
(寶蓮禪寺; ⌚9am-6pm; Lantau) This enormous temple complex contains the 26m-tall **Tian Tan Buddha statue** (天壇大佛; ⌚10am-5.30pm), the world's largest seated bronze Buddha statue (see p955). From Mui Wo, board bus 2 to **Ngong Ping**, a plateau 500m above sea level, where a cable-car system called **Ngong Ping 360** (昂平360纜車; www.np360.com.hk; Lantau; one-way/return HK$58/88; ⌚10am-6pm Mon-Fri, 9am-6.30pm Sat & Sun) whizzes you past breathtaking views to the monastery. Ngong Ping 360 has another terminal in **Tung Chung** (東涌), a two-minute walk from Tung Chung MTR station.

Tai O FISHING VILLAGE
(大澳; Map p472; Lantau) One of Hong Kong's oldest fishing villages, picturesque Tai O is famous for its **stilt houses**, **rope-tow ferry** and temple dedicated to Kwan Yu (God of War). It's reachable by bus 1 from Mui Wo, bus 11 from Tung Chung or bus 21 from Ngong Ping. Follow the smell of drying anchovies.

Laid-back **Lamma** (Map p472) has decent beaches, excellent walks and a plethora of restaurants in **Yung Shue Wan** and **Sok Kwu Wan**. A fun day involves taking the ferry to Yung Shue Wan, walking the easy 90-minute trail to Sok Kwu Wan and

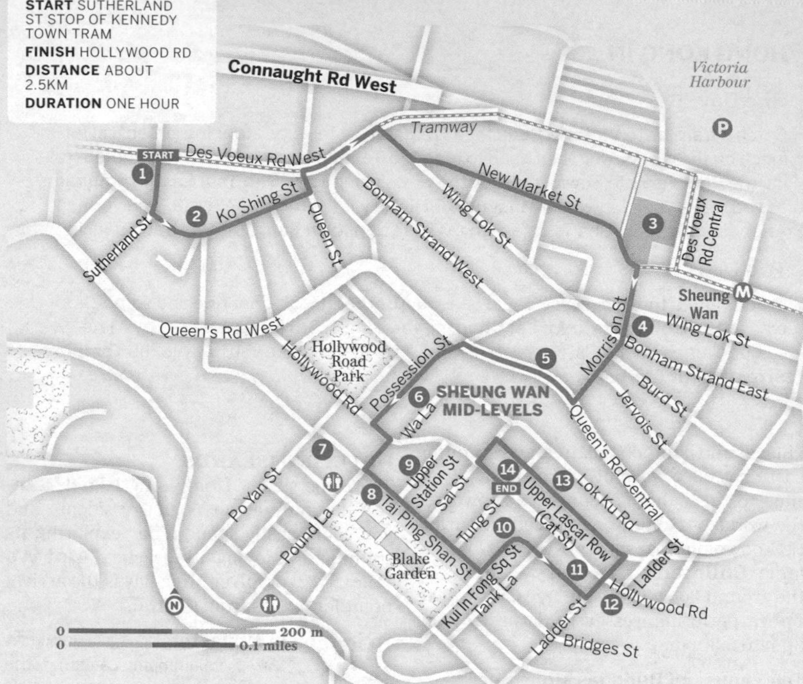

Walking Tour
Sheung Wan

A one-hour walk through Sheung Wan is a wonderful step back into Hong Kong's past. Begin the tour at the Sutherland St stop of the Kennedy Town tram. Have a look at (and sniff of) Des Voeux Rd West's 1 **dried seafood shops**, then turn up Ko Shing St, where there are 2 **herbal medicine wholesalers**. At the end of the street, walk northeast along Des Voeux Rd West and turn right onto New Market St, where you'll find 3 **Western Market** at the corner of Morrison St. Walk south along this street past Bonham Strand, which is lined with 4 **ginseng root sellers**, and turn right on Queen's Rd West. To the right you'll pass 5 **traditional shops** selling bird's nests (for soup) and paper funeral offerings (for the dead).

Cross Queen's Rd Central and turn left onto 6 **Possession St**, where the British flag was first planted in 1841.

Climbing Pound Lane to where it meets Tai Ping Shan St, look right to see 7 **Pak Sing Ancestral Hall**, then turn left to find 8 **Kwun Yam Temple** and 9 **Tai Sui Temple**.

A bit further on, turn left into Square St, where you'll pass 10 **Cloth Haven** (43-45 Square St), a weaving workshop, and 11 **funeral shops**. Turn left into Ladder St and you'll see 12 **Man Mo Temple**. Descend Ladder St to Upper Lascar Row, home of the 13 **Cat Street bazaar**. Go down the length of Cat St, then turn left into Lok Ku Rd. Another left takes you to 14 **Hollywood Rd**, with its antique shops and art galleries.

settling in for lunch at one of the seafood restaurants beside the water.

Dumbbell-shaped **Cheung Chau** (Map p472), with a harbour filled with fishing boats, a windsurfing centre, several temples and some bars and restaurants, also makes a fun day out. Not far away is **Peng Chau** (Map p472), the smallest and most traditional of the easily accessible islands.

Activities

The Hong Kong Tourism Board (HKTB) offers a range of fun and free activities, from feng shui classes through sunset cruises to taichi sessions, providing a window into local culture that's hard to find by yourself. For a full list of what's on, go to www.discoverhongkong.com and click on 'Attractions' or 'Touring'. The **Map Publications Centre** (香港地圖銷售處; Map p494; www.landsd.gov.hk/mapping/en/pro&ser/products.htm; 382 Nathan Rd, Yau Ma Tei; ⏲8.45am-5.30pm Mon-Fri) sells excellent maps detailing hiking and cycling trails. They can be bought online and at major post offices around town. Sporting buffs should contact the **South China Athletic Association** (南華體育會; Map p480; ☎2577 6932; www.scaa.org.hk; 5th fl, South China Sports Complex, 88 Caroline Hill Rd, Causeway Bay; visitor membership HK$50), which has facilities for any number of sports. Another handy website is www.hkoutdoors.com.

Martial Arts

Fightin' Fit MARTIAL ARTS SCHOOL
(Map p476; ☎2526 6648; www.fightinfit.com.hk; Ste 303, Peter Bldg, 56-62 Queen's Rd, Central; ⏲11am-9.30pm; Ⓜ Central, exit D) Various kinds of martial arts, including Wing Chun (see p976) and Thai boxing, are taught here.

Wan Kei Ho International Martial Arts Association MARTIAL ARTS SCHOOL
(Map p476; ☎2544 1368; www.kungfuwan.com; 3rd fl, Yue's House, 304 Des Voeux Rd Central, Sheung Wan; Ⓜ Sheung Wan, exit A) This place has a local and foreign following.

Hiking

Hong Kong is an excellent place to hike and the numerous trails on offer are all very attractive. The four main ones are **MacLehose Trail**, **Wilson Trail**, **Lantau Trail** and **Hong Kong Trail**. The famous **Dragon's Back Trail** is scenic and relatively easy.

For more information check out www.hkhiking.com/index.html (an English-speaking group organising regular hikes) and www.hkwalkers.net.

Cycling

Cycle tracks in Hong Kong are located predominantly in the New Territories, running from Sha Tin through Tai Po to Tai Mei Tuk (Map p472).

Bike rental:

Friendly Bike Shop (老友記單車; ☎2984 2278; Shop B, 13 Mui Wo Ferry Pier Rd, Lantau; ⏲10am-7pm Mon-Fri, to 8pm Sat & Sun; per day/hr HK$30/20)

Shun Lee Bicycle Co (☎2695 7195; 2a Lucky Plaza Commercial Complex, 1-15 Wang Pok St, Sha Tin; ⏲10am-7pm)

Wong Kei (☎2662 5200; Ting Kok Rd, Tai Mei Tuk)

Online resources:

Agriculture, Fisheries and Conservation Department (www.afcd.gov.hk) Details on mountain biking; click on 'Country & Marine Parks'.

Crazy Guy on Bike (www.crazyguyonabike.com/doc/Hongkong) This English website has almost everything you need.

Water Sports

Hong Kong's five government-run **water-sports centres** (www.lcsd.gov.hk/watersport/en/index.php) have canoes, windsurfing boards and other equipment for hire by certificate-holders. For wakeboarding, check out **Wakeboard** (☎3120 4102; frankie@islandwake.com; www.wakeboard.com.hk).

Golf

The **Hong Kong Golf Club** (www.hkgolfclub.org) welcomes nonmembers on weekdays at its **Fanling** (☎2670 1211; Lot No 1, Fan Kam Rd, Sheung Shui; Ⓜ Fanling) and **Deep Water Bay** (☎2812 7070; 19 Island Rd, Deep Water Bay; 🚌bus 6, 6A) venues. The scenic 36-hole **Jockey Club Kau Sai Chau Public Golf Course** (☎2791 3388; www.kscgolf.org.hk/index-e.asp; Kau Sai Chau, Sai Kung) is the territory's only public golf course. A ferry departs for Kau Sai Chau (every 20 minutes from 6.40am to 7pm weekdays, 6.40am to 9pm Friday to Sunday) from the pier near the Wai Man Rd car park.

Tours

Star Ferry (☎2118 6201; www.starferry.com.hk) runs a 60-minute **Harbour Tour** (day/night

LOCAL KNOWLEDGE

FRED YEUNG: ROCK CLIMBER, GRAFFITI ARTIST

Best Rock Climbing

On Tung Lung Chau (Map p472), where there's a technical wall, a sea gully and a big wall. Follow the path to the fort on the island and you'll see Holiday Store. The folks there will show you. All climbers stop there for noodles and supplies. A **ferry** (2560 9929) leaves Sai Wan Ho typhoon shelter for the island four to six times a day on weekends. On weekdays you can probably just show up at the typhoon shelter and haggle with sampan operators. Tai Tau Chau, near Shek O beach, also has excellent granite, some with bolted routes.

Best Graffiti

Hong Kong's graffiti hall of fame is a lane close to a school and one of the exits of Mong Kok East MTR station. You'll see throw-ups, stencils, pieces and wildstyle. There's also a pavilion at Hong Kong's most popular surf spot, **Big Wave Bay** (Map p472; M Shau Kei Wan station, exit A3, Shek O-bound minibus) featuring works that change every year. The **Jockey Club Creative Arts Centre** (p484) has graffiti on the fifth and sixth levels.

HK$55/110; 11.05am-9.05pm), beginning at Tsim Sha Tsui and stopping at Central, Wan Chai and Hung Hom. Get tickets at the piers.

Tours run by the **HKTB** (2508 1234; www.discoverhongkong.com; 9am-6pm):

Island Tour (half-/full day HK$350/490) Includes Man Mo Temple, the Peak, Aberdeen, Repulse Bay and Stanley Market.

Land Between Tour (half-/full day HK$350/450) Covers temples, villages and the China boundary.

Festivals & Events

Western and Chinese culture combine to create an interesting mix of cultural events and 17 official public holidays. However, determining the exact times can be tricky: some follow the Chinese lunar calendar, so the date changes each year. For a full schedule with exact dates see www.discoverhongkong.com.

Hong Kong Arts Festival ARTS
(www.hk.artsfestival.org) February to March.

Man Hong Kong International Literary Festival LITERATURE
(www.festival.org.hk) March.

Hong Kong Sevens RUGBY
(www.hksevens.com) Late March or early April.

Hong Kong International Film Festival FILM
(www.hkiff.org.hk) March to April.

Le French May Arts Festival ARTS
April to May.

Tin Hau Festival & Buddha's Birthday DEITIES' BIRTHDAYS
April or May.

International Dragon Boat Races DRAGON BOATS
(www.hkdba.com.hk) May to June.

Summer International Film Festival FILM
(www.hkiff.org.hk) August to September.

New Vision Arts Festival ARTS
(www.newvisionfestival.gov.hk) October to November, biennial.

Hong Kong International Jazz Festival JAZZ
(http://hkja.org/blog) November.

Hong Kong Photo Festival PHOTOGRAPHY
(www.hkphotofest.org) Biennial. Dates change; check the website.

Sleeping

Hong Kong offers the full gamut of accommodation, from cell-like spaces to palatial suites in some of the world's finest hotels. Compared with those in other cities in China, rooms are relatively expensive, though they can still be cheaper than their US or European counterparts. The rates listed here are the rack rates.

Most hotels are on Hong Kong Island between Central and Causeway Bay, and either side of Nathan Rd in Kowloon, where you'll also find the largest range of budget places. Most midrange and top-end hotels and a small number of budget places add 13% in taxes to the listed rates; check when you book.

The good news is that prices fall sharply during the shoulder and low seasons, particularly in the midrange and top-end categories, when you can get discounts of up to 60% if you book online, through a travel agent or with an agency such as the **Hong Kong Hotels Association** (HKHA; ☎2383 8380; www.hkha.org), which has reservation centres at the airport.

High seasons are March to early May (trade-fair season), October to November, and Chinese New Year (late January or February). Check the exact dates on www.discoverhongkong.com.

Unless specified otherwise, all rooms listed here have private bathrooms and air-conditioning, and all but the cheapest will have cable TV in English. Many places offer weekly and monthly rates.

HONG KONG ISLAND

Most of Hong Kong Island's top-end hotels are in Central and Admiralty, while Wan Chai and Sheung Wan cater to the midrange market. Causeway Bay has quite a few budget guesthouses that are a step up (in both price and quality) from their Tsim Sha Tsui counterparts.

TOP CHOICE **Upper House** BOUTIQUE HOTEL $$$
(奕居; Map p476; ☎2918 1838; www.upperhouse.com; Pacific Place, 88 Queensway, Admiralty; r from HK$2800, ste from HK$4500; @ 🛜; Ⓜ Admiralty, exit F) Every corner of this boutique hotel spells serenity – the understated and classy lobby, the sleek 'paperless' rooms, the elegant sculptures, and the manicured lawn where guests can join free yoga classes. There are plans for a rooftop pool. In the meantime, guests can pay to use the swimming facilities of hotels nearby.

Ice House STUDIO APARTMENT $$
(Map p476; ☎2836 7333; www.icehouse.com.hk; 38 Ice House St, Central; r HK$900-1050, low-season discounts of 20%; @; Ⓜ Central, exit G) The location, in the heart of Central and staggering distance from Lan Kwai Fong, and the 64 spacious, open-plan 'suites' make the Ice House excellent value. Each room has a kitchenette, a work desk and internet access.

Hotel LKF HOTEL $$$
(蘭桂芳酒店; Map p476; ☎3518 9688; www.hotel-lkf.com.hk; 33 Wyndham St, Central; r from HK$3500, low-season discounts of up to 50%; @; Ⓜ Central, exit D2) Right in the thick of the Lan Kwai Fong action (but far enough above it not to be disturbed by it), the stylish LKF offers spacious rooms in muted earth tones containing all the trimmings: fluffy dressing gowns, espresso machines, and free bed-time milk and cookies. Internet access is for the top three floors only.

Y-Loft Youth Square Hostel HOSTEL $$
(☎3721 8989; 238 Chai Wan Rd; tw/d/tr HK$600/750/990, ste HK$1200-1800, low-season discounts of 25%; @ 🛜; Ⓜ Chai Wan, exit A) If you don't mind living a little further away in Chai Wan (not Wan Chai!), you'll be rewarded with large, clean and cheerful rooms. Stanley is only 15 minutes away by bus from the 16X bus stop opposite the MTR station. To reach the hostel from exit A, go straight through the mall to the footbridge and take the first exit on your right. Reception's on the 12th floor.

Four Seasons Hotel LUXURY HOTEL $$$
(四季酒店; Map p476; ☎3196 8888; www.fourseasons.com/hongkong; IFC 3, 8 Finance St, Central; r from HK$4300, ste from HK$8800; @ 🛜 🏊; Ⓜ Tung Chung Line Hong Kong station, exit F) Everything about the Four Seasons is class, from the fine rooms and restaurants to the panoramic harbour views from its location in the International Financial Centre. There's also a great spa. But it's the sophisticated service that is most memorable.

Yesinn Hostel HOSTEL $
(www.yesinn.com; Flat B, 5th fl, Front Block, 294 King's Rd, Fortress Hill; dm without bathroom HK$99-199, per person s/d/tr from HK$268/159/119; @; Ⓜ Fortress Hill, exit B) Housed in an old building, Yesinn with its brightly coloured walls is a reasonable alternative to the cheap sleeps on Nathan Rd. But the eight-person dorms are small and there's no communal area.

Hong Kong Hostel HOSTEL $
(香港旅館; Map p480; ☎2392 6868; www.hostel.hk; Flat A2, 3rd fl, Paterson Bldg, 47 Paterson St, Causeway Bay; dm HK$150, s/d/tr HK$300/350/480, without bathroom HK$250/280/420; @) A good place to meet backpackers, with 110 rooms scattered across several floors. Although not spacious, they come with phone, TV and fridge. Standards do vary a bit, however, so look at a few.

Causeway Bay Guest House GUESTHOUSE $
(華生旅舍; Map p480; ☎2895 2013; www.cbgh.net; Flat B, 1st fl, Lai Yee Bldg, 44a-d Leighton Rd,

BEWARE: FAKE MONKS

Real monks in Hong Kong never solicit money. However, you may be approached in temples and even bars and shops by con artists in monks' habits who try to make you part with your money. The more aggressive ones may offer fake Buddhist amulets for sale, or force 'blessings' on you then pester you for a donation. When accosted, just say 'no' and ignore them.

For more on scams, see p991.

Causeway Bay; s HK$300-380, d HK$400-450, tr HK$510-600; 📶; Ⓜ Causeway Bay, exit A) If you want to save on accommodation to spend in the Causeway Bay shoppolopolis, this no-frills but clean seven-room guesthouse might be for you. The free wi-fi connection, however, is unstable. Enter from Leighton Lane.

Jia BOUTIQUE HOTEL **$$$**
(Map p480; ☎3196 9000; www.jiahongkong.com; 1-5 Irving St, Causeway Bay; r HK$2500, ste from HK$3500, low-season discounts of up to 40%; @📶; Ⓜ Causeway Bay, exit F) Inspired by French designer Philippe Starck, this boutique hotel is chic as hell, from the stunning staff uniforms and postmodern furnishings to the guests: models in sunglasses loitering in the lobby. Standard rooms are poky, but the service is smooth.

Traders Hotel BOUTIQUE HOTEL **$$**
(☎2974 1234; www.shangri-la.com/en/property/hongkong/traders; 508 Queen's Rd West, Western; r HK$800-1300; @📶🏊; 🚌bus 5 or 10 from Central) It's a 15-minute tram ride from Central in a rather ho-hum neighbourhood, but this stylish number offers good value, some harbour views, large rooms, chic furnishings, and a rooftop pool and gym.

Garden View YWCA HOTEL **$$**
(女青園景軒; Map p476; ☎2877 3737; http://hotel.ywca.org.hk; 1 MacDonnell Rd, Central; r HK$1550-1750, ste from HK$2350, low-season discounts of up to 50%; @📶🏊; 🚌green minibus 1A) Straddling the border of Central and Mid-Levels, the YWCA-run Garden View has fine views and is one of the better midrange places in Central. Rates include breakfast.

Bishop Lei International House HOTEL **$$**
(宏基國際賓館; Map p476; ☎2868 0828; www.bishopleihtl.com.hk; 4 Robinson Rd, Mid-Levels; r HK$1280-1880, ste from HK$2080, low-season discounts of up to 50%; @📶🏊; 🚌bus 23, 40) This 203-room hotel in Mid-Levels is not luxurious, but it does have polite staff, its own swimming pool and free wi-fi, and some rooms have quite spectacular views.

Central Park Hotel HOTEL **$$$**
(中環麗柏酒店; Map p476; ☎2850 8899; www.centralparkhotel.com.hk; 263 Hollywood Rd, Sheung Wan; r from HK$1900, ste from HK$5500, low-season discounts of up to 50%; @; Ⓜ Sheung Wan, exit A2) This 142-room affair has sleek, modern rooms that, while not tiny, seem bigger than they are through the effective use of mirrors. It's a short walk to Central.

Hotel Bonaparte HOTEL **$$**
(雅逸酒店; Map p480; ☎3518 6688; www.hotelbonaparte.com.hk; 11 Morrison Hill Rd, Wan Chai; r from HK$988; @📶; Ⓜ Wan Chai, exit A) They call the rooms cosy; we call them tiny. There are few frills to this place. The clinchers are the crisp new fixtures, low-season prices, the minibar and wi-fi freebies.

Noble Hostel HOSTEL **$**
(高富旅館; Map p480; ☎2576 6148; www.noblehostel.com.hk; Flat A3, 17th fl, Great George Bldg, 27 Paterson St, Causeway Bay; s/d/tw/tr HK$300/350/380/450; 📶; Ⓜ Causeway Bay, exit E) The 26 squeaky-clean rooms are a bit larger than others in this price range, and most have a fridge, although the decor looks decidedly tired.

Fleming BOUTIQUE HOTEL **$$$**
(芬名酒店; Map p480; ☎3607 2288; www.thefleming.com; 41 Fleming Rd, Wan Chai; r HK$1880-2980, low-season discounts of up to 50%; @📶; Ⓜ Wan Chai, exit A1) On a quiet road set back from all the Wan Chai night-time madness, the rooms at this boutique-y little place strike a good balance between smart minimalism and a cosy homeliness.

Alisan Guest House GUESTHOUSE **$**
(阿里山賓館; Map p480; ☎2838 0762; http://home.hkstar.com/~alisangh; Flat A, 5th fl, Hoito Ct, 23 Cannon St, Causeway Bay; s/d/tr HK$350/450/550; 📶; Ⓜ Causeway Bay, exit D1) Spread through several apartments, the rooms in this small family-run place are clean, the welcome warm and the advice good.

Charterhouse Hotel HOTEL **$$**
(利景酒店; Map p480; ☎2833 5566; www.charterhouse.com; 209-219 Wan Chai Rd, Wan

Chai; r HK$1540-2420, ste from HK$2640, low-season discounts of up to 55%; @; M Wan Chai, exit A3) Book online for big discounts on fairly comfortable rooms. Internet access on 'signature floor' only.

Wifi Boutique Hotel HOTEL $$
(星網酒店; Map p480; ☎2558 8939; www.wifihotel.com.hk; 366 Lockhart Rd, Wan Chai; r HK$1588-1988, ste from HK$2000, low-season discounts of up to 50%; 📶; M Causeway Bay, exit C) This hotel, located between Wan Chai and Causeway Bay, has 52 small but clean rooms.

KOWLOON

Kowloon has an incredible array of accommodation: from the Peninsula, the 'grand dame' of hotels, to its infamous neighbour, Chungking Mansions, plus plenty in between.

TOP CHOICE **Hyatt Regency Tsim Sha Tsui** LUXURY HOTEL $$$
(香港尖沙咀凱悅酒店; Map p492; ☎2311 1234; http://hongkong.tsimshatsui.hyatt.com; 18 Hanoi Rd, Tsim Sha Tsui; r HK$1500-2900, ste from HK$3300; @📶🏊; M Tsim Sha Tsui, exit D2) This Tsim Sha Tsui classic, reopened at this convenient address, features plush, medium-sized rooms, many with great views, and impeccable service. The photos of Tsim Sha Tsui captured by a local photographer are a refreshing touch.

Salisbury HOSTEL, HOTEL $$
(香港基督教青年會; Map p492; ☎2268 7888; www.ymcahk.org.hk; 41 Salisbury Rd, Tsim Sha Tsui; dm/s HK$240/750, d HK$800-1050, ste from HK$1500; @📶🏊; M Tsim Sha Tsui, exit E) Operated by the YMCA. The rooms here are simple, but the facilities and the five-star views are not. The location makes it great value. Budgeters who book ahead might get a bed in the four-bed dorms. However, no one can stay more than seven consecutive nights, and walk-in guests for the dorms aren't accepted if they've been in Hong Kong more than 10 days.

Hop Inn HOSTEL $
(樸樸旅舍; Map p492; ☎2881 7331; www.hopinn.hk; Flat A, 2nd fl, Hanyee Bldg, 19-21 Hankow Rd, Tsim Sha Tsui; s HK$350-450, d HK$480-610, tr HK$580-760; @; M Tsim Sha Tsui, exit A1) This guesthouse has a youthful vibe and nine spotless little rooms, each featuring illustrations by a Hong Kong artist. Our favourite is the first room by Gukzik Lau. Some rooms have no windows, but they're quieter than the ones that do.

Stanford Hillview Hotel HOTEL $$
(仕德福山景酒店; Map p492; ☎2722 7822; www.stanfordhillview.com; 13-17 Observatory Rd, Tsim Sha Tsui; s & d HK$1480-1680, ste from HK$2680, low-season discounts of up to 45%; 📶; M Tsim Sha Tsui, exit B1) At the eastern end of Knutsford Tce, the Stanford is a quality hotel in just about our favourite location in Tsim Sha Tsui, with little traffic noise but seconds from loads of bars and restaurants.

Royal Garden Hotel LUXURY HOTEL $$$
(帝苑酒店; Map p492; ☎2721 5215; www.rghk.com.hk; 69 Mody Rd, Tsim Sha Tsui East; s HK$2400-3400, d HK$2850-3550, ste from HK$4700; @📶🏊👪; M East Tsim Sha Tsui, exit P2) This often-overlooked hotel is one of the best equipped in Kowloon and offers solid value given the plushly appointed rooms, rooftop pool and putting green, fine restaurants and smart service.

TOP CHOICE **Peninsula Hong Kong** LUXURY HOTEL $$$
(香港半島酒店; Map p492; ☎2920 2888; www.peninsula.com; Salisbury Rd, Tsim Sha Tsui; r HK$4200-5800, ste from HK$6800; @📶🏊👪; M Tsim Sha Tsui, exit E) Hong Kong's colonial classic is pure elegance, with service and up-to-the-minute facilities to match. If you can afford it, the Pen is somewhere everyone should stay at least once.

Hotel InterContinental Hong Kong LUXURY HOTEL $$$
(香港洲際酒店; Map p492; ☎2721 1211; www.hongkong-ic.intercontinental.com; 18 Salisbury Rd, Tsim Sha Tsui; r HK$4700-6300, ste from HK$6800, low-season discounts of 20-25%; @📶🏊👪; M East Tsim Sha Tsui, exit J) It's getting on a bit, but the InterContinental still boasts the finest waterfront position in the

> **WANT MORE?**
>
> For in-depth information, reviews and recommendations at your fingertips,head to the Apple App Store to purchase Lonely Planet's *Hong Kong City Guide* iPhone app.
>
> Alternatively, head to **Lonely Planet** (www.lonelyplanet.com/china/hong-kong) for planning advice, author recommendations, traveller reviews and insider tips.

Kowloon

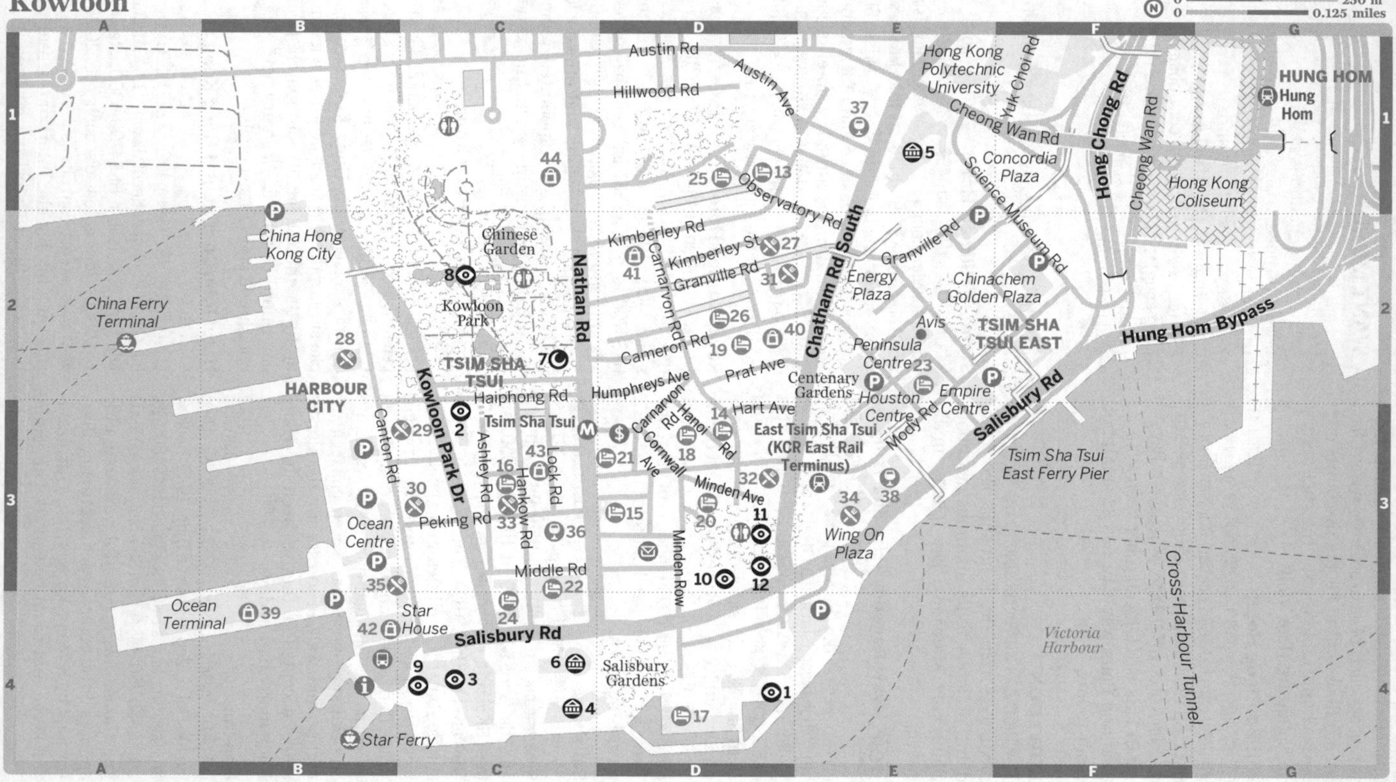
0 250 m
0 0.125 miles
HUNG HOM
Hung Hom
Hong Kong Coliseum
Cheong Wan Rd
Hong Chong Rd
Hung Hom Bypass
Cross-Harbour Tunnel
Hong Kong Polytechnic University
Yuk Choi Rd
Cheong Wan Rd
Concordia Plaza
Science Museum Rd
Granville Rd
Chinachem Golden Plaza
TSIM SHA TSUI EAST
Avis
Energy Plaza
Peninsula Centre
Centenary Gardens
Houston Centre
Empire Centre
Mody Rd
Salisbury Rd
Tsim Sha Tsui East Ferry Pier
Victoria Harbour
East Tsim Sha Tsui (KCR East Rail Terminus)
Wing On Plaza
Chatham Rd South
Austin Rd
Austin Ave
Hillwood Rd
Observatory Rd
Kimberley Rd
Kimberley St
Carnarvon Rd
Granville Rd
Cameron Rd
Prat Ave
Hart Ave
Humphreys Ave
Hanoi Rd
Cornwall Ave
Minden Ave
Minden Row
Nathan Rd
Chinese Garden
Kowloon Park
TSIM SHA TSUI
Haiphong Rd
Tsim Sha Tsui
Ashley Rd
Hankow Rd
Lock Rd
Peking Rd
Middle Rd
Kowloon Park Dr
Canton Rd
HARBOUR CITY
China Hong Kong City
China Ferry Terminal
Ocean Centre
Ocean Terminal
Star House
Salisbury Gardens
Star Ferry

Kowloon

territory, excellent service and a terrific spa. The view from the Lobby Lounge bar is unbeatable.

Acesite Knutsford Hotel HOTEL **$$**
(樂仕酒店; Map p492; ☎2377 1180; www.acesite-hotel.com; 8 Observatory Ct, Tsim Sha Tsui; s HK$1000, d HK$1200-1800, low-season discounts of up to 40%; ; Ⓜ Tsim Sha Tsui, exit B1) The 28 coffin-sized rooms here feel quite airy, thanks to savvy use of glass and whites. The service, by contrast, can be stuffy. The hotel is located in a quiet corner of Tsim Sha Tsui's residential quarter.

Golden Island Guesthouse GUESTHOUSE **$**
(金岛賓館; ☎9583 5051; www.gig.com.hk; Flat 1-2, 7th fl, Alhambra Bldg, 385 Nathan Rd; s/d/tw/tr from HK$220/300/350/450, low-season discounts of 20-30%; ; Ⓜ Yau Ma Tei, exit C) This 30-room guesthouse located in the down-at-heel Alhambra Building is a poor man's palace. All rooms come with showers, toiletries, TV and phone; some have keycards. English-speaking owner Jessie can book tickets and tours for you.

Booth Lodge HOSTEL **$**
(卜維廉賓館; Map p494; ☎2771 9266; http://boothlodge.salvation.org.hk; 11 Wing Sing Lane, Yau Ma Tei; s & tw incl breakfast HK$620-1500; Ⓜ Yau Ma Tei, exit C) This wedge-shaped, Salvation Army–run place is spartan and clean but fair value in the lower midrange. Standard rooms are about HK$500 out of season. Reception is on the 7th floor.

Yau Ma Tei

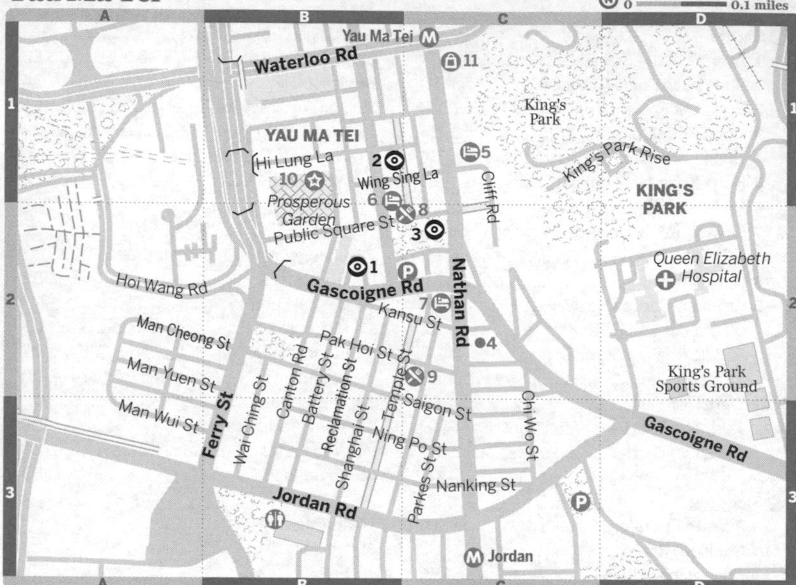

Minden BOUTIQUE HOTEL $$

(棉登酒店; Map p492; ☎2739 7777; www.theminden.com; 7 Minden Ave, Tsim Sha Tsui; r HK$900-1500, ste HK$2500; @; MTsim Sha Tsui, exit G) The boutique-ish Minden is centrally located, the rooms are comfortable and the lobby is packed with an eclectic mix of Asian and Western curios and furnishings.

Chelsea Hotel HOTEL $

(怡景酒店; Map p492; ☎2311 9511; www.chelseahotel.hk; 8a Hanoi Rd, Tsim Sha Tsui; r HK$700-900; wi-fi; MTsim Sha Tsui, exit D2) The rooms here are basic but pleasant, as is the service, and some on the 15th and 16th floors have glimpses of the harbour. Reception's on the 1st floor.

Cosmic Guest House GUESTHOUSE $

(宇宙賓館; Map p492; ☎2369 6669; www.cosmicguesthouse.com; Flat A1-A2 & F1-F4, 12th fl, Mirador Mansion, 58-62 Nathan Rd, Tsim Sha Tsui; s with/without bathroom from HK$160/120, tw from HK$220; wi-fi; MTsim Sha Tsui, exit D2) The sparkling-clean, quiet, friendly and secure Cosmic is a consistent favourite with travellers. Rooms are relatively bright and some rooms even have rain showers…wedged into 1-sq-metre bathrooms!

Yau Ma Tei

Sights

1 Jade Market B2
2 Temple Street Night Market B1
3 Tin Hau Temple C2

Activities, Courses & Tours

4 Map Publications Centre C2

Sleeping

5 Booth Lodge C1
6 Dorsett Seaview Hotel B1
7 Golden Island Guesthouse C2

Eating

8 Mido Cafe C2
9 Temple St Food Stalls C2

Entertainment

10 Broadway Cinematheque B1

Shopping

11 Protrek C1
Temple Street Night Market .... (see 9)

Park Guest House GUESTHOUSE $

(百樂賓館; Map p492; ☎2368 1689; fax 2367 7889; Flat A1, 15th fl, A Block, Chungking Mansions, 36-44 Nathan Rd, Tsim Sha Tsui; s/d

HK$200/260, r without bathroom HK$180; ; Tsim Sha Tsui, exit F) Small, clean and friendly, these rooms come with all the usual Chungking fare (TV, air-con, phone and a vague curry smell), plus a fridge.

Mei Lam Guest House GUESTHOUSE $
(美林賓館; Map p492; 2721 5278, 9095 1379; fax 2723 6168; Flat D1, 5th fl, Mirador Mansion, 62 Nathan Rd; s/d from HK$200/250; ; Tsim Sha Tsui, exit D2) A few notches above the usual standard, this excellent guesthouse has modern, comfortable rooms packed with extras including internet access.

World Wide Guest House GUESTHOUSE $
(環球賓館; Map p492; 2311 3550; wwgsthse@biznetvigator.com; Unit E1, 14th fl, Mirador Mansion, 58-62 Nathan Rd, Tsim Sha Tsui; s/d HK$250/350; @; Tsim Sha Tsui, exit F) This newish place has seven comfortable and larger-than-normal rooms, each with a broadband connection.

Man Hing Lung Hotel GUESTHOUSE $
(萬興隆酒店; Map p492; 2311 8807; www.manhinglung-hotel.com; Flat F2, 14th fl, Mirador Mansion, 58-62 Nathan Rd, Tsim Sha Tsui; s HK$120-150, d HK$150-200, tr HK$200-240; @; Tsim Sha Tsui, exit D2) The clinically clean and sparse atmosphere of the rooms is softened somewhat by the friendly owner and free internet access.

New Yan Yan Guest House GUESTHOUSE $
(新中華酒店; Map p492; 2366 8930, 9489 3891; fax 2721 0840; Flat E5, 12th fl, E Block, Chungking Mansions, 36-44 Nathan Rd, Tsim Sha Tsui; s HK$120-150, d HK$200-250; ; Tsim Sha Tsui, exit F) Clean, new fittings, friendly and reasonably priced for what you get. Internet access in the lobby.

Welcome Guest House GUESTHOUSE $
(惠康招待所; Map p492; 2721 7793; www.guesthousehk.net; Flat A5, 7th fl, A Block, Chungking Mansions, 36-44 Nathan Rd, Tsim Sha Tsui; s HK$160-200, d HK$260-300, s without shower HK$120; ; Tsim Sha Tsui, exit F) It's basic and a bit scruffy around the edges but worth a look for the price. Internet access in the lobby.

Chungking House GUESTHOUSE $
(鴻京酒店; Map p492; 2739 1600; www.chungkinghouse.com; reservations@chungkinghouse.com; 4th & 5th fl, A Block, Chungking Mansions, 36-44 Nathan Rd, Tsim Sha Tsui; s/d/q HK$200/250/500; Tsim Sha Tsui, exit F) This place covering two floors – with two receptions and a total of 80 rooms – is pretty swish by the standards of Chungking Mansions.

Star Guest House GUESTHOUSE $
(星華旅運社; Map p492; 2723 8951; www.starguesthouse.com.hk; 6th fl, 21 Cameron Rd, Tsim Sha Tsui; s/tw/tr HK$350/450/550; @; Tsim Sha Tsui, exit B2) Owned and run by the charismatic Charlie Chan, who can arrange almost anything. Has 18 small, clean rooms.

Lee Garden Guest House GUESTHOUSE $
(利園旅店; Map p492; 2367 2284; charliechan@iname.com; 8th fl, D Block, 36 Cameron Rd, Tsim Sha Tsui; s/tw/tr HK$350/450/550; @; Tsim Sha Tsui, exit B2) Sister property up the road from Star Guest House.

Dorsett Seaview Hotel HOTEL $$
(帝豪海景酒店; Map p494; 2782 0882; www.dorsettseaview.com.hk; 250 Shanghai St, Yau Ma Tei; s HK$480-1280, d HK$750-1450, ste from HK$1500; ; Yau Ma Tei, exit C) A clean, basic, well-located standby. Book online for the best rates.

NEW TERRITORIES

The New Territories do not offer travellers as many accommodation options as the urban areas, but there are both official and independent hostels here, usually in remote areas. The **Country & Marine Parks Authority** (1823) maintains 28 no-frills campsites in the New Territories and 11 in the Outlying Islands. They are free and are clearly labelled on the four main trail maps. Go to www.afcd.gov.hk and click on 'Country & Marine Parks'.

Tao Fong Shan Pilgrim's Hall HOSTEL $
(道風山雲水堂; 2691 2739; www.tfssu.org/pilgrim.html; 33 Tao Fong Shan Rd, Sha Tin; s/d with shared bathroom HK$250/380; East Rail Sha Tin station, exit B) This lovely 18-room place is perched on a peaceful hillside. Getting here is a challenge, so follow the directions from the website carefully (click on 'home', then 'location map') or take a cab (about HK$30) from Sha Tin MTR station.

Hyatt Regency Hong Kong LUXURY HOTEL $$$
(3723 1234; www.hongkong.shatin.hyatt.com; r HK$2500-3100, ste HK$3700-12700; @; East Rail University station, exit B) The Hyatt lives up to its name of being the poshest hotel in the New Territories. Rooms are nicely appointed, with most commanding views of the harbour or the hills. The Chinese restaurant **Sha Tin 18** (p499) is excellent.

MECCA OF CHEAP SLEEPS

Chungking Mansions (重慶大廈) has been synonymous with budget accommodation in Hong Kong for decades. The crumbling block on Nathan Rd is stacked with the city's cheapest hostels and guesthouses, in addition to curry joints and souvenir shops. Rooms at Chungking are usually minuscule and service rudimentary. But standards have risen in recent years and several guesthouses positively sparkle with new fittings. Even the lifts have been upgraded, though they're still painfully slow.

Mirador Mansion (美麗都大廈), its neighbour just up the street, also has a fair number of cheap sleeps.

OUTLYING ISLANDS

Lantau, Lamma and Cheung Chau all have decent accommodation. We think Lamma is the ideal place to stay if you're on a budget, with good-value small hotels and a relaxed vibe. For campers, the **Country & Marine Parks Authority** (☎1823) maintains nine sites on Lantau. Camping is prohibited on Hong Kong beaches.

Bali Holiday Resort STUDIOS, APARTMENTS **$**
(優閒渡假屋; ☎2982 4580; 8 Main St, Lamma; r from HK$280-380, apt from HK$560-760; 📶) An agency rather than a resort as such, Bali has about 30 studios and apartments sprinkled around the island. All have TVs, fridges and air-con, and some have sea views. Prices double on weekends. Apartments only have wi-fi.

Warwick Hotel HOTEL **$**
(華威酒店; ☎2981 0081; www.warwickhotel.com.hk; Cheung Chau Sports Rd, Tung Wan Beach, Cheung Chau; d HK$750-1000; 📶) This criminally ugly building has quiet, neutrally decorated rooms, some offering wonderful vistas across the sea to Lamma and Hong Kong Island. Wi-fi's available in the lobby only.

Eating

One of the world's greatest food cities, Hong Kong offers culinary excitement whether you're spending HK$20 on a bowl of noodles or megabucks on haute cuisine.

The best of China is well represented, be it Cantonese, Shanghainese, Northern or Sichuanese cuisine. What's more, the international fare on offer – French, Italian, Spanish, Japanese, Thai, Indian, Indonesian, fusion – is the finest and most diverse in all of China. There are also great vegetarian options.

Hong Kong is an expensive place to dine by regional Chinese standards, but cheaper than Sydney, London or New York, and with a more consistent quality of food and service than most eateries in mainland China.

While you're in Hong Kong do try dim sum, uniquely Cantonese dishes normally steamed and served for breakfast, brunch or lunch.

HONG KONG ISLAND

The island's best range of cuisines is in Central and Wan Chai.

TOP CHOICE **Luk Yu Teahouse** CANTONESE **$$**
(陸羽茶室; Map p476; ☎2523 5464; 24-26 Stanley St, Central; mains HK$100-350; ⏰7am-10pm; 👪; Ⓜ Central, exit D2) Hong Kong's most famous teahouse is known for its divine dim sum (available 7am to 5pm) and delectable Cantonese dishes. The elegant Eastern art deco furnishings are also much raved about. All this more than compensates for the sometimes cavalier service by the wrinkly waiters (though that too is a classic). Luk Yu comes recommended by the Michelin inspectors.

TOP CHOICE **Hang Zhou Restaurant** HANGZHOU **$$**
(杭州酒家; Map p480; ☎2591 1898; 1st fl, Chinachem Johnston Plaza, 178-188 Johnston Rd, Wan Chai; lunch HK$70-200, dinner HK$200-1800; ⏰11.30am-2.30pm & 5.30-10.30pm; Ⓜ Wan Chai, exit A5) A food critics' favourite, this establishment with one Michelin star excels at Hangzhou cooking, the delicate sister of Shanghainese cuisine. Dishes such as shrimp stir-fried with tea leaves show how the best culinary creations should engage all your senses.

Ser Wong Fun CANTONESE **$**
(蛇王芬; Map p476; ☎2543 1032; 30 Cochrane St, Central; meals HK$70-150; ⏰11am-10.30pm; Ⓜ Central, exit D1) This snake-soup specialist whips up old Cantonese dishes that are as mesmerising as its celebrated broth, and the packed tables attest to it. Many regulars come just for the homemade pork-liver sausage infused with rose wine – perfect over a bowl of immaculate white rice, on a red tablecloth. Booking advised.

TOP CHOICE **Pure Veggie House** VEGETARIAN CHINESE **$$**
(心齋; Map p476; 3rd fl, Coda Plaza, 51 Garden Rd, Admiralty; meals HK$150-250; ⏰11am-10pm; 🖉 👪; Ⓜ Admiralty, then bus 12A) Hong Kong's

best vegetarian restaurant shows how, in the hands of a master, a Chinese vegetarian menu doesn't have to read like the rundown of a meat-lookalike contest. All dishes and dim sum, some unique to this place, are delicious and MSG-free. The service is immaculate.

Tung Po Seafood Restaurant CANTONESE $
(☎2880 9399; 2nd fl, Municipal Services Bldg, 99 Java Rd, North Point; meals HK$80-180; ⏰5.30pm-12.30am, reservations 2.30-5.30pm; Ⓜ North Point, exit A1) This institution has revolutionised *dai pai dong* (hawker-style) cooking in Hong Kong. There's no end to the novelty in its menu, which has featured items such as steamed glutinous rice with duck jus. Even beer is served in big rice bowls, to be downed bandit style. Book ahead or go before 7pm.

Lin Heung Tea House CANTONESE $
(蓮香樓; Map p476; ☎2544 4556; 160-164 Wellington St, Sheung Wan; meals HK$120-300; ⏰6am-11pm, dim sum to 3.30pm; Ⓜ Sheung Wan, exit E2) This unpretentious teahouse, founded in 1926, is full of retirees with their noses to the paper and starry-eyed Gen-Xers hungry for the rough, tough (but good enough) Cantonese fare of days bygone.

West Villa CANTONESE $$
(西苑; Map p480; ☎2882 2110; Shops 101-102, 1st fl, Lee Gardens Two, 28 Yun Ping Rd, Causeway Bay; meals from HK$250; ⏰11am-midnight Mon-Sat, from 10am Sun; 👪; Ⓜ Causeway Bay, exit E) Though best known for its honey-lacquered *char siu* (叉燒; barbecued pork), this modern restaurant also makes tip-top dim sum and outstanding Cantonese dishes. Eat fast – ditherers and dawdlers are shown no mercy by the gruff waitresses. Book ahead.

L'Atelier de Joel Robuchon FRENCH $$$
(Map p476; ☎2166 9000; www.joel-robuchon.com; Shop 401, Landmark, Queen's Rd Central, Central; lunch HK$400-1500, dinner HK$560-1800; ⏰7.30-10am, noon-2.30pm & 6.30-10.30pm, no breakfast Sun; Ⓜ Central, exit F) We think this latest 'workshop' of the celebrity chef is everything it's cracked up to be. What's more, sampling its Michelin-starred wonders doesn't have to cost the earth. Go for breakfast or share a few tapas with a friend.

Life Cafe VEGETARIAN, WESTERN $
(Map p476; www.lifecafe.com.hk; 10 Shelley St, Central; salads HK$80-90, mains HK$80-105; ⏰9am-10pm; 🖉👪) Life serves fantastic vegan salads, cakes and dishes free of gluten, wheat, garlic – you name it – over three floors stylishly decked out in reclaimed teak and recycled copper-domed lamps. The ground-floor deli has guilt-free goodies for takeaway.

Classified the Cheese Room EUROPEAN $$
(Map p476; www.classifiedfoodshops.com.hk; 108 Hollywood Rd, Sheung Wan; meals HK$150-300; ⏰noon-11pm Mon-Fri, 10am-11pm Sat & Sun; 🚌bus 26) With a state-of-the-art walk-in ageing room showcasing over 20 varieties of cheese and a massive wine list, Classified is paradise for fans of all things fermented. The salads and pastas are also decent.

San Xi Lou SICHUANESE $$
(三希樓; Map p476; 7th fl Coda Plaza, 51 Garden Rd, Admiralty; meals HK$100-350; ⏰11am-10.30pm; Ⓜ Admiralty, then bus 12A) The fresh ingredients and the complexity of the spices should tell you this is Hong Kong's finest Sichuanese kitchen. If still in doubt, ask the Sichuanese expats at the neighbouring tables.

Yung Kee CANTONESE $$
(鏞記酒家; Map p476; www.yungkee.com.hk; 32-40 Wellington St, Central; meals HK$300-600; ⏰11am-11.30pm; Ⓜ Central, exit D2) Operating since 1942, Yung Kee is famous for its roast goose and dim sum (served 2pm to 5.30pm Monday to Saturday, 11am to 5.30pm Sunday), though everything in the phone book of a menu is good.

City Hall Maxim's Palace CANTONESE $
(大會堂美心皇宮; Map p476; ☎2521 1303; 3rd fl, Lower Block, Hong Kong City Hall, 1 Edinburgh Pl, Central; dim sum HK$30-60; ⏰11am-4.30pm Mon-Sat, from 9am Sun, 5.30-10.45pm Mon-Sun; 👪; Ⓜ Central, exit K) This is a typically Hong Kong dim sum experience, in a huge kitschy hall with hundreds of locals, seemingly as many dim sum choices, and views of harbour reclamation in progress.

Magushi JAPANESE $$
(真串; Map p476; www.magushi.com; 74 Peel St, Sheung Wan; lunch from HK$60, dinner HK$150-300; ⏰noon-2.30pm & 6-11.30pm Mon-Fri, 6-11.30pm Sat & Sun) The Japanese kebabs and sushi at this lively spot are well worth the steep trek up Peel St, but the dizzying sake collection could make your descent a perilous journey.

Nha Trang VIETNAMESE $
(芽莊; Map p476; ☎2581 9992; 88 Wellington St, Central; meals HK$70-180; ⏰noon-11pm; 🖉; 🚌bus 40M) The hipsters who queue for a table at this modern joint do so for the

SELF-CATERING

Hong Kong's two main supermarket chains **Park'nShop** (www.parknshop.com) and **Wellcome** (www.wellcome.com.hk) have so many outlets you're bound to run into a few. **ThreeSixty** (Map p476; www.threesixtyhk.com; Landmark, Central; ⏲8am-7.30pm Mon-Sat) has more organic choices but is on the pricey side. The gourmet **city'super** (Map p492; www.citysuper.com.hk; Shop 3001, Gateway Arcade, 25-27 Canton Rd, Harbour City, Tsim Sha Tsui; ⏲10am-10.30pm) has attractive but expensive produce. Branches include one in the **IFC Mall** (Map p476; www.citysuper.com.hk; Shop 1041-1049, IFC Mall, 8 Finance St, Central; ⏲10.30am-9.30pm).

appealing and affordable Vietnamese fare, not the crammed and clamorous surrounds.

Classified Mozzarella Bar EUROPEAN **$$**
(☎2528 3454; 31 Wing Fung St, Wan Chai; ⏲11am-midnight) has creamy Burrata, scrumptious tapas and over 150 bottles.

KOWLOON

There's plenty of choice in both cuisine and budget, especially in Tsim Sha Tsui. More local places can be found further north.

T'ang Court CANTONESE **$$$**
(唐閣; Map p492; ☎2375 1133; http://hongkong.langhamhotels.com; Langham Hotel, 8 Peking Rd, Tsim Sha Tsui; lunch HK$200-2000, dinner HK$360-2000; ⏲11am-2.30pm & 6-10.30pm Mon-Fri, noon-2.30pm & 6-10.30pm Sat & Sun; ; ⓂEast Tsim Sha Tsui, exit L4) As befitting a restaurant named after China's greatest dynasty, T'ang Court has honed its speciality, Cantonese cooking, into an art, whether it's baked oysters on the half-shell or an honest plate of greens. The atmosphere is plush and hushed, with deep-pile carpets and heavy silks – the only noise you'll hear is that of yourself talking. If that seems too formal, rest assured that the polished service will make you feel right at home, like an emperor in his palace. T'ang Court has two Michelin stars.

TOP CHOICE **Ye Shanghai** SHANGHAINESE **$$$**
(夜上海; Map p492; ☎2376 3322; www.elite-concepts.com; 6th fl, Marco Polo Hotel, Harbour City, Canton Rd, Tsim Sha Tsui; meals HK$300-600; ⏲11.30am-3pm & 6-11pm; ⓂEast Tsim Sha Tsui, exit L4) The name means 'Shànghǎi nights'. Dark woods and subtle lighting inspired by 1920s Shànghǎi fill the air with romance. The modern Shanghainese creations, which are lighter and easier on the eye than traditional Shanghainese fare, are also exquisite. The only exception to this Jiangnan harmony is the Cantonese dim sum being served at lunch, though that too is wonderful. Ye Shanghai has one Michelin star.

Spring Deer CHINESE **$**
(鹿鳴春飯店; Map p492; ☎2366 4012; 1st fl, 42 Mody Rd, Tsim Sha Tsui; meals HK$50-350; ⏲11am-2.30pm & 6-10.30pm; ⓂTsim Sha Tsui, exit N2) Hong Kong's most famous Peking duck is served here and the roast lamb is impressive, but the service can be about as welcoming as a Běijīng winter, c 1967. Spring Deer comes recommended by the Michelin inspectors. Booking essential.

Yung Kee Siu Choi Wong CANTONESE **$**
(容記小菜王; 108 Fuk Wa St, Sham Shui Po; meals HK$80-200; ⏲5.30pm-2am; ⓂSham Shui Po, exit B2) The owner Mr Yik's stints as a loan shark and chef to Filipino president Ferdinand Marcos have raised a few eyebrows, but anyone who's eaten at this shabby but magnificent place shouldn't be surprised at the Michelin laurel it received. The roast pork squares (燒腩肉; *siu naam yuk*) and fried cuttlefish lips (炸墨魚嘴; *ja mak yu jeui*) are executed with the precision and flair of a true master.

Sabatini ITALIAN **$$$**
(Map p492; ☎2733 2000; www.rghk.com.hk; 3rd fl, Royal Garden Hotel, 69 Mody Rd, Tsim Sha Tsui; lunch HK$200-800, dinner HK$600-900; ⏲noon-2.30pm & 6-11pm; ; ⓂEast Tsim Sha Tsui, exit P2) One of two branches of Sabatini Ristorante Italiano in Rome, this place serves up excellent Italian favourites in a jovial, faux-rustic setting. Want romance with your risotto? An avuncular Filipino trio will serenade you at your table till you're weak in the knees. Booking advised.

TOP CHOICE **Woodlands** VEGETARIAN, INDIAN **$**
(活蘭印度素食; Map p492; Upper Ground fl, 16 & 17 Wing On Plaza, 62 Mody Rd, Tsim Sha Tsui; meals HK$55-100; ⏲noon-3.30pm & 6.30-10.30pm; ; ⓂEast Tsim Sha Tsui, exit P1) Woodlands comes highly recommended for its excellent Indian fare (mostly South Indian) and modest charm. Dithering gluttons should choose the thali meal, a round metal tray with samplings of different curries, soup, rice and dessert.

Hutong CHINESE $$$
(胡同; Map p492; ☎3428 8342; 28th fl, 1 Peking Rd, Tsim Sha Tsui; lunch HK$250-400, dinner HK$400-1000; ⊙noon-2.30pm & 6pm-midnight; MTsim Sha Tsui, exit C1) Muted lighting and interiors just this side of kitsch lend Michelin-starred Hutong a dramatic air. Like the decor, the tasty contemporary dishes are a tad contrived, but never mind, the real gem is out the window – the Kowloon waterfront in all its splendour.

Mido Cafe CHINESE $
(美都餐室; Map p494; ☎2384 6402; 63 Temple St, Yau Ma Tei; meals HK$25-80; ⊙9am-10pm; MYau Ma Tei, exit B2) The arty types who frequent this 'tea cafe' or *cha chaan tang* (茶餐廳) c 1950 are lured by its mosaic tiles, latticework and old Hong Kong charm. The best tables are by windows overlooking Tin Hau Temple on the upper floor.

Changwon Korean Restaurant KOREAN $
(莊園韓國料理; Map p492; 1g Kimberly St, Tsim Sha Tsui; meals HK$120-300; ⊙noon-4am; ✎; MTsim Sha Tsui, exit B1) Solid staples and long opening hours make Changwon a good place to meet Korean expats and late-night revelers. There's a branch in **Causeway Bay** (Map p480; ☎2836 3877; 1st & 2nd fl, 500 Jaffe Rd, Causeway Bay; MCauseway Bay, exit C).

Din Tai Fung SHANGHAINESE $
(鼎泰豐; Map p492; www.dintaifung.com.tw; Shop 130, 3rd fl, 30 Canton Rd, Tsim Sha Tsui; meals HK$90-160, ⊙11.30am-10.30pm; ✎ⓘ; MMTR Tsim Sha Tsui, exit C1) Whether it's comfort food or a carb fix you're craving, the dumplings and noodles at this Michelin-starred Taiwanese chain will do the trick. Queues are the norm; no reservations.

Indonesia Restaurant INDONESIAN $
(印尼餐廳; Map p492; 66 Granville Rd, Tsim Sha Tsui; meals HK$80-200; ⊙noon-3pm & 5-11pm Mon-Fri, noon-11pm Sat & Sun; MTsim Sha Tsui, exit B1) Whether you're grabbing a snack from the ground-floor deli or plonking down for a feast, Indonesia delivers.

Cheong Fat THAI $
(昌發泰國粉麵屋; 27 South Wall Rd, Kowloon City; noodles from HK$25; ⊙11.30am-11.30pm; MKowloon Tong station, exit B2, then minibus 25M) Blasting music videos in this hole-in-the-wall set the rhythm as you slurp up the tasty if thirst-inducing Chiang Mai noodles.

NEW TERRITORIES

The New Territories has a smaller range of ethnic cuisines than Kowloon and Hong Kong but an abundance of seafood and local places.

Chuen Kee Seafood Restaurant CANTONESE $$
(全記海鮮菜館; 87-89 Man Nin St, Sai Kung; meals HK$200-400; ⊙7am-11pm; MEast Rail Sha Tin station, then bus 299) The granddaddy of Sai Kung's seafood restaurants, Michelin-lauded Chuen Kee flaunts its pedigree with rows of tanks stocked with live fish and crustaceans. Pick your meal from the display, agree on a price and have them cook it for you the way you want. If opting for the more affordable seafood set meals, expect slightly less amazing quality. There's a **branch** (☎2791 1195; 53 Hoi Pong St; ⊙11am-11pm) close by.

TOP CHOICE **Dah Wing Wah** WALLED VILLAGE $
(大榮華酒樓; ☎2476 9888; 2nd fl, Koon Wong Mansion, 2-6 On Ning Rd, Yuen Long; meals HK$80-250; ⊙6am-midnight; 🚌bus 968 or N968 from Tin Hau bus terminus) This Michelin-recommended oldie is *the* place to go for the walled-village cuisine of the New Territories. Local ingredients are sourced from small farms and enhanced with culinary insight. Must-tries include lemon-steamed mullet and smoked oysters. Cantonese dim sum is served throughout the day.

Sha Tin 18 NORTHERN CHINESE $$$
(沙田18; ☎3723 1234; www.hongkong.shatin.hyatt.com; Hyatt Regency Hong Kong, 18 Chak Cheung St, Sha Tin; meals HK$250-800; ⊙11.30am-3pm & 5.30-10.30pm; ✎ⓘ; MEast Rail University station) At this wonderful modern eatery, the Peking duck (24-hour advance booking required) with skin crisper than a whistle is arguably the best in town. But don't inhale the whole bird. The other delicacies are breathtaking too, as are the desserts and the views.

TOP CHOICE **Honeymoon Dessert** CHINESE DESSERTS $
(滿記甜品; www.honeymoon-dessert.com; 9-10a, B&C Po Tung Rd, Sai Kung; dishes HK$30; ⊙1pm-2.45am; ✎; MEast Rail Sha Tin station, then bus 299) Branches in Asia, and 20 locations in Hong Kong including **Sheung Wan** (Map p476; ☎2851 2606; Shop 4-8, ground fl, Western Market, 323 Des Voeux Rd Central; ⊙noon-midnight; MSheung Wan, exit C) attest to Honeymoon's appeal. The sweet soups

ONLY IN HONG KONG

Hong Kong chefs are a sophisticated bunch who move with ease between Chinese and Western kitchens. This has resulted in one-of-a-kind dining experiences ranging from the unusual to the unprecedented. All of the following places except for the first one come with Michelin recommendation.

ABC WESTERN $

(Map p476; ☎9278 8227; CF7, Queen St Cooked Food Market, 38 Des Voeux Rd West, Sheung Wan; meals HK$80-200; ⊙noon-2.30pm & 6.30-10pm Mon-Sat, evenings only Sun) Mediterranean fare served hawker-style in a Chinese food market. Booking advised for dinner.

Bo Innovation FUSION, MOLECULAR CUISINE $$$

(厨魔; Map p480; ☎2850 8371; www.boinnovation.com; 60 Johnston Rd; lunch HK$200-1080, dinner HK$680-1080; ⊙noon-2pm & 7-10pm Mon-Fri, 7-10pm Sat) Hong Kong's take on molecular cuisine deconstructs old Chinese flavours and assembles them in unexpected ways. Booking essential.

Olala NOODLES, SHANGHAINESE $$

(一碗麵; 33 St Francis St, Wan Chai; noodles HK$150; ⊙11.30am-10.30pm) Iberico ham, French clams and al dente strands make up Hong Kong's most expensive bowls of noodles, and they're delicious. At the end of Wing Fung St, make a left into Star St. Olala is at the corner of Star and Francis.

Tai Ping Koon HONG KONG–STYLE WESTERN $$

(太平館; Map p480; www.taipingkoon.com; 6 Pak Sha Rd, Causeway Bay; meals HK$70-250; ⊙11am-11.20pm; 👪) Nostalgic Hong Kong–style Western cuisine originating in the kitchens of white Russians. Try the borscht and baked pork chop over rice.

Tim Ho Wan DIM SUM $

(Shop 8, 2-20 Kwong Wa St, Mong Kok; meals HK$30-50; ⊙10am-9.15pm) A former Four Seasons dim sum chef recreates magic in the world's cheapest Michelin-starred eatery for those who'd wait for a table.

and fruit-based concoctions are indeed impressive.

OUTLYING ISLANDS

Lamma boasts the biggest choices in Yung Shue Wan and Sok Kwu Wan. There are also some decent choices on Lantau and fewer on Cheung Chau.

Lamcombe Seafood Restaurant CANTONESE $$

(南江海鮮酒樓; 47 Main St, Yung Shue Wan, Lamma; meals HK$120-300; ⊙11am-2.30pm & 5-10pm) Lammaites and island hoppers have been coming to good old Lamcombe for fried squid, steamed scallops and other seafood dishes for over a decade.

Stoep Restaurant MEDITERRANEAN $$

(32 Lower Cheung Sha Village, Lantau; mains HK$65-200; ⊙11am-10pm Tue-Sun; 🚌bus 1 or 2 from Mui Wo) Right on quiet Lower Cheung Sha Beach, the Stoep serves up meat, fish and South African barbecue and a chilled atmosphere.

Windsurfing Watersports Centre & Cafe WESTERN $

(滑浪風帆中心露天茶座; www.ccwindc.com.hk; 1 Hak Pai Rd, Cheung Chau; meals HK$80-200; ⊙10am-6pm) Feast on fish steak and fries at this balmy seaside cafe owned by the uncle of Hong Kong's only Olympic royalty, Lee Lai-shan.

Drinking

Lan Kwai Fong (LKF) in Central is synonymous with night life in Hong Kong, attracting everyone from expat and Chinese suits to travellers. In general, watering holes in Wan Chai are cheaper and more relaxed (some say seedier), though sleek new spots have been fast emerging around Star St. Drinking places in Kowloon tend to attract more locals. Most places offer discounts on drinks during happy hour, usually from late afternoon to early evening – 4pm to 8pm, say – but times vary from place to place.

HONG KONG ISLAND

TOP CHOICE Club 71 BAR

(七一吧; Map p476; Basement, 67 Hollywood Rd, Central; ⊙3pm-2am Mon-Sat, 6pm-1am Sun; bus 26) Named after a protest march that took place on 1 July 2003, this is one of the best drinking spots for nonposeurs. It's also a great place to meet Hong Kong's musicians, artists and writers (plus wannabes of all of the above). Club 71 is accessed via a small footpath off either Peel St, Aberdeen St or Wyndham St.

TOP CHOICE Sevva BAR

(Map p476; www.sevva.hk; 25th fl, Prince's Bldg, 10 Chater Rd, Central; ⊙noon-midnight Mon-Thu, to 2am Fri & Sat; M Central, exit H) If there was a million-dollar view in Hong Kong, it'd be the one from the balcony of this stylish number – iconic skyscrapers up so close you see their arteries of steel, with the harbour and Kowloon in the distance. At night, it takes your breath away, and Sevva's cocktails are a wonderful excuse to let it.

Tastings Wine Bar WINE BAR

(Map p476; www.tastings.hk; Basement, Yuen Yick Bldg, 27 & 29 Wellington St, Central; ⊙5pm-2am Mon-Sat; M Central, exit D2) The centrepiece of this cool, subterranean bar is a set of five sleek wine-dispensing machines from Italy. With a prepaid card, you can sample – by a sip, a half-glass or a glass – 40 vintages out of 160 on the bar's list.

8th Estate Winery WINERY $

(☎2518 0922; www.the8estatewinery.com; Room 306, 3rd fl, Harbour Industrial Centre, 10 Lee Hing St, Ap Lei Chau) The world's only fully functional winery inside an industrial building produces 100,000 bottles a year with imported grapes that are aged in oak drums. Public tastings from 2pm to 5pm almost every Saturday; open-house party from 5pm to 9pm every second Saturday of the month (HK$250 per person). Registration required. Take bus 90 from Exchange Sq in Central, get off at South Horizons, and cab it over (under HK$20).

Pawn GASTROPUB

(Map p480; 62 Johnston Rd, Wai Chai; ⊙11am-late; M Wan Chai, exit B2) Occupying a period building that used to house a century-old pawn shop, the Pawn serves a huge range of beers and wines from stylishly beaten-up sofas and cool terrace tables overlooking tram tracks.

Makumba MUSICAL BAR

(Map p476; www.makumba.com.hk; 48 Peel St, Central; ⊙6pm-late) Makumba is an inviting cavern saturated with earthy vibes and pulsating rhythms. A predominantly African crowd moves to music performed nightly by a Senegalese band or visiting artists.

Executive B.A.R. BAR

(Map p480; 27th fl, Bartlock Centre, 3 Yiu Wa St, Causeway Bay; ⊙5.30pm-3am Mon-Sat; M Causeway Bay, exit B) The legendary cocktails at this wonderfully understated address are each ceremoniously crafted by Ichiro, the Japanese owner.

Cafe Zambra CAFE

(Map p480; www.zambra.net/cafe.html; 239 Jaffe Rd, Wan Chai; coffee & snacks HK$50-100; ⊙7.30am-10pm; M Wan Chai, exit A1) For coffee-lovers, Zambra is a delightful alternative to franchise mediocrity.

KOWLOON

Phonograph BAR

(Map p492; Shop A&B, ground fl, 2 Austin Ave, Tsim Sha Tsui; ⊙6pm-4am; M Tsim Sha Tsui, exit B2) With dark, velvety interiors opening onto a quiet corner of Tsim Sha Tsui, Phonograph is a breath of fresh air on Kowloon's bar scene. Musicians and artist types come for the mellow vibe and eclectic music selection.

Felix BAR, RESTAURANT

(Map p492; 28th fl, Peninsula Hong Kong, Salisbury Rd, Tsim Sha Tsui; ⊙6pm-2am; M East Tsim Sha Tsui, exit L2) Designed by Philippe Starck, swanky Felix is where to head for amazing views and expensive drinks.

Delaney's IRISH PUB

(Map p492; Basement, Mary Bldg, 71-77 Peking Rd, Tsim Sha Tsui; ⊙8am-3am; M East Tsim Sha Tsui, exit D2) This popular Irish pub has the full Irish theme, including good craic most of the time. It's a good choice for watching sports.

Tapas Bar TAPAS BAR

(Map p492; www.shangri-la.com/en/property/hongkong/kowloonshangrila; Lobby, Kowloon Shangri-La, 64 Mody Rd, Tsim Sha Tsui East; ⊙3.30pm-1am; M East Tsim Sha Tsui, exit P1) Harbour views and bistro-style decor make this a great venue for relaxing, people watching, and if you're into posing, a bit of that too.

STUBBED OUT

In Hong Kong, smoking is banned in all restaurants, bars, shopping malls and museums – even at beaches and public parks – but you can light up in 'alfresco' areas. Some bars, however, risk getting fined to attract more customers during nonpeak hours. You'll know which ones they are by the ashtray they nonchalantly place on your table.

☆ Entertainment

Hong Kongers work hard and play harder. To find out what's on, pick up a copy of **HK Magazine** (http://hk-magazine.com), an entertainment listings magazine. It's free, appears on Friday and can be found in restaurants, bars and hotels. For more comprehensive listings buy the fortnightly **Time Out** (www.timeout.com.hk) from newsstands. Also worth checking out is the freebie **bc magazine** (www.bcmagazine.net).

The main ticket providers, **Urbtix** (☎2734 9009; www.urbtix.hk; ⏰10am-8pm), **Cityline** (☎2317 6666; www.cityline.com.hk) and **Hong Kong Ticketing** (☎3128 8288; www.hkticketing.com; ⏰10am-8pm), have among them tickets to every major event in Hong Kong. You can book through the websites or on the phone.

Cinema

Tickets can be bought through Cityline (for mainstream films) and Urbtix (for alternative screenings). If you're into arthouse films, check out **Broadway Cinematheque** (Map p494; ☎2338 3188; Prosperous Garden, 3 Public Square St, Yau Ma Tei; ⏰11.30am-10.30pm) of the Broadway Circuit. To book, go to www.cinema.com.hk and click on 'Cinematheque'.

Cantonese Opera

Hong Kong is one of the best places to watch Cantonese opera. **Sunbeam Theatre** (www.ua-sunbeam.com; 423 King's Rd, North Point) is dedicated to the art form. Performances are also being staged at **Ko Shan Theatre** (☎2330 5661; www.lcsd.gov.hk/CE/CulturalService/KST; 77 Ko Shan Rd, Hung Hom). The best way to book if you don't speak Cantonese is through the Urbtix or Cityline systems.

Live Music & Clubbing

TOP CHOICE **Peel Fresco** MUSIC BAR
(Map p476; www.peelfresco.com; 49 Peel St, Central; ⏰5pm-late Mon-Sat) This charming place has great live jazz six nights a week, with local and overseas acts performing next to huge Renaissance-style paintings. The action starts around 9.30pm, but go at 9pm to get a seat.

Tazmania Ballroom CLUB
(Map p476; www.tazmaniaballroom.com; 1st fl, LKF Tower, 33 Wyndham St, Central; ⏰5am-late; Ⓜ Central, exit D2) This sexy, futuristic lair hasn't forgotten how to be playful. At any one time, you'll see people dressed to the hilt smoking on the balcony, or in sweatpants playing pool at gold-plated tables.

Backstage Live Restaurant LIVE MUSIC
(Map p476; ☎2167 8985; www.backstagelive.hk/; 1st fl, Somptueux Central, 52-54 Wellington St, Central; incl 1 drink HK$150-250; ⏰11.30am-late Mon-Fri, 6.30pm-late Sat; Ⓜ Central, exit D1) For four or more nights a week, this restaurant hosts gigs in new indie, alternative and postpunk from Hong Kong and overseas. Check website for details.

Gecko Lounge MUSIC BAR
(Map p476; lower ground fl, 15-19 Hollywood Rd, Central; ⏰4pm-2am Mon-Thu, to 6am Fri, 6pm-6am Sat) Entered from Ezra's Lane off Cochrane St or Pottinger St, French-owned Gecko is an intimate lounge that attracts an easy-going, arty crowd. Live jazz on Tuesday and Wednesday.

Wanch LIVE MUSIC
(Map p480; 54 Jaffe Rd, Wan Chai; ⏰4pm-2am; Ⓜ Wan Chai, exit C) This small venue has live music (mostly rock and folk) seven nights a week from around 9pm, with the occasional solo guitarist thrown in.

Azure BAR
(Map p476; www.azure.hk; 29th fl, LKF Tower, 33 Wyndham St, Central; ⏰11am-1am Mon-Thu, to 3am Fri & Sat, to midnight Sun; Ⓜ Central, exit D2) Panoramic city views, loungey interiors and early closing times make Azure a pleasant venue for some easy dancing and drinking.

Gay & Lesbian Venues

For more venues and the latest events, try **Utopia Asia** (www.utopia-asia.com/hkbars.htm) or **Gay HK** (www.gayhk.com).

Propaganda CLUB
(Map p476; lower ground fl, 1 Hollywood Rd, Central; weekend cover HK$100; ⏰9pm-late Tue-Sat) Hong Kong's premier gay dance club. The weekend cover charge gets you into Works below on Friday. Enter from Ezra's Lane.

Works CLUB
(Map p476; 1st fl, 30-32 Wyndham St, Central; weekend cover HK$60-100; ⏲7pm-2am) Propaganda's sister club is a popular starting point for an evening on the town.

Shopping

It's not the bargain destination it was, but Hong Kong is crammed with retail space, making it a delight for shoppers.

If you prefer everything under one roof, here are two of the sleeker options:

IFC Mall (國際金融商場; Map p476; www.ifc.com.hk; 1 Harbour View St, Central; ⓂTung Chung Line Hong Kong station)

Pacific Place (太古廣場; Map p476; 88 Queensway, Admiralty; ⓂAdmiralty)

In Kowloon, head for:

Harbour City (海港城; Map p492; Canton Rd, Tsim Sha Tsui) An enormous complex.

K11 (Map p492; 18 Hanoi Rd, Tsim Sha Tsui; ⓂEast Tsim Sha Tsui, exit D2) Interesting shops and art spaces.

Citygate Outlets (東薈城名店倉; www.citygateoutlets.com.hk; 20 Tat Tung Rd, Tung Chung, Lantau; MTR Tung Chung Station, exit B) in Tung Chung, Lantau, specialises in out-of-season products at discounted prices, including sportswear, designer fashion, electrical appliances and travel gear.

For antiques and curios, Central's **Hollywood Rd** (Map p476) should be your first stop, while cheaper **Cat St** (Map p476), also in Central, specialises in younger (ie retro) items such as old postcards and Mao paraphernalia.

You can buy clothes you'll enjoy wearing for less than you'd pay at home in Hong Kong's malls. For cheap attire, try **Jardine's Bazaar** (渣甸街; Map p480) in Causeway Bay, and **Johnston Rd** (Map p480) in Wan Chai. In Kowloon, besides **Temple Street night market** (p481) try **Ladies Market** (女人街;Tung Choi St, Fa Yuen St & Sai Yeung Choi St, Mong Kok; ⏲noon-10.30pm; MTR Mong Kok exit B2) in Mong Kok.

Hong Kong is one of the best places in Asia to buy English-language books and the city's computer malls have some of the lowest prices on earth. Similarly, there are some fantastic camera stores, though most are *not* on Nathan Rd in Tsim Sha Tsui.

STREET MUSIC

For an unusual Hong Kong experience, catch one of the free-for-all, under-the-stars gigs thrown by eclectic musician Kung Chi-sing. One Friday every month the charismatic artist organises a **concert** (☎2582 0280; www.kungmusic.hk, www.hkac.org.hk; Hong Kong Arts Centre; ⏲6.30-9pm) outside the Arts Centre (Map p480) in Wan Chai. The colourful line-ups have included anything from alternative pop, indie rock, punk and jazz to Cantonese opera and Mozart. Mind you, this is not self-indulgent, anything-goes artistic diarrhoea. This is excellent, professional-quality music (Kung trained in classical music in the US) performed in an electrifying atmosphere. The concerts have attracted a loyal following that includes the Venezuelan and Canadian Consuls-General in Hong Kong. Check online for dates.

HONG KONG ISLAND

Central and Causeway Bay are the main shopping districts on Hong Kong Island.

TOP CHOICE **Horizon Plaza** FURNITURE
(海怡工貿中心; 2 Lee Wing St, Ap Lei Chau, Aberdeen; ⏲10am-7pm) The warehouses and factory outlets in this enormous plaza sell Western- and Chinese-style furniture and designer clothing at prices cheaper than what you'd find in the city. Most shops will pack and ship too. Get a directory from the lift lobby. Bus 90 from Central's Exchange Sq terminus takes you to Ap Lei Chau Estate bus terminus; from there take a cab.

Daydream Nation FASHION
(www.daydream-nation.com; 21 Wing Fung St, Star St, Wan Chai; ⏲noon-8.30pm; ⓂAdmiralty, exit F) Daydream Nation is a 'Vogue Talent 2010' brand created by a fashion designer and her musician brother. The highly wearable clothes come with a touch of theatricality. There are CDs for sale too.

TOP CHOICE **G.O.D.** LIFESTYLE
(住好啲; Map p480; www.god.com.hk; Leighton Centre, Sharp St East, Causeway Bay; ⏲noon-10pm; ⓂCauseway Bay) This spunky shop is where to go for really cool Hong Kong–style accessories and souvenirs. It

STAR FERRY

On a smoggy day, they're the only stars you'll see from Victoria Harbour. The iconic **Star Ferry** (天星小輪), founded in 1888, is a fleet of 12 passenger ferries (each named after a star) that plies Victoria Harbour between Hong Kong and Kowloon.

For a modest fare, you can cross the harbour on one of four routes. It's a little hard to imagine, therefore, that in 1966, thousands gathered here to protest against a five-cent fare increase. The protest eventually erupted into the 1966 Riot, the first in a series of important social protests leading to colonial reform.

The Star Ferry has borne witness to major events in Hong Kong history. In 1910, the Kowloon–Canton Railway was built near its Kowloon concourse, linking Hong Kong with the mainland. On Christmas Day 1941, the colonial governor, Sir Mark Aitchison Young, took the ferry to Tsim Sha Tsui, where he surrendered to the Japanese at the Peninsula Hotel.

In 2006, amid vehement opposition, the government tore down the old pier at Edinburgh Pl on Hong Kong Island. Taking over its functions is an ugly Edwardian replica at Piers 4–7 further west. The pier in Kowloon remains untouched.

has five stores in town, including one at the Jockey Club (p484).

Arch Angel Antiques ANTIQUES
(Map p476; 53-55 Hollywood Rd, Central; 9.30am-6.30pm; bus 26) This well-respected shop has knowledgable staff and a wide selection of antiques and curios, including many at affordable prices. Everything is authenticated.

Shanghai Tang CHINESE APPAREL
(上海灘; Map p476; 12 Pedder St, Central; 10am-8pm Mon-Sat, 11am-7pm Sun; M Central) If you fancy a cheongsam with a modern pattern or a lime-green mandarin jacket, this is the place to go.

Hong Kong Book Centre BOOKS
(Map p476; 2522 7046; www.hongkongbookcentre.com; Basement, On Lok Yuen Bldg, 25 Des Voeux Rd, Central; 9am-6.30pm Mon-Fri, to 5.30pm Sat; M Central) English-language publications.

Page One BOOKS
(葉壹堂; Map p480; Shop 922, 9th fl, Times Sq, 1 Matheson St, Causeway Bay; 10.30am-10pm Mon-Thu, to 10.30pm Fri-Sun; M Causeway Bay) Mostly English-language publications.

Wan Chai Computer Centre COMPUTERS
(灣仔電腦城; Map p480; 1st fl, Southorn Centre, 130-138 Hennessy Rd, Wan Chai; 10am-8pm Mon-Sat; M Wan Chai) A busy warren of dozens of computer shops just outside Wan Chai MTR. A safe bet.

Photo Scientific CAMERAS
(攝影科學; Map p476; 6 Stanley St, Central; 9am-7pm Mon-Sat; M Central) Professional photographers come here to shop and we've enjoyed years of good service and fair prices.

Protrek CAMPING GEAR
(Map p494; www.protrek.com.hk; 522 Nathan Rd, Yau Ma Tei; noon-8pm Mon-Sat; M Yau Ma Tei) This reliable place with branches all over town is your best bet for hiking and camping gear.

Mountain Folkcraft CRAFTS
(高山民藝; Map p476; 12 Wo On Lane, Central; 9.30am-6.30pm Mon-Sat; M Central, exit D1) This place sells bolts of batik, clothing, wood carvings, and papercuts made by ethnic minorities in Asia.

Dymocks BOOKS
(Map p476; Shop 2007-2011, 2nd fl, IFC Mall, 1 Harbour View St, Central; 9.30am-9pm; M Tung Chung Line Hong Kong station) Mostly English-language publications.

In Square COMPUTER MALL
(Map p480; 10th-12th fl, Windsor House, 311 Gloucester Rd, Causeway Bay; 11am-9pm; M Causeway Bay) Causeway Bay's best choice for computer gadgets has higher prices than most other places.

KOWLOON

Shopping in Kowloon is a mix of the down-at-heel and the glamorous; you can find just about anything – especially in Tsim Sha Tsui.

Ap Liu Street Flea Market GADGETS
(鴨寮街; Ap Liu St, Sham Shui Po; noon-midnight; M Sham Shui Po, exit A2) Close by Golden Computer Arcade, Ap Liu St has shops and stalls selling every electronic/electrical ap-

pliance you can imagine (new and used), from satellite dishes to cameras. It's very local.

Golden Computer Arcade & Golden Shopping Center COMPUTERS
(黄金電腦商場和高登電腦中心; www.goldenarcade.org; 146-152 Fuk Wa St, Sham Shui Po; ⌚11am-9pm; Ⓜ Sham Shui Po, exit D2) Housed in the same building opposite Sham Shui Po MTR station, these are *the* places to go for low-cost computers and peripherals if you're ready to brave the language barrier.

Yue Hwa Chinese Products Emporium CHINESE PRODUCTS
(裕華國貨; Map p492; 301-309 Nathan Rd, Yau Ma Tei; ⌚10am-10pm; Ⓜ Yau Ma Tei, exit D) This enormous place has seven floors of ceramics, furniture, souvenirs, clothing and traditional medicines.

Swindon Books BOOKS
(辰衝; Map p492; www.swindonbooks.com; 13 15 Lock Rd, Tsim Sha Tsui; ⌚10am-8pm Mon-Sat, 12.30-6.30pm Sun; Ⓜ Tsim Sha Tsui) Mostly English-language publications.

Onestop Photo Company CAMERAS
(忠誠; Map p492; Shop 2, ground fl, Champagne Ct, 18 Kimberley Rd, Tsim Sha Tsui; ⌚10.30am-8.30pm; Ⓜ Tsm Sha Tsui) Unusually for Tsim Sha Tsui, this camera shop has prices marked, but bargain anyway.

Initial FASHION
(Map p492; www.initialfashion.com; Shop 2, 48 Cameron Rd, Tsim Sha Tsui; ⌚11.30am-10.30pm; Ⓜ Tsim Sha Tsui) Initial's 10-plus branches carry stylish, multifunctional urbanwear.

Izzue FASHION
(Map p492; www.izzue.com; LG64, Silvercord Centre, 30 Canton Rd, Tsim Sha Tsui; ⌚noon-10pm; Ⓜ MTR Tsim Sha Tsui, exit C1) With close to 20 branches, Izzue sells casual wear designed for the young and hip.

Star Computer City COMPUTERS
(星光電腦城; Map p492; 2nd fl, Star House, 3 Salisbury Rd, Tsim Sha Tsui; ⌚10am-8pm; Ⓜ Tsim Sha Tsui) Conveniently near the Star Ferry Pier and hence relatively expensive, and only two dozen computer shops!

Mong Kok Computer Centre COMPUTERS
(旺角電腦中心; 8-8a Nelson St, Mong Kok; ⌚1-10pm; Ⓜ Mong Kok) Cheap, but language can be a barrier, and you'll see more finished products than computer components.

Information

Hong Kong is awash with free maps – the airport is full of them. The *Hong Kong Map*, distributed by the HKTB, is enough for most travellers.

Emergency

Fire, police & ambulance (☎999)

Internet Access

Internet cafes may be hard to come by, but wi-fi is widely available. Free wi-fi:

» Parks, public libraries, sports centres, museums, cooked-food markets, community halls, and government premises listed at www.gov.hk/en/theme/wifi/location.

» Over 30 MTR stations (see www.mtr.com.hk/eng/facilities/wifi.html).

» Hong Kong International Airport.

» McDonald's (www.mcdonalds.com.hk), Pacific Coffee (www.pacificcoffee.com) and Starbucks (www.starbucks.com.hk) outlets with purchase.

Media

Print Local and Asian editions printed locally: *South China Morning Post, The Standard, HK Magazine, BC Magazine, Time Out, USA Today, International Herald Tribune, Financial Times, Wall Street Journal Asia.*

English-language TV (terrestrial) & radio TVB Pearl, ATV World; BBC World Service, RTHK 3 and 4.

Medical Services

Medical care is of a high standard in Hong Kong (general enquiries, call ☎2300 6555), though private hospital care is costly. Hospitals with 24-hour emergency services:

Matilda International (明德國際醫院; 41 Mt Kellett Rd, Peak) Pricey private hospital atop Victoria Peak.

Prince of Wales (30-32 Ngan Shing St, Sha Tin) Public hospital in the New Territories.

Queen Elizabeth (伊利沙伯醫院; 30 Gascoigne Rd, Yau Ma Tei) Public hospital in Kowloon.

Money

The Hong Kong dollar is pegged to the US dollar at a rate of US$1 to HK$7.80.

ATMs Available throughout Hong Kong, including at the airport.

Banks Best exchange rates, but some levy commissions of HK$50 or more for each transaction.

Licensed moneychangers Abundant in tourist districts and ground floor of Chungking Mansions. **Wing Hoi Money Exchange** (ground fl, Shop No 9b, Mirador Arcade, 58 Nathan Rd, Tsim Sha Tsui; ⌚8.30am-8.30pm Mon-Sat, to

7pm Sun) in Mirador Mansion can change most major currencies and travellers cheques; rates at the airport are poor.

Post

The excellent **Hong Kong Post** (www.hongkongpost.com) offices:

General post office (中央郵政局; 2 Connaught Pl, Central; ⏲8am-6pm Mon-Sat, 9am-5pm Sun)

Tsim Sha Tsui post office (尖沙咀郵政局; ground & 1st fl, Hermes House, 10 Middle Rd, Tsim Sha Tsui; ⏲9am-6pm Mon-Sat, to 2pm Sun)

Telephone

Facts you should know before making calls in Hong Kong:

» All phone numbers have eight digits (except ☎800 toll-free numbers) and no area codes.

» Local calls are free on private phones and cost HK$1 for five minutes on pay phones.

» A phonecard, available at convenience stores, will let you make international direct-dial calls.

» A SIM card (from HK$50) with prepaid call time will connect you to the local mobile-phone network.

Some handy phone numbers:

International directory assistance (☎10015)

Local directory assistance (☎1081)

Reverse charge/collect calls (☎10010)

Weather & time (☎18501)

Tourist Information

The enterprising and efficient **HKTB** (香港旅遊發展局; ☎visitor hotline 9am-6pm 2508 1234; www.discoverhongkong.com) runs an immensely useful visitor hotline and excellent website. It also maintains Visitor Information and Service Centres:

Hong Kong International Airport (Buffer Halls A & B, Arrivals Level, Terminal 1; ⏲7am-11pm)

Hong Kong Island (The Peak Piazza; ⏲9am-9pm)

Kowloon (Star Ferry Concourse, Tsim Sha Tsui; ⏲8am-8pm)

Lo Wu (2nd fl, Arrival Hall, Lo Wu Terminal Bldg; ⏲8am-4pm) At the border to mainland China.

Travel Agencies

China Travel Service (中國旅行社; CTS; ☎2522 0450; www.ctshk.com; ground fl, China Travel Bldg, 77 Queen's Rd, Central; ⏲9am-6pm Mon-Fri, 9am-7.30pm Mon-Sat, 9.30am-5pm Sun)

Phoenix Services Agency (峯寧旅運社; ☎2722 7378; info@phoenixtrvl.com; Room 1404-5, 14th fl, Austin Tower, 22-26a Austin Ave, Tsim Sha Tsui; ⏲9am-6pm Mon-Fri, to 4pm Sat)

Getting There & Away

Air

Some 90 airlines operate between **Hong Kong International Airport** (HKG; ☎2181 8888; www.hkairport.com) and about 150 destinations worldwide. Competition keeps fares relatively low, and Hong Kong is a great place to find discounted tickets.

There are few bargain airfares between Hong Kong and China, however, as the government regulates the prices. Seats can be difficult to book due to the enormous volume of business travellers and Chinese tourists, so book well in advance.

However, if you're prepared to travel a couple of hours to Guǎngzhōu or Shēnzhèn, in nearby Guǎngdōng province, then you can find much cheaper flights. Shēnzhèn airport (see p557), in particular, has flights to just about everywhere in China. For an idea of price, check out www.elong.net.

See p995 for international airlines flying to/from Hong Kong.

Airline offices in Hong Kong:

Air China (www.airchina.hk)

Cathay Pacific (www.cathaypacific.com)

China Airlines (www.china-airlines.com)

China Southern (www.cs-air.com)

Dragonair (www.dragonair.com)

Hong Kong Express (www.hongkongexpress.com)

Boat

Regularly scheduled ferries link the **China Ferry Terminal** (中港碼頭; China Hong Kong City, 33 Canton Rd, Tsim Sha Tsui) in Kowloon and/or the **Hong Kong–Macau Ferry Terminal** (港澳碼頭; Shun Tak Centre, 200 Connaught Rd, Sheung Wan) on Hong Kong Island with a string of towns and cities on the Pearl River delta – but not central Guǎngzhōu or Shēnzhèn. For sea transport to/from Macau, see p530.

CMSE (☎2858 0909) has seven services daily between the Hong Kong–Macau Ferry Terminal and Shékǒu port (HK$110). **Chu Kong Passenger Transportation Co** (☎2858 3876; www.cksp.com.hk) runs seven ferries a day to Zhūhǎi from the China Ferry Terminal and eight from the Hong Kong–Macau Ferry Terminal (HK$178). Chu Kong also has ferries from the China Ferry Terminal to a number of other ports in southern Guǎngdōng province (from HK$195).

Hong Kong levies a HK$11 departure tax that is normally included in the ticket price.

Bus

For info on buses from the airport to mainland China, see the boxed text, p507. You can reach virtually any major destination in Guǎngdōng province by bus (HK$100 to HK$220).

CTS Express Coach (☎2764 9803; http://ctsbus.hkcts.com) Has the most extensive cross-border bus services to destinations in Guǎngdōng province.

Trans-Island Limousine Service (☎3193 9333; www.trans-island.com.hk) Has buses to a dozen destinations in Guǎngdōng province.

Train

You can get the latest train schedules and ticket prices from the MTR's excellent website, www.mtr.com.hk. Other handy train-related facts:

Immigration formalities at Hung Hom Completed before boarding, including checking your visa for China; arrive at station 45 minutes before departure.

Tickets Can be booked in advance at CTS, East Rail stations in Hung Hom, Mong Kok, Kowloon Tong and Sha Tin, and MTR Travel at Admiralty Station; tickets booked with credit card by phone (☎2947 7888) must be collected at least one hour before departure.

Trains to Guǎngzhōu, Shànghǎi, Běijīng and Zhàoqìng Daily from Hung Hom station; HK$235 to HK$934.

Trains to Shēnzhèn Board East Rail train at Hung Hom station or any East Rail station along the way, and ride it to Lo Wu; from Shēnzhèn you can take a local train or bus to Guǎngzhōu and beyond.

HKIA TO CHINA THE FAST WAY

A growing number of travellers are heading straight from Hong Kong International Airport (HKIA) to airports in Macau, Shēnzhèn and Guǎngzhōu.

Chu Kong Passenger Transportation Co (☎2858 3876; www.cksp.com.hk/eng/home.html) buses go from HKIA to Shēnzhèn airport (HK$295, 50 minutes, six times daily from 10am to 7.50pm); they also run to Macau, Shékǒu, Dōngguǎn, Zhūhǎi and Zhōngshān.

The following companies (all with counters at HKIA) have buses going to points in southern China (Dōngguǎn HK$200, Fóshān HK$220, Guǎngzhōu HK$250 and Shēnzhèn airport HK$180):

CTS Express Coach (☎2261 2147)

Eternal East Cross Border Coach (☎2261 0176)

Go Go Bus (☎2261 0886; www.gogobus.com)

Getting Around

Hong Kong's public-transport system is the envy of cities the world over. It's fast, easy to navigate, relatively inexpensive and ridiculously easy with the Octopus card payment system.

To/From the Airport

Airport Express (www.mtr.com.hk; 24/21/13min ride from Central/Kowloon/Tsing Yi HK$100/90/60) Fastest and costliest public route to the airport; most airlines allow Airport Express passengers to check in at the Central or Kowloon stations up to a day ahead of departure; trains depart from **Hong Kong Airport Express station** in Central every 12 minutes.

Bus (www.nwstbus.com.hk; fares HK$21-45) Services connect the airport with Lantau, the New Territories, Kowloon and Hong Kong Island.

Taxi To Central about HK$300 plus luggage charge of HK$5 per item.

Ferry For info on service to Shēnzhèn airport, see the boxed text above.

Bicycle

In quiet areas of the Outlying Islands or New Territories, a bike can be a lovely way of getting around as long as you don't mind a few hills. For rental info, see p487.

Car & Motorcycle

Hong Kong's maze of one-way streets and dizzying expressways isn't for the faint-hearted. But if you're hell-bent on ruining your holiday, **Avis** (☎2890 6988; Shop 46, ground fl, Peninsula Centre, 67 Mody Rd, Tsim Sha Tsui; ⏰8am-7pm Mon, 9am-7pm Tue-Fri, 9am-4pm Sat & Sun) will rent you a Honda Civic for HK$790/3500 a day/week with unlimited kilometres.

Public Transport

No more rummaging in your purse for small change:

Octopus card (www.octopuscards.com; HK$150, plus refundable deposit HK$50) Reusable 'smart card' that can be used on most forms of public transport and in a number of stores. To put money on your card, go to an add-value machine/ticket office at MTR stations, or 7-Eleven stores.

MTR Tourist 1-Day Pass (HK$55) This pass, allowing unlimited travel on the MTR for 24 hours, is good for short stays.

BUS Hong Kong's extensive **bus system** (fares HK$2.50-40; ⏰5.30/6am-midnight/12.30am), including a handful of night buses, will get you almost anywhere. Note that exact change or an

Octopus card is required. The HKTB has leaflets on the major bus routes. You can search bus routes and check fares online:

City Bus (www.citybus.com.hk)

First Bus (www.nwstbus.com.hk)

Kowloon Motor Bus (www.kmb.hk)

There are myriad bus stops and stations; major ones:

Central Bus Terminus (Exchange Sq) Gets you to the southern side of the island. Buses 6, 6A and 260 leave for Stanley and Repulse Bay, and buses 70 and 70P for Aberdeen.

Admiralty Above Admiralty MTR station. Gets you to the southern side of the island.

Star Ferry Pier Has buses to Hung Hom station and points in eastern and western Kowloon.

Other useful services are buses 73 and 973 from Repulse Bay to Aberdeen. Bus 9 from Shau Kei Wan MTR station (exit A3) goes to Shek O. Bus 299 from Sha Tin goes to Sai Kung. To explore the eastern side of the peninsula, take bus 94 from Sai Kung to Wong Shek pier.

PUBLIC LIGHT BUS 'Public light buses', better known as 'minibuses', have no more than 16 seats and come in two varieties:

With red roof/stripe Fares HK$2 to HK$20; supplement bus services. Get on or off almost anywhere – just yell *'ni do, m gói'* (here, please); pay with Octopus card/coins as you exit.

With green roof/stripe Operate on over 350 set routes and make designated stops.

CROSS-HARBOUR FERRY The **Star Ferry** (www.starferry.com.hk; from HK$2) operates on four routes:

Central–Hung Hom

Central–Tsim Sha Tsui

Wan Chai–Hung Hom

Wan Chai–Tsim Sha Tsui

OUTLYING ISLANDS FERRIES Schedules are posted at all ferry piers and on the ferry companies' websites, or ask for a pocket-sized timetable. Most ferries depart from the Outlying Islands Piers close to the IFC building in Central. The main companies serving the islands:

Hong Kong & Kowloon Ferry Co (www.hkkf.com.hk) Serves Lamma and Peng Chau.

New World First Ferry (NWFF; www.nwff.com.hk) Services to Lantau and Cheung Chau, and an interisland service connecting Peng Chau, Mui Wo (Lantau) and Cheung Chau.

TRAIN The **Mass Transit Railway** (MTR;www.mtr.com.hk; fares HK$4-26) runs 10 lines composing arguably the best railway service on earth – fast, convenient and always on time. You can buy individual tickets or use an Octopus card (slightly cheaper). Once you go past the turnstile, you must complete the journey within 150 minutes.

The MTR also runs overland services on two main lines and two smaller lines, offering excellent transport to the New Territories:

East Rail From Hung Hom station in Kowloon to Lo Wu (HK$33) and Lok Ma Chau, gateway to Shēnzhèn; a spur runs from Tai Wai to Wu Kai Sha.

Light Rail Fares HK$3.70 to HK$5.80. Operates on routes in western New Territories between Tuen Mun and Yuen Long, and feeds the West Rail.

West Rail From Hung Hom station to Tuen Mun via Yuen Long.

TRAM Hong Kong's century-old trams, operated by **Hong Kong Tramways Ltd** (www.hktramways.com; fares HK$2), comprise the only all double-decker wooden-sided tram fleet in the world. They operate on six overlapping routes, on 16km of track running east–west along the northern side of Hong Kong Island.

Taxi

Hong Kong is served by taxis of three colours:

Blue Serving Lantau; HK$13 flag fall, then HK$1.30 for every 200m.

Green Serving the New Territories; HK$14.50 flag fall, then HK$1.30 for every subsequent 200m.

Red Serving Hong Kong Island and Kowloon; HK$18 flag fall for the first 2km, then HK$1 for every additional 200m.

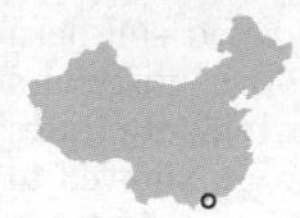

Macau

POPULATION: 549,500 / TELEPHONE CODE: 853

Includes »

Best Places to Eat

» Alfonso III (p525)

» Antonio (p525)

» Robuchon a Galera (p525)

» Café Nga Tim (p525)

» Lung Wah Tea House (p525)

Best Places to Stay

» Mandarin Oriental (p523)

» Pousada de Mong Há (p523)

» Pousada de São Tiago (p523)

» Pousada de Coloane (p524)

» Grand Hyatt Macau (p524)

Why Go?

The Chinese people have stood up and they're off to Macau. Chairman Mao (who coined the first half of that sentence) must be spinning in his glass coffin. Mainlanders can't get enough of this once Portuguese-administered backwater-turned-gambling-megaresort.

Such has been its explosive growth since 2002 that it is commonplace to refer to Macau as the Vegas of the East. It might be more appropriate to put that the other way round, since Macau has eclipsed its American rival in gambling income. And there are other things that Macau does better. Beyond the gaming halls, it offers cobblestoned streets punctuated with Chinese temples and baroque churches, pockets of greenery, a historic centre of Unesco World Heritage status, and balmy beaches.

Macau's history has also created a one-of-a-kind cuisine that celebrates the marriage of European, Latin American, African and Asian flavours.

When to Go

Macau

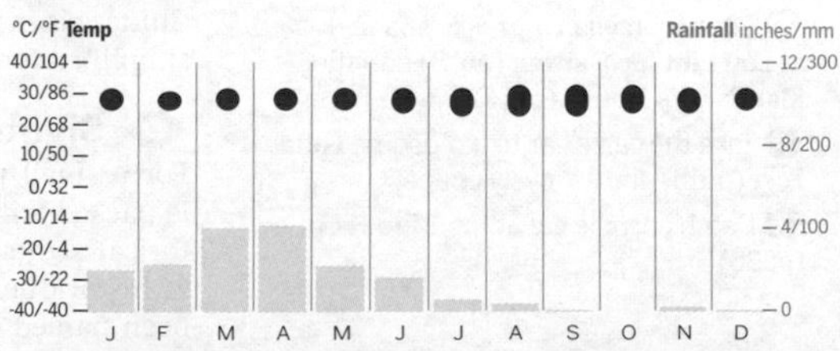

March–May Celebrate the arts, a sea goddess and a dragon as mist hangs over the Inner Harbour.

June–September Days in the shade of temples and dragonboats; nights aglow with fireworks.

October–February Music and Grand Prix in a high-octane run-up to Christmas and New Year.

Macau Highlights

1. Get context for your impressions at the **Macau Museum** (p511)
2. Explore the ethereal ruins of the very symbol of Macau at the **Church of St Paul** (p511)
3. Take a stroll in the old quarter around **Rua dos Ervanários** and **Rua de Nossa Senhora do Amparo** (p527)
4. Sample Macau's unique cuisine at **Alfonso III** (p525)
5. Lose yourself in mazelike spaces at **Lou Lim Ioc Garden** (p518) and the **Mandarin's House** (p514)
6. Take the cable car to handsome **Guia Fort** (p518) and its lovely chapel
7. Catch an indie gig at the **Blue Frog** (p526)

History

Portuguese galleons first visited southern China to trade in the early 16th century, and in 1557, as a reward for clearing out pirates endemic to the area, they were allowed to establish a tiny enclave in Macau. As trade with China grew, so did Macau, which became the principal centre for Portuguese trade with China, Japan and Southeast Asia. However, after the Opium Wars between the Chinese and the British, and the subsequent establishment of Hong Kong, Macau went into a long decline.

China's Cultural Revolution spilled over into the territory as riots broke out in 1966. The government reportedly proposed that Portugal should leave Macau forever but, fearing the economic shock that would have on Hong Kong, the Chinese refused the offer.

In 1999, under the Sino-Portuguese Joint Declaration, Macau was returned to China and designated a Special Administrative Region (SAR). Like Hong Kong, the pact ensures Macau a 'high degree of autonomy' in all matters (except defence and foreign affairs) for 50 years. The handover, however, did not change Macau as much as the termination of gambling monopoly in 2001. Casinos mushroomed, transforming the skyline of the city, and tourists from mainland China surged.

Language

Cantonese and Portuguese are the official languages of Macau, though few people speak Portuguese. English is harder to find here than in Hong Kong, but in most midrange and top-end hotels, casinos, restaurants and tourist zones you should be able to get by. Mandarin is reasonably well understood, though note that most written Chinese is in traditional characters, not the simplified forms used on the mainland.

Sights

For a small place (just 29 sq km), Macau is packed with important cultural and historical sights, including eight squares and 22 historic buildings, which have collectively been named the Historic Centre of Macau World Heritage Site by Unesco. Most of the sights are on the peninsula. At many, seniors aged over 60 years and children 11 years or under are admitted free – just ask. The **Macau Museums Pass** (MOP$25) allows entry to a half-dozen museums over a five-day period.

CENTRAL MACAU PENINSULA

Running from Avenida da Praia Grande to the Inner Harbour, Avenida de Almeida Ribeiro – or San Ma Lo (新馬路; New Thoroughfare) in Cantonese – is the peninsula's main thoroughfare and home to the charming **Largo do Senado** (Map p516), a black-and-white-tiled square close to major sights.

TOP CHOICE Ruins of the Church of St Paul RUINS

(大三巴牌坊; Ruinas de Igreja de São Paulo; Rua de São Paulo) A gateway to nowhere in the middle of the city is all that remains of the Church of St Paul, considered by some to be the greatest monument to Christianity in Asia. The church was designed by an Italian Jesuit and built in 1602 by Japanese Christian exiles and Chinese craftsmen. In 1835 a fire destroyed everything except the facade. Like much of Macau's colonial architecture, its European appearance belies the fascinating mix of influences (in this case, Chinese, Japanese, Indochinese) that contributed to its aesthetics. The gargoyles for instance are Chinese lions, the kind usually seen guarding entrances to temples – a daring interpretation by a Jesuit. Behind the ruins, there's a small **Museum of Sacred Art** (天主教藝術博物館; Museu de Arte Sacra; Rua de São Paulo; ⌚9am-6pm), and a crypt and ossuary.

TOP CHOICE Monte Fort & Macau Museum FORT, MUSEUM

(大炮台; Fortaleza do Monte; Map p516; admission free; ⌚7am-7pm Mon-Sun) Built by the Jesuits between 1617 and 1626, Monte Fort is accessible by escalator just east of the Church of St Paul. Barracks and storehouses were designed to allow the fort to survive a long siege, but the cannons were fired only once: during an aborted invasion by the Dutch in 1622. Now the ones on the south side are trained at Grand Lisboa Casino. On the outside of the south-eastern wall, about 6m from the ground and under a cannon, is a (sealed) rectangular opening. This former door was used by soldiers patrolling the old city wall which was lower than the fort and connected to it at a right angle. Housed in the fort is the remarkable **Macau Museum** (澳門博物館; Museu de Macau; Map p516; ☎2835 7911; www.macaumuseum.gov.mo; admission MOP$15; ⌚10am-5.30pm Tue-Sun), with exhibits on the history and traditions of Macau.

Church of St Dominic CHURCH

(聖母堂; Igreja de São Domingos; Map p516; Largo de São Domingos; ⌚10am-6pm) This lovely 17th-century baroque church occupies the site of a convent built by the Spanish Dominicans in 1587. It contains the **Treasury of Sacred Art** (聖物寶庫; Tresouro de Arte Sacra; Map p516; admission free; ⌚10am-6pm), an Aladdin's cave of ecclesiastical art, including dismembered relics and a skull, exhibited over three floors.

FREE Lou Kau Mansion HISTORIC MANSION

(盧家大屋; Casa de Lou Kau; Map p516; 7 Travessa da Sé; ⌚9am-7pm Tue-Sun) Built in 1889, this elegant Cantonese-style mansion with southern European elements belonged to a merchant who also commissioned the Lou Lim Ioc Garden (p518). Behind the grey facade, a maze of open and semi-enclosed spaces featuring stained-glass windows and flower-bird motifs mesmerise.

St Joseph's Seminary Church CHURCH

(聖若瑟修院及聖堂; Capela do Seminario São Jose; Map p516; Rua do Seminario; ⌚10am-5pm) One of Macau's most beautiful buildings and the best example of tropicalised baroque, the church was consecrated in 1758

PRICE INDICATORS

The following price indicators are used in this chapter:

Sleeping

$	less than MOP$700
$$	MOP$700 to MOP$2000
$$$	more than MOP$2000

Eating

$	less than MOP$200
$$	MOP$201 to MOP$400
$$$	more than MOP$400

MACAU PRIMER

Like Hong Kong's, Macau's political and economic systems are still significantly different from those of mainland China. See p988 for information on money, and p993 and p993 for details on visas. Prices in this chapter are quoted in patacas (MOP$) unless otherwise stated. The term 'Macanese' refers specifically to people of Portuguese descent who were born in Macau, or their traditions.

Macau Peninsula

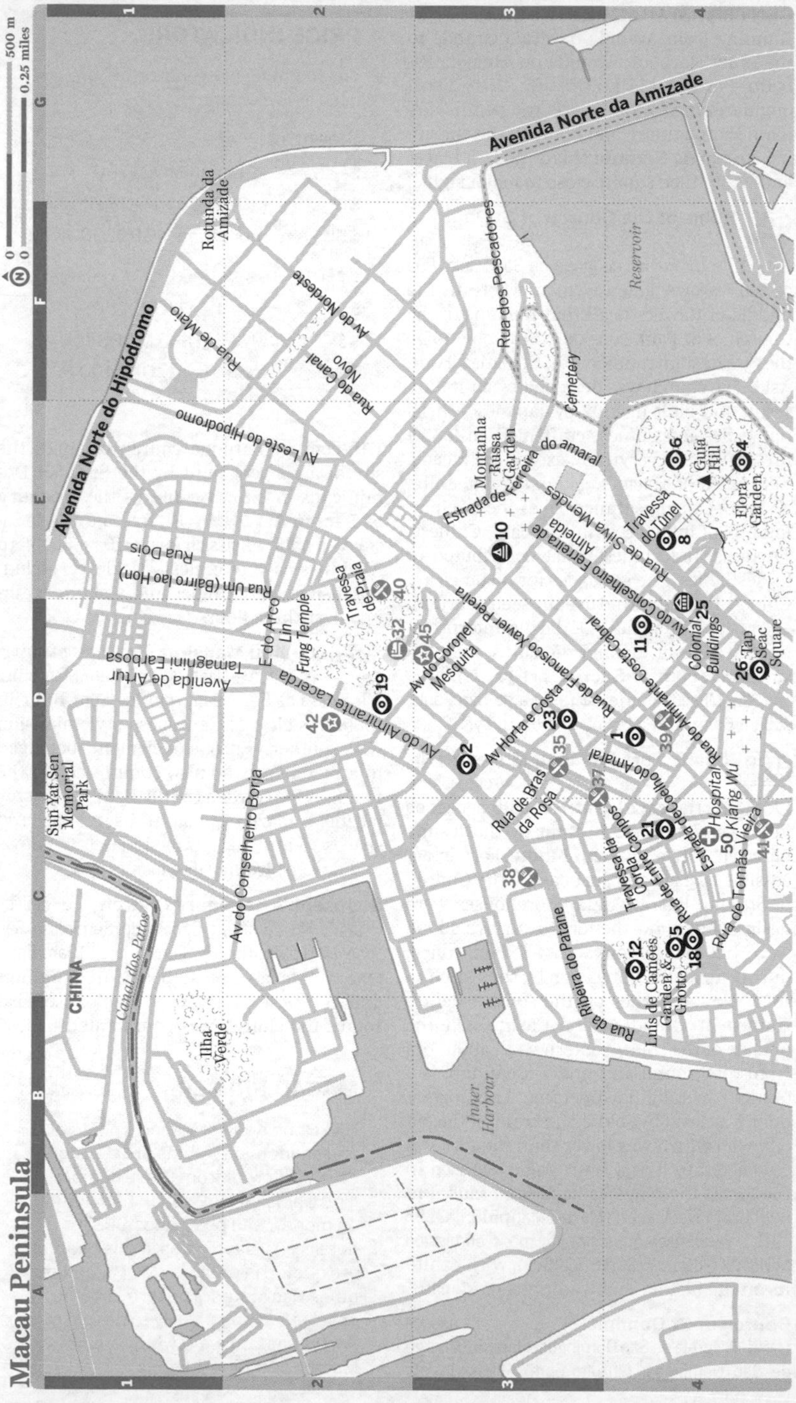

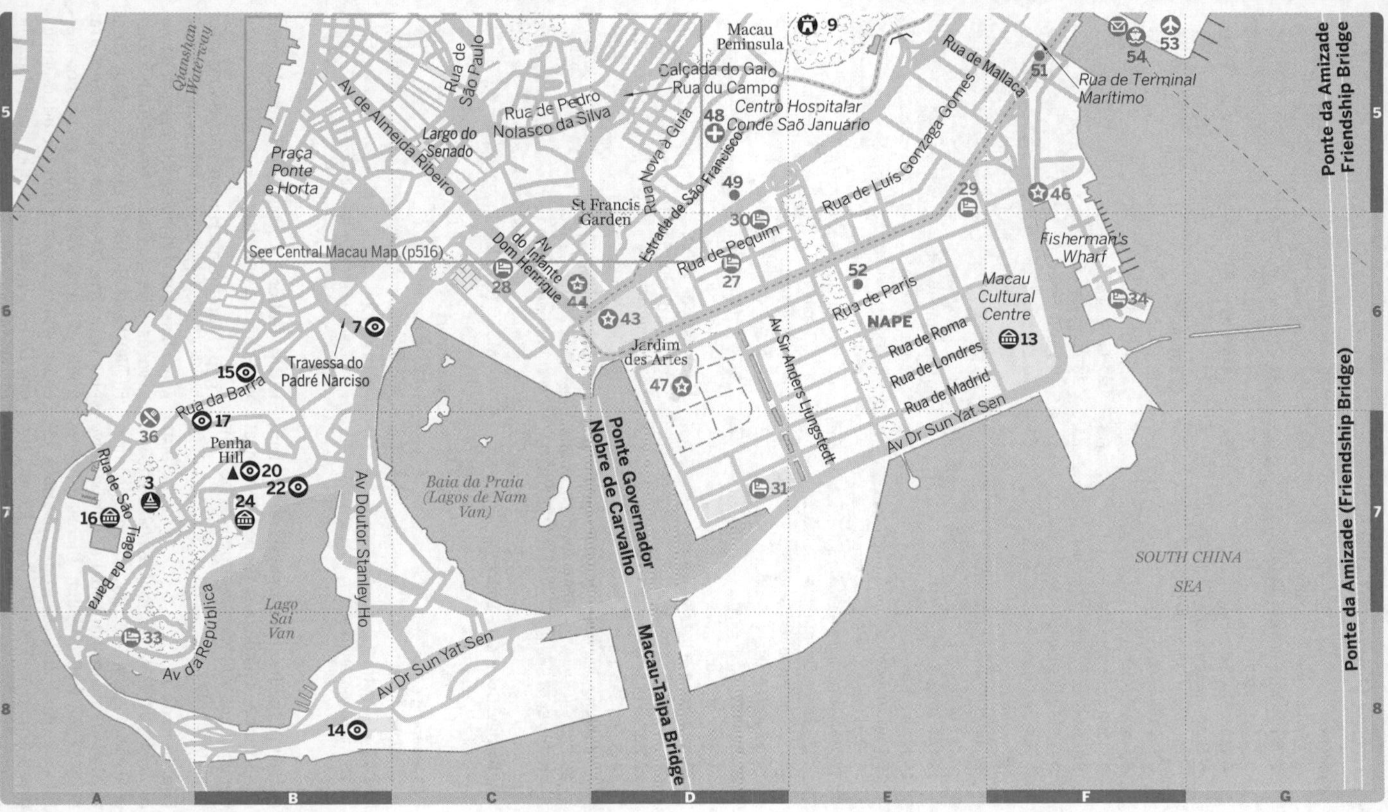
Macau Peninsula
9
Calçada do Gaio
Rua du Campo
Centro Hospitalar Conde Saõ Januário
48
Rua de Mallaca
51
Rua de Terminal Marítimo
54
53
Ponte da Amizade Friendship Bridge
Qianshan Waterway
Rua de São Paulo
Av de Almeida Ribeiro
Rua de Pedro Nolasco da Silva
Largo do Senado
Praça Ponte e Horta
Rua Nova à Guia
Estrada de São Francisco
49
Rua de Luís Gonzaga Gomes
29
46
St Francis Garden
30
Fisherman's Wharf
See Central Macau Map (p516)
Av do Infante Dom Henrique
Rua de Pequim
27
28
44
52
Rua de Paris
Macau Cultural Centre
34
43
NAPE
13
7
Jardim des Artes
Av Sir Anders Ljungstedt
Rua de Roma
Rua de Londres
Rua de Madrid
Travessa do Padré Narciso
15
47
Av Dr Sun Yat Sen
Rua da Barra
17
36
Penha Hill
20
22
Ponte Governador Nobre de Carvalho
3
Av Doutor Stanley Ho
Baia da Praia (Lagos de Nam Van)
31
24
16
Rua de São Tiago da Barra
SOUTH CHINA SEA
Lago Sai Van
33
Av da República
Macau-Taipa Bridge
Ponte da Amizade (Friendship Bridge)
Av Dr Sun Yat Sen
14
A
B
C
D
E
F
G
5
6
7
8

Macau Peninsula

Sights

1 AFA (Art for All Society) D4
2 Almirante Lacerda (Red Market) D3
3 A-Ma Temple A7
4 Cable Car Terminus E4
5 Casa Garden & Museu do Orient C4
Chapel of Our Lady of Guia (see 9)
Creative Macau (see 13)
6 Flora Garden E4
7 Government House B6
8 Guia Cable Car E4
9 Guia Fort & Lighthouse E5
10 Kun Iam Temple E3
11 Lou Lim Ioc Garden D4
12 Luís de Camões Garden & Grotto C4
13 Macau Museum of Art F6
14 Macau Tower B8
15 Mandarin's House B6
16 Maritime Museum A7
17 Moorish Barracks B7
Museu do Oriente (see 12)
18 Old Protestant Cemetery C4
19 Ox Warehouse D2
20 Penha Hill B7
21 Poor Space C4
22 Residence of the Portuguese Consul General B7
23 Rotunda de Caros da Maia D3
24 Santa Sancha Palace B7
Sr Wong Ieng Kuan Library (see 12)
25 Sun Yat Sen Memorial House D4
26 Tap Seac Square D4

Activities, Courses & Tours

Gray Line Tours (see 54)

Sleeping

27 Holiday Inn D6
28 Hotel Sintra C6
29 Mandarin Oriental E5
30 Metropark Hotel D6
31 MGM Grand Macau D7
32 Pousada de Mong Há D2
33 Pousada de Saõ Tiago A8
34 Rocks Hotel F6

Eating

35 Chat Yin D3
36 Litoral A7
37 Little Sweet House D3
38 Lung Wah Tea House C3
39 Nusantara Nam-yeong D4
40 O Porto E2
Robuchon a Galera (see 43)
41 Xina Cafe C4

Entertainment

42 Canidrome D2
43 Casino Lisboa D6
44 Grand Lisboa Casino C6
45 Live Music Association (XL Creation) D3
Macau Cultural Centre (see 13)
46 Nicole Fashion Club F5
47 Wynn Macau D6

Information

48 Centro Hospitalar Conde Saõ Januário D5
49 China Travel Service D5
50 Hospital Kiang Wu C4
51 Macau Immigration Department F5
MGTO (Ferry Terminal) (see 54)
MGTO (Guia Lighthouse) (see 9)

Transport

52 Air Macau E6
Avis Rent A Car (see 54)
53 Heliport F5
54 Macau Ferry Terminal F5

as part of the Jesuit seminary. It has a lemon-meringue facade, a scalloped canopy at the entrance and the first dome to be built in all of China.

Leal Senado SENATE
(民政總署大樓; Map p516; ☎2857 2233; 163 Av de Almeida Ribeiro) The 'Loyal Senate' is home to Macau's main municipal administrative body. If you walk through, there's a peaceful courtyard and the stately **Senate Library** (⊙1pm-7pm) out the back. Inside, the **IACM Gallery** (⊙9am-9pm Tue-Sun) holds well-curated exhibitions.

TOP CHOICE **Mandarin's House** HISTORIC RESIDENCE
(鄭家大屋; Caso do Mandarim; Map p512; www.wh.mo/mandarinhouse; 10 Travessa de Antonio da Silva; admission free; ⊙10am-5.30pm Fri-Tue) Built in 1869, this sprawling complex with over 60 rooms was the ancestral home of Zheng Guanying, an author-merchant whose readers had included emperors, Dr Sun Yatsen and Chairman Mao. The

stunning compound features a moon gate, a passageway for sedans, courtyards and halls, in a labyrinthine arrangement typical of certain Chinese architecture.

St Lazarus District NEIGHBOURHOOD

(瘋堂斜巷; Calçada da Igreja de São Lazaro) The highlight of this lovely neighbourhood with cobbled streets is the **Old Ladies' House** (仁慈堂婆仔屋; Albergue Santa Casa da Misericordia; Map p516; www.albcreativelab.com; 8 Calçada da Igreja de São Lazaro; ⌚noon-7pm Wed-Mon), which sheltered Portuguese refugees from Shànghǎi in WWII, and later, homeless elderly women. It's now run by an art group, and an exhibition hall sits where a funeral parlour used to be. Out front, there's a courtyard with gorgeous old trees.

Na Tcha Temple TEMPLE

(哪吒古廟; Templo de Na Tcha; Rua de São Paulo; ⌚8am-5pm) There's no better symbol of Macau's cultural diversity than this Chinese temple (c 1888), sitting quietly in the compound of the Ruins of the Church of St Paul. It's dedicated to the child god of war to halt the plague that was occurring at the time. Incidentally, the wall outside the temple, often said to be a section of the old city walls, is in fact the wall of the former St Paul's College.

Ox Warehouse FORMER SLAUGHTERHOUSE

(牛房倉庫; Map p512; http://oxwarehouse.blogspot.com; cnr Avs do Coronel Mesquita & Almirante Lacerda; ⌚noon-7pm Wed-Mon) This atmospheric former slaughterhouse is a happening art space featuring engagingly experiential exhibitions and performances.

Pawnshop Museum MUSEUM

(典當業展示館; Espaço Patrimonial – Uma Casa de Penhores Tradicional; Map p516; 396 Av de Almeida Ribeiro; admission MOP$5; ⌚10.30am-7pm, closed 1st Mon of month) Occupying the premises of a former pawnshop (c 1917), this quaint museum shows how this once-thriving business was run in Macau.

SOUTHERN MACAU PENINSULA

The southern Macau Peninsula features a number of old colonial houses and baroque churches that are best visited on foot.

Colonial Macau HISTORIC NEIGHBOURHOODS

From Avenida de Almeida Ribeiro, follow Calçada do Tronco Velho to the **Church of St Augustine** (聖奧斯定教堂; Igreja de Santo Agostinho; Map p516; Largo de Santo Agostinho; ⌚10am-6pm), dating from 1814. Facing the church is China's first Western theatre, the **Dom Pedro V Theatre** (崗頂劇院; Teatro Dom Pedro; Map p516; Calçada do Teatro). This 19th-century pastel-green building is not open to the public. Next you will see the **Church of St Lawrence** (聖老楞佐教堂; Igreja de São Lourenço; Rua da Imprensa Nacional; ⌚10am-6pm Tue-Sun, 1-2pm Mon) with its magnificent painted ceiling. Walk down Travessa do Padre Narciso to the pink **Government House** (特區政府總部; Sede do Goberno; Map p512; cnr Av da Praia Grande & Travessa do Padré Narciso), originally built for a Portuguese noble in 1849 and, for now, headquarters of the Macau SAR (Special Administrative Region) government. The oldest section of Macau is a short distance southwest of here, via the waterfront promenade **Avenida da República** (Map p512). Along this stretch you'll see several colonial villas and civic buildings that are not open to the public. These include the **residence of the Portuguese consul-general** (葡國駐澳門領事官邸; Consulado-Geral de Portugal em Macau; Map p512; Rua do Boa Vista), which was once the Hotel Bela Vista, one of the most storied hotels in Asia. Nearby is the ornate **Santa Sancha Palace** (禮賓府; Palacete de Santa Sancha; Map p512; Estrada de Santa Sancha), once the residence of Macau's Portuguese governors.

MACAU IN ONE DAY

Start in the **Largo do Senado** and wander up to the **Ruins of the Church of St Paul**. Spend an hour or so in the **Macau Museum** to give it all some context, before getting a feel for Macau's living history as you wander back through the tiny streets towards the Inner Harbour port and lunch at **Litoral**. After lunch take a look around the **A-Ma Temple** before jumping on a bus to sleepy **Coloane Village**. Take an easy stroll around here and bus it back via the **Cotai Strip** for an awe-inspiring look at the megaresorts. Have dinner at unpretentious **Alfonso III**, then, for contrast, head for the gaudy magnificence of the **Grand Lisboa casino**, before enjoying rooftop drinks at **Corner's Wine Bar & Tapas Cafe**. If you've still got the energy, saunter over to **Macau Soul** for live jazz.

Central Macau

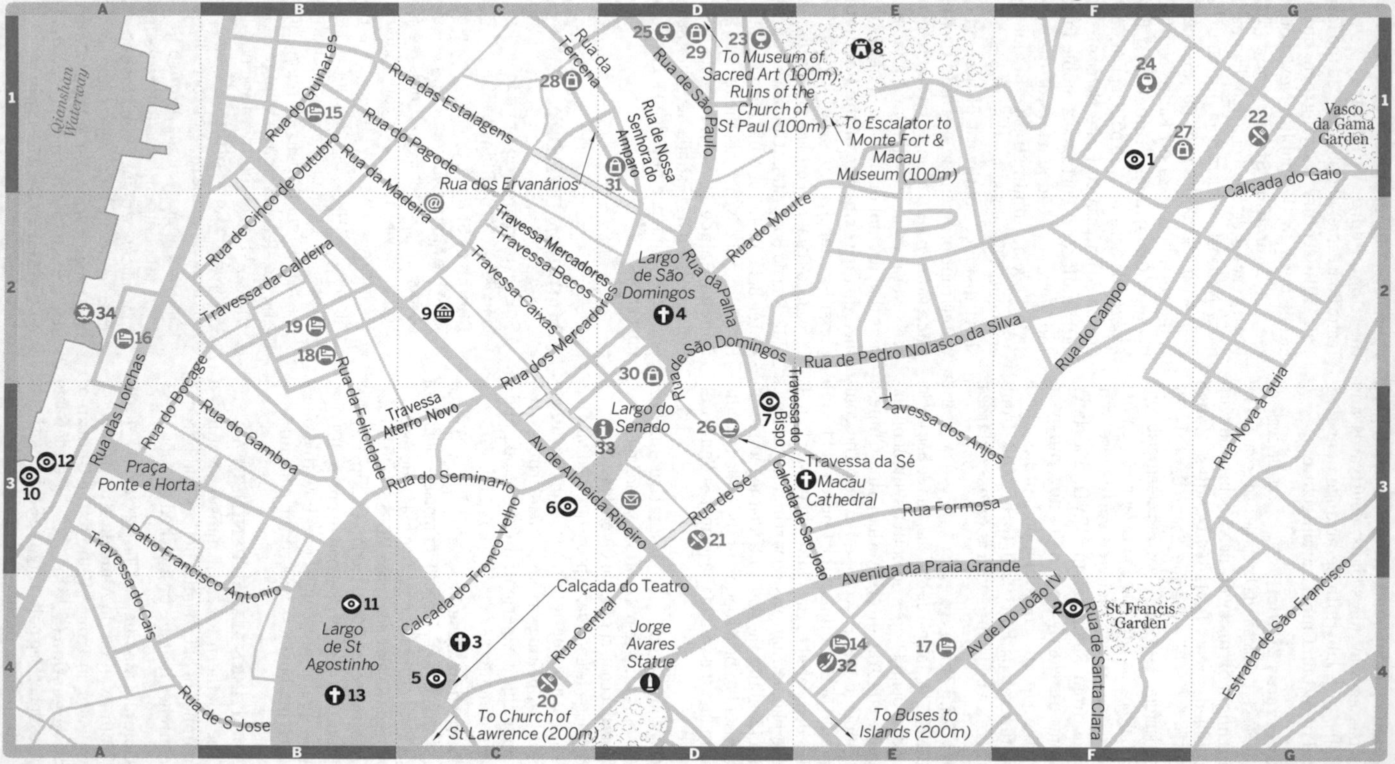

0 200 m
0 0.1 miles

Qianshan Waterway
Rua da Tercena
Rua de São Paulo
To Museum of Sacred Art (100m); Ruins of the Church of St Paul (100m)
To Escalator to Monte Fort & Macau Museum (100m)
Vasco da Gama Garden
Rua do Guinares
Rua das Estalagens
Rua do Pagode
Rua da Madeira
Rua de Nossa Senhora do Amparo
Rua dos Ervanários
Calçada do Gaio
Rua de Cinco de Outubro
Travessa da Caldeira
Travessa Mercadores
Travessa Becos
Travessa Caixas
Rua dos Mercadores
Largo de São Domingos
Rua da Palha
Rua do Moute
Rua de São Domingos
Rua de Pedro Nolasco da Silva
Rua do Campo
Rua Nova à Guia
Rua das Lorchas
Rua do Bocage
Rua do Gamboa
Rua da Felicidade
Travessa Aterro Novo
Largo do Senado
Travessa do Bispo
Travessa dos Anjos
Travessa da Sé
Macau Cathedral
Praça Ponte e Horta
Rua do Seminario
Av de Almeida Ribeiro
Rua de Sé
Calcada de Sao Joao
Rua Formosa
Patio Francisco Antonio
Travessa do Cais
Calçada do Tronco Velho
Calçada do Teatro
Avenida da Praia Grande
Largo de St Agostinho
Rua Central
Jorge Avares Statue
Av de Do João IV
St Francis Garden
Rua de Santa Clara
Estrada de São Francisco
Rua de S Jose
To Church of St Lawrence (200m)
To Buses to Islands (200m)

1 2 3 4 5 6 7 8 9 10 11 12 13 14 15 16 17 18 19 20 21 22 23 24 25 26 27 28 29 30 31 32 33 34

A B C D E F G
1 2 3 4

Central Macau

Sights

1 Albergue da Santa Casa da Misericórdia (Old Ladies' House) F1
2 Chinese Reading Room F4
3 Church of St Augustine C4
4 Church of St Dominic D2
5 Dom Pedro V Theatre C4
IACM Gallery .... (see 6)
6 Leal Senado C3
7 Lou Kau Mansion D3
Macau Museum .... (see 8)
8 Monte Fort E1
9 Pawnshop Museum C2
10 Pier 8 .... A3
Senate Library .... (see 6)
11 Sir Robert Ho Tung Library B4
12 South Sampan Pier A3
13 St Joseph's Seminary Church B4
Treasury of Sacred Art .... (see 4)

Sleeping

14 Augusters Lodge E4
15 East Asia Hotel B1
16 Macau Masters Hotel A2
17 New Nam Pan Hotel E4
18 San Va Hospedaria B2
19 Vila Universal B2

Eating

20 Alfonso III C4
21 Escada D3
22 Lai Kei Ice-cream G1

Drinking

23 Corner's Wine Bar & Tapas Cafe D1
24 Jabber F1
25 Macau Soul D1
26 Mactim Cafe D3

Shopping

27 Av Ateliê F1
28 Flea Market C1
Lines Lab .... (see 1)
29 Macau Creations D1
30 Pinto Livros D2
31 Traditional Shops D1

Information

32 Companhia de Telecomunicações de Macau (CTM) E4
33 MGTO (Largo do Senado) D3

Transport

34 Boats to Wānzái A2

TOP CHOICE **Macau Museum of Art** MUSEUM
(澳門藝術博物館; Museu de Arte de Macau; Map p512; www.artmuseum.gov.mo; Macau Cultural Centre, Av Xian Xing Hai; admission MOP$5, ⏲10am-6.30pm Tue-Sun) This vast, excellent museum houses rotating exhibits as well as permanent collections of works by established Chinese and Western artists such as George Chinnery (1774–1852), who spent most of his adult life in Macau painting. Also inside the Cultural Centre is **Creative Macau** (☎2875 3282; www.creativemacau.org.mo; ⏲2-7pm Mon-Sat), an art space featuring exhibitions, poetry readings and workshops.

A-Ma Temple TEMPLE
(媽閣廟; Templo de A-Ma; Map p512; Rue de São Tiago da Barra; ⏲10am-6pm) The A-Ma Temple is dedicated to A-Ma (better known as Tin Hau, the goddess of the sea), from which the name Macau is derived. Many believe that when the Portuguese asked the name of the place, they were told 'A-Ma Gau' (bay of A-Ma). In modern Cantonese, 'Macau' is Ou Mun (澳門), meaning 'gateway of the bay'.

Penha Hill SCENIC VIEWS
(主教山; Colina da Penha; Map p512) The views here are excellent, as are buildings such as Bishop's Palace, the Chapel of Our Lady of Penha (Capela de Nostra senora da Penha) and modernist villas.

Moorish Barracks BUILDING
(港務局大樓; Map p512; Capitania dos Portos; Barra Hill) Designed by an Italian, this lovely neoclassical building with Moorish influences is now the headquarters of the Macau Maritime Administration. Turn right as you leave A-Ma Temple; a 10-minute walk uphill will take you to the barracks.

Maritime Museum MUSEUM
(海事博物館; Museu Marítimo; Map p512; www.museumaritimo.gov.mo; 1 Largo do Pagode da Barra; admission MOP$10, Sun MOP$5; ⏲10am-5.30pm Wed-Mon) The Maritime Museum has interesting artefacts from Macau's

LOCAL KNOWLEDGE

FRANK LEI: PHOTOGRAPHER, ART DIRECTOR OF OX WAREHOUSE

Thanks to the thriving economy, the Portuguese influence, and better support given to artists, Macau's art scene is more vibrant than ever before.

Best Private Art Spaces

The Museu do Orient (p519) has good-quality, well-curated exhibitions.

AFA (Art for All Society) (p518), is another great choice. This active art group has a gallery and artist studios at its headquarters inside a textile factory. It also holds exhibitions all over town. **Comuna de Pedra** (石頭公社; ☎6628 0064; comunadepedra@hotmail.com; http://comunadepedra.blogspot.com) is a contemporary dance company that performs in Macau and overseas. Then of course, **Ox Warehouse** (p515), which I founded. Theatre group **Poor Space** (窮空間; Map p512; ☎2835 1572; http:poorspace.wordpress.com; Rua Espectacao Almeida, 3rd fl, flat A, Son Heng Bldg; ⏲1-7pm Wed-Sun) has a handicraft shop that doubles up as a stage.

seafaring past, a mock-up of a Hakka fishing village, and displays of dragon boats.

NORTHERN MACAU PENINSULA

The northern peninsula sees fewer tourists and is thus quite a good area to just wander around. The historic **Three Lamps** (三盞燈; *saam jaan dang*) district is known for its Southeast Asian – particularly Burmese – influences. It begins at Rotunda de Caros da Maia (Map p512), with the three street lamps that give it its name, and sprawls over several square blocks.

TOP CHOICE Guia Fort FORT
(東望洋山堡壘; Fortaleza de Guia; Map p512; ⏲9am-5.30pm) As the highest point on the Macau Peninsula, this fort affords panoramic views of the city and, on a clear day, across to the islands and China. At the top you'll find a **lighthouse**, built in 1865 and the oldest on the China coast, and the lovely **Chapel of Our Lady of Guia** (聖母雪地殿聖堂; Capela de Nossa Señora da Guia; Map p512; ⏲10am-5pm Tue-Sun), built in 1622 and retaining almost 100% of its original features, including one of the most valuable mural paintings in East Asia. Walk up or take the **Guia Cable Car** (東望洋山纜車; Teleférico da Guia; Map p512; one way/return MOP$3/5; ⏲8am-6pm Tue-Sun) that runs from the entrance to **Flora Garden** (二龍喉公園; Jardim da Flora; Map p512; Travessa do Túnel; ⏲7.30am-8.30pm), Macau's largest public park.

Lou Lim Ioc Garden GARDEN
(盧廉若公園; Jardim Lou Lim Ioc; Map p512; 10 Estrada de Adolfo de Loureiro; ⏲6am-9pm) A cool and shady Sūzhōu-style garden with pavilions, lotus ponds, bamboo groves, grottoes and a bridge with nine turns (to escape from evil spirits, who can only move in straight lines). You'll see locals practising taichi or playing Chinese musical instruments here.

Luís de Camões Garden & Grotto GARDEN
(白鴿巢公園(賈梅士公園; Jardim e Gruta de Luís de Camões; Map p512; ⏲6am-10pm) This relaxing park is dedicated to the one-eyed poet Luís de Camões (1524–80), who is said to have written part of his epic *Os Lusíadas* in Macau, though there is little evidence that he ever reached the city. **Sr Wong Leng Kuan Library** (see boxed text, p520) is inside the garden.

TOP CHOICE Kun Iam Temple TEMPLE
(觀音堂; Templo de Kun Iam; Map p512; Av do Coronel Mesquita; ⏲10am-6pm) Dating back four centuries, Kun Iam Temple is Macau's oldest and most interesting temple. The likeness of Kun Iam, the Goddess of Mercy, is in the main hall; to the left of the altar and behind glass is a statue of a bearded arhat rumoured to represent Marco Polo. The first treaty of trade and friendship between the USA and China was signed in the temple's terraced gardens in 1844.

AFA (Art for All Society) GALLERY
(全藝社; Map p512; ☎2836 6064; www.afamacau.com; 3rd fl, Lun Hing Knitting Factory, 45 Rua de Francisco Xavier Pereira; ⏲2.30-6pm Mon-Fri, 10am-6pm Sat & Sun) Don't miss this small gallery inside a knitting factory if you want to see Macau's best contemporary art. Founded by local artist James Chu, AFA also has a branch in Běijīng.

Tap Seac Square SQUARE
(塔石廣場; Map p512) Bold and beautiful, this new square lined with important historic architecture (Cultural Affairs Bureau, Central Library of Macau, Library for Macau's Historical Archives) was designed by Macanese architect Carlos Marreiros, who also created Tap Seac Health Centre (adjacent to Cultural Affairs Bureau), a contemporary interpretation of Macau's neoclassical buildings featuring a verandah and wavy glass suggestive of windblown *cheongsams* (one-piece Chinese dress for women) – a childhood memory of the architect.

FREE **Sun Yatsen Memorial House** MUSEUM
(國父紀念館; Casa Memorativa de Doutor Sun Yat Sen; Map p512; ☎2857 4064; 1 Rua de Silva Mendes; ⊙10am-5pm Wed-Mon) This neo-Moorish house commemorates Dr Sun Yatsen (1866–1925), founder of the Chinese republic. Dr Sun's brother funded its construction, Dr Sun's son built it, and his first wife, Lu Muzhen, lived there until she died. Dr Sun himself, interestingly, never lived in this house.

Museu do Oriente GALLERY
(東方基金會 博物館; Map p512; www.foriente.pt; 13 Praça de Luís de Camões; ⊙10am-5.30 Mon-Fri, 10am-7pm daily during special exhibitions) Housed in Casa Garden, the former headquarters of the British East India Company, this gallery mounts some of the best exhibitions of contemporary and ancient art in Macau.

Old Protestant Cemetery CEMETERY
(基督教墳場; Antigo Cemitério Protestante; Map p512; 15 Praça de Luís de Camões; ⊙8.30am-5.30pm) This cemetery was established in 1821 as the last resting place of (mostly Anglophone) Protestants. Among those interred here is Irish-born artist George Chinnery.

THE ISLANDS

Connected to the Macau mainland by three bridges and joined together by an ever-growing area of reclaimed land called Cotai, Coloane and, to a lesser extent, Taipa are oases of calm and greenery. By contrast, the Cotai Strip is development central, with megacasinos sprouting up.

TOP CHOICE **Taipa** ISLAND
(氹仔; Tam Chai in Cantonese; Map p521) Traditionally an island of duck farms and boat yards, Taipa is rapidly becoming urbanised and now houses hotels, a university, a racecourse, a stadium and an airport. But a parade of baroque churches, temples, overgrown esplanades and lethargic settlements mean it's still possible to experience the traditional charms of the island.

Taipa Village, in the north-central part of the island, is a window to the island's past. Here you'll find the stately **Taipa House Museum** (龍環葡韻; Casa Museum da Taipa; Map p521; Av da Praia; admission MOP$5; ⊙10am-5.30pm Tue-Sun), housed in five waterfront villas that give a sense of how the Macanese middle-class lived in the early 20th century. Also in the village is the **Church of Our Lady of Carmel** (嘉模聖母堂; Igreja de Nossa Senhora de Carmo; Map p521; Rue da Restauração) and temples including **Pak Tai Temple** (北帝廟; Templo Pak Tai; Map p521; Rua do Regedor).

The small **Taipa Flea Market** (Map p521; www.iacm.gov.mo; Bombeiros Square, Rua do Regedor & Rua das Gaivotas; ⊙11am-8pm Sun), organised for most parts of the year, is a good place to shop for souvenirs.

You can rent bicycles in Taipa Village from **Aluguer de Bicicletas** (Map p521; ☎2882 7975; 36 Largo Governador Tamagini Barbosa); there's no English sign but it's next to the Don Quixote restaurant.

TOP CHOICE **Coloane** ISLAND
(路環; Lo Wan in Cantonese; Map p522) A haven for pirates until the start of the 20th century, Coloane considerably larger than Taipa, is the only part of Macau that doesn't seem to be changing at a head-spinning rate, which is a relief.

All buses stop at the roundabout in Coloane Village on the western shore, which overlooks mainland China across the water. The main attraction in the village is the **Chapel of St Francis Xavier** (聖方濟各教堂; Capela de São Francisco Xavier; Map p522; Av de Cinco de Outubro; ⊙10am-8pm), built in 1928 and which contains a relic of the saint's arm bone. The village has some interesting temples, including the **Tam Kong Temple** (譚公廟; Templo Tam Kong; Map p522; Largo Tam Kong Miu; ⊙8.30am-6pm), where you'll find a dragon boat made of whale bone. To the north of the village on Estrada da Lai Chi Vun are photogenic **old junk-building sheds**, which have been the centre of a development-versus-preservation debate.

About 1.5km southeast of Coloane Village is **Cheoc Van Beach** (Bamboo Bay; Map p522); while larger and more popular **Hác Sá Beach** lies to the northeast.

MACAU'S INNER BEAUTIES

Between history and glitz, Macau offers those with a good eye some wonderful architecture.

Lovely Libraries

Macau's libraries show how tiny proportions can be beautiful.

Sir Robert Ho Tung Library (何東圖書館; Map p516; ☎2837 7117; 3 Largo de St Agostinho; ⏰10am-7pm Mon-Sat, 11am-7am Sun; @) This stunner comprises a 19th-century villa and a glass-and-steel extension rising above a back garden, with Piranesi-like bridges shooting out between the two.

Chinese Reading Room (八角亭; Map p516; Rua de Santa Clara; ⏰9am-noon & 7pm-midnight) A former drinks booth, known as 'Octagonal Pavilion' (c 1926) in Chinese.

Sr Wong Ieng Kuan Library (白鴿巢公園黃營均圖書館; Map p512; ☎2895 3075; Praça de Luís de Camões; ⏰8am-8pm, closed Mon; @) An oasis of calm between a boulder (which juts into its interior) and a banyan tree (which frames its entrance) in the Luís de Camões Garden.

Coloane Library (路環圖書館; Map p522; Rua de Cinco de Outubro, Coloane; ☎2888 2254; ⏰1-7pm Mon-Sat; @) A mini Grecian temple c 1917 with a pediment containing the word 'library' in Chinese and Portuguese.

Modernist Marvels

Macau's heritage of modernism is important but little known.

Pier 8 (8號碼頭; Map p512; Rua do Dr Lourenco Pereira Marquez) A fine example of Chinese modernism in grey 50 paces south from Macau Masters Hotel; best views are from the South Sampan Pier (南舢板碼頭; Map p512; Cais de Sampanas Sul) next door.

Penha Hill (p520) Bishop's Hill is littered with the stylish villas of the wealthy.

East Asia Hotel (東亞酒店; Map p516; cnr Rua do Guimares and Rua da Madeira) Chinese art deco in mint green; a little shabby, very chic.

Almirante Lacerda (紅街市大樓; Map p512; Mercado Almirante Lacerda; cnr Avs do Almirante Lacerda & Horta e Costa; ⏰7.30am-7.30pm) This art deco 'Red Market' houses a wet market.

Atop **Alto de Coloane** (170m), the 20m-high **A-Ma Statue** (媽祖像及媽閣廟; Estátua da Deusa A-Ma; Estrada do Alto de Coloane) represents the goddess who gave Macau its name. Hewn from white jade, it stands beside the enormous **Tian Hou Temple** (天后廟; ⏰8am-6pm) that forms the core of the ultra-touristy **A-Ma Cultural Village** (媽祖文化村). A **free shuttle** runs every 30 minutes (9am to 6pm) from the ornamental gate on Estrada de Seac Pai Van.

Activities

While Macau is no adventure paradise, it offers a taste of everything from spectator to extreme sport. For more ways besides the following to get those endorphins flowing, visit www.iacm.gov.mo (click 'facilities' for lists of trails and sport facilities).

Cycling

There are two cycling trails in Taipa. The longer **Taipa Grande trail** can be accessed via a paved road off the Estrada Colonel Nicolau de Mesquita, near the United Chinese Cemetery; whereas the **Taipa Pequena Trail** is reachable by way of Estrada Lou Lim Ieok, behind the Regency Hotel. Bicycles can be rented from a kiosk near the bus stop adjacent to the Museum of Taipa and Coloane History in Taipa Village.

Canidrome DOG RACING

(Map p512; www.macauyydog.com; Av do General Castelo Branco; admission MOP$10) Asia's only facility for greyhound racing, the Canidrome has races every Monday, Thursday, Saturday and Sunday at 7.30pm.

The Islands – Taipa

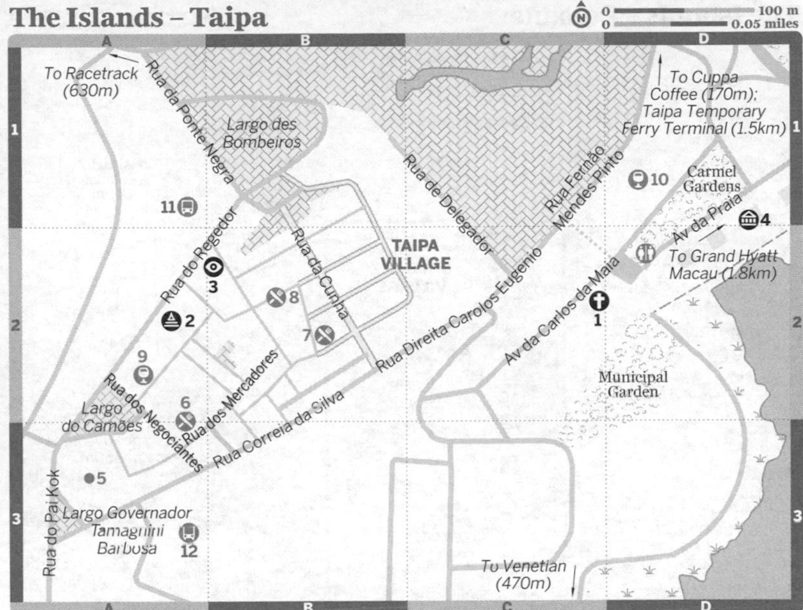

AJ Hackett ADVENTURE CLIMBS
(http://macau.ajhackett.com; ☎8988 8875) New Zealand–based AJ Hackett organises all kinds of adventure climbs up and around the Macau Tower.

Macau Motor Sports Club GO-KARTING
(☎2888 2126; http://macaummc.com; Estrada de Seac Pai Van, Coloane; per 15min MOP$180-220; ⏲11:30am-7pm Mon-Fri, 10.30am-8.30pm Sat & Sun) This club has a picturesque 1.2km professional go-karting circuit at the southern end of the Cotai Strip.

Macau Formula 3 Grand Prix CAR RACING
(☎2855 5555; www.macau.grandprix.gov.mo; practice days MOP$50, race days MOP$200-900) Macau's biggest sporting event of the year is held in the third week of November.

Hiking

Macau's hiking trails are not difficult and you can quickly get to a road to flag down a taxi if necessary. The longest one is the 8100m **Coloane Trail**, which begins in the mid-section of Estrada do Alto de Coloane and winds around the island. You can also make a detour to **Alto de Coloane** (170m) to see the A-Ma Statue. **Guia Hill** on the peninsula has a popular pedestrian trail. As you leave the fort, turn right on Estrada do Engenheiro Trigo.

The Islands – Taipa

Sights

1 Church of Our Lady of Carmel............C2
2 Pak Tai Temple............A2
3 Taipa Flea Market............B2
4 Taipa House Museum............D1

Activities, Courses & Tours

5 Aluguer de Bicicletas............A3

Eating

6 Antonio............A2
7 Mok Yee Kei............B2
8 O Santos............B2

Drinking

9 Old Taipa Tavern............A2
10 Portal............D1

Transport

11 Bus Stop............A1
12 Main Bus Stop............A3

Tours

Quality Tours, coach trips organised by the MGTO (Macau Government Tourist Office) and tendered to such agents as **Gray Line** (錦倫旅行社; Map p512; ☎2833 6611; Room 1015, ground fl, Macau Ferry Terminal;

MACAU TOURS

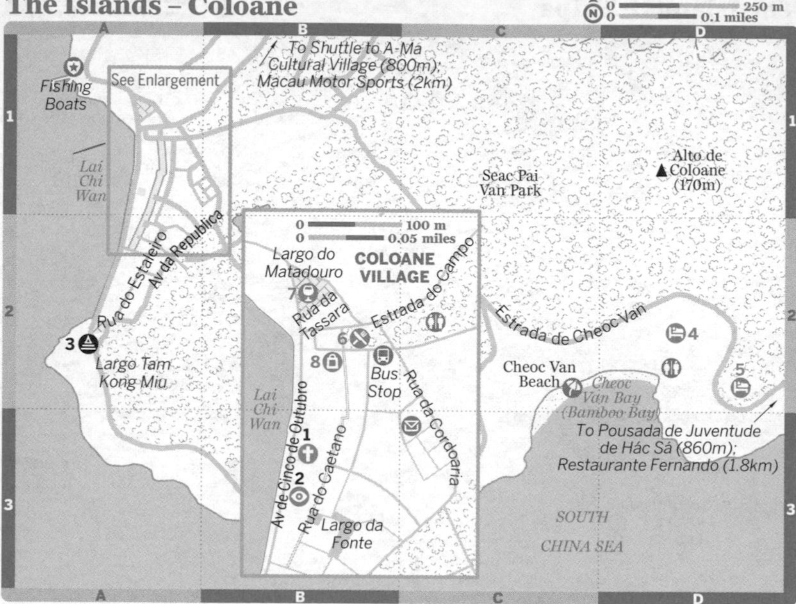

adult/child 3-11 MOP$118/108), take about five hours.

Festivals & Events

The mixing of two very different cultures for over 400 years has left Macau with a unique collection of festivals and cultural events. For exact dates, check www.macautourism.gov.mo or the individual event's website.

Lunar New Year LUNAR
Late January or early February.

Procession of the Passion of Our Lord RELIGIOUS
Takes place in February.

Macau Arts Festival ARTS
(www.icm.gov.mo/fam) Held in May.

A-Ma Festival CULTURAL
Held in May.

Feast of the Drunken Dragon CULTURAL
May or June.

Dragon Boat Festival DRAGON BOATS
Takes place in June.

International Fireworks Display Contest FIREWORKS
Held in September.

International Music Festival MUSIC
(www.icm.gov.mo/fimm) October and November.

Macau International Marathon MARATHON
(www.sport.gov.mo) First Sunday of December.

Macau Formula 3 Grand Prix RACING
(www.macau.grandprix.gov.mo) Third weekend in November.

Sleeping

New hotels spring up almost by the week, the vast majority aimed at the moneyed rather than budget travellers, so you have to look hard for decent cheap sleeps. For those with the cash there are some world-class options. Rates shoot up on Friday or Saturday, while during the week you can find some incredible deals at travel agencies, hotel websites and specialist sites such as www.macau.com. **Shun Tak Centre** (200 Connaught Rd, Sheung Wan) in Hong Kong, from where the Macau ferries depart, is also good, as are the booths in the arrivals hall of the Macau Ferry Terminal.

All rooms listed here have air-conditioning and bathroom unless otherwise stated. Most midrange and top-end hotels have shuttle buses from the ferry terminal.

MACAU PENINSULA

Cheap guesthouses occupy central Macau, around Rua das Lorchas and Avenida de

The Islands – Coloane

Almeida Ribeiro, with options aplenty on Rua da Felicidade, the hub of the former red-light district, while the top-end casino-hotels generally occupy the southeast and centre of town.

TOP CHOICE **Mandarin Oriental** LUXURY HOTEL $$$
(文華東方酒店; Map p512; ☎8805 8888; www.mandarinoriental.com/macau; Av Dr Sun Yat Sen; r MOP$3500-4900, ste from MOP$6100;) A great high-end option, the new Mandarin has everything associated with the brand – elegance, superlative service, comfy rooms and excellent facilities. Though not big in size, it's a refreshing contrast to the glossy casino-hotels.

San Va Hospedaria GUESTHOUSE $
(新華旅店; Map p516; ☎2857 3701; www.sanvahotel.com; 65-67 Rua da Felicidade; s MOP$100-160, d & tw MOP$120-180) Built in 1873, San Va is about the cheapest, most atmospheric lodging in town (Wong Kar-wai filmed parts of *2046* here). It's very basic, with tiny rooms, no air-con and shared bathrooms. At the time of research, a new wing was under construction.

TOP CHOICE **Pousada de Mong Há** INN $$
(望厦賓館; Map p512; ☎2851 5222; www.ift.edu.mo/pousada; Colina de Mong Há; s/d/ste incl breakfast MOP$680/960/1360, discounts of up to 30% midweek & low season;) This attractive Portuguese-style inn atop Mong Há Hill is an old barracks and is now run by tourism students. The rooms are simple, homely and squeaky clean. The rates are among the best in the city.

Pousada de São Tiago LUXURY HOTEL $$$
(聖地牙哥酒店; Map p512; ☎2837 8111; www.saotiago.com.mo; Fortaleza de São Tiago da Barra, Av da República; ste MOP$5800-9800, discounts of 35-50% low season;) The 'St James Inn', built into the ruins of a 17th-century fort, has 12 balconied suites with splendid views of the harbour. It's romantic, old-fashioned and expensive.

MGM Grand Macau LUXURY HOTEL $$$
(澳門美高梅酒店; Map p512; ☎8802 1888; www.mgmgrandmacau.com; Av Dr Sun Yat Sen; r/ste from MOP$3200/7800, discounts of 35-50% low season;) This casino-hotel has a youthful vibe and contemporary architecture featuring a baroque-inspired wave motif that's repeated inside the stylish rooms.

Hotel Sintra HOTEL $$
(新麗華酒店; Map p512; ☎2871 0111; www.hotelsintra.com; 58-62 Av de Do João IV; s & d MOP$1160-1760, ste from MOP$2360, discounts of up to 50% midweek) This centrally located three-star hotel is great value. The rooms are spotless and the staff polite. Our only complaint is the slow lift.

Rocks Hotel BOUTIQUE HOTEL $$$
(萊斯酒店; Map p512; ☎2295 6528; www.rockshotel.com.mo; Fisherman's Wharf; s & d MOP$1880-2580, ste from MOP$4080;) This elegant Victorian-style boutique hotel is set amid a tribal-hut African restaurant and casino. The rooms are decent and most have a view of the waterfront.

Holiday Inn HOTEL $$
(澳门假日酒店; Map p512; ☎2878 3333; www.macau.holiday-inn.com; 82-86 Rua de Pequim; s & d MOP$1000-1760, ste from MOP$2360, discounts of up to 40% low season;) True, there's a degree of chain-hotel blandness here, but standards are high and it's a solid-enough midrange option, given the lack of decent contenders in this category.

Metropark Hotel HOTEL $$
(澳門維景酒店; Map p512; ☎2878 1233; www.metroparkmacau.com; 199 Rua de Pequim; r MOP$1680-2300, ste from MOP$2300, discounts of up to 60% low season;) The Metropark is popular with visitors from Hong Kong, due to its huge low-season discounts. Rooms are clean, but the lobby is a madhouse and the facilities are mediocre.

New Nam Pan Hotel GUESTHOUSE $
(新南濱賓館; Map p516; ☎2848 2842, www.cnmacauhotel.com; 2nd fl, 8 Av de Do João

IV; s/d/tr/q MOP$280/380/480/580, plus MOP$100-200 weekends;) Central location, a rustic vibe and eight spotless rooms make New Nam Pan a good budget option.

Vila Universal GUESTHOUSE $
(大利迎賓館; Map p516; 2857 3247/5602; Cheng Peng Bldg, 73 Rua da Felicidade; s/d from MOP$280/350, plus MOP$50-80 weekends;) Fish tanks, seashell displays and yellow sofas in the lobby impart a homely atmosphere, but the 32 rooms, though clean and decent, are more impersonal.

Augusters Lodge GUESTHOUSE $
(Map p516; 2871 3242, 6664 5026; www.augusters.de; Flat 3J, Block 4, Kam Loi Bldg, 24 Rua do Dr Pedro Jose Lobo; dm from MOP$120 per person, 15% discount with advanced reservation;) Something of a backpackers' hub, this tiny, friendly guesthouse has basic but clean rooms with shared bathrooms and a kitchen. It's located above the CTM shop.

Macau Masters Hotel HOTEL $
(萬事發酒店; Map p516; 2893 7572; www.mastershotel-macau.com; 162 Rua das Lorchas; s/d from MOP$650/870;) A shabby exterior hides a smartly maintained hotel with small, well-equipped, if somewhat outmoded, rooms. Electricity supply is sometimes unstable.

THE ISLANDS

Taipa is changing fast, with several high-end international hotel chains opening up along the Cotai Strip. Coloane offers some great budget options, including two HI-affiliated hostels.

TOP CHOICE **Pousada de Coloane** HOTEL $$
(竹灣酒店; Map p522; 2882 2143; www.hotelpcoloane.com.mo; Estrada de Cheoc Van, Coloane; r from MOP$750, discounts of 20-40% low season;) This 30-room hotel with its Portuguese-style rooms (all with balconies and sea views) is excellent value. And the location above Cheoc Van Beach is about as chilled as you'll find. It's served by buses 25 and 26 A.

Grand Hyatt Macau LUXURY HOTEL $$$
(澳門君悅酒店; 8868 1234; http://macau.grand.hyatt.com; City of Dreams, Estrada do Istmo, Cotai; r MOP$1488-2688, ste MOP$1588-2788; @) The most tasteful of the casino-hotels on the Cotai Strip, the Grand Hyatt is part of the City of Dreams casino-shopping-performance complex. The massive rooms come with glass-and-marble showering areas and a full battery of technology. Take a cab or any of the shuttle buses going to City of Dreams to get here.

Pousada de Juventude de Cheoc Van HOSTEL $
(竹灣青年旅舍; Map p522; 2888 2024; Rua de António Francisco, Coloane; dm/d Sun-Fri MOP$40/70, Sat MOP$50/100) This clean hostel is on the eastern side of Cheoc Van Bay, below the Pousada de Coloane. It has a small kitchen and garden. Book through the **Education & Youth Services Department** (2855 5533; www.dsej.gov.mo). You must have an HI card or equivalent; men and women are separated.

Westin Resort Macau BUSINESS HOTEL $$$
(澳門威斯汀渡假酒店; 2887 1111; www.westin.com/macau; 1918 Estrada de Hác Sá, Coloane; r MOP$2200-2700, ste from MOP$5000, discounts of up to 50% low season; @) This sprawling resort overlooking the hills and Hác Sá Beach has rooms with sunny terraces, fancy showers and high-thread-count bedding. The '90s Californian decor is a tad dull, but you'll love the outdoor spa and the 'aquatic' driving range where you can shoot balls out into the sea.

Pousada de Juventude de Hác Sá HOSTEL $
(黑沙青年旅舍; 2888 2701; Rua de Hác Sá Long Chao Kok, Coloane; dm/d/q Sun-Fri MOP$40/50/70, Sat MOP$50/70/100) Same deal as the Cheoc Van hostel; at the southern end of Hác Sá Beach.

Eating

Browse a typically Macanese menu and you'll find an enticing stew of influences from Chinese and Asian cuisines, as well as from those of former Portuguese colonies in Africa, India and Latin America. Coconut, tamarind, chilli, jaggery (palm sugar) and shrimp paste can all feature. A famous Macanese speciality is *galinha africana* (African chicken), made with coconut, garlic and chillies. Other Macanese favourites include *casquinha* (stuffed crab), *minchi* (minced meat cooked with potatoes, onions and spices) and *serradura,* a milk pudding.

You'll find Portuguese dishes here too; popular ones include *salada de bacalhau* (dried salted cod salad), *arroz de pato* (rice with duck confit) and *leitão assado no forno* (roast suckling pig). While Macau's Chinese cuisine is good, most people come here to sample Macanese or Portuguese food.

Alfonso III MACANESE $

(亞豐素三世餐廳; Map p516; ☎2858 6272; 11a Rua Central; meals MOP$70-200; ⊙noon-3pm & 6-10.30pm Mon-Sat) With a diverse menu featuring liver and tripe dishes in addition to popular classics, all fabulously executed, it's clear this unpretentious eatery doesn't just cater for the weekend crowds. It's always packed with Macanese families, so book ahead.

TOP CHOICE **Antonio** PORTUGUESE $$$

(安東尼奧; Map p521; ☎2899 9998; www.antoniomacau.com; 3 Rua dos Negociantes, Taipa; starters MOP$100-255, mains MOP$150-300; ⊙noon-3pm & 6.30-10.30pm Mon-Fri, noon-10.30pm Sat & Sun) Dark mahogany set off by blue-and-white azulejo tiles prepare you for an authentic Portuguese meal at this Michelin-recommended restaurant known for whipping up a mean goat's cheese with honey (MOP$145) and a lavish seafood stew (MOP$480 for two people).

Robuchon a Galera FRENCH $$$

(Map p512; ☎2888 3888; www.hotelisboa.com; 3rd fl, Hotel Lisboa, 2-4 Av de Lisboa; set lunches MOP$398-638, set dinners MOP$1488-2100; ⊙noon-2.30pm, 6.30-10.30pm) Macau's only restaurant with three Michelin stars has everything that you associate with the Robuchon name: chic decor, fine Gallic creations and impeccable service. The wine list is beyond impressive.

O Santos MACANESE $

(山度士葡式餐廳; Map p521; 20 Rua da Cunha, Taipa; meals MOP$100-200; ⊙noon-3pm & 6.30-10.30pm) Despite its location on the touristy Rua da Cunha, charming O Santos keeps its standards up. Patrons have been coming back for the chicken and rice in blood (*arroz de cabidela;* MOP$98) and friendly banter with the owner, a former naval chef, for 20 years.

Litoral MACANESE $$

(海灣餐廳; Map p512; http://restaurante-litoral.com; 261a Rua do Almirante Sérgio; meals MOP$200-500; ⊙noon-3pm & 5.30-10.30pm) This famous joint serves solid Macanese and Portuguese fare, including delicious stews and baked rice dishes – many spun from the heirloom recipes of the matron Manuela, who runs the place.

Escada MACANESE $$

(大堂街八號葡國餐廳; Map p516; ☎2896 6900; www.yp.mo/escada; 8 Rua de Sé; starters MOP$48-128, mains MOP$80-200; ⊙noon-3pm & 6-10.30pm) Occupying a former town house, Escada has a few balcony tables that make for a romantic dinner. The signature African chicken (MOP$128) is excellent, but steer clear of the steaks. Book ahead.

Xina Cafe MEDITERRANEAN $

(Map p512; ☎2835 0489; 72b Rua de Tomãs Vieira; lunch dishes MOP$25-60, dinners per person MOP$250; ⊙11.30am-6.30pm Tue-Sun) 'China' serves simple salads and tapas during the day. In the evening, owner Pedro cooks superb, Mediterranean-style dinners for the lucky few who manage to land a seat at his table (you'll need to book in groups of six or more, two days in advance).

O Porto MACANESE $

(內港餐廳; Map p512; ☎2859 4643; 17 Travessa da Praia; mains MOP$65-110; ⊙12.30-2pm & 6.30-10.30pm, closed Wed) Not to be confused with O Porto Interior on Rua do Almirante Sérgio, this modest place near steps leading to Mong Há Hill serves reasonably priced Macanese dishes, with a few luxuries: checkered tablecloth, football paraphernalia and warm service.

TOP CHOICE **Lung Wah Tea House** CANTONESE $

(龍華茶樓; Map p512; ☎2857 4456; 3 Av do Almirante Lacerda; dim sum from MOP$14, tea MOP$10; ⊙7am-2pm; ⊖) There's grace in the retro furniture and the casual way it's thrown together in this airy Cantonese teahouse (c 1963) with a Michelin Bib Gourmand. Take a booth by windows overlooking the Almirante Lacerda (Red Market), where the teahouse buys its produce every day. There's no English menu; just point and take.

Restaurante Fernando MACANESE $

(法蘭度餐廳; www.fernando-restaurant.com; 9 Praia de Hác Sá, Coloane; mains MOP$55-160, rice dishes MOP$60-75; ⊙noon-9.30pm) A Macau institution famed for seafood and the perfect place for a protracted, boozy lunch by the sea.

Café Nga Tim MACANESE $

(雅憩花園餐廳; Map p522; 8 Rua do Caetano, Coloane; mains MOP$70-200; ⊙noon-1am) We love the Chinese-Portuguese food, the small-town atmosphere, the view of the Chapel of St Francis Xavier, the prices and the owner – a guitar-and erhu-strumming ex-cop named Feeling.

Chat Yin BURMESE $

(Map p512; 1 Rua de Bras da Rosa; noodles MOP$16-34; ⊙7.30am-6.30pm) Located in

SWEETS & TREATS

The streets of Macau are in no short supply of places for a welcome pick-me-up.

Mok Yee Kei (莫義記; Map p521; 9a Rua da Cunha, Taipa; desserts from MOP$9; ⏲8am-11pm) An 80-year-old shop known for homemade ice creams and puddings.

Little Sweet House (小甜甜; Map p512; Shop C, Wah Mei Bldg, 5a Travessa da Corda; desserts from MOP$9; ⏲8am-11pm) A neat little place serving crêpes and Chinese desserts.

Lai Kei Ice-cream (禮記雪糕; Map p516; 12-12a Av do Conselherio Ferrerira de Alemida; ice cream MOP$7-24; ⏲noon-7pm) A nostalgic soda fountain which dates from 1960s.

Nusantara Nam-yeong (南洋小食; Map p512; 86b Rua do Almirante Costa Cabral; snacks from MOP$10 for 3; ⏲noon-8pm) A family-run shop selling Indonesian snacks.

the Three Lamps district, this Burmese joint with minty-green stuccoed walls whips up a sumptuous Burmese fish soup with noodles and the hearts of banana trees.

Drinking

Macau's unique and atmospheric drinking places are far removed from the glitz of the Outer Harbor.

TOP CHOICE **Lord Stow's Cafe** CAFE
(澳門澳門安德魯餅店; Map p522; www.lordstow.com; Largo do Matadouro, Coloane Village; ⏲10am-6pm) This cosy cafe serves baked goodies from the famous bakery around the corner, including the popular *pastéis de nata* (scrumptious egg-custard tarts with a flaky crust), and cheesecake in unusual flavours such as green tea and black sesame.

Portal COCKTAIL BAR
(大門酒吧; Map p521; 86 Rua Direita Carlos Eugenio, Taipa; ⏲6.30pm-3am) Portal has an infectiously young vibe that makes you want to be a teen again – have cocktails for dinner (they're made by a professional mixologist by the way) and flirt with other teens. There's live music on weekends from 9.30pm.

Jabber CAFE
(Map p516; 34-38 Rua de São Roque; ⏲noon-7pm Tue-Fri, 3-7pm Sat & Sun) Located in the St Lazarus district, this sexy subterranean cafe with hot-pink walls belongs to a fashion designer who also lends her talent to the tasty and creative menu. Its cocktails will give you a nice afternoon buzz.

Old Taipa Tavern PUB
(好客鄉莊; Map p521; 21 Rua dos Negociantes, Taipa; ⏲11am-2am; 📶) Open shutter-doors and a location in the middle of Taipa Village make for great people-watching at this laid-back bar. Local bands perform on Mondays (8pm to midnight).

Corner's Wine Bar & Tapas Cafe BAR, CAFE
(大三巴角落餐廳; Map p516; 3 Travessa de São Paulo; ⏲cafe noon-5pm daily, bar 5pm-midnight Sun-Thu, to 1am Fri & Sat) This artsy rooftop bar has plush pink couches and stunning views of the St Paul ruins.

Cuppa Coffee CAFE
(104 Rua Fernão Mendes Pinto, Taipa; ⏲8am-8pm; 📶) Expect freshly baked bread, yummy sandwiches, great smoothies and decent coffees at this nifty cafe.

Mactim Cafe CAFE
(Map p516; Shop D, 1a Travessa do Meio, Largo do Senado; ⏲11.30am-9pm, closed Wed) This small French-style cafe serves decent coffees and cakes.

Entertainment

Macau's nightlife may be dominated by the ever-expanding casino scene, but a number of interesting live-music venues have also sprung up about town.

Blue Frog BAR
(藍蛙; ☎2882 8281; www.bluefrog.com.cn; Venetian Macao-Resort-Hotel, Estrada da Baía de N Senhora da Esperança, Taipa; ⏲11am-late) This bar inside the Venetian is a smoking stage for indie gigs. Almost every weekend, you'll see psych-rockers or synth-punkers who look completely out of place in a casino, smack in the middle of one, having the time of their lives. And it's awesome.

Macau Soul BAR
(澳感廊; Map p516; ☎2836 5182; www.macausoul.com; 31a Rua de São Paulo; ⏲9.30am-8.30pm Mon-Thu, 9.30am-midnight Fri-Sun) Huddled in the shadows of the Ruins of St Paul, Macau Soul is elegantly decked out

in woods and stained-glass windows, with a basement where blues bands perform to packed audiences. Opening hours vary, so phone ahead.

Live Music Association (XL Creation) LIVE-MUSIC VENUE
(Map p512; lmamusic@ymail.com; 10b Man Kei Industrial Bldg, 48 Av do Coronel Mesquita) This excellent but evasive dive in an industrial building features performances by indie bands on some nights. Email for the latest events, or join the Facebook group by the same name.

Wynn Macao CASINO
(永利澳門; Map p512; www.wynnmacau.com; Rua Cidade de Sintra) A gentlemen's club for punters, Wynn features interiors in solid browns interrupted impatiently by reds and golds. Presumably feng shui had a say too – the hotel sports a chip on its shoulder that's pointed at Grand Lisboa.

Grand Lisboa Casino CASINO
(新葡京; Map p512; www.grandlisboa.com; Av de Lisboa) This flaming-torch-shaped megastructure has become the landmark you navigate the streets by, outshining its sister next door, **Casino Lisboa** (葡京; 2-4 Av de Lisboa), once the best-known casino in Asia for its faded '60s glamour.

Venetian CASINO
(威尼斯人; www.venetianmacao.com; Estrada da Baía de N Senhora da Esperança, Taipa) Occupying the Cotai Strip, this ersatz Doge's Palace is a minimalist's nightmare – a vast hotel, gambling and shopping city within a city, that recreates Venetian icons, right down to the canals and singing gondoliers.

Nicole Fashion Club DANCE CLUB
(Map p512; Fisherman's Wharf; ⏲10pm-late) Pick your night here carefully: midweek it can be dead, but on a good night there's a decent mix of tunes, a glamorous crowd, and a fun vibe.

Shopping

Browsing through the shops in the old city, specifically on crumbly **Rua dos Ervanários** and **Rua de Nossa Senhora do Amparo** (Map p516) near the Ruins of St Paul, can be a great experience. There are shops selling stamps, jade, incense and goldfish. In the afternoon, flea-market vendors spread their wares on the ground.

You can also look for antiques or replicas at shops on or near **Rua de São Paulo, Rua das Estalagens** and **Rua de São António**. **Rua de Madeira** and **Rua dos Mercadores**, which lead up to **Rua da Tercena** and its **flea market** (Map p516) have stores selling mahjong tiles and bird cages. With their humble, one- or two-storey houses dating from agricultural times, these are lovely streets to walk around in, even if you don't buy anything.

In recent years many designers have set up shop in the city, particularly in the **St Lazarus district**.

Stores selling pork jerky, egg rolls and almond cookies are scattered all over town. Standards are pretty much the same, so just hop into the nearest one.

TOP CHOICE **Macau Creations** LIFESTYLE
(澳門佳作;Map p516; ☎2835 2954; www.macaucreations.com; 5a Rua da Ressurreicao; ⏲10am-10pm) Excellent Macau-themed

FREELOADING IN MACAU

So you've lost the shirt off your back but you still want to travel. Well, you probably can, if you're in Macau.

All big-name casinos have free shuttle service to and from the Macau Ferry Terminal, Taipa Ferry Terminal, the Border Gate, even the airport, with Venetian boasting an enormous fleet. Anyone can use these buses – no questions asked. What's more, some casinos have buses to each other. Combine that with walking and you're pretty much set.

Operating hours of these services fall between 9.30am and 11pm, and buses depart every three to 15 minutes. Check the casino websites or at the front desk.

If you're on a casino-bound route, don't forget to pick up your complimentary chip. A free spin may be just what's needed to land you a bed for the night. If it doesn't, don't lose heart. You can leave your bags at any casino-hotel for free even if your real pad is the pavement.

You know what they say: you find out who your real friends are when you're down and out.

BRIGHT LIGHTS, SIN CITY

Macau's seafront has turned into King Kong's playground, a space occupied by gargantuan monuments whose size makes it easy to imagine their downfall. Of course, casinos are no stranger to a city known as 'the Vegas of the East', but while previously there was only one landmark house of cards, now the sky's the limit. The change began when casino mogul Stanley Ho's monopoly ended in 2002 and Las Vegas operators set up shop in competition. There are at present some 30 casinos in Macau.

Over 80% of gamblers and 95% of high rollers come from mainland China. The latter play in members-only rooms where the total amount wagered on any given day can exceed a country's GDP, and where money allows you to do wonderful things like smash a chandelier with an ashtray and not pay for it. These VIP rooms are also assumed to be convenient sites for money laundering.

For recreational players, your closest brush with a casino's seedy side will probably be harassment by tip hustlers – scam artists who hang around tables acting like your new best friend. They can steal your chips, nag you for a cut and/or try to drag you off to a casino that will tip them for bringing clients.

All casinos operate 24 hours a day. Punters must be at least 18 years old and properly dressed (no shorts or flipflops).

clothes, stationery and memorabilia designed by 30 artists living in the city, including Russian Konstantin Bessmertny and Macanese Carlos Marreiros.

Pinto Livros BOOKS
(邊度有書; Map p516; http://blog.roodo.com/pintolivros; 1a Veng Heng Bldg, 31 Largo do Senado; ⏲11.30am-11pm) This upstairs reading room overlooking Largo do Senado has a decent selection of titles in art and culture, a few esoteric CDs and two resident cats.

Lines Lab FASHION
(Map p516; www.lineslab.com; Shop A3, 8 Calçada da Igreja de São Lazaro; ⏲1-8pm closed Mon) Two Lisbon-trained designers opened this boutique in the Old Ladies' House art space and created edgy Macau-inspired clothes and bags for it.

Av Ateliê HANDICRAFTS
(Map p516; 39a Rua Nova de São Lazaro; ⏲2.30-6pm Mon-Sat) This Portuguese-owned shop in the St Lazarus district sells handcrafted toys, bags and other pretty paraphernalia (MOP$60 to MOP$800). Cash only.

Asian Artefacts ANTIQUES
(Map p522; 9 Rua dos Negociantes, Coloane; ⏲10am-7pm) If you're serious about antiques, this shop in Coloane Village, with its before-and-after photos of restored pieces, is recommended.

ℹ Information

The Macau Government Tourist Office (MGTO) distributes the excellent (and free) *Macau Tourist Map*, with tourist sights and streets labelled in Portuguese and Chinese. Small inset maps highlight the Taipa and Coloane areas and show bus routes.

Emergency

Emergency tourist hotline (☎112) English-speaking staff.

Fire services (☎2857 2222)

Official emergency services (☎999)

Police (☎2857 3333)

Internet Access

Macau's few internet cafes come and go quickly. The good news is that wi-fi coverage is expanding. Most libraries, museums and some parks and squares have free wi-fi. See the website www.wifi.gov.mo/en/locations.html for an updated list. To enjoy mobile wi-fi, you can buy a prepaid phonecard (MOP$50 to MOP$130) or a mobile wireless broadband pass (MOP$120/220 for one/five days from CTM.

Internet Resources

Useful Macau websites:

Cityguide (www.cityguide.gov.mo) Practical information (eg transport).

GoMacau (www.gomacau.com) Latest information on hotels, flights, sights, entertainment and activities.

Macau Cultural Institute (www.icm.gov.mo) Macau's cultural offerings month by month.

Macau Government Tourist Office (www.macautourism.gov.mo) The best source of information for visiting Macau.

Macau Yellow Pages (www.yp.com.mo) Telephone directory with maps.

Medical Services

The first two hospitals listed here have 24-hour emergency services:

Centro Hospitalar Conde São Januário (山頂醫院; 2831 3731; Estrada do Visconde de São Januário) Southwest of Guia Fort.

Hospital Kiang Wu (鏡湖醫院; 2837 1333; Rua de Coelho do Amaral) Northeast of the ruins of the Church of St Paul.

University Hospital (2882 1838; www.uh.org.mo; Block H, Macau University of Science & Technology, Av Wai Long, Taipa; 9am-9pm Mon-Sat, to 5pm Sun) Western and Chinese medical services available.

Money

ATMs are everywhere, especially just outside the Hotel Lisboa, where you'll find half a dozen. Most allow you to choose between patacas and Hong Kong dollars.

You can change cash and travellers cheques at the banks lining Avenida da Praia Grande and Avenida de Almeida Ribeiro.

Post

China Post (中国邮政; Zhōngguó Yóuzhèng) Ferry terminal branch (10am-7pm Mon-Sat); Main post office (Av de Almeida Ribeiro; 9am-6pm Mon-Fri, to 1pm Sat) Little red vending machines dispense stamps throughout Macau. Poste restante service is available at counters 1 and 2 of the main post office.

Telephone

Some handy phone-related facts:

Local calls Free from private phones and most hotel telephones; calls from public payphones cost MOP$1 for five minutes.

Prepaid IDD/local cards (from MOP$50) Can be used in most mobile phones; purchase from CTM stores or the ferry terminal.

Some useful numbers:

International directory assistance (101)

Local directory assistance (181)

Weather (1311)

Tourist Information

The website www.macautourism.gov.mo/en/main/faq.php has a useful FAQ page on Macau. Also, pick up themed leaflets on Macau's sights and bilingual maps at outlets of the **Macau Government Tourist Office** (MGTO; 澳門旅遊局; 2831 5566; www.macautourism.gov.mo):

Guia Lighthouse (旅遊局東望洋燈塔分局; 2856 9808; 9am-1pm & 2.15-5.30pm)

Hong Kong (澳門政府旅遊局; 2857 2287; Room 336-337, Shun Tak Centre, 200 Connaught Rd, Sheung Wan; 9am-10pm)

Largo do Senado (旅遊諮詢處; 8397 1120; 9am-6pm)

Macau Ferry Terminal (旅遊局外港碼頭分局; 2872 6416; 9am-10pm)

Travel Agencies

China Travel Service (CTS; 中国旅行社; Zhōngguó Lǚxíngshè; 2870 0888; cts@cts.com.mo; Av do Dr Rodrigo, 207, Edifício Nam Kuong; 9am-5pm) China visas (MOP$285 plus photos) are available to most passport-holders in one day.

Getting There & Away

Air

For details of airlines, check the website of **Macau International Airport** (www.macau-airport.gov.mo); the airport itself is on Taipa. **Air Macau** (澳門航空; NX; www.airmacau.com.mo; ground fl, 398 Alameda Doutor Carlos d'Assumpção) has at least one flight a day to mainland cities, including Běijīng, Hángzhōu, Nánjīng and Shànghǎi, as well as to Taipei and Kaohsiung in Taiwan, and to Bangkok and Seoul.

Sky Shuttle (www.skyshuttlehk.com; Mon-Thu HK$2600, Fri-Sun HK$2800) runs a 15-minute helicopter shuttle between Macau and Hong Kong up to 54 times a day, 9am to 11pm.

Boat

TO CHINA **Yuet Tung Shipping Co** (2877 4478; MOP$129) Daily ferry from pier 11a, just off Rua das Lorchas, to Shékǒu in Shēnzhèn. The trip takes 80 minutes; the ferry leaves at 10am, 12.30pm, 6.15pm and 8.15pm, and returns at 8.15am, 9.45am, 11.45am and 6.30pm. Tickets can be bought up to three days in advance from pier 11a.

Sampans and ferries (MOP$12.50, departure tax MOP$20; hourly 8am-4pm) From a small pier near where Rua das Lorchas meets Rua do Dr Lourenço Pereira Marques to Wānzǎi.

TO HONG KONG Three ferry companies operate services to/from Hong Kong virtually 24 hours a day:

CotaiJet (www.cotaijet.com.mo; economy/superclass Mon-Fri MOP$142/244, Sat & Sun MOP$154/260, night crossing MOP$176/275) Every half-hour from 7am to 1am; runs between Taipa Ferry Terminal and Hong Kong's Hong Kong–Macau Ferry Terminal. A feeder shuttle bus service drops off at destinations on the Cotai Strip. Check the website for services to Hong Kong International Airport.

New World First Ferry (www.nwff.com.hk; economy/deluxe Mon-Fri HK$140/245, Sat & Sun HK$155/260, night crossing MOP$175/275) Every half-hour from 7am to 10.30pm. The 60–75-minute trip runs between Macau Ferry Terminal and Hong Kong's China Ferry Terminal.

TurboJet (www.turbojet.com.hk; economy/superclass Mon-Fri HK$142/244, Sat & Sun HK$154/260, night crossing HK$176/275) Has the most sailings; 55-minute trip; departs from **Hong Kong–Macau Ferry Terminal** (200 Connaught Rd, Sheung Wan) and from **Macau Ferry Terminal**. See the website for services to Hong Kong International Airport.

Bus

Macau is an easy gateway into China:

Border Gate (Portas de Cerco; ⏲7am-midnight) Take bus 3, 5, 9, 10, 18 or 25 and walk across.

Cotai Frontier Post (⏲9am-8pm) On the causeway linking Taipa and Coloane; allows visitors to cross Lotus Bridge by shuttle bus (HK$3) to Zhūhǎi; buses 15, 21, 25 and 26 drop you off at the crossing.

Macau International Airport (☎info 2888 1228) Buses to Guǎngzhōu and Dōngguǎn (both MOP$155, four hours).

Underground bus terminal near Border Gate (☎2893 3888) Kee Kwan Motor Rd Co has buses going to Guǎngzhōu (MOP$80, four hours, every 15 minutes from 8am to 9.40pm) and to Zhōngshān (MOP$23, 90 minutes, every 20 minutes from 8am to 8pm).

ℹ Getting Around

To/From the Airport

Airport bus AP1 (MOP$4.20) Airport to Macau Ferry Terminal and Border Gate; stops at major hotels en route. Runs every 15 minutes from 7am to midnight. Extra charge of MOP$3 for each large piece of luggage.

Airport buses MT1 and MT2 (MOP$4.20) Airport to Praça de Ferreira do Amaral near Casino Lisboa; from 7am to 10am, then 4pm to 8pm.

Buses 21 and 26 Airport to Coloane.

Bus 21 Airport to A-Ma Temple.

Taxi (about MOP$40) Airport to town centre.

Bicycle

Bikes can be rented in Taipa Village. You are not allowed to cross the Macau–Taipa bridges on a bicycle.

Car

Avis Rent A Car (www.avis.com.mo; Room 1022, ground fl, Macau Ferry Terminal) hires out cheap Smart City Coupes/Toyota Corollas (MOP$600 to MOP$850).

Public Transport

Macau has about 50 public bus and minibus routes, running from 6am to midnight. Fares cost MOP$3.20 on the peninsula, MOP$4.20 to Taipa, MOP$5 to Coloane Village and MOP$6.40 to Hác Sá Beach. Destinations are displayed in Portuguese and Chinese.

Macau Transmac Bus Co (www.transmac.com.mo) and **Macau TCM Bus Co** (www.tcm.com.mo) have information on routes and fares. The *Macau Tourist Map,* available at MGTO outlets, also has a list of both bus companies' routes and a pamphlet listing all bus routes.

Useful services on the peninsula include buses 3 and 3A, between the ferry terminal and city centre; buses 3 and 5, which go to the Border Gate; and bus 12, which runs from the ferry terminal, past Hotel Lisboa to Lou Lim Ioc Garden and Kun Iam Temple. Buses 21, 21A, 25 and 26A go to Taipa and Coloane.

Taxi

Not many taxi drivers speak English, so it can help to have your destination written in Chinese. Flag fall is MOP$13 (first 1.6km); then it's MOP$1.50 for each additional 230m. There's a MOP$5/2 surcharge to Coloane from Macau peninsula/Taipa, and a MOP$5 surcharge for journeys from the airport. Large bags cost an extra MOP$3. Call ☎2851 9519 or ☎2893 9939 for yellow radio taxis.

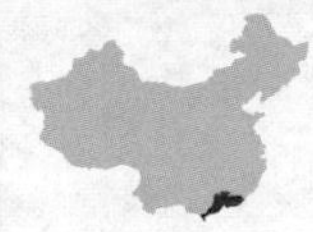

Guǎngdōng

POPULATION: 93 MILLION

Includes »

Best Places to Eat

» Bǐngshèng Restaurant (p541)

» Pànxī Restaurant (p541)

» Feng's Kitchen (p553)

» Wilber's (p541)

» Jīn Yuè Xuān (p559)

Best Places to Stay

» White Swan Hotel (p541)

» Orange House (p553)

» Shēnzhèn Loft Youth Hostel (p555)

Why Go?

Often hiding under the traveller's radar, Guǎngdōng's interesting history and natural beauty have yet to be discovered by most visitors, so you may have a plethora of colourful sights to yourself. Away from the cities, northern Guǎngdōng (广东) boasts some unspoiled, undulating landscape. The blue pine forests in Nánlǐng and the seldom-visited river valleys in Qīngyuǎn are absolutely stunning.

If it's architectural wonders you're after, Guǎngdōng also fits the bill nicely. The Unesco-crowned watchtowers in Kāipíng and the earthen Hakka roundhouses in Méizhōu will knock your socks off.

Historically, Guǎngdōng was the birthplace of reform and revolution, eventually changing the fate of modern China. On the highways and byways of the Pearl River Delta, you'll uncover the glory and sorrow of its revolutionary past.

Feeling peckish? The strong foodie culture here won't let you leave hungry – you can sample world-renowned dim sum prepared at its best.

When to Go

Guǎngzhōu

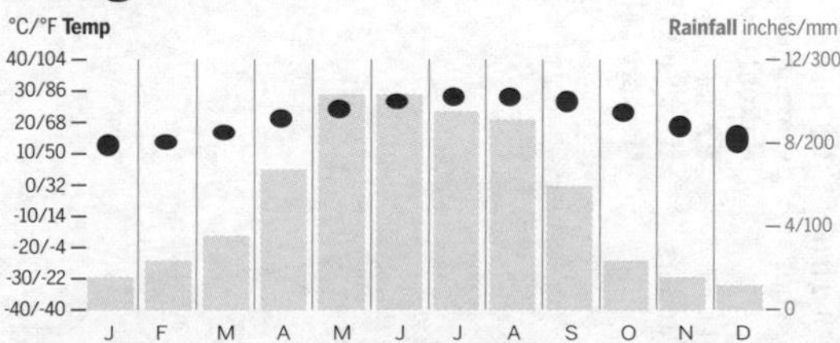

April–June Verdant paddy fields form a beautiful backdrop in the *diàolóu* villages in Kāipíng.

July–September Recharge your spirit in the lush, cool hill station in Nánlǐng.

October–December With the typhoons and heat gone, this is the best time to visit the region.

Guǎngdōng Highlights

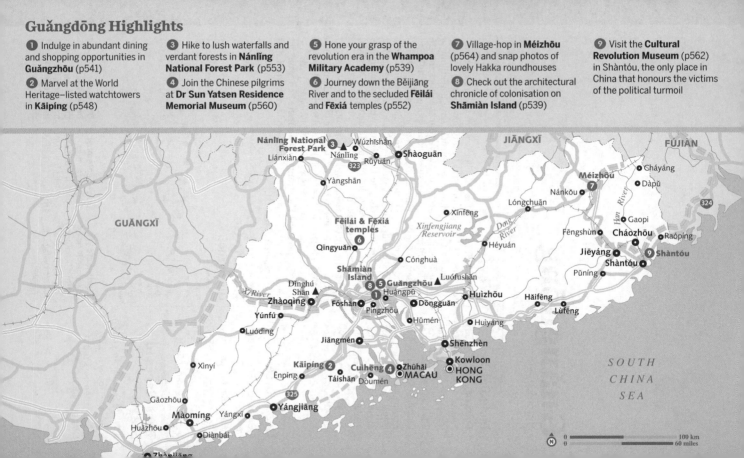

1. Indulge in abundant dining and shopping opportunities in **Guǎngzhōu** (p541)
2. Marvel at the World Heritage–listed watchtowers in **Kāipíng** (p548)
3. Hike to lush waterfalls and verdant forests in **Nánlǐng National Forest Park** (p553)
4. Join the Chinese pilgrims at **Dr Sun Yatsen Residence Memorial Museum** (p560)
5. Hone your grasp of the revolution era in the **Whampoa Military Academy** (p539)
6. Journey down the Běijiāng River and to the secluded **Fēilái** and **Fēxiá** temples (p552)
7. Village-hop in **Méizhōu** (p564) and snap photos of lovely Hakka roundhouses
8. Check out the architectural chronicle of colonisation on **Shāmiàn Island** (p539)
9. Visit the **Cultural Revolution Museum** (p562) in Shàntóu, the only place in China that honours the victims of the political turmoil

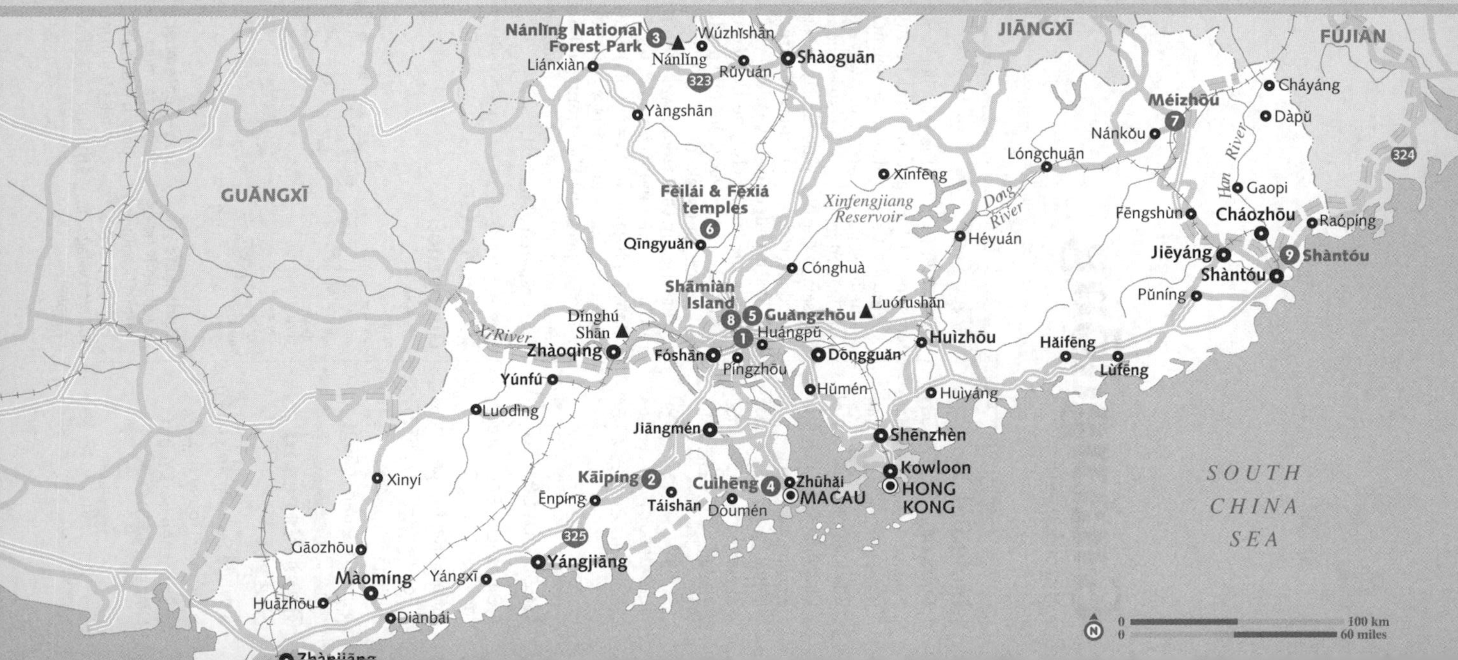

PRICE INDICATORS

The following price indicators are used in this chapter:

Sleeping

$	less than Y250
$$	Y250 to Y600
$$$	more than Y600

Eating

$	less than Y70
$$	Y70 to Y150
$$$	more than Y150

History

Guǎngdōng has had contact with the outside world for over a millennium. Among the first outsiders to make their way here were the Romans, who appeared as early as the 2nd century AD. By the Tang dynasty (AD 618–907), Arab merchants were visiting regularly and a sizeable trade with the Middle East and Southeast Asia had developed.

The first Europeans to settle here were the Portuguese in 1557. They were followed by the Jesuits in 1582, who established themselves at Zhàoqìng, west of Guǎngzhōu. The British came along in the 17th century and by 1685 merchant ships from the East India Company were calling at Guǎngzhōu. In 1757 an imperial edict gave the *cohong*, a local merchants' guild, a monopoly on China's trade with foreigners, who were restricted to Shāmiàn Island. Trade remained in China's favour until 1773, when the British shifted the balance by unloading 1000 chests of Bengal opium at Guǎngzhōu. Addiction swept China like wildfire, eventually leading to the Opium Wars.

In the 19th century Guǎngdōng was a hotbed of reform and revolt. During the Taiping Rebellion (1856–64), Hong Xiuquan, who claimed to be the younger brother of Jesus Christ, tried to overthrow the dynasty and establish his own 'Kingdom of Heavenly Peace', but was crushed with the help of foreign powers. Thereafter, Guǎngdōng became a base for political elites to sow revolutionary ideas. Among these elites were distinguished politicians like Kang Youwei, Liang Qichao and Sun Yatsen, who was born in Cuìhēng village and later became the first president of the Republic of China.

Twentieth-century Guǎngdōng saw its share of hardships and successes, being the headquarters of both the Nationalist and Communist parties and enduring untold suffering during the Cultural Revolution. After 1978, with Deng Xiaoping's 'open door' economic policy, Guǎngdōng became the first province to experience capitalism, with Shēnzhèn, Zhūhǎi and Shàntóu set up as Special Economic Zones. Guǎngdōng's continued economic success has made it a leading export centre for consumer goods.

Language

The vast majority of the people of Guǎngdōng speak Cantonese, a dialect distinct from Mandarin. Though it enjoys much less exalted status than the national language, Cantonese is older and sounds much better for reading classical poetry.

Guǎngzhōu 广州

☎020 / POP 12 MILLION

Guǎngzhōu, known to many in the West as Canton, is China's busiest transport and trade hub. You are likely to pass through it at least once to get to other parts of the country. Avoid visiting during Chinese New Year, which sees the largest annual human migration in the world.

History

The history of Guǎngzhōu is dominated by trade and revolution. Since the Tang dynasty (AD 618–907), it was China's most important southern port and the starting point for the Maritime Silk Road, an important route for shipping silk and other goods to the West. It was also a trading post for the Portuguese in the 16th century, and for the British in the 17th century.

The city was a stronghold of the republican forces after the fall of the Qing dynasty in 1911. Sun Yatsen led the Kuomintang (KMT; Nationalist Party) in Guǎngzhōu in the early 1920s to mount campaigns against the northern warlords. Later, Guǎngzhōu was also a centre of activity for the fledgling Chinese Communist Party (CCP), and Mao Zedong and other prominent communist leaders were based here in 1925–26.

Since liberation in 1949, Guǎngzhōu's only mission has been to make money. Even when China effectively cut itself off from

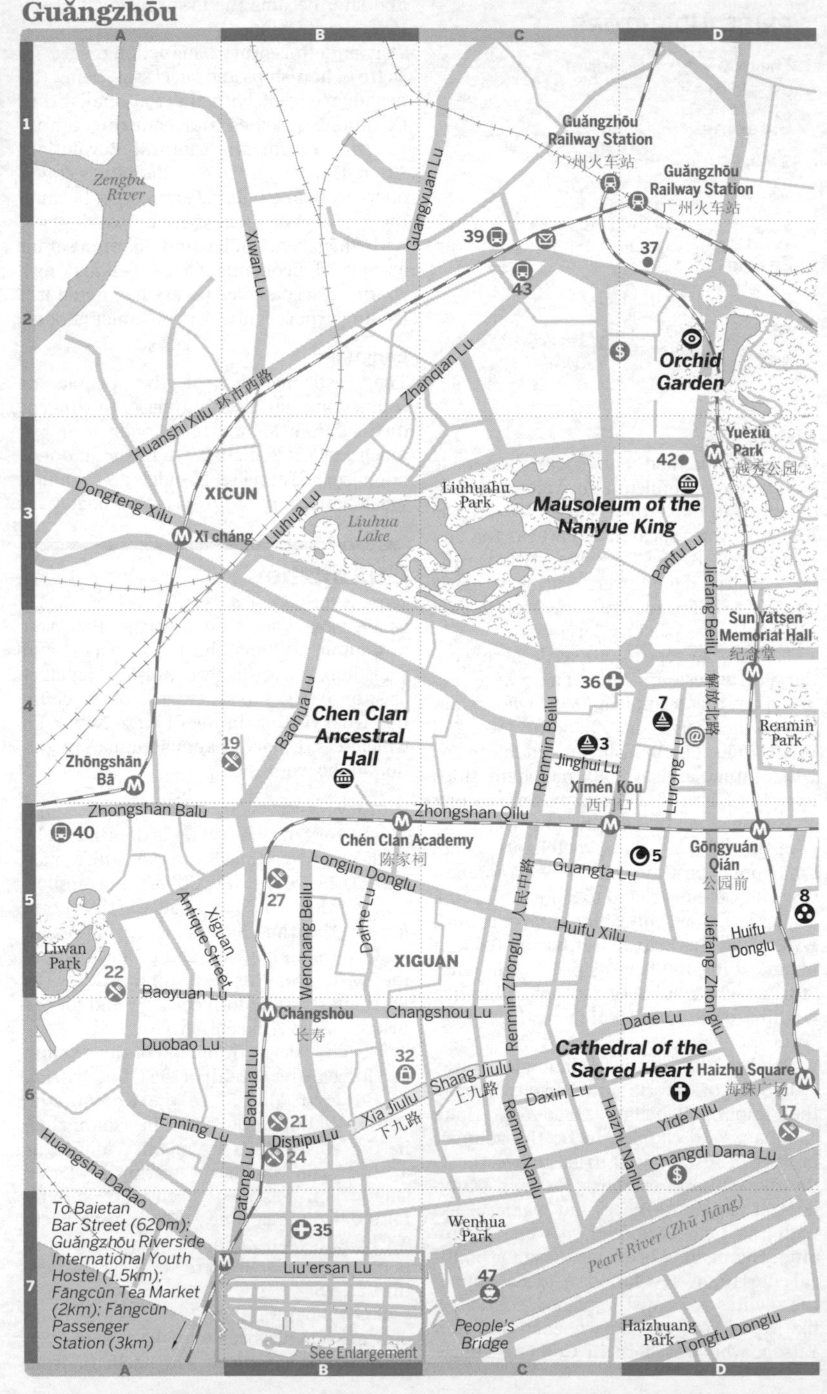

Zengbu River
Guǎngzhōu Railway Station
广州火车站
Guǎngzhōu Railway Station
广州火车站
Xiwan Lu
Guangyuan Lu
39
43
37
Orchid Garden
Zhanqian Lu
Huanshi Xilu 环市西路
Yuèxiù Park
越秀公园
42
Dongfeng Xilu
XICUN
Liuhuahu Park
Mausoleum of the Nanyue King
Xī cháng
Liuhua Lu
Liuhua Lake
Panfu Lu
Jiefang Beilu
Sun Yatsen Memorial Hall
纪念堂
36
7
Baohua Lu
Chen Clan Ancestral Hall
19
3
解放北路
Renmin Park
Zhōngshān Bā
Renmin Beilu
Jinghui Lu
Ximén Kōu
西门口
Liurong Lu
Zhongshan Balu
Zhongshan Qilu
40
Chén Clan Academy
陈家祠
Gōngyuán Qián
公园前
5
Longjin Donglu
27
Guangta Lu
人民中路
8
Antique Street
Xiguan
Wenchang Beilu
Daihe Lu
Huifu Xilu
Huifu Donglu
Liwan Park
22
XIGUAN
Renmin Zhonglu
Jiefang Zhonglu
Baoyuan Lu
Chángshòu
长寿
Changshou Lu
Dade Lu
Duobao Lu
Baohua Lu
32
Cathedral of the Sacred Heart
Haizhu Square
海珠广场
Shang Jiulu
上九路
Daxin Lu
Enning Lu
Xia Jiulu
下九路
Renmin Nanlu
Haizhu Nanlu
Yide Xilu
17
21
Dishipu Lu
24
Huangsha Dadao
Changdi Dama Lu
Datong Lu
To Baietan Bar Street (620m); Guǎngzhōu Riverside International Youth Hostel (1.5km); Fāngcūn Tea Market (2km); Fāngcūn Passenger Station (3km)
35
Wenhua Park
Pearl River (Zhū Jiāng)
Liu'ersan Lu
47
People's Bridge
Haizhuang Park
Tongfu Donglu
See Enlargement

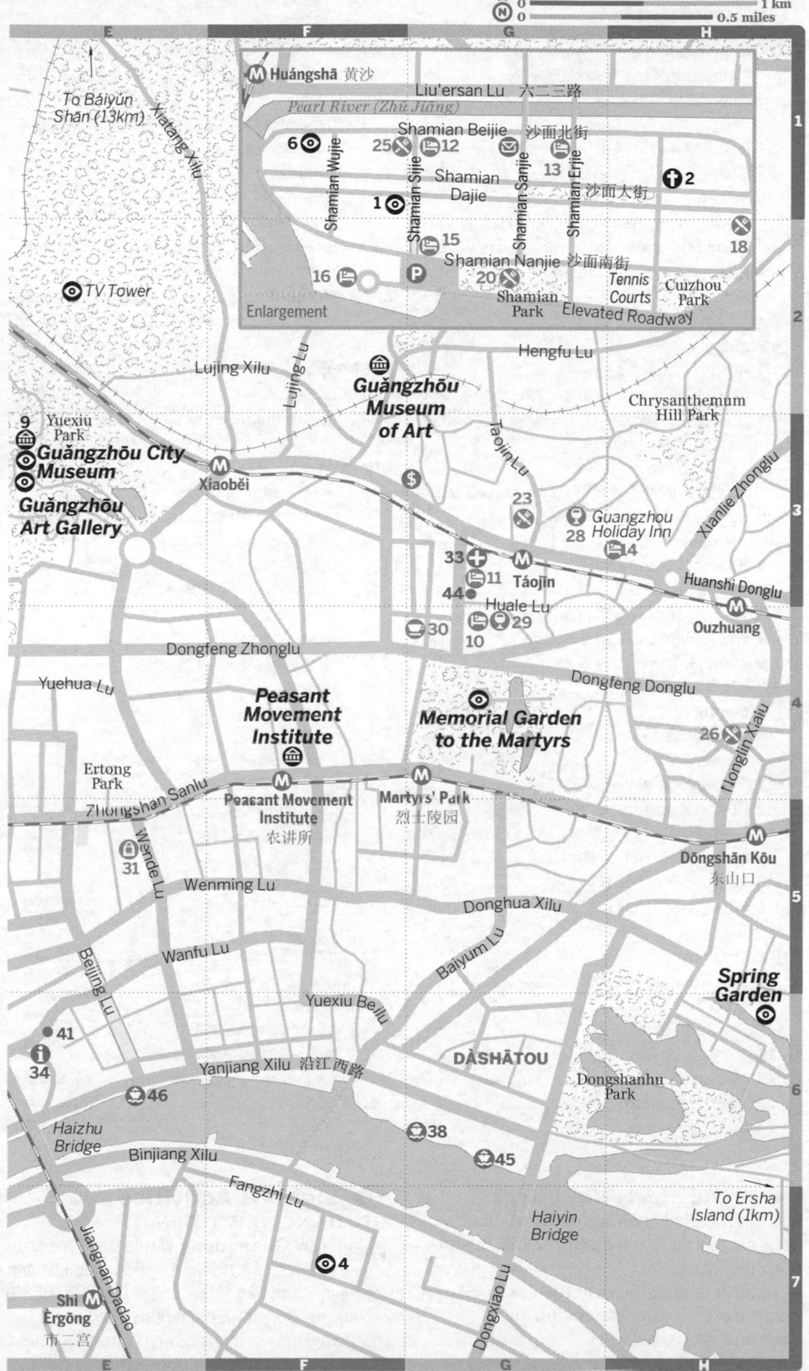
0 1 km
0 0.5 miles
Huángshā 黄沙
Liu'ersan Lu 六二三路
Pearl River (Zhū Jiāng)
Shamian Beijie 沙面北街
Shamian Wujie
Shamian Sijie
Shamian Dajie
Shamian Sanjie
Shamian Erjie
沙面大街
Shamian Nanjie 沙面南街
Tennis Courts
Cuizhou Park
Shamian Park
Elevated Roadway
Enlargement
To Báiyún Shān (13km)
Xiatang Xilu
TV Tower
Lujing Xilu
Lujing Lu
Guǎngzhōu Museum of Art
Hengfu Lu
Chrysanthemum Hill Park
Yuexiu Park
Guǎngzhōu City Museum
Guǎngzhōu Art Gallery
Xiaobĕi
Taojin Lu
Guangzhou Holiday Inn
Xianlie Zhonglu
Táojīn
Huale Lu
Huanshi Donglu
Ouzhuang
Dongfeng Zhonglu
Dongfeng Donglu
Yuehua Lu
Peasant Movement Institute
Memorial Garden to the Martyrs
Honglin Xialu
Ertong Park
Zhongshan Sanlu
Peasant Movement Institute
农讲所
Martyrs' Park
烈士陵园
Dōngshān Kōu
东山口
Wende Lu
Wenming Lu
Donghua Xilu
Wanfu Lu
Baiyum Lu
Beijing Lu
Spring Garden
Yuexiu Beilu
DÀSHĀTOU
Yanjiang Xilu 沿江西路
Dongshanhu Park
Haizhu Bridge
Binjiang Xilu
Fangzhi Lu
To Ersha Island (1km)
Haiyin Bridge
Jiangnan Dadao
Dongxiao Lu
Shì Èrgōng
市二宫
GUǍNGDŌNG GUǍNGZHŌU

Guǎngzhōu

Top Sights

Cathedral of the Sacred Heart D6
Chen Clan Ancestral Hall B4
Guǎngzhōu Art Gallery E3
Guǎngzhōu City Museum E3
Guǎngzhōu Museum of Art F2
Mausoleum of the Nanyue King D3
Memorial Garden to the Martyrs G4
Orchid Garden D2
Peasant Movement Institute F4
Spring Garden H6

Sights

1 Art 64 .... F1
2 Church of Our Lady of Lourdes H1
3 Guangxiao Temple C4
4 Memorial Museum of Generalissimo Sun Yatsen's Mansion F7
5 Mosque Dedicated to the Prophet D5
6 Shāmiàn Traditional Chinese Medical Center F1
7 Temple of the Six Banyan Trees D4
8 Water Gate D5
9 Zhènhǎi Tower E3

Sleeping

10 7 Days Inn G4
11 Garden Hotel G3
12 Guǎngdōng Victory Hotel G1
13 Guǎngdōng Victory Hotel (New Annexe) G1
14 Guǎngzhōu Holiday Inn H3
15 Guǎngzhōu Youth Hostel G2
16 White Swan Hotel F2

Eating

17 1920 Restaurant & Bar D6
18 Dolci Vita H2
19 Foo Yau Yuan B4
20 Lucy's G2
21 Nánxìn B6
22 Pànxī Restaurant A5
23 Sultan G3
24 Táo Táo Jū Restaurant B6
25 Thài Zhēn Cow & Bridge F1
26 Wilber's H4
27 Wuzhànjì B5

Drinking

28 Overseas Chinese Village G3
29 Paddy Field G4
30 People's Café G4

Entertainment

Bound .... (see 17)

Shopping

31 Wende Lu E5
32 Xiguan Antique Street B6

Information

33 Can-Am International Medical Centre G3
34 China Travel Service Guangzhou E6
35 Guǎngzhōu Hospital of Traditional Chinese Medicine B7
36 Guǎngzhōu No 1 People's Hospital C4

Transport

37 China Southern Airlines D2
38 Dashatou Wharf G6
39 Guangdong Long-Distance Bus Station C2
40 Guangfo Bus Station (Buses to Fóshan) A5
41 Hotel Landmark Canton E6
42 Japan Airlines D3
43 Liuhua Bus Station C2
44 Malaysia, Thai International, United and Vietnam Airlines G3
45 New Pier G6
46 Tiānzì Pier E6
47 Xidi Pier C7

the rest of the world after liberation, what was then called the Canton Trade Fair was the only forum in which China did business with the West.

In 2010 Guǎnzhōu held the Asian Games, resulting in major expansion of the city's road and metro network.

Sights & Activities

ZHUJIANG NEW TOWN

FREE **New Guangdong Museum** MUSEUM
(广东省博物馆新馆; Guǎngdōngshěng Bówùguǎn Xínguǎn; Map p538; ☎3804 6886; 2 Zhujiang Donglu; ⌚9am-5pm Tue-Sun) This spanking-new ultramodern museum next to the opera house occupies almost the en-

tire block by the waterfront. Its extensive collection illustrates the human and natural history of Guǎngdōng, as well as arts, literature and architecture. Take metro line 3 to Zhujiang New Town station, exit B1.

Mausoleum of the Nanyue King MAUSOLEUM
(南越王墓; Nányuèwáng Mù; Map p534; ☎8666 4920; 867 Jiefang Beilu; admission Y12, audioguide Y10; ⏲9am-5.30pm) A must on your itinerary in Guǎngdōng, this superb mausoleum from the 2000-year-old Nanyue kingdom, accidentally discovered in 1983, is now one of China's best museums.

The mausoleum houses the tomb of Zhao Mo, second king of Nanyue and grandson of the fabled Qin general Zhao Tuo, who was sent south by the emperor in 214 BC to quell unrest and established a sovereign state with Guǎngzhōu as its capital. Shortly after Zhao Mo's death, the Han plundered the kingdom, claiming the territory as their own. One of the mausoleum's highlights is Zhao Mo's burial suit, made of thousands of tiny jade tiles – jade was thought to preserve the body and make one immortal. The English audioguide is recommended.

Also related to the history of Nanyue kingdom are the recently excavated, surprisingly well preserved remnants of a Nanyue-era **water gate** (南越国水闸遗址 (光明广场); Nányuèguó Shuǐzhá Yízhǐ; basement, Metro Mall, Huifu Donglu; ⏲noon-6pm) in the basement of a shopping mall. The tiny museum here has excellent displays on the history of combating water woes in China.

Xīnhépǔ HISTORIC AREA
Ambling along the tree-lined streets in the neighbourhood of Xīnhépǔ (新河浦) on the southern edge of the historic Dōngshān area (东山区; Dōngshān Qū) is a pleasant retreat from the hustle and bustle of the city. Here, a cluster of colonial villas and churches built by the missionaries at the beginning of the 20th century are beautifully restored. During the republican era, the houses were private dwellings for the Kuomintang's high-ranking officials; now, they're private residences for local bigwigs. Only the three-storey **Spring Garden** (春园; Chūnyuán; Map p534; 24 Xinhepu Lu; admission free; ⏲9.30am-5pm) is open to the public. It was the former headquarters of the central committee of the CCP in 1923, and Mao Zedong also sojourned here during the party's third national congress. The site of this crucial meeting (where the Kuomintang and communists formed an alliance for the first time) is just a stone's throw from Spring Garden, and has been converted into a (boring) **museum** (Zhōnggòg Sāndà Huìzhǐ Jìniànguǎn; ☎8760 6531; 3 Xuguyuan Lu; admission Y5; ⏲9am-4.30pm) detailing the events.

To get here, take metro line 1 to Dōngshān Kōu station, exit A. Walk along Shuqian Lu to the south and follow the signs.

Yuèxiù Park PARK
(越秀公园; Yuèxiù Gōngyuán; Map p534; 13 Jiefang Beilu; admission Y5; ⏲6am-9pm) You'll find gardens, shaded wood paths, historical monuments and museums in this vast urban park. On top of a hill in the centre of the park is the red-walled, five-storey **Zhènhǎi Tower** (Zhènhǎi Lóu; Map p534), built in 1380. It was used as a watchtower to keep out the pirates who once pillaged China's coastal cities. In 1928 the tower was rebuilt to accommodate the **Guǎngzhōu City Museum** (广州市博物馆; Guǎngzhōushì Bówùguǎn; Map p534; ☎8355 0627; admission Y10; ⏲9am-5.30pm), which has an excellent collection of exhibits tracing the history of Guǎngzhōu from the Neolithic period. There are sweeping views of Guǎngzhōu from the top storey. On the east side of the tower is the **Guǎngzhōu Art Gallery** (Guǎngzhōu Měishùguǎn; Map p534). In addition to Cantonese embroidery and carved ivory decorations, it also has displays outlining Guǎngzhōu's trading history with the West. Take metro line 2 to Yuèxiù Gōngyuán station.

Orchid Garden GARDEN
(兰圃; Lán Pǔ; Map p534; Lanpu Lu; admission Y8, with tea tasting Y20; ⏲8am-6pm) Across from Yuèxiù Park off Jiefang Beilu is this charming garden famous for its blossoming orchids. With its winding paths, arched stone bridges and willow-fringed ponds, you may forget you're even in Guǎngzhōu. An old Muslim cemetery sits on the western edge of the park, supposedly the burial site of Abu Waqas, the uncle of the Prophet, who is credited with bringing Islam to China. The cemetery is closed to non-Muslims.

FREE **Peasant Movement Institute** HISTORIC SITE
(农民运动讲习所; Nóngmín Yùndòng Jiǎngxísuǒ; Map p534; ☎8333 3936; 42 Zhongshan Sanlu; ⏲9am-4.30pm Tue-Sun) The institute was established in 1924 by the CCP at the site of a former Confucian temple. Mao Zedong and Zhou Enlai both taught here, before the school closed in 1926. You can

East Guǎngzhōu

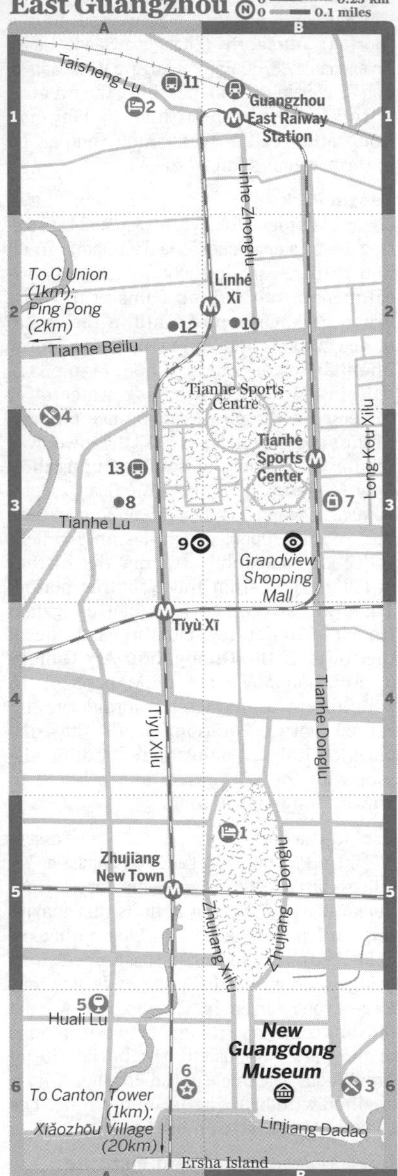

East Guǎngzhōu

Top Sights
New Guangdong Museum B6

Sleeping
1 Grant Hyatt Guǎngzhōu B5
2 Lilac International Suites A1

Eating
3 Bǐngshèng Restaurant B6
4 Nur Bostan A3

Drinking
5 Elaine's Garden A6

Entertainment
6 Guangzhou Opera House A6

Shopping
7 Computer Markets B3

Information
8 Newpage A3
9 Teem Plaza A3

Transport
10 Citic Plaza B2
11 Guangzhou Dongzhan Coach Station A1
12 Singapore Airlines A2
13 Tiānhé Dàxia` A3

see Mao Zedong's re-created personal quarters and even his bed. Take metro line 1 to Nóngjiǎng Suǒ station.

Memorial Garden to the Martyrs GARDEN
(烈士陵园; Lièshì Língyuán; Map p534; admission Y3; ⏲8am-7pm) East of the Institute on Zhongshan Sanlu, the garden commemorates those killed on 13 December 1927 under the orders of Chiang Kaishek. The massacre occurred when a small group of workers, led by the CCP, were gunned down by Kuomintang forces. Over 5000 lives were lost.

Guǎngzhōu Museum of Art MUSEUM
(广州艺术博物院; Guǎngzhōu Yìshù Bówùyuàn; Map p534; ☎8365 9337; 3 Luhu Lu; admission Y20; ⏲9am-5pm Tue-Fri, 9.30am-4.30pm Sat & Sun) The museum has an extensive collection of works, ranging from ancient to contemporary Chinese art and sculpture. Other interesting exhibits include a fantastic room on the top floor with displays of rare Tibetan tapestries. Take bus 10 or 63.

LIWAN DISTRICT

Chen Clan Ancestral Hall HISTORIC SITE
(陈家祠; Chénjiā Cí; Map p534; ☎8181 4559; 34 Enlongji Lu; admission Y10; ⏲8.30am-5.30pm) This enormous compound is an ancestral shrine, a Confucian school and a 'chamber of commerce' for the Chen clan, built in 1894

by the residents of 72 villages in Guǎngdōng; the Chen lineage is the predominant family. The complex encompasses 19 buildings of the traditional Lingnan style (southern Chinese style). All buildings contain exquisite carvings, statues and paintings, and are decorated with ornate scrollwork throughout. Take metro line 1 to Chénjiācí station.

Shāmiàn Island HISTORIC AREA

The leafy oasis of Shāmiàn Island (沙面岛; Shāmiàn Dǎo), which was acquired as a foreign concession in 1859 after the two Opium Wars, is a peaceful respite from the city. Back in the 19th century, the British and French were granted permission to set up their warehouses on this 'sand surface island'. The sandbank was connected to the mainland by several bridges, with iron gates that prohibited any Chinese from entering the island. Major renovation has restored some of the buildings to their original appearance, transforming them into chic restaurants and hotels.

Shamian Dajie is a tranquil stretch of gardens and trees. The Roman Catholic **Church of Our Lady of Lourdes** (天主教露德圣母堂; Tiānzhǔjiào Lùdé Shèngmǔ Táng; Map p534; Shamian Dajie; ⌚8am-6pm), built by the French in 1892, is on the eastern end of the thoroughfare. **Art 64** (☎8121 5176; Map p534; 64 Shamian Dajie; ⌚10am-7pm), a contemporary art gallery, is worth a visit.

Shāmiàn Traditional Chinese Medical Center (沙面国医馆; Shāmiàn Guóyīguǎn; Map p534; ☎8121 8383; 85-87 Shamian Beijie; ⌚11am-2am), at the western end of the island, is recommended by travellers for its massage (Y68 per hour).

To reach the island, take metro line 1 to Huángshā station.

Temple of the Six Banyan Trees BUDDHIST TEMPLE

(六榕寺; Liùróng Sì; Map p534; 87-89 Liurong Lu; admission Y15; ⌚8am-5pm) This Buddhist temple was built in AD 537 to enshrine Buddhist relics brought over from India. The relics were placed in the octagonal **Decorated Pagoda** (Huā Tǎ). The temple was given its current name by the exiled poet Su Dongpo in 1099, who commemorated the banyan trees in the courtyard with a poem. The banyan trees are long gone but you can see the characters *(liùróng)* he wrote hanging above the temple's gateway. To get here, take bus 56.

Guāngxiào Temple BUDDHIST TEMPLE

(光孝寺; Guāngxiào Chánsì; Map p534; 109 Jinghui Lu; admission Y5; ⌚6am-5pm) The 'Bright Filial Piety Temple', about 400m west of the Temple of the Six Banyan Trees, is the oldest temple in Guǎngzhōu, dating back to the 4th century. By the Tang dynasty it was well established as a centre of Buddhist learning in southern China. Bodhidarma, the founder of Zen Buddhism, once taught here.

Most of the current buildings date from the 19th century. The most impressive is the main hall, with its double eaves. Inside is a 10m-high statue of the Buddha. At the back of the hall sits an equally impressive statue of Guanyin, Goddess of Mercy. Take metro line 1 to Xīmén Kǒu station.

Mosque Dedicated to the Prophet MOSQUE

(怀圣寺; Huáishèng Sì; Map p534; ☎8333 3593; 56 Guangta Lu) The original building on the site of this mosque is thought to have been established in 627 by Abu Waqas, one of the Prophet Mohammed's uncles, making it the first of its kind in China. The present mosque dates from the Qing dynasty. Take metro line 1 to Xīmén Kǒu station.

Cathedral of the Sacred Heart CHURCH

(石室教堂; Shíshì Jiàotáng; Map p534; Yide Xilu) The French were granted permission to build this cathedral after the second Opium War. The twin-spired Roman Catholic cathedral was designed in the neo-Gothic style and built entirely of granite, with massive towers that reach a height of 48m. Take metro line 2 to Haizhu Sq.

Pearl River Cruises BOAT TRIP

The northern bank of the Pearl River is an interesting area, filled with people, markets and dilapidated buildings. It's a wonderful place for a morning or evening stroll, or Pearl River cruises (珠江游览船).

Guǎngzhōu Star Cruises Company (☎8333 2222) has nine evening cruises on the Pearl River (Y68 to Y128, 1½ hours) between 6.40pm and 8.50pm. Boats leave from the **Tiānzì Pier** (Tiānzì Mǎtou; Map p534; Beijing Lu), just east of Hǎizhū Bridge (Hǎizhū Qiáo; catch metro line 2 from Hǎizhū Guǎngchǎng station), and head down the river as far as Èrshā Island (Èrshā Dǎo) before turning back.

OTHER ISLANDS

FREE **Whampoa Military Academy** MUSEUM

(黄埔军校; Huángpǔ Jūnxiào; ☎8820 3564; ⌚9am-5pm Tue-Sun) Day tripping on

Chángzhōu Island (长洲岛; Chángzhōu Dǎo) is simply fun. Apart from a dozen of relatively undisturbed villages, the highlight on this island is this academy. Established in 1924 by the Kuomintang, it trained a number of military elites for both the Kuomintang and the CCP who went on to fight in many subsequent conflicts and civil wars. It was destroyed by the Japanese in 1938 and the present structure was restored in 1965. Today the complex houses a museum dedicated to the military history of modern China.

Take metro line 2 to Chìgǎng station, then exit C1. Board bus 262 on Xingang Zhonglu to Xīnzhōu pier (新洲码头; Xīnzhōu Mǎtou). Ferries (Y1.50) to the academy depart every 40 minutes past the hour from 6.40am to 8.40pm. Private boats can also take you there; expect to pay Y15 for the whole trip. Taking photos on the ferry is strictly prohibited, as it passes through a naval base.

FREE Memorial Museum of Generalissimo Sun Yatsen's Mansion HISTORIC SITE
(孙中山大元帅府; Sūn Zhōngshān Dàyuánshuài Fǔ; Map p534; ☎8900 2276; www.dyshf.com; 18 Dongsha Jie Fangzhi Lu; ⏲9am-5pm Tue-Sun) In Hǎizhū district, this beautiful Victorian mansion was where Sun Yatsen lived when he established governments in the then Canton in 1917 and 1923. Take metro line 2 to Shì Ĕrgōng station (the Second Workers Cultural Palace), and then take a taxi (Y9).

Guǎngdōng Museum of Art MUSEUM
(广东美术馆; Guǎngdōng Měishùguǎn; ☎8735 1468; www.gdmoa.org; 38 Yanyu Lu; admission Y15; ⏲9am-5pm Tue-Sun) At the southern end of Èrshā Island (Èrshā Dǎo), and founded in 1997, the museum often shows exhibits of contemporary Chinese artists and has been the site of the Guǎngzhōu Triennale, first held in 2003. Take bus 12, 18 or 89.

Guǎngdōng Overseas Chinese Museum MUSEUM
(广东华侨博物馆; Guǎngdōng Huáqiáo Bówùguǎn; Yide Xilu) This new museum opposite Guǎngdōng Museum of Art should be open by press time.

Canton Tower TOWER
(广洲电视观光塔;Guǎngzhōu Diànshì Guānguāng Tǎ; Yuejiang Xilu) The world's tallest TV tower (610m) is in Hǎizhū, immediately opposite Zhujiang New Town. Facilities include a rooftop observation deck, revolving restaurants and 4D cinemas.

Festivals & Events

The 15-day **Canton Trade Fair** (Zhōngguó Chūkǒu Shāngpǐn Jiāoyì Huì; ☎2608 8888; www.cantonfair.org.cn) has been held twice yearly, usually in April and October, since 1957. Apart from the Spring Festival (Chinese New Year) in late January/early February, this is the biggest event in Guǎngzhōu. The fair is held in complexes on Pázhōu Island (Pázhōu) south of the river.

Sleeping

Guǎngzhōu's choices in the budget and lower midrange are dreary. For those who want to splurge, there are plenty of excellent top-end and upper midrange hotels. They're expensive, especially during the Canton Trade Fair (usually in April and October). All hotels offer in-room broadband internet access.

YUÈXIÙ & TIĀNHÉ DISTRICTS

Garden Hotel HOTEL $$$
(花园酒店; Huāyuán Jiǔdiàn; Map p534; ☎8333 8989; www.thegardenhotel.com.cn; 368 Huanshi Donglu; 环市东路368号; s & d US$160-260, discounts of 20-30%; ❄@≋) One of the most popular upmarket hotels in Guǎngzhōu with waterfalls and cheery gardens at the back and on the 4th floor. Rooms are as classy as its lobby. Advanced bookings essential.

Grant Hyatt Guǎngzhōu HOTEL $$$
(广州富力君悦大酒店; Guǎngzhōu Fùlì Jūnyuè Dàjiǔdiàn; Map p538; ☎8396 1234; www.guangzhou.grand.hyatt.com; 12 Zhujiang Xilu; 珠江西路12号; r from Y1300; ❄@≋) This five-star addition to the new financial district in Guǎngzhōu has sparkling rooms with king-size beds, and the clever use of mirrors and glass in the bathroom provides a very enjoyable shower experience.

7 Days Inn HOTEL $
(Qītiān Liánsuǒ Jiǔdiàn; Map p534; ☎8364 4488; fax 8364 4477; 32 Huale Lu; 华乐路32号; r Y147-228; ❄@) This chain hotel is the cheapest decent option amid the five-star enclave in Yuèxiù (越秀) district. It's behind the Garden Hotel.

Lilac International Suites HOTEL $$
(广州莱乐可国际公寓酒店; Láilèkě Guójì Gōngyù Jiǔdiàn; Map p538; ☎6131 6888; www.lilacsuites.com; 1 Taisheng Lu; 泰盛路1号; s & d Y580, discounts of 50-60%; ❄@) Uncluttered and stylish rooms can be found in this small hotel just three-minutes' walk from Guǎngzhōu

east train station. It's behind McDonald's and Starbucks. Take exit B from the Guǎngzhōu Dōngzhàn metro station.

SHĀMIÀN ISLAND & FĀNGCŪN DISTRICTS

Shāmiàn Island is by far the quietest and most attractive area to stay in Guǎngzhōu. The riverfront area in Fāngcūn is a bit out of the way, but the gigantic tea market and decent nightlife options make staying there less isolated.

White Swan Hotel HOTEL **$$$**
(白天鹅宾馆; Báitiān'é Bīnguǎn; Map p534; ☎8188 6968; www.whiteswanhotel.com; 1 Shamian Nanjie; 沙面南街1号; s & d Y1300-1500, ste from Y3100; ❄@) This huge property on Shāmiàn is considered the most prestigious hotel in Guǎngzhōu, complete with a waterfall in the lobby and fish ponds. Rooms are classic and the outdoor pool offers some fine river views. There are several excellent restaurants and bars.

Guǎngdōng Victory Hotel HOTEL **$$**
(胜利宾馆; Shènglì Bīnguǎn; Map p534; ☎8121 6688; www.vhotel.com; 53 & 54 Shamian Beijie; 沙面北街53 & 54号; r from Y320; ❄@) There are two branches of the Victory Hotel on Shāmiàn Island: an older one at 54 Shamian Beijie (enter from 10 Shamian Sijie), with adequate rooms starting from Y320; and a newer wing (胜利宾馆 (新楼)) at 52 Shamian Nanjie with better-value doubles costing between Y480 and Y800.

Guǎngzhōu Riverside International Youth Hostel HOSTEL **$**
(广州江畔国际青年旅舍; Guǎngzhōu Jiāngpàn Guójì Qīngnián Lǚshè; ☎2239 2500; fax 2239 2548; 15 Changdi Jie; 长堤街15号; dm Y50, s Y108-138, d Y148-198, ste Y268; @) We've received both complaints (about the hygiene) and recommendations (about the location) from readers about this HI-affiliated hostel in Guǎngzhōu. At the time of research it was under renovation, so hopefully there'll be improvements after it gets a facelift. It's located at the east end of Bái'étán Bar St (白鹅潭酒吧街; Bái'étán Jiǔbā) in Fāngcūn. Take metro line 1 to Fāngcūn station and exit B1. Turn right and walk through the back lane next to the hospital and you'll reach tree-lined Luju Lu (陆居路). Turn left and walk along the road until you see the river. Then turn right and it's another five-minute walk. Ferries also depart frequently from Huángshā pier on Shāmiàn Island to Fāngcūn pier right in front of the hostel.

Guǎngzhōu Youth Hostel HOSTEL **$**
(广东鹅潭宾馆; Guǎngdōng Étán Bīnguǎn; Map p534; ☎8121 8606; fax 8121 8298; 2 Shamian Sijie; 沙面四街2号; dm Y60, s & d Y200-260; @) For the cheapest beds on Shāmiàn Island, head to this nondescript hostel. Backpacker ambience is nonexistent, but rooms are moderately clean.

Eating

Guǎngzhōu has a gastronomic culture and legendary cuisine. Dim sum, or yum cha as it's called in these parts, is the heart of Cantonese cuisine. You'll find yum cha served in restaurants around the city. In the Xīguān district, there are many tiny eateries featuring some locally well-known *Xīguān xiǎochī* (西关小吃; snacks and dessert), where you can bump elbows with the locals. Moreover, the large population of traders, migrants and expats means there are also many other types of Chinese restaurants, and a fair share of good restaurants serving international cuisines.

TOP CHOICE **Bǐngshèng Restaurant** SEAFOOD **$$**
(炳胜海鲜酒家; Bǐngshèng Hǎixiān Jiǔjiā; Map p538; ☎3803 5888; 2 Xiancun Lu; dishes from Y38; ⏲11am-midnight) This exquisite Cantonese restaurant surprises us every time we visit, and the price is right! Shùndé (a town south of Guǎngzhōu) cuisine is the speciality here, where freshwater fish is prepared in many different ways. The *dòufuhuā zhēngxiègāo* (豆腐花蒸蟹羔; bean curd with crab roe) and *hǎilú cìshēn* (海鲈刺身; sea bass sashimi) are outstandingly tasty. Also try the *cuìpí chāshāo* (脆皮叉烧; crispy barbecued pork). It has a handful of branches in town but the newest one in Zhujiang New Town is by far the best. No English menu; grab a Chinese friend to communicate.

Pànxī Restaurant DIM SUM **$$**
(泮溪酒家; Pànxī Jiǔjiā; Map p534; ☎8172 1328; 151 Longjin Xilu; dishes from Y36; ⏲7.30am-midnight; 📖) Housed in a majestic garden, this ginormous restaurant serves some of the best dim sum in town. It's also one of the all-time favourites for the elders in Guǎngzhōu. Wake up early. It's impossible to get a table after 8.30am.

Wilber's EUROPEAN **$$$**
(Map p534; ☎3761 1101; 62 Zhusigang Ermalu; ⏲11am-4pm & 5-9pm; 📖) Hidden away on the edge of Yuèxiù district, Wilber's gets

top marks for atmosphere and the food is not far behind. It's housed in an elegantly restored colonial villa with whitewashed walls and a leafy patio. Beautiful urbanites love having an alfresco lunch or sundowners here, and Wilber's sometimes turns into an indoor, gay-friendly drinking den.

Nur Bostan UIGHUR $
(Map p538; 160 Tianhe Jijie; mains Y28; ⏲9am-1am; 📋) With a sizeable Muslim community in town, there's no shortage of places for halal food. Nur Bostan is by far the best Uighur restaurant in town, cooking the most authentic and uncompromising dishes – *polo, laghman* and Xīnjiāng-style pancakes with lamb. Kebabs are grilled outside in front of diners. It's located behind the T Mall.

Táo Táo Jū Restaurant CANTONESE $$
(陶陶居; Táotáojū Jiǔjiā; Map p534; ☎8139 6111; 20 Dishipu Lu; dishes from Y35; ⏲6.45am-midnight; 📋) Arguably the most famous yum cha restaurant in town, this place is always packed during lunch hours. It's a pain if you're indecisive – the menu covers over 200 items! Try the trademark *táotáo jiāngcōng jī* (陶陶姜葱鸡; ginger and onion chicken).

Dolci Vita ITALIAN $$$
(Map p534; ☎8121 5407; 1 Shamian Dajie; mains from Y64; ⏲11.30am-11.30pm; 📋) Housed in a delightful Victorian villa, Dolci Vita has an enviable location on Shāmiàn Island and is the place for a special night out. It serves a good range of Italian fare, and the wine list is excellent.

1920 Restaurant & Bar GERMAN $$
(Map p534; ☎8333 6156; 183 Yanjiang Xilu; mains from Y35; ⏲11am-2am; 📋) Guǎngzhōu's expats highly recommend this German restaurant on the riverfront. Enjoy an imported beer (from Y30) on its patio. The menu includes sausages, meatballs and stuffed goose.

Thài Zhēn Cow & Bridge THAI $
(泰珍牛桥; Tàizhēn Niúqiáo; Map p534; 54 Shamian Beijie; mains Y58-78; ⏲11am-11pm; 📋) For the best Thai fare in Guǎngzhōu, head to this bizarrely named restaurant on Shāmiàn. The menu boasts the most extensive choices of curries and the desserts are superb.

Lucy's WESTERN $
(Lùsī Jiǔbā Cāntīng; Map p534; 3 Shamian Nanjie; mains Y28-40; ⏲11am-2am; 📋) This is quite a humble place compared with its glamorous neighbours like Dolci Vita, but it's popular with Western carnivores seeking comfort food. It's located in a park on Shāmiàn, a good spot for people-watching.

Sultan TURKISH $
(Map p534; 367 Huanshi Donglu; mains Y30; ⏲11am-11pm; 📋) All the wonders of a Turkish kitchen can be found in this sumptuously decorated yet reasonably priced restaurant: lentil soup, lamb shish kebab, feta cheese and rice pudding. It's behind the Friendship Store and is frequented by Middle East businessmen.

Nánxìn DESSERTS $
(南信; Map p534; 47 Dishipu Lu; dessert Y7-15; ⏲10am-midnight) A specialist in *Xīguān xiǎochī*, this busy restaurant is a very popular pit stop for Cantonese desserts. Try the steamed egg whites with milk (双皮奶; *shuāngpínǎi*).

Wǔzhànjì CANTONESE $
(伍湛记; Map p534; cnr Longjin Donglu & Liwan Lu; dishes Y5-13; ⏲6am-1am) Guǎngzhōu dining at its most simple: shabby surroundings but excellent steamed rice-flour rolls and congee. *Yuānyāng chángfěn* (鸳鸯肠粉; pork and beef roll) is always the locals' favourite.

Foo Yau Yuan VEGETARIAN $
(佛有缘; Fó Yǒu Yuán; Map p534; Liwan Lu; dishes from Y18; ⏲7am-3pm & 5pm-10pm) An unpretentious vegetarian restaurant recommended by readers. It's hidden in the Xìngfǔ Xīncūn (幸福新村) residential quarter.

Drinking

Cafe culture is growing slowly in Guǎngzhōu. You'll find some passable cafes along the roads and alleys west of the Garden Hotel and chains sprouting in Zhujiang New Town. Guǎngzhōu has a number of international-style bars where, in addition to downing chilled Tsingtao and imported beers, you can scarf down pizza or burgers, rice or noodles. Watering holes include the bars on **Bái'étán Bar Street** (白鹅潭酒吧街; Bái'étán Jiǔbā Jiē) along the Pearl River, next to the Riverside International Youth Hostel. The **Overseas Chinese Village** (Map p534) on Heping Lu and nearby Huanshi Donglu has a string of bars catering to foreigners and trendy locals.

People's Cafe CAFE
(Map p534; 35 Jianshe Wumalu; coffee from Y22, sandwiches Y30; ⏲7.30am-midnight) This popular cafe run by two Korean sisters has had a very smart facelift after its relocation.

Best are the homemade pastries and tasty sandwiches. At night it turns into a cheerful drinking spot.

Ping Pong BAR

(☎2829 6302; 60 Xianlie Donghenglu; ⏰6pm-2am) This speakeasy-like bohemian watering hole hosts live music from time to time and offers a mix of theatre and exhibitions. It's hard to find, though. Flag down a taxi and tell the driver to drop you at the rear entrance of Xīnghǎi Conservatory (Xīnghǎi Yīnyuè Xuéyuàn Hòumén; 星海音乐学院后门). And make sure the driver isn't taking you to Xīnghǎi Concert Hall on Èrshā Island!

C Union BAR

(喜窝 (城市会); Xǐ Wō; ☎3584 0144; 115 Shuiyin Lu; ⏰7pm-2am) An unpretentious but very busy boozer, C Union attracts a good mix of local college students and expats with its live music, from R&B to reggae. It's behind the Chéngshìhuì (城市会) building. Only accessible by taxi.

Paddy Field IRISH PUB

(Map p534; Westin Hotel, 6 Linhe Zhonglu; ⏰6.30pm-3am) Frequented for its top-notch beer, this famous Irish pub cranks up on Thursday for its salsa party.

Elaine's Garden CAFE

(Map p538; 107 Huali Lu, Zhujiang New Town; coffee from Y35; ⏰11am-midnight) If you want to rest your legs after visiting Guǎngdōng's giant museum, head to this tiny but elegantly decorated cafe and wine bar for a peaceful afternoon retreat.

☆ Entertainment

Grab a copy of *That's PRD* (http://guangzhou.urbanatomy.com), a free monthly magazine providing invaluable information on the entertainment happening around town. It's available at most major hotels and international-style bars.

The nightlife in Guǎngzhōu is growing fast, with new clubs springing up everywhere. Venues change fast, so check *That's PRD* for the latest info.

Bound CLUB

(Map p534; 3th fl, 183 Yanjiang Lu; ⏰7pm-7am) The latest place to hit Guǎngzhōu's club scene, Bound is an all-in-one club that boasts a restaurant and a lounge on the rooftop with fabulous night views of the Zhūjiāng River. Below is the dance floor with DJs pumping out music, a mixture of mainstream rock and hip-hop. Average drink prices and usually rocks till dawn.

Grand House CLUB

(☎8732 0368; 38 Yanyu Lu; ⏰7.30pm-3am) As its name suggests, this place is just grand: plush leather seating, floor-to-ceiling glass and trippy LED lights. Music ranges from blues to dance beats. There are two dance floors and two garden lounges facing the Pearl River promenade. Events and theme parties are held every week. It's behind the Guǎngdōng Museum of Art on Èrshā Island.

Guangzhou Opera House THEATRE

(Guǎngzhōu Dàjùyuàn; Map p538; ☎400 880 8922; www.chgoh.org; 1 Zhujiang Xilu) This brand-new 1800-seat opera house in Zhujiang New Town is Guǎngdōng's premier performance venue and China's third-largest theatre. See the website for upcoming gigs.

Xīnghǎi Concert Hall THEATRE

(星海音乐厅; Xīnghǎi Yīnyuè Tīng; ☎8735 2766; 33 Qingbo Lu) Home to the Guǎngzhōu Symphony Orchestra, the city's venue for classical music is on Èrshā Island.

Shopping

As a major trading and manufacturing hub in southern China, Guǎngzhōu has an overwhelming variety of goods on the market, and almost each market or area has its speciality. Prices are reasonably cheap.

Fāngcūn Tea Market TEA

(芳村茶叶市场; Fāngcūn Cháyè Shìchǎng; Fangcun Dadao) Tea connoisseurs will not leave this market in Fāngcūn empty-handed. This is a sprawling market with block after block of tea shops/malls selling tea and teawares on Fangcun Dadao. Most target wholesale traders but retail is often possible. Take exit C at the Fāngcūn metro stop.

Xīguān Antique Street ANTIQUES

(Xīguān Gǔwán Chéng; Lizhiwan Lu) This street in the Xīguān area has shops selling everything from ceramic teapots to Tibetan rugs. Even if you're not interested in loading up your pack with ceramic vases, it's still a wonderful place to wander and browse.

Wende Lu ART

Fine-art enthusiasts shouldn't miss the less touristy but equally interesting Wende Lu, east of Beijing Lu. An array of shops and galleries abound along the road, selling calligraphy, paintings and antique books.

Shangxia Jiulu CLOTHING

Literally 'Up Down Nine Street', this pedestrianised shopping street in one of the oldest parts of the city, where the buildings retain elements of both Western and Chinese architecture, is a good place to look for discounted clothing.

Computer Markets ELECTRONICS

(天河电脑城; Tiānhé Diànnǎo Chéng; Map p538; Tianhe Lu) If you're interested in electronics, make sure to investigate the computer malls and markets at the east end of Tianhe Lu.

Newpage BOOKS

(外文书店; Wàiwén Shūdiàn; ☎3886 4208; 4th fl, Guangzhou Book Centre, 123 Tianhe Lu; ⏲9.30am-9.30pm) Pricey imported English magazines, novels and guidebooks.

Other popular spots for discounted clothing and other merchandise include **Hǎizhū Sq** (Hǎizhū Guǎngchǎng), accessible by metro line 2 to Haizhu Sq station, and **Beijing Lu**, a 300m pedestrianised street crammed full of shops big and small selling virtually everything imaginable, easily reachable from the Gōngyuán Qián metro stop.

Information

Good maps of Guǎngzhōu in both English and Chinese can be found at newsstands. Bookshops also have a variety of maps for sale.

Internet Access

Most hotels provide free broadband internet access (网吧) and all Starbucks in Guǎngzhōu have free wi-fi.

Internet Cafe (极速网吧; Jísù Wǎngbā; 603 Jiefang Beilu;Y5 per hour;⏲24hr)

Internet Resources

Life of Guangzhou (www.lifeofguangzhou.com) A yellow pages for visitors and expats in Guǎngzhōu.

Medical Services

Can-Am International Medical Centre (加美国际医疗中心; Jiāměi Guójì Yīliáo Zhōngxīn; ☎8387 9057; 5th fl, Garden Tower, Garden Hotel, 368 Huanshi Donglu) Has English-speaking doctors on staff but it's necessary to call first.

Guǎngzhōu Hospital of Traditional Chinese Medicine (广州中医院; Guǎngzhōu Zhōngyīyuàn; ☎8188 6504; 16 Zhuji Lu) Offers acupuncture, herbal medicine and other traditional Chinese remedies.

Guǎngzhōu No 1 People's Hospital (广州第一人民医院; Guǎngzhōu Dìyī Rénmín Yīyuàn; 1 Panfu Lu) Has a medical clinic for foreigners on the 1st floor of the complex.

Money

American Express Guǎngzhōu (美国运通广州; Měiguó Yùntōng Guǎngzhōu; ☎8331 1611; fax 8331 1616; room 806, 8th fl, Main Tower, Guǎngdōng International Hotel, 339 Huanshi Donglu; ⏲9am-5.30pm Mon-Fri) Can cash and sell Amex travellers cheques.

Bank of China (中国银行; Zhōngguó Yínháng; ☎8334 0998; 698 Renmin Beilu; ⏲9am-6pm Mon-Fri, to 4pm Sat & Sun) Most branches change travellers cheques.

Post

China Post (中国邮政; Zhōngguó Yóuzhèng; Huanshi Xilu; ⏲8am-8pm) Conveniently located next to the train station.

Public Security Bureau

PSB (公安局; Gōng'ānjú; ☎8311 5800/5808; 155 Jean Annul; ⏲8-11.30am & 2.30-5pm) Helps with all 'aliens' needs. Between Dade Lu and Darin Lu.

Telephone

China Telecom (中国电信; Zhōngguó Diànxìn; ☎1000; 196 Huanshi Xilu; ⏲8am-6pm) The main branch is opposite the train station on the eastern side of Renmin Beilu.

Travel Agencies

Most hotels offer travel services that, for a small charge, can help you book tickets and tours.

China Travel Service (CTS; 广州中国旅行社; Zhōngguó Lǚxíngshè; ☎8333 6888; 8 Qiaoguang Lu; ⏲8.30am-6pm Mon-Fri, 9am-5pm Sat & Sun) Located next to Hotel Landmark Canton (华厦大酒店; Huáxià Dàjiǔdiàn), it offers various tours and books tickets.

Getting There & Away

Air

The Civil Aviation Administration of China (CAAC; Zhōngguó Mínháng) is represented by **China Southern Airlines** (中国南方航空; CZ; Zhōngguó Nánfāng Hángkōng; ☎800 820 6666, 8612 0330; www.cs-air.com; 181 Huanshi Lu; ⏲24hr). The office is southeast of the main train station. For general flight information ring ☎95539.

China Southern has frequent flights to major cities in China, including Guìlín (Y660), Shànghǎi (Y1280) and Běijīng (Y1700). International destinations served by China Southern include Amsterdam, Bangkok, Ho Chi Minh City, Jakarta, Kuala Lumpur, Los Angeles, Melbourne, Osaka, Paris, Penang, Singapore and Sydney.

Foreign airline offices in Guǎngzhōu:

Japan Airlines (日本航空; Rìběn Hángkōng; ☎3877 3868; fax 3877 3967; room 4601, Citic Plaza, 233 Tianhe Beilu)

Singapore Airlines (☎8755 6300; fax 8755 5518; room 2701-04, Metro Plaza, 183-187 Tianhe Beilu)

Thai Airways International (☎8365 2333; fax 8365 2488; G3, Garden Hotel, 368 Huanshi Donglu)

United Airlines (☎8333 8989, ext 3165; G05, Garden Hotel, 368 Huanshi Donglu)

Vietnam Airlines (☎8386 7093, ext 10; M04, Attic, Garden Hotel, 368 Huanshi Donglu)

Bus

Guǎngzhōu has many long-distance bus stations with services to all parts of Guǎngdōng, southern Fújiàn, eastern Guǎngxī and further afield. All of the following stations have frequent buses to Fóshān (Y18, 45 minutes), Kāipíng (Y62, two hours), Shēnzhèn (Y65, two hours) and Zhūhǎi (Y85, 2½ hours).

Fāngcūn Passenger Station (Fāngcūn Kèyùnzhàn; Huadi Dadao) In Fāngcūn district; accessible by metro (Kēngkǒu station).

Guǎngzhōu Dōngzhàn Coach Station (广州东站客运站; Guǎngzhōu dōngzhàn kèyùnzhàn; Linhe Xilu) Behind Guǎngzhōu east train station. Good for destinations within Guǎngdōng; departures aren't as frequent as from other stations.

Guǎngdōng long-distance bus station (广东省汽车客运站; Guǎngdōng shěng qìchē kèyùnzhàn; Huanshi Xilu) To the right of the train station. There's a smaller long-distance bus station (Guǎngzhōu shìqìchēzhàn) over the footbridge.

Liúhuā bus station (流花车站; Liúhuā chēzhàn) Across Huanshi Xilu in front of the train station.

Other destinations from the long-distance bus stations:

Cháozhōu Y160 to Y180, six hours, five daily (9.20am, 11.20am, 3.20pm, 6.20pm and 10.10pm)

Guìlín Y170, 13 hours,six daily (9.10am, 11.15am, 1pm, 8.30pm, 9.30pm and 11.30pm)

Hǎikǒu Y190 to Y260, 16 hours, 10 daily

Nánníng Y180, 15 hours, 10 daily

Qīngyuǎn Y35, two hours, every 20 minutes

Shàntóu Y150 to Y180, six hours, every 30 minutes

Sháoguān Y65 to Y70, 3½ to four hours, every 45 minutes

Xiàmén Y200, 10 hours, seven daily

Zhàoqìng Y45, 1½ hours, every 15 minutes

The easiest way to get to Hong Kong is by the deluxe buses that ply the Guǎngzhōu–Shēnzhèn freeway. Most top-end hotels have tickets (Y100, Y250 to Hong Kong International Airport, three hours, every 30 to 60 minutes). Direct buses through Zhūhǎi to Macau (Y65, 2½ hours) leave from the Hotel Landmark Canton and Garden Hotel.

Train

Guǎngzhōu's three major train stations serve destinations all over China. CTS, next to the Hotel Landmark Canton, books train tickets up to five days in advance for a service charge of Y20.

Guǎngzhōu main train station (Guǎngzhōu zhàn; Huanshi Xilu) – the oldest train station – is a chaotic and seething mass of humanity. To get there, catch metro line 2 to Guǎngzhōu Huǒchēzhàn station. Slower trains from here:

Lhasa Y896, 54 hours, one daily (12.19pm)

Sháoguān Y52, 2½ hours, frequent services

Zhàoqìng Y29, two hours, 18 daily

All pricey, super-fast high-speed trains leave from the new **Guǎngzhōu south station** (Guǎngzhōu nánzhàn; Shibi, Pānyú) in outlying Pānyú. Destinations:

Chángshā Y333, two hours, frequent services

Qīngyuǎn Y40, 22 minutes, 14 daily (7.32am to 7.28pm)

Sháoguān Y110, 45 minutes, frequent services

Wǔhān Y333 to Y490, four hours, frequent services

There's a light rail link to Zhūhǎi and the high-speed service to Shēnzhèn north station (25 minutes). The most reliable way to get to this far-flung station is to take metro line 2. It's a 45-minute ride from stop in the main train station. Or take one of the **south station express buses** (南站快线; Nánzhàn Kuàixiàn; Y15) that leave from several locations in Guǎngzhōu, including the Liúhuā bus station, Garden Hotel and Hotel Landmark Canton; the trip takes approximately 50 minutes. Tickets for trains leaving from the south station can be bought in other stations, but not vice versa.

Guǎngzhōu east station (Guǎngzhōu dōngzhàn) also serves long-distance destinations:

Běijīng Y443, 21½ hours, two daily (3.08pm and 6.05pm)

Shànghǎi Y367, 17 hours, one daily (6.11pm)

The station is used more for the frequent bullet trains to Shēnzhèn (Y75 to Y80, one hour, 6.32am to 10.52pm) and a dozen direct trains to Hung Hom, Hong Kong (Y186, HK$190, 1¾ hours, 8.19am to 9.32pm).

The separate **ticketing booths** (⏲7.30am-9pm) for trains to Hong Kong are on the 2nd floor. Take metro line 1 to Guǎngzhōu Dōngzhàn station.

Getting Around

Greater Guǎngzhōu extends some 20km east to west and north to south. The metro is the speediest and cleanest way to get around.

To/From the Airport

Guǎngzhōu's **Báiyún International Airport** (Báiyún Guójì Jīchǎng; www.baiyunairport.com) is 28km north of the city. Airport shuttle buses (Y17 to Y28, one hour, every 15 to 30 minutes, 7am to 10pm) leave from a half-dozen locations in the city, including the China Southern Airlines office near the main train station; Tiānhé Dàshà (天河大厦), not far from the east station; and Fāngcūn bus station. A taxi to/from the airport will cost about Y140.

Metro line 3, linking the airport's south terminal (Airport South station; Jīcháng Nán) and Guǎngzhōu east station is finally in service. The ride will take 45 minutes (Y12).

Public Transport

Guǎngzhōu has a large network of motor buses and BRT (Y2 to Y5). Unfortunately, the network is overstretched and buses are usually overcrowded.

METRO

Depending on the line, the metro runs from about 6.20am to just before 11pm. Fares are Y2 to Y12. A better deal for getting around is to buy a transit pass (*yáng chéng tōng;* 羊城通), which can be bought from kiosks inside the metro stations. Passes start at Y50 and require a Y30 deposit, which can be refunded in designated metro stations, including Dōngshānkǒu and Gōngyuàn Qián. The pass can be used for all public transport, including yellow taxis.

Currently, Guǎngzhōu has eight metro lines in full service. Free maps are available at all stations.

Taxi

Taxis are abundant on the streets of Guǎngzhōu but demand is high, particularly during the peak hours from 8am to 9am, and at lunch and dinnertime. Most taxi drivers in Guǎngzhōu are migrant workers (ie they don't know the city well). If possible, try to flag down the rare yellow or red cabs, which are driven by local drivers.

The flag fall is Y7, with an additional Y1 for a fuel surcharge. A trip from the main train station to Shāmiàn Island should cost between Y15 and Y20; from Guǎngzhōu east train station to the island is Y50 to Y60.

Around Guǎngzhōu

WHITE CLOUD HILLS 白云山

The **White Cloud Hills** (Báiyún Shān; admission Y5), in the northern suburbs of Guǎngzhōu, are an adjunct of the **Dàyú Range** (大庾岭; Dàyú Lǐng). There are more than 30 peaks, which were once dotted with temples and monasteries. It's a good hike up to the top, a refreshing escape from the polluted city below. **Star Touching Peak** (摩星岭; Móxīng Lǐng), at 382m, is the highest point in the hills.

Take bus 24 from Zhongshan Wulu, just south of Rénmín Gōngyuán, and alight at the terminal. The trip takes between half an hour and one hour.

XIǍOZHŌU VILLAGE 小洲村

In the southern part of the island of Hǎizhū, some 20km south of Tiānhé, is this ancient **water village** (Xiǎozhōu Cūn), where local artists find solace and inspiration from its beautiful landscape. The village is threaded by tree-lined canals and stone bridges, and dotted with oyster-shell houses. Some villagers' ancestral homes have been converted to artists' studios and galleries. The artist community is growing gradually, and performances, exhibitions and film screenings are held here regularly.

Take the metro line 2 to Kecun station (exit D), then board bus 252 (eastbound) and ask to get off at Xiǎozhōu Zhàn (小洲站; 14 stops).

Fóshān 佛山

☎0757 / POP 5.9 MILLION

Day trippers from Guǎngzhōu can easily get to this city adjacent to the provincial capital in an hour-long bus ride. Fóshān (literally 'Buddha Hill') is renowned for its ceramics, and metal work since the Ming dynasty. Today, the city is better known as the birthplace of Wong Fei Hung, a beloved 19th-century martial artist and acupuncturist, later immortalised in movies, including Jet Li's *Once Upon a Time in China* series.

Sights

Zǔ Miào TAOIST TEMPLE

(祖庙; ☎8229 3723; 21 Zumiao Lu; admission Y20; ⏲8.30am-6pm) The number one attraction in Fóshān, and founded in the 11th century, this complex is the premier temple in Guǎngdōng dedicated to Beidi (Pak Tai in Cantonese), a Taoist god of the north. Significantly, it's where Cantonese opera originated. You'll see an imposing statue of Beidi in the main hall and a huge open stage in front of the hall, where opera performances are still held during festivals as an offering

THE MAKING OF A NATIONAL LEGEND

Fóshān-born Wong Fei Hung (1847–1924) is one of the best-known folk heroes in China. Although an outstanding kung fu master in his lifetime, he didn't become widely known until his life story was combined with fiction in countless movies from 1949 to the present – most made in Hong Kong – in which he was portrayed as an upright master fighting against villains and lately as a hero fighting 'foreign devils' in the late Qing era. Sadly, Wong spent his later years in desolation and poverty, after his son was murdered and his martial-arts school in what was then Canton was destroyed by fire. Regardless, an astonishing 106 movies (and counting!) have celebrated this famous son of Fóshān, resulting in the world's longest movie series and the making of a national legend.

Another Fóshān hero is Ip Man (1893–1972), who rose to fame as a Wing Chun (a form of martial arts for self-defence) master at the outset of WWII. He later fled to Hong Kong in 1949 and founded a martial-arts school, the first time Wing Chun was taught openly with a curriculum (before that, the skills and techniques were passed down orally). One of his most notable disciples was Bruce Lee, who ultimately made Wing Chun one of the most popular forms of kung fu all around the globe. Ip Man was recently immortalised by a series of semi-biographical movies and TV series. *Wing Chun Warrior* by Ken Ing is an entertaining read about the stories of this kung fu master and his followers.

to the god. Today, the complex has two exhibition halls dedicated to Fóshān-born Kung Fu masters, Ip Man (Bruce Lee's martial arts guru) and Wong Fei Hung. To get there from Zǔmiào bus station, turn left to the intersection with Zumiao Lu and left again. It's about a 15-minute walk.

FREE **Rénshòu Temple** BUDDHIST TEMPLE
(仁寿寺; Rénshòu Sì; ☎8225 3053; 9 Zumiao Lu; ⌚8am-5pm) A short walk north of Zǔ Miào Temple is this former Ming monastery, which remains an active place of worship today. Inside, you'll find a seven-storey pagoda built in 1656, as well as the **Fóshān Folk Arts Studio**, famous for its intricately beautiful paper cuts. Behind the temple is a good vegetarian **restaurant** (dishes Y18-30; ⌚11am-2.30pm & 5-8.30pm; 📷).

Liang's Garden GARDEN
(梁园; Liáng Yuán; ☎8224 1279; Songfeng Lu; admission Y10; ⌚8.30am-5.30pm) This garden complex with its tranquil lotus pond, willow-lined pathways and carefully arranged rock formations dates from the 19th century. The elegantly restored family residences are a delight to explore. From Rénshòu Temple, walk north until you see a branch of the Bank of China across the road. Liang's Garden is another 300m north of the bank.

Nánfēng Ancient Kiln CERAMICS
(南风古灶; Nánfēng Gǔzào; ☎8271 1798; 6 Gaomiao Lu, Shíwān; admission Y25; ⌚9am-5.30pm) The trip to Fóshān is not complete without a visit to Shíwān (石湾), 2km southwest of downtown, China's most important ceramics production centre. The highlight is this kiln, which contains two early Ming 'dragon kilns' that are more than 30m long. Signs (in English) explain the four-day process from clay to glazed pot.

Getting There & Around

Fóshān's **Zǔmiào bus station** (Zǔmiào chēzhàn; Jianxin Lu) runs buses to Guǎngzhōu's long-distance bus stations near the old train station, Guǎngfó bus station (Guǎngfó Qìchēzhàn; Zhongshan Balu) and Fāngcūn bus station in Kēngkǒu, every 20 minutes between 6.45am and 11pm. The bus fare is Y15.

Destinations served from Fóshān's **long-distance bus station** (Fóshān shěng qìchēzhàn; Fenjiang Beilu), 400m south of the train station:

Shēnzhèn Y90 to Y110, 2½ hours, every 20 minutes

Zhūhǎi Y50 to Y65, two hours, every 20 minutes

Trains between Fóshān and Guǎngzhōu (Y10 to Y17, 30 minutes, 18 daily) are faster than buses, but there are fewer daily departures. The metro also runs between Guǎngzhōu station and Fóshān's Zǔmiào station (aka Ancestral Temple Station). The journey takes 30 minutes (Y5). There's a direct express train to Hung Hom, Hong Kong (Y245, three hours), with a daily departure at 16.13pm (10.42pm from Kowloon).

Both bus 101 and 109 (Y2) link the train station to Zǔ Miào and Shíwān. Taxis start at Y7; a taxi to Shíwān will cost around Y10.

Kāipíng 开平

✆0750 / POP 680,000

The town centre of Kāipíng (Hoi Ping in Cantonese), 140km southwest of Guǎngzhōu, is sleepy and scruffy, but don't let that disappoint you. The World Heritage–listed *diāolóu* (碉楼), a very photogenic cluster of flamboyant fortified residences and watchtowers scattered across the 20km periphery of Kāipíng, are one of the most arresting man-made attractions in Guǎngdōng.

Displaying an eclectic mix of European architectural styles from Roman to rococo, the towers were built in the early 20th century by villagers who were 'sold' as coolies to California and Southeast Asia. Those who made a fortune brought home exotic architectural styles and built the towers as fortresses, not only to show off their wealth, but also to keep out bandits, and later to protect residents from Japanese troops. Out of the approximately 3000 original *diāolóu*, only 1833 remain. Each was built with sturdy walls, iron gates and ports for defence and observation.

Sights

A combo ticket to Lì Garden and the villages of Mǎjiànglóng and Zìlì costs Y110; if you just visit Lì Garden and either one of the villages, it costs Y90.

Zìlì HISTORIC VILLAGE

(自力村; Zìlì Cūn; ⌚8.30am-5.30pm) The must-see attraction in Kāipíng is the village of Zìlì, 11km west of Kāipíng, which boasts the largest collection of *diāolóu*. Fifteen towers rise beautifully amid the paddy fields but only three towers, built in the 1920s, are open to the public. The tallest, **Míngshí Lóu** (铭石楼), the shorter **Yèshēng Jūlú** (叶生居庐) and the poetically named **Yúnhuàn Lóu** (云幻楼; literally Mist and Mirage) were once the most prosperous homes of the Fang clan, who made a bundle in Malaya and Chicago. On top of the buildings are four towers known as 'swallow nests', each with embrasures, cobblestones and a water cannon, which was used against bandits.

Next to the village is the noteworthy **Fang Clan's Dēng Lóu** (方氏灯楼; admission free), a five-storey tower built in 1920 and called Light Tower because of its powerful searchlight.

Lì Garden HISTORIC SITE

(立园; Lì Yuán; ⌚8.30am-5.30pm) About a 15-minute taxi ride from Kāipíng, Lì Garden is a villa complex constructed in 1936 by a Chinese emigrant to the United States. While it has no *diāolóu,* the decor reflects the Italianate styles of that era. Most of the splendidly decorated buildings are open to the public.

Other smaller but historically important collections of *diāolóu* include the oldest tower, **Yínglóng Lóu** (迎龙楼; admission free) in Sānménlǐ Village (三门里), and the fortified houses in **Mǎjiànglóng Village** (马降龙; Mǎjiànglóng).

Ruìshí Lóu HISTORIC SITES

(瑞石楼; admission Y20; ⌚9am-5pm Sat & Sun) One of the most marvellous of the towers is located behind Jǐnjiānglǐ Village (锦江里), 20km south of Kāipíng. Built in 1923, the privately owned tower has nine storeys with a Byzantine-style roof and Roman dome supported by elaborately decorated walls and pillars.

In nearby Nánxìng Village, **Nánxìng Xié Lóu** (南兴斜楼; Leaning Tower; admission free) was built in 1903 and tilts severely to one side, with its central axis over 2m off-centre.

Chìkǎn HISTORIC VILLAGE

The charming old town of Chìkǎn (赤坎), 10km southwest of Kāipíng, has an array of quaint old buildings called *qílóu* (骑楼) straddling the Tánjiāng River (潭江). Distinctive for their pillars and enclosed balconies, they were built by overseas Cantonese merchants in the 1920s, and are reminiscent of bygone Canton. You can get there by bus 4 from opposite Chángshā bus station or bus 6 from Yìcí bus station. A taxi costs around Y26 one way.

Fēngcǎi Hall HISTORIC SITE

(风采堂; Fēngcǎi Táng; admission Y5; ⌚9am-4.30pm) Not a typical ancestral hall, this compound was built by the Yu clan in 1906. Its structure retains an exquisite southern Chinese architectural style, but Western elements are eccentrically blended in its decor. The complex consists of six courtyards and 15 halls, and is hidden in a high school 1.5km south of Chángshā bus station across the Tánjiāng River. Take bus 2 from either bus station and ask to get off at Fēngcǎi Zhōngxué (风采中学).

PIGLETS FOR SALE

The mid-19th century saw Guǎngdōng and parts of Fújiàn in a state of despair, stalked by famine and revolts. Meanwhile, slavery was outlawed in most Western countries, creating a need to recruit cheap manpower for the labour-intensive exploitation of the New World. Conditions were ripe for many unskilled workers from Táishān (where Kāipíng is located) and elsewhere to seek opportunities for a better life in Europe and its colonies.

Disingenuous recruiters promised good pay and working conditions, but in reality the workers were shipped all the way to North and South America, Australia and Southeast Asia, only to work like slaves. Many people died before even arriving at their destinations, packed like sardines in the indescribably inhumane onboard environment, which was later described as a 'floating hell'. Those who survived worked as coolies under miserable conditions on the sugarcane fields of South America, on farms in Southeast Asia, and in goldmining and rail construction in the United States and Canada. The coolie trade was known in Cantonese as *maai ju jai* – 'selling piglets'.

From the mid-19th to early 20th centuries, 'piglet centres' were widely established in Hong Kong and Macau to recruit labourers: some nine million Chinese workers left home. Some were not reunited with their families for 30 years, and others never had the chance to return home alive. Of those who survived, however, a handful made a fortune, becoming wealthy *huáqiáo*, or 'overseas Chinese'.

The *huáqiáo*, transformed from piglets into a powerful community, brought home wealth and exotic ideas that were assimilated into their culture. More importantly, they played a quiet yet vital role in subsequent uprisings led or instigated by Sun Yatsen, with significant financial contributions and political participation, which finally led to the fall of the Qing in 1911.

Sleeping & Eating

Day tripping from Guǎngzhōu is possible, but staying overnight in Kāipíng will allow you to see more.

Seven Continent Hotel HOTEL $
(七洲商务酒店; Qīzhōu Shāngwù Jiǔdiàn; ☎222 8777; fax 220 6378; 4-6 Musha Lu; 幕沙路4-6号; s Y159, d Y179-199; ❄@) A reasonable option opposite Chángshā bus station.

Pan Tower Hotel HOTEL $$
(潭江半岛酒店; Tánjiāng Bàndǎo Jiǔdiàn; ☎233 3333; www.pantowerhotel.com; 2 Zhongyin Lu; 中银路4-6号; r Y800, discounts of 50-60%; ❄@) *The* place to stay in Kāipíng, with an excellent Cantonese restaurant. It's on an islet on the Tánjiāng River and only accessible by taxi (Y10 from Chángshā bus station, five minutes).

Lì Garden boasts a huge alfresco restaurant to the right of the entrance. No English menu. Try the mushroom-and-eel studded claypot rice (黄鳝煲仔饭; *huángshàn bāozǎi fàn;* Y30), a local speciality in Kāipíng. In Zìlì, villagers serve homemade dishes with fresh ingredients in their homes.

Getting There & Around

Buses to Kāipíng from Guǎngzhōu's Guǎngfó bus station (Y58, two hours, every 30 minutes from 7am to 8.30pm) will drop you off at one of two bus stations: the bigger **Yìcí bus station** (义祠总站; Yìcí Zǒngzhàn; ☎221 3126; Mucun Lu) or the more convenient **Chángshā bus station** (长沙汽车站; Chángshā Qìchēzhàn; ☎233 3442; Musha Lu). Both stations run frequent buses to Guǎngzhōu (Y55 to Y60), Shēnzhèn (Y90, 2½ hours) and Zhūhǎi (Y52 to Y71, 2½ hours) between 6.20am and 7.30pm. Yìcí bus station also has buses to Hong Kong (HK$150, four hours, 9.15am, 2pm and 4.10pm). Local buses 7 and 13 link the two stations, or it's Y8 by taxi.

Opposite Chángshā station (or in front of KFC, if you prefer), you can switch to local buses (Y4 to Y5) that go to Chìkǎn and some of the towers. The *diāolóu* are scattered throughout several counties. If you want to see most, if not all, of the above-mentioned towers, your best bet would be to hire a taxi for the whole day. You'll find taxi drivers waiting in front of Chángshā station to take you around. A full day will cost around Y350, but you can negotiate this rate.

Zhàoqìng 肇庆

☎0758 / POP 3.9 MILLION

Right by the Xī River (Xī Jiāng), the sleepy town of Zhàoqìng in western Guǎngdōng is bordered by lakes and a series of limestone formations in the north. This was where Italian Jesuit priest Mateo Ricci first set foot in China in 1583.

Sights

Seven Star Crags Park PARK
(七星岩公园; Qīxīng Yán Gōngyuán; ☎230 2838; admission Y60; ⏲8am-5.30pm) The main attraction in town, with concealed caves and grottoes among the limestone hills. Willow and kapok trees line the paths around **Star Lake** (Xīng Hú). It's beautiful, though hardly worthy of the hefty admission price.

City Walls HISTORIC SITE
The oldest part of Zhàoqìng is surrounded by its old city walls (古城; *gǔ chéng*), complete with fortifications. **River View Tower** (阅江楼; Yuèjiāng Lóu; ☎2232968; Jiangbin Zhonglu; admission free; ⏲8.30am-4.30pm) to the southeast houses the Zhàoqìng Museum, with exhibits of ink stones and boring illustrations of Zhàoqìng's revolutionary history. To its northwest is the **Cloud-Draped Tower** (披云楼; Pīyún Lóu; Songcheng Xilu).

Chóngxǐ Pagoda MONUMENT
(崇禧塔; Chóngxǐ Tǎ; Guta Nanlu; admission Y5; ⏲8.30am-5pm) Facing the river is this nine-storey Song-style pagoda. From the top there are terrific views of the river.

Sleeping

Ming Tien Inn HOTEL $
(名典商旅酒店; Míngdiǎn Shānglǚ Jiǔdiàn; ☎229 3333; fax 229 3888; 13 Duanzhou Silu; 端州四路13号; d Y438-538, discounts of 50-60% ❄@) Next to the long-distance bus station. Rooms are gleaming and smartly designed.

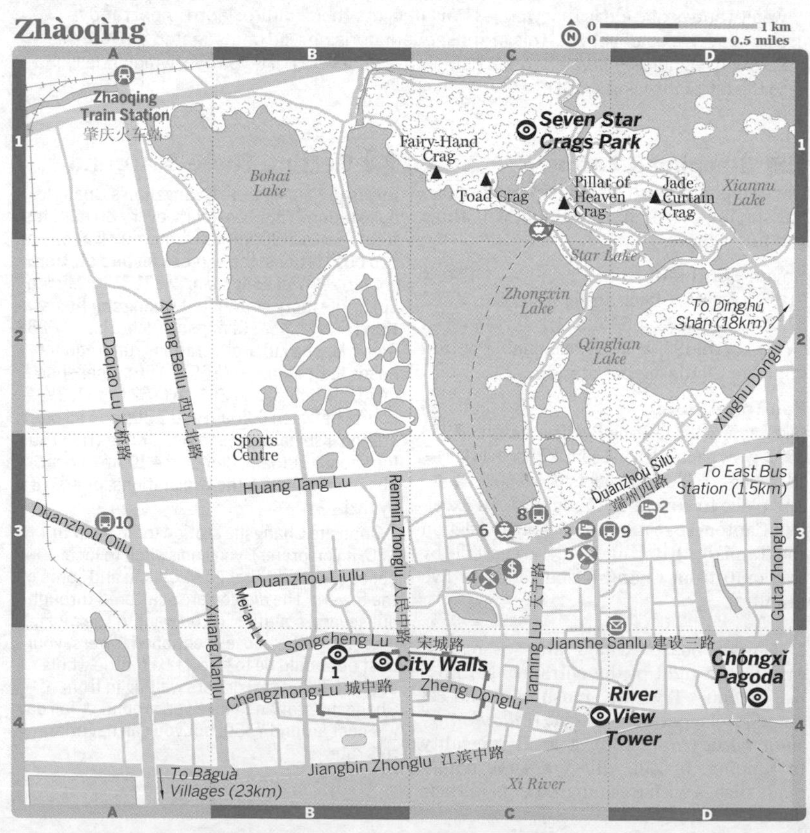

Star Lake Hotel HOTEL **$$**
(星湖大酒店; Xīnghú dàjiǔdiàn; ☎221 1138; www.starlakehotel.com; 37 Duanzhou Silu; 端州四路37号; d Y500-600, ste from Y880, discounts of 30%; ❄@) Housed in the tallest building in Zhàoqìng, this once clean but weary upper-range hotel had a complete facelift and should be ready to service by press time.

Eating

Glutinous rice dumplings (裹蒸粽; *guǒzhēngzòng*) are Zhàoqìng's culinary speciality. They're wrapped in bamboo leaves and may contain anything from peanuts to dried sausage and salted duck-egg yolk.

Seafood stalls fill the pavements of the northern stretch of **Wenming Lu** at night. Steamed Xī Jiāng *basa* fish (西江鮰鱼; Xījiāng Hānyú) is exceptionally delicious.

The restaurant in the **Dynasty Hotel** (皇朝酒店; Huángcháo Jiǔdiàn; ☎223 8238; 9 Duanzhou Wulu) is notable for its yum cha and other Cantonese specialities.

Information

Bank of China (中国银行; Zhōngguó Yínháng; Duanshou Wulu; ⏲9am-5pm Mon-Sat)

China Post (中国邮政; Zhōngguó Yóuzhèng; Jianshe Sanlu; ⏲9am-8pm)

Zhàoqìng

Top Sights

	Chóngxǐ Pagoda	D4
	City Walls	B4
	River View Tower	C4
	Seven Star Crags Park	C1

Sights

1	Cloud-Draped Tower	B4

Sleeping

2	Ming Tien Inn	D3
3	Star Lake Hotel	C3

Eating

4	Dynasty Hotel	C3
5	Restaurants & Food Stalls	C3

Transport

6	Boats to Seven Star Crags Park	C3
7	Ferry	C1
8	Local Bus Station (Buses to Dinghú Shan)	C3
9	Long-Distance Bus Station	D3
10	Qiaoxi Bus Station	A3

China Travel Service (CTS; 肇庆中国旅行社; Zhàoqìng Zhōngguó Lǚxíngshè; ☎226 8090; Duanzhou Wulu; ⏲8am-9pm)

Getting There & Away

Bus

Most destinations are served by the **long-distance bus station** (汽车客运总站; qìchē kèyùn zǒngzhàn; Duanzhou Silu), opposite the lake. Buses to Guǎngzhōu (Y46, 1½ hours), Shēnzhèn (Y100, three hours) and Zhūhǎi (Y75, four hours) are frequent. The bus to Guìlín (Y120, seven hours) in Guǎngxī province departs at 11.40am daily.

To catch a bus to Kāipíng (Y42, 2½ hours), head to the **east bus station** (城东客运站; Chèngdōng kèyùnzhàn; Duanzhou Sanlu), 1.5km east of the long-distance bus station.

Train

The fastest train to Guǎngzhōu (Y17 to Y36) takes two hours. Tickets booked at CTS or hotels include a Y10 service charge. A light rail linking Zhàoqìng to Guǎngzhōu (40 minutes) was scheduled for 2012.

The direct express train to Hung Hom, Hong Kong (HK$235, 4½ hours), departs at 3.10pm.

Getting Around

The **local bus station** (Duanzhou Silu) faces the lake just opposite Gateway Sq. Bus 12 links the train and long-distance bus stations with the ferry pier via the centre of town. A taxi to the train station from the centre costs about Y15.

Around Zhàoqìng

DǏNGHÚ SHĀN 鼎湖山

This 11.3-sq-km **reserve** (Mt Dingu; ☎0758-262 2510; 21 Paifang Lu; admission Y60), 18km northeast of Zhàoqìng, offers some good walks among lush vegetation, temples, waterfalls and pools.

Bǎodǐng Garden (宝鼎园; Bǎodǐng Yuán), at the reserve's northern edge, contains the **Nine Dragon Vessel** (Jiǔlóng Bǎodǐng), the world's largest *dǐng*, a ceremonial Chinese pot with two handles and three or four legs, unveiled for the millennium. A short distance to the southwest, a small boat (Y15) will ferry you to the tiny wooded island in **Dǐng Lake** (Dǐng Hú), where there's a butterfly preserve. **Qìngyún Temple** (庆云寺; Qìngyún Sì) is an enormous Buddhist complex of over 100 buildings. Don't miss the gilded statues of 500 Buddhist arhats (those who have achieved enlightenment and passed to nirvana at death), the rice pot capable of feeding 1000 people and the camellia planted in the central courtyard in 1685.

Bus 21 (Y4.50) goes to Dǐnghú Shān from the local bus station in Zhàoqìng. From the reserve's main entrance you can follow the main road north on foot or you can catch one of the electric carts (Y15) that make a loop around the reserve. A taxi from Zhàoqìng to the reserve will cost about Y60.

BĀGUÀ VILLAGES 八卦村

Two villages, exceptional for their shape and feng shui deployment, are not on the usual tourist trail but are great excursions from Zhàoqìng. Branded as Bāguà Cūn, **Líchá Cūn** (黎槎村; admission Y20; ⌚8.15am-5.30pm), 21km east of Zhàoqìng, is a 700-year-old octagonal village, built according to *bagua,* an octagonal symbol of Taoism that has eight trigrams representing changes in different phases of life. An aerial image of the village is displayed at the entrance. Houses radiate from a *taichi* (symbol of yin and yang in Taoism) on a central terrace, turning the village into a maze. Some houses here have the regionally distinctive 'wok-handle' roofs, symbolising wealth and status. Most villagers emigrated to Australia in the last decades and only the elders remain. Bus 315 (Y8, 40 minutes) goes to Líchá behind **Qiáoxī bus station** (Qiáoxī kèyùnzhàn; Duanzhou Qilu) in Zhàoqìng.

To the southeast of Zhàoqìng, **Xiǎngǎng Cūn** (蚬岗村) is another Ming-dynasty Bagua village. It's larger and livelier than Líchá, but villagers aren't used to outsiders, so expect curious eyes. There are 16 magnificently decorated ancestral halls, open only on the first and 15th days of the lunar months. Board bus 308 (Y9, one hour) at the Qiáoxī station in Zhàoqìng to get here.

Qīngyuǎn 清远

☎0763 / POP 3.9 MILLION

Sitting on the northern banks of the Běi River, the industrial town of Qīngyuǎn itself is not an obvious charmer, but this is where to set off for a sublime boat trip to the river valley surrounded by pine forests and deeply eroded canyons. The secluded temple in Fēilái and the monastery in Fēixiá, about 20km upstream from Qīngyuǎn, are the main attractions.

Boats leave from Qīngyuǎn's **Wǔyī dock** (五一码头; Wǔyī Mǎtóu), 15km east of town. The fixed rate is Y380, and the entire trip, from Fēilái onwards to Fēixiá and return, takes about four hours.

The first part of the trip takes you along the river past some mountain villages and ancient pagodas to the huge Buddhist temple complex of **Fēilái** (飞来; admission Y15), nestled at the foot of a steep mountain. Though Fēilái has been around for over 1400 years, the whole complex was destroyed by landslide in 1997 and subsequently rebuilt. The temple is serenely located in a pine forest; follow the narrow path through the forest to the mountaintop pavilion that offers terrific views of the river gorge below.

When your boat arrives at **Fēixiá** (飞霞; admission Y36), about 4km upstream, you'll be dropped off at stairs that lead upwards from the riverbank and onwards to the Taoist temple and monastery. To get to the temple, follow the stairs through the woods for about 20 minutes. Founded in the late 18th century, it's actually a complex of different halls, courtyards and pavilions connected by tree-lined paths. The imposing walls and mazes of dark corridors are both peaceful and spooky.

For accommodation, adjacent to the main bus station is **Royal Crown Hotel** (华冠大酒店; Huáguàn Dàjiǔdiàn; ☎387 8888; fax 387 8883; 8 Fengming Lu; 凤鸣路8号; d from Y288, discounts of 30-40%; ❄@), which has adequate rooms in a convenient location.

Fishermen at the dock serve meals on boats. Dinner for two, which includes freshly caught fish and wild vegetables, will cost about Y150.

ℹ Getting There & Around

It's possible to visit Fēilái and Fēixiá on a day trip from Guǎngzhōu if you catch one of the 10 high-speed trains from Guǎngzhōu south station that stop in Qīngyuǎn (Y40, 22 minutes). On arrival at Qīngyuǎn, it's just a 15-minute walk to Wǔyī dock (turn right once you leave the station).

Buses run about every 15 minutes from Guǎngzhōu's long-distance bus stations near the main train station (Y35, two hours) from 6.30am to 9pm. There are also buses from Shēnzhèn (Y95, three hours).

Qīngyuǎn's main bus station is about 4km south of the Běi River. Bus 9 (Y3, 35 minutes) links the main bus station to the train station, where you can walk to the dock. Alternatively, a taxi will cost around Y50.

Nánlǐng National Forest Park 南岭国家森林公园

☎0751 / POP 2000 / ELEV 1200M

Inhaled enough toxic fumes in the Pearl River Delta? Head north to Nánlǐng (Southern Mountains) to purify yourself. Lying 285km north of Guǎngzhōu, the Nánlǐng ranges stretch from Guǎngxī to Jiāngxī provinces, separating the Pearl River from the Yangzi River. The ranges in Guǎngdōng have been declared a **reserve** (Nánlǐng Guójiā Sēnlín Gōngyuán; ☎523 2038; www.eco-nanling.com; admission Y60; ⏲8am-6pm), preserving the old-growth blue pine forest. Though part of the forest was destroyed by a freak snowstorm in 2008, it still possesses its own beauty and offers some fine hikes.

Sights & Activities

Come here with your walking boots primed and ready for action. There are four trails, and most can be finished within two to three hours. The easiest is a 6km-long trail that follows a stream and leads you through **Water Valley** (亲水谷; Qīnshuǐgǔ), which includes verdant, steep-sided gorges and crystal-clear pools along the way.

A shorter but more interesting 3.5km trail will take you along a series of stunning **waterfalls** (瀑布长廊; Pùbù Chángláng). All along the trail you'll be spoiled by the sight, sound and feel of clear, cool mountain streams that tumble downward as frothy cascades and waterfalls.

The 12km-long trail to **Little Yellow Mountain** (小黄山; Xiǎo Huángshān) is a more challenging hike through an old-growth forest of endangered blue pines, a species unique to this part of Guǎngdōng. From the crest (1608m), the views of rolling mountain ranges are spectacular.

The longest (28km) and most difficult hike is the least-visited No 4 Trail (四号林道; Sìhào Líndào) to **Shíkēngkōng** (石坑空). At 1902m, Shíkēngkōng is the highest peak in Guǎngdōng and straddles the boundary between Guǎngdōng and Húnán.

The park entrance is at the southern end of the village of **Wúzhǐshān** (五指山), which is populated by forest rangers and small enough to cover on foot. Farmers from villages nearby do their weekly shopping and stock clearance at Wúzhǐshān's lively Sunday market. Staying in the Orange House in the village will allow you multiday access to the park. Keep the ticket and receipt, and get them stamped at the hotel.

From Wúzhǐshān it's another 6km drive or walk to the beginning of the trails to the waterfalls and Water Valley, and yet another 6km to Little Yellow Mountain. The best way is to hire a taxi from Wúzhǐshān. For between Y160 and Y200 you can hire a taxi for the whole day. Usually the driver will drop you at one end of the trail and wait for you at the other. A one-way trip to the lower entrance of the trail to Little Yellow Mountain is Y80.

No matter when you visit Nánlǐng, bring enough warm clothing, as the temperature drops dramatically at night on the mountain.

Sleeping & Eating

As camping inside the park is prohibited, the only option is to stay in Wúzhǐshān. There are a couple of *zhāodàisuǒs* (basic lodgings) where you can get a room from Y80. The campground next to the theatre/library not far from the Orange House hotel was closed at the time of research.

The market *(shìchǎng)* in the village has several food stalls where you can grab a bite.

Orange House BOUTIQUE HOTEL $$
(橙屋; Chéngwū; ☎523 2929; d Y398-489, discounts of 30-40% via www.ctrip.com; ❄@) *The* place to stay in Wúzhǐshān is the landmark Orange House, a refurbished, cheery boutique hotel with 32 comfortable rooms. Staff don't speak English. Advance booking is essential. The hotel also manages an air-con-free **Ranger House** (林舍; Línshè; tr Y198), equipped with eight spotless triple rooms right behind the Orange House.

Feng's Kitchen CANTONESE
(冯家菜; Féngjiācài; ☎523 2107) Mr Feng, a retired forest worker turned chef, serves delectable meals in his courtyard. Reservations are necessary.

Getting There & Away

Make your way to Sháoguān (韶关) before heading to Nánlǐng. High-speed trains (Y110, 45 minutes) leave from Guǎngzhōu south station for the new **Sháoguān train station** (韶关高铁站; Sháoguān Gāotiézhàn), 10km southwest of the east train station. From there, board bus 22 (terminating at the east train station) and ask the driver to drop you at **Xihe bus station** (西河汽车站; Xīhé Qìchēzhàn; Gongye Dong Lu). Buses to Wúzhǐshān (Y20, two hours) depart at 8.05am, 11.45am and 3.30pm daily.

Guǎngzhōu's main train station also has many northbound trains stopping over at **Sháoguān east station** (韶关东站; Sháoguān Dōngzhàn). They're cheaper but much slower (Y38 to Y58, 2½ hours). Buses to Wúzhǐshān leave from in front of the train station at 7.45am, 11.15am and 3.15pm.

Buses (Y70, four hours) leave Guǎngzhōu's long-distance bus stations for Sháoguān's Xihe bus station every 40 minutes between 6.50am and 8.30pm. If you miss the buses to Wúzhǐshān, don't despair. Catch a bus to Rǔyuán (乳源; Y10, one hour) that leaves from Xihe every 40 minutes. From Rǔyuán, three buses to Wúzhǐshān (Y10) leave at 9.05am, 12.45pm and 4.30pm, or you can hire a taxi (Y80 one way).

In Wúzhǐshān, buses to Sháoguān leave at 7.30am, 12.30pm and 3.30pm.

Shēnzhèn 深圳

0755 / POP 14 MILLION

China's wealthiest city and a 'Special Economic Zone' (SEZ), Shēnzhèn is the first port of call if you're coming from Hong Kong. The city draws a mix of businessmen, investors and migrant workers to its golden gates, all of them trying to find a place in China's economic miracle.

Shēnzhèn was no more than a backwater until it won the equivalent of the National Lottery and became a SEZ in 1980. Over the decades, developers have added a stock market, glistening skyscrapers and malls. Nowadays, there are debates of merging Shēnzhèn with Hong Kong, but this idea remains legally and politically infeasible.

Shēnzhèn used to be mostly about fake watches and handbags (and cheap massages). Recently, culture scenes are booming in the west of the city, making it a nicer place to explore than before. It's also a useful transport hub to other parts of China.

You can buy a five-day, Shēnzhèn-only visa (Y160 for most nationalities, Y469 for Brits; cash only) at the **Luóhú border** (Lo Wu; 9am-10.30pm), **Huángǎng** (9am-1pm & 2.30-5pm) and **Shékǒu** (8.45am-12.30pm &

Shēnzhèn

2.30-5.30pm). US citizens must buy a visa in advance in Macau or Hong Kong.

Sights

Shēnzhèn is known more for business than culture but finally there are some quality places to visit.

FREE **Shēnzhèn Museum** MUSEUM
(深圳博物馆新馆; Shēnzhèn Bówùguǎn Xīnguǎn; ☎8201 3036; www.shenzhenmuseum.com.cn; East Gate, Citizens' Centre, Fuzhong Sanlu, Futian; ⏲10am-6pm Tue-Sun) A good introduction to this incredible city is this hulking new complex. Through spectacular life-sized dioramas and massive interactive multimedia presentations, it showcases the city's short yet dynamic history of social transformation before and after Deng Xiaoping's policies of reform. Take metro line 4 to Shìmín Zhōngxīn station (Civic Centre Station), exit B.

FREE **OCT Contemporary Art Terminal** MUSEUM
(华侨城当代艺术中心; Huáqiáochéng Dāngdài Yìshù Zhōngxīn; ☎2691 1976; Enping Jie, Overseas Chinese Town; ⏲10am-5.30pm Tue-Sun) Out in 'Overseas Chinese Town' (OCT; Huáqiáochéng) this is an excellent museum with exhibits of international and local contemporary Chinese artists. The pub scene thrives here as well. To get there, take metro line 1 to Qiáochéng Dōng station, exit A. Turn right and walk 300m to the petrol station, then turn right again on Enping Jie.

Art Galleries GALLERIES
Just one metro stop from the Art Terminal are two galleries worth a visit. **He Xiangning Art Gallery** (何香凝美術館; Héxiāngníng Měishúguǎn; ☎2660 4540; www.hxnart.com; 9013 Shennan Lu; admission Y20, Fri free; ⏲10am-5.30pm Tue-Sun) has an esoteric collection of hybrid Japanese/Chinese water paintings by the legendary late master of modern Chinese art, He Xiangning. Pick up a pamphlet in English at the ticket office. Adjacent is the Water Cube–like **OCT Art & Design Gallery** (华美术馆; Huá Měishúguǎn; ☎3399 3111; www.oct-and.com; 9009 Shennan Lu; admission Y18; ⏲10am-5.30pm Tue-Sun), with a marvellous collection of works from mainland avant-garde designers. Take exit C from Huáqiáochéng station.

Window of the World PARK
(世界之窗; Shìjiè Zhīchuāng; ☎2660 8000; admission Y120; ⏲9am-10.30pm) Travellers with kids may consider visiting this theme park in the OCT, where diminutive famous monuments of the world are admired. This and other OCT theme parks can be reached by metro line 1 to the Window of the World station (Shìjiè Zhīchuāng Zhàn).

Shēnzhèn

Sleeping
1 Shangri-La Hotel.......B3

Eating
Laurel.......(see 7)
2 Laurel.......B3
3 Made in Kitchen.......B2
4 Muslim Hotel Restaurant.......D1

Entertainment
5 True Color.......B1

Shopping
6 Dōngmén Market.......B1
7 Luóhú Commercial City.......B4

Information
8 China Travel Service Shenzhen.......B1

Transport
9 Buses to Shékǒu.......B2
10 Local Bus Station.......B3
11 Local Minibuses.......B4
12 Luóhú Bus Station.......B3
13 Taxi Stands.......B3

Sleeping

Hotels in Shēnzhèn regularly slash up to 50% off the regular rack rates on weekdays, though you should always ask for a discount. This is also partially offset by the 10% or 15% tax/service charge levied by many hotels. All hotels provide in-room broadband.

Shēnzhèn Loft Youth Hostel HOSTEL $
(Shēnzhèn Qiáochéng Lǚyǒu Guójì Qīngnián Lǚshè; ☎8609 5773; www.yhachina.com; 3 Enping Jie, Huáqiáochéng; 华侨城恩平街3栋; dm Y60, d from Y148; ❄@) This HI hostel is the standard by which all hostels in China should be judged. It's located in the vibrant OCT Contemporary Art Terminal.

Shēnzhèn Vision Fashion Hotel BOUTIQUE HOTEL $$
(深圳视界风尚酒店; Shēnzhèn Shìjiè Fēngshàng Jiǔdiàn; ☎2558 2888; www.visionfashionhotel.com; 5018 Shennan Donglu; 深南东路5018号; d Y688-1880, discounts of 50-70%; ❄@) Inside a theatre complex is this new boutique hotel with many different interior designs

in its range of rooms. Some are chic, some bizarre. Its prime location and quiet environment make it very good value. Use Exit B of the Dàjùyuàn metro (Grand Theater Station).

Eating

With an influx of migrants, Shēnzhèn has an amazing culinary variety representing different styles of Chinese and international cuisines to soothe homesick bellies.

Laurel CANTONESE $$
(丹桂轩; Dānguì Xuān; meals Y50-180; ⏲7am-11pm) Century Plaza Hotel (☎8232 1888; 2nd fl, Century Plaza Hotel, 1 Chunfeng Lu); Luóhú (☎8232 3668; Shop 5010, 5th fl, Luóhú Commercial City) The main branch at the Century Plaza Hotel serves some of the best dim sum in town, though the Luóhú branch is a handy choice if you're shopping at Luóhú Commercial City.

Made in Kitchen FUSION $$
(厨房制造; Chúfáng Zhìzào; ☎8261 1639; 7th fl, Kingglory Plaza, 2028 Renmin Lu; appetisers Y8-88, mains Y48-208; ⏲9.30am-11.30pm) With a sleek ambience, this restaurant serves some of the best Asian fusion dishes. The menu is a feast for the eyes and palate, with over 400 diverse choices such as samosas, sashimi and steak.

Muslim Hotel Restaurant HALAL $
(穆斯林宾馆大餐馆; Mùsīlín Bīnguǎn Dàcānguǎn; ☎8225 9664; ground fl, Muslim Hotel, 2013 Wenjing Nanlu; dishes Y30-62; ⏲10am-11pm) Expect various beef and mutton dishes in this halal restaurant run by the Hui (Chinese Muslims). It's in a hotel done up like a mock mosque. Take minibus 430.

Drinking & Entertainment

There are a bunch of places around Citic City Plaza (中信城市广场; Zhōngxìn Chéngshì Guǎngchǎng) and COCO Park. Take the metro to Kēxué Guǎn (科学馆) and Gòuwù Gōngyuān (购物公园) respectively.

Hip cafes and pubs can also be found in the OCT Contemporary Art Terminal, including **Yīdù táng** (一渡堂; ☎8610 6046; Block F3, OCT-LOFT Art Terminal, Enping Lu, Huáqiáochéng; ⏲10am-2am), a warehouse turned Bohemian-style drinking haunt where rebellious local bands jam every night after 10pm.

Clubbers should check out the made-in-Shenzhen brand **True Color** (本色; Běnsè; ☎8230 1833; 4th fl, Golden World, 2001 Jiefang Lu; ⏲9am-1am), a long-time local favourite that attracts city slickers and trendy young adults alike with its watering-hole-plus-dance-floor formula.

And don't forget to pick up a free copy of *That's PRD* (http://shenzhen.urbanatomy.com) for a list of monthly events in the city, available in major hotels, bars and cafes.

Shopping

For many visitors to Shēnzhèn, shopping is a raison d'être. An invaluable book to guide you is *Shop in Shenzhen: An Insider's Guide* (HK$128/US$15) by Ellen McNally, available in bookshops throughout Hong Kong. You're guaranteed not to leave Shēnzhèn empty-handed, though the quality can vary.

Dàfēn Village PAINTINGS
You shouldn't miss Dàfēn Village (大芬村; Dàfēncūn) in Bùjí, Lónggǎng district. Even just walking around is an eye-opening experience. With 600 art-packed stores and 8000 skilled artists, this village generates thousands of freshly painted Van Goghs and any famous masterpiece you can imagine, every week. Bus 306 from Luóhú takes you to the village in an hour. A taxi ride costs around Y50.

Luóhú Commercial City MARKET
(罗湖商业城; Luóhú Shāngyè Chéng; ⏲6.30am-midnight) This overrated covered market greets visitors as they emerge from customs and immigration. You'll find five storeys of shopping insanity, with corridor after corridor of stalls selling knock-off handbags, clothing, wigs, knick-knacks, massages and DVDs.

Dōngmén Market MARKET
(东门市场; Dōngmén Shìchǎng) Another chaotic market popular for tailored suits and skirts, and cheap ready-to-wear clothes, with competitive prices. Be extremely careful of pickpockets. By metro, get off at Laojie station and leave from exit A.

Huáqiáng Běi ELECTRONICS
On the western edge of Luóhú district is Huáqiáng Běi (华强北), a living, breathing eBay for those on the hunt for electronics. The area abounds with blocks of buildings crammed with tiny booths selling the latest tech gadgets and computer components at rock-bottom prices. Take exit A at Huáqiánglù station.

Information

Bank of China (中国银行分行; Zhōngguó Yínháng; 2022 Jianshe Lu; ⌚8.30am-5pm Mon-Fri, 9am-4pm Sat & Sun)

China Post (中国邮政; Zhōngguó Yóuzhèng; 3040 Jianshe Lu; ⌚8am-8pm)

China Travel Service (CTS; 深圳中国旅行社; Zhōngguó Lǚxíngshè; ☎2519 2595; 3023 Renmin Nanlu; ⌚9am-6pm)

Great Land International Travel Service (巨邦国旅; Jùbāng Guóji Lǚxíngshè; ☎2515 5555; 3rd fl, Junting Hotel, 3085 Shennan Donglu; ⌚10am-6pm) Good for plane tickets.

HSBC (汇丰银行; Huìfēng Yínháng; ground fl, Shangri-La Hotel; 香格里拉大酒店; Xiānggélǐlā Dàjiǔdiàn, 1002 Jianshe Lu; ⌚9am-5pm Mon-Fri, 10am-6pm Sat)

Internet Cafe (网吧; 3023 Renmin Nanlu; Y5 per hour) Adjacent to CTS.

Public Security Bureau (PSB; 公安局; Gōng'ānjú; ☎2446 3999; 4018 Jiefang Lu)

SZ Party (www.shenzhenparty.com) For current events in Shēnzhèn.

Getting There & Away

Air

Shēnzhèn airport (Shēnzhèn Jīchǎng; ☎2777 6789; www.szairport.com) has flights to most major destinations around China.

Boat

Shékǒu port (☎2669 1213) runs ferries to several destinations. Ferry routes to Hong Kong:

Hong Kong International Airport Y260, 30 minutes, 14 daily (7.45am to 9pm)

Macau ferry pier in Central Y110, 50 minutes, six daily (7.45am, 10.15am, 11.45am, 2pm, 4.30pm & 7.15pm)

Tuen Mun Y38, 30 minutes, one daily (3.13pm)

Ferry routes to Macau:

Macau Ferry Terminal Y170, one hour, 10 daily (8.15am to 7.30pm)

Taipa Y170, 9.30am, one hour, two daily (12.15pm and 5.30pm)

Ferry routes to Zhūhǎi:

Jiuzhou Port Y95, one hour, every 30 minutes (7.30am to 8.30pm)

Fúyǒng ferry terminal (Fúyǒng kèyùnzhàn; ☎2345 5107) in Shēnzhèn airport runs ferries to Hong Kong and Macau:

Macau Ferry Terminal Y196, 70 minutes, six daily (8.45am to 5.30pm)

Skypier in Hong Kong Airport Y364, 40 minutes, six daily (8.30am to 6.30pm)

Bus

Regular intercity buses leave from **Luóhú bus station** (罗湖汽车站; Luóhú qìchēzhàn) under the shopping centre:

Cháozhōu Y150, 5½ hours, three daily (8.30am, 1.40pm and 8pm)

Guǎngzhōu Y60, two hours, every 10 minutes (6am to 10pm)

Shàntóu Y170, five hours, every 30 minutes (7.30am to 9.30pm)

Xiàmén Y240 to Y303, eight hours, six daily (9.30am, 11am, 7.30pm, 8.30pm, 9.30pm and 9.50pm)

Train

High-speed trains to Guǎngzhōu (25 minutes), Hángzhōu and Fúzhōu depart from the new Shenzhen North Station (深圳北站; Shēnzhèn Béizhàn) in Lónghuá, 16km northeast of Luóhú. They were scheduled to be in service by mid-2011. There are also frequent bullet trains (Y80 to Y100, 52 minutes) between Guǎngzhōu and Luóhú.

The MTR offers the most convenient transport to Shēnzhèn from Hong Kong (see p507).

Getting Around

To/From the Airport

Shēnzhèn's airport is 36km west of the city. A taxi from Lónghuá to the airport costs Y130 to Y150. Airport bus departures:

Huálián Hotel (华联大厦; Huálián Dàshà; Shennan Zhonglu) Y20, 40 minutes, every 20 minutes (6.20am to 9pm). Can be reached on bus 101 or Kēxué Guǎn metro Station (exit B2).

Shenzhen Train Station Y20, one hour, every 15 minutes (6.30am to 10pm) Buses leave from the local bus station east of the train station.

The metro spur line to the airport was expected to be completed by July 2011.

Public Transport

Shēnzhèn has two metro lines (tickets are Y2 to Y6). Line 1 (east–west) is the most useful for visitors, stretching from the Luóhú border crossing to Shenzhen University. Extensions to Shékǒu and the airport were to be completed by 2011. A south–north line serves Shenzhen North Station and Futian Port, where you can change to/from Lok Ma Chau station in Hong Kong.

Shēnzhèn has an efficient network of buses and minibuses (Y2 to Y4). From the train station bus 12 heads north, then west to Huáqiáng Běi, and bus 101 goes west to Window of the World. Bus 204 to Shékǒu leaves from a station north of the intersection of Jianshe Lu and Jiabin Lu.

Shēnzhèn Tōng (深圳通), a transit pass which can be bought in metro stations, is good for all public transports except taxis.

Taxi

The taxi flag fall is Y12.50 (Y16.10 from 11pm to 6am). It's then Y0.60 for every additional 250m.

Around Shēnzhèn

Visiting the timeless **Dàpéng Fortress** (大鹏所城; Dàpéng Sǔochéng; ☎0755-8431 5618; Dàpéng Town, Lónggǎng District; adult/student & senior Y20/10; ⏲10am-6pm) to the east of Shēnzhèn is a nice retreat from the teeming metropolis. This fortified town is best known as a key battle site in the Opium Wars of the 19th century. It's still a lively village with dwellings occupied by locals and migrants.

From Shēnzhèn, board bus 360 at Yínhú bus terminal (银湖汽车总站; Yínhú Qìchē Zǒngzhàn); buses 7 and 352 behind the train station will take you there. The journey takes about 90 minutes. Alight at Wángmǔ (王母) and change to minibus 966. It takes another 10 minutes to get to Dàpéng. Bus 360 runs until 7pm. A taxi from Luóhú costs Y170 (one way).

Zhūhǎi 珠海

☎0756 / POP 1.5 MILLION

Zhūhǎi, or Pearl Sea, is Shēnzhèn's little SEZ sister, and is close enough to Macau for a day trip. It's as laid-back as its neighbour Macau and has the fewest maniacal drivers in China.

Gǒngběi, which abuts the Macau border, to the south of the city, is the main tourist district, with lots of hotels, restaurants and shops. To the northeast is Jídà, the eastern part of which contains some large waterfront hotels and resorts as well as Jiǔzhōu Harbour (Jiǔzhōu Gǎng), where Hong Kong, Shēnzhèn and Guǎngdōng passenger ferries arrive and depart.

Visas (Y160 for most nationalities, Y469 for Brits) valid for three days are available at the border at 8.30am to 12.15pm, 1pm to

Zhūhǎi

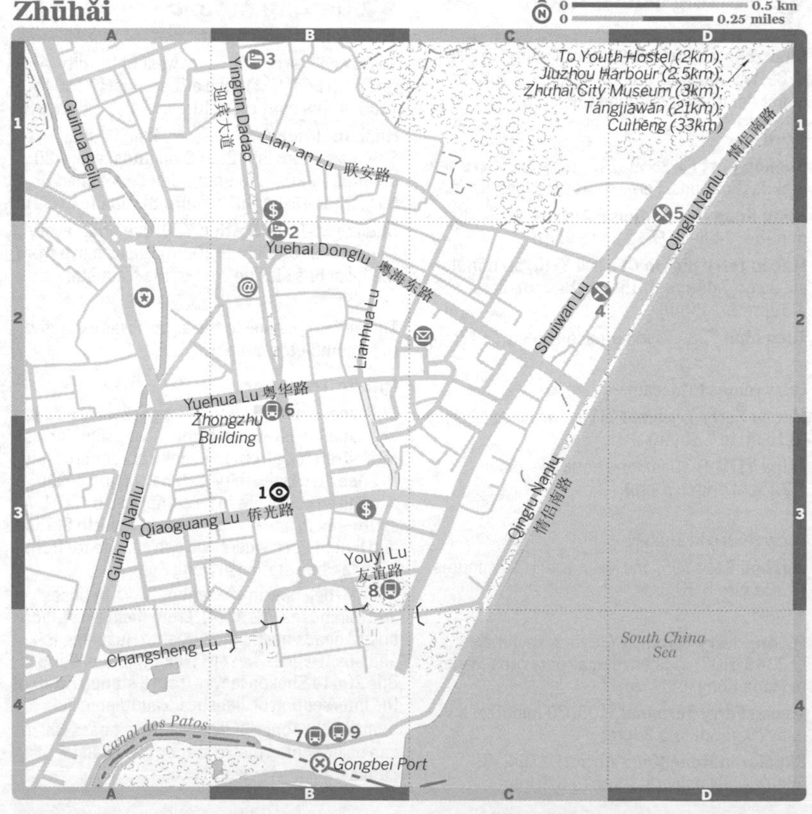

6.15pm and 7pm to 10.30pm. US citizens must buy a visa in advance in Macau or Hong Kong.

Sights

FREE **Zhūhǎi City Museum** MUSEUM
(珠海市博物馆; Zhūhǎishì Bówùguǎn; ☎332 4708; 191 Jingshan Lu; ⊙9am-5pm Tue-Sun) Downtown, the renovated City Museum in Jídà has 13 exhibition halls showing old photos of Zhūhǎi, as well as cannon batteries and stelae excavated around the city. The exhibits are not particularly attractive, but the meticulously arranged garden is charming amid the bustling downtown. From Gǒngběi take bus 2 on Yingbin Dadao. Bus 26 leaves from Jiǔzhoū Harbour.

Tángjiā Public Garden GARDEN
(唐家共乐园; Tángjiā Gònglèyuán; ☎338 8896; Eling, Tángjiāwān; adult/student Y10/5; ⊙8.30am-5.30pm) On the outskirts of Zhūhǎi are some lesser-known sites that have nonetheless played vital parts in Guǎngdōng history. To the north is the labyrinth-like Tángjiāwān (唐家湾), where this private estate of the first premier of the Republic of China, Tong Shaoyi, was created in 1900. Now it's a garden preserving various old-growth and rare species from south China.

FREE **Tángjiā Temple** BUDDHIST TEMPLE
(唐家三庙; Tángjiā Sānmiào; cnr Datong Lu & Xindizhi Jie, Tángjiāwān; ⊙8.30am-6pm) On your way to the Tángjiā Public Garden, detour to visit this 300-year-old temple. A highlight is the grim-looking Buddha statue brought from India when the temple was founded. Board bus 10 on Yingbin Dadao and alight at Tángjiā Market (Tángjiāshìchǎng).

Sleeping

There's little demand for budget accommodation as very few travellers stay in Zhūhǎi, apart from people on business.

Youth Hostel HOSTEL $
(国际青年学生旅馆; Guójì Qīngnián Xuéshēng Lǚguǎn; ☎7711 7712; www.zhuhai-holitel.com; 9 Shihua Donglu; 石花东路9号; dm Y60) Hidden away on the Zhūhǎi Holiday Resort (珠海度假村; Zhūhǎi Dùjiàcūn) grounds in Jídà, this hostel has two eight-bed dorms. Take bus 99 outside the Vanguard Department Store on Yingbin Dadao (eight stops).

Yindo Hotel HOTEL $$
(银都酒店; Yíndū Jiǔdiàn; ☎888 3388; fax 888 3311; cnr Yingbin Dadao & Yuehai Donglu; 迎宾大道与粤海东路交界; s & d Y860-1240, discounts of 40-50%; ❄@) A good-value midrange option very close to the border.

Eating & Drinking

The area of Gǒngběi near the Macau border has restaurants, bars and street hawkers. Night owls will find Zhuhai's nightlife passable, with a stack of pubs on Shuiwan Lu. Nearby, Lianhua Lu has a cluster of open bar booths straddling the road where drinks are cheap and streetwalkers rampant.

Rosa Chinensia DIM SUM $$
(月桂轩; Yuèguì Xuān; ☎818 3382; 2nd fl, 305 Qinglu Nanlu; dim sum Y8-28, dishes Y48-188; ⊙8am-5pm) If you can't get a table in Jīn Yuè Xuān, this is a good, affordable alternative. Apart from its many dim sum choices, it has a creative menu of Cantonese cuisine with a contemporary twist.

Jīn Yuè Xuān DIM SUM $$
(金悦轩; ☎813 3133; 1st-3rd fl, Block B, 265 Rihua Commercial Square, Qinglu Nanlu; meals Y100-130; ⊙9am-10pm) For the best dim sum and classic Cantonese cuisine in Zhūhǎi, head to this elegant restaurant well before 11am to score a table.

Information

Bank of China (中国银行; Zhōngguó Yínháng) Gǒngběi (cnr Yingbin Dadao & Yuehai Donglu; ⊙9am-5pm Mon-Fri, 10am-4pm Sat & Sun); Lianhua Lu (⊙8.30am-5pm Mon-Fri, 10am-4pm Sat & Sun)

China Post (中国邮政; Zhōngguó Yóuzhèng; 1041-1043 Yuehai Donglu; ⊙8am-8pm)

Zhūhǎi

Sights
1 Vanguard Department Store B3

Sleeping
2 Yindo Hotel B2
3 Zhuhai Overseas Chinese Hotel B1

Eating
4 Jin Yue Xuan C2
5 Rosa Chinensia D1

Transport
6 Airport Shuttle Bus B2
7 CTS Bus Station B4
8 Gongbei Long-Distance Bus Station B3
9 Kee Kwan Bus Station B4

China Travel Service (CTS; 中国旅行社; Zhōngguó Lǚxíngshè; ☎889 9072; 33 Yingbin Dadao; ⏰8am-8pm) Next door to the Zhūhǎi Overseas Chinese Hotel.

Internet Cafe (E-bar; E霸网吧; 1155 Yingbin Dadao; per hr Y5)

Public Security Bureau (PSB; 公安局; Gōng'ānjú; ☎864 2114; Guihua Nanlu, Gǒngběi)

Getting There & Away

Air

Zhūhǎi's airport serves various destinations in China, including Běijīng (Y1940), Shànghǎi (Y1400) and Chéngdū (Y1460).

Boat

Jetcats between Zhūhǎi and Hong Kong (Y165, 70 minutes) depart seven times a day between 8am and 5pm from **Jiǔzhōu Harbour** (九州港码头; Jiǔzhōu Gǎng Mǎtóu; ☎333 3359) for the China ferry terminal in Kowloon, and eight times a day from 9am to 9.30pm for the Macau ferry pier in Central.

A high-speed ferry operates between Jiǔzhōu Harbour and Shēnzhèn's port of Shékǒu (Y95, one hour). There are departures every half-hour between 8am and 9.30pm. They leave from Shékǒu every half-hour between 7.30am and 9.30pm. Local buses 3, 12, 25 and 26 all go to Jiǔzhōu Harbour.

Bus

Gǒngběi long-distance bus station (拱北长途汽车站; Gǒngběi chángtú qìchēzhàn; ☎888 5218; Youyi Lu), as well as **Kee Kwan bus station** (歧关汽车站; Qíguān Qìchēzhàn) and **CTS bus station** (中旅车站; Zhōnglǚ Chēzhàn), both below the shopping centre at Gǒngběi Port, are the most useful bus stations. All run regular buses between 6am and 10pm:

Fóshān Y90, three hours

Guǎngzhōu Y85, 2½ hours

Kāipíng Y80, 2½ hours

Shàntóu Y205 seven hours

Shēnzhèn Y100, 2½ hours

Zhàoqìng Y100, 4½ hours

Light Rail

A light rail that links Gǒngběi Port in Zhūhǎi to Guǎngzhōu south station (express train Y55, 29 minutes; regular train Y40, 75 minutes) is expected to be in service by mid-2011.

Getting Around

Zhūhǎi's airport is 43km southwest of the city. An airport shuttle bus (Y25) runs hourly between 6.30am and 9.30pm from outside the Zhōngzhū Building (Zhōngzhū Dàshà), on the corner of Yuehua Lu and Yingbin Dadao. A taxi costs about Y140. The light rail spur line from the city centre to the airport is scheduled to be completed by 2011.

Zhūhǎi has a clean, efficient and cheap bus system, with fares pegged at Y2.

Taxis have meters and the cost is Y10 for the first 3km, then Y0.60 for each additional 250m. To go from the Macau border to Jiǔzhōu Harbour costs around Y25.

Around Zhūhǎi

About 33km north of Zhūhǎi, the small village of **Cuìhēng** (翠亨) is a place of pilgrimage for Chinese of all political persuasions. This is the site of the **Dr Sun Yatsen Residence Memorial Museum** (孙中山故居纪念馆; Sūn Zhōngshān Gùjū Jìniànguǎn; ☎0760-550 1691; Cuiheng Dadao; admission free; ⏰9am-5pm), where the father of modern China was born in 1866 and returned to live with his parents for four years in 1892. The museum recreates the house (the original was torn down in 1913) where Sun grew up; the village compound includes a remarkable collection of furniture and objects from everyday life. Bilingual signs are available.

To reach the museum, board bus 10 from Yingbin Dadao in Zhūhǎi; alight at the terminus and change to bus 12. Or pay Y100 (one way) for a taxi from Gǒngběi.

Shàntóu 汕头

☎0754 / POP 4.9 MILLION

Shàntóu is seldom visited by travellers and it's extremely polluted, but you can use it as a base to explore some wonderful sights on its outskirts.

Most of the centre of Shàntóu lies on a peninsula, bordered to the south by the South China Sea and separated from the mainland to the west and north by a river and canals.

The people who live here and in Cháozhōu are largely Chiu Chow, and speak a dialect called Teochew (Chaoshan in Mandarin), which is completely different from Cantonese. It's the language of many of the Chinese who emigrated to Thailand and Cambodia.

A few old, derelict **colonial buildings** can be seen in the area bounded by Waima Lu, Minzu Lu and Shengping Lu.

History

As early as the 18th century, the East India Company had a station on an island outside the harbour of Shàntóu. By the mid-19th century it had grown into an important trading port known to the outside world as Swatow. The port was officially opened to foreign trade in 1860 under the Treaty of Tientsin, which ended the Second Opium War. Like Shēnzhèn and Zhūhǎi, Shàntóu was granted SEZ status in the 1980s.

Sleeping

Home Inn HOTEL $
(如家快捷酒店; Rújiā Kuàijié Jiǔdiàn; ☎8857 1588; fax 8856 0008; 88 Changping Lu; 长平路41号; d Y169-209, ❄@) The rooms in this chain hotel are cramped but clean. To get there, take buses 12, 24, 28 or 39 on Changping Lu (outside CTS bus station) and get off at Huìzhǎn Zhōngxīn (会展中心; five stops). Walk back 300m and look for a building brightly painted in yellow.

Meritus HOTEL $$
(汕头君华大酒店; Shàntóu Jūnhuá Dàjiǔdiàn; ☎8819 1188; www.meritusshantou.com; Jinsha Lu; 金沙东路; r Y1610-1840; ❄@) A favourite with business travellers, this is the best five-star place to stay in Shàntóu. Rates can drop as low as Y540. Free shuttles to the airport are available.

Eating

The Chiu Chow have a distinct cuisine that makes great use of seafood and accompanying sauces. A few specialities include *chiu jau lou sui ngoh* (潮州卤水鹅; Cháozhōu *lǔshuǐ'é;* Chiu Chow soy goose), *O luah* (蚝烙; *háolào;* oyster omelette) and *tong tso yi min* (糖醋伊面; *tángcù yīmiàn;* sweet-and-sour pan-fried egg noodles). And no meal is complete without thimble-sized cups of strong and bitter *gongfu cha,* a fermented oolong tea called Iron Bodhisattva.

Piāoxiāng Xiǎoshídiàn DUMPLINGS $
(☎8836 2960; 39 Guoping Lu; meals from Y15; ⌚7am-8pm) This Chiu Chow snack specialist is always a local favourite. Try the *O luah,* as well as different types of Chiu Chow dumplings, steamed or pan-fried. If your Chinese isn't up to it, let your fingers do the talking.

You can also sample the food in a frenetic **night market** (Fuping Lu) with an entire street of food stalls just west of Minzu Lu.

Information

Bank of China (Zhōngguó Yínháng; 98 Jinsha Lu; ⌚9am-5pm Mon-Fri)

China Post (中国邮政; Zhōngguó Yóuzhèng; Waima Lu; ⌚8am-6pm)

China Travel Service (CTS; 广州中国旅行社; Zhōngguó Lǚxíngshè; ☎863 6332; 41 Shanzhang Lu; ⌚8am-9.30pm) Bus and air tickets. Next to the Shàntóu Overseas Chinese Hotel.

Internet cafe (Lèfēi Wǎngbā; 乐飞网吧; Gongyuan Lu; per hr Y5; ⌚24hr)

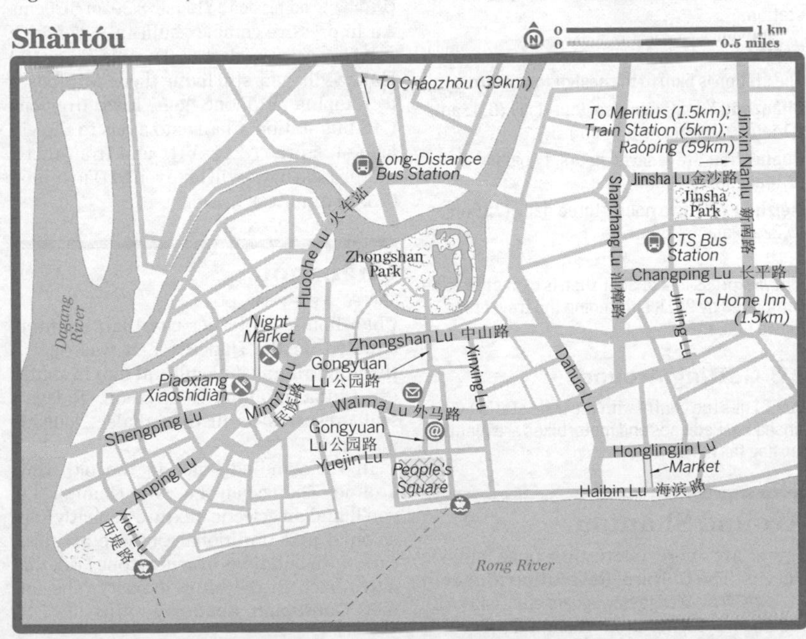

Getting There & Away

Air

Shàntóu airport, 13km northeast of the centre, has flights to Hong Kong (Y1290, three daily). Domestic destinations include Běijīng, Guǎngzhōu (Y660), Guìlín, Hǎikǒu, Nánjīng and Shànghǎi. From the airport, there's a shuttle bus to downtown (Y10) that meets every flight. A taxi costs about Y40 from the centre.

The existing airport will be closed by the end of 2011 and a new airport in Jiēyáng, 28km northwest of Shàntóu, will be in service.

Bus

Buses to Shàntóu will drop you at either the **central bus station** (Shàntóu zhōngxīngzhàn; Taishan Lu) next to the train station, the **long-distance bus station** (Shàntóu qìchē zǒngzhàn; Huoche Lu) or the more central **CTS bus station** (Zhōnglǔ Chēzhàn; cnr Shangzhang Lu & Changping Lu). All stations run regular buses:

Fúzhōu Y150, seven hours

Guǎngzhōu Y150, six hours

Shēnzhèn Y150, five hours

Xiàmén Y105, four hours

Buses to Hong Kong (Y200, six hours, 8.20am, 8.50am, 9.30am, 1pm and 2pm) leave from the CTS bus station, with tickets only available at the CTS. Minibuses to Cháozhōu (Y12, one hour) and Méizhōu (Y45, three hours) leave from a small office just south of the CTS station.

Train

The station is 5km to the east of the centre.

Cháozhōu Y8, 30 minutes, four daily (6.42am, 9.14am, 9.48am and 5.54pm)

Guǎngzhōu Y164, seven hours, two daily (9.14am and 9.48am)

Méizhōu Y29, two hours, three daily (7.15am, 10.22am and 6.26pm)

A new express link to Shēnzhèn is expected to be completed by 2011, shortening the travel time to two hours.

Getting Around

Bus 2 links the centre with the train station via Jinsha Lu. Pedicabs and motorbikes are plentiful; flag fall is Y5.

Around Shàntóu

Sights are more interesting once outside the city. The **Cultural Revolution Museum** (文革博物馆; Wēngé Bówùguǎn; admission Y10; ⌚9.30am-5.30pm), atop Tǎshān Park (塔山风景区; Tǎshānfēngjǐngqū) 25km north of the city centre, is a sobering reminder and so far the only museum in China honouring the victims of the revolution. Names, inscriptions and murals of the era are engraved on the walls, leaving many older-generation visitors in tears. There are no English explanations. To get there, take bus 18 on Jinsha Lu (Y6, eastbound) and get off at Túchéng Tǎshān (涂城塔山), or take bus 102 outside the long-distance bus station and get off at Tǎshān Lùkǒu (塔山路口). After this 45-minute bus ride, cross the road and walk another 800m to the entrance. There's another 2km walk uphill (take the path on the left).

Midway between Cháozhōu and Shàntóu you'll find **Chen Cihong Memorial Home** (陈慈黉故居; Chén Cíhóng Gùjū; admission Y16; ⌚8am-5.30pm), a residence of a wealthy Chinese businessman who made his fortune in the rice trade in Hong Kong and Thailand in the 19th century. The huge complex is an eccentric but aesthetically pleasing mix and match of Western architecture and Chinese feng shui. Board bus 103 from the east side of People's Sq in Shàntóu to get there.

Located in Raópíng (饶平), 59km northeast of Shàntóu, is China's largest octagonal-shaped Hakka adobe house, **Dàoyùnlóu** (道韵楼; admission Y10; ⌚8.30am-5.30pm). An impressive complex built in 1587 which used to accommodate 600 people, it has 100 Hakka villagers still living there. Minibuses to Raópíng (Y13, one hour) leave from the CTS bus station. Change to a bus to the village of Sānráo (三饶; Y11), and from there, motor-rickshaws will take you to Dàoyùnlóu (Y5, 10 minutes).

Cháozhōu 潮州

☎0768 / POP 2.5 MILLION

Cháozhōu is a prettier city than Shàntóu, situated on the Hán River. It was once a thriving trading and cultural hub in southern China, rivalling Guǎngzhōu. Today, it still preserves its distinct dialect, cuisine and opera.

In the winding lanes in the old town around Zhongshan Lu and Changli Lu, you'll find an eclectic mixture of neatly kept colonial and traditional Chinese architecture, with buildings bearing stonework that dates back to the Ming dynasty. The former **Confucian Academy** (海阳县儒学宫;

Hǎiyángxiàn Rúxué Gōng; Changli Lu; admission Y4; ⏲8am-5pm) is a good place to orientate yourself before setting off.

Kāiyuán Temple BUDDHIST TEMPLE
(开元寺; Kāiyuán Sì; admission Y5; ⏲6am-5pm) Cháozhōu's most famous attraction is this active temple. Built in AD 738, the temple was recently renovated to house more arhats, including a huge 1000-arm Guanyin.

City Wall HISTORIC SITE
The ramparts of Cháozhōu's old city wall (古城; *gǔ chéng*) offer great views of the city, running along the river for almost 2.5km and interrupted by four ornate fortifications, including **Guǎngjì Gate Tower** (广济门楼; Guǎngjì Ménlóu; admission Y10; ⏲9am-5.20pm), which displays the history of the construction of Guǎngjì Bridge.

Jao Tsung I Petite Ecole MUSEUM
(饶宗颐学术馆; Ráozōngyí Xuéshùguǎn; admission Y10; ⏲9am-5pm) Opposite the Xiàshuǐ Gate Tower (Xiàshuǐ Ménlóu) is this museum and exquisite Cháozhōu-style garden dedicated to the Sinologist Jao Tsung I.

Hánwén Temple TEMPLE
(韩文公祠; Hánwéngōng Cí; admission Y5) On the east bank of the Han, this temple commemorates the Tang-dynasty poet and philosopher Han Yu, who was banished to 'far-flung' Guǎngdōng for his outspoken views against Buddhism.

Sleeping & Eating

Cháozhōu is best visited as a day trip from Shàntóu. If you do decide to stay overnight, there are a few options.

Cháozhōu Hotel HOTEL $$$
(潮州宾馆; Cháozhōu Bīnguǎn; ☎233 3333; www.chaozhouhotel.com; cnr Chaofeng Lu & Yonghu Lu; 潮枫路与永护路交界; s/d Y618/718, discounts of 50%; ❄@) A couple of hundred yuan more will allow you more comfort in the elegantly decorated rooms of this hotel.

Home Inn HOTEL $
(如家快捷酒店; Rújiā Kuàijié Jiǔdiàn; ☎232 5666; fax 228 5595; 188 Kaiyuan Lu; 开元路188号; r Y139-179; ❄@) Behind KFC, this is the best budget option in town and should accept foreigners by press time.

Cháozhōu has a collection of eateries in the old town where you can try some local Chiu Chow dishes. Some superb dishes to try include steamed crab (清蒸蟹; Qīngzhēngxiè) and fish balls in soup (鱼丸汤; Yúwántāng). For snacks, make sure to head to the hole-in-the-wall **Hú Róng Quán** (胡荣泉; Taiping Lu; ⏲8am-late), a short walk north from Kāiyuán Temple. Moon cakes and the gooey lotus-paste buns are the top items here.

Getting There & Away

Buses link Cháozhōu's west bus station with Shàntóu (Y12, one hour). Buses also depart from here for Guǎngzhōu (Y178, 5½ hours), Méizhōu (Y50, two hours), Shēnzhèn (Y170, 4½ hours) and Xiàmén (Y80 to Y120, 3½ hours).

Cháozhōu's train station is 8km west of the centre; there are two trains a day to Guǎngzhōu (Y137 to Y167, 6½ hours), leaving at 9.47am and 10.22am. A taxi to the station costs Y15.

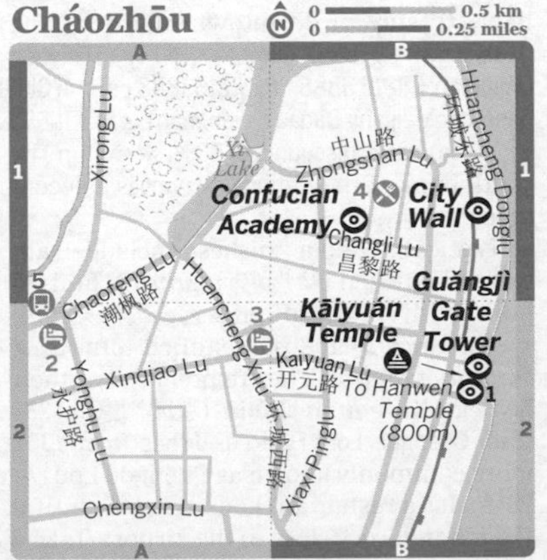

Cháozhōu

Top Sights

City Wall	B1
Confucian Academy	B1
Guǎngjì Gate Tower	B2
Kāiyuán Temple	B2

Sights

1 Jao Tsung I Petite Ecole	B2

Sleeping

2 Cháozhōu Hotel	A2
3 Home Inn	A2

Eating

4 Hú Róng Quán	B1

Transport

5 West Bus Station	A1

Méizhōu 梅州

☎0753 / POP 5 MILLION

Unlike its neighbour in Yǒngdìng County, across the border in Fújiàn province, Méizhōu, also populated by the Hakka (Kèjiā in Mandarin; 客家) people and with a landscape dotted by *tǔlóu* (roundhouses), is never in the spotlight. But the relative lack of tourism has preserved its character, one made even more unique by its overseas Hakka, who brought home exotic architectural ideas in the early 20th century. In addition to the earthy *tǔlóu,* you'll see a jumble of architectural wonders in different Hakka villages.

Sights

FREE **Hakka Museum** MUSEUM
(客家博物馆; Kèjiā Bówùguǎn; Dongshan Dadao; ⏲9am-5pm) Méizhōu, divided by Méijiāng River, is a manageable city and this museum in the Hakka Park (客家公园; Kèjiā Gōngyuán) on the north bank is a good warm-up to the culture of this Hakkaland. Bus 1 from Jiangnan Lu (eastbound) and bus 6 from the train station stop there.

Nánkǒu HISTORIC SITES
About 16km west of Méizhōu is the idyllic village of Nánkǒu (南口) , populated by the Pan clan who made a bundle in Indonesia and Hong Kong more than 100 years ago. The most eye-catching edifice here is **Nánhuá Yòulú** (南华又庐; admission Y5), built in 1904. The 118 rooms and nine wells are symmetrically arranged, and roofs are decorated with elaborated ornamentations. Next to it is the **Huànyún Lóu** (焕云楼), built in the same era with sturdy concrete (a symbol of wealth). The building was embellished with baroque decor and Doric columns. Although dilapidated, it still preserves a fading charm.

You'll also find a cluster of *Wéilóngwū,* the horse hoof-shaped *tǔlóu,* dotting the paddy fields in this village. The best-kept one is **Pan's ancestral house** (潘氏祖屋; Pānshì Zǔwū).

Getting to Nánkǒu is pretty straightforward. Take bus 9 from the **local bus terminal** (市公共汽车总站; Shì Gōnggòng Qìchēzhàn; cnr Meijiang Dadao & Xinzhong Lu), 1.5km south of the Tiányuán Hotel. Buses to Xìngníng (兴宁; Y10, every 20 minutes) that leave from the main bus station also pass through Nánkǒu. Once you get off, walk 1km further to the entrance of the village. Look for the Chinglish sign 'Qiao Xiang Cun Tourist Professional Village' on your left. The last bus back to Méizhōu is at 4.30pm. A taxi ride costs around Y30.

Liánfāng Lóu HISTORIC SITE
(联芳楼; admission Y5) Hidden in a village near the town of Báigōng, 14km east of Méizhōu, this magnificent mansion was previously owned by an Indonesian Hakka family in the 1930s. There are 98 rooms altogether, symmetrically arranged. Three balconies are flamboyantly decorated with mythical creatures from both the East and the West, complete with domes on the roofs.

Tài'ān Lóu HISTORIC SITE
(泰安楼; admission Y20) Further afield in Dàpu County (大埔), 70km east, this three-storey structure isn't a typical *tǔlóu.* First, it's square, and second, it's fortified by stone walls. Built in 1764, this stony dwelling boasts 200 rooms and 40 kitchens. It used to be home to 380 households, but now only eight families still live here.

Huā'è Lóu HISTORIC SITE
(花萼楼; admission Y40) The 400-year-old 'house of calyx', another 33km east, is the largest circular earthen castle in Guǎngdōng, complete with three rings. Interestingly, remnants of propaganda slogans of the Cultural Revolution are plentiful in this village.

If time allows, make a detour to the picturesque **terraced rape fields** in Píngshān Village (坪山村梯田; Píngshāncūn Tītián). It's a 30-minute ride to the northeast from Huā'è Lóu.

Sleeping & Eating

As the *tǔlóu* in this part of China are not ready to accommodate tourists yet, you're likely to stay in downtown Méizhōu. The **Tiányuán Hotel** (田园大酒店; Tiányuán Dàjiǔdiàn; ☎216 3888; www.2163888.com, in Chinese; cnr Meijiang Dadao & Jiangnan Lu; 江南路35号; r from Y368, discounts of 50%; ❄@), on the south bank of the Méjiāng River, is a decent place to stay.

Typtical Hakka dishes include salt-roasted chicken (盐焗鸡; *yánjú jī*), braised pork with mustard preserves (梅菜扣肉; *mécài kòuròu*) and pork-stuffed tofu (酿豆腐; *niàng dòufu*). They're prepared at their best at **Xīngyuán Jiǔjiā** (星园酒家; ☎233 1315; Chengde Lou, Fuqi Lu; dishes from Y30), more commonly known as Chéngdé Lóu (承德楼). It's a restaurant housed in a beautiful *Wéilóngwū* very close to the airport. Take a taxi (Y10) or a motor rickshaw (Y6) to get there from the city centre.

In the **Culture Park** (文化公园; Wénhuà Gōngyuán; Gongyuan Lu) on the north bank, the **night market** gets into full swing after 7.30pm.

Getting There & Away

Air

Méizhōu's airport is just 9km south of town. Guangzhou (Y700) and Hong Kong (Y1108; Mondays and Fridays) are the only destinations it serves. A taxi ride to the airport costs around Y15.

Bus

There are two bus stations: the **main bus station** (汽车总站; qìchē zǒngzhàn; Meizhou Dadao) north of the river and **Jiāngnán bus station** (江南汽车站; Jiángnán qìchēzhàn; Binfang Dadao) to the south. Most buses to Méizhōu will drop you at the main station, but don't be surprised if they don't.

Guǎngzhōu Y100, seven hours, 16 daily

Hong Kong Y120, six hours, three daily (8am, 11am and 3pm)

Shàntóu Y50 to Y56, three hours, hourly (9am to 9pm)

Shēnzhèn Y29, two hours, three daily (7.15am, 10.22am & 6.26pm)

Yǒngdìng Y40, three hours, two daily (6.30am & 4pm)

Train

The train station is located south of the town not far from the airport. There are three daily trains to Guǎngzhōu (Y118; 12.56am, 1.12am and 12.38pm) and Yǒngdīng (Y16; 12.43am, 1.04am and 3.01am).

Getting Around

Local bus 6 links the train station to both bus stations. Taxis in Méizhōu are cheap – anywhere within the city centre costs no more than Y10.

Apart from Nánkǒu, all of the above-mentioned sights are scattered in different villages and almost inaccessible by public transport. It makes more sense to hire a taxi for a day. Expect to pay Y300.

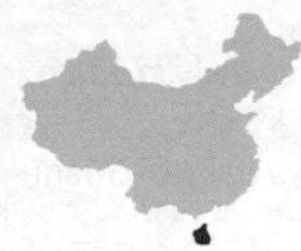

Hǎinán

POPULATION: 8.2 MILLION

Includes »

Best Places to Eat

» Áozhuāng Hǎixiān Chéng (p577)

» Holiday Inn of Jadeite Mountain City Restaurant (p574)

» Folk Jar Restaurant (p570)

» Pattaya Thai Cuisine (p580)

Best Places to Stay

» Bó'áo Inn (p576)

» Sunny Sanya Family Inn (p580)

» Resort InTime (p580)

» Sānyà Backpackers (p580)

Why Go?

China's largest tropical island boasts all the balmy weather, coconut palms and gold-sand beaches you could ask for. Down at Sānyà it's see-and-be-seen on the boardwalks or escape altogether at some of Asia's top luxury resorts. Thatched huts and banana pancakes haven't popped up anywhere yet, but there's a whiff of funkiness coming from the East Coast beachside towns, and the budding surf scene is helping to spread the gospel of chill-out.

Money's pouring into Hǎinán (海南) these days to ramp up the luxury quotient, and you can cruise on the new high-speed rail, but cycling is still the better way to get around. When you've had enough of a lathering on the coast, the cool central highlands are an ideal place to be on two wheels. The good roads, knockout mountain views, and concentration of Li and Miao, the island's first settlers, give the region an appealing distinction from the lowlands.

When to Go

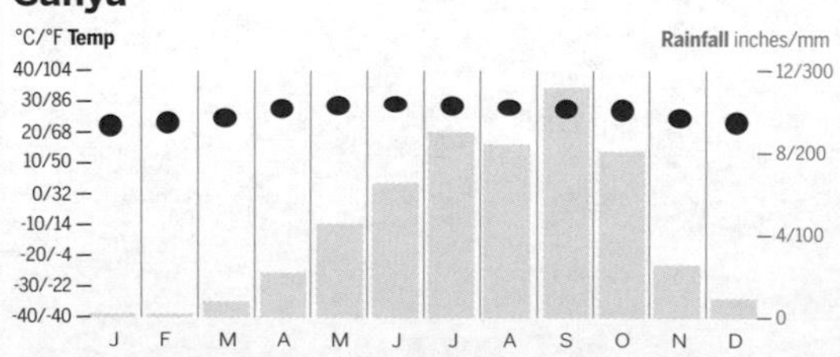

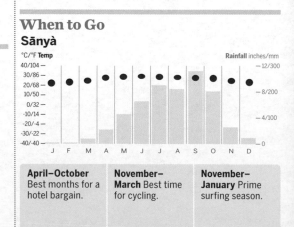

April–October Best months for a hotel bargain.

November–March Best time for cycling.

November–January Prime surfing season.

History

Until the economic boom of the last 30 years, Hăinán had been a backwater of the Chinese empire since the first Han settlements appeared on the coast almost 2000 years ago. Largely ignored by a series of dynasties, Hăinán was known as the 'tail of the dragon', 'the gate of hell', and a place best used as a repository for occasional high-profile exiles such as the poet Su Dongpo and the official Hai Rui.

More recently, China's first communist cell was formed here in the 1920s, and the island was heavily bombarded and finally occupied by the Japanese during WWII. Li and Han Chinese guerrillas waged an effective campaign to harass the Japanese forces but the retaliation was brutal – the Japanese executed a third of the island's male population. Even today among the younger generation, resentment over Japanese atrocities lingers.

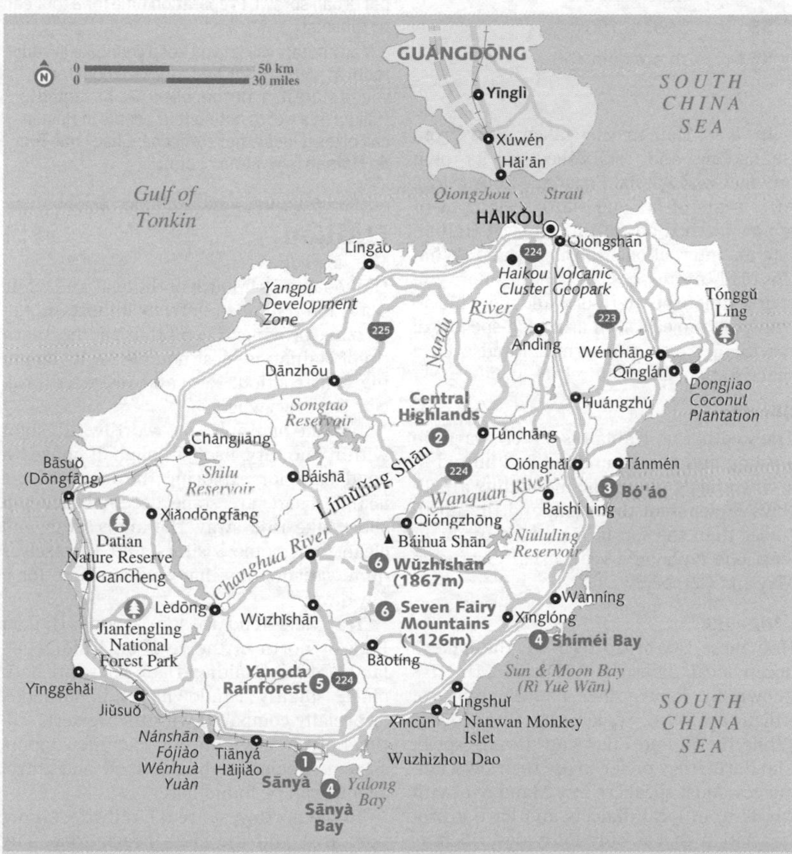

Hăinán Highlights

1. Soak up the sun, sand and cocktails at **Sānyà** (p578), China's top beach resort
2. Cycle the **Central Highlands** (p573), home of the Li and Miao
3. Explore the traditional villages and empty beaches around **Bó'áo** (p575)
4. Surf China's best waves at **Sānyà Bay** (p579) and **Shíméi Bay** (p577)
5. Hike through a tropical rainforest at **Yanoda** (p581)
6. Climb **Wŭzhǐshān** (p574) and **Seven Fairy Mountains** (p574), the most famous peaks on Hăinán

PRICE INDICATORS

The following price indicators are used in this chapter:

Sleeping

$	less than Y200
$$	Y200 to Y400
$$$	more than Y400

Eating

$	less than Y20
$$	Y20 to Y50
$$$	more than Y50

In 1988 Hǎinán was taken away from Guǎngdōng and established as its own province and Special Economic Zone (SEZ). After years of fits and starts, development is now focused on turning tropical Hǎinán into an 'international tourism island'. What this really means, besides building more golf courses, more beach resorts and more mega-transport projects such as a high-speed rail service, a cruise ship terminal and even a space station, is not entirely clear.

Climate

The weather on Hǎinán is largely warm in autumn and winter, and hot and humid in spring and summer. The mountains are always cooler than the coast, and the north cooler than the south. Hǎinán is hit by at least one typhoon a year, usually between May and October.

Language

Hǎinánese is a broad term for the baker's dozen local dialects of Hǎinán Mǐn (it's known by many other names), most of which are also spoken in Guǎngdōng. While the Li and Miao can usually speak Mandarin, they prefer to use their own languages. Most speakers mix Mandarin with words from local dialects and have a pronunciation that is only fairly described as wildly nonstandard.

Getting Around

Getting around most of Hǎinán is both cheap and easy. Hǎikǒu and Sānyà are linked by three main highways: the eastern expressway along the coast (only 3½ hours by bus); the central and much slower highway via Wǔzhǐshān; and the less popular western expressway. The main roads are great, bus services comfortable and departures regular. Buses come in two main classes: air conditioned and not.

At the time of writing, work on a high-speed rail line was under construction, scheduled to have 14 stops and linking Hǎikǒu to Sānyà (90 minutes) along the east coast.

BICYCLE

Hǎinán is a great destination for recreational touring. You're rarely more than an hour from a village with food and water, and never more than a few hours from a town with a decent hotel. At the same time, you'll find most of your riding is out in nature or touring pretty farming valleys, not urban sprawl. Preparation time for a tour can be minimal.

Many hotels will let you keep your bike in your room at night, or will find a locked room for you to store it in. Decent bikes can be rented in Hǎikǒu. It's worth noting that people in Hǎinán call bikes *dānchē*, not *zìxíngchē*. Check out **Tour de Hǎinán** (www.tohcr.com).

Hǎikǒu 海口

0898 / POP 830,000

Hǎikǒu means 'Mouth of the Sea', and while sea trade remains relatively important, the buzzing provincial capital at the northern tip of Hǎinán is most notable for its booming construction. New and restarted projects are everywhere.

Hǎikǒu has only one worthwhile sight within the city itself, though it makes a good base for exploring the north of the island. There are some decent beaches a short bike ride away, the air is fresh and clean, and some visitors find themselves quite satisfied just hanging out here for a few days.

Travellers tend to stay around Hǎikǒu Park or north of the river on Hǎidiàn Island (海甸岛; Hǎidiàn Dǎo). These are both older, slightly rundown neighbourhoods (especially compared with the western sections of the city), but all your life-support systems, including banks, food and travel agents, can be found here.

To the northwest are the railway station, port area and the city's beach zone. The main bus station and high-speed rail terminal is in the southwest of town. The airport is about 25km to the east.

Sights & Activities

Strolling along the river around Értóng Park is enjoyable, especially as the colourful wooden boats cruise in. A few kilometres west of the centre stretch kilometre after

HĂINÁN FARE

There is a huge variety of Chinese cuisine available in Hăinán. Fresh fruit and vegies are available everywhere, and unlike in much of China, they are grown under blue skies and in red soil free from industrial contamination.

There are myriad seafood dishes available, most of them using imported fish and crustaceans – Hăinán's fisheries having been largely fished out.

Don't forget to try Hăinán's own famous four dishes. They are pretty much a tourist thing now, but still worth asking for.

» **Dōngshān mutton** (东山羊; *dōngshān yáng*) A black-wool mountain goat fed camellias and orchids, and stewed, roasted or cooked in coconut milk, or used in soups.

» **Hélè crab** (和乐蟹; *hélè xiè*) Juicy crab, usually steamed but also roasted, from Hélè near Wànníng; it's best eaten in autumn.

» **Jiājī duck** (加积鸭; *jiājī yā*) To-die-for roast duck from Jiājī, near Qiónghăi.

» **Wénchāng chicken** (文昌鸡; *wénchāng jī*) Most famous of all and originally cooked up in coastal Wénchāng, this is succulent chicken raised on a diet of rice and peanuts.

kilometre of sandy beach. Take bus 37 from Értóng Park and get off anywhere.

FREE **Hăinán Museum** MUSEUM
(海南省博物馆; Hăinán Shěng Bówùguăn; 68 Guoxing Dadao; ⏲9am-4.30pm, closed Mon) This large complex of exhibition rooms should be your first stop when you arrive in Hăinán. The displays on ethnic minorities, as well as Hăinán's 20th-century history, which included fierce resistance against the Japanese and later Nationalists, are particularly informative. Most of the displays have English write-ups. Bus 43 and 48 from downtown stop outside the museum. It's on the far east side of town, close to the airport. A taxi will cost around Y30.

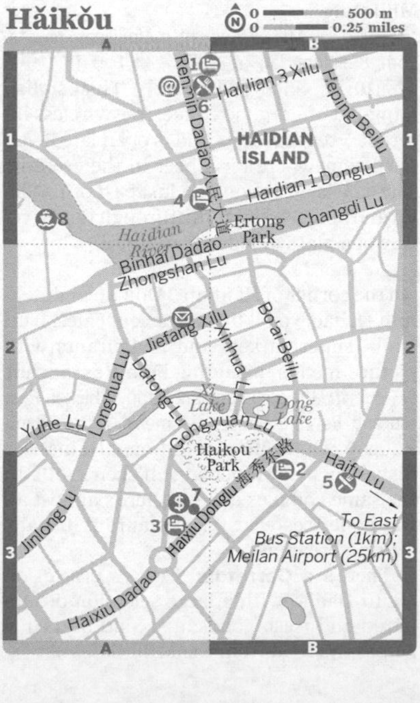

Sleeping

Unlike in the more seasonal Sānyà, prices in Hăikŏu tend to be greatly discounted from the published rates pretty much year-round. Only during major holidays might you get a rude shock.

Hăinán Mínháng Bīnguăn HOTEL $$
(海南民航宾馆; Hăinán Civil Aviation Hotel; ☎6650 6888; fax 6677 2610; 9 Haixiu Donglu; r Y160-200; @) The hotel's update still isn't setting any trends, but the inoffensive modern decor offers a cosy environment to

Hăikŏu

0 — 500 m
0 — 0.25 miles

Hăikŏu

Sleeping
1 Hăikŏu Banana Youth Hostel ... A1
2 Hăikŏu Bīnguăn ... B3
3 Hăinán Mínháng Bīnguăn ... A3
4 Jiāngwān Seaview Hotel ... A1

Eating
5 Carrefour ... B3
6 Fùlè Restaurant ... A1

Transport
7 China Southern Airlines ... A3
8 Xingang Ferry Terminal ... A1

START YOUR DAY THE HǍINÁN WAY

Getting started in the morning with a decent and cheap breakfast is often a challenge in China. On Hǎinán, in nearly every city, town and hovel, a local institution called Lǎobà Chá exists where you can get fresh coffee (NT4 a pot), meat-filled buns (包子; *bāozi*) and a host of sweet snacks. OK, healthwise it's not exactly muesli and yoghurt, but you can always supplement it with some fresh fruit picked up from the stall down the street.

Lǎobà Chá are easily recognised by their large bare interiors, or in smaller towns by their outdoor seating (usually under shady trees). If you can't find one, just ask a local.

unwind. The most expensive rooms have king-size beds, bright bathrooms and their own computers (though all rooms have broadband internet access). The location is good if you need to be downtown and near a lot of restaurants and shops. As a bonus, the airport shuttle bus (Y15) starts and ends here.

Hǎikǒu Bīnguǎn HOTEL $$$
(海口宾馆; Hǎikǒu Hotel; ☎6535 1234; www.haikouhotel.com; 4 Haixiu Donglu; r from Y688, discounts of 50-60%; @) Right in the middle of Hǎikǒu near the park, the Hǎikǒu Hotel offers slick service and attractive rooms. Service is excellent, as is the hotel's Chinese restaurant.

Jiāngwān Seaview Hotel HOTEL $$
(江湾海景大酒店; Jiāngwān Hǎijǐng Dàjiǔdiàn; 2 Haidian 1 Donglu; ☎6629 9111; www.jiangwanhaijing.com; r from Y588, discounts to under Y200) The good location by the river and equally good views from upper-level rooms are highlights for this otherwise fairly generic midrange. Staff are friendly but a little shy around Western guests.

Hǎikǒu Banana Youth Hostel HOSTEL $
(海口巴纳纳国际青年旅舍; Hǎikǒu Bānànà Qīngnián Lǚshè; ☎6628 6780; www.haikouhostel.com; 3 Dong, 6 Bieshu Liyuan Xiaoqu, 21 Renmin Dadao; 海甸岛人民大道21号梨园小区6号别墅3栋; dm/s/d Y50/120/180; @) Showing signs of weariness and weirdness far too early in its life, the Banana is a real hit-and-miss these days though it's still a great place for travel information. Expect the usual hostel amenities including laundry, internet, bike rentals, common areas and a bar-restaurant that serves Western breakfasts. If the owners aren't around don't expect much English to be spoken.

Eating & Drinking

A lot of evening eating is done in the refreshingly cool outdoors on practically every major street. Haixiu Donglu between the Hǎikǒu Bīnguǎn and Hǎinán Mínháng Bīnguǎn is chock-a-block full of cheap food stalls and fast-food joints. Small stands selling lemon drinks and teas are plentiful. *Liángchá* (cool tea) is a little medicinal in taste but locals swear it helps cool the body's fires on a hot day.

Folk Jar Restaurant HUNAN $$
(山间堂民间瓦缸煨汤馆; Shānjiāntáng Mínjiān Wǎgāng Wēitāngguǎn; Food Street; Jinlong Lu; 金龙路美食街; Y18-38; lunch & dinner)You'll expect prices to be much higher when you see the classy grey brick interior of this excellent Hunan restaurant. But the fiery dishes are quite reasonably priced and there's even a picture menu to help you choose. The restaurant is just west of Yu Sha Lu on busy Jinlong Lu, a hub of sorts for ethnic restaurants in Hǎikǒu.

Mǐlì Cafe CAFE
(米粒咖啡; Mǐlì Kāfēi; http://millicafe.niwota.com; 8 Jinlong Lu; 金龙路8号嘉华城市广场美景苑101房; 1pm-midnight) This stylish hang-out offers good coffee, free wireless internet, great desserts and is open late if you need somewhere for a beer in the evening. The cafe is off Jinlong Lu just east of Yu Sha Lu and accessed by going through the driveway of a glassy modern building.

On the corner of Haidian 3 Donglu and Renmin Dadao, you'll find a stack of cafes, fruit stalls, supermarkets and restaurants with picture menus, including **Fùlè Restaurant** (富乐鸡饭店; Fùlèjī Fàndiàn; Happy Chicken Restaurant; Renmin Dadao; set meals Y20; 8am-9.30pm), which offers traditional Hǎinánese dishes such as Wénchāng chicken (Y30). In the same complex as Fùlè there's almost always one Western-style restaurant (usually serving breakfast).

There's a **Carrefour** (家乐福; Jiālèfú) on Haifu Dadao with a large selection of prepared and fresh goods; a second branch is across the road from the Mǐlì Cafe.

Information

The annually published *Hăinán Island Guide Map* (Y6) has a good city map of Hăikŏu, which includes a map of all of Hăinán island on the back in addition to smaller maps of Sānyà and Bó'áo. The **Xīnhuá Bookstore** (新华书店l; Xīnhuá Shūdiàn; 10 Jiefang Xilu; ⏲9am-10pm) has good for maps if you are biking.

Many cafes around Guomao and Jinlong Lu have wireless internet access.

Bank of China (中国银行; Zhōngguó Yínháng; Datong Lu) Changes money and travellers cheques. ATM outlets that take foreign cards are plentiful around town.

Internet cafe (网吧; wăngbā; Renmin Dadao; per hr Y2-5; ⏲8am-midnight) Located about 100m north of the corner of Renmin Dadao and Haidian 3 Lu. Go up the stairs to the 2nd floor.

Getting There & Away

Air

Hăikŏu's **Měilán Airport** (www.mlairport.com) is well connected to most of China's major cities, including Hong Kong and Macau, with international flights to Bangkok, Singapore, Kuala Lumpur and Taipei. Low-season one-way domestic fares are cheap. Destinations include Běijīng (Y2250), Guăngzhōu (Y680) and Shànghăi (Y1660).

Bus

Buses from the **Xīngăng Passenger Ferry Terminal** (海口新港客运站; Hăikŏu Xīnggăng Kèyùn Zhàn; ☎6866 1943) run to Guăngzhōu (Y186, 12 hours, hourly).

Services also leave from the **south bus station** (汽车南站; 32 Nanhai Dadao):

Qióngzhōng Y37, three hours, hourly buses via the central highway

Sānyà Y77, 3½ hours, frequent services

Wŭzhĭshān Y83, four hours, seven daily via the east highway

Frequent buses leave from the **east bus station** (汽车东站; 148 Haifu Lu):

Qiónghăi Y26, 1½ hours, every 30 minutes

Wénchāng Y18, 1½ hours, frequent services

Train

The train station is far west of the city. Bus 37 (Y2) connects the train station and Értóng Park. Bus 50 (Y2) connects the train station with the south bus station, passing Hăikŏu Park.

Trains to/from Guăngzhōu (hard sleeper Y251 to Y270, 12 hours, 8.42pm and 10.03pm) are shunted onto a ferry to cross the Qióngzhōu Strait. Buy tickets at the train station or from the dedicated counter in the **China Southern Airlines** (中国南方航空; Zhōngguó Nánfāng Hángkōng; 9 Haixiu Dong Lu) office.

Getting Around

To/from the Airport

Měilán Airport is 25km southeast of the city centre. A shuttle bus (Y15, every 30 minutes) runs to/from Hăinán Mínháng Bīnguăn. A taxi costs Y60 (negotiated priced) to downtown. Negotiate the price when going to the airport by taxi; don't use the meter as it will be far more expensive.

Bicycle

Cycling around Hăikŏu is a great way to take in the beaches and rural scenery at the pace they deserve. You can rent bikes at the **Hăikŏu Banana Youth Hostel** (www.haikouhostel.com; 3 Dong, 6 Bieshu Liyuan Xiaoqu, 21 Renmin Dadao) for Y20 a day. For longer rentals to tour the island, visit **Hăinán Bike** (海南开拓者; Hăinán Kāituòzhě; ☎6656 7333; www.hnbike.cn; 2 Bin He Lu; 滨河路2号), off Jinlong Lu. The shop is a club for local bike enthusiasts but rents out bikes for Y30 a day (including helmet, Y1000 deposit).

High-Speed Rail

Running from Sānyà via the east coast, the new high-speed rail stops in Hăikŏu at the train station and south bus station.

Public Transport

Hăikŏu's centre is easy to walk around. The bus system (Y1 to Y2) is decent, though it often takes transfers to get around.

Taxi

Taxis charge Y10 for the first 2.6km. They're easy to spot, but difficult to catch on large roads because of barriers.

Around Hăikŏu

HĂIKŎU VOLCANIC CLUSTER GEOPARK 海口火山群世界地质公园

The geopark (Hăikŏu Huŏshānqún Shìjiè Dìzhì Gōngyuán) encompasses about 108 sq km of rural countryside in Shíshān township and features dozens of extinct volcanoes, lava tunnels and even an abandoned village made of lava stones. Minibuses from Hăikŏu will drop you off outside a spiffy **tourist park** (admission Y60; ⏲8.30am-5.30pm) that's worth a visit if you want to walk into a volcanic crater overgrown with lush vegetation.

From the park, catch a motorcycle taxi 2km to the **Seventy-Two Cave Lava Tunnel Protected Area** (七十二洞熔岩隧道保护区), more commonly known as Huŏshan

Dòng (Volcanic Cave). The tunnel is several hundred metres long, about 20m wide and 15m high.

While there isn't an official ticket booth outside, the local elders will ask you to pay Y1 to Y10 (depending on your numbers), plus another Y2 for a torch that will burn out long before you get through the tunnel. Think you don't need a torch, or a local guide? Think again. We can attest from personal experience that you'll get some heavy pressure from the ageing guardians if you don't cough up the dough.

Close to the tunnel entrance is **Huǒshān Cūn** (火山村; Volcanic Village). The abandoned village is made entirely out of lava stones and is very photogenic. You may also be asked to pay to enter here.

Getting There & Away

The geopark is about 15km from Hǎikǒu. To get there, first take a taxi to the T-intersection of Xiuying Xiaojie and Xiuying Dadao (秀英小街、英大道) and then catch one of the frequent minibuses (Y3, 30 minutes) to Shíshān County (Shíshān Zhèn; 石山镇) from the bus stop on the far side of Xiuying Dadao.

A taxi to the park costs Y50. Given the size of the area, and its proximity to Hǎikǒu, exploring by bicycle is best.

DŌNGJIĀO COCONUT PLANTATION 东郊椰林

The coconut plantation (Dōngjiāo Yēlín) takes up a big chunk of Wénchāng County on the northeast coast. It's more like a large farming community than a single plantation, and the cool palm-lined lanes and traditional villages really give the region a lot of character. Add in kilometres of long sandy beaches and you have a great place to hang out for a few days exploring or relaxing. In the low season you'll have the beaches virtually to yourself unless a student group has shown up to conquer the land. Those with a nose for history might find the WWII-era concrete bunkers dotted along the beach interesting.

Accommodation is provided by a couple of resorts. The **Hǎinán Prima Resort** (海南百莱玛度假酒店; ☎0898-6353 8222; www.hainanprimaresort.com; r/cabins from Y288/488) has bare rooms, and comfortable one- and two-storey wood chalets priced by size and proximity to the beach. All signs, menus and instruction boards are in English, though the slightly indifferent staff speak none. If the Prima isn't your bag, wander into the nearby village, where locals offer homestays.

If you continue down the main road that took you to the Prima Resort, a few rough kilometres later you'll reach a small dock where for Y6 you can hire an old wooden junk for a short tour of the **mangroves** (红树林; Hóng Shùlín). You can also get the captain to take you across the inlet where you can grab a taxi to Wénchāng.

Getting There & Away

BUS

Getting to the plantation is quite a trip. From Hǎikǒu's east or south bus station, buses leave for Wénchāng (文昌; Y17, 1½ hours, 73km) every 30 minutes. In Wénchāng, catch a minibus (Y7, one hour) heading directly to the plantation. After crossing an inlet on a ferry, it's 20 minutes to the Prima Resort.

The new high-speed rail will have a station in Wénchāng, and there are likely to be buses running directly to the plantation from here in the future.

CYCLING

Small-scale development is taking away much of the charm of Wénchāng County, but it's still an enjoyable one- or two-day ride from Hǎikǒu to Dōngjiāo. Given the size of the plantation, you really need your own transport if you plan to do anything other than hang out at the beach.

The fastest way (still about 100km) is to follow Highway 201 to Wénchāng and then cross the inlet to Dōngjiāo. A more interesting route from Hǎikǒu heads east to Yǎnhǎi (演海镇; Yǎnhǎi Zhèn), where you can catch an old wood junk (Y6, every 30 minutes) across the inlet to Pūqián (铺前镇; Pūqián Zhèn). You'll need a map and someone in Hǎikǒu to give you clear directions, and you can still expect to get lost a few times on the unmarked back roads. From Pūqián, follow Highway 203 for about 60km until you see the signs for the Dōngjiāo Yēlín turn-off. This route is around 130km.

If you don't fancy riding all the way from Hǎikǒu, or want to do this trip in one day, consider taking a taxi to Wénchāng (Y100) and starting from there.

TÓNGGǓ LǏNG 铜鼓岭

Tónggǔ Lǐng is the name of a small mountain and nature reserve on the northeast coast just north of the Dōngjiāo Coconut Plantation. There are great views up and down the coast from the top, and to the north is a long stretch of beach. There's no public transportation to the area. If you bike from the coconut plantation, expect to take around two hours. It's a nice ride through the rural backwaters of Hǎinán.

Central Highlands

0898

Hǎinán's reputation rests on its tropical beaches, but for many travellers it's in this region of dark green mountains and terraced rice-growing valleys that one makes genuine contact with the island's culture.

Until recently, Han Chinese had left almost no footprint here, and even today visible signs of Chinese culture, such as temples or shrines, are very rarely seen. Instead, the region is predominantly Li and Miao, minority ethnic groups who have lived a relatively primitive subsistence existence for most of their time on the island. Indeed, groups of Li living as hunter-gatherers were found in the mountainous interior of Hǎinán as recently as the 1930s. Today, they are by far the poorest people on Hǎinán.

Travelling in the region is easy, as a decent bus system links major and minor towns.

HǍIKǑU TO WǓZHǏSHĀN

五指山市 -琼中

Most buses reach Wǔzhǐshān in a few hours via the east coast highway. If you want to ply the central highway, head first to Qióngzhōng (Y37, three hours, 137km, hourly) and from there connect to Wǔzhǐshān (Y17, two hours, 96km, hourly).

Cycling this route is enjoyable (the highway has a good shoulder most of the way), and allows for endless side trips up small country roads and stops in tiny villages to chat with fruit vendors or the folks at a family-run restaurant. After a day riding through the lush Túnchāng County valley, the route climbs into some fine hill country around **Shíyùn** (什运). The village (32km southwest of Qióngzhōng) sits on a grassy shelf above a river and is worth a look around. Local cyclists recommend the 42km side trip from here up a wooded canyon to **Báishā** (白沙).

Returning to the central highway, you can look forward to a long climb (at least 10km), followed by a long fast descent into Wǔzhǐshān. A scenic side trip (think rice fields, green peaks and stone villages) involves turning at Máoyáng for Shuǐmǎn and continuing from Shuǐmǎn to Wǔzhǐshān via the back roads.

The major towns in this area are **Túnchāng** (屯昌) and **Qióngzhōng** (琼中), the latter a major settlement for the Miao. You'll find hotels and restaurants in both. Smaller villages have basic guesthouses, usually with no air-con. It you are continuing on from Wǔzhǐshān to Sānyà, the road is one long, steep downhill after the turn-off to Bǎotíng.

WǓZHǏSHĀN CITY (TŌNGSHÍ)

五指山市 (通什)

Once called Tōngzhá or Tōngshí, Wǔzhǐshān Shì was renamed after the famous nearby mountain, the highest point on the island and a symbol of Hǎinán. Though the size of a large town, Wǔzhǐshān is actually China's smallest city, having been given such status when it became the capital of the short-lived Li and Miao Autonomous Prefecture back in the 1980s.

Most travellers here are heading out to climb the mountain, or using the town as a base for exploring the region. Note that there's nowhere to change or withdraw money in Wǔzhǐshān, so bring what you need. There's an **internet cafe** (per hr Y2.50; 24hr) on the 2nd floor of the Jīnyuán Dàjiǔdiàn.

Sleeping & Eating

There are cheap restaurants all around the bus station area, as well as countless fruit stalls, bakeries, and cafes. Barbecue stalls set up in the evenings all over town.

Tong Shi Guo Ji Hotel HOTEL $
(通什国际大酒店; Tōngshí Guójì Dàjiǔdiàn; Haiyu Lu; d/tw Y128/260, discounts of 40%) This hotel is a big step up from other budget places in town (it has Western toilets for one thing) for only a few dollars more. The big twins (discounted to Y100 off-season) are worth paying a little more for their open views of the city and mountains. The hotel is a few blocks down from Jīnyuán Dàjiǔdiàn, just as the road starts to swing to the right to follow the river.

Jīnyuán Dàjiǔdiàn HOTEL $
(金源大酒店; 8662 2942; Haiyu Lu; r from Y78) A cheap and cheerful place directly opposite the bus station. Rooms are bland and have squat toilets, but are rather big and clean. The friendly staff will store luggage, including a bike, in a locked room off the lobby.

Zhèngzōng Lánzhōu Lāmiàn MUSLIM $
(正宗兰州拉面; Authentic Lanzhou Noodles; 海榆路; dishes Y5-20) Just a few doors down from the Jīnyuán Dàjiǔdiàn, this Hui Muslim restaurant sells a wide range of cheap but excellent noodle and lamb dishes. Try the *gānbànmiàn* (十伴面; Y7) a kind of

stir-fried spaghetti bolognaise with hand-pulled noodles.

Holiday Inn of Jadeite Mountain City Restaurant CHINESE **$$**
(五指山翡翠山城假日酒店; Wǔzhǐshān Fěicuì Shānchéng Jiàrì Jiǔdiàn; 2nd fl, 1 Shanzhuang Lu; dishes Y15-50, set meals Y20; ⏰7am-midnight) The Chinese food in this hotel restaurant is excellent but consider trying the famous Li dish *shuǐ mǎn yā* (boiled duck with rice and wine). Dim sum breakfasts are reasonably priced (average dish Y6). From the bus station, turn left and follow the road as it bends right to follow the river. The hotel and its big English sign is about 0.5km down on the right.

Getting There & Away

Buses from Wǔzhǐshān:

Báishā Y33, 2½ hours, two daily (8.30am and noon)

Bǎotíng Y9, 40 minutes, half-hourly (7am to 6pm)

Hǎikǒu Y83, four hours, seven daily (7.15am to 3.30pm)

Qióngzhōng Y17, two hours, hourly (6.30am to 5.30pm)

Sānyà Y23, 1½ hours, half-hourly (7am to 5.30pm)

Shuǐmǎn Y9, one hour, hourly (7am to 5pm)

Around Wǔzhǐshān

WǓZHǏSHĀN (FIVE FINGER MOUNTAIN) 五指山

The **mountain** (admission Y54; ⏰24hr) after which Wǔzhǐshān is named rises 1867m out of the centre of Hǎinán in a reserve 30km northeast of the city. As the highest peak in the land, it's naturally steeped in local lore: the five peaks, for example, are said to represent the Li people's five most powerful gods. Despite the name, however, from most angles the summit looks like a single volcanic peak or a cleft hoof.

The reserve is the source of the Wanquan (万泉河) and Changhua (昌化江) Rivers and protects a mixed forest containing 6.5% of all vascular plant species in China. It's a rich (though threatened) ecosystem and receives the highest rainfall in Hǎinán. The *average* humidity here is over 90%.

It's pretty much an all-day event to get out here and climb the mountain. Most people can get to the top of the second finger (the highest) in four hours, but be warned that although the path is clear, it's very steep and puts most hikers out of breath in minutes. Coming down is not much faster than going up, so give yourself six to eight hours to complete your climb.

The climb to the top takes you through two distinct vegetative zones. The broadleaf forest at the base is thick with bamboo and banyans, mixing with evergreens such as pine as the elevation rises and the temperature cools. The peak is often clouded in, so go as early as you can if you want to enjoy the views.

Wǔzhǐshān sits about 4km from the village of **Shuǐmǎn** (水满). The ride from Wǔzhǐshān to Shuǐmǎn (Y8, one hour, 35km) is a scenic one, passing traditional villages set among yellow terraced rice fields that are backed by rolling dark hills. There is no fixed schedule but buses run about every hour. In Wǔzhǐshān, buy your ticket on the buses, which usually leave from gate 10. Make sure to get a bus going to Shuǐmǎn via Nánshèng.

In Shuǐmǎn, motorcyclists will take you the remaining 3km for Y10, though you could easily walk it (there are signs in English pointing the way). Note that the last bus back to Wǔzhǐshān leaves Shuǐmǎn just past 6pm.

SEVEN FAIRY MOUNTAINS 七仙岭

About 39km southeast of Wǔzhǐshān is the small and conspicuously orderly Li town of **Bǎotíng** (保亭). While that orderliness may strike you as noteworthy after a few weeks spent travelling in China, the main reason to come here is to climb the Seven Fairy Mountains (Qī Xiān Lǐng; elevation 1126m), an eye-catching ridge comprised of jagged spear-like crags. The area is perhaps more famous among Chinese, however, for the hot-spring resorts popping up in the tropical forest.

Naruda Tropical Resort (君澜热带雨林温泉酒店; Jūnlán Rèdàiyǔlín Wēnquán Jiǔdiàn; ☎8388 8888; cabins from Y1380, discounts of 40-50%) is gorgeously laid out, with high-end wood cabins and outdoor pools tucked in quiet lanes that afford excellent views of the surrounding ridgeline.

The mountain entrance and hot spring area are 9km off the main road from Bǎotíng. It's a pretty ride on its own past lush tropical forests and small villages (in addition to a few massive resorts and a golf course). Tickets to climb Qī Xiān Lǐng can be purchased at a **ticket office** (per person Y30; ⏰from 7.30am) across from the entrance

THE LI & MIAO

Four main ethnic groups live on Hǎinán (though the government lists 39 in total). These include the first settlers of the island, the Li and Miao (H'mong), who today are found mostly in the forested areas covering the Límǔlǐng Shān (Mother of the Lí Mountain) range that stretches down the centre of the island. The Li probably migrated to Hǎinán from Fújiàn 3000 years ago and today number over one million.

Despite a long history of rebellion against the Chinese, the Li aided communist guerrillas on the island during the war with the Japanese. Perhaps for this reason the island's centre was made an 'autonomous' region after the communist takeover. The region hereafter would be self-governing, giving the marginalised Li and Miao communities a degree of control.

That situation, however, proved short-lived after newly empowered local politicians were done in for corruption and money-wasting on a scale remarkable even by Chinese standards. For evidence, look to the imposing and overly grand main building of Qióngzhōu University in Wǔzhǐshān, overlooking the city. This was to be the region's legislative assembly.

Like the Li, the Miao spread from southern China and now can be found across northern Vietnam, Laos and Thailand. Today there are some 60,000 Miao living on Hǎinán, occupying some of the most rugged terrain on the island.

to Naruda Tropical Resort. From the ticket office, continue up the road a few kilometres to the trailhead. From here, it's three to four hours to the top and back.

There are frequent buses to Bǎotíng from Wǔzhǐshān (Y9, 40 minutes). From Bǎotíng's bus station, catch a motorcycle taxi to the hot-spring area. It's Y15 to the hot-spring area but you'll have to negotiate if you want to be taken all the way to the trailhead.

The East Coast

☎0898

Hǎinán's east coast is a series of spectacular palm-lined beaches, long bays and headlands, most of which are unfortunately not usually visible from the main roads, not even at bicycle level. With the best beaches developed or being developed, there is little reason to make a special trip out here (to Bó'áo being the exception) unless you are surfing or wish to stay at a resort. Biking or motorcycling is another story, however, as there are endless deserted bays, small villages and rural roads to explore.

In the past, the east coast was the centre of Han settlement. If you are coming from the highlands you will start to notice temples, gravesites, shrines and other signs of Chinese culture dotting the landscape.

BÓ'ÁO 博鳌

This attractive little coastal town at the confluence of three rivers is famous as the site of the **Bó'áo Forum for Asia** (BFA), a yearly meet-up of top-level officials, academics and economists exclusively from the Asia region. For cyclists, Bó'áo is a natural stop along the coast, offering good accommodation and food. For all travellers, it's an unpretentious little beach town (with a usually deserted beach), surrounded by some of the prettiest countryside on Hǎinán.

Like much of Hǎinán, or China for that matter over the past few years, Bó'áo has been under the spell of the construction fairy. In the north of town, luxury apartments and villas are popping up with such abandon you'd think there was an actual demand for them. There isn't, and with competition from thousands of other units in Sānyà, Wénchāng and Hǎikǒu, the majority will likely remain empty.

Bó'áo covers a large area, though the 'downtown' blocks are tiny, essentially being two streets that intersect at a T-junction: Haibin Lu (海滨 路) runs north–south and Zhaobo Lu (朝博路) runs east–west.

Sights & Activities

Despite hosting the BFA every year, and despite the over-construction giving parts of town the look of a small Dubai, Bó'áo is still a rather rural place. Even a few blocks from the main junction are small villages of stone and brick buildings where locals dry rice in the middle of the lanes, and burn incense in small shrines to their local folk deities. **Nánqiáng Village** (南强村; Nánqiáng

Cūn) is one such place about 2km west of the main junction. About 30km northeast of Bó'áo is the little fishing village of **Tánmén** (潭门), where the local multicoloured wooden junks are made and repaired.

Beaches BEACHES

Bó'áo's beach is a few hundred metres east of the main road. To get there, head south down Haibin Lu. Turn left at the Jinjiang Hot Spring Hotel and follow the road as it swings right to drop you off at a **Matsu Temple** just off the beach. The river hits the sea here and a thin sandbar at the mouth is for some reason a popular place to boat out to.

If you plan to swim, head at least half a kilometre north to avoid dangerous currents. There's a lovely secluded section of beach past the Áozhuāng seafood area where it's just you, the sea and grazing black goats.

Cai Family Residence HISTORIC SITE

(蔡家大院; Càijiā Dàyuàn) If you have a bike, or some means of transport, head west out of town and when the road ends at a junction turn left (south) and cross a long bridge. From here, just follow your nose and either get off the main road onto the red-dirt country lanes or continue to the coast and head south. You'll pass through pineapple and rice fields, and some very picturesque villages.

Head right after crossing the bridge and in a few kilometres you'll reach the Cai Family Residence. This sprawling old mansion in **Liúkè Village** (留客村) was built in 1934 by several brothers who made their fortune in Indonesia in the rubber industry. As with many houses built by expat sons, it's a blend of Asian and Western styles. You'll find dragon heads, for example, but also classical statues.

The house was abandoned in 1937 after the Japanese invaded Hăinán, and later became a guerrilla outpost for resistance fighters. In 2006 the house was declared a heritage site and a decade-long restoration project is now under way. At the time of writing, you couldn't enter the building on your own; the well-connected Bó'áo Inn offers an excursion to the house by river boat, which includes a look inside.

Courtyard of Eastern Culture BUDDHIST TEMPLE

(东方文化苑; Dōngfāng Wénhuàyuàn) This modern Buddhist temple complex is well worth a few hours of exploring. Some highlights include a towering but finely detailed statue of the many-armed and many-headed Guanyin, a stunning pagoda and a two-storey **Lotus Centre** dedicated to the lotus symbol in Buddhism. Nicely, there are detailed English explanations inside.

A motorcycle taxi from town costs about Y5. You can easily walk back and take in some of the traditional villages along the way. The complex was closed at the time of writing but should be reopened by the time you read this.

Sleeping

TOP CHOICE **Bó'áo Inn** B&B $$

(博鳌客栈; Bó'áo Kèzhàn; ☎138 7627 1007; www.hainan-letsgo.com; r from Y385) The owners of this great little inn, an American expat and her Chinese husband, started it in part just to meet more travellers. So expect to be treated like family during your stay and to be doted on and plied with home-made meals and fresh-baked goodies (their banana bread is fantastic and becoming the stuff of backpacker legends). The husband, a local photojournalist, is also the perfect guide if you wish to explore minority villages and some truly out-of-the-way places. For cyclists who plan to stay the night on their tour of Hăinán, the owners offer 24-hour assistance via cell phone. It's a great service if your Chinese is a bit weak. The inn also offers bicycle rentals for local tours. Reservations for the inn must be made in advance.

Hăi Jĭng Wān Hotel HOTEL $

(海景湾宾馆; Hăijĭng Wān Bīnguăn; ☎6277 9558; r Y80-120) Want a huge, high-ceilinged room, with an open view? The modern, tile-floored rooms in this friendly family-run place are just the ticket (at least the top floors). The hotel is 150m west of the main junction on the south side of the road.

Eating

Because of its international status as the BFA, the town has a good range of Chinese restaurants dedicated to regional cuisine (Shāndōng, Húnán and Sìchuān; dishes Y8 to Y60). You'll see English signs out front and some now even have English or picture menus. On the main streets you'll find small grocery stores, and abundant fruit stands.

Áozhuāng Hăixiān Chéng SEAFOOD $$

(熬庄海鲜城) For seafood, head north out of town to this collection of seaside restaurants that's famous across the island. Just choose and point to what you want cooked up. Restaurants open around 9.30am and close when the last customers leave. You can walk here on the main road, or better yet along the seaside road starting at the Matsu temple, in about 30 minutes.

Shāndōng Dumplings NORTHERN CHINESE **$**
(山东水饺; Shāndōng Shuǐjiǎo; Zhaobo Lu; dumplings from Y15) Try Shāndōng Dumplings for good traditional northern food. You'll find it at the end of the row of shops and restaurants west of the main intersection.

Dōngběi Xiāng CHINESE **$$**
(东北香; Zhaobo Lu) Just 100m down from the main intersection. Among the other great dishes, try the steamed river fish *(bó'áo yú).*

Drinking

Lao Wood Coffee Rest Area CAFE
(老房子; Lǎo Fángzi; 61 Haibin Lu; drinks from Y18, 10am-2am,) The owner of this cafe, a local dancer and art administrator, literally had an old traditional stone house taken apart and reassembled on Bó'áo's main street to make his dream of opening a stylish cafe come true. The inside is chock-full of antiques and objets d'art, while out back is a small leafy garden.

Sea Story BAR
(海的故事; Hǎide Gùshì; 10am-10pm;) Another fantastic addition to Bó'áo, the ocean-facing Sea Story features an open driftwood interior with a funky beachcomber design: an old 5m-long fishing junk literally sits as the centrepiece just off the lobby. Outside, the breezy deck is an ideal spot for cocktails or even a meal in the evening. Loud music, karaoke and other intrusive noises or activities are banned. Sea Story is about 1km from the Matsu Temple along the seaside lane to the Áozhuāng seafood area.

Information

There is a **Bank of China** (中国银行; Zhōngguó Yínháng) two blocks north of the main junction, with an ATM that accepts foreign cards. Several **internet cafes** (网吧; wǎngbā; per hour Y3) operate near the main junction.

A decent map of the Bó'áo area can be found at the bottom of the general *Hǎinán Tourism Guide Map.*

Getting there & Away

First catch a bus from Hǎikǒu's east bus station to Qiónghǎi (琼海; fast/slow Y26/20, 1½ hours, 102km). Cross the street to the Kentucky Fried Chicken side, and look for the bus stop just down the road to the left. Catch minibus 2 to Bó'áo (Y3, frequent). Passengers get dropped off at the main junction in Bó'áo.

BǍISHÍ LǏNG 百石岭

An easy morning or all-day excursion from Bó'áo by bus or bike takes you to this scenic ridge with a citadel-like peak dominating the local skyline. You can reach the top in about an hour but the views carry across the plains and foothills of Qióngzhōng County. There are a few old temples on the ridge, and from the peak eagles can often be seen soaring on the updrafts just a few dozen metres away. There's a Y8 admission to climb the ridge and a couple of hot-spring resorts nearby to relax in afterwards if you're visiting in the cooler months.

To get to Bǎishí Lǐng by public transport, first take a bus to Qiónghǎi. Cross the road as you exit the station, turn left and walk one block. Catch minibus 1 (Y2) and about 15 minutes later get off at an intersection with a clear sign in English to Bǎishí Lǐng. Hail any passing motorcycle taxi (Y15) to take you the last 6km to the start of the hike.

The trip makes for a great loop of about 80km if you have a bike. In essence, you ride along the north side of the Wànquán River (万泉) to Shíbì (石壁), and then cross over and ride the south side back.

SHÍMÉI BAY & SUN & MOON BAY 石梅湾、日月湾

Shíméi Bay (Shíméi Wān) and Sun and Moon Bay (Rì Yuè Wān) are among the most stunning stretches of coastline on Hǎinán. Development of major resorts is proceeding apace but the beaches are still open to the public and offer some of China's best surfing waves from November to January. Dàdōnghǎi-based **Surfing Hǎinán** (www.surfinghainan.com) hosts an annual surf competition here every November, and offers lessons, board rentals and transportation (which is very inconvenient otherwise). Some hostels and hotels also offer day trips to the bays and you can ride out to them if you are biking the east coast. Unlike at Sānyà, the bay areas get a bit chilly and overcast in the winter months, and thin wet suits are needed for surfing.

LOCAL KNOWLEDGE

RECHARD LI: PHOTOJOURNALIST

Favourite Subjects

I like to aim at people's real life with my lens. I am most happy when I am with the local Hăinán people. I listen to their stories and record their life with my camera.

Of course, I like to shoot the beautiful places of Hăinán Island, too. Yángpŭ, on the west of the Island, where they make salt the traditional way; the fishermen's market at Tánmén; the sunsets on Sānyà beach; the volcanic village area outside Hăikŏu; and the Five Finger Mountain area (Wŭzhĭshān), especially in autumn.

Photographing Locals

There's no need to pay any money to take pictures of locals but sometimes they will stare directly at your lens, which makes you feel not very good and makes it hard to get a good picture. Try to have a local person ask the other locals what you would like them to do for your picture.

Hăinán's Most Iconic Image

A Li girl's smile.

Best Tip

Keep your lenses dry on the island, otherwise the wet weather will ruin them. Invest in a charcoal or silica gel pack and put it into your camera bag to absorb the moisture away from your camera.

Rechard Li is a newspaper photojournalist for the Hăinán Daily Group. A native of Héběi province, he has been living in Bó'áo with his American wife since 2005.

Sānyà 三亚

☎0898 / POP 490,000

China's premier beach community is a modern construction in every way – which makes the claim that it is the Hawaii of China a little suspect. Certainly, if you are hoping to be charmed by an indigenous culture closely tied to the sea – in addition to enjoying your beer, golden sand beaches and clear tropical blue waters, of course – you will be a bit disappointed. Sānyà is built just for fun.

While the full 40km or so of coastline dedicated to tourism is usually referred to as Sānyà, the region is actually made up of three distinct zones. Sānyà Bay is home to the bustling city centre and a long stretch of beach and hotels aimed at locals and mainland holidaymakers. Dàdōnghăi Bay, about 3km southeast, beyond the Lùhuítóu Peninsula, is where most Western travellers stay. In fact, it receives such a steady influx of Russian vacationers these days that almost all signs are in Cyrillic as well as Chinese. A further 15km east, at exclusive Yàlóng Bay, the beach is first-rate, as is the line of plush international resorts.

You'll find the bus station in the Sānyà Bay area on Jiefang Lu, the main drag. This road morphs into Yuya Lu as it heads into Dàdōnghăi Bay and Yàlóng Bay. The *Sānyà Tour Guide* map (Y6) is worth buying from hostels and hotels to get an overview of the area.

Like any tourist haven, Sānyà does have its irritations. The stalking taxi drivers, relatively high prices and usual menu of low-level scams (pickpocketing is particularly rampant) are the downsides.

Sights & Activities

Unsurprisingly for a beach resort, the vast majority of things to see and do revolve around sand, sea, shopping and after-hours entertainment.

Beaches BEACHES

The long sandy strip off the city centre at **Sānyà Bay** (三亚湾; Sānyà Wān) is the most relaxed of the three main beaches, and the one place you will really see people kicking back, laughing, playing and having a beachy old time. There's a long pathway for strolling in the cool evenings, and if the tide is out a little you can walk on the sand for many kilometres.

Dàdōnghǎi Bay (大东海湾; Dàdōnghǎi Wān) sports a wider beach than Sānyà and has a shaded boardwalk running along most of its length. The setting, in a deep blue bay with rocky headlands, is simply gorgeous but it does get busy here and people really seem to be trying too hard to enjoy themselves.

Some consider **Yàlóng Bay** (亚龙湾; Yàlóng Wān; Asian Dragon Bay; admission Y33; ⏲6.30am-6.30pm) to have the best beach.

Both Dàdōnghǎi and Yàlóng Bays offer a wide range of activities, including jetskiing, snorkelling and parasailing, but instruction is usually substandard and lifeguards on duty are not properly trained and of little use in an emergency. See Sānyà Backpackers for scuba lessons and rentals.

Surfing Hǎinán SURFING
(冲浪海南; Chōnglàng Hǎinán; ☎135 1980 0103; www.surfinghainan.com; Dàdōnghǎi; board rental/lessons per day Y200/350) From May to September, Dàdōnghǎi gets decent surfing waves, while nearby Shíméi Bay has prime conditions from November to January. You can rent boards from Surfing Hǎinán, which was started in 2008 by three surfers from China, Japan and the US. Lessons (including lunch) and multiday packages for the experienced are also available.

Surfing is just starting to gain a tiny following in China and so far the majority of surfers out on the waters are still Westerners. This is not the next Indonesia but as part-owner Brendan says, 'The best thing about surfing Hǎinán is that it's empty.' Beginners will find this a no-hassle spot to try a sport they've always been curious about.

Surfing Hǎinán also offers a fun 30-minute **breakfast paddle** (Y500) across Dàdōnghǎi to Yàlóng Bay that includes a buffet breakfast at one of the five-star resorts.

Surfing Sānyà is a bit tricky to find down on the unmarked back alleys of Dàdōnghǎi, so call when you arrive or take the first lane (the fruit street) as you head down Haiyun Lu off Yuya Lu. At the end, look for the blue cow head.

Sleeping

Dàdōnghǎi Bay is the place to head for midrange and budget lodgings. The top-end resorts are off the beach at Yàlóng Bay in a private area of palm-lined roads and landscaped grounds. Outside peak periods 30% to 60% discounts are common everywhere.

At the time of writing, the streets of Dàdōnghǎi were a mess as thousands of new apartment units were being added to the area.

Sunny Sanya Family Inn HOTEL $$
(红屋顶家庭旅馆; Hóngwūdǐng Jiātíng Lǚguǎn; ☎8820 9345; www.sunnysanya.com; 29 Haiyun

Sānyà

Sleeping
1 Blue Sky International Youth Hostel C1
2 Minhu Hotel B1
Resort In Time .... (see 5)
3 Sanya Backpackers B1
4 Sunny Sanya Family Inn A2

Eating
5 Pattaya Thai Cuisine A2

Sānyà

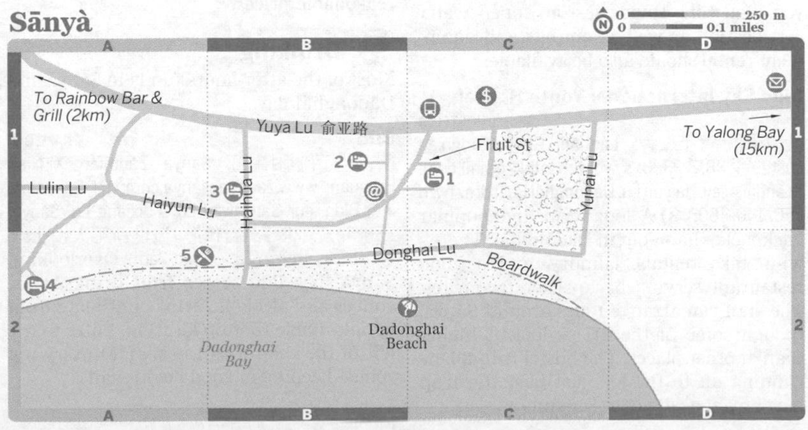

Lu, Dàdōnghǎi Bay; s/d with breakfast Y198/298; ☎) This cheerful little family-run hotel is just a minute's walk from the sea at the far end of the bay. Rooms are a bit small but bright and the tropical-beach-hut styling gives them a cosy rather than cramped feeling. Staff speak reasonably good English and can help arrange day trips out to Yanodaand Wǔzhǐshān. The on-site restaurant has excellent Chinese food at reasonable prices. Finding the inn the first time is a bit difficult so it's best to catch a taxi.

Resort In Time RESORT **$$$**
(湘投银泰度假酒店; Xiāngtóu Yíntài Dùjià Jiǔdiàn; ☎8821 0888; www.resortintime.com; Dàdōnghǎi Bay; r from Y1288; @) It feels a bit like you are entering a busy bus terminal when you walk in the lobby and head up the elevator to reception, but that's about the only thing pedestrian about this great little resort right by the beach. The hotel grounds are surprisingly large and leafy, and feature a barbecue area near the pool. The rooms aren't the most spacious but those with sea views are set at a perfect angle to take in the bay. Nonsmoking floors are available.

Sānyà Backpackers HOSTEL **$$**
(三亚背包度假屋; Sānyà Bēibāo Dùjià Wū; ☎8821 3963; www.sanyabackpackers.com; No 2 Type 1 Villa, Lu Ming Community, Haihua Lu, Dàdōnghǎi Bay; dm Y75-90, d/tw Y240/200;) The new kid on the hostel block, Sānyà is run by a Singaporean diving instructor who's trying to lift scuba standards in Hǎinán. The spic and span rooms are set in a stylish whitewashed building in a quiet residential compound off Haihua Lu. Sānyà was just getting set up at the time of writing but should have a rooftop bar and breakfast cafe by the time you read this. Diving lessons, open water certification as well as outings and equipment rental should also be available.

Blue Sky International Youth Hostel HOSTEL **$**
(蓝天国际青年旅舍; Lántiān Guójì Qīngnián Lǚshè; ☎8818 2320; sy.youthhostel@gmail.com; 1 Lanhai Alley, Haiyun Lu, Dàdōnghǎi Bay; dm/tw/d Y50/140/160;) A long-term and popular backpacker hang-out in Dàdōnghǎi. There's wi-fi, bike rentals, laundry, and a good restaurant serving backpacker favourites. The staff can arrange tours around Sānyà, though some of the prices looked higher than at other places. The hostel is in a lane running off to the left just past the fruit lane as you head down Haiyun Lu.

Minhu Hotel HOTEL **$**
(民和宾馆; Mínhé Bīnguǎn; ☎8821 2281; 12th fl, Haitianhuiyuan Bldg, 96 Yuya Lu, Dàdōnghǎi Bay; s/tw Y70/80) The rooms are cheap and basic but have unexpectedly good views over the ocean. The entrance is around the back of the Kai Yuan Hotel but it's easiest to approach from Haiyun Lu by turning right down a small alley almost adjacent to the fruit street.

Eating

The entire beachfront at Dàdǒnghǎi is one long strip of restaurants, bars, and cafes, most of which are overpriced and not terribly good, even if the overall atmosphere is cool, shady and scenic.

Rainbow Bar & Grill BAR & GRILL **$$**
(云博西餐酒吧; Yúnbó Xīcān Jiǔbā; www.rainbowbargrill.com; 1f Eadry Resort Hotel, Time Coast, Yuya Lu, Sānyà; mains Y30-55; 10am-late;) Rainbow serves spot-on Western favourites such as club sandwiches (Y45) and burgers, and features a pool table, dance floor and live music most nights. The location is by the river between Sānyà and Dàdōnghǎi.

Pattaya Thai Cuisine THAI **$$**
(芭堤雅泰式餐饮酒吧; Bādīyǎ Tàishì Cānyǐn Jiǔbā; dishes Y28-58; 10am-10pm) Serves some great Thai staples with a killer view over the bay. The location is on the boardwalk, behind Resort In Time. There's a picture menu.

Sunny Sanya Family Inn LOCAL CUISINE **$$**
(红屋顶家庭旅馆; Hóngwūdǐng Jiātíng Lǚguǎn; ☎8820 9345; www.sunnysanya.com; 29 Haiyun Lu, Dàdōnghǎi Bay; breakfast, lunch & dinner;) Has good local dishes, including a number of fresh seafood dishes, at very reasonable prices.

Drinking

Most of the after-hours fun is in Sānyà and Dàdōnghǎi Bay.

Bud CAFE, BAR
(三亚早苗休闲会馆; Sānyà Zǎomiáo Xiūxián Huìguǎn; www.zaomiaosanya.com; 11f Shenshixindi Bldg, cnr Sanyawan Lu & Jixiang Lu, Sānyà; 三亚市三亚晚路吉祥路口盛世新第大楼十一楼; drinks from Y22; 1pm-2am) Overlooking Sānyà Bay, Bud serves fruit drinks, teas, coffees and alcoholic drinks until late from its inimitable rooftop location. Enter to the left of the shop with the sign 'Military mu robust keeping in good health hall'.

Fat Daddy's BAR
(胖老巴; Pàng Lǎobā; cnr Sanyawan & Jinjiling Lu, Sānyà; 三亚市三亚晚路金鸡岭路口; drinks from Y20; ⏲11am-1am; 📶🍴) Just up the road from Bud is this ground-level bar with a leafy outdoor patio across from the beach, and a large indoor bar with pool tables. Folksy rock music is played loud and there's a big selection of cocktails and beers, including some Australian microbrews. Fat Daddy's is also popular for its generous steaks and pizzas.

Information

There is the full gamut of internet cafes, banks, travel agencies etc in Sānyà city as well as Dàdōnghǎi Bay. You can make international calls from a number of shops on Haiyun Lu.

Bank of China (中国银行; Zhōngguó Yínháng; Yuya Lu, Dàdōnghǎi Bay) Changes travellers cheques and has an ATM.

Internet cafe (网吧; wǎngbā; Haiyun Lu, Dàdōnghǎi Bay; per hr Y3; ⏲24hr)

Getting There & Away

Air

Sānyà's **Phoenix Airport** (www.sanyaairport.com) has international flights to Singapore, Hong Kong, Malaysia, Thailand, Taiwan and Japan, as well as to Běijīng (Y2310), Guǎngzhōu (Y780) and Shànghǎi (Y1830).

Bus

Frequent buses and minibuses to most parts of Hǎinán depart from the **long-distance bus station** (Jiefang Lu, Sānyà).

Hǎikǒu Y77, 3½ hours, regular services

Wǔzhǐshān Y23, two hours, regular services

Getting Around

Phoenix Airport is 25km from Dàdōnghǎi Bay. Shuttle bus 8 (Y8) leaves for the airport from Yuya Lu. A taxi should cost Y50.

Buses 2 and 8 (Y1, frequent) travel from Sānyà bus station to Dàdōnghǎi Bay. From Dàdōnghǎi Bay to Yàlóng Bay, catch bus 15 (Y5). Motorcycle sidecars charge Y3 to Y5 to most places.

Taxis charge Y5 for the first 2km. A taxi from Sānyà to Dàdōnghǎi Bay costs Y10 to Y15, and from Dàdōnghǎi Bay to Yàlóng Bay it's Y40.

Around Sānyà

YANODA RAINFOREST 呀诺达雨林

About 50% of Hǎinán is still densely forested, though much is under constant threat from development. A section of land between Sānyà and Wǔzhǐshān called **Yanoda Rainforest** (Yānuòdá Yǔlín; www.yanoda.com; admission Y188; ⏲9am-5pm) has been set aside as a reserve and park, and with its abundant banyans, bamboo, ficus, rattan and host of creepers and vines, it's a very fine example of a tropical rainforest. A wood boardwalk winds its way up through the forest, allowing you to get right under vines, around trees and over rocky patches.

To get to the reserve, make a reservation with your hotel in Sānyà the day before you want to visit. A free shuttle bus leaves from Resort InTime at around 9am and returns around 4pm. Admission includes a free (but lousy) buffet lunch.

If you've seen everything before 4pm, which is likely, head 1km down the road from the park to the central highway and hail any bus heading to Sānyà (Y8 to Y12).

To explore Hǎinán's forests without the crowds, head to Wǔzhǐshān, Bǎotíng or the very remote **Jiānfēnglǐng National Forest Park** (尖峰岭国家森林公园; Jiānfēnglǐng Guójiā Sēnlín Gōngyuán; www.jflpark.com), about 115km west of Sānyà. You need your own transportation to make this latter trip worthwhile, as it's a massive area. Hostels sometimes have day trips to Jiānfēnglǐng.

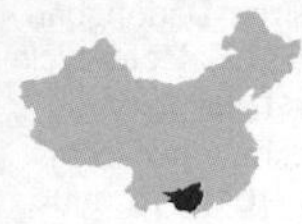

Guǎngxī

POPULATION: 50 MILLION

Includes »

Best Places to Eat

» Luna (p595)
» River Bar (p595)
» Āmóu Meǐshí (p600)

Best Places to Stay

» Jìngguān Mínglóu Hotel (p587)
» Yangshuo Village Inn (p594)
» Wànjiǐnglóu (p591)

Why Go?

Tell someone in China that you're heading to Guǎngxī (广西) and they'll seethe with envy. It's hard not to fall for this achingly beautiful province, which offers endless rewards for those with an outdoorsy temperament. The star attraction is the much-loved karst scenery in Guìlín and Yángshuò, where travellers can venture off by bicycle or hike through lush, green valleys.

Expect the mighty rush of the Détiān Waterfall, and the marvellous Chéngyáng Wind and Rain Bridge on the highlands, to dazzle you. A trek through the lofty Dragon's Backbone Rice Terraces gives you a glimpse into the distinct tradition of each village, populated by diverse minority groups like the Zhuang, Yao and Dong.

For less-active travellers, come and discover the secrets of the 2000-year-old Huāshān cliff murals in a peaceful boat journey on the Zuǒ River; or simply wander along the quaint old settlements in Běihǎi and savour its wonderful human landscape.

When to Go

Guìlín

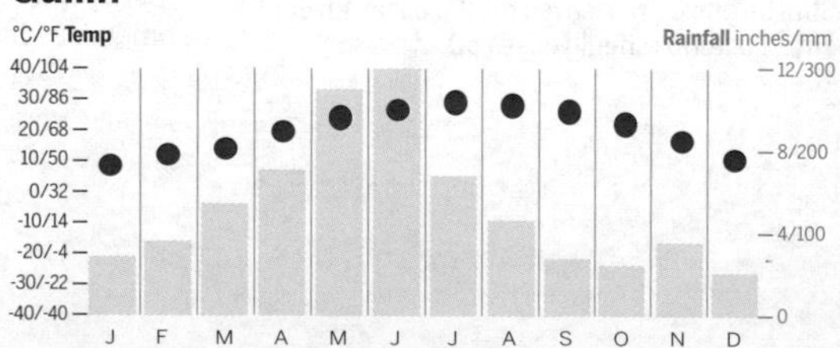

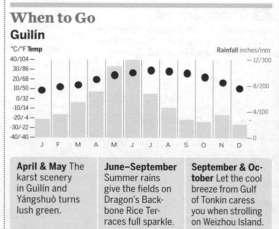

April & May The karst scenery in Guìlín and Yángshuò turns lush green.

June–September Summer rains give the fields on Dragon's Backbone Rice Terraces full sparkle.

September & October Let the cool breeze from Gulf of Tonkin caress you when strolling on Weizhou Island.

Guǎngxī Highlights

1. Lose yourself among the dramatic limestone scenery in **Yángshuò** (p592) when cycling alongside the Yùlóng River
2. Trek through China's most spectacular highland vistas at **Dragon's Backbone Rice Terraces** (p590)
3. Admire the striking **Chéngyáng Wind and Rain Bridge** (p591) near Sānjiāng and experience the rural pleasure around nearby paddies
4. Feel the spray of the **Détiān Waterfall** (p607) before village-hopping to **Míngshì Tiányuán** (p608)
5. Enjoy the puttering boat journey from Pānlóng to the 2000-year-old **Huāshān cliff murals** (p606)
6. Promenade through the 19th-century streets of the old town of **Běihǎi** (p602)
7. Take a breather on breezy **Wéizhōu Island** (p605), and marvel at its diverse coral communities by swimming or snorkelling

PRICE INDICATORS

The following price indicators are used in this chapter:

Sleeping

$	less than Y150
$$	Y150 to Y350
$$$	more than Y350

Eating

$	less than Y40
$$	Y40 to Y100
$$$	more than Y100

History

In 214 BC a Qin-dynasty army attempted to assimilate the Zhuang people, living in what is now called Guăngxī, into their newly formed Chinese empire. But while the eastern and southern parts submitted, the western extremes remained largely controlled by hill-tribe chieftains. The system was further complicated in the northern regions by the Yao and Miao tribespeople who had been driven from their homes in Húnán and Jiāngxī by the advance of the Han Chinese. Unlike the majority of the Zhuang, the Yao and Miao refused to be assimilated and remained in conflict with the Han for centuries.

Major tribal uprisings occurred in the 19th century, the most significant being the Taiping Rebellion (1850–64), which began in Guìpíng and became one of the bloodiest civil wars in human history.

Communist bases were set up in Guăngxī following the 1929 Baise Uprising led by Deng Xiaoping, although they were eventually destroyed by Kuomintang forces. And much of Guăngxī fell briefly under Japanese rule following highly destructive WWII invasions.

Today the Zhuang, China's largest minority group, make up 32% of Guăngxī's population, leading to the province being reconstituted in 1955 as the Guăngxī Zhuang Autonomous Region. As well as Zhuang, Miao and Yao, Guăngxī is home to significant numbers of Dong people.

Language

Travellers with a grasp of Mandarin *(pŭtōnghuà)* will have few problems navigating Guăngxī's vast sea of languages. Cantonese *(guăngdōnghuà)*, known as *báihuà* in these parts, is the language of choice in Nánníng, Chóngzuŏ, Píngxiáng and Dàxīn, but most people also understand Mandarin. Visitors will also hear a number of minority languages being spoken, such as Zhuang, Dong, Xiang, Hmong, Sui, Hakka, Jing (Vietnamese) and Yi.

The Zhuang romanisation system, looking like badly spelled Pinyin, is prominently displayed, while bilingual Chinese/Vietnamese signs can be seen in areas nearing Vietnam.

In Guìlín and Yángshuò, you'll come across locals with excellent knowledge of English.

Guìlín 桂林

0773 / POP 740,000

Whether you're going north to the highlands, or south to Yángshuò and beyond, Guìlín is where you're likely to spend a night or two. Set off alongside the tranquil Lí River (漓江; Lí Jiāng) for a good introduction to Guăngxī's dreamlike scenery, with its otherworldly karst topography as a backdrop. Many streets are embroidered with osmanthus trees, filling the air with a sweet fragrance.

The city's complete reliance on tourism means that it's well managed and clean, but you'll have to share it with the crowds, and admission fees to most sights soar. However, you'll see scenery that outstrips Guìlín in Yángshuò, so you won't miss too much if you skip sightseeing here.

With modern facilities and a high percentage of English-speaking locals, Guìlín is a convenient base to plan trips to the rest of the province.

Sights

Solitary Beauty Peak PARK

(独秀峰; Dúxiù Fēng; 1 Wangcheng; 王城1号; admission Y70; 7.30am-6pm) A peaceful, leafy retreat from the city centre, the entrance fee for this famous pinnacle includes admission to **Wáng Chéng** (王城), a 14th-century Ming prince's mansion, now home to Guăngxī Normal University (lucky students!). The 152m peak is a steep climb, but affords fine views of Guìlín. Buses 1 and 2 both stop nearby.

Reed Flute Cave CAVE

(芦笛岩; Lúdí Yán; admission Y90; 7.30am-6pm) Former US Secretary of State Henry

Kissinger described the cave as 'poetic', although chances are he didn't have the dulcet tones of a Chinese tour guide ringing in his ears when the thought came to him. The huge Reed Flute Cave is a garish but nonetheless impressive grotto housing multicoloured lighting and fantastic stalactites and stalagmites. The entrance was once distinguished by clumps of reeds used to fashion musical instruments, hence the name, and the enormous **Crystal Palace of the Dragon King** was used as an air-raid shelter during wars. It's tempting to slip away from the tour groups, but bring a torch, as the illuminations are often turned off as the crowds walk on. Bus 3 and free bus 58 both go here.

Seven Stars Park PARK

(七星公园; Qīxīng Gōngyuán; admission Y35, Seven Star Caves Y30; ⊙park 6am-9.30pm, caves 8am-5.30pm) One of China's original tourist attractions, first opening to sightseers during the Sui dynasty, the 137-hectare Seven Stars Park makes for some pleasant strolls. There are peaks to climb, caves to explore, lawns to picnic on and even wild monkeys to see; early evening on Moon Tooth Hill (月牙山; Yuèyá Shān) is your best bet. Skip the thoroughly depressing zoo.

To get here, walk, cycle or catch bus 10 or 11 from the train station. From the park, free bus 58 runs to Wave Subduing Hill, Folded Brocade Hill and Reed Flute Cave.

City Wall WALL REMNANTS

About 1km north of Folded Brocade Hill is the **East Gate** (东镇门; Dōngzhèn Mén), a part-reconstructed gateway flanked by crumbling sections of the original Song-dynasty city wall (城墙; *chéng qiáng*). Take bus 1, 2 or free bus 51 and get off at Dōngzhèn Lù, then turn right down the road of the same name. Alternatively it's a short walk or cycle north along the riverbank, just east of the entrance to Folded Brocade Hill. The gate lies on the northeast edge of **Mùlóng Lake Park** (木龙湖; Mùlóng Hú; admission Y10; ⊙9am-10pm), which houses a pretty reconstruction of a Song-dynasty pagoda (木龙塔; Mùlóng Tǎ) and is a picturesque setting for Chinese classical music performances, held at 8pm every evening.

On the northern shore of Róng Lake (榕湖; Róng Hú), and strikingly illuminated at night, the more centrally located **South Gate** (南门; Nán Mén) is the only surviving part of this section of the wall.

Sun & Moon Twin Pagodas PAGODAS

(日月双塔; Rìyuè Shuāng Tǎ; admission Y30; ⊙8.30am-10.30pm) Elegantly embellishing the scenery of **Shān Lake** (杉湖; Shān Hú), the Sun and Moon Twin Pagodas, beautifully illuminated at night, are the highlight of a stroll around Guìlín's two central lakes. The octagonal, seven-storey **Moon Pagoda** (月塔; Yuè Tǎ) is connected by an underwater tunnel to the 41m-high **Sun Pagoda** (日塔; Rì Tǎ), the world's tallest copper pagoda and one of the few pagodas anywhere in the world with a lift.

Other Hills HILLS

Just west of Solitary Beauty Peak is **Wave-Subduing Hill** (伏波山; Fúbō Shān; admission Y25; ⊙7am-6pm), which offers more great views as well as the chance to see Song- and Tang-dynasty Buddhist carvings etched into the walls of **Returned Pearl Cave** (还珠洞; Huánzhū Dòng). A short walk further north is **Folded Brocade Hill** (叠彩山; Diécǎi Shān; admission Y20; ⊙7am-6pm), where you can find arguably the best views of the city, some restored Ming-dynasty pavilions and, inside **Wind Cave** (风洞; Fēngdòng), another fine collection of Buddhist sculptures. Just south of the city centre is **Elephant Trunk Hill** (象鼻山; Xiàngbí Shān; admission Y40; ⊙7am-6.30pm), perhaps best viewed

RISING PEAKS

Scraping your jaw off the floor as you gape at the stunning karst peaks that attract mountains of tourists to Guǎngxī every year, it's hard to imagine how the view could get any better. In fact, the sheer beauty of this region may not yet have reached its pinnacle. The peaks here are the result of erosion from carbonic acid, created when rainwater reacts with carbon dioxide in the air. This erosion allowed cracks to open up in the limestone, which later widened to form caves whose tops eventually collapsed, leaving only their tall sides still standing. But because levels of carbonic acid here are lower in rainwater than they are in soil, the base of these dramatic peaks is being eroded at a greater rate than their bulk, the sides of which are too steep for soil to settle on. The result is that Guǎngxī's famous towering peaks are actually slowly growing taller.

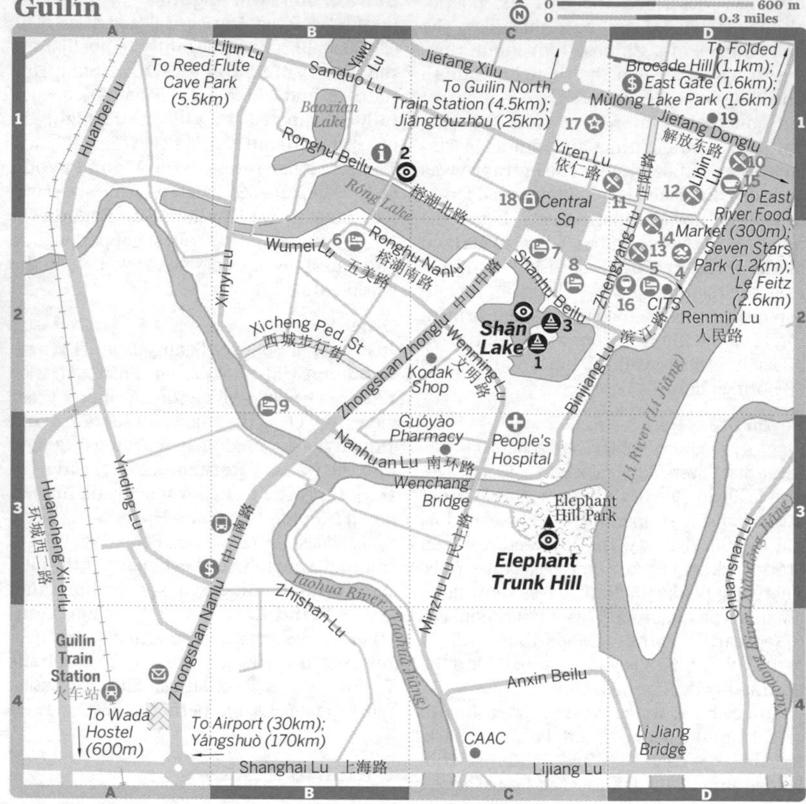

from one of the bamboo rafts (about Y5) that float down the Lí River.

Activities

Swimming in the Lí River is very popular in summer. If that's not clean enough for you, the **Sheraton** (喜来登酒店; Xǐláidēng Jiǔdiàn; ☎282 5588; 15 Binjiang Lu; 滨江路15号) has an outdoor pool (admission Y30).

Tours

The very popular Lí River trip from Guìlín to Yángshuò lasts about 4½ hours and includes a wonderfully scenic boat trip to Yángshuò, lunch, and a bus ride back to Guìlín. Expect to pay Y350 to Y450 for a boat with an English-speaking guide or Y245 for the Chinese version. China International Travel Service (CITS; 中国国际旅行社; Zhōngguó Guójì Lǚxíngshè), p589, can arrange it, as can pretty much every hotel and tourist information service centre in Guìlín.

Sleeping

Wada Hostel HOSTEL $
(瓦当旅舍; Wǎdāng Lǚshè; ☎215 4888; www.wada-hostel.com; 212 Huanchengxi Yilu; 环城西一路212号; dm Y15-Y35, d Y110; ❄@) This new hostel is a bit out from the action in the city centre but the useful bus 10 will connect you to most of the attractions. A plus is that all buses to Yángshuò stop at its main entrance. It has a comfortable bar and cafe, and various types of dorms with huge bunk beds. To get there from the train station, take the first right on Shanghai Lu. Go under the bridge and turn left at the intersection onto Huanchengxi Yilu. From there it's a 10-minute walk (600m) and the hostel is on the left.

Backstreet Youth Hostel HOSTEL $
(后街国际青年旅舍; Hòujiē Qīngnián Lǚshè; ☎281 9936; guilinhostel@hotmail.com; 3 Renmin Lu; 人民路3号; dm/d Y45/120; ❄@) The pros: rooms are big (even the dorms) and

Guìlín

Top Sights

Sights

Activities, Courses & Tours

Sleeping

Eating

Drinking

Entertainment

Shopping

Transport

decorated tastefully with wood furnishings, and the location is superb, with bars, restaurants and shops just a stone's throw away. The cons: Caucasian travellers are preferred here, and some of the rooms are smelly (check them out before paying).

Riverside Hostel INN $$
(九龙商务旅游酒店; Jiǔlóng Shāngwù Lǚyóu Jiǔdiàn; ☎258 0215; www.guilin-hostel.com; 6 Zhumu Xiang, Nanmen Qiao; 南门桥竹木巷6号; s & d Y100-220; ❄@) This cosy inn by the Táohuā River (桃花江) is highly recommended by travellers (especially couples). Staff are attentive and rooms are comfy. The tatami rooms fill up fast. Its three-room branch, **Lakeside Inn** (背包驿站; Bēibāo Yìzhàn; ☎280 6806; 1-1-2 Shanhu Beilu; 杉湖北路杉湖综合楼1-1-2号) by Shān Lake is equally good. Advance bookings by phone or via the website are essential.

Jìngguān Mínglóu Hotel HOTEL $$$
(静观茗楼度假酒店; Jìngguān Mínglóu Dùjià Jiǔdiàn; ☎228 3265; 9 Ronghu Nanlu; 榕湖南路9号; standard/deluxe d Y380/480, deluxe ste Y1380; ❄) If luxury chain hotels are not your cup of tea, book this one. This adorable hotel with stunning views of Róng Lake and Guìlín's surrounding karst scenery is simply exquisite. Reproduction antique Chinese furniture adorns the lobby and extends into the fabulous rooms. The friendly staff don't speak English and there's nowhere to eat here, but small restaurants and cafes line the lakeside, so you won't have far to walk.

Líjiāng Waterfall Hotel HOTEL $$$
(漓江大瀑布饭店; Líjiāng Dàpùbù Fàndiàn; ☎282 2881; www.waterfallguilin.com; 1 Shanhu Beilu; 杉湖北路1号; d without/with river view Y1320/1480, discounts of 10-30%; ⊖❄@≋) This top-notch hotel has first-class facilities, wonderfully accommodating staff and a general feeling of grandeur, particularly if you walk up to its magnificent 2nd-floor atrium. Some rooms have stunning views of the river and lakes. It's also the proud owner of the world's tallest man-made waterfall (45m high), turned on daily from 8.30pm to 8.45pm and best viewed from Central Sq.

Eating

Local specialities include Guìlín rice noodles (桂林米粉; Guìlín *mǐfěn*), beer duck (啤酒鸭; *píjiǔ yā*) and Guìlín snails (桂林田螺; Guìlín *tiánluó*), while the ubiquitous *chǎoguō fàn* (炒锅饭; claypot rice dishes; from Y6) make a great snack.

Cantonese and Western food are not uncommon in the city. The pedestrianised Zhengyang Lu and its surrounding lanes are the busiest dining area, while there's a cluster of fish restaurants on Nanhuan Lu, just east of Wenchang Bridge.

Zhèngyáng Tāngchéng SOUP $$
(正阳汤城; 8 Zhengyang Lu; dishes Y25-78; ⏲11.30am-3am; 🗐) Easily one of the most popular soup restaurants in the city serving local specialities. The alfresco dining area is a prime people-watching spot. We especially recommend the grilled Lí River fish and soup with sea bass and chrysanthemum.

Zhèngzōng Yóuzháwáng SNACKS $
(正宗油炸王; Yīren Lu; skewers from Y1.50; ⏲10.30am-2am) For late-night spicy, and we mean spicy, *má là chuàn* (麻辣串; spicy kebabs), you could do worse than this friendly hole-in-the-wall near the corner of Zhengyang Lu and Yiren Lu. No menu. No need. Just point, pay and eat. It's next to KFC.

Amani PIZZA $$
(阿玛尼; Āmǎní; ☎210 6351; Binjiang Lu; pizzas from Y38; ⏲10am-1am) Customers flock here for the tasty pizza, possibly the best in town. The laid-back setting makes this an easy place to while away the hours. It has a more hectic **branch** (☎280 9351; 159 Zhengyang Lu; ⏲10am-2am) on the pedestrianised street.

Fúji Chángfěnzhōu DIM SUM $
(福记肠粉粥; Yiren Lu; dishes from Y5.50-15; ⏲10am-midnight) A simple, neat, canteen-style restaurant that serves dim sum and light Cantonese meals. Porridge and steamed vermicelli rolls are the specialities here. Try the steamed roll with shrimp (鲜虾拉肠; *xiānxiā lācháng*) and minced pork congee with preserved egg (皮蛋瘦骨肉粥; *pídàn shòuròuzhōu*). No English menu. For dim sum you can pick from the cart.

Bǎiwèi Dumpling Restaurant DUMPLINGS $
(百味饺子馆; Bǎiwèi Jiǎoziguǎn; ☎210 6743; 9-5 Libin Lu; dishes from Y8; ⏲9.30am-10.30pm; 📋) This pocket-sized restaurant in an alley just off Yiren Lu is a dumpling lover's heaven. The minimum order is 20 pieces (Y0.30 to Y0.40 per piece). English menu now available.

Drinking & Entertainment

Guìlín's streets are dotted with trendy little cafes, while Zhengyang Lu has a short stretch of bars with outdoor seating.

Le Feitz BAR
(翡翠酒吧; Fěicuì Jiǔbā; ☎137 3773 4082; 1-8 Chaoyang Lu, University Residence; 朝阳路大学生公寓城1-8号; ⏲10am-midnight) Frequented by local college students and expats alike, Le Feitz is arguably the most popular Irish pub in Guilin. It has live music almost every evening. It's near the north gate of Guangxi Normal University (朝阳路师大北门; Cháoyáng Lù Shìdàběimén).

Joys Bar CLUB
(爵色酒吧; Juésè Jiǔbā; inside Guilin Culture Palace; 桂林文化宫内; ⏲9pm-2.30am) The sturdy wooden furnishing and velvet curtains give this Chinese-style club a classy yet unfussy feel. The clientele is mostly a trendy, 20ish local crowd, but it has started to attract a smattering of expats.

Paulaner BAR
(柏龙酒吧; Bólóng Jiǔbā; 2 Zhengyang Lu; ⏲4pm-1.30am) Prices surged after its recent facelift but it still serves the best German beer in town. The big-screen TV is still there for sports fans.

Little Italian CAFE
(这里; Zhèlǐ; 18 Binjiang Lu; ⏲10am-midnight; @) A pleasant, studenty place that offers great coffee and breakfast goodies. Free internet access.

Steam Coffee CAFE
(爱上咖啡; Àishàng Kāfēi; 10 Binjiang Lu; ⏲10am-midnight) One of several trendy cafes on this stretch of street and serves equally good coffee.

Shopping

Night Market MARKET
(夜市; Yèshì; Zhongshan Zhonglu; ⏲from 7pm) For souvenirs, check out Guìlín's night market, which runs along Zhongshan Zhonglu from Ronghu Beilu to Sanduo Lu.

East River Food Market MARKET
(东江市场; Dōngjiāng Shìchǎng; ⏲6am-8pm) On the way to Seven Stars Park, this bustling undercover market sells everything from fresh fruit and vegetables to live eels.

Information

Buy a map of Guìlín (桂林地图; Guìlín Dìtú) from bookshops or kiosks (Y6).

CD Burning & Internet Access

Many hostels have internet access and wi-fi.

Kodak shop (柯达商店; Kēdá shāngdiàn; 8 Zhongshan Zhonglu; ⏲8.30am-10.30pm) Burns CDs (刻光盘; *kè guāngpán*) for Y20 a disk. Located outside the Míngchéng Hotel (Míngchéng Jiǔdiàn).

Medical Services

Guóyào Pharmacy (国药大药房; Guóyào Dàyàofáng; 19 Nanhuan Lu; ⏲8am-8pm) Just around the corner from the People's Hospital.

People's Hospital (人民医院; Rénmín Yīyuàn; Wenming Lu)

Money

The **Bank of China** (中国银行; Zhōngguó Yínháng) branches on Zhongshan Nanlu (near the main bus station) and Jiefang Donglu change money and travellers cheques, give credit-card advances and have 24-hour ATMs.

Post

China Post (中国邮政; Zhōngguó Yóuzhèng; Zhongshan Beilu; ⏲8am-7pm) A large branch of China Post: it's 500m north of the roundabout of Jiefang Donglu. There's another handy branch by the train station.

Public Security Bureau

PSB (公安局; Gōng'ānjú; ☎582 3492; 16 Shijiayan Lu; ⏲8.30am-noon & 3-6pm Mon-Fri) Can extend visas. It's located by Xiǎodōng River and 500m south of the Seven Stars Park. A taxi ride from downtown will cost around Y18.

Telephone

You can buy IC and IP phonecards, and top up your mobile, at any number of corner shops displaying a small telephone sign. There's one (小卖店; Xiǎomài Diàn) beside Backstreet Youth Hostel.

Tourist Information

Guìlín Tourist Information Service Centre (桂林旅游咨询服务中心; Guìlín Lǚyóu Zīxún Fúwù Zhōngxīn; ☎280 0318; South Gate, Ronghu Beilu; ⏲8am-10pm) These helpful centres dot the city. There's a good one by the South Gate on Róng Lake.

Travel Agencies

China International Travel Service (CITS; 中国国际旅行社; Zhōngguó Guójì Lǚxíngshè; www.guilintrav.com; Binjiang Lu) Helpful staff. There are other branches everywhere.

Getting There & Away

Air

Air tickets can be bought from the **Civil Aviation Administration of China** (CAAC; 中国民航; Zhōngguó Mínháng; ☎384 7252; cnr Shanghai Lu & Anxin Beilu; ⏲7.30am-8.30pm). Direct flights to/from Guìlín include Běijīng (Y1440), Chéngdū (Y980), Chóngqìng (Y840), Hǎikǒu (Y890), Guǎngzhōu (Y990), Hong Kong (Xiānggǎng; Y1410), Kūnmíng (Y840), Shànghǎi (Y1300) and Xī'ān (Y1090).

International destinations include Seoul, Korea (Hànchéng; Y2185), and Osaka, Japan (Dàbǎn; Y3500).

Bus

Guìlín's **main bus station** (客运总站; Guìlín kèyùn zǒngzhàn; ☎382 2666; Zhongshan Nanlu) is north of the train station. There are regular buses to the following destinations:

Běihǎi Y172, seven hours, three daily (8.30am, 9.20am and 9pm)

Guǎngzhōu Y169, 9½ hours, six daily

Huángyáo Y47, five hours, three daily (9.10am, 1.10pm and 2.20pm)

Lóngshèng Y30, two hours, every 40 minutes

Nánníng Y98 to Y108, five hours, every 15 minutes

Sānjiāng Y33, four hours, hourly

Shēnzhèn Y252, 12 hours, two daily (1.20pm and 5.40pm)

Yángshuò Y15 to Y18, 1½ hours, every 15 minutes

Train

Few trains start in Guìlín, so it's often tough to find tickets, especially for hard sleepers. Buy them at least a couple of days in advance if possible. Most trains leave from Guìlín Station (桂林站; Guìlín Zhàn), but some may leave from Guìlín North Train Station (桂林北站; Guìlín Běizhàn), which is 9km north of the city centre.

Direct services include:

Běijīng Y416, 23 hours, four daily (1.56am, 1.28pm, 3.36pm and 7.02pm)

Chóngqìng Y272, 19 hours, one daily (8.42am)

Guǎngzhōu Y207, 12 hours, two daily (6.28pm and 9.23pm)

Kūnming Y281, 18 hours 30 minutes, three daily (3.34pm, 4.30pm and 4.56pm)

Nánníng Y65, five hours 30 minutes, regular services

Shànghǎi Y341, 22 hours, four daily (12.12pm, 2.05pm, 5.02pm and 5.33pm)

Xī'ān Y385, 27 hours, one daily (5.54pm)

Getting Around

To/From the Airport

Guìlín's Liǎngjiāng International Airport (两江国际机场; Liǎngjiāng Guójì Jīchǎng) is 30km west of the city. Half-hourly shuttle buses (Y20) run from the CAAC office between 6.30am and 9pm. From the airport, shuttle buses meet every arrival. A taxi costs about Y80 (40 minutes).

Bicycle

Guìlín's sights are all within cycling distance. Many hostels rent bicycles (about Y20 per day). For decent bikes with gears, head to **Ride Giant** (捷安特自行车; Jié'āntè Zìxíngchē; ☎286 1286; 16 Jiefang Donglu; 解放东路16号; ⏲9am-8.30pm). Bike rental is Y30 per day, although the deposit is a whopping Y500.

Bus

Buses numbered 51 to 58 are all free. The following are the most useful for tourists:

Bus 2 Runs past the train and main bus stations, Elephant Trunk Hill, Liberation Bridge and Folded Brocade Hill.

Bus 10 Goes from Wada Hostel to the train and bus stations, and Seven Stars Park.

Bus 51 Starts at the train station and heads north along the length of Zhongshan Lu and beyond.

Bus 58 Goes to Elephant Trunk Hill, Seven Stars Park, Wave Subduing Hill, Folded Brocade Hill and Reed Flute Cave.

Around Guìlín

The fascinating 1000-year-old village of **Jiāngtóuzhōu** (江头洲), whose 800 inhabitants are all surnamed Zhōu (周), is tucked away among farmland about 25km north of Guìlín. There's an unmistakable rustic charm, with ducks and chickens running freely through narrow, cobblestone alleyways, which in turn house weathered, grey-brick courtyard homes fronted by huge wooden gates. As you approach the village, you'll notice the ancient and misshapen arched **Hùlóng Bridge** (护龙桥; Hùlóng Qiáo), opposite which is a public noticeboard. Follow the alleyway alongside the noticeboard and just keep wandering.

The only place to stay is the basic **Láishānlǐ Fànzhuāng** (来山里饭庄; ☎0773-633 1676; tw without/with air-con Y50/70; ❄) on the corner of the main road from Jiǔwū, about 500m back from the village. You can also eat here.

Jiāngtóuzhōu is a two- to three-hour bike ride from Guìlín (see p596). Alternatively, take an orange minibus on the stretch of Zhongshan Beilu near Guìlín North Train Station to Língchuān (灵川; Y3, 30 minutes), then change to a bus to Jiǔwū (九屋; Y4, 35 minutes), from where it's a 15-minute walk to the village. Buses stop running around 5.30pm.

Dragon's Backbone Rice Terraces 龙脊梯田

☎0773

This part of Guǎngxī boasts stunning views of terraced paddy fields, and the clear standout is **Dragon's Backbone Rice Terraces** (Lóngjǐ Tītián; adult Y50). The rice fields rise up to 1000m high and are an amazing feat of farm engineering on hills dotted with minority villages. The best time to visit is after the summer rains, which leave the fields glistening with reflections. The fields turn golden just before harvesting (October), and become snow-white in winter (December). Avoid visiting in early spring (March), when the mountains are shrouded in mist.

Dàzhài (大寨) is a laid-back Yao village that has an idyllic rural allure with a bubbling stream (look out for the snakes in the water). The number of guesthouses has mushroomed in recent years, but it remains relatively unspoilt by tourism. Continue uphill to the village of **Tiántóuzhài** (田头寨) atop the mountain. It's a sublime place to marvel at the panoramic views of the terraces, not to mention the sunrise or a starry night sky. **Píng'ān** (平安), a beautiful 600-year-old Zhuang village, is the biggest settlement and most popular among tourists. It has the best facilities, but expect to share your experience with the masses.

Most locals here are Zhuang or Yao, but you'll also find Dong and Miao people in the area.

There's nowhere in this area to change money, not even in Lóngshèng, so come prepared.

Activities

You can take any number of short **walks** from each village to some fabulous viewing points, and to really get among the terraces there are great **hiking** opportunities. The four- to five-hour trek between the villages of Dàzhài and Píng'ān, passing through the villages of Tiántóuzhài and Zhōngliù (中六), is highly recommended. The route is clearly signposted, but if you want a local to guide you, there will be plenty of offers. Expect to pay Y30 to Y40.

Sleeping & Eating

You can stay in traditional wooden homes of minority villagers (offer locals around Y20 for a simple bed), but three in particular – Dàzhài, Tiántóuzhài and Píng'ān – are set up for tourists.

Nearly all guesthouses offer food, and most guesthouses and restaurants have English menus. Look out for *zhútǒng fàn* (竹筒饭; Y10), a rice meal barbecued inside large bamboo sticks.

DÀZHÀI

Minority Cafe & Inn GUESTHOUSE $
(龙脊咖啡店; Lóngjǐ Kāfēidiàn; ☎758 5605; r Y30-45) Perched above the village on the trail leading up to Tiántóuzhài, this small, friendly guesthouse has a cute terrace and an English menu (dishes Y10 to Y25). It's about a 20-minute walk (1km) uphill from the main gate.

Yínhé Lǚguǎn GUESTHOUSE $
(银河旅馆; ☎133 2473 5211; tw without/with bathroom Y60/80) Rooms are basic but clean and go for Y30 to Y50 most of the time. It's on the left of the stream just as you enter Dàzhài from the bus stop.

TIÁNTÓUZHÀI

TOP CHOICE **Wànjiǐnglóu** INN $
(万景楼; ☎758 5665; www.wanjinglou.com, in Chinese; tw Y70-90) This excellent guesthouse is located above Tiántóuzhài. Rooms with sweeping views don't have bathrooms (but rooms without views do). The staff don't speak English but are helpful enough. After you leave the village of Tiántóuzhài, take the path up to the right (the left is to Píng'ān). From there it's another 15-minutes' walk (about 800m) and the guesthouse is above Dazhai Hostel. It can arrange direct shuttle buses to/from Guìlín.

Jīntián Guesthouse GUESTHOUSE $
(金田酒店; Jīntián Jiǔdiàn; ☎758 5683; www.ljjtjd.com; r Y80-100, discounts of 10-30% weekdays) All rooms are adequately comfortable, and the owner, Hanna, speaks excellent English. It's on the left as you walk up the hill from Dàzhài.

PÍNG'ĀN

Wàngjǐ Peasant Family Happy FARM STAY $
(望脊农家乐; Wàngjǐ Nóngjiālè; ☎758 3262; beds per person Y20) This weirdly named family-run guesthouse offers a less comfortable, but friendly, alternative to the ski-resort chalet lookalikes elsewhere in Píng'ān. On the way up the hill, bear right after the concrete Countryside Inn, walk past the school and continue up to the end of the path. Shared bathrooms only. Now has an English menu (dishes Y12 to Y40).

Lóngyǐng Hotel HOTEL $$
(龙颖饭店; Lóngyǐng Fàndiàn; ☎758 3059; tw without/with air-con incl breakfast Y220/280; ❄@) Located near the top of the village, this is the best-quality option in Píng'ān. Decent rooms with air-con often go for Y120. The manager speaks English and there are terrific views from the terrace. A new branch next to Dazu Hotel, with cheaper rooms (Y70 to Y100), is now open.

ℹ Getting There & Away

Hotels in Tiántóuzhài, including Wànjiǐnglóu and **Quánjǐng Lóu** (全景楼; ☎758 5688), arrange direct **shuttle service** between Guìlín and Dàzhài for their guests. They also take other passengers if seats are available. The bus (Y40, three hours) usually leaves Guìlín train station at 8.30am. Reservations are a must. These private shuttles are run by villagers, so if you speak Chinese you can book directly with the drivers. Among them are **Mr Liu** (☎152 9585 8826) and **Mr Pan** (☎137 3737 7986). Buses return to Guìlín at 11.30am.

All hotels in Píng'ān provide a similar service. The bus (Y30) leaves Guìlín train station at 1pm and returns at 10am. Again, **reservations** (☎138 7735 0504) are necessary.

If you opt for **public transport**, take a bus to Lóngshèng (龙胜) and ask to get off at Hépíng (和平). From that road junction, minibuses trundle back and forth between Lóngshèng and the rice terraces, stopping there to pick up passengers to Dàzhài (Y8, 45 minutes, every 20 minutes, 7am to 6pm) and Píng'ān (Y7, 30 minutes, every 30 minutes between 7.40am and 5pm). Buses to Guìlín (Y27, 1½ hours, 6.30am to 7pm) also stop over there. To continue to Sānjiāng (Y15, 1½ hours, hourly between 7am and 6pm), you have to catch a bus from Lóngshèng bus station.

Sānjiāng 三江

☎0772 / POP 360,000

Sānjiāng is notoriously humdrum, but it's a jumping-off point to get to the idyllic Dong villages and the exquisite Chéngyáng Wind and Rain Bridge.

The 78m-long **Chéngyáng Wind and Rain Bridge** (程阳桥; Chéngyáng Qiáo; admission Y60) is one of more than 100 nail-less bridges in the area built by the Dong (they are renowned carpenters) at the turn of the last century from fir logs. It took 12 years to knock together and is a picture of elegance.

You can **swim** in the river by Chéngyáng Bridge, while the surrounding network of villages makes for great **walks**. Possible **bike rides** include the tough, three-hour climb to the remote hilltop village of Gāoyǒu (高友; see the boxed text, p592).

There are a number of places to stay in the charming village of **Mǎ'ān** (马鞍) behind Chéngyáng Bridge. For its great location by the river (wooden waterwheel in front of you, bridges to your left), the pick of the bunch is **Dong Village Hotel** (侗家旅馆; Dòngjiā Lǚguǎn; ☎858 2421; www.donghotel.com; s/d/tr Y50/60/90). Walk over the bridge from the bus stop and turn left. Just inside the village, the friendly **Yang's Guesthouse** (程阳客栈; Chéngyáng Kèzhàn; ☎858 3126; r Y50-70; @)

GREAT GUĂNGXĪ BIKE RIDES

Lí Valley Boat-'n'-Bike Combo

YÁNGSHUÒ TO XĪNGPÍNG & BACK (15KM BOAT, 20KM CYCLE, HALF-DAY)

Combine a river cruise from Yángshuò to Xīngpíng (p597) with a bike ride back along this glorious valley. Put your bike on a bamboo raft (Y170 to Y250, 1½ hours), then sit back and enjoy the view to the historic village of Xīngpíng. From here, cycle south, following the trail past the villages of Gŭpí Zhài (古皮寨), Qiáotóu Pù (桥头铺) and Dòngxīn (洞心) before reaching Fúlì (福利), 4km east of Yángshuò. Just past Fúlì take your bike on a ferry (Y5) across the Lí River, then continue past Dùtóu (渡头) and back to Yángshuō, crossing the river once more, this time over a bridge.

Dong Village Lung Buster

CHÉNGYÁNG BRIDGE TO GĀOYŎU VILLAGE (16KM, THREE HOURS)

This challenging trip starts at the elegant Chéngyáng Wind and Rain Bridge and ends with a muscle-stretching 6km climb to the hilltop village of Gāoyŏu (高有). From the bridge, follow the river along the 10km road to Línxī (林溪), passing the villages of Píngzhài (平寨), Dōngzhài (东寨), Dàzhài (大寨), Píngpŭ (平埔) and Guàndòng (冠洞). If you don't have the time or energy for the climb up to Gāoyŏu, lunch here and head back to Chéngyáng Bridge (two to three hours round trip). If your thighs are up to it, turn right in the village centre, soon leaving the paved road behind you, and after 1.5km, by a small wind-and-rain bridge, turn sharply right to begin the big ascent. The mountain views are stunning, but even without stopping for photos it will take about 1½ hours to reach Gāoyŏu, where, just before the drum tower, on your right, you'll find the family-run **Gāoyŏu Guesthouse** (高有客栈; Gāoyŏu Kèzhàn; r Y20). Meals (Y30) are available, but no English is spoken. The freewheel back to Chéngyáng takes about two hours.

has bikes (Y20 per day), English-speaking staff and free internet.

Getting There & Away

Most buses go to and from the **east bus station** (河东车站; *hédōng chēzhàn*), but buses to Chéngyáng Bridge go from the **west bus station** (河西车站; *héxī chēzhàn*), a 10-minute walk (about 500m, or a Y2 rickshaw ride) across the river. To get to the west bus station, turn right from the east bus station, right again over the river and right once more after you cross the river. Steps up to the ticket office are 20m on the left. Bring cash; there's nowhere to withdraw money.

Buses depart regularly from Sānjiāng east bus station for Lóngshèng (Y18, 1½ hours, 6.30am to 5.50pm) and Guìlín (Y40, 3½ hours), and four daily depart for Tōngdào in Húnán (Y20, 2½ hours, 7.20am, 8.30am, 12.35pm and 1.45pm). For Chéngyáng Bridge, take the half-hourly bus bound for Línxī (林溪) from Sānjiāng west bus station (Y6, 30 minutes, 7.30am to 5.30pm). Do not despair if you miss the last bus. Private minivans to Línxī wait on the main road outside the west bus station. The fare is the same as the buses but they won't leave until they're full. If you're in a hurry, expect to pay Y30 to Y40 for the whole thing.

Yángshuò 阳朔

0773 / POP 310,000

Seasoned travellers to Guăngxī spend as little time in Guìlín as possible, preferring to make Yángshuò their base, though many of these veterans will gripe about Yángshuò's lack of authenticity – 'too many tourists', they complain. Yes, parts of it are very Western indeed. Whether you find this influence of Western culture repulsive or attractive, it doesn't change the fact that Yángshuò is gorgeous.

Yángshuò's dramatic karst landscape is at times otherworldly. Take a leisurely bamboo-raft ride or cycle through the dreamy valleys and you'll see. There's also a host of well-run courses and activities to keep you occupied far beyond your original intended length of stay. Travelling with kids is easy here. It's one of the more family-friendly Chinese destinations, with English-speaking locals, well set-up hostels and food for the finicky.

Sights

Peaks & Hills WALKS, VIEWS

Yángshuò is surrounded by towering, leafy, limestone peaks. The most accessible is **Bìlián Peak** (碧莲峰; Bìlián Fēng; admission Y30), which overlooks Xi Jie (West St) and the Lí River, and can be climbed in about half an hour for some excellent views. **Yángshuò Park** (阳朔公园; Yángshuò Gōngyuán) is a short walk west of Xi Jie and where you'll find **Man Hill** (西郎山; Xīláng Shān), which supposedly resembles a young man bowing to a shy young girl represented by **Lady Hill** (小姑山; Xiǎogū Shān). **Dragon Head Hill** (龙头山; Lóngtóu Shān) is a short walk north of the town centre.

Activities

Rock Climbing CLIMBING

Yángshuò is fast becoming one of the hottest climbing destinations in Asia. There are eight major peaks in regular use, already providing more than 250 bolted climbs. More are being bolted every year. **China Climb** (中国攀岩; Zhōngguó Pānyán; ☎881 1033; www.chinaclimb.com; 45 Xianqian Jie; ⏰9am-9pm), located inside Lizard Lounge bar, is the biggest climbing club in China and the most professional outfit in town. It offers local advice for experienced climbers and fully guided, bolted climbs for beginners. Prices start at Y300 per person for a half-day climb, with everything included. Also ask here for information on renting kayaks (from Y150 per day).

Cycling CYCLING

There's no shortage of places to rent bikes (from Y15 per day), but for the best equipment and strong advice on possible trips, try **Bike Asia** (☎882 6521; www.bikeasia.com; 42 Guihua Lu; 桂花路42号; ⏰9am-6pm), above Bar 98. Bikes go for Y50 per day (deposit Y350), including safety helmet and map. English-speaking guides (from Y300) are available.

Courses

Once you've exhausted the splendid countryside, Yángshuò is a premier place to expand your skills with a course or two.

Yángshuò Taichi Health Centre TAICHI

(阳朔太极拳健康中心; Yángshuò Tàijíquán Jiànkāng Zhōngxīn; ☎890 0125; www.chinasouth-taichi.com; Baoquan Lu; classes per hr/week/month Y80/1500/4000; ⏰office 8-11.30am & 2.30-5.30pm) Runs classes for both the Yang and Chen styles of taichi. Cheap accommodation is available for students.

Omeida Chinese Academy CHINESE LANGUAGE

(欧美达书院; Ōuměidá Shūyuàn; ☎881 2233; www.omeida.com.cn; Pantao Lu) Has reader-recommended Chinese-language classes. It offers two-week classes (10 hours per week) for Y1000 and also hires English teachers.

Yángshuò

Activities, Courses & Tours

1	Bike Asia	C1
2	China Climb	C1
3	Cloud 9 Restaurant	B2

Sleeping

4	Hóngfú Palace Hotel	C2
5	Monkey Jane's Guesthouse	C1

Eating

	Le Vôtre	(see 4)
6	Pure Lotus Vegetarian Restaurant	C1

Drinking

	Bar 98	(see 1)
7	Ming Yuan	C1

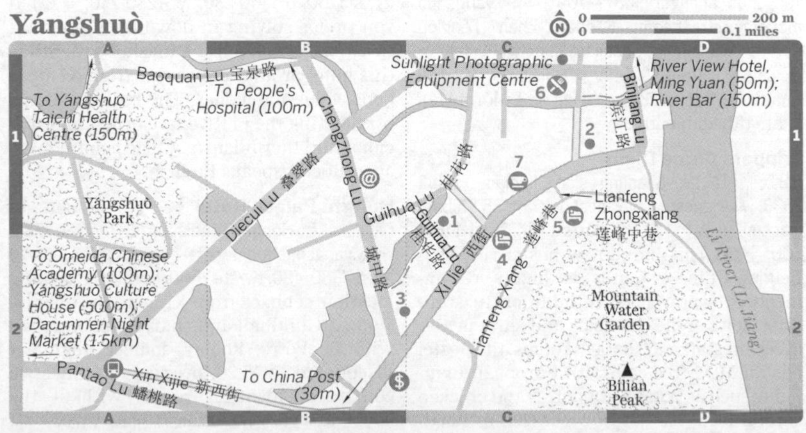

Cloud 9 Restaurant COOKING
(聚福楼; Jùfúlóu Fàndiàn; ☎881 3686; Chengzhong Lu) Runs two three-hour cooking courses a day, for around Y150 per person including market tour and lunch. Would-be chefs receive printouts of the recipes they've just messed up.

Sleeping

Yángshuò is teeming with hotels run by English-speaking staff, especially at the budget end of the market, and all provide internet access. While the Xi Jie neighbourhood has abundant options, some of the best lodgings are located on the outskirts of Yángshuò.

Yangshuo Village Inn BOUTIQUE HOTEL $$$
(听月楼; Tīngyuè Loú; ☎139 7836 9849; www.yangshuoguesthouse.com; Moon Hill Village; Yuèliàng Shān Lìcūn; 月亮山历村; d Y380-390, ste Y500; ❄) Located below Moon Hill (9km south of Yangshuo centre), the Village Inn is proud of its ecofriendly practices and high-quality services. Indeed, it exceeded all our expectations. Rooms with local handmade bamboo furniture are beyond fabulous, especially those in the tastefully renovated mudbrick farmhouse. Refillable water bottles are provided for guests to use. Staff are attentive and speak excellent English. The rooftop houses an Italian restaurant, Luna, with stunning views of Moon Hill. From Yángshuò bus station, take a minibus to Gāotiān (高田) and tell the driver to drop you at Lì Cūn (历村; Y5, every 15 minutes). A taxi from Xi Jie costs around Y30.

Its equally excellent sister hotel **Yangshuo Mountain Retreat** (阳朔胜地; Yángshuò Shèngdì; ☎877 7091; www.yangshuomountainretreat.com; Gāotián Zhèn Fēnglóu Cūnwěi Wánggōng Shānjiǎo; 高田镇凤楼村委王公山脚; r from Y500; ❄@), located by the beautiful Yùlóng River (遇龙河; Yùlóng Hé), is an affordable luxury.

Trippers Carpe Diem HOSTEL $$
(山景假日酒店; Shānjǐng Jiàrì Jiǔdiàn; ☎882 2533; www.guesthouseyangshuo.com; 35 Shibanqiaocun; 石板桥村35号; dm/s Y35/120, d Y160-300; ❄@) This brand-new hostel run by a Belgian-Chinese family is highly recommended by travellers. In addition to stunning views of the rice fields and karst peaks, excellent staff and spotless rooms, the hostel has an MSG-free cafe with European highlights such as potato croquettes and chicken cordon bleu. It's out of town (1.5km north of Xi Jie) but close enough to walk to. Walk along the river (upstream) for 15 minutes to Shíbǎnqiáo Village. A taxi from the bus station costs no more than Y20.

TOP CHOICE **Yangshuo Outside Inn** HOSTEL $
(荷兰饭店; Hélán Fàndiàn; ☎881 7109; www.yangshuo-outside.com; Cháolóng Village, Jìmǎ; 骥马朝龙村; dm/s Y50/100, d Y120-200; ❄@) Run by a Swiss family, this fabulous farmhouse-turned hostel surrounded by rural vistas is located 4km southwest of Yángshuò. The whole adobe complex is filled with rustic charm and a communal feel, which gives you a glimpse of rural life in China without compromising the standard of hygiene and comfort. An annexe with modern-furnished family suites (Y300 to Y500) was recently added. It's close to the Yùlóng River; a taxi here will cost Y25 or it's 20 minutes by bike. Check the website for directions and bookings.

Yángshuò Culture House GUESTHOUSE $
(阳朔文化小屋; Yángshuò Wénhuà Xiǎowū; ☎882 7750; www.yangshuo-study-travel.com; 110 Beisan Xiang, Chengxi Lu; 城西路北三巷110号; dm Y70, d & tw without/with bathroom Y70/80; ❄@) The pinewood rooms are nothing to write home about but they are bright and spacious. Owner Mr Wei can help organise activities and classes, but best of all he throws in three meals a day for free! It's about a 10-minute walk west of the bus station, along Chengxi Lu. Look out for the yellow sign on the right. This place gets booked up, so it's well worth making an online reservation.

River View Hotel HOTEL $$
(望江楼酒店; Wàngjiānglóu Jiǔdiàn; ☎882 2688; www.riverview.com.cn; 11 Binjiang Lu; 滨江路11号; s Y100, d Y100-230, tw Y230-250; ❄@) If you prefer staying in downtown but want to avoid the hubbub of Yángshuò's nightlife, this hotel around the corner from Xi Jie is good value for money. The balcony rooms overlooking the Lí River are bright and spacious, and they fill up fast. The helpful manager, Rocky, speaks English.

Hóngfú Palace Hotel HOTEL $$
(鸿福饭店; Hóngfú Fàndiàn; ☎137 3739 7888; www.yangshuohongfuhotel.com; 79 Xi Jie; 西街79号; d Y380-480, tw/ste Y660/880; ❄) Cracking location, set back from Xi Jie in the historic Jiangxi Guildhall and sharing its premises with Le Vôtre. Roomy doubles, regularly discounted to Y220, overlook a Qing-style courtyard. Identical rooms without the courtyard view go for as little as Y170.

Monkey Jane's Guesthouse HOSTEL $
(背包客栈; Bēibāo Kèzhàn; ☎882 1603; www.monkeyjane.pyksy.com; 28 Lianfeng Zhongxiang; 莲峰中巷28号; dm Y20, d without/with air-con Y60/80; ❄@) This famous hostel is perhaps more for those who want to party hard. Some travellers really enjoy the 'beer pong' game on its legendary rooftop bar (the views are jaw-dropping), while others find it crazy. The outer rooms are generally OK but others are gloomy and damp. Staff members are as friendly as ever, though.

Eating & Drinking

Local specialities include *píjiǔ yú* (啤酒鱼; beer fish) and *tiánluóniàng* (田螺酿; stuffed snails). Also look out for street vendors making and selling *jiāngtáng* (姜糖; ginger sweets; Y5 per bag) or those with copper kettles selling *hēi zhīma hú* (黑芝麻糊; Y3), a sweet syrupy drink made from sesame paste.

Dàcūnmén Night Market MARKET $
(大村门夜市; Dàcūnmén Yèshì; Pantao Lu; ⏰5pm-late) This night market is a culture-filled slice of nontourist Yángshuò life. Watch locals sniffing out the best spices or bartering for their snails, but be warned: it's not for the squeamish. Exotic tastes such as beer fish, dog hotpot, fish-head soup, frogs and snails can be found here. It's a 30-minute walk from Xi Jie. After you pass the gas station on Pantao Lu, look for the fire station on the left. Behind it is the night market.

Luna ITALIAN $$$
(☎139 7836 9849; Moon Hill Village; Yuèliàng Shān Lìcūn; 月亮山历村; dishes from Y38; ⏰7.30am-midnight) The spectacular views of Moon Hill definitely makes Luna worth a visit, but what really seems to keep customers coming are its organic salad, and exquisitely cooked pasta. The menu features a wide selection of Italian fare, and the wine list is impressive. It's located on the rooftop of Yangshuo Village Inn (p594).

Pure Lotus Vegetarian Restaurant CHINESE VEGETARIAN $$
(暗香蔬影素菜馆; Ànxiāng Shūyǐng Sùcàiguǎn; Diecui Lu; dishes from Y18-35; ⏰11am-2pm & 5-10pm; 🚭) If you've just been taking photos of dogs being skinned in the night market, this is the place to come to repair your damaged karma. Buddhist music creates an enchanting atmosphere in which to delve into Lotus' sumptuous menu. The tomatoes stuffed with tofu, potatoes and mushrooms (Y28) come highly recommended. There's a cute little terrace out back.

Le Vôtre FRENCH $$$
(乐德法式餐厅; Lèdé Fǎshì Cāntīng; 79 Xi Jie; dishes from Y38; ⏰8am-midnight) The first French restaurant in town, and still the best. This one shares its historic premises with the Hóngfú Palace Hotel. The interior, flanked by a dazzling array of Christian and Buddhist statues and hung with portraits of Chairman Mao, oozes an eccentric charm. The huge outdoor seating area draws big crowds, as do the fine menu and home-brewed beer (from Y25).

River Bar BAR $$
(漓湾酒吧; Líwān Jiǔbā; Binjiang Lu; drinks from Y25, dishes from Y28; ⏰5pm-late) It's all in the name – stunningly situated by Lí River, this outdoor bar has a hideaway vibe and provides sublime river views while you sip a bewildering array of cocktails. The varied menu includes steaks, pasta, kebabs, and a big list of teas and coffees.

Bar 98 BAR $$
(47 Guihua Lu; ⏰2pm late) First choice for many of Yángshuò's expat English teachers, this bar has no-nonsense ambience and a pool table. It keeps you entertained most weekdays: live music on Wednesday and Friday evenings, and a trivia quiz game on Tuesdays (after 9pm). All-day breakfasts and vegie burgers are served here.

Ming Yuan CAFE $
(明园咖啡; Míngyuán Kāfēi; ☎134 5736 9680; 50 Xi Jie; coffees from Y26; ⏰10am-midnight) If the constant bustle of Yángshuò gets too much, creep into this small cafe. The downstairs tables are a bit cramped, but it's still a quiet slice of civilisation and the cream of the crop for coffee, with a rich range of blends including some more obscure offerings. It recently opened a bigger, elegantly decorated **branch** (14 Binjiang Lu; ⏰8am-11pm) adjacent to River View Hotel.

Entertainment

Impressions Liú Sānjiě OUTDOOR PERFORMANCE $$
(印象刘三姐; Yìnxiàng Liú Sānjiě; ☎881 7783; tickets Y198-680; ⏰8-9pm) The top show in town is directed by moviemaker Zhang Yimou, the man who also directed the opening ceremony at the Běijīng Olympics. Six hundred performers, including local fishermen, take to the Li River each night.

MORE GREAT GUĂNGXĪ BIKE RIDES

Ancient Village Pursuit

GUÌLÍN TO JIĀNGTÓUZHŌU (25KM, 2½ HOURS)

Leave the city behind and take this relaxing, countryside spin to the 1000-year-old village of Jiāngtóuzhōu (p590). From the west gate of Solitary Beauty Peak, head north along Zhongshan Beilu for 1km, then turn left onto Huancheng Beiyilu (环城北一路) before taking the first right. Keep cycling north until you leave the suburb town of Dìngjiāng Zhèn (定江镇), then continue along the country lane for about 30 minutes (15km). When the road forks, bear right towards Tánxià Zhèn (潭下镇). At the Tánxià Zhèn junction, turn left then follow signs to Jiǔwū (九屋). Jiāngtóuzhōu is down a track on the right, just past Jiǔwū.

Yùlóng River Loop

YÁNGSHUÒ TO DRAGON BRIDGE & BACK (20KM ROUND TRIP, FOUR HOURS)

Soak up the rural charm as you follow the beautiful Yùlóng River past rice paddies, fish farms and water buffalo to the 600-year-old Dragon Bridge (p598). From Yángshuò, cycle along Pantao Lu and take the first main road on the left after the Farmers Trading Market. Continue straight, past the hospital on your right, and through the village of Jìmǎ (骥马) before following the road round to the right to reach the start of a bumpy track. Follow this all the way to Dragon Bridge (遇龙桥; Yùlóng Qiáo). Note: the last few hundred metres are on a main road. Cross the bridge and follow another track south for 20 minutes (around 8km) until it becomes a small, paved road, which eventually stops at the river's edge. Take a bamboo raft across the river (Y5), then turn left off a small paved road down a tiny pathway, which leads you back to the Jìmǎ village road.

Twelve surrounding karst peaks are illuminated as part of the show, which gets rave reviews from many travellers. Book at your hostel or hotel: hotels often arrange slight discounts.

 Shopping

Souvenir shops run the length of Xi Jie, while stalls set up daily along Binjiang Lu. Bargain your socks off.

 Information

Travel agencies are all over town, while backpacker-oriented cafes and bars, as well as most hotels, can often dispense good advice. Shop around for the best deals.

Touts are an almost constant nuisance in Yángshuò, but with perhaps a greater percentage of English speakers here than in any other place in China, there's little need for their services. Fend them off firmly but politely.

Bank of China (中国银行; Zhōngguó Yínháng; Xi Jie; ⌚9am-5pm) Foreign exchange and 24-hour ATM for international cards.

Café Too & Hostel (自游人旅店; Zìyóurén Lǚdiàn; ☎882 8342; 7 Chengzhong Lu; ⌚8am-midnight) Friendly, bite-sized cafe with fresh coffee, free internet and an impressive range of foreign-language books that you can swap.

China Post (中国邮政; Zhōngguó Yóuzhèng; Pantao Lu; ⌚8am-5pm) Has English-speaking staff and long-distance phone services.

People's Hospital (人民医院; Rénmín Yīyuàn; 26 Chengzhong Lu) English-speaking doctors available.

Public Security Bureau (PSB; 公安局; Gōng'ānjú; Chengbei Lu; ⌚8am-noon & 3-6pm summer, 2.30-5.30pm winter) Has several fluent English-speakers. Doesn't issue visa extensions. It's 100m east of People's Hospital.

Sunlight Photographic Equipment Centre (阳光照相器材店; Yángguān Zhaòxiàng qìcáidiàn; Xi Jie; ⌚8am-8pm) Burns CDs for Y15 per disc.

 Getting There & Away

Air

The closest airport is in Guìlín; see p589 for details of available flights. Your hotel should be able to organise taxi rides directly to the airport (about Y240, one hour).

Bus

Direct bus links:

Guìlín Y15 to Y18, one hour, every 10 minutes (6.45am to 8.30pm)

Nánníng Y121, 6½ hours, two daily (8am and 11.30am)

Shēnzhèn Y232, 13 hours, one daily (8.20pm)
Xīngpíng Y7, one hour, every 15 minutes (6.30am to 6pm)
Yángdī Y10, 30 minutes, every 20 minutes (6.30am to 6pm)

The bus from Guìlín to Huángyáo only stops in Yángshuò (Y35, three hours, 11.10am) if it's not full.

Train

Yángshuò has no train station, but train tickets for services from Guìlín and Nánníng can be bought from hotels and travel agencies around town. Expect to pay Y50 commission.

Getting Around

The best way to get around is by bicycle; you can rent one at almost all hostels, and from street-side outlets for Y15 per day. A deposit of Y200 is standard, but don't hand over your passport. For better-quality bikes, and sound advice on bike trips, head to **Bike Asia** (☎882 6521; www.bikeasia.com; 42 Guihua Lu; ⏲9am-6pm); for details, see p593.

Around Yángshuò

The highlight of a trip to Guǎngxī is to get out into the countryside of Yángshuò. There are weeks of exploring possibilities here, by bike, boat, foot or any combination thereof. Unfortunately, the local authority has plans to privatise the whole area. It's very likely that you'll be forced to pay admission fees just for entering the territory by the time you read this book.

The villages in the vicinity of Yángshuò, especially Xīngpíng, come alive on **market days**, which operate on a three-, six- and nine-day monthly cycle.

LÍ RIVER 漓江

There are also a number of picturesque, ancient villages to visit, and the river here far outstrips anything you'll see around Guìlín. Classic rural scenes of wallowing water buffalo and farmers tending to crops are dominated by a backdrop of prominent limestone peaks.

Xīngpíng (兴坪), the location of the photo on the back of Y20 banknotes, is more than 1000 years old and houses a number of historic residences. Most travellers base themselves here to explore the surrounding countryside. The HI-affiliated **This Old Place** (老地方; Lǎo Dìfang; ☎870 2887; www.topxingping.com; 5 Rongtan Lu; dm Y30-40, s Y60, d Y80-180) is an excellent place to stay. It has a cafe on Lao Jie. The stunning 16km-**hiking trail** between Xīngpíng and Yángdī (扬堤) takes around four to five hours to complete, crossing the river three times. The admission fee is Y16, which includes two ferry crossings. The last crossing is an extra Y4.

You can take a bus (Y8) from Yángshuò to Yángdī, then walk the trail to Xīngpíng before getting a raft (Y170) or bus (Y7, until 7pm) back. A raft between Xīngpíng and Yángdī is Y120.

Another fun option in this area is the boat-and-bike trip from Yángshuò to Xīngpíng and back (see p592).

Also very popular, and much closer to Yángshuò (about 9km east), is the historic village of **Fúlì** (福利), with its stone houses and cobbled lanes. Fúlì is famous in these parts for its handmade fans. You'll see them everywhere. It takes about an hour to get here by bike. First cycle south from Yángshuò before turning east over the bridge that takes you on towards Dùtou Village (渡头村; Dùtou Cūn). There, take your bike on the ferry (Y5) across the river. Fúlì is on the other side. There are also regular buses from Yángshuò to a drop-off point within walking distance of Fúlì (Y3, 15 minutes).

Around Yángshuò

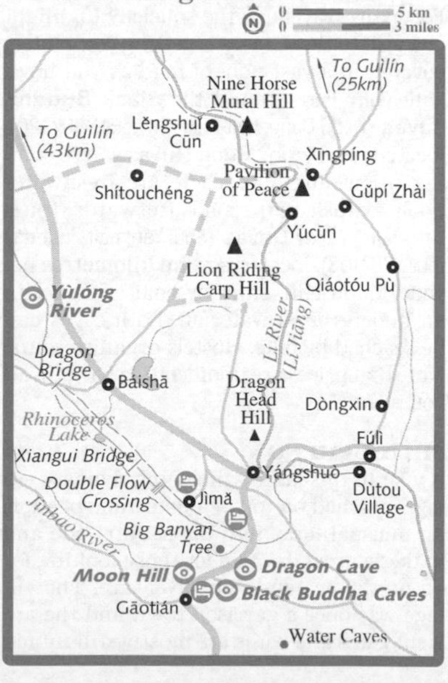

YÙLÓNG RIVER 遇龙河

The scenery along this smaller, quieter river, about 6km southwest of Yángshuò, is simply breathtaking. There are a number of great swimming spots and countless exploring possibilities. Just rent a bike and get out there.

One option is to aim for **Dragon Bridge** (遇龙桥; Yùlóng Qiáo), about 10km upstream. This 600-year-old stone arched bridge is among Guǎngxī's largest and comes with higgledy-piggledy steps and sides that lean inwards with age. Locals say the water under the bridge is 7m deep. It's certainly a great spot for a swim. For details of how to get here by bike, see the boxed text, p596. Alternatively, take a bus to Jīnbǎo (金宝) and ask to get off at the bridge (Y5, 35 minutes), just after Báishā (白沙).

MOON HILL 月亮山

For mind-blowing views of the surrounding countryside, head to the surreal limestone pinnacle **Moon Hill** (Yuèliàng Shān; admission Y15), famed for its moon-shaped hole. To get here by bike, take the main road south of Yángshuò towards the river and turn right onto the road about 200m before the bridge. Moon Hill is another 8km down the road on your right.

BLACK BUDDHA CAVES & WATER CAVES 黑佛洞、水岩

For many travellers, the squelchy highlight of a visit to these caves is getting completely covered in a vast pool of mud as you navigate your way around the **Black Buddha Caves** (Hēifó Dòng; half-/full-day tour Y80/120), located just before Moon Hill as you're coming from Yángshuò. There are freshwater pools to wash off the mud afterwards. Tours into the **Water Caves** (Shuǐ Yán; half-/full-day tour Y78/108), located several kilometres beyond Moon Hill, enter by boat and take in an underground waterfall. Both caves can be reached by bike. Hostels organise tours. Note that prices are unofficial, so bargain all you want.

SHÍTOUCHÉNG 石头城

A visit to this fascinating Qing-dynasty village, perched on top of a limestone peak, is an unusual foray into the countryside and makes a great day trip for those looking for an off-the-beaten-track adventure. The village was once a garrison town and the ancient gates and walls are mostly still intact. It's a steep 30- to 50-minute climb up the hill from the village's 'new town' to the 'old town' where the wall begins. Once at the top, it will take another four to five hours to walk around to all four of the main gates. Locals will show you around the stone ruins for about Y30.

To get here from Yángshuò, take any Guìlín-bound bus to Pútáo (Y5), from where a motorbike taxi (Y20) will take you the rest of the way to Shítouchéng. You should be able to arrange a motorbike ride back to Pútáo through one of the villagers. From there, you can flag down a southbound bus back to Yángshuò.

Huángyáo 黄姚

☎0774

Huángyáo is one of China's most high-profile villages, with many movies and TV series filmed there; Edward Norton's *The Painted Veil* is among them. The lovingly preserved 900-year-old **village** (adult Y68) is dotted with two dozen temples, a number of pavilions and clan halls, and an old stage (古戏台; *gǔ xìtái*). Bucolic charm permeates when you amble along the stone pathways. Two 500-year-old banyan trees wind their way up from the river's edge to the side of the village and make a lovely place to rest after wandering the streets.

Booker Inn (泊客驿站; Bókè Yìzhàn; ☎672 2586; 33 Yingsiu Jie; 迎秀街38号; r Y50; wi-fi) and **Chance** (偶然间; Ǒuránjiān; ☎672 2046; 33 Zhongxing Jie; 中兴街38号; dm & d Y80; wi-fi) on the other side of the river are particularly set up for backpackers. Both have rooms (shared bathrooms only) with wood furnishing, free wi-fi and a minibar. Huángyáo is famed for its *dòufu* (豆腐; tofu). Dine in the courtyard of **Guōjiā Dàyuàn** (郭家大院; 44 An Dongjie; 安东街44号), which does simply delicious *dòufu niàng* (豆腐酿; tofu slabs stuffed with minced pork and vegetables; Y20). Across the river, **Dàilóngqiáo Fānzhuāng** (带龙桥饭庄) has an English menu and serves similar dishes.

There are three direct buses daily from Guìlín (Y48, five hours, 9.15am, 1.10pm and 1.30pm); one goes via Yángshuò (Y35, three hours, 11.10am). The return from Huángyáo (Y50, 8.10am and 2.20pm) will drop you off in Yángshuò if you ask. From Guǎngdōng, it's possible to get to Huángyáo via Hèzhōu (贺州).

Nánníng 南宁

0771 / POP 7.1 MILLION

Like many provincial capitals in China, Nánníng is a bog-standard city with few sights of note. But at heart it's a fairly relaxed place to recharge your batteries before leaving for or coming back from Vietnam. Travel agencies and hostels can arrange Vietnam visas in one to three days and there's just about enough to keep you occupied while you wait.

Sights & Activities

FREE **Guǎngxī Provincial Museum** MUSEUM

(广西省博物馆; Guǎngxī Shěng Bówùguǎn; www.gxmuseum.com; Minzu Dadao; 9am-5pm Tue-Sun) This ugly, mammoth museum actually has a superb collection of ancient Dong bronze drums, some dating back more than 2000 years. They were used as sacrificial and ritual vessels as well as musical instruments, and the biggest is a whopping 165cm in diameter. In the leafy back garden are some full-size examples of Dong and Miao houses, and a nail-less Wind and Rain Bridge, which now houses an impressive restaurant, Āmóu Měishí.

Guǎngxī Medicinal Herb Botanical Garden GARDEN

(广西药用植物园; Guǎngxī Yàoyòng Zhíwùyuán; admission Y10; dawn-dusk) The fascinating subtropical Guǎngxī Medicinal Herb Botanical Garden is the largest medicinal botanical garden in China. More than 4000 medicinal plants from over 20 countries can be found here. Buses 22 and 81 from Cháoyáng Garden stop by the main gate. Buses 7 and 66 from the train station also go there.

Yōng River Bridge SWIMMING

The river at the southwestern end of the modern Yōng River Bridge (邕江桥; Yōngjiāng Qiáo) is a very popular swimming spot, particularly on summer evenings. For the less adventurous, nearby Yōngjiāng Hotel has a small outdoor pool (Y50).

Big groups of locals meet for a spot of **dancing** every evening in **Bīnjiāng Park** (滨江公园; Bīnjiāng Gōngyuán), just behind the riverbank where swimmers congregate. It's great to watch and anyone can join in.

On the eastern side of the bridge, just south of South Gate Market, is a small network of **alleyways**. Here you'll find some of Nánníng's older, low-rise housing, a stark contrast from the shiny shopping centres off nearby Chaoyang Lu, and an interesting place for a quiet stroll.

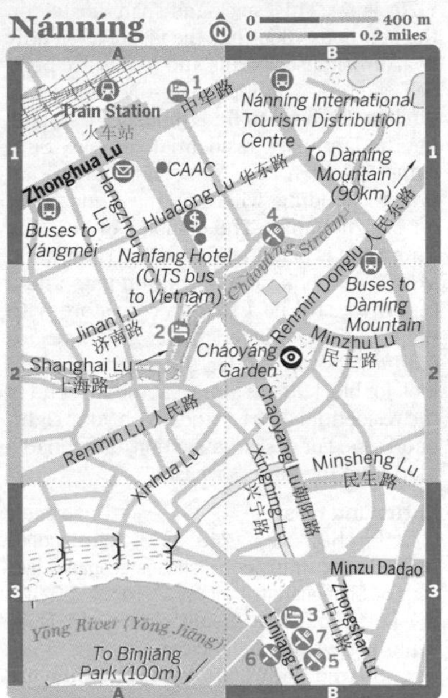

Nánníng

Sleeping

1 High-Class Hotel A1
2 Lotusland Hostel A2
3 Yōngjiāng Hotel B3

Eating

4 Farmers Market B1
5 South Gate Market B3
6 Xīngdǎo Hào B3
7 Xù Courtyard Restaurant B3

Sleeping

There's a cluster of budget hotels around the train station, displaying the price of their cheapest discounted rooms in oversized numbers on signs in the windows.

Nanning City Hostel HOSTEL $

(南宁市青年旅舍; Nánníngshì Qīngnián Lǚshè; 152 7771 7217; www.nanningcityhostel.bravehost.com; Apt 102, Block 12, Ou Jing Ting Yuan Community, 63-1 Minzu Dadao; 民族大道63-1号阳光一百欧景庭园E座12单元1102号; dm from Y60, s without bathroom Y70, double with bathroom

Y120; ❄@) This spick-and-span hostel on the penthouse floor has the feel of a friendly boarding house. Dorms and rooms are neat. Self-caterers will appreciate the communal kitchen. It's hard to find, though. First, look for the landmark residential complex Sunshine 100 (阳光一百, Yángguāng Yībái), an orange building with parking and shops, on Minzu Dadao. The complex of Ōu Jǐng Tíng Yuán is behind it (it's on the right-hand side). Then look for a black iron gate and a security guard next to a grocery store with the Chinese characters上水百货 *(shàngshuǐ bǎihuò)* above it. Enter the gated area and look for block 12. It's almost at the east end of the residential quarter and it's on your right-hand side. For easier navigation, download a map from the hostel's website.

Lotusland Hostel HOSTEL **$**
(荷逸居; Héyì Jū; ☎243 2592; lotuslandhostel@163.com; http://lotuslandhostel.spaces.live.com; 64 Shanghai Lu; 上海路64号; d/tw Y50/100 ❄) Lotusland is a hostel pioneer in Nánníng. Everything feels clean and spanking new. Shared bathrooms only, but they are sparkling. It's a relatively easy 15-minute walk (about 900m) from the train station. Vietnam visa application service is provided here with no additional costs. From Lángdōng bus station, take bus 6 or 213.

High-Class Hotel HOTEL **$$**
(海格拉斯大酒店; Hǎigélāsī Dàjiǔdiàn; ☎579 6888; 76 Zhonghua Lu; 中华路76号; d & tw Y388; ❄📶) Spacious doubles with spotless wooden floors, smart furniture, supportive mattresses and accommodating staff make this well-presented hotel the best choice in the train station area. Discounts bring rooms down to Y168 (Y178 with computer). All rooms have wi-fi.

Yōngjiāng Hotel HOTEL **$$$**
(邕江宾馆; Yōngjiāng Bīnguǎn; ☎218 0888; www.yjhotel.cn; 1 Linjiang Lu; 临江路1号; standard/deluxe d Y680/880, discounts of 50%; ❄@🏊) If you plump for the deluxe double, this welcoming five-star hotel overlooking the river is worth the splurge. Decor is luxurious yet modern, with chunky canvases hanging in the corridors and in some rooms. There's a delightful little teahouse, as well as a small, kidney-shaped outdoor pool.

Eating

The place to eat is Zhongshan Lu, a bustling street jam-packed with food stalls and small restaurants selling all manner of tasty fare, from squid kebabs (Y5) and *chòu dòufu* (臭豆腐; stinky tofu) to *lǎoyǒumiàn* (老友面; literally 'old friend' noodles). There's a cluster of cheap restaurants at the south end of Gonghe Lu, and you'll find simple restaurants around the train station selling breakfast *bāozi* (包子; dumplings; Y3) or Guìlín *mǐfěn* (桂林米粉; Guìlín noodles; Y3.50). For familiar Western fare and a sip of coffee or beer, there are a dozen cafes and bars in the Sunshine 100 complex on Minzu Dadao.

A great place for buying fruit and snacks is **South Gate Market** (南门市场; Nánmén Shìchǎng; ⏲5.30am-7pm), off Zhongshan Lu. Closer to the train station, on the north side of Cháoyáng Stream, is the small **Farmers Market** (农贸市场; Nóngmào Shìchǎng; ⏲5am-11pm), another excellent place for fresh fruit.

TOP CHOICE **Āmóu Meǐshí** GUǍNGXĪ **$$**
(阿谋美食; 21 Gucheng Lu; ⏲9am-9pm) Well, this is a chain but this branch really stands out. Housed on the picturesque Wind and Rain Bridge behind Guangxi Provincial Museum, this restaurant has a beautiful, leafy garden as its backdrop. It dishes out various tribal food of the region. You may not know those ethnic minorities, but you'll sure like their grub. Try the Miao's *zhūxiāng* fish (苗家竹香鱼; *miáojiā zhūxiāngyú;* Y68). Other mouth-watering dishes include roasted eggplant in Tai style (傣家茄子; *dǎijiā qiézi;* Y25) and shredded Lí River duck (手撕漓江鸭; *shǒusī líjiāngyā;* Y38). No English menu.

Xù Courtyard Restaurant SOUTHERN CHINESE **$$**
(旭园; Xù Yuán; Linjiang Lu; ⏲10.30am-9.30pm) This friendly restaurant is in a converted courtyard that dates back to 1892. It whips up some scrumptious dishes, including orange-peel-flavoured pork-rib wraps (橙皮纸包骨; *chéngpí zhǐbāogǔ;* Y48), secret-recipe roast duck (密制丁香鸭; *mìzhì dīngxiāngyā;* Y38 per half duck) and plum-marinated *huángfēng* fish (梅子黄蜂鱼; *méizi huángfēngyú;* Y38). Chinese-only menu, but some English is spoken.

Xīngdǎo Hào FISH **$**
(星岛号; Linjiang Lu; ⏲6pm-2am) Right on the river, with tables spread out across the deck of the now disused river-ferry wharf, this no-nonsense restaurant-cum-bar is a great spot for an evening meal, or even just a few beers. No English menu, but the *hóngshāo luófēi yú* (红烧罗非鱼; Y20), a Yōng River fish speciality, comes recommended. Beers from Y8.

Just For You CAFE **$$**
(为了你餐厅; Wèilenǐ Cāntīng; ☎571 2801; 61 Minzu Dadao, Sunshine 100, No 33 Shangye Jie; 民族大道61号阳光一百商业街33号; ⏰9am-midnight) If you want to meet up and yarn with other English speakers, head to Just For You. This cafe offers a range of American and Southeast Asian fare, and vegetarian pizza (Y38) is served. It's also a popular Chinese-dates-foreigners spot, located behind Sunshine 100.

Information

The useful *Street Map of Nanning* (南宁街道图; Nánníng Jiēdào Tú; Y4), in English and Chinese, can be found at bookshops and kiosks around town. Hawkers also sell it outside the train station.

Bank of China (中国银行; Zhōngguó Yínháng; Chaoyang Lu; ⏰9am-5pm Mon-Fri) Changes travellers cheques and gives credit-card advances. Other Bank of China branches around town have 24-hour ATMs that accept international bank cards.

China International Travel Service (CITS; 中国国际旅行社; Zhōngguó Guójì Lǚxíngshè; ☎232 3330; 76 Chaoyang Lu; ⏰7am-11pm) Has some English-speaking staff, issues one-month Vietnam visas (Y380) and sells bus tickets (Y150) to Hanoi (Hénèi).

China Post (中国邮政; Zhōngguó Yóuzhèng; Zhonghua Lu; ⏰8am-6pm) This handy branch is just across from the train station.

Public Security Bureau (PSB; 公安局; Gōng'ānjú; ☎280 1260; 10 Xiuling Lu Xierli; 秀灵路西二里10号; ⏰9am-4.30pm Mon-Fri) The foreign affairs office is about 2km north of the train station, off Xiuling Lu (秀灵路).

Getting There & Away

Air

Direct daily flights from Nánníng include Běijīng (Y1850), Shànghǎi (Y1660), Xī'ān (Y1800), Kūnmíng (Y630), Guǎngzhōu (Y730) and Hong Kong (Y1850). You can also fly to a number of other countries in Asia, including Vietnam (Yuènán; Y1950).

The **Civil Aviation Administration of China** (CAAC; 中国民航; Zhōngguó Mínháng; ☎243 1459; 82 Chaoyang Lu; ⏰24hr) sells tickets. The twice-hourly airport shuttle bus (Y15, 40 minutes, 5.30am to 10.30pm) leaves from outside this office. A taxi to the airport is about Y100.

Bus

All long-distance bus stations are inconveniently located on the outskirts of the city. The main one is **Lángdōng bus station** (琅东客运站; Lángdōng kèyùnzhàn; ☎550 8333), about 5km east of the city centre. Buses to pretty much everywhere leave from there, although be aware that you may be dropped at one of the other bus stations when arriving in Nánníng. It has a ticketing office in town on Chaoyang Lu near CAAC.

There are frequent daily services:

Běihǎi Y60, three hours, every 10 to 20 minutes (7am to 10.40pm)

Chóngzuǒ Y22, two hours, every 30 to 60 minutes (7.40am to 8.40pm)

Guǎngzhōu Y242, nine hours, 12 daily (9am to 11pm)

Guìlín Y100 to Y110, 4½ hours, every 15 to 30 minutes (7.30am to 11.30pm)

Píngxiáng Y68, 2½ hours, 16 daily (7.30am to 8.30pm)

There is one direct bus daily to Détiān Falls (Détiān Pùbù; Y50, 3½ hours, 7.40am). Other daily routes include Chóngqìng, Chéngdū, Hǎinán Dǎo, Shànghǎi and Hong Kong (Xiānggǎng).

Local buses 6 and 213 (45 minutes) go from Chaoyang Lu and Minzu Dadao to Lángdōng bus station.

Train

A number of daily trains go to Guìlín (Y32 to Y65, 4½ to 6½ hours), Kūnmíng (Y55 to Y113, 12½ to 14 hours) and Wǔhàn (Y126 to Y170, 15½ to 21 hours). Some other daily services:

Běihǎi Y22 to Y25, three hours, two daily (9.36am and 1.30pm)

Běijīng West Y276, 27 hours, one daily (9.10am)

Chéngdū Y199, 36½ hours, one daily (7.38pm)

Chóngqìng Y152, 27 hours, one daily (7.38pm)

Guǎngzhōu Y94 to Y106, 11½ to 14 hours, three daily (12.27am, 5.12am and 7.13pm)

Shànghǎi Y199/231, 31/28 hours, two daily (5.49am and 11.16am)

Xī'ān Y223, 33 hours, one daily (12.07pm)

Two daily trains go to Píngxiáng (Y17/15, 3½/5½ hours, 8am/10.30am) near the Vietnam border. Both stop at Chóngzuǒ (Y10/9, two/three hours) and Níngmíng (Y13/11, 2½ to four hours), but only the slow one stops at Píngxiáng's north train station.

Booth 16 in the train station sells international tickets to Hanoi (Y147). The train leaves at 6.45pm (11 hours). Bring your passport.

Getting Around

A number of buses, including bus 6 and 213, run the length of Chaoyang Lu and Minzu Dadao until around 11pm. A taxi ride from Lángdōng bus station to downtown is around Y30.

BORDER CROSSING: GETTING TO VIETNAM FROM NÁNNÍNG

There are seven daily buses to Hanoi (Hénèi, Vietnam; Y150, 7½ hours) via the Friendship Pass (友谊关; Yǒuyì Guān). Two departures (8am and 8.20am) leave from the Nánníng International Tourism Distribution Centre (南宁国际旅游集散中心; Nánníng Guójì Lǚyóu Jísàn Zhōngxīn), and four departures (8.40am, 9am, 10am and 1.40pm) leave from Lángdōng bus station. One bus run by CITS (Y150, 7.30am) leaves from Nanfang Hotel (南方酒店; Nánfāng Jiǔdiàn). Note that you'll have to get off the bus and walk across the border at Friendship Pass before boarding another bus to Hanoi.

The border is open from 8am to 8pm Chinese time; however, travellers have reported that passports aren't always stamped after around 4.30pm. China is one hour ahead of Vietnam.

For further information, head to shop.lonelyplanet.com to purchase a downloadable PDF of the Hanoi chapter from Lonely Planet's *Vietnam* guide.

Around Nánníng

YÁNGMĚI 扬美

This beautifully preserved **17th-century town** (admission Y10) on the Yōng River (邕江; Yōng Jiāng), 26km west of central Nánníng, makes a great day trip. You could easily spend a couple of hours wandering the cobbled streets and historic buildings.

Buses leave from behind Huátiān Guójì (华天国际), an office-block building on Huaqiang Lu (华强路) just west of Nánníng's train station, from around 8.30am to 4.30pm (Y10, 90 minutes, every 50 minutes) and return between the same times.

DÀMÍNG MOUNTAIN 大明山

About 90km northeast of Nánníng, the **Dàmíng Mountain Reserve** (大明山保护区; Dàmíng Shān Bǎohùqū; admission Y30) is home to more than 1700 species of plants. The average elevation is over 1200m, with Dàmíng Mountain, the highest peak, reaching 1760m. This is good hiking territory, with valleys, forests, scenic lookouts and waterfalls, but paths are poorly marked, so consider a guide.

You probably have to stay overnight in the small forestry village at the base of the mountain. **Dàmíng Shān Lóngténg Guesthouse** (大明山龙腾宾馆; Dàmíng Shān Lóngténg Bīnguǎn; ☎0771-139 7815 3459; r from Y150) has helpful staff, who can assist with arranging guides and transport up the mountain. Booking in advance is recommended. Try the room reservation hotline: ☎985 1122.

From Nánníng, two daily buses (Y25, two hours, 10.30am and 3.30pm) leave from a special bus stop on Renmin Donglu, just east of Cháoyáng Garden. The morning bus, however, won't leave unless there are at least 10 passengers, and neither bus will continue up the mountain beyond the ticket office for the final 27km unless there are enough people. Return buses are more frequent and run from Dàmíng Shān until around 5pm.

Běihǎi 北海

☎0779 / POP 560,000

Běihǎi (literally 'North Sea') is famed among Chinese tourists for its Silver Beach, dubbed 'the Number One beach on earth' in tourism brochures. It sure ain't southern Thailand, but it's still worth a visit. Much more charming is Běihǎi's quaint old quarter of colonnaded streets, where colonial-era architectural heritage has escaped the demolition ball. It's a rewarding area for a stroll.

Sights & Activities

Turning left from the long-distance bus station, along Beibuwan Lu, the road soon forks. The right fork (Heping Lu; 和平路) takes you to a Bank of China, the post office and on towards the old town. The left fork takes you past Zhōngshān Park, Tiānhóng Hotel and the central bus station, all on your left.

Old Town HISTORIC AREA

(老城; *lǎochéng*) Běihǎi's enchanting old town used to be a trading hub of old Běihǎi but is now a sleepy home of the city's older residents, who while away the hours playing mah jong and Chinese chess. It spreads east away from Sichuan Lu, with recently restored 19th-century *qilou* buildings (Chinese arcade houses) straddling the streets and alleys.

A few buildings of note include the attractive **former post office** (大清邮政北海

Bĕihăi

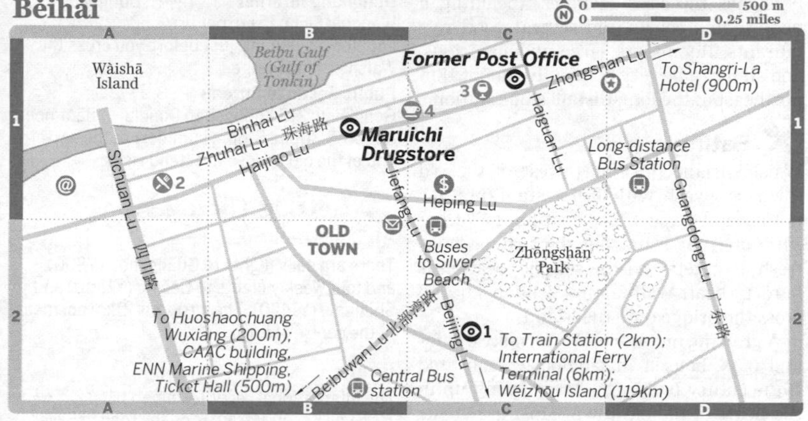

分局旧址; Dàqīng Yóuzhèng Běihăi Fēnjú Jiùzhǐ; cnr Zhongshan Donglu & Haiguan Lu; admission Y5), which now serves as a simple museum devoted to relics of the Qing-dynasty postal system; and the **Maruichi Drugstore** (丸一药房; Wányī Yàofáng; ☎203 9169; 104 Zhuhai Lu; ⏲8.30am-5.30pm), a site in the disguise of a pharmacy that allowed the Japanese to carry on espionage activities in the 1930s, which now houses a tiny national security museum (no English captions). The **former British Consulate Building** (英国领事馆旧址; Yīngguó Lǐngshìguăn Jiùzhǐ), within the grounds of a high school, is an imposing building with a cream-coloured edifice built in 1885.

The best place to start your stroll is at the western end of Zhuhai Lu (珠海路), off Sichuan Lu, just before the Wàishā Island bridge. Look for the small white arch inscribed with the Chinese characters 升平街 (Shengping Jie), the road's former name.

Silver Beach BEACH
(银滩; *yíntān*) This is what most Chinese tourists come to Běihăi for: Silver Beach, a long stretch of silvery-yellow sand with so-so waters, about 8km south of the city centre. There's a host of midrange, doll's-house-lookalike hotels and a number of places to eat, serving expensive but very fresh seafood. Take bus 3 (Y2) from the central bus station; it runs until 10pm.

Sleeping

From the central bus station, cross Sichuan Lu (四川路), which leads north to Wàishā Island (外沙岛; Wàishā Dăo), to reach Běihăi's cheapest accommodation, on

Bĕihăi

Top Sights
- Former Post Office C1
- Maruichi Drugstore B1

Sights
1 Former British Consulate Building C2

Eating
2 Old Town Coffee, Bar & Restaurant A1

Drinking
3 Aussino C1
4 Gāodì Coffee C1

Huoshaochuang Wuxiang (火烧床五巷), a small alley off Beibuwan Xilu, jam-packed with *zhāodàisuŏ* (招待所), simple guesthouses offering doubles/twins from Y30.

Most budget and midrange options in town are crappy. For an affordable luxury, stay in the Shangri-La.

Tiānhóng Hotel HOTEL $$
(天虹宾馆; Tiānhóng Bīnguăn; ☎221 0555; Beibuwan Lu; 北部湾路; d/tw Y188/258; ❄) This midrange hotel by the central bus station has bright, spacious rooms with dark-wood furniture, as well as friendly staff. Doubles and twins drop to Y100. Turn right from the bus station and it's on your right. No English sign.

Shangri-La Hotel HOTEL $$$
(香格里拉大饭店; Xiānggélǐlā Dàfàndiàn; ☎206 2288; 33 Chating Lu; 茶亭路33号; d with city/sea view from Y529/609; ❄@≋) Běihăi's best

hotel has top-class facilities, including a pool, tennis courts and several good restaurants. Rooms are large and luxurious, and staff can be very helpful. It's about 1km northeast of the long-distance bus station.

Eating

Wàishā Island, just northwest of the old town, is awash with fish restaurants. It's not cheap – expect to pay at least Y70 per *jīn* (600g) for fish – but the seafood is as fresh as it gets and the seaside location is hard to beat. Walk along Sichuan Lu and cross the bridge onto the island.

A growing number of Western-style cafes and bars, housed in fabulously renovated 19th-century buildings, have sprung up in the heart of the old town. Most are at the western end of Zhuhai Lu, off Sichuan Lu.

Old Town Coffee, Bar and Restaurant CAFE $
(老道咖啡; Lǎodào Kāfēi; ☎203 6652; 80 Zhuhai Lu; 珠海路80号; dishes from Y15; ⊙2.30pm-1.30am; wi-fi) Serves Chinese and Western food, fresh coffee (Y18) and beer (Y6), and has free wi-fi and English-speaking staff. Look out for the 'Backpacker' sign.

Gāodì Coffee CAFE $
(高地咖啡; Gāodì Kāfēi; ☎202 6586; 13 Zhuhai Lu; 珠海路13号; ⊙1pm-1am) Housed in an elegantly decorated red brick building, this cafe specialises in Vietnamese coffee (from Y30).

Drinking

Aussino WINE BAR $$
(富隆海创七号会所; Fùlóng Hǎichuàng Qīhào Huìsuǒ; ☎220 0800; 7 Zhuhai Lu; 珠海路110号; ⊙1pm-1am) The wine cellar is housed in a beautifully renovated, open-roofed building. It stocks an impressive selection of European wines. No English sign. Look for the misspelt 'Aussino Waild Wines' sign on the east end of the street.

Shopping

Xīnhuá Bookstore BOOKS
(新华书店; Xīnhuá Shūdiàn; ⊙8.30am-10pm) Inside a multistorey department store opposite the central bus station; you can buy a city map (地图; *dìtú;* Y5) here.

Information

Bank of China (中国银行; Zhōngguó Yínháng) Its 24-hour ATM accepts international cards.

China Post (邮局; Zhōngguó Yóuzhèng; ⊙8am-6pm)

Dōngháng Internet (东航网吧; Dōngháng Wǎngbā; Sichuan Lu; per hr Y1.50; ⊙24hr) Located on your left just before you cross the Wàishā Island bridge.

Public Security Bureau (PSB; 公安局; Gōng'ānjú; 213 Zhongshan Donglu; ⊙8am-noon & 2.30-5.30pm, 3-6pm summer) At the eastern end of the old town; can extend visas.

Getting There & Away

Air

There are daily flights to Guǎngzhōu (Y800), and four weekly flights to Běijīng (Y1800) and Shànghǎi (Y1420). The airport is 21km northeast of the centre of town.

Boat

The International Ferry Terminal (国际客运码头; Guójì Kèyùn Mǎtou) is on the road to Silver Beach (bus 3; Y2). One ferry daily (Y120 to Y280, 12 hours, 6pm) leaves for Hǎikǒu on Hǎinán Dǎo (p568). Three express ferries (Y120 to Y180, one hour 10 minutes, 8.30am, 11.15am and 4pm) leave daily for the nearby volcanic island of Wéizhōu. Ferries return to Běihǎi at 9.40am, 2.30pm and 5.15pm. The slow boats are no longer running.

Bus

Direct bus routes include Nánníng (Y60, three hours, regular) and Guìlín (Y180, seven hours, six daily).

Train

Two trains leave daily to Nánníng from Běihǎi train station (Y40, three hours), at 9.24am and 12.53pm. Coming the other way, the trains from Nánníng arrive in Běihǎi at 9.05am and 1.53pm. Tickets to onward destinations can be bought from the **train station ticket office** (⊙8.10am-noon & 2-5pm) for a Y5 fee.

Getting Around

To/From the Airport

Airport shuttle buses (Y10, 30 minutes) leave from outside the **Civil Aviation Administration of China** (CAAC; 中国民航; Zhōngguó Mínháng; ☎303 3757; Beibuwan Xilu; 北部湾西路; ⊙8am-10pm), a few hundred metres beyond Huoshaochuang Wuxiang, and connect with every flight. Flight tickets can also be bought here.

Bus

The two main bus stations, long-distance (客运总站; Kèyùn Zǒngzhàn) and central (北海信禾客运中心; Běihǎi Xìnhé Kèyùn Zhōngxīn), are both on Beibuwan Lu (北部湾路). Buses will drop you at either station.

From the central bus station, bus 2 (Y1) goes to the train station.

Pedal-powered Tricycles

In an encouraging attempt to fend off air pollution, authorities have put more than 600 pedal-powered tricycles into operation. Use them. From the central bus station, expect to pay Y1 to the long-distance bus station, Y3 to Huoshaochuang Wuxiang, Y5 to Wàishā Island, Zhuhai Lu or the Shangri-La Hotel, and Y10 to the train station.

Tickets for boats to Wéizhōu Island can be purchased from the International Ferry Terminal, or **ENN Marine Shipping Ticket Hall** (新奥海运售票大厅; Xīn'ào Hǎiyùn Shòupiào Dàtīng; ☎306 6829, 388 0711) in Huáměi Guǎngchǎng (华美广场). It's on Sichuan Lu near the inner section with Beihai Dadao. For the ferry schedule, see p604.

Around Běihǎi

WÉIZHŌU ISLAND 涠洲岛

With its friendly fishing families, the island of **Wéizhōu** (admission Y90) is a beach site not yet overwhelmed by throngs of tourists. The island is 36 nautical miles from Běihǎi and is China's largest volcanic island. Make this 6.5km-long and 6km-wide island a day trip.

Boats from Běihǎi pull into the new ferry pier in the northwest of the island. The main settlement **Nanwan Port** (南湾港; Nánwān Gǎng) is 5km south of the pier. To get there, it's Y5 by motor-rickshaw. The waters around Wéizhōu contain some of the most diverse coral communities in the area; ask in Nanwan Port about motorboat rides and diving opportunities. Beyond the island's beaches, caves, corals and dormant volcanic scenery, visitors will find a handful of historic sights awaiting exploration. Within Nanwan Port – the former volcanic nucleus of the island – is the **Three Old Women Temple** (三婆庙; Sānpó Miào), but of more interest are the two French-built churches on Wéizhōu. Built in 1853, the white-washed **Catholic Church** (天主堂; Tiānzhǔ Tāng) in Shèngtáng (盛塘) in the northeast of the island still attracts worshippers. The **Holy Mother Church** (圣母堂; Shèngmǔ Táng), built in 1880, is in the village of Chéngzǎi (城仔), roughly on the same latitude but closer to the ferry terminal.

The smaller **Xieyang Island** (斜阳岛; Xiéyáng Dǎo) sits in the sea 9 nautical miles to the southeast of Wéizhōu Island, and can be reached by boat from Nanwan Port.

If you miss the last boat back to Běihǎi, accommodation is available in Nanwan Port. The HI-affiliated **Piggybar** (猪仔吧; Zhūzǎibā; ☎139 0779 0533; piggybar.com, in Chinese; Nanwan Port; dm Y25-30, r Y60-80) has primitive facilities and very basic rooms. Bike rental (Y20 per day) is also available. For a reasonable degree of comfort, **Dishui Courtyard Hotel** (Dīshuǐjū; 滴水居; ☎329 9636; Dishui Village; Dishuicun; 滴水村; r Y150-190), to the west of the port, has some pleasant cabins.

Chóngzuǒ 崇左

☎0771 / POP 340,000

Situated beside a big loop in the Zuǒ River (左江; Zuǒ Jiāng), this unattractive city doesn't have much to see, except for the leaning pagoda and the ecology park, where you have the chance to see a rare species of monkey.

Sights & Activities

Across the river from the train station is a semi-restored section of the old city wall that follows the river for a short distance and makes a pleasant walk.

Chóngzuǒ Ecology Park NATURE RESERVE
(崇左生态公园; Chóngzuǒ Shēngtài Gōngyuán; ☎793 0222; admission Y80; ⏲9am-noon & 2-6pm) The modest-sized Chóngzuǒ Ecology Park, run by a Peking University research centre, is a sanctuary for the extremely rare white-headed leaf monkey (白头叶猴; *báitóu yèhóu*), indigenous to China. It's estimated that fewer than 1000 are in the wild, where there are about 590 of these highly endangered primates in this small but important nature reserve alone.

A simple walking trail (45 minutes) takes you in a loop around the park's karst hills, where the monkeys spend most of the day. This is also king cobra territory, so resist the temptation to stray from the path.

You'll have the best chance of seeing monkeys at dawn or dusk when they make their way up to or down from the hilltops. There's accommodation inside the park but special arrangement has to be made via the research centre. To get here, take a minibus (Y8, 45 minutes, 6.30am to 6.30pm) to Bǎnlì (板利) from the bus station. Tell your driver to drop you off at Shēngtài Gōngyuán.

Zuǒjiāng Leaning Pagoda PAGODA
(左江斜塔; Zuǒjiāng Xiétǎ; admission Y5; ⏲8.30am-5.30pm) Do not expect anything like the Tower of Pisa. But nevertheless, the whitewashed brick Zuǒjiāng Pagoda is photogenic enough. Built in 1621, it's one of

only eight of its kind in the world – leaning. Standing 18m tall, it's perched, lighthouse-like, on top of a rocky outcrop on Phoenix Lake. However, climbing the pagoda was impossible at the time of research, as the interior was damaged by a flood in 2009. To reach it, take bus 3 from the bus station (Y1.20, 20 minutes). Don't forget to tell the driver you're going to *xiétǎ*. A taxi is a fixed rate of Y20.

Sleeping & Eating

Hotels around the train and bus stations are shabby, but if you are just looking for a bed to sleep for a night there is no shortage of cheap hotels. Some offer beds for as little as Y30.

There are also plenty of cheap restaurants around both stations, offering simple, point-and-choose fried dishes for less than Y10. There's an enormous food market a few hundred metres west of the bus station underneath an ugly blue roof.

Yangguang Hotel HOTEL **$**
(阳光大酒店; Yángguāng Dàjiǔdiàn; ☎784 0501; fax 784 8498; 36 Jiangnan Lu; 江南路36号; s/d Y218/228, d with computer Y368; ❄) Just east of the train station, this hotel is the most decent one we found that offers reasonable two-star comfort with relatively clean rooms. Discounts bring singles and doubles down to Y70.

Information

Exiting the train station, you'll see **Xiūxián Internet** (休闲网吧; Xiūxián Wǎngbā; per hr Y2; ⏲24hr) on your right. There's a **Bank of China** with a 24-hour ATM accepting international cards next to the bus station. You can buy a city map (地图; *dìtú;* Y4) at both stations.

Getting There & Away

The train station is just south of the river on the east–west street of Jiang Nanlu (江南路). The bus station is about 1km further south on another east–west road, Yanshan Lu (沿山路). Just west of both stations, Xinmin Lu (新民路) connects these two roads. Turn left from the train station or right from the bus station to get to Xinmin Lu. Bus 2 (Y2) connects the stations, but takes only 10 minutes to walk.

Bus

Regular daily buses:

Dàxīn Y19, 1½ hours, every 30 minutes (6.20am to 4.55pm)

Nánníng Y46, 2½ hours, every 30 minutes (6.30am to 7.30pm)

Níngmíng Y19, 50 minutes, every 20 minutes (8.10am to 6pm)

Píngxiáng Y30, 80 minutes, every 20 minutes (8am to 6pm)

Train

Three trains leave daily for Nánníng (Y9 to Y20, one hour 52 minutes to three hours 22 minutes, 8.10am, 11.36am and 2.21pm). In the other direction, three trains leave daily for Píngxiáng, at 9.44am (Y14, one hour 46 minutes), 2.58pm (Y7, two hours 38 minutes) and 8.28pm (Y16, one hour and 43 minutes). The Píngxiáng trains stop at Níngmíng (Y10/6, 55 minutes/1¼ hours).

Zuǒ River Scenic Area
左江风景区

The chance of catching a glimpse of white-headed leaf monkeys in the wild, gaping at 170m-high ancient rock murals and puttering along a spectacular section of the Zuǒ River in a small wooden boat make this area, on the train line between Nánníng and Píngxiáng, well worth checking out.

The village of **Pānlóng** (攀龙) is the launch pad. Behind it, you'll find **Lǒngruì Nature Reserve** (陇瑞自然保护区; Lǒngruì Zìrán Bǎohùqū), home to forest-covered karst peaks, elusive monkeys and endless hiking opportunities. But be sure to get a permit (许可证; *xǔkězhèng*) from the police in the village before you head off into the hills.

Camping is no longer allowed here but just between Pānlóng and the nature reserve entrance there are some large wood cabins, set up for tour groups, where you can find decent accommodation for Y160. If that's too much like a holiday camp for you, you'll find basic rooms (Y70), and a great place to eat by the river, at **Nóngjiālè Restaurant** (农家乐餐馆; Nóngjiālè Cānguǎn), right beside the 100-year-old Guānyīn Temple (观音庙; Guānyīn Miào), about 200m from the ticketing office.

The main reason to come to Pānlóng, though, is to take a one-hour (one-way) boat trip past stunning, karst-rock scenery to the **Huāshān cliff murals** (花山岩画; Huāshān yánhuà). These crudely drawn depictions of ancient people and animals, painted in red on sheer cliff faces up to 172m above the river, are almost 2000 years old. They are apparently the work of the Luoyue people, ancestors of the Zhuang, but why they were painted is still a mystery. The admission fee (Y80) includes the boat fee if there are 10 or more visitors; otherwise you have to pay an extra Y120 to Y200 for the boat.

Getting There & Away

To get to Pānlóng, first catch a train or bus to Níngmíng (宁明). From the train station, take a motor-rickshaw (Y3 if full, Y20 if you're the only passenger, 30 minutes) to Mínzú Shānzhài (民族山寨), another name for Pānlóng. From Níngmíng bus station, take local bus 9 to Bǎihuò Dàlóu (百货大楼). From there, the same bus goes to Mínzú Shānzhài at 7.30am, 9am, 11.30am, 2pm and 4.30pm. Or you can take a rickshaw (Y20). Bus 9 returns once every two hours, with the last bus leaving Mínzú Shānzhài at 5pm.

Regular buses leave Níngmíng for Píngxiáng (Y9), Chóngzuǒ (Y18) and Nánníng (Y50), the last buses leaving at 6.45pm, 5.40pm and 7.40pm, respectively. Trains to Pínxiáng leave at 10.40am (Y10, 50 minutes) and 4.15pm (Y4, one hour 21 minutes).

Trains to Chóngzuǒ (Y4/10, 1½ hours/51 minutes) and Nánníng (Y26/12, two hours 53 minutes/four hours 26 minutes) leave at 1.26pm (fast train) and 9.59am (slow train).

Píngxiáng 凭祥

☎0771 / POP 110,000

Guǎngxī's gateway to Vietnam (Yuènán; 越南) is a modest market town with little in the way of tourist attractions, so there's no real reason to stay.

Turn right (south) out of the bus station to find the Bank of China (中国银行; Zhōngguó Yínháng), a couple of internet cafes (网吧; *wǎngbā*) and the north train station (北站; *běi zhàn*). For a quick bite to eat, turn left from the bus station, where there are a handful of noodles shops.

If you need accommodation, **Yǒuyì Bīnguǎn** (友谊宾馆; ☎853 6626; tw/tr Y70/80), located directly opposite the bus station, has acceptable rooms.

Only one train leaves from the north train station, Píngxiáng Beǐzhàn (冯祥北站), the 9.05am to Nánníng (Y15, 5½ hours), via Níngmíng (Y4) and Chóngzuǒ (Y7). From the north train station turn left after Zhongyue International Hotel and 360 Bar, and its bizarre motorbike sculpture, then take the first right to the bus station. A faster train leaves for Níngmíng (Y10), Chóngzuǒ (Y14) and Nánníng (Y30, 3½ hours) from the less central train station, Píngxiáng Zhàn (凭祥站), at 12.45pm. Motor-rickshaws (about Y5) link the two train stations.

GUIDEBOOK CONFISCATION WARNING

There are still reports of Lonely Planet's *China* being confiscated by border officials at Friendship Pass, or even by police on the streets in Píngxiáng. We advise you to photocopy vital information and put a cover over your guidebook just in case. Note that all bags are searched as you walk into the north train station. Once you leave Píngxiáng, you should have no problem.

From Píngxiáng bus station there are regular buses to Níngmíng (Y9, one hour) until 7pm, to Chóngzuǒ (Y30, one hour 20 minutes) until 6.40pm and to Nánníng (Y68, three hours) until 8pm.

Détiān Waterfall 德天瀑布

☎0771

Although it may not be Niagara Falls, **Détiān Waterfall** (Détiān Pùbù; www.detian.com), Asia's largest and the world's second-largest transnational waterfall, is absolutely sublime. Then there are the surrounding karst peaks and the added buzz of being on the Vietnamese border. Admission is Y80, but if you take the direct bus from Nánníng, the bus ticket will entitle you to a Y10 discount.

The water drops 40m in three stages, creating an elegant collection of cascades and small pools across a total width of 200m. Swimming is not allowed, but bamboo rafts (Y20) will take you right up to the spray. When we visited, guards were no longer allowing tourists to walk all the way to the 53rd boundary marker, despite signs pointing you in that direction. You can, though, climb Fort Mountain (银盘山; Yínpán Shān; 1½ hours) for stunning views of the area.

Outside the entrance gates there are guesthouses offering doubles with air-con for around Y60. **Détiān Kèzhàn** (德天客栈; ☎377 5201) is a decent option. Just inside the gates, **Détiān Shānzhuāng** (德天山庄; ☎377 3570; d & tw from Y500; ❄) has overpriced rooms with views of the falls. There are a number of very similar restaurants with very similar menus (Y30 per dish) just outside the gates. Détiān Shānzhuāng has its own pricier version.

BORDER CROSSING: GETTING TO VIETNAM FROM PÍNGXIÁNG

The Friendship Pass (友谊关; Yǒuyì Guān) border is located about 10km from Píngxiáng on the Chinese side, and a few kilometres from the obscure town of Dong Dang on the Vietnamese side; the nearest Vietnamese city (Liàngshān; Lang Son in Vietnamese) is 18km from Friendship Pass. The border is is open from 8am to 8pm Chinese time (China is one hour ahead of Vietnam), but some travellers have reported that passports aren't always stamped after around 4.30pm.

To get to the border crossing, take a motor-rickshaw or taxi (about Y25) from Píngxiáng. From there it's a 600m walk to the Vietnamese border post. Onward transport to Hanoi, located 164km southwest of the border, is by bus or train via Lang Son.

If you're heading into China from the Friendship Pass, catch a minibus to Píngxiáng bus station, from where there are regular onward buses. A word of caution: because train tickets to China are expensive in Hanoi, some travellers buy a ticket to Dong Dang, walk across the border and then buy a train ticket on the Chinese side. This isn't the best way, because it's several kilometres from Dong Dang to Friendship Pass, and you'll have to hire someone to take you by motorbike. If you're going by train, it's best to buy a ticket from Hanoi to Píngxiáng, and then in Píngxiáng buy a ticket to Nánníng or beyond.

Unless you catch the one direct bus, which departs from Nánníng's International Tourism Distribution Centre (one way/return Y50/90, 3½ hours, 7.40am) and stops en route at Landong bus station (8.30am), you will have to come via Dàxīn (大新), then Shuòlóng (硕龙), from either Nánníng or Chóngzuǒ. At Dàxīn, turn left from the bus station and walk for five to 10 minutes (about 600m) down Minsheng Jie (民生街) until you reach the traffic lights at the junction with Lunli Lu (伦理路). There on your right you'll see minibuses to Shuòlóng (Y10, one hour, last bus 6pm). At Shuòlóng you'll find minibuses (Y20 per vehicle) and motor-rickshaws (Y15 per vehicle) waiting under a big tree to take you the final 20 minutes to Détiān.

Coming back, the last bus leaves Shuòlóng for Dàxīn at around 4pm. There are regular buses from Dàxīn to Nánníng (Y40, 2½ hours) until 8.30pm and to Chóngzuǒ (Y20, 1½ hours) until 4.40pm. The direct bus from the falls to Nánníng leaves at 3.20pm.

Around Détiān Waterfall

From Shuòlóng it's possible to catch a minibus to **Míngshì Tiányuán** (明仕田园), a succession of scenic Zhuang villages 25km southeast of Shuòlóng. It's an unspoiled version of Yángshuò surrounded by jagged forest hills and emerald meandering rivers. There's no admission fee yet but signs of tourism are surfacing. **Ming Shi Mountain Village** (明仕山庄; Míngshì Shānzhuāng; ☎375 5028; gxmingshi@yahoo.cn; Kanxu Village; Kānxú Xiāng; 堪圩乡; d Y690-880, discounts of 50%) is a landmark and a beautiful resort where you can rent a bike (Y20 per hour) to explore the villages. Walking is an equally pleasant way to explore the valley. **Shānlǐrén Shēngtài Nóngjiālè** (山里人生态农家乐; ☎375 3532; Kanxu Village; Kānxúxiāng; 堪圩乡明仕村那乙屯; r Y80), a decent farm-stay 1km west of the resort, offers spacious double and fresh homemade meals. No English spoken.

To get there you can charter a van from Détiān (Y50) or Shuòlóng (Y25) directly. The minibus from Shuòlóng to Chóngzhuǒ (Y5, 8am) will drop you at Míngshì Tiányuán if you ask. If you're stuck in Shuòlóng, **Guan Kou Hotel** (Guānkǒu Dàjiǔdiàn; 关口大酒店; r 80), 200m east of the big tree, has basic rooms.

To leave, minibuses to Léipíng (雷平; Y6) pass through Mínshì's main road until 3pm. From Léipíng, buses go to Dàxīn; they stop running at 5pm.

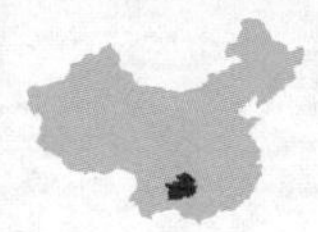

Guìzhōu

POPULATION: 36.7 MILLION

Includes »

Best Places to Eat

» Kǎilǐ Sour Fish Restaurant (p614)

» Sìhéyuàn (p614)

» Night Market in Kǎilǐ (p617)

Best Places to Stay

» Sheraton Hotel (p613)

» Guótài Dàjiǔdiàn (p617)

» Beautiful Harbor Hotel (p626)

Why Go?

Poor old Guìzhōu (贵州), always the short-end-of-the-stick southwest China province. A much-quoted proverb has it as a place 'without three *lǐ* of flat land, three days of fine weather, or three cents to rub together'. Ouch.

Certainly, pockets of Guìzhōu are desperately poor and you'll see clouds more often than the sun. The upside is that there's plenty of elbow room out in the simply stunning countryside, a sublime mix of undulating hills and carpets of forest, riven with rivers tumbling into magnificent waterfalls and down into spooky-thrilling karst cave networks.

As big a draw as the landscapes is Guìzhōu's extraordinary human mosaic. Almost 35% of the province's population is made up of over 18 ethnic minorities. They all contribute to Guìzhou's social butterfly calendar, which enjoys more folk festivals than any other province in China, and the welcome you'll get from the people more than makes up for the weather.

When to Go

Guìyáng

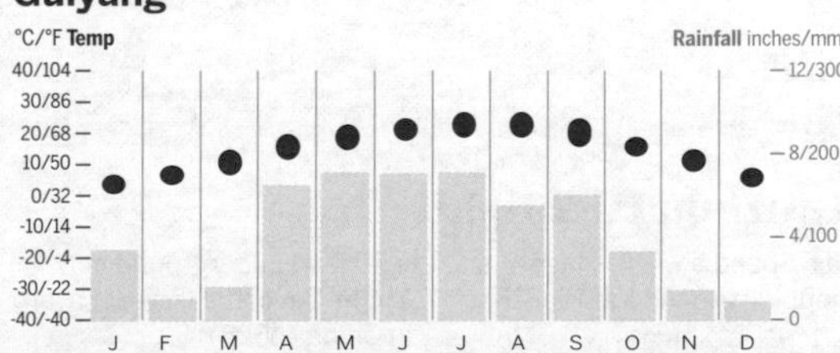

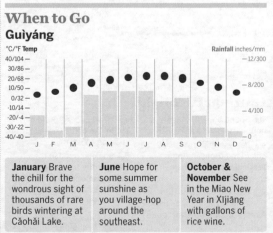

January Brave the chill for the wondrous sight of thousands of rare birds wintering at Cǎohǎi Lake.

June Hope for some summer sunshine as you village-hop around the southeast.

October & November See in the Miao New Year in Xījiāng with gallons of rice wine.

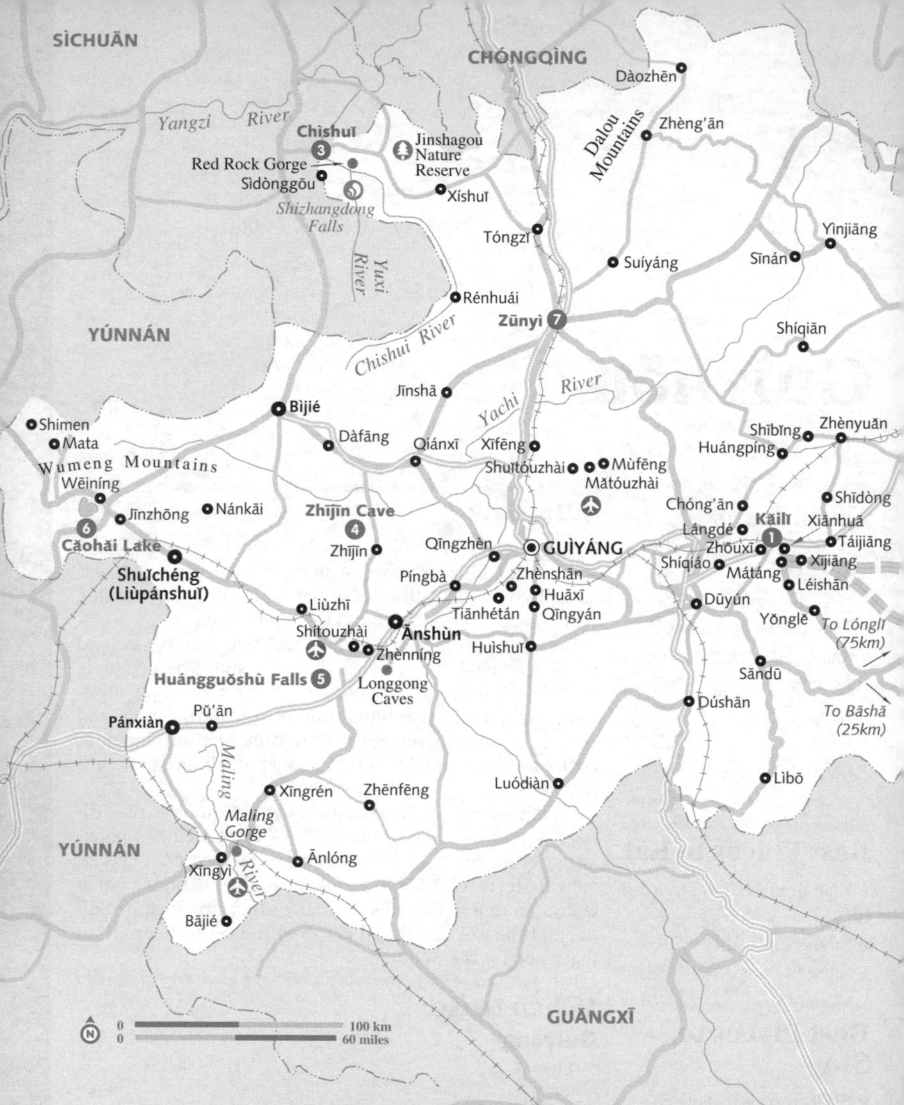

Guìzhōu Highlights

1 Spend a week village-hopping around **Kǎilǐ** (p618)

2 Party with the locals at one of the thousand-odd **festivals** (p619) held in Guìzhōu each year

3 Get way off the beaten track in the prehistoric fern forests around **Chìshuǐ** (p628)

4 Head underground at **Zhījīn Cave**, the largest cavern in China (p623)

5 Soak yourself in the mists at the thundering **Huángguǒshù Falls** (p623), China's largest waterfall

6 Escape the madding crowds and get up close with rare black cranes at remote **Cǎohǎi Lake** (p624)

7 Find fascinating CCP history and potent local firewater in **Zūnyì** (p624)

History

Chinese rulers set up an administration in this area as far back as the Han dynasty (206 BC–AD 220), but it was merely an attempt to maintain some measure of control over Guìzhōu's non-Han tribes.

It wasn't until the Sino-Japanese war, when the Kuomintang made Chóngqìng their wartime capital, that the development of Guìzhōu began. Most of this activity ceased at the end of WWII and industrialisation of the area wasn't revived until the Chinese Communist Party (CCP) began construction of the railways. Despite an expanding mining industry, Guìzhōu's GDP per capita remains the lowest in all China.

Climate

Guìzhōu has a temperate climate with an annual average temperature of 15°C. The coldest months are January and February, when temperatures dip to around 1°C. It simply always feels damp, mists are heavy and the sun rarely shines.

Language

Mandarin Chinese is spoken by the Han majority, although with a distinctive local accent. Thai and Lao are spoken by some, and Miao-Yao (Hmong-mien) dialects by the Miao and Yao.

Getting There & Away

AIR You can fly to more than 40 destinations within China from Guìyáng's airport, including all major Chinese cities. International destinations include Hong Kong, Singapore and Macau.

BUS Guìyáng and Chóngqìng are linked by an expressway. Another expressway from Guìyáng to Kūnmíng is nearing completion. Yúnnán is also accessible – less comfortably – by bus via Wēiníng in the west. Guǎngxī can be accessed through Cóngjiāng in the southeastern part of the province.

Within the province, many of the major sites are accessible via OK roads. However, secondary roads in the northeast, west and southeast are uniformly poor.

TRAIN Sleepers to Chéngdū in Sìchuān, Kūnmíng in Yúnnán and Guìlín are popular options.

Getting Around

Buses are by far the best bet for exploring Guìzhōu. New expressways have been built even in the more remote western areas of the province. However, roads between smaller cities and villages are still a work in progress – and there are many mountains and hills out there to wind around – so make sure you bring plenty of patience.

PRICE INDICATORS

The following price indicators are used in this chapter:

Sleeping

$	less than Y160
$$	Y160 to Y400
$$$	more than Y400

Eating

$	less than Y50
$$	Y50 to Y100
$$$	more than Y100

The train system links all major cities, but is generally slower and less convenient than buses.

CENTRAL GUÌZHŌU

The capital city Guìyáng dominates the central portion of the province. You'll likely have to spend a day or two here as you make your way around Guìzhōu.

Guìyáng 贵阳

0851 / POP 1.2 MILLION

While it will never win any beauty contests, or prizes for its tourist sights, Guìyáng (parts of it, anyway) is surprisingly modern and vibrant for the capital of China's poorest province. The riverside and Rénmín Sq provide enjoyable areas to wander, and there's fantastic street food, lively markets and disorienting, mazelike shopping areas. Most of the locals are chuffed to encounter foreigners and make them welcome.

Sights

Hóngfú Temple BUDDHIST TEMPLE

(弘福寺; Hóngfú Sì; admission Y2; 7am-6pm) Located in **Qiánlíng Park** (黔灵公园; Qiánlíng Gōngyuán; admission Y5; 24hr) in the north of the city, Hóngfú Temple is perched near the top of 1300m Qiánlíng Shān and dates back to the 17th century. It's an easy 40-minute walk to the temple, or there's a **cable car** (up/down Y15/20; 9am-5pm). The monastery has a vegetarian restaurant in the rear courtyard. From the train station area, take bus 2.

Guìyáng

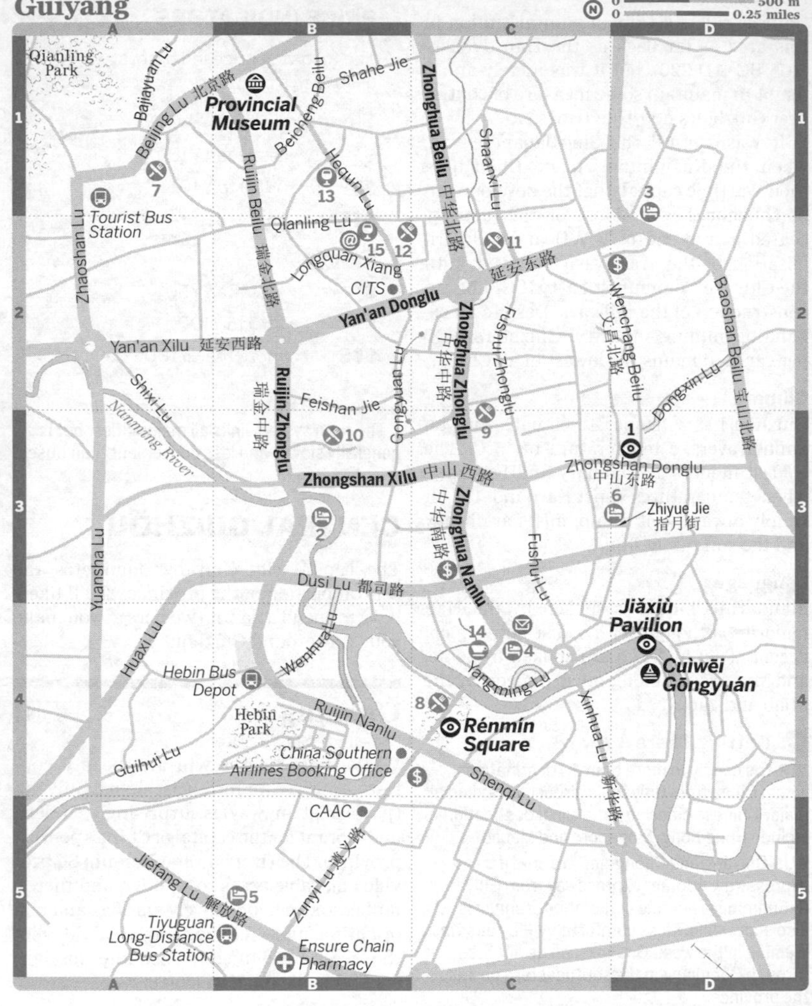

FREE Provincial Museum MUSEUM
(省博物馆; Shěng Bówùguǎn; Beijing Lu; ⏲9am-5pm Tue-Sun) The exhibits at this low-tech museum are a truly bizarre mix, with the ground floor given over to a seemingly random collection of firearms. Head to the 2nd floor instead for the section on Guìzhōu's minorities, which features traditional clothing and musical instruments. There are some English captions.

Other Sights HISTORIC SITES
Begin at **Rénmín Square** (人民广场; Rénmín Guǎngchǎng) and take a gander at one of the nation's largest Mao statues… as he salutes Wal-Mart across the street (guess which site the locals are visiting more?).

Walk north across the river, turn right (east) onto Yangming Lu, cross a roundabout, descend to the river and follow it to the triple-roofed **Jiǎxiù Pavilion** (甲秀楼; Jiǎxiù Lóu; admission Y2; ⏲8.30am-11pm), Guìyáng's most famous landmark

Across the river is **Cuìwēi Gōngyuán** (翠微公园; admission Y2; ⏲9am-11pm), an erstwhile Ming-dynasty temple which has picturesque pavilions and some pricey Miao souvenirs.

Guìyáng

Top Sights

Sights

Sleeping

Eating

Drinking

Backtrack across the bridge and walk north along Wenchang Beilu to another Ming-dynasty speciality: **Wénchāng Pavilion** (文昌阁; Wénchāng Gé), restored along with the city walls. There are always plenty of locals lounging around, chatting and snacking here.

Tours

Organised tours (in Chinese) to Huángguǒshù Falls and Lónggōng Caves leave daily from a special tourist bus station (旅游客运站; *lǚyóu kèyùnzhàn*) opposite Qiánlíng Park. Many of the hotels also organise day tours. CITS runs one-day tours to the caves and waterfall for Y270 per person. There are fewer tours (if they run at all) in the off season.

Festivals & Events

There are at least 1000 minority festivals in Guìzhōu each year (see the boxed text, p619). Check with CITS for details or do research ahead for dates, but even the locals don't know when they're happening till a month or so before.

Sleeping

Budding hoteliers should take note of the fact that Guìyáng's accommodation options are sadly limited, with a plethora of bland low and midrange places and a complete lack of genuine hostels or guesthouses.

Sheraton Hotel HOTEL **$$$**
(喜来登贵航酒店; Xǐláidēng Guìháng Jiǔdiàn; ☎588 8888; www.sheraton.com/guiyang; Zunyi Lu; 遵义路; d Y1580, discounts of up to 50%;) Sitting astride a downtown intersection like a colossus, the rooms here are Guìyáng's top digs. Huge, comfy beds, as well as a spa, gym, pool and Western and Chinese restaurants.

Jīnqiáo Fàndiàn HOTEL **$$**
(金桥酒店; Golden Bridge Hotel; ☎582 9958; 2 Ruijin Nanlu; 瑞金南路2号; s/d/tr Y358/398/428, discounts of 40-50%) The venerable Jīnqiáo is over 40 years old, a lifetime by Chinese hotel standards, and although it looks its age a bit, it still stands out from the midrange crowd, thanks to its distinctive wedding cake–style exterior (it's very neo-Stalinist) and its marble lobby. The spacious rooms are well kept, the staff helpful and discounts are often on offer.

Yìdū Youth Hostel HOTEL **$**
(逸都酒店; Yìdū Jiǔdiàn; ☎864 9777; fax 863 1799; 9 Zhiyue Jie; 指月街9号; 6-/10-bed dm Y50/40, s, d & tr Y368-428;) Despite the name, this isn't a real hostel. Instead, it's a midrange hotel with some dorm rooms, and guess which guests are at the bottom of the pecking order? The unenthusiastic staff are one reason, along with the lack of atmosphere, that this place gets mixed reviews. But the dorms are modern and clean. The entrance is down an alley off Wenchang Nanlu.

Mayflower Hostel HOTEL **$**
(澎湖湾酒店; Pénghúwān Jiǔdiàn; ☎674 3007; 16th fl, Jiaxinhuating Bldg, 176 Baoshan Beilu; 宝山北路176号嘉信华庭大厦16层; s, d & tr Y120-160;) Another one of Guìyáng's ersatz hostels, the Mayflower is spread across a couple of floors of an office building. Not all of the the rooms are in great condition, so check them first. The best have panoramic views of the city, a refreshing change from the often dire vistas offered by most Chinese hotels, and all come with some form of internet access, either ADSL or wi-fi.

Star Hotel HOTEL $

(兴瑜商务宾馆; Xīngyú Shāngwù Bīnguǎn; ☎595 2588; 192 Jiefang Lu; 解放路192号; s & d Y158; ❄@) Mahjong fans will like this place, as every room has a table to play at. Everyone else can marvel at finding a hotel with modern, clean and sizeable rooms so close to the bus and train stations.

Eating

Night markets (夜市; *yèshì*) aren't as ubiquitous as they once were in Guìyáng, but there are still plenty of options for those who like to eat al fresco. Start snooping along Shaanxi Lu; if you don't find what you like, wander over to the Hequn Lu/ Qianling Lu area. Still nothing? Try the one east of Ruijin Zhonglu along a tiny alley or the little stalls north of Rénmín Sq.

Do try the local versions of *shāguō fěn* (沙锅粉), a noodle and seafood, meat or vegetable combination placed in a casserole pot and fired over a flame of rocket-launch proportions. The deep-fried skewered potatoes dusted in chilli powder are the best in the province. You'll see vendors grilling thin rice pancakes – these are 'silk babies' (丝娃娃; *sīwáwa*), to which pickled veggies, sliced radish/bamboo and spicy vinegar sauce are added.

Bear in mind that they eat a lot of dog in Guìzhōu, so if you don't want to feast on man's best friend, learn how to say *wǒ bù chī gǒuròu* (I don't eat dog meat).

TOP CHOICE Kaili Sour Fish Restaurant ETHNIC MINORITY $$

(老凯俚酸汤鱼; Lǎo Kǎilǐ Suāntāngyú; ☎584 3665; 55 Shengfu Lu; mains from Y38; ⊙9.30am-midnight) Locals flock here because it specialises in the best *suāntāngyú* (酸汤鱼; sour fish soup) in town. A Miao delicacy that's Guìzhōu's most famous dish, the fish are chopped up or dumped whole in a bubbling hotpot. You then add the veggies of your choice and away you go. Great stuff. There's no English menu, but the waitresses will help you out.

Sìhéyuàn GUÌZHŌU $

(四合院; ☎682 5419; Qianling Xilu; mains from Y15; ⊙9am-10pm) Every Guìyáng local (and expat) knows this place – a boisterous, frenetic, labyrinthine spot with most typical local dishes you could imagine, all very tasty. It's tough to find – walk west along Qianling Xilu off Zhonghua Beilu and keep your eyes peeled for a Protestant church on the right; the restaurant is down a small alley opposite. No English menu.

Dongjia Family Restaurant ETHNIC MINORITY $

(侗家食府; Dòngjiā Shífǔ; ☎650 7186; 42 Beijing Lu; mains from Y23; ⊙9.30am-10pm) Specialising in minority cooking from all over Guìzhōu, this is a friendly joint with fake trees in the dining area to give it that authentic country feel. For once, the pictures in the book-sized menu don't lie; the food here is very nicely presented and comes in ample servings.

Drinking

There are plenty of spots for coffee around town. Hequn Lu, north of Qianling Lu, has a smattering of bars, as does Qianling Donglu. The main drinking action, though, takes place in the city's numerous KTV (karaoke) clubs.

People's Commune BAR

(人民公社文化主题酒吧; Rénmín Gōngshè Wénhuà Zhǔtí Jiǔbā; Zhujia Alley, Hequn Lu; beer from Y8; ⊙7am-2am) A friendly CCP-themed, bamboo-built bar, with an outside terrace, pictures of Mao and Zhou Enlai on the walls and patriotic songs on the jukebox. Only beer is served here, in utilitarian tin cups, as cocktails are far too bourgeois. It's down an alley on the west side of Hequn Lu, just before the junction with Qianling Xilu. Look for the sign.

Highlands Coffee CAFE

(高原咖啡; Gāoyuán Kāfēi; 1 Boai Lu Liu Dongjie; drinks from Y10; ⊙10am-11pm Mon-Sat, 3-11pm Sun) Run by a friendly American (with an equally welcoming staff), this is where you go for your coffee or speciality tea fix. The smoothies are just as good. It's tucked off Zunyi Lu close to Wal-Mart.

Information

Bank of China (中国银行; Zhōngguó Yínháng; near cnr Dusi Lu & Zhonghua Nanlu) Has an ATM and offers all services you need. Other branches can be found on the corner of Wenchang Beilu and Yan'an Donglu, and on Zunyi Lu near Rénmín Sq.

China International Travel Service (CITS; 中国国际旅行社; Zhōngguó Guójì Lǚxíngshè; ☎690 1706; www.gzcits.com; 7th fl, Longquan Bldg, 1 Hequn Lu; ⊙9am-6pm Mon-Fri) The helpful English- and German-speaking staff can provide information on local festivals. Guide quality is hit-and-miss, reportedly.

China Post (邮局; Zhōngguó Yóuzhèng; 46 Zhonghua Nanlu) Offers a poste restante service. China Telecom is next door.

Ensure Chain Pharmacy (一树药业连锁; Yīshù Yàoyè Liánsuǒ; cnr Zunyi Lu & Jiefang Lu; ⏲24hr) Near the train station.

Internet cafe (网吧; wǎngbā; Longquan Xiang; per hr Y3; ⏲24hr) There's another internet cafe opposite this one. It's down an alley off Hequn Lu.

Public Security Bureau (PSB; 公安局; Gōng'ānjú; ☎590 4509; Daying Lu; ⏲8.30am-noon & 2.30-5pm Mon-Fri) The staff don't see many foreigners here, but they seem pleasant enough.

Getting There & Away

Air

Airline offices in Guìyáng include the **Civil Aviation Administration of China** (CAAC; 中国民航; Zhōngguó Mínháng; 264 Zunyi Lu; ⏲8.30am-8.30pm) and **China Southern Airlines** (中国南方航空公司售票区; Zhōngguó Nánfāng Hángkōng Gōngsī Shòupiàoqū; cnr Zunyi Lu & Ruijin Nanlu).

Destinations include Běijīng (Y1560), Shànghǎi (Y1280), Guǎngzhōu (Y600), Guìlín (Y630), Chéngdū (Y500), Xī'ān (Y840), Kūnmíng (Y440) and Chóngqìng (Y590). International destinations include Singapore, Hong Kong and Macau.

Bus

At the time of writing, a brand-new **main long-distance bus station** (贵阳客车站; Guìyáng Kèchēzhàn) had just opened way out in the western suburbs on Jinyang Nanlu. It's a long haul from downtown. Take bus 208 from the Hébīn bus depot; a taxi will cost Y30 to Y35.

Ānshùn Y35, 1½ hours, every 30 minutes (7.30am to 7pm)

Chóngqìng Y110, five to six hours, every 40 minutes (7am to 7.30pm)

Guìlín, Y260, 10 to 11 hours, two daily (8pm and 9pm)

Huángguǒshù, Y50, 2½ hours, eight daily (8am to 3pm)

Wēiníng, Y90, six hours, two daily (9am and noon)

Zūnyì, Y65, 2½ hours, every 30 minutes (7.30am to 7.20pm)

Another bus station, **Tǐyùguǎn long-distance bus station** (体育馆长途车站; Tǐyùguǎn Chángtú Kèyùnzhàn), is close to the train station on Jiefang Lu. Buses go to the following places:

Ānshùn Y36, 1½ hours, every 15 minutes (7am to 10pm)

Kǎilǐ Y60, 2½ hours, every 20 to 30 minutes (7.30am to 7.30pm)

The **Hébīn Bus Depot** (河滨汽车站; Hébīn Qìchē Zhàn) west of Rénmín Sq has buses to closer suburban destinations.

Train

Guìyáng's gleaming train station has been upgraded, but it's easier (and quicker) to travel within Guìzhōu by bus. You can buy train tickets four days in advance.

The following prices are for hard sleepers:

Chéngdū Y135 to Y232, 12 to 23 hours, seven daily (12.38am, 4.03pm, 4.30pm, 4.50pm, 6.03pm, 6.10pm and 11.16pm)

Chóngqìng Y127, nine to 12 hours, 11 daily (12.38am to 11.16pm)

Guǎngzhōu (K66, fastest train) Y335, 20 hours, one daily (3.22pm)

Guìlín Y191, 12 hours, one daily (10.27pm)

Kǎilǐ Y14 to Y29, two to three hours, regular services (24 hours)

Kūnmíng Y157, 11 to 14 hours, 12 daily (24 hours)

Zūnyì Y12 to Y24, three to six hours, several daily (24 hours)

Getting Around

To/From the Airport

Airport buses depart from the CAAC office every 30 minutes (Y10, 8.30am to 7pm). A taxi from the airport will cost around Y60.

Bus

Buses 1 and 2 (Y1) do city tour loops from the train station, passing close to the main long-distance bus station. Bus 1 travels up Zhonghua Nanlu and heads westward along Beijing Lu.

Taxi

Taxi flagfall is Y10; late at night it increases to Y12.

Qīngyán 青岩

With its winding, stone-flagged streets and restored city walls, **Qīngyán** (admission Y30) makes a pleasant contrast to modern Guìyáng. A former Ming-era military outpost dating back to 1378, Qīngyán was once a traffic hub between the southwest provinces, leaving the village with Taoist temples and Buddhist monasteries rubbing up against Christian churches and menacing watchtowers.

Some of the places of worship are still active; make sure to visit the tranquil **Yíngxiáng Temple** (迎祥寺; Yíngxiáng Sì), on a side street populated by fortune tellers, and to compare the current, minimalist Catholic church with the now disused but much more impressive 19th-century original.

Qīngyán is about 30km south of Guìyáng and makes an easy day trip. Take bus 207 from the Hébīn Bus Depot to Huāxī (Y2, 45 minutes, every 20 minutes from 6.30am), and get off at the last stop. Then take the 210 (Y2, 20 minutes), which will drop you outside the north gate and the ticket office.

Zhènshān & Tiānhétán 镇山、天河潭

West of Qīngyán and around 25km southwest of Guìyáng, Zhènshān is a Bouyi village dating from the Ming dynasty, overlooking a picturesque reservoir. It's a lovely setting with fine architecture and sees far fewer tourists than Qīngyán. To get there, take bus 211 (Y2, 50 minutes, every 20 minutes from 6.30am) from the Hébīn Bus Depot and get off at Shíbǎn (石板); from there, it's a short hop on a minibus or even a motorcycle.

Just half a dozen or so kilometres beyond Zhènshān, bus 211 (Y70) continues to Tiānhétán, a worthy park if you haven't yet had enough of caves in Guìzhōu. The entrance fee includes boat rides to the caves. There are also some nice canals leading through Bouyi farming areas.

EASTERN GUÌZHŌU

More than a baker's dozen minority groups live in the gorgeous misty hills and river valleys east of Kǎilǐ; this area is truly a rare window on atypical life in China. Sure, some villages have been discovered big time and you'll hear incessant moaning about it from some travellers (as if they weren't tourists, too), but there are still endless places to lose yourself here. Booming country markets and festivals are held almost weekly.

China's largest Miao village, Xījiāng, and the remote Dong village of Zhàoxīng, in the southeast, are particularly popular. If you have time, consider visiting them as part of the back-door route into Guǎngxī. Outside Kǎilǐ there are no places to change money, so bring plenty of renminbi with you.

Kǎilǐ 凯里

☎0855 / POP 153,000

About 195km almost directly east of Guìyáng, Kǎilǐ is a compact, friendly town and really nothing more than a base for visiting minority villages or planning a back-door trip into Guǎngxī.

Sights & Activities

If you have time, visit **Dàgé Park** (大阁公园; Dàgé Gōngyuán; Big Pagoda Park) or **Jīnquánhú Park** (金泉湖公园; Jīquáhú Gōngyuán; Big Pagoda Park), which has a

TRADITIONAL GARMENTS

The variety of clothing among the minorities of Guìzhōu provides travellers with a daily visual feast. Clothes are as much a social and ethnic denominator as pure decoration. They also indicate whether or not a woman is married, and are a pointer to a woman's wealth and skills at weaving and embroidery.

Many women in remote areas still weave their own hemp and cotton cloth. Some families, especially in Dong areas, still ferment their own indigo paste as well, and you will also see this for sale in traditional markets. Many women will not attend festivals in the rain for fear that the dyes in their fabrics will run. Methods of producing indigo are greatly treasured and kept secret, but are increasingly threatened by the introduction of artificial chemical dyes.

Embroidery is central to minority costume and is a tradition passed down from mother to daughter. Designs include many important symbols and references to myths and history. Birds, fish and a variety of dragon motifs are popular. The highest quality work is often reserved for baby carriers, and many young girls work on these as they approach marrying age. Older women will often spend hundreds of hours embroidering their own funeral clothes.

Costumes move with the times. In larger towns, Miao women often substitute their embroidered smocks with a good woolly jumper (sweater) and their headdresses look suspiciously like mass-produced pink and yellow Chinese towels.

Dong-minority drum tower (dating from – whoa! – two decades ago). Also check out the **Minorities Museum** (贵州民族博物馆; Guìzhōu Mínzú Bówùguǎn; Ningbo Lu; admission free; ⏱9am-5pm) in the south of town, which, though it seems old, was recently relocated here and has some displays of minority clothing and artefacts.

Wu Min, also known as Louisa, a local Miao woman, runs **treks** to remote Miao and Dong villages that come highly recommended. She can also organise homestays, as well as arrange for visitors to study the Miao and Dong languages and learn local dances. She speaks good English. Contact her via email at wuminlouisa@gmail.com.

Festivals & Events

Markets and festivals are one of Guìzhōu's major attractions, and the profusion of them around Kǎilǐ makes this sleepy town the best place to base yourself for exploring them. For more festival details, see the boxed text, p619.

Sleeping

Guótài Dàjiǔdiàn HOTEL $$
(国泰大酒店; ☎826 9818; fax 826 9818; 6 Beijing Donglu; 北京东路6号; s & d Y258 288, discounts of up to 33%; ❄@) Smiling staff, a central location and good discounts make this a great midrange option. You can find places with more stars but they aren't usually worth the extra money.

Petroleum Hotel HOTEL $
(石油宾馆; Shíyóu Bīnguǎn; ☎823 4331; 44 Yingpan Donglu; 营盘东路44号; dm/s/d/tr Y40/80/100/120, discounts of 20-30%) This is a budget favourite despite the beaten-down rooms and very basic facilities. Off-season you might have the place to yourself; in summer you may need to call ahead (particularly during festivals).

New Century Hotel HOTEL $$
(新世纪大酒店; Xīnshìjì Dàjiǔdiàn; ☎826 0333; 1 Shaoshan Nanlu; 韶山南路1号; s Y238-288, d Y318, discounts of up to 33%; ❄@) Decent-sized rooms and generous discounts are available at this new-ish place slap in the middle of town. Avoid the noisy rooms at the front.

Eating

Kǎilǐ has some fantastic snack stalls lining its streets. Savoury crepes, potato patties, barbecues, tofu grills, noodles, hotpot, *shuǐjiǎo* (boiled dumplings) and wonton soup overflow at extremely reasonable prices. Make tracks for the **night market** (夜市; *yèshì*) just off Beijing Donglu, very close to the Guótài Dàjiǔdiàn, which is always packed with locals and stays open till the wee hours.

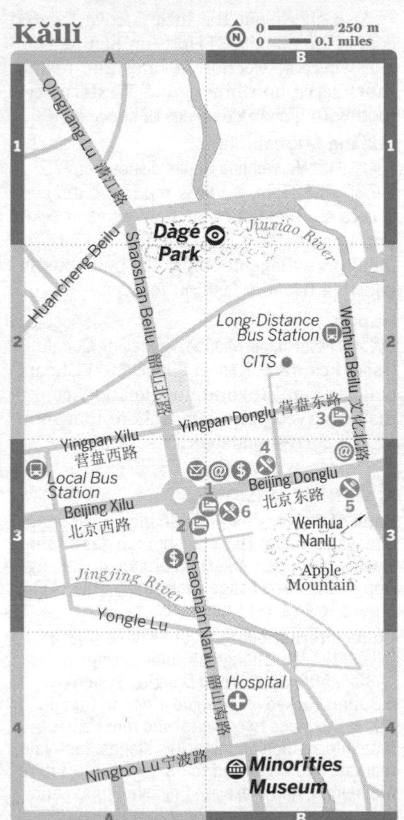

Kǎilǐ

Top Sights

Sleeping

Eating

Also check out the little alcove located east of the Ludujia Ri Hotel on Beijing Donglu, where a selection of cafes and restaurants serve up Chinese and Western-style food with varying degrees of success.

Lǐxiǎng Miànshídiàn NOODLES $
(理想面食店; Wenhua Nanlu; dishes from Y5; ⌚7.30am-7.30pm; 📵) This modest eatery serves simple dishes such as wonton soup and noodles, and is handy for a morning meal pre-village-hopping. It's been busily run in a friendly fashion forever.

Happy NOODLES $
(欢乐面吧; Huānlè Miànbā; 46 Beijing Donglu; dishes from Y8; ⌚11am-11.30pm; 📶📵) Cheap coffee (from Y10) and noodle and rice dishes served in an atmosphere that more or less corresponds with its name.

Information

Bank of China (中国银行; Zhōngguó Yínháng; Shaoshan Nanlu) This main branch has all services and an ATM. A second branch on Beijing Donglu will also change cash. Many other ATMs around town accept foreign cards.

China International Travel Service (CITS; 中国国际旅行社; Zhōngguó Guójì Lǚxíngshè; ☎822 2506; 53 Yingpan Donglu; ⌚9am-5.30pm) Tucked just behind Yingpan Donglu, this is the place to come for the most up-to-date information on minority villages, festivals, markets and organised tours. All the staff here are helpful, and there are English, French and Japanese speakers amongst them.

China Post (邮局; Zhōngguó Yóuzhèng; cnr Shaoshan Beilu & Beijing Donglu) You can make international phone calls on the 2nd floor.

Internet cafe (网吧; wǎngbā; cnr Wenhua Beilu & Beijing Donglu; per hr Y2; ⌚24hr) On the 2nd floor, with 400 computers and comfy chairs. There's another internet cafe on Beijing Donglu, almost opposite the Guótài Dàjiǔdiàn.

Public Security Bureau (PSB; 公安局; Gōng'ānjú; ☎853 6113; Beijing Donglu; ⌚8.30-11.30am & 2.30-5.30pm Mon-Fri) Deals with all passport and visa enquiries.

Getting There & Away

Bus

Kǎilǐ is served by five bus stations. The **long-distance bus station** (长途客运站) on Wenhua Beilu has departures to most destinations.

Cóngjiāng Y87, eight hours, six daily (7am to 2.30pm)

Guìyáng Y60, 2½ hours, every 20 minutes (7am to 8.30pm)

Jǐnpíng (锦屏; for Lónglǐ) Y75, five hours, 10 daily (6.20am to 2.50pm)

Léishān Y13.50, one hour, every 25 minutes (7am to 7pm)

Lìpíng Y95, seven hours, eight daily (7am to 3.30pm)

Róngjiāng Y65, 4½ hours, every 40 minutes (6.40am to 4.40pm)

Xījiāng Y24, 80 minutes, five daily (9am, 10.30am, 12.30pm, 2.30pm and 4.30pm)

If you can't find what you are looking for, try the **local bus station** (客运站) on Yingpan Lu, where several buses a day run to most surrounding villages, including Lángdé (Y10), Chóng'ān (Y11, one hour), Májiāng (Y10) and Huángpíng (Y13, 30 minutes).

For Shíqiáo (Y16, 90 minutes, several from 7am to 7pm), head to the **small local bus station** (往石桥的公交车), south of the long-distance bus station on Wenhua Nanlu. Yet another local station along the road to Táijiāng on the east side of town has departures to points east, such as Nánhuā.

Still another – whew! – is located north of the first-mentioned local bus station along Huancheng Beilu. This **local bus station** (往麻塘、舟溪的公交车) has departures for points north such as Mátáng (but also, inexplicably, south, such as Zhōuxī).

Train

Kǎilǐ's train station is a couple of kilometres north of town but departures are infrequent and the train service slow, apart from the trains to Guìyáng, which leave round the clock (Y14 to Y29, two to three hours).

For longer distances, it's worth stopping in Guìyáng to secure a reservation.

Getting Around

Bus fares cost Y1 in Kǎilǐ and almost all of the buses departing from the train station follow the same route: up Qingjiang Lu, past the long-distance bus station, along Beijing Donglu and down Shaoshan Nanlu to the Minorities Museum. For the train station, take bus 2.

Taxi flagfall is Y6.

Around Kǎilǐ

If you're village-hopping into Guǎngxī, which is lovely wherever you go, plan on spending about a week. Note that some of these villages are starting to charge entrance fees, so don't be surprised if you're hit up for a ticket.

An extraordinary number of markets are held in the villages surrounding Kǎilǐ. Xiānhuā has a huge market every six to seven days. Zhōuxī, Léishān and Táijiāng hold markets every six days. Check with the CITS in Kǎilǐ for the latest information.

XĪJIĀNG 西江

Ensconced snugly in the Léigōng Hills, **Xījiāng** (admission Y60) is thought to be the largest Miao village and is well known for its embroidery and silver ornaments (the Miao believe that silver can dispel evil spirits). It's one of those treasures – paddies, mists, wooden houses, water buffalo, the works.

Unsurprisingly, it is now a firm fixture on the tourist trail. There's now a performance square, English signposts, numerous souvenir shops and even an ATM that takes foreign cards. But old men still squat on the streets smoking pipes, the women do their washing in the river, and the pace of life remains that of a traditional village. The people are overwhelmingly friendly too; solo travellers can expect to be roped into any impromtu parties going on.

When the sun is shining, Xījiāng is simply idyllic. Head away from the village on the paths that weave their way through the rice paddies, side-stepping the farmers and water buffalo, and recharge your soul in the surrounding hills. There's a three-day trek from here to **Páiyáng** (排羊), a Miao village north of Xījiāng. This trail winds its way through some remote minority villages and lush scenery. You will probably find accommodation with locals en route, but you shouldn't expect it so come prepared to sleep under the stars.

Many families offer rooms with dinner for Y50; they'll find you, or simply ask. Otherwise, try the **Ukea Inn** (有家客栈; Yǒujiā Kèzhàn; ☎137 6551 9880; d Y80) on the main street, which has sparkly clean rooms with sit-down toilets.

From Kǎilǐ there are five buses a day to Xījiāng (Y24, 80 minutes). Returning to Kǎilǐ, buses leave at 8am, 9.30am, 11am, 1.30pm and 3.30pm. Alternatively, if you're heading south and east towards Guǎngxī, there are 12 buses a day to Léishān (Y10, 1½ hours, 6.30am to 5.40pm), from where you can head south towards Róngjiāng (榕江).

LÁNGDÉ 郎德

Superb extant Miao architecture and cobbled pathways naturally draw loads of tour buses for elaborate singing, dancing and reed flute performances in this village. But the commercialisation can't overcome the wondrousness of the locals. There's a terrific 15km trail along the Bālā River that will take you through several Miao villages.

About 20km outside Kǎilǐ, buses pass by Lángdé (Y10) on the way to Léishān. The village is 2km from the main road. Getting away, get out on the street and flag down a bus back to Kǎilǐ.

CELEBRATING WITH LOCALS, GUÌZHŌU-STYLE

Minority celebrations are lively events that can last for days at a time, and often include singing, dancing, horse racing and buffalo fighting.

One of the biggest is the **Lúshēng Festival**, held in either spring or autumn, depending on the village. The *lúshēng* is a reed instrument used by the Miao people. Other important festivals include the **Dragon Boat Festival**, **Hill-leaping Festival** and **Sharing the Sister's Meal Festival** (equivalent to Valentine's Day in the West). The **Miao New Year** is celebrated on the first four days of the 10th lunar month in Kǎilǐ, Guàdīng, Zhōuxī and other Miao areas. The **Fertility Festival** is celebrated only every 13 years (the next one's due in 2016).

All minority festivals follow the lunar calendar and so dates vary from year to year. They will also vary from village to village and shaman to shaman. CITS in Kǎilǐ can provide you with a list of local festivals.

LÉISHĀN 雷山

This village is usually used as a transit point, but you can also head to **Léigōng Shān** (雷公山; Leigong Mountain; admission Y30), at 2178m, which offers some interesting hiking. A newer road from here also leads to Lèlǐ (乐里), towards Róngjiāng. From Kǎilǐ, there are numerous buses to Léishān.

SHÍQIÁO 石桥

Shíqiáo means 'stone bridge' and you'll know why when you spy the lovely ones in this beautiful Miao town southwest of Kǎilǐ. The town was famed for its handmade paper, which, though not so apparent today, can still be seen. Even if you're not into paper, it's a great place to visit.

Shíqiáo buses (Y16, two hours) depart from a local bus station on Wenhua Nanlu in Kǎilǐ, south of the long-distance bus station.

MÁTÁNG 麻塘

This village around 30km from Kǎilǐ is home to the Gejia. Officially classified as a subgroup of the Miao minority, the Gejia have different customs, dress and language, and are renowned batik artisans; their traditional dress often features batik and embroidery. Mátáng has been dolled up for tourism – the inevitable performance square has materialised – and the women hawkers here are rather more persistent than in other villages.

The village is 2km from the main road and buses regularly run past the drop-off point in the direction of Chóng'ān (Y6) and Kǎilǐ (Y8). Just stand on the side of the road and flag down anything that comes your way.

LÓNGLǏ 隆里

Stranded in splendid isolation amidst fields and rice paddies near the border with Húnán, **Lónglǐ** (admission Y15) is a real oddity. For a start, it isn't a minority village. Instead, this former garrison town is populated by the descendants of Han soldiers sent to protect the empire from the pesky Miao. One of the province's 'eco-museums' (read, real-live village), it's fascinating for its extant architecture. Wander the narrow cobblestone streets and gander at the mostly wooden houses, some lovely courtyards, pavilions, temples and the town walls. The surrounding area looks prime for bike exploration, too.

Just outside the old town, **Lónglǐ Gǔchéng Jiǔdiàn** (隆里古城酒店; ☎08555 718 0018; r with/without bathroom Y60/40) is the only current accommodation choice and offers basic rooms with Chinese-style toilets.

Coming from Kǎilǐ is a bit tricky since there's no direct bus. First you have to take a bus to Jǐnpíng (锦屏; Y75, five hours, 10 buses daily, 6.20am to 2.50pm), then switch to another bus (Y13, 90 minutes, half-hourly or so from 7am to around 2pm).

BĀSHĀ 岜沙

Wander up the hill from Cóngjiāng (从江) and you'd swear Bāshā is a movie set depicting the Tang or Song eras – its men still wear period clothes, have daggers on their belts and shave their heads, leaving only a stylish topknot. When not farming, they can be found hunting with antique rifles. Meanwhile, the women parade in full Miao rig with their hair twisted into a curl on the top of their heads.

Quite why Bāshā is stuck in a timewarp is a mystery, as it's only 7.5km from very modern Cóngjiāng. Not even the locals can explain why they've retained their ancient customs so well. Nor is Bāshā undiscovered. A collection of six hamlets that sprawls across a beautiful valley, Chinese-English signs point the way to the various places of interest. It's best seen during a festival, even if that means more visitors, because most of the year the men are out in the fields during the day. But at any time, the surrounding countryside is superb.

Some rudimentary inns in the village offer beds for Y20. You might also be able to arrange a hunting trip with the men. Otherwise, you can stay in Cóngjiāng. The **Xīngyùe Bīnguǎn** (星月宾馆; ☎0855-641 8598; Jiangdong Lu; 江东路; d Y128; ❄@) has clean, spacious rooms and is just to the left of the bus station.

There's no bus to Bāshā and it's a very steep walk up to the village. Taxis in Cóngjiāng will try and sting you for Y40 for a one-way journey, but you should pay Y50 for a round-trip. It's best to get the driver to wait for you, as not much transportation hangs around the village.

ZHÀOXĪNG 肇兴

Perhaps the quintessential Dong village, packed with traditional wooden structures, several wind and rain bridges and five remarkable drum towers, Zhàoxīng is no longer the little-known paradise it once was. Its sheer uniqueness makes for a powerful draw, and the locals are certainly not complaining about the increase in visitors.

But the essential, amazing nature of Zhàoxīng hasn't changed. Yes, the restaurants on the main street have English menus, which is just as well as they eat rat (老鼠肉; *lǎoshǔ ròu*) in these parts, and there are now any number of quasi-inns and guesthouses offering rooms from Y50. But Zhàoxīng remains a working farming village, where most people still speak only their native Dong language and are extremely welcoming. The tour groups might swoop in on hit-and-run missions, but

Zhàoxīng remains a very easy place to while away a few days.

Nearby too, are Dong villages that are still tourist-free. Hike west out of Zhàoxīng from the bus station for an hour, up a steep hill and past some splendid rice terraces, and you're in equally friendly Jītáng (基塘), which has its own drum tower. Head the other way out of Zhàoxīng through the fields and two hours later you reach Táng'ān (堂安), a village so essentially Dong it's been named a living museum.

The **Wangjiang Lou Hostel** (望江楼客栈; Wàngjiānglóu Kèzhàn; ☎613 0269; d/tr Y50/60; ❄@) isn't a hostel, but is a family-run place by the river with nice wooden rooms with hot showers and sit-down toilets. The most modern digs in the village can be found at the **Zhàoxīng Bīnguǎn** (肇兴宾馆; ☎613 0899; s & d Y168-228; ❄), where rooms are spotless, with tiny gleaming bathrooms. It's a tour group haunt, so it's often booked out.

At the time of writing, the village was in the throes of major construction work, while the building of a nearby, long-delayed, new highway (which will cut journey times from Kǎilǐ in half) was in full swing. When it is all finished, sometime in 2011, expect there to be an admission fee to Zhàoxīng.

Until the new expressway opens, getting here from Kǎilǐ is a slog. First, you have to travel to Cóngjiāng (Y87, eight hours, six buses daily from 7am to 2.30pm) and then change for a bus to Zhàoxīng (Y18, 2½ hours, 7.30am and 1pm). From Lípíng (黎平) there are five buses a day (Y18, 3½ hours, 8.20am to 2.50pm).

Heading out of Zhàoxīng, there are two morning buses (Y18, 7.30am and midday) to Cóngjiāng and two buses a day to Sānjiāng (三江) in Guǎngxī (Y35, four hours, 8.30am and 11.30am). From there you can catch an onward bus to Guìlín. There are at least five buses daily to Lípíng.

WESTERN GUÌZHŌU

Birds, caves and waterfalls are the main attractions of this region. Outside Ānshùn, the thundering Huángguǒshù Falls is Guìzhōu's premier tourist attraction, while Zhījīn Cave is one of the largest in the world. Way out west, the town of Wēiníng has one of China's top birdwatching locations in Cǎohǎi Lake, and also offers a back-door route into Yúnnán.

Ānshùn 安顺

☎0853 / POP 449,000

Once a centre for tea and opium trading, Ānshùn remains the commercial hub of western Guìzhōu and is now most famous as a producer of batik, kitchen knives and the lethal Ānjiǔ brand of alcohol.

An undistinguished, grubby city, most travellers come here for the easy access to Huángguǒshù Falls or to head to Zhījīn Cave.

Sights

Fǔwén Miào CONFUCIAN TEMPLE
(府文庙; admission Y10; ⌚8.30am-6pm) Check out this dilapidated but charming Confucian temple with some stunningly intricate carvings, in the north of town.

FREE **Dōnglín Temple** BUDDHIST TEMPLE
(东林寺; Dōnglín Sì; ⌚7.30am-6pm) The resident Buddhist monks welcome visitors warmly to this temple, built in AD 1405 (during the Ming dynasty) and restored in 1668.

FREE **Lóngwáng Miào** BUDDHIST TEMPLE
(龙王庙; ⌚7.30am-5.30pm) Another working Buddhist temple. It's just off Zhonghua Beilu.

Sleeping

Sān Xīng Dàjiǔdiàn HOTEL $$
(三星大酒店; ☎329 4100; 18 Huangguoshu Dajie; 黄果树大街18号; s & d Y348-388, discounts of 60%; ❄) Fraying at the edges, but with big, clean rooms set around an atrium as a reminder of its glory days, the Sān Xīng is very handy for the bus and train stations. It's a decent deal in a city with few budget options.

Xīxiùshān Bīnguǎn HOTEL $$
(西秀山宾馆; ☎333 7888; fax 333 7668; 63 Zhonghua Nanlu; 中华南路63号; s/d Y288/588, discounts of 50%; ❄@) A tour group favourite, this cavernous place has two large wings so they can normally find a spare room. The wood-panelled best ones are very comfortable, with nice bathrooms.

Fènghuángshān Dàjiǔdiàn HOTEL $$
(凤凰山大酒店; Golden Phoenix Mountain Hotel; ☎322 5724; 58 Tashan Donglu; 塔山东路58号; d Y228-528, discounts of up to 40%; ❄@) The bathrooms can be iffy here, and the rooms are overstocked with furniture, but the staff are pleasant enough. Look for a building that

looks like a bank, with two lions standing guard outside. Big discounts are normally available.

Eating

Local speciality *qiáoliángfěn* (乔凉粉) is a spicy dish made from buckwheat noodles and preserved bean curd. A good on-the-run snack is *chōngchōng gāo* (冲冲糕), a cake made from steamed sticky rice with sesame and walnut seeds and sliced wax gourd.

By far the best place to eat is the **night market** (夜市; *yèshì*) on Gufu Jie. It's the most happening spot in Ānshùn, with the locals crowding out the many food tents and stalls that set up here. There's fantastic barbecued fish, as well as Uighur kebabs and endless noodle dishes.

Information

Bank of China (中国银行; Zhōngguó Yínháng; cnr Tashan Xilu & Zhonghua Nanlu) Offers all services and has an ATM. There are many other ATMs around town.

China Post (邮局; Zhōngguó Yóuzhèng; cnr Zhonghua Nanlu & Tashan Donglu) Look for it tucked next to the China Telecom building.

China Travel Service (CTS; 中国旅行社; Zhōngguó Lǚxíngshè; ☎322 4537; Tashan Donglu; ⊙9am-6pm Mon-Fri) Look for a blue sign with white Chinese characters.

Internet cafe (网吧; wǎngbā; Huangguoshu Dajie; per hr Y2.50; ⊙24hr) Opposite the Sān Xīng Dàjiǔdiàn. There's another one on Nanshui Lu off Zhonghua Nanlu.

Ānshùn

Top Sights

Sleeping

Eating

Getting There & Around

The **north bus station** (安顺客车北站) has buses to Zhījīn town (for Zhījīn Cave); go to the **west bus station** (客运西站) for Lónggōng Caves.

The **long-distance bus station** (长途客运站) on the corner of Huangguoshu Dajie and Zhonghua Nanlu has a handful of useful destinations:

Guìyáng Y35 to Y36, two hours, every 20 minutes (6am to 9pm)

Huángguǒshù Y13, one hour, every 20 minutes (7.30am to 7pm)

Kūnmíng Y120, 15 to 17 hours, three daily (9am, 10.40am and 4pm)

Another **long-distance bus station** (往中国东南的高快汽车站) in front of the train station has buses for provinces in the southeast of China.

It is still very hard to get sleeper reservations for trains from here; pick them up in Guìyáng instead. To Shuǐchéng (also known as Liùpánshuǐ, for Wēiníng) there is a daily train at 10.43am (Y12, four hours).

Minibus 1 zips around town from the train station and up Tashan Donglu. Bus 2 travels between the train station and the north bus station. Buses cost Y1. Taxi flagfall is Y6.

Around Ānshùn

LÓNGGŌNG CAVES 龙宫洞

The vast **Lónggōng** (Lónggōng Dòng; Dragon Palace; admission Y120; ⏲8.30am-5.30pm) cave network snakes through 20 hills. While some travellers enjoy drifting through the caves on rowboats with their subdued guides, others find the whole experience – coloured lights, cheesy music, tour groups – kitschy.

Lónggōng is 23km south of Ānshùn and an easy day trip. Local buses (Y8, 40 minutes) depart every hour from Ānshùn's west bus station from 8am. Returning, buses leave hourly until about 5pm.

ZHĪJĪN CAVE 织金洞

As the largest cave in China, and one of the biggest in the entire world at 10km long and up to 150m high, **Zhījīn Cave** (Zhījīn Dòng; admission Y135; ⏲8.30am-5.30pm) gets tourist accolades. *Lord of the Rings* has been used to describe the abstract landscape of spectacular shapes and spirals, often cathedral-like, reaching from the floor to the ceiling.

Tickets to the cave, which is 15km outside Zhījīn and 125km north of Ānshùn, include a compulsory 2½-hour Chinese-only tour (minimum 10 people). The tour covers some 6km of the cave, up steep, slippery steps at times, and there are English captions at the main points along the way. Solo travellers visiting outside of peak summer months or Chinese holidays should be prepared for what can be a tedious wait for enough people to roll up to form a group.

A long day trip from Ānshùn is just possible, but you need to be on the 7.25am bus to Zhījīn (Y30, 3½ hours), which leaves from Ānshùn's north bus station. Once there, hop a taxi (Y4) to the local bus station on Yuping Jie and catch one of the minibuses that leave regularly for the cave entrance (Y7, 50 minutes). Returning from the caves, buses leave regularly. The last bus back to Ānshùn heads out of Zhījīn at 5.30pm.

HUÁNGGUǑSHÙ FALLS 黄果树大瀑布

Disgorging from endless buses, a friendly invasion of frenetic tourists from all over China come to see the 77.8m-tall, 81m-wide **Huángguǒshù Falls** (Huángguǒshù Dàpùbù; Yellow Fruit Tree Falls; admission Mar-Oct Y180, Nov-Feb Y160; ⏲8.30am-5.30pm), making this Guìzhōu's number-one tourist attraction. From May to October especially, these falls really rock the local landscape with their cacophony, while mist-prism rainbows dance about **Rhinoceros Pool** below.

The cascades are actually part of a 450-sq-km cave and karst complex discovered when engineers explored the area in the 1980s to gauge the region's hydroelectric potential. There are paths around the falls through very pleasant scenery that take a few hours to cover.

Here's the beef: in the last four years the admission price has doubled. Not only that, but there's a compulsory Y50 fee for a bus ride from the ticket office to the actual park entrance. Compared to the far cheaper, less-visited and almost as spectacular Shízhàngdòng Waterfall in northern Guìzhōu, it smacks of serious price-gouging.

You can do Huángguǒshù Falls in a day trip from Guìyáng at a push, while it's an easy one from Ānshùn. There are accommodation options everywhere in Huángguǒshù village, but hotels are horribly overpriced. Expect little from **Huángguǒshù Gōngshāng Zhāodàisuǒ** (黄果树工商招待所; ☎359 2583; d/tr Y288/328), but with a discount it'll be your 'best' bet.

From Ānshùn, buses run every 20 minutes from the long-distance bus station at the corner of Zhonghua Nanlu and Huangguoshu Dajie. There are eight buses a day from Guìyáng to Huángguǒshù (Y50, 2½ hours, every 40 minutes from 8am) from the long-distance bus station on Jinyang Nanlu. The last bus heads back to Guìyáng at 4pm.

Wēiníng 威宁

☎0857 / POP 57,000

A dusty, scrappy place with a manic energy epitomised by the orange motorised rickshaws that career around town, Wēiníng is one of the top spots in the world for that most sedate of hobbies, birdwatching. The jewel-like Cǎohǎi Lake sits close to downtown and draws twitchers to observe wintering migratory birds, especially the rare black-necked crane. Wēiníng is also home to a large population of Hui (Muslim), Miao and Yi; a big market held every three or four days sees the town thronged with people from the surrounding minority villages.

Sights & Activities

Cǎohǎi Lake LAKE

(草海湖; Cǎohǎi Hú; Grass Sea Lake) Cǎohǎi Lake has a fragile history, having been drained during both the Great Leap Forward and the Cultural Revolution in hopes of producing farmland. It didn't work and the lake was refilled in 1980. Government tinkering with water levels in ensuing years impacted the local environment and villagers' livelihoods; officials have since enlisted locals to help with the lake's protection in an effort to remedy both problems. The 20-sq-km freshwater wetland has been a national nature reserve since 1992, but many environmental problems remain.

Black-necked cranes are the main attraction, but among the other 180 or so protected bird species are black and white storks, golden and imperial eagles, white-tailed sea eagles, Eurasian cranes and white spoonbills. The prime time to see them is from November to March.

There are lovely trails around much of the lake, but the best way to get close-up to the birds is to cruise around the lake on a punt. Buy tickets at the **ticket office** (per boat 1/2/3hr Y120/240/360; ⏲8.30am-5.30pm) at the end of the path leading to the lake, rather than from the touts lurking nearby.

To get to the lake it's a 45-minute walk southwest of downtown Wēiníng or a five-minute taxi ride (Y5).

Sleeping & Eating

Hēijǐnghè Bīnguǎn HOTEL **$$**
(黑颈鹤宾馆; ☎623 6888; Jianshe Donglu; s & d Y188-308, discounts of 30%; ❄@) Cramped rooms and cold in the winter, this is the self-proclaimed top choice in town. Don't expect too much. To get here, turn right out of the bus station; it's a block ahead on the left, set back from the road.

Cǎohǎi Jiàrì Jiǔdiàn HOTEL **$$**
(草海假日酒店; ☎623 1881; Caohai Lu; 草海路; s, d & tr per person Y358-388, discounts of 50-60%; ❄) Right by the lake, rooms here are big and comfortably furnished, and service has improved markedly. It's still not worth the price, but discounts make things more tolerable.

They eat a lot of noodles in Wēiníng; you will too. There are hole-in-the-wall places all over town.

Information

There's no place to change money in Wēiníng. An ATM on Jianshe Donglu, near the Hējǐnghè Bīnguǎn, should take foreign cards, but don't count on it. Opposite the bus station, above the China Mobile shop, there's a rough and ready **internet cafe** (per hr Y2; ⏲24hr).

Getting There & Away

Wēiníng is a seven-hour bus ride from Guìyáng (Y90, 9am and noon). You can also get here from Ānshùn. First take a bus to Shuǐchéng (水城; Y55, 3½ hours, every 50 minutes from 8.30am to 5.30pm), then transfer to a Wēiníng-bound bus (Y30, two hours, hourly from 7.50am).

Leaving Wēiníng, you can backtrack to Guìyáng (Y90, 9am, midday, 6pm) or take a bus south to Xuānwēi in Yúnnán (Y50, five hours, seven daily from 7.30am to 3.30pm). From Wēiníng, there is also a daily sleeper bus to Kūnmíng (Y108, 11 hours, 5pm).

Alternatively, take a bus to Zhāotōng (Y30, three hours, 8am, 1pm, 3.30pm), from where you can hop over to Xīchāng in southern Sìchuān and connect with the Kūnmíng–Chéngdū train line.

NORTHERN GUÌZHŌU

This is where things get a bit wild. Few foreigners venture north of Guìyáng; those that do will find that already incomprehensible accents get broader, roads more rugged and that a stray *lǎowài* (foreigner) can stop the traffic. Way up on the Sìchuān border, Chìshuǐ and its surrounding valleys, waterfalls and national parks are virgin territory for travellers, and utterly gorgeous. Further south, historic Zūnyì was the setting for a key moment in the rise of Mao Zedong and will delight CCP buffs. Combining both offers a little-travelled route into southern Sìchuān.

Zūnyì 遵义

☎0852 / POP 555,000

Get your delightfully earnest CCP history here, the location of the Zūnyì Conference, a meeting that shaped the nation's future in no small terms. Other than that, Zūnyì prefecture is the home of Maotai, the fiery clear liquor that's the closest thing to China's national drink, so this is the best spot to pick some up.

Sights

Communist History Sites HISTORIC SITES
Zūnyì's CCP sights have had some serious facelifts – as has the neighbourhood surrounding them, with much being knocked down to 'recreate' what it looked like in the 1930s (they must have had lots of clothes shops back then).

There are a dozen or so spots to see, but only a few are truly worthwhile. Admission is free to all of them, but you'll need to show your passport to get a ticket from the office by the Zūnyì Conference Site.

The **Zūnyì Conference Site** (遵义会议会址; Zūnyì Huìyì Huìzhǐ; ☎825 6866; Ziyin Lu; ⏲8.30am-5.30pm Mar-Oct, 8.30am-5pm Nov-Feb) is hands down the most-visited attraction and by far the most comprehensive. Set in a colonial-style house, there are rooms filled with CCP memorabilia, lots of photo exhibits (check out the floppy hair Mao was modelling back in the early 1930s), details about the Long March and the Conference, as well as the meeting rooms and living quarters of the bigwigs. Sadly, the only English captions are 'Don't Touch' and 'Please Keep Off the Grass'.

The **Red Army General Political Department** (红军总政治部旧址; Hóngjūn Zǒngzhèngzhìbù Jiùzhǐ), in a lane off Ziyin Lu, is close by in a courtyard residence, which shares the grounds with an attractive, disused **Catholic church** (天主教堂) left behind by French missionaries.

Opposite is the **Residence of Bo Gu** (博古旧居; Bógǔ Jiùjū), the general leader of the CCP Central Committee at the time of the Zunyi Conference. Nearby, the **State Bank of the Red Army** (红军银行; Hóngjūn Yínháng), which was closed for repairs at the time of writing, has some terrific money displays and decent English captions.

Temples BUDDHIST TEMPLES
Zūnyì has two active Buddhist temples. Built in the 1920s, the very well maintained **Xiāngshān Temple** (湘山寺; Xiangshān Sì) is situated on a small hill in a lively part of town. **Báiyún Temple** (白云寺; Báiyún Sì) is more rundown but still quite charming.

Sleeping

Beautiful Harbor Hotel HOTEL $$
(京腾丽湾酒店; Jīngténg Lìwān Jiǔdiàn; ☎864 9898; fax 865 4188; Beijing Lu; 北京路; s & d Y468-618, discounts of 50-60%; ❄@) A fine place to drop anchor, there are more expensive hotels in Zūnyì but none better. Modern, sensibly designed rooms, helpful staff, generous discounts, and it's only a few minutes' walk from the train and bus stations.

Jīnlóng Jiǔdiàn HOTEL $$
(金龙酒店; ☎823 1671; 45 Zhonghua Nanlu; 中华南路45号; s Y188, d Y208-328, discounts of 60%; ❄) Located on busy Zhonghua Nanlu,

Zūnyì

Top Sights
- Red Army General Political Department B1
- Residence of Bo Gu B1
- State Bank of the Red Army B1
- Zūnyì Conference Site B1

Sights
1 Báiyún Temple D1
2 Catholic Church B1
3 Xiāngshān Temple C2

Sleeping
4 Jīnlóng Jiǔdiàn C2
5 Xiāngshān Bīnguǎn B2

Eating
6 Grill Stalls C2
7 Grill Stalls C2

Drinking
8 Coffee Houses & Cafes D1

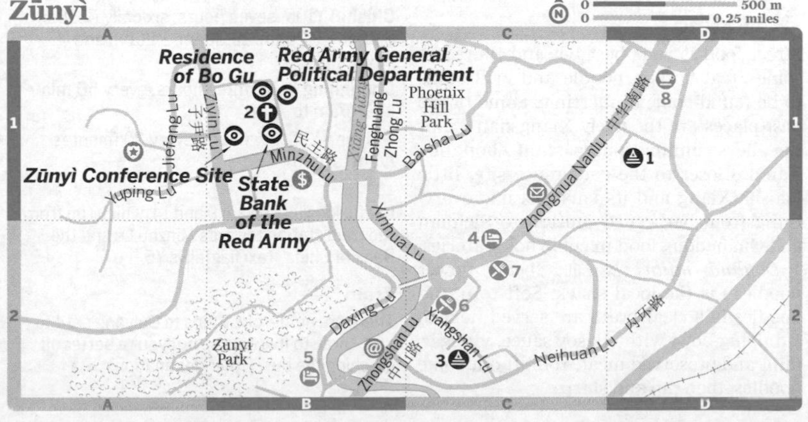

THE ZŪNYÌ CONFERENCE

On 16 October 1934, hemmed in the Jiāngxī soviet by Kuomintang forces, the communists set out on a Herculean, one-year, 9500km Long March from one end of China to the other. By mid-December they had reached Guìzhōu and marched on Zūnyì. Taking the town by surprise, the communists were able to take a breather.

From 15 to 18 January 1935, in the now-famous Zūnyì Conference, top leaders reviewed their Soviet-influenced strategies that had cost them their Jiāngxī base and many troops. Mao, until this time largely overshadowed by his contemporaries, was highly critical of the communists' strategy thus far, and the resolutions of the conference largely reflected his views. He was elected a full member of the ruling Standing Committee of the Politburo and Chief Assistant to Zhou Enlai in military planning, a pivotal factor in his rise to power.

and more or less equidistant between the sights and the train and bus stations, the Jinlong has rooms ranging from the poky and modest to the spacious and attractive. Discounts make the best ones a steal.

Xiāngshān Bīnguǎn HOTEL **$$**
(香山宾馆; ☎823 4444; Daxing Lu; 大兴路; s & d Y198-278; ❄@) Right on the river, a good place to escape the hustle of downtown Zūnyì. The rooms are a little dull, but clean and decent-sized. The staff are keen to help.

Eating

Street food is your best bet and there are some great hotpot, noodle and grill stalls to be found come dinnertime. Some of the best places are the lively Xiangshan Lu or the alleys running southeast off Zhonghua Nanlu. Closer to the conference site, little Laosha Xiang and its environs has everything from barbecued mutton to Sìchuān and Guǎngdōng food in cubbyhole eateries.

Dòuhuā miàn (豆花面; 'bean flower noodles') is the local snack. Soft tofu and noodles in a clear broth are served next to a dipping bowl with oil, soy sauce, vinegar, mint and preserved meat. You lift out some noodles, then dip and slurp.

Drinking

Zūnyì nightlife is generally shut up inside the giant KTV bars lining Zhonghua Beilu. There are a few bars on Aomen Lu, north of Zhonghua Beilu, close to the intersection with Shanghai Lu, as well as some pricey coffee places (咖啡馆; Kāfēi Guǎn) on Zhonghua Nanlu.

Information

Bank of China (中国银行; Zhōngguó Yínháng; Minzhu Lu) Zūnyì's main branch with a 24-hour ATM and currency and traveller cheque exchange. There are many other branches around town, including one on Dalian Lu around the corner from the Beautiful Harbour Hotel.

Beidouxing internet cafe (北斗星网吧; Běidǒuxīng wǎngbā; Zhongshan Lu; per hr Y3; ⏲24hr) Just opposite Neihuan Lu on the 2nd floor (look for the Pepsi sign). There's another decent one on the corner of Beijing Lu and Wenhua Lu, close to the bus and train station.

China Post (邮局; Zhōngguó Yóuzhèng; Zhonghua Nanlu; ⏲8am-8pm) You can make long-distance calls here, too.

Public Security Bureau (PSB; 公安局; Gōng'ānjú; Jinian Sq; ⏲8.30-11.30am & 2.30-5.30pm) Offers visa extensions.

Getting There & Around

Bus

Zūnyì has two bus stations. The main one is on Beijing Lu and is where Guìyáng buses arrive and depart. There are also buses here to Ānshùn and Chóngqìng.

Buses for Chìshuǐ leave from the newer **Máocǎopù Qìchēzhàn** (茅草铺汽车站) on Shenzhen Lu (there's a statue of Mao to wave you off). A taxi there from the main bus station is Y6.

Ānshùn Y92, 5½ hours, four daily (9am, 11am, 1.30pm and 3.30pm)

Chìshuǐ Y105, seven hours, six daily (7.20am, 8.30am, 9.20am, 10.30am, 1.20pm and 3.30pm)

Chóngqìng Y118, three hours, every 50 minutes (7am to 7pm)

Guìyáng Y65, 2½ hours, every 20 minutes (7am to 7pm)

Useful local buses are 9 and 14, which run from the train station towards Minzhu Lu and the Bank of China. Taxi flagfall is Y5.

Train

There are numerous trains to Guìyáng (Y14 to Y24, three to five hours), but you're better off catching the bus. Other destinations:

Chéngdū hard sleeper Y157, nine to 14 hours, two daily (2.41am and 8.57pm)

Chóngqìng hard sleeper Y98, six to 10 hours, 10 daily

Chìshuǐ 赤水

0852 / POP 50,000

Sitting right on the border with Sìchuān, Chìshuǐ was once a node for the transport of salt. Now, it's the gateway to some of the least-seen natural delights in the southwest. Just outside town are deep gorges and valleys flanked by towering cliffs hewn out of red sandstone, a profusion of waterfalls, as well as bamboo and fern forests that date back to the Jurassic Era.

While the locals are extremely friendly, there's nothing of intrinsic interest in Chìshuǐ itself, but it's the logical base for exploring the surrounding sights. The town sits on the east bank of the Chishui River (Chìshuǐ Hé). Cross the town's main bridge (Chìshuǐ Dàqiáo) to the other side and you're in Jiǔzhī (九支) in Sìchuān.

Note that it's not possible to change money in either Chìshuǐ or Jiǔzhī, so bring cash with you. There is a 24-hour ATM on the corner of Renmin Xilu, close to the bus station, that takes foreign cards, but don't rely on it.

Sleeping

You can find basic rooms for Y50 in places opposite the bus station on Renmin Xilu.

Chìshuǐ Kǎiyuè Bīnguǎn HOTEL $$
(赤水凯悦宾馆; 288 9888; West Inner Huanlu; 西内环路; s & d Y188-296, discounts of 60%;) A newish place with the best budget rooms in town. The rooms are big and clean and come with ADSL connections. Not all have sit-down toilets, so check them first.

Chìshuǐ Yuán Bīnguǎn HOTEL $$
(赤水源宾馆; 288 7798; 18 Renmin Beilu; 人民北路18号; s & d Y300-588; discounts of 30-50%;) This hotel is the town stalwart and remains a favourite with tour groups. The rooms are large and perfectly fine, if a little old-fashioned. The bathrooms are considerably plainer. Expect discounts, if it's not booked out.

Zhōngyuè Dàjiǔdiàn HOTEL $$
(中悦大酒店; 282 3888; 22 Nanzheng Jie; 南正街22号; s & d Y478-548, discounts of 30%;) The posh option. Comfortable rooms, proper showers and helpful staff, although they seem a little alarmed by foreigners, and discounts even in summer.

Eating

For food, head to the main drag of Renmin Xilu, where hole-in-the-wall eateries serve up noodle and rice dishes, different varieties of dumplings and the ever-present pig's feet, as well as various other animal organs. There are also streetfood stalls and supermarkets close to the bus station here. On Renmin Beilu, there are a few hotpot places.

Getting There & Away

Chìshuǐ has two bus stations. The **Qìchē Kèyùnzhàn** (汽车客运站) on Renmin Xilu handles most local destinations:

Chéngdū Y112, five hours, three daily (7.50am, 9.40am and 2.45pm)

Chóngqìng (Y102, 4½ hours, seven daily (6am to 5pm)

Shízhàngdòng Y10, six daily (6.50am to 4.20pm)

Sìdònggōu Y5.50, every 20 minutes (from 6.30am)

Zūnyì Y105, eight hours, six daily (6.10am to 3.40pm)

For Guìyáng (Y160, eight hours, 6.55am and 8.50am) and Jīnshāgōu (Y11.50, 1½ hours, 9.30am and 3.55pm), you need the **Lǚyóu Chēzhàn** (旅游车站) on Nan Jiao Lu by the river, a Y4 cab ride from Renmin Xilu. There are also two buses a day to Zūnyì (Y105, eight hours, 6.35am and 10.10am) from here.

Taxi flagfall is Y3.

Around Chìshuǐ

It's hard to imagine a more dramatic landscape. The locals claim that there are 4000 waterfalls in the area, and some are spectacular, but everywhere you look they're gushing into the rivers that run red because of the colour of the earth (Chìshuǐ means 'red water') and which cut through valleys and gorges covered in lush foliage. If that wasn't enough, there are huge forests of bamboo and alsophila plants, giant ferns that date back 200 million years and which were once the food of dinosaurs.

Given the spread-out nature of the sights, it's worth considering hiring a taxi or minibus to tour them all. Expect to pay Y200 to Y400 per day, depending on your bargaining skills.

SHÍZHÀNGDÒNG WATERFALL 十丈洞瀑布

Only a metre or so shorter than the much better-known, and visited, Huángguǒshù Falls, the 76m-high **Shízhàngdòng Waterfall** (Shízhàngdòng Pùbù; admission Y40; ⌚8am-4pm) explodes in a sea of spray as it crashes down. You can be 100m away and still get drenched if the wind is right.

About 40km from Chìshuǐ, six buses a day (Y10, one hour) run here from the bus station on Renmin Xilu starting at 6.50am. The bus will drop you in Shízhàngdòng village, from where it's a short walk to the ticket office. From there, it's a 30- to 40-minute walk up a road to the turn-off to the waterfall, or you can ride there on a buggy (Y20 return). There is another, more pleasant walk on the other side of the river to the falls. Doing the complete circuit takes three to four hours.

SÌDÒNGGŌU 四洞沟

This **valley** (admission Y30; ⌚8am-7pm) close to Chìshuǐ is forested with ancient ferns, as well as being dotted with waterfalls. Paths follow both sides of a river, with minifalls gushing down over them, and take you past four 'proper' waterfalls. The biggest and most impressive is the last one, the 60m-high **White Loong Pond Waterfall**. The cool thing here is that you can get really close to the falls, including being able to walk behind one. It takes about three hours to do the circuit, although there are plenty of trails leading off the main paths that will provide fun and games for intrepid hikers.

Sìdònggōu is the most touristy of Chìshuǐ's sights, but still not overly crowded, even in summer. Minibuses run here from the bus station on Chìshuǐ's Renmin Xilu (Y5.50, 30 minutes) and return when they have at least seven people on board.

JĪNSHĀGŌU NATURE RESERVE 金沙沟自然保护区

By far the least-visited of the sights in the area, this reserve (Jīnshāgōu Zìrán Bǎohùqū) was established to protect the alsophila ferns that grow in abundance here. It's also the site of a bamboo forest, known as the **Bamboo Sea** (竹海; zhúhǎi; admission Y25; ⌚8am-5pm), where you can trek through the trees in almost total isolation. The paths get very slippery when wet and there are lots of mosquitoes, so come armed with repellent.

To get here, catch the buses heading to Jīnshāgōu village from Chìshuǐ's Lǚyóu Chēzhàn (Y11.50, one hour). From there, you'll have to negotiate with the locals for a motorbike or minibus ride to the park entrance, which is another 20 minutes away. Expect to pay between Y30 and Y40 each way. Make sure to arrange a pick-up for your return; very little transport hangs around the park.

RED ROCK GORGE 红石野谷

Dotted with small waterfalls that make for a vivid contrast with the red sandstone cliffs of the **gorge** (Hóngshí Yěgǔ; admission Y30; ⌚8am-5pm), this is one of the more popular sights with local tourists. There are some good photo opportunities here, particularly if the sun is shining, when the red earth really stands out.

Minibuses run here from the bus station on Chìshuǐ's Renmin Xilu (Y6, 40 minutes, five daily from 8am to 4.30pm).

Chinese Opera, Běijīng (p84)
Chinese opera's colourful blend of singing, mime, dancing and acrobatics can be seen at the Cháoyáng Theatre (p85) in Běijīng.

RICHARD I'ANSON

1

5

KEREN SU

1. Rice Fields, Guǎngxī (p590)
Terraced rice fields around Guilín offer stunning views and great hiking opportunities.

2. Xiǎntōng Temple, Wǔtái Shān (p344)
The most captivating of a cluster of Buddhist temples in Shānxī's gorgeous mountainous, monastic enclave.

4

KEREN SU

3. Giant Panda, Ocean Park (p479)
Hong Kong's huge marine-themed amusement park is also home to some giant pandas.

4. Bamboo Sea, Sìchuān (p730)
A national park with swaying bamboo forest, walking trails and charming lakes and waterfalls.

5. Zhuang Woman, Guǎngxī (p582)
A visit to Guǎngxī's villages gives you a glimpse into the distinct traditions of the Zhuang people.

GEOFF STRINGER

Lángmùsì, Gānsù (p818)
Lángmùsì delights with colourful monastery buildings, flapping prayer flags and the mesmerising chanting of monks at twilight.

2. Éméi Shān, Sìchuān (p719)
China's sacred Buddhist mountain, Éméi Shān, offers cool, misty retreat in its ramshackle wooden temples.

3. Zhuang Girl, Guǎngxī (p582)
The Zhuang, China's largest minority group, make up 32% of Guǎngxī's population.

4. Red Panda, Sìchuān (p717)
Bìfēngxiá Panda Base is the world's largest collection of captive pandas, with more than 80 specimens.

KEREN SU

HUW JONES

CHRISTOPHER GROENHOUT

1. Stanley Market, Hong Kong (p479)
Hong Kong Island's Stanley Market is a maze of covered alleyways, best visited on weekdays.

2. The Bund, Shànghǎi (p165)
Early morning riverside scenes on the Bund as the city stirs from its slumber.

3. Jade Market, Hong Kong (p482)
Some 450 stalls in Kowloon sell all varieties and grades of jade, so make sure you know your nephrite from your jadeite.

4. Déhāng, Húnán (p462)

Verdant valleys around Déhāng are layered with terraced fields and flushed by waterfalls and clear streams.

5. Lama Temple, Běijīng (p57)

Dōngchéng district boasts the most renowned Tibetan Buddhist temple outside the historic lands of Tibet.

GREG ELMS

3

Lantern Festival, Shànghǎi (p183)
Paper lanterns in the streets mark the Lantern Festival celebrations which fall on the 15th day of the first lunar month.

Yúnnán

POPULATION: 46.7 MILLION

Includes »

Best Places to Eat

» Tángcháo Yīpǐn (p644)
» Cāng Ěr Chūn (p658)
» Silent Holy Stones (p676)
» Dai barbecue restaurants in Jǐnghóng (p694)
» Bo Bo's Cold Drinks Shop (p688)

Best Places to Stay

» Jade Emu (p657)
» Kevin's Trekker Inn (p676)
» Téngchōng International Youth Hostel (p683)
» Kūnmíng Cloudland Youth Hostel (p641)
» Green Lake Hotel (p641)
» DōngbāHotel (p663)

Why Go?

Once a place of banishment for disgraced officials (who must have arrived and chuckled at their inadvertent luck), Yúnnán (云南) offers a diversity of both people and landscapes that makes it a dream destination for travellers. If you have time to visit only one province in China, then it should be Yúnnán.

More than half of the country's ethnic minority groups reside here, providing an extraordinary glimpse into China's mixed salad of humanity. Then there's the hugely varied splendour of the land – triple-thick jungle sliced by the Mekong River in the south, soul-recharging glimpses of the sun over rice terraces in the central and southeastern regions, and towering, snow-capped mountains as you edge towards Tibet.

In one week you can sweat in the tropics and freeze in the Himalayas, and in between check out ancient towns. So however long you've given yourself in Yúnnán, double it. Trust us on this one.

When to Go

Kūnmíng

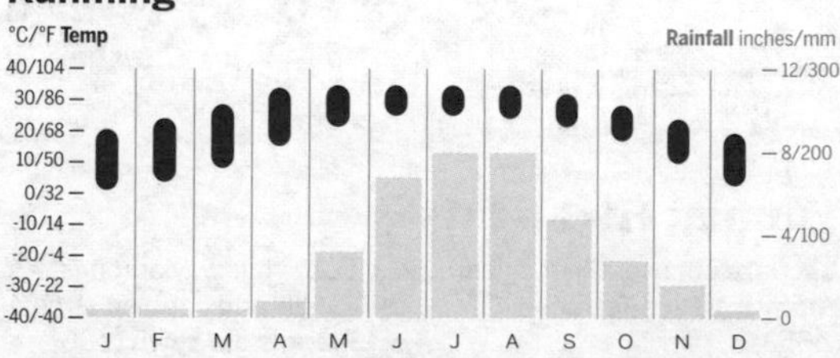

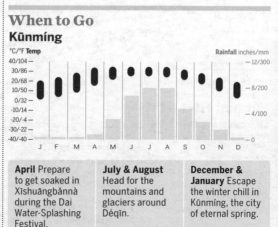

April Prepare to get soaked in Xīshuāngbǎnnà during the Dai Water-Splashing Festival.

July & August Head for the mountains and glaciers around Déqīn.

December & January Escape the winter chill in Kūnmíng, the city of eternal spring.

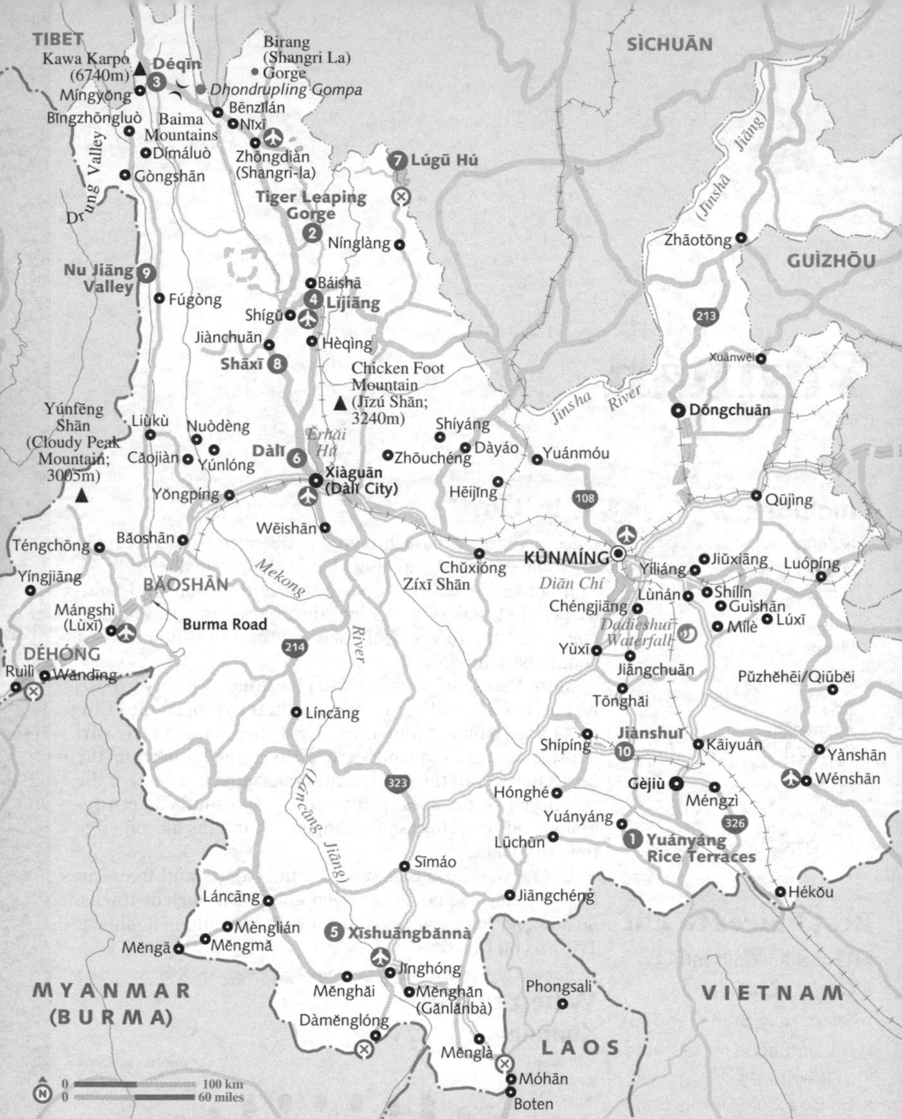

Yúnnán Highlights

1. Gaze out over the magical **Yuányáng Rice Terraces** (p652)
2. Test your legs and lungs trekking **Tiger Leaping Gorge** (p670)
3. Marvel at the peaks (and glacier) around **Déqīn** (p679)
4. Lose your way amongst the canals and cobbled streets of **Lìjiāng's old town** (p661)
5. Look for elephants and hike to minority villages in the jungle of **Xīshuāngbǎnnà** (p690)
6. Kick back in the cafes and bars of **Dàlǐ** (p658)
7. Laze around the shores of stunning **Lúgū Hú** (p673)
8. See how time has stood still in the former Tea-Horse Trail oasis of **Shāxī** (p669)
9. Get way off the map in the remote **Nù Jiāng Valley** (p681)
10. Check out the classic architecture in **Jiànshuǐ** (p650)

History

With its remote location, harsh terrain and diverse ethnic make-up, Yúnnán was once considered a backward place populated by barbarians.

The early Han emperors held tentative imperial power over the southwest and forged southern Silk Road trade routes to Burma. From the 7th to mid-13th century, though, two independent kingdoms, the Nanzhao and Dàlǐ, ruled and dominated the trade routes from China to India and Burma. It wasn't until the Mongols swept through that the southwest was integrated into the Chinese empire as Yúnnán. Even so, it remained an isolated frontier region, more closely aligned with Southeast Asia than China.

Today, Yúnnán is still a strategic jumping-off point to China's neighbours. Despite its geographical isolation, much of the province has modernised rapidly in recent years.

Climate

With its enormous range of geomorphology – 76.4m above sea level near Vietnam to 6740m in the Tibetan plateau (averaging around 2000m) – Yúnnán's diverse climate is part of its appeal. In the frozen northwestern region around Déqīn and Zhōngdiàn (Shangri-la), winters reach chilling lows of -12°C, but in the subtropical climate of Xīshuāngbǎnnà you can still walk around in a T-shirt in January.

Dàlǐ has an ideal temperature year-round, never dipping below 4°C in winter or above 25°C in summer, while the capital Kūnmíng has a pleasant climate where it can be downright springlike in the winter months and it's never too hot in the summer.

Language

In addition to Mandarin, the other major languages spoken in Yúnnán belong to the Tibeto-Burman family (eg the Naxi language) and the Sino-Tibetan family (eg the Lisu language).

Getting There & Around

AIR Kūnmíng is served by all Chinese airlines and has daily flights to most cities. International destinations are increasing all the time; Kūnmíng is busily building the fourth-largest airport in the country.

All major – and some obscure – tourist spots within Yúnnán are served by daily flights from Kūnmíng (and at times from other major Chinese cities). The northwest is linked by Zhōngdiàn (Shangri-la), Dàlǐ and Lìjiāng. Mángshì and Téngchōng in the southwest offer flights to the capital, and Jǐnghóng is Xīshuāngbǎnnà's primary air link.

Dàlǐ airport has flights to Kūnmíng, Jǐnghóng and Guǎngzhōu. From Lìjiāng there are daily flights to Běijīng, Shànghǎi, Chéngdū, Shēnzhèn and Guǎngzhōu. From Zhōngdiàn (Shangri-la) you can fly to Kūnmíng, Chéngdū, Lhasa, Guǎngzhōu, Shēnzhèn and Guìyáng. Destinations from Jǐnghóng include Lìjiāng, Dàlǐ, Shànghǎi and Guǎngzhōu. Mángshì and Téngchōng currently only have flights to Kūnmíng.

BOAT Water levels permitting, you can float between Thailand and Jǐnghóng in the south.

BUS Yúnnán leads the pack in southwest China in beaverishly building new expressways and highways. Expressways link Kūnmíng with Dàlǐ, east to Guìzhōu and Guǎngxī, southwest past Bǎoshan to Ruìlì (hopefully within the life of this edition) and past Jǐnghóng to the Laos border. An expressway is also being built from Kūnmíng to Hékǒu on the Vietnam border and beyond to Hanoi; it may be complete by 2012.

TRAIN Railways link Yúnnán to Guìzhōu, Guǎngxī, Sìchuān and beyond. In Yúnnán itself, development of the railways has been slower than elsewhere, due mostly to topographical interference. A daily train links Dàlǐ and Lìjiāng and will be travelling on to Zhōngdiàn (Shangri-la) by 2015.

PRICE INDICATORS

The following price indicators are used in this chapter:

Sleeping

$	less than Y160
$$	Y160 to Y300
$$$	more than Y300

Eating

$	less than Y20
$$	Y20 to Y50
$$$	more than Y50

CENTRAL YÚNNÁN

Kūnmíng 昆明

☎0871 / POP 1.1 MILLION

Kūnmíng, known as the 'Spring City' for its equable climate, is one of China's most laid-back and liveable cities, and an enjoyable place to spend a few days. Indeed, 'hurry up' doesn't seem to exist in the local vernacular. Sure, like other cities it has

TRANS-ASIA RAILWAY, MAYBE

In March 2010 the Chinese government announced that it was in negotiations to build three high-speed rail lines connecting it with the rest of Asia, Europe and the Middle East. One of those lines is set to link Kūnmíng with Singapore, via Vietnam, Thailand and Malaysia, as well as extending west to Myanmar (Burma) and India.

Sceptics, though, wonder if the lines will ever be built. After all, Běijīng said in 2006 that it was starting work on a different Trans-Asia rail network that would connect China with Southeast Asia and India. But so far, the only line definitely taking shape is one between Lashio in Myanmar (Burma) and the Yúnnán border town of Jiěgào, and there is no date yet for its completion.

The huge costs involved in laying high-speed tracks, ongoing niggles between China and its neighbours, and the fact that Běijīng wants the trains to run on the gauge Chinese trains use, mean it will likely be sometime yet before travellers can jump on a train in Kūnmíng and race south to Singapore at 320km/h-plus.

busily deconstructed much of its old neighbourhoods, and the number of cars on the roads increases inexorably. Yet, Kūnmíng has some intriguing temples and historic structures, while grand parks are nearby and the legendary Stone Forest is a day trip away.

History

The region of Kūnmíng has been inhabited for 2000 years, but it wasn't until WWII that the city really began to expand, when factories were established and refugees fleeing the Japanese poured in from eastern China. As the end point of the famous Burma Road, a 1000km haul from Lashio, in Myanmar (Burma), the city played a key role in the Sino-Japanese war. Renmin Xilu marks the tail end of the road.

Following the war, the city fell back into its usual role of overlooked and isolated provincial city. When China opened to the West, however, tourists really noticed the province, and Kūnmíng used its gateway status to the rest of Yúnnán to slowly become one of the loveliest cities in southwest China.

Sights & Activities

Yuántōng Temple BUDDHIST TEMPLE
(圆通寺; Yuántōng Sì; Yuantong Jie; admission Y6, surrounding park Y10; ⏲8am-5.20pm) This temple is the largest Buddhist complex in Kūnmíng and a draw for pilgrims. It's over 1000 years old and has been refurbished many times; the latest renovations were going on at the time of writing. To the rear a hall has been added, with a statue of Sakyamuni, a gift from Thailand's king. The good vegetarian restaurant (p645) here is to the left of the temple entrance.

Green Lake Park PARK
(翠湖公园; Cuìhú Gōngyuán; Cuihu Nanlu; ⏲6am-10pm) Come here to people-watch, practise taichi or just hang with the locals and stroll. The roads along the park are lined with wannabe trendy cafes, teahouses and shops. In November everyone in the city awaits the return of the local favourites, red-beaked seagulls; it's a treat watching people, er, 'flock' to the park when the first one shows up.

Yúnnán Provincial Museum MUSEUM
(云南省博物馆; Yúnnán Shěng Bówùguǎn; 118 Wuyi Lu; admission Y10; ⏲9am-4.30pm) Fresh off an aesthetic rehab, this museum has reasonable exhibitions on Diān Chí (Lake Dian) prehistoric and early cultures, and Yúnnán's minorities.

Chuàng Kù (The Loft) ART GALLERIES
West of downtown in a disused factory area known as Chuàng Kù (The Loft) (创库艺术主题社区) are a small number of galleries and cafes featuring modern Chinese artists and photographers. **Yuánshēng Art Space** (源生坊; Yuánshēngfáng; 101 Xiba Lu; ☎419 5697; ⏲9am-1.30am) is a gallery-bar-restaurant-theatre focusing on the province's ethnic groups. The cornerstone of sorts is **TC/G Nordica** (诺地卡; Nuòdìkǎ; ☎411 4692; www.tcgnordica.com/en; 101 Xiba Lu; ⏲5-11.30pm Mon, 11.30am-11pm Tue-Sat, noon-4pm Sun), best described as a gallery-exhibition hall-cultural centre – with, oddly, a restaurant serving Scandinavian and Chinese food. Not many taxi drivers know this place as The Loft; ask to go to 101 Xiba Lu.

Tang-Dynasty Pagodas HISTORIC SITES
These pagodas won't give you a 'wow!' moment, but you can hang with the old dudes getting haircuts, slurping tea and playing their endless mah jong games, south of Jinbi Lu. **West Pagoda** (西寺塔; Xīsì Tǎ; Dongsi Jie; admission free; ⏲9am-5pm) has surroundings a tad livelier; **East Pagoda** (东寺塔; Dōngsì Tǎ; 63 Shulin Jie; ⏲9am-5pm) smacks of a new edifice – it was rebuilt in the 19th century after either a Muslim revolt or an earthquake (foreign and Chinese sources conflict).

Mosques MOSQUE
The oldest of the lot, the 400-year-old **Nánchéng Mosque** (南城清真古寺; Nánchéng Qīngzhēn Gǔsì; 51 Zhengyi Lu), was ripped down in 1997 in order to build a larger version, which looks vaguely like a bad Las Vegas casino. And sadly, that's now about it for the area's once-thriving Muslim neighbourhood (ripped down *in toto* in 2007).

Sleeping

TOP CHOICE **Kūnmíng Cloudland Youth Hostel** YOUTH HOSTEL $
(昆明大脚氏青年旅社; Kūnmíng Dàjiǎoshì Qīngnián Lǚshè; ☎410 3777; 23 Zhuantang Lu; 篆塘路23号; 4-/6-/8-bed dm Y40/35/30, s/d without/with bathroom Y110/180; @📶) Run by some friendly inveterate backpackers who know the needs of travellers, Cloudland hasn't let standards slip over the years. The staff smile and hustle, there's a pleasant communal area to hang out in, and the rooms are bright, comfy and well kept. Wi-fi equipped. To get here from the train or long-distance bus station, take city bus 64 and get off at the Yúnnán Daily News stop (云南日报社站).

TOP CHOICE **Green Lake Hotel** HOTEL $$$
(翠湖宾馆; Cuìhú Bīnguǎn; ☎515 8888; www.greenlakehotel.com; 6 Cuihu Nanlu; 翠湖南路6号; d from Y1680, discounts from 30%; 🚭❄@🏊) Proud but subdued, this gentle giant of Kūnmíng *hôtellerie* history has a fabulous location, opposite Green Park, and has kept up with modernity and done so tastefully and with top-notch service. The panorama from the top floors is worth the price alone.

Hump Hostel YOUTH HOSTEL $
(驼峰客栈; Tuófēng Kèzhàn; ☎364 0359; Jinmabiji Sq, Jinbi Lu; 金碧路金马碧鸡广场; 4-/6-/8-/10-bed dm Y40/40/35/35, s/d without/with bathroom Y90/150; @) There's nothing bad about this popular place whatsoever except that its superlative draw – central location amidst dozens of Chinese-style bars, karaoke joints and restaurants – is also a drawback (yes, take earplugs). Dorms are big, there's a great terrace and around the corner the Hump Bar is the current hot spot for carousing in the wee hours.

Camellia Youth Hostel YOUTH HOSTEL $
(茶花国际青年旅舍; Cháhuā Guójì Qīngnián Lǚshè; ☎837 4638; newcamellia@gmail.com; 96 Dongfeng Donglu; 东风东路96号; dm Y40, s & d Y120; 🚭@) A spit apart but separate from the Camellia Hotel, this newly upgraded place is the most sedate hostel in town. The dorms are spotless and come with en suite bathrooms, the rooms are spacious and there's a gardenlike communal area.

To get here from the train station, take bus 2 or 23 to Dongfeng Donglu, then change to bus 5 heading east and get off at the second stop.

Camellia Hotel HOTEL $$
(茶花宾馆; Cháhuā Bīnguǎn; ☎316 3000; www.kmcamelliahotel.com; 96 Dongfeng Donglu; 东风东路96号; s & d Y388; ❄@) Recently refurbished with pleasant, smart rooms, the Camellia remains a solid midrange choice. It's also very convenient, thanks to the location and the presence of travel agencies and tour operators on the ground floor. The staff are helpful and efficient too.

Zhènzhuāng Guest House HISTORIC $$$
(震庄迎宾馆; Zhènzhuāng Yíngbīnguǎn; ☎310 0088; fax 313 9756; 514 Beijing Lu; 北京路514号; d/ste Y600/1200; ❄@) A fascinating place, this 1936 city-state of sprawling villas, ponds, gardens and trees covers 9 hectares in the heart of downtown (it was once the home of Yúnnán's governor). Rooms are lovely enough, with huge, comfy beds, but the grounds are even better; you can actually awaken to birds singing. The staff are wonderful but bemused by foreigners.

Sun Kiss HOTEL $
(阳光酒店; Yángguāng Jiǔdiàn; ☎805 9400; 252 Beijing Lu; 北京路252号; s/d Y158/168; ❄@) The bouncy staff give the impression that this new place, very handy for the train station, has indeed been blessed with a big smacker from the weather gods. Heart-shaped pillows and bright, modern rooms make it a real standout from the tired cheapies that surround it.

Kūnmíng Hotel HOTEL $$$
(昆明饭店; Kūnmíng Fàndiàn; ☎316 2063; www.kunminghotel.com.cn; 52 Dongfeng Donglu;

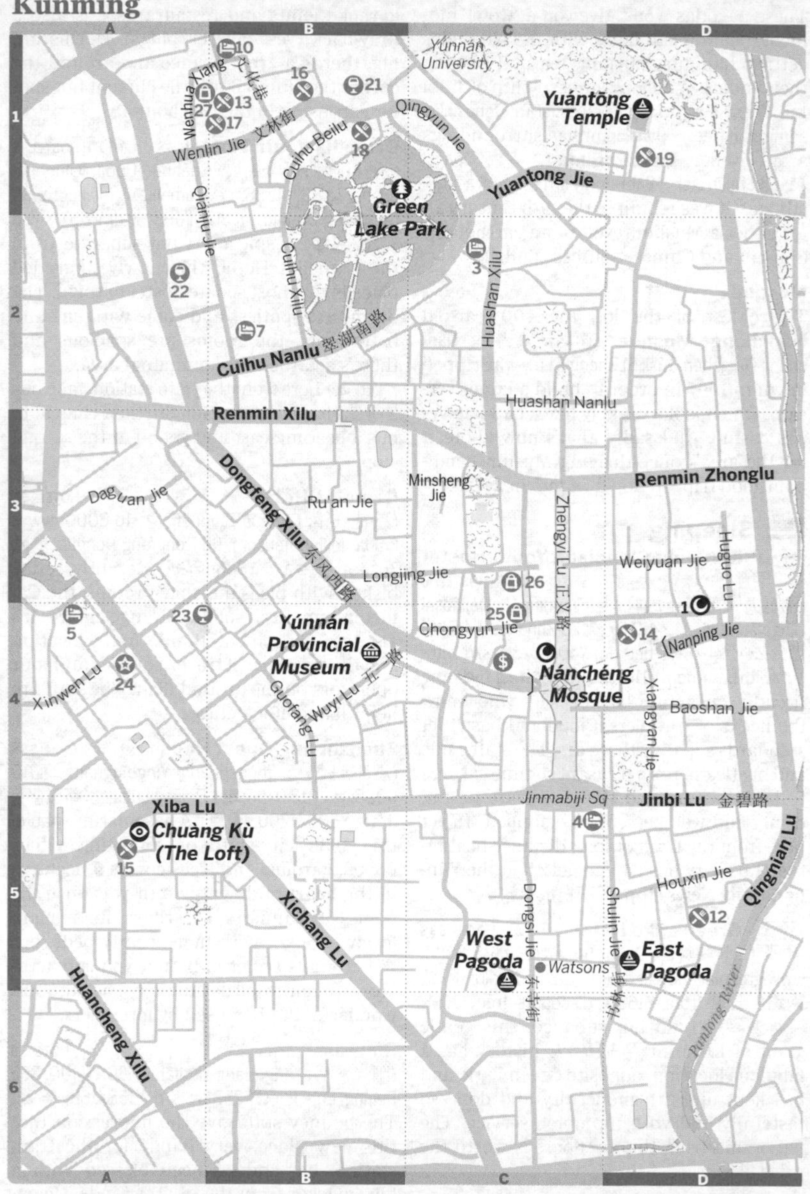

东风东路52号; s & d Y780, ste Y1419, discounts of 30%; ⊖❄@) A hangover from the 1950s, but the service has improved a lot since then. Professional staff and comfortable rooms, which are a good deal with the discounts sometimes given. Chinese and Western restaurants are also on-site.

Yúndà Bīnguǎn HOTEL **$$**
(云大宾馆; Yúnnán University Hotel; ☎503 4179; fax 503 4172; Wenhua Xiang; 文化巷; d & tw Y298-

Kūnmíng

Top Sights

Sights

Sleeping

Eating

Drinking

Entertainment

Shopping

468, discounts of 40%; ❄ @) Conveniently close to the restaurant/bar hub of Wenhua Xiang and Wenlin Jie, the Yúndà's rooms are not exciting but do the job. The hotel is divided into two, with the cheaper rooms in the wing across the road from the main entrance.

Míngtōng Hotel HOTEL $
(明通印象青年酒店; Míngtōng Yìnxiàng Qīngnián Jiǔdiàn; ☎312 8858; 94 Mingtong Xiang; 明通巷94号; d Y80-168, tr with shared bathroom Y100; @)

Tucked into an alley off Beijing Lu, this low-key 'youth hotel' has big, bright rooms and pleasant staff (though without much English). The en suite doubles are great value.

Kūnmíng Youth Hostel YOUTH HOSTEL **$**
(昆明国际青年旅舍; Kūnmíng Gúojì Qīngnián Lûshè; ☎517 5395; Yúnnán Provincial Library Annex, Cuihu Nanlu; 翠湖南路省图书馆侧楼; dm/s/d Y30/120/130; 📶) Mostly patronised by local travellers and considerably less busy than the other hostels in town, the facilities here are pretty basic. But the location is fine and there's wi-fi throughout. The entrance is off Qianju Jie; look for the small red YHA sign.

Eating

Kūnmíng is home to all of Yúnnán's fabulous foods. Noodles (rice or wheat) are absolutely the top quick food, usually served in a meat broth with a chilli sauce. You'll always find *pároù ěrsī* (扒肉饵丝), basically braised meat chunks laden atop noodles; toppings vary by shop but the best will have everything under the sun – even ground peanuts and fresh coriander.

Regional specialities are *qìguōjī* (汽锅鸡; herb-infused chicken cooked in an earthenware steampot and imbued with medicinal properties depending on the spices used – *chóngcǎo;* 虫草; caterpillar fungus, or pseudoginseng is one); *xuānweī huǒtuǐ* (宣威火腿; Yúnnán ham); *guòqiáo mǐxiàn (*过侨米线; across-the-bridge noodles); *rǔbǐng* (辱饼; goat's cheese); and various Muslim beef and mutton dishes.

Yúnnán is blessed with infinite varieties of mushrooms (蘑菇; *mógū*), of which many are rare and pricey in other provinces but delightfully common and dirt cheap here. Try *châshùgū* (茶树菇; tea tree mushrooms), which grow only in proximity to tea trees and are infused with their essence.

For all manner of foreign restaurants, including Korean, Japanese and Thai, head to Wenhua Xiang. For self-catering, try **Carrefour Supermarket** (家乐福超级市场; Jiālèfú; Nanping Jie), a branch of the popular French chain.

TOP CHOICE **Tángcháo Yīpǐn** YUNNAN **$$**
(唐朝一品; ☎515 1518; 18 Wenlin Jie; dishes from Y18; ⏲9am-9pm) Descend the stairs to this cosy courtyard restaurant for its very tasty array of just about every local dish you can think of. Get here early in the evening, before the most popular have been snapped up by eager locals. No English is spoken, but the picture menu will guide you. It's across the road from the Ganesh restaurant-bar; look for the red lanterns.

Hóng Dòu Yuán YUNNAN **$**
(红豆圆; 142 Wenlin Jie; dishes from Y10; ⏲11am-9pm) An old-school Chinese eaterie, with cigarette butts on the floor, a duck-your-head stairway and plastic-film-covered tables, this is a real locals hang-out on cosmopolitan Wenlin Jie. The food is excellent and will draw you back. Try regional specialities like the *táozá rǔbǐng* (fried goat's cheese and Yúnnán ham) and *liáng bái ròu* (peppery, tangy beef). Picture menu.

Déhóng Ruǎnjiā Dǎiwèi Yuán ETHNIC MINORITY **$**
(德宏阮家傣味园; ☎412 8519; 101 Xiba Lu; dishes from Y12; ⏲9am-9pm) Inside The Loft complex, this fine place serves up authentic, sour and spicy Dai cuisine in a laid-back atmosphere. Try the fantastic barbecued fish, and accompany it with a few glasses of the rice wine stored in giant vats awaiting your

ACROSS-THE-BRIDGE NOODLES

Yúnnán's best-known dish is 'across-the-bridge noodles' *(*过侨米线*; guòqiáo mǐxiàn).* You are provided with a bowl of very hot soup (stewed with chicken, duck and spare ribs) on which a thin layer of oil is floating, along with a side dish of raw pork slivers (in classier places this might be chicken or fish), vegetables and egg, and a bowl of rice noodles. Diners place all of the ingredients quickly into the soup bowl, where they are cooked by the steamy broth. Prices generally vary from Y5 to Y15, depending on the side dishes. It's usually worth getting these, because with only one or two condiments the soup lacks zest.

It is said the dish was created by a woman married to an imperial scholar. He decamped to an isolated island to study and she got creative with the hot meals she brought to him every day after crossing the bridge. This noodle dish was by far the most popular and christened 'across-the-bridge noodles' in honour of her daily commute.

attention. There's a small outside area and a picture menu.

1910 La Gare du Sud YUNNAN $$
(火车南站; Huǒchē Nánzhàn; ☎316 9486; dishes from Y22; ⊙11am-9pm; 📖) Offering Yúnnán specialities in a pleasant neocolonial-style atmosphere, this place is now a fave with both expats – it's the kind of place foreign students take their parents when they come to visit – and cashed-up locals. It's hidden down an alley off Chongshan Lu, south of Jinbi Lu.

Yùquánzhāi Vegetarian Restaurant VEGETARIAN $
(玉泉斋餐厅; Yùquánzhāi Cāntīng; 22 Yuantong Jie; dishes from Y18; ⊙10am-9pm) Popular with locals, monks and expats, head here for dishes that look and taste like meat but aren't. We like the Endless Buddha Force (assorted veggies and tofu), but all the dishes here are worth sampling.

Salvador's WESTERN $$
(萨尔瓦多咖啡馆; Sà'ěrwǎduō kāfēiguǎn; 76 Wenhua Xiang; sandwiches from Y15, mains from Y25; ⊙8am-11pm) Always busy with travellers and foreign students, Salvador's is now a Kūnmíng staple. With a Mexican/ Mediterranean food theme, as well as solid breakfasts, good coffee and a decent range of teas, it caters for all hours of the day. In the evening you can hang around the bar and watch as Kūnmíng's beautiful people parade along Wenhua Xiang.

Box Bar ITALIAN $$
(老夫子酒吧; Lǎofūzǐ Jiǔbā; 76 Wenhua Xiang; pizzas from Y25; ⊙11am-midnight) Cute cubbyhole of a restaurant run by two Italians whose big, sloppy pizzas are deservedly popular. Also has homemade lasagne and gelato. It's good for coffee or cocktails too.

Zhènxīng Fàndiàn YUNNAN $
(振兴饭店; Yúnnán Typical Local Food Restaurant; cnr Baita Lu & Dongfeng Donglu; dishes from Y12; ⊙24hr) A good introduction to Kūnmíng fare, especially for *guòqiáo mǐxiàn,* and handy for late-night eats. Pay upfront at the desk where the grumpy middle-aged ladies sit.

Drinking

Foreigners congregate in the bars on and around Wenhua Xiang, while Jinmabiji Sq is home to many Chinese-style bars and karaoke joints. The Kūndū Night Market area is also a club and bar zone. Just a stone's throw south of Xinwen Jie, **Uprock** (167 Xichang Lu; ⊙8am-late) maintains its status as the city's best-known club.

Ganesh BAR
(印象国; Yìnxiàng Guó; 156 Wenlin Jie; ⊙10am-2am) Foreign beers at reasonable prices! Great Indian food! Live football on the telly! Brits will love this place, but so it seems do most expats in Kūnmíng. The all-day thalis (meat or vegetarian, Y38) are a tremendous deal.

Halfway House BAR
(半山咖啡; Bànshān Kāfēi; ☎535 2702; Kunshi Lu; ⊙10.30am-3am) A locals' hang-out, but one without the 'let's order a bottle of Chivas and play dice games' silliness that can make Chinese bars an alienating, deafening and expensive experience. There's live music here every week. Just off Dongfeng Xilu, it's hard to spot.

Shopping

Yúnnán specialities are marble and batik from Dàlǐ, jade from Ruìlì, minority embroidery, musical instruments and spotted-brass utensils.

Some functional items that make good souvenirs include large bamboo water pipes for smoking angel-haired Yúnnán tobacco;

ONE-STOP SHOPPING

The **Flower & Bird Market** (花鸟市场; Huāniǎo Shìchǎng; Tongdao Jie), also known as *lǎo jiē* (old street), has shrunk dramatically in recent years and is now ominously hemmed in by encroaching modernity. Nor are flowers and birds the main draw here any more. Instead, strollers peruse stalls chock-full of jewellery, endless curios, knick-knacks and doo-das (the contents of someone's back hall often enough), some occasionally fine rugs and handmade clothing, and a hell of a lot of weird stuff.

One block west of the intersection of Guanghua Jie and the pedestrian-only Zhengyi Lu sits **Fú Lín Táng** (福林堂), the city's oldest pharmacy, which has been dishing out the *sānqì* (the legendary Yunnanese cure-all root mixed into tea; about Y20 to Y100 per gram) since 1857.

THE HUI

Wandering about Kūnmíng you will note its Hui (回; Chinese Muslim) residents. Of the province's approximately 550,000 Hui, Kūnmíng holds the lion's share.

In the 13th century Mongol forces swooped into the province to outflank the Song-dynasty troops and were followed by Muslim traders, builders and craftsmen. Yúnnán was the only region put under a Muslim leader immediately after Kublai Khan's armies arrived, when Sayyid Ajall was named governor in 1274.

Yúnnán's Muslims are rightfully proud of their legendary local boy done good Cheng Ho (Zheng He), the famed eunuch admiral who opened up the Chinese sea channels to the Middle East (and who some believe may actually have been the first to voyage to the Americas).

Heavy land taxes and disputes between Muslims and Han Chinese over local gold and silver mines triggered a Muslim uprising in 1855, which lasted until 1873. The Muslims chose Dàlǐ (Xiàguān) as their base and laid siege to Kūnmíng, overrunning the city briefly in 1863. Du Wenxiu, the Muslim leader, proclaimed his newly established Kingdom of the Pacified South (Nánpíng Guó) and took the name Sultan Suleyman. But success was short-lived and in 1873 Dàlǐ was taken by Qing forces and Du Wenxiu was captured and executed. Up to a million people died in Yúnnán alone, the death toll rising to 18 million nationwide. The uprisings were quelled, but they also had the lasting effect of eliciting sympathy from Burma and fomenting a passion for local culture among many of southwestern China's ethnic minorities, most of whom had supported the Hui.

and local herbal medicines, such as Yúnnán Báiyào (Yúnnán White Medicine), which is a blend of over 100 herbs and is highly prized by Chinese throughout the world.

Yunnanese tea is an excellent buy and comes in several varieties, from bowl-shaped bricks of smoked green tea called *tuóchá*, which have been around since at least Marco Polo's time, to leafy black tea that rivals some of India's best.

Tiānfú Famous Teas TEA
(天福茗茶; Tiānfú Míngchá; cnr Shangyi Jie & Beijing Lu; ⌚8.30am-10.30pm) Worth checking out.

Mandarin Books & CDs BOOKS
(52 Wenhua Xiang; ⌚9.30am-9.30pm) For guidebooks, novels, magazines and a selection of travel writing in English and other languages.

ℹ Information

For any and all information on the city, check out www.gokunming.com (it also covers parts of the rest of Yúnnán). You can also head to Lonely Planet (www.lonelyplanet.com/china/yunnan) for planning advice, author recommendations, traveller reviews and insider tips.

Maps (Y8) are available from the train/bus station areas and in hotels, but they're not much use to non-Chinese speakers.

Kūnmíng is one of the safest cities in China but, as always, take special precaution near the train and long-distance bus stations. Reports of pickpockets are not unheard of, and there have been a number of victims of drug-and-robs on overnight sleeper buses.

CD Burning

Kodak (柯达; Kēdá; 429 Beijing Lu; ⌚8.30am-10.30pm) Burns CDs for Y20. Most hostels will also do the same.

Internet Access

Every hotel and cafe frequented by travellers offers the internet (网吧) or wi-fi, either for free or around Y5 per hour; the city's zillion internet cafes charge Y2 to Y4 per hour.

Medical Services

Richland International Hospital (瑞奇德国际医院; Ruìqídé Guójì Yīyuàn; ☎574 1988; Beijing Lu) The first of its kind in Yúnnán, even if most of the doctors are Chinese, it's on the bottom three floors of the Shàngdū International building; Yanchang Xian extension near Jinxing Flyover.

Watsons (屈臣士; Qū Chén Shì; Dongsi Jie; ⌚9am-10pm) Western cosmetics and basic medicines. There are other branches around town.

Yán'ān Hospital (Yán'ān Yīyuàn; ☎317 7499, ext 311; 1st fl, block 6, Renmin Donglu) Has a foreigners' clinic.

Money

Some banks other than Bank of China have ATMs which should accept international cards.

Bank of China (中国银行; Zhōngguó Yínháng; 448 Renmin Donglu; ⌚9am-noon & 2-5pm)

Offers all necessary services and has an ATM. Branches are at Dongfeng Xilu and Huancheng Nanlu.

Post

China Post (国际邮局; Zhōngguó Yóuzhèng; 223 Beijing Lu) The main international office has a very efficient poste restante and parcel service (per letter Y3, ID required). It is also the city's Express Mail Service (EMS) and Western Union agent. Also on Dongfeng Donglu.

Public Security Bureau

(PSB; 公安局; Gōng'ānjú; 301 7878; 399 Beijing Lu; 9-11:30am & 1-5pm Mon-Fri) To visit the givers of visa extensions, head south-east of Government Sq to the corner of Shangyi Jie and Beijing Lu.

Another **PSB office** (571 7001; Jinxing Lu) is off Erhuan Beilu in northern Kūnmíng; take bus 3, 25 or 57.

Tourist Information

Many of the popular backpacker hotels and some of the cafes can assist with travel queries.

Tourist Complaint & Consultative Telephone (316 4961) Where you can complain about or report dodgy tourist operations.

Travel Agencies

China International Travel Service (CITS; 中国国际旅行社; Zhōngguó Guójì Lǚxíngshè; 1118 Huancheng Nanlu; 9am-6.30pm) A good source of information. Organises tours; English and French spoken. Another branch is at 322 Beijing Lu.

 Getting There & Away

Air

When Kūnmíng's new airport is finished (possibly in 2012), it will be China's fourth largest and include direct services to/from North America, Europe, Australia and throughout Asia. Kūnmíng has international flights to most major Asian cities, including Hong Kong (Y1550), Vientiane (Y1800), Yangon (Y2318) and Kuala Lumpur (Y3088).

China Eastern Airlines/Civil Aviation Administration of China (CAAC; Zhōngguó Mínháng; 28 Tuodong Lu; 8.30am-7.30pm) issues tickets for any Chinese airline but the office only offers discounts on certain flights.

Daily flights from Kūnmíng:

Běijīng Y1630
Chéngdū Y790
Chóngqìng Y710
Guǎngzhōu Y1010
Guìyáng Y440
Lhasa Y1960
Nánjīng Y1750
Nánníng Y630
Qīngdǎo Y1810
Shànghǎi Y1900
Shēnzhèn Y1050
Xī'ān Y1280

Destinations within Yúnnán:

Bǎoshān Y360
Jǐnghóng Y450
Lìjiāng Y420
Mángshì/Déhóng Y450
Xiàguān/Dàlǐ Y640
Zhōngdiàn (Shangri-la) Y500

Bus

In an effort to reduce traffic congestion, Kūnmíng's five bus stations have been relocated to the outskirts of the city.

Buses departing the **south bus station** (彩云北路南客运站; Cǎiyún Běilù Nán Kèyùnzhàn):

Jiànshuǐ Y78, 3½ hours, every 30 minutes (7.30am to 7.30pm)

Jǐnghóng Y198 to Y246, nine to 10 hours, hourly (8am to 3pm and 10pm)

Yuányáng Y132, 6½ hours, three daily (10.20am, 3pm and 7.30pm)

Buses departing the **west bus station** (马街西客运站; Mǎjiē Xī Kèyùnzhàn):

Bǎoshān Y169 to Y207, nine hours, every hour (8.30am to 10pm)

Dàlǐ Y100, four to five hours, every 20 minutes (7.30am to 7.30pm)

Lìjiāng Y180, 10 hours, every hour (7.30am to 7.30pm)

Ruìlì Y248, 12 hours, five daily (8.30am, 10.30am, 1pm, 5pm and 9pm)

Téngchōng Y214, 12 hours, four daily (9am, 9.50am, 6.30pm and 9pm)

Zhōngdiàn (Shangri-la) Y217, 12 hours, one daily (9am)

Buses departing the **east bus station** (白沙河东客运站; Báishāhé Dōng Kèyùnzhàn):

Hékǒu Y150, eight hours, four daily (9.40am to 7.30pm)

Shílín Y30 to Y35, two hours, every 30 minutes (8am to noon)

Allow plenty of time to get to the bus stations. Bus 154 runs to the south bus station from the train station, as does bus 80 to the west bus station and bus 60 to the east bus station. A taxi will cost Y35 to Y45.

BORDER CROSSINGS: GETTING TO LAOS & VIETNAM

Getting to Laos

A daily bus from Kūnmíng to Vientiane (Y486) leaves from the old main long-distance bus station, by the train station, at 5pm if there are enough passengers. By the time you read this, it may be leaving from the south bus station, so check. See p699 for more about the border crossing.

Getting to Vietnam

Apart from getting on a plane, the only way to get to Vietnam from Kūnmíng for now is by bus. Regular buses run from Kūnmíng's east bus station to the border town of Hékǒu.

A big by-the-way: official proceedings at this border crossing can be frustrating (and officials have been known to confiscate Lonely Planet guides because they show Taiwan as a different country to China). Just keep your cool.

On the Chinese side, the **border checkpoint** is technically open 8am to 11pm but don't bank on anything after 6pm. Set your watch when you cross the border – the time in China is one hour later than in Vietnam. Visas are unobtainable at the border crossing.

Train

You can buy train tickets up to 10 days in advance. The following prices are for hard-sleeper middle berths on the fastest train:

Běijīng Y558
Chéngdū Y248
Éméi town Y224
Guǎngzhōu Y341
Guìyáng Y157
Liùpánshuǐ Y106
Shànghǎi Y491
Xī'ān Y385

Two overnight trains run daily to Dàlǐ (Y67) but travel agents book these out well in advance, so it can be tough to get a berth at short notice. You have a slightly better chance for the day train at 9.26am.

 Getting Around

A subway is under construction and scheduled to open sometime in 2013.

To/From the Airport

Buses 52 and 103 run between the centre of town and the airport. A taxi will average Y20 to the dead centre of town.

Traffic jams aren't at Běijīng levels yet, but you may do a lot of waiting in taxis.

Bicycle

Many backpacker hotels and hostels rent bikes for around Y15 to Y20 per day.

Bus

Bus 63 runs from the east bus station to the Camellia Hotel and on to the main train station. Bus 2 runs from the train station to Government Sq (Dongfeng Guangchang) and then past the west bus station. Fares range from Y1 to Y4. The main city buses have no conductors and require exact change.

Around Kūnmíng

There are some grand sights within a 15km radius of Kūnmíng, but getting to most of them is time-consuming and you'll find most of them extremely crowded.

If you don't have much time, the Bamboo Temple (Qióngzhú Sì) and Xī Shān (Western Hills) are the most interesting. Both have decent transport connections. Diān Chí (Lake Dian) has terrific circular-tour possibilities of its own.

BAMBOO TEMPLE 筇竹寺

This serene **temple** (Qióngzhú Sì; admission Y6; ⏲8am-7pm) is definitely one to be visited by sculptors as much as by those interested in temple collecting. Raised during the Tang dynasty, it was rebuilt in the 19th century by master Sichuanese sculptor Li Guangxiu and his apprentices, who fashioned 500 *luóhàn* (arhats or noble ones).

Li and his mates pretty much went gonzo in their excruciating, eight-year attempt to perfectly represent human existence in statuary – a fascinating mishmash of superb realism and head-scratching exag-

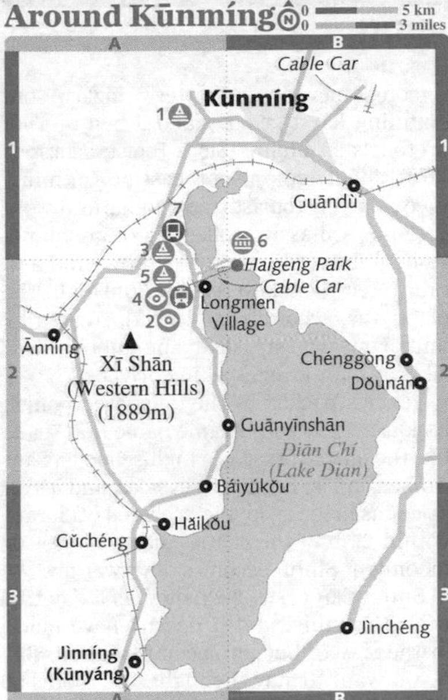

Around Kūnmíng

Sights

1 Bamboo Temple ... A1
2 Dragon Gate ... A2
3 Huátíng Temple ... A1
4 Sāngīng Gé ... A2
5 Tàihuá Temple ... A2
6 Yúnnán Nationalities Museum ... B1

Transport

7 Gāyáo Bus Station ... A1

gerated surrealism. How about the 70-odd surfing Buddhas, riding the waves on a variety of mounts – blue dogs, giant crabs, shrimp, turtles and unicorns? And this is cool: count the arhats one by one to the right until you reach your age – that is the one that best details your inner self.

So lifelike are the sculptures that they were considered in bad taste by Li Guangxiu's contemporaries (some of whom no doubt appeared in caricature), and upon the project's completion he disappeared into thin air.

The temple is about 12km northwest of Kūnmíng. The C61 bus (Y5, 40 minutes) runs there regularly from the eerily empty old west bus station. A taxi to the temple will cost around Y60.

Diān Chí 滇池

The shoreline of Diān Chí (Lake Dian), to the south of Kūnmíng, is dotted with settlements, farms and fishing enterprises; the western side is hilly, while the eastern side is flat country. The southern end of the lake, particularly the southeast, is industrial.

The lake is elongated – about 40km from north to south – and covers an area of 300 sq km. Plying the waters are *fānchuán* (pirate-sized junks with bamboo-battened canvas sails). It's mainly for scenic touring and hiking, and there are some fabulous aerial views from the ridges at Dragon Gate in Xī Shān.

XĪ SHĀN 西山

Kunmingites like to give you the local creed: 'If you haven't seen Xī Shān (the Western Hills), you haven't seen Kūnmíng'. Xī Shān is spread out across a long wedge of parkland on the western side of Diān Chí, and a day trip to this range, full of walking (some very steep sections), exploring and discovering all the temples and other cultural relics, is perfectly lovely. Its hills are also called the 'Sleeping Beauty Hills', a reference to the undulating contours, which are thought to resemble a reclining woman with tresses of hair flowing into the sea. (This is certainly more of a draw than the original 'Sleeping Buddha Hills'!)

It's a steepish approach from the north side. The hike from Gāoyáo bus station, at the foot of the hills, to Dragon Gate takes 2½ hours, though most people take a connecting bus from Gāoyáo to the top section. Alternatively, it is possible to cycle to the hills from the city centre in about an hour – to vary the trip, consider doing the return route across the dikes of upper Diān Chí.

At the foot of the climb, about 15km from Kūnmíng, is **Huátíng Temple** (华亭寺; Huátíng Sì; admission Y20; ⏲8am-6pm), a country temple of the Nanzhao kingdom believed to have been constructed in the 11th century. It's one of the largest in the province and its numerous halls have more arhats.

The road from Huátíng Temple winds 2km from here up to the Ming-dynasty **Tàihuá Temple** (太华寺; Tàihuá Sì; admission Y6; ⏲8am-6pm). The temple courtyard houses a fine collection of flowering trees, including magnolias and camellias.

Sānqīng Gé (三清阁), near the top of the mountain, was a country villa of a Yuan-dynasty prince, and was later turned into a temple dedicated to the three main Taoist deities (*sānqīng* refers to the highest level of Taoist 'enlightenment').

From near here you can catch a **chairlift** (one way/return Y25/50) if you want to skip the final ascent to the summit. Alternatively, a tourist tram takes passengers up to the Dragon Gate for Y5.

Further up, near the top of the mountain, is **Dragon Gate** (龙门; Lóng Mén; admission Y40). That quote about Xī Shān has a part two: 'And if you haven't seen Lóng Mén, you haven't seen Xī Shān'. This is a group of grottoes, sculptures, corridors and pavilions that were hacked from the cliff between 1781 and 1835 by a Taoist monk and coworkers, who must have been hanging up there by their fingertips. At least that's what the locals do when they visit, seeking out the most precarious perches for views of Diān Chí.

To get here, take bus 5 (Y1) from the Kūnmíng Hotel to the terminus at Liǎngjiāhé, and then change to bus 6 (Y1), which will take you to Gāoyáo bus station at the foot of the hills. Alternatively, minibuses (Y6) run from opposite Liǎngjiāhé and drop passengers at spots along the way.

Returning, you could also take the cable car across to Hǎigěng Park for Y40. From there, take the 94 bus or a taxi for the 3km or so to the Yúnnán Nationalities Village, opposite the Yúnnán Minorities Museum, where you can catch bus 44 (Y1, 40 minutes) to Kūnmíng's main train station.

YÚNNÁN NATIONALITIES MUSEUM 云南民族博物馆

On the northeast corner of the lake, the **Yúnnán Nationalities Museum** (Yúnnán Mínzú Bówùguǎn; admission Y10; 9am-4.30pm Tue-Sun) is reputedly the largest minorities museum in China, even if it doesn't have a whole lot on display. But the ground-floor exhibition of costumes is comprehensive and comes with proper English captions.

Across the road is the **Yúnnán Nationalities Village** (云南民族村; Yúnnán Mínzú Cūn; admission Y70; 8.30am-10pm). Walk through a tacky re-creation of an old Kūnmíng street to reach the 'village', where all-smiling, all-dancing minorities perform for mostly domestic tour groups. Skip it and head to Xīshuāngbǎnnà for the real thing instead.

Buses 24 and 44 (Y1) run to both the museum and village from the main train station.

Shílín 石林

0871

A conglomeration of utterly bizarre but stunning karst geology and a hell of a lot of tourists, **Shílín** (Stone Forest; admission Y175), about 120km southeast of Kūnmíng, is equal parts tourist trap and natural wonderland. A massive collection of grey limestone pillars split and eroded by wind and rainwater (the tallest reaches 30m high), the place was, according to legend, created by immortals who smashed a mountain into a labyrinth for lovers seeking privacy.

Yes, it's packed to the gills, every single rock is affixed with a lame name that reads like the purple prose of a high-schooler, Sani women can be persistent in sales, and it's all pricey as hell. Yet, idyllic, secluded walks are within 2km of the centre and by sunset or moonlight Shílín becomes otherworldly.

Shílín can easily be visited as a day trip from Kūnmíng, and it doesn't have much in the way of budget accommodation. But if you want to stay the night, the rooms at **Shílín Bìshǔyuán Bīnguǎn** (771 1088; d/tr Y300/360, discounts of 30%) are quiet and have good views over Shílín.

Near the main entrance is a cluster of restaurants and snack bars that are open from dawn to dusk. Check all prices before you order, as overcharging is not uncommon.

Sani song-and-dance evenings are organised when there are enough tourists. Shows normally start at around 8pm at a stage next to the minor stone forest but there are sometimes extra performances. There are also Sani performances at the same location during the day between 2pm and 3pm.

During the July/August **Torch Festival**, wrestling, bullfighting, singing and dancing are held at a natural outdoor amphitheatre by Hidden Lake south of Shílín.

Buses to Shílín (Y30 to Y35, two hours, every 30 minutes, 8am to noon) leave from the east bus station.

Jiànshuǐ 建水

0873 / POP 17,400

Jiànshuǐ is a charming town of old buildings, an enormous Confucian temple, a cave laden with swallows, and some of the best steampot cooking and barbecue you'll find in Yúnnán. The architecture is constantly being 'facelifted', but still retains much of its distinct character, and the locals, who are a mix of Han, Hui and Yi, are extremely friendly.

Known in ancient times as Bùtóu or Bādiàn (巴甸), Jiànshuǐ's history dates back to the Western Jin period, when it was under the auspices of the Ningzhou kingdom. It was handed around to other authorities until its most important days as part of the Tonghai Military Command of the Nanzhao kingdom. The Yuan dynasty established what would eventually become the contemporary town.

Sights

Classic architecture surrounds you in Jiànshuǐ, and not just in the old-style back alleys. Virtually every main street has a historically significant traditional structure. The architecture here is especially intriguing because of the obvious mixture of central plains and local styles. Many old buildings, despite official decrees positing them as state treasures, have been co-opted for other purposes and the trick – and the great fun – is trying to find them.

Note that you can buy a Y133 **through ticket** (通票; *tōngpiào*) that gets you into the Confucian Temple, the Zhu Family Garden and Swallow's Cavern. It's on sale at any of those places.

Confucian Temple CONFUCIAN TEMPLE
(文庙;Wénmiào; Linan Lu; admission Y60; ⊙8am-6.30pm) Jiànshuǐ's famous temple was modelled after the temple in Confucius' hometown of Qūfù (Shāndong province) and finished in 1285; it covers 7.5 hectares and is the third-largest Confucian temple in China. (Some locals employ a flurry of Byzantine mathematics to prove it's the largest; either way, Xué Lake, around which it sits, uses the Chinese word for 'sea' in its name!)

The temple has operated as a school for nearly 750 years and was so successful that over half of all Yúnnán's successful candidates in imperial examinations during this period came from Jiànshuǐ. Many of the names of buildings in Jiànshuǐ use the ideogram *wén*, or 'literacy'.

Zhu Family Garden HISTORIC SITE
(朱家花园; Zhūjiā Huāyuán; Hanlin Jie; admission Y50; ⊙8am-8pm) This spacious 20,000-sq-metre complex, a fascinating example of Qing-era one-upping-the-Joneses, comprises ancestral buildings, family homes, ponds and lovely gardens, and took 30 years to build (it's now partially converted into an atmospheric inn with Qing-style rooms for Y480). The Zhu family made its name through its mill and tavern, and dabbled in everything from tin in Gèjiù to opium in Hong Kong, eventually falling victim to the political chaos following the 1911 revolution.

Cháoyáng Gate HISTORIC SITE
(朝阳楼; Cháoyáng Lóu) Guarding the centre of town, Cháoyáng Gate, an imposing Ming edifice, was modelled on the Yellow Crane Tower in Wǔhàn and Yuèyáng Tower in Húnán, and bears more than a passing resemblance to the Gate of Heavenly Peace in Běijīng. There's no charge to walk up into the gate and admire the building and views; you'll find a wonderful traditional teahouse, often with local musicians playing.

Zhǐlín Sì BUDDHIST TEMPLE
(指林寺) The largest preserved wooden structure in Yúnnán, this monastery was built during the latter stages of the Yuan dynasty; its distinctive design feature is the brackets between columns and crossbeams.

Sleeping

Huáqīng Jiǔdiàn HOTEL $$
(华清酒店; ☎766 6166; 46 Hanlin Jie; 翰林街46号; s & d Y280-468, discounts of 40%; ❄@) Decorated in a neo-Qing-dynasty style, the rooms here are nicely set up and come with lovely, small terraces. The attached cafe-bar next door is an OK place for a coffee or evening drink. Obliging staff and discounts in quiet times complete the picture.

Lín'ān Inn INN $$
(临安客栈; Lín'ān Kèzhàn; ☎765 5866; 32 Hanlin Jie; 翰林街32号; d & tw Y198-218, discounts of 30%; ❄@) A prime location in the heart of the old town, but the biggest draw is the great communal outside area, which is very pleasant in the evening. Regular discounts make this a budget choice, but the rooms are a big step up from the cheapies. They'll cook for you too.

Garden Hotel HOTEL $
(花园宾馆;Huāyuán Bīnguǎn; ☎765 2310; 36 Lin'an Lu; 临安路36号; s & d with shared bathroom Y30, with private bathroom Y60-80; ❄) The largest of a number of no-frills places on Linan Lu. As the price suggests, the rooms are basic, but they are clean.

Eating

Jiànshuǐ is legendary for its *qìguō* (汽锅), a stew made in the county's famed earthenware pots and often infused with medicinal herbs. The cook may make use of the local speciality – grass sprout (*cǎoyá;* 草牙), also known as elephant's tooth grass root, which tastes like bamboo. Only found in Jiànshuǐ County, it's often used in broth or fried with liver or pork. Vegetarians might find a place that will substitute tofu.

You'll also find tons of places serving delicious *liáng miàn,* cold rice noodles served with sesame paste and tofu balls cooked on a grill.

Then there's glorious **Jiànshuǐ barbecue** (建水烧烤; Jiànshuǐ *shāokǎo*). Cubbyhole restaurants are filled with braziers roasting meats, veggies, tofu and perhaps goat's cheese. A perfect night out is a roasted meal under the Jiànshuǐ stars with friends. Try the intersection of Hanlin Jie and Lin'an Lu for barbecue places.

Information

There are **internet cafes** (山城网吧; wǎngbā; per hr Y2.50, ⌚24hr) on Yongning Jie, just south of Lin'an Lu, and on Hanlin Jie next to the Huáqīng Jiǔdiàn. There are a few ICBC ATMs around town that take foreign cards.

Getting There & Away

Jiànshuǐ has a couple of bus stations. The main one is 3km north of Cháoyáng Gate. For very local destinations, you need to head to the second small (regional) bus station a few minutes' walk west at the corner of Chaoyang Beilu and Beizheng Jie.

From the main station, there are buses continually leaving for Yuányáng (Y33, 2½ hours), but these go to Nánshà. For Xīnjiē and the rice terraces, there are six buses in the morning and one in the evening (Y39, four hours, from 6.50am to 8pm).

Frequent buses head to Kūnmíng (Y73, every 25 minutes, three to four hours, 7am to 7.35pm). Hékǒu-bound travellers have three morning buses (Y70, five hours, 6.40am, 8.16am, 10.57am). The masochistic can take one of the sleepers to Jǐnghóng (Y170, 17 hours), scheduled for 1.30pm and 4.30pm.

Around Jiànshuǐ

SWALLOW'S CAVERN 燕子洞

This freak of nature and ornithology is halfway between Jiànshuǐ and Gèjiù. The karst formations (the largest in Asia) are a lure, but what you'll want to see are the hundreds of thousands of swallows flying around in spring and summer. The **cave** (Yànzǐ Dòng; admission Y80; ⌚9am-5pm) is split into two – one high and dry, the other low and wet. The higher cave is so large that a three-storey pavilion and a tree fit inside. Plank walkways link up; the Lú River runs through the lower cave for about 8km and you can tour the caverns in 'dragon-boats'.

There's no direct bus, but the ones bound for Méngzì, Kāiyuán or Gèjiù which don't take the expressway pass the cavern (Y10, one hour).

TWIN DRAGON BRIDGE 双龙桥

This bridge (Shuānglóng Qiáo) across the confluence of the Lú and Tàchōng Rivers is 5km from the western edge of town. One of the 10 oldest in China, the bridge features 17 arches, so many that it took two periods of the Qing dynasty to complete the project. To get there, take minibus 4 from Jiànshuǐ's second bus station (Y2). Note that you have to ask the driver to tell you where to get off and then point you in the right direction. Bus 4 continues to **Huánglóng Sì** (黄龙寺), a small temple.

Yuányáng Rice Terraces 元阳梯田

☎0873 / POP 22,700

Picture hilltop villages, the only things visible above rolling fog and cloud banks, an artist's palette of colours at sunrise and sunset, spirit-recharging treks through centuries-old rice-covered hills, with a few water buffalo eyeing you contentedly nearby. Yes, it's hard not to become indulgent when describing these *tītián* (rice terraces), hewn from the rolling topography by the Hani over centuries. They cover roughly 12,500 hectares and are one of Yúnnán's most stunning sights.

Yuányáng is actually split into two: Nánshā, the new town, and Xīnjiē, the old town an hour's bus ride up a nearby hill. Either can be labelled Yuányáng, depending what map you use. Xīnjiē is the one you want, so make sure you get off there.

XĪNJIĒ 新街

Xīnjiē is a bit grubby, but it's a very friendly place and easy to use as a base of operations. The bus station is a minute's walk from Titian Sq, the town's hub.

Sights & Activities

The terraces around dozens of outlying villages have their own special characteristics. Ask at your accommodation for the best place to start your explorations, or just ask any photographers around where they're

THE HANI (AKHA) PEOPLE

The Hani (哈尼族, also known in adjacent countries as the Akha) are of Tibetan origin, but according to folklore they are descended from frogs' eyes. They are closely related to the Yi as a part of the Tibeto-Burman group; the language is Sino-Tibetan but uses Han characters for the written form.

They are mostly famed for their river valley rice terraces, especially in the Red River valley, between the Āiláo and Wúliàng Shān, where they cultivate rice, corn and the occasional poppy. There is a great variety in dress among the Hani, particularly between the Xīshuāngbǎnnà and the Hónghé Hani around Yuányáng. Hani women (especially the Aini, a subgroup of the Hani) wear headdresses of beads, feathers, coins and silver rings, some of which are made with French (Vietnamese), Burmese and Indian coins from the turn of the century.

The Hani have two animated New Year celebrations. The seven-day **Misezha** New Year festival takes place in the 10th month of the lunar calendar; this is preceded by the **Kuzhazha** god-worshipping celebration in the sixth lunar month, lasting three to six days. As part of the festivals, the Hani use an ox hide swing to symbolically ward off bad fortune and augur a favourable year ahead.

going for the perfect shot. We've been warmly welcomed wherever we wandered. Bilingual maps are available at all hotels in town. Bear in mind that the *tītián* are at their most extraordinary in winter when they are flooded with water which the light bounces off in spectacular fashion.

Duōyīshù (多依树), about 25km from Xīnjiē, has the most awesome sunrises and is the one you should not miss. **Quánfúzhuāng** (全福庄) is a less-crowded alternative and has easy access down to the terraces. For sunsets, **Bádá** (八达) and **Měngpǐn** (勐品), also known as **Lǎohǔzuǐ** (老虎嘴), can be mesmerising.

Commercialisation has come to the *tītián* and there are now charges for the most popular spots. A combined Y60 ticket gets you to Duōyīshù, Bádá and Quánfúzhuāng. For Měngpǐn/Lǎohǔzuǐ, the entrance fee is Y30.

Buses run to all the villages from the bus station, but you are much better off arranging your own transport, or hooking up with other travellers to split the cost of a sunrise–sunset drive. Minibuses and motorickshaws congregate around the Yúntī Shùnjié Dàjiǔdiàn and on the street west of the bus station. Expect to pay Y400 in peak season for a minibus. Less comfortable moto-rickshaws can be got for Y150 to Y200.

Several **markets** are worth visiting; check with Window of Yuányáng (see p654) for up-to-the-minute schedules.

Yuányáng Rice Terraces

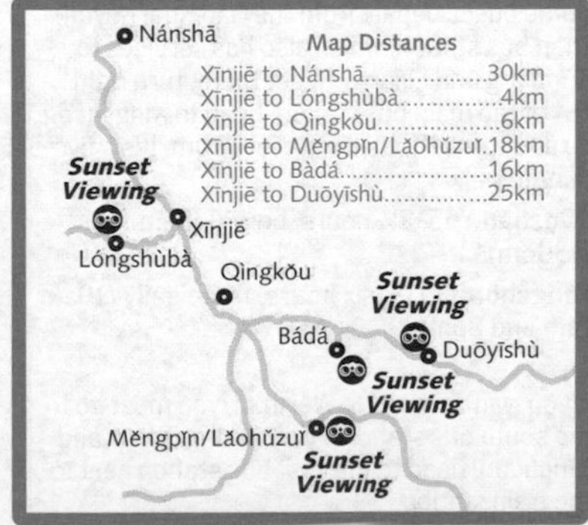

Sleeping & Eating

There are a number of places surrounding the bus station where rooms can be found for Y30 to Y100, depending on the level of comfort you desire. There are restaurants surrounding Titian Sq. Try **Liù Jūn Fàndiàn** (六军饭店; dishes from Y12; 8am-10pm), on the corner of the square closest to the bus station.

Sunny Guesthouse GUESTHOUSE $
(多依树阳光客栈; Duōyīshù Yángguāng Kèzhàn; 159 8737 1311; sunny-guesthouse@163.com; 10-/4-bed dm Y30/40; @) Surrounded by rice paddies in Duōyīshù's Pǔgāolǎo village, this is the place to come if you want to spend a few days walking in the area. Simple, fresh rooms (some with smashing terrace views), with shared shower, and they cook fine food too. Call first so you can arrange to be picked up.

Yúntī Shùnjié Dàjiǔdiàn HOTEL $$
(云梯顺捷大酒店; ☎562 4858; s/tr Y198/268) Just off Titian Sq and a few minutes from the bus station, this place has clean, compact rooms. Discounts bring the price down to Y100; a good deal.

Information

Agricultural Bank of China (中国农业银行; Zhōngguó Nóngyè Yínháng) Has an ATM that takes foreign cards and will change money, but won't touch travellers cheques. To find it, head down the stairs by the entrance to the Yúntī Shùnjié Dàjiǔdiàn and walk on for a couple of minutes; it's on the left-hand side.

Internet cafe (山城网吧; wǎngbā; per hr Y2.50-3; ⏲24hr) There are places close to the bus station and on Titian Sq near the Yúntī Shùnjié Dàjiǔdiàn.

Window of Yuányáng (☎562 3627; www.yuanyangwindow.com; @) Do visit this place, down the steps from the main square (on the 2nd floor of a building on your right). Associated with World Vision, staff here work in sustainable economic development in local villages. Volunteers – from Hong Kong – are very friendly and helpful. Great locally produced items are here, too (not to mention coffee!).

Getting There & Away

There are three buses daily from Kūnmíng to Yuányáng (Y128, 6½ hours, three daily at 10.20am, 3pm and 7.30pm); these return at 9.05am, 4pm and 6.30pm. Other destinations include Hékǒu (Y46, four hours).

You could forge on to Xīshuāngbǎnnà by taking the 7.30am bus to Lǜchūn (Y34, four hours), where you'll pray to get the Jiāngchéng bus at noon (Y34, five hours). If you miss it, try for a Sīmáo bus. By the time you arrive in Jiāngchéng, there'll be no more buses for the day, but you can stay the night and buses to Jǐnghóng (Y52, 8½ hours) start running at 6am.

Alternatively, backtrack to Jiànshuǐ (Y39, 3½ hours, six daily from 10.20am to 4.30pm) and catch the twice-daily Jǐnghóng sleepers (Y170, 17 hours, 1.30pm and 4.30pm) from there.

Xiàguān 下关

☎0872 / POP 138,000

Always remember: Xiàguān, the capital of Dàlǐ Prefecture, is also referred to as Dàlǐ (大理) on tickets, maps and buses. Coming from anywhere but northern Yúnnán, you'll likely have to stop off in Xiàguān to get to the 'real' Dàlǐ.

At the southern tip of Ěrhǎi Hú (Erhai Lake), about 400km west of Kūnmíng, this formerly important staging post on the Burma Road is still a key centre for transport. There is no reason to stay in Xiàguān and you only need to come here in order to catch a bus or train.

Information

Bank of China (Zhōngguó Yínháng; Jianshe Donglu) Changes money and travellers cheques, and has an ATM that accepts all major credit cards.

Public Security Bureau (PSB; 公安局; Gōng'ānjú; ☎214 2149; Tai'an Lu; ⏲8-11am & 2-5pm Mon-Fri) Handles all visa extensions for Xiàguān and Dàlǐ. Take bus 8 from Dàlǐ and ask to get off at the Shi Ji Middle School (世纪中学; Shìjì Zhōngxué).

Getting There & Away

AIR Xiàguān's airport is 15km from the town centre. The CAAC ticket office is inconveniently situated near the train station. No public buses run to the airport; taxis will cost Y50 from Xiàguān or Y100 from Dàlǐ. Three flights daily leave for Kūnmíng (Y640) and one or two to Xīshuāngbǎnnà (in peak seasons).

BUS Xiàguān's new main bus station, known as the Dàlǐ Express Bus Station (Kuàisù Kèyùnzhàn), is on Nan Jian Lu and is where most long-distance buses arrive and depart.

Jǐnghóng Y199, 17 hours, three daily (noon, 2pm and 8.30pm)

Kūnmíng Y100, five to six hours, every 20 minutes (7am to 7pm)

Mángshì (Lùxī) Y103, six to eight hours, two daily (10.30am and 6pm)

Ruìlì Y123 to Y187, 10 to 12 hours, two daily (8.30am and 8pm)

Buses from the north bus station, reached by bus 8 (Y2) or Y10 taxi ride:

Lìjiāng Y38, three hours, every 30 minutes (7am to 7pm)

Zhōngdiàn (Shangri-la) Y65, eight hours, every 30 minutes (7am to midday, then one at 8pm)

Some buses depart from the Gāo Kuài Kèyùnzhàn bus station, which also has services to Kūnmíng and Lìjiāng. To get there, turn right out of the main bus station, head to Xingsheng Lu and turn left, then walk for 100m. It's a five-minute walk.

Bǎoshān Y65, 2½ hours, hourly (8am to 6.30pm)

Téngchōng Y118, six hours, three daily (10am, 1pm and 8pm)

If you want to head to Wēishān, you must go to the south bus station. For Haǐdōng, Wāsè and Bīnchuān, head to the east bus station next to the train station.

Buses to Dàlǐ (Y2, 30 minutes) leave from outside the Gāo Kuài Kèyùnzhàn bus station. Bus 8 (Y2, 30 minutes) also runs from the train station, through the centre of Xiàguān to Dàlǐ's west gate. If you want to be sure, ask for Dàlǐ Gǔchéng (Dali Old City).

Tickets for nearly all destinations can (and sometimes should) be booked in Dàlǐ.

TRAIN There are two overnight sleeper trains from Kūnmíng's main train station at 10.30pm and 11pm, arriving in Xiàguān between 4am and 6am. Returning to Kūnmíng, overnight trains leave Xiàguān at 8.53pm and 10.20pm. There is one train daily to Lìjiāng at 5.12pm (Y15, two hours).

Bus 8 (Y2, 40 minutes) goes to downtown Xiàguān and on to Dàlǐ.

Jīzú Shān 鸡足山

Packed with temples and pagodas, this **Chicken Foot Mountain** (admission Y60) is a major attraction for Buddhist pilgrims – both Chinese and Tibetan. Most come for that rite of passage in China: a sunrise over a sacred mountain. Jīndǐng (金顶), the Golden Summit, is at a cool 3240m so make sure to bring warm clothing.

Sights & Activities

In the Qing dynasty there were approximately 100 temples on the mountain and somewhere in the vicinity of 5000 resident monks. Not today, but the many temples do include **Zhùshèng Temple** (祝圣寺; Zhùshèng Sì), the most important on the mountain, and about an hour's walk up from the bus stop at Shāzhǐ.

Just before the last ascent is the **Magnificent Head Gate** (华首门; Huáshǒu Mén). At the summit is **Lèngyán Pagoda** (楞严塔; Lèngyán Tǎ), a 13-tier Tang-dynasty pagoda that was restored in 1927.

A **cable car** (admission Y30) lifts you to the summit from the halfway point. Ubiquitous pony ride options exist – the touts will find you!

If you're travelling here via Bīnchuān, consider a stopover in **Zhoūchéng** (州城), once the administrative centre of the area and another of the important salt capitals. You can check out a 15th-century temple, ancient bridge and some residual old architecture.

Sleeping & Eating

Accommodation is available at the base of the mountain, about halfway up and on the summit at Golden Summit Temple (金顶寺; Jīndǐng Sì) – a sleeping bag might be a good idea. Prices average Y30 to Y40 per bed. Food gets expensive once you reach the summit.

Getting There & Away

From Xiàguān's east bus station, take a bus to Bīnchuān (Y11, two hours), from where you'll have to change for a bus or minibus to Shāzhǐ at the foot of the mountain (Y10, one hour).

Wēishān 巍山

0872 / POP 20,700

Some 55km or so south of Xiàguān, Wēishān is the heart of a region populated by Hui and Yi. It was once the nucleus of the powerful Nanzhao kingdom, and from here the Hui rebel Du Wenxiu led an army in revolt against the Qing in the 19th century. Today, it's an attractive small town of narrow streets lined with wooden houses, with drum towers at strategic points and a lovely backdrop of the surrounding hills.

The town's central point is the unmistakable **Gǒngcháng Lóu** (拱长楼; Gǒngcháng Tower). South from Gǒngcháng Lóu you'll come to **Mēnghuà Old Home** (蒙化老家; Mēnghuà Lǎojiā; admission Y6; 8am-9pm), the town's best-preserved slice of architecture.

Línyè Bīnguǎn (林业宾馆; 612 0761; 24 Xi Xin Jie; 西新街24号; s & d Y40-70;) is a hop, skip and a jump from Gǒngcháng Lóu and has big, newly decorated rooms. It's a Y4 ride from the bus station in a moto-rickshaw.

The only restaurants in the town are cubbyhole eateries. Head north or south of Gǒngcháng Lóu to find most of them. You may see people indulging in a local Yi speciality, baked tea.

Xiàguān's south bus station has buses (Y13, 1½ hours) to Wēishān from 6am to 6pm.

Around Wēishān

WĒIBǍO SHĀN 巍宝山

Eminently worthy **Wēibǎo Shān** (Wēibǎo Mountain; admission Y60), about 10km south of Wēishān, has a relatively easy hike to its peak at around 2500m. During the Ming and Qing dynasties it was the zenith of China's Taoism, and you'll find some superb Taoist murals; the most significant are at **Wénchāng Gōng** (文昌宫; Wénchāng Palace; No 3 on the entrance ticket) and **Chángchún Cave** (长春洞; Chángchūn Dòng; No 1 on the entrance ticket). Birders in particular love the mountain; the entire county is a node on an international birding flyway.

The only lodging on the mountain is the uninspired **Wēibǎo Shān Bīnguǎn** (巍宝山宾馆; ☎135 7725 2206; d Y40-180), near the main entrance, which has rooms in various states of repairs.

There are no buses here. Head to the street running east of Gǒngcháng Lóu in Wēishān to pick up a microvan to the mountain. Expect to pay Y60 for the round trip; you'll need the driver to wait for you.

Dàlǐ 大理

☎0872 / POP 40,000

Dàlǐ, the original funky banana-pancake backpacker hang-out in Yúnnán, was once *the* place to chill, with its stunning location sandwiched between mountains and Ěrhǎi Hú (Ěrhǎi Lake). Loafing here for a couple of weeks was an essential Yúnnán experience.

Today, though, Dàlǐ routinely gets bashed for being – you guessed it – too 'touristy'. Yes, much of the old has been garishly redone and, oh my goodness, have Chinese tour groups found the place. Then again, this sniffy attitude has resulted in fewer Westerners heading here, so you won't be as taken for granted as in years past. Forget the whingers, for there are fascinating possibilities for exploring, especially by bicycle and in the mountains above the lake, and getting to know the region's Bai culture.

History

Dàlǐ lies on the western edge of Ěrhǎi Hú at an altitude of 1900m, with a backdrop of the imposing 4000m-tall Cāng Shān (Green Mountains). For much of the five centuries in which Yúnnán governed its own affairs, Dàlǐ was the centre of operations, and the old city retains a historical atmosphere that is hard to come by in other parts of China.

The main inhabitants of the region are the Bai, who number about 1.5 million and are thought to have settled the area some 3000 years ago. In the early 8th century they succeeded in defeating the Tang imperial army before establishing the Nanzhao kingdom, which lasted until the Mongol hordes arrived in the mid-13th century.

Sights

Three Pagodas HISTORIC SITES

(三塔寺; Sān Tǎ Sì; adult/student incl Chongsheng Temple Y121/62; ⏲7am-7pm) Absolutely *the* symbol of the town/region, these pagodas 2km north of the north gate are among the oldest standing structures in southwestern China.

The tallest of the three, **Qiānxún Pagoda**, has 16 tiers that reach a height of 70m. It was originally erected in the mid-9th century by engineers from Xī'ān. It is flanked by two smaller 10-tiered pagodas, each of which are 42m high. While the price is cheeky considering you can't go inside the pagodas, **Chóngshèng Temple** (Chóngshèng Sì) behind them has been restored and converted into a relatively worthy museum.

FREE **Dàlǐ Museum** MUSEUM

(大理博物馆; Dàlǐ Shì Bówùguǎn; Fuxing Lu; ⏲8.30am-5.30pm) The museum houses a small collection of archaeological pieces relating to Bai history, including some fine figurines.

Catholic Church CHURCH

(off Renmin Lu) Also worth checking is Dàlǐ's Catholic Church. It dates back to 1927 and is a unique mix of Bai-style architecture and classic European church design. Mass is held here at 9am every Sunday.

Festivals & Events

Third Moon Fair CULTURAL FESTIVAL

Merrymaking – along with endless buying, selling and general horse-trading (but mostly merrymaking) – takes place during the Third Moon Fair (Sānyuè Jié), which begins on the 15th day of the third lunar month (usually April) and ends on the 21st day.

Three Temples Festival CULTURAL FESTIVAL

The Three Temples Festival (Ràosān Líng) is held between the 23rd and 25th days of the fourth lunar month (usually May). The first day involves a trip from Dàlǐ's south gate to Sacred Fountainhead Temple (Shèngyuán Sì) in Xǐzhōu. Here travellers stay up until dawn, dancing and singing, before moving on to Jīnguì Temple (Jīnguì Sì) and returning by way of Mǎjiǔyì Temple (Mǎjiǔyì) on the final day.

Torch Festival CULTURAL FESTIVAL

The Torch Festival (Huǒbǎ Jié) is held on the 24th day of the sixth lunar month (normally July) and is likely to be the best photo op in the province. Flaming torches are paraded at night through homes and fields.

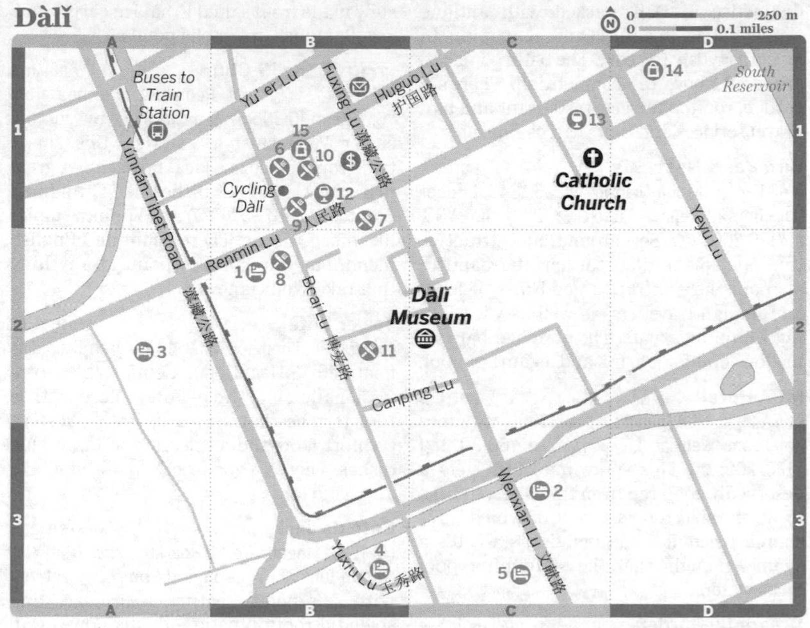

Dàlǐ

Top Sights
Catholic Church ... C1
Dàlǐ Museum ... C2

Sleeping
1 Bird Bar & Nest ... B2
2 Friends Guesthouse ... C3
3 Jade Emu ... A2
4 Jim's Tibetan Hotel ... B3
5 MCA Hotel ... C3

Eating
6 Café de Jack ... B1
7 Cāng Ěr Chūn ... B1
8 Jim's Peace Café ... B2
9 Sweet Tooth ... B1
10 Tower Café ... B1
11 Yī Rán Táng ... B2

Drinking
12 Bad Monkey ... B1
13 Daliba Vodka ... C1

Shopping
14 Bookworm ... D1
15 Mandarin Books & CDs ... B1

Sleeping

There's heaps of accommodation in Dàlǐ, but the popular places often fill up quickly during peak summer months.

TOP CHOICE **Jade Emu** YOUTH HOSTEL $
(金玉缘中澳国际青年旅舍; Jīnyùyuán Zhōng'ào Guójì Qīngnián Lǚshè; ☎267 7311; http://jade-emu.com; West Gate Village; 西门村; dm without/with bathroom Y25/30, s & d Y120-150; @) This Aussie-owned and run venture smack in the shadow of Cāng Shān (a five-minute walk from the old town) sets the standard for hostels in Dàlǐ. The staff here know what travellers want, the attention to detail is impressive and the only criticism is that the big and airy rooms are rather characterless. Around the corner, sister establishment **Jade Roo** copes with the overflow of travellers, with similar but slightly cheaper rooms.

Jim's Tibetan Hotel HOTEL $$
(吉姆和平酒店; Jímǔ Hépíng Jiǔdiàn; ☎267 7824; www.china-travel.nl; 13 Yuxiu Lu; 玉秀路13号; d Y280; @ 🛜) The rooms here are the most

distinctive in Dàlǐ, packed with antique Chinese-style furniture and managing to be both stylish and cosy. The bathrooms too are a cut above the competition. There's a garden, rooftop terrace, restaurant and bar. Travel services and tours can be booked.

Bird Bar & Nest HOTEL $
(鸟吧鸟窝; Niǎobā Niǎowō; ☎266 1843; birdbardali.com; 22 Renmin Lu; 人民路22号; dm Y30, s Y120-200; @) Set around an attractive tree- and plant-filled garden, the handful of rooms here attract a good mix of local and foreign travellers, as well as vacationing Kūnmíng expats. The attached bar is a mellow joint for a drink and a game of pool.

MCA Hotel HOTEL $
(MCA酒店; MCA Jiǔdiàn; ☎267 3666; www.mcahotel.com; Wenxian Lu; 文献路; d Y60-80, tr/f Y120/200; @) This sprawling outfit gets a deservedly good rep from travellers, thanks to its sizeable rooms, many of which have shared balconies, and obliging staff. It's a shame, though, that the swimming pool lacks water.

Dragonfly Garden GUESTHOUSE $
(蜻蜓花园; Qīngtíng Huāyuán; ☎269 1518; dragonflydali.com; Cáicūn wharf; 才村码头; dm Y30, log cabins s/d Y10/40, standard s & d Y80-100, r with mountain view Y150) On the edge of Ěrhǎi Hú, 5km or so from Dàlǐ, this bohemian place is not as popular as it once was, but remains a place to relax far from the madding crowds of the old town. The dorm and log cabin shared bathrooms are rough and ready, but the standard rooms are good value.

Friends Guesthouse GUESTHOUSE $
(大理古城三友客栈; Dàlǐ Gǔchéng Sānyǒu Kèzhàn; ☎266 2888; www.friendsdali.com; 2 Wenxian Lu; 文献路2号; dm Y20, s & d Y60-100; @) The choice for cheapo digs in the old town, this place has always been super-busy (and friendly) and has upgraded its facilities recently.

Eating

Bai food makes use of local flora and fauna – many of which are unrecognisable! Province wide, *ěr kuài* (饵块) are flattened and toasted rice 'cakes' with an assortment of toppings (or plain). 'Milk fan' (*rǔshàn;* 乳扇) may not sound appetising, but this 'aired' yogurt/milk mixture (it ends up as a long, thin sheet) is a local speciality and is often fried or melted atop other foods. This is distinct from *rǔbǐng*. Given Ěrhǎi Hú's proximity, try *shāguō yú* (沙锅鱼), a claypot fish casserole/stew made from salted Ěrhǎi Hú carp – and, as a Bai touch, magnolia petals.

TOP CHOICE **Cāng Ěr Chūn** YUNNAN $
(苍洱春; 84 Renmin Lu; dishes from Y6; ⊙9am-10.30pm) Surrounded by cookie-cutter Western-style eateries, this small, two-storey place is a local favourite. A great place for classic Bai dishes like Grandma's potato (*lǎo nǎi yángyù*) and Yunnan staples like *táozá rǔbǐng*. There's a limited English menu, but you can also point at anything that takes your fancy.

Tower Café WESTERN $$
(钟楼咖啡; Zhōnglóu Kāfēi; 44 Yangren Jie; mains from Y26; ⊙11am-11pm) Comfortable, professionally run, three-storey place with a roof terrace that serves up solid Western comfort food and a selection of tasty Thai dishes. There's a good range of foreign beer and wine too.

Café de Jack WESTERN $
(樱花格; Yīnghuā Gé; 82 Boai Lu; dishes from Y10; ⊙8am-1am; @) A capacious but cosy retreat with soft booth seating, a fireplace and splendid rooftop patio – this is now a Dàlǐ institution. Not all the dishes are equally good, but the lasagne and chocolate cake are standouts. Also has a limited but decent selection of Bai dishes.

Sweet Tooth CAFE $
(甜点屋; Tiándiǎn Wū; 52 Boai Lu; dishes from Y10; ⊙8.30am-10.30pm; @) Owned and run by a culinary arts graduate, the homemade ice cream and desserts here are simply inspiring. There's also fine coffee and proper English tea. As an added bonus, the cafe benefits local deaf culture.

Yī Rán Táng VEGETARIAN $
(一然堂; 20 Honglong Alley; dishes Y5; ⊙11.30am-1pm & 5.30-7pm) An altruistic, Buddhist-inspired, all-vegetarian buffet where you pay Y5 for a bowl of rice and whatever dishes the cooks have come up with on the day.

Jim's Peace Café TIBETAN $
(吉姆和平餐厅; Jímǔ Hépíng Cāntīng; 63 Boai Lu; mains Y18-32; ⊙7.30am-10pm) The Tibetan banquet (Y35; minimum four people) here is not to be missed, but there's also a wide range of Western and Chinese dishes on offer, including breakfasts.

Drinking

The Western-style restaurants double as bars. Also worth trying is **Daliba Vodka** (Dàlǐ Bā;

143 Renmin Lu; ⏲5.30pm-late), a cool bar off the main strip with a great selection of homemade flavoured vodkas, including Sichuan hotpot! Then there's the eternally happening, Brit-run **Bad Monkey** (坏猴子; Huài Hóuzi; Renmin Lu; ⏲9am-late), which brews its own beers in the nearby mountains, has occasional live music and endless drink specials.

Shopping

Dàlǐ is famous for its marble blue-and-white batik printed on cotton and silk.

The centre of town has a profusion of clothes shops. Most shopkeepers can also make clothes to your specifications – which will come as a relief when you see how small some of the items of ready-made clothing are.

Most of the 'silver' jewellery sold in Dàlǐ is really brass. For those roving sales ladies badgering you incessantly, don't feel bad to pay one-fifth of their asking price – that's what locals advise. For marble from street sellers, 40% to 50% is fair. In shops, two-thirds of the price is average. And don't fall for any 'expert' opinions; go back later on your own and deal.

A few more or less useful maps (Y12) can be picked up at hostels and restaurants around town. You can also find them at **Mandarin Books & CDs** (五华书苑; Wǔhuá Shūyuàn; Huguo Lu), along with guidebooks and novels in Chinese, English, French and German, as well as at the **Bookworm** (书呆子; Shūdāizi; 63 Renmin Lu), which also has books for exchange.

Information

On hikes around Cāng Shān there have been several reports of robbery of solo walkers (and violence has been increasing in these incidents). On the overnight sleeper bus from Kūnmíng, a bag is often pinched or razored. Mostly, though, you'll simply be pestered constantly by the middle-aged Bai women who control the local ganja trade.

All hostels and many hotels offer travel advice, arrange tours and book tickets for onward travel. There are also numerous travel agencies and cafes that will book bus tickets and offer all manner of tours. They can be expensive unless you can get a group together.

Internet cafes can be found along all the main streets (Y2 to Y2.50 per hour), but all hostels and hotels also offer online access.

Bank of China (中国银行; Zhōngguó Yínháng; Fuxing Lu) Changes cash and travellers cheques, and has an ATM that accepts all major credit cards.

China Minority Travel (chinaminoritytravel@gmail.com) Henriette, a Dutch expat, can offer a long list of trips, including tours to Muslim markets and Yi minority markets as well as through remote areas of Yúnnán and overland travel to Lhasa from Zhōngdiàn (Shangri-la) when it is allowed. Jim's Peace Café and Jim's Tibetan Hotel do work with her but she technically works from home, so send an email in advance.

China Post (中国邮政; Zhōngguó Yóuzhèng; cnr Fuxing Lu & Huguo Lu; ⏲8am-8pm)

Public Security Bureau (PSB; 公安局; Gōng'ānjú; 21 Tianbao Jie, Xiàguān; ⏲8-11am & 2-5pm Mon-Fri) Visas cannot be renewed in Dàlǐ, so you'll have to head to Xiàguān.

Getting There & Away

The golden rule: most buses advertised to Dàlǐ actually go to Xiàguān. Coming from Lìjiāng, Xiàguān-bound buses stop at the eastern end of Dàlǐ to let passengers off before continuing on to the north bus station.

From Kūnmíng's west bus station there are numerous buses to Dàlǐ (Y100, four to five hours, every 20 minutes from 7.30am to 7.30pm). Heading north, it's easiest to pick up a bus on the roads outside the west or east gates; buy your ticket in advance from your guesthouse or a travel agent and they'll make sure you get on the right one. (You could hail one yourself to save a surcharge but you're not guaranteed a seat.)

Buses run regularly to Shāpíng (Y7), Xǐzhōu (Y5) and other local destinations from outside the west gate.

Getting Around

From Dàlǐ, a taxi to Xiàguān airport takes 45 minutes and costs around Y100; to Xiàguān's train station it costs Y50.

Bikes are the best way to get around (Y20 to Y40 per day). You can't do better than **Cycling Dàlǐ** (cyclingdali.com; 55 Boai Lu; ⏲7.30am-8pm), which has solid bikes and offers loads of other travel services.

Buses (Y2, 30 minutes, marked 大理) run between the old town and Xiàguān from as early as 6.30am; get on along Yu'er Lu or where it meets the road one block west of Boai Lu (coming in it will drop you off along Boai Lu). Bus 8 runs between Dàlǐ and central Xiàguān (Y2, 30 minutes) on the way to the train station every 15 minutes from 6.30am.

Around Dàlǐ

Travellers have a **market** to go to nearly every day of the week. Every Monday at **Shāpíng** (沙坪), about 30km north of Dàlǐ, there is a colourful Bai market (Shāping

Gǎnjí). From 10am to 2.30pm you can buy everything from tobacco, melon seeds and noodles to meat, jewellery and wardrobes. In the ethnic clothing line, you can look at shirts, headdresses, embroidered shoes and money belts, as well as local batik. Remember, it's a compliment to be quoted insanely high prices, as it means you're welcome there; so bargain back – politely.

Regular buses to Shāpíng (Y7, one hour) leave from just outside the west gate. By bike, it will take about two hours at a good clip.

Markets also take place in **Shuānglǎng** (双廊; Tuesday), **Shābā** (沙巴; Wednesday), **Yòusuǒ** (右所; Friday morning, the largest in Yúnnán) and **Jiāngwěi** (江尾; Saturday). **Xǐzhōu** (喜州) and **Zhōuchéng** (州城) have daily morning and afternoon markets, respectively. **Wāsè** (挖色) also has a popular market every five days with trading from 9am to 4.30pm. Thanks to the lack of boats, travellers now have to slog to Xiàguān's east bus station for buses to Wāsè.

Many cafes and hotels in Dàlǐ offer tours or can arrange transportation to these markets for around Y150 for a half day.

ĚRHǍI HÚ 洱海湖

Ěrhǎi Hú (Ear-Shaped Lake) dominates the local psyche. The seventh-biggest freshwater lake in China, it sits at 1973m above sea level and covers 250 sq km; it's also dotted with trails perfect for bike rides and villages to visit. It's a 50-minute walk, a 15-minute bus ride or a 10-minute downhill zip on a bike from Dàlǐ.

Cáicūn (才村), a pleasant little village east of Dàlǐ (Y1 on bus 2), is the nexus of lake transport. Sadly, putt-putt local ferries are a distant memory. All boat travel is now on 'official' vessels. Expect to pay Y150 for a three-hour trip. That said, ask around at cafes and guesthouses – you may find someone who knows someone who…you know the drill.

Close to Wāsè are **Pǔtuó Dǎo** (普陀岛; Pǔtuó Island) and **Lesser Pǔtuó Temple** (小普陀寺; Xiǎopǔtuó Sì), set on an extremely photogenic rocky outcrop.

Roads now encircle the lake so it is possible to do a loop (or partial loop) of the lake by mountain bike. A great day's bike trip is from Dàlǐ to Shāpíng. Some hard-core cyclists continue right around the lake, stopping at other markets on the way. (However, the lack of boats means you're looking at an overnight stay or an extremely long ride in one day.) From Dàlǐ to Wāsè it's around 58km by road.

Plenty of cafes in Dàlǐ can arrange whatever else you dream up.

CĀNG SHĀN 苍山

This range of gorgeous peaks rises imposingly above Dàlǐ and offers the best legwork in the area. Most travellers head first for **Zhōnghé Temple** (中和寺; Zhōnghé Sì), a long, steep hike up the mountainside behind Dàlǐ; or take the **chairlift** (one way/return Y35/60) up **Zhōnghé Shān** (中和山; Zhōnghé Mountain; admission Y30; ⏲8am-6pm).

You can also hike up the mountain, a sweaty two to three hours for those in moderately good shape (but note the warning that there have been several reports of robbery of solo walkers). Walk about 200m north of the chairlift base to the riverbed (often dry). Follow the left bank for about 50m and walk through the cemetery, then follow the path zigzagging under the chairlift. When you reach some stone steps, you know you are near the top.

Branching out from either side of Zhōnghé Temple is a trail that winds along the face of the mountains, taking you in and out of steep, lush valleys and past streams and waterfalls. From the temple, it's an amazing 11km up-and-down hike south to **Gǎntōng Temple** (感通寺; Gǎntōng Sì), **Qīngbì Stream** (清碧溪; Qīngbì Xī) and/or **Guānyīn Pavilion** (观音堂; Guānyīn Táng), from where you can continue to the road and pick up a Dàlǐ-bound bus. There's also a **cable car** (one way/return Y50/80) between Qīngbì Stream and Gǎntōng Temple. If you buy your tickets for chairlifts from a travel agent or your guesthouse you can score a discount.

You can loaf in basic luxury at 2950m near Zhōnghé Temple at **Higherland Inn** (高地旅馆; Gāodì Lǚguǎn; ☎266 1599; www.higherland.com; dm Y30, d Y80-120). If you want to get away from the crowds in Dàlǐ, this is the place to do it. The hostel has fabulous views, regular barbecues and only a handful of rooms, which means it's an incredibly relaxing place to stay.

XǏZHŌU 喜洲

A trip to the old town of Xǐzhōu for a look at its well-preserved Bai architecture is lovely. You can catch a local bus from the south gate in Dàlǐ (Y3) or take a taxi (Y30 to Y35) to make the 18km trip, but a bicycle trip with an overnight stop in Xǐzhōu (there's accommodation in town) is also a good idea. From here, the interesting town of **Zhōuchéng** (州城) is 7km further north; it too has basic accommodation.

NORTHWEST YÚNNÁN

Lìjiāng 丽江

☎NEW TOWN 08891, OLD TOWN 0888 / POP OLD TOWN 40,000

How popular is this timelocked – if touristified – place? Lìjiāng's maze of cobbled streets, rickety (or rickety-looking, given gentrification) wooden buildings and gushing canals suck in around five million people a year. At times, the old town's tiny alleys can seem less like thoroughfares from ancient China than central London or New York at rush hour.

But remember the 80/20 rule: 80% of the tourists will be in 20% of the places. Get up early enough and more often than not you'll avoid the crowds. And if they do appear, that's the cue to beat a retreat into the delightful labyrinth of old streets, where soon enough it'll be just you again.

A UN World Heritage Site since 1999, Lìjiāng is a city of two halves: the old town and the very different and modern new town. The old town is where you'll be spending your time and it's a jumble of lanes that twist and turn. If you get lost, head upstream and you'll make your way back to the main square.

Sights

Note that the old town technically has a Y80 entrance fee. Nobody usually pays this, but you may be asked for it if you try to buy a ticket for other sights around town.

Old Town HISTORIC AREA

(古城) If a waterside location indeed engenders good fortune, then Lìjiāng is lucky, lucky, lucky. The old town is dissected by a web of arterylike canals that once brought the city's drinking water from Yuquan Spring, in what is now Black Dragon Pool Park. Several wells and pools are still in use around town (but hard to find). Where there are three pools, these were designated into pools for drinking, washing clothes and washing vegetables. A famous example of these is the **White Horse Dragon Pool** (白马龙潭; Báimǎlóng Tán; ⏲7am-10pm) in the deep south of the old town, where you can still see the odd local washing their veggies after buying them in the market.

The focus of the old town is the busy **Old Market Square** (四方街; Sìfāng Jiē). Once the haunt of Naxi traders, they've long since made way for tacky souvenir stalls. However, the view up the hill and the surrounding lanes are still extraordinary.

Now acting as sentinel of sorts for the town, the **Looking at the Past Pavilion** (望古楼; Wànggǔ Lóu; admission Y15; ⏲7am-9pm) has a unique design using dozens of four-storey pillars – culled from northern Yúnnán old-growth forests.

Black Dragon Pool Park SCENIC AREA

(黑龙潭公园; Hēilóngtán Gōngyuán; Xin Dajie; admission free with Y80 town entrance ticket; ⏲7am-

Lìjiāng

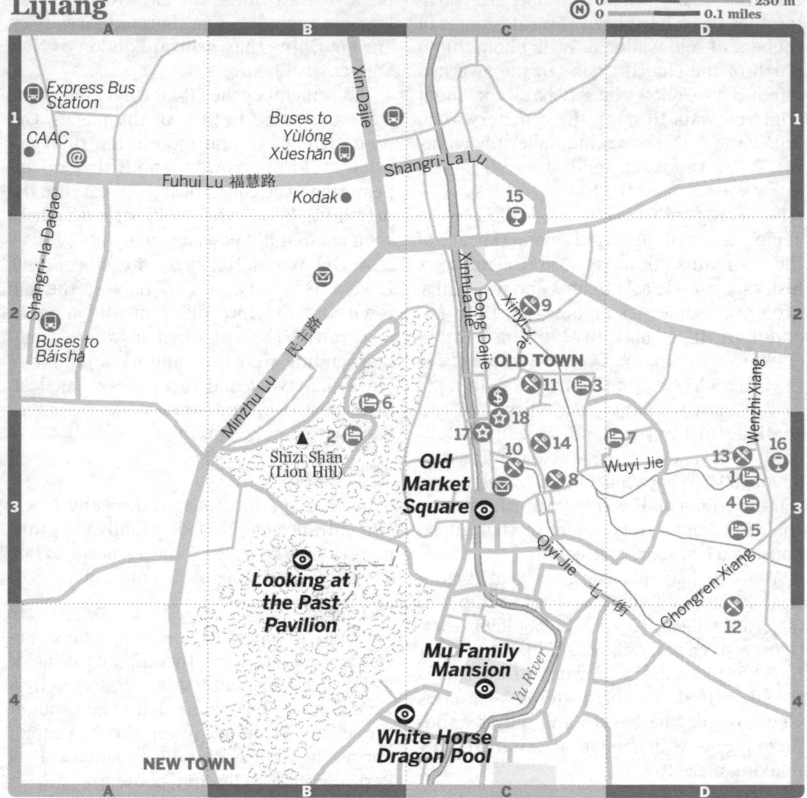

8.30pm) On the northern edge of town is the Black Dragon Pool Park; its view of Yùlóng Xuěshān (Jade Dragon Snow Mountain) is the most obligatory photo shoot in southwestern China. The **Dōngbā Research Institute** (东巴文化研究室; Dōngbā Wénhuà Yánjiūshì; ⌚8am-5pm Mon-Fri) is part of a renovated complex on the hillside here. You can see Naxi cultural artefacts and scrolls featuring a unique pictograph script.

Trails lead up **Xiàng Shān** (Elephant Hill) to a dilapidated gazebo and then across a spiny ridge past a communications centre and back down the other side, making a nice morning hike, but note the warning on p665.

The **Museum of Naxi Dongba Culture** (纳西东巴文化博物馆; Nàxī Dōngbā Wénhuà Bówùguǎn; admission free; ⌚9am-5pm) is at the park's northern entrance and is a decent introduction to traditional Naxi lifestyle and religion, complete with good English captions.

Mu Family Mansion HISTORIC SITE
(木氏土司府; Mùshì Tǔsīfǔ; admission Y60; ⌚8.30am-5.30pm) The former home of a Naxi chieftain, the Mu Family Mansion was heavily renovated (more like built from scratch) after the devasting earthquake that struck Lìjiāng in 1996. Mediocre captions do a poor job of introducing the Mu family but many travellers find the beautiful grounds reason enough to visit.

Festivals & Events

The 13th day of the third moon (late March or early April) is the traditional day to hold a **Fertility Festival**.

July brings the **Torch Festival** (Huǒbǎ Jié), also celebrated by the Bai in the Dàlǐ region and the Yi all over the southwest. The origin of this festival can be traced back to the intrigues of the Nanzhao kingdom, when the wife of a man burned to death by the king eluded the romantic

Lìjiāng

entreaties of the monarch by leaping into a fire.

Sleeping

Throw a stick and you'll hit a charming Naxi guesthouse in the old town. There are well over 700 places to stay in the old city, with more appearing all the time. In peak seasons (especially holidays), prices double (or more).

TOP CHOICE **Dōngbā Hotel** HOTEL $
(东巴客栈; Dōngbā Kèzhàn; ☎512 1975; www.dongbahotel.com; 109 Wenzhi Alley; 文治巷109号; s & d Y120-280; @) A family-style atmosphere (free laundry and tea and coffee), great staff, and cute rooms (some on two levels) with huge, comfy beds and nice bathrooms make this very well maintained inn a lovely place to stay. It gets a lot of repeat guests, which says it all.

Mama Naxi's Guesthouse GUESTHOUSE $
(古城香格韵客栈; Gǔchéng Xiānggéyùn Kèzhàn; ☎510 7713; 70 Wangjia Zhuang Lane, Wuyi Jie; 五一街文化巷70号; dm Y25-30, s & d Y60-150; @) With two guesthouses close to each other, named '1' and '3' ('2' is in Dàlǐ), which are always busy, the ever-energetic Mama is doing her best to corner the backpacker market in Lìjiāng. Certainly, she knows what travellers want, even if it not all of them like what they get. Head to '3' at 70 Wangjia Zhuang Lane for solid dorms, cramped

THE NAXI

Lìjiāng has been the base of the 286,000-strong Naxi (纳西; also spelt Nakhi and Nahi) minority for about the last 1400 years. The Naxi descend from ethnically Tibetan Qiang tribes and lived until recently in matrilineal families. Since local rulers were always male it wasn't truly matriarchal, but women still seemed to run the show.

The Naxi matriarchs maintained their hold over the men with flexible arrangements for love affairs. The *azhu* (friend) system allowed a couple to become lovers without setting up joint residence. Both partners would continue to live in their respective homes; the boyfriend would spend the nights at his girlfriend's house but return to live and work at his mother's house during the day. Any children born to the couple belonged to the woman, who was responsible for bringing them up. The man provided support, but once the relationship was over, so was the support. Children lived with their mothers and no special effort was made to recognise paternity. Women inherited all property and disputes were adjudicated by female elders.

There are strong matriarchal influences in the Naxi language. Nouns enlarge their meaning when the word for 'female' is added; conversely, the addition of the word for 'male' will decrease the meaning. For example, 'stone' plus 'female' conveys the idea of a boulder; 'stone' plus 'male' conveys the idea of a pebble.

but clean standard rooms, information-gathering, socialising and cheap eats. 'I', at 78 Wangjia Zhuang Lane (☎510 0700), is dorm-free and more peaceful.

Panba Hostel YOUTH HOSTEL $
(潘巴家院青年旅舍; Pānbā Jiāyuán Qīngnián Lǚshè; ☎511 9077; apan1125@hotmail.com; Wenming Xiang, Wuyi Jie; 五一街文明巷; dm Y25-35, s & d Y110-120; @) At the as yet undeveloped eastern end of Wuyi Jie, this increasingly popular place is a 15-minute walk from the centre of the old town, and so far from the tour group madness. The rooms are a decent size and come with shared balconies, while the solicitous staff get rave reviews. Book ahead.

Zen Garden Hotel HOTEL $$
(瑞和园酒店; Ruìhé Yuán Jiǔdiàn; ☎518 9799; www.zengardenhotel.com; 36 Xingren Lane, Wuyi Jie; 五一街兴仁下段36号; d/ste Y500/1200; @) As befits its name, this is a serene, hushed establishment. Run by a Naxi teacher and decorated with help from her artist brother, the furniture and design in the communal areas is tremendous, even if the rooms themselves are a little more functional than their price suggests.

Panorama Guesthouse GUESTHOUSE $
(黄山壹号客栈; Huángshān Yīhào Kèzhàn; ☎512 8784; 1 Upper Huangshan Lu; 黄山路上段1号; s & d Y100-180; @) The self-proclaimed first choice on the street and set around a little garden on winding Huangshan Lu, the 2nd- and 3rd-floor rooms here offer cool views over the old town, as does the cosy bar/communal area. The cheapest rooms come with squat toilets.

Jírì Guānjǐng Kèzhàn INN $
(吉日观景客栈; ☎888 1788; 55 Huangshan Lu; 黄山下段55号; s & d Y120-280; @) Another one of the increasing number of inns looming over Old Market Square, this has spacious, comfortable rooms, the more expensive of which come with great views and computers, as well as a cool, courtyard vibe.

Lìjiāng International Youth Hostel YOUTH HOSTEL $
(丽江老谢车马店; Lìjiāng Laǒxiè Chēmǎdiàn; ☎518 0124; 44 Mishi Xiang, Xinyi Jie; 新义街密士巷44号; dm Y25, s & d Y50-120, tr Y150-180; @) The dorms here are big (eight and 12 beds) and a bit run down, the rooms generic, but there's a great bar/communal area and the staff are helpful.

YÚNNÁN NORTHWEST YÚNNÁN

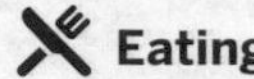

Eating

There are many, many eateries around the old town, and almost every menu will have both Chinese and Western dishes.

Bābā is the Lìjiāng local speciality – thick flatbreads of wheat, served plain or stuffed with meat, vegetables or sweets. There are always several 'Naxi' items on menus, including the famous 'Naxi omelette' and 'Naxi sandwich' (goat's cheese, tomato and fried egg between two pieces of local *bābā*). Try locally produced *yìnjiǔ*, a lychee-based wine with a 500-year history – it tastes like a decent semisweet sherry.

Mama Fu's YUNNAN $
(马马付餐厅; Mǎmǎfù Cāntīng; Mishi Xiang; dishes from Y18; ⏲9am-10.30pm) An original Lìjiāng culinary cornerstone from way back, alfresco dining here beside a tranquil stream provides one of the best people-watching opportunities in the old town. The Chinese dishes are very solid, especially the Naxi ones (try the *chǎo hǎicài*, a local vegetable speciality).

Ama Yi Naxi Snacks ETHNIC MINORITY $
(阿妈意纳西饮食院; Āmāyì Nàxī Yǐnshí Yuàn; www.ljamy.com; Wuyi Jie; dishes from Y22; ⏲10am-9.30pm) The name doesn't do justice to the small but very authentic selection of Naxi cuisine on offer at this calm courtyard restaurant. Fantastic mushroom dishes, as well as *zhútǒng fàn*, rice that comes packed in bamboo. It's down an alley off Wuyi Jie, close to the Stone Bridge.

Lamu's House of Tibet TIBETAN $
(西藏屋西餐馆; Xīzàngwū Xīcāntīng; 56 Xinyi Jie; dishes from Y18; ⏲7am-midnight; @) Lamu has been putting smiles and service before yuán for over a decade and, after a few relocations, she's finally nailed her spot in this casual pine-and-bamboo place on the north side of the old town. The upstairs is great for people-watching. It's a UN menu, but the Tibetan items are all you really need (though the Naxiburger rocks).

Well Bistro WESTERN $
(井卓餐馆; Jǐngzhuó Cānguǎn; 32 Mishi Xiang; dishes from Y10; ⏲8am-11pm; wi-fi) Laid-back and friendly, this is an oasis in a busy part of the old town and a great place to relax after a day's walking. Western breakfasts, burgers, pasta and pizza (from Y30), as well as rice and noodle dishes, and great coffee and proper booze. There's a book exchange here too and wi-fi.

KEEPING THE GOOD FORTUNE

An interesting local historical tidbit has it that the original Naxi chieftain, whose former home is the Mu Family Mansion, would not allow the old town to be girdled by a city wall because drawing a box around the Chinese character of his family name would change the character from *mù* (wood) to *kún* (surrounded, or hard pressed).

Tiān Hé Cāntīng YUNNAN $
(天和餐厅; 139 Wuyi Jie; dishes from Y10; ⊙7am-10.30pm) It's hard to find a neighbourhood-style restaurant in the old town, or one that doesn't also serve Western food, but this place hits the spot with a mix of Naxi dishes and Chinese staples like dumplings, hotpots and *gōng bǎo jī dīng*.

Petit Lìjiāng Bookcafé WESTERN $
(www.petitlijiang.com; 50 Chongren Xiang, Qiyi Jie; dishes from Y15; ⊙8.30am-10.30pm; @) Owners Mei and Olivier are great sources of travel information, and the food (a mix of classic Chinese and Western dishes) and atmosphere are fine (head upstairs for the best seats). The bookshop has a small but good collection of English- and French-language titles focusing on Yúnnán and elsewhere in China.

N's Kitchen WESTERN $
(二楼小厨; Èrlóu Xiǎochú; 17 Jishan Xiang, Xinyi Jie; dishes from Y22; ⊙9am-9pm; @) Clamber up the steep stairs for one of the best breakfasts in town, a monster burger and a cheery welcome. It's a good source of travel info too, as well as having mountain bikes for hire.

Drinking

Xinhua Jie, just off Old Market Square, is packed out with Chinese-style drinking dens. More amenable to Western tastes is expat hang-out **New Amsterdam** (小荷兰酒吧; Xiǎo Hélán Jiǔbā; 44 Block C, Yuhe Corridor; ⊙11am-late), run by a Dutch guy and his Chinese wife, with a happy hour between 5pm and 6pm, pub grub, pool and darts. Also worth checking is the Irish-owned **Stone the Crows** (130 Wuyi Jie; ⊙7pm-late), an endearingly ramshackle rooftop bar with great views over the old town.

☆ Entertainment

Naxi Orchestra MUSIC
(纳西古乐会; Nàxī Gǔyuè Huì; Naxi Music Academy; tickets Y120-160; ⊙performances 8pm) One of the few things you can do in the evening in Lìjiāng is attend performances of this orchestra inside a beautiful building in the old town. Not only are all two dozen or so members Naxi, but they play a type of Taoist temple music (known as *dòngjīng*) that has been lost elsewhere in China. The pieces they perform are said to be faithful renditions of music from the Han, Song and Tang dynasties, and are played on original instruments. Local historian of note Xuan Ke often speaks for the group at performances.

Dongba Palace MUSIC
(东巴宫; Dōngbā Gōng; Dong Dajie; tickets Y120-180; ⊙performances 7pm) This government run place has a less-authentic song-and-dance show.

Information

Crowded, narrow streets are a pickpocket's heaven. Solo women travellers have been mugged when walking alone at night in isolated areas of historic Lìjiāng. Xiàng Shān (Elephant Hill) in Black Dragon Pool Park (Hēilóngtán Gōngyuán) has been the spot of quite a few robberies.

Lìjiāng's cafes and backpacker inns are your best source of information on the area. There are no internet cafes in the old town, but all hostels and hotels have internet access and/or wi-fi, as do virtually all the cafes in town.

Bank of China (中国银行; Zhōngguó Yínháng; Dong Dajie) This branch is in the old town and has an ATM machine. There are other banks around town with ATMs too.

China International Travel Service (CITS; 中国国际旅行社; Zhōngguó Guójì Lǚxíngshè; 3rd fl, Lifang Bldg, cnr Fuhui Lu & Shangrila Dadao) Can arrange tours in and around Lìjiāng. The entrance is down an alley off Shangrila Dadao.

China Post (中国邮政; Zhōngguó Yóuzhèng; Minzhu Lu; ⊙8am-8pm) Offers EMS (Express Mail Service). Another post office is in the old town just north of Old Market Sq.

Eco-tours (www.ecotourchina.com) Run by Zhao Fan at the Café Buena Vista in Báishā; you can get information at **Lamu's House of Tibet** (56 Xinyi Jie). Check out Zhao Fan's maps of Lìjiāng-area cycling trails.

Kodak (柯达; Kēdá; Fuhui Lu) CD burning for Y20 per CD.

Public Security Bureau (PSB; 公安局; Gōng'ānjú; Fuhui Lu; ⊙8.30-11.30am & 2.30-5.30pm Mon-Fri) Is reputedly very speedy with visa extensions.

JOSEPH ROCK

Yúnnán has always been a hunting ground for famous, foreign plant-hunters such as Kingdon Ward and Joseph Rock (1884–1962). Rock lived in Lìjiāng between 1922 and 1949, becoming the world's leading expert on Naxi culture and local botany. Enigmatic and eccentric, he is remembered to this day; everywhere you go in northwestern Yúnnán you still hear that 'Luòkè' (Rock) passed through in (name the year).

Born in Austria, the withdrawn autodidact taught himself eight languages, including Sanskrit. After becoming the world's foremost authority on Hawaiian flora, the US Department of Agriculture, Harvard University and later *National Geographic* (he was their famed 'man in China') sponsored Rock's trips to collect flora for medicinal research. He devoted much of his life to studying Naxi culture, which he feared was being extinguished by the dominant Han culture.

Rock sent over 80,000 plant specimens from China – two were named after him – along with 1600 birds and 60 mammals. His caravans stretched for half a mile, and included dozens of servants, including a cook trained in Austrian cuisine, a portable darkroom, trains of pack horses, and hundreds of mercenaries for protection against bandits, not to mention the gold dinner service and collapsible bathtub.

Rock lived in Yùhú village (called Nguluko when he was there), outside Lìjiāng. Many of his possessions are now local family heirlooms.

The *Ancient Nakhi Kingdom of Southwest China* (1947) is Joseph Rock's definitive work. Immediately prior to his death, his Naxi dictionary was finally prepared for publishing. Take a look at *In China's Border Provinces: The Turbulent Career of Joseph Rock, Botanist-Explorer* (1974) by JB Sutton.

Getting There & Away

Air

Lìjiāng's airport is 25km east of town. Tickets can be booked at **CAAC** (中国民航; Zhōngguó Mínháng; cnr Fuhui Lu & Shangrila Dadao; ⏲8.30am-9pm). Most hotels in the old town also offer an air-ticket booking service.

From Lìjiāng there are oodles of daily flights to Kūnmíng (Y420), as well as daily flights to Chéngdū (Y790), Běijīng (Y2410), Shànghǎi (Y2430), Shēnzhèn (Y1630), Guǎngzhōu (Y1790) and Xīshuāngbǎnnà (Y790).

Bus

The main long-distance bus station (客运站; Kèyùnzhàn) is south of the old town; to get there, take bus 8 or 11 (Y1; the latter is faster) from along Minzhu Lu.

Kūnmíng Y170 to Y190, nine to 10 hours, regular services (9am, 10.30am, 11.30am, 2pm, 6.30pm and 9pm); sleeper Y164, nine hours, four daily (7pm, 8pm, 8.30pm and 9pm)

Lúgū Hú Y75, seven to eight hours, two daily (9am and 10am)

Nínglàng Y30, five hours, 14 daily (9am to 3.30pm)

Qiáotóu Y17, two hours, two daily (7.50am and 8.30am)

Xiàguān Y43 to Y69, 3½ hours, every 20 minutes (7am to 6.30pm)

Zhōngdiàn (Shangri-la) Y40, five hours, every 40 minutes (7.30am to 5pm)

In the north of town, the **express bus station** (高快客运站; Gāo Kuài Kèyùnzhàn; Shangrila Dadao) for Kūnmíng has daily departures:

Kūnmíng Y160 to Y170, six daily (8.30am, 10am, 11am, noon, 1.30pm and 8.30pm)

Lúgū Hú (Lúgū Lake) Y72, seven to eight hours, two daily (8.30am and 9.30am)

Zhōngdiàn (Shangri-la) Y61, five hours, four daily (8.30am, 9.30am, 1pm and 2.30pm)

Buses to Xiàguān run from both the long-distance station and the express bus station; the long-distance station has more services, however.

Train

There is one train daily to Dàlǐ at 9.58am (Y15, two hours) and one sleeper to Kūnmíng (Y92, nine hours) at 10.12pm.

Getting Around

Buses to the airport (Y15) leave from outside the CAAC office 90 minutes before flight departures. The long-distance bus station also has buses to the airport (Y7).

Taxis start at Y7 in the new town and are not allowed into the old town. Bike hire is available at most hostels and at N's Kitchen (Y30 per day).

Around Lìjiāng

It is possible to see most of Lìjiāng's environs on your own, but a few agencies offer half- or full-day tours, starting from Y200, plus fees.

There are a number of monasteries around Lìjiāng, all Tibetan in origin and belonging to the Karmapa (Red Hat) sect. Most were extensively damaged during the Cultural Revolution and there's not much monastic activity nowadays.

Jade Peak Monastery (玉峰寺; Yùfēng Sì) is on a hillside about 5km past Báishā. The last 3km of the track requires a steep climb. The monastery sits at the foot of Yùlóng Xuěshān (5500m) and was established in 1756. The monastery's main attraction nowadays is the **Camellia Tree of 10,000 Blossoms** (Wànduǒ Shānchá). Ten thousand might be something of an exaggeration, but locals claim that the tree produces at least 4000 blossoms between February and April. A monk on the grounds risked his life to keep the tree secretly watered during the Cultural Revolution.

Lìjiāng is also famed for its **temple frescoes**, most of which were painted during the 15th and 16th centuries by Tibetan, Naxi, Bai and Han artists; many were restored during the later Qing dynasty. They depict various Taoist, Chinese and Tibetan Buddhist themes and can be found on the interior walls of temples in the area. The Cultural Revolution did lots of ravaging here, keep in mind.

Frescoes can be found in Báishā and on the interior walls of **Dàjué Palace** (Dàjué Gōng) in the village of Lóngquán.

Báishā 白沙

Báishā is a small village on the plain north of Lìjiāng, near several old temples, and is one of the best day trips out of Lìjiāng, especially if you have a bike. Before Kublai Khan made it part of his Yuan empire (1271–1368), Báishā was the capital of the Naxi kingdom.

The 'star' attraction of Báishā is **Dr Ho Shi Xiu,** a legendary herbalist who was propelled to fame by the travel writer Bruce Chatwin when he mythologised him in a 1986 *New Yorker* story as the 'Taoist physician in the Jade Dragon Mountains of Lìjiāng'.

A sprightly 87 at the time of writing and still treating the ill every day with herbs collected from the nearby mountains, Dr Ho is very chatty (he speaks English, German and Japanese) and is happy to regale visitors with great stories about Joseph Rock (whom

Around Lìjiāng

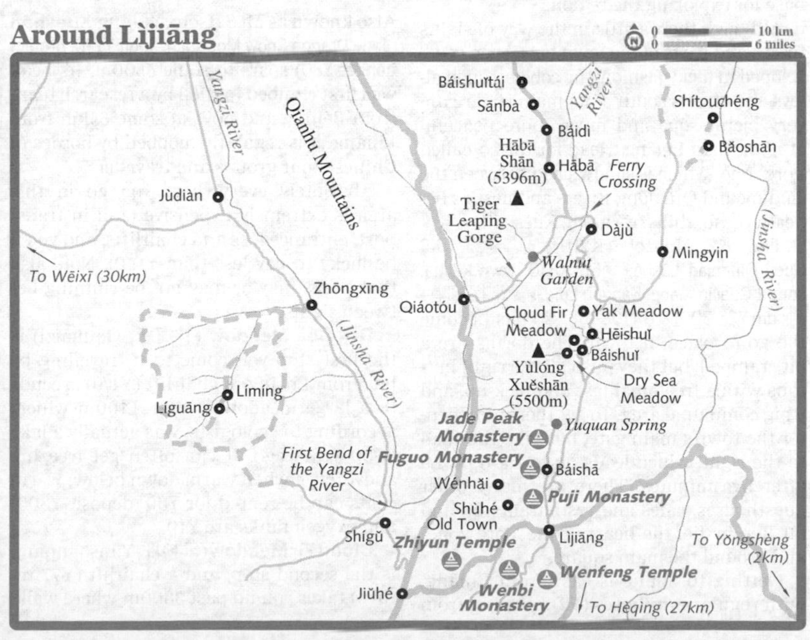

he knew as a young boy), Chatwin and the various other celebrities he has encountered down the years.

Almost directly opposite the clinic of Dr Ho's is **Café Buena Vista** (Nànà Wéisītǎ Jùlèbù; www.ecotourchina.com), a gallery-cum-cafe run by an artist. Café Buena Vista runs eco-tours and is a good place to get travel information.

There are a couple of frescoes worth seeing in town and the surrounding area. The best can be found in Báishā's **Dàbǎojī Palace** (大宝积宫;Dàbǎojī Gōng; admission Y15; ⌚8.30am-5.30pm), and at the neighbouring **Liúlí Temple** (Liúlí Diàn) and **Dàdìng Gé** (大蘸阁).

Báishā is an easy 20- to 30-minute bike ride from Lìjiāng. Otherwise, catch one of the frequent minibuses (Y3) from Shangri-la Dadao, about 500m south of Fuhui Lu. They return to Lìjiāng regularly.

Shùhé Old Town 束河古城

More rustic and tranquil than Lìjiāng, Shùhé Old Town (Shùhé Gǔchéng) is attracting increasing numbers of travellers looking to escape the crowds. A former staging post on the Tea-Horse Road that's just 4km from Lìjiāng, Shùhé can be done as a day trip, or makes a tempting alternative base for exploring the region.

Although there's little in the way of sights to see, and parts of the town have been redeveloped in tacky fashion, the cobblestoned alleys and streets south of its main square are very picturesque and much more peaceful at night than Lìjiāng. Head for the so-called 'core zone', which is sandwiched between the Jiǔdǐng and Qīnglóng Rivers and nestles beneath the foothills of Yùlóng Xuěshān.

The **K2 Hostel** (K2国际青年旅舍; K2 Guójì Qīngnián Lǚshè; ☎513 0110; www.k2yha.com; 1 Guailiu Xiang, Kangpu Lu; 康普路拐柳巷1号; dm Y25-30, s & d Y108-138; @) has become the go-to place in town. The dorms are a bit cramped, but they push all the right buttons with a free breakfast and pick-up, and a big communal area. To get there, don't enter the town's main gate, but take the road to the right, which leads on to Kangpu Lu after five minutes. There are many other guesthouses, cafes and restaurants on and off Renlin Jie, the heart of the 'core zone', and around the main square.

Getting to Shùhé is easy from Lìjiāng, with regular minibuses (Y2) running from the corner of Fuhui Lu and Shangrila Dadao.

At present, there is no admission charge, but that may change.

NAXI SCRIPT

The Naxi created a written language over 1000 years ago using an extraordinary system of pictographs – the only hieroglyphic language still in use. The most famous Naxi text is the Dongba classic *Creation*, and ancient copies of it and other texts can still be found in Lìjiāng, as well as in the archives of some US universities. The Dongba were Naxi shamans who were caretakers of the written language and mediators between the Naxi and the spirit world. The Dongba religion, itself an offshoot of Tibet's pre-Buddhist Bon religion, eventually developed into an amalgam of Tibetan Buddhism, Islam and Taoism.

Useful phrases in the Naxi language are *nuar lala* (hello) and *jiu bai sai* (thank you).

Yùlóng Xuěshān 玉龙雪山

Also known as Mt Satseto, **Yùlóng Xuěshān** (Jade Dragon Snow Mountain; adult Y190, protection fee Y80) soars to some 5500m. Its peak was first climbed in 1963 by a research team from Běijīng and now, at some 35km from Lìjiāng, it is regularly mobbed by hordes of Chinese tour groups and travellers.

Absolutely everywhere you go in this area is extremely expensive (add in transport, entrance fees and chairlifts, and you'll be lucky to pay less than Y450). Note also that buses may or may not be running between sights.

Dry Sea Meadow (甘海子; Gānhǎizi) is the first stop you come to if travelling by bus from Lìjiāng. A chairlift (Y170) ascends to a large meadow at over 4400m which, according to geologists, was actually a lake 2000 years ago. It can often get freezing above, even when warm down below; warm coats can be rented for Y30 (deposit Y300) and oxygen tanks are Y40.

Cloud Fir Meadow (云杉坪; Yúnshānpíng) is the second stop, and a chairlift (Y77 return) takes you up past 3300m where walkways lead to awesome glacier views. Horses can be hired here for Y80.

The views from above are impressive, but make sure you get here well before the first chair up at 8.30am. Unless you get a head start on the tour groups, prepare for up to an hour's wait to get either up or down the mountain.

Around 60km from Lìjiāng, or a 30-minute drive from Dry Sea Meadow, is **Yak Meadow** (牦牛坪; Máoniúpíng), where yet another chairlift (Y80) pulls visitors up to an altitude of 3500m. Here there are ample hiking opportunities near **Xuěhuā Hú** (雪花湖; Snowflake Lake). Crowds and long waits are almost unheard of here.

At the time of research, camping in the area was not prohibited, but it's better to check when you get there as regulations tend to change quicker than the cloud cover.

Minibuses (Y15 to Y20) sometimes leave for all three spots from near the intersection of Minzhu Lu and Fuhui Lu in Lìjiang. Returning to Lìjiāng, buses leave fairly regularly but check with your driver to find out what time the last bus will depart.

Shíbǎoshān 石宝山

About 75km southwest of Lìjiāng (or 110km northwest of Dàlǐ) are the **Stone Treasure Mountain Grottoes** (石宝山石窟; Shíbǎoshān Shíkū; admission Y30; ⏲dawn-dusk). The local tourism bureau loves to tout purported (but anonymous) scholars who compare them favourably with the grottoes of Dūnhuáng, Dàzú and Dàtóng. The most famous temple group, **Stone Bell** (石钟; Shízhōng), includes some of the best Bai stone carvings in southern China and offers insights into life at the Nanzhao court of the 9th century. (And some, er, rather racy sculptures of female genitalia.)

If you need accommodation, **Shíbǎoshān Bīnguǎn** (石宝山宾馆; ☎478 6093; d Y220; ❄) is nothing special. Otherwise, you're looking at extremely basic beds at Bǎoxiàng Sì Temple (宝相寺) halfway up the front of the mountain or Shìzhōng Temple (石钟寺; Shìzhōng Sì) halfway up the mountain's back side. These are often full.

To get here, take a bus to Jiànchuān, then hope for a shuttle van from in front of the bus station taking tourists to the mountain. If there is no shuttle van, take one headed towards Shāxī (Y8, 30 minutes) and get off at the entrance to the mountain, where you have a 2km hike uphill to the main entrance.

If you're coming from Dàlǐ on the old Dàlǐ–Lìjiāng road, you'll have to take a Jiànchuān-bound bus, then get off at the small village of Diānnán, about 8km south of Jiànchuān, where a narrow road branches southwest to the village of Shāxī, 23km away, and then catch a local van.

Shāxī 沙溪

☎0872

Arrive in **Shāxī** (admission Y20) and you enter a wormhole, every step harkening back to the clippety-clop of horses' hooves and shouts of traders.

Shāxī was once a crucial node on one of the old Tea-Horse Roads that stretched from Yúnnán to India. Only three caravan oases remain, Shāxī being the best preserved and the only one with a surviving market (held on Fridays).

The village's wooden houses, courtyards and narrow, winding streets make it a popular location for period Chinese movies and TV shows, but this is still a wonderfully sleepy place where nightlife means sitting out under the canopy of stars and listening to the frogs croaking in the rice paddies.

Sights

Sideng Jie (寺登街) is the ancient town street leading off the main road. The Y20 ticket to the village gets you admission to the multi frescoed **Xìngjiào Sì** (兴教寺; Xìngjiào Temple), the only Ming-dynasty Bai Buddhist temple, as well as the **Three Terraced Pavilion** (三层楼; Sāncénglóu), which has a prominent theatrical **stage** (古戏台; *gǔxìtái*), something of a rarity in rural China. The absolute highlight, however, is the **Ōuyáng Courtyard** (欧阳大院; Ōuyáng Dàyuàn), a superb example of three-in-one Bai folk architecture in which one wall protected three yards/residences (it's now an inn).

Exit the east gate and head south along the Huì River (惠江; Huì Jiāng) for five minutes, cross the ancient **Yùjīn Qiáo** (玉津桥; Yùjīn Bridge), and you're walking the same trail as the horse caravans. (If you look hard enough, you'll still be able to see hoofprints etched into the rock, or so the locals claim.)

Sleeping & Eating

A number of old courtyard homes on and off Sideng Jie have been converted into upmarket inns; there are also places offering beds from Y20.

THE TEA-HORSE ROAD

Less well-known than the Silk Road, but equally important in terms of trade and the movement of ideas, people and religions, the Tea-Horse Road (茶马古道; Chámǎgǔdào) linked southwest China with India via Tibet. A series of caravan routes, rather than a single road, which also went through parts of Sìchuān, Burma, Laos and Nepal, the trails started deep in the jungle of Xīshuāngbǎnnà. They then headed north through Dàlǐ and Lìjiāng and into the thin air of the Himalayan mountains on the way to the Tibetan capital Lhasa, before turning south to India and Burma.

Although archaeological finds indicate that stretches of the different routes were in use thousands of years ago, the road really began life in the Tang dynasty (AD 618–907). An increased appetite for tea in Tibet led to an arrangement with the Chinese imperial court to barter Yúnnán tea for the prized horses ridden by Tibetan warriors. By the Song dynasty (AD 960–1279), 20,000 horses a year were coming down the road to China, while in 1661 alone some 1.5 million kilos of tea headed to Tibet.

Sugar and salt were also carried by the caravans of horses, mules and yaks. Buddhist monks, Christian missionaries and foreign armies utilised the trails as well to move between Burma, India and China. In the 18th century the Chinese stopped trading for Tibetan horses and the road went into a slow decline. Its final glory days came during WWII, when it was a vital conduit for supplies from India for the allied troops fighting the Japanese in China. The advent of peace and the communist takeover of 1949 put an end to the road.

Some of the inns on Sideng Jie operate as cafes and restaurants, or try the hole-in-the-wall places on the village's main road.

Tea and Horse Caravan Trail Inn INN $
(古道客栈; Gǔdào Kèzhàn; ☎472 1051; 83 Sideng Jie; 寺登街83号; s & d without/with bathroom Y40/150, discounts of 30%) The cheap rooms at this friendly place are basic and clean, but the more expensive ones are a significant step up and come with comfy beds and big bathrooms, as well as being set around a pleasant garden area.

Dragonfly GUESTHOUSE $
(☎472 1464; shaxi-travel@hotmail.com; Duànjiādēng Village (段家登); s & d Y150) This small guesthouse 3km north of Shāxī is run by a friendly English teacher. It's popular, so book ahead.

Karma Cafe CAFE $$
(卡玛聚; Kǎ Mǎ Jù; Sideng Jie; dishes from Y12; ⏲8am-10pm) Has decent, and a few expensive Chinese and Tibetan dishes.

Trail Cafe CAFE $
(细语咖啡; Xìyǔ Kāfēi; 47 Sideng Jie; ⏲9am-10pm) The Trail Cafe is a cool spot for a coffee or drink.

Getting There & Away

From Jiànchuān, there are hourly buses (Y8, one hour) to Shāxī, or catch a shared minivan ride that also stops at Shíbǎo Shān.

Tiger Leaping Gorge 虎跳峡

☎0887

Gingerly stepping along a trail swept with scree to allow an old fellow with a donkey to pass; resting atop a rock, exhausted, looking up to see the fading sunlight dance between snow-shrouded peaks, then down to see the lingering rays dancing on the rippling waters a thousand metres away; feeling utterly exhilarated. That pretty much sums up **Tiger Leaping Gorge** (Hǔtiào Xiá; admission Y50), the unmissable trek of southwest China.

One of the deepest gorges in the world, it measures 16km long and is a giddy 3900m from the waters of the Jīnshā River (Jīnshā Jiāng) to the snowcapped mountains of Hābā Shān (Hābā Mountain) to the west and Yùlóng Xuěshān to the east, and, despite the odd danger, it's gorgeous almost every single step of the way.

At the time of writing, extensive roadworks in the area meant that the Y50 admission fee had been suspended. Expect it to rise when the road through the gorge reopens.

The gorge trek is not to be taken lightly. Even for those in good physical shape, it's a workout. The path constricts and crumbles; it certainly can wreck the knees. When it's raining (especially in July and August), landslides and swollen waterfalls can block the paths, in particular on the low road. (The best time to come is May and the start

Tiger Leaping Gorge

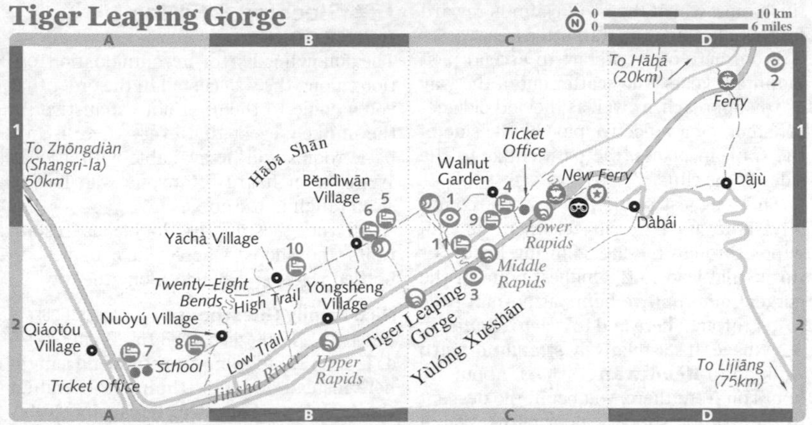

Tiger Leaping Gorge

Sights

1 Bamboo Forest C1
2 Pagoda D1
3 Tiger Leaping Stone C2

Sleeping

4 Chateau de Woody C1
5 Five Fingers Mountain Guesthouse B1
6 Halfway Guesthouse B2
7 Jane's Guesthouse A2
8 Naxi Family Guesthouse A2
9 Sean's Spring Guesthouse C1
10 Tea Horse Guesthouse B2
11 Tina's Guesthouse C2

of June, when the hills are afire with plant and flower life.)

A few people – including a handful of foreign travellers – have died in the gorge. Over the last decade, there have also been cases of travellers being assaulted on the trail. As always, it's safer in all ways not to do the trek alone.

Check with cafes and lodgings in Lìjiāng or Qiáotóu for trail and weather updates. Most have fairly detailed gorge maps; just remember they're not to scale and occasionally out of date.

Make sure you bring plenty of water on this hike – 2L to 3L is ideal – as well as plenty of sunscreen and lip balm.

Activities

There are two trails: the higher (the older route) and the lower, which follows the new road and is best avoided, unless you enjoy being enveloped in clouds of dust from passing tour buses and 4WDs. While the scenery is stunning wherever you are in the gorge, it's absolutely sublime from the high trail. Make sure you don't get too distracted by all that beauty, though, and so miss the arrows that help you avoid getting lost on the trail.

It's six hours to Běndìwān or a strenuous eight hours to Walnut Garden. It's much more fun, and a lot less exhausting, to do the trek over two days. By stopping overnight at one of the many guesthouses along the way, you'll have the time to appreciate the magnificent vistas on offer at almost every turn of the trail.

Ponies can be hired (their owners will find you) to take you to the gorge's highest point for between Y100 and Y150; it's not uncommon to see three generations of a family together, with the oldies on horseback and the young ones panting on foot behind them.

The following route starts at **Jane's Guesthouse**. Walk away from **Qiáotóu** (桥头), past the school, for five minutes or so, then head up the paved road branching to the left; there's an arrow to guide you. After about 2.5km on the road, you'll reach the **Sunrise Guesthouse**. It's here that the gorge trail proper starts and the serious climbing begins. Note that locals may try and hit you up for an additional 'fee' at this point, which they will claim is reward for them keeping the trail litter-free.

From here on, you start to ascend past mountain goats who scatter out of the way as you approach, as well as the odd old geezer smoking a reflective pipe by the side of the trail. In places, the path clings to the sides of the cliffs.

The toughest section of the trek comes after **Nuòyú** (诺余) village, when the trail winds through the 28 agonising bends, or turns, that lead to the highest point of the gorge. Count on five hours at normal pace to get through here and to reach **Yāchà** (牙叉) village. It's a relatively straightforward walk on to **Běndìwān** (本地湾). About 1½ hours on from there, you begin the descent to the road on slippery, poor paths. Watch your step here; if you twist an ankle, it's a long hop down.

After the path meets the road at **Tina's Guesthouse**, there's a good detour that leads down 40 minutes to the middle rapids and **Tiger Leaping Stone**, where a tiger is once said to have leapt across the Yangzi, thus giving the gorge its name.

From Tina's to **Walnut Garden** (核桃园), it is a further 40-minute walk along the road. A new alternative trail to Walnut Garden keeps high where the path descends to Tina's, crosses a stream and a 'bamboo forest' before descending into Walnut Garden.

The next day's walk is shorter at four to six hours. There are two ferries and so two route options to get to **Dàjù** (大具). After 45 minutes you'll see a red marker leading down to the new (winter) ferry (*xīn dùkǒu;* one way Y20); the descent includes one hairy section with a sheer drop.

Many trekkers call it a day when they reach the bottom and flag down anything heading back Qiáotóu. The road to Dàjù and the village itself is pretty uninteresting. If you do decide to go on, it's a hard climb to the car park, where you may have to register with the PSB (Gōng'ānjú).

The second, lesser-used option continues along the road from Walnut Garden until it reaches the permanent ferry crossing (Y20). From here paths lead to Dàjù, where there are two buses a day back to Lìjiāng (Y40, three hours, 7.30am and 1.30pm).

If you're doing the walk the other way round and heading for Qiáotóu, walk north through Dàjù, aiming for the white pagoda at the foot of the mountains.

Sleeping & Eating

IN THE GORGE

The following list of accommodation options along the way (listed in the order that you'll come to them) is not exhaustive. In the unlikely event that everywhere is full, basic rooms will be available with a local. We've never heard of anyone who had to sleep rough in the gorge.

All the guesthouses double as restaurants and shops, where you can pick up bottled water and snacks along the way.

Naxi Family Guesthouse GUESTHOUSE $
(纳西雅阁; Nàxī Kèzhàn; ☎880 6928; dm Y20, s & d Y120; @) Taking your time to spend a night here instead of double-timing it to Walnut Garden isn't a bad idea. It's an incredibly friendly, well-run place (organic veggies and wines, and the only internet access in the gorge), set around a pleasant courtyard.

Tea Horse Guesthouse GUESTHOUSE $
(茶马客栈; Chámǎ Kèzhàn; ☎139 8871 7292; dm Y20, s & d Y120) Just after Yāchà village, this bigger place has a great 'Naxi mama' running things, and even has a small spa and massage parlour where aching limbs can be eased.

Halfway Guesthouse GUESTHOUSE $
(中途客栈; Zhōngtú Kèzhàn, Běndìwān; ☎139 8870 0522; dm Y20, s & d Y120-150) Once a simple home to a guy collecting medicinal herbs and his family, this is now a busy-busy operation. The vistas here are awe inspiring and perhaps the best of any lodging in the gorge; the view from the communal toilets is worth the price of a bed alone.

Five Fingers Mountain Guesthouse GUESTHOUSE $
(五指客栈; Wǔzhǐ Kèzhàn; ☎139 8877 6286; dm/s Y25/50) An endearingly rustic place, where chickens run around and you're part of the family during your stay. The 200m climb up from the road to get here is a killer after five hours of walking, though.

Tina's Guesthouse GUESTHOUSE $
(中峡旅店; Zhōngxiá Lǚdiàn; ☎820 2258; tina999@live.cn; dm Y25, s & d Y60-280). It's a bit concrete-blocky and lacks the charm of other places on the mountain, but there are lots of beds and the location is perfect for those too knackered to make it to Walnut Garden.

Sean's Spring Guesthouse GUESTHOUSE $
(山泉客栈; Shānquán Kèzhàn; ☎820 2223; www.tigerleapinggorge.com; dm Y25, s & d Y60-200) One of the original guesthouses on the trail,

and still the spot for lively evenings and socialising. It's run by the eponymous Sean, a true character. Recently refurbished, the best rooms have great views of Yùlóng Xuěshān.

Chateau de Woody GUESTHOUSE **$**
(山白脸旅馆; Shānbáiliǎn Lǚguǎn; ☎139 8871 2705; s & d Y60) Another old-school gorge guesthouse, the rooms here all have views and bathrooms and are a very good deal. Across the road, the less-attractive modern extension has rooms for the same price.

QIÁOTÓU

Jane's Guesthouse GUESTHOUSE **$**
(峡谷行客栈; Xiágǔ Xíng Kèzhàn; ☎880 6570; dm Y20, s & d Y50-80; @) This two-storey place with tidy, clean rooms is where many people start their trek. The breakfasts here make for good walking fuel and it has left-luggage facilities (Y5 a bag).

Getting There & Away

From the Lìjiāng long-distance bus station, buses run to Zhōngdiàn (Shangri-la) every 40 minutes (7.30am to 5pm) and pass through Qiáotóu (Y21).

Returning to Lìjiāng from Qiáotóu, buses start running through from Zhōngdiàn (Shangri-la) at around 10am. The last one rolls through at around 7.40pm (Y20). The last bus to Zhōngdiàn (Shangri-la) passes through at around 7pm.

At the time of writing, there were no buses to Báishuǐtái from Lìjiāng. There is one bus a day from Zhōngdiàn (Shangri-la) to Báishuǐtái (Y25, three hours, 9.10am).

Eventually, new road building will result in paved roads connecting Qiáotóu, Walnut Garden and the settlement across the river from Dàjù, then north to connect Báishuǐtái and Zhōngdiàn (Shangri-la).

Tiger Leaping Gorge to Báishuǐtái

An adventurous add-on to the gorge trek is to continue north all the way to Hābā (哈巴) village and the limestone terraces of Báishuǐtái (白水台). This turns it into a four-day trek from Qiáotóu and from here you can travel on to Zhōngdiàn (Shangri-la). From Walnut Garden to Hābā, via Jiāngbiān (江边), is seven to eight hours. From here to the Yi village of Sānbà (三坝) is about the same, following trails. You could just follow the road and hitch with the occasional truck or tractor, but it's longer and less scenic. Some hardy mountain bikers have followed the trail. This is really only fun from north to south, elevations being what they are. The best way would be to hire a guide in Walnut Garden for around Y100 per day, depending on the number of people. For Y150 per day you should be able to get a horse and guide.

In Hābā most people stay at the **Hābā Snow Mountain Inn** (哈巴雪山客栈; Hābā Xuěshān Kèzhàn; ☎0887 886 6596; beds Y30; @). In Sānbà, beds can also be found for around Y25. From Sānbà there is an 8am bus to Zhōngdiàn (Shangri-la; Y40, five hours), or you could get off at the turn-off to Bìtǎ Hǎi (Emerald Pagoda Lake) and hike there.

If you plan to try the route alone, assume you'll need all provisions and equipment for extremes of weather. Ask for local advice before setting out.

Lúgū Hú 泸沽湖

☎0888

Straddling the remote Yúnnán-Sìchuān border, this **lake** (admission Y78) remains a laid-back, idyllic place that makes for a great getaway, even if it is more popular than it once was, especially with Chinese travellers. The ascent to the lake, which sits at 2690m, is via a spectacular switchback road and the first sight of the 50 sq km body of water, surrounded by lushly forested slopes, will take your breath away.

Villages are scattered around the outskirts of the lake, with **Luòshuǐ** (洛水) the biggest and most developed, and the one where the bus will drop you. As well as guesthouses, and a few cafes with English menus and Western food, there are the inevitable souvenir shops. Nevertheless, it's hardly a boomtown, with the dominant night-time sound being the lapping of the lake.

Most travellers move quickly to **Lǐgé** (里格), a much smaller village on the northwestern shore of the lake. Although guesthouses make up most of the place, along with restaurants serving succulent, but pricey, barbecue, the sights and nights here are lovely. If you want a less touristy experience, then you need to keep village-hopping around the lake to the Sìchuān side. At the moment, top votes for alternative locations are **Luòwǎ** (洛瓦) and **Wǔzhīluó** (五支罗).

The area is home to several Tibetan, Yi and Mosu (a Naxi subgroup) villages. The Mosu are the last practising matriarchal society in the world and many other Naxi customs lost in Lìjiāng are still in evidence here.

The best times to visit the lake are April to May, and September to October, when the weather is dry and mild. It's usually snowbound during the winter months.

Sights & Activities

From Luòshuǐ and Lǐgé you can punt about with local Mosu by dugout canoe – known by the Mosu as 'pig troughs' *(zhūcáo)*. Expect to head for **Lǐwùbǐ Dǎo** (里务比岛), the largest island (and throw a stone into Sìchuān). The second-largest island is **Hēiwǎé Dǎo** (黑瓦俄岛). Boat-trip prices vary wildly. If you're in a group of six to eight people, it's around Y30 per person.

FREE **Mosu Folk Custom Museum** MUSEUM
(摩俗民族博物馆; Mósú Mínzú Bówùguǎn; Luòshuǐ; ⏲9am-8pm) This museum in Luòshuǐ is set within the traditional home of a wealthy Mosu family, and the obligatory guide will show you around and explain how the matriarchal society functions. There is also an interesting collection of photos taken by Joseph Rock in the 1920s.

Zhāměi Temple MONASTERY
(扎美寺; Zhāměi Sì) On the outskirts of Yǒngníng, this is a Tibetan monastery with at least 20 lamas in residence. Admission is free, but a donation is expected. A private minivan costs Y10 per person for the half-hour ride, or you could opt to walk the 20km or so through pleasant scenery.

Sleeping & Eating

Hotels and guesthouses line the lakeside in Luòshuǐ and Lǐgé, with doubles from around Y50. Most have attached restaurants that serve traditional Mosu foods, including preserved pig's fat and salted sour fish – the latter being somewhat tastier than the former.

Yǎsé Dába Lǚxíngzhě Zhījiā HOTEL $
(雅瑟达吧旅行者之家; ☎588 1196; Lǐgé; s & d Y80-180; @) All the rooms at this Lǐgé retreat come with decent views, but the ones on the 2nd floor are tremendous. In the restaurant, try Lúgū Hú fish (泸沽湖鱼; *lúgū hú yú*) or sausage (香肠; *xiāngcháng*).

Ākè Dàjiǔdiàn HOTEL $
(阿客大酒店; ☎588 1167; Luòshuǐ; s & d without/with bathroom Y30/50; 📶) In Luòshuǐ and run by a friendly Mosu lady who can cook local dishes for you and arrange visits to traditional homes, the Ake has big, well-kept rooms and is just a few metres from the lake itself.

Húsī Teahouse YOUTH HOSTEL $
(湖思茶屋; Húsī Cháwū; ☎588 1170; www.husihostel.com; Luòshuǐ; dm Y30, s & d Y120-150; @) The granddaddy of all Lúgū Hú backpacker joints, this place in Luòshuǐ is functional (no private bathrooms) but clean and friendly. Some of the rooms come with floor-to-ceiling windows overlooking the lake.

Lao Shay Youth Hostel YOUTH HOSTEL $
(老谢车马店; Lǎoxiè Chēmǎdiàn; ☎588 1555; www.laoshay.com; Lǐgé; dm Y25, s, d & tr Y50-180; @) The staff here aren't the most helpful, but it's smack in the middle of Lǐgé, the best rooms have lake views and you can rent a bike for Y30 a day.

Getting There & Away

Lìjiāng's long-distance bus station has two direct buses a day to the lake (Y72, seven to eight hours, 9am and 10am) but buy your ticket at least one day in advance as it's often sold out. (The express bus station also has two buses a day at 8.30am and 9.30am for the same price.)

Alternatively, you can go to Nínglàng (宁蒗; Y30, four hours, 13 buses daily, 8am to 3.30pm), from where there's a daily bus to the lake (Y30, three to four hours, 12.30pm). For Lǐgé you'll have to change for a minibus in Luòshuǐ (Y15 per person).

Leaving Luòshuǐ, the direct buses to Lìjiāng leave daily at 10am, noon and 3.30pm. Again, tickets should be bought at least a day in advance. There are also two buses to Nínglàng at 10am and noon. From Nínglàng, there are plenty of buses to Lìjiāng and at least one a day to Xiàguān.

To Sìchuān, there's a daily bus to Xīchàng (西昌; Y95, seven to eight hours, 2pm), although it wasn't running at the time of writing due to road repairs.

Zhōngdiàn (Shangri-la) 中甸(香格里拉)

☎0887 / POP 120,000 / ELEV 3200M

Zhōngdiàn, which is now better known as Shangri-la (and also has the Tibetan name Gyalthang), is where you begin to breathe in the Tibetan world. That's if you can breathe at all, given its altitude.

Home to one of Yúnnán's most rewarding monasteries, Zhōngdiàn is also the last stop in Yúnnán for a rough five- or six-day journey to Chéngdū via the Tibetan townships and rugged terrain of western Sìchuān.

How times change. A mere decade ago, Zhōngdiàn was just a one-yak town. Pigs nibbled on garbage-strewn street corners; there was but one place to stay and pretty much nowhere to eat. Then, watching Lìjiāng and

Zhōngdiàn (Shangri-la)

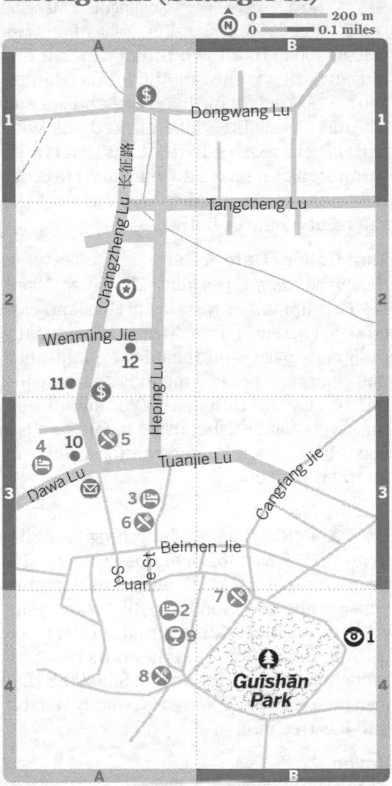

Zhōngdiàn (Shangri-la)

Top Sights
Guīshān Park....B4

Sights
1 Scripture Chamber....B4

Sleeping
2 Cobbler's Hill Inn....A4
3 Dragoncloud Guesthouse....A3
4 Kevin's Trekker Inn....A3

Eating
5 Noah Café....A3
6 N's Kitchen....A3
7 Silent Holy Stones....B4
8 Tara Gallery Café & Bar....A4

Drinking
9 Raven....A4

Information
CD Burning....(see 5)
Haiwei Trails....(see 9)
10 Khampa Caravan....A3
11 Kodak....A2

Transport
12 CAAC....A2

Dàli zoom into the tourism stratosphere, local and provincial officials declared the town/county the location of British writer James Hilton's fictional Shangri-la, described in his novel *The Lost Horizon*.

The result was a big jump in visitors, and the numbers are increasing all the time, as well as a building boom that continues to this day. But while the old town is doing its best to mimic Lìjiāng in its profusion of clothes and jewellery shops, Zhōngdiàn remains far less frenetic and an easy place to kick back for a few days.

Plan your visit for between March and October. During winter the city practically shuts down and transportation is often halted completely by snow storms.

In mid- to late June, the town hosts a horse-racing festival that sees several days of dancing, singing, eating and, of course, horse racing. Accommodation is tight at this time.

Sights

Zhōngdiàn is a wonderful place for getting off the beaten track, with plenty of trekking and horse-riding opportunities, as well as little-visited monasteries and villages. However, the remote sights are difficult to do independently given the lack of public transport.

Ganden Sumtseling Gompa MONASTERY
(松赞林寺; Sōngzànlín Si; admission Y85; ⏲7am-7pm) About an hour's walk north of town is this 300-year-old Tibetan monastery complex with around 600 monks. Extensive rebuilding (and a 150% jump in the ticket price in the last two years alone) has robbed the monastery of some of its charm, but it remains the most important in southwest China and is definitely worth the visit. Bus 3 runs here from anywhere along Changzheng Lu (Y1). You can sometimes avoid paying by coming after 5pm.

Old Town HISTORIC AREA
After checking out the monastery, everyone just wanders about the old town, specifically **Square Street** (Sifang Jie); from this branches a spider web of cobbled lanes and renovated buildings (some say tacky, others

say cool). You'll also see white stupas everywhere. Hidden within the old town is the **Scripture Chamber** (古城藏经堂; Gǔchéng Cángjīng Táng), a reconstructed temple that was previously used as a memorial to the Red Army. **Guīshān Park** (Guīshān Gōngyuán) is also nearby and has a temple at the top with some commanding views of the area.

Bǎijī Sì BUDDHIST TEMPLE
(百鸡寺; 100 Chickens Temple) For even better views, head to this delightfully named and little-visited temple. To get there, walk along Dawa Lu past Kevin's Trekker Inn and turn left at the big white stupa.

Just south of town and also overlooking the old town district is another monastery.

Sleeping

Despite Zhōngdiàn's often glacial night temperatures, many guesthouses are neither heated nor have 24-hour hot water. Most dorms in town are fairly basic too.

TOP CHOICE **Kevin's Trekker Inn** GUESTHOUSE $
(龙门客栈; Lóngmén Kèzhàn; ☎822 8178; www.kevintrekkerinn.com; 138 Dawa Lu; 达娃路138号; dm/tr Y25/120, d Y80-150; @) Kevin, a Yunnanese Bai, and his wife are charming, endlessly helpful and a fantastic source of local knowledge. Their guesthouse is cosy and comfortable, and the new roof terrace with views over the old town is a great addition. Book ahead, or miss out.

Dragoncloud Guesthouse GUESTHOUSE $
(龙行客栈; Lóngxíng Kèzhàn; ☎828 9250; www.dragoncloud.cn; 94 Beimen Jie, Jiantang Zhen; 建塘镇北门街94号; dm/s/d Y30/80/120; @) Set around a courtyard, the dorms here are spacious, if rudimentary, while the standard rooms come with modern bathrooms. During bouts of chill, you'll love the fireplace in the common area, which also has a pool table.

Cobbler's Hill Inn INN $
(皮匠坡老客栈; Píjiàngpō Lǎokèzhàn; ☎828 9894; www.sozhen.com; 7 Dianlaka Jie; 甸腊卡7号; s & d Y80-120) A three-plus-century-old building houses this creaky but charming inn with obliging owners. Check out a variety of rooms – dark but relaxing – the priciest of which sport some grand vistas and funky antique beds.

Eating & Drinking

There are dozens of places to eat offering Tibetan, Indian, Western and Chinese food.

TOP CHOICE **Silent Holy Stones** TIBETAN $
(静静的嘛呢石; Jìngjìngde Mānīshí; ☎152 8455 6908; 1 Zuobarui; dishes from Y16; ⏲10am-10pm) In a town full of Tibetan restaurants, this is the one the locals head to. With a real neighbourhood feel and a menu of Amdo specialities like minced yak with *tsampa* (the roasted barley flour that is a Tibetan staple), it's a treat. You'll need to order the whole goat in advance, otherwise try the yak meat momo or hotpot.

Tara Gallery Café & Bar TIBETAN $$
(No 29 Old Town; dishes from Y28; ⏲10am-10pm; @) This upmarket restaurant, bar and cafe (and art gallery) is a lovely, thoughtfully designed space, and includes a plant-filled 2nd-floor terrace. The menu is a tantalising mix of Tibetan, Indian and Yúnnán dishes; the seven-course Tibetan set meal (Y80) is a feast. It's also a relaxing spot for a coffee or an evening drink.

Noah Café WESTERN $
(挪亚咖啡; Nuóyà Kāfēi; Changzheng Lu; dishes from Y22; ⏲8am-10.30pm Tue-Sun; wi-fi) It's been around for a spell now, but Noah's has consistently good food, mostly Western but with some Chinese dishes, and good service, as well as wi-fi for Y4 an hour. Its sister establishment **N's Kitchen** (☎688 6500; 33 Beimen Jie; ⏲8am-10.30pm; wi-fi) is equally reliable and has free wi-fi.

Raven BAR
(乌鸦酒吧; Wūyā Jiǔbā; 19 Beimen Jie; ⏲10.30am-late) Owned by a Londoner, and with the comfy feel of a local boozer, this is the one place in Zhōngdiàn where you'll find English beers (along with decent coffee and proper English tea). Lounge on the sofas downstairs, or hit the pool table on the 2nd floor.

Information

Altitude sickness is a real problem here and most travellers need at least a couple of days to acclimatise. Brutal winter weather can bring the town to a complete standstill, so try to plan your visit for between March and October.

There are no internet cafes in the old town, but all hostels and hotels and most cafes have some sort of web access.

Agricultural Bank of China (中国农业银行; Zhōngguó Nóngyè Yínháng; cnr Changzheng Lu & Xiangyang Lu; ⏲8.30am-noon & 2.30-5.30pm Mon-Fri) Offers all services, but some travellers have reported difficulty using anything but cash. You can also try the ICBC ATM just north of Noah Café.

SHANGRI-LA – FACT & FICTION

At first it seemed like a typically overstated tourist campaign: 'Shangri-la Found'. Only they weren't kidding. In November 1997 'experts' had established with 'certainty' that the fabled 'Shangri-la' of James Hilton's 1933 bestseller *Lost Horizon* was, indeed, in Déqīn County.

Hilton's novel (later filmed by Frank Capra and starring Ronald Coleman, Jane Wyatt and John Gielgud) tells the story of four travellers who are hijacked and crash-land in a mountain utopia ruled by a 163-year-old holy man. This 'Shangri-la' is in the Valley of the Blue Moon, a beautiful fertile valley capped by a perfect pyramid peak, Mt Karakul. According to Hilton's book, Shangri-la is reached by travelling 'southwest from Peking for many months', and is found 'a few hundred kilometres from a world's end market town...where Chinese coolies from Yúnnán transfer their loads of tea to the Tibetans'.

The claim is based primarily on the fact that Déqīn's Kawa Karpo peak perfectly resembles the 'pyramid-shaped' landmark of Mt Karakul. Also, the county's blood-red valleys with three parallel rivers fit a valley from *Lost Horizon*.

One plausible theory is that Hilton, writing the novel in northwest London, based his descriptions of Shangri-la on articles by Joseph Rock that he had read in *National Geographic* magazine, detailing Rock's expeditions to remote parts of Lìjiāng, Mùlǐ and Déqīn. Others believe that Hilton's 'Shangri-la' may just have been a corruption of the word *Shambhala*, a mystical Buddhist paradise.

Tourism authorities wasted little time latching onto the Shangri-la phenomenon and today there are Shangri La hotels, travel agencies and a Shangri-la airport. Sensing that 'there's money in them thar Shangri-la hills', rival bids popped up around Yúnnán. Cízhōng in Wēxī County pointed out that its Catholic churches and Tibetan monasteries live side by side in the valley. One local was even told that she was the blood relative of one of the (fictional) characters! Meanwhile, Dàochéng, just over the border in Sìchuān, had a strong bid based around the pyramid peak of its mountain Channa Dorje and the fact that Rock wrote about the region in several articles. Then there's the town of Xiónggǔ, a Naxi village 40km from near Lìjiāng, which boasts a stone tablet from the Qing dynasty, naming the town 'Xianggeli', from where the name Shangri-la is derived.

Cynics have had a field day with this and the resulting hijacking of the concept, part of which was to establish tourism to replace logging, which had been banned.

Shangri-la is at its heart surely a metaphor. As a skinny-dipping Jane Wyatt says in the film version of the book: 'I'm sure there's a wish for Shangri-la in everyone's heart...'

Kodak (柯达; Kēdá; crn Changzheng Lu & Rongba Lu; per CD Y15; ⏲8am-11pm) CD burning. Noah's Cafe will also do this.

Haiwei Trails (www.haiweitrails.com; Raven, Beimen Jie) Foreign-run, it has a good philosophy towards local sustainable tourism, with over a decade of experience.

Khampa Caravan (康巴商道探险旅行社; Kāngbā Shāngdào Tànxiǎn Lǚxíngshè; www.khampacaravan.com; 2nd flr, cnr Dawa Lu & Changzheng Lu; ⏲9am-noon & 2-5.30pm Mon-Fri, 9am-noon Sat) Tibetan-run, this well-established outfit organises some excellent short or longer adventures that get good feedback and specialises in arranging travel into Tibet. The company also runs a lot of sustainable development programs within Tibetan communities. See www.shangrilaassociation.org for more details.

Public Security Bureau (PSB; 公安局; Gōng'ānjú; Changzheng Lu; ⏲8.30am-12.30pm & 2.30-5pm) Will extend visas.

Getting There & Away

Air

There are up to four flights daily to Kūnmíng (Y1000) and a daily flight to Lhasa in peak season. Flights for other domestic destinations also leave from the airport but are completely irregular and destinations change from week to week. You can enquire about your destination or buy tickets at **CAAC** (中国民航; Zhōngguó Mínháng;Wenming Jie).

The airport is 5km from town and is sometimes referred to as Díqìng or Deqen – there is currently no airport at Déqīn. Don't expect to see any taxis here; you'll be lucky if there's a shuttle bus. If the shuttle bus isn't there you'll have to negotiate with drivers or call your accommodation to try and arrange transport.

Bus

Destinations from Zhōngdiàn (Shangri-la):

Bǎishuǐtái Y25, three hours, one daily (9.10am)

Déqīn Y46, six to seven hours, four daily (7.20am to noon)

Dōngwàng Y49, seven to eight hours, one daily (7.30am)

Kūnmíng Y213, 11 hours, four daily (9am to 8pm)

Lìjiāng Y40, 4½ hours, hourly (8am to 5.40pm)

Xiàguān Y65, seven hours, every 30 minutes (7am to 12.30pm, then 7.30pm and 8pm)

Xiāngchéng Y75, eight hours, one daily (7.30am)

For Bēnzǐlán you can catch the Déqīn bus, which passes through Bēnzǐlán on the way.

If you're up for the bus-hopping trek to Chéngdū, in Sìchuān, you're looking at a minimum of five to six days' travel at some very high altitudes – you'll need warm clothes. The first stage of the trip is to Xiāngchéng in Sìchuān. From Xiāngchéng, your next destination is Lǐtáng, though if roads are bad you may be forced to stay overnight in Dàochéng. From Lǐtáng, it's on to Kāngdìng, from where you can make your way west towards Chéngdū.

Note that roads out of Zhōngdiàn can be temporarily blocked by snow at any time from November to March. Bring lots of warm clothes and a flexible itinerary.

Around Zhōngdiàn

The following is but a thumbnail sketch; many other sights – mountains, meadows, ponds, *chörtens* (Tibetan stupas) etc – await your exploration; just note that virtually everything either has or will have a pricey admission fee (those pesky chairlifts, especially).

Some 7km northwest of town you'll find the seasonal **Nàpà Hǎi** (纳帕海; Nàpà Lake; admission Y30), surrounded by a large grassy meadow. Between September and March there's myriad rare species, including the black-necked crane. Outside of these months, the lake dries up and there is little reason to visit.

Approximately 10km southeast of Zhōngdiàn (Shangri-la) is the **Tiānshēng Bridge** (天生桥; Tiānshēng Qiáo; admission Y15, hot springs Y85; ⏲9am-6pm Apr-Oct), a natural limestone formation, and, further southeast, the subterranean **Xiàgěi Hot Springs** (下给温泉; Xiàgěi Wēnquán; admission free, hot springs Y80; ⏲9am-late); for both places, ask at your accommodation for off-season hours. If you can arrange transport, en route is the **Great Treasure Temple** (大宝寺; Dàbǎo Sì), one of the earliest Buddhist temples in Yúnnán.

The above sites are wildly popular with Chinese tour groups, but many foreign travellers seem underwhelmed.

EMERALD PAGODA LAKE & SHǓDŪ HǍI 碧塔海、属都海

Some 25km east of Zhōngdiàn (Shangri-la), the bus to Sānbà can drop you along the highway for **Emerald Pagoda Lake** (Bìtǎ Hǎi; admission Y190), which is also known as Pǔdácuò (普达错), a Mandarinised-version of its Tibetan name. The lake is 8km down a trail (a half-hour by pony), and while the ticket price is laughably steep, there are other trails to the lake. A bike is useful for finding them; taxis will drop you at the ticket office.

Pony trips can be arranged at the lake. An intriguing sight in summer is the comatose fish that float unconscious for several minutes in the lake after feasting on azalea petals.

The whopping entrance fee is also due to the inclusion of **Shǔdū Hǎi**, another lake approximately 10km to the north. The name means 'Place Where Milk is Found' in Tibetan because its pastures are reputedly the most fertile in northwestern Yúnnán.

Getting to the lake(s) is tricky. You usually have to catch the bus to Sānbà, get off at the turn-off and hitch. Getting back you can wait (sometimes interminably) for a bus or hike to one of the entrances or main road and look out for taxis – but there may be none. A taxi will cost around Y200 for the return trip, including Shǔdū Hǎi.

BÁISHUǏTÁI 白水台

Báishuǐtái is a limestone deposit plateau 108km southeast of Zhōngdiàn (Shangri-la), with some breathtaking scenery and Tibetan villages en route. For good reason it has become probably the most popular backdoor route between Lìjiāng and Zhōngdiàn (Shangri-la). The **terraces** (admission Y30) – think of those in Pamukkale in Turkey or Huánglóng in Sìchuān – are lovely, but can be tough to access if rainfall has made trails slippery.

A couple of guesthouses at the nearby towns of Báidì and Sānbà have rooms with beds from Y30 to Y40.

GETTING TO TIBET

At the time of writing, it was not possible to travel overland to Tibet. That may well have changed by the time you read this. If it hasn't and you're tempted to try and sneak in, then think again. There were at least 11 checkpoints operating on the road between Zhōngdiàn (Shangri-la) and Lhasa in 2010; you will be caught, fined, detained and possibly deported.

It is possible to fly to Lhasa from Zhōngdiàn, but flights are cheaper from elsewhere (Kūnmíng and Chéngdū), and you'll need to be part of an organised group with all the necessary permits. By far the best people to talk to about Tibet travel in Zhōngdiàn are **Khampa Caravan** (康巴商道探险旅行社; Kāngbā Shāngdào Tànxiǎn Lǚxíngshè; ☎828 8648; www.khampacaravan.com).

In Kūnmíng, **Mr Chen's Tour** (陈先生旅游; Chénxiānshēng Lǚyóu; ☎316 6105; Room 105, Camellia Hotel, 154 Dongfeng Lu) has been organising Tibet travel for years, although some travellers report that his sales pitch is better than his trips.

From Zhojngdian there is a daily bus to Báishuǐtái at 9.10am (Y25). One adventurous option is to trek or hitch all the way from Báishuǐtái to Tiger Leaping Gorge.

BĒNZǏLÁN 奔子栏

Roughly halfway to Bēnzǐlán, and where the highway intersects with the road to Wēixī, consider hopping off in **Nǐxī** (尼西), famed for its pottery. Indeed, some three-quarters of the village's 100-plus families still make the 3km trek to and from local hills, where the clay is said to be sublime.

Benzilán makes an excellent base to explore the wonderful **Dhondrupling Gompa** (东竹林寺; Dōngzhúlín Sì), 22km from Bēnzilán, heading northwest along the main road.

Bēnzǐlán has plenty of restaurants and small hotels. All offer decent beds from Y30. **Duōwén Lǚguǎn** (bed Y30), around the bend in the northern end of town, is perhaps the best choice. This Tibetan-style place has a prayer wheel by the entrance and pleasant rooms.

To Bēnzǐlán, there is one bus a day at 2pm (Y20). Alternatively, take any bus between Zhōngdiàn (Shangri-la) and Déqīn.

Déqīn 德钦

☎0887 / POP 60,100 / ELEV 3550M

Mellifluously named Déqīn (that last syllable seems to ring, doesn't it?) lies in some of the most ruggedly gorgeous scenery in China. Snuggly cloud-high at an average altitude of 3550m, it rests in the near embrace of one of China's most magical mountains, **Kawa Karpo** (梅里雪山; often referred to as Méilǐ Xuěshān). At 6740m, it is Yúnnán's highest peak and straddles the Yúnnán-Tibet border.

A true border town, Déqīn is one of Yúnnán's last-outpost-before-Tibet entries, but from here you could also practically hike east to Sìchuān or southwest to Myanmar (Burma). Díqìng Prefecture was so isolated that it was never really controlled by anyone until the PLA (People's Liberation Army) arrived in force in 1957.

More than 80% of locals are Tibetan, though a dozen other minorities also live here, including one of the few settlements of non-Hui Muslims in China. The town, though, is seriously unattractive – you've come here for the environs, remember!

If you are travelling in winter, remember you are crossing some serious ranges – three times over 5000m – and at any time from mid-October to late spring, heavy snows can close the roads. Pack sensibly and plan for a snowbound emergency.

Confusingly, Déqīn is the name of the city and county; both are incorporated by the Díqìng Tibetan Autonomous Prefecture (迪庆藏族自治州). The county seat (and destination of the bus from Zhōngdiàn) is spelled both ways, but you'll also see other variations on signs, maps, whatever. Plus, remember well – as if you could forget – that Déqīn County is also referred to as 'Shangri-la' in an effort to keep tourist dollars flowing up from the other Shangri-la (the erstwhile Zhōngdiàn).

Most people make immediate tracks for Fēilái Sì. If you do have to plunk down in the town for the night, head south some 200m from the bus station to **Déqīn Tibet Hotel** (德钦楼; ☎841 2031; Déqīn Lóu; dm/d Y30/100), the best cheap place in town. It's basic but decently maintained, with some nice views from its rooftop.

From Zhōngdiàn (Shangri-la), buses leave four times daily for Déqīn between 7.20am and noon (Y46, four hours). They return from Déqīn on a similar schedule.

Around Déqīn

The Gelukpa (Yellow Hat) sect **Déqīn Gompa** (德钦寺) is 3km south of Déqīn. The young monks are friendly but there's not a lot to see.

FĒILÁI SÌ 飞来寺

Approximately 10km southwest of Déqīn is the small but interesting Tibetan **Fēilái Temple** (Fēilái Sì), or Naka Zhashi (or Trashi) Gompa in Tibetan, devoted to the spirit of Kawa Karpo. There's no charge but leave a donation. No photos are allowed inside the tiny hall.

Everyone comes here for the sublime views – particularly the sunrises – of the Méilǐ Xuěshān range, including 6740m-high Kawa Karpo (also known as Méilǐ Xuěshān or Tàizi Shān) and the even more beautiful peak to the south, 6054m-high **Miacimu** (神女; Shénnǚ in Chinese), whose spirit is the female counterpart of Kawa Karpo. Joseph Rock described Miacimu as 'the most glorious peak my eyes were ever privileged to see…like a castle of a dream, an ice palace of a fairy tale'. Locals come here to burn juniper incense to the wrathful spirit of the mountain.

Sadly, weather often as not does not cooperate, shrouding the peaks in mist. Winter is your best shot at a sunrise photo op.

Guesthouses come and go like the wind here; most lack a palpable sense of spirit and, often, basic amenities like running water and electricity. **Guānjǐng Tiāntáng** (观景天堂; ☎841 6466; d Y180) is overpriced but better than most.

To get here from Déqīn a taxi will cost you Y30. Alternatively, head out onto the road and try to flag down any vehicle that's heading your way.

MÍNGYǑNG GLACIER 明永冰川

Tumbling off the side of Kawa Karpo peak is the 12km-long **Míngyǒng Glacier** (Míngyǒng Bīngchuān; admission Y63). At over 13 sq km, it is not only the lowest glacier in China (around 2200m high) but also an oddity – a monsoon marine glacier, which basically translates as having an ecosystem that couldn't possibly be more diverse: tundra, taiga, broadleaf forest and meadow. A conservation area has been created around the base of the peak. It also hauls, moving an average of 530m per year. (Well, at least it used to – it's been slowing a great deal since 1995 and the direst projections say it will start receding and become snowless within 80 years.)

For thousands of years the mountain has been a pilgrimage site and you'll still

THE YŬBĒNG & KAWA KARPO TREKS

A trek to the fabulous **Yǔbēng Waterfall** (雨崩神瀑; Yǔbēng Shénpù) is right up there. At the bridge over the Mekong River to Míngyǒng Glacier, the road leads 6km to Xīdāng (西当) and another 3km or so to a hot spring. Then it's possible to arrange pony hire to take you 25km (four to six hours) to Yǔbēng villages (upper and lower), where there are half a dozen basic guesthouses, including **Mystic Waterfall Lodge** (神瀑客栈; Shénpù Kèzhàn; ☎0887 841 1082; dm/d Y20/100), run by a friendly guide named Aqinpu.

You could hike all the way here from Fēilái Sì using local roads and paths, or using a combination of bus/pony/hiking, the easiest of which would be to bus to Xīdāng, hire a pony (Y100) to the mountain pass two-thirds of the way to Yǔbēng (雨崩) village, then hike the rest of the way.

From Yǔbēng village, loads of treks lie out there. It's a three- to four-hour trip on foot or horseback to the waterfall. Or, you could head south to a fabulous lake (it's around 4350m high and not easy to find, so take a guide).

There is a 3pm (and usually 8am) minibus from Déqīn to Xīdāng (Y15) that returns the next morning at 8am (the other at 3pm). You could also use the Míngyǒng bus to get back to Déqīn as it passes by Xīdāng at around 3pm or 4pm. A taxi from Fēilái Sì to Xīdāng is around a whopping Y150.

Then there's the legendary Kawa Karpo *kora*, a 12-day pilgrim circumambulation of Méilǐ Xuěshān. However, half of it is in the Tibetan Autonomous Region, so you'll need a permit to do it; you'll definitely need a guide.

meet a few Tibetan pilgrims, some of whom circumambulate the mountain over seven days in autumn. Surrounding villages are known as 'heaven villages' because of the dense fog that hangs about in spring and summer, even permeating into homes.

Trails to the glacier lead up from Míngyǒng's central square marked by a new *chörten*. After 45 minutes a path splits off down to the (unimpressive) toe of the glacier. Continuing on, after another 45 minutes you get to the Tibetan **Tàizǐ Miào** (太子庙), where there is a **guesthouse** (d Y180). A further 30 minutes along the trail is **Lotus Temple** (莲花庙; Liánhuā Miào), which offers fantastic views of the glacier framed by prayer flags and *chörten*. Horses can also be hired to go up to the glacier (Y150).

If you're coming from Yǔbēng, you could also hike to Míngyǒng from Xīdāng in around three hours if you hoof it.

Beds in guesthouses are Y30 to Y40, toilet facilities are basic, and electricity is iffy. A handful of new hotels that claim to be midrange have gone up in the last half-decade, most of which are uninspiring but still cost Y100 to Y250 for a standard room with bathroom.

From Déqīn, minibuses to Míngyǒng leave regularly from the bridge near the market at the top end of town (Y15, one to two hours, 8am to 3pm or 4pm). You can also try to rent a car through your accommodation.

The road from Déqīn descends into the dramatic Mekong Gorge. Six kilometres before Míngyǒng the road crosses the Mekong River and branches off to Xīdāng. Nearby is a small temple, the Bǎishūlín Miào, and a *chörten*.

NÙ JIĀNG VALLEY

The 320km-long Nù Jiāng Valley (怒江大峡谷) is one of Yúnnán's best-kept secrets. The Nù Jiāng (known as the Salween in Myanmar (Burma); its name in Chinese means 'Raging River') is the second-longest river in Southeast Asia and one of only two undammed rivers in China. Sandwiched between the Gāolígòng Shān and Myanmar (Burma) to the west, Tibet to the north and the imposing Bìluó Shān to the east, the gorge holds nearly a quarter of China's flora and fauna species, and half of China's endangered species. The valley also has an exotic mix of Han, Nu, Lisu, Drung and Tibetan nationalities, and even the odd Burmese trader. And it's simply stunning – all of it.

Getting there is a pain. On a map, it seems a stone's throw from Déqīn in the province's northwest. Nope. All traffic enters via the Bǎoshān region. Once there, you trundle eight hours up the valley, marvelling at the scenery, and then head back the way you came. Plans have been announced to blast a road from Gòngshān in the northern part of the valley to Déqīn, and another from the village of Bǐngzhōngluò even further north into Tibet. Given the immense topographical challenges, these plans are a long way off.

Liùkù 六库

☎0886 / POP 17, 800

Liùkù is the lively, pleasant capital of the prefecture. Divided by the Nù Jiāng River, it's the main transport hub of the region, although it's of little intrinsic interest. You may have to register with a police checkpoint about 2km before entering the town.

Sleeping & Eating

There are many places on Chuancheng Lu close to the main bus station where you can find tired rooms for Y40 to Y80. The **Nù Jiāng Traffic Hotel** (怒江交通宾馆; Nùjiāng Jiāotōng Bīnguǎn; ☎362 0046; 141 Chuancheng Lu; 穿城路141号; s & d Y60-100; ❄) isn't the cheapest hotel in town, but the bathrooms don't smell and it's just around the corner from the bus station.

To eat, head to the riverbank, south of Renmin Lu, where loads of outdoor restaurants cook great barbecued fish.

Information

There's an **internet cafe** (山城网吧; wǎngbā; per hr Y3; ⏲8am-midnight) just south of Renmin Lu. You can't change money in Liùkù, but there are a few ATMs that take foreign cards.

Getting There & Away

Kūnmíng buses leave and depart from the main bus station on Xiang Yang Donglu, as do a few buses to and from Xiàguān. Most Xiàguān-bound buses depart from the town's other bus station on Jiang Yilu across the river:

Bǎoshān Y40, three to four hours, every 30 minutes (7.30am to 3pm)

Bǐngzhōngluò Y74, nine hours, one daily (8.20am)

Gòngshān Y65, eight hours, every 50 minutes (7am to 1pm)

Kūnmíng Y163 to Y245, 11 to 12 hours, five daily (8.30am, 7pm, 7.30pm, 8pm and 8.30pm)

Xiàguān Y67, five to six hours, every 40 minutes (6.20am to 2.20pm)

Bǐngzhōngluò 丙中洛

☎0886

The main reason to come to the Nù Jiāng Valley is to visit this isolated, friendly **village** (admission Y100), set in a beautiful, wide and fertile bowl. Just 35km south of Tibet and close to Myanmar (Burma), it's a great base for hikes into the surrounding mountains and valleys. The area is at its best in spring and early autumn. Don't even think about coming in the winter.

Potential short hops include heading south along the main road for 2km to the impressive 'first bend' of the Nù Jiāng River, or north along a track more than 15km long that passes through a host of villages. Longer three- or four-day treks include heading to the Tibetan village of Dímáluò (迪麻洛) and then onto Yànmén, where you can catch a bus to Déqīn.

A guide is pretty much essential. Tibetan trek leader Alou comes highly recommended. He's based at his bar, **Road to Tibet** (☎356 6182; aluo_luosang@yahoo.com.cn), just off the village main drag, although he's often away on treks so email him first. Another pricier option is Peter, a Lemao guide, who offers treks for Y250 a day. You can find him at **Nù Jiāng Baini Travel** (☎139 8853 9641; yangindali@yahoo.co.uk) on the main street. He speaks English and is a good source of local information, as well as renting mountain bikes for Y50 a day.

An **internet cafe** (per hr Y3; ⏲10am-midnight) is next to the **Road to Tibet** bar.

Sleeping & Eating

There's no reason to pay more than Y60 for a room in Bǐngzhōngluò. At the time of writing, the characterless **Yù Dòng Bīnguǎn** (玉洞宾馆; ☎358 1285; s & d Y80-180, discounts of 60%) on the main street was the best option. There are a few eating options on the main street.

Getting There & Away

There is one direct bus a day from Liùkù to Bǐngzhōngluò (Y74, nine hours, 8.20am). It returns from opposite the Yù Dòng Bīnguǎn at 8am. Otherwise, take a bus to Gòngshān (Y65, eight hours, seven daily, every 50 minutes from 7am to 1pm), where you can transfer to one of the regular buses that go back and forth to Bǐngzhōngluò (Y10, 1½ hours) until 5pm or 6pm.

From Gòngshān, there are 10 daily buses to Liùkù from 6.10am to 1pm.

Drung Valley 独龙江

Separated from the Nù Jiāng Valley by the high Gāolígòng Shān range and only reached by road in 1999, this is one of the remotest valleys in China and is home to the tiny Drung ethnic group, whose women still tattoo their faces. The Drung River actually flows out of China into Myanmar (Burma), where it eventually joins the Irrawaddy. There is a county guesthouse *(xiàn zhāodàisǔo)* in capital **Dúlóngjiāng**.

No buses run into the valley. You'll have to hire a minivan from Gòngshān for the rough 96km trip to Dúlóngjiāng. Beyond that, most travel is on foot. All travel is dicey in rainy weather and the road is closed if there's snow.

BǍOSHĀN REGION

Scrunched against Myanmar (Burma) and bisected by the wild Nù Jiāng, the Bǎoshān region (保山) has never seen too many wanderers passing through. That's difficult to understand, given its primary draws – the chance to immerse yourself in geothermally heated pools after days of traipsing around dormant volcanoes.

The eponymous capital is unremarkable; lovely Téngchōng (and its environs) is where it's at. The Téngchōng area is peppered with minority groups whose villages lie in and around the ancient fire mountains. Located to the west of the Gāolígòng Shān (Gaoligong Mountain) range, Téngchōng is also prime earthquake territory, having experienced 71 earthquakes measuring over five on the Richter scale since 1500.

As early as the 4th and 5th centuries BC (two centuries before the northern routes through central Asia were established), the Bǎoshān area was an important stop on the southern Silk Road – the Sìchuān-India route. The area did not come under Chinese control until the Han dynasty. In 1277 a huge battle was waged in the region between the 12,000 troops of Kublai Khan and 60,000 Burmese soldiers and their 2000 elephants. The Mongols won and went on to take Pagan.

THE NÙ JIĀNG DAM

In 2003 Unesco named the Nù Jiāng Valley a World Heritage Site, calling it one of the world's most precious ecosystems of its kind. Then, almost simultaneously, the Chinese government announced plans for a series of 13 dams along the Nù Jiāng. The project would theoretically produce more electricity than even the Three Gorges Dam.

Opposition was immediate. Unesco warned that such a project could warrant the area's delisting; it was joined in its opposition to the project by more than 70 international environmental groups. More amazing was local opposition; more than 50 prominent Chinese (from pop stars to business billionaires) spoke out against the dams. In a very rare example of people power succeeding in China, the government has since backed away from the plan, with Premier Wen Jiabao ordering more studies on the scheme's potential impact. Local politicians, though, remain keen for the project to go ahead and the area's future remains highly uncertain.

Téngchōng 腾冲

0875

With 20 volcanoes in the vicinity, lots of hot springs and great trekking potential, there's plenty to explore in this neck of the woods. And the city itself is a bit of an oddity – one of the few places in China that, though much of the old architecture has been demolished, remains a pleasant place to hang out, with oodles of green space (you can actually smell the flowers!) and a friendly, low-key populace.

Sights & Activities

Much of the old-time architecture is now gone, but some OK places for a random wander are still to be found.

Markets MARKETS

The backstreets running off Yingjiang Xilu sport a couple of small markets with splashes of colour and activity in the mornings. Walking along Fengshan Lu from Feicui Lu, the first side street on the left has a small **produce market** (产品市场; *chǎnpǐn shìchǎng*). Further down on the right is a large, covered **jade market** (珠宝玉器交易中心; *zhūbǎo yùqì jiāoyì zhōngxīn*), where you can sometimes see the carving process. Walk east along Yingjiang Xilu and you will come across a larger **produce market** on your right.

FREE **Láifēng Shān National Forest Park** PARK

(来凤山国家森林公园; Láifēng Shān Guójiā Sēnlín Gōngyuán; 8am-7pm) On the western edge of town, walk through lush pine forests of this park to **Láifēng Temple** (来凤寺; Láifèng Sì) or make the sweaty hike up to the summit, where a pagoda offers fine views.

Diéshuǐ Waterfall WATERFALL

(叠水瀑布; Diéshuǐ Pùbù; admission Y30) In the western suburbs of town, beside the **Xiānlè Temple** (仙乐寺; Xiānlè Sì), this is a good place for a picnic. The area makes a nice destination for a bike ride and you could easily combine it with a trip to **Héshùn** (和顺), a picturesque village 4km outside Téngchong.

Sleeping & Eating

There's no shortage of places to stay: bargain hard at any hotel.

TOP CHOICE **Téngchōng International Youth Hostel** YOUTH HOSTEL $

(腾冲国际青年旅舍; Téngchōng Guójì Qīngnián Lǚshè; 519 8677; tengchongyha2007@hotmail.com; Yuquanyuan; 玉泉园; dm/d Y25/140;) Fronting a redone public square just off the main road, this gem is one of the finest hostels in China. The dorms have great, thick mattresses, while the spacious standard rooms have sparkling bathrooms. The whole place is spotless and all the facilities, including wi-fi, you need are here. The obliging staff are an added bonus. It's a Y5 taxi ride from the long-distance bus station.

Xīnghuá Dàjiǔdiàn HOTEL $$

(兴华大酒店; 513 2688; 团坡小区7号; s & d Y160;) There are alarming, tiger-pattern carpets here, but the rooms themselves are comfortable, if generic. The location, northeast of Láifēng Shān National Forest Park, is handy in what is a spread-out town.

Fēnghuāng Jiǔdián HOTEL $

(风光酒店; 516 0699; Re Hai Lu; 热海路; s & d Y120;) Two blocks north from the long-distance bus station (on the right side of the

Téngchōng

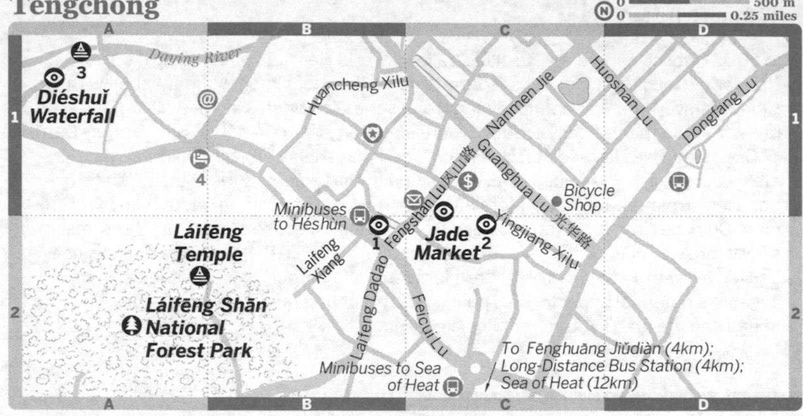

Téngchōng

Top Sights

Diéshuǐ Waterfall ... A1
Jade Market ... C1
Láifēng Shān National Forest Park ... A2
Láifēng Temple ... A2

Sights

1 Produce Market ... B2
2 Produce Market ... C2
3 Xiānlè Temple ... A1

Sleeping

4 Xīnghuá Dàjiǔdiàn ... A1

street), this hotel is not the cheapest of the many clustered here, but it has OK, clean rooms that come with broadband access.

There are many hole-in-the-wall eateries and barbecue places along Feicui Lu and elsewhere around town. At night, food stalls set up in the centre of town off Fengshan Lu.

Information

Bank of China (中国银行; Zhōngguó Yínháng; cnr Fengshan Lu & Yingjiang Xilu) Has a 24-hour ATM and will change cash and travellers cheques. There are other ATMs around town that take foreign cards too.

China Post (国际邮局; Zhōngguó Yóuzhèng; Fengshan Lu) Serves as post and telephone office.

Internet cafe (网吧; wǎngbā; 100m north of Xīnghuá Dàjiǔdiàn; per hr Y3) At the time of writing, internet cafes in Tèngchōng were not admitting foreigners.

Public Security Bureau (PSB; 公安局; Gōng'ānjú; Yingjiang Xilu; ⌚8.30-11.30am & 2.30-5.30pm Mon-Fri) Can help with visa extensions.

Getting There & Away

Air

Téngchōng's airport 12km south of town has a daily flight to Kūnmíng (Y1000).

Bus

The city's long-distance bus station is in the south of town.

Bǎoshān Y50, three hours, every 40 minutes (7.50am to 7pm)

Kūnmíng (express) Y234, 11 hours, one daily (9am); (sleeper) Y218, 12 hours, 10 daily (3.30pm to 8.10pm)

Xiàguān Y103, six to seven hours, two daily (10.30am and noon); (sleeper) Y108, six to seven hours, one daily (7.30pm)

Téngchōng's local bus station (客运站; Kèyùnzhàn) has frequent departures to local destinations:

Mángshì Y30, four hours, nine daily (7.30am to 4.30pm)

Ruìlì Y57, six hours, nine daily (7am to 3.50pm)

Buses to local destinations north of Téngchōng, such as Mǎzhàn, Gùdōng, Ruìdián, Diántān or Zìzhì, either leave from, or pass through, Huoshan Lu in the northeast of town. There's also an old local bus station on Dongfang Lu.

Getting Around

Téngchōng's environs make for some fine bike riding. You can hire a bike from a shop on Guanghua Lu or from the Téngchōng International Youth Hostel (both Y20 per day).

Bus 2 runs from the town centre to the long-distance bus station. Taxis charge Y5 to hop around town.

Around Téngchōng

Getting out to the sights is a bit tricky. Catching buses part of the way and hiking is one possibility, while some of the closer attractions can be reached by bicycle.

Your other option is to hire a van, which may be affordable if there are several of you; head down to the minibus stand just off the southern end of Huoshan Lu or to the minibus stand for the Sea of Heat in the south of town.

Some highlights of the region are the traditional villages that are scattered between Téngchōng and Yúnfēng Shān (Cloudy Peak Mountain). The relatively plentiful public transport along this route means that you can jump on and off minibuses to go exploring as the whim takes you.

HÉSHÙN 和顺

Southwest of town, **Héshùn** (admission Y80; ⏲8am-7pm) is well worth a visit. It has been set aside as a retirement village for overseas Chinese, but it's of more interest as a quiet, traditional Chinese village with cobbled streets. There are some great old buildings in the village, providing lots of photo opportunities. The village also has a small **museum** (博物馆; *bówùguǎn*) and a famous old **library** (图书馆; *túshūguǎn*). You can avoid buying a ticket by coming after 7pm, when the ticket office shuts.

The newish **Lao Shay Youth Hostel** (老谢车马店; Lǎoxiě Chēmǎdiàn; ☎515 8398; Cunjiawan; 寸家湾; dm Y20, d Y50-88; @) in the village (by the big banyan tree) is pleasant and set around a small courtyard.

Frequent minibuses leave Téngchōng from the corner of Feicui Lu and Laifeng Xiang (Y2), or you can pick them up opposite the Xīnghuá Dàjiǔdiàn. It's an easy bicycle ride out to the village but the ride back is an uphill slog.

YÚNFĒNG SHĀN 云峰山

A Taoist mountain dotted with 17th-century temples and monastic retreats, **Yúnfēng Shān** (Cloudy Peak Mountain; admission Y35) is 47km north of Téngchōng. At the time of writing, the **cable car** (one way/return Y30/50), from where it's a 20-minute walk to **Dàxióng Bǎodiàn** (大雄宝殿), a temple at the summit, was shut for repairs. **Lǔzǔ Diàn** (鲁祖殿), the temple second from the top, serves up solid vegetarian food at lunchtime. It's a quick walk down but it can be hard on the knees.

To get to the mountain, go to Huoshan Lu in Téngchōng and catch a bus to Gùdōng (Y15), and then a microbus from there to the turn-off (Y10). From the turn-off you have to hitch, or you could take the lovely walk past the village of Hépíng (和平) to the pretty villages just before the mountain. Hiring a vehicle from Téngchōng to take you on a return trip will cost about Y300.

VOLCANOES

Téngchōng County is renowned for its volcanoes, and although they have been behaving themselves for many centuries, the seismic and geothermal activity in the area indicates that they won't always continue to do so. The closest volcano to Téngchōng is **Mǎ'ān Shān** (马鞍山; Saddle Mountain), around 5km to the northwest. It's just south of the main road to Yíngjiāng.

Around 22km to the north of town, near the village of Mǎzhàn, is the most accessible cluster of **volcanoes** (admission Y40). The main central volcano is known as **Dàkōng Shān** (大空山; Big Empty Hill), which pretty much sums it up, and to the left of it is the black crater of **Hēikōng Shān** (黑空山; Black Empty Hill). You can haul yourself up the steps for views of the surrounding lava fields (long dormant).

Minibuses run frequently to Mǎzhàn (Y5) from along Huoshan Lu, or take a Gùdōng-bound minibus. From Mǎzhàn town it's a 10-minute walk or take a motortricycle (Y5) to the volcano area.

SEA OF HEAT 热海

A cluster of hot springs, geysers and streams about 12km southwest of Téngchōng that is rapidly being turned into an upmarket resort for domestic tourists, the **Sea of Heat** (Rèhǎi; admission Y60, pool access Y80; ⏲8am-11pm) features a couple of outdoor hot springs and a nice warm-water swimming pool along with indoor baths. Some of the springs here reach temperatures of 102°C (don't swim in these ones!).

The rooms at the **Yǎng Shēng Gé** (养生阁; ☎586 9700; s & d Y1600, ste Y3600) all come with their very own mini-spa complete with water piped from the hot springs. It's close to the ticket office. Alternatively, you can visit the **spa** right by the ticket office and take a dip for Y268. If you don't want to douse yourself, then it takes a pleasant hour or so to walk through the park.

Microbuses leave for the Sea of Heat (Y5) when full from the Dongfang Lu turn-off in the south of Téngchōng.

DÉHÓNG PREFECTURE

Déhóng Prefecture (德宏州; Déhóng Zhōu and Jingpo Autonomous Prefecture) juts into Myanmar (Burma) in the far west of Yúnnán. Once a backwater of backwaters, as trade grew, the region saw tourists flock in to experience its raucous border atmosphere.

That's dimmed quite a bit, but most Chinese tourists in Déhóng are still here for the trade from Myanmar (Burma) that comes through Ruìlì and Wǎndīng; Burmese jade is a popular commodity and countless other items are spirited over the border. The border with Myanmar (Burma) is punctuated by many crossings, some of them almost imperceptible, so be careful if you go wandering too close.

The most obvious minority groups in Déhóng are the Burmese (normally dressed in their traditional saronglike *longyi*), Dai and Jingpo (known in Myanmar (Burma) as the Kachin, a minority group long engaged in armed struggle against the Myanmar (Burmese) government). For information on etiquette for visiting temples in the region see the boxed text on p697.

Mángshì (Lùxī) 芒市(潞西)

0692 / POP 15,100

Mángshì is Déhóng's air hub. If you fly in from Kūnmíng, there are minibuses running directly from the airport to Ruìlì; your best bet is to jump onto one of these and head south. Leaving Mángshì, you might have to stay overnight. In which case just wander about the town and its few temples.

Chángjiāng Bīnguǎn (228 6055; 2 Weimin Lu; 为民路2号; d/tr Y160/240; ❄) is a standard hotel with standard rooms, while **Xīngjiàn Jiǔdiàn** (228 6788; Jianguo Lu; 建国路; d Y100; ❄@) is a newer place in a good location down the street from the bus station.

The best places to head for food are the point-and-choose places on Dongfeng Lu just west of the market or along Qingnian Lu.

The airport is 10km from the city, with daily flights between Mángshì and Kūnmíng (Y450). There are no buses to town, so a taxi will cost you Y25. Minibuses to Ruìlì (Y30, two hours) usually wait at the airport for incoming flights.

Buses leave **CAAC** (Wenhua Lu; 8.30am-noon & 2.30-6pm) for the airport around an hour before flight departures.

There are several bus stations in Mángshì. Both the long-distance bus station in the north of town and the southern bus station offer similar destinations, including Kūnmíng (Y195, 10 hours) at 10.30am, 6.30pm and 9pm.

A bus stand a block southwest of the southern bus stand has the most frequent departures to Wǎndīng (Y22) and Ruìlì (Y30, 7am to 8pm); they leave when full.

Ruìlì 瑞丽

0692

In the early 1980s, Deng Xiaoping rationalised the risks of China opening up to the outside world by saying, 'If you open the window, some flies naturally get in.' China's then leader probably didn't have Ruìlì in mind, but within a few years of trade with Myanmar (Burma) being allowed, the insects were swarming across the border and this tiny town had become Yúnnán's sin city.

Drugs, guns, gems, poached wildlife and smuggled goods of all kinds circulated, while brothels, casinos and some of the dodgiest nightclubs in China catered for the gangsters, newly flush import-export merchants and the voyeurs who flocked to Ruìlì in their wake.

Nowadays, visitors are more likely to stumble into a shopping mall than a den of thieves. But although the town has been cleaned up significantly since the late 1990s, on the surface at least, the mix of Han Chinese, minorities and Burmese traders is still intact, making for some great market action. And with its palm tree–lined streets, bicycle rickshaws and steamy climate, Ruìlì has a distinctly laid-back, Southeast Asian feel.

The minority villages nearby are also good reason to come; the stupas are in much better condition than those in Xīshuāngbǎnnà, and it's worth getting a bicycle and heading out to explore.

Ruìlì

Top Sights

Sleeping

Eating

Drinking

Another draw for travellers is Myanmar (Burma), which lies only a few kilometres away. Though individual tourists are not allowed to cross freely, organising permits to take you through the sensitive border area is becoming easier.

China is furiously building an expressway to link Kūnmíng with the border, while on the Myanmar (Burma) side new highways stretch all the way to Mandalay, making what had been a horrible five-day journey much more sane. One day, foreign travellers may be able to re-create the 'Southern Silk Route', of which Ruìlì and Mandalay were a part.

The city is actually fairly tame at night, although prostitution remains an enormous and obvious industry here. Drugs are also still a major problem; vehicles, including buses, leaving Ruìlì are often searched (if you're caught in possession of anything illegal, you're headed to Chinese prison). The easy availability of heroin in the recent past also means that Déhóng Prefecture has significant numbers of HIV/AIDS sufferers, from sharing needles, although there has been a decline in the number of new cases in the last few years. There's also a very nasty trade in trafficked women from Myanmar (Burma).

Sights

Think atmosphere rather than aesthetics. The huge **market** (市场; Shìchǎng) in the west of town is one of the most colourful and fun in Yúnnán; a real swirl of ethnicities, including Dai, Jingpo, Han and Burmese, as well as the odd Bangladeshi and Pakistani trader. Get here in the morning, when the stalls are lined with Burmese smokes, tofu wrapped in banana leaves, dodgy pharmaceuticals from Thailand, clothes, you name it. It's also a good place to grab lunch at one of the many snack stalls.

Also great for people-watching is Ruìlì's ever-expanding **jade market** (珠宝街; Zhūbǎo Jiē), the centre of town in all senses.

Sleeping

There are lots of hotels in Ruìlì, so it's generally a buyer's market; expect 50% discounts or more everywhere.

New Kǎitōng International Hotel HOTEL $$
(新凯通国际大酒店; Xīn Kǎitōng Guójì Dàjiǔdiàn; ☎415 7777; fax 415 6190; 150 Biancheng Lu; 边城路150号; s & d Y360; ❄@≈) In terms of service, this is a significant step up from other places in town, even if the rooms aren't too different. But it does have an outdoor swimming pool (Y10 for nonresidents) and snooker tables.

Bāshí Jiǔdiàn HOTEL $
(巴石酒店; ☎412 9088; cnr Renmin Lu & Nanmao Jie; 南卯街; s & d Y160; ❄) The staff here have been struck down by the stultifying, steamy atmosphere of Ruìlì and slumber most of the time. But you can normally grab one of the big rooms for a bargain Y50.

Ruìlì Bīnguǎn HOTEL $$
(瑞丽宾馆; ☎410 0899; 25 Jianshe Lu; 建设路25号; s & d Y220; ❄@) The best bet for comfort at a reasonable price, with spacious, well-kept rooms, all with ADSL, a quiet location and pleasant staff.

Eating & Drinking

Street stalls set up all over town come nightfall; just follow your nose.

TOP CHOICE **Bo Bo's Cold Drinks Shop** CAFE $
(步步冷饮店; Bùbù Lěngyǐndiàn; Xi'nan Lu; dishes from Y5; ⌚8am-1am) Busy from early to late, the *longyi*-clad Burmese waiters at this Ruìlì institution hustle as they serve up fantastic fruit juices, Burmese-style milky tea, ice cream and cakes, as well as simple but tasty rice and noodle dishes. There's a cool outside area at night, where you can quaff a Myanmar (Burma) lager under the stars.

Huáfēng Market STREET MARKET $
(华丰市场; Huáfēng Shìchǎng; off Jiegang Lu; ⌚6pm-late) A big outdoor food court that thrives once darkness descends, come here for Burmese and Chinese food, including superb barbecue dishes as well as the odd Thai delicacy. The food is all on display, so just pick and point.

Information

Bank of China (中国银行; Zhōngguó Yínháng; Nanmao Jie) Provides all the usual services and will cash travellers cheques for US dollars if you're headed to Myanmar (Burma). There are other ATMs around town that take foreign cards. You can also change/find US dollars at the Jade Market.

China Post (国际邮局; Zhōngguó Yóuzhèng; cnr Mengmao Lu & Renmin Lu) Despite (or perhaps because?) of its border location, sending any kind of package abroad from this post and telephone office is difficult, if not impossible.

Diélái Photograph Centre (蝶来摄影中心; Diélái Shèyǐng Zhōngxīn; Nanmao Jie) Can burn CDs for Y15 each. Keep an eye out for the big yellow Kodak sign.

Internet cafe (网吧; wǎngbā; cnr Nanmao Jie & Jiegang Lu; per hr Y3; ⌚24hr) At the time of writing, foreigners weren't allowed to use Ruìlì's internet cafes.

Public Security Bureau (PSB; 公安局; Gōng'ānjú; Jianshe Jie; ⌚8.30-11.30am & 2.30-5.30pm)

Getting There & Away

Plans are under way to extend Xiàguān's rail line to Ruìlì. An expressway from Bǎoshān to Ruìlì was being built at the time of writing, which will link Ruìlì to Xiàguān and on to Kūnmíng.

Air

Daily flights come from Kūnmíng via Mángshì, a two-hour drive away. You can buy tickets at **China Eastern Airlines** (东方航空公司; Dōngfāng Hángkōng Gōngsī; ☎411 1111; Renmin Lu; ⌚8.30am-6pm). Shuttle buses leave daily from the office, three hours before scheduled flights (Y60). You can also use the ticket office to book and reconfirm return flights – do so early.

Bus

Ruìlì has a long-distance bus station (长途客运站; Chángtú Kèyùnzhàn) in the centre of town and a north bus station, really more of a forecourt, at the top of Jiegang Lu. Head to the north bus station (汽车北站; Qìchē Běizhàn) if you're trying to get to Mángshì (Y30, last bus 6pm – they leave when full); for everything else, you're better off going to the long-distance station:

Bǎoshān Y72, six hours, every 30 to 40minutes (6am to 4pm)

Jǐnghóng Y293, 24 to 26 hours, one daily (9am)

Kūnmíng Y247, 12 to 15 hours, five daily (9am, 3pm, 6pm, 7pm and 8pm)

Téngchōng Y57, six hours, every 40 to 50 minutes (5.50am to 12.20pm)

Xiàguān Y122 to Y167, 11 to 12 hours, two daily (9am and 8pm)

For local destinations, minibuses leave from opposite the main bus station, or you can just flag one down in the street. Destinations include Wǎndīng (Y10), the border checkpoint at Jiěgào (Y10) and the village of Nóngdǎo (Y8). Buses to Zhāngfēng (Y11, one hour) leave from Xinjian Lu.

Getting Around

The most interesting day trips require a bicycle. Ask at your accommodation about the best place to rent one.

A flat rate for a taxi ride inside the city should be Y5, and up for negotiation from there. There are also cheaper motor and cycle rickshaws.

Around Ruìlì

Most of the sights around Ruìlì can be explored easily by bicycle. It's worth making frequent detours down the narrow paths leading off the main roads to visit minority villages. The people are friendly, and there are lots of photo opportunities. The *Tourism and Traffic Map of Ruìlì*, available from the Xīnhuá bookshop on Renmin Lu, shows the major roads and villages.

The shortest ride is to turn left at the corner north of China Post and continue out of the town proper into the little village of Měngmǎo. There are half a dozen Shan temples scattered about; the fun is in finding them.

GOLDEN DUCK PAGODA 弄安金鸭塔

In the outskirts of town to the southwest, on the main road, this pagoda (Nòng'ān Jīnyā Tǎ) is an attractive stupa set in a temple courtyard. It was established to mark the arrival of a pair of golden ducks that brought good fortune to what was previously an uninhabited marshy area.

TEMPLES

Just past Golden Duck Pagoda is a crossroads and a small wooden temple. The road to the right (west) leads to the villages of **Jiěxiàng** (姐相) and **Nóngdǎo** (弄岛), and on the way are a number of small temples, villages and stupas. None are spectacular but the village life is interesting and there are often small markets near the temples.

The first major Dai temple is **Hǎnshā Zhuāng Temple** (喊沙奘寺; Hǎnshā Zhuāng Sì), a fine wooden structure with a few resident monks. It's set a little off the road and a green tourism sign marks the turn-off. The surrounding Dai village is interesting.

Another 20 minutes or so further down the road, look out for a white stupa on the hillside to the right. This is **Léizhuāngxiāng** (雷装相), Ruìlì's oldest stupa, dating back to the middle of the Tang dynasty. There's a nunnery in the grounds of the stupa as well as fantastic views of the Ruìlì area. Once the stupa comes into view, take the next path to the right that cuts through the fields. You will see blue signs written in Chinese and Dai pointing the way through a couple of Dai villages. When you get to the market crossroads at the centre of the main village, take the right path. You'll need to push your bicycle for the last ascent to the stupa. In all, it should take you about 50 minutes to cycle here from Golden Duck Pagoda.

About 2km past the town of Jiěxiàng is **Děnghǎnnóng Zhuāng Temple** (等喊弄奘寺; Děnghǎnnóng Zhuāng Sì), a wooden Dai temple with pleasant surroundings.

It's possible to cycle all the way to Nóngdǎo, around 29km southwest of Ruìlì. There's a solitary hotel in town that has cheap doubles or you can return to Ruìlì on one of the frequent minibuses.

JIĚGÀO BORDER CHECKPOINT 姐告边检点

There's not much here but border fanatics will find the trip satisfying if only to marvel at how everything seems so relaxed on both sides of the – quite literally – bamboo curtain.

On a thumb of land jutting into Myanmar (Burma), Jiěgào is the main checkpoint for a steady stream of cross-border traffic. As with Ruìlì, this place has seen its popular casinos and other dens of iniquity replaced by cheap electronics shops and pricey restaurants.

To get here, continue straight ahead from Golden Duck Pagoda, cross the Myanmar (Burma) bridge over Ruìlì Jiāng and you will come to Jiěgào, about 7km from Ruìlì.

Shared red taxis with signs for Jiěgào (Y10) circle the centre of Ruìlì from dawn until late at night.

WǍNDĪNG BORDER CHECKPOINT 畹町边检站

East of Ruìlì lies Wǎndīng, a second checkpoint for crossing into Myanmar (Burma). Foreigners can't cross here, although it's something of a tradition to pester the border officials so that maybe one day they'll allow foreigners to cross. It's not as busy as Jiěgào, nor is it as interesting, but if you're a true borderholic then it's worth making the 30-minute drive just so you can take a photo and say you've been.

Staff at the foreign affairs office of the PSB, just across from the Chinese border checkpoint, seem quite easy-going, and look bored enough to have a chuckle at your request for permission to cross.

You could spend some time at the **Wǎndīng Forest Reserve** (畹町森林公园; Wǎndīng Sēnlín Gōngyuán; admission Y2). There are some pleasant walks.

Local places to stay might be able to provide information on **river trips** that include a barbecue lunch in a minority village. Prices vary depending on the number of participants, but you should be able to do one for from Y50 per person. Alternatively, it is possible to catch a lift on a boat with locals. Take a minibus in the direction of Mángshì and get off at the bridge that connects with the main Ruìlì–Mángshì road. Travellers have caught boats back to the second bridge closer to Ruìlì and then hitched back to Ruìlì or Wǎndīng. Some very strenuous haggling is required for boat trips.

Minibuses for Wǎndīng (Y10) leave Ruìlì when full, and vice versa.

BORDER CROSSING: GETTING TO MYANMAR (BURMA)

To cross from China into Myanmar (Burma), travellers must have the correct visa, travel permits and be part of an official 'group'. The group, which might consist entirely of yourself and no one else, will be escorted from Jiĕgào in China to Hsipaw in Myanmar (Burma), an eight-hour drive from the border. Once you reach Hsipaw you can wave goodbye to your guide and are free to travel on your own further south to Mandalay, Yangon and so on.

Ask around at the various travel agencies and tour operators located at the **Camellia Hotel** (茶花宾馆; Cháhuā Bīnguǎn; www.kmcamelliahotel.com; 96 Dongfeng Donglu) in Kūnmíng for the best deals. Remember, it's not possible to organise a visa for Myanmar (Burma) in Ruìlì and you will have to do this either at the embassy in Běijīng (see p985) or in Kūnmíng at the Myanmar consulate (p986).

GOLDEN PAGODA 姐勒金塔

A few kilometres to the east of Ruìlì on the road to Wǎndīng is the Golden Pagoda (Jiělè Jīntǎ), a fine structure that dates back 200 years.

BÀNGMÁHÈ 棒麻贺

Another possible cycling route takes you west of Ruìlì, past the old town of Měngmǎo, now a suburb of Ruìlì. After 4km, just past the village of Jiědōng (姐东), a turn-off north leads to Bàngmáhè village, a Jingpo settlement with a small waterfall nearby.

XĪSHUĀNGBĂNNÀ REGION

North of Myanmar (Burma) and Laos, Xīshuāngbǎnnà is the Chinese approximation of the original Thai name of Sip Sawng Panna (12 Rice-Growing Districts). The Xīshuāngbǎnnà region (西双版纳), better known as simply Bǎnnà, has become China's own mini-Thailand, attracting tourists looking for sunshine and water-splashing festivals, hikers readying for epic jungle treks, and burned-out locals and expats fleeing the cold and congestion of China's cities.

Still, Xīshuāngbǎnnà rarely feels overwhelmed by visitors – even the capital, Jǐnghóng, is basically an overgrown, somnolent town.

Environment

Xīshuāngbǎnnà has myriad plant and animal species, although recent scientific studies have shown the tropical rainforest areas of Bǎnnà are now acutely endangered. The jungle areas that remain contain dwindling numbers of wild tigers, leopards, elephants and golden-haired monkeys. The number of elephants has doubled to 250, up 100% from the early 1980s; the government now offers compensation to villagers whose crops have been destroyed by elephants, or who assist in wildlife conservation. In 1998 the government banned the hunting or processing of animals, but poaching is notoriously hard to control.

People

About one-third of the million-strong population of this region are Dai; another third or so are Han Chinese and the rest are a conglomerate of minorities that include the Hani, Lisu and Yao, as well as lesser-known hill tribes such as the Aini (a subgroup of the Hani), Jinuo, Bulang, Lahu and Wa.

Xīshuāngbǎnnà Dai Autonomous Prefecture, as it is known officially, is subdivided into the three counties of Jǐnghóng, Měnghǎi and Měnglà.

Climate

The region has two seasons: wet and dry. The wet season is between June and August, when it rains ferociously, although not every day. From September to February there is less rainfall, but thick fog descends during the late evening and doesn't lift until 10am or even later.

November to March sees temperatures average about 19°C. The hottest months of the year are from April to September, when you can expect an average of 25°C.

Festivals & Events

During festivals, booking same-day airline tickets to Jǐnghóng can be extremely difficult. Hotels in Jǐnghóng town are booked solid and prices usually triple. Most people end up commuting from a nearby Dai village. Festivities take place all over Xīshuāngbǎnnà, so you might be lucky further away from Jǐnghóng.

Xīshuāngbǎnnà

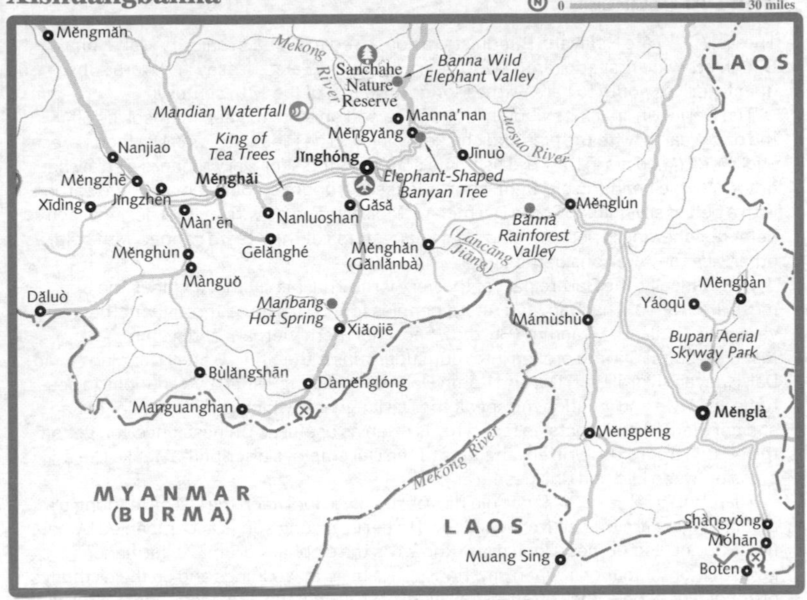

Tanpa Festival — CULTURAL FESTIVAL

In February, young boys are sent to the local temple for initiation as novice monks.

Tan Jing Festival — CULTURAL FESTIVAL

Between February and March, participants honour Buddhist texts housed in local temples.

Water-Splashing Festival — CULTURAL FESTIVAL

Held in mid-April, the Water-Splashing Festival washes away the dirt, sorrow and demons of the old year and brings in the happiness of the new. Jǐnghóng usually celebrates it from 13 to 15 April but dates in the surrounding villages vary. Foreigners get special attention, so prepare to be drenched all day. Remember, the wetter you get, the more luck you'll receive.

Closed-Door Festival — CULTURAL FESTIVAL

The farming season, July to October, is the time for the Closed-Door Festival (傣族关门节), when marriages or festivals are banned. Traditionally, this is also the time of year that men aged 20 or older are ordained as monks for a period of time. The season ends with the **Open-Door Festival**, when everyone lets their hair down again to celebrate the harvest.

Tan Ta Festival — CULTURAL FESTIVAL

This festival is held during the last 10-day period of October or November, with temple ceremonies, rocket launches from special towers and hot-air balloons. The rockets, which often contain lucky amulets, blast into the sky; those who find the amulets are assured of good luck.

Jǐnghóng 景洪

☎0691

Jǐnghóng – the 'City of Dawn' in the local Dai language – is the capital of Xīshuāngbǎnnà Prefecture, but don't take that too seriously. It's still a drowsy Mekong River jungle town as much as a city. Taller buildings are going up, neophyte tour groups run around in all directions (great people-watching fun, actually) but it's still a perfect representation of laid-back Bǎnnà.

In the summer, the low season, prepare yourself for searing heat and a sapping humidity that puts the entire city into an extended slow motion. If you've acclimatised to higher and nippier elevations in Yúnnán, you'll probably find yourself needing lots of midday siestas. During the winter months, though, the temperature is just perfect.

THE DAI PEOPLE

The Dai (傣族) are Hinayana Buddhists (as opposed to China's majority Mahayana Buddhists) who first appeared 2000 years ago in the Yangzi Valley and were subsequently driven south to here by the Mongol invasion of the 13th century.

The Dai live in spacious wooden houses, raised on stilts to keep themselves off the damp earth, with the pigs and chickens below. The most common Dai foods are sticky rice (*khao nio* in Dai) and fish. The common dress for Dai women is a straw hat or towel-wrap headdress, a tight, short blouse in a bright colour, and a printed sarong with a belt of silver links. Some Dai men tattoo their bodies with animal designs, and betel-nut chewing is popular. Many Dai youngsters get their teeth capped with gold, as otherwise they are considered ugly.

Linguistically, the Dai are part of the very large Thai family that includes the Siamese, Lao, Shan, Thai Dam and Ahom peoples found scattered throughout the river valleys of Thailand, Myanmar (Burma), Laos, northern Vietnam and Assam. The Xīshuāngbǎnnà Dai are broken into four subgroups – the Shui (Water) Dai, Han (Land) Dai, Huayao (Floral Belt) Dai and Kemu Dai – each distinguished by variations in costume, lifestyle and location. All speak the Dai language, which is quite similar to Lao and northern Thai dialects. In fact, Thai is often as useful as Chinese once you get off the beaten track. The written language of the Dai employs a script that looks like a cross between Lao and Burmese.

Zhang khap is the name for a solo narrative opera, for which the Dai have a long tradition. Singers are trained from childhood to perform long songs accompanied by native flute and sometimes a long drum known as the elephant drum. Performances are given at monk initiations, when new houses are built, at weddings and on the birthdays of important people; they often last all night. At the end, the audience shouts *'Shuay! Shuay!'* which is close to 'Hip, hip, hooray!' Even courtship is done via this singing. Some Dai phrases include *douzao li* (hello), *yindi* (thank you) and *goihan* (goodbye).

Sights & Activities

Tropical Flower & Plants Garden GARDENS
(热带花卉园; Rèdài Huāhuìyuán; 99 Jinghong Xilu; admission Y40; ⏲7.30am-6pm) This terrific botanic garden, west of the town centre, is one of Jǐnghóng's better attractions. Admission gets you into a series of gardens where you can view over 1000 different types of plant life. Take the path on the left-hand side as you enter the gardens to head towards the lovely tropical rainforest area.

Peacock Lake Park PARK
The artificial lake in the centre of town isn't much, but the small park (孔雀湖公园; Kǒngquè Hú Gōngyuán) next to it is pleasant. The English Language Corner takes place here every Sunday evening, so this is your chance to exchange views or to engage with the locals practising their English.

Blind Massage School MASSAGE
(盲人按摩; Mángrén Ànmó; cnr Mengle Dadao & Jingde Lu; ⏲9am-midnight) Jǐnghóng's oft-recommended Blind Massage School offers hour-long massages for Y40. Staff are extremely kind and travellers give it terrific reports. Head down the lane off Mengle Dadao and climb the stairs on your left up to the 2nd floor.

Sleeping

Manting Lu is lined with cheapies, where you can find bearable rooms from Y50. Outside of festival season, big discounts are normally on offer all over town.

Many Trees International Youth Hostel YOUTH HOSTEL $
(曼丽翠国际青年旅舍; Mànlìcuì Gúojì Qīngnián Lǚshè; ☎212 6210; 5 Manyun Xiang; 嘎兰中路曼允巷5号; dm Y30-35, d Y85-95; ❄📶) Jǐnghóng has been crying out for a proper hostel for years, now it has one. The dorms are smallish, but have en suite bathrooms; the doubles are a good deal for the price. There's wi-fi throughout and a cosy communal area. It's down an alley off Galan Zhonglu.

Popular Holiday Hotel HOTEL $$
(假日时尚酒店; Jiàrì Shíshàng Jiǔdiàn; ☎213 9001; 104 Galan Zhonglu; 嘎兰中路104号; d Y358; ❄@) Standing out from the three-star pack by virtue of its sizeable, light, clean and modern rooms, many of which come with computers, the optimistic name

Jǐnghóng

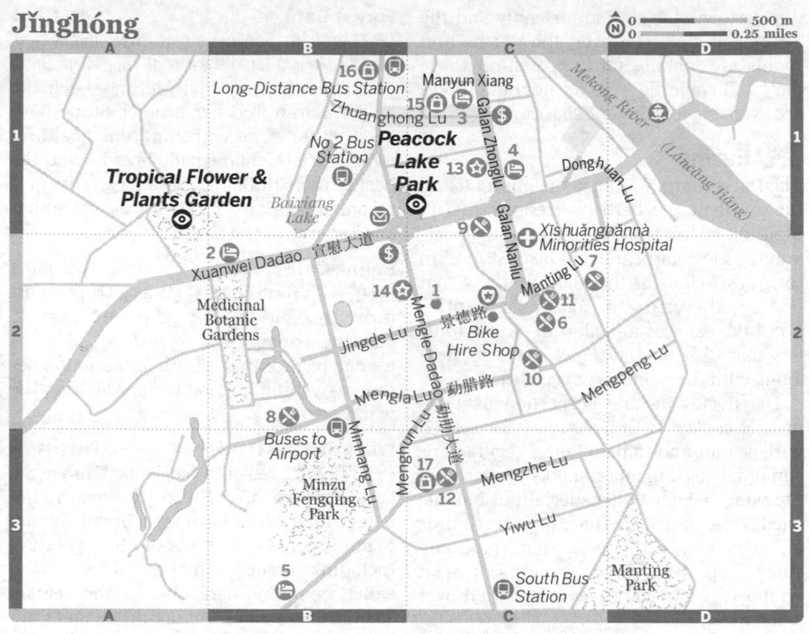

Jǐnghóng

Top Sights

Peacock Lake Park C1
Tropical Flower & Plants Garden A1

Activities, Courses & Tours

1 Blind Massage School C2

Sleeping

2 Bǎnnà College Hostel B2
3 Many Trees International Youth Hostel C1
4 Popular Holiday Hotel C1
5 Tai Garden Hotel B3

Eating

6 Bǎnnà Café C2
7 Dai BBQ Restaurants C2
8 Forest Café B2
9 Luō Luō Bīng Wū C1
10 Měiměi Café C2
11 Thai Restaurant C2
12 Wàngtiānshù Deli C3

Entertainment

13 Měngbālā Nàxī Arts Theatre C1
14 YES Disco B2

Shopping

15 Jade Market C1
16 Market B1
17 Xīshuāngbǎnnà Travel & Study Club C3

of this place is well justified. Ignore the listed prices; you should be able to get a room for Y100 to Y120 outside of festival time.

Tai Garden Hotel HOTEL $$$
(泰园酒店; Tàiyuán Jiǔdiàn; ☎216 6999; www.newtgh.com; 61 Minhang Lu; 民航路61号; d Y960 plus 15% tax, discounts of up to 60%; ❄@≋) Secluded and often eerily deserted in the low season, when rooms are hugely discounted, the Tai is a great escape from the tour group chaos. Fine grounds and a large and clean outdoor swimming pool (Y20 for nonguests) to cool off in add to its allure.

Bǎnnà College Hostel YOUTH HOSTEL $
(版纳学院; Bǎnnà Xuéyuàn; ☎213 8365; 93 Xuanwei Dadao; 宣慰大道93号; dm Y15-20, s/d Y60/70; ❄@) For yonks, this was *the* budget hang-out in Jǐnghóng. It's still the cheapest

digs in town, the staff are friendly and the location is fine. However, the dorms and rooms are looking fairly beaten-up these days and could do with an upgrade. Bikes are available for hire at Y25 a day.

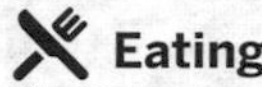

Eating

The Dai restaurants along Menghun Lu and the excellent Dai barbecue restaurants off Manting Lu are where you'll find the locals and the most authentic and tastiest food in town (as well as at the night markets that pop up all over town). You might want to avoid the eateries aimed at domestic tourists that dish up Dai dance performances along with their culinary specialities.

Dai dishes include barbecued fish, eel or beef cooked with lemongrass or served with peanut-and-tomato sauce. Vegetarians can order roast bamboo shoots prepared in the same fashion. Other specialities include fried river moss (better than it sounds and excellent with beer), spicy bamboo-shoot soup and *shāokǎo* (skewers of meat wrapped in banana leaves and grilled over wood fires).

Měiměi Café WESTERN $
(美美咖啡厅; Měiměi Kāfēitīng; Menglong Lu; dishes from Y15; ⌚8.30am-1am; 📶) You'll find it and you'll eat here. This is the original of all the Western-style cafes in town and still the best, thanks to its menu of burgers and sandwiches, pizza and pasta, and foreigner-friendly Chinese and Thai dishes. The owner Mei Mei is a great source of local info.

Luō Luō Bīng Wū NOODLES $
(啰啰冰屋; 96 Xuanwei Dadao; dishes from Y5; ⌚7.30am-10pm) Busy as long as it is open, the locals flock here for the cheap and tasty rice noodle and fried rice dishes, but especially for the fruit juices, shakes and Taiwanese-style shaved ice desserts that are perfect for cooling off. There's an open-air area out back.

Thai Restaurant THAI $
(泰国餐厅; Tàiguó Cāntīng; Manting Lu; mains from Y12; ⌚8am-9.30pm) If you're not making the trek overland to Southeast Asia, get your Thai fix at this ever-reliable open-air restaurant. It's not the most upmarket Thai place in town, but it's certainly the most popular and there's a huge range of dishes to choose from.

Forest Café WESTERN $
(森林咖啡屋; Sēnlín Kāfēiwū; www.forest-cafe.org; 23 Mengla Lu; dishes from Y8; ⌚9am-9pm) Almost as long as Mei Mei has been the owner, Sarah and her brother Stone have been at the Forest, dishing out healthful foods – try the homemade bread – and the best burgers in Bǎnnà. Sarah also gets rave recommendations for her treks. Another good source of travel tips.

Banna Cafe WESTERN $
(版纳咖啡; Bǎnnà Kāfēi; 1 Manting Lu; breakfast from Y25; ⌚7am-late) A good place for breakfast, this friendly, Dai-owned cafe also has a small terrace that is ideal for a sundowner or late-evening libation while watching the world go by.

Wàngtiānshù Deli WESTERN $
(望天树美食; Wàngtiānshù Měishí; 111 Mengzhe Lu; dishes from Y12; ⌚8.30am-10.30pm) Swiss-owned deli with European bread, homemade ice cream and lots of other goodies, including French wine and cheese, you won't find anywhere else in the region. There's also a small but decent menu of salads and steaks.

☆ Entertainment

Měngbālā Nàxī Arts Theatre THEATRE
(蒙巴拉纳西艺术宫; Měngbālā Nàxī Yìshùgōng; Galan Zhonglu; tickets Y160; ⌚8.10pm & 9.45pm) Wildly popular with tour groups, this theatre has nightly song and dance shows.

YES Disco CLUB
(迪斯科; Dísīkē; Mengle Dadao; admission free; ⌚8.30pm-late) Long-running, loud and always packed out with a young local crowd, YES is now a Jǐnghóng institution. Like all Chinese clubs, it's more about drinking than dancing.

Shopping

Market groupies can head to the fabulous fish and produce **market** tucked behind some modern buildings across from the long-distance bus station. The nearby **Jade Market** (玉市场; Yù Shìzhǎng; Zhuanghong Lu) features lots of Burmese and other South Asians hawking their goods alongside locals, and is fun for people-watching as well as shopping.

Information

Every once in a while we get reports from travellers regarding drug-and-rob incidents on the Kūnmíng–Jǐnghóng bus trip. Be friendly but aware, accept nothing, and never leave your stuff unattended when you hop off for a break.

Bank of China (中国银行; Zhōngguó Yínháng; Xuanwei Dadao) Changes travellers cheques and foreign currency, and has an ATM machine. There are other branches on Galan Zhonglu and Minhang Lu.

China Post (国际邮局; Zhōngguó Yóuzhèng; cnr Mengle Dadao & Xuanwei Dadao; ⏲8am-8.30pm) You can make international calls from here.

Internet cafes (山城网吧; wǎngbā; Manting Lu; per hr Y3) There are many internet cafes along this street.

Public Security Bureau (PSB; 公安局; Gōng'ānjú; Jingde Lu; ⏲8-11.30am & 3-5.30pm) Has a fairly speedy visa-extension service.

Xīshuāngbǎnnà MInorities Hospital (西双版纳民族医院; Xīshuāngbǎnnà Mínzú Yīyuàn; ☎213 0123; Galan Nanlu) The best bet for having an English speaker available.

Getting There & Away

Air

There are several flights a day to Kūnmíng (Y450) but in April (when the Water-Splashing Festival is held) you'll need to book tickets several days in advance to get either in or out.

In peak seasons you can hop on one or two flights daily to Dàlǐ (Y790) and/or Lìjiāng (Y680), along with semiregular flights to Shànghǎi (Y2250, daily) and Chéngdū (Y1350, three per week). There are travel agents all over town selling tickets.

Bus

The **long-distance bus station** (长途客运站; Chángtú Kèyùnzhàn; Minhang Lu) is the most useful for long-distance destinations, and also has a daily bus to Luang Nam Tha in Laos (Y78, seven hours, 10.40am).

Kūnmíng Y243, nine hours, 15 daily (8am to 9.50pm)

Lìjiāng Y334, 20 hours, one daily (2.30pm)

Ruìlì Y320, 26 hours, one daily (9am)

Xiàguān Y202 to Y261, 17 hours, four daily (12.30pm, 4.40pm, 5.30pm and 7.30pm)

If you want to explore Xīshuāngbǎnnà, go to the No 2 bus station (第二客运站; Dì'èr Kèyùnzhàn), also known as the Bǎnnà Bus Station.

Gǎnlǎnbà Y8.50, 40 minutes, every 30 minutes (7am to 7pm)

Měnghǎi Y15, 45 minutes, every 20 minutes (7am to 7.20pm)

Měnghùn Y16, 90 minutes, every 20 minutes (7am to 6.40pm)

BORDER CROSSING: GETTING TO THAILAND

The days of hitching rides on cargo boats to Laos and Thailand are long gone. Now, fast ferries leave Jǐnghóng on Tuesday, Thursday and Saturday for the seven-hour ride (Y800) to Chiang Saen in Thailand. Get there at 7.30am to start customs proceedings.

Travellers from most countries won't need a Thai visa unless they're planning on staying in the country longer than 30 days. The Thai consulate (p986) in Kūnmíng can issue a 60-day tourist visa for Y200. Visas take two days to process.

At the time of writing, these boats had been delayed by extremely low water levels; some claimed it was due to dam projects on the Mekong (yup, another day, another dam in China), while officials said it was 'seasonal'. Whatever – it had taken up to 15 hours!

Měnglà Y40, four hours, every 30 minutes (6.30am to 6.20pm)

Měnglún Y16, 90 minutes, every 20 minutes (7am to 6pm)

Měnyǎng Y10, 40 minutes, half-hourly (8am to 6pm)

Sānchàhé Y15, one hour, 10 daily (7.30am to 5pm)

Sīmáo Y41, two hours, every 30 minutes (6.30am to 7pm)

Head to the south bus station (客运南站; Kèyùn Nánzhàn), which mostly has departures to Kūnmíng, for buses to Dàměnglóng.

If you want to get to the Yuányáng Rice Terraces, first you'll have to take a bus to Jiāngchéng (江城; Y56, nine to 10 hours, 6.30am or 9.15am), stay there overnight and then hop on another bus to Lǜchūn (绿春; Y34, five hours), a nice Hani town with a good market, before hopping on a bus to Yuányáng (Y34, four hours). You could also take a bus from the main station to Shípíng (15 hours) or Jiànshuǐ (18 hours) and loop back if you're going to those places anyway.

Getting Around

The no 1 bus (Y2) runs to the airport, 5km south of the city, from a stop on Mengla Lu near the corner with Minhang Lu. A taxi will cost around Y20 but expect to be hit up for up to three times that amount during festivals.

Jǐnghóng is small enough that you can walk to most destinations, but a bike makes life easier and can be rented through most accommodation for Y25 to Y30 a day or from the **bike shop** (☎212 0125; ⏲8.30am-10pm) on Jingde Lu.

A taxi anywhere in town costs Y6.

Around Jǐnghóng

Trekking (or busing) to the endless minority villages is the draw. You can spend weeks, but even with limited time most destinations in Xīshuāngbǎnnà are only two or three hours away by bus. Note that to get to the most isolated villages, you'll often first have to take the bus to a primary (and uninteresting) village and stay overnight there, since only one bus per day – if that – travels to the tinier villages.

Market addicts can rejoice – it's an artist's palette of colours in outlying villages. The most popular markets seem to be the Thursday market in Xīdìng, then Měnghùn, followed by Měnghǎi.

Villages in the vicinity of Jǐnghóng can be reached by bicycle and this can be a good way to acclimatise yourself to the stifling heat. Many of them you will happen upon by chance. The most famous trek has always been the two- to three-hour ride to Měnghǎn (Gǎnlǎnbà); the ride can be hairy with traffic/pollution, but surrounding the village, it's sublime.

Take note: it can feel like every second village begins with the prefix 'Meng' and it isn't unheard of for travellers to end up at the wrong village entirely because of communication problems. Have your destination written down in script before you head off.

SĀNCHÀHÉ NATURE RESERVE

三岔河自然保护区

This nature reserve (Sānchàhé Zìrán Bǎohùqū), 48km north of Jǐnghóng, is one of five enormous forest reserves in southern Yúnnán. It has an area of nearly 1.5 million hectares; seriously, treat it with respect – you get off-trail here, you won't be found. The madding crowds head for **Bǎnnà Wild Elephant Valley** (版纳野象谷; Bǎnnà Yěxiànggǔ; admission Y65), named after the 50 or so wild elephants that live in the valley. The elephants are very retiring and rare are the travellers who have actually seen any of them. You will see monkeys, though, and it's worth a visit if you want to see something of the local forest. A 2km-long **cable car** (one way/return Y40/60) runs over the tree tops from the main entrance into the heart of the park, as does an elevated walkway.

There's a ho-hum **hotel** (d 240) at the main entrance; staying in the park is no

TREKKING IN XĪSHUĀNGBǍNNÀ

Treks around Xīshuāngbǎnnà used to be among the best in China – you'd be invited into a local's home to eat, sleep and drink *mǐjiǔ* (rice wine). Increasing numbers of visitors have changed this in places. Don't automatically expect a welcome mat and a free lunch just because you're a foreigner, but remember that throwing your money around could change the local economy.

If you do get invited into someone's home, try to establish whether payment is expected. If it's not, leave an offering (ask at the backpacker cafes what's considered appropriate) or leave modest gifts such as candles, matches, rice etc – even though the family may insist on nothing.

Also take care before heading off. It's a jungle out there, so go prepared, and make sure somebody knows where you are and when you should return. In the rainy season you'll need to be equipped with proper hiking shoes and waterproof gear. At any time you'll need water purification tablets, bottled water or a water bottle able to hold boiled water, as well as snacks and sunscreen.

Seriously consider taking a guide. You won't hear much Mandarin Chinese on the trail, let alone any English. Expect to pay around Y250 per day.

Forest Café (☎0691 898 5122; www.forest-cafe.org) in Jǐnghóng is a great place to start. Sarah, the owner, has years of experience leading treks and comes recommended. The **Měiměi Café** (☎0691 212 7324), also in Jǐnghóng, is also recommended.

Try the **Xīshuāngbǎnnà Travel & Study Club** (Xīshuāngbǎnnà Lǚxué Júlébù; ☎0691 213 1707; 19 Mengzhe Lu; ⏲8.30am-9pm) for trekking equipment; it also rents mountain bikes for Y40 a day.

longer an option. There are 10 buses daily to Sānchàhé (Y15, 1½ hours, 7.30am to 5pm).

MĚNGYǍNG 勐养

The much photographed **Elephant-Shaped Banyan Tree** (象形榕树; Xiàngxíng Róngshù) is the reason most people visit Měngyǎng, 34km northeast of Jǐnghóng on the road to Sīmáo. It's also a centre for the Hani, Floral-Belt Dai and Lahu, one of the poorest minorities in the region.

From Měngyǎng it's another 19km southeast to **Jīnuò** (基诺), which is home base for the Jinuo minority.

MĚNGHǍN (GǍNLǍNBÀ) 勐罕(橄榄坝)

A few years ago, Měnghǎn (or Gǎnlǎnbà as it's sometimes referred to) was a grand destination – you'd bike here and chill. Sadly, much of the main attraction – the lovely, friendly, somnolent village itself – has basically been roped off as a quasi minority theme park (and a pricey one at that) with tour buses, cacophonic dancing – the usual. That said, the environs of the village are still wondrous.

Sights

Dai Minority Park ANCIENT VILLAGE

(傣族园; Dàizúyuán; ☎0691 250 4099; Manting Lu; adult/student Y100/50) This was once the part of town that everyone came to this region to experience – especially for its classic temples and Dai families hosting visitors in their traditional homes. (It's now the aforementioned 'theme park'.) Tourists can spend the night in villagers' homes and partake in water-splashing 'festivals' twice a day. Despite the artificial nature of it all, some travellers have loved the experience.

For wonderful scenery along rivers and rice paddies, travellers recommend heading to the south of town, crossing the Mekong by ferry (Y2 with a bike), and then heading left (east). The last ferry returns at 7pm.

Sleeping & Eating

Beds in a Dai home within the park will cost between Y30 and Y50 per person. Food is extra. Beds are traditional Dai mats and are usually very comfortable. Most homes will also have showers for you. Restaurants inside the park are pricey and firmly aimed at tour groups.

Getting There & Away

Buses to Měnghǎn leave from Jǐnghóng's No 2 bus station (Y8.50, every 20 minutes, 7.15am to 7pm). From Měnghǎn's bus station, there are buses back to Jǐnghóng (Y8.50) every 20 minutes and two buses a day to Měnglún (Y9.50, one hour, 10am and 2pm).

It's possible to cycle from Jǐnghóng to Měnghǎn in a brisk two hours or a leisurely three hours, although the traffic can be heavy.

Getting Around

You can rent a mountain bike from one of several bicycle shops along Manting Lu (Y20 per day).

MĚNGLÚN 勐伦

East of Měnghǎn, Měnglún sports the **Tropical Plant Gardens** (热带植物园; Rèdài Zhíwùyuán; adult/student Y80/50; ⏰7.30am-midnight). The gardens are gorgeous and get some high marks from visitors.

To get there, turn left out of the bus station and then take the first left. Follow the road downhill and bear to the right and you'll reach the ticket office, which is just before a footbridge across the Mekong.

Your best bet for a clean bed in town is the **Chūnlín Bīnguǎn** (春林宾馆; ☎0691 871 5681; d Y50), which is close to the gardens' entrance.

From Jǐnghóng's No 2 bus station there are buses to Měnglún (Y16, 90 minutes, every 20 minutes, 6.30am to 6.20pm). Alternatively, Měnglún can be combined with a day trip to Měnghǎn.

From Měnglún, there are buses to Měnglà (Y24, 2½ hours, every 20 minutes, 8am to 6pm) and Jǐnghóng (Y16, 75 minutes, every 20 minutes, 6.30am to 7pm).

ETIQUETTE IN DAI TEMPLES

Around Dai temples the same rules apply as elsewhere: dress appropriately (no sleeveless tops or shorts); take off shoes before entering; don't take photos of monks or the inside of temples without permission; leave a donation if you do take any shots and consider leaving a token donation even if you don't – unlike in Thailand, these Buddhists receive no government assistance. It is polite to *'wai'* the monks as a greeting and remember to never rub anyone's head, raise yourself higher than a Buddha figure or point your feet at anyone. (This last point applies to secular buildings too. If you stay the night in a Dai household, it is good form to sleep with your feet pointing towards the door.)

THE JINUO PEOPLE

The Jinuo people (基诺族), sometimes known as the Youle, were officially 'discovered' as a minority in 1979 and are among the smallest groups – numbering between 12,000 and 18,000. They call themselves 'those who respect the uncle' and are thought to possibly have descended from the Qiang.

The women wear a white cowl, a cotton tunic with bright horizontal stripes and a tubular black skirt. Earlobe decoration is an elaborate custom – the larger the hole and the more flowers it can contain, the more beautiful the woman is considered. Teeth are sometimes painted black with the sap of the lacquer tree, which serves the dual dental purpose of beautifying the mouth and preventing tooth decay and halitosis.

Previously, the Jinuo lived in longhouses with as many as 27 families occupying rooms on either side of the central corridor. Each family had its own hearth, but the oldest man owned the largest hearth, which was always the closest to the door. Longhouses are rarely used now and the Jinuo seem to be quickly losing their distinctive way of life. The **Temaoke Festival** is held in Jinuo villages on the 6th to 8th of the second lunar month. During this festival you can witness elaborate rituals with the sacred Sun Drum.

MĚNGLÀ 勐腊

Měnglà: not the nicest send-off from China, nor the nicest first port of call. (Though the scenery north of town is gorgeous.) The only reason you should find yourself here is if you're crossing into (or coming from) Laos at Móhān. Depending on bus condition/road traffic/arrival time, you may be stuck here for the night.

At **Měnglà Bīnguǎn** (勐腊宾馆; ☎0691 812 2168; dm/d Y20/50) the dorm beds are spartan; the nicer doubles have their own balcony. It's near No 2 bus station. The **Jīnqiáo Dàjiǔdiàn** (金桥大酒店; ☎0691 812 4946; d Y50-70, tr Y80; ❄) is convenient for the north bus station just up the hill.

There is a **Bank of China** (中国银行; Zhōngguó Yínháng; ⏲8-11.30am & 3-6pm Mon-Fri) in the southern half of town that changes cash and travellers cheques but won't give cash advances on credit cards. To change renminbi back into US dollars, you'll need your original exchange receipts.

Měnglà has two bus stations. The northern long-distance bus station has buses to Kūnmíng (Y287, two or three, 8.30am to 11.30am). The No 2 bus station is in the southern part of town.

DÀMĚNGLÓNG 大勐龙

Dàměnglóng (just the latter two characters, 'Měnglóng', are written on buses) is a scrappy place with drowsy folks lolling about the dusty streets. Sights include some decent pagodas, but mostly you're here to traipse or bike through endless villages (ask about bike hire at the Huá Jié Bīnguǎn).

About 55km south of Jǐnghóng and a few kilometres from the Myanmar (Burma) border, the border crossing point (not open for foreigners) with Myanmar (Burma) has been designated as the entry point for a planned highway linking Thailand, Myanmar (Burma) and China, which should really liven things up around here if it ever gets built.

Sights

White Bamboo Shoot Pagoda BUDDHIST TEMPLE

(曼飞龙塔; Mànfēilóng Tǎ; admission Y5) Surrounded by jungle (watch out for stray snakes!), this pagoda dates back to 1204 and is Dàměnglóng's premier attraction. According to the legend, this pagoda's temple was built on the location of a hallowed footprint left behind by Sakyamuni Buddha, who is said to have visited Xīshuāngbǎnnà. If you have an interest in ancient footprints you can look for it in a niche below one of the nine stupas. The temple has been extensively renovated in recent years.

If you're in the area late October or early November, check the precise dates of the **Tan Ta Festival**. At this time, White Bamboo Shoot Pagoda is host to hundreds of locals whose celebrations include dancing, rocket launchings, paper balloons and so on.

The pagoda is easy to get to: just walk back along the main road towards Jǐnghóng for 2km until you reach a small village with a temple on your left. From here there's a path up the hill; it's about a 20-minute walk. There's often no one around to collect the entry fee. A moto-rickshaw from Dàměnglóng is Y10.

FREE **Black Pagoda** BUDDHIST TEMPLE
(黑塔; Hēi Tǎ) Just above the centre of town is a Dai monastery with a steep path beside it leading up to the Black Pagoda – you'll notice it when entering Dàměnglóng. The pagoda itself is actually gold, not black. Take a stroll up and have a chat with the four young monks in residence. The views of Dàměnglóng and surrounding countryside are more interesting than the temple itself.

Sleeping & Eating

Huá Jié Bīnguǎn HOTEL $
(华杰宾馆; ☎0691 274 2588; d Y50) Not very prepossessing, but the best option in town. To get here, turn right out of the bus station, then left up the hill and it's on the left-hand side, set back from the road.

There are simple Dai barbecue places scattered around the village. Try the ones close to the Black Pagoda.

Getting There & Away

Buses to Dàměnglóng (Y16, 90 minutes, every 20 minutes, 6.30am to 6.30pm) leave from Jǐnghóng's south bus station. Remember, the 'Da' character is sometimes not displayed. Buses for the return trip run on the same schedule.

Buses from Měnglà's No 2 station:

Jǐnghóng Y40, every 30 to 60 minutes (6.30am to 6.30pm)

Měnglún Y20 to Y25, every 20 minutes (6.40am to 7.30pm)

Móhān Y15, every 20 minutes (8am to 6pm)

XIǍOJIĒ 小街

The village of Xiǎojiē, about 15km north of Dàměnglóng, is surrounded by Bulang, Lahu and Hani villages. Lahu women shave their heads; apparently the younger ones aren't happy about this any more and hide their heads beneath caps. The Bulang are possibly descended from the Yi of northern Yúnnán. The women wear black turbans with silver decorations; many of the designs are of shells, fish and marine life.

There's plenty of room for exploration in this area, although be careful not to drift across the Burmese border.

MĚNGHǍI 勐海

This modern town is another potential base for exploring the countryside, although it's not as pleasant a place as Jǐnghóng. Grab a bike and head north for the most interesting pagodas and villages.

If you're passing through Měnghǎi, it's worth visiting the huge daily **produce market** that attracts members of the hill tribes. The best way to find it is to follow the early-morning crowds.

Buses run from Jǐnghóng's No 2 bus station to Měnghǎi (Y15, 45 minutes, every 20 minutes, 7am to 7.20pm). They return every 20 minutes or so too.

MĚNGHÙN 勐混

This quiet little village, about 26km southwest of Měnghǎi, has a colourful **Sunday market**. The town begins buzzing around 7am and the action lingers on through to midday. The swirl of hill tribespeople alone, with the women sporting fancy leggings, headdresses, earrings and bracelets, makes the trip worthwhile. Some travellers love it, while others decry the 'foreignisation' of locals.

There are several guesthouses, though none are remarkable. For Y50 you get a double with bathroom and TV, but no air-con.

BORDER CROSSING: GETTING TO LAOS

On-the-spot visas for Laos can be obtained at the border. The price will depend on your nationality (generally US$35 to US$40). The **Chinese checkpoint** (☎0691 812 2684; ⏲8am-5.30pm) is generally not much of an ordeal. Don't forget that Laos is an hour behind China.

A daily bus runs to Luang Nam Tha in Laos from Jǐnghóng (Y78, seven hours, 10.40am). Along with the bus to Vientiane from Kūnmíng (which leaves Kūnmíng at 5pm when there are enough passengers; Y486), it stops at Měnglà, but you're not guaranteed a seat.

No matter what anyone says, there should be no 'charge' to cross. Once your passport is stamped (double-check all stamps), you can jump on a tractor or truck to take you 3km into Laos for around Y5. Whatever you do, go early, in case things wrap up early on either side. There are guesthouses on both the Chinese and Lao sides; people generally change money on the Lao side.

BULANG PEOPLE

The Bulang people (布朗族) live mainly in the Bùlǎng, Xīdìng and Bādá mountains of Xīshuāngbǎnnà. They keep to the hills farming cotton, sugarcane and Pu'er tea, one of Yúnnán's most famous exports.

The men wear collarless jackets, loose black trousers and turbans of black or white cloth. They traditionally tattoo their arms, legs, chests and stomachs. The women wear simple, brightly coloured clothes and vibrant headdresses decorated with flowers. Avid betel-nut chewers, the women believe black teeth are beautiful.

Buses departing from Jǐnghóng for Měnghùn (Y16, 90 minutes, every 20 minutes, 7am to 6.40pm) run from the No 2 bus station.

From Měnghùn, minibuses run regularly to Měnghǎi (Y6, one hour), Xīdìng (Y12, 1½ hours, 7.10am and 4pm) and throughout the day to Jǐnghóng.

XĪDÌNG 西定

This sleepy hillside hamlet comes alive every Thursday for its weekly **market**, one of the best in the region. At other times you'll find Xīdìng almost deserted. If you want to see the market at its most interesting, you'll really have to get here the night before. There's a horrible hotel by the bus station; you're better off asking around and finding a bed with a local.

To get here by public transport you can either catch one of the two direct buses from Měnghǎi (Y12, 10.40am and 3.30pm) or travel via Měnghùn and change for a bus to Xīdìng. Buses from Xīdìng leave twice a day (Y11, 7.20am and 1pm) for Měnghùn. If you miss the bus you can always get a ride on a motorbike (Y30), a spectacular if hair-raising experience.

JǏNGZHĒN 景真

In the village of Jǐngzhēn, about 14km west of Měnghǎi, is the **Octagonal Pavilion** (八角亭; Bājiǎo Tíng; admission Y10; ⌚8am-6pm), first built in 1701. The original structure was severely damaged during the Cultural Revolution but renovated in 1978 and the ornate decoration is still impressive. The temple also operates as a monastic school. The paintings on the wall of the temple depict scenes from the Jataka, the life history of Buddha.

Frequent minibuses from the bus station in Měnghǎi go via Jǐngzhēn (Y6, 30 minutes).

Sìchuān

POPULATION: 84 MILLION

Includes »

Best Places to Eat

» Tibetan Restaurant (p738)

» Yùlín Chuànchuàn Xiāng (p711)

» Khampa Cafe & Arts Centre (p737)

» Ābù Lǔzī (p751)

» Tibetan Culture Dew (p733)

Best Places to Stay

» Zhuo Ma's (p750)

» Dala Gong Guesthouse (p739)

» Sim's Cozy Garden Hostel (p709)

» Lǐ Family Courtyard (p726)

» Jya Drolma and Gayla's Guesthouse (p736)

Why Go?

Like the seemingly magical theatre performances of *biànliǎn*, or 'face-changing', that originate here, Sìchuān (四川) is a land of many guises. Capital Chéngdū is quick to show off its slick, shiny, modern-China face, but you don't have to venture far to see a more traditional Sìchuān pose. The countryside around Chéngdū is scattered with alleyway-riddled ancient villages and lost-in-time teahouses, while mist-shrouded mountains creak with old wooden monasteries. Central Sìchuān is also home to the most famous face in all of China, that of the giant panda.

Head north, though, and you find a Chinese province posing as a region of alpine valleys and forested hills dotted with blue-green lakes and wonderful hiking trails.

And go west to witness Sìchuān's fabulous impression of Tibet. This is Kham, one of old Tibet's three traditional provinces; a vast landscape of high-plateau grasslands and snowcapped mountains where Tibetan culture still thrives.

When to Go

Chéngdū

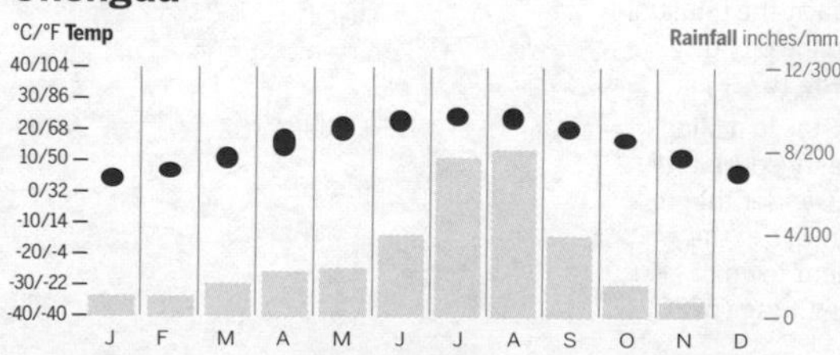

March–May Prime time for Chéngdū: not too humid; no summer rains yet; peach blossoms.

July & August Great time to visit the Tibetan areas; weather's warm and horse festivals abound.

June–October Head north, to brimming lakes, warm camping and stunning autumn forests.

Sìchuān Highlights

1. Get eye to eye with China's cuddliest national icon at Chéngdū's **Giant Panda Breeding Research Base** (p705)
2. Sleep in a monastery on the beautiful forested slopes of **Éméi Shān** (p719)
3. Join the new ecotourism program and be one of the first to go camping inside the stunning **Jiǔzhàigōu National Park** (p748)
4. Horse trek in the woods and mountains around the laid-back village of **Sōngpān** (p745)
5. Commune with Tibetan nomads on the gorgeous high-plateau grasslands around **Tǎgōng** (p736)
6. Feel Lilliputian at **Lèshān** (p722) as you stand beside the toenails of the world's largest Buddha statue
7. Visit ancient salt mines, dinosaur fossils and some of the best teahouses in China at the unusual riverside city of **Zìgòng** (p727)
8. Stay in a Ming-dynasty courtyard and wander the alleyways in the ancient town of **Lángzhōng** (p726)

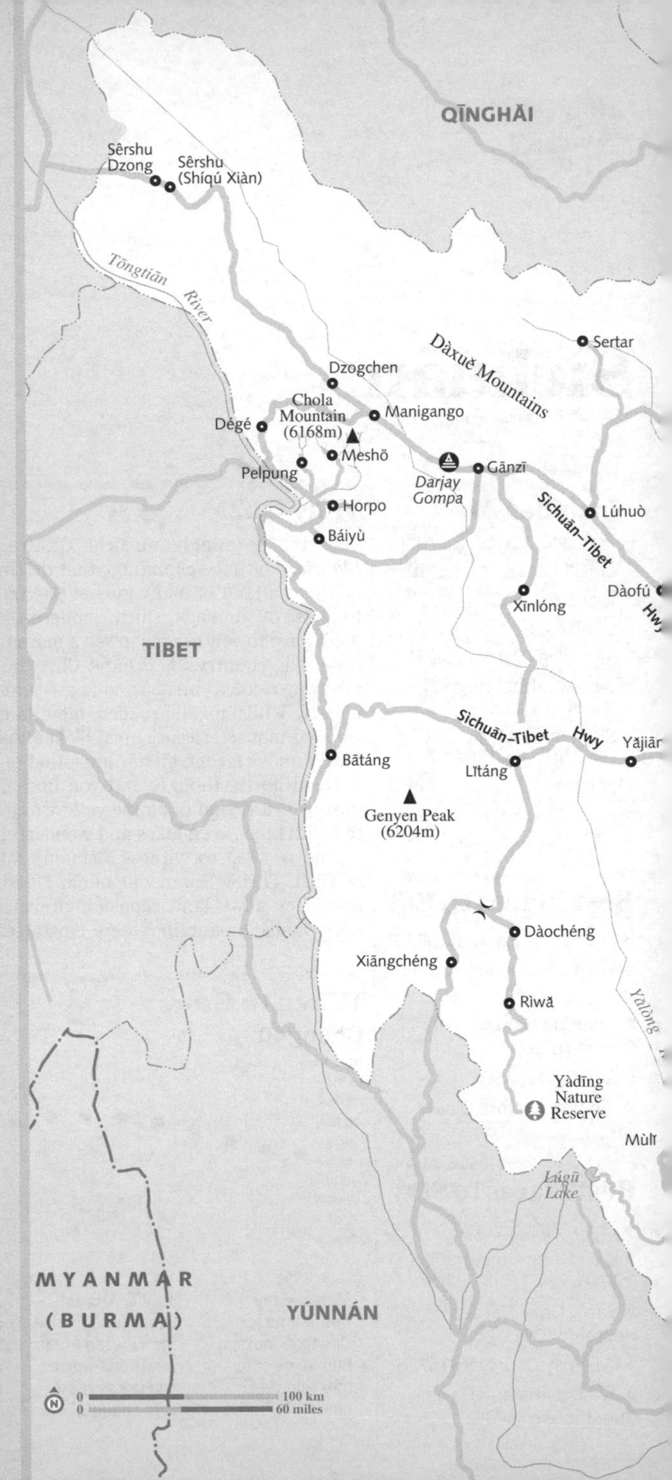

GĀNSÙ
Lǎngmùsì
Zöigê
3 Jiǔzhàigōu National Park
Nánpíng
Huánglóng National Park
Ābà
Hóngyuán
Jiuhuáng Airport
Chuānzhǔsì
4 Sōngpān
Xuěbǎo Mountain (5588m)
Qiónglái Mountains
Píngwǔ
Guǎngyuán
Zhāohuà
Mǎ'ěrkāng
Bāzhōng
Jiāngyóu
Màoxiàn
Wòlóng Nature Reserve
Wènchuān
Miányáng
Lángzhōng
8
Sìgūniang Shān (6250m)
Déyáng
Sìchuān Basin
Sānxīngduī
Guǎnghàn
Wòlóng
Dānbā
Qīngchéng Shān
1 CHÉNGDŪ
Nánchōng
Suìníng
Bàměi
Xīnjīn
5 Tǎgōng
Pínglè
Bìfēngxiá
Méishān
Kāngdìng (Dardo)
ndūqiáo
Yǎ'ān
Hóngyǎ
Chéngdū Expressway
Luǐ Jiāng
Éméi
Gònggā Shān (7556m)
Éméi Shān 2
6 Lèshān
Nèijiāng
Zìgòng 7
Shímián
Wūsīhé
Ebian
Tuōwū
Lúzhōu
Yíbīn
Chángníng
Chìshuǐ
Gǒngxiàn
Bamboo Sea
Měigū
Luòbiāo
Zhāojué
Xīchāng
Bùtuō
Luójì Mountain (4358m)
ányuán
Pǔgé
Jīnshā River
Pānzhīhuā (Jīnjiāng)

History

Sìchuān's early history was turbulent. The region was the site of various breakaway kingdoms, ever skirmishing with central authority, but it was finally wrestled into control and established as the capital of the Qin empire in the 3rd century BC. It was here that the kingdom of Shu (a name by which the province is still known) ruled as an independent state during the Three Kingdoms period (AD 220–80).

During the Warring States period (475–221 BC), local governor and famed engineer Li Bing managed to harness the flood-prone Mín River (岷江; Mín Jiāng) on the Chuānxī plain with his revolutionary weir system; the Dūjiāngyàn Irrigation Project (p717) still supplies Chéngdū with water, and still protects locals from floods, 2200 years after it was constructed! It's one reason why this part of China is known for being so fertile.

Another more recent factor was the efforts of Zhao Ziyang, governor of Sìchuān in 1975 and the province's first Communist Party secretary. After the tragic mistakes made during the Great Leap Forward (p922), when an estimated one-tenth of Sìchuān's population starved to death, Ziyang became the driving force behind agricultural and economic reforms that put Sìchuān back on the map. His 'Responsibility System', whereby plots of land were let out to individual farmers on the proviso that a portion of the crops be sold back to the government, was so successful it became the national model. This fertile land continues to produce more than 10% of the nation's grain, soybeans, pork and other crops.

Tragedy struck the region on 12 May 2008, when a devastating earthquake measuring 7.9 on the Richter scale hit the province's central region. According to some sources, it killed more than 88,000 people, many of them schoolchildren, and left millions more injured or homeless. For more on the rebuilding effort, see the boxed text, p711.

Language

Sichuanese is a Mandarin dialect, but the pronunciation is different enough that it's often difficult for those who speak standard Chinese to understand. One word visitors should know: instead of the oft-heard *méiyǒu* ('no'; literally 'don't have'), the Sichuanese say *méide*.

In addition to Mandarin, Sìchuān's other major languages belong to the Tibeto-Burman family and are spoken by Tibetans and the Yi.

PRICE INDICATORS

The following price indicators are used in this chapter:

Sleeping

$	less than Y200
$$	Y200 to Y600
$$$	more than Y600

Eating

$	less than Y30
$$	Y30 to Y50
$$$	more than Y50

Getting There & Around

AIR Chéngdū's airport is the largest in southwest China. Other smaller airports in Sìchuān that are useful for tourists include Jiǔzhàigōu, in the north, and Kāngdìng, in the west.

BUS Speedy expressways in eastern and southern Sìchuān make short trips from Chéngdū of many destinations.

Heading north of Chéngdū or anywhere west of Kāngdìng is a different story altogether. Road and weather conditions deteriorate rapidly and landslides that block the way are common. The scenery, though, can be spectacular.

You can travel to Gānsù province by bus, via Zöigě; to Qīnghǎi via Sěrshu or Ābà; and to Yúnnán via Xiāngchéng or Pānzhīhuā (Jīnjiāng).

Bus routes west into Tibet have historically been off limits to foreigners. You can often buy tickets, but once over the border, you'll probably get thrown off the bus, fined and sent back the way you came.

TRAIN Chéngdū is the main railway hub in China's southwest, with trains to pretty much anywhere, including Lhasa, provided you've arranged a travel permit in advance.

CENTRAL SÌCHUĀN

The province's laid-back capital city, Chéngdū, is where most travellers start their Sìchuān explorations, and it makes a great base for trips out to the region's top sights. This area is dotted with centuries-old towns and villages, Lángzhōng being the largest and best preserved, while lush, forested mountains make for great hiking, especially at Éméi Shān. Nearby Lèshān houses the world's largest Buddha statue, and then, of course, there are the pandas; practically impossible to see in the wild, they are made accessible here by some excellent wildlife reserves.

Chéngdū 成都

☎028 / POP 4.1 MILLION / ELEV 500M

On the face of it, Chéngdū has little appeal: it's flat, with no distinguishing natural features; the weather's grey and drizzly for much of the year; and the traffic's appalling. Yet somehow everyone comes away satisfied. Perhaps it's the wonderful teahouses found in the city's many parks and temples. Maybe it's the fabulous food, or the decent nightlife scene. It could simply be the pandas, of course. Who knows? Chances are, though, you'll be able to find out for yourself. Chéngdū is the transport hub for the whole of this region, so most travellers pass through this modern, fast-growing, yet surprisingly relaxed city at least once during their forays into China's southwest.

History

Chéngdū has seen the rise and fall of nearly a dozen independent kingdoms or dynasties since its founding in 316 BC; agricultural potential and strategic geography were key to its political power. Yet throughout history it has been equally well known for culture; not by accident did the Tang-dynasty poet Du Fu brush his strokes here.

Two walls were constructed in the Qin dynasty (221–206 BC) to create two adjacent city sections, both lying north of Brocade River (锦江; Jǐn Jiāng). Sadly, nothing remains of either after they were levelled in 1644 by rebel Zhang Xianzhong, who occupied the city, razed it to the ground, murdered most of its residents and then founded his own kingdom.

There's also nothing left of the once vast imperial palace, built in the Ming dynasty (1368–1644) on the site where Tianfu Sq and the Mao statue now stand. It covered 380,000 sq metres, more than half the size of Běijīng's Forbidden City, and one-fifth of Chéngdū's total area at the time, but was destroyed during the Cultural Revolution, the last of its magnificent gates finally disappearing in 1979.

These days the city is split by the Brocade River, a reminder of the city's silk brocade industry, which thrived during the Eastern Han dynasty (AD 25–220); from Chéngdū, the Southern Silk Road guided caravans to the known world.

By the time of the Tang dynasty (AD 618–907), the city had become a cornerstone of Chinese society. Three hundred years later, during the Song dynasty, Chéngdū began to issue the world's first paper money.

Sights

Giant Panda Breeding Research Base WILDLIFE RESERVE

(大熊猫繁殖研究中心; Dàxióngmāo Fánzhí Yánjiū Zhōngxīn; www.panda.org.cn; admission Y58; 🕗8am-6pm) One of Chéngdū's most popular tourist attractions, this reserve, 18km north of the city centre, is the easiest way to catch a glimpse of Sìchuān's most famous residents outside of a zoo. The enclosures here are large and kept in good condition.

Home to nearly 50 giant and red pandas, the base focuses on getting these sexually reluctant creatures to breed; March to May is the 'falling in love period', wink wink. If you visit in autumn or winter, you may see tiny newborns in the nursery.

There's a corny but informative 15-minute film about panda mating habits and an old-fashioned museum has detailed exhibits on panda evolution, habits, habitats and conservation efforts, all with English captions.

Try to visit the base in the morning, when the pandas are most active. Feeding takes place around 9.30am, although you'll see them eating in the late afternoon too. During the middle of the day they spend most of their time sleeping, particularly during the height of midsummer, when they sometimes disappear into their living quarters (air-conditioned, apparently).

Tourist bus 902 (Y2, one hour, frequent services 8am to 4pm) runs here from outside Traffic Inn, and goes past Sim's Cozy Garden Hostel en route. Last bus back is 6pm. All decent youth hostels run trips here, too, which cost more but get you to the base earlier.

Wénshū Temple BUDDHIST TEMPLE

(文殊院; Wénshū Yuàn; Renmin Zhonglu; admission Y5; 🕗6am-9pm) This Tang-dynasty monastery is dedicated to Wenshu (Manjushri), the Bodhisattva of Wisdom, and is Chéngdū's largest and best-preserved Buddhist temple. The air is redolent with incense, there's a low murmur of chanting, and despite frequent crowds of worshippers, there's still a sense of serenity and solitude. The temple's excellent **vegetarian restaurant** (文殊院素宴厅; Wénshūyuàn

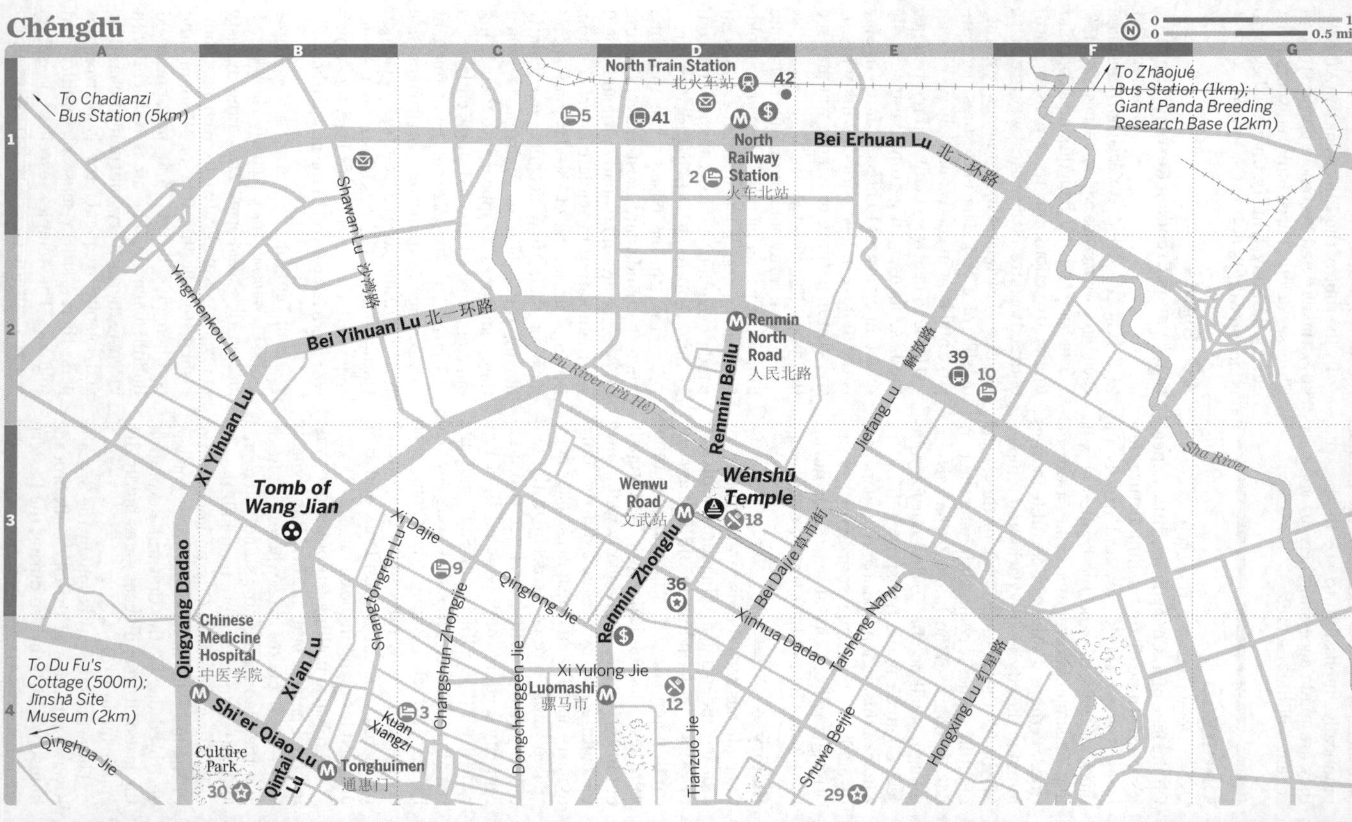
Chéngdū
0 1 km
0 0.5 miles
To Chadianzi Bus Station (5km)
To Zhāojué Bus Station (1km); Giant Panda Breeding Research Base (12km)
North Train Station
北火车站
42
5
41
North Railway Station
火车北站
2
Bei Erhuan Lu 北二环路
Shawan Lu 沙湾路
Yingmenkou Lu
Bei Yihuan Lu 北一环路
Renmin North Road
人民北路
Renmin Beilu
39
10
解放路
Jiefang Lu
Fu River (Fǔ Hé)
Sha River
Xi Yihuan Lu
Tomb of Wang Jian
Wénshū Temple
Wenwu Road
文武站
18
Xi Dajie
Bei Dajie 草市街
9
Qinglong Jie
Renmin Zhonglu
36
Xinhua Dadao
Taisheng Nanlu
Hongxing Lu 红星路
Qingyang Dadao
Chinese Medicine Hospital
中医学院
Xi'an Lu
Shangtongren Lu
Changshun Zhongjie
Dongchenggen Jie
Xi Yulong Jie
Luomashi
骡马市
12
Tianzuo Jie
Shuwa Beijie
29
To Du Fu's Cottage (500m); Jīnshā Site Museum (2km)
Qinghua Jie
Shi'er Qiao Lu
Qintai Lu
Culture Park
30
3
Kuan Xiangzi
Tonghuimen
通惠门

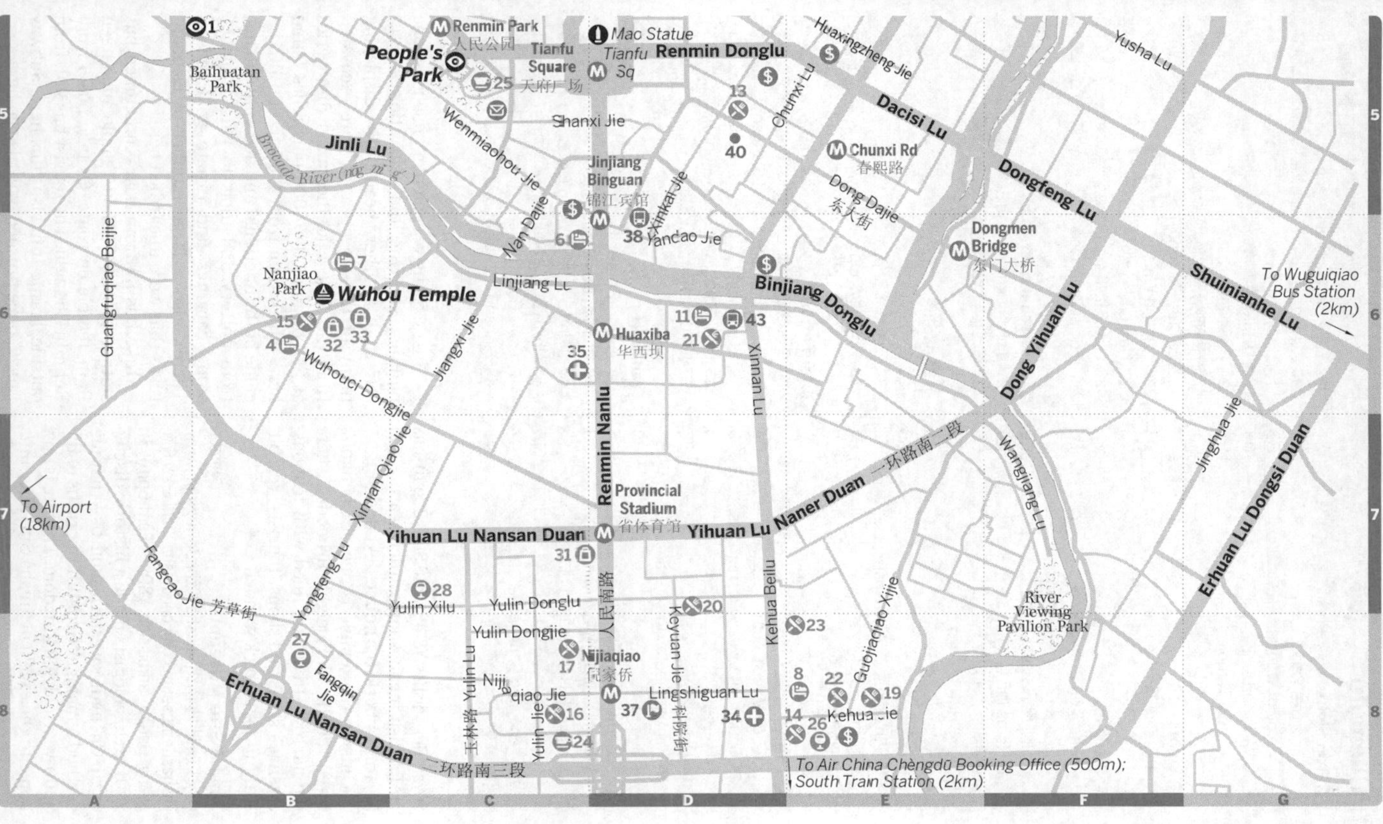

Renmin Park
人民公园
People's Park
Mao Statue
Tianfu Sq
Tianfu Square
天府广场
Renmin Donglu
Huaxingzheng Jie
Yusha Lu
Baihuatan Park
Shanxi Jie
Wenmiaohou Jie
Chunxi Lu
Dacisi Lu
Chunxi Rd
春熙路
Jinli Lu
Brocade River
Jinjiang Binguan
锦江宾馆
Xinkai Jie
Dong Dajie
东大街
Dongfeng Lu
Nan Dajie
Yancao Jie
Dongmen Bridge
东门大桥
Guangfuqiao Beijie
Nanjiao Park
Wǔhóu Temple
Linjiang Lu
Binjiang Donglu
Shuinianhe Lu
To Wuguiqiao Bus Station (2km)
Huaxiba
华西坝
Xinnan Lu
Dong Yihuan Lu
Wuhouci Dongjie
Jiangxi Jie
Renmin Nanlu
Ximian Qiao Jie
一环路南二段
Jinghua Jie
Wangjiang Lu
Provincial Stadium
省体育馆
Yihuan Lu Naner Duan
Erhuan Lu Dongsi Duan
To Airport (18km)
Yihuan Lu Nansan Duan
Fangcao Jie 芳草街
Yongfeng Lu
Yulin Xilu
Yulin Donglu
人民南路
Kehua Beilu
Guojiaqiao Xijie
River Viewing Pavilion Park
Yulin Dongjie
Keyuan Jie
Nijiaqiao
倪家桥
Fangqin Jie
Yulin Lu
玉林路
Nijiaqiao Jie
Lingshiguan Lu
科院街
Kehua Jie
Yulin Jie
Erhuan Lu Nansan Duan
二环路南三段
To Air China Chèngdū Booking Office (500m); South Train Station (2km)

Chéngdū

Top Sights
People's Park C5
Tomb of Wang Jian B3
Wénshū Temple D3
Wǔhóu Temple B6

Sights
1 Green Ram Temple B5

Sleeping
2 Chéngdū Grand Hotel D1
3 Dragon Town Guesthouse C4
4 Holly's Hostel B6
5 Home Inn C1
6 Jǐnjiāng Hotel C6
7 Jǐnlǐ Hotel B6
8 Kèhuāyuǎn Hotel E8
9 Loft C3
10 Sim's Cozy Garden Hostel E2
Traffic Hotel .... (see 11)
11 Traffic Inn D6

Eating
12 Chén Mápó Dòufu D4
13 Chuànchuànxiāng Restaurants D5
Highfly Cafe .... (see 11)
14 Huí Zhī Fèng E8
15 Kampa Tibetan Restaurant B6
16 Sultan C8
17 Tiāntiān Fàndiàn C8
18 Vegetarian Restaurant D3
19 Xīnjiāng Hóng Mǔdān Mùsīlín Kuàicān E8
20 Yángyáng Cānguǎn D7
21 Yùlín Chuànchuàn Xiāng D6
22 Yùlín Chuànchuàn Xiāng E8
23 Zígòng Càiguǎn E8

Drinking
24 Bookworm C8
25 Hè Ming Teahouse C5
Le Cafe Panam(e) .... (see 14)
26 Leg and Whistle E8
27 New Little Bar B8
28 Old Little Bar C7
Yuèlái Teahouse .... (see 29)

Entertainment
29 Jǐnjiāng Theatre E4
30 Shǔfēng Yǎyùn Teahouse B4

Shopping
31 52 Camp C7
32 Outdoor Shops B6
33 Tibetan Shops B6

Information
34 Global Doctor Chéngdū Clinic D8
35 No 4 Huáxī Hospital of Sichuan University C6
36 PSB (Foreign Affairs Section) D3
37 US Consulate D8

Transport
38 Airport Shuttle Bus D6
39 Beimen Bus Station E2
40 China Southern Airlines D5
41 North Bus Station D1
42 Train Ticket Office D1
43 Xīnnánmén Bus Station D6

Sùyàn Tīng; dishes Y8-48; ⏲10.30-8.30pm) has an English menu, some garden seating and an atmospheric **teahouse** next door.

Outside the temple is one of Chéngdū's three rebuilt 'old' neighbourhoods, where the narrow streets are lined with teahouses, snack stalls and shops. Touristy, yes, but still fun for a quick wander.

Jīnshā Site Museum MUSEUM
(金沙遗址博物馆; Jīnshā Yízhǐ Bówùguǎn; www.jinshasitemuseum.com; cnr Jinsha Yizhi Lu & Qingyang Dadao; admission Y80; ⏲8am-6pm) In 2001 archaeologists made a historic discovery in Chéngdū's western suburbs – they unearthed a major site containing ruins of the 3000-year-old Shu kingdom. The site is now home to the excellent Jīnshā Site Museum.

This expansive complex includes one building showing the excavation site itself and another beautifully displaying many of the objects that were excavated from the area. Like the earlier discoveries at Sānxīngduī, the 6000-plus relics found here, which date from 1200 to 600 BC, include both functional and decorative items, from pottery and tools to jade artefacts, stone carvings and ornate gold masks. There's also a large number of elephant tusks that were unearthed here.

Take bus 82 from near Xīnnánmén bus station, passing Wǔhóu Temple and Green Ram Temple en route. Or take bus 5 from Renmin Zhonglu. The tourist bus 901, from outside Traffic Inn, also runs here. Subway Line 2, once finished, will also go here.

Tomb of Wang Jian MAUSOLEUM
(王建墓; Wángjiàn Mù; Yongling Lu; admission Y20; ⏲8am-6pm) The only mausoleum excavated in China so far that features an above-ground tomb chamber, this slightly creepy vault honours Wang Jian (847–918), a general who came to power after the AD 907 collapse of the Tang dynasty and became emperor of the Shu kingdom. The tomb itself is decorated with carvings of 24 musicians all playing different instruments, considered to be the best surviving record of a Tang-dynasty musical troupe, while the statue of Wang Jian at the back of the tomb is thought to be the only existing lifelike sculpture of an ancient Chinese king.

FREE **People's Park** PARK
(人民公园; Rénmín Gōngyuán; ⏲6.30am-10pm) Particularly on weekends, People's Park is filled with locals dancing, singing, strolling and practising taichi. There are a number of teahouses here too; Hè Míng Teahouse is particularly popular.

Plopped in the middle of the park's bonsai and perennials (open 9am to 5pm) is the **Monument to the Martyrs of the Railway Protection Movement** (1911). This obelisk memorialises an uprising of the people against corrupt officers who pocketed cash intended for railway construction.

Green Ram Temple TAOIST TEMPLE
(青羊宫; Qīngyáng Gōng; admission Y10; ⏲8am-6pm) Located in **Culture Park** (Wénhuà Gōngyuán; ⏲7am-10pm), this is Chéngdū's oldest and most extensive Taoist temple. According to legend, stroking the bronze goat here can vanquish life's troubles. (The other, less goatlike goat combines features of all the Chinese zodiac animals.) Another highlight is an eight-sided pagoda, built without bolts or pegs.

Du Fu's Cottage FORMER RESIDENCE
(杜甫草堂; Dùfǔ Cǎotáng; 38 Qinghua Lu; admission Y60; ⏲8am-6.30pm) The revered Tang-dynasty poet, Du Fu (712–70) was born in Hénán, but lived in Chéngdū, in this thatched cottage, for four of his most prolific years. He wrote more than 200 poems whilst here, including one entitled 'My thatched hut was torn apart by the autumn wind'. The 10-hectare site is now part park, part museum.

Wǔhóu Temple TEMPLE
(武侯祠; Wǔhóu Cí; admission Y60; ⏲8am-6pm) Located in **Nánjiāo Park** (Nánjiāo Gōngyuán; ⏲6am-10pm) and surrounded by gardens with mossy cypresses draped over walkways, this temple honours several figures from the Three Kingdoms period, including Emperor Liu Bei and legendary military strategist Zhuge Liang, who was immortalised in one of the classics of Chinese literature, *Romance of the Three Kingdoms (Sān Guó Yǎnyì)*. Just east of the temple is **Jǐnlǐ Gǔjiē** (锦里古街) a gentrified 'new-old' district crammed with souvenir junk stalls and local snacks.

River Viewing Pavilion Park PARK
(望江楼公园; Wàngjiānglóu Gōngyuán; admission Y20; ⏲8am-6pm) Dedicated to celebrated Tang-dynasty female poet Xue Tao, this park is best known for its bamboo; it features over 150 varieties, from bonsai-sized potted plants to towering giants. If you're not interested in the Xue Tao exhibits, enter the park through the western gate (open from 6.30am to 9pm), where no admission is charged and you can still stroll among the bamboo. Buses 35 and 335 come here from the city centre.

Sleeping

TOP CHOICE **Sim's Cozy Garden Hostel**
YOUTH HOSTEL $
(老沈青年旅舍; Lǎoshěn Qīngnián Lǚshè; ☎8196 7573; www.gogosc.com; 211 Yihuan Lu Bei Siduan; 一环路北四段211号; dm Y30-40, s without/with bathroom Y80/120, d Y160-240;) This fabulous place sprawling its way around two lush garden courtyards is certainly the best hostel in Chéngdū, and quite possibly the best of its kind in China. Owners Sim and Maki (he's Singaporean, she's Japanese) are experienced travellers (they're great resources for travel in Sìchuān and Tibet) and welcoming hosts who take pride in getting all the details right, from lockable storage boxes in the dorms to DVD players and reading lamps in the doubles. Travellers can hang out in the gardens, the bar or the open-air terrace, and the restaurant serves decent food. The only downside is its relatively isolated location, but there's good bus information, as well as info on pretty much everything else, on the noticeboards. Take bus 28 from Xīnnánmén bus station.

Traffic Inn YOUTH HOSTEL $
(交通青年旅舍; Jiāotōng Qīngnián Lǚshè; ☎8545 0470; www.redcliffinn.cn; 6 Linjiang Zhonglu; 临江中路6号; dm Y20-30, s/d/tr without bathroom Y60/80/120, with bathroom Y140/160/210;) If Sim's wasn't so damn good, this place would be the best hostel in town. Rooms without private bathrooms are the best, with stripped-wood furniture, tiled

flooring and loads of space. The mosaic-tiled shared shower rooms are spotless, and the excellent **Highfly Cafe** (高飞咖啡; Gāofēi Kāfēi; ⊙7am-1am) with patio seating and free pool table is just round the back. Dorms and rooms with private bathrooms are housed in the adjoining **Traffic Hotel** (交通酒店; Jiāotōng Jiǔdiàn; ☎8545 1017), a good-quality Chinese budget hotel. Note: rooms with bathrooms are cheaper if you deal directly with the hotel rather than go through the youth hostel. There's good wi-fi connection in all rooms, staff members are very helpful and the location, close to Xīnnánmén bus station, couldn't be more convenient.

Loft YOUTH HOSTEL $
(四号工厂青年旅馆; Sìhào Gōngchǎng Qīngnián Lǚguǎn; ☎8626 5770; www.lofthostel.com; 4 Shangtongren Lu, Xiaotong Xiang; 小通巷上同仁路4号; dm Y40, tw without bathroom Y100, tw & d with bathroom Y180; ❄@☜) Chic boutique hotel meets youth hostel at this trendy converted printing factory. Cool details include exposed-brick walls and black-tiled bathrooms; laid-back staff members are pretty cool, too. A cafe serves Western food, and the relaxing common areas include a pool table, free internet access and an urban-style courtyard.

Jǐnlǐ Hotel HOTEL $$
(锦里客栈; Jǐnlǐ Kèzhàn; ☎6631 1335; 231 Wuhouci Dajie; 武侯祠大街231号; s/d Y480/560, discounts of around 40%; ❄) If you don't mind the touristy surroundings on the Jǐnlǐ shopping street near Wǔhóu Temple, this upmarket inn set in two courtyard-style buildings is a fun place to stay. Rooms mix traditional Chinese wooden furnishings with modern trappings such as white duvets and TVs.

Jǐnjiāng Hotel HOTEL $$$
(锦江宾馆; Jǐnjiāng Bīnguǎn; ☎8550 6050; www.jjhotel.com; 80 Renmin Nanlu; 人民南路二段80号; r from Y1587, discounts of around 50%; ❄@≋) Jǐnjiāng was Sìchuān's first-ever five-star hotel and, up until the late '70s, its nine-storey block was the tallest building in Chéngdū. There are more luxurious hotels in the city these days, but this one retains a certain charm that the bigger international chains lack. Guests are greeted by a string quartet in the lobby and staff members are both courteous and well turned out; especially the red-uniformed bell hops. Rooms are comfortable without being the height of luxury, but if they were good enough for Spanish tenor Plácido Domingo when he stayed here in 2009, they're probably good enough for you.

Holly's Hostel YOUTH HOSTEL $
(九龙鼎青年客栈; Jiǔlóngdǐng Qīngnián Kèzhàn; ☎8554 8131; hollyhostelcn@yahoo.com; 246 Wuhouci Dajie; 武侯祠大街246号; dm Y25-35, d without bathroom Y80, d/tw/tr with bathroom Y120/140/180; @☜) Rooms at this lovely little hostel tucked down a lane near the Tibetan quarter are a bit bland, but staff are friendly and there's a great roof-terrace cafe serving well-priced Chinese and Western food as well as fresh coffee (from Y10). There's also a free pool table, wi-fi and bikes for rent (per day Y20).

Kèhuāyuǎn Hotel HOTEL $$
(刻花苑宾馆; Kèhuāyuàn Bīnguǎn; ☎8546 2555; 141 Kehua Beilu; 科华北路141号; tw/d Y598/698, discounts of around 50%; ❄@) Large, smart comfortable rooms come with small but sparkling shower rooms. Staff members are friendly but speak little English. Laptop users can get online for free in all rooms. Cheaper rooms without windows are also available.

Dragon Town Guesthouse YOUTH HOSTEL $$
(龙堂客栈; Lóngtáng Kèzhàn; ☎8664 8408; www.dragontown.com.cn; 26 Kuan Xiangzi; 宽巷子26号; dm Y20-50, d/tw Y200/220; ❄@☜) It has let itself go in recent years and is starting to look a bit rundown, but the location in the newly reconstructed Kuānzhǎi Xiàngzi (宽窄巷子) area is still excellent. The alleys around here are full of trendy restaurants, cafes and boutique shops, and while most of the buildings are no more than five years old, some, including Dragon Town's, date back to the Qing dynasty. The hostel's courtyard with fish pond remains atmospheric but in general a lick of paint wouldn't go astray.

Chéngdū Grand Hotel HOTEL $$
(成都大酒店; Chéngdū Dàjiǔdiàn; ☎8317 3888; 29 North Renmin; 人民北路二段29号; d & tw Y400-560, discounts of around 50%; ❄@) This 23-storey old-school Chinese hotel with decent, internet-enabled rooms makes a comfortable choice if you need to be near the train station.

Eating

Cheap, quick snacks known as *xiǎo chī* (little eats) are a way of life here. Another favourite, although harder to find than it used to be, is *shāokǎo* (barbecue) – chilli-rubbed grilled skewers of meat, vegies and smoked tofu that used to be sold off street-market stalls but these days are restricted to small hole-in-the-wall restaurants or

REBUILDING QUAKE-STRICKEN COMMUNITIES

At 2.28pm on 12 May 2008, an earthquake measuring 7.9 on the Richter scale occurred along the Lóngménshān fault in Wènchuān County, 80km northwest of Chéngdū. The results were catastrophic: 88,000 people were killed, 375,000 injured, more than 33 million were affected, with 11 million left homeless and 1.5 million displaced.

The main tremor lasted for almost two minutes, causing the ground to shift about 10m in areas near the epicentre. Buildings were evacuated as far away as Běijīng and Bangkok.

Mountains were sliced apart. Rivers changed course. Landslides smothered roads and blocked rivers, creating 'quake' lakes. Whole towns were buried.

Almost 50,000 aftershocks were recorded within the first six months after the quake. Hundreds of thousands of homes that withstood the initial quake collapsed with the aftershocks.

Peter Goff, chairman of Sìchuān Quake Relief (www.sichuan-quake-relief.org), said China's immediate reaction was swift and impressive.

'Within 90 minutes of the quake Premier Wen Jiabao was on a plane to Chéngdū to oversee the recovery work,' he said. 'More than 150,000 Chinese troops and medics were mobilised within hours. The government announced that it would spend 1 trillion yuan (US$147 billion) to rebuild areas devastated by the earthquake over a three-year period, and most families who lost homes were given a grant of around Y20,000 (US$3000), about one-third the cost of a small rural house.'

Mr Goff said the authorities were quite rightly praised for their initial reaction, but it wasn't long before questions started to be asked.

'They were strongly criticised for the highly contentious issue of shoddy school construction,' he said. 'In numerous areas across the quake zone "tofu" schools toppled down while surrounding buildings remained intact, which led to parents accusing local officials and developers of corruption.

'To appease the parents, some special regulations were brought in. The one-child policy restrictions, for example, were lifted for parents whose child was either killed or severely injured in the disaster. And local officials offered bereaved parents compensation – usually about US$15,000 (Y100,000) – as long as they promised not to raise the issue again or to engage in any petitioning or protesting. Parents and volunteers who have protested or pushed the matter have been rounded up, detained and threatened by local officials.

'Another issue that is causing local concern is the matter of farmers being asked to give up their land and move into urban communities to make way for infrastructure redevelopment projects. This is part of a national urban–rural integration plan but it has been speeded up in Sìchuān as a result of the earthquake. Allegations abound of officials and developers offering inadequate compensation and using the quake reconstruction efforts as a pretext to increase their holdings.

'In terms of infrastructure there's no doubt the area will be better served than ever before when all the reconstruction projects are completed, but there is still a significant number of people who, physically or economically, are unable to rebuild their lives.'

temporary late-evening operations cooked on the back of bicycle-rickshaws.

Another popular Chéngdū speciality is *chuànchuàn xiāng,* the skewers version of the famous Chóngqìng hotpot *(huǒguō),* and just as spicy. *Chuànchuàn xiāng* is a quintessential Chéngdū eating experience and there are restaurants all over the city, including a bunch of pocket-sized ones on Shuwa Jie (暑袜街).

Several monasteries, including Wénshū Temple, Zhāojué Temple and Green Ram Temple, have vegetarian restaurants (dishes Y7 to Y20) that are generally open only for lunch. There's also a vegetarian restaurant at the **Monastery of Divine Light** (Bǎoguāng Sì; dishes from Y7; ⌚11am-1.30pm) in Xīndū.

TOP CHOICE **Yùlín Chuànchuàn Xiāng** HOTPOT **$** (玉林串串香; 2-3 Kehua Jie; 科华街2-3号; per skewer Y0.12 & Y1; ⌚11am-late) This lively open-fronted branch of the popular Yùlín chain is packed in the evenings with a hungry student crowd from nearby Sìchuān University. Choose your own skewers from a side room then cook them yourself in the boiling, spicy broth on your table. Staff will count up how many skewers you've eaten at the end of your meal. The garlic and chilli dipping sauce is Y3 extra. There's another, slightly smaller branch near Traffic Inn youth hostel.

Yángyáng Cānguǎn SICHUANESE **$**
(杨杨餐馆; 32 Jinyuan Xiang; 锦苑巷; dishes Y8-40; ⌚9am-9pm; 📵) Good-quality, inexpensive Sichuanese food with terrace seating, fast service and an English menu. Note, the English menu doesn't have prices, so you might want to ask for the Chinese menu *(zhōngwén càidān)* too.

Zìgòng Càiguǎn SICHUANESE **$$**
(自贡菜馆; 127-129 Kehua Beilu; 科华北路127—129号; dishes Y18-48; ⌚10am-11pm) You'll find all the usual Sichuanese favourites with the addition of some specialities from the southern town of Zìgòng, historically one of this region's three culinary centres (along with Chéngdū and Chóngqìng). Look for the characters for Zìgòng (自贡) written in brackets after dishes. Zìgōng food uses different types of chillies and peppers from standard Sìchuān fare, and often contains rabbit meat (兔肉; *tùròu*), fish (鱼肉; *yúròu*) or frog (田鸡; *tiánjī*). Dishes are spicy, as you'd expect, but not quite as blow-your-head-off spicy as in other parts of the province. There's a photo menu, but to get you started try Yùmǐ Nèntù (玉米嫩兔; Y25), boneless rabbit pieces and sweet corn in a mild sauce, or Tiàoshuǐ Tiánjī (跳水田鸡; Y45 per *jin*), frogs in a spicy ginger sauce. One *jīn* (Chinese weight, about 600g) is enough for one person.

Chén Mápó Dòufu SICHUANESE **$$$**
(陈麻婆豆腐; 2nd fl, 197 Xi Yulong Jie; dishes Y12-58; ⌚11.30am-9pm) This plush branch of the famous chain is a great place to sample *mápó dòufu* (small/large Y12/20) – soft, fresh bean curd with a fiery sauce of garlic, minced beef, salted soybean, chilli oil and Sìchuān pepper. It's one of Sìchuān's most famous dishes and this restaurant's speciality. Photo menu.

Xīnjiāng Hóng Mǔdān Mùsīlín Kuàicān MUSLIM **$**
(新疆红牡丹穆斯林快餐; cnr Kehua Jie & Guojiaqiao Xijie; dishes Y6-50; ⌚10am-11.30pm) This extremely popular Xīnjiāng restaurant beside Sìchuān University is a great place to sample the Uighur speciality *dàpánjī* (literally 'big plate chicken') – a massive portion of chicken, potatoes and peppers stewed in a savoury, spicy sauce. Even the 'small' plate (Y30) will serve two or three. When you're part-way through the meal, staff dump a pile of handmade noodles into your dish, perfect for sopping up the sauce. Lamb skewers (羊肉串; *yángròu chuàn;* Y1) and grilled naan bread (烤馕; *kǎo náng;* Y4) are good accompaniments. If you're eating solo, the *dīngdīng miàn* (丁丁面; Y6 to Y8) is a noodle dish worth sampling.

Huì Zhī Fèng BARBECUE **$$**
(惠之凤; Blue Caribbean Plaza, cnr Kehua Beilu & Kehua Jie; 科华北路143号蓝色加勒比广场; dishes Y8-28; ⌚11am-late; 📵) Chéngdū's answer to teppan-yaki and a great place to fill up before drinks on Kehua Jie. There are tables outside, but it's more fun to sit inside, around the giant horseshoe-shaped hotplate and watch the chef griddle the dishes you've just ordered. There's an English menu, but if you're looking for inspiration, the bacon-wrapped mushrooms (培根卷; *péigēn juǎn;* Y20) are divine. Two dishes per person are usually enough.

Tiāntiān Fàndiàn SICHUANESE **$$**
(天添饭店; 17 Yulin Dong Jie; 玉林东街17号; dishes Y8-58; ⌚9am-9.30pm) Specialises in duck dishes and stews, but has the whole range of classic Sichuanese dishes including a particularly delicious clay-pot mushroom dish (干锅茶树菇; *gānguō cháshùgū;* Y28). No English, but has a good photo menu.

Sultan MIDDLE EASTERN **$$**
(苏坦; Sūtǎn; 1 Yulin Nanjie, Dushi Jin'an Bldg; dishes Y8-58; ⌚11am-10pm; 📶) Friendly, easygoing Middle Eastern restaurant with lamb kebabs, hummus, warm naan and homemade yoghurt. You could linger over dark Turkish coffee (there's free wi-fi), sit outside on the sunny patio, or lounge in a private room piled with cushions and puff on a fruit-flavoured *sheesha* pipe (Y50). The entrance is on a side road just east of Yulin Nanjie.

Kampa Tibetan Restaurant TIBETAN **$**
(康巴藏餐; Kāngbā Zàngcān; off 246 Wuhouci Dajie; 武侯词大街246号附18; dishes Y8-28; ⌚8am-11pm; 📵) Small, friendly Tibetan-run restaurant next to Holly's Hostel serving tasty Tibetan classics like *tsampa* (porridge of roasted barley flour), yak meat and butter tea. English menu.

Drinking

Sìchuān represents the culture of tea better than anywhere else in China. The art of tea-drinking dates back 3000 years, and Sìchuān's teahouses have long been the centres of neighbourhood social life. They were, and still are, where people gossiped, played cards, watched opera performances, had haircuts and even had their ear wax removed! Today you'll find crowded teahouses all over Chéngdū, particularly in the city's parks and temple grounds. There are also some pleasant ones on the banks of the Brocade River. Tea is generally bought by the cup (Y5 to Y30) and is topped up for free as often as you like.

There's a decent number of bars and cafes here too. For the latest on Chéngdū's nightlife scene, pick up one of the city's expat magazines: *Chengdoo* or *More Chengdu*.

Hè Míng Teahouse TEAHOUSE

(鹤鸣茶馆; Hèmíng Cháguǎn; People's Park; teas Y10-25; ⌚7am-9pm) One of Chéngdū's most pleasant and popular spots to while away an afternoon over a bottomless cup of flower tea. The tea menu is in English. Having your ears cleaned (Y20) is optional.

Old Little Bar BAR

(小酒馆(玉林店); Xiǎo Jiǔguǎn (Yùlín Diàn); 55 Yulin Xilu; 玉林西路55号; beers from Y10; ⌚6pm-2am) Reportedly set up by China's rock legend Cui Jian, this is Chéngdū's most established rock bar. It no longer has live performances – go to New Little Bar for that – but still a cool place to hang out with music-loving locals.

New Little Bar BAR

(小酒馆(芳沁店); Xiǎo Jiǔguǎn (Fāngqìn Diàn); ☎8515 8790; Fangqin Jie, behind 47 Yongfeng Lu; 永丰路47号芳沁街; beers from Y10; ⌚6pm-2am) This small pub-like venue is *the* place in Chéngdū to catch local bands performing live. Bands play every Friday and Saturday, and occasionally on weekdays, usually from 8pm. Live music carries a cover charge of around Y30, depending on who's playing. Check expat magazine *Chengdoo* for monthly line-ups.

Bookworm CAFE

(老书虫; Lǎo Shūchóng; ☎8552 0177; www.chengdubookworm.com; 2-7 Yulin Donglu, 28 Renmin Nanlu; ⌚9am-1am) This excellent bookstore-cafe, with branches in Běijīng and Sūzhōu, is a peaceful spot for a drink or a coffee. It often hosts author talks, concerts and other events. Check its website for a schedule.

Le Cafe Panam(e) BAR

(巴黎酒吧; Bālí Jiǔbā; 2nd fl, Blue Caribbean Plaza, cnr Kehua Beilu & Kehua Jie; 科华北路143号蓝色加勒比广场2层; beers from Y10; ⌚5pm-4am) This hip French-owned bar is the coolest of a number of drinking venues in and around this small plaza.

Temple of Mercy TEAHOUSE

(大慈寺; Dàcí Sì; Dacisi Lu; admission Y3; ⌚10am-6pm) Most of Chéngdū's temples have teahouses; this one is a favourite for tea, mah jong and lazy afternoons in the sun.

Leg and Whistle BAR

(2nd fl, 19 Chuanda Huayuan Building, Kehua Jie; 科华街川大花园19号2层) Near Le Cafe Panam(e), this is the place to go to watch football.

Entertainment

Chéngdū is the home of Sìchuān opera, which dates back more than 250 years. It's nothing like Western opera; many performances feature slapstick, glass-shattering songs, men dressed as women, gymnastics and even fire breathing. An undoubted highlight is 'face-changing' (变脸; *biànliǎn*) in which performers swap masks, seemingly by magic.

Shǔfēng Yǎyùn Teahouse SÌCHUĀN OPERA

(蜀风雅韵; Shǔfēng Yǎyùn; ☎8776 4530; www.shufengyayun.com; Culture Park; tickets Y150-260) Located in Culture Park, this large teahouse puts on excellent shows that include music, puppetry, comedy, Sìchuān opera and the province's famed face-changing performances. Shows run nightly from 8pm to 9.30pm. If you come at around 7.30pm you can watch performers putting on their make-up. Kids might like to have their own faces painted (from Y100).

Jǐnjiāng Theatre SÌCHUĀN OPERA

(锦江剧场; Jǐnjiāng Jùchǎng; ☎8662 0019; 54 Huaxingzheng Jie; 华兴正街54号; tickets Y120-260; ⌚8-9.30pm) There are similar mixed-performance shows held daily at this renowned opera theatre. The adjoining **Yuèlái Teahouse** (悦来茶楼; Yuèlái Chálóu; teas Y6-15; ⌚8.30am-9.30pm) also has performances on its small stage every Saturday from 2pm to 5pm. Tickets for the teahouse shows cost Y20 to Y35.

Shopping

The main modern shopping district, filled with famous brands from around the world, is a part-pedestrianised area east of Tianfu Sq, between Zongfu Lu and Dong Dajie.

Southeast of Wǔhóu Temple is a small **Tibetan neighbourhood**. While it's not evident in the architecture, it is in the prayer flags, colourful scarves, beads and brass goods for sale. It's an interesting area for wandering.

Outdoor clothing and equipment are a big buy in Chéngdū, as many people head to Tibet or the western mountains. More outdoor shops line Wuhouci Dajie, opposite Wǔhóu Temple. Quality varies and fakes abound.

52 Camp OUTDOOR CLOTHING & EQUIPMENT
(户外用品商城; Hùwài Yòngpǐn Shāngchéng; Renmin Nanlu; 人民南路; ⌚9am-9.30pm) Stocks good-quality camping gear and clothing, including brands such as Karrimor and Columbia.

Information

Internet Access

All hotels and cafes we've reviewed here have internet access for laptop users. Most youth hostels and some top-end hotels also have computer terminals for guests. Internet cafes are plentiful; look for the characters 网吧 *(wǎngbā)*.

Wàntōng Wǎngbā (万通网吧; per hr Y4; ⌚24hr) Second floor of building in front of train station.

Xīnnánmén bus station (新南门汽车站; Xīnnánmén Qìchēzhàn; per hr Y3; ⌚24hr) Second-floor internet cafe.

Internet Resources

ChengduLiving (www.chengduliving.com) Smart, nicely designed website including well-written features, podcasts and reasonably active comments sections.

GoChengdoo (www.gochengdoo.com/en) Good introduction to the city from the guys behind Chèngdū's best expat mag, *Chengdoo*.

More Chengdu (www.morechengdu.com) OK website of the city's next-best English-language magazine. Good for restaurant listings.

Medical Services

Global Doctor Chéngdū Clinic (环球医生成都诊所; Huánqiú Yīshēng Chéngdū Zhěnsuǒ; ☎8528 3660, 24hr helpline 139 8225 6966; 2nd fl, 9-11 Lippo Tower Bldg, 62 Kehua Beilu; 科华北路62号力宝大夏2层9—11号; ⌚8.30am-6pm Mon-Fri) English-speaking doctors and a 24-hour English-language helpline.

No 4 Huáxī Hospital of Sìchuān University (华西第四医院; Huáxī Dìsì Yīyuàn; ☎8550 1570; Renmin Nanlu; 人民南路) The Huáxī hospital complex is Chéngdū's largest and gets good reports from expats. Many of the doctors and some staff members speak English.

Money

Most ATMs now accept foreign cards. We've marked some convenient ones on the map.

Bank of China (中国银行; Zhōngguó Yínháng; 35 Renmin Zhonglu, 2nd Section; 人民中路二段35号; ⌚8.30am-5.30pm Mon-Fri, to 5pm Sat & Sun) Changes money and travellers cheques, and offers cash advances on credit cards.

Post

China Post (中国邮政; Zhōngguó Yóuzhèng; North Train Station; 北火车站; ⌚8am-9pm summer, 8.30am-8pm winter) Handy branch outside train station; open later than most; can send parcels abroad.

Public Security Bureau

PSB (省公安厅外事科; Gōng'ānjú; ☎8640 7067; 391 Shuncheng Dajie; 391号顺成大街; ⌚9am-noon & 1-5pm Mon-Fri) Foreign affairs office on 2nd floor; extends visas in five working days. For faster service, try offices in Lèshān, Kāngdìng or, best of all, Sōngpān.

Tourist Information

Best sources for up-to-the-minute restaurant, bar and entertainment listings are free monthly magazines *Chengdoo* (www.gochengdoo.com) and *More Chengdu* (www.morechengdu.com). Look for copies at youth hostels or Western-friendly bars and cafes.

Tourist hotline (☎8292 8555) Free English-speaking hotline.

Travel Agencies

Skip the gazillion Chinese travel agencies around town and head straight to the travel desk at one of Chéngdū's many excellent youth hostels. Sim's is the pick of the bunch in terms of reliability.

Getting There & Away

Air

You can fly from Chéngdū to pretty much any other major Chinese city, while there are international flights to Bangkok, Kuala Lumpur, Singapore, Los Angeles, Vancouver, London, Amsterdam, Sydney, Melbourne, New Delhi, Bangalore and Seoul.

Many travellers choose to fly from here to Lhasa. Those without much time on their hands, but a bit of extra cash, might consider flying to smaller destinations within Sìchuān, such as Kāngdìng or Jiǔzhàigōu.

The best place to find cheap flights is nearly always www.elong.com. Also worth trying are www.ctrip.com and www.travelzen.com.

If for some reason you can't book online, try the airline offices in Chéngdū:

Air China Chéngdū Booking Office (国航世界中心; Guóháng Shìjiè Zhōngxīn; ☎24hr hotline 4008 100 999; 1 Hangkong Lu, off Renmin Nanlu; 人民南路4段航空路1号; ⊙8.30am-5pm)

China Southern Airlines (中国南方航空; Zhōngguó Nánfāng Hángkōng; ☎8666 3618; 278 Shangdong Dajie; ⊙8.30am-5.30pm)

Bus

The main bus station for tourists is Xīnnánmén (新南门), officially called the Tourism Passenger Transport Centre. The other two most useful are Chádiànzi (茶店子) and Běimén (北门). However, be prepared to be dropped at other bus stations when arriving in Chéngdū.

Destinations from Xīnnánmén include the following:

Dānbā Y128, nine hours, one daily (6.30am*)

Éméi Shān Y42, 2½ hours, every 30 minutes (7.20am to 7pm)

Huánglóngxi Y8, one hour, every 30 minutes (8.30am to 3.20pm)

Jiǔzhàigōu Y141, 10 hours, one daily (8am**)

Kāngdìng Y119 to Y129, seven hours, hourly (7.10am to 2.10pm)

Lèshān Y45, two hours, every 20 minutes (7.20am to 7.30pm)

Pínglè Y25, two hours, five daily (8.30am to 5.15pm)

Qīngchéng Shān Y20, 1½ hours, every 30 minutes (8.30am to 11am)

Yǎ'ān (for Bìfēngxiá) Y45, two hours, every 30 minutes (7.30am to 7pm)

Yíbīn Y79 to Y89, four hours, two daily (9.10am and 3.30pm)

* This is a Dàofú-bound bus, via Dānbā and Bàměi. You must buy a ticket to Bàměi (Y148), then ask the driver nicely for a Y20 refund because you want to get off early at Dānbā.

** Roads to Jiǔzhàigōu were under repair at the time of research, so expect this info to change.

Following are some of the destinations from Chádiànzi:

Jiǔzhàigōu Y121, 10 hours, two daily (7.20am and 9am)

Sōngpān Y136, 11 hours, three daily (6.30am, 7am and 7.30am)

The new tunnel-tastic route to Jiǔzhàigōu, via Sōngpān, should be open by the time you read this; it was reportedly set to cut journey times down to four or five hours! Check at Chéngdū hostels for the latest.

Destinations from Běimén include the following:

Lángzhōng Y94, five hours, hourly (7am to 6.30pm)

Yíbīn Y104, four hours, hourly (7.20am to 6.30pm)

Zìgōng Y80, three hours, hourly (7am to 7.30pm)

Train

The ticket office of Chéngdū North Train Station is in a separate building on your right as you approach the station. Hotels can book tickets for an extra fee. Example destinations and fares:

Běijīng West sleeper Y405/402/431, 26/32/30 hours, three daily (11.40am/10pm/11.49pm)

Chóngqìng seat Y98, two hours, hourly (8am to 7pm)

Éméi seat Y13 to Y24, two to three hours, eight daily (1pm to 9.30pm)

Kūnmíng sleeper Y153 to Y254, 19 to 24 hours, five daily (10am to 3.38pm)

Lhasa sleeper Y578, 44 hours, one daily (8.59pm)

Xī'ān seat/sleeper Y113/201, 13 to 18 hours, eight daily (11.40am to 9.41pm)

Xīníng sleeper Y300, 19/24 hours, two daily (12.10pm/8.59pm)

Yíbīn seat Y25 to Y51, 6½ hours, seven daily (8.39am to 11.10pm)

Zìgōng seat Y20 to Y41, 4½ to 5½ hours, seven daily (8.39am to 11.10pm)

ℹ Getting Around

To/From the Airport

Shuāngliú Airport is 18km west of the city. Bus 303 (Y10) is an airport shuttle (机场大巴; Jīchǎng Dàbā) that shadows flight times and travels from Yándào Jiē (盐道街) to the airport. Bus 300 runs a similar service between the airport and the North Train Station.

A taxi between the airport and the centre will cost Y50 to Y70, depending on how bad the traffic is. Most guesthouses offer airport pick-up services for slightly more than the taxi fare.

Bicycle

Chéngdū is nice and flat, although the traffic can be a strain on cyclists. Youth hostels rent out bikes for around Y20 per day. Make sure you use a lock.

Public Transport

BUS You can get almost anywhere in Chéngdū by bus, as long as you can decipher the labyrinthine bus routings. Stops are marked in Chinese and English, and most have posted route maps for the buses that stop there. Fares within the city are Y1 (一元) or Y2 (二元); the price is marked on the fare box.

Useful routes:

Bus 16 North Train Station–Renmin Lu–South Train Station

Bus 1 City centre–Wǔhóu Temple

Bus 81 Mao statue–Green Ram Temple

Bus 28 Xīnnánmén bus station–Běimén bus station

Bus 82 Chádiànzi bus station–Xīnnánmén bus station

Bus 49 Xīnnánmén bus station–Zhāojué bus station

Tourist Bus 902 Traffic Inn–Sim's–Panda Breeding Base

Tourist Bus 901 Traffic Inn–Wǔhóu Temple–People's Park–Jīnshā Site Museum

SUBWAY Chéngdū's first five subway lines were under construction at the time of research. The extremely handy Line 1, which links up with North Train Station before following the length of Renmin Lu, will be open by the time you read this. The east–west-running Line 2, which meets Line 1 at Tiānfǔ Sq before continuing west to Chádiànzì bus station, was due to open during the summer of 2011.

Taxi

Taxi flag fall is Y5 or Y7, depending on the quality of the car. The Y5 cabs add a Y1 fuel charge; Y7 cabs don't. All taxis are Y1 more expensive at night. At the time of research, rumour had it that taxi flag-fall prices were to be increased by Y2.

Around Chéngdū

SĀNXĪNGDUĪ MUSEUM 三星堆

The striking exhibits at the **Sānxīngduī Museum** (Sānxīngduī Bówùguǎn; admission Y82; ⌚8.30am-6pm) highlight archaeological finds that some Chinese archaeologists regard as even more important than Xī'ān's Terracotta Warriors.

Throughout the 20th century, farmers around the town of Guǎnghàn, 40km north of Chéngdū, continually unearthed intriguing pottery shards and other dirt-encrusted detritus. However, war, the lack of funds and other challenges prevented anyone from taking these discoveries seriously. Finally, in 1986, archaeologists launched a full-scale excavation and made a startling discovery: they unearthed a major site dating from the Shu kingdom, considered the cradle of Chinese civilisation, in the upper reaches of the Yangzi River (Cháng Jiāng).

The museum houses two buildings' worth of artefacts from this period, but the stars of its collections are dozens and dozens of bronze masks – so sophisticated that they wouldn't look out of place in a modern art gallery, yet they were crafted more than 4000 years ago. Most travellers will be satisfied with a half-day trip here, but art and archaeology buffs may want to linger for hours.

One morning bus (Y14, two hours, 8.30am) runs here direct from Chéngdū's Xīnnánmén bus station. Alternatively, there are regular buses from Chéngdū's Zhāojué station (Y12, two hours, 9am to 6.40pm) to Guǎnghàn, from where you can catch local bus 6 (Y2) for the remaining 10km to the site. There are no direct buses back to Chéngdū, so you'll have to go via Guǎnghàn.

QĪNGCHÉNG SHĀN 青城山

Covered in dripping-wet forests, the lush holy mountain of **Qīngchéng Shān** (Azure City Mountain; admission Y90) has been a Taoist retreat for more than 2000 years. Its beautiful trails are lined with ginkgo, plum and palm trees as well as caves, pavilions and gorgeous, centuries-old wooden temples, some of which you can stay overnight in.

The weather is generally better than at Éméi Shān, so the views are less likely to be obscured by mist, and with a summit of only 1600m, it's also a far easier climb; four hours up and down. There's a detailed map of the trails on the back of your entrance ticket and signs are in English too.

The new high-speed rail link means the mountain is now even more popular with Chéngdū day trippers, who can crowd some trails, particularly those near the entry and exit to the cable car (one way/return Y35/60). Some travellers prefer heading instead to **Qīngchéng Hòushān** (青城后山; Azure City Back Mountain), a more peaceful, less touristy area some 15km northwest of Qīngchéng Shān proper that has over 20km of hiking trails in a more natural environment. Buses and minibuses ply the road between the two mountains.

If you want to stay the night, two or three temples on the mountain welcome guests, including the fabulous **Shàngqīng Temple** (Shàngqīng Gōng; d with bathroom Y180 & Y280), a Qing-dynasty rebuild of the original Jin-dynasty temple set in the forest near the top of the mountain; it has a restaurant (dishes Y15 to Y25) and a teahouse (tea from Y5). The cheapest rooms (Y40 to Y100) are supposed to be reserved for pilgrims, but you may be able to land one if you ask sweetly.

SIX THINGS TO KNOW ABOUT PANDAS

» Pandas weren't discovered by the Western world until 1869, when French curate-naturalist Père Armand David brought a pelt back from China.

» There are now fewer than 1000 wild pandas, restricted to just five mountain ranges straddling the provinces of Sìchuān, Shaanxi (Shǎnxī) and Gānsù.

» About 99% of a wild panda's diet is made up of bamboo, but pandas have a carnivorous (meat-eating) ancestry and do, very occasionally, eat small rodents.

» Over the centuries, pandas have developed a 'thumb' – not a real thumb, but a modified wrist bone that enables them to strip bamboo leaves from their branches and to manipulate shoots and stems.

» Bamboo is very low in nutrients, so pandas need to spend around 16 hours a day munching through almost 40kg of the stuff in order to stay healthy.

» About every 25 years bamboos flower and die en masse, and the pandas must move to other feeding areas to survive. In the mid-1970s more than 130 pandas starved to death when bamboos flowered and died in Mín Shān, Sìchuān.

Snack stands are scattered along the mountain trails.

There are still direct morning buses to Qīngchéng Shān from Chéngdū's Xīnnánmén bus station (Y20, two hours, 8am to 11am, last bus back 6.30pm), but it's far preferable to take the high-speed rail link from Chéngdū's North Train Station (Y15, 50 minutes, 7.15am to 7.25pm, last train back 8.30pm). Bus 101 (Y2, five minutes) links the train station to the mountain.

Consider getting off the train one stop before Qīngchéng Shān to take a look at the **Dūjiāngyàn Irrigation Project** (都江堰水利工程; Dūjiāngyàn Shuǐlì Gōngchéng; admission Y90; ⏲8am-6pm). Constructed in the 3rd century BC to tame the fast-flowing Mín River, it's now a Unesco World Heritage Site.

BÌFĒNGXIÁ PANDA BASE

碧峰峡大熊猫基地

Established in 2003 under the direction of the Giant Panda Research Centre at Wòlóng, the **Bìfēngxiá Panda Base** (Bìfēngxiá Dàxióngmāo Jīdì; admission Y118, foreigner visitors Y60; ⏲8.30am-6pm), outside the city of Yǎ'ān (雅安), originally focused more on research than on tourism. However, after the Wòlóng Nature Reserve was severely damaged in the 2008 earthquake, all of its surviving pandas were moved to Bìfēngxiá, and the Yǎ'ān reserve began to receive an influx of tourists. It's now home to more than 80 pandas, the world's largest collection of captive pandas. At the time of research, the plan was to move some of the pandas back to Wòlóng once it had been rebuilt, sometime in 2012.

The Bìfēngxiá area is very spread out and spans a deep gorge and some stunning forest scenery, making for some lovely walks. The **panda centre** (☎0835 231 8145) is on the opposite side of the park from the entrance (there's a zoo too, which you can skip). The **ticket office** is inside Bìfēngxiá Dàjiǔdiàn, the large hotel in the main car park. At the time of research foreigners received a 50% discount. Be sure to bring your passport with you in case this excellent promotion is still running when you visit.

To get to the panda centre, 3km away from the ticket office, there's a free bus, but it's a pleasant half-hour walk. Alternatively, take the free lift (请云梯; *qǐngyúntī*) down to another section of the road below, and walk the long way round (90 minutes). Buses don't go this way round, so it's a more peaceful walk. There's more walking to be done on trails inside the panda centre, where the pandas are kept in OK enclosures similar to those at Chéngdū's Giant Panda Breeding Research Base. There's also an oh-so-cute 'panda kindergarten' enclosure; 13 baby pandas were born here the year before we visited, so there was plenty to coo about.

Bìfēngxiá is an easy day trip from Chéngdū, but you can stay in the park. Staff at the panda centre can help you arrange a room.

To get here, catch a bus from Xīnnánmén to Yǎ'ān. Get off just before the main bus station at the Tourist Bus Station (旅游车站; Lǚyoú Chēzhàn), where you'll find minibuses (Y5) waiting to take you the final 18km to the panda base. The last bus back to Chéngdū from the Tourist Bus Station leaves at 6.30pm.

PÍNGLÈ 平乐

A popular subject of paintings for Chinese art students, this ancient riverside village was originally a way station on the Southern Silk Road more than 2000 years ago. Modern life is encroaching, as are sellers of tourist trinkets, but enough old-town life remains for a pleasant day-long excursion from Chéngdū.

The buildings in the **old town** (古镇; *gǔzhèn*) date to the Ming and Qing dynasties, and locals still live in these old wooden houses lining the narrow streets on both sides of the river. The town's most venerable inhabitants, though, are its banyan trees, a dozen of which are more than 1000 years old. Don't miss the cutest of old stone passageways, called Fúhuì Street Water Gate (福惠街水门; Fúhuì Jiē Shuǐmén), which leads down to a river pathway housing two reconstructed wooden waterwheels and a couple of teahouses.

There are plenty of teahouses across the river too, where you can also board bamboo boats (Y50 per hour) or wander away from the water for a rural stroll in the decidedly untouristy surrounding farmland.

The old town has several small inns – look for signs saying 客栈 (*kèzhàn;* guesthouse) or 住宿 (*zhùsù;* lodgings) – although for most visitors a day trip will be sufficient. **Dàhé Kèzhàn** (大河客栈; 18-24 Changchong Jie; 长庆街18—24号; ☎8878 2830; r Y90), the first place by the river you reach from the bus station, has nice little rooms, with weenie private bathrooms. Restaurants are everywhere. Look out for the tasty steamed buns (Y0.50) made from either sweet corn (玉米馍; *yùmǐ mó*) or pumpkin (南瓜馍; *nánguā mó*).

Five daily buses for Pínglè leave from Chéngdū's Xīnnánmén bus station, returning at 7am, 1pm, 2.20pm, 3.20pm and 4.50pm. Walk out of Pínglè bus station and turn right for the old town.

LIǓ JIĀNG 柳江

The lovely pastoral setting is the main draw of this gorgeous village tucked away in the central Sìchuān countryside. The old town (古镇; *gǔzhèn*), with its narrow alleyways, wooden courtyard buildings and ancient banyan trees, straddles both sides of the Yángcūn River (杨村河; Yángcūn Hé) in a picture-perfect setting. In fact, after recent renovations, it's almost too perfect (you'll have a hard time picking out genuine old buildings here), and at weekends it becomes overrun by tourists all craving a piece of rural charm. Nevertheless, it's still a lovely spot for a lazy lunch or a trip to a teahouse. If you want to stay the night, the charming **Wàngjiāng Kèzhàn** (望江客栈; ☎139 0903 6203; Guzhen Laojie; 古镇老街; r Y80) has creaky wooden floorboards, basic rooms with shared bathrooms, and river views. If the crowds get too much, there's some excellent walking to be done in the surrounding countryside.

One fine option is the 3.5km uphill hike to Hóujiā Shānxiàng (侯家山巷). The start of the road here is close to the bus station and is marked by a wooden gateway. Once you've found that, just follow the road and signs past mooing cows, ploughing farmers, rice terraces, bamboo clumps and small tea plantations. On the road near the top is **Tiàowàng Wǎwū** (眺望瓦屋; ☎130 8838 1221; r Y80, dishes from Y5), a large renovated wooden courtyard building with simple twin rooms, friendly owners and fabulous views. You can grab a bowl of noodles (面; *miàn*) here or whatever rice dishes (饭; *fàn*) they happen to be cooking that day. Don't bother hiking any further up the hill, unless you want to bump into Chinese tourists ruining the ambience by belting out heavily amplified, out-of-tune karaoke songs at the modern three-storey hotel at the top of the mountain.

You can reach Liǔ Jiāng direct from Xīnnánmén bus station (Y46, three hours, 9am). The return bus leaves at 3pm. If that's full, there are regular buses to Hóngyǎ (洪雅), where you can change. Last bus from Hóngyǎ to Chéngdū is 5.20pm. If that's full, change at Méishān (眉山; last Chéngdū bus 6.50pm).

WÒLÓNG NATURE RESERVE 卧龙自然保护区

Formerly the largest of China's panda conservation centres, **Wòlóng Nature Reserve** (Wòlóng Zìrán Bǎohùqū), 140km northwest of Chéngdū, suffered extensive damage in the 2008 Sìchuān earthquake. At the time of research, the reserve remained closed to the public, and all of the pandas had been transferred to the Bìfēngxiá Panda Base near Yǎ'ān.

Wòlóng was scheduled to reopen to tourists, with at least some of its pandas back in place, in 2012. Check at hostels in Chéngdū for the latest.

Éméi Shān 峨眉山

☎0833 / ELEV 3099M

A cool, misty retreat from the Sìchuān basin's sweltering heat, stunning **Éméi Shān** (adult Y150) is one of China's four most famous Buddhist mountains (the others are Pǔtuóshān, Wǔtái Shān and Jiǔhuá Shān). Here you'll find fabulous forested mountain scenery, ramshackle wooden temples and macaques demanding tribute for safe passage. There's also the wonderful opportunity to spend the night in one of the many monasteries that dot the mountain range.

Éméi Shān has little of its original templework still remaining. Glittering Jīndǐng Temple (Jīndǐng Sì), with its brass tiling engraved with Tibetan script, was completely gutted by fire. Other temples suffered the same fate, and all were looted to various degrees during the war with Japan and the Cultural Revolution. Some do still go back a few years, though, with Wànnián Temple, the oldest, clocking in at a very respectable 1100 years old.

The waves of pilgrims, hawkers and, most of all, tourists during peak season eliminate much solitude, but the crowds hover largely around the areas closest to the cable cars and the major temples. Away from them, the pathways, lined with fir, pine and cedar trees, make for peaceful hiking. Lofty crags, cloud-kissing precipices, butterflies and azaleas together form a nature reserve, and the mountain joins Lèshān, Jiǔzhàigōu and Dūjiāngyàn Irrigation Project on Unesco's list of World Heritage Sites in Sìchuān.

When to Go

The best time to visit Éméi Shān is between May and October. Avoid the national holidays, when the number of visitors reaches epic proportions.

Snowfall generally begins around November on the upper slopes. In winter you can hire iron soles with spikes to deal with encrusted ice and snow, but trails can be extremely slippery.

Temperate zones start at 1000m. Cloud cover, mist and often-dense fog are prevalent year-round, interfering with views of the sunrise (and of the trail ahead). If you're very lucky, you'll be able to see Gònggā Shān (Gongga Mountain) to the west; if not, you'll have to settle for the less appealing Telecom tower – or perhaps just your hand in front of your face.

Some average temperatures:

	JANUARY	APRIL	JULY	OCTOBER
Éméi town	7°C	21°C	26°C	17°C
Summit	6°C	3°C	12°C	-1°C

> **WHAT TO BRING**
>
> You can buy all of the following in Bàoguó Village. Teddy Bear Hotel stores bags for free. Bàoguó bus station charges Y0.50 per hour.
>
> - ☐ Sturdy footwear or hiking boots (the stone paths can get very slippery)
> - ☐ Rain jacket with hood (it rains a lot on Éméi)
> - ☐ Extra jumper (it's chilly near the summit, especially in the evenings)
> - ☐ Walking stick (for knackered knees and monkey attacks)
> - ☐ Fixed-length umbrella (doubles as a walking stick)
> - ☐ Torch (if you stay on the mountain)
> - ☐ Fruit and snacks (to supplement all those instant noodles)
> - ☐ Toilet paper

Sights

Bàoguó Temple BUDDHIST MONASTERY

(报国寺; Bàoguó Sì; Declare Nation Temple; admission Y8) Constructed in the 16th century, this temple features beautiful gardens of rare plants, as well as a 3.5m-high porcelain Buddha dating back to 1415, which is housed near the Sutra Library.

Qīngyīn Pavilion BUDDHIST TEMPLE

(清音阁; Qīngyīn Gé) Named 'Pure Sound Pavilion' after the soothing sounds of the waters coursing around rock formations, this temple is built on an outcrop in the middle of a fast-flowing stream. Rest in one of the small pavilions here while you appreciate the natural 'music'.

'Ecological' Monkey Zone WILDLIFE AREA

Between Qīngyīn Pavilion and Hóngchūn Píng (Venerable Trees Terrace) is the first place most hikers encounter the mountain's infamous monkeys. Despite the area's 'ecological' moniker, attendants here alternately feed the monkeys and, when they get too aggressive, chase them away with sticks and slingshots.

Wànnián Temple BUDDHIST MONASTERY
(万年寺; Wànnián Sì; Long Life Monastery; admission Y10) Reconstructed in the 9th century, Wànnián Temple is the oldest surviving Éméi temple. It's dedicated to the man on the white elephant, the Bodhisattva Pǔxián (also known as Samantabhadra), the Buddhist Lord of Truth and protector of the mountain. This 8.5m-high **statue** cast in copper and bronze dates from AD 980 and weighs an estimated 62,000kg. If you can manage to rub the elephant's hind leg, good luck will be cast upon you. The statue is housed in **Brick Hall**, a domed building with small stupas on it and the only building left unharmed in a 1945 fire.

Elephant Bathing Pool BUDDHIST MONASTERY
(洗象池; Xǐxiàng Chí) According to legend, Elephant Bathing Pool is where Pǔxián flew his elephant in for a big scrub, but today there's not much of a pool to speak of. Being almost at the crossroads of both major trails, the temple here is often crowded with pilgrims.

Jīndǐng Temple BUDDHIST TEMPLE
(金顶寺; Jīndǐng Sì; Golden Summit Temple) The magnificent Jīndǐng Temple is at the Golden Summit (Jīn Dǐng; 3077m), commonly referred to as the mountain's highest peak. Covered with glazed tiles and surrounded by white marble balustrades, the renovated temple, which now occupies 1695 sq metres, is quite striking. In front of the temple, the unmissable 48m-tall golden statue **Multi-dimensional Samantabhadra** (十方普贤; Shífāng Pǔxián) honours mountain protector Puxian and was added in 2006.

The mountain's highest point is actually nearby **Wànfó Dǐng** (Ten Thousand Buddha Summit) at 3099m, but it has been closed to visitors for some years now.

Fúhǔ Temple BUDDHIST MONASTERY
(伏虎寺; Fúhǔ Sì; Crouching Tiger Monastery; admission Y6) Located about 1km from Bàoguó Temple, Fúhǔ Temple is hidden deep within the forest. It houses a 7m-high copper pagoda inscribed with Buddhist images and texts.

Xiānfēng Temple BUDDHIST MONASTERY
(仙峰寺; Xiānfēng Sì; Immortal Peak Monastery) Somewhat off the beaten track, this well-looked-after monastery is backed by rugged cliffs and surrounded by fantastic scenery.

Sleeping

ON THE MOUNTAIN

Almost all the temples on the mountain (with the notable exception of Jīndǐng Temple at the summit) offer cheap lodgings

Éméi Shān

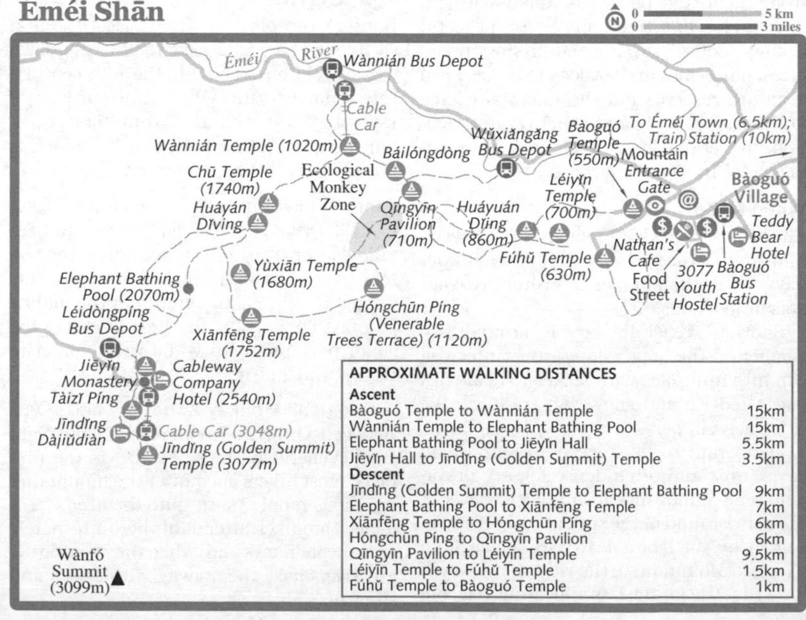

APPROXIMATE WALKING DISTANCES

Ascent	
Bàoguó Temple to Wànnián Temple	15km
Wànnián Temple to Elephant Bathing Pool	15km
Elephant Bathing Pool to Jiēyǐn Hall	5.5km
Jiēyǐn Hall to Jīndǐng (Golden Summit) Temple	3.5km
Descent	
Jīndǐng (Golden Summit) Temple to Elephant Bathing Pool	9km
Elephant Bathing Pool to Xiānfēng Temple	7km
Xiānfēng Temple to Hóngchūn Píng	6km
Hóngchūn Píng to Qīngyīn Pavilion	6km
Qīngyīn Pavilion to Léiyīn Temple	9.5km
Léiyīn Temple to Fúhǔ Temple	1.5km
Fúhǔ Temple to Bàoguó Temple	1km

POSSIBLE ROUTES

There are numerous options for tackling Éméi Shān with various combinations of buses, cable cars, hiking trails and monastery stop-offs. Here are four popular ones:

» **One day** Make use of buses and cable cars by taking a bus to Wànnián Temple (45 minutes), then hiking to the top (four hours) with the help of both cable cars before walking down to Léidòngpíng bus depot (1½ hours) and taking a bus back to Bàoguó Village (90 minutes).

» **Two days** Take the bus to Wànnián bus depot (45 minutes) then hike up via Chū Temple to the summit (five to six hours). On the way down, turn right a short distance past Elephant Bathing Pool and take the more scenic path, via Xiānfēng Temple, back to Wànnián bus depot (eight hours).

» **Two days** Take the bus to Léidòngpíng (90 minutes) then walk to the top (one to two hours) before making your long descent to Bàoguó Village (10 hours) via an overnight stay in a monastery.

» **Three days** Ditch the buses completely and simply hike up and down the whole mountain (about 20 hours in total). To mix things up, go via Wànnián Temple on the way up and via Xiānfēng Temple on the way down. While you're on the way down, start preparing yourself mentally for at least three to four days of jelly legs.

in dormitory-style accommodation with shared bathrooms but usually no showers. Some also have guesthouse-quality private rooms, sometimes with private bathrooms.

Xiānfēng Temple MONASTERY $
(仙峰寺; Xiānfēng Sì; dm & tw without bathroom Y30-260, tw with bathroom Y280) This pretty remote temple, with a lovely forested location backed by rugged cliffs, is set around a large shaded front courtyard and has a wonderfully peaceful atmosphere. There's a good range of rooms from dorms to pricier twins that have showers. Approximate walking time from foot/summit is six/four hours.

Yùxiān Temple MONASTERY $
(遇仙寺; Yùxiān Sì; dm/tw from Y30/80) Scenery wise this is one of the most spectacular places to stay – the views are stunning here. And considering how small the temple is, there's also a large choice of rooms, from basic dorms to private twins. It is very remote here, though, so could feel a little eerie if you're staying on your own. From foot/summit is seven/three hours.

Hóngchún Píng MONASTERY $
(洪椿坪; dm Y30-40, tw Y45-80) Arguably the smartest of the temples with accommodation, this place is another with a nice courtyard, making it a comfortable choice to spend some time in. Rooms are simple but decent. From foot/summit is three/seven hours.

Tàizǐ Píng MONASTERY $
(太子坪; dm Y30-40) What this quiet, ramshackle wooden temple lacks in comfort, it gains in charm. Expect extremely basic three-bed dorms with a cold-water sink for washing. From foot/summit is 9¼ hours/45 minutes.

There are also two hotels on the mountain, although standards are low considering the prices:

Jīndǐng Dàjiǔdiàn HOTEL
(金顶大酒店; ☎509 8088/77; tw/tr Y780/580, discounted to Y620/460) From foot/summit 9½ hours/30 minutes.

Cableway Company Hotel HOTEL
(索道公司招待所; Suǒdào Gōngsī Zhāodàisuǒ; ☎155 2030 0955; tr/tw Y150/260) From foot/summit 8½ hours/90minutes.

IN BÀOGUÓ VILLAGE

Teddy Bear Hotel YOUTH HOSTEL $$
(玩具熊酒店; Wánjùxióng Jiǔdiàn; ☎559 0135, 138 9068 1961; www.teddybear.com.cn; 43 Baoguo Lu; dm Y35, d & tw from Y260, tr Y180; ❄@📶) This 'backpacker central' place has cute, well-maintained rooms and English-speaking staff. The left-luggage service is free and there are massages available when you make it back down the mountain. Guests are also given an excellent hand-drawn map of the mountain trails for free. The cafe here serves OK Chinese and Western food and is a great place to swap tales of monkey attacks and sore knees. Standard

twins often slide to Y100. Call for a free pick-up from Éméi bus or train station.

3077 Youth Hostel YOUTH HOSTEL $
(峨眉3077青年旅社; Éméi Sānlíngqīqī Qīngnián Lǚshè; ☎559 1698; www.em3077.com; nr Língxiù Wēnquán Spa; 灵秀温泉附近; dm Y30, tw from Y80; ❄@📶) This new hostel is aimed primarily at Chinese backpackers, so English-speaking skills may not be quite as good as at Teddy Bear. However, with its large courtyard, wood-interior cafe-restaurant and cool bedroom furnishings it has a lot more character. Shared bathrooms only.

Eating

On the mountain, most temples have small dining halls, but you're never very far from one of the many trailside cafes that dot the mountain. Most serve simple noodle (面; *miàn*) or rice (饭; *fàn*) dishes as well as instant noodles (方便面; *fāngbiàn miàn*).

In Bàoguó Village, restaurants and supermarkets abound. Haochi Jie, or 'Food Street', is crammed with places to eat, many with outdoor seating.

A speciality breakfast snack here is the yellow buckwheat bun (荞麦粑; *qiáomài bā;* Y1).

Nathan's Cafe SICHUANESE $$
(梁山饭店; Liángshān Fàndiàn; Haochi Jie; 好吃街; dishes Y4-60; ⌚7am-10pm; 📋) With a small outdoor seating area on lively 'Food Street', this place does Western breakfasts, simple noodle dishes and all the Sìchuān classics. Some English spoken.

Information

Agricultural Bank of China (农业银行; Nóngyè Yínháng; ⌚9am-5pm) Has foreign exchange desk and foreign-friendly ATM. The ATM by Bàoguó bus station also accepts foreign cards.

Internet cafe (网吧; wǎngbā; per hr Y2; ⌚24hr) Walk five minutes north from mountain entrance then climb steps on right to level of road bridge. At top, turn right and walk 200m. Can also get online at youth hostels listed above.

Getting Around

Bàoguó (报国) Village is your gateway to the mountain. Buses from the village bus station travel to three bus depots on the mountain: Wǔxiǎngǎng (五显冈; Y20, 15 minutes), about a 20-minute walk below Qīngyīn Pavilion; Wànnián (万年;Y20, 45 minutes), below Wànnián Temple; and Léidòngpíng (雷洞坪; Y40, 90 minutes), a few minutes' walk from Jīngdǐng Cable Car.

Buses run roughly half-hourly from 6am to 5pm from 26 April to 31 October and from 7am to 4pm from 1 November to 25 April.

The last buses back down the mountain leave at 6pm (5pm in winter) from each of the three mountain bus depots. However, it is usually possible – especially during the summer – to get a seat on a private coach going back down the mountain. They keep running for at least an hour after the public buses stop. The ticket office at the mountain bus depots will help you get on one.

Getting There & Away

The town of Éméi (峨眉山市; Éméi Shān Shì) lies 6.5km east of the mountain Éméi Shān and is the transport hub for the mountain. All buses to Éméi Shān terminate here – at the new **Éméi Shān Passenger Traffic Centre** (峨眉山客运中心; Éméi Shān Kèyùn Zhōngxīn), directly opposite Éméi Train Station (峨眉火车站; Éméi Huǒchēzhàn). From here, it's a Y20 cab to Bàoguó Village, the gateway to the mountain. Alternatively, take Bus 1 (Y1) from outside Éméi bus station to Pēnshuǐ Chí (喷水池) bus stop, then take Bus 5 (Y1.50) from across the square to Bàoguó (报国).

Note, whilst it's not possible to travel direct to Bàoguó from most long-distance destinations, some long-distance buses do leave from Bàoguó (see below). If you want to head south to Zìgòng, you must leave from Éméi bus station (Y48, three hours, frequent services 7.50am to 3.30pm).

Buses from Bàoguó bus station include the following destinations:

Chéngdū Y45, 2½ hours, frequent services (8am to 6pm)

Chóngqìng Y115, six hours, one daily (8.30am)

Lèshān Y11, one hour, frequent services (8am to 5.30pm)

Train

Destinations from Éméi Train Station include the following:

Chéngdū seat Y24, 2½ hours, seven daily (5.53am to 11.28pm)

Kūnmíng sleeper Y224, 17 hours, three daily (3.35pm, 5.20pm and 6.16pm)

Xī'ān sleeper Y232, 19 hours, one daily (10.28am)

Lèshān 乐山

☎0833 / POP 156,000

With fingernails bigger than the average human, the world's tallest Buddha (see the boxed text, p955) draws plenty of tourists to this relaxed riverside town. It's an easy day

DON'T MISS

TOP 10 SÌCHUĀN TEAHOUSES

Sadly, in many parts of China, teahouses are shadows of their former selves. Not so in Sìchuān, where tea culture still thrives and where you'll find some of the country's best remaining teahouses (茶馆; *cháguǎn*) and tea gardens (茶园; *cháyuán*). Here are our favourites:

» **Wángyé Temple, Zìgòng** Housed in an ochre-coloured, 100-year-old temple overlooking Fǔxī River (釜溪河; Fǔxī Hé).

» **Huánhóu Palace, Zìgòng** Surely the most dramatic entrance gate to any teahouse in China?

» **Hèmíng Teahouse, People's Park, Chéngdū** Perfect people-watching material. Sip tea by the park lake, play cards or even get your ears de-waxed!

» **Tibetan Restaurant, Gānzī** A riot of reds, blues and golds, this friendly teahouse, run by a local nun, is *the* place for yak-butter tea in Gānzī.

» **Moon Reflection Tea Garden, Sōngpān** Beside the rushing waters of the Mín River and a favourite with mah jong–playing locals.

» **Any teahouse by the river, Pínglè** Order a pot of China's finest and sit beside a wooden Ming-dynasty building while you watch other tourists punt their way along the river on bamboo rafts.

» **Tibetan Culture Dew, Kāngdìng** Distinctly Chinese on the outside, but inside it's rustic-Tibetan, with stone walls and wood beams decorated in colourful prayer flags.

» **Shàngqīng Temple, Qīngchéng Shān** Inside a Qing-dynasty wooden temple near the summit of Qīngchéng Taoist mountain.

» **Yuèlái Teahouse, Chéngdū** Popular local teahouse that really comes into its own on Saturday afternoons when it holds intimate opera performances on a small stage.

» **River Viewing Pavilion Park, Chéngdū** Tea gardens set among 150 varieties of bamboo.

trip from Chéngdū or a convenient stopover en route to or from Éméi Shān.

While it's possible to see the Buddha and head onward the same day, Lèshān isn't a bad spot to hang out for a day or two. In the evenings, you can stroll the riverfront along Binhe Lu; in the large square near the intersection with Baita Jie, you may find fan dancers, ballroom dancers and even tango lessons under way.

Sights

Grand Buddha BUDDHIST SITE

(大佛; Dàfó; adult Y90; ⏲7.30am-6.30pm Apr-early Oct, 8am-5.30pm early Oct-Mar) Lèshān's pride and joy is the serene, 1200-year-old Grand Buddha carved into a cliff face overlooking the confluence of the Dàdù River (大渡河; Dàdù Hé) and the Mín River. And at 71m tall, he's definitely big. His ears stretch for 7m, his shoulders span 28m, and each of his big toes is 8.5m long.

A Buddhist monk called Haitong conceived the project in AD 713, hoping that the Buddha would calm the swift rivers and protect boatmen from lethal currents. The huge project wasn't completed until 90 years after Haitong's death but eventually, just as he had once wished, the river waters calmed. Locals say it was the Grand Buddha's calming effect. Sceptics say it was due to the lengthy construction process in which surplus rocks from the sculpting filled the river hollows.

Inside the body, hidden from view, is a water-drainage system to prevent weathering, although Dàfó is showing his age and soil erosion is an ongoing problem.

To fully appreciate the Buddha's magnitude, get an up-close look at his head, then descend the steep, winding stairway for the Lilliputian view. Avoid visiting on weekends or holidays, when traffic on the staircase can come to a complete standstill.

Admission to the Buddha includes access to a number of caves and temples on the grounds and to the **Máhàoyá Tombs Museum** (麻浩崖墓博物馆; Máhàoyámù Bówùguǎn), which has a modest collection

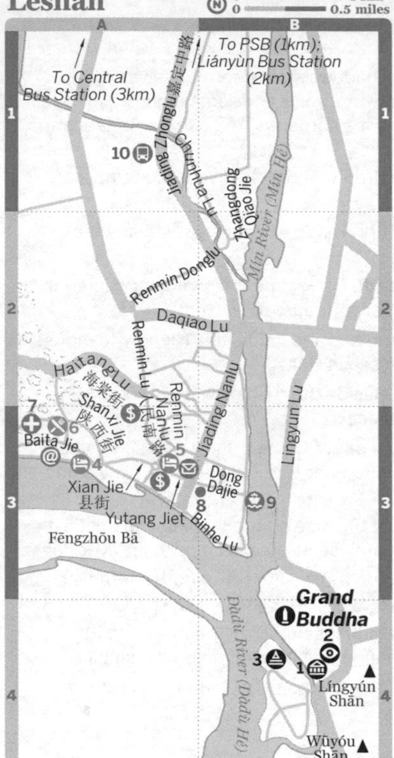

Lèshān

Top Sights

Grand Buddha B4

Sights

1 Máhàoyá Tombs Museum B4
2 Oriental Buddhist Theme Park B4
3 Wūyóu Temple B4

Sleeping

4 Jiāzhōu Hotel A3
5 Post & Telecommunication Hotel A3

Eating

6 Yang's Restaurant A3

Information

7 People's Hospital A3
8 Photo Shop B3

Transport

9 Ferry Dock B3
10 Xiàobà Bus Station A1

of tombs and burial artefacts dating from the Eastern Han dynasty (AD 25–220).

Also included in the ticket price is **Wūyóu Temple** (乌尤寺; Wūyóu Sì), which, like the Grand Buddha, dates from the Tang dynasty, with Ming and Qing renovations. This monastery also contains calligraphy, painting and artefacts, but the highlight is the hall of 1000 terracotta arhat (Buddhist celestial beings, similar to angels) displaying an incredible variety of postures and facial expressions – no two are alike. Also inside the 1909 **Luóhàn Hall**, where the arhat are housed, is a fantastic statue of **Avalokiteshvara**, the Sanskrit name of the Goddess of Mercy (Guanyin in Chinese).

One sight on the grounds that requires a separate ticket is the recently constructed **Oriental Buddhist Theme Park** (东方佛都; Dōngfāng Fódū; admission Y70), housing 3000 Buddha statues and figurines from around Asia, including a 170m-long reclining Buddha, said to be the world's longest.

Bus 13 (Y1) travels from Xiàobà bus station and loops through the town centre (you can catch it on Dong Dajie) before crossing the river to reach the Grand Buddha Scenic Area and Wūyóu Temple.

You could charge through the Grand Buddha area in a couple of hours, but allowing at least a half-day would be more relaxed.

Tours

Tour boats pass by for panoramic views of the Grand Buddha (hovering in front for about 10 minutes), which reveal two guardians in the cliff side, not visible from land. Large **tour boats** (Y50, 30 minutes) and smaller **speedboats** (Y50, 15 to 20 minutes) both leave regularly from the ferry dock (旅游船码头; *lǚyóuchuán mǎtóu*). They run from 7.30am to 6.30pm (1 April to 7 October) or from 8am to 5.30pm (8 October to 31 March).

The affable **Mr Yang** (☎211 2046, 130 3645 6184; richardyangmin@yahoo.com.cn; Yang's Restaurant, 2f 186 Baita Jie), of Yang's Restaurant fame, arranges a village visit as a day trip for foreign tourists that includes a calligraphy demonstration, an old-town tour and a visit to a local school. He charges Y200 per person including transport, lunch and his services as an English-speaking guide. Call ahead and he'll meet you at the bus station.

Sleeping & Eating

Jiāzhōu Hotel HOTEL $$
(嘉州宾馆; Jiāzhōu Bīnguǎn; ☎213 9888; 85 Baita Jie; 白塔街85号; r incl breakfast from Y360; ❄@) Rooms aren't quite as grand as the lobby suggests, but this place is more upmarket than most and makes for a very comfortable stay. Third-floor rooms and above have internet connection for laptop users, and many rooms, even some of the cheapies, have river views. Standard twins often go for Y220.

Post & Telecommunication Hotel HOTEL $
(邮电宾馆; Yóudiàn Bīnguǎn; ☎211 1788; 82 Yutang Jie; 玉堂街82号; tw incl breakfast Y148, with computer Y168; ❄@) The orange and peach colour scheme is a little garish, but this place is clean and quiet. It's set back from the street behind the post office (go through the car park to the hotel entrance).

Yang's Restaurant SICHUAN $
(杨家餐厅; Yángjiā Cāntīng; 2f 186 Baita Jie; 白塔街186号2层; dishes Y15-25; ⏲6-9pm) Octogenarian and travel guru Mr Yang and his wife run this small restaurant in the living room of their home. They serve simple but tasty local food and he may regale you with tales of his life while you eat.

Lots of small restaurants are hidden away on Lèshān's side streets. For dumplings, noodles and other quick bites, try Dong Dajie and the surrounding streets between the post office and the river. There are more small eateries and fruit stalls on Xian Jie west of the roundabout and along Baita Jie and Shanxi Jie.

Information

Bank of China (中国银行; Zhōngguó Yínháng; 16 Renmin Nanlu) Changes money and travellers cheques, offers cash advances on credit cards and has foreign-friendly ATM. Another ATM near the Post & Telecommunication Hotel.

China Post (中国邮政; Zhōngguó Yóuzhèng; 62 Yutang Jie)

Internet cafe (网吧; wǎngbā; per hr Y2; ⏲24hr) Opposite Yang's Restaurant; 2nd floor. There are others dotted around town. Just look for the characters 网吧.

People's Hospital (人民医院; Rénmín Yīyuàn; ☎211 9310, after-hr emergencies 211 9328; 238 Baita Jie) Has some English-speaking doctors.

Photo shop (世界图片社; Shìjiè Túpiànshè; 139 Dong Dajie; 东大街139号; ⏲9am-8.30pm) CD burning per disk Y10.

Public Security Bureau (PSB; 省公安厅外事科; Gōng'ānjú; ☎518 2555; 243 Jiading Beilu; 嘉定北路243号; ⏲9am-noon & 1-5pm Mon-Fri) Visa extensions in two days. North of town, on corner of Bailu Lu (百禄路); take Bus 1 (Y1) or a taxi (Y5 to Y6) from the centre.

Getting There & Around

Lèshān has three bus stations, all north of the centre. Buses from Chéngdū's Xīnnánmén station arrive at Xiàobà bus station (肖坝车站; Xiàobà chēzhàn), but Central bus station (乐山客运中心车站; Lèshān Kèyùn Zhōngxīn chēzhàn) is bigger and has more frequent services to more destinations. You may also be dropped at Liányùn bus station (联运车站; Liányùn chēzhàn).

Pedicab rides cost Y2 to Y5. Taxis start at a flat rate of Y3 for the first 3km.

Bus services from Xiàobà bus station include the following destinations:

Chéngdū Y45 to Y51, two hours, every 30 minutes (7am to 7pm)

Chóngqìng Y104, six hours, one daily (10.40am)

Éméi Shān (Bàoguó) Y11, one hour, every hour (8am to 5.30pm)

Éméi town (Éméi Shì) Y8, one hour, every 30 minutes (7am to 6.30pm)

Yǎ'ān Y55, two hours, three daily (9.30am, 1.50pm and 4.10pm)

Services from Central bus station include the following:

Chéngdū Y45 to Y51, two hours, every 20 minutes (7am to 7.25pm)

Chóngqìng Y104, six hours, hourly (7.10am to 4.30pm)

Éméi town Y8, one hour, every 15 minutes (8am to 6pm)

Jiājiāng Y7, one hour, every 40 minutes (7.30am to 6pm)

Kāngdìng Y129, eight hours, one daily (9.30am)

Local buses cost Y1. Some handy routes:

Bus 1 Liányùn bus station–PSB–Xiàobà bus station–town centre

Bus 6 Xiàobà bus station–town centre

Bus 13 Xiàobà bus station–town centre–Grand Buddha–Wūyóu Temple

Bus 9 Central bus station–Xiàobà bus station–town centre

Lángzhōng 阆中

☎0817 / POP 112,000

Seemingly endless black-tile roofs with swooping eaves overlooking the narrowest of alleys; flagstone streets lined with tiny shops; temples atop misty hills above a river. If you're looking for fast-disappearing 'old China' details like these, hop on a bus to the town of Lángzhōng, Sìchuān's capital city for 17 years during the Qing dynasty and home to the province's largest grouping of extant traditional architecture.

Despite Lángzhōng's increasing tourist development, the old town (古镇; *gǔzhèn*) is still largely home to locals who go about their day-to-day business – seamstresses working at sewing machines, herbalists dispensing medical treatments, and schoolchildren laughing and chattering through the lanes.

Sights

Lángzhōng's eclectic mix of sights showcases the town's rich history, allows visitors to walk through restored courtyard-style homes, and highlights the town's layout according to feng shui principles. Most attractions have an English-language overview sign, but inside, English captions vary from some to none. Most people will also be happy just wandering the alleys and gaping at the architecture – a blend of North China quadrangle and South China garden styles.

There's some good exploring to be done across the river, south of the old town. At the foot of one hill sits the sedate-looking **Grand Buddha** (大佛寺; Dàfó Sì), one of the largest Buddha statues in Sìchuān. Nearby, among Buddhist statuary, grottoes and caves littering the hillsides, is **No 1 Scholars Cave** (状元洞; Zhuàngyuán Dòng), where two legendary court officials crammed for their examinations.

For bird's-eye views of the town's rooftops and lanes, climb to the top of either of two towers: **Huáguāng Lóu** (华光楼; Dadong Jie; admission Y15), just past the Fēng Shuǐ Museum and rebuilt in 1867, or **Zhōngtiān Lóu** (中天楼; Wumiao Jie; admission Y10), a 2006 rebuild on the way to Zhāng Fēi Temple.

A Y80 combination ticket admits you to the towers and the three attractions listed below. You can buy individual tickets too. Many smaller sights charge admission as well, including some of the beautifully restored courtyard homes (typically around Y4); if you're not staying or stopping for lunch in a courtyard home, it's well worth a peek into at least one.

Zhāng Fēi Temple TEMPLE
(张飞庙; Zhāngfēi Miào; Xi Jie; admission Y40) This temple is the tomb of and shrine to local boy Zhang Fei, a respected general during the kingdom of Shu, who administered the kingdom from here. It's on Xi Jie (西街), a continuation of Wumiao Jie (武庙街).

Fēng Shuǐ Museum MUSEUM
(风水馆; Fēngshuǐ Guǎn; Dadong Jie; admission Y20) This museum includes a model of the town, illustrating its feng shui–inspired design. A helpful English-speaking guide is sometimes available here. It's next to Tiānyī Youth Hotel on Dadong Jie (大东街).

Gòng Yuàn HISTORIC BUILDINGS
(贡院; Xuedao Jie; admission Y35) Among the best-preserved imperial examination halls in China. On Xuedao Jiē (学道街), which is parallel to Wumiao Jie, one block north.

Sleeping

There are dozens of renovated courtyard guesthouses; look for signs saying 客栈 (*kèzhàn;* guesthouse) or 住宿 (*zhùsù;* lodgings).

TOP CHOICE **Lǐ Family Courtyard** COURTYARD $$
(李家大院; Lǐjiā Dàyuàn; ☎623 6500; 47 Wumiao Jie; 武庙街47号; r from Y368) You used to have to pay just to look inside this gorgeous 500-year-old courtyard home. Now you can stay in it! Immaculate twins and doubles, with dinky little bathrooms, are off three small courtyards and were going for Y128 when we were there. See p727 for directions to Wumiao Jie.

Tiānyī Youth Hotel GUESTHOUSE $
(天一青年旅舍; Tiānyī Qīngnián Lǚshè; ☎622 5501; 100 Dadong Jie; 大东街100号; d/tw without bathroom Y90/98, with bathroom Y188, discounts of 20%; @) If you want to improve your geomancy, settle into this inn beside the Fēng Shuǐ Museum. Each of the stylish doubles is inspired by a feng shui element: earth, wood, fire, metal or water. The shared-bathroom twins and doubles are simpler but still crisp and clean, with lots of natural wood. See p727 for directions to Dadong Jie.

Eating

Lángzhōng has long been one of China's major vinegar production centres – everything is pickled here! Otherwise, famed local fare includes *zhāngfēi niúròu* (张飞牛

肉; preserved water-buffalo beef) and *táng guōkuī* (糖锅盔; slightly sweetened pita-bread pockets; Y1).

There's an interesting **market** (市场; *shìchǎng*) off Dadong Jie where you can pick up fruit, vegetables and skinned pig's faces.

Zhāngfēi Zhuāngyuán SICHUAN $
(张飞庄园; ☎622 9659; 4 Wumiao Jie; 武庙街4号; dishes Y4-10; ⊙9am-8.30pm) The old town has plenty of noodle joints, but this large eatery with wooden tables and benches opens to the street. The ordinary beef noodles (牛肉面; *niúròu miàn;* Y5) are good, but you really should try the house special *zhāngfēi niúròu* (Y13 to Y15), which are delicious and come with side dishes of soup, cold beef slices and *xiáncài*, the local-speciality pickled vegetables.

☆ Entertainment

North Sìchuān Shadow Puppetry THEATRE
(川北皮影; Chuānběi Píyǐng; ☎623 8668; 67-69 Wumiao Jie; 武庙街67—69号; tickets Y10; ⊙8-10pm) Informal but fun 20-minute performances of north Sìchuān shadow puppetry are held in the small open-air courtyard here. They need at least four people for the show to start. It's a couple of doors down from Lǐ Family Courtyard.

Information

Along the river at the eastern end of the old town, a **tourist information centre** (游客中心; Yóukè Zhōngxīn) has flashy touch-screen computers illustrating the town's sights, and some staffers speak some English. For **street maps** (地图; *dìtú*), you can pick up better versions (free to Y10) at shops around town or at some tourist sights. Multilingual signs and maps are posted throughout the old town's streets.

The **Bank of China ATM** (cnr Dadong Jie & Neidong Jie) at the top end of Dadong Jie is foreign-card friendly and there's an **internet cafe** (网吧; wǎngbā; per hr Y3; ⊙8am-midnight) on Maojia Xiang (毛家巷) off Bailishu Jiē (百里树街), a lane just outside the old town running parallel to Dadong Jie.

Getting There & Away

Buses from Chéngdū's Běimén bus station arrive at Kèyùn Zhōngxīn Qìchēzhàn (客运中心汽车站), the main bus station here, which also serves Chóngqìng (Y109, five hours, 7.20am, 8.40am, 9.40am, 10.50am and 2pm). Buses returning to Chéngdū leave between 6.40am and 5.30pm.

Lángzhōng also has a smaller bus station, Bāshíjiǔ Duì (89队), which serves Guǎngyuán (Y49, four hours, 8am, 9am, noon and 2pm), from where you can catch trains north to Xī'ān or buses west to Jiǔzhàigōu. A local bus, labelled simply 89队 (*bāshíjiǔ duì;* Y2, 20 minutes), connects the two stations.

For the old town (古镇; *gǔzhèn*), get off this bus at the Rénmín Hospital stop (人民医院; Rénmín Yīyuàn). If you're coming from the main bus station, keep walking in the same direction the bus was going, then turn left at the first lights, onto Tianshanggong Jie (天上宫街) and keep walking straight. Dadong Jie will be on your left. Wumiao Jie will be straight on.

SOUTHERN SÌCHUĀN

Not often on the radar of foreign tourists, steamy southern Sìchuān is for those who prefer things a little offbeat. Quirky sights here include dinosaur fossils, ancient cliff-face hanging coffins and a bamboo forest. It's also home to some of China's very best teahouses.

Zìgòng 自贡

☎0813 / POP 693,000

This intriguing, rarely visited riverside city has been an important centre of Chinese salt production for almost 2000 years. Remnants of that industry make up part of an unconventional list of sights that includes the world's deepest traditional salt well and Asia's first dinosaur museum. Zìgòng is also the undisputed king of Sìchuān teahouses, so there's plenty of opportunity to while away the hours here if you fancy putting your feet up for a day.

Sights

Salt Industry History Museum MUSEUM
(盐业历史博物馆; Yányè Lìshǐ Bówùguǎn; 89 Dongxing Si; 东兴寺89号; admission Y20; ⊙8.30am-5pm) This absorbing museum, housed in a beautiful 270-year-old guildhall, is devoted to the region's salt industry and does an excellent job of telling the story through old photographs, good English captions and a modest collection of exhibits. The building itself, though, built by Shaanxi salt merchants in 1736, threatens to steal the show with its cool stone courtyards, intricate woodcarvings and wonderful swooping eaves.

To get here from the hotels, walk down the hill and turn left onto Jiefang Lu (解放路). The museum will be on your right after about 500m.

Shēnhǎi Salt Well SALT WELL
(燊海井; Shēnhǎi Jǐng; ☎510 1721; 289 Da'an Jie; 大安街289号; admission Y20; ⏲8.30am-5pm) This 1001m-deep artesian salt well was the world's deepest well when it was built in 1835 and it remains the deepest salt well ever drilled using the traditional mining technique of percussion drilling.

Many of the original parts, including a 20m-high wooden derrick that towers above the tiny 20cm-wide mouth of the well, are still intact, and the well still operates as a salt provider, although on a much smaller scale than before. Nine salt cauldrons are still in operation and visitors can see them bubbling away beside rows of the 2ft-high blocks of salt that came from them.

There are excellent English captions explaining how bamboo was once used for brine pipes, how buffaloes used to turn the heavy winch (an electric motor is used these days) and how tofu was added to the brine to help separate impurities.

Take bus 5 or 35 (Y1) from opposite the Róngguāng Business Hotel. Bus 35 continues to the Dinosaur Museum.

Dinosaur Museum MUSEUM
(恐龙馆; Kǒnglóng Guǎn; ☎580 1235; 238 Dashan Pu, Da'an District; 大安区大山铺238号; admission Y42; ⏲8.30am-5.30pm) As if a still-working ancient salt well wasn't quirky enough, Zìgòng is also home to Asia's first museum dedicated entirely to dinosaurs. Built on top of an excavation site, which has

WORTH A TRIP

SÌCHUĀN'S MYSTERIOUS HANGING COFFINS

Travellers looking to get off the beaten track might want to consider a trip to the remote corner of southeast Sìchuān, home to one of the province's most unusual and most mysterious sights: the Hanging Coffins of the ancient Bo people. The origins and eventual disappearance of the Bo continue to baffle archaeologists. It is thought they may be distant relatives of the Tujia, who can still be found scattered around the Three Gorges area, particularly in southwestern Húběi and northwestern Húnán. However, almost everything we know about the Bo has been gleaned from the sites of their coffins, which can still be found resting on wooden stakes, hammered into the side of cliffs up to 1000 years ago.

We know, for instance, from crude paintings found on some of the cliff faces, that the Bo were keen horsemen with a sharp social divide. Adult skeletons that have been recovered have also shown that the Bo knocked out their own teeth whilst still alive, although exactly why they practised this custom is still unknown.

There are hanging coffins at a few sites in this part of China, but at **Luòbiāo** (洛表) the **hanging coffins** (悬棺; xuánguān; admission Y20; ⏲8am-6pm) are found in greater numbers than elsewhere and are reasonably accessible.

At one time there were more than 300 coffins here, although about one-third have fallen to the ground as their support stakes gradually rotted away.

There's a small, free-to-enter museum just inside the site entrance with old photos and a coffin you can inspect up close. About 100m on, you'll find a large collection of coffins with steps leading up to a better vantage point. About 2km further on is another impressive collection of coffins.

One of the reasons this place is so rarely visited is that it's a pain in the neck to get here. First you need to get to the grim coal-mining town of Gǒngxiàn (珙县), which you can reach on buses from either Yíbīn (Y20, one hour, every 20 minutes from 6.30am to 7pm) or Chángníng (Y10.50 or Y13, one hour, frequent services from 5.50am to 6.10pm) near the Bamboo Sea. At Gǒngxiàn, catch a bus to Luòbiāo (Y15, two hours 45 minutes, every 20 minutes from 6am to 5pm), from where you can walk (40 minutes; take the right fork) or take a motorcycle taxi (Y5) to the entrance. The last bus back to Gǒngxiàn leaves at 5.20pm.

Locals say the area is at its most photogenic first thing in the morning as the sun rises opposite the cliffs, so you may want to consider arriving the evening before and staying at one of the cheap guesthouses by the bus station. The coffins are Luòbiāo's only tourist sight but you could fill any spare time with walks around the fabulous surrounding countryside.

one of the world's largest concentrations of dinosaur fossils, this museum has a fabulous collection of reassembled skeletons as well as half-buried dinosaur bones left in situ for visitors to see.

Dinosaur fossils started being discovered here in 1972 and their high numbers baffled archaeologists at first. It is now believed the skeletons were dumped here en masse from other sites in the region by huge floods.

Take bus 35 (Y1, 30 minutes) from opposite Róngguāng Business Hotel.

Sleeping

Róngguāng Business Hotel HOTEL $$
(容光商务酒店; Róngguāng Shāngwù Jiǔdiàn; ☎211 9999; 25 Ziyou Lu; 自由路25号; tw & d incl breakfast Y288-328; ❄@) Large, smart rooms with friendly staff, internet access for laptop users and free-to-use computers on the 4th floor, where you also get your free buffet breakfast. Rooms are discounted to Y120 and Y160. To get here, take bus 1 or 35 from the bus station or bus 34 from the train station.

Xióngfēi Holiday Hotel HOTEL $$$
(雄飞假日酒店; Xióngfēi Jiàrì Jiǔdiàn; ☎211 8888; 193 Jiefang Lu; 解放路193号; r from Y600; ❄@) For a bit more class, although not a lot more comfort in the standard rooms, try this upmarket place a few doors down from Róngguāng Business Hotel on the corner of Ziyou Lu and Jiefang Lu. Rooms were going for half-price when we were here.

Eating & Drinking

Evenings here are all about *shāokǎo* (烧烤; barbecue), with stalls spilling onto the pavement around Róngguāng Business Hotel as well as elsewhere around town. Zìgòng locals love their rabbit meat (兔肉; *tùròu*) and the skewers on offer include rabbit.

If you fancy a break from fiery Sìchuān cuisine, try the small dumplings restaurant, just up the hill from Róngguāng, which does delicious Tiānjīn-style boiled dumplings (小龙包; *xiǎolóng bāo;* Y4 per basket) and rice porridge (稀饭; *xīfàn;* Y1) and is open from 6am to 8pm. Look for the piles of bamboo baskets.

TOP CHOICE **Wángyé Temple** TEAHOUSE $
(王爷庙; Wángyé Miào; Binjiang Lu; 滨江路; teas from Y4, dishes Y8-20; ⌚8.30am-11pm) There are many wonderful teahouses in Zìgòng, particularly along the river, but this one, housed within the ochre-coloured walls of a 100-year-old temple, is one of the nicest you'll find anywhere in Sìchuān. Perched above the Fǔxī River (釜溪河; Fǔxī Hé), it sits opposite Fǎzàng Temple (法藏寺; Fǎzàng Sì). Apparently, the pair were built to ensure safe passage for cargo boats transporting salt downstream. Now locals hang out here, drink tea, play cards and admire the river view. It's also a fine spot for lunch, with all the usual Sìchuān favourites as well as rabbit hotpot (鲜锅兔; *xiānguō tù;* Y50) and a tasty fried rabbit dish (小煎兔; *xiǎojiān tù;* Y16), although food is only served between 11am and 1pm. From the hotels listed above, walk down to the river, turn left and follow the river for about 750m.

Huánhóu Palace TEAHOUSE $
(桓侯宫; Huánhóu Gōng; Zhonghua Lu; 中华路; teas Y4-8; ⌚8.30am-8pm) Another fabulous Zìgòng teahouse, this one is housed inside an 1868 butchers guildhall with a dramatic stone facade, wood-beamed courtyard interior and old stone stage. It's on your left as you walk towards the salt museum from the hotels listed above.

TOP FIVE SICHUANESE DISHES

» *gōngbào jīdīng* (宫爆鸡丁; spicy chicken with peanuts)

» *gānbiān sìjìdòu* (干煸四季豆; dry-fried green beans)

» *mápó dòufu* (麻婆豆腐; pock-marked Mother Chen's bean curd)

» *shuǐzhǔ yú* (水煮鱼; boiled fish in a fiery sauce)

» *huíguō ròu* (回锅肉; boiled and stir-fried pork with salty and hot sauce)

Information

Bank of China (中国银行; Zhōngguó Yínháng; Ziyou Lu) Foreign-friendly ATM next to Róngguāng Business Hotel.

Internet cafe (网吧; wǎngbā; per hr Y1.50; ⌚24hr) Up an alley beside the bank.

Getting There & Around

Bus

Destinations from Zìgòng bus station include the following:

Chéngdū Y60 to Y75, 3½ hours, every 30 minutes (6.30am to 7pm)

Chóngqìng Y74, 3½ hours, frequent services (6.40am to 6.30pm)

Éméi Shān Y48, 3½ hours, frequent services (6.10am to 5pm)

Lèshān Y41, three hours, frequent services (6.10am to 5pm)

Yíbīn Y26, one hour, every 30 minutes (7.30am to 7pm)

Local Buses

To get to either of the hotels we list here, walk out of the bus station, turn right and walk 200m to the first bus stop. Then take bus 1 or 35 (Y1) six stops to Shízì Kǒu (十字口) bus stop. The hotels are opposite and down the hill a bit from the bus stop. From the train station, take bus 34 (Y1) to Bīnjiāng Lù (滨江路) bus stop. From there, walk back 100m and turn left up Ziyou Lu.

Train

Destinations from the train station include the following:

Chéngdū seat Y20 to Y41, six to seven hours, three daily (9.26am, 9.40am and 10.05am)

Chóngqìng seat Y25 to Y29, seven hours, two daily (8.27am and 2.10pm)

Kúnmíng sleeper Y207/126, 16/18½ hours, two daily (fast 3.13pm, slow 8.02pm)

Yíbīn seat Y5.50 to Y13, 1½ hours, 11 daily (3.49am to 11.03pm)

Yíbīn 宜宾

This relatively modern, mid-sized Chinese city has little in the way of tourist sights but acts as a travel hub for trips to the Bamboo Sea and the Hanging Coffins.

The good-value **Jīngmào Hotel** (经贸宾馆; Jīngmào Bīnguǎn; ☎0831-701 0888; 108 Minzhu Lu; 民主路108号; tw Y258-308; @), where discounts bring rates down to Y130 to Y150, is a smart choice in the centre of town.

The lanes behind the hotel are lined with **barbecue stalls** (烧烤; *shāokǎo*) every evening. In the daytime, look for *ránmiàn* (然面), a delicious fried noodle dish and a local favourite.

On the 2nd floor of the building next to Jīngmào Hotel is an **internet cafe** (per hour Y2; ⏲24hr). For a foreign-friendly **ATM**, turn right out of the hotel, then right again at the lights. Bank of China will be on your right before you reach the river.

ℹ Getting There & Around

Bus

Most travellers will arrive in Yíbīn at the new Gāokè bus station (高客站; Gāokè zhàn), north of the centre. Take bus 4 (Y1, 10 minutes) into town and get off at Xùfǔ Shāngchéng (叙府商城) bus stop on Renmin Lu (人民路). Turn right at the lights ahead of you and Jīngmào Hotel will be on your left.

Continue on bus 4 to get to Nánkè bus station (南客站; Nánkè Zhàn) for buses to the Bamboo Sea (竹海; Zhúhǎi; Y20, 90 minutes, 9.30am and 10am) and the Hanging Coffins in Luòbiǎo (洛表; Y32, three hours, 2.05pm). If you miss the direct buses to the Bamboo Sea, go via Chángníng (长宁, Y13.50, one hour, every 15 minutes from 6.45am to 7.30pm). If the direct Luòbiǎo bus isn't convenient, go via Gǒngxiàn (珙县, Y16, one hour, every 20 minutes from 6.30am to 7pm).

Consider visiting the Hanging Coffins from the Bamboo Sea, as buses from Chángníng go to Gǒngxiàn.

Buses from Yíbīn's Gāokè bus station include the following destinations:

Chéngdū Y90 to Y106, four hours, frequent services (7.30am to 7pm)

Chóngqìng Y96 to Y108, four hours, frequent services (6.50am to 7pm)

Éméi Shān Y78, 4½ hours, three daily (8.20am, 12.10pm and 1.10pm)

Lèshān Y68, four hours, five daily (9am, 10.40am, 11.20am, 2.20pm and 4.10pm)

Zìgòng Y26, one hour, frequent services (7.30am to 7pm)

Train

Bus 11 links the train station with Gāokè bus station and passes by the end of Renmin Lu. Trains leaving from Yíbīn train station (火车站; *huǒchē zhàn*) include the following destinations:

Chéngdū seat Y25 to Y51, 7½ to nine hours, three daily (8am, 8.08am and 8.28am)

Chóngqìng seat Y31 to Y36, nine hours, two daily (6.34am and 12.35pm)

Kúnmíng sleeper Y117/191, 17/15 hours, two daily (slow 4.45pm, fast 9.28pm)

Zìgòng seat Y5.50 to Y13, 1½ hours, 11 daily (1.10am to 3.40pm)

Bamboo Sea 蜀南竹海

Swaths of swaying bamboo forest, well-marked walking trails and a handful of charming lakes and waterfalls make south Sìchuān's Bamboo Sea, or **Shǔnán Zhúhǎi** (adult Y90), a worthwhile detour for those heading south.

There are more than 30 types of bamboo across this 120-sq-km national park and the scenery is gorgeous enough to have attracted many a TV and film director.

The villages of **Wànlǐng** (万岭), near the west gate, and **Wànlǐ** (万里), near the east gate, are the main two settlements inside the park and your best bet for a base. Both have walking options nearby, but one possibility is to hike between the two. It's about 11km if you follow the road the whole way, but various loops within scenic areas mean you'll probably end up walking a lot more than that. Expect to take at least half a day. Two possible **cable car** (索道; *suǒdào*) rides can shorten your walking distances considerably, and are a great way to see the forest from another angle.

From Wànlǐng, it takes about 20 minutes to reach the **Guānguāng cable car** (观光索道; Guānguāng Suǒdào, one way/return Y30/40; ⏲8am-5pm), a 25-minute trip which takes you over some stunning bamboo forests. There's a nice forest loop you can walk (about one hour) just beyond the entrance to the cable car. Once you've ridden the cable car, turn right as you exit to reach the 10-minute **Dàxiágǔ cable car** (大峡谷索道; Dàxiágǔ Suǒdào; one way/return Y20/30; ⏲8.30am-5.30pm), which crosses a dramatic gorge and leads into another scenic area with a number of trails, some of which pass by two lakes. Leaving this area, head for Sānhé Jiè (三合界), a junction where you can find accommodation. Turn right here for the final 30-minute walk to Wànlǐ village.

Two waterfalls near Wànlǐ are worth a look. To get to **Rainbow Falls** (七彩飞瀑; Qīcǎi Fēipù), either follow the lake by the village or turn right before it and walk along the road for about 1km to the signposted main gate. You can continue down past these falls to **Golden Dragon Falls** (金龙瀑布; Jīnlóng Pùbù). This is off the tourist maps so pretty quiet, although you do have to pay Y10 to an enterprising old man for right of passage. You can climb back up to the main road through a wonderfully peaceful bamboo forest.

If you're hiking you'll pass numerous guesthouses and hotels along the way. In Wànlǐng, try **Chéngbīnlóu Jiǔdiàn** (承宾楼酒店; ☎0831-498 0104; s/tw Y180/200, discounted to Y60/80). Wànlǐ also has plenty of accommodation, but for somewhere more tranquil walk 1km beyond Wànlǐ to **Zhúyùn Shānzhuāng** (竹韵山庄; ☎497 9001, 138 9092 5673; r from Y360), opposite the main gate to Rainbow Falls. It backs onto a quiet lake, and spotless rooms with private bathroom were going for Y60 when we were here.

All guesthouses and hotels do food too. It's generally pretty good, although more expensive than outside the park. Alternatively, look out for one of the cheap noodle restaurants (面馆; *miànguǎn*) in Wànlǐng or Wànlǐ.

ℹ Getting There & Around

There's a **map** on the back of your entrance ticket, and you can get hold of maps in the park, but the easiest to use and most detailed maps are the ones drawn on wooden boards throughout the park. Take a photo of one to guide you. All the main sights are signposted too.

Motorbike taxis can take you between the two main villages (around Y50, 45 minutes) if you decide not to walk.

Bus

Buses into the park stop at the west gate to allow you to get off and buy your entrance ticket, before passing through Wànlǐng then terminating at Wànlǐ.

There are two direct buses from Wànlǐ back to Yíbīn (Y20, 90 minutes, 7am and 1.10pm), although times can change, so check when you get here. Both pass Wànlǐng (30 minutes) and, if you ask, will drop you at the junction for Chángníng (one hour), where you can change for Gǒngxiàn to get to the Hanging Coffins.

WESTERN SÌCHUĀN

North and west of Chéngdū, green tea becomes butter tea, Confucianism yields to Buddhism and gumdrop hills leap into jagged snowy peaks. Welcome to Tibet, in all but name.

This part of Sìchuān makes up a large chunk of what Tibetans refer to as Kham (in Chinese 康巴; Kāngbā), one of old Tibet's three traditional provinces, and is home to the Khampas, a Tibetan ethnic group known throughout Tibetan history for being fierce warriors.

Western Sìchuān experiences up to 200 freezing days per year, but summers can be blistering by day and the high altitude invites particularly bad sunburn.

Kāngdìng (Dardo) 康定

☎0836 / POP 82,000 / ELEV 2616M

Coming from the Chéngdū area, there are two main gateways into Tibetan Sìchuān. One option is Dānbā, but by far the most popular is Kāngdìng, and for many travellers this will be their first taste of the Tibetan world.

BRING PLENTY OF CHINESE CASH

At the time of research it was impossible to change money or travellers cheques, get advances on credit cards or use ATMs with foreign bank cards anywhere in western Sìchuān apart from Kāngdìng. The one handy anomaly was the ATM in Xiāngchéng, near the border with Yúnnán, which accepted VISA cards.

The town has long been a trade centre between Chinese and Tibetan cultures and you'll find elements of both here.

Set in a steep river valley at the confluence of the raging Zhéduō and Yǎlā Rivers (known as the Dar and Tse in Tibetan), with the towering Gònggā Shān (7556m) beyond, Kāngdìng is famous throughout China for a popular love song inspired by the town's surrounding scenery.

Sights

Monasteries MONASTERIES

There are several small monasteries in and around Kāngdìng. The central **Ānjué Temple** (安觉寺; Ānjué Sì; Ngachu Gompa in Tibetan) dates back to 1652 and was built under the direction of the fifth Dalai Lama.

Nánwú Temple (南无寺; Nánwú Sì) belongs to the Gelugpa (Yellow Hat) sect of Tibetan Buddhism and is the most active monastery in the area. It also affords good views of Kāngdìng and the valley. Walk south along the main road, cross the river and keep going for about 200m until you see a rusty old sign (in traditional Chinese characters: 南無寺) for the monastery on your right. Follow that track uphill, beside a stream, and the monastery will be on your right.

Nearby, about 100m further along the main road, is **Jīngāng Temple** (金刚寺; Jīngāng Sì), a 400-year-old Nyingma monastery set around a lawned courtyard. Turn right at the sign for Knapsack Inn.

Other Sights SCENIC AREAS

You can head up **Pǎomǎ Shān** (admission Y50) for excellent views of Kāngdìng and the surrounding mountains and valleys. The ascent takes you past oodles of prayer flags, several Buddhist temples and up to a white *chörten* (Tibetan stupa). Avoid hiking alone, as a British tourist was murdered here in 2000 and one or two muggings have been reported.

Two sets of steps lead up the hill, or you can take the **cable car** (索道; suǒdào; one way/return Y20/30). By the entrance to the cable car is a small **Tibetan museum** (admission Y30; ⏰8am-6pm).

Èrdào Bridge Hot Springs HOT SPRINGS

(二道温泉; Èrdào Wēnquán; admission Y10-120; ⏰7am-midnight) About 5km north of Kāngdìng, these springs are a pleasant 45-minute walk along the Yǎlā River, or take a cab (Y8).

Festivals & Events

Kāngdìng's biggest annual festival, the **Walking Around the Mountain Festival** (Zhuànshānjié), takes place on Pǎomǎ Shān on the eighth day of the fourth lunar month (normally in May) to commemorate the birthday of the Historical Buddha, Sakyamuni. White-and-blue Tibetan tents cover the hillside and there's wrestling, horse racing and visitors from all over western Sìchuān.

Sleeping

Yōngzhū Hotel GUESTHOUSE $

(拥珠驿栈; Yōngzhū Yìzhàn; ☎283 2381, 159 8373 8188; dm Y30-40, d Y120-160) Hidden in a lane beside Kāngdìng Hotel off Guangming Lu, this small, friendly guesthouse has comfortable, well-kept rooms, including three- and four-bed dorms, decorated with colourful Tibetan furnishings and built around an inner atrium. There's 24-hour hot water in both the common and private bathrooms.

Kāngdìng Hotel HOTEL $$

(康定宾馆; Kāngdìng Bīnguǎn; ☎283 2077; 25 Guangming Lu; 光明路25号; r from Y360; ❄@) For something more comfortable, this decent midranger, right beside Ānjué Temple, had standard twins going for Y240 when we were there.

Dēngbā Hostel YOUTH HOSTEL $

(登巴客栈; Dēngbā Kèzhàn; ☎282 3009; 6 Bei'er Xiang; 西大街北二巷; dm/s/tw Y25/30/60; @📶) Tatty but very welcoming hostel with small rooms. Common showers and toilets only. Self-service laundry and bike rental (per day Y20 to Y30). Off Xo Dajie.

Two hostels that were closed at the time of research, but which generally get good reviews from travellers:

Zhilam Hostel HOSTEL $$

(汇道客栈; Huìdào Kèzhàn; ☎283 1100; www.zhilamhostel.com; Bái Tǔkǎn Cūn; 白土坎村;

Kāngdìng (Dardo)

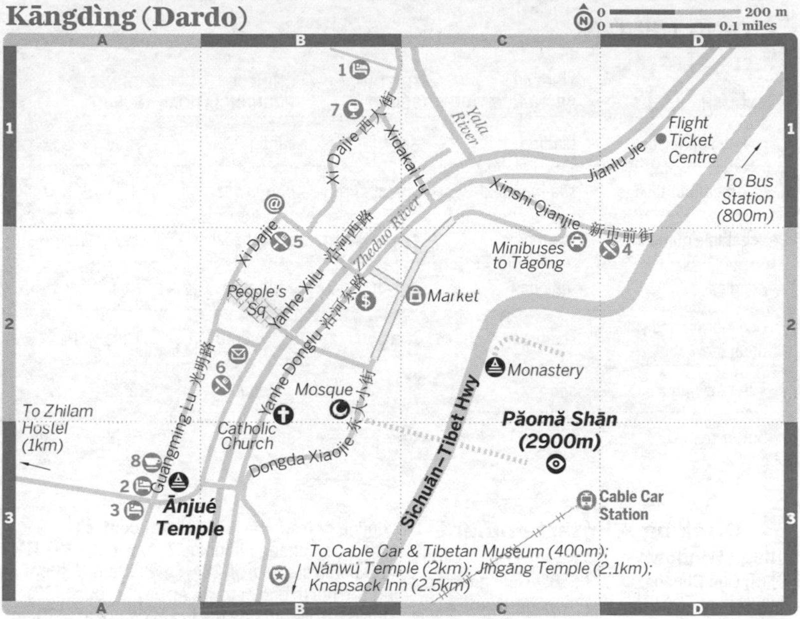

Kāngdìng (Dardo)

Top Sights
- Ānjué Temple A3
- Pǎomǎ Shān (2900m) C3

Sleeping
- 1 Dēngbā Hostel B1
- 2 Kāngdìng Hotel A3
- 3 Yōngzhū Hotel A3

Eating
- 4 Ā'Rè Tibetan Restaurant D2
- 5 Barbecue Stalls B2
- 6 Tibetan Culture Dew B2

Drinking
- 7 Happiness in Heaven B1
- 8 Village Window A3

dm/d Oct-Apr Y35/260, May-Sep Y60/450; @) American-run; it's a 10-minute walk up the lane beyond Yōngzhū Hotel.

Knapsack Inn HOSTEL $
(背包客栈; Bēibāo Kèzhàn; 283 8377; dm Y25-35, d without bathroom Y80; @) Next door to Jīngāng Temple.

Eating

On mild evenings, Sìchuān **barbecue stalls** set up around the northeast corner of People's Sq.

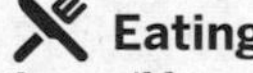
Tibetan Culture Dew TIBETAN $
(西藏雨; Xīzàng Yǔ; 158 0836 6530; Yanhe Xilu; 沿河西路; dishes Y15-38; 11am-11pm) Hang out with the yak-butter-tea-sipping locals at this lovely teahouse/restaurant with a rustic stone-and-wood interior decorated with colourful Tibetan prayer flags. There are all sorts of tea if you don't like the yak-butter variety, plus coffee and beer. The English menu is limited, but includes *tsampa,* Tibetan yoghurt, a few yak-meat dishes and some delicious dumplings.

Ā'Rè Tibetan Restaurant TIBETAN $$
(阿热藏餐; Ā'rè Zàngcān; 669 6777; Xinshi Qianjie; 新市前街; dishes Y12-78; 9am-10pm;) Bigger menu and more of a proper restaurant than Tibetan Culture Dew, this place does tasty soups, *tsampa* and yak-meat dishes including a whole yak hoof, if that sort of thing takes your fancy. English menu.

EATING TIBETAN

ENGLISH	TIBETAN PRONUNCIATION	TIBETAN SCRIPT	CHINESE PRONUNCIATION	CHINESE SCRIPT
roasted barley flour	*tsampa*	རྩམ་པ།	*zānbā*	糌粑
yak-meat dumplings	*sha-momo*	ཤ་མོག་མོག	*niúròu bāozi*	牛肉包子
vegetable dumplings	*tse-momo*	ཚལ་མོག་མོག	*sùcài bāozi*	素菜包子
noodles	*thuk-pa*	ཐུག་པ།	*zàngmiàn*	藏面
rice, potato and yak-meat stew	*shamdra*	ཤ་འབྲས།	*gālí niúròu fàn*	咖喱牛肉饭
Tibetan yoghurt	*sho*	ཞོ།	*suānnǎi*	酸奶
butter tea	*bo-cha*	བོད་ཇ།	*sūyóu chá*	酥油茶

Drinking & Entertainment

Village Window CAFE $
(村窗; Cūn Chuāng; ☎283 5665; Guangming Lu; 光明路; coffees from Y10; ⊙noon-11pm; @⊡) The coolest of the new cafes in town, this Tibetan-run place, adorned with books and ornaments, does fresh coffee, various teas, beer and snacks. You can use the internet for free, if you order a drink. English menu.

Happiness in Heaven TIBETAN DANCE HALL $
(天地吉祥; Tiāndì Jíyàng; Xi Dajie; 西大街; drinks from Y20; ⊙7pm-midnight) Traditional Tibetan and Chinese songs, including the famous 'Kāngdìng Love Song' (康定情歌; Kāngdìng Qínggē), are performed to ear-splitting techno beats and appreciative audiences, and you can get up and dance once the performances are finished.

Information

ATM (自动柜员机; Zìdòng Guìyuán Jī; Yanhe Donglu) China Construction Bank ATM. One of a few around town that takes foreign cards.

Internet café (网吧; wǎngbā; per hr Y3; ⊙24hr)

Public Security Bureau (PSB; 公安局; Gōng'ānjú; ☎281 1415; Dongda Xiaojie; ⊙8.30am-noon & 2.30-5.30pm) Next-day visa-extension service.

Getting There & Away

Air

Kāngdìng Airport only serves Chéngdū (35 minutes), and only has one daily flight (8.13am). Tickets cost around Y1000 before discounts, but can often be had for Y500 or less. Buy them online or from the **flight ticket centre** (机场售票中心; Jīchǎng Shòupiào Zhōngxīn; ☎287 1111; 28 Jianlu Jie; 箭炉街28号; ⊙8.30am-5.30pm) at the north end of town. An airport bus (Y22) leaves from outside the ticket centre at 6.30am.

Bus

The bus station is a 10-minute walk north of the centre. Minibuses to all destinations listed here leave from outside the bus station. Ones to Tǎgōng are cheaper from Xinshi Qianjie. Remember: private hire – *bāochē* (包车); shared vehicle – *pīnchē* (拼车).

Bātáng Y142.50, 12 hours, one daily (6am)

Chéngdū Y121 to Y131, eight hours, hourly (6am to 4pm)

Dānbā Y46, three hours, two daily (7am and 3.30pm)

Dégé Y176, 16 hours, one daily (6am)

Gānzī Y113, 11 hours, one daily (6am)

Lèshān Y113, seven hours, one daily (7am)

Lǐtáng Y87.50, eight hours, one daily (6.30am)

Tǎgōng Y39, three hours, one daily (6am)

Xīchāng Y103.50, eight hours, one daily (6am)

Dānbā 丹巴

☎0836 / POP 58,200 / ELEV 1800M

This friendly town, set in a dramatic gorge overlooking the confluence of three rushing rivers, makes a nice alternative to Kāngdìng as a gateway into Tibetan Sìchuān.

The hills surrounding Dānbā contain clusters of fascinating ancient watchtowers and a number of picturesque Tibetan villages, some offering homestays.

Sights

Qiāng Watchtowers RUINS
(羌族碉楼; Qiāngzú Diāolóu) These ancient stone towers, nestled incongruously among village homes on hillsides overlooking the Dàdù River, were built by the Qiang people between 700 and 1200 years ago. The towers range from 20m to 60m in height and were used as places of worship and to store valuable goods as well as to signal warnings of would-be attackers. They were built with a number of inner wooden storeys, which have since disintegrated, and entrances that were some metres above ground. One enterprising family in **Suōpō** (梭坡; the nearest village to Dānbā with watchtowers) has rebuilt the wooden levels of the tower next to their home and allows visitors to climb up the inside from their rooftop, for a small fee, of course (Y15). Don't worry about finding them. They, or a 'friend' of theirs, will find you.

To get to Suōpō, turn left out of Zháxī Zhuōkāng Backpackers Hostel and walk along the river for about 30 minutes. Turn down the track beside the small police station then cross the suspension bridge and keep walking up to the village. Look for stone steps under some large trees up to your left, just after you reach the village's first couple of buildings. These steps lead to the nearest towers.

Tibetan Villages VILLAGES
(藏寨; Zàngzhài) There are a number of pretty Tibetan villages in the hills round here but Dānba's pride and joy is **Jiǎjū** (甲居; admission Y30), 7km northwest of town and perched on top of a multiswitchback track that winds its way up a steep river gorge. Being named 'Best Village in China' by Chinese *National Geographic* in 2005 was probably going a bit far, but with its fruit trees, its charming Tibetan stone houses and its remote location, Jiǎjū is certainly worth the trip.

One of a number of stone houses that has been converted into a homestay is the excellent **Liǎngkē Shù** (两棵树; ☎8807 199, 135 6868 5278; dm inc meals Y50), with simple dormitories decorated with traditional Tibetan furniture, a pleasant central courtyard and stunning views. The owner can arrange trips into the fabulous surrounding countryside. To get here, take a shared minivan (Y5) from the Bāměi end of Dānbā. A private taxi costs Y40 one way.

Another popular homestay village is **Zhōnglù** (中路; admission Y20), 13km from town, but you'll need to take a taxi (Y80).

Sleeping & Eating

Local specialities include aromatic pigs trotters (香猪蹄; *xiāng zhūtuǐ*), cured pork (腊肉; *là ròu*) and a prized fish dish called *shí bāzi* (石巴子), which will set you back about Y200 per *jīn*. In Chéngdū it costs more than Y1000! A number of small restaurants by the bus station open early for breakfast noodles (面; *miàn*) or dumplings (小龙包子; *xiǎolóng bāozi*).

Zháxī Zhuōkāng Backpackers Hostel HOTEL $
(扎西卓康青年旅舍; Zháxī Zhuōkāng Qīngnián Lǚshè; ☎352 1806; 35 Sanchahe Nanlu; 三岔河南路35号; dm Y20-30, tw without/with bathroom Y60/80; @) Despite being more hotel than youth hostel, this place is still traveller central in Dānbā. You'll receive a friendly welcome and there's free internet in the lobby, but the rooms are standard budget-hotel jobs. It's a 25-minute walk from the bus station (walk down to the river, turn right and keep going) or Y5 in a cab.

Wǎnglǎo Wǔ SÌCHUĀN $$
(王老五; dishes Y15-40; ⊙noon-11pm) Across the street from Zháxī Zhuōkāng Backpackers Hostel, this decent 2nd-floor Sichuanese restaurant rustles up all the usual Sìchuān favourites plus some excellent cured-pork dishes. Try the cured pork with green chillies (腊肉青椒; *làròu qīngjiāo;* Y25) or the mushrooms with pork slices (木耳肉片; *mù'ěr ròupiàn;* Y15). If you can't afford the *shí bāzi* (石巴子; Y240 per *jīn*), try the ordinary braised river fish (红烧鱼; *hóngshāo yú;* Y30 to Y40 per *jīn*). No English menu.

Information

Jiarong Buxing Jie is a pedestrian-only shopping street that you pass on the walk between the bus station and Zháxī Zhuōkāng Backpackers Hostel. At its east end, in one of the last buildings on the left, is an **internet cafe** (网吧; wǎngbā; 26 Jiarong Buxing Jie; per hr Y3; ⊙8am-midnight).

Getting There & Away

For Tǎgōng, take a minibus (Y50, three hours) from the west end of town, via Bāměi (Y30, two hours). Bus destinations include the following:

Chéngdū Y120, nine hours, two daily (6.20am and 6.30am)

Gānzī Y97, nine hours, one daily (7am)

Kāngdìng Y45, four hours, two daily (6.20am and 3pm)

Mǎ'ěrkāng Y44, six hours, one daily (7.30am)

TIBET BORDER CLOSED

At the time of research, foreigners were forbidden from travelling overland from Sìchuān into Tibet proper because Tibet's far eastern prefecture of Chamdo, which borders Sìchuān, was completely off limits. Check the Tibet branch of Lonely Planet's online forum, **Thorn Tree** (www.lonelyplanet.com/thorntree), for the latest information.

Sìchuān–Tibet Highway (Northern Route)

The legendary Sìchuān–Tibet Hwy splits in two just west of Kāngdìng. The northern route is 300km longer than the southern route, and is generally less travelled. You'll pass awesome high-plateau grasslands and traditional Tibetan communities with their remote monasteries and motorcycle-riding yak herders.

Crossing Chola Mountain, the highest pass (5050m) this side of Lhasa, takes you to Dégé and the border with the TAR (Tibetan Autonomous Region), or Tibet proper. You can also take this route to head north into Qīnghǎi province via Sěrshu.

You *must* come prepared with warm clothing; even in midsummer, it can be very cold at higher elevations. Remember that bus services can be erratic – this is no place to be in a hurry.

TĂGŌNG 塔公

0836 / POP 8000 / ELEV 3750M

The small Tibetan village of Tăgōng and its beautiful surrounding grasslands offer plenty of excuses to linger. As well as an important monastery and a fascinating nearby nunnery, there's also horse trekking and hiking, and travellers give rave reviews to the Tibetan homestays here.

Take time to adjust to the altitude if you're coming from lower terrain to the east.

Sights

Tăgōng Monastery BUDDHIST MONASTERY

(塔公寺; Tăgōng Sì; admission Y20) The story goes that when Princess Wencheng, the Chinese bride-to-be of Tibetan king Songtsen Gampo, was on her way to Lhasa in the 7th century, a precious statue of Jowo Sakyamuni Buddha toppled off one of the carts in her entourage. A replica of the statue was carved on the spot where it landed and a temple then built around it. You'll find the statue in the right-hand hall here. The original, which is the most revered Buddha image in all of Tibet, is housed in Lhasa's Jokhang Temple.

Also note the beautiful 1000-armed Chenresig (Avalokiteshvara) in the hall to the left. And don't miss the impressive collection of over 100 *chörtens* behind the monastery.

Activities

Horse trekking (per person per day Y250) and guided **grassland hikes** (per person per day Y150) can be arranged with Angela at Khampa Cafe & Arts Centre. Prices are all-inclusive. She will also point you in the right direction if you want to hike out into the grasslands on your own.

Festivals

Like many places in this part of Tibetan Sìchuān, Tăgōng holds an annual **horse-racing festival** *(sàimǎhuì)* during the fifth lunar month (usually early July), which features thousands of Tibetan herdsmen and Tibetan opera.

Sleeping

Angela at Khampa Cafe & Arts Centre can arrange **Tibetan homestays** (per person per night Y40). The homestays get particularly good reviews from travellers.

Jya Drolma and Gayla's Guesthouse GUESTHOUSE $

(266 6056; dm Y25, tw without bathroom Y50) Bedrooms here – even the dorms – are a riot of golds, reds and blues, with elaborately painted ceilings and walls. There are common toilets on each floor and one shower with 24-hour hot water. Look for the English sign on the opposite side of the square from the monastery. No English spoken, but a very friendly welcome.

Snowland Guesthouse GUESTHOUSE $

(雪城旅社; Xuěchéng Lǚshè; 286 6098, 130 5645 7979; tagongsally@yahoo.com; dm from Y10, s without bathroom Y20, tw with bathroom Y80) This long-standing backpacker hangout, right beside Tăgōng Monastery, has less character than Gayla's but is still a fine choice. Sally, who also runs the adjacent cafe-restaurant, speaks a bit of English.

WORTH A TRIP

HÉPÍNG FĂHÙI NUNNERY

Lama Tsemper was a revered local hermit who spent much of his life meditating in a cave about two hours' walk across the grasslands from Tăgōng. Local nuns would bring him food and generally look after him so that when, just before his death in the 1980s, he requested a temple be built here, it was decided to build a nunnery too. **Hépíng Făhuì** (和平法会), known locally as *ani gompa* (nunnery, in Tibetan), is now home to around 500 nuns and more than 100 monks and is a fascinating place to visit.

Lama Tsemper's remains are in a *chörten* (Tibetan stupa) inside the original **cave**; you may have to ask a nun to unlock the door to look inside. Below the cave is the **temple**, and a huge **mani wall** (a wall made from prayer stones), as big as the temple itself, which has its own *kora* circuit that attracts many pilgrims.

From the mani wall, you can see a hill, covered in thousands of prayer flags, where **sky burials** take place. Some families donate the deceased's possessions to the nunnery, and these genuine Tibetan family heirlooms can actually be bought in the small **convenience shop** at the foot of the hill. Next to the shop is a **canteen** (noodles Y6, tsampa Y6, butter tea Y8) with a simple **guesthouse** (dm Y20) upstairs.

Getting to *ani gompa* across the grasslands is half the fun. Walk north out of town as far as the Golden Temple; 100m past the temple, turn right down a track. You'll be able to see the golden roof of a monastic school way off in the distance to your left. The nunnery is beside this. But first, continue along the track, crossing the river bridge, and keep walking until the track starts to lead away from the monastic school. That's your cue to head off-piste, over the grasslands, dodging yaks, horses and the occasional wild rabbit en route. The nunnery is to the left of the monastic school. The track linking the two leads to the mani wall and then on down to the guesthouse. If you continue past the nunnery you'll eventually get back to the main road, where you may be able to hitch a lift back to Tăgōng.

Eating

TOP CHOICE Khampa Cafe & Arts Centre TIBETAN, WESTERN $

(☎136 8449 3301; http://definitelynomadic.com; dishes Y9-28; ⊙8am-11pm) Run by Angela, a super-helpful American woman, and her Tibetan husband Djarga, this fantastic new cafe serves authentic Tibetan cuisine as well as Westernised Tibetan dishes (think yak burger) and straightforward Western food, including good breakfasts. The fresh coffee is excellent, as is the yak-butter tea, and there should be wi-fi up and running by the time you read this. They also sell beautiful clothes, handicrafts and jewellery handmade by locals from various parts of western Sìchuān and Tibet. Next door to Tăgōng Monastery.

Sally's Kham Restaurant TIBETAN, WESTERN, CHINESE $

(☎139 0564 7979; tagongsally@yahoo.com; dishes Y3-35; ⊙8am-10pm) This spit-and-sawdust cafe-restaurant serves Tibetan, Western and Chinese food and is another good place to meet travellers. Sally, who speaks OK English, can help with travel information.

Getting There & Away

A bus from Gānzī to Kāngdìng (Y40, two hours, 7.30am) passes Tăgōng Monastery, but you might not get a seat. Alternatively, take a shared minivan (Y50). Note, you might struggle to find fellow passengers after about 10am.

To get to Lǐtáng, take the Kāngdìng bus or a shared minivan to Xīndūqiáo (新都桥; Y15, one hour), from where you can flag down the Kāngdìng–Lǐtáng bus (Y64, seven hours), which passes by at around 9am, or a minibus (Y80).

For Dānbā, take a shared minivan to Bāměi (八美; Y20, one hour), then switch minivans (Y30, two hours).

For Gānzī (Y80, eight hours), you can try to snag a seat on the bus from Kāngdìng, which passes here between 9am and 10am. You may be able to arrange a shared minivan too.

GĀNZĪ 甘孜

☎0836 / POP 61,400 / ELEV 3394M

This dusty but lively market town in a picturesque valley surrounded by snowcapped mountains is the capital of the Gānzī (Garzě) Autonomous Prefecture and is populated mostly by Tibetans.

Gānzī is a handy intermediate stop between Sěrshu and Kāngdìng or on the way west to Dégé and beyond. It's easy to spend a couple of days here exploring the beautiful countryside, which is scattered with Tibetan villages and monasteries. Photo opportunities abound.

Sights

North of the town's Tibetan quarter, **Gānzī Temple** (甘孜寺; Gānzī Sì; Garzě Gompa in Tibetan; admission Y15) is the region's largest monastery, dating back more than 500 years and glimmering with blinding quantities of gold. Encased on the walls of the main hall are hundreds of small golden Sakyamunis. In a smaller hall just west of the main hall is an awe-inspiring statue of Jampa (Maitreya or Future Buddha), dressed in a giant silk robe. The views into the mountains from here are fantastic.

The monastery is about a 25- to 30-minute walk from the bus station. Turn left out of the station and keep going until you reach the Tibetan neighbourhood. Then wind your way uphill around the clay and wooden houses.

Sleeping & Eating

Jīntàiyáng Bīnguǎn HOTEL $
(金太阳宾馆; ☎752 5479; 53 Jiefang Jie; 解放街53号; r without bathroom Y30-50, with bathroom Y80; wi-fi) Simple but clean rooms around a courtyard out back. Round-the-clock hot water, even in the common bathrooms, and, believe it or not, wi-fi (not the quickest, mind)! Turn left out of the station and it's on your left. Another building off Chuanzang Lu houses smarter twins with private bathrooms that usually go for Y100; it also has wi-fi. Turn left out of the station, take the first right and it's on your left through an archway.

Golden Yak Hotel HOTEL $
(金牦牛酒店; Jīnmáoniú Jiǔdiàn; ☎752 2353; Dajin Tan; 打金滩; r without/with hot water Y60/150) This dependable chain has branches at a number of bus stations in western Sìchuān. This particular one has a main building at the back of the bus station forecourt, with standard doubles discounted to Y120, and a separate building across the forecourt housing enormous but slightly shabby twin rooms with bathrooms but no hot water.

TOP CHOICE **Tibetan Restaurant** TIBETAN $
(藏餐馆; Zàngcānguǎn; 2nd fl, 47 Dajin Tan; 打金滩47号2层; dishes Y10-35; 7am-11pm; menu) This wonderfully decorated teahouse/restaurant, just across from the bus station, is run by a local nun and is the main Tibetan hang-out in town. Sip butter tea, tuck into hearty plates of yak meat and get your hands covered in dough as you attempt to mix your own *tsampa*. English menu.

Information

Internet cafe (网吧; wǎngbā; per hr Y4; 24hr) Turn left out of the bus station and take the second road on your right; it's on the 2nd floor.

Getting There & Away

A bus to Dégé (Y66, eight to 10 hours), via Manigango (Y30, three hours), passes through here at 9am, but it's often full. Minibuses ply the same route for Y10 to Y20 more, but leave before the bus arrives (between 7.30am and 8.30am). After 9am it's hard to find fellow passengers, so you'll either have to fork out for the whole minibus or hitch.

Scheduled bus services run to the following destinations:

Chéngdū Y220, 18 hours, one daily (6am)
Dānbā Y99, nine hours, one daily (6.30am)
Kāngdìng Y115, 11 hours, one daily (6.30am)
Sěrshu Y101, six hours, one daily (6.30am)
Yùshù Y146, 13 hours, one daily (6am)

AROUND GĀNZĪ

There are a number of Tibetan villages and monasteries in the fabulous countryside west of Gānzī.

Perched attractively on a hill up a rutted dirt track, **Beri Gompa** (白利寺; Báilì Sì) is a mid-sized monastery about 15km west of town, on the road to Dégé. On sunny days, its gold top sparkles against the deep-blue sky. The scenery from Gānzī to here is stunning, so you might consider hiking to the monastery and back from Gānzī. Bring a packed lunch. Turn left out of the bus station then take the first left; follow the road over the bridge then along the river all the way, passing plenty of Tibetan villages and temples en route. Otherwise, hitch a ride on any Dégé-bound vehicle.

Further along the same road, about 30km from Gānzī, is **Darjay Gompa** (大金寺; Dàjīn Sì). This monastery was once home to more than 3000 monks. Many were killed during the Cultural Revolution. Others escaped to India. Nowadays, around 300 monks reside here. They spend much of their time having animated debates in the courtyard outside the main hall. Inside the hall, you'll find large photos of the 14th Dalai Lama and, right at the back, a row of impressive 3m-tall Buddha images. You

WORTH A TRIP

DALA GONG GUESTHOUSE

Travellers who are sick of staying in dusty market towns, and only seeing this area's drop-dead-gorgeous scenery through the window of a bus, will adore **Dala Gong Guesthouse** (dm Y30).

A 10-minute walk from **Darjay Gompa**, one of the area's most revered monasteries, the small temple of Dala Gong is home to three friendly monks who welcome guests to share their mudbrick wood-beamed living quarters set among the prettiest scenery you can imagine – snowcapped mountains to one side; rolling grasslands and a river to the other. Climb up onto the roof for 360-degree views and to plot your next hike to one of the nearby villages, monasteries or mountains.

Accommodation was dormitory-only when we stayed, and as basic as it gets, but two small modern blocks were being built in the courtyard at the time of research, promising private rooms with bathrooms (Y100) and, wait for it...hot water! We shall see.

If, as we suspect, the showers are cold, fear not; there are some free-to-use, open-air **hot springs** five minutes' walk away over the other side of the river. Locals use them to wash themselves, their children, their clothes and sometimes even their motorbikes, but there's plenty of room for everyone, so squeeze in.

The only food options are eating with the monks (offer them whatever money you feel is right). If you tire of eating *tsampa* (porridge of roasted barley flour) three times a day, there's a small **shop** (⊙8am-9pm) on the main road outside the monastery, which sells drinks, snacks and instant noodles.

To get to the guesthouse from Darjay Gompa, walk for 10 minutes along the only track that leads away from the back entrance of the monastery.

may have to get one of the monks to unlock the door to the hall.

Travellers who wish to stay the night here and soak up the sumptuous scenery should consider the wonderful but simple **Dala Gong Guesthouse**, a 10-minute walk from the monastery and just a short stroll from some **hot springs**.

To get to Darjay Gompa from Gānzī, either grab a seat on the Dégé-bound bus (Y10, 45 minutes, 8.30am) or take a minibus (Y30). Note, the bus is often full and the shared minibuses leave before it (around 7.30am). A private taxi will cost at least Y50. Keen hikers could consider walking here but it will take a whole day. Walk to Beri Gompa and just keep going.

MANIGANGO 马尼干戈

☎0836 / ELEV 3800M

There's not much going on in this dusty two-street town halfway between Gānzī and Dégé. Nearby, though, is the stunning turquoise lake, Yilhun Lha-tso, while the large monastery, Dzogchen Gompa, isn't too far away on the road north to Yùshù.

The town is known in Chinese as Yùlóng or Mǎnígāngē, but it's most commonly referred to by its Tibetan name, Manigango.

Sleeping & Eating

Manigange Pani Hotel HOTEL $
(马尼干戈怕尼酒店; Mǎnígāngē Pàní Jiǔdiàn; dm Y10-20, tw without/with bathroom Y80/160) This good hotel has become the town's centre of gravity, with its car park used as the unofficial bus station and its buffet-style restaurant the most popular lunch stop for passing motorists. Sleeping-wise there are rooms for everyone; from dirt-cheap five-bed dorms to really quite decent twins with private bathrooms, and hot water (8pm to 11pm only), that go for Y130 when it's quiet. The **restaurant** (vegetable/meat dishes Y10/15; ⊙7am-11pm) has an easy-to-order, point-and-choose buffet with surprisingly good results.

Qīngzhēn Gānsù Líntán Fàndiàn MUSLIM $
(清真甘肃临潭饭店; noodles from Y8; ⊙8am-11pm) This popular Muslim restaurant run by a friendly guy from Gānsù province makes a nice change from Sichuanese or Tibetan. No menu, but noodle dishes on offer include beef noodle squares (牛肉面片; *niúròu miànpiàn;* Y8) and glass noodles with beef (牛肉粉条; *niúròu fěntiáo;* Y8). The *shǒuzhuā yángròu* (手抓羊肉; Y35 per *jīn*) is the restaurant's speciality lamb dish. One *jīn* is enough for one person. Located at the town crossroads.

Information

Internet cafe (网吧; wǎngbā; per hr Y5; noon-11pm) Located 100m along the lane opposite Manigange Pani Hotel.

Getting There & Away

A daily bus to Dégé (Y40, three to four hours) passes through Manigango at about 11am, but is often full. Going the other way, there are usually some empty seats on the Gānzī-bound bus (Y30, three to four hours), which passes by at a similar time. Catch both from Manigange Pani Hotel. A bus from Gānzī, heading for Sěrshu (Y80, seven hours), passes by the crossroads at around 8.30am.

Plenty of minibuses congregate outside Manigange Pani Hotel waiting to scoop up bus-less passengers.

YILHUN LHA-TSO 新路海

The fabulous turquoise-blue waters of this holy alpine **lake** (Xīnlù Hǎi; admission Y20), 13km southwest of Manigango, are the main reason most travellers stop in this area. The stunning lake is bordered by *chörten* and dozens of rock carvings, and is framed by snowcapped mountains. You can walk an hour or two up the left (east) side of the lakeshore for views of the nearby glacier.

This is also a great place to camp – some travellers have even slept in caves here – although you'll need to bring your own tent and guard against mosquitoes. Monks from Darjay Gompa sometimes camp here during the summer in colourful Tibetan nomad tents.

To get here, either nab a seat in a Dégé-bound minibus (Y20), hitch a ride or hike. The lake is a five-minute walk from the main road, along a signposted track. Motorbikes (Y20) wait to take you back to Manigango.

DZOGCHEN GOMPA 竹庆佛学院

This important Nyingmapa **monastery** (Zhúqìng Fóxuéyuàn), 50km north of Manigango, has a stunning location at the foot of a glacial valley. The recently reconstructed monastery was founded in 1684 and is the home of the Dzogchen school, the most popular form of Tibetan Buddhism in the West. Several hundred monks live here.

The site includes the small town, 1.5km off the road, which has a few shops, *chörten* and a chapel with huge prayer wheels. Up the small gorge is the main monastery and 1km further is the *shedra* (monastic college). The college offers beds for Y15 per night, though you need a sleeping bag and your own food.

Buses to Yùshù and Sěrshu run daily past Dzogchen, but in practice it's easier to hitch. Make sure you set out in the morning, as there is little traffic on the roads come the afternoon. Hiring a taxi in Manigango will cost at least Y200/300 one way/return. The road crosses over the Muri La Pass (4633m), so make sure you have warm clothes, especially if you're hitching in the back of a truck.

DÉGÉ 德格

0836 / POP 58,600 / ELEV 3270M

Your bumpy bus rides just got bumpier. Dégé is cut off from the rest of western Sìchuān by the towering Chola Mountain (6168m), and to get here from the east you will probably have to endure a highly uncomfortable, slightly scary three-hour minibus ride along a dirt track that goes up and over the 5050m-high Tro La (Chola) Pass. Here, Tibetans on board will throw coloured prayer paper out the window and chant something that you can only hope will help carry you all to safety.

Unless you've managed to secure the correct permits to enter the rarely travelled Chamdo prefecture of Tibet proper, the main reason you'll have made the arduous trek out here is to see Dégé's famous printing monastery, one of this region's stellar sights.

Sights

TOP CHOICE **Bakong Scripture Printing Press & Monastery** BUDDHIST MONASTERY

(德格印经院; Dégé Yìnjīngyuàn; www.degeparkhang.org; admission Y50; 8.30am-noon & 2-6.30pm) This striking 18th-century monastery houses one of western Sìchuān's star attractions: a fascinating printing press that still uses traditional woodblock printing methods and which houses an astonishing 70% of Tibet's literary heritage.

There are more than 217,000 engraved blocks of Tibetan scriptures here from all the Tibetan Buddhist orders, including Bön. These texts include ancient works about astronomy, geography, music, medicine and Buddhist classics, including two of the most important Tibetan sutras. A history of Indian Buddhism comprising 555 woodblock plates is the only surviving copy in the world (written in Hindi, Sanskrit and Tibetan).

Within the monastery, dozens of workers hand-produce over 2500 prints to order each day, as ink, paper and blocks fly through the workers' hands at lightning speed. In one side room you'll find an older crowd of printers who produce larger and more complex prints of Tibetan gods on paper or coloured cloth.

You can also examine storage chambers, paper-cutting rooms and the main hall of the monastery itself, protected from fire and earthquakes by the guardian goddess Drölma (Tara). There are some nice murals in the two ground-floor chapels, so bring a torch.

You aren't allowed to take photos in the storerooms or the main hall, but the workers were happy for us to snap away while they worked frantically to meet their quota.

To get here, turn right out of the bus station then left over the bridge and keep walking up the hill.

Other Monasteries BUDDHIST MONASTERIES
If you continue following the road up the hill beyond the printing house, you'll reach the recently renovated 1000-year-old **Gonchen Monastery**.

High in the mountains to the south and east of Dégé are several other monasteries, including **Pelpung Gompa**, **Dzongsar Gompa** and **Pewar Gompa**. To head out this way, try to get a seat in a minibus leaving from outside the bus station.

Sleeping & Eating

Héxié Hotel HOTEL **$$**
(和谐旅馆; Héxié Lǚguǎn; ☎822 6111; Chamashang Jie; 茶马上街; tw Y200-250) A friendly Tibetan-run hotel with a homely feel to it. Spacious carpeted rooms come with coat stand, hot-water flask and pinewood table and chairs, while the comfy beds have clean sheets and warm puffy duvets. Bathrooms are shared but have 24-hour hot-water showers. Best of all are the discounts. Rooms normally go for Y60, and sometimes for as little as Y40, making this the best-value stay in Dégé. Turn left out of the bus station and it's on your left after about five minutes' walk.

Róngmài Ángzhā Bīnguǎn HOTEL **$**
(绒麦昂扎宾馆; Chamashang Jie; 茶马上街; dm Y30, tw from Y188) The private rooms with showers, some overlooking the river, are of decent quality and can be nabbed for Y120. The three-bed dorms are clean and reasonably spacious, and come with a TV. The common bathrooms, though, don't have showers. On the right before Héxié Hotel.

Kāngbā Zàngcān TIBETAN FOOD **$**
(康巴藏餐; Chamashang Jie; 茶马上街; dishes Y10-35; ⏲noon-midnight) The decor is half Tibetan, half African safari, but the food and the clientele are as Tibetan as it gets. There's butter tea (Y10), Tibetan yoghurt (Y5), yak-meat *momos* (Y10) and various yak-meat dishes including a hearty yak pie (牛肉饼; *níuròu bǐng;* Y20). *Tsampa* (Y5) isn't on the menu, but is of course available. No English menu. No English sign. No English spoken. Turn left out of the bus station and it's on your right; on the 2nd floor.

There are several small restaurants and **noodle shops** near the bus station.

Information

Internet cafe (网吧; wǎngbā; per hr Y3; ⏲8.30am-midnight) Turn right out of the bus station, left over the bridge and down steps to your right. Entrance is just past the pool hall.

Getting There & Away

Just one daily eastbound bus leaves from here, at 7.30am, heading for Kāngdìng (Y179, next-day arrival) via Manigango (Y41, three hours), Gānzī (Y68, six hours) and Lúhuò, where it stops for the night. Otherwise, there are minibuses.

There's normally a daily bus to Jomda (江达; Jiāngdá) in Tibet proper, from where you can catch onward transport to Chamdo and Lhasa, but foreigners haven't been allowed to ride public transport in Chamdo prefecture for many years, so you will almost certainly have to have prearranged a private vehicle in advance if you want to cross the border here. You will, of course, need a Tibet permit.

A shared minivan from Dégé to Lhasa costs around Y600 per person and take two days.

SĚRSHU (SHÍQÚ) 石渠

☎0836 / POP 60,000 / ELEV 4100M

There are two places commonly called Sěrshu (or Sershul): the traditional monastery town of Sěrshu Dzong to the west and the modern county town of Sěrshu (Shíqú Xiàn), 30km to the east, which has more lodgings and transport connections.

While you'll probably stop in Shíqú Xiàn en route between Manigango and Yùshù in Qīnghǎi, the huge monastery of Sěrshu Dzong and its intensely Tibetan village is far more interesting and well worth a stopover.

It's home to hundreds of monks and has two assembly halls, a Maitreya chapel, several modern chapels and a *shedra*, with a *kora* encircling the lot. The road west from here towards Qīnghǎi is classic yak and nomad country, passing several long *mani* (prayer) walls and dozens of black yak-hair tents in summer.

It's pretty high here, so be alert for signs of altitude sickness.

Sleeping & Eating

In Sĕrshu Dzong you can stay at the **monastery guesthouse** (色须寺刚京饭店; sèxū sì gāngjīng fàndiàn; dm Y10-20, tw per bed Y40-50).

In Shíqú Xiàn, Tibetan-run **Gésà'ĕr Jiŭdiàn** (格萨尔酒店; tw/tr per bed Y20, d Y50) has acceptable cheapies, although the shared bathroom is nothing more than a row of pit toilets. Coming from the direction of Manigango, take the first left after the post office and look for the big green building. Reception is on the 2nd floor along with a very popular Tibetan restaurant. The only place we could find with showers was **Shangdeenyma Hotel** (香德尼玛大酒店; Xiāngdénímă Dàjiŭdiàn; ☎862 2888; tr/d/tw Y242/246/288) in an imposing Tibetan-style building set back from the main street. The cheaper triples and doubles have common bathrooms and go for Y180. The standard twins with private bathrooms go for Y200. Make sure the hot water is working before splashing out for a room.

There are plenty of small restaurants – noodle joints as well as Tibetan teahouses – on and off the main road. The most comfortable place to get your fix of *momo*, *tsampa* and butter tea is the Gésà'ĕr Jiŭdiàn's colourful **Tibetan restaurant** (dishes Y8-35; ⏲10am-11pm).

Getting There & Away

The small bus station at the far east end of Shíqú Xiàn has a 7am and a 12.30pm bus to Gānzī (Y99, eight hours), via Manigango (Y77, four hours). The 12.30pm bus is a through bus from Qīnghăi province so isn't always punctual.

Buses to Yùshù (Y40, five hours) weren't running at the time of research because of the earthquake earlier in the year, but previously there had been an 8am bus, leaving from the even smaller bus station at the far west end of town, and a bus from Gānzī that passed through town at around 3pm.

The Yùshù-bound buses will let you off at Sĕrshu Dzong. Alternatively, it's Y20 in a shared minivan. The 12.30pm through bus to Gānzī passes through Sĕrshu Dzong at around 11am.

Sìchuān–Tibet Highway (Southern Route)

Travel here takes you through vast grasslands dotted with Tibetan block homes and contentedly grazing yaks, while majestic peaks tower beyond. While journeying along this 2140km route is slightly easier than taking the northern route, it's still not for the faint-hearted; road conditions can be pretty poor, and high altitude is just as much a factor here as it is further north. However, Kāngdìng–Lĭtáng–Xiāngchéng–Zhōngdiàn (Shangri-la) has become a very popular route into Yúnnán.

As in the rest of western Sìchuān, warm clothing is a must here, and be on the lookout for signs of altitude sickness.

LĬTÁNG 理塘

☎0836 / POP 51,300 / ELEV 4014M

Lĭtáng claims to be the world's highest town. It isn't. That accolade is shared by Wēnquán in Qīnghăi province and La Rinconada in Peru, both of which stand at a wheeze-inducing 5100m. Nevertheless, at a dizzying altitude of 4014m, Lĭtáng is still exceptionally high, so be sure to look out for signs of altitude sickness.

The surrounding scenery will certainly leave you breathless, and there are great opportunities to get out and see it – whether by horse, motorbike or simply hiking – making this a decent place to spend a couple of days.

Lĭtáng is famed as the birthplace of the seventh and 10th Dalai Lamas, but the town's large monastery, Chöde Gompa, is the most absorbing sight.

Sights & Activities

Chöde Gompa MONASTERY

(长青春科尔寺; Chángqīngchūn Kē'ĕr Sì) At the northern end of town, the large Chöde Gompa is a Tibetan monastery built for the third Dalai Lama. Inside is a statue of Sakyamuni that is believed to have been carried from Lhasa by foot. Don't miss climbing onto the roof of the furthest right of the three main halls for great views of the Tibetan homes leading up to the monastery and the grasslands and mountains beyond. Monks climb up here every day to sound the temple's long horns. To get here, walk past the post office, turn left at the end of the road then take the first right.

Báită Gōngyuán CHÖRTEN

(白塔公园) Worshippers seem to be perpetually circling Báită Gōngyuán as they recite mantras and spin prayer wheels. You can join the locals hanging out in the surrounding park. Turn left out of the bus station and just keep walking.

If you keep walking past Báită Gōngyuán, there are **hot springs** (温泉; wēnquán; admission Y15) 4km west of the centre.

Outdoor Activities OUTDOOR ACTIVITIES

Hiking opportunities abound outside of town. The hills behind the monastery are one fine option. For more ideas, talk to Mr Zheng at Tiāntiān Restaurant or to the English-speaking managers at either Potala Inn or Peace Guesthouse.

Potala Inn can also help organise **horse trekking**, while Peace Guesthouse can arrange renting **motorbikes** for the day.

Lǐtáng has a **sky burial** site just behind the monastery. If you do attend a sky burial, be sure to remember exactly what you are watching and treat the ceremony, and all those involved, with the utmost respect. For more details, ask Longlife, the manager of Peace Guesthouse, or Mr Zheng at Tiāntiān Restaurant.

Festivals & Events

One of the biggest and most colourful Tibetan festivals, the annual **Lǐtáng Horse Festival** includes horse racing, stunt riding, dance competitions and an arts-and-crafts fair.

Sadly, the event was cancelled in 2008, 2009 and 2010 due to political protests as well as disputes over race results, which spiralled into fighting. It usually starts on 1 August and lasts several days, but check at the hostels in Kāngdìng or Chéngdū for the current situation.

Sleeping & Eating

TOP CHOICE **Potala Inn** YOUTH HOSTEL $
(布达拉大酒店; Bùdálā Dàjiǔdiàn; ☎532 2533; dm Y25-35, tw Y140-180; @ wi-fi) Run by an English-speaking Tibetan woman called Metok, this large hostel has a mixed bag of rooms, ranging from basic bunk-bed dorms to Tibetan-style twins with private bathroom. Pretty much everything is on offer here – hiking, horse trekking, sky-burial visits, bike rental – but what makes this place stand out from the crowd is its excellent wi-fi-enabled 2nd-floor cafe, which wouldn't seem out of place in Běijīng. Those without laptops can get online on the ground floor (per hour Y4). Turn left from the bus station and it's on the right, set back from the main street.

Peace Guesthouse YOUTH HOSTEL $
(和平酒店; Hépíng Jiǔdiàn; ☎532 1100, 152 8360 5821; dm/tw Y20/40; @ wi-fi) A favourite with Israeli travellers, this friendly no-nonsense hostel, run by helpful English-speaking manager Longlife, has large, clean, albeit basic rooms, and a small cafe. Turn right out of the bus station and walk 50m up the hill.

Tiāntiān Restaurant CHINESE, WESTERN $
(天天饭食; Tiāntiān Fànshí; ☎135 4146 7941; 108 Xingfu Donglu; 幸福东路108号; dishes Y12-40; ⏰7.30am-11pm; wi-fi, English menu) The ever-friendly, English-speaking, ace chef Mr Zheng has moved his popular travellers' haven across the road to a larger location. Look for the Lonely Planet logo. The same good food – a mix of Chinese, Tibetan and Western – is on offer, as is the excellent fresh coffee and reliable travel advice. English menu. Turn left out of the bus station and it's on the left.

Snow Mountain Restaurant TIBETAN $
(宫呷雪山民族特餐; Gōnggā Xuěshān Mínzú Tècān; 222 Xingfu Donglu; 幸福东路222号; dishes Y10-40; ⏰6.30am-11pm; English menu) For more-authentic Tibetan food, try this simple place with English menu. It's between the bus station and Tiāntiān Restaurant.

Information

China Post (中国邮政; Zhōngguó Yóuzhèng; Tuanjie Lu; ⏰9-11.30am & 2-5.30pm) Turn left out of bus station then right at main crossroads.

Internet cafe (网吧; wǎngbā; Tuanjie Lu; per hr Y5; ⏰8.30am-midnight) Next to post office.

Getting There & Away

Lǐtáng's bus station, at the town's eastern end, has buses to the destinations shown below. Times are unpredictable, so double-check. It's normally easy to bag Kāngdìng or Xīndūqiáo tickets (same bus) but the others are through buses, so are often full by the time they get here. Minibuses hang around outside the bus station to save the day. There's an OK road north to Gānzī, but no public buses ply the route.

Destinations and fares:

Bātáng Y63, 3½ hours, one daily (around 3pm)

Dàochéng Y49, four hours, one daily (around 1.30pm)

Kāngdìng Y87, eight hours, one daily (6.30am)

Xiāngchéng Y66, five hours, one daily (around 1.30pm)

Xīndūqiáo Y63, six hours, one daily (6.30am)

BĀTÁNG 巴塘

☎0836 / ELEV 2589M

Just 32km from the Tibet border, Bātáng (or Bathang in Tibetan) is one of Sìchuān's main gateways into Tibet proper. Foreigners will need to have all their paperwork in order, of course, but it is easy to catch minibuses from here to Markham or even Lhasa. Bātáng itself has a welcoming monastery, while outside the town are lovely suburbs of ochre-coloured Tibetan houses.

Bātáng is much lower than surrounding areas; when it's late winter in Lǐtáng, it's already spring here.

The Gelugpa sect **Chöde Gaden Pendeling Monastery** (康宁寺; Kāngníng Sì) was undergoing heavy renovations at the time of research but is usually well worth a visit. There are three rooms behind the main hall: a protector chapel, giant statue of Jampa and a 10,000 Buddha room. Up some stairs via a separate entrance is a room for the Panchen Lama, lined with photos of exiled local lamas who now reside in India. Most images here are new but one upstairs statue of Sakyamuni is claimed to be 2000 years old. Continue down the hill from Jīnsuì Bīnguǎn.

There are some fine walks around town, including a lovely Tibetan hillside village, a riverside *chörten* and a hilltop, covered in prayer flags, offering views of the town.

Hotels and restaurants abound. **Jīnsuì Bīnguǎn** (金穗宾馆; ☎562 2700; 1 Ba'an Lu; 巴安路1号5附; dm Y30, tw without/with bathroom Y100/280, discounted to Y60/100) is an old standby with basic rooms. Ones at the back are quieter and face Tibetan homes. Turn left out of the bus station and take the first right after the hard-to-miss golden eagle. Nicer is **Xuěchéng Zhāxī Bīnguǎn** (雪城扎西宾馆; ☎562 3222; cnr Minguang Lu & Bakang Dadao; 巴康达到和民光路; tr/tw Y180/380, discounted to Y100/180; ❄) with its grand Tibetan-style lobby leading to the best rooms in town. Turn left out of the bus station then right at the golden eagle statue.

On mild evenings you can find excellent roadside Sìchuān **barbecues** (烧烤; shāokǎo; per skewer Y0.50-1). For something more Tibetan, try **Xuěyǔ Zàngcān** (雪雨藏餐; dishes from Y5; ⏲8.30am-11pm). Turn left out of the bus station and it's on your left.

There's an **internet cafe** (网吧; wǎngbā; per hr Y3; ⏲9am-midnight) diagonally opposite Xuěchéng Zháxī Bīnguǎn.

ℹ Getting There & Away

All public buses are eastbound and leave Bātáng bus station at 6am. You can go to Lǐtáng (Y58, 3½ hours), Xīndūqiáo (Y121, 10½ hours), Kāngdìng (Y140, 12 hours) and even Chéngdū (Y245, one day). The Chéngdū bus isn't a sleeper, though.

Tibet proper is served by shared minibuses, which congregate at the crossroads just down from Jīnsuì Bīnguǎn. Markham (芒康; Mángkāng; Y50, 2½ hours) and Lhasa (拉萨; Lāsà; Y500, two days) are popular destinations.

XIĀNGCHÉNG 乡城

☎0836 / ELEV 2836M

The small, modern town centre of Xiāngchéng has a sprinkling of Tibetan homes and a fine monastery commanding wonderful views of the surrounding villages, some of which contain ancient stone watchtowers. The main reason for coming here, though, is to travel to or from Zhōngdiàn (Shangri-la) in Yúnnán province.

Note: apart from in Kāngdìng, this is the only place in western Sìchuān where you can withdraw cash with a foreign bank card. Load up!

Xiāngchéng's attractive **monastery** (admission Y15) was completely rebuilt by hand by local carpenters, carvers and painters. It's at the opposite end of town from the bus station: just after Zhāxī Hotel, turn left onto Shuoqu Jie (硕曲街); at the end of the road climb the steps, turn right and follow the dirt track all the way.

Xiāngchéng's main street has plenty of lodgings and restaurants; turn left from the bus station to head into town. Near the station, on your left through a car-park courtyard, **Xiāngbālā Seven Lakes Hotel** (七湖宾馆; Qīhú Bīnguǎn; ☎189 9047 5516; tw without/with bathroom Y40/60) has basic rooms and friendly staff. More comfortable is **Zhāxī Hotel** (扎西大酒店; Zhāxī Dàjiǔdiàn; ☎582 6111; tw Y260), which discounts good-quality doubles to Y140. It's on the right at the top end of town.

One quirky place to eat and drink is **Zhāpí Chéng** (扎啤城; Draft Beer City; beers Y6-8, dishes Y8-30; ⏲5pm-2am), which resembles a German beer hall (wooden benches, jugs of beer) but which serves very tasty, distinctly Chinese cold snacks (spicy duck neck, rabbit head, pig's trotters), as well as a more substantial and equally delicious barbecued fish dish (烤鱼; *kǎoyú;* around Y30). There are four types of draught beer, the best being the standard lager (黄啤; *huángpí;* Y6) and the stout (黑啤; *hēipí;* Y8). It's on the right before Zhāxī Hotel.

Next to the beer hall is an Agricultural Bank of China **ATM** that accepts Visa cards. Behind this block is an **internet cafe** (网吧; wǎngbā; per hr Y4; ⏲9.30am-midnight).

ℹ Getting There & Away

From Xiāngchéng there's a morning bus to Zhōngdiàn (Shangri-la; Y85, eight hours, 6am). Going the other way, you can catch a bus to Kāngdìng (Y146, 12 hours, 6am), but note: you won't be sold tickets on this bus for Lǐtáng even though it's en route. You will have to travel by shared minibus (Y70, four to five hours).

NORTHERN SÌCHUĀN

Hiking, or even camping, in the stunning Jiǔzhàigōu National Park or heading out on horseback around Sōngpān are how most travellers experience the carpets of alpine forest, swaths of grasslands, icy lakes and snow-topped mountains of northern Sìchuān. You can also travel north from here into Gānsù, Shaanxi or even Qīnghǎi.

The main roads heading north to this area from Chéngdū suffered severe damage in the 2008 earthquake and bus routes were still being affected by road repairs more than two years after the disaster. Get an update on the situation before you set out from Chéngdū.

Sōngpān 松潘

☎0837 / POP 71,650 / ELEV 2800M

Horse trekking into the woods and mountains is the main draw of this laid-back historic town, but the hiking's good too and there's a reasonably strong backpacker vibe, which makes Sōngpān a good place to catch up on the latest travel tales.

Note, in midwinter (December to March) Sōngpān shuts down almost completely. Many guesthouses and restaurants, including Emma's Kitchen, are closed then. However, horse trekking is still possible.

Sights

Sōngpān's part-rebuilt **town wall** may be less than 10 years old but its **ancient gates** are original Ming-dynasty structures going back some 600 years. Note the horse carvings at the foot of the two south gates, half swallowed up by the ever-rising level of the road. The only original part of the **old wall** is by the rebuilt West Gate, which overlooks the town from its hillside perch.

Two wooden **covered bridges** (古松桥; Gǔsōng Qiáo), the bases of which are genuinely old, span the Mín River. On the western side of the river is **Guānyīn Gé** (观音阁), a small temple near the start of a hillside trail that offers good views over Sōngpān.

Activities

Horse Trekking HORSE TREKKING

One of the most popular ways to experience the idyllic mountain forests and emerald-

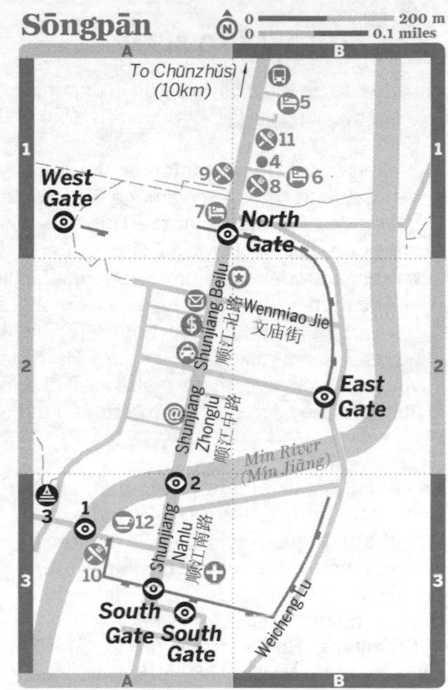

Sōngpān

Top Sights
- East Gate ... B2
- North Gate ... A1
- South Gate ... A3
- South Gate ... A3
- West Gate ... A1

Sights
1. Covered Bridge ... A3
2. Covered Bridge ... A3
3. Guānyīn Gé ... A3

Activities, Courses & Tours
4. Shùnjiāng Horse Treks ... B1

Sleeping
5. Old House ... B1
6. Shùnjiāng Guesthouse ... B1
7. Sun River International Hotel ... A1

Eating
8. Emma's Kitchen ... B1
9. Lánzhōu Niúròumiàn ... A1
10. Móunì Tibetan Restaurant ... A3
11. Song in the Mountain ... B1

Drinking
12. Teahouses ... A3

THE WAY TO XĪ'ĀN

For those on their way to Xī'ān in Shaanxi province, the most direct way to get there overland is via the mid-sized town of **Guǎngyuán** (广元), which is on the main Chéngdū–Xī'ān train line.

China's only female emperor, Wu Zetian, was born in Guǎngyuán during the Tang dynasty, and she is feted among the temples, pavilions and 1000-odd statues lining the modest cliffs at **Huángzé Temple** (皇泽寺; Huángzé Sì; admission Y50), on the west bank of Jiālíng Hé. However, Guǎngyuán is also the site of China's largest nuclear-weapons-grade plutonium production facility, so nobody really lingers here.

And there's no need to. There are nine trains a day, running pretty much every hour from 4.38pm right through until 3am. The 4.38pm (T8) is an express, and takes eight hours. The rest take 10 or 11 hours. Hard sleepers cost Y139. A seat should be Y76. If you get stuck here, there are loads of cheap hotels around the bus and train stations. Just don't expect anything too comfortable.

green lakes surrounding Sōngpān is by joining up with a horse trek. Guides take you through pristine valleys and forests aboard a not-so-big, very tame horse. Many people rate this experience as a highlight of their Sìchuān travels.

Shùnjiāng Horse Treks (顺江旅游马队; Shùnjiāng Lǚyóu Mǎduì; ☎880 9118) have been catering horse treks to tourists for years. The majority of travellers are happy, but now and again some report somewhat apathetic guides. On offer is anything from one- to 14-day treks and trips can be tailored to suit you.

One of the most popular treks is a three- or four-day trek to **Ice Mountain** (雪玉顶; Xuěyùdǐng), a spectacular trip through unspoilt scenery.

Rates are around Y220 per person per day, all-inclusive. The guides take care of everything: you won't touch a tent pole or a cooking pot unless you want to. The only additional charge is entrance to the different sites and national parks visited on some of the trips, but you'll be warned of these before you set out.

As food consists mainly of green vegetables, potatoes and bread, you may want to take along some extra snacks for variety.

Hiking HIKING

The surrounding hills are equally good for hiking. One option is to hike up to the only remaining part of the original town wall, by West Gate. It takes around one hour. There are three paths up, meaning you can complete a round trip. One starts beside the stream by Lánzhōu Niúròumiàn Muslim restaurant. Another leads up the hill from the post office, while a third is accessed via Guānyīn Gé temple. It's also possible to hike for about two hours to Shàngníbā Monastery (上泥巴寺庙; Shàngníbā Sìmiào) in the eastern hills.

Sleeping

Shùnjiāng Guesthouse GUESTHOUSE $

(顺江自助旅馆; Shùnjiāng Zìzhù Lǚguǎn; ☎723 1064; Shunjiang Beilu; 顺江北路; dm Y25, tw & d Y80) The owners of Shùnjiāng Horse Treks company run this smart guesthouse with simple rooms around an open courtyard. It can be freezing here in cold weather, but bathrooms have heat lamps and 24-hour hot water, and beds come with electric blankets.

Old House GUESTHOUSE $

(古韵客栈; Gǔyùn Kèzhàn; ☎172 31368; Shunjiang Beilu; 顺江北路; dm/s/tw Y30/80/100; @ wi-fi) Very handy for the bus station, this attractive old-style three-storey wooden building has small but clean rooms off an interior courtyard. English-speaking staff, 24-hour hot water and wi-fi, a rarity in these parts.

Sun River International Hotel HOTEL $$

(太阳河国际大酒店; Tàiyánghé Guójì Dàjiǔdiàn; ☎723 9888; Shunjiang Beilu; 顺江北路; tw & d Y880-980) Ignore the ridiculous rack rates here. Discounts are such that standard twins tend to go for Y160. And for Y250 to Y350 you can get very smart double rooms with internet access.

Eating

Sōngpān has an excellent assortment of breads – big crusty loaves, Tibetan flatbread and sweet breads made and sold fresh all day at stalls along Shunjiang Zhonglu. The same road is also lined with small restaurants and noodle shops.

TOP CHOICE **Emma's Kitchen** WESTERN $$
(小欧洲西餐厅; Xiǎo Ōuzhōu Xīcāntīng; Shunjiang Beilu; ☎880 2958; mains Y8-40; ⏰7.30am-late; @) Sōngpān's main travellers' hang-out is this laid-back cafe that serves fresh coffee, pizza and other Western fare, along with some Chinese dishes. Emma is exceedingly helpful and can sort out almost anything from laundry to travel information. Also has internet (per hour Y6) and CD burning (per disk Y15).

A couple of doors along, **Song in the Mountain**, run by the helpful Sarah Yang, has a similar menu (minus the fresh coffee) with similar prices.

Móunì Tibetan Restaurant TIBETAN $$
(牟尼藏餐; Móuní Zàngcān; ☎723 3929; mains Y10-55; ⏰8am-7pm) The English menu is limited but the location, in a lovely garden by the river, is worth the visit. By Mín River off Shunjiang Nanlu.

Lánzhōu Niúròumlàn MUSLIM $
(兰州牛肉面; Shunjiang Beilu; dishes from Y5; ⏰7am 9.30pm) For fresh noodles, try this unassuming restaurant. Pulled noodles (Lāmiàn; 拉面; Y6) are the speciality.

Drinking

Along the Mín River (岷江; Mín Jiāng), on the southern edge of town, are several small **teahouses** (tea from Y5) where you can while away the afternoon with the locals. **Moon Reflection Tea Garden** (映月茶园; Yìngyuè Cháyuán; ⏰8am-6pm) is a particular favourite with tile-clinking mah jong players.

Information

Agricultural Bank of China (中国农业银行; Nóngyè Yínháng; Shunjiang Beilu) Foreign-friendly ATM.

China Post (中国邮政; Zhōngguó Yóuzhèng; Shunjiang Beilu; ⏰9-11.30am & 2-5.30pm)

Public Security Bureau (PSB; 公安局; Gōng'ānjú; ☎723 3778; Shunjiang Beilu; ⏰8.30am-noon & 3-6pm) Can renew visas in one day.

Tōngtiānhé internet cafe (通天河网吧; Tōngtiānhé Wǎngbā; Shunjiang Zhonglu; per hr Y3; ⏰24hr) Upstairs in an alley off the main street. No English sign.

Getting There & Away

Air

See Jiǔzhàigōu section (p751) for information on flying to this area. There's no public transport between Sōngpān and the airport. A taxi should be around Y100.

Bus

Buses leaving from Sōngpān bus station (客运站; kèyùnzhàn) are detailed below. Note, bus times and prices change slightly depending on the season, so double-check. Buses to Chéngdū were still using the longer, more expensive route via Jiǔzhàigōu at the time of research, which took almost 14 hours and cost Y175. The shorter route, which was damaged by the 2008 earthquake, should have reopened by the time you read this. For Lángmùsì and the overland route into Gānsù province, you'll need to change at Zöigě.

Chéngdū Y88, eight hours, two daily (6am and 6.30am)

Huánglóng National Park Y24, two hours, one daily (6am)

Jiǔzhàigōu Y30, 2½ hours, two daily (7am and 1pm)

Zöigě Y42, three hours, two daily (10am and 2.30pm)

Huánglóng National Park 黄龙景区

A trip to this **national park** (Huánglóng Jǐngqū; Yellow Dragon Valley; www.huanglong.com; adult Y200; ⏰7am-6pm) is essentially a very expensive three-hour walk up and down one small valley. The valley, however, is stunning, and its terraced, coloured limestone ponds of blues, turquoises, yellows and greens are exquisite. So, if you can spare the cash, this place is well worth seeing. Interspersed with waterfalls and backed by the 5588m Xuěbǎo Peak (雪宝鼎; Xuěbǎo Dǐng), this string of shimmering ponds stretches down the valley where yellow-tinged calcium carbonate and limestone deposits help create the water's sparkle, particularly on sunny days. Note: in winter much of the water is frozen solid and many of the ponds are dried up. It's best to come between May and October, and preferably in July and August.

The most spectacular ponds, called **Wǔcǎichí** (五彩池; Five-coloured Pool), are behind **Huánglóng Temple** (黄龙寺; Huánglóng Sì) at the top of the park. You can reach them in about 90 minutes, although you may need more time if the altitude bothers you; the highest pools are at 3553m. You can also take a **cable car** (索道; suǒdào; Y80) most of the way to the top.

Huánglóng doesn't draw nearly the crowds that Jiǔzhàigōu does, but it's an increasingly popular tour destination. For a more peaceful visit, arrive first thing in the morning before the tour groups roll in. As

THE ROAD TO GĀNSÙ

Those heading north into Gānsù province will need to bus-hop their way from Sōngpān. First stop is **Zöigě** (in Chinese 若尔盖; Ruò'ěrgài), a small, dusty Tibetan town set among the remote plateau grasslands and with a distinct frontier-town feel to it. The grasslands here burst into life with wildflowers in late summer, and it's possible to arrange horse trekking, although facilities aren't as good as in Sōngpān, and English-language skills among those organising them are pretty much nonexistent.

Shǔguāng Bīnguǎn (曙光宾馆; ☎0837-229 2988; tw Y100) has decent rooms with private bathroom. Turn left out of the bus station and walk 100m. There are plenty of eating options on this road (Shuguang Jie) too.

Zöigě buses go to Sōngpān (Y42, three hours, 10am and 2.30pm) and Lángmùsì (p818; Y21, two hours, 2.30pm), an enchanting monastery town that straddles the Sìchuān–Gānsù border and from where you can catch onward transport towards Lánzhōu.

Be aware that altitudes are high out here (Zöigě is at 3500m) and temperatures often plummet to uncomfortable levels. In winter, snow sometimes renders roads unpassable, so buses can be sporadic.

you hike up, stay to the right to go directly to Wǔcǎichí (follow the signs that say 'Way Up'), so you can appreciate the main attraction ahead of the crowds. Then as you descend, detour onto the 'sightseeing paths' to take in the rest of the pools and waterfalls.

By the park entrance is a modern **visitor centre** with restaurant, teahouse and free left-luggage room. You can pick up a free English-language leaflet with a map of the park here. There are a couple of expensive tour-group hotels by the entrance, but you can't stay in the park, so most independent travellers day trip here from Sōngpān or Jiǔzhàigōu. There are a couple of canteens on the way up the valley, and vendors selling snacks, but this is great picnic territory so you might want to bring your own food. There's free oxygen available at certain points of the climb.

From Sōngpān, the 6am Píngwǔ-bound bus stops here (Y25, 90 minutes), although at peak times a slightly later bus is sometimes added to the schedule. Normally only one bus makes the return journey. It's supposed to pass Huánglońg at 2pm, although at the time of research it was more like 4pm. Alternatively, a bus bound for Jiǔzhàigōu (Y40, three hours) leaves Huánglóng at 3pm and goes via Chuānzhǔ Sì (川主寺; Y25, one hour), from where you can take a shared taxi to Sōngpān (Y10).

If you arrive at Jiǔhuáng Airport in the morning, you can catch an airport bus to Jiǔzhàigōu (Y100), which stops off here long enough for you to tour the park.

Jiǔzhàigōu National Park 九寨沟风景名胜区

☎0837 / POP 62,000 / ELEV 2000M

The stunning Unesco World Heritage Site of **Jiǔzhàigōu National Park** (Jiǔzhàigōu Fēngjǐng Míngshèngqū; Nine Village Valley National Park; www.jiuzhai.com; admission May–mid-Nov Y220, mid-Nov–Apr Y80, shuttle bus Y90; ⏲7am-6pm) is one of Sìchuān's star attractions. An incredible 1.5 million people visit the park every year to gawp at its famous bluer-than-blue lakes, its rushing waterfalls and its deep green trees backed by snowy mountains. Add into the mix, kilometres of well-maintained walking trails and newly launched ecotourism camping trips, and you'll begin to get a feel for Jiǔzhàigōu's charms.

The best time to visit is September through to November, when you're most likely to have clear skies and (particularly in October) blazing autumn colours to contrast with the turquoise lakes. Summer is the busiest but rainiest time. Spring can be cold but still pleasant, and winter, if you're prepared for frigid temperatures, brings dramatic ice-coated trees and frozen-in-place waterfalls (as well as lower prices).

Jiǔzhàigōu means 'Nine Village Valley' and refers to the region's nine Tibetan villages. According to legend, Jiǔzhàigōu was created when a jealous devil caused the goddess Wunosemo to drop her magic mirror, a present from her lover the warlord god Dage. The mirror dropped to the ground and shattered into 118 shimmering turquoise lakes.

Sights

Lakes & Waterfalls SCENIC SITES

The main road follows Zécháwā River (Zéchāwā Hé) up Shùzhēng Valley, as it runs past Héyè Village (Héyè Cūn) to **Sparkling Lake** (火花海; Huǒhuā Hǎi), the first in a series of lakes filled by the **Shùzhēng Waterfall** (树正瀑布; Shùzhēng Pùbù).

A walking trail begins north of Sparkling Lake and runs along the eastern edge of the river up to **Nuòrìlǎng Waterfall** (诺日朗瀑布; Nuòrìlǎng Pùbù). Here, the road branches in two, with the eastern road leading to **Long Lake** (长海; Cháng Hǎi) and **Five-Coloured Pool** (五彩池; Wǔcǎi Chí) and the western road to **Swan Lake** (天鹅海; Tiān'é Hǎi). The western route has a greater concentration of attractions, most of which are accessible from the quiet forest trail leading from **Mirror Lake** (镜海; Jìnghǎi) to **Panda Lake** (熊猫海; Xióngmāo Hǎi). Views from this trail are particularly good, especially of **Pearl Beach Waterfall** (珍珠滩瀑布; Zhēnzhūtān Pùbù).

The eastern route is almost better done by bus as the narrow road sees a great deal of traffic and there are fewer 'sights'. Nevertheless, the two lakes at the far end, Long Lake and Five-coloured Pool, are both well worth a visit.

From the park entrance to Nuòrìlǎng Waterfall is about 14km. It's a further 17.5km along the western road to Swan Lake and another couple of kilometres on to the **Virgin Forest**. It's about 18km up the eastern road from Nuòrìlǎng Waterfall to Long Lake.

Zhārú Temple TEMPLE

The first official site inside the park proper is the Tibetan Zhārú Temple (扎如寺; Zhārú Sì; Zaru Gompa in Tibetan), in the Zhārú Valley. The bus doesn't stop here, but it's only a short walk from the ticket office; go left at the first fork off the main road.

Activities

As part of an excellent new **ecotourism program** (☎773 7811; ecotourism@jiuzhai.com; Visitors Centre; 1-/2-/3-day hikes Y380/760/1580) visitors can now hike along and even camp (if you're on one of the official guided eco tours) inside the Zhārú Valley, just east of the main tourist valley. This is an extremely rare opportunity in China and numbers are strictly limited so it's advisable to email or phone ahead, especially if you want to camp. Prices include park entrance fees, English-speaking guides, all camping equipment

Jiǔzhàigōu

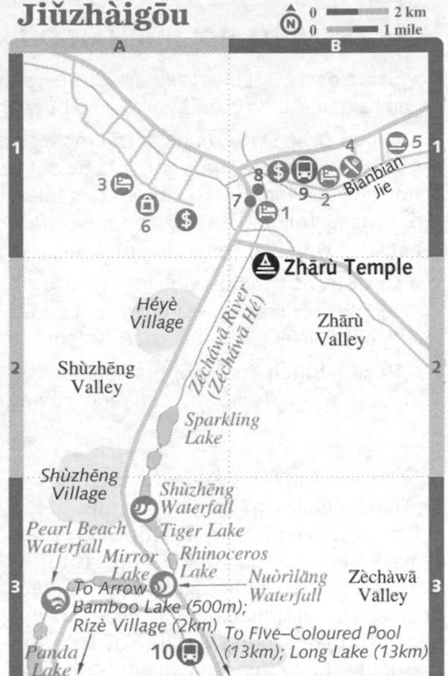

Jiǔzhàigōu

Top Sights

Zhārù Temple B2

Sleeping

1 Jiǔzhàigōu Grand Hotel D1
2 MCA Chalets B1
3 Self-Tour Youth Hostel A1

Eating

4 Ābù Lǔzī B1

Drinking

5 Star Cafe B1

Shopping

6 Kodak Shop A1

Information

7 Park Entrance B1
8 Visitors Centre & Tickets B1

Transport

9 Bus Station B1
10 Nuòrìlǎng Bus Station A3

and main meals, although you may want to bring along some fruit and snacks. The multiday hikes include a day in the main park without a guide. Check the park

HOW TO 'DO' JIǓZHÀIGŌU

» **Start early** Get into the park as close to the 7am opening as you can. Not only will you have more time, but you'll also beat the later-sleeping tour groups.

» **Go up first** Since much of the most spectacular scenery is in the park's higher reaches, you'll see the highlights first if you take the bus to the top and walk or ride down. Head first to either Long Lake or Swan Lake, work your way down to the Nuòrìlǎng junction, then go up the other fork. Later in the day, you can see the lakes between Nuòrìlǎng and the entrance.

» **Get out of the bus** Walking trails run throughout the park, and by walking, you'll steer clear of the biggest crowds. The walking trails are generally on the opposite side of the lakes from the road, so you'll have more peace and quiet, too.

» **Pack a lunch** Dining options inside the park are limited and expensive. If you bring your own food, you can picnic away from the hordes.

website or ask at the Visitors Centre (游客中心; Yóukè Zhōngxīn) for more details.

For those who like to do things on their own, there are great hiking opportunities all over this area, although be sure to steer clear of the national park itself. One option is to hike around the hills near Zhuo Ma's homestay; Zhuo Ma can advise you on where's good.

Sleeping

There's an almost endless supply of hotels around Péngfēng Village (彭丰村; Péngfēng Cūn) and Bianbian Jie (although Bianbian Jie tends to close down in winter), so don't worry if the options listed here are full. Apart from at the youth hostels, where discounts are rare, expect prices close to rack rates only during high season (July and August) and major national holidays. Staying inside the park is not allowed any more, although villagers may still offer you a bed.

TOP CHOICE **Zhuo Ma's** HOMESTAY $
(卓玛; Zhuómǎ; ☎135 6878 3012; www.zhuomajiuzhaigou.hostel.com; beds Y180) A genuine Tibetan homestay, this beautifully decorated wood cabin in a tiny village about 10km up the valley from the main park has three simple rooms and a wonderfully accommodating family. The lovely Zhuo Ma speaks some English and is on hand to welcome foreign guests. Her mother *(amma)* is the host and cooks the meals along with Zhuo Ma's brother Ke Zhu, a Lhasa-trained chef who prepares the food at the family's restaurant, Ābù Lǔzī. There's a common bathroom with shower, and prices include three meals a day.

If rooms are full, Zhuo Ma's neighbours offer spillover accommodation, although without a shower. It costs around Y50 to get here in a taxi from Péngfēng Village. If you're coming from Sōngpān you could ask the driver to drop you on the main road at Shānsì Village (山四寨; Shānsì Zhài). Zhuo Ma's is about a 15-minute walk up a dirt track from there. Any problems, just call Zhuo Ma.

Self-tour Youth Hostel YOUTH HOSTEL $
(自游青年旅舍; Zìyóu Qīngnián Lǚshè; ☎776 4617; www.57jzg.com; Péngfēng Village; 彭丰村; Péngfēng Cūn; dm/d/tw/tr Y30/70/80/90; @ wi-fi) There are five or six very similar youth hostels within 100m of each other in Péngfēng Village. This one is the nearest to the park entrance and one of the cheapest. It also rents mountain bikes (Y10 per two hours). Rooms are bigger here than in other hostels, although they lack character. Wi-fi doesn't extend into the rooms.

Jiǔzhàigōu Grand Hotel HOTEL $$$
(九寨沟贵宾楼饭店; Jiǔzhàigōu Guìbīnlóu Fàndiàn; ☎773 9066, 773 5555; r incl breakfast from Y680) You can't beat the location, just behind the park entrance gate. The rooms themselves are run-of-the-mill midrange units, but some have views of either the mountains or the small river that runs alongside the hotel. Rates usually start at just over Y200 and include breakfast.

MCA Chalets HOTEL $$
(国际乡村客栈; Guójì Xiāngcūn Kèzhàn; ☎773 9818, 136 7837 7715; Bianbian Jie; 边边街; r Y200-600) Has a range of rooms in a number of buildings along the pleasant river promenade known as Bianbian Jie. Prices often drop to around the Y100 mark.

Eating & Drinking

Péngfēng Village and Bianbian Jie are stuffed full with cheap restaurants. Inside the park, you can buy pricey water and snacks in the villages. Otherwise, there's a restaurant at the Nuòrìlǎng junction.

TOP CHOICE **Ābù Lǔzī** TIBETAN **$$**
(阿布鲁孜; Ābù Lǔzī Fēngqíng Zàngcānba; ☎139 9042 1118, 135 6878 3012; www.abuluzi.com; 11 Bianbian Jie; 边边街11号; dishes Y22-58; ⏲dinner only;) The only genuine Tibetan restaurant in Jiǔzhàigōu, this place, run by the same family who run Zhuo Ma's homestay, has a limited but excellent menu which is in English and has photos.

Star Cafe CAFE **$**
(太白楼; Tàibái Lóu; ☎773 9839; 23 Bianbian Jie; 边边街23号; coffees Y10-30, food & snacks Y5-36; ⏲noon-late;) The coolest hang-out in town, Star Cafe has a good selection of fresh coffee, beers and spirits and some OK food. There's also wi-fi and patio seating by the river.

Information

An **ATM** (自动柜员机; Zìdòng Guìyuán Jī) at the park entrance accepts foreign cards, as does the China Construction Bank and Agricultural Bank of China, where you can also change cash.

There's a number of **internet cafes** (网吧; *wǎngbā*) in Péngfēng Village, which also has a **Kodak shop** (柯达; Kēdá) where you can burn CDs (Y20 per disk).

The park has an excellent English-language website at www.jiuzhai.com. You can also get information from the Visitors Centre at the park entrance.

Getting There & Away

Air

More than a dozen daily flights link Chéngdū with Jiǔzhàigōu Airport (officially called Jiǔhuáng Airport). Other direct flights include Běijīng, Shànghǎi, Hángzhōu, Chóngqìng, Kúnmíng and Xī'ān.

Buses to Jiǔzhàigōu (Y45, 1½ hours) meet arriving flights. A taxi from the airport is about Y200.

There's also an airport bus that stops first at Huánglóng National Park, waiting long enough for passengers to tour the park, and then continues on to Jiǔzhàigōu (Y100).

Bus

The new tunnel-tastic route from Jiǔzhàigōu to Chéngdū, via Sōngpān, should be open by the time you read this and was reportedly set to cut journey times down to four or five hours! Check www.jiuzhai.com for the latest. At the time of research, buses leaving from Jiǔzhàigōu bus station (汽车站; Qìchēzhàn) included the following:

Chéngdū Y140, 10 hours, two daily (7.30am and 8am)

Guǎngyuán Y90, nine hours, one daily (6.30am)

Huánglóng National Park Y40, three hours, two daily (6.30am and 7am)

Lánzhōu Y223, 11 hours, one daily (7am)

Sōngpān Y30, two hours, one daily (7.30am)

Getting Around

Hop-on/hop-off buses (Y90) travel within the park itself, and are pretty much essential because of the size of the park. They stop at almost all the sights listed here.

Outside the park, there's no public bus service. To get around you have to walk, cycle or take a taxi. You can rent adequate mountain bikes from Self-tour Youth Hostel. Taxi fares begin at Y5.

Chóngqìng

POPULATION: 5 MILLION

Includes »

Best Places to Eat

» Shùnfēng 123 (p759)

» Yèfù Huǒguō (p759)

» *Shāokǎo* street barbecues (p759)

» Onboard an evening river cruise (p754)

» Gǔzhèn Jiǔdàwǎn in Sōngji Village (p765)

Best Places to Stay

» Tina's Hostel (p757)

» Sunrise Míngqīng Hostel (p757)

» Any village guesthouse in Zhōngshān (p764)

» Sunrise Backpack Hostel (p757)

» Huílóng Kèzhàn in Láitān Village (p764)

Why Go?

Some visitors are attracted by the cliffside location overlooking the iconic Yangzi River (Cháng Jiāng); others by the eye-wateringly spicy food that the locals are so proud of. Others still love the gritty atmosphere down by the docks with their 'bangbang' army of porters and old steel ships, while some tourists come here simply to climb aboard boats heading for the awe-inspiring Three Gorges on what is arguably China's most spectacular river cruise. Whatever the reason for coming, most visitors tend to agree there's a unique feel to Chóngqìng (重庆), an allure not found in other major Chinese cities.

True, the weather's awful. This is the City of Fog; it rains much of the time, is as polluted as almost anywhere in China and is a furnace come midsummer. But like its signature dish, the chilli-filled fire broth known as hotpot, Chóngqìng emits a certain spice that many people just can't resist.

When to Go

Chóngqìng

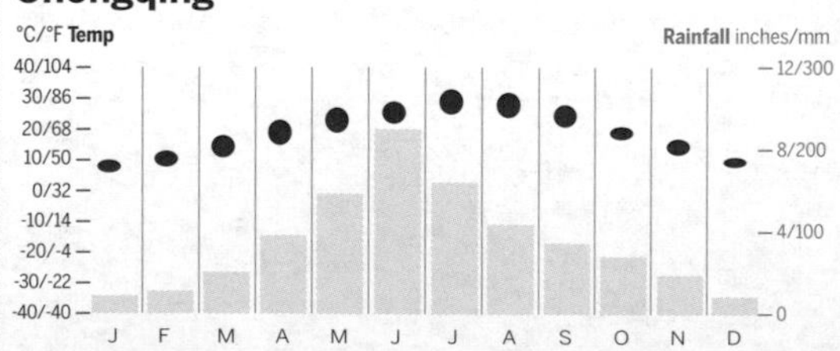

April & May Winter chill has lifted; full force of summer sweat-box yet to arrive; but still rainy.

July & August Only if you love it hot; temperatures top 40°C and the city resembles a steam bath.

September & October Like spring: more manageable temperatures, but worth carrying an umbrella.

Chóngqìng Highlights

1 Relax aboard a **Yangzi River Cruise** (p766) as it makes its way downstream to the awesome Three Gorges

2 Gasp in awe at the exquisite artwork inside the **Dàzú Buddhist Caves** (p763)

3 Tuck in to the world's spiciest **hotpot** (p759) at Yèfù Huǒguō

4 Pull up a stool and sample the delights of *shāokǎo*, Chóngqìng's delicious **streetside barbecues** (p759)

5 See traditional wooden stilt housing in the ancient riverside village of **Zhōngshān** (p764)

6 Squeeze your way through Chóngqìng's fascinating network of **hillside alleyways**

7 Wander the cobblestones, or just chill in a teahouse in the Ming-dynasty village of **Sōngji** (p765)

History

Stone tools unearthed along the Yangzi River valleys showed that humans lived in this region two million years ago. In recent times, however, it wasn't until the 1930s, following the Japanese invasion, that Chóngqìng began to make its mark. From 1938 to 1945, the city (previously known as Chungking) became the Kuomintang's wartime capital. It was here that representatives of the Chinese Communist Party (CCP), including Zhou Enlai, acted as 'liaisons' between the Kuomintang and the communists headquartered at Yán'ān, in Shaanxi province.

Refugees from all over China flooded in during WWII, swelling the population to over two million. In a city overstrained, with its bomb-shattered houses, these wartime residents must have found their new home's name somewhat ironic: Chóngqìng means 'double happiness' or 'repeated good luck'.

In 1997 Chóngqìng separated from Sìchuān province and became a municipality under the direct control of the central government. Billions of yuán have gone into its development, launching a major construction surge that shows no sign of slowing. In 2010 the Chinese government announced Chóngqìng's Liǎngjiāng district would follow the likes of Pǔdōng in Shànghǎi, Bīnhǎi in Tiānjīn and Shēnzhèn in Guǎngdōng province by becoming China's latest special economic zone (SEZ), with preferential tax, investment, trade and land policies.

Chóngqìng is sometimes mistakenly referred to as the biggest city in the world. It isn't. Figures for the whole municipality's population top 32 million, but these are made up of a number of towns and cities. The city of Chóngqìng itself has a mere five million, for now.

Language

In addition to standard Mandarin Chinese, Chóngqìng residents also speak Sichuanese. It's a Mandarin dialect, but pronunciation is different enough that it's often difficult for those who speak standard Chinese to understand. One word visitors should know: instead of the oft-heard *méiyǒu* ('no'; literally, 'don't have'), the Sichuanese say *méide*.

PRICE INDICATORS

The following price indicators are used in this chapter:

Sleeping

$	less than Y200
$$	Y200 to Y500
$$$	more than Y500

Eating

$	less than Y40
$$	Y40 to Y80
$$$	more than Y80

Sights & Activities

Arhat Temple BUDDHIST TEMPLE
(罗汉寺; Luóhàn Sì; Map p756; Luohan Si Jie; 罗汉寺街; admission Y10; ⏲8am-5pm) Built around 1000 years ago, this still-active temple is now sandwiched between skyscrapers. A notable feature is the corridor flanked by intricate rock carvings found just after you enter the complex, but the main attraction here is Arhat Hall (罗汉堂; Luóhàn Táng), off to your right just after the corridor, which contains 500 terracotta arhats (a Buddhist term for those who have achieved enlightenment and who pass to nirvana at death). Between the stone-carvings corridor and the temple proper there is a reasonably priced **vegetarian restaurant** (dishes Y12-35; ⏲10am-5pm) with a photo menu.

Húguǎng Guild Hall MUSEUM
(湖广会馆; Húguǎng Huìguǎn; Map p756; ☎6393 0287; Dongshuimen Zhengjie; 东水门正街; admission Y30; ⏲9am-6pm, tickets not sold after 5pm) You could spend several hours poking around the beautifully restored buildings in this gorgeous museum complex, which once served as a community headquarters for immigrants from the Hú (Húnán and Húběi) and Guǎng (Guǎngdōng and Guǎngxī) provinces who arrived in Chóngqìng several hundred years ago. There are rooms filled with artwork and furniture, a **temple**, a **teahouse** and several stages for Chinese **opera performances**. Free-to-watch rehearsals of Yuèjù (operatic style originating from Zhèjiāng province) and Jīngjù (Běijīng Opera) are held every Thursday and Saturday, usually between 3pm and 6pm.

River Cruises RIVER CRUISES
Chóngqìng looks best from the water, especially at night when the city flashes with neon. Two-hour river cruises (游船; Map p756) leave nightly from Cháotiānmén Dock at around 7pm. Buy tickets as you board the boats rather than from agencies

or hotels. Most boats offer very similar trips and serve food on board for an extra cost. If you're stuck for choice, **Jīnbì Huīhuáng** (金碧辉煌; per person Y68; dinner from Y30; ⏲7pm), noticeable by its neon-gold crown, has been recommended by readers.

Chóngqìng Science & Technology Museum MUSEUM
(重庆科技馆; Chóngqìng Kējìguǎn; ☎6186 3051; 7 Xi Dajie, Jiangbei District; 江北成西大街7号; admission Y40; ⏲9.30am-5pm Tue-Sun) Located opposite the eye-catching Chóngqìng Grand Theatre and housed in its own impressive state-of-the-art building, this new museum overlooking the Jiālíng River has plenty of interactive games and gadgets to keep the kids occupied for an hour or two. They'll also enjoy the IMAX theatre (Y30) and even the cable car ride just to get here. Pleasant **gardens** behind the museum contain two 100-year-old churches and make a nice picnic spot.

Cíqìkǒu Ancient Town OLD TOWN
(磁器口古镇; Cíqìkǒu Gǔzhèn) The opportunity to glimpse slices of old Chóngqìng makes it worth riding out to this part of town, on the Jiālíng River west of the centre. Most of the buildings, many dating to the late Ming dynasty, have been restored for tourists, and the main drag can feel like a carnival, but away from the central street, a living, working village remains. You can easily lose yourself in its narrow lanes, peeking into homes and tiny storefronts. And there's plenty to eat here, both in the alleys and overlooking the river.

It's also worth poking your head inside **Bǎolún Sì** (宝轮寺; admission Y5; ⏲7am-6pm), one of Cíqìkǒu's only remaining temples. Its main building is more than 1000 years old.

Take bus 503 (40 minutes) from Cháotiānmén. It stops at the Càiyuánbà bus station, from where you can also catch bus 808. Bus 215 (one hour) meanders here from the Liberation Monument. A taxi costs about Y30.

FREE **Three Gorges Museum** MUSEUM
(三峡博物馆; Sānxiá Bówùguǎn; Map p759; 236 Renmin Lu; ⏲9am-5pm Tue-Sun, last entry 4pm) This sleek museum showcases the history of settlement in the Chóngqìng region. A 1st-floor exhibition about the Three Gorges includes a model of the dam, and upstairs you can learn more about southwest China's minority cultures through their clothing and artwork. Some exhibits have better English captions than others, but the artefacts are well presented throughout.

Although admission is free, you need a ticket from the booth outside on the square.

From the Dàxīgōu light rail station, the museum is about a 15-minute walk west along Renmin Lu.

Cable Car Trips CABLE CAR
A ride on either the **Yangzi River Cable Car** (Chángjiāng suǒdào; Map p756; tickets Y5; ⏲7am-10pm) or the **Jiālíng River Cable Car** (Jiālíngjiāng suǒdào; Map p756; tickets Y5; ⏲10am-9pm) gives you a bird's-eye view of the murky waters. Both are within walking distance of the Liberation Monument. The Yangzi ride drops you off near the modern, riverside bar-and-restaurant strip on Nan'an Binjiang Lu. The Jiālíng ride takes you to the eye-catching Chóngqìng Grand Theatre and the Science Museum.

CHÓNGQÌNG'S STILT HOUSING

Once a striking feature of the Chóngqìng skyline, stilt houses (吊脚楼; *diàojiǎo lóu*) were, in many ways, the predecessor to the modern skyscraper; sprawling vertically rather than horizontally to save space. Their design also served to keep family units in close quarters despite the uneven terrain of hilly Chóngqìng. They were built on a bamboo or fir frame that was fitted into bore holes drilled into the mountainside, and their thin walls were stuffed with straw and coated with mud to allow for cooling ventilation in a city that swelters in summer.

Modernisation has turned stilt housing into a symbol of poverty and as a result they have all but disappeared in the city centre. A wonderful exception is the tall, rickety-looking wooden building to your left as you stand at the top of the Eighteen Steps Lane viewing platform. And many stilt houses still survive in the villages around Chóngqìng municipality, with some fine examples in the alleyways of Sōngji and particularly by the river in Zhōngshān.

Chóngqìng City (East)

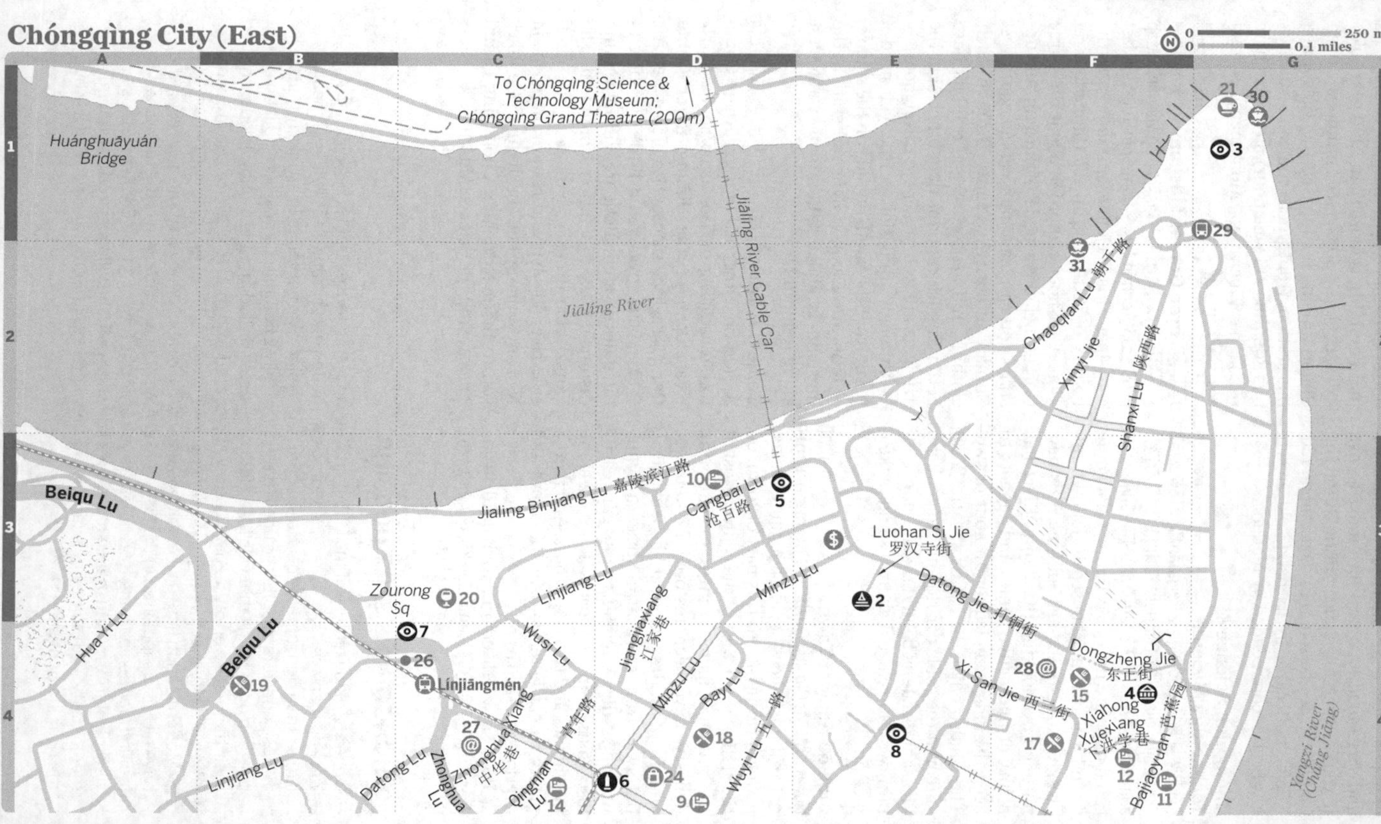

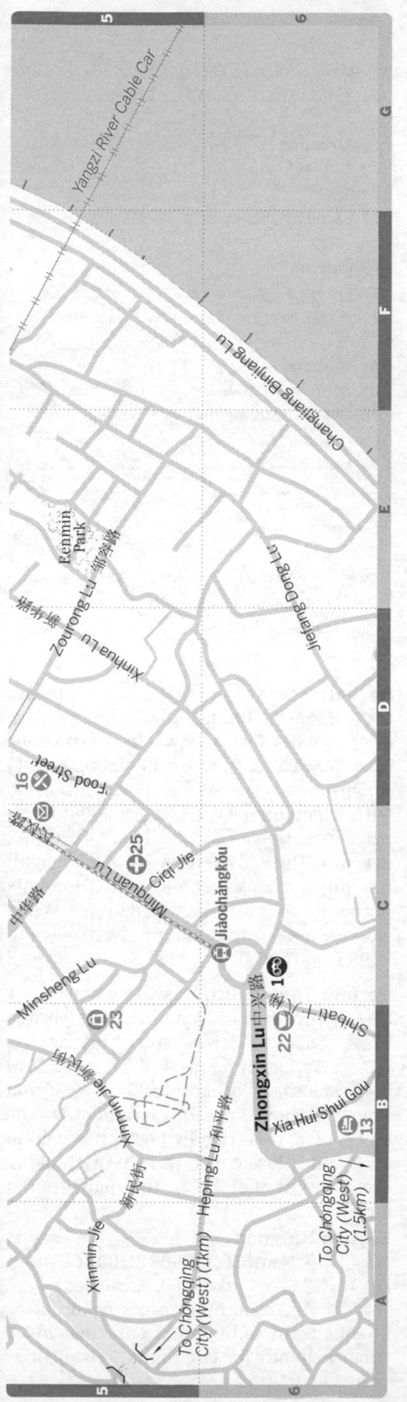

FREE **Pípá Mountain Park** PARK

(枇杷山公园; Pípá Shān Gōngyuán; Map p759; ⌚6am-10pm) For views of the city skyline, climb 345m Pípá Mountain Park, the highest point on the Chóngqìng peninsula. During the day, residents bring their songbirds to the park for air and group warbling.

Sleeping

TOP CHOICE **Tina's Hostel** YOUTH HOSTEL $

(老街客栈; Lǎo Jiē Kèzhàn; Map p756; ☎8621 9188; www.cqhostel.com; Ganzibao Alley, off Zhongxing Lu; 中兴路柑子堡; dm Y25-45, r from Y100; ❄@📶) Perched above the street-market alleys surrounding Eighteen Steps Lane (十八梯; Shíbātī), where Chóngqìng's few remaining stilt houses can still be found, Tina's is perfect for exploring the grittier side of the city. Its rooftop terrace, with free pool table, makes a wonderful vantage point before you dive in to the old town. Some rooms suffer slightly from damp but all are neat and bathrooms are clean if a little cramped. Staff members are welcoming and speak good English. There's free pick-up from the train station, or take the sky train to Jiàochǎngkǒu and walk down the hill on Zhongxing Lu until you see a sign for Tina's on your left.

Sunrise Míngqīng Hostel COURTYARD $$

(尚悦明清客栈; Shàngyuè Míngqīng Kèzhàn; Map p756; ☎6393 1579; www.srising.com; 23 Xiahong Xuexiang (down steps from 26 Jiefang Donglu); 下洪学巷23号 (解放东路26中对面); dm Y59, d Y199-399, ste Y999, discounts to 30%; ❄@📶) Despite the name, and the fact that it has a couple of dorms, this gorgeous 300-year-old courtyard place isn't really a hostel. Rooms are beautifully decorated with dark-wood furniture and have cute little modern bathrooms. The courtyard has its own fish-pond and the Qing-dynasty building has the same beautiful yellow walls and stone gateways as next-door Húguǎng Guild Hall. It's great fun getting here too, down a tiny alley from Jiefang Dong Lu. There's no restaurant or bar.

Sunrise Backpack Hostel YOUTH HOSTEL $

(尚悦背包客栈; Shàngyuè Bēibāo Kèzhàn; Map p756; ☎6391 1980; www.srising.com; 2 Bajiaoyuan; 芭蕉园2号; dm Y35-50, s Y89, tw from Y130; ❄@📶) There's bags of old-world charm in this recently renovated stilt-style building, and rooms are excellent value. Ones overlooking the river (and the main road below) have huge windows and are big and bright, but the traffic noise is constant.

Chóngqìng City (East)

Sights
1 18 Steps Lane Viewing Platform ... C6
2 Arhat Temple ... E3
3 Cháotiānmén Sq ... G1
4 Húguǎng Guild Hall ... F4
5 Jiālíng River Cable Car ... D3
6 Liberation Monument ... D4
7 Línjiāng Pái Decorative Arch ... C4
8 Yangzi River Cable Car ... E4

Sleeping
9 Harbour Plaza ... D4
10 Hóngyádòng Dàjiǔdiàn ... D3
11 Sunrise Backpack Hostel ... F4
12 Sunrise Míngqīng Hostel ... F4
13 Tina's Hostel ... B6
14 Xīnhuá Hotel ... C4

Eating
15 Barbecue Stalls ... F4
16 Hǎochī Jiē Xiǎopáidàng ... D5
17 Shānchéng Lǎohuǒguō ... F4
18 Shùnfēng 123 ... D4
Wàngwàngxiān Yācháng Huǒguō (see 17)
19 Yèfù Huǒguō ... B4

Drinking
20 Cici Park ... C3
21 Ile Cafe ... G1
22 Lǎojiē Shíbātī Chálóu ... B6

Shopping
23 Flower & Bird Market ... B5
24 Kodak Express ... D4

Information
25 24hr Pharmacy ... C5
26 China International Travel Service ... C4
Harbour Plaza Travel Centre ... (see 9)
27 Huīhuī Wǎngba ... C4
28 Yìjìng Wǎngba ... F4

Transport
29 Cháotiānmén Bus Stop ... G1
30 River Cruises ... G1
31 Three Gorges Ferry Port & Ticket Hall ... F2

Ones overlooking the charming alleyway out the front are quieter, but darker. The alleys round here are perfect for wandering, but be prepared for lots of steps! It's right by Húguǎng Guild Hall, or slightly further down from Sunrise Míngqìng Hostel.

Xīnhuá Hotel HOTEL **$$**
(新华酒店; Xīnhuá Jiǔdiàn; Map p756; ☎6355 7777; 9 Qingnian Lu; 青年路9号; tw from Y460, discounted to Y328; ❄@) Elegant, low-lit interior with spacious, well-equipped rooms (TV, fridge, safe) and good-sized bathrooms with separate shower and tub. A stone's throw from Liberation Monument so about as central as it gets.

Hóngyádòng Dàjiǔdiàn HOTEL **$$$**
(洪崖洞大酒店; Map p756; ☎6399 2888; 56 Cangbai Lu; 沧白路56号; d from Y518, ste from Y998, 40% discount is typical; ❄@) This huge complex hugging the cliffside overlooking Jiālíng River comes with restaurants, bars, shopping streets, a theatre and this pretty decent hotel. The whole complex is new, and the rooms are clean and modern, but it's been built in the style of Chóngqìng's once ubiquitous stilt buildings so some find it a little twee.

Harbour Plaza HOTEL **$$$**
(重庆海逸酒店; Chóngqìng Hǎiyì Jiǔdiàn; Map p756; ☎6370 0888; www.harbour-plaza.com/hpcq; Wuyi Lu; 五一路; r from Y1300; ❄@≋) Rooms are spacious, elegant and come with widescreen TV, fridge, safe and internet connection (Y80 per day). Otherwise, decent bathrooms come with a very small tub which doubles as a shower. Discounts border on the ridiculous sometimes. When we were here, standard twins were down to Y498 from Y1600.

Perfect Time Youth Hostel YOUTH HOSTEL **$**
(纯真年代青年旅舍; Chúnzhēn Niándài Qīngnián Lǚshè; ☎6547 7008; www.hostelchongqing.com; 2 Zhong Jie, Cíqìkǒu; 磁器口正街2号; dm Y30, tw Y140, with shared bathroom Y80; @wifi) If you fancy the charms of Cíqìkǒu rather than the city centre, this friendly hostel has helpful staff and a lovely cafe terrace overlooking the river. At the end of the main tourist strip.

Fùyuàn Bīnguǎn HOTEL **$$**
(富苑宾馆; Map p759; ☎6903 3111; 12 Caiyuan Lu; 菜袁路12号; r from Y260, discounted to Y148; ❄@) Around the corner from Càiyuánbà train and bus stations, this old-timer is handy for late-night arrivals or early departures.

Eating

Chóngqìng is all about **hotpot** (火锅; *huǒguō*): a fiery cauldron of head-burning chillies (辣椒; *làjiāo*) and mouth-numbing Sìchuān peppers (花椒; *huājiāo*) into which is dipped deliciously fresh ingredients, from vegetables and tofu to all types of fish and meat. It's a dish best sampled with a group of friends. Indeed, hotpot restaurants tend to be among the liveliest you'll find. But don't underestimate a hotpot's bite. This part of China is renowned for spicy food, and it doesn't come spicier than hotpot.

Another great thing to sample in Chóngqìng are the **street barbecues** (烧烤; *shāokǎo*), the perfect point-and-eat street food. Just choose your skewers, hand them over and wait for them to come back spiced and grilled. The junction where Datong Jie meets Shanxi Lu is a good spot, but you'll find *shāokǎo* all over the city.

For cheap noodle joints, try the Flower and Bird Market (p761).

TOP CHOICE **Shùnfēng 123** SICHUANESE $$
(顺风123; Shùnfēng Yāo Èr Sān; Map p756; Dàbùhùi Shopping Centre, West Bldg, 3rd fl, Jiěfàngbēi; 大部会西楼商厦三楼; dishes Y10-50; ⏲10am-midnight) Mouth-wateringly good, high-quality Sichuanese food, with some pan-Asian dishes too, at the Jiěfàngbēi branch of one of Chóngqìng's best-value high-end restaurants. Everything here is tasty, but we loved the *jiāowáng chánzuǐ tù* (椒王馋嘴兔; rabbit and peppers; Y38) and the *shānhú xiā* (珊瑚虾; coral shrimp; Y36). For dessert, don't miss the *mìzhì chāshāo sū* (秘制叉烧酥; secret-recipe meat-filled pastries; Y3 each). Enter through a lift accessed from Bayi Lu (八一路).

Yèfù Huǒguō HOTPOT $
(夜富火锅; Map p756; Beiqu Lu, 15 Linjiangmen; 临江门15号北区路; dishes Y3-15; ⏲9am-4am) Seats are of the plastic stool variety, and if you're fussy about hygiene you might want to consider somewhere else, but if you truly love hotpot, welcome to Heaven. Here you'll find quite possibly the spiciest hotpot on the planet, and Yèfù's fire broth will leave you practically hallucinating if you're not careful. Unless you're hardcore, insist on '*wēi là*' (微辣; mildly spicy), although even that will be *very* spicy. The delicious xiànzhá sūròu (现炸酥肉; deep-fried pork) is already cooked. Everything else needs to be dunked. From Línjiāngmén station (临江

HOW SPICY CAN YOU GO?

- *jiā má jiā là* (加嘛加辣; extra, extra spicy)
- *zuì là* (最辣; top-level spice)
- *zhōng là* (中辣; mid-level spice)
- *wēi là* (微辣; mildly spicy)
- *bù là* (不辣; not spicy – note that in Chóngqìng this will still be spicy)

Chóngqìng City (West)

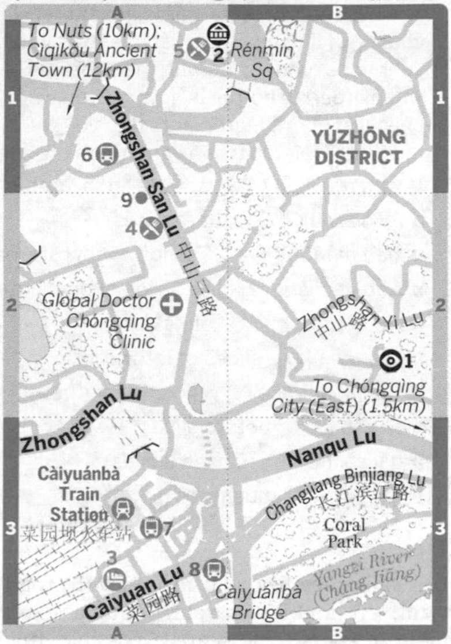

Chóngqìng City (West)

Sights
1 Pípá Mountain Park B2
2 Three Gorges Museum A1

Sleeping
3 Fùyuàn Bīnguǎn A3

Eating
4 Dòngtíngxiān Huǒguō A2
5 Made in Kitchen A1

Transport
6 Airport Shuttle Bus A1
7 Càiyuánbà Bus Station A3
8 Càiyuánbà Old Station A3
9 Chóngqìng Civil Aviation Ticket Centre A2

HOTPOT MENU

The best hotpot restaurants are entirely local affairs so you have about as much chance of finding an English menu as you have of being able to eat the thing without your nose running. As with many dishes in Chóngqìng, the first thing to establish when ordering hotpot is how hot you want it (see p759). Then you'll be given a menu checklist of raw ingredients that you will later cook in your pot. Here are some of our favourites for you to look out for on the menu:

» *yángròu juǎn* (羊肉卷; wafer-thin lamb slices)

» *féi niúròu* (肥牛肉; beef slices)

» *xiān máodǔ* (鲜毛肚; strips of cow stomach)

» *xiān yācháng* (鲜鸭肠; strips of duck intestine)

» *lǎo dòufu* (老豆腐; tofu slabs)

» *ǒu piàn* (藕片; slices of lotus root)

» *xiān huánghuā* (鲜黄花; chrysanthemum stalks)

» *tǔ dòu* (土豆; potato slices)

» *bǎi cài* (百菜; cabbage leaves)

» *mù'ěr* (木耳; mushroom)

门), walk along Beiqu Lu, following the road right, left, and it's on your left up a small flight of stairs (blue sign). If possible, line your stomach with lead before you come.

Hǎochī Jiē Xiǎopáidàng SICHUANESE **$**
(好吃街小排档; Map p756; Food Street; 好吃街; dishes Y18-38; ⌚11am-9.30pm) A trip to Food Street, a bustling restaurant strip near Liberation Monument (解放碑; Jiěfàng Bēi), should be done at least once, and this place is one of the liveliest here. It specialises in *gānguō* (干锅; literally 'dry pot'; Y32 to Y38), a clay pot of herbs and spices plus a main ingredient of your choice – anything from fragrant chicken (飘香鸡; *piāoxiāng jī*) and spare ribs (排骨; *páigǔ*) to pig intestine (肥肠; *féicháng*). The Sìchuān-pepper chicken (花椒鸡; *huājiāo jī*) is a great dish for those who are starting to become addicted to Chóngqìng's favourite mouth-numbing peppercorn, while plain fried green vegetable dishes such as *xiǎobái cài* (小白菜; cabbage) or *kōngxīn cài* (空心菜; water spinach) make good mouth-cooling accompaniments.

Shānchéng Lǎohuǒguō HOTPOT **$**
(山城老火锅; Map p756; 24 Daomenkou, Jiefang Donglu; 解放东路到门口24号; dipping ingredients Y2-15, sauce Y3; ⌚4.30-11pm) Tables with wooden benches and an often raucous atmosphere full of locals make this a great down-to-earth place in which to sample Chóngqìng's signature dish.

Made in Kitchen CHINESE-WESTERN **$$$**
(厨房制造; Chúfáng Zhìzào; Map p759; ☎6363 6228; Three Gorges Museum, 236 Renmin Lu; 人民路236号三峡博物馆; dishes Y20-100; ⌚11am-10pm) Fine dining with excellent service and a fabulous menu, including a good choice of imported wines. Located underneath the Three Gorges Museum; the entrance is down to the left as you face the museum entrance.

Dòngtíngxiān Huǒguō HOTPOT **$**
(洞亭鲜火锅; Map p759; 149 Zhongshan Sanlu; 中山三路149号; dipping ingredients Y2-20, dipping sauce Y5; ⌚10.30am-midnight) The explosive qualities of Chóngqìng hotpot are well documented, so, just to be safe, why not sample yours in a wartime bomb shelter? This is the most popular of three small restaurants housed in converted bunkers that were cut into the rocks on one side of Zhongshan Sanlu. Like all the best hotpot places it's a no-nonsense affair, with stools for seats, but the hotpot's good so who cares?

Wàngwàngxiān Yācháng Huǒguō HOTPOT **$**
(旺旺鲜鸭肠火锅; Map p756; 26 Daomenkou, Jiefang Donglu; 解放东路到门口26号; dipping ingredients Y2-12, sauce Y3; ⌚9.30am-midnight) Has a similar atmosphere and menu as Shānchéng Lǎohuǒguō, although it specialises in duck intestine (鸭肠; *yācháng*).

Drinking

As well as the places listed, there's a string of upmarket riverside bars (酒吧; *jiǔbā*), cafes and restaurants on Nán'àn Bīnjiāng

Lù (南岸滨江路). Take the cable car over the Yangzi, then walk down to the river and turn left. From there, walk 15 minutes along the river or hop on any bus for one stop. The cable car stops running at 10pm.

TOP CHOICE **Cici Park** BAR
(西西公园; Map p756; Xīxī Gōngyuán; 2 Linjiang Lu; 临江路2号; beer from Y15; ⏲7pm-4am) The most laidback bar in Chóngqìng, Cici's has chilled-out music and loungey, bohemian furnishings with outdoor seating on the square too. Beers are affordable, mixers start at Y25 and there's local plum wine (梅子酒; *méizi jiǔ*; Y10) that comes in a cute bottle with a thimble cup. It's on a big open square on the roof of a small shopping complex beside the renovated city gate Línjiāng Pái (临江牌).

TOP CHOICE **Lǎojiē Shíbātī Chálóu** TEAHOUSE
(老街十八梯茶楼; Map p756; 1 Zhongxin Lu; 中心路1号; tea from Y30, beer from Y10; ⏲10am-8pm) There's been a teahouse on this spot for more than 600 years and walking in here is like stepping into an antiques shop, with its wooden interior, period photos and fabulous furniture. The views are cool too as you look over one of the oldest parts of town, a maze of winding market lanes that can be accessed by walking down the teahouse's namesake alley, Eighteen Steps Lane (十八梯; Shíbātī).

Nuts CLUB
(坚果; Jiānguǒ Jùlèbù; www.douban.com/host/nutsclub, in Chinese; Shaozhong Lu, Shapingba District; 沙坪坝区沙中路; beer from Y5; ⏲8pm-2am) This pint-sized club is the best place to see local bands playing live. It's right by Chóngqìng University so gets a decent crowd in. Live music tends to be weekends only, from 8pm to 10pm, and usually carries a Y30 cover charge. After that it's DJs.

Ile Cafe CAFE
(屿咖啡酒廊; Map p756; Yǔkāfēi Jiǔláng; Cháotiānmén Sq; 朝天门广场; beer & coffee from Y28; ⏲10.30am-2am) If it was anywhere else in Chóngqìng this otherwise ordinary bar-cafe would be overpriced, but you pay for the location: a patio perch, overlooking the Yangzi River docks. It's down one level from the main square.

Shopping

Chóngqìng's modern shopping district is centred on Liberation Monument. For souvenirs, try the unashamedly touristy third floor of **Hóngyádòng** (56 Cangbai Lu; 沧白路56号), below the hotel of the same name.

> **STREETSIDE BARBECUE: TOP FIVE**
>
> » *dòufu pí* (豆腐皮; tofu skin)
>
> » *xiǎo mántou* (小馒头; mini steamed rolls)
>
> » *niángāo* (年糕; sticky rice cake)
>
> » *qiézi* (茄子; eggplant/aubergine)
>
> » *jiǔcài* (韭菜; leek)

Flower & Bird Market MARKET
(花鸟市场; Huāniǎo Shìchǎng; Map p756; ⏲dawn-dusk) The birds have long since flown, but the fragrant flowers and herbs that fill the alleys here lend a burst of colour to Chóngqìng's greyer days. Noodle joints also dot the lanes.

Lǎo Chóngqìng Huàfāng ARTWORK
(老重庆画坊; 13 Huangjueping Yixiang, Cíqìkǒu; 磁器口黄桷坪一巷13号; ⏲8.30am-7pm) Funky impressions of old Chóngqìng that make great souvenirs of the city. You can pay thousands for some of the original paintings here, but small prints start at Y10. It's on the main strip in Cíqìkǒu Ancient Town.

Kodak Express PHOTOGRAPHY
(柯达; Kēdá; Bayi Lu; 八一路; CD burning Y15) Opposite Metropolitan Plaza, just north of Zourong Lu.

Information

Internet Access

There are internet cafes all over the city. Look for the characters 网吧 *(wǎngbā)*.

Huīhuī Wǎngbā (辉辉网吧; Map p756; 1st fl, 20-40 Zhonghua Xiang; 中华巷20－40号2层; per hr Y2.50; ⏲24hr)

Yìjìng Wǎngbā (忆镜网吧; Map p756; Shanxi Lu; 陕西路; per hr Y2.50; ⏲24hr)

Internet Resources

Chóngqìng Expat Club (www.cqexpat.com) The best of a sorry bunch of English-language websites about Chóngqìng.

Medical Services

24-hour pharmacy (药店; Yàodiàn; Map p756; 63 Minquan Lu; 民权路63号; ⏲24hr) Western medicine, ground floor; Chinese medicine, 1st floor.

Global Doctor Chóngqìng Clinic (环球医生重庆诊所; Huánqiú Yīshēng Chóngqìng Zhěnsuǒ; Map p759; ☎8903 8837; Suite 701, 7th fl, Office

Tower, Hilton Hotel, 139 Zhongshan Sanlu; 中山三路139号希尔顿酒店商务楼7层701室; ⊙9am-5pm Mon-Fri) A 24-hour emergency service is available by dialling the general clinic number.

Money

Most of the ATMs around town now accept foreign cards.

Bank of China (中国银行; Zhōngguó Yínháng; Map p756; 104 Minzu Lu; 民族路104号; ⊙9am-noon & 1.30-5pm Mon-Fri) Changes money and travellers cheques, and gives advances on credit cards. Foreign-friendly ATM.

Post & Telephone

China Post (中国邮政; Zhōngguó Yóuzhèng; Minquan Lu; 民权路; ⊙9am-7pm) You can top up your Chinese phone and buy SIM cards at the China Mobile store (open 9am to 9pm) on the 1st floor.

Public Security Bureau

PSB (公安局; Gōng'ānjú; ☎6396 1994; 555 Huanglong Lu; 黄龙路555号; ⊙9am-noon & 1-5pm) Extends visas. Accessed from Zǐwēi Zhīlù (紫薇支路). Take Bus 461 from Cháotiānmén to last stop.

Travel Agencies

Tina's Hostel and Perfect Time Youth Hostel can arrange tours of all types and have better English-language speakers than the following.

China International Travel Service (CITS; 中国国际旅行社; Zhōngguó Guójì Lǚxíngshè; Map p756; ☎6387 6537; 8th fl, 151 Zourong Lu; 邹容路151号; ⊙9am-6pm) Friendly English-speaking staff can arrange train tickets (Y30 commission), flights and Three Gorges cruises.

Harbour Plaza Travel Centre (海逸旅游中心; Hǎiyì Lǚyóu Zhōngxīn; Map p756; ☎6370 0888; 3rd fl, Harbour Plaza, Wuyi Lu; ⊙7.50am-11pm) Staff speak OK English and can book air tickets and Three Gorges tours.

Getting There & Away

Air

Chóngqìng's Jiāngběi Airport (重庆江北飞机场) is 25km north of the city centre. As always, it's easiest to book online. Try www.elong.com or www.ctrip.com. Alternatively, buy tickets at the **Chóngqìng Civil Aviation Ticket Centre** (重庆机场机票销售中心; Chóngqìng Jīchǎng Jīpiào Xiāoshòu Zhōngxīn; Map p759; ☎6385 1105; 161 Zhongshan San Lu; 中山三路161号; ⊙8.30am-8pm). Because of the new high-speed rail link, there are no longer flights between Chóngqìng and Chéngdū. Direct flights:

Běijīng Y1660, 2½ hours

Kúnmíng Y780, 70 minutes

Shànghǎi Y1590, 2½ hours

Xī'ān Y770, 90 minutes

Wǔhàn Y890, 90 minutes

Boat

Chóngqìng is the starting point for hugely popular cruises down the Yangzi River through the magnificent Three Gorges. For all the details, see p766.

Bus

Chóngqìng has several long-distance bus stations, but most buses use **Càiyuánbà Bus Station** (菜园坝老站; Càiyuánbà) beside the main (old) train station. Destinations:

Chéngdū Y110 to Y120, four hours, every hour (8am to 8pm)

Dàzú Y51, 2½ hours, every 30 minutes (6.30am to 9pm)

Héchuān Y31, 80 minutes, every 30 minutes (6.30am to 8.30pm)

Jiāngjīn Y23, 70 minutes, every 30 minutes (6.40am to 8pm) Leaves from Càiyuánbà Old Station.

Yǒngchuān Y33, 90 minutes, every 20 minutes (6.30am to 9.20pm)

Train

New, faster trains, including the bullet train to and from Chéngdū, use Chóngqìng's new **North Station** (北站; Běizhàn), but many others still use the older train station at **Càiyuánbà** (菜园坝). Plenty of local buses link both train stations, including 419, 611 and 168. Train destinations:

Běijīng sleeper Y416, 24 and 29 hours, two daily (11am and 11.42pm)

***Chéngdū** seat Y98, two hours, 11 daily (8am to 7.30pm)

***Guìlín** sleeper Y169, 20 hours, one daily (9.01pm)

Kūnmíng sleeper Y254, 19 to 20 hours, two daily (9.21am and 2.11pm)

Lhasa sleeper Y619, 45 hours, every other day (7.55pm)

***Shànghǎi** sleeper Y423, 28 hours, one daily (8am)

***Xī'ān** sleeper Y112 to Y185, 12 hours, three daily (10.08am, 11.12am and 5.57pm)

*From North Station; the others leave from Càiyuánbà.

Getting Around

Airport

The **airport shuttle bus** (机场大巴; *jīchǎng dàbā*) meets all arriving planes (Y15, 45 minutes) and takes you to a small road off Zhōngshān Sānlù (中山三路), via a couple of stops in the north of the city. Bus 461 goes from Zhōngshān Sānlù to Cháotiānmén (朝天门). To get to the sky train, turn left onto Zhongshan Sanlu and go straight

THE TOUGHEST PORTERS IN CHINA

Ever since the first Chóngqìng-ers couldn't bear the thought of carrying their buckets of water from the river up to their cliffside homes, there's been a need for a special kind of porter. A porter who can lift more than his bodyweight and lug that load up and down hills all day long. A porter who can't use a trolley like in other cities, or a bike or a rickshaw, but instead works on foot using only the cheapest of tools: a bamboo pole, or 'bangbang', and a length of rope.

Known as the Bangbang Army, these porters have been bearing the city's weights on their shoulders for hundreds of years, but their numbers really exploded in the 1990s when the government began resettling millions who lived along the Yangzi River. Many came from the countryside with little education and no relevant skills, and soon became part of the 100,000-strong workforce. Unregulated and poor, 'bangbang' porters earn around Y30 per day to work in one of China's hottest, hilliest cities, lugging heavy loads up and down steep hills. When you consider some of the wealth that's been pumped into the city in recent years (just look across the river at the Grand Theatre), it's perhaps surprising that this age-old trade still thrives. But for now, at least, the Bangbang Army continues to be an integral feature of the alleyway-riddled areas that link this fast modernising city to its old docks.

over the large roundabout. Niújiǎotuó (牛角沱) station will be on your left. Buses to the airport run from 6am to 8pm. A taxi is around Y50.

Bus

Local bus fares are Y1 or Y2. Useful routes:

Bus 120 Cháotiānmén–Càiyuánbà Train Station

Bus 461 Cháotiānmén–Zhongshan Sanlu (for airport bus)

Bus 462 Zhongshan Sanlu (airport bus)–Liberation Monument

Bus 419 North Train Station–Càiyuánbà Train Station

Bus 105 North Train Station–Línjiāngmén (near Liberation Monument)

Bus 141 North Train Station–Cháotiānmén

Subway

Chóngqìng's first subway line (Line 2) is actually an overground **Light Rail** (轻轨; qīngguǐ; Y2-4; ⏲6.30am-10.30pm) for most of its length, but burrows underground at its eastern end where Línjiāngmén and Jiàochǎngkǒu stations are both walking distance from Liberation Monument.

Lines 1 and 3 were due to open in 2011 and will be mostly underground. Line 1 will link Cháotiānmén with the western district of Shāpíngbà. Line 3 will link the two train stations. Extensions for both these lines are planned for 2013, linking Line 1 with Cíqìkǒu Ancient Town and Line 3 with the airport.

Taxi

Fares start at Y5. A taxi from Jiěfàngbēi to Nuts Club should cost around Y35.

AROUND CHÓNGQÌNG

Dàzú Buddhist Caves 大足石窟

The fabulous rock carvings of Dàzú (Dàzú Shíkū) are a Unesco World Heritage Site and one of China's four great Buddhist cave sculpture sites, along with those at Dūnhuáng, Luòyáng and Dàtóng. The Dàzú sculptures are the most recent of the four, but some believe the artwork here to be the best of all.

Scattered over roughly 40 sites are thousands of cliff carvings and statues (with Buddhist, Taoist and Confucian influences), dating from the Tang dynasty (9th century) to the Song dynasty (13th century). The main groupings are at Treasured Summit Hill and North Hill.

Sights

Treasured Summit Hill ROCK CARVINGS
(宝顶山; Bǎodǐng Shān; admission Y120, combination ticket with North Hill Y170; ⏲8.30am-6pm) Of the extensive sculptures at this site, the centrepiece is a 31m-long, 5m-high reclining Buddha depicted entering nirvana, with the torso sunk into the cliff face. Next to the Buddha, with a temple built around her for protection, is a mesmerising gold Avalokiteshvara (or Guānyīn, the Goddess of Mercy; see the boxed text, p935). Her 1007 individual arms fan out around her, entwined and reaching for the skies. Each hand has

an eye, the symbol of wisdom. It is believed these sculptures were completed over roughly 70 years, between 1174 and 1252.

Treasured Summit Hill differs from other cave sites in that it incorporates some of the area's natural features – a sculpture next to the reclining Buddha, for example, makes use of an underground spring.

The site is about 15km northeast of Dàzú town and is accessed on a bus from Dàzú's new bus station (新站; *xīnzhàn*; Y4, 25 minutes, until midday). Buses from Chóngqìng drop you at Dàzú's old bus station (老站; *lǎozhàn*). To get from old to new, turn right out of the old station, then immediately left at the crossroads and keep walking for five to 10 minutes. Then turn left over the canal and take the first left. It's Y5 in a cycle rickshaw. Once at the site, it's a 10-minute walk from where the bus drops you off, past numerous **restaurants**, **guesthouses** and **souvenir stalls**, to the entrance to the sculptures. Buses returning from Treasured Summit Hill run until 6pm, but may drop you at Dōngguānzhàn bus stop, from where you can take local Bus 1 to Dàzú's old station, or a Y5 cycle rickshaw to the new station.

North Hill ROCK CARVINGS

(北山; Běi Shān; admission Y90; ⌚8.30am-6pm) This site, originally a military camp, contains some of the region's earliest carvings. The dark niches hold several hundred statues, although the collection is smaller than at Treasured Summit Hill and some are in poor condition.

North Hill is about a 30-minute hike – up many steps – from Dàzú town; aim straight for the pagoda visible from the old bus station.

Sleeping & Eating

You can easily visit Dàzú as a day trip from Chóngqìng. If you decide to stay overnight, try the standard midrange **Dàzú Bīnguǎn** (大足宾馆; ☎4372 1888; Longgang Longzhonglu; 龙岗龙中路; d Y300), which gives small discounts. It's 200m past the Dàzú's new bus station, on your left and set back from the road (龙中路; Lóngzhǒng Lù).

If you turn left out of the hotel and left again onto Bǐnhé Jiā (滨河街) you'll reach a roundabout, near which there are plenty of restaurants and street stalls serving noodles, dumplings and other light bites. Turning left at the roundabout, you'll cross a river where there are some teahouses. You can also continue this way to the old bus station.

Getting There & Away

Buses from Dàzú old station:

Chóngqìng Y51, 2½ hours, every 30 minutes (6.30am to 6pm

Yǒngchuān (for Sōngji) Y21, 90 minutes, every 45 minutes (7.10am to 5.40pm)

Buses from Dàzú new station:

Chéngdū Y84, four hours, four daily (7.15am, 8.55am, 9.50am and 2pm)

Héchuān (for Láitān) Y20, 2½ hours, four daily (8am, 10.20am, 2pm and 5.10pm)

Zhōngshān 中山

Chóngqìng's once ubiquitous stilt-style homes are an endangered species these days, but trek out to this gorgeous riverside village and you'll find plenty of them to gawp at. The old town (古镇; Gǔzhèn) is essentially one long street lined with wooden homes on stilts above the riverbank. Be sure to walk down to the river and look up at the houses to see their support structures.

Many residents of these old houses have turned their living rooms into storefronts. While some hawk souvenir trinkets, others sell locally made products such as chilli sauce or jugs of rice wine. Popular snacks include squares of grilled, spice-rubbed tofu, and sweet doughy rice cakes filled with ground nuts.

Above the river are several restaurants and teahouses, where you can have lunch or simply snooze in a lounge chair, as well as a couple of basic guesthouses (beds from Y30) which, although low on luxury, are great places to stay thanks to the cracking riverside location. It's possible, though, to visit Zhōngshān in a day trip from Chóngqìng.

To get here from Chóngqìng, change buses at Jiāngjīn (江津), from where buses leave for Zhōngshān (Y10 to Y13, two hours, roughly every 30 minutes from 8.40am to 4.30pm). The last bus back to Jiāngjīn is 4.20pm. The last bus from Jiāngjīn back to Chóngqìng is 7pm.

Láitān 涞滩

The main attraction in this ancient walled village overlooking the Qú River is a towering **Buddha** (二佛寺; Èrfó Sì; admission Y20) carved into a hillside and surrounded by more than 1000 mini-statues. The Buddha dates to the 12th or 13th century. At roughly

14m tall, it pales in comparison to the giant Buddha at Lèshān, but it's still quite impressive – and far less visited.

A short walk from the Buddha is the village **temple** (admission Y5), which is still in use.

Allow time to wander around the village, which is more than 1000 years old, checking out the small shops and eateries. Láitān *mǐjiǔ* (米酒; rice wine) is a local speciality.

Although it is possible to visit Láitān in a day trip from Chóngqìng, some people might like to stay the night within the village walls at the neat and tidy **Huílóng Kèzhàn** (回笼客栈; ☎023-4256 1999; r Y120, discounted to Y100). There's nothing special about the guesthouse itself (although it's clean and well looked after), but staying here gives you the chance to experience the nontouristy side of this ancient village, once all the day trippers have left.

From Chóngqìng, change buses at Héchuān, from where there are three direct buses to Láitān (Y10, 50 minutes, 10.16am, 1.40pm and 4.10pm) as well as regular buses to Lóngshì (Y9.50, 45 minutes). From Lóngshì, minibuses (Y2, five minutes) leave for Láitān from outside the bus station.

The last bus back to Chóngqìng from Héchuān is 6pm.

Sōngji 松溉

Cobblestone alleyways housing temples, teahouses, old gateways and some wonderful courtyard homes are perfect for aimless strolls in this still lived-in Ming-dynasty village on the banks of the Yangzi River.

If you're looking for a focus, seek out the **Chén Family Compound** (陈家大院; Chén Jiā Dàyuàn; admission Y2), the historic home of the village's most prominent family. This sprawling structure once contained more than 100 rooms. What remains of the compound is much smaller, but its walls are extensively decorated with family photos and memorabilia. Actor Joan Chén (Bernardo Bertolucci's *The Last Emperor* and Ang Lee's *Lust, Caution*) is the family member best known outside China.

On a bluff above the river, about a 20-minute walk from the old town, is the **Dōngyù Temple** (东狱庙; Dōngyù Miào), home to a 9.5m-tall Buddha and some gruesome dioramas depicting various hells (impaling, scalding, having your tongue ripped out).

Sōngshān Bīnguǎn (松山宾馆; ☎023-4954 6078; r from Y80; ❄) has smart clean doubles, some with river views. Nearby **Gǔzhèn Jiǔdàwǎn** (古镇九大碗; dishes Y15-30; ⏲9am-8pm) is a nicely renovated old courtyard that has been turned into a restaurant-cum-teahouse. There's a selection of Chinese teas here plus a well-priced menu of mostly Sichuanese dishes. To guide yourself around the lanes, take a photo of the large wooden bilingual map at the entrance to the old town (古镇; *gǔzhèn*), just down towards the river from where the bus drops you.

To get to Sōngji, catch a bus to Yongchuān, from where minibuses to Songji (Y9, 70 minutes) leave every 20 minutes. The last bus back to Yǒngchuān leaves Sōngji at about 5.30pm. The last bus from Yǒngchuān to Chóngqìng leaves at 6.50pm.

Cruising the Yangzi

Includes »

Travel in China is often a terrestrial and sedentary experience, with agonising bus rides, colossal freeways, traffic jams, dusty mountain roads, marathon train journeys and daily victories hard won over stupefying distances. Half of the 'China Experience' can be the unavoidable grind of getting from A to B (sometimes via C and D, if there are no direct buses). Much of the other half is recuperating from the first half. So the Yangzi Cruise – on China's longest and most scenically impressive river – enjoys special significance as a trip where the destination is irrelevant compared to the greater drama of the journey. It's an occasion to put the travel schedule on ice, hang up one's hat and admire an astonishing panorama sliding past.

When to Go

December–March The low season; rates are cheaper and the journey is more serene

April & May The best weather, but the highest prices and rowdiest crowds

October & November Cooler climes but the crowds are back

The Three Gorges

Few river panoramas have inspired as much awe as the Three Gorges (三峡; Sānxiá). Well-travelled Tang-dynasty poets and men of letters have gone weak-kneed before them. Voluble emperors and hard-boiled communist party VIPs have been rendered speechless. Flotillas of sightseers have megapixelled their way from Chóngqìng to Yíchāng. For as long as many Yangzi boat hands can remember, the Three Gorges have been a member of the prestigious China Tour triumvirate, rubbing shoulders with the Terracotta Warriors and the Great Wall.

Yet the gorges these days get mixed press. Some travellers have their socks well and truly blown away; others arrive in Yíchāng scratching their heads and wondering what all the fuss was about. The route's natural scenery is certainly way

FAST FACTS

» The Three Gorges Dam is the world's largest man-made generator of electric power from a renewable source.

» The Three Gorges Dam is designed to withstand an earthquake of 7 on the Richter scale.

» Plans for the Three Gorges Dam date from 1919, when Sun Yatsen (Sun Zhongshan) saw its huge potential for power generation.

» The Yangzi River will deposit over 500 million tons of silt every year into the reservoir behind the dam.

» The Yangzi River has caused hundreds of catastrophic floods, including the disastrous inundation of 1931, in which an estimated 145,000 people died.

more dramatic than its historical sights, often crammed with historical allusions obscure to all but Chinese minds; temples and so forth along the way can be crowded, while uniform riverine towns and settlements are modern-looking rather than twee and charming. To some, the gorges' dramatic appearance can become rather repetitive, especially overlong Xīlíng Gorge (Xīlíng Xiá). The reservoir built up behind the Three Gorges Dam – a body of water almost the length of England – has certainly taken its toll as much more is now inundated.

But if you don't expect to swoon at every bend in the river, journeying downriver is a stimulating and relaxing adventure, not least because of the change of pace and perspective.

Apart from bringing some binoculars with you, here are four handy tips to maximise your enjoyment of the Three Gorges:

» Try to ensure the Three Gorges aren't one of just three things on your China tour

» Disregard the roar of a marketing machine selling the Three Gorges like there was no tomorrow

» Treat the journey as an occasion to unwind from the effort of getting around China

» Take along a good read

If you don't have the time for the *Three Gorges* Director's Cut, hop on the hydrofoil and jet down for the shorter and edited (but perhaps equally enjoyable) highlights version.

The River

The journey puts you adrift on China's mightiest – and the world's third-longest – river, the gushing 6300km Yangzi (长江; Cháng Jiāng). Starting life as trickles of snow melt in the Tánggǔlā Shān of southwestern Qīnghǎi, the river then spills from Tibet, swells through seven Chinese provinces, sucks in water from hundreds of tributaries and powerfully rolls into the Pacific Ocean north of Shànghǎi. En route, it surges past some of China's greatest cities: supersized Chóngqìng, Wǔhàn and Nánjīng.

The Effects of the Dam

The dwarfing chasms of rock, sculpted over aeons by the irresistible volume of water, are the Yangzi River's most fabled length. Yet the construction of the controversial and record-breaking Three Gorges Dam cloaked the gorges in as much uncertainty as their famous mists: have the gorges been humbled or can they somehow shrug off the rising waters? In brief, the gorges have been undoubtedly affected by the rising waters. The peaks are not as towering as they once were, nor are the flooded chasms through which boats travel as narrow and pinched. The effect is more evident to seasoned boat hands or repeat visitors who are more inclined to repeat the 'you should have seen them in the old days' mantra, accompanied by a knowing look. But for first-timers the gorges still put together a dramatic show when the highlights arrive (but prepare for some lengthy intervals between performances).

THE ROUTE

Apocryphally the handiwork of the Great Yu (see p249), a legendary architect of the river, the gorges – Qútáng, Wū and Xīlíng – commence just east of Fèngjié in Chóngqìng and level out west of Yíchāng in Húběi province, a distance of around 200km. The principal route for those cruising the Yangzi River is therefore between the megalopolis of Chóngqìng and humdrum Yíchāng downstream.

The route can be travelled in either direction, but most passengers journey

Yangzi River (Cháng Jiāng)

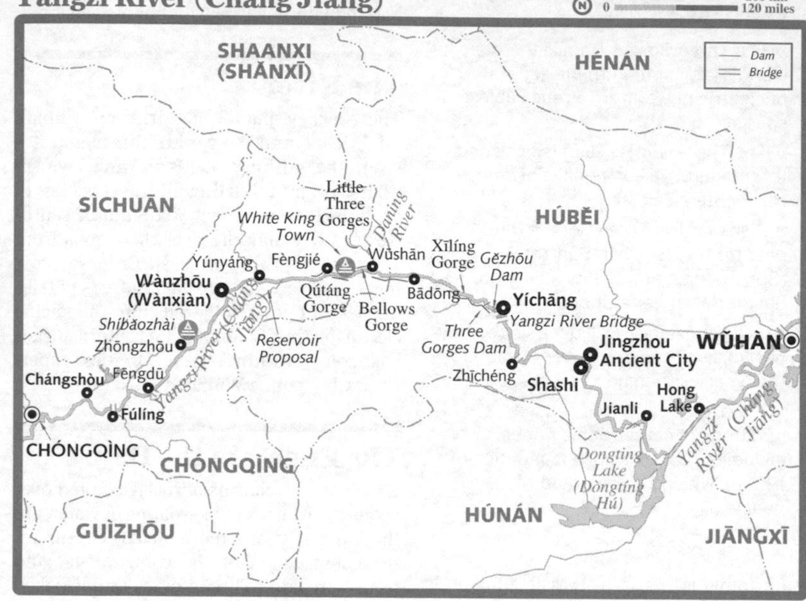

downstream from the 'City of Fog' Chóngqìng to Yíchāng. Some vessels soldier on beyond Yíchāng as far as Shànghǎi, but the riverside scenery becomes distinctly ho-hum beyond Yíchāng.

Vessels stop at many of the towns between Chóngqìng and Yíchāng that can also be reached by road, so taking the bus can speed up your journey. If you buy your ticket from an agency, ensure you're not charged upfront for the sights along the way, as you may not want to visit them all and some of the entrance fees are as steep as the surrounding inclines. The only ticket really worth buying in advance is for the popular Little Three Gorges tour, which is often full (see p769).

Chóngqìng to Wànzhōu

重庆 – 万州

The initial stretch is slow-going and unremarkable, although the dismal view of factories gradually gives way to attractive terraced countryside and the occasional small town.

Passing the drowned town of Fúlíng (涪陵), the first port of call is at **Fēngdū** (丰都), 170km from Chóngqìng. Long nicknamed the **City of Ghosts** (鬼城; Guǐchéng), the town is just that: inundated in 2009, its residents were moved across the river. This is the stepping-off point for crowds to clamber up – or take the cable car (Y20) up – **Míng Shān** (名山; admission Y60), with its theme-park crop of ghost-focused temples.

Drifting through the county of Zhōngzhōu, the boat takes around three hours to arrive at **Shíbǎozhài** (石宝寨; Stone Treasure Stockade; admission Y80; ⏲8am-4pm) on the northern bank of the river. A 12-storey, 56m-high wooden pagoda built on a huge, river-water-encircled rock bluff, the structure originally dates to the reign of Qing-dynasty emperor Kangxi (1662–1722). Your boat may stop for rapid expeditions up to the tower and for climbs into its interior.

Most morning boats moor for the night at partially inundated **Wànzhōu** (万州; also called Wànxiàn). Travellers aiming to get from A to B as fast as possible while taking in the gorges can skip the Chóngqìng to Wànzhōu section by hopping on a three-hour bus and then taking either the hydrofoil or a passenger ship from the Wànzhōu jetty.

Wànzhōu to Yíchāng

万州–宜昌

Boats departing from Wànzhōu soon pass the relocated **Zhāng Fēi Temple** (张飞庙;

Zhāngfēi Miào; admission Y20), where short disembarkations may be made. Yúnyáng (云阳), a modern town strung out along the northern bank of the river, is typical of many utilitarian settlements. Boats drift on past ragged islets, some carpeted with small patchworks of fields, and alongside riverbanks striated with terraced slopes, rising like green ribbons up the inclines.

The ancient town of **Fèngjié** (奉节), capital of the state of Kui during the periods known as the 'Spring and Autumn' (722–481 BC) and 'Warring States' (475–221 BC), overlooks Qútáng Gorge, the first of the three gorges. The town – where most ships and hydrofoils berth – is also the entrance point to half-submerged **White King Town** (白帝城; Báidìchéng; admission Y50), where the King of Shu, Liu Bei, entrusted his son and kingdom to Zhu Geliang, as chronicled in *The Romance of the Three Kingdoms*.

Qútáng Gorge (瞿塘峡; Qútáng Xiá) – also known as Kui Gorge (夔峡; Kuí Xiá) – rises dramatically into view, towering into huge vertiginous slabs of rock, its cliffs jutting out in jagged and triangular chunks. The shortest and narrowest of the three gorges, 8km-long Qútáng Gorge is over almost as abruptly as it starts, but is considered by many to be the most awe-inspiring. The gorge offers a dizzying perspective onto huge strata and vast sheets of rock despite having some of its power robbed by the rising waters. On the northern bank is **Bellows Gorge** (风箱峡; Fēngxiāng Xiá), where nine coffins were discovered, possibly placed here by an ancient tribe.

After Qútáng Gorge the terrain folds into a 20km stretch of low-lying land before boats pull in at the riverside town of **Wūshān** (巫山), situated high above the river. Many boats stop at Wūshān for five to six hours so passengers can transfer to smaller tour boats for trips along the **Little Three Gorges** (小三峡; Xiǎo Sānxiá; tickets Y150-200) on the Dàníng River (大宁河; Dàníng Hé). The landscape is gorgeous, and some travellers insist that the narrow gorges are more impressive than their larger namesakes.

Back on the Yangzi River, boats pull away from Wūshān to enter the penultimate Wū Gorge, under a bright-red bridge. Some of the cultivated fields on the slopes overhanging the river reach almost illogical angles.

Wū Gorge (巫峡; Wū Xiá) – the Gorge of Witches – is stunning, cloaked in green and carpeted in shrubs, its cliffs frequently disappearing into ethereal layers of mist. About 40km in length, its towering cliffs are topped by sharp, jagged peaks on the northern bank. A total of 12 peaks cluster on either side, including **Goddess Peak** (神女峰; Shénnǚ Fēng) and **Peak of the Immortals** (集仙峰; Jíxiān Fēng). If you're fortunate, you'll catch the sunrise over Goddess Peak.

Boats continue floating eastward out of Wū Gorge and into Húběi province, past the mouth of **Shénnóng Stream** (神农溪; Shénnóng Xī) and the town of Bādōng (巴东) on the southern bank, along a 45km section before reaching the last of the three gorges.

At 80km, **Xīlíng Gorge** (西陵峡; Xīlíng Xiá) is the longest and perhaps least impressive gorge; sections of the gorge in the west have been submerged. Note the slow-moving cargo vessels, including long freight ships loaded with mounds of coal, ploughing downriver to Shànghǎi. The gorge was traditionally the most hazardous, where hidden shoals and reefs routinely holed vessels, but it has long been tamed, even though river traffic slows when the fog reduces visibility.

The monumental **Three Gorges Dam** (三峡大坝; Sānxiá Dàbà; admission Y105) looms up and boats stop so passengers can shuttle across to the dam's observation deck for a bird's-eye view of this mammoth project. Hydrofoils from Chóngqìng and Yíchāng pull in here for passengers to disembark. Boats continue and pass through the locks of the Gězhou Dam (葛洲坝; Gězhōu Bà) before completing the journey 30km downstream to Yíchāng.

BOATS & TICKETS

The growth of speedier expressways sees fewer passenger boats nosing all the way down from Chóngqìng to Nánjīng or Shànghǎi, so most cruises focus on the Three Gorges. In Chóngqìng, most hotels, hostels and travel agents can sell you a trip, some on the luxury cruise ships aimed primarily at Western tourists. You can also buy tickets for the ordinary ferries at the **ferry port ticket hall** (重庆港售票大厅; Chóngqìnggǎng Shòupiào Dàtīng; ⌚6am-10pm), accessed from under the bridge on Chaoqian Lu (朝千路) in Chóngqìng. An option is **Chongqing Port International Travel Service** (重庆港国际旅行社; Chóngqìng Gǎng Guójì Lǚxíngshè; ☎023-6618 3683; www.cqpits.com.cn; 18 Xinyi Jie), where staff speak English. Travel agents and hotels in Yíchāng

BEST TOP-END CRUISES

» **Viking River Cruises** (www.vikingrivercruises.com) Very luxurious cruise, offering five-day cruises from Chóngqìng to Wǔhàn, as part of a larger 12-day tour of China; complete tour £1995.

» **Orient Royal Cruises** (www.orientroyalcruise.com; ☎027 8576 9988; Wǔhàn) Good spoken English from guides, comfy cabins, decent restaurant and bar, excursions. Four-day Chóngqìng–Yíchāng journey or five-day Yíchāng–Chóngqìng voyage. Prices from Y6230 per person.

» **Victoria Cruises** (www.victoriacruises.com) Comfortable four- to five-day Chóngqìng–Yíchāng and Yíchāng–Chóngqìng route; excellent English-speaking guides. From $470 (winter price) plus $65 for shore excursions.

also sell cruise tickets for the upstream journey; for the passenger ferry and hydrofoil, buy tickets at **Yíchāng Ferry Terminal** (宜昌港客运站; Yíchāng Gǎng Kèyùnzhàn; ☎696 6166; Yanjing Dadao). In Yíchāng, **China International Travel Service** (CITS; 中国国际旅行社; Zhōngguó Guójì Lǚxíngshè; ☎625 3088; Yunji Lu; ⏲8.30am-5.30pm) can arrange tickets.

Luxury Cruises

The most luxurious passage is on international-standard cruise ships, where maximum comfort and visibility accompany a leisurely agenda. Trips include shore visits to all the major sights (Three Gorges Dam, Little Three Gorges et al), allowing time to tour the attractions (often secondary to the scenery). Cabins have air-con, TV (perhaps satellite), fridge/minibar and perhaps more. These vessels are ideal for travellers with time, money and negligible Chinese skills. The average duration for such a cruise is three nights and three to four days.

Tourist Boats

Typically departing from Chóngqìng at around 9pm, Chinese tourist cruise ships usually take around 2½ days to reach Yíchāng. Some Chinese cruise ships stop at all the sights; others stop at just a few (or none at all). They are less professional than the luxury tour cruises and are more aimed at domestic travellers (Chinese food, little spoken English). It is possible to book packages that take you first by bus to Wànzhōu from Chóngqìng, where you board a vessel for the rest of the trip.

The following details are for cruise ships that do not stop at the tourist sights:

1st class Y1042, two-bed cabin with shower

2nd class upper/lower bunk Y483/530, four-bed cabins

3rd class upper/lower bunk Y317/347, six-bed cabins

The following details are for vessels that stop at six tourist sights:

1st class Y1525, two-bed cabin with shower

2nd class upper/lower bunk Y992/1060, four-bed cabins

3rd class from Y620, six-bed cabins

Passenger Ships

A further alternative is to board a straightforward passenger ship from Chóngqìng to Yíchāng. They are cheap, but can be disappointing: you will sail through the first two gorges in the dead of night and only catch the last gorge. Stops are frequent but hasty and they pass tourist sights by. Journeys take 36 hours (38 hours from Yíchāng to Chóngqìng). Shared toilets and showers can be grotty. Meals on board are average, so take along your own food and drinks. Functional accommodation costs the following:

1st class (一等; *yīděng*) Y800, twin cabin

2nd class (二等; *èrděng*) Y490 to Y510

3rd class (三等; *sānděng*) Y400 to Y424

4th class (四等; *sìděng*) Y302 to Y332, 8-bed dorm

In theory, you can buy tickets on the day of travel, but booking one or two days in advance is recommended. Fares tend to be similar whether you buy them from an agency or direct from the ticket hall, but it's worth shopping around to check. If buying a ticket through an agent, ensure you know exactly what the price includes.

Hydrofoil

Hydrofoils are the fastest route through the gorges, although the direct Chóngqìng–Yíchāng hydrofoil service runs no more. Hydrofoils depart hourly from Wànzhōu (Y410, including a bus from Chóngqìng to Wànzhōu, or Y300 for the hydrofoil ticket only) downriver, running to the hydrofoil terminal west of Yíchāng. The journey takes 10 hours: three hours for the bus trip from Chóngqìng to Wànzhōu, six hours for the hydrofoil journey from Wànzhōu to Yíchāng and an hour by bus from the Yíchāng hydrofoil terminal into town. Note that Wànzhōu is also called Wànxiàn (万县). You can also pick up the hydrofoil to/from Yíchāng to/from Fēngjié (Y220, hourly) and Wūshān (Y190, hourly).

Hydrofoils are passenger vessels and are not geared towards tourists, so there's no outside seating. Visibility is OK (albeit through perspex windows), but if you stand by the door you can get a good view. For those who find a day of gorge-viewing sufficient, hydrofoils are ideal, but tourist sights are skipped. Food and refreshments are served, but it's a good idea to take along your own snacks and drinks as the food is humdrum. Hydrofoils make regular but very brief stops at towns along the river for embarkation and disembarkation; check when the boat is leaving if disembarking.

Xīnjiāng

POPULATION: 20.3 MILLION

Includes »

Best Places to Eat

- » Aroma (p778)
- » May Flower (p777)
- » Altun Orda (p790)

Best Places to Stay

- » In a yurt at Tiān Chí (p781)
- » Kashgar Old Town Youth Hostel (p789)
- » Jīnzhànghán Grasslands Camp (p859)
- » Yema International Business Clubhouse (p777)

Why Go?

The old Chinese proverb 'Heaven is high and the Emperor is far away' could well have been spoken about Xīnjiāng (新疆), China's far-flung and restive western frontier. Xīnjiāng and distant Běijīng have been at odds since time immemorial, but the cultural differences between the two are just what make this province so unique for travellers. Central Asian culture is still very much alive in the Uighur homeland, from the spicy kebabs to the austere sounds of muqam and devotion to Islam. For anyone interested in an Arabian Nights adventure there is much to experience, including ghost cities, camel treks, nomad camps and spice bazaars. Equally awesome are the landscapes, ranging from the scorching Taklamakan Desert to the mighty Tiān Shān (Heaven) Mountains. Perhaps the best reason to come is the chance to experience the heart of the Silk Road, to walk in the footsteps of Marco Polo and gaze into the past of this diverse route that once served as the superhighway of the Asian continent.

When to Go

Ürümqi

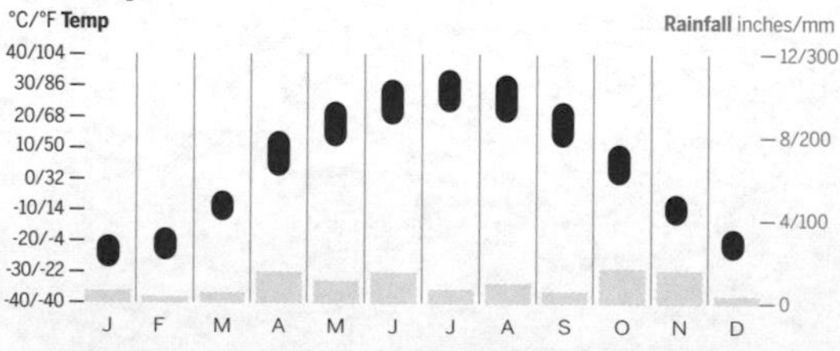

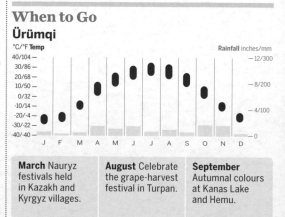

March Nauryz festivals held in Kazakh and Kyrgyz villages.

August Celebrate the grape-harvest festival in Turpan.

September Autumnal colours at Kanas Lake and Hemu.

History

By the end of the 2nd century BC the Han had pushed their borders west into what is now Xīnjiāng. Military garrisons were established along the trade routes and silk flowed out of the empire in return for strong Ferghana horses. In the 7th century the Tang dynasty reasserted the imperial rule that had been lost following the collapse of the Han, but the sway of the Tang dynasty was never absolute. The Uighurs held quite a bit of control throughout the 8th century, and the An Lushan rebellion (AD 755–63) sapped the imperial strength even more.

It was during Kharakhanid rule in the 10th to 12th centuries that Islam took hold

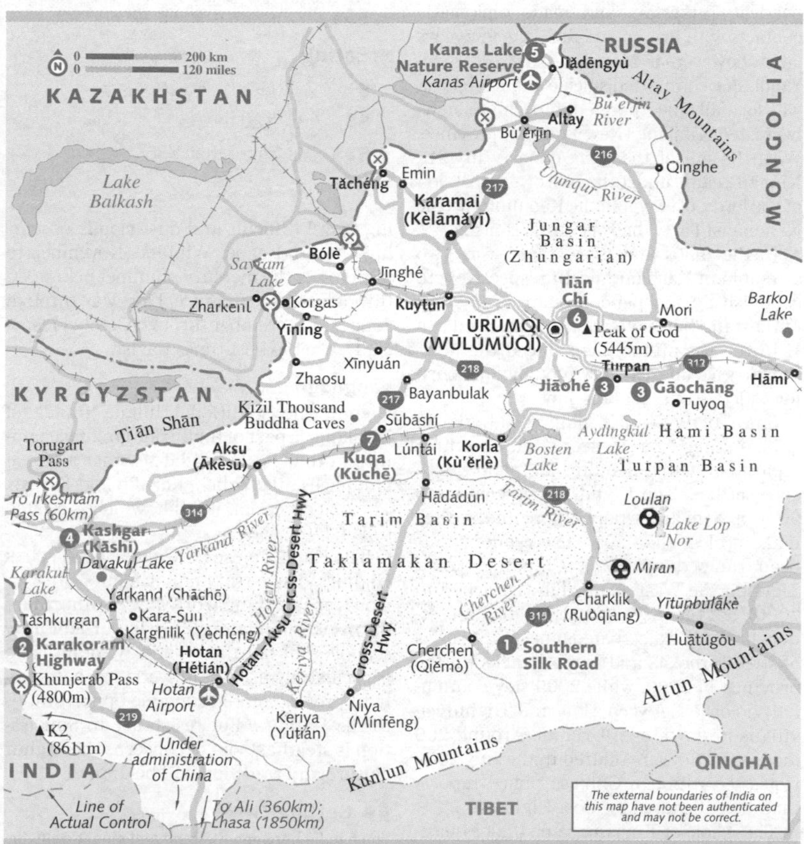

Xīnjiāng Highlights

1. Follow the route of Marco Polo and explore the **Southern Silk Road** (p794), a string of ancient cities along the fringes of the Taklamakan Desert
2. Intoxicate yourself in the dramatic high-altitude scenery of the **Karakoram Highway** (p792)
3. Explore the ancient ruined cities of **Jiāohé** (p784) and **Gāochāng** (p784), near the oasis town of Turpan
4. Haggle for a fat-tailed sheep at the Sunday livestock market in timeless **Kashgar** (p786)
5. Trekk by foot or horse over the spectacular Altai mountains from Hémù to **Kanas Lake Nature Reserve** (p799)
6. Spend a night at gorgeous **Tiān Chí** (p781), perfect for horse treks and hiking
7. Pause on the Northern Silk Road at **Kuqa** (p785), for its authentic food bazaar and nearby Kizil Thousand Buddha Caves

in Xīnjiāng. In 1219, Yīlí (Ili), Hotan and Kashgar fell to the Mongols; Timur, of Turkic origin, had control over Kashgaria in the late 14th century for a few years. Thereafter, the Mongols regained their control over the region until the mid-18th century, when the Manchu army marched into Kashgar.

In 1865 a Kokandi officer named Yaqub Beg seized Kashgaria, proclaimed an independent Turkestan, and made diplomatic contacts with Britain and Russia. A few years later, however, a Manchu army returned, Yaqub Beg committed suicide and Kashgaria was formally incorporated into China's newly created Xīnjiāng (New Frontier) province. With the fall of the Qing dynasty in 1911, Xīnjiāng came under the rule of a succession of warlords, over whom the Kuomintang (the Nationalist Party) had very little control.

In the 1930s and 1940s there were two attempts in Kashgar and Ili respectively to establish an independent state of Eastern Turkestan, but both were short-lived. In 1946 the Kuomintang convinced the Muslims to give up their new republic in return for a pledge of real autonomy.

Since 1949, China's main social goal in Xīnjiāng has been to keep a lid on ethnic separatism while flooding the region with Han settlers. The Uighurs once composed 90% of Xīnjiāng's population; today they make up less than 50%. The economy has been ramped up under China's ongoing 'Develop the West' campaign (launched in 2000), but the increased arrival of Han settlers has only exacerbated tensions. A series of street protests and bomb attacks hit the province in 2008, while 2009 saw communal violence between Han and Uighur civilians in downtown Ürümqi. Around 200 died and 1700 were injured in the July 2009 riots, according to Chinese police reports (numbers disputed by most Uighurs).

The whole of Xīnjiāng came under quasi-martial law in 2009, with thousands of Uighurs arrested; among the regulations was an internet black-out that lasted for 10 months. Armed soldiers patrolling the streets remains a fairly regular sight in Xīnjiāng.

Climate

Xīnjiāng's climate is one of extremes. Turpan is the hottest spot in the country – up to 47°C in summer (June to August), when the Tarim and Jungar Basins aren't much cooler. As daunting as the heat may seem, spring (April and May) is not a particularly good time to visit, with frequent sandstorms making travel difficult and dust clouds obscuring the landscape. Winters (November to March) see the mercury plummet below 0°C throughout the province. Late May through June and September through October (especially) are the best times to visit.

Language

Uighur, the traditional lingua franca of Xīnjiāng, is part of the Turkic language family and thus fairly similar to other regional languages, like Uzbek, Kazakh and Kyrgyz. The one exception is Tajik, which is related to Persian.

The Han Chinese in Xīnjiāng don't speak Uighur. Vice versa, many Uighurs can't, or won't, speak Mandarin. Now learning Mandarin is mandatory in Uighur-language schools (but not the other way round), and is exclusively used in universities, nominally to provide more economic opportunities to the Uighurs. But resistance to Sinicisation is steadfast, out of concerns the Uighur culture and tradition will be diluted.

PRICE INDICATORS

The following price indicators are used in this chapter:

Sleeping

$	less than Y150
$$	Y150 to Y230
$$$	more than Y230

Eating

$	less than Y20
$$	Y20 to Y35
$$$	more than Y35

Getting There & Away

You can fly between Xīnjiāng and most domestic cities, Central Asia and a couple of cities further afield, including Moscow and Tehran; for details, see p779.

There are overland border crossings with Pakistan (Khunjerab Pass), Kyrgyzstan (Irkeshtam and Torugart Passes) and Kazakhstan (Korgas, Ālāshānkǒu, Tǎchéng and Jímùnǎi). The Kulma Pass to Tajikistan may open to foreign travel in the coming years; see p793 for more.

All of these border crossings are by bus, except Ālāshānkǒu, China's only rail link to Central Asia.

Heading back into mainland China, the obvious route is the train running through Gānsù. More rugged approaches are along the southern Silk

Road from Charklik to Qīnghǎi, and Karghilik to Ali (Tibet).

Getting Around

The railway coming from Gānsù splits in two near Turpan, with one branch heading west through Ürümqi to Kazakhstan, and the other going southwest to Kashgar. Rail lines to Yīníng and Hotan should be finished by 2011 or 2012.

Buses go to the same destinations as the train and are slightly cheaper (and occasionally faster). On-board entertainment usually includes kung-fu film marathons cranked to maximum volume.

Flying around the province can save time, especially between the major cities. All flights go through Ürümqi. Bear in mind, though, that flights are sometimes cancelled for lack of passengers or due to bad weather.

CENTRAL XĪNJIĀNG

Ürümqi 乌鲁木齐

0991 / POP 2.5 MILLION

Ürümqi's two and half million residents live in a city that sprawls 20km across a fertile plain in the shadow of the Tiān Shān. High-rise apartments form a modern skyline and at ground level this city heaves with traffic, noise and all manner of commerce. Any thoughts of spotting wandering camels and ancient caravanserais will soon be dashed.

As a fast-growing Central Asian hub the city does business with clients from Běijīng to Baku and plays host to a curious mix of people, including burly Russian traders, Han migrants and wispy-bearded Uighurs trying to make sense of it all.

Ürümqi is not a historic city, but there is still plenty to see and do; the provincial museum is excellent and there is a lively Uighur quarter with a colourful market and mosque. Many travellers end up hanging around for either a Kazakh or Kyrgyz visa. If you're killing time, consider a side trip to Tiān Chí or Turpan, or possibly both.

Sights & Activities

FREE Xīnjiāng Autonomous Region Museum MUSEUM
(新疆自治区博物馆; Xīnjiāng Zìzhìqū Bówùguǎn; 132 Xibei Lu; 10am-6pm Tue-Sun) The massive Xīnjiāng Autonomous Region Museum, with 10 halls, is a must for Silk Road aficionados. The highlight is the locally famous 'Loulan Beauty' of Indo-European ancestry, one of the desert-mummified bodies that became a Uighur independence symbol in the 1990s. Other exhibits include Buddhist frescoes from the Kizil Thousand Buddha Caves (p786) and an introduction to all of the province's minorities. From the Hongshan intersection, take bus 7 for four stops and ask to get off at the museum *(bówùguǎn)*.

Èrdàoqiáo Market & International Bazaar BAZAAR
The Uighur market, Èrdàoqiáo Market (Èrdàoqiáo Shìchǎng), and the International Bazaar (Guójì Dàbāzhá), have undergone extensive 'redevelopment' in recent years. The carpenters and blacksmiths that once worked in the nearby alleys have all but vanished and the target customers are no longer Uighur traders but Chinese tour groups, who arrive in droves. Planted in the bazaar is a replica of the Bukhara Minaret in Uzbekistan. This one, of course, has an **elevator** (Y20) to the top. The area is bursting with restaurants, snack stalls and souvenir stands, plus the odd camel brought in for tourist photos. The non-traditional has also arrived in the form of a KFC and Carrefour supermarket. It's worth visiting at night when the entire complex is bathed in bright lights and neon.

Hóngshān Swimming Pool SWIMMING POOL
(红山游泳池; Hóngshān Yóuyǒngchí; 214 Binhe Nanlu; admission Y10; 10.30am-9.30pm) Beat the summer heat at this pool, located behind the Parkson Shopping Mall. Men are not allowed to wear baggy swimsuits; you have to don the skimpy spandex variety favoured by Chinese swimmers. Shops selling bathing suits are located around the corner.

People's Park PARK
(Rénmín Gōngyuán; admission Y5; 7.30am-dusk) A green oasis. Has north and south entrances.

Hóngshān Park PARK
(Hóngshān Gōngyuán; admission Y10; dawn-dusk) More of an amusement park, with better views than People's Park. Also has north and south entrances.

Sleeping

Xīnjiāng Màitián International Youth Hostel HOSTEL $
(麦田国际青年旅舍; Xīnjiāng Màitián Guójì Qīngnián Lǚshè; 459 1488; www.xjmaitian.com; 726 Youhao Nanlu; 友好南路726号; dm/r Y40/150; @) Behind the Parkson Shopping Mall (Yǒuhǎo Bǎishèng Gòuwùzhōngxīn),

Ürümqi

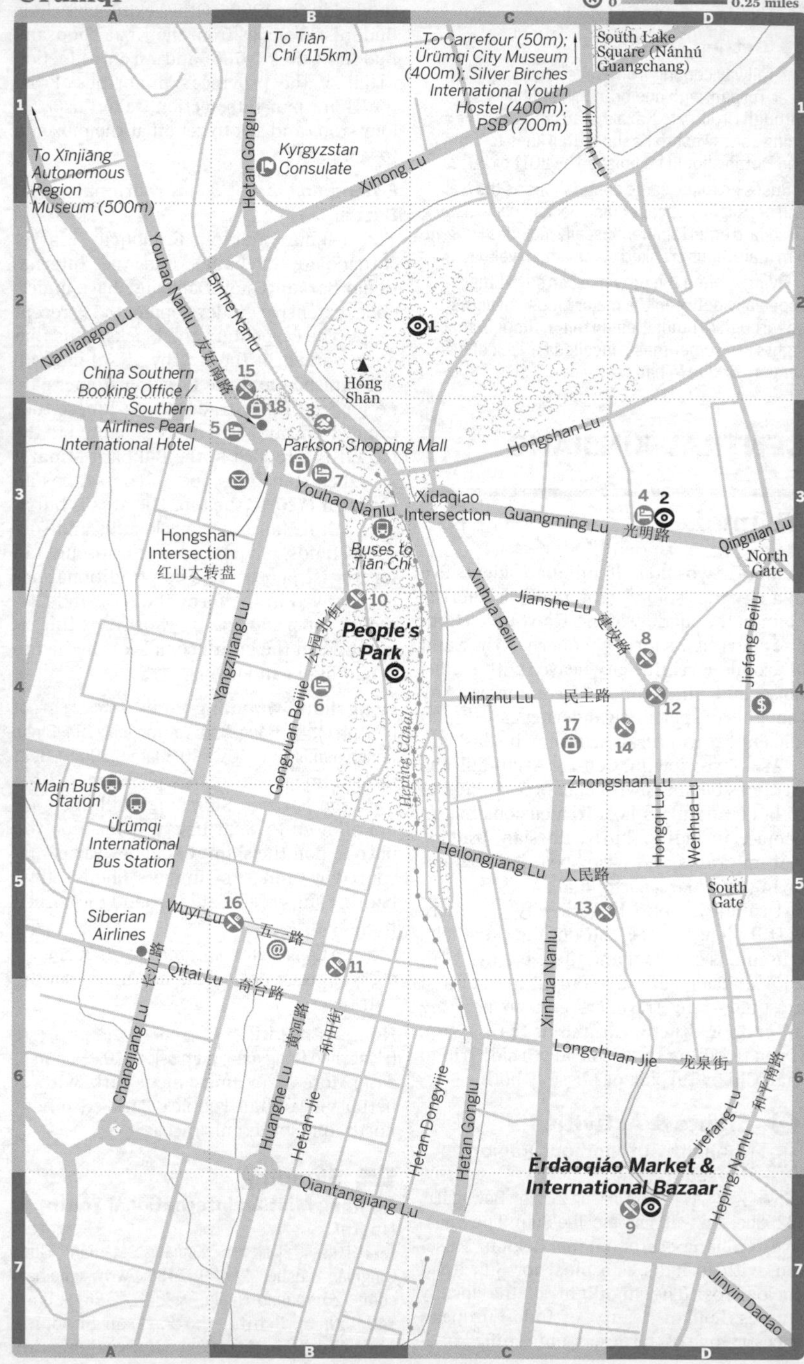

0 500 m
0 0.25 miles
To Tiān Chí (115km)
To Carrefour (50m); Ürümqi City Museum (400m); Silver Birches International Youth Hostel (400m); PSB (700m)
South Lake Square (Nánhú Guangchang)
To Xīnjiāng Autonomous Region Museum (500m)
Kyrgyzstan Consulate
Hetan Gonglu
Xihong Lu
Xinmin Lu
Youhao Nanlu
Binhe Nanlu
Nanliangpo Lu
Hóng Shān
China Southern Booking Office / Southern Airlines Pearl International Hotel
Parkson Shopping Mall
Hongshan Lu
Xidaqiao Intersection
Guangming Lu 光明路
Qingnian Lu
North Gate
Hongshan Intersection 红山大转盘
Buses to Tiān Chí
Jianshe Lu 建设路
People's Park
Yangzijiang Lu
Gongyuan Beijie 公园北街
Xinhua Beilu
Minzhu Lu 民主路
Jiefang Beilu
Heping Canal
Zhongshan Lu
Hongqi Lu
Wenhua Lu
Main Bus Station
Ürümqi International Bus Station
Heilongjiang Lu 人民路
South Gate
Siberian Airlines
Wuyi Lu 五一路
Qitai Lu 奇台路
长江路
Xinhua Nanlu
Longchuan Jie 龙泉街
黄河路
和田街
Changjiang Lu
Huanghe Lu
Hetian Jie
Hetan Dongyijie
Hetan Gonglu
Jiefang Lu
和平南路
Heping Nanlu
Èrdàoqiáo Market & International Bazaar
Qiantangjiang Lu
Jinyin Dadao

Ürümqi

Top Sights

Èrdàoqiáo Market & International Bazaar D7
People's Park B4

Sights

1 Hóngshān Park C2
2 Western International Travel Service D3

Activities, Courses & Tours

3 Hóngshān Swimming Pool B3

Sleeping

4 Bógédá Bīnguǎn D3
5 Pea Fowl Mansions B3
6 Sùbā Jiǔdiàn B4
7 Xīnjiāng Màitián International Youth Hostel B3

Eating

8 Aroma D4
9 Carrefour D7
10 Fubar B4
11 May Flower B5
12 Rénmín Dìanyǐng Yuàn D4
13 Texas Cafe C5
14 Vine Coffeehouse D4
15 Wúshàng Vegetarian Restaurant B2
16 Wǔyī Night Market B5

Shopping

17 Foreign Languages Bookshop C4
18 Outdoor Gear B3

centrally located Màitián has doubles and dorms, some with private bathrooms. The shared bathrooms and the lounge are pretty grotty, but the rooms do get a regular cleaning. It's a popular option in this price range and you may need to book ahead.

Silver Birches International Youth Hostel HOSTEL $
(白桦林国际青年旅舍; Báihuàlín Guójì Qīngnián Lǚshè; ☎481 1428; www.yhaxinjiang.com; 186 Nanhu Nanlu; 南湖南路186号; dm/tw Y45/120; @) The English-speaking staff at this hostel are very friendly and can help organise trips and onward transport. On the downside, the hostel itself is dark and poorly maintained. It's not in the centre but does have a peaceful location near a park and night market. From Rénmín Guǎngchǎng you can take bus 104 and get off at South Lake Sq (Nánhú Guǎngchǎng).

Pea Fowl Mansions HOTEL $$
(孔雀大厦; Kǒngquè Dàshà; ☎452 2988; 489 Youhao Nanlu; 友好南路489号; tw from Y288, discounts of 40%; ❄) If you can overlook the peeling paint, loose wallpaper and generally scruffy appearance this is an OK place to stay in the city centre. Big discounts are usually available. It's right by Hongshan intersection, the drop-off point for airport buses.

Bógédá Bīnguǎn HOTEL $$$
(博格达宾馆; ☎886 3910; fax 886 5769; 253 Guangming Lu; 光明路253号; tw Y388, low-season discounts of 40%; ❄@) This hotel has a fairly drab facade, but the interior has been remodelled in a tasteful fashion, with marble floors, jade sculptures and Chinese art hanging from the walls. Rooms are well maintained and have excellent bathrooms. The travel agency here (Western International Travel Service, p779) comes recommended.

Yema International Business Clubhouse HOTEL $$$
(Yěmǎ Gúojì Shāngwù Huìguǎn; 野马国际商务会馆; ☎768 8888; www.xyyema.com; 158 Kunming Lu; 昆明路158号; d incl breakfast Y298-698; ❄@) This elegant high-rise hotel has a sauna, cafe, art gallery, wine bar and restaurant. It even has its own zoo with rare animals including Przewalski horses (wild horses indigenous to Central Asia). There are a range of rooms, from less expensive doubles in an annexe to larger rooms in the main tower. The hotel is located north of the city, next to the Kazakhstan embassy.

Sùbā Jiǔdiàn HOTEL $$$
(速8酒店; Super 8 Hotel; ☎559 0666; www.super8.com.cn; 140 Gongyuan Beijie; 公园北街140号; tw incl breakfast Y218-308; ❄🛜) Quietly located behind People's Park, this chain hotel has nothing surprising, but it represents good value with its ultra-neat rooms and free breakfast.

Eating & Drinking

Ürümqi's dining scene is surprisingly cosmopolitan. Regional Chinese cuisine is good here; Jianshe Lu has the largest selection of restaurants, ranging from Uighur staples to affordable Korean. During July and August markets are awash in fresh fruit.

TOP CHOICE **May Flower** UIGHUR $$$
(五月花; Wǔyuèhuā; cnr Wuyi Lu & Hetian Jie; meals Y25-55; ⏲11am-midnight) From the delicious Uighur cuisine to the pleasant faux-courtyard setting, May Flower is a feast for the senses. Try the speciality, *polo*

WHICH TIME IS IT?

Making an appointment in Xīnjiāng is not just a matter of asking what time, but inevitably ends with a strange but required question – 'which time?' All of China officially runs on Běijīng time (*Běijīng shíjiān*). Xīnjiāng, several time zones removed from Běijīng, however, runs duelling clocks: while the Chinese tend to stick to the official Běijīng time, the ethnic minorities set their clocks to unofficial Xīnjiāng time (*Xīnjiāng shíjiān*), two hours behind Běijīng time. Thus 9am Běijīng time is 7am Xīnjiāng time. Most government-run services, such as the bank, post office, bus station and airlines, run on Běijīng time. To cater to the time difference, government offices and other institutions generally operate from 10am to 1.30pm and from 4pm to 8pm. Unless otherwise stated, we use Běijīng time in this chapter.

(rice pilaf; *zhuāfàn*), along with a few sticks of shish kebab and a glass of pomegranate juice, then sit back and enjoy the traditional live music (8pm).

Aroma MALTESE **$$$**
(啊诺玛西餐厅; Ānuòmǎ Xīcāntīng; 196 Jianshe Lu; meals Y35-65; ⌚noon-midnight) A Maltese chef who somehow washed up in Ürümqi runs this delectable restaurant. Pizzas, pastas, risotto and steaks are on the menu – everything is made to perfection. It's opposite the Laiyuan Hotel.

Vine Coffeehouse CARIBBEAN **$$$**
(德曼咖啡屋; Démàn Kāfēiwū; 65 Minzhu Lu; meals Y25-50; ⌚1.30-11.30pm, closed Mon; ⊖) Run by the friendly Arlette from Curaçao, this fine cafe brings you savoury West Indian cuisine in a Caribbean atmosphere. Dishes are flavourful and the chocolate cake is divine, but portions are a tad small. It's down a side street on the left.

Fubar PUB GRUB **$$$**
(福吧; Fúbā; www.fubarchina.com; 40 Gongyuan Beijie; meal & beer Y35-65; ⌚11am-2am; ☎) Fubar is run by two expats, an Irishman and a Japanese-American; both are happy to pull a pint for bedraggled Silk Road travellers. The menu consists of classic pub grub, with tasty pizzas, burgers and frothy glasses of imported beer (Y35 to Y50). Young expat teachers and volunteers congregate here, making this a good place to get information on activities around Ürümqi.

Texas Cafe TEX-MEX **$$**
(德克萨斯西餐厅; Dékèsàsī Xīcāntīng; Mashi Xiao Qiu; meals Y30-60; ⌚1.30-11.30pm, closed Mon) This cowboy-themed place serves great Tex-Mex treats including nachos, fajitas, burritos and steaks. It's located on a little alley known locally as Grape St (Pútáo Chánglàng; 葡萄长廊). The owner is a native Texan, so you know it's authentic.

Wúshàng Vegetarian Restaurant VEGETARIAN **$**
(无尚素食府; Wúshàng Sùshífǔ; Youhao Lu; dishes from Y15; ⌚11am-9.30pm; ✎) This vegetarian Chinese restaurant has a popular local following. Try the sautéed broccoli (*xī lán huā*) or tofu noodles (*hóngyóu dòufupí*). From the China Southern Airlines office walk north for two minutes and make a right turn after the Outdoor Gear shop down a little alley; pass a gate and look for the orange sign on the right.

The animated night markets with shish kebabs and handmade noodles are also worth a gander. The most thriving by far is the **Wǔyī night market** (Wǔyī Li); bus 51 from Hongshan intersection to south bus station stops at its entrance on Changjiang Lu. (Tell the driver *'Wǔyī yèshì'*.) Another great outdoor market is located at **Rénmín Diànyǐng Yuàn** (人民电影院).

In Èrdàoqiáo Market and near Silver Birches International Youth Hostel are Carrefour (加乐福; *Jiālèfú*) centres – great for fresh fruit; both have cafeterias for tasty freshly made (and cheap) food.

Shopping

Foreign Languages Bookshop BOOKS
(外文书店; Wàiwén Shūdiàn; Xinhua Beilu; ⌚10.30am-8pm) Just south of Minzhu Lu.

Outdoor Gear OUTDOOR EQUIPMENT
(☎450 8611; 70 Youhao Nanlu) Sells tents, sleeping bags, stoves and gas canisters. Also rents sleeping bags (Y10 per night) and tents (Y25 per night).

Information

Bank of China (中国银行; Zhōngguó Yínháng; cnr Jiefang Beilu & Dongfeng Lu; ⌚9.30am-7pm Mon-Fri, 11am-5pm Sat & Sun) Can handle most transactions and has an ATM (and at other branches).

UIGHUR FOOD

Uighur cuisine includes all the trusty Central Asian standbys, such as kebabs, *polo* and *chuchura* (dumplings), but has benefited from Chinese influence to make it the most enjoyable region of Central Asia in which to eat.

Uighurs boast endless varieties of *laghman* (pulled noodles; *lāmiàn* in Chinese), though the usual topping is a combination of mutton, peppers, tomatoes, eggplant and garlic shoots. *Suoman* are noodles fried with tomatoes, peppers, garlic and meat. *Suoman gush siz* are the vegetarian variety. *Suoman* can be quite spicy, so ask for *laza siz* (without peppers) if you prefer a milder version.

Kebabs are another staple and are generally of a much better standard than the ropey *kawaps* of the Central Asian republics. *Jiger* (liver) kebabs are the low-fat variety. *Tonor* kebabs are larger and baked in an oven *tonor* – tandoori style.

Nan (breads) are a particular speciality, especially when straight out of the oven and sprinkled with poppy seeds, sesame seeds or fennel. They make a great plate for a round of kebabs.

Other snacks include *serik ash* (yellow, meatless noodles), *nokot* (chickpeas), *pintang* (meat and vegetable soup) and *gang pan* (rice with vegetables and meat). Most travellers understandably steer clear of *opke*, a broth of bobbing goat's heads and coiled, stuffed intestines.

Samsas (baked mutton dumplings) are available everywhere, but the meat-to-fat ratio varies wildly. Hotan and Kashgar offer huge meat pies called *daman* or *gosh girde*.

For dessert try *morozhenoe* (vanilla ice cream churned in iced wooden barrels), *matang* (walnut fruit loaf), *kharsen meghriz* (fried dough balls filled with sugar, raisins and walnuts) or *dogh* (sometimes known as *doghap*), a delicious mix of shaved ice, syrup, yoghurt and iced water. As with all ice-based food, try the latter with caution. *Tangzaza* are triangles of glutinous rice wrapped in bamboo leaves covered in syrup. Damn good stuff.

Xīnjiāng is justly famous for its fruit, whether it be *uruk* (apricots), *uzum* (grapes), *tawuz* (watermelon), *khoghun* (sweet melon) or *yimish* (raisins). The best grapes come from Turpan; the sweetest melons from Hāmì.

Meals are washed down with *kok chai* (green tea), often laced with nutmeg or rose petals.

China International Travel Service (CITS; 中国国际旅行社; Zhōngguó Guójì Lǚxíngshè; ☎282 1428; www.xinjiangtour.com; 33 Renmin Lu; ⊙10am-7.30pm Mon-Fri) This office runs standard tours around the province and can supply a driver and English-speaking guide.

China Post (中国邮政; Zhōngguó Yóuzhèng; Hongshan intersection; ⊙9.30am-8.30pm) The main branch handles all international parcels.

Join Internet Cafe (聚异网吧; Jùyì Wǎngbā; 190 Wuyi Lu; per hr Y2; ⊙24hr)

Public Security Bureau (PSB; 公安局; Gōng'ānjú; ☎281 0452, ext 3456; Kelamayi Donglu; ⊙10am-1.30pm & 4-6pm Mon-Fri) Not much hassle renewing visas here.

Western International Travel Service (大西部国际旅行社; Dàxībù Gúojì Lǚxíngshè; ☎885 0256; Bógédá Bīnguǎn, 253 Guangming Lu) This agency has the best rates around for trips to Kanas Lake. It can also secure cheap airline tickets.

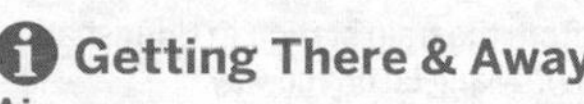

Getting There & Away

Air

International flights include Almaty (Kazakhstan), Bishkek and Osh (Kyrgyzstan), Baku (Azerbaijan), Istanbul (Turkey), Islamabad (Pakistan), Moscow (Russia), Dushanbe (Tajikistan), Tashkent (Uzbekistan), Khovd (Mongolia) and Tehran (Iran). Some of these are seasonal and many are suspended for no real reason. New international flights are constantly being proposed but not always realised.

There are four primary international airline offices in town:

AeroMongolia [☎15022923901; www.aeromongolia.mn) Has a weekly flight to Khovd (Mongolia) on Thursdays, one way fare is US$173. The flight continues to Ulaanbaatar on the same day. There is no office but they do have a representative at the airport. This flight is new and definitely subject to change.

Azerbaijan Airlines (☎258 3526; 876 Dawan Beilu) Also southeast of town in the Xī Yù Bīnguǎn, room 526, in the older block.

Kyrgyzstan Airlines (☎582 8061; 876 Dawan Beilu) Southeast of town in the Xī Yù Bīnguǎn (西域宾馆), room 215.

Siberian Airlines (☎286 2326; Changjiang Lu) In the Ramada Inn.

CAAC (Zhōngguó Mínháng; ☎464 7188; 133 Nanhu Nanlu) has a booking office in the ChengJian Mansion, right across the street from Silver Birches International Youth Hostel. It flies to Běijīng (Y1050), Chéngdū (1110) and Chóngqìng (Y940).

China Southern (Nánfāng Hángkōng Shòupiàochù; ☎95539; 576 Youhao Nanlu) has a booking office in the Southern Airlines Pearl International Hotel. It flies to Lánzhōu (Y1690), Guǎngzhōu (Y2220) and Shànghǎi (Y2150), among other destinations.

Destinations within Xīnjiāng include Altay (Ālètài), Hotan (Hétián), Kashgar (Kāshí), Kuqa (Kùchē), Tǎchéng and Yīníng.

Bus

Two long-distance bus stations in Ürümqi serve northern and southern destinations. The **main bus station** (碾子沟汽车站; niǎnzigōu chángtú qìchēzhàn; Heilongjiang Lu) has sleeper buses to:

Bù'ěrjīn Y150 to Y160, 13 hours, two daily (11.15am and 8.10pm)

Tǎchéng Y142 to Y152, 11 to 12 hours, five daily (10am, 11am, noon, 6.20pm and 7.50pm)

Yīníng Y160 to Y170, 11 to 14 hours, almost hourly (9am to 9pm)

Bus 2 runs from the train station to Hongshan, passing Heilongjiang Lu on the way.

The **south bus station** *(nánjiāo kèyùnzhàn)* has frequent departures for:

Turpan Y41, 2½ hours

Kuqa Y135 to Y185, 11 to 14 hours

Kashgar Y220 to Y235, 24 hours

Hotan Y255 to Y360, 20 to 26 hours, crossing the Taklamakan Desert. For the fastest journey, ask for the express bus (*tèkuài chē;* 特快车).

There is also a once-daily bus that travels to Cherchen (Y246 to Y269) on the southern Silk Road, via Korla (Y185 to Y202), departing at 7pm.

Bus 1 runs between Xīdàqiáo and the south bus station, bus 109 will get you there from Hongshan intersection, and bus 104 will get you here from the South Lake Square.

Train

The province is building several new rail lines. Numerous trains serve Lánzhōu; the T296 is the best choice. There is a **train booking office** (huǒchē shòupiàochù; 77 Xinmin Lu; commission Y5; ⌚7.30am-9pm) in the city centre. Destinations (hard/soft sleeper):

Běijīng (T70) Y652/1006, 42 hours, one daily (8.03pm)

Chéngdū (K454) Y552/854, 49 hours, one daily (2.05pm)

Kashgar (K9786) Y345/529, 24 hours, one daily (10am)

Kuqa (5806) Y126/211, 15 hours, one daily (10.12pm)

Lánzhōu (T296) Y390/600, 21 hours, one daily (3pm)

Shànghǎi (T54) Y699/1079, 44 hours, one daily (5.20pm)

Yīníng (5815) Y151/234, 11 hours, one daily (9.10pm)

BORDER CROSSING: GETTING TO KAZAKHSTAN

If you have a Kazakhstan visa, you can go to Almaty (upper/lower bunk Y400/420, 24 hours) in Kazakhstan via Korgas by buses departing from Ürümqi International bus station (☎587 8637; Wūlǔmùqí Guójì yùnshū qìchēzhàn), behind the main bus station. There are departures at 5pm every day except Saturday. A longer but more pleasant trip would be to travel to Almaty via Yīníng.

Trains currently depart Ürümqi twice weekly for Almaty, Kazakhstan (via Ālāshānkǒu) on Monday and Saturday at midnight. The journey takes a slow 32 hours, six of which are spent at Chinese and Kazakh customs. Tickets start at around Y850 and can only be purchased in the lobby of the Xiāngyǒu Jiǔdiàn (next to the train station), at the **booking office** (往阿拉木图火车票售票处; Huǒchēpiào Shòupiàochù; ⌚10am-1pm & 3.30-6pm Sat, Mon, Wed & Thu). You will need to already have a Kazakhstan visa.

A new rail line to Yīníng opened in 2010. Another line to Altay is under construction.

At the time of writing you could get a 30-day visitor visa at the Kazakhstan consulate (see p987) for about Y140. The visa takes five days to be issued. The Kazakhs are notorious for changing their visa requirements.

Yīníng (K9789) Y162/245, 10½ hours, one daily (22.54pm)

Xī'ān (1044) Y287/494, 34 hours, one daily (11.46pm)

Getting Around

The airport is 16km from the Hongshan intersection; a taxi costs about Y40. An airport bus (Y10) runs straight south through town to the train station. In the city centre, an airport shuttle (Y10, free for China Southern passengers) leaves from the Southern Airlines Pearl International Hotel hourly from 6am to 10pm. You'll need to arrive 15 minutes early to catch the shuttle.

Useful buses (Y1) include bus 7, which runs up Xinhua Lu through the Xidaqiao and Hongshan intersections, linking the city centre with the main post office; and bus 2, which runs from the train station through the Hongshan intersection and way up along Beijing Lu. Buses 1 and 51 go from the south bus station to Xidaqiao and Hongshan intersections respectively, and the latter continues to its last stop 2km south of the airport terminal. Bus 8 runs from the train station along Heilongjiang Lu to the Minzhu Lu traffic circle.

Giant Bike Shop (Jíe'āntè Zìxíngchē Háng; ☎888 9917; 415 Xinmen Lu), about 200m south of Xinmen Jie, near Huangda Guangchang bus stop, sells bike parts and rents bikes for Y30 to Y60 per day.

Tiān Chí 天池

Two thousand metres up in the Tiān Shān range is **Tiān Chí** (Heaven Lake, admission Y100), a small, long, steely-blue lake nestled below the view-grabbing 5445m Peak of God (Bógédá Fēng). Scattered across the spruce-covered slopes are Kazakh yurts and lots of sheep. It was a paradise described in Vikram Seth's wonderful travelogue *From Heaven Lake,* but it's a bit overhyped now; multitudinous tourists and excessive facilities make the lake area no longer heavenly. Despite this, plenty of backcountry is still out here.

Horse treks offer some stunning views of the Tiān Shān range. The horse guides will find you once you arrive at the lake. Treks can also be organised at the yurt camps. From the top of the cable car, paths lead further into the mountains; one hike is 9.3km and the other is 7.9km (signs point the way).

Regardless of the temperature in Ürümqi, take warm clothes and rain gear, as the weather can be unpredictable. For information on hiking in the Tiān Shān range, contact the **Xiǎo Yáng Jǔntuán hiking group** (小羊军团; ☎0991-460 7239), or the group organiser **Fei Fei** (☎139 9994 2887). The group has tents and sleeping bags for hire. You may also be able to join one of their trips into the mountains (usually on weekends in summer).

In late May Kazakhs set up yurts around the lake for tourists (Y50 per person with three meals); **Rashit** (☎138 9964 1550; www.rashityurt.com) is the most popular host for backpackers. The yurts near the ticket office also take boarders (Y50 without meals). Alternatively, you can camp here. It's best to bring food as there is not much in the area. The yurt owners sometimes require ID, so make sure to bring your passport.

Tourist buses to the Tiān Chí car park leave Ürümqi from 9am to 9.30am from the north gate of People's Park and return between 5pm and 6pm. Most stop at the hotels (including Silver Birches) to pick up passengers before leaving town. In the low season they may not run at all. The return fare is Y50 and the trip takes about 2½ hours. The drivers may charge the full fare even if you are just taking the bus one way. Note that the tourist bus stops at a number of tourist bazaars and breaks 1½ hours for lunch; you can avoid this by going on public transport. From the northern bus station take a bus to Fūkāng (阜康) for Y15, then switch to a bus or share taxi (Y16) to the lake.

From the car park, there's a chairlift (Y35 return) or bus (Y35 return), but it's best to take the 45-minute hike to the lake. The path starts left of the chairlift. There are actually two paths, so you can take one up and the other down.

Turpan 吐鲁番

☎0995 / POP 57,900

Turpan is the Death Valley of China. In July and August temperatures soar to 40°C and force the local population into a state of semi-torpor. At 154m below sea level, it's the second-lowest depression in the world and the hottest spot in China – the highest recorded temperature here was 49.6°C!

But just as the heat seems to make life unbearable, the ground water and fertile soil of the Turpan depression make this a veritable oasis in the desert. The remains of several ancient cities in the area prove that humans discovered this fact long ago. The ruins plus some quaint villages, mosques and desert scenery make the visit worthwhile.

Turpan

Top Sights

Turpan Museum B2

Sleeping

1 Dōngfāng Jiǔdiàn A2
2 Jiāotōng Bīnguǎn A2
3 Tǔlǔfān Bīnguǎn B2
4 Xīzhōu Dàjiǔdiàn B1

Eating

5 Bazaar A2
John's Information Café .... (see 3)

Transport

Bicycle Rental .... (see 3)
6 Long-Distance Bus Station A2

While the surrounding sights are unique, the modern town of Turpan is a fairly recent creation and of little interest to travellers. Most of your time will likely be spent touring the surrounding sights.

History

Settlements in the Turpan Basin predate the Han dynasty; the inhabitants have ranged from Indo-Europeans (possibly Tocharians related to the mummies in Ürümqi's museum) to the Chinese and Uighurs.

In the mid-9th century the ancestors of the Uighurs were forced from their homeland in Mongolia, with one group eventually settling in Gāochāng (Khocho). The city was the Uighur capital until 1250, and saw the Uighurs transform from nomads to farmers, and from Manicheans to Buddhists and eventually Muslims.

Sights

Emin Minaret MINARET

(额敏塔; Émǐn Tǎ; admission Y30; dawn-dusk) Emin Hoja, a Turpan general, founded this splendid Afghan-style structure in 1777. Also known as Sūgōng Tǎ, its 15 simple brick motifs, including flowers and waves, leap from the structure. Unfortunately, the minaret is closed. Unless you have a burning desire to get up close, it's possible to snap a photograph of the minaret from the entrance without paying the admission fee.

Biking or strolling the 3km to get there is half the fun, the dusty, tree-lined streets an evocative – and fascinating – glimpse into 'old' Turpan. If the heat is too much, hop on bus 6 from the corner of Gaochang Lu and Laocheng Lu.

FREE **Turpan Museum** MUSEUM

(吐鲁番博物馆; Tǔlǔfān Bówùguǎn; Laocheng Lu; 10.30am-7pm) Touted as the 'second-largest museum in Xīnjiāng' (the first is in Ürümqi), the museum houses a bountiful collection of relics found at archaeological sites in the Turpan Basin, as well as a hall of dinosaur fossils. Pop in here before signing up for a tour; the photos of nearby sites might help you decide what you'd like to visit.

City Mosque MOSQUE

There are several mosques in town. The most active of them, City Mosque (清真寺; Qīngzhēn Sì), is on the western outskirts about 3km from the town centre.

Sleeping

Tǔlǔfān Bīnguǎn HOTEL $

(吐鲁番宾馆; 856 8888; tlfbg@126.com; 2 Qingnian Nanlu; 青年南路2号; dm Y50, d incl breakfast Y280, discounts of 30%;) The white-tile exterior of the Turpan Hotel is uninspiring, but things improve when you enter the quaint lobby, decorated with colourful Uighur motifs. The small dorm rooms are grotty and dark. The private doubles are clean and decent value. The swimming pool was closed when we visited.

Dōngfāng Jiǔdiàn HOTEL $

(东方酒店; 626 8228; 324 Laocheng Lu; 老城路324号; d/tr Y200/260, discounts of 50%;) This place has a clean, air-conditioned lobby, but the rooms upstairs are a little old and musty. Mattresses are rock hard and the smell of smoke is pervasive. Still, you'll have a hard time finding a cheaper room and they are better than the dorms at the Tǔlǔfān Bīnguǎn.

Xīzhōu Dàjiǔdiàn HOTEL $$$
(西州大酒店; ☎855 4000; 882 Qingnian Beilu; 青年北路882号; tw incl breakfast Y480, discounts of 40%; ❄@) The Xīzhōu is a clean and friendly three-star option with an ugly pink-and-white exterior. Some rooms have internet-enabled computers.

Jiāotōng Bīnguǎn HOTEL $
(交通宾馆; ☎853 1320; 125 Laocheng Lu; 老城路125号; ❄) This place was under renovation at the time of research but might be worth checking out. It's next to the bus station.

Eating

Head to the food court at the **bazaar** *(shìchǎng)* for Uighur cooking, though finding the stalls – not the handful on the main alley – requires a bit of patience. The fresh 'pull noodles' *(sozoup laghman)* are excellent.

In addition to the lively market surrounding Public Sq, dinner choices include a string of restaurants that set up tables under the trees on Qingnian Lu. *Laghman* and Chinese dishes cost Y5 to Y10.

John's Information Café RESTAURANT $
(☎150 2626 8966; Qingnian Nanlu; dishes from Y10; ⏲7am-10pm; @📋) This place has a quiet location in the backyard of the Tǔlǔfān Bīnguǎn. Western and Chinese meals are offered, but there is a fair amount of crossover – the pasta we ordered was filled with Chinese spices, peppers and chillies. The ice-cream sundae was a treat in Tupan's blistering heat. The name is somewhat misleading as there is little in the way of traveller information.

Information

Bank of China (中国银行; Zhōngguó Yínháng; Laocheng Lu; ⏲9.30am-12.30pm & 4.30-7.30pm) Can change cash and travellers cheques.

China Post (中国邮政; Zhōngguó Yóuzhèng; Laocheng Lu; ⏲10am-8pm) West of the Bank of China.

Internet cafe (网吧; wǎngbā; Gaochang Lu; per hr Y2) On the west side of Public Sq, near the food stalls.

Public Security Bureau (PSB;公安局; Gōng'ānjú; Gaochang Lu) North of the city centre; will likely refer you to the capital.

Getting There & Away

The nearest train station is at Dàhéyán (大河沿), 54km north of Turpan. You can buy tickets in Turpan at the **train booking office** (火车售票处; huǒchē shòupiàochù; Laocheng Lu, opposite Dongfang Jiudian; commission Y5; ⏲7.30am-9pm), located inside a China Mobile office.

From the **long-distance bus station** (长途汽车站; Chángtú Qìchēzhàn; Laocheng Lu), minibuses to Dàhéyán (Y7.5, one hour) run approximately every 30 minutes between 8.30am and 8pm. The last bus tends to sell out, so buy your ticket early. If you miss the bus, shared taxis run to Dàhéyán (per person Y15) from a lot behind the bus station.

Buses to Ürümqi (Y41, 2½ hours) run every 20 minutes between 7.30am and 8.30pm. There is one daily bus at 1pm to Kashgar (Y206, 22 hours) via Kuqa (Y118, 13 hours). A bus to Hāmì (Y70, seven hours) departs at 10.30am; it continues to Dūnhuáng (Y140, 12 to 14 hours) in Gānsù.

Getting Around

Public transport around Turpan is by taxi, minibus or bicycle. Bicycles (about Y5 per hour), available from John's Information Café, are most convenient for the town itself.

Around Turpan

Some of Turpan's surrounding sights are fascinating and others are a waste of time. Turpan's long-distance bus station has buses going to some of the spots, but it doesn't save you much. The easiest way to see them is on a custom tour – local drivers *will* find you and you can choose what you want to see. For four people, figure on paying Y50 to Y70 per person.

You can bypass the **Astana Graves** (阿斯塔那古墓区; Āsītǎnà Gǔmùqū; admission Y20) and the **Bezeklik Caves** (柏孜克里克千佛洞; Bózīkèlǐkè Qiānfó Dòng; admission Y20), both essentially empty. The latter is famous for having many of its distinctive murals cut out of the rock face by German archaeologists in 1905. Some buses stop at **Grape Valley** (葡萄沟; Pútáo Gōu; admission Y60) for lunch, but besides the September harvest – when it's spectacular – it's underwhelming.

Two possible additions to tours include a **karez** (坎儿井; kǎn'ērjǐng; admission Y40), a type of underground aqueduct particular to Central Asia – and **Aydingkul Lake** (艾丁湖; Àidīng Hú; admission Y10), the second-lowest lake in the world. Be forewarned that it's more of a muddy, salt-encrusted flat than a lake.

You'll be gone for the day, so don't underestimate the desert sun. Hot – damn hot. Essential survival gear includes a water bottle, sunscreen, sunglasses and a hat.

TUYOQ 吐峪沟

Set in a green valley fringed by the Flaming Mountains, the mud-constructed village **Tuyoq** (Tǔyùgōu; admission Y30) offers a glimpse at 'traditional' Uighur life and architecture (traditional as long as you overlook the entry fee and gate). Tuyoq has been a pilgrimage site for Muslims for centuries, and the devout claim that seven trips here equal one trip to Mecca. On the hillside above the village (near the road) is the *mazar*, or symbolic **tomb** (admission Y20) of the first Uighur Muslim. Though damaged in the Cultural Revolution, it's still the object of pilgrimage. Don't leave town without trying some of the locally produced chilled mulberry juice (Y10 per bottle), available near the tomb entrance.

Up the gorge is a series of Buddhist caves dating back to the 3rd century AD. These were closed at the time of research, due to instability of the walls.

Tuyoq is often looped into a tour with the Flaming Mountains and Bezeklik Caves.

JIĀOHÉ RUINS 交河故城

Also called Yarkhoto, **Jiāohé** (admission Y40) was established by the Chinese as a garrison town during the Han dynasty. It's one of the world's largest (6500 residents lived here), oldest and best-preserved ancient cities. A main road cuts through the city; at the end is a large monastery with Buddhist figures still visible.

The ruins (Jiāohé Gùchéng) are 8km west of Turpan. About 1km before the ruins on the right is the **Uighur Old Village** (维吾尔古村; Wéiwú'ěr Gǔcūn; admission Y35) that describes traditional life of the Uighur people in the Turpan Desert. It's well worth visiting as part of a tour to the ruins.

It's possible to cycle to the ruins from Turpan (see p783 for hire info).

GĀOCHĀNG (KHOCHO) RUINS 高昌故城

Originally settled in the 1st century BC, **Gāochāng** (admission Y40) rose to power in the 7th century during the Tang dynasty. Also known as Khocho, or sometimes Kharakhoja, it became the Uighur capital in AD 850 and a major staging post on the Silk Road until it burnt in the 14th century. Texts in classical Uighur, Sanskrit, Chinese and Tibetan have all been unearthed here, as well as evidence of a Nestorian church and a significant Manichean community – a dualistic Persian religion that borrowed figures from Christianity, Buddhism and Hinduism.

Though the earthen city walls, once 12m thick, are clearly visible, not much else at Gāochāng ruins (Gāochāng Gùchéng) is left standing other than a large Buddhist monastery in the southwest. To the north, adjacent to an adobe pagoda, is a two-storey structure (half underground), purportedly the ancient palace.

FLAMING MOUNTAINS 火焰山

Around Bezeklik Caves and Tuyoq are the **Flaming Mountains** (Huǒyàn Shān; admission Y40), the midday appearance of which is aptly compared to multicoloured tongues of fire. The Flaming Mountains were immortalised in the Chinese classic *Journey to the West* (see p956) as a mountainous inferno that the monk Xuan Zang had to pass through. Luckily for Xuan Zang, his travel buddy, Sun Wukong (the Monkey King), used a magic fan to extinguish the blaze.

Compare it to the Uighur version, in which a hero slays a child-eating dragon living within the mountains (its blood, hence, is the colouring) and slices it into eight pieces, which each represent a valley here.

You can clamber around in places, but only in the early morning – and don't forget your fan.

Hāmì (Kumul) 哈密

☎0902 / POP 365,000

Hāmì, with its delicious melons, was a much-anticipated stop on the Silk Road for ancient travellers looking for some R&R. Marco Polo described another claim to fame; according to local custom men allowed passing caravanmen to bunk down with their wives. No such tradition exists today (so far as we could tell), but Hāmì is still worth a stop; there are enough sights to keep you busy for a day and the town is a convenient halfway point between Ürümqi and Dūnhuáng.

The main site in Hāmì (also known as Kumul) is the **Hāmì Kings Mausoleum** (哈密王陵; Hāmì Wánglíng; Huancheng Lu; admission Y40; ⏲9am-8pm), a complex that contains the tombs of nine generations of Hāmì kings. Across the street, the **Hāmì Museum** (哈密博物馆; Hāmì Bówùguǎn; Huancheng Lu; admission free; ⏲9am-1pm & 4-7pm) features dinosaur fossils found in the region plus exhibits of Hāmì's unique culture and history. The adjacent building is the **Kumul Muqam Heritage Centre** (哈密木卡姆传

承中心; Hāmì Mùkǎmǔ Chuánchéng Zhōngxīn; admission Y15; ⏲9am-1pm & 4-7pm), which focuses specifically on Uighur music. Groups of four or more people are usually treated to a short concert. Opposite the Heritage Centre, the **Mansion of the Hāmì Kings** (哈密回王府; Hāmì Huíwāng Fǔ; admission Y40; ⏲9am-6pm) is a tacky reconstruction of an earlier palace and not worth the admission price. The tombs are 5km south of the train station; a taxi is about Y10.

If the summer heat of Hāmì is unbearable, take a day trip out to the cooler climes of **Barkol Lake** (巴里坤湖; Bālǐkūn Hú), on the north side of the Tiān Shān. Kazakh herders set up their yurts here in summer and offer horse riding for Y10 per hour. To reach the yurts first take a bus from Hāmì's main bus station to Bālǐkūn town (Y22, 2½ hours, hourly between 8.30am and 7pm). From Bālǐcūn it's 16km to the yurts. A return taxi starts at Y50. Along the route from Hāmì keep an eye out for the remains of ancient beacon towers, slowly disintegrating by the roadside.

Hāmì has a number of hotels and restaurants around the train station. One decent option is the **Jiǔchóngtiān Bīnguǎn** (九重天宾馆; ☎231 5656; 4 Tianshan Lu; d Y120-160), which has a mix of older and renovated rooms. With your back to the train station, it's just 50m straight ahead, on the right.

A **Bank of China** (中国银行; Zhōngguó Yínháng; Guangchang Beilu) is located just north of the main square (Renmin Guangchang).

Long-distance buses depart from a station located 200m east of the Hāmì Kings Mausoleum. Buses to Turpan (Y83, six hours) depart at 10am, 11am and 1.30pm. Buses to Ürümqi (Y103, nine hours) go every two hours, although the hard sleeper train (Y149) will prove more comfortable.

Kuqa 库车

☎0997 / POP 45,000

Grimy, dusty Kuqa (Kùchē) was once a thriving city-state and centre of Buddhism on the ancient Silk Road. Here Kumarajiva (AD 344?–413), the first great translator of Buddhist sutras from Sanskrit into Chinese, was born to an Indian father and Kuqean princess, before later being abducted to Liángzhóu and then Cháng'ān to manage translations of the Buddhist canon. When the 7th-century monk Xuan Zang passed through, he recorded that two enormous 30m-high Buddha statues flanked Kuqa's western gate, and that the nearby monasteries held over 5000 monks.

The bus station is east of town on Tianshan Lu, and the train station a further 5km southeast.

Sights

Qiuci Palace MUSEUM
(库车王府; Kùchē Wángfǔ; Linji Lu; admission Y55; ⏲9am-8.30pm) Located in the old town is the newly restored (ie rebuilt) Qiuci Palace, bestowed by Emperor Qianlong of the Qing dynasty and the residence of the kings of Qiuci until the early 20th century. The **Qiuci Museum** housed here has a wonderful collection of Buddhism-related frescos (some are replicas) and human remains from the ruins nearby. Behind the museum, the ancestral hall displays the history of the Qiuci kings and photos of the life of the last king, Dawud Mahsut, who still survives.

Take bus 1 on Tianshan Lu and get off at the last stop, then walk 1km further.

Bazaar & Mosque BAZAAR & MOSQUE
Every Friday a large **bazaar** (巴扎; Lǎochéng Bāzā) is held about 2.5km west of town, next to a bridge on Renmin Lu. It's nothing to rival Kashgar's, but is free of tour buses. A small **mosque** (清真寺; Qīngzhēn Sì) 150m further west draws a throng of worshippers on Friday afternoon. North of here through the old town is an awesome but less animated **Great Mosque** (清真大寺; Qīngzhēn Dàsì; admission Y15).

To get here from the new town, take buses 1 or 3 from Tianshan Lu.

Qiūcí Ancient City Ruins RUINS
These **ruins** (龟兹故城; Qiūcí Gùchéng), located on the main road, are all that is left of the capital of Qiūcí. It's a 20-minute walk northwest of the main intersection where Tianshan Lu forks in two, or bus 4 will take you there. Expect, well, not much.

Sleeping & Eating

Jiāotōng Bīnguǎn HOTEL $
(交通宾馆; Traffic Hotel; ☎712 2682; 87 Tianshan Lu; 天山路87号; s & tw Y40-150; ❄) Located next to the bus station, this place has a few different rooms, from cramped, airless singles to large doubles (a few with air con). Rooms are ratty and depressing, but if you're looking for dirt cheap, this is your best bet. Hot water runs after 9pm.

Kùchē Bīnguǎn HOTEL **$$**
(库车宾馆; ☎712 2901; 76 Jiefang Lu; 解放路76号; tw incl breakfast Y488-788, discounts of 60%; ❄) Kuqa's main hotel has airy, bright and fairly spacious rooms. After the discount rooms go for as low as Y140. Located near the city centre, it's easiest to catch a taxi here.

The best place to get a bite to eat is at the bazaar just off Tianshan Zhonglu (at the bottom end of Youyi Lu). Kebabs, noodles and *samsas* (mutton dumplings) are served hot and fresh. The best meals are to be had at the first stall on the left, marked with a sign that says 'Islam'.

Information

Bank of China (中国银行; Zhōngguó Yínháng; 25 Tianshan Donglu; ⏲9.30am-8pm)

Internet cafe (网吧; wǎngbā; cnr Wenhua Lu & Youyi Lu; per hr Y2) At the main intersection (east of the Xīnhuá bookstore).

Getting There & Away

AIR The airport east of the city has daily flights to Ürümqi (Y870). A taxi there costs Y5. **China Southern** (南航售票处; Nánháng Shòupiàochù; ☎712 9390) has a booking office next to Mínháng Bīnguǎn (民航宾馆) on Wenhua Zhonglu.

BUS The bus station has a variety of sleepers heading east to Ürümqi (Y165 to Y185, 10 to 17 hours). For Kashgar (Y151, 16 hours) you have to wait for a sleeper from Ürümqi to pass and hope that it has berths. There are frequent connections to Aksu (Y42, four hours), where you can connect to Kashgar. A daily bus to Hotan (Y160 to Y177, eight hours) departs at 2pm.

At the time of writing no buses were running to Yīníng. Even if bus service resumes, it's unlikely you'd get a ticket as Hwy 217 is off-limits to foreigners.

TRAIN There is a **train booking office** (huǒchē shòupiàochù; Youyi Lu; commission Y5; ⏲9.30am-1pm & 3.30-5pm) located next to the Jīnqiáo Jiǔdiàn (金桥酒店), about 200m north of the Xinhua bookstore. The K9787 to Kashgar (seat/sleeper Y99/183) leaves inconveniently at 1.54am. There are more convenient trains to Ürümqi (seat/sleeper Y116/215), including the 5808 at 7.14pm and the K9788 at 9.59pm. The 5807 to Aksu leaves at 3.10pm. Bus 6 runs along Tianshan Lu to the train station.

Getting Around

Taxi rides are a standard Y5 per trip, while pedicabs, tractors and donkey carts are generally Y1 to Y3, depending on the distance you want to travel.

Around Kuqa

KIZIL THOUSAND BUDDHA CAVES 克孜尔千佛洞

Seventy-five kilometres northwest of Kuqa are the **Kizil Thousand Buddha Caves** (Kèzī'ěr Qiānfó Dòng; admission Y55; ⏲daylight), an important site in Central Asian studies, with a wondrous mix of art and religion dated as early as the 3rd century. Historians suggest the early art of the Mògāo Caves at Dūnhuáng (p828), where Buddhism bloomed later than at Kuqa, was inspired by those in Kizil.

Of the more than 230 caves here, 10 are open to the public, and most are in poor shape. One cave was stripped by Western archaeologists, while the others have been defaced by both Muslims and Red Guards.

More interesting is the hike through the desert canyon to the spring Qiānlèi Quán (千泪泉). If you forgo the caves, admission is only Y10, but it's a long way to drive just to go hiking. A return taxi will cost around Y200 and takes 1½ hours.

ANCIENT CITY RUINS 苏巴什故城

There are several ruined cities in the Kuqa region, but these consist of no more than a few crumbling walls. The most famous is **Sūbāshí** (admission Y25; ⏲daylight), 23km northeast of Kuqa. A taxi to Sūbāshí and back costs about Y60.

SOUTHWEST XĪNJIĀNG – KASHGARIA

The Uighurs' heartland is Kashgaria, the rough-but-mellifluous-sounding historical name for the western Tarim Basin. Consisting of a ring of oases lined with poplar trees, it was a major Silk Road hub and has bristled with activity for over 2000 years, with the weekly bazaars remaining the centre of life here to this day.

Kashgar 喀什

☎0998 / POP 340,000

The westernmost metropolis of China's New Frontier, Kashgar (Kāshí) has been the epicentre of cultural conflict and cooperation for over two millennia.

Modernity has swept in like a sandstorm. The highways and railroads that connect it to the rest of China have brought waves of

SLOWLY ALONG THE SILK ROAD

If you are cycling along the Silk Road or just catching lifts between towns you may end up in one or more transit points, such as Korla (库尔勒), Lúntái (轮台) or Aksu (阿克苏). Bear these tips in mind as you travel through these cities:

If you need a place to crash, nearly every bus station in Xīnjiāng has an attached hotel that accepts foreigners. They all have the same name: Traffic Hotel (Jiāotōng Bīnguǎn; 交通宾馆) and will usually offer an en suite for Y70 to Y90. Notably, the Traffic Hotel in Korla is an excellent deal. The exception is Aksu, where the best deal is the Jiāngnán Kuàijié Jiǔdiàn (疆南快捷酒店), located 200m northwest of the central bus station.

A trip on the cross-desert highway is a quick way to reach Hotan by bus, but the route is risky on a bike. Distances between towns/rest stops are vast and sandstorms can be downright deadly. For sane people, the journey can really only be made with a support vehicle. A cheaper option is to load your bike onto a bus and then pick up the trail in Hotan.

Han migrant workers. Taxis and motorbikes are everywhere, and much of the old city is being bulldozed in the name of 'progress'.

Yet, in the face of these changes, the spirit of Kashgar lives on. The great-grandsons of craftsmen and artisans still hammer and chisel away in side alleys; everything sellable is hawked and haggled over boisterously; and not a few donkey carts still trundle their way through the crowds. And the Sunday market is the real deal, no matter how many tour buses roll up.

So soak it in for a few days, eat a few kebabs, chat with a local medicine man in a back alley, and prepare your trip along the southern Silk Road to Hotan, over the Torugart or Irkeshtam Passes to Kyrgyzstan or south up the stunning Karakoram Hwy to Pakistan.

Sights

Sunday Market BAZAAR

(星期天市场; Yengi Bazaar; Xīngqītiān Shìchǎng; Aizirete Lu; daily) A Uighur primer: *'Boish-boish!'* means 'Coming through!' You'd best hip yourself to this phrase, or risk being ploughed over by a push cart at the Sunday Market, which, despite its name, is open every day. Step carefully through the jam-packed entrance and allow your five senses guide you through the market; the pungent smell of cumin, the sight of scorpions in a jar, the sound of muqam from tinny radios, the taste of hot samsas and the feel of soft sheepskin caps are delightful, and overwhelming. A section on the northern side of the market contains everything of interest to foreign visitors, including the spice market, musical instruments, fur caps, kitschy souvenirs and carpets (see p790). A taxi to the Sunday Market is Y5.

If you miss the Sunday Market, don't despair: there are plenty of other markets in Xīnjiāng to visit. Try the Sunday market in Hotan (p796), the Monday market in Upal (p792), the Tuesday market in Charbagh (p795) or the Friday bazaar in Kuqa (p785).

Livestock Market BAZAAR

(动物市场; Mal Bazaar; Dòngwù Shìchǎng; 8am-6pm Sun) No visit to Kashgar is complete without a trip to the Livestock Bazaar and since it only occurs once a week (on Sunday) you'll need to plan accordingly. The day begins with Uighur farmers and herders trekking into the city from the nearby village. By lunchtime just about every sellable sheep, camel, horse, cow and donkey within 50km has been squeezed through the bazaar gates. Trading is swift and boisterous between the swarthy old traders; animals are carefully inspected and haggling is done with finger motions. Happy buyers then stuff their sheep in the back of a taxi or truck and lurch away. It's dusty, smelly, crowded, disorientating and wonderful all at once. The big tour buses usually arrive in the morning so plan an afternoon visit.

A taxi to the market is Y12. Otherwise, bus 8 runs from Id Kah Mosque.

Old Town OLD TOWN

Sprawling on both sides of Jiefang Lu are roads full of Uighur shops and narrow alleys lined with adobe houses right out of an early-20th-century picture book. Houses range in age from 50 to 500 years old and the lanes twist haphazardly through neighbourhoods where Kashgaris have lived and worked for centuries. It's a great place for

Kashgar

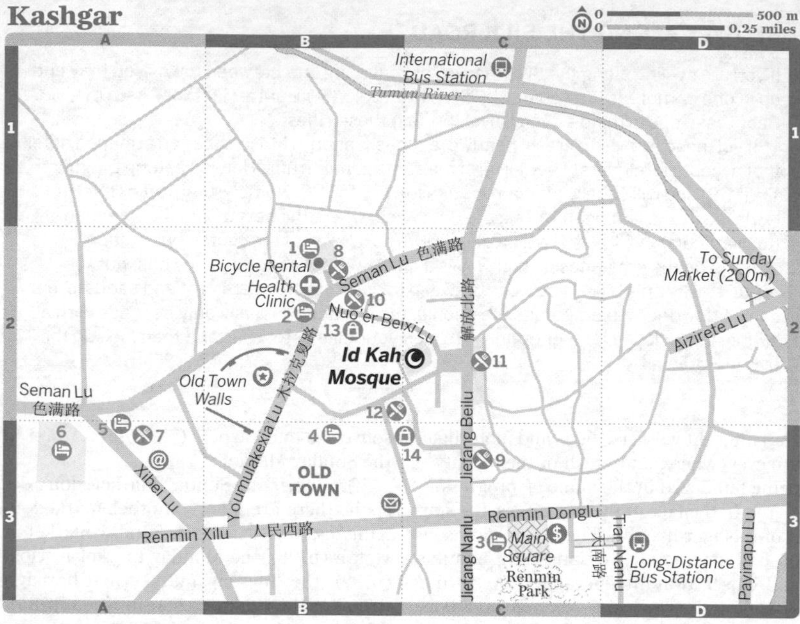

Kashgar

strolling, peeking through gates, chatting up the locals and admiring the craftsmen as they create their wares.

The Chinese government has shown little affection for the old town, however, and has spent the past two decades knocking it down, block by block. During our short stay we witnessed dozens of old homes bulldozed.

The old neighbourhoods that do remain tend to be hard to spot because they lie behind the high modern tower blocks along the main boulevards. Check out the streets southeast of the Night Market or the craft stalls on the street north of the post office. Avoid the residential area to the east, which has been turned into a tourist trap and requires a ticket to enter.

At the eastern end of Seman Lu stands a 10m-high section of the old town walls, which are at least 500 years old.

Id Kah Mosque MOSQUE

(艾提尕尔清真寺; Ài Tígă'ěr Qīngzhēn Sì; admission Y20) The yellow-tiled Id Kah Mosque, which dates from 1442, is the heart of the city – and not just geographically. Enormous, its courtyard and gardens can hold 20,000 people during the annual Qurban Baiyram celebrations.

Non-Muslims may enter, but Fridays are usually no-go. Dress modestly, including a headscarf for women. Take off your shoes if entering carpeted areas and be discreet when taking photos.

Abakh Hoja Tomb TOMB

(香妃墓; Abakh Hoja Maziri; Xiāngfēimù; admission Y30; ⊙daylight) On the northeastern outskirts of town is the Abakh Hoja Tomb, covered in splendidly mismatched glazed tiles and best known among Uighurs as the resting place of Abakh Hoja, one of Kashgar's more popular rulers. Purportedly among others interred is Ikparhan, his granddaughter. Known as Xiang Fei (Fragrant Concubine), she led the Uighurs in revolt, was defeated and ended up Emperor Qianlong's concubine. Take bus 20 from the main square (Renmin Guangchang) heading east until the last stop. A taxi is Y10.

Ha Noi Ruins & Mor Pagoda RUINS

(罕诺依古城; Hǎnnuòyī Gǔchéng; admission Y15; ⊙daylight) At the end of a 45km drive northeast of town are the Ha Noi Ruins, a Tang dynasty town built in the 7th century and abandoned in the 12th century. Little remains beside a solid pyramid-like structure and the huge Mor Pagoda (莫尔佛塔; Mù'ěr Fótǎ).

Flag down any taxi in town. A round trip, including waiting time, is Y100 to Y150.

Shipton's Arch (Tushuk Tash) NATURAL ARCH

This natural rock arch (天洞; Tiāndòng) is reputedly the tallest on earth, an incredible 1200m high. The first Westerner to describe it was British mountaineer Eric Shipton during his visit to the region in 1947. Successive expeditions attempted to find it without success until a team from National Geographic rediscovered the arch in 2000. The arch, located 80km northwest of Kashgar, receives few visitors. Kashgar-based tour operators can organise day or overnight trips. The journey involves one hour over paved highway, one hour over a rough 4WD-only track and then 30 minutes of steep climbing. The ascent to the arch involves climbing up ladders to an elevation of 2800m; bring sturdy shoes, warm clothing, snacks and water.

Tours

John's Café, Abdul Wahab, and Kashgar Guide organise multiday trips; see p791. Popular trips include trekking to Muztagh Ata and camel tours through the Taklamakan Desert. For a challenge, consider biking the Karakoram Hwy.

Sleeping

Accommodation can be tighter on the days preceding the Sunday Market. In the low season you should be able to coax out some discounts.

Eden Hotel HOTEL $$

(海尔巴格大饭店; Hǎiěrbāgé Dàfàndiàn; ☎266 4444; 148 Seman Lu; 色满路148号; d Y280 discounts 20%; ❄@) Eden is a brand new, mid-range hotel located next to Qinibag. Rooms have internet, the staff speaks English and there's an attached Turkish restaurant. Finishing touches were still being made when we visited but it has since opened and received positive reports from travellers. Price include breakfast.

Sèmǎn Bīnguǎn HOTEL $

(色满宾馆; ☎258 2129; fax 258 2861; 337 Seman Lu; 色满路337号; dm Y30-40, tw Y100-380; @) A labyrinthine complex with myriad rooms. Dorms are OK, but the toilets and showers could do with a clean. More expensive (but gaudy) rooms are in the former Russian consulate out the back. The staff are very friendly and helpful.

Kashgar Old Town Youth Hostel HOSTEL $

(喀什老城青年旅舍; Kāshí Lǎochéng Qīngnían Lǚshè; ☎282 3262, 135 6537 2911; www.pamirinn.com; 233 Wusitangboyi Lu; 吾斯塘博依路233号; dm Y35, r Y70-80; @🛜) Nestled in the old city, this atmospheric place is set around a courtyard where overlanders hang out in the afternoon sun, swapping stories and travel info. The dorm rooms are a bit bare and the beds are rock hard, but staff speak English. In high season you need to book well in advance to get your hands on a private room.

Màitián Youth Hostel HOSTEL $

(麦田国际青年旅舍; Màitián Guójì Qīngnián Lǚshè; ☎262 0595; www.yhaks.com; Remin Donglu Nan 1 Xiang; 人民东路南一巷; dm Y30, tw from Y120) This hostel east of East Lake (Dōnghú) seems to only open its doors in high season, so call ahead before rocking up. Bus 16 heading east on Renmin Lu takes you there; get off just after the bridge, then head south for 300m down the alley named Renmin Donglu Nan 1 Xiang.

Chini Bagh Hotel HOTEL $$

(其尼瓦克宾馆; Qíníwǎkè Bīnguǎn; ☎298 2103; fax 298 2299; 93 Seman Lu; 色满路93号; dm Y35-50, tw Y70-280; ❄@) The Chini Bagh, immortalised in William Dalrymple's travelogue *In Xanadu,* is located on the grounds of the former British consulate. It has several buildings that contain an eclectic collection of rooms, from dingy dorms to clean midrange rooms and a new five-star complex. The compound also has a clutch of travel agents and nearby restaurants.

Sahar Hotel BUDGET HOTEL **$**
(色哈尔宾馆; Sèhā'ěr Bīnguǎn; ☎258 1122; 348 Seman Lu; 色满路348号; d Y60) A friendly but dowdy hotel whose customers are mostly Pakistani, Tajik and Uighur traders. The hotel offers some of the cheapest private rooms available to foreigners.

International Hotel HOTEL **$$$**
(中西亚国际大酒店; Zhōngxīyà Guójì Dàjiǔdiàn; ☎280 2222; fax 280 2266; 8 Renmin Donglu; 人民东路8号; tw incl breakfast Y598, discounts of 20%; ❄@) Next to the Main Sq, this four-star hotel is the most upmarket option in Kashgar. Rooms from the upper floors have sweeping views of Kashgar.

Eating

In restaurants, *suoman, suoman gush siz* and *polo* (see the boxed text, p779) are all recommended. For snacks, tea and local company, visit the **Uighur Teahouse** (茶馆; Cháguǎn) at the main crossroads in the old town.

Night Market MARKET **$**
(夜市; yèshì; meals from Y8; ⏲8pm-midnight Xīnjiāng time) The night market opposite the Id Kah Mosque (in the alleys east of Jiefang Beilu) is another good place to sample local fare. Vendors sell chickpeas, kebabs, breads, boiled goat heads and tasty desserts.

Karakorum Café CAFE **$$**
(87 Seman Lu; mains from Y28; ⏲9am-11pm summer, noon-11pm winter; @📶) Smart-looking cafe serving Western-style breakfasts, salads, sandwiches, desserts and coffee. The warmed banana nut muffins are outstanding. Another attraction is the bathroom, possibly the best in all of Xīnjiāng.

Fubar PUB **$$**
(福吧; Fúbā; www.fubarchina.com; 120 Seman Lu; mains from Y25; ⏲8.30am-2am summer, noon-2am winter; 📶) Grab a beer here and relax on the roof garden in the evening (well, Xīnjiāng time) after a long, sweaty day. Like its flagship in Ürümqi, this watering hole serves imported alcohol and authentic Western food.

Gallery Café CAFE **$$$**
(☎152 9290 3517; coffee Y8-30, meals Y20-80; ⏲2pm-11pm; 📶) This American and Canadian cafe serves pizzas, drinks and desserts. Grab a seat by the window and watch life pass by on the alley, or head upstairs to relax on the sofas in an artsy setting. To find it, walk down Jiefang Beilu for 100m (from Renmin Xilu) and turn right at the first alley, just past the Nuran Restaurant. The cafe is a few steps down on the right.

Altun Orda RESTAURANT **$$**
(金噢尔大特色菜; Jīn'ào'ěrdà Tèsècài; Xibei Lu; dishes from Y25) A sumptuously designed restaurant, famous for its roasted mutton (Y55). Other tasty dishes include *ghoush nan* (meat pie) and *mirizlig manta* (pastry with raisins and walnuts).

John's Cafe CAFE **$$**
(银提扎尔餐厅; Yíntízhā'ěr Cāntīng; www.johncafe.net; 337 Seman Lu; mains from Y20) In the courtyard of Sèmǎn Bīnguǎn, this is a popular hang-out, offering both Western (pricey) and Chinese (cheaper) dishes. There's another branch in the Chini Bagh Hotel.

Shopping

For serious shopping go to the old town, ready to bargain. Be aware that Sunday Market prices tend to be higher. Hats, teapot sets, copper and brass ware, and Uighur knives are among the souvenirs you'll find around town.

Local Uighur carpet dealer **Elvis** (☎138 9913 6195; elvisablimit@yahoo.com), aka Ablimit Ghopor, speaks English and can help you understand the intricacies of the Kashgar carpet market. A proud connoisseur of *muqam* (Uighur traditional music), he can help you sample it. A jack-of-all-trades, Elvis also helps to organise trips in and around Kashgar.

Sunday Market MARKET
(星期天市场; Yengi Bazaar; Xīngqītiān Shìchǎng; Aizirete Lu; ⏲daily) Most carpet dealers display their wares at the Sunday Market pavilion. The rugs here are made of everything from silk to synthetics. The brightly coloured felt *shyrdakhs* from Kyrgyzstan are a good buy; don't pay more than Y450 for a large one. The best regional carpets were once made in Hotan, but these days the designs are modern and finding traditional designs can be difficult. Also, some carpets are actually manufactured in the factories in Tiānjīn. Be careful when you shop.

Hotan Carpet Shop CARPETS
(Nuo'er Beixi Lu; www.hotancarpet.com) Reliable carpet dealer Abdullah was born into a family of carpet weavers and

CARPET BUYING TIPS

When carpet shopping, bear in the mind the following tips.

» Traditional carpets are coloured with vegetable dyes, although most carpet makers use chemical dyes today.

» Silk carpets are more expensive than wool carpets. Because they are delicate and pricey Uighurs often hang them on the wall rather than placing them on the floor.

» To spot a fake, turn the carpet over and look at the bottom. If the top and bottom look completely different it's probably not authentic. If the pattern on the bottom resembles the pattern on the top, it's real. If the pattern on the bottom is clear and detailed, this indicates that the knots are closer together, indicating a better quality carpet.

» The best carpets are made from young sheep wool taken in late spring.

» Classic designs including the Khotan Pomegranate carpet, which features small red pomegranates, and the Khotan three medallion carpet which features circular designs and other geometric shapes.

See www.elvisabalimit.jozan.net and www.hotancarpet.com for more information.

knows his stuff. His shop is on the lane between the Eden Hotel and the Id Kah Mosque.

Uighur Musical Instrument Factory MUSICAL INSTRUMENTS
(Kumudai'erwazha Lu) You'll find long-necked stringed instruments running the gamut from souvenirs to collectors' items. If any traditional performances are on, owner Mohammed will know where to find them. This family-run place is on the street north of the post office.

Information

Travellers have lost money or passports to pickpockets at the Sunday Market and even on local buses, so keep yours tucked away.

Some foreign women walking the streets alone have been sexually harassed. The Muslim Uighur women dress in long skirts and heavy stockings like the Uighur women in Ürümqi and Turpan, but here one sees more female faces hidden behind veils of brown gauze. It is wise for women travellers to dress as would be appropriate in any Muslim country, covering arms and legs.

Internet Access

Several of the hotels and restaurants listed above offer wi-fi.

Internet cafe (网吧; wǎngbā; Seman Lu) Near the Altun Orda Restaurant.

Laundry

There is a laundry service and dry cleaner *(gānxǐ diàn)* just north of the Chini Bagh Hotel complex.

Medical Services

Health clinic (诊所; zhěnsuǒ; Seman Lu) Located below the CITS office in the Chini Bagh Hotel complex. Can administer first aid and medicines. Some staff speak English.

People's Hospital (Rénmín Yīyuàn; Jiefang Beilu) North of the river.

Money

Bank of China (中国银行; Zhōngguó Yínháng; Main Sq; ⌚9.30am-1.30pm & 4-7.30pm) Changes travellers cheques and cash and has a 24 hour ATM. You can also sell yuan back into US dollars at the foreign exchange desk if you have exchange receipts; this is a good idea if you are headed to Tashkurgan, where the bank hours are erratic.

Post

China Post (中国邮政; Zhōngguó Yóuzhèng; 40 Renmin Xilu; ⌚9.30am-8pm) The 2nd floor handles all foreign letters and packages.

Public Security Bureau

PSB (公安局; Gōng'ānjú; 111 Youmulakexia Lu; ⌚9.30am-1.30pm & 4-8pm) You can extend your visa here.

Travel Agencies

Kashgar has no shortage of travel agents; some fly-by-night, others reliable.

Abdul Wahab (☎220 4012; abdultour@yahoo.com; www.silkroadinn.com; 337 Seman Lu) One of the best operating out of the Sèmǎn Bīnguǎn.

CITS (中国国际旅行社; Zhōngguó Guójì Lǚxíngshè; ☎298 3156; Seman Lu) Located at the Chini Bagh Hotel complex; contact Mohammed Yusuf.

John's Cafe (约翰中西餐厅; Yuēhàn Zhōngxī Cāntīng; ☎258 1186; www.johncafe.net; 337 Seman Lu) An established operator; contact John at the Sèmǎn Bīnguǎn.

Kashgar Guide (☎295 1029; www.kashgarguide.com; 148 Seman Lu) Run by Imam Husan, this is another good choice operating out of the Eden Hotel. It organises bookings, transport and excursions, and can link you up with other budget-minded travellers to help share costs.

Getting There & Away

It's imperative when you buy tickets in Kashgar to verify 'which time' the ticket is for (see p778). It should be Běijīng time, but this isn't always the case.

AIR There are seven daily flights to Ürümqi (Y1230), which are sometimes cancelled due to poor turnout or sandstorms. A handy **Air Ticket Agent** (Jīpiao Daīshòuchù; ☎296 6666; 8 Renmin Donglu) is located at the International Hotel.

BUS Domestic buses use the **long-distance bus station** (喀什站; kāshí zhàn; Tian Nanlu). There are six buses for Hotan (Y89, seven to 10 hours) between 9am and 9.30pm, but it's more enjoyable to stop off in Yengisar (Y8, 1½ hours), Yarkand (Y26, three hours) or Karghilik (Y35.50, four hours). Buses to these towns run hourly.

Sleeper buses to Ürümqi (Y229 to Y248, 24 hours) depart from the international bus station between 7.50am and 7.30pm. From the same station you can get a bus to Kuqa (Y140 to Y150, 12 hours) at 4pm or 7pm.

CAR You can hire 4WDs (four to six passengers) and minibuses (eight to 12 passengers) from John's Cafe or CITS (see p791). Rates for a 4WD to meet/drop you off at Torugart Pass average US$180 to US$240, which includes transportation, guide and permits (min two-day wait, though three is more likely). Food and lodging are extra, and the driver pays for his own. From Torugart to Naryn a taxi costs around US$140.

TRAIN Daily trains to Ürümqi depart at 8.18am and 1.16pm and take 32 and 24 hours, respectively. Lower-berth sleeper tickets on the faster train are Y345. The line to Hotan is expected to be completed by 2011. You can buy tickets from the **train booking office** (huǒchē shòupiàochù; Tian Nanlu; commission Y5; ⏲9.30am-1pm & 3-7pm) at the long-distance bus station.

Getting Around

TO/FROM THE AIRPORT The airport is 13km northeast of the town centre. One shuttle bus (Y10) meets all incoming flights. Just tell the driver your destination in town. A taxi should cost the same. From the Main Sq, bus 2 goes directly to the airport.

BICYCLE A bicycle is the cheapest and most versatile way to get around Kashgar. Mountain bikes can be hired at the Chini Bagh Hotel for Y50 per day (or Y25 for a half-day). The **Giant Bike Shop** (捷安特自行车行; Jié'āntè Zìxíngchē Háng; ☎640 1616; 37 Jiangkang Lu) also rents bikes for Y30 per day. It's located 1.5km south of town opposite the Three Fortune Hotel (三运宾馆; Sānyùn Bīnguǎn).

BUS Useful bus routes are buses 2 (Jiefang Lu to the international bus station and the airport), 9 (international bus station to the Chini Bagh Hotel and Sèmǎn Bīnguǎn), 8 (Id Kah Mosque to the Livestock Market), 20 (post office to Abakh Hoja Tomb) and 28 (Id Kah Mosque to the train station). The fare is Y1.

TAXI Taxis are metered and the flag fall is Y5. Anywhere in town shouldn't cost more than Y14.

Karakoram Highway 中巴公路

The Karakoram Hwy (KKH; Zhōngbā Gōnglù) over the Khunjerab Pass (4800m) is the gateway to Pakistan. For centuries this route was used by caravans plodding down the Silk Road. Khunjerab means 'valley of blood' – local bandits used to take advantage of the terrain to slaughter merchants and plunder caravans.

Facilities en route are being gradually improved, but take warm clothing, food and drink on board with you – once stowed on the bus roof it's unavailable. Check the state of the highway well ahead of time. In 2010 a massive landslide on the Pakistani side blocked a river and created a new 20km-long lake that submerged the highway, causing disaster for the people of the Hunza Valley and big headaches for travellers. Check Lonely Planet's **Thorn Tree** (www.lonelyplanet.com/thorntree) for updates.

Even if you don't plan to go to Pakistan, it's still worth heading up the highway at least to Tashkurgan. It's possible to do this as a day trip but highly recommended that you spend a night or two up in these gorgeous mountains. Some travellers hire bikes in Kashgar, get a lift up to Tashkurgan and cycle back for an exciting three-day journey.

KASHGAR TO TASHKURGAN

Travelling up the KKH to Tashkurgan is a highlight of Kashgaria. The journey begins with a one-hour drive through agricultural plains to **Upal** (Wùpà'ěr in Chinese), where most vehicles stop for breakfast. There's a great weekly market here every Monday. You can also see the **Tomb of Mahmud Kashgari**, an 11th-century scholar and writer be-

BORDER CROSSING: GETTING TO KYRGYZSTAN, PAKISTAN & TAJIKISTAN

To Kyrgyzstan

There are two passes into Kyrgyzstan: the Torugart Pass, which leads to Bishkek, and the Irkeshtam Pass, which goes to Osh. Getting to Osh (Y470, two days) is straightforward, with a bus leaving Kashgar's **international bus station** (国际汽车站; guójì qìchēzhàn; Jiefang Beilu) on Thursday (and perhaps Monday if demand warrants it) at 9am. Another option is to hire a taxi up to the border, which will probably cost around Y300.

Crossing the Torugart requires more red tape. What you require on the Chinese side is a *xǔkězhèng* permit from the PSB entry-exit section in Ürümqi. Most agents in Kashgar can get this; two of the most popular options now are with **CITS** (中国国际旅行社; Zhōngguó Guójì Lǚxíngshè; ☎298 3156; Seman Lu) or **John's Cafe** (约翰中西餐厅; Yuēhàn Zhōngxī Cāntīng; ☎258 1186; www.johncafe.net; 337 Seman Lu). For prices, see p792. Most likely you will need to have pre-arranged transport on the Kyrgyz side, which travel agents can arrange with their contacts in Naryn or Bishkek.

You must already have a Kyrgyzstan visa.

To Pakistan

Buses to/from Sost (Y270 plus Y2 per bag, two days) in Pakistan leave Kashgar's **international bus station** (国际汽车站; guójì qìchēzhàn; Jiefang Beilu) daily at noon. However, if there are fewer than 10 passengers the bus may not depart until the following day. The 500km trip stops overnight at Tashkurgan, where customs procedures are conducted. Bring water, snacks and warm clothes as nights can be cold year-round. If you are already in Tashkurgan, there is a morning bus to Sost for Y230.

If buses have stopped for the season but you're desperate to cross the border, Pakistani traders may have space in a truck or chartered bus. You can also hire a taxi or a 4WD from one of the tour outfits.

To Tajikistan

The Kulma Pass (4362m), linking Kashgar with Murghob (via Tashkurgan), opened in 2004, with three monthly buses making the trip. At the time of writing the pass was not open to foreign travellers; go to **Travel Tajikistan** (www.traveltajikistan.com/road rail/road.html) for the latest updates.

loved by Uighurs. The tomb is about 2.5km from the market on the edge of Upal hill.

Two hours from Kashgar you enter the canyon of the Ghez River (Ghez Darya in Uighur), with wine-red sandstone walls at its lower end. Ghez itself is just a checkpost; photographing soldiers or buildings is strictly prohibited. Upstream, the road is cut into the sheer rock walls. At the top of the canyon, 3½ hours above the plain, is a huge wet plateau ringed with sand dunes, aptly called Kumtagh (Sand Mountain) by locals.

Soon Kongur Mountain (Gōnggé'ěr Shān; 7719m) rises up on the left side of the road. Next Muztagh Ata Mountain (Mùshìtǎgé Shān; 7546m) comes into view. The main stopping point for views is **Karakul Lake** (admission Y50), a glittering mirror of glacial peaks 194km from Kashgar. From here you can hike into the hills or circumnavigate the lake. Most settlements as far as Karakul are Kyrgyz. It's well worth exploring the mountains beyond the lake. Kashgar Guide (p791) can organise five-day trekking tours around the lake and to the Muztagh Ata base camp (4500m), sleeping in tents and yurts along the way. The trek (US$50 to US$70 per day) includes food, permits, guide and even a camel that will haul your gear. At the lake you'll find a restaurant, formal yurt accommodation (Y50), camping spots (Y20) and horse riding (Y50).

The journey continues on through some stunning scenery – high mountain pastures with grazing camels and yaks tended by yurt-dwelling Tajiks. The final major town on the Chinese side is Tashkurgan at 3600m. Tashkurgan consists of a couple of main shopping streets and a small market.

Officially, the border opens on 15 April and closes on 31 October. However, the border can open late or close early depending on conditions at Khunjerab Pass. Travel formalities are performed at Sost, on the Pakistan border, and visas are available here (but check this ahead of time as the situation could change). The Chinese customs and immigration formalities are done at Tashkurgan (technically 3km down the road towards Pakistan). Then it's 126km to the last checkpost at Khunjerab Pass, the actual border, where your documents are checked again before you head into Pakistan.

Tashkurgan is a small town and you could easily kill a couple of hours wandering its streets and small market. On the outskirts of town, close to the river, is the **Stone City** (石头城; Shítóuchéng, admission Y8), which has a murky past but is believed to be a 1400-year-old fort built by a Tajik king of the Kyrpana kingdom. It was one of the filming locations for the movie *Kite Runner*. The river valley below is dotted with Tajik yurts in summer; it's worth slogging through the boggy grassland to reach some of the yurts and meet the welcoming shepherd families. The views from the floor of the river valley are spectacular. Some travellers head up to the Khunjerab Pass for a photo opportunity on the actual border. Note that you need a border permit (available in Kashgar), which most tour agencies can arrange.

Sleeping

There are several small hotels in Tashkurgan.

Jiāotōng Bīnguǎn HOTEL $
(交通宾馆; ☎0998-342 1192; dm/d Y15/80) Next to the bus station; has some scruffy doubles and cheap dorms with stinky bathrooms.

Crown Inn HOTEL $$$
(皇冠大酒店; ☎0998-342 2888; 1 Pamir Lu; d incl breakfast Y400-450; @ 📶) Singapore-run plush hotel that offers comfortable, bright rooms and a Western breakfast.

Getting There & Away

The bus leaves for Sost (Y250) at 10am from Tashkurgan. There is one bus going back to Kashgar (Y54) at 9.30am; if you miss it, a share taxi is around Y60 per person.

It's possible to reach Tashkurgan from Kashgar in a shared vehicle (per person Y80). These depart from the **Tashkurgan Administration Office** (塔什库尔干办事处; Tăshíkù'ěrgān Bànshìchù; 166 Xiyu Dadao Lu; 西域大道166号) in Kashgar. Otherwise, try the daily bus from the bus station leaving at 8.30am (Y51.50, six hours).

From Kashgar it's 118km to the Ghez checkpoint, 194km to Karakul Lake, 283km to Tashkurgan and 380km to the Pakistani border.

SOUTHERN SILK ROAD

The Silk Road east of Kashgar splits into two threads in the face of the huge Taklamakan Desert. The northern thread follows the modern road and railway to Kuqa and Turpan. The southern road charts a more remote course between desert sands and the huge Pamir and Kunlun mountain ranges.

No jaw-dropping sights, but the journey takes you about as far into the Uighur heartland as you can get. It's possible to visit the southern towns as a multiday trip from Kashgar before crossing the Taklamakan Desert to Ürümqi, or as part of a rugged backdoor route into Tibet or Qīnghǎi.

Yengisar 英吉沙

The tiny town of Yengisar (Yīngjíshā) is synonymous with knife production. A lesser-known but more sensitive fact is it's the birthplace of the Uighur's icon of nationalism, Isa Yusuf Alptekin (1901–95), the leader of the First East Turkestan Republic in Kashgar who died in exile in Istanbul.

There are dozens of knife shops here, most of them strung along the highway in ugly strip-mall fashion. Ask for the 'knife factories' (小刀厂; *xiǎodāochǎng* in Chinese; *pichak chilik karakhana* in Uighur). Each worker makes the blade, handle and inlays himself, using only the most basic of tools. To get there from the main bus station, hop in a taxi (Y5) for the 3km trip to the knife shops. They are right on the main road, so you'd even pass them on the way to Yarkand. Note that knives are prohibited in check-in luggage, so you'll have to ship them home.

Buses pass through the town regularly en route to Yarkand (Y18, 1½ hours) and Kashgar (Y8, 1½ hours).

Yarkand 莎车

At the end of a major trade route from British India, over the Khunjerab Pass from Leh, Yarkand (Shāchē) was for centuries an important caravan town and centre for Hindu tradesmen and moneylenders.

The town is known for the dead. Tombs honouring royalty are the primary draw, the most famous of which is the tomb of Ammanisahan, a Uighur queen and musician famed for her work collecting the Uighur *muqam*.

In the alleys of the intriguing old town, craftsmen still work their wares – noisily and sweatily – with ball-pen hammers and grindstones.

Modern Yarkand is split into a Chinese new town and an Uighur old town. Take a right upon exiting the bus station to get to the main avenue. Once there, take another right and flag down any public bus, which will take you past the Shāchē Bīnguǎn, 1km east of the bus station; the old town and the Altun Mosque complex are 1km further.

Sights

The main attractions are in the old town. Use the **Altun Mosque complex** (阿勒屯清真寺; Ālètún Qīngzhēn Sì) as a landmark. It's on a small street off the main avenue. The **Mausoleum of Ammanisahan** is beside it. Across the prayer hall of the mosque is the **mazar** where the members of the royal family in Yarkand were buried between the 16th and 17th centuries. Admission to these places is Y15. To visit the town's sprawling, overgrown cemetery, go out the back door of the mosque and turn right (you can also get there from an alley heading off the main road). There is no charge to enter this complex. To get to the old town, take a left off the main avenue as if heading to the mosque, then take the first right down a dirt lane and keep going.

Yarkand also has a **Sunday Market**, smaller than those of Kashgar or Hotan. The market is held a block north of the Altun Mosque.

Sleeping & Eating

Xīnshèng Bīnguǎn HOTEL $
(新盛宾馆; ☎852 7555; 4 Xincheng Lu; 新城路4号; tw/tr Y120/140) This place has smoky, scruffy rooms and is overpriced compared to the Subhi Altun, but you may be able to bargain the price down a bit. It's on the main road, just outside the gates of the Shāchē Bīnguǎn.

Sūbìyí Ālètún Bīnguǎn HOTEL $
(苏碧怡阿勒屯宾馆; ☎851 2222; cnr A'Letun Lu & Laocheng Lu; 阿勒屯路和老城路的十字路口; tw/tr Y120/180) This new hotel has very clean rooms at competitive rates in a nice location near the old town, a one-minute walk from the Altun Mosque complex.

The old town has tempting noodle shops with patrons sitting on *kangs* (long sleeping platforms) instead of chairs.

Getting There & Around

Buses leave half-hourly for Kashgar (Y26, three hours), Yengisar (Y18, 1½ hours) and Karghilik (Y10, one hour). There are four daily buses at noon, 2pm, 4pm and 6pm to Hotan (Y50 to Y59, six hours), and six daily to Ürümqi (Y238 to Y257, 24 hours).

From the bus station, public buses (Y0.50) will take you 2km to the old town and Altun Mosque complex.

Karghilik 叶城

Karghilik (Yèchéng) is of importance to travellers as the springboard of legendary Hwy 219, the Xīnjiāng–Tibet highway that leads to Ali in Tibet.

The main attraction here is the 15th-century **Friday Mosque** (Jama Masjid) and covered bazaar at its front. The traditional adobe-walled backstreets of the old town spread south behind the mosque.

The town of **Charbagh**, located 10 minutes' drive towards Yarkand, has a large market on Tuesday.

Sleeping & Eating

The PSB, hoping to corral foreigners, all of whom they assume are sneaking into Tibet, only allows you to stay in one of the following options.

Jiāotōng Bīnguǎn BUDGET HOTEL $
(交通宾馆; ☎728 5540; 1 Jiaotong Lu; 交通路1号; dm/s Y50/80, tw Y160-180) The Traffic Hotel has a newer modern block with reasonably clean double rooms and some grimmer dorms. The area around the station is pretty chaotic during the day, so keep an eye on your stuff if walking around the neighbourhood.

Qiáogēlǐfēng Dēngshān Bīnguǎn HOTEL $$
(乔戈里峰登山宾馆; ☎748 5000; 9180 Línggōnglǐ; 零公里9180号; tw Y120-368; ❄) The 'K2 Hotel' is the better place to stay and closer to the Tibetan Antelope bus station if you're headed to Tibet. Board bus 2 outside the bus station or take a taxi for Y10. It's 6km from the bus station.

There are busy Uighur eateries outside the Friday Mosque and 24-hour food stalls across from the bus station.

Getting There & Away

Buses to Yarkand (Y10) and Kashgar (Y34, four hours) leave every half-hour until 8.30pm. Every two hours there is a bus to Hotan (Y34, five hours) until 8.30pm.

The 1100km-long road to Ali, in western Tibet, branches off from the main Kashgar–Hotan road 6km east of Karghilik. A bus makes the trip twice a week, but at the time of writing foreigners were not allowed to use it. The only way to (legally) take the highway is by organising a Land Cruiser tour with an agent in Lhasa. See Lonely Planet's *Tibet* guide for details.

Hotan 和田

0903 / POP 104,900

Hotan has long been known as the epicentre of the Central Asian and Chinese jade trade. Locally unearthed jade artefacts have been dated to around 5000 BC and it is believed that Hotan (Hétián; also known as Khotan) attracted Chinese traders long before they headed westward in search of Central Asia's horses.

The Hotanese also uncovered the secret of Chinese silk by the 5th century AD and later established themselves as the region's foremost carpet weavers.

Today Hotan is largely a Chinese city, but it still has some fascinating old neighbourhoods and an authentic market. While the architecture is not as refined as you'll see in Kashgar, Hotan feels more genuine. You can visit some carpet and silk factories, but what may make the 500km-long slog from Kashgar worthwhile is the fantastic Sunday Market, the largest and least visited in Xīnjiāng.

Beijing Xilu is the main east–west axis running past the enormous main square (Tuánjié Guǎngchǎng). The bank is to the southwest of the square, while the PSB, hotels and bus stations are north from here. The Jade Dragon Kashgar River runs several kilometres east of town.

Sights

Rows of shops along Beijing Lu have a huge selection of jade pulled from the Jade Dragon Kashgar River. Sadly, overdredging for gemstones has already devastated the riverbed, so buying jade here only encourages more digging.

Sunday Market MARKET

Hotan's most popular attraction is its weekly Sunday market (星期天市场; sometimes on Friday as well). The colourful market swamps the northeast part of town and reaches fever pitch between noon and 2pm Xīnjiāng time. The most interesting parts to head for are the *gillam* (carpet) bazaar, which also has a selection of atlas silks, the *doppi* (skullcap) bazaar and the livestock bazaar.

FREE **Carpet Factory** TRADITIONAL CARPET MAKING

On the eastern bank of the Jade Dragon Kashgar River is this small factory (地毯厂; dìtǎn chǎng; gillam karakhana in Uighur). Even with up to 10 weavers, 1 sq metre of wool carpet takes 20 days to complete. To get here, take bus 10 outside the bus station and get off at the last stop.

Silk Workshop TRADITIONAL SILK MAKING

(Jíyàxiāng; admission Y5) Past the carpet factory, southeast of Hotan, is the small town of Jíyàxiāng (吉亚乡), a traditional centre for silk production. You can look around the fascinating workshop (*sīchóuchǎng;* atlas karakhana in Uighur) to see how the silk is spun, dyed and woven using traditional methods. A return trip by taxi to the workshop, taking in the carpet factory, costs Y60.

Imam Asim TOMB, CEMETERY

About 10km beyond Jíyàxiāng lie an interesting cemetery and the Imam Asim (Tomb of Four Imams), reached by a paved road. It's a popular pilgrimage site, particularly during the month of May. The cemetery lies on the edge of the Taklamakan Desert, so coming out here is a good opportunity to enjoy the desert scenery and slide down the sand dunes. The best day to visit is Thursday, when a festive market springs up by the roadside, about 2km before the tomb.

FREE **Hotan Cultural Museum** MUSEUM

(和田博物馆; Hétián Bówùguǎn; Beijing Xilu; 9.30am-1.30pm & 4-7.30pm, closed Wed) West of town is the regional Hotan Cultural Museum. The main attractions are two 1500-year-old Indo-European mummies from the ancient city ruins around Hotan. Take buses 2 or 6 from the town centre to get here.

Melikawat Ruins RUINS

(古城; Mǎlìkèwǎtè Gǔchéng; admission Y10) The deserts around Hotan are peppered with the faint remains of abandoned cities. The most interesting are those of Melikawat, 25km south of town, a Tang-dynasty settlement with wind-eroded walls, the remains

Hotan

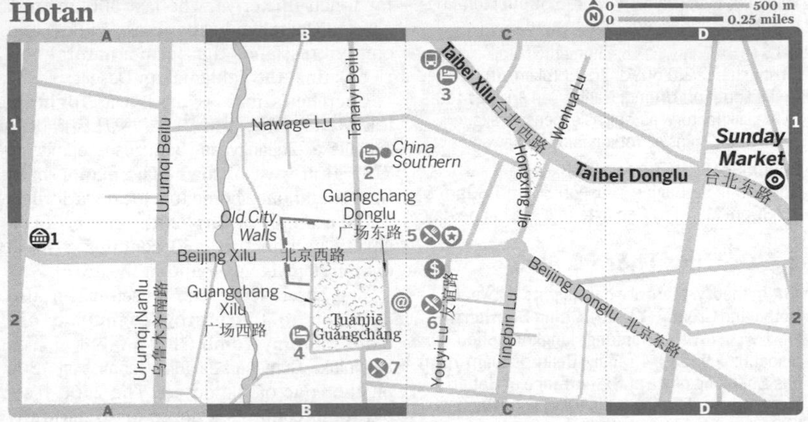

Hotan

Top Sights

Sunday Market D1

Sights

1 Hotan Cultural Museum A2

Sleeping

2 Hétián Yíngbīnguǎn B1

3 Jiāotōng Bīnguǎn C1

4 Yùdū Dàjiǔdiàn B2

Eating

5 Chinese Night Market C2

6 Marco's Dream Cafe C2

7 Uighur Night Market B2

of pottery kilns, Buddhist stupas and scattered potsherds. Some scholars believe Melikawat was a capital city of the Yutian state (206 BC–AD907), an Indo-European civilisation that thrived during the height of the Silk Road epoch. A taxi should cost about Y100 to Melikawat.

Rawaq Pagoda is another interesting sight, but you'll need a permit (Y450) to visit; contact CITS for assistance.

Sleeping & Eating

Jiāotōng Bīnguǎn BUDGET HOTEL $

(交通宾馆; ☎203 2700; Taibei Xilu; 台北西路; d without/with bathroom Y70/140; ❄) Attached to the bus station, this Jiāotōng Bīnguǎn is worn out but popular with budget travellers. The shared bathrooms are awful, so consider the en suite rooms, sometimes discounted to Y90.

Hétián Yíngbīnguǎn HOTEL $$

(和田迎宾馆; ☎202 2824; fax 202 3688; 4 Tanaiyi Beilu; 塔乃依北路4号; dm Y30, tw incl breakfast Y120-368; ❄) The dorms and cheaper rooms are in the old wing. Rooms in the main building have been renovated.

Yùdū Dàjiǔdiàn HOTEL $$

(玉都大酒店; ☎202 9999; Guangchang Xilu; 北京西路75号; tw from Y148) The 'Jade Capital' is quiet and clean, on the west side of the main square. Rooms are featureless but neat. A cluster of eating outlets is nearby.

Marco's Dream Cafe CAFE $

(☎152 9266 1017; yklmlan@yahoo.co.uk; Youyi Lu; 友谊路; 📶) This Malaysian-run restaurant serves a nice range of Western dishes including salads, shepherd's pie and pepper steak. A roast dinner is prepared on Sunday. The friendly owners speak English and can provide travel advice.

Uighur night market MARKET $

(维族人夜市; Wéizúrén Yèshì; Guangchang Donglu) On the street south of the square; a good place to grab a kebab.

Chinese night market MARKET $

(中式夜市; Zhōngshì Yèshì; Beijing Xilu) This tiny market is just next to the PSB.

Information

There's an internet cafe on the 2nd floor in a building on the east side of the square.

Bank of China (中国银行; Zhōngguó Yínháng; cnr Urumqi Nanlu & Aqiale Lu; ⏲9.30am-1.30pm & 4-8pm Mon-Fri) Cashes travellers cheques.

China Construction Bank (中国建设银行; Zhōngguó Jiànshè Yínháng; cnr Beijing Lu &

Youyi Lu; ⌚9.30am-1pm & 4-6.30pm Mon-Fri) Has ATMs that accept foreign cards.

CITS (中国国际旅行社; Zhōngguó Guójì Lǚxíngshè; ☎251 6090; 3F, 23 Tuken Lu) Located to the south off Urumqi Nanlu. Can arrange tours to the silk factory, as well as expensive excursions to the ruins at Yotkan and Melikawat.

Public Security Bureau (PSB;公安局; Gōng'ānjú; 92 Beijing Xilu; ⌚9.30am-1.30pm & 4-7.30pm Mon-Fri) Can extend visas in one day.

Getting There & Away

AIR In theory, there are daily flights between Hotan and Ürümqi (Y1250). **China Southern** (南方航空售票处; Nánfāng Hángkōng Shòupiàochù; ☎95539; 4 Tanaiyi Beilu; ⌚10am-7pm) has a booking office at the entrance of Hétián Yíngbīnguǎn. The airport is 10km southwest of town; a taxi there costs Y20.

BUS There are two bus stations (客运站; *kèyùnzhàn*) in Hotan. Most buses leave from the one on Taipei Xilu. For destinations east of Niya, head to the east bus station 2km east of downtown.

There are nine buses to Kashgar (Y67 to Y93, seven to 10 hours) from 9.30am to 10pm. These buses also stop at Karghilik (Y34, five hours) and Yarkand (Y42, six hours).

Buses to Ürümqi (Y257 to Y387, 25 hours) head straight across the desert on one of two cross-desert highways. Express buses usually take the newer Hotan–Aksu road, but it's difficult to know which road your bus will take until you get on board and ask the driver. A daily bus to Kuqa (Y160 to Y177, eight hours) departs at 2pm.

If you are continuing on the southern Silk Road, take the 10.30am bus to Cherchen (Y100 to Y147, 10 hours). There are also buses every two hours to Niya (Y40 to Y53, five hours).

Getting Around

Bus 10 runs from the **bus station** (客运站; kèyùnzhàn; Taibei Xilu) past the Sunday Market to the east bus station, 2km away. Taxis in town cost a flat Y5.

Hotan to Golmud 和田至格尔木

To continue east along the southern Silk Road, you'll need to catch the 10.30am bus (Y101 to Y142) to **Cherchen** (且末; Qiěmò), 580km away. Buses leave from Hotan's east bus station (东站; *dōng zhàn*); bus 10 runs to the east bus station from Hotan's bus station. The journey to Cherchen takes nine to 10 hours and goes via Keriya (于田; Yútián) and Niya (民丰; Mínfēng). The bus stops for lunch in Keriya. The last 300km from Niya to Cherchen heads across endless and empty grasslands that form a natural barrier against the Taklamakan Desert.

Cherchen's main sight is the **Toghraklek Manor Museum** (托乎拉克庄园博物馆; Tuōhūlākè Zhuāngyuán Bówùguǎn; admission Y20), 4km west of town. The manor, built in 1911 and once home to a local warlord, is a fine example of early-20th century Kashgarian architecture and contains a small exhibit of artefacts found in the area.

The caretaker at the museum can also take you to the nearby **Zaghunluq Ancient Mummy Tomb** (扎滚鲁克古墓群景点; Zāgǔnlǔkè Gǔmùqún Jǐngdiǎn; admission Y30), on the edge of the desert. The 2600-year-old tomb contains a dozen or so naturally mummified bodies, still sporting shreds of colourful clothing. Photography is prohibited in the tomb.

At Cherchen, the **Jiāotōng Bīnguǎn** (交通宾馆; ☎0996-762 7088; d/tr Y80/90; ❄) in the bus-station complex has dirty and depressing rooms. Better options include the **Kūnyù Bīnguǎn** (昆玉宾馆; ☎0996-762 6555; Tuanjie Beilu; d Y100) next to the town square or the **Mùzītāgé Bīnguǎn** (木孜塔格宾馆; ☎0996-762 5150; d incl breakfast Y150), about 300m west of the square, next to the airport (it's also called the Qiěmò Bīnguǎn). To find the town square, walk 650m west of the bus station and turn right at the first set of traffic lights. The square is about 200m from the intersection. A taxi to the hotels costs Y5.

From Cherchen there is a bus at 7pm to Ürümqi (Y246, 18 hours) and a 10am bus to Korla (Y124, 10 hours); both of these go via the Cross-Desert Hwy. The bus to Hotan (Y100) leaves at 10am.

Continuing east, a daily bus (Y76, four hours) heads another 320km east to Charklik (若羌; Ruòqiāng), departing at 10.30am. Charklik is a modern Chinese city, but there are several ancient ruined cities nearby. The most famous is **Luolan**, located some 260km northeast of Charklik, but you'll probably have to join a very pricey group tour to visit as permits can run into the thousands of dollars. The ruined fortress of **Miran** is closer, located just 7km southeast of the modern town of Miran (which is 85km northwest of Charklik). It's also cheaper – group permits cost around Y400 to Y500. Contact CITS in Ürümqi for help with permits.

From Charklik you can complete the Taklamakan loop by taking a bus to Korla (Y83, six to seven hours, 10am, noon, 2pm and 6pm).

Alternatively, you can continue east to **Golmud** in Qīnghǎi. No bus goes all the way to Golmud, so you will probably first have to get a bus or minivan to Yītūnbùlākè (依吞布拉克; Y95, four to six hours) on the Xīnjiāng–Qīnghǎi border. Asbestos mining is the main industry here and Yītūnbùlākè is essentially an environmental catastrophe; expect a rough ride across some hell-on-earth landscapes and bring a scarf to cover your mouth. These vehicles depart when full (six people); almost every day a jeep goes in summer. Next you need to catch the daily bus or any passing vehicle to Huātǔgōu (花土沟), about 66km away, in Qīnghǎi. From Huātǔgōu you can catch a daily public bus to Golmud (Y175, 12 to 17 hours) or Xīníng (Y225, 24 to 28 hours).

The route to Golmud is plagued by washouts and landslides, so don't go this way if you're in a hurry.

NORTHERN XĪNJIĀNG

This region of thick evergreen forests, rushing rivers and isolated mountain ranges is historically home to pastoral nomads. It was closed to foreigners until the 1990s, due to the proximity of the Russian, Mongolian and Kazakhstan borders, which were considered sensitive. Its delicate environment – both politically and ecologically – means you should keep your travel low impact.

Bù'ěrjīn 布尔津

☎0906 / POP 60,000

Bù'ěrjīn, 620km north of Ürümqi, marks the end of the desert and the beginning of the grasslands and mountains to the north. The town's population is mainly Kazakh, but there are also Russians, Han, Uighurs and Tuva Mongolians.

Tourism is a growing industry here and local authorities have spruced up the town with parks, brick sidewalks and pastel-painted buildings. In summer, you'll also be confronted with swarms of biting insects around dusk, so stock up on insect repellent, available in local shops.

Sleeping & Eating

Jiāotōng Bīnguǎn BUDGET HOTEL $
(交通宾馆; ☎652 2643; Wenming Lu; 文明路; tw from Y80) At the lower end of the price range, this remains the most convenient cheapie for foreigners, especially if you need to catch a shared taxi to Kanas Lake in the morning.

Shénxiān Wān Dàjiǔdiàn HOTEL $$
(神仙湾大酒店; ☎652 1325; 5 Shenhu Lu; 神湖路5号; tw Y140) The Immortal Bay Hotel has clean rooms and an efficient staff that are willing to negotiate the price. From the bus station, turn left and then right at the first intersection. It's about 200m down on the left.

Night market MARKET $
(yèshì; Hebin Lu; mains from Y10; ⊙7pm-midnight) Specialising in grilled fish, fresh yoghurt and *kvas* (a yeast brew popular in Russia), this night market is located near the river and makes for very atmospheric dining. To find it, walk south on Youyifeng Lu and keep going until the street dead ends. It's on the right. A second night market is in the alley opposite the People's Hospital (人民医院; Rénmín Yīyuàn), between Youyifeng Lu and Kanasi Lu.

Information

Industrial & Commercial Bank (ICBC; Zhōngguó Gōngshāng Yínháng; Huancheng Nanlu; ⊙10am-1.30pm & 4-6.30pm) Changes major currencies.

Internet cafe (网吧; ⊙9am-midnight) No sign; located at the western end of the smaller night market.

Public Security Bureau (PSB; 公安局; Gōng'ānjú; cnr Yueliangwan Lu & Youyifeng Lu) Can supply you with a permit for a closed area.

Getting There & Away

There are buses to Ürümqi (Y145 to Y163, 13 hours) at 10am and 8pm and hourly buses to Altay (Ālètài; Y21, 1½ hours) between 10am and 7pm. Six daily buses also run to Jímùnǎi (Y16, two hours) on the border with Kazakhstan.

Altay has an airport with daily flights to/from Ürümqi (Y950). A rail line from Ürümqi to Altay is under construction.

Kanas Lake Nature Reserve 哈纳斯湖自然保护区

The stunning Kanas Lake is a long finger lake found in the southernmost reaches of the Siberian taiga ecosystem, pinched in between Mongolia, Russia and Kazakhstan. Most of the local inhabitants are Kazakh or Tuvan. Chinese tourists (and the occasional foreigner) descend on the place like locusts in summer, but with a little effort it's still possible to escape the crowds. Many come hoping for a cameo by the Kanas Lake Monster, China's Nessie, who has long figured in stories around yurt campfires to scare the kids. She appears every year or two, bringing loads of journalists and conspiracy hounds.

Sights & Activities

About 160km from Bù'ěrjīn the road comes to an end at Jiǎdēngyù, basically a collection of hotels near the entrance to the **Kanas Lake Nature Reserve** (Hānàsī Hú Zìrán Bǎohùqū; adult/student Y150/120). Buy a ticket and board a tourist bus (per person Y90, unlimited rides), which carries you 16km up the canyon to a tourist base. The journey takes one hour and includes three photo stops along the way, including Crouching Dragon Bay (卧龙湾; Wòlóng Wān), Moon Bay (月亮湾; Yuèliàng Wān) and Immortal Bay (神仙湾; Shénxiān Wān).

At the tourist base you can change buses to take you the final 2km to Kanas Lake. The old Tuva village lines the road, just past the tourist base. (The new Tuva village is 2km to the west, across the river.) From the final stop it's a five-minute walk to the lake. At the lakeshore you can take a speedboat ride (Y120, 40 minutes) halfway up the lake. A boardwalk along the shore takes you 4.5km up the side of the lake to a vantage point. It's also possible to walk downstream from the dock along the river. The bus terminus is also the starting point for thrilling white water–rafting trips (Y200, 40 minutes).

A great day hike is to the lookout point, **Guānyú Pavilion** (观鱼亭; Guānyú Tíng; 2030m). It's a long, ambling walk from the village; from the top are superb panoramas of the lake and nearby grasslands. It's possible to reach the pavilion by horse – horsemen in the village offer the trip for Y150 (plus another Y150 for the guide). The easiest way up is by bus (Y40/60 one way/return) from the new Tuva village. The bus gets close to the top, from where you walk 1066 steps to the pavilion. The bus trip takes 15 minutes, while the walk up the steps is 20 to 30 minutes.

There are similar landscapes in the neighbouring **Bai Kaba** (Báihābā; admission Y60) village. A taxi from Kanas Lake is Y150. Unfortunately, it was closed to foreigners at the time of research, so check the situation before planning a trip here.

Note that the entry ticket and bus ticket are good for two days, in case you spend the first night outside the park gates. Once you are in the park, no one checks your ticket, so you can stay as long as you like and use the hop on, hop off bus service to get between the lake and village.

A more awe-inspiring and adventurous route to the reserve is a two-day horse trek from the valley of **Hémù** (禾木; student/adult Y48/60), 70km southeast of Kanas Lake, via Karakol (Black Lake). It's costly, though: a guide is Y200 per day, horse rental is Y150 per day, and you also have to pay for the guide's horse. You can save money by trekking in on foot. From Hemu it's a seven- to 10-hour walk to Black Lake. After camping by the lake, walk along the south shore and then continue west for six to seven hours to the old Tuva village. You must be completely self-sufficient with food, tent and sleeping bag. Guides usually do not bring their own food or equipment and may rely on you. On day two you won't find much water on the trail, so load up at Black Lake before setting off. The bus fee is waived if you enter this way, but someone may track you down and charge you for an admission ticket.

You can reach Hémù by bus from Bù'ěrjīn (Y50, five hours), but the journey is slow as the driver stops frequently to run errands for himself and the passengers. It's faster to get a shared taxi; just make sure it will take you all the way to the village and not just to the gate where you pay the admission fee, which is some 20km before the village. A bus (Y200) is available from the gate at Jiǎdēngyù; the price includes the admission ticket to Hémù.

The whole area is only accessible from mid-May to mid-October, with ice and snow making transport difficult at other times.

Tours

The four-day trip out of Ürümqi with Western International Travel Service (p779) in the Bógédá Bīnguǎn is an excellent deal. For Y650 you get an air-con minibus (only 10 hours to Bù'ěrjīn), two nights in Bù'ěrjīn, a park entrance ticket and one night's lodging at the lake. This company operates some of the facilities and activities in the park, including the rafting and boating trips.

Sleeping & Eating

The best place to stay is at a homestay in the old or the new Tuva village. There are several homestays but none have signs, so you'll have to ask around. The homestays are basic, usually just a spare bedroom. You pay Y50 for a bed plus about Y15 to Y20 per meal.

One option is the guesthouse owned by a Tuvan man, **Banzan** (☎135 6518 7064), who lives about 200m past the school (学校; *xuéxiào*) in the old Tuva village near the main road about 2km before the lake. Banzan's family are performers, so you may get to see some traditional singing and dancing. Look for the fading green sign with the picture of a man playing the flute.

In the new village across the river, ask for **Hadala Beka** (☎137 7905 4663), who has a guesthouse with three rooms. To find it on your own, first go to the new village, walk down the main road and look for the large solar panels on your left. The guesthouse is on the far side of the solar panels.

If you need running water and flush toilets, there are a couple of hotels at the tourist base. Try the **Lánhú Bīnguǎn** (Blue Lake Hotel; 蓝湖宾馆; ☎0906-632 6008; r Y200-480), located in a yurt-shaped building near the bus parking lot.

While camping is off limits, it's unlikely that anyone will look for you. Food in the reserve is expensive and monotonous; bring your own supplies.

In Hemu, you can stay at the **Lantian International Youth Hostel** (交通宾馆; ☎0991-886 8118; www.yhahm.com; dm Y50, d Y120), a rustic wood-cabin hostel and comfortable base for exploring the village and nearby mountains.

Getting There & Away

See the Tours section also.

AIR The brand-new Kanas airport, 50km south of the reserve, has flights to and from Ürümqi (Y1130, one hour) in summer (July and August). A shuttle (Y40) meets all incoming flights.

BUS There is no public bus to the reserve, but two buses per day go to Hémù (Y50) at 10am and 4pm. The buses leave outside the bus station at Bù'ěrjīn and the village school in Hémù respectively.

TAXI A share taxi to the reserve is Y60 per person or Y240 for the whole thing. The 160km trip takes two to three hours. Rates to Hémù cost the same. Taxi drivers *will* look for you at Bù'ěrjīn's bus station.

Yīníng 伊宁

☎0999 / POP 240,000

Located on the historic border between the Chinese and Russian empires, Yīníng (Gulja) has long been subject to a tug-of-war between the two sides. The city was occupied by Russian troops between 1872 and 1881, and in 1962 there were major Sino-Soviet clashes along the Ili River (Yīlí Hé). There is little reason to go out of your way for Yīníng, but you may end up passing though on your way to Kazakhstan.

The heart of the city is People's Sq (Rénmín Guǎngchǎng). The bus station is at the northeast end of Jiefang Lu, the main thoroughfare through town. An **internet café** (网吧; Yingbin Lu; ⏲24hr) is located on the 2nd floor above the Agricultural Bank (from the Yīlí Bīnguǎn walk east about 200m).

If you've got an interest in Manchu history it's worth taking a ride out to the Ili Valley (Yīlí Gǔ; 伊犁谷), home to some 20,000 Xibe (Xībózú), who were dispatched by the Qing government to safeguard and settle the region during the 18th century. This is the only place in China where you'll find a population capable of reading and writing Manchurian, which otherwise died out when the Manchus were assimilated into Chinese culture. You can visit the Lamaist temple **Jingyuǎn Sì** (靖远寺; admission Y10), outside nondescript Qapaqal (Chábùchá'ěr). Minibuses to Qapaqal (Y3, 30 minutes) depart from the Yīníng bus station.

Sleeping & Eating

Yīlí Bīnguǎn HOTEL **$$**

(☎802 3799; fax 802 4964; 8 Yingbin Lu; 迎宾路8; tw Y150-400) Its rooms aren't always the fanciest, but this place certainly has character. You are greeted at the entrance by a bust of Lenin, beyond which is a veritable forest filled with chirping birds, winding roads and old Soviet buildings. Banging doors aside, it's the quietest place in town. The Zixiangge Coffee Club, just inside the gate, is good for a Western-style meal.

Just to the south of town is a long line of **open-air restaurants** and **teahouses** where you can sit and watch the mighty Ili River (Ili Daria in Uighur, Yīlí Hé in Chinese) slide by. To get there, hop on bus 2 and get off at the last stop, just before the bridge over the river.

Getting There & Away

From the **main bus station** *(qìchēzhàn)* there are buses to Ürümqi (Y160 to Y190, 11 to 14 hours), Bólè (Y44, four hours) and Korla (Y190 to Y205, 18 hours). Note that Hwy 217 is closed to foreigners, so there is no chance of a shortcut to Kuqa.

For Almaty (Y150, 12 hours), buses depart from a parking lot on Yingayati Lu, about 1km northeast of Renmin Sq. You must already have a Kazakhstan visa.

The railway to Yīníng was completed in 2010. There are two daily trains to Ürümqi, the 5816 (hard/soft sleeper Y151/234) at 8.50pm and the K9790 (hard/soft sleeper Y162/245) at 11pm. The journey is around 11 hours. The station is 8km northwest of the city centre; buses 10, 16, 201 and 401 go there.

There are several flights a day to Ürümqi (Y600); tickets are available from the **Xinjiang Airport Group** (☎803 1888), which has an office by the gate of the Yīlí Bīnguǎn.

Bólè 博乐

Close to the border with Kazakhstan, Bólè (Bortala in Mongolian) is the centre of a Mongolian autonomous county and the jumping-off point for Sayram Lake. Just as the Xibe were sent to guard the border in the Ili Valley, Chahar Mongols (from Inner Mongolia) were dispatched to this plateau by the Qing government to defend the border. They simply never went home. Xibu Guangchang (西部广场), the town square, is a gathering place for Mongolian, Kazakh and Uighur craftsmen and artists. The town also has a Mongolian Buddhist **monastery** (Zhèn Yuǎn Sì), built in 1984, and a **museum** that describes the unique melting pot of peoples in the area.

The best way to reach Bólè is by overnight train 5801 (hard/soft sleeper Y115/175, 11 hours, 10.55pm). Buses (Y10, 45 minutes) wait at the station to take you into the city. From Bólè there are hourly buses to Ürümqi (Y100) or you can take the train, departing at 9.30pm.

Around Bólè

The vast **Sayram Lake** (塞里木湖; Sàilǐmù Hú), 120km north of Yīníng and 90km west of Bólè, is an excellent spot to explore the Tiān Shān range. The lake is especially colourful during June and July, when the alpine flowers are in full bloom.

While there is some food around, the selection is pricey and limited, so take what you need. In the height of summer, there are Kazakh yurts (about Y40 per night including three meals) scattered around the lake willing to take boarders. Admission to the lake is Y40.

By bus, Sayram Lake is two hours from Bólè or three hours from Yīníng; any bus passing between the two cities can drop you by the lake. They usually stop at its southwestern corner, where you'll find horses for hire and plenty of yurt accommodation in summer. At the time of research the road was under construction, so most of the yurts had moved further up the hillside.

Coming from Yīníng, the last section of road is a spectacular series of mountain switchbacks. A new set of bridges and tunnels was being constructed at the time of research and when complete will significantly shorten travel times.

Gānsù

POPULATION: 26.4 MILLION

Includes »

Best Places to Eat

» Oasis (p826)

» Talo Restaurant (p819)

» Nomad Restaurant (p815)

» Yuánjì Làzhī Ròujiāmó (p820)

Best Places to Stay

» Overseas Tibetan Hotel (p815)

» Lángmùsì Hotel (p818)

» Ziyunge Hotel (p820)

» Dune Guesthouse (p826)

Why Go?

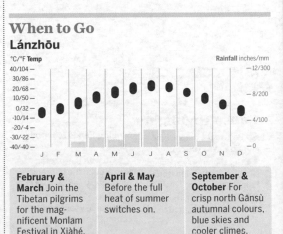

Synonymous with the Silk Road, the slender province of Gānsù flows east to west along the Hexi Corridor, the gap through which all manner of goods once streamed from China to Central Asia. The constant flow of commerce left Buddhist statues, beacon towers, forts, chunks of the Great Wall and ancient trading towns in its wake.

Gānsù (甘肃) offers an entrancingly rich cultural and geographic diversity. Historians immerse themselves in Silk Road lore, art aficionados swoon before the wealth of Buddhist paintings and sculptures, while adventurers hike to glaciers and tread along paths well worn by Tibetan nomads. The ethnic diversity is astonishing: in Línxià, the local Hui Muslims act as though the silk route lives on; in Xiàhé and Lángmùsì, a pronounced Tibetan disposition holds sway, while other minority groups such as the Bao'an and Dongxiang join in the colourful minority patchwork.

When to Go

Lánzhōu

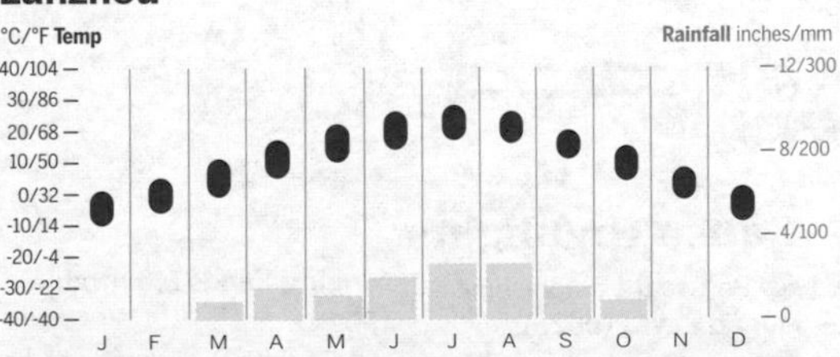

February & March Join the Tibetan pilgrims for the magnificent Monlam Festival in Xiàhé.

April & May Before the full heat of summer switches on.

September & October For crisp north Gānsù autumnal colours, blue skies and cooler climes.

History

Although the Qin dynasty had a toehold on eastern Gānsù, the first significant push west along the Hexi Corridor came with the Han dynasty. An imperial envoy, Chang Ch'ien, was dispatched to seek trading partners and returned with detailed reports of Central Asia and the route that would become known as the Silk Road. The Han extended the Great Wall through the Hexi Corridor, expanding their empire in the process. As trade along the Silk Road grew, so did the small way stations set up along its route; these grew into towns and cities that form the major population centres of modern Gānsù. The stream of traders from lands east and west also left their mark in the incredible diversity of modern Gānsù. The Buddhist grottoes at Mogao, Màijī Shān and elsewhere are testament to the

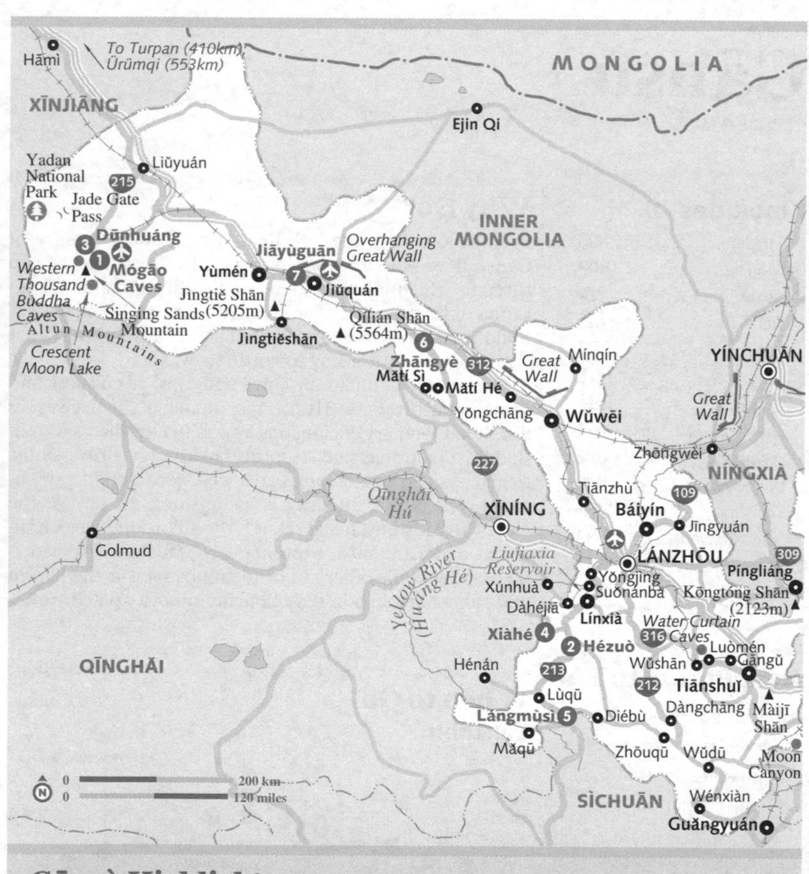

Gānsù Highlights

1. Peruse the astonishing **Mògāo Caves** (p828)
2. Get thoroughly spooked climbing Hézuò's **Milarepa Palace** (p817)
3. Camp beneath the stars amid the vast dunes of the **Singing Sands Mountain** (p830)
4. Go with the Tibetan flow around the **Labrang Monastery** (p812) *kora* in Xiàhé
5. Hike to your heart's content through the fantastic scenery around **Lángmùsì** (p818)
6. Stand head to head with the vast **Sleeping Buddha** of Zhāngyè (p821)
7. Feel the Gobi wind in your hair as you stand on the ramparts of **Jiāyùguān Fort** (p824)

PRICE INDICATORS

The following price indicators are used in this chapter:

Sleeping

$	less than Y200
$$	Y200 to Y500
$$$	more than Y500

Eating

$	less than Y40
$$	Y40 to Y100
$$$	more than Y100

great flourishing of religious and artistic schools along the Silk Road.

The mixing of cultures in Gānsù eventually led to serious tensions, which culminated in the Muslim rebellions of 1862 to 1877. The conflict left millions dead and virtually wiped out Gānsù's Muslim population. Ethnic tensions have never really left the province; in March 2008, pro-Tibetan demonstrations in Xiàhé led to riots. Lethal mud slides after heavy rain in August 2010 led to the deaths of hundreds of villagers in Zhōuqū (south Gānsù).

Climate

Gānsù rarely sees any rain, and dust storms can whip up, particularly in the spring. Winters are nippy from November to March.

Language

Gānsù has its own group of regional Chinese dialects, loosely known as Gansuhua (part of the northwestern Lanyin Mandarin family). On the borders of Qīnghǎi and Sìchuān there is a significant Tibetan population speaking the Tibetan Amdo dialect.

Getting There & Around

Lánzhōu has flights around the country; other airports such as Dūnhuáng and Jiāyùguān only have a handful of flights to major cities, with fewer flights in the winter.

Train is the best way to connect the province's Silk Road sights and continue along the popular rail routes to Xīnjiāng or Xī'ān. For southern Gānsù you are largely at the mercy of (sometimes painfully slow) buses.

LÁNZHŌU & SOUTHERN GĀNSÙ

Lánzhōu is a major transportation hub employed by most travellers as a springboard for elsewhere. The Tibetan-inhabited areas around Xiàhé and Lángmùsì are the principal enticements – perfect stopovers for overlanders heading to or from Sìchuān.

Lánzhōu 兰州

0931 / POP 3.2 MILLION

Roughly at China's cartographic bullseye, Gānsù's elongated capital marks the halfway point for overlanders trekking across the country. The city sprawls in an inelegant east–west concrete melange for over 20km along the southern banks of the Yellow River (Huáng Hé). Growing up on a strategic stretch of the river, and sitting between competing Chinese and Central Asian empires, Lánzhōu frequently changed hands. Trapped between mountains, Lánzhōu has frequent bad-air days when a grey sun sets anaemically over a hazy city.

Sights

FREE **Gānsù Provincial Museum** MUSEUM
(甘肃省博物馆; Gānsù Shěng Bówùguǎn; Xijin Xilu; audio guide for Silk Road exhibition Y10; 9am-5pm Tue-Sun) This sparkling museum has an intriguing collection of Silk Road artefacts, including inscribed Han-dynasty **wooden tablets** used to relay messages along the Silk Road and a graceful Eastern Han (25 BC–AD 220) bronze horse galloping upon the back of a swallow. The latter, known as the **'Flying Horse of Wuwei'**, was unearthed at Léitái and is much reproduced across northwestern China. Unearthed 120km northeast of Lánzhōu, a 2nd-century-BC **silver plate** depicting Bacchus, the Greco-Roman god of wine, may set your mind pondering. Among other items on view are **Persian coins**, some lovely **Bodhisattva statues** from Tiāntīshān and a collection of dinosaur skeletons upstairs, where you will also find a cafe. Bus 1 goes here.

White Cloud Temple TAOIST TEMPLE
(白云观; Báiyún Guàn; Binhe Zhonglu; 7am-5.30pm) This largely rebuilt Qing-dynasty Taoist temple is an oasis of reverential calm at the heart of the city. About 20 black-clad bearded **monks** inhabit the place – several of them are qualified to

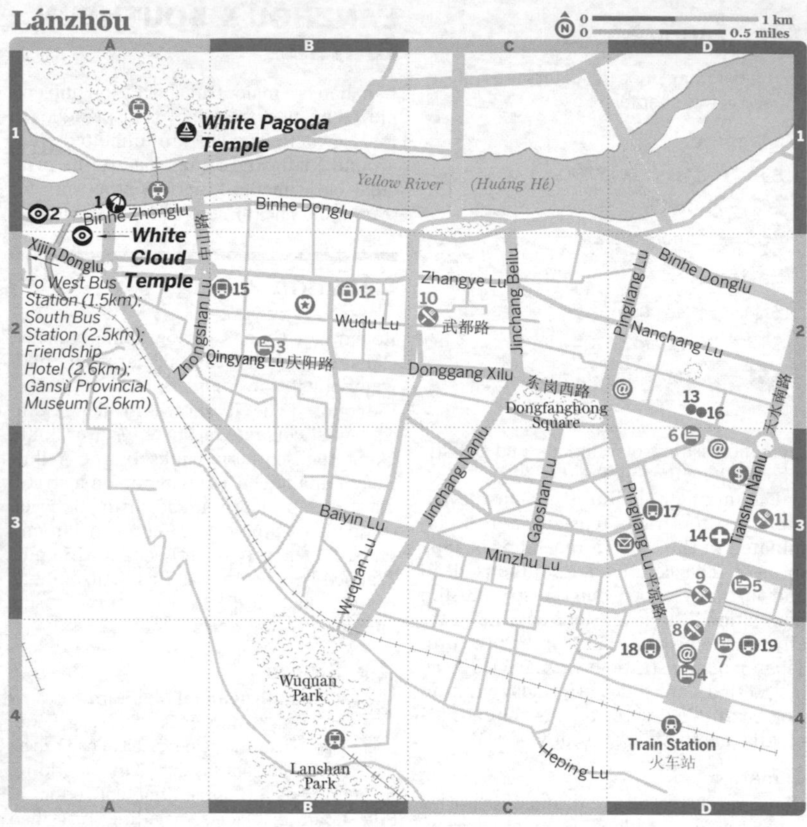

Lánzhōu

Top Sights

White Cloud Temple ... A2

White Pagoda Temple ... A1

Sights

1 Beach ... A1

2 Water Wheels ... A1

Sleeping

3 Grand Soluxe Hotel Gānsù ... B2

4 Huálián Bīnguǎn ... D4

5 Jǐnjiāng Inn ... D3

6 JJ Sun Hotel ... D3

7 Zǐjīnghuā Jiǔdiàn ... D4

Eating

8 Héjiāhé ... D4

9 Hézhèng Lù Night Market Entrance ... D3

10 Jiànjūn Niúròumiàn ... C2

11 Néngrénjù ... D3

Shopping

12 Foreign Languages Bookshop ... B2

Information

13 Gānsù Airport Booking Office ... D2

14 Lǎobǎixìng Pharmacy ... D3

Transport

15 Bus 111 to South Bus Station ... B2

16 China Eastern Airlines ... D2

17 East Bus Station ... D3

18 Main Long-Distance Bus Station ... D4

19 Tiānshuǐ Bus Station ... D4

read fortunes; other **soothsayers** in eccentric attire and antique glasses muster outside the temple.

White Pagoda Hill PARK
(白塔山; Báitǎ Shān; admission Y6; ⏲6.30am-8.30pm summer) This park is on the northern bank of the Yellow River. At its zenith is **White Pagoda Temple** (白塔寺; Báitǎ Sì), originally built during the Yuan dynasty (1206–1368), from where there are good views across the city. A **cable car** (incl park ticket up/down/return Y25/15/30) spans the river; the terminal is just to the west of Zhōngshān Bridge. Bus 34 or 137 comes here from in front of the train station on Tianshui Nanlu.

Water wheels WATER WHEELS
(水车园; Shuǐchē yuán; admission Y4) A short stroll from White Cloud Temple are these two huge copies of irrigation devices that once lined the Yellow River.

Beach BEACH
East of the water wheels, this beach (河滩; Hétān) area is bursting on weekends with volleyball games, kites, speedboats and coracle raft trips (Y30 to Y40) across the chocolate-coloured river.

Sleeping

The most practical area to base yourself is in the east, home of the train station; always fish for discounts. Most budget hostels near the train station won't accept foreigners.

JJ Sun Hotel HOTEL $$$
(锦江阳光酒店; Jǐnjiāng Yángguāng Jiǔdiàn; ☎880 5511; www.jjsunhotel.com; 589 Donggang Xilu; 东岗西路589号; tw/s Y800/900, discounts of 30%; ❄@) This good four-star choice has well-groomed, spacious and affordable rooms that are larger than those at the Grand Soluxe and come with very clean bathrooms. Pleasant wood-panelled restaurant on 2nd floor.

Zǐjīnghuā Jiǔdiàn HOTEL $$
(紫荆花酒店; Bauhinia Hotel; ☎863 8918; 36 Tianshui Nanlu; 天水南路36号; tw & d Y388-400, tr Y380, discounts of up to 70%; ❄) Once you get beyond the depressing ground-floor bar and dawdling lifts, rooms are good and discounts fab. Aim for a south-facing corner room, which nets you extra space and good mountain views at this colossal tower hotel near the train station.

Grand Soluxe Hotel Gānsù HOTEL $$$
(甘肃阳光大酒店; Gānsù Yángguāng Dàjiǔdiàn; ☎460 8888; www.sunshineplaza.com.cn; 428 Qingyang Lu; 庆阳路428号; d Y1060-1480, discounts of 40%; ❄@) The gilded lobby is brash, but overall this is a reasonably luxurious 'five-star' option overseen by pleasant staff. Business kings are small with shower (no bath), but well turned out and good value with discounts; elite kings are larger.

Friendship Hotel HOTEL $
(友谊宾馆; Yǒuyì Bīnguǎn; ☎268 9169; 16 Xijin Xilu; 西津西路16号; old wing tw Y60, with bathroom Y108-280, new wing tw Y380; ❄) The old-fashioned cheapo rooms with wood floorboards but no shower feel like a boarding school – or an asylum – but are decent and good value. The Y108 rooms are vast but crummy. For better rooms, head to the Jiābīn Lóu (Guest Hall), where much more pleasant doubles await. Although there's a tennis court and green grounds to the rear, the architecture is best described as 'Great Wall of Kitsch'.

Huálián Bīnguǎn HOTEL $
(华联宾馆; ☎499 2000; 7-9 Tianshui Nanlu; 天水南路7-9号; d Y189, tr Y319, discounts of 40-50%;❄) This 360-room monster has comfortable, slightly scruffy rooms and a big lobby with a travel agency. The staff are friendly and speak English, but you'll have to put up with some traffic noise and slow lifts; discounts are attractive. It's right opposite the train station, with a handy internet cafe located next door. Trips to Bǐnglíng Sì arranged (Y198).

Jǐnjiāng Inn HOTEL $
(锦江之星; Jǐnjiāng Zhīxīng; ☎861 7333; 182 Tianshui Lu; 天水路182号; tw & d Y189; ❄@) Neat and tidy express business-style hotel around 1km north of the train station with unfussy, compact and well-maintained rooms and snappy service. No discounts, but great value.

Eating & Drinking

Lánzhōu enjoys nationwide fame for its *niúròumiàn* (牛肉面), beef noodle soup that's spicy enough to make you snort. Two handy phrases are *'jiā ròu'* (加肉; add beef) and *'bùyào làjiāo'* (不要辣椒; without chillies).

Hézhèng Lù night market MARKET $
(和政路夜市场入口; Hézhèng Lù Yèshìchǎng Rùkǒu) This bustling market, extending

from Tianshui Lu to Pingliang Lu, is terrific for savouring the flavours of the northwest. The mix of Hui, Han and Uighur stalls offers everything from goat's head soup to steamed snails, *ròujiābǐng* (肉夹饼; mutton served inside a 'pocket' of flat bread), lamb dishes seasoned with cumin, *dàpánjī* (large plate of spicy chicken and potatoes), Sìchuān hole-in-the-wall outfits, dumplings, spare-rib noodles and more.

Néngrénjù HOTPOT **$$**
(能仁聚; 216 Tianshui Lu; hotpot for 2 Y50; ⏲11am-10pm; 🗐) Tasty Běijīng-style traditional lamb hotpot (涮羊肉; *shùan yángròu*) spot where you swiftly scald wafer-thin strips of lamb to bleach out the colour before dunking in sesame sauce; great for group dining with beers but also good solo; ensure you check your bill carefully, though.

Jiànjūn Niúròumiàn NOODLES **$**
(建军牛肉面; 234 Jingning Lu; meals Y7; ⏲6am-5pm) This popular restaurant makes an early start but shuts early. Grab a ticket from the desk at front and exchange it with kitchen staff, who will ladle you out a huge, filling and sweltering bowl of delicious beef noodles (牛肉面; *niúròumiàn*), eye-rollingly spiced up with chilli and coriander.

Héjiāhé CHINESE FAST FOOD **$**
(和家和; Tianshui Nanlu; meals Y20; ⏲6am-11pm) Convenient, bright and unfussy fast-food restaurant with a helpful photo menu and range of quickly delivered dishes, including *hóngshāoròu fàn* (红烧肉饭; braised pork and rice; Y15) and *nǎichá* (奶茶; bubble tea; Y4.50).

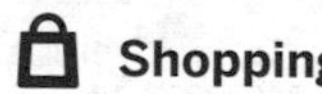

Shopping

Foreign Languages Bookshop BOOKS
(外文书店; Wàiwén Shūdiàn; 35 Zhangye Lu; ⏲8.30am-6.30pm) In the centre of town.

Information

Bank of China (中国银行; Zhōngguó Yínháng; Tianshui Lu; ⏲8.30am-noon & 2.30-6pm Mon-Fri) Has an indoor ATM.

China International Travel Service (CITS; 中国国际旅行社; Zhōngguó Guójì Lǚxíngshè; ☎232 3048; www.citsgs.com; Xijin Xilu) Small office next to Gansu Provincial Museum.

China Post (中国邮政; Zhōngguó Yóuzhèng; cnr Minzhu Lu & Pingliang Lu; ⏲8am-7pm)

Hóngchén Internet Cafe (宏晨网吧; Hóngchén Wǎngbā; per hr Y2.5; ⏲24hr) On the 2nd floor, next to Huálián Bīnguǎn.

Internet cafe (网吧; wǎngbā; 2nd fl, 449 Donggang Xilu; per hr Y2; ⏲24hr)

Internet cafe (网吧; wǎngbā; per hr Y2; ⏲24hr) Next to No 710 Donggang Xilu, in between Kodak Express outlet and Bank of China.

Lǎobǎixìng Pharmacy (老百姓大药房; Lǎobǎixìng Dàyàofáng; Tianshui Lu; ⏲24hr) Evening service, knock on door.

Public Security Bureau (PSB; 公安局; Gōng'ānjú; 482 Wudu Lu; ⏲8.30-11.30am & 2.30-5.30pm Mon-Fri) The foreign-affairs branch is located on the ground floor, next to a giant Orwellian tower. Visa extensions are generally granted on the same day; one photo required. At the time of writing the office was being refurbished and a temporary office was at 52 Huangheyan Nanbinhe Lu.

Western Travel Service (西部旅行社; Xībù Lǚxíngshè; ☎885 0529; 486 Donggang Xilu) Located on the 2nd floor of the west wing of Lánzhōu Fàndiàn. Has English-speaking staff and offers competitively priced tours and ticket bookings.

Getting There & Away

Air

Among other cities, Lánzhōu has flights to Běijīng (Y1340), Dūnhuáng (Y1260), Jiāyùguān (Y1080), Kūnmíng (Y1410), Shànghǎi (Y1750) and Xī'ān (Y600). Book tickets from:

China Eastern Airlines (东方航空公司; Zhōngguó Dōngháng Hángkōng; ☎882 1964; 586 Donggang Xilu; ⏲office 8.30am-7.30pm, phone line 24hr)

Gānsù Airport Booking Office (甘肃机场售票中心; Gānsù Jīchǎng Shòupiào Zhōngxīn; ☎888 9666; 520 Donggang Xilu; ⏲8.30am-9pm) Can book all air tickets at discounted prices.

Bus

Lánzhōu has several bus stations, all with departures for Xīníng. The **main long-distance bus station** (长途车站; chángtú chēzhàn; Pingliang Lu) and the **south bus station** (汽车南站; qìchē nánzhàn; Langongping Lu) are the most useful.

The following services depart from the main long-distance bus station:

Píngliáng Y82, five to six hours, hourly (7.30am to 5pm)

Tiānshuǐ Y71.50, four hours, every 30 minutes (7am to 6pm)

Xīníng Y58, three hours, every 30 minutes (7.10am to 8.10pm)

Yínchuān Y120, six hours, every two hours (7.20am to 3.20pm)

GETTING TO GĀNNÁN

At the time of writing, the authorities were still twitchy about individual travellers taking buses southwest to Línxià, Hézuò, Xiàhé and Lángmùsì, so travellers buying tickets to these destinations at the south bus station were required to provide a photocopy of their passport information page and visa page. The ticket office could not provide these, so you had to supply them yourself; a shop left out of the bus station and across the road can photocopy your passport for you, but if you are taking an early bus get this done beforehand somewhere else as the shop may not be open. Be aware that this regulation may have changed by the time you read this.

The following services depart from the south bus station:

Hézuò Y32, four hours, every 30 minutes (7am to 4.30pm)

Lángmùsì Y73, eight hours, two daily (8.30am and 9.30am)

Línxià Y30, three hours, every 30 minutes (7am to 7pm)

Xiàhé Y45.50, six hours, three daily (7.30am, 8.30am and 2pm)

Zhāngyè Y100, 12 hours, one daily (6pm)

The **west bus station** (汽车西站; qìchē xīzhàn; Xijin Xilu) has departures to Liújiāxiá (Y10.50, two hours, every 20 minutes 7am to 6pm); for Bǐnglíng Sì, see p809. The **east bus station** (汽车东站; qìchē dōngzhàn; ☎841 8411; Pingliang Lu) has sleepers to Zhāngyè and Jiāyùguān, Tiānshuǐ (Y71.5) and Píngliáng (Y82 to Y98, regular, five to six hours).

Hidden off the main street, the **Tiānshuǐ bus station** (天水汽车站; Tiānshuǐ Qìchēzhàn; Tianshui Lu) has buses for eastern Gānsù, including Luòmén (Y50, four hours).

Train

Lánzhōu is the major rail link for trains heading to and from western China. Departing from Lánzhōu, the T9205 (Y49, 7.29am) is a handy two-tier train that stops in Wǔwēi; it departs Wǔwēi at 10.19am to continue to Zhāngyè (Y41, two hours) and Jiāyùguān. There are also overnight trains to:

Dūnhuáng Y263, 12 hours

Jiāyùguān Y178, 10 hours

Turpan Y369, 22 hours

You can continue west to Ürümqi (Y390, 24 hours); east is to Xī'ān (hard sleeper Y175). In summer buy your onward tickets a couple of days in advance to guarantee a sleeper berth.

A soft seat in one of the double-decker express trains is by far the most civilised way to get to Xīníng (hard/soft seat Y33/50, 3½ hours). Trains depart at 10.50am and 7pm.

For details on trains to Lhasa, see p890.

Getting Around

The airport is 70km north of the city. **Airport buses** (☎896 8555) leave every hour from 8am to 7pm just west of the China Eastern Airlines office three hours before scheduled flight departures. The trip costs Y30 and takes 70 minutes. A taxi costs around Y120, or Y30 per seat. Lánzhōu badly needs a metro system.

Useful bus routes:

Buses 1, 6, 31 and 137 From the train station to the west bus station and the Friendship Hotel via Xiguan Shizi.

Bus 111 From Zhongshan Lu (at the Xiguan Shizi stop; 去汽车南站的111路公交车) to the south bus station.

Buses 7 and 10 From the train station up the length of Tianshui Nanlu before heading west and east, respectively.

Public buses cost Y1; taxis are Y7 for the first 3km. A taxi from the train station to the south bus station costs Y20.

Bǐnglíng Sì 炳灵寺

Due to its relative inaccessibility, **Bǐnglíng Sì** (adult/student Y50/25) is one of the few Buddhist grottoes in China to survive the tumultuous 20th century unscathed. Over a period spanning 1600 years, sculptors dangling from ropes carved 183 niches and sculptures into the porous rock along the dramatic canyon walls. Today the cliffs are isolated by the waters of the Liújiāxiá Reservoir (Liújiāxiá Shuǐkù) on the Yellow River. All considered, come here for a nice day out rather than for the cave art alone, which doesn't compare to somewhere like Dūnhuáng.

As with other Silk Road grottoes, wealthy patrons, often traders along the route west, sponsored the development of Bǐnglíng Sì, which reached its height during the prosperous Tang dynasty. The star of the caves is the 27m-high seated **statue of Maitreya**, the future Buddha, but some of the smaller, sway-hipped Bodhisattvas and guardians, bearing an obvious Indian influence, are equally exquisite. Photos are allowed. Art buffs can climb the staircase to Tang-dynasty caves 169 and 172 for an extra fee of Y300.

If you've hired your own boat, and thus have more time at the site, you can take a jeep (Y40) or hike 2.5km further up the impressive canyon to a small **Tibetan monastery**.

Note that from November to March, water levels may be too low to visit the caves, so check before setting off.

Western Travel Service (Xībù Lǚxíngshè; ☎0931-885 0529; 486 Donggang Xilu) in Lánzhōu can organise a visit to the caves for two people for Y340 per person.

You can visit Bǐnglíng Sì as a day trip from Lánzhōu or en route to Línxià. Frequent buses from Lánzhōu's west bus station (Y12, two hours) run past the Liújiāxiá Reservoir, and will drop you 500m from the boat ticket office.

The going rates for a covered speedboat (seating up to eight people) are Y400 for the one-hour journey. The boat ticket office is good at hooking up independent travellers with small groups, which will make the price around Y65 to Y80 per person. For this you'll get about 1½ hours at the site, which is really a minimum. Private operators close to the dam will pester you with similar rates, and sometimes even cheaper speedboats (Y200). For those that have the time, the ferry (May to October) is just Y30 for a return trip, but it is a pretty dreary seven-hour return trip! Make sure you bring snacks, sunscreen, cold drinks and a couple of paperbacks.

If you're heading to Línxià after the caves, you can arrange for a speedboat to drop you off at Liánhuātái (莲花台) on the way back. From there, minibuses will taxi you on to Línxià (Y10, one hour).

Línxià 临夏

☎0930 / POP 203,200

The bus from Lánzhōu descends after a while into a highly fertile valley before pulling into this slow-moving and lazy Silk Road town where residents carry on as though the camel caravans are just over the horizon. Han China runs out of steam and hits the buffers here: in this overt stronghold of Chinese Islam, the skyline is dominated by onion-domed mosques. Among the goods for sale you'll spot gourds, daggers, saddlery, carpets, textiles and oversized spectacles, as well as Muslim and Buddhist religious paraphernalia. Also noticeable are more Western songs on the radio and far fewer excruciating 'hulloos' from roadside quipsters. Línxià isn't quite a destination in itself, but many travellers break up the trip to or from Xiàhé here and it's a great place to get fed, watered, rested and recharged.

Sights

Wànshòu Temple TAOIST TEMPLE
(万寿观; Wànshòu Guàn; admission Y10; ⏲7am-8pm) If you have a bit of time to kill, this cedar-scented temple extends seven levels up the hillside at the northwest fringe of Línxià. Along the cliffs you can visit other surrounding temples overlooking the city. Take bus 6 to the west bus station and head for the nine-storey pagoda on the ridge located opposite.

Sleeping & Eating

Shuǐquán Bīnguǎn HOTEL $
(水泉宾馆; ☎631 4968; 68 Jiefang Nanlu; 解放南路68号; s/d/tr with shared bathroom Y20/40/60, d with shower Y60-80; ❄) This cheapie in front of the Shuǐquán Mosque is handy for the bus station and has fine, clean and spacious rooms, but beds and pillows are hard. Light sleepers may get jolted by the early-morning call to prayer. Rooms on the street side get the most sunlight. Heading out of the south bus station, turn right and walk 200m.

Línxià Fàndiàn HOTEL $
(临夏饭店; ☎623 0081; 9 Hongyuan Lu; 红园路9号; tw from Y180; ❄) The new block has the better, pricier rooms, while the cheaper ones are in the old block. It's not in the most exciting part of town, about 800m east of the west bus station.

Shuǐquán Cāntīng MUSLIM $
(水泉餐厅; Jiefang Nanlu; meals Y25-50; ⏲7.30am-9.30pm) Handily tucked away by the hotel of the same name, this is a good place for a plate of spicy *dàpánjī* (大盘鸡; chicken with green and red peppers and potato in an oily chilli sauce; medium/large Y50/60); we recommend going for a medium plate unless you have a horse-like hunger or there are three of you. It can be a bit of a wait, but when it arrives the dish is a real feast.

Beidajie Yèshì NIGHT MARKET

At this market just west of Zhongxin Guangchang (中心广场; Centre Sq), you can sit down alfresco for lamb kebabs (Y0.70 each) and watch vendors fire up tasty *shā guō* (砂锅; minihotpots; Y8) on sheets of flame from around 7pm.

Come evening, street vendors dole out *shā guō* and hot snacks at other strategically placed main intersections.

Information

Bank of China (中国银行; Zhōngguó Yínháng; Jiefang Lu; ⌚8.30am-noon & 2.30-6pm Mon-Fri) On left-hand side of Jiefang Lu around 100m north of Sāndàoqiáo Guǎngchǎng (三道桥广场); 24hr ATM.

Ránqíng Internet Bar (燃情岁月; Ránqíng Suìyuè; Jiefang Lu; per hr Y3.50; ⌚24hr) On the 2nd floor behind the Héngshēng Hotel (Héngshēng Bīnguǎn) just before Zhongxin Guangchang.

Getting There & Away

Línxià has three long-distance bus stations: **south** *(nán zhàn)*, **west** *(xī zhàn)* and **east** *(dōng zhàn)*. You may dropped off at the west bus station but it is of little use otherwise. The east station is handy for Dōngxiāng and also has buses to Liújiāxiá (Y16, three hours, every 30 minutes 8am to 4pm). Bus 6 links the south and the west bus stations, or a taxi is Y4.

The following services depart from the **south bus station**:

Hézuò, Y20, two hours, every 30 minutes (6am to 5pm)

Lánzhōu, Y29.50, three hours, every 20 minutes (7.30am to 5.30pm)

Tiānshuǐ, Y80, 10 hours, one daily (6.20am)

Xiàhé, Y19, two hours, every 30 minutes (6.30am to 5pm)

Xīníng, Y56, eight hours, one daily (6am)

One interesting route is to the Mèngdá Nature Reserve (p872) in Qīnghǎi. The fastest way to the reserve is to catch transport to Dàhéjiā (p811) and charter a taxi (Y40) for the last 15km.

If you're on the slow road to Qīnghǎi, buses to Xúnhuà (Y30, 3½ hours, 8am to 3pm) leave every hour or two from a courtyard behind the Tiānhé Fàndiàn (天河饭店), reachable by walking 350m northeast from the south bus station to the first intersection, Sandaoqiao Guangchang (三道桥广场), then turning right and walking 350m to the hotel. From Xúnhuà you'll find onward transport to Xīníng or Tóngrén.

Suǒnánbà (Dōngxiāng) 锁南坝(东乡)

☎0930 / POP 12,000

Spilling over a ridge high above Línxià and home to both Hui and Dongxiang minorities, this little market town's only street is a hive of activity, with locals trading wares and occasional shepherds shooing flocks about. The town is called Suǒnánbà, while the surrounding county is Dōngxiāng, but some people also call the town Dōngxiāng.

The Dongxiang people speak an Altaic language and are believed to be descendants of 13th-century immigrants from Central Asia, moved forcibly to China after Kublai Khan's Middle East conquest.

The local **museum** (东乡博物馆; Dōngxiāng Bówùguǎn; ☎712 3286; ⌚8.30am-5pm) has an ethnographic room with traditional clothing, saddles and bronze items, much of it resembling items used by Mongols; you may have to ask staff to unlock the small exhibition halls. The museum is on the 3rd and 4th floors of the enormous pink-and-orange building opposite the bus station. Captions are in Chinese.

Frequent minibuses (Y5, 40 minutes, 6am to 8pm) head up on the pleasant journey past terraced fields from Línxià's east bus station. To continue to Lánzhōu (Y18, two hours), buses leave Suǒnánbà on the hour from the top of the hill (at the T-junction) between 8am and 4pm. The bus only turns up at the last minute, as the driver spends about 30 minutes trawling the main road looking for passengers.

Dàhéjiā 大河家

☎0930 / POP 4500

With sweeping views over the Yellow River, towering red cliffs and (in summer) verdant green terraces, Dàhéjiā is a kaleidoscope of colour. The surrounding area is home to a significant population of Bao'an (保安族), Muslims who speak a Mongolic language. The Bao'an are famed for producing knives and share cultural traits with the Hui and Dongxiang. Their Mongol roots come out during summer festivals, when it is possible to see displays of wrestling and horse riding.

A 12km loop road from Dàhéjiā goes out to the peaceful Bao'an villages of **Gānhétán** (甘和谈), **Méipó** (媒婆) and **Dàdūn** (大敦).

You can walk to the villages in about 40 minutes or hire a taxi (Y30).

Unless you have a special interest in minority culture in China, Dàhéjiā is a bit far for a side trip. However, the town is worth visiting if you're travelling on the road between Línxià and Xīníng. The **Sānlián Bīnguǎn** (三联宾馆; ☎139 9309 7599; dm Y20-30, tw with bathroom Y50-88) is a decent Hui-run hotel in town, near the Yellow River bridge.

Most buses between Línxià and Xīníng will stop here. From Línxià you can also catch an hourly minibus (Y18, two hours, 7am to 4.30pm) from the *dàxīqìchēzhàn* (大西汽车站), which is different to the regular west bus station.

Xiàhé 夏河

☎0941 / POP 70,000

The alluring monastic town of Xiàhé attracts an astonishing band of visitors, from backpack-laden students, insatiable wanderers, shaven-headed Buddhist nuns, Tibetan nomads in their most colourful finest, camera-toting tour groups and dusty, itinerant beggars. Most visitors are rural Tibetans, whose purpose is to pray, prostrate themselves and seek spiritual fulfilment at holy Labrang monastery (Lābǔléng Sì).

In a beautiful mountain valley at 2920m above sea level, Xiàhé has a certain rhythm about it and visitors quickly tap into its fluid motions. The rising sun sends pilgrims out to circle the 3km *kora* (pilgrim path) that rings the monastery. Crimson-clad monks shuffle into the temples to chant morning prayers. It's easy to get swept up in the action, but some of the best moments come as you relax in a cosy teahouse, hands warmed by a hot bowl of yak tea.

The area was long part of the Tibetan region of Amdo. As a microcosm of southwestern Gānsù, the area's three principal ethnic groups are represented in Xiàhé. In rough terms, Xiàhé's population is 50% Tibetan, 40% Han and 10% Hui. Labrang Monastery marks the division between Xiàhé's mainly Han and Hui Chinese eastern quarter and the scruffy Tibetan village to the west.

Despite Xiàhé's ostensible tranquillity, these ethnic groups don't necessarily mix peacefully. The Tibetan community maintains a strong solidarity with their brethren on the plateau, and demonstrations and rioting here in the wake of the 2008 riots in Lhasa led to the region's being closed to individual travellers till early 2010.

Sights

Labrang Monastery TIBETAN MONASTERY
(拉卜楞寺; Lābǔléng Sì; admission Y40) Even the most illustrious of China's other incense-wreathed temples pale in comparison with the vast magnitude of this astounding complex. The palpable spiritual energy that emanates from this sacred monastery is only matched by the potent veneration brought by its unending flow of Tibetan pilgrims. Even if Tibet is not on your itinerary, the monastery sufficiently conveys the esoteric mystique of its devout persuasions, leaving indelible impressions of a deeply sacred domain.

The monastery is one of the six major Tibetan monasteries of the Gelugpa order (Yellow Hat sect of Tibetan Buddhism). The others are Ganden, Sera and Drepung Monasteries near Lhasa; Tashilhunpo Monastery in Shigatse; and Kumbum (Tǎ'ěr Sì; p868) near Xīníng, Qīnghǎi.

Labrang monastery was founded in 1709 by Ngagong Tsunde (E'angzongzhe in Chinese), the first-generation Jamyang (a line of reincarnated Rinpoches or living Buddhas ranking third in importance after the Dalai and Panchen Lamas), from nearby Gānjiā. At its peak the monastery housed nearly 4000 monks, but their ranks greatly declined during the Cultural Revolution. Numbers are recovering, and are currently restricted to 1200 monks, drawn from Qīnghǎi, Gānsù, Sìchuān and Inner Mongolia.

With its endless squeaking prayer wheels, hawks circling overhead and the deep throb of Tibetan trumpets resonating from the surrounding hills, Labrang is a monastery in the entire sense of the word. In addition to the chapels, residences, golden-roofed temple halls and living quarters for the monks, Labrang is also home to six *tratsang* (monastic colleges or institutes), exploring esoteric Buddhism, theology, medicine, astrology and law. Many of the chapel halls are illuminated in a yellow glow by yak butter lamps, their strong-smelling fuel scooped out from voluminous tubs.

Xiàhé

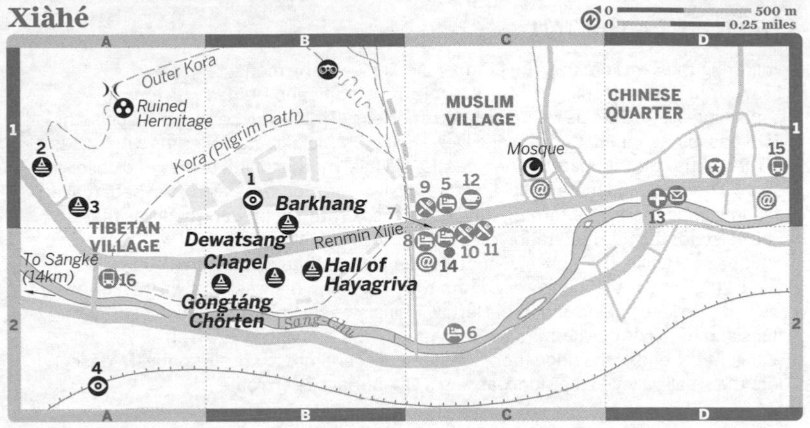

Xiàhé

Top Sights
Barkhang ... B1
Dewatsang Chapel ... B2
Gòngtáng Chörten ... B2
Hall of Hayagriva ... B2

Sights
1 Monastery Ticket Office ... B1
2 Ngakpa Gompa ... A1
3 Nunnery ... A1
4 Thangka Display Terrace ... A2

Sleeping
5 Labrang Baoma Hotel ... C1
6 Labrang Red Rock International Hostel ... C2
7 Overseas Tibetan Hotel ... C2
8 Tara Guesthouse ... C2

Eating
Everest Café ... (see 7)
9 Nomad Restaurant ... C1
10 Snowy Mountain Café ... C2
11 Tsewong's Cafe ... C2

Drinking
12 Teahouses ... C1

Information
13 Déshèngtáng Pharmacy ... D1
14 OT Travels & Tours ... C2

Transport
15 Bus Station ... D1
16 Buses to Dájiǔtān ... A2

The only way to visit the interior of these buildings is with a tour, which generally includes the **Institute of Medicine**, the **Manjushri Temple**, the **Serkung** (Golden Temple) and the main **Prayer Hall** (Grand Sutra Hall), plus a **museum** of relics and yak-butter sculptures. English tours (Y40) of the monastery leave the ticket office (售票处; Shòupiàochù) around 10.15am and 3.15pm; take the morning tour if you can as there's more to see. An alternative is to latch on to a Chinese tour. Even better is to show up at around 6am or 7am to be with the monks. At dusk the hillside resonates with the throaty sound of sutras being chanted behind the wooden doors.

The rest of the monastery can be explored by walking the *kora* (see the boxed text, p814) and although many of the temple halls are padlocked shut, there are a couple of separate smaller chapels you can visit. Over three floors, the **Barkhang** (admission Y10; 9am-noon & 2-5pm) is the monastery's traditional printing press (with rows upon rows of over 20,000 wood blocks for printing) and is well worth a visit. Photos are allowed.

Its interior illuminated by a combination of yak-butter lamps and electric light bulbs by the thousand, the 31m-tall **Gòngtáng Chörten** (贡唐宝塔; Gòngtáng Bǎotǎ; admission Y10) is a spectacular stupa with lovely

WALK LIKE A TIBETAN

Following the 3km *kora* (pilgrim path) encircling Labrang monastery is perhaps the best approach to grasping its layout, scale and significance. Lined with long rows of squeaking prayer wheels, white-washed *chörtens* (Tibetan stupas) and chapels, the *kora* passes Gòngtáng Chörten and Dewatsang Chapel. Tibetan pilgrims with beads in their hands and sunhats on their heads, old folk, mothers with babies and children, shabby nomads and more walk in meditative fashion clockwise along the path (called *zhuǎnjìngdào*, 'scripture-turning way' in Chinese), rotating prayer wheels as they go. Look also for the tiny meditation cells on the northern hillside.

For a short hike, the more strenuous outer *kora* path takes about an hour and climbs high above the monastery. From the nunnery in the west of town, make your way up the ridge behind and to the left, winding steeply uphill to a bunch of prayer flags and the ruins of a hermitage. The views of the monastery open up as you go along. At the end of the ridge there's a steep descent into town; alternatively, descend into the small valley to the side, passing a sky-burial site en route.

interior murals and fantastic views from the roof onto a landscape dotted with the port-red figures of monks. At the rear of the stupa is a **Sleeping Buddha** (卧佛; Wòfó) depicting Sakyamuni on the cusp of entering nirvana.

The **Dewatsang Chapel** (德哇仓文殊佛殿; Déwācāng Wénshū Fódiàn; admission Y10), built in 1814, ranges over four floors and houses a vast 12m-statue of Manjushri (Wenshu) and thousands of Buddhas in cabinets around the walls. The **Hall of Hayagriva** (马头明王殿; Mǎtóu Míngwáng Diàn; Hall of Horse-head Buddha), destroyed during the Cultural Revolution, was reopened in 2007. Containing vivid and bright murals, the hall also encapsulates a startlingly fierce 12m-high effigy of Hayagriva – a wrathful manifestation of the usually calm Avalokiteshvara (Guanyin) – with six arms and three faces.

Access to the rest of the monastery area is free, and you can easily spend several hours just walking around and soaking up the atmosphere in the endless maze of mud-packed walls. The Tibetan greeting, in the local Amdo dialect, is '*Cho day mo?*' (How do you do?) – a great icebreaker.

The best morning views of the monastery come from the **Thangka Display Terrace**, a popular picnic spot, or the forested hills south of the main town.

Nunnery BUDDHIST NUNNERY

This welcoming nunnery (*ani gompa* in Tibetan, 尼姑庵, *nígū'ān* in Chinese) is on the hill above the Tibetan part of town.

Ngakpa Gompa BUDDHIST MONASTERY

(红教寺; Hóngjiào Sì; admission Y5) Next door is the small Nyingmapa (Red Hat) school monastery, whose lay monks wear striking red and white robes and long, braided hair.

Tours

Lohsang at the OT Travels & Tours is excellent for information and tours of the surrounding area. Tsewong's Cafe is also a great resource for travellers, with a variety of tours and loads of info.

Festivals & Events

Festivals are central to the calendar for both the devotional monks and the nomads who stream into town from the grasslands in multicoloured splendour. Tibetans use a lunar calendar, so dates for individual festivals vary from year to year.

Monlam (Great Prayer) Festival BUDDHIST

This festival starts three days after the Tibetan New Year, which is usually in February or early March. On the morning of the 13th day of the festival, more than 100 monks carry a huge *thangka* (sacred painting on cloth) of the Buddha, measuring more than 30m by 20m, and unfurl it on the hill facing the monastery. This is accompanied by spectacular processions and prayer assemblies.

On the 14th day there is an all-day session of Cham dances performed by 35 masked dancers, with Yama, the lord of death, playing the leading role. On the 15th day there is an evening display of butter lanterns and sculptures. On the 16th day the Maitreya statue is paraded around the monastery.

During the second month (usually starting in March or early April) there are several interesting festivals, with a procession of monastery relics on the seventh day.

Sleeping

Overseas Tibetan Hotel HOTEL $
(华侨饭店; Huáqiáo Fàndiàn; ☎712 2642; www.overseastibetanhotel.com; 77 Renmin Xijie; 人民西街77号; dm Y20, d Y160-200; @) Well-run and bustling place, owned by the energetic and bouncy Jesuit-educated Lohsang, a likeable Tibetan with faultless English who runs the *kora* most mornings. Dorms are simple; pricier doubles are well laid out and attractive, coming with a bathroom. Also here are the Everest Cafe, internet access (Y5 per hour), bike hire and a travel agency.

Labrang Red Rock International Hostel HOSTEL $
(拉卜楞红石国际青年旅馆; Lābǔléng Hǒngshí Guójì Qíngnián Lǚguǎn; ☎712 3698; labranghongshi@yahoo.cn; 253 Yagetang; 雅鸽搪253号; 8/4-bed dm Y30/35, d Y100; @) This Tibetan-themed, very quiet hostel has varnished pine-wood rooms, solar-powered hot showers, a restaurant and bar area and a beautiful display of *thangka*. Doubles are clean and spacious. YHA card holders get a discount; internet is Y5 per hour. Walk past the Tara Guesthouse and turn left before the bridge.

Tara Guesthouse GUESTHOUSE $
(卓玛旅社; Zhuōmǎ Lǚshè; ☎712 1274; tseringtara@aol.com; 268 Yagetang; 雅鸽搪268号; dm Y10-30, s/tw Y30/50) This long-time budget place is run by monks from Sìchuān and has small, comfortable *kang* rooms (shared shower room, no phone) arranged around a courtyard and frugal dorms. There's a terrace with great views over the monastery; hot water is solar powered. English is well spoken at the front desk.

Labrang Baoma Hotel HOTEL $$
(拉卜楞宝马宾馆; Lābǔléng Bǎomǎ Bīnguǎn; ☎712 1078; www.labranghotel.com; 77 Renmin Xijie; 人民西街77号; 4-bed dm Y40, s/d Y290/280, discounts of 45%; @) Pleasant and vibrantly colourful hotel with friendly staff, nice interior courtyard and comfortable ensuite doubles. Bike hire and laundry.

Eating & Drinking

For those of you who can't make it to Tibet, Xiàhé is an opportunity to develop an appetite for the flavours of the Land of Snows, whether it's *momo* (boiled dumplings), *tsampa* (a porridge of roasted barley flour), yak-milk yoghurt, or throat-warming glasses of the local firewater. For Chinese or Hui dishes, try the restaurants around the bus station; cake shops round out the picture.

Nomad Restaurant TIBETAN $
(牧民齐全饭庄; Mùmín Qíquán Fànzhuāng; dishes Y5-25) With its great service and commanding views of the monastery and *kora* route, get into the swing of things with some hot yak milk (Y4), boiled yak meat (Y35), a bowl of *tsampa* (Y8), a plate of *momo* (Y10), vegetable hotpot (Y18) and a volatile shot of Nomad barley alcohol (Y6). It's on the 3rd floor, just before the monastery walls.

Snowy Mountain Cafe CAFE-RESTAURANT $
(雪山咖啡馆; Xuěshān Kāfēiguǎn; ☎139 9309 1241; www.snowymtncafe.com; dishes Y4-8) Popular upstairs foreign-owned spot for international dishes with a strong menu ranging from omelettes (cheese omelette Y12) to spag bolognese (Y25), winning pizzas (cheese Y32), Bistec a lo Pobre (steak with fried potatoes, onions and eggs; Y35) and beyond. It's also a good place for hoovering up travel information or organising plane and train tickets.

Tsewong's Cafe CAFE $
(泽旺小吃; CàixiàngZéwàng Kāfēiguǎn; ☎138 9397 9763; tsewongscafe@yahoo.com.cn; dishes Y20-50; ⏲9am-late) Switched-on traveller cafe with much-loved pizzas (Y38 to Y48) and kebabs (more like a Turkish İskender kebab, with tomatoes, yoghurt and bread), *tsampa* (Y10), a simple Chinese menu plus coffee, internet access and ticketing (Y50 per ticket).

Everest Cafe CAFE, RESTAURANT $
(77 Renmin Xijie; 人民西街77号; ⏲7am-late) Popular spot for breakfast (Y20), lunch or a late-night beer; attached to the Overseas Tibetan Hotel.

Shopping

Xiàhé is excellent for Tibetan handicrafts, so why not don a cowboy hat or a Tibetan trilby, wrap yourself in a *chuba* (Tibetan cloak), light up some juniper incense, wrap your head in a furry yellow monk's hat, jump into a pair of monk's boots, flap a prayer flag or shell out for brocaded silks, Tibetan cloth, Tibetan-style tents or a silver teapot? Stacks of handicraft shops line the upper part of the main road, before the monastery walls.

 Information

It's not possible to change travellers cheques in Xiàhé.

China Post (中国邮政; Zhōngguó Yóuzhèng; ⊙8am-6pm)

Déshèngtáng Pharmacy (德盛堂药店; Déshèngtáng Yàodiàn; ⊙8.30am-8pm) Western, Chinese and Tibetan medicine; just west of post office.

Industrial & Commercial Bank of China (ICBC; 工商银行; Gōngshāng Yínháng) Has an ATM and changes US dollars.

Lèlè Wǎngbā (乐乐网吧; per hr Y3; ⊙24hr) Internet access diagonally across from the bus station, in an off-street courtyard.

OT Travels & Tours (☎712 2642; othotel@public.lz.gs.cn) This reliable travel agency at the Overseas Tibetan Hotel can arrange cars and guides to nearby sights. Contact Losang.

Phoenix Internet Bar (凤凰网络; Fènghuáng Wǎngluò; per hr Y3; ⊙8am-11pm) South of Tara Guesthouse.

Public Security Bureau (PSB;公安局; Gōng'ānjú; ☎333 8010; ⊙9am-noon & 3-6pm Mon-Fri) Does not handle visa extensions; you'll need to go to Hézuò, Línxià or Sōngpān.

Xùnjié Wǎngbā (迅捷网吧; per hr Y3; ⊙24hr) Near the mosque.

 Getting There & Away

There is no airport in Xiàhé, nor do trains run there, but it's regularly serviced by bus. Most travellers head on to either Lánzhōu or Sìchuān; the road less travelled takes you over the mountains to Tóngrén in Qīnghǎi.

The following bus services depart from Xiàhé.

Hézuò Y14, one hour, every 30 minutes (6.30am to 5.30pm)

Lángmùsì Y46.50, four hours, one daily (7.40am)

Lánzhōu Y49.50, 4½ hours, four daily (6.30am, 7.30am, 2.30pm and 8.30pm)

Línxià Y20, three hours, every 30 minutes (6am to 5.30pm)

Tóngrén Y25, five hours, one daily (6.30am)

Xīníng Y60, seven hours, one daily (6.10am)

If you can't get a direct ticket to/from Lánzhōu, take a bus to Línxià and change there. Allow time for the journey from Línxià, which can be a real test: the driver may dawdle for an hour for fares, insist on crawling by the side of the road to fill the final seat, stop at an abattoir so an animal carcass can be flung on board and then stop at checkpoints.

 Getting Around

Most hotels and restaurants hire bikes for Y10 to Y15 per day. Taxis cost Y1 to Y2 per seat for a short trip around town, including to the bus station or monastery.

Around Xiàhé

SĀNGKĒ GRASSLANDS 桑科草原

Expanses of open grassland where Tibetans graze yak herds around the village of Sāngkē (桑科) reward trips along the river 14km up the valley from Xiàhé. Development has turned the area into a small circus, complete with touristy horse rides and fake tourist yurts, but you can keep going to more distant and pristine grasslands in the direction of Amchog. You can cycle up to Sāngkē in about one hour. The twice-daily bus to Dájiǔtān (达久滩; Y10) from Xiàhé passes by Sāngkē, but timings mean you have to hitch back. A minivan costs about Y30 return.

GĀNJIĀ GRASSLANDS 甘加草原

For more adventure, the Gānjiā Grasslands (Gānjiā Cǎoyuán), 34km from Xiàhé, are far less developed and offer a great day trip from Xiàhé.

The bumpy road crosses the Naren-Ka pass before quickly descending into wide grasslands. Past Gānjiā Xiàn village, a side road climbs 12km to **Trakkar Gompa** (白石崖寺; Báishíyá Sì; admission Y15), a monastery of 90 monks set against a backdrop of vertical rock formations. A 10-minute walk behind the monastery is the **Nekhang** (白石崖溶洞; Báishí Yá Róng dòng; admission Y20), a cave complex where pilgrims lower themselves down ropes and ladders into two sacred underground chambers. A Dutch traveller fell to his death here in 2006, and to prevent the same fate we advise avoiding this place; your driver will probably suggest the same.

From Trakkar it's a short drive to the impressive, 2000-year-old, Han-dynasty village of **Bājiǎo** (八角; Karnang in Tibetan; admission Y10), the remarkable 12-sided walls of which now shelter a small village. From here it's a short 5km diversion to the renovated **Tseway Gompa** (佐海寺; Zuǒhǎi Sì; admission Y10), one of the few Bön monasteries in Gānsù. There are great views of Bājiǎo from the ridge behind the monastery.

It is also possible to hike over several days from the grasslands to 4636m-high **Dálǐjiā Shān** (达里加山; Dálǐjiā Mountain), but you will need to be well equipped for the camping trek; Xúnhuà-bound travellers from Línxià can get off the bus from Línxià at the Dálǐjiā mountain pass (达里加山口; Dálǐjiā Shānkǒu), from where you can trek up to the peak. Summer is the best season for such treks as you have more daylight hours, but note that the last Xúnhuà-bound bus will come through the pass at around 4pm, so you will need to hitch on to Xúnhuà if you miss it (or take camping gear). Alternatively, continue walking in the direction of Xúnhuà for around 15km to **Dàowéi Tibetan Village** (道帏藏族乡; Dàowéi Zàngzú Xiāng; also called Guru), where you may find a bed for the night, or take a minibus from Dàowéi to the larger Báizhuāng Village (白庄乡; Báizhuāng Xiāng), which has hotels. Dàowéi itself has a local monastery and is beautifully surrounded by climbable mountains.

OT Travels & Tours and Tsewong's Cafe, both in Xiàhé, can advise on all of these trips and arrange a car for four people and an English-speaking guide for around Y250 for the day; they can also arrange fun camping trips for overnighting on the grasslands.

Hézuò 合作

☎0941 / POP 76,000

The booming regional capital of Gānnán (甘南) prefecture, Hézuò is a transit point for travellers plying the excellent overland route between Gānsù and Sìchuān provinces. The city is also the sight of the incredible Milarepa Palace, a bewitching Tibetan temple ranging spectacularly over nine floors.

Sights

Milarepa Palace TIBETAN TEMPLE

(九层佛阁; Sekhar Gutok; Jiǔcéng Fógé; admission Y20; ⏲7.30am-6pm) About 2km from the bus station along the main road towards Xiàhé is this towering temple, ringed by prayer wheels. The port-coloured building is highly unusual in the Tibetan world. It's really worth buying the entrance ticket to investigate the incredible interior (remove your shoes), where a sacred meteorite is also housed. The ground-floor hall is a powerful spectacle, a galaxy of Bodhisattvas, Buddhist statues and celestial figures gloomily illuminated by yak-butter lamps. Climb upstairs to a further staggering display of lamas and living Buddhas on the 2nd floor; more deities muster on the 4th floor. An unsettling array of fearsome, blue and turquoise tantric effigies awaits on the 6th floor. Make your way to the 8th floor for further effigies of Sakyamuni and Guanyin and views over the hills and town. The town's main monastery, **Tso Gompa** (admission Y20; ⏲9am-6pm), is next door. Bus 1 runs here from the centre of town.

Sleeping & Eating

For not-bad chicken burgers, try Màidíbǎo (麦迪堡) just north of the main square.

With Xiàhé just an hour to the north there is little reason to stay here, and cheap hotels are loath to take foreigners. If you get stuck, the **Gānnán Fàndiàn** (甘南饭店; ☎821 4733; Maqu Xilu; 玛曲西路; d Y150-240, tr Y300, discounts of 15%; ❄) has decent, clean and bright doubles with shower; it's located on the southwest corner of the main square.

Information

The post office is north of the square on Renmin Jie.

China Construction Bank (中国建设银行; Zhōngguó Jiànshè Yínháng) On the square south of the bus station; changes money.

Internet cafe (网吧; wǎngbā; Renmin Jie; per hr Y2.50; ⏲24hr) North of the square on Renmin Jie.

Public Security Bureau (PSB; 公安局; Gōng'ānjú; ⏲8.30am-noon & 2.30-5pm) Turn right out of the bus station onto Sāngqū Xīlù (桑曲西路); the PSB visa office is around 50m along on your left.

Getting There & Away

Hézuò is where buses from Zöigě (Ruò'ěrgài), in Sìchuān, and Xiàhé meet. Most buses to Lángmùsì go from the south bus station. The **central main bus station** has buses to:

Lángmùsì Y32.5, three hours, one daily (9am)

Lánzhōu Y32 to Y60, four hours, regular services (6.30am to 4.30pm)

Línxià Y20, 1½ hours, every 30 minutes

Xiàhé Y14, one hour, every 30 minutes

From the **south bus station** there are buses to:

Lángmùsì Y32.50, three hours, three daily (7am, 10.20am and 12.20pm)

Zöigě Y55, 3½ hours, one daily (7.30am)

A taxi between the two bus stations costs Y2 per person, or take bus 1 (Y1).

Lángmùsì 郎木寺

☎0941 / POP 3000

Straddling the border between Sìchuān and Gānsù is Lángmùsì (Taktsang Lhamo in Tibetan), an alpine Amdo Tibetan village nestled among steep grassy meadows, evergreen forests of slender pine trees brushing the sky, crumbling stupas, piles of mani stones and snow-clad peaks. Lovely and moist compared to the lowlands, Lángmùsì is a delightful place, surrounded by countless red and white monastery buildings, flapping prayer flags and the mesmerising sound of monks chanting at twilight.

Sights

The White Dragon River (白龙江; Báilóng Jiāng) divides the town in two.

Kerti Gompa TIBETAN MONASTERY

(格尔底寺; Géěrdǐ Sì; admission valid 3 days Y15) Rising up on the Sìchuān side of the river is this monastery – otherwise dubbed the Sìchuān Monastery – built in 1413, home to around 700 monks and composed of five temples and colleges. A short walk from the monastery stand small pavilions built over a brook whose waters power a round-the-clock revolving of prayer wheels housed inside (the *ne plus ultra* of holiness)!

Serti Gompa TIBETAN MONASTERY

(赛赤寺; Sàichì Sì; admission Y20) On the Gānsù side, higher up the hill, is this smaller monastery with its golden- and silver-roofed halls. The monastery dates from 1748 and is also simply referred to as Gānsù Monastery. Views are lovely from here. Like its cousin across the border in Sìchuān, the monastery is best visited in the morning (7am to 8am and 10.30am to 1pm) and late afternoon (6pm to 8pm).

Activities

Bountiful hiking opportunities radiate in almost every direction. Southwest of Kerti Gompa is **Namo Gorge** (纳摩大峡谷; Nàmó Dàxiágǔ), which makes for a superlative 90-minute (return) hike. The gorge contains several sacred grottoes, one dedicated to the Tibetan goddess Palden Lhamo, the other known as the **Fairy Cave** (仙女洞; Xiānnǚ Dòng), which gives the town its Tibetan name (*lángmù* meaning fairy). Cross rickety bridges flung over the gushing stream, trek past piles of mani stones and prayer flags and hike on into a splendid ravine. After about 30 minutes of clambering over rocks you reach a grassy plain surrounded by towering peaks.

Another popular trek is the hike along the White Dragon River to the **river's source** (白龙江源头; Báilóng Jiāng Yuántóu) where Chinese hikers go in search of *chóngcǎo* (虫草), a coveted herb used in Chinese medicine.

A lovely walk heads out over the hills from Sertri Gompa to the small village of **Jíkēhé Cūn** (吉科合村); if you can ignore the mountainous backdrop, it's not unlike a jaunt across England's South Downs.

It's also possible to trek up **Red Stone Mountain** (红石崖; Hóngshí Yá) right next to the village.

Lángmùsì Tibetan Horse Trekking (☎667 1504; www.langmusi.net), across from the Lángmùsì Bīnguǎn, runs guided horse treks from one to four days, overnighting at nomads' tents en route, with the option of climbing nearby **Huágàishén Shān** (华盖神山). Prices start from around Y180 per day.

Kelsang at the Lángmùsì Bīnguǎn can arrange guides (Y150 per day) for hikes up the gorge behind Kerti Gompa, and transport (Y100 to Y150) for a trip to some **hot springs** (admission Y5) outside town.

Festivals & Events

If you are in the area in late July, head out to Mǎqǔ (玛曲) to see the **annual horse races**. The dates change each year, so try contacting the Lángmùsì Bīnguǎn to find out when it is being held. Mǎqǔ is 67km west of Lángmùsì. Travellers cafes and hotels in Lángmùsì can arrange transport to the town.

Sleeping

Lángmùsì Hotel HOTEL $$$

(☎667 1555; d Y666-699, tr Y700, discounts of up to 70%) With an over-the-top Tibetan-style lobby, this friendly four-storey place is the best in Lángmùsì, with very pleasant, clean and spacious standard doubles with bathrooms; the Tibetan-style deluxe rooms are virtually identical apart from carpets and ceiling pattern (but have showers). Excellent discounts. It's on the road south towards Kerti Gompa.

Lángmùsì Bīnguǎn HOTEL $
(郎木寺宾馆; ☎667 1086; tibetanyakboy@yahoo.co.uk; dm Y30, tw with shower Y160-180, discounts of 30-50%) English-speaking staff here are very friendly and rooms with shower are fine, making this an OK place. If you prefer something more rustic, owner Kelsang can arrange for a homestay with a Tibetan family in a nearby village for Y70 per night.

Xiùfēng Bīnguǎn HOTEL $
(秀峰宾馆; ☎667 1020; dm Y20, d Y100-120) Undergoing renovation and expansion at the time of writing, this pleasant place off the main street is run by a friendly Hui family and should have new doubles added by the time you read this.

Nomads Youth Hostel HOSTEL $
(旅朋青年旅社; Lǚpéng Qīngnián Lǚshè; ☎667 1460; dm/d Y20/50) Popular with Chinese backpackers, this friendly place on the main street has scruffy and basic dorms, doubles with shared toilet, homely foyer and bar. Can arrange treks.

Sànà Bīnguǎn HOTEL $
(萨娜宾馆; ☎667 1062; d Y60-160, tr per bed Y30) Another friendly place, accessed through the back of a shop on the main road.

Eating

Talo Restaurant RESTAURANT $
(达老餐厅; Dálǎo Cāntīng; ☎825 5666) Decorated with yak skulls, prayer flags and *tangka*, this friendly upstairs Tibetan restaurant has a great menu embracing pancakes (Y12), apple rings (Y20), a host of Tibetan dishes and other heart-warming food. Overlooking the main street, it's a great place for a beer. There's a smarter restaurant attached for more variety.

Several backpacker cafes offer similar menus, with big burgers, tasty pies and hot coffee; these include **Lesha's Restaurant** (☎667 1179) – on the main street – and **Ali's Restaurant** (☎667 1090), just before the bridge on the way to Sertri Gompa. At the time of research, Lángmùsì Tibetan Horse Trekking was planning to open an internet-equipped restaurant-cafe across the road.

Information

There is nowhere to change money, so come with cash. At the time of writing there was no public internet access and the only internet cafe, on the other side of the road from the Lángmùsì Bīnguǎn, was shut; ask at Lángmùsì Tibetan Horse Trekking for the latest. The PSB (公安局; Gōngānjú) is just down from the Lángmùsì Hotel. You can burn photos onto CDs at **Lángmùsì Tibetan Horse Trekking** (⊙9am-9pm) for Y10.

Getting There & Away

There's one daily bus to Zöigě (Ruò'ěrgài; Y22, one hour) at 7am and three daily buses to Hézuò (Y32.5, three hours), departing at 6.30am, 7am and noon. For Sōngpān you have to overnight in Zöigě or hire a car (Y800).

If you don't take a direct bus to Lángmùsì, you'll have to get off at the intersection 4km from the town, from where minivans ferry passengers into town for Y2.

HEXI CORRIDOR

Bound by the Qílián Shān range to the south and the Mǎzōng (Horse's Mane) and Lóngshǒu (Dragon's Head) ranges to the north, the narrow strip of land that is Hexi Corridor (河西走廊; Héxī Zǒuláng), around which the province is formed, was once the sole western passage in and out of the Middle Kingdom.

Wǔwēi 武威

☎0936 / POP 509,000

Wǔwēi stands at the strategic eastern end of the Hexi Corridor. It was from here, two millennia prior, that the emperors of China launched their expeditionary forces into the unknown west, eventually leading them to Jiāyùguān and beyond. Temples, tombs and traditional gates hint at Wǔwēi's Silk Road past, and the city is rapidly modernising around a glossy central square.

Sights

Léitái Sì TEMPLE
(雷台寺; admission Y50; ⊙8am-6pm) The pride and joy of the city, the bronze **Flying Horse of Wǔwēi** (飞马) was discovered here in 1969 and has since been adopted as the unofficial symbol of Gānsù. It was found in a secret tomb beneath this temple, built on top of steep earthen ramparts. While it's a thrill to explore a 2000-year-old tomb, there is precious little inside. The Flying Horse is now displayed in the Gānsù Provincial Museum (p805). The site is located 1.2km

north of Wénhuà Guǎngchǎng (文化广场; Culture Sq).

Confucius Temple CONFUCIAN TEMPLE
(文庙; Wénmiào; admission Y31; ⏲7.30am-6pm) This Ming-era temple has quiet gardens and stele-filled pavilions. The most important stele features the extinct Xīxià language carved into one side and a Chinese translation on the other: a sort of Rosetta stone, the stele has allowed researchers to understand the once unintelligible Xīxià texts. The stele is now housed in a small **museum** (⏲8.30am-6pm) across the street (shut for renovation at the time of writing); your ticket for the Confucius Temple allows you inside. To reach the temple, walk south from the main square to the reconstructed South Gate (南门), then turn left just before the gate and walk east for 650m to the temple.

Kumarajiva Pagoda BUDDHIST PAGODA
Located 400m north of Wénhuà Guǎngchǎng, this pagoda (罗什寺塔; Luóshísì Tǎ) is a brick structure originally dating to 488. Dedicated to the great translator of Buddhist sutras (whose tongue was buried beneath the pagoda), the pagoda was toppled during the great earthquake in 1927 and rebuilt. Pilgrims circumambulate the pagoda in clockwise fashion.

Ancient Bell Tower HISTORIC SITE
(古钟楼; Gǔzhōng Lóu; admission Y10) This bell tower is pretty much all that survives of **Dàyún Temple** (大云寺古钟楼; Dàyúnsì Gǔzhōnglóu; admission Y5; ⏲8am-6pm), which was levelled by the great tremor of 1927. The flattened area around the temple looks like another earthquake has struck. From the square walk 250m north to the first intersection, then turn right (east) and walk 800m to the tower.

Hǎizàng Temple BUDDHIST TEMPLE
(海藏寺; Hǎizàng Sì; admission Y10) A short trip on bus 5 (Y2) outside town, this temple is a fascinating active monastery. The **Three Sages Hall** (Sānshèng Diàn) contains a 'hermaphroditic Guanyin'; dating to the Ming dynasty, the venerably old **Wúliàng Palace** (Wúliàng Diàn) was once used to store sutras but now houses a reclining Buddha in a glass cabinet. An absorbing feature is the minute pavilion to the right of the Wuliang Palace containing a **well** whose 'magic waters' (神水; *shénshuǐ*) are connected by subterranean streams to a Holy Lake (圣湖; Shènghú) in the Potala Palace in Lhasa. Drinking the well's waters is said to cure myriad ailments.

Sleeping & Eating

Ziyunge Hotel HOTEL $$
(紫云阁酒店; Zǐyúngé Jiǔdiàn; ☎225 3888; Mingqing Fanggu Wenhua Jie; 明清仿古文化街; s/d/tr Y198/280/218, discounts of 30%; ❄) Just east of South Gate, this great hotel has excellent, comfortable and spacious rooms with shower (and hairdryer) and new furnishings. You can often net a standard double for around Y120.

Yuánjì Làzhī Ròujiāmó SHǍNXĪ $
(袁记腊汁肉夹馍; Mingqing Fanggu Wenhua Jie; ⏲7.30am-9pm; meals Y12) Not far from the Ziyunge Hotel, this busy little restaurant serves some simply scrumptious *ròujiāmó* (called the 'Chinese hamburger'; Y4) from Shǎnxī province and bowls of tasty hundun (Y3). Don't be put off by the plastic seats; the food is excellent.

Information

Bank of China (中国银行; Zhōngguó Yínháng) West end of the pedestrian shopping street (步行商业街; Bùxíng Shāngyè Jiē); can change money.

Internet cafe (网吧; Wǎngbā; per hr Y2; ⏲24hr) West end of the pedestrian shopping street running west from Wénhuà Guǎngchǎng.

Public Security Bureau (PSB;公安局; Gōng'ānjú) On Dong Dajie, east of Wénhuà Guǎngchǎng.

Getting There, Away & Around

Bus

From the **west bus station** (汽车西站), located 1.5km southwest of Cultural Sq, express buses run to:

Jiāyùguān Y86, seven hours, one daily (7.30pm)

Lánzhōu Y51, three hours, every 15 minutes (6am to 6pm)

Zhāngyè Y51, 3½ hours, hourly (7.50am to 5pm)

Train

Trains depart hourly to Zhāngyè (Y40). For Lánzhōu (Y45 to Y52) take the T296 express at 8.20am or the K592 at 8.20pm. Departing from Lánzhōu at 7.29am, the T9205 (Y49) is a handy two-tier train that stops in Wǔwēi; it departs Wǔwēi at 10.19am to continue to Zhāngyè (Y41, two hours) and Jiāyùguān.

The N857 and K591 are overnight trains to Dūnhuáng (Y118). The 7520 departs for

Zhōngwèi (Y22) at 8.44am. A train ticket booking office (火车票代售点; Huǒchēpiào Dàishòudiǎn) is located at 26 Nanguan Xilu, west of the South Gate.

The station is located 3.5km south of Wénhuà Guǎngchǎng; the two are connected by buses 1 and 2 (Y1). Taxis start at Y3.

Zhāngyè 张掖

☎0936 / POP 260,000

Colourful Zhāngyè, with its colossal Buddha, pagodas, traditional Chinese-style pedestrian streets and unique cliff temples at nearby Mǎtí Sì, makes for an absorbing Silk Road stopover. Marco Polo certainly enjoyed it – the great traveller stayed here for a year on his way to the court of Kublai Khan. Local authorities have honoured Polo's legacy by erecting a statue of the man; it stands near a quirky street lined with mock-Venetian architecture.

Sights

The sad remnants of Zhāngyè's earthen **city walls** can be seen on Beihuan Lu.

Great Buddha Temple BUDDHIST TEMPLE
(大佛寺; Dàfó Sì; ☎821 9671; adult/student Y41/21; ⏲8am-6pm) Originally dating to 1098 (Western Xia dynasty), this excellent temple contains an astonishing 35m-long sleeping Buddha – China's largest of this variety (see p955) – surrounded by mouldering clay arhats and Qing-dynasty murals. Take a good look at the main hall and the woodwork, including the doors – it's one of the few wooden structures from this era still standing in China. A colony of bats squeaks high up in its rafters along with flitting flocks of swallows. Until the 1960s, small children would clamber into the huge Buddha and play around inside his tummy. The stairs to the floor above are, sadly, inaccessible. Out the back is the impressive white **earth stupa** (土塔; *tǔ tǎ*) dating from the Ming dynasty, when this vast temple complex was called Hóngrén Temple (弘仁寺; Hóngrén Sì).

Wooden Pagoda BUDDHIST PAGODA
(木塔; Mùtǎ; admission Y5; ⏲7.30am-6.30pm) In the main square one block north of the Great Buddha Temple, this pagoda is a brick and wooden structure that was first built in AD 528. Note that this pagoda represents wood as the earth stupa represents earth in the Chinese theory of the five elements (wood, earth, water, fire and metal).

Sleeping & Eating

To eat, head 300m west of the drum tower and look for Mingqing Jie (明清街), an alley of faux-Qing architecture lined with dozens of clean, friendly restaurants.

Liángmào Bīnguǎn HOTEL $
(粮贸宾馆; ☎825 2398; Dong Jie Shizi; 东街什字; dm Y18, s Y88, tw Y68-88, tr Y158, business d Y158; ❄) This seven-storey hotel has a wide range of clean, airy rooms strung out along curved corridors. It's 900m east of the drum tower.

Xīnyuán Bīnguǎn HOTEL $
(馨园宾馆; ☎825 1766; Beishuiqiao Jie; 北水桥街; tw with shared shower Y90, s Y140, d Y120-140, discounts of 40%; ❄) This place has OK rooms and a good location in the western half of town near the Marco Polo statue, although the staff is rather slack.

Information

Several internet cafes can be found on Jīnmài Pedestrian St (金脉步行街; Jīnmài Bùxíng Jiē) just east of the drum tower.

Bank of China (中国银行; Zhōngguó Yínháng) At Dong Jie and 168 Xianfu Jie. Both branches have ATM and can change travellers cheques.

Shèngdá Internet Cafe (盛达网吧; Shèngdá Wǎngbā; Xijie; per hr Y2.50; ⏲8am-midnight) East of junction between Mingqing Jie and Xijie.

Getting There & Around

Bus

The town has three bus stations, in the south, east and west. The **west bus station** (xī zhàn; ☎821 0597) has the most frequent departures:

Dūnhuáng Y108, 12 hours, two in the morning (7.50am and 11.30am), then two sleepers

Golmud 5.30pm

Jiāyùguān Y50.50, 3½ hours, hourly (9.30am to 5.10pm)

Lánzhōu Y98.50, eight hours, hourly (7am to 1.30pm, sleepers after that)

Wǔwēi Y51, 3½ hours, every 30 minutes (7.20am to 5pm)

Xīníng Y60.50, seven hours, two daily (7am and 6pm)

Train

Departing from Lánzhōu at 7.29am, the two-tier T9205 arrives in Zhāngyè at 12.29pm before proceeding to Jiāyùguān; another fast train departs for Jiāyùguān at 8pm. While arriving by train is no problem, departures are limited. The **train ticket office** (12 Oushi Jie; 欧式街12

号; ⏲8am-4pm) near the Marco Polo statue can book sleepers on the N857 to Dūnhuáng (hard sleeper Y160, 6¼ hours, 12.20am) and train N852 to Lánzhōu (hard sleeper Y94, 11 hours, 11.18pm). From Lánzhōu it's best to take the train as only night buses run.

A taxi to/from the train station is Y10, or take bus 1 (Y1). The station is 7km northeast of the city centre. Buses 4 and 13 run past the west bus station. Taxis start at Y4.

Mǎtí Sì 马蹄寺

The temples at **Mǎtí Sì** (Horse Hoof Monastery; admission Y45), built miraculously into the sandstone cliff (between the 5th and 14th centuries), are reached via twisting staircases, balconies, narrow passages and platforms that will leave your head spinning. Tibetan monks administer the place and locals will offer you horses for riding in the surrounding hills.

There are several good day hikes around here, including the five-hour loop through pine forest and talus fields to the **Línsōng Waterfall** (临松瀑布; Línsōng Pùbù) and back down past **'Sword Split Stone'** (剑劈石; Jiànpīshí). For unrivalled panoramas, take the elevatorlike ascent of the ridge behind the **white chörten** at Sānshísāntiān Shíkū (三十三天石窟).

The **Wòlóng Shānzhuāng** (卧龙山庄; dm/tw Y20/100) at Mǎtí Sì is a good place to stay. If you're adequately prepared for camping, some overnight trips are also possible.

Buses leave every 30 minutes from Zhāngyè's south bus station for the crossroads village of Mǎtí Hé (马蹄河, Y11, 1½ hours, 6.40am to 5.40pm), from where you can catch a minibus or taxi (Y20) for the final 7km or so. Direct buses to Mǎtí Sì depart at 3.40pm, and you might find a direct bus on weekend mornings. The last bus back from Mǎtí Hé leaves at 4.30pm.

Jiāyùguān 嘉峪关

☎0937 / POP 170,000

You approach Jiāyùguān through the forbidding lunar landscape of north Gānsù. It's a fitting setting, as Jiāyùguān marks the symbolic end of the Great Wall, the western gateway of China proper and, for imperial Chinese, the beginning of the back of beyond. One of the defining points of the Silk Road, a Ming-dynasty fort was erected here in 1372 and Jiāyùguān came to be colloquially known as the 'mouth' of China, while the narrow Hexi Corridor, leading back towards the *nèidì* (inner lands), was dubbed the 'throat'.

You'll need plenty of imagination to conjure up visions of the Silk Road, as modern Jiāyùguān is a city of straight roads and identikit blocks, almost as if airlifted into position from North Korea. But the Jiāyùguān Fort is an essential part of Silk Road lore and most certainly worth a visit.

Sleeping

It's possible to spend the night at the fort at the **Taihe Country Villa** (☎639 6622).

Yíngbīn Hotel HOTEL $
(迎宾宾馆; Yíngbīn Bīnguǎn; ☎620 1751; tw/tr without shower Y60/70, s/d/tw Y100/100/120) Bright inside with fine rooms (although the bathrooms look like they belong in an asylum), this place is good value and well located for restaurants and transport.

Jiāyùguān Bīnguǎn HOTEL $$$
(嘉峪关宾馆; ☎620 1588; 1 Xinhua Beilu; 新华北路1号; s Y668-780, d Y768, ste Y1880, discounts of 30-40%; ❄@) Rooms are pleasant and reasonably modern with bathroom and computer; there are also a sauna, small gym, ticket agent and good service.

Liángshijú Zhāodàisuǒ GUESTHOUSE $
(粮食局招待所; ☎622 6293; 2nd fl, 24 Xinhua Zhonglu; s/tw without shower Y40/58, tw Y68) Just by the hospital, this clean and well-run guesthouse is central and good value.

Jīnyè Bīnguǎn HOTEL $
(金叶宾馆; ☎620 1333; 12 Lanxin Xilu; 兰新西路12号; d Y100-180, tr Y120, discounts of 40%; ❄) The ensuite rooms are good value at this clean and quiet hotel with a useful location by the bus station.

Eating

For cake, croissant and coffee, try branches of the bakery Aili.

Āmílái Niúyángròu Fěntāngguǎn LAMB NOODLES $
(阿迷来牛羊肉粉汤馆; Shengli Nanlu; 胜利南路; ⏲7am-2.30pm & 4-9pm) Excellent and filling bowls of *jiāgōng yángròu fěntāng* (加工羊肉粉汤; lamb and vermicelli soup; Y14) – chuck in a *bǐng* (饼; flat bread; Y0.50) and you've a meal. There's no English sign, but hunt out the red and green sign around 200m south of the intersection with Hekou Xilu.

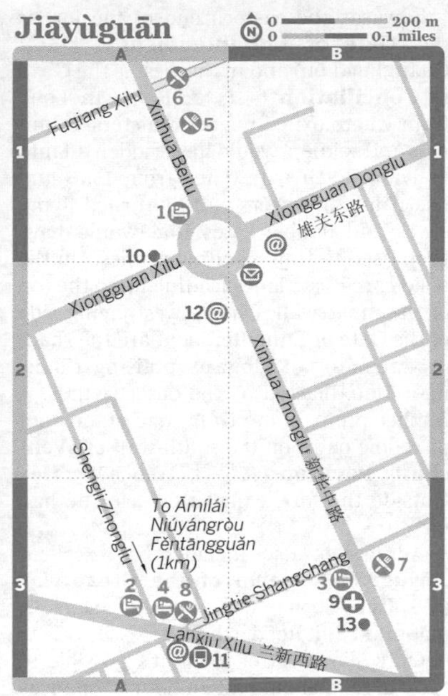

Jiāyùguān

Sleeping

1 Jiāyùguān Bīnguǎn A1
2 Jīnyè Bīnguǎn A3
3 Liángshijú Zhāodàisuǒ B3
4 Yíngbīn Hotel A3

Eating

5 Àilǐ A1
6 Fùqiáng Market Entrance A1
7 Jìngtiě Xiǎochīchéng B3
8 Liuyuan Restaurant A3

Information

9 People's No 1 Hospital B3

Transport

10 Bicycle Hire A1
11 Bus Station A3
12 Jiāyùguān Airport Ticket Office A2
13 Train Booking Office B3

Liuyuan Restaurant SÌCHUĀN $

(苑中苑酒店; Yuànzhōngyuàn Jiǔdiàn; Lanxin Xilu; dishes from Y15; 📋) Directly across from the bus station is this classy Sìchuān restaurant.

Fùqiáng Market MARKET $

For a fast, hot meal, try the food stalls at this market (富强市场; Fùqiáng Shìchǎng), north of the traffic circle.

Jìngtiě Xiǎochīchéng MARKET $

(镜铁小吃城; Jingtie Market; ⌚10am-10pm) Also try this busy place, off Xinhua Zhonglu, where you can load up on lamb kebabs (Y10), lamb ribs (Y10), beer (Y3), *ròujiāmó*, wonton soup, dumplings, roast duck and more.

Information

Bank of China (中国银行; Zhōngguó Yínháng; Xinhua Zhonglu; ⌚9.30am-5.30pm Mon-Fri, 10am-4pm Sat & Sun) Has an ATM and can change money. It's south of Lanxin Xilu intersection.

China Post (中国邮政; Zhōngguó Yóuzhèng; cnr Xinhua Zhonglu & Xiongguan Donglu; ⌚8.30am-7pm Mon-Fri, 10am-6pm Sat & Sun) At the traffic circle in the centre of town.

Jiāxiáng Internet Cafe (嘉祥网吧; Jiāxiáng Wǎngbā; Xiongguan Donglu; per hr Y4; ⌚24hr) Pricey.

People's No 1 Hospital (第一人民医院; Dìyī Rénmín Yīyuàn; Xinhua Zhonglu)

Public Security Bureau (PSB;公安局; Gōng'ānjú; ☎631 6927, ext 2039; 312 Guodao; ⌚8.30am-noon & 2.30-6pm Mon-Fri) At the southern edge of town, diagonally opposite the stadium. Visa extensions available.

Xīnjùdiǎn Internet Cafe (新聚典网络; Xīnjùdiǎn Wǎngluò; per hr Y2; ⌚24hr)

Getting There & Away

Air

Book air tickets at the **Jiāyùguān Airport Ticket Office** (嘉峪关机场售票处; Jiāyùguān Jīchǎng Shòupiàochù; Minhang Dasha, Xinhua Zhonglu; ⌚8am-7.10pm). Jiāyùguān's airport is 13km from town, offering flights to Běijīng (Y1880), Lánzhōu (Y1080), Shànghǎi (Y2190) and Xī'ān (Y1210).

Bus

Jiāyùguān's bus station (汽车站; Qìchēzhàn) is by a busy four-way junction on Lanxin Xilu, next to the main budget hotels. Doubling as a billiards hall, the station has buses to:

Dūnhuáng Y70, five hours, four daily (9am to 2.30pm)

Lánzhōu Y150.50, 12 hours, three daily (2.30pm, 4.30pm and 6.30pm), all sleepers

Wǔwēi Y96, seven hours, five daily (2.30pm to 8.30pm)

Zhāngyè Y44 to Y50.50, 3½ hours, every 30 minutes (7am to 3pm)

Train

Departing from Lánzhōu at 7.29am, the two-tier T9205 arrives in Jiāyùguān at 2.43pm. From Jiāyùguān there are daytime trains to:

Dūnhuáng Y28, four hours

Zhāngyè Y22, three hours

There are a couple of sleeper trains to:

Lánzhōu Y180, nine hours

Ürümqi Y220, 15 hours

Purchase tickets at the **train booking office** (火车站售票处; huǒchēzhàn shòupiàochù; 28 Xinhua Zhonglu; ⌚8am-4.30pm Mon-Fri, to 4pm Sat & Sun) near the hospital, next to the China Construction Bank.

Jiāyùguān's Luhua train station is 5km south of the town centre. Bus 1 runs here from Xinhua Zhonglu (Y1). A taxi costs Y10.

 Getting Around

Bikes are good for reaching some surrounding attractions. The gatekeeper at the Jiǔgāng Bīnguǎn (出租自行车; Chūzū Zìxíngchē) hires them for Y20 per day (Y400 deposit).

One airport bus (Y10) runs daily at 11am from the Jiāyùguān Airport Ticket Office to the airport; a taxi will cost around Y40.

Bus 2 (Y1) runs from the train station to the bus station.

Around Jiāyùguān

A taxi to the Wei Jin Tombs, Jiāyùguān Fort and the Overhanging Great Wall should cost you no more than Y100 for a half-day; if you just go to the fort and Overhanging Great Wall, figure on Y50.

JIĀYÙGUĀN FORT 嘉峪关城楼

One of the classic images of western China, the **Jiāyùguān Fort** (Jiāyùguān Chénglóu; May-Oct/Nov-Apr Y100/80; ⌚8.30am-7.30pm) guards the pass between the snowcapped Qílián Shān peaks and Hēi Shān (Black Mountains) of the Mǎzōng Shān range. The admission ticket also grants you access to the First Beacon Platform of the Great Wall and the Overhanging Great Wall.

Built in 1372, the fort was christened the 'Impregnable Defile Under Heaven'. Although the Chinese often controlled territory far beyond the Jiāyùguān area, this was the last major stronghold of imperial China – the end of the 'civilised world', beyond which lay only desert demons and the barbarian armies of Central Asia.

Towards the eastern end of the fort is the **Gate of Enlightenment** (光化楼; Guānghuá Lóu) and in the west is the **Gate of Conciliation** (柔远楼; Róuyuǎn Lóu), from where exiled poets, ministers, criminals and soldiers would have ridden off into oblivion. Each gate dates from 1506 and has 17m-high towers with upturned flying eaves and double gates that would have been used to trap invading armies. On the inside are horse lanes leading up to the top of the inner wall. On the west-facing side of the Gate of Enlightenment are the shadowy remains of **slogans** praising Chairman Mao, blasted by the desert winds. A further prolix quote from Mao stands out in yellow paint on the south wall of **Wenchang Pavilion** (文昌阁; Wénchāng Gé). Outside the fort, camel rides can be had for Y10.

Admission also includes an excellent **Jiāyùguān Museum of the Great Wall** (⌚8.30am-7.30pm), with photos, artefacts, maps and Silk Road exhibits.

Only 5km west of town, it's possible to cycle here in about half an hour. A one-way taxi trip to the fort costs about Y10.

OVERHANGING GREAT WALL 悬壁长城

Running north from Jiāyùguān, this section of **wall** (Xuánbì Chángchéng; adult/student Y21/11; ⌚8.30am-dusk) is believed to have been first constructed in 1539, though this reconstruction dates from 1987. It's quite an energetic hike up to excellent views of the desert and the glittering snow-capped peaks in the distance. A **smaller section of wall** (admission Y25) is next door, but this one is included in the Jiāyùguān Fort ticket. Both sections of wall are 9km from the fort. A taxi is around Y50 return from town.

FIRST BEACON PLATFORM OF THE GREAT WALL 长城第一墩

Atop a 82m-high cliff overlooking the Taolai River, the remains of this **beacon platform** (Chángchéng Dìyī Dūn; admission Y21; ⌚9am-5pm) are not much to look at (they resemble a shaped pile of dirt), but the views over the river in their dramatic gorge are impressive and you can walk alongside attached vestiges of the Great Wall. Descend to the subterranean viewing platform above the river or sweep across it on a pulley for Y31. Admission is included in the Jiāyùguān Fort ticket. A taxi from town is around Y35 return.

WEI JIN TOMBS 新城魏晋墓

These **tombs** (Xīnchéng Wèijìnmù; admission Y35; ⏲sunrise-sunset) date from approximately AD 220–420 (the Wei and Western Jin periods) and contain extraordinarily fresh brick wall paintings depicting scenes from everyday life, from making tea to picking mulberries for silk production. There are literally thousands of tombs in the desert 20km east of Jiāyùguān, but only one is currently open to visitors, that of a husband and wife. The small **museum** is also worth a look. You can preview some of the painted bricks at the Jiāyùguān Fort museum. A taxi will cost around Y50.

JULY 1ST GLACIER 七一冰川

About 90km southwest of Jiāyùguān, the **July 1st Glacier** (Qīyī Bīngchuān; admission Y51) sits high in the Qílián Shān range at 4300m. It is reached via the train to the iron-ore town of Jìngtiěshān (镜铁山; Y10), departing from Jiāyùguān's Luhua train station at 8am. It's a scenic three-hour train trip to Jìngtiěshān, where you can hire a taxi to the glacier (return Y120, 20km). Hikers can walk a 5km trail alongside the glacier. Icy winter weather grinds transport to a halt from November to March. In summer it's a great place to come to escape the heat of the desert below, but if you come in the spring or autumn it can be a cold and forbidding place – the glacier fills the rocky valley and there is little life up here. Global warming is having an effect on the glacier, which has retreated 50m in recent years.

You could theoretically do this in one day, but it's better to stay the night in Jìngtiěshān, where there is a cheap and basic hostel *(zhāodàisuǒ)*. This will leave you with enough time the next morning to hire a taxi up to **Tiān'é Hú** (return Y50) and the Tibetan village of **Qíqīng**. Return trains depart around 1.46pm from Jìngtiěshān. A return taxi to the glacier from Jiāyùguān costs around Y400 (nine hours).

Dūnhuáng 敦煌

✆0937 / POP 156,000

The fertile Dūnhuáng oasis has long been a refuge for weary Silk Road travellers. Most visitors only stayed long enough to swap a camel and have a feed; others settled down and built the forts, towers and magnificent cave temples that are now scattered over the surrounding area. These sites, along with some dwarfing sand dunes and desertscapes, make Dūnhuáng a magnificent place, despite its remoteness. The low-rise

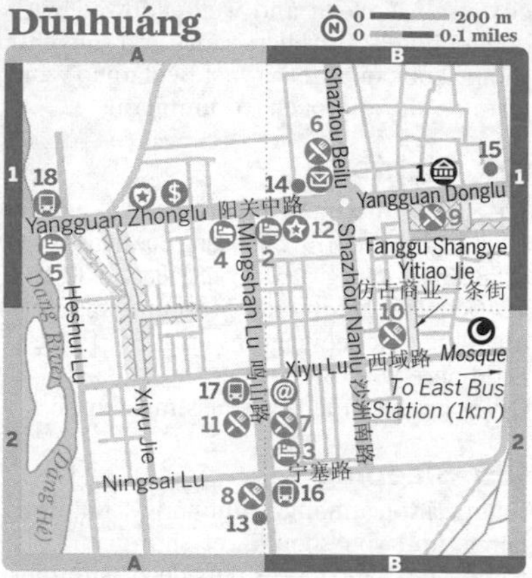

Dūnhuáng

Sights

1 Dūnhuáng Museum ... B1

Sleeping

2 Dūnhuáng Legend Hotel ... B1
3 Fēitiān Bīnguǎn ... B2
4 Gōngyì Měishù Zhāodàisuǒ ... A1
5 Grand Soluxe Hotel Dūnhuáng ... A1

Eating

6 Bǎilèjī ... B1
7 Charley Johng's Café ... B2
John's Information Cafe ... (see 3)
8 Làzhi Ròujiāmó ... A2
9 Night Market ... B1
10 Oasis ... B2
11 Shirley's Café ... A2
Zhèngzōng Lánzhōu Niúròumiàn ... (see 7)

Entertainment

12 Dūnhuáng Theatre ... B1

Information

Fēitiān Travel Service ... (see 3)
13 Train Booking Office ... A2

Transport

14 Air Ticket Office ... B1
15 CAAC ... B1
16 Long-Distance Bus Station ... B2
17 Minibus Stand ... A2
18 Minibuses to Nánhú ... A1

city itself is clean and well-endowed with budget hotels, travellers' cafes and souvenir shops. Look out for the vast Běidàqiáo wind farm on the approach to Dūnhuáng.

Sights

FREE **Dūnhuáng Museum** MUSEUM
(敦煌博物馆; Dūnhuáng Bówùguǎn; ☎882 2981; Yangguan Donglu; ⊙8am-6.30pm Apr-Oct) The Dūnhuáng Museum is largely unchanged since opening in 1984; there's little here you can't see at the Mògāo Caves or the Jade Gate Pass museum.

Sleeping

Competition among Dūnhuáng's hotels is fierce, and you should get significant discounts (50% or more) outside of summer. Unless stated otherwise, the following are open year-round. At the time of writing, Charley Johng's Cafe was about to open its own hotel near the mosque; dorms were to be in the Y35 to Y40 price range, with doubles at around Y150. Ask at the cafe.

Dune Guesthouse GUESTHOUSE $
(敦煌月泉山庄; Dūnhuáng Yuèquán Shānzhuāng; ☎388 2411; dm Y30, tents Y40 , d Y100, huts Y100-250) This excellent chilled-out backpacker retreat is right by Singing Sands Mountain (p830); it's run by the folks at Charley Johng's Cafe, so make enquiries there first. Cabins are out the back among the fruit trees. Tents and sleeping bags (Y20) are also for rent; sunhats and parasols are free. From the minibus 3 terminus walk north a short way, take the first turning left on the other side of the road past the vines and follow the signs.

Silk Road Dūnhuáng Hotel HOTEL $$
(敦煌山庄; Dūnhuáng Shānzhuāng; ☎888 2088; www.dunhuangresort.com; Dunyue Lu; 敦月路; dm Y80, d Y350-1200, discounts of 20%; ❄) Around 2km from Singing Sands Mountain, this four-star resort-style outfit is tastefully designed with Central Asian rugs, a cool stone floor and Chinese antiques. Four-bed dorms are in the student building way round the back, and the cheaper doubles (with bathrooms) are in the 'Professional Quarters'; both come with views of the dunes. Pricier accommodation is in the main building; there are also courtyard villa suites. A taxi from town costs Y10, or take minibus 3 (Y1).

Dūnhuáng Legend Hotel HOTEL $$$
(敦煌飞天大酒店; Dūnhuáng Fēitiān Dàjiǔdiàn; ☎8885 3999; www.dhlegendhotel.com; 2 Mingshan Lu; 鸣山路2号; d Y698-888, discounts of 40%; ❄@) Rooms at this four-star Chinese-oriented hotel are well furnished and good value with discount, but standard doubles only come with shower. No Western breakfasts.

Grand Soluxe Hotel Dūnhuáng HOTEL $$$
(敦煌阳光沙州大酒店; Dūnhuáng Yángguāng Shāzhōu Dàjiǔdiàn; ☎886 2888; 31 Yangguan Zhonglu; 阳关中路31号; tw & d Y860, ste Y1600, discounts of 40%; @❄) Opened in 2008, this pleasant hotel has comfortable and elegant rooms decorated with Chinese motifs and looking out over the river in a striking and modern building. Broadband included.

Fēitiān Bīnguǎn HOTEL $$
(飞天宾馆; ☎882 2337; 22 Mingshan Lu; 鸣山路22号; dm Y40, s/d/tr/ste Y320/320/388/788, discounts of 50%; ❄) This longstanding two-star hotel has a good location and decent rooms with dark wood furnishings. Hot water only from 7am to 10am and evenings. It's closed in winter.

Gōngyì Měishù Zhāodàisuǒ GUESTHOUSE $
(工艺美术招待所; ☎884 0919; 14 Yangguan Zhonglu; 阳关中路14号; d without shower Y40) On 3rd floor in courtyard opposite China Construction Bank off Yangguan Zhonglu. Friendly place with simple but cheap doubles.

Eating & Drinking

Several Western travellers' cafes can be found in town with dishes in the Y10 to Y20 mark. In addition to providing internet access and bike hire, these are good spots to exchange information with other travellers.

Oasis CAFE $
(☎150 0937 6021; Fanggu Shangye Yitiao Jie; ⊙3pm-11pm Tue-Sun) Surely the best milk shakes (Y12; blueberry, peach, kiwifruit and more) in northwest China and some of the finest coffee too, including the endless coffee (Y18), perfect for an everlasting caffeine rush. There're good smoothies (Y10) as well at this relaxing, chilled-out spot run by an Oklahoman. Pristine loo too.

Night Market STREET MARKET $$
(夜市; Yèshì; ⊙till 2am) Lively spot off Yangguan Donglu with singing, music bands and roast lamb by the platter (Y40 per *jīn*). There are loads of Sìchuān, Korean noodles,

claypot, barbecue and Lánzhōu noodles outfits here, so just take your pick. Look out for cooling cups of *xìngpíshuǐ* (杏皮水; Y5, apricot juice).

Làzhī Ròujiāmó RÒUJIĀMÓ $
(腊汁肉夹馍; Mingshan Lu; ⏲10am-10pm) The plastic flowers and tacky furniture won't win any awards, but this place does some very tasty *ròujiāmó* (肉夹馍; Y5 to Y6) – the famous 'Chinese hamburger' from Shaanxi province.

Zhèngzōng Lánzhōu Niúròumiàn NOODLES $
(正宗兰州牛肉面; Mingshan Lu; meals Y15; ⏲7am-10pm) One of several places you can hoover up a bowl of tasty and filling *hóngshāo niúròumiàn* (红烧牛肉面; noodles with braised beef; Y12); it's a short walk north of the Fēitiān Bīnguǎn.

Zhāixīng Gé BAR
(摘星阁; Silk Road Dunhuang Hotel; Dunyue Lu; ⏲6.30am-2pm & 4.30pm-midnight) Tremendous spot for a rooftop sundowner gazing out over the golden sand dunes; although at Y30 for a small bottle of beer, it may be worth tanking up first at the far, far cheaper (but viewless) Silk Road Alehouse (丝路酒坊) bar outside.

Charley Johng's Cafe CAFE $
(查理约翰咖啡馆; Chálǐ Yuēhàn Kāfēitīng; ☎388 2411; dhzhzh@public.lz.gs.cn; 21 Mingshan Lu) Western snacks and dishes.

John's Information Cafe CAFE $
(约翰旅游信息咖啡厅; Yuēhàn Lǚyóu Xìnxī Kāfēitīng; ☎882 7000; johncafe@hotmail.com; Fēitiān Bīnguǎn, 22 Mingshan Lu) Al fresco seating, Western dishes, English-speaking staff.

Shirley's Cafe CAFE $
(谢里斯咖啡馆; Xièlǐsī Kāfēiguǎn) Simple cafe with Western dishes.

Bǎilèjī FAST FOOD $
(百乐基; Shazhou Beilu; ⏲10am-11pm) Fast food.

☆ Entertainment

Dunhuang Goddess (敦煌神女; Dūnhuáng Shénnǚ; tickets Y180; ⏲8.30pm) is an 80-minute acrobatic dramatisation of stories on the walls of the Mògāo Caves. It's held at the **Dūnhuáng Theatre** (敦煌大剧院; Dūnhuáng Dàjùyuàn); English subtitles are provided.

Information

Ask at any of the Western cafes in town for tourist info; they can also help with tours from camel rides to overnight camping excursions. Internet access at Shirley's Cafe is Y6 per hour.

Bank of China (中国银行; Zhōngguó Yínháng; Yangguan Zhonglu; ⏲8am-noon & 3-6.30pm) Has an ATM and changes travellers cheques.

China Post (中国邮政; Zhōngguó Yóuzhèng; cnr Yangguan Zhonglu & Shazhou Beilu; ⏲8am-7pm) Located in the China Telecom building on the main traffic circle.

Fēitiān Travel Service (飞天旅行社; Fēitiān Lǚxíngshè; ☎882 2726, ext 8619; Fēitiān Bīnguǎn, 22 Mingshan Lu) Can arrange buses to Mògāo, local tours and car hire.

Liányǒu Wǎngbā (连友网吧; cnr Mingshan Lu & Xinjiang Lu; per hr Y4; ⏲8am-midnight) Internet access.

Public Security Bureau (PSB; 公安局; Gōng'ānjú; ☎886 2071; Yangguan Zhonglu; ⏲8am-noon & 3-6.30pm Mon-Fri) Two days needed for visa extension.

Getting There & Away

Air

Apart from November to March, when there are only flights to/from Lánzhōu and Xī'ān, there are regular flights to/from Běijīng (Y1880), Lánzhōu (Y1150), Shànghǎi (Y2550), Ürümqi (Y710) and Xī'ān (Y1680).

Seats can be booked at the **Civil Aviation Administration of China** (CAAC; 民航售票处; Zhōngguó Mínháng; ☎882 2389; 12 Yangguan Donglu; ⏲8am-noon & 2-8pm) or at the **air ticket office** (☎883 0008) in the lobby of the Yóuzhèng Bīnguǎn (邮政宾馆), west of China Post.

Bus

Arriving in Dūnhuáng you may be dropped off at a station just south of Yǒuhǎo Bīnguǎn. The bus to Ürümqi may stop in Turpan (Y150); otherwise, you'll need to take a bus to Hāmì (Y70, 8am and 2pm) from the **east bus station** on Sanwei Lu and change; buses to Liǔyuán (柳园; Y20, eight per day 8am to 6.30pm) also go from here. Dūnhuáng's main **long-distance bus station** (长途汽车站; Zhángtú Qìchēzhàn; ☎885 3746) has buses to:

Golmud Y90, nine hours, two daily (9am and 7.30pm)

Jiāyùguān Y60, five hours, two daily (8.30am and 9.30am), plus a sleeper for Y80 at 10.30am

Lánzhōu Y214, 17 hours, three daily (8am, 10.30am and 2pm), all sleepers

Urumqi Y185, 14 hours, one daily (6pm). Sleeper

Wǔwēi Y160, three daily (8am, 10.30am and 2pm), all sleepers

Zhāngyè Y120, three daily (8am, 10.30am and 2pm), all sleepers

Train

For Lánzhōu (Y268, 14 hours), take the K592 departing at 9.39am or the N858 departing at 9.25pm. For Ürümqi (Y249, 14 hours) take train T216 departing at 8.16pm. The same train also stops in Turpan (Y180, 12 hours). For Běijīng West, you'll have to take the bus to Liǔyuán first.

The station is 10km east of town. You can purchase tickets at the **train booking office** (铁路售票处; tiělù shòupiàochù; ☎595 9592; 31 Mingshan Lu; ⏲8am-4pm summer, to 3.30pm winter), south of Ningsai Lu, for a commission of Y5.

Getting Around

You can hire bikes from the travellers cafes for Y1 per hour. Getting to some of the outlying sights by bike is possible, but hard work at the height of summer.

To charter a ride for the sights around town, the minibus stand (小公共汽车站; Xiǎogōnggòng Qìchēzhàn) across from the Jiàrì Dàjiǔdiàn on Mingshan Lu is one place to start negotiations.

Dūnhuáng's airport is 13km east of town; taxis cost Y20. The train station is on the same road as the airport. Taxis start at Y5.

Around Dūnhuáng

Most people visit the Mògāo Caves in the morning, followed by the Míngshā Shān sand dunes in the late afternoon.

MÒGĀO CAVES 莫高窟

The Mògāo Caves (Mògāo Kū) are, simply put, one of the greatest repositories of Buddhist art in the world. At its peak, the site housed 18 monasteries, over 1400 monks and nuns, and countless artists, translators and calligraphers. Wealthy traders and important officials were the primary donors responsible for creating new caves, as caravans made the long detour past Mògāo to pray or give thanks for a safe journey through the treacherous wastelands to the west. The traditional date ascribed to the founding of the first cave is AD 366.

The caves fell into disuse after the collapse of the Yuan dynasty and were largely forgotten until the early 20th century, when they were 'rediscovered' by a string of foreign explorers (see p829).

Entrance to the **caves** (☎886 9060; low/high season Y80/160; ⏲8.30am-6pm May-Oct, 9am-5.30pm Nov-Apr, tickets sold till 1hr before closing) is strictly controlled – it's impossible to visit them on your own. The general admission ticket grants you a two-hour tour of 10 caves, including the infamous Library Cave (No 17; see the boxed text, p829) and a related exhibit containing rare fragments of manuscripts in classical Uighur and Manichean. Excellent English-speaking guides (Y20) are always available, and you can generally arrange tours in many other languages as well.

Of the 492 caves, 20 'open' caves are rotated fairly regularly, so recommendations are useless, but tours always include the two **big Buddhas**, 34.5m and 26m tall respectively. It's also possible to visit 12 of the more unusual caves for an additional fee; prices range from Y100 (No 217, early Tang) to Y500 (No 465, tantric art). Note that in some of the caves later frescoes may cover earlier wall paintings.

A torch (flashlight) is imperative – those used by the guides are weak, so bring your own if possible. Photography is strictly prohibited everywhere within the fenced-off caves area. Note that if it's raining, snowing or sand storming, the caves will be closed.

After the tour it's well worth visiting the **Dūnhuáng Research Centre**, where eight more caves, each representative of a different period, have been flawlessly reproduced, along with selected murals.

If you have a special interest in the site, check out the **International Dūnhuáng Project** (http://idp.bl.uk), an online database of digitalised manuscripts from the Library Cave at Mògāo.

Sights

Northern Wei, Western Wei & Northern Zhou Caves BUDDHIST CAVES

The earliest caves are distinctly Indian in style and iconography. All contain a central pillar, representing a stupa (symbolically containing the ashes of the Buddha), which the devout would circle in prayer. Paint was derived from malachite (green), cinnabar (red) and lapis lazuli (blue), expensive minerals imported from Central Asia.

The art of this period is characterised by its attempt to depict the spirituality of those who had transcended the material world through their asceticism. The Wei statues are slim, ethereal figures with finely chiselled features and comparatively large heads. The Northern Zhou figures have ghostly white eyes. Don't be fooled by the thick, black modernist strokes – it's the

SILK ROAD RAIDERS

In 1900, the self-appointed guardian of the Mògāo Caves, Wang Yuanlu, discovered a hidden library filled with tens of thousands of immaculately preserved manuscripts and paintings, dating as far back as AD 406.

It's hard to describe the exact magnitude of the discovery, but stuffed into the tiny room were texts in rare Central Asian languages, military reports, music scores, medical prescriptions, Confucian and Taoist classics, and Buddhist sutras copied by some of the greatest names in Chinese calligraphy – not to mention the oldest printed book in existence, the *Diamond Sutra* (AD 868). In short, it was an incalculable amount of original source material regarding Chinese, Central Asian and Buddhist history.

Word of the discovery quickly spread and Wang Yuanlu, suddenly the most popular bloke in town, was courted by rival archaeologists Auriel Stein and Paul Pelliot, among others. Following much pressure to sell the cache, Wang Yuanlu finally relented and parted with an enormous horde of treasure. During his watch close to 20,000 of the cave's priceless manuscripts were whisked off to Europe for the paltry sum of UK£220.

Still today, Chinese intellectuals bitter at the sacking of the caves deride Stein, Pelliot and other 'foreign devils' for making off with a national treasure. Defenders of the explorers point out that had the items been left alone they may have been lost during the ensuing civil war or the Cultural Revolution.

oxidisation of lead in the paint, not some forerunner of Picasso.

Sui Caves — BUDDHIST CAVES

The Sui dynasty (AD 581–618) began when a general of Chinese or mixed Chinese-Tuoba origin usurped the throne of the Northern Zhou dynasty and reunited northern and southern China for the first time in 360 years.

The Sui dynasty was short-lived and very much a transition between the Wei and Tang periods. This can be seen in the Sui caves: the graceful Indian curves in the Buddha and Bodhisattva figures start to give way to the more rigid style of Chinese sculpture.

Tang Caves — BUDDHIST CAVES

During the Tang dynasty (AD 618–907), China pushed its borders westward as far as Lake Balkash in today's Kazakhstan. Trade expanded and foreign merchants and people of diverse religions streamed into Cháng'ān, the Tang capital.

This was Mògāo's high point. Painting and sculpture techniques became much more refined, and some important aesthetic developments, notably the sex change (from male to female) of Guanyin and the flying apsaras, took place. The beautiful murals depicting the Buddhist Western Paradise offer rare insights into the court life, music, dress and architecture of Tang China.

Some 230 caves were carved during the Tang dynasty, including two impressive grottoes containing enormous, seated Buddha figures. Originally open to the elements, the statue of Maitreya in cave 96 (believed to represent Empress Wu Zetian, who used Buddhism to consolidate her power) is a towering 34.5m tall, making it the world's third-largest Buddha. The Buddhas were carved from the top down using scaffolding, the anchor holes of which are still visible.

Post-Tang Caves — BUDDHIST CAVES

Following the Tang dynasty, the economy around Dūnhuáng went into decline, and the luxury and vigour typical of Tang painting began to be replaced by simpler drawing techniques and flatter figures. The mysterious Western Xia kingdom, which controlled most of Gānsù from 983 to 1227, made a number of additions to the caves at Mògāo and began to introduce Tibetan influences.

Getting There & Away

The Mògāo Caves are 25km (30 minutes) southeast from Dūnhuáng. A green bus (one way Y8) starts waiting at around 8am and leaves at 8.30am from the intersection across from the Dūnhuáng Hotel; it returns at noon, which isn't really enough time at the caves. A return taxi costs from Y100 to Y150 for a day.

Some people ride out to the caves on a bicycle, but be warned that half the ride is through total desert – hot work in summer.

WESTERN THOUSAND BUDDHA CAVES 西千佛洞

These little-visited **caves** (Xī Qiānfó Dòng; admission Y40; ⏲7am-5.30pm), 35km west of Dūnhuáng, range from the Northern Wei to the Tang dynasties. There are 16 caves hidden in the cliff face of the Dǎng Hé gorge, of which six are open to the public. The art may not compare to Mògāo, but the lack of crowds is more restful – although some (eg cave 15) may require an additional fee. Afterwards, wander off on a walk through the desert canyon.

The caves are best reached by taxi (Y60 return) or minibus. Alternatively, catch a bus to Nánhú (南湖; 40 minutes) from the intersection of Heshui Lu and Yangguan Zhonglu in Dūnhuáng, and ask the driver to drop you off at the turn-off to the caves, from where it's a 10-minute walk across the desert.

SINGING SANDS MOUNTAIN & CRESCENT MOON LAKE 鸣沙山、月牙泉

Six kilometres south of Dūnhuáng at **Singing Sands Mountain** (Míngshā Shān; low/high season Y80/120; ⏲6am-10pm), the desert meets the oasis in most spectacular fashion. From here it's easy to see how Dūnhuáng gained its moniker 'Shāzhōu' (Town of Sand). The climb to the top of the dunes – the highest peak swells to 1715m – is sweaty work, but the view across the undulating desert sands and green poplar trees below is awesome. Hire a pair of bright orange shoe protectors (防沙靴; *fángshāxuē;* Y10) or just shake your shoes out later.

At the base of the colossal dunes is a famous yet underwhelming pond, **Crescent Moon Lake** (Yuèyáquán). The dunes are a no-holds-barred tourist playpen, with **camel rides** (Y80 for a one-hour ride), **dune buggies** (Y150), **'dune surfing'** (sand sliding; Y15 to Y20), **paragliding** (jumping off the dunes with a chute on your back; Y60), **archery** (Y1 per arrow) and even **microlighting**. But if your sole interest is in appreciating the dunes in peace, it's not hard to hike away from the action.

You can ride a bike to the dunes in around 20 minutes. Minibus 3 (Y1) shuttles between Dūnhuáng and the dunes from 7.30am to 10pm, departing from opposite the Yǒuhǎo Bīnguǎn. A taxi costs Y10 one way. Most people head out here at about 6pm when the weather starts to cool down.

Western cafes in town offer overnight camel trips to the dunes; Charley Johng's, for example, charges Y300 per person for an overnight stay in a tent and camel rides (with the ever-popular Mr Li); there are also five- to eight-day expeditions out to the Jade Gate Pass, Liuyuan and even as far as Lop Nor in the deserts of Xīnjiāng.

YĂDĀN NATIONAL PARK & JADE GATE PASS 雅丹国家地质公园、玉门关

The weird, eroded desert landscape of **Yădān National Park** (Yǎdān Guójiā Dìzhì Gōngyuán; incl tour Y60) is 180km northwest of Dūnhuáng, in the middle of the Gobi Desert's awesome nothingness. A former lake bed that eroded in spectacular fashion some 12,000 years ago, the strange rock formations provided the backdrop to the last scenes of Zhang Yimou's film *Hero*. The desert landscape is dramatic, but you can only tour the site on a group minibus, so there's little scope to explore on your own.

To get to Yǎdān you have to pass by (and buy a ticket to) the **Jade Gate Pass** (Yùmén Guān; admission Y45), 102km from Dūnhuáng. Both this and the **South Pass** (阳关; Yáng Guān), 78km west of Dūnhuáng, were originally military stations, part of the Han-dynasty series of beacon towers that extended to the garrison town of Loulan in Xīnjiāng. For caravans travelling westward, the Jade Gate marked the beginning of the northern route to Turpan, while the South Pass was the start of the southern route through Miran. The Jade Gate derived its name from the important traffic in Khotanese jade.

The entry fee includes a small **museum** (with scraps of real Silk Road silk); a nearby section of **Han-dynasty Great Wall**, built in 101 BC and impressive for its antiquity and refreshing lack of restoration; and the ruined city walls of **Hécāng Chéng**, 15km away on a side road.

The only way to get out here is to hire a car for a long day trip to take in Yǎdān, the Jade Gate and the Western Thousand Buddha Caves. Fēitiān Travel Service (see p827) organises air-conditioned cars for about Y450; you might get a minivan for around Y350.

EASTERN GĀNSÙ

Most travellers speed through eastern Gānsù, catching mere glimpses from the train window as they shuttle between Lánzhōu and Xī'ān. This is a shame because the area contains some spectacular Silk Road remnants at Màijī Shān and the Water Curtain Caves, as well as a handsome regional hub in Tiānshuǐ. Moon Canyon, in the far southern part of the province, is the hidden gem of the region.

Tiānshuǐ 天水

☎0938 / POP 450,000

Tiānshuǐ's splendid Buddhist caves at Màijī Shān entice a consistent flow of visitors to one of Gānsù's more attractive and laid-back cities. Industrial growth has sent the place on an outwards sprawl, but the old downtown of Tiānshuǐ (known as Qínchéng) has remained pleasantly low-rise and locals pass the time playing a lot of pool.

Tiānshuǐ is actually two separate towns 15km apart – the gritty railhead sprawl, known as Běidào (北道), and the central commercial area to the west, known as Qínchéng (秦城) – lashed together by a long freeway. Màijī Shān is 35km south of Běidào.

Sights

Tiānshuǐ's main draw is the grottoes at Màijī Shān, but if you have time to kill you could explore the other sights.

Fúxī Temple TEMPLE
(伏羲庙; Fúxī Miào; off Jiefang Lu, Qincheng; admission Y30; ⏲8am-6pm) Cracked during the Sìchuān earthquake of 2008, this Ming-dynasty temple was begun in 1483. The main hall is one of the most elaborate structures in Gānsù, with intricate wooden door panels and original paintings of the 64 hexagrams (varying combinations of the eight trigrams used in the I Ching) on the ceiling.

One of the mythic progenitors of the Chinese people, leaf-clad Fúxī was reputedly a local of Chenji (present-day Tiānshuǐ) who introduced the domestication of animals, hunting and the eight trigrams (used for divination) to early Chinese civilisation. A pleasant pedestrian area filled with itinerant musicians, wood carvers and souvenir stalls has been built at the front of the temple.

Yùquán Temple TAOIST TEMPLE
(玉泉观; Yùquán Guàn; Renmin Xilu, Qincheng; adult/student Y20/10; ⏲7.30am-6.30pm) Ascending in layers up the hillside above Qínchéng, this Taoist temple is a pleasant, green and rambling shrine. Of note are the ancient cypress trees, some more than 1000 years old.

Sleeping

Tiānshuǐ has plenty of accommodation, with discounts of up to 40% pretty standard. Cheap guesthouses *(zhāodàisuǒ)* can be found on Yima Lu in Běidào. A good alternative is to spend the night by Màijī Shān, a far more rural experience.

QINCHENG

Tiānshuǐ Dàjiǔdiàn HOTEL $
(天水大酒店; ☎828 9999; 1 Qincheng Dazhong Nanlu; 秦城大众南路1号; d without bathroom Y90, with bathroom Y146-190, tr Y97, discounts of 40%; ❄) The bargain but battle-scarred *pǔtōng* (economy) rooms with shared bathroom are great for budget seekers, with hot showers down the hall. It's right at the commercial heart of town, next to KFC.

BEIDAO

Dōng'ān Fàndiàn HOTEL $
(东安饭店; ☎261 3333; Yima Lu; 一马路; tw Y168, discounts of 40%; ❄) Very comfortable, with double-glazed windows, quality furnishings and good bathrooms with phone and hairdryer, this is a great three-star option 50m east of the train station. Excellent value.

Wànhuì Zhāodàisuǒ GUESTHOUSE $
(万汇招待所; ☎492 7976; Yima Lu; 一马路; tw Y35-80) This serviceable Běidào guesthouse four shops west of the post office has frugal cheapies and better standard rooms. Reception's on the 3rd floor.

Eating

Tiānshuǐ is famed for its *miànpí* (面皮) noodles, which can be found everywhere. In Qínchéng, good claypot, Sìchuān and noodle snack stalls stuff Xiaochi Jie (小吃街; Snack St), while fruit and walnut sellers cram Guangming Xiang, east and south of the Tiānshuǐ Dàjiǔdiàn.

Tasty *ròujiāmó* and other fine snack food in Běidào fills Erma Lu, the pedestrian alley south of the train station. For chicken burgers, a branch of the fast-food chain Dico's can be found on Erma Lu.

Běidào Qīngzhēn Lǎozìhào Niúròu Miànguǎn NOODLES $

(北道清真老字号牛肉面馆; Erma Lu, Beidao; meals Y8; ⌚24hr) Get a ticket from the kiosk out front and collect your beef noodles (*niúròumiàn;* Y4) and flatbread (*shāobǐng;* Y0.50) from the kitchen window at this place with a 30-year history. The noodles are excellent, infused with dollops of scarlet-red chilli oil. For extra meat, ask for *jiāròu niúròumiàn* (加肉牛肉面; Y7). There's no English sign, but it's obliquely opposite a branch of ICBC bank.

Information

Perhaps it's the bad air, but chemists (药房; *yàofáng*) are simply everywhere.

Bank of China (中国银行; Zhōngguó Yínháng) Běidào (⌚8.30am-noon & 2.30-5.30pm); Qínchéng (Minzhu Donglu) The Běidào branch is opposite the train station and has Forex and ATM.

China Post (中国邮政; Zhōngguó Yóuzhèng; ⌚8am-6pm) Qínchéng (Ziyou Lu); Běidào (Yima Lu)

Huáxīng Internet Cafe (华兴网吧; Huáxīng Wǎngbā; Yima Lu, Běidào; per hr Y2; ⌚24hr)

Industrial & Commercial Bank of China (工商银行; Gōngshāng Yínháng; Lantian City Plaza; Qínchéng) Has 24-hour ATM.

Tianle Internet Cafe (天乐网吧; Tiānlè Wǎngbā; Xiaochi Jie; Qínchéng; per hr Y1.50; ⌚24hr) Up steps west off Xiaochi Jie.

Getting There & Away

Bus

Buses from the **long-distance bus station** in Qínchéng run to:

Baoji Y48, two hours, regular services

Gāngǔ Y12, 90 minutes, every 20 minutes

Hanzhong Y88, seven to eight hours, one daily (6am)

Huīxiàn Y30, three hours, hourly

Lánzhōu Y55 to Y67, four hours, every 20 minutes

Línxià Y80, seven hours, one daily (6.30am)

Luòmén Y18, two hours, two daily (6.30am and 2.30pm)

Píngliáng Y70, five hours, four daily (6am, 7am, 8am and 9.30am)

Xī'ān Y100, 4½ hours, hourly

Yínchuān Y148, 12 hours, two daily (6am and 2.30pm)

Buses to Lánzhōu also depart throughout the day from the forecourt of the train station in Běidào. There are also two morning departures a day from here to Huīxiàn.

Train

Tiānshuǐ is on the Xī'ān–Lánzhōu railway line; there are dozens of daily trains in either direction. If you arrive early, you can visit Màijī Shān as a day trip, avoiding the need to stay overnight in Tiānshuǐ.

From Tiānshuǐ it's four to six hours to either Lánzhōu (hard seat Y62) or Xī'ān (Y61).

Getting Around

Taxis shuttle passengers between Qínchéng (from the Tiānshuǐ Dàjiǔdiàn and long-distance bus station) and the train station in Běidào for Y10. Alternatively, take the much slower bus 1 or 6 (Y3, 40 minutes) from Dazhong Lu.

Around Tiānshuǐ

MÀIJĪ SHĀN 麦积山

Set among wild and lush green hills southeast of Tiānshuǐ, the riveting grottoes of Màijī Shān (Haystack Mountain) are some of China's most famous Buddhist rock carvings. The solitary, tree-capped rock sticks up from the verdant, rolling landscape like a vast Chinese haystack, hence the name.

Sights

Màijī Shān CAVES

(adult/student Y70/35; ⌚8am-6pm) The cliff sides are riddled with niches and statues carved principally during the Northern Wei and Zhou dynasties (AD 386–581), with later additions. Vertigo-inducing catwalks and steep spiral stairways cling to the cliff face, affording close-ups of the art.

It's not certain just how the artists managed to clamber so high; one theory is that they created piles from blocks of wood reaching to the top of the mountain before moving down, gradually removing them as they descended. A number of the statues were slightly damaged by the Sìchuān earthquake of 2008 but have been repaired.

A considerable amount of pigment still clings to many of the statues – a lot of which are actually made of clay rather than hewn from rock – although you frequently have to climb up steps to peer at them through tight mesh grills. Also in many caves there is no natural illumination, so the figures of the Bodhisattvas sit hunched in the gloom or the frescoes are indiscernible. Much, though, is clearly visible and most of the more impressive sculptures decorate the upper walkways, especially at cave 4.

The entire undertaking is rounded off with a crescent of hawker stalls.

An English-speaking guide charges Y150 for the day. It's possible to view normally closed caves (eg Cave 133 and Cave 1) for an extra fee of Y500 per group.

Cave 13

Within the hard-to-miss Sui-dynasty trinity of **Buddha and Bodhisattvas** is the largest statue on the mountain: the cave's central effigy of Buddha tops out at 15.7m. When the statue was restored three decades ago, a handwritten copy of the *Sutra of Golden Light* was discovered within the Buddha's fan.

Cave 4

This cave's marvellous seven niches are large grottoes originally dating from the Northern Wei, with later additions from the Sui, Tang and Song. Note the powerful guardian figures, typical of torsional, muscular and fierce Tang-dynasty examples. The radiant-looking Bodhisattvas are simply exquisite, while swallows flit out from the overhanging rock above.

Cave 3

Also called the 1000 Buddha Corridor, this cave features an impressive hall past twin rows of solemn-faced Buddhas (actually 297 carvings all told). Note the lower row is far more weathered and damaged.

Cave 155

The oldest statues can be found here.

Cave 148

The figures here are among those displaying the influence of the Gandhara style, which arrived in China from India along the Silk Road.

Cave 144

The statues here are almost completely weathered away.

Cave 54

A quantity of the graffiti defacing some statues is also reasonably old – the characters daubed here are full form.

Cave 59

The largely indistinct 1200-character testament on the wall of this cave dates from 1035, recording the monies collected for restoring the statues.

The admission ticket includes entry to a small **botanic garden** *(zhíwùyuán)*. You only need around an hour or so for the grottoes and afterwards a hike up nearby **Xiāngjí Shān** (香积山) is lovely, with opportunities to break off into the woods which are full of birds and wildlife. At the base of the mountain is **Ruiying Monastery** (瑞应寺; Ruìyìng Sì; Y10).

Sleeping

There are several places where you can spend the night, including the **Arboretum Hotel** within the botanic garden.

Zhōuyú Nóngjiālè FARMSTEAD **$**
(周于农家乐; ☎139 1963 5896; beds Y20, d Y40) Tucked away in the woods, this place has simple but very cheap rooms in a farmstead environment; it also has heated *kàng* beds for winter and can cook up meals. To find the farmstead, take the path up to Xiāngjí Shān for around 600m; it's on the right.

Getting There & Away

Minibus 34 (Y5, 40 minutes) leaves every seven minutes from in front of the Tiānshuǐ train station. It may drop you at the crossroads, 5km before the site, from where a taxi van will cost Y5 per seat to the ticket office. You can walk the last 2km to 3km from the ticket office to the caves or take the tour buggy (*guāngguān che;* Y10). Horses can also be hired for Y20. A taxi from Tiānshuǐ costs around Y100 return. On the way back you may find the occasional minibus 34 waiting to fill up for the return trip (Y6).

Moon Canyon 月亮峡

Tucked in a hidden corner of southeastern Gānsù is the pristine wilderness of **Moon Canyon** (Yuèliàng Xiá; admission Y20), with its rushing rivers and towering rock walls, and the surrounding Three Beaches National Park (三滩自然保护区; Sāntān Zìrán Bǎohùqū).

At the entrance to the valley is **Moon Canyon Retreat** (月亮峡度假村; Yuèliàng Xiá Dùjiàcūn; ☎755 7888; www.threebeaches.com; dm/tents/cabins Y50/100/120, tw Y220; ⏲Apr-Oct), with four spartan but low-impact lodges.

A new road leads 15km up to the village of Yánpíng (严坪), where there are half a dozen **homestays** (农家乐; nóngjiālè; dm Y10), marked by tourism signs. Accommodation is basic but friendly, and local dishes are available. There is one shop in the village, so bring some snacks.

For those with camping equipment, it's a five-hour hike up to the Sāntān (Three Beaches); one possible three-day trek is to the purported **old-growth forest** (原始森林; *yuánshǐ sēnlín*) upstream. Jeeps ferry (mainly Chinese) tourists up to the first pool (Y250 return) but not beyond.

Moon Canyon is on the Chéngdū–Xī'ān rail line near the village of Jiālíng (嘉陵). There is only one stop per day in either direction (both at around 1pm) – the closest major rail links are Guǎngyuán (Sìchuān) and Bǎojī (Shaanxi). Frequent buses run between Tiānshuǐ and Huīxiàn (徽县; Y30, three hours), from where you can hire a minivan (Y60) for the final 26km. Alternatively, take a minibus from Huīxiàn on to Jiālíng and then hire a minivan (Y20) or walk the 6km from there.

Gāngǔ 甘谷

☎0938

If you're Buddha-hopping across Gānsù, stop off at this village and make the one-hour hike up the hillside to an impressive carved image of **Sakyamuni** (complete with moustache). The path along the ridge is easy to follow and there are numerous little shrines along the way. The Buddha is easily visible from the road that runs past the town. Gāngǔ is 65km west of Tiānshuǐ and 30km east of Luòmén; local buses and trains between the two will stop here.

Water Curtain Caves 水帘洞

☎0938

The **Water Curtain Caves** (Shuǐlián Dòng; admission Y25; ⏰7am-7pm) are an embodiment of that classic image of China – Taoist and Buddhist temples sheltered by steep cliffs and the majestic image of a carved Buddha guarding the vacant canyons below. The caves are 17km north of **Luòmén** (洛门), a town on the main road between Lánzhōu and Tiānshuǐ.

The main sight is **Lāshāo Sì** (拉稍寺), an overhanging cliff sheltering an amazingly vibrant 31m-high painted figure of Sakyamuni seated cross-legged upon a throne of lotus petals, lions, deer and elephants. The bas-relief carving and accompanying mint-green and salmon coloured frescoes were completed in the Northern Wei dynasty (AD 386–534). The secondary sights here are the eponymous Taoist temple of **Shuǐlián Dòng**, a short walk uphill, and the faded remnants of the **Thousand Buddha Cave** (千佛洞; Qiānfó Dòng), a 10-minute walk up a side valley.

Minibuses in Luòmén will take you the 17km to the Water Curtain Caves for Y60 return; a motor tricycle is cheaper at around Y35. Half the road was washed out a few years back, so any vehicle you take needs to be sturdy enough for the rough journey (and getting here may well be impossible after heavy rain).

Luòmén is on the Lánzhōu–Xī'ān rail line, but only a couple of trains per day stop here. Two direct buses leave from Tiānshuǐ's long-distance bus station (in Qínchéng; two hours, Y18) at 6.30am and 2.30pm; otherwise change buses in Gāngǔ (甘谷). From Luòmén it's a 20-minute minibus ride (Y2) on to Wǔshān (武山) and then a short bus ride to Lǒngxī (陇西), from where there are frequent trains to/from Lánzhōu.

The only place to stay is the decent **Luòmén Bīnguǎn** (洛门宾馆; ☎322 7668; tw Y80).

Píngliáng 平凉

☎0933 / POP 106,800

A booming Chinese midsized town, Píngliáng is a logical base for visits to the nearby holy mountain of Kōngtóng Shān. The train station is in the northeastern part of town and the main bus station in the far western part. They are connected by Xi Dajie and Dong Dajie, home to the town's major hotels, restaurants and shops.

The **Píngliáng Bīnguǎn** (平凉宾馆; ☎825 3988; 86 Xi Dajie; 西大街86号; tw Y200-268) is a large midrange place in the town centre. Next door, the **Qīnghuá Bīnguǎn** (清华宾馆; ☎823 4241; 90 Xi Dajie; 西大街90号; dm Y25-35, d Y90) is a friendly budget option.

About 200m west of the Píngliáng Bīnguǎn is the Sìzhōng Alley market (Sìzhōng Xiàng shìchǎng), with numerous restaurants and stalls.

The following services depart from Píngliáng's main bus station, in the western part of town:

Gùyuán Y7 to Y18, 1½ hours, hourly (8.20am to 5pm)

Lánzhōu Y90, five hours, hourly (7am to 4.50pm)

Tiānshuǐ Y54, seven hours, two daily (6.40am and 8.50am).

Xī'ān Y70, six hours, five daily (7.40am to 3pm)

Yán'ān Y106, nine hours, one daily (6am)

For Tiānshuǐ there are more frequent departures from the east bus station *(qìchē dōngzhàn)*.

Getting to Píngliáng is easiest by train. There are overnight trains to Lánzhōu (train N855; Y103, 11 hours), Xī'ān (train 2586; Y66, seven hours) and Yínchuān (train K361; Y122, 8½ hours).

Around Píngliáng

KŌNGTÓNG SHĀN 崆峒山

On the border of Níngxià in the Liùpán Shān (六盘山) range, **Kōngtóng Shān** (winter/summer Y60/120; ⌚8am-6.30pm) is one of the 12 principal peaks in the Taoist universe. It was first mentioned by the philosopher Zhuangzi (399–295 BC), and illustrious visitors have included none other than the Yellow Emperor. Numerous paths lead over the hilltop past dozens of picturesque temples to the summit at over 2100m.

The main entrance is on the north side of the mountain. You can make a nice loop trip by descending via the steps on the mountain's south side and taking a taxi from the base. If you'd rather not walk, a **cable car** (suǒdào; return Y30) spans the reservoir on the south side to the top of the cliffs.

There is accommodation and food on the mountain at the **Kōngtóng Shānzhuāng** (崆峒山庄; dm Y40-60, tw Y240; ⌚closed Nov-Apr).

Kōngtóng Shān is 11km west of Píngliáng. You might find a minibus (Y5) situated on the opposite side of the park across from the main bus station, or you can hire a minivan for Y20/40 one way/return. Both will drop you close to the ticket office, where you need to pay for a separate vehicle to take you the 3.5km up to the mountain (per person/car Y10/50).

Níngxià

POPULATION: 5.9 MILLION

Includes »

Best Places to Eat

» Bái Gōng (p840)

» Xiānhè Lóu (p840)

» Zhōngwèi Night Market (p844)

Best Places to Stay

» Jīxiáng Xīxià International Youth Hostel (p840)

» In a tent while camel trekking in the Tengger Desert (p845)

» Zhōngwèi Dàjiǔdiàn (p843)

Why Go?

Níngxià (宁夏) is a raw landscape of stark mountains and dusty plains sliced in two by the Yellow River (Huáng Hé). There is a distinct *Grapes of Wrath* feel to the place as Hui peasants till the yellow earth, clinging to a centuries-old lifestyle despite the constant threat of drought and floods. While such images don't necessarily translate into glowing tourist brochures, thousands of years of history have left some unique sites worth visiting.

In ancient times Níngxià lay on the front line between the nomads of Mongolia and the settled Chinese to the south. At various times the region was part of Chinese and nomadic empires, and the great puzzle of history has left ancient rock carvings, Buddhist statues and the royal tombs of the Xixia. At Níngxià's heart lies the Yellow River and no visit is complete without a float down its silty waters. Best of all, the province sees few visitors, so when visiting these sites you feel as though you have the place to yourself.

When to Go

Yínchuān

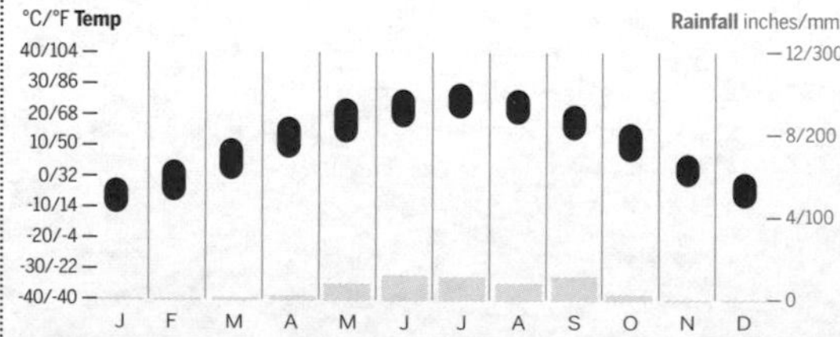

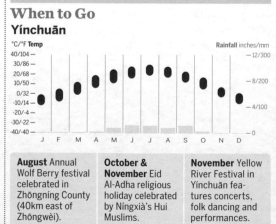

August Annual Wolf Berry festival celebrated in Zhōngníng County (40km east of Zhōngwèi).

October & November Eid Al-Adha religious holiday celebrated by Níngxià's Hui Muslims.

November Yellow River Festival in Yínchuān features concerts, folk dancing and performances.

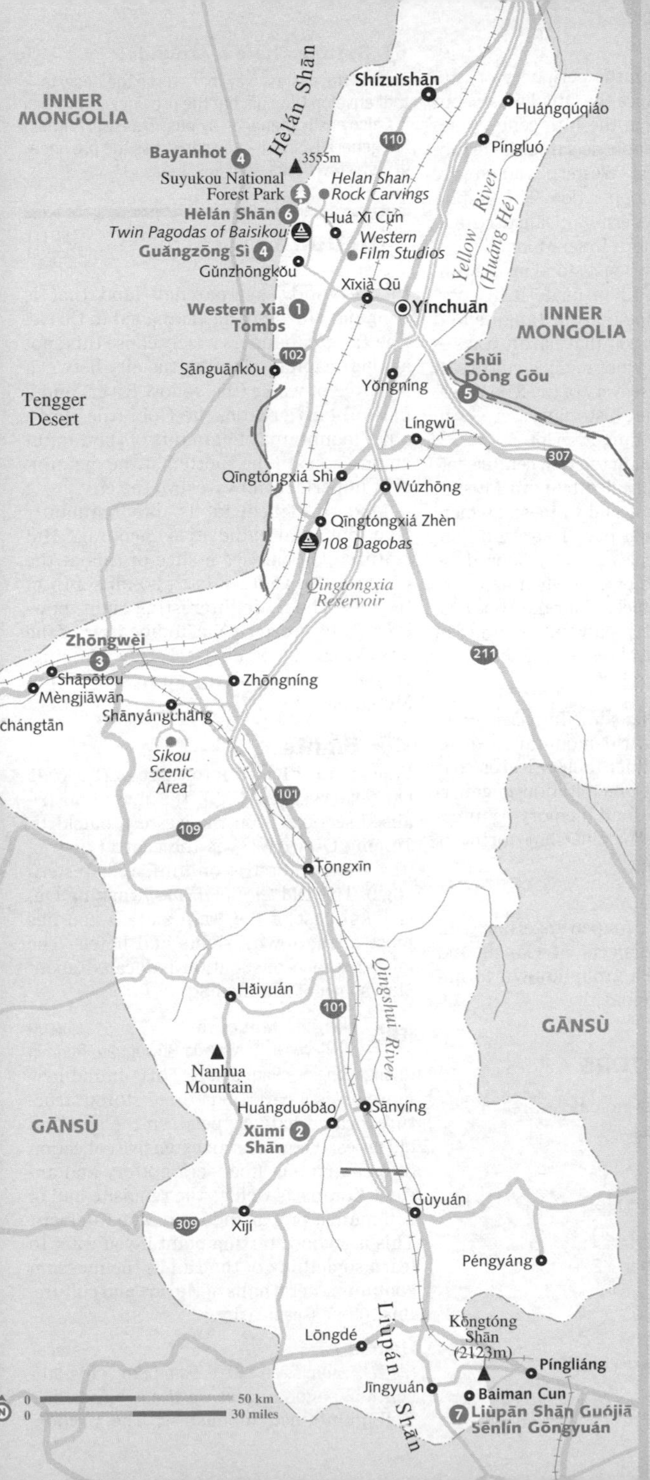

Níngxià Highlights

1 Visit the imperial **Western Xia Tombs** (p841) outside Yínchuān, one of the few reminders of this long-extinct culture

2 Explore the little-visited Buddhist grottoes at **Xūmí Shān** (p845)

3 Unwind in the tourist town of **Zhōngwèi** (p843), with its utterly weird haunted house under Gāo Temple and nearby desert activities including rafting and camel trekking

4 Get a taste of Mongol culture at the lonely sites in and around Bayanhot, including **Guǎngzōng Sì** (p843) and **Yánfú Sì** (p843)

5 Explore the tunnels, trap doors and hidden weapons at **Shǔi Dòng Gōu** (p842), at a portion of the Great Wall

6 See the sights at **Hèlán Shān** (p841), including rock carvings, pagodas, hiking trails and the Western Film Studios

7 Journey to **Liùpān Shān Guójiā Sēnlín Gōngyuán** (p845), in southern Níngxià, where Ghengis Khan finally bit the dust

History

Níngxià had been on the periphery of Chinese empires ever since the Qin dynasty, but it took centre stage in the 10th century AD when the Tangut people declared the establishment of the Xixia (Western Xia) empire in the face of Song opposition. The empire was composed of modern-day Gānsù, Níngxià, Shaanxi and western Inner Mongolia, but it quickly collapsed when it stood up to Mongol forces. Genghis Khan made it his personal mission to wipe out the Tanguts and did such a thorough job that hardly a trace remains of the once vibrant Xixia culture. It was only with the discovery of the Xīxià stele in Wǔwēi (p820) that historians were even able to decipher the Tangut script.

The Mongol retreat in the 14th century left a void that was soon filled by both Muslim traders from the west and Chinese farmers from the east. Tensions had always run high between the two peoples, but Mao offered the Muslim Hui an olive branch when he chose the province as a homeland for the Hui. Like Tibet and Xīnjiāng, it is only 'autonomous' in name, with real control vested in Běijīng.

Climate

Part of the Loess Plateau, Níngxià is composed primarily of arid mountain ranges and highlands. Summer temperatures soar during the day, and precipitation is generally no more than a fond memory. Winters are long and often freezing, but spring is lovely, though blustery.

Language

Níngxià's dialect is grouped together with the northwestern dialects of Gānsù and Qīnghǎi, an umbrella group known to linguists as Lanyin Mandarin.

PRICE INDICATORS

The following price indicators are used in this chapter:

Sleeping

$	less than Y150
$$	Y150 to Y220
$$$	more than Y220

Eating

$	less than Y20
$$	Y20 to Y35
$$$	more than Y35

Getting There & Around

Train is the easiest way to traverse the deserts that envelop Níngxià, but the province is so small it's also easily managed by bus. Transport times are generally short – you can cross the province in just a few hours.

Yínchuān 银川

0951 / POP 1.2 MILLION

In the windy, sun-parched land that is Níngxià, Yínchuān has managed to thrive. The Tangut founders wisely chose this spot as their capital, planting the city between a source of water (the Yellow River) and a natural barrier from the Gobi (the Hèlán Shān mountains). Remnants of the Tangut empire can still be spotted at the magnificent imperial tombs west of the city.

Modern Yínchuān is predominantly Han, but local authorities encourage Hui culture; you can see a slice of this at the Chinese Hui Culture Park 20km south of the city. The more interesting sight, however, is the Western Xia Tombs west of the city. Yínchuān is also a handy jumping-off point for longer trips to western Inner Mongolia.

Sights

Yínchuān is divided into three parts. Xīxià Qū (西夏区; New City), the new industrialised section, is on the western outskirts. Jīnfèng Qū (金凤区) is the central district (the train station is on Jīnfèng's western edge). The Old City (兴庆区; Xìngqìng Qū) is 12km east of the train station and has most of the town's sights and hotels. The long-distance bus station is located about 5km south of Nanmen Sq.

FREE **Níngxià Museum** MUSEUM
(宁夏博物馆; Níngxià Bówùguǎn; Renmin Guangchang; 9am-5pm) This brand-new museum is a cavernous three-storey structure located halfway between the new and old cities. It contains an extensive collection of rock art, Silk Road–era pottery and ancient Korans as well as the requisite hall of communist propaganda and Mao fun facts. This is a good starting point if you want to learn something of the Hui as the museum contains several halls of Hui art and culture. Bus 102 passes nearby.

Hǎibǎo Tǎ PAGODA
(海宝塔; admission Y10; 9am-5pm) This 5th-century pagoda is set on the grounds of a well-maintained monastery. The pagoda,

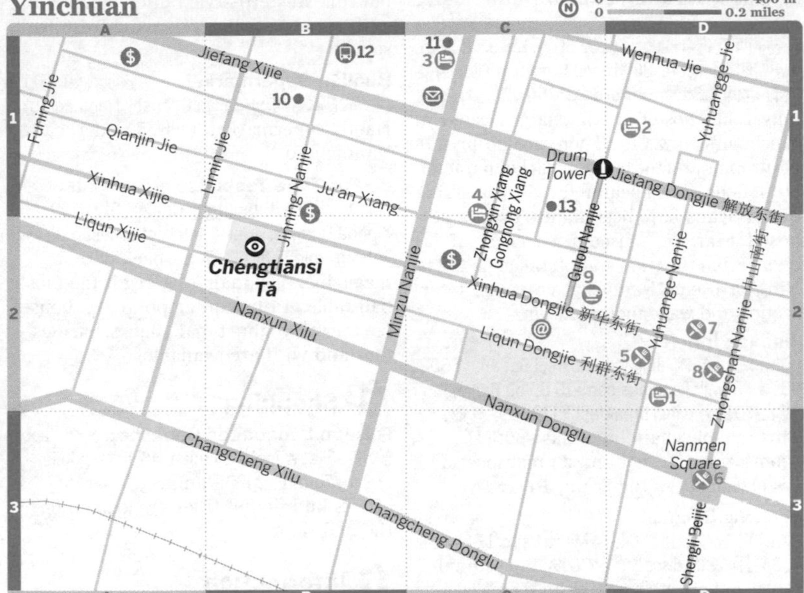

also known as Běi Tǎ (North Pagoda), was toppled by an earthquake in 1739 and rebuilt in 1771 in the original style. From the top of the nine-storey structure you get fine views of the Hèlán Shān range to the west and the Yellow River to the east. Take minibus 20 north on Jinning Beijie for five stops to the Běitǎ Lùkǒu (北塔路口) and then walk north for 15 minutes, or take a taxi (Y5).

Chéngtiānsì Tǎ PAGODA

(承天寺塔) Also known as Xī Tǎ (西塔; West Pagoda), the pagoda was closed for renovation at the time of research, but when it opens you should be able to climb to the top via 13 tiers of steepish stairs.

Sleeping

There are lots of places to stay in the Old City centre, but don't expect any great deals – most places are rundown, overpriced or a combination thereof. The following places all offer discounts of 20% to 30% from the rates listed here.

Yuānhēng Dàjiǔdiàn HOTEL $

(元亨大酒店; ☎602 9998; Zhongxin Xiang; 中心巷; r Y100) This is one of the best deals in the Old City. Although the rooms are nothing fancy and the building is slowly deteriorating, you can't beat the price. It's located on a quiet alley away from busy boulevards.

Yínchuān

Top Sights

Chéngtiānsì Tǎ B2

Sleeping

1 Dōngfāng Dàfàndiàn D2
2 Jǐnjiāng Inn D1
3 Mínháng Bīnguǎn C1
4 Yuānhēng Dàjiǔdiàn C1

Eating

5 Bái Gōng D2
6 Huálián Supermarket D3
7 Napoli D2
8 Xiānhè Lóu D2

Drinking

9 Be For Time Teahouse C2

Information

10 Foreign Languages Bookshop B1

Transport

11 China Air Express C1
12 Minibus 20 .... B1
13 Train Booking Office C1

Jīxiáng Xīxià International Youth Hostel YOUTH HOSTEL **$**
(吉祥西夏青年旅舍; ☎202 3021, 138 9518 3021; www.jxhostel.com; 86 Xixiaqu Huaiyuan Xilu; 西夏区怀远西街86号; dm/s/d Y35/50/80; @) The only youth hostel in Níngxià is located in Yínchuān's New City. There are no private bathrooms and the building lacks character, but it does have a helpful, English-speaking owner. Plans have been laid to open a new hostel near the museum, so check if it's open. From the train station take bus 102 to Ningxia Daxue Nanmeng, cross the intersection and walk another 200m.

Jǐnjiāng Inn CHAIN HOTEL **$$**
(锦江之星旅馆; Jǐnjiāng Zhīxīng Lǚguǎn; ☎602 9966; www.jinjianginns.com; 15 Gulou Beijie; 鼓楼北街15号; d incl breakfast Y179-199; ❄@) This reliable chain hotel has spotless rooms, free internet and a great location. It's just north of the Drum Tower.

Mínháng Bīnguǎn HOTEL **$$**
(民航宾馆; ☎604 2968; 34 Minzu Beijie; 民族北街34号; r Y218, discounts of 30%) A lower-mid-range option with small, clean rooms overlooking a quiet street and a string of cake shops. The sign outside says CAAC Hotel.

Dōngfāng Dàfàndiàn BUDGET HOTEL **$**
(东方大饭店; ☎382 3366; 192 Liqun Dongjie; 利群东街192号; tw Y100) Its rooms are tiny and you may have to try a few beds before getting one that is comfortable. On the upside, it's clean, secure and one of the cheapest places around.

Eating & Drinking

Bái Gōng DIM SUM **$$**
(白宫; 84 Yuhuange Nanjie; dishes from Y10-15; ⏲24hr) Waiters here push around carts piled high with all forms of delicious steamed dumplings and buns. It offers good variety for solo travellers (and easy ordering), but you may need to order half a dozen dishes to quench your appetite.

Xiānhè Lóu CHINESE **$$**
(仙鹤楼; 118 Zhongshan Nanjie; dishes Y12-22) You can't go wrong here, with great *kǎoyángpái* (烤羊排; barbecued ribs) and *jīngjiàng ròusī* (京酱肉丝; soy pork), which you wrap up in little pancakes. Check out the *shuǐjiǎo* (boiled ravioli-style dumplings) production line in the southern of the two branches here (they're located about 30m apart).

Napoli WESTERN **$$$**
(那波理; Nàbōlǐ; 195 Xinhua Dongjie; buffet Y48) Take a break from noodle stalls and try out this Western-style buffet, complete with rare treats like pizza and fresh fruit salad.

Huálián Supermarket SUPERMARKET **$**
(北京华联超市; Huálián Chāoshì; Nanmen Sq) Handy supermarket located underneath Nanmen Sq.

Be For Time Teahouse TEA, COFFEE
(避风塘茶楼; Bìfēngtáng Chálóu; 5th fl, 99 Xinhua Dongjie; drink & internet access Y18; ⏲10am-midnight; wi-fi) Kick back with a magazine, play mah jong or hit the foosball table at this contemporary teahouse. Ice cream, yoghurt, bar snacks, various teas and wi-fi are available.

Shopping

Foreign Languages Bookshop BOOKS
(外文书店; Wàiwén Shūdiàn; 46 Jiefang Xijie; ⏲9am-7pm) English-language current-affairs and fiction titles are located on the 2nd floor.

Information

Bank of China (中国银行; Zhōngguó Yínháng; 170 Jiefang Xijie; ⏲8am-noon & 2.30-6pm) You can change travellers cheques and use the ATM at this main branch. Other branches change cash only.

China Comfort International Travel Service (CCT; 康辉旅游; Kāng Huī Lǚyóu; ☎504 5678; www.chinasilkroadtour.com; 317 Jiefang Xijie; ⏲8.30am-noon & 2.30-6pm Mon-Fri) Organises desert trips, rafting and permits for Ējìnà Qí.

China Post (中国邮政; Zhōngguó Yóuzhèng; cnr Jiefang Xijie & Minzu Beijie)

Internet cafe (网吧; wǎngbā; Xinhua Dongjie; per hr Y2; ⏲8am-11pm) Centrally located, down a courtyard.

Public Security Bureau (PSB; 公安局; Gōng'ānjú; 472 Beijing Donglu; ⏲8.30am-noon & 2.30-6.30pm Mon-Fri) For visa extensions. Take bus 3 from the Drum Tower.

Getting There & Away

Air

Yínchuān's main ticket office of the **Civil Aviation Administration of China** (CAAC; 中国民航; Zhōngguó Mínháng; ☎691 3456; 540 Changcheng Donglu; ⏲8am-6pm) is located just south of Nanmen Sq. You can also buy tickets from **China Air Express** (民航快递; Mínháng Kuàidì; ☎401 3333; 36 Minzu Beijie).

Flights connect Yínchuān with Běijīng (Y1190), Chéngdū (Y1210), Guǎngzhōu (Y1990),

Shànghǎi (Y1600), Ürümqi (Y1450) and Xī'ān (Y670), among other destinations.

Bus

The bus station is located 5km south of Nanmen Sq on the road to Zhōngwèi. Bus departure times from the long-distance bus station:

Bayanhot Y26, two hours, half-hourly (6.30am to 6.30pm)

Gùyuán (express) Y80, five hours, half-hourly (7.30am to 5pm)

Lánzhōu Y120, six hours, hourly (8.05am to 5pm)

Xī'ān Y169, eight to 10 hours, five daily (8.30am to 2.30pm)

Yán'ān Y136, eight to nine hours, five daily (7.20am to 1pm)

Zhōngwèi (express) Y46, two to three hours, hourly (8.30am to 5.30pm)

For some northern destinations you may be referred to the northern bus station (北门车站; *běimén chēzhàn*); to get there from the long-distance bus station hop on bus 3 (Y1).

There are frequent *kuaike* (express buses) to Zhōngwèi and Gùyuán. These are recommended over the much slower local buses which stop at every village to pick up and drop off passengers.

Train

Yínchuān is on the Lánzhōu–Běijīng railway line, which runs via Hohhot (11 hours) and Dàtóng (13 hours) before reaching Běijīng (19 hours). If you're heading for Lánzhōu (hard sleeper Y131, 8½ hours), the handy overnight train K915 leaves at 10.20pm. For Xī'ān (14 hours), try train 2587 (hard sleeper Y185) leaving at 5.42pm, or train K359 (Y197) leaving at 7.50pm. The train station is in Xīxià Qū, about 12km west of the Old City centre.

There's a **train booking office** (火车售票处; huǒchē shòupiàochù; 15 Gongnong Xiang; commission Y5; ⏲8am-noon & 3.30-5pm) in the Old City, just south of the Drum Tower.

ℹ Getting Around

The airport is 25km from the Old City centre; buses (Y15) leave from in front of the CAAC office (opposite). A taxi to/from the airport costs around Y40.

Between 6am and 11.30pm bus 1 (Y1) runs from the long-distance bus station to Nanmen Sq in the Old City, along Jiefang Jie and then on to the train station in Xīxià Qū. Count on a minimum 30- to 40-minute trip.

Taxis cost Y5 for the first 3km. A taxi between the train station and the Old City costs Y20 to Y30.

Around Yínchuān

WESTERN XIA TOMBS 西夏王陵

The **Western Xia Tombs** (Xīxià Wánglíng; admission Y60; ⏲8am-7pm), which look like giant scoops of ice cream melting in the desert, are Níngxià's most famous sight. The first tombs were built a millennium ago by the Western Xia's first ruler, Li Yuanhao. There are nine imperial tombs, plus 200 lesser tombs, in an area of 50 sq km. The 23m-tall main tomb was originally built as an octagonal seven-storey wooden pagoda, but all that remains is the large earthen core. Permits, usually organised through local tour operators, are required to visit other tombs in the area.

The examples of Buddhist art in the good site **museum** offer a rare glimpse into the ephemeral Western Xia culture, and point to clear artistic influences from neighbouring Tibet and Central Asia.

The tombs are 33km west of Yínchuan. A return taxi costs around Y90. You could take bus 2 to its terminus in Xīxià Qū and then take a cheaper taxi (Y15 each way) from there. In summer you might just find a direct bus from Yínchuān's long-distance bus station. The site is also on the road towards Bayanhot, if you are headed that way.

HÈLÁN SHĀN 贺兰山

The rugged Hèlán Mountains long proved an effective barrier against both nomadic invaders and the harsh Gobi winds. It was the preferred burial site for Xixia monarchs, and the foothills are today peppered with graves and honorific temples. You can combine a trip here with a visit to the Western Xia Tombs.

All the sites in the mountain range are easily visited by taxi; the nearest village is Huá Xī Cūn (华西村), 40km from the Yínchuān train station. From the village it's 13km to the **Twin Pagodas of Bàisìkǒu** (拜寺口双塔; Bàisìkǒu Shuāngtǎ; admission Y10), which are 13 and 14 storeys high and decorated with Buddha statuettes.

About 10km north of the pagodas is a boulder-strewn gorge filled with **rock carvings** (贺兰山岩画; Hèlánshān Yánhuà; admission Y60) thought to date back 10,000 years. There are over 2000 pictographs, depicting animals, hunting scenes and faces, including one (so local guides like to claim) of an alien. The ticket price includes entry to a museum and a ride in a golf cart to the

THE HUI

The Hui (回族) are in some respects one of the country's more unusual minority groups. Scattered throughout most provinces of China, their various communities generally have little in common except Islam. And if the idea of a communist government using religion to define ethnicity seems like a paradox, even stranger is the fact that nearly 80% of the Hui live outside of their own designated autonomous region.

The Hui are the ultimate melting-pot people. The origins of these Chinese Muslims date back over a thousand years to a time when trade thrived between China and the Middle East and Central Asia. Arab traders arriving by boat and via the Silk Road intermarried with the local women. Their descendants have distinctly Chinese facial features but adhere to Central Asian culture and religious beliefs, such as the practising of Islam and a disdain for pork.

Most Hui men wear white skull caps, while women don headscarves and occasionally a veil. While Chinese language and writing are almost universal among the Hui, the educated can also read Arabic and will have studied the Koran. These languages have proven useful skills in recent years, as Chinese corporations on the coast are hiring Hui to act as translators for Arab businessmen coming to China.

Today China's 10 million Hui are scattered across the country, with the highest concentrations in Gānsù, Níngxià and Shaanxi. True to their origins as traders and caravanserai operators, many Hui are still engaged in small business, transport and hotel management.

valley containing the rock carvings. Don't miss the images of the Rastafarian-like sun god (climb the side steps up the hill). The pictographs are the only remnants of early nomadic tribes who lived in the steppes north of China.

On the way back to Yínchuān, you can stop at the **Western Film Studios** (镇北堡西部影城; Zhènběibǎo Xībù Yǐngchéng; admission Y60; ⏲8am-6pm), where the famed Chinese film *Red Sorghum* was shot. The fortress and old city movie sets are phoney but fun.

If you have a bit more time to spend, there are hiking trails into the mountains. A good place to start is **Sūyùkǒu National Forest Park** (苏峪口国家森林公园; Sūyùkǒu Guójiā Sēnlín Gōngyuán; per person/car Y60/10, museum Y25) – you can hike up the trails from the car park or take the cable car (up/down Y50/30) straight up to cool pine-covered hills.

To explore the area, first take a minibus from the train station to Huá Xī Cūn (华西村); from here taxis can take you to the surrounding sites for around Y80. Starting from Yínchuān, it's possible to loop in these sites with a visit to the Western Xia Tombs for around Y300.

SHǓI DÒNG GŌU 水洞沟

Shǔi Dòng Gōu (☎130 3799 2234; admission Y48; ⏲8am-6pm) is an archaeological site 25km east of Yínchuān, right on the border with Inner Mongolia. The site is divided into two parts; the first contains a Ming-era section of the Great Wall and a new museum that resembles Jabba the Hut's bunker. The second section, 2km away and reached by minibus, consists of a fortress with an elaborate network of underground tunnels once used by Chinese soldiers defending the Great Wall. The renovated tunnels include trap doors, false passages and booby traps. The admission price includes the guided tour and transport between the various sites.

Two buses per hour run past Shǔi Dòng Gōu (Y9) from Yínchuān's northern bus station. Let the driver know where you are going and he'll let you off near the gate.

BAYANHOT 阿拉善左旗

Bayanhot (Ālāshàn Zuǒqí), 105km from Yínchuān, is a burgeoning Chinese city with Mongol roots. The original Mongol town was centred on the small 18th-century Yánfū Sì (Buyan Arudikh in Mongolian) monastery and the adjoining home of the local prince, the Alashan Qin Wang.

Bayanhot means 'Rich City' in Mongolian and for good reason. The Mongols that live here are particularly active in the trade of rare and precious minerals. On weekends the pavement in front of the museum is crowded with locals dealing the stones, making this a good time to visit the town.

The temple, **Yánfú Sì** (延福寺; admission Y5; ⌚8am-noon & 2-6pm), was completed in 1742 and was once populated by 200 lamas; it now houses around 30. Morning services, especially on weekends, attract the local Mongol community. Next door is the local museum, **Ālāshàn Bówùguǎn** (阿拉善博物馆; admission Y8; ⌚8am-noon & 2-6pm), a Qing-era complex of buildings and courtyards that was once home to the Alashan Qin Wang. Photos of the last prince (1903–68) and his family, plus some of their personal effects, are prominent exhibits. There is also a good collection of *thangkas* (painted scrolls), as well as exhibits on Mongol ethnography and local wildlife.

Frequent buses depart from Yínchuān's long-distance bus station for Bayanhot (Y26, two hours) between 6.30am and 6pm. From Bayanhot there are three daily buses to Ējìnà Qí (Y95, eight hours) at 8am, 8.20am and 9.20am. One daily bus goes to Āláshàn Yòuqí (Y78, six hours) at 7.10am. If you plan on heading to Ējìnà Qí from here you'll need a PSB-issued permit, which can be arranged by travel agents in Yínchuān.

AROUND BAYANHOT

A large temple complex 38km southeast of Bayanhot, **Guǎngzōng Sì** (广宗寺; admission Y21; ⌚8am-6pm) was once one of the largest monasteries in Mongolia. The main prayer hall, Gandan Danjaling Sum, contains the remains of the sixth Dalai Lama (inside the golden stupa in the middle of the room). The monastery (called Baruun Khuree in Mongolian, which means 'West Camp') was demolished in the Cultural Revolution, but the temples have since been rebuilt with concrete. About 70 monks now pray here. There are good walking trails in the mountains behind the complex; take the path to the right of the main temple and follow the concrete path for one hour to a grassy plateau with stunning views.

To get to the monastery, travel 17km back towards Yínchuān, take the obvious turnoff and travel 21km east. A taxi from Bayanhot back to Yínchuān with a stop at the monastery will cost Y180.

When you eventually head back to Yínchuān, look out for the crumbling, yet still mighty, remains of the Great Wall at **Sānguānkǒu** (三关口). This is a great place to get out of your vehicle and hike along the wall. Some bits are up to 10m high and 3m wide.

Zhōngwèi 中卫

☎0955 / POP 1 MILLION

Zhōngwèi easily wins the prize for Níngxià's best-looking city. In the 1990s the town was tapped for tourist development and its streets, alleys and squares were renovated in the traditional Chinese style. While the redevelopment has been a little neglected, Zhōngwèi remains an attractive and relaxing destination; it's also well endowed with moderately priced hotels and restaurants. Zhōngwèi is also a good base for a trip up the Yellow River or further afield to the Tengger Desert (Ténggélǐ Shāmò), where you can go camel trekking.

Sights

Gāo Temple TEMPLE

(高庙; Gāo Miào; Gulou Beijie; admission Y20; ⌚8am-6.30pm) This eclectic, multipurpose temple has at various times catered to the needs of Buddhism, Confucianism and Taoism. It's still a hodgepodge of architectural styles, but the revitalised Buddhist deities have muscled out the original Taoists and Confucians.

The real oddity is the former **bomb shelter**, built beneath the temple during the Cultural Revolution and later converted into a Buddhist hell-haunted house. The eerie, dimly lit tunnels echo with the haunting screams of the damned. Try not to get too freaked out.

Sleeping

A nice alternative to staying in town is the desert guesthouse at Shāpōtóu (see p845).

Fēngmào Yuán Jiǔdiàn HOTEL $$

(丰茂源酒店; ☎709 1555; 65 Changcheng Donglu; 长城东路65号; tw Y168, discounts of 40-60%) This place has small rooms with modern showers and flat-panel TVs. Rooms could be better maintained, but you often get a good discount (down to Y78 in low season). If it doesn't suit, this road has a dozen more hotels of similar standard and price.

Zhōngwèi Dàjiǔdiàn HOTEL $$$

(中卫大酒店; ☎702 5555; 53 Gulou Beijie; 鼓楼北街53号; tw Y388, discounts of 40-60%; ❄) This midrange hotel has a large, welcoming lobby and clean rooms that are a great deal if you can get the discount rate, sometimes as low as Y138.

Xīngxiáng Bīnguǎn BUDGET HOTEL $

(兴祥宾馆; ☎701 9970; 61 Changcheng Donglu; 长城东路61号; dm Y50, tw Y130-150, discounts

Zhōngwèi

Sights

1 Gāo Temple B1

Sleeping

2 Fēngmào Yuán Jiǔdiàn B1

3 Xīngxiáng Bīnguǎn B1

4 Zhōngwèi Dàjiǔdiàn B1

Eating

5 Night Market A2

6 Westland Coffee Shop A2

Drinking

7 Italian Bar B2

of 30%) Rooms here are scruffy and dim, but this is one of the cheapest hotels in town and convenient for the train station.

Eating & Drinking

Night Market MARKET $

(夜市; yèshì; Xiangyang Buxingjie; dishes Y15-25) Known locally as the 'Snack Street' (小吃街; Xiaǒchī Jiē), this is one of the best places to dine. There are lots of cheap eats; two favourites are *ròujiāmó* (肉夹馍; fried pork or beef stuffed in pita bread, sometimes with green peppers and cumin) and *shāguō* (砂锅; minihotpot). A nearby side alley is jam-packed with bars and small clubs.

Italian Bar BAR

(意调酒吧; Yìdiào Jiǔbā; Gulou Beijie; ⏲1pm-1am) This small, somewhat grungy bar serves up Y8 beers to a local crowd. Expect to be invited in for a round of drinks. From here you could take your pub crawl to the bars near the Night Market.

Westland Coffee Shop WESTERN $$

(西岸咖啡; Xī'àn Kāfēi; Xinlong Beijie; meals from Y25; ⏲9am-midnight) Western-style place offering reasonable pizza, pasta and steaks. Finish off your meal with a tasty banana split (Y12). The sign outside says 'Coffee Tea B&F'.

Information

Bank of China (中国银行; Zhōngguó Yínháng; cnr Gulou Beijie & Gulou Dongjie; ⏲9am-5pm) Has an ATM.

China Post (中国邮政; Zhōngguó Yóuzhèng; Gulou Xijie)

Níngxià Desert Travel Service (宁夏沙漠旅行社; Níngxià Shāmò Lǚxíngshè; 宁夏沙漠旅行社; ☎702 7776, 137 3950 1113; www.nxdesert.com; Gulou Nanjie) Pricey but professional outfit for camel and rafting trips (see p845). Contact the English-speaking manager Billy. The office is 1.5km south of the Drum Tower.

Public Security Bureau (PSB; 公安局; Gōng'ānjú; ☎706 0597; Silou Dong Nanjie; ⏲8.30am-noon & 2.30-5pm) It's about 4km south of the Drum Tower.

Sàiqī Wǎngbā (赛期网吧; Gulou Beijie; per hr Y2.50; ⏲24hr) Internet cafe, located on the same alley as the Italian Bar.

Getting There & Away

Bus

The long-distance bus station (长途汽车站; *chángtú qìchēzhàn)* is 2.5km east of the Drum Tower, on the southern side of Dong Dajie. Take bus 1 or a taxi (Y4). Frequent buses to Yínchuān (Y46, three hours) leave every half-hour from 6.30am to 6pm; express buses (Y46, two hours) make the trip six times daily. To get to Gùyuán, you'll need to first get to Zhōngníng (Y11, one hour) and change there. For Lánzhōu (Y50), a night bus departs from the Drum Tower at 11pm.

Train

From Zhōngwèi you can catch trains heading to the north, south and southeast. By express train it will take you 2½ hours to reach Yínchuān, six hours to Lánzhōu (train K43; 9.39am) and 12 hours to Xī'ān (train 2586; 9.07pm). For Gùyuán (3½ hours) take the Xī'ān train.

Around Zhōngwèi

SHĀPŌTÓU 沙坡头

The desert playground of **Shāpōtóu** (admission Y90; ⏲7am-5.30pm), 17km west of Zhōngwèi, lies on the fringes of the Tengger Desert, at the dramatic convergence of desert dunes, the Yellow River and lush farmlands. It's based around the Shāpōtóu Desert Research Centre, which was founded in 1956 to battle the ever-increasing problem of desertification in China's northwest.

Shāpōtóu has become something of a desert amusement park, with camel rides (Y30), speed boats (Y80 to Y120), zip lines (Y80), bungee jumps (Y210), sand sleds (Y30) and a climbing wall (Y30). The scenery is impressive but heavily commercialised.

A traditional mode of transport on the Yellow River for centuries was the *yángpí fázi* (leather raft), made from sheep or cattle skins soaked in oil and brine and then inflated. Touts at Shāpōtóu offer motorboat rides up to Shuāngshīshān (双狮山) for Y100 per person, from where you can raft back downstream.

A day trip up the river to a working water wheel at Běichángtān (北长滩), some 70km west from Zhōngwèi, costs around Y300.

Shāpō Shānzhuāng (沙坡山庄; ☎0955-768 9073; r Y150; ⏲Apr-Oct) is a basic but comfortable hotel near the dunes. Meals are available.

There are frequent public minibuses (去沙坡头的中巴) between Zhōngwèi and the main entrance of Shāpōtóu (Y5, 45 minutes), petering out around 6.30pm. They leave from the south side of Zhōngwèi's People's Sq, stopping briefly at the Gulou Beijie and Changcheng Xilu intersection in Zhōngwèi. A taxi costs Y30/50 one way/return.

TENGGER DESERT 腾格里沙漠

If you've ever fancied playing Lawrence of Arabia, make a trek out to the Tengger Desert, a mystical landscape of shifting sand dunes and the occasional herd of two-humped camels. Shāpōtóu lies on the southern fringe, but it's definitely worth avoiding the crowds to head deeper into the desert. The sun can be fierce out here, so make sure to bring a hat, sunglasses and plenty of water. Nights are cool, so bring a warm layer.

Níngxià Desert Travel Service in Zhōngwèi offers overnight camel treks through the desert with a visit to the Great Wall for around Y250 to Y350 per person per day. The price includes transport, food and guide. Your guide may even bring along a sand sled for a session of sunset sand surfing. Drinking beers around the campfire under a starry sky tops off the experience. The desert trek can be combined with a rafting trip down the Yellow River.

Gùyuán & Around 固原

☎0954

Gùyuán, on the border of southern Níngxià, is a poor city in sharp contrast to moneyed cousins Zhōngwèi and Yínchuān up north. Tourists are a rare sight in these parts, yet visitors who make it here will find uniqueness in its majority Hui presence. Streets and markets are filled with wispy-bearded men wearing white skull caps, haggling over everything from melons to car parts. It is particularly lively in the late afternoon, when farmers from neighbouring villages stream into town for shopping trips.

Sights & Activities

Xūmí Shān CAVES

(须弥山; admission Y30) These Buddhist grottoes some 50km northwest of the city are the highlight of southern Níngxià. Xūmí is the Chinese transliteration of the Sanskrit word *sumeru,* a Buddhist paradise.

Cut into the five adjacent sandstone hills are 132 caves housing more than 300 Buddhist statues dating back 1400 years, from the Northern Wei to the Sui and Tang dynasties. Cave 5 contains Xūmí Shān's largest statue, a colossal Maitreya (future Buddha), standing 20.6m high. Further uphill, the best statues are protected by the Yuánguāng Temples (caves 45 and 46; 6th century) and Xiànggúo (cave 51; 7th century), where you can walk around the interior and examine the artwork up close – amazingly, the paint on several of the statues has yet to wear away.

To reach the caves, take a bus from Gùyuán to Sānyíng (三营; Y6, one hour), on the main road 40km north of Gùyuán near the Xūmí Shān turn-off. These buses depart from Wenhua Jie, opposite the Huá Shèng Bīnguǎn. From Sānyíng you can hop on a minibus to Huángduóbǎo (Y3 when full) and then hitch or hire a minibus for the 9km to the caves. A minibus from Sānyíng to Xūmí Shān is the best bet at Y50 return. The curator at the caves has a motorbike and can give you a ride back to Sānyíng if you need a lift. A basic guesthouse (dorms Y30) is located near the entrance.

Liùpān Shān Guójiā Sēnlín Gōngyuán PROTECTED AREA

(六盘山国家森林公园; Liupan Mountain National Forest Park; admission Y40, car Y20) Southern Níngxià's other highlight, Liùpān Shān, is where some believe Ghengis Khan died in

1227. Now it's a protected area, with an information centre and a walking trail that leads 3km up a side valley to a waterfall. About 5km further up the main valley past the info centre is a clearing with some stone troughs and tables that locals say was used by the Mongols during their stay. According to legend, Ghengis fell ill and came to the mountain to ingest medicinal plants native to the area. He perished on its slopes. If you are keen on retracing the steps of Ghengis Khan, Liùpān Shān is a must-see, but for the uninvolved traveller it's not an essential stop.

To get here, take a bus from Gùyuán to Jīngyuán (泾源; Y20, one hour) and then hire a taxi for the final 18km to the reserve (Y80 return). A taxi all the way from Gùyuán will cost Y250. **Níngxià Shénzhōu Lǚxíngshè** (宁夏神州旅行社; ☎204 1559), located on the 2nd floor of the Liùpánshān Bīnguǎn, can organise a car and guide for Y350.

Gùyuán Museum MUSEUM
(固原博物馆; Gùyuán bówùguǎn; Xicheng Lu; admission Y20; ⏲8am-noon & 2-6pm Tue-Fri, 9am-4pm Sat & Sun) Has some artefacts from the Mongol period (Ghengis Khan died not far from here in 1227).

Sleeping & Eating

Liùpánshān Bīnguǎn HOTEL $$
(六盘山宾馆; ☎202 0005; 77 Zhongshan Jie; 中山街77号; tw Y180, discounts of 25%) This landmark hotel has two wings; foreigners will be directed to the rear annexe on Zhongshang Jie. Rooms are clean and quiet but starting to fall apart in places. The restaurant caters to large groups of drunken businessmen, who may invite you over for a tipple. Dishes big enough for two people cost around Y40, but solo travellers can ask for a half portion.

Huá Shèng Bīnguǎn BUDGET HOTEL $
(华盛宾馆; ☎203 3166; Wenhua Jie; 文化街; dm/d Y60/100) The basic hotel has badly stained carpets and tatty rooms, but it's one of the cheapest in the city centre. It's located next to the Night Market.

Night Market MARKET $
This market (小吃城; Xiǎochī Chéng) on Wenhua Jie specialises in hotpot (砂锅; *shāguō*). It's next to the Huá Shèng Bīnguǎn.

Getting There & Away

Gùyuán is on the Zhōngwèi–Bǎojī railway line, with trains to Xī'ān (eight hours), Yínchuān (six hours) and Lánzhōu (10 hours), but sleeper tickets are near impossible to get, and the majority of trains depart in the middle of the night. If you can get it, the 9.44pm overnight to Lánzhōu (train N855) is handy. To get to the train station you'll need to take bus 1 or a taxi (Y5).

Express buses from the long-distance bus station:

Lánzhōu Y90, nine hours, one daily (8am)
Tiānshuǐ Y60, seven hours, one daily (6am)
Xī'ān Y90, seven hours, one daily (8.10am)
Yínchuān Y80, 4½ hours, every 30 minutes (9am to 5.30pm)

There are also frequent buses to Píngliáng (Y20, 1½ hours) and Jīngyuán (Y20, one hour). Express buses are a little pricier but infinitely faster than the painfully slow local buses.

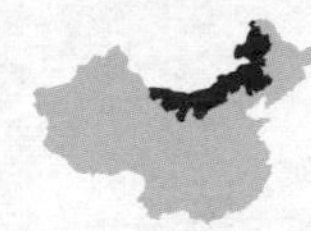

Inner Mongolia

POPULATION: 24.5 MILLION

Includes »

Best Places to Eat

» Xiǎoféiyáng Huǒguōchéng (p918)

» With a family of herders (p925)

» Yellow Street in Hohhot (p918)

Best Places to Stay

» Anda Guesthouse (p916)

» Nèi Měnggǔ Fàndiàn (p916)

» Jīnzhànghán Grasslands Camp (p925)

Why Go?

Mongolia. The word alone stirs up visions of nomadic herders, thundering horses, and of course, the man who needs no introduction – Genghis Khan. The Mongols conquered half the known world in the 13th century and while their empire is long gone, visitors are still drawn to this magical land wrapped up in both myth and legend.

Travellers heading north of the Great Wall half expect to see the Mongol hordes galloping along. The reality is quite different as 21st-century Inner Mongolia (内蒙古; Nèi Měnggǔ) is a wholly different place. The south of the province, which receives the most visitors, is industrialised and very much within the realm of China's modern economic miracle. The Mongolia of your dreams exists off the tourist route, amid the sands of the Badain Jaran Desert or the grassy plains of Hǎilā'ěr. Some effort is required to reach these areas but the spectacular scenery and hospitable Mongolian herders make it worthwhile.

When to Go

Hohhot

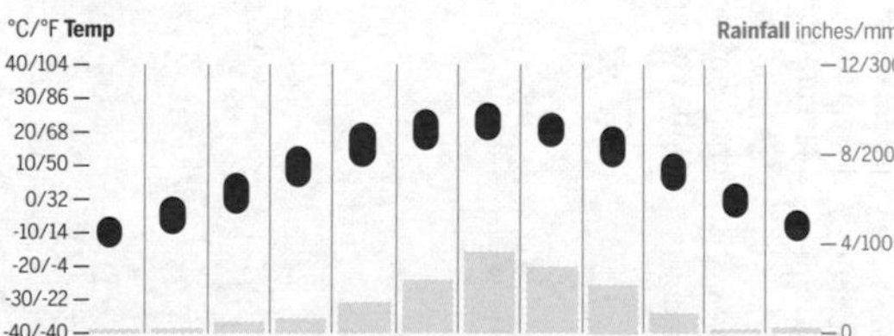

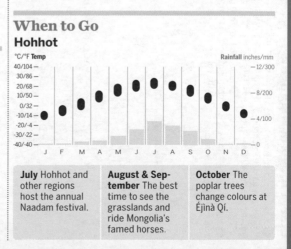

July Hohhot and other regions host the annual Naadam festival.

August & September The best time to see the grasslands and ride Mongolia's famed horses.

October The poplar trees change colours at Éjìnà Qí.

Inner Mongolia Highlights

1. Saddle up and go for a horse ride around the glorious grasslands near **Hǎilā'ěr** (p922)
2. Wander amid the ancient walls of **Shàng-Dū** (Xanadu; p922) and contemplate the lost greatness of Kublai Khan's pleasure dome
3. Listen to the groaning chants of Mongolian monks at the colourful monasteries of **Dà Zhào** (p916) and **Xílìtú Zhào** (p916) in Hohhot
4. Journey across the desert and into the mountains to explore the legendary **Cave Temple** (p922) in little-visited Dèngkǒu County
5. Mount a camel and set off across the dunes of the **Badain Jaran Desert** (p923)
6. Mingle with the Chinese-speaking ethnic Russians at the unique village of **Shì Wěi** (p925) near the Russian border

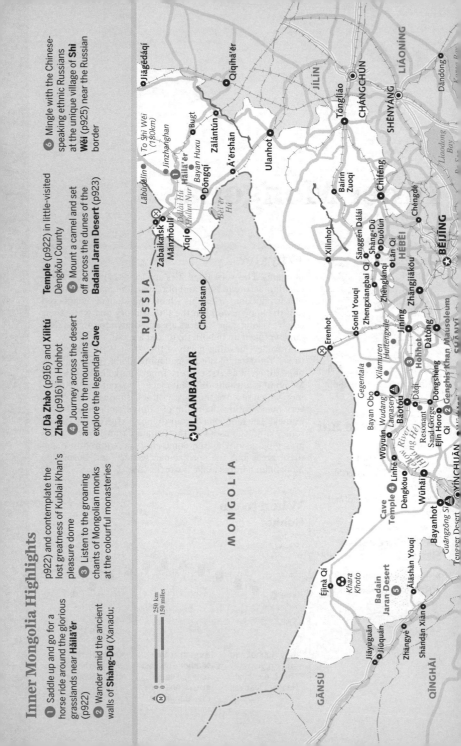

History

The nomadic tribes of the northern steppes have always been at odds with the agrarian Chinese. Seeking a solution to the constant skirmishes with the numerous Xiongnu clans, the first emperor of the Qin dynasty (221–207 BC), Qin Shi Huang, began building the Great Wall to keep them out. Throughout its history, the wall acted more like a speed bump than an actual barrier to the northern hordes.

Genghis Khan and grandson Kublai rumbled through in the 13th century, unifying the scattered Mongol tribes, conquering China and then most of the Eurasian continent, founding an empire that stretched from Vietnam to Hungary. The subjugation of Western Europe was only called off when Genghis Khan's successor, Ögedei, died in 1241.

The Mongols eventually moved their capital from Karakorum in Mongolia to Běijīng (called Dàdū by the Mongols), and after conquering southern China in 1279, Kublai Khan became the first emperor of the Yuan dynasty.

By the end of the 14th century, however, a series of incompetent rulers led to the disintegration of the Mongol Empire. The Mongols again became a collection of disorganised roaming tribes, warring among themselves and occasionally raiding China, until the Qing emperors finally gained control in the 18th century.

A divide-and-conquer policy by the Qing led to the creation of an 'Inner' and 'Outer' Mongolia. The Qing opened up Inner Mongolia to Han farmers, and waves of newcomers arrived to cultivate the landscape. Outer Mongolia was spared this policy; with backing from the USSR, it gained full independence in 1921, leaving Inner Mongolia in the hands of China's Nationalists.

The Chinese government established the Inner Mongolia Autonomous Region in 1947 and has tried hard to assimilate the Mongolians, who make up about 15% of Inner Mongolia's total population. (Most of the other 85% are Han Chinese, with a smattering of Hui, Manchu, Daur and Ewenki.)

Inner Mongolia's economy has been turned upside down in recent decades. In the late 1970s the government launched a campaign to settle nomadic herders, who for centuries had followed their herds of sheep, cattle, horses, goats and camels. Geologists have since discovered underground riches; coal mining and steel production have taken over as the prime economic movers.

Inner Mongolia's 17% growth rate is the highest in China but it has come at a great environmental cost. The coal industry has turned over pastureland at alarming rates and desertification is the root cause of dust storms that envelope Běijīng each spring. It was primarily coal trucks from Inner Mongolia that caused the headline-making 100km-long traffic jam in the summer of 2010. The region around Hǎilā'ěr has been spared heavy industry and the economy here is largely based on cattle ranching and tourism.

Climate

Siberian blizzards and cold air currents rake the Mongolian plains from November to March. June to August brings pleasant temperatures, but in the west it gets scorchingly hot during the day. Pack warm clothing for spring (March to May) and autumn (September to November).

The best time to visit is between July and September, particularly to see the grasslands, which are green only in summer. Make sure you bring warm, windproof clothing, as even in midsummer it's often windy, and evening temperatures can dip to 10°C or below.

Language

The Mongolian language is part of the Altaic linguistic family, which includes the Central Asian Turkic languages and the now defunct Manchurian. Although the vertical Mongolian script (written left to right) adorns street signs, almost everyone speaks standard Mandarin.

PRICE INDICATORS

The following price indicators are used in this chapter:

Sleeping

$	less than Y170
$$	Y170 to Y250
$$$	more than Y250

Eating

$	less than Y20
$$	Y20 to Y35
$$$	more than Y35

Getting There & Away

Inner Mongolia borders Mongolia and Russia. There are border crossings at Erenhot (Mongolia) and Mǎnzhōulǐ (Russia), which are stopovers on the Trans-Mongolian and Trans-Manchurian Railways, respectively. To Mongolia, you can also catch a local train to Erenhot, cross the border and take another local train to Ulaanbaatar (with the appropriate visa). Possible air connections include Hohhot to Ulaanbaatar or Hǎilā'ěr to Choibalsan (eastern Mongolia).

Hohhot 呼和浩特

0471 / POP 1.14 MILLION

The capital of Inner Mongolia is a relatively prosperous city that was founded by Altan Khan in the 16th century. Hohhot (Hūhéhàotè or Hūshì) means 'Blue City' in Mongolian, apparently a reference to the arching blue skies over the grasslands. Streets are attractively tree-lined and there is a handful of interesting temples and pagodas in the town – enough to keep you busy for a day or two before descending to the hinterlands. Try to plan your visit for late July, when the Naadam festivities occur at nearby Gegentala.

Sights

Wǔtǎ Pagoda PAGODA

(五塔寺; Wǔtǎ Sì; Wutasi Houjie; admission Y30; 8am-5.30pm) This striking, Indian-influenced, five-tiered pagoda was completed in 1732. Its main claim to fame is the Mongolian star chart around the back, though the engraving of the Diamond Sutra (in Sanskrit, Tibetan and Mongolian), extending around the entire base of the structure, is in much better condition. Bus 1 runs by the pagoda.

Dà Zhào MONASTERY

(大召; Danan Jie; admission Y30; 8am-6.30pm) Dà Zhào is a large, well-maintained lamasery that is still used as a temple. In the sacred main prayer hall, you may come upon groups of Mongol monks chanting and praying (usually at 9am).

Xílìtú Zhào MONASTERY

(席力图召; Danan Jie; admission Y10; 8am-7.30pm) Across the main boulevard is this simpler monastery, the purported stomping ground of Hohhot's 11th Living Buddha (he actually works elsewhere). Monks chant at 9am and 3pm.

Souvenir Shops SHOPS

(表记店铺; Biǎojì Diànpù) To the west of Dà Zhào, an original Qing-era street is jam-packed with souvenir shops. South of Dà Zhào is a kitschy open-air shopping plaza done up as a *hútòng* (narrow alleyway). At the end of this street is the enormous new temple complex **Guānyīn Sì** (观音寺) with its oversized stupa (佛塔), which the locals circumambulate.

Great Mosque MOSQUE

(清真大寺; Qīngzhēn Dàsì; 28 Tongdao Beilu) North of the old town is the Great Mosque. Built in the Chinese style, it dates from the Qing dynasty with later expansions. Check it out after dark when the flashing neon lights that cover the minaret make it look like a Las Vegas casino. You can look around as long as you don't enter the prayer hall.

FREE **Inner Mongolia Museum** MUSEUM

(内蒙古博物院; Nèi Měnggǔ Bówùyuàn; Xinhua Dongdajie; 9am-5.30pm Tue-Sun) This massive new museum with a sloping roof is meant to resemble the vast steppes of Mongolia. It contains a range of exhibits, from dinosaurs and Genghis Khan all the way up to space-age rockets and the latest mining excavators. Take bus 3 from Xinhua Dajie or pay Y10 for a cab.

Horse-Racing Grounds HORSE RACING

(赛马场; Sàimǎchǎng; Hulunbei'er Lu; admission Y1; 7am-9pm) Horse lovers may want to visit these racing grounds to watch races and other horse-riding sports, such as steeplechase and polo. Ask at hotels in town for a schedule of events and races. The Horse-Racing Grounds are on Hulunbei'er Lu, about 4km north of the train station.

Festivals & Events

The week-long summer festival known as **Naadam** features traditional Mongolian sports such as archery, wrestling and horse racing. It takes place at Gegentala from 25 to 31 July. You could organise a taxi to get you out there or do the trip through one of the local tours, available through most hotels.

Sleeping

TOP CHOICE **Anda Guesthouse** GUESTHOUSE $

(安达旅馆; Āndá Lǔguǎn; 691 8039, 159 475 19807; andaguesthouse@hotmail.com; Qiao Kao Xijie; 桥靠西街; dm/d Y60/160; @) This place is developing a good reputation among backpackers, thanks to its

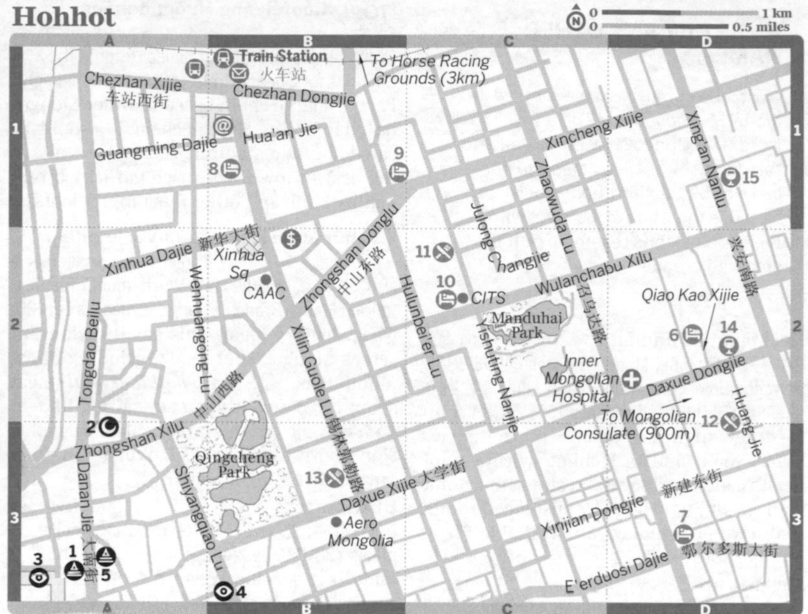

friendly, English-speaking staff and cosy atmosphere. The bathrooms could do with some renovation but the dorms and doubles are clean and brightly lit. Kitchen facilities are available and it has a lounge and courtyard. The staff are eager to show off Mongolian culture and can organise non-touristy trips outside the city. The guesthouse is reasonably central but hard to find as it's located down an unmarked alley and has no formal address or signboard. It's best to call ahead and get a pick-up from the train station. If you want to search for it, start by taking bus 2, 37 or 61 to the Inner Mongolia Hospital (内蒙古医院大楼A座; Nèi Měnggǔ Yīyuàn Dàlóu A zuò) then walking west for six minutes on Qiao Kao Xijie. Look for the shop called 'Man Yi Beauty Salonm' (sic) and take the little alley across the street. Walk to the end of the alley and turn left.

Bīnyuè International Hostel HOSTEL **$**
(宾悦国际青年旅舍; Bīnyuè Guójì Qīngnián Lǔshè; ☎660 5666; fax 431 0808; 52 Zhaowuda Lu; 昭乌达路52号; dm/d Y50/150; ❄) This large hostel is a bit scruffy and the beds are rock hard but doubles are comfortable and some dorm rooms have private bathrooms. From the train station, take bus 34 southeast to Normal University (师范大学; Shīfàn Dàxué); the hotel tower is a half-block further south. The hostel is behind the main hotel.

Hohhot

Sights
1 Dà Zhào A3
2 Great Mosque A3
3 Souvenir Shops A3
4 Wuta Pagoda B3
5 Xílìtú Zhào A3

Sleeping
6 Anda Guesthouse D2
7 Bīnyuè International Hostel D3
8 Hūhéhàotè Tiělù Bīnguǎn B1
9 Jǐnjiāng Inn B1
10 Nèi Měnggǔ Fàndiàn C2

Eating
11 UBC Coffee C2
12 Wūzhūmùqìn Naǐchágǔan Sì Fēndìan D2
13 Xiǎoféiyáng Huǒguōchéng B3

Drinking
14 Andai D2
15 Náirè Jiǔbā D1

A YURT BY ANY OTHER NAME...

'Yurt', the common name for traditional Mongolian tents, is a Turkish word. The Mongolian word is *ger,* and the Chinese call them '*Měnggǔ bāo*' – literally 'Mongolian buns' – perhaps because the white structures with their conical tops resemble puffy steamed breads.

Nèi Měnggǔ Fàndiàn HOTEL $$$
(内蒙古饭店; Inner Mongolia Hotel; ☎693 8888; www.nmghotel.com; Wulanchabu Xilu; 乌兰察布西路; d Y660-960, discounts 15%; ❄≋) This 14-storey high-rise is one of the nicest hotels you'll find in Hohhot, with a pool, health centre and several restaurants. Some staff speak English. A few misplaced rooms that have no windows are available for as low as Y280.

Jǐnjiāng Inn HOTEL $$
(锦江之星旅馆; Jǐnjiāng Zhīxīng Lǚguǎn; ☎666 8000; www.jinjianginns.com; 61 Xinhua Dajie; 新华大街61号; s/d Y179/200; ❄@) Ultra-efficient chain hotel that has spotless, if somewhat bland, rooms. Free internet is available in the lobby.

Hūhéhàotè Tiělù Bīnguǎn HOTEL $
(呼和浩特铁路宾馆; Hohhot Railway Hotel; ☎225 4001; 131 Xilin Guole Beilu; 锡林郭勒北路131号; d incl breakfast Y168; ❄) This midrange hotel is conveniently located between the train station and Xinhua Sq. Rooms are small but have air-con.

Eating

Mongolia's notable culinary contribution is *huǒguō* (火锅; hotpot), a refined version, so the story goes, of the stew originally cooked in soldiers' helmets. Mutton (羊肉; *yángròu*), noodles (面; *miàn*), tofu (豆腐; *dòufu*), mushrooms (蘑菇; *mógu*) and other veggies are added to the bubbling cauldron.

For an excellent selection of Mongolian and Chinese restaurants, head down to Huáng Jiē (Yellow Street; 黄街), also known as 'Shar Jie' in Mongolian, which is lined with about 40 small eateries. Mongolian meals, including hotpot and kebabs, are also available at the horse-racing grounds on the city's north side (bus route 24).

TOP CHOICE **Xiǎoféiyáng Huǒguōchéng** MONGOLIAN HOTPOT $$
(小肥羊火锅城; Little Fat Sheep Hotpot City; Xilin Guole Lu; for 2 people from Y40; ⏲11am-midnight) Part of a large chain based in Inner Mongolia, Xiǎoféiyáng Huǒguōchéng is a sophisticated hotpot restaurant that makes some of the best in town, with rich garlicky broth, quality lamb and other fresh ingredients.

Wūzhūmùqìn Nǎichágǔan Sì Fēndìan TRADITIONAL MONGOLIAN $
(乌珠穆沁奶茶馆四分店; Wuzhumuqin Tea Restaurant Fourth Branch; Huang Jie; meals from Y20; ⏲7am-2pm & 5-10pm) This small restaurant serves Mongol 'soul food', including *bāozi* (dumplings; 蒙古包子), *makhtei shul* (meat soup; 肉汤) and *suutei tsai* (salty milk tea; 奶茶). Look for the large yellow and blue sign above the door. FYI: Wuzhumuqin is an area in Xilingol region.

UBC Coffee WESTERN $$$
(上岛咖啡; Shàngdǎo Kāfēi; Yishuting Nanjie; meals Y30-150; ⏲9am-1.30am) Coffee shop and diner serving Western food such as sandwiches, steaks and milkshakes, plus Asian fusion dishes.

Drinking

Andai BAR
(安歌儿; Āngē'ěr; 11 Qiao Kao Xijie; beers Y12; ⏲8pm-1am) Mongolian dive bar with cheap suds and live music, starting most nights at 10pm.

Information

Bank of China (中国银行; Zhōngguó Yínháng; Xinhua Dajie) 24-hour ATM available.

China International Travel Service (CITS; 中国国际旅行社; Zhōngguó Guójì Lǚxíngshè; ☎620 0673; www.citsim.com, in Chinese; Yishuting Nanjie) Offers grasslands tours mainly geared towards the Chinese market. It's on the 1st floor of a building behind the Nèi Měnggǔ Fàndiàn.

Foreign Languages Bookshop (外文书店; Wàiwén Shūdiàn; 58 Xinhua Dajie)

Jīnpái Internet Cafe (金牌网吧; Jīnpái Wǎngbā; Xilin Guole Lu; per hr Y4.5; ⏲24hr) Large internet cafe about 200m south of the train station.

China Post (中国邮政; Zhōngguó Yóuzhèng; Chezhan Dongjie) To the left as you exit the train station.

Public Security Bureau (PSB; 公安局; Gōng'ānjú; Chilechuan Dajie; ⏲8.30am-noon & 2.30-5pm Mon-Fri) For visa extensions and other enquiries, the foreign-affairs bureau is to the left of the main building, outside the gated compound.

BORDER CROSSING: GETTING TO MONGOLIA

Hohhot is a reasonable departure point for trips northwards into Mongolia. Two direct trains a week run between Hohhot and Ulaanbaatar (hard/soft sleeper Y970/1480), the Mongolian capital, on Monday and Friday at 10.05pm. The same train stops in Erenhot (二连浩特; Èrliánhàotè; hard/soft sleeper Y82/127, eight hours), at the Mongolian border. Erenhot is listed on Chinese train timetables as Èrlián (二连).

There are also five daily buses to Erenhot (Y88, six hours), the first at 8am. From here you can catch a jeep across the border (about Y50) and continue to Ulaanbaatar on the daily 5.50pm local train.

Aero Mongolia (空蒙古; Kōng Měnggǔ ; ☎138 4818 7711; www.aeromongolia.mn; 36 Daxue Xiji) flies from Hohhot to Mongolia on Monday, Wednesday and Friday for around Y1460. The schedule changes periodically so check the website for updates (note that the Wednesday flight is usually suspended in winter). The office is located in the Xuéfǔ Kāngdū building, tower A, Room 806 (学府康都A座806号).

If you need a visa, head for the **Mongolian consulate** (蒙古领事馆; Měnggǔ Lǐngshìguǎn; no phone; 5 Dongying Nanjie, 东影南街5马; ⏲8.30am-12.30pm Mon, Tue & Thu). Most travellers can get a 30-day visa, although some are only given 21 days. The visa costs Y260 and takes four days to process. A rush visa (Y446) can be given on the same day. US citizens do not need a visa to visit Mongolia. To find the consulate, travel east on Daxue Dongjie, turn left on Dongying Nanjie and look for the consulate 200m on the left.

Note that there is also a consulate in **Erenhot** (Měnggǔ Lǐngshìguǎn; ☎0479-753 9200; Bldg 1206; ⏲8.30am-4.30pm Mon-Fri). To find the consulate from the bus station, walk east a half block to the T-junction and make left. Walk north along this road (Youyi Beilu) for 10 minutes until you see the red, blue and yellow Mongolian flags on your left. A 30-day rush tourist visa (Y495) can be issued on the same day you drop it off.

Getting There & Away

Air

The **Civil Aviation Administration of China** (中国民航公司; CAAC; Zhōngguó Mínháng; ☎696 4103; Xilin Guole Lu) is on the south side of Xinhua Sq. Daily flight destinations (routes are reduced in winter) include Běijīng (Y480), Xī'ān (Y930), Hǎilā'ěr (Y2170), Manzhouli (Y2020), Chifeng (Y1240), Xilinhot (Y830), Ürümqi (Y1400) and Shànghǎi (Y1250).

Bus

Buses from Hohhot go to the following:

Bāotóu Y35, two hours, every 30 minutes (6.40am to 7.30pm)

Běijīng Y150, six to eight hours, 15 daily (7.30am to 7.30pm)

Dàtóng Y57, four hours, hourly (7.20am to 5.40pm)

Dōngshèng Y59, three hours, every 30 minutes (7.20am to 6pm)

Train

From Hohhot, express trains go to the following:

Bāotóu Y47, two hours, 16 daily

Běijīng hard/soft sleeper Y170/254, 10 hours, 17 daily

Dàtóng hard/soft sleeper Y98/142, four hours, 20 daily

Xilinhot hard/soft sleeper Y125/204, 11 hours, one daily

Yínchuān hard/soft sleeper Y175/264, nine hours, five daily

Sleeper tickets, especially to Běijīng, can be hard to come by in July and August; CITS or hotel travel desks can book sleepers for a Y30 commission.

Getting Around

Useful bus routes include bus 1, which runs from the train station to the old part of the city, via Zhongshan Xilu; bus 33, which runs east on Xinhua Dajie from the train station; bus 5, which plies the length of Xilin Guole Lu; and bus 24 to the horse-racing grounds. Tickets for local buses are Y1.

Hohhot's airport is 15km east of the city. The airport bus (Y5) leaves from the CAAC office; a taxi (flag fall Y6) will cost about Y35.

Around Hohhot

In the middle of the fields, 7km east of the airport (about 22km from Hohhot), is **Bái Tǎ** (白塔; White Pagoda; admission Y35), a striking seven-storey octagonal tower built during the Liao dynasty. A steep, double-barrelled staircase leads to a small shrine room at the top. Few travellers come here so you feel like you have the place to yourself. A taxi from Hohhot will cost around Y60 to Y70 return.

About 110km north of Hohhot is the grassland area of **Xilamuren** (Xīlāmùrén), with dozens of yurt camps that cater mainly to the Chinese market. Sadly, nearby mining operations have accelerated infrastructure development, so don't come this way if you are looking for a true wilderness experience. Xilamuren is worth considering if you want to try your luck on a Mongolian horse but if you are hoping for a traditional Mongolian experience you'll need to look elsewhere.

If you want to avoid the tourist camps at Xilamuren (and they are touristy), Anda Guesthouse (p916) in Hohhot can set you up at the home of a local family; day trips start from Y220 (including one meal) or Y340 for an overnight trip (including three meals). Horse riding is about Y50 per hour. If you want to visit the area on your own take a bus (Y20) or taxi (Y200) to the small tourist village of Zhàohé (召河), from where the yurt camps can be reached on foot.

There are more camps at **Gegentala** (Gěgěntălā) and **Huitengxile** (Huīténgxīlè). Both are two to 2½ hours from Hohhot but these don't offer any advantages over Xilamuren. Tour operators like CITS usually take their groups to Gegentala, especially for Naadam. If you have more time, skip this grassland area and head for more remote spots like Xilingol, Hăilā'ĕr or independent Mongolia.

Bāotóu 包头

0472 / POP 2.43 MILLION

Bāotóu sprawls across more than 20km of dusty landscape, much of it industrialised and polluted. Unless you have a particular interest in steel production, there is little reason to stop, although the city does act as a transit point for sights such as Wŭdāng Lamasery and Genghis Khan's Mausoleum.

Bāotóu is divided into eastern and western sections. Most travellers stay in the eastern district (Dōnghé), because it's a useful transit hub. The western districts include the areas of Kūndūlún and Qīngshān.

The train station in the western area is called Bāotóu train station (Bāotóu Zhàn); in the eastern area it's East Bāotóu train station (Bāotóu Dōngzhàn).

Sleeping & Eating

Xīhú Fàndiàn HOTEL $$
(West Lake Hotel; 418 7101; 10 Nanmenwai Dajie; 南门外大街10号; dm Y35, d Y170-230, discounts 30%;) A decent midrange pick within walking distance of the East Bāotóu train station.

Bīnlì Jiŭdiàn HOTEL $$
(696 0000; 19 Nanmenwai Dajie; 南门外大街19号; d incl breakfast Y200-250, discounts 30%;) This place has flashy rooms done up in chrome, glass and warm woods. It's located 900m north of the train station, at the corner of the first main intersection.

Xiáng Yúnjū BUDGET RESTAURANT $
(10 Nanmenwai Dajie; dishes Y6-20; 9am-10pm) Small, friendly joint about 100m up the road from the Xīhú Fàndiàn. Portions are reasonably sized for solo travellers.

Hóngfŭ Dàfàndiàn RESTAURANT $$
(19 Nanmenwai Dajie; buffet dishes Y6-18; 9am-9.30pm) Attached to the Bīnlì Jiŭdiàn, this sophisticated eatery has a buffet that makes ordering easy.

Information

There's an internet cafe across the street from Xīhú Fàndiàn.

Bank of China (中国银行; Zhōngguó Yínháng; Yizhong Xilu; 8am-5.30pm) From the East Bāotóu train station, walk north and make the first left onto Yizhong Xilu. The bank is about 500m down on the right. It has a 24-hour ATM.

Pénglái Chāoshíkōng Wăngluò (Pénglái Space Time Internet; Nanmenwai Dajie; per hr Y3; 24hr) Located opposite the Xīhú Fàndiàn.

China Post (中国邮政; Zhōngguó Yóuzhèng; off Nanmenwai Dajie; 8am-5.30pm)

Public Security Bureau (PSB; 公安局; Gōng'ānjú; Gangtie Dajie; 8.30-11.30am & 2.30-5pm Mon-Fri) In a futuristic tower east of the Bank of China in West Bāotóu.

Getting There & Away

Air

An **air ticket office** (Tiānyì hángkōng shòupiàochù; 412 2222; 20 Nanmenwai Dajie) is located opposite the 'Meet All' Shopping Centre (which is one building north of the Bīnlì Jiŭdiàn). Flights connect Bāotóu with Bĕijīng (Y660).

Bus

Bus times from East Bāotóu bus station:

Dōngshèng, Y31, 1½ hours, every 20 to 30 minutes (7.30am to 6pm)

Hohhot, Y35, two to three hours, every 20 to 30 minutes (6.30am to 7.30pm)

Yán'ān (Shaanxi), Y141, eight hours, two daily (1pm and 5pm)

Yúlín (Shaanxi), Y75, five hours, eight daily (6.10am to 3.30pm)

From West Bāotóu, buses leave from the intersection of Tuanjie Dajie and Baiyun E'bo Lu.

Train

Frequent trains between Hohhot and Bāotóu (hard/soft sleeper Y51/73, two hours) stop at both the east and west stations. Clarify with an attendant which station you have arrived at when coming into Bāotóu. Often travellers get off at West Bāotóu when they intended to go to East Bāotóu. Other destinations:

Běijīng hard/soft sleeper Y111/184, 13 hours, 13 daily

Yínchuān hard/soft sleeper Y86/127, seven hours, five daily

Tàiyuán hard/soft sleeper Y111/184, 14 hours, two daily

Lánzhōu hard/soft sleeper Y142/225, 15 hours, three daily

Getting Around

The airport is 2km south of the East Bāotóu train station. In spite of the short distance, taxis will ask around Y30 for the one-way journey.

Bus 5 (Y2) takes 45 minutes to shuttle between Bāotóu's two districts. In East Bāotóu, you can catch this bus on Nanmenwai Dajie near the train station. Some bus 5 services run express between the east and west sides in 30 to 35 minutes.

A taxi between the east and west districts costs Y30 to Y40.

Around Bāotóu

WŬDĀNG LAMASERY 五当召

Lying on the pilgrim route from Tibet to Outer Mongolia, this **monastery** (Wǔdāng Zhào; admission Y45; ⏲8am-6.30pm) saw considerable foot traffic from the time of its establishment in 1749. At its height it was the largest monastery in Inner Mongolia, housing 1200 monks belonging to the Gelugpa sect of Tibetan Buddhism. There are about 40 monks today. To get a good feel for the place, you could spend the night at the pilgrims' hostel and get up early for the monks' morning prayers. The admission ticket also lets you inside a small **Mongol ethnography museum**.

The monastery is 67km northeast of Bāotóu. A direct air-con bus (Y10, 1½ hours) departs from the bus parking lot in front of East Bāotóu's train station around 9.30am and leaves the monastery around 1pm. Alternatively, bus 7 (Y10, one hour), from the same parking lot, goes to Shíguǎi (石拐), 40km from Bāotóu. From Shíguǎi you can hire a taxi to the monastery (Y50 return). Note that the conductor on bus 7 might charge you around Y40 but this will include the price of the taxi to the monastery, which they organise for you.

Genghis Khan Mausoleum 成吉思汗陵园

Located 130km south of Bāotóu, in the middle of absolutely nowhere, is the **Genghis Khan Mausoleum** (Chéngjí Sīhán Língyuán; admission Y80; ⏲8am-6pm), China's tribute to the great Mongol warlord.

The first thing to know about this place is that old Genghis was not buried here, making the mausoleum part of the name somewhat irrelevant. The historical basis for this place dates back to an old Mongol tradition of worshipping Genghis Khan's personal effects, including his saddle, bow and other items. Kublai Khan established the cult and handed over care for the objects to the Darhats, a Mongol clan. Darhat elders kept the relics inside eight white tents, which could be moved in times of warfare.

In the early 1950s China's new communist government decided to build a permanent site for the relics and constructed the triple-domed building at Ejin Horo. By then most of the relics had been lost or stolen and whatever was left was destroyed during the Cultural Revolution (the saddles, bows and other items you'll see are all replicas). After a stint as a salt warehouse, the building was restored in 1979. Today many of the guards at the site still claim descent from the Darhat clan.

The mausoleum is 25km south of Ejin Horo Qi (伊金霍洛旗; Yījīn Huòluò Qí), where you can find transport to get here.

From Ejin Horo Qi (locals call it 'Yi Qi'), buses will let you off at a small tourist village with a handful of shops and hotels. From the roundabout at the tourist village you can catch a taxi (Y15) the final 5km to the mausoleum.

From Bāotóu there is one bus per day (Y37; 6.10am) to Ejin Horo Qi, from where there are plenty of buses heading south towards the mausoleum, most continuing towards Yúlín (榆林). Locals also know the mausoleum as Chénglíng (成陵).

If you can't get the 6.10am bus, take a frequent bus instead to Dōngshèng (东胜) where you can transfer to Ejin Horo Qi. From Hohhot there are direct buses to Dōngshèng. To return, take a cab back to the main highway and flag down any Dōngshèng-bound bus. Buses should pass by regularly till about 5pm; after that you can get a taxi from the roundabout.

Cave Temple 阿桂庙

The remote, little-visited **Cave Temple** (Āguì Miào; admission free; ⌚7am-6pm) is one of the oldest monasteries in Inner Mongolia. Construction began in the mid-17th century and was expanded in 1831 by the famed Outer Mongolian monks, Danzan Ravjaa. The temples were destroyed during the Cultural Revolution but have since been rebuilt. Look out for the most holy relic, a statue of Padmasambhava in the main hall, said to be fashioned by Padmasambhava himself. About 20 monks live here and one will probably tote you around the cave temples (and may offer you a bowl of mutton soup if you arrive in time for lunch).

The monastery is 90km from the city of Dèngkǒu (磴口). The only way to get here is by taxi (Y250 including waiting time). The 90-minute ride is over fairly rough roads and the final 6km winds up a narrow defile in the Langshan mountains.

Dèngkǒu is a minor stop of the Bāotóu–Yínchūan railway (most trains stop in the middle of the night). Long-haul express buses don't stop here; the nearest main bus terminal is in Línhé (临河). It's possible to get a bus from Bāotóu to Línhé (Y62, four hours), then take a local bus to Dèngkǒu (Y14, one hour). Travelling by bus from Yínchūan is less convenient; the driver will pull to the side of the expressway where you slide down the embankment to an access road below the highway. From here you'll need to hitch the last few kilometres to Dèngkǒu.

Shàng-Dū (Xanadu) 上都

Marco Polo made it his final stop and Samuel Taylor Coleridge immortalised it in Western minds as the ultimate pleasure palace. Today Xanadu, or **Shàng-Dū** (元上都遗址; Yuán Shàngdū yízhǐ; admission Y30; ⌚7am-6pm), is little more than a vast prairie with vague remnants of once mighty walls, but in days of yore it was indeed one of the most wonderful places on Earth.

Construction of the city started in 1252 and lasted four years. Yet its lifespan was relatively brief, being overrun by Ming forces in 1369. Little is visible today although it's easy to make out the city walls, about 1.5km from the gate and ticket window. After passing through the outer wall, continue another 500m to inner ramparts. A golf car can take you the whole way for Y10.

There are a few different approaches to Shàng-Dū. From Hohhot, the best option is to take the daily K502 train to Sānggēn Dálái (soft sleeper Y205, eight hours), departing at noon. From Sānggēn Dálái (桑根达来) you can get a shared taxi (Y120), 52km south to the small city of Lánqí (蓝旗). Lánqí has a museum dedicated to Shàng-Dū (under renovation at the time of research), and an enormous plaza with a statue of Kublai Khan. From Lánqí it's an easy 27km taxi ride (Y150 return) to Shàng-Dū. If you are coming from Běijīng (275km due south), take a bus to the city of Duōlún (多伦), which is 36km east of Shàng-Dū. From Duōlún, you can take a taxi to the site and then move onto Lánqí. Heading to Hohhot, take train 1814 at 10.16am from Sānggēn Dálái.

For handy accommodation in the area, try **Yuán Shàngdū Xiàgōng Dàjiǔdiàn** (元上都夏宫大酒店; Zhèn Téngfēi Lù; ☎0479-4227666; r Y100), a Mongol-themed hotel in Lánqí, next to the museum. The lobby is notable for containing numerous maps and drawings of Xanadu.

Hǎilā'ěr 海拉尔

☎0470 / POP 236,000

Hǎilā'ěr is the largest city in the northern arm of Inner Mongolia and thus a hub for transport and industry. Although the city itself is rather ordinary, it's definitely worth stopping for the chance to visit the Hūlúnbèi'ěr Grasslands, a vast expanse of prairie that begins just outside the city.

In the grasslands around Hǎilā'ěr are several tourist 'yurt camps' where you can eat, listen to traditional music and sometimes stay the night. Although they're not places where Mongolians actually live, you can still learn a bit about Mongolian culture, and the settings on the wide-open prairies

WORTH A TRIP

INNER MONGOLIA'S FAR WEST

The golden deserts, shimmering lakes and ruined cities of western Inner Mongolia are not easily visited independently, but with some logistical help this region can make for some great off-the-beaten-track adventures.

One destination is **Khara Khoto** (Black City; in Chinese Hēichéng, 黑城; admission Y80; ⌚8am-7pm), a ruined Tangut city built in 1032 and captured by Genghis Khan in 1226 (his last great battle). Khara Khoto continued to thrive under Mongol occupation, but in 1372 an upstart Ming battalion starved the city of its water source, killing everyone inside. Six hundred years of dust storms nearly buried the city, until the Russian explorer PK Kozlov excavated and mapped the site, and recovered hundreds of Tangut-era texts (kept at the Institute of Oriental Manuscripts in St Petersburg). The remains of Khara Khoto, located about 25km southeast of Éjìnà Qí (额济纳旗), are barely visible today. The allure here is the remoteness of the site and surrounding natural beauty. A great time to visit is late September to early October when the poplar trees are changing colours; but be warned that every hotel room in Éjìnà Qí will be booked out at this time.

The second tourist drawcard in these parts is the remote but stunning **Badain Jaran Desert** (巴丹吉林沙漠; Bādānjílín Shāmò), a mysterious landscape of desert lakes, Buddhist temples and towering dunes. The dunes here are the tallest in the world, some topping 380m (incredibly, the same height as the Empire State Building). The closest town in the region, Ālāshàn Yòuqí (阿拉善右旗), is a 30-minute drive from the dunes. **Badanjalin Travel Service** (☎0483-602 1618; smtxlvyou.2008@hotmail.com), in the town, organises camel treks and jeep tours for around Y1000 per day. Chéngdū-based **Navo Tours** (☎028-8611 7722; www.navo-tour.com) runs tours here (as well as to Khara Khoto) with English-speaking guides.

This part of Inner Mongolia is highly militarised (a rocket launch site is nearby) and travel permits are required for the road between Jiǔquán and Éjìnà Qí, as well as Khara Khoto itself and the Badain Jaran Desert. Travel agents need five to 10 days to organise the necessary permits.

The closest rail links are Jiǔquán and Zhāngyè in Gānsù province. However, public transport between Gānsù and Inner Mongolia is limited. A daily bus travels between Ālāshàn Yòuqí and Shāndān Xiàn (山丹县), but the best connections start with other Inner Mongolian towns such as Bayanhot. There are daily buses from Bayanhot to both Éjìnà Qí and Ālāshàn Yòuqí.

Besides Badanjalin Travel Service and Navo Tours, tour operators in Hohhot, Yínchuān and Zhōngwèi can organise a seven- to 10-day trip to these places for around Y8000 per person.

are striking. For a more authentic (if more rustic) experience, you can stay with local families in the grasslands, although this is easiest to organise if you speak a bit of Mandarin (or Mongolian).

The main square is on Zhongyang Dajie, near Xingan Lu. Hotels and services are conveniently located near the main square. A pedestrian street, Buxing Jie, contains several souvenir shops run by Mongolians. Meeting the owners is a good way to tap into the Mongolian community. Just past Buxing Jie is a recreated Qing-era *hutong*, completed in 2010; it includes a replica of a government office, now a small **museum** (admission Y20; ⌚9am-6pm).

Sights

Ewenki Museum MUSEUM
(鄂温克博物馆; Èwēnkè Bówùguǎn; admission Y10; ⌚8.30am-noon & 2.30-5.30pm) Roughly 20,000 Ewenki people live in northern Inner Mongolia, most in the Hulunbei'er Grasslands surrounding Hǎilā'ěr. At this modern museum, you can glimpse some of their history and culture. The Ewenki have traditionally been herders, hunters and farmers; they're one of the few peoples in China to raise reindeer.

The museum is on the southeastern edge of town. Bus 3 (Y1) runs here from the main square; a taxi will cost Y25 to Y30 (return). The museum is on the road to the Bayan

Huxu Grasslands, so you could stop here on your way out of town.

Underground Fortress HISTORIC FORT
(海拉尔要塞遗址; Hǎilā'ěr Yàosài Yízhǐ; admission Y60) In the mid-1930s, during the Japanese occupation of Manchuria, this network of tunnels was constructed in the grasslands north of Hǎilā'ěr. The site now contains a museum, monuments and plenty of old tanks lying around. Inside the freezing, spooky tunnels you can peek into 'rooms' where soldiers bunked.

The site is 4km northwest of the train station. A taxi between the tunnels and the town centre costs about Y30 (return). You'll need an hour to see the site. The tunnels are on the road to Jīnzhànghán, so you might negotiate a stop here en route.

Festivals & Events

The Hǎilā'ěr **Naadam** (sports festival) is held annually from 1 to 3 August. You'll see plenty of wrestling, horse racing and archery.

Sleeping & Eating

TOP CHOICE **Tiānxìn Business Hotel** HOTEL $$
(天信商务酒店; Tiānxìn Shāngwù Jiǔdiàn; ☎835 3588; 7 Tianxin Xiaoqu; 天信小区7号; d Y200-400; ❄) This hotel has two parts: a Y300-per-night wing (with a big sign in English) and a smaller **annexe** (☎835 3675), about 50m down the alley, with rooms for Y150. Rooms in the annexe were recently renovated and have clean, modern bathrooms. It has a good central location and a price to suit most budgets. It's down a small lane 100m south of the main roundabout, just off Buxing Jie.

Bèi'ěr Dàjiǔdiàn HOTEL $$
(贝尔大酒店; Bei'er Hotel; ☎835 8455; fax 833 4960; 36 Zhongyang Dajie; 中央大街36号; d incl breakfast Y320-480; ❄) This midrange place has a big, welcoming lobby and English-speaking staff. There are different wings for different budgets.

Huá Róng Jiàrì Jiǔdiàn HOTEL $$$
(Sinowell Holiday Hotel; ☎832 9999; fax 832 2160; 15 Qiaotou Jie; 桥头街15号; r incl breakfast Y400-680; ❄) This local landmark is a veritable skyscraper in central Hǎilā'ěr. It has a selection of rooms from midrange to the high end. English is spoken and there's an air ticket office and a travel agency.

Moongun Choloo MONGOLIAN RESTAURANT $
(Tianxin Xiaoqu; light meals Y15-25; ⏲7am-10pm) Below the Tiānxìn Business Hotel annexe (just down the alley from the main building), this cheap Mongolian cafe serves fresh yoghurt, *buuz* (dumplings) and *airag* (fermented mare's milk). It's a good place to meet Buriat Mongols.

Chuānjiāo Xīngǎng Huǒguō HOTPOT RESTAURANT $$
(川骄新港火锅; Xingan Donglu; 2-person hotpot from Y80; ⏲11am-11pm) A good place for Inner Mongolian hotpot. Located one block east of Bèi'ěr Dàjiǔdiàn.

Information

Bank of China (中国银行; Zhōngguó Yínháng; Xingan Donglu at Zhongyang Dajie) Next door to Bèi'ěr Dàjiǔdiàn in the centre of town.

China International Travel Service (CITS; 中国国际旅行社; Zhōngguó Guójì Lǚxíngshè; ☎822 4017; fax 822 1728; 22 Alihe Lu) In Hédōng (east of the river), on the 2nd floor of Běiyuán Bīnguǎn.

Internet cafe (网吧; wǎngbā; lower level, cnr Zhongyang Dajie & Xingan Xilu; per hr Y2) Diagonally opposite the Bèi'ěr Dàjiǔdiàn.

China Post (国际邮局; Zhōngguó Yóuzhèng; Zhongyang Dajie at Yueju Xilu) Post and telephone office.

Public Security Bureau (PSB; Gōng'ānjú; Alihe Lu) Opposite CITS in Hédōng.

Getting There & Away

Hulunbuir Aviation Travel (中国民航公司; Zhōngguó Mínháng; ☎834 6071; Dong Dajie, off Qiaotou Dajie) is near the bridge. There are direct daily flights from Hǎilā'ěr to Běijīng (Y950, two hours) and Hohhot (Y1310, 2¼ hours). CITS and hotel ticket agencies also book flights.

EZ Nis (☎0470 8215 2228; www.eznis airways.com), a Mongolian airline, flies to Mongolia two or three times per week, stopping in Choibalsan (US$74) and Ulaanbaatar (US$198). If you plan to fly to Ulaanbaatar you can just buy the ticket online. If you want to stop in Choibalsan you need to get special permission from Mongolian immigration. EZ Nis can organise this in two days (email its office in Ulaanbaatar).

From the **long-distance bus station** (长途车站; Chángtú Qìchēzhàn; Jinxinzi Lu, off Chezhan Jie), there are regular buses to Mǎnzhōulǐ (Y31, three hours) between 7.30am and 6pm.

Several daily trains go to Mǎnzhōulǐ (Y26, three to 3½ hours). There are daily trains between Hǎilā'ěr and Hā'ěrbīn (hard/soft sleeper Y125/200, 11 hours), Qíqíhā'ěr (Y116/179, eight to nine hours) and Běijīng (Y319/506, 28 hours).

The train station is in the northwestern part of town. A taxi to the city-centre hotels is Y12.

Getting Around

There is no airport bus, but you can take a taxi to the airport for around Y25. Taxi sharks wait for new arrivals and ask Y60 to get from the airport to town. If you can't bargain them down you could walk 3km to the edge of town and hail a taxi.

Bus 7 runs from the train station past the bus station to Bèi'ěr Dàjiǔdiàn. Bus 1 runs from Hédōng to the train station. Taxi fares start at Y6.

Around Hǎilā'ěr

JĪNZHÀNGHÁN GRASSLANDS

金帐汗草原

Set along a winding river about 40km north of Hǎilā'ěr, this **grasslands camp** (Jīnzhànghán Cǎoyuán; ☎133 2700 0919; ⏲Jun-early Oct) is designed for tourists, and has a spectacular setting. You can occupy an hour or so looking around and sipping milk tea, spend the day horse riding (per hour Y150) or hiking, or come for an evening of dinner, singing and dancing.

If you want to stay the night, you can sleep in one of the **yurts** (per person Y80). There's no indoor plumbing but there is a toilet hut.

To get here, you'll have to hire a taxi from Hǎilā'ěr (about Y120 return, 40 minutes).

About 2km before the main camp there are a couple of unsigned family-run camps. Prices for food, accommodation and horse rental are about half what you pay at Jīnzhànghán, but they are rather less organised.

SHÌ WĚI

室韦

This small Russian village of log cabins and rutted roads is right on the Éěrgǔnà River, which marks the border with Russia. Little happens in town but it's fun to sample some of the Russian food on offer and stroll along the riverbank (look for the Russian village on the opposite bank). The backcountry road here, through scattered elm forests, is another reason to visit.

Decades of intermarriage between the Russians and Chinese has produced some unique-looking locals. While most people are a blend between the two races, a few could easily pass for pure-blood Russians. Speaking with some of them reveals that while they may look European, their mother tongue is indeed Mandarin. Many families have turned their homes into guesthouses and you can get a room in a private house for about Y50 to Y100. Homestays include **Lisa** (⏲139 4708 3113), **Marsha** (☎139 4700 9617) and **Donia** (☎138 4705 6927).

To reach Shì Wěi from Hǎilā'ěr, first travel to Lābùdálín (拉布达林; Y27, two hours); buses leave every 40 minutes from 6.50am. From Lābùdálín (sometimes called Éěrgǔnà) there are two buses per day heading to Shì Wěi (Y35, three hours), departing at 9.30am and 3.30pm. Buses return to Lābùdálín at 8.30am and 9am. A taxi from Lābùdálín and back is Y300.

SOUTH OF HǍILĀ'ĚR

The road south from Hǎilā'ěr leads 170km southwest to **Dōngqí** (东旗), known as Zuun Khoshuu in Mongolian. While in town you may spot dusty traders from Mongolia (the town is just 25km north of the border). Note that Dōngqí is listed on maps as Xīnbā'ěr Hǔ Zuǒqí (新巴尔虎左旗).

About 18km northwest of Dōngqí is the recently renovated **Ganjur Monastery** (甘珠尔). Founded in 1771, the monastery was the largest in Hulunbuir Banner (*banner* is a Qing-era administrative term; similar to a county). Today it is home to 13 monks and situated in very scenic surrounds. A basic **yurt camp** (蒙古包宿营; ménggǔbao sùyíng; per night Y100) is located near the gate of the monastery.

Heading west from the monastery, the road leads through vast grasslands (with the occasional yurt-dwelling herder family) for about 105km to **Xīqí** (西旗), which Mongols refer to as Baruun Khoshuu. The small city is inhabited largely by Barga people (a Mongolian clan). From here it's 23km on a rough track to the shores of Dálài Hú, where you'll find more yurt camps at a beach called **Huángjīn Hǎi'àn** (黄金海岸). Foreigners need a permit for Xīqí. Note that on maps, Xīqí is listed as Xīnbā'ěr Hǔ Yòuqí (新巴尔虎右旗).

There are hourly buses from Hǎilā'ěr to Dōngqí (Y26, two hours) from 8am. Travel between Dōngqí and Xīqí is best done in a taxi so you can stop at the lake, monastery and yurts en route. It is Y100 between the towns, plus another Y100 for a trip to the lake.

Alternatively, if you are heading east, the back roads lead from Dōngqí to Ā'ěrshān. A bus (Y43, three hours) leaves at 8.30am, or you could take a direct bus from Hǎilā'ěr (Y66, five hours) at 6.30am or 8.40am. There is good hiking in the hills around Ā'ěrshān (阿尔山). From the town you could hire a taxi (per day Y180) to take you into the beautiful **Āʼěrshān National Forest Park** (阿尔山国家森林公园; Āʼěrshān Guójiā Sēlín Gōngyuán; admission Y125). Āʼěrshān is about 190km southeast of Dōngqí and 370km from Hǎilāʼěr. It is connected by train to Ulanhot (Wūlánhàotè).

Mǎnzhōulǐ 满洲里

0470 / POP 55,400

This laissez-faire border city, where the Trans-Siberian Railway crosses from China to Russia, is a pastel-painted boomtown of shops, hotels and restaurants catering to the Russian market. Unless you look Asian, expect shopkeepers to greet you in Russian. Mǎnzhōulǐ is modernising at lightning speed, but a few Russian-built log houses still line Yidao Jie.

Mǎnzhōulǐ is small enough to get around on foot. From the train station to the town centre, it's a 10-minute walk. Turn right immediately as you exit the station, then right again to cross the footbridge. You'll come off the bridge near the corner of Yidao Jie and Zhongsu Lu.

Sights

Besides the Russian traders, Mǎnzhōulǐ's main attraction is **Hūlún Hú** (呼伦湖; admission Y30), one of the largest lakes in China. Called Dalai Nuur (Ocean Lake) in Mongolian, it unexpectedly pops out of the grasslands like an enormous inland sea. You can go fishing here or simply stroll along the rocky lakeshore. The easiest way to get to Hūlún Hú, 39km southeast of Mǎnzhōulǐ, is to hire a taxi (about Y200 return).

Halfway between the city and the Russian border is a bizarre **park** filled with giant Russian Matryoshka dolls, many with portraits of famous historical figures, from Albert Einstein to Michael Jordan. The largest doll is a Russian-style restaurant. Next to the park is a **museum** of Russian art.

Sleeping

There must be 100 hotels and guesthouses in Mǎnzhōulǐ, all within walking distance of each other. Signs are in Russian – гостиница *(gastinitsa)* is the Russian word for 'hotel'. Likewise, there are plenty of restaurants, so just wander around a bit and see what takes your fancy.

TOP CHOICE **Fēngzéyuán Lǚdiàn** GUESTHOUSE $
(丰泽源旅店; 225 4099, 139 4709 3443; Yidao Jie; 一道街; d Y100; @) Located inside a restored Russian log cabin (painted yellow and green), this friendly guesthouse has clean rooms with computers. Coming off the pedestrian bridge from the train station it's the first building in front of you, next to the statue of Zhou Enlai. From the bus station, walk 200m east and turn right when you see Zhou Enlai. Don't confuse this with the nearby Jīxiáng Lǚguǎn, which looks very similar but is closer to the road. The Fēngzéyuán is cleaner, better maintained, friendlier and cheaper than its nearby rival.

Wéiduōlìyà Jiǔdiàn HOTEL $$
(维多利亚酒店; 391 9999; 116 Erdao Jie; 二道街116号; d Y380; wi-fi) The Victoria Hotel is a 28-storey tower with glass elevator, sweeping views of the city and modern rooms. If they are not busy you might get a room for as low as Y200. It's opposite Guójì Fàndiàn.

Chénglín Bīnguǎn HOTEL $$
(城林宾馆; 623 8866; Sidao Jie; 四道街; r Y160) Solid midrange hotel with good prices. It's a block east of the main square at Sidao Jie and Haiguan Lu.

Eating

Barguuzin BURIAT RESTAURANT $$
(巴图敖其尔; Bātú Áoqíʼěr; 622 0121; cnr Erdao Jie & Zhongsu Lu; dishes Y10-30; 6.30am-midnight) Run by Buriat Mongols from Russia, this place specialises in Mongolian and Russian cuisine. It's located about 40m west of the giant mushroom on Zhongsu Lu, below street level. If you still can't find it, ask around for '*Buriatskaya Kukhnya*' (Buriat food).

BORDER CROSSING: GETTING TO RUSSIA

Buses to Zabaikalsk (Y65), over the Russian border, depart eight times daily between 7.50am and 1.30pm, but they tend to be much slower than the private cars (because the Chinese traders on your bus will take ages to get through customs). In Mǎnzhōulǐ you could ask around for a ride from a Russian trader (Russians get through faster). Otherwise, take a taxi to the border (Y20), 9km from town, and get a ride across from there with a Russian driver.

Information

Bank of China (中国银行; Zhōngguó Yínháng; Yidao Jie) Near the junction with Haiguan Lu.

China International Travel Service (CITS; 中国国际旅行社; Zhōngguó Guójì Lǚxíngshè; ☎622 8319; 35 Erdao Jie; ⌚8.30am-noon & 2.30-5pm Mon-Fri) On the 1st floor of Guójì Fàndiàn (International Hotel). Sells train tickets for Chinese cities.

Internet cafe (网吧; wǎngbā; Yidao Jie; per hr Y3; ⌚24hr) About 50m east of the Jīxiáng Lǚguǎn.

China Post (国际邮局; Zhōngguó Yóuzhèng; cnr Haiguan Jie & Sidao Jie) Post and telephone office.

Public Security Bureau (PSB; 公安局; Gōng'ānjú; cnr Sandao Jie & Shulin Lu)

Getting There & Around

Mǎnzhōulǐ has a small airport on the edge of town; a taxi to the airport will take about 15 minutes. There are daily flights to Běijīng (Y2100, 2¼ hours) and, in summer, to Hohhot (Y2020, 2½ hours).

You can reach Mǎnzhōulǐ by train from Hǎilā'ěr (Y26, three to 3½ hours, 10 daily), Hā'ěrbīn (hard/soft sleeper Y208/324, 13 hours, six daily) or Qíqíhā'ěr (hard/soft sleeper Y175/264, 11 hours, three daily).

Taxis charge Y10 from the station to the centre. Otherwise, most trips around town are Y7.

Buses leave all day for Hǎilā'ěr (Y31, three hours) from the long-distance bus station on Yidao Jie, west of Míngzhū Fàndiàn.

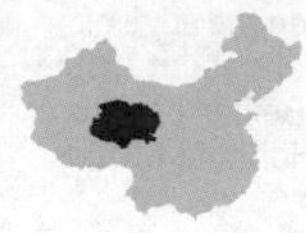

Qīnghǎi

POPULATION: 5.4 MILLION

Includes »

Best Places to Eat

» Black Tent (p932)

» Yīpǐnguó Nóngzhuāng (p939)

» Qing Xiang Yuan Farmhouse (p939)

» Qīnghǎi Tǔ Huǒguō (p932)

Best Places to Drink

» Rebkong Teahouse (p937)

» Greenhouse (p932)

» On the bank of the Yellow River (p939)

» Black Tent (p932)

» Sūjī Nímǎ (p932)

Why Go?

Big, bold and beautifully barren, Qīnghǎi (青海), larger than any European country, occupies a vast swathe of the northeastern chunk of the Tibetan plateau. In fact, as far as Tibetans are concerned, this isn't China at all; it's Amdo, one of old Tibet's three traditional provinces, and much of what you'll experience here will seem very much Tibetan rather than Chinese; there are monasteries galore, yaks by the hundred and nomads camped out across high-altitude grasslands.

Rough-and-ready Qīnghǎi is classic off-the-beaten-track territory, often with that last-frontier feel to it. Travelling around is both inconvenient and uncomfortable, and you can go for days without meeting another tourist. But those wonderful moments of solitude, those middle-of-nowhere high-plateau vistas and the chance to discover some of the more remote communities of China's ethnic minorities make the long bus rides, the cold weather, and the often head-achingly high altitude well worth bearing.

When to Go

Xīníng

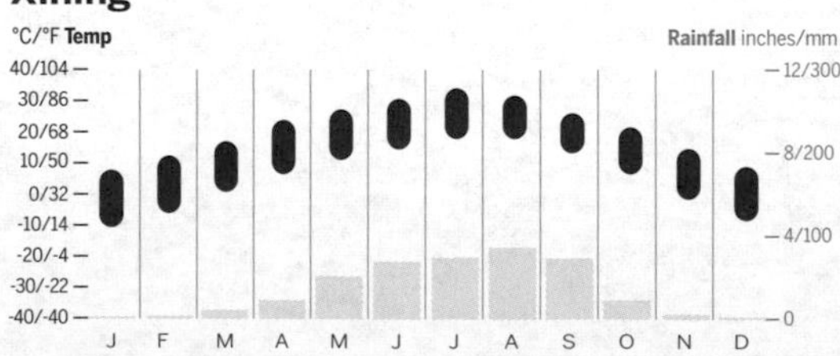

January & February Tibetan New Year (Losar), with lots of pilgrims and celebrations at monasteries.

July–September Grasslands at their greenest; landscape dotted with nomad tents.

September Safest and most comfortable time for trekking around Mt Amnye Machen.

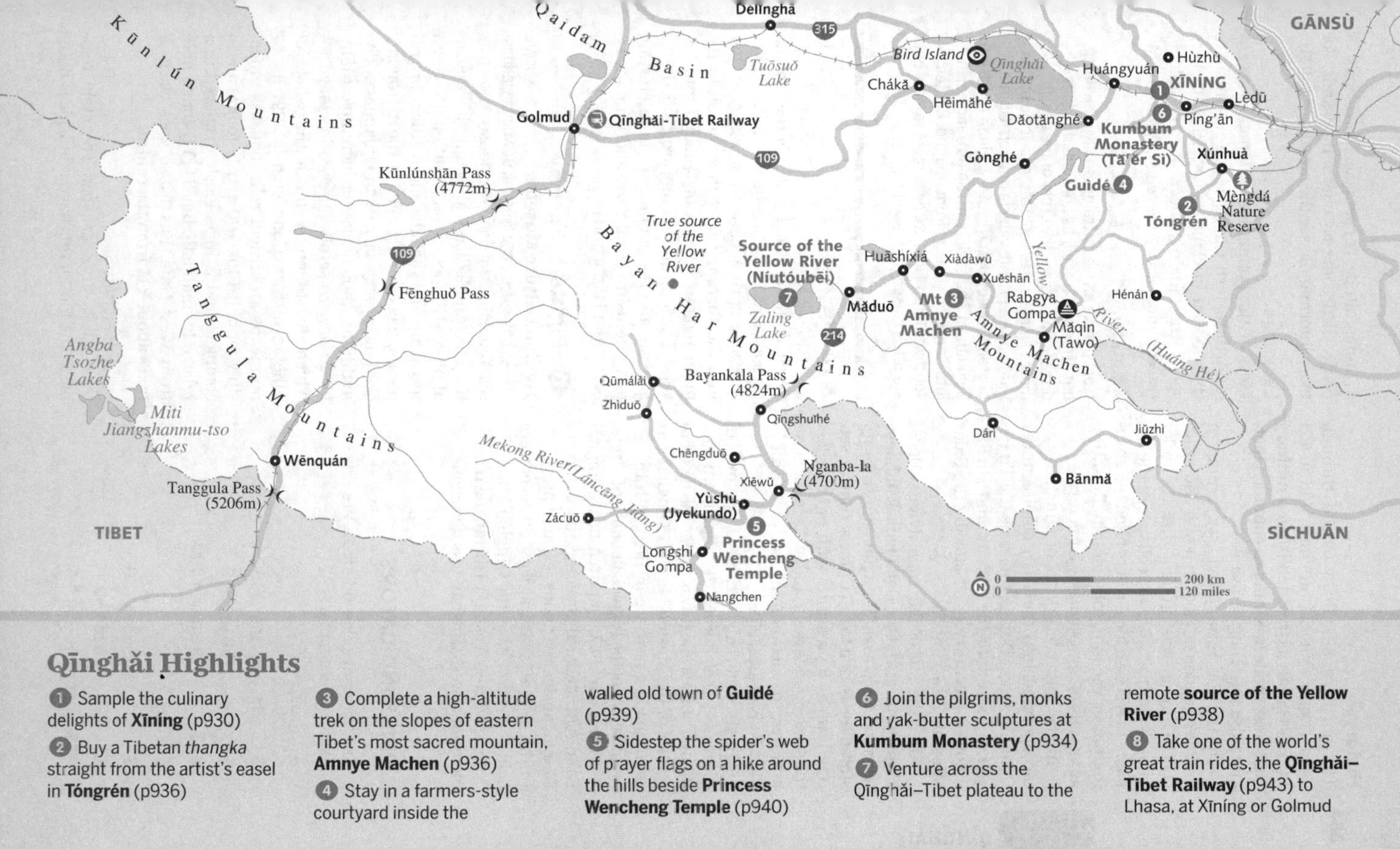

Qīnghǎi Highlights

1 Sample the culinary delights of **Xīníng** (p930)

2 Buy a Tibetan *thangka* straight from the artist's easel in **Tóngrén** (p936)

3 Complete a high-altitude trek on the slopes of eastern Tibet's most sacred mountain, **Amnye Machen** (p936)

4 Stay in a farmers-style courtyard inside the walled old town of **Guìdé** (p939)

5 Sidestep the spider's web of prayer flags on a hike around the hills beside **Princess Wencheng Temple** (p940)

6 Join the pilgrims, monks and yak-butter sculptures at **Kumbum Monastery** (p934)

7 Venture across the Qīnghǎi–Tibet plateau to the remote **source of the Yellow River** (p938)

8 Take one of the world's great train rides, the **Qīnghǎi–Tibet Railway** (p943) to Lhasa, at Xīníng or Golmud

History

The northern Silk Road passed through what is now Qīnghǎi province, and in 121 BC the Han dynasty established a military base near modern Xīníng to counter Tibetan raids on trading caravans.

During the Yarlung dynasty, a time of great expansion of Tibetan power and influence, Qīnghǎi was brought directly under Lhasa's control. After the collapse of the dynasty in AD 842, local rulers filled the ensuing power vacuum, some nominally acting as vassals of Song-dynasty emperors.

In the 13th century all of Qīnghǎi was incorporated into the Yuan empire under Genghis Khan. During this time the Tǔ began to move into the area around Hùzhù, followed a century or so later by the Salar Muslims into Xúnhuà.

After the fall of the Yuan dynasty, local Mongol rulers and the Dalai Lamas in Lhasa wrestled for power. The Qing emperors restored the region to full Chinese control, setting it up as a prefecture with more or less the same boundaries as today. As in the past, however, they left administrative control in the hands of local elites.

Qīnghǎi officially became a province of China in 1929 during the republican era, though at the time it was under the de facto control of the Muslim Ma clan. Qīnghǎi was again made a province in 1949 with the establishment of the People's Republic of China.

In the late 1950s an area near Qīnghǎi Lake (Qīnghǎi Hú) became the centre of China's nuclear weapons research program. In the next 40 years, at least 30 tests were held at a secret base, the Qīnghǎi Mine.

In April 2010, Yùshù, a Tibetan town in remote southwest Qīnghǎi, was devastated by a 7.1-magnitude earthquake. Thousands of people died, some say tens of thousands. For more information, see the boxed text (p941).

PRICE INDICATORS

The following price indicators are used in this chapter:

Sleeping

$	less than Y150
$$	Y150 to Y300
$$$	more than Y300

Eating

$	less than Y30
$$	Y30 to Y50
$$$	more than Y50

Language

Most of the population in Qīnghǎi speaks a northwestern Chinese dialect similar to that spoken in Gānsù. Most Tibetans here speak the Amdo dialect. It's possible to travel almost everywhere using Mandarin.

Getting There & Around

Most people arrive by train, usually into Xīníng, but after that train lines are limited so long-distance buses are the order of the day. In more remote areas you'll often have no option but to hire a private vehicle or hitch. Off-the-beaten-track overland routes include south into Sìchuān, at Aba or Sěrshu (Shíqú), and north into Gānsù or Xīnjiāng from Golmud. Routes southwest into Tibet are even more remote but are often closed to foreigners.

Xīníng 西宁

0971 / POP 2.1 MILLION / ELEV 2275M

Perched on the eastern edge of the Tibetan plateau, this lively provincial capital makes a perfect springboard from which to dive into the surrounding sights and on to the more remote regions of Qīnghǎi and beyond. The food and lodging are good, the air is fresh, and the populace is an interesting mix of Muslim (Huí, Salar and Uighur), Tibetan and Hàn Chinese.

Sights

Tibetan Culture Museum MUSEUM

(藏文化博物馆; Zàng Wénhuà Bówùguǎn; admission Y60; 9.30am-5pm) Previously known as the Tibetan Medicine Museum, this unusual place still focuses on traditional Tibetan medicine and includes old medical instruments, bags, scrolls and, in the astronomy section, a very large sand mandala. The highlight, though, is the incredible 618m-long *thangka* scroll – the world's longest – which charts pretty much the whole of Tibetan history. Completed in 1997 it's by no means an ancient relic, but it is unfeasibly long. It took 400 artists four years to complete and is ingeniously displayed in a relatively small hall. Bus 34 (Y1) comes here from West Gate. Bus 1 also goes close. A taxi's about Y15 from the centre.

FREE **Běichán Sì** TEMPLE

(北禅寺; 8am-4pm) The main temple at the foot of this barren hillside is nothing special but halfway up the steep climb to the top you pass cave temples and shrines that are thought to be 1700 years old. A pagoda, and great views of the city await you at the top. Turn left after you pass under the railway line and follow the road round to the temple entrance, or take a Y6 cab.

FREE **Qīnghǎi Provincial Museum** MUSEUM
(青海省博物馆; Qīnghǎi Shěng Bówùguǎn; Xīnníng Sq, 58 Xiguan Dajie; 新宁广场西关大街58号; ⏲9am-4.30pm Mon-Sat) Scaled down in recent years, but still has some nice pieces recovered from excavations in Qīnghǎi. The Tibetan carpet exhibition is worth seeing. Bus 1 goes here, or take bus 22 from Dongguan Dajie.

Great Mosque MOSQUE
(清真大寺; Qīngzhēn Dàsì; 25 Dongguan Dajie; admission Y15; ⏲7am-8pm) About one-third of Xīníng's population is Muslim and there are more than 80 mosques across the city. But this is the big one. In fact, it's one of the largest mosques in China. Friday lunchtime prayers regularly attract 50,000 worshippers who spill out onto the streets before and afterwards. And during Ramadan as many as 300,000 come here to pray. Non-Muslims can't enter the main prayer hall, but can stroll around the grounds. The mosque was first built during the late 14th century and has since been restored.

FREE **Golden Stupa Temple** BUDDHIST TEMPLE
(金塔寺; Jīntǎ Sì; 19 Hongjuesi Jie; 宏觉寺街19号; ⏲8am-4pm) Small temple named after long-destroyed golden *chörten* (Tibetan stupa). Used as place of study by monks at Kumbum Monastery.

City Wall RUIN
(城墙; Chéngqiáng; Kunlun Zhonglu; 昆仑中路) One or two isolated sections of Xīníng's old city wall still remain, the most accessible being a short stretch on Kunlun Zhonglu.

Sleeping

Lete Youth Hostel YOUTH HOSTEL $
(理体青年旅舍; Lǐtǐ Qīngnián Lǚshè; ☎820 2080; http://xnlete.googlepages.com; 16th fl, Bldg No 5, International Village Apartments, 2-32 Jiancai Xiang; 建材巷2-32号国际村公寓5号楼16层; dm Y30-35, s/d Y40/80, d with bathroom Y120; @📶) This friendly hostel has the best backpacker vibe in Xīníng and is a great place to get the low-down on travelling in Qīnghǎi and on to Tibet. The modern, multifloor layout includes cafe/bar, widescreen TVs, laundry, kitchen and a small terrace that you can sleep out on in summer (Y10). Rooms are clean, bright and spacious, although singles are tiny. Staff members speak good English and the travel agency Tibetan Connections is two floors up. One black mark: the showers are either cold, or a trickle.

Chéng Lín Hotel HOTEL $$
(成林大厦; Chénglín Dàshà; ☎491 1199; Dong Dajie; 东大街; tw/d Y260/280; ❄) Spacious, well turned out rooms with ensuite shower come with dark-wood furniture, TV and kettle and are great value after discounts. Twins were going for Y133 when we were there. No internet in the rooms, but there's an internet cafe (per hour Y2 to Y4) on the third floor. Limited English.

Jiànyín Hotel HOTEL $$$
(建银宾馆; Jiànyín Bīnguǎn; ☎826 1539; 55 Xi Dajie; 西大街55号; d/tw Y468/668; ❄@) There are fancier hotels in town, but we like the old-school feel to this place with its gaudy maroon and gold carpets snaking through gloomy corridors. The rooms themselves are bright and spacious (although bathrooms are pokey) and come with a computer (Y20 extra) or just internet access (per hour Y2.40). Staff are friendly and discounts are superb; twins can drop to Y300.

Sunshine Pagoda International Youth Hostel YOUTH HOSTEL $
(塔顶阳光国际青年旅舍; Tǎdǐng Yángguāng Guójì Qīngnián Lǚshè; ☎821 5571; www.tdyg-inn.com; Wenmiao Square 3rd fl, off Wenhua Jie; 文华街文庙广场3层; dm Y35-55, r Y80; @📶) More popular with Chinese travellers than Westerners, this OK hostel is in the thick of the action if it's drinking you're after. Rooms are basic but tidy and there's a cosy cafe area.

Eating

Xīníng has a great range of food. Try the Tibetan district around the train station for cheap Tibetan fare. For Muslim food head to Dongguan Dajie, near the Great Mosque, or the northern stretch of Nan Xiaojie. For snacks, try one of the cheap barbecue places (烧烤; *shǎokǎo*) on Xiao Xinjie that stay open until the early hours, or head to Mo Jia Jie Market (墨家街市场; Mòjiājiā Shìchǎng) where you can also sample a local favourite: spicy cold noodles (酿皮; *niàng pí*; Y4).

Xīníng

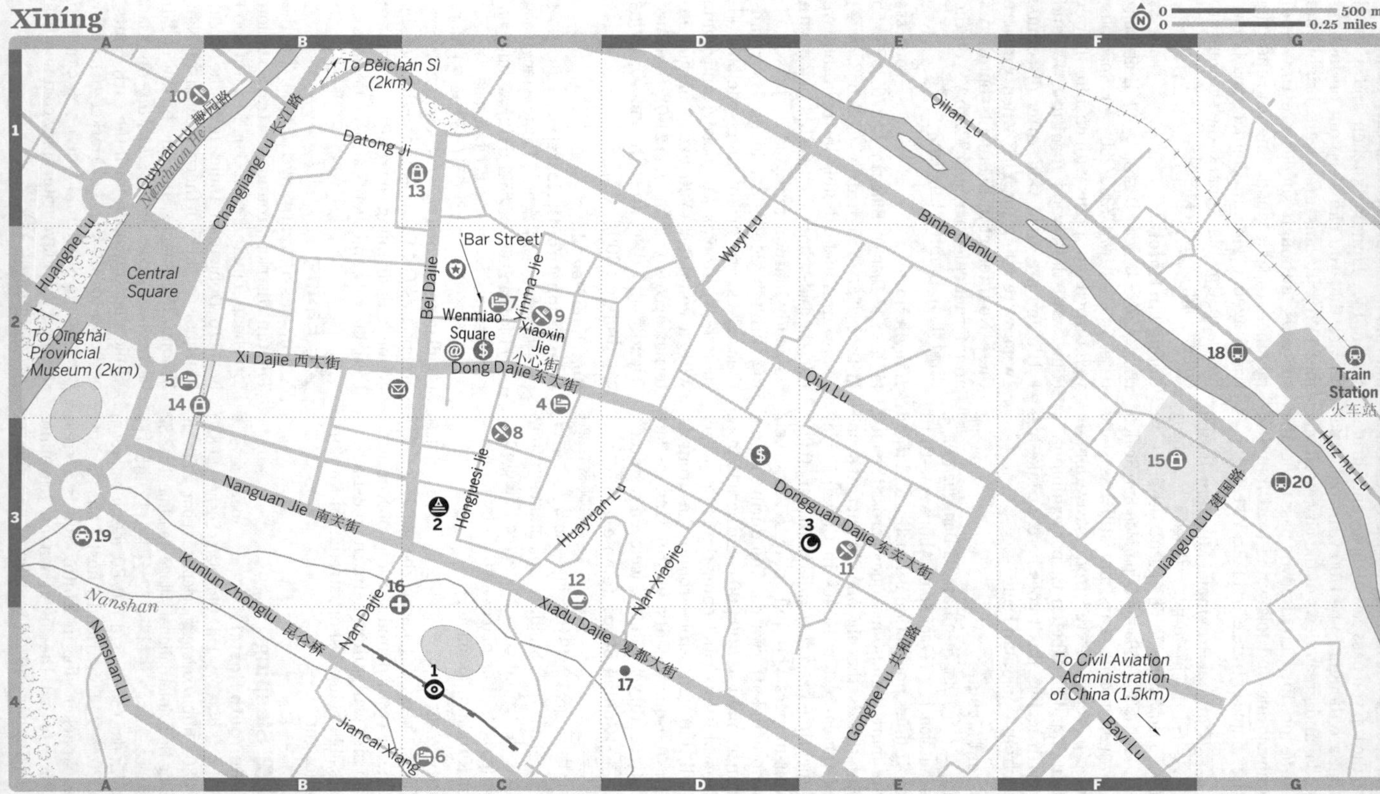
To Běichán Sì (2km)
Quyuan Lu
Nanchuan He
Changjiang Lu 长江路
Datong Ji
Huanghe Lu
Central Square
To Qīnghǎi Provincial Museum (2km)
'Bar Street'
Bei Dajie
Yinma Jie
Wenmiao Square
Xiaoxin Jie 小心街
Xi Dajie 西大街
Dong Dajie 东大街
Hongjuesi Jie
Nanguan Jie 南关街
Kunlun Zhonglu 昆仑桥
Nanshan
Nanshan Lu
Nan Dajie
Jiancai Xiang
Huayuan Lu
Nan Xiaojie
Xiadu Dajie 夏都大街
Wuyi Lu
Qiyi Lu
Binhe Nanlu
Qilian Lu
Dongguan Dajie 东关大街
Gonghe Lu 共和路
Jianguo Lu 建国路
Huz hu Lu
Train Station 火车站
To Civil Aviation Administration of China (1.5km)
Bayi Lu
500 m
0.25 miles

Xīníng

Sights

1 City Wall C4
2 Golden Stupa Temple C3
3 Great Mosque E3

Sleeping

4 Chéng Lín Hotel C2
5 Jiànyín Hotel A2
6 Lete Youth Hostel C4
7 Sunshine Pagoda International Youth Hostel C2

Eating

Black Tent .... (see 7)
8 Mo Jia Jie Market C3
9 Qīnghǎi Tǔ Huǒguō C2
10 Sūjī Nímǎ A1
11 Zhènyà Niúròu Miàn E3

Drinking

12 Greenhouse C3

Shopping

13 Amdo Café C1
14 Shuǐjǐng Xiàng Market A2
15 Tibetan Market F3

Information

16 Qīnghǎi Red Cross Hospital B3
17 Snow Lion Tours D4
Tibetan Connections .... (see 6)

Transport

18 Buses to Kumbum Monastery G2
19 Taxis to Kumbum Monastery A3
20 Xīníng Bus Station G3

Black Tent TIBETAN $$
(黑帐房藏餐吧; Hēizhàngfáng Zàngcānbā; ☎823 4029; 18 Wenmiao Sq, 3rd fl; 文庙广场18号3层; dishes Y15-40; ⏲9.30am-10.30pm; 📄) Authentic Tibetan nosh, including *tsampa* (roasted barley; Y17), *momo* (dumplings; Y25 to Y30) and yak-butter yoghurt (Y12) as well as some tasty Nepalese dishes. Also serves yak-butter tea (per pot Y20) and Qīnghǎi's favourite local tipple, barley wine (青稞酒; *qīngkē jiǔ*).

Qīnghǎi Tǔ Huǒguō HOTPOT $
(青海土火锅; ☎491 0881; 31 Yinma Jie; pots Y58/78/98; ⏲11am-10pm) Unlike its fiery Chóngqìng cousin, Qīnghǎi's chilli-less hotpot, which comes in attractive copper pots, won't burn your head off when you eat it. This place has three different pot sizes, all of which include 10 different ingredients. If you can read Chinese, you can add more from the menu. The Y58 version is plenty for two or three people. Dipping sauces – either chilli (香辣; *xiǎnglà*) or garlic (蒜泥; *suànní*) – are Y2 extra.

Sūjī Nímǎ TIBETAN $$$
(苏姬尼玛风情宫; Sūjī Nímǎ Fēngqíng Gōng; ☎610 2288; Quyuan Lu (off Huanghe Lu); 趣园路(黄河路); dishes Y30-80, beer from Y15; ⏲3pm-midnight) The main reason to come to this canal-side restaurant is to watch the evening performances of Tibetan dancing (9.30pm to midnight) which are free as long as you buy drinks or a meal. The Tibetan food is also very good. There's no English menu but the *kāngbā níupái* (康巴牛排; Khampa beef steak; Y58) and *zàngxiāng mèntǔjī* (藏乡焖土鸡; Tibetan clay pot chicken; Y46) are highly recommended.

Zhènyà Niúròu Miàn MUSLIM $
(震亚牛肉面; 24 Dongguan Dajie; noodles Y5/6.5; ⏲9am-10pm) Join the local Muslim population for their noodle fix at this busy place by the Great Mosque. There's no menu, but there are only two dishes: beef noodles (牛肉面; *niúròu miàn*; Y5) and minced-meat noodles (干拌面; *gān bànmiàn*; Y6.50). A small peppery soup (酸汤; *suān tāng*) comes free.

Drinking

If you like your bars to come with loud music, neon lights, booth seating and scantily clad waitresses head to Xīníng's so-called **bar street** (酒吧街; jiǔ bā jiē; beer from Y6); three floors of bars, cafes and restaurants are set around Confucius Temple Sq (文庙广场; Wénmiào Guǎngchǎng) off Wenhua Jie.

Greenhouse CAFE
(古林房咖啡; Gǔlínfáng Kāfēi; 222-22 Xiadu Dajie; 夏都大街222-22号; coffee from Y13; ⏲8am-10.30pm; 📶) Rustic split-level wood interior and easily the best coffee in town. Also serves smoothies (Y20) and snacks (Y4 to Y25).

Shopping

In the lively Tibetan market (西藏市场; Xīzàng Guǎngchǎng) near the train station you'll find stall after stall selling traditional fabrics and clothing.

Amdo Café HANDICRAFTS
(安多咖啡屋; Ānduō Kāfēiwū; ☎821 3127; Datong Jie; ⏲9am-6pm Mon-Sat; 📶) Profits from the lovely handmade Tibetan gifts (from Y6) sold here go back to the local

craftswomen. There's also decent coffee (from Y8).

Shuǐjǐng Xiàng Market SOUVENIRS
(水井巷商场; Shuǐjǐng Xiàng Shāngchǎng; ⌚9am-6pm) Lively market running north-south between Xi Dajie and Nanguan Jie.

Information

Bank of China (中国银行; Zhōngguó Yínháng; ⌚9am-5pm Mon-Fri, 10am-4pm Sat & Sun) Branches on Dongguan Dajie, Dong Dajie and next to CAAC on Bayi Lu all change cash and travellers cheques and have foreign-friendly ATMs.

Post office (中国邮政; Zhōngguó Yóuzhèng; Da Shizi, cnr Xi Dajie & Nan Dajie; ⌚8.30am-6pm)

Public Security Bureau (PSB; 公安局; Gōng'ānjú; 35 Bei Dajie; ⌚8.30-11.30am & 2.30-5.30pm Mon-Fri) Can extend visas.

Qīnghǎi Red Cross Hospital (青海红十字医院; Qīnghǎi Hóngshízì Yīyuàn; ☎824 7545; Nan Dajie) English-speaking doctors available. Outpatients (门诊部; *ménzhěn bù*) has a 24-hour pharmacy (药店; *yàodiàn*).

Snow Lion Tours (☎134 3932 9243; www.snowliontours.com; Suite 601, Unit 4, Bldg 35, International Village, off Xiadu Dajie; 夏都大街际村35号楼4单元601室) Run by knowledgeable English-speaking Tibetan guy; arranges treks, camping with nomads and Tibet permits.

Tiāntángniǎo Internet (天堂鸟网铬; Tiāntángniǎo wǎnggè; Dong Dajie; per hr Y2-3.50; ⌚24hr) Second and 3rd floor.

Tibetan Connections (☎820 3271; www.tibetanconnections.com; 2-32 Jian Cai Xiang, International Village Bldg 5, 18th fl) Foreign-managed agency organising treks, camp-outs and cultural tours in Qīnghǎi, as well as Lhasa train tickets and permits. Above Lete Youth Hostel.

Getting There & Away

Air

Flights include Běijīng (Y1550), Chéngdū (Y1090), Shànghǎi (Y1950), Golmud (Y1420, three weekly) and Xī'ān (Y720). There are no direct flights to Lhasa. You must fly via Chéngdū.

The **Civil Aviation Administration of China** (CAAC; 中国民航; Zhōngguó Mínháng; ☎813 3333; 32 Bayi Xilu; ⌚8.30am-5.30pm) has a booking office on the eastern edge of town.

Bus

Destinations from **Xīníng Bus Station** (车站; chēzhàn):

Bānmǎ Y160, 15 hours, one daily (4pm)

Lánzhōu Y56, three hours, every 30 minutes (7.20am to 6.30pm)

Mǎqìn (Tawo) Y100, 12 hours, three daily (8.45am seats only, 5pm and 6pm sleepers)

Píng'ān Y6.80, one hour, every seven minutes (7am to 6.30pm)

Tóngrén Y32.50, four hours, every 30 minutes (7.30am to 5pm)

Xiàhé Y50, six hours, one daily (7.15am)

Xúnhuà Y30, five hours, every 30 minutes (7.20am to 4.20pm)

Yùshù sleeper Y175, 16 to 17 hours, six daily

Zhāngyè slow bus/fast bus Y97/Y59, six hours/eight hours, two/three daily (9am and 3pm/7.30am, 5.30pm and 6.30pm)

Train

Lhasa-bound trains pass through Xīníng (Y395, 25 hours, six daily from 2.56pm to 7.40pm) on their way towards the now world-famous **Qīnghǎi–Tibet Railway** stretch of China's rail network, but the K9801 (2.56pm) actually starts here, so is usually easier to get tickets for. You will, of course, need all your Tibet papers in order. Other destinations from Xīníng train station (火车站; huǒchē zhàn) include the following:

Běijīng sleeper Y416, 22 to 24 hours, two daily (10.19am and 12.02pm)

Chéngdū sleeper Y300, 25 and 20½ hours, two daily (9.24am and 11.48am)

Golmud seat/sleeper Y113/201, 9½ hours, eight daily (2.56pm to 10pm)

Lánzhōu Y33, 2½ hours, 17 daily (8am to 10.20pm)

Xī'ān seat/sleeper Y116/207, 10½ to 12½ hours, nine daily (9am to 10.20pm)

Getting Around

The airport is 27km east of the city. Shuttle buses (Y21, 30 minutes) leave roughly two hours before flights from the CAAC office on Bayi Lu.

Handy Bus 1 (Y1) runs from the train station and along Dongguan Dajie to Central Sq before heading north to the Tibetan Culture Museum. Taxis are Y6 for the first 3km and Y1.20 per kilometre thereafter.

Around Xīníng

KUMBUM MONASTERY (TǍ'ĚR SÌ) 塔尔寺

One of the great monasteries of the Gelugpa (Yellow Hat) sect of Tibetan Buddhism, the **Kumbum Monastery** (Tǎ'ěr Sì; admission Y80; ⌚8.30am-6pm) is in the small town of Huángzhōng (湟中), 26km south of Xīníng. It was built in 1577 on hallowed ground – the birthplace of Tsongkhapa, founder of the Gelugpa sect.

BIRD-WATCHING AT QĪNGHǍI LAKE

China's largest lake, Qīnghǎi Lake (青海湖; Qīnghǎi Hú; Lake Kokonor; elevation 3600m) has become an over-touristy big-draw destination for large tour groups, but bird-watchers may still enjoy a trip here.

Bird Island (鸟岛; Niǎo Dǎo; admission Y115), on the western side of the lake, about 300km from Xīníng, is worth visiting from March to early June. The island (now in fact a peninsula) is the breeding ground for thousands of wild geese, gulls, cormorants, sandpipers, extremely rare black-necked cranes and other bird species. Perhaps the most interesting are the bar-headed geese that migrate over the Himalaya to spend winter on the Indian plains, and have been spotted flying at altitudes of 10,000m.

The closest accommodation to Bird Island is **Niǎo Dǎo Bīnguǎn** (鸟岛宾馆; ☎0970-865 5098; r with breakfast from Y380). You are still 16km from the island here, but you should be able to hire a taxi (Y50 return). Camping is another option.

Every travel agency in Xīníng offers trips to Qīnghǎi Lake. At the time of research, Tibetan Connections was offering a two-day camping trip for Y700 (transport costs only). You could get to the lake much more cheaply if you hired a private minivan or taxi from Xīníng with a group of travellers.

It's of enormous historical significance, and hundreds of monks still live here but, perhaps because it's such a big tourist draw for this part of Qīnghǎi, the atmosphere pales into comparison with other monasteries in Amdo. The artwork and architecture, however, remain impressive.

Nine temples are open, each with its own characteristics. The most important is the **Grand Hall of Golden Tiles** (大金瓦殿; Dàjīnwǎ Diàn), where an 11m-high *chörten* marks the spot of Tsongkhapa's birth. You'll see pilgrims walking circuits of the building and prostrating outside the entrance. Also worth seeking out is the **Yak Butter Scripture Temple** (酥油画馆; Sūyóuhuà Guǎn) which houses sculptures of human figures, animals and landscapes carved out of yak butter.

Buses to Huángzhōng (Y3, 45 minutes) leave every six minutes from the small bus station opposite Xīníng train station, starting at 7am. The bus you want doesn't have a number so look above the front windscreen for the characters: 西宁火车站一专线一湟中汽车站 (Xīníng train station to Huángzhōng bus station). Get off at the last stop and keep walking up the hill to the monastery. The last bus back is at 7pm. Shared taxis (拼车; *pīnchē*; Y8 per seat, 30 minutes) leave from the southeast corner of Kunlun Bridge.

YÒUNÍNG SÌ 佑宁寺

Well known throughout the Tibetan world, but rarely visited by tourists, this sprawling 17th-century hillside monastery in the Hùzhù Tǔzú (互助土族) Autonomous County is also considered one of the greats of the Gelugpa order.

Famous for its academies of medicine and astrology, its scholars and its living Buddhas *(tulku)*, Yòuníng Sì (Rgolung in Tibetan) was instrumental in solidifying Gelugpa dominance over the Amdo region. The monastery was founded by the Mongolian 4th Dalai Lama, and over time became a religious centre for the local Tǔ (themselves a distant Mongolian people). At its height, over 7000 monks resided here; these days there are probably less than 200, all of whom are Tǔ.

The monastery lies at the edge of a forested valley, and many chapels perch wondrously on the sides of a cliff face. Give yourself a couple of hours to explore the whole picturesque area.

The easiest way to the monastery is to take a bus to Píng'ān (Y6.80, one hour), then hire a taxi (one way/return Y50/90, 30 minutes). For just over Y200 you should be able to include a visit to the birthplace of the 14th Dalai Lama, but make sure you're clear on how long you want to spend at each place. It is possible to bus it from Píng'ān, but it involves a lot of waiting: take a bus bound for Hùzhù (互助) but get off at the turn-off for Yòuníng Sì (Yòuníng Sì lùkǒu) then wave down a bus to the monastery. The monastery is about 25km north of Píng'ān.

BIRTHPLACE OF THE 14TH DALAI LAMA 达赖故居

About 30km southeast of the town of Píng'ān, in the remote, sleepy village of Taktser (红崖村; Hóngyá Cūn), set in a ring of high snow-brushed mountains, is the birthplace of the 14th Dalai Lama (Dálài gùjū). The building is open to foreign visitors only when there are no political tensions in Tibet, and it's been closed to foreigners during March and April in recent years because of a number of sensitive dates during those months.

Assuming you are allowed in, you'll be able to visit the room where his Holiness was born (marked by a golden *chörten*), as well as a restored chapel that contains his former bed and throne. A side room displays some old family photos, including those of the Dalai Lama's parents, sister and brothers.

The Dalai Lama last visited here in 1955 en route to Běijīng to meet with Chairman Mao. The previous (13th) Dalai Lama paused here en route to Labrang just long enough to predict his own next reincarnation. You can spot the building (No 055) by its large wooden gate tied with *katags* (white ceremonial scarves).

Take a bus to Píng'ān (Y6.80, one hour) then take a cab (Y150 return; 50 minutes).

Tóngrén (Repkong) 同仁

☎0973

For several centuries now, the villages outside the monastery town of Tóngrén (Repkong in Tibetan) have been famous for producing some of the Tibetan world's best *thangkas* (Tibetan sacred art) and painted statues, so much so that an entire school of Tibetan art is named after the town. Visiting the Wútún Sì monastery not only gives you a chance to meet the artists, but also to purchase a painting or two, fresh off the easel.

Tóngrén is set on the slopes of the wide and fertile Gu-chu river valley. The local populace is a mix of Tibetans and Tǔ. The valley and surrounding hills are easily explored on foot.

Everything in town is walking distance from the five-way junction by Repkong Bridge (热贡桥; Règòng Qiáo). If you have your back to the bridge, take the first right to the bus station (50m), the second right to Tóngrén Holiday Hotel (500m), go straight on for Zhongshan Lu and turn left for Rongwo Gonchen Gompa (750m).

Sights

Rongwo Gonchen Gompa MONASTERY

(隆务寺; Dehelong NanLu; 德合隆南路; admission Y50) Tóngrén's main monastery (Lóngwù Sì) is a huge and rambling maze of renovated chapels and monks' residences,

TREKKING ON SACRED MT AMNYE MACHEN

The 6282m peak of Machen Kangri, or Mt Amnye Machen (阿尼玛卿山; Ānímǎqīng Shān), is Amdo's most sacred mountain – it's eastern Tibet's equivalent to Mt Kailash in western Tibet. Tibetan pilgrims travel for weeks to circumambulate the peak, believing it to be home to the protector deity Machen Pomra. The circuit's sacred geography and wild mountain scenery make it a fantastic, though adventurous, trekking destination.

The full circuit takes a week, or five days on a horse, though tourists often limit themselves to a half circuit. Several monasteries lie alongside the route.

With almost all of the route above 4000m, and the highest pass hitting 4600m, it's essential to acclimatise before setting off, preferably by spending a night or two at nearby Mǎqìn (Tawo; 3760m). You can make a good excursion 70km north of town to **Rabgya Gompa** (拉加寺; Lājiā Sì), an important branch of Tibet's Sera Monastery. The best months to trek are May to October, though be prepared for snow early and late in the season.

Most trekkers will be on an organised tour. The travel agencies we list in Xīníng (p932) can arrange trips, including English-speaking Tibetan guides. Expect to pay around US$75 per person per day, all-inclusive.

If you decide to head out on your own, take the bus to Mǎqìn (Tawo) and then hitch or hire a minivan out to Xuěshān (雪山), the traditional starting point of the *kora* (pilgrim path), where you may be able to find a guide, but don't count on it.

dating from 1301. It's well worth a wander, and you'll need one or two hours to see everything. Your ticket includes entry into six main halls, although you may be able to take a peek inside others too. There are more than 500 resident monks and every day dozens of them go into the courtyard outside the Hall of Bodhisattva Manjusri to take part in animated, hand-clapping debates. There's a map in English on a wooden board just inside the main gate.

Wútún Sì MONASTERY

Sengeshong village, 6km from Tóngrén, is the place to head if you're interested in Tibetan art. There are two monasteries, collectively known as **Wútún Sì** (吾屯寺), that are divided into an **Upper (Yango) Monastery** (上寺; Shàng Sì; admission Y10), closest to town, and a **Lower (Mango) Monastery** (下寺; Xià Sì; admission Y10). The monks will show you around whatever chapels happen to be open and then take you to a showroom or workshop. The resident artists are no amateurs – commissions for their work come in all the way from Lhasa, and prices aren't cheap. Artwork at the Upper Monastery is of an exceptionally high quality, but expect to pay hundreds of rénmínbì for the smallest *thangka,* thousands for a poster-sized one and tens or even hundreds of thousands for the largest pieces. Remember, though, that an A4-sized *thangka* takes one artist at least a month to complete, and larger pieces take two artists up to a year to finish. Around the more touristy Lower Monastery there are more showrooms and you'll find cheaper versions here (from Y300), although the quality is still high.

The Lower Monastery is easily recognisable by eight large *chörten* out front. While there, check out the 100-year-old Jampa Lhakhang (Jampa Temple) and the new chapels dedicated to Chenresig and Tsongkhapa.

The Upper Monastery includes a massive modern *chörten* as well as the old *dukhang* (assembly hall) and the new chapel dedicated to Maitreya (Shampa in Amdo dialect). The interior murals here (painted by local artists) are superb.

To get here, take a minibus (Y2 per seat) from outside Tóngrén bus station ticket office. The walk back from here is pleasant.

Gomar Gompa MONASTERY

(郭麻日寺; admission Y10) Across the Gu-chu river valley from Wútún Sì is the mysterious 400-year-old Gomar Gompa (Guōmárì Sì), a charming monastery that resembles a medieval walled village. There are 130 monks in residence living in whitewashed mud-walled courtyards and there are a few temples you can visit. The huge *chörten* outside the monastery entrance was built in the 1980s and is the biggest in Amdo. You can climb it, but remember to always walk clockwise. There are photos of the 14th Dalai Lama at the top.

To get here, turn left down a side road as you pass the last of the eight *chörten* outside Wútún Sì's Lower Monastery. Follow the road 1km across the river and turn right at the end on a main road. Then head up the track towards the giant *chörten*. Further up the valley is **Gasar Gompa**, marked by its own distinctive eight *chörtens*.

Sleeping & Eating

Tóngrén Holiday Hotel HOTEL $$

(同仁假日宾馆; Tóngrén Jiàrì Bīnguǎn; ☎872 8277; Dehelong Beilu; 德合隆北路; tw & d from Y198) Along with Yúnlóng Hotel opposite, this is the most comfortable place to stay in town. Rooms are clean, bright and spacious, and discounts bring standard ones down to Y120.

Huángnán Bīnguǎn HOTEL $

(黄南宾馆; ☎872 2293; 18 Zhongshan Lu; 中山路18号; dm Y20, tw without/with bathroom Y110/130) For something cheaper, but grottier, try this OK place on Zhongshan Lu. Twins with bathroom usually go for Y80. Note, the common bathrooms don't have showers. It's on the left as you walk away from the bridge.

TOP CHOICE **Rebkong Teahouse** TIBETAN $

(热贡茶艺; Règòng Cháyì; Zhongshan Lu; dishes Y12-35; ⌚8.30am-11pm; 📋) There are a few Tibetan teahouses in town but this is hands down the coolest. There's a small range of well-presented Tibetan dishes as well as snacks (from Y3), tea (including yak-butter tea; Y12), fresh coffee (from Y10) and beers (from Y6). Some English is spoken. It's at the far end of Zhongshan Lu from the bridge. First floor.

Information

China Construction Bank ATM (建设银行; Jiànshè Yínháng; Zhongshan Lu; 中山路) Foreign-card friendly.

Internet cafe (网吧; wǎngbā; per hr Y3; ⌚24hr) Opposite bank, inside China Telecom building.

Getting There & Around

The scenery on the road from Xīníng is awesome as it follows a tributary of the Yellow River through steep-sided gorges, but the way out to Xiàhé is even better, passing dramatic red rock scenery and the impressive Gartse Gompa, where local Tibetan herders board the bus to sell fresh yoghurt. Buses from **Tóngrén Bus Station** include the following:

Línxià Y36.50, three hours, two daily (7.30am and 8am)

Xiàhé Y25, three hours, one daily (8am)

Xīníng Y31, four hours, every 40 minutes (7.20am to 5pm)

Xúnhuà Y15, two hours, four daily (9.30am, 11am, 1pm and 3pm)

Around Tóngrén

A nice side trip from Tóngrén is to **Xúnhuà** (循化), a town in the Xúnhuà Salar Autonomous County, about 75km northeast of Tóngrén. The Salar Muslims have their origins in Samarkand and speak an isolated Turkic language, giving the region a Central Asian feel (and cuisine).

About 30km from Xúnhuà is Heaven Lake (Tiān Chí) at **Mèngdá Nature Reserve** (孟达国家自然保护区; Mèngdá Guójiā Zìrán Bǎohùqū; admission Y50; ⌚7am-6pm). The tiny lake is sacred for both Salar Muslims and Tibetan Buddhists, and is much hyped locally. There are, in truth, more picturesque lakes around Qīnghǎi, but the road to the reserve – which follows the coppery-green Yellow River as it cuts its way through a fantastically scenic gorge of rust-red cliffs – is worth the trip alone. You'll find stunning photo opportunities around every turn.

From the main gate of the reserve, you can ride horses (Y50, 30 minutes) to the lake or take a gas-powered buggy (free) to a small parking area, then walk the rest of the way.

To get the reserve you'll need to hire a taxi from outside Xúnhuà bus station. Expect to pay at least Y80 return, including waiting time. There are plenty of noodle restaurants opposite the bus station. *Miàn piàn* (面片; noodle squares; Y5) is a local favourite. If you get stuck here, **Jiāotōng Bīnguǎn** (交通宾馆; ☎0972-881 2615; d/tw Y188/228), beside the bus station, has comfortable rooms often discounted to less than Y100.

There are four buses a day back to Tóngrén (Y15, 2½ hours, 9am, 11am, 1pm, 2pm), six to Línxià (Y23, three hours, 8am, 9am, 10am, 11.30am, 1pm, 3pm) and buses every 20 minutes to Xīníng (Y25, four hours, 7am to 4pm).

THE SOURCE OF THE YELLOW RIVER

For an adventurous side-trip into remote Qīnghǎi, and a chance to experience some stunning, barren, high-plateau scenery, head towards Zaling Lake (扎陵湖; Zālíng Hú) where it's possible to find the source of arguably China's most revered waterway, the Yellow River.

The scenery around the two lakes here, and en route, is awesome. Wildlife you may spot includes foxes, marmots, eagles, antelope and, of course, plenty of yaks. There's nowhere to stay or eat, so most people visit the lake as a day trip from the two-street town of Mǎduō (玛多). It is possible to camp here in the summer but you'll need to be completely self-sufficient.

Remember this area, including Mǎduō (4260m), is over 4000m high so altitude sickness is a real risk. Consider coming from Yùshù (3680m) rather than Xīníng (2275m) so you don't have to ascend too much in one go.

In Mǎduō it's easy to find Land Cruisers to take you to the lake and back (Y800 per vehicle; three hours one way). Just left of Mǎduō bus station is **Liángyóu Bīnguǎn** (粮油宾馆; ☎0975 834 5048; s/tw Y128/168) with clean, simple rooms and shared bathroom.

Note, the widely accepted source of the Yellow River, which is marked by an engraved stone tablet, is actually just the most accessible of a number of sources. Locals, and your driver, will refer to it as *niútóubēi* (牛头碑). If you want to get to the very-hard-to-find true source of the Yellow River (黄河源头; Huánghé yuántóu) you'll need a two-day round trip from Mǎduō (sleeping in the jeep) and it will cost around Y3000 per vehicle, assuming you can find a driver willing to take you.

The bus back to Xīníng from Mǎduō leaves at 7.30am.

Guìdé 贵德

So often a dreary muddy brown, the Yellow River (黄河; Huáng Hé) sparkles a jade shade of green as it powers its way past historical Guìdé. Sitting on the riverbank here at sunset, with a beer in hand, is a great way to end the day. The old town (古城; *gǔchéng*), still largely enclosed within its crumbling 10m-high mud walls, also makes for a pleasant stroll and is a good base for your stay.

Sights

The focal point of the old town is **Jade Emperor Temple** (玉皇阁; Yùhuáng Gé; admission Y25; ⏲8.30am-6pm), a small complex first built in 1592 and restored most recently in 2001. It includes a three-storey pagoda, which can be climbed for good views, and a Confucius Temple (文庙; Wén Miào). The square beside it contains the small **Museum of Guìdé County** (admission free with temple ticket; ⏲8.30am-6pm) which houses a handful of interesting Ming and Qing artefacts recovered from the local area, but lacks English captions.

Around the back of the old town is Jìngǎng Xiàn (进港线), a dirt track that leads down to the **Yellow River**. A large suspension bridge was being built at its far end at the time of research. Once finished, it will open up the chance to explore the far side of the river. Until then, walk left from the bridge, with the river on your right until you find a nice spot. If you continue for about 2km you'll reach the huge, recently built wooden **water wheel** (水车; *shuǐchē*) by a paved riverbank area that's popular with locals.

If your legs need a rest after all that walking, hop in a taxi (Y15 to Y20 one way) to Guìdé's **hot springs** (温泉; *wēnquán*), known locally as rèshuǐ gōu (热水沟), which are a 13km-drive from town past some mightily impressive barren scenery. Here you can join the local Tibetans for a free outdoor bath. There are four or five small pools and everyone just piles in. It's not for the shy.

Sleeping & Eating

Another highlight of a stay in Guìdé is bunking up for the night in a farmers-style courtyard (农家院; *nóngjiā yuàn*). There are a handful in and around the old town offering good food and basic rooms set around a shaded garden. None have showers, but there are plenty of modern hotels that do if you can't live without one.

The delightful **Yīpǐnguó Nóngzhuāng** (伊品国农庄; ☎0974 855 4465; beds per person Y20; dishes Y15-75) is inside the old town, in the small lane to the right of the square as you're facing the pagoda. Just behind the old town walls, on the corner of the road leading down to the river is the equally cute **Qīng Xiāng Yuán Farmhouse** (清香源农庄; Qīngxiāngyuán Nóngzhuāng; ☎0974 855 4271; beds per person Y30; dishes Y10-60).

Information

China Construction Bank ATM (建设银行; Jiànshè Yínháng; 14 Yingbin Xilu, 迎宾西路) Accepts foreign cards. Turn left from the bus station and keep going.

Internet cafes (网吧; wǎngbā) On both Yingbing Xilu and Bei Dajie.

Getting There & Around

The old town is 1.5km from the bus station. Turn left out of the station on Yingbing Xilu, then left again along Xi Jie and left once more down Bei Dajie and it will be directly in front of you. Three-wheel motorised rickshaws ply the streets of Guìdé. Most short trips cost Y5.

There are regular buses back to Xīníng (Y25, 3½ hours, from 7.40am to 5.40pm). Annoyingly the Xīníng–Mǎqìn bus doesn't stop here as it passes through, so you have to go back to Xīníng if you want to head south from here on public transport.

Yùshù (Jyekundo) 玉树

☎0976 / ELEV 3680M

Up until the spring of 2010, Yùshù (Jyekundo in Tibetan) and its surrounding areas seemed to be becoming one of Qīnghǎi's hottest new adventure-travel destinations. This very remote, but exceptionally friendly town, whose population was 97% Tibetan, offered one of the best opportunities for visitors to experience genuine, undiluted Tibetan culture. And the surrounding area was dotted with dozens of impressive monasteries, famous pilgrim sites and gorgeous wooded valleys that cried out for exploration. All that changed at 7.49am on 14 April, when a 7.1-magnitutude earthquake devastated the town, leaving much of it in ruins and, according to official accounts, killing 2698 people (although some believe the true figure across the whole region to be more like 20,000). For more, see the boxed text (p941).

The slow task of rebuilding the town was already well underway when this book was being researched. And we feel travellers can play a small part in helping Yùshù recover by pumping tourist dollars into the local community.

However, it was impossible for us to gauge how quickly and to what extent the town would recover, so we recommend that before you decide to visit, you check the latest, either with hostels in Xīníng, or online through Lonely Planet's Thorn Tree forum (www.lonelyplanet.com/thorntree).

Sights & Activities

First built in 1398, the **Jyekundo Dondrubling Monastery** (Jiégǔ Sì) suffered heavy damage from the earthquake (the main prayer hall was completely destroyed and a number of resident monks were killed), but at the time of research it was hoped it could be repaired and remain in its original, dramatic location in a natural bowl overlooking the town. It's possible to walk here from town via the atmospheric **mani lhakhang** (chapel containing a large prayer wheel).

The hard-to-miss statue in Yùshù's central square represents King Gesar of Ling, a revered Tibetan warrior-god whose epic deeds are remembered in the world's longest epic poem of the same name. It was undamaged by the earthquake.

Festivals & Events

Traditionally, every 25 July, for three days, Yùshù would burst at the seams as tens of thousands of Tibetans swaggered into town for the horse festival. The 2010 event was cancelled because of the earthquake, so double-check the latest before you make this part of your itinerary.

Getting There & Away

Air

Yùshù Bātáng Airport is 25km south of town. At the time of research there were three weekly flights to Xīníng and one to Xī'ān. Before the earthquake, there had been plans to open routes to Chéngdū and Lhasa, but these had been put on hold.

Bus

A the time of research, daily bus services for Xīníng, Sěrshu (Shíqú), Gānzī, Kāngdìng and Chéngdū had resumed.

Minivans were leaving throughout the day from various parts of town to other, even more remote parts of Yùshù prefecture such as Chēngduō (称多; Trindu), Qūmálái (曲麻莱; Chumarleb), Zhìduō (治多; Drido), Nángqiān (囊谦; Nangchen) and Záduō (杂多; Dzado).

Around Yùshù

SENG-ZE GYANAK MANI WALL

嘛尼石城

Just outside Yùshù, on the road to Xiēwǔ, is what is thought to be the world's largest *mani* wall, the Seng-ze Gyanak Mani (Mānī Shíchéng). *Mani* walls are piles of stones with Buddhist mantras carved or painted on them. Founded in 1715, the Seng-ze Gyanak Mani is said to now consist of an estimated two billion mantras, piled one on top of the other over hundreds of square metres. It's an astonishing sight that grows more and more marvellous as you circumambulate the wall with the pilgrims, turn dozens of prayer wheels, and head into the pile itself for a moment of quiet reflection.

Sadly, Seng-ze Gyanak Mani suffered heavy damage from the Yùshù earthquake, but was not completely destroyed and the plan was to repair it on its original site, 3km east of Yùshù in Xīnzhài (新寨) village.

PRINCESS WENCHENG TEMPLE

文成公主庙

History credits the Tang-dynasty Chinese Princess Wencheng as instrumental in converting her husband and Tibetan king, Songtsen Gampo, to Buddhism in the 7th century. In a valley 20km south of Yùshù, a famous temple (Wénchéng Gōngzhǔ Miào) marks the spot where the princess (and possibly the king) paused for a month en route from Xī'ān to Lhasa.

The inner chapel has a rock carving (supposedly self-arising) of Vairocana (Nampa Namse in Tibetan), the Buddha of primordial wisdom, which allegedly dates from the 8th century. To the left is a statue of King Songtsen Gampo.

The temple, which suffered minor damage from the Yùshù earthquake, is small, and few linger in it long, but allow time to explore the nearby hills. Here a sprawling spider's web of blue, red, yellow, white and pink prayer flags runs up the slopes, down the slopes and over the ravine, covering every inch of land, and is one of the most extraordinary sights imaginable.

A steep trail (a popular *kora* route for pilgrims) ascends from the end of the row of eight *chörtens* to the left of the temple. At the end of the trail head up the grassy side valley for some great hiking and stunning open views.

Minibuses run here from Yùshù.

SURVIVING THE YÙSHÙ EARTHQUAKE

Jamin York, an American who has lived for many years on the Tibetan plateau, was living in Yùshù (Jyekundo) in 2010 with his wife and two young sons when the town was devastated by a massive earthquake that destroyed most of the buildings and killed thousands of people. Jamin, his wife and his youngest son, who was just 18 months old at the time, had been woken by a much smaller earthquake at around 4am and had been unable to get back to sleep. Then, at 7.49am, the 7.1-magnitude earthquake struck.

'Our 3rd-floor apartment began to shake violently,' he said. 'My wife and younger son were in the living room and were tossed across the room, hitting the concrete floor. My older son (three years old) was in the back bedroom, still asleep, while I was near the front door of our apartment. My wife quickly grabbed our younger son off the floor and staggered to the doorway. I ran to the back bedroom, navigating my way through shattered glass, overturned furniture and broken water pipes, to get our older son. My wife and I, each with a child in hand, opened the door of our apartment where we were met by a neighbour running down the stairs who graciously took our older son from us and helped us out of the building.

'The air was filled with dust, making it impossible to see more than 15 or 20 metres. As the dust began to settle, though, we realised this was a major earthquake. People were screaming all around us for help. Injured people, some quite severe, were crawling out to the road from the twisted mess that was once their home. Most of the buildings around us were completely destroyed. Many had fallen all the way down while others were still standing, but had extensive cracks and holes. We stood, in a state of shock in the freezing morning wind, wondering what to do next.

'Fortunately our 4WD vehicle was undamaged so for the next hour my family and I sat inside it trying to put together a plan. There were several small aftershocks so our biggest concern was finding a safe, open area to be in. We saw that hundreds of people were walking towards Gesar Sq in the middle of town, so we followed them. As we drove to the square, most of the buildings along the way were heavily damaged. Thousands of injured people lined the road and we saw many who had been killed. The town of Jyekundo, as I knew it, was gone. The entire area was destroyed.

'A friend of ours found us and offered to look after my family while I went back to our apartment to try and get some necessities – we had no food, water or adequate clothing for the bitterly cold weather. I walked roughly 1km back to our complex. Along the way, I passed a makeshift hospital. A van pulled up and two guys were carrying a man to one of the handful of nurses who was helping the injured. I decided to lend a hand. When I began to help carry the man, I realized that he was already dead. There were close to 75 people in the makeshift hospital, but half of them were already dead. It was turning into a makeshift morgue.

'The police soon asked everyone in town to move out to the horse festival grounds on the far west end of town. When we arrived, we saw that thousands of people were already there, most with just the clothes they had on their backs. Most people lost all of their possessions. Everyone we talked to had lost at least one loved one, if not more. After spending over seven hours in the earthquake zone, we finally heard a report that the highway to Xīníng was open. We spent the next two days driving back to the city, thankful to be alive.'

NANGCHEN 囊谦

The scenic county of Nangchen (Nángqiān), a former Tibetan kingdom, is the end of the line for most travellers. While some attempt to continue across the Qinghai–Tibet border into Riwoche and Chamdo, without the proper permits (and guide and driver) you are most likely to be turned back (and fined). In any case, the drive here and back to Yùshù is scenic enough, and the charming little county capital of Sharda (3550m) about as off-the-beaten-path as you can get.

Minivans and the odd Land Cruiser leave for Nangchen from Yùshù when full. The paved road to Nangchen goes over three

WORTH A TRIP

MONASTERIES AROUND YÙSHÙ

The road from Yùshù to Xiāwǔ is dotted with monasteries set among beautiful landscapes, perfect for hiking. Worth visiting is **Sebda Gompa** (赛巴寺; Sàibǎ Sì), about 15km from Yùshù. The main assembly hall at the monastery is impressive, but most surprising is the new chapel featuring a huge 18m statue of Guru Rinpoche, with smaller statues of his various manifestations on either side. The adjacent **ethnographic museum** (admission Y10) has some offbeat gems like traditional clothing, swords and stuffed animals. If you have more time you can explore the ruins of the old monastery on the ridge behind the *gompa* or do some great hiking in the opposite valley.

At Xiāwǔ village, by the turn-off to Sěrshu, is the Sakyapa-school **Drogon Gompa** (歇武寺; Xiāwǔ Sì), in a fine hillside location. Atop the hill is the scary *gönkhang* (protector chapel), adorned with snarling stuffed wolves and Tantric masks. Only men may enter this chapel.

Minivans ply the route between Yùshù and Xiāwǔ from where you should be able to get onward transport to Sěrshu .

passes and via **Lungshi Gompa** (龙西寺; Lóngxī Sì) en route.

In Sharda, you can find basic accommodation at the **Sān Jiāng Yuán Bīnguǎn** (三江源宾馆; ☎159 0976 6903; d/tr without bathroom Y80/210, d with bathroom Y150). There are no common showers, but ask the owner politely and he may open up the shower in a double room if the place isn't busy.

Golmud 格尔木

☎0979 / POP 200,000 / ELEV 2800M

No tourist sights, little in the way of entertainment and located 150km away from… well…anything, the small town of Golmud (Gé'ěrmù) exists for most travellers simply as a transportation hub for Lhasa, Dūnhuáng (in Gānsù) and Huātǔgōu (on the way to Xīnjiāng).

Sleeping

Very few of Golmud's many hotels accept foreigners. The following are exceptions.

Golmud Mansions HOTEL $$
(格尔木大厦; Gé'ěrmù Dàshà; ☎845 0968; 33 Yingbin Lu; 迎宾路33号; d & tw from Y218; @) A decent choice if you need to be close to the train station, standard rooms are big, clean and comfortable and can be nabbed for Y198. Better quality rooms with internet access cost an extra Y70. The triple-bed dorms (Y298 before discounts) have no common showers.

Dōngfāng Hotel HOTEL $
(东方宾馆; Dōngfāng Bīnguǎn; ☎841 0011; 7 Bayi Lu; 八一路7号; d & tw from Y216) In the more lively end of town, Dōngfāng has neat and tidy rooms that go for Y108 after discounts and some staff who speak a bit of English.

Eating & Drinking

Bayi Lu and Kunlun Lu are lined with small restaurants, as is the train station area.

Ālán Cāntīng MUSLIM $
(阿兰餐厅; 48-1 Bayi Lu; dishes Y5-48; ⏲8.30am-9pm) Great noodles (Y5 to Y10). Try *gānbàn miàn* (干拌面; spaghetti-style noodles with meat sauce; Y6) or *niúròu miàn* (牛肉面; beef noodles; Y5). Has other dishes in a separate photo menu.

Xiāngsìhǎi Xiǎochǎo SICHUANESE $
(香四海小炒; Kunlun Lu; dishes Y12-40; ⏲10am-10pm) Well-run restaurant across from main gate of Golmud Hotel. Part picture menu.

Dio Coffee CAFE
(迪欧咖啡; Dí'ōu Kāfēi; Yuhong Xiang; 育红巷; ⏲9am-1.30am; coffee/tea from Y28/Y20; wi-fi) Get your laptop out, order a latte and forget for a moment that you were ever in Qīnghǎi.

Information

Bank of China (中国银行; Zhōngguó Yínháng; cnr Kunlun Lu & Chaidamu Lu; ⏲9am-5pm Mon-Fri, 10am-4.30pm Sat & Sun) Changes travellers cheques and cash. Foreign-friendly ATM.

CAAC (机场售票处; Jīchǎng Shòupiàochù; ☎24hr booking line 842 3333; Chaidamu Lu; ⏲8.30am-6pm) The place to come for flight tickets if you don't book online.

China International Travel Service (CITS;中国国际旅行社; Zhōngguó Guójì Lǚxíngshè; ☎849

Golmud

Golmud

Sleeping

1 Dōngfāng Hotel B1
2 Golmud Mansions B3

Eating

3 Ālán Cāntīng B1
4 Xiāngsìhǎi Xiǎochǎo A2

Drinking

5 Dio Coffee B2

6275; 60 Bayi Zhonglu, 4th fl; 八一中路60号4层; ⌚8.30am-6pm Mon-Fri) The only place in town that can arrange Tibet permits. At the time of research they were only sold as part of all-inclusive tours. No CITS sign outside. Look instead for the characters 中国旅游 (Zhōngguó Lǚyóu; China Travel).

China Post (中国邮政; Zhōngguó Yóuzhèng; Chaidamu Lu; ⌚9am-5.30pm)

Public Security Bureau (PSB; 公安局; Gōng'ānjú; 6 Chaidamu Lu; ⌚8am-noon & 2.30-5pm Mon-Fri) Can extend visas, and sells Dūnhuáng permits (lǚxíng zhèng; Y50).

Ruìqīng Internet (Ruìqīng Wǎngluò; Bayi Lu; 八一路; per hr Y2; ⌚24hr) Next to Dōngfāng Hotel. No English sign.

Getting There & Away

Air

Only four flights a week (Monday, Wednesday, Friday and Sunday) leave Golmud airport. They all first go to Xīníng (Y1400 before discounts), then to Xī'ān. Taxis are the only way to get to the airport (Y20, 30 minutes).

Bus

There are two daily buses to Dūnhuáng (Y93/Y108, eight to nine hours, 9am/6pm). The evening one is a sleeper. At the time of research, foreigners still needed to first buy a Dūnhuáng travel permit (旅行证; lǚxíng zhèng; Y50) from Golmud PSB. Likewise, there are two daily buses to Huātǔgōu (Y97/Y125, five hours, 10.30am/midday), the second again being a sleeper (just in case you fancy an afternoon nap). From Huātǔgōu you can catch buses to Charklik (Ruòqiāng) in Xīnjiāng.

These days most people prefer to take the train to Lhasa, but there is still one bus a day that leaves from the **Tibet Bus Station** (西藏汽车站; Xīzàng Qìchēzhàn; 157 1979 5134; 11 Yanqiao Zhonglu) between 11am and 2pm (they decide the evening before). It takes 16 to 18 hours. If you're Chinese, a ticket costs Y240. If you're not, it costs Y1000! That doesn't include your Tibet permit which, if you haven't prearranged, you must get through CITS.

Train

Golmud marks the start of the **Qīnghǎi–Tibet Railway**, although most passengers get on their Lhasa-bound train earlier down the line in places such as Xīníng, Chéngdū or Běijīng. As with anywhere, you'll need your Tibet permit to be in order to use the Lhasa train. Trains tend to pass through Golmud late in the evening or at night. Destinations include the following:

XĪNÍNG Y201, 10 hours, eight daily from 9pm to 2.19am

LÁNZHŌU Y242, 12 hours, six daily from 9.50pm to 2.19am

LHASA Y254, 15hours, seven daily from 12.40am to 5.48am

Getting Around

Bus 1 (Y1) runs from the train station to the junction with Bayi Lu and Kunlun Zhonglu. Bus 2 (Y1) goes from the Tibet Bus Station along Bayi Lu and eventually on to the train station. Taxis start at Y5.

Tibet

Includes »

Best Places to Eat

» Snowland Restaurant (p887)

» Third Eye Restaurant (p896)

» Friendship Snowland Restaurant (p893)

Best Places to Stay

» Nomad's tents at Everest Base Camp (p898)

» Yabshi Phunkhang (p886)

» Kyichu Hotel (p886)

Why Go?

Though never exactly a Shangri La, Tibet has nonetheless held the imagination of Western spiritual seekers, adventurers and intrepid travellers for centuries. Double the size of France, and home to a mere three million people, the 'roof of the world' promises incredible high-altitude scenery, awe-inspiring monastic cities, epic road trips and a beautiful, unique Himalayan culture that has endured a half-century of assault and hardship.

Extremely popular with Chinese travellers and with one of the fastest growth rates in China, much of Tibet is changing fast, with new paved roads, airports and a railway spur planned for the coming years. The magic of old Tibet is still there, you just to have to work a bit harder to find it these days.

When to Go

Lhasa

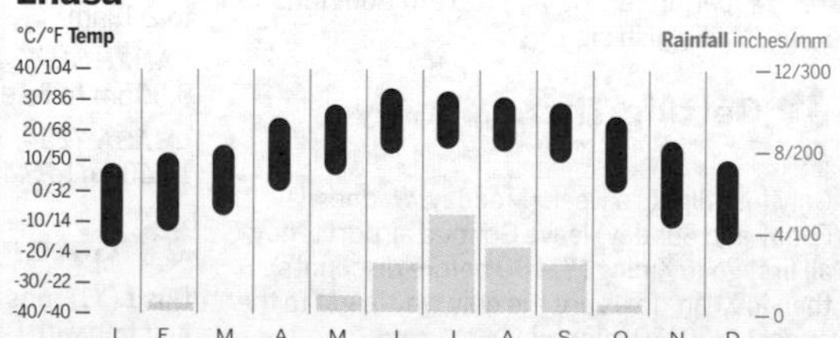

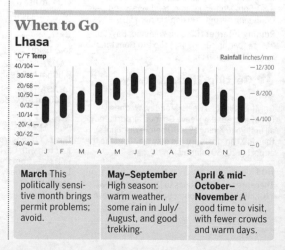

March This politically sensitive month brings permit problems; avoid.

May–September High season: warm weather, some rain in July/August, and good trekking.

April & mid-October–November A good time to visit, with fewer crowds and warm days.

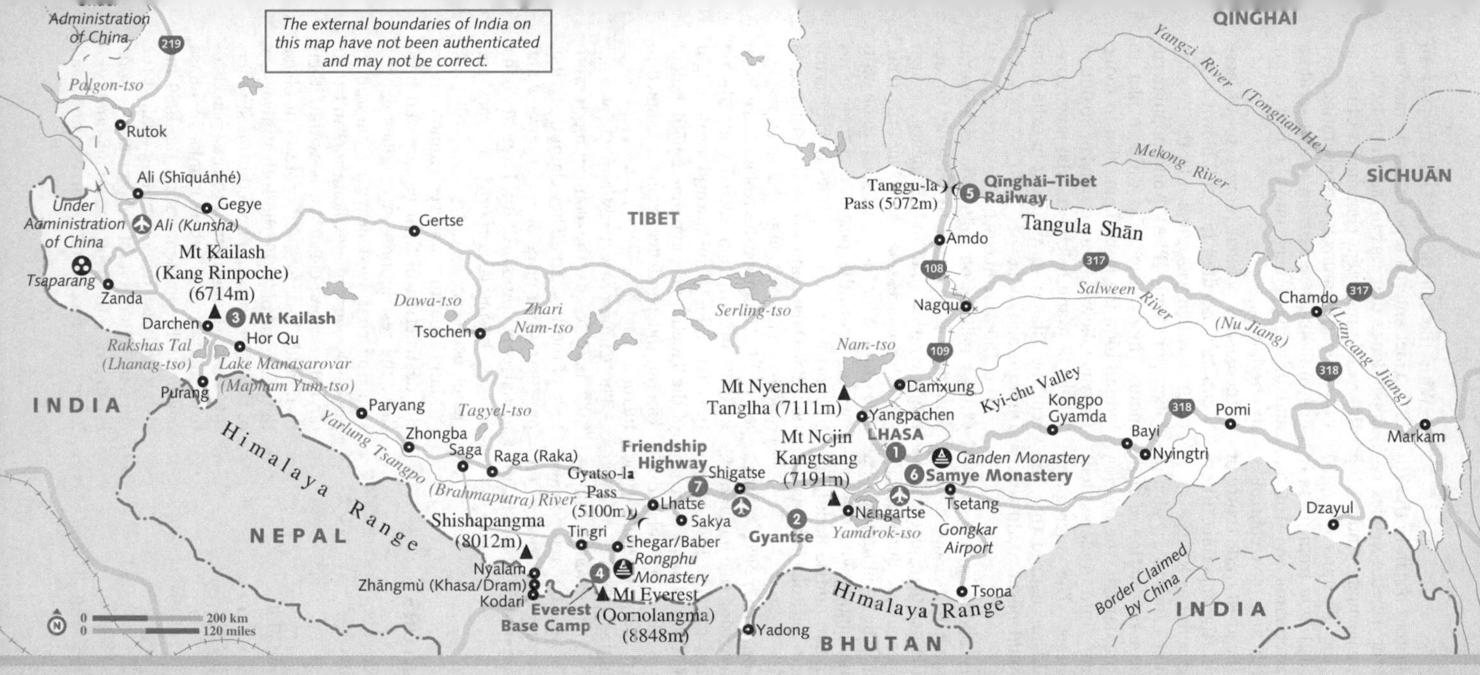

Tibet Highlights

1 Mix with pilgrims and travellers in the Potala Palace, Jokhang Temple and Barkhor circuit in **Lhasa** (p882)

2 Count the murals in the 108 chapels of the **Gyantse Kumbum** (p894), a nine-storey *chörten* (Tibetan stupa)

3 Follow fellow pilgrims on the three-day *kora* (pilgrim circuit) around **Mt Kailash** (p901)

4 Rouse yourself from a yak-wool tent to catch the first light upon the world's highest peak from **Everest Base Camp** (p898)

5 See why Tibet is the 'roof of the world' as you ride the **Qīnghǎi–Tibet Railway** (p890)

6 Take a ferry across the Yarlung Tsangpo to the **Samye Monastery** (p893)

7 Take the 4WD trip along the **Friendship Highway** (p893) from Lhasa to Kathmandu

History

Recorded Tibetan history began in the 7th century AD, when the Tibetan armies began to assemble a great empire. Under King Songtsen Gampo, the Tibetans occupied Nepal and collected tribute from parts of Yúnnán. Shortly afterwards the Tibetan armies moved north and took control of the Silk Road and the great trade centre of Kashgar, even sacking the imperial Chinese city of Cháng'ān (present-day Xī'ān).

Tibetan expansion came to an abrupt halt in 842 with the assassination of anti-Buddhist King Langdarma; the region subsequently broke into independent feuding principalities. The increasing influence of Buddhism ensured that the Tibetan armies would never again leave their high plateau.

By the 7th century, Buddhism had spread through Tibet, though it had taken on a unique form, as it adopted many of the rituals of Bön (the indigenous pre-Buddhist belief system of Tibet). The combination of a traditional animistic religion with the esoteric practices of Indian tantric Buddhism proved a very potent spiritual formula for the Tibetans.

From the 13th century, power politics began to play an increasing role in religion. In 1641, the Gelugpa ('Yellow Hat' order) used the support of Mongol troops to crush the Sakyapa, their rivals. It was also during this time of partisan struggle that the Gelugpa leader adopted the title of Dalai Lama (Ocean of Wisdom), given to him by the Mongols. From here on out, religion and politics in Tibet became inextricably entwined and both were presided over by the Dalai Lama.

PRICE INDICATORS

The following price indicators are used in this chapter:

Sleeping

$	less than Y130
$$	Y130 to Y400
$$$	more than Y400

Eating

$	less than Y30
$$	Y30 to Y80
$$$	more than Y80

With the fall of the Qing dynasty in 1911, Tibet entered a period of de facto independence that was to last until 1950. In this year a resurgent communist China invaded Tibet, claiming it was 'liberating' over one million Tibetans from feudal serfdom and bringing it back into the fold of the motherland.

Increasing popular unrest to Chinese occupation resulted in a full-blown revolt in 1959, which was crushed by the People's Liberation Army (PLA). Amid popular rumours (likely true) of a Chinese plot to kidnap him, the Dalai Lama fled to India. He was followed by an exodus of 80,000 of Tibet's best and brightest, who now represent the Tibetan government-in-exile from Dharamsala, India.

The Dalai Lama, who has referred to China's policies on migration as 'cultural genocide', is resigned to pushing for autonomy rather than independence, though even that concession has borne little fruit. The Chinese for their part seem to be waiting for him to die, positioning themselves to control the future politics of reincarnation. The Dalai Lama's tireless insistence on a non-violent solution to the Tibet problem led to him winning the Nobel Peace Prize in 1989, but although global sympathy on the part of the Western world for the plight of the Tibetan people remains high, talk of Tibetan independence seems consigned to history.

The Chinese are truly baffled by what they perceive as the continuing ingratitude of the Tibetans. They claim that Tibet pre-1950 was a place of abject poverty and feudal exploitation. China brought roads, schools, hospitals, airports, factories and rising incomes.

Many Tibetans, however, cannot forgive the destruction of their culture and heritage, the restrictions on religious expression, the continued heavy military/police presence, economic exploitation and their obvious second-class status within their own land. The riots and protests in Lhasa in the spring of 2008 (the 49th anniversary of the 1959 uprising) brought this simmering dissatisfaction out into the open. Protests that started when monks in Lhasa began both commemorating the 1959 uprising and also demonstrating against the current detention of fellow monks soon escalated into demonstrations and violence after reports of the arrests and beatings of protesting monks. Lhasa erupted into full-scale riots and protests spread to other Tibetan areas in Gānsù, Sìchuān and Qīnghǎi provinces. The Chinese response to the protests was predictable: arrest, imprisonment and an increased police presence in many monasteries. Armed riot police continue to occupy street corners in Lhasa's old town.

As immigration and breakneck modernisation continue, the government is gambling that economic advances will diffuse the Tibetans' religious and political aspirations. It's a policy that is working in the rest of China. It remains to be seen whether Tibetans will be so easily bought.

Climate

Most of Tibet is a high-altitude desert plateau at more than 4000m and many passes exceed 5000m. Days in summer (June to September) are warm, sunny and dry, and you can expect some rainfall in southern Tibet in the evenings, but temperatures drop quickly after dark. Sunlight is very strong at these altitudes, so bring plenty of high-factor sunscreen and lip balm.

Language

Most urban Tibetans speak Mandarin in addition to Tibetan. Even in the countryside you can get by with basic Mandarin in most restaurants and hotels, since they are normally run by Mandarin-speaking Han or Hui Chinese. That said, Tibetans are extremely pleased when foreign visitors at least greet them in Tibetan, so it's well worth learning a few phrases. In Lhasa and Shigatse, it is easy to get by with English at the more popular restaurants and hotels.

Getting There & Away

NEPAL ROUTE The 865km road connecting Lhasa with Kathmandu is known as the Friendship Highway (see p893). The main means of transport for foreigners is a rented vehicle.

When travelling from Nepal to Lhasa, foreigners generally arrange transport and permits through agencies in Kathmandu. Be careful with whom you organise your trip – the vast majority of complaints about Tibet that we receive have been about budget trips from Kathmandu. The most common option is a seven-day overland budget tour, which run two or three times a week and cost from US$350, plus visa fees and return flight costs (around US$400). There are also fly-in, fly-out options.

Regardless of what the agency says, you will probably end up in a bus with travellers with other companies. Accommodation en route is pretty simple. Most agencies advertising in Thamel are agents only; they don't actually run the trips. The better agencies in Kathmandu include the following:

Ecotrek (☎01-4423207; www.ecotrek.com.np, www.ecotreknepl.com; Thamel)

Explore Nepal Richa Tours & Travel (☎01-4423064; www.explorenepalricha.com; 2nd fl, Namche Bazaar Bldg, Tri Devi Marg, Thamel)

Green Hill Tours (☎01-4700803; www.greenhill-tours.com; Thamel)

Royal Mount Trekking (☎01-4241452; www.royaltibet.com; Durbar Marg)

Tashi Delek Nepal Treks & Expeditions (☎01-4410746; www.tashidelektreks.com.np; Thamel)

Whatever you do, when coming from Nepal do *not* underestimate the sudden rise in elevation; altitude sickness is very common. It is especially not recommended to visit Everest Base Camp within a few days of leaving Kathmandu.

Heading to Nepal, you will arrange a 4WD trip as part of your Tibet tour.

The **Nepalese Consulate-General** (尼泊尔领事馆; Níbó'ěr Lǐngshìguǎn; Map p884; ☎0891-681 5744; www.nepalembassy.org.cn; 13 Luobulingka Beilu; ⏲10am-12.30pm Mon-Fri) in Lhasa issues visas in 24 hours. The current fee for a 15-/30-/90-day visa is Y175/280/700. Bring a visa photo. It's also possible to obtain visas at Kodari, the Nepalese border town (see p900).

QĪNGHǍI ROUTE Now that the railway connects Lhasa with Qīnghǎi, there is no reason to suffer the long ride on the sleeper bus from Golmud. Bear in mind that it is much harder to get train tickets *to* Lhasa than *from* Lhasa, so flying in and taking a train out makes sense – see p890 for details.

OTHER ROUTES Between Lhasa and Sìchuān, Yúnnán and Xīnjiāng provinces are some of the wildest, highest and most remote routes in the world. It's generally possible to enter and leave Tibet via these routes if you are travelling with an organised tour and have the proper permits. In 2010, permits were impossible to obtain for overland routes through eastern Tibet, but these should reopen soon.

If you try to sneak in, note that the authorities sometimes come down very heavily on travellers and the drivers giving them a lift. At the very least be aware that you are putting anyone who gives you a ride at risk of being fined and losing a driving licence.

TIBET TRAVEL RESTRICTIONS

Troubled Tibet is essentially part of China, yet in many ways separate from it. Travel regulations here differ markedly from the rest of the nation; tourists currently need to arrange a tour in order to visit any place in the Tibetan Autonomous Region (TAR).

Travel regulations are in constant flux in Tibet and travel infrastructure is changing at a rapid rate. Be sure to check current regulations with travel companies and check the designated Tibet branch of the **Lonely Planet Thorn Tree** (http://thorntreelonelyplanet.com).

Travellers to Tibet face much tighter restrictions than in other parts of China. Authorities would say this is for tourists' protection, though it has more to do with foreigners' tendency to sympathise with the Tibetan cause and bear witness to political tensions. Recent restrictions forbid foreigners from visiting a Tibetan home or staying overnight in a monastery.

At the time of research:

» Foreign travellers need a Tibet Tourism Bureau (TTB) permit to get into Tibet and an Alien Travel Permit (and other permits) to travel outside Lhasa.

» To get these permits you need to pre-book an itinerary, a guide for your entire stay and transport for outside Lhasa with an agency, before travelling to Tibet.

» You can be a 'group' of any size (including a group of one) but you'll find 4WD rates cheapest if you travel in a group of three or four.

» To get on a plane or train to Lhasa you need to show your TTB permit. For the plane you need the original, so your agency will courier that to you at an address in China (normally a hostel). A printout/copy is currently acceptable for the train.

» You don't need to book transport for your time in Lhasa but you do need to visit the main monasteries with a guide.

» For travel outside Lhasa you will need to pre-arrange transport hire (normally a 4WD). You cannot travel outside Lhasa independently and cannot take public transport. In case this changes, we have included basic information on public transport.

» Most agencies charge around Y600 for permits, Y250 per day for a guide and anywhere from US$80 to US$150 per day for 4WD hire (not per person). Many agencies let you book your own accommodation.

» Travel from Nepal to Tibet brings its own complications, since foreigners can only travel on a group visa (a separate piece of paper), which is only valid from two to three weeks and is almost impossible to extend. If you already have a Chinese visa in your passport it will be cancelled. Group visas cost US$58 and take 10 days, or you can pay US$118 for express service. US citizens pay a surcharge. See p890.

Getting Around

These days almost all foreigners travel around Tibet in a rented 4WD. Public buses outside Lhasa are off limits to foreigners, and bus stations generally won't sell you a ticket.

As for cycling – it's possible, but currently expensive, as you still need a guide and transport, even if you're not travelling in it! Cyclists in Tibet have died from road accidents, hypothermia and pneumonia. Tibet is not the place to learn the ins and outs of long-distance cycling – do your training elsewhere. For experienced cyclists, the Lhasa–Kathmandu trip is one of the world's great rides. Check out *Tibet Overland: A Route and Planning Guide for Mountain Bikers and Other Overlanders* by Kym McConnell, and www.tibetoverland.com.

Lhasa ལྷ་ས་ 拉萨

☎0891 / POP 400,000 / ELEV 3650M

Lhasa is the traditional political and spiritual centre of the Tibetan world. Despite rampant Chinese-led modernisation Tibet's premodern and sacred heritage survives in the form of the grand Potala Palace (former seat of the Dalai Lama), the ancient Jokhang Temple (Tibet's first and most holy), the great monastic centres of Sera, Drepung and Ganden, and the city's countless other smaller temples, hermitages, caves, sacred rocks, pilgrim paths, and prayer-flag-bedecked hilltops.

The companies listed here can arrange tours and permits for Tibet and are used to dealing with individual travellers.

Lhasa

» **Tibet F.I.T. Travel** (☎634 9239; www.tibetfit.com; lhakpa88@yahoo.com; 2nd fl, Snowland Hotel, 4 Zangyiyuan Lu) Contact Lhakpa Tsering.

» **Namchen Tours** (www.shangrilatours.com) Based at Barkhor Namchen House, p887, in Lhasa's old town.

» **China International Travel Service** (CITS; 中国国际旅行社; Zhōngguó Guójì Lǚxíngshè; ☎691 2080; tibetanintibet@yahoo.cn; Zangyiyuan Lu) Contact Tenzin.

» **Shigatse Travels** (☎633 0489; www.shigatsetravels.com; Yak Hotel, 100 Beijing Donglu) Higher-end tours.

» **Snow Lion Tours** (☎134 3932 9243; www.snowliontours.com; 1 Danjielin Lu) Contact Wangden Tsering, with a branch in Xīníng and an office in Běijīng.

» **Spinn Café** (☎136 5952 3997; www.cafespinn.com; 135 Beijing Donglu) Contact Kong/Pazu.

Other Cities in China

» **Leo Hostel** (广聚元饭店; Guǎngjùyuán Fàndiàn; Map p48; ☎10-8660 8923; www.leohostel.com; 52 Dazhalan Xijie, Qiánmēn, Běijīng)

» **Tibetan Connections** (☎135 1973 7734; www.tibetanconnections.com; 16th fl, Bldg No 5, International Village Apartments, 2-32 Jiancai Xiang) Recommended.

» **Sim's Cozy Travel** (☎028-8335 5322, 133 9819 5552; www.gogosc.com; Sim's Cozy Guest House, Chéngdū) Popular agency and hostel (p709) in Chéngdū.

» **Wind Horse Adventure Tours** (☎971-613 1358; www.windhorseadventuretours.com; 19 Nan Dajie, Xīníng) Contact Tashi Phuntsok.

For overland trips from Yúnnán, consult companies such as **Khampa Caravan** (康巴商道探险旅行社; Kāngbā Shāngdào Tànxiǎn Lǚxíngshè; www.khampacaravan.com), p677 and **Haiwei Trails** (www.haiweitrails.com), p677, in Zhōngdiàn, and **China Minority Travel** (www.china-travel.nl) in Dàlǐ, p659.

See also our Itineraries chapter for a permit-free alternative way to see Tibetan lands.

In Lhasa, the colour, humour and religious devotion of the immensely likeable Tibetan people is as much of a highlight as the big sights. This is also one of Asia's best people-watching towns, and the old town is one of the most fascinating to explore.

Lhasa is a pretty comfortable travellers' destination these days. There are dozens of good budget and midrange hotels and no shortage of excellent inexpensive restaurants. English is not widely spoken, but you'll have no trouble in the more popular hotels, restaurants, cafes and travel agencies. Lhasa is also currently the only place in Tibet where you have a certain freedom to explore without your guide, plus it's cheaper than the rest of Tibet because you don't need to hire transport.

Lhasa divides clearly into a sprawling Chinese section to the west and a much smaller but infinitely more interesting Tibetan old town in the east, centred on the wonderful Barkhor area. The latter has the best food and accommodation and is easily the best place to be based.

Sights

In addition to the main sights listed here, Lhasa's old town is worth exploring for its backstreet temples, craft shops and interesting Muslim neighbourhood.

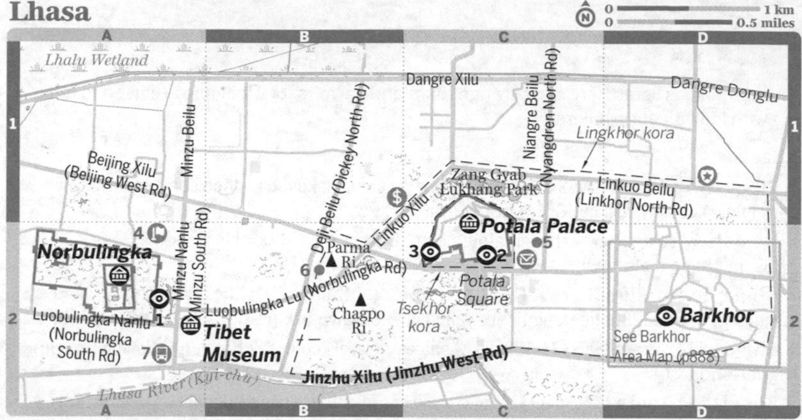

Barkhor

PILGRIM CIRCUIT

(བར་འཁོར་ ; 八廓; Bākuò; Map p888) It's impossible not to be swept up in the wondrous tide of humanity that is the Barkhor, a *kora* (pilgrim circuit) that winds clockwise around the periphery of the Jokhang Temple. You'll swear it possesses some spiritual centrifugal force, as every time you approach within 50m, you somehow get sucked right in and gladly wind up making the whole circuit again! Spiritual souvenirs and pilgrim accessories line the entire circuit, with stalls selling prayer flags, amulets, turquoise jewellery, Tibetan boots, cowboy hats, yak butter and juniper incense. It's the perfect place to start your explorations of Lhasa, and the last spot you'll want to see before you bid the city farewell.

The crowd of pilgrims is captivating. Braided-haired Khambas from eastern Tibet swagger in huge *chubas* (cloaks) with ornate daggers; and Amdowa nomads from the northeast wear ragged sheepskins or, for women, incredibly ornate braids and coral headpieces.

Jokhang Temple

TEMPLE

(ཇོ་ཁང་ ; 大昭寺; Dàzhāo Sì; Map p888; admission Y85; ⏲inner chapels 8am-12.30pm) The 1300-year-old Jokhang Temple is the spiritual heart of Tibet: the continuous waves of awestruck pilgrims prostrating themselves outside are testament to its timeless allure.

The Jokhang was originally built to house an image of Buddha brought to Tibet by King Songtsen Gampo's Nepalese wife. However, another image, the Jowa Sakyamuni, was later moved here by the king's other wife (the Chinese Princess Wencheng), and it is this image that gives the Jokhang both its name and spiritual potency: Jokhang means 'chapel of the Jowo' and the central golden Buddha here is the most revered in all of Tibet.

The two-storeyed Jokhang is best visited in the morning, though the crowds of yak-butter-spooning pilgrims can be thick. Access is possible in the afternoon through a side entrance but the interior chapels are often shut and there are no pilgrims.

Potala Palace

PALACE

(པོ་ཏ་ལ་ ; 布达拉宫; Bùdálā Gōng; Map p884; admission Y100; ⏲9.30am-3pm before 1 May, 9am-3.30pm after 1 May, interior chapels close 4.30pm) The magnificent Potala Palace, once the seat of the Tibetan government and the winter residence of the Dalai Lamas, is Lhasa's cardinal landmark. Your first sight of its towering, fortress-like walls is a moment you'll remember for a long time.

An architectural wonder even by modern standards, the palace rises 13 storeys from 130m-high Marpo Ri (Red Hill) and contains more than a thousand rooms. Pilgrims and tourists alike shuffle down through the three storeys, trying to take in the magnificent chapels and prayer halls.

The first recorded use of the site dates from the 7th century AD, when King Songtsen Gampo built a palace here. Construction of the present structure began during the reign of the fifth Dalai Lama in 1645 and took divisions of labourers and artisans more than 50 years to complete. It is impressive enough to have caused Zhou

Lhasa

Top Sights

- Barkhor D2
- Norbulingka A2
- Potala Palace C2
- Tibet Museum A2

Sights

- 1 Norbulingka Ticket Office A2
- 2 Potala South Entrance C2
- 3 Potala Ticket Booth C2

Information

- 4 Nepali Consulate-General A2

Transport

- 5 CAAC & Buses to Airport C2
- 6 City Train Ticket Office B2
- 7 Western (Main) Bus Station A2

Enlai to send his own troops to protect it from the Red Guards during the Cultural Revolution.

The layout of the Potala Palace includes the rooftop **White Palace** (the eastern part of the building), used for the living quarters of the Dalai Lama, and the central **Red Palace**, used for religious functions. The most stunning chapels of the Red Palace house the jewel-bedecked golden *chörten* (Tibetan stupa) tombs of several previous Dalai Lamas. The apartments of the 13th and 14th Dalai Lamas, in the White Palace, offer a more personal insight into life in the palace. Grand aesthetics and history aside, however, one can't help noticing that today it is essentially an empty shell, notably missing its main occupant, the Dalai Lama, and a cavernous memorial to what once was.

Visiting the Potala

Tickets for the Potala are limited. The day before you wish to visit, take your passport and head to the far southwest exit (yes, exit) and look for the **ticket booth** just inside the gate. After showing your passport you will receive a free ticket voucher with a time stamped on it.

The next day, be at the **south entrance** 30 minutes before the time on the voucher (tour groups use the southeast entrance). After a security check, follow the other visitors to the stairs up into the palace. Halfway up you'll pass the actual ticket booth. Note that if you arrive later than the time on your voucher (or if you forget your voucher) you can be refused a ticket. Photography isn't allowed inside the chapels.

Norbulingka SUMMER PALACE

(ནོར་བུ་གླིང་ཁ་; 罗布林卡; Luóbùlínkǎ; Minzu Lu; Map p884; admission Y60; 9am-6.30pm) About 3km west of the Potala Palace is the Norbulingka, the former summer residence of the Dalai Lama. The pleasant park contains several palaces and chapels, the highlight of which is the **New Summer Palace** (Takten Migyü Podrang), built by the current (14th) Dalai Lama, but it's not really worth the entry fee.

FREE **Tibet Museum** MUSEUM

(འགྲེམས་སྟོན་ཁང་; 西藏博物馆; Xīzàng Bówùguǎn; Map p884; Minzu Nanlu; 9am-6.30pm) This museum has some interesting displays, if you can filter out the Chinese propaganda. Starting with the prehistory of Tibet, the multiple halls cover everything from weapons and musical instruments, to folk handicrafts and fine ancient *thangkas* (Tibetan sacred art). Look for the 18th-century golden urn (exhibit No 310) used by the Chinese to recognise their version of the Panchen Lama. A useful handheld audio self-touring device is available for Y20.

Activities

Raft Tibet RAFTING, HORSE RIDING

(Map p888; 136 3890 0332; www.windhorsetibet.com; Zangyiyuan Lu) Tibet Wind Horse Adventure offers half-/one-/two-day (Y600/760/1520) rafting trips between June and October, as well as day trips on horseback (Y760).

Festivals & Events

Tibetan festivals are held according to the Tibetan lunar calendar, which usually lags at least a month behind the West's Gregorian calendar. The following is a brief selection of Lhasa's major festivals.

Losar Festival

Taking place in the first week of the first lunar month (February), there are performances of Tibetan opera, prayer ceremonies at the Jokhang and Nechung Monastery, and the streets are thronged with Tibetans dressed in their finest.

Saga Dawa

The 15th day (full moon) of the fourth lunar month (May/June) sees huge numbers of pilgrims walking the Lingkhor pilgrim circuit.

LHASA'S PILGRIM CIRCUITS

Lhasa's four main *koras* (pilgrim circuits) are well worth walking, especially during the Saga Dawa festival, when the distinction between tourist and pilgrim can become very fine. Remember always to proceed clockwise.

» **Nangkhor** Encircles the inner precincts of the Jokhang.

» **Barkhor** Traces the outskirts of the Jokhang.

» **Lingkhor** You can join the 8km-long circuit anywhere, but the most interesting section is from the southeastern old town to the Potala Palace.

» **Potala Kora (Tsekhor)** An almost continuous circuit of prayer wheels, *chörtens* (Tibetan stupas), rock paintings and chapels encircles the Potala Palace.

Worship of the Buddha

During the second week of the fifth lunar month (June), the parks of Lhasa, in particular the Norbulingka, are crowded with picnickers.

Drepung Festival

The 30th day of the sixth lunar month (July) is celebrated with the hanging at dawn of a huge *thangka* at Drepung Monastery. Lamas and monks perform opera in the main courtyard.

Shötun Festival

The first week of the seventh lunar month (August) sees the unveiling of a giant *thangka* at Drepung Monastery, then moves down to Sera and down to the Norbulingka for performances of *lhamo* (Tibetan opera) and some epic picnics.

Palden Lhamo

The 15th day of the 10th lunar month (being November) has a procession around the Barkhor circuit bearing Palden Lhamo, protective deity of the Jokhang Temple.

Tsongkhapa Festival

Much respect is shown to Tsongkhapa, the founder of the Gelugpa order, on the anniversary of his death on the 25th of the 10th lunar month (December). Check for processions and monk dances at the monasteries at Ganden, Sera and Drepung.

Sleeping

Backpacker hotels listed here have (lower-end) midrange rooms that are decent for a small budget-traveller splurge. Several more top-end hotels are planned to open in Lhasa over the coming years.

Yak Hotel HOTEL **$$**
(亚宾馆; Yà Bīnguǎn; Map p888; ☎630 0008; 100 Beijing Donglu; dm Y30-40, d with bathroom Y450-650, VIP r Y880, discounts of 30-50%; ❄@) Once a backpacker favourite, the Yak is still one of Lhasa's most popular hotels, but it's now firmly midrange. Best bets are the Tibetan-style back-block rooms (Y600), the larger but noisier deluxe rooms overlooking the street (Y650), or the plush VIP rooms *(guìbīnlóu)*, all discounted to between Y380 and Y450. Reservations are recommended.

TOP CHOICE **Kyichu Hotel** HOTEL **$$**
(吉曲饭店; Jíqǔ Fàndiàn; Map p888; ☎633 1541; www.kyichuhotel.com; 149/18 Beijing Donglu; standard/deluxe r Y280/320; ❄📶@) The recently renovated Kyichu is a well-run place that's popular with repeat travellers to Tibet. Rooms are pleasant, with Tibetan carpets, but the real selling points are the excellent service and peaceful garden courtyard (with wi-fi and espresso coffee). Ask for a garden-view room at the back, as these are the quietest. Reservations are recommended. Credit cards accepted.

Rama Kharpo HOTEL **$**
(热玛嘎布宾馆; Rèmǎ Gābù Bīnguǎn; Map p888; ☎634 6963; www.lhasabarkhor.com; 5 Ongto Shingka Lam; dm/r Y25/150; 📶) This easily missed place is hidden deep in the old town near the Muslim quarter. Both dorm and en suite rooms are comfortable and the dark but pleasant cafe is a great meeting place, serving beer, breakfasts and simple food.

TOP CHOICE **Yabshi Phunkhang** BOUTIQUE **$$$**
(尧西平康; Yáoxī Píngkāng; Map p888; ☎632 8885; www.yabshiphunkhang.com; Beijing Donglu; deluxe r/ste Y1000/1800, discounts of up to 60%;❄📶) Architectural integrity is rare in Lhasa these days, which makes the four-year restoration of this mid-19th-century mansion all the more impressive. The collection of 21 large, well-equipped rooms linked by lovely courtyards and sitting areas is both stylish and very Tibetan. It's a great romantic top-end choice.

Dhood Gu Hotel HOTEL **$$**
(敦固宾馆; Dūngù Bīnguǎn; Map p888; ☎632 2555; www.dhodguhotel.com; 19 Shasarsu Lu;

冲赛康夏莎苏19号; s/d/ste incl breakfast Y280/300/520; @) Staff are a little cool at this three-star Nepalese-run hotel, but the old-quarter location and ornate Tibetan-style decor are great. Head to the rooftop bar if your room lacks a view.

House of Shambhala BOUTIQUE $$$
(香巴拉府; Xiāngbālā Fǔ; Map p888; ☎632 6533; www.shambhalaserai.com; 7 Jiri Erxiang; 吉日二巷7号; d incl breakfast Y675-1015; @) It can take a bit of hunting to locate Lhasa's first boutique hotel, but once you see the mustard-coloured exterior, and impressive wooden doors, you'll know you're there. The hotel's 10 rooms sport a funky Tibetan design, with liberal use of wood, stone, silk, and antique furnishings. From the fabulous rooftop terrace the views over the old quarter can really take you back in time. A 17-room annexe, the **Shambhala Palace**, is hidden deeper in the old town.

Barkhor Namchen House GUESTHOUSE $
(八廓龙乾家庭旅馆; Bākuò Lóngqián Jiātíng Lûguǎn; Map p888; ☎679 0125; www.tibetnamchen.com; dm Y25, s Y60-70, d Y70; @) This small backstreet Tibetan-style guesthouse is a good budget choice. The old-town location is near perfect, the staff are friendly, and the Asian-style bathrooms and communal hot showers are superclean. Rooms are fairly small and some have limited natural light (ask for an upper-floor room), but you can head to the good rooftop restaurant for fine views.

Gorkha Hotel HOTEL $$
(郭尔喀饭店; Guò'ěrkā Fàndiàn; Map p888; ☎627 1992; tibetgorkha7@hotmail.com; 45 Linkuo Nanlu; 林廓南路45号; tr without bathroom per bed Y50-80, r/ste Y280/300; @) This atmospheric Nepali-Tibetan venture housed the Nepali consulate in the 1950s and still boasts traditional architecture. Rooms vary, so look at a few (the suites are perfect for families). It's in the south of the old town, near several lovely old temples.

Snowland Hotel HOTEL $
(雪域宾馆; Xuěyù Bīnguǎn; Map p888; ☎632 3687; snowlandhotel@gmail.com; 4 Zangyiyuan Lu/Mentsikhang Lam; 藏医院4号路; dm/d Y20/60, d standard/deluxe with bathroom Y100/150; @) Don't bother with the budget rooms in this old-timer, but do take a look at the slightly beaten-up en suite rooms; the deluxe rooms are some of the best value in town. The location next to Barkhor Sq is perfect. Check the water pressure and mattresses before committing.

Eating

The staple diet in Tibet is *tsampa* (porridge of roasted barley flour) and *bö cha* (yak-butter tea). Tibetans mix the two in their hands to create doughlike balls. *Momos* (dumplings filled with vegetables or yak meat) and *thugpa* (noodles with meat) are also local comfort food. Variations include *thanthuk* (fried noodle squares) as well as *shemdre* (rice, potato and yak-meat curry).

Lhasa is filled with restaurants serving a range of excellent Nepalese, Chinese, Tibetan and Western dishes. Unless noted otherwise, the places listed here are open for breakfast, lunch and dinner.

Tashi I WESTERN $
(Map p888; cnr Zangyiyuan Lu & Beijing Donglu; dishes Y10-25; ⏲8am-10pm; 📋) This old standard feels like a slice of old Tibet and is a mellow place to hang out. Try the *bobi* (chapatti-like unleavened bread), which comes with seasoned cream cheese and fried vegetables or meat.

New Mandala Restaurant NEPALI $$
(新满斋餐厅; Xīnmǎnzhāi Cāntīng; Map p888; Zangyiyuan Lu; dishes Y20-35; 📋) Excellent views over the Barkhor. The Nepali set meals are excellent and it's a great place to people watch over a cold beer. The menu is the standard mix of Western, Nepali and Chinese food.

Snowland Restaurant WESTERN $$
(雪域餐厅; Xuěyù Cāntīng; Map p888; Zangyiyuan Lu; dishes Y25-40; ⏲8am-10pm; 📋) Attached to the Snowland Hotel, this well-run restaurant serves a mix of excellent Continental and Nepali food in very civilised surroundings. The Indian dishes are particularly good and the cakes (discounted after 9pm) are easily the best in town. Try the gourmet-quality 'yak' cheese.

UNDER PRESSURE

If you fly into Lhasa, take care when reopening things such as tubes of sunscreen or even jars of Coffee-mate from a local shop, as the change in pressure can cause messy explosions of volcanic proportions.

Barkhor Area

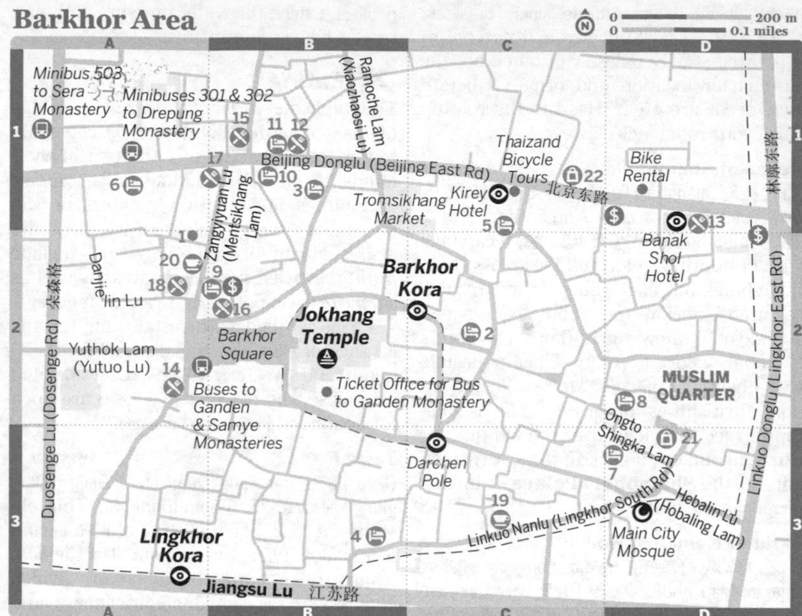

Woeser Zedroe Tibetan Restaurant

TIBETAN $

(光明泽缀藏餐馆; Guāngmíng Zézhuì Zàngcānguǎn; Map p888; Zangyiyuan Lu; mains Y6-28; lunch & dinner;) This is where visiting and local Tibetans come to fill up after a visit to the Jokhang. Add some pleasant traditional seating and a perfect location to the Tibetan vibe and it's a logical lunch stop. The *momos* are recommended, especially the fried yak meat or cheese varieties.

Pentoc Tibetan Restaurant

TIBETAN $

(Map p888; dishes Y10-15;) For something more authentically Tibetan, charming English-speaking Pentoc runs this local teahouse restaurant after working in Tashi I for many years. It's a good place to try homemade Tibetan standards, such as *momos*, *thugpa*, *shemdre* (rice, potato and yak meat), plus butter tea, *chang* (barley beer) and even *dal bhat* (lentils and rice). It's 20m down an alleyway off Beijing Donglu, on the left.

Nam-tso Restaurant

WESTERN $

(Map p888; 8 Beijing Donglu; mains Y20-30, set breakfasts Y27;) Alfresco dining under the Tibetan stars is possible on the rooftop of the Banak Shol hotel. And the sizzlers, yak burgers and Western breakfasts served here are worth every kuài.

Dunya Restaurant

WESTERN $$

(Map p888; 633 3374; www.dunyarestaurant.com; 100 Beijing Donglu; dishes Y30-65;) With its classy decor, wide-ranging dishes and interesting specials, this foreign-run eatery is popular with travellers who need something reassuringly familiar.

Drinking

Tibetans consume large quantities of *chang* (a tangy alcoholic drink derived from fermented barley) and *bö cha*. The other major beverage is *cha ngamo* (sweet milky tea). Hole-in-the-wall Tibetan teahouses can be found all over the old town.

Ani Sangkhung Nunnery Teahouse

TEAHOUSE

(Map p888; 29 Linkuo Nanlu; tea Y2-8; 8am-5pm) If you're exploring the old town and need a break, make a beeline for this bustling teahouse in the courtyard of Lhasa's most important (and most politically active) nunnery. The nuns do a great job and the location is superb.

Summit Café

CAFE

(顶峰咖啡店; Dǐngfēng Kāfēidiàn; Map p888; coffees Y15-25; 7.30am-11pm; @) Off Zangyiyuan Lu, the courtyard of the Shangbala Hotel is the place to head for

Barkhor Area

Top Sights

Barkhor Kora C2
Jokhang Temple B2
Lingkhor Kora A3

Activities, Courses & Tours

1 Raft Tibet (Tibet Wind Horse Adventure) A2

Sleeping

2 Barkhor Namchen House C2
3 Dhood Gu Hotel B1
4 Gorkha Hotel B3
5 House of Shambhala C1
6 Kyichu Hotel A1
7 Rama Kharpo D3
8 Shambhala Palace D2
9 Snowland Hotel B2
10 Yabshi Phunkhang B1
11 Yak Hotel B1

Eating

12 Dunya Restaurant B1
13 Nam-tso Restaurant D1
14 New Mandala Restaurant A2
15 Pentoc Tibetan Restaurant B1
16 Snowland Restaurant B2
17 Tashi I B1
18 Woeser Zedroe Tibetan Restaurant A2

Drinking

19 Ani Sangkhung Nunnery Teahouse C3
Dunya Bar .... (see 12)
20 Summit Café A2

Shopping

21 Lhasa Villages Handicrafts D3
22 Outlook Outdoor Equipment C1

Lhasa's best espresso hit. There's cosy seating, wi-fi, excellent coffee and great deserts.

Dunya Bar BAR
(Map p888; www.dunyarestaurant.com; 100 Beijing Donglu; bottled beers Y15; noon-midnight;) This classy bar above the restaurant of the same name has a nice balcony and screens major sports events.

Shopping

Whether it's prayer wheels, *thangkas,* sunhats or imported muesli, you shouldn't have a problem finding it in Lhasa. The Barkhor circuit is especially good for buying souvenirs. Most of this stuff is mass-produced in Nepal. Haggle, haggle, haggle.

Lhasa Villages Handicrafts HANDICRAFTS
(Map p888; 633 0898; www.tibetcraft.com; 11 Chaktsal Ganglu; 10am-7pm) A wander through the Tibetan old town leads to this excellent shop established to bolster local handicrafts in the face of rising Nepali and Chinese imports. Quality and prices are top end, and you can watch local craftspeople at work in the courtyard. The shop (formerly known as Dropenling) is a little tricky to find, but as you get nearer you'll see signs pointing the way. Ask about the two-hour walking tours of old-town craft workshops.

Outlook Outdoor Equipment OUTDOOR GEAR
(Kàn Fēngyún Biànhuàn Yuǎnjìng; Map p888; 634 5589; 11 Beijing Donglu) The best of many local shops selling Chinese-made Gore-Tex jackets, fleeces, sleeping bags, stoves, tents and mats, and it also rents out equipment.

Information

Internet Access

The most popular **Internet cafes** (网吧; wǎngbā; per hr Y3-5) are at the Yak and Snowland hotels. If you have a laptop, the Summit Café and Rama Kharpo and Yabshi Phunkhang hotels offer free wi-fi.

Medical Services

Military Hospital (西藏军区总医院; Xīzàng Jūnqū Zǒngyīyuàn; 625 3120; Niangre Beilu) Near the Sera Monastery.

Money

Bank of China (中国银行; Zhōngguó Yínháng; Map p884; Linkuo Xilu; 9am-1pm & 3.30-6.30pm Mon-Fri, 10.30am-4pm Sat & Sun) Offers credit-card advances, bank transfers and foreign exchange, plus a 24-hour ATM.

Bank of China (branch) (中国银行; Zhōngguó Yínháng; Map p888; Beijing Donglu; 10am-4.30pm Mon-Fri, 11am-3.30pm Sat & Sun) The most conveniently located bank changes cash and travellers cheques, and has an ATM. It's between the Banak Shol and Kirey hotels.

China Construction Bank ATM (中国建设银行; Zhōngguó Jiànshè Yínháng; Map p888;

Zangyiyuan Lu) Conveniently located 24-hour ATM next to the Snowland Hotel.

Post

China Post (中国邮政; Zhōngguó Yóuzhèng; Map p884; Beijing Donglu; ⏲9am-8pm Mon-Sat, 10am-6pm Sun) Buy stamps from the counter in the far-left corner. It's east of the Potala Palace.

Public Security Bureau

Lhasa City PSB (拉萨市公安局; Lāsà Shì Gōng'ānjú; Map p884; ☎624 8154; 17 Linkuo Beilu; ⏲9am-12.30pm & 3.30-6pm Mon-Fri) Visa extensions of up to a week are given, but only a day or two before your visa expires and only if you are on a tour. Other offices are not interested in seeing you.

Telephone

Several private phone booths on Zangyiyuan Lu and Beijing Donglu offer cheap international calls. Look for the 'Telephone Supermarket' (国际公话超市; Guójì Gōnghuà Chāoshì) signs.

Travel Agencies

See the boxed text, p883 for a list of agencies in Lhasa that can arrange your tour and TTB (Tibet Tourism Bureau) permit.

Getting There & Away

Air

It's generally possible to buy flights to Lhasa online on sites such as www.expedia.com, www.ctrip.com and www.elong.net. If buying in person, you will need to show your TTB permit; Air China won't sell you a ticket without a permit.

Leaving Lhasa is a lot simpler, as tickets can be purchased (and changed) without hassle from the **Civil Aviation Administration of China** (CAAC; 中国民航; Zhōngguó Mínháng; Map p884; ☎633 3446; 1 Niangre Lu; ⏲9am-6.30pm). Flight connections continue to all major destinations in China and even Hong Kong. Note that tickets are often discounted by up to 30%.

Flights to/from Lhasa include the following destinations:

Ali Y2500, two weekly

Běijīng (via Chéngdū) Y2520, seven weekly

Chéngdū Y1590, 60 to 70 weekly

Chóngqìng Y1720, seven weekly

Guǎngzhōu (via Chóngqìng) Y2590, two weekly

Kathmandu Y2970 (US$379 from Kathmandu), three to four weekly

Kūnmíng (via Zhōngdiàn), Y2050, seven weekly

Shànghǎi Pǔdōng (via Xī'ān), Y2850, two weekly

Xī'ān Y1740, four weekly

Zhōngdiàn Y1470, seven weekly (summer only)

Bus

Tickets for the sleeper buses from Lhasa to Golmud (Y220, 24 hours) can be bought at the **long-distance bus station** (Map p884). Most sane people will take the train or fly out.

Destinations around Tibet are a little trickier, as foreigners are currently not allowed to travel by public transport. Should this change, there are buses from the long-distance station to Shigatse, Gyantse and beyond.

Train

The **Qīnghǎi–Tibet Railway** has been the world's highest train ride since starting operations in 2006. With the line topping the 5072m Tanggu-la Pass, and with 80% of the Golmud to Lhasa stretch being over 4000m, the railway is one impressive piece of engineering. Its 160km of bridges and elevated track were built over permafrost, so sections of cooling pipes had to be inserted in places to help keep the boggy ground frozen in summer. The cost? A cool US$4.1 billion, and with planned extensions to Shigatse currently under construction, this figure is set to grow.

The Chinese are rightfully swollen with pride over this engineering marvel, while the Tibetans aren't quite so sure. The railway will bring cheaper (Chinese-made) goods and greater economic growth, but it will also increase Han migration, delivering one million passengers to Lhasa every year. What the line does best is staple Tibet ever more firmly to the rest of China.

At the time of writing, foreign travellers needed a copy of their TTB permit in order to buy a train ticket and board the train to Lhasa. On board all passengers have access to piped-in oxygen through a special socket located next to each seat or berth. Additional oxygen is also pumped into compartments between Golmud and Lhasa, although the cabins are not actually pressurised.

Soft-sleeper berths come with individual TVs, and speakers in each cabin make periodic travel announcements in Chinese and English about the train, its construction and sights along the way. Other than these additions, the trains are similar to most others in China, though schedules are at least designed so as to let you take in the best scenery during daylight hours.

You can buy train tickets up to 10 days in advance at the Lhasa **train station ticket office** (⏲7am-10pm), at the train station on the southwest edge of town, or the more centrally located **city ticket office** (火车票代售处; Huǒchēpiào Dàishòuchù; Map p884; Deji Beilu; ⏲9-11.30am & 1-5pm). Trains to Lhasa arrive in the evening; trains from Lhasa depart between 7.30am and 1.30pm.

A luxury joint-venture train, the *Tangula Express*, is planned but currently on hold. If it happens, you can expect glass observation cars, dining by Kempinski, luxury cabins with showers and a tariff of around US$1000 a day.

Trains to Lhasa, and fares (hard seat/hard sleeper/soft sleeper; sleeper fares are for lower berths):

From **Běijīng West** (T27), Y389/813/1262, 48 hours, one daily (9.30pm)

From **Chéngdū** (T22/23), Y331/712/1104, 48 hours, one daily (6.18pm)

From **Chóngqìng** (T222/3), Y355/754/1168, 48 hours, one every other day (7.20pm)

From **Guǎngzhōu** (T264/5), Y451/923/1530, 58 hours, one every other day (1.07pm)

From **Lánzhōu** (K917), Y242/552/854, 30 hours, one every other day (4.45pm)

From **Shànghǎi** (T164/5), Y406/845/1314, 52 hours, one every other day (4.11pm)

From **Xīníng** (K917), Y226/523/810, 27 hours, one daily (4.45pm)

Getting Around

To/From the Airport

Gongkar airport is 65km from Lhasa. Most tourists are picked up by their guide as part of their tour.

Airport buses (Y25, 75 minutes) leave up to 10 times a day between 7.30am and 1.30pm from the courtyard in front of the CAAC building. Tickets are sold on the bus, so show up early to guarantee a seat. Buses greet all incoming flights.

A taxi to the airport costs between Y150 and Y200.

Bicycle

A good option for getting around Lhasa once you have acclimatised is to hire a bike. There are a couple of bike-rental places opposite the Banak Shol hotel, or you can hire quality mountain bikes from **Thaizand Bicycle Tours** (Map p888; ☎691 0898; thaizand@hotmail.com; Kirey Hotel, 105 Beijing Donglu) for Y40 to Y80 per day, with a helmet and pads.

Minibus

Privately run minibuses (Y2) travel frequently between Beijing Donglu and western Lhasa.

Taxi

Taxis charge a standard fare of Y10 to anywhere within the city. Few Chinese drivers know the Tibetan names for even the major sites. Bicycle-rickshaws should charge around Y5 for short trips but require endless haggling.

Around Lhasa

DREPUNG MONASTERY འབྲས་སྤུངས་ 哲蚌寺

A preternaturally spiritual 1½-hour-long *kora* around this 15th-century **monastery** (Zhébàng Sì; admission Y50; ⏲9.30am-5.30pm), 8km west of Lhasa, is among the highlights of a trip to Tibet. Along with Sera and Ganden Monasteries, Drepung functioned as one of the three 'pillars of the Tibetan state' and this one was purportedly the largest monastery in the world, with around 7000 resident monks at its peak. Drepung means 'rice heap', a reference to the white buildings dotting the hillside.

The kings of Tsang and the Mongols savaged the place regularly, though, oddly, the Red Guards pretty much left it alone during the Cultural Revolution. With concerted rebuilding, this monastic village once again resembles its proud former self and around 600 monks reside here. At lunchtime you can see the novices bringing in buckets of *tsampa* and yak-butter tea. In the afternoons you can often see Tibetan-style religious debating (lots of hand slapping and gesticulating). The best way to visit the monastery is to follow the pilgrim groups or the yellow signs.

Nearby **Nechung Monastery** (admission Y10; ⏲8.30am-5pm), a 10-minute walk downhill, was once the home of the Tibetan state oracle and is worth a visit.

Minibus Nos 301, 302 and 303 (Y2) run from Beijing Donglu to the foot of the Drepung hill, from where a coach (Y1) runs up to the monastery. A taxi from the Barkhor area is Y30. There is a Y10 to Y20 charge per chapel for photography.

SERA MONASTERY སེ་ར་དགོན་པ་ 色拉寺

About 5km north of Lhasa, this **monastery** (Sèlā Sì; admission Y55; ⏲9am-5pm) was founded in 1419 by a disciple of Tsongkhapa and was, along with Drepung Monastery, one of Lhasa's two great Gelugpa monasteries.

About 600 monks are now in residence, well down from an original population of around 5000. The half-dozen main colleges feature spectacular prayer halls and chapels. Equally interesting is the monk debating that takes place from 3.30pm to 5pm in a garden next to the assembly hall in the centre of the monastery. As at Drepung, there's a fine hour-long *kora* path around the exterior of the monastery.

VISITING MONASTERIES & TEMPLES

Most monasteries and temples extend a warm welcome to foreign guests, and in remote areas will often offer a place to stay for the night, depending on government travel restrictions. Please maintain this good faith by observing the following courtesies:

» Always circumambulate monasteries, chapels and other religious objects clockwise, thus keeping shrines and *chörtens* (Tibetan stupas) to your right.

» Don't touch or remove anything on an altar and don't take prayer flags or *mani* (prayer) stones.

» Don't take photos during a prayer meeting. At other times always ask permission to take a photo, especially when using a flash. The larger monasteries charge photography fees, though some monks will allow you to take a quick photo for free. If they won't, there's no point getting angry – you don't know what pressures they may be under.

» Don't wear shorts or short skirts in a monastery, and take your hat off when you go into a chapel.

» Don't smoke in a monastery.

» If you have a guide, try to ensure that he or she is Tibetan, as Chinese guides invariably know little about Tibetan Buddhism or monastery history.

» Be aware that women are generally not allowed in protector chapels *(gönkhang)*.

Minibus 503 (Y2) runs to Sera from Duosenge Lu, or it's a 30-minute bicycle ride from central Lhasa. There is a Y15 to Y30 fee per chapel for photography, and it's Y850 for video.

From Sera Monastery it's possible to take a taxi or walk northwest for another hour to little-visited **Pabonka Monastery**. Built in the 7th century by King Songtsen Gampo, this is one of the most ancient Buddhist sites in the Lhasa region.

GANDEN MONASTERY དགའ་ལྡན་ 甘丹寺

About 40km east of Lhasa, this **monastery** (Gāndān Sì; admission Y45; ⌚dawn-dusk), founded in 1417 by Tsongkhapa, was the first Gelugpa monastery. Still the order's heart and soul, it's the one out-of-Lhasa sight to choose if your time is limited. Two *koras* offer astounding views over the braided Kyichu Valley and you'll probably meet more pilgrims here than anywhere else.

Some 400 monks have returned and extensive reconstruction has been under way for some time now, alongside a strong police presence. There is a Y20 fee per chapel for photography; Y1500 for video.

Pilgrim buses leave for Ganden Monastery (Y25 return) between 6am and 7am from Barkhor Sq, returning around 1.30pm. Tourists can sometimes take the bus if their guide accompanies them; otherwise 4WD hire costs around Y400.

NAM-TSO གནམ་མཚོ་ 纳木错

The waters of sacred **Nam-tso** (Nàmùcuò; adult Y120), the second-largest salt lake in China, are an almost transcendent turquoise blue and shimmer in the rarefied air of 4730m. Geographically part of the Changtang Plateau, the lake is bordered to the north by the Taánggǔlā Shān range and to the southeast by 7111m Nyenchen Tanglha peak.

The scenery is breathtaking but so is the altitude: 1100m higher than Lhasa. Do not rush here but instead count on a week in Lhasa at the minimum to avoid acute mountain sickness (AMS); see p1013.

Most travellers head for **Tashi Do Monastery** in the southeastern corner of the lake. There are some fine walks in the area, as well as a short but pilgrim-packed *kora*. Half a dozen charmless metal **guesthouses** (dm Y30-50, r Y120-160) offer food and accommodation around the monastery between April and October, though the site is starting to seriously suffer from overvisitation. Bedding is provided but nights here can be very cold.

Nam-tso is 195km north of Lhasa, a four-hour paved drive over the high (5190m) Largen-la. Even if independent travel returns, there is no public transport to the lake.

SAMYE MONASTERY

བསམ་ཡས་དགོན་པ་ 桑耶寺

About 170km southeast of Lhasa, on the north bank of the Yarlung Tsangpo (Brahmaputra) River is **Samye Monastery** (Sāngyē Sì; admission Y40; ⏲8am-5.30pm), the first monastery in Tibet. Founded in AD 775 by King Trisong Detsen, Samye is famed not just for its pivotal history, but its unique mandala design: the main hall, or Ütse, represents Mt Meru, the centre of the universe, while the outer temples represent the oceans, continents, subcontinents and other features of the Buddhist cosmology.

Simple accommodation is available at the **Monastery Guesthouse** (☎0891-783 6666; dm Y50, d with bathroom Y150), outside the monastery walls and with the best doubles in town. The monastery restaurant serves mediocre *momos* with lots of local atmosphere. The **Friendship Snowland Restaurant** (☎136-1893 2819; meals Y14-40; ⏲8am-midnight), outside the east gate, serves better Chinese and Tibetan dishes, banana pancakes and milky tea. Dorm rooms (Y30) with real mattresses (not foam) are available upstairs. There are several other decent accommodation options nearby, including the friendly **Dawa Guesthouse** (达瓦家庭旅馆; Dáwā Jiātíng Lǚguǎn; ☎799 5171; dm Y30).

If you are heading to Everest Base Camp or the Nepal border, a visit here will only add one day to your itinerary. If the rules on independent travel relax, you may be able to catch the daily pilgrim minibus in the morning from Barkhor Sq in Lhasa.

You may have to detour briefly to the nearby town of Tsetang (泽当; Zédāng) for your guide to pick up a required travel permit.

The Friendship Highway

The 865km route between Kathmandu and Lhasa, known as the Friendship Highway, offers without a doubt one of the world's great overland routes. At times sublime, at times unnerving, at times nauseating (the highest point is the Gyatso-la Pass at 5100m), it's the yellow-brick road of Tibet, leading to some of the most magical destinations on the plateau.

For the sake of simplicity, we've included the side route from Lhasa to Shigatse via Yamdrok-tso and Gyantse under the Friendship Highway heading. This is the route most travellers take between the two towns and it's by far the more scenic and attraction-packed.

YAMDROK-TSO

ཡར་འབྲོག་མཚོ་ 羊卓雍错

On the direct road between Gyantse and Lhasa, you'll probably catch your first sight of coiling Yamdrok-tso (Yángzhuō Yōngcuò; 4488m) from the summit of the Kamba-la pass (4794m). The lake lies several hundred metres below the road, and in clear weather is a fabulous shade of deep turquoise. Far in the northwest distance is the huge massif of Mt Nojin Kangtsang (7191m).

The small town of **Nangartse** along the way has some basic accommodation and several restaurants but most people overnight in Gyantse. A 20-minute drive or a two-hour walk from Nangartse brings you to **Samding Monastery** (admission Y20), a charming place with scenic views of the surrounding area and lake.

GANDEN TO SAMYE TREK

One of the most popular – but not the easiest – treks in Tibet is the four- to five-day hike from Ganden Monastery to Samye Monastery, an 80km wilderness walk connecting two of Tibet's most important monasteries. It begins less than 50km from Lhasa and takes you over the high passes of the Shuga-la (5250m) and Chitu-la (5100m). Along the way are subalpine lakes, dwarf forests and meadows, all at high altitude, so it shouldn't be underestimated.

Obviously, know before you go: this means the land and the capabilities of your mind and body. The situation for getting permits for trekking is the same as for normal travel in Tibet (see boxed text, p883). Some agencies will let you arrange your own ad hoc trek (ie horse hire and food), as long as you take a guide and arrange transport to and from the trailheads; others require a fully supported trek. **Tibet Wind Horse Adventure** (☎0891-683 3009; www.windhorsetibet.com; Zangyiyuan Lu, Lhasa) is one of the most professional trekking agencies in Lhasa, though it's not the cheapest. For further details, see the trekking chapter of Lonely Planet's *Tibet* guide.

DON'T MISS

GYANTSE KUMBUM

The one unmissable sight in Gyantse, the spectacular Gyantse Kumbum (literally '100,000 Images Stupa') is the largest *chörten* (Tibetan stupa) in Tibet. A pilgrim path spirals up the inside of the monumental nine-tiered structure, built in the 15th century by a local prince, passing 108 chapels, each filled with masterful original murals. Bring a torch (flashlight) if you want to examine them in detail.

From Nangartse to Gyantse you cross the 4960m Karo-la, site of the highest battle in British imperial history in 1903–1904, where glaciers spill off the side peaks beside a popular viewpoint.

GYANTSE རྒྱལ་རྩེ 江孜

0892 / ELEV 3980M

The traditional town of Gyantse (Jiāngzī) is famed for its monumental nine-tiered *chörten,* long considered one of Tibet's architectural wonders. Historically, the town was at the centre of a thriving trans-Himalayan wood and wool trade, and Gyantse carpets were considered the best in Tibet. These days, Gyantse remains one of the least Chinese-influenced settlements, and wandering the backstreets affords a rare picture of traditional urban Tibetan life.

Sights & Activities

In the fourth lunar month (early June to mid-July) the town hosts a great **horse-racing** and **archery festival**.

Pelkhor Chöde Monastery MONASTERY
(白居寺; Báijūsì; admission Y40; 9am-6pm, some chapels closed 1-3pm) The high red-walled compound of this monastery, founded in 1418, once encircled 15 monasteries from three different orders of Tibetan Buddhism. The surviving **assembly hall** (straight ahead as you enter the compound) is worth a lingering visit for the fine murals, statues and butter-lamp-lit atmosphere. Just beside the assembly hall is the **Gyantse Kumbum**.

Gyantse Dzong FORT
(Old Fort; 817 2116; admission Y40; 8.30am-8.30pm) Gyantse Dzong towers above Gyantse on a finlike outcrop, and has outstanding views of the Pelkhor Chöde Monastery and surrounding valley. The fort was taken by the British in 1904 during their invasion of Tibet. Entry is via the gate north of the main intersection, or drive up from the back side.

Sleeping

Gyantse is a popular stop for 4WD tours and has a decent range of accommodation and food along north–south Yingxiong Nanlu.

Jiànzàng Hotel HOTEL $$
(建藏饭店; Jiànzàng Fàndiàn; Yingxiong Nanlu; 英雄南路; 817 3720; tr per bed Y50, d Y180-200) Long a popular place with 4WD groups, the smallish but modern rooms come with bathroom and 24-hour hot water. Prices start high but are open to negotiation. The 2nd-floor restaurant is a decent option for breakfast or a cup of tea. The manager featured in the recent BBC documentary 'A Year in Tibet'.

Zōngshān Hotel HOTEL $$
(宗山饭店; Zōngshān Fàndiàn; 817 5555; 1 Weiguo Lu; d incl breakfast Y520, discounts of 50-70%; @) With 24-hour hot water, clean Western-style rooms and discounted rates of Y140 to Y160 a room, this is a solid-value midrange option. A top-floor restaurant (dishes Y15 to Y40) offers almost 360-degree views of Gyantse.

Wutse Hotel HOTEL $$
(乌孜饭店; Wūzī Fàndiàn; 817 2909; Yingxiong Nanlu) This popular place was undergoing renovations at the time of research but is worth a look.

Eating

Yak Restaurant WESTERN, TIBETAN $$
(亚美食餐厅; Yà Měishí Cāntīng; Yingxiong Nanlu; mains Y15-35; 7am-11pm;) The Yak offers backpacker treats such as French toast (Y15), pizza, yak burgers, sizzlers (dishes served on a hot, sizzling plate) and Western breakfasts. The owner prides herself on her French cuisine, so have a go at the yak-liver paté or yak bourguignon.

Tashi Restaurant INDIAN, WESTERN $$
(扎西餐厅; Zhāxī Cāntīng; Yingxiong Nanlu; mains Y15-40; 7.30am-11pm;) This Nepali-run place (a branch of Tashi in Shigatse) whips up tasty and filling Indian fare. It also has the usual range of Western breakfasts, Italian and Chinese food. The decor is Tibetan but the Indian movies and Nepali music give it a subcontinental vibe.

Gyantse Kitchen

TIBETAN, INTERNATIONAL $$

(江孜厨房; Jiāngzī Chúfáng; Shanghai Zhonglu; dishes Y15-40; 7am-midnight;) This local favourite serves Western, Tibetan and Indian food, plus unique fusion dishes such as yak pizza. The friendly owner, who may join you for a drink, donates a portion of his income to support poor families in Gyantse.

Getting There & Away

Most people visit Gyantse as part of a trip to the Nepal border, Mt Everest, or out west to Mt Kailash. Should the permit situation change, there are plenty of minibuses (1½ hours) and taxis (one hour) for the 90km trip between Shigatse and Gyantse.

SHIGATSE གཞིས་ཀ་རྩེ་ 日喀则

0892 / POP 80,000 / ELEV 3840M

Shigatse (Rìkāzé) is the second-largest city in Tibet, and like Lhasa has two distinct faces: a Tibetan one and a Chinese one. The Tibetan section, running northeast of the high-walled Tashilhunpo Monastery, is filled with whitewashed compounds, dusty alleys and prayer-wheel-spinning pilgrims. The Chinese section is thoroughly modern and is where you'll find most restaurants and hotels and other life-support systems.

History

As the traditional capital of the central Tsang region, Shigatse was long a rival with Lhasa for political control of the country. The Tsang kings and later governors exercised their power from the imposing heights of the (recently rebuilt) Shigatse Dzong. Since the time of the Mongol sponsorship of the Gelugpa order, Shigatse has been the seat of the Panchen Lamas, the second-highest-ranking lamas in Tibet. Their centre was and remains the Tashilhunpo Monastery.

Sights

Tashilhunpo Monastery

MONASTERY

(བཀྲ་ཤིས་ལྷུན་པོ་དགོན་; 扎什伦布寺; Zhāshílúnbù Sì; admission Y55; 9am-7pm summer, 10am-noon & 3.30-6pm winter) The seat of the Panchen Lama and one of Tibetan culture's six great Gelugpa institutions (along with Drepung, Sera and Ganden monasteries in Lhasa; as well as Kumbum and Labrang in Qīnghǎi and Gānsù provinces, respectively). Built in 1447 by a nephew of Tsongkhapa, the monastery is the size of a small village, and lends itself to a half-day or more of exploration and discovery.

In addition to the mesmerising statue of Jampa (Maitreya) Buddha (at nearly 27m high it's the largest gilded statue in the world) in the Temple of the Maitreya, the monastery is famed for the opulent tombs of the fourth and 10th Panchen Lamas. The former saw 85kg of gold and masses of jewels used in its construction. Despite the spectacle, some travellers don't like the atmosphere at Tashilhunpo, conjecturing that some of the monks are in cahoots with the authorities.

A delightful hour-long *kora* starts at the southwest corner of the outer wall and quickly heads into the hills for open views over the monastery and city. The Potala-like structure to the east is the rebuilt **Shigatse Dzong** (fortress). It's currently empty but a museum/gallery is planned.

Sleeping

Shigatse has a good range of hotels, most offering rooms with private bathroom (with hot shower).

Gang Gyan Shigatse Orchard Hotel

HOTEL $$

(日喀则刚坚宾馆; Rìkāzé Gāngjiān Bīnguǎn; 882 0777; 77 Zhufeng Lu; tr without bathroom Y188, d with bathroom Y368, discounts of 60%) Right next to the traditional-carpet factory and just 100m from Tashilhunpo Monastery, the location here can't be beat. Rooms are large and comfortably furnished. The shared bathrooms are clean but the shower water supply is iffy, a problem the rooms with private bathrooms don't share.

Tenzin Hotel

HOTEL $$

(旦增宾馆; Dànzēng Bīngǔan; 882 2018; 8 Bangjiakong Lu; 帮加孔路8号; dm Y40, d/tr without bathroom Y180/120, d with bathroom Y220, discounts of 30%) This place has long been popular with both 4WD tours and budget travellers. It's a bit noisy on the lower floors but the clean rooms, old-town location and views from the roof more than make up for this. The shared bathrooms usually have 24-hour hot water. The restaurant (dishes Y15 to Y35) serves up pretty tasty Tibetan, Chinese and Nepalese fare when the chef is in residence.

Eating

There are dozens of Chinese restaurants around town, and a number of Tibetan places along Qingdao Lu.

Shigatse

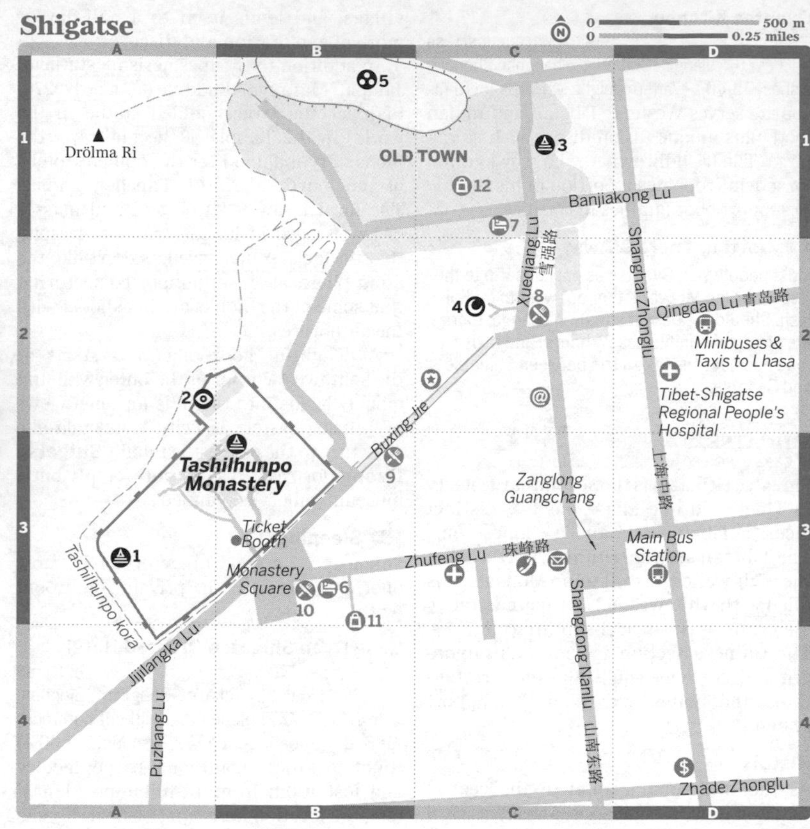

Songtsen Tibetan Restaurant INTERNATIONAL **$$**
(松赞西藏餐厅; Sōngzàn Xīzàng Cāntīng; Buxing Jie; dishes Y20-40; ⌚8am-10pm; 📋) This popular Western-style place does hearty breakfasts. It has a great location on the pedestrian-only street, offering views of the pilgrims ambling past as you dine on good Indian, Nepalese, Tibetan or Western fare.

Third Eye Restaurant NEPALI **$$**
(Zhufeng Lu; dishes Y10-30; ⌚7.30am-10.30pm; 📋) There's a great ambience inside this Nepali-run place, with monks sipping butter tea under *thangkas*, as travellers tuck into spicy Indian dishes.

Gongkar Tibetan Restaurant TIBETAN **$**
(贡嘎山美味藏餐厅; Gònggā Shān Měiwèi Zàngcāntīng; Xueqiang Lu; dishes Y10-20; 📋) This popular local hang-out features the standard *momos* and noodle dishes, in addition to some easy-to-resist dishes such as yak-tongue soup.

Shopping

The **Tibetan market** in front of the Tenzin Hotel is a good place to pick up souvenirs such as prayer wheels, rosaries and *thangkas*. There are also dozens of souvenir and craft shops along Qingdao Lu. Bargain hard.

Tibet Gang Gyen Carpet Factory CARPETS
(西藏刚坚地毯厂; Xīzàng Gāngjiān Dìtǎn Chǎng; www.tibetgang-gyencarpet.com; 9 Zhufeng Lu; ⌚9am-1pm & 3-7pm) This Tibetan–French joint venture hires and trains impoverished women to weave high-quality 100% Tibetan wool carpets. You can watch carpets being made on the premises and the factory will ship internationally. The entrance is just east of the Gang Gyan Shigatse Orchard Hotel.

Information

The cheapest places to make calls are the many private telephone booths around town.

Bank of China (中国银行; Zhōngguó Yínháng; Shanghai Zhonglu; ⌚9am-6.30pm Mon-Fri,

Shigatse

Top Sights

Tashilhunpo Monastery B3

Sights

1 Chörten A3
2 Festival Thangka Wall A2
3 Mani Lhakhang C1
4 Mosque C2
5 Shigatse Dzong B1

Sleeping

6 Gang Gyan Shigatse Orchard Hotel B3
7 Tenzin Hotel C1

Eating

8 Gongkar Tibetan Restaurant C2
9 Songtsen Tibetan Restaurant B3
Tenzin Restaurant .... (see 7)
10 Third Eye Restaurant B3

Shopping

11 Tibet Gang Gyen Carpet Factory B3
12 Tibetan Market C1

10am-5pm Sat & Sun) Changes travellers cheques and cash and gives credit-card advances. There's a 24-hour ATM outside.

China Post (中国邮政; Zhōngguó Yóuzhèng; cnr Shandong Lu & Zhufeng Lu; ⏲9am-6.30pm)

China Telecom (中国电信; Zhōngguó Diànxìn; Zhufeng Lu; ⏲9am-6.30pm Mon-Fri, 9.30am-6.30pm Sat & Sun) Phone calls and fax service, with an internet cafe (网吧; *wǎngbā*) above.

Public Security Bureau (PSB; 公安局; Gōng'ānjú; Qingdao Lu; ⏲9.30am-12.30pm & 3.30-6.30pm Mon-Fri) Group travellers headed to Western Tibet may have to wait for their guide to pick up a travel permit here.

Tiān Lè Internet Bar (天乐网吧; Tiānlè Wǎngbā; Shandong Lu; per hr Y5; ⏲24hr) Good connection speeds and window seats for those who need a little fresh air.

Getting There & Around

Currently all foreigners have to prearrange transport as part of their tour. If this changes, minibuses (six to seven hours) and shared taxis (five hours) leave for Lhasa from a stand on Qingdao Lu on the eastern side of Shigatse. Minivans and taxis to Gyantse run when full from outside the main bus station and there are also buses to Saga, Sakya, Lhatse and various other points down the Friendship Highway.

A taxi anywhere in Shigatse costs Y10.

Shigatse's Peace Airport, 50km east of the city, is due to open in 2011.

SAKYA ས་སྐྱ་ 萨迦

☎0892 / ELEV 4280M

In the 13th century, the monastic town of Sakya (Sàjiā) emerged as an important centre of scholarship. With Mongol military support, the Sakya lamas became rulers of all Tibet. Their rule was short-lived, but Sakya remained a powerful municipality. Even today the local colouring of buildings – ash grey with red and white vertical stripes – symbolises both the Rigsum Gonpo (the trinity of Bodhisattvas) and Sakya authority.

Sights

Sakya Monastery MONASTERY

(admission Y45; ⏲9am-6pm) The southern section of the Sakya Monastery, built in 1268, is a massive fortresslike compound, with high defensive walls. Inside, the dimly lit assembly hall exudes a sanctity few others can rival. The northern section of the monastery, on the other side of the Trum-chu (Trum River) has been mostly reduced to picturesque ruins, though restoration work is ongoing and it's worth some exploration.

Sleeping & Eating

Manasarovar Sakya Hotel HOTEL $$

(神湖萨迦宾馆; Shénhú Sàjiā Bīnguǎn; ☎824 2222; Gesang Zhonglu; dm Y20-30, d/tr Y280/380, discounts of 20-30%) There is a mix of rooms in this rambling hotel; the ones that overlook the road are probably best. The thick walls keep the place cold and dark but rooms are comfortable enough and some have en suite hot showers. The eight-bed dorm rooms are OK; one includes a bathroom. There are superb views from the hotel's rooftop and good Western dishes in the rather charmless restaurant.

Sakya Lowa Family Hotel GUESTHOUSE $

(萨迦镇鲁蛙家庭旅馆; Sàjiā Zhèn Lǔwā Jiātíng Lǚguǎn; ☎824 2156; Baogang Beilu; per person Y50) The Lowa is a family-run guesthouse with basic but clean rooms. Walls are brightly painted and accented with traditional motifs, but there are no showers. It's east of the Manasarovar Sakya Hotel.

Sakya Monastery Restaurant TIBETAN FOOD $

(萨迦寺餐厅; Sàjiā Sì Cāntīng; dishes Y7-15) This restaurant is owned by the monastery and serves up fried rice, *thugpa* and steaming glasses of *cha ngamo*.

Getting There & Away

Sakya is 25km off the Friendship Highway. Most people stay overnight at Sakya en route to the Everest region. There is one daily minibus between Shigatse and Sakya.

RONGPHU MONASTERY & EVEREST BASE CAMP

རོང་པོ་ཆེ་དགོན་པ་ ཇོ་མོ་གླང་མའི་ག་ཤམ་འོག་

绒布寺、珠峰

Before heading to the Nepal border, or as part of a five-day excursion from Lhasa, many travellers make the diversion to iconic **Everest Base Camp** (EBC; 5150m). The clear vistas (if you are lucky) up a glacial valley to the sheer North Face are far superior to anything you'll see in Nepal. Everest is known locally as Chomolungma (sometimes spelt Qomolangma), or as Zhūfēng in Chinese.

Private vehicles can drive on a gravel road to **Rongphu Monastery** (the highest in the world), and then proceed just a few kilometres more to a small collection of nomad tents set near a China Post kiosk (the highest post office in the world). From here it's a one-hour walk or shuttle-bus ride (Y25) up a winding dirt road to EBC.

Food and lodging are pretty limited up here (though the mobile phone reception is great!). The **Monastery Guesthouse** (dm Y40, tw per bed Y80) at Rongphu was under renovation in 2010. The ugly two-star hotel nearby is laughably overpriced. The most popular option is to stay in the **nomad tents** (per person Y40) and these actually offer the warmest and most comfortable bedding: those yak-dung stoves put out a fantastic amount of heat! Even so, a sleeping bag is an excellent idea. Simple meals and even canned beer are available inside all the tents. Keep your belongings locked in your vehicle. Because EBC is a prime target for political protests, the Chinese army maintains a strong presence up here.

EBC is about 90km off the Friendship Highway on a dirt road over the 5050m Pang-la. Before you set off you'll need to stop in **Baber** (Báibā; 白坝), or New Tingri; 4250m) – or Old Tingri if coming from Nepal – to pay the Qomolangma National Park entrance fee of Y400 per vehicle, plus Y180 per passenger. Clarify with your agency whether you are expected to pay for both your vehicle and your guide.

If you need to spend the night in Baber the **Kangjong Hotel** (雪域宾馆; Xuěyù Bīnguǎn; ☎139 8992 3995; d without/with bathroom Y100/220) is one of several good options. The attached Tibetan-style **restaurant** (dishes Y10-15) serves tasty hot meals and is a cosy place to kick back with a thermos of sweet tea. The hotel is in the middle of town at the crossroads to Shegar.

TINGRI TO ZHĀNGMÙ

དིང་རི་ 定日

འགྲམ་ 樟木

The huddle of mudbrick buildings that comprises the old village of **Tingri** (Dìngrì; 4250m) has recently expanded about a kilometre down the Friendship Highway. The views of the towering Himalayan peaks of Mt Everest (8848m) and Cho Oyu (8153m) across the sweeping plain make up for the ramshackle feel.

Ruins on the hill overlooking Tingri are all that remain of the **Tingri Dzong**. This fort was destroyed in a late-18th-century Nepalese invasion. Many more ruins on the plains between Shegar and Tingri shared the same history.

There are several Tibetan guesthouses and restaurants on the main highway, including the **Tingri Snowland Hotel** (定日雪域饭店; Dìngrì Xuěyù Fàndiàn; ☎152 0802 7313; s/d Y60/70) in the far west of the strip, which has great views. Rooms are basic but bright and clean and there are hot showers (Y10).

From Tingri down to **Zhāngmù** on the Nepal border is an easy half-day's drive of just under 200km. If you are coming the other way you should break the trip into two days to aid acclimatisation. The highest point along the paved road is the Tong-la pass (4950m), 95km from Tingri.

The one-street town of Nyalam (Nièlāmù) is about 30km from the Nepal border and a usual overnight spot for 4WD trips from Nepal. There are several decent hotels, including the new **Shishapangma Guesthouse** (希夏邦马旅馆; Xīxiàbāngmǎ Lǚguǎn; ☎0892-8277 2191; dm/tr Y40/200) located at the very edge of town, at the top of the hill on the Zhāngmù side.

After Nyalam, the road drops like a stone into a lush, deep misty gorge lined with spectacular waterfalls, many of which are hundreds of metres high. You can feel the air getting thicker as you descend towards the subcontinent.

ZHĀNGMÙ

འགྲམ་ 樟木

☎0892 / ELEV 2250M

The frenetic border town of Zhāngmù (Khasa in Nepalese, Dram in Tibetan) hangs from the slopes above the tortuous final kilometres of the Friendship Highway. The smells of curry and incense float in the air, and the babbling sound of fast-flowing streams cuts through the traffic noise. After time on the high plateau, it's either a feast for the senses, or an unwelcome assault on the meditative mood you've been cultivating for the past weeks.

Sleeping & Eating

Sherpa Hotel HOTEL $$
(夏尔巴酒店; Xià'ěrbā Jiǔdiàn; ☎874 2098; d/tr without bathroom Y80/120, d with bathroom Y200) The pink-painted rooms are clean (if a little small) at this friendly hotel and hot water is available most of the time. The two bars at street level can be noisy but the back rooms remain fairly quiet. The rooms that face the valley afford spectacular views. The restaurant food is some of the best in town (dishes Y15 to Y40).

Zhāngmù Bīnguǎn HOTEL $$$
(樟木宾馆; ☎874 2221; d/tr Y480/580, deluxe r Y680, discounts of 15%) The modern rooms in this government-run hotel are luxurious by Tibetan standards, and the back rooms have great mountain views, but it's overpriced and the management is a bit snooty.

Base Camp Restaurant INTERNATIONAL FOOD $$
(大本营餐厅; Dàběnyíng Cāntīng; Ground fl, Gang Gyen Hotel; dishes Y20-45; 9am-midnight;) Looking a little like a Western sports bar (except with oxygen tanks and climbing gear instead of footballs and jerseys), this popular establishment serves a full range of Nepali, Chinese, Tibetan and Western mains, including steaks and breakfast foods. The curries are thick and delicious.

Information

The **Bank of China** (中国银行; Zhōngguó Yínháng; 9.30am-1.30pm & 3.30-6.30pm Mon-Fri, 11am-2pm Sat & Sun), up the hill, will change cash and travellers cheques into yuán, and also yuán into US dollars, euros or UK pounds if you have an exchange receipt (ie the receipt you get when you change foreign currency into yuán). It doesn't deal in Nepalese rupees; for those go to the moneychangers that operate openly in front of the Zhāngmù Hotel.

Western Tibet

Tibet's far wild west, known in Tibetan as Ngari, has few permanent settlers, but is nevertheless a lodestone to a billion pilgrims from three major religions (Buddhism, Hinduism and Jainism). They are drawn to the twin spiritual power places of Mt Kailash and Lake Manasarovar, two of the most legendary and far-flung destinations in the world.

Ngari is a blunt, expansive realm of salt lakes, Martian-style deserts, grassy steppes and towering snowcapped mountains. It's a mesmerising landscape, but also intensely remote: a few tents and herd of yaks may be all the signs of human existence one comes across in half a day's drive. It's a week-long, dusty, bumpy drive to Kailash – but then, perhaps some journeys shouldn't be too easy.

Warm clothes are essential on any trip to the region, even in summer, and a sleeping bag is recommended. The three-day *kora* around Mt Kailash can be done without a tent but bringing one will give you added flexibility and comfort. Accommodation along the way ranges from basic guesthouses to chilly hotel rooms. Few have attached bathrooms but most towns have at least one public bathhouse. Most towns now have well-stocked supermarkets, internet cafes and Chinese restaurants, though it's still worth bringing along a few treats, such as peanuts, chocolate bars and dehydrated food from home.

The only places to change money in Ngari are banks in Ali, and it's much easier to change US dollars as cash rather than travellers cheques. It's best just to bring what you expect to spend in renminbi.

When to Go

May, June and from mid-September to early October are probably the best times for travel in the region. During the summer months of July and August rains can temporarily wash out roads. The Drölma-la pass on the Mt Kailash *kora* is usually blocked with snow from late October or early November until early April. The festival of Saga Dawa (see p885) during May or June brings hundreds of pilgrims and tourists to the mountain.

Permits

You'll need a fistful of permits to visit Ngari: a TTB permit, Alien Travel Permit, military permit, foreign affairs permit etc. The travel agency that organises your 4WD trip will arrange these but will need a week, preferably two, to do so.

BORDER CROSSING: GETTING TO NEPAL

After filling in an exit and health form at **Chinese immigration** (⌚9.30am-6.30pm, sometimes closed 1.30-3.30pm) in Zhāngmù, access to Nepal is via the Friendship Bridge and Kodari, around 8km below Zhāngmù. Your 4WD should take you the distance, or cars and trucks offer rides across this stretch of no man's land for Y10.

At **Nepali immigration** (⌚8.30am-4pm) in Kodari, you can get a visa for the same price as in Lhasa (US$25/40/100 for a 15-/30-/90-day visa, or the equivalent in rupees, plus one passport photo), though it is sensible to get one beforehand in Lhasa just to be safe; see p890 for details. Note that Nepal is 2¼ hours behind Chinese time.

There are four daily buses to Kathmandu (Rs 240 to Rs 280, 4½ hours) – the 1.30pm is express – or take a bus to Barabise (Rs 65, three hours) and change. The easier option is to share a private vehicle with other travellers. Drivers will be outside immigration waiting to haggle. A ride to Kathmandu (four to five hours) costs Rs 3000 per car (Rs 800 per seat) but you'll struggle to find a driver after 5pm.

For further information, head to shop.lonelyplanet.com to purchase a downloadable PDF of the Kathmandu chapter from Lonely Planet's *Nepal* guide.

Getting There & Away

Four-wheel-drive trips to Mt Kailash require around 14 days if just taking the southern route, or 21 days for a loop combining both the northern and southern routes. Add on three days to explore the Guge Kingdom at Tsaparang. One good option is to exit at Zhāngmù, detouring from Saga to the Friendship Highway via the lake of Peiku-tso.

There is bus service along the northern route from Lhasa to Ali and on to Yèchéng in Xīnjiāng but foreigners are not permitted to take these.

SOUTHERN ROUTE

From Lhasa there are two routes to Ngari, the southern being the quicker option if you're headed straight for Mt Kailash. Both routes follow the paved Friendship Highway as far as the town of **Lhatse** (拉孜; Lāzī), where there are several hotels, including the **Lhatse Tibetan Farmers Hotel** (拉孜农民旅馆; Lāzī Nóngmíń Lǔguǎn; ☎832 2333; d without/with bathroom Y35/130), which also features a cosy Tibet-style restaurant.

After Lhatse, both routes continue on a mostly paved road to the hamlet of **Raga**. After this the routes split, with the southern one heading directly northwest towards Darchen. There are simple **guesthouses** (dm Y30) in Raga but most groups continue 60km to the larger military town of **Saga** (萨嘎; Sàgá), which has internet cafes and hot public showers. The **Saga Hotel** (萨嘎宾馆; Sàgá Bīnguǎn; ☎0892-820 2888; d/tr with bathroom Y420/360; ❄@) is right at the town crossroads and has hot showers and Western bathrooms. Tibetan guesthouses such as the cosy **Bo Tie The Clan Hotel** (Bodo Dronkhang; 博扎家族旅馆; Bózhá Jiāzú Lǔguǎn; dm Y30 per bed) are a 10-minute walk (800m) north of the centre.

Once the current road upgrading has finished you will be able to reach Darchen in one long day (490km) from Saga but until then most groups split the bouncy, scenic ride into two days. This also helps with the acclimatisation process. After Lhatse you never drop below 4000m.

In grubby **Paryang** (帕羊; Pàyáng), the **Shishapangma Hotel** (希夏邦马宾馆; Xīxiàbāngmǎ Bīnguǎn; dm/d per bed Y40/100) is popular with Indian pilgrims. The central **Tashi Hotel** (扎西旅馆; Zhāxī Lǔguǎn; dm Y30) is a smaller, simpler Tibetan-style place. From Paryang to Darchen is 245km.

NORTHERN ROUTE

The northern route splits from the southern at the little hamlet of Raga, heading almost due north. From here it's 3½ days to Ali and then another day to Darchen, but the reward for the extra mileage is passing through some of the most epic scenery on the planet. There are vast grasslands, massive turquoise salt lakes, dry-as-bones badlands, and mountain ranges coloured purple, red and green. Small herds of wild asses and Tibetan antelope are often spotted near the road, as are yak and sheep and their nomad herders.

After Raga, it's a full day's drive (235km) to **Tsochen** (措勤; Cuòqín), via spectacular Tagyel-tso. The **Friendship Feria Hotel** (友谊宾馆; Yǒuyì Bīnguǎn; ☎0897-261 2308; d/tr/q without bathroom Y120/150/200) is at the beginning of town on the left, before the petrol station. Rooms are clean and there's plenty of hot and cold water in drums, with outside pit toilets. The town has electricity between 7pm and 1am. You will have to register at the local PSB office.

After Tsochen it's a shorter day's drive to **Gertse** (改则; Gǎizé), a dull town, where most 4WD groups stay in the **Xīnqìxiàng Zhāodàisuǒ** (新气象招待所; r without bathroom Y120), with spacious rooms for one to four people, all at the same price. There are plenty of good Sìchuān and Muslim restaurants on the main strip and a couple of **public showers** (淋浴; línyù; showers Y10). On the southern outskirts is a long strip of photogenic whitewashed *chörtens* and prayer flags that draws pilgrims in the evening.

After Gertse the next stop is **Gegye** (革吉; Géjí), a midsized army town where the best place to stay is the **Shuǐlì Bīnguǎn** (水利宾馆; ☎0897-263 2146; cnr Yanhu Lu & Hebei Lu; r Y100), with clean rooms and shared indoor squat toilets.

ALI ཨ་ལི་ 阿里

From Gegye to **Ali** (Ālǐ), the largest town in Ngari, it's only a few hours' drive along the infant Indus River, but most groups spend the night in Ali to freshen up after many days without showers, and stock up on supplies.

The **Agricultural Bank of China** (中国农业银行; Zhōngguó Nóngyè Yínháng; ⏲10am-7pm Mon-Fri), near the army post, west of the roundabout, will change US dollars, euros and UK pounds (cash only) and has an ATM. **Gésāng Wǎngchéng** (格桑网城; Shiquanhe Zhonglu; per hr Y10; ⏲24hr) east of the roundabout, offers internet access.

Half a kilometre east of the traffic circle, the decent **Shénhú Bīnguǎn** (神湖宾馆; ☎136-3897 7982; s/d without bathroom Y50/80, s/d with bathroom Y150/140) is a good first choice, owned by the Yak Hotel in Lhasa. The **Heng Yuan Guesthouse** (恒远宾馆; Héngyuǎn Bīnguǎn; ☎282 8288; s/d with bathroom Y120/140, tr without bathroom Y150) on the main roundabout has decent rooms in the main building (avoid the back courtyard rooms) but chaotic management. The PSB usually prevents foreigners from staying in the cheaper hotels.

For a taste of Central Asia, head to the popular Uighur restaurant (*ashkhana* in Turkic), 100m north of the main roundabout, for great nan bread, *suoman* (fried noodle squares) and mutton kebabs.

Ali's Kunsha airport opened in 2010, about 50km south of the city, with two or three weekly flights to Lhasa (Y2400) and on to Chéngdū.

MT KAILASH གངས་རིན་པོ་ཆེ་ 冈仁波斋峰

Known in Tibetan as Kang Rinpoche, or 'Precious Jewel of Snow', the hulking pyramidal shaped Mt Kailash (Gāng Rénbōzhāi Fēng; 6714m) seldom needs to be pointed out to travellers: it just dominates the landscape. For Buddhists, Kailash is the abode of Demchok, a wrathful manifestation of Sakyamuni. For Hindus it is the domain of Shiva, the Destroyer and Transformer.

It's not hard to see why Kailash became associated long ago with the myth of a great mountain, the navel of the world. A little more surprising is that this mountain was said to be the source of the four major rivers of Asia: and most astonishing that the legends are more or less true. The drainage system around Kailash and Lake Manasarovar is in fact the source of the Karnali (a major tributary of the Ganges), the Brahmaputra,

ALTITUDE SICKNESS

Altitude sickness (or acute mountain sickness, AMS) is no joke and it is quite common to discover that the nice travellers you met on the way into Lhasa have left the next day, sick as a dog (or worse) from the change in altitude. While medicines such as Diamox can certainly help (see p1013), it's best to avoid shocking your system, by rising in altitude gradually.

The train allows for slightly better acclimatisation than the flight but most people experience only minor symptoms (headaches, breathlessness) when flying in to Lhasa (3600m), as long as they take things easy for their first couple of days. The key is to ascend gradually, preferably less than 500m per day. Spend up to a week in and around Lhasa before heading to higher elevations like Nam-tso or Western Tibet and don't even think about heading straight to Everest Base Camp (5150m) from Kathmandu (1300m), even if you stay overnight in Nyalam (3750m) en route.

If you are really concerned about AMS, spend some time at higher elevations in western Sìchuān or Nepal before travelling to Lhasa.

WORTH A TRIP

THE LOST KINGDOM OF GUGE

One worthwhile detour from either Ali or Darchen is to the surreal ruins of the **Guge Kingdom** at **Tsaparang** (admission Y200). The ruins, which seem to grow like a honeycomb out of the barren hills, were once the centre of one of Tibet's most prosperous kingdoms. The tunnels and caves are great fun to explore and the chapels offer superb examples of Kashmiri-influenced mural art. A trip here will add three days to your itinerary, but is worth it to see some outstanding scenery and one of Asia's little-known wonders.

From either Ali or Darchen it's a day's drive to **Zanda** (札达; Zhádá), the nearest town to Tsaparang (18km away), and home to spectacular Thöling Monastery.

Indus and Sutlej Rivers. A visit to Kailash puts you squarely in one of the geographical and spiritual centres of the world.

Activities

Many pilgrims are often happy enough just to gaze at the southern face of Kailash (scarred in such a way that it resembles a swastika – a Buddhist and Hindu symbol of spiritual strength). But for Tibetans and most foreign travellers the purpose of coming here is to complete a *kora* around the mountain.

The *kora* begins in grubby **Darchen** (塔尔钦; Tǎ'ěrqīn; 4560m), and takes (on average) three days to complete (though most Tibetans do it in one long 15-hour day). The *kora* is not a climb to the top, but a walk around the central peak. The highest point is the 5630m Drölma-la pass, though no point is below 4600m.

The first day is a 20km walk (six to seven hours) from Darchen to Dira-puk Monastery. The ascent is minimal, which allows you to take your time and enjoy the otherworldly landscape of the Lha-chu river valley. The second day is the hardest, as it involves the ascent to the Drölma-la pass, the steep descent down the pass to the Lham-chu Khir river valley, and hike to the Zutul-puk Monastery. Expect to take eight hours or more to complete this 18km stretch. The final day is a relatively simple 14km (three hours) walk back to Darchen.

Any reasonably fit and acclimatised person should be able to complete the three-day walk, but come prepared with warm and waterproof clothing and equipment. Local guides and porters are available in Darchen for Y120 a day. Larger groups often hire yaks to carry their supplies.

Travellers must register with the **Public Security Bureau** (PSB; 公安局; Gōng'ānjú) in Darchen and pay Y200 for a joint Kailash and Manasarovar entry fee.

Sleeping & Eating

At the end of each day's walk there is accommodation (Y40 to Y60) at the local monasteries or in a nearby guesthouse, though it's advisable to carry a tent if walking during July and August or the popular Saga Dawa festival. Instant noodles, tea and beer are available at nomad tents along the way, but bring hot drinks and snacks with you.

Most travellers spend a night in Darchen before and after the *kora*. Guesthouses offer basic accommodation (no running water, outdoor pit toilets). There are a couple of supermarkets and a public shower; internet might be available by the time you read this.

Pilgrim Hotel GUESTHOUSE
(朝圣宾馆; Cháoshèng Bīnguǎn; ☎0897-298 0833; dm Y60; @) Donates part of its profits to local monasteries.

Lhasa Holyland Guesthouse GUESTHOUSE
(拉萨圣地康桑旅馆; Lāsà Shèngdì Kāngsāng Lǚguǎn; ☎139-8907 0818; dm Y60-70) Houses the local PSB office.

Darchen Aid the Poor Programme Hotel TIBETAN FOOD
(塔尔青利民扶贫宾馆; Tǎ'ěrqīng Lìmín Fúpín Bīnguǎn; mains Y10-25) This cosy Tibetan-style restaurant is our favourite place to eat; also has decent rooms.

LAKE MANASAROVAR

མཚོ་མ་ཕམ་ 玛旁雄错

After their *kora*, most travellers head to Lake Manasarovar (Mǎpáng Xióngcuò), or Mapham Yum-tso (Victorious Lake) in Tibetan, to rest and gaze across the sapphire-blue waters at a perfect snowcapped mountain backdrop. The lake is the most venerated in Tibet, and has its own five-day *kora*.

Picturesque **Chiu village**, sight of the Chiu Monastery, overlooks the northwestern shore of the lake, and here you'll find a half-dozen identical friendly **guesthouses** (dm Y50), some right down at the water's edge. Basic meals are available.

Understand China

population per sq km

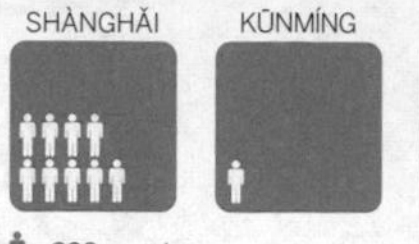

China Today

» Population: 1.34 billion

» GDP (PPP): $8.75 trillion

» GDP per capita: $6600

» Labour force: 813 million

» Unemployment: 4.3%

» Highest point: Mount Everest (8848m)

» Annual alcohol consumption (per person): 5.2L

China Superpower?

For decades, the world has been awestruck by China's potential. Gazing into the statistics of growth, it's all too easy to fall in with those who perceive China as an emergent superpower. The picture is even easier to see with a West crippled by austerity measures. Books such as *When China Rules the World* by Martin Jacques triumphantly declare the establishment of a new world order.

China's apparent ability to shrug off the financial crisis (despite a downturn in exports) through a massive stimulus package revealed a robust resilience to ride out the worst. Despite a slowing in the rate of economic growth, the Chinese economy continues to expand at a rate of around 10% and the growing middle-classes are upbeat. China has it sewn up, say the pundits.

From a Western perspective, there is understandable agreement. China can be both ultramodern (space missions, the Pudong skyline, Maglev trains) and very powerful (a vast standing army, a gigantic economy), despite only three decades of growth. Naysayers discern a coming crash, initiated perhaps by the pricking of a property market bubble, Japan 1990s-style, and a subsequent cascade downwards, but just as many pundits are optimistic, insisting that the only way is up.

China's more balanced perspective is that it is a developing nation, and a vast difference in magnitude separates it from being a superpower. It is wise to remember that China's per capita GDP puts it roughly on a level with Namibia. China possesses colossal latent power by virtue of its size and huge population, but these dimensions have also hampered equal growth across the nation. Inequality in China is among the most extreme in the world, something perhaps unforgivable

Top Books

When a Billion Chinese Jump (Jonathan Watts) China's environmental travails under the microscope, and it's not pretty.

The Rape of Nanking (Iris Chang) Puts into perspective China's deep-rooted ambivalence towards its island neighbour, Japan.

Diary of a Madman and Other Stories (Lu Xun) Astonishing tales from the father of modern Chinese fiction.

belief systems
(% of population)

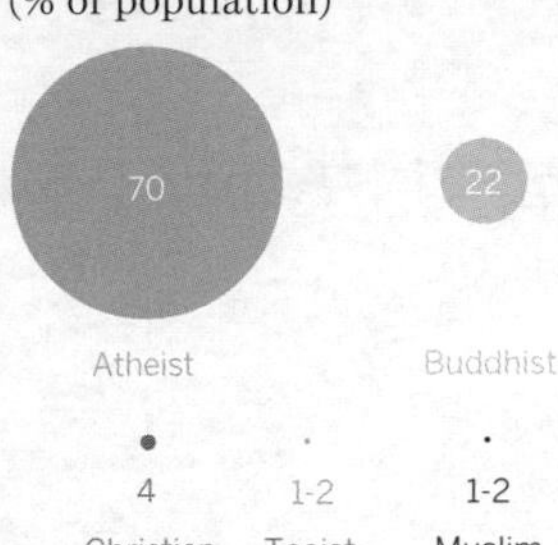

if China were 100 people

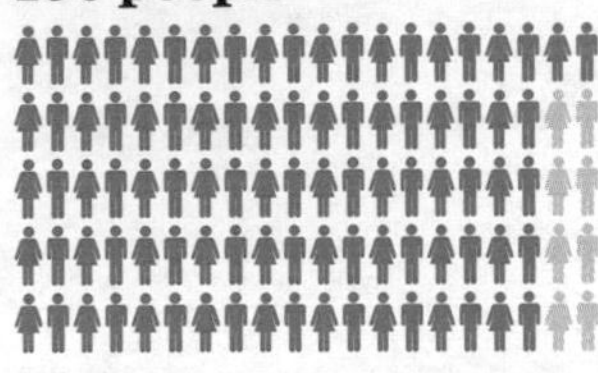

for a communist government. The urban middle class is growing rapidly, but most of China remains rural and poor.

China dazzles in its big cities, but often lacks even the most basic equipment and systems. The Dàlián oil spill (p288) in July 2010 came in the same week that China overtook the US as the world's largest energy consumer making the nation a superpower at least in oil dependency terms. But the ensuing clean-up operation saw a ragtag navy of fishing boats tackling the spill, as workers used their bare hands, straw mats, pots and stockings full of human hair to battle the oil. What the world saw was the vast and poorly equipped mobilisation of one of China's greatest resources – its people – to tackle the spill. It worked, but it wasn't modern.

China is a growing power but has yet to commission its first aircraft carrier and is unable to project conventional military power far beyond its borders. The nation is also tentative about assuming a leadership role either in the Far East or on the world stage, partly because the US remains powerful in the Pacific region and also because China remains focused on, if not obsessed with, domestic concerns (and Taiwan).

Harmony

The Chinese leadership under Hu Jintao has taken pains to stress 'harmony' throughout society, as part of China's formula of a 'peaceful rise'. Mocked by many Chinese, the vapid notion of 'harmony' is being sold across the nation at a time when China is undergoing a phenomenal period of social stress. Some analysts suggest that ostensible harmony is easier to achieve in authoritarian states like China, because the press is muffled, free speech disallowed and dissent quashed. The 11-year sentencing of Liu Xiaobo for his democratic agenda in Charter 08 is only

Top Films

Still Life (Jia Zhangke; 2005) Bleak and hauntingly beautiful portrayal of a family devastated by the construction of the Three Gorges Dam.

Raise the Red Lantern (Zhang Yimou; 1991) The exquisitely fashioned tragedy from the sumptuous palette of the Fifth Generation.

harmonious in the sense he has been silenced, perhaps explaining why Běijīng reacted with such venom to his Nobel Peace Prize in 2010.

The laws of social entropy apply in China as elsewhere, however, and tensions inevitably ripple across the surface of society, or suddenly explode with eye-blinking ferocity. A series of bizarre kindergarten massacres in 2010 shocked the nation. Many Chinese called for greater understanding of those afflicted by mental health problems, a malady that carries great stigma in Chinese society. Others pointed to agonising dysfunction at the heart of modern Chinese society.

Ethnic relations are also prickly. The underlying tensions that ignited deadly riots in Tibet in 2008 and Xīnjiāng in 2009 are perhaps yet to be fully addressed, although Běijīng believes a combination of investment and blaming separatists and outsiders is the solution.

As a poke in the eye to those who saw China's growing middle class as a democratising influence, evidence suggests Běijīng is becoming less tolerant of dissent. Lawyers, human rights advocates and democracy activists who attempt to organise resistance to Běijīng's authority routinely face charges of endangering national security.

Meanwhile, morale is low in the ranks of Western businessmen in China as they bridle under regulations designed to protect local businesses.

A certain fragility exists in China's increasing sense of confidence and growing self-assurance. Some of this transmutes into a worrying nationalism, which is particularly appealing to young Chinese who perhaps lack other ideologies they can believe in.

Dos & Don'ts

» Never, ever fight to settle the bill if your Chinese host is determined to pay.

» Take off your shoes when visiting a Chinese person's home, or offer to.

» Never give a clock as a gift as it has morbid overtones.

Myths

» The Chinese are hard-working – for sure, but don't expect service with a smile at the train station ticket office.

» The Chinese are communists – some are, more aren't.

» You can see the Great Wall from space – motorways would be more visible as they're far wider.

History

The epic sweep of China's history paints a perhaps deceiving impression of long epochs of peace occasionally convulsed by break-up, internecine division or external attack. Yet China has, for much of its history, been in conflict either internally or with outsiders. Although China's size and shape has also continuously changed – from tiny beginnings by the Yellow River (Huáng Hé) to the subcontinent of today – an uninterrupted thread of history runs from its earliest roots to the full flowering of Chinese civilisation. Powerful links connect the Chinese of today with their ancestors 5000 or 6000 years ago, creating the longest-lasting civilisation on earth.

From Oracle Bones to Confucius

The earliest 'Chinese' dynasty, the Shang, was long considered apocryphal. However, archaeological evidence – cattle bones and turtle shells in Hénán covered in mysterious scratches, recognised by a scholar as an early form of Chinese writing – proved that a society known as the Shang developed in central China from around 1766 BC. The area it controlled was tiny – perhaps 200km across – but Chinese historians have argued that the Shang was the first Chinese dynasty. By using Chinese writing on 'oracle bones', the dynasty marked its connection with the Chinese civilisation of the present day.

Sometime between 1050 and 1045 BC, a neighbouring group known as the Zhou conquered Shang territory. The Zhou was one of many states competing for power in the next few hundred years, but developments during this period created some of the key sources of Chinese culture that would last till the present day. A constant theme of the first millennium BC was conflict, particularly the periods known as the 'Spring and Autumn' (722–481 BC) and 'Warring States' (475–221 BC).

The Chinese world in the 5th century BC was both warlike and intellectually fertile, rather like ancient Greece during the same period.

Ban Zhao was the most famous woman scholar in early China. Dating from the late 1st century AD, her work *Lessons for Women* advocated chastity and modesty as favoured female qualities.

TIMELINE

c 4000 BC

Archaeological evidence for the first settlements along the Yellow River (Huáng Hé). Even today, the river remains a central cultural reference point for the Chinese.

c 1700 BC

Craftsmen of the Shang dynasty master the production of bronzeware, in one of the first examples of multiple production in history. The bronzes were ritual vessels.

c 600 BC

Laotzu (Laozi), founder of Taoism, is supposedly born. The folk religion of Taoism coexisted with later introductions such as Buddhism, a reflection of Chinese religion's syncretic, rather than exclusive, nature.

From this disorder emerged the thinking of Confucius (551–479 BC), whose system of thought and ethics underpinned Chinese culture for 2500 years (see p141). A wandering teacher, Confucius gave lessons in personal behaviour and statecraft, advocating an ordered and ethical society obedient towards hierarchies. Confucius' desire for an ordered and ethical world seems a far cry from the warfare of the time he lived in.

So far, some 7000 soldiers in the famous Terracotta Army have been found near Xī'ān. The great tomb of the first emperor still remains unexcavated, although it is thought to have been looted soon after it was built.

Early Empires

The Warring States period ended decisively in 221 BC. The Qin kingdom conquered other states in the central Chinese region and Qin Shi Huang declared himself emperor. The first in a line of rulers that would last until 1912, later histories portrayed Qin Shi Huang as particularly cruel and tyrannical, but the distinction is dubious as the ensuing Han dynasty (206 BC–AD 220) adopted many of the short-lived Qin's practices of government.

Qin Shi Huang oversaw vast public works projects, including walls built by some 300,000 men, connecting defences into what would become the Great Wall. He unified the currency, measurements and written language, providing the basis for a cohesive state.

Establishing a trend that would echo through Chinese history, a peasant, Liu Bang, rose up and conquered China, founding the Han dynasty. The dynasty is so important that the name Hàn (汉; 漢) still refers to ethnic Chinese. Critical to the centralisation of power, Emperor Wu (140–87 BC) institutionalised Confucian norms in government.

CONFUCIUS TEMPLES 文庙

Despite the rechampioning of the Shāndōng sage as a lynchpin of CCP (Chinese Communist Party) efforts to create a 'harmonious' society, Confucian temples *(wénmiào)* remain passive and inanimate places (unless it's Kǒngzi's birthday). This, however, is part of their appeal: they are peaceful, unhurried and often silent.

» Confucius Temple, Qūfù (p142): the mother of all patriarchal temples, in Qūfù, Confucius' birthplace

» Confucius Temple, Běijīng (p58): China's second largest Confucius temple and a haven of peace in Běijīng

» Confucius Temple, Jiànshuǐ (p651): locals insist it's China's biggest

» Confucius Temple, Píngyáo (p350): housing Píngyáo's oldest building in one of China's most magnificent old towns

» Confucius Temple, Tài Shān (p139): not such an amazing temple, but its location atop one of China's most famous mountains is peerless

551 BC

The birth of Confucius. Collected in *The Analects*, his ideas of an ethical, ordered society that operated through hierarchy and self-development would dominate Chinese culture until the early 20th century.

KRZYSZTOF DYDYNSKI

» Confucius (p141) statue

214 BC

Emperor Qin indentures thousands of labourers to link existing city walls into one Great Wall, made of tamped earth. The stone-clad bastion dates from the Ming dynasty.

c 100 BC

The Silk Road between China and the Middle East means that Chinese goods become known in places as far off as Rome.

RUINS

Many of China's historical artefacts may be in a state of perpetual ruin, but some vestiges get top-billing:

» Ruins of the Church of St Paul (p511): China's most sublime architectural wreck

» Jiànkòu Great Wall (p103): no other section of the Great Wall does the tumble-down look in such dramatic fashion

» Great Fountain Ruins (p69): sublime tangle of Jesuit-designed stonework

» Xanadu (p856): a vivid imagination is required to conjure up impressions of Kublai Khan's pleasure palace

» Ming City Wall Ruins Park (p58): Běijīng's last section of Ming city wall

Promoting merit as well as order, he was the first leader to experiment with examinations for entry into the bureaucracy, but his dynasty was plagued by economic troubles, as estate owners controlled more and more land. Indeed, the issue of land ownership would be a constant problem throughout Chinese history, to today. Endemic economic problems and the inability to exercise control over a growing empire led to the collapse and downfall of the Han. Social problems included an uprising by Taoists (known as the Yellow Turbans). Upheaval would become a constant refrain in later Chinese dynasties.

The Han demonstrated clearly that China is fundamentally a Eurasian power in its relations with neighbouring peoples. To the north, the Xiongnu (a name given to various nomadic tribes of Central Asia) posed the greatest threat to China. Diplomatic links were also formed with Central Asian tribes, and the great Chinese explorer Zhang Qian provided the authorities with information on the possibilities of trade and alliances in northern India. During the same period, Chinese influence percolated into areas that would later become known as Vietnam and Korea.

Parts of the Grand Canal still function as a waterway and other sections are being enlisted as elements of the south–north water diversion project (p972).

Disunity Restored

Between the early 3rd and late 6th centuries AD, north China witnessed a succession of rival kingdoms vying for power while a potent division formed between north and south. Riven by warfare, the north was controlled by non-Chinese rule, most successfully by the Northern Wei dynasty (386–534), founded by the Tuoba, a northern people who embraced Buddhism and left behind some of China's finest Buddhist art, including the famous caves outside Dūnhuáng (p828). A succession of rival regimes followed until nobleman Yang Jian (d 604) reunified China

c 100 BC

Buddhism first arrives in China from India. This religious system ends up thoroughly assimilated into Chinese culture and is now more powerful in China than in its country of origin.

AD 755–763

An Lushan rebels against the Tang court. Although his rebellion is put down, the court cedes immense military and fiscal power to provincial leaders, a recurring problem through Chinese history.

874

The Huang Chao rebellion breaks out, which will help reduce the Tang empire to chaos and lead to the fall of the capital in 907.

c 1000

The major premodern inventions – paper, printing, gunpowder, compass – are commonly used in China. The economy begins to commercialise and create a countrywide market system.

under the fleeting Sui dynasty (581–618). His son Sui Yangdi contributed greatly to the unification of south and north through construction of the Grand Canal, which was later extended and remained the empire's most important communication route between south and north until the late 19th century. After instigating three unsuccessful incursions onto Korean soil, resulting in disastrous military setbacks, Sui Yangdi faced revolt on the streets and was assassinated in 618 by one of his high officials.

Evidence from Han tombs suggests that a popular item of cuisine was a thick vegetable and meat stew, and that flavour enhancers such as soy sauce and honey were also used.

The Tang: China Looks West

The Tang rule (618–907) was an outward-looking time, when China embraced the culture of its neighbours – marriage to Central Asian people or wearing Indian-influenced clothes was part of the era's cosmopolitan élan – and distant nations that reached China via the Silk Road. The Chinese nostalgically regard the Tang as their cultural zenith. The output of the Tang poets is still regarded as China's finest, as is Tang sculpture, while its legal code became a standard for the whole East Asian region.

The Tang was founded by the Sui general Li Yuan, his achievements consolidated by his son Taizong (626–49). Cháng'ān (modern Xī'ān) became the world's most dazzling capital, with its own cosmopolitan foreign quarter, a population of a million, a market where merchants from as far away as Persia mingled with locals and an astonishing city wall that eventually enveloped 83 sq km. The city exemplified the Tang devotion to Buddhism, with some 91 temples recorded in the city in 722, but a tolerance of and even absorption with foreign cultures allowed alien faiths a foothold, including Nestorian Christianity, Manichaeism, Islam, Judaism and Zoroastrianism.

Taizong was succeeded by a unique figure: Chinese history's sole reigning woman emperor, Wu Zetian (625–705). Under her leadership the empire reached its greatest extent, spreading well north of the Great

HISTORY BOOKS

» *The City of Heavenly Tranquillity: Beijing in the History of China* (Jasper Becker; 2009): Becker's authoritative and heartbreaking rendering of Běijīng's transformation from magnificent Ming capital to communist-capitalist hybrid

» *The Penguin History of Modern China: The Fall and Rise of a Great Power 1850–2008* (Jonathan Fenby): highly readable account of the paroxysms of modern Chinese history

» *China, A History* (John Key; 2008): an accessible and well-written journey through Middle Kingdom history

1215
Genghis Khan conquers Běijīng as part of his creation of a massive Eurasian empire under Mongol rule. The Mongols overstretch themselves, however, and neglect good governance.

1286
The Grand Canal is extended to Běijīng. Over time, the canal becomes a major artery for the transport of grain, salt and other important commodities between north and south China.

1298–99
Marco Polo writes his famous account of his travels to China. Inconsistencies in his story have led some scholars to doubt whether he ever went to China at all.

1368
Zhu Yuanzhang founds the Ming dynasty and tries to impose a rigid Confucian social order on the entire population. However, China is now too commercialised for the policy to work.

Wall and far west into inner Asia. Her strong promotion of Buddhism, however, alienated her from the Confucian officials and in 705 she was forced to abdicate in favour of Xuanzong, who would preside over the greatest disaster in the Tang's history: the rebellion of An Lushan.

Xuanzong appointed minorities from the frontiers as generals, in the belief that they were so far removed from the political system and society that ideas of rebellion or coups would not enter their minds. Nevertheless, it was An Lushan, a general of Sogdian-Turkic parentage, who took advantage of his command in north China to make a bid for imperial power. The fighting lasted from 755 to 763, and although An Lushan was defeated, the Tang's control over China was destroyed forever. It had ceded huge amounts of military and tax-collecting power to provincial leaders to enable them to defeat the rebels, and in doing so dissipated its own power. This was a permanent change in the relationship between the government and the provinces; previous to 755, the government had an idea of who owned what land throughout the empire, but after that date the central government's control was permanently weakened. Even today, the dilemma has not been fully resolved.

In its last century, the Tang withdrew from its former openness, turning more strongly to Confucianism, while Buddhism was outlawed by Emperor Wuzong from 842 to 845. The ban was later modified, but Buddhism never regained its previous power and prestige. The Tang decline was marked by imperial frailty, growing insurgencies, upheaval and chaos.

EUNUCHS

The Tang saw the first major rise to power of eunuchs. Often from ethnic minority groups, they were brought to the capital and given positions within the imperial palace. In many dynasties they had real influence.

Open Markets, Bound Feet

Further disunity – the fragmentary-sounding Five Dynasties or Ten Kingdoms period – followed the fall of the Tang until the Northern Song dynasty (960–1127) was established. The Song dynasty existed in a state of constant conflict with its northern neighbours. The Northern Song was a rather small empire coexisting with the non Chinese Liao dynasty (which controlled a belt of Chinese territory south of the Great Wall that now marked China's northern border) and less happily with the Western Xia, another non-Chinese power that pressed hard on the northwestern provinces. In 1126 the Song lost its capital, Kāifēng, to a third non-Chinese people, the Jurchen (previously an ally against the Liao). The Song was driven to its southern capital of Hángzhōu for the period of the Southern Song (1127–1279), yet the period was culturally rich and economically prosperous.

The full institution of a system of examinations for entry into the Chinese bureaucracy was brought to fruition during the Song. At a time when brute force decided who was in control in much of medieval Europe, young Chinese men sat tests on the Confucian classics, obtaining

1406

Ming Emperor Yongle begins construction of the 800 buildings of the Forbidden City. This complex, along with much of the Great Wall, shows the style and size of late-imperial architecture.

1557

The Portuguese establish a permanent trade base in Macau, the first of the European outposts that will eventually lead to imperialist dominance of China from the mid-19th century.

c 1600

The period of China's dominance as the world's greatest economy begins to end. By 1800 European economies are industrialising and clearly dominant.

1644

Běijīng falls to peasant rebel Li Zicheng and the last Ming emperor Chongzhen hangs himself in Jǐngshān Park; the Qing dynasty is established.

The features of the largest Buddhist statue in the Ancestor Worshipping Cave at the Lóngmén Caves outside Luòyáng are supposedly based on Tang female emperor Wu Zetian, a famous champion of Buddhism.

office if successful (most were not). The system was heavily biased towards the rich, but was remarkable in its rationalisation of authority, and lasted for centuries. The classical texts set for the examinations became central to the transmission of a sense of elite Chinese culture, even though in later centuries the system's rigidity failed to adapt to social and intellectual change.

China's economy prospered during the Song rule, as cash crops and handicraft products became far more central to the economy, and a genuinely China-wide market emerged, which would become even stronger during the Ming and Qing dynasties. The sciences and arts also flourished under the Song, with intellectual and technical advances across many disciplines. Kāifēng emerged as an eminent centre of politics, commerce and culture.

The cultural quirk of foot binding appears to have emerged during the Song. It is still unknown how the custom of binding up a girl's feet in cloths so that they would never grow larger than the size of a fist began, yet for much of the next few centuries, it became a Chinese social norm.

Mongols to Ming

The fall of the Song reinforced notions of China's Eurasian location and growing external threats. Genghis Khan (1167–1227) was beginning his rise to power, turning his sights on China; he took Běijīng in 1215, destroying and rebuilding it; his successors seized Hángzhōu, the Southern Song capital, in 1276. The court fled and, in 1279, Southern Song resistance finally expired. Kublai Khan, grandson of Genghis, now reigned over all of China as emperor of the Yuan dynasty. Under Kublai, the entire population was divided into categories of Han, Mongol and foreigner, with the top administrative posts reserved for Mongols, even though the examination system was revived in 1315. The latter decision unexpectedly strengthened the role of local landed elites:

HISTORY MUSEUMS

» Hong Kong Museum of History (p481): one of the former British territory's best museums: a colourful narrative supported by imaginative displays

» Shànghǎi History Museum (p178): excellent chronicle of Shànghǎi's colourful journey from 'Little Sūzhōu' to 'Whore of the Orient' and beyond

» Macau Museum (p511): the ex-Portuguese territory's fascinating history brought vividly to life

» Shaanxi History Museum (p362): eye-opening chronicle of ancient Chang'an

1689
The Treaty of Nerchinsk is signed, delineating the border between China and Russia: this is the first modern border agreement in Chinese history, as well as the longest lasting.

1793
British diplomat Lord Macartney visits Běijīng with British industrial products, but is told by the Qianlong emperor that China has no need of his products.

1823
The British are swapping roughly 7000 chests of opium annually – with about 140 pounds of opium per chest, enough to supply one million addicts – compared to 1000 chests in 1773.

1839
The Qing official Lin Zexu demands that British traders at Guǎngzhōu hand over 20,000 chests of opium, leading the British to provoke the First Opium War in retaliation.

since elite Chinese could not advance in the bureaucracy, they decided to spend more time tending their large estates instead. Another innovation was the use of paper money, although overprinting created a problem with inflation.

The Mongols ultimately proved less able at governance than warfare, their empire succumbing to rebellion within a century and eventual vanquishment. Ruling as Ming emperor Hongwu, Zhu Yuanzhang established his capital in Nánjīng, but by the early 15th century the court had begun to move back to Běijīng, where a hugely ambitious reconstruction project was inaugurated by Emperor Yongle (r 1403–24), building the Forbidden City and devising the layout of the city we see today.

Although the Ming tried to impose a traditional social structure in which people stuck to hereditary occupations, the era was in fact one of great commercial growth and social change. Women became subject to stricter social norms (for instance, widow remarriage was frowned upon) but female literacy also grew. Publishing, via woodblock technology, burgeoned and the novel appeared.

Emperor Yongle, having usurped power from his nephew, was keen to establish his own legitimacy. In 1405 he launched the first of seven great maritime expeditions. Led by the eunuch general Zheng He (1371–1433), the fleet consisted of more than 60 large vessels and 255 smaller ones, carrying nearly 28,000 men. The fourth and fifth expeditions departed in 1413 and 1417, and travelled as far as the present Middle East. The great achievement of these voyages was to bring tribute missions to the capital, including two embassies from Egypt. Yet ultimately, they were a dead end, motivated by Yongle's vanity to outdo his father, not for the purpose of conquest nor the establishment of a settled trade network. The emperors after Yongle had little interest in continuing the voyages, and China dropped anchor on its global maritime explorations.

The Great Wall was re-engineered and clad in brick while ships also arrived from Europe, presaging an overseas threat that would develop from entirely different directions. Traders were quickly followed by missionaries, and the Jesuits, led by the formidable Matteo Ricci, made their way inland and established a presence at court. Ricci learned fluent Chinese and spent years agonising over how Christian tenets could be made attractive in a Confucian society with very different norms. The Portuguese presence linked China directly to trade with the New World, which had opened up in the 16th century. New crops, such as potatoes, maize, cotton and tobacco, were introduced, further stimulating the commercial economy. Merchants often lived opulent lives, building fine private gardens (as in Sūzhōu) and buying delicate flowers and fruits.

CHINESE JEWS

Little if anything remains of the synagogue in the Song capital of Kāifēng, but the city once harboured the country's largest population of Chinese Jews, some of whom survive to this day.

1842

The Treaty of Nánjīng concludes the first Opium War. China is forced to hand over Hong Kong island to the British and open up five Chinese ports to foreign trade.

HUW JONES

» Victoria Harbour (p481), Hong Kong

1856

Hong Xiuquan claims to be Jesus' younger brother and starts the Taiping uprising. With the simultaneous Nian and Muslim uprisings, the Taiping greatly undermines the authority of the Qing dynasty.

The Ming was eventually undermined by internal power struggles. Natural disasters, including drought and famine, combined with a menace from the north. The Manchu, a nomadic warlike people, saw the turmoil within China and invaded.

The Qing: the Path to Dynastic Dissolution

After conquering just a small part of China and assuming control in the disarray, the Manchu named their new dynasty the Qing (1644–1911). Once ensconced in the (now torched) Forbidden City, the Manchu realised they needed to adapt their nomadic way of life to suit the agricultural civilisation of China. Threats from inner Asia were neutralised by

A BEASTLY AFFAIR

In February 2009, China was in uproar about the sale of two bronze animal heads by the auction house Christie's. The saga was the latest twist and turn in a story stretching back to 1860, when the Old Summer Palace in Běijīng was torched by Anglo-French troops at the end of the Second Opium War and the animal heads were pilfered.

The 12 heads belonged to a dozen statues with human bodies and animal heads (representing the 12 animals of the Chinese zodiac) that jetted water from their mouths in 12 two-hour sequences, part of an elaborate structure called the Hǎiyàntáng.

Four of the original 12 animal heads have been repatriated (by being bought at auction or donated) and can be seen at the Poly Art Museum (p65). Of the eight still abroad, the rat and rabbit heads became the focus of a powerful Chinese sense of injustice in 2009 when they appeared at Christie's.

A convincing moral argument exists that the animal heads should be returned to China; however, others pointed to the lack of conclusive evidence that the animal heads had been stolen by French or British troops; the possibility also existed, others argued, that they had been plundered by Chinese for sale abroad to international clients.

The animal heads are perhaps a peculiar choice of national ire for the Chinese, considering they are evidently Western in fashion, designed by the Jesuit minds which also fashioned the Western palace buildings at the Old Summer Palace. It has also been suggested that the Empress Dowager disliked the heads so much that she had them removed; if that story is true, where were they stored? Although the Old Summer Palace was certainly torched by the French and the British, there are also indications that some Chinese also joined in the looting, eager to get back at Manchu rule.

What is evident is that the ruins, and the animal heads, have become eternal symbols of China's humiliation at the hands of the foreign powers, and icons that increasingly resonate as the country assumes a more central role in international affairs.

1882

Shànghǎi is electrified by the British-founded Shanghai Electric Company. Shànghǎi's first electricity-producing plant generates 654kw and the Bund is illuminated by electric light the following year.

GREG ELMS

» The Bund (p165), Shànghǎi

1898

Emperor Guangxu permits major reforms, including new rights for women, but is thwarted by the Dowager Empress Cixi, who has many reformers arrested and executed.

1898

The New Territories adjoining Kowloon in Hong Kong are leased to the British for 99 years, eventually returning, along with the rest of Hong Kong, in 1997.

incorporating the Qing homeland of Manchuria into the empire, as well as that of the Mongols, whom they had subordinated. Like the Mongols before them, the conquering Manchu found themselves in charge of a civilisation whose government they had defeated, but whose cultural power far exceeded their own. The result was quite contradictory: on the one hand, Qing rulers took great pains to win the allegiance of high officials and cultural figures by displaying a familiarity and respect for traditional Chinese culture; on the other hand, the Manchu rulers were at great pains to remain distinct. They enforced strict rules of social separation between the Han and Manchu, and tried to maintain – not always very successfully – a culture that reminded the Manchu of their nomadic warrior past. The Qing flourished most greatly under three emperors who ruled for a total of 135 years: Kangxi, Yongzheng and Qianlong.

PUBLISHING

Mass publishing, using woodblock printing, took off during the Ming dynasty. Among the bestsellers of the era were swashbuckling novels such as *The Water Margin* and *The Romance of the Three Kingdoms*.

Much of the map of China that we know today derives from the Qing period. Territorial expansion and expeditions to regions of Central Asia spread Chinese power and culture further than ever. The expansion of the 18th century was fuelled by economic and social changes. The discovery of the New World by Europeans in the 15th century led to a new global market in American food crops, such as chillies and sweet potatoes, allowing food crops to be grown in more barren regions, where wheat and rice had not flourished. In the 18th century, the Chinese population doubled from around 150 million to 300 million people.

Historians now take very seriously the idea that in the 18th century China was among the most advanced economies in the world. The impact of imperialism would help commence China's slide down the table, but the seeds of decay had been sown long before the Opium Wars of the 1840s. Put simply, as China's size expanded, its state remained too small. China's dynasty failed to expand the size of government to cope with the new realities of a larger China.

War & Reform

For the Manchu, the single most devastating incident was not the Opium Wars, but the far more destructive anti-Qing Taiping War of 1856–64, an insurgency motivated partly by a foreign credo (Christianity). Established by Hakka leader Hong Xiuquan, the Heavenly Kingdom of Great Peace (Taiping Tianguo) banned opium and intermingling between the sexes, made moves to redistribute property and was fiercely anti-Manchu. The Qing eventually reconquered the Taiping capital at Nánjīng, but upwards of 20 million Chinese died in the uprising.

The events that finally brought the dynasty down, however, came in quick succession. Foreign imperialist incursions continued and Western

1900

The Hanlin Academy in Běijīng – centre of Chinese learning and literature – is accidentally torched by Chinese troops during the Boxer Rebellion, destroying its priceless collection of books.

1904–05

The Russo-Japanese War is fought entirely on Chinese territory. The victory of Japan is the first triumph by an Asian power over a European one.

1905

Major reforms in the late Qing, including the abolition of the 1000-year-long tradition of examinations in the Confucian classics to enter the Chinese bureaucracy.

1908

Two-year-old Puyi ascends the throne as China's last emperor. Local elites and new classes such as businessmen no longer support the dynasty, leading to its ultimate downfall.

In the 18th century, the Chinese used an early form of vaccination against smallpox that required not an injection, but instead the blowing of serum up the patient's nose.

powers nibbled away at China's coastline; Shànghǎi, Qīngdǎo, Tiānjīn, Gǔlàng Yǔ, Shàntóu, Yāntái, Wēihǎi, Níngbō and Běihǎi would all either fall under semicolonial rule or enclose foreign concessions. Hong Kong was a British colony and Macau was administered by the Portuguese. Attempts at self-strengthening – involving attempts to produce armaments and Western-style military technology – were dealt a brutal blow by the Sino-Japanese War of 1894–95. Fought over control of Korea, it ended with the humiliating destruction of the new Qing navy. Not only was Chinese influence in Korea lost, but Taiwan was ceded to Japan.

Japan itself was a powerful Asian example of reform. In 1868 Japan's rulers, unnerved by ever-greater foreign encroachment, had overthrown the centuries-old system of the Shōgun, who acted as regent for the emperor. An all-out program of modernisation, including a new army, constitution, educational system and railway network was undertaken, all of which gave Chinese reformers a lot to ponder.

One of the boldest proposals for reform, which drew heavily on the Japanese model, was the program put forward in 1898 by reformers including the political thinker Kang Youwei (1858–1927). However, in September 1898 the reforms were abruptly halted, as the Dowager Empress Cixi, fearful of a coup, placed the emperor under house arrest and executed several of the leading advocates of change. Two years later, Cixi made a decision that helped to seal the Qing's fate. In 1900 north China was convulsed by attacks from a group of peasant rebels whose martial arts techniques led them to be labelled the Boxers, and who wanted to expel the foreigners and kill any Chinese Christian converts. In a major misjudgement, the dynasty declared in June that it supported the Boxers. Eventually, a multinational foreign army forced its way into China and defeated the uprising which had besieged the foreign Legation Quarter in Běijīng. The imperial powers

OLD TOWNS & VILLAGES 古镇

For strong shades of historic China, make a beeline for the following old towns (*gǔzhèn*):

» Píngyáo (p349): the best preserved of China's ancient walled towns

» Fènghuáng (p464): exquisite riverside setting, pagodas, temples, covered bridges and ancient city wall

» Hóngcūn (p385): gorgeous Huīzhōu village embedded in the lovely south Ānhuī countryside

» Tiánluókēng Tǔlóu Cluster (p271): overnight in a photogenic Hakka roundhouse

» Shāxī (p669): flee modern China along Yúnnán's ancient Tea-Horse Rd

1911

Revolution spreads across China as local governments withdraw support for the dynasty, and instead support a republic under the presidency of Sun Yatsen (fundraising in the US at the time).

1912

Yuan Shikai, leader of China's most powerful regional army, goes to the Qing court to announce that the game is up: on 12 February the last emperor, six-year-old Puyi, abdicates.

1915

Japan makes the '21 demands', which would give it massive political, economic and trading rights in parts of China. Europe's attention is distracted by WWI.

1916

Yuan Shikai tries to declare himself emperor. He is forced to withdraw and remain president, but dies of uremia later that year. China splits into areas ruled by rival militarists.

FOREIGN CONCESSIONS & COLONIES

China's coastline is dotted with a string of foreign concession towns that ooze charm and a sensation of 19th- and early-20th-century grandeur.

» Shànghǎi, French Concession (p173): Shànghǎi's most stylish concession goes to the French

» Gǔlàng Yǔ, Xiàmén (p267): thoroughly charming colonial remains on a beautiful island setting

» Qīngdǎo: wander the German district for cobbled streets and Teutonic architecture (p146)

» Hong Kong: Heung Gong – 'Fragrant Harbour' (p470): outstanding ex-colonial cachet on the Guǎngdōng coast

» Macau (p509): an unforgettable cocktail of Cantonese and Portuguese flavour

» Shāmiàn Island (p539): gentrified and leafy lozenge of Guǎngzhōu sand, decorated with a handsome crop of buildings and streets

then demanded huge financial compensation from the Qing. In 1902 the dynasty reacted by implementing the Xinzheng (New Governance) reforms. This set of reforms, now half-forgotten in contemporary China, looks remarkably progressive, even set against the standards of the present day.

The Cantonese revolutionary Sun Yatsen (1866–1925) remains one of the few modern historical figures respected in both China and Taiwan. Sun and his Revolutionary League made multiple attempts to undermine Qing rule in the late 19th century, raising sponsorship and support from a wide-ranging combination of the Chinese diaspora, the newly emergent middle class, and traditional secret societies. In practice, his own attempts to end Qing rule were unsuccessful, but his reputation as a patriotic figure dedicated to a modern republic gained him high prestige among many of the emerging middle-class elites in China, though much less among the key military leaders.

To show that he was familiar with classical Chinese culture, emperor Kangxi sponsored a great encyclopaedia of Chinese culture, which is still read by scholars today.

The end of the Qing dynasty arrived swiftly. Throughout China's southwest, popular feeling against the dynasty had been fuelled by reports that railway rights in the region were being sold to foreigners. A local uprising in the city of Wǔhàn in October 1911 was discovered early, leading the rebels to take over command in the city and hastily declare independence from the Qing dynasty. Within a space of days, then weeks, most of China's provinces did likewise. Provincial assemblies across China declared themselves in favour of a republic, with Sun

1925
The shooting of striking factory workers on 30 May in Shànghǎi by foreign-controlled police inflames Nationalist passions, giving hope to the Kuomintang party, now regrouping in Guǎngzhōu.

1926
The Northern Expedition: Kuomintang and communists unite under Soviet advice to unite China by force, then establish a Kuomintang government.

1927
The Kuomintang leader Chiang Kaishek turns on the communists in Shànghǎi and Guǎngzhōu, having thousands killed and forcing the communists to turn to a rural-based strategy.

1930s
Cosmopolitan Shànghǎi is the world's fifth-largest city (and the largest city in the Far East), supporting a polyglot population of four million people.

Yatsen (who was not even in China at the time) as their candidate for president.

The Republic: Instability & Ideas

Life stories in China went through unimaginable transformations in the early 20th century. Henrietta Harrison's *The Man Awakened from Dreams* (2005) and Robert Bickers' *Empire Made Me* (2003) grippingly describe these changes for a rural scholar and a Shànghǎi policeman.

The Republic of China lasted less than 40 years on the mainland and continues to be regarded as a dark chapter in modern Chinese history, when the country was under threat from what many described as 'imperialism from without and warlordism from within'. Yet there was also breathing room for new ideas and culture. In terms of freedom of speech and cultural production, the republic was a much richer time than any subsequent era in Chinese history. Yet the period was certainly marked by repeated disasters, rather like the almost contemporaneous Weimar Republic in Germany.

Sun Yatsen returned to China and only briefly served as president, before having to make way for militarist leader Yuan Shikai. In 1912 China held its first general election, and it was Sun's newly established Kuomintang (Nationalist; Guómíndǎng, literally 'Party of the National People') party that emerged as the largest grouping. Parliamentary democracy did not last long, as the Kuomintang itself was outlawed by Yuan, and Sun had to flee into exile in Japan. However, after Yuan's death in 1916, the country split into rival regions ruled by militarist warlord-leaders. Supposedly 'national' governments in Běijīng often controlled only parts of northern or eastern China and had no real claim to control over the rest of the country. Also, in reality, the foreign powers still had control over much of China's domestic and international situation. Britain, France, the US and the other Western powers showed little desire to lose those rights, such as extraterritoriality and tariff control.

The city of Shànghǎi became the focal point for the contradictions of Chinese modernity. By the early 20th century, Shànghǎi was a wonder not just of China, but of the world, with skyscrapers, art deco apartment blocks, neon lights, women (and men) in outrageous new fashions, and a vibrant, commercially minded, take-no-prisoners atmosphere. The racism that accompanied imperialism was visible every day, as Europeans kept themselves separate from the Chinese. Yet the glamour of modernity was undeniable too, as workers flocked from rural areas to make a living in the city, and Chinese intellectuals sought out French fashion, British architecture and American movies. In the prewar period, Shànghǎi had more millionaires than anywhere else in China, yet its inequalities and squalor also inspired the first congress of the Chinese Communist Party (CCP).

The militarist government that held power in Běijīng in 1917 provided 96,000 Chinese who served on the Western Front in Europe, not as sol-

1930

Chiang's Kuomintang government achieves 'tariff autonomy': for the first time in nearly 90 years, China regains the power to tax imports freely, an essential part of fiscal stability.

1931

Japan invades Manchuria (northeast China), provoking an international crisis and forcing Chiang to consider anti-Japanese, as well as anticommunist, strategies.

1932

War breaks out in the streets of Shànghǎi in February–March, a sign that conflict between the two great powers of East Asia, China and Japan, may be coming soon.

1935

Mao Zedong begins his rise to paramount power at the conference at Zūnyì, held in the middle of the Long March to the northwest, on the run from the Kuomintang.

diers but digging trenches and doing hard manual labour. This involvement in WWI led to one of the most important events in China's modern history: the student demonstrations of 4 May 1919.

Double-dealing by the Western Allies and Chinese politicians who had made secret deals with Japan led to an unwelcome discovery for the Chinese diplomats at the Paris Peace Conference in 1919. Germany had been defeated, but its Chinese territories – such as Qīngdǎo – were not to be returned to China but would instead go to Japan. Five days later, on 4 May 1919, some 3000 students gathered in central Běijīng, in front of the Gate of Heavenly Peace, and then marched to the house of a Chinese government minister closely associated with Japan. Once there, they broke in and destroyed the house. This event, over in a few hours, became a legend.

The student demonstration came to symbolise a much wider shift in Chinese society and politics. The May Fourth Movement, as it became known, was associated closely with the New Culture, underpinned by the exciting ideas of 'Mr Science' and 'Mr Democracy'. In literature, a May Fourth generation of authors wrote works attacking the Confucianism that they felt had brought China to its current crisis, and explored new issues of sexuality and self-development. The CCP, later mastermind of the world's largest peasant revolution, was founded in the intellectual turmoil of the movement, many of its founding figures associated with Peking University, such as Chen Duxiu (dean of humanities), Li Dazhao (head librarian) and the young Mao Zedong, a mere library assistant (see p456).

FOREIGN POWERS

Běijīng's Foreign Legation quarter east of Tiān'ānmén Sq still contains the old embassy buildings, churches, post offices and banks of the foreign powers of the late 19th and early 20th centuries.

The Northern Expedition

After years of vainly seeking international support for his cause, Sun Yatsen found allies in the newly formed Soviet Russia. The Soviets ordered the fledgling CCP to ally itself with the much larger 'bourgeois' party, the Kuomintang. Their alliance was attractive to Sun: the Soviets would provide political training, military assistance and finance. From their base in Guǎngzhōu, the Kuomintang and CCP trained together from 1923, in preparation for their mission to reunite China.

Sun died of cancer in 1925. The succession battle in the party coincided with a surge in antiforeign feeling that accompanied the May Thirtieth Incident. Under Soviet advice, the Kuomintang and CCP prepared for their 'Northern Expedition', the big 1926 push north that was supposed to finally unite China. In 1926–27, the Soviet-trained National Revolutionary Army made its way slowly north, fighting, bribing or persuading its opponents into accepting Kuomintang control. The most powerful military figure turned out to be an officer from Zhèjiāng

1937

The Japanese and Chinese clash at Wanping, near Běijīng, on 7 July, sparking the conflict that the Chinese call the 'War of Resistance', which only ends in 1945.

PHIL WEYMOUTH

» Sculpture depicting the 'War of Resistance', Běijīng

1938

Former prime minister Wang Jingwei announces he has gone over to Japan. He later inaugurates a 'restored' Kuomintang government with Japan holding the whip hand over government.

named Chiang Kaishek (1887–1975). Trained in Moscow, Chiang moved steadily forward and finally captured the great prize, Shànghǎi, in March 1927. However, a horrific surprise was in store for his communist allies. The Soviet advisers had not impressed Chiang and he was convinced their intention was to take power in alliance with the Kuomintang as a prelude to seizing control themselves. Instead, Chiang struck first. Using local thugs and soldiers, Chiang organised a lightning strike by rounding up CCP activists and union leaders in Shànghǎi and killing thousands of them.

Kuomintang Rule

Chiang Kaishek's Kuomintang government officially came to power in 1928 through a combination of military force and popular support. Marked by corruption, it suppressed political dissent with great ruthlessness. Yet Chiang's government also kick-started a major industrialisation effort, greatly augmented China's transport infrastructure and successfully renegotiated what many Chinese called 'unequal treaties' with Western powers. In its first two years, the Kuomintang doubled the length of highways in China and increased the number of students studying engineering. The government never really controlled more than a few (very important) provinces in the east, however, and China remained significantly disunited. Regional militarists continued to control much of western China; the Japanese invaded and occupied Manchuria in 1931; and the communists re-established themselves in the northwest.

COMMUNISM

Chiang's New Life Movement and the Chinese Communist Party ideology were attempts to mobilise society through renewal of the individual. But only the communists advocated class war.

In 1934 Chiang Kaishek launched his own ideological counter-argument to communism: the New Life Movement. This was supposed to be a complete spiritual renewal of the nation, through a modernised version of traditional Confucian values, such as propriety, righteousness and loyalty. The New Life Movement demanded that the renewed citizens of the nation must wear frugal but clean clothes, consume products made in China rather than seek luxurious foreign goods, and behave in a hygienic manner. Yet Chiang's ideology never had much success. Against a background of massive agricultural and fiscal crisis, prescriptions about what to wear and how to behave lacked popular appeal.

The new policies did relatively little to change the everyday life for the population in the countryside, where more than 80% of China's people lived. Some rural reforms were undertaken, including the establishment of rural cooperatives, but their effects were small. The Nationalist Party also found itself unable to collect taxes in an honest and transparent way.

1939

On 3–4 May Japanese carpet bombing devastates the temporary Chinese capital of Chóngqìng. From 1938 to 1943, Chóngqìng is one of the world's most heavily bombed cities.

1941

In the base area at Yán'ān (Shaanxi), the 'Rectification' program begins, remoulding the Communist Party into an ideology shaped principally by Mao Zedong.

1941

The Japanese attack the US at Pearl Harbor. China becomes a formal ally of the US, USSR and Britain in WWII, but is treated as a secondary partner at best.

1943

Chiang Kaishek negotiates an agreement with the Allies that, when Japan is defeated, Western imperial privileges in China will end forever, marking the twilight of Western imperialist power in China.

The Long March

The communists had not stood still and after Chiang's treachery, most of what remained of the CCP fled to the countryside. A major centre of activity was the base area in impoverished Jiāngxī province, where the party began to try out systems of government that would eventually bring them to power. However, by 1934, Chiang's previously ineffective 'Extermination Campaigns' were making the CCP's position in Jiāngxī untenable. The CCP commenced its Long March, travelling over 6400km. Four thousand of the original 80,000 communists who set out eventually arrived, exhausted, in Shaanxi (Shǎnxī) province in the northwest, far out of the reach of the Kuomintang. It seemed possible that within a matter of months, however, Chiang would attack again and wipe them out.

The approach of war saved the CCP. There was growing public discontent at Chiang Kaishek's seeming unwillingness to fight the Japanese. In fact, this perception was unfair. The Kuomintang had undertaken retraining of key regiments in the army under German advice, and also started to plan for a wartime economy from 1931, spurred on by the Japanese invasion of Manchuria. However, events came to a head in December 1936, when the militarist leader of Manchuria (General Zhang Xueliang) and the CCP kidnapped Chiang. As a condition of his release, Chiang agreed to an openly declared United Front: the Kuomintang and communists would put aside their differences and join forces against Japan.

Exact mortality figures have never been worked out, but the minimum number of deaths in China during WWII appears to be around 15 million, with some 80 million Chinese becoming refugees.

War & the Kuomintang

China's status as a major participant in WWII is often overlooked or forgotten in the West. The Japanese invasion of China, which began in 1937, was merciless, with the notorious Nanjing Massacre (also known as the Rape of Nánjīng; see p210) just one of a series of war crimes committed by the Japanese Army during its conquest of eastern China. The government had to operate in exile from the far southwestern hinterland of China, as its area of greatest strength and prosperity, China's eastern seaboard, was lost to Japanese occupation.

In China itself, it is now acknowledged that both the Kuomintang and the communists had important roles to play in defeating Japan. Chiang, not Mao, was the internationally acknowledged leader of China during this period, and despite his government's multitude flaws, he maintained resistance to the end. However, his government was also increasingly trapped, having retreated to Sìchuān province and a temporary capital at Chóngqìng. Safe from land attack by Japan, the city still found itself under siege, subjected to some of the heaviest bombing

1946

Communists and the Kuomintang fail to form a coalition government, plunging China back into civil war. Communist organisation, morale and ideology all prove key to the communist victory.

1949

Mao Zedong stands on top of the Gate of Heavenly Peace in Běijīng on 1 October, and announces the formation of the PRC, saying 'The Chinese people have stood up'.

MANFRED GOTTSCHALK

» Gate of Heavenly Peace (p53), Běijīng

in the war. From 1940, supply routes were cut off as the road to Burma was closed by Britain, under pressure from Japan, and Vichy France closed connections to Vietnam. Although the US and Britain brought China on board as an ally against Japan after Pearl Harbor on 7 December 1941, the Allied 'Europe First' strategy meant that China was always treated as a secondary theatre of war. Chiang Kaishek's corruption and leadership qualities were heavily criticised, and while these accusations were not groundless, without Chinese Kuomintang armies (which kept one million Japanese troops bogged down in China for eight years), the Allies' war in the Pacific would have been far harder. The communists had an important role as guerrilla fighters, but did far less fighting in battle than the Kuomintang.

MAO ZEDONG

Mao Zedong is one of the most intriguing figures of 20th-century history. Philip Short's *Mao: A Life* (1999) is the most detailed and thoughtful recent account of his life in English.

The real winners from WWII, however, were the communists. They undertook important guerrilla campaigns against the Japanese across northern and eastern China, but the really key changes were taking place in the bleak, dusty hill country centred on the small town of Yán'ān, capital of the CCP's largest base area. The 'Yán'ān way' that developed in those years solidified many CCP policies: land reform involving redistribution of land to the peasants, lower taxes, a self-sufficient economy, ideological education and, underpinning it all, the CCP's military force, the Red Army. By the end of the war with Japan, the communist areas had expanded massively, with some 900,000 troops in the Red Army, and party membership at a new high of 1.2 million.

Above all, the war with Japan had helped the communists come back from the brink of the disaster they had faced at the end of the Long March. The Kuomintang and communists plunged into civil war in 1946 and after three long years the CCP won. On 1 October 1949 in Běijīng, Mao declared the establishment of the People's Republic of China. The cult of Mao's personality, which began with the sinisterly named Rectification movements during the war, would culminate in the disastrous Cultural Revolution of the 1960s.

Mao's China

Mao's China desired, above all, to exercise ideological control over its population. It called itself 'New China', with the idea that the whole citizenry, down to the remotest peasants, should find a role in the new politics and society. The success of Mao's military and political tactics also meant that the country was, for the first time since the 19th century, united under a strong central government.

Most Westerners – and Western influences – were swiftly removed from the country. The US refused to recognise the new state at all. However, China had decided, in Mao's phrase, to 'lean to one side' and ally

1950

China joins the Korean War, helping Mao to consolidate his regime with mass campaigns that inspire (or terrify) the population.

1957

A brief period of liberalisation under the 'Hundred Flowers Movement'. However, criticisms of the regime lead Mao to crack down and imprison or exile thousands of dissidents.

1958

The Taiwan Straits Crisis. Mao's government fires missiles near islands under the control of Taiwan in an attempt to prevent rapprochement between the US and USSR in the Cold War.

1962

The Great Leap Forward causes mass starvation. Politburo members Liu Shaoqi and Deng Xiaoping reintroduce limited market reforms, which will lead to their condemnation during the Cultural Revolution.

itself with the Soviet Union in the still-emerging Cold War. The 1950s marked the high point of Soviet influence on Chinese politics and culture. However, the decade also saw rising tension between the Chinese and the Soviets, fuelled in part by Khrushchev's condemnation of Stalin (which Mao took, in part, as a criticism of his own cult of personality). Sino-Soviet differences came to a head in 1960 with the withdrawal of Soviet technical assistance from China, and relations remained frosty until the 1980s.

Mao's experiences had convinced him that only violent change could shake up the relationship between landlords and their tenants, or capitalists and their employees, in a China that was still highly traditional. The first year of the regime saw some 40% of the land redistributed to poor peasants. At the same time, some one million or so people condemned as 'landlords' were persecuted and killed. The joy of liberation was real for many Chinese; but campaigns of terror were also real and the early 1950s were no golden age.

As relations with the Soviets broke down in the mid-1950s, the CCP leaders' thoughts turned to economic self-sufficiency. Mao, supported by Politburo colleagues, proposed the policy known as the Great Leap Forward (Dàyuèjìn), a highly ambitious plan to harness the power of socialist economics to boost production of steel, coal and electricity. Agriculture was to reach an ever-higher level of collectivisation. Family structures were broken up as communal dining halls were established: people were urged to eat their fill, as the new agricultural methods would ensure plenty for all, year after year.

However, the Great Leap Forward was a monumental failure. Its lack of economic realism caused a massive famine and at least 20 million deaths. Yet the return to a semimarket economy in 1962, after the Leap had comprehensively ended, did not dampen Mao's enthusiasm for revolutionary renewal. This led to the last and most fanatical of the campaigns that marked Mao's China: the Cultural Revolution of 1966–76.

Ding Ling's novel *The Sun Shines on the Sanggan River* (1948) gives a graphic account of the violence, as well as the joy, that greeted land reform (ie redistribution) in China in the early 1950s.

Cultural Revolution

Mao had become increasingly concerned that post-Leap China was slipping into 'economism' – a complacent satisfaction with rising standards of living that would blunt people's revolutionary fervour. Mao was particularly concerned that the young generation might grow up with a dimmed spirit of revolution. For these reasons, Mao decided that a massive campaign of ideological renewal, in which he would attack his own party, must be launched.

Still the dominant figure in the CCP, Mao used his prestige to undermine his own colleagues. In summer 1966, prominent posters in large,

1966

The Cultural Revolution breaks out, and Red Guards demonstrate in cities across China. The movement is marked by a fetish for violence as a catalyst for transforming society.

1972

US President Richard Nixon visits China, marking a major rapprochement during the Cold War, and the start of full diplomatic relations between the two countries.

1973

Deng Xiaoping returns to power as deputy premier. The modernising faction in the party fights with the Gang of Four, who support the continuing Cultural Revolution.

1976

Mao Zedong dies, aged 83. The Gang of Four are arrested by his successor and put on trial, where they are blamed for all the disasters of the Cultural Revolution.

handwritten characters appeared at prominent sites, including Peking University, demanding that figures such as Liu Shaoqi (president of the PRC) and Deng Xiaoping (senior Politburo member) must be condemned as 'takers of the capitalist road'. Top leaders suddenly disappeared from sight, only to be replaced by unknowns, such as Mao's wife Jiang Qing and her associates, later dubbed the 'Gang of Four'. Meanwhile, an all-pervasive cult of Mao's personality took over. One million youths at a time, known as Red Guards, would flock to hear Mao in Tiān'ānmén Sq. Posters and pictures of Mao were everywhere. The Red Guards were not ashamed to admit that their tactics were violent. Immense violence permeated throughout society: teachers, intellectuals and landlords were killed in their thousands.

The Soviets withdrew all assistance from the PRC in 1960, leaving the great bridge across the Yangzi River at Nánjīng half-built. It became a point of pride for Chinese engineers to finish the job without foreign help.

While Mao initiated and supported the Cultural Revolution, it was also genuinely popular among many young people (who had less to lose). However, police authority effectively disappeared, creative activity came to a virtual standstill and academic research was grounded.

The Cultural Revolution could not last. Worried by the increasing violence, the army forced the Red Guards off the streets in 1969. The early 1970s saw a remarkable rapprochement between the US and China: the former was desperate to extricate itself from the quagmire of the Vietnam war; the latter terrified of an attack from the now-hostile USSR. Secretive diplomatic manoeuvres led, eventually,

SLOGANEERING

In communist China, political slogans were always one of the first instruments to hand in the propaganda department's ample tool chest. Typically painted in vermillion letters on walls, banners or posters, communist slogans were punchy, formulaic, systematic and unsophisticated. Their language was forthright and simple, appealing directly to the masses. The emphasis on rote learning in Chinese education gave slogans added authority and easy memorability while their appearance everywhere reinforced the ever-presence and watchfulness of the communist state. During the Cultural Revolution they became increasingly violent and intimidating. Slogans from this period survive fitfully around China, including in the following places, although many have either been scrubbed out or buried beneath cement or plaster.

» Nánjiēcūn (p406): literally everywhere

» Chuāndǐxià (p97): on external house walls in the village

» 798 Art District, Běijīng (p68): throughout the district

» Huā'è Lóu (p564): Hakka roundhouse in eastern Guǎngdōng

» Jiāyùguān Fort (p824): in yellow letters and ghostly shadows on buildings and walls

1980

The one-child policy is enforced. The state adopts it as a means of reducing the population, but at the same time imposes unprecedented control over the personal liberty of women.

TIM MAKINS

» Chinese family sightseeing in Běijīng

1987

The Last Emperor, filmed in the Forbidden City, collects an Oscar for Best Picture, and marks a new openness in China towards the outside world.

to the official visit of US President Richard Nixon to China in 1972, which began the reopening of China to the West. Slowly, the Cultural Revolution began to cool down, but its brutal legacy survives today. Those guilty of murder and violence re-entered society with little or no judgment while today's CCP discourages analysis and debate of the 'decade of chaos'.

Reform

Mao died in 1976, to be succeeded by the little-known Hua Guofeng (1921–2008). Within two years, Hua had been outmanoeuvred by the greatest survivor of 20th-century Chinese politics, Deng Xiaoping. Deng had been purged twice during the Cultural Revolution, but after Mao's death he was able to reach supreme leadership in the CCP with a radical program. In particular, Deng recognised that the Cultural Revolution had been highly damaging economically to China. Deng enlisted a policy slogan originally invented by Mao's pragmatic prime minister, Zhou Enlai – the 'Four Modernisations'. The party's task would be to set China on the right path in four areas: agriculture, industry, science and technology, and national defence.

During the Cultural Revolution, some 2.2 billion Chairman Mao badges were cast. Read *Mao's Last Revolution* (2006) by Roderick MacFarquhar and Michael Schoenhals for the history; see Zhang Yimou's film *To Live* (1994) to understand the emotions.

To make this policy work, many of the assumptions of the Mao era were abandoned. The first, highly symbolic move of the 'reform era' (as the post-1978 period is known) was the breaking down of the collective farms. Farmers were able to sell a proportion of their crops on the free market, and urban and rural areas were also encouraged to establish small local enterprises. 'To get rich is glorious,' Deng declared, adding, 'it doesn't matter if some areas get rich first.' As part of this encouragement of entrepreneurship, Deng designated four areas on China's coast as Special Economic Zones (SEZs), which would be particularly attractive to foreign investors.

Politics was kept on a much shorter rein than the economy, however. Deng was relaxed about a certain amount of ideological impurity, but some other members of the leadership were concerned by the materialism in reform-era China. They supported campaigns of 'anti-spiritual pollution', in which influences from the capitalist world were condemned. Yet inevitably the overall movement seemed to be towards a freer, market-oriented society.

The new freedoms that the urban middle classes enjoyed created the appetite for more. After student protests demanding further opening up of the party in 1985–86, the prime minister (and relative liberal) Hu Yaobang was forced to resign in 1987 and take responsibility for allowing social forces to get out of control. He was replaced as general secretary by Zhao Ziyang, who was more conservative politically, although an economic reformer. In April 1989 Hu Yaobang died, and

1988

The daring series *River Elegy (Héshāng)* is broadcast on national TV. It is a devastating indictment of dictatorship and Mao's rule in particular, and is banned in China after 1989.

1989

Hundreds of civilians are killed by Chinese troops in the streets around Tiān'ānmén Sq. No official reassessment has been made, but rumours persist of deep internal conflict within the party.

1997

Hong Kong is returned to the People's Republic of China. Widespread fears that China will interfere directly in its government prove wrong, but politics becomes more sensitive to Běijīng.

2001

China joins the World Trade Organization, giving it a seat at the top table that decides global norms on economics and finance.

students around China used the occasion of his death to organise protests against the continuing role of the CCP in public life. At Peking University, the breeding ground of the May Fourth demonstrations of 1919, students declared the need for 'science and democracy', the modernising watchwords of 80 years earlier, to be revived.

In spring 1989 Tiān'ānmén Sq was the scene of an unprecedented demonstration. At its height, nearly a million Chinese workers and students, in a rare cross-class alliance, filled the space in front of the Gate of Heavenly Peace, with the CCP profoundly embarrassed to have the world's media record such events. By June 1989 the numbers in the square had dwindled to only thousands, but those who remained showed no signs of moving. Martial law was imposed and on the night of 3 June, tanks and armoured personnel carriers were sent in. The death toll has never been officially confirmed, but it seems likely to have been in the high hundreds or even more. Hundreds of people associated with the movement were arrested, imprisoned or forced to flee to the West.

For some three years, China's politics were almost frozen, but in 1992 Deng, the man who had sent in the tanks, made his last grand public gesture. That year, he undertook what Chinese political insiders called his 'southern tour', or *nánxún*. By visiting Shēnzhèn, Deng indicated that the economic policies of reform were not going to be abandoned. The massive growth rates that the Chinese economy has posted ever since have justified his decision. Deng also made another significant choice: grooming Jiang Zemin – the mayor of Shànghǎi, who had peacefully dissolved demonstrations in Shànghǎi in a way that the authorities in Běijīng had not – as his successor by appointing him as general secretary of the party in 1989.

FILM

One product of the new freedom of the 1980s was a revived Chinese film industry. *Red Sorghum*, the first film directed by Zhang Yimou, was a searingly erotic film of a type that had not been seen since 1949.

21st-Century China

Since 2002, President Hu Jintao and Prime Minister Wen Jiabao have made more efforts to deal with the inequality and poverty in the countryside, but this remains a major concern, along with reform of the CCP itself.

China has placed scientific development at the centre of its quest for growth, sending students abroad in their tens of thousands to study science and technology, and develop a core of scientific knowledge within China itself.

As a permanent member of the UN Security Council and in its quest for economic and diplomatic influence in Africa and South America, China has a powerful international role. It is, however, hesitant to assume a more influential position in international affairs. China's preference for remaining neutral but friendly and business-like may also be

2004

The world's first commercially operating Maglev train begins scorching a trail across Shànghǎi's Pǔdōng District.

CHRISTOPHER HERWIG

» Maglev high-speed train (p203), Shànghǎi

2006

The Three Gorges Dam is completed. Significant parts of the landscape of western China are lost beneath the waters, but energy is also provided for the expanding Chinese economy.

tested: crises such as the ever-volatile North Korean situation, Iran's nuclear ambitions and the scramble for mineral resources in Africa and energy resources around the globe mean that China is having to make hard choices about which nations it wishes to favour.

Nationalism has become a popular rallying cry at home. This does not necessarily mean xenophobia or antiforeign sentiment, although anti-Japanese feelings are easily roused. It is clear, however, that China's own people consider that the country's moment has arrived, and that they must oppose attempts – whether by the West or Japan – to prevent it taking centre stage in the region. Its long history has, for now, begun to bring China back to the prominence it once enjoyed.

Chinese communist politics are often hard to understand. A lively guide written by a former diplomat is Kerry Brown's *Struggling Giant: China in the 21st Century* (2007).

2008
Běijīng hosts the 2008 Summer Olympic Games and Paralympics. The Games go smoothly and are widely considered to be a great success in burnishing China's image overseas.

2008
Violent riots in Lhasa, Tibet, again put the uneasy region centre stage. Protests spread to other Tibetan areas in Gānsù, Sìchuān and Qīnghǎi provinces.

2009
July riots in Ürümqi leave hundreds dead as interethnic violence flares between Uighurs and Han Chinese. Běijīng floods the region with soldiers and implements a 10-month internet blackout.

2010
A huge 7.1-magnitude earthquake in the Qīnghǎi region of the far west flattens the remote town of Yùshù in April, killing thousands.

The People of China

Despite being the world's most populous nation – the stamping ground of roughly one-fifth of humanity – China is often regarded as being largely homogenous, at least from a remote Western perspective. This is probably because Han Chinese – the majority ethnic type in this energetic and bustling nation – constitute over nine-tenths of the population. But rather like Chinese cuisine, and of course the nation's mystifying linguistic Babel, you only have to get your travelling shoes on and you encounter a vibrant and expectation-defying patchwork and mixed salad of ethnicities.

Ethnic Makeup

Han Chinese – the predominant clan in China and the nation's 56th recognised ethnic group – make up the lion's share of China's people, 92% of the total figure. Because Han civilisation is the dominant culture of the land, when we think of China – from its writing system to its visual arts, calligraphy, literature and politics – we associate it with Han culture.

The Han Chinese are distributed throughout China but predominantly concentrate along the Yellow River, Yangzi River and Pearl River basins. A glance at the map of China, however, reveals that these core heartland regions of Han China are fragments of contemporary China's massive expanse. The colossal regions of Tibet, Qīnghǎi, Xīnjiāng, Inner Mongolia and the three provinces of the northeast (Manchuria) are all historically non-Han regions, areas of which remain essentially non-Han today.

Many of these regions are peopled by some of the remaining 8% of the population: China's 55 other ethnic minorities, known collectively as *shǎoshù mínzú* (少数民族; minority nationals). The largest minority groups in China include the Zhuang (壮族), Manchu (满族; Man zu), Miao (苗族), Uighur (维吾尔族; Weiwu'er zu), Yi (彝族), Tujia (土家族), Tibetan (藏族; Zang zu), Hui (回族), Mongolian (蒙古族; Menggu zu),

CHINA DEMOGRAPHICS

- Population: 1.34 billion
- Birth rate: 12.17 births per 1000 people
- Percentage of people over 65 years of age: 8.6%
- Urbanisation rate: 2.7%
- Sex ratio (under age of 15): 1.17 (boys to girls)
- Life expectancy: 74.5 years

ETHNIC RELATIONS

As with most fractious features of Chinese society, Běijīng goes to superhuman lengths to present China's ethnic relations as 'harmonious'. Newspapers, TV reports, museum exhibitions and ethnic performances tirelessly depict tribes of joyful minorities. It is part of the deintellectualisation of sensitive issues which bashes the square peg of China's ethnic relations into a seemingly round hole.

The chemistry between China's ethnic minorities and the Han majority (who wield the political and often the business power) is certainly more complex than 'harmonious'. Like an occasionally unhappy marriage, composure can be maintained on the outside, with an effort of will. When ethnic relations swiftly unravel – with occasionally shocking violence – Běijīng prefers to publicly blame 'outside forces' instead of addressing domestic causes. One of the responses to the Tibet disturbances of 2008 and the vicious Ürümqi riots of 2009 was to flood the areas with troops. Troops tend to stay in place, so they become part of the long-term stick-rather-than-carrot solution. Ürümqi also found itself without internet access for 10 months, a sign of Běijīng's distrust of access to electronic information.

Buyi (布依族), Dong (侗族), Yao (瑶族), Korean (朝鲜族; Chaoxian zu), Bai (白族), Hani (哈尼族), Li (黎族), Kazak (哈萨克族; Hasake zu) and Dai (傣族). Population sizes differ dramatically, from the sizeable Zhuang in Guǎngxī to small numbers of Menba (门巴族) in Tibet. Ethnic labelling can be quite fluid: the roundhouse-building Hakka (客家; Kejia) were once regarded as a separate minority, but are today considered to be Han Chinese.

China's minorities tend to cluster along border regions, in the north west, the west, the southwest, the north and northeast of China, but are also distributed throughout the country. Some people are found in just one area (such as the Hani in Yúnnán); others, such as the Muslim Hui (p842), are found across China.

Wedged into the southwest corner of China between Tibet, Myanmar (Burma), Vietnam and Laos, fecund Yúnnán province alone is home to over 20 ethnic groups, making it one of the most ethnically diverse provinces in the country. See that chapter for an introduction to the minority peoples of the region.

The Chinese Character

As a race, the Han Chinese are quite reserved. Shaped by Confucian principles, the Chinese of today's China are thoughtful and discreet, but also very pragmatic. Conservative and somewhat introverted, they favour dark clothing over bright or loud colours.

Chinese people (apart from the Shanghainese, some Chinese may insist) are very generous. Don't be surprised if a Chinese person you have just met on a train invites you for a meal in the dining carriage. They will probably insist on paying, in which case do not attempt to thwart their efforts. The Chinese also simply adore children and are particularly warm to them.

The Chinese are also an exceptionally proud people. They are proud of their civilisation and history, their written language and their inventions and achievements. This pride rarely comes across as arrogance or self-assurance, however, and is frequently tinged with a lack of confidence. The Chinese may, for example, be very proud of the railway to Tibet or of China's newfound world status, but there is little self-satisfaction in the nation's opaque political culture or manifest corruption.

The modern Chinese character has been shaped by recent political realities, and while Chinese people have always been reserved and

NAXI

The Naxi created a written language over 1000 years ago using an extraordinary system of pictographs – the only hieroglyphic language still in use today.

circumspect, in today's China they may appear even more prudent. While Chinese people are often very honest and frank about certain things (asking your age and how much you earn or expressing a dislike for Japan), they can be painfully tight-lipped on other subjects (such as the relevance of free speech in the context of China). All of this makes the Chinese appear rather complicated, despite their reputation for being straightforward.

Women in China

Chairman Mao once said that women hold up half the sky. Women in today's China officially share complete equality with men; in reality, however, as with other nations that profess sexual equality, the reality is often far different. Chinese women do not enjoy strong political representation; the Chinese Communist Party is a largely patriarchal (and aged) organisation. Iconic political leaders from the early days of the Chinese Communist Party were all men and the influential echelons of the party remain a largely male domain.

For an academic look at internal colonisation and Han perspectives on minority regions, read *Frontier People: Han Settlers in Minority Areas of China* by Mette Halskov Hansen.

High-profile, successful Chinese women are very much in the public eye, but the relative lack of career opportunities for females in other fields also indicates a continuing bias against women in employment. Women in today's China enjoy more freedom than ever before and a revolution in their status has taken place since 1949, but sexual discrimination in the workplace survives.

In traditional China, an ideal woman's behaviour was governed by the 'three obediences and four virtues' of Confucian (p936) thought. The three obediences were: submission to the father before marriage, husband after marriage and sons in the case of widows. The four virtues were propriety in behaviour, demeanour, speech and employment.

The Communist Party after 1949 tried to outlaw old customs and put women on equal footing with men. They abolished arranged marriages and encouraged women to get an education and join the workforce. Pictures from this time show sturdy, ruddy-cheeked women with short cropped hair and overalls, a far cry from the corpulent palace ladies of the Tang or the pale, willowy beauties featured in later traditional paintings. In their quest for equality, the Communist Party successfully desexualised women in the 1950s and '60s, manufacturing a further

WHO'S IN THE MIDDLE?

China's middle class (*zhōng chǎn*) is a controversial subject: for starters, no one agrees on how it should be defined. China's State Information Centre takes a numbers approach, identifying the middle class as those whose annual income is between US$7300 and US$73,000 (Y50,000 and Y500,000). International banks and market research groups tend to raise the bar slightly higher, identifying the minimum cut-off at US$10,000 (Y68,382) and looking at factors such as whether or not households own a car, apartment, eat out regularly and so on.

Other economists, however, are less enthusiastic. Dragonomics, which publishes the *China Economic Quarterly,* believes that middle class is a misleading term; many Chinese described as such are in fact considerably poorer than their counterparts in developed countries. Their study argues that the country consists of 'consuming China' – 110 million people living in the Běijīng, Shànghǎi and Guǎngzhōu metropolitan areas – and 'surviving China' – everyone else. But however you define it, everyone does agree that the middle class – or the consumers – are on the rise. According to the state, over half of China's urban population will have an annual income of over $7300 by 2025.

CHINA'S ONE-CHILD POLICY

The 'one-child policy' (actually a misnomer) was railroaded into effect in 1979 in a bid to keep China's population to one billion by the year 2000; the latest government estimate claims the population will peak at 1.5 billion in 2033. The policy was originally harshly implemented but rural revolt led to a softer stance; nonetheless, it has generated much bad feeling between local officials and the rural population. All non-Han minorities are exempt from the one-child policy.

Rural families are now allowed to have two children if the first child is a girl, but some have upwards of three or four kids. Additional children often result in fines and families having to shoulder the cost of education themselves, without government assistance. Official stated policy opposes forced abortion or sterilisation, but allegations of coercion continue as local officials strive to meet population targets. The government is taking steps to punish officials who force women to undergo inhumane sterilisation procedures. Families who do abide by the one-child policy will often go to great lengths to make sure their child is male. In parts of China, this is creating a serious imbalance of the sexes – in 2007, 111 boys were born for every 100 girls. That could mean that by 2020, over 30 million men may be unable to find spouses.

form of imprisonment that contemporary Chinese women regard with disdain.

Women's improved social status today has meant that more women are putting off marriage until their late 20s or early 30s, choosing instead to focus on education and career opportunities. This has been enhanced by the rapid rise in house prices, further encouraging women to leave marriage (and having children) till a later age. Equipped with a good education and a high salary, they have high expectations of their future husbands (some of whom may be wary of courting girls with doctorates, in case they are outshone). Premarital sex and cohabitation before marriage are increasingly common in larger cities and lack the stigma they had several years ago.

Again, there is a strong rural–urban divide and all is not well down on the farm. Urban women are far more optimistic and freer, while women from rural areas, where traditional beliefs are at their strongest, fight an uphill battle against discrimination. Rural China is heavily weighted against girls, where a marked preference for baby boys over baby girls exists. This has resulted in an imbalance between China's population of men to women, a consequence of female foeticide, selective abortions and even infanticide. China's women are more likely to commit suicide than men (bucking the global trend), while rural Chinese women are up to five times as likely to kill themselves. When one considers the fact that most of the Chinese population lives in rural areas, the problem comes into frightening perspective.

The law can also be vicious, with handcuffed prostitutes shamefully paraded in public. Very few women smoke in public and do so in private, revealing a taboo in this area.

Chinese suspicions of most '-isms' and avoidance of collective action not proscribed by the authorities perhaps contribute to the scarcity of a feminist movement in China.

Lifestyle

The people of China today enjoy a far more diverse set of lifestyles than at any other time in their history. Beyond ethnic differences, the big divide is between the city and the countryside. The culture of the big city – with its bars, white-collar jobs, desirable schools, dynamism and cosmopolitan flair – stands in marked contrast to rural China, where little may have changed in the past three decades. Many of China's cities – take Tiānjīn (p107), for example – are clearly international in aspiration, but the countryside remains deeply poor, especially in the southwest. China calls itself a 'developing country', which it is, but tremendous imbalances divide fully developed areas from regions that have seen little development.

Further polarisations include the generation gap. A vivid absence of sympathy exists between youngsters and their parent's, and in particular their grandparent's, generation. This misunderstanding can, in a Western context, be explained by youthful rebellion and nonconformity. Chinese youths, however, are generally more conformist than their Western counterparts; what is more evident is the juxtaposition of two completely opposing political cultures and generations, one that was communist and the other which is staunchly materialist and ideology-free.

Religion & Beliefs

Despite the pragmatic nature of the Chinese people, ideas have always possessed a particular volatility and potency in China. Communism itself is – or was – a forceful ideology that briefly assumed immense authority over the minds of China's citizens. The Taiping Rebellion of the 19th century fused Christianity with revolutionary principles of social organisation, almost sweeping away the Qing dynasty in the process and leaving 20 million dead in its horrifying 20-year spasm. The momentary incandescence of the Boxer Rebellion drew upon a volatile cocktail of martial arts practices and superstition, fused with xenophobia. The chaos of the Cultural Revolution is perhaps further suggestion of what can happen when ideas are allowed the full supremacy they seek.

The Chinese Communist Party (CCP) today remains fearful of ideas and beliefs that compromise its primacy. Proselytising is not permitted, religious organisation is regulated and organisations such as Falun Gong can be banned. Nonetheless, worship and religious practice is generally permitted and China's spiritual world provides a vivid and colourful backdrop to contemporary Chinese life.

During the Cultural Revolution, many Christian churches around China served as warehouses or factories, and were gradually rehabilitated in the 1980s.

Religion Today

An estimated 400 million Chinese adhere to a particular faith in today's China. Although the CCP made strident efforts after 1949 to supplant religious worship with a nationwide fervour for the secular philosophy of communism, it long ago gave up attempting to force its will. Middle aged and elderly Chinese once zealously believed in Mao Zedong's ideology, but the central tenets of that era – Marxist-Leninist collectivism and progress towards a communist society – were abandoned in favour of once heretical economic reform.

With Chinese society showing signs of stress, however, religion is enjoying an upswing as the people return to religion for spiritual solace at a time of great change and dislocation. The hopeless, poor and destitute may turn to religion as they feel abandoned by communism and the safety nets it once offered. Yet the educated and prosperous are similarly turning to religion for a sense of guidance and direction.

Religious belief in China is generally marked by great tolerance. Although faiths are quite distinct, some crossover and convergence exists between Buddhism, Taoism and Confucianism, and you may discover shrines where all three faiths have a presence. Guanyin, the Buddhist Goddess of Mercy, has an equivalent in Tianhou, the Taoist goddess and protector of fisher folk, and the two goddesses appear interchangeable. You may encounter other symbioses too: elements of Taoism and Buddhism can be discerned in the thinking of some Chinese Christians.

China's oldest surviving Buddhist temple is the White Horse Temple in Luòyáng; other Buddhist temples may well have existed but have since vanished.

Buddhism

Although not an indigenous faith, Buddhism (Fó Jiào) is the religion most deeply associated with China, Tibet and Chinatowns abroad.

Buddhism's peak has long waned but the faith still exercises a powerful influence over the spiritual persona of China. Many Chinese may not be regular temple goers but they possess an interest in Buddhism; they may merely be 'cultural Buddhists', with a fondness for Buddhist civilisation.

Chinese towns with any history should have several Buddhist temples, but the number is well down on pre-1949 figures. The small town of Zhèngdìng (p115), for example, has four Buddhist temples, but at one time had eight. Běijīng once had hundreds of Buddhist temples, compared to the 20 or so you can find today.

Some of China's greatest surviving artistic achievements are Buddhist in inspiration. The largest and most ancient repository of Chinese, Central Asian and Tibetan Buddhist artwork can be found at the Mogao Caves in Gānsù (p828), while the carved Buddhist caves at both Lóngmén and Yúngāng are spectacular pieces of religious and creative heritage.

Origins

Founded in ancient India around the 5th century BC, Buddhism teaches that all of life is suffering, and that the cause of this anguish is desire, itself rooted in sensation and attachment. Suffering can only be overcome by following the eightfold path, a set of guidelines for moral behaviour, meditation and wisdom. Those who have freed themselves from suffering and the wheel of rebirth are said to have attained nirvana or enlightenment. The term Buddha generally refers to the historical founder of Buddhism, Siddhartha Gautama, but is also sometimes used to denote those who have achieved enlightenment.

Siddhartha Gautama left no writings; the sutras that make up the Buddhist canon were compiled many years after his death.

SACRED MOUNTAINS

Beyond Tibet, China has four sacred Buddhist mountains, each one the home of a specific Bodhisattva. The two most famous mountains are Wǔtái Shān and Éméi Shān, respectively ruled over by Wenshu and Puxiang.

Buddhism in China

Like other faiths such as Christianity, Nestorianism, Islam and Judaism, Buddhism originally reached China via the Silk Road. The earliest recorded Buddhist temple in China proper dates back to the 1st century AD, but it was not until the 4th century when a period of warlordism coupled with nomadic invasions plunged the country into disarray, that Buddhism gained mass appeal. Buddhism's sudden growth during this period is often attributed to its sophisticated ideas concerning the afterlife (such as karma and reincarnation), a dimension unaddressed by either Confucianism or Taoism. At a time when existence was especially precarious, spiritual transcendence was understandably popular.

As Buddhism converged with Taoist philosophy (through terminology used in translation) and popular religion (through practice), it went on to develop into something distinct from the original Indian tradition. The most famous example is the esoteric Chan school (Zen in Japanese), which originated sometime in the 5th or 6th century, and focused on attaining enlightenment through meditation. Chan was novel not only in its unorthodox teaching methods, but also because it made enlightenment possible for laypeople outside the monastic system. It rose to prominence during the Tang and Song dynasties, after which the centre of practice moved to Japan. Other major Buddhist sects in China include Tiantai (based on the teachings of the Lotus Sutra) and Pure Land, a faith-based teaching that requires simple devotion, such as reciting the Amitabha Buddha's name, in order to gain rebirth in paradise. Today, Pure Land Buddhism is the most common.

Buddhist Schools

Regardless of its various forms, most Buddhism in China belongs to the Mahayana school, which holds that since all existence is one, the fate of the individual is linked to the fate of others. Thus, Bodhisattvas – those who have already achieved enlightenment but have chosen to remain on earth – continue to work for the liberation of all other sentient beings. The most popular Bodhisattva in China is Guanyin, the Goddess of Mercy.

Ethnic Tibetans and Mongols within the PRC practise a unique form of Mahayana Buddhism known as Tibetan or Tantric Buddhism (Lǎma Jiào). Tibetan Buddhism, sometimes called Vajrayana or 'thunderbolt vehicle', has been practised since the early 7th century AD and is influenced by Tibet's pre-Buddhist Bon religion, which relied on priests or shamans to placate spirits, gods and demons. Generally speaking, it is much more mystical than other forms of Buddhism, relying heavily on mudras (ritual postures), mantras (sacred speech), yantras (sacred art) and secret initiation rites. Priests called lamas are believed to be reincarnations of highly evolved beings; the Dalai Lama is the supreme patriarch of Tibetan Buddhism.

Taoism

A home-grown philosophy-cum-religion, Taoism is also perhaps the hardest of all China's faiths to grasp. Controversial, paradoxical, and – like the Tao itself – impossible to pin down, it is a natural counterpoint to rigid Confucianist order and responsibility.

GUANYIN 观音

The boundlessly compassionate countenance of Guanyin, the Buddhist Goddess of Mercy, can be encountered in temples across China. The goddess (more strictly a Bodhisattva or a Buddha-to-be) goes under a variety of aliases: Guanshiyin (literally 'Observing the Cries of the World') is her formal name, but she is also called Guanzizai, Guanyin Dashi and Guanyin Pusa, or, in Sanskrit, Avalokiteshvara. Known as Kannon in Japan and Guanyam in Cantonese, Guanyin shoulders the grief of the world and dispenses mercy and compassion. Christians will note a semblance to the Virgin Mary in the aura surrounding the goddess, which at least partially explains why Christianity has found a slot in the Chinese consciousness.

In Tibetan Buddhism, her earthly presence manifests itself in the Dalai Lama, and her home is the Potala Palace (p884) in Lhasa. In China, her abode is the island of Pǔtuóshān (p253) in Zhèjiāng province, the first two syllables of which derive from the name of her palace in Lhasa.

In temples throughout China, Guanyin is often found at the very rear of the main hall, facing north (most of the other divinities, apart from Weituo, face south). She typically has her own little shrine and stands on the head of a big fish, holding a lotus in her hand. On other occasions, she has her own hall, often towards the rear of the temple.

The goddess (who in earlier dynasties appears to be male rather than female) is often surrounded by little effigies of the *luóhàn* (or *arhat*; those freed from the cycle of rebirth), who scamper about; the Guānyīn Pavilion (p660) outside Dàlǐ is a good example of this. Guanyin also appears in a variety of forms, often with just two arms, but sometimes also in a multi-armed form (as at the Pǔníng Temple in Chéngdé; p121). The 11-faced Guanyin, the fierce horse-head Guanyin, the Songzi Guanyin (literally 'Offering Son Guanyin') and the Dripping Water Guanyin are just some of her myriad manifestations. She was also a favourite subject for *déhuà* (white-glazed porcelain) figures, which are typically very elegant.

Taoism predates Buddhism in China and much of its religious culture connects to a distant animism and shamanism, despite the purity of its philosophical school. In its earliest and simplest form, Taoism draws from *The Classic of the Way and its Power* (Taote Jing; Dàodé Jìng), penned by the sagacious Laotzu (Laozi; c 580–500 BC) who left his writings with the gatekeeper of a pass as he headed west on the back of an ox. Some Chinese believe his wanderings took him to a distant land in the west where he became Buddha.

The Classic of the Way and its Power is a work of astonishing insight and sublime beauty. Devoid of a god-like being or deity, Laotzu's writings instead endeavour to address the unknowable and indescribable principle of the universe which he calls Dao (*dào;* 道), or 'the Way'. This way is the way or method by which the universe operates, so it can be understood to be a universal or cosmic principle.

The Chinese verb for 'to know' is *zhīdào* (知道), literally 'know the *dao*' or 'to know the way', indicating a possible Taoist etymology.

The opening lines of *The Classic of the Way and its Power* confess, however, that the treatise may fail in its task: 道可道非常道, 名可名非常名; 'The way that can be spoken of is not the real way, the name that can be named is not the true name'. Despite this disclaimer, the 5000-character book, completed in terse classical Chinese, somehow communicates the nebulous power and authority of 'the Way'. The book remains the seminal text of Taoism, and Taoist purists see little need to look beyond its revelations.

One of Taoism's most beguiling precepts, *wúwéi* (inaction) champions the allowing of things to naturally occur without interference. The principle is enthusiastically pursued by students of Taiji Quan, Wuji Quan and other soft martial arts (p974) who seek to equal nothingness in their bid to lead an opponent to defeat himself.

Confucianism

The very core of Chinese society for the past two millennia, Confucianism (Rújiā Sīxiǎng) is a humanist philosophy that strives for social harmony and the common good. In China, its influence can be seen in everything from the emphasis on education and respect for elders to the patriarchal role of the government.

The Qin emperor Qinshi Huangdi ordered an infamous burning of Confucian writings and buried Confucians scholars alive.

Confucianism is based upon the teachings of Confucius (Kǒngzǐ; see p141), a 6th-century-BC philosopher who lived during a period of constant warfare and social upheaval. While Confucianism changed considerably throughout the centuries, some of the principal ideas remained the same – namely an emphasis on five basic hierarchical relationships: father-son, ruler-subject, husband-wife, elder-younger, and friend-friend. Confucius believed that if each individual carried out his or her proper role in society (ie, a son served his father respectfully while a father provided for his son, a subject served his ruler respectfully while a ruler provided for his subject, and so on) social order would be achieved. Confucius' disciples later gathered his ideas in the form of short aphorisms and conversations, forming the work known as *The Analects* (Lúnyǔ).

Early Confucian philosophy was further developed by Mencius (Mèngzǐ) and Xunzi, both of whom provided a theoretical and practical foundation for many of Confucius' moral concepts. In the 2nd century BC, Confucianism became the official ideology of the Han dynasty, thereby gaining mainstream acceptance for the first time. This was of major importance and resulted in the formation of an educated elite that served both the government as bureaucrats and the common people as exemplars of moral action. During the rule of the Tang dynasty an official examination system was created, which, in theory, made the imperial government a true meritocracy. However, this also contributed to an ossification of Confucianism, as the ideology grew increasingly mired in the weight of its own tradition, focusing exclusively on a core set of texts.

Nonetheless, influential figures sporadically reinterpreted the philosophy – in particular Zhu Xi (1130–1200) who brought in elements of Buddhism and Taoism to create Neo Confucianism (Lǐxué or Dàoxué) – and it remained a dominant social force up until the 1911 Revolution toppled the imperial bureaucracy. In the 20th century, intellectuals decried Confucian thought as an obstacle to modernisation and Mao further levelled the sage in his denunciation of 'the Four Olds'. But feudal faults notwithstanding, Confucius' call for social harmony has again resurfaced in government propaganda.

Believing he was the son of God and brother of Jesus Christ, Hakka rebel Hong Xiuquan led the bloody and tumultuous pseudo-Christian Taiping Rebellion against the Qing dynasty from 1856 to 1864.

Christianity

The explosion of interest in Christianity in China over recent years is unprecedented except for the wholesale conversions that accompanied the tumultuous rebellion of the pseudo-Christian Taiping in the 19th century. That Chinese Christians made up a considerable proportion of the volunteers helping with relief efforts after the huge Sìchuān earthquake of May 2008 indicates the increasing penetration of the religion into modern Chinese society.

Christianity first arrived in China with the Nestorians, a sect from ancient Persia that spilt with the Byzantine Church in 431 AD, who arrived in China via the Silk Road in the 7th century. A celebrated tablet in Xī'ān (p361) records their arrival. Much later, in the 16th century, the Jesuits arrived and were popular figures at the imperial court, although they made few converts.

Large numbers of Catholic and Protestant missionaries established themselves in the 19th century, but left after the establishment of the PRC in 1949. Christianity is perhaps uniquely placed to expand in China today due to its industrious work ethic, associations with first-world nations, its emphasis on human rights and charitable work. Some estimates point to as many as 100 million Christians in China. However, the exact population is hard to calculate as many groups – outside the four official Christian organisations – lead a strict underground existence (in what are called 'house churches') out of fear of a political clampdown.

In 2003, former Běijīng bureau chief of Time magazine David Aikman wrote *Jesus in Beijing: How Christianity is Transforming China and Changing the Global Balance of Power*, in which he predicts almost one third of Chinese turning to Christianity within 30 years.

Islam

Islam (Yīsīlán Jiào) in China dates to the 7th century, when it was first brought to China by Arab and Persian traders along the Silk Road. Later, during the Mongol Yuan dynasty, maritime trade increased, bringing new waves of merchants to China's coastal regions, particularly the port cities of Guǎngzhōu and Quánzhōu. The descendants of these groups – now scattered across the country – gradually integrated into Han culture, and are today distinguished primarily by their religion. In Chinese, they are referred to as the Hui.

Other Muslim groups include the Uighurs, Kazaks, Kyrgyz, Tajiks and Uzbeks, who live principally in the border areas of the northwest. It is estimated that 1.5% to 3% of Chinese today are Muslim.

Kāifēng in Hénán province is home to the largest community of Jews in China. The religious beliefs and customs of Judaism (Yóutài Jiào) have died out, yet the descendants of the original Jews still consider themselves Jewish.

Communism

Ironically (or perhaps intentionally), Mao Zedong, while struggling to uproot feudal superstition and religious belief, sprung to godlike status in China through his personality cult. In the China of today, Mao retains a semi-deified aura.

Communism sits awkwardly with the economic trajectory of China over the past 30 years. Once a philosophy forged in the white-hot crucible of civil war, revolution and the patriotic fervour to create a nation free from foreign interference, communism had largely run its credible course by the 1960s. By the death of Mao Zedong in 1976, the political philosophy had repeatedly brought the nation to catastrophe, with the Hundred Flowers Movement, the Great Leap Forward and the disastrous violence of the Cultural Revolution.

The Chinese for 'comrade' is *tóngzhì* (同志), a term still used by elderly Chinese. Younger Chinese use it rarely, as it also means 'homosexual' or 'gay'.

Communism remains the official guiding principle of the CCP. However, young communist aspirants are far less likely to be ideologues than pragmatists seeking to advance within the party structure. In real terms, many argue that communism has become an adjunct to the survival of the CCP.

Communism in China owes something to Confucianism. Confucius' philosophy largely concerns itself with the affairs of man and human society and the relationship between rulers and the ruled, rather than the supernatural world. Establishing a rigid framework for human conduct, the culture of Confucianism has been requisitioned by communists seeking to establish authority over society.

With the collapse of the Soviet Union in 1989, Běijīng became aware of the dangers of popular power and sought to maintain the coherence and strength of the state. This has meant that the CCP still seeks to impose itself firmly on the consciousness of Chinese people through patriotic education, propaganda, censorship, nationalism and the building of a strong nation.

Communism also has considerable nostalgia value for elderly Chinese who bemoan the loss of values in modern-day China and pine for the days when they felt more secure and society was more egalitarian. Chairman Mao's portrait still hangs in abundance across China, from drum towers in Guǎngxī province to restaurants in Běijīng, testament to a generation of Chinese who still revere the communist leader.

NATIONALISM

In today's China, '-isms' (主义; *zhǔyì* or 'doctrines') are often frowned upon. Any *zhǔyì* may suggest a personal focus that the CCP would prefer people channel into hard work instead. 'Intellectualism' is suspect as it may clash with political taboos. 'Idealism' is non-pragmatic and potentially destructive, as Maoism showed.

Many argue that China's one-party state has reduced thinking across the spectrum via propaganda and censorship, dumbing-down and an educational system that emphasises patriotic education. This has, however, helped spawn another '-ism': nationalism.

Nationalism is not restricted to Chinese youth but it is this generation – with no experience of the Cultural Revolution's terrifying excesses – which most closely identifies with its message. The *fènqīng* (angry youth) has been swept along with China's rise; while they are no lovers of the CCP, they yearn for a stronger China that can stand up to 'foreign interference' and dictate its own terms.

The CCP actively encourages strong patriotism, but is nervous about its transformation into nationalism and its potential for disturbance. Much nationalism in the PRC has little to do with the CCP but everything to do with China; while the CCP has struggled at length to identify itself with China's civilisation and core values, it has been only partially successful. With China's tendency to get quickly swept along by passions, nationalism is an often unseen but quite potent force in today's China.

Animism

Around 3% of China's population is animist, a primordial religious belief akin to shamanism. Animists see the world as a living being, with rocks, trees, mountains and people all containing spirits that need to live in harmony. If this harmony is disrupted, restoration of this balance is attempted by a shaman who is empowered to mediate between the human and spirit world. Animism is most widely believed by minority groups and exists in a multitude of forms, some of which have been influenced by Buddhism and other religions.

Chinese Cuisine

While weighing up the immensity of China, it's also worth recalling that this is a land simply obsessed with food. Food plays a central and prominent role in both Chinese society and the national psyche. Work, play, romance, business and the family all revolve around food. Meals are occasions to clinch deals, strike up new friendships, rekindle old ones and fall in love. When people meet, a common Chinese greeting is '*Nǐ chīfàn le ma*?' – 'Have you eaten yet?'. All you need to fully explore this tasty domain is a pair of chopsticks, an explorative palate and a passion for the unusual and unexpected.

Real Chinese Food

Your very first impressions of China were quite possibly via your taste buds. Chinatowns the world over teem with the aromas of Chinese cuisine, ferried overseas by China's versatile and hard-working cooks. Chinese food is a wholesome point of contact – and a very tasty one at that – between an immigrant Chinese population and local people. Chinatowns across the globe swarm with diners on Sundays looking to 'yum cha' and heartily feast on dim sum.

Did you know that chilli peppers arrived in China from Peru and Mexico during the rule of the Ming dynasty?

But what you see – and taste – abroad is usually just a wafer-thin slice of a very hefty and wholesome pie. Chinese cuisine in the West is culled from the cookbook of an emigrant community that largely emerged from China's southern seaboard. In a similar vein, the sing-song melodies of Cantonese was for decades the most-heard dialect in the world's Chinatowns, even though the dialect is hardly representative of the Chinese language. So although you may be hard pressed to avoid dim sum and *cha siu* in your local Chinatown, finding more 'obscure' specialties from Yúnnán, the Northeast or Xīnjiāng can be a tough task. If you do happen upon dishes from other parts of China, they may all be curiously Cantonese in flavour. Local Chinatown 'Szechuan' cooking is even further from the authentic eye-watering western cuisine of Sìchuān than its curious spelling. The Peking duck at your local restaurant is at best a distant and second-rate cousin of the authentic article crisply fired up over fruit tree wood in the ovens of Běijīng *kǎoyādiàn* (roast duck restaurants). Běijīng chefs wouldn't go near them with a barge pole.

To get an idea of the size of its diverse menu, remember that China is not that much smaller than Europe. Just as Europe is a patchwork of different nation states, languages, cultural traditions and climates, China is similarly a smorgasbord of dialects, languages, ethnic minorities and often extreme geographic and climatic differences. Your average Tibetan nomad has never eaten dim sum and probably never will. Inner Mongolian herdsmen are not famed for their love of hairy crabs from Shànghǎi. The sheer size of the land, the strength of local culture and differences in geography and altitude means there can be little in common between the cuisines of Xīnjiāng and Tibet, even though they are adjacent to each other. Eating your way around China is one of the best ways to journey the land, so pack a sense of culinary adventure along with your travelling boots!

Regional Cooking

China's immense geographical, topographical and climatic disparities combined with millennia of local cooking traditions have forged China's various schools of cuisine. While many regions proudly lay claim to their own distinctive style of cooking and considerable shades exist in between, China is traditionally carved up into four principal schools: northern, eastern, western and southern.

The development of China's varied regional cuisines has been influenced by the climate, abundance of certain crops and animals, the type of terrain, proximity to the sea and last, but not least, the influence of neighbouring nations and the import of ingredients and aromas. Naturally sea fish and seafood is prevalent in coastal regions of China, while in Inner Mongolia and Xīnjiāng there is a dependence on meat such as beef and lamb.

Of their various cooking schools, the Chinese traditionally say '南甜北咸东辣西酸' or 'Sweet in the south, salty in the north, hot in the east and sour in the west'. It's a massive generalisation, but as with most generalisations, there's more than a grain of truth.

Flash-frying in hot peanut or vegetable oil is a typical sight in streetside restaurants, markets or the kitchens of even the best establishments. The technique evolved due to the historical scarcity of fuel, so meat and vegetables could be cut into small chunks and fried exceedingly quickly at a high temperature.

TRAVEL YOUR TASTE BUDS

China is such a gourmand's paradise you won't know when to stop. In the north, fill up on a tasty dish of wontons *(húndún)*, stuffed with juicy leeks and minced pork or Mongolian hotpot *(ménggǔ huǒguō)*, a hearty brew of mutton, onions and cabbage.

China's arid northwest locals can pop a bowl of noodles topped with sliced donkey meat *(lǘròu huáng miàn)* under your nose or sizzling lamb kebobs *(kǎo yángròu)* in your fingers. Stop by Xī'ān for warming bowls of mutton broth and shredded flat bread *(yángròu pàomó)*. A bowl of Lánzhōu hand-pulled noodles *(lā miàn)* is a meal in itself.

In case you're pining for something sweet and savoury, head to Shànghǎi for delicious honey-smoked carp *(mìzhī xūnyú)* or a tongue-tingling plate of hot and sour squid *(suānlà yóuyú)*. Cleanse your palate with a glass of heady Shàoxīng yellow wine *(Shàoxīng huángjiǔ)* or the more delicate flavours of Dragonwell tea *(lóngjǐng chá)*. It may not exactly give you wings, but a dish of Huángshān braised pigeon *(Huángshān zhāngā)* will definitely give you the stamina to clamber up the misty inclines of Huángshān.

Some like it hot, and little comes hotter than the fiery flavours of Sìchuān. Begin with mouth-numbing mapo tofu *(mápó dòufu)*, followed by the celebrated spicy chicken with peanuts *(gōngbào jīdīng)*. If the smoke still isn't coming out of your ears, fish smothered in chilli *(shuǐzhǔ yú)* should have you breathing fire. Alternatively, test your mettle with a volcanic Chóngqìng hotpot.

In the south, relax with morning dim sum in Guǎngzhōu or a bowl of Cantonese snake soup (*shé gēng*) in one of the city's boisterous night markets. While in Macau, taste the Macanese dish *porco à alentejana*, a mouthwatering casserole of pork and clams.

And wherever you go in China you'll be pursued by the toe-curling smell of stinky tofu (*chòu dòufu*) — trust us, it tastes better than it smells.

Northern School

In the dry north Chinese wheat belt there's an accent on millet, sorghum, maize, barley and wheat rather than rice (which requires an abundance of water). With a more down-to-earth spectrum of flavours rather than the finer and sweeter aromas of southern cooking, northern cooking is rich and wholesome. Filling breads – such as *mántou* (馒头) or *bǐng* (饼; flat breads) – are steamed, baked or fried while noodles may form the basis of any northern meal, although the ubiquitous availability of rice means it can always be found. Northern cuisine is frequently quite salty, and appetising dumplings (饺子; *jiǎozi*) are widely eaten.

PASTA

Legend credits Marco Polo with bringing pasta to Italy from China in 1295.

Northern cooking has a reputation in other parts of China for being rather pedestrian and unsophisticated, but it is filling and appetising and particularly well suited to the harsh and hardy winter climate.

Note, however, that Shāndōng cuisine – *lǔcài* (鲁菜) – is also one of the eight great Chinese cooking traditions, so the northern school is far from peripheral. Furthermore, with Běijīng the principal capital through the Yuan, Ming and Qing dynasties, Imperial cooking is also a chief characteristic of the northern school. Peking Duck is Běijīng's signature dish, served with typical northern ingredients – pancakes, spring onions and fermented bean paste. You can find it all over China, but it's only true to form in the capital, roasted in ovens fired up with fruit tree wood.

The influence of Manchurian cooking and the cold climate of the three northeastern provinces – Liǎoníng, Jílì'n and Hēilóngjiāng – have left a legacy of rich and hearty stews, dense breads and dumplings. The cooking of the nomadic Mongolians has also left a pronounced mark on northern meat cooking, especially in the Mongolian hotpot and the Mongolian barbecue. Milk from nomadic herds of cattle, goats and horses has also made its way into northern cuisine, as yoghurts for example.

Meat roasting is also more common in the north than in other parts of China. Meats in northern China are braised until falling off the bone, or are slathered with spices and barbecued until smoky. Pungent garlic, chives and spring onions are used with abandon, and are also used raw.

Hallmark northern dishes:

PINYIN	SCRIPT	ENGLISH
Běijīng kǎoyā	北京烤鸭	Peking duck
jiāo zhá yángròu	焦炸羊肉	deep-fried mutton
qīng xiāng shāo jī	清香烧鸡	chicken wrapped in lotus leaf
shuàn yángròu	涮羊肉	lamb hotpot
mántou	馒头	steamed buns
jiǎozi	饺子	dumplings
ròu bāozi	肉包子	steamed meat buns
sān měi dòufu	三美豆腐	sliced bean curd with Chinese cabbage
sì xǐ wánzi	四喜丸子	steamed and fried pork, shrimp and bamboo shoot balls
yuán bào lǐ jí	芫爆里脊	stir-fried pork tenderloin with coriander
zào liū sān bái	糟溜三白	stir-fried chicken, fish and bamboo shoots

Southern School

The southern Chinese – particularly the Cantonese – spearheaded successive waves of immigration overseas, leaving an aromatic constellation of Chinatowns around the world as outposts of the Chinese culinary empire. Consequently, this is the school of cooking most Westerners are very familiar with, even though, being modified to suit local tastes, it is quite different from the southern cooking of China. Cantonese cooking (粤菜; *yuècài*) is also further from the Western palate than many richer-tasting northern Chinese dishes.

The regional joshing continues: non-southern Chinese accuse southern cooking of lacking flavour. Indeed, Cantonese restaurants can be thin on the ground in China outside Cantonese-speaking areas. Cantonese restaurants, when you do find them, are frequently vast aircraft-hanger size dim sum restaurants or hotel restaurants, rather than hole-in-the-wall diners (although these can be found).

Southern cooking may lack the richness and saltiness of northern cooking, but instead more subtle aromas are tempted to the surface. The Cantonese astutely believe that good cooking does not require much flavouring, for it is the *xiān* (natural freshness) of the ingredients that mark a truly high-grade dish. Hence the near obsessive attention paid to the freshness of ingredients in southern cuisine.

The hallmark dish is dim sum (点心; Mandarin: *diǎnxīn*), the signature dining experience of every Chinatown the world over and a standard Sunday institution. Yum cha (literally 'drink tea') – another name for dim sum dining – in Guǎngzhōu and Hong Kong can actually be enjoyed any day of the week. Dishes – often in steamers – are wheeled around on trolleys so you can see what you want to order.

Rice is the primary staple of southern cooking. Sparkling paddy fields glitter across southern China; the humid climate, plentiful rainfall and well-irrigated land means that rice has been farmed in the south since the Chinese first populated the region during the Han dynasty (206 BC–AD 220).

Southern-school dishes:

PINYIN	SCRIPT	ENGLISH
bái zhuó xiā	白灼虾	blanched prawns with shredded scallions
dōngjiāng yánjú jī	东江盐焗鸡	salt-baked chicken
gāli jī	咖喱鸡	curried chicken
háoyóu niúròu	蚝油牛肉	beef with oyster sauce
kǎo rǔzhū	烤乳猪	crispy suckling pig
mì zhī chāshāo	密汁叉烧	roast pork with honey
shé ròu	蛇肉	snake
tángcù lǐjī/ gǔlǎo ròu	糖醋里脊/ 咕老肉	sweet and sour pork fillets
tángcù páigǔ	糖醋排骨	sweet and sour spare ribs

Western School

The cuisine of landlocked Western China, a region heavily populated by ethnic minorities, enters an entirely different spectrum of flavours and sensations. The trademark ingredient of the western school is the fiercely hot red chilli, a potent firecracker of a herb. Aniseed, coriander, garlic and peppercorns are also thrown in to give dishes that extra pungency.

At www.chinavista.com/culture/cuisine/recipes.html there's a great collection of Chinese recipes divided by province.

The standout cuisine of the western school is fiery Sìchuān (川菜; *chuāncài*), renowned for its eye-watering peppery aromas. One of the herbs that differentiates Sìchuān cooking from other spicy cuisines is the use of 'flower pepper' *(huājiāo)*, a numbing peppercorn-like herb that floods the mouth with an anaesthetising fragrance. Meat, particu-

HITTING THE HOT SPOT

The Sìchuān hotpot (p760) sets foreheads streaming and tummies aquiver all over China from sultry Hǎinán Island to the frigid borderlands of Hēilóngjiāng. It is a fierce and smouldering concoction, bursting with fire and boiling with volcanic flavour.

The Mongolian hotpot is a very different and more subtle creature indeed. Mutton or lamb is the principal meat in a Mongolian hotpot, with scalded strips of meat rescued from the boiling soup and doused in thick sauces, especially sesame sauce (芝麻酱; *zhīmajiàng*). Vegetables – cabbage, mushrooms and potatoes – are also cast into the boiling froth and eaten when soft. The hotpot dates to when Mongolian soldiers would use their helmets as a pot, heating them up over a fire with broth, meat, vegetables and condiments.

larly in Húnán, is marinated, pickled or otherwise processed before cooking, which is generally by stir or explode-frying.

Sìchuān restaurants are everywhere in China, swarming around train stations, squeezed away down food streets or squished into street markets with wobbly stools and rickety tables parked out front. Across the land, legions of *xiǎochī* (hole-in-the-wall diners) are Sìchuān restaurants dishing up spicy standbys. A Sìchuān dish you can find cooked up by chefs across China is the delicious sour cabbage fish soup (酸菜鱼; *suāncàiyú*; wholesome fish chunks in a spicy broth). The Chóngqìng hotpot is a force to be reckoned with but must be approached with a stiff upper lip (and copious amounts of liquid refreshment). Húnán food (湘菜; *xiāngcài*) is similarly extremely spicy but without the numbing sensations of Sìchuān cooking. Communist firebrand Mao Zedong was a Húnán native who liked his dishes off-the-scale, like his politics.

For the lowdown on Muslim Uighur cuisine from China's northwest, see the boxed text (p779).

Other western-school dishes:

PINYIN	SCRIPT	ENGLISH
gōngbào jīdīng	宫爆鸡丁	spicy chicken with peanuts
shuǐ zhǔ niúròu	水煮牛肉	spicy fried and boiled beef
shuǐzhǔyú	水煮鱼	fried and boiled fish, garlic sprouts and celery
dāndanmiàn	担担面	spicy noodles
huíguō ròu	回锅肉	boiled and stir-fried pork with salty and hot sauce
Chóngqìng huǒguō	重庆火锅	Chóngqìng hotpot
suāncàiyú	酸菜鱼	sour cabbage fish soup
yú xiāng ròusī	鱼香肉丝	fish-flavour pork strips
bàngbàng jī	棒棒鸡	shredded chicken in a hot pepper and sesame sauce
gānshāo yán lǐ	干烧岩鲤	stewed carp with ham and hot and sweet sauce
málà dòufu	麻辣豆腐	spicy tofu
zhàcài ròusī	榨菜肉丝	stir-fried pork or beef tenderloin with tuber mustard
zhāngchá yā	樟茶鸭	camphor tea duck

Eastern School

The eastern school of Chinese cuisine derives from a fecund and fertile region of China, cut by waterways and canals, dotted with lakes, fringed by a long coastline and nourished by a subtropical climate. Jiāngsū province itself – one of the core regions of the eastern school – is famed as the Land of Fish and Rice, a tribute to its abundance of food and produce. The region was also historically prosperous and in today's export-oriented economy, today's eastern provinces are among China's wealthiest. This combination of riches and bountiful food created a culture of epicurism and gastronomic appreciation.

The Song dynasty saw the blossoming of the restaurant industry here; in Hángzhōu, the southern Song dynasty capital, restaurants and teahouses accounted for two-thirds of the city's business during a splendidly rich cultural era. At this time, one of Hángzhōu's most famous dishes – *dōngpō ròu* (named after the celebrated poet and governor of Hángzhōu, Su Dongpo) – achieved fame.

Generally more oily and sweeter than other Chinese schools, the eastern school revels in fish and seafood, reflecting of its geographical proximity to major rivers and the sea. Fish is usually *qīngzhēng* (清蒸; steamed) but can be stir-fried, pan-fried or grilled. Hairy crabs *(dàzháxiè)* are a Shànghǎi speciality between October and December. Eaten with soy, ginger and vinegar and downed with warm Shàoxīng wine, the best crabs come from Yangcheng Lake. The crab is believed to increase the body's *yīn* (coldness), so *yang* (warmth) is added by imbibing lukewarm rice wine with it. It is also usual to eat male and female crabs together.

As with Cantonese food, freshness is a key ingredient in the cuisine and sauces and seasonings are only employed to augment essential flavours. Stir-frying and steaming are also used, the latter with Shànghǎi's famous *xiǎolóngbāo*, steamer buns filled with nuggets of pork or crab swimming in a scalding meat broth. Learning how to devour these carefully without the meat juice squirting everywhere and scalding the roof of your mouth (or blinding your neighbour) requires some – quite enjoyable – practice.

Chinese Cuisine by Susana Foo features enlightening Chinese recipes adapted for Western ingredients.

China's best soy sauce is also produced in the eastern provinces, and the technique of braising meat using soy sauce, sugar and spices was perfected here. Meat cooked in this manner takes on a dark mauve hue auspiciously described as 'red', a colour associated with good fortune. '*Nóngyóu chìjiàng* means 'rich oil and red sauces', a defining characteristic of the cuisine', says Jereme Leung of Shànghǎi's Whampoa Club. 'Soy sauce from the region is the hardest thing to substitute when trying to produce this characteristic abroad.'

Famous dishes from the eastern school:

PINYIN	SCRIPT	ENGLISH
jiāng cōng chǎo xiè	姜葱炒蟹	stir-fried crab with ginger and scallions
xiǎolóngbāo	小笼包	steamer buns
mìzhī xūnyú	蜜汁熏鱼	honey-smoked carp
níng shì shànyú	宁式鳝鱼	stir-fried eel with onion
qiézhī yúkuài	茄汁鱼块	fish fillet in tomato sauce
qīng zhēng guìyú	清蒸鳜鱼	steamed Mandarin fish
sōngzǐ guìyú	松子鳜鱼	Mandarin fish with pine nuts
suānlà yóuyú	酸辣鱿鱼	hot and sour squid
yóubào xiārén	油爆虾仁	fried shrimp
zhá hēi lǐyú	炸黑鲤鱼	fried black carp
zhá yúwán	炸鱼丸	fish balls

Dining: the Ins & Outs

Chinese Restaurants

Restaurants in China serve scrumptious food, but finding eateries with any sense of warmth or charm can be a real task outside the big cities. With their huge round tables and thousand-candle-power electric lights, large banqueting-style restaurants are impersonal, with little sense of intimacy or romance. Waiting staff can be both intrusive and snobbish and are rarely trained to give you breathing space. Don't be surprised if your waitress stands nearby, staring at you as you experiment with your rudimentary chopstick techniques. At the lower end of the scale are the cheap Chinese restaurants, where diners leave chicken bones on the tabletop, loudly slurp their noodles, chain-smoke and shout into mobiles. At each extreme, the food is the focal point of the meal and that is what diners are there for. Many restaurants charge for the pre-packed moist tissues which may be handed to you; you are not charged if you refuse them. Always check your bill carefully as foreigners may be overcharged in some restaurants.

Zòngzi (dumplings made of glutinous rice wrapped in bamboo or reed leaves) are eaten during the Dragon Boat festival.

Dining Times

The Chinese eat early. Lunch usually commences from around 11.30am, either self-cooked or a takeaway at home, or in a street-side restaurant. Rushed urban diners may just grab a sandwich, a fast-food burger or a lunchbox (合饭; *héfàn*). Dinner usually kicks off from around 6pm. Reflecting these dining times, some restaurants open at around 11am to close for an afternoon break at about 2.30pm before opening again at around 5pm and closing in the late evening. Chinese diners don't hang around at the end of dinner parties or banquets: they may suddenly rise en masse and depart with little warning, leaving you wondering what happened.

Menus

In Běijīng, Shànghǎi and other large cities, you may be proudly presented with an English menu (英文菜谱; Yīngwén Càipǔ). In lesser towns and out in the sticks, don't expect anything other than a Chinese-language menu and a hovering waitress with zero English. The best is undoubtedly the ever-handy photo menu, even though what's pictured on the menu may be a very distant relative of what appears on your table. If you like the look of what other diners are eating, just point over with your chopsticks (我要那个; *wǒ yào nèi gè;* 'I want that' – a very handy phrase). Alternatively, pop into the kitchen and point out the meats and vegetables you would like to eat.

The ever-elusive English language menu, if you locate one, may also be misfiring. In the run up to the Běijīng Olympic Games in 2008, the authorities attempted to standardise English translations of Chinese menus throughout the city. The plan was to rid English menus citywide of such lost-in-translation bloopers as 'government abused chicken' *(gōngbào jīdīng),* 'grilled enema', 'potato wire' and other surreal dishes. Quite how successful this campaign was is open to question.

TIPPING

Tipping is never done at cheap restaurants in mainland China. Smart, international restaurants will encourage tipping but it is not obligatory and it's uncertain whether waiting staff receive their tips at the end of the night. Hotel restaurants automatically add a 15% service charge and some high-end restaurants may do the same.

CHOPSTICKS

Sooner or later you may need to start twiddling those fiddly chopsticks (筷子; *kuàizi*), and it's worth coming to China primed, if not totally prepared. Much Chinese food is cooked in small bite-size chunks, arriving on the table in communal dishes. Being already sliced up, there is little need for a knife, so chopsticks are perfectly suited to Chinese cuisine.

In smarter restaurants you will receive a pair of white plastic imitation ivory chopsticks that will come wrapped in its own paper sheath. You may also have a chopstick rest. Cheaper restaurants still equip diners with throwaway bamboo chopsticks which are incredibly wasteful. China gets through 45 billion pairs annually: a lot of bamboo. Don't worry about not mastering chopsticks; even Chinese diners have occasional problems with slippery button mushrooms, recalcitrant peanuts or evasive broccoli. You can practise at home with a pair of pencils! Some restaurants also use metal chopsticks, but these are quite rare. Some travellers invest in a pair of their own chopsticks, which is a good idea if you are concerned about the wastefulness of using bamboo chopsticks or have concerns regarding hygiene.

Whatever type you use, don't point them at people and don't stick them upright in bowls of rice; it's a portent of death.

Desserts & Sweets

The Chinese do not generally eat dessert, but fruit – typically watermelon *(xīguā)* or oranges *(chéng)* – often concludes a meal. Ice cream can be ordered in some places, but in general sweet desserts *(tiánpǐn)* are consumed as snacks and are seldom available in restaurants.

Table Manners

Chinese meal times are generally relaxed affairs with no strict rules of etiquette. Meals can commence in Confucian vein before spiralling into total Taoist mayhem, fuelled by incessant toasts with *báijiǔ* (a white spirit) or beer and furious smoking by the men.

Meals typically unfold with one person ordering on behalf of a group. When a group dines, a selection of dishes is ordered for everyone to share rather than individual diners ordering a dish just for themselves. As they arrive, dishes are placed communally in the centre of the table or on a lazy Susan which may be revolved by the host so that the principal guest gets first choice of whatever dish arrives. Soup may arrive midway through the meal or at the end. Rice often arrives at the end of the meal; if you would like it earlier, just ask.

It is good form to fill your neighbours' tea cups or beer glasses when they are empty. Show your appreciation to the pourer by gently tapping your middle finger on the table. To serve yourself tea or any other drink without serving others first is bad form. When your teapot needs a refill, signal this to the waiter by taking the lid off the pot.

It's best to wait until someone announces a toast before drinking your beer; if you want to get a quick shot in, propose a toast to the host. The Chinese do in fact toast each other much more than in the West, often each time they drink. A toast is conducted by raising your glass in both hands in the direction of the toastee and crying out *gānbēi*, literally 'dry the glass', which is the cue to drain your glass in one hit. This can be quite a challenge if your drink is 65% *báijiǔ*, and your glass is rapidly refilled to the meniscus after you drain it, in preparation for the next toast.

Smokers can light up during the meal, unless you are in the no-smoking area of a restaurant. Depending on the restaurant, smokers may

CHINA'S COOKING OIL SCANDAL

In 2010, diners in China were appalled to discover that one in 10 meals cooked in Chinese restaurants was prepared with cooking oil dredged up from sewers and drains. Oil is lavishly employed in Chinese cooking and generates considerable waste.

This waste oil (地沟油; *dìgōuyóu*) is harvested by night soil collectors who scoop out the solidified oil from drains near restaurants and sell it on for around Y300 a barrel. The oil is then processed, sold to restaurant owners and it re-enters the food chain. It is a stomach-churningly lucrative industry. Quoting a professor from Wuhan Polytechnic University, *The China Youth Daily* revealed that up to three million tons of waste oil is recycled annually in China, or around 10% of all cooking oil consumed. The processed waste oil retails for around half the price of ordinary cooking oil but is sometimes mixed in with ordinary cooking oil prior to being sold. Once used again, there is nothing to stop the waste oil from being harvested afresh for further recycling. At present no regulations preventing the recycling of waste oil exist in China, so the industry is set to grow further.

smoke through the entire meal. If you are a smoker, ensure you hand around your cigarettes to others as that is standard procedure (cigarettes are generally cheap in China).

Last but not least, never insist to the last on paying for the bill if someone is tenaciously determined on paying – usually the person who invited you to dinner. By all means offer, but then raise your hands in mock surrender when resistance is met; to pay for a meal when another person is determined to pay is to make them lose face.

Chinese toothpick etiquette is similar to that found in other Asian nations: one hand excavates with the toothpick, while the other hand shields the mouth.

Street Food

Snacking your way around China is a fine way to sample the different flavours of the land while on the move. Most towns have a street market or a night market (夜市; *yèshì*) for good-value snacks and meals so you can either take away or park yourself on a wobbly stool and grab a beer. Street markets such as Kāifēng's boisterous night market (p419) abound with choices you may not find in restaurants. Vocal vendors will be forcing their tasty creations on you but you can also see what people are buying, so all you have to do is join the queue and point.

Eating with Kids

As with travelling with children in China, dining out with kids can be a challenge. Budget eateries won't have kids' menus; nor will they have booster seats. Smarter restaurants may supply these but it can be touch and go. Children will be shrieking to go instantly to McDonalds or KFC. In large cities you will be able to find more restaurants switched on to the needs of families, especially Western restaurants that may have a play area, kids menu, activities, booster seats and other paraphernalia.

Breakfast

Breakfast in China is generally light, simple and over-and-done-with quickly. The meal may merely consist of a bowl of rice porridge (粥; *zhōu*) or its watery cousin, rice gruel (稀饭; *xīfàn*). Pickles, boiled eggs, steamed buns, fried peanuts and deep-fried dough sticks (油条; *yóutiáo*) are also popular, washed down with warm soybean milk. Breakfast at your Chinese hotel may consist of some or all of these. Coffee is rarely drunk at breakfast time, unless the family is modern, urban and middle class, but it's easy to find cafes, especially in large towns. Sliced bread (面包; *miànbāo*) was once rare but is increasingly common, as is butter (黄油; *huángyóu*).

Vegetarianism

If you'd rather chew on a legume than a leg of lamb, it can be hard going trying to find truly vegetarian dishes. China's history of famine and poverty means the consumption of meat has always been a sign of status, and is symbolic of health and wealth. Eating meat is also considered to enhance male virility, so vegetarian men raise eyebrows. Partly as a result of this, there is virtually no vegetarian movement in China, although Chinese may forgo meat for Buddhist reasons. For the same reasons, they may avoid meat on certain days of the month but remain carnivorous at other times. As a Westerner, trying to explain your secular and ethical reasons for not eating meat may inspire bemusement.

When trying to pursue a vegetarian diet in China, you will find that vegetables are often fried in animal-based oils, while vegetable soups may be made with chicken or beef stock, so simply choosing vegetable items on the menu is ineffective. In Běijīng and Shànghǎi you will, however, find a generous crop of vegetarian restaurants to choose from alongside outfits such as Element Fresh (p82) which have a decent range of healthy vegetarian options.

Out of the large cities, you may be hard pressed to find a vegetarian restaurant. Your best bet may be to head to a sizeable active Buddhist temple or monastery, where you could well find a Buddhist vegetarian restaurant that is open to the public. Buddhist vegetarian food typically consists of 'mock meat' dishes created from tofu, wheat gluten, potato and other vegetables. Some of the dishes are almost works of art, with vegetarian ingredients sculpted to look like spare ribs or fried chicken. Sometimes the chefs go to great lengths to create 'bones' from carrots and lotus roots. Some of the more famous vegetarian dishes include vegetarian 'ham', braised vegetarian 'shrimp' and sweet and sour 'fish'.

If you want to say 'I am a vegetarian' in Chinese, the phrase to use is 我吃素 *(wǒ chī sù)*.

Tea

An old Chinese saying identifies tea as one of the seven basic necessities of life, along with fuel, oil, rice, salt, soy sauce and vinegar. The Chinese were the first to cultivate tea, and the art of brewing and drinking tea has been popular since Tang times (AD 618–907).

Interestingly, tea was once used as a form of currency in China.

China has three main types of tea: green tea (*lǜ chá*), black tea (*hóng chá*) and *wūlóng* (a semifermented tea, halfway between black and green tea). In addition, there are other variations, including jasmine *(cháshuǐ)* and chrysanthemum *(júhuā chá)*. Some famous regional teas of China are Fújiàn's *tiě guānyīn*, *pǔ'ěr* from Yúnnán and Zhèjiāng's *lóngjǐng* tea. Eight-treasure tea *(bābǎo chá)* consists of rock sugar, dates, nuts and tea combined in a cup; it makes a delicious treat. Tea is to the Chinese what fine wine is to the French, a beloved beverage savoured for its fine aroma, distinctive flavour and pleasing aftertaste.

Alcoholic Drinks

If tea is the most popular drink in China, then beer (啤酒; *píjiǔ*) is surely second. Many towns and cities have their own brewery and label, although a remarkable feat of socialist standardisation ensures a striking similarity in flavour and strength. You can drink bathtubs of the stuff and still navigate a straight line. If you want your beer cold, ask for *liáng de* (凉的) and if you want it truly arctic, call for *bīngzhèn de* (冰镇的).

The best-known beer is Tsingtao, made with Laoshan mineral water, which lends it a sparkling quality. It's originally a German beer since the town of Qīngdǎo (formerly spelled 'Tsingtao') was once a German concession and the Chinese inherited the brewery (see the boxed text, p150), which dates to 1903, along with Bavarian beer-making ways. Experts claim that draught *(zhāpí)* Tsingtao is superior to the bottled variety, although the very best can be bought by the bag on the streets of Qīngdǎo.

Several foreign beers are also brewed in China. If you crave variety, many of the bars listed in this book should have a selection of foreign imported beers; prices will be high, however.

Also look out for black beer from Xīnjiāng and dark beers from other local breweries (eg Reeb beer in Shànghǎi) which offer more bite. Rather more alternative beers include Inner Mongolian milk beer and pineapple beer from Běijīng.

China has cultivated vines and produced wine for an estimated 4000 years.

China has cultivated vines and produced wine for an estimated 4000 years. The word 'wine' gets rather loosely translated – many Chinese 'wines' are in fact spirits that will have you wincing. Milder rice wine is intended mainly for cooking rather than drinking but is often drunk warm. Chinese wine-producing techniques differ from those of the West: Western producers try to prevent oxidation in their wines, but oxidation produces a flavour that Chinese tipplers find desirable and go to great lengths to achieve. Chinese diners are also keen on wines with different herbs and other materials soaked in them, which they drink for their health and for restorative or aphrodisiac qualities.

Wine with dead bees, pickled snakes or lizards is desirable for its alleged tonic properties – in general, the more poisonous the creature, the more potent the tonic effects. Maotai, a favourite of Chinese drinkers, is a spirit called *báijiǔ* made from sorghum (a type of millet) and used for toasts at banquets. The cheap alternative is Erguotou, distilled in Běijīng but available all over China; look out for the Red Star (Hongxing) brand to avoid being hit by moonshine that will bring on a thundering hangover. *Báijiǔ* ranges across the alcohol spectrum from milder forms to around 65% proof. In its fiercer forms, the drink is highly volatile, liable to remove the roof of your mouth and turn your legs to rubber.

Arts & Architecture

China is custodian of one of the world's richest cultural and artistic legacies. Until the 20th century, China's arts were deeply conservative and resistant to change; in the last hundred years revolutions in technique and content have fashioned a dramatic transformation. Despite this evolution, China's arts – whatever the period – remain united by a common aesthetic that taps into the very soul and essence of the nation.

Aesthetics

In reflection of the Chinese character, Chinese aesthetics have traditionally been marked by restraint and understatement, a preference for oblique references over direct explanation, vagueness in place of specificity and an avoidance of the obvious and a fondness for the subtle. Traditional Chinese aesthetics sought to cultivate a more reserved artistic impulse and these principles compellingly find their way into virtually every Chinese art form, from painting to sculpture, ceramics, calligraphy, film, poetry and literature.

The most abstract calligraphic form is grass hand script *(caoshū)*, which even Chinese people have difficulty reading.

Calligraphy

Although calligraphy (书法; *shūfǎ*) has a place among most languages that employ alphabets, the art of calligraphy in China is taken to unusual heights of intricacy and beauty. Although Chinese calligraphy is beautiful in its own right, the complex infatuation Chinese people have for their written language helps elucidate their great respect for the art of calligraphy.

To understand how perfectly suited written Chinese is for calligraphy, it is vital to grasp how written Chinese works. A word in English represents a sound alone; a written character in Chinese combines both sound and a picture. Indeed, the sound element of a Chinese character – when present – is often auxiliary to the presentation of a visual image, even if abstract.

Furthermore, although some Chinese characters were simplified in the 1950s as part of a literacy drive, most characters have remained unchanged for thousands of years. This longevity stems from the pictorial nature of Chinese characters. As characters are essentially images, they inadequately reflect changes in spoken Chinese over time. A phonetic written language such as English alters over the centuries to reflect changes in the sound of the language. Being pictographic, Chinese cannot easily do this, so while the spoken language has transformed over the centuries, the written language remained more static. Indeed, one only has to look at the diversity of Chinese dialects – which all use the same written characters – to grasp that Chinese characters must essentially be pictorial.

As Chinese calligraphers are engaged therefore in representing pictures, it is simpler to fathom why calligraphy in China is considered so vital among the arts. This also explains why Chinese calligraphy is the trickiest of China's arts to comprehend for Western visitors, unless they have a sound understanding of written Chinese. The beauty of a Chinese character may be partially appreciated by a Western audience, but for a full understanding it is also essential to understand the meaning of the character in context.

BRUSHSTROKES

The character 永, which means 'eternal', contains the five fundamental brushstrokes necessary to master calligraphy.

There are five main calligraphic scripts – seal script, clerical script, semicursive script, cursive script and standard script – each of which reflects the style of writing of a specific era. Seal script, the oldest and most complex, was the official writing system during the Qin dynasty and has been employed ever since in the carving of the seals and name 'chops' that are used to stamp documents. Expert calligraphers have a preference for using full-form characters *(fántǐzì)* rather than their simplified variants *(jiǎntǐzì)*.

Painting

Traditional Painting

Unlike Chinese calligraphy, no 'insider' knowledge is required to fully admire traditional Chinese painting. Despite its symbolism, obscure references and the occasional abstruse hand of Chinese philosophy, Chinese painting is largely accessible. For this reason, traditional Chinese paintings – especially landscapes – have long been treasured in the West for their beauty.

As described in Xie He's 6th-century-AD treatise, the *Six Principles of Painting*, the chief aim of Chinese painting is to capture the innate essence or spirit *(qì)* of a subject and endow it with vitality. The brush line, varying in thickness and tone, was the second principle (referred to as the 'bone method') and is the defining technique of Chinese painting. Traditionally, it was imagined that brushwork quality could reveal the artist's moral character. As a general rule, painters were less concerned with achieving outward resemblance (that was the third principle) than with conveying intrinsic qualities.

Early painters dwelled on the human figure and moral teachings, while also conjuring up scenes from everyday life. By the time of the Tang dynasty, a new genre, known as landscape painting, had begun to flower. Reaching full bloom during the Song and Yuan dynasties, landscape painting meditated on the environment around man. Towering mountains, ethereal mists, open spaces, trees and rivers, and light and dark were all exquisitely presented in ink washes on silk. Landscape paintings attempted to capture the metaphysical and the absolute, drawing the viewer into a particular realm where the philosophies of Taoism and Buddhism found expression. Man is typically a small and almost insignificant subtext to the performance. The dream-like painting sought to draw the viewer in rather than impose itself on him or her.

On a technical level, the success of landscapes depended on the artists' skill in capturing light and atmosphere. Blank, open spaces devoid of colour create light-filled voids, contrasting with the darkness of mountain folds, filling the painting with *qì* and vaporous vitality. Specific emotions are not aroused but instead nebulous sensations permeate. Painting and classical poetry often went hand in hand, best exemplified by the work of Tang-dynasty poet/artist Wang Wei (699–759).

Modern Art

After 1949, classical Chinese techniques had been abandoned and foreign artistic techniques imported wholesale. Washes on silk were replaced with oil on canvas and China's traditional obsession with the mysterious and ineffable made way for attention to detail and realism.

By 1970, Chinese artists had aspired to master the skills of socialist-realism, a vibrant communist-endorsed style that drew from European neo-classical art, the lifelike canvases of Jacques Louis David and the output of Soviet Union painters. Saturated with political symbolism and propaganda, the blunt artistic style was produced on an industrial scale.

The entire trajectory of Chinese painting – which had evolved in glacial increments over the centuries – had been redirected virtually overnight. Vaporous landscapes, in which people played an incidental role, had been replaced with hard-edged panoramas dominated by communists. Traditional Taoist and Buddhist philosophy was overturned; man was now a master of nature, which would bend to his will. Dreamy vistas were out; smoke stacks, red tractors and muscled peasants were in.

Human activity in these paintings was directed towards the glory of the communist revolution and the individual artistic temperament was subscripted to the service of the state. The communist vision conceived of man as the governor of his destiny; art was just another foot soldier in the quest. Dumbed-down, Chinese art became art for the masses.

Consultant designer of the Bird's Nest, Chinese artist Ai Weiwei later distanced himself from the stadium, saying it was a 'pretend smile' of bad taste; the artist has become a thorn in the side of the Chinese authorities.

It was only with the death of Mao Zedong in September 1976 that the shadow of the Cultural Revolution – when Chinese aesthetics were conditioned by the threat of violence – began its retreat. The individual artistic temperament was once again allowed freedom to explore inner persuasions. Painters such as Luo Zhongli employed the realist techniques gleaned from China's art academies to depict the harsh realities etched in the faces of contemporary peasants. Others escaped the suffocating confines of socialist realism to navigate new horizons. A voracious appetite for Western art introduced fresh concepts and ideas. The ambiguity of exact meaning in the fine arts also offered a degree of protection from state censors.

One group of artists, the Stars, found retrospective inspiration in Picasso and German Expressionism. The ephemeral group had a lasting impact on the development of Chinese art in the 1980s and 1990s, paving the way for the New Wave movement that emerged in 1985. New Wave artists were greatly influenced by Western art, especially the iconoclastic Marcel Duchamp. In true nihilist style, the New Wave artist Huang Yongping destroyed his works at exhibitions, in an effort to escape from the notion of 'art'. Political realities became instant subject matter as performance artists wrapped themselves in plastic or tape to symbolise the repressive realities of modern-day China.

The Tiān'ānmén Square protests in 1989 fostered a long-lasting cynicism that permeated artworks with loss, loneliness and social isolation. An exodus of artists to the West commenced. A long-lasting liaison with pop art generated ironic commentary on the increasingly consumerist nature of Chinese society and the bankruptcy of political ideology. Cynical realists Fang Lijun and Yue Minjun fashioned grotesque portraits that conveyed hollowness and mock joviality, tinged with despair.

For in-depth articles and reviews of contemporary Chinese arts and artists, click on www.newchineseart.com, run by the Shànghǎi-based gallery Art Scene China.

Much Chinese art since 1990 has dwelled obsessively on contemporary socio-economic realities, with consumer culture, materialism, urbanisation and social change a repetitive and tiring focus. More universal themes have become apparent, however, as the art scene has matured. Meanwhile, many artists who left China in the 1990s have returned, setting up private studios and galleries. Government censorship remains, but artists are branching out into other areas and moving away from overtly political content and China-specific concerns.

In 2007, Zhang Xiaogang's paintings, the most famous of which are monochromatic Cultural Revolution–era family-style portraits, earned nearly US$57 million in auctions, the second-highest amount among living artists anywhere. In 2008 Christie's in Hong Kong sold Zeng Fanzhi's painting *Mask Series 1996 No. 6* (featuring masked members of China's communist youth organisation, the Young Pioneers) for US$9.7 million, which is the highest price yet paid for a contemporary Chinese artwork.

Major art festivals in China include Běijīng's 798 International Art Festival (May), China International Gallery Exposition (October) and Běijīng Biennale (October 2011); the Shànghǎi Biennale (September to November 2012); Guǎngzhōu Triennial (September to November 2011); and Hong Kong's one-day Clockenflap festival (no set dates).

In 2010, a Qing dynasty Chinese vase sold for £53.1 million after being discovered in the attic of a house in north-west London and put up for auction.

Ceramics

China's very first vessels – dating back over 8000 years – were simple handcrafted earthenware pottery, primarily used for religious purposes. The invention of the pottery wheel during the late Neolithic period, however, led to a dramatic technological and artistic leap.

Over the centuries, Chinese potters perfected their craft, introducing many new exciting styles and techniques. The spellbinding artwork of the Terracotta Warriors in Xī'ān reveals a highly developed level of technical skill achieved by Qin-dynasty craftsmen. Periods of artistic development, under the cosmopolitan Tang dynasty, for example, prompted further stylistic advances. The Tang dynasty 'three-colour ware' is a much admired type of ceramic from this period, noted for its vivid yellow, green and white glaze. Demand for lovely blue-green celadons grew in countries as distant as Egypt and Persia.

The Yuan dynasty saw the first development of China's standout 'blue-and-white' *(qīnghuā)* porcelain. Cobalt blue paint, from Persia, was applied as an underglaze directly to white porcelain with a brush, the vessel was covered with another transparent glaze, and fired. This technique was perfected during the Ming and such ceramics became hugely popular all over the world, eventually acquiring the name 'Chinaware', whether produced in China or not.

Although many different kilns were established over China, the most famous was at Jǐngdézhèn in Jiāngxī province, where royal porcelain was fired up.

During the Qing dynasty, porcelain techniques were further refined and developed, showing superb craftsmanship and ingenuity. British and European consumers dominated the export market, displaying an insatiable appetite for Chinese vases and bowls decorated with flowers and landscapes. The Qing is also known for its stunning monochromatic ware, especially the ox-blood vases and highly meticulous imperial yellow bowls, and enamel decorated porcelain. The Qing is also notable for its elaborate and highly decorative wares.

The traditional Chinese character for poetry 詩 *(shī)* consists of 'words' 言 (the meaning element) placed next to a 'temple' 寺 (the sound element).

Jǐngdézhèn remains an excellent place to visit ceramic workshops and purchase various types of ceramic wares, from Mao statues to traditional glazed urns. The Shànghǎi Museum has a premier collection of porcelain, while several independent retailers in Běijīng and Shànghǎi also sell more modish and creative pieces.

Sculpture

The earliest sculpture in China dates to the Zhou and Shang dynasties, when small clay and wooden figures were commonly placed in tombs to protect the dead and guide them on their way to heaven.

With the arrival of Buddhism, sculpture turned towards spiritual figures and themes, with sculptors frequently enrolled in huge carving projects for the worship of Sakyamuni. Influences also arrived along the

Silk Road from abroad, bringing styles from as far afield as Greece and Persia, via India. The magnificent Buddhist caves at Yúngāng in Shānxī province date back to the 5th century and betray Indian influence.

Chisellers also began work on the Lóngmén Caves in Hénán province at the end of the 5th century. The earliest effigies are similar in style to those at Yúngāng, revealing Indian influence and more other-worldliness in their facial expressions. Later cave sculptures at Lóngmén were completed during the Tang dynasty and reveal a more Chinese style.

The most superlative examples are at the Mògāo Caves at Dūnhuáng in Gānsù province, where well-preserved Indian and Central Asian style sculptures, particularly of the Tang dynasty, carry overtly Chinese characteristics – many statues feature long, fluid bodies and have warmer, more refined facial features.

The Shànghǎi Museum has a splendid collection of Buddhist sculpture, as does Capital Museum and the Poly Art Museum, both in Běijīng.

Beyond China's grottoes, other mesmerising Chinese sculpture hides away in temples across China. The colossal statue of Guanyin in Pǔníng Temple in Chéngdé is a staggering sight, carved from five different types of wood and towering over 22m in height. Shuānglín Temple outside Píngyáo in Shānxī province is famed for its painted statues from the Song and Yuan dynasties.

For a translation of Tang dynasty verse, try to find a copy of Vikram Seth's *Three Chinese Poets*.

Literature

Classical Poetry

From the Han dynasty through the Song dynasty, Chinese poetry was the primary means of literary expression for the educated elite and is still considered China's most sophisticated literary genre.

Even more so than classical Chinese, classical poetry employs a vastly pared down syntax (articles, prepositions, plurals and sometimes even the subject are implicit) to maximise brevity and to ensure each line has an equal number of characters (and therefore syllables). The use of rhyme, parallel couplets, word play, harmony, literary allusion and assonance were all of central importance. Classical poems aim to conjure up a 'painting' through which the poet could evoke his or her emotion. The written character is also an important part of this representation, as each character is a picture in itself, so images are partially conjured up by their effective employment.

China's earliest collection of poems is the *Book of Songs* (Shījìng; also called the Classic of Poetry), apocryphally collated by Confucius and dat-

BATTLE OF THE BUDDHAS

Hands down China's largest Buddha gazes out over the confluence of the waters of the Dàdù River and the Mín River at Lèshān in Sìchuān. When the even bigger Buddha at Bamyan in Afghanistan was demolished by the Taliban, the Lèshān Buddha enjoyed instantaneous promotion to the top spot as the world's largest. The Buddha in the Great Buddha Temple at Zhāngyè in Gānsù province may not take it lying down, though: he is China's largest 'housed reclining Buddha'. Chinese children once climbed inside him to scamper about within his cavernous tummy.

Lounging around in second place is the reclining Buddha in the Mògāo Caves, China's second largest. The vast reclining Buddha at Lèshān is a whopping 170m long and the world's largest 'alfresco' reclining Buddha. Bristling with limbs, the Thousand Arm Guanyin statue in the Pǔníng Temple's Mahayana Hall in Chéngdé also stands up to be counted: she's the largest wooden statue in China (and possibly the world). Not to be outdone, Hong Kong fights for its niche with the Tian Tan Buddha Statue, the world's 'largest outdoor seated bronze Buddha statue'.

ing to the sixth century BC. One of the five classics, the *Book of Songs* contains over 300 delightful poems infused with pastoral themes and folk rhythms.

The Song of Chu (Chǔcí), contains poems by Qu Yuan (c 340–278 BC), China's greatest early poet and author of *Li Sao* (The Lament). Another of China's most famous poets was Tao Yuanming (365–427), much loved for the unfussiness of his landscape verse.

Classical poetry matured into a golden age during the Tang dynasty (618–907), when trade with the outside world burgeoned and China prospered. It was also a time of stunning artistic invention and creativity, reflected in the poetry of the day. Li Bai (Li Po; the Taoist), Du Fu (Tu Fu; the Confucian), Wang Wei (the Buddhist) and Bai Juyi (the Populist – he purportedly rewrote all poems his servants were unable to understand) were all Tang poets. Other great poets of this era include Meng Haoran, Liu Zongyuan and Li Shangying. Li Bai in particular is much-loved by the Chinese for his Taoist eccentricities and devotion to nature and wine, while Du Fu is admired for his more restrained and occasionally maudlin eloquence. At the start of the Tang dynasty a type of strict eight-line verse called *lǜshī* appeared, which brought structure and symmetry to classical poetry.

During the Song dynasty a more romantic lyric poetry called *cí* emerged – originally lyrics intended to be set to music. Su Shi (Su Dongpo), Li Qingzhao and Ou Yangxiu are some of the most famous poets from this era.

With the rapid decline of classical literature in the early 20th century, Chinese verse came under the revolutionising influence of Western poetic devices and techniques, an acquisition that permanently changed its complexion.

DIVINATION

The *I Ching* (Yìjīng; Book of Changes) is the oldest Chinese text and is used for divination. It is comprised of 64 hexagrams, composed of broken and continuous lines, that represent a balance of opposites (yin and yang), the inevitability of change and the evolution of events.

Classical Novels

Until the early 20th century, classical literature (古文; *gǔwén*) had been the principal form of writing in China for thousands of years. A breed of purely literary writing, classical Chinese employed a stripped-down form of written Chinese that did not reflect the way people actually spoke or thought. Its grammar differed from the syntax of spoken Chinese and it employed numerous obscure Chinese characters. Classical Chinese maintained divisions between educated and uneducated Chinese, putting literature beyond the reach of the common person and fashioning a cliquey lingua franca for Confucian officials and scholars.

Classical novels evolved from the popular folktales and dramas that entertained the lower classes. During the Ming dynasty they were penned in a semi-vernacular (or 'vulgar') language, and are often irreverently funny and full of action-packed fights.

The best-known novel outside China is *Journey to the West* (Xīyóu Jì) – more commonly known as *Monkey*. Written in the 16th century, it follows the misadventures of a cowardly Buddhist monk (Tripitaka; a stand-in for the real-life pilgrim Xuan Zang) and his companions – a rebellious monkey, lecherous pig-man and exiled monster-immortal – on a pilgrimage to India. In 2007 a Chinese director collaborated with the creators of the virtual band Gorillaz to transform the story into a circus opera that has played to considerable international acclaim.

The Water Margin/Outlaws of the Marsh/All Men Are Brothers (Shuǐhǔ Zhuàn) is, on the surface, an excellent tale of honourable bandits and corrupt officials along the lines of Robin Hood. On a deeper level, though, it is a reminder to Confucian officials of their right to rebel when faced with a morally suspect government (at least one emperor officially banned it).

Modern Literature

Classical Chinese maintained its authority over literary minds till the early 20th century, until it came under the influence of the West.

Torch-bearing author Lu Xun wrote his short story *Diary of a Madman* in 1918. It was revolutionary stuff. The opening paragraph of Lu's seminal and shocking fable is conceived in classical (archaic) language. The stultified introduction – peppered with archaic characters and the excruciatingly pared-down grammar of classical Chinese – presents itself as one solid block of text, without new paragraphs or indentation. The passage concludes abruptly and the reader is confronted with colloquial and vernacular Chinese *(báihuà)*: 今天晚上, 很好的月光 (*jīntiān wǎnshàng, hěnhǎo de yuèguāng*; 'Tonight there is good moonlight.').

The story continues in modern Chinese to its conclusion. For Lu Xun to write his short story in the spoken vernacular was explosive, as Chinese people were finally able to read language as it was spoken. Magnifying the power of the story was its subject matter: the diary's narrator is convinced those around him are cannibals (a metaphor for the self-consuming nature of traditional, Confucian society). *Diary of a Madman* is a haunting and unsettling work, raising doubts as to the real madness of its narrator and concluding with lines that offer a glimmer of salvation. From this moment on, mainstream Chinese literature would be written as it was thought and spoken: Chinese writing had been instantaneously modernised.

The Book and the Sword by Jin Yong/Louis Cha (2004) is China's most celebrated martial-arts novelist's first book. The martial-arts genre *(wǔxiá xiǎoshuō)* is a direct descendant of the classical novel.

Other notable contemporaries of Lu Xun include Ba Jin (*Family*; 1931), Mao Dun (*Midnight*; 1933), Lao She (*Rickshaw Boy/Camel Xiangzi*; 1936) and the modernist playwright Cao Yu (*Thunderstorm*). Lu Xun and Ba Jin translated a great deal of foreign literature into Chinese.

Few contemporary voices have been translated into English, but there's enough material to keep a serious reader busy. The provocative Mo Yan (*Life and Death Are Wearing Me Out*; 2008), Yu Hua (*To Live*; 1992) and Su Tong (*Rice*; 1995) have written momentous historical novels set in the 20th century; all are excellent, though not for the faint of heart. Zhu Wen mocks the get-rich movement in his brilliantly funny short stories, published in English as *I Love Dollars and Other Stories of China* (2007). It's a vivid and comic portrayal of the absurdities of everyday China.

'Hooligan author' Wang Shuo (*Please Don't Call Me Human*; 2000) remains China's best-selling author with his political satires and convincing depictions of urban slackers. Chun Sue (*Beijing Doll*; 2004) and Mian Mian (*Candy*; 2003) examine the dark urban underbellies of Běijīng and Shànghǎi, respectively. Alai (*Red Poppies*; 2002), an ethnic Tibetan, made waves by writing in Chinese about early-20th-century Tibetan Sìchuān – whatever your politics, it's both insightful and a page-turner. Émigré Ma Jian (*Red Dust*; 2004) writes more politically critical work; his debut was a Kerouacian tale of wandering China as a spiritual pollutant in the 1980s. China's most renowned dissident writer, Gao Xingjian, won the Nobel Prize for Literature in 2000 for his novel *Soul Mountain*, an account of his travels along the Yangzi after being misdiagnosed with lung cancer. All of his work has been banned in the PRC since 1989.

Wolf Totem (2009) by Jiang Rong is an astonishing look at life on the grasslands of Inner Mongolia during the Cultural Revolution and the impact of modern culture on an ancient way of life.

Controversial blogger Han Han catapulted himself into the literary spotlight with his novel *Triple Door*, a searing critique of China's educational system.

Film

The moving image in the Middle Kingdom dates to 1896, when Spaniard Galen Bocca unveiled a film projector and blew the socks off wide-eyed crowds in a Shànghǎi teahouse. Shànghǎi's cosmopolitan verve and exotic looks would make it the capital of China's film industry, but China's very first movie – *Conquering Jun Mountain* (an excerpt from a piece of Beijing Opera) – was actually filmed in Běijīng in 1905.

In *The Vagrants* (2009), author Yi Yunli fashions a wonderfully written, bleak and disturbing portrait of dissent and oppression in a Chinese town in 1979.

Shànghǎi opened its first cinema in 1908. In those days, cinema owners would cannily run the film for a few minutes, stop it and collect money from the audience before allowing the film to continue. The golden age of Shànghǎi film-making came in the 1930s when the city had over 140 film companies. Its apogee arrived in 1937 with the release of *Street Angel*, a powerful drama about two sisters who flee the Japanese in northeast China and end up as prostitutes in Shànghǎi; and *Crossroads*, a clever comedy about four unemployed graduates. Japanese control of China eventually brought the industry to a standstill and sent many film-makers packing.

China's film industry was stymied after the Communist Revolution, which sent film-makers scurrying to Hong Kong and Taiwan, where they played key roles in building up the local film industries that flourished there. Cinematic production in China was co-opted to glorify communism and generate patriotic propaganda. The days of the Cultural Revolution (1966–76) were particularly dark. Between 1966 and

NON-NATIVE TONGUES

Beyond translations of famous Chinese works, an accessible corpus of literature exists from Chinese émigrés conceiving works in English and French.

» *Wild Swans* (Jung Chang; 1992) Prize-winning autobiographical saga about three generations of Chinese women struggling to survive the tumultuous events of 20th-century China. Chang is also the co-author of the controversial best-selling biography *Mao: The Unknown Story* (2005).

» *Balzac and the Little Seamstress* (Dai Sijie; 2000) Two teenagers find a secret cache of Western novels during the Cultural Revolution, helping them – and the local tailor's daughter – to escape from the tediousness of rural re-education. Originally written in French.

» *A Concise Chinese-English Dictionary for Lovers* (Guo Xiaolu; 2007) Written deliberately in Chinglish, Guo humorously recounts the experiences of a Chinese girl sent to London to study.

» *Ocean of Words* (1996), *Waiting* (1999), *The Bridegroom* (2000), *The Crazed* (2002), *War Trash*, *A Free Life* (2007) The most prolific of the diaspora writers, Ha Jin has won both the National Book Award (USA) and the PEN/Faulkner Award (among others).

» *A Thousand Years of Good Prayers* (Yiyun Li; 2006) Prize-winning short stories depicting the lives of everyday Chinese caught up in the changes of the past two decades.

» *Red Azalea* (1994), *Becoming Madame Mao* (2000), *Wild Ginger* (2002), *Empress Orchid* (2004), *The Last Empress* (2007) Anchee Min spins fiction out of the life stories of some of China's most ambitious (and least-loved) women.

» *Death of a Red Heroine* (2000), *A Loyal Character Dancer* (2002), *When Red is Black* (2004), *A Case of Two Cities* (2006), *Red Mandarin Dress* (2007), *The Mao Case* (2009) Qiu Xiaolong's insightful Inspector Chen novels feature a literary-minded cop and a vivid street-level portrayal of changing Shànghǎi.

» *The Girl Who Played Go* (Shan Sa; 2001) A local girl in Japanese-occupied Manchuria and an undercover Japanese soldier match wits in an epic game of go *(wéiqí)* and in the process fall fatally in love. Originally written in French.

» *The People's Republic of Desire* (Annie Wang; 2006) A candid exploration of sexuality in modern Běijīng.

» *On the Smell of an Oily Rag* (Yu Ouyang; 2008) Clever cross-cultural observances from a Chinese émigré living in Australia.

1972, just eight movies were made on the mainland, as the film industry was effectively shut down.

It wasn't until two years after the death of Mao Zedong that the Běijīng Film Academy, China's premier film school, reopened in September 1978. Its first intake of students included Zhang Yimou, Chen Kaige and Tian Zhuangzhuang – masterminds of the celebrated 'Fifth Generation'. The cinematic output of the Fifth Generation signalled an escape from the dour, colourless and proletarian Mao era, and a second glittering golden age of Chinese film-making arrived in the 1980s and 1990s with their lush and lavish tragedies. A bleak but beautifully shot tale of a Chinese Communist Party cadre who travels to a remote village in Shaanxi province to collect folk songs, Chen Kaige's *Yellow Earth* aroused little interest in China but proved a sensation when released in the West in 1985.

A worker in a foot-massage parlour is raped by her boss, setting in motion a series of devastating consequences for both of them in Li Yu's *Lost in Beijing* (2007).

It was followed by Zhang's *Red Sorghum*, which introduced Gong Li and Jiang Wen to the world. Gong became the poster girl of Chinese cinema in the 1990s and the first international movie star to emerge from the mainland. Jiang, the Marlon Brando of Chinese film, has proved both a durable leading man and an innovative, controversial director of award-winning films such as *In the Heat of the Sun* and *Devils on the Doorstep*.

Rich, seminal works such as *Farewell My Concubine* (1993; Chen Kaige) and *Raise the Red Lantern* (1991; Zhang Yimou) were garlanded with praise, receiving standing ovations and winning major film awards. Their directors were the darlings of Cannes; Western cinema-goers were entranced. Many Chinese cinema-goers also admired their artistry, but some saw Fifth Generation output as pandering to the Western market.

In 1993, Tian Zhuangzhuang made the brilliant *The Blue Kite*. A heartbreaking account of the life of one Běijīng family during the Cultural Revolution, it so enraged the censors that Tian was banned from making films for years.

The 2010 remake of *The Karate Kid*, starring Jackie Chan, is set in Běijīng and authentically conveys the city despite having nothing to do with karate.

Each generation charts its own course and the ensuing Sixth Generation – graduating from the Běijīng Film Academy post Tiān'ānmén Square protests – was no different. Sixth Generation film directors eschewed the luxurious beauty of their forebears, and sought to capture the angst and grit of modern urban Chinese life. Their independent, low-budget works put an entirely different and more cynical spin on mainland Chinese film-making, but their darker subject matter and harsh film style (frequently in black and white) left many Western viewers cold.

Independent film-making found an influential precedent with Zhang Yuan's 1990 debut *Mama*. Zhang is also acclaimed for his candid and gritty documentary-style *Beijing Bastards* (1993). *The Days*, directed by Wang Xiaoshui, follows a couple drifting apart in the wake of the Tiān'ānmén Square protests. Wang also directed the excellent *Beijing Bicycle* (2001), inspired by De Sica's *Bicycle Thieves*.

Jia Zhangke has emerged as the most acclaimed of China's new film-makers. His meditative and compassionate look at the social impact of the construction of the Three Gorges Dam on local people, *Still Life* (2006), scooped the Golden Lion at the 2006 Venice Film Festival.

In a protectionist move, Běijīng caps the number of foreign films that can be shown annually in cinemas to around 20. Yet the film industry in China still has to outmanoeuvre taboos. Directors still walk on eggshells and even oblique criticism of the authorities remains hazardous. Many Chinese directors seek sanctuary in the highly popular historical and martial-arts epics starring Andy Lau, Jet Li and Samo Hong, but these may have increasingly limited appeal abroad, while contemporary Chinese TV dramas are often wooden and clunky, hobbled by creative hesitancy.

Wong Kar Wai's outstanding *Chungking Express* (1994) and *In the Mood for Love* (2000) are examples of Hong Kong movie-making at its very best.

Architecture

Traditional Architecture

Four principal styles governed traditional Chinese architecture: imperial, religious, residential and recreational. The imperial style was naturally the most grandiose, overseeing the design of buildings employed by successive dynastic rulers; the religious style was employed for the construction of temples, monasteries and pagodas, while the residential and recreational style took care of the design of houses and private gardens.

Whatever the style, Chinese buildings traditionally followed a similar basic ground plan, consisting of a symmetrical layout oriented around a central axis – ideally running north–south, to conform with basic feng shui *(fēngshuǐ)* dictates and to maximise sunshine – with an enclosed courtyard *(yuàn)* flanked by buildings on all sides.

In many aspects, imperial palaces are glorified courtyard homes (south-facing, a sequence of courtyards, side halls and perhaps a garden at the rear) completed on a different scale. Apart from the size, the main dissimilarity would be guard towers on the walls and possibly a moat, imperial yellow roof tiles, ornate dragon carvings (signifying the emperor), the repetitive use of the number nine and the presence of temples.

Many residential quarters of the well-to-do, and temples or halls within imperial palaces were protected by a spirit wall *(yǐngbì)* at their entrance, designed to thwart bad spirits, but also to put a stop to prying eyes. Despite the loss of countless spirit walls, China remains dotted with them, often obsolete as the buildings they once shielded have vanished. Dàtóng's Nine Dragon Screen is a spectacular example.

Behind the entrance in palaces and wealthier residential buildings stood a public hall; behind this was the private living quarters, erected around another courtyard with a garden; most buildings were constructed as one-storey edifices. A sense of harmony prevailed over the entire design, ordered by symmetry and a certain reserve, which also meant that no one particular structure took precedence. Compounds were enlarged simply by adding more courtyards.

Religious Architecture

Chinese Buddhist, Taoist and Confucian temples tend to follow a strict, schematic pattern. All temples are laid out on a north–south axis in a series of halls, with the main door of each hall facing south.

Chinese temples are very different from Christian churches, with a sequence of halls and buildings interspersed with breezy open-air courtyards. The roofless courtyards allow the weather to permeate within the temple and also permits the *qì* (气) to circulate, dispersing stale air and allowing incense to be burned.

Building boom: China consumes roughly 50% of the world's concrete and 36% of its steel.

Buddhist Temples

Once you have cracked the logic of Buddhist temples, you can discover how most temples conform to a predictable pattern.

The first hall and access portal to the temple is generally the Hall of Heavenly Kings, where a sedentary, central statue of the tubby Bodhisattva Maitreya is flanked by the ferocious Four Heavenly Kings. Behind you'll find the first courtyard, where the Drum Tower and Bell

Tower may rise to the east and west and smoking braziers may also be positioned.

The main hall is often the Great Treasure Hall sheltering glittering statues of the past, present and future Buddhas, seated in a row. This is the main focal point for worshippers at the temple. On the east and west interior wall of the hall are often 18 *luóhàn* (arhat) in two lines, either as statues or paintings. In some temples, they gather in a throng of 500, housed in a separate hall. A statue of Guanyin (the Goddess of Mercy) frequently stands at the rear of the main hall, facing north, atop a fish's head or a rocky outcrop. The goddess may also be venerated in her own hall and occasionally presents herself with a huge fan of arms, in her 'Thousand Arm' incarnation. The awesome effigy of Guanyin in the Mahayana Hall at Pǔníng Temple in Chéngdé is the supreme example.

The rear hall may be where the sutras (Buddhist scriptures) were once stored, in which case it will be called the Sutra Storing Building. A pagoda may rise above the main halls or may be the only surviving fragment of an otherwise destroyed temple. Conceived to house the remains of Buddha and later other Buddhist relics, pagodas were also used for storing sutras, religious artefacts and documents.

Taoist Temples

Taoist shrines are more nether-worldly than Buddhist shrines, although the basic layout echoes Buddhist temples. Decorated with a distinct set of motifs, including the *bāguà* (eight trigrams) formations, reflected in eight-sided pavilions and halls and the Taiji yin/yang *(yīn/yáng)* diagram. Effigies of Laotzu, the Jade Emperor and other characters popularly associated with Taoist myth, such as the Eight Immortals and the God of Wealth, are customary.

Taoist temple entrances are often guarded by Taoist door gods, similar to Buddhist temples; the main hall is usually called the Hall of the Three Clear Ones, devoted to a triumvirate of Taoist deities.

Taoist monks (and nuns) are easily distinguished from their shaven-headed Buddhist confrères by their long hair, twisted into topknots, straight trousers and squarish jackets.

In China, tower blocks are only built to last for 25 to 30 years. In 2009, a newly-built Shànghǎi tower block collapsed, killing one worker and raising further concerns about quality control.

Confucian Temples

Confucian temples bristle with steles celebrating local scholars, some supported on the backs of *bìxì* (mythical tortoise-looking dragons). A statue of Kongzi (Confucius) usually resides in the main hall, overseeing rows of musical instruments and flanked by disciples. A mythical animal, the *qílín* (a statue exists at the Summer Palace in Běijīng), is commonly seen. The *qílín* was a hybrid animal that appeared on earth only in times of harmony. The largest Confucian temple in China is at Qūfù in Shāndōng, Confucius' birthplace.

Modern Architecture

China is one of today's most exciting nations for breaking the architectural mould, ripping up the rule book, risk taking and a healthy but chancy dose of leaping-before-looking. Architecturally in today's China, anything goes. You only have to look at the Pǔdōng skyline to witness a melange of competing modern designs, some dramatic, inspiring and novel, others cheesy and rash. The skyline represents a nation brimming over with confidence and newfound zeal, but overhung with awkwardness.

If modern architecture in China is regarded as anything post-1949, then China has ridden a roller-coaster ride of styles and fashions. In Běijīng, stand between the Great Hall of the People (1959) and the National Centre for the Performing Arts (2008) and weigh up how far

ART DECO IN SHÀNGHǍI

Fans of art deco must visit Shànghǎi. The reign of art deco is one of the city's architectural high-water marks and the city boasts more art deco buildings than any other city, from the drawing boards of the French firm Leonard, Veysseyre and Kruze and others. Largely emptied of foreigners in 1949, Shànghǎi largely kept its historic villas and buildings intact, including its fabulous art deco monuments. The Peace Hotel, Bank of China building, Cathay Theatre, Green House, Paramount Ballroom, Broadway Mansions, Liza Building, Savoy Apartments, Picardie Apartments and Majestic Theatre are all art deco gems. For a comprehensive low-down on the style, hunt down a copy of *Shanghai Art Deco* by Deke Erh and Tess Johnston.

China has travelled in the past 50 years. Interestingly, neither building possesses evident Chinese motifs; both are united by foreign styling, Soviet design for the former and French imagination for the latter. The same applies to the complex form of Běijīng's CCTV Building, where a continuous loop through horizontal and vertical planes required some audacious engineering.

While much of the country's interior still lacks the financial muscle necessary to consider anything beyond simple functionality, the coastal areas are widely regarded as an architect's dreamland – no design is too outrageous to be built, zoning laws have been scrapped and the labour force is large and inexpensive. Planning permission can be simple to arrange – often all it requires is sufficient *guānxī* (connections).

Many of the top names in international architecture – IM Pei, Rem Koolhaas, Norman Foster, Kengo Kuma, Jean-Marie Charpentier, Herzog & de Meuron – have all designed at least one building in China in the past decade. Other impressive examples of modern architecture include the National Stadium (aka the 'Bird's Nest'), the National Aquatics Center (aka the 'Water Cube') and Běijīng South train station, all in Běijīng; the art deco–esque Jīnmào Tower, the towering Shànghǎi World Financial Center, Tomorrow Square and South Railway Station in Shànghǎi; and the new Sūzhōu Museum in Sūzhōu, a stunning fusion of geometric lines and classical Chinese garden design. The Bank of China Tower remains an iconic piece of architecture, as is the HSBC Building, both in Hong Kong's Central district.

Gardens

Originally designed as either imperial parks or as private compounds attached to a residence, Chinese gardens are entirely different in concept from European garden design. Like an ink painting, Chinese garden design was rooted in the Chinese notion of the natural world and humankind's place within it. While European gardens emphasised colour, flowers, grass and either a geometrical precision or a semi-wild abandonment to nature, Chinese gardens instead aimed to recreate the constituent parts of nature, from mountains and hills to lakes, ponds and vegetation. Colours are largely subdued while the size of the garden is typically small and enclosed.

In Tàiyuán, the World Trade Hotel is a rather tasteless downsized reproduction of New York's former towers.

A vibrant focus is devoted to the arrangements of rocks and rockeries, the placing of ponds and the use of foliage, small trees and shrubs. Pavilions, walkways, corridors and bridges bring in human features, however these are never dominant or overbearing and instead complement the picture. Man is an element of the garden but his presence is as an observer and participant rather than as a central focus or force.

The landscapes of a traditional Chinese painting are always central to a successful garden. Windows may find themselves strategically placed to frame a particular view, and in private compounds, plants were often selectively grown against a backdrop of whitewashed walls, which recalled the empty space of a painting. Mountains *(shān)* and water *(shuǐ)* are essential components of traditional paintings and find themselves replicated in garden design through rockeries and fish-filled ponds. The play of light is similarly a vital ingredient, playing off water surfaces, reflecting from white walls and casting shadows.

Another important feature of gardens is symbolism. Plants were chosen as much for their symbolic meaning as their beauty (the pine for longevity, the peony for nobility), and the giant eroded rocks suggest mountains as well as the changing, indefinable nature of the Tao. Likewise, the names of gardens and halls are often literary allusions to ideals expressed in classical poetry.

Yet there is also a sense of artificiality in Chinese gardens. The hand of Confucian man is always recognisable, no matter how successfully the garden reproduces a Chinese landscape. This strong artificiality is very recognisable in modern Chinese parks, which derive from traditional garden design. Concrete paths, walkways, hard-edged borders, artificial ponds and regularly planted trees are typical of modern Chinese parks. Park goers in today's parks in China are guided in definite directions by paths, rather than being encouraged to wander at random. Nature is recreated, but from the artificial viewpoint of man rather than through encouraging the original landscape to reveal itself.

Gardens were particularly prevalent in southeastern China south of the Yangzi River, notably in Hángzhōu, Yángzhōu and Sūzhōu.

China's Landscapes

The Land

The world's third-largest country – roughly the same size as the USA – China covers a colossal 9.5-million sq km, only surpassed in area by Russia and Canada. Straddling natural environments as diverse as subarctic tundra in the north and tropical rainforests in the south, the land embraces the world's highest mountain range and one of its hottest deserts in the west to the steamy, typhoon-lashed coastline of the South China Sea. Fragmenting this epic landscape is a colossal web of waterways, including one of the world's mightiest rivers – the Yangzi (长江; Cháng Jiāng).

Mountains

China's terrain is in large parts mountainous and hilly, commencing in dramatically precipitous fashion in the vast and sparsely populated Tibetan west and levelling out gradually towards the fertile, well-watered, populous and wealthy provinces of eastern China.

This mountainous disposition sculpts so many of China's natural scenic wonders, from the glittering Dragon's Backbone Rice Terraces of Guǎngxī to the exhilaration of Mt Everest, the stunning beauty of Jiǔzhàigōu National Park in Sìchuān, the ethereal peaks of misty Huángshān in Ānhuī, the vertiginous inclines of Huà Shān in Shaanxi (Shǎnxī), the divine karst geology of Yángshuò in Guǎngxī and the volcanic drama of Heaven Lake in Jílín.

Frozen reservoirs of water, China's glaciers – 15% of the world's ice mass – have depleted by around 20% since the mid-1960s and at current rates are set to vanish by 2100.

Averaging 4500m above sea level, the Tibet-Qīnghǎi region's highest peaks thrust up in the Himalayan mountain range along its southern rim, where mountains average about 6000m above sea level, with 40 peaks rising dizzyingly to 7000m or more. Also known as the planet's 'third pole', this is where the world's highest peak, Mt Everest – called Zhūmùlǎngmǎfēng by the Chinese – thrusts up jaggedly from the Tibet-Nepal border. Low temperatures, high winds and intense solar radiation (p881) are regional characteristics.

This vast high-altitude region (Tibet alone constitutes one-eighth of China's landmass) is home to an astonishing 37,000 glaciers, the third-largest mass of ice on the planet after the Arctic and Antarctic. This colossal body of frozen water ensures that the Tibet-Qīnghǎi region is the source of many of China's largest rivers, including the Yellow (Huáng Hé), Mekong (Láncāng Jiāng), Salween (Nù Jiāng) Rivers and, of course, the mighty Yangzi, all of whose headwaters are fed by snowmelt from here. Global warming, however, is eating into this glacial mass: by some estimates, 40% of the region's glaciers will have disappeared by 2050, resulting in flooding in the short term and growing aridity in the long term.

Tibet is also an immense storehouse of mineral wealth, helping to clarify its Chinese name (西藏; Xīzàng; 'Western Treasure House'). Deep within the mountains of Tibet lie enormous deposits of gold, copper, uranium, lithium, lead and other valuable minerals and ores.

This mountainous disposition finds repeated refrain throughout China, albeit on a less dramatic scale, as the land continually wrinkles into spectacular mountain ranges. China's hills and mountains may form a dramatic and sublime backdrop, but they generate huge agricultural complications. Many farmers cultivate small plots of land assiduously eked out in patchworks of land squashed between hillsides, mountain cliffs and ravines, in the demanding effort to feed 20% of the world's population with just 10% of its arable land. Only 15% of China's land can be cultivated; up hillside gradients, the inclines are valiantly levelled off, wherever possible, into bands of productive terraced fields.

Official state estimates predict one-seventh of China's population may need to be resettled due to growing desertification in the north of China.

Deserts

China contains head-spinningly vast – and growing – desert regions that occupy almost a fifth of the country's landmass, largely in its mighty northwest. These are inhospitably sandy and rocky expanses where summers are torturously hot and winters bone-numbingly cold. North towards Kazakhstan and Kyrgyzstan from the plateaus of Tibet and Qīnghǎi lies Xīnjiang's Tarim Basin, the largest inland basin in the world. This is the location of the mercilessly thirsty Taklamakan Desert – China's largest desert and the world's second largest mass of sand after the Sahara Desert. China's biggest shifting salt lake, Lop Nur (the site of China's nuclear bomb tests) is also here.

The harsh environment shares many topographical features in common with the neighbouring nations of Afghanistan, Kyrgyzstan and Kazakhstan and is almost the exact opposite of China's lush and well-watered southern provinces. But despite the scorching aridity of China's northwestern desert regions, their mountains (the mighty Tiān Shān, Altai, Pamir and Kunlun ranges) contain vast supplies of water, largely in the form of snow and ice.

Northeast of the Tarim Basin is Ürümqi, the world's furthest city from the sea. The Tarim Basin is bordered to the north by the lofty Tiān Shān range – home to the glittering mountain lake of Tiān Chí – and to the west by the mighty Pamirs, which border Pakistan. Also in Xīnjiāng is China's hot spot, the Turpan Basin, known as the 'Oasis of Fire' and entering the record books as China's lowest-lying region and the world's second-deepest depression after the Dead Sea in Israel. China's most

MOUNTAINS, MYTH & MAGIC

Steeped in legend and superstition and infused with spirits and deities, China's mountains have long been cherished by devout bands of Taoists and Buddhists who erected temples and founded monastic communities on their slopes. Mt Kailash and many other peaks in Tibet are powerfully associated with Buddhist divinities and Bodhisattvas, drawing legions of pilgrims and worshippers to complete a *kora* (pilgrim path) around their slopes. Outside Tibet, each of China's five sacred Buddhist mountains has its ruling Bodhisattva, whose presence permeates their shrines, gullies and peaks. In Pǔtuóshān it is the merciful Guanyin (see the boxed text, p935) who is worshipped; in Wǔtái Shān, erudite Wenshu (Manjushri) is the presiding deity. Huà Shān, Sōng Shān, Wǔdāng Shān and other Taoist peaks are famed for the recluses who retreated to their crags and caves to cultivate 'internal power' and devise mind-boggling martial-arts skills (p974).

famous desert is of course the Gobi, although most of it lies outside the country's borders.

The Silk Road into China steered its epic course through this entire region, ferrying caravans of camels laden with merchandise, languages, philosophies, customs and peoples from the far-flung lands of the Middle East. Today the region is rich in fossil fuels, containing one-third of China's known gas and oil reserves as well as vast and unexploited coal deposits.

East of Xīnjiāng extend the epic grasslands and steppes of Inner Mongolia in a huge and elongated belt of land that stretches to the region once called Manchuria.

WIND FARMS

China has earmarked a staggering US$140 billion for an ambitious program of wind farms; ranging from Xīnjiāng province to Jiāngsū province in the east, the huge wind farms are due for completion in 2020.

Rivers & Plains

The other major region comprises roughly 45% of the country and contains 95% of the population. This densely populated part of China descends like a staircase from west to east, from the inhospitable high plateaus of Tibet and Qīnghǎi to the fertile but largely featureless plains and basins of the great rivers that drain the high ranges. As a general rule of thumb, as you head east towards the seaboard, provinces become wealthier.

These plains are the most important agricultural areas of the country and the most heavily populated. It's hard to imagine, but the plains have largely been laid down by siltation by the Yangzi and other great rivers over many millennia. The process continues: the Yangzi alone deposits millions of tonnes of silt annually and land at the river mouth is growing at a rate of 100m a year. Hardly any significant stands of natural vegetation remain in this area, although several mountain ranges are still forested and provide oases for wildlife and native plants.

The Yellow River, about 5460km long and the second-longest river in China, is often touted as the birthplace of Chinese civilisation. China's longest river, the Yangzi, is one of the longest rivers in the world. Its watershed of almost 2 million sq km – 20% of China's land mass – supports 400 million people. Dropping from its source high on the Tibetan plateau, it runs for 6300km to the sea, of which the last few hundred kilometres is across virtually flat alluvial plains. The Yangzi has been an important thoroughfare for humans for centuries, used throughout China's history for trade and transport; it even has its own unique wildlife, but all this has been threatened by the controversial Three Gorges Dam Project. The dam will generate power and is supposed to thwart the Yangzi's propensity to flood – floodwaters periodically inundate millions of hectares and destroy hundreds of thousands of lives.

Wildlife

China's vast size, diverse topography and climatic disparities support an astonishing range of habitats for a wide-ranging diversity of animal life. Scattered from steamy tropical rainforests in the deep southwest to subarctic wilderness in the far north, from the precipitous mountains of Tibet to the low-lying deserts of the northwest and the huge Yangzi River, China's wild animals comprise nearly 400 species of mammal (including some of the world's rarest and most charismatic species), more than 1300 bird species, 424 reptile species and over 300 species of amphibian. The Tibetan plateau alone is the habitat of over 500 species of birds, while half of the animal species in the northern hemisphere can be found in China.

It is unlikely you will see many of these creatures in their natural habitat unless you are a specialist, or have a lot of time, patience, persistence, determination and luck. If you go looking for large animals in the wild on the off chance, your chances of glimpsing one are virtually nil. But there are plenty of pristine reserves within relatively easy reach of travellers' destinations such as Chéngdū in and Xī'ān. More and more visitors are including visits to protected areas as part of their itinerary for a look at China's elusive wildlife residents – outside of China's rather pitiful zoos.

Eleven Siberian tigers starved to death at the Shenyang Forest wild-animal zoo in China's northeast in 2010, underscoring concerns about the treatment of tigers in China.

Mammals

China's towering mountain ranges form natural refuges for wildlife, many of which are now protected in parks and reserves that have escaped the depredations of loggers and dam-builders. The barren high plains of the Tibetan plateau are home to several large animals, such as the *chiru* (Tibetan antelope), Tibetan wild ass, wild sheep and goats, and wolves. In theory, many of these animals are protected but in practice poaching and hunting still threaten their survival.

The beautiful and retiring snow leopard, which normally inhabits the highest parts of the most remote mountain ranges, sports a luxuriant coat of fur against the cold. It preys on mammals as large as mountain goats, but is unfortunately persecuted for allegedly killing livestock.

The Himalayan foothills of western Sìchuān support the greatest diversity of mammals in China. Aside from giant pandas, other mammals found in this region include the panda's small cousin, the raccoon-like red panda, as well as Asiatic black bears and leopards. Among the grazers are golden takin, a large goatlike antelope with a yellowish coat and a reputation for being cantankerous, argali sheep and various deer species, including the diminutive mouse deer.

The sparsely populated northeastern provinces abutting Siberia are inhabited by reindeer, moose, musk deer, bears, sables and Manchurian tigers. Overall, China is unusually well endowed with big and small cats. The world's largest tiger, the Manchurian Tiger *(Dōngběihǔ)* – also known as the Siberian Tiger (see the boxed text, p327) – only numbers a few hundred in the wild, its remote habitat being one of its principal saviours. Three species of leopard can be found, including the beautiful clouded leopard of tropical rainforests, plus several species of small cat, such as the Asiatic golden cat and a rare endemic species, the Chinese mountain cat.

Rainforests are famous for their diversity of wildlife, and the tropical south of Yúnnán province, particularly the area around Xīshuāngbǎnnà, is one of the richest in China. These forests support Indochinese tigers and herds of Asiatic elephants.

The wild mammals you are most likely to see are several species of monkey. The large and precocious Père David's macaque is common at Éméi Shān in Sìchuān, where bands often intimidate people into handing over their picnics; macaques can also be seen on Hǎinán's Monkey Island. Several other monkey species are rare and endangered, including the beautiful golden monkey of the southwestern mountains and the snub-nosed monkey of the Yúnnán rainforests. But by far the most endangered is the Hǎinán gibbon, numbering just a few dozen individuals on Hǎinán island thanks to massive forest clearance.

Changqing Nature Reserve in Shaanxi province is well worth a visit for its relatively unspoilt montane forest and the chance to see giant pandas in the wild. Find out more at www.cqpanda.com.

The giant panda is western Sìchuān's most famous denizen, but the animal's solitary nature makes it extremely hard to observe in the wild, and even today, after decades of intensive research and total protection in dedicated reserves, sightings are rare. A census revised the world population of this amazing and appealing animal upwards after an estimated 39 pandas were located in Wánglǎng Nature Reserve in Sìchuān. Another positive development has been the 'bamboo tunnel', an area of reforestation designed to act as a corridor for the pandas to move between two fragmented patches of forest.

Birds

Most of the wildlife you'll see will be birds, and with more than 1300 species recorded, including about 100 endemic or near-endemic species, China offers some great bird-watching opportunities. Spring is usually the best time to see them, when deciduous foliage buds, migrants return from their wintering grounds and nesting gets into full swing. BirdLife International (www.birdlife.org/regional/asia), the worldwide bird conservation organisation, recognises 12 Endemic Bird Areas (EBAs) in China, nine of which are wholly within the country and three are shared with neighbouring countries.

At www.cnbirds.com, China Birding is an excellent resource for overwintering sites, migration routes, the geographical distribution of your feathered friends in China as well as lots of excellent photos.

Although the range of birds is huge, China is a centre of endemicity for several species and these are usually the ones that visiting birders will seek out. Most famous are the pheasant family, of which China boasts 62 species, including many endemic or near-endemic species.

Other families well represented in China include the laughing thrushes, with 36 species; parrotbills, which are almost confined to China and its near neighbours; and many members of the jay family. The crested ibis is a pinkish bird that feeds on invertebrates in the rice paddies, and was once found from central China to Japan.

Among China's more famous large birds are cranes, and nine of the world's 14 species have been recorded here. In Jiāngxī province, on the lower Yangzi, a vast series of shallow lakes and lagoons was formed by stranded overflow from Yangzi flooding. The largest of these is Póyáng Lake, although it is only a few metres deep and drains during winter. Vast numbers of waterfowl and other birds inhabit these swamps year-round, including ducks, geese, herons and egrets. Although it is difficult to get to, birders are increasingly drawn to the area in winter, when many of the lakes dry up and attract flocks of up to five crane species, including the endangered, pure white Siberian crane.

Parts of China are now established on the itineraries of global ecotour companies. Check websites such as www.eurobirding.com for bird-watchers' trip reports and more information on bird-watching in China. Recommended destinations include Zhālóng Nature Reserve, one of several vast wetlands in Hēilóngjiāng province. Visit in summer to see breeding storks, cranes and flocks of wildfowl before they fly south for the winter. Běidàihé, on the coast of the China Sea, is well known for migratory birds on passage. Other breeding grounds and wetlands include Qīnghǎi Hú in Qīnghǎi, Cǎohǎi Lake in Guìzhōu, Jiǔzhàigōu in Sìchuān and Mai Po Marsh in Hong Kong. For the latter, the Hong Kong Bird Watching Society (www.hkbws.org.hk) organises regular outings and publishes a newsletter in English.

In reflection of its water woes, China has developed the world's most intensive cloud-seeding program.

Most bird-watchers and bird tours head straight for Sìchuān, which offers superb birding in sites such as Wòlóng. Here, several spectacular pheasants, including golden, blood and kalij pheasants, live on the steep forested hillsides surrounding the main road. As the road climbs towards Beilanshan Pass, higher-altitude species such as eared pheasants and the spectacular Chinese monal may be seen. Alpine meadows host smaller birds, and the rocky scree slopes at the pass hold partridges, the beautiful grandala and the mighty lammergeier (bearded vulture), with a 2m wingspan.

Reptiles & Amphibians

The Chinese alligator – known as the 'muddy dragon' – is one of the smallest of the world's crocodilians, measuring only 2m in length, and is harmless to humans. Owing to habitat clearance and intense pressure to turn its wetlands to agriculture along the lower Yangzi, fewer than 130 of these crocs still exist in the wild. A captive breeding program has been successful, but as yet there are few options for releasing this rare reptile back into the wild.

The cold, rushing rivers of the southwestern mountains are home to the world's largest amphibian, the giant salamander. This enormous amphibian can reach 1m in length and feeds on small aquatic animals. Unfortunately, it is now critically endangered in the wild and, like so many other animals, hunted for food. More than 300 other species of frog and salamander occur in China's waterways and wetlands, and preying on them is a variety of snakes, including cobras and vipers. One of China's more unusual national parks is Snake Island, near Dàlián in Liáoníng province. This 800-hectare dot in the China Sea is uninhabited by people, but supports an estimated 130,000 Pallas' pit vipers, an extraordinary concentration of snakes that prey on migrating birds that land on the island every spring and autumn in huge numbers. By eating several birds each season, the snakes can subsist on lizards and invertebrates for the rest of the year until migration time comes round again.

Plants

China is home to more than 32,000 species of seed plant and 2500 species of forest tree, plus an extraordinary plant diversity that includes some famous 'living fossils' – a diversity so great that Jílín province in the semifrigid north and Hǎinán province in the tropical south share few plant species. Many reserves still remain where intact vegetation ecosystems can be seen firsthand, but few parts of the country have escaped human impact. Deforestation continues apace in many regions and vast areas are under cultivation with monocultures such as rice.

Bamboo comprises 99% of the giant panda's diet, and it spends up to 16 hours a day feeding, during which time it may eat up to 20kg of bamboo shoots, stems and leaves.

Apart from rice, the plant probably most often associated with China and Chinese culture is bamboo, of which China boasts some 300 species. Bamboos grow in many parts of China, but bamboo forests were once so extensive that they enabled the evolution of the giant panda, which eats virtually nothing else, and a suite of small mammals, birds and insects that live in bamboo thickets. Most of these useful species are found in the subtropical areas south of the Yangzi, and the best surviving thickets are in southwestern provinces such as Sìchuān.

Many plants commonly cultivated in Western gardens today originated in China, among them the ginkgo tree, a famous 'living fossil' whose unmistakable imprint has been found in rocks 270 million years old. The unique and increasingly rare dove tree or paper tree, whose greatly enlarged white bracts look like a flock of doves, grows only in the deciduous forests of the southwest.

THE YANGZI DOLPHIN

The Yangzi floodway was big enough to favour the evolution of distinct large river creatures, including the Yangzi dolphin *(baiji)* and Chinese alligator, both now desperately endangered. The Yangzi dolphin, one of just a few freshwater dolphin species in the world (others occur in the Ganges and Amazon River systems) and by far the rarest, migrated to the Yangzi River from the Pacific Ocean over 20 million years ago and adapted itself to its freshwater habitat. The dolphin largely lost the use of its eyes in the gloomy Yangzi waters and instead steered a course through the river using a form of sonar.

From being quite commonplace – around 6000 dolphins still lived in the Yangzi River during the 1950s – numbers fell drastically during the three decades of explosive economic growth from the 1970s, and the last confirmed sighting was in 2002. The creature is a victim – one of many – of human activity in the region, succumbing to drowning in fishing nets and lethal injuries from ships' propellers.

Deciduous forests cover mid-altitudes in the mountains, and are characterised by oaks, hemlocks and aspens, with a leafy understorey that springs to life after the winter snows have melted. Among the more famous blooms of the understorey are rhododendrons and azaleas, and many species of each grow naturally in China's mountain ranges. Best viewed in spring, some species flower right through summer; one of the best places to see them is at Sìchuān's Wòlóng Nature Reserve. Both rhododendrons and azaleas grow in distinct bands at various heights on the mountainsides, which are recognisable as you drive through the reserve to the high mountain passes. At the very highest elevations, the alpine meadows grazed by yaks are often dotted with showy and colourful blooms.

The World Health Organization estimates that air pollution causes more than 650,000 fatal illnesses per year in China, while more than 95,000 die annually from consuming polluted drinking water.

Deforestation has levelled huge tracts of China's once vast and beautiful primeval forests. At the end of the 19th century, 70% of China's northeast was still forest. Unsustainable clear-cutting in the 20th century – especially during the rapacious Great Leap Forward – was not banned there until the mid-1980s, by which time only 5% of old-growth woodland remained. Logging controls were more strictly enforced after the great floods of 1998, when deforestation was identified as contributing to the floodwaters. Since then a vigorous replanting campaign was launched to once again cover huge tracts of China with trees, but these cannot restore the rich biodiversity that once existed.

Endangered Species

Almost every large mammal you can think of in China has crept onto the endangered species list, as well as many of the so-called 'lower' animals and plants. The snow leopard, Indochinese tiger, chiru antelope, crested ibis, Asiatic elephant, red-crowned crane and black-crowned crane are all endangered.

Deforestation, pollution, hunting and trapping for fur, body parts and sport are all culprits. The Convention on International Trade in Threatened and Endangered Species (CITES) records legal trade in live reptiles and parrots, and astonishingly high numbers of reptile and wild cat skins. The number of such products collected or sold unofficially is anyone's guess.

EATEN TO EXTINCTION

China's taste for exotic animals is helping drive many to extinction. In 2007 a deserted ship containing 5000 rare creatures was discovered floating off south China. The cargo included 44 leatherback turtles, over 2500 monitor lizards, 31 pangolins and a large consignment of bear paws. It is assumed the cargo was heading for the restaurants of south China. In 2010 another ship containing hundreds of dead pangolins was found. As a result of voracious demand for exotic meat in China, species such as the pangolin have vanished from China and neighbouring countries, so traffickers have turned to Malaysia and other Southeast Asian nations, where populations are also rapidly dwindling.

Snakes feature prominently on China's menus – more than 10,000 tonnes of serpents are dished up every year to diners – and in traditional Chinese medicine, as snake parts are believed to restore health and boost sexual prowess. The venom of dangerous species such as vipers is particularly sought for medicine. The situation is so dire that no fewer than 43 of China's 200 snake species are said to be endangered. Nature, however, has a way of fighting back and the depletion of snake numbers leads pretty quickly to an increase in rodent numbers, with resulting crop destruction.

TOP BOOKS ON CHINA'S ENVIRONMENT

» *When a Billion Chinese Jump* (2010) Jonathan Watts' sober and engaging study of China's environmental concerns.

» *The River Runs Black: The Environmental Challenge to China's Future* (2004) Elizabeth Economy's frightening look at the unhappy marriage between breakneck economic production and environmental degradation.

» *The China Price: The True Cost of Chinese Competitive Advantage* (2008) Alexandra Harney's telling glimpse behind the figures of China's economic rise.

» *China's Water Crisis* (2004) Ma Jun rolls up his sleeves to examine the sources of China's water woes.

» *Mao's War Against Nature* (2001) Judith Shapiro looks at the ideological confrontation between communism and the environment.

Despite the threats, a number of rare animal species cling to survival in the wild. Notable among them are the Chinese alligator in Ānhuī, the giant salamander in the fast-running waters of the Yangzi and Yellow Rivers, the Yangzi River dolphin in the lower and middle reaches of the river (although there have been no sightings since 2002), and the pink dolphin of the Hong Kong islands of Sha Chau and Lung Kwu Chau. The giant panda is confined to the fauna-rich valleys and ranges of Sìchuān, but your best chances for sighting one is in Chéngdū's Giant Panda Breeding Research Base. You may be lucky enough to chance upon a golden monkey in the mountains of Sìchuān, Yúnnán and Guìzhōu.

Intensive monoculture farmland cultivation, the reclaiming of wetlands, river damming, industrial and rural waste, and desertification are reducing unprotected forest areas and making the survival of many of these species increasingly precarious. Although there are laws against killing or capturing rare wildlife, their struggle for survival is further complicated as many remain on the most-wanted lists for traditional Chinese medicine and dinner delicacies. In Tibet, the *chiru* antelope has long been hunted for a fleece that provides a lucrative type of wool. Despite conservation efforts, poaching still continues in an area that is hard to effectively monitor due to its size and a lack of human resources.

The Environment

China may be vast, but with two-thirds of the land either mountain, desert or uncultivable, the remaining third is overwhelmed by the people of the world's most populous nation. For social and political reasons, China is only now experiencing its – and the world's – most rapid period of urbanisation in history, so the city often impinges in inescapable fashion.

Deforestation and overgrazing have accelerated the desertification of vast areas of China, particularly in the western provinces. Deserts now cover almost one-fifth of the country and China's dustbowl is the world's largest, swallowing up 200 sq km of arable land every month.

For decades China neglected the environment as it was costly to protect; environmental concerns were parked on the back-burner to be dealt with once the national economy had developed. China embarked on a course of development first, clean up later. The costs of such procrastination may, however, return to haunt Běijīng. The World Bank calculates the annual cost of pollution alone in China at almost 6% of the national GDP; when all forms of environmental damage are incorporated, the figure leaps as high as 12%, meaning China's environmental costs may outweigh economic growth. This alone should be enough to focus minds.

In 2010 China overtook the USA as the world's largest energy consumer; in the same year the nation replaced Japan as the world's second-largest economy and is tipped to overtake the USA by 2030 (some say by 2020).

A Greener China?

The debacle of the 2009 climate summit in Copenhagen painted China as an obstinate deal-breaker. China is paradoxically painfully aware of its accelerated desertification, growing water shortages, shrinking glaciers, increasingly acidic rain and progressively polluted environment, but remains unclear whether or how to fully champion the development of greener and cleaner energy sources.

Evidence of ambitious and bold thinking is easy to find: in 2010 China announced it would pour billions into developing electric and hybrid vehicles; Běijīng is committing itself to overtaking Europe in investment in renewable energy by 2020; the construction of wind farms (in blustery Gānsù, for example) continues apace; and China leads the world in production of solar cells.

Běijīng has pledged US$6.8 billion to plant a 'green wall' of millions of trees along 5700km to halt the encroaching desert sands.

Its authoritarian system of governance allows China to railroad through daring initiatives. However, this same government is also fond of reaching for the familiar tools in its workshop, relying heavily on technological 'solutions' and huge engineering programs to combat environmental problems. For example, China is attempting to engineer itself out of its water crisis by diverting some of the waters of the Yangzi River to thirsty north China, when devising more manageable solutions to water use may be more advisable for a sustainable future.

Some greener initiatives, such as the Three Gorges Dam, sport green credentials in some areas (no greenhouse gases, renewable energy source, small carbon footprint) but are environmentally unsound in others (water-polluting, seismic effects, local climate change). Other initiatives may also be little more than hype, as China learns to twiddle the 'soft power' knobs in a public relations exercise with an increasingly attentive outside world. The world's first ecologically sustainable city at

SOUTH–NORTH WATER DIVERSION PROJECT

Water is the lifeblood of economic and agricultural growth, but as China only possesses around 7% of the world's water resources (with almost 20% of its population), the liquid is an increasingly precious resource.

In a region of low rainfall, north China is facing a grim water crisis. Farmers are draining aquifers that have taken thousands of years to accumulate, while Chinese industry is using three to 10 times more water per unit of production than developed nations. Meanwhile, water usage in large cities such as Běijīng and Tiānjīn continues to climb as migrants move in from rural areas. By some estimates, the aquifers of north China may only have another 30 years of life left.

The Chinese Communist Party (CCP) remains hypnotised by monumental engineering projects as solutions. To combat the water crisis, the CCP embarked on the construction of the US$62 billion South–North Water Diversion Project, a vast network of rivers, canals and lakes lashing north and south. The logic is to divert surplus water from the Yangzi River to the dwindling and long overexploited Yellow River.

The project has been snared by complications. There are concerns that pollution in the Yangzi River waters will become progressively concentrated as water is extracted, while Yangzi cities such as Nánjīng and Wǔhàn are increasingly anxious they will be left with less water. Alarm has also arisen at the pollution in channels – including the Grand Canal, which linked Hángzhōu with north China – earmarked to take the diverted waters. There are worries that these polluted reaches are almost untreatable, making elements of the project unviable.

Critics also argue that the project, which will involve the mass relocation of hundreds of thousands of people, will not address the fundamental issue of China's water woes – the absence of policies for the sustainable use of water as a precious resource.

Dōngtān on Chongming Island at the mouth of the Yangzi River was projected to house 25,000 people by the time of the 2010 World Expo. There was considerable international press attention when the idea was launched, but the city has yet to be built.

One of China's main quandaries is coal. China's coal-fired growth comes at a time when the effort to tackle global warming has become a chief global priority. Coal is cheap, easy to extract and remains China's number one energy source, generating almost 70% of power requirements. Huge untapped reserves in the northwest await exploitation, vast coalfields in Inner Mongolia are now being mined and the economics of coal mining in China make it a cheap and reliable fuel source. Nonetheless, coal is an unrenewable resource and experts predict China's reserves will be depleted within a century. But with energy requirements booming in step with economic growth, it is unlikely China will shake off its increasing addiction to the fuel that has created some of the most polluted cities on the planet.

One of the aims of the Three Gorges Dam is to help prevent flooding on the Yangzi River. The river has caused hundreds of catastrophic floods, including the disastrous inundation of 1931, in which an estimated 145,000 died.

The Martial Arts of China

Unlike Western fighting arts – Savate, kickboxing, boxing, wrestling etc – Chinese martial arts are deeply impregnated with religious and philosophical values. And, some might add, a morsel or two of magic. Many eminent exponents of *gōngfū* (功夫) were devout monks or religious recluses who drew inspiration from Buddhism and Taoism and sought a mystical communion with the natural world around them. Their arts were not leisurely pursuits but were closely entangled with the meaning and purpose of their lives.

Several Chinese styles of *gōngfū* include drunken sets, where the student mimics the supple movements of an inebriate.

Often misinterpreted, *gōngfū* teaches an approach to life that stresses patience, endurance, magnanimity and humility. For those who truly take to the Chinese martial arts, it's a rewarding journey with a unique destination. When two people discover they share an interest in martial arts, it's the cue for an endless exchange of techniques and anecdotes. It's a club mentality for members only.

Styles & Schools

China lays claim to a bewildering range of martial-arts styles. There's the flamboyant and showy, inspired by the movements of animals or insects (such as Praying Mantis Boxing), but there are also schools more empirically built upon the science of human movement (eg Wing Chun). Some pugilists stress a mentalist approach (eg Xingyi Quan) although others put their money on physical power (White Eyebrow Boxing). On the more obscure fringes are the esoteric arts, abounding with metaphysical feats, arcane practices and closely guarded techniques.

Many fighting styles were once secretively handed down for generations within families and it is only relatively recently that outsiders have been accepted as students. Some schools, especially the more obscure of styles, have died out partly because of their exclusivity.

Some styles have found themselves divided into competing factions, each laying claim to the original teachings and techniques. Such styles may find themselves in a state of schism, where the original principles have become either distorted or lost. Other styles though became part of the mainstream and flourished; Wing Chun in particular has been elevated into a globally recognised art, largely due to its associations with Bruce Lee (even though he ultimately developed his own style).

Unlike with Taekwondo or Karate-do, there is frequently no international regulatory body that oversees the syllabus, tournaments or grading requirements for China's individual martial arts. Consequently students of China's myriad martial arts may be rather unsure of where they stand or what level they have attained. With no standard syllabus, it is often down to the individual teacher to decide what to teach his or her student, and how quickly. A teacher of Five Ancestors Boxing (Wǔzúquán) may communicate the art in whatever increments he deems appropriate, but may only disclose the top-drawer skills that are crucial for success to his most trusted disciples.

Hard School

Although there is considerable blurring between the two camps, Chinese martial arts are often distinguished between hard and soft schools. Typically aligned with Buddhism, the hard or 'external' (外家; *wàijiā*) school tends to be more vigorous, athletic and focussed on the development of power. Many of these styles are related to Shàolín Boxing *(shàolín quánfǎ)* and the Shàolín Temple in Hénán province.

Shàolín Boxing is forever associated with Bodhidharma, an ascetic Indian Buddhist monk who visited the Shàolín Temple and added a series of breathing and physical exercises to the Shàolín monk's sedentary meditations. The Shàolín monk's legendary endeavours and fearsome physical skills became known throughout China and beyond. Famous external schools include White Eyebrow Boxing, Long Boxing and Tiger Boxing.

Soft School

Usually inspired by Taoism, the soft or 'internal' Chinese school (内家; nèijiā) develops pliancy and softness as a weapon against hard force. Taichi (Taiji Quan) is the best known soft school, famed for its slow and lithe movements and an emphasis on cultivating *qì* (energy). Attacks are met with yielding movements that smother the attacking force and lead the aggressor off balance. Adept taichi students are able to cause considerable damage to an attacker, although the road to mastery is a long and difficult one, involving a re-education of physical movement and suppression of one's instinct to tense up when threatened. Other soft schools include the circular moves of Bāguà Zhǎng and the linear boxing patterns of Xingyi Quan, based on five basic punches – each linked to one of the five elements of Chinese philosophy – and the movements of 12 animals.

Forms

Most students of Chinese martial arts – hard or soft – learn forms (套路; *tàolu*), a series of movements linked together into a pattern, which embody the principal punches and kicks of the style. In essence, forms are unwritten compendiums of the style, to ensure passage from one generation to the next. The number and complexity of forms varies from style to style: taichi may only have one form, although it may be very lengthy (the long form of the Yang style takes around 20 minutes to perform). Five Ancestors Boxing has dozens of forms, while Wing Chun only has three empty-hand forms.

A Malaysian Five Ancestors master once broke the leg of a Thai boxer, with his finger!

Qìgōng

Closely linked to both the hard and especially the soft martial-arts schools is the practice of *qìgōng*, a technique for cultivating and circulating *qì* around the body. *Qì* can be developed for use in fighting to protect the body (eg iron-shirt *qìgōng*), as a source of power or for curative and health-giving purposes.

Martial Arts Case Study: Bāguà Zhǎng

One of the more esoteric and obscure of the soft Taoist martial arts, Bāguà Zhǎng (八卦掌;Eight Trigram Boxing, also known as Pa-kua) is also one of the most intriguing. The Bāguà Zhǎng student wheels around in a circle, rapidly changing direction and speed, occasionally thrusting out a palm strike.

Bāguà Zhǎng draws its inspiration from the trigrams (an arrangement of three broken and unbroken lines) of the classic *Book of Changes* (Yìjīng or I Ching), the ancient oracle used for divination. The trigrams are typically arranged in circular form and it is this pattern that is traced out by the Bāguà Zhǎng exponent. Training commences by just walking the circle so the student gradually becomes infused with its patterns and rhythms.

A hallmark of the style is the exclusive use of the palm, not the fist, as the principal weapon. This may seem curious and perhaps even ineffectual, but in fact the palm can transmit a lot of power – consider a thrusting palm strike to the chin, for example. The palm is also better protected than the fist as it is cushioned by muscle. The fist also has to transfer its power through a multitude of bones that need to be correctly aligned to avoid damage while the palm sits at the end of the wrist. Consider hitting a brick wall as hard as you can with your palm (and then imagine doing it with your fist!). In fact, Bāguà Zhǎng fighters were feared among Chinese boxers for their ferocity and unorthodox moves.

The student must become proficient in the subterfuge, evasion, speed and unpredictability that are hallmarks of Bāguà Zhǎng. Force is generally not met with force, but deflected by the circular movements manifested in students through their meditations upon the circle. Circular forms – arcing, twisting, twining and spinning – are the mainstay of all movements, radiating from the waist.

Despite being dated by historians to the 19th century, Bāguà Zhǎng is quite probably a very ancient art. Beneath the Taoist overlay, the movements and patterns of the art suggest a possibly animistic origin, which gives the art its timeless rhythms.

Martial Arts Case Study: Wing Chun

Conceived by a Buddhist nun called Ng Mui from the Shàolín Temple who taught her skills to a young girl called Wing Chun (詠春), Wing Chun (Yǒng Chūn) is a fast and dynamic system of fighting that promises quick results for novices. This was the style that taught Bruce Lee how to move and, although he ultimately moved away from it to develop his own style, Wing Chun had an enormous influence on the Hong Kong fighter and actor.

Wing Chun emphasises speed rather than strength. Evasion, rapid strikes and low kicks are the hallmarks of the style. Forms are simple and direct, dispensing with the pretty flourishes that clutter other styles.

The art can perhaps best be described as scientific. There are none of the animal forms that make other styles so exciting and mysterious. Instead, Wing Chun is built around its centre line theory, which draws an imaginary line down the human body and centres all attacks and blocks along that line. The line runs through the sensitive regions: eyes, nose, mouth, throat, heart, solar plexus and groin and any blow on these points is debilitating and dangerous.

The three empty hand forms – which look bizarre to non-initiates – train arm and leg movements that both attack and defend this line. None of the blocks stray beyond the width of the shoulders, as this is the limit of possible attacks, and punches follow the same theory. Punches are delivered with great speed in a straight line, along the shortest distance between puncher and punched. All of this gives Wing Chun its distinctive simplicity.

A two-person training routine called *chi sau* (sticky hands) teaches the student how to be soft and relaxed in response to attacks, as pliancy

IRON PALM

Praying Mantis master Fan Yook Tung once killed two stampeding bulls with an iron-palm technique.

generates more speed. Weapons in the Wing Chun arsenal include the lethal twin Wing Chun butterfly knives and an extremely long pole, which requires considerable strength to handle with skill.

Courses & Books

Martial-arts courses can be found in abundance across China, from Běijīng, Hong Kong, Shànghǎi, Wǔdāng Shān in Húběi, Yángshuò in Guǎngxī and the Shàolín Temple in Hénán. See under Courses in these sections for more.

Try to track down a copy of John F Gilbey's *The Way of a Warrior*, a tongue-in-cheek, well-written and riveting account of the Oriental fighting arts.

Survival Guide

Directory A–Z

Accommodation

Accommodation in China has undergone a revolution in recent years. Whether you are looking for rustic homesteads, homestays, youth hostels, student dormitories, guesthouses, courtyard lodgings, boutique hotels or five-star towers, the choice is growing by the day.

Rooms & Prices

Most rooms in China are twins, with two single beds. **Single rooms** (单间; *dānjiān*) are rarer. **Double rooms** (双人房、 标准间; *shuāng rén fáng* or *biāozhǔn jiān*) will often be twins, but hotels may also have large-bed rooms (大床房; *dàchuáng fáng*), which are rooms with a large single bed. **Suites** (套房; *tàofáng*) are available at most midrange and top-end hotels. **Dorms** (多人房; *duōrénfáng*) are usually, but not always, available at youth hostels (and at a few hotels). All rooms in this book come with private bathroom/shower room, unless otherwise stated.

Accommodation in this book is divided by price category, identified by the symbols $ (budget), $$ (midrange) or $$$ (top end); accommodation prices vary across China, so refer to each chapter for that region's budget breakdown, identified at the start of the chapter. Generally speaking, hostels, guesthouses and one- to two-star hotels fall into the budget category; midrange hotels are typically three to four stars, while top-end hotels are four to five stars.

You usually have to check out by noon. If you check out between noon and 6pm you will be charged 50% of the room price; after 6pm you have to pay for another full night.

Booking Online

Booking online can secure good prices on rooms, and should be the first place you look. You can get a substantial discount (up to 50% off the walk-in rate) by booking through an online agency, although some simply offer rates you can get from the hotels or youth hostels yourself. Airports at major cities often have hotel-booking counters that offer discounted rates.

Useful accommodation websites:

Asia Hotels (www.asia-hotels.com)

China Hotels (www.china-hotelguide.com)

Redflag (www.redflag.info)

SinoHotel (www.sinohotel.com)

Tripadvisor (www.tripadvisor.com) Excellent source of accommodation reviews.

Once in China, book discounted rooms on the following sites:

Ctrip (☎800 820 6666; www.english.ctrip.com)

Elong (☎800 810 1010; www.elong.com)

Checking In

At check-in you will need your passport; a registration form will ask what type of visa you have. For most travellers, the visa will be L; for a full list of visa categories, see p992. A deposit (押金; *yājīn*) is required at most hotels; this will be paid either with cash or by providing your credit-card details. If your deposit is paid in cash, you will be given a receipt.

Camping

There are few places where you can legally camp and as most of China's flatland is put to agricultural use, you will largely be limited to remote, hilly regions. Camping is more feasible in wilder

BOOK YOUR STAY ONLINE

For more accommodation reviews by Lonely Planet authors, check out hotels.lonelyplanet.com/China. You'll find independent reviews, as well as recommendations on the best places to stay. Best of all, you can book online.

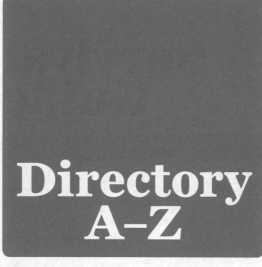

HOTEL DISCOUNTS

Always ignore the rack rate and ask for the discounted price or bargain for a room, as discounts apply in generally all but youth hostels (except for hostel members) and the cheapest accommodation; you can do this in person at reception, or book online. Apart from during the busy holiday periods (the first week of May and October, and Chinese New Year), rooms should be priced well below the rack rate and rarely booked out. Discounts of 10% to 50% off the tariff rate (30% is typical) are the norm, available by simply asking at reception, by phoning in advance to reserve a room or by booking online at Ctrip. We have listed both the rack rate and the discount you should expect to receive at each hotel, where they apply.

and less populated parts of west China. In certain destinations with camping possibilities, travel agencies and hotels will arrange overnight camping trips or multiday treks, in which case camping equipment will be supplied.

Courtyard Hotels

Largely confined to Běijīng, courtyard hotels have rapidly mushroomed. Arranged around traditional *sìhéyuàn* (courtyards), rooms are usually on ground level. Courtyard hotels are charming and romantic, but are often expensive and rooms are small, in keeping with the dimensions of courtyard residences. Facilities will be limited so don't expect a swimming pool, gym or subterranean garage.

Guesthouses

The cheapest of the cheap are China's ubiquitous guesthouses (招待所; *zhāodàisuǒ*). Often found clustering near train or bus stations but also dotted around cities and towns, not all guesthouses accept foreigners. Many are on the 2nd floor above street level, accessed by a crummy flight of steps (look out for the signs). Reception is usually a simple counter, staffed by the owner in everyday clothes, mop in hand and fag in mouth. Rooms (doubles, twins, triples, quads) are primitive and grey, with tiled floors and possibly a shower room or shabby bathroom; showers may be communal. There may be air-con and/or a dated TV. Guesthouses do not tend to have restaurants and are more commonly used by men than women.

Other terms for guesthouses:

» 旅店 *(lǚdiàn)*

» 旅馆 *(lǚguǎn)*

» 有房 means 'rooms available'

» 今日有房 means 'rooms available today'

» 住宿 *(zhùsù)* means 'accommodation'

Homesteads

In more rural destinations, small towns and villages, you should be able to find a homestead (农家; *nóngjiā*). The owner of the house will have a handful of rooms that cost in the region of Y50 (bargaining is possible); you will not need to register. The owner will be more than happy to cook up meals for you as well, but may try to coax you into eating the most expensive on offer, generally free-range chicken *(tǔjī)* or pork. Showers and toilets are generally communal.

Hostels

If you're looking for efficiently run budget accommodation, turn to China's youth hostel sector. **Hostelling International** (☎400 886 0808; www.yhachina.com) hostels are generally well run, with a growing network of member hostels. **Utels hostels** are generally inferior and not as widespread; some may also not take foreigners. You may discover other private youth hostels scattered around China that are unaffiliated; standards at these may be variable.

Youth hostels are typically staffed by youthful English-speakers who are also well informed on local sightseeing. The foreigner-friendly vibe in youth hostels stands in marked contrast to Chinese hotels that are often unaware of Western requirements. They are also superb for meeting like-minded travellers. Double rooms in youth hostels are often better than midrange equivalents, often just as comfortable and better located, and levels of service may be superior. Many offer wi-fi, while most have at least one internet terminal (free perhaps, free for 30 minutes or roughly Y5 to Y10 per hour). Laundry, book-lending, kitchen facilities, bike rental, lockers, noticeboard, bar and cafe should all be available.

Dorms usually cost between Y40 and Y55 (discount of around Y5 for members). They typically come with bunk beds but may have standard beds. Most dorms won't have an en suite shower, though some do; they should have air-con. Many hostels also have doubles, singles, twins and maybe even family rooms; prices vary but are often around Y150 to Y250 for a double, again with discounts for members. Hostels can arrange ticketing or help you book a room in another affiliated youth hostel. Book

HOTEL HASSLES

About a decade ago, an upbeat official announcement insisted foreigners would be able to stay at any hotel of their choosing. Today, however, foreign travellers still find themselves routinely barred from cheap hotels, even if they speak Chinese. The official line is that this is for the security and safety of 'foreign guests', and the Public Security Bureau (PSB) decides which hotels or guesthouses are safe. Many 'foreign guests', however, argue that they should be allowed to decide whether a place is safe or not and choose accordingly. In fact, many guesthouses that refuse foreigners are quite safe, but foreigners are directed to more expensive midrange hotels. The list of hotels that accept foreigners varies: during our last visit to Chéngdé, for example, budget hotels that were once fine for foreigners were off limits.

In China's poorly regulated hotel industry, reverse-racism is also inflicted on Chinese travellers. Some hotels and hostels aimed at Westerners do not accept Chinese guests, recommending instead they find somewhere else to spend the night. These hotels seek to separate Westerners and Chinese, to create a Westerner-only atmosphere that fundamentally conflicts with the purpose of visiting China in the first place. Chinese-looking guests need to be warned that they may be told to find a room elsewhere.

If you are really keen to stay in one particular hostel, it may be a good idea to phone the hostel beforehand and book your room in English.

ahead (online if possible) as rooms are frequently booked out, especially at weekends or the busy holiday periods.

Hotels

Hotels are called *bīnguǎn* (宾馆), *jiǔdiàn* (酒店), *dàjiǔdiàn* (大酒店), *fàndiàn* (饭店) or *dàfàndiàn* (大饭店) in Chinese.

Hotels vary wildly in quality within the same budget bracket. The star rating system employed in China can be misleading: hotels are frequently awarded four or five stars when they are patently a star lower in ranking. A Chinese-run 'five star' hotel may have achieved its ranking by installing an unimpressive swimming pool or by supplying gifts and lavish dinners to inspectors. Deficiencies may not be immediately apparent, so explore and make an inspection of the overall quality of the hotel. Viewing the room up front pays dividends. English skills are often poor, even in some five-star hotels; sometimes they are non-existent.

Practically all hotels will change money for guests, and most midrange and top-end hotels accept credit cards. All hotel rooms are subject to a 10% or 15% service charge. Most hotels in the midrange bracket will have broadband internet access and may have wi-fi.

The Chinese method of designating floors is the same as that used in the USA, but different from, say, that used in Australia. What would be the ground floor in Australia is the 1st floor in China, the 1st is the 2nd, and so on.

Temples & Monasteries

Some temples and monasteries (especially on China's sacred mountains) provide accommodation. They are cheap, but ascetic, and may not have running water or electricity.

University Accommodation

Some universities provide cheap and basic accommodation either in their foreign-student dormitory buildings (留学生楼; *liúxuéshēng lóu*) or more expensive rooms at their experts' building (专家楼; *zhuānjiā lóu*), where visiting teachers often stay.

TWO STARS

Apart from at youth hostels, budget accommodation can be found in hotels rated two

HOTEL TIPS

» Ask your hotel concierge for a local map

» The standard of English is often better at youth hostels than at midrange or high-end hotels

» Your hotel can help with ticketing, for a commission

» See the Accommodation section of the Language chapter for a handy primer of Chinese phrases

» Almost every hotel has a left-luggage room, which should be free if you are a guest in the hotel

» Always bargain for a room

EXPRESS BUSINESS HOTELS

Clean and natty express business chains have expanded across China, offering lower-midrange comfort, good hygiene and convenience. They are often centrally located and generally purpose-built, with smallish Ikea-kitted rooms and no wardrobes in their standard doubles. Some of these chains offer membership schemes that bring rates down.

Home Inn (☎800 820 3333; www.homeinns.com)
Jinjiang Inn (www.jinjianginns.com)
Motel 168 (www.motel168.com)

stars or unranked. Expect basic facilities, possibly grimy bathrooms or shower rooms, threadbare carpets, very basic or non-existent English-language skills at reception and a simple restaurant or none at all. All two-star hotel rooms should come with air-conditioning and TV, but may not have telephones or internet access, so ask beforehand. Rooms may have water coolers or a thermos flask (in old establishments). If it's an old-fashioned place, you may find a *fúwùyua'n* (female assistant) on each floor. Breakfast, if available, may consist of boiled eggs, rice porridge, pickled vegetables and so forth.

THREE TO FOUR STARS

Three- to four-star hotels offer comfort and a greater measure of flair than two-star hotels; they are also often bland and uninspiring. When making a choice, opt for Sino-foreign joint-venture hotels over Chinese-owned hotels wherever possible. Opt for newer establishments, as three- to four-star hotels rapidly get set in their ways. Staff should speak some English, but language skills can be highly mechanical, even at reception. There should be a Western restaurant and a bar (if it's a three-star hotel, expect it to be cheesy).

Rooms in three- to four-star hotels all have a bathroom or shower room, air-con and telephone; they should also come with a kettle (and coffee sachets), water cooler, safe and minibar. Rooms may also have satellite TV, cable TV or an in-house movie channel, and broadband internet connection. No-smoking rooms should be available; the hotel may have a health centre or gym. You may receive a free newspaper slipped under your door, at best perhaps the anodyne *China Daily*. A Western breakfast may be available, certainly at four-star establishments.

In large cities such as Běijīng and Shànghǎi, a growing number of courtyard and boutique hotels fall within this category, offering a more personal level of service, a more intimate environment in which to stay and perhaps a more unique sense of personality and style.

FIVE STARS

China has very few independent hotels of real distinction, so it's generally advisable to select chain hotels that offer a proven standard of international excellence. Shangri-La, Marriott, Hilton, St Regis, Ritz-Carlton, Marco Polo and Hyatt all have a presence in China and can generally be relied upon for high standards of service and comfort.

Some Chinese-owned hotels display five stars when they are, at best, four stars, so be warned (however, the tariff should be cheaper). Five-star hotels should have top-quality recreational, shopping and sport facilities (including swimming pool, health centre or gym and tennis courts), and a wide selection of Chinese and international dining options and a decent bar.

Five-star hotel rooms will have a kettle (and coffee sachets), safe, minibar, satellite or cable TV, broadband internet connection, wi-fi, iPod dock perhaps, both shower and bath, free newspaper (typically the *International Herald Tribune*) and nightly turndown service. No-smoking rooms will be available, as will Western breakfasts. Superior comfort should also be available on executive floors, which typically provide business facilities, free drinks upon arrival and in the afternoon, and complimentary breakfast. Service should be top-notch and English *should* be spoken well, although prepare for the worst.

Most top end hotels list their room rates in US dollars, but you will have to pay in local currency.

Activities

Grab copies of expat magazines in Běijīng, Hong Kong, Guǎngzhōu and Shànghǎi for information on activities such as running, cycling, football, cricket, swimming, ice skating, skateboarding and waterskiing.

Golf

There are almost 200 golf courses in China; Běijīng alone has more than a dozen, and others can be found in destinations ranging from Guǎngzhōu to Shànghǎi. For details of well-known golf courses, check out **World Golf** (www.worldgolf.com/courses/chinagcs.html).

Hiking

Hiking is an excellent way to see some of China's most dramatic landscapes; see p319 for some suggested routes. Outfits in China, such as **Wildchina** (www.wildchina.com), offer a host of dramatic treks in remote parts of the country.

Horse Riding

Horse-riding expeditions aimed at tourists can be found in Xīnjiāng, Gānsù, Inner Mongolia, Sìchuān and beyond. In particular, Lángmùsì in Gānsù offers good horse-trekking opportunities, while horse riding around Sōngpān in Sìchuān is popular.

A growing number of equestrian clubs can be found in the big cities; check the classified pages of expat mags for details.

Martial Arts

See the Martial Arts of China chapter (p974) for information on martial arts.

Rock Climbing

Rock climbing is popular in Yángshuò in Guǎngxī, where increasing numbers of foreigners are seeking out the region's bolted climbs. Rock climbing is also popular in Hong Kong (see the boxed text, p488).

Skiing

It is not worth going to China for a skiing holiday, but if you're visiting during the winter months, northeast China has downhill skiing in Jílín and Hēilóngjiāng.

Business Hours

China officially has a five-day working week. Banks, offices and government departments are open Monday to Friday, roughly from around 9am until 5pm or 6pm; some may close for two hours in the middle of the day. Many banks also open on Saturdays and may also open on Sundays. Post offices are generally open seven days a week.

Saturday and Sunday are public holidays. Most museums stay open on weekends and may make up for this by closing for one day during the week.

Travel agencies and foreign-exchange counters in tourist hotels are usually open seven days a week. Department stores, shopping malls and shops are generally open from 10am to 10pm, seven days a week.

Parks tend to open soon after sunrise and close at twilight.

Internet cafes are typically open 24 hours, but some open at 8am and close at midnight.

Restaurants are generally open from around 10.30am to midnight, but some shut at around 2pm and reopen at 5pm or 6pm; others open early for breakfast. The Chinese eat much earlier than Westerners, lunching at around midday and dining at about 6pm. Many bars open in the late afternoon and shut around midnight or later.

Children

Children will be more comfortable in the large cities of Hong Kong, Běijīng and Shànghǎi (see the boxed text, p187), and are likely to feel out of place in smaller towns and in the wilds. Before you pack the buckets and spades, remember that, with the exception of Hǎinán, China has a dreary selection of beaches.

Practicalities

Baby food and milk powder are widely available in supermarkets, as are basics like nappies, baby wipes, bottles, medicine, dummies and other paraphernalia. Few cheap restaurants have baby chairs, and finding baby-changing rooms is next to impossible.

Be prepared for long train and bus rides or plane journeys and their associated difficulties.

For train travel, children shorter than 1.4m can get a hard sleeper for 75% of the full price or a half-price hard seat. Children shorter than 1.1m ride free, but you have to hold them the entire journey.

If you're taking a stroller with you, prepare for the inconvenience of uneven pavements littered with bicycles and other objects. Escalators at metro stations are often up only.

Many sights and museums have children's admission prices, which usually apply to children under 1.1m or 1.3m in height. Infants under the age of two fly for 10% of the full airfare, while children between the ages of two and 11 pay half the full price for domestic flights and 75% of the adult price for international flights.

Always ensure that your child carries a form of ID and a hotel card in case they get lost.

Ask a doctor specialising in travel medicine for information on recommended immunisations for your child.

For more information on travelling with children, consult the following:

» *Travel with Children* (Brigitte Barta et al)

» *Travelling Abroad with Children* (Samantha Gore-Lyons)

» *Take the Kids Travelling* (Helen Truszkowski)

» *Backpacking with Babies and Small Children* (Goldie Silverman)

» *Adventuring with Children* (Nan Jeffrey)

Customs Regulations

Chinese customs generally pay tourists little attention. There are clearly marked 'green channels' and 'red channels' at the airport. Some travellers have had their Lonely Planet guides confiscated at the (usually Vietnam) border (see the boxed text, p607).

Duty free, you're allowed to import 400 cigarettes or the equivalent in tobacco products; 1.5L of alcohol; 50g of gold or silver; and a camera, video camera and similar items for personal use only. Importation of fresh fruit and cold cuts is prohibited.

You can legally only bring in or take out Y6000 in Chinese currency, although there are no restrictions on foreign currency (but declare any cash exceeding US$5000 or its equivalent in another currency).

You are not allowed to import or export illegal drugs, or animals and plants (including seeds). Pirated DVDs and CDs are illegal exports from China as well as illegal imports into most other countries – if found they will be confiscated. You can take Chinese medicine up to a value of Y300 when you depart China.

Objects considered to be antiques require a certificate and a red seal to clear customs when leaving China. Anything made before 1949 is considered an antique, and if it was made before 1795 it cannot legally be taken out of the country. To get the proper certificate and red seal, your antiques must be inspected by the **Relics Bureau** (Wénwù Jú; ☎010-6401 9714, no English spoken) in Běijīng.

Discount Cards

Seniors over the age of 65 are frequently eligible for a discount, so make sure you take your passport when visiting sights as proof of age.

An **International Student Identity Card** (ISIC; €12) can net students half-price discounts at many sights. Firstly examine the ticket price board at sights to see whether students are eligible for a discount and then, forcefully if necessary, insist on a discount.

Embassies & Consulates

Embassies

There are two main embassy compounds in Běijīng – **Jiànguóménwài** and **Sānlǐtún** (Map p66). Embassies are open from 9am to noon and 1.30pm to 4pm Monday to Friday, but visa departments are often only open in the morning. For visas, you need to phone up to make an appointment.

Australia (☎010-5140 4111; www.china.embassy.gov.au; 21 Dongzhimenwai Dajie)

Canada (☎010-5139 4000; fax 010-6532 4072; www.canada.org.cn; 19 Dongzhimenwai Dajie)

France (☎010-8532 8080; fax 010-6532 4757; www.ambafrance-cn.org; 3 Sanlitun Dongsanjie)

Germany (☎010-8532 9000; fax 010-6532 5336; www.peking.diplo.de; 17 Dongzhimenwai Dajie)

India (☎010-6532 1908; fax 010-6532 4684; www.indianembassy.org.cn; 1 Ritan Donglu)

Ireland (☎010-6532 2691; fax 010-6532 6857; www.embassyofireland.cn; 3 Ritan Donglu)

Kazakhstan (☎010-6532 6182; fax 010-6532 6183; 9 Sanlitun Dongliujie)

Laos (☎010-6532 1224; 11 Sanlitun Dongsijie)

Mongolia (☎010-6532 1203; fax 010-6532 5045; www.mongolembassychina.org; 2 Xiushui Beijie)

Myanmar (☎010-6532 0351; fax 010-6532 4208; www.myanmarembassy.com/chinese; 6 Dongzhimenwai Dajie)

Nepal (☎010-6532 1795; fax 010-6532 3251; www.nepalembassy.org.cn; 1 Sanlitun Xi Liujie)

Netherlands (☎010-8532 0200; fax 010-8532 0300; www.hollandinchina.org; 4 Liangmahe Nanlu)

New Zealand (☎010-8532 7000; fax 010-6532 4317; www.nzembassy.com/china; 1 Ritan Dong Erjie)

North Korea (☎010-6532 1186; fax 010-6532 6056; 11 Ritan Beilu)

Pakistan (☎010-6532 2504/2558; fax 010-6532 2715; 1 Dongzhimenwai Dajie)

Russia (☎010-6532 1381; fax 010-6532 4851; www.russia.org.cn; 4 Dongzhimen Beizhongjie)

UK (☎010-5192 4000; fax 010-5192 4239; http://ukinchina.fco.gov.uk; 11 Guanghua Lu)

USA (☎010-8531 3000; fax 010- 8531 4200; http://beijing.usembassy-china.org.cn; 55 Anjialou Lu)

Vietnam (☎010-6532 1155; fax 010-6532 5720; www.vnemba.org.cn; 32 Guanghua Lu)

Consulates

CHÉNGDŪ

France (☎028-6666 6060; 30th fl, Times Sq, 2 Zongtongfu Lu)

Germany (☎028-8528 0800; 25th fl, Western Tower, 19 Renmin Nanlu 4th Section)

Pakistan (☎028-8526 8316; 8th fl, Western Tower, 19 Renmin Nanlu 4th Section)

South Korea (☎028-8616 5800; 19th fl, Tianfu Oasis Tower, 2 Xianan Dajie)

USA (☎028-8558 3992; 4 Lingshiguan Lu)

CHÓNGQÌNG

Canada (☎023-6373 8007; 17th fl, Metropolitan Tower, Zourong Lu)

UK (☎023-6369 1500; 28th fl, Metropolitan Tower, Zourong Lu)

GUǍNGZHŌU

Australia (☎020-3814 0111; fax 020-3814 0112; 12th fl, Development Centre, 3 Liujiang Dadao)

PRACTICALITIES

» There are four types of plugs – three-pronged angled pins, three-pronged round pins, two flat pins or two narrow round pins. Electricity is 220 volts, 50 cycles AC.

» The standard English-language newspaper is the *China Daily* (www.chinadaily.com.cn). China's largest circulation Chinese-language daily is the *People's Daily (Rénmín Rìbào)*. It has an English-language edition on www.english.peopledaily.com.cn. Imported English-language newspapers can be bought from five-star hotel bookshops.

» Listen to the **BBC World Service** (www.bbc.co.uk/worldservice/tuning) or **Voice of America** (www.voa.gov); however, the websites can be jammed. Chinese Central TV (CCTV) has an English language channel – CCTV9. Your hotel may have ESPN, Star Sports, CNN or BBC News 24.

» China officially subscribes to the international metric system, but you will encounter the ancient Chinese weights and measures system that features the *liǎng* (tael, 37.5g) and the *jīn* (catty, 0.6kg). There are 10 *liǎng* to the *jīn*.

Canada (☎020-8611 6100; fax 020-8611 6196; Room 801, China Hotel Office Tower, Liuhua Lu)

France (☎020-2829 2000; fax 020-2829 2001; Room 810, 8th fl, Main Tower, Guangdong International Hotel, 339 Huanshi Donglu)

Germany (☎020-8313 0000; fax 020-8516 8133; 14th fl, Main Tower, Yuehai Tianhe Bldg, 208 Tianhe Lu)

India (☎020-8550 1501; 14th fl, Skyframe Tower, 8 Linhe Zhonglu)

Netherlands (☎020-3813 2200; fax 020-3813 2299; Teem Tower, 208 Tianhe Lu)

New Zealand (☎020-8667 0253; Room 1055, China Hotel Office Tower, Liuhua Lu)

Russia (☎020-8518 5001; 26a Fazhan Zhongxin Bldg, 3 Linjiang Dadao)

UK (☎020-8314 3000; fax 020-8332 7509; 2nd fl, Main Tower, Guangdong International Hotel, 339 Huanshi Donglu)

USA (☎020-8121 8000; fax 020-8121 8428; 5th fl, Tianyu Garden, 136-142 Linhe Zhonglu)

HOHHOT

Mongolia (Ménggǔ Lǐngshìguǎn; ☎0471-492 3819; Unit 1, Bldg 5, Wulan Residential Compound)

HONG KONG

Australia (☎852-2827 8881; 23rd fl, Harbour Centre, 25 Harbour Rd, Wan Chai)

Canada (☎852-2810 4321; 11-14th fl, Tower I, Exchange Sq, 8 Connaught Pl, Central)

France (☎852-3196 6100; 26th fl, Tower II, Admiralty Centre, 18 Harcourt Rd, Admiralty)

Germany (☎852-2105 8788; 21st fl, United Centre, 95 Queensway, Admiralty)

India (☎852-2528 4018; 26a United Centre, 95 Queensway, Admiralty)

Ireland (☎852-2527 4897; 1408 Two Pacific Pl, 88 Queensway, Admiralty)

Laos (☎852-2544 1186; 14th fl, Arion Commercial Centre, 2-12 Queen's Rd West, Sheung Wan)

Nepal (☎852-2369 7813; 715 China Aerospace Tower, Concordia Plaza, 1 Science Museum Rd, Tsim Sha Tsui)

Netherlands (☎852-2522 5127; Room 5702, 57th fl, Cheung Kong Centre, 2 Queen's Rd, Central)

New Zealand (☎852-2877 4488, 2525 5044; Room 6508, 65th fl, Central Plaza, 18 Harbour Rd, Wan Chai)

Russia (☎852-2877 7188; 21st fl, Sun Hung Kai Centre, 30 Harbour Rd, Wan Chai)

UK (☎852-2901 3000; 1 Supreme Court Rd, Admiralty)

USA (☎852-2523 9011; 26 Garden Rd, Central)

Vietnam (☎852-2591 4510; vnconsul@netvigator.com; 15th fl, Great Smart Tower, 230 Wan Chai Rd, Wan Chai)

KŪNMÍNG

Laos (☎0871-316 8916; Ground fl, Kunming Diplomat Compound, 6800 Caiyun Beilu)

Myanmar (☎0871-364 1268; B504 Longyuan Haozhai, 166 Weiyuan Jie)

Thailand (☎0871-316 8961; fax 0871-316 6891; Ground fl, South Wing, Kunming Hotel, 145 Dongfeng Donglu)

Vietnam (☎0871-352 2669; 2nd fl, Kai Wah International Hotel, 157 Beijing Lu)

LHASA

Nepal (☎0891-681 5744; fax 0891-683 6890; 13 Norbulingka Lu) On a side street between the Lhasa Hotel and Norbulingka.

QĪNGDǍO

Japan (☎0532-8090 0001; fax 0532-8090 0009; 59 Xianggang Donglu)

South Korea (☎0532-8897 6001; fax 0532-8897 6005; 8 Qinling Lu)

SHÀNGHǍI

Australia (☎021-2215 5200; www.shanghai.china.embassy.gov.au; 22nd fl, CITIC Sq, 1168 West Nanjing Rd)

Canada (☎021-3279 2800; www.shanghai.gc.ca; Suite 604, West Tower, Shànghǎi Centre, 1376 Nanjing Xilu)

France (☎021-6103 2200; www.consulfrance-shanghai.org; 2nd fl, 689 Guangdong Lu)

Germany (☎021-3401 0106; www.shanghai.diplo.de; 181 Yongfu Lu)

India (☎021-6275 8881; 1008 Shanghai International Trade Centre, 2201 Yan'an Xilu)

Ireland (☎021-6279 8729; 700a Shànghǎi Centre, 1376 Nanjing Xilu)

Japan (☎021-5257 4766; www.shanghai.cn.emb-japan.go.jp; 8 Wanshan Lu)

Nepal (☎021-6272 0259; 16a, 669 Beijing Xilu)

Netherlands (☎021-2208 7288; 10th fl, Tower B, Dawning Center, 500 Hongbaoshi Lu)

New Zealand (☎021-5407 5858; 16th fl, The Centre, 989 Changle Lu)

Russia (☎021-6324 8383; fax 021-6324 2682; 20 Huangpu Lu)

UK (☎021-3279 2000; fax 021-6279 7651; Room 319, 3rd fl, Shànghǎi Centre, 1376 Nanjing Xilu)

USA (http://shanghai.usembassy-china.org.cn) French Concession (☎021-6279 7662; 1469 Huaihai Zhonglu); Jìng'ān (☎021-3217 4650, after-hours emergency number for US citizens 021-6433 3936; 8th fl, Westgate Tower, 1038 West Nanjing Rd)

SHĚNYÁNG

France (☎024-2319 0000; fax 024-2319 0001; 34 Nanshisan Weilu)

North Korea (☎024-8690 3451; fax 024-8690 3482; 37 Beiling Dajie) North Korea visas are more likely to be obtained at the North Korean embassy in Běijīng.

Russia (☎024-2322 3927; fax 024-2322 3907; 31 Nanshisan Weilu)

South Korea (☎024-2385 3388; 37 Nanshisan Weilu)

USA (☎024-2322 1198; fax 024-2323 1465; 52 Shisi Weilu)

ÜRÜMQI

Kazakhstan (Hāsàkèsītǎn Lǐngshìguǎn; ☎0991-381 5796; 31 Kunming Lu) If you're applying for a visa, show up early and don't expect calls to be taken. A taxi here will cost about Y30. If you take bus 2 to Xiǎo Xī Gōu, turn right at the first intersection and then again five minutes later; this will put you on Kunming Lu. From there it's a five-minute walk.

WǓHÀN

France (☎027-6579 7900; fax 027-8577 8426; Rooms 1701-1708, Wuhan International Trade Center, 568 Jianshe Dadao)

Gay & Lesbian Travellers

Despite China's florid homosexual traditions, the puritanical overseers of the Chinese Communist Party (CCP) have worked tirelessly to suppress them. Greater tolerance exists in the big cities than in the more conservative countryside. However, even in urban areas, gay and lesbian visitors should not be too open about their sexual orientation in public. You will often see Chinese same-sex friends holding hands or putting their arms around each other, but this usually has no sexual connotation.

Utopia (www.utopia-asia.com/tipschin.htm) has tips on travelling in China and a complete listing of gay bars nationwide. Useful publications include the *Spartacus International Gay Guide* (Bruno Gmunder Verlag), a best-selling guide for gay travellers.

Insurance

A travel-insurance policy to cover theft, loss, trip cancellation and medical problems is a good idea. Travel agents can sort this out for you, although it is often cheaper to find good deals with an insurer online or with a broker. Worldwide travel insurance is available at www.lonelyplanet.com/travel_services. You can buy, extend and claim online anytime – even if you're already on the road.

Some policies specifically exclude 'dangerous activities' such as scuba diving, skiing and even trekking. A locally acquired motorcycle licence is not valid under some policies. Check that the policy covers ambulances or an emergency flight home.

Paying for your airline ticket with a credit card often provides limited travel accident insurance – ask your credit-card company what it's prepared to cover.

You may prefer a policy that pays doctors or hospitals directly rather than reimbursing you for expenditures after the fact. If you have to claim later, ensure you keep all documentation.

See also the Insurance section (p1009) in the Health chapter.

Internet Access

China's clumsy tango with the internet continues to raise eyebrows abroad. The number of internet-cafe licences is strictly controlled, users need to show ID before going online and in some internet cafes (网吧; *wǎngbā*) – eg in Běijīng – you will be digitally photographed (by a camera in an innocuous metal box on the registration counter). Rules are rigorously enforced in big cities such as Běijīng, but are more relaxed in small towns. At the time of writing, however, internet cafes in some regions of China were insisting users provide a valid Chinese ID (impossible for foreign travellers to produce).

Up to 10% of websites are traditionally inaccessible in China due to censorship. If you're checking emails, reading foreign newspapers online and chatting with friends, China's internet cafes are generally trouble-free, even though access to some newspapers and other links can suddenly vanish. Video-sharing sites have also come under control.

Internet cafes are listed under the Information section for destinations throughout the book. In large cities and towns, the area around the train station is generally a good place to find internet cafes.

Rates at internet cafes should be around Y2 to Y5 per hour for a standard, no-frills outlet. There are usually different priced zones, with the common area (普通区; *pǔtōng qū*) the cheapest. Rates also vary depending on what time you go online; daytime is cheapest, night-time is more expensive. Deposits of Y10 are sometimes required.

Internet-cafe opening hours can be 8am to midnight or, more commonly, 24 hours.

Youth hostels and other backpacker hotels should have internet access in common areas; if access is not gratis, rates will be around Y5 per hour. Many midrange and top-end hotels provide free broadband internet access as standard; many also have wi-fi areas. Throughout this book the internet icon (@) is used in hotel reviews to indicate the presence of an internet cafe or a terminal where you can get online; wi-fi areas are indicated with a wi-fi icon (wi-fi).

Many cafe chains and tourist hotels now have broadband wi-fi access.

Language Courses

When searching for Chinese-language schools, weigh up the fees and syllabus carefully as many outfits charge expensive fees while using teaching methods that may not suit Westerners. Most schools just teach Mandarin as it is the lingua franca of the entire nation, but other schools also offer classes in Cantonese. Also think about where you would like to study: Běijīng may sound enticing as the Běijīng accent has such cachet, but it will be years before you can successfully mimic the intonation, while a course in a delightful setting such as Yángshuò in Guǎngxī province may be more memorable an experience.

Legal Matters

Anyone under the age of 18 is considered a minor; the minimum age at which you can drive is also 18. The age of consent for marriage is 22 for men and 20 for women. There is no minimum age restricting the consumption of alcohol or use of cigarettes.

China's laws against the use of illegal drugs are harsh, and foreign nationals have been executed for drug offences (trafficking in more than 50g of heroin can result in the death penalty); in 2009 a British citizen was executed for smuggling drugs (despite protestations that he was mentally impaired). The Chinese criminal justice system does not ensure a fair trial and defendants are not presumed innocent until proven guilty. Note that China conducts more judicial executions than the rest of the world put together – up to 10,000 per year (27 per day) according to some estimates. If arrested, most foreign citizens have the right to contact their embassy.

Money

Consult the Need to Know chapter (p18) for a table of exchange rates.

The Chinese currency is the renminbi (RMB), or 'people's money'. The basic unit of RMB is the yuán (元; Y), which is divided into 10 jiǎo (角), which is again divided into 10 fēn (分). Colloquially, the yuán is referred to as kuài and jiǎo as máo (毛). The fēn has so little value these days that it is rarely used.

The Bank of China issues RMB bills in denominations of Y1, Y2, Y5, Y10, Y20, Y50 and Y100. Coins come in denominations of Y1, 5 jiǎo, 1 jiǎo and 5 fēn. Paper versions of the coins remain in circulation.

Hong Kong's currency is the Hong Kong dollar (HK$). The Hong Kong dollar is divided into 100 cents. Bills are issued in denominations of HK$10, HK$20, HK$50, HK$100, HK$500 and HK$1000. Copper coins are worth 50c, 20c and 10c, while the $5, $2 and $1 coins are silver and the $10 coin is nickel and bronze. The Hong Kong dollar is pegged to the US dollar at a rate of US$1 to HK$7.80, though it is allowed to fluctuate a little.

Macau's currency is the pataca (MOP$), which is divided into 100 avos. Bills are issued in denominations of MOP$10, MOP$20, MOP$50, MOP$100, MOP$500 and MOP$1000. There are copper coins worth 10, 20 and 50 avos and silver-coloured MOP$1, MOP$2, MOP$5 and MOP$10 coins. The pataca is pegged to the Hong Kong dollar at a rate of MOP$103.20 to HK$100. In effect, the two currencies are interchangeable and Hong Kong dollars, including coins, are accepted in Macau. Chinese renminbi is also accepted in many places in Macau at one-to-one. You can't spend patacas anywhere else, however, so use them before you leave Macau. Prices quoted in this book are in yuán unless otherwise stated.

ATMs

Bank of China and the Industrial & Commercial Bank of

China (ICBC) 24-hour ATMs are plentiful, and you can use Visa, MasterCard, Cirrus, Maestro Plus and American Express to withdraw cash. All ATMs accepting international cards have dual language ability. The network is largely found in sizeable towns and cities. If you plan on staying in China for a long period, it is advisable to open an account at a bank with a nationwide network of ATMs, such as the Bank of China. In larger cities, you will be able to find HSBC and Citibank ATMs.

The exchange rate on ATM withdrawals is similar to that for credit cards, but there is a maximum daily withdrawal amount.

ATMs are listed in the Information sections of destinations throughout this book. To have money wired from abroad, visit Western Union or Moneygram (www.moneygram.com).

Credit Cards

Credit is not big in China. The older generation doesn't like debt, however short-term. Although it is increasingly fashionable for young Chinese to use credit cards, numbers remain low compared to the West. Banks like Bank of China, ICBC, China Construction Bank and Zhaoshang Bank all issue credit cards and are trying to encourage the Chinese to spend. In large tourist towns such as Běijīng, credit cards are relatively straightforward to use, but don't expect to be able to use them everywhere, and always carry enough cash; the exception is in Hong Kong, where international credit cards are accepted almost everywhere (although some shops may try to add a surcharge to offset the commission charged by credit companies, which can range from 2.5% to 7%).

Where they are accepted, credit cards often deliver a slightly better exchange rate than in banks. Money can also be withdrawn at certain ATMs in large cities on credit cards such as Visa, MasterCard and Amex. Credit cards generally can't be used to buy train tickets, but Civil Aviation Administration of China (CAAC; 中国民航; Zhōngguó Mínháng) offices readily accept international Visa cards for buying air tickets.

Moneychangers

It's best to wait till you reach China to exchange money as the exchange rate will be better. Foreign currency and travellers cheques can be changed at border crossings, international airports, branches of the Bank of China, tourist hotels and some large department stores; hours of operation for foreign-exchange counters are 8am to 7pm (later at hotels). Top-end hotels will generally change money for hotel guests only. The official rate is given almost everywhere and the exchange charge is standardised, so there is little need to shop around for the best deal.

Australian, Canadian, US, UK, Hong Kong and Japanese currencies and the euro can be changed in China. In some backwaters, it may be hard to change lesser-known currencies; US dollars are still the easiest to change.

Keep at least a few of your exchange receipts. You will need them if you want to exchange any remaining RMB you have at the end of your trip.

Tipping

Almost no one in China (including Hong Kong and Macau) asks for tips. Tipping used to be refused in restaurants, but nowadays many midrange and top-end eateries include their own (often huge) service charge; cheap restaurants do not expect a tip. Taxi drivers throughout China do not ask for or expect tips.

Travellers Cheques

These are worth taking with you if you are principally travelling in large cities and tourist areas. Travellers cheques cannot be used everywhere, however; as with credit cards, always ensure you carry enough ready cash. You should have no problem cashing travellers cheques at tourist hotels, but they are of little use in budget hotels and restaurants. Bear in mind that most hotels will only cash the cheques of guests. If cashing them at banks, aim for the larger banks such as the Bank of China or ICBC. Some banks won't change travellers cheques at the weekend.

Cheques from most of the world's leading banks and issuing agencies are now accepted in China; stick to the major companies such as Thomas Cook, Amex and Visa, however. In big cities travellers cheques are accepted in almost any currency, but in smaller destinations it's best to stick to big currencies such as US dollars or UK pounds. Keep your exchange receipts so you can change your money back to its original currency when you leave.

Passports

You must have a passport with you at all times; it is the most basic travel document and all hotels (and some internet cafes) will insist on seeing it. The Chinese government requires that your passport be valid for at least six months after the expiry date of your visa. You will need at least one entire blank page in your passport for the visa.

Take an ID card with your photo in case you lose your passport. Even better, make photocopies of your passport – your embassy may need these before issuing a new one. You should also report the loss to the local Public Security Bureau (PSB). Be careful who you pass your passport to, as you may never see it again.

Long-stay visitors should register their passport with their embassy.

Post

The international postal service is efficient, and airmail letters and postcards will probably take between five and 10 days to reach their destinations. Domestic post is swift – perhaps one or two days from Guǎngzhōu to Běijīng. Intracity post may be delivered the same day it's sent.

Postcards to overseas destinations cost Y4.50, and airmail letters up to 20g cost Y5 to Y7 to all overseas destinations except Taiwan and Hong Kong and Macau (Y1.50); domestic letters cost Y0.80 and postcards Y0.50. As elsewhere, China charges extra for registered mail, but it offers cheaper postal rates for printed matter, small packets, parcels, bulk mailings and so on.

China Post operates an express mail service (EMS) that is fast, reliable and ensures that the package is sent by registered post. Parcels sent to domestic destinations by EMS cost Y20 (up to 200g; Y5 for each additional 200g). International EMS charges vary according to country; sample minimum rates (parcels up to 500g) include Y164 to Australia, Y184 to the USA and Y224 to the UK. Not all branches of China Post have EMS.

Major tourist hotels have branch post offices where you can send letters, packets and parcels, but you may only be able to post printed matter. Other parcels may need to be sent from the town's main post office, where a contents check will occur and a customs form will be attached to the parcel. Even at cheap hotels you can usually post letters from the front desk.

In major cities, private carriers such as **United Parcel Service** (☎800 820 8388; www.ups.com/content/cn), **DHL** (Dūnháo; ☎800 810 8000; www.cn.dhl.com), **Federal Express** (Liánbāng Kuàidì; ☎800 988 1888; http://fedex.com/cn) and **TNT Skypak** (☎800 820 9868; www.tnt.com/express/zh_cn) have a pick-up service as well as drop-off centres; call their offices for details.

If you are sending items abroad, take them unpacked with you to the post office to be inspected; an appropriate box or envelope will be found for you. Most post offices offer materials for packaging (including padded envelopes, boxes and heavy brown paper), for which you'll be charged. Don't take your own packaging as it will probably be refused. If you have a receipt for the goods, put it in the box when you're mailing it, since the parcel may be opened again by customs further down the line.

Public Holidays

You may get the impression it's Christmas all year round, judging by the pictures of Santa Claus that cling to restaurant walls across the land, whatever the season. The People's Republic of China has 11 national holidays, as follows. Hong Kong and Macau have different holidays; see p488 and p522, respectively, for more information.

New Year's Day 1 January

Chinese New Year 23 January 2012, 10 February 2013

International Women's Day 8 March

Tomb Sweeping Festival 5 April

International Labour Day 1 May

Youth Day 4 May

International Children's Day 1 June

Birthday of the Chinese Communist Party 1 July

Anniversary of the Founding of the People's Liberation Army 1 August

Moon Festival end of September

National Day 1 October

Many of the above are nominal holidays that do not result in leave. The 1 May holiday is a three-day holiday, while National Day marks a week-long holiday from 1 October; the Chinese New Year is also a week-long holiday for many. It's not a great idea to arrive in China or go travelling during these holidays as things tend to grind to a halt. Hotel prices all over China rapidly shoot up during the May and October holiday periods.

Safe Travel

Crime

Travellers are more often the victims of petty economic crime, such as theft, than serious crime. Although an American was stabbed to death in broad daylight in Běijīng in 2008, such crimes are rare. Foreigners are natural targets for pickpockets and thieves – keep your wits about you and make it difficult for thieves to get at your belongings. Incidences of crime increase around the Chinese New Year.

High-risk areas in China are train and bus stations, city and long-distance buses (especially sleeper buses), hard-seat train carriages and public toilets. Don't leave anything of value in your bicycle basket.

Hotels are generally safe and some have attendants on every floor. Dormitories obviously require more care. Don't be overly trusting of your fellow travellers; some of them are considerably less than honest. All hotels have safes and storage areas for valuables – use them.

Carry as much cash as you need and keep the rest in travellers cheques. Obviously you will need to equip yourself with more cash if you're travelling to remote areas, as you may not be able to cash your travellers cheques; take a money belt for your cash, passport and credit cards.

Foreigners have been attacked or killed for their valuables, especially in more rural locations, so be vigilant at all times. Travelling solo carries obvious risks; it's advisable to travel with someone else or in a small group. Female travellers in particular should avoid travelling solo. Even in Běijīng, single women taking taxis have been taken to remote areas and robbed by taxi drivers, so don't assume anywhere is safe.

LOSS REPORTS

If something of yours is stolen, report it immediately to the nearest Foreign Affairs Branch of the PSB. Staff will ask you to fill in a loss report before investigating the case.

If you have travel insurance it is essential to obtain a loss report so you can claim compensation. Be prepared to spend many hours, perhaps even several days, organising it. Make a copy of your passport in case of loss or theft.

Scams

Con artists are not just increasingly widespread in China – methods are becoming ever more audacious. Well-dressed girls flock along Shànghǎi's East Nanjing Rd and Běijīng's Wangfujing Dajie, dragging single men to expensive cafes or Chinese teahouses, leaving them to foot monstrous bills. 'Poor' art students haunt similar neighbourhoods, press-ganging foreigners into art exhibitions where they are coerced into buying trashy art.

Also watch out for itinerant Buddhist monks preying on foreigners for alms. They approach visitors and, after asking them to sign a book, ask for a donation to a temple along the 'give-as-much-as-you-see-fit' line. Another common tactic is for the monk to give you a Buddhist talisman, and then ask for a donation (see the boxed text, p490). Just refuse. Travellers can feel pressured into giving money, and it can also be hard to work out if the monks are genuine or not. This also happens when you walk into a temple and a monk asks you to take a seat and sign a book and then asks for a donation for the rebuilding of one of the temple halls. This is not a scam as such but it is an underhand way of extracting money from foreigners who feel pressured into making a donation.

Also watch out for dodgy tours to the Great Wall (see the boxed text, p101), especially the Bādálǐng section. Also be on your guard against fake alcohol, especially if the cocktail tariff in the bar is too good to be true.

Taxi scams at Běijīng's Capital Airport are legendary; always join the queue at the taxi rank and insist that the taxi driver uses his or her meter. Try to avoid pedicabs and motorised three wheelers wherever possible; we receive a litany of complaints against pedicab drivers who originally agree on a price and then insist on an alternative figure (sometimes 10 times the sum) once arriving at the destination.

There's a plague of dishonest businesses and enterprises: the travel agency you phoned may just be a gang of card-playing sharks cooped up in a cigarette-smoke-filled hotel room.

Be alert at all times if you decide to change money on the black market, which we can't recommend. Those buying black-market train tickets should be aware that not only is this illegal but also that the date, time, destination and ticket type (eg soft sleeper) may be incorrect.

Not a scam as such, but always be alert to being ripped off: foreigners are ripped off without mercy. Exercise caution especially when goods do not have a price label (most of the time). Always examine your restaurant bill carefully for hidden extras.

Transport

China's roads kill without mercy. Traffic accidents are the major cause of death in China for people aged between 15 and 45, and the World Health Organization (WHO) estimates there are 600 traffic deaths per day. At long-distance bus stations across China you may be subjected to posters graphically portraying victims of road crashes; then when you get on the bus you find there are no seatbelts (most of the time) or the seatbelts are virtually unusable through neglect, inextricably stuffed beneath the seat. If you insist on wearing a seatbelt everyone looks at you as if you are quite insane. Outside of the big cities, taxis are unlikely to have rear seatbelts fitted; the taxi driver is bound by law to wear one, but most of the time he will just drape it uselessly across his chest if traffic police are in the vicinity.

Your greatest danger in China will almost certainly be crossing the road, so develop 360-degree vision and a sixth sense. Crossing only when it is safe to do so could perch you at the side of the road in perpetuity, but don't imitate the local tendency to cross without looking. Note that cars can frequently turn on red lights in China, so the green 'walk now' man does not mean it is safe to cross.

Telephone

If making a domestic call, look out for very cheap public phones at newspaper stands (报刊亭; *bàokāntíng*) and hole-in-the-wall shops (小卖部; *xiǎomàibù*); you make your call and then pay the owner. Domestic and international long-distance phone calls can also be made from main telecommunications offices and 'phone bars' (话吧; *huàbā*). Cardless international calls are expensive and it's far cheaper to use an IP card.

Area codes for all cities, towns and destinations appear in the relevant chapters.

Mobile Phones

China Mobile outlets can sell you a SIM card, which will cost from Y60 to Y100 depending on the phone number and will include Y50 of credit. When this runs out, you can top up the number by buying a credit-charging card *(chōngzhí kǎ)* from China Mobile outlets and some newspaper stands.

Phonecards

If you wish to make international calls, it is much cheaper to use an IP card. International calls on IP cards (IP卡; IP *kǎ*) are Y1.80 per minute to the USA or Canada, Y1.50 per minute to Hong Kong, Macau and Taiwan, and Y3.20 to all other countries; domestic long-distance calls are Y0.30 per minute. You dial a local number, then punch in your account number, followed by a pin number and finally the number you wish to call. English-language service is usually available. IP cards can be found at newspaper kiosks, hole-in-the-wall shops, internet cafes and from any China Telecom office, although in some cities they can be hard to find. Some IP cards can only be used locally, while others can be used nationwide, so it is important to buy the right card (and check the expiry date).

Visas

Applying for Visas

FOR CHINA

Apart from citizens of Japan, Singapore and Brunei, all visitors to China require a visa, which covers the whole of China, although there remain restricted areas that require an additional permit from the PSB. Permits are also required for travel to Tibet (see the boxed text, p883), a region that the authorities can suddenly bar foreigners from entering.

Your passport must be valid for at least six months after the expiry date of your visa and you'll need at least one entire blank page in your passport for the visa.

At the time of writing, prices for a standard 30-day visa were as follows:

» £30 for UK citizens
» US$140 for US citizens
» US$30 for citizens of other nations

Double-entry visas:

» £45 for UK citizens
» US$140 for US citizens
» US$45 for all other nationals

Six-month multiple-entry visas:

» £90 for UK citizens
» US$140 for US citizens
» US$60 for all other nationals

A standard 30-day single-entry visa can be issued from most Chinese embassies abroad in three to five working days. Express visas cost twice the usual fee. In some countries (eg the UK and the US), the visa service has been outsourced from the Chinese embassy to a Chinese Visa Application Service Centre, which levies an extra administration fee. In the case of the UK, a single-entry visa costs £30, but the standard administration charge levied by the centre is a further £35.25, making visa applications expensive.

A standard 30-day visa is activated on the date you enter China, and must be used within three months of the date of issue. Sixty-day and 90-day travel visas are harder to get. To stay longer, you can extend your visa in China.

Visa applications require a completed application form (available at the embassy or downloaded from its website) and at least one photo (normally 51mm x 51mm). You normally pay for your visa when you collect it. A visa mailed to you will take up to three weeks. In the US and Canada, mailed visa applications have to go via a visa agent, at extra cost. In the US, many people use the **China Visa Service Center** (☎in the USA 800 799 6560; www.mychinavisa.com), which offers prompt service. The procedure takes around 10 to 14 days.

Hong Kong is a good place to pick up a China visa. China Travel Service (CTS) will be able to obtain one for you, or you can apply directly to the **Visa Office of the People's Republic of China** (Map p480; ☎3413 2300; 7th fl, Lower Block, China Resources Centre, 26 Harbour Rd, Wan Chai; ⊙9am-noon & 2-5pm Mon-Fri). Visas processed here in one/two/three days cost HK$400/300/150. Double-entry visas are HK$220, while six-month/one-year multiple-entry visas are HK$400/600 (plus HK$150/250 for express/urgent service). Be aware that American and UK passport holders must pay considerably more for their visas. You must supply two photos.

Five-day visas (Y160 for most nationalities, Y469 for British, US citizens excluded) are available at the Luóhú border crossing between Hong Kong and Shēnzhèn, valid for Shēnzhèn only.

Three-day visas are also available at the Macau–Zhūhǎi border (Y160 for most nationalities, Y469 for British, US citizens excluded). US citizens have to buy a visa in advance in Macau or Hong Kong.

Be aware that political events can suddenly make visas more difficult to procure or renew.

When asked about your itinerary on the application form, list standard tourist destinations; if you are considering going to Tibet or western Xīnjiāng, just leave it off the form. The list you give is not binding. Those working in media or journalism may want to profess a different occupation; otherwise, a visa may be refused or a shorter length of stay than that requested may be given. There are eight categories of visas (for most travellers, an L visa will be issued):

TYPE	ENGLISH NAME	CHINESE NAME
C	flight attendant	*chéngwù* 乘务
D	resident	*dìngjū* 定居
F	business or student	*fǎngwèn* 访问
G	transit	*guòjìng* 过境
J	journalist	*jìzhě* 记者
L	travel	*lǚxíng* 旅行
X	long-term student	*liúxué* 留学
Z	working	*gōngzuò* 工作

FOR HONG KONG

At the time of writing, most visitors to Hong Kong, including citizens of the EU, Australia, New Zealand, the USA and Canada, could enter and stay for 90 days without a visa. British passport holders get 180 days, while South Africans are allowed to stay 30 days visa-free. If you require a visa, apply at a Chinese embassy or consulate before arriving. If you visit Hong Kong from China, you will need to either have a multiple-entry visa to re-enter China or a new visa.

FOR MACAU

Most travellers, including citizens of the EU, Australia, New Zealand, the USA, Canada and South Africa, can enter Macau without a visa for between 30 and 90 days. Most other nationalities can get a 30-day visa on arrival, which will cost MOP$100/50/200 per adult/child under 12/family. If you're visiting Macau from China and plan to re-enter China, you will need to be on a multiple-entry visa.

Visa Extensions

FOR CHINA

The Foreign Affairs Branch of the local PSB deals with visa extensions.

First-time extensions of 30 days are usually easy to obtain on single-entry tourist visas; further extensions are harder to get, and may only give you another week. Travellers report generous extensions in provincial towns, but don't bank on this. Popping across to Hong Kong to apply for a new tourist visa is another option.

Extensions to single-entry visas vary in price, depending on your nationality. At the time of writing, US travellers paid Y185, Canadians Y165, UK citizens Y160 and Australians Y100. Expect to wait up to five days for your visa extension to be processed.

The penalty for overstaying your visa in China is up to Y500 per day. Some travellers have reported having trouble with officials who read the 'valid until' date on their visa incorrectly. For a one-month travel (L) visa, the 'valid until' date is the date by which you must enter the country (within three months of the date the visa was issued), not the date upon which your visa expires.

FOR HONG KONG

For tourist-visa extensions, inquire at the **Hong Kong Immigration Department** (Map p480; ☎2852 3047; www.immd.gov.hk; 2nd fl, Immigration Tower, 7 Gloucester Rd, Wan Chai; ⌚8.45am-4.30pm Mon-Fri, 9-11.30am Sat). Extensions (HK$160) are not readily granted unless there are extenuating circumstances such as illness.

FOR MACAU

If your visa expires, you can obtain a single one-month extension from the **Macau Immigration Department** (Map p512; ☎2872 5488; Ground fl, Travessa da Amizade; ⌚9am-5pm Mon-Fri).

Residence Permits

The 'green card' is a residence permit, issued to English teachers, foreign expats and long-term students who live in China. Green cards are issued for a period of six months to one year and must be renewed annually. Besides needing all the right paperwork, you must also pass a health exam, for which there is a charge. Families are automatically included once the permit is issued, but there is a fee for each family member. If you lose your card, you'll pay a hefty fee to have it replaced.

Volunteering

Large numbers of Westerners work in China with international development charities such as **VSO** (www.vso.org.uk), which can provide you with useful experience and the chance to learn Chinese.

Global Vision International (GVI; www.gvi.co.uk) Teaching in China.

Global Volunteer Network (www.globalvolunteernetwork.org) Connecting people with communities in need.

Joy in Action (JIA; www.jia-workcamp.org) Establishing work camps in places in need in south China.

World Teach (www.worldteach.org) Volunteer teachers.

Transport

GETTING THERE & AWAY

Flights, tours and rail tickets can be booked online at www.lonelyplanet.com/bookings.

Entering China

No particular difficulties exist for travellers entering China. The main requirements are a passport that's valid for travel for six months after the expiry date of your visa and a visa (see p992). As a general rule, visas cannot be obtained at the border (apart from five-day visas for Shēnzhèn at the Hong Kong–Shēnzhèn border and three-day visas at the Zhūhǎi–Macau border). In general, visas are not required for Hong Kong or Macau; if you enter Hong Kong or Macau from China and wish to re-enter China, you'll need either a multiple-entry visa or a new visa. For travel to Tibet, see the boxed text on p883. Chinese immigration officers are scrupulous and highly bureaucratic, but not overly officious. Travellers arriving in China will be given a health declaration form and an arrivals form to complete.

Air

Airports

Hong Kong, Běijīng and Shànghǎi are China's principal international air gateways.

Báiyún International Airport (CAN; Xīnbáiyún Jīchǎng; ☎020-36066999) In Guǎngzhōu; receiving an increasing number of international flights.

Capital Airport (PEK; Shǒudū Jīchǎng; ☎010-6454 1100; http://en.bcia.com.cn) Běijīng's international airport; three terminals.

Hong Kong International Airport (HKG; ☎852-2181 8888; www.hkairport.com) Located at Chek Lap Kok on Lantau island in the west of the territory.

Hóngqiáo Airport (SHA; Hóngqiáo Jīchǎng; ☎021-6268 8899/3659) In Shànghǎi's west; domestic flights.

Pǔdōng International Airport (PVG; Pǔdōng Guójì Jīchǎng; ☎021-96990; http://www.shanghaiairport.com) In Shànghǎi's east; international flights.

Airlines flying to/from China

The following list comprises airlines flying into Běijīng, Hong Kong, Shànghǎi, Kūnmíng and Macau; for all other cities, see the relevant destination section.

Aeroflot Russian Airlines (SU; www.aeroflot.ru) Běijīng (☎010-6500 2412); Hong Kong (☎852-2537 2611); Shànghǎi (☎021-6279 8033)

Air Canada (AC; www.aircanada.ca) Běijīng (☎010-6468 2001); Hong Kong (☎852-2867 8111); Shànghǎi (☎021-6279 2999)

Air China (CA; www.airchina.com.cn) Běijīng (☎4008 100 999); Hong Kong (☎852-3970 9000); Shànghǎi (☎021 5239 7227)

Air France (AF; www.airfrance.com) Běijīng (☎010-6588 1388); Hong Kong (☎852-2501 9433); Shànghǎi (☎4008 808 808)

Air Macau (NX; www.airmacau.com.mo) Běijīng (☎010-6515 8988); Macau (☎853-396 5555); Shànghǎi (☎021-6248 1110)

Air New Zealand (NZ; ☎in Hong Kong 852-2862 8988; www.airnewzealand.com)

AirAsia (FD; ☎in Macau 853-2886 1388; www.airasia.com)

Alitalia (AZ; www.alitalia.com) Běijīng (☎010-6501 4861); Shànghǎi (☎021-6103 1133)

All Nippon Airways (NH; www.ana.co.jp) Běijīng (☎800 820 1122); Hong Kong (☎852-2810 7100); Shànghǎi (☎021-5696 2525)

American Airlines (AA; www.aa.com) Běijīng (☎010-5879 7600); Shànghǎi (☎021-6375 8686)

Asiana Airlines (OZ; www.us.flyasiana.com) Běijīng (☎010-6468 4000); Hong Kong (☎852-2523 8585); Shànghǎi (☎4006 508 000)

Austrian Airlines (OS; www.aua.com) Běijīng (☎010-6462 2161); Shànghǎi (☎021-6340 3411)

British Airways (BA; www.british-airways.com) Běijīng (☎010 6512 4070); Hong

Kong (☎852-3071 5083); Shànghǎi (☎1080 0440 0031)

Cathay Pacific (CX; www.cathaypacific.com) Běijīng (☎010-8486 8532); Hong Kong (☎852-2747 1888)

China Airlines (CI; ☎in Hong Kong 852-2868 2299; www.china-airlines.com)

China Eastern Airlines (MU; www.ce-air.com) Běijīng (☎010-6602 4070); Hong Kong (☎852-2861 1898); Shànghǎi (☎021-95108)

China Southern Airlines (CZ; www.cs-air.com) Běijīng (☎010-950 333); Hong Kong (☎852-2929 5033); Shànghǎi (☎021-950 333)

Dragonair (KA; www.dragonair.com) Běijīng (☎010-6518 2533); Hong Kong (☎852-3193 3888); Kūnmíng (☎0871-356 1208/9); Shànghǎi (☎021-6375 6375)

El Al Israel Airlines (LY; www.elal.co.il) Běijīng (☎010-6597 4512); Hong Kong (☎852-2380 3362)

Emirates Airline (EK; ☎in Hong Kong 852-2801 8777; www.emirates.com)

Ethiopian Airlines (ET; ☎in Hong Kong 852-2117 0223; www.flyethiopian.com)

EVA Airways (BR; www.evaair.com) Hong Kong (☎852-2380 3362); Macau (☎853-2872 6866)

Garuda Indonesia (GA; www.garuda-indonesia.com) Běijīng (☎010-6505 2901); Hong Kong (☎852-2840 0000)

Hong Kong Airlines (HX; ☎in Hong Kong 852-2155 1888; www.hkairlines.com)

Iran Air (IR; ☎in Běijīng 010-6512 4945; www.iranair.com)

Japan Airlines (JL; www.jal.com) Běijīng (☎010-6513 0822); Hong Kong (☎852-2523 0081); Shànghǎi (☎021-6288 3000) Also flies to Qīngdǎo, Dàlián and Xiàmén.

Kenya Airways (KQ; ☎in Hong Kong 852-3678 2000; www.kenya-airways.com)

KLM (KL; www.klm.nl) Běijīng (☎010-6505 3505); Hong Kong (☎852-2808 2168); Shànghǎi (☎4008 808 222)

Korean Air (KE; www.koreanair.com) Běijīng (☎010-8453 8137); Hong Kong (☎852-2366 2001); Shànghǎi (☎021-6275 2000) Also flies to Qīngdǎo and Shěnyáng.

Koryo Air (JS; ☎in Běijīng 010-6501 1557)

Lao Airlines (QV; ☎in Kūnmíng 0871-312 5748; www.laoairlines.com)

Lufthansa Airlines (LH; www.lufthansa.com) Běijīng (☎010-6468 8838); Shànghǎi (☎021-5352 4999)

Malaysia Airlines (MH; www.malaysia-airlines.com.my) Běijīng (☎010-6505 2681); Hong Kong (☎852-2916 0088); Kūnmíng (☎0871-316 5888); Shànghǎi (☎021-6279 8607)

MIAT Mongolian Airlines (OM; ☎in Běijīng 010-6507 9297; www.miat.com)

Nepal Airlines (TG; www.royalnepal-airlines.com) Běijīng (☎010-6505 5071); Hong Kong (☎852-2375 2180); Shànghǎi (☎021-6270 8352)

Northwest Airlines (NW; www.nwa.com) Běijīng (☎010-6505 1353); Hong Kong (☎852-2810 4288); Shànghǎi (☎4008 140 081)

Pakistan International Airlines (PK; www.piac.com.pk) Běijīng (☎010-6505 1681); Hong Kong (☎852-2366 4770)

Philippine Airlines (PR; ☎in Hong Kong 852-2301 9300; www.philippineairlines.com)

Qantas Airways (QF; www.qantas.com.au) Běijīng (☎010-6567 9006); Hong Kong (☎852-2822 9000); Shànghǎi (☎021-6145 0188)

Qatar Airways (QR; ☎in Hong Kong 852-2868 9833; www.qatarairways.com)

Scandinavian Airlines (SK; www.sas.dk) Běijīng (☎010-8527 6100); Shànghǎi (☎021-5228 5001)

Shanghai Airlines (www.shanghai-air.com) Hong Kong (☎852-3586 2238); Shànghǎi (☎021-6255 0550, 800 620 8888)

Singapore Airlines (SQ; www.singaporeair.com) Běijīng (☎010-6505 2233); Hong Kong (☎852-2520 2233); Shànghǎi (☎021-6288 7999)

Swiss International Airlines (LX; ☎in Hong Kong 852-3002 1330; www.swiss.com)

Thai Airways International (TG; www.thaiairways.com) Běijīng (☎010-6460 8899); Hong Kong (☎852-2179 7777); Kūnmíng (☎0871-351 1515); Shànghǎi (☎021-8515 0088)

Tiger Airways (TR; ☎in Hong Kong 852-2116 8730; www.tigerairways.com)

Trans Asia Airways (GE; ☎in Macau 853-2870 3438/1777; www.tna.com.tw)

United Airlines (UA; www.ual.com) Běijīng (☎010-6463 1111); Hong Kong (☎852-2810 4888); Shànghǎi (☎021-3311 4567)

Uzbekistan Airways (HY; www.uzairways.com) Běijīng (☎010-6500 6442); Shànghǎi (☎021-6307 1896)

Vietnam Airlines (VN; ☎in Hong Kong 852-2810 4896; www.vietnamair.com.vn)

Virgin Atlantic (VS; www.virgin-atlantic.com) Hong Kong (☎852-2532 6060); Shànghǎi (☎021-5353 4600)

Viva Macau (ZG; www.flyvivamacau.com)

Tickets

The cheapest tickets to Hong Kong and China can often be found either online or in discount agencies in Chinatowns around the world. Budget and student-travel agents offer cheap tickets, but the real bargains are with agents that deal with the Chinese, who regularly return home. Airfares to China peak between June and September.

The cheapest flights to China are with airlines requiring a stopover at the home airport, such as Air France to

Běijīng via Paris, or Malaysia Airlines to Běijīng via Kuala Lumpur.

The best direct ticket deals are available from China's international carriers, such as China Eastern.

The cheapest available airline ticket is called an APEX (advance purchase excursion) ticket, although this type of ticket includes expensive penalties for cancellation and changing dates of travel. For browsing and buying tickets on the internet, try **Fly China** (www.flychina.com).

To bid for last-minute tickets online, try **Skyauction** (www.skyauction.com). **Priceline** (www.priceline.com) aims to match the ticket price to your budget.

Discounted air-courier tickets are a possibility, but they carry restrictions. As a courier, you transport documents or freight internationally and see it through customs, so you usually have to sacrifice your baggage allowance. Generally trips are on fixed round-trip tickets and offer an inflexible period in the destination country. For more information, check out organisations such as **Courier Association** (www.aircourier.org) and **International Association of Air Travel Couriers** (IAATC; www.courier.org).

Australia

From Australia, Hong Kong is a popular gateway. However, fares from Australia to Hong Kong are generally not that much cheaper than fares to Běijīng or Shànghǎi.

Flight Centre (☎133 133; www.flightcentre.com.au) Offices throughout Australia.

STA Travel (☎1300 733 035; www.statravel.com.au) Offices in all major cities and many university campuses.

Canada

Browse agency ads in the *Globe & Mail*, the *Toronto Star*, the *Montreal Gazette* and the *Vancouver Sun*. From Canada, fares to Hong Kong are often higher than those to Běijīng. Air Canada has daily flights to Běijīng and Shànghǎi from Vancouver. Air Canada, Air China and China Eastern Airlines sometimes run supercheap fares.

Expedia (www.expedia.ca) Online bookings.

M's Travel (☎604 232 0288; www.mstravel.ca/english) Discount tickets to China, its main customers are overseas Chinese.

Travel CUTS (☎1866 246 9762; www.travelcuts.com) Canada's national student travel agency; offices in all major cities.

Travelocity (☎877 282 2925; www.travelocity.ca)

Continental Europe

Generally there is not much variation in airfare prices from the main European cities. The major airlines and travel agents usually have a number of deals on offer, so shop around. **STA Travel** (www.statravel.com) and **Nouvelles Frontières** (www.nouvelles-frontieres.fr) have branches throughout Europe.

Some recommended agencies:

CTS Viaggi (☎in Italy 02 584 751; www. cts.it)

ISSTA (☎in the Netherlands 020 618 8031; www.isstadirect.nl)

Voyages Wasteels (☎in France 01 42 61 69 87; www.wasteels.fr)

Japan

Daily flights operate between Tokyo and Běijīng, as well as regular flights between Osaka and Běijīng. Daily flights link Shànghǎi to Tokyo and Osaka, and there are flights from Japan to other major cities in China, including Dàlián and Qīngdǎo.

STA Travel (☎in Tokyo 03-5391 2922; www.statravel.co.jp)

New Zealand

Flight Centre (☎0800 24 35 44; www.flightcentre.co.nz)

STA Travel (☎0800 474 400; www.statravel.co.nz)

Singapore

Chinatown Point Shopping Centre on New Bridge Rd has a good selection of travel agents.

STA Travel (☎6737 7188; www.statravel.com.sg) Three offices in Singapore.

CLIMATE CHANGE & TRAVEL

Every form of transport that relies on carbon-based fuel generates CO_2, the main cause of human-induced climate change. Modern travel is dependent on aeroplanes, which might use less fuel per kilometre per person than most cars but travel much greater distances. The altitude at which aircraft emit gases (including CO_2) and particles also contributes to their climate change impact. Many websites offer 'carbon calculators' that allow people to estimate the carbon emissions generated by their journey and, for those who wish to do so, to offset the impact of the greenhouse gases emitted with contributions to portfolios of climate-friendly initiatives throughout the world. Lonely Planet offsets the carbon footprint of all staff and author travel.

South Korea

Xanadu Travel (☎02-795 7771; fax 02-797 7667; www.xanadu.co.kr) Good discount travel agency in Seoul.

Thailand

STA Travel (☎02-236 0262; www.statravel.co.th; Room 1406, 14th fl, Wall Street Tower, 33/70 Surawong Rd) Good and reliable place to start.

UK & Ireland

Discount air travel is big business in London. Advertisements for many travel agencies appear in the travel pages of the weekend broadsheet newspapers, and in *Time Out*, the *Evening Standard* and *TNT*. The cheapest flights include KLM to China via Amsterdam, Air France via Paris or Singapore Airlines via Singapore.

Travel agents in London's Chinatown dealing with flights to China:

Jade Travel (☎0870 898 8928; www.jadetravel.co.uk; 5 Newport Pl)

Omega Travel (☎0844 493 8888; www.omegatravel.ltd.uk; 53 Charing Cross Rd)

Reliance Tours Ltd (☎0800 018 0503; www.reliance-tours.co.uk; 12-13 Little Newport St)

Sagitta Travel Agency (☎0870 077 8888; www.sagitta-tvl.com; 9 Little Newport St)

USA

Discount travel agents in the USA are known as consolidators. San Francisco is the ticket-consolidator capital of America, although some good deals can also be found in Los Angeles, New York and other big cities. Consolidators can be found through the *Yellow Pages* or the travel sections of major daily newspapers.

Air Brokers International (☎1 800 883 3273; www.airbrokers.com)

INTERNATIONAL TRAIN ROUTES

The number of international train routes to China is limited, but visionary plans are being hatched to lash China and Europe tighter together. Within 15 years, express trains may be racing from Běijīng to London on high-speed tracks in 48 hours as part of a vast Chinese £65-billion project aiming to complete three transnational high-speed routes: to Singapore from Kūnmíng (see the boxed text, p640), to Berlin from Běijīng, and the rest of Europe and Eastern Europe via Moscow.

In addition to the **Trans-Siberian** and **Trans-Mongolia rail services**, the following trains run international routes:

- » Hung Hom station in **Kowloon** (Jiǔlóng; Hong Kong; www.throughtrain.kcrc.com; p507) to **Guǎngzhōu**, **Shànghǎi** and **Běijīng**
- » **Pyongyang** (North Korea) to **Běijīng** (p93)
- » **Almaty** (Kazakhstan) to **Ürümqi** (p780)
- » **Běijīng** to **Ulaanbaatar** (p93)
- » **Běijīng** to **Hanoi** (p93)

STA Travel (☎800 781 4040; www.sta-travel.com) Offices in most major US cities.

Vietnam

Air China and Vietnam Airlines fly between Ho Chi Minh City and Běijīng; China Southern Airlines flights are via Guǎngzhōu. Shanghai Airlines has five flights weekly to Ho Chi Minh City from Shànghǎi.

From Běijīng to Hanoi there are two flights weekly with either China Southern Airlines or Vietnam Airlines.

Land

China shares borders with Afghanistan, Bhutan, India, Kazakhstan, Kyrgyzstan, Laos, Mongolia, Myanmar, Nepal, North Korea, Pakistan, Russia, Tajikistan and Vietnam; the borders with Afghanistan, Bhutan and India are closed. There are also official border crossings between China and its special administrative regions, Hong Kong and Macau; see p506 and p530, respectively, for overland transport details.

Lonely Planet *China* guides can be confiscated by officials, primarily at the Vietnam–China border (see the boxed text, p607).

Kazakhstan

Border crossings from Ürümqi to Kazakhstan are via border posts at Korgas (p780), Ālāshànkǒu (p780), Tǎchéng (p774) and Jímùnǎi (p774). Ensure you have a valid Kazakhstan visa (obtainable, at the time of writing, in Ürümqi, or from Běijīng) or China visa.

Apart from Ālāshànkǒu, which links China and Kazakhstan via train, all border crossings are by bus; you can generally get a bike over, however. Two trains weekly also run between Ürümqi and Almaty (p780).

Remember that borders open and close frequently due to changes in government policy; additionally, many are only open when the weather permits. It's always best to check with the Public Security Bureau (PSB; Gōng'ānjú) in Ürümqi for the official line.

Kyrgyzstan

There are two routes between China and Kyrgyzstan: one between Kashgar and Osh, via the Irkeshtam Pass; and one between Kashgar and Bishkek, via the dramatic 3752m Torugart Pass. See p793 for details.

Laos

From the Měnglà district in China's southern Yúnnán province, you can enter Laos via Boten in Luang Nam Tha province; see p699. A daily bus runs between Vientiane and Kūnmíng (see p648), and also from Jǐnghóng to Luang Nam Tha in Laos.

You can now get an on-the-spot visa for Laos at the border, the price of which depends on your nationality (although you cannot get a China visa here).

Mongolia

From Běijīng, the Trans-Mongolian Railway trains and the K23 trains (see p93) travel to Ulaanbaatar. Two trains weekly run between Hohhot and Ulaanbaatar, and there are also buses between Hohhot and the border town of Erenhot; see p853 for details.

Myanmar (Burma)

The famous Burma Road runs from Kūnmíng in Yúnnán province to the Burmese city of Lashio. The road is open to travellers carrying permits for the region north of Lashio, although you can legally cross the border in only one direction – from the Chinese side (Jiěgào) into Myanmar. See p690 for more details on journeying to Myanmar. Myanmar visas can only be arranged in Kūnmíng or Běijīng.

Nepal

The 865km road connecting Lhasa with Kathmandu is known as the Friendship Hwy (p893). It's a spectacular trip across the Tibetan plateau, the highest point being Gyatso-la Pass (5100m).

Visas for Nepal can be obtained in Lhasa, or even at the border at Kodari. See p881 for practical information about the journey, and p900 for information about the border crossing, including transport from Kodari to Kathmandu.

When travelling from Nepal to Tibet, foreigners still have to arrange transport through tour agencies in Kathmandu. Access to Tibet can, however, be restricted for months at a time without warning.

North Korea

Visas for North Korea are difficult to arrange, and at the time of writing it was impossible for US and South Korean citizens. Those interested in travelling to North Korea from Běijīng should contact Nicholas Bonner or Simon Cockerell at **Koryo Tours** (☎010-6416 7544; www.koryogroup.com; 27 Beisanlitun Nan, Běijīng).

There are five weekly flights and four international express trains (K27 and K28) between Běijīng and Pyongyang.

Pakistan

The exciting trip on the Karakoram Hwy (p792), said to be the world's highest public international highway, is an excellent way to get to or from Chinese Central Asia. There are buses from Kashgar for the two-day trip to the Pakistani town of Sost via Tashkurgan when the pass is open; see p793.

Russia

A once-weekly train runs from Hā'ěrbīn to Vladivostok via Suífēnhé (see p330); the train runs twice-weekly in the other direction.

The Trans-Mongolian and Trans-Manchurian branches of the Trans-Siberian Railway run from Běijīng to Moscow.

There's a border crossing 9km from Mǎnzhōulǐ; see p860. There is also a border crossing at Hēihé (p334).

Tajikistan

At the time of writing, the Kulma Pass, linking Kashgar with Murghob, was not open to foreign travellers. See p793 for more.

Vietnam

Visas are unobtainable at the border crossings; Vietnam visas can be acquired in Běijīng (p985), Kūnmíng (p986) and Nánníng (p601). Chinese visas can be obtained in Hanoi.

FRIENDSHIP PASS

China's busiest border with Vietnam is at the obscure Vietnamese town of Dong Dang, 164km northeast of Hanoi. The closest Chinese town to the border is Píngxiáng in Guǎngxī province, about 10km north of the actual border gate. See p608 for information about the border crossing, and for transport between Píngxiáng and Vietnam. There are also seven Hanoi-bound buses from Nánníng, running via the Friendship Pass; see p602 for details.

HÉKǑU

The Hékǒu–Lao Cai border crossing is 468km from Kūnmíng and 294km from Hanoi. At the time of writing, the only way to reach Vietnam via Hékǒu was by bus from Kūnmíng; see p648.

MONG CAI

A third, but little-known border crossing is at Mong Cai in the northeast corner of the country, just opposite the Chinese city of Dōngxīng and around 200km south of Nánníng.

There are also two weekly trains from Běijīng to Hanoi; see p93 for details.

TRAVELLING THE TRANS-SIBERIAN RAILWAY

Rolling out of Europe and into Asia, through eight time zones and over 9289km of taiga, steppe and desert, the Trans-Siberian Railway and its connecting routes constitute one of the most famous and most romantic of the world's great train journeys.

There are, in fact, three railways. The 'true' **Trans-Siberian** line runs from Moscow to Vladivostok. But the routes traditionally referred to as the Trans-Siberian Railway are the two branches that veer off the main line in eastern Siberia for Běijīng.

Since the first option excludes China, most readers of this book will be choosing between the **Trans-Mongolian** and the **Trans-Manchurian** railway lines. The Trans-Mongolian route (Běijīng to Moscow, 7865km) is faster, but it requires an additional visa and another border crossing – the positive side is that will you also get to see some of the Mongolian countryside. The Trans-Manchurian route is longer (Běijīng to Moscow, 9025km).

See Lonely Planet's *Trans-Siberian Railway* for further details. Another useful source of information is **Seat 61** (www.seat61.com/Trans-Siberian.htm).

Routes

TRANS-MONGOLIAN RAILWAY

Trains offer deluxe two-berth compartments (which come with a shared shower), 1st-class four-berth compartments and 2nd-class four-berth compartments. Tickets for 2nd-class/deluxe compartments cost from around Y3737/Y5501 to Moscow, Y1128/1619 to Ulaanbaatar and Y2661/3909 to Novosibirsk. Ticket prices are cheaper if you are travelling in a group.

» From **Běijīng**: train K3 leaves Běijīng on its five-day journey to Moscow at 7.45am every Wednesday, passing through Dàtóng, Ulaanbaatar and Novosibirsk, arriving in Moscow the following Monday at 2.28pm.

» From **Moscow**: train K4 leaves at 10.03pm on Tuesdays arriving in Běijīng on the following Monday at 2.04pm. Departure and arrival times may fluctuate slightly.

TRANS-MANCHURIAN RAILWAY

Trains have 1st-class two-berth compartments and 2nd-class four-berth compartments; prices are similar to those on the Trans-Mongolian Railway.

» From **Běijīng**: train K19 departs Běijīng at 10.56pm on Saturday (arriving in Moscow the following Friday at 5.57pm) before arriving at the border post Mǎnzhōulǐ, 2347km

River

Fast ferries leave Jǐnghóng in Yúnnán three times a week for the seven-hour trip to Chiang Saen in Thailand (see p695).

Sea

Japan

There are weekly ferries between Osaka and Shànghǎi (see p201). From Tiānjīn (Tánggū), a weekly ferry runs to Kōbe in Japan; see p112. There are also twice-weekly boats from Qīngdǎo to Shimonoseki; see p155.

Check in two hours before departure for international sailings.

South Korea

International ferries connect the South Korean port of Incheon with Wēihǎi, Qīngdǎo (p155), Yāntái (p159), Tiānjīn (Tánggū; p112), Dàlián (p291) and Dāndōng (p296). There are also boats between Qīngdǎo and Gunsan (p155).

In Seoul, tickets for any boats to China can be bought from the **International Union Travel Agency** (☎822-777 6722; Room 707, 7th fl, Daehan Ilbo Bldg, 340 Taepyonglo 2-ga, Chung-gu). In China, tickets can be bought cheaply at the pier, or from China International Travel Service (CITS; Zhōngguó Guójì Lǚxíngshè) for a very steep premium.

To reach the International Passenger Terminal from Seoul, take the Seoul–Incheon commuter train (subway line 1 from the city centre) and get off at the Dongincheon station. The train journey takes 50 minutes. From Dongincheon station it's either a 45-minute walk or five-minute taxi ride to the ferry terminal.

GETTING AROUND

Air

Despite being a land of vast distances, it's quite straightforward to navigate your way from Běijīng. Zabaykal'sk is the Russian border post; from here, the train continues to Tarskaya, where it connects with the Trans-Siberian line.

» From **Moscow**: train K20 leaves Moscow at 11.58pm every Friday, arriving in Běijīng the following Friday at 5.31am. Departure and arrival times may fluctuate slightly.

Visas

Travellers will need Russian and Mongolian visas for the Trans-Mongolian Railway, as well as a Chinese visa. These can often be arranged along with your ticket by travel agents such as China International Travel Service (CITS).

Mongolian visas take three to five days to process, coming as two-day **transit visas** (US$15) or 30-day **tourist visas** (US$30). A transit visa is easy to get (present a through ticket and a visa for your onward destination). The situation regarding visas changes regularly, so check with a Mongolian embassy or consulate. All Mongolian embassies shut for the week of National Day (Naadam), which officially falls around 11 to 13 July.

Russian transit visas (one-week/three-day/one-day process US$50/80/120) are valid for 10 days if you take the train, but will only give you three or four days in Moscow at the end of your journey. You need one photo, your passport and the exact amount in US dollars. You will also need a valid entry visa for a third country plus a through ticket from Russia to the third country. You can also obtain a 30-day Russian tourist visa, but the process is complicated.

Buying Tickets

In Běijīng, tickets can be conveniently purchased from **CITS** (Zhōngguó Guójì Lǚxíngshè; ☎010 6512 0507; www.cits.com.cn; Beijing International Hotel, 9 Jianguomen Neidajie). **Monkey Business Shrine** (www.monkeyshrine.com; Youyi Youth Hostel, 43 Beisanlitun Lu) in Běijīng also arranges trips, and has an informative website with a downloadable brochure. There's another **branch** (☎852-2723 1376; Liberty Mansion, Kowloon) in Hong Kong.

Abroad, tickets and sometimes visas can be arranged through an agency:

Intourist Travel (www.intourist.com) With branches in the UK, USA, Canada, Finland and Poland.

Russia Experience (☎020-8566 8846; www.trans-siberian.co.uk; Research House, Fraser Rd, Perivale, Middlesex, England)

White Nights (☎/fax 1800 490 5008; www.wnights.com; 610 Sierra Dr, Sacramento, CA, USA)

terrestrially around China by rail (p1005) and bus if you have time; if you are in more of a rush, get airborne.

China's air network is extensive and growing. China's civil aviation fleet is expected to triple in size over the next two decades; airports are constantly being built and upgraded all over the land. Air safety and quality have improved considerably, but the speed of change is generating problems: China has a shortage of qualified pilots and an investigation in 2010 exposed 200 airline pilots with falsified information on their CVs.

Shuttle buses often run from **Civil Aviation Administration of China** (CAAC; Zhōngguó Mínháng) offices in towns and cities throughout China to the airport; see the Getting Around sections of relevant chapters. For domestic flights, arrive at the airport one hour before departure.

Remember to keep your baggage receipt label on your ticket as you will need to show it when you collect your luggage. Planes vary in style and comfort. You may get a hot meal, or just a small piece of cake and an airline souvenir. On-board announcements are delivered in Chinese and English.

Airlines in China

The CAAC is the civil aviation authority for numerous airlines:

Air China (☎in Běijīng 4008 100 999; www.airchina.com.cn)

China Eastern Airlines (☎in Shànghǎi 95530; www.ce-air.com)

China Southern Airlines (☎in Guǎngzhōu 95539; www.cs-air.com) Serves a web of air routes, including Běijīng, Shànghǎi, Xī'ān and Tiānjīn.

Hainan Airlines (☎in Hǎinán 950718; www.hnair.com)

Shandong Airlines (☎in Jǐnán 96777; www.shandongair.com.cn)

Shanghai Airlines (☎in Shànghǎi 1010 5858; www.shanghai-air.com)

Shenzhen Airlines (☎in Shēnzhèn 95080; www.shenzhenair.com)

Sichuan Airlines (☎in Chéngdū 4008 300 999; www.scal.com.cn)

Spring Airlines (☎in Shànghǎi 800 820 6222; www.china-sss.com) Has connections between Shànghǎi and tourist destinations such as Qīngdǎo, Guìlín, Xiàmén and Sānyà. No food or drink served on board.

Some of the above airlines also have subsidiary airlines. Not all Chinese airline websites have English-language capability. Airline schedules and airfares are listed within the relevant chapters.

The CAAC publishes a combined international and domestic timetable in both English and Chinese in April and November each year. This timetable can be bought at some airports and CAAC offices in China. Individual airlines also publish timetables, which you can buy from ticket offices throughout China.

Tickets

Except during major festivals and holidays, tickets are easy to purchase, with an oversupply of airline seats. Tickets can be purchased from branches of the CAAC nationwide, airline offices, travel agents or the travel desk of your hotel; travel agents will usually offer a better discount than airline offices. Discounts are common, except when flying into large cities such as Shànghǎi and Běijīng on the weekend, when the full fare can be the norm; prices quoted in this book are the full fare. To book online and obtain good discounts, visit www.Ctrip.com, www.elong.com or www.9588.com. Fares are calculated according to one-way travel, with return tickets simply costing twice the single fare.

You can use credit cards at most CAAC offices and travel agents. Departure tax is included in the ticket price.

Bicycle

Except in seriously bike-free hilly cities such as Chóngqìng, bicycles (自行车; *zìxíngchē*) are an excellent method for getting around China's cities and tourist sights. They can also be invaluable for exploring the countryside surrounding towns such as Yángshuò.

Hire

Bicycle-hire outlets that cater to travellers can be found in many but not all traveller centres; addresses are listed in destination chapters. Most youth hostels rent out bicycles, as do many hotels, although the latter are more expensive.

Bikes can be hired by the day or by the hour and it's also possible to hire for more than one day. Rental rates vary depending on where you find yourself, but rates start at around Y10 to Y15 per day in cities such as Běijīng.

Most hire outlets will ask you for a deposit of anything up to Y500 (get a receipt); you'll also need to leave some sort of ID.

Touring

Cycling through China allows you to go when you want, to see what you want and at your own pace. It can also be an extremely cheap, as well as a highly authentic, way to see the land.

You will have virtually unlimited freedom of movement but, considering the size of China, you will need to combine your cycling days with trips by train, bus, boat, taxi or even planes, especially if you want to avoid particularly steep regions, or areas where the roads are poor or the climate is cold.

Bikechina (www.bikechina.com) is a good source of information for cyclists coming to China. The Yángshuò-based company offers tours around southwest China, ranging from one-day bike tours of Chéngdū to five-day round trips from Chéngdū to Dānbā and eight-day trips around Yúnnán.

A basic packing list for cyclists includes a good bicycle-repair kit, sunscreen and other protection from the sun, waterproofs, fluorescent strips and camping equipment. Ensure you have adequate clothing, as many routes will be taking you to considerable altitude. Road maps in Chinese are essential for asking locals for directions.

Boat

Boat services within China are limited. They're most common in coastal areas, where you are likely to use a boat to reach offshore islands such as Pǔtuóshān or Hǎinán, or the islands off Hong Kong. The Yāntái–Dàlián ferry will probably survive because it saves hundreds of kilometres of overland travel.

The best-known river trip is the three-day boat ride along the Yangzi (Cháng Jiāng) from Chóngqìng to Yíchāng (p766). The Lí River (Lí Jiāng) boat trip from Guìlín to Yángshuò (p586) is a popular tourist ride.

Hong Kong employs a veritable navy of vessels that connect with the territory's myriad islands, and a number of popular boats run between the territory and other parts of China, including Macau, Zhūhǎi, Shékǒu (for Shēnzhèn) and Zhōngshān. See p506 for details.

Boat tickets can be purchased from passenger ferry terminals or through travel agents.

Bus

Long-distance bus (长途公共汽车; *chángtú gōnggòng qìchē*) services are extensive and reach places you cannot get to by train; with

the increasing number of intercity highways, journeys are getting quicker. Tickets are cheaper and easier to get than train tickets.

However, tickets are getting more expensive, breakdowns can be a hassle, and some rural roads and provincial routes (especially in the southwest, Tibet and the northwest) remain in bad condition. Precipitous drops, pot holes, dangerous road surfaces and reckless drivers mean accidents remain common. Long-distance journeys can also be cramped and noisy, with Hong Kong films and cacophonous karaoke looped on overhead TVs. Drivers continuously lean on the horn. In such conditions, taking an MP3 player is crucial for one's sanity. Astonishingly, seat belts are a rarity in many provinces; if you find one knotted in a cat's cradle beneath your seat, it may look like it's been used to clean a wheel axle.

Routes between large cities sport larger, cleaner and more comfortable fleets of private buses, some equipped with toilets; shorter and more far-flung routes still rely on rattling minibuses into which as many fares as possible are crammed. On countless routes, buses wait till they fill up before leaving or exasperatingly trawl the streets looking for fares.

Sleeper buses (卧铺客车; *wòpù kèchē*) ply popular long-haul routes, costing around double the price of a normal bus service. Bunks can be short, however, and buses claustrophobic.

Take plenty of warm clothes on buses to high-altitude destinations in winter. A breakdown in frozen conditions can prove lethal for those unprepared. Take a lot of extra water on routes across areas such as the Taklamakan Desert.

Bus journey times given throughout this book should be used as a rough guide only. You can estimate times for bus journeys on nonhighway routes by calculating the distance against a speed of 25km per hour.

All cities and most towns have one or more **long-distance bus station** (长途汽车站; *chángtú qìchēzhàn*), generally located in relation to the direction the bus heads in. Tickets are easy to purchase; often just turn up at the bus station and buy your ticket there and then, rather than booking in advance. Booking in advance, however, can secure you a better seat, as many buses have numbered seats; the earlier you buy your ticket, the closer to the front of the bus you will sit.

In many cities, the train station forecourt doubles as a bus station.

Car & Motorcycle

Driving Licence

To drive in Hong Kong and Macau, you will need an International Driving Permit. Foreigners can drive motorcycles if they are residents in China and have an official Chinese motorcycle licence.

Hire

Both Běijīng's Capital Airport or Shànghǎi's Pǔdōng International Airport have a **Vehicle Administration Office** (车管所; chēguǎnsuǒ; ☎6453 0010, 9am-6pm Mon-Sun) where you can have a temporary three-month driving licence issued. This will involve checking your driving licence and a simple medical exam (including an eyesight test). You will need this licence before you can hire a car from **Hertz** (☎800-988-1336), which has branches at Capital Airport and Pǔdōng International Airport. Hire cars from Hertz start from Y450 per day (up to 150km per day; Y20000 deposit). **Avis** (☎400 882 1119) also has a growing network around China, with car rental starting from Y200 per day (Y5000 deposit). See the Hong Kong and Macau chapters for details on car hire in each of those territories.

Road Rules

Cars in China drive on the right-hand side of the road. Even skilled drivers will be unprepared for China's roads: in the cities, cars lunge from all angles and chaos abounds.

Local Transport

Long-distance transport in China is good, but local transport is not so efficient. The choice of local transport is diverse but vehicles can be slow and overburdened, and the network confusing for visitors. Hiring a car is often impractical, while hiring a bike can be inadequate. Unless the town is small, walking is often too tiring. On the plus side, local transport is cheap, and taxis are usually ubiquitous and affordable.

Bus

Bus services are extensive and fares inexpensive but vehicles are often packed; navigation is tricky for non-Chinese speakers as bus routes at bus stops are generally listed in Chinese, without Pinyin. Traffic can be slow. In Běijīng and Shànghǎi, stops will be announced in English.

Maps of Chinese cities and bus routes are available from hawkers outside train stations. Ascending a bus, point to your destination on the map and the conductor (seated near the door) will sell you the right ticket. They usually tell you where to disembark, provided they remember. Buses with snowflake motifs are air-conditioned.

Metro & Light Rail

Going underground is fast, efficient and cheap; most networks are either very new or relatively new and can be found in a rapidly growing number of cities.

Taxi

Taxis (出租汽车; *chūzū qìchē*) are cheap, plentiful and easy to find. Congregation points include train and long-distance bus stations.

Taxi drivers rarely speak any English so have your destination written down in characters.

To use the same driver again, ask for his card (名片; *míngpiàn*). Taxis can be hired for a single trip or on a daily basis.

Taxi rates per kilometre are clearly marked on a sticker on the rear side window of the taxi; flag fall varies from city to city, and also depends upon the size and quality of the vehicle. Rates are listed in the Getting Around section of destinations.

Most taxis have meters but they may only be switched on in larger towns and cities. If the meter is not used (on an excursion out of town, for example), negotiate a price before you set off and write the fare down. If you want the meter used, ask for *dǎbiǎo* (打表). Ask for a receipt (发票; *fāpiào*); if you leave something in the taxi, the taxi number is printed on the receipt so it can be located.

To share a car or minibus (ie paying per seat), ask to *pīnchē* (拼车); if you want to pay for the whole car, it's *bāochē* (包车).

Other Local Transport

An often bewildering variety of ramshackle transport options exists across China. **Motor tricycles** are enclosed three-wheeled vehicles that congregate outside train and bus stations. Pedal-powered **tricycles** also muster outside train and bus stations and cruise the streets.

Motorbike riders also offer lifts in some towns for what should be half the price of a regular taxi. You must wear a helmet – the driver will provide one.

For all of the above agree on a price in advance (preferably have it written down). Prices can compare with taxis, so check fares beforehand and bargain.

China by Train

Trains are the best way to travel around China in reasonable speed and comfort, despite crowding. They are also adventurous, exciting, fun, practical and efficient, and ticket prices are reasonable to boot. Colossal investment over recent years has put the rail network at the heart of China's rapid modernisation drive. You don't have to be a trainspotter to find China's railways an enthralling subculture – you also get to meet the Chinese people at their most relaxed and sociable.

The Chinese Train Network

One of the world's most extensive rail networks, passenger railways cover every province in China, including the insular bastion of Hǎinán, finally breached in the closing months of 2010. In line with China's frantic economic development and the pressures of transporting 1.4 billion people across one of the world's largest nations, expansion of China's rail network over the past decade has been astonishing.

The railway to Lhasa in Tibet began running in 2006, despite scepticism that it could ever be laid, so now you can climb aboard a train in Běijīng or Shànghǎi and alight in Tibet's capital. Thousands of miles of track are laid every year across China and new express train series are being continuously launched to shrink China's vast distances. Brand-new state-of-the-art train stations are also incessantly appearing, such as Wēnzhōu's impressive new south station (like a vast aircraft hangar, cooled with hundreds of air-conditioning nozzles), many to serve high-speed links.

With the simultaneous advent of high-speed D-, G-, Z- and C-class express trains, getting between major cities as a traveller is increasingly a breeze. An ultra-high-speed railway is being built between Běijīng and Shànghǎi, with trains due to begin running in 2011.

For international trains to China, see the Transport chapter (p995).

Trains

Chinese train numbers are usually prefixed by a letter, designating the category of train. The fastest, most luxurious and expensive intercity trains are the streamlined, high-speed 'C', 'D' and 'G' trains, which rapidly shuttle between major cities, such as Běijīng and Tiānjīn and Běijīng and Shànghǎi.

With their modern looks, 200km/h to 250km/h D-class trains are also referred to as 'harmonious class' ('harmony' is the Chinese Communist Party's latest fix-all word). The wide-bodied trains breathlessly glide around China at the apex of speed and comfort. Temperature-regulated 1st-class carriages have mobile and laptop chargers, seats are two abreast with ample legroom and TV sets showing peaceful programs. Doors between carriages are opened with electric buttons.

C- and G-class trains are even faster, with the speediest expected to reach 380km/h; by 2012 G-class trains will convey passengers from Běijīng to Kūnmíng in 12 hours (instead of the current 47 hours). In 2011 G-class trains were set to start shuttling passengers from Běijīng to Shànghǎi in a mere four hours. Overnight Z-class trains are not as fast but are still express and very comfortable; rather down the pecking order are T- and K-class trains, which are older and more basic.

There are also numbered trains that do not commence with a letter; these are *pǔkuài* (普快) or *pǔkè* (普客) trains, the most unsophisticated.

Ticket Types

It is possible to **upgrade** (补票; *bǔpiào*) your ticket once aboard your train. If

TRAIN CATEGORIES

CATEGORY	MEANING	TYPE
C	*chengji gāosù*	ultra-high-speed express
D	*dòngchē, héxiè hào*	high-speed express
G	*gāotiě*	high-speed
K	*kuàisù* (快速)	fast train
T	*tèkuài* (特快)	express
Z	*zhídá tèkuài* (直达特快)	direct express (overnight)

you have a standing ticket, for example, find the conductor and upgrade to a hard seat, soft seat, hard sleeper or soft sleeper (if there are any available).

Soft Sleeper

Soft sleepers (软卧; *ruǎn wò*) are very comfortable, with four air-conditioned bunks in a closed compartment. Soft-sleeper tickets cost much more than hard-sleeper tickets; however, soft sleepers often sell out, so book early. Soft sleepers vary between trains and the best are on the more recent D- and Z-class trains.

All Z-class trains are soft-sleeper trains, with very comfortable, up-to-date berths. A few T-class trains also offer two-berth compartments, with their own toilet. Tickets on upper berths are slightly cheaper than lower berths.

Hard Sleeper

Hard sleepers (硬卧; *yìng wò*) are available on slower and less-modern T-, K- and N-class trains, as well as trains without a letter prefix. Carriages consist of doorless compartments with half a dozen bunks in three tiers; sheets, pillows and blankets are provided. It does very nicely as an overnight hotel. There is a small price difference between berths, with the lowest bunk (下铺; *xiàpù*) the most expensive and the highest bunk (上铺; *shàngpù*) the cheapest. The middle bunk (中铺; *zhōngpù*) is good, as all and sundry invade the lower berth to use it as a seat during the day, while the top one has little headroom and puts you near the speakers.

As with all other classes, smoking is prohibited. Lights and speakers go out at around 10pm. Each compartment is equipped with its own hot-water flask, filled by an attendant. Hard-sleeper tickets are the most difficult of all to buy; you almost always need to buy these a few days in advance.

Seats

Soft-seat class (软座; *ruǎn zuò*) is more comfortable but not nearly as common as hard-seat class. First-class (一等; *yīděng*) and 2nd-class (二等; *èrděng*) soft seats are available in D-, C- and G-class high-speed trains. First class comes with TVs, mobile phone and laptop charging points, and seats arranged two abreast.

Second-class soft seats are also very comfortable; staff are very courteous throughout. Overcrowding is not permitted. On older trains, soft-seat carriages are often double-decker, and are not as plush as the faster and more modern high-speed express trains.

Hard-seat class (硬座; *yìng zuò*) is not available on the faster and plusher C-, D- and G-class trains, and is only found on T-, K- and N-class trains and trains without a number prefix; a handful of Z-class trains have hard seat. Hard-seat class generally has padded seats, but it's hard on your sanity; often unclean and noisy, and painful on the long haul. Since hard seat is the only class most locals can afford, it's packed to the gills.

You should get a ticket with an assigned seat number, but if seats have sold out, ask for a **standing ticket** (无座、站票; *wúzuò* or *zhànpiào*), which gets you on the train, where you may find a seat or can upgrade; otherwise you will have to stand in the carriage or between carriages (with the smokers). Hard-seat sections on newer trains are air-conditioned and less crowded.

Travelling by Train

Trains are generally highly punctual in China and also generally a safe way to travel, with few accidents. Train stations are often conveniently close to the centre of town. Travelling on sleeper berths at night often means you can frequently arrive at your destination first thing in the morning, saving a night's hotel accommodation.

Think ahead, get your tickets early and you can sleep your way around a lot of China. Don't leave it till the very last minute to board your train, as queues outside the main train station entrance (进站口; *jìnzhànkǒu*) can be shocking. You are required to pass your bags through a security scanner at the train station entrance.

On long train trips, load up with snacks, food and drinks for the journey. Trolleys of food and drink are wheeled along carriages during the trip, but prices are high and the selection is limited. For tea and noodles, flasks of hot water are provided in each sleeper compartment. You can also load up on mineral water and snacks at stations, where hawkers sell items from platform stalls. Long-distance trains should have a **canteen carriage** (餐厅车厢; *cāntīng chēxiāng*) where you can buy cooked food and beer from a limited menu; they are sometimes open through the night.

In each class of sleeper, linen is clean and changed for each journey; beds are generally bedbug-free. Staff rarely speak English, except sometimes on the high-speed express trains.

On a nonsleeper, ask a member of staff or a fellow passenger to tell you when your station arrives.

If taking a sleeper train, you will be required to exchange your paper ticket for a plastic or metal card with your bunk number on it. The conductor then knows when you are due to disembark, so you can be woken in time and have your ticket returned to you. Hold on to your paper ticket as it may be inspected at the train station exit.

Ticketing

Buying Tickets

The Achilles heel of China's overburdened rail system, buying tickets can be a real pain.

Never aim to get a hard-sleeper (or increasingly, soft sleeper) ticket on the day of travel – plan ahead. Most tickets can be booked in advance between two and 10 days prior to your intended date of departure. Buying hard-seat tickets at short notice is usually no hassle, but it may be a standing ticket rather than a numbered seat. Tickets can only be purchased with cash.

Most tickets are one way only, with prices calculated per kilometre and adjustments made depending on class of train, availability of air-con, type of sleeper and bunk positioning. If you want to buy tickets for a train between two destinations beyond the city you are buying your ticket in, it is often better to go to an independent ticket office that charges a commission.

Tickets for hard sleepers are usually obtainable in major cities, but are trickier to buy in quiet backwaters. As with air travel, buying tickets around the Chinese New Year and during the 1 May and 1 October holiday periods can be very hard, and prices increase on some routes.

Touts swarm around train stations selling black-market tickets; this can be a way of getting scarce tickets, but foreigners frequently get ripped off.

RAILING AGAINST RAIL

The Chinese have travelled by train (火车; *huǒchē*; literally 'fire vehicle') for decades like absolute naturals, but it was far from love at first sight. Railways were strongly resisted in the 19th century for fear they disturbed ancestors' graves and obstructed feng shui; Běijīng was also anxious that railroads would accelerate the military domination of China by foreign powers. China's first railway (1875) ran from Shànghǎi to Wúsōng at the mouth of the Yangzi River, operating for a few brief years before encountering stiff local resistance, being torn up and being shipped to Taiwan.

Ticket Offices

Ticket offices (售票厅; *shòupiàotīng*) at train stations are usually to one side of the main train station entrance. Ticket sales are automated on very few routes. There may be a window (look for the sign) manned by someone with basic English skills; otherwise join the queue at one of the other windows.

Try and get to the station early but always prepare to queue for up to half an hour to get your ticket; you may queue for 20 minutes and when you reach the window it may shut temporarily. Some stations are surprisingly well run, others are bedlam. Take your passport in case you are asked for it when buying a ticket.

Alternatively, independent train ticket offices usually exist elsewhere in town where tickets can be purchased without the same kind of queues, for a Y5 commission; such outlets are listed in towns and cities within destination chapters. Your hotel will also be able to rustle up a ticket for you for a commission, and so can a travel agent.

Telephone booking services exist, but operate only in Chinese.

Tickets can also be bought online at **China Trip Advisor** (www.chinatripadvisor.com) or **China Train Timetable** (www.china-train-ticket.com), but it's cheaper to buy your ticket at the station. For trains from Hong Kong to Shànghǎi, Guǎngzhōu or Běijīng, tickets can be ordered online at no mark up from **KCRC** (www.mtr.com.hk).

To get a **refund** (退票; *tuìpiào*) on an unused ticket, windows exist at large train stations where you can get 80% of the ticket value back.

Timetables

Paperback train timetables for the entire country (Y7) are published every April and October, but are available in Chinese only. Even to Chinese readers, their Byzantine layout is taxing. You can download an annual English translation for a fee from www.chinatt.org. Online English-language timetables:

China Highlights (www.chinahighlights.com)

China Train Timetable (www.china-train-ticket.com)

China Travel Guide (www.chinatravelguide.com)

Internet Resources

Seat 61 (www.seat61.com/China.htm)

Shike (www.shike.org.cn, in Chinese)

Tielu (www.tielu.org, in Chinese)

Health

China is a reasonably healthy country to travel in, but some health issues should be noted. Pre-existing medical conditions and accidental injury (especially traffic accidents) account for most life-threatening problems, but becoming ill in some way is not unusual. Outside of the major cities, medical care is often inadequate, and food- and waterborne diseases are common. Malaria is still present in some parts of the country, and altitude sickness can be a problem, particularly in Tibet.

In case of accident or illness, it's best just to get a taxi and go to hospital directly.

The following advice is a general guide only and does not replace the advice of a doctor trained in travel medicine.

BEFORE YOU GO

» Pack medications in their original, clearly labelled containers.

» If you take any regular medication, bring double your needs in case of loss or theft.

» Take a signed and dated letter from your physician describing your medical conditions and medications (using generic names).

» If carrying syringes or needles, ensure you have a physician's letter documenting their medical necessity.

» If you have a heart condition, bring a copy of your ECG taken just prior to travelling.

» Get your teeth checked before you travel.

» If you wear glasses, take a spare pair and your prescription.

In China you can buy some medications over the counter without a doctor's prescription, but not all, and in general it is not advisable to buy medications locally without a doctor's advice. Fake medications and poorly stored or out-of-date drugs are also common, so try and take your own.

Insurance

» Even if you are fit and healthy, don't travel without health insurance – accidents happen.

» Declare any existing medical conditions you have (the insurance company *will* check if your problem is pre-existing and will not cover you if it is undeclared).

» You may require extra cover for adventure activities such as rock climbing or skiing.

» If you're uninsured, emergency evacuation is expensive; bills of more than US$100,000 are not uncommon.

» Ensure you keep all documentation related to any medical expenses you incur.

Recommended Vaccinations

Specialised travel-medicine clinics stock all available vaccines and can give specific recommendations for your trip. The doctors will consider your vaccination history, the length of your trip, activities you may undertake and underlying medical conditions, such as pregnancy.

» Visit a doctor six to eight weeks before departure, as most vaccines don't produce immunity until at least two weeks after they're given.

» Ask your doctor for an International Certificate of Vaccination (otherwise known as the 'yellow booklet'), listing all vaccinations received.

» The only vaccine required by international regulations is yellow fever.

Proof of vaccination against yellow fever is only required if you have visited a country in the yellow-fever zone within the six days prior to entering China. If you are travelling to China directly from South America or Africa, check with a travel clinic as to whether you need yellow-fever vaccination.

Medical Checklist

Recommended items for a personal medical kit:

- » Antibacterial cream, eg mucipirocin
- » Antibiotics for diarrhoea, including norfloxacin, ciprofloxacin or azithromycin for bacterial diarrhoea; or tinidazole for giardia or amoebic dysentery
- » Antibiotics for skin infections, eg amoxicillin/clavulanate or cephalexin
- » Antifungal cream, eg clotrimazole
- » Antihistamine, eg cetrizine for daytime and promethazine for night-time
- » Anti-inflammatory, eg ibuprofen
- » Antiseptic, eg Betadine
- » Antispasmodic for stomach cramps, eg Buscopan
- » Decongestant, eg pseudoephedrine
- » Diamox if going to high altitudes
- » Elastoplasts, bandages, gauze, thermometer (but not mercury), sterile needles and syringes, safety pins and tweezers
- » Indigestion tablets, such as Quick-Eze or Mylanta
- » Insect repellent containing DEET
- » Iodine tablets to purify water (unless you're pregnant or have a thyroid problem)
- » Laxative, eg coloxyl
- » Oral-rehydration solution (eg Gastrolyte) for diarrhoea, diarrhoea 'stopper' (eg loperamide) and antinausea medication (eg prochlorperazine)
- » Paracetamol
- » Permethrin to impregnate clothing and mosquito nets
- » Steroid cream for rashes, eg 1% to 2% hydrocortisone
- » Sunscreen
- » Thrush (vaginal yeast infection) treatment, eg clotrimazole pessaries or Diflucan tablet
- » Urinary-infection treatment, eg Ural

Websites

Centers for Disease Control & Prevention (CDC; www.cdc.gov)

Lonely Planet (www.lonelyplanet.com)

MD Travel Health (www.mdtravelhealth.com) Provides complete travel-health recommendations for every country; updated daily.

World Health Organization (WHO; www.who.int/ith) Publishes the excellent *International Travel & Health*, revised annually and available online at no cost.

Further Reading

Healthy Travel – Asia & India (Lonely Planet) Handy pocket size, packed with useful information.

Traveller's Health by Dr Richard Dawood.

Travelling Well (www.travellingwell.com.au) by Dr Deborah Mills.

IN CHINA

Availability of Health Care

Good clinics catering to travellers can be found in major cities. They are more expensive than local facilities but you may feel more comfortable dealing with a Western-trained doctor who speaks your language. These clinics usually have a good understanding of the best local hospital facilities and close contacts with insurance companies should you need evacuation.

Self-treatment may be appropriate if your problem is minor (eg traveller's diarrhoea), you are carrying the relevant medication and you cannot attend a clinic. If you think you may have a serious disease, especially malaria, do not waste time – get to the nearest quality facility. To find the nearest reliable medical facility, contact your insurance company or your embassy.

Infectious Diseases

Dengue

This mosquito-borne disease occurs in some parts of southern China. There is no vaccine so avoid mosquito bites. The dengue-carrying mosquito bites day and night, so use insect-avoidance measures at all times. Symptoms include high fever, severe headache and body ache. Some people develop a rash and diarrhoea. There is no specific treatment – just rest and paracetamol. Do not take aspirin. See a doctor to be diagnosed and monitored.

Hepatitis A

A problem throughout China, this food- and waterborne virus infects the liver, causing jaundice (yellow skin and eyes), nausea and lethargy. There is no specific treatment for hepatitis A; you just need to allow time for the liver to heal. All travellers to China should be vaccinated.

Hepatitis B

The only sexually transmitted disease that can be prevented by vaccination, hepatitis B is spread by contact with infected body fluids. The long-term consequences can include liver cancer and cirrhosis. All travellers to China should be vaccinated.

Japanese B Encephalitis

A rare disease in travellers; however, vaccination is recommended if you're in rural areas for over a month during summer months, or if you're spending more than three months in the country. No treatment available;

HEALTH ADVISORIES

It's usually a good idea to consult your government's travel-health website before departure, if one is available.

Australia (www.dfat.gov.au/travel)
Canada (www.travelhealth.gc.ca)
New Zealand (www.mfat.govt.nz/travel)
UK (www.dh.gov.uk) Search for travel in the site index.
USA (www.cdc.gov/travel)

one-third of infected people die, another third suffer permanent brain damage.

Malaria

For such a serious and potentially deadly disease, an enormous amount of misinformation exists concerning malaria. Before you travel, ensure you seek medical advice to see if you need antimalaria medication and receive the right medication and dosage for you.

Malaria has been nearly eradicated in China; it is not generally a risk for visitors to the cities and most tourist areas. It is found mainly in rural areas in the southwestern region bordering Myanmar, Laos and Vietnam – principally Hǎinán, Yúnnán and Guǎngxī. More limited risk exists in remote rural areas of Fújiàn, Guǎngdōng, Guìzhōu and Sìchuān. Generally, medication is only advised if you are visiting rural Hǎinán, Yúnnán or Guǎngxī.

Malaria is caused by a parasite transmitted by the bite of an infected mosquito. The most important symptom of malaria is fever, but general symptoms such as headache, diarrhoea, cough or chills may also occur. Diagnosis can only be made by taking a blood sample.

To prevent malaria, avoid mosquitoes and take antimalaria medications. Most people who catch malaria are taking inadequate or no antimalaria medication.

Always take these insect-avoidance measures in order to help prevent all insect-borne diseases (not just malaria):

» Use an insect repellent containing DEET on exposed skin. You can wash this off at night, as long as you are sleeping under a mosquito net. Natural repellents such as citronella can be effective, but require more frequent application than products containing DEET.
» Sleep under a mosquito net impregnated with permethrin.
» Choose accommodation with screens and fans (if it's not air-conditioned).
» Impregnate clothing with permethrin in high-risk areas.
» Wear long sleeves and trousers in light colours.
» Use mosquito coils.
» Spray your room with insect repellent before going out for your evening meal.

Rabies

An increasingly common problem in China, this fatal disease is spread by the bite or lick of an infected animal, most commonly a dog. Seek medical advice immediately after any animal bite and commence postexposure treatment. The pretravel vaccination means the post-bite treatment is greatly simplified.

If an animal bites you:

» Gently wash the wound with soap and water, and apply an iodine-based antiseptic.
» If you are not prevaccinated, you will need to receive rabies immunoglobulin as soon as possible, followed by a series of five vaccines over the next month. Those who have been prevaccinated require only two shots of vaccine after a bite.
» Contact your insurance company to locate the nearest clinic stocking rabies immunoglobulin and vaccine.

Immunoglobulin is often unavailable outside of major centres, but it's crucial that you get to a clinic that has immunoglobulin as soon as possible if you have had a bite that has broken the skin.

Schistosomiasis (Bilharzia)

This disease is found in the central Yangzi River (Cháng Jiāng) basin, carried in water by minute worms that infect certain varieties of freshwater snail found in rivers, streams, lakes and, particularly, behind dams. The infection often causes no symptoms until the disease is well established (several months to years after exposure); any resulting damage to internal organs is irreversible.

The main method of prevention is avoiding swimming or bathing in fresh water where bilharzia is present. A blood test is the most reliable way to diagnose the disease, but the test will not show positive until weeks after exposure. Effective treatment is available.

Typhoid

Typhoid is a serious bacterial infection spread via food and water. Symptoms include headaches, a high and slowly progressive fever, perhaps accompanied by a dry cough and stomach pain. Vaccination is not 100% effective, so still be careful what you eat and drink. All travellers spending more than a week in China should be vaccinated.

RECOMMENDED VACCINATIONS

The World Health Organization (WHO) recommends the following vaccinations for travellers to China:

Adult diphtheria and tetanus (ADT) Single booster recommended if you've not received one in the previous 10 years. Side effects include sore arm and fever. A new ADT vaccine that immunises against pertussis (whooping cough) is also available and may be recommended by your doctor.

Hepatitis A Provides almost 100% protection for up to a year; a booster after 12 months provides at least another 20 years' protection. Mild side effects such as a headache and sore arm occur in 5% to 10% of people.

Hepatitis B Now considered routine for most travellers. Given as three shots over six months; a rapid schedule is also available. There is also a combined vaccination with Hepatitis A. Side effects are mild and uncommon, usually a headache and sore arm. Lifetime protection results in 95% of people.

Measles, mumps and rubella (MMR) Two doses of MMR is recommended unless you have had the diseases. Occasionally a rash and a flulike illness can develop a week after receiving the vaccine. Many adults under 40 require a booster.

Typhoid Recommended unless your trip is less than a week. The vaccine offers around 70% protection, lasts for two to three years and comes as a single shot. Tablets are also available; however, the injection is usually recommended as it has fewer side effects. A sore arm and fever may occur. A vaccine combining Hepatitis A and typhoid in a single shot is now available.

Varicella If you haven't had chickenpox, discuss this vaccination with your doctor.

The following immunisations are recommended for travellers spending more than one month in the country or those at special risk:

Influenza A single shot lasts one year and is recommended for those over 65 years of age or with underlying medical conditions such as heart or lung disease.

Japanese B encephalitis A series of three injections with a booster after two years. Recommended if spending more than one month in rural areas in the summer months, or more than three months in the country.

Pneumonia A single injection with a booster after five years is recommended for all travellers over 65 years of age or with underlying medical conditions that compromise immunity, such as heart or lung disease, cancer or HIV.

Rabies Three injections in all. A booster after one year will then provide 10 years' protection. Side effects are rare – occasionally a headache and sore arm.

Tuberculosis A complex issue. High-risk adult long-term travellers are usually recommended to have a TB skin test before and after travel, rather than vaccination. Only one vaccine is given in a lifetime. Children under five spending more than three months in China should be vaccinated.

Pregnant women and children should receive advice from a doctor who specialises in travel medicine.

Traveller's Diarrhoea

Traveller's diarrhoea is by far the most common problem affecting travellers – between 30% and 50% of people will suffer from it within two weeks of starting their trip. In most cases, traveller's diarrhoea is caused by bacteria and responds promptly to treatment with antibiotics.

Treatment consists of staying well hydrated; rehydration solutions such as Gastrolyte are best. Antibiotics such as norfloxacin, ciprofloxacin or azithromycin will kill the bacteria quickly. Loperamide is just a 'stopper' and doesn't cure the problem; it can be helpful, however, for long bus rides. Don't take loperamide if you have a fever, or blood in your stools. Seek medical attention quickly if you do not respond to an appropriate antibiotic.

» Eat only at busy restaurants with a high turnover of customers.

» Eat only freshly cooked food.

» Avoid food that has been sitting around in buffets.

» Peel all fruit, cook vegetables and soak salads in iodine water for at least 20 minutes.

Amoebic Dysentery

Amoebic dysentery is actually rare in travellers and is overdiagnosed. Symptoms are similar to bacterial diarrhoea – fever, bloody diarrhoea and generally feeling unwell. Always seek reliable medical care if you have blood in your diarrhoea. Treatment involves two drugs: tinidazole or metronidazole to kill the parasite in your gut, and then a second drug to kill the cysts. If amoebic dysentery is left untreated, complications such as liver or gut abscesses can occur.

Giardiasis

Giardiasis is a parasite relatively common in travellers. Symptoms include nausea, bloating, excess gas, fatigue and intermittent diarrhoea. 'Eggy' burps are often attributed solely to giardia, but are not specific to the parasite. Giardiasis will eventually go away if left untreated, but this can take months. The treatment of choice is tinidazole, with metronidazole a second option.

Intestinal Worms

These parasites are most common in rural, tropical areas. Some may be ingested in food such as undercooked meat (eg tapeworms) and some enter through your skin (eg hookworms). Infestations may not show up for some time, and although they are generally not serious, some can cause severe health problems later if left untreated. Consider having a stool test when you return home.

Environmental Hazards

Air Pollution

Air pollution is a significant problem in many Chinese cities. People with underlying respiratory conditions should seek advice from their doctor prior to travel to ensure they have adequate medications in case their condition worsens. Take treatments such as throat lozenges, and cough and cold tablets.

Altitude Sickness

There are bus journeys in Tibet, Qīnghǎi and Xīnjiāng where the road goes over 5000m. Acclimatising to such extreme elevations takes several weeks at least, but most travellers come up from sea level very fast – a bad move! Acute mountain sickness (AMS) results from a rapid ascent to altitudes above 2700m. It usually commences within 24 to 48 hours of arriving at altitude, and symptoms include headache, nausea, fatigue and loss of appetite (feeling much like a hangover).

If you have altitude sickness, the cardinal rule is that you must not go higher as you are sure to get sicker and could develop one of the more severe and potentially deadly forms of the disease: high-altitude pulmonary oedema (HAPE) and high-altitude cerebral oedema (HACE). Both are medical emergencies and, as there are no rescue facilities similar to those in the Nepal Himalaya, prevention is the best policy.

AMS can be prevented by 'graded ascent'; it is recommended that once you are above 3000m you ascend a maximum of 300m daily with an extra rest day every 1000m. You can also use a medication called Diamox as a prevention or treatment for AMS, but you should discuss this first with a doctor experienced in altitude medicine. Diamox should not be taken by people with a sulphur drug allergy.

If you have altitude sickness, rest where you are for a day or two until your symptoms resolve. You can then carry on, but ensure you follow the graded-ascent guidelines. If symptoms get worse, descend immediately before you are faced with a life-threatening situation. There is no way of predicting who will suffer from AMS, but certain factors predispose you to it: rapid ascent, carrying a heavy load, and having a seemingly minor illness such as a chest infection or diarrhoea. Make sure you drink at least 3L of noncaffeinated drinks daily to stay well hydrated. The sun is intense at altitude so take care with sun protection.

Heat Exhaustion

Dehydration or salt deficiency can cause heat exhaustion. Take time to acclimatise to high temperatures, drink sufficient liquids and avoid physically demanding activity.

Salt deficiency is characterised by fatigue, lethargy, headaches, giddiness and muscle cramps; salt tablets may help, adding extra salt to your food is better.

Hypothermia

Be particularly aware of the dangers of trekking at high altitudes or simply taking a long bus trip over mountains. In Tibet it can go from being mildly warm to blisteringly cold in minutes – blizzards can appear from nowhere.

Progress from very cold to dangerously cold can be rapid due to a combination of wind, wet clothing, fatigue and hunger, even if the air temperature is above freezing. Dress in layers; silk, wool and some artificial fibres are all good insulating materials. A hat is important, as a lot of heat is lost through the head. A strong, waterproof outer layer (and a space blanket for emergencies) is essential. Carry basic supplies, including food containing simple sugars, and fluid to drink.

Symptoms of hypothermia are exhaustion, numb skin (particularly the toes and fingers), shivering, slurred speech, irrational or

DRINKING WATER

Follow these tips to avoid becoming ill.

» Never drink tap water.

» Bottled water is generally safe – check the seal is intact at purchase.

» Avoid ice.

» Avoid fresh juices – they may have been watered down.

» Boiling water is the most efficient method of purifying it.

» The best chemical purifier is iodine. It should not be used by pregnant women or those with thyroid problems.

» Water filters should also filter out viruses. Ensure your filter has a chemical barrier such as iodine and a pore size of less than 4 microns.

violent behaviour, lethargy, stumbling, dizzy spells, muscle cramps and violent bursts of energy.

To treat mild hypothermia, first get the person out of the wind and/or rain, remove their clothing if it's wet, and replace it with dry, warm clothing. Give them hot liquids – not alcohol – and high-calorie, easily digestible food. Early recognition and treatment of mild hypothermia is the only way to prevent severe hypothermia, a critical condition that requires medical attention.

Insect Bites & Stings

Bedbugs don't carry disease but their bites are very itchy. Treat the itch with an antihistamine.

Lice inhabit various parts of the human body, most commonly the head and pubic areas. Transmission is via close contact with an affected person. Lice can be difficult to treat; you may need numerous applications of an antilice shampoo such as permethrin. Pubic lice (crab lice) are usually contracted from sexual contact.

Ticks are contracted by walking in rural areas, and are commonly found behind the ears, on the belly and in armpits. If you have had a tick bite and experience symptoms such as a rash, fever or muscle aches, see a doctor. Doxycycline prevents some tick-borne diseases.

Women's Health

Pregnant women should receive specialised advice before travelling. The ideal time to travel is in the second trimester (between 14 and 28 weeks), when the risk of pregnancy-related problems is at its lowest and pregnant women generally feel at their best. During the first trimester, miscarriage is a risk; in the third trimester, complications such as premature labour and high blood pressure are possible. Travel with a companion and carry a list of quality medical facilities for your destination, ensuring you continue your standard antenatal care at these facilities. Avoid rural areas with poor transport and medical facilities. Most of all, ensure travel insurance covers all pregnancy-related possibilities, including premature labour.

Malaria is a high-risk disease in pregnancy. The World Health Organization recommends that pregnant women do not travel to areas with chloroquine-resistant malaria.

Traveller's diarrhoea can quickly lead to dehydration and result in inadequate blood flow to the placenta. Many drugs used to treat various diarrhoea bugs are not recommended in pregnancy. Azithromycin is considered safe.

Heat, humidity and antibiotics can all contribute to thrush. Treatment is with antifungal creams and pessaries such as clotrimazole. A practical alternative is a single tablet of fluconazole (Diflucan). Urinary-tract infections can be precipitated by dehydration or long bus journeys without toilet stops; bring suitable antibiotics.

Supplies of sanitary products may not be readily available in rural areas. Birth-control options may be limited, so bring adequate supplies of your own form of contraception.

Language

WANT MORE?

For in-depth language information and handy phrases, check out Lonely Planet's *China Phrasebook*. You'll find it at **shop.lonelyplanet.com**, or you can buy Lonely Planet's iPhone phrasebooks at the Apple App Store.

The official language of China is the dialect spoken in Běijīng. It is usually referred to in the west as Mandarin, but the Chinese call it Pǔtōnghuà (common speech). Pǔtōnghuà is variously referred to as Hànyǔ (the Han language), Guóyǔ (the national language) or Zhōngwén or Zhōngguóhuà (Chinese).

Discounting its ethnic minority languages, China has eight major dialect groups: Pǔtōnghuà (Mandarin), Yue (Cantonese), Wu (Shanghainese), Minbei (Fuzhou), Minnan (Hokkien-Taiwanese), Xiang, Gan and Hakka. These dialects also divide into subdialects.

With the exception of the western and southernmost provinces, most of the population speaks Mandarin, although there are regional accents.

Writing

Chinese is often referred to as a language of pictographs. Many of the basic Chinese characters are in fact highly stylised pictures of what they represent, but most (around 90%) are compounds of a 'meaning' element and a 'sound' element.

It is commonly felt that a well-educated, contemporary Chinese person might know and use between 6000 and 8000 characters. To read a Chinese newspaper you will need to know 2000 to 3000 characters, but 1200 to 1500 would be enough to get the gist.

Theoretically, all Chinese dialects share the same written system. In practice, Cantonese adds about 3000 specialised characters of its own and many of the dialects don't have a written form at all.

MANDARIN

Pinyin & Pronunciation

In 1958 the Chinese adopted a system of writing their language using the Roman alphabet. It's known as Pinyin. The original idea was to eventually do away with Chinese characters. However, tradition dies hard, and the idea has been abandoned.

Pinyin is often used on shop fronts, street signs and advertising billboards. Don't expect all Chinese people to be able to use Pinyin, however. In the countryside and the smaller towns you may not see a single Pinyin sign anywhere, so unless you speak Chinese you'll need a phrasebook with Chinese characters.

In this chapter we've provided Pinyin alonside the Mandarin script.

Vowels

a	as in 'father'
ai	as in 'aisle'
ao	as the 'ow' in 'cow'
e	as in 'her', with no 'r' sound
ei	as in 'weigh'
i	as the 'ee' in 'meet' (or like a light 'r' as in 'Grrr!' after c, ch, r, s, sh, z or zh)
ian	as the word 'yen'
ie	as the English word 'yeah'
o	as in 'or', with no 'r' sound
ou	as the 'oa' in 'boat'
u	as in 'flute'
ui	as the word 'way'
uo	like a 'w' followed by 'o'
yu/ü	like 'ee' with lips pursed

Consonants

c	as the 'ts' in 'bits'
ch	as in 'chop', but with the tongue curled up and back
h	as in 'hay', but articulated from farther back in the throat
q	as the 'ch' in 'cheese'
sh	as in 'ship', but with the tongue curled up and back
x	as in 'ship'
z	as the 'ds' in 'suds'
zh	as the 'j' in 'judge' but with the tongue curled up and back

The only consonants that occur at the end of a syllable are n, ng and r.

In Pinyin, apostrophes are occasionally used to separate syllables in order to prevent ambiguity, eg the word píng'ān can be written with an apostrophe after the 'g' to prevent it being pronounced as pín'gān.

Tones

Chinese is a language with a large number of words with the same pronunciation but a different meaning. What distinguishes these homophones is their 'tonal' quality – the raising and the lowering of pitch on certain syllables. Mandarin employs four tones – high, rising, falling-rising and falling, plus a fifth 'neutral' tone that you can all but ignore. Tones are important for distinguishing meaning of words – eg the word ma has four different meanings according to tone, as shown below. Tones are indicated in Pinyin by the following accent marks on vowels:

high tone	mā (mother)
rising tone	má (hemp, numb)
falling-rising tone	mǎ (horse)
falling tone	mà (scold, swear)

Basics

When asking a question it is polite to start with qǐng wèn – literally, 'may I ask?'.

Hello.	你好。	Nǐhǎo.
Goodbye.	再见。	Zàijiàn.
How are you?	你好吗？	Nǐhǎo ma?
Fine. And you?	好。你呢？	Hǎo. Nǐ ne?
Excuse me.		
(to get attention)	劳驾。	Láojià.
(to get past)	借光。	Jièguāng.
Sorry.	对不起。	Duìbùqǐ.
Yes./No.	是。/不是。	Shì./Bùshì.
Please ...	请……	Qǐng ...
Thank you.	谢谢你。	Xièxie nǐ.
You're welcome.	不客气。	Bù kèqi.

KEY PATTERNS – MANDARIN

To get by in Mandarin, mix and match these simple patterns with words of your choice:

How much is (the deposit)?	
（押金）多少？	(Yājīn) duōshǎo?
Do you have (a room)?	
有没有（房）？	Yǒuméiyǒu (fáng)?
Is there (heating)?	
有（暖气）吗？	Yóu (nuǎnqì) ma?
I'd like (that one).	
我要（那个）。	Wǒ yào (nàge).
Please give me (the menu).	
请给我（菜单）。	Qǐng gěiwǒ (càidān).
Can I (sit here)?	
我能（坐这儿）吗？	Wǒ néng (zuòzhèr) ma?
I need (a can opener).	
我想要（一个开罐器）。	Wǒ xiǎngyào (yīge kāiguàn qì).
Do we need (a guide)?	
需要（向导）吗？	Xūyào (xiàngdǎo) ma?
I have (a reservation).	
我有（预订）。	Wǒ yǒu (yùdìng).
I'm (a doctor).	
我（是医生）。	Wǒ (shì yīshēng).

What's your name?	
你叫什么名字？	Nǐ jiào shénme míngzi?
My name is ...	
我叫……	Wǒ jiào ...
Do you speak English?	
你会说英文吗？	Nǐ huìshuō Yīngwén ma?
I don't understand.	
我不明白。	Wǒ bù míngbái.

Accommodation

Do you have a single/double room?	
有没有（单人/套）房？	Yǒuméiyǒu (dānrén/tào) fáng?
How much is it per night/person?	
每天/人多少钱？	Měi tiān/rén duōshǎo qián?

campsite	露营地	lùyíngdì
guesthouse	宾馆	bīnguǎn
hostel	招待所	zhāodàisuǒ
hotel	酒店	jiǔdiàn
air-con	空调	kōngtiáo
bathroom	浴室	yùshì
bed	床	chuáng
cot	张婴儿床	zhāng yīng'ér chuáng
window	窗	chuāng

Signs – Mandarin

入口	Rùkǒu	**Entrance**
出口	Chūkǒu	**Exit**
问讯处	Wènxùnchù	**Information**
开	Kāi	**Open**
关	Guān	**Closed**
禁止	Jìnzhǐ	**Prohibited**
厕所	Cèsuǒ	**Toilets**
男	Nán	**Men**
女	Nǚ	**Women**

Directions

Where's (a bank)?
(银行)在哪儿? (Yínháng) zài nǎr?

What is the address?
地址在哪儿? Dìzhǐ zài nǎr?

Could you write the address, please?
能不能请你把地址写下来? Néngbunéng qǐng nǐ bǎ dìzhǐ xiě xiàlái?

Can you show me where it is on the map?
请帮我找它在地图上的位置。 Qǐng bāngwǒ zhǎo tā zài dìtú shàng de wèizhi.

Go straight ahead.
一直走。 Yīzhí zǒu.

at the traffic lights
在红绿灯 zài hónglǜdēng

behind	背面	bèimiàn
far	远	yuǎn
in front of ...	……的前面	... de qiánmian
near	近	jìn
next to	旁边	pángbiān
on the corner	拐角	guǎijiǎo
opposite	对面	duìmiàn
Turn left.	左转。	Zuǒ zhuǎn.
Turn right.	右转。	Yòu zhuǎn.

Eating & Drinking

What would you recommend?
有什么菜可以推荐的? Yǒu shénme cài kěyǐ tuījiàn de?

What's in that dish?
这道菜用什么东西做的? Zhèdào cài yòng shénme dōngxi zuòde?

That was delicious!
真好吃! Zhēn hǎochī!

The bill, please!
买单! Mǎidān!

Cheers!
干杯! Gānbēi!

I'd like to reserve a table for ...	我想预订一张……的桌子。	Wǒ xiǎng yùdìng yīzhāng ... de zhuōzi.
(eight) o'clock	（八）点钟	(bā)diǎn zhōng
(two) people	（两个）人	(liǎngge) rén

I don't eat ...	我不吃……	Wǒ bùchī ...
fish	鱼	yú
nuts	果仁	guǒrén
poultry	家禽	jiāqín
red meat	牛羊肉	niúyángròu

Key Words

appetisers	凉菜	liángcài
bar	酒吧	jiǔbā
bottle	瓶子	píngzi
bowl	碗	wǎn
breakfast	早饭	zǎofàn
cafe	咖啡屋	kāfēiwū
chidren's menu	儿童菜单	értóng càidān
(too) cold	(太)凉	(tài) liáng
dinner	晚饭	wǎntàn
dish (food)	盘	pán
food	食品	shípǐn
fork	叉子	chazi
glass	杯子	bēizi
halal	清真	qīngzhēn
highchair	高凳	gāodèng
hot (warm)	热	rè
knife	刀	dāo
kosher	犹太	yóutài
local specialties	地方小吃	dìfāng xiǎochī
lunch	午饭	wǔfàn
main courses	主菜	zhǔ cài
market	菜市	càishì
menu (in English)	(英文)菜单	(Yīngwén) càidān
plate	碟子	diézi
restaurant	餐馆	cānguǎn
(too) spicy	(太)辣	(tài) là
spoon	勺	sháo
vegetarian food	素食食品	sùshí shípín

Meat & Fish

beef	牛肉	niúròu
chicken	鸡肉	jīròu
duck	鸭	yā
fish	鱼	yú

lamb	羊肉	yángròu
pork	猪肉	zhūròu
seafood	海鲜	hǎixiān

Fruit & Vegetables

apple	苹果	píngguǒ
banana	香蕉	xiāngjiāo
bok choy	小白菜	xiǎo báicài
carrot	胡萝卜	húluóbo
celery	芹菜	qíncài
cucumber	黄瓜	huánggua
'dragon eyes'	龙眼	lóngyǎn
fruit	水果	shuǐguǒ
grape	葡萄	pútáo
green beans	扁豆	biǎndòu
guava	石榴	shíliu
lychee	荔枝	lìzhī
mango	芒果	mángguǒ
mushroom	蘑菇	mógū
onion	洋葱	yáng cōng
orange	橙子	chéngzi
pear	梨	lí
pineapple	凤梨	fènglí
plum	梅子	méizi
potato	土豆	tǔdòu
radish	萝卜	luóbo
spring onion	小葱	xiǎo cōng
sweet potato	地瓜	dìguā
vegetable	蔬菜	shūcài
watermelon	西瓜	xīguā

Other

bread	面包	miànbāo
butter	黄油	huángyóu
egg	蛋	dàn
herbs/spices	香料	xiāngliào
pepper	胡椒粉	hújiāo fěn
salt	盐	yán
soy sauce	酱油	jiàngyóu
sugar	砂糖	shātáng
tofu	豆腐	dòufu
vinegar	醋	cù
vegetable oil	菜油	càiyóu

Question Words – Mandarin

How?	怎么?	Zěnme?
What?	什么?	Shénme?
When?	什么时候	Shénme shíhòu?
Where?	哪儿	Nǎr?
Which?	哪个	Nǎge?
Who?	谁?	Shuí?
Why?	为什么?	Wèishénme?

Drinks

beer	啤酒	píjiǔ
Chinese spirits	白酒	báijiǔ
coffee	咖啡	kāfēi
(orange) juice	(橙)汁	(chéng) zhī
milk	牛奶	niúnǎi
mineral water	矿泉水	kuàngquán shuǐ
red wine	红葡萄酒	hóng pútáo jiǔ
rice wine	米酒	mǐjiǔ
soft drink	汽水	qìshuǐ
tea	茶	chá
(boiled) water	(开)水	(kāi) shuǐ
white wine	白葡萄酒	bái pútáo jiǔ
yoghurt	酸奶	suānnǎi

Emergencies

Help!	救命!	Jiùmìng!
I'm lost.	我迷路了。	Wǒ mílù le.
Go away!	走开!	Zǒukāi!

There's been an accident!
出事了! Chūshì le!

Call a doctor!
请叫医生来! Qǐng jiào yīshēng lái!

Call the police!
请叫警察! Qǐng jiào jǐngchá!

I'm ill.
我生病了。 Wǒ shēngbìng le.

It hurts here.
这里痛。 Zhèlǐ tòng.

I'm allergic to (antibiotics).
我对(抗菌素)过敏。 Wǒ duì (kàngjūnsù) guòmǐn.

Shopping & Services

I'd like to buy ...
我想买…… Wǒ xiǎng mǎi ...

I'm just looking.
我先看看。 Wǒ xiān kànkan.

Can I look at it?
我能看看吗? Wǒ néng kànkan ma?

I don't like it.
我不喜欢。 Wǒ bù xǐhuan.

Numbers – Mandarin

1	一	yī
2	二/两	èr/liǎng
3	三	sān
4	四	sì
5	五	wǔ
6	六	liù
7	七	qī
8	八	bā
9	九	jiǔ
10	十	shí
20	二十	èrshí
30	三十	sānshí
40	四十	sìshí
50	五十	wǔshí
60	六十	liùshí
70	七十	qīshí
80	八十	bāshí
90	九十	jiǔshí
100	一百	yībǎi
1000	一千	yīqiān

How much is it?
多少钱？ Duōshǎo qián?

That's too expensive!
太贵了！ Tàiguì le!

Can you lower the price?
能便宜一点吗？ Néng piányi yīdiǎn ma?

There's a mistake in the bill.
帐单上有问题。 Zhàngdān shàng yǒu wèntí.

ATM	自动取款机	zìdòng qǔkuǎn jī
credit card	信用卡	xìnyòng kǎ
internet cafe	网吧	wǎngbā
post office	邮局	yóujú
tourist office	旅行店	lǚxíng diàn

Time & Dates

What time is it?
现在几点钟？ Xiànzài jǐdiǎn zhōng?

It's (10) o'clock.
(十)点钟。 (Shí)diǎn zhōng.

Half past (10).
(十)点三十分。 (Shí)diǎn sānshífēn.

morning	早上	zǎoshang
afternoon	下午	xiàwǔ
evening	晚上	wǎnshàng
yesterday	昨天	zuótiān
today	今天	jīntiān
tomorrow	明天	míngtiān

Monday	星期一	xīngqī yī
Tuesday	星期二	xīngqī èr
Wednesday	星期三	xīngqī sān
Thursday	星期四	xīngqī sì
Friday	星期五	xīngqī wǔ
Saturday	星期六	xīngqī liù
Sunday	星期天	xīngqī tiān

January	一月	yīyuè
February	二月	èryuè
March	三月	sānyuè
April	四月	sìyuè
May	五月	wǔyuè
June	六月	liùyuè
July	七月	qīyuè
August	八月	bāyuè
September	九月	jiǔyuè
October	十月	shíyuè
November	十一月	shíyīyuè
December	十二月	shí'èryuè

Transport

Public Transport

boat	船	chuán
bus (city)	大巴	dàbā
bus (intercity)	长途车	chángtú chē
plane	飞机	fēijī
taxi	出租车	chūzū chē
train	火车	huǒchē
tram	电车	diànchē

I want to go to ...
我要去…… Wǒ yào qù ...

Does it stop at (Hāěrbīn)?
在(哈尔滨)能下车吗？ Zài (Hā'ěrbīn) néng xià chē ma?

What time does it leave?
几点钟出发？ Jǐdiǎnzhōng chūfā?

What time does it get to (Hángzhōu)?
几点钟到(杭州)？ Jǐdiǎnzhōng dào (Hángzhōu)?

Can you tell me when we get to (Hángzhōu)?
到了(杭州)请叫我，好吗？ Dàole (Hángzhōu) qǐng jiào wǒ, hǎoma?

I want to get off here.
我想这儿下车。 Wǒ xiǎng zhèr xiàchē.

When's the ... (bus)?	……(车)几点走?	... (chē) jǐdiǎn zǒu?
first	首趟	Shǒutàng
last	末趟	Mòtàng
next	下一趟	Xià yītàng

A ... ticket to (Dàlián).	一张到(大连)的……票。	Yīzhāng dào (Dàlián) de ... piào.
1st-class	头等	tóuděng
2nd-class	二等	èrděng
one-way	单程	dānchéng
return	双程	shuāngchéng

aisle seat	走廊的座位	zǒuláng de zuòwèi
cancelled	取消	qǔxiāo
delayed	晚点	wǎndiǎn
platform	站台	zhàntái
ticket office	售票处	shòupiàochù
timetable	时刻表	shíkè biǎo
train station	火车站	huǒchēzhàn
window seat	窗户的座位	chuānghu de zuòwèi

Driving & Cycling

bicycle pump	打气筒	dǎqìtóng
child seat	婴儿座	yīng'érzuò
diesel	柴油	cháiyóu
helmet	头盔	tóukuī
mechanic	机修工	jīxiūgōng
petrol/gas	汽油	qìyóu
service station	加油站	jiāyóu zhàn

I'd like to hire a ...	我要租一辆……	Wǒ yào zū yīliàng ...
4WD	四轮驱动	sìlún qūdòng
bicycle	自行车	zìxíngchē
car	汽车	qìchē
motorcycle	摩托车	mótuochē

Does this road lead to ...?
这条路到……吗? Zhè tiáo lù dào ... ma?

How long can I park here?
这儿可以停多久? Zhèr kěyi tíng duōjiǔ?

The car has broken down (at ...).
汽车是(在……)坏的。Qìchē shì (zài ...) huài de.

I have a flat tyre.
轮胎瘪了。 Lúntāi biě le.

I've run out of petrol.
没有汽油了。 Méiyou qìyóu le.

CANTONESE

Cantonese is still the most popular dialect in Hong Kong, Guǎngzhōu and the surrounding area. Cantonese speakers can read Chinese characters, but will pronounce many of the characters differently from a Mandarin speaker.

Several systems of Romanisation for Cantonese script exist, and no single one has emerged as an official standard. In this chapter we use Lonely Planet's pronunciation guide designed for maximum accuracy with minimum complexity.

Pronunciation

Vowels

a	as the 'u' in 'but'
ai	as in 'aisle' (short sound)
au	as the 'ou' in 'out'
ay	as in 'pay'
eu	as the 'er' in 'fern'
eui	as in French *feuille* (eu with i)
ew	as in 'blew' (short and pronounced with tightened lips)
i	as the 'ee' in 'deep'
iu	as the 'yu' in 'yuletide'
o	as in 'go'
oy	as in 'boy'
u	as in 'put'
ui	as in French *oui*

Consonants

In Cantonese, the ng sound can appear at the start of a word. Practise by saying 'sing along' slowly and then do away with the 'si'.

Note that words ending with the consonant sounds p, t, and k must be clipped in Cantonese. You can hear this in English as well – say 'pit' and 'tip' and listen to how much shorter the 'p' sound is in 'tip'.

Many Cantonese speakers, particularly young people, replace an 'n' sound with an 'l' if a word begins with it – ná̱y (you), is often heard as lá̱y. Where relevant, this change is reflected in our pronunciation guide.

Tones

Tones in Cantonese fall on vowels (a, e, i, o, u) and on n. The same word pronounced with different tones can have a very different meaning, eg gwa̱t (dig up) and gwàt (bones). Our pronunciation guide shows six tones, divided into high and low pitch groups. High-pitch tones involve tightening the vocal muscles to get a higher note, whereas lower-pitch tones are made by relaxing the vocal chords to get a lower note. The tones are indicated with the following accent marks:

à	high
á	high rising
a	level
à̱	low falling
á̱	low rising
a̱	low

Basics

Hello.	哈佬 。	hàa·ló
Goodbye.	再見 。	joy·gin
How are you?	你幾好啊嗎？	láy gáy hó à maa
Fine.	幾好 。	gáy hó
Excuse me. (to get attention)	對唔住 。	deui·ǹg·jew
Excuse me. (to get past)	唔該借借 。	ǹg·gòy je·je
Sorry.	對唔住 。	deui·ǹg·jew
Yes./No.	係 。/不係 。	hai/ǹg·hai
Please ...	唔該……	ǹg·gòy ...
Thank you.	多謝 。	dàw·je
You're welcome.	唔駛客氣 。	ǹg·sái haak·hay

What's your name?
你叫乜嘢名？ láy giu màt·yé méng aa

My name is ...
我叫…… ngáw giu ...

Do you speak (English)?
你識唔識講(英文)啊？ láy sìk·ǹg·sìk gáwng (yìng·mán) aa

I don't understand.
我唔明 。 ngáw ǹg mìng

Accommodation

campsite	營地	yìng·day
guesthouse	賓館	bàn·gún
hostel	招待所	jiù·doy·sáw
hotel	酒店	jáu·dim

Do you have a ... room?	有冇……房？	yáu·mó ... fáwng
single	單人	dàan·yàn
double	雙人	sèung·yàn

How much is it per ...?	一……幾多錢？	yàt ... gáy·dàw chín
night	晚	máan
person	個人	gaw yàn

air-con	空調 (HK) 冷氣 (China)	hùng·tiù láang·hay
bathroom	沖涼房	chùng·lèung·fáwng
bed	床	chàwng
cot	BB床	bi·bì chàwng
window	窗	chèung

KEY PATTERNS – CANTONESE

To get by in Cantonese, mix and match these simple patterns with words of your choice:

When's (the next tour)?
(下個旅遊團係)幾時？ (haa·gaw léui·yàu·tèwn hai) gáy·sì

Where's (the station)?
(車站)喺邊度？ (chè·jaam) hái·bìn·do

Where can I (buy a padlock)?
邊度可以(買倒鎖)？ bìn·do háw·yí (máai dó sáw)

Do you have (a map)?
有冇(地圖)？ yáu·mó (day·tò)

I need (a mechanic).
我要(個整車師傅)。 ngáw yiu (gaw jíng·chè sì·fú)

I'd like (a taxi).
我想(坐的士) 。 ngáw séung (cháw dìk·sí)

Can I (get a stand-by ticket)?
可唔可以(買張後補飛)呀？ háw·ǹg·háw·yí (máai jèung hau·bó fày) aa

Could you please (write it down)?
唔該你(寫落嚟)? ǹg·gòy láy (sé lawk lài)

Do I need (to book)?
駛唔駛(定飛先)呀？ sái·ǹg·sái (deng·fày sìn) aa

I have (a reservation).
我(預定)咗 。 ngáw (yew·deng) jáw

Directions

Where's ...?	……喺邊度？	... hái bìn·do
What's the address?	地址係？	day·jí hai
behind	後面	hau·min
far	遠	yéwn
left	左邊	jáw·bìn
near ...	……附近	... fu·gan
next to ...	……旁邊	... pàwng·bìn
on the corner	十字路口	sap·ji·lo·háu
opposite	對面	deui·min
right	右邊	yau·bìn
straight ahead	前面	chìn·min
traffic lights	紅綠燈	hùng·luk·dàng

Eating & Drinking

What would you recommend?
有乜嘢好介紹？ yáu màt·yé hó gaai·siu

What's in that dish?
呢道菜有啲乜嘢？ lày do choy yáu dì màt·yé

That was delicious.
真好味 。 jàn hó·may

I'd like the bill, please.
唔該我要埋單 。 ǹg·gòy ngáw yiu màai·dàan

Cheers!
乾杯！ gàwn·buì

I'd like to book a table for ...	我想訂張檯，……嘅。	ngáw séung deng jèung tóy ... ge
(eight) o'clock	(八)點鐘	(baat) dím·jùng
(two) people	(兩)位	(léung) wái

I don't eat ...	我唔吃……	ngáw ǹg sik ...
fish	魚	yéw
nuts	果仁	gwáw·yàn
poultry	雞鴨鵝	gài ngaap ngàw
red meat	牛羊肉	ngàu yèung yuk

Key Words

appetisers	涼盤	lèung·pún
baby food	嬰兒食品	yìng·yi sik·bán
bar	酒吧	jáu·bàa
bottle	樽	jèun
bowl	碗	wún
breakfast	早餐	jó·chàan
cafe	咖啡屋	gaa·fè·ngùk
children's menu	個小童菜單	gaw siú·tung choy·dàan
(too) cold	(太)凍	(taai) dung
dinner	晚飯	máan·faan
food	食物	sik·mat
fork	叉	chàa
glass	杯	buì
halal	清真	chìng·jàn
high chair	高凳	gò·dang
hot (warm)	熱	yit
knife	刀	dò
kosher	猶太	yàu·tàai
local specialities	地方小食	day·fàwng siú·sik
lunch	午餐	ńg·chàan
market	街市 (HK) 市場 (China)	gàai·sí sí·chèung
main courses	主菜	jéw·choy
menu (in English)	(英文)菜單	(yìng·màn) choy·dàan
plate	碟	díp
restaurant	酒樓	jáu·làu
(too) spicy	(太)辣	(taai) laat
spoon	羹	gàng
supermarket	超市	chiù·sí
vegetarian food	齋食品	jàai sik·bán

Meat & Fish

beef	牛肉	ngàu·yuk
chicken	雞肉	gài·yuk
duck	鴨	ngaap
fish	魚	yéw
lamb	羊肉	yèung·yuk
pork	豬肉	jèw·yuk
seafood	海鮮	hóy·sìn

Fruit & Vegetables

apple	蘋果	ping·gwáw
banana	香蕉	hèung·jiù
cabbage	白菜	baak·choy
carrot	紅蘿蔔	hùng·làw·baak
celery	芹菜	kàn·choy
cucumber	青瓜	chèng·gwàa
fruit	水果	séui·gwáw
grapes	葡提子	pò·tài·jí
green beans	扁荳	bín·dau
lemon	檸檬	lìng·mùng
lettuce	生菜	sàang·choy
mushroom	蘑菇	màw·gù
onion(s)	洋蔥	yèung·chùng
orange	橙	cháang
peach	桃	tó
pear	梨	láy
pineapple	菠蘿	bàw·làw
plum	梅	muì
potato	薯仔	sèw·jái
spinach	菠菜	bàw·choy
tomato	番茄	fàan·ké
vegetable	蔬菜	sàw·choy

Other

bread	麵包	min·bàau
butter	牛油	ngàu·yàu
egg	蛋	dáan

Signs – Cantonese

入口	**Entrance**
出口	**Exit**
廁所	**Toilets**
男	**Men**
女	**Women**

Question Words – Cantonese

How?	點樣?	dím·yéung
What?	乜嘢?	màt·yé
When?	幾時?	gáy·sì
Where?	邊度?	bìn·do
Who?	邊個?	bìnz·gaw
Why?	點解?	dím·gáai

herbs/spices	香料	hèung·liú
pepper	胡椒粉	wù·jiù·fán
rice	白飯	baak·faan
salt	鹽	yìm
soy sauce	豉油	si·yàu
sugar	砂糖	sàa·tàwng
vegetable oil	菜油	choy·yàu
vinegar	醋	cho

Drinks

beer	啤酒	bè·jáu
coffee	咖啡	gaa·fè
juice	果汁	gwáw·jàp
milk	牛奶	ngàu·láai
mineral water	礦泉水	kawng·chèwn·séui
red wine	紅葡萄酒	hùng·pò·tò·jáu
tea	茶	chàa
white wine	白葡萄酒	baak·pò·tò·jáu

Emergencies

Help!	救命!	gau·meng
I'm lost.	我蕩失路。	ngáw dawng·sàk·lo
Go away!	走開!	jáu·hòy

There's been an accident!
有意外! yáu yi·ngoy

Call a doctor!
快啲叫醫生! faai·dì giu yì·sàng

Call the police!
快啲叫警察! faai·dì giu gíng·chaat

I'm sick.
我病咗。 ngáw beng·jáw

I'm allergic to ...
我對……過敏。 ngáw deui ... gaw·mán

Shopping & Services

I'd like to buy ...
我想買…… ngáw séung máai ...

I'm just looking.
睇下。 tái haa

Can I look at it?
我可唔可以睇下? ngáw háw·ǹg·háw·yí tái haa

How much is it?
幾多錢? gáy·dàw chín

That's too expensive!
太貴啦! taai gwai laa

Can you lower the price?
可唔可以平啲呀? háw·ǹg·háw·yí pèng dì aa

There's a mistake in the bill.
帳單錯咗。 jeung·dàan chaw jáw

ATM	自動提款機	ji·dung tài·fún·gày
credit card	信用卡	seun·yung·kàat
internet cafe	網吧	máwng·bàa
post office	郵局	yàu·gúk
tourist office	旅行社	léui·hàng·sé

Time & Dates

What time is it?	而家幾點鐘?	yì·gàa gáy·dím·jùng
It's (10) o'clock.	(十)點鐘。	(sap)·dím·jùng
Half past (10).	(十)點半。	(sap)·dím bun

morning	朝早	jiù·jó
afternoon	下晝	haa·jau
evening	夜晚	ye·máan
yesterday	寢日	kàm·yat
today	今日	gàm·yat
tomorrow	听日	tìng·yat

Monday	星期一	sìng·kày·yàt
Tuesday	星期二	sìng·kày·yi
Wednesday	星期三	sìng·kày·sàam
Thursday	星期四	sìng·kày·say
Friday	星期五	sìng·kày·ńg
Saturday	星期六	sìng·kày·luk
Sunday	星期日	sìng·kày·yat

January	一月	yàt·yewt
February	二月	yi·yewt
March	三月	sàam·yewt
April	四月	say·yewt
May	五月	ńg·yewt
June	六月	luk·yewt
July	七月	chàt·yewt
August	八月	baat·yewt
September	九月	gáu·yewt
October	十月	sap·yewt
November	十一月	sap·yàt·yewt
December	十二月	sap·yi·yewt

Transport

Public Transport

boat	船	sèwn
bus	巴士 (HK)	bàa·sí
	公共汽車 (China)	gùng·gung hay·chè
plane	飛機	fày·gày
taxi	的士	dìk·sí
train	火車	fáw·chè
tram	電車	din·chè

Does it stop at (Mong Kok)?
會唔會喺(旺角)停呀？ wui·ng·wui hái (wawng·gawk) ting aa

What time does it leave?
幾點鐘出發？ gáy·dím jùng chèut·faa

What time does it get to (Shunde)?
幾點鐘到(順德)？ gáy·dím jùng do (seun·dàk)

What's the next stop?
下個站叫乜名？ haa·gaw jaam giu màt méng

Please tell me when we get to (Guangzhou).
到(廣州)嘅時候，唔該叫聲我。 do (gwáwng·jàu) ge si·hau ng·gòy giu sèng ngáw

I'd like to get off at (Panyu).
我要喺(番禺)落車。 ngáw yiu hái (pùn·yèw) lawk·chè

Numbers – Cantonese

1	一	yàt
2	二	yi
3	三	sàam
4	四	say
5	五	ńg
6	六	luk
7	七	chàt
8	八	baat
9	九	gáu
10	十	sap
20	二十	yi·sap
30	三十	sàam·sap
40	四十	say·sap
50	五十	ńg·sap
60	六十	luk·sap
70	七十	chàt·sap
80	八十	baat·sap
90	九十	gáu·sap
100	一百	yàt·baak
1000	一千	yàt·chìn

When's the ... (bus)?	……(巴士)幾點開？	... (bàa·sí) gáy dím hòy
first	頭班	tàu·bàan
last	尾班	máy·bàan
next	下一班	haa·yàt·bàan

A ... ticket to (Panyu).	一張去(番禺)嘅……飛。	yàt jèung heui (pùn·yèw) ge ... fày
1st-class	頭等	tàu·dáng
2nd-class	二等	yi·dáng
one-way	單程	dàan·ching
return	雙程	sèung·ching

aisle	路邊	lo·bìn
cancelled	取消	chéui·sìu
delayed	押後	ngaat·hau
platform	月台	yéwt·tòy
ticket window	售票處	sau·piu·chew
timetable	時間表	si·gaan·biú
train station	火車站	fó·chè·jaam
window	窗口	chèung·háu

Driving & Cycling

I'd like to hire a ...	我想租架……	ngáw séung jò gaa ...
4WD	4WD	fàw·wiù·jàai·fù
bicycle	單車	dàan·chè
car	車	chè
motorcycle	電單車	din·dàan·chè

baby seat	BB座	bi·bì jaw
diesel	柴油	chàai·yàu
helmet	頭盔	táu·kwài
mechanic	修車師傅	sàu·chè sì·fú
petrol/gas	汽油	hay·yàu
service station	加油站	gàa·yàu·jàam

Is this the road to (Mong Kok)?
呢條路係唔係去(旺角)㗎？ lày tiu lo hai·ng·hai heui (wawng·gawk) gaa

How long can I park here?
我喺呢度可以停幾耐？ ngáw hái lày·do háw·yí ting gáy·loy

The (car/motorbike) has broken down at (...).
架(車/電單車)係(……)壞咗。 gaa (chè/din·dàan·chè) hái (...) waai jáw

I have a flat tyre.
我爆咗呔。 ngáw baau·jáw tàai

I've run out of petrol.
我冇晒油。 ngáw mó saai yáu

TIBETAN

Tibetan is spoken by around six million people, mainly in Tibet but also in Nepal, India, Bhutan and Pakistan. In urban areas almost all Tibetans also speak Mandarin.

Most sounds in Tibetan are similar to those found in English, so if you read our coloured pronunciation guides as if they were English, you'll be understood. Note that the symbol â is pronounced as the 'a' in 'ago', ö as the 'er' in 'her', and ü as the 'u' in 'flute' but with a raised tongue.

When a vowel is followed by n, m or ng, this indicates a nasalised sound (pronounced with air escaping through the nose). When a consonant is followed by h, the consonant is aspirated (ie accompanied by a puff of air).

Basics

There are no words in Tibetan that are the direct equivalents of English 'yes' and 'no'. Although it won't always be completely correct, you'll be understood if you use la ong for 'yes' and la men for 'no'.

Hello.	བཀྲ་ཤིས་བདེ་ལེགས།	ta·shi de·lek
Goodbye.		
(if staying)	ག་ལེར་ཕེབས།	ka·lee pay
(if leaving)	ག་ལེར་བཞུགས།	ka·lee shu
Excuse me.	དགོངས་དག	gong·da
Sorry.	དགོངས་དག	gong·da
Please.	ཐུགས་རྗེ་གཟིགས།	tu jay sig
Thank you.	ཐུགས་རྗེ་ཆེ།	tu·jay·chay

How are you?
ཁྱེད་རང་སྐུ་གཟུགས་ kay·râng ku·su
བདེ་པོ་ཡིན་པས། de·po yin·bay

Fine. And you?
བདེ་པོ་ཡིན། ཁྱེད་རང་ཡང་ de·bo·yin kay·râng·yâng
སྐུ་གཟུགས་བདེ་པོ་ཡིན་པས། ku·su de·po yin·bay

What's your name?
ཁྱེད་རང་གི་མཚན་ལ་ kay·râng·gi tsen·lâ
ག་རེ་རེད། kâ·ray·ray

My name is ...
ངའི་མིང་ལ་ ... རེད། ngay·ming·la ... ray

Do you speak English?
ཁྱེད་རང་དབྱིན་ཇི་སྐད་ kay·râng in·ji·kay
ཤེས་ཀྱི་ཡོད་པས། shing·gi yö·bay

I don't understand.
ཧ་གོ་མ་སོང་། ha ko ma song

Accommodation

I'm looking for a ...	... གཅིག་མིག་ བལྟ་གི་ཡོད།	...·chig mig ta·gi·yö
campsite	གུར་བརྒྱབ་ནས་ སྡོད་སའི་ས་ཆ	gur gyâb·nay dö·say sa·cha
guesthouse	མགྲོན་ཁང་	drön·khâng
hotel	འགྲུལ་ཁང་	drü·khâng

I'd like to book a room.
ཁང་མིག་ཅིག་གླ་དགོས་ཡོད། khâng·mi·chig la gö·yö

How much for one night?
མཚན་གཅིག་ལ་གོང་ tsen chig·la gong
ག་ཚད་རེད། kâ·tsay ray

I'd like to stay with a Tibetan family.
ང་བོད་པའི་མི་ཚང་ nga bö·pay mi·tsâng
མཉམ་དུ་བསྡད་འདོད་ཡོད། nyâm·do den·dö yö

I need some hot water.
ང་ལ་ཆུ་ཚ་པོ་དགོས། nga·la chu tsa·po gö

Directions

Where is ...?
... ག་པར་ཡོད་རེད། ... ka·bah yö·ray

Numbers – Tibetan

1	༡	chig
2	༢	nyi
3	༣	soom
4	༤	shi
5	༥	nga
6	༦	doog
7	༧	dün
8	༨	gye
9	༩	gu
10	༡༠	chu
20	༢༠	nyi·shu
30	༣༠	soom·chu
40	༤༠	shib·chu
50	༥༠	ngâb·chu
60	༦༠	doog·chu
70	༧༠	dün·chu
80	༨༠	gyay·chu
90	༩༠	goob·chu
100	༡༠༠	gya
1000	༡༠༠༠	chig·tong

Can you show me (on the map)?
(ས་བཀྲ་འདི་ནང་) (sâp·ta di·nâng)
སྟོན་གནང་དང་། tön nâng·da

Turn left/right.
གཡོན་ལ་/གཡས་ལ་ yön·la/yeh·la
སྐྱོགས་གནང་། kyog·nâng

behind ...	… རྒྱབ་ལ་	... gyâb·lâ
in front of ...	… མདུན་ལ་	... dün·lâ
near (to) ...	… འཁྲིས་ལ་	... tee·lâ
opposite ...	… ཕར་ཕྱོགས་ལ་	... pha·chog·lâ
straight ahead	ཁ་ཐུག་འགྲོ།	ka·toog·do

Eating & Drinking

What do you recommend?
ཁྱེད་རང་ཁྱེད་ན་ག་རེ་ kay·râng chay·na kâ·ray
ཡག་གི་རེད། yâ·gi·ray

What's in that dish?
ཁ་ལག་ཕ་གི་ནང་ག་རེ་ kha·la pha·gi·nâng kâ·ray
ཡོད་རེད། yö·ray

I'm vegetarian.
ང་ཤ་མི་ཟ་མཁན་ཡིན། nga sha mi·sa·ken yin

That meal was delicious.
ཁ་ལག་ཞིམ་པོ་ཞེ་དྲགས་ kha·la shim·bu shay·ta
བྱུང་། choong

breakfast	ཞོགས་སྐད་ཁ་ལག་	shog·kay kha·la
coffee	ཇ་ཀོ་ཕི་	cha ka·bi
dinner	དགོང་དག་ཁ་ལག་	gong·da kha·la
fish	ཉ་ཤ་	nya·sha
food	ཁ་ལག་	kha·la
fruit	ཤིང་ཏོག་	shing·tog
juice	ཁུ་བ་	khu·wa
lunch	ཉིན་གུང་ ཁ་ལག་	nyin·goong kha·la
meat	ཤ་	sha
milk	འོ་མ་	oh·ma
restaurant	ཟ་ཁང་	sa·khâng
tea	ཇ་	cha
vegetable	སྔོ་ཚལ་	ngo·tsay
(boiled) water	ཆུ་ (འཁོལ་མ་)	chu (khö·ma)

Emergencies

Call ...	… སྐད་ གཏོང་དང་།	... kay tong·da
a doctor	ཨེམ་ཆི་	ahm·chi
the police	སྐོར་སྲུང་བ་	kor·soong·wa
Help!	རོགས་གནང་དང་།	rog nâng·da
Go away!	ཕར་རྒྱུགས།	phâh gyook

I'm lost.
ང་ལམ་ཀ་བརླགས་ཤག nga lâm·ga la·sha

I'm allergic to ...
ངར་ … ཕོགས་ཀྱི་ཡོད། ngah ... pho·gi·yö

Shopping & Services

Do you have any ... ?
ཁྱེད་རང་ལ་ … kay·râng·la ...
བཙོང་ཡག་ཡོད་པས། tsong·ya yö·bay

How much is it?
གོང་ག་ཚད་རེད། gong kâ·tsay ray

It's too expensive.
གོང་ཆེ་དྲགས་ཤག gong chay·ta·sha

I'll give you ...
ངས་ … སྤྲད་དགོས། ngay ... tay go

bank	དངུལ་ཁང་	ngü·khâng
post office	སྦྲག་ཁང་	da·khâng
tourist office	ཡུལ་སྐོར་ སྐྱོ་འཆམ་པའི་ ལས་ཁུངས་	yu·kor to·châm·pay lay·khoong

Time & Dates

What time it is?
ད་ལྟ་ཆུ་ཚོད་ག་ཚད་རེད། tân·da chu·tsö kâ·tsay·ray

It's half past (two).
ཆུ་ཚོད་ (གཉིས་) དང་ chu·tsö (nyi)·dâng
ཕྱེད་ཀ་རེད། chay·ka ray

It's (two) o'clock.
ཆུ་ཚོད་ (གཉིས་) པ་རེད། chu·tsö (nyi)·pa ray

yesterday	ཁ་སང་	kay·sa
today	དེ་རིང་	te·ring
tomorrow	སང་ཉིན་	sa·nyin
Monday	གཟའ་ཟླ་བ་	sa da·wa
Tuesday	གཟའ་མིག་དམར་	sa mig·ma
Wednesday	གཟའ་ལྷག་པ་	sa lhâg·bâ
Thursday	གཟའ་ཕུར་བུ་	sa phu·bu
Friday	གཟའ་པ་སངས་	sa pa·sâng
Saturday	གཟའ་སྤེན་པ་	sa pem·pa
Sunday	གཟའ་ཉི་མ་	sa nyi·mâ

Transport

Where is this	... འདི་ག་པར་	... ka·bah
... going?	འགྲོ་གི་རེད།	doh·gi ray
boat	གྲུ་གཟིངས་	dru·zing
bus	སྤྱི་སྤྱོད་	chi·chö
	གླང་འཁོར་	lâng·kho
plane	གནམ་གྲུ་	nâm·du
I'd like to	ང་ ... གཅིག་	nga ... chig
hire a ...	གཡར་འདོད་ཡོད།	yar dhö·yö
car	མོ་ཊ་	mo·ta
donkey	བོང་བུ་	boong·gu
landcruiser	ལེན་ཀྲུ་རུ་ས་	len ku·ru·sa
pack animals	ཁལ་སེམས་ཅན་/	kel sem·chen/
	ཁལ་མ་	kel·ma
porter	དོ་པོ་ཁུར་མཁན་	doh·po khu·khen
yak	གཡག་	yak

How much is it daily/weekly?
ཉིན་/བདུན་ཕྲག་རེ་རེར་ nyin/dun·tâg ray·ray
གོང་ག་ཚད་རེད། gong kâ·tsay ray

Does this road lead to ...?
ལམ་ཀ་འདི་ ... lâm·ga·di ...
འགྲོ་ཡག་རེད་པས། doh·ya re·bay

Can I get there on foot?
པ་གིར་གོམ་པ་བརྒྱབ་ནས་ pha·gay gom·pa gyâb·nay
སླེབས་ཐུབ་ཀྱི་རེད་པས། leb thoob·ki re·bay

UIGHUR

Uighur is spoken all over Xīnjiāng and in parts of Kyrgyzstan and Uzbekistan. In China, written Uighur uses Arabic script. The phrases in this chapter reflect the Kashgar dialect.

In our pronunciation guides, stressed syllables are indicated by italics. Most consonant sounds in Uighur are the same as in English, though note that h is pronounced with a puff of air. The vowels are:

a	as in 'hat'
aa	as the 'a' in 'father'
ee	as in 'sleep', but produced back in the throat
o	as in 'go'
ö	as the 'e' in 'her', but pronounced with rounded lips
u	as in 'put'
ü	as the 'i' in 'bit' with the lips rounded and pushed forward

Basics

Hello.	ئەسسالامۇ	as·saa·laa·*mu*
	ئەلەيكۇم.	a·lay·*kom*
Goodbye.	خەير-خوش.	hayr·*hosh*
Excuse me.	گۆرۇچەك گە	ka·chü·*rüng ga*
	قانداق	kaan·*daak*
	باردۇ؟	baar·i·du
Sorry.	گۆرۇچەك.	ka·chü·*rüng*
Yes.	ھەئە.	ee·a·*a*
No.	ياق.	yaak
Please.	مەرھەممەت.	ma·ree·am·*mat*
Thank you.	رەخمەت سىزگە.	rah·*mat* siz·ga

How are you?
قانداق kaan·*daak*
ئەھۋالىڭىز؟ a·ee·vaa·*li*·ngiz

Fine. And you?
ياخشى، سىزچۇ؟ yaah·*shi* siz·*chu*

What's your name?
سىزنىڭ siz·*ning*
ئىسمىڭىز نىمە؟ is·mi·*ngiz* ni·*ma*

My name is ...
مېنىڭ ئىسمىم ... mi·*ning* is·*mim* ...

Do you speak English?
سىز ئىنگىلىزچە siz ing·gi·lis·*ka*
بىلەمسىز؟ bi·*lam*·siz

I don't understand.
چۈشەنمىدىم. man chu·*shan*·mi·dim

Accommodation

I'd like to book a room.
مەن ياتاق زاكاس قىلماقچى ئىدىم. man yaa·*taak* zaa·*kaas* kil·maak·*chi* i·*dim*

How much is it per night/person?
ھەربىر كۈنلىكى/ ئادەمگە نەچچە پۇل؟ ee·*ar* bir kün·li·*ki*/ aa·*dam*·gee nach·*cha* pool

double room	قوش كىشلىك ياتاق	kosh kish·*lik* yaa·*taak*
hotel	مېھمانخانا	mee·maan·*haa*·naa
single room	بىر كىشلىك ياتاق	bir kish·*lik* yaa·*taak*

Directions

Can you show me on the map?
ماڭا بۇ يەرنىڭ خەرىتىدىكى ئورنىنى كۆرسىتىپ بېرەمسىز؟ maa·*ngaa* bu *yar*·ning ha·ri·*ti*·di·*ki* or·ni·*ni* kör·si·*tip* bi·ram·*siz*

Numbers – Uighur

1	بىر	bir
2	ئىككى	ik·ki
3	ئۈچ	üch
4	تۆت	töt
5	بەش	bash
6	ئالتە	aal·*ta*
7	يەتتە	yat·*ta*
8	سەككىز	sak·*kiz*
9	توققۇز	tok·*kuz*
10	ئون	on
20	يىگىرمە	yi·*gir*·ma
30	ئوتتۇز	ot·*tuz*
40	قىرىق	ki·*rik*
50	ئەللىك	al·*lik*
60	ئاتمىش	at·*mish*
70	يەتمىش	yat·*mish*
80	سەكسەن	sak·*san*
90	توقسان	tok·*saan*
100	بىر يۈز	bir yüz
1000	بىر مىڭ	bir mng

Turn right/left.
ئوڭغا/سولغا قايرىلىپ. ong·*raa*/sol·*raa* kaay·ri·*lip*

It's straight ahead.
ئۇدۇل ئالدىغا مېڭىپ. u·*dul* aal·*di*·raa me·*ngip*

Where is ...?	... نەدە؟	... na·*da*
behind ...	... ئارقىدا	... aar·*ki*·daa
in front of ...	... ئالدىدا	... aal·*di*·daa
near ...	... ئەتراپىدا	... at·raa·*pi*·daa
on the corner	نىڭ بۇلۇڭىدا	ning bu·lu·*ngi*·daa
opposite	... نىڭ قارشى تەرىپىدە	... ning kaar·*shi* ta·ri·*pi*·da

Eating & Drinking

What would you recommend?
قانداق قورومنى تەۋسىيە قىلىسىز؟ kaan·*daak* ko·rum·*ni* tav·si·*ya* ki·*li*·siz

Do you have vegetarian food?
كۆكتاتلىق يىمەكلىكلەر بارمۇ؟ kök·taat·*lik* yi·mak·lik·*lar* baar·*mu*

What's in that dish?
بۇ قورومىنىڭ خۇرۇچلىرى نىمە؟ bu ko·ro·mi·*ning* hu·ruch·*li*·ri ni·*ma*

That was delicious.
شۇنداق يېيىشلىك بوپتۇ. shoon·*daak* yi·*yish*·lik bop·*too*

coffee	قەھۋە	ka·ee·*va*
eggs	تۇخۇم	tu·*hoom*
fish	بېلىق	be·*lik*
food	يىمەكلىك	yi·mak·*lik*
fruit	مېۋە	mi·*va*
(orange) juice	ئەپلىسىن	ap·*li*·sin
meat	گۆش	gösh
milk	سۈت	süt
nuts	مېغىز	me·*riz*
tea	چاي	chaay
vegetable	كۆكتات	*kök*·taat
(boiled) water	(قايناق) سۇ	(kaay·*naak*) soo

breakfast	ئەتتىگەنلىك تاماق	a·ti·gan·*lik* taa·*maak*
lunch	چۈشلۈك تاماق	chüsh·*lük* taa·*maak*
dinner	كەچلىك تاماق	kach·*lik* taa·*maak*
restaurant	تاماقخانا	taa·maak·haa·*naa*
teahouse	چايخانا	chaay·haa·*naa*

Emergencies

Help!	قۇتقۇزۇڭلار!	kut·ku·zung·*laar*
Go away!	يوقال!	yo·*kaal*
doctor	دوختۇر	doh·*toor*
police	ساقچى	saak·*chi*

I'm lost.
مەن ئىزىپ قالدىم. — man e·*zip* kaal·*dim*

I'm allergic to ...
ماڭا ... رىئاكسىيە قىلىدۇ. — maa·*ngaa* ... ri·*aak*·si·ya ki·li·*doo*

Shopping & Services

I'd like to buy ...
مىنىڭ ... نى سىتىۋالغۇم بار. — mi·*ning* ... ni sc *ti* vaal·room baar

Can I look at it?
كۆرۈپ باقسام بولامدۇ؟ — kö·*rüp* baak·*saam* bo·laam·*doo*

How much is it?
قانچە پۇل؟ — kaan·*cha* pool

That's too expensive.
بەك قىممەتكەن. — bak *kim*·mat·kan

I'll give you ...
سىزگە ... بىرەي. — siz·*ga* ... *bi*·ray

ATM	ئاپتوماتىك پۇل ئىلىش ماشىنىسى	aap·to·maa·*tik* pool e·*lish* maa·*shi*·ni·si
credit card	ئىناۋەتلىك كارتوچكىسى	i·naa·*vat*·lik kaar·*toch*·ki·si
post office	پوچتىخانا	*posh*·taa·haa·naa
tourist office	ساياھەت ئىدارىسى	saa·yaa·*ee*·at i·*daa*·ri·si

Time & Dates

What time is it?
ھازىر سائەت قانچە بولدى؟ — ee·aa·*zir* saa·*at* kan·*cha* bol·*di*

It's (10) o'clock.
سائەت (ئون) بولدى. — saa·*at* (on) bol·*di*

Half past (10).
(ئون) يىرىم بولدى. — (on) ye·*rim* bol·*di*

yesterday	تۆنۈگۈن	tü·nü·*gün*
today	بۈگۈن	bü·*gün*
tomorrow	ئەتە	a·*ta*

Monday	دۈشەنبە	dü·shan·*ba*
Tuesday	سەيشەنبە	say·shan·*ba*
Wednesday	چارشەنبە	chaar·shan·*ba*
Thursday	پەيشەنبە	pay·shan·*ba*
Friday	جۈمە	jü·*ma*
Saturday	شەنبە	shan·*ba*
Sunday	يەكشەنبە	yak·shan·*ba*

Transport

Is this the road to (Kashgar)?
بۇ (قەشقەر)گە بارىدىغان يولمۇ؟ — bo (kash·*kar*)·ga baa·ri·di·*haan* yol·*mu*

Can I get there on foot?
ئۇيەرگە پىيادى بارغىلى بولامدۇ؟ — u yar·ga pi·*yaa*·da bar·*ri*·li boo·*laam*·du

airplane	ئايروپىلان	aay·roo·pi·*laan*
airport	ئايدۇرۇم	aay·*doo*·room
bicycle	ۋەلسىپىت	val·si·*pit*
boat	كىمە	ki·*ma*
bus	ئاپتوبۇس	aap·too·*boos*
bus stop	ئاپتوبۇس بىكىتى	aap·*too*·boos bi·ki·*ti*
motorcycle	موتوسىكلىت	mo·to·si·ki·*lit*
one-way ticket	بىر يوللۇق بىلەت	bir yol·*look* bi·*lat*
return ticket	قايتىپ كىلىش بىلىتى	kaay·*tip* ki·*lish* be·li·*ti*
train	پويىز	po·*yiz*
train station	بىكەت	bi·*kat*

MONGOLIAN

Mongolian has an estimated 10 million speakers worldwide. The standard Mongolian in the Inner Mongolia Autonomous Region of China is based on the Chahar dialect and written using a cursive script in vertical lines (ie from top to bottom), read from left to right. So if you want to ask a local to read the script in this section, just turn the book 90 degrees clockwise. Our coloured pronunciation guides, however, should simply be read the same way you read English.

In the pronunciation guides, stressed syllables are indicated by italics. Most consonant sounds in Mongolian are the same as in English, though note that r in Mongolian is a hard, trilled sound, kh is pronounced as the 'ch' in the Scottish *loch*, and z as in 'lads'. As for the vowels, ē is pronounced as in 'there', ô as in 'alone', ö as 'e' with rounded lips, öö as a slightly longer ö, u as in 'cut' and ŭ as in 'good'.

Basics

Hello.
sēn bēn nô

Goodbye.
ba·yur·*tē*

Excuse me./Sorry.
ôch·*lē*·rē

Yes./No.
teem/oo·*gway*

Thank you.
ba·yur·*laa*

How are you?
sēn bēn nô

Fine. And you?
sēn sēn
sēn nô

What's your name?
tan·*nē* *al*·dur

My name is ...
min·*nee* nur ...

Do you speak English?
ta *ang*·gul hul
mu·tun nô

I don't understand.
bee *oil*·og·sun·gway

Accommodation

Where's a hotel?
joch·*deen* *bô*·tul
haa bēkh vē

Numbers – Mongolian

1	nig
2	*hoi*·yur
3	gŭ·*roo*
4	dŭ·*ro*
5	tav
6	jŭr·*gaa*
7	dol·*lô*
8	nēm
9	yis
10	*a*·ra·oo
20	hur
30	gŭch
40	dŭch
50	teb
60	jir
70	dal
80	nai
90	yir
100	jô
1000	myang

I'd like to book a room, please.
bee nig ŭr·*röö*
jakh·*aal*·dakh san·*naa*·tē

How much is it per night/person?
nig *ho*·nug/hoon
hut·tee jôs vē

single room ganch *hoo*·nē ŭr·*röö*

double room *hoi*·yur *hoo*·nē ŭr·*röö*

Directions

Where's ...?
... haa bēkh vē

Can you show me on the map?
oon·*ee* *gaj*·rin
jir·rug döör *nad*·ad
jaaj *ŭg*·gŭn nô

It's straight ahead.
shôt *ya*·vun

Turn left.
joonsh·ön

Turn right.
ba·*rônsh*·ön

behind *ar*·dun

in front of *oom*·nun

near oi·rul·*chô*

on the corner *ŭn*·chŭgt bēn

opposite *us*·rug *tal*·dun

Eating & Drinking

I'd like to see the menu.
tsay·dan ŭj·jee·*yöö*

What would you recommend?
und *ya*·mar *sē*·khun hôl bēkh vē

What are the local specialities?
und *ya*·mar onch *ga*·rul·tē vē

What's in that dish?
yoo·gur *hee*·dug vē

I'm a vegetarian.
boo *saa*·yô

That was delicious!
mash *amt*·tē

Can we have the bill?
dang·*saan* bod·dee·*yöö*

breakfast ŭg·*löö*·geen hôl

coffee kôt

dinner ö·*röö*·geen hôl

eggs *ŭn*·dug

fish *jag*·gas

food hôl

fruit *ji*·mus

kumiss *chu*·gu

lunch ŭd·*een* hôl

meat makh

milk soo

restaurant *hô*·lung gur

tea chē

teahouse *chē*·geen *mŭkh*·lukh

vegetable nog·*gô*

(boiled) water (*bo*·chil·sun) ŭs

yoghurt *e*·rug

Emergencies

Help!
em av·*raa*

I'm ill.
bee ŭvd·chikh·*löö*

I'm allergic to ...
bee ... *i*·duj bolkh gway *nad*·ud *taa*·rukh·gway

doctor umch

lost *göö*·sun

police chag·*daa*

Shopping & Services

I'd like to buy ...
bee ... *a*·vukh san·*naa*·tē

Can I look at it?
bee ŭ·jij *bol*·un nô

How much is it?
hut·tee jôs vē

That's too expensive.
mash ŭn·*tē*

I'll give you ...
tand ... ŭg·gee·*yöö*

ATM tee kwan jee

credit card it·gum·*jeen* kaart

market jakh dul·*goor*

post office *shô*·dang tob·*chô*

Time & Dates

What time is it?
hut·tee chag bolj bēkh vē

It's (10) o'clock.
(*ar*·bun) chag bolj bēn

Half past (10).
(*ar*·bun) chag *ha*·gas

yesterday *oo*·chig·dur

today oo·*noo*·dur

tomorrow mar·*gaash*

Monday	ga·rug·*een nig*·un
Tuesday	ga·rug·*een* hoir
Wednesday	ga·rug·*een* *gŭr*·bun
Thursday	ga·rug·*een* *dŭr*·bun
Friday	ga·rug·*een ta*·vun
Saturday	ga·rug·*een* jur·*gaa*
Sunday	ga·rug·*een ŭd*·dur

Transport

Is this the road to ...?
un bol ... *ya*·vukh jam mŭn nô

Can I get there on foot?
bee *yav*·gun o·chij *bol*·un nô

Where can I hire a horse?
haa·naas mur tŭr·öös·ulj *bol*·ukh vē

How much is it per hour?
nig chag *hut*·tee jôs vē

Can I change horses?
bee mur·*öön* sol·*lee*·yô *bol*·un nô

Can I have a guide?
jamch olj ŭgch *bol*·un nô

airport	*nis*·gul·een *bô*·tul
bicycle	dŭ·*gway*
boat	jab
bus	*neet*·in *ma*·shin *tur*·rug
bus stop	jog·*sôl*
motorcycle	*mo*·tur
plane	*nis*·gul
reins	jol·*lô*
return ticket	yavj *ha*·rikh bil·*lēt*
saddle	um·*ööl*
stirrup	dŭ·*röö*
train	galt *tur*·rug
train station	*galt tur*·gun ŭr·*töö*

GLOSSARY

apsara – Buddhist celestial being
arhat – Buddhist, especially a monk, who has achieved enlightenment and passes to nirvana at death

běi – north; the other points of the compass are *dōng* (east), *nán* (south) and *xī* (west)
biānjiè – border
biéshù – villa
bīnguǎn – hotel
bìxì – mythical tortoiselike dragon
Bodhisattva – one worthy of nirvana who remains on earth to help others attain enlightenment
Bön – pre-Buddhist indigenous faith of Tibet
bówùguǎn – museum

CAAC – Civil Aviation Administration of China
cadre – Chinese government bureaucrat
cāntīng – restaurant
cǎoyuán – grasslands
CCP – Chinese Communist Party
chau – land mass
chéngshì – city
chí – lake, pool
chop – carved name seal that acts as a signature
chörten – Tibetan *stupa*
CITS – China International Travel Service
cūn – village

dàdào – boulevard
dàfàndiàn – large hotel
dàjiē – avenue
dàjiǔdiàn – large hotel
dǎo – island
dàpùbù – large waterfall
dàqiáo – large bridge
dàshà – hotel, building
dàxué – university
déhuà – white-glazed porcelain
dìtiě – subway
dōng – east; the other points of the compass are *běi* (north), *nán* (south) and *xī* (west)
dòng – cave
dòngwùyuán – zoo

fàndiàn – hotel, restaurant
fēng – peak
fēngjǐngqū – scenic area

gé – pavilion, temple
gompa – monastery
gōng – palace
gōngyuán – park
gōu – gorge, valley
guān – pass
gùjū – house, home, residence

hǎi – sea
hǎitān – beach
Hakka – Chinese ethnic group

Han – China's main ethnic group
hé – river
hú – lake
huáqiáo – overseas Chinese
Hui – ethnic Chinese Muslims
huǒchēzhàn – train station
huǒshān – volcano
hútòng – a narrow alleyway

jiāng – river
jiǎo – unit of *renminbi;* 10 jiǎo equals 1 *yuán*
jiàotáng – church
jīchǎng – airport
jiē – street
jié – festival
jīn – unit of weight; 1 *jīn* equals 600g
jīngjù – Beijing opera
jìniànbēi – memorial
jìniànguǎn – memorial hall
jiǔdiàn – hotel
jū – residence, home
junk – originally referred to Chinese fishing and war vessels with square sails; now applies to various types of boating craft

kang – raised sleeping platform
karakhana – workshop, factory
KCR – Kowloon–Canton Railway
kora – pilgrim circuit
Kuomintang – Chiang Kaishek's Nationalist Party; now one of Taiwan's major political parties

lama – a Buddhist priest of the Tantric or Lamaist school; a title bestowed on monks of particularly high spiritual attainment
lǐlòng – Shànghǎi alleyway
lín – forest
líng – tomb
lìshǐ – history
lóu – tower
LRT – Light Rail Transit
lù – road
lǚguǎn – guest house
luóhàn – Buddhist, especially a monk, who has achieved enlightenment and passes to nirvana at death; see also *arhat*

mah jong – popular Chinese card game for four people; played with engraved tiles
mǎtou – dock
mén – gate
ménpiào – entrance ticket
Miao – ethnic group living in Guìzhōu
miào – temple
MTR – Mass Transit Railway
mù – tomb

nán – south; the other points of the compass are *běi* (north), *dōng* (east) and *xī* (west)

páilou – decorative archway
Pinyin – the official system for transliterating Chinese script into roman characters
PLA – People's Liberation Army
Politburo – the 25-member supreme policy-making authority of the Chinese Communist Party
PRC – People's Republic of China
PSB – Public Security Bureau; the arm of the police force set up to deal with foreigners
pùbù – waterfall

qì – life force
qiáo – bridge
qìchēzhàn – bus station

rénmín – people, people's
renminbi – literally 'people's money'; the formal name for the currency of China, the basic unit of which is the *yuán*; shortened to RMB

sampan – small motorised launch
sānlún mótuōchē – motor tricycle
sānlúnchē – pedal-powered tricycle
SAR – Special Administrative Region
sēnlín – forest
shān – mountain
shāngdiàn – shop, store
shěng – province, provincial
shì – city
shí – rock
shìchǎng – market
shíkū – grotto
shíkùmén – literally 'stone-gate house'; type of 19th-century Shànghǎi residence
shòupiàochù – ticket office
shuǐkù – reservoir
sì – temple, monastery
sìhéyuàn – traditional courtyard house
stupa – usually used as reliquaries for the cremated remains of important *lamas*

tǎ – pagoda
thangka – Tibetan sacred art
tíng – pavilion

wān – bay
wǎngbā – internet café
wēnquán – hot springs

xī – west; the other points of the compass are *dōng* (east), *běi* (north) and *nán* (south)
xī – small stream, brook
xiá – gorge
xiàn – county
xuěshān – snow mountain

yá – cliff
yán – rock or crag
yóujú – post office
yuán – basic unit of *renminbi*
yuán – garden

zhào – lamasery
zhāodàisuǒ – guest house
zhíwùyuán – botanic gardens
zhōng – middle
Zhōngguó – China
zìrán bǎohùqū – nature reserve

behind the scenes

SEND US YOUR FEEDBACK

We love to hear from travellers – your comments keep us on our toes and help make our books better. Our well-travelled team reads every word on what you loved or loathed about this book. Although we cannot reply individually to postal submissions, we always guarantee that your feedback goes straight to the appropriate authors, in time for the next edition. Each person who sends us information is thanked in the next edition – and the most useful submissions are rewarded with a free book.

Visit **lonelyplanet.com/contact** to submit your updates and suggestions or to ask for help. Our award-winning website also features inspirational travel stories, news and discussions.

Note: We may edit, reproduce and incorporate your comments in Lonely Planet products such as guidebooks, websites and digital products, so let us know if you don't want your comments reproduced or your name acknowledged. For a copy of our privacy policy visit lonelyplanet.com/privacy.

OUR READERS

Many thanks to the travellers who used the last edition and wrote to us with helpful hints, useful advice and interesting anecdotes:

A Avais Akhtar, Nancy Aki, Amdoboy, Sebastian Arabito, Ben Archer, Gregory Aroney **B** Kevin Bao, Malcolm Battle, Sebastien Beauchamps, Andrea Biggi, Bastiaan Bijl, Diego Bonifacino, Robert Brandl, Michael Breede, Sander Breedeveld, Melissa Bromwich, Robert Brooks, Sarah Bullen, Wolf Burian, Brian Burk **C** Steve Cannings, Sabina Carlsson, Ans & Bas Castelein-de Groot, Javier Castro Guinea, Nate Cavalieri, Anita Chakraborty, Kaung Chiau Lew, Yangs Chuyuan, Sue Colley, Samantha Cook, Madeline Corrigan **D** Peter Dahler, David Daily, Liam D'Arcy-Brown, Melanie Davison, Fabien De Vel, Maria De Lange, Susannah Deane, Joseph Distler, Jeff Ditter, Chris Dronen **E** Phillip Ekkels, Jeff Emmett, Brian Engel, Caroline English, Helen Ennis **F** Carina Fabisak, Zhang Fan, Richard Forsyth, Clive Foss, Bonnie Fox, Caroline Frances-King, Kathleen Freed, Tizian Fritz **G** Dave G, Klaus Gabriel, Barbara Gallagher, Pierre Gallant, Bernd Gammerl, Adrian Gaunt, Will George, Jonas Gerson, Yotam Gingold, Aaron Glick, Matthew Gollings, Yuri Gorelik, Dianna Graham, Chretien Gregoire, Patrick Gross, Martin Grznar, Heiko Günther, Rani Gustafson **H** Michael Haas, Lance Hall, Tim Harford-Cross, Linda Harries, Pierre Heisbourg, Barbara Heusi, Steven Heywood, Stephen Hoare-Vance, Laura Hornikx, Luke Howie, Spencer Humiston, Scott Humm, Andrew Humphrey, Dagmar Hussel **I** Jon Ingleson, Jeannie Ivanov **J** Bradwell Jackson, Ralpha Jacobson, Guillaume Jacques, Andrea James, Aleksandra Järvinen, Cai Jinming, Job Jobsen, Robert John, Eva Johnson, Steve Jomphe, Peter Jost, Joyce **K** Kyra Kane, Carol Kempe, Matthew Kennedy, David Kerkhoff, Niels Kibshede, Amanda King, Janis Kirpitis, Suzanne Klein, Tim Klink, Kelly Knowles, Miriam Kochman, Nina Kubik-Cheng **L** David Lamb, Winona Landis, Bregje Laumans, Ines Laura, Paul Lavender, Allison Leathart, Winston Lee, Julian Lees, Rhonda Lerner, Oliver Lewis, Dr Yngve Lööf, Amanda Love, Jerome Luepkes, Steven Lum **M** Rodney Mantle, Katharina Markgraf, Mizio Matteucci, Virginia Medinilla, Michiel Mertens, Tomer Metz, Michelle, Robert Molesworth, Ulrike Morrenth, Jens Müller, Ami Muranetz **N** Kester Newill, Dennis Nicoll **O** Lucie Ohankova, Justin O'Hearn, Russell Osborne, Kristel Ouwehand **P** Riccardo Paccapelo, Marcus Pailing, Col Palmer, Eva Papadopoulou, Terence Parker, Gavin Parnaby, John Pascoe, Daniel Paulsen, Woo Peiyi, Jonathan & Noa Perry, Bianca Peters, Emma Petrini, Claire Phillips, John Pinger, Igor Polakovic, Jan Polatschek, Jiri Preclik, Anthony

Pugh, Wayne Purcell **R** Rahmat Rahardja Ong, David Ramirez, Stefan Ratschan, Ron Read, Anthony Reindl, Toby Robertson, Ian Roger, Martin Röjdmark, Frank Roosen **S** Radim Sarapatka, Maddy Savitt, Jeannette Schönau, Heiko Schultz, Henry Scott, Serena, Amit Shachaf, Bella Shah, Rolf Siebert, Siham, Ruth Simister, Stephen Smart, Susan Snoeks, Brechtje Spreeuwers, Kurt Stecker, Prasan Stianrapopangs, Chantal Stieber, Lorenz Stoehr, Meaghan Stolk, Dan Straw **T** Craig Tafel, Noreen Tai, Shohei Takashiro, Caroline Theyse, Marianne Tihon, Annika Tiko, Franciska Tillema, Tom, Martina Tomassini, Yves Traynard, Dana Trytten, Ben Tuff **U** Nathalie Unterbrink **V** Adrienne Van Gelder, Filip Van Den Heuvel, Jolanda Van Dongen, Jos Van Der Horst, René Van Gurp, Tessa Van Gelderen, Cecilia Vázquez Ramírez, Jimena Velasco, Danny Verheij, Ruben Versmessen, Andrea Votavova, Otto Vroege **W** Robert W Rae, Andreas Wachaja, Felix Wagner, Clive Walker, Cheryl Wallace, Eimhin Walsh, Peter Williams, Steve Wilson, Daniel Wong **Y** Curtis Yallop, John Young, Wen Yu Ho **Z** Gottfried Zantke, Gail Zohar, Norbert Zussy

AUTHOR THANKS

Damian Harper

Thanks to Emily Wolman and the staff at Lonely Planet; also thanks to my co-authors. Gratitude as always to Daisy, Timothy Jiafu and Emma Jiale. On the road thanks to everyone who helped out and offered encouragement, especially Mr Sun (sorry, didn't get your first name!), Xie Jianguo and Jamie Chen.

Piera Chen

A warm thank you to William Lee, Frank Lei, Fred Yeung, Venessa Cheah, Yvonne Ieong, Freddie Hai, Jacqueline Chu and Olivia Aires for enriching my research. Thanks also to my parents and my brother, whose memories of Macau and Hong Kong inspired me in rather unexpected ways, and to Susanna Eusantos for taking care of my daughter. As always, much love and gratitude to Sze Pang-cheung, my husband.

Chung Wah Chow

Heartfelt thanks to Leo Liu, Yang Liyan, Emmanuelle Maillard, Kara Jenkinson, Ronald van der Weerd and Einat Keinan in Guǎngxī; Wanny Liang, Christy Cai, Tom Bird, Trey and Hera Menefee, David Abrahamson, Chiu Yi Ting and Angelo Chiu in Guǎngdōng. Thanks also to Leona Wong and Brian Glucroft for keeping me company; and to Daniel McCrohan for keeping the chapter in good shape. Special thanks to Antoine Godde and Sarah Chan for your invaluable help and support.

Min Dai

Thanks as ever to Damian for his invaluable help. Thanks also to Margaux, Li Jianjun, Liu Meina, Sansan, Jiafu and Jiale for their support; much gratitude also to the residents of Píngyáo for such a great trip. A debt of thanks to the friendly Wǔtáishān monk who lent me his umbrella and the ever-so-friendly inhabitants of Nánjiēcūn for doing things differently.

THIS BOOK

This 12th edition of Lonely Planet's *China* was researched and written by a team of stellar authors, led by Damian Harper, who also coordinated and contributed to the 11th edition. The guidebook was commissioned in Lonely Planet's Oakland office and produced by the following:

Commissioning Editor Emily K Wolman
Coordinating Editors Dianne Schallmeiner, Branislava Vladisavljevic
Coordinating Cartographers David Kemp, Peter Shields
Coordinating Layout Designer Yvonne Bischofberger
Managing Editors Sasha Baskett, Liz Heynes, Annelies Mertens
Managing Cartographers David Connolly, Hunor Csutoros, Alison Lyall
Managing Layout Designers Jane Hart, Indra Kilfoyle, Celia Wood
Assisting Editors Susie Ashworth, Janet Austin, Sarah Bailey, Carolyn Boicos, Andrea Dobbin, Trent Holden, Kim Hutchins, Alan Murphy, Alison Ridgway, Helen Yeates
Assisting Cartographers Anita Banh, Enes Bašić, András Bogdanovits, Ildikó Bogdanovits, Valeska Cañas, Diana Duggan, Corey Hutchison, Anthony Phelan, Andy Rojas, Andrew Smith, Brendan Streager
Assisting Layout Designers Mazzy Prinsep, Jessica Rose, Jacqui Saunders, Kerrianne Southway
Cover Research Naomi Parker
Internal Image Research Aude Vauconsant

Thanks to Mark Adams, Imogen Bannister, Xiao Bianr, Rebecca Chau, Stefanie Di Trocchio, Janine Eberle, Michael Essex, Joshua Geoghegan, Mark Germanchis, Michelle Glynn, Lauren Hunt, Laura Jane, David Kemp, Nic Lehman, Tim Lu, John Mazzocchi, Daniel Moore, Wayne Murphy, Adrian Persoglia, Piers Pickard, Averil Robertson, Lachlan Ross, Michael Ruff, Julie Sheridan, Laura Stansfeld, John Taufa, Sam Trafford, Juan Winata, Nick Wood

David Eimer

Special gratitude goes to Li Xinying for her help and patience. Thanks to Chris Taylor in Kūnmíng for the Daliv tips and the old school Lonely Planet stories, as well as to the Bird Bar crew for proving that the grass is always greener in Yúnnán. As ever, thanks to the many people who provided insights along the way, whether knowingly or unwittingly.

Robert Kelly

A warm thanks to Damian Harper, and Emily Wolman at Lonely Planet. To all the gang in Hǎinán who have gone from contacts to friends, my best to you all. As always, deepest thanks to Huei-ming, Kate and Sean for holding down the fort while I was away. And a final dedication to my beloved sister Dawn, who passed away during this project, but who loved my work and was always thrilled to receive phone calls 'from the strangest places'.

Michael Kohn

So many people along the way made my research easier. Thanks to the crew at Fubar, especially Hiroshi Kuwae, Manus McMathuna and Elizabeth Arnold. Travel partners along the way included Vijay, Vivian and Sayaka, cyclists Adam and Cat (congrats on the nuptials), and Yakov (the pious one). Help also arrived from Xiao Sheng (Ürümqi), Moon (Kashgar) YK and Liman Tan (Hotan) and Zorigoo (Hohhot). In Lonely Planet–land, thanks to coordinating author Damian Harper for encouragement. Behind the scenes, thanks to editors Emily Wolman and Liz Heynes. As ever, thanks to Baigal and little Molly, who make coming home the best part of the trip.

Shawn Low

Thanks to Emily for entrusting me with this gig and to Damian for guidance. Thanks to Di Schallmeiner for coordinating and all the Lonely Planet crew for their hard work on this kick-ass book. On the road, thanks goes to Húyùe, Dāndān, Huáhóng, Choi Lee, Joshua Maddox and his crew. Howie and Christine: big thumbs up too for the hospitality. And of course, my dearest Wency, for her patience, support, assistance and excellent Mandarin.

Bradley Mayhew

Thanks to Bill of Tibetan Connections and to Tenzin, Xiaojin and Lumbum in Lhasa. Cheers to Andre and Alyson for a fine trip out to Western Tibet and to Tibet co-author Mike Kohn who supplied much of the research for this chapter. Thanks to Tashi at Yabshi Phunkang, to Lobsang for help as always, to Nyima and Tashi at Dropenling and to Liz Heynes and Emily Wolman for helping with style issues.

Daniel McCrohan

Thanks to Wangden Tsering (Xīníng), Steve Wilson, Wang Li, Daniel Lotinga (all Chóngqìng), Peter Goff (Chéngdù), Amanda and Josh Henck (Jiǔzhàigōu) and Angela Lankford (Tǎgōng). Extra big thanks to Gong Ying (Chóngqìng) and Kieran Fitzgerald (Jiǔzhàigōu). And gigantic thanks to Jamin York (Yùshù), Tom Herbert and Isabel Brough (both Chéngdù). Love, as always, to all my family in the UK and to my newfound family in Belgium/Holland/Greece. Extra special love to Taotao, Dudu and Yoyo.

Christopher Pitts

As always, thanks to everyone who offered valuable insight or provided company along the way. In Shànghǎi, much gratitude is owed to Gerald Neumann. Thanks to fellow authors Damian Harper and Daniel McCrohan, as well as all who work behind the scenes. Particular thanks as well to Anne-Marie and Patrick for helping out with the kids, and my mum and dad, who, in hindsight, did an exemplary job raising us. Finally, love to Perrine, Elliot and Céleste – what would I do without you?

ACKNOWLEDGMENTS

Climate map data adapted from Peel MC, Finlayson BL & McMahon TA (2007) 'Updated World Map of the Köppen-Geiger Climate Classification', *Hydrology and Earth System Sciences*, 11, 163344.

Cover photograph: Great Wall/Panorama Stock/IPhotolibrary. Many of the images in this guide are available for licensing from Lonely Planet Images: www.lonelyplanetimages.com.

index

000 Map pages
000 Photo pages

C

000 Map pages
000 Photo pages

000 Map pages
000 Photo pages

I

M

000 Map pages
000 Photo pages

000 Map pages
000 Photo pages

T

000 Map pages
000 Photo pages

how to use this book

These symbols will help you find the listings you want:

- Sights
- Activities
- Courses
- Tours
- Festivals & Events
- Sleeping
- Eating
- Drinking
- Entertainment
- Shopping
- Information/ Transport

These symbols give you the vital information for each listing:

- Telephone Numbers
- Opening Hours
- Parking
- Nonsmoking
- Air-Conditioning
- Internet Access
- Wi-Fi Access
- Swimming Pool
- Vegetarian Selection
- English-Language Menu
- Family-Friendly
- Pet-Friendly
- Bus
- Ferry
- Metro
- Subway
- London Tube
- Tram
- Train

Reviews are organised by author preference.

Look out for these icons:

TOP CHOICE Our author's recommendation

FREE No payment required

A green or sustainable option

Our authors have nominated these places as demonstrating a strong commitment to sustainability – for example by supporting local communities and producers, operating in an environmentally friendly way, or supporting conservation projects.

Map Legend

Sights
- Beach
- Buddhist
- Castle
- Christian
- Hindu
- Islamic
- Jewish
- Monument
- Museum/Gallery
- Ruin
- Winery/Vineyard
- Zoo
- Other Sight

Activities, Courses & Tours
- Diving/Snorkelling
- Canoeing/Kayaking
- Skiing
- Surfing
- Swimming/Pool
- Walking
- Windsurfing
- Other Activity/ Course/Tour

Sleeping
- Sleeping
- Camping

Eating
- Eating

Drinking
- Drinking
- Cafe

Entertainment
- Entertainment

Shopping
- Shopping

Information
- Bank
- Embassy/ Consulate
- Hospital/Medical
- Internet
- Police
- Post Office
- Telephone
- Toilet
- Tourist Information
- Other Information

Transport
- Airport
- Border Crossing
- Bus
- Cable Car/ Funicular
- Cycling
- Ferry
- Metro
- Monorail
- Parking
- Petrol Station
- Taxi
- Train/Railway
- Tram
- Other Transport

Routes
- Tollway
- Freeway
- Primary
- Secondary
- Tertiary
- Lane
- Unsealed Road
- Plaza/Mall
- Steps
- Tunnel
- Pedestrian Overpass
- Walking Tour
- Walking Tour Detour
- Path

Geographic
- Hut/Shelter
- Lighthouse
- Lookout
- Mountain/Volcano
- Oasis
- Park
- Pass
- Picnic Area
- Waterfall

Population
- Capital (National)
- Capital (State/Province)
- City/Large Town
- Town/Village

Boundaries
- International
- State/Province
- Disputed
- Regional/Suburb
- Marine Park
- Cliff
- Wall

Hydrography
- River, Creek
- Intermittent River
- Swamp/Mangrove
- Reef
- Canal
- Water
- Dry/Salt/ Intermittent Lake
- Glacier

Areas
- Beach/Desert
- Cemetery (Christian)
- Cemetery (Other)
- Park/Forest
- Sportsground
- Sight (Building)
- Top Sight (Building)

David Eimer

Shaanxi (Shǎnxī), Húnán, Guìzhōu, Yúnnán David first came to China in 1988. Since then, he has travelled across the country, from the far west to the Russian and Korean borders in the northeast, through the south and southwest and along the eastern coast. After stints as a journalist in LA and London, he succumbed to his fascination with China in 2005 and moved to Běijīng. As well as contributing to newspapers and magazines, David worked on the last edition of *China* for Lonely Planet, has co-authored the *Beijing* and *Shanghai* city guides and wrote the most recent *Beijing Encounter*.

Robert Kelly

Liáoníng, Jílín, Hēilóngjiāng, Hǎinán Ever since he learned that his dad's airline job meant he could fly for peanuts, Robert has been travelling. He first landed in China in the mid-80s, and has popped around Asia ever since, eventually settling down in Taiwan 15 years ago. For this book, Robert researched the very southern point and the very northern tip of China. If there was ever a perfect lesson in the need to avoid summaries and stereotypes when talking about China, this was it. This is Robert's sixth title for Lonely Planet.

Michael Kohn

Xīnjiāng, Níngxià, Inner Mongolia Michael grew up in Northern California and made his first trip to China in 1994. He jumped ship in Hong Kong, went to Tibet and later hiked along the Great Wall. Michael has returned to China a dozen times. This is his second tour of duty on Lonely Planet's *China* guide. He has also updated Lonely Planet guides to Tibet, Central Asia and Mongolia and has written two books of his own. Michael is currently based in Ulaanbaatar. His work can be read online at www.michaelkohn.us.

Shawn Low

Shāndōng, Jiāngsū, Fújiàn, Ānhuī Shawn left his Singapore home for Melbourne and made his way into Lonely Planet as a book editor. Since then, he's done a stint as a commissioning editor, authored guides to Singapore and Southeast Asia, and is now Lonely Planet's Asia-Pacific Travel Editor. His fascination with China began after he was dispatched to Yúnnán to host an episode of National Geographic & Lonely Planet's *Roads Less Travelled*. Returning to China as an author felt like an obvious thing to do – so he did.

Bradley Mayhew

Tibet A mountain junkie, Bradley has been visiting the Tibetan plateau for 20 years, since studying Chinese at Oxford University. Bradley has coordinated the last four editions of the *Tibet* guide and is also the co-author of Lonely Planet's *Bhutan*, *Nepal*, *Trekking in the Nepal Himalaya* and *Central Asia*, as well as the *Odyssey Guide to Uzbekistan*. He has lectured on Central Asia to the Royal Geographical Society and was the subject of a Arte/SWR documentary retracing the route of Marco Polo. See what he's up to at www.bradleymayhew.blogspot.com.

Daniel McCrohan

Sìchuān, Chóngqìng, Qīnghǎi Daniel trained as journalist in the UK and worked for several years on newspapers before turning to travel writing. An Asia fanatic, he travelled extensively throughout the continent for more than 15 years before settling down in China in 2005. He now lives with his wife and their children in a courtyard home in one of Běijīng's *hútòng* (alleyways). Daniel has worked on Lonely Planet guides to China, India, Shànghǎi and Tibet. He also worked as a presenter for the Lonely Planet TV series *Best in China*. Find him on www.danielmccrohan.com.

Christopher Pitts

Shànghǎi, Jiāngxī A Philadelphia native, Chris started off his university years studying classical Chinese poetry before a week in 1990s Shànghǎi (en route to school in Kūnmíng) abruptly changed his focus to the idiosyncracies of modern China. After spending several years in Asia memorising Chinese characters, he abruptly traded it all in and moved to Paris, where he currently lives with his family, Perrine, Elliot and Céleste. He works as a freelance writer, editor and translator for various publishers. Visit his website at www.christopherpitts.net.

OUR STORY

A beat-up old car, a few dollars in the pocket and a sense of adventure. In 1972 that's all Tony and Maureen Wheeler needed for the trip of a lifetime – across Europe and Asia overland to Australia. It took several months, and at the end – broke but inspired – they sat at their kitchen table writing and stapling together their first travel guide, *Across Asia on the Cheap*. Within a week they'd sold 1500 copies. Lonely Planet was born.

Today, Lonely Planet has offices in Melbourne, London and Oakland, with more than 600 staff and writers. We share Tony's belief that 'a great guidebook should do three things: inform, educate and amuse'.

OUR WRITERS

Damian Harper

Coordinating author, Běijīng, Journey to the Great Wall, Tiānjīn & Héběi, Cruising the Yangzi, Gānsù After graduating with a degree in Chinese (modern and classical) from London's School of Oriental and African Studies, Damian moved to pre-handover Hong Kong. He then embarked on an epic nine-province journey for the 6th edition of Lonely Planet's *China*. Since then he has worked on five further editions and has worked in Shànghǎi and Běijīng (developing a Mandarin accent somewhere between the two), contributing to multiple editions of the Lonely Planet *Beijing* and *Shanghai* city guides.

Piera Chen

Hong Kong, Macau Piera has been travelling to Macau since she was six. Over the years, while working in Hong Kong, it was poetry readings, *fado* (Portuguese music) concerts, and a masterfully executed *pato de cabidela* (duck stewed in its own blood) that kept luring her back. For this book, she spoke to insiders of the casino industry, and for both the Hong Kong and Macau chapters, she scoured the streets for indie music dives, art spaces, and other unpolished gems. Piera also co-authored the 14th Lonely Planet *Hong Kong & Macau* city guide.

Chung Wah Chow

Guǎngdōng, Guǎngxī Chung Wah is a Hong Kong native who has travelled extensively in the mainland. The sheer diversity of China's languages has always fascinated her. Cantonese, Hakka, Tai, Uighur, Teochew and Hokkien – she loves them all. With an advanced degree in translation studies, a penchant for travel and discovering new sounds and words, Chung Wah merged her talents by becoming a travel writer. She contributed to the previous Lonely Planet edition of *China* and co-authored Lonely Planet's *Hong Kong & Macau* city guide.

Min Dai

Zhèjiāng, Shānxī, Hénán, Húběi Min Dai grew up in the old town of balmy Qīngdǎo on the Shāndōng coast before studying for four years at Běijīng Normal University. She moved to London in the mid-1990s but her seaside roots see her holidaying occasionally in Brighton, Hastings, Margate and even Bournemouth. Min Dai has also lived in Shànghǎi, Běijīng, Hong Kong and Singapore and returns to China frequently to visit family and friends and to journey across her homeland. Married with two children, Min Dai has worked on two editions of Lonely Planet's *China*.

OVER PAGE MORE WRITERS

Published by Lonely Planet Publications Pty Ltd
ABN 36 005 607 983
12th edition – May 2011
ISBN 978 1 74179 589 9

10 9 8 7 6 5 4 3 2 1
Printed in Singapore